Collectors' Info

COLLECTIBLES
PRICE GUIDE
1994 Edition

YOUR GUIDE TO CURRENT PRICES
FOR LIMITED EDITION

Plates ❖ Figurines ❖ Bells ❖ Graphics
Ornaments ❖ Dolls ❖ Steins

Collectors' Information Bureau
5065 Shoreline Road
Barrington, Illinois 60010
(708) 842-2200

ACKNOWLEDGMENTS

The staff of the Collectors' Information Bureau would like to express our deep appreciation to our distinguished panel of limited edition retailers and secondary market experts, whose knowledge and dedication to the collectibles industry have helped make this book possible. Although we would like to recognize them by name, they have agreed that to be singled out in this manner may hinder their ability to maintain an unbiased view of the marketplace.

STAFF

Editorial and Administrative Management

Debra Ley
Rita Vander Meulen
Cindy Zagumny

Research and Development

Carol Van Elderen
Jessica Gazda
Susan Knappen
Courtney Lawrence

Design and Graphics

Lynnda White
Kristin Wiley - Wright Design

Printing

William C. Brown Communications

Printed in the United States of America.

ISBN: 0-930785-16-9 Collectors' Information Bureau

ISBN: 0-87069-715-3 Wallace-Homestead Book Company

❖ CONTENTS ❖

❖ INTRODUCTION ❖

Welcome to the 1994 edition of the *Collectibles Price Guide!* This comprehensive, up-to-date index is published each spring by the Collectors' Information Bureau and reports on current primary and secondary market retail prices for limited edition figurines, cottages, plates, dolls, bells, Christmas ornaments, graphics and steins.

The Guide, now in its fourth edition, is considered one of the most authoritative and comprehensive price guides available today, listing over 35,000 current market prices. It is an ideal resource for collectors to use in establishing the value of their collections for insurance purposes. It is also a useful guide for those collectors who decide to buy or sell a retired collectible on the secondary market.

How We Obtain Our Prices

The *Collectibles Price Guide* is the result of an extensive cooperative effort between the Collectors' Information Bureau's in-house research and development staff and our national panel of limited edition retailers and secondary market dealers. A very systematic procedure for gathering and reporting prices has been developed and refined over the years in order to provide collectors with the most accurate and timely information possible.

The process begins with the C.I.B. research and development staff gathering up-to-date information from collectibles manufacturers on new items as well as those which have been "retired." This information is entered into a computer and copies are mailed to the C.I.B.'s panel of retailers and exchanges across the United States.

Members of this panel are carefully screened by C.I.B. management for their in-depth knowledge of the marketplace, their stature within the collectibles field, and their dedication to meeting the information needs of collectors everywhere. Through mail and telephone surveys, the panel works with our in-house researchers as a cooperative team to report and analyze actual sales transactions.

Based on these findings, which are checked and rechecked, a price is determined for each entry in which there has been trading activity. Where prices for some items may vary throughout the country, we provide a price range showing a "low" and a "high." All prices are for items in mint condition.

The secondary market in collectibles is a vast, ever-changing market. Some collectibles maintain a steady value for years, while prices for others go up and down so quickly it would be impossible to provide a completely up-to-date price in a printed book. That's why it's very important for anyone who uses the *Collectibles Price Guide* – or any of the other price indexes on the market – to think of it as a general guideline only. Also remember that prices quoted are retail prices, which means that they are the prices which these retail stores or secondary market exchanges have confirmed in a sales transaction, including their profit.

The Secondary Market — What It Is And How It Works

When a collectible is introduced by a manufacturer and made available to collectors, it is first sold on the "primary" market. This means that the item is sold at its original retail price through limited edition retailers or directly through the manufacturer by direct mail or other means.

Eventually, the collectible may be "sold out," meaning that the manufacturers and retailers no longer have the item available to sell to collectors at the original retail price. In these cases, collectors who still wish to buy the piece have only one option: to purchase it from someone who already owns it and to pay the price the current market will bear. In other words, the collectible must be purchased on the "secondary" market.

The price of a collectible on the secondary market is determined solely by supply and demand. There may be many new buyers who wish to acquire a "sold out" piece that is in short supply, in which case the secondary market price for that particular collectible will rise. Likewise, if there is little or no demand for a particular piece, the price will decrease accordingly.

Collectors should also be aware that prices can – and do – fluctuate on the secondary market, sometimes quite dramatically. For example, when collectors feel that a particular item has reached its highest value, the demand for that piece may decrease – and so will the price. When this happens, the demand may again increase as collectors take advantage of the lower price.

Buying And Selling On The Secondary Market

Collectors often ask if they should buy multiples of collectible items in the hope of selling them – and making a profit – if the piece rises on the secondary market. In fact, very few collectibles experts encourage people to purchase collectibles for investment purposes. No one can predict which "sold out" collectibles will increase in value on the secondary market. Some collectibles may go up in value, and others may go down.

In addition, there are those collectibles which sell out, but never generate enough demand to increase their value over their original primary market price. Other collectibles peak quickly after being sold out. And still others rise in value slowly over a long period of time.

When purchasing collectibles, the best strategy is to simply buy what you love – for the joy of acquiring a beautiful piece of artwork that will warm your heart whenever you look at it...to enhance the beauty of your home...or to create a special family tradition that can be passed along from generation to generation. If your favorite collectibles rise in value over time, so much the better. But most experts agree that it should never be your primary motivation for buying.

Still, many collectors enjoy buying and selling on the secondary market – and you can, too, if you approach it with some knowledge of how it operates. That way, you can be sure of participating in a fair and equitable transaction, whether you're buying or selling a piece.

The first step in becoming familiar with the secondary market is to study the market dynamics and trends, and to consult price guides, such as this one. That way, you can get a good "feel" for what's happening in the market. In fact, many collectors keep a reference library of past editions of our *Collectibles Price Guides* so that they can follow secondary market trends over a period of time.

Once you have decided to buy or sell a retired collectible on the secondary market, there are several ways you can go about it. You may wish to work with a collectible retailer who specializes in the secondary market or a collector "exchange." Or, you may want to participate in a "swap and sell" meet or auction.

A collectibles retailer who specializes in the secondary market will act as a broker and handle secondary market transactions by taking items on consignment or purchasing them outright. Others will match up buyers and sellers – often using a computer database or filing system. In most cases, a commission or brokerage fee will be charged to a seller, which can range from 10% to 50%.

Collector "exchanges" are businesses exclusively dedicated to matching up buyers and sellers on the secondary market. Acting as a "middleman" in a collectible transaction, the exchange guarantees that the buyer will receive an item that is in mint condition. The seller is assured of prompt payment for the collectible that is sold.

Each exchange operates differently, with most adding a brokerage fee – usually 10% to 35% – to the asking price. Some exchanges may also charge a membership fee or listing fee, so it is a good idea to ask about commission rates before listing with a particular exchange.

Collectors also have an opportunity to buy and sell collectibles directly to each other at "swap and sell" meets and auctions. National collector conventions and local collector clubs and retailers often organize swap meets, where collectors can rent table space to sell retired collectibles. Many of these gatherings are advertised in publications dedicated to collecting.

Buyer — And Seller — Beware!

Collectors who decide to jump into the secondary market often find to their surprise that it can take quite a while to sell a particular collectible – or to locate a collectible that they wish to purchase. Perhaps a particular collectible they want to buy is in great demand, or the one they wish to sell is too readily available.

Even in the best of circumstances, buying or selling a retired collectible takes some time. Several weeks can go by for the process to be completed. Prospective buyers and sellers must be contacted, the item for sale must be examined to confirm its authenticity and condition, and money must be exchanged.

Collectors who want to sell large collections must be equally, if not more, patient. Selling a large collection in its entirety can be especially challenging, simply because there are not many individuals, retailers, and exchanges who can afford to buy a whole collection at once. Sometimes dealers will take a large collection on consignment and pay collectors, taking a sales commission, as individual items are sold.

As you can see, there are many factors to consider as you get more involved in the secondary market. The Collectors' Information Bureau offers a variety of publications that will help you learn more about your collecting hobby and this dynamic, ever-changing market, including the *Collectibles Market Guide and Price Index*, the *Directory to Limited Edition Collectible Stores*, and the *Directory to Secondary Market Retailers*.

You may also wish to subscribe to the "C.I.B. Report," our quarterly newsletter filled with news and information on the latest collectibles. You'll find these publications described in greater detail in the following pages.

WOULD YOU LIKE TO LEARN MORE ABOUT COLLECTIBLES?

The Collectors' Information Bureau Is Here To Help!

Would you like to become a more knowledgeable collector? Are you interested in finding out more about the secondary market? Are you curious about finding out where you can buy and sell retired pieces? Do you want the latest news and information on collectibles right at your fingertips?

You'll find the answers to all these questions – and more – inside the books created just for you by the Collectors' Information Bureau. You'll find page after page of the most accurate and up-to-date information on limited edition plates, figurines, cottages, bells, graphics, ornaments, dolls and steins. And you'll also find the information you need on limited edition collectibles and retail stores in your area and around the country.

Since 1982, the Collectors' Information Bureau – a trade organization with nearly 80 member companies – has reached out to thousands of collectors across the country and around the world. Today, we're proud to remain your most trusted source for limited edition collectibles information.

The Collectors' Information Bureau can help you find even more pleasure in your collecting hobby as you build your library of up-to-date, authoritative resources.

COLLECTIBLES MARKET GUIDE & PRICE INDEX — ELEVENTH EDITION

This big, beautiful resource book, with 32 pages of full color photography, is perhaps the most comprehensive guide to collecting available today. In more than 600 pages, you'll find just about everything you need to know about collecting. Beginning collectors will appreciate learning about all the aspects of the fun and exciting world of collectibles, and experienced hobbyists will find new insights and ideas on every page.

Chapter after fascinating chapter provides you with a wealth of information on decorating with your collectibles, insuring your collection against loss and theft, collector clubs, artists and manufacturers, and much, much more. The book also includes a 184-page price index.

Collectibles Price Guide

Published each spring as a mid-year update to the Price Index, the *Collectibles Price Guide* reports on current primary and secondary market retail prices for limited edition plates, figurines, cottages, bells, graphics, ornaments, dolls and steins.

This up-to-date index is considered one of the most authoritative and comprehensive price guides available today, listing over 35,000 current market prices. It is a helpful resource in establishing the value of your collection for insurance purposes and can be a useful guide, if you decide to buy or sell retired collectibles on the secondary market.

Directory to Secondary Market Retailers

Here is a comprehensive, up-to-date guide to buying and selling limited edition collectibles that are available only on the secondary market. Featuring more than 200 of today's most respected secondary market dealers and exchanges nationwide, this handy paperback gives you all the information you need to reach the people you need to be in touch with when buying and selling retired collectibles.

Listings for the collectible stores appear alphabetically, and each includes such information as:

- ❖ Name, address, telephone number (FAX where applicable) of the secondary market retailer or exchange
- ❖ Store hours
- ❖ Secondary market lines
- ❖ Secondary market terms
- ❖ Business history

Two comprehensive indexes – one by location and one by collectible line – makes this book a convenient, easy-to-use reference whenever you need to find the right secondary market retailer or exchange.

Directory to Limited Edition Collectible Stores

This directory features hundreds of collectible stores across the United States and in Canada for collectors who wish to purchase collectibles nationwide by phone, mail, or in person. Entries are listed by state and include store name, address, telephone number, store hours, collectibles lines, possible secondary market leads, as well as shipping, layaway, and special terms. Plus, a comprehensive, easy-to-use index lets you find the information you need instantly.

The "C.I.B. Report"

You'll get all the latest collectibles news in the "C.I.B. Report." Each issue of this quarterly newsletter brings you the information you need to help make collecting even more fun and exciting. You'll enjoy page after page of new product introductions, collectors club activities, artist open houses, product retirement announcements, convention news...and much, much more! When you subscribe to the "C.I.B. Report," you won't have to worry about missing a single issue of this fun, informative newsletter.

Books published by the Collectors' Information Bureau may be purchased at your local bookstore, collectibles retailer, or directly through the C.I.B.

For more information, contact the Collectors' Information Bureau at:

5065 Shoreline Road, Suite 200
Barrington, Illinois 60010
(708) 842-2200

❖ THE COMPANY WE KEEP ❖

1994 C.I.B. Membership

Kurt S. Adler, Inc.
1107 Broadway
New York, NY 10010

Anheuser-Busch, Inc.
Retail Sales Department
2700 South Broadway
St. Louis, MO 63118

Annalee Mobilitee Dolls, Inc.
Box 708 Reservoir Road
Meredith, NH 03253

Armani
c/o Miller Import Corp.
300 Mac Lane
Keasbey, NJ 08832

Artaffects, Ltd.
P.O. Box 98
Staten Island, NY 10307

The Ashton-Drake Galleries
9200 N. Maryland Avenue
Niles, IL 60714

BAND Creations
28427 N. Ballard
Lake Forest, IL 60045

Marty Bell Fine Art, Inc.
9314 Eton Avenue
Chatsworth, CA 91311

The Bradford Exchange
9333 Milwaukee Avenue
Niles, IL 60714

Brandywine Collectibles
2413 Wolftrap Rd.
Yorktown, VA 23692

Byers' Choice Ltd.
P.O. Box 158
Chalfont, PA 18914

Rick Cain Studios
619 S. Main Street
Gainesville, FL 32601

Calabar Creations
1941 S. Vineyard Ave.
Ontario, CA 91761

Cast Art Industries, Inc.
1120 California Ave.
Corona, CA 91719

The Cat's Meow/ F J Designs
2163 Great Trails Drive
Wooster, OH 44691

Christopher Radko
Planetarium Station
P.O. Box 770
New York, NY 10024

Classic Collectables by
Uniquely Yours
P.O. Box 16861
Philadelphia, PA 19142

Creart
4517 Manzanillo Drive
Austin, TX 78749

C.U.I., Inc./Classic Carolina
Collections/Dram Tree
1502 North 23rd Street
Wilmington, NC 28405

Department 56, Inc.
P.O. Box 44456
Eden Prairie, MN 55344-1456

The Walt Disney Company
500 South Buena Vista Street
Burbank, CA 91521-6876

Duncan Royale
1141 So. Acacia Avenue
Fullerton, CA 92631

Dynasty Dolls
c/o Cardinal Inc.
P.O. Box 99
400 Markley Street
Port Reading, NJ 07064

The Fenton Art Glass Company
700 Elizabeth Street
Williamstown, WV 26187

Fitz and Floyd
Heirloom Collectibles Division
P.O. Box 516125
Dallas, TX 75251-6125

Flambro Imports
1530 Ellsworth Industrial Drive
Atlanta, GA 30318

The Franklin Mint
Franklin Center, PA 19091

Fraser International
5990 N. Belt E, Building 606
Humble, TX 77396

Margaret Furlong Designs
210 State Street
Salem, OR 97301

GANZ
908 Niagara Falls Blvd.
North Tonawanda, NY 14120-2060

Gartlan USA, Inc.
1951 Old Cuthbert Road
Cherry Hill, NJ 08034

Georgetown Collection
866 Spring Street
Westbrook, ME 04092

Goebel
Goebel Plaza
P.O. Box 10, Rte. 31
Pennington, NJ 08534-0010

Great American Taylor
Collectible Corp.
Drawer 249
Southern Pines, NC 28388

The Greenwich Workshop
30 Lindeman Drive
Trumbull, CT 06611

Hallmark Cards, Inc.
P.O. Box 412734
Kansas City, MO 64141-2734

The Hamilton Collection*
4810 Executive Park Court
Jacksonville, FL 32216-6069

Hand & Hammer Silversmiths
Hand & Hammer Collectors' Club
2610 Morse Lane
Woodbridge, VA 22192

Harbour Lights
8130 La Mesa Blvd.
La Mesa, CA 91941

Hawthorne Architectural Register
9210 N. Maryland Avenue
Niles, IL 60714

John Hine Studios, Inc.
4456 Campbell Road
P.O. Box 800667
Houston, TX 77280-0667

Historical Miniatures
95 Hathaway Street, C-10
Providence, RI 02907

M.I. Hummel Club*
Division of Goebel Art GmbH
Goebel Plaza
P.O. Box 11
Pennington, NJ 08534-0011

Iris Arc Crystal
114 East Haley St.
Santa Barbara, CA 93101

LCS Products & Services Corp.
8240 Ronda Drive
Canton, MI 48187

Ladie and Friends, Inc.
220 North Main Street
Sellersville, PA 18960

The Lance Corporation
321 Central Street
Hudson, MA 01749

The Lawton Doll Company
548 North First
Turlock, CA 95380

Ron Lee's World of Clowns
2180 Agate Court
Simi Valley, CA 93065

George Z. Lefton Co.
3622 S. Morgan St.
Chicago, IL 60609

LEGENDS
2665D Park Center Drive
Simi Valley, CA 93065

Lenox Collections
1170 Wheeler Way
Langhorne, PA 19047

Lightpost Publishing
Ten Almaden Blvd. 9th Floor
San Jose, CA 95113

Lilliput Lane Limited c/o Lilliput Incorporated
9052 Old Annapolis Road
Columbia, MD 21045

Lladro Collectors Society
43 W. 57th Street
New York, NY 10019

Seymour Mann, Inc.
225 Fifth Avenue,
Showroom #102
New York, NY 10010

Maruri U.S.A.
7541 Woodman Place
Van Nuys, CA 91405

June McKenna Collectibles Inc.
P.O. Box 846
Ashland, VA 23005

Michael's Limited
P.O. Box 217
Redmond, WA 98078-0217

Midwest of Cannon Falls
32057 64th Avenue, P.O. Box 20
Cannon Falls, MN 55009-0020

Miss Martha Originals, Inc.
P.O. Box 5038
Glencoe, AL 35905

Old World Christmas
P.O. Box 8000
Spokane, WA 99203

PenDelfin Sales Inc.
750 Ensminger Road #108
Box 884
Tonawanda, NY 14150

Possible Dreams
6 Perry Drive
Foxboro, MA 02035

Precious Art/Panton
110 E. Ellsworth Road
Ann Arbor, MI 48108

R.R. Creations
P.O. Box 8707
Pratt, KS 67124

Rawcliffe Corporation
155 Public Street
Providence, RI 02903

Reco International Corp.*
150 Haven Avenue
Port Washington, NY 11050

Roman, Inc.*
555 Lawrence Avenue
Roselle, IL 60172-1599

Royal Copenhagen/Bing & Grondahl
27 Holland Ave.
White Plains, NY 10603

Royal Doulton
700 Cottontail Lane
Somerset, NJ 08873

Sarah's Attic
126-1/2 West Broad
P.O. Box 448
Chesaning, MI 48616

Shelia's Inc.
P.O. Box 31028
Charleston, SC 29417

Summerhill Crystal
P.O. Box 1479
Fairfield, IA 52556

Swarovski America Ltd.
2 Slater Road
Cranston, RI 02920

United Design Corporation
P.O. Box 1200
Noble, OK 73068

VickiLane
3233 NE Cadet
Portland, OR 97220

WACO Products Corp.
One North Corporate Drive
Riverdale, NJ 07457-0160

World Gallery of Dolls & Collectibles
P.O. Box 581
Great Falls, VA 22066

***Charter Member**

❖ Collectors' Information Bureau ❖

PRICE INDEX 1994

Limited Edition: Plates ❖ Figurines ❖ Bells ❖ Graphics ❖ Ornaments ❖ Dolls ❖ Steins

This index includes several thousand of the most widely traded limited editions in today's collectibles market. It is based on interviews with about 300 of the most experienced and informed limited edition dealers in the United States, as well as several independent market advisors.

HOW TO USE THIS INDEX

Listings are set up using the following format:

Company		Series			
Number	Name	Artist	Edition Limit	Issue Price	Quote
❶ Enesco Corporation		❷ Retired Precious Moments Figurines			
79-13-002	Praise the Lord Anyhow-E1374B	S. Butcher	Retrd.	8.00	75-125.00
❸❹❺	❻	❼	❽	❾	❿

❶ Company = Company Name

❷ Retired Precious Moments Figurines = Series Name

❸ 79 = 1979 (year of issue)

❹ 13 = Series number for Enesco Corporation. This number indicates that this series is the 13th listed for this particular company. Each series is assigned a series number.

❺ 002 = Item Number within series. For example, this is the second listing within the series. Each item has a sequential number within its series.

❻ Praise the Lord Anyhow-E1374B = Proper title of the collectible. Many titles also include the model number for further identification purposes.

❼ S. Butcher = Artists' name. The first initial and last name is indicated most often, however a studio name may also be designated in this lot. (Example: Walt Disney).

❽ Retrd. = Retired. In this case, the collectible is no longer available. The edition limit category generally refers to the number of items created with the same name and decoration. Edition limits may indicate a specific number (i.e. 10,000) or the number of firing days for plates (i.e. 100-day, the capacity of the manufacturer to produce collectibles during a given firing period). Refer to "Open," "Suspd.," "Annual," and "Yr. Iss." under "Terms and Abbreviations" below.

❾ 8.00 = Issue Price in U.S. Dollars

❿ 75-125.00 = Current Quote Price reflected may show a price or price range. Quotes are based on interviews with retailers across the country, who provide their actual sales transactions.

A Special Note to All Precious Moments Collectors: *Each ENESCO Precious Moments subject is engraved with a special annual mark. This emblem changes with each production year. The Collector value for each piece varies because of these distinctive yearly markings. Our pricing reflects an average for all years.*

A Special Note to All Hallmark Keepsake Ornament Collectors: *All quotes in this section are for ornaments in mint condition in their original box.*

A Special Note to All Department 56 Collectors: *Year of Introduction indicates the year in which the piece was designed, sculpted and copyrighted. It is possible these pieces may not be available to the collectors until the following calendar year.*

TERMS AND ABBREVIATIONS

Annual = Issued once a year

Closed = An item or series no longer in production

N/A = Not Available

Open = Not limited by number or time, available until manufacturer stops production, "retires" or "closes" the item or series

Retrd. = Retired

S/O = Sold Out

Set = Refers to two or more items issued together for a single price

Suspd. = Suspended (not currently being produced: may be produced in the future)

Undis. = Undisclosed

Unkn. = Unknown

Yr. Iss. = Year of issue (limited to a calendar year) 28-day, 10-day, etc., limited to this number of production (or firing) days, usually not consecutive

BELLS

Company / Number	Name	Series / Artist	Edition Limit	Issue Price	Quote
ANRI		**ANRI Wooden Christmas Bells**			
76-01-001	Christmas	J. Ferrandiz	Yr.Iss.	6.00	50.00
77-01-002	Christmas	J. Ferrandiz	Yr.Iss.	7.00	40-42.00
78-01-003	Christmas	J. Ferrandiz	Yr.Iss.	10.00	40.00
79-01-004	Christmas	J. Ferrandiz	Yr.Iss.	13.00	25-30.00
80-01-005	The Christmas King	J. Ferrandiz	Yr.Iss.	17.50	18.50
81-01-006	Lighting The Way	J. Ferrandiz	Yr.Iss.	18.50	18.50
82-01-007	Caring	J. Ferrandiz	Yr.Iss.	18.50	18.50
83-01-008	Behold	J. Ferrandiz	Yr.Iss.	18.50	18.50
85-01-009	Nature's Dream	J. Ferrandiz	Yr.Iss.	18.50	18.50
ANRI		**Juan Ferrandiz Musical Christmas Bells**			
76-02-001	Christmas	J. Ferrandiz	Yr.Iss.	25.00	80.00
77-02-002	Christmas	J. Ferrandiz	Yr.Iss.	25.00	80.00
78-02-003	Christmas	J. Ferrandiz	Yr.Iss.	35.00	75.00
79-02-004	Christmas	J. Ferrandiz	Yr.Iss.	47.50	60.00
80-02-005	Little Drummer Boy	J. Ferrandiz	Yr.Iss.	60.00	63.00
81-02-006	The Good Shepherd Boy	J. Ferrandiz	Yr.Iss.	63.00	63.00
82-02-007	Spreading the Word	J. Ferrandiz	Yr.Iss.	63.00	63.00
83-02-008	Companions	J. Ferrandiz	Yr.Iss.	63.00	63.00
84-02-009	With Love	J. Ferrandiz	Yr.Iss.	55.00	55.00
Artaffects		**Bells**			
87-01-001	Newborn Bell	R. Sauber	Unkn.	25.00	25.00
87-01-002	Motherhood Bell	R. Sauber	Unkn.	25.00	25.00
87-01-003	Sweet Sixteen Bell	R. Sauber	Unkn.	25.00	25.00
87-01-004	The Wedding Bell (White)	R. Sauber	Unkn.	25.00	25.00
87-01-005	The Wedding Bell (Silver)	R. Sauber	Unkn.	25.00	25.00
87-01-006	The Wedding Bell (Gold)	R. Sauber	Unkn.	25.00	25.00
Artaffects		**Bride Belles Figurine Bells**			
88-02-001	Caroline	R. Sauber	Unkn.	27.50	27.50
88-02-002	Jacqueline	R. Sauber	Unkn.	27.50	27.50
88-02-003	Elizabeth	R. Sauber	Unkn.	27.50	27.50
88-02-004	Emily	R. Sauber	Unkn.	27.50	27.50
88-02-005	Meredith	R. Sauber	Unkn.	27.50	27.50
88-02-006	Laura	R. Sauber	Unkn.	27.50	27.50
88-02-007	Sarah	R. Sauber	Unkn.	27.50	27.50
88-02-008	Rebecca	R. Sauber	Unkn.	27.50	27.50
88-02-009	Groom	R. Sauber	Unkn.	22.50	22.50
Artaffects		**Indian Brave Annual Bell**			
89-03-001	Christmas Pow-Pow	G. Perillo	Closed	24.50	30.00
90-03-002	Christmas Bells	G. Perillo	Closed	24.50	24.50
Artaffects		**Indian Princess Annual Bell**			
89-04-001	The Little Princess	G. Perillo	Closed	24.50	30.00
90-04-002	Little Madonna	G. Perillo	Closed	24.50	24.50
Artists of the World		**DeGrazia Bells**			
80-01-001	Los Ninos	T. DeGrazia	7,500	40.00	95.00
80-01-002	Festival of Lights	T. DeGrazia	5,000	40.00	85.00
Band Creations		**Celebrations**			
94-01-001	Deck the Halls, Christmas SC62026	T. Rubel	Open	15.00	15.00
94-01-002	L'Amour, Valentine's Day SC62027	T. Rubel	Open	15.00	15.00
94-01-003	Lucky Lady, St. Patrick's Day SC62028	T. Rubel	Open	15.00	15.00
94-01-004	My Someone Special, Mother's Day SC62029	T. Rubel	Open	15.00	15.00
94-01-005	Always on the Ball, Father's Day SC62030	T. Rubel	Open	15.00	15.00
94-01-006	Hop To It, Easter SC62031	T. Rubel	Open	15.00	15.00
94-01-007	It's Only Me, Halloween SC62032	T. Rubel	Open	15.00	15.00
94-01-008	Bountiful Bear, Thanksgiving SC62033	T. Rubel	Open	15.00	15.00
94-01-009	With Honors, Graduation SC62034	T. Rubel	Open	15.00	15.00
94-01-010	Best Friends, First Date SC62035	T. Rubel	Open	15.00	15.00
94-01-011	Happy Days, Anniversary SC62036	T. Rubel	Open	15.00	15.00
94-01-012	Another Year, Birthday SC62037	T. Rubel	Open	15.00	15.00
Band Creations		**Christmas Animals**			
94-02-001	Horse SC22029	T. Rubel	Open	6.00	6.00
94-02-002	Bear SC22030	T. Rubel	Open	6.00	6.00
94-02-003	Elephant SC22031	T. Rubel	Open	6.00	6.00
94-02-004	Dalmation SC22032	T. Rubel	Open	6.00	6.00
94-02-005	Rabbit SC22033	T. Rubel	Open	6.00	6.00
94-02-006	Moose SC22034	T. Rubel	Open	6.00	6.00
Belleek		**Belleek Bells**			
88-01-001	Bell, 1st Edition	Belleek	Yr.Iss.	38.00	38.00
89-01-002	Tower, 2nd Edition	Belleek	Yr.Iss.	35.00	35.00
90-01-003	Leprechaun, 3rd Edition	Belleek	Yr.Iss.	30.00	30.00
91-01-004	Church, 4th Edition	Belleek	Yr.Iss.	32.00	32.00
92-01-005	Cottage, 5th Edition	Belleek	Yr.Iss.	30.00	30.00
93-01-006	Pub, 6th Edition	Belleek	Yr.Iss.	30.00	30.00
Belleek		**Twelve Days of Christmas**			
91-02-001	A Partridge in a Pear Tree	Belleek	Yr.Iss.	30.00	30.00
92-02-002	Two Turtle Doves	Belleek	Yr.Iss.	30.00	30.00
93-02-003	Three French Hens	Belleek	Yr.Iss.	30.00	30.00
94-02-004	Four Calling Birds	Belleek	Yr.Iss.	30.00	30.00
Bing & Grondahl		**Annual Christmas Bell**			
80-01-001	Christmas in the Woods	H. Thelander	Yr.Iss.	39.50	39.50
81-01-002	Christmas Peace	H. Thelander	Yr.Iss.	42.50	42.50
82-01-003	The Christmas Tree	H. Thelander	Yr.Iss.	45.00	45.00
83-01-004	Christmas in the Old Town	E. Jensen	Yr.Iss.	45.00	45.00
84-01-005	The Christmas Letter	E. Jensen	Yr.Iss.	45.00	45.00
85-01-006	Christmas Eve at the Farmhouse	E. Jensen	Yr.Iss.	45.00	45.00
86-01-007	Silent Night, Holy Night	E. Jensen	Yr.Iss.	45.00	45.00
87-01-008	The Snowman's Christmas Eve	E. Jensen	Yr.Iss.	47.50	47.50
88-01-009	The Old Poet's Christmas	E. Jensen	Yr.Iss.	49.50	49.50
89-01-010	Christmas Anchorage	E. Jensen	Yr.Iss.	52.00	52.00
90-01-011	Changing of the Guards	E. Jensen	Yr.Iss.	55.00	55.00
91-01-012	The Copenhagen Stock Exchange at Christmas	E. Jensen	Yr.Iss.	59.50	59.50
92-01-013	Christmas At the Rectory	J. Steensen	Yr.Iss.	62.50	62.50
93-01-014	Father Christmas in Copenhagen	J. Steensen	Yr.Iss.	62.50	62.50
94-01-015	A Day At The Deer Park	J. Nielsen	Yr.Iss.	62.50	62.50
Bing & Grondahl		**Christmas in America Bell**			
88-02-001	Christmas Eve in Williamsburg	J. Woodson	Yr.Iss.	27.50	100.00
89-02-002	Christmas Eve at the White House	J. Woodson	Yr.Iss.	29.00	75.00
90-02-003	Christmas Eve at the Capitol	J. Woodson	Yr.Iss.	30.00	30.00
91-02-004	Independence Hall	J. Woodson	Yr.Iss.	35.00	35.00
92-02-005	Christmas in San Francisco	J. Woodson	Yr.Iss.	37.50	37.50
93-02-006	Coming Home For Christmas	J. Woodson	Yr.Iss.	37.50	37.50
94-02-007	Christmas Eve in Alaska	J. Woodson	Yr.Iss.	37.50	37.50
C.U.I./Carolina Collection/Dram Tree		**Sterling Classic**			
91-01-001	Small Tortoiseshell	J. Harris	10,000	100.00	100.00
91-01-002	Swallowtail	J. Harris	10,000	100.00	100.00
91-01-003	Camberwell Beauty	J. Harris	10,000	100.00	100.00
91-01-004	Large Blue	J. Harris	10,000	100.00	100.00
91-01-005	Peacock	J. Harris	10,000	100.00	100.00
91-01-006	Clouded Yellow	J. Harris	10,000	100.00	100.00
91-01-007	Mouse	J. Harris	10,000	100.00	100.00
91-01-008	Kingfisher	J. Harris	10,000	100.00	100.00
91-01-009	Barn Owl	J. Harris	10,000	100.00	100.00
Enesco Corporation		**Precious Moments Annual Bells**			
83-01-001	Surrounded With Joy-E-0522	S. Butcher	Retrd.	18.00	54-75.00
82-01-002	I'll Play My Drum for Him-E-2358	S. Butcher	Retrd.	17.00	60-85.00
84-01-003	Wishing You a Merry Christmas-E-5393	S. Butcher	Retrd.	19.00	41-55.00
81-01-004	Let the Heavens Rejoice-E-5622	S. Butcher	Retrd.	15.00	165-180.
85-01-005	God Sent His Love-15873	S. Butcher	Retrd.	19.00	38-43.00
86-01-006	Wishing You a Cozy Christmas-102318	S. Butcher	Retrd.	20.00	40.00
87-01-007	Love is the Best Gift of All-109835	S. Butcher	Retrd.	22.50	30-44.00
88-01-008	Time To Wish You a Merry Christmas-115304	S. Butcher	Retrd.	25.00	40-45.00
89-01-009	Oh Holy Night-522821	S. Butcher	Retrd.	25.00	39-45.00
90-01-010	Once Upon A Holy Night-523828	S. Butcher	Retrd.	25.00	30-35.00
91-01-011	May Your Christmas Be Merry-524182	S. Butcher	Retrd.	25.00	39.00
92-01-012	But The Greatest Of These Is Love-527726	S. Butcher	Retrd.	25.00	25-35.00
93-01-013	Wishing You The Sweetest Christmas -530174	S. Butcher	Yr.Iss.	25.00	25.00
Enesco Corporation		**Precious Moments Various Bells**			
81-02-001	Jesus Loves Me-E-5208	S. Butcher	Suspd.	15.00	40-50.00
81-02-002	Jesus Loves Me-E-5209	S. Butcher	Suspd.	15.00	40-60.00
81-02-003	Prayer Changes Things-E-5210	S. Butcher	Suspd.	15.00	40-60.00
81-02-004	God Understands-E-5211	S. Butcher	Retrd.	15.00	55-75.00
81-02-005	We Have Seen His Star-E-5620	S. Butcher	Suspd.	15.00	40-50.00
81-02-006	Jesus Is Born-E-5623	S. Butcher	Suspd.	15.00	40-55.00
82-02-007	The Lord Bless You and Keep You-E-7175	S. Butcher	Suspd.	17.00	35-38.00
82-02-008	The Lord Bless You and Keep You-E-7176	S. Butcher	Suspd.	17.00	40-55.00
82-02-009	The Lord Bless You and Keep You- E-7179	S. Butcher	Suspd.	22.50	34-59.00
82-02-010	Mother Sew Dear-E-7181	S. Butcher	Suspd.	17.00	35-50.00
82-02-011	The Purr-fect Grandma-E-7183	S. Butcher	Suspd.	17.00	35-54.00
Enesco Corporation		**Memories of Yesterday Bell**			
94-03-001	Time For Bed-525243	M. Attwell	Open	25.00	25.00
Enesco/Hamilton Gifts Ltd.		**Bells**			
92-01-001	Susanna 999377	M. Humphrey	Open	22.50	22.50
92-01-002	Sarah 999385	M. Humphrey	Open	22.50	22.50
92-01-003	Hollies For You 996095	M. Humphrey	Open	22.50	22.50
Fenton Art Glass Company		**Connoisseur Bell Collection**			
83-01-001	Bell, Burmese Handpainted	Fenton	Closed	50.00	50.00
83-01-002	Craftsman Bell, White Satin Carnival	Fenton	Closed	25.00	25.00
84-01-003	Bell, Famous Women's Ruby Satin Irid.	Fenton	Closed	25.00	25.00
85-01-004	Bell, 6 1/2" Burmese, Handpainted	Fenton	Closed	55.00	55.00
86-01-005	Bell, Burmese-Shells	Fenton	Closed	60.00	60.00
88-01-006	Bell, 7" Wisteria	Fenton	Closed	45.00	45.00
89-01-007	Bell, Handpainted Rosalene Satin	Fenton	Closed	50.00	50.00
91-01-008	Bell, 7" Roses on Rosalene	Fenton	Closed	50.00	50.00
Fitz and Floyd, Inc.		**Annual Christmas Bell**			
94-01-001	Night Before Christmas	V. Balcou	Yr.Iss.	25.00	25.00
Fitz and Floyd, Inc.		**Heirloom Collection**			
94-02-001	Reindeer	R. Havins	Yr.Iss.	25.00	25.00
Goebel/Schmid		**M.I. Hummel Collectibles Annual Bells**			
78-01-001	Let's Sing 700	M. I. Hummel	Closed	50.00	45-150.00
79-01-002	Farewell 701	M. I. Hummel	Closed	70.00	25-165.00
80-01-003	Thoughtful 702	M. I. Hummel	Closed	85.00	28-85.00
81-01-004	In Tune 703	M. I. Hummel	Closed	85.00	35-85.00
82-01-005	She Loves Me, She Loves Me Not 704	M. I. Hummel	Closed	90.00	75-150.00
83-01-006	Knit One 705	M. I. Hummel	Closed	90.00	58-105.00
84-01-007	Mountaineer 706	M. I. Hummel	Closed	90.00	78-96.00
85-01-008	Sweet Song 707	M. I. Hummel	Closed	90.00	72-90.00
86-01-009	Sing Along 708	M. I. Hummel	Closed	100.00	72-108.00
87-01-010	With Loving Greetings 709	M. I. Hummel	Closed	110.00	144.00
88-01-011	Busy Student 710	M. I. Hummel	Closed	120.00	72-120.00
89-01-012	Latest News 711	M. I. Hummel	Closed	135.00	72-135.00
90-01-013	What's New? 712	M. I. Hummel	Closed	140.00	140-200.
91-01-014	Favorite Pet 713	M. I. Hummel	Closed	150.00	165-200.
92-01-015	Whistler's Duet 714	M. I. Hummel	Closed	160.00	149-160.00
Gorham		**Various**			
75-01-001	Sweet Song So Young	N. Rockwell	Annual	19.50	50.00
75-01-002	Santa's Helpers	N. Rockwell	Annual	19.50	30.00
75-01-003	Tavern Sign Painter	N. Rockwell	Annual	19.50	30.00
76-01-004	Flowers in Tender Bloom	N. Rockwell	Annual	19.50	40.00
76-01-005	Snow Sculpture	N. Rockwell	Annual	19.50	45.00
77-01-006	Fondly Do We Remember	N. Rockwell	Annual	19.50	55.00
77-01-007	Chilling Chore (Christmas)	N. Rockwell	Annual	19.50	35.00
78-01-008	Gaily Sharing Vintage Times	N. Rockwell	Annual	22.50	22.50
78-01-009	Gay Blades (Christmas)	N. Rockwell	Annual	22.50	22.50
79-01-010	Beguiling Buttercup	N. Rockwell	Annual	24.50	26.50
79-01-011	A Boy Meets His Dog (Christmas)	N. Rockwell	Annual	24.50	30.00
80-01-012	Flying High	N. Rockwell	Annual	27.50	27.50
80-01-013	Chilly Reception (Christmas)	N. Rockwell	Annual	27.50	27.50
81-01-014	Sweet Serenade	N. Rockwell	Annual	27.50	27.50
81-01-015	Ski Skills (Christmas)	N. Rockwell	Annual	27.50	27.50
82-01-016	Young Mans Fancy	N. Rockwell	Annual	29.50	29.50
82-01-017	Coal Season's Coming	N. Rockwell	Annual	29.50	29.50
83-01-018	Christmas Medley	N. Rockwell	Annual	29.50	29.50
83-01-019	The Milkmaid	N. Rockwell	Annual	29.50	29.50
84-01-020	Tiny Tim	N. Rockwell	Annual	29.50	29.50
84-01-021	Young Love	N. Rockwell	Annual	29.50	29.50
84-01-022	Marriage License	N. Rockwell	Annual	32.50	32.50
84-01-023	Yarn Spinner	N. Rockwell	5,000	32.50	32.50
85-01-024	Yuletide Reflections	N. Rockwell	5,000	32.50	32.50
86-01-025	Home For The Holidays	N. Rockwell	5,000	32.50	32.50
86-01-026	On Top of the World	N. Rockwell	5,000	32.50	32.50
87-01-027	Merry Christmas Grandma	N. Rockwell	5,000	32.50	32.50
87-01-028	The Artist	N. Rockwell	5,000	32.50	32.50
88-01-029	The Homecoming	N. Rockwell	15,000	37.50	37.50

BELLS

Number	Name	Artist	Edition Limit	Issue Price	Quote
Gorham		**Currier & Ives - Mini Bells**			
76-02-001	Christmas Sleigh Ride	Currier & Ives	Annual	9.95	35.00
77-02-002	American Homestead	Currier & Ives	Annual	9.95	25.00
78-02-003	Yule Logs	Currier & Ives	Annual	12.95	20.00
79-02-004	Sleigh Ride	Currier & Ives	Annual	14.95	20.00
80-02-005	Christmas in the Country	Currier & Ives	Annual	14.95	20.00
81-02-006	Christmas Tree	Currier & Ives	Annual	14.95	17.50
82-02-007	Christmas Visitation	Currier & Ives	Annual	16.50	17.50
83-02-008	Winter Wonderland	Currier & Ives	Annual	16.50	17.50
84-02-009	Hitching Up	Currier & Ives	Annual	16.50	17.50
85-02-010	Skaters Holiday	Currier & Ives	Annual	17.50	17.50
86-02-011	Central Park in Winter	Currier & Ives	Annual	17.50	17.50
87-02-012	Early Winter	Currier & Ives	Annual	19.00	19.00
Gorham		**Mini Bells**			
81-03-001	Tiny Tim	N. Rockwell	Annual	19.75	19.75
82-03-002	Planning Christmas Visit	N. Rockwell	Annual	20.00	20.00
Dave Grossman Designs		**Norman Rockwell Collection**			
75-01-001	Faces of Christmas NRB-75	Rockwell-Inspired	Retrd.	12.50	35.00
76-01-002	Drum for Tommy NRB-76	Rockwell-Inspired	Retrd.	12.00	30.00
76-01-003	Ben Franklin (Bicentennial)	Rockwell-Inspired	Retrd.	12.50	25.00
80-01-004	Leapfrog NRB-80	Rockwell-Inspired	Retrd.	50.00	60.00
Hallmark Galleries		**Enchanted Garden**			
92-01-001	Fairy Bunny (porcelain)	E. Richardson	9,500	35.00	35.00
Kirk Stieff		**Musical Bells**			
77-01-001	Annual Bell 1977	Kirk Stieff	Closed	17.95	40-120.00
78-01-002	Annual Bell 1978	Kirk Stieff	Closed	17.95	75.00
79-01-003	Annual Bell 1979	Kirk Stieff	Closed	17.95	50.00
80-01-004	Annual Bell 1980	Kirk Stieff	Closed	19.95	50.00
81-01-005	Annual Bell 1981	Kirk Stieff	Closed	19.95	60.00
82-01-006	Annual Bell 1982	Kirk Stieff	Closed	19.95	60-120.00
83-01-007	Annual Bell 1983	Kirk Stieff	Closed	19.95	50-60.00
84-01-008	Annual Bell 1984	Kirk Stieff	Closed	19.95	40.00
85-01-009	Annual Bell 1985	Kirk Stieff	Closed	19.95	40.00
86-01-010	Annual Bell 1986	Kirk Stieff	Closed	19.95	40-50.00
87-01-011	Annual Bell 1987	Kirk Stieff	Closed	19.95	30.00
88-01-012	Annual Bell 1988	Kirk Stieff	Closed	22.50	35-45.00
89-01-013	Annual Bell 1989	Kirk Stieff	Closed	25.00	25.00
90-01-014	Annual Bell 1990	Kirk Stieff	Closed	27.00	27.00
91-01-015	Annual Bell 1991	Kirk Stieff	Closed	28.00	28.00
92-01-016	Annual Bell 1992	Kirk Stieff	Closed	30.00	30.00
93-01-017	Annual Bell 1993	Kirk Stieff	Open	30.00	30.00
Kirk Stieff		**Bell**			
92-02-001	Santa's Workshop Christmas Bell	Kirk Stieff	3,000	40.00	40.00
93-02-002	Santa's Reindeer Bell	Kirk Stieff	Open	30.00	30.00
Lance Corporation		**Hudson Pewter Bicentennial Bells**			
74-01-001	Benjamin Franklin	P.W. Baston	Closed	Unkn.	75-100.00
74-01-002	Thomas Jefferson	P.W. Baston	Closed	Unkn.	75-100.00
74-01-003	George Washington	P.W. Baston	Closed	Unkn.	75-100.00
74-01-004	John Adams	P.W. Baston	Closed	Unkn.	75-100.00
74-01-005	James Madison	P.W. Baston	Closed	Unkn.	75-100.00
Lenox China		**Songs of Christmas**			
91-01-001	We Wish You a Merry Christmas	Unknown	Yr.Iss.	49.00	49.00
92-01-002	Deck the Halls	Unknown	Yr.Iss.	49.00	49.00
93-01-003	Jingle Bells	Unknown	Yr.Iss.	57.00	57.00
Lenox Collections		**Crystal Christmas Bell**			
81-01-001	Partridge in a Pear Tree	Lenox	15,000	55.00	55.00
82-01-002	Holy Family Bell	Lenox	15,000	55.00	55.00
83-01-003	Three Wise Men	Lenox	15,000	55.00	55.00
84-01-004	Dove Bell	Lenox	15,000	57.00	57.00
85-01-005	Santa Claus Bell	Lenox	15,000	57.00	57.00
86-01-006	Dashing Through the Snow Bell	Lenox	15,000	64.00	64.00
87-01-007	Heralding Angel Bell	Lenox	15,000	76.00	76.00
91-01-008	Celestial Harpist	Lenox	15,000	75.00	75.00
Lenox Collections		**Bird Bells**			
91-02-001	Bluebird	Unknown	Open	57.00	57.00
91-02-002	Hummingbird	Unknown	Open	57.00	57.00
91-02-003	Chickadee	Unknown	Open	57.00	57.00
92-02-004	Robin Bell	Unknown	Open	57.00	57.00
Lenox Collections		**Carousel Bell**			
92-03-001	Carousel Horse	Unknown	Open	45.00	45.00
Lladro		**Lladro Christmas Bell**			
87-01-001	Christmas Bell - L5458M	Lladro	Annual	29.50	41-175.00
88-01-002	Christmas Bell - L5525M	Lladro	Annual	32.50	23-97.00
89-01-003	Christmas Bell - L5616M	Lladro	Annual	32.50	70-95.00
90-01-004	Christmas Bell - L5641M	Lladro	Annual	35.00	30-70.00
91-01-005	Christmas Bell - L5803M	Lladro	Annual	37.50	37.50-70.00
92-01-006	Christmas Bell - L5913M	Lladro	Annual	37.50	40-70.00
93-01-007	Christmas Bell - L6010M	Lladro	Annual	37.50	40-70.00
94-01-008	Christmas Bell - L7542M	Lladro	Annual	39.50	40.00
Midwest of Cannon Falls		**The Littlest Angel Collection**			
94-01-001	Angel with Wreath Bell 11632-6	Midwest	Open	12.50	12.50
Old World Christmas		**Porcelain Christmas**			
88-01-001	First Edition Santa Bell	E.M. Merck	Retrd.	10.00	10.00
89-01-002	Second Edition Santa Bell	E.M. Merck	Retrd.	10.00	10.00
Reco International		**Special Occasions**			
89-01-001	The Wedding	S. Kuck	Open	15.00	15.00
Reco International		**Special Occasions-Wedding**			
91-02-001	From This Day Forward	C. Micarelli	Open	15.00	15.00
91-02-002	To Have And To Hold	C. Micarelli	Open	15.00	15.00
Reed & Barton		**Noel Musical Bells**			
80-01-001	1980 Bell	Reed & Barton	Closed	20.00	50.00
81-01-002	1981 Bell	Reed & Barton	Closed	22.50	45.00
82-01-003	1982 Bell	Reed & Barton	Closed	22.50	40.00
83-01-004	1983 Bell	Reed & Barton	Closed	22.50	45.00
84-01-005	1984 Bell	Reed & Barton	Closed	22.50	50.00
85-01-006	1985 Bell	Reed & Barton	Closed	25.00	40.00
86-01-007	1986 Bell	Reed & Barton	Closed	25.00	35-45.00
87-01-008	1987 Bell	Reed & Barton	Closed	25.00	30-45.00
88-01-009	1988 Bell	Reed & Barton	Closed	25.00	27.50-40.00
89-01-010	1989 Bell	Reed & Barton	Closed	25.00	27.50
90-01-011	1990 Bell	Reed & Barton	Closed	27.50	30.00
91-01-012	1991 Bell	Reed & Barton	Closed	30.00	30.00
92-01-013	1992 Bell	Reed & Barton	Closed	30.00	30.00
93-01-014	1993 Bell	Reed & Barton	Yr.Iss.	30.00	30.00
94-01-015	1994 Bell	Reed & Barton	Yr.Iss.	30.00	30.00
Reed & Barton		**Yuletide Bell**			
81-02-001	Yuletide Holiday	Reed & Barton	Closed	14.00	14.00
82-02-002	Little Shepherd	Reed & Barton	Closed	14.00	14.00
83-02-003	Perfect Angel	Reed & Barton	Closed	15.00	15.00
84-02-004	Drummer Boy	Reed & Barton	Closed	15.00	15.00
85-02-005	Caroler	Reed & Barton	Closed	16.50	16.50
86-02-006	Night Before Christmas	Reed & Barton	Closed	16.50	16.50
87-02-007	Jolly St. Nick	Reed & Barton	Closed	16.50	16.50
88-02-008	Christmas Morning	Reed & Barton	Closed	16.50	16.50
89-02-009	The Bell Ringer	Reed & Barton	Closed	16.50	16.50
90-02-010	The Wreath Bearer	Reed & Barton	Closed	18.50	18.50
91-02-011	A Special Gift	Reed & Barton	Closed	22.50	22.50
92-02-012	My Special Friend	Reed & Barton	Closed	22.50	22.50
93-02-013	My Christmas Present	Reed & Barton	Yr.Iss.	22.50	22.50
94-02-014	1994 Yuletide Bell	Reed & Barton	Yr.Iss.	22.50	22.50
River Shore		**Rockwell Children Series I**			
77-01-001	School Play	N. Rockwell	7,500	30.00	75.00
77-01-002	First Day of School	N. Rockwell	7,500	30.00	75.00
77-01-003	Football Hero	N. Rockwell	7,500	30.00	75.00
77-01-004	Flowers for Mother	N. Rockwell	7,500	30.00	60.00
River Shore		**Rockwell Children Series II**			
78-02-001	Dressing Up	N. Rockwell	15,000	35.00	50.00
78-02-002	Future All American	N. Rockwell	15,000	35.00	52.00
78-02-003	Garden Girl	N. Rockwell	15,000	35.00	40.00
78-02-004	Five Cents A Glass	N. Rockwell	15,000	35.00	40.00
River Shore		**Norman Rockwell Single Issues**			
81-03-001	Looking Out to Sea	N. Rockwell	7,000	45.00	95.00
81-03-002	Spring Flowers	N. Rockwell	347	175.00	175.00
81-03-003	Grandpa's Guardian	N. Rockwell	7,000	45.00	45.00
Roman, Inc.		**The Masterpiece Collection**			
79-01-001	Adoration	F. Lippe	Open	20.00	20.00
80-01-002	Madonna with Grapes	P. Mignard	Open	25.00	25.00
81-01-003	The Holy Family	G. Notti	Open	25.00	25.00
82-01-004	Madonna of the Streets	R. Ferruzzi	Open	25.00	25.00
Roman, Inc.		**F. Hook Bells**			
85-02-001	Beach Buddies	F. Hook	15,000	25.00	27.50
86-02-002	Sounds of the Sea	F. Hook	15,000	25.00	27.50
87-02-003	Bear Hug	F. Hook	15,000	25.00	27.50
Roman, Inc.		**Annual Fontanini Christmas Crystal Bell**			
91-03-001	1991 Bell	E. Simonetti	Closed	30.00	30.00
92-03-002	1992 Bell	E. Simonetti	Closed	30.00	30.00
93-03-003	1993 Bell	E. Simonetti	Yr.Iss.	30.00	30.00
Roman, Inc.		**Annual Nativity Bell**			
90-04-001	Nativity	I. Spencer	Closed	15.00	15.00
91-04-002	Flight Into Egypt	I. Spencer	Closed	15.00	15.00
92-04-003	Gloria in Excelsis Deo	I. Spencer	Closed	15.00	15.00
93-04-004	Three Kings of Orient	I. Spencer	Yr.Iss.	15.00	15.00
Royal Copenhagen		**Christmas**			
92-01-001	The Queen's Carriage	S. Vestergaard	Closed	69.50	69.50
93-01-002	Christmas Guests	S. Vestergaard	Yr.Iss.	62.50	62.50
94-01-003	Christmas Shopping	S. Vestergaard	Yr.Iss.	62.50	62.50
Schmid		**Berta Hummel Christmas Bells**			
72-01-001	Angel with Flute	B. Hummel	Yr.Iss.	20.00	75.00
73-01-002	Nativity	B. Hummel	Yr.Iss.	15.00	80.00
74-01-003	The Guardian Angel	B. Hummel	Yr.Iss.	17.50	45.00
75-01-004	The Christmas Child	B. Hummel	Yr.Iss.	22.50	45.00
76-01-005	Sacred Journey	B. Hummel	Yr.Iss.	22.50	25.00
77-01-006	Herald Angel	B. Hummel	Yr.Iss.	22.50	50.00
78-01-007	Heavenly Trio	B. Hummel	Yr.Iss.	27.50	40.00
79-01-008	Starlight Angel	B. Hummel	Yr.Iss.	38.00	45.00
80-01-009	Parade into Toyland	B. Hummel	Yr.Iss.	45.00	55.00
81-01-010	A Time to Remember	B. Hummel	Yr.Iss.	45.00	55.00
82-01-011	Angelic Procession	B. Hummel	Yr.Iss.	45.00	50.00
83-01-012	Angelic Messenger	B. Hummel	Yr.Iss.	45.00	55.00
84-01-013	A Gift from Heaven	B. Hummel	Yr.Iss.	45.00	75.00
85-01-014	Heavenly Light	B. Hummel	Yr.Iss.	45.00	75.00
86-01-015	Tell the Heavens	B. Hummel	Yr.Iss.	45.00	45.00
87-01-016	Angelic Gifts	B. Hummel	Yr.Iss.	47.50	47.50
88-01-017	Cheerful Cherubs	B. Hummel	Yr.Iss.	52.50	55.00
89-01-018	Angelic Musician	B. Hummel	Yr.Iss.	53.00	55.00
90-01-019	Angel's Light	B. Hummel	Yr.Iss.	53.00	53.00
91-01-020	Message From Above	B. Hummel	5,000	58.00	58.00
92-01-021	Sweet Blessings	B. Hummel	5,000	65.00	65.00
93-01-022	Silent Wonder	B. Hummel	5,000	58.00	58.00
Schmid		**Berta Hummel Mother's Day Bells**			
76-02-001	Devotion for Mothers	B. Hummel	Yr.Iss.	22.50	55.00
77-02-002	Moonlight Return	B. Hummel	Yr.Iss.	22.50	45.00
78-02-003	Afternoon Stroll	B. Hummel	Yr.Iss.	27.50	45.00
79-02-004	Cherub's Gift	B. Hummel	Yr.Iss.	38.00	45.00
80-02-005	Mother's Little Helper	B. Hummel	Yr.Iss.	45.00	45.00
81-02-006	Playtime	B. Hummel	Yr.Iss.	45.00	45.00
82-02-007	The Flower Basket	B. Hummel	Yr.Iss.	45.00	45.00
83-02-008	Spring Bouquet	B. Hummel	Yr.Iss.	45.00	45.00
84-02-009	A Joy to Share	B. Hummel	Yr.Iss.	45.00	45.00
Schmid		**The Littlest Light**			
93-03-001	The Littlest Light	B. Hummel	Open	15.00	15.00
Schmid		**Peanuts Annual Bells**			
79-04-001	A Special Letter	C. Schulz	10,000	15.00	25.00
80-04-002	Waiting For Santa	C. Schulz	10,000	15.00	25.00
81-04-003	Mission For Mom	C. Schulz	10,000	17.50	20.00
82-04-004	Perfect Performance	C. Schulz	10,000	18.50	18.50
83-04-005	Peanuts in Concert	C. Schulz	10,000	12.50	12.50
84-04-006	Snoopy and the Beagle Scouts	C. Schulz	10,000	12.50	12.50

BELLS/CHRISTMAS ORNAMENTS

Company / Number	Name	Series / Artist	Edition Limit	Issue Price	Quote
Schmid		**Peanuts Christmas Bells**			
75-05-001	Woodstock, Santa Claus	C. Schulz	Yr.Iss.	10.00	25.00
76-05-002	Woodstock's Christmas	C. Schulz	Yr.Iss.	10.00	25.00
77-05-003	Deck the Doghouse	C. Schulz	Yr.Iss.	10.00	20.00
78-05-004	Filling the Stocking	C. Schulz	Yr.Iss.	13.00	15.00
Schmid		**Peanuts Mother's Day Bells**			
73-06-001	Mom?	C. Schulz	Yr.Iss.	5.00	15.00
74-06-002	Snoopy/Woodstock/Parade	C. Schulz	Yr.Iss.	5.00	15.00
76-06-003	Linus and Snoopy	C. Schulz	Yr.Iss.	10.00	15.00
77-06-004	Dear Mom	C. Schulz	Yr.Iss.	10.00	15.00
78-06-005	Thoughts That Count	C. Schulz	Yr.Iss.	13.00	15.00
Schmid		**Peanuts Special Edition Bell**			
76-07-001	Bi-Centennial	C. Schulz	Yr.Iss.	10.00	20.00
Schmid		**Disney Annuals**			
85-08-001	Snow Biz	Disney Studios	10,000	16.50	16.50
86-08-002	Tree for Two	Disney Studios	10,000	16.50	16.50
87-08-003	Merry Mouse Medley	Disney Studios	10,000	17.50	17.50
88-08-004	Warm Winter Ride	Disney Studios	10,000	19.50	19.50
89-08-005	Merry Mickey Claus	Disney Studios	10,000	23.00	23.00
90-08-006	Holly Jolly Christmas	Disney Studios	10,000	26.50	26.50
91-08-007	Mickey & Minnie's Rockin' Christmas	Disney Studios	10,000	26.50	26.50
Schmid		**Lowell Davis Mini Bell**			
92-09-001	New Day	L. Davis	Yr.Iss.	10.00	10.00
Schmid/B.F.A.		**RFD Bell**			
79-01-001	Blossom	L. Davis	Closed	65.00	300-400.
79-01-002	Kate	L. Davis	Closed	65.00	300-400.
79-01-003	Willy	L. Davis	Closed	65.00	400.00
79-01-004	Caruso	L. Davis	Closed	65.00	300.00
79-01-005	Wilbur	L. Davis	Closed	65.00	300-350.
79-01-006	Old Blue Lead	L. Davis	Closed	65.00	275-300.
80-01-007	Cow Bell "Blossom"	L. Davis	Open	65.00	65.00
80-01-008	Mule Bell "Kate"	L. Davis	Open	65.00	65.00
80-01-009	Goat Bell "Willy"	L. Davis	Open	65.00	65.00
80-01-010	Rooster Bell "Caruso"	L. Davis	Open	65.00	65.00
80-01-011	Pig Bell "Wilbur"	L. Davis	Open	65.00	65.00
80-01-012	Dog Bell "Old Blue and Lead"	L. Davis	Open	65.00	65.00

CHRISTMAS ORNAMENTS

Company / Number	Name	Series / Artist	Edition Limit	Issue Price	Quote
Kurt S. Adler Inc.		**Fabriché™ Ornament Series**			
92-01-001	Hugs And Kisses W1560	KS. Adler	Open	22.00	22.00
92-01-002	Hello Little One! W1561	KS. Adler	Open	22.00	22.00
92-01-003	Not a Creature Was Stirring W1563	KS. Adler	Open	22.00	22.00
92-01-004	Merry Chrismouse W1565	KS. Adler	Open	10.00	10.00
92-01-005	Christmas in the Air W1593	KS. Adler	Open	35.50	35.50
92-01-006	An Apron Full of Love W1594	M. Rothenberg	Open	27.00	27.00
93-01-007	Master Toymaker W1595	KS. Adler	Open	27.00	27.00
93-01-008	Homeward Bound W1596	KS. Adler	Open	27.00	27.00
93-01-009	Par For the Claus W1625	KS. Adler	Open	27.00	27.00
93-01-010	Santa With List W1510	KS. Adler	Open	20.00	20.00
94-01-011	Cookies For Santa W1639	KS. Adler	Open	28.00	28.00
94-01-012	All Star Santa W1665	KS. Adler	Open	27.00	27.00
94-01-011	Santa's Fishtales W1666	KS. Adler	Open	29.00	29.00
94-01-012	Firefighting Friends W1668	KS. Adler	Open	28.00	28.00
94-01-013	Checking His List W1634	KS. Adler	Open	23.50	23.50
94-01-014	Holiday Flight W1637	Smithsonian	Open	45.00	45.00
Kurt S. Adler Inc.		**Smithsonian Museum Fabriché™ Ornament Series**			
92-02-001	Holiday Drive W1580	KSA/Smithsonian	Open	38.00	38.00
92-02-002	Santa On a Bicycle W1547	KSA/Smithsonian	Open	31.00	31.00
Kurt S. Adler Inc.		**Steinbach Ornament Series**			
92-03-001	The King's Guards ES300	KS. Adler	Retrd.	27.00	27.00
Kurt S. Adler Inc.		**Christmas in Chelsea Collection**			
92-04-001	Allison Sitting in Chair W2812	J. Mostrom	Open	25.50	25.50
92-04-002	Christina W2812	J. Mostrom	Open	25.50	25.50
92-04-003	Holly W2709	J. Mostrom	Open	21.00	21.00
92-04-004	Christopher W2709	J. Mostrom	Open	21.00	21.00
92-04-005	Amanda W2709	J. Mostrom	Open	21.00	21.00
92-04-006	Peony W2728	J. Mostrom	Open	20.00	20.00
92-04-007	Delphinium W2728	J. Mostrom	Open	20.00	20.00
92-04-008	Rose W2728	J. Mostrom	Open	20.00	20.00
92-04-009	Holly Hock W2728	J. Mostrom	Open	20.00	20.00
92-04-010	Amy W2729	J. Mostrom	Retrd.	21.00	21.00
92-04-011	Allison W2729	J. Mostrom	Retrd.	21.00	21.00
94-04-012	Alice, Marguerite W2973	J. Mostrom	Open	28.00	28.00
94-04-013	Guardian Angel With Baby W2974	J. Mostrom	Open	31.00	31.00
Kurt S. Adler Inc.		**Royal Heritage Collection**			
93-05-001	Nicholas W2923	J. Mostrom	Open	25.50	25.50
93-05-002	Patina W2923	J. Mostrom	Open	25.50	25.50
93-05-003	Sasha W2923	J. Mostrom	Open	25.50	25.50
93-05-004	Anastasia W2922	J. Mostrom	Open	28.00	28.00
93-05-005	Elizabeth W2924	J. Mostrom	Open	25.50	25.50
93-05-006	Charles W2924	J. Mostrom	Open	25.50	25.50
93-05-007	Caroline W2924	J. Mostrom	Open	25.50	25.50
93-05-008	Joella W2979	J. Mostrom	Retrd.	27.00	27.00
93-05-009	Kelly W2979	J. Mostrom	Retrd.	27.00	27.00
94-05-010	Snow Princess W2971	J. Mostrom	Open	28.00	28.00
94-05-011	Ice Fairy, Winter Fairy W2972	J. Mostrom	Open	25.50	25.50
Kurt S. Adler Inc.		**Cornhusk Mice Ornament Series**			
93-06-001	Nutcracker Suite Fantasy Cornhusk Mice W2885	M. Rothenberg	Open	15.50	15.50
93-06-002	Ballerina Cornhusk Mice W2700	M. Rothenberg	Open	13.50	13.50
94-06-003	Little Pocahontas, Indian Brave W2950	M. Rothenberg	Open	18.00	18.00
94-06-004	Cowboy W2951	M. Rothenberg	Open	18.00	18.00
94-06-005	Drosselmeir Fairy, Mouse King W2949	M. Rothenberg	Open	16.00	16.00
94-06-006	Clara, Prince W2948	M. Rothenberg	Open	16.00	16.00
94-06-007	3" Father Christmas Ornament W2976	M. Rothenberg	Open	18.00	18.00
94-06-008	9" Father Christmas Ornament W2982	M. Rothenberg	Open	25.00	25.00
Kurt S. Adler Inc.		**Smithsonian Museum Carousel Ornament Series**			
87-07-001	The Antique Carousel Goat S3027/1	KSA/Smithsonian	Retrd.	14.50	14.50
87-07-002	The Antique Carousel Bunny S3027/2	KSA/Smithsonian	Retrd.	14.50	14.50
88-07-003	The Antique Carousel Horse S3027/3	KSA/Smithsonian	Retrd.	14.50	14.50
88-07-004	The Antique Carousel Giraffe S3027/4	KSA/Smithsonian	Retrd.	14.50	14.50
89-07-005	The Antique Carousel Lion S3027/5	KSA/Smithsonian	Retrd.	14.50	15.00
89-07-006	The Antique Carousel Cat S3027/6	KSA/Smithsonian	Retrd.	14.50	15.00
90-07-007	The Antique Carousel Zebra S3027/7	KSA/Smithsonian	Open	14.50	15.00
90-07-008	The Antique Carousel Seahorse S3027/8	KSA/Smithsonian	Open	14.50	15.00
91-07-009	The Antique Carousel Rooster S3027/9	KSA/Smithsonian	Retrd.	14.50	15.00
91-07-010	The Antique Carousel Horse S3027/10	KSA/Smithsonian	Open	14.50	15.00
92-07-011	The Antique Carousel Elephant S3027/11	KSA/Smithsonian	Open	14.50	15.00
92-07-012	The Antique Carousel Camel S3027/12	KSA/Smithsonian	Open	15.00	15.00
93-07-013	The Antique Carousel Tiger S3027/13	KSA/Smithsonian	Open	15.00	15.00
93-07-014	The Antique Carousel Horse S3027/14	KSA/Smithsonian	Open	15.00	15.00
94-07-013	The Antique Carousel Reindeer S3027/15	KSA/Smithsonian	Open	15.50	15.50
94-07-014	The Antique Carousel Pig S3027/16	KSA/Smithsonian	Open	15.50	15.50
Kurt S. Adler Inc.		**Little Dickens**			
94-08-001	Little Scrooge in Bathrobe W2959	J. Mostrom	Open	30.00	30.00
94-08-002	Little Scrooge in Overcoat W2960	J. Mostrom	Open	30.00	30.00
94-08-003	Little Bob Crachit W2961	J. Mostrom	Open	30.00	30.00
94-08-004	Little Mrs. Crachit W2962	J. Mostrom	Open	27.00	27.00
94-08-005	Little Tiny Tim W2963	J. Mostrom	Open	22.50	22.50
94-08-006	Little Marley's Ghost W2964	J. Mostrom	Open	33.50	33.50
Kurt S. Adler Inc.		**International Christmas**			
94-09-001	Poland-Marissa, Hedwig W2965	J. Mostrom	Open	27.00	27.00
94-09-002	Scotland-Bonnie, Douglas W2966	J. Mostrom	Open	27.00	27.00
94-09-003	Eskimo-Atom, Ukpik W2967	J. Mostrom	Open	28.00	28.00
94-09-004	Spain-Maria, Miguel W2968	J. Mostrom	Open	27.00	27.00
94-09-005	Germany-Katerina, Hans W2969	J. Mostrom	Open	27.00	27.00
94-09-006	Native American-White Dove, Little Wolf -W2970	J. Mostrom	Open	28.00	28.00
Kurt S. Adler Inc.		**Night Before Christmas**			
94-10-001	Cathy, Johnny	J. Mostrom	Open	24.00	24.00
All God's Children		**Christmas Ornaments**			
87-01-001	Cameo Ornaments (set of 12)- D1912	M. Holcombe	Retrd.	144.00	1200.00
87-01-002	Doll Ornaments (set of 24) - D1924	M. Holcombe	Retrd.	336.00	2000-2400.
93-01-003	Santa with Scooty-1571	M. Holcombe	Open	22.50	22.50
All God's Children		**Angel Dumpling**			
93-02-001	Eric-1570	M. Holcombe	Open	22.50	22.50
Anheuser-Busch, Inc.		**A & Eagle Collector Ornament Series**			
91-01-001	Budweiser Girl-Circa 1890's N3178	A.-Busch, Inc.	Open	15.00	15.00
92-01-002	1893 Columbian Exposition N3649	A.-Busch, Inc.	Open	15.00	15.00
93-01-003	Greatest Triumph N4089	A.-Busch, Inc.	Open	15.00	15.00
Anheuser-Busch, Inc.		**Christmas Ornaments**			
92-02-001	Clydesdales Mini Plate Ornaments N3650 (3 pc. set)	S. Sampson	Open	23.00	23.00
93-02-002	Budweiser Six-Pack Mini Plate Ornaments N4220	M. Urdahl	Open	10.00	10.00
Annalee Mobilitee		**Christmas Ornaments**			
85-01-001	Clown Head	A. Thorndike	5,701	6.95	175.00
92-01-002	3" Skier	A. Thorndike	8,332	14.45	175.00
93-01-003	Pepi Herman Crystal Ornament (artist proof)	A. Thorndike	1	N/A	750.00
93-01-004	Tree Top Star w/ 3" Angel (artist proof)	A. Thorndike	1	N/A	300.00
ANRI		**Ferandiz Message Collection**			
89-01-001	Let the Heavens Ring	J. Ferrandiz	1,000	215.00	215.00
90-01-002	Hear The Angels Sing	J. Ferrandiz	1,000	225.00	225.00
ANRI		**Ferrandiz Woodcarvings**			
88-02-001	Heavenly Drummer	J. Ferrandiz	1,000	175.00	225.00
89-02-002	Heavenly Strings	J. Ferrandiz	1,000	190.00	190.00
ANRI		**Disney Four Star Collection**			
89-03-001	Maestro Mickey	Disney Studios	Yr.Iss.	25.00	25.00
90-03-002	Minnie Mouse	Disney Studios	Yr.Iss.	25.00	25.00
Armani		**Christmas**			
91-01-001	1991 Christmas Ornament 799A	G. Armani	Retrd.	11.50	11.50
92-01-002	1992 Christmas Ornament 788F	G. Armani	Retrd.	23.50	23.50
93-01-003	1993 Christmas Ornament 892P	G. Armani	Retrd.	25.00	25.00
94-01-004	1994 Christmas Ornament 801P	G. Armani	Yr.Iss.	25.00	25.00
Artaffects		**Annual Christmas Ornaments**			
85-01-001	Papoose Ornament	G. Perillo	Unkn.	14.00	65.00
86-01-002	Christmas Cactus	G. Perillo	Unkn.	15.00	50.00
87-01-003	Annual Ornament	G. Perillo	Unkn.	15.00	35.00
88-01-004	Annual Ornament	G. Perillo	Yr.Iss.	17.50	25.00
89-01-005	Annual Ornament	G. Perillo	Yr.Iss.	17.50	25.00
90-01-006	Annual Ornament	G. Perillo	Yr.Iss.	19.50	19.50
91-01-007	Annual Ornament	G. Perillo	Yr.Iss.	19.50	19.50
Artaffects		**Annual Bell Ornaments**			
85-02-001	Home Sweet Wigwam	G. Perillo	Yr.Iss.	14.00	14.00
86-02-002	Peek-A-Boo	G. Perillo	Yr.Iss.	15.00	15.00
87-02-003	Annual Bell Ornament	G. Perillo	Yr.Iss.	15.00	15.00
88-02-004	Annual Bell Ornament	G. Perillo	Yr.Iss.	17.50	17.50
89-02-005	Annual Bell Ornament	G. Perillo	Yr.Iss.	17.50	17.50
90-02-006	Annual Bell Ornament	G. Perillo	Yr.Iss.	17.50	17.50
91-02-007	Annual Bell Ornament	G. Perillo	Yr.Iss.	19.50	19.50
Artaffects		**Sagebrush Kids Bell Ornaments**			
87-03-001	The Fiddler	G. Perillo	Open	9.00	9.00
87-03-002	The Harpist	G. Perillo	Open	9.00	9.00
87-03-003	Christmas Horn	G. Perillo	Open	9.00	9.00
87-03-004	The Gift	G. Perillo	Open	9.00	9.00
87-03-005	Christmas Candle	G. Perillo	Open	9.00	9.00
87-03-006	The Carolers	G. Perillo	Open	9.00	9.00
Artaffects		**Kachina Ornaments**			
91-04-001	Sun Kachina	G. Perillo	Open	17.50	17.50
91-04-002	Old Kachina	G. Perillo	Open	17.50	17.50
91-04-003	Snow Kachina	G. Perillo	Open	17.50	17.50
91-04-004	Dawn Kachina	G. Perillo	Open	17.50	17.50
91-04-005	Kachina Mother	G. Perillo	Open	17.50	17.50
91-04-006	Totem Kachina	G. Perillo	Open	17.50	17.50
Artaffects		**Sagebrush Kids Collection**			
91-05-001	Tee-Pee Ornament	G. Perillo	Open	15.00	15.00
91-05-002	Tee-Pee Ornament	G. Perillo	Open	15.00	15.00
91-05-003	Shield Ornament	G. Perillo	Open	15.00	15.00
91-05-004	Moccasin Ornament	G. Perillo	Open	15.00	15.00

CHRISTMAS ORNAMENTS

Company		Series			
Number	**Name**	**Artist**	**Edition Limit**	**Issue Price**	**Quote**
Artaffects		**Simple Wonders**			
91-06-001	Kim	C. Roeda	Open	22.50	22.50
91-06-002	Brittany	C. Roeda	Open	22.50	22.50
91-06-003	Nicole	C. Roeda	Open	22.50	22.50
91-06-004	Megan	C. Roeda	Open	22.50	22.50
91-06-005	Little Feather	C. Roeda	Open	22.50	22.50
91-06-006	Ashley	C. Roeda	Open	22.50	22.50
92-06-007	Sweet Surprise	C. Roeda	Retrd.	15.00	15.00
94-06-008	Deck the Halls (White)	C. Roeda	Yr.Iss.	15.00	15.00
94-06-009	Deck the Halls (Black)	C. Roeda	Yr.Iss.	15.00	15.00
Artists of the World		**De Grazia Annual Ornaments**			
86-01-001	Pima. Indian Drummer Boy	T. De Grazia	Yr.Iss.	27.50	375-475.
87-01-002	White Dove	T. De Grazia	Yr.Iss.	29.50	125-150.
88-01-003	Flower Girl	T. De Grazia	Yr.Iss.	32.50	75-95.00
89-01-004	Flower Boy	T. De Grazia	Yr.Iss.	35.00	67.50-75.00
90-01-005	Pink Papoose	T. De Grazia	Yr.Iss.	35.00	65-95.00
90-01-006	Merry Little Indian	T. De Grazia	10,000	87.50	95-125.00
91-01-007	Christmas Prayer	T. De Grazia	Yr.Iss.	49.50	95.00
92-01-008	Bearing Gift	T. De Grazia	Yr.Iss.	55.00	67.50
93-01-009	Lighting the Way	T. De Grazia	Yr.Iss.	57.50	67.50
94-01-010	Warm Wishes	T. De Grazia	Yr.Iss.	65.00	65.00
95-01-011	Little Prayer	T. De Grazia	Yr.Iss.	49.50	49.50
Band Creations		**Li'l Velvets Magical Christmas**			
94-01-001	Rocking Horse SC42040	T. Rubel	Open	12.00	12.00
94-01-002	Big Cheese SC42055	T. Rubel	Open	12.00	12.00
94-01-003	Stocking Stuffer SC42056	T. Rubel	Open	12.00	12.00
94-01-004	Over the Moon SC42057	T. Rubel	Open	12.00	12.00
94-01-005	Baby's First Christmas SC42056	T. Rubel	Open	12.00	12.00
Band Creations		**Christmas Animals (Glass Balls)**			
94-02-001	Horse SC22000	T. Rubel	Open	3.00	3.00
94-02-002	Bear SC22001	T. Rubel	Open	3.00	3.00
94-02-003	Elephant SC22002	T. Rubel	Open	3.00	3.00
94-02-004	Dalmatian SC22003	T. Rubel	Open	3.00	3.00
94-02-005	Pig SC22004	T. Rubel	Open	3.00	3.00
94-02-006	Moose SC22005	T. Rubel	Open	3.00	3.00
94-02-007	Penguin SC22006	T. Rubel	Open	3.00	3.00
94-02-008	Panda SC22007	T. Rubel	Open	3.00	3.00
94-02-009	Giraffe SC22008	T. Rubel	Open	3.00	3.00
94-02-010	Rabbit SC22009	T. Rubel	Open	3.00	3.00
94-02-011	Fawn SC22010	T. Rubel	Open	3.00	3.00
Band Creations		**Angel Tree Toppers**			
94-03-001	Garland Angel SC52016	T. Rubel	Open	45.00	45.00
94-03-002	Wreath Angel SC52017	T. Rubel	Open	45.00	45.00
Band Creations		**Angel Ornaments**			
94-04-001	Garland Angel SC52018	T. Rubel	Open	15.00	15.00
94-04-002	Wreath Angel SC52019	T. Rubel	Open	15.00	15.00
Band Creations		**Santa Claus Ornaments**			
94-05-001	Tannenbaum SC52007	T. Rubel	Open	10.00	10.00
94-05-002	Tannenbaum Head SC52010	T. Rubel	Open	10.00	10.00
94-05-003	Spirit SC52008	T. Rubel	Open	10.00	10.00
94-05-004	Spirit Head SC52011	T. Rubel	Open	10.00	10.00
94-05-005	Cornucopia SC52009	T. Rubel	Open	10.00	10.00
94-05-006	Cornucopia Head SC52012	T. Rubel	Open	10.00	10.00
Band Creations		**Candyland Mountain Ornaments**			
94-06-001	Lion SC82000	T. Rubel	Open	8.00	8.00
94-06-002	Bear SC82001	T. Rubel	Open	8.00	8.00
94-06-003	Duck SC82002	T. Rubel	Open	8.00	8.00
94-06-004	Elephant SC82003	T. Rubel	Open	8.00	8.00
94-06-005	Stork SC82004	T. Rubel	Open	8.00	8.00
94-06-006	Cat SC82005	T. Rubel	Open	8.00	8.00
94-06-007	Dog SC82006	T. Rubel	Open	8.00	8.00
94-06-008	Mouse SC82007	T. Rubel	Open	8.00	8.00
Band Creations		**Candyland Mountain Ornaments (Glass Balls)**			
94-07-001	Lion SC82016	T. Rubel	Open	3.00	3.00
94-07-002	Bear SC82017	T. Rubel	Open	3.00	3.00
94-07-003	Duck SC82018	T. Rubel	Open	3.00	3.00
94-07-004	Elephant SC82019	T. Rubel	Open	3.00	3.00
94-07-005	Stork SC82020	T. Rubel	Open	3.00	3.00
94-07-006	Cat SC82021	T. Rubel	Open	3.00	3.00
94-07-007	Dog SC82022	T. Rubel	Open	3.00	3.00
94-07-008	Mouse SC82023	T. Rubel	Open	3.00	3.00
Band Creations		**Santa's Animal Kingdom**			
94-08-001	Poly Ornament SC12007	T. Rubel	Open	10.00	10.00
94-08-002	Glass ball Ornament SC12012	T. Rubel	Open	6.00	6.00
Bing & Grondahl		**Christmas**			
85-01-001	Christmas Eve at the Farmhouse	E. Jensen	Closed	19.50	19.50
86-01-002	Silent Night, Holy Night	E. Jensen	Closed	19.50	25.00
87-01-003	The Snowman's Chrismtas Eve	E. Jensen	Closed	22.50	22.50
88-01-004	In the King's Garden	E. Jensen	Closed	25.00	25.00
89-01-005	Christmas Anchorage	E. Jensen	Closed	27.00	27.00
90-01-006	Changing of the Guards	E. Jensen	Closed	32.50	35.00
91-01-007	Copenhagen Stock Exchange	E. Jensen	Closed	34.50	34.50
92-01-008	Christmas at the Rectory	J. Steensen	Closed	36.50	36.50
93-01-009	Father Christmas in Copenhagen	J. Nielson	Closed	36.50	36.50
94-01-010	A Day at the Deer Park	J. Nielson	Yr.Iss.	36.50	36.50
Bing & Grondahl		**Christmas In America**			
86-02-001	Christmas Eve in Williamsburg	J. Woodson	Closed	12.50	90-150.00
87-02-002	Christmas Eve at the White House	J. Woodson	Closed	15.00	15-60.00
88-02-003	Christmas Eve at Rockefeller Center	J. Woodson	Closed	18.50	18.50
89-02-004	Christmas in New England	J. Woodson	Closed	20.00	20-35.00
90-02-005	Christmas Eve at the Capitol	J. Woodson	Closed	20.00	25-45.00
91-02-006	Independence Hall	J. Woodson	Closed	23.50	23.50
92-02-007	Christmas in San Francisco	J. Woodson	Closed	25.00	25.00
93-02-008	Coming Home For Christmas	J. Woodson	Closed	25.00	25.00
94-02-009	Christmas Eve in Alaska	J. Woodson	Yr.Iss.	25.00	25.00
Bing & Grondahl		**Santa Claus**			
89-03-001	Santa's Workshop	H. Hansen	Yr.Iss.	20.00	20.00
90-03-002	Santa's Sleigh	H. Hansen	Yr.Iss.	20.00	20.00
91-03-003	The Journey	H. Hansen	Yr.Iss.	23.50	23.50-45.00
92-03-004	Santa's Arrival	H. Hansen	Yr.Iss.	25.00	25.00
93-03-005	Santa's Gifts	H. Hansen	Yr.Iss.	25.00	25.00
94-03-006	Christmas Stories	H. Hansen	Yr.Iss.	25.00	25.00

Company		Series			
Number	**Name**	**Artist**	**Edition Limit**	**Issue Price**	**Quote**
Brandywine Collectables		**Williamsburg Ornaments**			
88-01-001	Bootmaker	M. Whiting	Closed	9.00	9.00
88-01-002	Apothocary	M. Whiting	Closed	9.00	9.00
88-01-003	Wigmaker	M. Whiting	Closed	9.00	9.00
88-01-004	Nicolson Shop	M. Whiting	Closed	9.00	9.00
88-01-005	Tarpley's Store	M. Whiting	Closed	9.00	9.00
88-01-006	Finnie Quarter	M. Whiting	Closed	9.00	9.00
89-01-004	Cole Shop	M. Whiting	Closed	9.00	9.00
89-01-005	Gunsmith	M. Whiting	Closed	9.00	9.00
89-01-006	Windmill	M. Whiting	Closed	9.00	9.00
89-01-007	Music Teacher	M. Whiting	Closed	9.00	9.00
Brandywine Collectables		**Custom Collection**			
89-02-001	Lorain Lighthouse	M. Whiting	Closed	9.00	9.00
91-02-002	Smithfield VA. Courthouse	M. Whiting	Closed	9.00	9.00
Carriage House: See Margaret Furlong Designs					
Cast Art Industries		**Dreamsicles Ornaments**			
92-01-001	Cherub With Moon-DX260	K. Haynes	Closed	6.00	6.00
92-01-002	Praying Cherub-DX261	K. Haynes	Closed	6.00	6.00
92-01-003	Cherub With Star-DX262	K. Haynes	Closed	6.00	6.00
92-01-004	Cherub On Cloud-DX263	K. Haynes	Closed	6.00	6.00
92-01-005	Bunny-DX270	K. Haynes	Closed	6.00	6.00
92-01-006	Piggy-DX271	K. Haynes	Closed	6.00	6.00
92-01-007	Raccoon-DX272	K. Haynes	Closed	6.00	6.00
92-01-008	Squirrel-DX273	K. Haynes	Closed	6.00	6.00
92-01-009	Bear-DX274	K. Haynes	Closed	6.00	6.00
92-01-010	Lamb-DX275	K. Haynes	Closed	6.00	6.00
The Cat's Meow		**Christmas Ornaments**			
85-01-001	Rutledge House	F. Jones	Retrd.	4.00	N/A
85-01-002	Bancroft House	F. Jones	Retrd.	4.00	N/A
85-01-003	Grayling House	F. Jones	Retrd.	4.00	N/A
85-01-004	School	F. Jones	Retrd.	4.00	N/A
85-01-005	Chapel	F. Jones	Retrd.	4.00	N/A
85-01-006	Morton House	F. Jones	Retrd.	4.00	N/A
The Cat's Meow		**Christmas Ornaments**			
87-02-001	Globe Corner Bookstore	F. Jones	Retrd.	5.00	26-50.00
87-02-002	District #17 School	F. Jones	Retrd.	5.00	26-50.00
87-02-003	Kennedy Birthplace	F. Jones	Retrd.	5.00	26-75.00
87-02-004	Blacksmith Shop	F. Jones	Retrd.	5.00	26-50.00
87-02-005	Set/4	F. Jones	Retrd.	20.00	105-200.
Cazenovia Abroad		**Christmas Ornaments**			
68-01-001	Teddy Bear-P101TB	Unknown	Unkn.	9.00	34-45.00
68-01-002	Elephant-P102E	Unknown	Unkn.	9.00	34-45.00
68-01-003	Duck-P103D	Unknown	Unkn.	9.00	34-45.00
68-01-004	Bunny-P104B	Unknown	Unkn.	9.00	34-45.00
68-01-005	Cat-P105C	Unknown	Unkn.	9.00	34-45.00
68-01-006	Rooster-P106R	Unknown	Unkn.	10.00	34-45.00
68-01-007	Standing Angel-P107SA	Unknown	Unkn.	9.00	39-52.50
68-01-008	Tiptoe Angel-P108TTA	Unknown	Unkn.	10.00	34-45.00
69-01-009	Fawn-P109F	Unknown	Unkn.	12.00	45.00
70-01-010	Snow Man-P110SM	Unknown	Unkn.	12.00	45.00
70-01-011	Peace-P111P	Unknown	Unkn.	12.00	45.00
70-01-012	Porky-P112PK	Unknown	Unkn.	15.00	45.00
71-01-013	Kneeling Angel-P113KA	Unknown	Unkn.	15.00	48-65.00
72-01-014	Rocking Horse-P114RH	Unknown	Unkn.	15.00	48-65.00
73-01-015	Treetop Angel-P115TOP	Unknown	Unkn.	10.00	37-50.00
74-01-016	Owl-P116O	Unknown	Unkn.	15.00	45.00
75-01-017	Star-P117ST	Unknown	Unkn.	15.00	45.00
76-01-018	Hatching Chick-P118CH	Unknown	Unkn.	15.00	45.00
77-01-019	Raggedy Ann-P119RA	Unknown	Unkn.	17.50	39-52.50
78-01-020	Shell-P120SH	Unknown	Unkn.	20.00	34-45.00
79-01-021	Toy Soldier-P121TS	Unknown	Unkn.	20.00	34-45.00
80-01-022	Burro-P122BU	Unknown	Unkn.	20.00	34-45.00
81-01-023	Clown-P123CL	Unknown	Unkn.	25.00	34-45.00
82-01-024	Rebecca-P124RE	Unknown	Unkn.	25.00	34-45.00
83-01-025	Raggedy Andy-P125AND	Unknown	Unkn.	27.50	39-52.50
83-01-026	Mouse-P126MO	Unknown	Unkn.	27.50	39-52.50
84-01-027	Cherub-P127CB	Unknown	Unkn.	30.00	39-52.50
85-01-028	Shaggy Dog-P132SD	Unknown	Unkn.	45.00	50.00
86-01-029	Peter Rabbit-P133PR	Unknown	Unkn.	50.00	50.00
86-01-030	Big Sister-P134BS	Unknown	Unkn.	60.00	60.00
86-01-031	Little Brother-P135LB	Unknown	Unkn.	55.00	55.00
87-01-032	Lamb-P136LA	Unknown	Unkn.	60.00	60.00
87-01-033	Sea Horse-P137SE	Unknown	Unkn.	35.00	26-35.00
88-01-034	Partridge-P138PA	Unknown	Unkn.	70.00	70.00
88-01-035	Squirrel-P139SQ	Unknown	Unkn.	70.00	70.00
84-01-036	Reindeer & Sleigh-H100	Unknown	Unkn.	1250.00	1500.00
89-01-037	Swan-P140SW	Unknown	Open	45.00	45.00
90-01-038	Moravian Star-P141PS	Unknown	Open	65.00	65.00
91-01-039	Hedgehog-P142HH	Unknown	Open	65.00	65.00
91-01-040	Bunny Rabbit-P143BR	Unknown	Open	65.00	65.00
91-01-041	Angel-P144A	Unknown	Open	63.00	63.00
92-01-042	Humpty Dumpty-P145HD	Unknown	Open	70.00	70.00
Cazenovia Abroad		**Carousel**			
91-02-001	Flag Horse-A301CFH	Herschell-Spillman	2,649	75.00	75.00
91-02-002	Fishing Cat-A302CFH	Cernigliaro	2,649	75.00	75.00
91-02-003	Flirting Rabbit-A303CFH	Cernigliaro	2,649	75.00	75.00
92-02-004	Sneaky Tiger-A304LST	C. Looff	2,649	82.50	82.50
92-02-005	Spillman Polar Bear-A305HPB	Herschell-Spillman	2,649	82.50	82.50
92-02-006	Rose Horse-A306PRH	C.W. Parker	2,649	82.50	82.50
94-02-007	Flying Mane Jumping-A307LFM	Illions	2,649	82.50	82.50
94-02-008	Pig-A308DP	Cernigliaro	2,649	82.50	82.50
94-02-009	Zebra-A309DZ	Cernigliaro	2,649	82.50	82.50
Cazenovia Abroad		**Twelve Days of Christmas**			
94-03-001	Partridge in a Pear Tree A401PP	J. Kall	Open	85.00	85.00
94-03-002	Two Turtle Doves A402TT	J. Kall	Open	85.00	85.00
94-03-003	Three French Hens A403TF	J. Kall	Open	85.00	85.00
Christopher Radko		**1987 Holiday Collection**			
87-01-001	Circle of Santas 8811	C. Radko	Retrd.	16.95	48.00
87-01-002	Royal Porcelain 8812	C. Radko	Retrd.	16.95	48.00
87-01-003	Simply Cartiere 8817	C. Radko	Retrd.	16.95	48.00
87-01-004	Baby Balloon 8832	C. Radko	Retrd.	7.95	25.00
87-01-005	Grecian Column 8842	C. Radko	Retrd.	9.95	30.00
87-01-006	Ripples on Oval 8844	C. Radko	Retrd.	6.00	15.00
87-01-007	Satin Scepter 8847	C. Radko	Retrd.	8.95	30.00
87-01-008	Double Royal Drop 8856	C. Radko	Retrd.	25.00	70.00

CHRISTMAS ORNAMENTS

Company		Series			
Number	Name	Artist	Edition Limit	Issue Price	Quote
87-01-009	Royal Diadem 8860	C. Radko	Retrd.	25.00	70.00
87-01-010	Mushroom in Winter 8862	C. Radko	Retrd.	12.00	40.00
87-01-011	Birdhouse 8873	C. Radko	Retrd.	10.00	30.00
87-01-012	Striped Balloon 8877	C. Radko	Retrd.	16.95	60.00
Christopher Radko		**1988 Holiday Collection**			
88-02-001	Faberge Oval 3	C. Radko	Retrd.	15.00	30.00
88-02-002	Celestial 4	C. Radko	Retrd.	15.00	35.00
88-02-003	Royal Porcelain 12	C. Radko	Retrd.	16.00	35.00
88-02-004	Gilded Leaves 13	C. Radko	Retrd.	16.00	30.00
88-02-005	Stained Glass 16	C. Radko	Retrd.	16.00	32.00
88-02-006	Alpine Flowers 22	C. Radko	Retrd.	16.00	30.00
88-02-007	Christmas Fanfare 50	C. Radko	Retrd.	15.00	35.00
88-02-008	Double Royal Star 56	C. Radko	Retrd.	23.00	60.00
88-02-009	Mushroom Winter 62	C. Radko	Retrd.	10.00	30.00
88-02-010	Crown Jewels 74	C. Radko	Retrd.	15.00	30.00
Christopher Radko		**1989 Holiday Collection**			
89-03-001	Lilac Sparkle 9-7	C. Radko	Retrd.	17.00	30.00
89-03-002	Alpine Flowers 9-43	C. Radko	Retrd.	17.00	30.00
89-03-003	Seahorse 9-54	C. Radko	Retrd.	10.00	30.00
89-03-004	Charlie Chaplin 9-55	C. Radko	Retrd.	8.50	18.95
89-03-005	Kim Ono 9-57	C. Radko	Retrd.	6.50	24.00
89-03-006	Joey Clown (light pink) 9-58	C. Radko	Retrd.	9.00	45.00
89-03-007	Walrus 9-63	C. Radko	Retrd.	8.00	45.00
89-03-008	Shy Rabbit 9-66	C. Radko	Retrd.	7.00	50.00
89-03-009	Fisher Frog 9-65	C. Radko	Retrd.	7.00	40.00
89-03-010	Shy Kitten 9-66	C. Radko	Retrd.	7.00	7.00
89-03-011	Hurricane Lamp 9-67	C. Radko	Retrd.	7.00	21.00
89-03-012	Parachute 9-68	C. Radko	Retrd.	6.50	20.00
89-03-013	Grecian Urn 9-69	C. Radko	Retrd.	12.95	35.00
89-03-014	Double Top 9-71	C. Radko	Retrd.	7.00	20.00
89-03-015	Serpent 9-72	C. Radko	Retrd.	7.00	17.50
89-03-016	Small Reflector 9-76	C. Radko	Retrd.	7.50	27.50
89-03-017	King Arthur (Lt. Blue) 9-103	C. Radko	Retrd.	12.00	N/A
Christopher Radko		**1990 Holiday Collection**			
90-04-001	Yarn Fight 23	C. Radko	Retrd.	18.00	35.00
90-04-002	Early Winter 24	C. Radko	Retrd.	10.00	29.95
90-04-003	Fat Lady 35	C. Radko	Retrd.	7.00	20.00
90-04-004	Dublin Pipe 40	C. Radko	Retrd.	14.00	50.00
90-04-005	Snowman on Ball 45	C. Radko	Retrd.	14.00	24.00
90-04-006	Angel on Harp 46	C. Radko	Retrd.	9.00	35.00
90-04-007	Lullaby 47	C. Radko	Retrd.	9.00	20.00
90-04-008	Golden Puppy 53	C. Radko	Retrd.	8.00	45.00
90-04-009	Crowned Prince 56	C. Radko	Retrd.	7.00	45.00
90-04-010	Tuxedo Penguin 57	C. Radko	Retrd.	8.00	N/A
90-04-011	Walrus 59	C. Radko	Retrd.	8.50	30.00
90-04-012	Mother Goose (blue bonnet/pink shawl) 52	C. Radko	Retrd.	10.00	N/A
90-04-013	Smiling Kite 63	C. Radko	Retrd.	14.00	45.00
90-04-014	Conch Shell 65	C. Radko	Retrd.	9.00	25.00
90-04-015	Roly Poly Santa (Red bottom) 69	C. Radko	Retrd.	13.00	45.00
90-04-016	King Arthur (Red) 72	C. Radko	Retrd.	16.00	N/A
90-04-017	Peacock (on snowball) 74	C. Radko	Retrd.	18.00	50.00
90-04-018	Silent Movie (black hat) 75	C. Radko	Retrd.	8.50	20.00
90-04-019	Father Christmas 76	C. Radko	Retrd.	7.00	15.00
90-04-020	Happy Gnome 77	C. Radko	Retrd.	8.00	40.00
90-04-021	Small Nautilus Shell 78	C. Radko	Retrd.	7.00	22.00
90-04-022	Kim Ono 79	C. Radko	Retrd.	6.00	6.00
90-04-023	Ballooning Santa 85	C. Radko	Retrd.	20.00	60.00
90-04-024	Emerald City 92	C. Radko	Retrd.	7.50	16-40.00
90-04-025	Maracca 94	C. Radko	Retrd.	8.95	45.00
90-04-026	Rose Lamp 96	C. Radko	Retrd.	14.00	50.00
Christopher Radko		**1991 Holiday Collection**			
91-05-001	Harvest 3	C. Radko	Retrd.	13.50	24.50
92-05-002	Chimney Santa 12	C. Radko	Retrd.	14.50	25.00
91-05-003	Shirley 15	C. Radko	Retrd.	16.00	36.00
91-05-004	Cosette 16	C. Radko	Retrd.	16.00	25.00
91-05-005	Altar Boy 18	C. Radko	Retrd.	16.00	31.00
91-05-006	Dutch Boy 27	C. Radko	Retrd.	11.00	30.00
91-05-007	Dutch Girl 28	C. Radko	Retrd.	11.00	30.00
91-05-008	Dawn & Dust 34	C. Radko	Retrd.	14.00	24.50
91-05-009	Hatching Duck 35	C. Radko	Retrd.	14.00	50.00
91-05-010	Proud Peacock 37	C. Radko	Retrd.	23.00	36.40
91-05-011	Woodland Santa 38	C. Radko	Retrd.	14.00	29.00
91-05-012	Fruit in Balloon 40	C. Radko	Retrd.	22.00	45.00
91-05-013	Aztec Bird 41	C. Radko	Retrd.	20.00	49.00
91-05-014	Apache 42	C. Radko	Retrd.	8.50	24.50
91-05-015	Sally Ann 43	C. Radko	Retrd.	8.00	25.00
91-05-016	Tabby 46	C. Radko	Retrd.	8.00	49.00
92-05-017	Bowery Kid 50	C. Radko	Retrd.	14.50	25.00
91-05-018	Prince on Ball (pink/blue/green) 51	C. Radko	Retrd.	15.00	45.00
91-05-019	Sleepy Time Santa 52	C. Radko	Retrd.	15.00	40.00
91-05-020	Tulip Fairy 63	C. Radko	Retrd.	16.00	N/A
91-05-021	Anchor America 65	C. Radko	Retrd.	21.50	38.00
91-05-022	Sunshine 67	C. Radko	Retrd.	22.00	39.95
91-05-023	Aspen 76	C. Radko	Retrd.	20.50	N/A
91-05-024	Florentine 83	C. Radko	Retrd.	22.00	39.95
91-05-025	Her Purse 88	C. Radko	Retrd.	10.00	26.50
91-05-026	Dapper Shoe 89	C. Radko	Retrd.	10.00	22.50-35.00
91-05-027	Flower Child 90	C. Radko	Retrd.	13.00	40.00
91-05-028	Rainbow Bird 92	C. Radko	Retrd.	16.00	25.00
91-05-029	King Arthur (Blue) 95	C. Radko	Retrd.	18.50	N/A
91-05-030	Raspberry & Lime 96	C. Radko	Retrd.	12.00	50.00
91-05-031	Einstein Kite 98	C. Radko	Retrd.	20.00	32.00
91-05-032	Melon Slice 99	C. Radko	Retrd.	18.00	30.40
91-05-033	Madonna & Child 103	C. Radko	Retrd.	15.00	35.00
92-05-034	Chance Encounter 104	C. Radko	Retrd.	13.50	N/A
91-05-035	Sitting Bull 107	C. Radko	Retrd.	16.00	34.00
91-05-036	Jemima's Child 111	C. Radko	Retrd.	16.00	45.00
91-05-037	By the Nile 124	C. Radko	Retrd.	21.50	39.50
91-05-038	Olympiad 125	C. Radko	Retrd.	22.00	39.50
91-05-039	Vienna 1901 127	C. Radko	Retrd.	21.50	N/A
91-05-040	Red Star 129	C. Radko	Retrd.	21.50	39.95
91-05-041	Blue Rainbow 136	C. Radko	Retrd.	21.50	39.95
91-05-042	All Weather Santa 137	C. Radko	Retrd.	32.00	69.95
91-05-043	Star Quilt 139	C. Radko	Retrd.	21.50	39.95
91-05-044	Aztec 141	C. Radko	Retrd.	21.50	39.95
Christopher Radko		**1992 Holiday Collection**			
92-06-001	Mother Goose 37	C. Radko	Retrd.	15.00	25.00
92-06-002	Virgin Mary 46	C. Radko	Retrd.	20.00	25.00
92-06-003	Cheerful Sun 50	C. Radko	Retrd.	18.00	24.50

Company		Series			
Number	Name	Artist	Edition Limit	Issue Price	Quote
92-06-004	Little League 53	C. Radko	Retrd.	20.00	25-35.00
92-06-005	Circus lady 54	C. Radko	Retrd.	12.00	15.00
92-06-006	Her Slipper 56	C. Radko	Retrd.	17.00	22.00
92-06-007	Tulip Fairy 57	C. Radko	Retrd.	18.00	23-30.00
92-06-008	Clown Snake 62	C. Radko	Retrd.	22.00	27.00
92-06-009	Pierre Winterberry 64	C. Radko	Retrd.	17.00	25.00
92-06-010	Barbie's Mom 69	C. Radko	Retrd.	26.00	26.00
92-06-011	Diva 73	C. Radko	Retrd.	17.00	21-25.00
92-06-012	Harlequin Tier Drop 74	C. Radko	Retrd.	18.00	45.00
92-06-013	Downhill Racer 76	C. Radko	Retrd.	34.00	42.00
92-06-014	Royal Septor 77	C. Radko	Retrd.	36.00	45.00
92-06-015	Rainbow Parasol 90	C. Radko	Retrd.	30.00	N/A
92-06-016	Seahorse 92	C. Radko	Retrd.	20.00	25.00
92-06-017	Sitting Bull 93	C. Radko	Retrd.	23.00	45.00
92-06-018	Cowboy Santa 94	C. Radko	Retrd.	24.00	N/A
92-06-019	Folk Art Set 95	C. Radko	Retrd.	10.00	13.00
92-06-020	Serpents of Paradise 97	C. Radko	Retrd.	13.00	16-19.00
92-06-021	Candy Trumpet man (red) 98	C. Radko	Retrd.	27.00	33-45.00
92-06-022	Jumbo 99	C. Radko	Retrd.	31.00	35.30
92-06-023	Two Sided Santa Reflector 102	C. Radko	Retrd.	28.00	35.00
92-06-024	Forest Friends 103	C. Radko	Retrd.	14.00	17.50
92-06-025	Santa in Winter White 106	C. Radko	Retrd.	28.00	36.95
92-06-026	St. Nickcicle 107	C. Radko	Retrd.	26.00	33.00
92-06-027	Primary Colors 108	C. Radko	Retrd.	30.00	42.50
92-06-028	Tropical Fish 109	C. Radko	Retrd.	17.00	17.00
92-06-029	Stardust Joey 110	C. Radko	Retrd.	16.00	25.00
92-06-030	Russian Imperial 112	C. Radko	Retrd.	25.00	31.50
92-06-031	Choir Boy 114	C. Radko	Retrd.	24.00	30.00
92-06-032	Dolly Madison 115	C. Radko	Retrd.	17.00	21.00
92-06-033	Butterfly Bouquet 119	C. Radko	Retrd.	27.00	33.00
92-06-034	Aspen 120	C. Radko	Retrd.	26.00	33.00
92-06-035	Victorian Santa & Angel Balloon 122	C. Radko	Retrd.	68.00	91.00
92-06-036	Christmas Cardinals 123	C. Radko	Retrd.	26.00	33.00
92-06-037	Delft Design 124	C. Radko	Retrd.	26.50	35.00
92-06-038	Ziegfeld Follies 126	C. Radko	Retrd.	27.00	40.00
92-06-039	Ice Poppies 127	C. Radko	Retrd.	26.00	32.00
92-06-040	Vienna 1901 128	C. Radko	Retrd.	27.00	40.00
92-06-041	Celestial 129	C. Radko	Retrd.	26.00	40.00
92-06-042	Russian Star 130	C. Radko	Retrd.	26.00	32-40.00
92-06-043	Florentine 131	C. Radko	Retrd.	27.00	40.00
92-06-044	Sputniks 134	C. Radko	Retrd.	25.50	32.00
92-06-045	Elf Reflectors 136	C. Radko	Retrd.	28.00	36.00
92-06-046	Merry Christmas Maiden 137	C. Radko	Retrd.	26.00	N/A
92-06-047	By the Nile 139	C. Radko	Retrd.	27.00	33-40.00
92-06-048	Elephant on Parade 141	C. Radko	Retrd.	26.00	33-35.00
92-06-049	Christmas Rose 143	C. Radko	Retrd.	25.50	32.00
92-06-050	King of Prussia 149	C. Radko	Retrd.	27.00	33-35.00
92-06-051	Neopolitan Angels 152	C. Radko	Retrd.	27.00	33.00
92-06-052	Winter Wonderland 156	C. Radko	Retrd.	26.00	33.00
92-06-053	Pink Lace 158	C. Radko	Retrd.	28.00	36.00
92-06-054	Chevron 160	C. Radko	Retrd.	28.00	35.00
92-06-055	Tiffany Bright 161	C. Radko	Retrd.	28.00	N/A
92-06-056	Alpine Flowers 162	C. Radko	Retrd.	28.00	36.00
92-06-057	Norweigian Princess 170	C. Radko	Retrd.	15.00	22.00
92-06-058	Floral Cascade Tier Drop 175	C. Radko	Retrd.	32.00	41-45.00
92-06-059	Star of Wonder 177	C. Radko	Retrd.	27.00	35.00
92-06-060	Thunderbolt 178	C. Radko	Retrd.	60.00	59.95
92-06-061	Elephant Reflector 181	C. Radko	Retrd.	17.00	25.00
92-06-062	Faith, Hope & Love 183	C. Radko	Retrd.	12.00	N/A
92-06-063	Gabriel's Trumpets 188	C. Radko	Retrd.	20.00	25.00
92-06-064	Harold Lloyd Reflector 218	C. Radko	Retrd.	70.00	100.00
92-06-065	To Grandma's House 239	C. Radko	Retrd.	20.00	N/A
92-06-066	Ice Pear 241	C. Radko	Retrd.	20.00	26.00
Christopher Radko		**1993 Holiday Collection**			
93-07-001	Tweeter 94	C. Radko	Retrd.	3.20	6.00
93-07-002	Waddles 95	C. Radko	Retrd.	3.80	11.00
93-07-003	Monkey Man 97	C. Radko	Retrd.	16.00	16.00
93-07-004	Snowday Santa 98	C. Radko	Retrd.	20.00	27.00
93-07-005	Beyond the Stars 108	C. Radko	Retrd.	18.50	20.00
93-07-006	Polar Bears 112A	C. Radko	Retrd.	15.50	14.50
93-07-007	Blue Top 114	C. Radko	Retrd.	16.00	16.00
93-07-008	Tuxedo Santa 117	C. Radko	Retrd.	21.90	29.00
93-07-009	Mr. & Mrs. Claus 121	C. Radko	Retrd.	17.90	18.00
93-07-010	Angel of Peace 132	C. Radko	Retrd.	17.00	24.00
93-07-011	Saraband 140	C. Radko	Retrd.	27.80	35.00
93-07-012	Cinderella's Bluebirds 145	C. Radko	Retrd.	25.90	26.00
93-07-013	Pennsylvania Dutch 146	C. Radko	Retrd.	26.80	33.00
93-07-014	Deco Snowfall 147	C. Radko	Retrd.	26.80	33.00
93-07-015	French Rose 152	C. Radko	Retrd.	26.60	27-33.00
93-07-016	Rainbow Reflector 154	C. Radko	Retrd.	26.60	35.00
93-07-017	Serenade Pink 157	C. Radko	Retrd.	26.80	35.00
93-07-018	Cold Fish 158	C. Radko	Retrd.	25.80	26.00
93-07-019	Winterbirds 164	C. Radko	Retrd.	26.80	27.00
93-07-020	Little Doggie 180	C. Radko	Retrd.	7.00	15.00
93-07-021	Center Ring (Exclusive) 192	C. Radko	Retrd.	30.80	38.00
93-07-022	Downhill Racer 195	C. Radko	Retrd.	30.00	36.00
93-07-023	Sweetheart 202	C. Radko	Retrd.	16.00	18.00
93-07-024	Star Children 208	C. Radko	Retrd.	18.00	25.00
93-07-025	Monterey 209	C. Radko	Retrd.	27.90	22.00
93-07-026	One Small Leap 222	C. Radko	Retrd.	26.00	33.00
93-07-027	Centurian 224	C. Radko	Retrd.	25.50	30.50
93-07-028	Light in the Windows 229	C. Radko	Retrd.	24.50	29.50
93-07-029	V.I.P. 230	C. Radko	Retrd.	23.00	23.00
93-07-030	Grecian Urn 231	C. Radko	Retrd.	23.00	23.00
93-07-031	English Kitchen 234	C. Radko	Retrd.	26.00	28.00
93-07-032	Stocking Stuffers 236	C. Radko	Retrd.	16.00	23.00
93-07-033	Aladdin's Lamp 237	C. Radko	Retrd.	20.00	27.00
93-07-034	Auld Lang Syne 246	C. Radko	Retrd.	15.00	22.00
93-07-035	SnowDance 247	C. Radko	Retrd.	29.00	36.00
93-07-036	Circus Seal 249	C. Radko	Retrd.	28.00	35.00
93-07-037	Forest Friends 250	C. Radko	Retrd.	28.00	35.00
93-07-038	Emperor's Pet 253	C. Radko	Retrd.	22.00	29.00
93-07-039	Pagoda 258	C. Radko	Retrd.	8.00	15.00
93-07-040	Grandpa Bear 260	C. Radko	Retrd.	12.80	13-20.00
93-07-041	Geisha Girls 261	C. Radko	Retrd.	11.90	12-19.00
93-07-042	Mushroom Elf 267	C. Radko	Retrd.	17.90	25.00
93-07-043	Shy Rabbit 280	C. Radko	Retrd.	13.90	21.00
93-07-044	Monterey 290	C. Radko	Retrd.	15.00	15-22.00
93-07-045	Bell House Boy 291	C. Radko	Retrd.	21.00	28.00
93-07-045	Chimney Sweep Bell 294	C. Radko	Retrd.	26.00	28.00
93-07-046	Majestic Reflector 312	C. Radko	Retrd.	70.00	70.00
93-07-047	Calla Lilly 314	C. Radko	Retrd.	12.90	20.00
93-07-048	Rose Pointe Finial 323	C. Radko	Retrd.	34.00	34.00

CHRISTMAS ORNAMENTS

Company		Series			
Number	**Name**	**Artist**	**Edition Limit**	**Issue Price**	**Quote**
93-07-049	Bishop of Myra 327	C. Radko	Retrd.	19.90	27.00
93-07-050	Sloopy Snowman 328	C. Radko	Retrd.	19.90	27.00
93-07-051	Texas Star 338	C. Radko	Retrd.	7.50	8.00
93-07-052	Sail by Starlight 339	C. Radko	Retrd.	11.80	14-19.00
93-07-053	Enchanted Gardens 341	C. Radko	Retrd.	5.50	13.00
93-07-054	Christmas Stars 342	C. Radko	Retrd.	14.00	21.00
93-07-055	Pompadour 344	C. Radko	Retrd.	8.80	11.00
93-07-056	Littlest Snowman Ltd. 347	C. Radko	Retrd.	13.90	22.00
93-07-057	Starlight Santa 348	C. Radko	Retrd.	20.00	19.00
93-07-058	Honey Bear 352	C. Radko	Retrd.	13.90	21.00
93-07-059	U-Boat 353	C. Radko	Retrd.	15.50	23.00
93-07-060	Little Eskimo 355	C. Radko	Retrd.	13.90	21.00
93-07-061	Apache 357	C. Radko	Retrd.	13.90	14-21.00
93-07-062	Gypsy Girl 371	C. Radko	Retrd.	16.00	18-23.00
93-07-063	Kitty Rattle 374	C. Radko	Retrd.	17.80	25.00
93-07-064	Smithy 378	C. Radko	Retrd.	17.90	25.00
93-07-065	Purse 389	C. Radko	Retrd.	15.60	16.00
93-07-066	Quartet 392	C. Radko	Retrd.	3.60	11.00
93-07-067	Spider & the Fly 393	C. Radko	Retrd.	6.40	14.00
93-07-068	Ice Star Santa 405	C. Radko	Retrd.	38.00	47.00
93-07-069	Evening Star Santa 409	C. Radko	Retrd.	59.00	85.00
93-07-070	Alpine Village 420	C. Radko	Retrd.	23.80	35.00
93-07-071	Holiday Spice 422	C. Radko	Retrd.	24.00	24.00
Christopher Radko		**Christopher Radko Family of Collectors**			
93-08-001	Angels We Have Heard on High SP1	C. Radko	Retrd.	50.00	50.00
94-08-002	Starbuck Santa SP3	C. Radko	Yr.Iss.	75.00	75.00
Christopher Radko		**Twelve Days of Christmas**			
93-09-001	Partridge in a Pear Tree SP2	C. Radko	5,000	35.00	75.00
94-09-002	Two Turtle Doves SP4	C. Radko	10,000	28.00	28.00
Christopher Radko		**Aids Awareness**			
93-10-001	A Shy Rabbit's Heart 462	C. Radko	Retrd.	15.00	22.00
94-10-002	Frosty Cares SP5	C. Radko	Yr.Iss.	25.00	25.00
Christopher Radko		**Pediatrics Cancer Research**			
94-11-001	A Gifted Santa 70	C. Radko	Yr.Iss.	25.00	25.00
Cybis		**Christmas Collection**			
83-01-001	1983 Holiday Bell	Cybis	Yr.Iss.	145.00	1000.00
84-01-002	1984 Holiday Ball	Cybis	Yr.Iss.	145.00	700.00
85-01-003	1985 Holiday Angel	Cybis	Yr.Iss.	75.00	500.00
86-01-004	1986 Holiday Cherub Ornament	Cybis	Yr.Iss.	75.00	500.00
87-01-005	1987 Heavenly Angels	Cybis	Yr.Iss.	95.00	400.00
88-01-006	1988 Holiday Ornament	Cybis	Yr.Iss.	95.00	375.00
Department 56		**Snowbabies Ornaments**			
86-01-001	Sitting, Lite-Up, Clip-On, 7952-9	Department 56	Closed	7.00	25-35.00
86-01-002	Crawling, Lite-Up, Clip-On, 7953-7	Department 56	Closed	7.00	18-28.00
86-01-003	Winged, Lite-Up, Clip-On, 7954-5	Department 56	Closed	7.00	35-44.00
86-01-004	Snowbaby on Brass Ribbon, 7961-8	Department 56	Closed	8.00	100.00
87-01-005	Moon Beams, 7951-0	Department 56	Open	7.50	7.50
87-01-006	Snowbaby Adrift Lite-Up, Clip-On, 7969-3	Department 56	Closed	8.50	60-75.00
87-01-007	Mini, Winged Pair, Lite-Up, Clip-On, 7976-6	Department 56	Open	9.00	9.00
88-01-008	Twinkle Little Star, 7980-4	Department 56	Closed	7.00	72-81.00
89-01-009	Noel, 7988-0	Department 56	Open	7.50	7.50
89-01-010	Surprise, 7989-8	Department 56	Open	12.00	12.00
89-01-011	Star Bright, 7990-1	Department 56	Open	7.50	7.50
90-01-012	Rock-A-Bye Baby, 7939-1	Depatrment 56	Open	7.00	7.00
90-01-013	Penguin, Lite-Up, Clip-On, 7940-5	Department 56	Closed	5.00	11-18.00
90-01-014	Polar Bear, Lite-Up, Clip-On, 7941-3	Department 56	Closed	5.00	9-18.00
91-01-015	Swinging On a Star, 6810-1	Department 56	Open	9.50	9.50
91-01-016	My First Star, 6811-0	Department 56	Open	7.00	7.00
92-01-017	Snowbabies Icicle With Star, 6825-0	Department 56	Open	16.00	16.00
92-01-018	Starry, Starry Night, 6830-6	Department 56	Open	12.50	12.50
93-01-019	Wee...This is Fun!, 6847-0	Department 56	Open	13.50	13.50
93-01-020	Sprinkling Stars in the Sky, 6848-9	Department 56	Open	12.50	12.50
Department 56		**CCP Ornaments-Flat**			
86-02-001	Christmas Carol Houses, set of 3 (6504-8)	Department 56	Closed	13.00	35-45.00
86-02-002	Fezziwig's Warehouse	Department 56	Closed	4.35	N/A
86-02-003	Scrooge and Marley Countinghouse	Department 56	Closed	4.35	N/A
86-02-004	The Cottage of Bob Cratchit & Tiny Tim	Department 56	Closed	4.35	N/A
86-02-005	New England Village, set of 7 (6536-6)	Department 56	Closed	25.00	275-325.
86-02-006	Apothecary Shop	Department 56	Closed	3.50	15-25.00
86-02-007	General Store	Department 56	Closed	3.50	12-45.00
86-02-008	Nathaniel Bingham Fabrics	Department 56	Closed	3.50	10-20.00
86-02-009	Livery Stable & Boot Shop	Department 56	Closed	3.50	10-15.00
86-02-010	Steeple Church	Department 56	Closed	3.50	15-115.00
86-02-011	Brick Town Hall	Department 56	Closed	3.50	15-50.00
86-02-012	Red Schoolhouse	Department 56	Closed	3.50	15-60.00
Department 56		**Christmas Carol Character Ornaments-Flat**			
86-03-001	Christmas Carol Characters, set of 3(6505-6)	Department 56	Closed	13.00	30-42.00
86-03-002	Bob Cratchit & Tiny Tim	Department 56	Closed	4.35	25-30.00
86-03-003	Scrooge	Department 56	Closed	4.35	25-30.00
86-03-004	Poulterer	Department 56	Closed	4.35	25-30.00
Department 56		**Village Light-Up Ornaments**			
85-04-001	Dickens' Village, set of 8 (6521-8)	Department 56	Closed	48.00	195.00
85-04-002	Crowntree Inn	Department 56	Closed	6.00	21-40.00
85-04-003	Candle Shop	Department 56	Closed	6.00	14-35.00
85-04-004	Green Grocer	Department 56	Closed	6.00	23-35.00
85-04-005	Golden Swan Baker	Department 56	Closed	6.00	17-30.00
85-04-006	Bean and Son Smithy Shop	Department 56	Closed	6.00	15-25.00
85-04-007	Abel Beesley Butcher	Department 56	Closed	6.00	17-25.00
85-04-008	Jones & Co. Brush & Basket Shop	Department 56	Closed	6.00	30-40.00
85-04-009	Dickens' Village Church	Department 56	Closed	6.00	42.00
87-04-010	Dickens' Village, set of 6 (6520-0)	Department 56	Closed	36.00	100-165.
87-04-011	Blythe Pond Mill House	Department 56	Closed	6.00	30-55.00
87-04-012	Barley Bree Farmhouse	Department 56	Closed	6.00	15-30.00
87-04-013	The Old Curiosity Shop	Department 56	Closed	6.00	15-36.00
87-04-014	Kenilworth Castle	Department 56	Closed	6.00	56-82.00
87-04-015	Brick Abbey	Department 56	Closed	6.00	77-110.00
87-04-016	Chesterton Manor House	Department 56	Closed	6.00	25-60.00
87-04-017	Dickens' Village, set of 14 (6521-8, 6520-0)	Department 56	Closed	84.00	325-350.
87-04-018	Christmas Carol Cottages, set of 3 (6513-7)	Department 56	Closed	16.95	44-80.00
87-04-019	Fezziwig's Warehouse	Department 56	Closed	6.00	25-30.00
87-04-020	Scrooge & Marley Countinghouse	Department 56	Closed	6.00	15-25.00
87-04-021	The Cottage of Bob Cratchit & Tiny Tim	Department 56	Closed	6.00	15-25.00
86-04-022	New England Village, set of 7 (6533-1)	Department 56	Closed	42.00	325.00
86-04-023	Apothecary Shop	Department 56	Closed	6.00	18-25.00
86-04-024	General Store	Department 56	Closed	6.00	54-60.00

Company		Series			
Number	**Name**	**Artist**	**Edition Limit**	**Issue Price**	**Quote**
86-04-025	Nathaniel Bingham Fabrics	Department 56	Closed	6.00	30-40.00
86-04-026	Livery Stable & Boot Shop	Department 56	Closed	6.00	24-35.00
86-04-027	Steeple Church	Department 56	Closed	6.00	125-150.
86-04-028	Brick Town Hall	Department 56	Closed	6.00	45-50.00
86-04-029	Red Schoolhouse	Department 56	Closed	6.00	65-78.00
87-04-030	New England Village, set of 6 (6534-0)	Department 56	Closed	36.00	200-275.
87-04-031	Timber Knoll Log Cabin	Department 56	Closed	6.00	108-135.
87-04-032	Smythe Woolen Mill	Department 56	Closed	6.00	168.00
87-04-033	Jacob Adams Farmhouse	Department 56	Closed	6.00	58.00
87-04-034	Jacob Adams Barn	Department 56	Closed	6.00	78.00
87-04-035	Craggy Cove Lighthouse	Department 56	Closed	6.00	100-140.
87-04-036	Weston Train Station	Department 56	Closed	6.00	57.00
87-04-037	New England Village, set of 13 (6533-1, 6534-0)	Department 56	Closed	78.00	495-775.
Department 56		**Miscellaneous Ornaments**			
84-05-001	Dickens 2-sided Tin Ornaments, set of 6 (6522-6)	Department 56	Closed	12.00	165-260.
84-05-002	Crowntree Inn	Department 56	Closed	2.00	45.00
84-05-003	Green Grocer	Department 56	Closed	2.00	45.00
84-05-004	Golden Swan Baker	Department 56	Closed	2.00	45.00
84-05-005	Bean and Son Smithy Shop	Department 56	Closed	2.00	45.00
84-05-006	Abel Beesley Butcher	Department 56	Closed	2.00	45.00
84-05-007	Jones & Co. Brush & Basket Shop	Department 56	Closed	2.00	45.00
88-05-008	Christmas Carol- Scrooge's Head (5912-9)	Department 56	Closed	12.95	30-35.00
88-05-009	Christmas Carol- Tiny Tim's Head (5913-7)	Department 56	Closed	10.00	22-40.00
88-05-010	Christmas Carol- Bob & Mrs. Cratchit (5914-5)	Department 56	Closed	18.00	33-44.00
88-05-011	Balsam Bell Brass Dickens' Candlestick (6244-8)	Department 56	Closed	3.00	10.00
83-05-012	Snow Village Wood Ornaments, set of 6 (5099-7)	Department 56	Closed	30.00	N/A
83-05-013	Gabled House	Department 56	Closed	5.00	N/A
83-05-014	Swiss Chalet	Department 56	Closed	5.00	N/A
83-05-015	Countryside Church	Department 56	Closed	5.00	150.00
83-05-016	Carriage House	Department 56	Closed	5.00	N/A
83-05-017	Centennial House	Department 56	Closed	5.00	150.00
83-05-018	Pioneer Church	Department 56	Closed	5.00	N/A
Duncan Royale		**History Of Santa Claus**			
92-01-001	Santa I (set of 12)	Duncan Royale	Open	144.00	144.00
92-01-002	Santa II (set of 12)	Duncan Royale	Open	144.00	144.00
Enesco Corporation		**Precious Moments Ornaments**			
83-01-001	Surround Us With Joy-E-0513	S. Butcher	Yr.Iss.	9.00	60-65.00
83-01-002	Mother Sew Dear-E-0514	S. Butcher	Open	9.00	16-25.00
83-01-003	To A Special Dad-E-0515	S. Butcher	Suspd.	9.00	30.00
83-01-004	The Purr-fect Grandma-E-0516	S. Butcher	Open	9.00	16-25.00
83-01-005	The Perfect Grandpa-E-0517	S. Butcher	Suspd.	9.00	25-40.00
83-01-006	Blessed Are The Pure In Heart -E-0518	S. Butcher	Yr.Iss.	9.00	40-55.00
83-01-007	O Come All Ye Faithful-E-0531	S. Butcher	Suspd.	10.00	45-60.00
83-01-008	Let Heaven And Nature Sing-E-0532	S. Butcher	Retrd.	9.00	35-45.50
83-01-009	Tell Me The Story Of Jesus-E-0533	S. Butcher	Suspd.	9.00	35-55.00
83-01-010	To Thee With Love-E-0534	S. Butcher	Retrd.	9.00	40-65.00
83-01-011	Love Is Patient-E-0535	S. Butcher	Suspd.	9.00	40-55.00
83-01-012	Love Is Patient-E-0536	S. Butcher	Suspd.	9.00	35-70.00
83-01-013	Jesus Is The Light That Shines- E-0537	S. Butcher	Suspd.	9.00	45-60.00
82-01-014	Joy To The World-E-2343	S. Butcher	Suspd.	9.00	35-66.00
82-01-015	I'll Play My Drum For Him-E-2359	S. Butcher	Yr.Iss.	9.00	100-170.
82-01-016	Baby's First Christmas-E-2362	S. Butcher	Suspd.	9.00	25-70.00
82-01-017	The First Noel-E-2367	S. Butcher	Suspd.	9.00	45-66.00
82-01-018	The First Noel-E-2368	S. Butcher	Retrd.	9.00	40-60.00
82-01-019	Dropping In For Christmas-E-2369	S. Butcher	Retrd.	9.00	36-70.00
82-01-020	Unicorn-E-2371	S. Butcher	Retrd.	10.00	45-75.00
82-01-021	Baby's First Christmas-E-2372	S. Butcher	Suspd.	9.00	35-45.00
82-01-022	Dropping Over For Christmas-E-2376	S. Butcher	Retrd.	9.00	45-59.00
82-01-023	Mouse With Cheese-E-2381	S. Butcher	Suspd.	9.00	75-125.00
82-01-024	Our First Christmas Together-E-2385	S. Butcher	Suspd.	10.00	15-55.00
82-01-025	Camel, Donkey & Cow (3 pc. set)-E2386	S. Butcher	Suspd.	25.00	55-90.00
84-01-026	Wishing You A Merry Christmas-E-5387	S. Butcher	Yr.Iss.	10.00	37.50-45.00
84-01-027	Joy To The World-E-5388	S. Butcher	Retrd.	10.00	40-55.00
84-01-028	Peace On Earth-E-5389	S. Butcher	Suspd.	10.00	30-45.00
84-01-029	May God Bless You With A Perfect Holiday Season-E-5390	S. Butcher	Suspd.	10.00	25-30.00
84-01-030	Love Is Kind-E-5391	S. Butcher	Suspd.	10.00	30-50.00
84-01-031	Blessed Are The Pure In Heart-E-5392	S. Butcher	Yr.Iss.	10.00	40.00
81-01-032	But Love Goes On Forever-E-5627	S. Butcher	Suspd.	6.00	70-135.00
81-01-033	But Love Goes On Forever-E-5628	S. Butcher	Suspd.	6.00	60-150.00
81-01-034	Let The Heavens Rejoice-E-5629	S. Butcher	Yr.Iss.	6.00	200-250.
81-01-035	Unto Us A Child Is Born-E-5630	S. Butcher	Suspd.	6.00	40-65.00
81-01-036	Baby's First Christmas-E-5631	S. Butcher	Suspd.	6.00	45-60.00
81-01-037	Baby's First Christmas-E-5632	S. Butcher	Suspd.	6.00	45-70.00
81-01-038	Come Let Us Adore Him (4pc. set)-E-5633	S. Butcher	Suspd.	22.00	75-115.00
81-01-039	Wee Three Kings (3pc. set)-E-5634	S. Butcher	Suspd.	19.00	100-129.
81-01-040	We Have Seen His Star-E-6120	S. Butcher	Retrd.	6.00	55-80.00
85-01-041	Have A Heavenly Christmas-12416	S. Butcher	Open	12.00	17.50-30.00
85-01-042	God Sent His Love-15768	S. Butcher	Yr.Iss.	10.00	30-75.00
85-01-043	May Your Christmas Be Happy-15822	S. Butcher	Suspd.	10.00	30-48.00
85-01-044	Happiness Is The Lord-15830	S. Butcher	Suspd.	10.00	20-37.00
85-01-045	May Your Christmas Be Delightful-15849	S. Butcher	Suspd.	10.00	15-35.00
85-01-046	Honk If You Love Jesus-15857	S. Butcher	Suspd.	10.00	15-27.00
85-01-047	Baby's First Christmas-15903	S. Butcher	Yr.Iss.	10.00	42.00
85-01-048	Baby's First Christmas-15911	S. Butcher	Yr.Iss.	10.00	30-45.00
86-01-049	Shepherd of Love-102288	S. Butcher	Suspd.	10.00	20-40.00
86-01-050	Wishing You A Cozy Christmas-102326	S. Butcher	Yr.Iss.	10.00	30-40.00
86-01-051	Our First Christmas Together-102350	S. Butcher	Yr.Iss.	10.00	15-39.00
86-01-052	Trust And Obey-102377	S. Butcher	Open	10.00	16-35.00
86-01-053	Love Rescued Me-102385	S. Butcher	Open	10.00	16-35.00
86-01-054	Angel Of Mercy-102407	S. Butcher	Open	10.00	15-35.00
86-01-055	It's A Perfect Boy-102415	S. Butcher	Suspd.	10.00	25-40.00
86-01-056	Lord Keep Me On My Toes-102423	S. Butcher	Retrd.	10.00	35-40.00
86-01-057	Serve With A Smile-102431	S. Butcher	Suspd.	10.00	20-35.00
86-01-058	Serve With A Smile-102458	S. Butcher	Suspd.	10.00	20-45.00
86-01-059	Reindeer-102466	S. Butcher	Yr.Iss.	11.00	190-275.
86-01-060	Rocking Horse-102474	S. Butcher	Suspd.	10.00	19-29.00
86-01-061	Baby's First Christmas-102504	S. Butcher	Yr.Iss.	10.00	25-40.00
86-01-062	Baby's First Christmas-102512	S. Butcher	Yr.Iss.	10.00	25-35.00
87-01-063	Bear The Good News Of Christmas-104515	S. Butcher	Yr.Iss.	12.50	25-35.00
87-01-064	Baby's First Christmas-109401	S. Butcher	Yr.Iss.	12.00	35-55.00
87-01-065	Baby's First Christmas-109428	S. Butcher	Yr.Iss.	12.00	35-45.00
87-01-066	Love Is The Best Gift Of All-109770	S. Butcher	Yr.Iss.	11.00	35-50.00
87-01-067	I'm A Possibility-111120	S. Butcher	Suspd.	11.00	30-49.00
87-01-068	You Have Touched So Many Hearts-112356	S. Butcher	Open	11.00	16-30.00
87-01-069	Waddle I Do Without You-112364	S. Butcher	Open	11.00	16-39.00

CHRISTMAS ORNAMENTS

Company		Series			
Number	**Name**	**Artist**	**Edition Limit**	**Issue Price**	**Quote**
87-01-070	I'm Sending You A White Christmas-112372	S. Butcher	Suspd.	11.00	20-25.00
87-01-071	He Cleansed My Soul-112380	S. Butcher	Open	12.00	16-25.00
87-01-072	Our First Christmas Together-112399	S. Butcher	Yr.Iss.	11.00	25-35.00
88-01-073	To My Forever Friend-113956	S. Butcher	Open	16.00	20-35.00
88-01-074	Smile Along The Way-113964	S. Butcher	Suspd.	15.00	20.00
88-01-075	God Sent You Just In Time-113972	S. Butcher	Suspd.	13.50	25-35.00
88-01-076	Rejoice O Earth-113980	S. Butcher	Retrd.	13.50	25-50.00
88-01-077	Cheers To The Leader-113999	S. Butcher	Suspd.	13.50	25-35.00
88-01-078	My Love Will Never Let You Go-114006	S. Butcher	Suspd.	13.50	25-35.00
88-01-079	Baby's First Christmas-115282	S. Butcher	Yr.Iss.	15.00	25-35.00
88-01-080	Time To Wish You A Merry Christmas -115320	S. Butcher	Yr.Iss.	13.00	45-60.00
88-01-081	Our First Christmas Together-520233	S. Butcher	Yr.Iss.	13.00	20-35.00
88-01-082	Baby's First Christmas-520241	S. Butcher	Yr.Iss.	15.00	22-40.00
88-01-083	You Are My Gift Come True-520276	S. Butcher	Yr.Iss.	12.50	25-50.00
88-01-084	Hang On For The Holly Days-520292	S. Butcher	Yr.Iss.	13.00	25-45.00
89-01-085	Christmas is Ruff Without You-520462	S. Butcher	Yr.Iss.	13.00	35.00
89-01-086	May All Your Christmases Be White-521302 (dated)	S. Butcher	Yr.Iss.	15.00	16.00
90-01-087	Dashing Through the Snow-521574	S. Butcher	Open	15.00	16.00
89-01-088	Our First Christmas Together-521588	S. Butcher	Yr.Iss.	17.50	35.00
90-01-089	Don't Let the Holidays Get You Down-521590	S. Butcher	Open	15.00	16.00
89-01-090	Oh Holy Night-522848	S. Butcher	Yr.Iss.	13.50	35.00
89-01-091	Make A Joyful Noise-522910	S. Butcher	Open	15.00	16.00
89-01-092	Love One Another-522929	S. Butcher	Open	17.50	20-25.00
89-01-093	I Believe In The Old Rugged Cross-522953	S. Butcher	Open	15.00	30.00
89-01-094	Peace On Earth-523062	S. Butcher	Yr.Iss.	25.00	75-130.00
89-01-095	Baby's First Christmas-523194	S. Butcher	Yr.Iss.	15.00	30.00
89-01-096	Baby's First Christmas-523208	S. Butcher	Yr.Iss.	15.00	30.00
90-01-097	Dashing Through The Snow-521574	S. Butcher	Open	15.00	15-18.00
90-01-098	Baby's First Christmas-523798	S. Butcher	Yr.Iss.	15.00	25.00
90-01-099	Baby's First Christmas-523771	S. Butcher	Yr.Iss.	15.00	25.00
90-01-100	Once Upon A Holy Night-523852	S. Butcher	Yr.Iss.	15.00	24-30.00
90-01-101	Don't Let the Holidays Get You Down-521590	S. Butcher	Open	15.00	15.00
90-01-102	Wishing You A Purr-fect Holiday-520497	S. Butcher	Yr.Iss.	15.00	20-35.00
90-01-103	Friends Never Drift Apart-522937	S. Butcher	Open	17.50	17.50
90-01-104	Our First Christmas Together-525324	S. Butcher	Yr.Iss.	17.50	20-35.00
90-01-105	Glide Through The Holidays-521566	S. Butcher	Retrd.	13.50	125-150.
90-01-106	May Your Christmas Be A Happy Home-523704	S. Butcher	Yr.Iss.	27.50	35-75.00
91-01-107	Our First Christmas Together-522945	S. Butcher	Yr.Iss.	17.50	25.00
91-01-108	Happy Trails Is Trusting Jesus-523224	S. Butcher	Open	15.00	16.00
91-01-109	The Good Lord Always Delivers-527165	S. Butcher	Suspd.	15.00	15.00
91-01-110	Sno-Bunny Falls For You Like I Do-520438	S. Butcher	Yr.Iss.	15.00	25-35.00
91-01-111	Baby's First Christmas (Girl)-527092	S. Butcher	Yr.Iss.	15.00	20.00
91-01-112	Baby's First Christmas (Boy)-527084	S. Butcher	Yr.Iss.	15.00	25.00
91-01-113	May Your Christmas Be Merry (Ornament On Base)-526940	S. Butcher	Yr.Iss.	30.00	30-45.00
91-01-114	May Your Christmas Be Merry-524174	S. Butcher	Yr.Iss.	15.00	25.00
92-01-115	Baby's First Christmas-527475	S. Butcher	Yr.Iss.	15.00	15.00
92-01-116	Baby's First Christmas-527483	S. Butcher	Yr.Iss.	15.00	15.00
92-01-117	But The Greatest of These Is Love-527696	S. Butcher	Yr.Iss.	15.00	15-25.00
92-01-118	Our First Christmas-528870	S. Butcher	Yr.Iss.	17.50	17.50
92-01-119	But The Greatest of These Is Love-527734 (Ornament on Base)	S. Butcher	Yr.Iss.	30.00	30-40.00
92-01-120	Good Friends Are For Always-524131	S. Butcher	Open	15.00	16.00
92-01-121	Lord, Keep Me On My Toes-525332	S. Butcher	Open	15.00	16.00
92-01-122	I'm Nuts About You-520411	S. Butcher	Yr.Iss.	15.00	15-25.00
93-01-123	Wishing You the Sweetest Christmas-530190	S. Butcher	Yr.Iss.	30.00	30.00
93-01-124	Wishing You the Sweetest Christmas-530212	S. Butcher	Yr.Iss.	15.00	15.00
93-01-125	Loving, Caring And Sharing Along The Way -PM040 (Club Appreciation Members Only)	S. Butcher	Yr.Iss.	12.50	12.50
93-01-126	15 Years Tweet Music Together-530840 (15th Anniversary Commemorative Ornament)	S. Butcher	Yr.Iss.	15.00	15-50.00
93-01-127	Our First Christmas Together-530506	S. Butcher	Yr.Iss.	17.50	17.50
93-01-128	Share in The Warmth of Christmas-527211	S. Butcher	Open	15.00	16.00
93-01-129	It's So Uplifting to Have a Friend Like You -528846	S. Butcher	Open	16.00	16.00
93-01-130	Slow Down & Enjoy The Holidays-520489	S. Butcher	Yr.Iss.	16.00	16.00
93-01-131	Baby's First Christmas-530859	S. Butcher	Yr.Iss.	15.00	15.00
93-01-132	Baby's First Christmas-530867	S. Butcher	Yr.Iss.	15.00	15.00
93-01-133	Sugartown Chapel Ornament-530484	S. Butcher	Yr.Iss.	17.50	17.50
Enesco Corporation		**Precious Moments DSR Open House Weekend Ornaments**			
92-02-001	1992 -The Magic Starts With You-529648	S. Butcher	Retrd.	16.00	25.00
93-02-002	1993 -An Event For All Seasons-529974	S. Butcher	Yr.Iss.	15.00	15.00
Enesco Corporation		**Precious Moments Easter Seal Commemorative Ornaments**			
94-03-001	It's No Secret What God Can Do-244570	S. Butcher	Yr.Iss.	6.50	6.50
Enesco Corporation		**Memories of Yesterday Ornaments**			
88-02-001	Baby's First Christmas 1988-520373	M. Attwell	Yr.Iss.	13.50	25-30.00
88-02-002	Special Delivery! 1988-520381	M. Attwell	Yr.Iss.	13.50	25-38.00
89-02-003	Baby's First Christmas-522465	M. Attwell	Open	15.00	15-20.00
89-02-004	Christmas Together-522562	M. Attwell	Open	15.00	15-25.00
89-02-005	A Surprise for Santa-522473 (1989)	M. Attwell	Yr.Iss.	13.50	20-30.00
90-02-006	Time For Bed-524638	M. Attwell	Yr.Iss.	15.00	15-30.00
90-02-007	New Moon-524646	M. Attwell	Open	15.00	15-25.00
90-02-008	Moonstruck-524794	M. Attwell	Retrd.	15.00	15-25.00
91-02-009	Just Watchin' Over You-525421	M. Attwell	Open	17.50	17.50
91-02-010	Lucky Me-525448	M. Attwell	Retrd.	16.00	20.00
91-02-011	Lucky You-525847	M. Attwell	Retrd.	16.00	20.00
91-02-012	Star Fishin'-525820	M. Attwell	Open	16.00	16.00
91-02-013	S'no Use Lookin' Back Now!-527181(dated)	M. Attwell	Yr.Iss.	17.50	28.00
92-02-014	Merry Christmas, Little Boo-Boo-528803	M. Attwell	Open	37.50	37.50
92-02-015	I'll Fly Along To See You Soon-525804 (1992 Dated Bisque)	M. Attwell	Yr.Iss.	16.00	18.00
92-02-016	Mommy, I Teared It-527041 (Five Year Anniversary Limited Edition)	M. Attwell	Yr.Iss.	15.00	20.00
92-02-017	Star Light, Star Bright-528838	M. Attwell	Open	16.00	16.00
92-02-018	Swinging Together-580481 (1992 Dated Artplas)	M. Attwell	Yr.Iss.	17.50	22.00
92-02-019	Sailin' With My Friends-587575 (Artplas)	M. Attwell	Open	25.00	25.00
93-02-020	Wish I Could Fly To You-525790 (dated)	M. Attwell	Yr.Iss.	16.00	16.00
93-02-021	May All Your Finest Dreams Come True -528811	M. Attwell	Open	16.00	16.00
93-02-022	Bringing Good Wishes Your Way-592846 (Artplas)	M. Attwell	Open	25.00	25.00
94-02-023	Give Yourself a Hug From Me!-529109 ('94 Dated)	M. Attwell	Yr. Iss.	17.50	17.50
94-02-024	Just Dreaming of You-524786	M. Attwell	Open	16.00	16.00
94-02-025	'Bout Time I Came Along to See You-592854 (Artplas)	M. Attwell	Open	8.75	8.75

Company		Series			
Number	**Name**	**Artist**	**Edition Limit**	**Issue Price**	**Quote**
Enesco Corporation		**Memories of Yesterday Society Member's Only Ornament**			
92-03-001	With Luck And A Friend, I's In Heaven-MY922	M. Attwell	Yr.Iss.	16.00	32.00
93-03-002	I'm Bringing Good Luck-Wherever You Are -MY932	M. Attwell	Yr.Iss.	16.00	22.00
Enesco Corporation		**Memories of Yesterday Event Item Only**			
93-04-001	How 'Bout A Little Kiss?-527068	Enesco	Yr.Iss.	16.50	50.00
Enesco Corporation		**Enesco Treasury of Christmas Ornaments**			
83-04-001	Wide Open Throttle-E-0242	Enesco	3-Yr.	12.00	35.00
83-04-002	Baby's First Christmas-E-0271	Enesco	Yr.Iss.	6.00	N/A
83-04-003	Grandchild's First Christmas-E-0272	Enesco	Yr.Iss.	5.00	N/A
83-04-004	Baby's First Christmas-E-0273	Enesco	3-Yr.	9.00	N/A
83-04-005	Toy Drum Teddy-E-0274	Enesco	4-Yr.	9.00	N/A
83-04-006	Watching At The Window-E-0275	Enesco	3-Yr.	13.00	N/A
83-04-007	To A Special Teacher-E-0276	Enesco	7-Yr.	5.00	15.00
83-04-008	Toy Shop-E-0277	Enesco	7-Yr.	8.00	50.00
83-04-009	Carousel Horse-E-0278	Enesco	7-Yr.	9.00	20.00
81-04-010	Look Out Below-E-6135	Enesco	2-Yr.	6.00	N/A
82-04-011	Flyin' Santa Christmas Special 1982-E-6136	Enesco	Yr.Iss.	9.00	75.00
81-04-012	Flyin' Santa Christmas Special 1981-E-6136	Enesco	Yr.Iss.	9.00	N/A
81-04-013	Sawin' Elf Helper-E-6138	Enesco	2-Yr.	6.00	40.00
81-04-014	Snow Shoe-In Santa-E-6139	Enesco	2-Yr.	6.00	35.00
81-04-015	Baby's First Christmas 1981-E-6145	Enesco	Yr.Iss.	6.00	N/A
81-04-016	Our Hero-E-6146	Enesco	2-Yr.	4.00	N/A
81-04-017	Whoops-E-6147	Enesco	2-Yr.	3.50	N/A
81-04-018	Whoops, It's 1981-E-6148	Enesco	Yr.Iss.	7.50	75.00
81-04-019	Not A Creature Was Stirring-E-6149	Enesco	2-Yr.	4.00	25.00
84-04-020	Joy To The World-E-6209	Enesco	2-Yr.	9.00	35.00
84-04-021	Letter To Santa-E-6210	Enesco	2-Yr.	5.00	30.00
84-04-022	Lucy & Me Photo Frames-E-6211	Enesco	3-Yr.	5.00	N/A
84-04-023	Lucy & Me Photo Frames-E-6211	Enesco	3-Yr.	5.00	N/A
84-04-024	Lucy & Me Photo Frames-E-6211	Enesco	3-Yr.	5.00	N/A
84-04-025	Lucy & Me Photo Frames-E-6211	Enesco	3-Yr.	5.00	N/A
84-04-026	Lucy & Me Photo Frames-E-6211	Enesco	3-Yr.	5.00	N/A
84-04-027	Lucy & Me Photo Frames-E-6211	Enesco	3-Yr.	5.00	N/A
84-04-028	Baby's First Christmas 1984-E-6212	Gilmore	Yr.Iss.	10.00	30.00
84-04-029	Merry Christmas Mother-E-6213	Enesco	3-Yr.	10.00	30.00
84-04-030	Baby's First Christmas 1984-E-6215	Enesco	Yr.Iss.	6.00	N/A
84-04-031	Ferris Wheel Mice-E-6216	Enesco	2-Yr.	9.00	30.00
84-04-032	Cuckoo Clock-E-6217	Enesco	2-Yr.	8.00	40.00
84-04-033	Muppet Babies Baby's First Christmas-E6222	J. Henson	Yr.Iss.	10.00	45.00
84-04-034	Muppet Babies Baby's First Christmas-E6223	J. Henson	Yr.Iss.	10.00	45.00
84-04-035	Garfield Hark! The Herald Angel-E-6224	J. Davis	2-Yr.	7.50	35.00
84-04-036	Fun in Santa's Sleigh-E-6225	J. Davis	2-Yr.	12.00	35.00
84-04-037	"Deer!" Odie-E-6226	J. Davis	2-Yr.	6.00	30.00
84-04-038	Garfield The Snow Cat-E-6227	J. Davis	2-Yr.	12.00	35.00
84-04-039	Peek-A-Bear Baby's First Christmas-E-6228	Enesco	3-Yr.	10.00	N/A
84-04-040	Peek-A-Bear Baby's First Christmas-E-6229	Enesco	3-Yr.	9.00	N/A
84-04-041	Owl Be Home For Christmas-E-6230	Enesco	2-Yr.	10.00	23.00
84-04-042	Santa's Trolley-E-6231	Enesco	3-Yr.	11.00	50.00
84-04-043	Holiday Penguin-E-6240	Enesco	3-Yr.	1.50	15-20.00
84-04-044	Little Drummer-E-6241	Enesco	5-Yr.	2.00	N/A
84-04-045	Happy Holidays-E-6248	Enesco	2-Yr.	2.00	N/A
84-04-046	Christmas Nest-E-6249	Enesco	2-Yr.	3.00	25.00
84-04-047	Bunny's Christmas Stocking-E-6251	Enesco	Yr.Iss.	2.00	15.00
84-04-048	Santa On Ice-E-6252	Enesco	3-Yr.	2.50	25.00
84-04-049	Treasured Memories The New Sled-E-6256	Enesco	2-Yr.	7.00	N/A
84-04-050	Up On The House Top-E-6280	Enesco	6-Yr.	9.00	N/A
84-04-051	Penguins On Ice-E-6280	Enesco	2-Yr.	7.50	N/A
84-04-052	Grandchild's First Christmas 1984-E-6286	Enesco	Yr.Iss.	5.00	N/A
84-04-053	Grandchild's First Christmas1984-E-6286	Enesco	Yr.Iss.	5.00	N/A
84-04-054	Godchild's First Christmas-E-6287	Enesco	3-Yr.	7.00	N/A
84-04-055	Santa In The Box-E-6292	Enesco	2-Yr.	6.00	N/A
84-04-056	Carousel Horse-E-6913	Enesco	2-Yr.	1.50	N/A
83-04-057	Arctic Charmer-E-6945	Enesco	2-Yr.	7.00	N/A
82-04-058	Victorian Sleigh-E-6946	Enesco	4-Yr.	9.00	15.00
83-04-059	Wing-A-Ding Angel-E-6948	Enesco	3-Yr.	7.00	50.00
82-04-060	A Saviour Is Born This Day-E-6949	Enesco	8-Yr.	4.00	12-20.00
82-04-061	Crescent Santa-E-6950	Gilmore	4-Yr.	10.00	50.00
82-04-062	Baby's First Christmas 1982-E-6952	Enesco	Yr.Iss.	10.00	N/A
82-04-063	Polar Bear Fun Whoops,It's 1982-E-6953	Enesco	Yr.Iss.	10.00	75.00
82-04-064	Holiday Skier-E-6954	J. Davis	5-Yr.	7.00	N/A
82-04-065	Toy Soldier 1982-E-6957	Enesco	Yr.Iss.	6.50	N/A
82-04-066	Merry Christmas Grandma-E-6975	Enesco	3-Yr.	5.00	N/A
82-04-067	Carousel Horses-E-6958	Enesco	3-Yr.	8.00	20-40.00
82-04-068	Dear Santa-E-6959	Gilmore	8-Yr.	10.00	17.00
82-04-069	Penguin Power-E-6977	Enesco	2-Yr.	6.00	15.00
82-04-070	Bunny Winter Playground 1982-E-6978	Enesco	Yr.Iss.	10.00	N/A
82-04-071	Baby's First Christmas 1982-E-6979	Enesco	Yr.Iss.	10.00	N/A
83-04-072	Carousel Horses-E-6980	Enesco	4-Yr.	8.00	N/A
82-04-073	Grandchild's First Christmas 1982-E-6983	Enesco	Yr.Iss.	5.00	73.00
82-04-074	Merry Christmas Teacher-E-6984	Enesco	4-Yr.	7.00	N/A
83-04-075	Garfield Cuts The Ice-E-8771	J. Davis	3-Yr.	6.00	45.00
84-04-076	A Stocking Full For 1984-E-8773	J. Davis	Yr.Iss.	6.00	N/A
83-04-077	Stocking Full For 1983-E-8773	J. Davis	Yr.Iss.	6.00	N/A
85-04-078	Santa Claus Balloon-55794	Enesco	Yr.Iss.	8.50	20.00
85-04-079	Carousel Reindeer-55808	Enesco	4-Yr.	12.00	35-40.00
85-04-080	Angel In Flight-55816	Enesco	4-Yr.	8.00	20.00
85-04-081	Christmas Penguin-55824	Enesco	4-Yr.	7.50	35.00
85-04-082	Merry Christmas Godchild-55832	Gilmore	5-Yr.	8.00	N/A
85-04-083	Baby's First Christmas-55840	Enesco	2-Yr.	15.00	N/A
85-04-084	Old Fashioned Rocking Horse-55859	Enesco	2-Yr.	10.00	15.00
85-04-085	Child's Second Christmas-55867	Enesco	5-Yr.	11.00	N/A
85-04-086	Fishing For Stars-55875	Enesco	5-Yr.	9.00	20.00
85-04-087	Baby Blocks-55883	Enesco	2-Yr.	12.00	N/A
85-04-088	Christmas Toy Chest-55891	Enesco	5-Yr.	10.00	N/A
85-04-089	Grandchild's First Ornament-55921	Enesco	5-Yr.	7.00	8.00
85-04-090	Joy Photo Frame-55956	Enesco	Yr.Iss.	6.00	N/A
85-04-091	We Three Kings-55964	Enesco	Yr.Iss.	4.50	20.00
85-04-092	The Night Before Christmas-55972	Enesco	2-Yr.	5.00	N/A
85-04-093	Baby's First Christmas 1985-55980	Enesco	Yr.Iss.	6.00	N/A
85-04-094	Baby Rattle Photo Frame-56006	Enesco	2-Yr.	5.00	N/A
85-04-095	Baby's First Christmas 1985-56014	Gilmore	Yr.Iss.	10.00	N/A
85-04-096	Christmas Plane Ride-56049	L. Rigg	6-Yr.	10.00	N/A
85-04-097	Scottie Celebrating Christmas-56065	Enesco	5-Yr.	7.50	25.00
85-04-098	North Pole Native-56073	Enesco	2-Yr.	9.00	N/A
85-04-099	Skating Walrus-56081	Enesco	2-Yr.	9.00	20.00
85-04-100	Ski Time-56111	J. Davis	Yr.Iss.	13.00	N/A
85-04-101	North Pole Express-56138	J. Davis	Yr.Iss.	12.00	N/A
85-04-102	Merry Christmas Mother-56146	J. Davis	Yr.Iss.	8.50	N/A
85-04-103	Hoppy Christmas-56154	J. Davis	Yr.Iss.	8.50	N/A
85-04-104	Merry Christmas Teacher-56170	J. Davis	Yr.Iss.	6.00	N/A
85-04-105	Garfield-In-The-Box-56189	J. Davis	Yr.Iss.	6.50	25.00

CHRISTMAS ORNAMENTS

Company		Series			
Number	Name	Artist	Edition Limit	Issue Price	Quote
85-04-106	Merry Christmas Grandma-56197	Enesco	Yr.Iss.	7.00	N/A
85-04-107	Christmas Lights-56200	Enesco	2-Yr.	8.00	N/A
85-04-108	Victorian Doll House-56251	Enesco	Yr.Iss.	13.00	40.00
85-04-109	Tobaoggan Ride-56286	Enesco	4-Yr.	6.00	N/A
85-04-110	Look Out Below-56375	Enesco	Yr.Iss.	8.50	40.00
85-04-111	Flying Santa Christmas Special-56383	Enesco	2-Yr.	10.00	N/A
85-04-112	Sawin Elf Helper-56391	Enesco	Yr.Iss.	8.00	N/A
85-04-113	Snow Shoe-In Santa-56405	Enesco	Yr.Iss.	8.00	50.00
85-04-114	Our Hero-56413	Enesco	Yr.Iss.	5.50	N/A
85-04-115	Not A Creaturxe Was Stirring-56421	Enesco	2-Yr.	4.00	N/A
85-04-116	Merry Christmas Teacher-56448	Enesco	Yr.Iss.	9.00	N/A
85-04-117	A Stocking Full For 1985-56464	J. Davis	Yr.Iss.	6.00	25.00
85-04-118	St. Nicholas Circa 1910-56659	Enesco	5-Yr.	6.00	15.00
85-04-119	Christmas Tree Photo Frame-56871	Enesco	4-Yr.	10.00	N/A
90-04-120	Deck The Halls-566063	Enesco	3-Yr.	12.50	N/A
88-04-121	Making A Point-489212	G.G. Santiago	3-Yr.	10.00	N/A
88-04-122	Mouse Upon A Pipe-489220	G.G. Santiago	2-Yr.	10.00	12.00
88-04-123	North Pole Deadline-489387	Enesco	3-Yr.	13.50	N/A
88-04-124	Christmas Pin-Up-489409	Enesco	2-Yr.	11.00	18.00
88-04-125	Airmail For Teacher-489425	Gilmore	3-Yr.	13.50	N/A
86-04-126	1st Christmas Together 1986-551171	Enesco	Yr.Iss.	9.00	15-35.00
86-04-127	Elf Stringing Popcorn-551198	Enesco	4-Yr.	10.00	20-30.00
86-04-128	Christmas Scottie-551201	Enesco	4-Yr.	7.00	15-30.00
86-04-129	Santa and Child-551236	Enesco	4-Yr.	13.50	25-50.00
86-04-130	The Christmas Angel-551244	Enesco	4-Yr.	22.50	40-50.00
86-04-131	Carousel Unicorn-551252	Gilmore	4-Yr.	12.00	30-40.00
86-04-132	Have a Heavenly Holiday-551260	Enesco	4-Yr.	9.00	N/A
86-04-133	Siamese Kitten-551279	Enesco	4-Yr.	9.00	25.00
86-04-134	Old Fashioned Doll House-551287	Enesco	4-Yr.	15.00	N/A
86-04-135	Holiday Fisherman-551309	Enesco	3-Yr.	8.00	N/A
86-04-136	Antique Toy-551317	Enesco	3-Yr.	9.00	N/A
86-04-137	Time For Christmas-551325	Gilmore	4-Yr.	13.00	N/A
86-04-138	Christmas Calendar-551333	Enesco	2-Yr.	7.00	N/A
86-04-139	Merry Christmas-551341	Gilmore	3-Yr.	8.00	45.00
86-04-140	The Santa Claus Shoppe Circa1905-551562	J. Grossman	4-Yr.	8.00	15.00
86-04-141	Baby Bear Sleigh-551651	Gilmore	3-Yr.	9.00	30.00
86-04-142	Baby's First Christmas 1986-551678	Gilmore	Yr.Iss.	10.00	20.00
86-04-143	First Christmas Together-551708	Enesco	3-Yr.	6.00	10.00
86-04-144	Baby's First Christmas-551716	Enesco	3-Yr.	5.50	10.00
86-04-145	Baby's First Christmas 1986-551724	Enesco	Yr.Iss.	6.50	30.00
86-04-146	Peek-A-Bear Grandchild's First Christmas-552004	Enesco	Yr.Iss.	6.00	23.00
86-04-147	Peek-A-Bear Present-552089	Enesco	4-Yr.	2.50	N/A
86-04-148	Peek-A-Bear Present-552089	Enesco	4-Yr.	2.50	N/A
86-04-149	Peek-A-Bear Present-552089	Enesco	4-Yr.	2.50	N/A
86-04-150	Peek-A-Bear Present-552089	Enesco	4-Yr.	2.50	N/A
86-04-151	Merry Christmas 1986-552186	L. Rigg	Yr.Iss.	8.00	N/A
86-04-152	Merry Christmas 1986-552534	L. Rigg	Yr.Iss.	8.00	N/A
86-04-153	Lucy & Me Christmas Tree-552542	L. Rigg	3-Yr.	7.00	25.00
86-04-154	Santa's Helpers-552607	Enesco	3-Yr.	2.50	N/A
86-04-155	My Special Friend-552615	Enesco	3-Yr.	6.00	N/A
86-04-156	Christmas Wishes From Panda-552623	Enesco	3-Yr.	6.00	N/A
86-04-157	Lucy & Me Ski Time-552658	L. Rigg	2-Yr.	6.50	30.00
86-04-158	Merry Christmas Teacher-552666	Enesco	3-Yr.	6.50	N/A
86-04-159	Country Cousins Merry Christmas, Mom-552704	Enesco	3-Yr.	7.00	23.00
86-04-160	Country Cousins Merry Christmas, Dad-552704	Enesco	3-Yr.	7.00	23.00
86-04-161	Country Cousins Merry Christmas, Mom-552712	Enesco	4-Yr.	7.00	23.00
86-04-162	Country Cousins Merry Christmas, Dad-552712	Enesco	4-Yr.	7.00	25.00
86-04-163	Grandmother's Little Angel-552747	Enesco	4-Yr.	8.00	N/A
87-04-164	Puppy's 1st Christmas-552909	Enesco	2-Yr.	4.00	N/A
87-04-165	Kitty's 1st Christmas-552917	Enesco	2-Yr.	4.00	25.00
87-04-166	Merry Christmas Puppy-552925	Enesco	2-Yr.	3.50	N/A
87-04-167	Merry Christmas Kitty-552933	Enesco	2-Yr.	3.50	N/A
86-04-168	I Love My Grandparents-553263	Enesco	Yr.Iss.	6.00	N/A
86-04-169	Merry Christmas Mom & Dad-553271	Enesco	Yr.Iss.	6.00	N/A
86-04-170	S. Claus Hollycopter-553344	Enesco	4-Yr.	13.50	35.00
86-04-171	From Our House To Your House-553360	Enesco	3-Yr.	15.00	40.00
86-04-172	Christmas Rattle-553379	Enesco	3-Yr.	8.00	35.00
86-04-173	Bah, Humbug!-553387	Enesco	4-Yr.	9.00	N/A
86-04-174	God Bless Us Everyone-553395	Enesco	4-Yr.	10.00	15.00
87-04-175	Carousel Mobile-553409	Enesco	3-Yr.	15.00	50.00
86-04-176	Holiday Train-553417	Enesco	4-Yr.	10.00	N/A
86-04-177	Lighten Up!-553603	J. Davis	5-Yr.	10.00	N/A
86-04-178	Gift Wrap Odie-553611	J. Davis	Yr.Iss.	7.00	20.00
86-04-179	Merry Christmas-553646	Enesco	4-Yr.	8.00	N/A
87-04-180	M.V.B. (Most Valuable Bear)-554219	Enesco	2-Yr.	3.00	N/A
87-04-181	M.V.B. (Most Valuable Bear)-554219	Enesco	2-Yr.	3.00	N/A
87-04-182	M.V.B. (Most Valuable Bear)-554219	Enesco	2-Yr.	3.00	N/A
87-04-183	M.V.B. (Most Valuable Bear)-554219	Enesco	2-Yr.	3.00	N/A
88-04-184	1st Christmas Together-554537	Gilmore	3-Yr.	15.00	N/A
88-04-185	An Eye On Christmas-554545	Gilmore	3-Yr.	22.50	50.00
88-04-186	A Mouse Check-554553	Gilmore	3-Yr.	13.50	45.00
88-04-187	Merry Christmas Engine-554561	Enesco	2-Yr.	22.50	35.00
89-04-188	Sardine Express-554588	Gilmore	2-Yr.	17.50	30.00
88-04-189	1st Christmas Together 1988-554596	Enesco	Yr.Iss.	10.00	N/A
88-04-190	Forever Friends-554626	Gilmore	2-Yr.	12.00	23.00
88-04-191	Santa's Survey-554642	Enesco	2-Yr.	35.00	75-100.00
89-04-192	Old Town's Church-554871	Gilmore	2-Yr.	17.50	20.00
88-04-193	A Chipmunk Holiday-554898	Gilmore	3-Yr.	11.00	N/A
88-04-194	Christmas Is Coming-554901	Enesco	3-Yr.	12.00	12.00
88-04-195	Baby's First Christmas 1988-554928	Enesco	Yr.Iss.	7.50	N/A
88-04-196	Baby's First Christmas 1988-554936	Gilmore	Yr.Iss.	10.00	N/A
88-04-197	The Christmas Train-554944	Enesco	3-Yr.	15.00	N/A
88-04-198	Li'l Drummer Bear-554952	Gilmore	3-Yr.	12.00	30.00
87-04-199	Baby's First Christmas-555061	Enesco	3-Yr.	12.00	N/A
87-04-200	Baby's First Christmas-555088	Enesco	3-Yr.	7.50	15.00
87-04-201	Baby's First Christmas-555118	Enesco	3-Yr.	6.00	N/A
87-04-202	Sugar Plum Bearies-555193	Enesco	2-Yr.	4.50	N/A
87-04-203	Garfield Merry Kissmas-555215	J. Davis	3-Yr.	8.50	30.00
87-04-204	Sleigh Away-555401	Enesco	3-Yr.	12.00	N/A
87-04-205	Merry Christmas 1987-555428	L. Rigg	Yr.Iss.	8.00	N/A
87-04-206	Merry Christmas 1987-555436	L. Rigg	Yr.Iss.	8.00	N/A
87-04-207	Lucy & Me Storybook Bear-555444	L. Rigg	3-Yr.	6.50	N/A
87-04-208	Time For Christmas-555452	L. Rigg	3-Yr.	12.00	20.00
87-04-209	Lucy & Me Angel On A Cloud-555487	L. Rigg	3-Yr.	8.00	35.00
87-04-210	Teddy's Stocking-555940	Gilmore	3-Yr.	10.00	N/A
87-04-211	Kitty's Jack-In-The-Box-555959	Enesco	3-Yr.	11.00	30.00
87-04-212	Merry Christmas Teacher-555967	Enesco	3-Yr.	7.50	N/A
87-04-213	Mouse In A Mitten-555975	Enesco	3-Yr.	7.50	N/A
87-04-214	Boy On A Rocking Horse-555983	Enesco	3-Yr.	12.00	18.00

Company		Series			
Number	Name	Artist	Edition Limit	Issue Price	Quote
87-04-215	Peek-A-Bear Letter To Santa-555991	Enesco	2-Yr.	8.00	30.00
87-04-216	Garfield Sugar Plum Fairy-556009	J. Davis	3-Yr.	8.50	20.00
87-04-217	Garfield The Nutcracker-556017	J. Davis	4-Yr.	8.50	35.00
87-04-218	Home Sweet Home-556033	M. Gilmore	3-Yr.	15.00	45-55.00
87-04-219	Baby's First Christmas-556041	Enesco	4-Yr.	10.00	20.00
87-04-220	Little Sailor Elf-556068	Enesco	3-Yr.	10.00	28.00
87-04-221	Carousel Goose-556076	Enesco	3-Yr.	17.00	40.00
87-04-222	Night Caps-556084	Enesco	2-Yr.	5.50	N/A
87-04-223	Night Caps-556084	Enesco	2-Yr.	5.50	N/A
87-04-224	Night Caps-556084	Enesco	2-Yr.	5.50	N/A
87-04-225	Night Caps-556084	Enesco	2-Yr.	5.50	N/A
87-04-226	Rocking Horse Past Joys-556157	Enesco	3-Yr.	10.00	20.00
87-04-227	Partridge In A Pear Tree-556173	Gilmore	3-Yr.	9.00	35.00
87-04-228	Carousel Lion-556025	M. Gilmore	3-Yr.	12.00	25.00
87-04-229	Skating Santa 1987-556211	Enesco	Yr.Iss.	13.50	75.00
87-04-230	Baby's First Christmas 1987-556238	Gilmore	Yr.Iss.	10.00	N/A
87-04-231	Baby's First Christmas 1987-556254	Enesco	Yr.Iss.	7.00	N/A
87-04-232	Teddy's Suspenders-556262	Enesco	4-Yr.	8.50	19.00
87-04-233	Baby's First Christmas 1987-556297	Enesco	Yr.Iss.	2.00	N/A
87-04-234	Baby's First Christmas 1987-556297	Enesco	Yr.Iss.	2.00	N/A
87-04-235	Beary Christmas Family-556300	Enesco	2-Yr.	2.00	N/A
87-04-236	Beary Christmas Family-556300	Enesco	2-Yr.	2.00	N/A
87-04-237	Beary Christmas Family-556300	Enesco	2-Yr.	2.00	N/A
87-04-238	Beary Christmas Family-556300	Enesco	2-Yr.	2.00	N/A
87-04-239	Beary Christmas Family-556300	Enesco	2-Yr.	2.00	N/A
87-04-240	Beary Christmas Family-556300	Enesco	2-Yr.	2.00	N/A
87-04-241	Merry ChristmasTeacher-556319	Enesco	2-Yr.	2.00	N/A
87-04-242	Merry ChristmasTeacher-556319	Enesco	2-Yr.	2.00	N/A
87-04-243	Merry ChristmasTeacher-556319	Enesco	2-Yr.	2.00	N/A
87-04-244	Merry ChristmasTeacher-556319	Enesco	2-Yr.	2.00	N/A
87-04-245	1st ChristmasTogether 1987-556335	Enesco	Yr.Iss.	9.00	18.00
87-04-246	Country Cousins Katie Goes Ice Skating-556304	Enesco	3-Yr.	8.00	30.00
87-04-247	Country Cousins Scooter Snowman-556386	Enesco	3-Yr.	8.00	30.00
87-04-248	Santa's List-556394	Enesco	3-Yr.	7.00	23.00
87-04-249	Kitty's Bed-556408	Enesco	3-Yr.	12.00	30.00
87-04-250	Grandchild's First Christmas-556416	Enesco	3-Yr.	10.00	N/A
87-04-251	Two Turtledoves-556432	Gilmore	3-Yr.	9.00	30.00
87-04-252	Three French Hens-556440	Gilmore	3-Yr.	9.00	30.00
88-04-253	Four Calling Birds-556459	Gilmore	3-Yr.	11.00	30.00
87-04-254	Teddy Takes A Spin-556467	Enesco	4-Yr.	13.00	35.00
87-04-255	Tiny Toy Thimble Mobile-556475	Enesco	2-Yr.	12.00	35.00
87-04-256	Bucket O'Love-556491	Enesco	2-Yr.	2.50	N/A
87-04-257	Bucket O'Love-556491	Enesco	2-Yr.	2.50	N/A
87-04-258	Puppy Love-556505	Enesco	3-Yr.	6.00	N/A
87-04-259	Peek-A-Bear My Special Friend-556513	Enesco	4-Yr.	6.00	30.00
87-04-260	Our First Christmas Together-556548	Enesco	3-Yr.	13.00	20.00
87-04-261	Three Little Bears-556556	Enesco	3-Yr.	7.50	15.00
87-04-262	Lucy & Me Mailbox Bear-556564	L. Rigg	4-Yr.	3.00	N/A
87-04-263	Twinkle Bear-556572	Gilmore	3-Yr.	8.00	N/A
87-04-264	I'm Dreaming Of A Bright Christmas-556602	Enesco	2-Yr.	2.50	N/A
87-04-265	I'm Dreaming Of A Bright Christmas-556602	Enesco	2-Yr.	2.50	N/A
87-04-266	Christmas Train-557196	Enesco	3-Yr.	10.00	N/A
88-04-267	Dairy Christmas-557501	M. Cook	2-Yr.	10.00	30.00
88-04-268	Merry Christmas 1988-557595	L. Rigg	Yr.Iss.	10.00	N/A
88-04-269	Merry Christmas 1988-557609	L. Rigg	Yr.Iss.	10.00	N/A
88-04-270	Toy Chest Keepsake-558206	L. Rigg	3-Yr.	12.50	30.00
88-04-271	Teddy Bear Greetings-558214	L. Rigg	3-Yr.	8.00	30.00
88-04-272	Jester Bear-558222	L. Rigg	2-Yr.	8.00	N/A
88-04-273	Night-Watch Cat-558362	J. Davis	3-Yr.	13.00	35.00
88-04-274	Christmas Thim-bell-558389	Enesco	Yr.Iss.	4.00	30.00
88-04-275	Christmas Thim-bell-558389	Enesco	Yr.Iss.	4.00	N/A
88-04-276	Christmas Thim-bell-558389	Enesco	Yr.Iss.	4.00	N/A
88-04-277	Christmas Thim-bell-558389	Enesco	Yr.Iss.	4.00	N/A
88-04-278	Baby's First Christmas-558397	D. Parker	3-Yr.	16.00	N/A
88-04-279	Christmas Tradition-558400	Gilmore	2-Yr.	10.00	25.00
88-04-280	Stocking Story-558419	G.G. Santiago	3-Yr.	10.00	23.00
88-04-281	Winter Tale-558427	G.G. Santiago	2-Yr.	6.00	N/A
88-04-282	Party Mouse-558435	G.G. Santiago	3-Yr.	12.00	30.00
88-04-283	Christmas Watch-558443	G.G. Santiago	2-Yr.	11.00	14.00
88-04-284	Christmas Vacation-558451	G.G. Santiago	3-Yr.	8.00	23.00
88-04-285	Sweet Cherub-558478	G.G. Santiago	3-Yr.	7.00	8.00
88-04-286	Time Out-558486	G.G. Santiago	2-Yr.	11.00	N/A
88-04-287	The Ice Fairy-558516	G.G. Santiago	3-Yr.	23.00	45-55.00
88-04-288	Santa Turtle-558559	Enesco	2-Yr.	10.00	35.00
88-04-289	The Teddy Bear Ball-558567	Enesco	3-Yr.	10.00	20.00
88-04-290	Turtle Greetings-558583	Enesco	2-Yr.	8.50	25.00
88-04-291	Happy Howladays-558605	Enesco	Yr.Iss.	7.00	15.00
88-04-292	Special Delivery-558699	J. Davis	3-Yr.	9.00	30.00
88-04-293	Deer Garfield-558702	J. Davis	3-Yr.	12.00	30.00
88-04-294	Garfield Bags O' Fun-558761	J. Davis	Yr.Iss.	3.30	N/A
88-04-295	Garfield Bags O' Fun-558761	J. Davis	Yr.Iss.	3.30	N/A
88-04-296	Garfield Bags O' Fun-558761	J. Davis	Yr.Iss.	3.30	N/A
88-04-297	Garfield Bags O' Fun-558761	J. Davis	Yr.Iss.	3.30	N/A
88-04-298	Gramophone Keepsake-558818	Enesco	2-Yr.	13.00	20.00
88-04-299	North Pole Lineman-558834	Gilmore	2-Yr.	10.00	50.00
88-04-300	Five Golden Rings-559121	Gilmore	3-Yr.	11.00	25.00
88-04-301	Six Geese A-Laying-559148	Gilmore	3-Yr.	11.00	25.00
88-04-302	Pretty Baby-559156	R. Morehead	3-Yr.	12.50	25.00
88-04-303	Old Fashioned Angel-559164	R. Morehead	3-Yr.	12.50	20.00
88-04-304	Two For Tea-559776	Gilmore	3-Yr.	20.00	35-40.00
88-04-305	Merry Christmas Grandpa-560065	Enesco	3-Yr.	8.00	N/A
90-04-306	Reeling In The Holidays-560405	M. Cook	2-Yr.	8.00	15.00
91-04-307	Walkin' With My Baby-561029	M. Cook	2-Yr.	10.00	N/A
89-04-308	Scrub-A-Dub Chipmunk-561037	M. Cook	2-Yr.	8.00	20.00
89-04-309	Christmas Cook-Out-561045	M. Cook	2-Yr.	9.00	20.00
89-04-310	Sparkles-561843	S. Zimnicki	3-Yr.	17.50	25-27.50
89-04-311	Bunkie-561835	S. Zimnicki	3-Yr.	22.50	30.00
89-04-312	Popper-561878	S. Zimnicki	3-Yr.	12.00	25.00
89-04-313	Seven Swans A-Swimming-562742	Gilmore	3-Yr.	12.00	23.00
89-04-314	Eight Maids A-Milking-562750	Gilmore	3-Yr.	12.00	23.00
89-04-315	Nine Dancers Dancing-562769	Gilmore	3-Yr.	15.00	23.00
89-04-316	Baby's First Christmas 1989-562807	Enesco	Yr.Iss.	8.00	20.00
89-04-317	Baby's First Christmas 1989-562815	Gilmore	Yr.Iss.	10.00	N/A
89-04-318	First Christmas Together 1989-562823	Enesco	Yr.Iss.	11.00	N/A
89-04-319	Travelin' Trike-562882	Gilmore	3-Yr.	15.00	15.00
89-04-320	Victorian Sleigh Ride-562890	Enesco	3-Yr.	22.50	22.50
91-04-321	Santa Delivers Love-562904	Gilmore	2-Yr.	17.50	17.50
89-04-322	Chestnut Roastin'-562912	Gilmore	2-Yr.	13.00	13.00
90-04-323	Th-Ink-In' Of You-562920	Gilmore	2-Yr.	20.00	30.00
89-04-324	Ye Olde Puppet Show-562939	Enesco	2-Yr.	17.50	17.50
89-04-325	Static In The Attic-562947	Enesco	2-Yr.	13.00	25.00
89-04-326	Mistle-Toast 1989-562963	Gilmore	Yr.Iss.	15.00	25.00
89-04-327	Merry Christmas Pops-562971	Gilmore	3-Yr.	12.00	12.00

CHRISTMAS ORNAMENTS

Company		Series			
Number	Name	Artist	Edition Limit	Issue Price	Quote
90-04-328	North Pole Or Bust-562998	Gilmore	2-Yr.	25.00	25.00
89-04-329	By The Light Of The Moon-563005	Gilmore	3-Yr.	12.00	24.00
90-04-330	Stickin' To It-563013	Gilmore	2-Yr.	10.00	12.00
89-04-331	Christmas Cookin'-563048	Gilmore	3-Yr.	22.50	25.00
89-04-332	All Set For Santa-563080	Gilmore	3-Yr.	17.50	25.00
90-04-333	Santa's Sweets-563196	Gilmore	2-Yr.	20.00	20.00
90-04-334	Purr-Fect Pals-563218	Enesco	2-Yr.	8.00	8.00
89-04-335	The Pause That Refreshes-563226	Enesco	3-Yr.	15.00	37.50-45.00
89-04-336	Ho-Ho Holiday Scrooge-563234	J. Davis	3-Yr.	13.50	30.00
89-04-337	God Bless Us Everyone-563242	J. Davis	3-Yr.	13.50	30.00
89-04-338	Scrooge With The Spirit-563250	J. Davis	3-Yr.	13.50	30.00
89-04-339	A Chains Of Pace For Odie-563269	J. Davis	3-Yr.	12.00	25.00
90-04-340	Jingle Bell Rock 1990-563390	G. Armgardt	Yr.Iss.	13.50	30.00
90-04-341	Joy Ridin'-563463	J. Davis	2-Yr.	15.00	30.00
89-04-342	Just What I Wanted-563668	M. Peters	3-Yr.	13.50	13.50
89-04-343	Pucker Up!-563676	M. Peters	3-Yr.	11.00	11.00
89-04-344	What's The Bright Idea-563684	M. Peters	3-Yr.	13.50	13.50
90-04-345	Fleas Navidad-563978	M. Peters	3-Yr.	13.50	25.00
90-04-346	Tweet Greetings-564044	J. Davis	2-Yr.	15.00	15.00
90-04-347	Trouble On 3 Wheels-564052	J. Davis	3-Yr.	20.00	35.00
89-04-348	Mine, All Mine!-564079	J. Davis	Yr.Iss.	15.00	33.00
89-04-349	Star of Stars-564389	J. Jonik	3-Yr.	9.00	15.00
90-04-350	Hang Onto Your Hat-564397	J. Jonik	3-Yr.	8.00	15.00
90-04-351	Fireplace Frolic-564435	N. Teiber	2-Yr.	25.00	40.00
89-04-352	Hoe! Hoe! Hoe!-564761	Enesco	Yr.Iss.	20.00	40.00
91-04-353	Double Scoop Snowmouse-564796	M. Cook	3-Yr.	13.50	13.50
90-04-354	Christmas Is Magic-564826	M. Cook	2-Yr.	10.00	10.00
90-04-355	Lighting Up Christmas-564834	M. Cook	2-Yr.	10.00	10.00
89-04-356	Feliz Navidad! 1989-564842	M. Cook	Yr.Iss.	11.00	25.00
89-04-357	Spreading Christmas Joy-564850	M. Cook	3-Yr.	10.00	10.00
89-04-358	Yuletide Tree House-564915	J. Jonik	3-Yr.	20.00	20.00
90-04-359	Brewnig Warm Wishes-564974	Enesco	2-Yr.	10.00	10.00
90-04-360	Yippie-I-Yuletide-564982	K. Hahn	3-Yr.	15.00	15.00
90-04-361	Coffee Break-564990	K. Hahn	3-Yr.	15.00	15.00
90-04-362	You're Sew Special-565008	K. Hahn	Yr.Iss.	20.00	35.00
89-04-363	Full House Mouse-565016	K. Hahn	2-Yr.	13.50	25.00
89-04-364	I Feel Pretty-565024	K. Hahn	3-Yr.	20.00	30.00
90-04-365	Warmest Wishes-565032	K. Hahn	3-Yr.	15.00	15.00
90-04-366	Baby's Christmas Feast-565040	K. Hahn	3-Yr.	13.50	13.50
90-04-367	Bumper Car Santa-565083	G.G. Santiago	Yr.Iss.	20.00	25.00
89-04-368	Special Delivery(Proof Ed.)-565091	G.G. Santiago	Yr.Iss.	12.00	15.00
90-04-369	Ho! Ho! Yo-Yo!(Proof Ed.)-565105	G.G. Santiago	Yr.Iss.	12.00	15.00
89-04-370	Weightin' For Santa-565148	G.G. Santiago	3-Yr.	7.50	7.50
89-04-371	Holly Fairy-565199	C.M. Baker	Yr.Iss.	15.00	45.00
90-04-372	The Christmas Tree Fairy-565202	C.M. Baker	Yr.Iss.	15.00	40.00
89-04-373	Christmas 1989-565210	L. Rigg	Yr.Iss.	12.00	38.00
89-04-374	Top Of The Class-565237	L. Rigg	3-Yr.	11.00	11.00
89-04-375	Deck The Hogs-565490	M. Cook	2-Yr.	12.00	14.00
89-04-376	Pinata Ridin'-565504	M. Cook	2-Yr.	11.00	N/A
89-04-377	Hangin' In There 1989-565598	K. Wise	Yr.Iss.	10.00	19.50
90-04-378	Meow-y Christmas 1990-565601	K. Wise	Yr.Iss.	10.00	15.00
90-04-379	Seaman's Greetings-566047	Enesco	2-Yr.	11.00	18.00
90-04-380	Hang In There-566055	Enesco	3-Yr.	13.50	13.50
91-04-381	Pedal Pushin' Santa-566071	Enesco	Yr.Iss.	20.00	30.00
90-04-382	Merry Christmas Teacher-566098	Enesco	2-Yr.	11.00	11.00
90-04-383	Festive Flight-566101	Enesco	2-Yr.	11.00	11.00
90-04-384	Santa's Suitcase-566160	Enesco	3-Yr.	25.00	25.00
89-04-385	The Purr-Fect Fit!-566462	Enesco	3-Yr.	15.00	35.00
90-04-386	Tumbles 1990-566519	S. Zimnicki	Yr.Iss.	16.00	40.00
90-04-387	Twiddles-566551	S. Zimnicki	3-Yr.	15.00	30.00
91-04-388	Snuffy-566578	S. Zimnicki	3-Yr.	17.50	17.50
90-04-389	All Aboard-567671	Gilmore	2-Yr.	17.50	17.50
89-04-390	Gone With The Wind-567698	Enesco	Yr.Iss.	13.50	45.00
89-04-391	Dorothy-567760	Enesco	Yr.Iss.	12.00	45.00
89-04-392	The Tin Man-567779	Enesco	Yr.Iss.	12.00	30.00
89-04-393	The Cowardly Lion-567787	Enesco	Yr.Iss.	12.00	30.00
89-04-394	The Scarecrow-567795	Enesco	Yr.Iss.	12.00	30.00
90-04-395	Happy Holiday Readings-568104	Enesco	2-Yr.	8.00	8.00
89-04-396	Christmas 1989-568325	L. Rigg	Yr.Iss.	12.00	N/A
91-04-397	Holiday Ahoy-568368	Enesco	2-Yr.	12.50	12.50
91-04-398	Christmas Countdown-568376	Enesco	3-Yr.	20.00	20.00
89-04-399	Clara-568406	Enesco	Yr.Iss.	12.50	20.00
90-04-400	The Nutcracker-568414	Enesco	Yr.Iss.	12.50	30.00
91-04-401	Clara's Prince-568422	Enesco	Yr.Iss.	12.50	18.00
89-04-402	Santa's Little Reindear-568430	Enesco	2-Yr.	15.00	25.00
91-04-403	Tuba Totin' Teddy-568449	Enesco	3-Yr.	15.00	15.00
90-04-404	A Calling Home At Christmas-568457	Enesco	2-Yr.	15.00	15.00
91-04-405	Love Is The Secret Ingredient-568562	L. Rigg	2-Yr.	15.00	15.00
90-04-406	A Spoonful of Love-568570	L. Rigg	2-Yr.	10.00	10.00
90-04-407	Christmas Swingtime 1990-568597	L. Rigg	Yr.Iss.	13.00	N/A
90-04-408	Christmas Swingtime 1990-568600	L. Rigg	Yr.Iss.	13.00	N/A
90-04-409	Bearing Holiday Wishes-568619	L. Rigg	3-Yr.	22.50	22.50
90-04-410	Smitch-570184	S. Zimnicki	3-Yr.	22.50	22.50
91-04-411	Twinkle & Sprinkle-570206	S. Zimnicki	3-Yr.	22.50	22.50
90-04-412	Blinkie-570214	S. Zimnicki	3-Yr.	15.00	15.00
90-04-413	Have A Coke And A Smile™-571512	Enesco	3-Yr.	15.00	30.00
90-04-414	Fleece Navidad-571903	M. Cook	2-Yr.	13.50	25.00
90-04-415	Have a Navaho-Ho-Ho 1990-571970	M. Cook	Yr.Iss.	15.00	17.50
90-04-416	Cheers 1990-572411	T. Wilson	Yr.Iss.	13.50	N/A
90-04-417	A Night Before Christmas-572438	T. Wilson	2-Yr.	17.50	17.50
90-04-418	Merry Kissmas-572446	T. Wilson	2-Yr.	10.00	30.00
91-04-419	Here Comes Santa Paws-572535	J. Davis	3-Yr.	20.00	20.00
90-04-420	Frosty Garfield 1990-572551	J. Davis	Yr.Iss.	13.50	15.00
90-04-421	Pop Goes The Odie-572578	J. Davis	2-Yr.	15.00	30.00
91-04-422	Sweet Beams-572586	J. Davis	2-Yr.	13.50	13.50
90-04-423	An Apple A Day-572594	J. Davis	2-Yr.	12.00	12.00
90-04-424	Dear Santa-572608	J. Davis	3-Yr.	17.00	17.00
91-04-425	Have A Ball This Christmas-572616	J. Davis	Yr.Iss.	15.00	15.00
90-04-426	Oh Shoosh!-572624	J. Davis	3-Yr.	17.00	17.00
90-04-427	Little Red Riding Cat-572632	J. Davis	Yr.Iss.	13.50	33.00
91-04-428	All Decked Out-572659	J. Davis	2-Yr.	13.50	13.50
90-04-429	Over The Rooftops-572721	J. Davis	2-Yr.	17.50	28-35.00
90-04-430	Garfield NFL Los Angeles Rams-572764	J. Davis	2-Yr.	12.50	12.50
90-04-431	Garfield NFLCincinnati Bengals-573000	J. Davis	2-Yr.	12.50	12.50
90-04-432	Garfield NFLCleveland Browns-573019	J. Davis	2-Yr.	12.50	12.50
90-04-433	Garfield NFL Houston Oiliers-573027	J. Davis	2-Yr.	12.50	12.50
90-04-434	Garfield NFL Pittsburg Steelers-573035	J. Davis	2-Yr.	12.50	12.50
90-04-435	Garfield NFL Denver Broncos-573043	J. Davis	2-Yr.	12.50	12.50
90-04-436	Garfield NFLKansas City Chiefs-573051	J. Davis	2-Yr.	12.50	12.50
90-04-437	Garfield NFL Los Angeles Raiders-573078	J. Davis	2-Yr.	12.50	12.50
90-04-438	Garfield NFL San Diego Chargers-573086	J. Davis	2-Yr.	12.50	12.50
90-04-439	Garfield NFL Seattle Seahawks-573094	J. Davis	2-Yr.	12.50	12.50
90-04-440	Garfield NFL Buffalo Bills-573108	J. Davis	2-Yr.	12.50	12.50
90-04-441	Garfield NFL Indianapolis Colts-573116	J. Davis	2-Yr.	12.50	12.50
90-04-442	Garfield NFL Miami Dolphins-573124	J. Davis	2-Yr.	12.50	12.50
90-04-443	Garfield NFL New England Patriots-573132	J. Davis	2-Yr.	12.50	12.50
90-04-444	Garfield NFL New York Jets-573140	J. Davis	2-Yr.	12.50	12.50
90-04-445	Garfield NFL Atlanta Falcons-573159	J. Davis	2-Yr.	12.50	12.50
90-04-446	Garfield NFL New Orleans Saints-573167	J. Davis	2-Yr.	12.50	12.50
90-04-447	Garfield NFL San Francisco 49ers-573175	J. Davis	2-Yr.	12.50	12.50
90-04-448	Garfield NFL Dallas Cowboys-573183	J. Davis	2-Yr.	12.50	12.50
90-04-449	Garfield NFL New York Giants-573191	J. Davis	2-Yr.	12.50	12.50
90-04-450	Garfield NFL Philadelphia Eagles-573205	J. Davis	2-Yr.	12.50	12.50
90-04-451	Garfield NFL Phoenix Cardinals-573213	J. Davis	2-Yr.	12.50	12.50
90-04-452	Garfield NFL Washington Redskins-573221	J. Davis	2-Yr.	12.50	12.50
90-04-453	Garfield NFL Chicago Bears-573248	J. Davis	2-Yr.	12.50	12.50
90-04-454	Garfield NFL Detroit Lions-573256	J. Davis	2-Yr.	12.50	12.50
90-04-455	Garfield NFL Green Bay Packers-573264	J. Davis	2-Yr.	12.50	12.50
90-04-456	Garfield NFLMinnesota Vikings-573272	J. Davis	2-Yr.	12.50	12.50
90-04-457	Garfield NFL Tampa Bay Buccaneers-573280	J. Davis	2-Yr.	12.50	12.50
91-04-458	Tea For Two-573299	K. Hahn	3-Yr.	30.00	50.00
91-04-459	Hot Stuff Santa-573523	Enesco	Yr.Iss.	25.00	30.00
90-04-460	Merry Moustronauts-573558	M. Cook	3-Yr.	20.00	40.00
91-04-461	Santa Wings It-573612	J. Jonik	3-Yr.	13.00	13.00
90-04-462	All Eye Want For Christmas-573647	Gilmore	3-Yr.	27.50	45.00
90-04-463	Stuck On You-573655	Gilmore	2-Yr.	12.50	12.50
90-04-464	Professor Michael Bear, The One Bear Band-573663	Gilmore	3-Yr.	22.50	28.00
90-04-465	A Caroling Wee Go-573671	Gilmore	3-Yr.	12.00	12.00
90-04-466	Merry Mailman-573698	Gilmore	2-Yr.	15.00	30.00
90-04-467	Deck The Halls-573701	Gilmore	3-Yr.	22.50	25.00
90-04-468	You're Wheel Special-573728	Gilmore	3-Yr.	15.00	15.00
91-04-469	Come Let Us Adore Him-573736	Gilmore	2-Yr.	9.00	9.00
91-04-470	Moon Beam Dreams-573760	Gilmore	3-Yr.	12.00	12.00
91-04-471	A Song For Santa-573779	Gilmore	3-Yr.	25.00	25.00
90-04-472	Warmest Wishes-573825	Gilmore	Yr.Iss.	17.50	24.50
91-04-473	Kurious Kitty-573868	Gilmore	3-Yr.	17.50	17.50
90-04-474	Old Mother Mouse-573922	Gilmore	2-Yr.	17.50	20-32.00
90-04-475	Railroad Repairs-573930	Gilmore	2-Yr.	12.50	25.00
90-04-476	Ten Lords A-Leaping-573949	Gilmore	3-Yr.	15.00	23.00
90-04-477	Eleven Drummers Drumming-573957	Gilmore	3-Yr.	15.00	23.00
90-04-478	Twelve Pipers Piping-573965	Gilmore	3-Yr.	15.00	23.00
90-04-479	Baby's First Christmas 1990-573973	Gilmore	Yr.Iss.	10.00	N/A
90-04-480	Baby's First Christmas 1990-573981	Gilmore	Yr.Iss.	12.00	N/A
91-04-481	Peter, Peter Pumpkin Eater-574015	Gilmore	2-Yr.	20.00	30.00
90-04-482	Little Jack Horner-574058	Gilmore	2-Yr.	17.50	24.00
91-04-483	Mary, Mary Quite Contrary-574066	Gilmore	2-Yr.	22.50	32.50
91-04-484	Through The Years-574252	Gilmore	Yr.Iss.	17.50	17.50
91-04-485	Holiday Wing Ding-574333	Enesco	3-Yr.	22.50	22.50
91-04-486	North Pole Here I Come-574597	Enesco	3-Yr.	10.00	10.00
91-04-487	Christmas Caboose-574856	Gilmore	2-Yr.	25.00	30.00
90-04-488	Bubble Trouble-575038	K. Hahn	3-Yr.	20.00	35.00
91-04-489	Merry Mother-To-Be-575046	K. Hahn	3-Yr.	13.50	13.50
90-04-490	A Holiday 'Scent' Sation-575054	K. Hahn	3-Yr.	15.00	25.00
90-04-491	Catch Of The Day-575070	K. Hahn	3-Yr.	25.00	25.00
90-04-492	Don't Open 'Til Christmas-575089	K. Hahn	3-Yr.	17.50	17.50
90-04-493	I Can't Weight 'Til Christmas-575119	K. Hahn	3-Yr.	16.50	30.00
91-04-494	Deck The Halls-575127	K. Hahn	2-Yr.	15.00	25.00
90-04-495	Mouse House-575186	Enesco	3-Yr.	16.00	16.00
91-04-496	Dream A Little Dream-575593	Enesco	2-Yr.	17.50	17.50
91-04-497	Christmas Two-gether-575615	L. Rigg	3-Yr.	22.50	22.50
91-04-498	Christmas Trimmings-575631	Gilmore	2-Yr.	17.00	17.00
91-04-499	Gumball Wizard-575658	Gilmore	2-Yr.	13.00	13.00
91-04-500	Crystal Ball Christmas-575666	Gilmore	2-Yr.	22.50	22.50
90-04-501	Old King Cole-575682	Gilmore	2-Yr.	20.00	28.50
91-04-502	Tom, Tom The Piper's Son-575690	Gilmore	2-Yr.	15.00	33.00
91-04-503	Tire-d Little Bear-575852	L. Rigg	Yr.Iss.	12.50	12.50
90-04-504	Baby Bear Christmas 1990-575860	L. Rigg	Yr.Iss.	12.00	28.00
91-04-505	Crank Up The Carols-575887	L. Rigg	2-Yr.	17.50	17.50
90-04-506	Beary Christmas 1990-576158	L. Rigg	Yr.Iss.	12.00	12.00
91-04-507	Christmas Swingtime 1991-576166	L. Rigg	Yr.Iss.	13.00	13.00
91-04-508	Christmas Swingtime 1991-576174	L. Rigg	Yr.Iss.	13.00	13.00
91-04-509	Christmas Cutie-576182	Enesco	3-Yr.	13.50	13.50
91-04-510	Meow Mates-576220	Enesco	3-Yr.	12.00	12.00
91-04-511	Frosty The Snowman™-576425	Enesco	3-Yr.	15.00	15.00
91-04-512	Ris-ski Business-576719	T. Wilson	2-Yr.	10.00	10.00
91-04-513	Pinocchio-577391	J. Davis	3-Yr.	15.00	15.00
90-04-514	Yuletide Ride 1990-577502	Gilmore	Yr.Iss.	13.50	13.50
90-04-515	Tons of Toys-577510	Enesco	Yr.Iss.	13.00	13.00
90-04-516	McHappy Holidays-577529	Enesco	2-Yr.	17.50	24.50
90-04-517	Heading For Happy Holidays-577537	Enesco	3-Yr.	17.50	17.50
90-04-518	'Twas The Night Before Christmas-577545	Enesco	3-Yr.	17.50	17.50
90-04-519	Over One Million Holiday Wishes!-577553	Enesco	Yr.Iss.	17.50	23.00
90-04-520	You Malt My Heart-577596	Enesco	2-Yr.	25.00	25.00
91-04-521	All I Want For Christmas-577618	Enesco	2-Yr.	20.00	20.00
91-04-522	Things Go Better With Coke™-580597	Enesco	3-Yr.	17.00	17.00
91-04-523	Christmas To Go-580600	M. Cook	Yr.Iss.	22.50	22.50
91-04-524	Have A Mariachi Christmas-580619	M. Cook	2-Yr.	13.50	13.50
91-04-525	Christmas Is In The Air-581453	Enesco	Yr.Iss.	15.00	15.00
91-04-526	Holiday Treats-581542	Enesco	Yr.Iss.	17.50	17.50
91-04-527	Christmas Is My Goal-581550	Enesco	2-Yr.	17.50	17.50
91-04-528	A Quarter Pounder With Cheer®-581569	Enesco	3-Yr.	20.00	20.00
91-04-529	From The Same Mold-581798	Gilmore	3-Yr.	17.00	17.00
91-04-530	The Glow Of Christmas-581801	Enesco	2-Yr.	20.00	20.00
91-04-531	All Caught Up In Christmas-583537	Enesco	2-Yr.	10.00	10.00
91-04-532	Lights..Camera..Kissmas!-583626	Gilmore	Yr.Iss.	15.00	15.00
91-04-533	Sweet Steed-583634	Gilmore	3-Yr.	15.00	15.00
91-04-534	Dreamin' Of A White Christmas-583669	Gilmore	2-Yr.	15.00	15.00
91-04-535	Merry Millimeters-583677	Gilmore	3-Yr.	17.00	17.00
91-04-536	Here's The Scoop-583693	Enesco	2-Yr.	13.50	20.00
91-04-537	Happy Meal® On Wheels-583715	Enesco	3-Yr.	22.50	22.50
91-04-538	Christmas Kayak-583723	Enesco	2-Yr.	13.50	13.50
91-04-539	Marilyn Monroe-583774	Enesco	Yr.Iss.	20.00	20.00
91-04-540	A Christmas Carol-583928	Gilmore	3-Yr.	22.50	22.50
91-04-541	Checking It Twice-583936	Enesco	2-Yr.	25.00	25.00
91-04-542	Merry Christmas Go-Round-585203	J. Davis	3-Yr.	20.00	20.00
91-04-543	Holiday Hideout-585270	J. Davis	2-Yr.	15.00	15.00
91-04-544	Our Most Precious Gift-585726	Enesco	Yr.Iss.	17.50	17.50
91-04-545	Christmas Cheer-585769	Enesco	2-Yr.	13.50	13.50
91-04-546	Fired Up For Christmas-586587	Gilmore	2-Yr.	32.50	32.50
91-04-547	One Foggy Christmas Eve-586625	Gilmore	3-Yr.	30.00	30.00
91-04-548	For A Purr-fect Mom-586641	Gilmore	Yr.Iss.	12.00	12.00
91-04-549	For A Special Dad-586668	Gilmore	Yr.Iss.	17.50	17.50
91-04-550	With Love-586676	Gilmore	Yr.Iss.	13.00	13.00
91-04-551	For A Purr-fect Aunt-586692	Gilmore	Yr.Iss.	12.00	12.00
91-04-552	For A Dog-Gone Great Uncle-586706	Gilmore	Yr.Iss.	12.00	12.00
91-04-553	Peddling Fun-586714	Gilmore	Yr.Iss.	16.00	16.00
91-04-554	Special Keepsakes-586722	Gilmore	Yr.Iss.	13.50	13.50

CHRISTMAS ORNAMENTS

Company Number	Name	Series Artist	Edition Limit	Issue Price	Quote
91-04-555	Hats Off To Christmas-586757	K. Hahn	Yr.Iss.	22.50	22.50
91-04-556	Baby's First Christmas 1991-586935	Enesco	Yr.Iss.	12.50	12.50
91-04-557	Jugglin' The Holidays-587028	Enesco	2-Yr.	13.00	13.00
91-04-558	Santa's Steed-587044	Enesco	Yr.Iss.	15.00	15.00
91-04-559	A Decade of Treasures-587052	Gilmore	Yr.Iss.	37.50	75.00
91-04-560	Mr. Mailmouse-587109	Gilmore	2-Yr.	17.00	17.00
91-04-561	Starry Eyed Santa-587176	Enesco	2-Yr.	15.00	15.00
91-04-562	Lighting The Way-588776	Enesco	2-Yr.	20.00	20.00
91-04-563	Rudolph-588784	Enesco	2-Yr.	17.50	17.50
89-04-564	Tea For Two-693758	N. Teiber	2-Yr.	12.50	14.00
90-04-565	Holiday Tea Toast-694770	N. Teiber	2-Yr.	13.50	13.50
91-04-566	It's Tea-lightful-694789	Enesco	2-Yr.	13.50	13.50
89-04-567	Tea Time-694797	N. Teiber	2-Yr.	12.50	N/A
89-04-568	Bottom's Up 1989-830003	Enesco	Yr.Iss.	11.00	11.00
90-04-569	Sweetest Greetings 1990-830011	Gilmore	Yr.Iss.	10.00	10.00
90-04-570	First Class Christmas-830038	Gilmore	3-Yr.	10.00	10.00
89-04-571	Caught In The Act-830046	Gilmore	3-Yr.	12.50	12.50
89-04-572	Readin' & Ridin'-830054	Gilmore	3-Yr.	13.50	13.50
91-04-573	Beary Merry Mailman-830151	L. Rigg	3-Yr.	13.50	13.50
90-04-574	Here's Looking at You!-830259	Gilmore	2-Yr.	17.50	17.50
91-04-575	Stamper-830267	S. Zimnicki	Yr.Iss.	13.50	13.50
91-04-576	Santa's Key Man-830461	Gilmore	2-Yr.	11.00	11.00
91-04-577	Tie-dings Of Joy-830488	Gilmore	Yr.Iss.	12.00	12.00
91-04-578	Have a Cool Yule-830496	Gilmore	3-Yr.	12.00	12.00
90-04-579	Slots of Luck-830518	K. Hahn	2-Yr.	13.50	45-60.00
91-04-580	Straight To Santa-830534	J. Davis	2-Yr.	13.50	13.50
91-04-581	Letters To Santa-830925	Gilmore	2-Yr.	15.00	15.00
91-04-582	Sneaking Santa's Snack-830933	Gilmore	3-Yr.	13.00	13.00
91-04-583	Aiming For The Holidays-830941	Gilmore	2-Yr.	12.00	12.00
91-04-584	Ode To Joy-830968	Gilmore	3-Yr.	10.00	10.00
91-04-585	Fittin' Mittens-830976	Gilmore	3-Yr.	12.00	12.00
91-04-586	The Finishing Touch-831530	Gilmore	Yr.Iss.	10.00	10.00
91-04-587	A Real Classic-831603	Gilmore	Yr.Iss.	10.00	10.00
91-04-588	Christmas Fills The Air-831921	Gilmore	3-Yr.	12.00	12.00
91-04-589	Deck The Halls-860573	M. Peters	3-Yr.	12.00	12.00
91-04-590	Bathing Beauty-860581	K. Hahn	3-Yr.	13.50	35.00
92-04-591	Sparky & Buffer-561851	S. Zimnicki	3-Yr.	25.00	25.00
92-04-592	Moonlight Swing-568627	L. Rigg	3-Yr.	15.00	15.00
92-04-593	Carver-570192	S. Zimnicki	Yr.Iss.	17.50	17.50
92-04-594	A Rockin' GARFIELD Christmas-572527	J. Davis	2-Yr.	17.50	17.50
92-04-595	The Nutcracker-574023	Gilmore	3-Yr.	25.00	25.00
92-04-596	Humpty Dumpty-574244	Gilmore	2-Yr.	25.00	25.00
92-04-597	Music Mice-Tro!-575143	Enesco	2-Yr.	12.00	12.00
92-04-598	On Target Two-Gether-575623	Enesco	Yr.Iss.	17.00	17.00
92-04-599	Rock-A-Bye Baby-575704	Gilmore	2-Yr.	13.50	13.50
92-04-600	Queen of Hearts-575712	Gilmore	2-Yr.	17.50	17.50
92-04-601	Tasty Tidings-575836	L. Rigg	Yr.Iss.	13.50	13.50
92-04-602	Bearly Sleepy-578029	Gilmore	Yr.Iss.	17.50	17.50
92-04-603	Spreading Sweet Joy-580465	Enesco	Yr.Iss.	13.50	13.50
92-04-604	Ring My Bell-580740	J. Davis	Yr.Iss.	13.50	13.50
92-04-605	4 x 4 Holiday Fun-580783	J. Davis	2-Yr.	20.00	20.00
92-04-606	The Holidays Are A Hit-581577	Enesco	2-Yr.	17.50	17.50
92-04-607	Tip Top Tidings-581828	Enesco	2-Yr.	13.00	13.00
92-04-608	Christmas Lifts The Spirits-582018	Enesco	2-Yr.	25.00	25.00
92-04-609	A Pound Of Good Cheers-582034	Enesco	2-Yr.	17.50	17.50
92-04-610	Sweet as Cane Be-583642	Gilmore	3-Yr.	15.00	15.00
92-04-611	Sundae Ride-583707	Enesco	2-Yr.	20.00	20.00
92-04-612	The Cold, Crisp Taste Of Coke™-583766	Enesco	3-Yr.	17.00	17.00
92-04-613	Sew Christmasy-583820	Enesco	3-Yr.	25.00	25.00
92-04-614	Catch A Falling Star-583944	Gilmore	2-Yr.	15.00	15.00
92-04-615	Swingin' Christmas-584096	Enesco	2-Yr.	15.00	15.00
92-04-616	Mc Ho, Ho, Ho-585181	Enesco	3-Yr.	22.50	22.50
92-04-617	Holiday On Ice-585254	J. Davis	3-Yr.	17.50	17.50
92-04-618	Fast Track Cat-585289	J. Davis	3-Yr.	17.50	17.50
92-04-619	Holiday Cat Napping-585319	J. Davis	2-Yr.	20.00	20.00
92-04-620	The Finishing Touches-585610	T. Wilson	2-Yr.	17.50	17.50
92-04-621	Jolly Ol' Gent-585645	J. Jonik	3-Yr.	13.50	13.50
92-04-622	A Child's Christmas-586358	Enesco	3-Yr.	25.00	25.00
92-04-623	Festive Fiddlers-586501	Enesco	Yr.Iss.	20.00	25.00
92-04-624	La Luminaria-586579	M. Cook	2-Yr.	13.50	13.50
92-04-625	Cozy Chrismas Carriage-586730	Gilmore	2-Yr.	22.50	22.50
92-04-626	Small Fry's First Christmas-586749	Enesco	2-Yr.	17.00	17.00
92-04-627	Friendships Preserved-586765	K. Hahn	Yr.Iss.	22.50	22.50
92-04-628	Window Wish List-586854	Gilmore	2-Yr.	30.00	30.00
92-04-629	Through The Years-586862	Gilmore	Yr.Iss.	17.50	17.50
92-04-630	Baby's First Christmas 1992-586943	Enesco	Yr.Iss.	12.50	12.50
92-04-631	Firehouse Friends-586951	Gilmore	Yr.Iss.	22.50	22.50
92-04-632	Bubble Buddy-586978	Gilmore	2-Yr.	13.50	13.50
92-04-633	The Warmth Of The Season-586994	Enesco	2-Yr.	20.00	20.00
92-04-634	It's A Go For Christmas-587095	Gilmore	2-Yr.	15.00	15.00
92-04-635	Post-Mouster General-587117	Gilmore	2-Yr.	20.00	20.00
92-04-636	To A Deer Baby-587168	Enesco	Yr.Iss.	18.50	18.50
92-04-637	Moon Watch-587184	Enesco	2-Yr.	20.00	20.00
92-04-638	Guten Cheers-587192	Enesco	Yr.Iss.	22.50	22.50
92-04-639	Put On A Happy Face-588237	Enesco	2-Yr.	15.00	15.00
92-04-640	Beginning To Look A Lot Like Christmas-588253	Enesco	2-Yr.	15.00	15.00
92-04-641	A Christmas Toast-588261	Enesco	2-Yr.	20.00	20.00
92-04-642	Merry Mistle-Toad-588288	Enesco	2-Yr.	15.00	15.00
92-04-643	Tic-Tac-Mistle-Toe-588296	Enesco	3-Yr.	23.00	23.00
92-04-644	Heaven Sent-588423	J. Penchoff	2-Yr.	12.50	12.50
92-04-645	Holiday Happenings-588555	Gilmore	3-Yr.	30.00	30.00
92-04-646	Seed-son's Greetings-588571	Gilmore	3-Yr.	27.00	27.00
92-04-647	Santa's Midnight Snack-588598	Gilmore	2-Yr.	20.00	20.00
92-04-648	Trunk Of Treasures-588636	Enesco	Yr.Iss.	20.00	30.00
92-04-649	Festive Newsflash-588792	Enesco	2-Yr.	17.50	17.50
92-04-650	A-B-C-Son's Greetings-588806	Enesco	2-Yr.	16.50	16.50
92-04-651	Hoppy Holidays-588814	Enesco	Yr.Iss.	13.50	13.50
92-04-652	Fireside Friends-588830	Enesco	2-Yr.	20.00	20.00
92-04-653	Christmas Eve-mergency-588849	Enesco	2-Yr.	27.00	27.00
92-04-654	A Sure Sign Of Christmas-588857	Enesco	2-Yr.	22.50	22.50
92-04-655	Holidays Give Me A Lift-588865	Enesco	2-Yr.	30.00	30.00
92-04-656	Yule Tide Together-588903	Enesco	2-Yr.	20.00	20.00
92-04-657	Have A Soup-er Christmas-588911	Enesco	2-Yr.	17.50	17.50
92-04-658	Christmas Cure-Alls-588938	Enesco	2-Yr.	20.00	20.00
92-04-659	Dial 'S' For Santa-589373	Enesco	2-Yr.	25.00	25.00
92-04-660	Joy To The Whirled-589551	K. Hahn	2-Yr.	20.00	20.00
92-04-661	Merry Make-Over-589586	K. Hahn	3-Yr.	20.00	20.00
92-04-662	Campin' Companions-590282	K. Hahn	3-Yr.	20.00	20.00
92-04-663	Fur-Ever Friends-590797	Gilmore	2-Yr.	13.50	13.50
92-04-664	Tee-rific Holidays-590827	Enesco	3-Yr.	25.00	25.00
92-04-665	Spinning Christmas Dreams-590908	K. Hahn	3-Yr.	22.50	22.50
92-04-666	Christmas Trimmin'-590932	Enesco	3-Yr.	17.00	17.00
92-04-667	Wrappin' Up Warm Wishes-593141	Enesco	Yr.Iss.	17.50	17.50
92-04-668	Christmas Biz-593168	Enesco	2-Yr.	22.50	22.50
92-04-669	Holiday Take-Out-593508	Enesco	Yr.Iss.	17.50	17.50
92-04-670	A Christmas Yarn-593516	Gilmore	Yr.Iss.	20.00	20.00
92-04-671	Treasure The Earth-593826	K. Hahn	2-Yr.	25.00	25.00
92-04-672	Toyful' Rudolph-593982	Enesco	2-Yr.	22.50	22.50
92-04-673	Take A Chance On The Holidays-594075	Enesco	3-Yr.	20.00	20.00
92-04-674	Lights..Camera..Christmas!-594369	Enesco	3-Yr.	20.00	20.00
92-04-675	Spirited Stallion-594407	Enesco	Yr.Iss.	15.00	15.00
92-04-676	A Watchful Eye-595713	Enesco	Yr.Iss.	15.00	15.00
92-04-677	Good Catch-595721	Enesco	Yr.Iss.	12.50	12.50
92-04-678	Squirrelin' It Away-595748	K. Hahn	Yr.Iss.	12.00	12.00
92-04-679	Checkin' His List-595756	Enesco	Yr.Iss.	12.50	12.50
92-04-680	Christmas Cat Nappin'	Enesco	Yr.Iss.	12.00	12.00
92-04-681	Bless Our Home-595772	Enesco	Yr.Iss.	12.00	12.00
92-04-682	Salute the Season-595780	K. Hahn	Yr.Iss.	12.00	12.00
92-04-683	Fired Up For Christmas-595799	Enesco	Yr.Iss.	12.00	12.00
92-04-684	Speedin' Mr. Snowman-595802	M. Rhyner	Yr.Iss.	12.00	12.00
92-04-685	Merry Christmas Mother Earth-595810	K. Hahn	Yr.Iss.	11.00	11.00
92-04-686	Wear The Season With A Smile-595829	Enesco	Yr.Iss.	10.00	10.00
92-04-687	Jesus Loves Me-595837	K. Hahn	Yr.Iss.	10.00	10.00
92-04-688	Merry Kisses-831166	Enesco	2-Yr.	17.50	17.50
92-04-689	Christmas Is In The Air-831174	Enesco	2-Yr.	25.00	25.00
92-04-690	To The Point-831182	Gilmore	2-Yr.	13.50	13.50
92-04-691	Poppin' Hoppin' Holidays-831263	Gilmore	Yr.Iss.	25.00	25.00
92-04-692	Tankful Tidings-831271	Gilmore	2-Yr.	30.00	30.00
92-04-693	Ginger-Bred Greetings-831581	Gilmore	Yr.Iss.	12.00	12.00
92-04-694	A Gold Star For Teacher-831948	Gilmore	3-Yr.	15.00	15.00
92-04-695	A Tall Order-832758	Gilmore	3-Yr.	12.00	12.00
92-04-696	Candlelight Serenade-832766	Gilmore	2-Yr.	12.00	12.00
92-04-697	Holiday Glow Puppet Show-832774	Gilmore	3-Yr.	15.00	15.00
92-04-698	Christopher Columouse-832782	Gilmore	Yr.Iss.	12.00	12.00
92-04-699	Cartin' Home Holiday Treats-832790	Enesco	2-Yr.	13.50	13.50
92-04-700	Making Tracks To Santa-832804	Gilmore	2-Yr.	15.00	15.00
92-04-701	Special Delivery-832812	Enesco	2-Yr.	12.00	12.00
92-04-702	A Mug Full Of Love-832928	Gilmore	Yr.Iss.	13.50	13.50
92-04-703	Have A Cool Christmas-832944	Gilmore	Yr.Iss.	13.50	13.50
92-04-704	Knitten' Kittens-832952	Gilmore	Yr.Iss.	17.50	17.50
92-04-705	Holiday Honors-833029	Gilmore	Yr.Iss.	15.00	15.00
92-04-706	Christmas Nite Cap-834424	Gilmore	3-Yr.	13.50	13.50
92-04-707	North Pole Peppermint Patrol-840157	Gilmore	2-Yr.	25.00	25.00
92-04-708	A Boot-iful Christmas-840165	Gilmore	Yr.Iss.	20.00	20.00
92-04-709	Watching For Santa-840432	Enesco	2-Yr.	25.00	25.00
92-04-710	Special Delivery-840440	Enesco	Yr.Iss.	22.50	22.50
93-04-711	I'm Dreaming of a White-Out Christmas -566144	Enesco	2-Yr.	22.50	22.50
93-04-712	Born To Shop-572942	Enesco	Yr.Iss.	26.50	26.50
93-04-713	Toy To The World-575763	Enesco	2-Yr.	25.00	25.00
93-04-714	Bearly Balanced-580724	Enesco	Yr.Iss.	15.00	15.00
93-04-715	Joyeux Noel-582026	Enesco	2-Yr.	24.50	24.50
93-04-716	Holiday Mew-Sic-582107	Enesco	2-Yr.	20.00	20.00
93-04-717	Santa's Magic Ride-582115	Enesco	2-Yr.	24.00	24.00
93-04-718	Warm And Hearty Wishes-582344	Enesco	Yr.Iss.	17.50	17.50
93-04-719	Cool Yule-582352	Enesco	Yr.Iss.	12.00	12.00
93-04-720	Have A Holly Jell-O Christmas-582387	Enesco	Yr.Iss.	19.50	45.00
93-04-721	Festive Firemen-582565	Gilmore	2-Yr.	17.00	17.00
93-04-722	Light Up Your Holidays With Coke-583758	Enesco	Yr.Iss.	27.50	27.50
93-04-723	Pool Hall-idays-584851	Enesco	2-Yr.	19.00	19.90
93-04-724	Bah Humbug-585394	Davis	Yr.Iss.	15.00	15.00
93-04-725	Chimer-585777	Zimnicki	Yr.Iss.	25.00	25.00
93-04-726	Sweet Whiskered Wishes-585807	Enesco	Yr.Iss.	17.00	17.00
93-04-727	Grade "A" Wishes From Garfield -585823	Davis	2-Yr.	20.00	20.00
93-04-728	Tree For Two-586781	Gilmore	2-Yr.	17.50	17.50
93-04-729	A Bright Idea-586803	Gilmore	2-Yr.	22.50	22.50
93-04-730	Baby's First Christmas 1993-585823	Gilmore	Yr.Iss.	17.50	17.50
93-04-731	My Special Christmas-586900	Gilmore	Yr.Iss.	17.50	17.50
93-04-732	Baby's First Christmas Dinner-587001	Enesco	Yr.Iss.	12.00	12.00
93-04-733	A Pause For Claus-588318	Enesco	2-Yr.	22.50	22.50
93-04-734	Not A Creature Was Stirring...-588663	Gilmore	2-Yr.	27.50	27.50
93-04-735	Terrific Toys-588644	Enesco	Yr.Iss.	20.00	20.00
93-04-736	Christmas Dancer-588652	Enesco	Yr.Iss.	15.00	15.00
93-04-737	Countin' On A Merry Christmas-588954	Enesco	2-Yr.	22.50	22.50
93-04-738	To My Gem-589004	Enesco	Yr.Iss.	27.50	27.50
93-04-739	Christmas Mall Call-589012	Enesco	2-Yr.	20.00	20.00
93-04-740	Spreading Joy-589047	Enesco	2-Yr.	27.50	27.50
93-04-741	Pitter-Patter Post Office-589055	Enesco	2-Yr.	20.00	20.00
93-04-742	Happy Haul-idays-589098	Enesco	2-Yr.	30.00	30.00
93-04-743	Hot Off ThePress-589292	Enesco	2-Yr.	27.50	27.50
93-04-744	Designed With You In Mind-589306	Enesco	2-Yr.	16.00	16.00
93-04-745	Seeing Is Believing-589381	Gilmore	2-Yr.	20.00	20.00
93-04-746	Roundin' Up Christmas Together-590800	Enesco	Yr.Iss.	25.00	25.00
93-04-747	Toasty Tidings-590940	Enesco	2-Yr.	20.00	20.00
93-04-748	Focusing On Christmas-590983	Gilmore	2-Yr.	27.50	27.50
93-04-749	Dunk The Halls-591009	Enesco	2-Yr.	18.50	18.50
93-04-750	Mice Capades-591386	Hahn	2-Yr.	26.50	26.50
93-04-751	25 Points For Christmas-591750	Enesco	Yr.Iss.	25.00	25.00
93-04-752	Carving Christmas Wishes-592625	Gilmore	2-Yr.	25.00	25.00
93-04-753	Celebrating With A Splash-592692	Enesco	Yr.Iss.	17.00	17.00
93-04-754	Slimmin' Santa-592722	Enesco	Yr.Iss.	18.50	18.50
93-04-755	Plane Ol' Holiday Fun-592773	Enesco	Yr.Iss.	27.50	27.50
93-04-756	Smooth Move, Mom-593176	Enesco	Yr.Iss.	20.00	20.00
93-04-757	Tool TIme, Yule TIme-593192	Enesco	Yr.Iss.	18.50	18.50
93-04-758	Speedy-593370	Zimnicki	2-Yr.	25.00	25.00
93-04-759	On Your Mark, Set, Is That To Go?-593524	Enesco	Yr.Iss.	13.50	13.50
93-04-760	Do Not Open 'Til Christmas-593737	Hahn	2-Yr.	15.00	15.00
93-04-761	Greetings In Stereo-593745	Hahn	Yr.Iss.	19.50	19.50
93-04-762	Tangled Up For Christmas-593974	Enesco	2-Yr.	14.50	14.50
93-04-763	Sweet Season's Eatings-594202	Enesco	Yr.Iss.	22.50	22.50
93-04-764	Have A Darn Good Christmas-594229	Gilmore	2-Yr.	21.00	21.00
93-04-765	The Sweetest Ride-594253	Gilmore	2-Yr.	18.50	18.50
93-04-766	Lights...Camera...Christmas-594369	Enesco	Yr.Iss.	20.00	20.00
93-04-767	Have A Cheery Christmas, Sister-594687	Enesco	Yr.Iss.	13.50	13.50
93-04-768	Say Cheese-594962	Gilmore	2-Yr.	13.50	13.50
93-04-769	Christmas Kicks-594989	Enesco	Yr.Iss.	17.50	17.50
93-04-770	Time For Santa-594997	Gilmore	2-Yr.	17.50	17.50
93-04-771	Holiday Orders-595004	Enesco	Yr.Iss.	20.00	20.00
93-04-772	T'Was The Night Before Christmas-595012	Enesco	Yr.Iss.	22.50	22.50
93-04-773	Sugar Chef Shoppe-595055	Gilmore	2-Yr.	23.50	23.50
93-04-774	Merry Mc-Choo-Choo-595063	Enesco	Yr.Iss.	30.00	30.00
93-04-775	Basketful Of Friendship-595098	Enesco	Yr.Iss.	20.00	20.00
93-04-776	Rockin' With Santa-595195	Enesco	2-Yr.	13.50	13.50
93-04-777	Christmas-To-Go-595217	Enesco	Yr.Iss.	25.50	25.50
93-04-778	Sleddin' Mr. Snowman-595275	Enesco	2-Yr.	13.00	13.00
93-04-779	A Kick Out Of Christmas-595373	Enesco	2-Yr.	10.00	10.00
93-04-780	Friends Through Thick And Thin-595381	Enesco	2-Yr.	10.00	10.00

CHRISTMAS ORNAMENTS

Number	Name	Artist	Edition Limit	Issue Price	Quote
93-04-781	See-Saw Sweethearts-595403	Enesco	2-Yr.	10.00	10.00
93-04-782	Special Delivery For Santa-595411	Enesco	2-Yr.	10.00	10.00
93-04-783	Top Marks For Teacher-595438	Enesco	2-Yr.	10.00	10.00
93-04-784	Home Tweet Home-595446	Enesco	2-Yr.	10.00	10.00
93-04-785	Clownin' Around-595454	Enesco	2-Yr.	10.00	10.00
93-04-786	Heart Filled Dreams-595462	Enesco	2-Yr.	10.00	10.00
93-04-787	Merry Christmas Baby-595470	Enesco	2-Yr.	10.00	10.00
93-04-788	Your A Hit With Me, Brother-595535	Hahn	Yr.Iss.	10.00	10.00
93-04-789	For A Sharp Uncle-595543	Enesco	Yr.Iss.	10.00	10.00
93-04-790	Paint Your Holidays Bright-595551	Hahn	2-Yr.	10.00	10.00
93-04-791	Goofy "Goals" For It-596019	Enesco	Yr.Iss.	15.00	15.00
93-04-792	Goofy Slam Dunk'-598027	Enesco	Yr.Iss.	15.00	15.00
93-04-793	Goofy Scores Again-598035	Enesco	Yr.Iss.	15.00	15.00
93-04-794	Goofy About Football'-596043	Enesco	Yr.Iss.	15.00	15.00
93-04-795	You Got To Treasure The Holidays, Man' -596051	Enesco	Yr.Iss.	25.00	25.00
93-04-796	Ariel's Under-The-Sea Tree-596078	Enesco	Yr.Iss.	22.50	22.50
93-04-797	Here Comes Santa Claws-596086	Enesco	Yr.Iss.	22.50	22.50
93-04-798	You're Tea-Lighting, Mom!-596094	Enesco	Yr.Iss.	20.00	20.00
93-04-799	Hearts A Glow-596108	Enesco	Yr.Iss.	18.50	18.50
93-04-800	Love's Sweet Dance-596116	Enesco	Yr.Iss.	29.50	29.50
93-04-801	Holiday Wishes-596124	Enesco	Yr.Iss.	17.50	17.50
93-04-802	Hangin Out For The Holidays-596132	Enesco	Yr.Iss.	15.00	15.00
93-04-803	Magic Carpet Ride-596140	Enesco	Yr.Iss.	25.00	25.00
93-04-804	Holiday Treasures-596159	Enesco	Yr.Iss.	18.50	18.50
93-04-805	Happily Ever After-596167	Enesco	Yr.Iss.	25.00	25.00
93-04-806	The Fairest Of Them All-596175	Enesco	Yr.Iss.	20.00	20.00
93-04-807	December 25...Dear Diary-596809	Hahn	2-Yr.	10.00	10.00
93-04-808	Wheel Merry Wishes-596930	Hahn	2-Yr.	15.00	15.00
93-04-809	Good Grounds For Christmas-596957	Hahn	Yr.Iss.	24.50	24.50
93-04-810	Ducking The Season's Rush-597597	Enesco	Yr.Iss.	17.50	17.50
93-04-811	Here Comes Rudolph®-597686	Enesco	2-Yr.	17.50	17.50
93-04-812	It's Beginning To Look A Lot Like Christmas -597694	Enesco	Yr.Iss.	22.50	22.50
93-04-813	Christmas In The Making-597716	Enesco	Yr.Iss.	20.00	20.00
93-04-814	Mickey's Holiday Treasure-597759	Enesco	Yr.Iss.	12.00	12.00
93-04-815	Dream Wheels-597856	Enesco	Yr.Iss.	29.50	29.50
93-04-816	All You Add Is Love-598429	Enesco	Yr.Iss.	18.50	18.50
93-04-817	Goofy About Skiing-598631	Enesco	Yr.Iss.	22.50	22.50
93-04-818	A Toast Ladled With Love-830828	Hahn	2-Yr.	15.00	15.00
93-04-819	Christmas Is In The Air-831174	Enesco	2-Yr.	25.00	25.00
93-04-820	Delivered to The Nick In Time-831808	Gilmore	2-Yr.	13.50	13.50
93-04-821	Sneaking A Peek-831840	Gilmore	2-Yr.	10.00	10.00
93-04-822	Jewel Box Ballet-831859	Hahn	2-Yr.	20.00	20.00
93-04-823	A Mistle-Tow-831867	Gilmore	2-Yr.	15.00	15.00
93-04-824	Grandma's Liddle Griddle-832936	Gilmore	Yr.Iss.	10.00	10.00
93-04-825	To A Grade "A" Teacher-833037	Gilmore	2-Yr.	10.00	10.00
93-04-826	Have A Cool Christmas-834467	Gilmore	2-Yr.	10.00	10.00
93-04-827	For A Star Aunt-834556	Gilmore	Yr.Iss.	12.00	12.00
93-04-828	Watching For Santa-840432	Enesco	2-Yr.	25.00	25.00
Enesco/Hamilton Gifts Ltd.		**Maud Humphrey Bogart Ornaments**			
89-01-001	Sarah H1367	M. Humphrey	19,500	35.00	38.00
90-01-002	Victoria H1365	M. Humphrey	19,500	35.00	38.00
90-01-003	Michelle H1370	M. Humphrey	19,500	35.00	38.00
90-01-004	Catherine H1366	M. Humphrey	19,500	35.00	38.00
90-01-005	Gretchen H1369	M. Humphrey	19,500	35.00	38.00
90-01-006	Rebecca H5513	M. Humphrey	19,500	35.00	38.00
91-01-007	Cleaning House-915084	M. Humphrey	Open	24.00	24.00
91-01-008	Gift of Love-915092	M. Humphrey	Open	24.00	24.00
91-01-009	My First Dance-915106	M. Humphrey	Open	24.00	24.00
91-01-010	Special Friends-915114	M. Humphrey	Open	24.00	24.00
91-01-011	Susanna-915122	M. Humphrey	Open	24.00	24.00
91-01-012	Sarah-915165	M. Humphrey	Open	24.00	24.00
92-01-013	Hollies For You-915726	M. Humphrey	Closed	24.00	24.00
93-01-014	Tidings of Joy-915483	M. Humphrey	Open	27.50	1127.50
Enesco/Hamilton Gifts Ltd.		**Cherished Teddies**			
89-02-001	Bear In Stocking, dated	P. Hillman	Yr.Iss.	16.00	36.00
Fitz and Floyd, Inc.		**Fitz and Floyd Annual Christmas Ornaments**			
91-01-001	Plaid Teddy	M. Collins	Closed	15.00	15.00
92-01-002	Nutcracker Sweets	R. Havins	Closed	18.00	18.00
93-01-003	A Christmas Carol, Dickens	T. Kerr	7,500	18.00	18.00
94-01-004	Night Before Christmas	V. Balcou	7,500	18.00	18.00
Fitz and Floyd, Inc.		**Fitz and Floyd's Baby First Christmas**			
92-02-001	Rock-A-Bye Teddy	M. Collins	Closed	18.00	18.00
93-02-002	Li'l Angel	M. Collins	Closed	18.00	18.00
94-02-003	Bundles of Joy	M. Collins	Yr.Iss.	18.00	18.00
Fitz and Floyd, Inc.		**Our First Christmas**			
93-03-001	Christmas at Our House	M. Collins	Closed	18.00	18.00
93-03-002	The Honey Bunnies	M. Collins	Closed	18.00	18.00
94-03-003	Home for the Holidays	M. Collins	Yr.Iss.	18.00	18.00
94-03-004	Bear Huggs	M. Collins	Yr.Iss.	18.00	18.00
Fitz and Floyd, Inc.		**Heirloom Collection**			
92-04-001	Plaid Teddy with Star	M. Collins	Retrd.	15.00	15.00
92-04-002	Plaid Teddy with Gift	M. Collins	Retrd.	15.00	15.00
92-04-003	Partridge and Pear Tree	Averitt	Retrd.	15.00	15.00
92-04-004	Elf with Teddy Bear	V. Balcou	Retrd.	15.00	15.00
92-04-005	St. Nicholas Medallion, large	T. Kerr	Retrd.	18.00	18.00
92-04-006	St. Nicholas Medallion, small	T. Kerr	Retrd.	14.00	14.00
92-04-007	Holiday Cat	V. Balcou	Retrd.	15.00	15.00
92-04-008	"Merry Christmas" Elf	V. Balcou	Open	15.00	15.00
92-04-009	Elf with Candy Cane	V. Balcou	Open	15.00	15.00
92-04-010	Plaid Teddy in Wagon	M. Collins	Open	15.00	15.00
93-04-011	Christmas Quilt	M. Collins	Open	15.00	15.00
94-04-012	Kris Kringle	R. Havins	Open	15.00	15.00
94-04-013	Reindeer	R. Havins	Open	15.00	15.00
Flambro Imports		**Emmett Kelly Jr. Christmas Ornaments**			
89-01-001	65th Birthday	Undis.	Closed	24.00	40-100.00
90-01-002	30 Years Of Clowning	Undis.	Closed	30.00	125.00
91-01-003	EKJ With Stocking And Toys	Undis.	Closed	30.00	50.00
92-01-004	Home For Christmas	Undis.	Closed	24.00	30.00
93-01-005	Christmas Mail	Undis.	Closed	25.00	50.00
94-01-006	'70 Birthday Commemorative	Undis.	Yr.Iss.	24.00	24.00
Flambro Imports		**Raggedy Ann and Andy Ornaments**			
89-02-002	Raggedy Andy w/Gift Stocking	Undis.	Closed	13.50	18.00
89-02-002	Raggedy Andy w/Candy Cane	Undis.	Closed	13.50	18.00

Number	Name	Artist	Edition Limit	Issue Price	Quote
Margaret Furlong Designs		**Musical Series**			
80-01-001	The Caroler	M. Furlong	Closed	50.00	100-125.
81-01-002	The Lyrist	M. Furlong	Closed	45.00	75-100.00
82-01-003	The Lutist	M. Furlong	Closed	45.00	75-100.00
83-01-004	The Concertinist	M. Furlong	Closed	45.00	75.00
84-01-005	The Herald Angel	M. Furlong	Closed	45.00	75-100.00
Margaret Furlong Designs		**Annual Ornaments**			
80-02-001	3" Trumpeter Angel	M. Furlong	Closed	12.00	12.00
80-02-002	4" Trumpeter Angel	M. Furlong	Closed	21.00	21.00
82-02-003	3" Star Angel	M. Furlong	Closed	12.00	12.00
82-02-004	4" Star Angel	M. Furlong	Closed	21.00	21.00
Margaret Furlong Designs		**Gifts from God**			
85-03-001	The Charis Angel	M. Furlong	Closed	45.00	250.00
86-03-002	The Hallelujah Angel	M. Furlong	Closed	45.00	250.00
87-03-003	The Angel of Light	M. Furlong	Closed	45.00	100.00
88-03-004	The Celestial Angel	M. Furlong	Closed	45.00	100-150.
89-03-005	Coronation Angel	M. Furlong	Closed	45.00	75-125.00
Margaret Furlong Designs		**Joyeux Noel**			
90-04-001	Celebration Angel	M. Furlong	10,000	45.00	45-55.00
91-04-002	Thanksgiving Angel	M. Furlong	10,000	45.00	45.00
92-04-003	Joyeux Noel Angel	M. Furlong	10,000	45.00	45.00
93-04-004	Star of Bethlehem Angel	M. Furlong	10,000	45.00	45.00
94-04-005	Messiah Angel	M. Furlong	10,000	45.00	45.00
Ganz/Little Cheesers		**The Christmas Collection**			
92-01-001	Santa Cheeser Ornament	GDA/Thammavongsa	Open	14.00	14.00
92-01-002	Jenny Butterfield Ornament	GDA/Thammavongsa	Open	17.00	17.00
92-01-003	Myrtle Meadowmouse Ornament	GDA/Thammavongsa	Open	15.00	15.00
92-01-004	Little Truffle Ornament	GDA/Thammavongsa	Open	9.50	9.50
92-01-005	Jeremy With Teddy Bear Ornament	GDA/Thammavongsa	Open	13.00	13.00
92-01-006	Abner Appleton Ornament	GDA/Thammavongsa	Open	15.00	15.00
93-01-007	Baby's First X'mas Ornament	C. Thammavongsa	Open	12.50	12.50
93-01-008	Little Stocking Stuffer Ornament	C. Thammavongsa	Open	10.50	10.50
93-01-009	Our First Christmas Together Ornament	C. Thammavongsa	Open	18.50	18.50
93-01-010	Dashing Through the Snow Ornament	C. Thammavongsa	Open	11.00	11.00
93-01-011	Santa's Little Helper Ornament	C. Thammavongsa	Open	11.00	11.00
93-01-012	Skating Into Your Heart Ornament	C. Thammavongsa	Open	10.00	10.00
93-01-013	Medley Meadowmouse X'mas Bell Ornament	C. Thammavongsa	Open	17.00	17.00
Goebel		**Co-Boy Annual Ornaments**			
86-01-001	Coboy with Wreath	G. Skrobek	Closed	18.00	25.00
87-01-002	Coboy with Candy Cane	G. Skrobek	Closed	25.00	25.00
88-01-003	Coboy with Tree	G. Skrobek	Closed	30.00	30.00
Goebel		**Charlot Byj Annual Ornaments**			
86-02-001	Santa Lucia Angel	Charlot Byj	Closed	18.00	25.00
87-02-002	Christmas Pageant	Charlot Byj	Closed	20.00	20.00
88-02-003	Angel with Sheet Music	Charlot Byj	Closed	22.00	22.00
Goebel		**Charlot Byj Baby Ornaments**			
86-03-001	Baby Ornament	Charlot Byj	Closed	18.00	18.00
87-03-002	Baby Snow	Charlot Byj	Closed	20.00	20.00
88-03-003	Baby's 1st Stocking	Charlot Byj	Closed	27.50	27.50
Goebel		**Annual Ornaments**			
78-04-001	Santa (white)	Goebel	Closed	7.50	12.00
78-04-002	Santa (color)	Goebel	Closed	15.00	17-50.00
79-04-003	Angel/Tree (white)	Goebel	Closed	8.00	13.00
79-04-004	Angel/Tree (color)	Goebel	Closed	16.00	18-45.00
80-04-005	Mrs. Santa (white)	Goebel	Closed	9.00	14.00
80-04-006	Mrs. Santa (color)	Goebel	Closed	17.00	17-40.00
81-04-007	The Nutcracker (white)	Goebel	Closed	10.00	10.00
81-04-008	The Nutcracker (color)	Goebel	Closed	18.00	18-35.00
82-04-009	Santa in Chimney (white)	Goebel	Closed	10.00	10.00
82-04-010	Santa in Chimney (color)	Goebel	Closed	18.00	18.00
83-04-011	Clown (white)	Goebel	Closed	10.00	10.00
83-04-012	Clown (color)	Goebel	Closed	18.00	18-35.00
84-04-013	Snowman (white)	Goebel	Closed	10.00	10.00
84-04-014	Snowman (color)	Goebel	Closed	18.00	18-35.00
85-04-015	Angel (white)	Goebel	Closed	9.00	9.00
85-04-016	Angel (color)	Goebel	Closed	18.00	18-35.00
86-04-017	Drummer Boy (white)	Goebel	Closed	9.00	9.00
86-04-018	Drummer Boy (color)	Goebel	Closed	18.00	18.00
87-04-019	Rocking Horse (white)	Goebel	Closed	10.00	10.00
87-04-020	Rocking Horse (color)	Goebel	Closed	20.00	20.00
88-04-021	Doll (white)	Goebel	Closed	12.50	12.50
88-04-022	Doll (color)	Goebel	Closed	22.50	22.50
89-04-023	Dove (white)	Goebel	Closed	12.50	12.50
89-04-024	Dove (color)	Goebel	Closed	20.00	20.00
90-04-025	Girl In Sleigh	Goebel	Closed	30.00	30.00
91-04-026	Baby On Moon	Goebel	Closed	35.00	35.00
Goebel		**Christmas Ornaments**			
87-05-001	Three Angels with Toys-(Set)	Goebel	Open	30.00	30.00
87-05-002	Three Angels with Instruments-(Set)	Goebel	Open	30.00	30.00
88-05-003	Snowman	Goebel	Open	10.00	10.00
88-05-004	Santa's Boot	Goebel	Open	7.50	7.50
88-05-005	Saint Nick	Goebel	Open	15.00	15.00
88-05-006	Nutcracker	Goebel	Open	15.00	15.00
86-05-007	Teddy Bear - Red Hat	Goebel	Open	5.00	5.00
86-05-008	Teddy Bear - Red Scarf	Goebel	Open	5.00	5.00
86-05-009	Teddy Bear - Red Boots	Goebel	Open	5.00	5.00
86-05-010	Angel - Red with Song	Goebel	Open	6.00	6.00
86-05-011	Angel - Red with Book	Goebel	Open	6.00	6.00
86-05-012	Angel - Red with Bell	Goebel	Open	6.00	6.00
86-05-013	Angel with Lantern (color)	Goebel	Open	8.00	8.00
86-05-014	Angel with Lantern (white)	Goebel	Open	6.00	6.00
86-05-015	Angel with Horn (color)	Goebel	Open	8.00	8.00
86-05-016	Angel with Horn (white)	Goebel	Open	6.00	6.00
86-05-017	Angel with Lute (color)	Goebel	Open	8.00	8.00
86-05-018	Angel with Lute (white)	Goebel	Open	6.00	6.00
88-05-019	Angel with Toy Teddy Bear	Goebel	Open	10.00	10.00
88-05-020	Angel with Toy Rocking Horse	Goebel	Open	10.00	10.00
88-05-021	Angel with Toy Train	Goebel	Open	10.00	10.00
88-05-022	Angel with Toys-(Set of three)	Goebel	Open	30.00	30.00
88-05-023	Angel with Banjo	Goebel	Open	10.00	10.00
88-05-024	Angel with Accordian	Goebel	Open	10.00	10.00
88-05-025	Angel with Violin	Goebel	Open	10.00	10.00
88-05-026	Angel with Music Set	Goebel	Open	30.00	30.00

CHRISTMAS ORNAMENTS

Number	Name	Artist	Edition Limit	Issue Price	Quote
Goebel/M.I. Hummel	**M.I. Hummel Annual Figurine Ornaments**				
88-01-001	Flying High 452	M.I. Hummel	Closed	75.00	125-135.
89-01-002	Love From Above 481	M.I. Hummel	Closed	75.00	80-135.00
90-01-003	Peace on Earth 484	M.I. Hummel	Closed	80.00	85-105.00
91-01-004	Angelic Guide 571	M.I. Hummel	Closed	95.00	95.00
92-01-005	Light Up The Night 622	M.I. Hummel	Closed	100.00	100.00
93-01-006	Herald on High 623	M.I. Hummel	Closed	155.00	155.00
Goebel/M.I. Hummel	**M.I. Hummel Collectibles Christmas Bell Ornaments**				
89-02-001	Ride Into Christmas 775	M.I. Hummel	Closed	35.00	35-85.00
90-02-002	Letter to Santa Claus 776	M.I. Hummel	Closed	37.50	37.50-50.00
91-02-003	Hear Ye, Hear Ye 777	M.I. Hummel	Closed	39.50	39.50
92-02-004	Harmony in Four Parts 778	M.I. Hummel	Closed	50.00	50.00
93-02-005	Celestial Musician 779	M.I. Hummel	Closed	50.00	50.00
94-02-006	Festival Harmony w/Mandolin 780	M.I. Hummel	Yr.Iss.	50.00	50.00
Goebel/M.I. Hummel	**M.I. Hummel Collectibles Miniature Ornaments**				
93-03-001	Celestial Musician 646	M.I. Hummel	Open	90.00	90.00
94-03-002	Festival Harmony w/Mandolin 647	M.I. Hummel	Open	95.00	95.00
Gorham	**Archive Collectible**				
88-01-001	Victorian Heart	Gorham	Open	50.00	50.00
89-01-002	Victorian Wreath	Gorham	Open	50.00	50.00
90-01-003	Elizabethan Cupid	Gorham	Open	60.00	60.00
91-01-004	Baroque Angels	Gorham	Open	55.00	55.00
92-01-005	Madonna and Child	Gorham	Yr.Iss.	50.00	50.00
93-01-006	Angel With Mandolin	Gorham	Open	50.00	50.00
Gorham	**Annual Snowflake Ornaments**				
70-02-001	Sterling Snowflake	Gorham	Closed	10.00	240.00
71-02-002	Sterling Snowflake	Gorham	Closed	10.00	55.00
72-02-003	Sterling Snowflake	Gorham	Closed	10.00	55.00
73-02-004	Sterling Snowflake	Gorham	Closed	10.95	75.00
74-02-005	Sterling Snowflake	Gorham	Closed	17.50	50.00
75-02-006	Sterling Snowflake	Gorham	Closed	17.50	30-75.00
76-02-007	Sterling Snowflake	Gorham	Closed	20.00	40-80.00
77-02-008	Sterling Snowflake	Gorham	Closed	22.50	30-70.00
78-02-009	Sterling Snowflake	Gorham	Closed	22.50	40-70.00
79-02-010	Sterling Snowflake	Gorham	Closed	32.80	40-70.00
80-02-011	Silverplated Snowflake	Gorham	Closed	15.00	75.00
81-02-012	Sterling Snowflake	Gorham	Closed	50.00	75.00
82-02-013	Sterling Snowflake	Gorham	Closed	37.50	45-80.00
83-02-014	Sterling Snowflake	Gorham	Closed	45.00	50.00
84-02-015	Sterling Snowflake	Gorham	Closed	45.00	50.00
85-02-016	Sterling Snowflake	Gorham	Closed	45.00	50-75.00
86-02-017	Sterling Snowflake	Gorham	Closed	45.00	45-65.00
87-02-018	Sterling Snowflake	Gorham	Closed	50.00	65.00
88-02-019	Sterling Snowflake	Gorham	Closed	50.00	50.00
89-02-020	Sterling Snowflake	Gorham	Closed	50.00	50.00
90-02-021	Sterling Snowflake	Gorham	Closed	50.00	50.00
91-02-022	Sterling Snowflake	Gorham	Closed	55.00	55.00
92-02-023	Sterling Snowflake	Gorham	Closed	50.00	38-50.00
93-02-024	Sterling Snowflake	Gorham	Yr.Iss.	50.00	50.00
Gorham	**Annual Crystal Ornaments**				
85-03-001	Crystal Ornament	Gorham	Closed	22.00	22.00
86-03-002	Crystal Ornament	Gorham	Closed	25.00	25.00
87-03-003	Crystal Ornament	Gorham	Closed	25.00	25.00
88-03-004	Crystal Ornament	Gorham	Closed	28.00	28.00
89-03-005	Crystal Ornament	Gorham	Closed	28.00	28.00
90-03-006	Crystal Ornament	Gorham	Closed	30.00	30.00
91-03-007	Crystal Ornament	Gorham	Closed	35.00	35.00
92-03-008	Crystal Ornament	Gorham	Closed	32.50	32.50
93-03-009	Crystal Ornament	Gorham	Yr.Iss.	32.50	32.50
Gorham	**Baby's First Christmas Crystal**				
91-04-001	Baby's First Rocking Horse	Gorham	Open	35.00	35.00
Dave Grossman Creations	**Emmett Kelly Annual Figurine Ornaments**				
86-01-001	A Christmas Carol	B. Leighton Jones	Closed	12.00	12.00
87-01-002	Christmas Wreath	B. Leighton Jones	Closed	14.00	14.00
88-01-003	Christmas Dinner	B. Leighton Jones	Closed	15.00	15.00
89-01-004	Christmas Feast	B. Leighton Jones	Closed	15.00	15.00
90-01-005	Just What I Needed	B. Leighton Jones	Closed	15.00	15.00
91-01-006	Emmett the Snowman	B. Leighton Jones	Closed	15.00	25-30.00
92-01-007	Christmas Tunes	B. Leighton Jones	Closed	15.00	15.00
93-01-008	Downhill EKX-93	B. Leighton Jones	Closed	20.00	20.00
94-01-009	Holiday Skater EKX-94	B. Leighton Jones	Yr.Iss.	20.00	20.00
Dave Grossman Creations	**Gone With the Wind Ornaments**				
87-02-001	Tara	D. Geenty	Closed	15.00	45.00
87-02-002	Rhett	D. Geenty	Closed	15.00	45.00
87-02-003	Scarlett	D. Geenty	Closed	15.00	45.00
87-02-004	Ashley	D. Geenty	Closed	15.00	45.00
88-02-005	Rhett and Scarlett	D. Geenty	Closed	20.00	40.00
89-02-006	Mammy	D. Geenty	Closed	20.00	20.00
90-02-007	Scarlett (Red Dress)	D. Geenty	Closed	20.00	20.00
91-02-008	Prissy	R. Brown	Closed	20.00	20.00
92-02-009	Scarlett (Green Dress)	Rockwell-Inspired	Closed	20.00	20.00
93-02-010	Rhett (White Suit) GWO-93	Rockwell-Inspired	Closed	20.00	20.00
94-02-011	Scarlett GWO-94	Rockwell-Inspired	Yr.Iss.	20.00	20.00
94-02-012	Gold Plated GWO-00	Rockwell-Inspired	Open	13.00	13.00
94-02-013	Limited Edition GWO-94	Rockwell-Inspired	Yr.Iss.	25.00	25.00
Dave Grossman Creations	**Norman Rockwell Collection-Annual Rockwell Figurine Ornaments**				
78-03-001	Caroler NRX-03	Rockwell-Inspired	Retrd.	15.00	45.00
79-03-002	Drum for Tommy NRX-24	Rockwell-Inspired	Retrd.	20.00	30.00
80-03-003	Santa's Good Boys NRX-37	Rockwell-Inspired	Retrd.	20.00	30.00
81-03-004	Letters to Santa NRX-39	Rockwell-Inspired	Retrd.	20.00	30.00
82-03-005	Cornettist NRX-32	Rockwell-Inspired	Retrd.	20.00	30.00
83-03-006	Fiddler NRX-83	Rockwell-Inspired	Retrd.	20.00	30.00
84-03-007	Christmas Bounty NRX-84	Rockwell-Inspired	Retrd.	20.00	30.00
85-03-008	Jolly Coachman NRX-85	Rockwell-Inspired	Retrd.	20.00	30.00
86-03-009	Grandpa on Rocking Horse NRX-86	Rockwell-Inspired	Retrd.	20.00	30.00
87-03-010	Skating Lesson NRX-87	Rockwell-Inspired	Retrd.	20.00	30.00
88-03-011	Big Moment NRX-88	Rockwell-Inspired	Retrd.	20.00	25.00
89-03-012	Discovery NRX-89	Rockwell-Inspired	Retrd.	20.00	20.00
90-03-013	Bringing Home The Tree NRX-90	Rockwell-Inspired	Retrd.	20.00	20.00
91-03-014	Downhill Daring B NRX-91	Rockwell-Inspired	Retrd.	20.00	20.00
92-03-015	On The Ice	Rockwell-Inspired	Retrd.	20.00	20.00
93-03-016	Granps NRX-93	Rockwell-Inspired	Retrd.	24.00	24.00
93-03-017	Marriage License First Christmas Together NRX-m1	Rockwell-Inspired	Retrd.	30.00	30.00
94-03-018	Merry Christmas NRX-94	Rockwell-Inspired	Yr.Iss.	24.00	24.00
Dave Grossman Creations	**Norman Rockwell Collection-Annual Rockwell Ball Ornaments**				
75-04-001	Santa with Feather Quill NRO-01	Rockwell-Inspired	Retrd.	3.50	25.00
76-04-002	Santa at Globe NRO-02	Rockwell-Inspired	Retrd.	4.00	25.00
77-04-003	Grandpa on Rocking Horse NRO-03	Rockwell-Inspired	Retrd.	4.00	12.00
78-04-004	Santa with Map NRO-04	Rockwell-Inspired	Retrd.	4.50	12.00
79-04-005	Santa at Desk with Mail Bag NRO-05	Rockwell-Inspired	Retrd.	5.00	12.00
80-04-006	Santa Asleep with Toys NRO-06	Rockwell-Inspired	Retrd.	5.00	10.00
81-04-007	Santa with Boy on Finger NRO-07	Rockwell-Inspired	Retrd.	5.00	10.00
82-04-008	Santa Face on Winter Scene NRO-08	Rockwell-Inspired	Retrd.	5.00	10.00
83-04-009	Coachman with Whip NRO-9	Rockwell-Inspired	Retrd.	5.00	10.00
84-04-010	Christmas Bounty Man NRO-10	Rockwell-Inspired	Retrd.	5.00	10.00
85-04-011	Old English Trio NRO-11	Rockwell-Inspired	Retrd.	5.00	10.00
86-04-012	Tiny Tim on Shoulder NRO-12	Rockwell-Inspired	Retrd.	5.00	10.00
87-04-013	Skating Lesson NRO-13	Rockwell-Inspired	Retrd.	5.00	10.00
88-04-014	Big Moment NRO-14	Rockwell-Inspired	Retrd.	5.50	6.00
89-04-015	Discovery NRO-15	Rockwell-Inspired	Retrd.	6.00	6.00
90-04-016	Bringing Home The Tree NRO-16	Rockwell-Inspired	Retrd.	6.00	6.00
91-04-017	Downhill Daring NRO-17	Rockwell-Inspired	Retrd.	6.00	6.00
92-04-018	On The Ice NRO-18	Rockwell-Inspired	Retrd.	6.00	6.00
93-04-019	Granps NRO-19	Rockwell-Inspired	Retrd.	6.00	6.00
94-04-020	Triple Self Portrait-Commemorative NRO-20	Rockwell-Inspired	Yr.Iss.	6.00	6.00
Dave Grossman Designs	**Norman Rockwell Collection-Character Doll Ornaments**				
83-01-001	Doctor and Doll NRD-01	Rockwell-Inspired	Retrd.	20.00	30.00
83-01-002	Lovers NRD-02	Rockwell-Inspired	Retrd.	20.00	30.00
83-01-003	Samplers NRD-03	Rockwell-Inspired	Retrd.	20.00	30.00
Hallmark Galleries	**Enchanted Garden**				
92-01-001	Neighborhood Dreamer	E. Richardson	19,500	15.00	15.00
Hallmark Keepsake Ornaments	**1973 Hallmark Keepsake Collection**				
73-01-001	Betsey Clark 250XHD100-2	Keepsake	Yr.Iss.	2.50	85.00
73-01-002	Betsey Clark-First Edition 250XHD 110-2	Keepsake	Yr.Iss.	2.50	125.00
73-01-003	Manger Scene 250XHD102-2	Keepsake	Yr.Iss.	2.50	75.00
73-01-004	Christmas Is Love 250XHD106-2	Keepsake	Yr.Iss.	2.50	80.00
73-01-005	Santa with Elves 250XHD101-5	Keepsake	Yr.Iss.	2.50	75-85.00
73-01-006	Elves 250XHD103-5	Keepsake	Yr.Iss.	2.50	75.00
Hallmark Keepsake Ornaments	**1973 Keepsake Yarn Ornaments**				
73-02-001	Mr. Santa 125XHD74-5	Keepsake	Yr.Iss.	1.25	27.50
73-02-002	Mrs. Santa 125XHD75-2	Keepsake	Yr.Iss.	1.25	22.50
73-02-003	Mr. Snowman 125XHD76-5	Keepsake	Yr.Iss.	1.25	24.50
73-02-004	Mrs. Snowman 125XHD77-2	Keepsake	Yr.Iss.	1.25	22.50
73-02-005	Angel 125XHD78-5	Keepsake	Yr.Iss.	1.25	27.50
73-02-006	Elf 125XHD79-2	Keepsake	Yr.Iss.	1.25	24.50
73-02-007	Choir Boy 125XHD80-5	Keepsake	Yr.Iss.	1.25	27.50
73-02-008	Soldier 100XHD81-2	Keepsake	Yr.Iss.	1.00	22.00
73-02-009	Little Girl 125XHD82-5	Keepsake	Yr.Iss.	1.25	22.50
73-02-010	Boy Caroler 125XHD83-2	Keepsake	Yr.Iss.	1.25	29.50
73-02-011	Green Girl 125XHD84-5	Keepsake	Yr.Iss.	1.25	22.50
73-02-012	Blue Girl 125XHD85-2	Keepsake	Yr.Iss.	1.25	22.50
Hallmark Keepsake Ornaments	**1974 Hallmark Keepsake Collection**				
74-03-001	Norman Rockwell 250QX111-1	Keepsake	Yr.Iss.	2.50	80.00
74-03-002	Norman Rockwell 250QX106-1	Keepsake	Yr.Iss.	2.50	45-75.00
74-03-003	Betsey Clark-Second Edition 250QX 108-1	Keepsake	Yr.Iss.	2.50	45-78.00
74-03-004	Charmers 250QX109-1	Keepsake	Yr.Iss.	2.50	25-52.00
74-03-005	Snowgoose 250QX107-1	Keepsake	Yr.Iss.	2.50	75.00
74-03-006	Angel 250QX110-1	Keepsake	Yr.Iss.	2.50	65.00
74-03-007	Raggedy Ann and Andy(4/set) 450QX114-1	Keepsake	Yr.Iss.	4.50	75.00
74-03-008	Little Miracles (Set of 4) 450QX115-1	Keepsake	Yr.Iss.	4.50	55.00
74-03-009	Buttons & Bo (Set of 2) 350QX113-1	Keepsake	Yr.Iss.	3.50	50.00
74-03-010	Currier & Ives (Set of 2) 350QX112-1	Keepsake	Yr.Iss.	3.50	50.00
Hallmark Keepsake Ornaments	**1974 Keepsake Yarn Ornaments**				
74-04-001	Mrs. Santa 150QX100-1	Keepsake	Yr.Iss.	1.50	22.50
74-04-002	Elf 150QX101-1	Keepsake	Yr.Iss.	1.50	22.50
74-04-003	Soldier 150QX102-1	Keepsake	Yr.Iss.	1.50	21.50
74-04-004	Angel 150QX103-1	Keepsake	Yr.Iss.	1.50	27.50
74-04-005	Snowman 150QX104-1	Keepsake	Yr.Iss.	1.50	22.50
74-04-006	Santa 150QX105-1	Keepsake	Yr.Iss.	1.50	23.50
Hallmark Keepsake Ornaments	**1975 Keepsake Property Ornaments**				
75-05-001	Betsey Clark (Set of 4) 450QX168-1	Keepsake	Yr.Iss.	4.50	25-50.00
75-05-002	Betsey Clark (Set of 2) 350QX167-1	Keepsake	Yr.Iss.	3.50	40.00
75-05-003	Betsey Clark 250QX163-1	Keepsake	Yr.Iss.	2.50	36-40.00
75-05-004	Betsey Clark-Third Ed. 300QX133-1	Keepsake	Yr.Iss.	3.00	55-85.00
75-05-005	Currier & Ives (Set of 2) 250QX164-1	Keepsake	Yr.Iss.	2.50	16-40.00
75-05-006	Currier & Ives (Set of 2) 400QX137-1	Keepsake	Yr.Iss.	4.00	35-40.00
75-05-007	Raggedy Ann and Andy(2/set) 400QX 138-1	Keepsake	Yr.Iss.	4.00	65.00
75-05-008	Raggedy Ann 250QX165-1	Keepsake	Yr.Iss.	2.50	50.00
75-05-009	Norman Rockwell 250QX166-1	Keepsake	Yr.Iss.	2.50	75.00
75-05-010	Norman Rockwell 300QX134-1	Keepsake	Yr.Iss.	3.00	75.00
75-05-011	Charmers 300QX135-1	Keepsake	Yr.Iss.	3.00	20-40.00
75-05-012	Marty Links 300QX136-1	Keepsake	Yr.Iss.	3.00	35.00
75-05-013	Buttons & Bo (Set of 4) 500QX139-1	Keepsake	Yr.Iss.	5.00	30-47.50
75-05-014	Little Miracles (Set of 4) 500QX140-1	Keepsake	Yr.Iss.	5.00	30-50.00
Hallmark Keepsake Ornaments	**1975 Keepsake Yarn Ornaments**				
75-06-001	Raggedy Ann 175QX121-1	Keepsake	Yr.Iss.	1.75	35.00
75-06-002	Raggedy Andy 175QX122-1	Keepsake	Yr.Iss.	1.75	39.50
75-06-003	Drummer Boy 175QX123-1	Keepsake	Yr.Iss.	1.75	24.50
75-06-004	Santa 175QX124-1	Keepsake	Yr.Iss.	1.75	15-22.50
75-06-005	Mrs. Santa 175QX125-1	Keepsake	Yr.Iss.	1.75	21.50
75-06-006	Little Girl 175QX126-1	Keepsake	Yr.Iss.	1.75	19.50
Hallmark Keepsake Ornaments	**1975 Handcrafted Ornaments: Nostalgia**				
75-07-001	Locomotive (dated) 350QX127-1	Keepsake	Yr.Iss.	3.50	175.00
75-07-002	Rocking Horse 350QX128-1	Keepsake	Yr.Iss.	3.50	100-175.
75-07-003	Santa & Sleigh 350QX129-1	Keepsake	Yr.Iss.	3.50	200-275.
75-07-004	Drummer Boy 350QX130-1	Keepsake	Yr.Iss.	3.50	150.00
75-07-005	Peace on Earth (dated) 350QX131-1	Keepsake	Yr.Iss.	3.50	125-175.
75-07-006	Joy 350QX132-1	Keepsake	Yr.Iss.	3.50	175-275.
Hallmark Keepsake Ornaments	**1975 Handcrafted Ornaments: Adorable**				
75-08-001	Santa 250QX155-1	Keepsake	Yr.Iss.	2.50	85.00
75-08-002	Mrs. Santa 250QX156-1	Keepsake	Yr.Iss.	2.50	85.00
75-08-003	Betsey Clark 250QX157-1	Keepsake	Yr.Iss.	2.50	350.00
75-08-004	Raggedy Ann 250QX159-1	Keepsake	Yr.Iss.	2.50	225.00
75-08-005	Raggedy Andy 250QX160-1	Keepsake	Yr.Iss.	2.50	400.00
75-08-006	Drummer Boy 250QX161-1	Keepsake	Yr.Iss.	2.50	325.00

CHRISTMAS ORNAMENTS

Company Number	Name	Series Artist	Edition Limit	Issue Price	Quote
Hallmark Keepsake Ornaments	**1976 First Commemorative Ornament**				
76-09-001	Baby's First Christmas 250QX211-1	Keepsake	Yr.Iss.	2.50	30-95.00
Hallmark Keepsake Ornaments	**1976 Bicentennial Commemoratives**				
76-10-001	Bicentennial '76 Commemorative 250QX211-1	Keepsake	Yr.Iss.	2.50	75.00
76-10-002	Bicentennial Charmers 300QX198-1	Keepsake	Yr.Iss.	3.00	60.00
76-10-003	Colonial Children (Set of 2) 4 400QX 208-1	Keepsake	Yr.Iss.	4.00	40-65.00
Hallmark Keepsake Ornaments	**1976 Property Ornaments**				
76-11-001	Betsey Clark-Fourth Ed.300QX 195-1	Keepsake	Yr.Iss.	3.00	175.00
76-11-002	Betsey Clark 250QX210-1	Keepsake	Yr.Iss.	2.50	38-42.00
76-11-003	Betsey Clark (Set of 3) 450QX218-1	Keepsake	Yr.Iss.	4.50	50.00
76-11-004	Currier & Ives 250QX209-1	Keepsake	Yr.Iss.	2.50	40.00
76-11-005	Currier & Ives 300QX197-1	Keepsake	Yr.Iss.	3.00	42.00
76-11-006	Norman Rockwell 300QX196-1	Keepsake	Yr.Iss.	3.00	65.00
76-11-007	Rudolph and Santa 250QX213-1	Keepsake	Yr.Iss.	2.50	65-95.00
76-11-008	Raggedy Ann 250QX212-1	Keepsake	Yr.Iss.	2.50	65.00
76-11-009	Marty Links (Set of 2) 400QX207-1	Keepsake	Yr.Iss.	4.00	45.00
76-11-010	Happy the Snowman (Set of 2) 350QX216-1	Keepsake	Yr.Iss.	3.50	55.00
76-11-011	Charmers (Set of 2) 350QX215-1	Keepsake	Yr.Iss.	3.50	75.00
Hallmark Keepsake Ornaments	**1976 Decorative Ball Ornaments**				
76-12-001	Chickadees 225QX204-1	Keepsake	Yr.Iss.	2.25	50.00
76-12-002	Cardinals 225QX205-1	Keepsake	Yr.Iss.	2.25	55.00
Hallmark Keepsake Ornaments	**1976 Handcrafted Ornaments: Yesteryears**				
76-13-001	Train 500QX181-1	Keepsake	Yr.Iss.	5.00	125.00
76-13-002	Santa 500QX182-1	Keepsake	Yr.Iss.	5.00	175.00
76-13-003	Partridge 500QX183-1	Keepsake	Yr.Iss.	5.00	125.00
76-13-004	Drummer Boy 500QX184-1	Keepsake	Yr.Iss.	5.00	128-135.00
Hallmark Keepsake Ornaments	**1976 Handcrafted Ornaments: Twirl-Abouts**				
76-14-001	Angel 450QX171-1	Keepsake	Yr.Iss.	4.50	150-175.00
76-14-002	Santa 450QX172-1	Keepsake	Yr.Iss.	4.50	90-125.00
76-14-003	Soldier 450QX173-1	Keepsake	Yr.Iss.	4.50	80-120.00
76-14-004	Partridge 450QX174-1	Keepsake	Yr.Iss.	4.50	195.00
Hallmark Keepsake Ornaments	**1976 Handcrafted Ornaments: Tree Treats**				
76-15-001	Shepherd 300QX175-1	Keepsake	Yr.Iss.	3.00	90-150.00
76-15-002	Angel 300QX176-1	Keepsake	Yr.Iss.	3.00	125-195.
76-15-003	Santa 300QX177-1	Keepsake	Yr.Iss.	3.00	150-225.
76-15-004	Reindeer 300QX 178-1	Keepsake	Yr.Iss.	3.00	150.00
Hallmark Keepsake Ornaments	**1976 Handcrafted Ornaments: Nostalgia**				
76-16-001	Rocking Horse 400QX128-1	Keepsake	Yr.Iss.	3.50	160.00
76-16-002	Drummer Boy 400QX130-1	Keepsake	Yr.Iss.	3.50	155.00
76-16-003	Locomotive 400QX222-1	Keepsake	Yr.Iss.	3.50	185.00
76-16-004	Peace on Earth 400QX223-1	Keepsake	Yr.Iss.	3.50	195.00
Hallmark Keepsake Ornaments	**1976 Yarn Ornaments**				
76-17-001	Raggedy Ann 175QX121-1	Keepsake	Yr.Iss.	1.75	35.00
76-17-002	Raggedy Andy 175QX122-1	Keepsake	Yr.Iss.	1.75	39.50
76-17-003	Drummer Boy 175QX123-1	Keepsake	Yr.Iss.	1.75	22.50
76-17-004	Santa 175QX124-1	Keepsake	Yr.Iss.	1.75	23.50
76-17-005	Mrs. Santa 175QX125-1	Keepsake	Yr.Iss.	1.75	21.50
76-17-006	Caroler 175QX126-1	Keepsake	Yr.Iss.	1.75	27.50
Hallmark Keepsake Ornaments	**1977 Commemoratives**				
77-18-001	Baby's First Christmas 350QX131-5	Keepsake	Yr.Iss.	3.50	35-59.50
77-18-002	Granddaughter 350QX208-2	Keepsake	Yr.Iss.	3.50	150.00
77-18-003	Grandson 350QX209-5	Keepsake	Yr.Iss.	3.50	150.00
77-18-004	Mother 350QX261-5	Keepsake	Yr.Iss.	3.50	75.00
77-18-005	Grandmother 350QX260-2	Keepsake	Yr.Iss.	3.50	150.00
77-18-006	First Christmas Together 350QX132-2	Keepsake	Yr.Iss.	3.50	75.00
77-18-007	Love 350QX262-2	Keepsake	Yr.Iss.	3.50	95.00
77-18-008	For Your New Home 350QX263-5	Keepsake	Yr.Iss.	3.50	120.00
Hallmark Keepsake Ornaments	**1977 Property Ornaments**				
77-19-001	Charmers 350QX153-5	Keepsake	Yr.Iss.	3.50	50.00
77-19-002	Currier & Ives 350QX130-2	Keepsake	Yr.Iss.	3.50	55.00
77-19-003	Norman Rockwell 350QX151-5	Keepsake	Yr.Iss.	3.50	70.00
77-19-004	Disney 350QX133-5	Keepsake	Yr.Iss.	3.50	35-55.00
77-19-005	Disney (Set of 2) 400QX137-5	Keepsake	Yr.Iss.	4.00	75.00
77-19-006	Betsey Clark -Fifth Ed. 350QX264-2	Keepsake	Yr.Iss.	3.50	550.00
77-19-007	Grandma Moses 350QX150-2	Keepsake	Yr.Iss.	3.50	175.00
Hallmark Keepsake Ornaments	**1977 Peanuts Collection**				
77-20-001	Peanuts 250QX162-2	Keepsake	Yr.Iss.	2.50	65.00
77-20-002	Peanuts 350QX135-5	Keepsake	Yr.Iss.	3.50	55.00
77-20-003	Peanuts (Set of 2) 400QX163-5	Keepsake	Yr.Iss.	4.00	65.00
Hallmark Keepsake Ornaments	**1977 Christmas Expressions Collection**				
77-21-001	Bell 350QX154-2	Keepsake	Yr.Iss.	3.50	65.00
77-21-002	Ornaments 350QX155-5	Keepsake	Yr.Iss.	3.50	65.00
77-21-003	Mandolin 350QX157-5	Keepsake	Yr.Iss.	3.50	65.00
77-21-004	Wreath 350QX156-2	Keepsake	Yr.Iss.	3.50	65.00
Hallmark Keepsake Ornaments	**1977 The Beauty of America Collection**				
77-22-001	Mountains 250QX158-2	Keepsake	Yr.Iss.	2.50	30-55.00
77-22-002	Desert 250QX159-5	Keepsake	Yr.Iss.	2.50	30-55.00
77-22-003	Seashore 250QX160-2	Keepsake	Yr.Iss.	2.50	30-50.00
77-22-004	Wharf 250QX161-5	Keepsake	Yr.Iss.	2.50	30-50.00
Hallmark Keepsake Ornaments	**1977 Decorative Ball Ornaments**				
77-23-001	Rabbit 250QX139-5	Keepsake	Yr.Iss.	2.50	95.00
77-23-002	Squirrel 250QX138-2	Keepsake	Yr.Iss.	2.50	115.00
77-23-003	Christmas Mouse 250QX134-2	Keepsake	Yr.Iss.	3.50	85.00
77-23-004	Stained Glass 250QX152-2	Keepsake	Yr.Iss.	3.50	65.00
Hallmark Keepsake Ornaments	**1977 Colors of Christmas**				
77-24-001	Bell 350QX200-2	Keepsake	Yr.Iss.	3.50	35-55.00
77-24-002	Joy 350QX201-5	Keepsake	Yr.Iss.	3.50	35-60.00
77-24-003	Wreath 350QX202-2	Keepsake	Yr.Iss.	3.50	25-55.00
77-24-004	Candle 350QX203-5	Keepsake	Yr.Iss.	3.50	75.00
Hallmark Keepsake Ornaments	**1977 Holiday Highlights**				
77-25-001	Joy 350QX310-2	Keepsake	Yr.Iss.	3.50	25-55.00
77-25-002	Peace on Earth 350QX311-5	Keepsake	Yr.Iss.	3.50	45-75.00
77-25-003	Drummer Boy 350QX312-2	Keepsake	Yr.Iss.	3.50	70.00
77-25-004	Star 350QX313-5	Keepsake	Yr.Iss.	3.50	40.00
Hallmark Keepsake Ornaments	**1977 Twirl-About Collection**				
77-26-001	Snowman 450QX190-2	Keepsake	Yr.Iss.	4.50	55-65.00
77-26-002	Weather House 600QX191-5	Keepsake	Yr.Iss.	6.00	125.00
77-26-003	Bellringer 600QX192-2	Keepsake	Yr.Iss.	6.00	50-65.00
77-26-004	Della Robia Wreath 450QX193-5	Keepsake	Yr.Iss.	4.50	85-135.00
Hallmark Keepsake Ornaments	**1977 Metal Ornaments**				
77-27-001	Snowflake Collection (Set of 4)500QX 210-2	Keepsake	Yr.Iss.	5.00	95.00
Hallmark Keepsake Ornaments	**1977 Nostalgia Collection**				
77-28-001	Angel 500QX182-2	Keepsake	Yr.Iss.	5.00	125.00
77-28-002	Toys 500QX183-5	Keepsake	Yr.Iss.	5.00	110-145.
77-28-003	Antique Car 500QX180-2	Keepsake	Yr.Iss.	5.00	45-75.00
77-28-004	Nativity 500QX181-5	Keepsake	Yr.Iss.	5.00	130-175.
Hallmark Keepsake Ornaments	**1977 Yesteryears Collection**				
77-29-001	Angel 600QX172-2	Keepsake	Yr.Iss.	6.00	100-125.00
77-29-002	Reindeer 600QX173-5	Keepsake	Yr.Iss.	6.00	85.00
77-29-003	Jack-in-the-Box 600QX171-5	Keepsake	Yr.Iss.	6.00	100-125.00
77-29-004	House 600QX170-2	Keepsake	Yr.Iss.	6.00	85-115.00
Hallmark Keepsake Ornaments	**1977 Cloth Doll Ornaments**				
77-30-001	Angel 175QX220-2	Keepsake	Yr.Iss.	1.75	40-65.00
77-30-002	Santa 175QX221-5	Keepsake	Yr.Iss.	1.75	40-95.00
Hallmark Keepsake Ornaments	**1978 Commemoratives**				
78-31-001	Baby's First Christmas 350QX200-3	Keepsake	Yr.Iss.	3.50	50-75.00
78-31-002	Granddaughter 350QX216-3	Keepsake	Yr.Iss.	3.50	50.00
78-31-003	Grandson 350QX215-6	Keepsake	Yr.Iss.	3.50	50.00
78-31-004	First Christmas Together 350QX218-3	Keepsake	Yr.Iss.	3.50	45-55.00
78-31-005	25th Christmas Together 350QX269-3	Keepsake	Yr.Iss.	3.50	15-30.00
78-31-006	Love 350QX268-3	Keepsake	Yr.Iss.	3.50	50.00
78-31-007	Grandmother 350QX267-6	Keepsake	Yr.Iss.	3.50	50.00
78-31-008	Mother 350QX266-3	Keepsake	Yr.Iss.	3.50	27.00
78-31-009	For Your New Home 350QX217-6	Keepsake	Yr.Iss.	3.50	75.00
Hallmark Keepsake Ornaments	**1978 Peanuts Collection**				
78-32-001	Peanuts 250QX204-3	Keepsake	Yr.Iss.	2.50	50.00
78-32-002	Peanuts 350QX205-6	Keepsake	Yr.Iss.	3.50	75.00
78-32-003	Peanuts 350QX206-3	Keepsake	Yr.Iss.	3.50	50.00
78-32-004	Peanuts 250QX203-6	Keepsake	Yr.Iss.	2.50	50.00
Hallmark Keepsake Ornaments	**1978 Property Ornaments**				
78-33-001	Betsey Clark-Sixth Edition 350QX 201-6	Keepsake	Yr.Iss.	3.50	55.00
78-33-002	Joan Walsh Anglund 350QX221-6	Keepsake	Yr.Iss.	3.50	50-85.00
78-33-003	Spencer Sparrow 350QX219-6	Keepsake	Yr.Iss.	3.50	50.00
78-33-004	Disney 350QX207-6	Keepsake	Yr.Iss.	3.50	75.00
Hallmark Keepsake Ornaments	**1978 Decorative Ball Ornaments**				
78-34-001	Merry Christmas (Santa) 350QX202-3	Keepsake	Yr.Iss.	3.50	50.00
78-34-002	Hallmark's Antique Card Collection Design 350QX 220-3	Keepsake	Yr.Iss.	3.50	30-55.00
78-34-003	Yesterday's Toys 350QX250-3	Keepsake	Yr.Iss.	3.50	55.00
78-34-004	Nativity 350QX253-6	Keepsake	Yr.Iss.	3.50	150.00
78-34-005	The Quail 350QX251-6	Keepsake	Yr.Iss.	3.50	10-40.00
78-34-006	Drummer Boy 350QX252-3	Keepsake	Yr.Iss.	3.50	55.00
78-34-007	Joy 350QX254-3	Keepsake	Yr.Iss.	3.50	50.00
Hallmark Keepsake Ornaments	**1978 Holiday Highlights**				
78-35-001	Santa 350QX307-6	Keepsake	Yr.Iss.	3.50	95.00
78-35-002	Snowflake 350QX308-3	Keepsake	Yr.Iss.	3.50	50.00
78-35-003	Nativity 350QX309-6	Keepsake	Yr.Iss.	3.50	95.00
78-35-004	Dove 350QX310-3	Keepsake	Yr.Iss.	3.50	125.00
Hallmark Keepsake Ornaments	**1978 Holiday Chimes**				
78-36-001	Reindeer Chimes 450QX320-3	Keepsake	Yr.Iss.	4.50	60.00
Hallmark Keepsake Ornaments	**1978 Little Trimmers**				
78-37-001	Thimble Series (Mouse)-First Ed.250QX133-6	Keepsake	Yr.Iss.	2.50	225-300.
78-37-002	Santa 250QX135-6	Keepsake	Yr.Iss.	2.50	55-75.00
78-37-003	Praying Angel 250QX134-3	Keepsake	Yr.Iss.	2.50	95.00
78-37-004	Drummer Boy 250QX136-3	Keepsake	Yr.Iss.	2.50	75-85.00
78-37-005	Set of 4 - 250QX355-6	Keepsake	Yr.Iss.	10.00	400.00
Hallmark Keepsake Ornaments	**1978 Colors of Christmas**				
78-38-001	Merry Christmas 350QX355-6	Keepsake	Yr.Iss.	3.50	80.00
78-38-002	Locomotive 350QX356-3	Keepsake	Yr.Iss.	3.50	75.00
78-38-003	Angel 350QX354-3	Keepsake	Yr.Iss.	3.50	35-55.00
78-38-004	Candle 350QX357-6	Keepsake	Yr.Iss.	3.50	125.00
Hallmark Keepsake Ornaments	**1978 Handcrafted Ornaments**				
78-39-001	Dove 450QX190-3	Keepsake	Yr.Iss.	4.50	85.00
78-39-002	Holly and Poinsettia Ball 600QX147-6	Keepsake	Yr.Iss.	6.00	85.00
78-39-003	Schneeberg Bell 800QX152-3	Keepsake	Yr.Iss.	8.00	199.00
78-39-004	Angels 800QX150-3	Keepsake	Yr.Iss.	8.00	325-400.
78-39-005	Carrousel Series-First Edition600QX 146-3	Keepsake	Yr.Iss.	6.00	350-400.
78-39-006	Joy 450QX138-3	Keepsake	Yr.Iss.	4.50	80.00
78-39-007	Angel 400QX139-6	Keepsake	Yr.Iss.	4.50	85.00
78-39-008	Calico Mouse 450QX137-6	Keepsake	Yr.Iss.	4.50	160-200.
78-39-009	Red Cardinal 450QX144-3	Keepsake	Yr.Iss.	4.50	150-175.
78-39-010	Panorama Ball 600QX145-6	Keepsake	Yr.Iss.	6.00	90-135.00
78-39-011	Skating Raccoon 600QX142-3	Keepsake	Yr.Iss.	6.00	75-95.00
78-39-012	Rocking Horse 600QX148-3	Keepsake	Yr.Iss.	6.00	65-95.00
78-39-013	Animal Home 600QX149-6	Keepsake	Yr.Iss.	6.00	150-175.
Hallmark Keepsake Ornaments	**1978 Yarn Collection**				
78-40-001	Green Boy 200QX123-1	Keepsake	Yr.Iss.	2.00	20.00
78-40-002	Mrs. Claus 200QX125-1	Keepsake	Yr.Iss.	2.00	19.50
78-40-003	Green Girl 200QX126-1	Keepsake	Yr.Iss.	2.00	17.50
78-40-004	Mr. Claus 200QX340-3	Keepsake	Yr.Iss.	2.00	20.00
Hallmark Keepsake Ornaments	**1979 Commemoratives**				
79-41-001	Baby's First Christmas 350QX208-7	Keepsake	Yr.Iss.	3.50	18.00
79-41-002	Baby's First Christmas 800QX154-7	Keepsake	Yr.Iss.	8.00	135-175.
79-41-003	Grandson 350QX210-7	Keepsake	Yr.Iss.	3.50	20.00
79-41-004	Granddaughter 350QX211-9	Keepsake	Yr.Iss.	3.50	28.00
79-41-005	Mother 350QX251-9	Keepsake	Yr.Iss.	3.50	15.00
79-41-006	Grandmother 350QX252-7	Keepsake	Yr.Iss.	3.50	14.50
79-41-007	Our First Christmas Together350-QX 209-9	Keepsake	Yr.Iss.	3.50	45.00
79-41-008	Our Twenty-Fifth Anniversary350QX 250-7	Keepsake	Yr.Iss.	3.50	15-19.00
79-41-009	Love 350QX258-7	Keepsake	Yr.Iss.	3.50	30.00
79-41-010	Friendship 350QX203-9	Keepsake	Yr.Iss.	3.50	17.50
79-41-011	Teacher 350QX213-9	Keepsake	Yr.Iss.	3.50	10-18.00
79-41-012	New Home 350QX212-7	Keepsake	Yr.Iss.	3.50	40.00

Company Number	Name	Series Artist	Edition Limit	Issue Price	Quote
Hallmark Keepsake Ornaments		**1979 Property Ornaments**			
79-42-001	Betsey Clark-Seventh Edition350QX 201-9	Keepsake	Yr.Iss.	3.50	29.50
79-42-002	Peanuts (Time to Trim) 350QX202-7	Keepsake	Yr.Iss.	3.50	25.00
79-42-003	Spencer Sparrow 350QX200-7	Keepsake	Yr.Iss.	3.50	30.00
79-42-004	Joan Walsh Anglund 350QX205-9	Keepsake	Yr.Iss.	3.50	25-35.00
79-42-005	Winnie-the-Pooh 350QX206-7	Keepsake	Yr.Iss.	3.50	35.00
79-42-006	Mary Hamilton 350QX254-7	Keepsake	Yr.Iss.	3.50	15-30.00
Hallmark Keepsake Ornaments		**1979 Decorative Ball Ornaments**			
79-43-001	Night Before Christmas 350QX214-7	Keepsake	Yr.Iss.	3.50	29.50
79-43-002	Christmas Chickadees 350QX204-7	Keepsake	Yr.Iss.	3.50	29.00
79-43-003	Behold the Star 350QX255-9	Keepsake	Yr.Iss.	3.50	35-45.00
79-43-004	Christmas Traditions 350QX253-9	Keepsake	Yr.Iss.	3.50	32.50
79-43-005	Christmas Collage 350QX257-9	Keepsake	Yr.Iss.	3.50	30.00
79-43-006	Black Angel 350QX207-9	Keepsake	Yr.Iss.	3.50	10-20.00
79-43-007	The Light of Christmas 350QX256-7	Keepsake	Yr.Iss.	3.50	23.00
Hallmark Keepsake Ornaments		**1979 Holiday Highlights**			
79-44-001	Christmas Angel 350QX300-7	Keepsake	Yr.Iss.	3.50	85.00
79-44-002	Snowflake 350QX301-9	Keepsake	Yr.Iss.	3.50	40.00
79-44-003	Christmas Tree 350QX302-7	Keepsake	Yr.Iss.	3.50	75.00
79-44-004	Christmas Cheer 350QX303-9	Keepsake	Yr.Iss.	3.50	55.00
79-44-005	Love 350QX304-7	Keepsake	Yr.Iss.	3.50	87.50
Hallmark Keepsake Ornaments		**1979 Colors of Christmas**			
79-45-001	Words of Christmas 350QX350-7	Keepsake	Yr.Iss.	3.50	85.00
79-45-002	Holiday Wreath 350QX353-9	Keepsake	Yr.Iss.	3.50	39.50
79-45-003	Partridge in a Pear Tree 350QX351-9	Keepsake	Yr.Iss.	3.50	36-45.00
79-45-004	Star Over Bethlehem 350QX352-7	Keepsake	Yr.Iss.	3.50	65.00
Hallmark Keepsake Ornaments		**1979 Little Trimmer Collection**			
79-46-001	Thimble Series-Mouse 300QX133-6	Keepsake	Yr.Iss.	3.00	150-225.
79-46-002	Santa 300QX135-6	Keepsake	Yr.Iss.	3.00	55.00
79-46-003	A Matchless Christmas 400QX132-7	Keepsake	Yr.Iss.	4.00	75.00
79-46-004	Angel Delight 300QX130-7	Keepsake	Yr.Iss.	3.00	100.00
Hallmark Keepsake Ornaments		**1979 Handcrafted Ornaments**			
79-47-001	Holiday Scrimshaw 400QX152-7	Keepsake	Yr.Iss.	4.00	180.00
79-47-002	Christmas Heart 650QX140-7	Keepsake	Yr.Iss.	6.50	95.00
79-47-003	Christmas Eve Surprise 650QX157-9	Keepsake	Yr.Iss.	6.50	55.00
79-47-004	Santa's Here 500QX138-7	Keepsake	Yr.Iss.	5.00	50-65.00
79-47-005	Raccoon 650QX142-3	Keepsake	Yr.Iss.	6.50	85.00
79-47-006	The Downhill Run 650QX145-9	Keepsake	Yr.Iss.	6.50	135-150.
79-47-007	The Drummer Boy 800QX143-9	Keepsake	Yr.Iss.	8.00	125.00
79-47-008	Outdoor Fun 800QX150-7	Keepsake	Yr.Iss.	8.00	100-150.
79-47-009	A Christmas Treat 500QX134-7	Keepsake	Yr.Iss.	5.00	85.00
79-47-010	The Skating Snowman 500QX139-9	Keepsake	Yr.Iss.	5.00	40-85.00
79-47-011	Christmas is for Children 500QX135-9	Keepsake	Yr.Iss.	5.00	83-95.00
79-47-012	Ready for Christmas 650QX133-9	Keepsake	Yr.Iss.	6.50	150.00
Hallmark Keepsake Ornaments		**1979 Collectible Series**			
79-48-001	Carousel-Second Edition 650QX146-7	Keepsake	Yr.Iss.	6.50	150-200.
79-48-002	Thimble-Second Edition 300QX131-9	Keepsake	Yr.Iss.	3.00	150-195.
79-48-003	Snoopy and Friends 800QX141-9	Keepsake	Yr.Iss.	8.00	125.00
79-48-004	Here Comes Santa-First Edition 900QX 155-9	Keepsake	Yr.Iss.	9.00	595.00
79-48-005	Bellringer-First Edition 10QX147-9	Keepsake	Yr.Iss.	10.00	325-400.
Hallmark Keepsake Ornaments		**1979 Holiday Chimes**			
79-49-001	Reindeer Chimes 450QX320-3	Keepsake	Yr.Iss.	4.50	75.00
79-49-002	Star Chimes 450QX137-9	Keepsake	Yr.Iss.	4.50	75.00
Hallmark Keepsake Ornaments		**1979 Sewn Trimmers**			
79-50-001	The Rocking Horse 200QX340-7	Keepsake	Yr.Iss.	2.00	15.00
79-50-002	Merry Santa 200QX342-7	Keepsake	Yr.Iss.	2.00	15.00
79-50-003	Stuffed Full Stocking 200QX341-9	Keepsake	Yr.Iss.	2.00	19.00
79-50-004	Angel Music 200QX343-9	Keepsake	Yr.Iss.	2.00	17.50
Hallmark Keepsake Ornaments		**1980 Commemoratives**			
80-51-001	Baby's First Christmas 400QX200-1	Keepsake	Yr.Iss.	4.00	20-40.00
80-51-002	Black Baby's First Christmas 400QX 229-4	Keepsake	Yr.Iss.	4.00	20-25.00
80-51-003	Baby's First Christmas 12QX156-1	Keepsake	Yr.Iss.	12.00	40-45.00
80-51-004	Grandson 400QX201-4	Keepsake	Yr.Iss.	4.00	25.00
80-51-005	Granddaughter 400QX202-1	Keepsake	Yr.Iss.	4.00	25.00
80-51-006	Son 400QX211-4	Keepsake	Yr.Iss.	4.00	17.00
80-51-007	Daughter 400QX212-1	Keepsake	Yr.Iss.	4.00	29.50
80-51-008	Dad 400QX214-1	Keepsake	Yr.Iss.	4.00	15.00
80-51-009	Mother 400QX203-4	Keepsake	Yr.Iss.	4.00	13.50
80-51-010	Mother and Dad 400QX230-1	Keepsake	Yr.Iss.	4.00	12.00
80-51-011	Grandmother 400QX204-1	Keepsake	Yr.Iss.	4.00	15.00
80-51-012	Grandfather 400QX231-4	Keepsake	Yr.Iss.	4.00	13.50
80-51-013	Grandparents 400QX213-4	Keepsake	Yr.Iss.	4.00	49.00
80-51-014	25th Christmas Together 400QX206-1	Keepsake	Yr.Iss.	4.00	12.50
80-51-015	First Christmas Together 400QX205-4	Keepsake	Yr.Iss.	4.00	15-25.00
80-51-016	Christmas Love 400QX207-4	Keepsake	Yr.Iss.	4.00	15.00
80-51-017	Friendship 400QX208-1	Keepsake	Yr.Iss.	4.00	16.00
80-51-018	Christmas at Home 400QX210-1	Keepsake	Yr.Iss.	4.00	29.00
80-51-019	Teacher 400QX209-4	Keepsake	Yr.Iss.	4.00	13.00
80-51-020	Love 400QX302-1	Keepsake	Yr.Iss.	4.00	50.00
80-51-021	Beauty of Friendship 400QX303-4	Keepsake	Yr.Iss.	4.00	55.00
80-51-022	First Christmas Together 400QX305-4	Keepsake	Yr.Iss.	4.00	25-55.00
80-51-023	Mother 400QX304-1	Keepsake	Yr.Iss.	4.00	35.00
Hallmark Keepsake Ornaments		**1980 Property Ornaments**			
80-52-001	Betsey Clark-Eighth Edition 400QX 215-4	Keepsake	Yr.Iss.	4.00	29.50
80-52-002	Betsey Clark 650QX307-4	Keepsake	Yr.Iss.	6.50	65.00
80-52-003	Betsey Clark's Christmas 750QX194-4	Keepsake	Yr.Iss.	7.50	25.00
80-52-004	Peanuts 400QX216-1	Keepsake	Yr.Iss.	4.00	20-25.00
80-52-005	Joan Walsh Anglund 400QX217-4	Keepsake	Yr.Iss.	4.00	21.00
80-52-006	Disney 400QX218-1	Keepsake	Yr.Iss.	4.00	25.00
80-52-007	Mary Hamilton 400QX219-4	Keepsake	Yr.Iss.	4.00	21-80.00
80-52-008	Muppets 400QX220-1	Keepsake	Yr.Iss.	4.00	25-37.50
80-52-009	Marty Links 400QX221-4	Keepsake	Yr.Iss.	4.00	15.00
Hallmark Keepsake Ornaments		**1980 Decorative Ball Ornaments**			
80-53-001	Christmas Choir 400QX228-1	Keepsake	Yr.Iss.	4.00	150.00
80-53-002	Nativity 400QX225-4	Keepsake	Yr.Iss.	4.00	125.00
80-53-003	Christmas Time 400QX226-1	Keepsake	Yr.Iss.	4.00	20.00
80-53-004	Santa's Workshop 400QX223-4	Keepsake	Yr.Iss.	4.00	15-30.00
80-53-005	Happy Christmas 400QX222-1	Keepsake	Yr.Iss.	4.00	28-40.00
80-53-006	Jolly Santa 400QX227-4	Keepsake	Yr.Iss.	4.00	30.00
80-53-007	Christmas Cardinals 400QX224-1	Keepsake	Yr.Iss.	4.00	35.00
Hallmark Keepsake Ornaments		**1980 Holiday Highlights**			
80-54-001	Three Wise Men 400QX300-1	Keepsake	Yr.Iss.	4.00	22.50
80-54-002	Wreath 400QX301-4	Keepsake	Yr.Iss.	4.00	85.00
Hallmark Keepsake Ornaments		**1980 Colors of Christmas**			
80-55-001	Joy 400QX350-1	Keepsake	Yr.Iss.	4.00	25.00
Hallmark Keepsake Ornaments		**1980 Frosted Images**			
80-56-001	Drummer Boy 400QX309-4	Keepsake	Yr.Iss.	4.00	10-20.00
80-56-002	Santa 400QX310-1	Keepsake	Yr.Iss.	4.00	20.00
80-56-003	Dove 400QX308-1	Keepsake	Yr.Iss.	4.00	25-35.00
Hallmark Keepsake Ornaments		**1980 Little Trimmers**			
80-57-001	Clothespin Soldier 350QX134-1	Keepsake	Yr.Iss.	3.50	30-45.00
80-57-002	Christmas Teddy 250QX135-4	Keepsake	Yr.Iss.	2.50	125.00
80-57-003	Merry Redbird 350QX160-1	Keepsake	Yr.Iss.	3.50	55.00
80-57-004	Swingin' on a Star 400QX130-1	Keepsake	Yr.Iss.	4.00	60-75.00
80-57-005	Christmas Owl 400QX131-4	Keepsake	Yr.Iss.	4.00	45.00
80-57-006	Thimble Series-A Christmas Salute 400QX 131-9	Keepsake	Yr.Iss.	4.00	150.00
Hallmark Keepsake Ornaments		**1980 Handcrafted Ornaments**			
80-58-001	The Snowflake Swing 400QX133-4	Keepsake	Yr.Iss.	4.00	45.00
80-58-002	Santa 1980 550QX146-1	Keepsake	Yr.Iss.	5.50	95.00
80-58-003	Drummer Boy 550QX147-4	Keepsake	Yr.Iss.	5.50	65-95.00
80-58-004	Christmas is for Children 550QX135-9	Keepsake	Yr.Iss.	5.50	95.00
80-58-005	A Christmas Treat 550QX134-7	Keepsake	Yr.Iss.	5.50	75.00
80-58-006	Skating Snowman 550QX139-9	Keepsake	Yr.Iss.	5.50	75.00
80-58-007	A Heavenly Nap 650QX139-4	Keepsake	Yr.Iss.	6.50	50.00
80-58-008	Heavenly Sounds 750QX152-1	Keepsake	Yr.Iss.	7.50	90.00
80-58-009	Caroling Bear 750QX140-1	Keepsake	Yr.Iss.	7.50	150.00
80-58-010	Santa's Flight 550QX138-1	Keepsake	Yr.Iss.	5.50	95.00
80-58-011	The Animals' Christmas 800QX150-1	Keepsake	Yr.Iss.	8.00	55.00
80-58-012	A Spot of Christmas Cheer 800QX 153-4	Keepsake	Yr.Iss.	8.00	160.00
80-58-013	Elfin Antics 900QX142-1	Keepsake	Yr.Iss.	9.00	225.00
80-58-014	A Christmas Vigil 900QX144-1	Keepsake	Yr.Iss.	9.00	110.00
Hallmark Keepsake Ornaments		**1980 Special Editions**			
80-59-001	Heavenly Minstrel 15QX156-7	Keepsake	Yr.Iss.	15.00	350-375.
80-59-002	Checking it Twice 20QX158-4	Keepsake	Yr.Iss.	20.00	175-195.
Hallmark Keepsake Ornaments		**1980 Holiday Chimes**			
80-60-001	Snowflake Chimes 550QX165-4	Keepsake	Yr.Iss.	5.50	30.00
80-60-002	Reindeer Chimes 550QX320-3	Keepsake	Yr.Iss.	5.50	55.00
80-60-003	Santa Mobile 550QX136-1	Keepsake	Yr.Iss.	5.50	60.00
Hallmark Keepsake Ornaments		**1980 Collectible Series**			
80-61-001	Norman Rockwell-First Edition650QX 306-1	Keepsake	Yr.Iss.	6.50	150-225.
80-61-002	Frosty Friends-First Edition650QX 137-4	Keepsake	Yr.Iss.	6.50	595-600.
80-61-003	Snoopy & Friends-Second Ed. 900QX 154-1	Keepsake	Yr.Iss.	9.00	95.00
80-61-004	Carrousel-Third Edition 750QX141-4	Keepsake	Yr.Iss.	7.50	155.00
80-61-005	Thimble-Third Edition 400QX132-1	Keepsake	Yr.Iss.	4.00	150-175.
80-61-006	Here Comes Santa-Second Ed.12QX 143-4	Keepsake	Yr.Iss.	12.00	250.00
80-61-007	The Bellringers-Second Edition15QX 157-4	Keepsake	Yr.Iss.	15.00	55-75.00
Hallmark Keepsake Ornaments		**1980 Yarn Ornaments**			
80-62-001	Santa 300QX161-4	Keepsake	Yr.Iss.	3.00	20.00
80-62-002	Angel 300QX162-1	Keepsake	Yr.Iss.	3.00	20.00
80-62-003	Snowman 300QX163-4	Keepsake	Yr.Iss.	3.00	20.00
80-62-004	Soldier 300QX164-1	Keepsake	Yr.Iss.	3.00	20.00
Hallmark Keepsake Ornaments		**1981 Commemoratives**			
81-63-001	Baby's First Christmas-Girl450QX 600-2	Keepsake	Yr.Iss.	4.50	15.00
81-63-002	Baby's First Christmas-Boy450QX 601-5	Keepsake	Yr.Iss.	4.50	15.00
81-63-003	Baby's First Christmas-Black450QX 602-2	Keepsake	Yr.Iss.	4.50	17.50
81-63-004	Baby's First Christmas 550QX516-2	Keepsake	Yr.Iss.	5.50	29.50
81-63-005	Baby's First Christmas 850QX513-5	Keepsake	Yr.Iss.	8.50	15.50
81-63-006	Baby's First Christmas 1300QX440-2	Keepsake	Yr.Iss.	13.00	55.00
81-63-007	Godchild 450QX603-5	Keepsake	Yr.Iss.	4.50	12.50
81-63-008	Grandson 450QX604-2	Keepsake	Yr.Iss.	4.50	23.00
81-63-009	Granddaughter 450QX605-5	Keepsake	Yr.Iss.	4.50	25.00
81-63-010	Daughter 450QX607-5	Keepsake	Yr.Iss.	4.50	15-25.00
81-63-011	Son 450QX606-2	Keepsake	Yr.Iss.	4.50	15-25.00
81-63-012	Mother 450QX608-2	Keepsake	Yr.Iss.	4.50	19.00
81-63-013	Father 450QX609-5	Keepsake	Yr.Iss.	4.50	12-15.00
81-63-014	Mother and Dad 450QX700-2	Keepsake	Yr.Iss.	4.50	12.50
81-63-015	Friendship 450QX704-2	Keepsake	Yr.Iss.	4.50	12.50-26.00
81-63-016	The Gift of Love 450QX705-5	Keepsake	Yr.Iss.	4.50	17.50
81-63-017	Home 450QX709-5	Keepsake	Yr.Iss.	4.50	14.50
81-63-018	Teacher 450QX800-2	Keepsake	Yr.Iss.	4.50	12.00
81-63-019	Grandfather 450QX701-5	Keepsake	Yr.Iss.	4.50	12.00
81-63-020	Grandmother 450QX702-2	Keepsake	Yr.Iss.	4.50	12.50
81-63-021	Grandparents 450QX703-5	Keepsake	Yr.Iss.	4.50	12.00
81-63-022	First Christmas Together 450QX706-2	Keepsake	Yr.Iss.	4.50	25.00
81-63-023	25th Christmas Together 450QX707-5	Keepsake	Yr.Iss.	4.50	15.00
81-63-024	50th Christmas 450QX708-2	Keepsake	Yr.Iss.	4.50	12.00
81-63-025	Love 550QX502-2	Keepsake	Yr.Iss.	5.50	19.50
81-63-026	Friendship 550QX503-5	Keepsake	Yr.Iss.	5.50	29.50
81-63-027	First Christmas Together 550QX505-5	Keepsake	Yr.Iss.	5.50	22.50
81-63-028	25th Christmas Together 550QX504-2	Keepsake	Yr.Iss.	5.50	19.50
Hallmark Keepsake Ornaments		**1981 Property Ornaments**			
81-65-001	Betsey Clark Cameo 850QX512-2	Keepsake	Yr.Iss.	8.50	30.00
81-65-002	Betsey Clark 900QX423-5	Keepsake	Yr.Iss.	9.00	30-65.00
81-65-003	Betsey Clark-Ninth Edition450QX 802-2	Keepsake	Yr.Iss.	4.50	25.00
81-65-004	Muppets 450QX807-5	Keepsake	Yr.Iss.	4.50	25-35.00
81-65-005	Kermit the Frog 900QX424-2	Keepsake	Yr.Iss.	9.00	80-95.00
81-65-006	The Divine Miss Piggy 1200QX425-5	Keepsake	Yr.Iss.	12.00	95.00
81-65-007	Mary Hamilton 450QX806-2	Keepsake	Yr.Iss.	4.50	19.50
81-65-008	Marty Links 450QX808-2	Keepsake	Yr.Iss.	4.50	15.00
81-65-009	Peanuts 450QX803-5	Keepsake	Yr.Iss.	4.50	25.00
81-65-010	Joan Walsh Anglund 450QX804-2	Keepsake	Yr.Iss.	4.50	15.00
81-65-011	Disney 450QX805-5	Keepsake	Yr.Iss.	4.50	22.00
Hallmark Keepsake Ornaments		**1981 Decorative Ball Ornaments**			
81-66-001	Christmas 1981 450QX809-5	Keepsake	Yr.Iss.	4.50	25.00
81-66-002	Christmas Magic 450QX810-2	Keepsake	Yr.Iss.	4.50	19.50
81-66-003	Traditional (Black Santa) 450QX801-5	Keepsake	Yr.Iss.	4.50	50-95.00
81-66-004	Let Us Adore Him 450QX811-5	Keepsake	Yr.Iss.	4.50	50.00
81-66-005	Santa's Coming 450QX812-2	Keepsake	Yr.Iss.	4.50	19.50
81-66-006	Christmas in the Forest 450QX813-5	Keepsake	Yr.Iss.	4.50	175.00
81-66-007	Merry Christmas 450QX814-2	Keepsake	Yr.Iss.	4.50	17.50
81-66-008	Santa's Surprise 450QX815-5	Keepsake	Yr.Iss.	4.50	19.50

CHRISTMAS ORNAMENTS

Company Number	Name	Series Artist	Edition Limit	Issue Price	Quote
Hallmark Keepsake Ornaments		**1981 Crown Classics**			
81-67-001	Angel 450QX507-5	Keepsake	Yr.Iss.	4.50	25.00
81-67-002	Tree Photoholder 550QX515-5	Keepsake	Yr.Iss.	5.50	25.00
81-67-003	Unicorn 850QX516-5	Keepsake	Yr.Iss.	8.50	23.00
Hallmark Keepsake Ornaments		**1981 Frosted Images**			
81-68-001	Mouse 400QX508-2	Keepsake	Yr.Iss.	4.00	20.00
81-68-002	Angel 400QX509-5	Keepsake	Yr.Iss.	4.00	45-65.00
81-68-003	Snowman 400QX510-2	Keepsake	Yr.Iss.	4.00	25.00
Hallmark Keepsake Ornaments		**1981 Holiday Highlights**			
81-69-001	Shepherd Scene 550QX500-2	Keepsake	Yr.Iss.	5.50	20-25.00
81-69-002	Christmas Star 550QX501-5	Keepsake	Yr.Iss.	5.50	10-24.50
Hallmark Keepsake Ornaments		**1981 Little Trimmers**			
81-70-001	Puppy Love 350QX406-2	Keepsake	Yr.Iss.	3.50	30-40.00
81-70-002	Jolly Snowman 350QX407-5	Keepsake	Yr.Iss.	3.50	50.00
81-70-003	Perky Penguin 350QX409-5	Keepsake	Yr.Iss.	3.50	45-60.00
81-70-004	Clothespin Drummer Boy 450QX408-2	Keepsake	Yr.Iss.	4.50	45.00
81-70-005	The Stocking Mouse 450QX412-2	Keepsake	Yr.Iss.	4.50	60.00
Hallmark Keepsake Ornaments		**1981 Hand Crafted Ornaments**			
81-71-001	Space Santa 650QX430-2	Keepsake	Yr.Iss.	6.50	80-125.00
81-71-002	Candyville Express 750QX418-2	Keepsake	Yr.Iss.	7.50	125.00
81-71-003	Ice Fairy 650QX431-5	Keepsake	Yr.Iss.	6.50	65-85.00
81-71-004	Star Swing 550QX421-5	Keepsake	Yr.Iss.	5.50	50.00
81-71-005	A Heavenly Nap 650QX139-4	Keepsake	Yr.Iss.	6.50	49.50
81-71-006	Dough Angel 550QX139-6	Keepsake	Yr.Iss.	5.50	80.00
81-71-007	Topsy-Turvy Tunes 750QX429-5	Keepsake	Yr.Iss.	7.50	65.00
81-71-008	A Well-Stocked Stocking 900QX154-7	Keepsake	Yr.Iss.	9.00	60.00
81-71-009	The Friendly Fiddler 800QX434-2	Keepsake	Yr.Iss.	8.00	45-75.00
81-71-010	The Ice Sculptor 800QX432-2	Keepsake	Yr.Iss.	8.00	65.00
81-71-011	Christmas Dreams 1200QX437-5	Keepsake	Yr.Iss.	12.00	225.00
81-71-012	Christmas Fantasy 1300QX155-4	Keepsake	Yr.Iss.	13.00	75.00
81-71-013	Sailing Santa 1300QX439-5	Keepsake	Yr.Iss.	13.00	175.00
81-71-014	Love and Joy 900QX425-2	Keepsake	Yr.Iss.	9.00	95.00
81-71-015	Drummer Boy 250QX148-1	Keepsake	Yr.Iss.	2.50	50.00
81-71-016	St. Nicholas 550QX446-2	Keepsake	Yr.Iss.	5.50	35-50.00
81-71-017	Mr. & Mrs. Claus 1200QX448-5	Keepsake	Yr.Iss.	12.00	125-150.
81-71-018	Checking It Twice 2250QX158-4	Keepsake	Yr.Iss.	22.50	195.00
Hallmark Keepsake Ornaments		**1981 Holiday Chimes**			
81-72-001	Snowman Chimes 550QX445-5	Keepsake	Yr.Iss.	5.50	25.00
81-72-002	Santa Mobile 550QX136-1	Keepsake	Yr.Iss.	5.50	40.00
81-72-003	Snowflake Chimes 550QX165-4	Keepsake	Yr.Iss.	5.50	25.00
Hallmark Keepsake Ornaments		**1981 Collectible Series**			
81-73-001	Rocking Horse - 1st Edition900QX 422-2	Keepsake	Yr.Iss.	9.00	550-595.
81-73-002	Bellringer - 3rd Edition 1500QX441-5	Keepsake	Yr.Iss.	15.00	85-95.00
81-73-003	Norman Rockwell - 2nd Edition850QX 511-5	Keepsake	Yr.Iss.	8.50	30-45.00
81-73-004	Here Comes Santa - 3rd Ed.1300QX 438-2	Keepsake	Yr.Iss.	13.00	225-245.
81-73-005	Carrousel - 4th Edition 900QX427-5	Keepsake	Yr.Iss.	9.00	75-95.00
81-73-006	Snoopy and Friends - 3rd Ed.1200QX 436-2	Keepsake	Yr.Iss.	12.00	75.00
81-73-007	Thimble - 4th Edition 450QX413-5	Keepsake	Yr.Iss.	4.50	125.00
81-73-008	Frosty Friends - 2nd Edition800QX433-5	Keepsake	Yr.Iss.	8.00	350-425.
Hallmark Keepsake Ornaments		**1981 Fabric Ornaments**			
81-74-001	Cardinal Cutie 300QX400-2	Keepsake	Yr.Iss.	3.00	19.00
81-74-002	Peppermint Mouse 300QX401-5	Keepsake	Yr.Iss.	3.00	32.50
81-74-003	Gingham Dog 300QX402-2	Keepsake	Yr.Iss.	3.00	15.00
81-74-004	Calico Kitty 300QX403-5	Keepsake	Yr.Iss.	3.00	5-15.00
Hallmark Keepsake Ornaments		**1981 Plush Animals**			
81-75-001	Christmas Teddy 500QX404-2	Keepsake	Yr.Iss.	5.50	22-25.00
81-75-002	Raccoon Tunes 550QX405-5	Keepsake	Yr.Iss.	5.50	22-25.00
Hallmark Keepsake Ornaments		**1982 Commemoratives**			
82-76-001	Baby's First Christmas-Photoholder 650QX 312-6	Keepsake	Yr.Iss.	6.50	24.50
82-76-002	Baby's First Christmas 1300QX455-3	Keepsake	Yr.Iss.	13.00	30.00
82-76-003	Baby's First Christmas (Boy)450QX 216-3	Keepsake	Yr.Iss.	4.50	15.00
82-76-004	Baby's First Christmas (Girl)450QX 207-3	Keepsake	Yr.Iss.	4.50	15.00
82-76-005	Godchild 450QX222-6	Keepsake	Yr.Iss.	4.50	17.50
82-76-006	Grandson 450QX224-6	Keepsake	Yr.Iss.	4.50	17.50
82-76-007	Granddaughter 450QX224-3	Keepsake	Yr.Iss.	4.50	20-30.00
82-76-008	Son 450QX204-3	Keepsake	Yr.Iss.	4.50	25.00
82-76-009	Daughter 450QX204-6	Keepsake	Yr.Iss.	4.50	25.50
82-76-010	Father 450QX205-6	Keepsake	Yr.Iss.	4.50	14-24.00
82-76-011	Mother 450QX205-3	Keepsake	Yr.Iss.	4.50	15.00
82-76-012	Mother and Dad 450QX222-3	Keepsake	Yr.Iss.	4.50	12.00
82-76-013	Sister 450QX208-3	Keepsake	Yr.Iss.	4.50	22.50
82-76-014	Grandmother 450QX200-3	Keepsake	Yr.Iss.	4.50	12.00
82-76-015	Grandfather 450QX207-6	Keepsake	Yr.Iss.	4.50	12-24.00
82-76-016	Grandparents 450QX214-6	Keepsake	Yr.Iss.	4.50	12.00
82-76-017	First Christmas Together 850QX306-6	Keepsake	Yr.Iss.	8.50	35.00
82-76-018	First Christmas Together 450QX211-3	Keepsake	Yr.Iss.	4.50	20.00
82-76-019	First Christmas Together-Locket 1500QX 456-3	Keepsake	Yr.Iss.	15.00	45.00
82-76-020	Christmas Memories 650QX311-6	Keepsake	Yr.Iss.	6.50	19.50
82-76-021	Teacher 450QX214-3	Keepsake	Yr.Iss.	4.50	10.00
82-76-022	New Home 450QX212-6	Keepsake	Yr.Iss.	4.50	19.00
82-76-023	Teacher 650QX312-3	Keepsake	Yr.Iss.	6.50	15.00
82-76-024	25th Christmas Together 450QX211-6	Keepsake	Yr.Iss.	4.50	14.00
82-76-025	50th Christmas Together 450QX212-3	Keepsake	Yr.Iss.	4.50	14-24.00
82-76-026	Moments of Love 450QX209-3	Keepsake	Yr.Iss.	4.50	14.00
82-76-027	Love 450QX209-6	Keepsake	Yr.Iss.	4.50	15.00
82-76-028	Friendship 450QX208-6	Keepsake	Yr.Iss.	4.50	15.00
82-76-029	Teacher-Apple 550QX301-6	Keepsake	Yr.Iss.	5.50	15.00
82-76-030	Baby's First Christmas 550QX302-3	Keepsake	Yr.Iss.	5.50	20.00
82-76-031	First Christmas Together 550QX302-6	Keepsake	Yr.Iss.	5.50	20.00
82-76-032	Love 550QX304-3	Keepsake	Yr.Iss.	5.50	27.00
82-76-033	Friendship 550QX304-6	Keepsake	Yr.Iss.	5.50	24.50
Hallmark Keepsake Ornaments		**1982 Property Ornaments**			
82-77-001	Miss Piggy and Kermit 450QX218-3	Keepsake	Yr.Iss.	4.50	40.00
82-77-002	Muppets Party 450QX218-6	Keepsake	Yr.Iss.	4.50	40.00
82-77-003	Kermit the Frog 1100QX495-6	Keepsake	Yr.Iss.	11.00	75-95.00
82-77-004	The Divine Miss Piggy 1200QX425-5	Keepsake	Yr.Iss.	12.00	125.00
82-77-005	Betsey Clark 850QX305-6	Keepsake	Yr.Iss.	8.50	24.50
82-77-006	Norman Rockwell-3rd ed.850QX305-3	Keepsake	Yr.Iss.	8.50	18-36.00
82-77-007	Betsey Clark-10th edition450QX215-6	Keepsake	Yr.Iss.	4.50	29.50
82-77-008	Norman Rockwell 450QX202-3	Keepsake	Yr.Iss.	4.50	16-29.50
82-77-009	Peanuts 450QX200-6	Keepsake	Yr.Iss.	4.50	25.00
82-77-010	Disney 450QX217-3	Keepsake	Yr.Iss.	4.50	30-35.00
82-77-011	Mary Hamilton 450QX217-6	Keepsake	Yr.Iss.	4.50	17-21.00
82-77-012	Joan Walsh Anglund 450QX219-3	Keepsake	Yr.Iss.	4.50	18-27.00
Hallmark Keepsake Ornaments		**1982 Designer Keepsakes**			
82-78-001	Old World Angels 450QX226-3	Keepsake	Yr.Iss.	4.50	19.50
82-78-002	Patterns of Christmas 450QX226-6	Keepsake	Yr.Iss.	4.50	22.50
82-78-003	Old Fashioned Christmas 450QX227-6	Keepsake	Yr.Iss.	4.50	39.50
82-78-004	Stained Glass 450QX228-3	Keepsake	Yr.Iss.	4.50	19.50
82-78-005	Merry Christmas 450QX225-6	Keepsake	Yr.Iss.	4.50	15.00
82-78-006	Twelve Days of Christmas 450QX203-6	Keepsake	Yr.Iss.	4.50	39.50
Hallmark Keepsake Ornaments		**1982 Decorative Ball Ornaments**			
82-79-001	Christmas Angel 450QX220-6	Keepsake	Yr.Iss.	4.50	18.00
82-79-002	Santa 450QX221-6	Keepsake	Yr.Iss.	4.50	19.00
82-79-003	Currier & Ives 450QX201-3	Keepsake	Yr.Iss.	4.50	16.00
82-79-004	Season for Caring 450QX221-3	Keepsake	Yr.Iss.	4.50	20.00
Hallmark Keepsake Ornaments		**1982 Colors of Christmas**			
82-80-001	Nativity 450QX308-3	Keepsake	Yr.Iss.	4.50	40-46.00
82-80-002	Santa's Flight 450QX308-6	Keepsake	Yr.Iss.	4.50	25.00
Hallmark Keepsake Ornaments		**1982 Ice Sculptures**			
82-81-001	Snowy Seal 400QX300-6	Keepsake	Yr.Iss.	4.00	20-23.00
82-81-002	Arctic Penguin 400QX300-3	Keepsake	Yr.Iss.	4.00	12-19.50
Hallmark Keepsake Ornaments		**1982 Holiday Highlights**			
82-82-001	Christmas Sleigh 550QX309-3	Keepsake	Yr.Iss.	5.50	75.00
82-82-002	Angel 550QX309-6	Keepsake	Yr.Iss.	5.50	20-25.00
82-82-003	Christmas Magic 550QX311-3	Keepsake	Yr.Iss.	5.50	27.50
Hallmark Keepsake Ornaments		**1982 Handcrafted Ornaments**			
82-83-001	Three Kings 850QX307-3	Keepsake	Yr.Iss.	8.50	22.50
82-83-002	Baroque Angel 1500QX456-6	Keepsake	Yr.Iss.	15.00	150.00
82-83-003	Cloisonne Angel 1200QX145-4	Keepsake	Yr.Iss.	12.00	95.00
Hallmark Keepsake Ornaments		**1982 Brass Ornaments**			
82-84-001	Santa and Reindeer 900QX467-6	Keepsake	Yr.Iss.	9.00	45-50.00
82-84-002	Brass Bell 1200QX460-6	Keepsake	Yr.Iss.	12.00	15-22.50
82-84-003	Santa's Sleigh 900QX478-6	Keepsake	Yr.Iss.	9.00	24-30.00
Hallmark Keepsake Ornaments		**1982 Handcrafted Ornaments**			
82-85-001	The Spirit of Christmas 1000QX452-6	Keepsake	Yr.Iss.	10.00	125.00
82-85-002	Jogging Santa 800QX457-6	Keepsake	Yr.Iss.	8.00	35-45.00
82-85-003	Santa Bell 1500QX148-7	Keepsake	Yr.Iss.	15.00	60.00
82-85-004	Santa's Workshop 1000QX450-3	Keepsake	Yr.Iss.	10.00	85.00
82-85-005	Cycling Santa 2000QX435-5	Keepsake	Yr.Iss.	20.00	95.00
82-85-006	Christmas Fantasy 1300QX155-4	Keepsake	Yr.Iss.	13.00	59.00
82-85-007	Cowboy Snowman 800QX480-6	Keepsake	Yr.Iss.	8.00	45-50.00
82-85-008	Pinecone Home 800QX461-3	Keepsake	Yr.Iss.	8.00	90.00
82-85-009	Raccoon Surprises 900QX479-3	Keepsake	Yr.Iss.	9.00	150-175.
82-85-010	Elfin Artist 900QX457-3	Keepsake	Yr.Iss.	9.00	37.50-45.00
82-85-011	Ice Sculptor 800QX432-2	Keepsake	Yr.Iss.	8.00	75.00
82-85-012	Tin Soldier 650QX483-6	Keepsake	Yr.Iss.	6.50	39.50
82-85-013	Peeking Elf 650QX419-5	Keepsake	Yr.Iss.	6.50	32.50
82-85-014	Jolly Christmas Tree 650QX465-3	Keepsake	Yr.Iss.	6.50	75.00
82-85-015	Embroidered Tree - 650QX494-6	Keepsake	Yr.Iss.	6.50	25.00
Hallmark Keepsake Ornaments		**1982 Little Trimmers**			
82-86-001	Cookie Mouse 450QX454-6	Keepsake	Yr.Iss.	4.50	38.00
82-86-002	Musical Angel 550QX459-6	Keepsake	Yr.Iss.	5.50	100-125.
82-86-003	Merry Moose 550QX415-5	Keepsake	Yr.Iss.	5.50	25.00
82-86-004	Christmas Owl 450QX131-4	Keepsake	Yr.Iss.	4.50	35.00
82-86-005	Dove Love 450QX462-3	Keepsake	Yr.Iss.	4.50	55.00
82-86-006	Perky Penguin 400QX409-5	Keepsake	Yr.Iss.	4.00	35.00
82-86-007	Christmas Kitten 400QX454-3	Keepsake	Yr.Iss.	4.00	32.00
82-86-008	Jingling Teddy 400QX477-6	Keepsake	Yr.Iss.	4.00	40-48.00
Hallmark Keepsake Ornaments		**1982 Collectible Series**			
82-87-001	Holiday Wildlife-1st Ed. 700QX 313-3	Keepsake	Yr.Iss.	7.00	325-450.
82-87-002	Tin Locomotive-1st Ed. 1300QX 460-3	Keepsake	Yr.Iss.	13.00	475-525.
82-87-003	Clothespin Soldier-1st Ed. 500QX 458-3	Keepsake	Yr.Iss.	5.00	95-125.00
82-87-004	The Bellringer-4th Ed. 1500QX 455-6	Keepsake	Yr.Iss.	15.00	75-100.00
82-87-005	Carrousel Series-5th Ed. 1000QX 478-3	Keepsake	Yr.Iss.	10.00	80-100.00
82-87-006	Snoopy and Friends-4th Ed.1000QX 478-3	Keepsake	Yr.Iss.	13.00	85.00
82-87-007	Here Comes Santa-4th Edition 1500QX 464-3	Keepsake	Yr.Iss.	15.00	95-125.00
82-87-008	Rocking Horse-2nd Ed. 1000QX 502-3	Keepsake	Yr.Iss.	10.00	300-325.
82-87-009	Thimble-5th Edition 500QX451-3	Keepsake	Yr.Iss.	5.00	35-50.00
82-87-010	Frosty Friends-3rd Ed. 800QX 452-3	Keepsake	Yr.Iss.	8.00	135.00
Hallmark Keepsake Ornaments		**1982 Holiday Chimes**			
82-88-001	Tree Chimes 550QX484-6	Keepsake	Yr.Iss.	5.50	49.00
82-88-002	Bell Chimes 550QX494-3	Keepsake	Yr.Iss.	5.50	30.00
Hallmark Keepsake Ornaments		**1983 Commemoratives**			
83-89-001	Baby's First Christmas 750QX301-9	Keepsake	Yr.Iss.	7.50	15.00
83-89-002	Baby's First Christmas 1400QX402-7	Keepsake	Yr.Iss.	14.00	25.00
83-89-003	Baby's First Christmas 450QX200-7	Keepsake	Yr.Iss.	4.50	15.00
83-89-004	Baby's First Christmas 450QX200-9	Keepsake	Yr.Iss.	4.50	15.00
83-89-005	Baby's First Christmas 700QX302-9	Keepsake	Yr.Iss.	7.00	25.00
83-89-006	Grandchild's First Christmas400Q 430-9	Keepsake	Yr.Iss.	14.00	34.50
83-89-007	Child's Third Christmas 450QX226-9	Keepsake	Yr.Iss.	4.50	19.00
83-89-008	Grandchild's First Christmas600QX 312-9	Keepsake	Yr.Iss.	6.00	20.00
83-89-009	Baby's Second Christmas 450QX226-7	Keepsake	Yr.Iss.	4.50	25.00
83-89-010	Granddaughter 450QX202-7	Keepsake	Yr.Iss.	4.50	22.50
83-89-011	Grandson 450QX201-9	Keepsake	Yr.Iss.	4.50	15-22.50
83-89-012	Son 450QX202-9	Keepsake	Yr.Iss.	4.50	24.50
83-89-013	Daughter 450QX203-7	Keepsake	Yr.Iss.	4.50	12.00
83-89-014	Godchild 450QX201-7	Keepsake	Yr.Iss.	4.50	14.00
83-89-015	Grandmother 450QX205-7	Keepsake	Yr.Iss.	4.50	14.00
83-89-016	Mom and Dad 650QX429-7	Keepsake	Yr.Iss.	6.50	17.50
83-89-017	Sister 450QX206-9	Keepsake	Yr.Iss.	4.50	17.00
83-89-018	Grandparents 650QX429-9	Keepsake	Yr.Iss.	6.50	14.50
83-89-019	First Christmas Together 450QX208-9	Keepsake	Yr.Iss.	4.50	20.00
83-89-020	First Christmas Together 600QX310-7	Keepsake	Yr.Iss.	6.00	30-39.50
83-89-021	First Christmas Together 750QX301-7	Keepsake	Yr.Iss.	7.50	20.00
83-89-022	First Christmas Together- Brass Locket 1500QX 432-9	Keepsake	Yr.Iss.	15.00	30.00
83-89-023	Love Is a Song 450QX223-9	Keepsake	Yr.Iss.	4.50	20-25.00
83-89-024	Love 1300QX422-7	Keepsake	Yr.Iss.	13.00	29.50
83-89-025	Love 600QX310-9	Keepsake	Yr.Iss.	6.00	35.00
83-89-026	Love 450QX207-9	Keepsake	Yr.Iss.	4.50	25.00
83-89-027	Teacher 600QX304-9	Keepsake	Yr.Iss.	6.00	10.00
83-89-028	First Christmas Together 600QX306-9	Keepsake	Yr.Iss.	6.00	15-20.00
83-89-029	Friendship 600QX305-9	Keepsake	Yr.Iss.	6.00	14.50

CHRISTMAS ORNAMENTS

Company Number	Name	Series Artist	Edition Limit	Issue Price	Quote
83-89-030	Love 600QX305-7	Keepsake	Yr.Iss.	6.00	13.00
83-89-031	Mother 600Qx306-7	Keepsake	Yr.Iss.	6.00	14.50
83-89-032	25th Christmas Together 450QX224-7	Keepsake	Yr.Iss.	4.50	17.00
83-89-033	Teacher 450QX224-9	Keepsake	Yr.Iss.	4.50	14-20.00
83-89-034	Friendship 450QX207-7	Keepsake	Yr.Iss.	4.50	15.00
83-89-035	New Home 450QX210-7	Keepsake	Yr.Iss.	4.50	15.00
83-89-036	Tenth Christmas Together 650QX430-7	Keepsake	Yr.Iss.	6.50	20.00
Hallmark Keepsake Ornaments		**1983 Property Ornaments**			
83-90-001	Betsey Clark 650QX404-7	Keepsake	Yr.Iss.	6.50	29.50
83-90-002	Betsey Clark 900QX440-1	Keepsake	Yr.Iss.	9.00	27.50
83-90-003	Betsey Clark-11th Edition 450QX211-9	Keepsake	Yr.Iss.	4.50	30-50.00
83-90-004	Peanuts 450QX212-7	Keepsake	Yr.Iss.	4.50	17.50-24.00
83-90-005	Disney 450QX212-9	Keepsake	Yr.Iss.	4.50	30-50.00
83-90-006	Shirt Tales 450QX214-9	Keepsake	Yr.Iss.	4.50	22.50
83-90-007	Mary Hamilton 450QX213-7	Keepsake	Yr.Iss.	4.50	39.50
83-90-008	Miss Piggy 1300QX405-7	Keepsake	Yr.Iss.	13.00	195.00
83-90-009	The Muppets 450QX214-7	Keepsake	Yr.Iss.	4.50	50.00
83-90-010	Kermit the Frog 1100QX495-6	Keepsake	Yr.Iss.	11.00	35.00
83-90-011	Norman Rockwell-4th Edition750QX 300-7	Keepsake	Yr.Iss.	7.50	30-40.00
83-90-012	Norman Rockwell 450QX215-7	Keepsake	Yr.Iss.	4.50	42.50
Hallmark Keepsake Ornaments		**1983 Decorative Ball Ornaments**			
83-91-001	Currier & Ives 450QX215-9	Keepsake	Yr.Iss.	4.50	15-17.00
83-91-002	Christmas Joy 450QX216-9	Keepsake	Yr.Iss.	4.50	22.50
83-91-003	Here Comes Santa 450QX217-7	Keepsake	Yr.Iss.	4.50	40.00
83-91-004	Oriental Butterflies 450QX218-7	Keepsake	Yr.Iss.	4.50	15-20.00
83-91-005	Angels 500QX219-7	Keepsake	Yr.Iss.	5.00	22.00
83-91-006	Season's Greeting 450QX219-9	Keepsake	Yr.Iss.	4.50	20.00
83-91-007	1983 450QX220-9	Keepsake	Yr.Iss.	4.50	19.00
83-91-008	The Wise Men 450QX220-7	Keepsake	Yr.Iss.	4.50	30-39.50
83-91-009	Christmas Wonderland 450QX221-9	Keepsake	Yr.Iss.	4.50	95.00
83-91-010	An Old Fashioned Christmas450QX 2217-9	Keepsake	Yr.Iss.	4.50	15.00
83-91-011	The Annunciation 450QX216-7	Keepsake	Yr.Iss.	4.50	22.50
Hallmark Keepsake Ornaments		**1983 Holiday Highlights**			
83-92-001	Christmas Stocking 600Qx303-9	Keepsake	Yr.Iss.	6.00	39.50
83-92-002	Star of Peace 600QX304-7	Keepsake	Yr.Iss.	6.00	15.00
83-92-003	Time for Sharing 600QX307-7	Keepsake	Yr.Iss.	6.00	22-35.00
Hallmark Keepsake Ornaments		**1983 Crown Classics**			
83-93-001	Enameled Christmas Wreath 900QX 311-9	Keepsake	Yr.Iss.	9.00	12.50
83-93-002	Memories to Treasure 700QX303-7	Keepsake	Yr.Iss.	7.00	22.00
83-93-003	Mother and Child 750QX302-7	Keepsake	Yr.Iss.	7.50	34.50
Hallmark Keepsake Ornaments		**1983 Holiday Sculptures**			
83-94-001	Santa 400Qx308-7	Keepsake	Yr.Iss.	4.00	22-33.00
83-94-002	Heart 400QX307-9	Keepsake	Yr.Iss.	4.00	35-49.50
Hallmark Keepsake Ornaments		**1983 Handcrafted Ornaments**			
83-95-001	Embroidered Stocking 650QX479-6	Keepsake	Yr.Iss.	6.50	12-20.00
83-95-002	Embroidered Heart 650QX421-7	Keepsake	Yr.Iss.	6.50	19.50
83-95-003	Scrimshaw Reindeer 800QX424-9	Keepsake	Yr.Iss.	8.00	32.50
83-95-004	Jack Frost 900QX407-9	Keepsake	Yr.Iss.	9.00	40.00
83-95-005	Unicorn 1000QX426-7	Keepsake	Yr.Iss.	10.00	58-63.00
83-95-006	Porcelain Doll, Diana 900QX423-7	Keepsake	Yr.Iss.	9.00	20-30.00
83-95-007	Brass Santa 900QX423-9	Keepsake	Yr.Iss.	9.00	19.00
83-95-008	Santa's on His Way 1000QX426-9	Keepsake	Yr.Iss.	10.00	30-37.00
83-95-009	Old-Fashioned Santa 1100QX409-9	Keepsake	Yr.Iss.	11.00	55.00
83-95-010	Cycling Santa 2000QX435-5	Keepsake	Yr.Iss.	20.00	150.00
83-95-011	Santa's Workshop 1000QX450-3	Keepsake	Yr.Iss.	10.00	60.00
83-95-012	Ski Lift Santa 800QX418-7	Keepsake	Yr.Iss.	8.00	65.00
83-95-013	Hitchhiking Santa 800QX424-7	Keepsake	Yr.Iss.	8.00	39.50
83-95-014	Mountain Climbing Santa 650QX407-7	Keepsake	Yr.Iss.	6.50	34.50
83-95-015	Jolly Santa 350QX425-9	Keepsake	Yr.Iss.	3.50	35.00
83-95-016	Santa's Many Faces 600QX311-6	Keepsake	Yr.Iss.	6.00	30.00
83-95-017	Baroque Angels 1300QX422-9	Keepsake	Yr.Iss.	13.00	45-58.00
83-95-018	Madonna and Child 1200QX428-7	Keepsake	Yr.Iss.	12.00	18-39.50
83-95-019	Mouse on Cheese 650QX413-7	Keepsake	Yr.Iss.	6.50	45-48.00
83-95-020	Peppermint Penguin 650QX408-9	Keepsake	Yr.Iss.	6.50	35-48.00
83-95-021	Skating Rabbit 800QX409-7	Keepsake	Yr.Iss.	8.00	35-49.50
83-95-022	Skiing Fox 800QX420-7	Keepsake	Yr.Iss.	8.00	25.00
83-95-023	Mouse in Bell 1000QX419-7	Keepsake	Yr.Iss.	10.00	55-65.00
83-95-024	Mailbox Kitten 650QX415-7	Keepsake	Yr.Iss.	6.50	60.00
83-95-025	Tin Rocking Horse 650QX414-9	Keepsake	Yr.Iss.	6.50	40-43.00
83-95-026	Bell Wreath 650QX420-9	Keepsake	Yr.Iss.	6.50	27.50
83-95-027	Angel Messenger 650QX408-7	Keepsake	Yr.Iss.	6.50	95.00
83-95-028	Holiday Puppy 350QX412-7	Keepsake	Yr.Iss.	3.50	26-30.00
83-95-029	Rainbow Angel 550QX416-7	Keepsake	Yr.Iss.	5.50	85.00
83-95-030	Sneaker Mouse 450QX400-9	Keepsake	Yr.Iss.	4.50	30-45.00
83-95-031	Christmas Koala 400QX419-9	Keepsake	Yr.Iss.	4.00	24.00
83-95-032	Caroling Owl 450QX411-7	Keepsake	Yr.Iss.	4.50	39.50
83-95-033	Christmas Kitten 400QX454-3	Keepsake	Yr.Iss.	4.00	35.00
Hallmark Keepsake Ornaments		**1983 Collectible Series**			
83-96-001	The Bellringer-5th Edition1500QX 403-9	Keepsake	Yr.Iss.	15.00	110-135.
83-96-002	Holiday Wildlife-2nd Edition 700QX 309-9	Keepsake	Yr.Iss.	7.00	40-45.00
83-96-003	Here Comes Santa-5th Edition1300QX 403-7	Keepsake	Yr.Iss.	13.00	80-195.00
83-96-004	Snoopy and Friends-5th Ed.1300QX 416-9	Keepsake	Yr.Iss.	13.00	75.00
83-96-005	Carrousel-6th Edition 1100QX401-9	Keepsake	Yr.Iss.	11.00	47.50
83-96-006	Porcelain Bear-1st Edition700QX 428-9	Keepsake	Yr.Iss.	7.00	75.00
83-96-007	Clothespin Soldier-2nd Edition500QX 402-9	Keepsake	Yr.Iss.	5.00	25.00
83-96-008	Rocking Horse-3rd Edition1000QX 417-7	Keepsake	Yr.Iss.	10.00	80-200.00
83-96-009	Frosty Friends-4th Edition800QX 400-7	Keepsake	Yr.Iss.	8.00	65-185.00
83-96-010	Thimble - 6th Edition 500QX401-7	Keepsake	Yr.Iss.	5.00	35-45.00
83-96-011	Tin Locomotive - 2nd Edition1300QX 404-9	Keepsake	Yr.Iss.	13.00	200.00
Hallmark Keepsake Ornaments		**1984 Commemoratives**			
84-97-001	Baby's First Christmas 1600QX904-1	Keepsake	Yr.Iss.	16.00	40-55.00
84-97-002	Baby's First Christmas 1400QX438-1	Keepsake	Yr.Iss.	14.00	28-30.00
84-97-003	Baby's First Christmas 700QX300-1	Keepsake	Yr.Iss.	7.00	15.00
84-97-004	Baby's First Christmas 600QX340-1	Keepsake	Yr.Iss.	6.00	25-37.50
84-97-005	Baby's First Christmas-Boy450QX 240-4	Keepsake	Yr.Iss.	4.50	15.00
84-97-006	Baby's First Christmas-Girl450QX 340-1	Keepsake	Yr.Iss.	4.50	15.00
84-97-007	Baby's Second Christmas 450QX241-1	Keepsake	Yr.Iss.	4.50	18.00
84-97-008	Child's Third Christmas 450QX261-1	Keepsake	Yr.Iss.	4.50	15.00
84-97-009	Grandchild's First Christmas110QX 460-1	Keepsake	Yr.Iss.	11.00	15-33.00
84-97-010	Grandchild's First Christmas450QX 257-4	Keepsake	Yr.Iss.	4.50	14.00
84-97-011	Godchild 450QX242-1	Keepsake	Yr.Iss.	4.50	15.00
84-97-012	Grandson 450QX242-4	Keepsake	Yr.Iss.	4.50	20.00
84-97-013	Granddaughter 450QX243-1	Keepsake	Yr.Iss.	4.50	20.00
84-97-014	Grandparents 450QX256-1	Keepsake	Yr.Iss.	4.50	15.00
84-97-015	Grandmother 450QX244-1	Keepsake	Yr.Iss.	4.50	15.00
84-97-016	Father 600QX257-1	Keepsake	Yr.Iss.	6.00	12.00
84-97-017	Mother 600QX343-4	Keepsake	Yr.Iss.	6.00	12.50
84-97-018	Mother and Dad 650QX258-1	Keepsake	Yr.Iss.	6.50	17.00
84-97-019	Sister 650QX259-4	Keepsake	Yr.Iss.	6.50	10-15.00
84-97-020	Daughter 450QX244-4	Keepsake	Yr.Iss.	4.50	20-24.50
84-97-021	Son 450QX243-4	Keepsake	Yr.Iss.	4.50	20-25.00
84-97-022	The Miracle of Love 600QX342-4	Keepsake	Yr.Iss.	6.00	29.50
84-97-023	First Christmas Together 600QX342-1	Keepsake	Yr.Iss.	6.00	20.00
84-97-024	First Christmas Together 1600QX904-4	Keepsake	Yr.Iss.	16.00	45.00
84-97-025	First Christmas Together 1500QX436-4	Keepsake	Yr.Iss.	15.00	30.00
84-97-026	First Christmas Together 750QX340-4	Keepsake	Yr.Iss.	7.50	20.00
84-97-027	First Christmas Together 450QX245-1	Keepsake	Yr.Iss.	4.50	20.00
84-97-028	Heartful of Love 1000QX443-4	Keepsake	Yr.Iss.	10.00	45.00
84-97-029	Love...the Spirit of Christmas450QX 247-4	Keepsake	Yr.Iss.	4.50	18.00
84-97-030	Love 450QX255-4	Keepsake	Yr.Iss.	4.50	14.50
84-97-031	Ten Years Together 650QX258-4	Keepsake	Yr.Iss.	6.50	19.50
84-97-032	Twenty-Five Years Together650QX 259-1	Keepsake	Yr.Iss.	6.50	19.50
84-97-033	Gratitude 600QX344-4	Keepsake	Yr.Iss.	6.00	10.00
84-97-034	The Fun of Friendship 600QX343-1	Keepsake	Yr.Iss.	6.00	32.50
84-97-035	Friendship 450QX248-1	Keepsake	Yr.Iss.	4.50	15-24.00
84-97-036	A Gift of Friendship 450QX260-4	Keepsake	Yr.Iss.	4.50	15.00
84-97-037	New Home 450QX245-4	Keepsake	Yr.Iss.	4.50	60-107.50
84-97-038	From Our Home to Yours 450QX248-4	Keepsake	Yr.Iss.	4.50	12.00
84-97-039	Teacher 450QX249-1	Keepsake	Yr.Iss.	4.50	13-15.00
84-97-040	Baby-sitter 450QX253-1	Keepsake	Yr.Iss.	4.50	12.50
Hallmark Keepsake Ornaments		**1984 Property Ornaments**			
84-98-001	Betsey Clark Angel 900QX462-4	Keepsake	Yr.Iss.	9.00	20-29.50
84-98-002	Katybeth 900QX463-1	Keepsake	Yr.Iss.	9.00	18-25.00
84-98-003	Peanuts 450QX252-1	Keepsake	Yr.Iss.	4.50	20-25.00
84-98-004	Disney 450QX250-4	Keepsake	Yr.Iss.	4.50	25-33.00
84-98-005	The Muppets 450QX251-4	Keepsake	Yr.Iss.	4.50	29.50
84-98-006	Norman Rockwell 450QX251-4	Keepsake	Yr.Iss.	4.50	20.00
84-98-007	Currier & Ives 450QX250-1	Keepsake	Yr.Iss.	4.50	15-20.00
84-98-008	Shirt Tales 450QX252-4	Keepsake	Yr.Iss.	4.50	20-25.00
84-98-009	Snoopy and Woodstock 750QX439-1	Keepsake	Yr.Iss.	7.50	40-75.00
84-98-010	Muffin 550QX442-1	Keepsake	Yr.Iss.	5.50	20-30.00
84-98-011	Kit 550QX453-4	Keepsake	Yr.Iss.	5.50	20-30.00
Hallmark Keepsake Ornaments		**1984 Traditional Ornaments**			
84-99-001	White Christmas 1600QX905-1	Keepsake	Yr.Iss.	16.00	65-95.00
84-99-002	Twelve Days of Christmas1500QX 415-9	Keepsake	Yr.Iss.	15.00	95.00
84-99-003	Gift of Music 1500QX451-1	Keepsake	Yr.Iss.	15.00	65.00
84-99-004	Amanda 900QX432-1	Keepsake	Yr.Iss.	9.00	20-29.50
84-99-005	Holiday Jester 1100QX437-4	Keepsake	Yr.Iss.	11.00	25-33.00
84-99-006	Uncle Sam 600QX449-1	Keepsake	Yr.Iss.	6.00	29.25
84-99-007	Chickadee 600QX451-4	Keepsake	Yr.Iss.	6.00	30-37.50
84-99-008	Cuckoo Clock 1000QX455-1	Keepsake	Yr.Iss.	10.00	40-50.00
84-99-009	Alpine Elf 600QX452-1	Keepsake	Yr.Iss.	6.00	37.50
84-99-010	Nostalgic Sled 600QX442-4	Keepsake	Yr.Iss.	6.00	24.50
84-99-011	Santa Sulky Driver 900QX436-1	Keepsake	Yr.Iss.	9.00	32.50
84-99-012	Old Fashioned Rocking Horse750QX 346-4	Keepsake	Yr.Iss.	7.50	17.50
84-99-013	Madonna and Child 600QX344-1	Keepsake	Yr.Iss.	6.00	20-40.00
84-99-014	Holiday Friendship 1300QX445-1	Keepsake	Yr.Iss.	13.00	24.50
84-99-015	Peace on Earth 750QX341-4	Keepsake	Yr.Iss.	7.50	20-23.00
84-99-016	A Savior is Born 450X254-1	Keepsake	Yr.Iss.	4.50	19.50
84-99-017	Holiday Starburst 500QX253-4	Keepsake	Yr.Iss.	5.00	20.00
84-99-018	Santa 750QX458-4	Keepsake	Yr.Iss.	7.50	14.50
84-99-019	Needlepoint Wreath 650QX459-4	Keepsake	Yr.Iss.	6.50	10-15.00
84-99-020	Christmas Memories Photoholder 650QX 300-4	Keepsake	Yr.Iss.	6.50	24.50
Hallmark Keepsake Ornaments		**1984 Holiday Humor**			
84-100-001	Bell Ringer Squirrel 1000QX443-1	Keepsake	Yr.Iss.	10.00	25-35.00
84-100-002	Raccoon's Christmas 900QX447-7	Keepsake	Yr.Iss.	9.00	40-58.00
84-100-003	Three Kittens in a Mitten 800QX431-1	Keepsake	Yr.Iss.	8.00	32.50
84-100-004	Marathon Santa 800QX456-4	Keepsake	Yr.Iss.	8.00	40-50.00
84-100-005	Santa Star 550QX450-4	Keepsake	Yr.Iss.	5.50	30-40.00
84-100-006	Snowmobile Santa 650QX431-4	Keepsake	Yr.Iss.	6.50	30-35.00
84-100-007	Snowshoe Penguin 650QX453-1	Keepsake	Yr.Iss.	6.50	40-50.00
84-100-008	Christmas Owl 600QX444-1	Keepsake	Yr.Iss.	6.00	25-30.00
84-100-009	Musical Angel 550QX434-4	Keepsake	Yr.Iss.	5.50	43-60.00
84-100-010	Napping Mouse 550QX435-1	Keepsake	Yr.Iss.	5.50	40.00
84-100-011	Roller Skating Rabbit 500QX457-1	Keepsake	Yr.Iss.	5.00	17.50
84-100-012	Frisbee Puppy 500QX444-4	Keepsake	Yr.Iss.	5.00	44.50
84-100-013	Reindeer Racetrack 450QX254-4	Keepsake	Yr.Iss.	4.50	16.00
84-100-014	A Christmas Prayer 450QX246-1	Keepsake	Yr.Iss.	4.50	16.00
84-100-015	Flights of Fantasy 450QX256-4	Keepsake	Yr.Iss.	4.50	12-20.00
84-100-016	Polar Bear Drummer 450QX430-1	Keepsake	Yr.Iss.	4.50	20-35.00
84-100-017	Santa Mouse 450QX433-4	Keepsake	Yr.Iss.	4.50	37.50
84-100-018	Snowy Seal 400QX450-1	Keepsake	Yr.Iss.	4.00	14-19.00
84-100-019	Fortune Cookie Elf 450Q452-4	Keepsake	Yr.Iss.	4.50	39.50
84-100-020	Peppermint 1984 450Q452-1	Keepsake	Yr.Iss.	4.50	40.00
84-100-021	Mountain Climbing Santa 650QX407-7	Keepsake	Yr.Iss.	6.50	34.50
Hallmark Keepsake Ornaments		**1984 Limited Edition**			
84-101-001	Classical Angel 2750QX459-1	Keepsake	Yr.Iss.	27.50	110.00
Hallmark Keepsake Ornaments		**1984 Collectible Series**			
84-102-001	Nostalgic Houses and Shops-1st Edition 1300QX 448-1	Keepsake	Yr.Iss.	13.00	145-200.
84-102-002	Wood Childhood Ornaments- 1st Edition 650QX 439-4	Keepsake	Yr.Iss.	6.50	35.00
84-102-003	The Twelve Days of Christmas- 1st Edition 600QX 3484	Keepsake	Yr.Iss.	6.00	260-275.
84-102-004	Art Masterpiece - 1st Edition650QX 349-4	Keepsake	Yr.Iss.	6.50	13-25.00
84-102-005	Porcelain Bear - 2nd Edition700QX 454-1	Keepsake	Yr.Iss.	7.00	30-45.00
84-102-006	Tin Locomotive - 3rd Edition1400QX 440-4	Keepsake	Yr.Iss.	14.00	55.00
84-102-007	Clothespin Soldier -3rd Edition 500QX 447-1	Keepsake	Yr.Iss.	5.00	20-33.00
84-102-008	Holiday Wildlife - 3rd Edition 725QX 347-4	Keepsake	Yr.Iss.	7.25	20.00
84-102-009	Rocking Horse - 4th Edition 1000QX 435-4	Keepsake	Yr.Iss.	10.00	50-57.50
84-102-010	Frosty Friends -5th Edition 800QX 437-1	Keepsake	Yr.Iss.	8.00	52.50-55.00
84-102-011	Norman Rockwell - 5th Edition750QX 341-1	Keepsake	Yr.Iss.	7.50	20-35.00
84-102-012	Here Comes Santa -6th Edition1300QX 438-4	Keepsake	Yr.Iss.	13.00	60.00
84-102-013	The Bellringer - 6th & Final Ed.1500QX 438-4	Keepsake	Yr.Iss.	15.00	45.00
84-102-014	Thimble - 7th Edition 500QX430-4	Keepsake	Yr.Iss.	5.00	30-44.00
84-102-015	Betsey Clark - 12th Edition500QX 249-4	Keepsake	Yr.Iss.	5.00	25.00
Hallmark Keepsake Ornaments		**1984 Keepsake Magic Ornaments**			
84-103-001	Village Church 1500QLX702-1	Keepsake	Yr.Iss.	15.00	50.00
84-103-002	Sugarplum Cottage 1100QLX701-1	Keepsake	Yr.Iss.	11.00	45-52.00
84-103-003	City Lights 1000QLX701-4	Keepsake	Yr.Iss.	10.00	45-50.00
84-103-004	Santa's Workshop 1300QLX700-4	Keepsake	Yr.Iss.	13.00	50-62.50
84-103-005	Santa's Arrival 1300QLX702-4	Keepsake	Yr.Iss.	13.00	50-65.00
84-103-006	Nativity 1200 QLX700-1	Keepsake	Yr.Iss.	12.00	28.00

Company / Number	Series / Name	Artist	Edition Limit	Issue Price	Quote
84-103-007	Stained Glass 800QLX703-1	Keepsake	Yr.Iss.	8.00	19.50
84-103-008	Christmas in the Forest 800QLX703-4	Keepsake	Yr.Iss.	8.00	15-19.50
84-103-009	Brass Carrousel 900QLX707-1	Keepsake	Yr.Iss.	9.00	55-85.00
84-103-010	All Are Precious 800QLX704-1	Keepsake	Yr.Iss.	8.00	15-25.00
Hallmark Keepsake Ornaments	**1985 Commemoratives**				
85-104-001	Baby's First Christmas 1600QX499-5	Keepsake	Yr.Iss.	16.00	40.00
85-104-002	Baby's First Christmas 1500QX499-2	Keepsake	Yr.Iss.	15.00	40.00
85-104-003	Baby Locket 1600QX401-2	Keepsake	Yr.Iss.	16.00	35-38.00
85-104-004	Baby's First Christmas 575QX370-2	Keepsake	Yr.Iss.	5.75	20.00
85-104-005	Baby's First Christmas 700QX478-2	Keepsake	Yr.Iss.	7.00	14.50
85-104-006	Baby's First Christmas 500QX260-2	Keepsake	Yr.Iss.	5.00	15.00
85-104-007	Baby's Second Christmas 600QX478-5	Keepsake	Yr.Iss.	6.00	29.50
85-104-008	Child's Third Christmas 600QX475-5	Keepsake	Yr.Iss.	6.00	28-31.00
85-104-009	Grandchild's First Christmas500QX 260-5	Keepsake	Yr.Iss.	5.00	15.00
85-104-010	Grandchild's First Christmas1100QX 495-5	Keepsake	Yr.Iss.	11.00	24.00
85-104-011	Grandparents 700QX380-5	Keepsake	Yr.Iss.	7.00	10.00
85-104-012	Niece 575QX520-5	Keepsake	Yr.Iss.	5.75	10.50
85-104-013	Mother 675QX372-2	Keepsake	Yr.Iss.	6.75	10.00
85-104-014	Mother and Dad 775QX509-2	Keepsake	Yr.Iss.	7.75	18.50
85-104-015	Father 650QX376-2	Keepsake	Yr.Iss.	6.50	11-13.00
85-104-016	Sister 725QX506-5	Keepsake	Yr.Iss.	7.25	10-14.50
85-104-017	Daughter 550QX503-2	Keepsake	Yr.Iss.	5.50	12-15.00
85-104-018	Godchild 675QX380-2	Keepsake	Yr.Iss.	6.75	8-10.00
85-104-019	Son 550QX502-5	Keepsake	Yr.Iss.	5.50	42.50
85-104-020	Grandmother 475QX262-5	Keepsake	Yr.Iss.	4.75	15-23.00
85-104-021	Grandson 475QX262-2	Keepsake	Yr.Iss.	4.75	24.50
85-104-022	Granddaughter 475QX263-5	Keepsake	Yr.Iss.	4.75	11-25.00
85-104-023	First Christmas Together 1675QX400-5	Keepsake	Yr.Iss.	16.75	30.00
85-104-024	Love at Christmas 575QX371-5	Keepsake	Yr.Iss.	5.75	37.50
85-104-025	First Christmas Together 675QX370-5	Keepsake	Yr.Iss.	6.75	10.00
85-104-026	First Christmas Together 1300QX493-5	Keepsake	Yr.Iss.	13.00	30.00
85-104-027	Holiday Heart 800QX498-2	Keepsake	Yr.Iss.	8.00	25.00
85-104-028	First Christmas Together 800QX507-2	Keepsake	Yr.Iss.	8.00	13.00
85-104-029	Heart Full of Love 675QX378-2	Keepsake	Yr.Iss.	6.75	8-10.00
85-104-030	First Christmas Together 475QX261-2	Keepsake	Yr.Iss.	4.75	20.00
85-104-031	Twenty-Five Years Together800QX 500-5	Keepsake	Yr.Iss.	8.00	10-20.00
85-104-032	Friendship 775QX506-2	Keepsake	Yr.Iss.	7.75	10.00
85-104-033	Friendship 675QX378-5	Keepsake	Yr.Iss.	6.75	9.50
85-104-034	From Our House to Yours 775QX520-2	Keepsake	Yr.Iss.	7.75	11.00
85-104-035	Teacher 600QX505-2	Keepsake	Yr.Iss.	6.00	10-19.50
85-104-036	With Appreciation 675QX375-2	Keepsake	Yr.Iss.	6.75	9.50
85-104-037	Special Friends 575QX372-5	Keepsake	Yr.Iss.	5.75	10.00
85-104-038	New Home 475QX269-5	Keepsake	Yr.Iss.	4.75	25.00
85-104-039	Baby-sitter 475QX264-2	Keepsake	Yr.Iss.	4.75	10.00
85-104-040	Good Friends 475QX265-2	Keepsake	Yr.Iss.	4.75	22.50
Hallmark Keepsake Ornaments	**1985 Property Ornaments**				
85-105-001	Snoopy and Woodstock 750QX491-5	Keepsake	Yr.Iss.	7.50	31.50-55.00
85-105-002	Muffin the Angel 575QX483-5	Keepsake	Yr.Iss.	5.75	24.00
85-105-003	Kit the Shepherd 575QX484-5	Keepsake	Yr.Iss.	5.75	24.00
85-105-004	Betsey Clark 850QX508-5	Keepsake	Yr.Iss.	8.50	22.50
85-105-005	Hugga Bunch 500QX271-5	Keepsake	Yr.Iss.	5.00	19.50
85-105-006	Fraggle Rock Holiday 475QX265-5	Keepsake	Yr.Iss.	4.75	10.00
85-105-007	Peanuts 475QX266-5	Keepsake	Yr.Iss.	4.75	19.50-25.00
85-105-008	Norman Rockwell 475QX266-2	Keepsake	Yr.Iss.	4.75	20-23.00
85-105-009	Rainbow Brite and Friends 475QX 268-2	Keepsake	Yr.Iss.	4.75	20.00
85-105-010	A Disney Christmas 475QX271-2	Keepsake	Yr.Iss.	4.75	22.50
85-105-011	Merry Shirt Tales 475QX267-2	Keepsake	Yr.Iss.	4.75	19.00
Hallmark Keepsake Ornaments	**1985 Traditional Ornaments**				
85-106-001	Porcelain Bird 650QX479-5	Keepsake	Yr.Iss.	6.50	30-40.00
85-106-002	Sewn Photoholder 700QX379-5	Keepsake	Yr.Iss.	7.00	22.50
85-106-003	Candle Cameo 675QX374-2	Keepsake	Yr.Iss.	6.75	10-15.00
85-106-004	Santa Pipe 950QX494-2	Keepsake	Yr.Iss.	9.50	22.50
85-106-005	Old-Fashioned Wreath 750QX373-5	Keepsake	Yr.Iss.	7.50	19.50
85-106-006	Peaceful Kingdom 575QX373-2	Keepsake	Yr.Iss.	5.75	15-18.00
85-106-007	Christmas Treats 550QX507-5	Keepsake	Yr.Iss.	5.50	15-24.00
85-106-008	The Spirit of Santa Claus -Special Ed. 2250QX 498-5	Keepsake	Yr.Iss.	22.50	70-95.00
85-106-009	Nostalgic Sled 600QX442-4	Keepsake	Yr.Iss.	6.00	19.50
Hallmark Keepsake Ornaments	**1985 Holiday Humor**				
85-107-001	Night Before Christmas 1300QX449-4	Keepsake	Yr.Iss.	13.00	32-45.00
85-107-002	Nativity Scene 475QX264-5	Keepsake	Yr.Iss.	4.75	25.00
85-107-003	Santa's Ski Trip 1200QX496-2	Keepsake	Yr.Iss.	12.00	55.00
85-107-004	Mouse Wagon 575QX476-2	Keepsake	Yr.Iss.	5.75	50-57.00
85-107-005	Children in the Shoe 950QX490-5	Keepsake	Yr.Iss.	9.50	35-50.00
85-107-006	Do Not Disturb Bear 775QX481-2	Keepsake	Yr.Iss.	7.75	20.00
85-107-007	Sun and Fun Santa 775QX492-2	Keepsake	Yr.Iss.	7.75	35.00
85-107-008	Bottlecap Fun Bunnies 775QX481-5	Keepsake	Yr.Iss.	7.75	33-45.00
85-107-009	Lamb in Legwarmers 700QX480-2	Keepsake	Yr.Iss.	7.00	18-20.00
85-107-010	Candy Apple Mouse 750QX470-5	Keepsake	Yr.Iss.	6.50	42.50-55.00
85-107-011	Skateboard Raccoon 650QX473-2	Keepsake	Yr.Iss.	6.50	36.50
85-107-012	Stardust Angel 575QX475-2	Keepsake	Yr.Iss.	5.75	35-38.00
85-107-013	Soccer Beaver 650QX477-5	Keepsake	Yr.Iss.	6.50	24.50
85-107-014	Beary Smooth Ride 650QX480-5	Keepsake	Yr.Iss.	6.50	15.00
85-107-015	Swinging Angel Bell 1100QX492-5	Keepsake	Yr.Iss.	11.00	25-37.00
85-107-016	Doggy in a Stocking 550QX474-2	Keepsake	Yr.Iss.	5.50	27.00
85-107-017	Engineering Mouse 550QX473-5	Keepsake	Yr.Iss.	5.50	20-25.00
85-107-018	Kitty Mischief 500QX474-5	Keepsake	Yr.Iss.	5.00	20-25.00
85-107-019	Baker Elf 575QX491-2	Keepsake	Yr.Iss.	5.75	20.00
85-107-020	Ice-Skating Owl 500QX476-5	Keepsake	Yr.Iss.	5.00	25.00
85-107-021	Dapper Penguin 500QX477-2	Keepsake	Yr.Iss.	5.00	20-28.00
85-107-022	Trumpet Panda 450QX471-2	Keepsake	Yr.Iss.	4.50	22-30.00
85-107-023	Merry Mouse 450QX403-2	Keepsake	Yr.Iss.	4.50	18-22.00
85-107-024	Snow-Pitching Snowman 450QX470-2	Keepsake	Yr.Iss.	4.50	20-32.00
85-107-025	Three Kittens in a Mitten 800QX431-1	Keepsake	Yr.Iss.	8.00	34.50
85-107-026	Roller Skating Rabbit 500QX457-1	Keepsake	Yr.Iss.	5.00	19.00
85-107-027	Snowy Seal 400QX450-1	Keepsake	Yr.Iss.	4.00	16.00
Hallmark Keepsake Ornaments	**1985 Country Christmas Collection**				
85-108-001	Old-Fashioned Doll 1450QX519-5	Keepsake	Yr.Iss.	14.50	30-35.00
85-108-002	Country Goose 775QX518-5	Keepsake	Yr.Iss.	7.75	15-23.00
85-108-003	Rocking Horse Memories1000QX518-2	Keepsake	Yr.Iss.	10.00	12.00
85-108-004	Whirligig Santa 1250QX519-2	Keepsake	Yr.Iss.	12.50	20-25.00
85-108-005	Sheep at Christmas 825QX517-5	Keepsake	Yr.Iss.	8.25	20-30.00
Hallmark Keepsake Ornaments	**1985 Heirloom Christmas Collection**				
85-109-001	Keepsake Basket 1500QX514-5	Keepsake	Yr.Iss.	15.00	19-24.00
85-109-002	Victorian Lady 950QX513-2	Keepsake	Yr.Iss.	9.50	20-25.00
85-109-003	Charming Angel 975QX512-5	Keepsake	Yr.Iss.	9.75	24.50
85-109-004	Lacy Heart 875QX511-2	Keepsake	Yr.Iss.	8.75	28-30.00
85-109-005	Snowflake 650QX510-5	Keepsake	Yr.Iss.	6.50	20-25.00
Hallmark Keepsake Ornaments	**1985 Limited Edition**				
85-110-001	Heavenly Trumpeter 2750QX405-2	Keepsake	Yr.Iss.	27.50	95-100.00
Hallmark Keepsake Ornaments	**1985 Collectible Series**				
85-111-001	Windows of the World-1st Ed.975QX490-2	Keepsake	Yr.Iss.	9.75	75-95.00
85-111-002	Miniature Creche-1st Ed.875QX482-5	Keepsake	Yr.Iss.	8.75	25-60.00
85-111-003	Nostalgic Houses and Shops-Second Ed.-1375QX497-5	Keepsake	Yr.Iss.	13.75	75.00
85-111-004	Art Masterpiece-2nd Ed.675QX377-2	Keepsake	Yr.Iss.	6.75	20.00
85-111-005	Wood Childhood Ornaments-2nd Ed. 700QX472-2	Keepsake	Yr.Iss.	7.00	31-45.00
85-111-006	Twelve Days of Christmas-2nd Ed. 650QX371-2	Keepsake	Yr.Iss.	6.50	75.00
85-111-007	Porcelain Bear-3rd Ed.750QX479-2	Keepsake	Yr.Iss.	7.50	35-46.00
85-111-008	Tin Locomotive-4th Ed.1475QX497-2	Keepsake	Yr.Iss.	14.75	50.00
85-111-009	Holiday Wildlife-4th Ed.750QX376-5	Keepsake	Yr.Iss.	7.50	15.00
85-111-010	Clothespin Soldier-4th Ed.550QX471-5	Keepsake	Yr.Iss.	5.50	22-24.50
85-111-011	Rocking Horse-5th Ed.1075QX493-2	Keepsake	Yr.Iss.	10.75	50.00
85-111-012	Norman Rockwell-6th Ed.750QX374-5	Keepsake	Yr.Iss.	7.50	28-30.00
85-111-013	Here Comes Santa-6th Ed.1400QX496-5	Keepsake	Yr.Iss.	14.00	65.00
85-111-014	Frosty Friends-6th Ed.850QX482-2	Keepsake	Yr.Iss.	8.50	50.00
85-111-015	Betsey Clark-13th & final Ed.500QX263-2	Keepsake	Yr.Iss.	5.00	25-30.00
85-111-016	Thimble-8th Ed.550QX472-5	Keepsake	Yr.Iss.	5.50	30-37.00
Hallmark Keepsake Ornaments	**1985 Keepsake Magic Ornaments**				
85-112-001	Baby's First Christmas 1650QLX700-5	Keepsake	Yr.Iss.	16.50	40.00
85-112-002	Katybeth 1075QLX710-2	Keepsake	Yr.Iss.	10.75	35-47.50
85-112-003	Chris Mouse-1st edition1250QLX703-2	Keepsake	Yr.Iss.	12.50	65.00
85-112-004	Swiss Cheese Lane 1300QLX706-5	Keepsake	Yr.Iss.	13.00	45-78.00
85-112-005	Mr. and Mrs. Santa 1450QLX705-2	Keepsake	Yr.Iss.	14.50	40.00
85-112-006	Little Red Schoolhouse 1575QLX711-2	Keepsake	Yr.Iss.	15.75	50.00
85-112-007	Love Wreath 850QLX702-5	Keepsake	Yr.Iss.	8.50	30.00
85-112-008	Christmas Eve Visit 1200QLX710-5	Keepsake	Yr.Iss.	12.00	25-27.50
85-112-009	Season of Beauty 800QLX712-2	Keepsake	Yr.Iss.	8.00	20-30.00
Hallmark Keepsake Ornaments	**1986 Commemoratives**				
86-113-001	Baby's First Christmas 900QX412-6	Keepsake	Yr.Iss.	9.00	35-38.00
86-113-002	Baby's First Christmas Photoholder 800QX379-2	Keepsake	Yr.Iss.	8.00	15.00
86-113-003	Baby's First Christmas 600QX380-3	Keepsake	Yr.Iss.	6.00	20-25.00
86-113-004	Baby's First Christmas 550QX271-3	Keepsake	Yr.Iss.	5.50	15.00
86-113-005	Grandchild's First Christmas1000QX411-6	Keepsake	Yr.Iss.	10.00	16.00
86-113-006	Baby's Second Christmas 650QX413-3	Keepsake	Yr.Iss.	6.50	27.50
86-113-007	Child's Third Christmas 650QX413-6	Keepsake	Yr.Iss.	6.50	15.00
86-113-008	Baby Locket 1600QX412-3	Keepsake	Yr.Iss.	16.00	30.00
86-113-009	Husband 800QX383-6	Keepsake	Yr.Iss.	8.00	15.00
86-113-010	Sister 675QX380-6	Keepsake	Yr.Iss.	6.75	10.00
86-113-011	Mother and Dad 750QX431-6	Keepsake	Yr.Iss.	7.50	17.50
86-113-012	Mother 700QX382-6	Keepsake	Yr.Iss.	7.00	15.00
86-113-013	Father 650QX431-3	Keepsake	Yr.Iss.	6.50	13.00
86-113-014	Daughter 575QX430-6	Keepsake	Yr.Iss.	5.75	25.00
86-113-015	Son 575QX430-3	Keepsake	Yr.Iss.	5.75	20.00
86-113-016	Niece 600QX426-6	Keepsake	Yr.Iss.	6.00	10.00
86-113-017	Nephew 675QX381-3	Keepsake	Yr.Iss.	6.25	12.50
86-113-018	Grandmother 475QX274-3	Keepsake	Yr.Iss.	4.75	18.00
86-113-019	Grandparents 750QX432-3	Keepsake	Yr.Iss.	7.50	17.00
86-113-020	Granddaughter 475QX273-6	Keepsake	Yr.Iss.	4.75	15-22.50
86-113-021	Grandson 475QX273-3	Keepsake	Yr.Iss.	4.75	20.00
86-113-022	Godchild 475QX271-6	Keepsake	Yr.Iss.	4.75	10-14.50
86-113-023	First Christmas Together 1600QX400-3	Keepsake	Yr.Iss.	16.00	27.50
86-113-024	First Christmas Together 1200QX409-6	Keepsake	Yr.Iss.	12.00	30.00
86-113-025	First Christmas Together 7000QX379-3	Keepsake	Yr.Iss.	7.00	20.00
86-113-026	First Christmas Together 475QX270-3	Keepsake	Yr.Iss.	4.75	16-25.00
86-113-027	Ten Years Together 750QX401-3	Keepsake	Yr.Iss.	7.50	24.50
86-113-028	Twenty-Five Years Together800QX410-3	Keepsake	Yr.Iss.	8.00	24.50
86-113-029	Fifty Years Together 1000QX400-6	Keepsake	Yr.Iss.	10.00	18.00
86-113-030	Loving Memories 900QX409-3	Keepsake	Yr.Iss.	9.00	13-34.50
86-113-031	Timeless Love 600QX379-6	Keepsake	Yr.Iss.	6.00	24.50
86-113-032	Sweetheart 1100QX408-6	Keepsake	Yr.Iss.	11.00	27.00
86-113-033	Season of the Heart 4750QX270-6	Keepsake	Yr.Iss.	4.75	12.50
86-113-034	Friendship Greeting 800QX427-3	Keepsake	Yr.Iss.	8.00	15.00
86-113-035	Joy of Friends 675QX382-3	Keepsake	Yr.Iss.	6.75	12.50
86-113-036	Friendship's Gift 600QX381-6	Keepsake	Yr.Iss.	6.00	12.00
86-113-037	From Our Home to Yours 600QX383-3	Keepsake	Yr.Iss.	6.00	12.00
86-113-038	Gratitude 600QX432-6	Keepsake	Yr.Iss.	6.00	9.50
86-113-039	Friends Are Fun 475QX272-3	Keepsake	Yr.Iss.	4.75	30.00
86-113-040	New Home 475QX274-6	Keepsake	Yr.Iss.	4.75	11.25
86-113-041	Teacher 475QX275-3	Keepsake	Yr.Iss.	4.75	12.00
86-113-042	Baby-Sitter 475QX275-6	Keepsake	Yr.Iss.	4.75	10.00
Hallmark Keepsake Ornaments	**1986 Property Ornaments**				
86-114-001	The Statue of Liberty 600QX384-3	Keepsake	Yr.Iss.	6.00	15-33.00
86-114-002	Snoopy and Woodstock 800QX434-6	Keepsake	Yr.Iss.	8.00	30-38.00
86-114-003	Heathcliff 750QX436-3	Keepsake	Yr.Iss.	7.50	28-31.00
86-114-004	Katybeth 700QX435-3	Keepsake	Yr.Iss.	7.00	22.50
86-114-005	Paddington Bear 600QX435-6	Keepsake	Yr.Iss.	6.00	22.00
86-114-006	Norman Rockwell 475QX276-3	Keepsake	Yr.Iss.	4.75	20.00
86-114-007	Peanuts 475QX276-6	Keepsake	Yr.Iss.	4.75	18.00
86-114-008	Shirt Tales Parade 475QX277-3	Keepsake	Yr.Iss.	4.75	14.50
Hallmark Keepsake Ornaments	**1986 Holiday Humor**				
86-115-001	Santa's Hot Tub 1200QX426-3	Keepsake	Yr.Iss.	12.00	35.00
86-115-002	Playful Possum 1100QX425-3	Keepsake	Yr.Iss.	11.00	35.00
86-115-003	Treetop Trio 975QX424-6	Keepsake	Yr.Iss.	11.00	24-29.50
86-115-004	Wynken, Blynken and Nod 975QX424-6	Keepsake	Yr.Iss.	9.75	32.00
86-115-005	Acorn Inn 850QX424-3	Keepsake	Yr.Iss.	8.50	23-30.00
86-115-006	Touchdown Santa 800QX423-3	Keepsake	Yr.Iss.	8.00	40-43.00
86-115-007	Snow Buddies 800QX423-6	Keepsake	Yr.Iss.	8.00	32.50
86-115-008	Open Me First 725QX422-6	Keepsake	Yr.Iss.	7.25	20.00
86-115-009	Rah Rah Rabbit 700QX421-6	Keepsake	Yr.Iss.	7.00	39.50
86-115-010	Tipping the Scales 675QX418-6	Keepsake	Yr.Iss.	6.75	20-27.50
86-115-011	Li'l Jingler 675QX419-3	Keepsake	Yr.Iss.	6.75	26-35.50
86-115-012	Ski Tripper 675QX420-6	Keepsake	Yr.Iss.	6.75	23-27.00
86-115-013	Popcorn Mouse 675QX421-3	Keepsake	Yr.Iss.	6.75	28-47.00
86-115-014	Puppy's Best Friend 650QX420-3	Keepsake	Yr.Iss.	6.50	27.50
86-115-015	Happy Christmas to Owl 600QX418-3	Keepsake	Yr.Iss.	6.00	18-25.00
86-115-016	Walnut Shell Rider 600QX419-6	Keepsake	Yr.Iss.	6.00	24.00
86-115-017	Heavenly Dreamer 575QX417-3	Keepsake	Yr.Iss.	5.75	27-35.00
86-115-018	Mouse in the Moon 550QX416-6	Keepsake	Yr.Iss.	5.50	20-28.00
86-115-019	Merry Koala 500QX415-3	Keepsake	Yr.Iss.	5.00	18.00
86-115-020	Chatty Penguin 575QX417-6	Keepsake	Yr.Iss.	5.75	19.00
86-115-021	Special Delivery 500QX415-6	Keepsake	Yr.Iss.	5.00	24.50
86-115-022	Jolly Hiker 500QX483-2	Keepsake	Yr.Iss.	5.00	20-30.00
86-115-023	Cookies for Santa 450QX414-6	Keepsake	Yr.Iss.	4.50	15-25.00

Company Number	Name	Series Artist	Edition Limit	Issue Price	Quote
86-115-024	Merry Mouse 450QX403-2	Keepsake	Yr.Iss.	4.50	22.00
86-115-025	Skateboard Raccoon 650QX473-2	Keepsake	Yr.Iss.	6.50	39.50
86-115-026	Beary Smooth Ride 650QX480-5	Keepsake	Yr.Iss.	6.50	19.50
86-115-027	Snow-Pitching Snowman 450QX470-2	Keepsake	Yr.Iss.	4.50	22.50
86-115-028	Kitty Mischief 500QX474-5	Keepsake	Yr.Iss.	5.00	24.50
86-115-029	Soccer Beaver 650QX477-5	Keepsake	Yr.Iss.	6.50	24.50
86-115-030	Do Not Disturb Bear 775QX481-2	Keepsake	Yr.Iss.	7.75	15-24.50
Hallmark Keepsake Ornaments		**1986 Special Edition**			
86-116-001	Jolly St. Nick 2250QX429-6	Keepsake	Yr.Iss.	22.50	50.00
Hallmark Keepsake Ornaments		**1986 Limited Edition**			
86-117-001	Magical Unicorn 2750QX429-3	Keepsake	Yr.Iss.	27.50	100.00
Hallmark Keepsake Ornaments		**1986 Christmas Medley Collection**			
86-118-001	Joyful Carolers 975QX513-6	Keepsake	Yr.Iss.	9.75	30-40.00
86-118-002	Festive Treble Clef 875QX513-3	Keepsake	Yr.Iss.	8.75	27.50
86-118-003	Favorite Tin Drum 850QX514-3	Keepsake	Yr.Iss.	8.50	30.00
86-118-004	Christmas Guitar 700QX512-6	Keepsake	Yr.Iss.	7.00	18-25.00
86-118-005	Holiday Horn 800QX514-6	Keepsake	Yr.Iss.	8.00	29.50
Hallmark Keepsake Ornaments		**1986 Country Treasures Collection**			
86-119-001	Country Sleigh 1000QX511-3	Keepsake	Yr.Iss.	10.00	23-30.00
86-119-002	Remembering Christmas 865QX510-6	Keepsake	Yr.Iss.	8.75	25-30.00
86-119-003	Little Drummers 1250QX511-6	Keepsake	Yr.Iss.	12.50	28-35.00
86-119-004	Nutcracker Santa 1000QX512-3	Keepsake	Yr.Iss.	10.00	38-45.00
86-119-005	Welcome, Christmas 825QX510-3	Keepsake	Yr.Iss.	8.25	30-35.00
Hallmark Keepsake Ornaments		**1986 Traditional Ornaments**			
86-120-001	Holiday Jingle Bell 1600QX404-6	Keepsake	Yr.Iss.	16.00	25.00
86-120-002	Memories to Cherish 750QX427-6	Keepsake	Yr.Iss.	7.50	24.50
86-120-003	Bluebird 725QX428-3	Keepsake	Yr.Iss.	7.25	45-49.50
86-120-004	Glowing Christmas Tree 700QX428-6	Keepsake	Yr.Iss.	7.00	12.75
86-120-005	Heirloom Snowflake 675QX515-3	Keepsake	Yr.Iss.	6.75	19-22.00
86-120-006	Christmas Beauty 600QX322-3	Keepsake	Yr.Iss.	6.00	10.00
86-120-007	Star Brighteners 600QX322-6	Keepsake	Yr.Iss.	6.00	16.50
86-120-008	The Magi 475QX272-6	Keepsake	Yr.Iss.	4.75	12.75
86-120-009	Mary Emmerling: American Country Collection 795QX275-2	Keepsake	Yr.Iss.	7.95	25.00
Hallmark Keepsake Ornaments		**1986 Collectible Series**			
86-121-001	Mr. and Mrs. Claus-1st Edition1300QX402-6	Keepsake	Yr.Iss.	13.00	70-90.00
86-121-002	Reindeer Champs-1st Edition750QX422-3	Keepsake	Yr.Iss.	7.50	110.00
86-121-003	Betsey Clark: Home for Christmas-1st Edition 500QX277-6	Keepsake	Yr.Iss.	5.00	25.00
86-121-004	Windows of the World-2nd Ed.1000QX408-3	Keepsake	Yr.Iss.	10.00	25-35.00
86-121-005	Miniature Creche-2nd Edition900QX407-6	Keepsake	Yr.Iss.	9.00	48-60.00
86-121-006	Nostalgic Houses and Shops-3rd Edition 1375QX403-3	Keepsake	Yr.Iss.	13.75	175-200.
86-121-007	Wood Childhood Ornaments-3rd Edition 750QX407-3	Keepsake	Yr.Iss.	7.50	29.50
86-121-008	Twelve Days of Christmas-3rd Edition 650QX378-6	Keepsake	Yr.Iss.	6.50	27-40.00
86-121-009	Art Masterpiece-3rd & Final Ed. 675QX350-6	Keepsake	Yr.Iss.	6.75	13-24.50
86-121-010	Porcelain Bear-4th Edition 775QX405-6	Keepsake	Yr.Iss.	7.75	25-41.00
86-121-011	Tin Locomotive-5th Edition 1475QX403-6	Keepsake	Yr.Iss.	14.75	55.00
86-121-012	Holiday Wildlife-5th Edition 750QX321-6	Keepsake	Yr.Iss.	7.50	15.00
86-121-013	Clothespin Soldier-5th Edition 550QX406-3	Keepsake	Yr.Iss.	5.50	23-29.50
86-121-014	Rocking Horse-6th Edition 1075QX401-6	Keepsake	Yr.Iss.	10.75	45.00
86-121-015	Norman Rockwell-7th Edition 775QX321-3	Keepsake	Yr.Iss.	7.75	18-26.00
86-121-016	Frosty Friends-7th Edition 850QX405-3	Keepsake	Yr.Iss.	8.50	40-65.00
86-121-017	Here Comes Santa-8th Edition 1400QX404-3	Keepsake	Yr.Iss.	14.00	50-54.50
86-121-018	Thimble-9th Edition 575QX406-6	Keepsake	Yr.Iss.	5.75	20-33.00
Hallmark Keepsake Ornaments		**1986 Lighted Ornament Collection**			
86-122-001	Baby's First Christmas1950QLX710-3	Keepsake	Yr.Iss.	19.50	35.00
86-122-002	First Christmas Together2200QLX707-3	Keepsake	Yr.Iss.	14.00	39.50
86-122-003	Santa and Sparky-1st Edition2200QLX703-3	Keepsake	Yr.Iss.	22.00	75-125.00
86-122-004	Christmas Classics-1st Edition1750QLX704-3	Keepsake	Yr.Iss.	17.50	55-85.00
86-122-005	Chris Mouse-2nd Edition1300QLX705-6	Keepsake	Yr.Iss.	13.00	67.50-85.00
86-122-006	Village Express 2450QLX707-2	Keepsake	Yr.Iss.	24.50	85-110.00
86-122-007	Christmas Sleigh Ride 2450QLX701-2	Keepsake	Yr.Iss.	24.50	90-115.00
86-122-008	Santa's On His Way 1500QLX711-5	Keepsake	Yr.Iss.	15.00	69.50
86-122-009	General Store 1575QLX705-3	Keepsake	Yr.Iss.	15.75	50-60.00
86-122-010	Gentle Blessings 1500QLX708-3	Keepsake	Yr.Iss.	15.00	150-175.
86-122-011	Keep on Glowin' 1000QLX707-6	Keepsake	Yr.Iss.	10.00	49.50
86-122-012	Santa's Snack 1000QLX706-6	Keepsake	Yr.Iss.	10.00	40-56.00
86-122-013	Merry Christmas Bell 850QLX709-3	Keepsake	Yr.Iss.	8.50	20-25.00
86-122-014	Sharing Friendship 850QLX706-3	Keepsake	Yr.Iss.	8.50	22-25.00
86-122-015	Mr. and Mrs. Santa 1450QLX705-2	Keepsake	Yr.Iss.	14.50	65-95.00
86-122-016	Sugarplum Cottage 1100QLX701-1	Keepsake	Yr.Iss.	11.00	45.00
Hallmark Keepsake Ornaments		**1987 Commemoratives**			
87-123-001	Baby's First Christmas 975QX411-3	Keepsake	Yr.Iss.	9.75	25.00
87-123-002	Baby's First Christmas Photoholder 750QX4661-9	Keepsake	Yr.Iss.	7.50	29.50
87-123-003	Baby's First Christmas 600QX372-9	Keepsake	Yr.Iss.	6.00	20.00
87-123-004	Baby's First Christmas-Baby Girl 475QX274-7	Keepsake	Yr.Iss.	4.75	15.00
87-123-005	Baby's First Christmas-Baby Boy475QX274-9	Keepsake	Yr.Iss.	4.75	15.00
87-123-006	Grandchild's First Christmas900QX460-9	Keepsake	Yr.Iss.	9.00	24.50
87-123-007	Baby's Second Christmas 575QX460-7	Keepsake	Yr.Iss.	5.75	22.50
87-123-008	Child's Third Christmas 575QX459-9	Keepsake	Yr.Iss.	5.75	25-28.00
87-123-009	Baby Locket 1500QX461-7	Keepsake	Yr.Iss.	15.00	25-29.50
87-123-010	Mother and Dad 700QX462-7	Keepsake	Yr.Iss.	7.00	18.00
87-123-011	Mother 650QX373-7	Keepsake	Yr.Iss.	6.50	8.00
87-123-012	Dad 600QX462-9	Keepsake	Yr.Iss.	6.00	40-46.00
87-123-013	Husband 700QX373-9	Keepsake	Yr.Iss.	7.00	12.00
87-123-014	Sister 600QX474-7	Keepsake	Yr.Iss.	6.00	15.00
87-123-015	Daughter 575QX463-7	Keepsake	Yr.Iss.	5.75	20.00
87-123-016	Son 575QX463-9	Keepsake	Yr.Iss.	5.75	19.50
87-123-017	Niece 475QX275-9	Keepsake	Yr.Iss.	4.75	12.50
87-123-018	Grandmother 475QX277-9	Keepsake	Yr.Iss.	4.75	12.50
87-123-019	Grandparents 475QX277-7	Keepsake	Yr.Iss.	4.75	15-17.50
87-123-020	Grandson 475QX276-9	Keepsake	Yr.Iss.	4.75	15.00
87-123-021	Granddaughter 600QX374-7	Keepsake	Yr.Iss.	6.00	7-15.00
87-123-022	Godchild 475QX276-7	Keepsake	Yr.Iss.	4.75	10-15.00
87-123-023	First Christmas Together 1500QX446-9	Keepsake	Yr.Iss.	15.00	20-30.00
87-123-024	First Christmas Together 950QX446-7	Keepsake	Yr.Iss.	9.50	30.00
87-123-025	First Christmas Together 800QX445-9	Keepsake	Yr.Iss.	8.00	21-27.50
87-123-026	First Christmas Together 650QX371-9	Keepsake	Yr.Iss.	6.50	20.00
87-123-027	First Christmas Together 475QX272-9	Keepsake	Yr.Iss.	4.75	20.00
87-123-028	Ten Years Together 700QX444-7	Keepsake	Yr.Iss.	7.00	24.50
87-123-029	Twenty-Five Years Together750QX443-9	Keepsake	Yr.Iss.	7.50	24.50

Company Number	Name	Series Artist	Edition Limit	Issue Price	Quote
87-123-030	Fifty Years Together 800QX443-7	Keepsake	Yr.Iss.	8.00	22.50
87-123-031	Word of Love 800QX447-7	Keepsake	Yr.Iss.	8.00	20-30.00
87-123-032	Heart in Blossom 600QX372-7	Keepsake	Yr.Iss.	6.00	24.50
87-123-033	Sweetheart 1100QX447-9	Keepsake	Yr.Iss.	11.00	20-30.00
87-123-034	Love is Everywhere 475QX278-7	Keepsake	Yr.Iss.	4.75	19.50
87-123-035	Holiday Greetings 600QX375-7	Keepsake	Yr.Iss.	6.00	12.75
87-123-036	Warmth of Friendship 600QX375-9	Keepsake	Yr.Iss.	6.00	12.00
87-123-037	Time for Friends 475QX280-7	Keepsake	Yr.Iss.	4.75	17.00
87-123-038	From Our Home to Yours 475QX279-9	Keepsake	Yr.Iss.	4.75	12.00
87-123-039	New Home 600QX376-7	Keepsake	Yr.Iss.	6.00	29.50
87-123-040	Babysitter 475QX279-7	Keepsake	Yr.Iss.	4.75	12.00
87-123-041	Teacher 575QX466-7	Keepsake	Yr.Iss.	5.75	19.50
Hallmark Keepsake Ornaments		**1987 Holiday Humor**			
87-124-001	Snoopy and Woodstock 725QX472-9	Keepsake	Yr.Iss.	7.25	20-25.00
87-124-002	Bright Christmas Dreams 725QX440-7	Keepsake	Yr.Iss.	7.25	60-90.00
87-124-003	Joy Ride 1150QX440-7	Keepsake	Yr.Iss.	11.50	40.00
87-124-004	Pretty Kitten 1100QX448-9	Keepsake	Yr.Iss.	11.00	34.50
87-124-005	Santa at the Bat 775QX457-9	Keepsake	Yr.Iss.	7.75	16-30.00
87-124-006	Jogging Through the Snow725QX457-7	Keepsake	Yr.Iss.	7.25	24.50
87-124-007	Jack Frosting 700QX449-9	Keepsake	Yr.Iss.	7.00	27.50-30.00
87-124-008	Raccoon Biker 700QX458-7	Keepsake	Yr.Iss.	7.00	25.00
87-124-009	Treetop Dreams 675QX459-7	Keepsake	Yr.Iss.	6.75	15-25.00
87-124-010	Night Before Christmas 650QX451-7	Keepsake	Yr.Iss.	6.50	22-33.00
87-124-011	"Owliday" Wish 650QX455-9	Keepsake	Yr.Iss.	6.50	20-25.00
87-124-012	Let It Snow 650QX458-9	Keepsake	Yr.Iss.	6.50	17.50-22.00
87-124-013	Hot Dogger 650QX471-9	Keepsake	Yr.Iss.	6.50	24.00
87-124-014	Spots 'n Stripes 550QX452-9	Keepsake	Yr.Iss.	5.50	20-27.00
87-124-015	Seasoned Greetings 625QX454-9	Keepsake	Yr.Iss.	6.25	10-32.50
87-124-016	Chocolate Chipmunk 600QX456-7	Keepsake	Yr.Iss.	6.00	30-40.00
87-124-017	Fudge Forever 500QX449-7	Keepsake	Yr.Iss.	5.00	25-35.00
87-124-018	Sleepy Santa 625QX450-7	Keepsake	Yr.Iss.	6.25	30-33.00
87-124-019	Reindoggy 575QX452-7	Keepsake	Yr.Iss.	5.75	25.00
87-124-020	Christmas Cuddle 575QX453-7	Keepsake	Yr.Iss.	5.75	25-35.00
87-124-021	Paddington Bear 550QX472-7	Keepsake	Yr.Iss.	5.50	25.00
87-124-022	Nature's Decorations 475QX273-9	Keepsake	Yr.Iss.	4.75	25-33.00
87-124-023	Dr. Seuss: The Grinch's Christmas 475QX278-3	Keepsake	Yr.Iss.	4.75	30.00
87-124-024	Jammie Pies 475QX283-9	Keepsake	Yr.Iss.	4.75	14.50
87-124-025	Peanuts 475QX281-9	Keepsake	Yr.Iss.	4.75	29.50
87-124-026	Happy Santa 475QX456-9	Keepsake	Yr.Iss.	4.75	29.50
87-124-027	Icy Treat 450QX450-9	Keepsake	Yr.Iss.	4.50	20-25.00
87-124-028	Mouse in the Moon 550QX416-6	Keepsake	Yr.Iss.	5.50	21.00
87-124-029	L'il Jingler 675QX419-3	Keepsake	Yr.Iss.	6.75	27.50
87-124-030	Walnut Shell Rider 600QX419-6	Keepsake	Yr.Iss.	6.00	18.00
87-124-031	Treetop Trio 1100QX425-6	Keepsake	Yr.Iss.	11.00	25.00
87-124-032	Jolly Hiker 500QX483-2	Keepsake	Yr.Iss.	5.00	17.50
87-124-033	Merry Koala 500QX415-3	Keepsake	Yr.Iss.	5.00	15-17.00
Hallmark Keepsake Ornaments		**1987 Old-Fashioned Christmas Collection**			
87-125-001	Nostalgic Rocker 650QX468-9	Keepsake	Yr.Iss.	6.50	29.50
87-125-002	Little Whittler 600QX469-9	Keepsake	Yr.Iss.	6.00	25-33.00
87-125-003	Country Wreath 575QX470-9	Keepsake	Yr.Iss.	5.75	25-29.50
87-125-004	In a Nutshell 550QX469-7	Keepsake	Yr.Iss.	5.50	32.50
87-125-005	Folk Art Santa 525QX474-9	Keepsake	Yr.Iss.	5.25	25-35.00
Hallmark Keepsake Ornaments		**1987 Christmas Pizzazz Collection**			
87-126-001	Doc Holiday 800QX467-7	Keepsake	Yr.Iss.	8.00	32.00
87-126-002	Christmas Fun Puzzle 800QX467-9	Keepsake	Yr.Iss.	8.00	24.50
87-126-003	Jolly Follies 850QX466-9	Keepsake	Yr.Iss.	8.50	20-30.00
87-126-004	St. Louie Nick 775QX453-9	Keepsake	Yr.Iss.	7.75	22.00
87-126-005	Holiday Hourglass 800QX470-7	Keepsake	Yr.Iss.	8.00	20-23.00
87-126-006	Mistletoad 700QX468-7	Keepsake	Yr.Iss.	7.00	20-30.00
87-126-007	Happy Holidata 650QX471-7	Keepsake	Yr.Iss.	6.50	20-30.00
Hallmark Keepsake Ornaments		**1987 Traditional Ornaments**			
87-127-001	Goldfinch 700QX464-9	Keepsake	Yr.Iss.	7.00	32.00
87-127-002	Heavenly Harmony 1500QX465-9	Keepsake	Yr.Iss.	15.00	33-35.00
87-127-003	Special Memories Photoholder675QX 464-7	Keepsake	Yr.Iss.	6.75	22.50
87-127-004	Joyous Angels 775QX465-7	Keepsake	Yr.Iss.	7.75	25-30.00
87-127-005	Promise of Peace 650QX374-9	Keepsake	Yr.Iss.	6.50	24.50
87-127-006	Christmas Keys 575QX473-9	Keepsake	Yr.Iss.	5.75	29.50
87-127-007	I Remember Santa 475QX278-9	Keepsake	Yr.Iss.	4.75	22-25.00
87-127-008	Norman Rockwell: Christmas Scenes 475QX282-7	Keepsake	Yr.Iss.	4.75	23-25.00
87-127-009	Currier & Ives: American Farm Scene 475QX282-9	Keepsake	Yr.Iss.	4.75	15-22.50
Hallmark Keepsake Ornaments		**1987 Limited Edition**			
87-128-001	Christmas Time Mime 2750QX442-9	Keepsake	Yr.Iss.	27.50	35-60.00
87-128-002	Christmas is Gentle 1750QX444-9	Keepsake	Yr.Iss.	17.50	40-75.00
Hallmark Keepsake Ornaments		**1987 Special Edition**			
87-129-001	Favorite Santa 2250QX445-7	Keepsake	Yr.Iss.	22.50	45-47.00
Hallmark Keepsake Ornaments		**1987 Artists' Favorites**			
87-130-001	Three Men in a Tub 800QX454-7	Keepsake	Yr.Iss.	8.00	20.00
87-130-002	Wee Chimney Sweep 625QX451-9	Keepsake	Yr.Iss.	6.25	25-30.00
87-130-003	December Showers 550QX448-7	Keepsake	Yr.Iss.	5.50	25-35.00
87-130-004	Beary Special 475QX455-7	Keepsake	Yr.Iss.	4.75	17.50
Hallmark Keepsake Ornaments		**1987 Collectible Series**			
87-131-001	Holiday Heirloom-1st Ed./limited ed. 2500QX485-7	Keepsake	Yr.Iss.	25.00	35-50.00
87-131-002	Collector's Plate-1st Edition 800QX481-7	Keepsake	Yr.Iss.	8.00	45.00
87-131-003	Mr. and Mrs. Claus-2nd Edition 2nd Edition 132QX483-7	Keepsake	Yr.Iss.	13.25	40-45.00
87-131-004	Reindeer Champs-2nd Edition 750QX480-9	Keepsake	Yr.Iss.	7.50	40.00
87-131-005	Betsey Clark: Home for Christmas-2nd edition 500QX272-7	Keepsake	Yr.Iss.	5.00	15-25.00
87-131-006	Windows of the World-3rd Edition 1000QX482-7	Keepsake	Yr.Iss.	10.00	20-46.00
87-131-007	Miniature Creche -3rd Edition 900QX481-9	Keepsake	Yr.Iss.	9.00	30.00
87-131-008	Nostalgic Houses and Shops-4th Edition 483QX483-9	Keepsake	Yr.Iss.	14.00	59.50
87-131-009	Twelve Days of Christmas-4th Edition 650QX370-9	Keepsake	Yr.Iss.	6.50	25.00
87-131-010	Wood Childhood Ornaments-4th Edition 750QX441-7	Keepsake	Yr.Iss.	7.50	24.50
87-131-011	Porcelain Bear-5th Edition 775QX442-7	Keepsake	Yr.Iss.	7.75	29.50
87-131-012	Tin Locomotive-6th Edition 1475QX484-9	Keepsake	Yr.Iss.	14.75	58.00

Company		Series			
Number	**Name**	**Artist**	**Edition Limit**	**Issue Price**	**Quote**
87-131-013	Holiday Wildlife -6th Edition 750QX371-7	Keepsake	Yr.Iss.	7.50	15.00
87-131-014	Clothespin Soldier-6th & Final Ed. 550QX480-7	Keepsake	Yr.Iss.	5.50	15.00
87-131-015	Frosty Friends -8th Edition 850QX440-9	Keepsake	Yr.Iss.	8.50	40-55.00
87-131-016	Rocking Horse-7th Edition1075QX482-9	Keepsake	Yr.Iss.	10.75	40-45.00
87-131-017	Norman Rockwell-8th Edition775QX370-7	Keepsake	Yr.Iss.	7.75	15-30.00
87-131-018	Here Comes Santa-9th Edition 1400QX484-7	Keepsake	Yr.Iss.	14.00	45.00
87-131-019	Thimble-10th Edition 575QX441-9	Keepsake	Yr.Iss.	5.75	29.50
Hallmark Keepsake Ornaments		**1987 Keepsake Magic Ornaments**			
87-132-001	Baby's First Christmas 1350QLX704-9	Keepsake	Yr.Iss.	13.50	30-35.00
87-132-002	First Christmas Together 1150QLX708-7	Keepsake	Yr.Iss.	11.50	40.00
87-132-003	Santa and Sparky-2nd Edition1950QLX701-9	Keepsake	Yr.Iss.	19.50	60-75.00
87-132-004	Christmas Classics-2nd Ed.1600ZLX702-9	Keepsake	Yr.Iss.	16.00	55-75.00
87-132-005	Chris Mouse-3rd Edition1100QLX705-7	Keepsake	Yr.Iss.	11.00	45-50.00
87-132-006	Christmas Morning 2450QLX701-3	Keepsake	Yr.Iss.	24.50	40-50.00
87-132-007	Loving Holiday 2200QLX701-6	Keepsake	Yr.Iss.	22.00	52.50
87-132-008	Angelic Messengers 1875QLX711-3	Keepsake	Yr.Iss.	18.75	45-68.00
87-132-009	Good Cheer Blimp 1600QLX704-6	Keepsake	Yr.Iss.	16.00	49-51.00
87-132-010	Train Station 1275QLX703-9	Keepsake	Yr.Iss.	12.75	50-60.00
87-132-011	Keeping Cozy 1175QLX704-7	Keepsake	Yr.Iss.	11.75	34.50
87-132-012	Lacy Brass Snowflake 1150QLX709-7	Keepsake	Yr.Iss.	11.50	25.00
87-132-013	Meowy Christmas I 1000QLX708-9	Keepsake	Yr.Iss.	10.00	62.50
87-132-014	Memories are Forever Photoholder 850QLX706-7	Keepsake	Yr.Iss.	8.50	27.50
87-132-015	Season for Friendship 850QLX706-9	Keepsake	Yr.Iss.	8.50	19.50
87-132-016	Bright Noel 700QLX705-9	Keepsake	Yr.Iss.	7.00	29.50
Hallmark Keepsake Ornaments		**1987 Keepsake Collector's Club**			
87-133-001	Wreath of Memories QXC580-9	Keepsake	Yr.Iss.	Unkn.	45-75.00
87-133-002	Carrousel Reindeer QXC580-7	Keepsake	Yr.Iss.	Unkn.	45-65.00
Hallmark Keepsake Ornaments		**1988 Commemoratives**			
88-134-001	Baby's First Christmas 975QX470-1	Keepsake	Yr.Iss.	9.75	30.00
88-134-002	Baby's First Christmas 750QX470-4	Keepsake	Yr.Iss.	7.50	20.00
88-134-003	Baby's First Christmas 600QX372-1	Keepsake	Yr.Iss.	6.00	15.00
88-134-004	Baby's Second Christmas 600QX471-1	Keepsake	Yr.Iss.	6.00	20-30.00
88-134-005	Child's Third Christmas 600QX471-4	Keepsake	Yr.Iss.	6.00	20.00
88-134-006	Baby's First Christmas (Boy)475QX272-1	Keepsake	Yr.Iss.	4.75	15.00
88-134-007	Baby's First Christmas (Girl)475QX272-4	Keepsake	Yr.Iss.	4.75	15-26.00
88-134-008	Mother and Dad 800QX414-4	Keepsake	Yr.Iss.	8.00	20.00
88-134-009	Sister 800QX499-4	Keepsake	Yr.Iss.	8.00	10.00
88-134-010	Dad 700QX414-1	Keepsake	Yr.Iss.	7.00	15-26.00
88-134-011	Mother 650QX375-1	Keepsake	Yr.Iss.	6.50	10-13.00
88-134-012	Daughter 575QX415-1	Keepsake	Yr.Iss.	5.75	36-45.00
88-134-013	Son 575QX415-4	Keepsake	Yr.Iss.	5.75	30.00
88-134-014	Grandmother 475QX276-4	Keepsake	Yr.Iss.	4.75	13-15.00
88-134-015	Grandparents 475QX277-1	Keepsake	Yr.Iss.	4.75	15.00
88-134-016	Granddaughter 475QX277-4	Keepsake	Yr.Iss.	4.75	10-20.00
88-134-017	Grandson 475QX278-1	Keepsake	Yr.Iss.	4.75	15-19.50
88-134-018	Godchild 475QX278-4	Keepsake	Yr.Iss.	4.75	6-22.50
88-134-019	Sweetheart 975QX490-1	Keepsake	Yr.Iss.	9.75	20-27.00
88-134-020	First Christmas Together 900QX489-4	Keepsake	Yr.Iss.	9.00	28.00
88-134-021	First Christmas Together 675QX373-1	Keepsake	Yr.Iss.	6.75	20.00
88-134-022	Twenty-Five Years Together 675QX373-4	Keepsake	Yr.Iss.	6.75	13.50
88-134-023	Fifty Years Together 675QX374-1	Keepsake	Yr.Iss.	6.75	19.00
88-134-024	Love Fills the Heart 600QX374-4	Keepsake	Yr.Iss.	6.00	19.50
88-134-025	First Christmas Together 475QX274-1	Keepsake	Yr.Iss.	4.75	25.00
88-134-026	Five Years Together 475QX274-4	Keepsake	Yr.Iss.	4.75	19.50
88-134-027	Ten Years Together 475QX275-1	Keepsake	Yr.Iss.	4.75	15-25.00
88-134-028	Love Grows 475QX275-4	Keepsake	Yr.Iss.	4.75	19.00
88-134-029	Spirit of Christmas 475QX276-1	Keepsake	Yr.Iss.	4.75	15.50
88-134-030	Year to Remember 700QX416-4	Keepsake	Yr.Iss.	7.00	14.50
88-134-031	Teacher 625QX417-1	Keepsake	Yr.Iss.	6.25	16.50
88-134-032	Gratitude 600QX375-4	Keepsake	Yr.Iss.	6.00	12.00
88-134-033	New Home 600QX376-1	Keepsake	Yr.Iss.	6.00	19.50
88-134-034	Babysitter 475QX279-1	Keepsake	Yr.Iss.	4.75	10.50
88-134-035	From Our Home to Yours 475QX279-4	Keepsake	Yr.Iss.	4.75	12.00
Hallmark Keepsake Ornaments		**1988 Hallmark Handcrafted Ornaments**			
88-135-001	Peanuts 475QX280-1	Keepsake	Yr.Iss.	4.75	24.50
88-135-002	Jingle Bell Clown 1500QX477-4	Keepsake	Yr.Iss.	15.00	27.50
88-135-003	Travels with Santa 1000QX477-1	Keepsake	Yr.Iss.	10.00	25-32.50
88-135-004	Goin' Cross-Country 850QX476-4	Keepsake	Yr.Iss.	8.50	18-24.00
88-135-005	Winter Fun 850QX478-1	Keepsake	Yr.Iss.	8.50	20-25.00
88-135-006	Go For The Gold 800QX417-4	Keepsake	Yr.Iss.	8.00	20-26.50
88-135-007	Party Line 875QX476-1	Keepsake	Yr.Iss.	8.75	20-27.00
88-135-008	Soft Landing 700QX475-1	Keepsake	Yr.Iss.	7.00	18.00
88-135-009	Feliz Navidad 675QX416-1	Keepsake	Yr.Iss.	6.75	28-30.00
88-135-010	Squeaky Clean 675QX475-4	Keepsake	Yr.Iss.	6.75	25-27.00
88-135-011	Christmas Memories 650QX372-4	Keepsake	Yr.Iss.	6.50	19.50
88-135-012	Purrfect Snuggle 625QX474-4	Keepsake	Yr.Iss.	6.25	25.00
88-135-013	Snoopy and Woodstock 600QX474-1	Keepsake	Yr.Iss.	6.00	25-30.00
88-135-014	The Town Crier 550QX473-4	Keepsake	Yr.Iss.	5.50	17-25.00
88-135-015	Christmas Scenes 475QX273-1	Keepsake	Yr.Iss.	4.75	17.50
88-135-016	Jolly Walrus 450QX473-1	Keepsake	Yr.Iss.	4.50	22.50
88-135-017	Slipper Spaniel 450QX472-4	Keepsake	Yr.Iss.	4.50	15-20.00
88-135-018	Arctic Tenor 400QX472-1	Keepsake	Yr.Iss.	4.00	15-17.00
88-135-019	Christmas Cuckoo 800QX480-1	Keepsake	Yr.Iss.	8.00	22.50
88-135-020	Peek-a-boo Kittens 750QX487-1	Keepsake	Yr.Iss.	7.50	15-20.00
88-135-021	Cool Juggler 650QX487-4	Keepsake	Yr.Iss.	6.50	17.00
88-135-022	Sweet Star 500QX418-4	Keepsake	Yr.Iss.	5.00	15-27.00
88-135-023	Hoe-Hoe-Hoel 500QX422-1	Keepsake	Yr.Iss.	5.00	15-23.00
88-135-024	Nick the Kick 500QX422-4	Keepsake	Yr.Iss.	5.00	18.00
88-135-025	Holiday Hero 500QX423-1	Keepsake	Yr.Iss.	5.00	15.50
88-135-026	Polar Bowler 500QX478-1	Keepsake	Yr.Iss.	5.00	17.00
88-135-027	Par for Santa 500QX479-1	Keepsake	Yr.Iss.	5.00	17.00
88-135-028	Gone Fishing 500QX479-4	Keepsake	Yr.Iss.	5.00	14.00
88-135-029	Kiss the Claus 500QX486-1	Keepsake	Yr.Iss.	5.00	17.00
88-135-030	Love Santa 500QX486-4	Keepsake	Yr.Iss.	5.00	17.00
88-135-031	Teeny Taster 475QX418-1	Keepsake	Yr.Iss.	4.75	20-35.00
88-135-032	Filled with Fudge 475QX419-1	Keepsake	Yr.Iss.	4.75	20.00
88-135-033	Santa Flamingo 475QX483-4	Keepsake	Yr.Iss.	4.75	25-30.00
88-135-034	Kiss from Santa 450QX482-1	Keepsake	Yr.Iss.	4.50	15-25.00
88-135-035	Oreo 400QX481-4	Keepsake	Yr.Iss.	4.00	20-25.00
88-135-036	Noah's Ark 850QX490-4	Keepsake	Yr.Iss.	8.50	20.00
88-135-037	Sailing! Sailing! 850QX491-1	Keepsake	Yr.Iss.	8.50	18.00
88-135-038	Americana Drum 775QX488-1	Keepsake	Yr.Iss.	7.75	19.80
88-135-039	Kringle Portrait 750QX496-1	Keepsake	Yr.Iss.	7.50	23-30.00
88-135-040	Uncle Sam Nutcracker 700QX488-4	Keepsake	Yr.Iss.	7.00	15.00
88-135-041	Kringle Tree 650QX495-4	Keepsake	Yr.Iss.	6.50	32-37.00
88-135-042	Glowing Wreath 600QX492-1	Keepsake	Yr.Iss.	6.00	14.50
88-135-043	Sparkling Tree 600QX483-1	Keepsake	Yr.Iss.	6.00	8-15.00
88-135-044	Shiny Sleigh 575QX492-4	Keepsake	Yr.Iss.	5.75	15.00

Company		Series			
Number	**Name**	**Artist**	**Edition Limit**	**Issue Price**	**Quote**
88-135-045	Kringle Moon 550QX495-1	Keepsake	Yr.Iss.	5.00	17-27.50
88-135-046	Loving Bear 475QX493-4	Keepsake	Yr.Iss.	4.75	19.50
88-135-047	Christmas Cardinal 475QX494-1	Keepsake	Yr.Iss.	4.75	20.00
88-135-048	Starry Angel 475494-4	Keepsake	Yr.Iss.	4.75	14.50
88-135-049	Old-Fashioned School House 400QX497-1	Keepsake	Yr.Iss.	4.00	16.50
88-135-050	Old-Fashioned Church 400QX498-1	Keepsake	Yr.Iss.	4.00	16.50
Hallmark Keepsake Ornaments		**1988 Special Edition**			
88-136-001	The Wonderful Santacycle 2250QX411-4	Keepsake	Yr.Iss.	22.50	48-50.00
Hallmark Keepsake Ornaments		**1988 Artist Favorites**			
88-137-001	Little Jack Horner 800QX408-1	Keepsake	Yr.Iss.	8.00	25-28.00
88-137-002	Merry-Mint Unicorn 850QX423-4	Keepsake	Yr.Iss.	8.50	15-20.00
88-137-003	Midnight Snack 600QX410-4	Keepsake	Yr.Iss.	6.00	20-26.00
88-137-004	Cymbals of Christmas 550QX411-1	Keepsake	Yr.Iss.	5.50	25-28.00
88-137-005	Baby Redbird 500QX410-1	Keepsake	Yr.Iss.	5.00	15-20.00
88-137-006	Very Strawbeary 475QX409-1	Keepsake	Yr.Iss.	4.75	17-25.00
Hallmark Keepsake Ornaments		**1988 Collectible Series**			
88-138-001	Holiday Heirloom-Second Ed.2500QX406-4	Keepsake	Yr.Iss.	25.00	30-50.00
88-138-002	Tin Locomotive-Seventh Ed.1475QX400-4	Keepsake	Yr.Iss.	14.75	40.00
88-138-003	Nostalgic Houses and Shops-Fifth Edition -1450QX401-4	Keepsake	Yr.Iss.	14.50	40-50.00
88-138-004	Here Comes Santa-Tenth Ed.1400QX400-1	Keepsake	Yr.Iss.	14.00	33-43.00
88-138-005	Mr. and Mrs. Claus-Third Ed.1300QX401-1	Keepsake	Yr.Iss.	13.00	38-45.00
88-138-006	Rocking Horse-Eighth Ed.1075QX402-4	Keepsake	Yr.Iss.	10.75	30-40.00
88-138-007	Windows of the World-Fourth Edition 1000QX402-1	Keepsake	Yr.Iss.	10.00	20-36.00
88-138-008	Frosty Friends-Ninth Ed.875QX403-1	Keepsake	Yr.Iss.	8.75	48.00
88-138-009	Miniature Creche-Fourth Ed.850QX403-4	Keepsake	Yr.Iss.	8.50	12-24.50
88-138-010	Porcelain Bear-Sixth Ed.800QX404-4	Keepsake	Yr.Iss.	8.00	37-48.00
88-138-011	Collector's Plate-Second Ed.800QX406-1	Keepsake	Yr.Iss.	8.00	35.00
88-138-012	Norman Rockwell-Ninth Ed.775QX370-4	Keepsake	Yr.Iss.	7.75	18-24.00
88-138-013	Holiday Wildlife-Seventh Ed.775QX371-1	Keepsake	Yr.Iss.	7.75	15.00
88-138-014	Wood Childhood-Fifth Ed.750QX404-1	Keepsake	Yr.Iss.	7.50	24.50
88-138-015	Reindeer Champs-Third Ed.750QX405-1	Keepsake	Yr.Iss.	7.50	35.00
88-138-016	Five Golden Rings-Fifth Ed.650QX371-4	Keepsake	Yr.Iss.	6.50	20-23.00
88-138-017	Thimble-Eleventh Ed.575QX405-4	Keepsake	Yr.Iss.	5.75	15.00
88-138-018	Mary's Angels-First Ed.500QX407-4	Keepsake	Yr.Iss.	5.00	32.50-45.00
88-138-019	Betsey Clark: Home for Christmas-Third Edition 500QX271-4	Keepsake	Yr.Iss.	5.00	20-23.00
Hallmark Keepsake Ornaments		**1988 Keepsake Magic Ornaments**			
88-139-001	Baby's First Christmas 2400QLX718-4	Keepsake	Yr.Iss.	24.00	38-45.00
88-139-002	First Christmas Together 1200QLX702-7	Keepsake	Yr.Iss.	12.00	35.00
88-139-003	Santa and Sparky-Third Ed.1950QLX719-1	Keepsake	Yr.Iss.	19.50	30-50.00
88-139-004	Christmas Classics-Third Ed.1500QLX716-1	Keepsake	Yr.Iss.	15.00	30-50.00
88-139-005	Chris Mouse-Fourth Ed.875QLX715-4	Keepsake	Yr.Iss.	8.75	40-50.00
88-139-006	Country Express 2450QLX721-1	Keepsake	Yr.Iss.	24.50	35-77.00
88-139-007	Kringle's Toy Shop 2450QLX701-7	Keepsake	Yr.Iss.	24.50	45-55.00
88-139-008	Parade of the Toys 2200QLX719-4	Keepsake	Yr.Iss.	22.00	30-49.50
88-139-009	Last-Minute Hug 1950QLX718-1	Keepsake	Yr.Iss.	19.50	35-58.00
88-139-010	Skater's Waltz 1950QLX720-1	Keepsake	Yr.Iss.	19.50	49.50
88-139-011	Kitty Capers 1300QLX716-4	Keepsake	Yr.Iss.	13.00	38.25
88-139-012	Christmas is Magic 1200QLX717-1	Keepsake	Yr.Iss.	12.00	49.50
88-139-013	Heavenly Glow 1175QLX711-4	Keepsake	Yr.Iss.	11.75	16-29.00
88-139-014	Radiant Tree 1175QLX712-1	Keepsake	Yr.Iss.	11.75	22-25.00
88-139-015	Festive Feeder 1150QLX720-4	Keepsake	Yr.Iss.	11.50	44.50
88-139-016	Circling the Globe 1050QLX712-4	Keepsake	Yr.Iss.	10.50	28-37.00
88-139-017	Bearly Reaching 950QLX715-1	Keepsake	Yr.Iss.	9.50	30-33.00
88-139-018	Moonlit Nap 875QLX713-4	Keepsake	Yr.Iss.	8.75	24.50
88-139-019	Tree of Friendship 850QLX710-4	Keepsake	Yr.Iss.	8.50	22.50
88-139-020	Song of Christmas 850QLX711-1	Keepsake	Yr.Iss.	8.50	20-23.00
Hallmark Keepsake Ornaments		**1988 Keepsake Miniature Ornaments**			
88-140-001	Baby's First Christmas	Keepsake	Yr.Iss.	6.00	8.00
88-140-002	First Christmas Together	Keepsake	Yr.Iss.	4.00	20.00
88-140-003	Mother	Keepsake	Yr.Iss.	3.00	9.00
88-140-004	Friends Share Joy	Keepsake	Yr.Iss.	2.00	15.00
88-140-005	Love is Forever	Keepsake	Yr.Iss.	2.00	15.00
88-140-006	Holy Family	Keepsake	Yr.Iss.	8.50	15-21.00
88-140-007	Sweet Dreams	Keepsake	Yr.Iss.	7.00	23-26.00
88-140-008	Skater's Waltz	Keepsake	Yr.Iss.	7.00	10-22.00
88-140-009	Little Drummer Boy	Keepsake	Yr.Iss.	4.50	20-26.50
88-140-010	Three Little Kitties	Keepsake	Yr.Iss.	6.00	18.50
88-140-011	Snuggly Skater	Keepsake	Yr.Iss.	4.50	20-27.50
88-140-012	Happy Santa	Keepsake	Yr.Iss.	4.50	15-20.00
88-140-013	Sneaker Mouse	Keepsake	Yr.Iss.	4.00	20-22.00
88-140-014	Country Wreath	Keepsake	Yr.Iss.	4.00	12.00
88-140-015	Joyous Heart	Keepsake	Yr.Iss.	3.50	25-30.00
88-140-016	Candy Cane Elf	Keepsake	Yr.Iss.	3.00	20-22.00
88-140-017	Folk Art Lamb	Keepsake	Yr.Iss.	2.50	19.50
88-140-018	Folk Art Reindeer	Keepsake	Yr.Iss.	2.50	19.50
88-140-019	Gentle Angel	Keepsake	Yr.Iss.	2.00	19.50
88-140-020	Brass Star	Keepsake	Yr.Iss.	1.50	20-28.00
88-140-021	Brass Angel	Keepsake	Yr.Iss.	1.50	19.50
88-140-022	Brass Tree	Keepsake	Yr.Iss.	1.50	19.50
88-140-023	Jolly St. Nick	Keepsake	Yr.Iss.	8.00	28-37.00
88-140-024	Family Home-First Edition	Keepsake	Yr.Iss.	8.50	30-45.00
88-140-025	Kittens in Toyland-First Edition	Keepsake	Yr.Iss.	5.00	25.00
88-140-026	Rocking Horse-First Edition	Keepsake	Yr.Iss.	4.50	25.00
88-140-027	Penguin Pal-First Edition	Keepsake	Yr.Iss.	3.75	25-30.00
Hallmark Keepsake Ornaments		**1988 Hallmark Keepsake Ornament Collector's Club**			
88-141-001	Our Clubhouse QXC580-4	Keepsake	Yr.Iss.	Unkn.	42-50.00
88-141-002	Sleighful of Dreams 800QC580-1	Keepsake	Yr.Iss.	8.00	55-75.00
88-141-003	Holiday Heirloom-Second Edition 2500QXC406-4	Keepsake	Yr.Iss.	25.00	30-65.00
88-141-004	Christmas is Sharing 1750QXC407-1	Keepsake	Yr.Iss.	17.50	37.50
88-141-005	Angelic Minstrel 2750QXC408-4	Keepsake	Yr.Iss.	27.50	35.00
88-141-006	Hold on Tight QXC570-4	Keepsake	Yr.Iss.	Unkn.	60-80.00
Hallmark Keepsake Ornaments		**1989 Commemoratives**			
89-142-001	Baby's First Christmas Photoholder 625QX468-2	Keepsake	Yr.Iss.	6.25	25.00
89-142-002	Baby's First Christmas-Baby Girl475QX272-2	Keepsake	Yr.Iss.	4.75	10-18.00
89-142-003	Baby's First Christmas-Baby Boy475QX272-5	Keepsake	Yr.Iss.	4.75	12.50
89-142-004	Baby's First Christmas 675QX381-5	Keepsake	Yr.Iss.	6.75	10-20.00
89-142-005	Granddaughter's First Christmas 675QX382-2	Keepsake	Yr.Iss.	6.75	15.00
89-142-006	Grandson's First Christmas 675QX382-5	Keepsake	Yr.Iss.	6.75	15.00
89-142-007	Baby's First Christmas 725QX449-2	Keepsake	Yr.Iss.	7.25	32.50-55.00
89-142-008	Baby's Second Christmas 675QX449-5	Keepsake	Yr.Iss.	6.75	25.00
89-142-009	Baby's Third Christmas 675QX469-5	Keepsake	Yr.Iss.	6.75	18-20.00

Number	Name	Artist	Edition Limit	Issue Price	Quote
89-142-010	Baby's Fourth Christmas 675QX543-2	Keepsake	Yr.Iss.	6.75	20.00
89-142-011	Baby's Fifth Christmas 675QX543-5	Keepsake	Yr.Iss.	6.75	20.00
89-142-012	Mother 975QX440-5	Keepsake	Yr.Iss.	9.75	20.00
89-142-013	Mom and Dad 975QX442-5	Keepsake	Yr.Iss.	9.75	15.00
89-142-014	Dad 725QX442-5	Keepsake	Yr.Iss.	7.25	20.00
89-142-015	Sister 475QX279-2	Keepsake	Yr.Iss.	4.75	15-22.00
89-142-016	Grandparents 475QX277-2	Keepsake	Yr.Iss.	4.75	12.00
89-142-017	Grandmother 475QX277-5	Keepsake	Yr.Iss.	4.75	12.00
89-142-018	Granddaughter 475QX278	Keepsake	Yr.Iss.	4.75	15.00
89-142-019	Grandson 475QX278-5	Keepsake	Yr.Iss.	4.75	14-24.00
89-142-020	Godchild 625QX311-2	Keepsake	Yr.Iss.	6.25	12.00
89-142-021	Sweetheart 975QX486-5	Keepsake	Yr.Iss.	9.75	22.00
89-142-022	First Christmas Together 675QX485-2	Keepsake	Yr.Iss.	9.75	19.50
89-142-023	First Christmas Together 675QX383-2	Keepsake	Yr.Iss.	6.75	20.00
89-142-024	First Christmas Together 475QX273-2	Keepsake	Yr.Iss.	4.75	15.00
89-142-025	Five Years Together 475QX273-5	Keepsake	Yr.Iss.	4.75	19.50
89-142-026	Ten Years Together 475QX274-2	Keepsake	Yr.Iss.	4.75	19.50
89-142-027	Twenty-five Years Together Photoholder 875QX485-5	Keepsake	Yr.Iss.	8.75	12-17.50
89-142-028	Forty Years Together Photoholder 875QX545-2	Keepsake	Yr.Iss.	8.75	9-17.50
89-142-029	Fifty Years Together Photoholder 875QX486-2	Keepsake	Yr.Iss.	8.75	17.50
89-142-030	Language of Love 625QX383-5	Keepsake	Yr.Iss.	6.25	16.50
89-142-031	World of Love 475QX274-5	Keepsake	Yr.Iss.	4.75	16.50
89-142-032	Friendship Time 975QX413-2	Keepsake	Yr.Iss.	9.75	32.50
89-142-033	Teacher 575QX412-5	Keepsake	Yr.Iss.	5.75	24.50
89-142-034	New Home 475QX275-5	Keepsake	Yr.Iss.	4.75	15.00
89-142-035	Festive Year 775QX384-2	Keepsake	Yr.Iss.	7.75	15.00
89-142-036	Gratitude 675QX385-2	Keepsake	Yr.Iss.	6.75	13.50
89-142-037	From Our Home to Yours 625QX384-5	Keepsake	Yr.Iss.	6.25	12.50
89-142-038	Daughter 625QX443-2	Keepsake	Yr.Iss.	6.25	15.00
89-142-039	Son 625QX444-5	Keepsake	Yr.Iss.	6.25	15.00
89-142-040	Brother 625QX445-2	Keepsake	Yr.Iss.	6.25	15.00

Hallmark Keepsake Ornaments — 1989 Holiday Traditions

Number	Name	Artist	Edition Limit	Issue Price	Quote
89-143-001	Joyful Trio 975QX437-2	Keepsake	Yr.Iss.	9.75	20-26.00
89-143-002	Old-World Gnome 775QX434-5	Keepsake	Yr.Iss.	7.75	20-30.00
89-143-003	Hoppy Holidays 775QX469-2	Keepsake	Yr.Iss.	7.75	17.50
89-143-004	The First Christmas 775QX547-5	Keepsake	Yr.Iss.	7.75	15.50
89-143-005	Gentle Fawn 775QX548-5	Keepsake	Yr.Iss.	7.75	15.00
89-143-006	Spencer Sparrow, Esq. 675QX431-2	Keepsake	Yr.Iss.	6.75	20.00
89-143-007	Snoopy and Woodstock 675QX433-2	Keepsake	Yr.Iss.	6.75	35.00
89-143-008	Sweet Memories Photoholder 675QX438-5	Keepsake	Yr.Iss.	6.75	19.00
89-143-009	Stocking Kitten 675QX456-5	Keepsake	Yr.Iss.	6.75	11-15.00
89-143-010	George Washington Bicentennial 625QX386-2	Keepsake	Yr.Iss.	6.25	15.00
89-143-011	Feliz Navidad 675QX439-2	Keepsake	Yr.Iss.	6.75	19.50
89-143-012	Cranberry Bunny 575QX426-2	Keepsake	Yr.Iss.	5.75	14.50
89-143-013	Deer Disguise 575QX426-5	Keepsake	Yr.Iss.	5.75	24.50
89-143-014	Paddington Bear 575QX429-2	Keepsake	Yr.Iss.	5.75	20-28.00
89-143-015	Snowplow Santa 575QX420-5	Keepsake	Yr.Iss.	5.75	15.50
89-143-016	Kristy Claus 575QX424-5	Keepsake	Yr.Iss.	5.75	11.50
89-143-017	Here's the Pitch 575QX545-5	Keepsake	Yr.Iss.	5.75	13.50
89-143-018	North Pole Jogger 575QX546-2	Keepsake	Yr.Iss.	5.75	13.50
89-143-019	Camera Claus 575QX546-5	Keepsake	Yr.Iss.	5.75	15.50
89-143-020	Sea Santa 575QX415-2	Keepsake	Yr.Iss.	5.75	13.50
89-143-021	Gym Dandy 575QX418-5	Keepsake	Yr.Iss.	5.75	15.50
89-143-022	On the Links 575QX419-2	Keepsake	Yr.Iss.	5.75	14.50
89-143-023	Special Delivery 525QX432-5	Keepsake	Yr.Iss.	5.25	15.00
89-143-024	Hang in There 525QX430-5	Keepsake	Yr.Iss.	5.25	25-34.50
89-143-025	Owliday Greetings 400QX436-5	Keepsake	Yr.Iss.	4.00	15.00
89-143-026	Norman Rockwell 475QX276-2	Keepsake	Yr.Iss.	4.75	19.50
89-143-027	A Charlie Brown Christmas 475QX276-5	Keepsake	Yr.Iss.	4.75	25-30.00
89-143-028	Party Line 875QX476-1	Keepsake	Yr.Iss.	8.75	26.50
89-143-029	Peek-a-Boo Kitties 750QX487-1	Keepsake	Yr.Iss.	7.50	17-22.00
89-143-030	Polar Bowler 575QX478-4	Keepsake	Yr.Iss.	5.75	17.00
89-143-031	Gone Fishing 575QX479-4	Keepsake	Yr.Iss.	5.75	17.00
89-143-032	Teeny Taster 475QX418-1	Keepsake	Yr.Iss.	4.75	17.00
89-143-033	A Kiss™ From Santa 450QX482-1	Keepsake	Yr.Iss.	4.50	19.50
89-143-034	Oreo® Chocolate Sandwich Cookies 400QX481-4	Keepsake	Yr.Iss.	4.00	15.00

Hallmark Keepsake Ornaments — 1989 New Attractions

Number	Name	Artist	Edition Limit	Issue Price	Quote
89-144-001	Sparkling Snowflake 775QX547-2	Keepsake	Yr.Iss.	7.75	22-25.00
89-144-002	Festive Angel 675QX463-5	Keepsake	Yr.Iss.	6.75	18-22.00
89-144-003	Graceful Swan 675QX464-2	Keepsake	Yr.Iss.	6.75	18-22.00
89-144-004	Nostalgic Lamb 675QX466-5	Keepsake	Yr.Iss.	6.75	13.50
89-144-005	Horse Weathervane 575QX463-2	Keepsake	Yr.Iss.	5.75	14.50
89-144-006	Rooster Weathervane 575QX467-5	Keepsake	Yr.Iss.	5.75	10-14.00
89-144-007	Country Cat 625QX467-2	Keepsake	Yr.Iss.	6.25	15-17.00
89-144-008	Nutshell Holiday 575QX465-2	Keepsake	Yr.Iss.	5.75	20-27.50
89-144-009	Nutshell Dreams 575QX465-5	Keepsake	Yr.Iss.	5.75	20-27.50
89-144-010	Nutshell Workshop 575QX487-2	Keepsake	Yr.Iss.	5.75	20-27.50
89-144-011	Claus Construction 775QX488-5	Keepsake	Yr.Iss.	7.75	15-20.00
89-144-012	Cactus Cowboy 675QX411-2	Keepsake	Yr.Iss.	6.75	35.00
89-144-013	Rodney Reindeer 675QX407-2	Keepsake	Yr.Iss.	6.75	13.50
89-144-014	Let's Play 725QX488-2	Keepsake	Yr.Iss.	7.25	25.00
89-144-015	TV Break 625QX409-2	Keepsake	Yr.Iss.	6.25	15.50
89-144-016	Balancing Elf 675QX489-5	Keepsake	Yr.Iss.	6.75	22.50
89-144-017	Wiggly Snowman 675QX489-2	Keepsake	Yr.Iss.	6.75	24.50
89-144-018	Cool Swing 625QX487-5	Keepsake	Yr.Iss.	6.25	30.00
89-144-019	Goin' South 425QX410-5	Keepsake	Yr.Iss.	4.25	24.50-30.00
89-144-020	Peppermint Clown 2475QX450-5	Keepsake	Yr.Iss.	24.75	28-35.00

Hallmark Keepsake Ornaments — 1989 Artists' Favorites

Number	Name	Artist	Edition Limit	Issue Price	Quote
89-145-001	Merry-Go-Round Unicorn 1075QX447-2	Keepsake	Yr.Iss.	10.75	15-20.00
89-145-002	Carousel Zebra 925QX451-5	Keepsake	Yr.Iss.	9.25	19.50
89-145-003	Mail Call 875QX452-2	Keepsake	Yr.Iss.	8.75	20-30.00
89-145-004	Baby Partridge 675QX452-5	Keepsake	Yr.Iss.	6.75	15-18.00
89-145-005	Playful Angel 675QX453-5	Keepsake	Yr.Iss.	6.75	15-22.00
89-145-006	Cherry Jubilee 500QX453-2	Keepsake	Yr.Iss.	5.00	15.00
89-145-007	Bear-i-Tone 475QX454-2	Keepsake	Yr.Iss.	4.75	14.50

Hallmark Keepsake Ornaments — 1989 Special Edition

Number	Name	Artist	Edition Limit	Issue Price	Quote
89-146-001	The Ornament Express 2200QX580-5	Keepsake	Yr.Iss.	22.00	35-53.00

Hallmark Keepsake Ornaments — 1989 Collectible Series

Number	Name	Artist	Edition Limit	Issue Price	Quote
89-147-001	Christmas Kitty-First Ed.1475QX544-5	Keepsake	Yr.Iss.	14.75	20.00
89-147-002	Winter Surprise-First Ed.1075QX427-2	Keepsake	Yr.Iss.	10.75	25.00
89-147-003	Hark! It's Herald-First Ed.675QX455-5	Keepsake	Yr.Iss.	6.75	15-20.00
89-147-004	Crayola Crayon-First Ed.875QX435-2	Keepsake	Yr.Iss.	8.75	30-55.00
89-147-005	The Gift Bringers-First Ed.500QX279-5	Keepsake	Yr.Iss.	5.00	20-30.00
89-147-006	Mary's Angels-Second Ed.575QX454-5	Keepsake	Yr.Iss.	5.75	35-55.00
89-147-007	Collector's Plate-Third Ed.825QX461-2	Keepsake	Yr.Iss.	8.25	30.00
89-147-008	Mr. and Mrs. Claus-Fourth Ed.1325QX457-5	Keepsake	Yr.Iss.	13.25	35.50-40.00
89-147-009	Reindeer Champs-Fourth Ed.775QX456-2	Keepsake	Yr.Iss.	7.75	15-30.00
89-147-010	Betsey Clark: Home for Christmas-Fourth Edition 500QX230-2	Keepsake	Yr.Iss.	5.00	12.50
89-147-011	Windows of the World-Fifth Ed.1075QX462-5	Keepsake	Yr.Iss.	10.75	17.50
89-147-012	Miniature Creche-Fifth Ed.925QX459-2	Keepsake	Yr.Iss.	9.25	16-20.00
89-147-013	Nostalgic Houses and Shops-Sixth Edition 1425QX458-2	Keepsake	Yr.Iss.	14.25	35.00
89-147-014	Wood Childhood Ornaments-Sixth Edition 775QX459-5	Keepsake	Yr.Iss.	7.75	20-22.00
89-147-015	Twelve Days of Christmas-Sixth Ed. 675QX381-2	Keepsake	Yr.Iss.	6.75	12.50-20.00
89-147-016	Porcelain Bear-Seventh Ed.875QX461-5	Keepsake	Yr.Iss.	8.75	15.00
89-147-017	Tin Locomotive-Eighth Ed.1475QX460-2	Keepsake	Yr.Iss.	14.75	25.00
89-147-018	Rocking Horse-Ninth Ed.1075QX462-2	Keepsake	Yr.Iss.	10.75	30.00
89-147-019	Frosty Friends-Tenth Ed.925QX457-2	Keepsake	Yr.Iss.	9.25	25-50.00
89-147-020	Here Comes Santa-Eleventh Ed.1475QX458-5	Keepsake	Yr.Iss.	14.75	35.00
89-147-021	Thimble-Twelfth Edition 575QX455-2	Keepsake	Yr.Iss.	5.75	12-18.00

Hallmark Keepsake Ornaments — 1989 Keepsake Magic Collection

Number	Name	Artist	Edition Limit	Issue Price	Quote
89-148-001	Baby's First Christmas 3000QLX727-2	Keepsake	Yr.Iss.	30.00	50-55.00
89-148-002	First Christmas Together1750QLX734-2	Keepsake	Yr.Iss.	17.50	35.00
89-148-003	Forest Frolics-First Edition2450QLX728-2	Keepsake	Yr.Iss.	24.50	85.00
89-148-004	Christmas Classics-Fourth Ed.1350QLX724-2	Keepsake	Yr.Iss.	13.50	25-30.00
89-148-005	Chris Mouse-Fifth Edition 950QLX722-5	Keepsake	Yr.Iss.	9.50	40-45.00
89-148-006	Joyous Carolers 3000QLX729-5	Keepsake	Yr.Iss.	30.00	60.00
89-148-007	Tiny Tinker 1950QLX717-4	Keepsake	Yr.Iss.	19.50	40.00
89-148-008	Rudolph the Red-Nosed Reindeer 1950QLX725-2	Keepsake	Yr.Iss.	19.50	40-50.00
89-148-009	Loving Spoonful 1950QLX726-2	Keepsake	Yr.Iss.	19.50	32.50
89-148-010	Holiday Bell 1750QLX722-2	Keepsake	Yr.Iss.	17.50	35.00
89-148-011	Busy Beaver 1750QLX724-5	Keepsake	Yr.Iss.	17.50	40.00
89-148-012	Backstage Bear 1350QLX721-5	Keepsake	Yr.Iss.	13.50	30-38.00
89-148-013	The Animals Speak 1350QLX723-2	Keepsake	Yr.Iss.	13.50	50.00
89-148-014	Angel Melody 950QLX720-2	Keepsake	Yr.Iss.	9.50	15-17.00
89-148-015	Unicorn Fantasy 950QLX723-5	Keepsake	Yr.Iss.	9.50	16-19.00
89-148-016	Moonlit Nap 875QLX713-4	Keepsake	Yr.Iss.	8.75	22.50
89-148-017	Kringle's Toy Shop 2450QLX701-7	Keepsake	Yr.Iss.	24.50	40-60.00
89-148-018	Metro Express 2800QLX727-5	Keepsake	Yr.Iss.	28.00	70-75.00
89-148-019	Spirit of St. Nick 2450QLX728-5	Keepsake	Yr.Iss.	24.50	65.00

Hallmark Keepsake Ornaments — 1989 Keepsake Miniature Ornaments

Number	Name	Artist	Edition Limit	Issue Price	Quote
89-149-001	Baby's First Christmas 600QXM573-2	Keepsake	Yr.Iss.	6.00	12.00
89-149-002	Mother 600QXM564-5	Keepsake	Yr.Iss.	6.00	10.00
89-149-003	First Christmas Together 850QXM564-2	Keepsake	Yr.Iss.	8.50	10.00
89-149-004	Lovebirds 600QXM563-5	Keepsake	Yr.Iss.	6.00	14.50
89-149-005	Special Friend 450QXM565-2	Keepsake	Yr.Iss.	4.50	14.00
89-149-006	Sharing a Ride 850QXM576-5	Keepsake	Yr.Iss.	8.50	15.00
89-149-007	Little Star Bringer 600QXM562-2	Keepsake	Yr.Iss.	6.00	18-32.00
89-149-008	Santa's Roadster 600QXM566-5	Keepsake	Yr.Iss.	6.00	15-25.00
89-149-009	Load of Cheer 600QXM574-5	Keepsake	Yr.Iss.	6.00	18-20.00
89-149-010	Slow Motion 600QXM575-2	Keepsake	Yr.Iss.	6.00	16.50
89-149-011	Merry Seal 600QXM575-5	Keepsake	Yr.Iss.	6.00	15.00
89-149-012	Starlit Mouse 450QXM565-5	Keepsake	Yr.Iss.	4.50	12-22.00
89-149-013	Little Soldier 450QXM567-5	Keepsake	Yr.Iss.	4.50	10.00
89-149-014	Acorn Squirrel 450QXM568-2	Keepsake	Yr.Iss.	4.50	12.00
89-149-015	Happy Bluebird 450QXM566-2	Keepsake	Yr.Iss.	4.50	10-21.00
89-149-016	Stocking Pal 450QXM567-2	Keepsake	Yr.Iss.	4.50	10-15.00
89-149-017	Scrimshaw Reindeer 450QXM568-5	Keepsake	Yr.Iss.	4.50	8-10.00
89-149-018	Folk Art Bunny 450QXM569-2	Keepsake	Yr.Iss.	4.50	12.00
89-149-019	Brass Snowflake 450QXM570-2	Keepsake	Yr.Iss.	4.50	8-14.00
89-149-020	Pinecone Basket 450QXM573-4	Keepsake	Yr.Iss.	4.50	8-40.00
89-149-021	Strollin' Snowman 450QXM574-2	Keepsake	Yr.Iss.	4.50	9.00
89-149-022	Brass Partridge 300QXM572-5	Keepsake	Yr.Iss.	3.00	5-12.00
89-149-023	Cozy Skater 450QXM573-5	Keepsake	Yr.Iss.	4.50	10-20.00
89-149-024	Old-World Santa 300QXM569-5	Keepsake	Yr.Iss.	3.00	6.00
89-149-025	Roly-Poly Ram 300QXM570-5	Keepsake	Yr.Iss.	3.00	10-15.00
89-149-026	Roly-Poly Pig 300QXM571-2	Keepsake	Yr.Iss.	3.00	8-10.00
89-149-027	Puppy Cart 300QXM571-5	Keepsake	Yr.Iss.	3.00	15.00
89-149-028	Kitty Cart 300QXM572-2	Keepsake	Yr.Iss.	3.00	8-15.00
89-149-029	Holiday Deer 300QXM577-2	Keepsake	Yr.Iss.	3.00	12.00
89-149-030	Bunny Hug 300QXM577-5	Keepsake	Yr.Iss.	3.00	11.00
89-149-031	Rejoice 300QXM578-2	Keepsake	Yr.Iss.	3.00	10.00
89-149-032	Holy Family 850QXM561-1	Keepsake	Yr.Iss.	8.50	14.50
89-149-033	Three Little Kitties 600QXM569-4	Keepsake	Yr.Iss.	6.00	18.50
89-149-034	Country Wreath 450QXM573-1	Keepsake	Yr.Iss.	4.50	12.00
89-149-035	Noel R.R.-First Edition 850QXM576-2	Keepsake	Yr.Iss.	8.50	20.00
89-149-036	The Kringles-First Edition600QXM562-2	Keepsake	Yr.Iss.	6.00	10-15.00
89-149-037	Old English Village-Second Ed.850QXM561-5	Keepsake	Yr.Iss.	8.50	17.00
89-149-038	Penguin Pal-Second Ed.450QXM560-2	Keepsake	Yr.Iss.	4.50	20-37.00
89-149-039	Rocking Horse-Second Ed. 450QXM560-5	Keepsake	Yr.Iss.	4.50	15.00
89-149-040	Kittens in Toyland-Second Ed.450QXM561-2	Keepsake	Yr.Iss.	4.50	15-20.00
89-149-041	Santa's Magic Ride 850QXM563-2	Keepsake	Yr.Iss.	8.50	15-20.00

Hallmark Keepsake Ornaments — 1989 Hallmark Keepsake Ornament Collector's Club

Number	Name	Artist	Edition Limit	Issue Price	Quote
89-150-001	Visit from Santa QXC580-2	Keepsake	Yr.Iss.	Unkn.	50.00
89-150-002	Collect a Dream 900QXC428-5	Keepsake	Yr.Iss.	9.00	40-65.00
89-150-003	Christmas is Peaceful 1850QXC451-2	Keepsake	Yr.Iss.	18.50	45.00
89-150-004	Noelle 1975QXC448-3	Keepsake	Yr.Iss.	19.75	32.00
89-150-005	Holiday Heirloom-Third Ed.2500QXC460-5	Keepsake	Yr.Iss.	25.00	35-44.00
89-150-006	Sitting Purrty QXC581-2	Keepsake	Yr.Iss.	Unkn.	45-54.00

Hallmark Keepsake Ornaments — 1990 Commemoratives

Number	Name	Artist	Edition Limit	Issue Price	Quote
90-151-001	Baby's First Christmas 975QX4853	Keepsake	Yr.Iss.	9.75	15.00
90-151-002	Baby's First Christmas 675QX3036	Keepsake	Yr.Iss.	6.75	10.00
90-151-003	Baby's First Christmas-Baby Boy475QX2063	Keepsake	Yr.Iss.	4.75	15-24.00
90-151-004	Baby's First Christmas-Baby Girl475QX2066	Keepsake	Yr.Iss.	4.75	15.00
90-151-005	Baby's First Christmas-Photo Holder 775QX4843	Keepsake	Yr.Iss.	7.75	16-20.00
90-151-006	Granddaughter's First Christmas675QX3106	Keepsake	Yr.Iss.	6.75	13.50
90-151-007	Mom-to-Be 575QX4916	Keepsake	Yr.Iss.	5.75	20-25.00
90-151-008	Grandson's First Christmas 675QX3063	Keepsake	Yr.Iss.	6.75	13.50
90-151-009	Dad-to-Be 575QX4913	Keepsake	Yr.Iss.	5.75	20-22.00
90-151-010	Baby's First Christmas 775QX4856	Keepsake	Yr.Iss.	7.75	20.00
90-151-011	Baby's Second Christmas 675QX4683	Keepsake	Yr.Iss.	6.75	20.00
90-151-012	Child's Third Christmas 675QX4866	Keepsake	Yr.Iss.	6.75	15.00
90-151-013	Child's Fourth Christmas 675QX4873	Keepsake	Yr.Iss.	6.75	15.00
90-151-014	Child's Fifth Christmas 675QX4876	Keepsake	Yr.Iss.	6.75	15.00
90-151-015	Sweetheart 1175QX4893	Keepsake	Yr.Iss.	11.75	20-23.00
90-151-016	Our First Christmas Together 975QX4883	Keepsake	Yr.Iss.	9.75	15.00
90-151-017	Our First Christmas Together -Photo Holder Ornament 775QX4886	Keepsake	Yr.Iss.	7.75	15.50

Company Number	Name	Series Artist	Edition Limit	Issue Price	Quote
90-151-018	Our First Christmas Together 675QX3146	Keepsake	Yr.Iss.	6.75	15-20.00
90-151-019	Our First Christmas Together 475QX2136	Keepsake	Yr.Iss.	4.75	12-15.00
90-151-020	Time for Love 475QX2133	Keepsake	Yr.Iss.	4.75	16.00
90-151-021	Peaceful Kingdom 475QX2106	Keepsake	Yr.Iss.	4.75	12.00
90-151-022	Jesus Loves Me 675QX3156	Keepsake	Yr.Iss.	6.75	13.50
90-151-023	Five Years Together 475QX2103	Keepsake	Yr.Iss.	4.75	15.00
90-151-024	Ten Years Together 475QX2153	Keepsake	Yr.Iss.	4.75	13-15.00
90-151-025	Twenty-Five Years Together 975QX4896	Keepsake	Yr.Iss.	9.75	19.50
90-151-026	Forty Years Together 975QX4903	Keepsake	Yr.Iss.	9.75	19.50
90-151-027	Fifty Years Together 975QX4906	Keepsake	Yr.Iss.	9.75	19.50
90-151-028	Mother 875QX4536	Keepsake	Yr.Iss.	8.75	15.50
90-151-029	Dad 675QX4533	Keepsake	Yr.Iss.	6.75	18.00
90-151-030	Mom and Dad 875QX4593	Keepsake	Yr.Iss.	8.75	20.00
90-151-031	Grandmother 475QX2236	Keepsake	Yr.Iss.	4.75	15.00
90-151-032	Grandparents 475QX2253	Keepsake	Yr.Iss.	4.75	10.00
90-151-033	Godchild 675QX3167	Keepsake	Yr.Iss.	6.75	14-21.00
90-151-034	Son 575QX4516	Keepsake	Yr.Iss.	5.75	15.00
90-151-035	Daughter 575QX4496	Keepsake	Yr.Iss.	5.75	15.00
90-151-036	Brother 575QX4493	Keepsake	Yr.Iss.	5.75	10.00
90-151-037	Sister 475QX2273	Keepsake	Yr.Iss.	4.75	17.50
90-151-038	Grandson 475QX2293	Keepsake	Yr.Iss.	4.75	12-18.00
90-151-039	Granddaughter 475QX2286	Keepsake	Yr.Iss.	4.75	15-29.00
90-151-040	Friendship Kitten 675QX4142	Keepsake	Yr.Iss.	6.75	20-22.00
90-151-041	New Home 675QX4343	Keepsake	Yr.Iss.	6.75	15.00
90-151-042	Across The Miles 675QX3173	Keepsake	Yr.Iss.	6.75	13.50-17.50
90-151-043	From Our Home to Yours 475QX2166	Keepsake	Yr.Iss.	4.75	9.50
90-151-044	Teacher 775QX4483	Keepsake	Yr.Iss.	7.75	15.50
90-151-045	Copy of Cheer 775QX4486	Keepsake	Yr.Iss.	7.75	15.50
90-151-046	Child Care Giver 675QX3166	Keepsake	Yr.Iss.	6.75	13.50
Hallmark Keepsake Ornaments		**1990 New Attractions**			
90-152-001	S. Claus Taxi 1175QX4686	Keepsake	Yr.Iss.	11.75	25-30.00
90-152-002	Coyote Carols 875QX4993	Keepsake	Yr.Iss.	8.75	19.50
90-152-003	King Klaus 775QX4106	Keepsake	Yr.Iss.	7.75	18-28.00
90-152-004	Hot Dogger 775QX4976	Keepsake	Yr.Iss.	7.75	18-29.00
90-152-005	Poolside Walrus 775QX4986	Keepsake	Yr.Iss.	7.75	15.50
90-152-006	Three Little Piggies 775QX4996	Keepsake	Yr.Iss.	7.75	16-28.00
90-152-007	Billboard Bunny 775QX5196	Keepsake	Yr.Iss.	7.75	10-15.50
90-152-008	Mooy Christmas 675QX4933	Keepsake	Yr.Iss.	6.75	20-25.00
90-152-009	Pepperoni Mouse 675QX4973	Keepsake	Yr.Iss.	6.75	20.00
90-152-010	Santa Schnoz 675QX4983	Keepsake	Yr.Iss.	6.75	20-28.00
90-152-011	Cozy Goose 575QX4966	Keepsake	Yr.Iss.	5.75	12.25
90-152-012	Two Peas in a Pod 475QX4926	Keepsake	Yr.Iss.	4.75	25.00
90-152-013	Chiming In 975QX4366	Keepsake	Yr.Iss.	9.75	23-30.00
90-152-014	Christmas Croc 775QX4373	Keepsake	Yr.Iss.	7.75	15.50
90-152-015	Born to Dance 775QX5043	Keepsake	Yr.Iss.	7.75	15-24.00
90-152-016	Stocking Pals 1075QX5493	Keepsake	Yr.Iss.	10.75	22.00
90-152-017	Home for the Owlidays 675QX5183	Keepsake	Yr.Iss.	6.75	14-21.00
90-152-018	Baby Unicorn 975QX5486	Keepsake	Yr.Iss.	9.75	19.50
90-152-019	Spoon Rider 975QX5496	Keepsake	Yr.Iss.	9.75	20-24.00
90-152-020	Lovable Dears 875QX5476	Keepsake	Yr.Iss.	8.75	11-17.50
90-152-021	Meow Mart 775QX4446	Keepsake	Yr.Iss.	7.75	20.00
90-152-022	Perfect Catch 775QX4693	Keepsake	Yr.Iss.	7.75	16-26.00
90-152-023	Nutshell Chat 675QX5193	Keepsake	Yr.Iss.	6.75	13-21.00
90-152-024	Gingerbread Elf 575QX5033	Keepsake	Yr.Iss.	5.75	10.00
90-152-025	Stitches of Joy 775QX5186	Keepsake	Yr.Iss.	7.75	11.25
90-152-026	Little Drummer Boy 775QX5233	Keepsake	Yr.Iss.	7.75	20-29.00
90-152-027	Goose Cart 775QX5236	Keepsake	Yr.Iss.	7.75	16-23.00
90-152-028	Holiday Cardinals 775QX5243	Keepsake	Yr.Iss.	7.75	15-18.00
90-152-029	Christmas Partridge 775QX5246	Keepsake	Yr.Iss.	7.75	15.50
90-152-030	Joy is in the Air 775QX5503	Keepsake	Yr.Iss.	7.75	18-30.00
90-152-031	Happy Voices 675QX4645	Keepsake	Yr.Iss.	6.75	14.50
90-152-032	Jolly Dolphin 675QX4683	Keepsake	Yr.Iss.	6.75	28-35.00
90-152-033	Long Winter's Nap 675QX4703	Keepsake	Yr.Iss.	6.75	17.50
90-152-034	Hang in There 675QX4713	Keepsake	Yr.Iss.	6.75	14-24.00
90-152-035	Kitty's Best Pal 675QX4716	Keepsake	Yr.Iss.	6.75	20-22.50
90-152-036	SNOOPY and WOODSTOCK 675QX4723	Keepsake	Yr.Iss.	6.75	15.00
90-152-037	Beary Good Deal 675QX4733	Keepsake	Yr.Iss.	6.75	13.50
90-152-038	Country Angel 675QX5046	Keepsake	Yr.Iss.	6.75	150.00
90-152-039	Feliz Navidad 675QX5173	Keepsake	Yr.Iss.	6.75	15-32.00
90-152-040	Bearback Rider 975QX5483	Keepsake	Yr.Iss.	9.75	20-27.00
90-152-041	Polar Sport 775QX5156	Keepsake	Yr.Iss.	7.75	15.50
90-152-042	Polar Pair 575QX4626	Keepsake	Yr.Iss.	5.75	15.00
90-152-043	Polar Video 575QX4633	Keepsake	Yr.Iss.	5.75	12-19.00
90-152-044	Polar V.I.P. 575QX4663	Keepsake	Yr.Iss.	5.75	11.50
90-152-045	Polar TV 775QX5166	Keepsake	Yr.Iss.	7.75	15.00
90-152-046	Polar Jogger 575QX4666	Keepsake	Yr.Iss.	5.75	12-19.00
90-152-047	Garfield 475QX2303	Keepsake	Yr.Iss.	4.75	18-20.00
90-152-048	Peanuts 475QX2233	Keepsake	Yr.Iss.	4.75	20.00
90-152-049	Norman Rockwell Art 475QX2296	Keepsake	Yr.Iss.	4.75	15.00
Hallmark Keepsake Ornaments		**1990 Artists' Favorites**			
90-153-001	Donder's Diner 1375QX4823	Keepsake	Yr.Iss.	13.75	18-39.00
90-153-002	Welcome, Santa 1175QX4773	Keepsake	Yr.Iss.	11.75	19-23.00
90-153-003	Happy Woodcutter 975QX4763	Keepsake	Yr.Iss.	9.75	20-26.00
90-153-004	Angel Kitty 875QX4746	Keepsake	Yr.Iss.	8.75	15-20.00
90-153-005	Gentle Dreamers 875QX4756	Keepsake	Yr.Iss.	8.75	30.00
90-153-006	Mouseboat 775QX4753	Keepsake	Yr.Iss.	7.75	15-23.00
Hallmark Keepsake Ornaments		**1990 Special Edition**			
90-154-001	Dickens Caroler Bell-Mr. Ashbourne 2175QX5056	Keepsake	Yr.Iss.	21.75	35-45.00
Hallmark Keepsake Ornaments		**1990 Collectible Series**			
90-155-001	Merry Olde Santa-First Edition 1475QX4736	Keepsake	Yr.Iss.	14.75	45-74.50
90-155-002	Greatest Story-First Edition 1275QX4656	Keepsake	Yr.Iss.	12.75	15.00
90-155-003	Heart of Christmas-First Edition 1375QX4726	Keepsake	Yr.Iss.	13.75	40-75.00
90-155-004	Fabulous Decade-First Edition 775QX4466	Keepsake	Yr.Iss.	7.75	20-44.00
90-155-005	Christmas Kitty-Second Edition 1475QX4506	Keepsake	Yr.Iss.	14.75	20-32.00
90-155-006	Winter Surprise-Second Edition 1075QX4443	Keepsake	Yr.Iss.	10.75	25-33.00
90-155-007	CRAYOLA Crayon-Bright Moving Colors-Second Edition 875QX4586	Keepsake	Yr.Iss.	8.75	25-40.00
90-155-008	Hark! It's Herald-Second Edition 675QX4463	Keepsake	Yr.Iss.	6.75	11-20.00
90-155-009	The Gift Bringers-St. Lucia-Second Edition 500QX2803	Keepsake	Yr.Iss.	5.00	8-20.00
90-155-010	Mary's Angels-Rosebud-Third Edition 575QX4423	Keepsake	Yr.Iss.	5.75	25-37.00
90-155-011	Cookies for Santa-Fourth Edition 875QX4436	Keepsake	Yr.Iss.	8.75	25.00
90-155-012	Popcorn Party-Fifth Edition 1375QX4393	Keepsake	Yr.Iss.	13.75	40.00
90-155-013	Reindeer Champs-Comet-Fifth Edition 775QX4433	Keepsake	Yr.Iss.	7.75	9-18.00
90-155-014	Betsey Clark: Home for Christmas-Fifth Edition 500QX2033	Keepsake	Yr.Iss.	5.00	10-17.50

Company Number	Name	Series Artist	Edition Limit	Issue Price	Quote
90-155-015	Holiday Home-Seventh Edition 1475QX4696	Keepsake	Yr.Iss.	14.75	35-40.00
90-155-016	Seven Swans A-Swimming-Seventh Edition 675QX3033	Keepsake	Yr.Iss.	6.75	15.00
90-155-017	Rocking Horse-Tenth Edition 1075QX4646	Keepsake	Yr.Iss.	10.75	50-57.50
90-155-018	Frosty Friends-Eleventh Edition 975QX4396	Keepsake	Yr.Iss.	9.75	20-32.00
90-155-019	Festive Surrey-Twelfth Edition 1475QX4923	Keepsake	Yr.Iss.	14.75	20-34.50
90-155-020	Irish-Sixth Edition 1075QX4636	Keepsake	Yr.Iss.	10.75	15-22.00
90-155-021	Cinnamon Bear-Eighth Edition 875QX4426	Keepsake	Yr.Iss.	8.75	15-32.00
Hallmark Keepsake Ornaments		**1990 Keepsake Magic Ornaments**			
90-156-001	Children's Express 2800QLX7243	Keepsake	Yr.Iss.	28.00	55-76.00
90-156-002	Hop 'N Pop Popper 2000QLX7353	Keepsake	Yr.Iss.	20.00	55-89.00
90-156-003	Baby's First Christmas 2800QLX7246	Keepsake	Yr.Iss.	28.00	50-59.00
90-156-004	Christmas Memories 2500QLX7276	Keepsake	Yr.Iss.	25.00	40-55.00
90-156-005	Forest Frolics 2500QLX7236	Keepsake	Yr.Iss.	25.00	60-75.00
90-156-006	Santa's Ho-Ho-Hoedown 2500QLX7256	Keepsake	Yr.Iss.	25.00	50-65.00
90-156-007	Mrs. Santa's Kitchen 2500QLX7263	Keepsake	Yr.Iss.	25.00	55-60.00
90-156-008	Song and Dance 2000QLX7253	Keepsake	Yr.Iss.	20.00	65.00
90-156-009	Elfin Whittler 2000QLX7265	Keepsake	Yr.Iss.	20.00	25-45.00
90-156-010	Deer Crossing 1800QLX7213	Keepsake	Yr.Iss.	18.00	40-45.00
90-156-011	Our First Christmas Together 1800QLX7255	Keepsake	Yr.Iss.	18.00	40-45.00
90-156-012	Holiday Flash 1800QLX7333	Keepsake	Yr.Iss.	18.00	36.00
90-156-013	Starship Christmas 1800QLX7336	Keepsake	Yr.Iss.	18.00	30-45.00
90-156-014	Partridges in a Pear 1400QLX7212	Keepsake	Yr.Iss.	14.00	28.00
90-156-015	Letter to Santa 1400QLX7226	Keepsake	Yr.Iss.	14.00	18-34.00
90-156-016	Starlight Angel 1400QLX7306	Keepsake	Yr.Iss.	14.00	19-28.00
90-156-017	The Littlest Angel 1400QLX7303	Keepsake	Yr.Iss.	14.00	28.00
90-156-018	Blessings of Love 1400QLX7363	Keepsake	Yr.Iss.	14.00	35-54.00
90-156-019	Chris Mouse Wreath 1000QLX7296	Keepsake	Yr.Iss.	10.00	28-39.00
90-156-020	Beary Short Nap 1000QLX7326	Keepsake	Yr.Iss.	10.00	20-23.00
90-156-021	Elf of the Year 1000QLX7356	Keepsake	Yr.Iss.	10.00	20-26.00
Hallmark Keepsake Ornaments		**1990 Keepsake Miniature Ornaments**			
90-157-001	Thimble Bells 600QXM5543	Keepsake	Yr.Iss.	6.00	15-30.00
90-157-002	Nature's Angels 450QMX5733	Keepsake	Yr.Iss.	4.50	10.00
90-157-003	Cloisonne Poinsettia 1050QMX5533	Keepsake	Yr.Iss.	10.50	15.00
90-157-004	Coal Car 850QXM5756	Keepsake	Yr.Iss.	8.50	15-25.00
90-157-005	School 850QXM5763	Keepsake	Yr.Iss.	8.50	15-30.00
90-157-006	The Kringles 600QXM5753	Keepsake	Yr.Iss.	6.00	12-30.00
90-157-007	Kittens in Toyland 450QXM5736	Keepsake	Yr.Iss.	4.50	30.00
90-157-008	Rocking Horse 450QXM5743	Keepsake	Yr.Iss.	4.50	15-20.00
90-157-009	Penguin Pal 450QXM5746	Keepsake	Yr.Iss.	4.50	10.00
90-157-010	Santa's Streetcar 850QQXM5766	Keepsake	Yr.Iss.	8.50	17.00
90-157-011	Snow Angel 600QXM5773	Keepsake	Yr.Iss.	6.00	10-12.00
90-157-012	Baby's First Christmas 850QXM5703	Keepsake	Yr.Iss.	8.50	7.00
90-157-013	Grandchild's First Christmas 600QXM5723	Keepsake	Yr.Iss.	6.00	7.00
90-157-014	Special Friends 600QXM5726	Keepsake	Yr.Iss.	6.00	10-14.00
90-157-015	Mother 450QXM5716	Keepsake	Yr.Iss.	4.50	12-19.00
90-157-016	Warm Memories 450QXM5713	Keepsake	Yr.Iss.	4.50	10-19.00
90-157-017	First Christmas Together 600QXM5536	Keepsake	Yr.Iss.	6.00	7.00
90-157-018	Loving Hearts 300QXM5523	Keepsake	Yr.Iss.	3.00	6-14.00
90-157-019	Stringing Along 850QXM5606	Keepsake	Yr.Iss.	8.50	17.00
90-157-020	Santa's Journey 850QXM5826	Keepsake	Yr.Iss.	8.50	25.00
90-157-021	Wee Nutcracker 850QXM5843	Keepsake	Yr.Iss.	8.50	20.00
90-157-022	Bear Hug 600QXM5633	Keepsake	Yr.Iss.	6.00	12-20.00
90-157-023	Acorn Wreath 600QXM5686	Keepsake	Yr.Iss.	6.00	12.00
90-157-024	Puppy Love 600QXM5666	Keepsake	Yr.Iss.	6.00	12.00
90-157-025	Madonna and Child 600QXM5643	Keepsake	Yr.Iss.	6.00	12.00
90-157-026	Basket Buddy 600QXM5696	Keepsake	Yr.Iss.	6.00	12.00
90-157-027	Ruby Reindeer 600QXM5816	Keepsake	Yr.Iss.	6.00	12.00
90-157-028	Perfect Fit 450QXM5516	Keepsake	Yr.Iss.	4.50	13-18.00
90-157-029	Panda's Surprise 450QXM5616	Keepsake	Yr.Iss.	4.50	13.50
90-157-030	Stamp Collector 450QXM5623	Keepsake	Yr.Iss.	4.50	10.00
90-157-031	Christmas Dove 450QXM5636	Keepsake	Yr.Iss.	4.50	12-19.00
90-157-032	Type of Joy 450QXM5646	Keepsake	Yr.Iss.	4.50	12-17.00
90-157-033	Teacher 450QXM5653	Keepsake	Yr.Iss.	4.50	10-17.00
90-157-034	Air Santa 450QXM5656	Keepsake	Yr.Iss.	4.50	9-13.00
90-157-035	Sweet Slumber 450QXM5663	Keepsake	Yr.Iss.	4.50	12-15.00
90-157-036	Busy Carver 450QXM5673	Keepsake	Yr.Iss.	4.50	10.00
90-157-037	Lion and Lamb 450QXM5676	Keepsake	Yr.Iss.	4.50	15-19.00
90-157-038	Going Sledding 450QXM5683	Keepsake	Yr.Iss.	4.50	9.50
90-157-039	Country Heart 450QXM5693	Keepsake	Yr.Iss.	4.50	10-19.00
90-157-040	Nativity 450QXM5706	Keepsake	Yr.Iss.	4.50	10-13.00
90-157-041	Holiday Cardinal 300QXM5526	Keepsake	Yr.Iss.	3.00	9-12.00
90-157-042	Brass Bouquet 600QMX5776	Keepsake	Yr.Iss.	6.00	6.50
90-157-043	Brass Santa 300QXM5786	Keepsake	Yr.Iss.	3.00	7-15.00
90-157-044	Brass Horn 300QXM5793	Keepsake	Yr.Iss.	3.00	12.00
90-157-045	Brass Peace 300QXM5796	Keepsake	Yr.Iss.	3.00	7.00
90-157-046	Brass Year 300QXM5833	Keepsake	Yr.Iss.	3.00	7.00
Hallmark Keepsake Ornaments		**1990 Limited Edition**			
90-158-001	Dove of Peace 2475QXC447-6	Keepsake	25,400	24.75	55.00
90-158-002	Christmas Limited1975 QXC476-6	Keepsake	38,700	19.75	65-85.00
90-158-003	Sugar Plum Fairy 2775QXC447-3	Keepsake	25,400	27.75	45-60.00
Hallmark Keepsake Ornaments		**1990 Keepsake Collector's Club**			
90-159-001	Club Hollow QXC445-6	Keepsake	Yr.Iss.	Unkn.	30-46.00
90-159-002	Crown Prince QXC560-3	Keepsake	Yr.Iss.	Unkn.	30-40.00
90-159-003	Armful of Joy 800QXC445-3	Keepsake	Yr.Iss.	8.00	45-50.00
Hallmark Keepsake Ornaments		**1991 Commemoratives**			
91-160-001	Baby's First Christmas 1775QX5107	Keepsake	Yr.Iss.	17.75	25-42.50
91-160-002	Baby's First Christmas-Baby Boy475QX2217	Keepsake	Yr.Iss.	4.75	10-18.00
91-160-003	Baby's First Christmas-Baby Girl475QX2227	Keepsake	Yr.Iss.	4.75	10.00
91-160-004	Baby's First Christmas-Photo Holder 775QX4869	Keepsake	Yr.Iss.	7.75	12-20.00
91-160-005	Mom-to-Be 575QX4877	Keepsake	Yr.Iss.	5.75	15.00
91-160-006	Dad-to-Be 575QX4879	Keepsake	Yr.Iss.	5.75	15.00
91-160-007	Grandson's First Christmas 675QX5117	Keepsake	Yr.Iss.	6.75	10.00
91-160-008	Granddaughter's First Christmas 675QX5119	Keepsake	Yr.Iss.	6.75	10.00
91-160-009	A Child's Christmas 975QX4887	Keepsake	Yr.Iss.	9.75	15.50
91-160-010	Baby's First Christmas 775QX4889	Keepsake	Yr.Iss.	7.75	18-29.50
91-160-011	Baby's Second Christmas 675QX4897	Keepsake	Yr.Iss.	6.75	11.25-20.00
91-160-012	Child's Third Christmas 675QX4899	Keepsake	Yr.Iss.	6.75	15.00
91-160-013	Child's Fourth Christmas 675QX4907	Keepsake	Yr.Iss.	6.75	15.00
91-160-014	Child's Fifth Christmas 675QX4909	Keepsake	Yr.Iss.	6.75	15.00
91-160-015	Sweetheart 975QX4957	Keepsake	Yr.Iss.	9.75	17.50
91-160-016	Our First Christmas Together-Photo Holder 875QX4917	Keepsake	Yr.Iss.	8.75	15.00
91-160-017	Our First Christmas Together 875QX4919	Keepsake	Yr.Iss.	8.75	20.00
91-160-018	Our First Christmas Together 675QX3139	Keepsake	Yr.Iss.	6.75	15.00
91-160-019	Our First Christmas Together 475QX2229	Keepsake	Yr.Iss.	4.75	15-20.00
91-160-020	Under the Mistletoe 875QX4949	Keepsake	Yr.Iss.	8.75	20.00
91-160-021	Jesus Loves Me 775QX3147	Keepsake	Yr.Iss.	7.75	15.50

Company Number	Name	Series Artist	Edition Limit	Issue Price	Quote
91-160-022	Five Years Together 775QX4927	Keepsake	Yr.Iss.	7.75	15.50
91-160-023	Ten Years Together 775QX4929	Keepsake	Yr.Iss.	7.75	15.50
91-160-024	Twenty -Five Years Together 875QX4937	Keepsake	Yr.Iss.	8.75	19.50
91-160-025	Forty Years Together 775QX4939	Keepsake	Yr.Iss.	7.75	19.50
91-160-026	Fifty Years Together 875QX4947	Keepsake	Yr.Iss.	8.75	16-20.00
91-160-027	Mother 975QX5457	Keepsake	Yr.Iss.	9.75	15.00
91-160-028	Dad 775QX5127	Keepsake	Yr.Iss.	7.75	19.50
91-160-029	Mom and Dad 975QX5467	Keepsake	Yr.Iss.	9.75	22.00
91-160-030	Grandmother 475QX2307	Keepsake	Yr.Iss.	4.75	10-15.50
91-160-031	Grandparents 475QX2309	Keepsake	Yr.Iss.	4.75	10.00
91-160-032	Godchild 675QX5489	Keepsake	Yr.Iss.	6.75	15.50
91-160-033	Son 575QX5469	Keepsake	Yr.Iss.	5.75	12.00
91-160-034	Daughter 575QX5477	Keepsake	Yr.Iss.	5.75	12.00
91-160-035	Brother 675QX5479	Keepsake	Yr.Iss.	6.75	12.00
91-160-036	Sister 675QX5487	Keepsake	Yr.Iss.	6.75	19.50-29.00
91-160-037	Grandson 475QX2297	Keepsake	Yr.Iss.	4.75	15.50
91-160-038	Granddaughter 475QX2299	Keepsake	Yr.Iss.	4.75	16-22.00
91-160-039	Friends Are Fun 975QX5289	Keepsake	Yr.Iss.	9.75	17-20.00
91-160-040	Extra-Special Friends 475QX2279	Keepsake	Yr.Iss.	4.75	15.50
91-160-041	New Home 675QX5449	Keepsake	Yr.Iss.	6.75	15.00
91-160-042	Across the Miles 675QX3157	Keepsake	Yr.Iss.	6.75	15.50
91-160-043	From Our Home to Yours 475QX2287	Keepsake	Yr.Iss.	4.75	12.50
91-160-044	Terrific Teacher 675QX5309	Keepsake	Yr.Iss.	6.75	13.50
91-160-045	Teacher 475QX2289	Keepsake	Yr.Iss.	4.75	14-25.00
91-160-046	Gift of Joy 875QX5319	Keepsake	Yr.Iss.	8.75	19.50
91-160-047	The Big Cheese 675QX5327	Keepsake	Yr.Iss.	6.75	10.00
Hallmark Keepsake Ornaments		**1991 New Attractions**			
91-161-001	Winnie-the Pooh 975QX5569	Keepsake	Yr.Iss.	9.75	37.50-55.00
91-161-002	Piglet and Eeyore 975QX5577	Keepsake	Yr.Iss.	9.75	45.00
91-161-003	Christopher Robin 975QX5579	Keepsake	Yr.Iss.	9.75	40.00
91-161-004	Rabbit 975QX5607	Keepsake	Yr.Iss.	9.75	20-30.00
91-161-005	Tigger 975QX5609	Keepsake	Yr.Iss.	9.75	95-100.00
91-161-006	Kanga and Roo 975QX5617	Keepsake	Yr.Iss.	9.75	40.00
91-161-007	Look Out Below 875QX4959	Keepsake	Yr.Iss.	8.75	17.50-22.00
91-161-008	Yule Logger 875QX4967	Keepsake	Yr.Iss.	8.75	17.50-22.00
91-161-009	Glee Club Bears 87566QX4969	Keepsake	Yr.Iss.	8.75	24.00
91-161-010	Plum Delightful 875QX4977	Keepsake	Yr.Iss.	8.75	20.00
91-161-011	Snow Twins 875QX4979	Keepsake	Yr.Iss.	8.75	25.00
91-161-012	Loving Stitches 875QX4987	Keepsake	Yr.Iss.	8.75	35.00
91-161-013	Fanfare Bear 875QX5337	Keepsake	Yr.Iss.	8.75	25.00
91-161-014	Mrs. Cratchit 1375QX4999	Keepsake	Yr.Iss.	13.75	23-38.00
91-161-015	Merry Carolers 2975QX4799	Keepsake	Yr.Iss.	29.75	49.50
91-161-016	Ebenezer Scrooge 1375QX4989	Keepsake	Yr.Iss.	13.75	27.50
91-161-017	Bob Cratchit 1375QX4997	Keepsake	Yr.Iss.	13.75	22.50
91-161-018	Tiny Tim 1075QX5037	Keepsake	Yr.Iss.	10.75	23-33.00
91-161-019	Evergreen Inn 875QX5389	Keepsake	Yr.Iss.	8.75	15.50
91-161-020	Santa's Studio 875QX5397	Keepsake	Yr.Iss.	8.75	15.50
91-161-021	Holiday Cafe 875QX5399	Keepsake	Yr.Iss.	8.75	15.50
91-161-022	Jolly Wolly Santa 775QX5419	Keepsake	Yr.Iss.	7.75	15-26.50
91-161-023	Jolly Wolly Snowman 775QX5427	Keepsake	Yr.Iss.	7.75	15-22.50
91-161-024	Jolly Wolly Soldier 775QX5429	Keepsake	Yr.Iss.	7.75	15-22.50
91-161-025	Partridge in a Pear Tree 975QX5297	Keepsake	Yr.Iss.	9.75	19.50
91-161-026	Christmas Welcome 975QX5299	Keepsake	Yr.Iss.	9.75	19.50
91-161-027	Night Before Christmas 975QX5307	Keepsake	Yr.Iss.	9.75	18-25.00
91-161-028	SNOOPY and WOODSTOCK 675QX5197	Keepsake	Yr.Iss.	6.75	12.50-24.50
91-161-029	PEANUTS 500QX2257	Keepsake	Yr.Iss.	5.00	10-22.50
91-161-030	GARFIELD 775QX5177	Keepsake	Yr.Iss.	7.75	20.00
91-161-031	Norman Rockwell Art 500QX2259	Keepsake	Yr.Iss.	5.00	16.00
91-161-032	Mary Engelbreit 475QX2237	Keepsake	Yr.Iss.	4.75	19.50
91-161-033	Up 'N'Down Journey 975QX5047	Keepsake	Yr.Iss.	9.75	23-25.00
91-161-034	Old-Fashioned Sled 875QX4317	Keepsake	Yr.Iss.	8.75	20-26.00
91-161-035	Folk Art Reindeer 875QX5359	Keepsake	Yr.Iss.	8.75	15.50
91-161-036	Sweet Talk 875QX5367	Keepsake	Yr.Iss.	8.75	12.50
91-161-037	Snowy Owl 775QX5269	Keepsake	Yr.Iss.	7.75	20.00
91-161-038	Dinoclaus 775QX5277	Keepsake	Yr.Iss.	7.75	19.50
91-161-039	Basket Bell Players 775QX5377	Keepsake	Yr.Iss.	7.75	16-25.00
91-161-040	Nutshell Nativity 675QX5176	Keepsake	Yr.Iss.	6.75	20-28.00
91-161-041	Cuddly Lamb 675QX5199	Keepsake	Yr.Iss.	6.75	19.50
91-161-042	Feliz Navidad 675QX5279	Keepsake	Yr.Iss.	6.75	13.50
91-161-043	Polar Classic 675QX5287	Keepsake	Yr.Iss.	6.75	17.50
91-161-044	All-Star 675QX5329	Keepsake	Yr.Iss.	6.75	18-26.00
91-161-045	Chilly Chap 675QX5339	Keepsake	Yr.Iss.	6.75	15-20.00
91-161-046	On a Roll 675QX5347	Keepsake	Yr.Iss.	6.75	20-26.00
91-161-047	Joyous Memories-Photoholder 675QX5369	Keepsake	Yr.Iss.	6.75	17.50
91-161-048	Ski Lift Bunny 675QX5447	Keepsake	Yr.Iss.	6.75	15.50
91-161-049	Nutty Squirrel 575QX4833	Keepsake	Yr.Iss.	5.75	15.50
91-161-050	Notes of Cheer 575QX5357	Keepsake	Yr.Iss.	5.75	15.50
Hallmark Keepsake Ornaments		**1991 Artists' Favorites**			
91-162-001	Polar Circus Wagon 1375QX4399	Keepsake	Yr.Iss.	13.75	30-35.00
91-162-002	Noah's Ark 1375QX4867	Keepsake	Yr.Iss.	13.75	25-39.50
91-162-003	Santa Sailor 975QX4389	Keepsake	Yr.Iss.	9.75	15-22.00
91-162-004	Hooked on Santa 775QX4109	Keepsake	Yr.Iss.	7.75	15-28.00
91-162-005	Fiddlin' Around 775QX4387	Keepsake	Yr.Iss.	7.75	15-18.00
91-162-006	Tramp and Laddie 775QX4397	Keepsake	Yr.Iss.	7.75	15.00
Hallmark Keepsake Ornaments		**1991 Special Edition**			
91-163-001	Dickens Caroler Bell-Mrs. Beaumont -2175QX5039	Keepsake	Yr.Iss.	21.75	32.50-49.50
Hallmark Keepsake Ornaments		**1991 Collectible Series**			
91-164-001	1957 Corvette-First Edition1275QX4319	Keepsake	Yr.Iss.	12.75	95-195.00
91-164-002	Peace on Earth-Italy First Ed. 1175QX5129	Keepsake	Yr.Iss.	11.75	15-34.50
91-164-003	Heavenly Angels-First Edition 775QX4367	Keepsake	Yr.Iss.	7.75	20.00
91-164-004	Puppy Love-First Edition 775QX5379	Keepsake	Yr.Iss.	7.75	25-47.50
91-164-005	Merry Olde Santa-Second Ed. 1475QX4359	Keepsake	Yr.Iss.	14.75	40-75.00
91-164-006	Heart of Christmas-Second Ed. 1375QX4357	Keepsake	Yr.Iss.	13.75	20-25.00
91-164-007	Greatest Story-Second Edition 1275QX4129	Keepsake	Yr.Iss.	12.75	25.50
91-164-008	Fabulous Decade-Second Ed. 775QX4119	Keepsake	Yr.Iss.	7.75	20-22.50
91-164-009	Winter Surprise-Third Ed. 1075QX4277	Keepsake	Yr.Iss.	10.75	15.00
91-164-010	CRAYOLA CRAYON-Bright Vibrant Carols-Third Edition 975QX4219	Keepsake	Yr.Iss.	9.75	20-38.00
91-164-011	Hark! It's Herald Third Edition 675QX4379	Keepsake	Yr.Iss.	6.75	12-32.00
91-164-012	The Gift Bringers-Christkind Third Edition 500QX2117	Keepsake	Yr.Iss.	5.00	15.00
91-164-013	Mary's Angels-Iris Fourth Ed. 675QX4279	Keepsake	Yr.Iss.	6.75	16-40.00
91-164-014	Let It Snow! Fifth Ediiton 875QX4369	Keepsake	Yr.Iss.	8.75	20-25.00
91-164-015	Checking His List Sixth Edition 1375QX4339	Keepsake	Yr.Iss.	13.75	25-30.00
91-164-016	Reindeer Champ-Cupid Sixth Ed. 775QX4347	Keepsake	Yr.Iss.	7.75	15-33.00
91-164-017	Fire Station-Eigth Edition 1475QX4139	Keepsake	Yr.Iss.	14.75	26-35.00
91-164-018	Eight Maids A-Milking-Eigth Ed. 675QX3089	Keepsake	Yr.Iss.	6.75	10-15.00
91-164-019	Rocking Horse-11th Ed. 1075QX4147	Keepsake	Yr.Iss.	10.75	20.00
91-164-020	Frosty Friends-Twelfth Edition 975QX4327	Keepsake	Yr.Iss.	9.75	25-39.50
91-164-021	Santa's Antique Car-13th Ed. 1475QX4349	Keepsake	Yr.Iss.	14.75	28-33.00
91-164-022	Christmas Kitty-Third Edition 1475QX4377	Keepsake	Yr.Iss.	14.75	20-32.00
91-164-023	Betsey Clark: Home for Christmas Sixth Edition 500QX2109	Keepsake	Yr.Iss.	5.00	10.00
Hallmark Keepsake Ornaments		**1991 Keepsake Magic Ornaments**			
91-165-001	PEANUTS 1800QLX7229	Keepsake	Yr.Iss.	18.00	40-55.00
91-165-002	Santa Special 4000QLX7167	Keepsake	Yr.Iss.	40.00	65-80.00
91-165-003	Salvation Army Band 3000QLX7273	Keepsake	Yr.Iss.	30.00	55-77.50
91-165-004	Forest Frolics 2500QLX7219	Keepsake	Yr.Iss.	25.00	55-69.50
91-165-005	Chris Mouse Mail 1000QLX7207	Keepsake	Yr.Iss.	10.00	25-39.50
91-165-006	Arctic Dome 2500QLX7117	Keepsake	Yr.Iss.	25.00	49.50
91-165-007	Baby's First Christmas 3000QLX7247	Keepsake	Yr.Iss.	30.00	55-90.00
91-165-008	Bringing Home the Tree-2800QLX7249	Keepsake	Yr.Iss.	28.00	55.50
91-165-009	Ski Trip 2800QLX7266	Keepsake	Yr.Iss.	28.00	45-60.00
91-165-010	Kringles's Bumper Cars-2500QLX7119	Keepsake	Yr.Iss.	25.00	49.50
91-165-011	Our First Christmas Together-2500QXL7137	Keepsake	Yr.Iss.	25.00	35.00
91-165-012	Jingle Bears 2500QLX7323	Keepsake	Yr.Iss.	25.00	49.50
91-165-013	Toyland Tower 2000QLX7129	Keepsake	Yr.Iss.	20.00	35-49.50
91-165-014	Mole Family Home 2000QLX7149	Keepsake	Yr.Iss.	20.00	40-46.00
91-165-015	Starship Enterprise 2000QLX7199	Keepsake	Yr.Iss.	20.00	175-300.
91-165-016	It's A Wonderful Life 2000QLX7237	Keepsake	Yr.Iss.	20.00	50-75.00
91-165-017	Sparkling Angel 1800QLX7157	Keepsake	Yr.Iss.	18.00	29.50
91-165-018	Santa's Hot Line 1800QLX7159	Keepsake	Yr.Iss.	18.00	30-42.50
91-165-019	Father Christmas 1400QLX7147	Keepsake	Yr.Iss.	14.00	30.00
91-165-020	Holiday Glow 1400QLX7177	Keepsake	Yr.Iss.	14.00	30-35.00
91-165-021	Festive Brass Church 1400QLX7179	Keepsake	Yr.Iss.	14.00	24.50
91-165-022	Friendship Tree 1000QLX7169	Keepsake	Yr.Iss.	10.00	25-33.00
91-165-023	Elfin Engineer 1000QLX7209	Keepsake	Yr.Iss.	10.00	19.50
91-165-024	Angel of Light 3000QLT7239	Keepsake	Yr.Iss.	30.00	59.50
Hallmark Keepsake Ornaments		**1991 Keepsake Miniature Ornaments**			
91-166-001	Woodland Babies 600QXM5667	Keepsake	Yr.Iss.	6.00	10.00
91-166-002	Thimble Bells-Second Edition 600QXM5659	Keepsake	Yr.Iss.	6.00	12.00
91-166-003	Nature's Angels-Second Ed. 450QXM5657	Keepsake	Yr.Iss.	4.50	10.00
91-166-004	Passenger Car-Third Ed. 850QXM5649	Keepsake	Yr.Iss.	8.50	12.00
91-166-005	The Kringles-Third Edition 6000QXM5647	Keepsake	Yr.Iss.	6.00	12-25.00
91-166-006	Inn-Fourth Edition 850QXM5627	Keepsake	Yr.Iss.	8.50	14.00
91-166-007	Rocking Horse-Fourth Ed. 450QXM5637	Keepsake	Yr.Iss.	4.50	9.00
91-166-008	Kittens in Toyland-Fourth Ed. 450QXM5639	Keepsake	Yr.Iss.	4.50	12-24.00
91-166-009	Penquin Pal-Fourth Ed. 450QXM5629	Keepsake	Yr.Iss.	4.50	10-17.50
91-166-010	Ring-A-Ding Elf 850QXM5669	Keepsake	Yr.Iss.	8.50	18-28.00
91-166-011	Lulu & Family 600QXM5677	Keepsake	Yr.Iss.	6.00	20.00
91-166-012	Silvery Santa 975QXM5679	Keepsake	Yr.Iss.	9.75	20-23.00
91-166-013	Heavenly Minstrel 975QXM5687	Keepsake	Yr.Iss.	9.75	20-31.00
91-166-014	Tiny Tea Party Set of 6 2900QXM5827	Keepsake	Yr.Iss.	29.00	92-135.00
91-166-015	Special Friends 850QXM5797	Keepsake	Yr.Iss.	8.50	19.50
91-166-016	Mom 600QXM5699	Keepsake	Yr.Iss.	6.00	20-27.00
91-166-017	Baby's First Christmas 600QXM5799	Keepsake	Yr.Iss.	6.00	9.00
91-166-018	Our First Christmas Together 600QXM5819	Keepsake	Yr.Iss.	6.00	10.00
91-166-019	Key to Love 450QXM5689	Keepsake	Yr.Iss.	4.50	10-19.50
91-166-020	Grandchild's First Christmas 450QXM5697	Keepsake	Yr.Iss.	4.50	7.00
91-166-021	Treeland Trio 850QXM5899	Keepsake	Yr.Iss.	8.50	19.50
91-166-022	Wee Toymaker 850QXM5967	Keepsake	Yr.Iss.	8.50	17.50
91-166-023	Feliz Navidad 600QXM5887	Keepsake	Yr.Iss.	6.00	18-23.00
91-166-024	Top Hatter 600QXM5889	Keepsake	Yr.Iss.	6.00	20-26.00
91-166-025	Upbeat Bear 600QXM5907	Keepsake	Yr.Iss.	6.00	15-20.00
91-166-026	Friendly Fawn 600QXM5947	Keepsake	Yr.Iss.	6.00	12.50-19.50
91-166-027	Caring Shepherd 600QXM5949	Keepsake	Yr.Iss.	6.00	19.50
91-166-028	Cardinal Cameo 600QXM5957	Keepsake	Yr.Iss.	6.00	18-26.00
91-166-029	Courier Turtle 450QXM5857	Keepsake	Yr.Iss.	4.50	17.50
91-166-030	Fly By 450QXM5859	Keepsake	Yr.Iss.	4.50	19.50
91-166-031	Love Is Born 600QXM5959	Keepsake	Yr.Iss.	6.00	19.50
91-166-032	Cool 'n' Sweet 450QXM5867	Keepsake	Yr.Iss.	4.50	15-23.00
91-166-033	All Aboard 450QXM5869	Keepsake	Yr.Iss.	4.50	19.50
91-166-034	Bright Boxers 450QXM5877	Keepsake	Yr.Iss.	4.50	17.50
91-166-035	Li'l Popper 450QXM5897	Keepsake	Yr.Iss.	4.50	15-20.00
91-166-036	Kitty in a Mitty 450QXM5879	Keepsake	Yr.Iss.	4.50	14.50
91-166-037	Seaside Otter 450QXM5909	Keepsake	Yr.Iss.	4.50	14.50
91-166-038	Fancy Wreath 450QXM5917	Keepsake	Yr.Iss.	4.50	17.50
91-166-039	N. Pole Buddy 450QXM5927	Keepsake	Yr.Iss.	4.50	22.50
91-166-040	Vision of Santa 450QXM5937	Keepsake	Yr.Iss.	4.50	18-23.00
91-166-041	Busy Bear 450QXM5939	Keepsake	Yr.Iss.	4.50	12.50
91-166-042	Country Sleigh 450QXM5999	Keepsake	Yr.Iss.	4.50	10-15.00
91-166-043	Brass Church 300QXM5979	Keepsake	Yr.Iss.	3.00	10-19.00
91-166-044	Brass Soldier 300QXM5987	Keepsake	Yr.Iss.	3.00	9.50
91-166-045	Noel 300QXM5989	Keepsake	Yr.Iss.	3.00	12.50
91-166-046	Holiday Snowflake 300QXM5997	Keepsake	Yr.Iss.	3.00	12.50
Hallmark Keepsake Ornaments		**1991 Club Limited Editions**			
91-167-001	Secrets for Santa 2375QXC4797	Keepsake	28,700	23.75	50.00
91-167-002	Galloping Into Christmas 1975QXC4779	Keepsake	28,400	19.75	55.00
Hallmark Keepsake Ornaments		**1991 Keepsake Collector's Club**			
91-168-001	Hidden Treasure/Li'l Keeper 1500QXC4769	Keepsake	Yr.Iss.	15.00	30.00
91-168-002	Beary Artistic 1000QXC7259	Keepsake	Yr.Iss.	10.00	30.00
Hallmark Keepsake Ornaments		**1992 Collectible Series**			
92-169-001	Tobin Fraley Carousel-First Ed. 2800QX4891	Keepsake	Yr.Iss.	28.00	38-75.00
92-169-002	Owliver-First Ed. 775QX4544	Keepsake	Yr.Iss.	7.75	15-19.50
92-169-003	Betsey's Country Christmas-First Ed. 500QX2104	Keepsake	Yr.Iss.	5.00	5 .00
92-169-004	1966 Mustang-Second Ed. 1275QX4284	Keepsake	Yr.Iss.	12.75	25-45.00
92-169-005	Peace On Earth-Spain Second Ed. 1175QX5174	Keepsake	Yr.Iss.	11.75	20-25.00
92-169-006	Heavenly Angels-Second Ed.775QX4454	Keepsake	Yr.Iss.	7.75	17.50
92-169-007	Puppy Love-Second Ed. 775QX4484	Keepsake	Yr.Iss.	7.75	20-39.50
92-169-008	Merry Olde Santa-Third Ed. 1475QX4414	Keepsake	Yr.Iss.	14.75	35.00
92-169-009	Heart of Christmas-Third Ed. 1375QX4411	Keepsake	Yr.Iss.	13.75	20.00
92-169-010	Fabulous Decade-Third Ed. 775QX4244	Keepsake	Yr.Iss.	7.75	12.50-25.00
92-169-011	CRAYOLA CRAYON-Bright Colors Fourth Ed. 975QX4264	Keepsake	Yr.Iss.	9.75	15.00
92-169-012	The Gift Bringers-Kolyada Fourth Ed. 500QX2124	Keepsake	Yr.Iss.	5.00	5.00
92-169-013	Mary's Angels-Lily Fifth Ed. 675QX4274	Keepsake	Yr.Iss.	6.75	30-49.50
92-169-014	Gift Exchange Seventh Ed. 1475QX4294	Keepsake	Yr.Iss.	14.75	25.00
92-169-015	Reindeer Champs-Donder Seventh Ed. 875QX5284	Keepsake	Yr.Iss.	8.75	25.00
92-169-016	Five-and-Ten-Cent Store Ninth Ed. 1475QX4254	Keepsake	Yr.Iss.	14.75	20-25.00
92-169-017	Nine Ladies Dancing Ninth Ed. 675QX3031	Keepsake	Yr.Iss.	6.75	6.75
92-169-018	Rocking Horse Twelfth Ed. 1075QX4261	Keepsake	Yr.Iss.	10.75	20.00
92-169-019	Frosty Friends 13th Ed. 975QX4291	Keepsake	Yr.Iss.	9.75	15.00
92-169-020	Kringle Tours 14th Ed. 1475QX4341	Keepsake	Yr.Iss.	14.75	20.00

CHRISTMAS ORNAMENTS

Company Number	Name	Series Artist	Edition Limit	Issue Price	Quote
92-169-021	Greatest Story Third Ed. 1275QX4251	Keepsake	Yr.Iss.	12.75	20.00
92-169-022	Winter Surprise Fourth Ed. 1175QX4271	Keepsake	Yr.Iss.	11.75	20-32.50
92-169-023	Hark! It's Herald Fourth Ed. 775QX4464	Keepsake	Yr.Iss.	7.75	10.00
92-169-024	Sweet Holiday Harmony Sixth Ed. 875QX4461	Keepsake	Yr.Iss.	8.75	17.50
Hallmark Keepsake Ornaments		**1992 Artists' Favorites**			
92-170-001	Mother Goose 1375QX4984	Keepsake	Yr.Iss.	13.75	30.00
92-170-002	Elfin Marionette1175QX5931	Keepsake	Yr.Iss.	11.75	11.75
92-170-003	Polar Post 875QX4914	Keepsake	Yr.Iss.	8.75	8.75
92-170-004	Turtle Dreams 875QX4991	Keepsake	Yr.Iss.	8.75	13.50
92-170-005	Uncle Art's Ice Cream 875QX5001	Keepsake	Yr.Iss.	8.75	8.75
92-170-006	Stocked With Joy 775QX5934	Keepsake	Yr.Iss.	7.75	7.75
Hallmark Keepsake Ornaments		**1992 Special Edition**			
92-171-001	Dickens Caroler Bell-Lord Chadwick Third Ed. 2175QX4554	Keepsake	Yr.Iss.	21.75	44.00
Hallmark Keepsake Ornaments		**1992 Commemoratives**			
92-172-001	Baby's First Christmas1875QX4581	Keepsake	Yr.Iss.	18.75	25-39.50
92-172-002	Baby's First Christmas 775QX4641	Keepsake	Yr.Iss.	7.75	12.00
92-172-003	Baby's First Christmas-Baby Girl 475QX2204	Keepsake	Yr.Iss.	4.75	4.75
92-172-004	Baby's First Christmas-Baby Boy 475QX2191	Keepsake	Yr.Iss.	4.75	4.75
92-172-005	For My Grandma 775QX5184	Keepsake	Yr.Iss.	7.75	7.75
92-172-006	A Child's Christmas 975QX4574	Keepsake	Yr.Iss.	9.75	12.00
92-172-007	Grandson's First Christmas 675QX4621	Keepsake	Yr.Iss.	6.75	6.75
92-172-008	Grandaughter's First Christmas 675QX4634	Keepsake	Yr.Iss.	6.75	6.75
92-172-009	Mom-to-Be 675QX4614	Keepsake	Yr.Iss.	6.75	12.00
92-172-010	Dad-to-Be 675QX4611	Keepsake	Yr.Iss.	6.75	12.00
92-172-011	Baby's First Christmas 775QX4644	Keepsake	Yr.Iss.	7.75	15.00
92-172-012	Baby's Second Christmas 675QX4651	Keepsake	Yr.Iss.	6.75	15.00
92-172-013	Child's Third Christmas 675QX4654	Keepsake	Yr.Iss.	6.75	15.00
92-172-014	Child's Fourth Christmas 675QX4661	Keepsake	Yr.Iss.	6.75	15.00
92-172-015	Child's Fifth Christmas 675QX4664	Keepsake	Yr.Iss.	6.75	12.00
92-172-016	For The One I Love 975QX4884	Keepsake	Yr.Iss.	9.75	9.75
92-172-017	Our First Christmas Together 975QX5061	Keepsake	Yr.Iss.	9.75	20.00
92-172-018	Out First Christmas Together 875QX4694	Keepsake	Yr.Iss.	8.75	8.75
92-172-019	Our First Christmas Together 675QX3011	Keepsake	Yr.Iss.	6.75	6.75
92-172-020	Love To Skate 875QX4841	Keepsake	Yr.Iss.	8.75	8.75
92-172-021	Anniversary Year 975QX4851	Keepsake	Yr.Iss.	9.75	9.75
92-172-022	Dad 775QX4674	Keepsake	Yr.Iss.	7.75	10-15.00
92-172-023	Mom 775QX5164	Keepsake	Yr.Iss.	7.75	7.75
92-172-024	Brother 675QX4684	Keepsake	Yr.Iss.	6.75	15.00
92-172-025	Sister 675QX4681	Keepsake	Yr.Iss.	6.75	15.00
92-172-026	Son 675QX5024	Keepsake	Yr.Iss.	6.75	12.00
92-172-027	Daughter 675QX5031	Keepsake	Yr.Iss.	6.75	12.00
92-172-028	Mom and Dad 975QX4671	Keepsake	Yr.Iss.	9.75	30-36.00
92-172-029	Grandparents 475QX2004	Keepsake	Yr.Iss.	4.75	4.75
92-172-030	Grandmother 475QX2011	Keepsake	Yr.Iss.	4.75	4.75
92-172-031	Godchild 675QX5941	Keepsake	Yr.Iss.	6.75	9.00
92-172-032	Grandaughter 675QX5604	Keepsake	Yr.Iss.	6.75	6.75
92-172-033	Grandson 675QX5611	Keepsake	Yr.Iss.	6.75	12.00
92-172-034	Friendship Line 975QX5034	Keepsake	Yr.Iss.	9.75	20.00
92-172-035	Friendly Greetings 775QX5041	Keepsake	Yr.Iss.	7.75	7.75
92-172-036	New Home 875QX5191	Keepsake	Yr.Iss.	8.75	15.00
92-172-037	Across the Miles 675QX3044	Keepsake	Yr.Iss.	6.75	6.75
92-172-038	From Our Home To yours 475QX2131	Keepsake	Yr.Iss.	4.75	4.75
92-172-039	Secret Pal 775QX5424	Keepsake	Yr.Iss.	7.75	8.00
92-172-040	Teacher 475QX2264	Keepsake	Yr.Iss.	4.75	4.75
92-172-041	World-Class Teacher 775QX5054	Keepsake	Yr.Iss.	7.75	7.75
92-172-042	V. P. of Important Stuff 675QX5051	Keepsake	Yr.Iss.	6.75	6.75
92-172-043	Holiday Memo 775QX5044	Keepsake	Yr.Iss.	7.75	11.25
92-172-044	Special Dog 775QX5421	Keepsake	Yr.Iss.	7.75	27.50
92-172-045	Special Cat 775QX5414	Keepsake	Yr.Iss.	7.75	27.50
Hallmark Keepsake Ornaments		**1992 New Attractions**			
92-173-001	Eric the Baker 875QX5244	Keepsake	Yr.Iss.	8.75	8.75
92-173-002	Otto the Carpenter 875QX5254	Keepsake	Yr.Iss.	8.75	8.75
92-173-003	Max the Tailor 875QX5251	Keepsake	Yr.Iss.	8.75	8.75
92-173-004	Franz the Artist 875QX5261	Keepsake	Yr.Iss.	8.75	8.75
92-173-005	Freida the Animals' Friend 875QX5264	Keepsake	Yr.Iss.	8.75	8.75
92-173-006	Ludwig the Musician 875QX5281	Keepsake	Yr.Iss.	8.75	8.75
92-173-007	Silver Star 2800QX5324	Keepsake	Yr.Iss.	28.00	59.50
92-173-008	Locomotive 975QX5311	Keepsake	Yr.Iss.	9.75	25.00
92-173-009	Coal Car 975QX5401	Keepsake	Yr.Iss.	9.75	15.00
92-173-010	Stock Car 975QX5314	Keepsake	Yr.Iss.	9.75	15.00
92-173-011	Caboose 975QX5321	Keepsake	Yr.Iss.	9.75	15.00
92-173-012	Gone Wishin' 875QX5171	Keepsake	Yr.Iss.	8.75	22.00
92-173-013	Skiing 'Round 875QX5214	Keepsake	Yr.Iss.	8.75	8.75
92-173-014	North Pole Fire Fighter 975QX5104	Keepsake	Yr.Iss.	9.75	20-30.00
92-173-015	Rapid Delivery 875QX5094	Keepsake	Yr.Iss.	8.75	8.75
92-173-016	Green Thumb Santa 775QX5101	Keepsake	Yr.Iss.	7.75	7.75
92-173-017	Golf's a Ball 675QX5984	Keepsake	Yr.Iss.	6.75	12.50
92-173-018	A Santa-Full! 975QX5991	Keepsake	Yr.Iss.	9.75	20.00
92-173-019	Tasty Christmas 975QX5994	Keepsake	Yr.Iss.	9.75	15.00
92-173-020	Santa's Roundup 875QX5084	Keepsake	Yr.Iss.	8.75	8.75
92-173-021	Deck the Hogs 875QX5204	Keepsake	Yr.Iss.	8.75	20.00
92-173-022	Patridge In a Pear Tree 875QX5234	Keepsake	Yr.Iss.	8.75	8.75
92-173-023	Spirit of Christmas Stress 875QX5231	Keepsake	Yr.Iss.	8.75	20.00
92-173-024	Please Pause Here 1475QX5291	Keepsake	Yr.Iss.	14.75	25-35.00
92-173-025	SNOOPY® and WOODSTOCK 875QX5954	Keepsake	Yr.Iss.	8.75	15.00
92-173-026	Mary Engelbreit Santa Jolly Wolly 775QX5224	Keepsake	Yr.Iss.	7.75	7.75
92-173-027	GARFIELD 775QX5374	Keepsake	Yr.Iss.	7.75	7.75
92-173-028	Norman Rockwell Art 500QX2224	Keepsake	Yr.Iss.	5.00	5.00
92-173-029	PEANUTS® 500QX2244	Keepsake	Yr.Iss.	5.00	30.00
92-173-030	Owl 975QX5614	Keepsake	Yr.Iss.	9.75	20.00
92-173-031	Santa Maria 1275QX5074	Keepsake	Yr.Iss.	12.75	17.50
92-173-032	Fun on a Big Scale 1075QX5134	Keepsake	Yr.Iss.	10.75	16.00
92-173-033	Genius at Work 1075QX5371	Keepsake	Yr.Iss.	10.75	20.00
92-173-034	Hello-Ho-Ho 975QX5141	Keepsake	Yr.Iss.	9.75	14.50
92-173-035	Cheerful Santa 975QX5154	Keepsake	Yr.Iss.	9.75	25-35.00
92-173-036	Memories to Cherish 1075QX5161	Keepsake	Yr.Iss.	10.75	10.75
92-173-037	Tread Bear 875QX5091	Keepsake	Yr.Iss.	8.75	8.75
92-173-038	Merry "Swiss" Mouse 775QX5114	Keepsake	Yr.Iss.	7.75	10.00
92-173-039	Honest George 775QX5064	Keepsake	Yr.Iss.	7.75	7.75
92-173-040	Bear Bell Champ 775QX5071	Keepsake	Yr.Iss.	7.75	7.75
92-173-041	Egg Nog Nest 775QX5121	Keepsake	Yr.Iss.	7.75	7.75
92-173-042	Jesus Loves Me 775QX3024	Keepsake	Yr.Iss.	7.75	7.75
92-173-043	Loving Shepherd 775QX5151	Keepsake	Yr.Iss.	7.75	7.75
92-173-044	Toboggan Tail 775QX5459	Keepsake	Yr.Iss.	7.75	7.75
92-173-045	Down-Under Holiday 775QX5144	Keepsake	Yr.Iss.	7.75	7.75
92-173-046	Holiday Wishes 775QX5131	Keepsake	Yr.Iss.	7.75	7.75
92-173-047	Feliz Navidad 675QX5181	Keepsake	Yr.Iss.	6.75	6.75

Company Number	Name	Series Artist	Edition Limit	Issue Price	Quote
92-173-048	Holiday Teatime 1475QX5431	Keepsake	Yr.Iss.	14.75	20-29.50
92-173-049	Santa's Hook Shot 1275QX5434	Keepsake	Yr.Iss.	12.75	25-29.50
92-173-050	Cool Fliers 1075QX5474	Keepsake	Yr.Iss.	10.75	10.75
92-173-051	Elvis 1495QX562-4	Keepsake	Yr.Iss.	14.95	30.00
Hallmark Keepsake Ornaments		**1992 Magic Ornaments**			
92-174-001	PEANUTS-Second Ed. 1800QLX7214	Keepsake	Yr.Iss.	18.00	30-52.50
92-174-002	Forest Frolics-Fourth Ed. 2800QLX7254	Keepsake	Yr.Iss.	28.00	28.00
92-174-003	Chris Mouse Tales-Eighth Ed. 1200QLX7074	Keepsake	Yr.Iss.	12.00	20-29.50
92-174-004	Santa Special 4000QLX7167	Keepsake	Yr.Iss.	40.00	55-80.00
92-174-005	Continental Express 3200QLX7264	Keepsake	Yr.Iss.	32.00	32-39.50
92-174-006	Look! It's Santa 1400QLX7094	Keepsake	Yr.Iss.	14.00	32.00
92-174-007	The Dancing Nutcracker 3000QLX7261	Keepsake	Yr.Iss.	30.00	30.00
92-174-008	Enchanted Clock 3000QLX7274	Keepsake	Yr.Iss.	30.00	30.00
92-174-009	Christmas Parade 3000QLX7271	Keepsake	Yr.Iss.	30.00	30.00
92-174-010	Good Sledding Ahead 2800QLX7244	Keepsake	Yr.Iss.	28.00	57.50
92-174-011	Yuletide Rider 2800QLX7314	Keepsake	Yr.Iss.	28.00	57.50
92-174-012	Santa's Answering Machine 2200QLX7241	Keepsake	Yr.Iss.	22.00	22.00
92-174-013	Baby's First Christmas 2200QLX7281	Keepsake	Yr.Iss.	22.00	89-95.00
92-174-014	Out First Christmas Together 2000QLX7221	Keepsake	Yr.Iss.	20.00	35.00
92-174-015	Santa Sub 1800QLX7321	Keepsake	Yr.Iss.	18.00	18.00
92-174-016	Lighting the Way 1800QLX7231	Keepsake	Yr.Iss.	18.00	18.00
92-174-017	Under Construction 1800QLX7324	Keepsake	Yr.Iss.	18.00	31.50-42.50
92-174-018	Feathered Friends 1400QLX7091	Keepsake	Yr.Iss.	14.00	14.00
92-174-019	Watch Owls 1200QLX7084	Keepsake	Yr.Iss.	12.00	12.00
92-174-020	Nut Sweet Nut 1000QLX7081	Keepsake	Yr.Iss.	10.00	10.00
92-174-021	Angel Of Light 3000QLT7239	Keepsake	Yr.Iss.	30.00	30.00
92-174-022	Shuttlecraft Galileo 2400QLX733-1	Keepsake	Yr.Iss.	24.00	24-42.50
Hallmark Keepsake Ornaments		**1992 Miniature Ornaments**			
92-175-001	The Night Before Christmas 1375QXM5541	Keepsake	Yr.Iss.	13.75	20-34.50
92-175-002	The Bearymores-First Ed. 575QXM5544	Keepsake	Yr.Iss.	5.75	10.00
92-175-003	Woodland Babies-Second Ed. 600QXM5444	Keepsake	Yr.Iss.	6.00	9.00
92-175-004	Thimble Bells-Third Ed. 600QXM5461	Keepsake	Yr.Iss.	6.00	12.00
92-175-005	Nature's Angels-Third Ed. 450QXM5451	Keepsake	Yr.Iss.	4.50	10.00
92-175-006	Box Car-Fourth Ed/Noel R.R. 700QXM5441	Keepsake	Yr.Iss.	7.00	12.00
92-175-007	The Kringles-Fourth Ed. 600QXM5381	Keepsake	Yr.Iss.	6.00	10.00
92-175-008	Church-Fifth Ed./Old English V. 700QXM5384	Keepsake	Yr.Iss.	7.00	13.00
92-175-009	Rocking Horse-Fifth Ed. 450QXM5454	Keepsake	Yr.Iss.	4.50	9.00
92-175-010	Kittens in Toyland-Fifth Ed. 450QXM5391	Keepsake	Yr.Iss.	4.50	14.00
92-175-011	Feeding Time 575QXM5481	Keepsake	Yr.Iss.	5.75	8.00
92-175-012	Black-Capped Chickadee 300QXM5484	Keepsake	Yr.Iss.	3.00	6.00
92-175-013	Holiday Holly 975QXM5364	Keepsake	Yr.Iss.	9.75	9.75
92-175-014	Harmony Trio-Set of Three 1175QXM5471	Keepsake	Yr.Iss.	11.75	23.75
92-175-015	Grandchild's First Christmas 575QXM5501	Keepsake	Yr.Iss.	5.75	8.00
92-175-016	Baby's First Christmas 450QXM5494	Keepsake	Yr.Iss.	4.50	10.00
92-175-017	Mom 450QXM5504	Keepsake	Yr.Iss.	4.50	4.50
92-175-018	Grandma 450QXM5514	Keepsake	Yr.Iss.	4.50	4.50
92-175-019	Friends Are Tops 450QXM5521	Keepsake	Yr.Iss.	4.50	4.50
92-175-020	A+ Teacher 375QXM5511	Keepsake	Yr.Iss.	3.75	3.75
92-175-021	Inside Story 725QXM5881	Keepsake	Yr.Iss.	7.25	7.25
92-175-022	Holiday Splash 575QXM5834	Keepsake	Yr.Iss.	5.75	10.00
92-175-023	Christmas Copter 575QXM5844	Keepsake	Yr.Iss.	5.75	6.00
92-175-024	"Coca-Cola" Santa 575QXM5884	Keepsake	Yr.Iss.	5.75	10-15.00
92-175-025	Wee Three Kings 575QXM5531	Keepsake	Yr.Iss.	5.75	10.00
92-175-026	Angelic Harpist 450QXM5524	Keepsake	Yr.Iss.	4.50	9.00
92-175-027	Polar Polka 450QXM5534	Keepsake	Yr.Iss.	4.50	9.00
92-175-028	Buck-A-Roo 450QXM5814	Keepsake	Yr.Iss.	4.50	8.00
92-175-029	Ski For Two 450QXM5821	Keepsake	Yr.Iss.	4.50	4.50
92-175-030	Hoop It Up 450QXM5831	Keepsake	Yr.Iss.	4.50	10.00
92-175-031	Visions Of Acorns 450QXM5851	Keepsake	Yr.Iss.	4.50	4.50
92-175-032	Friendly Tin Soldier 450QXM5874	Keepsake	Yr.Iss.	4.50	10.00
92-175-033	Bright Stringers 375QXM5841	Keepsake	Yr.Iss.	3.75	7.00
92-175-034	Fast Finish 375QXM5301	Keepsake	Yr.Iss.	3.75	3.75
92-175-035	Cozy Kayak 375QXM5551	Keepsake	Yr.Iss.	3.75	6.00
92-175-036	Snug Kitty 375QXM5554	Keepsake	Yr.Iss.	3.75	8.00
92-175-037	Snowshoe Bunny 375QXM5564	Keepsake	Yr.Iss.	3.75	3.75
92-175-038	Gerbil Inc. 375QXM5924	Keepsake	Yr.Iss.	3.75	3.75
92-175-039	Hickory, Dickory, Dock 375QXM5861	Keepsake	Yr.Iss.	3.75	3.75
92-175-040	Going Places 375QXM5871	Keepsake	Yr.Iss.	3.75	3.75
92-175-041	Minted For Santa 375QXM5854	Keepsake	Yr.Iss.	3.75	3.75
92-175-042	Cool Uncle Sam 300QXM5561	Keepsake	Yr.Iss.	3.00	8.00
92-175-043	Perfect Balance 300QXM5571	Keepsake	Yr.Iss.	3.00	3.00
92-175-044	Puppet Show 300QXM5574	Keepsake	Yr.Iss.	3.00	3.00
92-175-045	Christmas Bonus 300QXM5811	Keepsake	Yr.Iss.	3.00	5.00
92-175-046	Spunky Monkey 300QXM5921	Keepsake	Yr.Iss.	3.00	3.00
92-175-047	Little Town of Bethlehem 300QXM5864	Keepsake	Yr.Iss.	3.00	3.00
92-175-048	Sew Sew Tiny (set of 6) 2900QXM5794	Keepsake	Yr.Iss.	29.00	32.50
Hallmark Keepsake Ornaments		**1992 Easter Ornaments**			
92-176-001	Easter Parade-First Ed. 675QEO8301	Keepsake	Yr.Iss.	6.75	6.75
92-176-002	Egg in Sports-First Ed. 675QEO9341	Keepsake	Yr.Iss.	6.75	6.75
Hallmark Keepsake Ornaments		**1992 Collectors' Club**			
92-176-001	Santa's Club List 1500QXC7291	Keepsake	Yr.Iss.	15.00	15.00
92-176-002	Rodney Takes Flight 975QXC5081	Keepsake	Yr.Iss.	9.75	22.00
92-176-003	Chipmunk Parcel Service 675QXC5194	Keepsake	Yr.Iss.	6.75	6.75
Hallmark Keepsake Ornaments		**1992 Limited Edition Ornaments**			
92-177-001	Victorian Skater (w/ base) 2500QXC4067	Keepsake	14,700	25.00	35.00
92-177-002	Christmas Treasures 2200QXC5464	Keepsake	15,500	22.00	22.00
Hallmark Keepsake Ornaments		**1993 Anniversary Edition**			
93-178-001	Tannenbaum's Dept. Store 2600QX5612	Keepsake	Yr.Iss.	26.00	45.00
93-178-002	Shopping With Santa 2400QX5675	Keepsake	Yr.Iss.	24.00	24.00
93-178-003	Frosty Friends 2000QX5682	Keepsake	Yr.Iss.	20.00	45.00
93-178-004	Glowing Pewter Wreath 1875QX5302	Keepsake	Yr.Iss.	18.75	18.75
Hallmark Keepsake Ornaments		**1993 Collectible Series**			
93-179-001	Humpty-Dumpty-First Ed. 1375QX5282	Keepsake	Yr.Iss.	13.75	27.50
93-179-002	U.S. Christmas Stamps-First Ed. 1075QX5292	Keepsake	Yr.Iss.	10.75	10.75
93-179-003	Peanuts-First Ed. 975QX5315	Keepsake	Yr.Iss.	9.75	30.00
93-179-004	Tobin Fraley Carousel-Second Ed. 2800QX5502	Keepsake	Yr.Iss.	28.00	30.00
93-179-005	Owliver-Second Ed. 775QX5425	Keepsake	Yr.Iss.	7.75	7.75
93-179-006	Betsey's Country Christmas-Second Ed. 500QX2062	Keepsake	Yr.Iss.	5.00	5.00
93-179-007	1956 Ford Thunderbird-Third Ed. 1275QX5275	Keepsake	Yr.Iss.	12.75	25.00
93-179-008	Puppy Love-Third Ed. 775QX5045	Keepsake	Yr.Iss.	7.75	7.75
93-179-009	Heart Of Christmas-Fourth Ed. 1475QX4482	Keepsake	Yr.Iss.	14.75	14.75
93-179-010	Merry Olde Santa-Fourth Ed. 1475QX4842	Keepsake	Yr.Iss.	14.75	30.00
93-179-011	Fabulous Decade-Fouth Ed. 775QX4475	Keepsake	Yr.Iss.	7.75	15.00

Number	Name	Artist	Edition Limit	Issue Price	Quote
93-179-012	CRAYOLA CRAYON-Bright Shining Castle Fifth Ed. 1075QX4422	Keepsake	Yr.Iss.	10.75	10.75
93-179-013	Mary's Angels-Ivy-Sixth Ed. 675QX4282	Keepsake	Yr.Iss.	6.75	15.00
93-179-014	A Fitting Moment-Eighth Ed. 1475QX4202	Keepsake	Yr.Iss.	14.75	14.75
93-179-015	Cozy Home-Tenth Ed. 1475QX4175	Keepsake	Yr.Iss.	14.75	25.00
93-179-016	Ten Lords A-Leaping-Tenth Ed. 675QX3012	Keepsake	Yr.Iss.	6.75	6.75
93-179-017	Rocking Horse-13th Ed. 1075QX4162	Keepsake	Yr.Iss.	10.75	20.00
93-179-018	Frosty Friends-14th Ed. 975QX4142	Keepsake	Yr.Iss.	9.75	25.00
93-179-019	Happy Haul-idays-15th Ed. 1475QX4102	Keepsake	Yr.Iss.	14.75	30.00
93-179-020	Peace On Earth-Poland-Third Ed. 1175QX5242	Keepsake	Yr.Iss.	11.75	15.00
93-179-021	Heavenly Angels-Third Ed. 775QX4945	Keepsake	Yr.Iss.	7.75	12.00
93-179-022	The Gift Bringers-The Magi-Fifth Ed. 500QX2065	Keepsake	Yr.Iss.	5.00	12.00
93-179-023	Reindeer Champs-Blitzen-Eighth Ed. 875QX4331	Keepsake	Yr.Iss.	8.75	8.75
93-179-024	Barbie 1475QX5725	Keepsake	Yr.Iss.	14.75	30-100.00
Hallmark Keepsake Ornaments		**1993 Artists' Favorites**			
93-180-001	On Her Toes 875QX5265	Keepsake	Yr.Iss.	8.75	8.75
93-180-002	Wake-Up Call 875QX5262	Keepsake	Yr.Iss.	8.75	8.75
93-180-003	Howling Good Time 975QX5255	Keepsake	Yr.Iss.	9.75	9.75
93-180-004	Bird Watcher 975QX5252	Keepsake	Yr.Iss.	9.75	9.75
93-180-005	Peek-a-Boo Tree 1075QX5245	Keepsake	Yr.Iss.	10.75	20.00
Hallmark Keepsake Ornaments		**1993 Special Editions**			
93-181-001	Julianne and Teddy 2175QX5295	Keepsake	Yr.Iss.	21.75	35.00
93-181-002	Dickens Caroler Bell-Lady Daphne-Fourth Ed. 2175QX5505	Keepsake	Yr.Iss.	21.75	21.75
Hallmark Keepsake Ornaments		**1993 Commemoratives**			
93-182-001	Baby's First Christmas 1875QX5512	Keepsake	Yr.Iss.	18.75	18.75
93-182-002	Baby's First Christmas 1075QX5515	Keepsake	Yr.Iss.	10.75	10.75
93-182-003	Baby's First Christmas-Baby Girl 475QX2092	Keepsake	Yr.Iss.	4.75	4.75
93-182-004	Baby's First Christmas-Baby Boy 475QX2105	Keepsake	Yr.Iss.	4.75	4.75
93-182-005	Baby's First Christmas 775QX5522	Keepsake	Yr.Iss.	7.75	7.75
93-182-006	A Child's Christmas 975QX5882	Keepsake	Yr.Iss.	9.75	9.75
93-182-007	Grandchild's First Christmas 675QX5552	Keepsake	Yr.Iss.	6.75	6.75
93-182-008	To My Grandma 775QX5555	Keepsake	Yr.Iss.	7.75	7.75
93-182-009	Mom-to-Be 675QX5535	Keepsake	Yr.Iss.	6.75	6.75
93-182-010	Dad-to-Be 675QX5532	Keepsake	Yr.Iss.	6.75	6.75
93-182-011	Baby's First Christmas 775QX5525	Keepsake	Yr.Iss.	7.75	15.00
93-182-012	Baby's Second Christmas 675QX5992	Keepsake	Yr.Iss.	6.75	15.00
93-182-013	Child's Third Christmas 675QX5995	Keepsake	Yr.Iss.	6.75	15.00
93-182-014	Child's Fourth Christmas 675QX5215	Keepsake	Yr.Iss.	6.75	15.00
93-182-015	Child's Fifth Christmas 675QX5222	Keepsake	Yr.Iss.	6.75	15.00
93-182-016	Our First Christmas Together 1875QX5955	Keepsake	Yr.Iss.	18.75	18.75
93-182-017	Our First Christmas Together 975QX5642	Keepsake	Yr.Iss.	9.75	15.00
93-182-018	Our First Christmas Together 875QX5952	Keepsake	Yr.Iss.	8.75	8.75
93-182-019	Our First Christmas Together 675QX3015	Keepsake	Yr.Iss.	6.75	12.00
93-182-020	Our Christmas Together 1075QX5942	Keepsake	Yr.Iss.	10.75	10.75
93-182-021	Strange and Wonderful Love 875QX5965	Keepsake	Yr.Iss.	8.75	8.75
93-182-022	Anniversary Year 975QX5972	Keepsake	Yr.Iss.	9.75	9.75
93-182-023	Mom and Dad 975QX5845	Keepsake	Yr.Iss.	9.75	15.00
93-182-024	Dad 775QX5855	Keepsake	Yr.Iss.	7.75	15.00
93-182-025	Mom 775QX5852	Keepsake	Yr.Iss.	7.75	15.00
93-182-026	Son 675QX5865	Keepsake	Yr.Iss.	6.75	6.75
93-182-027	Daughter 675QX5872	Keepsake	Yr.Iss.	6.75	6.75
93-182-028	Brother 675QX5542	Keepsake	Yr.Iss.	6.75	12.00
93-182-029	Sister 675QX5545	Keepsake	Yr.Iss.	6.75	15.00
93-182-030	Sister to Sister 975QX5885	Keepsake	Yr.Iss.	9.75	24-35.00
93-182-031	Our Family 775QX5892	Keepsake	Yr.Iss.	7.75	7.75
93-182-032	Niece 675QX5732	Keepsake	Yr.Iss.	6.75	6.75
93-182-033	Nephew 675QX5735	Keepsake	Yr.Iss.	6.75	6.75
93-182-034	Grandparents 475QX2085	Keepsake	Yr.Iss.	4.75	4.75
93-182-035	Grandmother 675QX5665	Keepsake	Yr.Iss.	6.75	6.75
93-182-036	Granddaughter 675QX5635	Keepsake	Yr.Iss.	6.75	6.75
93-182-037	Grandson 675QX5632	Keepsake	Yr.Iss.	6.75	6.75
93-182-038	Godchild 875QX5875	Keepsake	Yr.Iss.	8.75	8.75
93-182-039	Special Cat 775QX5235	Keepsake	Yr.Iss.	7.75	7.75
93-182-040	Special Dog 775QX5962	Keepsake	Yr.Iss.	7.75	7.75
93-182-041	Warm and Special Friends 1075QX5895	Keepsake	Yr.Iss.	10.75	10.75
93-182-042	Across the Miles 875QX5912	Keepsake	Yr.Iss.	8.75	8.75
93-182-043	New Home 775QX5905	Keepsake	Yr.Iss.	7.75	7.75
93-182-044	Apple for Teacher 775QX5902	Keepsake	Yr.Iss.	7.75	7.75
93-182-045	Star Teacher 575QX5645	Keepsake	Yr.Iss.	5.75	5.75
93-182-046	Coach 675QX5935	Keepsake	Yr.Iss.	6.75	6.75
93-182-047	People Friendly 875QX5932	Keepsake	Yr.Iss.	8.75	8.75
93-182-048	Top Banana 775QX5925	Keepsake	Yr.Iss.	7.75	7.75
Hallmark Keepsake Ornaments		**1993 New Attractions**			
93-183-001	Sylvester and Tweety 975QX5405	Keepsake	Yr.Iss.	9.75	20-25.00
93-183-002	Bugs Bunny 875QX5412	Keepsake	Yr.Iss.	8.75	8.75
93-183-003	Elmer Fudd 875QX5495	Keepsake	Yr.Iss.	8.75	8.75
93-183-004	Porky Pig 875QX5652	Keepsake	Yr.Iss.	8.75	8.75
93-183-005	Winnie the Pooh 975QX5715	Keepsake	Yr.Iss.	9.75	9.75
93-183-006	Kanga and Roo 975QX5672	Keepsake	Yr.Iss.	9.75	9.75
93-183-007	Owl 975QX5695	Keepsake	Yr.Iss.	9.75	9.75
93-183-008	Rabbit 975QX5702	Keepsake	Yr.Iss.	9.75	9.75
93-183-009	Tigger and Piglet 975QX5705	Keepsake	Yr.Iss.	9.75	20-30.00
93-183-010	Eeyore 975QX5712	Keepsake	Yr.Iss.	9.75	9.75
93-183-011	Tin Hot Air Balloon 775QX5615	Keepsake	Yr.Iss.	7.75	7.75
93-183-012	Tin Airplane 775QX5622	Keepsake	Yr.Iss.	7.75	18.00
93-183-013	Tin Blimp 775QX5625	Keepsake	Yr.Iss.	7.75	7.75
93-183-014	Making Waves 975QX5775	Keepsake	Yr.Iss.	9.75	9.75
93-183-015	Putt-Putt Penguin 975QX5795	Keepsake	Yr.Iss.	9.75	9.75
93-183-016	Icicle Bicycle 975QX5835	Keepsake	Yr.Iss.	9.75	9.75
93-183-017	Big on Gardening 975QX5842	Keepsake	Yr.Iss.	9.75	9.75
93-183-018	Fills the Bill 875QX5572	Keepsake	Yr.Iss.	8.75	8.75
93-183-019	Perfect Match 875QX5772	Keepsake	Yr.Iss.	8.75	8.75
93-183-020	Home For Christmas 775QX5562	Keepsake	Yr.Iss.	7.75	7.75
93-183-021	Bowling For ZZZ's 775QX5565	Keepsake	Yr.Iss.	7.75	7.75
93-183-022	Dunkin' Roo 775QX5575	Keepsake	Yr.Iss.	7.75	7.75
93-183-023	Beary Gifted 775QX5762	Keepsake	Yr.Iss.	7.75	7.75
93-183-024	Snowbird 775QX5765	Keepsake	Yr.Iss.	7.75	7.75
93-183-025	Christmas Break 775QX5825	Keepsake	Yr.Iss.	7.75	7.75
93-183-026	Quick As A Fox 875QX5792	Keepsake	Yr.Iss.	8.75	8.75
93-183-027	Faithful Fire Fighter 775QX5782	Keepsake	Yr.Iss.	7.75	7.75
93-183-028	Caring Nurse 675QX5785	Keepsake	Yr.Iss.	6.75	12.00
93-183-029	Star Of Wonder 675QX5982	Keepsake	Yr.Iss.	6.75	25.00
93-183-030	He Is Born 975QX5362	Keepsake	Yr.Iss.	9.75	9.75
93-183-031	Water Bed Snooze 975QX5375	Keepsake	Yr.Iss.	9.75	9.75
93-183-032	Room For One More 875QX5382	Keepsake	Yr.Iss.	8.75	20-30.00
93-183-033	Maxine 875QX5385	Keepsake	Yr.Iss.	8.75	8.75
93-183-034	Superman 1275QX5752	Keepsake	Yr.Iss.	12.75	12.75
93-183-035	The Pink Panther 1275QX5755	Keepsake	Yr.Iss.	12.75	12.75
93-183-036	PEANUTS 500QX2072	Keepsake	Yr.Iss.	5.00	5.00
93-183-037	One-Elf Marching Band 1275QX5342	Keepsake	Yr.Iss.	12.75	12.75
93-183-038	Curly 'n' Kingly 1075QX5285	Keepsake	Yr.Iss.	10.75	10.75
93-183-039	That's Entertainment 875QX5345	Keepsake	Yr.Iss.	8.75	8.75
93-183-040	Big Roller 875QX5352	Keepsake	Yr.Iss.	8.75	8.75
93-183-041	Snow Bear Angel 775QX5355	Keepsake	Yr.Iss.	7.75	7.75
93-183-042	Playful Pals 1475QX5742	Keepsake	Yr.Iss.	14.75	14.75
93-183-043	Lou Rankin Polar Bear 975QX5745	Keepsake	Yr.Iss.	9.75	9.75
93-183-044	Mary Engelbreit 500QX2075	Keepsake	Yr.Iss.	5.00	5.00
93-183-045	Look For Wonder 1275QX5685	Keepsake	Yr.Iss.	12.75	12.75
93-183-046	Peep Inside 1375QX5322	Keepsake	Yr.Iss.	13.75	13.75
93-183-047	Silvery Noel 1275QX5305	Keepsake	Yr.Iss.	12.75	12.75
93-183-048	Snowy Hideaway 975QX5312	Keepsake	Yr.Iss.	9.75	9.75
93-183-049	Makin' Music 975QX5325	Keepsake	Yr.Iss.	9.75	9.75
93-183-050	Smile! It's Christmas 975QX5335	Keepsake	Yr.Iss.	9.75	9.75
93-183-051	High Top-Purr 875QX5332	Keepsake	Yr.Iss.	8.75	8.75
93-183-052	Feliz Navidad 875QX5365	Keepsake	Yr.Iss.	9.75	9.75
93-183-053	Ready For Fun 775QX5124	Keepsake	Yr.Iss.	7.75	7.75
93-183-054	Clever Cookie 775QX5662	Keepsake	Yr.Iss.	7.75	45.00
93-183-055	Little Drummer Boy 875QX5372	Keepsake	Yr.Iss.	8.75	8.75
93-183-056	Popping Good Times 1475QX5392	Keepsake	Yr.Iss.	14.75	14.75
93-183-057	The Swat Team 1275QX5395	Keepsake	Yr.Iss.	12.75	12.75
93-183-058	Great Connections 1075QX5402	Keepsake	Yr.Iss.	10.75	10.75
Hallmark Keepsake Ornaments		**1993 Keepsake Magic Ornaments**			
93-184-001	PEANUTS-Third Ed. 1800QLX7155	Keepsake	Yr.Iss.	18.00	35.00
93-184-002	Forest Frolics-Fifth Ed. 2500QLX7165	Keepsake	Yr.Iss.	25.00	25.00
93-184-003	Chris Mouse Flight-Ninth Ed. 1200QLX7152	Keepsake	Yr.Iss.	12.00	15.00
93-184-004	Road Runner and Wile E. Coyote 3000QLX7415	Keepsake	Yr.Iss.	30.00	30.00
93-184-005	Winnie The Pooh 2400QLX7422	Keepsake	Yr.Iss.	24.00	24.00
93-184-006	Home On The Range 3200QLX7395	Keepsake	Yr.Iss.	32.00	32.00
93-184-007	Santa's Workshop 2800QLX7375	Keepsake	Yr.Iss.	28.00	28.00
93-184-008	Last-Minute Shopping 2800QLX7385	Keepsake	Yr.Iss.	28.00	28.00
93-184-009	Bells Are Ringing 2800QLX7402	Keepsake	Yr.Iss.	28.00	28.00
93-184-010	Baby's First Christmas 2200QLX7365	Keepsake	Yr.Iss.	22.00	40.00
93-184-011	Our First Christmas Together 2000QLX7355	Keepsake	Yr.Iss.	20.00	35.00
93-184-012	North Pole Merrython 2500QLX7392	Keepsake	Yr.Iss.	25.00	25.00
93-184-013	Song Of The Chimes 2500QLX7405	Keepsake	Yr.Iss.	25.00	25.00
93-184-014	Radio News Flash 2200QLX7362	Keepsake	Yr.Iss.	22.00	22.00
93-184-015	Dollhouse Dreams 2200QLX7372	Keepsake	Yr.Iss.	22.00	22.00
93-184-016	The Lamplighter 1800QLX7192	Keepsake	Yr.Iss.	18.00	25.00
93-184-017	Dog's Best Friend 1200QLX7172	Keepsake	Yr.Iss.	12.00	12.00
93-184-018	Santa's Snow-Getter 1800QLX7352	Keepsake	Yr.Iss.	18.00	18.00
93-184-019	Raiding The Fridge1600QLX7185	Keepsake	Yr.Iss.	16.00	16.00
Hallmark Keepsake Ornaments		**1993 Miniature Ornaments**			
93-185-001	On The Road-First Ed. 575QXM4002	Keepsake	Yr.Iss.	5.75	5.75
93-185-002	March Of The Teddy Bears-First Ed. 450QXM4005	Keepsake	Yr.Iss.	4.50	12.00
93-185-003	The Bearymores-Second Ed. 575QXM5125	Keepsake	Yr.Iss.	5.75	5.75
93-185-004	The Night Before Christmas-Second Ed. 4505QXM5115	Keepsake	Yr.Iss.	4.50	15.00
93-185-005	Nature's Angels-Fourth Ed. 450QXM5122	Keepsake	Yr.Iss.	4.50	4.50
93-185-006	Flatbed Car-Fifth Ed.700QXM5105	Keepsake	Yr.Iss.	7.00	12.00
93-185-007	Toy Shop-Sixth Ed. 700QXM5132	Keepsake	Yr.Iss.	7.00	7.00
93-185-008	Rocking Horse-Sixth Ed. 450QXM5112	Keepsake	Yr.Iss.	4.50	4.50
93-185-009	Woodland Babies-Third Ed. 575QXM5102	Keepsake	Yr.Iss.	5.75	5.75
93-185-010	The Kringles-Fifth Ed. 575QXM5135	Keepsake	Yr.Iss.	5.75	5.75
93-185-011	Thimble Bells-Fourth Ed. 575QXM5142	Keepsake	Yr.Iss.	5.75	10.00
93-185-012	Baby's First Christmas 575QXM5145	Keepsake	Yr.Iss.	5.75	5.75
93-185-013	Snuggle Birds 575QXM5182	Keepsake	Yr.Iss.	5.75	5.75
93-185-014	Mom 450QXM5155	Keepsake	Yr.Iss.	4.50	10.00
93-185-015	Grandma 450QXM5162	Keepsake	Yr.Iss.	4.50	4.50
93-185-016	Special Friends 450QXM5165	Keepsake	Yr.Iss.	4.50	4.50
93-185-017	Secret Pals 375QXM5172	Keepsake	Yr.Iss.	3.75	3.75
93-185-018	Tiny Green Thumbs, Set of 6, 2900QXM4032	Keepsake	Yr.Iss.	29.00	29.00
93-185-019	'Round The Mountain 725QXM4025	Keepsake	Yr.Iss.	7.25	7.25
93-185-020	Christmas Castle 575QXM4085	Keepsake	Yr.Iss.	5.75	5.75
93-185-021	Cloisonne Snowflake 975QXM4012	Keepsake	Yr.Iss.	9.75	9.75
93-185-022	Visions Of Sugarplums 725QXM4022	Keepsake	Yr.Iss.	7.25	7.25
93-185-023	Monkey Melody 575QXM4092	Keepsake	Yr.Iss.	5.75	5.75
93-185-024	Crystal Angel 975QXM4015	Keepsake	Yr.Iss.	9.75	30-35.00
93-185-025	Pull Out A Plum 575QXM4095	Keepsake	Yr.Iss.	5.75	5.75
93-185-026	Refreshing Flight 575QXM4112	Keepsake	Yr.Iss.	5.75	5.75
93-185-027	North Pole Fire Truck 475QXM4105	Keepsake	Yr.Iss.	4.75	4.75
93-185-028	Merry Mascot 375QXM4042	Keepsake	Yr.Iss.	3.75	3.75
93-185-029	Pear-Shaped Tones 375QXM4052	Keepsake	Yr.Iss.	3.75	3.75
93-185-030	I Dream Of Santa 375QXM4055	Keepsake	Yr.Iss.	3.75	3.75
93-185-031	Country Fiddling 375QXM4062	Keepsake	Yr.Iss.	3.75	3.75
93-185-032	Cheese Please 375QXM4072	Keepsake	Yr.Iss.	3.75	3.75
93-185-033	Ears To Pals 375QXM4075	Keepsake	Yr.Iss.	3.75	3.75
93-185-034	Into The Woods 375QXM4045	Keepsake	Yr.Iss.	3.75	3.75
93-185-035	Learning To Skate 300QXM4122	Keepsake	Yr.Iss.	3.00	3.00
93-185-036	Lighting A Path 300QXM4115	Keepsake	Yr.Iss.	3.00	3.00
Hallmark Keepsake Ornaments		**1993 Easter Ornaments**			
93-186-001	Springtime Bonnets-First Ed. 775QEO8322	Keepsake	Yr.Iss.	7.75	7.75
93-186-002	Easter Parade-Second Ed. 675QEO8325	Keepsake	Yr.Iss.	6.75	6.75
93-186-003	Egg in Sports-Second Ed. 675QEO8332	Keepsake	Yr.Iss.	6.75	6.75
Hallmark Keepsake Ornaments		**1993 Keepsake Collector's Club**			
93-186-001	Trimmed With Memories 1200QXC5432	Keepsake	Yr.Iss.	12.00	12.00
93-186-002	It's In The Mail 1000QXC5272	Keepsake	Yr.Iss.	10.00	10.00
Hallmark Keepsake Ornaments		**1993 Limited Edition Ornaments**			
93-187-001	Sharing Christmas 2000QXC5435	Keepsake	16,500	20.00	20.00
93-187-002	Gentle Tidings 2500QXC5442	Keepsake	17,500	25.00	25.00
Hallmark Keepsake Ornaments		**1994 Collectible Series**			
94-188-001	Betsey's Country Christmas-Third Ed. 500QX2403	Keepsake	Yr.Iss.	5.00	5.00
94-188-002	Pipers Piping-Eleventh Ed. 695QX3183	Keepsake	Yr.Iss.	6.95	6.95
94-188-003	Rocking Horse-Fourteenth Ed. 1095QX5016	Keepsake	Yr.Iss.	10.95	10.95
94-188-004	PEANUTS-Lucy-Second Ed. 995QX5203	Keepsake	Yr.Iss.	9.95	9.95
94-188-005	Postage Stamp-Second Ed. 1095QX5206	Keepsake	Yr.Iss.	10.95	10.95
94-188-006	Hey Diddle Diddle-Second Ed. 1395QX5213	Keepsake	Yr.Iss.	13.95	13.95
94-188-007	Tobin Fraley Carousel-Third Ed. 2800QX5223	Keepsake	Yr.Iss.	28.00	28.00
94-188-008	Owliver-Third Ed. 795QX5226	Keepsake	Yr.Iss.	7.95	7.95
94-188-009	Puppy Love-Fourth Ed. 795QX5253	Keepsake	Yr.Iss.	7.95	7.95
94-188-010	Merry Olde Santa-Fifth Ed. 1495QX5256	Keepsake	Yr.Iss.	14.95	14.95
94-188-011	Fabulous Decade-Fifth Ed. 795QX5263	Keepsake	Yr.Iss.	7.95	7.95

CHRISTMAS ORNAMENTS

Company		Series			
Number	**Name**	**Artist**	**Edition Limit**	**Issue Price**	**Quote**
94-188-012	Heart of Christmas-Fifth Ed. 1495QX5266	Keepsake	Yr.Iss.	14.95	14.95
94-188-013	CRAYOLA CRAYON-Fort w/Bear on Swing-Sixth Ed. 1095QX5273	Keepsake	Yr.Iss.	10.95	10.95
94-188-014	Mary's Angels-Jasmine Blk. Angel-7th Ed. 695QX5276	Keepsake	Yr.Iss.	6.95	6.95
94-188-015	Exchanging Mittens-Ninth Ed. 1495QX5283	Keepsake	Yr.Iss.	14.95	14.95
94-188-016	Drug Store/Shoe Shop-11th Ed. 1495QX5286	Keepsake	Yr.Iss.	14.95	14.95
94-188-017	Frosty Friends-Fifteenth Ed. 995QX5293	Keepsake	Yr.Iss.	9.95	9.95
94-188-018	Santa on Tractor-Sixteenth Ed. 1495QX5296	Keepsake	Yr.Iss.	14.95	14.95
94-188-019	Cats/Kittens-First Ed. 795QX5313	Keepsake	Yr.Iss.	7.95	7.95
94-188-020	Train-Engine-First Ed. 1895QX5316	Keepsake	Yr.Iss.	18.95	18.95
94-188-021	Baseball Hall Heros-Babe Ruth-First Ed. 1295QX5323	Keepsake	Yr.Iss.	12.95	12.95
94-188-022	1957 Chevy-Fourth Ed. 1295QX5422	Keepsake	Yr.Iss.	12.95	12.95
94-188-023	Pedal Car-First Ed. 1395QX5426	Keepsake	Yr.Iss.	13.95	13.95
Hallmark Keepsake Ornaments		**1994 Artists' Favorites**			
94-189-001	Horse and Rooster 895QX5396	Keepsake	Yr.Iss.	8.95	8.95
94-189-002	Squirrel Painting Mailbox/Scaffold 895QX5403	Keepsake	Yr.Iss.	8.95	8.95
94-189-003	Santa Pushing Lawn Mower 895QX5413	Keepsake	Yr.Iss.	8.95	8.95
94-189-004	Cat on Sailboat 895QX5416	Keepsake	Yr.Iss.	8.95	8.95
94-189-005	Angel and a Manger 1295QX5423	Keepsake	Yr.Iss.	12.95	12.95
Hallmark Keepsake Ornaments		**1994 Special Edition**			
94-190-001	Doll with Bear 2175QX4813	Keepsake	Yr.Iss.	21.75	21.75
Hallmark Keepsake Ornaments		**1994 Commemoratives**			
94-191-001	Baby's First Christmas 1895QX5633	Keepsake	Yr.Iss.	18.95	18.95
94-191-002	Baby's First Christmas 1295QX5743	Keepsake	Yr.Iss.	12.95	12.95
94-191-003	Baby's First Christmas-Baby Girl 500QX2433	Keepsake	Yr.Iss.	5.00	5.00
94-191-004	Baby's First Christmas-Baby Boy 500QX2436	Keepsake	Yr.Iss.	5.00	5.00
94-191-005	Baby's First Christmas Photo 795QX5636	Keepsake	Yr.Iss.	7.95	7.95
94-191-006	Baby's First Christmas 795QX5713	Keepsake	Yr.Iss.	7.95	7.95
94-191-007	Baby's Second Christmas 795QX5716	Keepsake	Yr.Iss.	7.95	7.95
94-191-008	Child's Third Christmas 695QX5723	Keepsake	Yr.Iss.	6.95	6.95
94-191-009	Child's Fourth Christmas 695QX5726	Keepsake	Yr.Iss.	6.95	6.95
94-191-010	Child's Fifth Christmas 695QX5733	Keepsake	Yr.Iss.	6.95	6.95
94-191-011	Grandchild's First Christmas 795QX5676	Keepsake	Yr.Iss.	7.95	7.95
94-191-012	Dad-To-Be 795QX5473	Keepsake	Yr.Iss.	7.95	7.95
94-191-013	Mom-To-Be 795QX5506	Keepsake	Yr.Iss.	7.95	7.95
94-191-014	Grandma Photo 695QX5613	Keepsake	Yr.Iss.	6.95	6.95
94-191-015	Our First Christmas Together 695QX3186	Keepsake	Yr.Iss.	6.95	6.95
94-191-016	Our First Christmas Together 995QX4816	Keepsake	Yr.Iss.	9.95	9.95
94-191-017	Our First Christmas Together 995QX5643	Keepsake	Yr.Iss.	9.95	9.95
94-191-018	Our First Christmas Together 1895QX5706	Keepsake	Yr.Iss.	18.95	18.95
94-191-019	Our First Christmas Together Photo 895QX565	Keepsake	Yr.Iss.	8.95	8.95
94-191-020	General Love 895QX5646	Keepsake	Yr.Iss.	8.95	8.95
94-191-021	Anniversary Year 1095QX5683	Keepsake	Yr.Iss.	10.95	10.95
94-191-022	Godparents 500QX2423	Keepsake	Yr.Iss.	5.00	5.00
94-191-023	Grandparents 500QX2426	Keepsake	Yr.Iss.	5.00	5.00
94-191-024	Godchild 895QX4453	Keepsake	Yr.Iss.	8.95	8.95
94-191-025	Dad 795QX5463	Keepsake	Yr.Iss.	7.95	7.95
94-191-026	Mom 795QX5466	Keepsake	Yr.Iss.	7.95	7.95
94-191-027	Sister 695QX5513	Keepsake	Yr.Iss.	6.95	6.95
94-191-028	Brother 695QX5516	Keepsake	Yr.Iss.	6.95	6.95
94-191-029	Granddaughter 695QX5523	Keepsake	Yr.Iss.	6.95	6.95
94-191-030	Grandson 695QX5526	Keepsake	Yr.Iss.	6.95	6.95
94-191-031	Sister to Sister 995QX5533	Keepsake	Yr.Iss.	9.95	9.95
94-191-032	Niece 795QX5543	Keepsake	Yr.Iss.	7.95	7.95
94-191-033	Nephew 795QX5546	Keepsake	Yr.Iss.	7.95	7.95
94-191-034	Our Family 795QX5576	Keepsake	Yr.Iss.	7.95	7.95
94-191-035	Special Dog 795QX5603	Keepsake	Yr.Iss.	7.95	7.95
94-191-036	Special Cat 795QX5606	Keepsake	Yr.Iss.	7.95	7.95
94-191-037	Grandpa 795QX5616	Keepsake	Yr.Iss.	7.95	7.95
94-191-038	Daughter 695QX5623	Keepsake	Yr.Iss.	6.95	6.95
94-191-039	Son 695QX5626	Keepsake	Yr.Iss.	6.95	6.95
94-191-040	Mom and Dad 995QX5666	Keepsake	Yr.Iss.	9.95	9.95
94-191-041	Grandmother 795QX5673	Keepsake	Yr.Iss.	7.95	7.95
94-191-042	Across the Miles 895QX5656	Keepsake	Yr.Iss.	8.95	8.95
94-191-043	New Home 895QX5663	Keepsake	Yr.Iss.	8.95	8.95
94-191-044	Friendship 895QX5686	Keepsake	Yr.Iss.	8.95	8.95
94-191-045	Friendship 1095QX5693	Keepsake	Yr.Iss.	10.95	10.95
94-191-046	Secret Santa 795QX5736	Keepsake	Yr.Iss.	7.95	7.95
Hallmark Keepsake Ornaments		**1994 New Attractions**			
94-192-001	Norman Rockwell 500QX2413	Keepsake	Yr.Iss.	5.00	5.00
94-192-002	Mary Engelbreit 500QX2416	Keepsake	Yr.Iss.	5.00	5.00
94-192-003	Beatrix Potter 500QX2443	Keepsake	Yr.Iss.	5.00	5.00
94-192-004	HERSHEYS 1095QX4766	Keepsake	Yr.Iss.	10.95	10.95
94-192-005	Flintstones 1495QX5003	Keepsake	Yr.Iss.	14.95	14.95
94-192-006	Speedy Gonzalez 895QX5343	Keepsake	Yr.Iss.	8.95	8.95
94-192-007	Yosemite Sam 895QX5346	Keepsake	Yr.Iss.	8.95	8.95
94-192-008	COCA-COLA Santa 1495QX5356	Keepsake	Yr.Iss.	14.95	14.95
94-192-009	Beatles Gift Set 4800QX5373	Keepsake	Yr.Iss.	48.00	48.00
94-192-010	Daffy Duck 895QX5415	Keepsake	Yr.Iss.	8.95	8.95
94-192-011	Dorothy and Toto 1095QX5433	Keepsake	Yr.Iss.	10.95	10.95
94-192-012	Scarecrow 995QX5436	Keepsake	Yr.Iss.	9.95	9.95
94-192-013	Tin Man 995QX5443	Keepsake	Yr.Iss.	9.95	9.95
94-192-014	Cowardly Lion 995QX5446	Keepsake	Yr.Iss.	9.95	9.95
94-192-015	LEGO'S 1095QX5453	Keepsake	Yr.Iss.	10.95	10.95
94-192-016	Lou Rankin Seal 995QX5456	Keepsake	Yr.Iss.	9.95	9.95
94-192-017	Coyote and Road Runner 1295QX5602	Keepsake	Yr.Iss.	12.95	12.95
94-192-018	Tasmanian Devil 895QX5605	Keepsake	Yr.Iss.	8.95	8.95
94-192-019	Winnie the Pooh/Tigger 1295QX5746	Keepsake	Yr.Iss.	12.95	12.95
94-192-020	Garfield 1295QX5753	Keepsake	Yr.Iss.	12.95	12.95
94-192-021	Batman 1295QX5853	Keepsake	Yr.Iss.	12.95	12.95
94-192-022	Musician 1095QX5773	Keepsake	Yr.Iss.	10.95	10.95
94-192-023	Tourist 895QX5846	Keepsake	Yr.Iss.	8.95	8.95
94-192-024	Bowling 895QX5856	Keepsake	Yr.Iss.	8.95	8.95
94-192-025	Tennis 795QX5863	Keepsake	Yr.Iss.	7.95	7.95
94-192-026	Skiing 895QX5866	Keepsake	Yr.Iss.	8.95	8.95
94-192-027	Basketball 795QX5873	Keepsake	Yr.Iss.	7.95	7.95
94-192-028	Baseball 795QX5876	Keepsake	Yr.Iss.	7.95	7.95
94-192-029	Boating 795QX5886	Keepsake	Yr.Iss.	7.95	7.95
94-192-030	Artist 795QX5893	Keepsake	Yr.Iss.	7.95	7.95
94-192-031	Fishing 895QX5913	Keepsake	Yr.Iss.	8.95	8.95
94-192-032	Soccer 795QX5916	Keepsake	Yr.Iss.	7.95	7.95
94-192-033	Football 895QX5923	Keepsake	Yr.Iss.	8.95	8.95
94-192-034	Golf 795QX5926	Keepsake	Yr.Iss.	7.95	7.95
94-192-035	Business 995QX5696	Keepsake	Yr.Iss.	9.95	9.95
94-192-036	Boss 795QX5703	Keepsake	Yr.Iss.	7.95	7.95
94-192-037	Teacher 795QX5766	Keepsake	Yr.Iss.	7.95	7.95
94-192-038	Doctor 895QX5823	Keepsake	Yr.Iss.	8.95	8.95
94-192-039	Policeman 895QX5826	Keepsake	Yr.Iss.	8.95	8.95
94-192-040	Mailman 795QX5833	Keepsake	Yr.Iss.	7.95	7.95
94-192-041	Fireman 795QX5843	Keepsake	Yr.Iss.	7.95	7.95
94-192-042	Teacher 695QX5836	Keepsake	Yr.Iss.	6.95	6.95
94-192-043	Care Giver 795QX5906	Keepsake	Yr.Iss.	7.95	7.95
94-192-044	Coach 795QX5933	Keepsake	Yr.Iss.	7.95	7.95
94-192-045	Nurse 695QX5973	Keepsake	Yr.Iss.	6.95	6.95
94-192-046	Winter Gnome 995QX5976	Keepsake	Yr.Iss.	9.95	9.95
94-192-047	Spring Gnome 995QX5983	Keepsake	Yr.Iss.	9.95	9.95
94-192-048	Summer Gnome 995QX5986	Keepsake	Yr.Iss.	9.95	9.95
94-192-049	Fall Gnome 995QX5993	Keepsake	Yr.Iss.	9.95	9.95
94-192-050	Shoebox w/ Cat 895QX5816	Keepsake	Yr.Iss.	8.95	8.95
94-192-051	Angel Hare 895QX5896	Keepsake	Yr.Iss.	8.95	8.95
94-192-052	"Peace on Earth" Santa 795QX5953	Keepsake	Yr.Iss.	7.95	7.95
94-192-053	Ethnic Children Snowflake 1095QX4406	Keepsake	Yr.Iss.	10.95	10.95
94-192-054	Choir Girl 895QX4473	Keepsake	Yr.Iss.	8.95	8.95
94-192-055	Feliz Navidad 895QX5793	Keepsake	Yr.Iss.	8.95	8.95
94-192-056	German Bear 1095QX5796	Keepsake	Yr.Iss.	10.95	10.95
94-192-057	Jackalope 895QX5756	Keepsake	Yr.Iss.	8.95	8.95
94-192-058	Pink Flamingo 995QX5763	Keepsake	Yr.Iss.	9.95	9.95
94-192-059	Shepherd w/ Lamb 895QX5536	Keepsake	Yr.Iss.	8.95	8.95
94-192-060	Inspirational Wood-Lion & Lamb 795QX5813	Keepsake	Yr.Iss.	7.95	7.95
94-192-061	Kittens Decorating Cookies (2) 1095QX5803	Keepsake	Yr.Iss.	10.95	10.95
94-192-062	Mice Writing Letter to Santa 1495QX5806	Keepsake	Yr.Iss.	14.95	14.95
94-192-063	Kissing Chipmunks w/ Mistletoe (2) 1295QX5996	Keepsake	Yr.Iss.	12.95	12.95
94-192-064	Candy Jar w/ Mouse 895QX5776	Keepsake	Yr.Iss.	8.95	8.95
94-192-065	Jingle Bell Band 1095QX5783	Keepsake	Yr.Iss.	10.95	10.95
94-192-066	Santa w/ Reindeer on Bike 1295QX5786	Keepsake	Yr.Iss.	12.95	12.95
94-192-067	Santa on Magic Carpet 795QX5883	Keepsake	Yr.Iss.	7.95	7.95
94-192-068	Red Bird on Ice Skates 795QX5946	Keepsake	Yr.Iss.	7.95	7.95
Hallmark Keepsake Ornaments		**1994 Keepsake Magic Ornaments**			
94-193-001	Cute Nativity 1600QLX7383	Keepsake	Yr.Iss.	16.00	16.00
94-193-002	Chris Mouse-Lite Jelly-10th Ed. 1200QLX7393	Keepsake	Yr.Iss.	12.00	12.00
94-193-003	Holiday Trolley 2000QLX7413	Keepsake	Yr.Iss.	20.00	20.00
94-193-004	Lighthouse 1800QLX7376	Keepsake	Yr.Iss.	18.00	18.00
94-193-005	Candy Miner 2000QLX7403	Keepsake	Yr.Iss.	20.00	20.00
94-193-006	PEANUTS-4th Ed. 2000QLX7406	Keepsake	Yr.Iss.	20.00	20.00
94-193-007	Maxine 2000QLX7503	Keepsake	Yr.Iss.	20.00	20.00
94-193-008	Puppy in Basket 2000QLX7423	Keepsake	Yr.Iss.	20.00	20.00
94-193-009	Talking Santa Head 2800QLX7426	Keepsake	Yr.Iss.	28.00	28.00
94-193-010	Spanish Hat w/ Character 2800QLX7433	Keepsake	Yr.Iss.	28.00	28.00
94-193-011	Winnie the Pooh 3200QLX7493	Keepsake	Yr.Iss.	32.00	32.00
94-193-012	Forest Frolics-6th Ed. 2800QLX7436	Keepsake	Yr.Iss.	28.00	28.00
94-193-013	Dancing Santa 2200QLX7416	Keepsake	Yr.Iss.	22.00	22.00
94-193-014	Clock w/ Pendulum 2400QLX7443	Keepsake	Yr.Iss.	24.00	24.00
94-193-015	Gingerbread House-Premier 4400QLX7382	Keepsake	Yr.Iss.	44.00	44.00
94-193-016	White Christmas 2800QLX7463	Keepsake	Yr.Iss.	28.00	28.00
94-193-017	Baby's First Christmas 2000QLX7466	Keepsake	Yr.Iss.	20.00	20.00
94-193-018	Santa Caliope 2400QLX7473	Keepsake	Yr.Iss.	24.00	24.00
94-193-019	25th Anniversary 2400QLX7486	Keepsake	Yr.Iss.	24.00	24.00
94-193-020	Tobin Fraley-First Ed. 3200QLX7496	Keepsake	Yr.Iss.	32.00	32.00
94-193-021	STAR TREK (special Issue) 2400QLX7386	Keepsake	Yr.Iss.	24.00	24.00
94-193-022	Barney 2400QLX7506	Keepsake	Yr.Iss.	24.00	24.00
94-193-023	Mufasa/Sarabi/Simba 3200QLX7513	Keepsake	Yr.Iss.	32.00	32.00
Hallmark Keepsake Ornaments		**1994 Miniature Ornaments**			
94-194-001	Mini Car-2nd Ed. 575QXM5103	Keepsake	Yr.Iss.	5.75	5.75
94-194-002	Drummer-2nd Ed. 450QXM5106	Keepsake	Yr.Iss.	4.50	4.50
94-194-003	Stock Car-6th Ed. 700QXM5113	Keepsake	Yr.Iss.	7.00	7.00
94-194-004	Rocking Horse-7th Ed. 450QXM5116	Keepsake	Yr.Iss.	4.50	4.50
94-194-005	Night Before Christmas-3rd Ed. 450QXM5123	Keepsake	Yr.Iss.	4.50	4.56
94-194-006	Nature's Angels-5th Ed. 450QXM5126	Keepsake	Yr.Iss.	4.50	4.50
94-194-007	The Bearymores-3rd Ed. 575QXM5133	Keepsake	Yr.Iss.	5.75	5.75
94-194-008	Hat Shop-7th Ed. 700QXM5143	Keepsake	Yr.Iss.	7.00	7.00
94-194-009	Baker Nutcracker-First Ed. 575QXM5146	Keepsake	Yr.Iss.	5.75	5.75
94-194-010	Old World Santa-First Ed. 600QXM5153	Keepsake	Yr.Iss.	6.00	6.00
94-194-011	Gingerbread Cookies 575QXM5166	Keepsake	Yr.Iss.	5.75	5.75
94-194-012	Bear on Scooter 675QXM5173	Keepsake	Yr.Iss.	6.75	6.75
94-194-013	Noah's Ark (special edition) 2450QXM4106	Keepsake	Yr.Iss.	24.50	24.50
94-194-014	Reindeer w/ Jewels 975QXM4026	Keepsake	Yr.Iss.	9.75	9.75
94-194-015	Mice Baking,set/6 2900QXM4033	Keepsake	Yr.Iss.	29.00	29.00
94-194-016	Babs Bunny 575QXM4116	Keepsake	Yr.Iss.	5.75	5.75
94-194-017	Plucky Duck 575QXM4123	Keepsake	Yr.Iss.	5.75	5.75
94-194-018	Hampton 575QXM4126	Keepsake	Yr.Iss.	5.75	5.75
94-194-019	Dizzy Devil 575QXM4133	Keepsake	Yr.Iss.	5.75	5.75
94-194-020	Elf Pouring COKE 575QXM5156	Keepsake	Yr.Iss.	5.75	5.75
94-194-021	Buster Bunny 575QXM5163	Keepsake	Yr.Iss.	5.75	5.75
94-194-022	Baby's First Christmas 575QXM4003	Keepsake	Yr.Iss.	5.75	5.75
94-194-023	General Love 575QXM4006	Keepsake	Yr.Iss.	5.75	5.75
94-194-024	Mom 450QXM4013	Keepsake	Yr.Iss.	4.50	4.50
94-194-025	Special Friends 450QXM4016	Keepsake	Yr.Iss.	4.50	4.50
94-194-026	Mary and Joseph 575QXM4036	Keepsake	Yr.Iss.	5.75	5.75
94-194-027	Baby in Manger 450QXM4043	Keepsake	Yr.Iss.	4.50	4.50
94-194-028	Doll and Bear 725QXM4046	Keepsake	Yr.Iss.	7.25	7.25
94-194-029	Santa w/ Toys 575QXM4053	Keepsake	Yr.Iss.	5.75	5.75
94-194-030	Carousel Horse 775QXM4056	Keepsake	Yr.Iss.	7.75	7.75
94-194-031	Elf Stringing Popcorn 450QXM4063	Keepsake	Yr.Iss.	4.50	4.50
94-194-032	Cherub 375QXM4066	Keepsake	Yr.Iss.	3.75	3.75
94-194-033	Santa's Sleigh 575QXM4073	Keepsake	Yr.Iss.	5.75	5.75
94-194-034	Bear w/ Bottle Brush Tree 475QXM4076	Keepsake	Yr.Iss.	4.75	4.75
94-194-035	Beaver and Tree 375QXM4086	Keepsake	Yr.Iss.	3.75	3.75
94-194-036	Jolly Wolly Snowman 375QXM4093	Keepsake	Yr.Iss.	3.75	3.75
94-194-037	Mouse Sleeping 300QXM4096	Keepsake	Yr.Iss.	3.00	3.00
94-194-038	Mouse on Button 375QXM4103	Keepsake	Yr.Iss.	3.75	3.75
Hallmark Keepsake Ornaments		**1994 Easter Ornaments**			
94-195-001	Sweet as Sugar 875QEO8086	A. Rogers	Yr.Iss.	8.75	8.75
94-195-002	Egg Car-First Ed. 775QEO8093	K. Crow	Yr.Iss.	7.75	7.75
94-195-003	Springtime Bonnets-2nd Ed. 775QEO8096	R. Bishop	Yr.Iss.	7.75	7.75
94-195-004	Golf-3rd Ed. 675QEO8133	B. Seidler	Yr.Iss.	6.75	6.75
94-195-005	Horn-3rd Ed. 675QEO8136	D. Rhodus	Yr.Iss.	6.75	6.75
94-195-006	Yummy Recipe 775QEO8143	A. Rogers	Yr.Iss.	7.75	7.75
94-195-007	Sunny Bunny Garden, set/3 1500QEO8146	E. Seale	Yr.Iss.	15.00	15.00
94-195-008	Baby's First Easter 675QEO8153	J. Francis	Yr.Iss.	6.75	6.75
94-195-009	Daughter 575QEO8156	T. Andrews	Yr.Iss.	5.75	5.75
94-195-010	Son 575QEO8163	T. Andrews	Yr.Iss.	5.75	5.75
94-195-011	CRAYOLA CRAYON-Colorful Spring 775QEO8166	K. Crow	Yr.Iss.	7.75	7.75
94-195-012	PEANUTS 775QEO8176	D. Unruh	Yr.Iss.	7.75	7.75
94-195-013	Divine Duet 675QEO8183	L. Votruba	Yr.Iss.	6.75	6.75

Company / Number	Name	Series / Artist	Edition Limit	Issue Price	Quote
94-195-014	Treetop Cottage 975QE08186	L. Sickman	Yr.Iss.	9.75	9.75
94-195-015	Easter Art Show 775QE08193	L. Votruba	Yr.Iss.	7.75	7.75
94-195-016	Sweet Easter Wishes Tender Touches 875QE08196	L. Votruba	Yr.Iss.	8.75	8.75
94-195-017	Peeping Out 675QE08203	D. Unruh	Yr.Iss.	6.75	6.75
94-195-018	Joyful Lamb 575QE08206	D. Unruh	Yr.Iss.	5.75	5.75
94-195-019	Riding a Breeze 575QE08213	D. Palmiter	Yr.Iss.	5.75	5.75
94-195-020	Carrot Trimmers 500QE08226	Hallmark	Yr.Iss.	5.00	5.00
Hallmark Keepsake Ornaments		**1994 Personalized Ornaments**			
94-196-001	Etch-A-Sketch 1075QP6006	Keepsake	Yr.Iss.	10.75	10.75
94-196-002	Fishing Basket 1475QP6023	Keepsake	Yr.Iss.	14.75	14.75
94-196-003	Heart Carved on Tree 1475QP6036	Keepsake	Yr.Iss.	14.75	14.75
94-196-004	Computer w/ "Mouse" 1275QP6046	Keepsake	Yr.Iss.	12.75	12.75
94-196-005	Reindeer Rooters 1475QP6056	Keepsake	Yr.Iss.	14.75	14.75
94-196-006	Mouse w/ Book 1275QP6066	Keepsake	Yr.Iss.	12.75	12.75
94-196-007	Cookie w/ Chipmunk 1075QP6073	Keepsake	Yr.Iss.	10.75	10.75
94-196-008	Cordless Phone 2950QXR6116	Keepsake	Yr.Iss.	29.50	29.50
94-196-009	Santa Says 1475QP6005	Keepsake	Yr.Iss.	14.75	14.75
94-196-010	Goin' Golfin' 1275QP6012	Keepsake	Yr.Iss.	12.75	12.75
94-196-011	Mailbox Delivery 1475QP6015	Keepsake	Yr.Iss.	14.75	14.75
94-196-012	On the Billboard 1275QP6022	Keepsake	Yr.Iss.	12.75	12.75
94-196-013	Photo Album 1275QP6025	Keepsake	Yr.Iss.	12.75	12.75
94-196-014	Playing Ball 1275QP6032	Keepsake	Yr.Iss.	12.75	12.75
94-196-015	Baby Block 1475QP6035	Keepsake	Yr.Iss.	14.75	14.75
Hallmark Keepsake Ornaments		**1994 Special Issues**			
94-197-001	Holiday Barbie #2 1495QX5216	Keepsake	Yr.Iss.	14.95	14.95
94-197-002	Barbie #1-Nostalgic 1495QX5006	Keepsake	Yr.Iss.	14.95	14.95
94-197-003	Simba/Nala-Lion King (2) 1295QX5303	Keepsake	Yr.Iss.	12.95	12.95
94-197-004	Timon/Pumbaa-Lion King 895QX5366	Keepsake	Yr.Iss.	8.95	8.95
94-197-005	Mufasa/Simba-Lion King 1495QX5406	Keepsake	Yr.Iss.	14.95	14.95
94-197-006	Barney 995QX5966	Keepsake	Yr.Iss.	9.95	9.95
Hallmark Keepsake Ornaments		**1994 Premiere Event**			
94-198-001	Tender T. Bear Decorating Tree 1500QX5336	Keepsake	Yr.Iss.	15.00	15.00
Hallmark Keepsake Ornaments		**1994 Keepsake Collector's Club**			
94-199-001	Happy Collecting 300QXC4803	Keepsake	Yr.Iss.	3.00	3.00
94-199-002	Sweet Bouquet 850QXC4806	Keepsake	Yr.Iss.	8.50	8.50
94-199-003	Holiday Pursuit 1175QXC4823	Keepsake	Yr.Iss.	11.75	11.75
94-199-004	First Hello 500QXC4846	Keepsake	Yr.Iss.	5.00	5.00
94-199-005	On Cloud Nine 1200QXC4853	Keepsake	Yr.Iss.	12.00	12.00
94-199-006	Mrs. Claus' Cupboard 5500QXC4843	Keepsake	Yr.Iss.	55.00	55.00
94-199-007	Tilling Time 500QXC8256	Keepsake	Yr.Iss.	5.00	5.00
Hallmark Keepsake Ornaments		**1994 Limited Editions**			
94-200-001	Jolly Holly Santa 2200QXC4833	Keepsake	N/A	22.00	22.00
94-200-002	Majestic Deer 2500QXC4836	Keepsake	N/A	25.00	25.00
Hallmark Keepsake Showcase Ornaments		**1994 Old World Silver Collection**			
94-01-001	Silver Poinsettias 2475QK1006	Keepsake	Yr.Iss.	24.75	24.75
94-01-002	Silver Snowflakes 2475QK1016	Keepsake	Yr.Iss.	24.75	24.75
94-01-003	Silver Bows 2475QK1023	Keepsake	Yr.Iss.	24.75	24.75
94-01-004	Silver Bells 2475QK1026	Keepsake	Yr.Iss.	24.75	24.75
Hallmark Keepsake Showcase Ornaments		**1994 Folk Art Americana Collection**			
94-02-001	Catching 40 Winks 1500QK1183	Keepsake	Yr.Iss.	15.00	15.00
94-02-002	Rarin' to Go 1500QK1193	Keepsake	Yr.Iss.	15.00	15.00
94-02-003	Going to Town 1575QK1166	Keepsake	Yr.Iss.	15.75	15.75
94-02-004	Racing Through the Snow 1575QK1173	Keepsake	Yr.Iss.	15.75	15.75
94-02-005	Roundup Time 1675QK1176	Keepsake	Yr.Iss.	16.75	16.75
Hallmark Keepsake Showcase Ornaments		**1994 Crystal Holidays Collection**			
94-03-001	Sapphire Skaters 2500QK1073	Keepsake	Yr.Iss.	25.00	25.00
94-03-002	Amethyst Forest 2500QK1076	Keepsake	Yr.Iss.	25.00	25.00
94-03-003	Emerald Sleigh Ride 2750QK1066	Keepsake	Yr.Iss.	27.50	27.50
94-03-004	Topaz Memories 3000QK1056	Keepsake	Yr.Iss.	30.00	30.00
94-03-005	Ruby Santa 3000QK1063	Keepsake	Yr.Iss.	30.00	30.00
Hallmark Keepsake Showcase Ornaments		**1994 Crackleware Ceramic Collection**			
94-04-001	Graceful Fawn 1075QK1033	Keepsake	Yr.Iss.	10.75	10.75
94-04-002	Joyful Lamb 1075QK1036	Keepsake	Yr.Iss.	10.75	10.75
94-04-003	Peaceful Dove 1075QK1043	Keepsake	Yr.Iss.	10.75	10.75
94-04-004	Jolly Santa 1075QK1046	Keepsake	Yr.Iss.	10.75	10.75
94-04-005	Dapper Snowman 1075QK1053	Keepsake	Yr.Iss.	10.75	10.75
Hand & Hammer		**Hand & Hammer Ornaments**			
80-01-001	Icicle 009	De Matteo	490	25.00	30.00
81-01-002	Roundel 109	De Matteo	220	25.00	45.00
81-01-003	Gabriel with Liberty Cap 301	De Matteo	275	25.00	50.00
81-01-004	Gabriel 320	De Matteo	Suspd.	25.00	32.00
82-01-005	Fleur de Lys Angel 343	De Matteo	320	28.00	35.00
82-01-006	Madonna & Child 388	De Matteo	175	28.00	50.00
84-01-007	Beardsley Angel 398	De Matteo	Open	28.00	48.00
82-01-008	Carved Heart 425	De Matteo	Suspd.	29.00	48.00
82-01-009	Straw Star 448	De Matteo	590	25.00	40.00
83-01-010	Fire Angel 473	De Matteo	315	25.00	28-36.00
83-01-011	Indian 494	De Matteo	190	29.00	50.00
83-01-012	Pollock Angel 502	De Matteo	Suspd.	35.00	50.00
83-01-013	Calligraphic Deer 511	De Matteo	Suspd.	25.00	29.00
83-01-014	Egyptian Cat 521	De Matteo	Unkn.	13.00	13.00
83-01-015	Dove 522	De Matteo	Unkn.	13.00	13.00
83-01-016	Sargent Angel 523	De Matteo	690	29.00	34.00
83-01-017	Cherub 528	De Matteo	295	29.00	50.00
83-01-018	Japanese Snowflake 534	De Matteo	350	29.00	35.00
83-01-019	Sunburst 543	De Matteo	Unkn.	13.00	50.00
83-01-020	Wise Man 549	De Matteo	Suspd.	29.00	36.00
84-01-021	Freer Star 553	De Matteo	Unkn.	13.00	30.00
84-01-022	Pineapple 558	De Matteo	Suspd.	30.00	38.00
84-01-023	Crescent Angel 559	De Matteo	Suspd.	30.00	32.00
84-01-024	Rosette 571	De Matteo	220	32.00	50.00
84-01-025	Nine Hearts 572	De Matteo	275	34.00	50.00
84-01-026	USHS 1984 Angel 574	De Matteo	Suspd.	35.00	50.00
84-01-027	Wreath 575	De Matteo	Unkn.	13.00	30.00
84-01-028	Praying Angel 576	De Matteo	Suspd.	29.00	30.00
84-01-029	Rocking Horse 581	De Matteo	Unkn.	13.00	13.00
84-01-030	Bunny 582	De Matteo	Unkn.	13.00	30.00
84-01-031	Ibex 584	De Matteo	400	29.00	50.00
84-01-032	Bird & Cherub 588	De Matteo	Unkn.	13.00	30.00
84-01-033	Wild Swan 592	De Matteo	Suspd.	35.00	50.00
84-01-034	Moravian Star 595	De Matteo	Open	38.00	50.00
84-01-035	Manger 601	De Matteo	Suspd.	29.00	32.00
84-01-036	Mt. Vernon Weathervane 602	De Matteo	Suspd.	32.00	39.00

Company / Number	Name	Series / Artist	Edition Limit	Issue Price	Quote
85-01-037	Peacock 603	De Matteo	470	34.00	37.00
85-01-038	Model A Ford 604	De Matteo	Unkn.	13.00	30.00
85-01-039	Crane 606	De Matteo	150	39.00	50.00
85-01-040	Angel 607	De Matteo	225	36.00	50.00
85-01-041	Militiaman 608	De Matteo	460	25.00	30.00
85-01-042	Nutcracker 609	De Matteo	510	30.00	50.00
85-01-043	Liberty Bell 611	De Matteo	Suspd.	32.00	40.00
85-01-044	Angel 612	De Matteo	217	32.00	50.00
85-01-045	Abigail 613	De Matteo	500	32.00	50.00
85-01-046	Audubon Swallow 614	De Matteo	Suspd.	48.00	60.00
85-01-047	Audubon Bluebird 615	De Matteo	Suspd.	48.00	60.00
85-01-048	Guardian Angel 616	De Matteo	1,340	35.00	39.00
85-01-049	Shepherd 617	De Matteo	1,770	35.00	39.00
85-01-050	Carousel Pony 618	De Matteo	Unkn.	13.00	13.00
85-01-051	Art Deco Deer 620	De Matteo	Suspd.	34.00	38.00
85-01-052	Halley's Comet 621	De Matteo	432	35.00	50.00
85-01-053	Mermaid 622	De Matteo	Suspd.	35.00	39.00
85-01-054	George Washington 629	De Matteo	Suspd.	35.00	39.00
85-01-055	USHS Madonna 630	De Matteo	Suspd.	35.00	50.00
85-01-056	USHS Bluebird 631	De Matteo	Suspd.	29.00	50.00
85-01-057	USHS Swallow 632	De Matteo	Suspd.	29.00	50.00
85-01-058	Grasshopper 634	De Matteo	Open	32.00	39.00
85-01-059	Hosanna 635	De Matteo	715	32.00	50.00
85-01-060	Teddy 637	De Matteo	Suspd.	37.00	40.00
85-01-061	Herald Angel 641	De Matteo	Suspd.	36.00	40.00
85-01-062	Cherub 642	De Matteo	815	37.00	37.00
85-01-063	Butterfly 646	De Matteo	Suspd.	39.00	39.00
85-01-064	French Quarter Heart 647	De Matteo	Open	37.00	36.00
85-01-065	Samantha 648	De Matteo	Suspd.	35.00	36.00
85-01-066	Eagle 652	De Matteo	375	30.00	50.00
85-01-067	Piazza 653	De Matteo	Suspd.	32.00	50.00
85-01-068	Camel 655	De Matteo	Unkn.	13.00	30.00
85-01-069	Reindeer 656	De Matteo	Unkn.	13.00	30.00
85-01-070	Lafarge Angel 658	De Matteo	Suspd.	32.00	50.00
85-01-071	Family 659	De Matteo	915	32.00	40.00
85-01-072	Unicorn 660	De Matteo	Suspd.	37.00	37.00
85-01-073	Old North Church 661	De Matteo	Open	35.00	39.00
85-01-074	Madonna 666	De Matteo	227	35.00	50.00
85-01-075	Bicycle 669	De Matteo	Unkn.	13.00	30.00
85-01-076	St. Nicholas 670	De Matteo	Unkn.	13.00	30.00
86-01-077	Nativity 679	De Matteo	Suspd.	36.00	38.00
86-01-078	Winged Dove 680	De Matteo	Suspd.	35.00	36.00
86-01-079	Nutcracker 681	De Matteo	1,356	37.00	37.00
86-01-080	Phaeton 683	De Matteo	Unkn.	13.00	13.00
86-01-081	Archangel 684	De Matteo	Suspd.	29.00	30.00
86-01-082	Teddy Bear 685	De Matteo	Suspd.	38.00	40.00
86-01-083	Hallelujah 686	De Matteo	Unkn.	38.00	38.00
86-01-084	Bear Claus 692	De Matteo	Unkn.	13.00	13.00
86-01-085	Prancer 698	De Matteo	Open	38.00	38.00
86-01-086	USHS Angel 703	De Matteo	Suspd.	35.00	50.00
86-01-087	Teddy 707	De Matteo	Unkn.	13.00	30.00
86-01-088	Christmas Tree 708	De Matteo	Unkn.	13.00	13.00
86-01-089	Lafarge Angel 710	De Matteo	Suspd.	31.00	50.00
86-01-090	Salem Lamb 712	De Matteo	Suspd.	32.00	40.00
86-01-091	Snowflake 713	De Matteo	Suspd.	36.00	40.00
86-01-092	Wreath 714	De Matteo	Suspd.	36.00	38.00
86-01-093	Santa Skates 715	De Matteo	Suspd.	36.00	36.00
86-01-094	Nightingale 716	De Matteo	Suspd.	35.00	50.00
86-01-095	Mother Goose 719	De Matteo	Open	34.00	40.00
86-01-096	Kringle Bear 723	De Matteo	Unkn.	13.00	30.00
86-01-097	Victorian Santa 724	De Matteo	250	32.00	35.00
87-01-098	Noel 731	De Matteo	Open	38.00	38.00
87-01-099	Naptime 732	J. Walpole	Suspd.	32.00	32.00
87-01-100	Hunting Horn 738	De Matteo	Open	37.00	37.00
87-01-101	Santa Star 739	J. Walpole	Suspd.	32.00	32.00
87-01-102	Sweetheart Star 740	De Matteo	Suspd.	39.50	39.50
87-01-103	Santa 741	De Matteo	Unkn.	13.00	13.00
87-01-104	Pegasus 745	De Matteo	Unkn.	13.00	13.00
87-01-105	Snow Queen 746	De Matteo	Suspd.	35.00	39.00
87-01-106	Dove 747	De Matteo	Unkn.	13.00	13.00
87-01-107	USHS Gloria Angel 748	De Matteo	Suspd.	39.00	50.00
87-01-108	Angel with Lyre 750	De Matteo	Suspd.	32.00	40.00
87-01-109	Santa and Sleigh 751	De Matteo	Suspd.	32.00	40.00
87-01-110	Reindeer 752	De Matteo	Open	38.00	38.00
87-01-111	Snowman 753	De Matteo	825	38.00	38.00
87-01-112	Cat 754	De Matteo	Open	37.00	37.00
87-01-113	Clipper Ship 756	De Matteo	Suspd.	35.00	35.00
87-01-114	Ride a Cock Horse 757	De Matteo	Suspd.	34.00	39.00
87-01-115	Art Deco Angel 765	De Matteo	Suspd.	38.00	40.00
87-01-116	Old Ironsides 767	De Matteo	Open	35.00	39.00
87-01-117	First Christmas 771	De Matteo	Unkn.	13.00	13.00
87-01-118	Stocking 772	De Matteo	Unkn.	13.00	13.00
88-01-119	Drummer Bear 773	De Matteo	Unkn.	13.00	13.00
88-01-120	Stocking 774	De Matteo	Unkn.	13.00	13.00
87-01-121	Minuteman 776	De Matteo	Suspd.	35.00	40.00
87-01-122	Buffalo 777	De Matteo	Suspd.	36.00	36.00
88-01-123	Star of the East 785	De Matteo	Suspd.	35.00	35.00
88-01-124	Dove 786	De Matteo	112	36.00	50.00
88-01-125	Madonna 787	De Matteo	600	35.00	35.00
88-01-126	Magi 788	De Matteo	Suspd.	39.50	39.50
88-01-127	Jack in the Box 789	De Matteo	Suspd.	39.50	39.50
88-01-128	Skaters 790	De Matteo	Suspd.	39.50	39.50
88-01-129	Angel 797	De Matteo	Unkn.	13.00	13.00
88-01-130	Christmas Tree 798	De Matteo	Unkn.	13.00	13.00
88-01-131	Thumbelina 803	De Matteo	Suspd.	35.00	40.00
88-01-132	Star 806	De Matteo	311	50.00	150.00
88-01-133	Madonna 809	De Matteo	15	39.00	50.00
89-01-134	Carousel Horse 811	De Matteo	2,150	34.00	34.00
88-01-135	Bank 812	De Matteo	400	40.00	40.00
88-01-136	Santa with Scroll 814	De Matteo	250	34.00	37.00
88-01-137	Madonna 815	De Matteo	Suspd.	39.00	50.00
88-01-138	Rabbit 816	De Matteo	Unkn.	13.00	13.00
88-01-139	Buggy 817	De Matteo	Unkn.	13.00	13.00
88-01-140	Angel 818	De Matteo	Suspd.	32.00	40.00
88-01-141	Boston State House 819	De Matteo	Open	34.00	40.00
88-01-142	US Capitol 820	De Matteo	Open	38.00	40.00
88-01-143	Nativity 821	De Matteo	Suspd.	32.00	39.00
88-01-144	Old King Cole 824	De Matteo	Suspd.	34.00	39.00
88-01-145	Stocking 827	De Matteo	Unkn.	13.00	13.00
88-01-146	Conn. State House 833	De Matteo	Open	38.00	38.00
88-01-147	Sleigh 834	De Matteo	Open	34.00	38.00
89-01-148	Stocking Bear 835	De Matteo	Unkn.	13.00	13.00
88-01-149	Night Before Xmas Col. 841	De Matteo	10,000	160.00	160.00
89-01-150	First Christmas 842	De Matteo	Unkn.	13.00	13.00

Company Number	Name	Series Artist	Edition Limit	Issue Price	Quote
89-01-151	Locket Bear 844	De Matteo	Unkn.	25.00	25.00
88-01-152	Cable Car 848	De Matteo	Open	38.00	38.00
88-01-153	Star 854	De Matteo	275	32.00	35.00
89-01-154	Santa 1989 856	De Matteo	1,715	35.00	35.00
89-01-155	Goose 857	De Matteo	650	37.00	37.00
89-01-156	Presidential Seal 858	De Matteo	500	39.00	39.00
88-01-157	Eiffel Tower 861	De Matteo	225	38.00	40.00
88-01-158	Coronado 864	De Matteo	Suspd.	38.00	38.00
90-01-159	Carousel Horse 866	De Matteo	1,915	38.00	38.00
90-01-160	Joy 867	De Matteo	1,140	36.00	36.00
90-01-161	Goose & Wreath 868	De Matteo	Open	37.00	37.00
90-01-162	1990 Santa 869	De Matteo	2,250	38.00	38.00
90-01-163	Cardinals 870	De Matteo	Open	39.00	39.00
90-01-164	Angel with Star 871	De Matteo	Open	38.00	38.00
89-01-165	Nutcracker 1989 872	De Matteo	1,790	38.00	38.00
89-01-166	USHS Angel 1989 901	De Matteo	Suspd.	38.00	38.00
89-01-167	Swan Boat 904	De Matteo	Open	38.00	38.00
89-01-168	MFA Noel 905	De Matteo	Suspd.	36.00	42.00
89-01-169	MFA Angel w/Tree 906	De Matteo	Suspd.	36.00	42.00
89-01-170	MFA Durer Snowflake 907	De Matteo	2,000	36.00	42.00
89-01-171	Independence Hall 908	De Matteo	Open	38.00	38.00
90-01-172	Cat on Pillow 915	De Matteo	Unkn.	13.00	13.00
90-01-173	Mouse w/Candy Cane 916	De Matteo	Unkn.	13.00	13.00
89-01-174	L&T Ugly Duckling 917	De Matteo	Suspd.	38.00	38.00
90-01-175	Farmhouse 919	De Matteo	Suspd.	37.00	37.00
90-01-176	Covered Bridge 920	De Matteo	Suspd.	37.00	37.00
90-01-177	Church 921	De Matteo	Suspd.	37.00	37.00
90-01-178	Mill 922	De Matteo	Suspd.	37.00	37.00
90-01-179	Currier & Ives Set -Victorian Village 923	De Matteo	2,000	140.00	140.00
90-01-180	Santa & Reindeer 929	De Matteo	395	39.00	43.00
90-01-181	Christmas Seal 931	De Matteo	Unkn.	25.00	25.00
89-01-182	Bugle Bear 935	De Matteo	Unkn.	12.00	12.00
89-01-183	Jack in the Box Bear 936	De Matteo	Unkn.	12.00	12.00
89-01-184	MFA LaFarge Angel set 937	De Matteo	Suspd.	98.00	98.00
90-01-185	First Christmas Bear 940	De Matteo	Suspd.	35.00	35.00
90-01-186	Santa in the Moon 941	De Matteo	Suspd.	38.00	38.00
90-01-187	Mole & Rat Wind in Will 944	De Matteo	Open	36.00	36.00
90-01-188	Toad Wind in Willows 945	De Matteo	Open	38.00	38.00
90-01-189	Merry Christmas Locket 948	De Matteo	Unkn.	25.00	25.00
90-01-190	Teddy Bear Locket 949	De Matteo	Unkn.	25.00	25.00
89-01-191	Barnesville Buggy 1989 950	De Matteo	Unkn.	13.00	13.00
89-01-192	Victorian Heart 954	De Matteo	Unkn.	13.00	13.00
89-01-193	Stocking Bear 955	De Matteo	Unkn.	12.00	12.00
89-01-194	Stocking w/Toys 956	De Matteo	Unkn.	12.00	12.00
90-01-195	Teddy Bear w/Heart 957	De Matteo	Unkn.	13.00	13.00
90-01-196	Clown w/Dog 958	De Matteo	Unkn.	13.00	13.00
90-01-197	Heart Angel 959	De Matteo	Suspd.	39.00	39.00
90-01-198	Carriage 960	De Matteo	Unkn.	13.00	13.00
90-01-199	Blake Angel 961	De Matteo	Unkn.	36.00	36.00
90-01-200	Colonial Capitol 965	De Matteo	Open	39.00	39.00
90-01-201	Governor's Palace 966	De Matteo	Open	39.00	39.00
90-01-202	Cockatoo 969	De Matteo	Unkn.	13.00	13.00
90-01-203	Father Christmas 970	De Matteo	Suspd.	36.00	36.00
90-01-204	Old Fashioned Santa 971	De Matteo	Suspd.	36.00	36.00
90-01-205	Patriotic Santa 972	De Matteo	Suspd.	36.00	36.00
90-01-206	Santa in Balloon 973	De Matteo	Suspd.	36.00	36.00
90-01-207	Santa on Reindeer 974	De Matteo	Suspd.	36.00	36.00
90-01-208	Santa UpTo Date 975	De Matteo	Suspd.	36.00	36.00
90-01-209	Presidential Homes 990	De Matteo	Open	350.00	350.00
90-01-210	Mrs. Rabbit 991	De Matteo	Open	39.50	39.50
90-01-211	Jeremy Fisher 992	De Matteo	Open	39.50	39.50
90-01-212	Peter Rabbit 993	De Matteo	Open	39.50	39.50
90-01-213	Peter's First Christmas 994	De Matteo	Suspd.	39.50	39.50
90-01-214	Flopsy Bunnies 995	De Matteo	Suspd.	39.50	39.50
90-01-215	First Baptist Angel 997	De Matteo	200	35.00	35.00
91-01-216	I Love Santa 998	De Matteo	Open	36.00	36.00
90-01-217	1990 Peter Rabbit 1018	De Matteo	4,315	39.50	39.50
90-01-218	Peter Rabbit Locket Ornament 1019	De Matteo	Unkn.	30.00	30.00
90-01-219	Jemima Puddleduck 1020	De Matteo	Unkn.	30.00	30.00
90-01-220	Landing Duck 1021	De Matteo	Unkn.	13.00	13.00
90-01-221	White Tail Deer 1022	De Matteo	Unkn.	13.00	13.00
90-01-222	Elk 1023	De Matteo	Unkn.	13.00	13.00
90-01-223	Angel With Violin 1024	De Matteo	Suspd.	39.00	39.00
91-01-224	Carousel Horse 1025	De Matteo	Open	38.00	38.00
91-01-225	Angel With Horn 1026	De Matteo	Open	32.00	32.00
90-01-226	Conestoga Wagon 1027	De Matteo	Open	38.00	38.00
90-01-227	Liberty Bell 1028	De Matteo	Open	38.00	38.00
90-01-228	The Boston Light 1032	De Matteo	Open	39.50	39.50
90-01-229	1990 Snowflake 1033	De Matteo	1,415	36.00	38.00
90-01-230	Pegasus 1037	De Matteo	Suspd.	35.00	35.00
90-01-231	Angels 1039	De Matteo	Suspd.	36.00	36.00
90-01-232	Beardsley Angel 1040	De Matteo	Suspd.	34.00	34.00
90-01-233	Georgia State Capitol 1042	De Matteo	2,000	39.50	39.50
90-01-234	N. Carolina State Capitol 1043	De Matteo	2,000	39.50	39.50
90-01-235	Florida State Capitol 1044	De Matteo	2,000	39.50	39.50
90-01-236	S. Carolina State Capitol 1045	De Matteo	2,000	39.50	39.50
90-01-237	Joy 1047	De Matteo	Suspd.	39.00	39.00
90-01-238	Steadfast Tin Soldier 1050	De Matteo	Suspd.	36.00	36.00
91-01-239	Cow Jumped Over The Moon 1055	De Matteo	Suspd.	38.00	38.00
91-01-240	1991 Santa 1056	De Matteo	3,750	38.00	38.00
90-01-241	USHS Angel 1990 1061	De Matteo	Suspd.	39.00	39.00
90-01-242	San Francisco Row House 1071	De Matteo	Open	39.50	39.50
91-01-243	Mommy & Baby Seal 1075	De Matteo	Suspd.	36.00	36.00
91-01-244	Mommy & Baby Wolves 1076	De Matteo	Suspd.	36.00	36.00
91-01-245	Mommy & Baby Koala Bear 1077	De Matteo	Suspd.	36.00	36.00
91-01-246	Mommy & Baby Kangaroo 1078	De Matteo	Suspd.	36.00	36.00
91-01-247	Mommy & Baby Panda Bear 1079	De Matteo	Suspd.	36.00	36.00
91-01-248	Large Jemima Puddleduck 1083	De Matteo	Open	49.50	49.50
90-01-249	Ferrel's Angel 1990 1084	De Matteo	Unkn.	15.00	15.00
91-01-250	Olivers Rocking Horse 1085	De Matteo	Open	37.00	37.00
91-01-251	Mrs. Rabbit 1991 1086	De Matteo	Suspd.	39.50	39.50
91-01-252	Tailor of Gloucester 1087	De Matteo	Open	39.50	39.50
91-01-253	Pig Robinson 1090	De Matteo	Open	39.50	39.50
91-01-254	Appley Dapply 1091	De Matteo	Open	39.50	39.50
91-01-255	Peter Rabbit With Book 1093	De Matteo	Open	39.50	39.50
90-01-256	Koala San Diego Zoo 1095	De Matteo	Open	36.00	36.00
90-01-257	Locomotive 1100	De Matteo	Suspd.	39.00	39.00
90-01-258	Montpelier 1113	De Matteo	Open	36.00	36.00
90-01-259	Ducklings 1114	De Matteo	Open	38.00	38.00
91-01-260	Large Peter Rabbit 1116	De Matteo	Open	49.50	49.50
91-01-261	Large Tailor of Gloucester 1117	De Matteo	Open	49.50	49.50
91-01-262	Nativity 1118	De Matteo	Open	38.00	38.00
91-01-263	Alice 1119	De Matteo	Open	39.00	39.00
91-01-264	Mad Tea Party 1120	De Matteo	Open	39.00	39.00
91-01-265	White Rabbit 1121	De Matteo	Open	39.00	39.00
91-01-266	Queen of Hearts 1122	De Matteo	Open	39.00	39.00
91-01-267	Waiting For Santa 1123	De Matteo	Open	38.00	38.00
90-01-268	Ember 1124	De Matteo	120	N/A	N/A
91-01-269	USHS Angel 1991 1139	De Matteo	Suspd.	38.00	38.00
91-01-270	Columbus 1140	De Matteo	1,500	39.00	39.00
91-01-271	The Voyages Of Columbus 1141	De Matteo	1,500	39.00	39.00
91-01-272	Precious Planet 1142	De Matteo	2,000	120.00	120.00
91-01-273	MFA Snowflake 1991 1143	De Matteo	Suspd.	36.00	36.00
91-01-274	Fir Tree 1145	De Matteo	Open	39.00	39.00
91-01-275	Nutcracker 1151	De Matteo	Open	49.50	49.50
91-01-276	Paul Revere 1158	De Matteo	Open	39.00	39.00
91-01-277	Alice in Wonderland 1159	De Matteo	Open	140.00	140.00
91-01-278	Nutcracker 1183	De Matteo	Open	38.00	38.00
91-01-279	Nutrcracker Suite 1184	De Matteo	Open	38.00	38.00
91-01-280	Gus 1195	De Matteo	200	N/A	N/A
91-01-281	San Francisco Heart 1196	De Matteo	Open	39.00	39.00
92-01-282	Xmas Tree & Heart 1162	De Matteo	Suspd.	36.00	36.00
92-01-283	Andrea 1163	De Matteo	Suspd.	36.00	36.00
92-01-284	Joy 1164	De Matteo	Open	39.50	39.50
92-01-285	Unicorn 1165	De Matteo	Suspd.	36.00	36.00
92-01-286	Noah's Ark 1166	De Matteo	Open	36.00	36.00
92-01-287	Jemima Puddleduck 1992 1167	De Matteo	Suspd.	39.50	39.50
92-01-288	Mrs. Rabbit 1181	De Matteo	Open	39.50	39.50
92-01-289	Round Teapot 1206	De Matteo	Open	49.50	49.50
92-01-290	Revere Teapot 1207	De Matteo	Open	49.50	49.50
92-01-291	Chocolate Pot 1208	De Matteo	Open	49.50	49.50
92-01-292	Angel W/ Double Horn 1212	De Matteo	2,000	49.50	49.50
92-01-293	Angel 1213	De Matteo	2,000	39.00	39.00
92-01-294	Della Robbia Ornament 1219	De Matteo	Open	39.00	39.00
92-01-295	Fairy Tale Angel 1222	De Matteo	Open	36.00	36.00
92-01-296	Parrot 1233	De Matteo	Open	37.00	37.00
92-01-297	St. John Lion 1235	De Matteo	10,000	39.00	39.00
92-01-298	St. John Angel 1236	De Matteo	10,000	39.00	39.00
92-01-299	Scrooge 1241	De Matteo	Open	36.00	36.00
92-01-300	Bob & Tiny Tim 1242	De Matteo	Open	36.00	36.00
92-01-301	Marley's Ghost 1243	De Matteo	Open	36.00	36.00
92-01-302	Mrs. Cratchit 1244	De Matteo	Open	36.00	36.00
92-01-303	America At Peace 1245	De Matteo	2,000	85.00	85.00
92-01-304	MFA Snowflake 1246	De Matteo	Open	39.00	39.00
92-01-305	Princess & The Pea 1247	De Matteo	Open	39.00	39.00
92-01-306	Dorothy 1284	De Matteo	Open	36.00	36.00
92-01-307	Tin Man 1285	De Matteo	Open	36.00	36.00
92-01-308	Scarecrow 1286	De Matteo	Open	36.00	36.00
92-01-309	Cowardly Lion 1287	De Matteo	Open	36.00	36.00
92-01-310	Heart of Christmas 1301	De Matteo	500	39.00	39.00
93-01-311	Angel Bell 1312	De Matteo	Open	38.00	38.00
93-01-312	Clara with Nutcracker 1316	De Matteo	Open	38.00	38.00
93-01-313	Carousel Horse 1993 1321	De Matteo	Yr.Iss.	38.00	38.00
93-01-314	Lion and Lamb 1322	De Matteo	Open	38.00	38.00
93-01-315	Mrs. Rabbit 1993 1325	De Matteo	Yr.Iss	39.50	39.50
93-01-316	Peace 1327	De Matteo	Open	36.00	36.00
93-01-317	Partridge & Pear 1328	De Matteo	Open	38.00	38.00
93-01-318	Violin 1340	De Matteo	Unkn.	39.50	39.50
93-01-319	Angel 1342	De Matteo	Open	38.00	38.00
93-01-320	Zig Zag Tree 1343	De Matteo	Open	39.00	39.00
93-01-321	Beantown 1344	De Matteo	Open	38.00	38.00
93-01-322	Creche 1351	De Matteo	Open	38.00	38.00
93-01-323	Celebrate America 1352	De Matteo	Open	38.00	38.00
93-01-324	Cheer Mouse 1359	De Matteo	Open	39.00	39.00
93-01-325	Window 1360	De Matteo	Open	38.00	38.00
93-01-326	Cable Car to the Stars 1363	De Matteo	Open	39.00	39.00
93-01-327	Public Garden 1370	De Matteo	Open	38.00	38.00
93-01-328	Peter Rabit 100th 1383	De Matteo	Yr.Iss.	39.50	39.50
93-01-329	Snowflake 1993 1394	De Matteo	Yr.Iss.	40.00	40.00
93-01-330	Xmas Tree 1395	De Matteo	Open	40.00	40.00
93-01-331	Puss In Boots 1396	De Matteo	Open	40.00	40.00
93-01-332	Gurgling Cod 1397	De Matteo	Open	50.00	50.00
93-01-333	Mouse King 1398	De Matteo	Open	38.00	38.00
93-01-334	Faneuil Hall 1399	De Matteo	Open	39.00	39.00
93-01-335	Angel 1993 1405	De Matteo	Yr.Iss.	45.00	45.00
93-01-336	Faneuil Hall 1412	De Matteo	Open	39.50	39.50
94-01-337	Golden Gate Bridge 1429	De Matteo	Open	39.50	39.50
94-01-338	Beatrix Potter Noel 1438	De Matteo	Open	39.50	39.50
94-01-339	Emperor 1439	De Matteo	Open	38.00	38.00
94-01-340	Heart of Christmas 1440	De Matteo	Open	39.00	39.00
94-01-341	Canterbury Star 1441	De Matteo	Open	35.00	35.00
94-01-342	Marmion Angels 1443	De Matteo	Open	50.00	50.00
94-01-343	1994 Peter Rabbit 1444	De Matteo	Yr.Iss.	39.50	39.50
94-01-344	Cardinal & Holly 1445	De Matteo	Open	38.00	38.00
94-01-345	R.E. Lee Monument 1446	De Matteo	Open	39.00	39.00
94-01-346	Weld Boathouse 1447	De Matteo	Open	39.00	39.00
94-01-347	1994 Star 1462	De Matteo	Yr.Iss.	39.50	39.50
94-01-348	Holly 1472	De Matteo	Open	38.00	38.00
94-01-349	Noel 1477	De Matteo	Open	38.00	38.00
94-01-350	Two Turtle Doves 1478	De Matteo	Open	38.00	38.00
94-01-351	Angel With Star 1480	De Matteo	Open	38.00	38.00
94-01-352	Heralding Angel 1481	De Matteo	Open	39.00	39.00
94-01-353	Marengo 1482	De Matteo	Open	39.00	39.00
94-01-354	1994 Snowflake 1486	De Matteo	Yr.Iss.	39.00	39.00
Hand & Hammer		**Annual Ornaments**			
87-02-001	Silver Bells 737	De Matteo	2,700	38.00	50.00
88-02-002	Silver Bells 792	De Matteo	3,150	39.50	39.50
89-02-003	Silver Bells 843	De Matteo	3,150	39.50	39.50
90-02-004	Silver Bells 865	De Matteo	3,615	39.00	39.00
90-02-005	Silver Bells Rev. 964	De Matteo	4,490	39.00	39.00
91-02-006	Silver Bells 1080	De Matteo	4,100	39.50	39.50
92-02-007	Silver Bells 1148	De Matteo	4,100	39.50	39.50
93-02-008	Silver Bells 1311	De Matteo	Yr.Iss.	39.50	39.50
94-02-009	Silver Bells 1463	De Matteo	Yr.Iss.	39.50	39.50
John Hine N.A. Ltd.		**David Winter Ornaments**			
91-01-001	Scrooge's Counting House	D. Winter	Closed	15.00	23.00
91-01-002	Hogmanay	D. Winter	Closed	15.00	23.00
91-01-003	A Christmas Carol	D. Winter	Closed	15.00	23.00
91-01-004	Mister Fezziwig's Emporium	D. Winter	Closed	15.00	23.00
91-01-005	Set	D. Winter	Closed	60.00	52-125.00
92-01-006	Fairytale Castle	D. Winter	Closed	15.00	15-23.00
92-01-007	Fred's Home	D. Winter	Closed	15.00	15-23.00
92-01-008	Suffolk House	D. Winter	Closed	15.00	15-23.00
92-01-009	Tudor Manor	D. Winter	Closed	15.00	15-23.00
92-01-010	Set	D. Winter	Closed	60.00	35-90.00
93-01-011	Scrooge's School	J. Hine Studios	Closed	15.00	15.00

CHRISTMAS ORNAMENTS

Company Number	Name	Series Artist	Edition Limit	Issue Price	Quote
93-01-012	Will O The Wisp	J. Hine Studios	Closed	15.00	15.00
93-01-013	The Grange	J. Hine Studios	Closed	15.00	15.00
93-01-014	Tom Fool's	J. Hine Studios	Closed	15.00	15.00
93-01-015	Set	J. Hine Studios	Closed	60.00	60.00
Iris Arc Crystal		**Christmas Ornaments**			
84-01-001	1984 Merry Christmas Ornament	P. Hale	Retrd.	28.00	28.00
85-01-002	1985 Noel Ornament	P. Hale	Retrd.	28.00	28.00
86-01-003	1986 Noel Christmas Ornament	P. Hale	Retrd.	30.00	30.00
87-01-004	1987 Angel Christmas Ornament	P. Hale	Retrd.	30.00	30.00
88-01-005	1988 Merry Christmas Ornament	P. Hale	Retrd.	30.00	30.00
89-01-006	1989 Christmas Ornament	P. Hale	Retrd.	30.00	30.00
90-01-007	1990 Reindeer Christmas Ornament	M. Goena	Retrd.	30.00	30.00
91-01-008	1991 Santa Christmas Ornament	M. Goena	Retrd.	35.00	35.00
92-01-009	1992 Angel Christmas Ornament	M. Goena	Retrd.	30.00	30.00
93-01-010	1993 Dove Christmas Ornament	M. Goena	Retrd.	35.00	35.00
Kirk Stieff		**Colonial Williamsburg**			
83-01-001	Tree Top Star, silverplate	D. Bacorn	Closed	29.50	29.50
87-01-002	Rocking Horse, silverplate	D. Bacorn	Closed	19.95	30.00
87-01-003	Tin Drum, silverplate	D. Bacorn	Closed	19.95	30.00
88-01-004	Lamb, silverplate	D. Bacorn	Closed	19.95	22.00
88-01-005	Unicorn, silverplate	D. Bacorn	Closed	22.00	22.00
89-01-006	Doll ornament, silverplate	D. Bacorn	Closed	22.00	22.00
92-01-007	Court House	D. Bacorn	Open	10.00	10.00
92-01-008	Prentis Store	D. Bacorn	Open	10.00	10.00
92-01-009	Wythe House	D. Bacorn	Open	10.00	10.00
93-01-010	Governors Palace	D. Bacorn	Open	10.00	10.00
Kirk Stieff		**Twelve Days of Christmas**			
85-02-001	Partridge in a Pear Tree	J. Barata	Closed	9.95	10.95
85-02-002	Two Turtle Doves	J. Barata	Closed	9.95	10.95
86-02-003	Three French Hens	J. Barata	Closed	9.95	10.95
86-02-004	Four Calling Birds	J. Barata	Closed	9.95	10.95
87-02-005	Five Golden Rings	J. Barata	Closed	9.95	10.95
87-02-006	Six Geese-A-Laying	J. Barata	Closed	9.95	10.95
88-02-007	Seven Swans-A-Swimming	J. Barata	Closed	9.95	10.95
88-02-008	Eight Maids-A-Milking	J. Barata	Closed	9.95	10.95
89-02-009	Nine Ladies Dancing	J. Barata	Closed	10.95	10.95
89-02-010	Ten Lords-a-Leaping	J. Barata	Closed	10.95	10.95
Kirk Stieff		**The Nutcracker Stained Glass Ornaments**			
86-03-001	Clara's Gift	Kirk Stieff	Closed	17.50	17.50
86-03-002	The Battle	Kirk Stieff	Closed	17.50	17.50
86-03-003	The Nutcracker Prince	Kirk Stieff	Closed	17.50	17.50
86-03-004	The Sugar Plum Fairy	Kirk Stieff	Closed	17.50	17.50
86-03-005	Set of Four	Kirk Stieff	Closed	69.95	69.95
Kirk Stieff		**Kirk Stieff Ornaments**			
84-04-001	Unicorn	D. Bacorn	Closed	17.50	19.95
83-04-002	Charleston Locomotive	D. Bacorn	Closed	17.50	19.95
86-04-003	Icicle, sterling silver	D. Bacorn	Closed	35.00	50.00
89-04-004	Smithsonian Carousel Horse	Kirk Stieff	Closed	50.00	50.00
89-04-005	Smithsonian Carousel Seahorse	Kirk Stieff	Closed	50.00	50.00
90-04-006	Toy Ship	Kirk Stieff	Closed	23.00	23.00
92-04-007	Repoussé Wreath	J. Ferraioli	Open	13.00	13.00
92-04-008	Repoussé Angel	J. Ferraioli	Open	13.00	13.00
92-04-009	Cat and Ornament	D. Bacorn	Open	10.00	10.00
92-04-010	Guardian Angel	J. Ferraioli	Open	13.00	13.00
93-04-011	Cat with Ribbon	D. Bacorn	Open	12.00	12.00
93-04-012	Bell with Ribbon	D. Bacorn	Open	12.00	12.00
93-04-013	Wreath with Ribbon	D. Bacorn	Open	12.00	12.00
93-04-014	Baby's Christmas	D. Bacorn	Open	12.00	12.00
93-04-015	French Horn	D. Bacorn	Open	12.00	12.00
93-04-016	Mouse and Ornament	D. Bacorn	Open	10.00	10.00
93-04-017	First Christmas Together	D. Bacorn	Open	10.00	10.00
Lance Corporation		**Sebastian Christmas Ornaments**			
43-01-001	Madonna of the Chair	P.W. Baston	Closed	2.00	150-200.
81-01-002	Santa Claus	P.W. Baston	Closed	28.50	30.00
82-01-003	Madonna of the Chair (Reissue of '43)	P.W. Baston	Closed	15.00	30-45.00
85-01-004	Home for the Holidays	P.W. Baston Jr.	Closed	10.00	12.50
86-01-005	Holiday Sleigh Ride	P.W. Baston Jr.	Closed	10.00	12.50
87-01-006	Santa	P.W. Baston Jr.	Closed	10.00	12.50
88-01-007	Decorating the Tree	P.W. Baston Jr.	Closed	12.50	12.50
89-01-008	Final Preparations for Christmas	P.W. Baston Jr.	Closed	13.90	13.90
90-01-009	Stuffing the Stockings	P.W. Baston Jr.	Closed	14.00	14.00
91-01-010	Merry Christmas	P.W. Baston Jr.	Closed	14.50	14.50
92-01-011	Final Check	P.W. Baston Jr.	Closed	14.50	14.50
93-01-012	Ethnic Santa	P.W. Baston Jr.	Closed	12.50	12.50
93-01-013	Caroling With Santa	P.W. Baston Jr.	Annual	15.00	15.00
Lenox China		**Annual Ornaments**			
82-01-001	1982 Ornament	Lenox	Yr.Iss.	30.00	50-90.00
83-01-002	1983 Ornament	Lenox	Yr.Iss.	35.00	75.00
84-01-003	1984 Ornament	Lenox	Yr.Iss.	38.00	65.00
85-01-004	1985 Ornament	Lenox	Yr.Iss.	37.50	60.00
86-01-005	1986 Ornament	Lenox	Yr.Iss.	38.50	50.00
87-01-006	1987 Ornament	Lenox	Yr.Iss.	39.00	45.00
88-01-007	1988 Ornament	Lenox	Yr.Iss.	39.00	45.00
89-01-008	1989 Ornament	Lenox	Yr.Iss.	39.00	39.00
90-01-009	1990 Ornament	Lenox	Yr.Iss.	42.00	42.00
91-01-010	1991 Ornament	Lenox	Yr.Iss.	39.00	39.00
92-01-011	1992 Ornament	Lenox	Yr.Iss.	39.00	39.00
93-01-012	1993 Ornament	Lenox	Yr.Iss.	39.00	39.00
Lenox China		**Days of Christmas**			
87-02-001	Partridge	Lenox	Open	22.50	22.50
88-02-002	Two Turtle Doves	Lenox	Open	22.50	22.50
89-02-003	Three French Hens	Lenox	Open	22.50	22.50
90-02-004	Four Calling Birds	Lenox	Open	25.00	25.00
91-02-005	Five Golden Rings	Lenox	Open	25.00	25.00
92-02-006	Six Geese a-Laying	Lenox	Open	25.00	25.00
93-02-007	Seven Swans	Lenox	Open	26.00	26.00
Lenox China		**Yuletide**			
85-03-001	Teddy Bear	Lenox	Closed	18.00	18.00
85-03-002	Christmas Tree	Lenox	Open	18.00	18.00
89-03-003	Santa with Tree	Lenox	Closed	18.00	18.00
89-03-004	Angel with Horn	Lenox	Open	18.00	18.00
90-03-005	Dove	Lenox	Open	19.50	19.50
91-03-006	Snowman	Lenox	Open	19.50	19.50
92-03-007	Goose	Lenox	Open	19.50	19.50
93-03-008	Cardinal	Lenox	Open	19.50	19.50

Company Number	Name	Series Artist	Edition Limit	Issue Price	Quote
Lenox China		**Carved**			
87-04-001	Portrait Wreath	Lenox	Closed	21.00	21.00
89-04-002	Georgian Frame	Lenox	Open	25.00	25.00
Lenox China		**Renaissance Angels**			
87-05-001	Angel with Trumpet	Lenox	Closed	21.00	21.00
87-05-002	Angel with Violin	Lenox	Closed	21.00	21.00
87-05-003	Angel with Mandolin	Lenox	Closed	21.00	21.00
Lenox China		**Golden Renaissance Angels**			
91-06-001	Angel with Trumpet	Lenox	Open	25.00	25.00
91-06-002	Angel with Violin	Lenox	Open	25.00	25.00
91-06-003	Angel with Mandolin	Lenox	Open	25.00	25.00
Lenox China		**Nativity**			
89-07-001	Mary & Child	Lenox	Closed	21.00	21.00
89-07-002	Joseph	Lenox	Closed	21.00	21.00
90-07-003	Melchior	Lenox	Closed	22.00	22.00
90-07-004	Gaspar	Lenox	Closed	22.00	22.00
90-07-005	Balthazar	Lenox	Closed	22.00	22.00
Lenox China		**Commemoratives**			
89-08-001	First Christmas Together (Dated)	Lenox	Yr.Iss.	22.50	25.00
89-08-002	Baby's First Christmas (Dated)	Lenox	Yr.Iss.	22.50	25.00
Lenox China		**Holiday Homecoming**			
88-09-001	Hearth	Lenox	Closed	22.50	22.50
89-09-002	Door (Dated)	Lenox	Closed	22.50	22.50
90-09-003	Hutch	Lenox	Open	25.00	25.00
91-09-004	Window (Dated)	Lenox	Yr.Iss.	25.00	25.00
92-09-005	Stove (Dated)	Lenox	Yr.Iss.	25.00	25.00
93-09-006	Clock	Lenox	Yr.Iss.	26.00	26.00
Lenox China		**Santa's Portraits**			
89-10-001	Santa's Visit	Lenox	Open	27.00	27.00
90-10-002	Santa With Garland	Lenox	Open	29.00	29.00
90-10-003	Santa's Ride	Lenox	Open	29.00	29.00
91-10-004	Santa And Child	Lenox	Open	29.00	29.00
92-10-005	Santa in Chimney	Lenox	Open	29.00	29.00
93-10-006	Santa Filling Stocking	Lenox	Open	29.00	29.00
Lenox China		**Lenox Christmas Village**			
89-11-001	Village Church	Lenox	Open	39.00	45.00
90-11-002	Village Inn	Lenox	Open	39.00	45.00
91-11-003	Village Town Hall (Dated)	Lenox	Yr.Iss.	39.00	45.00
92-11-004	Sweet Shop (Dated)	Lenox	Yr.Iss.	39.00	45.00
Lenox China		**Yuletide Express**			
88-12-001	Locomotive	Lenox	Open	39.00	39.00
89-12-002	Caboose	Lenox	Open	39.00	90.00
90-12-003	Passenger Car	Lenox	Open	39.00	39.00
91-12-004	Dining Car (Dated)	Lenox	Yr.Iss.	39.00	39.00
92-12-005	Tender Car (Dated)	Lenox	Yr.Iss.	39.00	39.00
Lenox China		**Renaissance Angel Treetopper**			
89-13-001	Angel Treetopper	Lenox	Closed	100.00	100.00
Lenox China		**Victorian Homes**			
90-14-001	Sheffield Manor	Lenox	Open	25.00	25.00
91-14-002	Cambridge Manor	Lenox	Open	25.00	25.00
92-14-003	Pembroke Manor	Lenox	Open	26.00	26.00
Lenox China		**Lenox Christmas Keepsakes**			
90-15-001	Swan	Lenox	Open	42.00	42.00
90-15-002	Rocking Horse	Lenox	Open	42.00	42.00
91-15-003	Sleigh	Lenox	Open	42.00	42.00
92-15-004	Fire Engine	Lenox	Open	42.00	42.00
Lenox China		**Victorian Lace**			
91-16-001	Christmas Tree	Lenox	Open	25.00	25.00
91-16-002	Fan	Lenox	Open	25.00	25.00
Lenox China		**Cathedral Portraits**			
91-17-001	15th Century Madonna & Child	Botticelli	Open	29.00	29.00
91-17-002	16th Century Madonna & Child	Raphael	Open	29.00	29.00
Lenox Collections		**The Christmas Carousel**			
89-01-001	White Horse	Lenox	Open	19.50	19.50
89-01-002	Zebra	Lenox	Open	19.50	19.50
89-01-003	Lion	Lenox	Open	19.50	19.50
89-01-004	Sea Horse	Lenox	Open	19.50	19.50
89-01-005	Pinto	Lenox	Open	19.50	19.50
89-01-006	Goat	Lenox	Open	19.50	19.50
89-01-007	Reindeer	Lenox	Open	19.50	19.50
89-01-008	Polar Bear	Lenox	Open	19.50	19.50
89-01-009	Hare	Lenox	Open	19.50	19.50
89-01-010	Elephant	Lenox	Open	19.50	19.50
89-01-011	Swan	Lenox	Open	19.50	19.50
89-01-012	Unicorn	Lenox	Open	19.50	19.50
89-01-013	Palomino	Lenox	Open	19.50	19.50
89-01-014	Black Horse	Lenox	Open	19.50	19.50
89-01-015	Cat	Lenox	Open	19.50	19.50
89-01-016	Tiger	Lenox	Open	19.50	19.50
90-01-017	Camel	Lenox	Open	19.50	19.50
90-01-018	Rooster	Lenox	Open	19.50	19.50
90-01-019	Giraffe	Lenox	Open	19.50	19.50
90-01-020	Panda	Lenox	Open	19.50	19.50
90-01-021	Frog	Lenox	Open	19.50	19.50
90-01-022	Pig	Lenox	Open	19.50	19.50
90-01-023	St. Bernard	Lenox	Open	19.50	19.50
90-01-024	Medieval Horse	Lenox	Open	19.50	19.50
90-01-025	Set of 24	Lenox	Open	468.00	468.00
Lenox Crystal		**Crystal Ball Ornaments**			
84-01-001	Deep Cut Ball	Lenox	Yr.Iss.	35.00	50.00
85-01-002	Cut Ball	Lenox	Yr.Iss.	35.00	50.00
86-01-003	Cut Ball	Lenox	Yr.Iss.	35.00	45.00
87-01-004	Cut Ball	Lenox	Yr.Iss.	29.00	29.00
88-01-005	Christmas Lights Ball	Lenox	Yr.Iss.	30.00	30.00
89-01-006	Starlight Ornament	Lenox	Open	34.00	34.00
89-01-007	Crystal Lights Ornaments	Lenox	Open	30.00	30.00
91-01-008	Crystal Abbey Ball	Lenox	Open	45.00	45.00
91-01-009	Crystal Starlight Ball-Blue	Lenox	Open	45.00	45.00
91-01-010	Crystal Starlight Ball-Red	Lenox	Open	45.00	45.00

CHRISTMAS ORNAMENTS

Company Number	Name	Series Artist	Edition Limit	Issue Price	Quote
91-01-011	Crystal Starlight Ball-Green	Lenox	Open	45.00	45.00
92-01-012	Crystal Optika	Lenox	Open	37.00	37.00
Lenox Crystal		**Annual Bell Series**			
87-02-001	Partridge Bell	Lenox	Yr.Iss.	45.00	45.00
88-02-002	Angel Bell	Lenox	Open	45.00	45.00
89-02-003	St. Nicholas Bell	Lenox	Open	45.00	45.00
90-02-004	Christmas Tree Bell	Lenox	Open	49.00	49.00
91-02-005	Teddy Bear Bell	Lenox	Yr.Iss.	49.00	49.00
92-02-006	Snowman Bell	Lenox	Yr.Iss.	49.00	49.00
Lenox Crystal		**Crystal Ornaments**			
89-03-001	Candlelight Bell	Lenox	Open	38.00	38.00
89-03-002	Annual Christmas Tree	Lenox	Yr.Iss.	26.00	26.00
89-03-003	Crystal Icicle	Lenox	Open	30.00	30.00
89-03-004	Our First Christmas	Lenox	Yr.Iss.	26.00	26.00
89-03-005	Baby's First Christmas	Lenox	Yr.Iss	26.00	26.00
89-03-006	Nativity	Lenox	Open	26.00	26.00
89-03-007	Snowflake	Lenox	Open	32.00	32.00
89-03-008	Christmas Lights Tree Top Ornament	Lenox	Open	55.00	55.00
90-03-009	Our First Christmas-1990	Lenox	Yr.Iss.	32.00	32.00
90-03-010	Baby's First Christmas-1990	Lenox	Yr.Iss.	30.00	30.00
90-03-011	Candy Cane	Lenox	Open	30.00	30.00
90-03-012	Christmas Tree-1990	Lenox	Yr.Iss.	30.00	30.00
90-03-013	Christmas Goose	Lenox	Open	29.00	29.00
91-03-014	Our First Christmas-1991	Lenox	Yr.Iss.	29.00	29.00
91-03-015	Baby's First Christmas-1991	Lenox	Yr.Iss.	29.00	29.00
91-03-016	Christmas Tree-1991	Lenox	Yr.Iss.	29.00	29.00
91-03-017	Christmas Stocking	Lenox	Open	29.00	29.00
91-03-018	Angel Pendent	Lenox	Open	29.00	29.00
91-03-019	Bird-Clear	Lenox	Open	29.00	29.00
91-03-020	Bird-Blue	Lenox	Open	29.00	29.00
91-03-021	Bird-Red	Lenox	Open	29.00	29.00
91-03-022	Bird-Green	Lenox	Open	29.00	29.00
91-03-023	Herald Angel-Clear	Lenox	Open	29.00	29.00
91-03-024	Herald Angel-Blue	Lenox	Open	29.00	29.00
91-03-025	Herald Angel-Red	Lenox	Open	29.00	29.00
91-03-026	Herald Angel-Green	Lenox	Open	29.00	29.00
91-03-027	Dove	Lenox	Open	32.00	32.00
91-03-028	Snowman	Lenox	Open	32.00	32.00
91-03-029	Abbey Treetopper	Lenox	Open	54.00	54.00
Lilliput Lane Ltd.		**Christmas Ornaments**			
92-01-001	Mistletoe Cottage	Lilliput Lane	Closed	27.50	27.50
93-01-002	Robin Cottage	Lilliput Lane	Yr.Iss.	35.00	35.00
94-01-003	Ivy House	Lilliput Lane	Yr.Iss.	35.00	35.00
Lladro		**Miniature Ornaments**			
88-01-001	Miniature Angels-L1604G (Set of 3)	Lladro	Yr.Iss.	75.00	125-150.
89-01-002	Holy Family-L5657G (Set of 3)	Lladro	Yr.Iss.	79.50	175.00
90-01-003	Three Kings-L5729G (Set of 3)	Lladro	Yr Iss.	87.50	150.00
91-01-004	Holy Shepherds-L5809G	Lladro	Yr.Iss.	97.50	90.00
93-01-005	Nativity Trio-L6095G	Lladro	Yr.Iss.	115.00	115-150.
Lladro		**Annual Ornaments**			
88-02-001	Christmas Ball-L1603M	Lladro	Yr.Iss.	60.00	65.00
89-02-002	Christmas Ball-L5656M	Lladro	Yr.Iss.	65.00	85-100.00
90-02-003	Christmas Ball-L5730M	Lladro	Yr Iss.	70.00	75-90.00
91-02-004	Christmas Ball-L5829M	Lladro	Yr.Iss.	52.00	52-90.00
92-02-005	Christmas Ball-L5914M	Lladro	Yr.Iss.	52.00	52-90.00
93-02-006	Christmas Ball-L6009M	Lladro	Yr.Iss.	54.00	54.00
Lladro		**Tree Topper Ornaments**			
90-03-001	Angel Tree Topper-L5719G-Blue	Lladro	Yr.Iss.	115.00	180-300.
91-03-002	Angel Tree Topper-L5831G-Pink	Lladro	Yr.Iss.	115.00	142.00
92-03-003	Angel Tree Topper-L5875G-Green	Lladro	Yr.Iss.	120.00	225.00
93-03-004	Angel Tree Topper-L5962G-Lavender	Lladro	Yr.Iss.	125.00	180.00
Lladro		**Ornaments**			
92-04-001	Snowman-L5841G	Lladro	Yr.Iss.	50.00	52.00
92-04-002	Santa-L5842G	Lladro	Yr.Iss.	55.00	57.00
92-04-003	Baby's First-1992-L5922G	Lladro	Yr.Iss.	55.00	55.00
92-04-004	Our First-1992-L5923G	Lladro	Yr.Iss.	50.00	50.00
92-04-005	Elf Ornament-L5938G	Lladro	Yr.Iss.	50.00	52.00
92-04-006	Mrs. Claus-L5939G	Lladro	Yr.Iss.	55.00	57.00
92-04-007	Christmas Morning-L5940G	Lladro	Yr.Iss.	97.50	108.00
93-04-008	Nativity Lamb-L5969G	Lladro	Yr.Iss.	85.00	85.00
93-04-009	Baby's First 1993-L6037G	Lladro	Yr.Iss.	57.00	57.00
93-04-010	Our First-L6038G	Lladro	Yr.Iss.	52.00	52.00
Lladro		**Angel Orchestra**			
91-05-001	Heavenly Harpist-15830	Lladro	Yr.Iss.	135.00	144-162.
92-05-002	Angelic Cymbalist-5876	Lladro	Yr.Iss.	140.00	225.00
93-05-003	Angelic Melody-L5963G	Lladro	Yr.Iss.	145.00	168.00
Seymour Mann Inc.		**Christmas Collection**			
85-01-001	Angel Wall XMAS-523	J. White	Closed	12.00	12.00
86-01-002	Cupid Head XMAS-53	J. White	Open	25.00	25.00
86-01-003	Santa XMAS-384	J. White	Closed	7.50	7.50
89-01-004	Christmas Cat in Teacup XMAS-660	J. White	Closed	13.50	13.50
91-01-005	Floral Plaque XMAS-911	J. White	Open	10.00	10.00
91-01-006	Flower Basket XMAS-912	J. White	Open	10.00	10.00
90-01-007	Cupid CPD-5	J. White	Open	13.50	13.50
90-01-008	Cupid CPD-6	J. White	Open	13.50	13.50
90-01-009	Doll Tree Topper OM-124	J. White	Closed	85.00	85.00
90-01-010	Hat w/ Streamers OM-116	J. White	Closed	20.00	20.00
90-01-011	Heartlace OM-119	J. White	Closed	12.00	12.00
90-01-012	Lace Ball OM-120	J. White	Closed	10.00	10.00
90-01-013	Tassel OM-118	J. White	Closed	7.50	7.50
91-01-014	Elf w/ Reindeer CJ-422	Jaimy	Open	9.00	9.00
91-01-015	Elves w/ Mail CJ-464	J. White	Open	30.00	30.00
91-01-016	Flat Red Santa CJ-115R	Jaimy	Open	2.88	2.88
91-01-017	Flat Santa CJ-115	Jaimy	Closed	7.50	7.50
91-01-018	Santas, set of 6 CJ-12	Jaimy	Closed	60.00	60.00
94-01-020	Santa w/ Candle CBU-300	J. White	Open	40.00	40.00
94-01-021	Santa w/ Lamb CBU-301	J. White	Open	40.00	40.00
94-01-022	Santa w/ Stick CBU-302	J. White	Open	40.00	40.00
94-01-023	Santa w/ Lantern CBU-303	J. White	Open	40.00	40.00
94-01-024	Santa w/ Children CBU-304	J. White	Open	40.00	40.00
94-01-025	Santa w/ Child CBU-305	J. White	Open	40.00	40.00
94-01-026	Santa w/ Sled CBU-306	J. White	Open	40.00	40.00
94-01-027	Santa w/ List CBU-307	J. White	Open	40.00	40.00

Company Number	Name	Series Artist	Edition Limit	Issue Price	Quote
Seymour Mann Inc.		**Gingerbread Christmas Collection**			
91-02-001	Gingerbread Angel CJ-411	J. Sauerbrey	Open	7.50	7.50
91-02-002	Gingerbread House CJ-416	J. Sauerbrey	Open	7.50	7.50
91-02-003	Gingerbread Man CJ-415	J. Sauerbrey	Open	7.50	7.50
91-02-004	Gingerbread Mouse/Boot CJ-409	J. Sauerbrey	Open	7.50	7.50
91-02-005	Gingerbread Mrs. Claus CJ-414	J. Sauerbrey	Open	7.50	7.50
91-02-006	Gingerbread Reindeer CJ-410	J. Sauerbrey	Open	7.50	7.50
91-02-007	Gingerbread Santa CJ-408	J. Sauerbrey	Open	7.50	7.50
91-02-008	Gingerbread Sleigh CJ-406	J. Sauerbrey	Open	7.50	7.50
91-02-009	Gingerbread Snowman CJ-412	J. Sauerbrey	Open	7.50	7.50
91-02-010	Gingerbread Tree CJ-407	J. Sauerbrey	Open	7.50	7.50
Seymour Mann Inc.		**Victorian Christmas Collection**			
91-03-001	Couple Against Wind CJ-420	Jaimy	Open	15.00	15.00
Seymour Mann Inc.		**Christmas Lite-Up Houses**			
94-04-001	Set/10 Lite-up Houses XMR-10	L. Sciola	Open	95.00	95.00
94-04-002	Set/10 Lite-up Houses XMR-11	L. Sciola	Open	95.00	95.00
94-04-003	Lite-up Restaurant XMR-20	L. Sciola	Open	30.00	30.00
94-04-004	Lite-up Church XMR-21	L. Sciola	Open	30.00	30.00
94-04-005	Lite-up Mansion XMR-23	L. Sciola	Open	30.00	30.00
94-04-006	Lite-up Library XMR-24	L. Sciola	Open	30.00	30.00
94-04-007	Lite-up Country House	L. Sciola	Open	30.00	30.00
June McKenna Collectibles, Inc.		**Flatback Ornaments**			
82-01-001	Santa With Toys	J. McKenna	Closed	14.00	50-80.00
82-01-002	Mama Bear, Blue Cape	J. McKenna	Closed	12.00	75-125.00
82-01-003	Papa Bear, Red Cape	J. McKenna	Closed	12.00	100-275.
82-01-004	Baby Bear, Teeshirt	J. McKenna	Closed	11.00	75-200.00
82-01-005	Candy Cane	J. McKenna	Closed	10.00	250.00
82-01-006	Colonial Man, available in 2 colors	J. McKenna	Closed	12.00	100-125.
82-01-007	Colonial Woman, available in 2 colors	J. McKenna	Closed	12.00	85-100.00
82-01-008	Kate Greenaway Boy	J. McKenna	Closed	12.00	300-500.
82-01-009	Kate Greenaway Girl	J. McKenna	Closed	12.00	350-500.
82-01-010	Angel With Toys	J. McKenna	Closed	14.00	95.00
83-01-011	Grandma, available in 4 colors	J. McKenna	Closed	12.00	65.00
83-01-012	Grandpa, available in 4 colors	J. McKenna	Closed	12.00	65.00
83-01-013	Mother Bear in Dress, available in 2 colors	J. McKenna	Closed	12.00	65.00
83-01-014	Father Bear in Suit, available in 2 colors	J. McKenna	Closed	12.00	65.00
83-01-015	Baby Bear in Vest, available in 2 colors	J. McKenna	Closed	11.00	85.00
83-01-016	Raggedy Ann	J. McKenna	Closed	12.00	175.00
83-01-017	Raggedy Andy	J. McKenna	Closed	12.00	175.00
83-01-018	St. Nick With Lantern	J. McKenna	Closed	14.00	50-75.00
83-01-019	Gloria Angel	J. McKenna	Closed	14.00	350-500.
83-01-020	Baby, available in 2 colors	J. McKenna	Closed	11.00	85.00
84-01-021	Angel with Horn	J. McKenna	Closed	14.00	95.00
84-01-022	Mr. Claus	J. McKenna	Closed	14.00	65.00
84-01-023	Mrs. Claus	J. McKenna	Closed	14.00	65.00
84-01-024	Country Boy, available in 2 colors	J. McKenna	Closed	12.00	60-85.00
84-01-025	Country Girl, available in 2 colors	J. McKenna	Closed	12.00	60-85.00
84-01-026	Old World Santa, available in 3 colors	J. McKenna	Closed	14.00	50-95.00
85-01-027	Bride	J. McKenna	Closed	25.00	200.00
85-01-028	Groom	J. McKenna	Closed	25.00	200.00
85-01-029	Baby Pig	J. McKenna	Closed	11.00	65.00
85-01-030	Father Pig	J. McKenna	Closed	12.00	65.00
85-01-031	Mother Pig	J. McKenna	Closed	12.00	65.00
85-01-032	Amish Man	J. McKenna	Closed	13.00	50-275.00
85-01-033	Amish Woman	J. McKenna	Closed	13.00	50-275.00
85-01-034	Primitive Santa	J. McKenna	Closed	17.00	75-150.00
86-01-035	Amish Boy	J. McKenna	Closed	13.00	65-275.00
86-01-036	Amish Girl	J. McKenna	Closed	13.00	65-275.00
86-01-037	Santa with Bells, green	J. McKenna	Closed	14.00	200-400.
86-01-038	Santa with Bells, blue	J. McKenna	Closed	14.00	55.00
86-01-039	Santa with Bear	J. McKenna	Closed	14.00	40.00
86-01-040	Santa with Bag	J. McKenna	Closed	16.00	30-40.00
88-01-041	Elizabeth, sill sitter	J. McKenna	Closed	20.00	200-300.
88-01-042	Guardian Angel	J. McKenna	Closed	16.00	40.00
88-01-043	1776 Santa	J. McKenna	Closed	17.00	40.00
88-01-044	Santa With Book (blue & red)	J. McKenna	Closed	17.00	40-110.00
88-01-045	Santa With Toys	J. McKenna	Closed	17.00	40.00
88-01-046	Santa With Wreath	J. McKenna	Closed	17.00	40.00
89-01-047	Glorious Angel	J. McKenna	Open	17.00	17.00
89-01-048	Santa With Staff	J. McKenna	Closed	17.00	40.00
89-01-049	Santa With Tree	J. McKenna	Closed	17.00	40.00
89-01-050	Winking Santa	J. McKenna	Closed	17.00	40.00
90-01-051	Ho Ho Ho	J. McKenna	Closed	17.00	40.00
90-01-052	Elf Jeffrey	J. McKenna	Closed	17.00	40.00
90-01-053	Harvest Santa	J. McKenna	Closed	17.00	40.00
91-01-054	Santa With Lights, black or white	J. McKenna	Closed	20.00	45.00
91-01-055	Santa With Banner	J. McKenna	Closed	20.00	20.00
91-01-056	Elf Joey	J. McKenna	Closed	20.00	20.00
91-01-057	Boy Angel	J. McKenna	Closed	20.00	20.00
91-01-058	Girl Angel	J. McKenna	Closed	20.00	30.00
92-01-059	Santa With Basket	J. McKenna	Closed	25.00	30.00
92-01-060	Santa With Sack	J. McKenna	Closed	25.00	30.00
92-01-061	Northpole News	J. McKenna	Closed	25.00	30.00
92-01-062	Elf Scotty	J. McKenna	Closed	25.00	30.00
92-01-063	Praying Angel	J. McKenna	Closed	25.00	30.00
93-01-064	Old Lamplighter	J. McKenna	Open	30.00	30.00
93-01-065	Christmas Treat	J. McKenna	Open	30.00	30.00
93-01-066	Final Notes	J. McKenna	Open	30.00	30.00
93-01-067	Elf Bernie	J. McKenna	Open	30.00	30.00
93-01-068	Angel of Peace- white or pink	J. McKenna	Open	30.00	30.00
94-01-069	Elf-Ricky	J. McKenna	Open	30.00	30.00
94-01-070	Snow Showers	J. McKenna	Open	30.00	30.00
94-01-071	Nutcracker	J. McKenna	Open	30.00	30.00
94-01-072	Ringing in Christmas	J. McKenna	Open	30.00	30.00
94-01-073	Santa with Pipe	J. McKenna	Open	30.00	30.00
94-01-074	Elf-Tammy	J. McKenna	Open	30.00	30.00
94-01-075	Mrs. Klaus	J. McKenna	Open	30.00	30.00
Midwest of Cannon Falls		**Wendt und Kuhn Ornaments**			
78-01-001	Angel Clip-on Ornament 07296	Wendt/Kuhn	Open	20.00	21.00
89-01-002	Trumpeting Angel Ornament,2 asst. 94029	Wendt/Kuhn	Open	14.00	15.00
91-01-003	Angel in Ring Ornament 12089	Wendt/Kuhn	Open	12.00	12.50
94-01-004	Angel on Moon, Star, 12 asst. 12945-6	Wendt/Kuhn	Open	20.00	20.00
Midwest of Cannon Falls		**Heritage Santa Collection Ornaments**			
90-02-001	Scanda Klaus Fabric Mache 05208	Midwest	Retrd.	18.00	18.00
90-02-002	Herr Kristmas Fabric Mache 05216	Midwest	Retrd.	18.00	18.00
90-02-003	MacNicholas Fabric Mache 05224	Midwest	Retrd.	18.00	18.00
90-02-004	Papa Frost Fabric Mache 05232	Midwest	Retrd.	18.00	18.00
91-02-005	Scanda Klaus Dimensional 29414	Midwest	Open	11.50	11.50
91-02-006	Herr Kristmas Dimensional 29422	Midwest	Open	11.50	11.50

Number	Name	Artist	Edition Limit	Issue Price	Quote
Company		Series			
91-02-007	MacNicholas Dimensional 29430	Midwest	Open	11.50	11.50
91-02-008	Papa Frost Dimensional 29448	Midwest	Retrd.	11.50	11.50
91-02-009	Father Christmas Dimensional 29456	Midwest	Open	11.50	11.50
91-02-010	Santa Niccolo Dimensional 29464	Midwest	Open	11.50	11.50
92-02-011	Santa Nykolai Dimensional 67745	Midwest	Open	11.50	11.50
92-02-012	Pere Noel Dimensional 67739	Midwest	Open	11.50	11.50
93-02-013	Santa España Dimensional 73766	Midwest	Open	11.50	11.50
93-02-014	Santa O'Nicholas Dimensional 73773	Midwest	Open	11.50	11.50
Midwest of Cannon Falls		**Leo R. Smith III Collection**			
94-03-001	Flying Woodsman Santa 11921-1	L.R. Smith	2,500	35.00	35.00
Midwest of Cannon Falls		**Farmyard Buddies**			
94-04-001	Curly, Corky and Clover Bearin' Gifts, 3 asst. 11790-3	Midwest	Open	7.50	7.50
94-04-002	Curly, Corky and Clover Snow Fun, 2 asst. 11796-5	Midwest	Open	13.50	13.50
94-04-003	Curly, Clover and Corky Hangin' Around, 3 asst. 11791-0	Midwest	Open	7.50	7.50
94-04-004	Clover and Corky Santa's Helpers, 2 asst. 11793-4	Midwest	Open	7.00	7.00
Midwest of Cannon Falls		**The Littlest Angel Collection**			
94-05-001	Flying Angel Wafer, 2 asst. 11624-1	Midwest	Open	7.50	7.50
94-05-002	Angel with Lamb 11625-8	Midwest	Yr. Iss.	8.00	8.00
94-05-003	Angel with Lamb and Dove, 2 asst. 11629-6	Midwest	Open	10.50	10.50
Midwest of Cannon Falls		**MouseKins Figurines**			
94-06-001	Grey and Burroughs Children Dressed as Angels, 4 asst. 12126-9	Midwest	Open	9.00	9.00
94-06-002	Santa Mouse Riding the Cardinal Delivering Gifts 12131-3	Midwest	Open	12.00	12.00
94-06-003	Heathcliff Grey Swinging on a Coo Coo Clock 12132-0	Midwest	Yr.Iss.	12.00	12.00
94-06-004	Sterling and Prudence Grey Carrying Goodies, 2 asst. 12136-8	Midwest	Open	9.50	9.50
94-06-005	Nicholas and Florence Burroughs Preparing for Christmas, 2 asst. 12129-0	Midwest	Open	9.50	9.50
94-06-006	Heather and Heathcliff Holding Cheese, 2 asst. 12138-2	Midwest	Open	9.50	9.50
94-06-007	J.D. and Holly Burroughs with Letter to Santa, 2 asst. 12139-9	Midwest	Open	9.50	9.50
94-06-008	Santa Mouse Enjoying Holiday Treats, 2 asst. 12140-5	Midwest	Open	9.50	9.50
Midwest of Cannon Falls		**Folk Art Gallery Collection**			
94-07-001	Santa's Birdhouse 11477-3	P. Schifferl	Open	22.00	22.00
94-07-002	Winter Fun Bear 11475-9	L. Schifferl	Open	20.00	20.00
94-07-003	Icicle Elf 11473-5	L. Schifferl	Open	11.00	11.00
94-07-004	Santa Riding High 11478-0	L. Schifferl	Open	24.00	24.00
94-07-005	Folk Style Rocking Horse 11474-2	L. Schifferl	Open	16.00	16.00
94-07-006	Starlight Santa 11476-6	P. Schifferl	Open	22.00	22.00
94-07-007	Folk Heart Santa 11481-0	P. Schifferl	Open	30.00	30.00
94-07-008	The Big Catch 11463-6	R. Tate	Open	10.00	10.00
94-07-009	Patriotic Whirligig Bear 11462-9	R. Tate	Open	8.00	8.00
94-07-010	Old World Santa, 3 asst. 11464-3	R. Tate	Open	10.00	10.00
94-07-011	Star Struck Santa 11428-5	R. Jones	Open	9.00	9.00
94-07-012	Heartwarming Snowman 11427-8	R. Jones	Open	10.00	10.00
94-07-013	Whistlin' Santa 12977-7	R. Jones	Open	12.00	12.00
94-07-014	Ho Ho Ho Santa 12065-1	Origin by Sticks	Open	21.00	21.00
94-07-015	Santa Bearing Gifts 12064-4	Origin by Sticks	Open	22.00	22.00
94-07-016	Angel on High 12061-3	Origin by Sticks	Open	12.00	12.00
94-07-017	Sign of Wonder, 2 asst. 12063-7	Origin by Sticks	Open	21.00	21.00
94-07-018	Heavenly Angel 11419-3	S. Hale	Open	11.00	11.00
94-07-019	Starbright Elves, 2 asst. 11421-6	S. Hale	Open	17.00	17.00
94-07-020	Santa of the Stars 11420-9	S. Hale	Open	16.00	16.00
Old World Christmas		**Angel & Female**			
86-01-001	Little Red Riding Hood 1001	E.M. Merck	Retrd.	9.90	11.75
86-01-002	Pink Angel with Wings 1002	E.M. Merck	Retrd.	8.90	8.90
86-01-003	Mrs. Santa Claus 1003	E.M. Merck	Retrd.	8.90	10.25
86-01-004	Clip-on Angel with Wings 1004	E.M. Merck	Open	10.25	10.25
87-01-005	Large Burgundy Angel with Wings 1005	E.M. Merck	Open	12.95	12.95
87-01-006	Mushroom Girl 1006	E.M. Merck	Open	9.25	9.25
87-01-007	Girl on Snowball with Teddy 1007	E.M. Merck	Open	9.25	9.25
87-01-008	Pastel Angel with Horn (A) 1008	E.M. Merck	Open	7.00	7.00
87-01-009	Girl in Grapes 1010	E.M. Merck	Retrd.	8.45	8.45
85-01-010	Small Girl with Tree 101029	E.M. Merck	Open	5.85	5.85
85-01-011	Gold Girl with Tree 1010306	E.M. Merck	Open	8.25	8.25
85-01-012	Red Girl with Tree 1010309	E.M. Merck	Open	8.25	8.25
85-01-013	Victorian Girl 101035	E.M. Merck	Retrd.	5.30	5.30
85-01-014	Light Blue Angel with Wings 101052	E.M. Merck	Retrd.	9.25	9.25
85-01-015	Caroling Girl 101062	E.M. Merck	Retrd.	6.65	6.65
85-01-016	Girl with Flowers 101069	E.M. Merck	Retrd.	7.45	7.45
88-01-017	Miss Liberty 1011	E.M. Merck	Open	10.35	10.35
88-01-018	Large Blue Angel 1012	E.M. Merck	Open	13.40	13.40
88-01-019	Large Doll Head 1013	E.M. Merck	Open	11.60	11.60
88-01-020	Girl Under Tree 1014	E.M. Merck	Open	7.80	7.80
88-01-021	Baby in Bunting 1015	E.M. Merck	Retrd.	7.65	13.95
88-01-022	Madonna with Child 1016	E.M. Merck	Open	12.75	12.75
88-01-023	Nativity 1017	E.M. Merck	Open	10.50	10.50
88-01-024	Victorian Angel 1018	E.M. Merck	Open	8.35	8.35
88-01-025	Pilgrim Girl 1019	E.M. Merck	Open	9.25	9.25
88-01-026	Little Witch 1020	E.M. Merck	Open	8.35	8.35
89-01-027	Irish Lassie 1021	E.M. Merck	Open	8.35	8.35
90-01-028	Small Girl Head 1022	E.M. Merck	Open	7.00	7.00
90-01-029	Angel Holding Star 1023	E.M. Merck	Open	7.80	7.80
90-01-030	Girl with Black Cat 1024	E.M. Merck	Open	9.25	9.25
90-01-031	Praying Girl 1025	E.M. Merck	Retrd.	7.80	7.80
90-01-032	Antique Style Doll Head 1026	E.M. Merck	Open	8.45	8.45
90-01-033	Miniature Mrs. Claus 1027	E.M. Merck	Open	4.95	4.95
90-01-034	Angel on Disc 1028	E.M. Merck	Retrd.	11.70	11.70
90-01-035	Heralding Angel 1029	E.M. Merck	Open	7.80	7.80
90-01-036	Girl in Polka Dot Dress 1030	E.M. Merck	Open	12.60	12.60
91-01-037	Baroque Angel 1031	E.M. Merck	Open	12.95	12.95
91-01-038	Praying Angel with Wings 1032	E.M. Merck	Open	8.55	8.55
85-01-039	Doll Head 103209	E.M. Merck	Retrd.	4.95	6.40
91-01-040	Angel of Peace 1033	E.M. Merck	Open	9.25	9.25
91-01-041	Cherub 1034	E.M. Merck	Open	8.80	8.80
91-01-042	Blue Praying Angel With Wings 1035	E.M. Merck	Open	8.25	8.25
91-01-043	Baby Jesus 1036	E.M. Merck	Open	9.25	9.25
91-01-044	Little Tyrolean Girl 1037	E.M. Merck	Open	7.00	7.00
92-01-045	Madonna 1038	E.M. Merck	Open	7.55	7.55

Number	Name	Artist	Edition Limit	Issue Price	Quote
Company		Series			
92-01-046	Shy Girl 1039	E.M. Merck	Open	9.90	9.90
92-01-047	Garden Girl 1040	E.M. Merck	Open	8.25	8.25
92-01-048	Thumbelina 1041	E.M. Merck	Open	10.25	10.25
92-01-049	Honey Child 1042	E.M. Merck	Open	7.45	7.45
85-01-050	Girl in Blue Dress 1042227	E.M. Merck	Open	7.00	7.00
92-01-051	Guardian Angel 1043	E.M. Merck	Open	8.25	8.25
92-01-052	Angel on Form 1044	E.M. Merck	Open	9.70	9.70
92-01-053	Girl with White Kitty 1045	E.M. Merck	Open	9.25	9.25
93-01-054	Small Blue Angel 1046	E.M. Merck	Open	6.65	6.65
93-01-055	Triplets in Bed 1051	E.M. Merck	Open	6.65	6.65
93-01-056	Red Riding Hood 1053	E.M. Merck	Open	7.55	7.55
93-01-057	Christmas Girl 1054	E.M. Merck	Open	6.55	6.55
93-01-058	Girl on Bell 1055	E.M. Merck	Open	8.75	8.75
93-01-059	Madonna & Child on Form 1056	E.M. Merck	Open	9.80	9.80
93-01-060	Chubby Mushroom Girl 1057	E.M. Merck	Open	8.00	8.00
93-01-061	Purple Angel with Star 1058	E.M. Merck	Open	8.70	8.70
93-01-062	Frau Schneemann 1059	E.M. Merck	Open	16.90	16.90
93-01-063	Angel Above Celestial Ball 1060	E.M. Merck	Open	41.00	41.00
93-01-064	Ballerina 1061	E.M. Merck	Open	14.50	14.50
94-01-065	Mermaid 1062	E.M. Merck	Open	38.90	38.90
94-01-066	Water Baby 1063	E.M. Merck	Open	8.25	8.25
94-01-067	Heidi and Peter 1064	E.M. Merck	Open	11.90	11.90
94-01-068	Nuremberg Angel 1065	E.M. Merck	Open	8.25	8.25
94-01-069	Mary 1066	E.M. Merck	Open	8.25	8.25
94-01-070	Oma 1067	E.M. Merck	Open	11.45	11.45
94-01-071	Heavenly Angel 1068	E.M. Merck	Open	11.00	11.00
94-01-072	Christmas Cutie 1069	E.M. Merck	Open	6.50	6.50
94-01-073	Double-Sided Egg Baby 1070	E.M. Merck	Open	7.25	7.25
94-01-074	Heidi 1071	E.M. Merck	Open	9.50	9.50
Old World Christmas		**Animals**			
86-02-001	Hungry Rabbit 1201	E.M. Merck	Open	8.55	8.55
86-02-002	Playing Cat 1202	E.M. Merck	Open	8.80	8.80
86-02-003	Bear in Crib 1203	E.M. Merck	Open	9.00	9.00
86-02-004	Cat in Bag 1204	E.M. Merck	Open	9.00	9.00
86-02-005	Monkey 1205	E.M. Merck	Open	5.85	5.85
86-02-006	Sitting Dog with Pipe 1206	E.M. Merck	Open	7.80	7.80
86-02-007	Smiling Dog 1207	E.M. Merck	Open	7.80	7.80
86-02-008	Honey Bear (A) 1208	E.M. Merck	Open	5.20	5.20
86-02-009	Cinnamon Bear 1209	E.M. Merck	Open	5.20	5.20
84-02-010	Kitten 121004	E.M. Merck	Open	7.00	7.00
84-02-011	Three-Sided: Owl, Dog, Cat 121009	E.M. Merck	Open	8.55	8.55
84-02-012	Puppy 121010	E.M. Merck	Open	7.00	7.00
84-02-013	Black Cat 121016	E.M. Merck	Open	9.00	9.00
84-02-014	Circus Dog 121021	E.M. Merck	Open	9.00	9.00
85-02-015	Snail 121041	E.M. Merck	Retrd.	6.65	7.95
85-02-016	Pink Pig 121042	E.M. Merck	Open	7.80	7.80
85-02-017	Frog 121068	E.M. Merck	Open	5.85	5.85
85-02-018	Rainbow Trout 121070	E.M. Merck	Open	6.75	6.75
85-02-019	Large Three-Sided Head 121088	E.M. Merck	Open	12.95	12.95
85-02-020	Large Teddy Bear 121089	E.M. Merck	Retrd.	12.75	15.95
85-02-021	Small Bunny 121090	E.M. Merck	Open	5.20	5.20
87-02-022	Mouse 1211	E.M. Merck	Open	9.90	9.90
85-02-023	Cat in Show 121103	E.M. Merck	Open	7.80	7.80
88-02-024	Lucky Pig 1212	E.M. Merck	Open	8.80	8.80
88-02-025	Jumbo Elephant 1213	E.M. Merck	Open	9.25	9.25
89-02-026	Large Fish 1214	E.M. Merck	Retrd.	6.65	7.25
89-02-027	Lady Bug 1215	E.M. Merck	Open	7.65	7.65
89-02-028	Calico Kitten 1217	E.M. Merck	Open	9.90	9.90
89-02-029	Teddy Bear with Bow 1218	E.M. Merck	Retrd.	6.65	6.65
89-02-030	Rabbit in Tree 1219	E.M. Merck	Open	8.35	8.35
89-02-031	White Kitty 1220	E.M. Merck	Retrd.	7.45	7.45
89-02-032	Cat and the Fiddle 1221	E.M. Merck	Open	7.80	7.80
89-02-033	King Charles Spaniel 1222	E.M. Merck	Open	9.90	9.90
89-02-034	Fat Fish 1223	E.M. Merck	Open	5.85	5.85
89-02-035	Small Goldfish 1224	E.M. Merck	Open	2.25	2.25
90-02-036	Small Squirrel 1225	E.M. Merck	Open	5.75	5.75
90-02-037	Teddy Bear with Bow 1226	E.M. Merck	Open	5.75	5.75
90-02-038	Pink Poodle 1227	E.M. Merck	Open	8.80	8.80
90-02-039	Sitting Black Cat 1228	E.M. Merck	Open	7.00	7.00
90-02-040	Assorted Tropical Fish 1229	E.M. Merck	Open	6.75	6.75
90-02-041	Two Kittens in Basket 1230	E.M. Merck	Open	8.10	8.10
90-02-042	Red Butterfly on Form 1231	E.M. Merck	Open	8.55	8.55
90-02-043	West Highland Terrrier 1232	E.M. Merck	Retrd.	7.45	7.45
90-02-044	Weather Frog 1233	E.M. Merck	Open	8.80	8.80
90-02-045	Pastel Fish 1234	E.M. Merck	Open	6.65	6.65
85-02-046	Grey Elephant 123420	E.M. Merck	Open	7.00	7.00
85-02-047	Matte Gold Bear with Heart 1234356	E.M. Merck	Open	7.00	7.00
90-02-048	Baby Bear with Milk Bottle 1235	E.M. Merck	Open	4.95	4.95
90-02-049	Mama Bear 1236	E.M. Merck	Open	9.90	9.90
90-02-050	Papa Bear 1237	E.M. Merck	Open	10.35	10.35
85-02-051	Butterfly on Form 1237447	E.M. Merck	Open	7.80	7.80
91-02-052	Kitten in Slipper 1240	E.M. Merck	Open	9.25	9.25
91-02-053	Large Puppy with Basket 1241	E.M. Merck	Retrd.	12.60	13.25
91-02-054	Panda Bear 1242	E.M. Merck	Open	9.25	9.25
91-02-055	Crocodile 1243	E.M. Merck	Open	7.35	7.35
91-02-056	Rabbit on Heart 1244	E.M. Merck	Open	8.00	8.00
91-02-057	Lobster 1245	E.M. Merck	Open	7.35	7.35
91-02-058	Sitting Puppy 1246	E.M. Merck	Open	6.75	6.75
91-02-059	Christmas Butterfly 1247	E.M. Merck	Open	7.00	7.00
91-02-060	Christmas Carp 1248	E.M. Merck	Open	7.00	7.00
91-02-061	Goldfish 1249	E.M. Merck	Open	7.00	7.00
92-02-062	Proud Pug 1250	E.M. Merck	Open	9.25	9.25
92-02-063	Lion 1251	E.M. Merck	Open	6.45	6.45
92-02-064	Frog on Lily Pad 1252	E.M. Merck	Open	6.65	6.65
92-02-065	Dog with Trumpet 1253	E.M. Merck	Open	9.25	9.25
92-02-066	Large Lady Bug 1254	E.M. Merck	Open	9.25	9.25
92-02-067	Salmon with Tail 1255	E.M. Merck	Open	9.25	9.25
93-02-068	Velveteen Rabbit 1256	E.M. Merck	Open	5.75	5.75
93-02-069	Sugar Bear 1257	E.M. Merck	Open	8.25	8.25
93-02-070	Monkey with Apple 1258	E.M. Merck	Open	8.80	8.80
93-02-071	Miniature Frog 1259	E.M. Merck	Open	3.50	3.50
93-02-072	Cat in House 1260	E.M. Merck	Open	7.65	7.65
93-02-073	Large Teddy Bear 1261	E.M. Merck	Open	15.65	15.65
93-02-074	Large Frog 1262	E.M. Merck	Open	7.90	7.90
93-02-075	Grizzly Bear 1265	E.M. Merck	Open	8.35	8.35
93-02-076	Buster 1266	E.M. Merck	Open	8.35	8.35
93-02-077	Brilliant Butterfly 1267	E.M. Merck	Open	10.70	10.70
93-02-078	Pastel Butterfly 1268	E.M. Merck	Open	8.45	8.45
93-02-079	Brilliant Butterfly on Form 1271	E.M. Merck	Open	7.25	7.25
93-02-080	Specked Trout 1272	E.M. Merck	Open	7.00	7.00
93-02-081	Sea Serpent 1273	E.M. Merck	Open	14.65	14.65
93-02-082	Frog with Banjo on Ball 1274	E.M. Merck	Open	18.50	18.50
93-02-083	Polar Bear on Icicle 1275	E.M. Merck	Open	18.50	18.50

CHRISTMAS ORNAMENTS

Company / Number	Name	Series / Artist	Edition Limit	Issue Price	Quote
93-02-084	My Darling 1276	E.M. Merck	Open	6.30	6.30
93-02-085	Circus Elephant on Ball 1277	E.M. Merck	Open	12.00	12.00
93-02-086	Circus Dog On Ball 1278	E.M. Merck	Open	13.20	13.20
93-02-087	Bear Above Reflector 1279	E.M. Merck	Open	33.75	33.75
93-02-088	Very Large Christmas Mouse 1280	E.M. Merck	Open	72.50	72.50
93-02-089	Very Large Christmas Bear 1281	E.M. Merck	Open	72.50	72.50
94-02-090	Sea Horse 1282	E.M. Merck	Open	14.50	14.50
94-02-091	Seal on Ball 1283	E.M. Merck	Open	24.50	24.50
94-02-092	Cow Jumping Over the Moon 1284	E.M. Merck	Open	27.75	27.75
94-02-093	Large Lion 1285	E.M. Merck	Open	19.85	19.85
94-02-094	Large Christmas Mouse 1286	E.M. Merck	Open	44.40	44.40
94-02-095	Large Christmas Bear 1287	E.M. Merck	Open	44.40	44.40
94-02-096	Frog Prince 1288	E.M. Merck	Open	8.10	8.10
94-02-097	Grasshopper 1289	E.M. Merck	Open	10.00	10.00
94-02-098	Ted 1290	E.M. Merck	Open	7.65	7.65
94-02-099	Woodland Squirrel 1291	E.M. Merck	Open	21.00	21.00
94-02-100	Spark Plug 1292	E.M. Merck	Open	14.00	14.00
94-02-101	Tony 1293	E.M. Merck	Open	17.65	17.65
Old World Christmas		**Bead Garlands**			
93-03-001	Clown & Drum Garland 1301	E.M. Merck	Open	55.00	55.00
93-03-002	Fruit Garland 1302	E.M. Merck	Open	55.00	55.00
93-03-003	Celestial Garland 1303	E.M. Merck	Open	55.00	55.00
93-03-004	Pickle Garland 1304	E.M. Merck	Open	55.00	55.00
93-03-005	Frog and Fish Garland 1305	E.M. Merck	Yr.Iss.	55.00	55.00
93-03-006	Angel Garland 1306	E.M. Merck	Open	55.00	55.00
93-03-007	Teddy Bear & Heart Garland 1307	E.M. Merck	Open	55.00	55.00
93-03-008	Santa Garland 1308	E.M. Merck	Yr.Iss.	55.00	55.00
94-03-009	Stars and Stripes Garland 1309	E.M. Merck	Open	55.00	55.00
94-03-010	Christmas Train 1310	E.M. Merck	Open	45.00	45.00
94-03-011	Woodland Christmas Garland 1311	E.M. Merck	Open	65.00	65.00
94-03-012	Floral Garland 1312	E.M. Merck	Open	65.00	65.00
94-03-013	North Pole Garland 1313	E.M. Merck	Open	65.00	65.00
Old World Christmas		**Assortment Ornaments**			
89-04-001	Twelve Assorted Miniature Forms 1402	E.M. Merck	Open	37.00	37.00
89-04-002	Set of 12 Assorted Small Forms 1403	E.M. Merck	Open	42.50	42.50
90-04-003	Assorted Shiny Miniature Forms 1404	E.M. Merck	Open	37.50	37.50
90-04-004	Assorted Miniature Figurals 1405	E.M. Merck	Open	60.00	60.00
92-04-005	Assorted Floral Miniatures 1406	E.M. Merck	Open	55.00	55.00
85-04-006	6 pc Display set, Santa 141039	E.M. Merck	Open	32.50	32.50
86-04-007	Replica of Antique Mold 1411	E.M. Merck	Open	40.00	40.00
Old World Christmas		**Collector's Editions**			
90-05-001	Night Before Christmas Ball 1501	E.M. Merck	500	72.50	72.50
91-05-002	Santa's Visit 1502	E.M. Merck	500	72.50	72.50
92-05-003	Santa's Departure 1503	E.M. Merck	500	72.50	72.50
92-05-004	Nutcracker Ornament 1510	E.M. Merck	2,000	33.75	49.95
93-05-005	Hansel and Gretal 1511	E.M. Merck	2,400	45.00	46.95
92-05-006	Santa with Tinsel Wire 1521	E.M. Merck	Retrd.	55.00	55.00
92-05-007	Angel with Tinsel Wire 1522	E.M. Merck	Retrd.	55.00	55.00
92-05-008	Snowman with Tinsel Wire 1523	E.M. Merck	Retrd.	32.50	32.50
92-05-009	Dresden Santa with Tinsel Wire 1525	E.M. Merck	Open	21.50	21.50
92-05-010	Angel on Swan with Tinsel Wire 1526	E.M. Merck	Open	21.50	21.50
92-05-011	Angel on Balloon 1527	E.M. Merck	Open	22.50	22.50
92-05-012	Cherub Above Ball 1528	E.M. Merck	Open	23.65	23.65
92-05-013	Father Christmas on Balloon 1529	E.M. Merck	Open	22.50	22.50
92-05-014	Very Large Mushroom with Flower 1530	E.M. Merck	Open	59.50	59.50
92-05-015	Very Large Ball with Reflectors 1531	E.M. Merck	Open	59.50	59.50
92-05-016	Very Large Ball with Icicle Drop 1532	E.M. Merck	Open	59.50	59.50
92-05-017	Very Large Drop with Reflectors 1533	E.M. Merck	Open	59.50	59.50
87-05-018	Very Large Icicle 1534	E.M. Merck	Open	59.50	59.50
92-05-019	Flying Peacock with Wings 1550	E.M. Merck	Open	22.50	22.50
92-05-020	Flying Songbird with Wings 1551	E.M. Merck	Open	21.75	21.75
92-05-021	Brilliant Peacock with Wings 1552	E.M. Merck	Open	23.00	23.00
92-05-022	Nightingale with Wings 1553	E.M. Merck	Open	21.00	21.00
93-05-023	Angel with Wings 1556	E.M. Merck	Retrd.	12.50	12.50
93-05-024	Guardian Angel with Wire 1562	E.M. Merck	Open	20.00	20.00
93-05-025	Heavenly Angel 1563	E.M. Merck	Open	20.00	20.00
93-05-026	Victorian Santa on Heart 1564	E.M. Merck	Open	12.95	12.95
93-05-027	Scrap Victorian Santa on Balloon 1565	E.M. Merck	Open	50.00	50.00
93-05-028	Scrap Victorian Angel on Balloon 1566	E.M. Merck	Open	50.00	50.00
93-05-029	Santa with Hot Air Balloon 1570	E.M. Merck	Open	38.85	38.85
93-05-030	Christmas Heart 1593	E.M. Merck	Yr.Iss.	10.00	10.00
94-05-031	Assorted Pumpkin People 1580	E.M. Merck	Open	19.75	19.75
Old World Christmas		**Hanging Birds**			
86-06-001	Owl on Form 1601	E.M. Merck	Open	11.00	11.00
86-06-002	Songbirds on Ball 1602	E.M. Merck	Open	9.25	9.25
86-06-003	Rooster on Form 1603	E.M. Merck	Retrd.	6.65	6.65
86-06-004	Large Owl with Stein 1604	E.M. Merck	Retrd.	10.00	17.95
86-06-005	Swan on Form 1605	E.M. Merck	Open	8.35	8.35
86-06-006	Parrot in Cage 1606	E.M. Merck	Open	7.45	7.45
86-06-007	Small Owl 1607	E.M. Merck	Open	5.75	5.75
86-06-008	Standing Owl 1608	E.M. Merck	Open	8.90	8.90
87-06-009	Fat Rooster 1610	E.M. Merck	Open	10.35	10.35
84-06-010	Cock Robin 161012	E.M. Merck	Open	7.00	7.00
84-06-011	Chick in Egg 161013	E.M. Merck	Open	8.25	8.25
85-06-012	Turkey 161058	E.M. Merck	Retrd.	8.00	8.00
85-06-013	Fancy Peacock 161066	E.M. Merck	Open	9.25	9.25
85-06-014	Cardinal with Wings 161098	E.M. Merck	Open	10.95	10.95
88-06-015	Bird House 1611	E.M. Merck	Open	10.35	10.35
85-06-016	Blue Bird with Wings 161100	E.M. Merck	Retrd.	7.65	7.65
88-06-017	Swans on Lake 1612	E.M. Merck	Open	7.80	7.80
90-06-018	Duck 1613	E.M. Merck	Open	6.20	6.20
90-06-019	Songbird on Form 1614	E.M. Merck	Open	8.80	8.80
90-06-020	Turkey 1615	E.M. Merck	Open	9.00	9.00
90-06-021	Wise Owl 1616	E.M. Merck	Open	8.35	8.35
91-06-022	Large Parrot on Ball 1617	E.M. Merck	Open	11.00	11.00
91-06-023	Songbird on Heart (A) 1618	E.M. Merck	Retrd.	8.25	8.25
91-06-024	Chick on Form 1619	E.M. Merck	Retrd.	8.00	8.00
92-06-025	Birdie 1620	E.M. Merck	Open	8.80	8.80
92-06-026	Gentleman Chick 1621	E.M. Merck	Open	7.65	7.65
92-06-027	Snowy Owl 1622	E.M. Merck	Open	6.00	6.00
92-06-028	Exotic Bird 1623	E.M. Merck	Open	10.35	10.35
92-06-029	Large German Songbird 1624	E.M. Merck	Open	11.25	11.25
92-06-030	Brilliant Hanging Snowbird 1625	E.M. Merck	Open	9.80	9.80
92-06-031	Messenger Bird 1626	E.M. Merck	Open	6.75	6.75
93-06-032	Cardinal on Form 1627	E.M. Merck	Open	7.55	7.55
93-06-024	Stork with Baby 1628	E.M. Merck	Open	9.60	9.60
93-06-025	Rooster at Hen House 1629	E.M. Merck	Open	10.25	10.25
93-06-026	Hanging Pastel Bird 1630	E.M. Merck	Open	10.50	10.50
93-06-027	Hanging Parrot 1631	E.M. Merck	Open	9.60	9.60
93-06-028	Parrot on Reflector 1632	E.M. Merck	Open	12.25	12.25
94-06-029	Royal Swan 1633	E.M. Merck	Open	27.75	27.75
94-06-030	Bird in Nest 1634	E.M. Merck	Open	19.90	19.90
Old World Christmas		**Clip-On Birds**			
86-07-001	Bird in Nest 1801	E.M. Merck	Open	10.35	10.35
86-07-002	Clip-On Rooster 1802	E.M. Merck	Retrd.	8.00	12.95
86-07-003	Gold Bird with Tinsel Tail 1803	E.M. Merck	Open	7.45	7.45
86-07-004	Parrot 1804	E.M. Merck	Open	8.35	8.35
87-07-005	White Cockatoo 1805	E.M. Merck	Open	7.80	7.80
87-07-006	Red Bird with Medallion 1806	E.M. Merck	Open	7.80	7.80
87-07-007	Shiny Gold Bird 1807	E.M. Merck	Open	5.55	5.55
87-07-008	Goldfinch 1808	E.M. Merck	Open	8.55	8.55
87-07-009	Small Purple Bird 1809	E.M. Merck	Open	7.00	7.00
87-07-010	Red Snowbird 1810	E.M. Merck	Retrd.	8.70	8.70
84-07-011	Large Cockatoo 181025	E.M. Merck	Open	13.95	13.95
85-07-012	Fancy Peacock 181073	E.M. Merck	Retrd.	13.50	13.50
85-07-013	Fat Songbird 181074	E.M. Merck	Open	7.80	7.80
85-07-014	Fantasy Bird with Tinsel Tail 181075	E.M. Merck	Open	8.00	8.00
85-07-015	Nuthatch 181076	E.M. Merck	Open	7.00	7.00
85-07-016	Cockatoo 181077	E.M. Merck	Open	8.55	8.55
85-07-017	Blue Bird 181078	E.M. Merck	Open	6.65	6.65
85-07-018	Snowbird 181080	E.M. Merck	Retrd.	8.00	8.00
85-07-019	Shiny Red Songbird 181081	E.M. Merck	Open	5.75	5.75
85-07-020	Pink Bird with Blue Wings 181082	E.M. Merck	Open	5.55	5.55
85-07-021	Nightingale 181083	E.M. Merck	Open	5.55	5.55
85-07-022	Large Goldfinch 181085	E.M. Merck	Open	9.25	9.25
85-07-023	Magnificent Songbird 181086	E.M. Merck	Open	13.95	13.95
85-07-024	Fancy Pink Peacock 181096	E.M. Merck	Open	13.95	13.95
85-07-025	Songbird with Topnotch 181099	E.M. Merck	Open	10.35	10.35
87-07-026	Lilac Bird 1811	E.M. Merck	Open	8.70	8.70
85-07-027	Bird of Pradise 181101	E.M. Merck	Open	7.80	7.80
87-07-028	Red Breasted Songbird 1812	E.M. Merck	Open	9.25	9.25
87-07-029	Fat Burgundy Bird 1813	E.M. Merck	Open	7.80	7.80
87-07-030	Partridge 1814	E.M. Merck	Open	8.80	8.80
87-07-031	Royal Songbird 1815	E.M. Merck	Open	12.75	12.75
87-07-032	Snow Owl 1816	E.M. Merck	Open	9.90	9.90
87-07-033	Robin 1819	E.M. Merck	Retrd.	8.80	10.25
89-07-034	Rainbow Parrot 1820	E.M. Merck	Open	12.60	12.60
90-07-035	Large Robin 1821	E.M. Merck	Open	10.35	10.35
90-07-036	Cardinal 1822	E.M. Merck	Open	9.90	9.90
90-07-037	Small Red-Headed Songbird 1823	E.M. Merck	Open	7.00	7.00
90-07-038	Christmas Bird 1824	E.M. Merck	Open	7.00	7.00
90-07-039	Miniature Peacock 1825	E.M. Merck	Open	8.35	8.35
90-07-040	Tropical Parrot 1826	E.M. Merck	Open	10.35	10.35
90-07-041	Large Pastel Bird 1827	E.M. Merck	Open	10.70	10.70
90-07-042	Miniature Parrot 1828	E.M. Merck	Open	8.45	8.45
90-07-043	Barn Owl 1829	E.M. Merck	Open	9.00	9.00
91-07-044	Large Peacock with Crown 1830	E.M. Merck	Open	13.95	13.95
91-07-045	Rooster 1831	E.M. Merck	Open	10.50	10.50
91-07-046	Festive Bird 1832	E.M. Merck	Open	7.00	7.00
91-07-047	Silly Bird 1833	E.M. Merck	Open	6.75	6.75
91-07-048	Canary 1834	E.M. Merck	Open	7.35	7.35
91-07-049	Bavarian Finch 1835	E.M. Merck	Open	9.25	9.25
91-07-050	Brilliant Snowbird 1836	E.M. Merck	Open	12.95	12.95
91-07-051	Advent Bird 1837	E.M. Merck	Open	8.00	8.00
91-07-052	Cockatiel 1838	E.M. Merck	Open	9.25	9.25
91-07-053	Alpine Bird 1839	E.M. Merck	Open	7.35	7.35
92-07-054	Forest Finch 1840	E.M. Merck	Open	8.00	8.00
92-07-055	Brilliant Songbird 1841	E.M. Merck	Open	7.35	7.35
92-07-056	Large Nightingale 1842	E.M. Merck	Open	8.00	8.00
92-07-057	Christmas Finch 1843	E.M. Merck	Open	7.65	7.65
92-07-058	Small Gull 1844	E.M. Merck	Open	4.95	4.95
92-07-059	Blue Bird with Topnotch 1845	E.M. Merck	Open	9.45	9.45
92-07-060	Large Woodpecker 1846	E.M. Merck	Open	11.15	11.15
92-07-061	Pastel Canary 1847	E.M. Merck	Open	7.65	7.65
92-07-062	Merry Songbird 1848	E.M. Merck	Open	7.90	7.90
93-07-063	Holiday Finch 1849	E.M. Merck	Open	10.60	10.60
93-07-064	King Fisher 1850	E.M. Merck	Open	10.00	10.00
93-07-065	Woodland Finch 1851	E.M. Merck	Open	7.55	7.55
93-07-066	Carnival Canary 1852	E.M. Merck	Open	9.45	9.45
93-07-067	Festive Sparrow 1853	E.M. Merck	Open	6.00	6.00
93-07-068	Tropical Songbird 1854	E.M. Merck	Open	7.55	7.55
93-07-069	Woodland Songbird 1855	E.M. Merck	Open	7.55	7.55
93-07-070	Love Birds 1856	E.M. Merck	Open	10.25	10.25
94-07-071	Regal Peacock 1857	E.M. Merck	Open	17.75	17.75
94-07-072	Woodland Peacock 1858	E.M. Merck	Open	12.00	12.00
94-07-073	Assorted Miniature Songbird 1859	E.M. Merck	Open	4.00	4.00
94-07-074	Magnificent Peacock 1860	E.M. Merck	Open	17.75	17.75
85-07-075	Gold Peacock, Tinsel Tail 1872016	E.M. Merck	Open	8.25	8.25
85-07-076	Large Peacock 187206	E.M. Merck	Open	10.35	10.35
85-07-077	Medium Peacock with Tinsel Tail 187215	E.M. Merck	Open	9.00	9.00
Old World Christmas		**Butterflies**			
87-08-001	Butterfly, White with Red 1901	E.M. Merck	Retrd.	20.95	26.75
87-08-002	Butterfly, White with Blue 1902	E.M. Merck	Retrd.	20.95	20.95
87-08-003	Butterfly, Red with Cream 1903	E.M. Merck	Retrd.	20.95	26.75
87-08-004	Butterfly, Orange with Orange 1904	E.M. Merck	Retrd.	20.95	26.75
87-08-005	Butterfly, Blue with Blue 1905	E.M. Merck	Retrd.	20.95	20.95
87-08-006	Butterfly, Gold with Gold 1906	E.M. Merck	Retrd.	20.95	20.95
Old World Christmas		**Churches & Houses**			
86-09-001	Gingerbread House (A) 2001	E.M. Merck	Retrd.	6.55	9.75
86-09-002	Farm House 2003	E.M. Merck	Open	8.45	8.45
86-09-003	House with Peacock 2004	E.M. Merck	Retrd.	7.45	7.45
86-09-004	House with Blue Roof 2005	E.M. Merck	Open	7.65	7.65
86-09-005	Windmill on Form 2006	E.M. Merck	Retrd.	7.45	13.95
88-09-006	Large Cathedral 2007	E.M. Merck	Open	9.80	9.80
88-09-007	Church/Tree on Form 2008	E.M. Merck	Open	8.35	8.35
88-09-008	Gingerbread House 2009	E.M. Merck	Open	9.00	9.00
88-09-009	Santa's House 2010	E.M. Merck	Open	8.00	8.00
85-09-010	Square House 201040	E.M. Merck	Open	7.80	7.80
85-09-011	Rathaus 201051	E.M. Merck	Retrd.	7.00	7.00
85-09-012	Bavarian House 201059	E.M. Merck	Open	8.00	8.00
85-09-013	Mill 201094	E.M. Merck	Retrd.	9.45	15.95
90-09-014	Garden House with Gnome 2011	E.M. Merck	Retrd.	7.80	7.80
90-09-015	Miniature House 2012	E.M. Merck	Open	4.95	4.95
90-09-016	Lighthouse 2013	E.M. Merck	Open	7.90	7.90
90-09-017	Christmas Chalet 2014	E.M. Merck	Open	8.00	8.00
90-09-018	Small Cathedral 2015	E.M. Merck	Open	8.00	8.00
90-09-019	Fairy Tale House 2016	E.M. Merck	Open	9.25	9.25
90-09-020	Matte Cream Church 2017	E.M. Merck	Open	8.00	8.00
90-09-021	Church on Disc 2018	E.M. Merck	Open	12.50	12.50
91-09-022	Thatched Cottage 2019	E.M. Merck	Open	7.35	7.35
91-09-023	Christmas Shop 2020	E.M. Merck	Open	9.45	9.45

CHRISTMAS ORNAMENTS

Company Number	Name	Series Artist	Edition Limit	Issue Price	Quote
91-09-024	Old Town Scene 2021	E.M. Merck	Open	9.25	9.25
91-09-025	Farm Cottage 2022	E.M. Merck	Open	8.55	8.55
91-09-026	Large Lighthouse/Mill 2023	E.M. Merck	Open	11.00	11.00
91-09-027	Mission with Sea Gull 2024	E.M. Merck	Open	9.45	9.45
91-09-028	Country Cottage 2025	E.M. Merck	Open	8.80	8.80
92-09-029	Mill House 2026	E.M. Merck	Open	8.35	8.35
92-09-030	Watch Tower 2027	E.M. Merck	Open	9.25	9.25
92-09-031	Rose Cottage 2028	E.M. Merck	Open	7.00	7.00
93-09-032	Castle Tower 2029	E.M. Merck	Open	9.45	9.45
93-09-033	Church on Bell 2030	E.M. Merck	Open	11.00	11.00
88-09-034	Matte White Church 203010	E.M. Merck	Open	7.80	7.80
93-09-035	Turkish Tea House 2031	E.M. Merck	Open	6.75	6.75
93-09-036	Bunny House 2032	E.M. Merck	Open	8.45	8.45
93-09-037	Barn 2033	E.M. Merck	Open	9.80	9.80
93-09-038	Large Windmill 2034	E.M. Merck	Open	13.20	13.20
94-09-039	Victorian Windmill 2035	E.M. Merck	Open	12.25	12.25
85-09-040	Matte Cream Church 206790-2	E.M. Merck	Retrd.	6.45	6.45
Old World Christmas		**Celestial Figures**			
86-10-001	Shooting Star on Ball 2201	E.M. Merck	Retrd.	6.65	10.25
87-10-002	Blue Man in the Moon 2203	E.M. Merck	Open	8.45	8.45
90-10-003	Shining Sun 2204	E.M. Merck	Open	7.00	7.00
91-10-004	Shining Star (A) 2205	E.M. Merck	Open	7.00	7.00
92-10-005	Blue Moon 2206	E.M. Merck	Open	7.00	7.00
92-10-006	Old Sol 2207	E.M. Merck	Open	7.55	7.55
92-10-007	Confetti Star 2208	E.M. Merck	Open	8.00	8.00
93-10-008	Comet on Form 2209	E.M. Merck	Open	7.65	7.65
93-10-009	Brilliant Star on Form 2210	E.M. Merck	Open	8.70	8.70
85-10-010	Sun/Moon 221027	E.M. Merck	Retrd.	7.00	7.00
85-10-011	Man in the Moon 221062	E.M. Merck	Open	7.00	7.00
93-10-012	High Noon 2211	E.M. Merck	Open	5.65	5.65
94-10-013	Assorted Shiny Stars 2212	E.M. Merck	Open	4.85	4.84
94-10-014	Midnight Moon 2213	E.M. Merck	Open	8.25	8.25
85-10-015	Large Gold Star with Glitter 2237139	E.M. Merck	Retrd.	7.00	7.00
Old World Christmas		**Clowns & Male Figures**			
86-11-001	Indian in Canoe 2401	E.M. Merck	Open	10.95	10.95
86-11-002	Aviator 2402	E.M. Merck	Open	7.80	7.80
86-11-003	500,000 Clown 2403	E.M. Merck	Open	10.80	10.80
86-11-004	Sailor Head 2404	E.M. Merck	Retrd.	7.45	12.95
86-11-005	Baby 2405	E.M. Merck	Retrd.	6.75	6.75
86-11-006	Pixie with Accordion 2406	E.M. Merck	Retrd.	4.95	4.95
86-11-007	Clown with Banjo 2407	E.M. Merck	Open	7.00	7.00
86-11-008	Clown with Drum 2408	E.M. Merck	Open	10.35	10.35
86-11-009	Clown with Accordion 2409	E.M. Merck	Open	10.35	10.35
86-11-010	Clown with Saxophone 2410	E.M. Merck	Open	10.35	10.35
84-11-011	Keystone Cop 241003	E.M. Merck	Open	9.90	9.90
84-11-012	Clown Playing Bass Fiddle 241005	E.M. Merck	Open	7.80	7.80
84-11-013	Clown in Stocking 241006	E.M. Merck	Retrd.	6.65	7.95
84-11-014	Indian Chief with Peace Pipe 241008	E.M. Merck	Open	7.45	7.45
84-11-015	'Shorty Clown' 241011	E.M. Merck	Retrd.	5.65	5.65
84-11-016	Roly-Poly Keystone Cop 241015	E.M. Merck	Retrd.	9.90	14.95
84-11-017	Scotsman 241017	E.M. Merck	Retrd.	6.20	13.95
84-11-018	'Stop' Keystone Cop 241019	E.M. Merck	Retrd.	6.65	16.95
84-11-019	Large Roly-Poly Clown 241024	E.M. Merck	Open	10.95	10.95
85-11-020	Small Fat Boy 241028	E.M. Merck	Open	5.55	5.55
85-11-021	Boy on Toy Car 241031	E.M. Merck	Open	8.45	8.45
85-11-022	Boy in Yellow Sweater 241032	E.M. Merck	Retrd.	7.00	7.00
85-11-023	Waiter in Tuxedo 241047	E.M. Merck	Retrd.	7.00	14.95
86-11-024	Boy Head with Stocking Cap 2411	E.M. Merck	Retrd.	5.30	7.25
86-11-025	Clown Head in Drum 2412	E.M. Merck	Open	10.25	10.25
86-11-026	Uncle Sam 2413	E.M. Merck	Open	10.80	10.80
86-11-027	Farm Boy 2414	E.M. Merck	Retrd.	4.95	6.50
86-11-028	School Boy 2415	E.M. Merck	Retrd.	4.95	7.25
86-11-029	Clip-on Boy Head 2416	E.M. Merck	Retrd.	6.45	6.45
86-11-030	Gnome Under Mushroom 2417	E.M. Merck	Retrd.	7.00	7.00
86-11-031	Clown Head with Burgundy Hat 2418	E.M. Merck	Open	7.00	7.00
86-11-032	Jester 2419	E.M. Merck	Open	7.45	7.45
87-11-033	Jolly Snowman 2420	E.M. Merck	Open	8.00	8.00
87-11-034	King 2421	E.M. Merck	Open	10.60	10.60
87-11-035	Clown in Red Stocking 2423	E.M. Merck	Open	8.00	8.00
87-11-036	Punch 2424	E.M. Merck	Open	8.70	8.70
87-11-037	Mr. Big Nose 2426	E.M. Merck	Retrd.	8.00	9.25
87-11-038	Scrooge 2427	E.M. Merck	Open	8.55	8.55
87-11-039	Bavarian with Hat 2428	E.M. Merck	Open	12.60	12.60
87-11-040	Jolly Clown Head 2429	E.M. Merck	Open	12.95	12.95
88-11-041	Mushroom Gnome 2430	E.M. Merck	Retrd.	6.20	6.20
88-11-042	Gnome in Tree 2431	E.M. Merck	Open	7.80	7.80
88-11-043	Harpo 2432	E.M. Merck	Retrd.	6.20	14.95
89-11-044	Dwarf with Shovel 2433	E.M. Merck	Open	7.00	7.00
85-11-045	Dutch Boy 243321	E.M. Merck	Retrd.	7.55	11.50
89-11-046	Frosty 2434	E.M. Merck	Open	7.00	7.00
89-11-047	Leprechaun 2435	E.M. Merck	Open	7.65	7.65
89-11-048	Small Clown Head 2436	E.M. Merck	Retrd.	6.65	6.65
89-11-049	Snowman with Broom 2437	E.M. Merck	Open	6.45	6.45
90-11-050	Devil Head 2438	E.M. Merck	Open	8.80	8.80
90-11-051	Black Boy 2439	E.M. Merck	Open	9.00	9.00
90-11-052	Scout 2440	E.M. Merck	Open	9.25	9.25
90-11-053	Dwarf 2441	E.M. Merck	Open	7.00	7.00
90-11-054	English Bobby 2442	E.M. Merck	Open	8.80	8.80
85-11-055	Fat Boy with Sweater & Cap 2442265	E.M. Merck	Open	5.85	5.85
90-11-056	Jolly Accordion Player 2443	E.M. Merck	Open	8.25	8.25
90-11-057	Clown on Ball 2444	E.M. Merck	Open	8.25	8.25
90-11-058	Snowman on Reflector 2445	E.M. Merck	Retrd.	10.35	10.95
90-11-059	Merry Wanderer 2446	E.M. Merck	Open	12.30	12.30
92-11-060	Snowman in Chimney 2447	E.M. Merck	Open	10.50	10.50
92-11-061	Garden Gnome 2448	E.M. Merck	Open	10.50	10.50
92-11-062	Baker 2449	E.M. Merck	Open	8.35	8.35
92-11-063	Bavarian 2450	E.M. Merck	Open	9.25	9.25
92-11-064	Pirate 2451	E.M. Merck	Open	7.45	7.45
92-11-065	Circus Clown 2452	E.M. Merck	Open	7.90	7.90
93-11-066	Winking Leprechaun 2453	E.M. Merck	Open	6.55	6.55
93-11-067	Boxer 2454	E.M. Merck	Open	7.20	7.20
93-11-068	Chimney Sweep 2455	E.M. Merck	Open	7.55	7.55
93-11-069	Santa's Helper 2456	E.M. Merck	Open	6.00	6.00
93-11-070	Sailor 2457	E.M. Merck	Open	7.55	7.55
93-11-071	Bacchus 2458	E.M. Merck	Open	6.65	6.65
93-11-072	Pinocchio 2459	E.M. Merck	Open	9.90	9.90
93-11-073	Jesus 2460	E.M. Merck	Open	7.65	7.65
93-11-074	Turquoise Clown 2461	E.M. Merck	Open	6.45	6.45
93-11-075	Small Snowman 2462	E.M. Merck	Open	6.00	6.00
93-11-076	Small Jester 2463	E.M. Merck	Open	7.35	7.35
93-11-077	Miniature Clown 2464	E.M. Merck	Open	6.00	6.00
93-11-078	Humpty Dumpty 2465	E.M. Merck	Open	8.55	8.55

Company Number	Name	Series Artist	Edition Limit	Issue Price	Quote
93-11-079	Large Sad Clown 2466	E.M. Merck	Open	13.40	13.40
93-11-080	Monk 2467	E.M. Merck	Open	7.90	7.90
85-11-081	Fat Standing Clown 246852	E.M. Merck	Open	6.55	6.55
93-11-082	Snowman on Icicle 2469	E.M. Merck	Open	15.45	15.45
93-11-083	Clown Above Ball 2470	E.M. Merck	Open	42.00	42.00
94-11-084	Jack Horner 2471	E.M. Merck	Open	6.50	6.50
94-11-085	Child in Manger 2472	E.M. Merck	Open	7.75	7.75
94-11-086	Hot Shot 2473	E.M. Merck	Open	11.00	11.00
94-11-087	My Buddy 2474	E.M. Merck	Open	7.75	7.75
94-11-088	Jesus on Form 2475	E.M. Merck	Open	17.65	17.65
94-11-089	Merlin 2476	E.M. Merck	Open	17.65	17.65
94-11-090	Joseph 2477	E.M. Merck	Open	8.25	8.25
94-11-091	Roly-Poly 2478	E.M. Merck	Open	24.00	24.00
94-11-092	Razzle-Dazzle 2479	E.M. Merck	Open	17.65	17.65
94-11-093	Show Time 2480	E.M. Merck	Open	18.90	18.90
94-11-094	John Bull 2481	E.M. Merck	Open	9.35	9.35
94-11-095	King Ludwig 2482	E.M. Merck	Open	12.75	12.75
94-11-096	Marley 2483	E.M. Merck	Open	7.75	7.75
Old World Christmas		**Fruits & Vegetables**			
86-12-001	Pumpkin Head 2801	E.M. Merck	Open	7.35	7.35
86-12-002	Carrot with Leaf 2802	E.M. Merck	Open	7.35	7.35
86-12-003	Large Acorn 2803	E.M. Merck	Open	6.65	6.65
86-12-004	Large Walnut 2804	E.M. Merck	Open	3.60	3.60
86-12-005	Pear with Face 2805	E.M. Merck	Open	7.00	7.00
86-12-006	Strawberry 2806	E.M. Merck	Open	4.75	4.75
86-12-007	Grapes with Green Glitter 2807	E.M. Merck	Open	4.75	4.75
86-12-008	Small Pear with Leaf 2808	E.M. Merck	Open	4.75	4.75
86-12-009	Pear with Leaf 2809	E.M. Merck	Open	5.55	5.55
87-12-010	Onion 2810	E.M. Merck	5,000	8.25	19.95
84-12-011	Pickle 281018	E.M. Merck	Open	7.00	7.00
84-12-012	Banana 281020	E.M. Merck	Open	8.00	8.00
84-12-013	Mr. Pear 281023	E.M. Merck	Retrd.	6.75	6.75
84-12-014	Large Matte Corn 281033	E.M. Merck	Open	9.25	9.25
85-12-015	Grapes on Form 281038	E.M. Merck	Retrd.	7.00	7.00
85-12-016	Very Large Strawberry 281050	E.M. Merck	Open	9.25	9.25
85-12-017	Large Basket of Grapes 281053	E.M. Merck	Open	10.35	10.35
85-12-018	Mr. Apple 281071	E.M. Merck	Retrd.	6.20	8.95
85-12-019	Large Pear with Leaf 281072	E.M. Merck	Open	7.35	7.35
87-12-020	Potato 2811	E.M. Merck	Open	8.45	8.45
87-12-021	Green Pepper 2812	E.M. Merck	Open	8.00	8.00
87-12-022	Plum With Leaf 2813	E.M. Merck	Open	7.35	7.35
87-12-023	Small Apple With Leaf 2814	E.M. Merck	Open	5.75	5.75
88-12-024	Small Tomato 2815	E.M. Merck	Open	4.00	4.00
88-12-025	Miniature Grapes 2816	E.M. Merck	Open	3.00	3.00
88-12-026	Gold Walnut 2817	E.M. Merck	Open	2.00	2.00
89-12-027	Shiny Corn 2818	E.M. Merck	Open	5.50	5.50
89-12-028	Small Matte Corn 2819	E.M. Merck	Open	4.50	4.50
89-12-029	Cucumber 2820	E.M. Merck	Retrd.	6.65	6.65
89-12-030	Large Frosted Strawberry 2821	E.M. Merck	Open	6.00	6.00
89-12-031	Berry 2822	E.M. Merck	Open	2.70	2.70
89-12-032	Gurken 2823	E.M. Merck	Open	2.70	2.70
90-12-033	Cherries on Form 2825	E.M. Merck	Retrd.	9.00	9.50
90-12-034	Large Red Apple 2828	E.M. Merck	Open	8.55	8.55
90-12-035	Large Golden Apple 2829	E.M. Merck	Open	8.55	8.55
90-12-036	Apricot 2831	E.M. Merck	Open	6.55	6.55
90-12-037	Sweet Pickle 2833	E.M. Merck	Open	4.50	4.50
90-12-038	White Grapes 2834	E.M. Merck	Open	6.75	6.75
90-12-039	Raspberry 2835	E.M. Merck	Retrd.	6.20	6.20
90-12-040	Strawberry Cluster 2836	E.M. Merck	Open	5.20	5.20
90-12-041	Apples on Form 2837	E.M. Merck	Open	9.00	9.00
85-12-042	Purple Grapes 283765	E.M. Merck	Open	5.75	5.75
90-12-043	Fruit Basket 2838	E.M. Merck	Open	7.80	7.80
90-12-044	Lime 2839	E.M. Merck	Open	3.50	3.50
90-12-045	Gold Grapes 2840	E.M. Merck	Open	6.75	6.75
90-12-046	Large Strawberry with Flower 2841	E.M. Merck	Retrd.	10.50	10.50
85-12-047	Small Purple Grapes 2841047	E.M. Merck	Open	4.00	4.00
85-12-048	Large Strawberry 2841432	E.M. Merck	Retrd.	4.20	4.20
90-12-049	Fruits on Form 2842	E.M. Merck	Open	10.35	10.35
90-12-050	Watermelon Slice 2844	E.M. Merck	Open	11.00	11.00
90-12-051	Fancy Strawberry 2845	E.M. Merck	Open	5.55	5.55
90-12-052	Peach 2846	E.M. Merck	Open	7.65	7.65
91-12-053	Very Large Pear 2847	E.M. Merck	Retrd.	10.60	10.60
91-12-054	Very Large Apple 2848	E.M. Merck	Retrd.	10.60	10.60
91-12-055	Large Fruit Basket 2849	E.M. Merck	Open	12.50	12.50
91-12-056	Double Mushroom 2850	E.M. Merck	Open	6.65	6.65
91-12-057	Strawberries/Flower on Form 2851	E.M. Merck	Open	8.55	8.55
91-12-058	Large Purple Grapes with Leaves 2852	E.M. Merck	Open	6.75	6.75
91-12-059	Red Pepper 2853	E.M. Merck	Open	9.45	9.45
91-12-060	Harvest Grapes 2854	E.M. Merck	Open	9.25	9.25
91-12-061	Large Raspberry 2855	E.M. Merck	Open	7.90	7.90
92-12-062	Shiny Red Apple 2856	E.M. Merck	Open	6.55	6.55
92-12-063	Orange 2857	E.M. Merck	Open	7.00	7.00
92-12-064	Large Tomato 2858	E.M. Merck	Open	7.45	7.45
92-12-065	Fruit Basket on Form 2859	E.M. Merck	Open	9.25	9.25
92-12-066	Candied Apple 2860	E.M. Merck	Open	8.70	8.70
92-12-067	Sugar Plum 2861	E.M. Merck	Open	7.55	7.55
92-12-068	Sugar Lemon 2862	E.M. Merck	Open	7.45	7.45
92-12-069	Sugar Pear 2863	E.M. Merck	Open	7.00	7.00
92-12-070	Sugar Strawberry 2864	E.M. Merck	Open	7.65	7.65
92-12-071	Sugar Grapes 2865	E.M. Merck	Open	7.45	7.45
93-12-072	Sugar Harvest Grapes 2866	E.M. Merck	Open	9.70	9.70
93-12-073	Sugar Raspberry 2867	E.M. Merck	Open	8.55	8.55
93-12-074	Chestnut 2869	E.M. Merck	Open	6.00	6.00
93-12-075	Pear Face 2871	E.M. Merck	Open	8.35	8.35
85-12-076	Large Strawberry with Glitter 287282	E.M. Merck	Open	6.45	6.45
93-12-077	Mushroom Face 2873	E.M. Merck	Open	5.85	5.85
93-12-078	Apple Tree 2874	E.M. Merck	Open	8.90	8.90
93-12-079	Pea Pod 2875	E.M. Merck	Open	9.60	9.60
93-12-080	Asparagus 2876	E.M. Merck	Open	10.60	10.60
93-12-081	Large Cornucopia 2877	E.M. Merck	Open	25.00	25.00
93-12-082	Garlic 2878	E.M. Merck	Open	7.00	7.00
93-12-083	Translucent Grapes with 18KT Gold 2879	E.M. Merck	Open	7.25	7.25
93-12-084	Miniature Mushrooms 2880	E.M. Merck	Open	4.00	4.00
93-12-085	Large Sugar Pear 2881	E.M. Merck	Open	12.95	12.95
93-12-086	Large Candied Apple 2882	E.M. Merck	Open	12.95	12.95
94-12-087	New Potato 2883	E.M. Merck	Open	5.80	5.80
94-12-088	Apple Slice 2884	E.M. Merck	Open	9.45	9.45
94-12-089	Orange Slice 2885	E.M. Merck	Open	9.45	9.45
94-12-090	French Carrot 2886	E.M. Merck	Open	4.45	4.45
94-12-091	Grapes with Butterfly 2887	E.M. Merck	Open	9.50	9.50
Old World Christmas		**Hearts**			
86-13-001	Small Gold Heart with Star 3001	E.M. Merck	Retrd.	2.85	4.25

CHRISTMAS ORNAMENTS

Company Number	Name	Series Artist	Edition Limit	Issue Price	Quote
86-13-002	Small Red Heart with Star 3002	E.M. Merck	Open	2.95	2.95
87-13-003	Heart with Ribbon 3003	E.M. Merck	Open	8.45	8.45
87-13-004	Burgundy Heart with Glitter 3004	E.M. Merck	Open	6.75	6.75
88-13-005	Valentine 3005	E.M. Merck	Open	5.75	5.75
88-13-006	Large Red Glitter Heart 3006	E.M. Merck	Open	8.45	8.45
89-13-007	Strawberry Heart 3007	E.M. Merck	Open	3.00	3.00
89-13-008	Double Heart 3008	E.M. Merck	Open	3.00	3.00
89-13-009	Smooth Heart 3009	E.M. Merck	Open	2.25	2.25
92-13-010	Heart with Flowers 3010	E.M. Merck	Retrd.	8.80	9.50
92-13-011	Scrap Angel on Heart (A) 3011	E.M. Merck	Open	8.35	8.35
93-13-012	Frost Red Translucent Heart 3012	E.M. Merck	Open	6.45	6.45
93-13-013	Merry Christmas Heart 3013	E.M. Merck	Open	7.20	7.20
85-13-014	Pink Heart with Glitter 306767	E.M. Merck	Open	6.75	6.75
85-13-015	Large Matte Red Heart 306925	E.M. Merck	Open	5.30	5.30
Old World Christmas		**Household Items**			
86-14-001	Red Stocking 3201	E.M. Merck	Retrd.	9.00	9.00
86-14-002	Cuckoo Clock 3202	E.M. Merck	Open	9.25	9.25
86-14-003	Black Stocking 3203	E.M. Merck	Retrd.	9.45	15.95
88-14-004	Wine Barrel 3204	E.M. Merck	Retrd.	7.00	9.75
88-14-005	Baby's Shoe 3205	E.M. Merck	Open	7.35	7.35
91-14-006	Money Bag 3206	E.M. Merck	Open	7.00	7.00
91-14-007	Pipe (A) 3207	E.M. Merck	Open	9.00	9.00
91-14-008	Small Cuckoo Clock 3209	E.M. Merck	Open	7.00	7.00
91-14-009	Small Wine Barrel 3210	E.M. Merck	Retrd.	6.30	6.30
85-14-010	Wall Clock 321060	E.M. Merck	Open	11.00	11.00
85-14-011	Clip-On Candle 321063	E.M. Merck	Open	12.95	12.95
85-14-012	Pastel Umbrella (A) 321091	E.M. Merck	Retrd.	11.00	11.00
85-14-013	Fancy Coffee Pot 321092	E.M. Merck	Open	13.95	13.95
85-14-014	Lady's Fan 321093	E.M. Merck	Open	6.65	6.65
85-14-015	Large Purse 321095	E.M. Merck	Open	7.00	7.00
92-14-016	Flapper Purse 3211	E.M. Merck	Open	9.25	9.25
85-14-017	Very Large Pink Umbrella 321103	E.M. Merck	Retrd.	29.50	29.50
93-14-018	Christmas Shoe 3212	E.M. Merck	Open	8.25	8.25
93-14-019	Fancy Teapot 3213	E.M. Merck	Open	8.75	8.75
93-14-020	Beer Stein 3214	E.M. Merck	Open	10.95	10.95
93-14-021	Fancy Purse 3215	E.M. Merck	Open	6.00	6.00
93-14-022	Elegant Chocolate Pot 3216	E.M. Merck	Open	12.85	12.85
85-14-023	Pocket Watch 326729	E.M. Merck	Open	5.85	5.85
Old World Christmas		**Icicles**			
88-15-001	Long Champagne Icicle 3401	E.M. Merck	Retrd.	7.25	7.25
85-15-002	Long Silver Icicle 3450380	E.M. Merck	Open.	7.00	7.00
Old World Christmas		**Miscellaneous Forms**			
86-15-001	Flower Basket 3601	E.M. Merck	Open	10.25	10.25
87-15-002	Stars on Form (A) 3602	E.M. Merck	Open	12.95	12.95
88-15-003	Ice Cream Cone with Glitter 3604	E.M. Merck	Open	13.40	13.40
88-15-004	Clip-On Tulip (A) 3605	E.M. Merck	Open	8.70	8.70
88-15-005	Skull 3606	E.M. Merck	Open	7.35	7.35
89-15-006	Red Rose on Form 3607	E.M. Merck	Open	5.85	5.85
89-15-007	Morning Glories 3608	E.M. Merck	Open	8.90	8.90
89-15-008	Flower with Butterfly 3609	E.M. Merck	Retrd.	9.75	10.95
89-15-009	Flower Bouquet in Basket 3610	E.M. Merck	Open	9.45	9.45
89-15-010	Christmas Lantern 3611	E.M. Merck	Open	7.80	7.80
89-15-011	Mr. Sunflower 3612	E.M. Merck	Open	7.80	7.80
89-15-012	Victorian Keepsake 3613	E.M. Merck	Open	9.25	9.25
89-15-013	Edelweiss 3614	E.M. Merck	Open	3.00	3.00
89-15-014	Ribbed Ball with Roses 3615	E.M. Merck	Open	3.00	3.00
89-15-015	Rose 3616	E.M. Merck	Open	2.40	2.40
89-15-016	Shiny Red Clip-On Tulip 3617	E.M. Merck	Retrd.	7.45	7.45
90-15-017	Edelweiss on Form 3618	E.M. Merck	Open	8.25	8.25
90-15-018	Poinsettias 3619	E.M. Merck	Open	9.90	9.90
90-15-019	Assorted Christmas Stars 3620	E.M. Merck	Open	7.00	7.00
90-15-020	Shamrock on Form 3621	E.M. Merck	Open	5.55	5.55
90-15-021	Large Snowflake 3622	E.M. Merck	Open	13.00	13.00
90-15-022	Pink Sea Shell 3623	E.M. Merck	Open	7.00	7.00
90-15-023	Sunburst 3624	E.M. Merck	Retrd.	8.00	8.00
90-15-024	Large Sea Shell 3625	E.M. Merck	Open	8.35	8.35
90-15-025	Assorted Christmas Flowers 3626	E.M. Merck	Open	8.00	8.00
90-15-026	Assorted Pastel Fantasy Forms 3627	E.M. Merck	Open	6.25	6.25
90-15-027	Clip-On Pink Rose 3628	E.M. Merck	Open	9.25	9.25
90-15-028	Large Conical Shell 3629	E.M. Merck	Retrd.	8.70	9.50
90-15-029	Poinsettia Blossom 3630	E.M. Merck	Open	11.60	11.60
92-15-030	Poinsettia on Form 3631	E.M. Merck	Open	7.35	7.35
92-15-031	Christmas Shamrock 3632	E.M. Merck	Open	9.25	9.25
92-15-032	Large Ribbed Ball with Roses 3633	E.M. Merck	Open	7.00	7.00
92-15-033	Christmas Ball with Roses 3634	E.M. Merck	Open	9.45	9.45
92-15-034	Fantasy Christmas Form 3635	E.M. Merck	Open	9.00	9.00
92-15-035	Assorted Spirals 3636	E.M. Merck	Open	8.25	8.25
92-15-036	Pansy 3637	E.M. Merck	Open	7.35	7.35
85-15-037	Ice Cream Cone 3637164	E.M. Merck	Retrd.	8.90	14.50
92-15-038	Basket of Roses 3638	E.M. Merck	Open	11.00	11.00
92-15-039	Garden Flowers 3639	E.M. Merck	Open	9.00	9.00
92-15-040	Assorted Northern Stars 3640	E.M. Merck	Open	6.20	6.20
92-15-041	Snowflake on Form 3641	E.M. Merck	Open	6.75	6.75
93-15-042	Crown 3642	E.M. Merck	Open	8.90	8.90
93-15-043	Lucky Shamrock 3643	E.M. Merck	Retrd.	7.80	9.25
93-15-044	Merry Christmas Ball 3645	E.M. Merck	Open	7.45	7.45
93-15-045	Large Conical Shell 3646	E.M. Merck	Open	7.35	7.35
93-15-046	Assorted Fantasy Form with Wire 3650	E.M. Merck	Open	20.00	20.00
85-15-047	Pink Rose with Glitter 366828	E.M. Merck	Open	4.95	4.95
Old World Christmas		**Musical Instruments**			
86-16-001	Cello 3801	E.M. Merck	Open	6.65	6.65
87-16-002	Guitar 3802	E.M. Merck	Open	6.65	6.65
88-16-003	Large Drum 3803	E.M. Merck	Open	10.35	10.35
88-16-004	Large Bell with Acorns 3804	E.M. Merck	Open	9.00	9.00
89-16-005	Bell with Flowers 3805	E.M. Merck	Open	5.85	5.85
89-16-006	Christmas Bells on From 3806	E.M. Merck	Open	8.35	8.35
90-16-007	Large Christmas Bell 3808	E.M. Merck	Open	10.35	10.35
90-16-008	Lyre 3809	E.M. Merck	Open	8.35	8.35
90-16-009	Zither 3810	E.M. Merck	Open	8.35	8.35
90-16-010	Large Cello 3811	E.M. Merck	Open	8.35	8.35
90-16-011	Large Banjo 3812	E.M. Merck	Open	8.35	8.35
90-16-012	Large Mandolin 3813	E.M. Merck	Open	8.35	8.35
90-16-013	Accordion 3814	E.M. Merck	Open	8.35	8.35
90-16-014	Small Fancy Drum 3815	E.M. Merck	Open	7.80	7.80
90-16-015	Assorted Snow Bells 3816	E.M. Merck	Open	6.65	6.65
90-16-016	Toy Drum 3817	E.M. Merck	Open	9.25	9.25
93-16-017	Large Bell with Holly 3819	E.M. Merck	Open	50.00	50.00
88-16-018	Clip-On Drum 383534	E.M. Merck	Open	8.00	8.00
Old World Christmas		**Santas**			
86-17-001	Santa Under Tree 4001	E.M. Merck	Open	10.35	10.35
86-17-002	Santa On Cone 4002	E.M. Merck	Retrd.	7.90	8.75
86-17-003	Santa On Carriage 4003	E.M. Merck	Retrd.	10.00	13.95
86-17-004	Santa In Chimney 4005	E.M. Merck	Open	8.70	8.70
86-17-005	Father Christmas Head 4006	E.M. Merck	Open	7.80	7.80
86-17-006	Green Clip-On Santa 4007	E.M. Merck	Open	7.80	7.80
86-17-007	St. Nicholas Head 4008	E.M. Merck	Open	6.65	6.65
86-17-008	Santa with Glued-On Tree 4009	E.M. Merck	Open	9.00	9.00
86-17-009	Small Blue Santa 4010	E.M. Merck	Open	5.40	5.40
84-17-010	Large Santa In Basket 401001	E.M. Merck	Open	12.95	12.95
84-17-011	Roly-Poly Santa 401002	E.M. Merck	Open	7.90	7.90
84-17-012	Old Father Christmas Head 401007	E.M. Merck	Open	7.00	7.00
84-17-013	Small Old-Fashioned Santa 401022	E.M. Merck	Open	6.65	6.65
85-17-014	Santa and Tree on Form 401026	E.M. Merck	Open	9.25	9.25
85-17-015	Father Christmas with Tree 401039	E.M. Merck	Open	8.00	8.00
85-17-016	Jolly Father Christmas 401043	E.M. Merck	Open	7.00	7.00
85-17-017	Gold Father Christmas 401045	E.M. Merck	Open	7.45	7.45
85-17-018	Blue Father Christmas 4010498	E.M. Merck	Open	8.00	8.00
85-17-019	Pink Father Christmas 4010499	E.M. Merck	Open	8.00	8.00
85-17-020	Santa in Tree 401054	E.M. Merck	Open	7.45	7.45
85-17-021	Large Santa with Tree 401055	E.M. Merck	Open	12.60	12.60
85-17-022	Parachuting Santa 401056	E.M. Merck	Open	8.00	8.00
85-17-023	Standing Santa 401057	E.M. Merck	Open	11.00	11.00
85-17-024	St. Nicholas on Horse 401064	E.M. Merck	Open	13.95	13.95
85-17-025	Small Santa with Pack 401065	E.M. Merck	Open	5.40	5.40
85-17-026	Matte Santa Head 401087	E.M. Merck	Open	8.00	8.00
86-17-027	Pink Clip-On Santa 4011	E.M. Merck	Open	8.35	8.35
85-17-028	Small Santa in Basket 401105	E.M. Merck	Open	9.25	9.25
87-17-029	Matte Red Roly-Poly Santa 4012	E.M. Merck	Open	7.90	7.90
87-17-030	Burgundy Father Christmas 4013	E.M. Merck	Open	7.80	7.80
87-17-031	Burgundy Santa Claus 4014	E.M. Merck	Open	13.95	13.95
87-17-032	Very Large Santa Head 4015	E.M. Merck	Open	13.95	13.95
87-17-033	Jolly Santa Head 4016	E.M. Merck	Open	8.80	8.80
87-17-034	Santa in Airplane 4017	E.M. Merck	Open	13.95	13.95
87-17-035	Santa Above Ball 4018	E.M. Merck	Open	13.95	13.95
89-17-036	Old-Fashioned Santa (A) 4019	E.M. Merck	Open	5.75	5.75
89-17-037	St Nicholas 4020	E.M. Merck	Open	10.00	10.00
89-17-038	Victorian Santa 4021	E.M. Merck	Open	8.45	8.45
89-17-039	Victorian Santa Head 4022	E.M. Merck	Open	8.35	8.35
89-17-040	Santa Hiding in Tree 4023	E.M. Merck	Open	11.00	11.00
89-17-041	Father Christmas 4024	E.M. Merck	Open	4.25	4.25
89-17-042	Santa 4025	E.M. Merck	Open	4.50	4.50
90-17-043	White Clip-On Santa 4026	E.M. Merck	Open	7.35	7.35
90-17-044	Small Victorian Santa Head 4027	E.M. Merck	Open	7.35	7.35
90-17-045	Blue Victorian St. Nick 4028	E.M. Merck	Retrd.	9.95	9.95
90-17-046	Light Blue St. Nicholas 4029	E.M. Merck	Open	6.45	6.45
90-17-047	Clip-On Victorian St. Nick 4030	E.M. Merck	Open	11.00	11.00
90-17-048	Weihnachtsmann with Tree 4031	E.M. Merck	Open	10.50	10.50
90-17-049	Miniature Santa 4032	E.M. Merck	Open	4.95	4.95
85-17-050	Father Christmas Head 403223	E.M. Merck	Open	7.80	7.80
85-17-051	Father Christmas with Basket 403224	E.M. Merck	Open	7.80	7.80
90-17-052	Snowy Santa 4033	E.M. Merck	Open	10.95	10.95
90-17-053	Weihnachtsmann 4034	E.M. Merck	Open	9.00	9.00
90-17-054	Round Jolly Santa Head 4035	E.M. Merck	Open	11.00	11.00
90-17-055	Father Christmas with Toys 4036	E.M. Merck	Open	13.95	13.95
90-17-056	Very Large Belznickel 4037	E.M. Merck	Open	22.50	22.50
90-17-057	Very Large St. Nick Head 4038	E.M. Merck	Open	22.50	22.50
90-17-058	Festive Santa Head 4039	E.M. Merck	Open	11.00	11.00
90-17-059	Old-Fashioned St. Nicholas 4040	E.M. Merck	Open	11.00	11.00
90-17-060	Old St. Nick with Toys 4041	E.M. Merck	Open	13.95	13.95
90-17-061	Large Weihnachtsmann 4042	E.M. Merck	Open	10.25	10.25
90-17-062	Victorian Scrap Santa 4043	E.M. Merck	Retrd.	9.70	9.70
90-17-063	Old Bavarian Santa 4044	E.M. Merck	Open	12.50	12.50
90-17-064	Victorian Father Christmas 4045	E.M. Merck	Open	10.00	10.00
90-17-065	Father Christmas on Form 4046	E.M. Merck	Open	11.00	11.00
91-17-066	Alpine Santa 4047	E.M. Merck	Open	7.00	7.00
91-17-067	Santa in Mushroom 4048	E.M. Merck	Open	8.70	8.70
92-17-068	Small Santa on Form 4049	E.M. Merck	Open	8.00	8.00
92-17-069	Roaring 20s Santa 4050	E.M. Merck	Open	10.00	10.00
92-17-070	Frontier Santa with Tree 4051	E.M. Merck	Open	11.00	11.00
92-17-071	Gold Weihnachtsmann 4052	E.M. Merck	Open	9.80	9.80
92-17-072	Old Swiss Santa 4053	E.M. Merck	Open	12.50	12.50
92-17-073	Round Santa Head 4054	E.M. Merck	Open	9.00	9.00
92-17-074	Belznickel 4055	E.M. Merck	Open	12.50	12.50
93-17-075	Snowy Purple Santa 4056	E.M. Merck	Open	7.35	7.35
93-17-076	Santa in Sleigh 4057	E.M. Merck	Open	14.65	14.65
93-17-077	Santa in Walnut 4058	E.M. Merck	Open	7.00	7.00
93-17-078	Santa in Chimney 4059	E.M. Merck	Open	12.50	12.50
93-17-079	Purple Belznickel 4060	E.M. Merck	Open	12.50	12.50
93-17-080	Frosty Santa 4061	E.M. Merck	Open	10.25	10.25
93-17-081	Woodland Santa 4062	E.M. Merck	Open	9.35	9.35
93-17-082	Purple Father Christmas 4063	E.M. Merck	Open	8.35	8.35
93-17-083	Large Father Christmas Head 4066	E.M. Merck	Open	22.50	22.50
93-17-084	Blue St. Nick 4067	E.M. Merck	Open	10.00	10.00
93-17-085	Old World Santa 4068	E.M. Merck	Open	11.00	11.00
93-17-086	Santa Above Reflector 4069	E.M. Merck	Open	40.00	40.00
85-17-087	Santa in Chimney 406912	E.M. Merck	Retrd.	11.00	11.00
93-17-088	Santa with Staff 4070	E.M. Merck	Open	10.95	10.95
93-17-089	Very Large Roly-Poly Santa 4071	E.M. Merck	Open	50.00	50.00
93-17-090	Santa Above Bell 4072	E.M. Merck	Open	36.00	36.00
94-17-091	Old World Santa Head 4074	E.M. Merck	Open	6.50	6.50
94-17-092	Double-Sided Santa Head 4075	E.M. Merck	Open	8.00	8.00
94-17-093	Very Merry Santa 4076	E.M. Merck	Open	7.35	7.35
94-17-094	Old-Fashioned St. Nick 4077	E.M. Merck	Open	9.25	9.25
94-17-095	Victorian Father Christmas 4078	E.M. Merck	Open	7.35	7.35
94-17-096	Santa's Shop 4079	E.M. Merck	Open	13.25	13.25
94-17-097	Father Christmas with Chenile 4080	E.M. Merck	Open	10.80	10.80
Old World Christmas		**Reflectors**			
86-18-001	Star Pattern Reflector (A) 4201	E.M. Merck	Open	9.25	9.25
86-18-002	Pink Reflector 4202	E.M. Merck	Open	9.50	9.50
86-18-003	Horseshoe Reflector 4203	E.M. Merck	Retrd.	7.80	7.80
87-18-004	Large Drop with Indents (A) 4204	E.M. Merck	Open	12.85	12.85
90-18-005	Strawberry in Reflector 4205	E.M. Merck	Open	9.25	9.25
90-18-006	Assorted Reflectors with Diamonds 4206	E.M. Merck	Open	9.95	9.95
90-18-007	Assorted 6 cm Reflectors 4207	E.M. Merck	Open	7.00	7.00
91-18-008	Peacock in Reflector 4208	E.M. Merck	Open	9.25	9.25
91-18-009	Pears in Reflector 4209	E.M. Merck	Open	9.25	9.25
92-18-010	Shining Sun Reflector 4210	E.M. Merck	Open	9.00	9.00
92-18-011	Poinsettia in Reflector 4211	E.M. Merck	Open	9.00	9.00
92-18-012	Flower in Reflector 4212	E.M. Merck	Open	9.25	9.25
92-18-013	Mushrooms in Reflector (A) 4213	E.M. Merck	Open	9.90	9.90
92-18-014	Scrap Santa in Reflector 4214	E.M. Merck	Retrd.	8.80	9.95

Company / Number	Name	Series / Artist	Edition Limit	Issue Price	Quote
93-18-015	Reflector with Tinsel Wire 4215	E.M. Merck	Open	20.00	20.00
94-18-016	Small Fantasy Form 4216	E.M. Merck	Open	22.00	22.00
94-18-017	Reflector on Icicle 4217	E.M. Merck	Open	27.75	27.75
Old World Christmas		**Toys**			
86-19-001	Large Nutcracker 4401	E.M. Merck	Open	13.50	13.50
86-19-002	Small Nutcracker 4402	E.M. Merck	Open	10.00	10.00
86-19-003	Dumb-Dumb 4403	E.M. Merck	Retrd.	6.45	12.95
86-19-004	Soccer Ball 4404	E.M. Merck	Open	7.00	7.00
88-19-005	Nutcracker Guard 4405	E.M. Merck	Open	8.50	8.50
90-19-006	Lucky Dice 4406	E.M. Merck	Open	7.00	7.00
90-19-007	Large Fancy Carousel 4407	E.M. Merck	Open	12.75	12.75
90-19-008	Rocking Horse/Tree on Form 4408	E.M. Merck	Open	12.95	12.95
90-19-009	Large Doll Buggy with Doll 4409	E.M. Merck	Open	11.50	11.50
93-19-010	Stocking with Toys 4410	E.M. Merck	Open	13.50	13.50
93-19-011	Cornucopia of Toys 4411	E.M. Merck	Open	9.50	9.50
85-19-012	Doll Buggy with Doll 4437138	E.M. Merck	Open	7.00	7.00
85-19-013	Small Carousel 446836	E.M. Merck	Open	7.00	7.00
Old World Christmas		**Transportation**			
86-20-001	Rolls Royce 4601	E.M. Merck	Retrd.	7.90	15.95
88-20-002	Cable Car 4602	E.M. Merck	Retrd.	8.45	14.95
90-20-003	Fire Truck 4603	E.M. Merck	Open	8.25	8.25
90-20-004	Old-Time Limousine 4604	E.M. Merck	Open	9.00	9.00
90-20-005	Large Zeppelin 4605	E.M. Merck	Open	8.25	8.25
90-20-006	Fancy Steam Locomotive 4606	E.M. Merck	Open	10.35	10.35
92-20-007	Commemorative Airship 4607	E.M. Merck	Open	9.25	9.25
92-20-008	Locomotive/Tree on Form 4608	E.M. Merck	Open	12.95	12.95
92-20-009	Race Car 4609	E.M. Merck	Open	7.00	7.00
93-20-010	Gold Car 4610	E.M. Merck	Open	9.80	9.80
85-20-011	Cable Car 461067	E.M. Merck	Retrd.	6.55	14.95
85-20-012	Locomotive 461069	E.M. Merck	Retrd.	7.00	7.00
93-20-013	Ocean Liner 4611	E.M. Merck	Open	9.45	9.45
93-20-014	Small Locomotive 4612	E.M. Merck	Open	9.80	9.80
93-20-015	Gray Zeppelin 4613	E.M. Merck	Open	6.75	6.75
85-20-016	Old-Fashioned Car 463747	E.M. Merck	Retrd.	6.25	6.25
85-20-017	Zeppelin 467265	E.M. Merck	Open	7.00	7.00
Old World Christmas		**Trees & Cones**			
86-21-001	Small Red & Gold Cones (A) 4801	E.M. Merck	Open	3.75	3.75
88-21-002	Large Mauve & Champagne Cone 4802	E.M. Merck	Retrd.	11.85	11.85
88-21-003	Smal Fir Cone (A) 4803	E.M. Merck	Open	4.50	4.50
89-21-004	Assorted Pearl Cones 4804	E.M. Merck	Open	3.85	3.85
89-21-005	Pine Cone Santa 4805	E.M. Merck	Open	4.75	4.75
90-21-006	Small Pine Cones with Leaves (A) 4806	E.M. Merck	Open	5.25	5.25
90-21-007	Assorted Shiny Cones 4807	E.M. Merck	Open	6.55	6.55
90-21-008	Assorted Pine Cones with Leaves 4809	E.M. Merck	Open	6.75	6.75
90-21-009	Multi-Colored Cone 4810	E.M. Merck	Open	7.00	7.00
85-21-010	Green Tree with Glitter 481044	E.M. Merck	Open	4.50	4.50
85-21-011	Fir Cone With Glitter 481046	E.M. Merck	Open	6.45	6.45
90-21-012	Pine Cone Man 4811	E.M. Merck	Open	8.25	8.25
90-21-013	Multi-Colored Tree 4812	E.M. Merck	Open	5.55	5.55
90-21-014	Fir Tree 4813	E.M. Merck	Open	7.00	7.00
90-21-015	Small Christmas Tree 4814	E.M. Merck	Open	4.95	4.95
90-21-016	Large Christmas Tree 4815	E.M. Merck	Open	8.00	8.00
92-21-017	Tree With Eagle 4816	E.M. Merck	Open	7.00	7.00
93-21-018	Sugar Cone 4817	E.M. Merck	Open	7.55	7.55
85-21-019	Very Large Red & Gold Cones 483612	E.M. Merck	Open	7.00	7.00
85-21-020	Medium Gold Cone w/Glitter 486712-5	E.M. Merck	Open	3.85	3.85
94-21-021	Matte Gold Cone with Snow 486866	E.M. Merck	Open	4.85	4.85
Old World Christmas		**Tree Tops**			
86-22-001	Red Santa 5001	E.M. Merck	Open	37.50	37.50
86-22-002	Blue Santa 5002	E.M. Merck	Open	37.50	37.50
86-22-003	Burgundy Angel 5003	E.M. Merck	Open	47.50	47.50
86-22-004	Blue Angel 5004	E.M. Merck	Open	47.50	47.50
86-22-005	Two Angels 5005	E.M. Merck	Open	47.50	47.50
87-22-006	Angel w/Crown 5007	E.M. Merck	Retrd.	50.00	50.00
87-22-007	Santa in Indent 5008	E.M. Merck	Open	25.00	25.00
87-22-008	Star Reflector 5010	E.M. Merck	Open	25.00	25.00
87-22-009	Heart Reflector 5011	E.M. Merck	Open	25.00	25.00
92-22-010	Large Tree Top w/Cherubs 5012	E.M. Merck	Open	57.50	57.50
92-22-011	Miniature Reflector 5013	E.M. Merck	Open	15.00	15.00
92-22-012	Large Spire w/Reflectors 5014	E.M. Merck	Open	69.50	69.50
92-22-013	Large Tree Top w/Roses 5015	E.M. Merck	Open	47.50	47.50
92-22-014	Fancy Spiral Tree Top 5016	E.M. Merck	Open	47.50	47.50
93-22-015	Very Large Reflector 5017	E.M. Merck	Open	65.00	65.00
85-22-016	Fancy Gold Spire w/Bells 5062-66	E.M. Merck	Retrd.	32.00	32.00
85-22-017	Fancy Red Spire w/Bells 5062-69	E.M. Merck	Retrd.	32.00	32.00
85-22-018	Santa Head Tree Top 506345	E.M. Merck	Open	19.35	19.35
Old World Christmas		**Light Covers**			
93-23-001	Doll Head 5202	E.M. Merck	Open	5.65	5.65
93-23-002	Peacock 5203	E.M. Merck	Open	5.65	5.65
93-23-003	Sugar Strawberry 5251	E.M. Merck	Open	5.65	5.65
93-23-004	Sugar Plum 5253	E.M. Merck	Open	5.65	5.65
93-23-005	Sugar Fruit Basket 5256	E.M. Merck	Open	5.65	5.65
93-23-006	Frosty Snowman 5270	E.M. Merck	Open	5.65	5.65
93-23-007	Frosty Cone 5271	E.M. Merck	Open	5.65	5.65
93-23-008	Frosty Icicle 5272	E.M. Merck	Open	5.65	5.65
93-23-009	Frosty Tree 5273	E.M. Merck	Open	5.65	5.65
93-23-010	Assorted Frosty Bell 5275	E.M. Merck	Open	5.65	5.65
93-23-011	Frosty Acorn 5276	E.M. Merck	Open	5.65	5.65
93-23-012	Frosty Red Rose 5277	E.M. Merck	Open	5.65	5.65
84-23-013	Gnome 529001-1	E.M. Merck	Retrd.	1.60	4.50
84-23-014	Snowman 519001-2	E.M. Merck	Retrd.	2.50	4.50
84-23-015	Standing Santa 529001-3	E.M. Merck	Retrd.	3.00	4.50
84-23-016	Mrs. Claus 529001-4	E.M. Merck	Retrd.	1.60	4.50
84-23-017	Clown 529001-5	E.M. Merck	Retrd.	1.60	4.50
84-23-018	Assorted Animals, set of 6 529003	E.M. Merck	Retrd.	10.35	27.00
84-23-019	Owl 529003-2	E.M. Merck	Retrd.	1.60	4.50
84-23-020	Bear 519003-3	E.M. Merck	Retrd.	2.50	4.50
84-23-021	Elephant 529003-4	E.M. Merck	Retrd.	1.60	4.50
84-23-022	Hedgehog 529003-5	E.M. Merck	Retrd.	1.60	4.50
84-23-023	Peacock 519003-6	E.M. Merck	Retrd.	2.70	2.70
84-23-024	Assorted Figurals, set of 6 529005	E.M. Merck	Retrd.	10.35	27.00
84-23-025	Flower Basket 529005-1	E.M. Merck	Retrd.	1.60	1.60
84-23-026	House 529005-2	E.M. Merck	Retrd.	1.60	4.50
84-23-027	Carousel 529005-3	E.M. Merck	Retrd.	2.70	4.50
84-23-028	Santa Head 529005-4	E.M. Merck	Retrd.	2.70	4.50
84-23-029	Santa on Heart 529005-5	E.M. Merck	Retrd.	3.00	4.50
84-23-030	Church on Ball 529005-6	E.M. Merck	Retrd.	2.50	4.50
84-23-031	3 Men in a Tub 529007-1	E.M. Merck	Retrd.	1.60	4.50
84-23-032	Queen of Heart 529007-3	E.M. Merck	Retrd.	2.70	4.50
84-23-033	Lil' Boy Blue 529007-5	E.M. Merck	Retrd.	1.60	1.60
85-23-034	Assorted Heads, set of 6 529009	E.M. Merck	Retrd.	10.35	27.00
85-23-035	Clown Head 529009-1	E.M. Merck	Retrd.	1.60	4.50
85-23-036	Red Riding Hood 529009-2	E.M. Merck	Retrd.	1.60	4.50
85-23-037	Santa Head 529009-3	E.M. Merck	Retrd.	3.00	4.50
85-23-038	Doll Head 529009-4	E.M. Merck	Retrd.	1.60	4.50
85-23-039	Father Christmas 529009-5	E.M. Merck	Retrd.	3.00	4.50
85-23-040	Lil' Rascal Head 529009-6	E.M. Merck	Retrd.	1.60	4.50
85-23-041	Assorted Fruit, set of 6 529011	E.M. Merck	Retrd.	20.00	27.00
85-23-042	Pear 529011-1	E.M. Merck	Retrd.	3.00	4.50
85-23-043	Strawberry 529011-2	E.M. Merck	Retrd.	3.00	4.50
85-23-044	Grapes 529011-3	E.M. Merck	Retrd.	3.00	4.50
85-23-045	Pineapple 529011-4	E.M. Merck	Retrd.	3.00	4.50
85-23-046	Apple 529011-5	E.M. Merck	Retrd.	3.00	4.50
85-23-047	Orange 529011-6	E.M. Merck	Open	3.00	3.00
85-23-048	Soldiers, set of 6 529013	E.M. Merck	Retrd.	17.95	27.00
85-23-049	Soldier with Drum 529013-1	E.M. Merck	Retrd.	2.70	4.50
85-23-050	Soldier with Gun 529013-2	E.M. Merck	Retrd.	2.70	4.50
85-23-051	King 529013-3	E.M. Merck	Retrd.	2.70	4.50
85-23-052	Assorted Santas, set of 6 529015	E.M. Merck	Retrd.	20.00	27.00
85-23-053	Santa with Tree 529015-3	E.M. Merck	Retrd.	3.00	4.50
85-23-054	Roly-Poly Santa 529015-6	E.M. Merck	Retrd.	3.00	4.50
85-23-055	Nutcracker Suite Figures, set of 6 529017	E.M. Merck	Retrd.	19.00	27.00
85-23-056	Clara-The Doll 529017-1	E.M. Merck	Retrd.	2.70	4.50
85-23-057	Marie-The Girl 529017-3	E.M. Merck	Retrd.	2.70	4.50
85-23-058	Nutcracker 529017-4	E.M. Merck	Retrd.	2.70	4.50
85-23-059	Mouse King 529017-5	E.M. Merck	Retrd.	2.70	4.50
85-23-060	Sugar Plum Fairy 529017-6	E.M. Merck	Retrd.	2.70	4.50
85-23-061	Transportation Set 529019	E.M. Merck	Retrd.	17.90	27.00
85-23-062	Tug Boat 529019-1	E.M. Merck	Retrd.	2.70	4.50
85-23-063	Balloon 529019-2	E.M. Merck	Retrd.	2.70	4.50
85-23-064	Automobile 529019-3	E.M. Merck	Retrd.	2.70	4.50
85-23-065	Locomotive 529019-4	E.M. Merck	Retrd.	2.70	4.50
85-23-066	Cable Car 529019-5	E.M. Merck	Retrd.	2.70	4.50
85-23-067	School Bus 529019-6	E.M. Merck	Retrd.	2.70	4.50
86-23-068	Assorted Bells, set of 6 529023	E.M. Merck	Retrd.	22.50	27.00
86-23-069	Tree on Bell 529023-1	E.M. Merck	Retrd.	3.95	4.50
86-23-070	Teddy Bear 529023-2	E.M. Merck	Retrd.	3.95	4.50
86-23-071	Santa on Bell 529023-3	E.M. Merck	Retrd.	3.95	4.50
86-23-072	Rocking Horse on Bell 529023-4	E.M. Merck	Retrd.	3.95	4.50
86-23-073	Angel on Bell 529023-5	E.M. Merck	Retrd.	3.95	4.50
86-23-074	Nutcracker on Bell 529023-6	E.M. Merck	Retrd.	3.95	4.50
86-23-075	Assorted Easter Eggs 529031-1	E.M. Merck	Retrd.	3.00	4.50
86-23-076	Hen in Basket 529033-1	E.M. Merck	Retrd.	3.60	4.50
86-23-077	Rabbit in Egg 529033-2	E.M. Merck	Retrd.	3.60	4.50
86-23-078	Chick 529033-3	E.M. Merck	Retrd.	3.60	4.50
86-23-079	Bunny 529033-4	E.M. Merck	Retrd.	3.60	4.50
86-23-080	Chick in Egg 529033-5	E.M. Merck	Retrd.	3.60	4.50
86-23-081	Bunny in Basket 529033-6	E.M. Merck	Retrd.	3.60	4.50
86-23-082	Teddy Bears, set of 6 529041	E.M. Merck	Retrd.	25.00	27.00
86-23-083	Teddy Bear with Candy Cane 529041-1	E.M. Merck	Retrd.	3.95	3.95
86-23-084	Teddy Bear with Red Heart 529041-2	E.M. Merck	Retrd.	3.95	3.95
86-23-085	Teddy Bear with Tree 529041-3	E.M. Merck	Retrd.	3.95	4.50
86-23-086	Teddy Bear with Nightshirt 529041-4	E.M. Merck	Open	3.95	3.95
86-23-087	Teddy Bear with Ball 529041-5	E.M. Merck	Open	3.95	3.95
86-23-088	Teddy Bear with Vest 529041-6	E.M. Merck	Open	3.95	3.95
86-23-089	Assorted Alphabet Blocks 529043-1	E.M. Merck	Retrd.	4.50	4.95
86-23-090	Assorted Roses, set of 6 529045	E.M. Merck	Retrd.	22.50	27.00
86-23-091	Assorted Red Roses 529045-1	E.M. Merck	Retrd.	3.95	4.50
86-23-092	Assorted Yellow Roses 529045-2	E.M. Merck	Retrd.	3.95	4.50
86-23-093	Assorted Pink Roses 529045-3	E.M. Merck	Retrd.	3.95	4.50
86-23-094	Assorted Peach Roses 529045-4	E.M. Merck	Retrd.	3.95	4.50
86-23-095	Father Christmas Set 529047	E.M. Merck	Retrd.	25.00	27.00
86-23-096	Red Father Christmas 529047-1	E.M. Merck	Retrd.	3.95	4.50
86-23-097	Green Father Christmas 529047-2	E.M. Merck	Retrd.	3.95	4.50
86-23-098	Blue Father Christmas 529047-3	E.M. Merck	Retrd.	3.95	4.50
86-23-099	Red Father Christmas 529047-4	E.M. Merck	Retrd.	3.95	4.50
86-23-100	White Father Christmas 529047-5	E.M. Merck	Retrd.	3.95	4.50
86-23-101	Purple Father Christmas 529047-6	E.M. Merck	Retrd.	3.95	4.50
88-23-102	Thanksgiving, set of 6 529049	E.M. Merck	Retrd.	25.00	27.00
88-23-103	Cornucopia 529049-1	E.M. Merck	Retrd.	3.95	4.50
88-23-104	Turkey 529049-2	E.M. Merck	Retrd.	3.95	4.50
88-23-105	Pilgrim Boy 529049-3	E.M. Merck	Retrd.	3.95	4.50
88-23-106	Pilgrim Girl 529049-4	E.M. Merck	Retrd.	3.95	4.50
88-23-107	Indian 529049-5	E.M. Merck	Retrd.	3.95	3.95
88-23-108	Ear of Corn 529049-6	E.M. Merck	Retrd.	3.95	3.95
88-23-109	Toy, set of 6 529051	E.M. Merck	Retrd.	25.00	27.00
88-23-110	Drum 529051-1	E.M. Merck	Retrd.	3.95	4.50
88-23-111	Doll 529051-2	E.M. Merck	Open	3.95	3.95
88-23-112	Stocking 529051-3	E.M. Merck	Retrd.	3.95	3.95
88-23-113	Christmas Tree 529051-4	E.M. Merck	Retrd.	3.95	4.50
88-23-114	Teddy Bear 529051-5	E.M. Merck	Retrd.	3.95	4.50
88-23-115	Clown 529051-6	E.M. Merck	Retrd.	3.95	4.50
88-23-116	Christmas Carol 529053	E.M. Merck	Retrd.	25.00	27.00
88-23-117	Assorted Fast Food 529055-1	E.M. Merck	Retrd.	3.95	4.50
88-23-118	Assorted Birds 529057-1	E.M. Merck	Retrd.	3.95	4.50
85-23-119	Six Red & White Hearts 529201	E.M. Merck	Retrd.	15.00	15.00
85-23-120	Red Heart 529201-1	E.M. Merck	Retrd.	2.85	4.50
85-23-121	White Heart 529201-2	E.M. Merck	Retrd.	2.85	4.50
85-23-122	Pink Heart 529201-3	E.M. Merck	Retrd.	2.85	4.50
85-23-123	Clear Icicles, set of 6 529205	E.M. Merck	Retrd.	20.00	27.00
85-23-124	Clear Icicle 529205-1	E.M. Merck	Retrd.	3.50	3.50
85-23-125	Pastel Icicles 529207	E.M. Merck	Retrd.	N/A	N/A
89-23-126	Assorted Fir Cone 529209-1	E.M. Merck	Retrd.	2.85	4.50
91-23-127	Assorted Spun Glass Globe 529213-1	E.M. Merck	Retrd.	3.50	4.50
89-23-128	Assorted Sea Shells 529301-4	E.M. Merck	Retrd.	3.50	3.50
89-23-129	Panda 529303-1	E.M. Merck	Open	6.45	6.45
89-23-130	Squirrel 529303-2	E.M. Merck	Open	6.45	6.45
89-23-131	Kitten 529303-3	E.M. Merck	Retrd.	6.45	6.45
89-23-132	Puppy 529303-4	E.M. Merck	Open	6.45	6.45
89-23-133	Swan 529303-5	E.M. Merck	Open	6.45	6.45
89-23-134	Frog 529303-6	E.M. Merck	Retrd.	6.45	6.45
92-23-135	Six Snowmen 529305	E.M. Merck	Retrd.	29.00	32.95
91-23-136	Assorted Snowmen 529305-1	E.M. Merck	Retrd.	5.55	5.55
Old World Christmas		**Halloween Light Covers**			
87-24-001	Six Halloween Light Covers 9221	E.M. Merck	Open	25.00	25.00
87-24-002	Jack O'Lantern 9221-1	E.M. Merck	Retrd.	3.95	4.50
87-24-003	Ghost w/Pumpkin 9221-2	E.M. Merck	Open	3.95	3.95
87-24-004	Scarecrow 9221-3	E.M. Merck	Retrd.	3.95	4.50
87-24-005	Witch Head 9221-4	E.M. Merck	Retrd.	3.95	4.50
87-24-006	Sad Pumpkin 9221-5	E.M. Merck	Retrd.	3.95	4.50
87-24-007	Skull 9221-6	E.M. Merck	Open	3.95	3.95
87-24-008	Six Halloween Light Covers 9223	E.M. Merck	Retrd.	25.90	27.00

Company / Number	Name	Series / Artist	Edition Limit	Issue Price	Quote
87-24-009	Haunted House 9223-1	E.M. Merck	Open	3.95	3.95
87-24-010	Smiling Cat 9223-2	E.M. Merck	Retrd.	3.95	4.50
87-24-011	Standing Witch 9223-3	E.M. Merck	Open	3.95	3.95
87-24-012	Smiling Ghost 9223-4	E.M. Merck	Open	3.95	3.95
87-24-013	Devil 9223-5	E.M. Merck	Retrd.	3.95	3.95
87-24-014	Pumpkin w/Top Hat 9223-6	E.M. Merck	Open	3.95	3.95
89-24-015	Spider 9241-1	E.M. Merck	Open	7.65	7.65
89-24-016	Witch Head 9241-2	E.M. Merck	Open	7.65	7.65
89-24-017	Dancing Scarecrow 9241-3	E.M. Merck	Open	7.65	7.65
89-24-018	Wizard 9241-4	E.M. Merck	Retrd.	7.65	9.50
89-24-019	Man in the Moon 9241-5	E.M. Merck	Retrd.	7.65	9.50
89-24-020	Pumpkin Face 9241-6	E.M. Merck	Open	7.65	7.65
Old World Christmas		**Easter**			
88-25-001	Gentleman Rabbit 9301	E.M. Merck	Retrd.	25.00	25.00
88-25-002	Gentleman Chick 9311	E.M. Merck	Retrd.	22.50	22.50
88-25-003	Lady Chick 9312	E.M. Merck	Retrd.	22.50	22.50
Old World Christmas		**Easter Light Covers**			
88-26-001	Assorted Easter Egg 9331-1	E.M. Merck	Retrd.	3.95	4.50
88-26-002	Hen in Basket 9333-1	E.M. Merck	Open	4.20	4.20
88-26-003	Rabbit in Egg 9333-2	E.M. Merck	Open	4.20	4.20
88-26-004	Chick 9333-3	E.M. Merck	Open	4.20	4.20
88-26-005	Bunny 9333-4	E.M. Merck	Open	4.20	4.20
88-26-006	Chick in Egg 9333-5	E.M. Merck	Open	4.20	4.20
88-26-007	Bunny in Basket 9333-6	E.M. Merck	Open	4.20	4.20
88-26-008	Assorted Pastel Egg 9335-1	E.M. Merck	Open	2.95	2.95
Old World Christmas		**Porcelain Christmas**			
87-27-001	Father Christmas (A) 9404	E.M. Merck	Retrd.	11.00	11.00
87-27-002	Father Christmas w/Cape 9405	E.M. Merck	Retrd.	11.00	11.00
87-27-003	Father Christmas w/Toys 9406	E.M. Merck	Retrd.	11.00	11.00
87-27-004	Santa Head 9410	E.M. Merck	Retrd.	6.55	6.55
87-27-005	Lighted Angel Tree Top 9420	E.M. Merck	Retrd.	29.50	29.50
89-27-006	Rocking Horse 9431	E.M. Merck	Open	6.65	6.65
89-27-007	Santa 9432	E.M. Merck	Open	6.65	6.65
89-27-008	Hummingbird 9433	E.M. Merck	Open	6.65	6.65
89-27-009	Teddy Bear 9434	E.M. Merck	Open	6.65	6.65
89-27-010	Angel 9435	E.M. Merck	Open	6.65	6.65
89-27-011	Nutcracker 9436	E.M. Merck	Open	6.65	6.65
87-27-012	Roly-Poly Santa 9441	E.M. Merck	Retrd.	6.75	8.65
88-27-013	Bunnies on Skies 9494	E.M. Merck	Retrd.	10.00	10.00
88-27-014	Bear on Skates 9495	E.M. Merck	Retrd.	10.00	10.00
88-27-015	Penguin w/Gifts 9496	E.M. Merck	Retrd.	10.00	10.00
Old World Christmas		**Collector Club**			
92-28-001	Mr. & Mrs. Claus set 1490	E.M. Merck	Retrd.	Gift	N/A
92-28-002	Glass Christmas Maidens, set of 4, 1491	E.M. Merck	Retrd.	35.00	39.95
92-28-003	Dresdener Drummer Nutcracker 7258	E.M. Merck	Retrd.	110.00	110.00
94-28-004	Santa in Moon 1492	E.M. Merck	12/94	Gift	N/A
94-28-005	Large Santa in Chimney 1493	E.M. Merck	12/94	42.50	42.50
Orrefors		**Christmas Ornaments**			
84-01-001	Dove	O. Alberius	Yr.Iss.	30.00	45.00
85-01-002	Angel	O. Alberius	Yr.Iss.	30.00	40.00
86-01-003	Reindeer	O. Alberius	Yr.Iss.	30.00	40.00
87-01-004	Snowman	O. Alberius	Yr.Iss.	30.00	40.00
88-01-005	Sleigh	O. Alberius	Yr.Iss.	30.00	40.00
89-01-006	Christmas Tree "1989"	O. Alberius	Yr.Iss.	35.00	40.00
90-01-007	Holly Leaves And Berries	O. Alberius	Yr.Iss.	35.00	40.00
91-01-008	Stocking	O. Alberius	Yr.Iss.	40.00	40.00
92-01-009	Star	O. Alberius	Yr.Iss.	35.00	40.00
93-01-010	Bell	O. Alberius	Yr.Iss.	35.00	40.00
93-01-011	Baby's1st Christmas	O. Alberius	Yr.Iss.	40.00	40.00
94-01-012	Rocking Horse	O. Alberius	Yr.Iss.	40.00	40.00
Rawcliffe Corporation		**Bubble Fairy™ Ornaments**			
93-01-001	"Joy" Hanging Baby Bubble Fairy RF156	J. deStefano	Open	40.00	40.00
93-01-002	"Blessing" Hanging Baby Bubble Fairy RF157	J. deStefano	Open	40.00	40.00
93-01-003	"Wonder" Hanging Baby Bubble Fairy RF158	J. deStefano	Open	40.00	40.00
93-01-004	"Sweetness" Hanging Baby Bubble Fairy RF159	J. deStefano	Open	40.00	40.00
92-01-005	"Holly" Hanging Baby Bubble Fairy RF160	J. deStefano	Open	40.00	40.00
Reco International		**The Reco Angel Collection Hang-Ups**			
87-01-001	Innocence	J. McClelland	Open	7.50	7.50
87-01-002	Harmony	J. McClelland	Open	7.50	7.50
87-01-003	Love	J. McClelland	Open	7.50	7.50
87-01-004	Gloria	J. McClelland	Open	7.50	7.50
87-01-005	Devotion	J. McClelland	Open	7.50	7.50
87-01-006	Joy	J. McClelland	Open	7.50	7.50
87-01-007	Adoration	J. McClelland	Open	10.00	10.00
87-01-008	Peace	J. McClelland	Open	10.00	10.00
87-01-009	Serenity	J. McClelland	Open	10.00	10.00
87-01-010	Hope	J. McClelland	Open	10.00	10.00
Reco International		**The Reco Ornament Collection**			
88-02-001	Billy	S. Kuck	Yr.Iss.	15.00	15.00
88-02-002	Lisa	S. Kuck	Yr.Iss.	15.00	15.00
89-02-003	Heather	S. Kuck	Yr.Iss.	15.00	15.00
89-02-004	Timothy	S. Kuck	Yr.Iss.	15.00	15.00
90-02-005	Amy	S. Kuck	Yr.Iss.	15.00	15.00
90-02-006	Johnny	S. Kuck	Yr.Iss.	15.00	15.00
90-02-007	Peace On Earth	S. Kuck	17,500	17.50	17.50
Reed & Barton		**Christmas Cross**			
71-01-001	Sterling Silver-1971	Reed & Barton	Closed	10.00	140.00
71-01-002	24Kt. Gold over Sterling-V1971	Reed & Barton	Closed	17.50	225.00
72-01-003	Sterling Silver-1972	Reed & Barton	Closed	10.00	60-125.00
72-01-004	24Kt. Gold over Sterling-V1972	Reed & Barton	Closed	17.50	65-105.
73-01-005	Sterling Silver-1973	Reed & Barton	Closed	10.00	60.00
73-01-006	24Kt. Gold over Sterling-V1973	Reed & Barton	Closed	17.50	55-65.00
74-01-007	Sterling Silver-1974	Reed & Barton	Closed	12.95	40-60.00
74-01-008	24Kt. Gold over Sterling-V1974	Reed & Barton	Closed	20.00	50-60.00
75-01-009	Sterling Silver-1975	Reed & Barton	Closed	12.95	35-55.00
75-01-010	24Kt. Gold over Sterling-V1975	Reed & Barton	Closed	20.00	45-50.00
76-01-011	Sterling Silver-1976	Reed & Barton	Closed	13.95	45-55.00
76-01-012	24Kt. Gold over Sterling-V1976	Reed & Barton	Closed	19.95	45-50.00
77-01-013	Sterling Silver-1977	Reed & Barton	Closed	15.00	35-55.00
77-01-014	24Kt. Gold over Sterling-V1977	Reed & Barton	Closed	18.50	45-50.00
78-01-015	Sterling Silver-1978	Reed & Barton	Closed	16.00	40-65.00
78-01-016	24Kt. Gold over Sterling-V1978	Reed & Barton	Closed	20.00	45-55.00
79-01-017	Sterling Silver-1979	Reed & Barton	Closed	20.00	45-60.00
79-01-018	24Kt. Gold over Sterling-V1979	Reed & Barton	Closed	24.00	32-57.00

Company / Number	Name	Series / Artist	Edition Limit	Issue Price	Quote
80-01-019	Sterling Silver-1980	Reed & Barton	Closed	35.00	55.00
80-01-020	24Kt. Gold over Sterling-V1980	Reed & Barton	Closed	40.00	45-50.00
81-01-021	Sterling Silver-1981	Reed & Barton	Closed	35.00	45.00
81-01-022	24Kt. Gold over Sterling-V1981	Reed & Barton	Closed	40.00	45.00
82-01-023	Sterling Silver-1982	Reed & Barton	Closed	35.00	50-70.00
82-01-024	24Kt. Gold over Sterling-V1982	Reed & Barton	Closed	40.00	45.00
83-01-025	Sterling Silver-1983	Reed & Barton	Closed	35.00	55.00
83-01-026	24Kt. Gold over Sterling-V1983	Reed & Barton	Closed	40.00	40-45.00
84-01-027	Sterling Silver-1984	Reed & Barton	Closed	35.00	45.00
84-01-028	24Kt. Gold over Sterling-V1984	Reed & Barton	Closed	45.00	45.00
85-01-029	Sterling Silver-1985	Reed & Barton	Closed	35.00	40-65.00
85-01-030	24Kt. Gold over Sterling-V1985	Reed & Barton	Closed	40.00	40.00
86-01-031	Sterling Silver-1986	Reed & Barton	Closed	38.50	38.50
86-01-032	24Kt. Gold over Sterling-V1986	Reed & Barton	Closed	40.00	40.00
87-01-033	Sterling Silver-1987	Reed & Barton	Closed	35.00	35.00
87-01-034	24Kt. Gold over Sterling-V1987	Reed & Barton	Closed	40.00	40.00
88-01-035	Sterling Silver-1988	Reed & Barton	Closed	35.00	40.00
88-01-036	24Kt. Gold over Sterling-V1988	Reed & Barton	Closed	40.00	40.00
89-01-037	Sterling Silver-1989	Reed & Barton	Closed	35.00	35-55.00
89-01-038	24Kt. Gold over Sterling-V1989	Reed & Barton	Closed	40.00	40.00
90-01-039	Sterling Silver-1990	Reed & Barton	Closed	40.00	35.00
90-01-040	24Kt. Gold over Sterling-1990	Reed & Barton	Closed	45.00	45.00
91-01-041	Sterling Silver-1991	Reed & Barton	Closed	40.00	35.00
91-01-042	24Kt. Gold over Sterling-1991	Reed & Barton	Closed	45.00	45.00
92-01-043	Sterling Silver-1992	Reed & Barton	Closed	40.00	40.00
92-01-044	24Kt. Gold over Sterling-1992	Reed & Barton	Closed	45.00	45.00
93-01-045	Sterling Silver-1993	Reed & Barton	Yr.Iss.	40.00	40.00
93-01-046	24Kt. Gold over Sterling-1993	Reed & Barton	Yr.Iss.	45.00	45.00
94-01-047	Sterling Silver-1994	Reed & Barton	Yr.Iss.	40.00	40.00
94-01-048	24Kt. Gold over Sterling-1994	Reed & Barton	Yr.Iss.	45.00	45.00
Reed & Barton		**Holly Ball**			
76-02-001	1976 Silver plated	Reed & Barton	Closed	13.95	50.00
77-02-002	1977 Silver plated	Reed & Barton	Closed	15.00	35.00
78-02-003	1978 Silver plated	Reed & Barton	Closed	15.00	40.00
79-02-004	1979 Silver plated	Reed & Barton	Closed	15.00	35.00
Reed & Barton		**Holly Bell**			
80-03-001	1980 Bell	Reed & Barton	Closed	22.50	40.00
80-03-002	Bell, gold plate, V1980	Reed & Barton	Closed	25.00	45.00
81-03-003	1981 Bell	Reed & Barton	Closed	22.50	35.00
81-03-004	Bell, gold plate, V1981	Reed & Barton	Closed	27.50	35.00
82-03-005	1982 Bell	Reed & Barton	Closed	22.50	35.00
82-03-006	Bell, gold plate, V1982	Reed & Barton	Closed	27.50	35.00
83-03-007	1983 Bell	Reed & Barton	Closed	23.50	40.00
83-03-008	Bell, gold plate, V1983	Reed & Barton	Closed	30.00	35.00
84-03-009	1984 Bell	Reed & Barton	Closed	25.00	30.00
84-03-010	Bell, gold plate, V1984	Reed & Barton	Closed	28.50	35.00
85-03-011	1985 Bell	Reed & Barton	Closed	25.00	35.00
85-03-012	Bell, gold plate, V1985	Reed & Barton	Closed	28.50	28.50
86-03-013	1986 Bell	Reed & Barton	Closed	25.00	35.00
86-03-014	Bell, gold plate, V1986	Reed & Barton	Closed	28.50	32.50
87-03-015	1987 Bell	Reed & Barton	Closed	27.50	30.00
87-03-016	Bell, gold plate, V1987	Reed & Barton	Closed	30.00	30.00
88-03-017	1988 Bell	Reed & Barton	Closed	27.50	30-40.00
88-03-018	Bell, gold plate, V1988	Reed & Barton	Closed	30.00	30.00
89-03-019	1989 Bell	Reed & Barton	Closed	27.50	35.00
89-03-020	Bell, gold plate, V1989	Reed & Barton	Closed	30.00	30.00
90-03-021	Bell, gold plate, V1990	Reed & Barton	Closed	30.00	30.00
90-03-022	1990 Bell	Reed & Barton	Closed	27.50	35.00
91-03-023	Bell, gold plate, V1991	Reed & Barton	Closed	30.00	30.00
91-03-024	1991 Bell	Reed & Barton	Closed	27.50	27.50
92-03-025	Bell, gold plate, V1992	Reed & Barton	Closed	30.00	30.00
92-03-026	Bell, silver plate, 1992	Reed & Barton	Closed	27.50	27.50
93-03-027	Bell, gold plate, V1993	Reed & Barton	Yr.Iss.	27.50	27.50
93-03-028	Bell, silver plate, 1993	Reed & Barton	Yr.Iss.	30.00	30.00
94-03-029	Bell, gold plate, 1994	Reed & Barton	Yr.Iss.	30.00	30.00
94-03-030	Bell, silver plate, 1994	Reed & Barton	Yr.Iss.	27.50	27.50
Reed & Barton		**12 Days of Christmas**			
83-04-001	Partridge in a Pear Tree	Reed & Barton	Closed	16.50	20.00
83-04-002	Turtle Doves	Reed & Barton	Closed	16.50	20.00
84-04-003	French Hens	Reed & Barton	Closed	18.50	20.00
84-04-004	Calling Birds	Reed & Barton	Closed	18.50	20.00
85-04-005	Gold Rings	Reed & Barton	Closed	20.00	20.00
85-04-006	Geese A'Laying	Reed & Barton	Closed	20.00	20.00
86-04-007	Swans A'Swimming	Reed & Barton	Closed	20.00	20.00
86-04-008	Maids A'Milking	Reed & Barton	Closed	20.00	20.00
87-04-009	Ladies Dancing	Reed & Barton	Closed	20.00	20.00
87-04-010	Lords A'Leaping	Reed & Barton	Closed	20.00	20.00
88-04-011	Pipers Piping	Reed & Barton	Closed	20.00	35.00
88-04-012	Drummers Drumming	Reed & Barton	Closed	20.00	20.00
Reed & Barton		**12 Days of Christmas Sterling and Lead Crystal**			
88-05-001	Partridge in a Pear Tree	Reed & Barton	Closed	25.00	27.50
89-05-002	Two Turtle Doves	Reed & Barton	Closed	25.00	27.50
90-05-003	French Hens	Reed & Barton	Closed	27.50	27.50
91-05-004	Colly birds	Reed & Barton	Closed	27.50	27.50
92-05-005	Five Golden Rings	Reed & Barton	Closed	27.50	27.50
93-05-006	Six French Hens	Reed & Barton	Yr.Iss.	27.50	27.50
94-05-007	Swans A 'Swimming	Reed & Barton	Yr.Iss.	27.50	27.50
94-05-008	Eight Maids A Milking	Reed & Barton	Yr.Iss.	27.50	27.50
Reed & Barton		**Carousel Horse**			
88-06-001	Silverplate-1988	Reed & Barton	Closed	13.50	13.50
88-06-002	Gold-covered-1988	Reed & Barton	Closed	15.00	15.00
89-06-003	Silverplate-1989	Reed & Barton	Closed	13.50	13.50
89-06-004	Gold-covered-1989	Reed & Barton	Closed	15.00	15.00
90-06-005	Silverplate-1990	Reed & Barton	Closed	13.50	13.50
90-06-006	Gold-covered-1990	Reed & Barton	Closed	15.00	15.00
91-06-007	Silverplate-1991	Reed & Barton	Closed	13.50	13.50
91-06-008	Gold-covered-1991	Reed & Barton	Closed	15.00	15.00
92-06-009	Silverplate-1992	Reed & Barton	Closed	13.50	13.50
92-06-010	Gold-covered-1992	Reed & Barton	Closed	15.00	15.00
93-06-011	Silverplate-1993	Reed & Barton	Closed	13.50	13.50
93-06-012	Gold-covered-1993	Reed & Barton	Closed	15.00	15.00
94-06-013	Silverplate-1994	Reed & Barton	Yr.Iss.	13.50	13.50
94-06-014	Gold-covered-1994	Reed & Barton	Yr.Iss.	15.00	15.00
Roman, Inc.		**The Discovery of America**			
91-01-001	Kitstopher Kolumbus	I. Spencer	1,992	15.00	15.00
91-01-002	Queen Kitsabella	I. Spencer	1,992	15.00	15.00

CHRISTMAS ORNAMENTS

Number	Name	Artist	Edition Limit	Issue Price	Quote
Company		**Series**			
Roman, Inc.		**Fontanini Annual Christmas Ornaments**			
91-02-001	1991 Annual (Girl)	E. Simonetti	Yr.Iss.	8.50	8.50
91-02-002	1991 Annual (Boy)	E. Simonetti	Yr.Iss.	8.50	8.50
92-02-003	1992 Annual (Girl)	E. Simonetti	Yr.Iss.	8.50	8.50
92-02-004	1992 Annual (Boy)	E. Simonetti	Yr.Iss.	8.50	8.50
93-02-005	1993 Annual (Girl)	E. Simonetti	Yr.Iss.	8.50	8.50
93-02-006	1993 Annual (Boy)	E. Simonetti	Yr.Iss.	8.50	8.50
Roman, Inc.		**Museum Collection of Angela Tripi**			
94-03-001	1994 Annual Angel Ornament	A. Tripi	2,500	49.50	49.50
Roman, Inc.		**Catnippers**			
88-04-001	Christmas Mourning	I. Spencer	Open	15.00	15.00
88-04-002	Ring A Ding-Ding	I. Spencer	Open	15.00	15.00
88-04-003	Puss in Berries	I. Spencer	Open	15.00	15.00
89-04-004	Bow Brummel	I. Spencer	Open	15.00	15.00
89-04-005	Happy Holidaze	I. Spencer	Open	15.00	15.00
89-04-006	Sandy Claws	I. Spencer	Open	15.00	15.00
90-04-007	Sock It to Me Santa	I. Spencer	Open	15.00	15.00
90-04-008	Stuck on Christmas	I. Spencer	Open	15.00	15.00
90-04-009	Felix Navidad	I. Spencer	Open	15.00	15.00
91-04-010	Meowy Christmas	I. Spencer	Open	15.00	15.00
91-04-011	Christmas Knight	I. Spencer	Open	15.00	15.00
91-04-012	Faux Paw	I. Spencer	Open	15.00	15.00
91-04-013	Snow Biz	I. Spencer	Open	15.00	15.00
91-04-014	Holly Days Are Happy Days	I. Spencer	Open	15.00	15.00
91-04-015	Pawtridge in a Purr Tree	I. Spencer	Open	15.00	15.00
Roman, Inc.		**Millenium Ornament**			
93-05-001	Silent Night	M. Lucchesi	20,000	20.00	20.00
93-05-002	The Annunciation	M. Lucchesi	20,000	20.00	20.00
93-05-003	Peace On Earth	M. Lucchesi	20,000	20.00	20.00
Royal Copenhagen		**Christmas**			
80-01-001	Bringing Home the Tree	K. Lange	Annual	19.50	19.50
81-01-002	Admiring Christmas Tree	K. Lange	Annual	19.50	19.50
82-01-003	Waiting For Christmas	K. Lange	Annual	19.50	19.50
83-01-004	Merry Christmas	K. Lange	Annual	19.50	19.50
84-01-005	Jingle Bells	K. Lange	Annual	19.50	19.50
85-01-006	Snowman	K. Lange	Annual	19.50	19.50
86-01-007	Christmas Vacation	K. Lange	Annual	19.50	19.50
87-01-008	Winter Birds	S. Vestergaard	Annual	19.50	19.50
88-01-009	Christmas Eve in Copenhagen	S. Vestergaard	Annual	19.50	19.50
89-01-010	The Old Skating Pond	S. Vestergaard	Annual	19.50	19.50
90-01-011	Christmas in Tivoli	S. Vestergaard	Annual	19.50	19.50
91-01-012	The Festival of Santa Lucia	S. Vestergaard	Annual	39.50	39.50
92-01-013	The Queen's Carriage	S. Vestergaard	Annual	36.50	36.50
93-01-014	Christmas Guests	S. Vestergaard	Annual	36.50	36.50
94-01-015	Christmas Shopping	S. Vestergaard	Annual	36.50	36.50
Royal Copenhagen		**Christmas in Denmark**			
91-02-001	Bringing Home the Tree	H. Hansen	Annual	25.00	25.00
92-02-002	Christmas Shopping	H. Hansen	Annual	25.00	25.00
93-02-003	The Skating Party	H. Hansen	Annual	25.00	25.00
94-02-004	The Sleigh Ride	H. Hansen	Annual	25.00	25.00
Royal Copenhagen		**Georg Jensen Gold-Plated Ornament**			
84-03-001	Christmas Bell	G. Jensen	Annual	30.00	50.00
85-03-002	Jingle Bell	G. Jensen	Annual	35.00	50.00
86-03-003	Christmas of Heart	G. Jensen	Annual	35.00	50.00
87-03-004	Snowflakes	G. Jensen	Annual	39.50	50.00
88-03-005	Holly	G. Jensen	Annual	39.50	50.00
89-03-006	Angel Bright	G. Jensen	Annual	42.50	50.00
90-03-007	Christmas Basket	G. Jensen	Annual	49.50	50.00
91-03-008	Christmas Deer	G. Jensen	Annual	49.50	50.00
92-03-009	The Robin's Nest	G. Jensen	Annual	65.00	65.00
93-03-010	Christmas Star	G. Jensen	Annual	65.00	65.00
94-03-011	Mistletoe	G. Jensen	Annual	65.00	65.00
Royal Copenhagen		**Crystal Ball Ornaments**			
93-04-001	N/A	A. Sofi-Romme	Annual	19.50	19.50
94-04-002	Holly	A. Sofi-Romme	Annual	19.50	19.50
Royal Doulton		**Bunnykins**			
91-01-001	Santa Bunny	Unknown	N/A	19.00	19.00
92-01-002	Caroling	Unknown	N/A	19.00	19.00
Royal Doulton		**Christmas Ornaments**			
93-02-001	Together for Christmas	Unknown	N/A	20.00	20.00
Royal Orleans		**Ornaments**			
84-01-001	Jimmy	J. Hagara	2-Yr.	10.00	N/A
84-01-002	Jenny	J. Hagara	2-Yr.	10.00	N/A
84-01-003	Lisa	J. Hagara	2-Yr.	10.00	N/A
84-01-004	Anne	J. Hagara	2-Yr.	10.00	N/A
Sarah's Attic, Inc.		**Holiday Ornaments**			
87-01-001	Bare Bottom Baby 2061	Sarah's Attic	Closed	10.00	10.00
87-01-002	Goose w/Wreath 3010	Sarah's Attic	Closed	8.00	8.00
87-01-003	Reba Rabbit w/Bonnet 3011	Sarah's Attic	Closed	8.00	8.00
87-01-004	Rayburn Rabbit w/Carrot 3012	Sarah's Attic	Closed	8.00	8.00
87-01-005	Reggie Rabbit w/Scarf 3013	Sarah's Attic	Closed	8.00	8.00
87-01-006	Girl Angel with Fur/Muff 3014	Sarah's Attic	Closed	8.00	8.00
87-01-007	Boy Angel with Fur/Muff 3015	Sarah's Attic	Closed	8.00	8.00
87-01-008	Angel Head/Wings 3016	Sarah's Attic	Closed	8.00	8.00
87-01-009	Angel Head Hands 3017	Sarah's Attic	Closed	8.00	8.00
87-01-010	Santa Head 3/4 View 3018	Sarah's Attic	Closed	8.00	8.00
87-01-011	Santa Head Full View 3019	Sarah's Attic	Closed	8.00	8.00
87-01-012	Santa with Basket 3020	Sarah's Attic	Closed	9.00	9.00
87-01-013	Ruthie Rabbit 3021	Sarah's Attic	Closed	8.00	8.00
87-01-014	Mini Santa 5406	Sarah's Attic	Closed	9.00	9.00
87-01-015	Corky 5409	Sarah's Attic	Closed	12.00	12.00
87-01-016	Clementine 5410	Sarah's Attic	Closed	12.00	12.00
87-01-017	Amber 5411	Sarah's Attic	Closed	12.00	12.00
87-01-018	Archie 5412	Sarah's Attic	Closed	12.00	12.00
87-01-019	Blondie 5413	Sarah's Attic	Closed	14.00	14.00
87-01-020	Butch 5414	Sarah's Attic	Closed	14.00	14.00
87-01-021	Stocking 5800	Sarah's Attic	Closed	8.00	8.00
88-01-022	Alex Bear 2062	Sarah's Attic	Closed	11.00	11.00
88-01-023	Amelia Bear 2063	Sarah's Attic	Closed	9.00	9.00
88-01-024	Abbee Bear 2064	Sarah's Attic	Closed	8.00	8.00
88-01-025	Ashbee Bear 2065	Sarah's Attic	Closed	8.00	8.00
88-01-026	Sitting Matt 2066	Sarah's Attic	Closed	12.00	12.00
88-01-027	Sitting Maggie 2067	Sarah's Attic	Closed	12.00	12.00
88-01-028	Benni Bear 2078	Sarah's Attic	Closed	8.00	8.00
88-01-029	Mini Matt 2107	Sarah's Attic	Closed	10.00	10.00
88-01-030	Mini Maggie 2108	Sarah's Attic	Closed	10.00	10.00
88-01-031	White Rabbit 2273	Sarah's Attic	Closed	9.00	9.00
88-01-032	Brown Rabbit 2275	Sarah's Attic	Closed	9.00	9.00
88-01-033	Cocker w/Pup-White 2277	Sarah's Attic	Closed	8.00	8.00
88-01-034	Cocker w/Pup-Brown 2278	Sarah's Attic	Closed	8.00	8.00
88-01-035	Kitten Diaper-White 2279	Sarah's Attic	Closed	8.00	8.00
88-01-036	Kitten Diaper-Brown 2280	Sarah's Attic	Closed	8.00	8.00
88-01-037	Bunny w/Wreath-Brown 2282	Sarah's Attic	Closed	6.00	6.00
88-01-038	Matt w/Puppy 3055	Sarah's Attic	Closed	12.00	12.00
88-01-039	Maggie w/Bunny 3056	Sarah's Attic	Closed	12.00	12.00
88-01-040	Cow w/Wreath 3057	Sarah's Attic	Closed	10.00	10.00
88-01-041	Pig 3058	Sarah's Attic	Closed	12.00	12.00
88-01-042	Cat w/Bonnet 3060	Sarah's Attic	Closed	10.00	10.00
88-01-043	Santa Mouse 3062	Sarah's Attic	Closed	10.00	10.00
88-01-044	Hooded Santa 3064	Sarah's Attic	Closed	8.00	8.00
88-01-045	Santa w/Pouch 3065	Sarah's Attic	Closed	8.00	8.00
88-01-046	Daisy Angel 3066	Sarah's Attic	Closed	8.00	8.00
88-01-047	Victorian Angel 3067	Sarah's Attic	Closed	7.00	7.00
88-01-048	Cat 6261	Sarah's Attic	Closed	6.00	6.00
88-01-049	Sheep 6263	Sarah's Attic	Closed	8.00	8.00
89-01-050	Brown Cow 2222	Sarah's Attic	Closed	10.00	10.00
89-01-051	Jolly 3206	Sarah's Attic	Closed	15.00	15.00
89-01-052	Christmas Wonder 3207	Sarah's Attic	Closed	20.00	20.00
90-01-053	Toby-Christmas 3279	Sarah's Attic	Closed	20.00	20.00
90-01-054	Star of Christmas 3280	Sarah's Attic	Closed	20.00	20.00
90-01-055	Packy-Bear on Package 3281	Sarah's Attic	Closed	20.00	20.00
90-01-056	Heavenly Family 3282	Sarah's Attic	Closed	32.00	32.00
90-01-057	Gala Angel w/Wreath 3283	Sarah's Attic	Closed	25.00	25.00
90-01-058	Burr Snowman 3284	Sarah's Attic	Closed	18.00	18.00
90-01-059	Abner Rabbit 3285	Sarah's Attic	Closed	17.00	17.00
90-01-060	Blessed Christmas 3286	Sarah's Attic	Closed	23.00	23.00
90-01-061	Spirit of Christmas 3287	Sarah's Attic	Closed	21.00	21.00
90-01-062	Peter Angel 3288	Sarah's Attic	Closed	25.00	25.00
90-01-063	Nutmeg Skates 3289	Sarah's Attic	Closed	17.00	17.00
90-01-064	Rosalee 3290	Sarah's Attic	Closed	27.00	27.00
94-01-065	Jolly Santa 4165	Sarah's Attic	12/94	14.50	14.50
94-01-066	America 4166	Sarah's Attic	12/94	14.50	14.50
94-01-067	Tillie 4167	Sarah's Attic	12/94	14.50	14.50
94-01-068	Bear 4168	Sarah's Attic	12/94	14.50	14.50
94-01-069	Snowball Rabbit 4169	Sarah's Attic	12/94	14.50	14.50
94-01-070	Love 4170	Sarah's Attic	12/94	14.50	14.50
94-01-071	Merry Santa 4171	Sarah's Attic	12/94	14.50	14.50
94-01-072	Angelle 4172	Sarah's Attic	12/94	14.50	14.50
94-01-073	School Days 4173	Sarah's Attic	12/94	14.50	14.50
94-01-074	Willie 4174	Sarah's Attic	12/94	14.50	14.50
94-01-075	Kiah 4175	Sarah's Attic	12/94	14.50	14.50
94-01-076	Chilly 4176	Sarah's Attic	12/94	14.50	14.50
94-01-077	Kiah (Gold) 4182	Sarah's Attic	12/94	14.50	14.50
94-01-078	Angelle (Gold) 4183	Sarah's Attic	12/94	14.50	14.50
Sarah's Attic, Inc.		**Santas Of The Month Ornaments**			
88-02-001	Jan. Mini Santa 2200	Sarah's Attic	Closed	16.00	21.00
88-02-002	Feb. Mini Santa 2201	Sarah's Attic	Closed	16.00	21.00
88-02-003	March Mini Santa 2202	Sarah's Attic	Closed	16.00	21.00
88-02-004	April Mini Santa 2203	Sarah's Attic	Closed	16.00	21.00
88-02-005	May Mini Santa 2204	Sarah's Attic	Closed	16.00	21.00
88-02-006	June Mini Santa 2205	Sarah's Attic	Closed	16.00	21.00
88-02-007	July Mini Santa 2206	Sarah's Attic	Closed	16.00	21.00
88-02-008	Aug. Mini Santa 2207	Sarah's Attic	Closed	16.00	21.00
88-02-009	Sept. Mini Santa 2208	Sarah's Attic	Closed	16.00	21.00
88-02-010	Oct. Mini Santa 2209	Sarah's Attic	Closed	16.00	21.00
88-02-011	Nov. Mini Santa 2210	Sarah's Attic	Closed	16.00	21.00
88-02-012	Dec.Mini Santa 2211	Sarah's Attic	Closed	16.00	21.00
Schmid		**Lowell Davis Country Christmas**			
83-01-001	Mailbox	L. Davis	Yr.Iss.	17.50	45-75.00
84-01-002	Cat in Boot	L. Davis	Yr.Iss.	17.50	60-65.00
85-01-003	Pig in Trough	L. Davis	Yr.Iss.	17.50	50-75.00
86-01-004	Church	L. Davis	Yr.Iss.	17.50	35-55.00
87-01-005	Blossom	L. Davis	Yr.Iss.	19.50	25-60.00
88-01-006	Wisteria	L. Davis	Yr.Iss.	19.50	25-50.00
89-01-007	Wren	L. Davis	Yr.Iss.	19.50	30-47.50
90-01-008	Wintering Deer	L. Davis	Yr.Iss.	19.50	30.00
91-01-009	Church at Red Oak II	L. Davis	Yr.Iss.	25.00	25.00
92-01-010	Born On A Starry Night	L. Davis	Yr.Iss.	25.00	25.00
93-01-011	Waiting for Mr. Lowell	L. Davis	Yr.Iss.	20.00	20.00
Schmid		**Lowell Davis Glass Ornaments**			
86-02-001	Christmas at Red Oak	L. Davis	Yr.Iss.	5.00	7-10.00
87-02-002	Blossom's Gift	L. Davis	Yr.Iss.	5.50	12.00
88-02-003	Hope Mom Likes It	L. Davis	Yr.Iss.	5.00	10.00
89-02-004	Peter and the Wren	L. Davis	Yr.Iss.	6.50	8.00
90-02-005	Wintering Deer	L. Davis	Yr.Iss.	6.50	6.50
91-02-006	Christmas at Red Oak II	L. Davis	Yr.Iss.	7.50	7.50
92-02-007	Born On A Starry Night Ball	L. Davis	Yr.Iss.	7.50	7.50
93-02-008	Waiting for Mr. Lowell	L. Davis	Yr.Iss.	7.50	7.50
Schmid		**Kitty Cucumber Annual**			
89-03-001	Ring Around the Rosie	M. Lillemoe	Yr.Iss.	25.00	25.00
90-03-002	Swan Lake	M. Lillemoe	Yr.Iss.	12.00	12.00
91-03-003	Tea Party	M. Lillemoe	Yr.Iss.	12.00	24.00
92-03-004	Dance 'Round the Maypole	M. Lillemoe	Yr.Iss.	10.00	10.00
Schmid		**Disney Annual**			
85-04-001	Snow Biz	Disney Studios	Yr.Iss.	8.50	20.00
86-04-002	Tree for Two	Disney Studios	Yr.Iss.	8.50	15.00
87-04-003	Merry Mouse Medley	Disney Studios	Yr.Iss.	8.50	10.00
88-04-004	Warm Winter Ride	Disney Studios	Yr.Iss.	11.00	45.00
89-04-005	Merry Mickey Claus	Disney Studios	Yr.Iss.	11.00	11.00
90-04-006	Holly Jolly Christmas	Disney Studios	Yr.Iss.	13.50	30.00
91-04-007	Mickey & Minnie's Rockin' Christmas	Disney Studios	Yr.Iss.	13.50	13.50
Sculpture Workshop Designs		**Annual**			
85-01-001	The Return of the Christmas Comet	F. Kreitchet	7,500	39.00	100.00
86-01-002	Liberty/Peace	F. Kreitchet	7,500	49.00	150.00
87-01-003	Christmas at Home	F. Kreitchet	2,500	57.00	90.00
88-01-004	Christmas Doves	F. Kreitchet	2,500	57.00	80.00
89-01-005	Santa's Reindeer	F. Kreitchet	2,500	60.00	75.00
90-01-006	Joyful Angels	F. Kreitchet	2,500	75.00	75.00
91-01-007	Angel & Shepherds	F. Krietchet	2,500	75.00	75.00

CHRISTMAS ORNAMENTS

Company		Series			
Number	**Name**	**Artist**	**Edition Limit**	**Issue Price**	**Quote**
Sculpture Workshop Designs		**Annual-Special Commemorative**			
87-02-001	The Bicentennial of the U.S. Constitution	F. Kreitchet	200	95.00	250.00
89-02-002	The Presidential Signatures	F. Kreitchet	200	95.00	125.00
91-02-003	The U.S. Bill of Rights	F. Kreitchet	200	150.00	150.00
Sculpture Workshop Designs		**Santa Series**			
92-03-001	Forever Santa	F. Kreitchet	2,500	68.00	68.00
93-03-002	Mrs. Claus	F. Kreitchet	2,500	68.00	68.00
Swarovski America Ltd.		**Holiday Ornaments**			
86-01-001	Small Angel/Noel	Unknown	Yr.Iss.	18.00	18.00
86-01-002	Small Bell/Merry Christmas	Unknown	Yr.Iss.	18.00	18.00
86-01-003	Small Dove/Peace	Unknown	Yr.Iss.	18.00	18.00
86-01-004	Small Holly/Merry Christmas	Unknown	Yr.Iss.	18.00	18.00
86-01-005	Small Snowflake	Unknown	Yr.Iss.	18.00	18.00
86-01-006	Medium Snowflake	Unknown	Yr.Iss.	22.50	22.50
86-01-007	Medium Bell/Merry Christmas	Unknown	Yr.Iss.	22.50	22.50
86-01-008	Medium Angel/Joyeux Noel	Unknown	Yr.Iss.	22.50	22.50
86-01-009	Large Angel/Noel	Unknown	Yr.Iss.	35.00	35.00
86-01-010	Large Partridge/Merry Christmas	Unknown	Yr.Iss.	35.00	35.00
87-01-011	1987 Holiday Etching-Candle	Unknown	Yr.Iss.	20.00	75-115.00
88-01-012	1988 Holiday Etching-Wreath	Unknown	Yr.Iss.	25.00	50-85.00
89-01-013	1989 Holiday Etching-Dove	Unknown	Yr.Iss.	35.00	65-100.00
90-01-014	1990 Holiday Etching	Unknown	Yr.Iss.	25.00	100.00
91-01-015	1991 Holiday Ornament	Unknown	Yr.Iss.	35.00	40-60.00
92-01-016	1992 Holiday Ornament	Unknown	Yr.Iss.	37.50	150-250.
93-01-017	1993 Holiday Ornament	Unknown	Yr.Iss.	37.50	37.50
Towle Silversmiths		**Sterling Twelve Days of Christmas Medallions**			
71-01-001	Partridge in Pear Tree	Towle	15,000	20.00	240.00
72-01-002	Two Turtle Doves	Towle	45,000	20.00	75.00
73-01-003	Three French Hens	Towle	75,000	20.00	30-100.00
74-01-004	Four Mockingbirds	Towle	60,000	30.00	30-100.00
75-01-005	Five Golden Rings	Towle	60,000	30.00	35-65.00
76-01-006	Six Geese-a-Laying	Towle	60,000	30.00	45-90.00
77-01-007	Seven Swans-a-Swimming	Towle	60,000	35.00	30-50.00
78-01-008	Eight Maids-a-Milking	Towle	60,000	37.00	45-75.00
79-01-009	Nine Ladies Dancing	Towle	40,000	Unkn.	40-60.00
80-01-010	Ten Lords-a-Leaping	Towle	25,000	76.00	40-50.00
81-01-011	Eleven Pipers Piping	Towle	25,000	50.00	40-50.00
82-01-012	Twelve Drummers Drumming	Towle	20,000	35.00	35-50.00
Towle Silversmiths		**Songs of Christmas Medallions**			
78-02-001	Silent Night Medallion	Towle	25,000	35.00	60.00
79-02-002	Deck The Halls	Towle	5,000	Unkn.	50.00
80-02-003	Jingle Bells	Towle	5,000	52.50	60.00
81-02-004	Hark the Hearld Angels Sing	Towle	5,000	52.50	60.00
82-02-005	O Christmas Tree	Towle	2,000	35.00	50.00
83-02-006	Silver Bells	Towle	2,500	40.00	60.00
84-02-007	Let It Snow	Towle	6,500	30.00	50.00
85-02-008	Chestnuts Roasting on Open Fire	Towle	3,000	35.00	50.00
86-02-009	It Came Upon a Midnight Clear	Towle	3,500	35.00	45.00
87-02-010	White Christmas	Towle	3,500	35.00	45.00
Towle Silversmiths		**Sterling Nativity Medallion**			
88-03-001	Angel Gabriel	Towle	7,500	40.00	50-60.00
89-03-002	The Journey	Towle	7,500	40.00	55.00
90-03-003	No Room at the Inn	Towle	7,500	40.00	45.00
91-03-004	Tidings of Joy	Towle	N/A	40.00	45.00
92-03-005	Star of Bethlehem	Towle	N/A	40.00	40.00
93-03-006	Mother and Child	Towle	N/A	40.00	40.00
94-03-007	Three Wisemen	Towle	N/A	40.00	40.00
Towle Silversmiths		**Remembrance Collection**			
90-04-001	Old Master Snowflake -1990	Towle	N/A	40.00	50-60.00
91-04-002	Old Master Snowflake-1991	Towle	N/A	40.00	55.00
92-04-003	Old Master Snowflake-1992	Towle	N/A	40.00	45.00
93-04-004	Old Master Snowflake-1993	Towle	N/A	40.00	45.00
94-04-005	Old Master Snowflake-1994	Towle	N/A	40.00	40.00
Towle Silversmiths		**Christmas Angel**			
91-05-001	1991 Angel	Towle	N/A	45.00	45.00
92-05-002	1992 Angel	Towle	N/A	45.00	45.00
93-05-003	1993 Angel	Towle	N/A	45.00	45.00
94-05-004	1994 Angel	Towle	N/A	45.00	45.00
United Design Corporation		**Angels Collection-Tree Ornaments™**			
90-01-001	Crystal Angel IBO-401	P.J. Jonas	Retrd.	20.00	20.00
90-01-002	Rose of Sharon IBO-402	P.J. Jonas	Retrd.	20.00	20.00
90-01-003	Star Glory IBO-403	P.J. Jonas	Retrd.	15.00	15.00
90-01-004	Victorian Angel IBO-404	P.J. Jonas	Retrd.	15.00	15.00
90-01-005	Crystal Angel, ivory IBO-405	P.J. Jonas	Open	20.00	20.00
90-01-006	Rose of Sharon, ivory IBO-406	P.J. Jonas	Open	20.00	20.00
90-01-007	Star Glory, ivory IBO-407	P.J. Jonas	Open	15.00	20.00
90-01-008	Victorian Angel, ivory IBO-408	P.J. Jonas	Open	15.00	20.00
91-01-009	Victorian Cupid, ivory IBO-409	P.J. Jonas	Open	15.00	20.00
91-01-010	Rosetti Angel, ivory IBO-410	P.J. Jonas	Open	20.00	24.00
91-01-011	Angel Waif, ivory IBO-411	P.J. Jonas	Open	15.00	20.00
91-01-012	Peace Descending, ivory IBO-412	P.J. Jonas	Open	20.00	20.00
91-01-013	Girl Cupid w/Rose, ivory IBO-413	S. Bradford	Open	15.00	20.00
91-01-014	Fra Angelico Drummer, blue IBO-414	S. Bradford	Open	20.00	20.00
91-01-015	Fra Angelico Drummer, ivory IBO-420	S. Bradford	Open	20.00	20.00
92-01-016	Angel and Tambourine IBO-422	S. Bradford	Open	20.00	20.00
92-01-017	St. Francis and Critters IBO-423	S. Bradford	Open	20.00	20.00
92-01-018	Mary and Dove IBO-424	S. Bradford	Open	20.00	20.00
92-01-019	Angel and Tambourine, ivory IBO-425	S. Bradford	Open	20.00	20.00
93-01-020	Angel Baby w/ Bunny IBO-426	D. Newburn	Open	22.50	24.00
93-01-021	Stars & Lace IBO-427	P.J. Jonas	Open	18.00	20.00
93-01-022	Heavenly Harmony IBO-428	P.J. Jonas	Open	25.00	30.00
93-01-023	Renaissance Angel IBO-429	P.J. Jonas	Open	24.00	24.00
93-01-024	Little Angel IBO-430	D. Newburn	Open	18.00	20.00
93-01-025	Renaissance Angel, crimson IBO-431	P.J. Jonas	Open	24.00	24.00
93-01-026	Stars & Lace, Emerald IBO-432	P.J. Jonas	Open	18.00	20.00
93-01-027	Heavenly Harmony, crimson IBO-433	P.J. Jonas	Open	22.00	30.00
93-01-028	Rosetti Angel, crimson IBO-434	P.J. Jonas	Open	20.00	24.00
93-01-029	Victorian Angel, plum IBO-435	P.J. Jonas	Open	18.00	20.00
93-01-030	Peace Descending, crimson IBO-436	P.J. Jonas	Open	20.00	20.00
93-01-031	Angle Waif, plum IBO-437	P.J. Jonas	Open	20.00	20.00
93-01-032	Star Glory, crimson IBO-438	P.J. Jonas	Open	20.00	20.00
93-01-033	Rose of Sharon, crimson IBO-439	P.J. Jonas	Open	20.00	20.00
93-01-034	Victorian Cupid, crimson IBO-440	P.J. Jonas	Open	15.00	20.00
93-01-035	Little Angel, crimson IBO-445	D. Newburn	Open	18.00	20.00
93-01-036	Crystal Angel, emerald IBO-446	P.J. Jonas	Open	20.00	20.00
94-01-037	Star Flight IBO-447	P.J. Jonas	Open	10.00	10.00
94-01-038	Music and Grace IBO-448	P.J. Jonas	Open	12.00	12.00
94-01-039	Music and Grace, crimson IBO-449	P.J. Jonas	Open	12.00	12.00
94-01-040	Musical Flight IBO-450	P.J. Jonas	Open	13.50	13.50
94-01-041	Musical Flight, crimson IBO-451	P.J. Jonas	Open	13.50	13.50
VickiLane		**Sweet Thumpkins**			
94-01-001	Secrets Out	V. Anderson	Yr.Iss.	14.50	14.50
Wallace Silversmiths		**Annual Silverplated Bells**			
71-01-001	1st Edition Sleigh Bell	Wallace	Closed	12.95	150.00
72-01-002	2nd Edition Sleigh Bell	Wallace	Closed	12.95	140-500.
73-01-003	3rd Edition Sleigh Bell	Wallace	Closed	12.95	140.00
74-01-004	4th Edition Sleigh Bell	Wallace	Closed	13.95	100-300.
75-01-005	5th Edition Sleigh Bell	Wallace	Closed	13.95	250.00
76-01-006	6th Edition Sleigh Bell	Wallace	Closed	13.95	300.00
77-01-007	7th Edition Sleigh Bell	Wallace	Closed	14.95	150.00
78-01-008	8th Edition Sleigh Bell	Wallace	Closed	14.95	85.00
79-01-009	9th Edition Sleigh Bell	Wallace	Closed	15.95	110.00
80-01-010	10th Edition Sleigh Bell	Wallace	Closed	18.95	50.00
81-01-011	11th Edition Sleigh Bell	Wallace	Closed	18.95	60.00
82-01-012	12th Edition Sleigh Bell	Wallace	Closed	19.95	80.00
83-01-013	13th Edition Sleigh Bell	Wallace	Closed	19.95	80.00
84-01-014	14th Edition Sleigh Bell	Wallace	Closed	21.95	75.00
85-01-015	15th Edition Sleigh Bell	Wallace	Closed	21.95	45-75.00
86-01-016	16th Edition Sleigh Bell	Wallace	Closed	21.95	35.00
87-01-017	17th Edition Sleigh Bell	Wallace	Closed	21.99	30.00
88-01-018	18th Edition Sleigh Bell	Wallace	Closed	21.99	30.00
89-01-019	19th Edition Sleigh Bell	Wallace	Closed	24.99	25.00
90-01-020	20th Edition Sleigh Bell	Wallace	Closed	25.00	25.00
90-01-021	Special Edition Sleigh Bell, gold	Wallace	Closed	35.00	35-50.00
92-01-022	22th Edition Sleigh Bell	Wallace	Closed	25.00	25.00
93-01-023	23rd Edition Sleigh Bell	Wallace	Closed	25.00	25.00
94-01-024	24th Edition Sleigh Bell	Wallace	Open	25.00	25.00
94-01-025	Sleigh Bell, gold	Wallace	Open	35.00	35.00
93-01-026	Santa Bel	Wallace	Open	25.00	25.00
94-01-027	Santa Bell (Holding Toy Sack)	Wallace	Open	25.00	25.00
Wallace Silversmiths		**Candy Canes**			
81-02-001	Peppermint	Wallace	Closed	8.95	225.00
82-02-002	Wintergreen	Wallace	Closed	9.95	60.00
83-02-003	Cinnamon	Wallace	Closed	10.95	50.00
84-02-004	Clove	Wallace	Closed	10.95	50.00
85-02-005	Dove Motif	Wallace	Closed	11.95	50.00
86-02-006	Bell Motif	Wallace	Closed	11.95	80.00
87-02-007	Teddy Bear Motif	Wallace	Closed	12.95	50.00
88-02-008	Christmas Rose	Wallace	Closed	13.99	25-45.00
89-02-009	Christmas Candle	Wallace	Closed	14.99	35.00
90-02-010	Reindeer	Wallace	Closed	16.00	20.00
91-02-011	Christmas Goose	Wallace	Closed	16.00	20.00
92-02-012	Angel	Wallace	Closed	16.00	16.00
93-02-013	Snowmen	Wallace	Closed	16.00	16.00
94-02-014	Canes	Wallace	Open	16.00	16.00
Wallace Silversmiths		**Grande Baroque 12 Day Series**			
88-03-001	Partridge	Wallace	Closed	39.99	55.00
89-03-002	Two Turtle Doves	Wallace	Closed	39.99	50.00
90-03-003	Three French Hens	Wallace	Closed	40.00	40.00
91-03-004	Four Colly Birds	Wallace	Closed	40.00	40.00
92-03-005	Five Golden Rings	Wallace	Closed	40.00	40.00
93-03-006	Six Geese-A-Laying	Wallace	Closed	40.00	40.00
94-03-007	Seven Swans A Swimming	Wallace	Open	40.00	40.00
Wallace Silversmiths		**Cathedral Ornaments**			
88-04-001	1988-1st Edition	Wallace	Closed	24.99	60.00
89-04-002	1989-2nd Edition	Wallace	Closed	24.99	55.00
90-04-003	1990-3rd Edition	Wallace	Closed	25.00	50.00
Wallace Silversmiths		**24K Goldplate Sculptures**			
88-05-001	Dove	Wallace	Closed	15.99	15.99
88-05-002	Candy Cane	Wallace	Closed	15.99	15.99
88-05-003	Christmas Tree	Wallace	Closed	15.99	15.99
88-05-004	Angel	Wallace	Closed	15.99	15.99
88-05-005	Nativity Scene	Wallace	Closed	15.99	15.99
88-05-006	Snowflake	Wallace	Closed	15.99	15.99
93-05-007	Ringing Bells	Wallace	Closed	10.00	10.00
93-05-008	Carousel	Wallace	Closed	10.00	10.00
93-05-009	Stocking	Wallace	Closed	10.00	10.00
93-05-010	Wreath	Wallace	Closed	10.00	10.00
93-05-011	Tree	Wallace	Closed	10.00	10.00
93-05-012	Dove	Wallace	Closed	10.00	10.00
94-05-013	Mother & Child	Wallace	Open	16.00	16.00
94-05-014	Peace Dove	Wallace	Open	16.00	16.00
Wallace Silversmiths		**Annual Pewter Bells**			
92-06-001	Angel	Wallace	Closed	25.00	25.00
93-06-002	Santa Holding List	Wallace	Yr.Iss.	25.00	25.00
Wallace Silversmiths		**Pewter Ornaments**			
XX-07-001	Toy Soldier	Wallace	Closed	9.99	9.99
XX-07-002	Gingerbread House	Wallace	Closed	9.99	9.99
XX-07-003	Teddy Bear	Wallace	Closed	9.99	9.99
XX-07-004	Rocking Horse	Wallace	Closed	9.99	9.99
XX-07-005	Dove	Wallace	Closed	9.99	9.99
XX-07-006	Candy Cane	Wallace	Closed	9.99	9.99
89-07-007	Wreath	Wallace	Closed	9.99	9.99
89-07-008	Angel with Candles	Wallace	Closed	9.99	9.99
89-07-009	Teddy Bear	Wallace	Closed	9.99	9.99
89-07-010	Cherub with Horn	Wallace	Closed	9.99	9.99
89-07-011	Santa	Wallace	Closed	9.99	9.99
93-07-012	Stocking	Wallace	Open	10.00	10.00
93-07-013	Wreath	Wallace	Open	10.00	10.00
93-07-014	Christmas Tree	Wallace	Open	10.00	10.00
94-07-015	Santa	Wallace	Open	10.00	10.00
94-07-016	Teddy Bear	Wallace	Open	10.00	10.00
94-07-017	Train	Wallace	Open	10.00	10.00
94-07-018	Toy Soldier	Wallace	Open	10.00	10.00
94-07-019	Snowman	Wallace	Open	10.00	10.00
Waterford Wedgwood U.S.A.		**Waterford Crystal Christmas Ornaments**			
78-01-001	1978 Ornament	Waterford	Annual	25.00	105.00
79-01-002	1979 Ornament	Waterford	Annual	28.00	80.00
80-01-003	1980 Ornament	Waterford	Annual	28.00	60.00
81-01-004	1981 Ornament	Waterford	Annual	28.00	44.50
82-01-005	1982 Ornament	Waterford	Annual	28.00	50.00

Company Number	Name	Series Artist	Edition Limit	Issue Price	Quote
83-01-006	1983 Ornament	Waterford	Annual	28.00	50.00
84-01-007	1984 Ornament	Waterford	Annual	28.00	50.00
85-01-008	1985 Ornament	Waterford	Annual	28.00	80.00
86-01-009	1986 Ornament	Waterford	Annual	28.00	50.00
87-01-010	1987 Ornament	Waterford	Annual	29.00	40.00
88-01-011	1988 Ornament	Waterford	Annual	30.00	40.00
89-01-012	1989 Ornament	Waterford	Annual	32.00	40.00
Waterford Wedgwood U.S.A.		**Wedgwood Christmas Ornaments**			
88-02-001	Jasper Christmas Tree Ornament	Wedgwood	Open	20.00	28.00
89-02-002	Jasper Angel Ornament	Wedgwood	Open	25.00	28.00
90-02-003	Jasper Santa Claus Ornament	Wedgwood	Open	28.00	28.00
91-02-004	Jasper Wreath Ornament	Wedgwood	Open	28.00	28.00
92-02-005	Jasper Stocking Ornament	Wedgwood	Open	25.00	25.00
93-02-006	Jasper Santa's Sleigh	Wedgwood	Open	25.00	25.00

DOLLS

Company Number	Name	Series Artist	Edition Limit	Issue Price	Quote
Kurt S. Adler Inc.		**Royal Heritage Collection**			
93-01-001	Anastasia J5746	J. Mostrom	3,000	125.00	125.00
93-01-002	Medieval King of Christmas W2981	J. Mostrom	2,000	390.00	390.00
93-01-003	Good King Wenceslas W2928	J. Mostrom	2,000	130.00	130.00
94-01-004	Sasha on Skates J5749	J. Mostrom	3,000	130.00	130.00
94-01-005	Nicholas on Skates J5750	J. Mostrom	3,000	120.00	120.00
Annalee Mobilitee Dolls		**Assorted Dolls**			
50-01-001	10" Boy Building Boat	A. Thorndike	N/A	9.95	1200.00
50-01-002	Cellist	A. Thorndike	N/A	N/A	5250.00
50-01-003	10" Christmas Girl	A. Thorndike	N/A	N/A	2350.00
50-01-004	10" Elf	A. Thorndike	N/A	N/A	900.00
50-01-005	12" Santa on Water Skis	A. Thorndike	1	N/A	3050.00
50-01-006	10" Square Dancers (Boy and Girl)	A. Thorndike	N/A	9.95	2100.00
54-01-007	26" Elf	A. Thorndike	N/A	9.95	550.00
54-01-008	10" Spring Girl	A. Thorndike	N/A	N/A	2350.00
55-01-009	14" Fireman	A. Thorndike	N/A	N/A	4750.00
56-01-010	10" Boy Building Boat	A. Thorndike	N/A	N/A	1550.00
57-01-011	10" Baby Angel	A. Thorndike	N/A	8.95	525.00
59-01-012	10" Girl and Boy on Tandem Bike	A. Thorndike	N/A	20.95	2200.00
59-01-013	10" Wood Sprite	A. Thorndike	N/A	N/A	750.00
60-01-014	7" Angel w/ Paper Wings	A. Thorndike	N/A	N/A	400.00
60-01-015	Boy Head	A. Thorndike	1	N/A	650-800.
60-01-016	10" Elf	A. Thorndike	N/A	N/A	400.00
60-01-017	29" Fur Trim Santa	A. Thorndike	N/A	N/A	1000.00
60-01-018	Girl Head	A. Thorndike	1	N/A	700-2400.
60-01-019	Head Pin	A. Thorndike	N/A	N/A	200.00
60-01-020	10" Impski	A. Thorndike	N/A	3.95	500.00
60-01-021	Man Head Pin-on	A. Thorndike	N/A	N/A	800.00
60-01-022	Mouse Head Pin-On	A. Thorndike	N/A	1.00	250.00
62-01-023	7" Baby Angel on Cloud	A. Thorndike	N/A	2.45	400-675.
63-01-024	Baby Angel Head w/ Santa Hat	A. Thorndike	N/A	1.00	350.00
63-01-025	10" Ballerina	A. Thorndike	N/A	5.95	1350.00
63-01-026	Bath Puff (yellow)	A. Thorndike	N/A	1.95	325.00
63-01-027	10" Elf	A. Thorndike	N/A	N/A	350.00
63-01-028	10" Friar	A. Thorndike	N/A	2.95	500.00
63-01-029	26" Friar	A. Thorndike	N/A	14.95	2500.00
63-01-031	7" Santa w/ Fur Trimmed Suit	A. Thorndike	N/A	2.95	400.00
63-01-032	5" Wee Skis	A. Thorndike	N/A	3.95	450.00
64-01-033	7" Boudoir Puff Baby Angel	A. Thorndike	N/A	3.95	400.00
64-01-034	18" Santa Kid	A. Thorndike	N/A	6.95	450.00
65-01-035	7" Christmas Dumb Bunny	A. Thorndike	N/A	3.95	775.00
65-01-036	7" Gnome w/ Vest	A. Thorndike	N/A	2.45	675.00
65-01-037	10" Golfer Boy Doll	A. Thorndike	N/A	9.95	700.00
65-01-038	7" Hangover Mouse	A. Thorndike	N/A	3.95	375.00
65-01-039	7" M/M Indoor Santa	A. Thorndike	N/A	5.95	500.00
65-01-040	10" Monk w/ Christmas Tree Planting	A. Thorndike	N/A	2.95	450.00
65-01-041	10" Reindeer	A. Thorndike	N/A	4.95	425.00
65-01-042	7" Singing Mouse	A. Thorndike	N/A	3.95	450.00
66-01-043	10" Go-Go Boy	A. Thorndike	N/A	3.95	350.00
66-01-044	10" Workshop Elf	A. Thorndike	N/A	N/A	425.00
67-01-045	7" Ballerina Mouse	A. Thorndike	N/A	3.95	450.00
67-01-046	10" Carnaby Street Boy	A. Thorndike	N/A	3.95	400.00
67-01-047	10" Elf w/ Skis and Poles	A. Thorndike	48	2.95	425-900.
67-01-048	7" Mrs. Holly Mouse	A. Thorndike	N/A	3.95	350.00
67-01-049	10" Surfer Girl	A. Thorndike	N/A	5.95	625.00
68-01-050	7" Baby in Christmas Bag	A. Thorndike	N/A	2.95	350.00
68-01-051	12" Gnome w/ Gay Apron	A. Thorndike	N/A	5.95	900.00
68-01-052	29" Mrs. Indoor Santa	A. Thorndike	N/A	16.95	475.00
68-01-053	7" Patches Pam Baby	A. Thorndike	N/A	2.95	600.00
69-01-054	12" Nightshirt Boy Mouse	A. Thorndike	N/A	9.95	550.00
69-01-055	7" Santa w/ Oversized Bag	A. Thorndike	N/A	3.95	350.00
70-01-056	7" Artist Mouse	A. Thorndike	298	3.95	400.00
70-01-057	7" Bartender Mouse	A. Thorndike	289	3.95	400.00
70-01-058	18" Bride and Groom Frogs	A. Thorndike	1	23.95	1400.00
70-01-059	7" Bunny (yellow)	A. Thorndike	3,215	3.95	375.00
70-01-060	10" Casualty Ski Elf w/ Crutch & Leg in Cast	A. Thorndike	2,.818	4.50	600.00
70-01-061	7" Christmas Baby on Hat Box	A. Thorndike	1,894	2.95	350.00
70-01-062	16" Christmas Wreath w/ Santa Head	A. Thorndike	1,662	9.95	375.00
70-01-063	10" Monk w/ Skis and Poles	A. Thorndike	1,386	3.95	350.00
70-01-064	22" Monkey (chartreuse)	A. Thorndike	70	10.95	725.00
70-01-065	7" Sherriff Mouse	A. Thorndike	11	3.95	650.00
71-01-066	10" Frog	A. Thorndike	427	2.95	400.00
71-01-067	3" Reindeer Head	A. Thorndike	N/A	1.00	200.00
71-01-068	7" Santa w/ Skis and Poles	A. Thorndike	N/A	5.45	300.00
71-01-069	10" Ski Elf	A. Thorndike	1,262	3.95	275.00
71-01-070	7" Santa Mailman	A. Thorndike	8,296	5.50	375.00
71-01-071	Snowman Head Pin-on	A. Thorndike	4,040	1.00	200.00
71-01-072	Snowman Kid	A. Thorndike	1,374	3.95	450.00
71-01-073	7" Swimmer Mouse w/ Inner Tube	A. Thorndike	267	3.95	325.00
72-01-074	16" Democratic Donkey	A. Thorndike	219	12.95	1600.00
72-01-075	10" Democratic Donkey	A. Thorndike	861	3.95	450.00
72-01-076	16" Elephant (Republican)	A. Thorndike	230	12.95	800.00
72-01-077	29" Mrs. Snow Woman w/ Cardholder Skirt	A. Thorndike	331	19.95	700.00
72-01-078	7" Santa on Ski-Bob w/ Oversized Bag	A. Thorndike	7,590	7.95	400.00
72-01-079	7" Secretary Mouse	A. Thorndike	727	3.95	500.00
73-01-080	18" Christmas Panda	A. Thorndike	437	10.50	600.00
74-01-081	7" Camper in Tent Mouse	A. Thorndike	468	5.45	325.00
74-01-082	7" Carpenter Mouse	A. Thorndike	2,687	5.45	275.00
74-01-083	7" Gardener Mouse	A. Thorndike	485	5.45	400.00
74-01-084	7" Hunter Mouse w/ Bird	A. Thorndike	690	5.45	325.00
74-01-085	Leprechaun Place Card Holder	A. Thorndike	240	1.20	225.00
74-01-086	10" Leprechaun w/ Sack	A. Thorndike	8,834	5.45	350.00
74-01-087	29" Motorized See-Saw Bunny Set	A. Thorndike	43	250.00	1600.00

Company Number	Name	Series Artist	Edition Limit	Issue Price	Quote
74-01-088	7" Sloppy Painter Mouse	A. Thorndike	349	5.45	550.00
75-01-089	10" Colonial Drummer Boy	A. Thorndike	1,846	5.95	375.00
75-01-090	8" Lamb	A. Thorndike	234	8.95	450.00
75-01-091	18" Yankee Doodle Dandy w/ 18" Horse	A. Thorndike	437	28.95	900.00
76-01-092	7" Needlework Mouse	A. Thorndike	3,566	6.95	400.00
76-01-093	7" Ski Mouse	A. Thorndike	10,375	6.95	225.00
76-01-094	18" Uncle Sam	A. Thorndike	345	16.95	500.00
77-01-095	7" Christmas Mouse in Santa's Mitten	A. Thorndike	15,916	7.95	175.00
77-01-096	7" Hobo Mouse	A. Thorndike	1,004	5.95	275.00
77-01-097	29" Mr. Santa Mouse w/ Sack	A. Thorndike	704	49.95	800.00
77-01-098	29" Mrs. Santa Mouse w/ Muff	A. Thorndike	571	49.95	800.00
77-01-099	8" Rooster	A. Thorndike	1,642	5.95	350.00
77-01-100	42" Scarecrow	A. Thorndike	365	61.95	2050.00
78-01-101	7" Airplane Pilot Mouse	A. Thorndike	2,308	6.95	425.00
78-01-102	29" Caroller Mouse	A. Thorndike	658	49.95	775.00
78-01-103	7" Carpenter Mouse	A. Thorndike	1,494	6.95	350.00
78-01-104	10" Elf w/ Planter	A. Thorndike	1,978	6.95	275.00
78-01-105	18" Pilgrim Boy	A. Thorndike	1,213	14.95	275.00
78-01-106	7" Santa w/ 10" Reindeer Trimming Christmas Tree	A. Thorndike	1,621	18.45	425.00
79-01-107	7" Ballerina	A. Thorndike	4,700	7.45	275.00
79-01-108	7" Gardener Mouse	A. Thorndike	1,939	7.95	325.00
79-01-109	7" Quilting Mouse	A. Thorndike	213	N/A	375.00
79-01-110	7" Skateboard Mouse	A. Thorndike	1,821	7.95	275.00
80-01-111	18" Ballerina Bunny	A. Thorndike	7,069	27.95	425.00
80-01-112	10" Balloon w/ Two 10" Frogs	A. Thorndike	837	49.95	850.00
80-01-113	10" Boy on Raft	A. Thorndike	1,087	28.95	325.00
80-01-114	42" Clown	A. Thorndike	224	74.95	700.00
80-01-115	8" Girl BBQ Pig	A. Thorndike	3,854	9.95	175.00
80-01-116	7" Hockey Mouse	A. Thorndike	2,477	9.95	300.00
81-01-117	18" Butterfly w/ 10" Elf	A. Thorndike	2,507	27.95	275.00
81-01-118	22" Christmas Giraffe w/ 10" Elf	A. Thorndike	1,377	44.00	825.00
81-01-119	7" I'm Late Bunny	A. Thorndike	100	N/A	475.00
81-01-120	10" Jack Frost Elf w/ 5" Snowflake (artist proof)	A. Thorndike	5,950	31.95	325.00
81-01-121	22" Sun Mobile	A. Thorndike	3,003	36.95	475.00
82-01-122	7" Cowboy Mouse	A. Thorndike	3,776	12.95	300.00
82-01-123	7" Cowgirl Mouse	A. Thorndike	3,116	12.95	300.00
82-01-124	10" Cyrano de Bergerac	A. Thorndike	35	N/A	2300.00
82-01-125	7" Wood Chopper Mouse	A. Thorndike	1,910	11.95	375.00
83-01-126	7" Angel w/ Musical Instrument on Music Box	A. Thorndike	N/A	29.95	425.00
83-01-127	5" Easter Parade Girl Bunny w/ Music Box	A. Thorndike	1,167	29.95	400.00
84-01-128	7" Angel on Star	A. Thorndike	772	32.95	475.00
84-01-129	18" Aerobic Girl	A. Thorndike	622	35.95	375.00
84-01-130	7" Boy w/ Firecracker	A. Thorndike	1,893	19.95	400.00
84-01-131	5" E.P. Boy Bunny	A. Thorndike	2,583	11.95	200.00
84-01-132	5" E.P. Girl Bunny	A. Thorndike	2,790	11.95	200.00
84-01-133	18" E.P. Girl Bunny	A. Thorndike	2,952	35.95	350.00
84-01-134	18" Fawn w/ Wreath	A. Thorndike	2,080	32.95	375.00
85-01-135	18" Ballerina Bear	A. Thorndike	918	39.95	275.00
85-01-136	7" Cookie Boy Logo Doll	A. Thorndike	3,562	15.00	675.00
85-01-137	7" Dress-Up Boy	A. Thorndike	1,174	18.95	225.00
85-01-138	7" Dress-Up Girl	A. Thorndike	1,536	18.95	225.00
85-01-139	7" Hockey Player Kid	A. Thorndike	1,578	18.95	400.00
85-01-140	7" Kid w/ Kite	A. Thorndike	1,084	17.95	300.00
86-01-141	7" Witch Mouse w/ Pumpkin Balloon	A. Thorndike	868	59.95	300.00
87-01-142	3" Baby Witch	A. Thorndike	3,645	13.95	275.00
87-01-143	7" BBQ Mouse	A. Thorndike	1,798	17.95	300.00
87-01-144	3" Bride and Groom	A. Thorndike	1,053	38.95	375.00
87-01-145	7" Bunny in 10" Carrot Balloon	A. Thorndike	624	49.95	375.00
87-01-146	7" Hangover Mouse	A. Thorndike	1,548	13.95	175.00
87-01-147	18" Special Mrs. Santa (special order)	A. Thorndike	341	N/A	400.00
87-01-148	10" State Trooper (#642)	A. Thorndike	511	134.00	500.00
87-01-149	18" Workshop Santa (special order)	A. Thorndike	1,001	N/A	450.00
89-01-150	10" Abraham Lincoln (artist proof)	A. Thorndike	1	N/A	1200.00
89-01-151	7" Polar Bear Cub (artist proof)	A. Thorndike	1	N/A	350.00
89-01-152	7" Polar Bear Cub	A. Thorndike	3,000	37.50	300.00
89-01-153	7" Robin Hood Mouse (artist proof)	A. Thorndike	1	N/A	350.00
89-01-154	10" Three Bunnies w/ Maypole	A. Thorndike	647	189.95	600.00
90-01-155	15" Christmas Dragon	A. Thorndike	448	49.95	400.00
90-01-156	7" Friar Tuck Mouse (artist proof)	A. Thorndike	1	N/A	350.00
90-01-157	7" Maid Marion Mouse (artist proof)	A. Thorndike	1	N/A	350.00
90-01-158	10" Nativity Set (artist proof)	A. Thorndike	1	N/A	700.00
90-01-159	10" Wise Men w/ Camel (artist proof)	A. Thorndike	1	N/A	600.00
91-01-160	10" Aviator Frog WW II (artist proof)	A. Thorndike	1	N/A	350.00
91-01-161	7" Fun in the Sun Kid	A. Thorndike	300	80.00	300.00
91-01-162	7" Santa in Tub w/ Rubber Duckie	A. Thorndike	5,373	33.95	200.00
91-01-163	7" Sheriff Mouse (artist proof)	A. Thorndike	1	N/A	650.00
91-01-164	10" Victory Ski Doll	A. Thorndike	1,192	49.50	350.00
91-01-165	3" Water Baby in Pond Lily	A. Thorndike	3,720	14.95	175.00
91-01-166	10" Wise Men (artist proof)	A. Thorndike	1	N/A	550.00
92-01-167	10" Baseball Player (artist proof)	A. Thorndike	1	N/A	425.00
92-01-168	10" Baseball Pitcher (artist proof)	A. Thorndike	1	N/A	425.00
92-01-169	7" Disney Kid	A. Thorndike	300	59.95	400.00
92-01-170	7" Hot Shot Businessman Kid (artist proof)	A. Thorndike	1	N/A	800.00
93-01-171	7"Airplane Boy (one of a kind)	A. Thorndike	1	N/A	900.00
93-01-172	7" Baby Bunny w/ Baby Bottle (artist proof)	A. Thorndike	1	N/A	450.00
93-01-173	10" Baseball Catcher (artist proof)	A. Thorndike	1	N/A	425.00
93-01-174	7" Boy Cutting His Hair (one of a kind)	A. Thorndike	1	N/A	1000.00
93-01-175	7" Bride Mouse (artist proof)	A. Thorndike	1	N/A	400.00
93-01-176	10" Christa McAuliffe Skier (artist proof)	A. Thorndike	1	N/A	625.00
93-01-177	30" Country Girl Bunny w/ Basket (artist proof)	A. Thorndike	1	N/A	700.00
93-01-178	10" E.P. Shopping Ostrich (artist proof)	A. Thorndike	1	N/A	450.00
93-01-179	10" Farmer w/ Rooster (artist proof)	A. Thorndike	1	N/A	1000.00
93-01-180	7" Flying Angel (artist proof)	A. Thorndike	1	N/A	400.00
93-01-181	7" Girl Building Snowman (artist proof)	A. Thorndike	1	N/A	500.00
93-01-182	12" Girl Scarecrow (artist proof)	A. Thorndike	1	N/A	650.00
93-01-183	7" Groom Mouse (artist proof)	A. Thorndike	1	N/A	400.00
93-01-184	7" Habitat Mouse (artist proof)	A. Thorndike	1	N/A	500.00
93-01-185	7" Hershey Kid (artist proof)	A. Thorndike	1	N/A	1000.00
93-01-186	10" Hobo Clown (artist proof)	A. Thorndike	1	N/A	550.00
93-01-187	7" Hot Shot Business Girl (artist proof)	A. Thorndike	1	N/A	450.00
93-01-188	7" Ice Cream Logo Kid (white, artist proof)	A. Thorndike	1	N/A	650.00
93-01-189	7" Ice Cream Logo Kid (yellow, artist proof)	A. Thorndike	1	N/A	750.00
93-01-190	7" Mississippi Levee Mouse (artist proof)	A. Thorndike	341	N/A	400.00
93-01-191	7" Mr. Old World Santa (artist proof)	A. Thorndike	1	N/A	425.00

Company / Number	Name	Series / Artist	Edition Limit	Issue Price	Quote
93-01-192	7" Mrs. Old World Santa (artist proof)	A. Thorndike	1	N/A	425.00
93-01-193	7" Naughty Angel w/ Black Eye (artist proof)	A. Thorndike	1	N/A	500.00
93-01-194	10" Nun (one of a kind)	A. Thorndike	1	N/A	900.00
93-01-195	5" Old World Caroler Boy (artist proof)	A. Thorndike	1	N/A	350-400.
93-01-196	5" Old World Caroler Girl (artist proof)	A. Thorndike	1	N/A	350-400.
93-01-197	18" Old World Reindeer w/ Bells (artist proof)	A. Thorndike	1	N/A	450.00
93-01-198	10" Pony Express (artist proof)	A. Thorndike	1	N/A	1800.00
93-01-199	7" Scuba Diving Mouse (one of a kind)	A. Thorndike	1	N/A	1000.00
93-01-200	7" Thanksgiving Boy (artist proof)	A. Thorndike	1	N/A	650.00
93-01-201	10" Window Shopper Ostrich (artist proof)	A. Thorndike	1	N/A	500.00
93-01-202	12" Witch Kid (one of a kind)	A. Thorndike	1	N/A	900.00
94-01-203	7" Auction Mouse (artist proof)	A. Thorndike	1	N/A	750.00
94-01-204	10" Ballerina Bear (one of a kind)	A. Thorndike	1	N/A	1100.00
94-01-205	10" Basket ball Player (black, artist proof)	A. Thorndike	1	N/A	550.00
94-01-206	10" Basketball Player (white, artist proof)	A. Thorndike	1	N/A	550.00
94-01-207	7" Candy Kiss Kid (one of a kind)	A. Thorndike	1	N/A	2250.00
94-01-208	7" Cheerleader Girl (artist proof)	A. Thorndike	1	N/A	650.00
94-01-209	7" Clown Mouse (one of a kind)	A. Thorndike	1	N/A	1050.00
94-01-210	7" Cocktail Mouse (one of a kind)	A. Thorndike	1	N/A	1100.00
94-01-211	10" Country Girl Bear (one of a kind)	A. Thorndike	1	N/A	925.00
94-01-212	7" Football Mouse (artist proof)	A. Thorndike	1	N/A	750.00
94-01-213	7" Girl w/ Teddy Bear (artist proof)	A. Thorndike	1	N/A	650.00
94-01-214	7" Hot Shot Business Girl (artist proof)	A. Thorndike	1	N/A	700.00
94-01-215	7" Jail House Mouse (artist proof)	A. Thorndike	1	N/A	650.00
94-01-216	10" M/M Santa Skating Music Box (artist proof)	A. Thorndike	1	N/A	900.00
94-01-217	10" Mrs. Santa "Last Minute Mending" (artist proof)	A. Thorndike	1	N/A	650.00
94-01-218	10" Old World Santa w/ Skis (artist proof)	A. Thorndike	1	N/A	800.00
94-01-219	7" Policeman Mouse (artist proof)	A. Thorndike	1	N/A	750.00
94-01-220	7" Santa w/ Dove (one of a kind)	A. Thorndike	1	N/A	1250.00
94-01-221	7" Scottish Lad (artist proof)	A. Thorndike	1	N/A	675.00
94-01-222	7" Valentine Girl w/ Card (artist proof)	A. Thorndike	1	N/A	750.00
94-01-223	10" White St. Nicholas (artist proof)	A. Thorndike	1	N/A	650.00
ANRI		**Disney Dolls**			
89-01-001	Mickey Mouse, 14"	Disney Studios	Closed	850.00	895.00
89-01-002	Minnie Mouse, 14"	Disney Studios	Closed	850.00	895.00
89-01-003	Pinocchio, 14"	Disney Studios	Closed	850.00	895.00
90-01-004	Donald Duck, 14"	Disney Studios	Closed	895.00	895.00
90-01-005	Daisy Duck, 14"	Disney Studios	Closed	895.00	895.00
ANRI		**Sarah Kay Dolls**			
88-02-001	Jennifer, 14"	S. Kay	Closed	500.00	500.00
88-02-002	Rebecca, 14"	S. Kay	Closed	500.00	500.00
88-02-003	Sarah, 14"	S. Kay	Closed	500.00	500.00
88-02-004	Katherine, 14"	S. Kay	Closed	500.00	500.00
88-02-005	Martha, 14"	S. Kay	Closed	500.00	500.00
88-02-006	Emily, 14"	S. Kay	Closed	500.00	500.00
88-02-007	Rachael, 14"	S. Kay	Closed	500.00	500.00
88-02-008	Victoria, 14"	S. Kay	Closed	500.00	500.00
89-02-009	Bride to Love And To Cherish	S. Kay	Closed	750.00	790.00
89-02-010	Groom With This Ring Doll	S. Kay	Closed	550.00	730.00
89-02-011	Charlotte (Blue)	S. Kay	Closed	550.00	575.00
89-02-012	Henry	S. Kay	Closed	550.00	575.00
89-02-013	Elizabeth (Patchwork)	S. Kay	Closed	550.00	575.00
89-02-014	Helen (Brown)	S. Kay	Closed	550.00	575.00
89-02-015	Eleanor (Floral)	S. Kay	Closed	550.00	575.00
89-02-016	Mary (Red)	S. Kay	Closed	550.00	575.00
90-02-017	Polly, 14"	S. Kay	Closed	575.00	680.00
90-02-018	Christina, 14"	S. Kay	Closed	575.00	730.00
90-02-019	Faith, 14"	S. Kay	Closed	575.00	685.00
90-02-020	Sophie, 14"	S. Kay	Closed	575.00	660.00
91-02-021	Jessica, 7"	S. Kay	Closed	300.00	300.00
91-02-022	Michelle, 7"	S. Kay	Closed	300.00	300.00
91-02-023	Peggy, 7"	S. Kay	Closed	300.00	300.00
91-02-024	Annie, 7"	S. Kay	Closed	300.00	300.00
91-02-025	Susan, 7"	S. Kay	Closed	300.00	300.00
91-02-026	Julie, 7"	S. Kay	Closed	300.00	300.00
91-02-027	Janine, 14"	S. Kay	Closed	750.00	750.00
91-02-028	Patricia, 14"	S. Kay	Closed	730.00	730.00
ANRI		**Ferrandiz Dolls**			
89-03-001	Gabriel, 14"	J. Ferrandiz	Closed	550.00	575.00
89-03-002	Maria, 14"	J. Ferrandiz	Closed	550.00	575.00
90-03-003	Margarite, 14"	J. Ferrandiz	Closed	575.00	730.00
90-03-004	Philipe, 14"	J. Ferrandiz	Closed	575.00	680.00
91-03-005	Carmen, 14"	J. Ferrandiz	Closed	730.00	730.00
91-03-006	Fernando, 14"	J. Ferrandiz	Closed	730.00	730.00
91-03-007	Miguel, 7"	J. Ferrandiz	Closed	300.00	300.00
91-03-008	Juanita, 7"	J. Ferrandiz	Closed	300.00	300.00
Artaffects		**Perillo Doll Collection**			
86-01-001	Morning Star (17-1/2")	G. Perillo	1,000	250.00	250.00
88-01-002	Sunflower (12")	G. Perillo	2,500	175.00	175.00
Artaffects		**Art Doll Collection**			
90-02-001	Little Dove (12")	G. Perillo	5,000	175.00	175.00
90-02-002	Straight Arrow (12")	G. Perillo	5,000	175.00	175.00
Artaffects		**Children of the Plains**			
92-03-001	Brave and Free (10" seated)	G. Perillo	Open	111.00	111.00
93-03-002	Song of Sioux (10" seated)	G. Perillo	Open	111.00	111.00
93-03-003	Gentle Shepherd (13" standing)	G. Perillo	Open	111.00	111.00
93-03-004	Bird Song (13" standing)	G. Perillo	Open	111.00	111.00
94-03-005	Cactus Flower	G. Perillo	Open	111.00	111.00
94-03-006	Pathfinder	G. Perillo	Open	111.00	111.00
94-03-007	Princess of the Sun	G. Perillo	Open	111.00	111.00
94-03-008	Little Friend	G. Perillo	Open	111.00	111.00
Artaffects		**Ruffles and Rhymes Doll Collection**			
93-04-001	Little Bo Peep (15" High)	Artaffects Studio	Open	89.00	89.00
94-04-002	Little Bo Peep	Artaffects Studio	Open	106.80	106.80
Artaffects		**Country Musicians Collection**			
94-05-001	Danny	Artaffects Studio	Open	118.00	118.00

Company / Number	Name	Series / Artist	Edition Limit	Issue Price	Quote
Ashton-Drake Galleries		**Yolanda's Picture - Perfect Babies**			
85-01-001	Jason	Y. Bello	Closed	48.00	500-1400.
86-01-002	Heather	Y. Bello	Closed	48.00	145-475.
87-01-003	Jennifer	Y. Bello	Closed	58.00	296-550.
87-01-004	Matthew	Y. Bello	Closed	58.00	95-325.
87-01-005	Sarah	Y. Bello	Closed	58.00	58-325.
88-01-006	Amanda	Y. Bello	Closed	63.00	125-275.
89-01-007	Jessica	Y. Bello	Closed	63.00	63-195.
90-01-008	Michael	Y. Bello	Closed	63.00	119-275.
90-01-009	Lisa	Y. Bello	Closed	63.00	77-175.
91-01-010	Emily	Y. Bello	Closed	63.00	63-110.
91-01-011	Danielle	Y. Bello	Closed	69.00	80-150.00
Ashton-Drake Galleries		**Children of Mother Goose**			
87-02-001	Little Bo Peep	Y. Bello	Closed	58.00	200-450.
87-02-002	Mary Had a Little Lamb	Y. Bello	Closed	58.00	145-325.
88-02-003	Little Jack Horner	Y. Bello	Closed	63.00	145.00
89-02-004	Miss Muffet	Y. Bello	Closed	63.00	63-275.00
Ashton-Drake Galleries		**Yolanda's Lullaby Babies**			
91-03-001	Christy (Rock-a-Bye)	Y. Bello	Closed	69.00	69-90.00
92-03-002	Joey (Twinkle, Twinkle)	Y. Bello	Closed	69.00	69.00
93-03-003	Amy (Brahms Lullaby)	Y. Bello	Closed	75.00	75.00
93-03-004	Eddie (Teddy Bear Lullaby)	Y. Bello	Closed	75.00	75.00
93-03-005	Jacob (Silent Night)	Y. Bello	Closed	75.00	75.00
94-03-006	Bonnie (You Are My Sunshine)	Y. Bello	12/94	80.00	80.00
Ashton-Drake Galleries		**Moments To Remember**			
91-04-001	Justin	Y. Bello	Closed	75.00	75-150.00
92-04-002	Jill	Y. Bello	Closed	75.00	75-95.00
93-04-003	Brandon (Ring Bearer)	Y. Bello	Closed	79.95	79.95
93-04-004	Suzanne (Flower Girl)	Y. Bello	Closed	79.95	79.95
Ashton-Drake Galleries		**Yolanda's Precious Playmates**			
92-05-001	David	Y. Bello	Closed	69.95	69.95
93-05-002	Paul	Y. Bello	Closed	69.95	69.95-125.00
94-05-003	Johnny	Y. Bello	12/94	69.95	69.95
Ashton-Drake Galleries		**Parade of American Fashion**			
87-06-001	The Glamour of the Gibson Girl	Stevens/Siegel	Closed	77.00	195-200.
88-06-002	The Southern Belle	Stevens/Siegel	Closed	77.00	125-225.
90-06-003	Victorian Lady	Stevens/Siegel	Closed	82.00	82-125.00
91-06-004	Romantic Lady	Stevens/Siegel	Closed	85.00	85-90.00
Ashton-Drake Galleries		**Heroines from the Fairy Tale Forests**			
88-07-001	Little Red Riding Hood	D. Effner	Closed	68.00	150-325.
89-07-002	Goldilocks	D. Effner	Closed	68.00	68-225.00
90-07-003	Snow White	D. Effner	Closed	73.00	95-195.00
91-07-004	Rapunzel	D. Effner	Closed	79.00	90-125.00
92-07-005	Cinderella	D. Effner	Closed	79.00	80-225.00
93-07-006	Cinderella (Ballgown)	D. Effner	Closed	79.95	80.00
Ashton-Drake Galleries		**International Festival of Toys and Tots**			
89-08-001	Chen, a Little Boy of China	K. Hippensteel	Closed	78.00	125-325.
89-08-002	Natasha	K. Hippensteel	Closed	78.00	78-200.00
90-08-003	Molly	K. Hippensteel	Closed	83.00	83.00
91-08-004	Hans	K. Hippensteel	Closed	88.00	88-100.00
92-08-005	Miki, Eskimo	K. Hippensteel	Closed	88.00	88-145.00
Ashton-Drake Galleries		**Born To Be Famous**			
89-09-001	Little Sherlock	K. Hippensteel	Closed	87.00	95-350.00
90-09-002	Little Florence Nightingale	K. Hippensteel	Closed	87.00	87-100.00
91-09-003	Little Davey Crockett	K. Hippensteel	Closed	92.00	92.00
92-09-004	Little Christopher Columbus	K. Hippensteel	Closed	95.00	95-150.00
Ashton-Drake Galleries		**Baby Book Treasures**			
90-10-001	Elizabeth's Homecoming	K. Hippensteel	Closed	58.00	80.00
91-10-002	Catherine's Christening	K. Hippensteel	Closed	58.00	58.00
91-10-003	Christopher's First Smile	K. Hippensteel	Closed	63.00	63-110.00
Ashton-Drake Galleries		**Growing Young Minds**			
91-11-001	Alex	K. Hippensteel	Closed	79.00	79.00
Ashton-Drake Galleries		**Happiness Is...**			
91-12-001	Patricia (My First Tooth)	K. Hippensteel	Closed	69.00	85-125.00
92-12-002	Crystal (Feeding Myself)	K. Hippensteel	Closed	69.95	69.95-95.00
93-12-003	Brittany (Blowing Kisses)	K. Hippensteel	Closed	69.95	69.95-95.00
93-12-004	Joy (My First Christmas)	K. Hippensteel	Closed	69.95	69.95
94-12-005	Candy Cane (Holly)	K. Hippensteel	12/95	69.95	69.95
94-12-006	Patrick (My First Playmate)	K. Hippensteel	12/95	69.95	69.95
Ashton-Drake Galleries		**Cindy's Playhouse Pals**			
89-13-001	Meagan	C. McClure	Closed	87.00	125-200.
89-13-002	Shelly	C. McClure	Closed	87.00	87-150.00
90-13-003	Ryan	C. McClure	Closed	89.00	89-125.00
91-13-004	Samantha	C. McClure	Closed	89.00	89-100.00
Ashton-Drake Galleries		**A Children's Circus**			
90-14-001	Tommy The Clown	J. McClelland	Closed	78.00	78-100.00
91-14-002	Katie The Tightrope Walker	J. McClelland	Closed	78.00	78.00
91-14-003	Johnnie The Strongman	J. McClelland	Closed	83.00	83.00
92-14-004	Maggie The Animal Trainer	J. McClelland	Closed	83.00	83.00
Ashton-Drake Galleries		**Maude Fangel's Cover Babies**			
91-15-001	Peek-A-Boo Peter	Fangel-Inspired	Closed	73.00	73-150.00
91-15-002	Benjamin's Ball	Fangel-Inspired	Closed	73.00	73.00
Ashton-Drake Galleries		**Amish Blessings**			
90-16-001	Rebeccah	J. Good-Kruger	Closed	68.00	75-149.00
91-16-002	Rachel	J. Good-Kruger	Closed	69.00	75-225.00
91-16-003	Adam	J. Good-Kruger	Closed	75.00	75-195.00
92-16-004	Ruth	J. Good-Kruger	Closed	75.00	75-145.00
92-16-005	Eli	J. Good-Kruger	Closed	79.95	100-195.
93-16-006	Sarah	J. Good-Kruger	12/94	79.95	79.95
Ashton-Drake Galleries		**Polly's Tea Party**			
90-17-001	Polly	S. Krey	Closed	78.00	100-160.
91-17-002	Lizzie	S. Krey	Closed	79.00	79.00
92-17-003	Annie	S. Krey	Closed	83.00	83.00
Ashton-Drake Galleries		**Yesterday's Dreams**			
90-18-001	Andy	M. Oldenburg	Closed	68.00	68-85.00
91-18-002	Janey	M. Oldenburg	Closed	69.00	69.00

Company / Number	Name	Series / Artist	Edition Limit	Issue Price	Quote
Ashton-Drake Galleries		**My Closest Friend**			
91-19-001	Boo Bear 'N Me	J. Goodyear	Closed	78.00	100-225.
91-19-002	Me and My Blankie	J. Goodyear	Closed	79.00	95-165.00
92-19-003	My Secret Pal (Robbie)	J. Goodyear	Closed	85.00	85.00
92-19-004	My Beary Best Friend	J. Goodyear	Closed	79.95	79.95
Ashton-Drake Galleries		**The Littlest Clowns**			
91-20-001	Sparkles	M. Tretter	Closed	63.00	80-100.00
91-20-002	Bubbles	M. Tretter	Closed	65.00	65-125.00
91-20-003	Smooch	M. Tretter	Closed	69.00	69-125.00
92-20-004	Daisy	M. Tretter	Closed	69.95	69.95
Ashton Drake Galleries		**Romantic Flower Maidens**			
88-21-001	Rose, Who is Love	M. Roderick	Closed	87.00	125-175.
89-21-002	Daisy	M. Roderick	Closed	87.00	125-150.
90-21-003	Violet	M. Roderick	Closed	92.00	125-150.
90-21-004	Lily	M. Roderick	Closed	92.00	104-175.
Ashton-Drake Galleries		**Precious Memories of Motherhood**			
89-22-001	Loving Steps	S. Kuck	Closed	125.00	125-146.
90-22-002	Lullaby	S. Kuck	Closed	125.00	125-195.
91-22-003	Expectant Moments	S. Kuck	Closed	149.00	125-295.
92-22-004	Bedtime	S. Kuck	Closed	149.95	149.95-186.
Ashton-Drake Galleries		**Classic Brides of The Century**			
90-23-001	Flora, The 1900s Bride	E. Williams	Closed	145.00	145.00
91-23-002	Jennifer, The 1980s Bride	E. Williams	Closed	149.00	149.00
93-23-003	Kathleen, The 1930s Bride	E. Williams	Closed	149.95	149.95
Ashton-Drake Galleries		**My Fair Lady**			
91-24-001	Eliza at Ascot	P. Ryan Brooks	Closed	125.00	225-345.
Ashton-Drake Galleries		**The King & I**			
91-25-001	Shall We Dance?	P. Ryan Brooks	Closed	175.00	295.00
Ashton-Drake Galleries		**Stepping Out**			
91-26-001	Millie	Akers/Girardi	Closed	99.00	200-225.
Ashton-Drake Galleries		**Year Book Memories**			
91-27-001	Peggy Sue	Akers/Girardi	Closed	87.00	87.00
93-27-002	Going Steady (Patty Jo)	Akers/Girardi	12/94	89.95	89.95
93-27-003	Prom Queen (Betty Jean)	Akers/Girardi	12/94	92.00	92.00
Ashton-Drake Galleries		**Winterfest**			
91-28-001	Brian	S. Sherwood	Closed	89.00	140-145.
92-28-002	Michelle	S. Sherwood	Closed	89.95	195.00
93-28-003	Bradley	S. Sherwood	Closed	89.95	89.95
Ashton-Drake Galleries		**Dianna Effner's Mother Goose**			
90-29-001	Mary, Mary, Quite Contrary	D. Effner	Closed	78.00	125-250.
91-29-002	The Little Girl With The Curl (Horrid)	D. Effner	Closed	79.00	100-275.
91-29-003	The Little Girl With The Curl (Good)	D. Effner	Closed	79.00	80-151.00
92-29-004	Little Boy Blue	D. Effner	Closed	85.00	85.00
93-29-005	Snips & Snails	D. Effner	12/94	85.00	85.00
93-29-006	Sugar & Spice	D. Effner	12/94	89.95	89.95
93-29-007	Curly Locks	D. Effner	12/95	89.95	89.95
Ashton-Drake Galleries		**A Child's Garden of Verses**			
91-30-001	Nathan (The Land of Nod)	J. Singer	Closed	79.00	79.00
93-30-002	My Toy Soldiers	J. Singer	Closed	79.95	79.95
93-30-003	Picture Books in Winter	J. Singer	Closed	85.00	85.00
93-30-004	My Ship & I	J. Singer	Closed	85.00	85.00
Ashton-Drake Galleries		**Down The Garden Path**			
91-31-001	Rosemary	P. Coffer	Closed	79.00	79.00
91-31-002	Angelica	P. Coffer	Closed	85.00	85.00
93-31-003	Amanda by the Shore	P. Coffer	Closed	89.95	89.95
Ashton-Drake Galleries		**Beautiful Dreamers**			
92-32-001	Katrina	G. Rademann	Closed	89.00	95.00
92-32-002	Nicolette	G. Rademann	Closed	89.95	89.95
93-32-003	Brigitte	G. Rademann	Closed	94.00	94.00
93-32-004	Isabella	G. Rademann	Closed	94.00	94.00
93-32-005	Gabrielle	G. Rademann	12/94	94.00	94.00
Ashton-Drake Galleries		**Great Moments From Hollywood**			
91-33-001	Shall We Dance?	P. Brooks	Closed	175.00	275-325.
Ashton-Drake Galleries		**International Spirit Of Christmas**			
89-34-001	American Santa	F. Wick	Closed	125.00	125.00
Ashton-Drake Galleries		**From The Heart**			
92-35-001	Carolin	T. Menzenbach	Closed	79.95	97-125.00
92-35-002	Erik	T. Menzenbach	Closed	79.95	125.00
Ashton-Drake Galleries		**Little House On The Prairie**			
92-36-001	Laura	J. Ibarolle	Closed	79.95	79.95
93-36-002	Mary Ingalls	J. Ibarolle	Closed	79.95	79.95
93-36-003	Nellie Olson	J. Ibarolle	Closed	85.00	85.00
93-36-004	Almanzo	J. Ibarolle	Closed	85.00	85.00
94-36-005	Carrie	J. Ibarolle	12/94	85.00	85.00
94-36-006	Ma Ingalls	J. Ibarolle	12/95	90.00	90.00
94-36-007	Pa Ingalls	J. Ibarolle	12/95	90.00	90.00
Ashton-Drake Galleries		**Rockwell Christmas**			
90-37-001	Scotty Plays Santa	Rockwell-Inspired	Closed	48.00	48.00
91-37-002	Scotty Gets His Tree	Rockwell-Inspired	Closed	59.00	59.00
93-37-003	Merry Christmas Grandma	Rockwell-Inspired	Closed	59.95	59.95
Ashton-Drake Galleries		**Holy Hunt's Bonnet Babies**			
91-38-001	Missy (Grandma's Little Girl)	H. Hunt	Closed	69.00	69.00
92-38-002	Susie (Somebody Loves Me)	H. Hunt	Closed	69.00	95.00
Ashton-Drake Galleries		**Heavenly Inspirations**			
92-39-001	Every Cloud Has a Silver Lining	C. McClure	Closed	59.95	59.95
93-39-002	Wish Upon A Star	C. McClure	Closed	59.95	59.95
94-39-003	Sweet Dreams	C. McClure	12/94	65.00	65.00
94-39-004	Luck at the End of Rainbow	C. McClure	12/94	65.00	65.00
94-39-005	Sunshine	C. McClure	12/94	69.95	69.95
94-39-006	Pennies From Heaven	C. McClure	12/95	69.95	69.95
Ashton-Drake Galleries		**Elvis: Lifetime Of A Legend**			
92-40-001	'68 Comeback Special	L. Di Leo	Closed	99.95	99.95
94-40-002	King of Las Vegas	L. Di Leo	12/94	99.95	99.95
Ashton-Drake Galleries		**Caught In The Act**			
92-41-001	Stevie, Catch Me If You Can	M. Tretter	Closed	49.95	49.95
93-41-002	Kelly, Don't I Look Pretty?	M. Tretter	Closed	49.95	49.95
94-41-003	Mikey (Look It Floats)	M. Tretter	12/94	55.00	55.00
94-41-004	Nickie (Cookie Jar)	M. Tretter	12/95	59.95	59.95
94-41-005	Becky (Kleenex Box)	M. Tretter	12/95	59.95	59.95
Ashton-Drake Galleries		**Your Heart's Desire**			
91-42-001	Julia	M. Stauber	Closed	99.00	99-295.00
Ashton-Drake Galleries		**My Heart Belongs To Daddy**			
92-43-001	Peanut	J. Singer	Closed	49.95	49.95
92-43-002	Pumpkin	J. Singer	Closed	49.95	49.95
94-43-003	Princess	J. Singer	12/94	59.95	59.95
Ashton-Drake Galleries		**Yolanda's Playtime Babies**			
93-44-001	Todd	Y. Bello	Closed	59.95	59.95
93-44-002	Lindsey	Y. Bello	12/94	59.95	59.95
93-44-003	Shawna	Y. Bello	12/94	59.95	59.95
Ashton-Drake Galleries		**Little Bits**			
93-45-001	Lil Bit of Sunshine	G. Rademann	12/94	39.95	39.95
93-45-002	Lil Bit of Love	G. Rademann	12/94	39.95	39.95
94-45-003	Lil Bit of Tenderness	G. Rademann	12/94	39.95	39.95
94-45-004	Lil Bit of Innocence	G. Rademann	12/94	39.95	39.95
Ashton-Drake Galleries		**Victorian Lace**			
93-46-001	Alicia	C. Layton	12/94	79.95	79.95
94-46-002	Colleen	C. Layton	12/95	79.95	79.95
94-46-003	Olivia	C. Layton	12/95	79.95	79.95
Ashton-Drake Galleries		**Father's Touch**			
93-47-001	2 A.M. Feeding	L. Di Leo	12/94	99.95	99.95
94-47-002	Come To Daddy	W. Hanson	12/95	99.95	99.95
Ashton-Drake Galleries		**Boys Will Be Boys**			
93-48-001	Fire's Out	J. Singer	Closed	69.95	69.95
93-48-002	Say Ah!	J. Singer	12/94	69.95	69.95
Ashton-Drake Galleries		**Lasting Traditions**			
93-49-001	Something Old	W. Hanson	12/94	69.95	69.95
94-49-002	Finishing Touch	W. Hanson	12/94	69.95	69.95
94-49-003	Mother's Pearls	W. Hanson	12/95	79.95	79.95
Ashton-Drake Galleries		**Joys of Summer**			
93-50-001	Tickles	K. Hippensteel	Closed	49.95	49.95
93-50-002	Little Squirt	K. Hippensteel	Closed	49.95	49.95
94-50-003	Yummy	K. Hippensteel	12/94	55.00	55.00
94-50-004	Havin' A Ball	K. Hippensteel	12/94	55.00	55.00
94-50-005	Lil' Scoop	K. Hippensteel	12/94	55.00	55.00
Ashton-Drake Galleries		**A Sense of Discovery**			
93-51-001	Sweetie (Sense of Discovery)	K. Hippensteel	Closed	59.95	59.95
Ashton-Drake Galleries		**I Want Mommy**			
93-52-001	Timmy (Mommy I'm Sleepy)	K. Hippensteel	Closed	59.95	59.95
93-52-002	Tommy (Mommy I'm Sorry)	K. Hippensteel	Closed	59.95	59.95
94-52-003	Up Mommy (Tammy)	K. Hippensteel	12/94	65.00	65.00
Ashton-Drake Galleries		**Lots Of Love**			
93-53-001	Hannah Needs A Hug	T. Menzenbach	Closed	49.95	49.95
93-53-002	Kaitlyn	T. Menzenbach	12/94	49.95	49.95
94-53-003	Nicole	T. Menzenbach	12/95	49.95	49.95
Ashton-Drake Galleries		**Peek A Boo**			
93-54-001	Where's Jamie?	J. Goodyear	Closed	69.95	69.95
Ashton-Drake Galleries		**Look At Me**			
93-55-001	Rose Marie	L. Di Leo	Closed	49.95	49.95
94-55-002	Ann Marie	L. Di Leo	12/94	49.95	49.95
94-55-003	Lisa Marie	L. Di Leo	12/95	55.00	55.00
Ashton-Drake Galleries		**Wishful Thinking**			
93-56-001	Danny (Pet Shop)	M. Tretter	12/94	79.95	79.95
Ashton-Drake Galleries		**Children Of The Sun**			
93-57-001	Little Flower	M. Severino	12/94	69.95	69.95
93-57-002	Desert Star	M. Severino	12/95	69.95	69.95
Ashton-Drake Galleries		**Sooo Big**			
93-58-001	Jimmy	M. Tretter	12/94	59.95	59.95
94-58-002	Kimmy	M. Tretter	12/95	59.95	59.95
Ashton-Drake Galleries		**Two Much To Handle**			
93-59-001	Julie (Flowers For Mommy)	K. Hippensteel	12/94	59.95	59.95
93-59-002	Kevin (Clean Hands)	K. Hippensteel	12/95	59.95	59.95
Ashton-Drake Galleries		**Little Handfuls**			
93-60-001	Ricky	M. Severino	12/94	39.95	39.95
93-60-002	Abby	M. Severino	12/95	39.95	39.95
Ashton-Drake Galleries		**Yolanda's Heaven Scent Babies**			
93-61-001	Meagan Rose	Y. Bello	12/94	49.95	49.95
93-61-002	Daisy Anne	Y. Bello	12/94	49.95	49.95
93-61-003	Morning Glory	Y. Bello	12/95	49.95	49.95
Ashton-Drake Galleries		**As Cute As Can Be**			
93-62-001	Sugar Plum	D. Effner	12/94	49.95	49.95
94-62-002	Puppy Love	D. Effner	12/95	49.95	49.95
Ashton-Drake Galleries		**1993 Special Edition Tour**			
93-63-001	Miguel	Y. Bello	Closed	69.95	69.95
93-63-002	Rosa	Y. Bello	Closed	69.95	69.95
Ashton-Drake Galleries		**Tumbling Tots**			
93-64-001	Roly Poly Polly	K. Hippensteel	12/94	69.95	69.95
94-64-002	Handstand Harry	K. Hippensteel	12/95	69.95	69.95
Ashton-Drake Galleries		**Young Love**			
93-65-001	First Kiss	J.W. Smith	12/94	118.00	118.00
93-65-002	Buttercups	J.W. Smith	12/94	Set	Set
Ashton-Drake Galleries		**Gustafson's Fairy Tales**			
93-66-001	Goldilocks and Three Bears	S. Gustafson	12/94	129.95	129.95

Company Number	Name	Series Artist	Edition Limit	Issue Price	Quote
Ashton-Drake Galleries		**Barely Yours**			
94-67-001	Cute as a Button	T. Tomescu	12/95	79.95	79.95
Ashton-Drake Galleries		**Baby Talk**			
94-68-001	All Gone	Good-Krueger	12/95	49.95	49.95
94-68-002	Bye-Bye	Good-Krueger	12/95	49.95	49.95
Ashton-Drake Galleries		**Lawton's Nursery Rhymes**			
94-69-001	Little Bo Peep	W. Lawton	12/95	79.95	79.95
Ashton-Drake Galleries		**Rockwell Friend For Life**			
94-70-001	Wrapped Up in Xmas	N. Rockwell	12/95	69.95	69.95
Ashton-Drake Galleries		**In the Good 'Ol Summertime**			
94-71-001	Along the Boardwalk (Ella)	W. Lawton	12/95	69.95	69.95
94-71-002	Meet Me at the Fair	W. Lawton	12/95	69.95	69.95
Ashton-Drake Galleries		**The American Dream**			
94-72-001	Patience	J. Kovacik	12/95	79.95	79.95
94-72-002	Hope	J. Kovacik	12/95	79.95	79.95
Ashton-Drake Galleries		**Season of Dreams**			
94-73-001	Autumn Breeze	G. Rademann	12/95	79.95	79.95
Ashton-Drake Galleries		**Oh Holy Night**			
94-74-001	The Holy Family (Jesus, Mary, Joseph)	Good-Krueger	12/95	129.95	129.95
Ashton-Drake Galleries		**Nursery Newborns**			
94-75-001	It's A Boy	J. Wolf	12/95	79.95	79.95
94-75-002	It's A Girl	J. Wolf	12/95	79.95	79.95
Ashton-Drake Galleries		**Let's Play Mother Goose**			
94-76-001	Cow Jumped Over the Moon	K. Hippensteel	12/95	69.95	69.95
94-76-002	Hickory, Dickory, Dock	K. Hippensteel	12/95	69.95	69.95
Ashton-Drake Galleries		**Happy Thoughts**			
94-77-001	Laughter is the Best Medicine	K. Hippensteel	12/95	59.95	59.95
Ashton-Drake Galleries		**Memories of Yesterday**			
94-78-001	A Friend in Need	M. Attwell	12/95	59.95	59.95
Band Creations		**Pat Wilson's Original Santas**			
92-01-001	Victorian Father Christmas	P. Wilson	200	370.00	370.00
92-01-002	Victorian Long Beard	P. Wilson	200	370.00	370.00
92-01-003	Victorian, white	P. Wilson	200	370.00	370.00
92-01-004	Seaside Santa, large	P. Wilson	200	370.00	370.00
92-01-005	Long Beard, small	P. Wilson	200	170.00	170.00
92-01-006	Seaside Santa, small	P. Wilson	200	170.00	170.00
92-01-007	Victorian, small	P. Wilson	200	170.00	170.00
Band Creations		**Nature's Woods**			
94-02-001	18" Snow Queen	M. Attwell	6,500	195.00	195.00
The Collectables Inc.		**The Collectibles Inc. Dolls**			
86-01-001	Tatiana	P. Parkins	1,000	270.00	675.00
87-01-002	Tasha	P. Parkins	1,000	290.00	1400.00
87-01-003	Storytime By Sarah Jane	P. Parkins	1,000	330.00	475-525.
89-01-004	Michelle	P. Parkins	250	270.00	400-450.
89-01-005	Welcome Home	D. Effner	1,000	330.00	475-675.
90-01-006	Lizbeth Ann	D. Effner	1,000	420.00	420.00
90-01-007	Bassinet Baby	P. Parkins	2,000	130.00	375-425.
90-01-008	Danielle	P. Parkins	1,000	400.00	475.00
90-01-009	In Your Easter Bonnet	P. Parkins	1,000	350.00	350.00
91-01-010	Yvette	P. Parkins	300	580.00	580.00
91-01-011	Lauren	P. Parkins	S/O	490.00	490.00
91-01-012	Bethany	P. Parkins	Closed	450.00	450.00
91-01-013	Natasha	P. Parkins	Closed	510.00	510.00
91-01-014	Adrianna	P. Parkins	Closed	1350.00	1350.00
91-01-015	Kelsie	P. Parkins	500	320.00	320.00
92-01-016	Karlie	P. Parkins	500	380.00	380.00
92-01-017	Marissa	P. Parkins	300	350.00	350.00
92-01-018	Shelley	P. Parkins	300	450.00	450.00
92-01-019	Angel on My Shoulder (Lillianne w/CeCe)	P. Parkins	500	530.00	530.00
92-01-020	Molly	P. Parkins	450	350.00	350.00
92-01-021	Matia	P. Parkins	250	190.00	190.00
92-01-022	Marty	P. Parkins	250	190.00	190.00
92-01-023	Missy	P. Parkins	Open	59.00	59.00
93-01-024	Haley	P. Parkins	500	330.00	330.00
93-01-025	Maggie	P. Parkins	500	330.00	330.00
93-01-026	Amber	P. Parkins	500	330.00	330.00
93-01-027	Little Dumpling (Black)	P. Parkins	500	190.00	190.00
93-01-028	Little Dumpling (White)	P. Parkins	500	190.00	190.00
The Collectables Inc.		**Mother's Little Treasures**			
85-02-001	1st Edition	D. Effner	1,000	380.00	700.00
90-02-002	2nd Edition	D. Effner	1,000	440.00	475-595.
The Collectables Inc.		**Yesterday's Child**			
82-03-001	Jason And Jessica	D. Effner	1,000	150.00	300.00
82-03-002	Cleo	D. Effner	1,000	180.00	250.00
82-03-003	Columbine	D. Effner	1,000	180.00	250.00
83-03-004	Chad And Charity	D. Effner	1,000	190.00	190.00
83-03-005	Noel	D. Effner	1,000	190.00	240.00
84-03-006	Kevin And Karissa	D. Effner	1,000	190.00	250-300.
84-03-007	Rebecca	D. Effner	1,000	250.00	250-300.
86-03-008	Todd And Tiffany	D. Effner	1,000	220.00	250.00
86-03-009	Ashley	P. Parkins	1,000	220.00	275.00
The Collectables Inc.		**Cherished Memories**			
86-04-001	Amy and Andrew	P. Parkins	1,000	220.00	325.00
88-04-002	Jennifer	P. Parkins	1,000	380.00	500-600.
88-04-003	Brittany	P. Parkins	1,000	240.00	300.00
88-04-004	Heather	P. Parkins	1,000	280.00	300-350.
88-04-005	Leigh Ann And Leland	P. Parkins	1,000	250.00	250-300.
88-04-006	Tea Time	D. Effner	1,000	380.00	450.00
90-04-007	Cassandra	P. Parkins	Closed	500.00	550.00
89-04-008	Generations	P. Parkins	1,000	480.00	500.00
90-04-009	Twinkles	P. Parkins	Closed	170.00	275.00
The Collectables Inc.		**Fairy**			
88-05-001	Tabatha	P. Parkins	1,500	370.00	400-450.

Company Number	Name	Series Artist	Edition Limit	Issue Price	Quote
The Collectables Inc.		**Butterfly Babies**			
89-06-001	Belinda	P. Parkins	Closed	270.00	375.00
90-06-002	Willow	P. Parkins	Closed	240.00	375.00
92-06-003	Laticia	P. Parkins	500	320.00	320.00
The Collectables Inc.		**Enchanted Children**			
90-07-001	Kristin	P. Parkins	S/O	550.00	650.00
90-07-002	Tiffy	P. Parkins	S/O	370.00	500.00
90-07-003	Kara	P. Parkins	Closed	550.00	550.00
90-07-004	Katlin	P. Parkins	Closed	550.00	550.00
The Collectables Inc.		**Collector's Club Doll**			
91-08-001	Mandy	P. Parkins	Closed	360.00	360.00
92-08-002	Kallie	P. Parkins	Closed	410.00	410.00
93-08-003	Mommy and Me	P. Parkins	Closed	810.00	810.00
94-08-004	Krystal	P. Parkins	Yr.Iss.	380.00	380.00
The Collectables Inc.		**Angel Series**			
92-09-001	Angel on My Shoulder	P. Parkins	Closed	530.00	530.00
93-09-002	My Guardian Angel	P. Parkins	500	590.00	590.00
Department 56		**Heritage Village Doll Collection**			
87-01-001	Christmas Carol Dolls1000-6 4/set (Tiny Tim, Bob Crachet, Mrs. Crachet, Scrooge)	Department 56	250	1500.00	1500.00
87-01-002	Christmas Carol Dolls5907-2 4/set (Tiny Tim, Bob Crachet, Mrs. Crachet, Scrooge)	Department 56	Open	250.00	250.00
88-01-003	Christmas Carol Dolls1001-4 4/set (Tiny Tim, Bob Crachet, Mrs. Crachet, Scrooge)	Department 56	350	1600.00	1600.00
88-01-004	Mr. & Mrs. Fezziwig 5594-8-Set of 2	Department 56	Open	172.00	172.00
Department 56		**Snowbabies Dolls**			
88-02-001	Allison & Duncan- Set of 2, 7730-5	Department 56	Closed	200.00	660-695.
Dolls by Jerri		**Dolls by Jerri**			
84-01-001	Clara	J. McCloud	1,000	320.00	1200-1500.
84-01-002	Emily	J. McCloud	1,000	330.00	2400-3500.
85-01-003	Scotty	J. McCloud	1,000	340.00	1200-2000.
85-01-004	Uncle Joe	J. McCloud	1,000	160.00	250-300.
85-01-005	Miss Nanny	J. McCloud	1,000	160.00	250-300.
85-01-006	Bride	J. McCloud	1,000	350.00	350-400.
86-01-007	David-2 Years Old	J. McCloud	1,000	330.00	550.00
86-01-008	Princess and the Unicorn	J. McCloud	1,000	370.00	370.00
86-01-009	Charlotte	J. McCloud	1,000	330.00	450-500.
86-01-010	Cane	J. McCloud	1,000	350.00	1200.00
86-01-011	Clown-David 3 Yrs. Old	J. McCloud	1,000	340.00	450.00
86-01-012	Tammy	J. McCloud	1,000	350.00	900.00
86-01-013	Samantha	J. McCloud	1,000	350.00	500.00
86-01-014	Elizabeth	J. McCloud	1,000	340.00	340.00
86-01-015	Audrey	J. McCloud	300	550.00	550.00
86-01-016	Yvonne	J. McCloud	300	500.00	500.00
86-01-017	Annabelle	J. McCloud	300	600.00	600.00
86-01-018	Ashley	J. McCloud	1,000	350.00	450-500.
86-01-019	Allison	J. McCloud	1,000	350.00	450-500.
86-01-020	Nobody	J. McCloud	1,000	350.00	550.00
86-01-021	Somebody	J. McCloud	1,000	350.00	550.00
86-01-022	Danielle	J. McCloud	1,000	350.00	500.00
86-01-023	Helenjean	J. McCloud	1,000	350.00	500-550.
86-01-024	David-Magician	J. McCloud	1,000	350.00	350-500.
86-01-025	Amber	J. McCloud	1,000	350.00	875.00
86-01-026	Joy	J. McCloud	1,000	350.00	350.00
86-01-027	Mary Beth	J. McCloud	1,000	350.00	350.00
86-01-028	Jacqueline	J. McCloud	300	500.00	500.00
86-01-029	Lucianna	J. McCloud	300	500.00	500.00
86-01-030	Bridgette	J. McCloud	300	500.00	500.00
86-01-031	The Fool	J. McCloud	1,000	350.00	350.00
86-01-032	Alfalfa	J. McCloud	1,000	350.00	350.00
85-01-033	Candy	J. McCloud	1,000	340.00	1000-2000.
82-01-034	Baby David	J. McCloud	538	290.00	2000.00
88-01-035	Holly	J. McCloud	1,000	370.00	750-825.
89-01-036	Laura Lee	J. McCloud	1,000	370.00	575.00
XX-01-037	Boy	J. McCloud	1,000	350.00	425.00
XX-01-038	Uncle Remus	J. McCloud	500	290.00	400-450.
XX-01-039	Gina	J. McCloud	1,000	350.00	475.00
XX-01-040	Laura	J. McCloud	1,000	350.00	425-500.
89-01-041	Goose Girl, Guild	J. McCloud	Closed	300.00	700-875.
XX-01-042	Little Bo Peep	J. McCloud	1,000	340.00	395-450.
XX-01-043	Little Miss Muffet	J. McCloud	1,000	340.00	395-450.
XX-01-044	Megan	J. McCloud	750	420.00	550.00
XX-01-045	Denise	J. McCloud	1,000	380.00	550.00
XX-01-046	Meredith	J. McCloud	750	430.00	600.00
XX-01-047	Goldilocks	J. McCloud	1,000	370.00	450-600.
XX-01-048	Jamie	J. McCloud	800	380.00	450.00
Dynasty Doll		**Annual**			
89-01-001	Amber	Unknown	Retrd.	90.00	90.00
90-01-002	Marcella	Unknown	Retrd.	90.00	90.00
91-01-003	Butterfly Princess	Unknown	Retrd.	110.00	110.00
93-01-004	Annual Bride	H. Tertsakian	Retrd.	190.00	190.00
93-01-005	Ariel	Unknown	Retrd.	120.00	120.00
94-01-006	Annual Bride	H. Tertsakian	Yr. Iss.	200.00	200.00
Dynasty Doll		**Christmas**			
87-02-001	Merrie	Unknown	Retrd.	60.00	60.00
88-02-002	Noel	Unknown	Retrd.	80.00	80.00
90-02-003	Faith	Unknown	Retrd.	110.00	110.00
91-02-004	Joy	Unknown	Retrd.	125.00	125.00
93-02-005	Genevieve	Unknown	Retrd.	164.00	164.00
Dynasty Doll		**Ballerina Series**			
91-03-001	Masha-Nutcracker	Lee Po Nan	Retrd.	190.00	190.00
93-03-002	Tina Ballerina	K. Henderson	Open	175.00	175.00
Dynasty Doll		**Anna Collection**			
92-04-002	Communion Girl	G. Hoyt	Open	125.00	125.00
Dynasty Doll		**Dynasty Collection**			
91-05-001	Lana	Unknown	Open	85.00	85.00
93-05-002	Tami	M. Cohen	7,500	190.00	190.00
93-05-003	Tory	M. Cohen	7,500	190.00	190.00
93-05-004	Juliet	G. Tepper	2,500	160.00	160.00
93-05-005	Heather	G. Tepper	2,500	160.00	160.00
93-05-006	Antoinette	H. Tertsakian	5,000	190.00	190.00
93-05-007	Catherine	H. Tertsakian	5,000	190.00	190.00

Company / Number	Name	Series / Artist	Edition Limit	Issue Price	Quote
93-05-008	Katy	M. Cohen	Retrd.	135.00	135.00
93-05-009	Nicole	Unknown	3,500	135.00	135.00
93-05-010	Carley	G. Hoyt	Open	120.00	120.00
93-05-011	Megan	Unknown	3,500	150.00	150.00
93-05-012	Julie	K. Henderson	Retrd.	175.00	175.00
94-05-013	Christina	Unknown	3,500	200.00	200.00
94-05-014	Kelsey	S. Kelsey	1,500	225.00	225.00
94-05-015	Rebecca	Unknown	1,500	175.00	175.00
94-05-016	Amy	Unknown	1,500	175.00	175.00
94-05-017	Amelia	G. Hoyt	1,500	170.00	170.00
94-05-018	Laurelyn	Unknown	2,000	180.00	180.00
94-05-019	Gabrielle	S. Kelsey	1,500	180.00	180.00
Dynasty Doll		**Indian Collection**			
92-06-001	Pocahontas	Unknown	Retrd.	95.00	105.00
94-06-002	Chief Eagle's Wing	Unknown	3,500	165.00	165.00
94-06-003	Spring Winds and Little Wolf	Unknown	3,500	120.00	120.00
Dynasty Doll		**Uta Brauser's City Kids**			
93-07-001	Jamaal	U. Brauser	5,000	220.00	220.00
93-07-002	Kadeem	U. Brauser	3,500	195.00	195.00
93-07-003	Mirambi	U. Brauser	5,000	190.00	190.00
93-07-004	Rickia	U. Brauser	3,500	170.00	170.00
93-07-005	Tisha	U. Brauser	3,500	170.00	170.00
Dynasty Doll		**Victorians**			
94-08-001	Danielle	H. Tertsakian	2,500	195.00	195.00
94-08-002	Beverly	H. Tertsakian	1,500	195.00	195.00
94-08-003	Margaret	H. Tertsakian	1,500	195.00	195.00
94-08-004	Winifred	H. Tertsakian	1,500	195.00	195.00
Elke's Originals, Ltd.		**Elke Hutchens**			
89-01-001	Annabelle	E. Hutchens	250	575.00	1500.00
90-01-002	Aubra	E. Hutchens	250	575.00	900.00
90-01-003	Aurora	E. Hutchens	250	595.00	900.00
91-01-004	Alicia	E. Hutchens	250	595.00	600.00
91-01-005	Braelyn	E. Hutchens	400	595.00	1150-1500.
91-01-006	Bellinda	E. Hutchens	400	595.00	750-800.
91-01-007	Brianna	E. Hutchens	400	595.00	1000.00
92-01-008	Bethany	E. Hutchens	400	595.00	700-800.
92-01-009	Cecilia	E. Hutchens	435	635.00	900.00
92-01-010	Cherie	E. Hutchens	435	635.00	900.00
92-01-011	Charles	E. Hutchens	435	635.00	500-600.
92-01-012	Clarissa	E. Hutchens	435	635.00	800-900.
93-01-013	Daphne	E. Hutchens	435	675.00	600.00
93-01-014	Deidre	E. Hutchens	435	675.00	600.00
93-01-015	Desirée	E. Hutchens	435	675.00	600.00
90-01-016	Kricket	E. Hutchens	500	575.00	500.00
92-01-017	Laurakaye	E. Hutchens	435	550.00	550.00
90-01-018	Little Liebchen	E. Hutchens	250	475.00	1000.00
90-01-019	Victoria	E. Hutchens	500	645.00	645.00
Enesco Corporation		**Precious Moments Dolls**			
81-01-001	Mikey, 18"- E-6214B	S. Butcher	Suspd.	150.00	225.00
81-01-002	Debbie, 18"- E-6214G	S. Butcher	Suspd.	150.00	235.00
82-01-003	Cubby, 18"- E-7267B	S. Butcher	5,000	200.00	540.00
82-01-004	Tammy, 18"- E-7267G	S. Butcher	5,000	300.00	540.00
83-01-005	Katie Lynne, 16"- E-0539	S. Butcher	Suspd.	165.00	175-185.
84-01-006	Mother Sew Dear, 18"- E-2850	S. Butcher	Retrd.	350.00	350-375.
84-01-007	Kristy, 12"- E-2851	S. Butcher	Suspd.	150.00	185.00
84-01-008	Timmy, 12"- E-5397	S. Butcher	Open	125.00	150-175.
85-01-009	Aaron, 12"- 12424	S. Butcher	Suspd.	135.00	150.00
85-01-010	Bethany, 12"- 12432	S. Butcher	Suspd.	135.00	150.00
85-01-011	P.D., 7"- 12475	S. Butcher	Suspd.	50.00	54-75.00
85-01-012	Trish, 7" - 12483	S. Butcher	Suspd.	50.00	54.00
86-01-013	Bong Bong, 13" - 100455	S. Butcher	12,000	150.00	198-250.
86-01-014	Candy, 13" - 100463	S. Butcher	12,000	150.00	350.00
86-01-015	Connie, 12" - 102253	S. Butcher	7,500	160.00	240.00
87-01-016	Angie, The Angel of Mercy - 12491	S. Butcher	12,500	160.00	250.00
90-01-017	The Voice of Spring - 408786	S. Butcher	2-Yr.	150.00	150.00
90-01-018	Summer's Joy - 408794	S. Butcher	2-Yr.	150.00	150.00
90-01-019	Autumn's Praise - 408808	S. Butcher	2-Yr.	150.00	150.00
90-01-020	Winter's Song - 408816	S. Butcher	2-Yr.	150.00	150.00
91-01-021	You Have Touched So Many Hearts- 427527	S. Butcher	2-Yr.	90.00	90.00
91-01-022	May You Have An Old Fashioned Christmas - 417785	S. Butcher	2-Yr.	150.00	150.00
91-01-023	The Eyes Of The Lord Are Upon You (Boy Action Muscial) - 429570	S. Butcher	Open	65.00	65.00
91-01-024	The Eyes Of The Lord Are Upon You (Girl Action Musical) - 429589	S. Butcher	Open	65.00	65.00
Enesco Corporation		**Precious Moments-Jack-In-The-Boxes**			
91-02-001	You Have Touched So Many Hearts-422282	S. Butcher	2 Yr.	175.00	175.00
91-02-002	May You Have An Old Fashioned Christmas- 417777	S. Butcher	2 Yr.	200.00	200.00
Enesco Corporation		**Jack-In-The-Boxes-4 Seasons**			
90-03-001	Voice of Spring-408735	S. Butcher	2 Yr.	200.00	200.00
90-03-002	Summer's Joy-408743	S. Butcher	2 Yr.	200.00	200.00
90-03-003	Autumn's Praise-408751	S. Butcher	2 Yr.	200.00	200.00
90-03-004	Winter's Song-408778	S. Butcher	2 Yr.	200.00	200.00
Enesco/Hamilton Gifts Ltd.		**Maud Humphrey Bogart Porcelain Dolls**			
91-01-001	Sarah H5617	M. Humphrey	Open	37.00	37.00
91-01-002	Susanna H5648	M. Humphrey	Open	37.00	37.00
91-01-003	My First Party H5686	M. Humphrey	Open	135.00	135.00
91-01-004	Playing Bride H5618	M. Humphrey	Open	135.00	135.00
Fitz and Floyd, Inc.		**Bloomers Floppy Folks™**			
92-01-001	Peony	M. Collins	Open	50.00	50.00
92-01-002	Bloomer	M. Collins	Open	50.00	50.00
Fitz and Floyd, Inc.		**Halloween Hoedown Floppy Folks™**			
92-02-001	Wanda Witch	R. Havins	Open	50.00	50.00
92-02-002	Hazel Witch	R. Havins	Open	50.00	50.00
92-02-003	Pumpkin Patch	R. Havins	Open	50.00	50.00
92-02-004	Halloween Kat	R. Havins	Open	50.00	50.00
92-02-005	Drac-in-the-Box	R. Havins	Retrd.	60.00	60.00
Fitz and Floyd, Inc.		**Wonderland Floppy Folks™**			
93-03-001	The Mad Hatter	R. Havins	3,000	60.00	60.00
93-03-002	The Cheshire Cat	R. Havins	3,000	60.00	60.00
93-03-003	The White Rabbit	R. Havins	3,000	60.00	60.00
Fitz and Floyd, Inc.		**Christmas Floppy Folks™**			
93-04-001	Santa Claus	V. Balcou	Open	65.00	65.00
93-04-002	Santa's Reindeer	V. Balcou	Open	65.00	65.00
93-04-003	Santa's Helper	V. Balcou	Open	65.00	65.00
Fitz and Floyd, Inc.		**Dinosaur Floppy Folks™**			
94-05-001	Mama Saurus	R. Havins	Open	55.00	55.00
94-05-002	Papa Saurus	R. Havins	Open	55.00	55.00
94-05-003	Junior Saurus	R. Havins	Open	55.00	55.00
Ganz/Little Cheesers		**Cheeserville Picnic Collection**			
92-01-001	Sweet Cicely Musical Doll In Basket	G.D.A. Group	Open	85.00	85.00
Georgetown Collection, Inc.		**Nursery Babies**			
90-01-001	Baby Bunting	T. DeHetre	Closed	118.20	195.00
90-01-002	Patty Cake	T. DeHetre	Closed	118.20	118.20
91-01-003	Diddle, Diddle	T. DeHetre	Closed	118.20	118.20
91-01-004	Little Girl	T. DeHetre	100-day	118.20	118.20
91-01-005	This Little Piggy	T. DeHetre	100-day	118.20	118.20
91-01-006	Rock-A-Bye Baby	T. DeHetre	100-day	118.20	118.20
Georgetown Collection, Inc.		**Baby Kisses**			
92-02-001	Michelle	T. DeHetre	100-day	118.60	118.60
Georgetown Collection, Inc.		**Let's Play**			
92-03-001	Peek-A-Boo Beckie	T. DeHetre	100-day	118.60	118.60
92-03-002	Eentsy Weentsy Willie	T. DeHetre	100-day	118.60	118.60
Georgetown Collection, Inc.		**Sugar & Spice**			
91-04-001	Little Sweetheart	L. Mason	100-day	118.25	118.25
91-04-002	Red Hot Pepper	L. Mason	100-day	118.25	118.25
92-04-003	Little Sunshine	L. Mason	100-day	141.10	141.10
Georgetown Collection, Inc.		**American Diary Dolls**			
90-05-001	Jennie Cooper	L. Mason	100-day	129.25	129.25
91-05-002	Bridget Quinn	L. Mason	100-day	129.25	129.25
91-05-003	Christina Merovina	L. Mason	100-day	129.25	129.25
91-05-004	Many Stars	L. Mason	100-day	129.25	129.25
92-05-005	Rachel Williams	L. Mason	100-day	129.25	129.25
92-05-006	Tulu	L. Mason	100-day	129.25	129.25
93-05-007	Sarah Turner	L. Mason	100-day	130.00	130.00
Georgetown Collection, Inc.		**Little Lovers**			
90-06-001	Laura	B. Deval	Closed	139.20	139.20
89-06-002	Katie	B. Deval	Closed	139.20	139.20
88-06-003	Emma	B. Deval	Closed	139.20	139.20
89-06-004	Megan	B. Deval	Closed	138.00	160.00
Georgetown Collection, Inc.		**Small Wonders**			
90-07-001	Corey	B. Deval	100-day	97.60	97.60
91-07-002	Abbey	B. Deval	100-day	97.60	97.60
92-07-003	Sarah	B. Deval	100-day	97.60	97.60
Georgetown Collection, Inc.		**Faerie Princess**			
89-08-001	Faerie Princess	B. Deval	Closed	248.00	248.00
Georgetown Collection, Inc.		**Miss Ashley**			
89-09-001	Miss Ashley	P. Thompson	Closed	228.00	228.00
Georgetown Collection, Inc.		**Tansie**			
88-10-001	Tansie	P. Coffer	Closed	81.00	81.00
Georgetown Collection, Inc.		**Kindergarten Kids**			
92-11-001	Nikki	V. Walker	100-day	129.60	129.60
Georgetown Collection, Inc.		**Portraits of Perfection**			
93-12-001	Peaches & Cream	A. Timmerman	100-day	149.60	149.60
93-12-002	Sweet Strawberry	A. Timmerman	100-day	149.60	149.60
93-12-003	Apple Dumpling	A. Timmerman	100-day	149.60	149.60
94-12-004	Blackberry Blossom	A. Timmerman	100-day	149.60	149.60
Georgetown Collection, Inc.		**Hearts in Song**			
92-13-001	Grace	J. Galperin	100-day	149.60	149.60
93-13-001	Michael	J. Galperin	100-day	150.00	150.00
Georgetown Collection, Inc.		**Children of the Great Spirit**			
93-14-001	Buffalo Child	C. Theroux	100-day	140.00	140.00
93-14-002	Winter Baby	C. Theroux	100-day	160.00	160.00
94-14-003	Golden Flower	C. Theroux	100-day	130.00	130.00
Georgetown Collection, Inc.		**Russian Fairy Tales Dolls**			
93-15-001	Vasilisa	B. Deval	100-day	190.00	190.00
Georgetown Collection, Inc.		**Linda's Little Ladies**			
93-16-001	Shannon's Holiday	L. Mason	100-day	169.95	169.95
Georgetown Collection, Inc.		**Faraway Friends**			
93-17-001	Kristin	S. Skille	100-day	140.00	140.00
94-17-002	Dara	S. Skille	100-day	140.00	140.00
Georgetown Collection, Inc.		**Georgetown Collection**			
93-18-001	Quick Fox	L. Mason	100-day	138.95	138.95
Georgetown Collection, Inc.		**Victorian Innocence**			
94-19-001	Annabelle	L. Mason	100-day	130.00	130.00
Goebel		**Victoria Ashlea Originals**			
88-01-001	Campbell Kid-Girl-758700	B. Ball	Closed	13.80	13.80
88-01-002	Campbell Kid-Boy-758701	B. Ball	Closed	13.80	13.80
84-01-003	Claude-901032	B. Ball	Closed	110.00	225.00
84-01-004	Claudette-901033	B. Ball	Closed	110.00	225.00
84-01-005	Henri-901035	B. Ball	Closed	100.00	200.00
84-01-006	Henrietta-901036	B. Ball	Closed	100.00	200.00
84-01-007	Jeannie-901062	B. Ball	Closed	200.00	550.00
84-01-008	Victoria-901068	B. Ball	Closed	200.00	1500.00
84-01-009	Laura-901106	B. Ball	Closed	300.00	575.00
83-01-010	Deborah-901107	B. Ball	Closed	220.00	400.00
84-01-011	Barbara-901108	B. Ball	Closed	57.00	110.00
84-01-012	Diana-901119	B. Ball	Closed	55.00	135.00
84-01-013	Clown-901136	B. Ball	Closed	90.00	120.00
84-01-014	Sabina-901155	B. Ball	Closed	75.00	N/A
85-01-015	Dorothy-901157	B. Ball	Closed	130.00	275.00
85-01-016	Claire-901158	B. Ball	Closed	115.00	160.00
85-01-017	Adele-901172	B. Ball	Closed	145.00	275.00

DOLLS

Company Number	Name	Series Artist	Edition Limit	Issue Price	Quote
85-01-018	Roxanne-901174	B. Ball	Closed	155.00	275.00
86-01-019	Gina-901176	B. Ball	Closed	300.00	300.00
86-01-020	Cat/Kitty Cheerful Gr Dr-901179	B. Ball	Closed	60.00	60.00
85-01-021	Garnet-901183	B. Ball	Closed	160.00	295.00
86-01-022	Pepper Rust Dr/Appr-901184	B. Ball	Closed	125.00	200.00
86-01-023	Patty Artic Flower Print-901185	B. Ball	Closed	140.00	140.00
87-01-024	Lillian-901199	B. Ball	Closed	85.00	100.00
87-01-025	Suzanne-901200	B. Ball	Closed	85.00	100.00
87-01-026	Kitty Cuddles-901201	B. Ball	Closed	65.00	65.00
87-01-027	Bonnie Pouty-901207	B. Ball	Closed	100.00	100.00
87-01-028	Amanda Pouty-901209	B. Ball	Closed	150.00	215.00
87-01-029	Tiffany Pouty-901211	B. Ball	Closed	120.00	160.00
87-01-030	Alice-901212	B. Ball	Closed	95.00	135.00
88-01-031	Elizabeth-901214	B. Ball	Closed	90.00	90.00
87-01-032	Bride Allison-901218	B. Ball	Closed	180.00	180.00
87-01-033	Dominique-901219	B. Ball	Closed	170.00	225.00
87-01-034	Sarah-901220	B. Ball	Closed	350.00	350.00
87-01-035	Tasha-901221	B. Ball	Closed	115.00	130.00
87-01-036	Michelle-901222	B. Ball	Closed	90.00	90.00
87-01-037	Nicole-901225	B. Ball	Closed	575.00	575.00
87-01-038	Clementine-901226	B. Ball	Closed	75.00	75.00
87-01-039	Catanova-901227	B. Ball	Closed	75.00	75.00
87-01-040	Caitlin-901228	B. Ball	Closed	260.00	260.00
88-01-041	Christina-901229	B. Ball	Closed	350.00	400.00
88-01-042	Melissa-901230	B. Ball	Closed	110.00	110.00
82-01-043	Marie-901231	B. Ball	Closed	95.00	95.00
82-01-044	Trudy-901232	B. Ball	Closed	100.00	100.00
82-01-045	Holly-901233	B. Ball	Closed	160.00	200.00
88-01-046	Brandon-901234	B. Ball	Closed	90.00	90.00
88-01-047	Ashley-901235	B. Ball	Closed	110.00	110.00
88-01-048	April-901239	B. Ball	Closed	225.00	225.00
88-01-049	Sandy-901240	K. Kennedy	Closed	115.00	115.00
88-01-050	Erin-901241	B. Ball	Closed	170.00	170.00
88-01-051	Catherine-901242	B. Ball	Closed	240.00	240.00
88-01-052	Susan-901243	B. Ball	Closed	100.00	100.00
88-01-053	Paulette-901244	B. Ball	Closed	90.00	90.00
88-01-054	Bernice-901245	B. Ball	Closed	90.00	90.00
88-01-055	Ellen-901246	B. Ball	Closed	100.00	100.00
88-01-056	Cat Maude-901247	B. Ball	Closed	85.00	85.00
88-01-057	Jennifer-901248	B. Ball	Closed	150.00	150.00
90-01-058	Helene-901249	K. Kennedy	Closed	160.00	160.00
89-01-059	Ashlea-901250	B. Ball	Closed	550.00	550.00
90-01-060	Matthew-901251	B. Ball	Closed	100.00	100.00
89-01-061	Marissa-901252	K. Kennedy	Closed	225.00	225.00
89-01-062	Holly-901254	B. Ball	Closed	180.00	180.00
89-01-063	Valerie-901255	B. Ball	Closed	175.00	175.00
90-01-064	Justine-901256	B. Ball	Closed	200.00	200.00
89-01-065	Claudia-901257	K. Kennedy	Closed	225.00	225.00
90-01-066	Rebecca-901258	B. Ball	Closed	250.00	250.00
89-01-067	Megan-901260	B. Ball	Closed	120.00	120.00
90-01-068	Carolyn-901261	K. Kennedy	Closed	200.00	200.00
90-01-069	Amy-901262	B. Ball	Closed	110.00	110.00
89-01-070	Lindsey-901263	B. Ball	Closed	100.00	100.00
90-01-071	Heidi-901266	B. Ball	2,000	150.00	150.00
84-01-072	Tobie-912023	B. Ball	Closed	30.00	30.00
84-01-073	Sheila-912060	B. Ball	Closed	75.00	135.00
84-01-074	Jamie-912061	B. Ball	Closed	65.00	100.00
85-01-075	Michelle-912066	B. Ball	Closed	100.00	225.00
85-01-076	Phyllis-912067	B. Ball	Closed	60.00	60.00
85-01-077	Clown Casey-912078	B. Ball	Closed	40.00	40.00
85-01-078	Clown Jody-912079	B. Ball	Closed	100.00	150.00
85-01-079	Clown Christie-912084	B. Ball	Closed	60.00	90.00
85-01-080	Chauncey-912085	B. Ball	Closed	75.00	110.00
86-01-081	Baby Lauren Pink-912086	B. Ball	Closed	120.00	120.00
85-01-082	Rosalind-912087	B. Ball	Closed	145.00	225.00
86-01-083	Clown Cyd-912093	B. Ball	Closed	70.00	70.00
82-01-084	Charleen-912094	B. Ball	Closed	65.00	65.00
86-01-085	Clown Christabel-912095	B. Ball	Closed	100.00	150.00
86-01-086	Clown Clarabella-912096	B. Ball	Closed	80.00	80.00
86-01-087	Baby Brock Beige Dress-912103	B. Ball	Closed	60.00	60.00
86-01-088	Clown Calypso-912104	B. Ball	Closed	70.00	70.00
86-01-089	Girl Frog Freda-912105	B. Ball	Closed	20.00	20.00
86-01-090	Googley German Astrid-912109	B. Ball	Closed	60.00	60.00
86-01-091	Clown Clarissa-912123	B. Ball	Closed	75.00	110.00
86-01-092	Baby Courtney-912124	B. Ball	Closed	120.00	120.00
85-01-093	Mary-912126	B. Ball	Closed	60.00	90.00
86-01-094	Clown Lollipop-912127	B. Ball	Closed	125.00	225.00
86-01-095	Clown Cat Cadwalader-912132	B. Ball	Closed	55.00	55.00
86-01-096	Clown Kitten-Cleo-912133	B. Ball	Closed	50.00	50.00
85-01-097	Millie-912135	B. Ball	Closed	70.00	125.00
85-01-098	Lynn-912144	B. Ball	Closed	90.00	135.00
86-01-099	Ashley-912147	B. Ball	Closed	125.00	125.00
87-01-100	Megan-912148	B. Ball	Closed	70.00	70.00
87-01-101	Joy-912155	B. Ball	Closed	50.00	50.00
87-01-102	Kittle Cat-912167	B. Ball	Closed	55.00	55.00
87-01-103	Christine-912168	B. Ball	Closed	75.00	75.00
87-01-104	Noel-912170	B. Ball	Closed	125.00	125.00
87-01-105	Sophia-912173	B. Ball	Closed	40.00	40.00
87-01-106	Julia-912174	B. Ball	Closed	80.00	80.00
87-01-107	Clown Champagne-912180	B. Ball	Closed	95.00	95.00
82-01-108	Clown Jolly-912181	B. Ball	Closed	70.00	70.00
87-01-109	Baby Doll-912184	B. Ball	Closed	75.00	75.00
87-01-110	Baby Lindsay-912190	B. Ball	Closed	80.00	80.00
87-01-111	Caroline-912191	B. Ball	Closed	80.00	80.00
87-01-112	Jacqueline-912192	B. Ball	Closed	80.00	80.00
87-01-113	Jessica-912195	B. Ball	Closed	120.00	135.00
87-01-114	Doreen-912198	B. Ball	Closed	75.00	75.00
88-01-115	Clown Cotton Candy-912199	B. Ball	Closed	67.00	67.00
88-01-116	Baby Daryl-912200	B. Ball	Closed	85.00	85.00
88-01-117	Angelica-912204	B. Ball	Closed	150.00	150.00
88-01-118	Karen-912205	B. Ball	Closed	200.00	250.00
88-01-119	Polly-912206	B. Ball	Closed	100.00	125.00
88-01-120	Brittany-912207	B. Ball	Closed	130.00	145.00
88-01-121	Melissa-912208	B. Ball	Closed	125.00	125.00
88-01-122	Baby Jennifer-912210	B. Ball	Closed	75.00	75.00
88-01-123	Molly-912211	K. Kennedy	Closed	75.00	75.00
88-01-124	Lauren-912212	B. Ball	Closed	110.00	110.00
88-01-125	Anne-912213	B. Ball	Closed	130.00	150.00
89-01-126	Alexa-912214	B. Ball	Closed	195.00	195.00
88-01-127	Diana-912218	B. Ball	Closed	270.00	270.00
88-01-128	Sarah w/Pillow-912219	B. Ball	Closed	105.00	105.00
88-01-129	Betty Doll-912220	B. Ball	Closed	90.00	90.00
88-01-130	Jennifer-912221	B. Ball	Closed	80.00	80.00
88-01-131	Baby Katie-912222	B. Ball	Closed	70.00	70.00
88-01-132	Maritta Spanish-912224	B. Ball	Closed	140.00	140.00
88-01-133	Laura-912225	B. Ball	Closed	135.00	135.00
88-01-134	Crystal-912226	B. Ball	Closed	75.00	75.00
88-01-135	Jesse-912231	B. Ball	1,000	110.00	115.00
88-01-136	Whitney Blk-912232	B. Ball	1,000	62.50	65.00
88-01-137	Goldilocks-912234	K. Kennedy	Closed	65.00	65.00
88-01-138	Snow White-912235	K. Kennedy	Closed	65.00	65.00
88-01-139	Stephanie-912238	B. Ball	Closed	200.00	200.00
88-01-140	Morgan-912239	K. Kennedy	Closed	75.00	75.00
XX-01-141	Charity-912244	B. Ball	Closed	70.00	70.00
88-01-142	Renae-912245	B. Ball	Closed	120.00	120.00
88-01-143	Amanda-912246	B. Ball	Closed	180.00	180.00
88-01-144	Heather-912247	B. Ball	Closed	135.00	150.00
89-01-145	Merry-912249	B. Ball	Closed	200.00	200.00
90-01-146	January Birthstone Doll-912250	K. Kennedy	Closed	25.00	25.00
90-01-147	February Birthstone Doll-912251	K. Kennedy	Closed	25.00	25.00
90-01-148	March Birthstone Doll-912252	K. Kennedy	Closed	25.00	25.00
90-01-149	April Birthstone Doll-912253	K. Kennedy	Closed	25.00	25.00
90-01-150	May Birthstone Doll-912254	K. Kennedy	Closed	25.00	25.00
90-01-151	June Birthstone Doll-912255	K. Kennedy	Closed	25.00	25.00
90-01-152	July Birthstone Doll-912256	K. Kennedy	Closed	25.00	25.00
90-01-153	August Birthstone Doll-912257	K. Kennedy	Closed	25.00	25.00
90-01-154	September Birthstone Doll-912258	K. Kennedy	Closed	25.00	25.00
90-01-155	October Birthstone Doll-912259	K. Kennedy	Closed	25.00	25.00
90-01-156	November Birthstone Doll-912260	K. Kennedy	Closed	25.00	25.00
90-01-157	December Birthstone Doll-912261	K. Kennedy	Closed	25.00	25.00
89-01-158	Tammy-912264	B. Ball	Closed	110.00	110.00
89-01-159	Maria-912265	B. Ball	Closed	90.00	90.00
89-01-160	Nancy-912266	B. Ball	Closed	110.00	110.00
89-01-161	Pinky Clown-912268	K. Kennedy	Closed	70.00	75.00
89-01-162	Margot-912269	B. Ball	Closed	110.00	110.00
89-01-163	Jingles-912271	B. Ball	Closed	60.00	60.00
89-01-164	Vanessa-912272	B. Ball	Closed	110.00	110.00
89-01-165	Alexandria-912273	B. Ball	Closed	275.00	275.00
89-01-166	Lisa-912275	B. Ball	Closed	160.00	160.00
89-01-167	Loni-912276	B. Ball	Closed	125.00	130.00
89-01-168	Diana Bride-912277	B. Ball	Closed	180.00	180.00
90-01-169	Annabelle-912278	B. Ball	Closed	200.00	200.00
89-01-170	Sara-912279	B. Ball	Closed	175.00	175.00
89-01-171	Terry-912281	B. Ball	2,000	125.00	130.00
89-01-172	Sigrid-912282	B. Ball	Closed	145.00	145.00
89-01-173	Missy-912283	B. Ball	Closed	110.00	115.00
89-01-174	Melanie-912284	K. Kennedy	Closed	135.00	135.00
89-01-175	Kristin-912285	K. Kennedy	Closed	90.00	95.00
89-01-176	Suzanne-912286	B. Ball	Closed	120.00	120.00
90-01-177	Ginny-912287	K. Kennedy	Closed	140.00	140.00
89-01-178	Candace-912288	K. Kennedy	Closed	70.00	70.00
89-01-179	Joy-912289	K. Kennedy	Closed	110.00	110.00
90-01-180	Licorice-912290	B. Ball	Closed	75.00	75.00
89-01-181	Jimmy Baby w/ Pillow-912291	K. Kennedy	Closed	165.00	165.00
89-01-182	Hope Baby w/ Pillow-912292	B. Ball	Closed	110.00	110.00
90-01-183	Fluffer-912293	B. Ball	Closed	135.00	140.00
90-01-184	Marshmallow-912294	K. Kennedy	Closed	75.00	75.00
89-01-185	Suzy-912295	B. Ball	Closed	110.00	110.00
90-01-186	Alice-912296	K. Kennedy	Closed	65.00	65.00
90-01-187	Baryshnicat-912298	K. Kennedy	Closed	25.00	25.00
90-01-188	Tasha-912299	K. Kennedy	Closed	25.00	25.00
90-01-189	Priscilla-912300	B. Ball	Closed	185.00	190.00
90-01-190	Mrs. Katz-912301	B. Ball	Closed	140.00	145.00
89-01-200	Pamela-912302	B. Ball	Closed	95.00	95.00
89-01-201	Emily-912303	B. Ball	Closed	150.00	150.00
90-01-202	Brandy-912304	K. Kennedy	Closed	150.00	150.00
90-01-203	Sheri-912305	K. Kennedy	Closed	115.00	115.00
90-01-204	Gigi-912306	K. Kennedy	Closed	150.00	150.00
90-01-205	Joanne-912307	K. Kennedy	Closed	165.00	165.00
89-01-206	Melinda-912309	K. Kennedy	Closed	70.00	70.00
90-01-207	Bettina-912310	B. Ball	Closed	100.00	105.00
90-01-208	Stephanie-912312	B. Ball	Closed	150.00	150.00
90-01-209	Amie-912313	K. Kennedy	Closed	150.00	150.00
90-01-210	Samantha-912314	B. Ball	Closed	185.00	190.00
90-01-211	Tracie-912315	B. Ball	Closed	125.00	125.00
90-01-212	Paula-912316	B. Ball	Closed	100.00	100.00
90-01-213	Debra-912319	K. Kennedy	Closed	120.00	120.00
90-01-214	Robin-912321	B. Ball	Closed	160.00	165.00
90-01-215	Heather-912322	B. Ball	Closed	150.00	150.00
90-01-216	Jillian-912323	B. Ball	Closed	150.00	150.00
90-01-217	Angela-912324	K. Kennedy	Closed	130.00	135.00
90-01-218	Penny-912325	K. Kennedy	Closed	130.00	130.00
90-01-219	Tiffany-912326	K. Kennedy	Closed	180.00	180.00
90-01-220	Susie-912328	B. Ball	Closed	115.00	120.00
90-01-221	Jacqueline-912329	K. Kennedy	Closed	136.00	140.00
90-01-222	Kelly-912331	B. Ball	Closed	95.00	95.00
90-01-223	Annette-912333	K. Kennedy	Closed	85.00	85.00
90-01-224	Julia-912334	K. Kennedy	Closed	85.00	85.00
90-01-225	Monique-912335	K. Kennedy	Closed	85.00	85.00
90-01-226	Monica-912336	K. Kennedy	Closed	100.00	105.00
90-01-227	Helga-912337	B. Ball	Closed	325.00	325.00
90-01-228	Sheena-912338	B. Ball	Closed	115.00	115.00
90-01-229	Kimberly-912341	B. Ball	1,000	140.00	145.00
84-01-230	Amelia-933006	B. Ball	Closed	100.00	100.00
84-01-231	Stephanie-933012	B. Ball	Closed	115.00	115.00
92-01-232	Wendy-912330	K. Kennedy	1,000	125.00	130.00
92-01-233	Margaret-912354	K. Kennedy	Closed	150.00	150.00
92-01-234	Cassandra-912355	K. Kennedy	1,000	165.00	165.00
92-01-235	Noelle-912360	K. Kennedy	1,000	165.00	170.00
92-01-236	Kelli-912361	B. Ball	1,000	160.00	165.00
92-01-237	Ashley-911004	B. Ball	2,000	99.00	105.00
92-01-238	Lauren-912363	K. Kennedy	1,000	190.00	195.00
92-01-239	Denise-912362	K. Kennedy	1,000	145.00	150.00
92-01-240	Kris-912345	K. Kennedy	Closed	160.00	160.00
92-01-241	Hilary-912353	B. Ball	Closed	130.00	135.00
92-01-242	Toni-912367	K. Kennedy	Closed	120.00	120.00
92-01-243	Angelica-912339	B. Ball	1,000	145.00	145.00
92-01-244	Marjorie-912357	B. Ball	Closed	135.00	135.00
92-01-245	Brittany-912365	K. Kennedy	Closed	140.00	145.00
92-01-246	Allison-912358	B. Ball	Closed	160.00	165.00
92-01-247	Jenny-912374	K. Kennedy	Closed	150.00	150.00
92-01-248	Holly Belle-912380	B. Ball	500	125.00	125.00
92-01-249	Michelle-912381	K. Kennedy	500	175.00	175.00
92-01-250	Tamika-912382	B. Ball	500	185.00	185.00
92-01-251	Sherise-912383	K. Kennedy	500	145.00	145.00
92-01-252	Cindy-912384	B. Ball	1,000	185.00	190.00
92-01-253	Tulip-912385	K. Kennedy	500	145.00	145.00
92-01-254	Carol-912387	K. Kennedy	1,000	140.00	140.00

Number	Name	Artist	Edition Limit	Issue Price	Quote
92-01-255	Alicia-912388	B. Ball	500	135.00	135.00
92-01-256	Iris-912389	K. Kennedy	500	165.00	165.00
92-01-257	Betsy-912390	B. Ball	500	150.00	150.00
92-01-258	Trudie-912391	B. Ball	500	135.00	135.00
92-01-259	Dottie-912393	K. Kennedy	1,000	160.00	160.00
93-01-260	Sarah-912408	B. Ball	2,000	40.00	40.00
93-01-261	Amanda-912409	B. Ball	2,000	40.00	40.00
93-01-262	Jessica-912410	B. Ball	2,000	40.00	40.00
93-01-263	Nicole-912411	B. Ball	2,000	40.00	40.00
93-01-264	Katie-912412	B. Ball	2,000	40.00	40.00
93-01-265	Lauren-912413	B. Ball	2,000	40.00	40.00
93-01-266	Beth-912430	K. Kennedy	2,000	45.00	45.00
93-01-267	Nadine-912431	K. Kennedy	2,000	45.00	45.00
93-01-268	Leslie-912432	K. Kennedy	2,000	45.00	45.00
93-01-269	Kaylee-912433	K. Kennedy	2,000	45.00	45.00
93-01-270	Shannon-912434	K. Kennedy	2,000	45.00	45.00
93-01-271	Julie-912435	K. Kennedy	2,000	45.00	45.00
93-01-272	January-Garnet-912394	K. Kennedy	2,500	29.50	29.50
93-01-273	February-Amethyst-912395	K. Kennedy	2,500	29.50	29.50
93-01-274	March-Aquamarine-912396	K. Kennedy	2,500	29.50	29.50
93-01-275	April-Diamond-912397	K. Kennedy	2,500	29.50	29.50
93-01-276	May-Emerald-912398	K. Kennedy	2,500	29.50	29.50
93-01-277	June-Lt. Amethyst-912399	K. Kennedy	2,500	29.50	29.50
93-01-278	July-Ruby-912400	K. Kennedy	2,500	29.50	29.50
93-01-279	August-Peridot-912401	K. Kennedy	2,500	29.50	29.50
93-01-280	September-Sapphire-912402	K. Kennedy	2,500	29.50	29.50
93-01-281	October-Rose Stone-912403	K. Kennedy	2,500	29.50	29.50
93-01-282	November-Topaz-912404	K. Kennedy	2,500	29.50	29.50
93-01-283	December-Zircon-912405	K. Kennedy	2,500	29.50	29.50
Goebel		**Victoria Ashlea Originals-Tiny Tot School Girls**			
94-02-001	Shawna- 912449	K. Kennedy	2,000	47.50	47.50
94-02-002	Christin- 912450	K. Kennedy	2,000	47.50	47.50
94-02-003	Patricia- 912453	K. Kennedy	2,000	47.50	47.50
94-02-004	Monique- 912455	K. Kennedy	2,000	47.50	47.50
94-02-005	Andrea- 12456	K. Kennedy	2,000	47.50	47.50
94-02-006	Susan- 12457	K. Kennedy	2,000	47.50	47.50
Goebel		**Victoria Ashlea Originals-Tiny Tot Clowns**			
94-03-001	Lisa	K. Kennedy	2,000	45.00	45.00
94-03-002	Stacy	K. Kennedy	2,000	45.00	45.00
94-03-003	Megan	K. Kennedy	2,000	45.00	45.00
94-03-004	Danielle	K. Kennedy	2,000	45.00	45.00
94-03-005	Marie	K. Kennedy	2,000	45.00	45.00
94-03-006	Lindsey	K. Kennedy	2,000	45.00	45.00
Goebel/M.I. Hummel		**M. I. Hummel Collectible Dolls**			
64-01-001	Gretel 1901	M. I. Hummel	Closed	55.00	125.00
64-01-002	Hansel 1902	M. I. Hummel	Closed	55.00	110.00
64-01-003	Rosa-Blue Baby 1904/B	M. I. Hummel	Closed	45.00	85.00
64-01-004	Rosa-Pink Baby 1904/P	M. I. Hummel	Closed	45.00	75.00
64-01-005	Little Knitter 1905	M. I. Hummel	Closed	55.00	75.00
64-01-006	Merry Wanderer 1906	M. I. Hummel	Closed	55.00	90.00
64-01-007	Chimney Sweep 1908	M. I. Hummel	Closed	55.00	110.00
64-01-008	School Girl 1909	M. I. Hummel	Closed	55.00	75.00
64-01-009	School Boy 1910	M. I. Hummel	Closed	55.00	80.00
64-01-010	Goose Girl 1914	M. I. Hummel	Closed	55.00	80.00
64-01-011	For Father 1917	M. I. Hummel	Closed	55.00	90.00
64-01-012	Merry Wanderer 1925	M. I. Hummel	Closed	55.00	110.00
64-01-013	Lost Stocking 1926	M. I. Hummel	Closed	55.00	75.00
64-01-014	Visiting and Invalid 1927	M. I. Hummel	Closed	55.00	75.00
64-01-015	On Secret Path 1928	M. I. Hummel	Closed	55.00	80.00
Goebel/M.I. Hummel		**M. I. Hummel Porcelain Dolls**			
84-02-001	Birthday Serenade/Boy	M. I. Hummel	Closed	225.00	250-300.
84-02-002	Birthday Serenade/Girl	M. I. Hummel	Closed	225.00	250-300.
84-02-003	On Holiday	M. I. Hummel	Closed	225.00	250-300.
84-02-004	Postman	M. I. Hummel	Closed	225.00	250-300.
85-02-005	Carnival	M. I. Hummel	Closed	225.00	250-300.
85-02-006	Easter Greetings	M. I. Hummel	Closed	225.00	250-300.
85-02-007	Lost Sheep	M. I. Hummel	Closed	225.00	250-300.
85-02-008	Signs of Spring	M. I. Hummel	Closed	225.00	250-300.
Good-Kruger		**Limited Edition**			
90-01-001	Daydream	J. Good-Kruger	Retrd.	199.00	250.00
90-01-002	Annie-Rose	J. Good-Kruger	Retrd.	219.00	350-500.
90-01-003	Cozy	J. Good-Kruger	Retrd.	179.00	275-375.
90-01-004	Alice	J. Good-Kruger	Retrd.	250.00	250.00
90-01-005	Christmas Cookie	J. Good-Kruger	Open	199.00	199.00
90-01-006	Sue-Lynn	J. Good-Kruger	Retrd.	240.00	300.00
91-01-007	Teachers Pet	J. Good-Kruger	Retrd.	199.00	250.00
91-01-008	Moppett	J. Good-Kruger	Retrd.	179.00	295.00
91-01-009	Victorian Christmas	J. Good-Kruger	Retrd.	219.00	275.00
91-01-010	Johnny-Lynn	J. Good-Kruger	Retrd.	240.00	280.00
92-01-011	Jeepers Creepers (Porcelain)	J. Good-Kruger	Retrd.	725.00	800.00
92-01-012	Anne	J. Good-Kruger	Retrd.	240.00	280-500.
Gorham		**Gorham Dolls**			
81-01-001	Jillian, 16"	S. Stone Aiken	Closed	200.00	350-475.
81-01-002	Alexandria, 18"	S. Stone Aiken	Closed	250.00	550-575.
81-01-003	Christopher, 19"	S. Stone Aiken	Closed	250.00	750-950.
81-01-004	Stephanie, 18"	S. Stone Aiken	Closed	250.00	1650-2100.
81-01-005	Cecile, 16"	S. Stone Aiken	Closed	200.00	700-950.
81-01-006	Christina, 16"	S. Stone Aiken	Closed	200.00	400-475.
81-01-007	Danielle, 14"	S. Stone Aiken	Closed	150.00	300-375.
81-01-008	Melinda, 14"	S. Stone Aiken	Closed	150.00	300-375.
81-01-009	Elena, 14"	S. Stone Aiken	Closed	150.00	600-750.
81-01-010	Rosemond, 18"	S. Stone Aiken	Closed	250.00	650-750.
82-01-011	Mlle. Monique, 12"	S. Stone Aiken	Closed	125.00	300.00
82-01-012	Mlle. Jeanette, 12"	S. Stone Aiken	Closed	125.00	175-225.
82-01-013	Mlle. Lucille, 12"	S. Stone Aiken	Closed	125.00	275-475.
82-01-014	Benjamin, 18"	S. Stone Aiken	Closed	200.00	550-600.
82-01-015	Ellice, 18"	S. Stone Aiken	Closed	200.00	550-600.
82-01-016	Corrine, 21"	S. Stone Aiken	Closed	250.00	400-600.
82-01-017	Baby in Blue Dress, 12"	S. Stone Aiken	Closed	150.00	350-375.
82-01-018	Baby in Apricot Dress, 16"	S. Stone Aiken	Closed	175.00	375.00
82-01-019	Baby in White Dress, 18"	Gorham	Closed	250.00	395.00
82-01-020	Melanie, 23"	S. Stone Aiken	Closed	300.00	650-725.
82-01-021	Jeremy, 23"	S. Stone Aiken	Closed	300.00	750-800.
82-01-022	Mlle. Yvonne, 12"	Unknown	Closed	125.00	275-450.
82-01-023	M. Anton, 12"	Unknown	Closed	125.00	195.00
82-01-024	Mlle. Marsella, 12"	Unknown	Closed	125.00	295.00
82-01-025	Kristin, 23"	S. Stone Aiken	Closed	300.00	550-700.
83-01-026	Jennifer, 19" Bridal Doll	S. Stone Aiken	Closed	325.00	700-825.
85-01-027	Linda, 19"	S. Stone Aiken	Closed	275.00	400-475.
85-01-028	Odette, 19"	S. Stone Aiken	Closed	250.00	450-475.
85-01-029	Amelia, 19"	S. Stone Aiken	Closed	275.00	325-400.
85-01-030	Nanette, 19"	S. Stone Aiken	Closed	275.00	325-400.
85-01-031	Alexander, 19"	S. Stone Aiken	Closed	275.00	400-500.
85-01-032	Gabrielle, 19"	S. Stone Aiken	Closed	225.00	400-450.
86-01-033	Julia, 16"	S. Stone Aiken	Closed	225.00	375-425.
86-01-034	Lauren, 14"	S. Stone Aiken	Closed	175.00	375-450.
86-01-035	Emily, 14"	S. Stone Aiken	Closed	175.00	375-450.
86-01-036	Fleur, 19"	S. Stone Aiken	Closed	300.00	400-500.
87-01-037	Juliet	S. Stone Aiken	Closed	325.00	400-450.
86-01-038	Meredith	S. Stone Aiken	Closed	295.00	350-400.
86-01-039	Alissa	S. Stone Aiken	Closed	245.00	300-375.
86-01-040	Jessica	S. Stone Aiken	Closed	195.00	275-350.
Gorham		**Limited Edition Dolls**			
82-02-001	Allison, 19"	S. Stone Aiken	Closed	300.00	4800.00
83-02-002	Ashley, 19"	S. Stone Aiken	Closed	350.00	1200.00
84-02-003	Nicole, 19"	S. Stone Aiken	Closed	350.00	1000.00
84-02-004	Holly (Christmas), 19"	S. Stone Aiken	Closed	300.00	750-900.
85-02-005	Lydia,19"	S. Stone Aiken	Closed	550.00	1800.00
85-02-006	Joy (Christmas), 19"	S. Stone Aiken	Closed	350.00	500-725.
86-02-007	Noel (Christmas), 19"	S. Stone Aiken	Closed	400.00	700-800.
87-02-008	Jacqueline, 19"	S. Stone Aiken	Closed	500.00	600-850.
87-02-009	Merrie (Christmas), 19"	S. Stone Aiken	Closed	500.00	795.00
88-02-010	Andrew, 19"	S. Stone Aiken	Closed	475.00	625-850.
88-02-011	Christa (Christmas), 19"	S. Stone Aiken	Closed	550.00	1500.00
90-02-012	Amey (10th Anniversary Edition)	S. Stone Aiken	Closed	650.00	750-1100.
Gorham		**Gorham Holly Hobbie Childhood Memories**			
85-03-001	Mother's Helper	Holly Hobbie	Closed	45.00	125.00
85-03-002	Best Friends	Holly Hobbie	Closed	45.00	125.00
85-03-003	First Day of School	Holly Hobbie	Closed	45.00	125.00
85-03-004	Christmas Wishes	Holly Hobbie	Closed	45.00	125.00
Gorham		**Gorham Holly Hobbie For All Seasons**			
84-04-001	Summer Holly 12"	Holly Hobbie	Closed	42.50	195.00
84-04-002	Fall Holly 12"	Holly Hobbie	Closed	42.50	195.00
84-04-003	Winter Holly 12"	Holly Hobbie	Closed	42.50	195.00
84-04-004	Spring Holly 12"	Holly Hobbie	Closed	42.50	195.00
Gorham		**Holly Hobbie**			
83-05-001	Blue Girl, 14"	Holly Hobbie	Closed	80.00	325.00
83-05-002	Christmas Morning, 14"	Holly Hobbie	Closed	80.00	275.00
83-05-003	Heather, 14"	Holly Hobbie	Closed	80.00	275.00
83-05-004	Little Amy, 14"	Holly Hobbie	Closed	80.00	275.00
83-05-005	Robbie, 14"	Holly Hobbie	Closed	80.00	275.00
83-05-006	Sweet Valentine, 16"	Holly Hobbie	Closed	100.00	350.00
83-05-007	Yesterday's Memories, 18"	Holly Hobbie	Closed	125.00	450.00
83-05-008	Sunday Best, 18"	Holly Hobbie	Closed	115.00	350.00
83-05-009	Blue Girl, 18"	Holly Hobbie	Closed	115.00	395.00
Gorham		**Little Women**			
83-06-001	Beth, 16"	S. Stone Aiken	Closed	225.00	575.00
83-06-002	Amy, 16"	S. Stone Aiken	Closed	225.00	575.00
83-06-003	Meg, 19"	S. Stone Aiken	Closed	275.00	695.00
83-06-004	Jo, 19"	S. Stone Aiken	Closed	275.00	675.00
Gorham		**Kezi Doll For All Seasons**			
85-07-001	Ariel 16"	Kezi	Closed	135.00	500.00
85-07-002	Aubrey 16"	Kezi	Closed	135.00	500.00
85-07-003	Amber 16"	Kezi	Closed	135.00	500.00
85-07-004	Adrienne 16"	Kezi	Closed	135.00	500-525.
Gorham		**Kezi Golden Gifts**			
84-08-001	Faith 18"	Kezi	Closed	95.00	195-225.
84-08-002	Felicity 18"	Kezi	Closed	95.00	195.00
84-08-003	Patience 18"	Kezi	Closed	95.00	195.00
84-08-004	Prudence 18"	Kezi	Closed	85.00	195.00
84-08-005	Hope 16"	Kezi	Closed	85.00	175-225.
84-08-006	Grace 16"	Kezi	Closed	85.00	175.00
84-08-007	Charity 16"	Kezi	Closed	85.00	175-195.
84-08-008	Merrie 16"	Kezi	Closed	85.00	175-195.
Gorham		**Limited Edition Sister Set**			
88-09-001	Kathleen	S. Stone Aiken	Closed	550.00	750-950.
88-09-002	Katelin	S. Stone Aiken	Set	Set	Set
Gorham		**Southern Belles**			
85-10-001	Amanda, 19"	S. Stone Aiken	Closed	300.00	950.00
86-10-002	Veronica, 19"	S. Stone Aiken	Closed	325.00	750.00
87-10-003	Rachel, 19"	S. Stone Aiken	Closed	375.00	825.00
88-10-004	Cassie, 19"	S. Stone Aiken	Closed	500.00	700.00
Gorham		**Valentine Ladies**			
87-11-001	Jane	P. Valentine	Closed	145.00	350-400.
87-11-002	Lee Ann	P. Valentine	Closed	145.00	325.00
87-11-003	Elizabeth	P. Valentine	Closed	145.00	450.00
87-11-004	Rebecca	P. Valentine	Closed	145.00	325.00
87-11-005	Patrice	P. Valentine	Closed	145.00	325.00
87-11-006	Anabella	P. Valentine	Closed	145.00	395-425.
87-11-007	Sylvia	P. Valentine	Closed	160.00	350.00
87-11-008	Rosanne	P. Valentine	Closed	145.00	325.00
87-11-009	Marianna	P. Valentine	Closed	160.00	400.00
88-11-010	Maria Theresa	P. Valentine	Closed	225.00	350.00
88-11-011	Priscilla	P. Valentine	Closed	195.00	325.00
88-11-012	Judith Anne	P. Valentine	Closed	195.00	325.00
88-11-013	Felicia	P. Valentine	Closed	225.00	395.00
89-11-014	Julianna	P. Valentine	Closed	225.00	275-325.
89-11-015	Rose	P. Valentine	Closed	225.00	275-325.
Gorham		**Precious as Pearls**			
86-12-001	Colette	S. Stone Aiken	Closed	400.00	1500-1650.
87-12-002	Charlotte	S. Stone Aiken	Closed	425.00	795-895.
88-12-003	Chloe	S. Stone Aiken	Closed	525.00	925.00
89-12-004	Cassandra	S. Stone Aiken	Closed	525.00	1300-1500.
XX-12-005	Set	S. Stone Aiken	Closed	1875.00	4200.00
Gorham		**Gorham Baby Doll Collection**			
87-13-001	Christening Day	Aiken/Matthews	Closed	245.00	295.00
87-13-002	Leslie	Aiken/Matthews	Closed	245.00	325.00
87-13-003	Matthew	Aiken/Matthews	Closed	245.00	285.00

DOLLS

Company / Number	Name	Series / Artist	Edition Limit	Issue Price	Quote
Gorham		**Beverly Port Designer Collection**			
87-14-001	Silver Bell 17"	B. Port	Closed	175.00	295.00
87-14-002	Kristobear Kringle 17"	B. Port	Closed	200.00	325.00
87-14-003	Tedwina Kimelina Bearkin 10"	B. Port	Closed	95.00	150.00
87-14-004	Christopher Paul Bearkin 10"	B. Port	Closed	95.00	150.00
87-14-005	Molly Melinda Bearkin 10"	B. Port	Closed	95.00	150.00
87-14-006	Tedward Jonathan Bearkin 10"	B. Port	Closed	95.00	150.00
88-14-007	Baery Mab 9-1/2"	B. Port	Closed	110.00	150.00
88-14-008	Miss Emily 18"	B. Port	Closed	350.00	450.00
88-14-009	T.R. 28-1/2"	B. Port	Closed	400.00	600.00
88-14-010	The Amazing Calliope Merriweather 17"	B. Port	Closed	275.00	425.00
88-14-011	Hollybeary Kringle 15"	B. Port	Closed	350.00	395.00
88-14-012	Theodore B. Bear 14"	B. Port	Closed	175.00	195.00
Gorham		**Bonnets & Bows**			
88-15-001	Belinda	B. Gerardi	Closed	195.00	450.00
88-15-002	Annemarie	B. Gerardi	Closed	195.00	450.00
88-15-003	Allessandra	B. Gerardi	Closed	195.00	395-550.
88-15-004	Lisette	B. Gerardi	Closed	285.00	495-550.
88-15-005	Bettina	B. Gerardi	Closed	285.00	495-550.
88-15-006	Ellie	B. Gerardi	Closed	285.00	495-550.
88-15-007	Alicia	B. Gerardi	Closed	385.00	800-975.
88-15-008	Bethany	B. Gerardi	Closed	385.00	1350-1500.
88-15-009	Jesse	B. Gerardi	Closed	525.00	800-850.
88-15-010	Francie	B. Gerardi	Closed	625.00	895-975.
Gorham		**Small Wonders**			
88-16-001	Patina	B. Gerardi	Closed	265.00	265.00
88-16-002	Madeline	B. Gerardi	Closed	365.00	365.00
88-16-003	Marguerite	B. Gerardi	Closed	425.00	425.00
Gorham		**Joyful Years**			
89-17-001	William	B. Gerardi	Closed	295.00	375.00
89-17-002	Katrina	B. Gerardi	Closed	295.00	375.00
Gorham		**Victorian Cameo Collection**			
90-18-001	Victoria	B. Gerardi	1,500	375.00	375.00
91-18-002	Alexandra	B. Gerardi	Closed	375.00	375.00
Gorham		**Children Of Christmas**			
89-19-001	Clara, 16"	S. Stone Aiken	Closed	325.00	675-850.
90-19-002	Natalie, 16"	S. Stone Aiken	1,500	350.00	395-450.
91-19-003	Emily	S. Stone Aiken	1,500	375.00	375-475.
92-19-004	Virginia	S. Stone Aiken	1,500	375.00	375-475.
Gorham		**Les Belles Bebes Collection**			
91-20-001	Cherie	S. Stone Aiken	Closed	375.00	500-600.
91-20-002	Desiree	S. Stone Aiken	1,500	375.00	375-475.
93-20-003	Camille	S. Stone Aiken	1,500	375.00	375-475.
Gorham		**Childhood Memories**			
91-21-001	Amanda	D. Valenza	Closed	98.00	98-150.00
91-21-002	Kimberly	D. Valenza	Closed	98.00	98-150.00
91-21-003	Jessica Anne's Playtime	D. Valenza	Closed	98.00	98-150.00
91-21-004	Jennifer	D. Valenza	Closed	98.00	98-150.00
Gorham		**Gifts of the Garden**			
91-22-001	Priscilla	S. Stone Aiken	Closed	125.00	200.00
91-22-002	Lauren	S. Stone Aiken	Closed	125.00	200.00
91-22-003	Irene	S. Stone Aiken	Closed	125.00	200.00
91-22-004	Valerie	S. Stone Aiken	Closed	125.00	200.00
91-22-005	Deborah	S. Stone Aiken	Closed	125.00	200.00
91-22-006	Alisa	S. Stone Aiken	Closed	125.00	200.00
91-22-007	Maria	S. Stone Aiken	Closed	125.00	200.00
91-22-008	Joelle (Christmas)	S. Stone Aiken	Closed	150.00	200.00
91-22-009	Holly (Christmas)	S. Stone Aiken	Closed	150.00	200.00
Gorham		**Dolls of the Month**			
91-23-001	Miss January	Gorham	Closed	79.00	125.00
91-23-002	Miss February	Gorham	Closed	79.00	125.00
91-23-003	Miss March	Gorham	Closed	79.00	125.00
91-23-004	Miss April	Gorham	Closed	79.00	125.00
91-23-005	Miss May	Gorham	Closed	79.00	125.00
91-23-006	Miss June	Gorham	Closed	79.00	125.00
91-23-007	Miss July	Gorham	Closed	79.00	125.00
91-23-008	Miss August	Gorham	Closed	79.00	125.00
91-23-009	Miss September	Gorham	Closed	79.00	125.00
91-23-010	Miss October	Gorham	Closed	79.00	125.00
91-23-011	Miss November	Gorham	Closed	79.00	125.00
91-23-012	Miss December	Gorham	Closed	79.00	125.00
Gorham		**Legendary Heroines**			
91-24-001	Jane Eyre	S. Stone Aiken	1,500	245.00	245.00
91-24-002	Guinevere	S. Stone Aiken	1,500	245.00	245.00
91-24-003	Juliet	S. Stone Aiken	1,500	245.00	245.00
91-24-004	Lara	S. Stone Aiken	1,500	245.00	245.00
Gorham		**Gift of Dreams**			
91-25-001	Samantha	Young/Gerardi	Closed	495.00	495.00
91-25-002	Katherine	Young/Gerardi	Closed	495.00	495.00
91-25-003	Melissa	Young/Gerardi	Closed	495.00	495.00
91-25-004	Elizabeth	Young/Gerardi	Closed	495.00	495.00
91-25-005	Christina (Christmas)	Young/Gerardi	Closed	695.00	695.00
Gorham		**The Friendship Dolls**			
91-26-001	Peggy-The American Traveler	P. Seaman	Closed	98.00	98.00
91-26-002	Meagan-The Irish Traveler	L. O'Connor	Closed	98.00	98.00
91-26-003	Angela-The Italian Traveler	S. Nappo	Closed	98.00	98.00
91-26-004	Kinuko-The Japanese Traveler	S. Ueki	Closed	98.00	98.00
Gorham		**Special Moments**			
91-27-001	Baby's First Christmas	E. Worrell	Closed	135.00	135-275.
92-27-002	Baby's First Steps	E. Worrell	Closed	135.00	135-225.
Gorham		**Dollie And Me**			
91-28-001	Dollie's First Steps	J. Pilallis	Closed	160.00	160.00
Gorham		**The Victorian Collection**			
92-29-001	Victoria's Jubilee	E. Woodhouse	Yr.Iss.	295.00	295.00
Gorham		**Days Of The Week**			
92-30-001	Monday's Child	R./L. Schrubbe	Open	98.00	98.00
92-30-002	Tuesday's Child	R./L. Schrubbe	Open	98.00	98.00
92-30-003	Wednesday's Child	R./L. Schrubbe	Open	98.00	98.00
92-30-004	Thurday's Child	R./L. Schrubbe	Open	98.00	98.00
92-30-005	Friday's Child	R./L. Schrubbe	Open	98.00	98.00
92-30-006	Saturday's Child	R./L. Schrubbe	Open	98.00	98.00
92-30-007	Sunday's Child	R./L. Schrubbe	Open	98.00	98.00
Gorham		**Times To Treasure**			
90-31-001	Storytime	L. Di Leo	Closed	195.00	195.00
91-31-002	Bedtime	L. Di Leo	Closed	195.00	195.00
93-31-003	Playtime	L. Di Leo	Closed	195.00	195.00
Gorham		**Victorian Children**			
92-32-001	Sara's Tea Time	S. Stone Aiken	1,000	495.00	495.00
93-32-002	Catching Butterflies	S. Stone Aiken	1,000	495.00	495.00
Gorham		**Bride Dolls**			
93-33-001	Susannah's Wedding Day	D. Valenza	9,500	295.00	295.00
Gorham		**Carousel Dolls**			
93-34-001	Ribbons And Roses	C. Shafer	Closed	119.00	119.00
Gorham		**Pillow Baby Dolls**			
93-35-001	Sitting Pretty	L. Gordon	Closed	39.00	39.00
93-35-002	Tickling Toes	L. Gordon	Open	39.00	39.00
93-35-003	On the Move	L. Gordon	Open	39.00	39.00
Gorham		**Victorian Flower Girls**			
93-36-001	Rose	J. Pillalis	Open	95.00	95.00
Gorham		**Celebrations Of Childhood**			
92-37-001	Happy Birthday Amy	L. Di Leo	Closed	160.00	160.00
Gorham		**Littlest Angel Dolls**			
92-38-001	Merriel	L. Di Leo	Closed	49.50	49.50
Gorham		**Puppy Love Dolls**			
92-39-001	Katie And Kyle	R./ L. Schrubbe	Open	119.00	119.00
Gorham		**Daydreamer Dolls**			
92-40-001	Heather's Daydream	S. Stone Aiken	Closed	119.00	119.00
Gorham		**Bonnet Babies**			
93-41-001	Chelsea's Bonnet	M. Sirko	Open	95.00	95.00
Gorham		**Imaginary People**			
93-42-001	Melinda, The Tooth Fairy	R. Tonner	2,900	95.00	95.00
Gorham		**International Babies**			
93-43-001	Natalia's Matrioshka	R. Tonner	Open	95.00	95.00
Gorham		**Nature's Bounty**			
93-44-001	Jamie's Fruitful Harvest	R. Tonner	Open	95.00	95.00
Gorham		**Portrait Perfect Victorian Dolls**			
93-45-001	Pretty in Peach	R. Tonner	2,900	119.00	119.00
Gorham		**Sporting Kids**			
93-46-001	Up At Bat	R. Schrubbe	Open	49.50	49.50
Gorham		**Tender Hearts**			
93-47-001	Saying Grace	M. Murphy	Open	119.00	119.00
Gorham		**Christmas Traditions**			
93-48-001	Trimming the Tree	S. Stone Aiken	2,500	295.00	295.00
Gorham		**Christmas Treasures**			
93-49-001	Chrissy	S. Stone Aiken	Open	150.00	150.00
H & G Studios, Inc.		**Brenda Burke Dolls**			
89-01-001	Arabelle	B. Burke	500	695.00	1400.00
89-01-002	Angelica	B. Burke	50	1495.00	3000.00
89-01-003	Adelaine	B. Burke	25	1795.00	3600.00
89-01-004	Amanda	B. Burke	25	1995.00	6000.00
89-01-005	Alicia	B. Burke	125	895.00	1800.00
89-01-006	Alexandra	B. Burke	125	995.00	2000.00
89-01-007	Bethany	B. Burke	45	2995.00	2995.00
89-01-008	Beatrice	B. Burke	85	2395.00	2395.00
89-01-009	Brittany	B. Burke	75	2695.00	2695.00
90-01-010	Belinda	B. Burke	12	3695.00	3695.00
91-01-011	Tender Love	B. Burke	25	3295.00	3295.00
91-01-012	Sleigh Ride	B. Burke	20	3695.00	3695.00
91-01-013	Charlotte	B. Burke	20	2395.00	2395.00
91-01-014	Clarissa	B. Burke	15	3595.00	3595.00
92-01-015	Dorothea	B. Burke	500	395.00	395.00
93-01-016	Melissa	B. Burke	1	7750.00	7750.00
93-01-017	Giovanna	B. Burke	1	7800.00	7800.00
Hallmark Galleries		**Victorian Memories**			
92-01-001	Daisy -plush bear	J. Greene	2,500	85.00	85.00
92-01-002	Bear-plush bear	J. Greene	9,500	35.00	35.00
92-01-003	Abner	J. Greene	4,500	110.00	110.00
92-01-004	Seth-plush bear	J. Greene	9,500	40.00	40.00
92-01-005	Katherine	J. Greene	1,200	150.00	150.00
92-01-006	Abigail	J. Greene	4,500	125.00	125.00
92-01-007	Olivia	J. Greene	4,500	125.00	125.00
92-01-008	Teddy -plush bear	J. Greene	9,500	45.00	45.00
92-01-009	Alice	J. Greene	4,500	125.00	125.00
92-01-010	Bunny B-plush rabbit	J. Greene	9,500	35.00	35.00
92-01-011	Emma/miniature doll	J. Greene	9,500	25.00	25.00
93-01-012	Hannah	J. Greene	2,500	130.00	130.00
93-01-013	Baby Doll Beatrice	J. Greene	9,500	20.00	20.00
94-01-014	Plush Teddy Boy Walter 7500QHG1033	J. Greene	4,500	75.00	75.00
94-01-015	Mini Boy Doll Thomas 2800QHG1035	J. Greene	9,500	28.00	28.00
94-01-016	Mini Jointed Bear Jesse 1200QHG1038	J. Greene	9,500	12.00	12.00
Hamilton Collection		**Songs of the Seasons Hakata Doll Collection**			
85-01-001	Winter Song Maiden	T. Murakami	9,800	75.00	75.00
85-01-002	Spring Song Maiden	T. Murakami	9,800	75.00	75.00
85-01-003	Summer Song Maiden	T. Murakami	9,800	75.00	75.00
85-01-004	Autumn Song Maiden	T. Murakami	9,800	75.00	75.00
Hamilton Collection		**Dolls of America's Colonial Heritage**			
86-02-001	Katrina	A. Elekfy	Open	55.00	55.00
86-02-002	Nicole	A. Elekfy	Open	55.00	55.00
87-02-003	Maria	A. Elekfy	Open	55.00	55.00

DOLLS

Number	Name	Artist	Edition Limit	Issue Price	Quote
Company		**Series**			
87-02-004	Priscilla	A. Elekfy	Open	55.00	55.00
87-02-005	Colleen	A. Elekfy	Open	55.00	55.00
88-02-006	Gretchen	A. Elekfy	Open	55.00	55.00
Hamilton Collection		**Star Trek Doll Collection**			
88-03-001	Mr. Spock	E. Daub	Closed	75.00	150.00
88-03-002	Captain Kirk	E. Daub	Closed	75.00	175.00
89-03-003	Dr. Mc Coy	E. Daub	Closed	75.00	200.00
89-03-004	Scotty	E. Daub	Closed	75.00	150.00
90-03-005	Sulu	E. Daub	Closed	75.00	150.00
90-03-006	Chekov	E. Daub	Closed	75.00	150.00
91-03-007	Uhura	E. Daub	Closed	75.00	150.00
Hamilton Collection		**The Antique Doll Collection**			
89-04-001	Nicole	Unknown	Closed	195.00	425.00
90-04-002	Colette	Unknown	Open	195.00	195.00
91-04-003	Lisette	Unknown	Open	195.00	195.00
91-04-004	Katrina	Unknown	Open	195.00	195.00
Hamilton Collection		**The Bessie Pease Gutmann Doll Collection**			
89-05-001	Love is Blind	B.P. Gutmann	Closed	135.00	135-225.
89-05-002	He Won't Bite	B.P. Gutmann	Closed	135.00	135.00
91-05-003	Virginia	B.P. Gutmann	Open	135.00	135.00
91-05-004	First Dancing Lesson	B.P. Gutmann	Open	195.00	195.00
91-05-005	Good Morning	B.P. Gutmann	Open	195.00	195.00
91-05-006	Love At First Sight	B.P. Gutmann	Open	195.00	195.00
Hamilton Collection		**The Maud Humphrey Bogart Doll Collection**			
89-06-001	Playing Bride	M.H. Bogart	Closed	135.00	135-175.
90-06-002	First Party	M.H. Bogart	Closed	135.00	135.00
90-06-003	The First Lesson	M.H. Bogart	Closed	135.00	149.00
91-06-004	Seamstress	M.H. Bogart	Closed	135.00	149.00
91-06-005	Little Captive	M.H. Bogart	Open	135.00	135.00
92-06-006	Kitty's Bath	M.H. Bogart	Open	135.00	135.00
Hamilton Collection		**Connie Walser Derek Baby Doll**			
90-07-001	Jessica	C.W. Derek	Closed	155.00	300-350.
91-07-002	Sara	C.W. Derek	Closed	155.00	155-225.
91-07-003	Andrew	C.W. Derek	Open	155.00	155.00
91-07-004	Amanda	C.W. Derek	Open	155.00	155.00
92-07-005	Samantha	C.W. Derek	Open	155.00	155.00
Hamilton Collection		**I Love Lucy (Vinyl)**			
88-08-001	Ethel	Unknown	Closed	40.00	210.00
88-08-002	Fred	Unknown	Closed	40.00	139.00
90-08-003	Lucy	Unknown	Closed	40.00	135.00
91-08-004	Ricky	Unknown	Closed	40.00	135-210.
92-08-005	Queen of the Gypsies	Unknown	Open	40.00	40.00
92-08-006	Vitameatavegamin	Unknown	Open	40.00	40.00
Hamilton Collection		**I Love Lucy (Porcelain)**			
90-08-001	Lucy	Unknown	Closed	95.00	195-250.
91-08-002	Ricky	Unknown	Closed	95.00	350.00
92-08-003	Queen of the Gypsies	Unknown	Closed	95.00	195.00
92-08-004	Vitameatavegamin	Unknown	Closed	95.00	195.00
Hamilton Collection		**Russian Czarra Dolls**			
91-09-001	Alexandra	Unknown	Closed	295.00	350.00
Hamilton Collection		**Storyboook Dolls**			
91-10-001	Alice in Wonderland	L. Di Leo	Open	75.00	75.00
Hamilton Collection		**International Children**			
91-11-001	Miko	C. Woodie	Closed	49.50	80.00
91-11-002	Anastasia	C. Woodie	Open	49.50	49.50
91-11-003	Angelina	C. Woodie	Open	49.50	49.50
92-11-004	Lian	C. Woodie	Open	49.50	49.50
92-11-005	Monique	C. Woodie	Open	49.50	49.50
92-11-006	Lisa	C. Woodie	Open	49.50	49.50
Hamilton Collection		**Central Park Skaters**			
91-12-001	Central Park Skaters	Unknown	Open	245.00	245.00
Hamilton Collection		**Jane Zidjunas Toddler Dolls**			
91-13-001	Jennifer	J. Zidjunas	Open	135.00	135.00
91-13-002	Megan	J. Zidjunas	Open	135.00	135.00
92-13-003	Kimberly	J. Zidjunas	Open	135.00	135.00
92-13-004	Amy	J. Zidjunas	Open	135.00	135.00
Hamilton Collection		**Jane Zidjunas Party Dolls**			
91-14-001	Kelly	J. Zidjunas	Open	135.00	135.00
92-14-002	Katie	J. Zidjunas	Open	135.00	135.00
93-14-003	Meredith	J. Zidjunas	Open	135.00	135.00
Hamilton Collection		**The Royal Beauty Dolls**			
91-15-001	Chen Mai	Unknown	Open	195.00	195.00
Hamilton Collection		**Abbie Williams Doll Collection**			
92-16-001	Molly	A. Williams	Closed	155.00	200.00
Hamilton Collection		**Zolan Dolls**			
91-17-001	A Christmas Prayer	D. Zolan	Open	95.00	95.00
92-17-002	Winter Angel	D. Zolan	Open	95.00	95.00
92-17-003	Rainy Day Pals	D. Zolan	Open	95.00	95.00
92-17-004	Quiet Time	D. Zolan	Open	95.00	95.00
93-17-005	For You	D. Zolan	Open	95.00	95.00
93-17-006	The Thinker	D. Zolan	Open	95.00	95.00
Hamilton Collection		**Baby Portrait Dolls**			
91-18-001	Melissa	B. Parker	Open	135.00	135.00
92-18-002	Jenna	B. Parker	Open	135.00	135.00
92-18-003	Bethany	B. Parker	Open	135.00	135.00
93-18-004	Mindy	B. Parker	Open	135.00	135.00
Hamilton Collection		**Helen Kish Dolls**			
91-19-001	Ashley	H. Kish	Closed	135.00	150-200.
92-19-002	Elizabeth	H. Kish	Closed	135.00	135.00
92-19-003	Hannah	H. Kish	Open	135.00	135.00
93-19-004	Margaret	H. Kish	Open	135.00	135.00
Hamilton Collection		**Picnic In The Park**			
91-20-001	Rebecca	J. Esteban	Open	155.00	155.00
92-20-002	Emily	J. Esteban	Open	155.00	155.00
92-20-003	Victoria	J. Esteban	Open	155.00	155.00
93-20-004	Benjamin	J. Esteban	Open	155.00	155.00
Hamilton Collection		**Bride Dolls**			
91-21-001	Portrait of Innocence	Unknown	Open	195.00	225.00
92-21-002	Portrait of Loveliness	Unknown	Open	195.00	225.00
Hamilton Collection		**Maud Humphrey Bogart Dolls**			
92-22-001	Playing Bridesmaid	Unknown	Closed	195.00	225.00
Hamilton Collection		**Year Round Fun**			
92-23-001	Allison	D. Schurig	Open	95.00	95.00
93-23-002	Christy	D. Schurig	Open	95.00	95.00
93-23-003	Paula	D. Schurig	Open	95.00	95.00
Hamilton Collection		**Laura Cobabe Dolls**			
92-24-001	Amber	L. Cobabe	Open	195.00	195.00
92-24-002	Brooke	L. Cobabe	Open	195.00	195.00
Hamilton Collection		**Belles of the Countryside**			
92-25-001	Erin	C. Heath Orange	Open	135.00	135.00
92-25-002	Rose	C. Heath Orange	Open	135.00	135.00
93-25-003	Lorna	C. Heath Orange	Open	135.00	135.00
Hamilton Collection		**Dolls By Kay McKee**			
92-26-001	Shy Violet	K. McKee	Open	135.00	135.00
92-26-002	Robin	K. McKee	Open	135.00	135.00
93-26-003	Katie Did It!	K. McKee	Open	135.00	135.00
93-26-004	Ryan	K. McKee	Open	135.00	135.00
Hamilton Collection		**Parker-Levi Toddlers**			
92-27-001	Courtney	B. Parker	Open	135.00	135.00
92-27-002	Melody	B. Parker	Open	135.00	135.00
Hamilton Collection		**Parkins Treasures**			
92-28-001	Tiffany	P. Parkins	Closed	55.00	55-79.00
92-28-002	Dorothy	P. Parkins	Closed	55.00	55-69.00
93-28-003	Charlotte	P. Parkins	Open	55.00	55.00
93-28-004	Cynthia	P. Parkins	Open	55.00	55.00
Hamilton Collection		**I'm So Proud Doll Collection**			
92-29-001	Christina	L. Cobabe	Open	95.00	95.00
93-29-002	Jill	L. Cobabe	Open	95.00	95.00
Hamilton Collection		**Through The Eyes of Virginia Turner**			
92-30-001	Michelle	V. Turner	Open	95.00	95.00
92-30-002	Danielle	V. Turner	Open	95.00	95.00
93-30-003	Wendy	V. Turner	Open	95.00	95.00
Hamilton Collection		**Santa's Little Helpers**			
92-31-001	Nicholas	C.W. Derek	Open	155.00	155.00
93-31-002	Hope	C.W. Derek	Open	155.00	155.00
Hamilton Collection		**Victorian Treasures**			
92-32-001	Katherine	C.W. Derek	Open	155.00	155.00
93-32-002	Madeline	C.W. Derek	Open	155.00	155.00
Hamilton Collection		**Daddy's Little Girls**			
92-33-001	Lindsay	M. Snyder	Open	95.00	95.00
93-33-002	Cassie	M. Snyder	Open	95.00	95.00
93-33-003	Dana	M. Snyder	Open	95.00	95.00
Hamilton Collection		**Proud Indian Nation**			
92-34-001	Navajo Little One	N/A	Open	95.00	95.00
93-34-002	Dressed Up For The Pow Wow	N/A	Open	95.00	95.00
93-34-003	Autumn Treat	N/A	Open	95.00	95.00
Hamilton Collection		**Holiday Carollers**			
92-35-001	Joy	U. Lepp	Open	155.00	155.00
93-35-002	Noel	U. Lepp	Open	155.00	155.00
Hamilton Collection		**Joke Grobben Dolls**			
92-36-001	Heather	J. Grobben	Open	69.00	69.00
93-36-002	Kathleen	U. Lepp	Open	95.00	95.00
93-36-003	Brianna	U. Lepp	Open	95.00	95.00
Hamilton Collection		**Treasured Toddlers**			
92-37-001	Whitney	V. Turner	Open	95.00	95.00
93-37-002	Natalie	V. Turner	Open	95.00	95.00
Hamilton Collection		**Children To Cherish**			
91-38-001	A GIft of Innocence	N/A	Yr.Iss.	135.00	135.00
91-38-002	A GIft of Beauty	N/A	Open	135.00	135.00
Hamilton Collection		**Wooden Dolls**			
91-39-001	Gretchen	N/A	9,850	225.00	225-250.
91-39-002	Heidi	N/A	9,850	225.00	225.00
Hamilton Collection		**Little Rascals™**			
92-40-001	Spanky	S./J. Hoffman	Open	75.00	75.00
93-40-002	Alfalfa	S./J. Hoffman	Open	75.00	75.00
Hamilton Collection		**Littlest Members of the Wedding**			
93-41-001	Matthew & Melanie	J. Esteban	Open	195.00	195.00
Hamilton Collection		**Toddler Days Doll Collection**			
92-42-001	Erica	D. Schurig	Open	95.00	95.00
93-42-002	Darlene	D. Schrig	Open	95.00	95.00
Hamilton Collection		**Cindy Marschner Dolls**			
93-43-001	Shannon	C. Marscher	Open	95.00	95.00
93-43-002	Julie	C. Marscher	Open	95.00	95.00
93-43-003	Kayla	C. Marscher	Open	95.00	95.00
Hamilton Collection		**Dolls by Autumn Berwick**			
93-44-001	Laura	A. Berwick	Open	135.00	135.00
Hamilton Collection		**Laura Cobabe Dolls II**			
93-45-001	Kristen	L. Cobabe	Open	75.00	75.00
Hamilton Collection		**Brooks Wooden Dolls**			
93-46-001	Waiting For Santa	P. Ryan Brooks	Open	135.00	135.00
93-46-002	Are You the Easter Bunny?	P. Ryan Brooks	15,000	135.00	135.00

Number	Name	Artist	Edition Limit	Issue Price	Quote
Company		**Series**			
Hamilton Collection		**Zolan Double Dolls**			
93-47-001	First Kiss	N/A	Open	135.00	135.00
Hamilton Collection		**Parkins Portraits**			
93-48-001	Lauren	P. Parkins	Open	79.00	79.00
93-48-002	Kelsey	P. Parkins	Open	79.00	79.00
Hamilton Collection		**First Recital**			
93-49-001	Hillary	N/A	Open	135.00	135.00
Hamilton Collection		**Join The Parade**			
92-50-001	Betsy	N/A	Open	55.00	55.00
Hamilton Collection		**Catherine Mather Dolls**			
93-51-001	Justine	C. Mather	15,000	195.00	195.00
Hamilton Collection		**Phyllis Parkins Dolls**			
92-52-001	Swan Princess	P. Parkins	9,850	195.00	195.00
Hamilton Collection		**Annual Connossieur Doll**			
92-53-001	Lara	N/A	7,450	295.00	295-495.
Hamilton Collection		**A Child's Menagerie**			
93-54-001	Becky	B. Van Boxel	Open	69.00	69.00
93-54-002	Carrie	B. Van Boxel	Open	69.00	69.00
Hamilton Collection		**Connie Walser Derek Dolls**			
92-55-001	Baby Jessica	C. W. Derek	Open	75.00	75.00
93-55-002	Baby Sara	C. W. Derek	Open	75.00	75.00
Hamilton Collection		**Connie Walser Derek Baby Dolls II**			
92-56-001	Stephanie	C.W. Derek	Open	95.00	95.00
92-56-002	Beth	C.W. Derek	Open	95.00	95.00
Hamilton Collection		**Kay McKee Klowns**			
93-57-001	The Dreamer	K. McKee	15,000	155.00	155.00
Hamilton Collection		**Sandra Kuck Dolls**			
93-58-001	A Kiss Goodnight	S. Kuck	Open	79.00	79.00
Edna Hibel Studios		**Child's Fancy**			
85-01-001	Jennie's Lady Jennifer	E. Hibel	Closed	395.00	2000.00
87-01-002	Wendy's Lady Gwenolyn	E. Hibel	Closed	495.00	900.00
88-01-003	Sami's Lady Samantha	E. Hibel	Closed	495.00	625.00
89-01-004	Sassee's Lady Sarah	E. Hibel	Closed	495.00	635.00
Edna Hibel Studios		**Grandma's Attic**			
87-02-001	Alice	E. Hibel	Closed	129.00	375.00
88-02-002	Martha	E. Hibel	Closed	139.00	400.00
89-02-003	Melanie	E. Hibel	Closed	139.00	180.00
91-02-004	Katie	E. Hibel	Closed	139.00	145.00
Annette Himstedt: see Timeless Creations					
Ladie and Friends™		**The Family and Friends of Lizzie High®**			
85-01-001	Lizzie High®-1100	B.K. Wisber	Open	30.00	37.00
85-01-002	Sabina Valentine (First Edition)-1101	B.K. Wisber	Closed	30.00	48.00
88-01-003	Sabina Valentine (Second Edition)-1101	B.K. Wisber	Open	40.00	42.00
85-01-004	Nettie Brown (First Edition)-1102	B.K. Wisber	Closed	30.00	43.00
88-01-005	Nettie Brown (Second Edition)-1102	B.K. Wisber	Open	36.00	38.00
85-01-006	Emma High-1103	B.K. Wisber	Closed	30.00	42.00
85-01-007	Rebecca Bowman (First Edition)-1104	B.K. Wisber	Closed	30.00	42.00
89-01-008	Rebecca Bowman (Second Edition)-1104	B.K. Wisber	Open	56.00	59.00
85-01-009	Mary Valentine-1105	B.K. Wisber	Closed	30.00	42.00
85-01-010	Wendel Bowman (First Edition)-1106	B.K. Wisber	Closed	30.00	42.00
92-01-011	Wendel Bowman (Second Edition)-1106	B.K. Wisber	Open	60.00	61.00
85-01-012	Russell Dunn-1107	B.K. Wisber	Closed	30.00	42.00
85-01-013	Luther Bowman (First Edition)-1108	B.K. Wisber	Closed	30.00	42.00
93-01-014	Luther Bowman (Second Edition)-1108	B.K. Wisber	Open	60.00	60.00
85-01-015	Elizabeth Sweetland (First Edition)-1109	B.K. Wisber	Closed	30.00	42.00
91-01-016	Elizabeth Sweetland (Second Edition)-1109	B.K. Wisber	Open	56.00	57.00
85-01-017	Christian Bowman-1110	B.K. Wisber	Closed	30.00	42.00
85-01-018	Amanda High (First Edition)-1111	B.K. Wisber	Closed	30.00	42.00
90-01-019	Amanda High (Second Edition)-1111	B.K. Wisber	Open	54.00	57.00
85-01-020	Louella Valentine-1112	B.K. Wisber	Closed	30.00	42.00
85-01-021	Peter Valentine-1113	B.K. Wisber	Closed	30.00	72.00
85-01-022	Nettie Brown (Christmas)-1114	B.K. Wisber	Closed	30.00	42.00
85-01-023	Cora High-1115	B.K. Wisber	Closed	30.00	42.00
85-01-024	Ida Valentine-1116	B.K. Wisber	Closed	30.00	42.00
85-01-025	Martin Bowman-1117	B.K. Wisber	Closed	30.00	43.00
85-01-026	Esther Dunn (First Edition)-1127	B.K. Wisber	Closed	45.00	60.00
91-01-027	Esther Dunn (SecondEdition)-1127	B.K. Wisber	Open	60.00	61.00
91-01-028	Cynthia High-1127A	B.K. Wisber	Open	60.00	61.00
85-01-029	Benjamin Bowman-1129	B.K. Wisber	Closed	30.00	40.00
85-01-030	Flossie High (First Edition)-1128	B.K. Wisber	Closed	45.00	62.00
89-01-031	Flossie High (Second Edition)-1128	B.K. Wisber	Open	54.00	56.00
85-01-032	Hannah Brown-1131	B.K. Wisber	Closed	45.00	60.00
85-01-033	Benjamin Bowman (Santa)-1134	B.K. Wisber	Open	34.00	40.00
85-01-034	Katrina Valentine-1135	B.K. Wisber	Closed	30.00	42.00
86-01-035	Grace Valentine (First Edition)-1146	B.K. Wisber	Closed	32.00	42.00
90-01-036	Grace Valentine (Second Edition)-1146	B.K. Wisber	Open	48.00	49.00
86-01-037	Juliet Valentine (First Edition)-1147	B.K. Wisber	Closed	32.00	42.00
90-01-038	Juliet Valentine (Second Edition)-1147	B.K. Wisber	Open	48.00	50.00
86-01-039	Alice Valentine-1148	B.K. Wisber	Closed	32.00	42.00
86-01-040	Susanna Bowman-1149	B.K. Wisber	Closed	45.00	58.00
86-01-041	Annie Bowman (First Edition)-1150	B.K. Wisber	Closed	32.00	42.00
93-01-042	Annie Bowman (Second Edition)-1150	B.K. Wisber	Open	68.00	68.00
86-01-043	Martha High-1151	B.K. Wisber	Closed	32.00	42.00
86-01-044	Dora High (First Edition)-1152	B.K. Wisber	Closed	30.00	41.00
92-01-045	Dora High (Second Edition)-1152	B.K. Wisber	Closed	48.00	48.00
86-01-046	Delia Valentine-1153	B.K. Wisber	Closed	32.00	42.00
86-01-047	Sara Valentine-1154	B.K. Wisber	Closed	32.00	38.00
86-01-048	Sally Bowman-1155	B.K. Wisber	Closed	32.00	42.00
86-01-049	Tillie Brown-1156	B.K. Wisber	Closed	32.00	42.00
86-01-050	Andrew Brown-1157	B.K. Wisber	Closed	45.00	58.00
86-01-051	Edward Bowman (First Edition)-1158	B.K. Wisber	Closed	45.00	58.00
94-01-052	Edward Bowman (Second Edition)-1158	B.K. Wisber	Open	76.00	76.00
86-01-053	Thomas Bowman-1159	B.K. Wisber	Closed	30.00	41.00
86-01-054	Maggie High-1160	B.K. Wisber	Closed	30.00	41.00
86-01-055	Karl Valentine-1161	B.K. Wisber	Closed	30.00	72.00
86-01-056	Willie Bowman-1162	B.K. Wisber	Closed	30.00	41.00
86-01-057	Sadie Valentine-1163	B.K. Wisber	Open	45.00	48.00
86-01-058	Sophie Valentine-1164	B.K. Wisber	Closed	45.00	58.00
86-01-059	Katie Bowman-1178	B.K. Wisber	Closed	36.00	39.00

Number	Name	Artist	Edition Limit	Issue Price	Quote
Company		**Series**			
86-01-060	Cassie Yocum (First Edition)-1179	B.K. Wisber	Closed	36.00	42.00
92-01-061	Cassie Yocum (Second Edition)-1179	B.K. Wisber	Open	80.00	80.00
86-01-062	Jillian Bowman-1180	B.K. Wisber	Closed	34.00	42.00
86-01-063	Jenny Valentine-1181	B.K. Wisber	Closed	34.00	42.00
86-01-064	Christopher High-1182	B.K. Wisber	Closed	34.00	42.00
86-01-065	Marland Valentine-1183	B.K. Wisber	Closed	33.00	100.00
86-01-066	Marie Valentine (First Edition)-1184	B.K. Wisber	Closed	47.00	58.00
92-01-067	Marie Valentine (Second Edition)-1184	B.K. Wisber	Open	68.00	69.00
86-01-068	Emily Bowman (First Edition)-1185	B.K. Wisber	Closed	34.00	34.00
90-01-069	Emily Bowman (Second Edition)-1185	B.K. Wisber	Open	48.00	49.00
86-01-070	Matthew Yocum-1186	B.K. Wisber	Closed	33.00	42.00
86-01-071	Madaleine Valentine (First Edition)-1187	B.K. Wisber	Closed	34.00	42.00
89-01-072	Madaleine Valentine (Second Edition)-1187	B.K. Wisber	Open	37.00	80.00
86-01-073	Rachel Bowman (First Edition)-1188	B.K. Wisber	Closed	34.00	42.00
89-01-074	Rachel Bowman (Second Edition)-1188	B.K. Wisber	Open	34.00	37.00
86-01-075	Molly Yocum (First Edition)-1189	B.K. Wisber	Closed	34.00	43.00
89-01-076	Molly Yocum(Second Edition)-1189	B.K. Wisber	Open	39.00	41.00
86-01-077	Carrie High (First Edition)-1190	B.K. Wisber	Closed	45.00	43.00
89-01-078	Carrie High (Second Edition)-1190	B.K. Wisber	Open	46.00	72.00
86-01-079	William Valentine-1191	B.K. Wisber	Closed	36.00	80.00
86-01-080	Jeremy Bowman-1192	B.K. Wisber	Closed	36.00	44.00
86-01-081	Marisa Valentine (w/ Brother Petey)-1194	B.K. Wisber	Open	45.00	49.00
86-01-082	Marisa Valentine (alone)-1194A	B.K. Wisber	Open	33.00	38.00
86-01-083	David Yocum-1195	B.K. Wisber	Open	33.00	36.00
86-01-084	Little Ghosts-1197	B.K. Wisber	Open	15.00	18.00
87-01-085	Johanna Valentine-1198	B.K. Wisber	Closed	37.00	42.00
87-01-086	Abigail Bowman-1199	B.K. Wisber	Closed	40.00	45.00
87-01-087	Naomi Valentine-1200	B.K. Wisber	Closed	40.00	44.00
87-01-088	Amy Bowman-1201	B.K. Wisber	Closed	37.00	41.00
87-01-089	Addie High-1202	B.K. Wisber	Open	37.00	41.00
87-01-090	The Wedding (Bride)-1203	B.K. Wisber	Open	37.00	40.00
87-01-091	The Wedding (Groom)-1203A	B.K. Wisber	Open	34.00	36.00
87-01-092	The Flower Girl-1204	B.K. Wisber	Open	17.00	23.00
87-01-093	Olivia High-1205	B.K. Wisber	Open	37.00	41.00
87-01-094	Imogene Bowman-1206	B.K. Wisber	Closed	37.00	40.00
87-01-095	Rebecca's Mother-1207	B.K. Wisber	Open	37.00	42.00
87-01-096	Penelope High-1208	B.K. Wisber	Closed	40.00	49.00
87-01-097	Margaret Bowman-1213	B.K. Wisber	Open	35.00	41.00
87-01-098	Patsy Bowman-1214	B.K. Wisber	Open	50.00	52.00
87-01-099	Ramona Brown-1215	B.K. Wisber	Closed	40.00	50.00
87-01-100	Gretchen High-1216	B.K. Wisber	Open	40.00	44.00
87-01-101	Cat on Chair-1217	B.K. Wisber	Closed	16.00	20.00
87-01-102	Katie and Barney-1219	B.K. Wisber	Open	38.00	41.00
87-01-103	Melanie Bowman (First Edition)-1220	B.K. Wisber	Closed	36.00	36.00
92-01-104	Melanie Bowman (Second Edition)-1220	B.K. Wisber	Open	46.00	47.00
87-01-105	Charles Bowman (First Edition)-1221	B.K. Wisber	Closed	34.00	42.00
92-01-106	Charles Bowman (Second Edition)-1221	B.K. Wisber	Open	46.00	47.00
87-01-107	Bridget Bowman-1222	B.K. Wisber	Closed	40.00	46.00
87-01-108	Laura Valentine-1223	B.K. Wisber	Open	36.00	39.00
87-01-109	Santa Claus (sitting)-1224	B.K. Wisber	Closed	50.00	61.00
87-01-110	Little Witch-1225	B.K. Wisber	Open	17.00	22.00
87-01-111	Priscilla High-1226	B.K. Wisber	Open	56.00	61.00
88-01-112	Megan Valentine-1227	B.K. Wisber	Closed	44.00	48.00
87-01-113	Pauline Bowman-1228	B.K. Wisber	Open	44.00	48.00
88-01-114	Allison Bowman-1229	B.K. Wisber	Open	56.00	59.00
88-01-115	Jacob High-1230	B.K. Wisber	Open	44.00	46.00
88-01-116	Janie Valentine-1231	B.K. Wisber	Open	37.00	41.00
88-01-117	Ruth Anne Bowman-1232	B.K. Wisber	Open	44.00	46.00
88-01-118	Daphne Bowman-1235	B.K. Wisber	Open	38.00	40.00
88-01-119	Mary Ellen Valentine-1236	B.K. Wisber	Open	40.00	43.00
88-01-120	Kinch Bowman-1237	B.K. Wisber	Open	47.00	49.00
88-01-121	Samantha Bowman-1238	B.K. Wisber	Open	47.00	49.00
88-01-122	Hattie Bowman-1239	B.K. Wisber	Open	40.00	44.00
88-01-123	Eunice High-1240	B.K. Wisber	Closed	56.00	58.00
88-01-124	Bess High-1241	B.K. Wisber	Open	45.00	48.00
88-01-125	Betsy Valentine-1245	B.K. Wisber	Open	42.00	43.00
88-01-126	Phoebe High-1246	B.K. Wisber	Closed	48.00	59.00
89-01-127	Vanessa High-1247	B.K. Wisber	Open	45.00	48.00
89-01-128	Amelia High-1248	B.K. Wisber	Open	45.00	48.00
89-01-129	Victoria Bowman-1249	B.K. Wisber	Open	40.00	42.00
89-01-130	Johann Bowman-1250	B.K. Wisber	Open	40.00	42.00
89-01-131	Emmy Lou Valentine-1251	B.K. Wisber	Open	45.00	47.00
89-01-132	Peggy Bowman-1252	B.K. Wisber	Open	58.00	60.00
89-01-133	Jessica High (with Mother)-1253	B.K. Wisber	Open	58.00	60.00
89-01-134	Jessica High (alone)-1253A	B.K. Wisber	Open	20.00	23.00
89-01-135	Jason High (with Mother)-1254	B.K. Wisber	Open	58.00	60.00
89-01-136	Jason High (alone)-1254A	B.K. Wisber	Open	20.00	23.00
89-01-137	Lucy Bowman-1255	B.K. Wisber	Open	45.00	47.00
89-01-138	Miriam High-1256	B.K. Wisber	Open	46.00	48.00
89-01-139	Santa (with Tub)-1257	B.K. Wisber	Open	58.00	61.00
89-01-140	Mrs. Claus-1258	B.K. Wisber	Open	42.00	44.00
90-01-141	Marlene Valentine-1259	B.K. Wisber	Open	48.00	50.00
90-01-142	Albert Valentine-1260	B.K. Wisber	Open	42.00	44.00
90-01-143	Nancy Bowman-1261	B.K. Wisber	Open	48.00	50.00
91-01-144	Annabelle Bowman-1267	B.K. Wisber	Open	68.00	69.00
91-01-145	Michael Bowman-1268	B.K. Wisber	Open	52.00	53.00
91-01-146	Trudy Valentine-1269	B.K. Wisber	Open	64.00	65.00
91-01-147	The Department Store Santa-1270	B.K. Wisber	Open	76.00	77.00
91-01-148	Santa's Helper-1271	B.K. Wisber	Open	52.00	53.00
91-01-149	Barbara Helen-1274	B.K. Wisber	Open	58.00	59.00
92-01-150	Edwin Bowman-1281	B.K. Wisber	Open	70.00	71.00
92-01-151	Carol Anne Bowman-1282	B.K. Wisber	Open	70.00	71.00
92-01-152	Joseph Valentine-1283	B.K. Wisber	Open	62.00	63.00
92-01-153	Natalie Valentine-1284	B.K. Wisber	Open	62.00	63.00
92-01-154	Kathryn Bowman (Limited Edition)-1285	B.K. Wisber	3,000	140.00	140.00
92-01-155	Wendy Bowman-1293	B.K. Wisber	Open	78.00	79.00
93-01-156	Christmas Tree w/Cats-1293A	B.K. Wisber	Open	42.00	42.00
92-01-157	Timothy Bowman-1294	B.K. Wisber	Open	56.00	57.00
92-01-158	Joanie Valentine-1295	B.K. Wisber	Open	48.00	49.00
93-01-159	Justine Valentine-1302	B.K. Wisber	Open	84.00	84.00
93-01-160	Pearl Bowman-1303	B.K. Wisber	Open	56.00	56.00
92-01-161	Ashley Bowman-1304	B.K. Wisber	Open	48.00	48.00
92-01-162	Francis Bowman-1305	B.K. Wisber	Open	48.00	48.00
93-01-163	Penny Valentine-1308	B.K. Wisber	Open	60.00	60.00
93-01-164	Santa Claus-1311	B.K. Wisber	Open	48.00	48.00
93-01-165	Mommy-1312	B.K. Wisber	Open	48.00	48.00
94-01-166	Josie Valentine-1322	B.K. Wisber	Open	76.00	76.00
94-01-167	Bonnie Valentine-1323	B.K. Wisber	Open	35.00	35.00
94-01-168	Jamie Bowman-1324	B.K. Wisber	Open	35.00	35.00
94-01-169	Elsie Bowman-1325	B.K. Wisber	Open	64.00	64.00
Ladie and Friends™		**The Little Ones™**			
85-02-001	White Girl (First Edition)-1130	B.K. Wisber	Closed	15.00	26.00
85-02-002	Black Girl (First Edition)-1130	B.K. Wisber	Closed	15.00	26.00

Company Number	Name	Series Artist	Edition Limit	Issue Price	Quote
85-02-003	White Boy (First Edition)-1130	B.K. Wisber	Closed	15.00	26.00
85-02-004	Black Boy (First Edition)-1130	B.K. Wisber	Closed	15.00	26.00
89-02-005	White Girl-pastels (Second Edition)-1130D	B.K. Wisber	Closed	20.00	23.00
89-02-006	Black Girl-pastels (Second Edition)-1130E	B.K. Wisber	Closed	20.00	23.00
89-02-007	White Girl-country color (2nd Edition)-1130F	B.K. Wisber	Closed	20.00	23.00
89-02-008	Black Girl-country color(2nd Edition)-1130G	B.K. Wisber	Closed	20.00	23.00
89-02-009	White Boy (Second Edition)-1130H	B.K. Wisber	Closed	20.00	23.00
89-02-010	Black Boy (Second Edition)-1130I	B.K. Wisber	Closed	20.00	23.00
92-02-011	Little One w/Beach Bucket-1275	B.K. Wisber	Open	26.00	27.00
92-02-012	Little One w/Easter Eggs-1276	B.K. Wisber	Open	26.00	27.00
92-02-013	Little One wApples-1277	B.K. Wisber	Open	26.00	27.00
92-02-014	Little One w/Kitten and Yarn-1278	B.K. Wisber	Open	34.00	35.00
92-02-015	Little One w/Birthday Gift-1279	B.K. Wisber	Open	26.00	27.00
92-02-016	Little One w/Kitten and Milk-1280	B.K. Wisber	Open	32.00	33.00
92-02-017	Little One Reading-1286	B.K. Wisber	Open	36.00	37.00
92-02-018	Little One w/Christmas Lights-1287	B.K. Wisber	Open	34.00	35.00
92-02-019	Little One w/Snowman-1288	B.K. Wisber	Open	36.00	37.00
92-02-020	Little One w/Sled-1289	B.K. Wisber	Open	30.00	31.00
92-02-021	Little One Clown-1290	B.K. Wisber	Open	32.00	33.00
92-02-022	Little One w/Valentine-1291	B.K. Wisber	Open	30.00	31.00
92-02-023	Little One Girl w/Easter Flowers-1296	B.K. Wisber	Open	34.00	34.00
93-02-024	Little One Bunny-1297	B.K. Wisber	Open	36.00	36.00
93-02-025	Little One 4th of July Girl-1298	B.K. Wisber	Open	30.00	30.00
93-02-026	Little One w/Spinning Wheel-1299	B.K. Wisber	Open	36.00	36.00
93-02-027	Little One w/Mop-1300	B.K. Wisber	Open	36.00	36.00
92-02-028	Little One Boy w/Easter Flowers-1306	B.K. Wisber	Open	30.00	30.00
93-02-029	Little One 4th of July Boy-1307	B.K. Wisber	Open	28.00	28.00
93-02-030	Little One w/Violin-1319	B.K. Wisber	Open	28.00	28.00
93-02-031	Little One Picnicking-1320	B.K. Wisber	Open	34.00	34.00
93-02-032	Little One Ballerina-1321	B.K. Wisber	Open	40.00	40.00
94-02-033	Little One Girl Dying Eggs-1326	B.K. Wisber	Open	30.00	30.00
94-02-034	Little One Boy Dying Eggs-1327	B.K. Wisber	Open	30.00	30.00
94-02-035	Little One Nurse-1328	B.K. Wisber	Open	40.00	40.00
94-02-036	Little One Teacher-1329	B.K. Wisber	Open	38.00	38.00
Ladie and Friends™		**The Little Ones™ at Christmas**			
90-03-001	Little One w/Basket of Greens-1263	B.K. Wisber	Open	22.00	25.00
90-03-002	Little One w/Cookie-1264	B.K. Wisber	Open	22.00	25.00
90-03-003	Little One w/Tree Garland-1265	B.K. Wisber	Open	22.00	25.00
90-03-004	Little One w/Gift-1266	B.K. Wisber	Open	22.00	25.00
91-03-005	White Girl w/Santa Photo-1272	B.K. Wisber	Open	24.00	27.00
91-03-006	Black Girl w/Santa Photo-1272A	B.K. Wisber	Open	24.00	27.00
91-03-007	White Boy w/Santa Photo-1273	B.K. Wisber	Open	24.00	27.00
91-03-008	Black Boy w/Santa Photo-1273A	B.K. Wisber	Open	24.00	27.00
93-03-009	Boy Peeking w/Tree-1313	B.K. Wisber	Open	60.00	60.00
93-03-010	Boy Peeking (Alone)-1314	B.K. Wisber	Open	22.00	22.00
93-03-011	Girl Peeking w/Tree-1315	B.K. Wisber	Open	60.00	60.00
93-03-012	Girl Peeking (Alone)-1316	B.K. Wisber	Open	22.00	22.00
93-03-013	Little One with Baking Table-1317	B.K. Wisber	Open	38.00	38.00
93-03-014	Little One with Note for Santa-1318	B.K. Wisber	Open	36.00	36.00
Ladie and Friends™		**The Pawtuckets™ of Sweet Briar Lane**			
86-04-001	Aunt Minnie Pawtucket™ (First Edition)-1136	B.K. Wisber	Closed	45.00	60.00
93-04-002	Aunt Minnie Pawtucket™-1136 (Second Edition)	B.K. Wisber	Open	72.00	72.00
93-04-003	Flossie Pawtucket™-1136A	B.K. Wisber	Open	33.00	33.00
86-04-004	Grammy Pawtucket™ (First Edition)-1137	B.K. Wisber	Closed	32.00	40.00
94-04-005	Grammy Pawtucket™ (Second Edition)-1137	B.K. Wisber	Open	68.00	68.00
86-04-006	Uncle Harley Pawtucket™ (First Edition)-1138	B.K. Wisber	Closed	32.00	43.00
94-04-007	Uncle Harley Pawtucket™-1138 (Second Edition)	B.K. Wisber	Open	74.00	74.00
86-04-008	Sister Flora Pawtucket™-1139	B.K. Wisber	Closed	32.00	90.00
86-04-009	Brother Noah Pawtucket™-1140	B.K. Wisber	Closed	32.00	43.00
86-04-010	Aunt Lillian Pawtucket™ (First Edition)-1141	B.K. Wisber	Closed	32.00	43.00
94-04-011	Aunt Lillian Pawtucket™ -1141 (Second Edition)	B.K. Wisber	Open	58.00	58.00
94-04-013	Pawtucket™ Bunny Hutch-1141A	B.K. Wisber	Open	38.00	38.00
86-04-014	Mama Pawtucket™ (First Edition)-1142	B.K. Wisber	Closed	34.00	44.00
94-04-015	Mama Pawtucket™ (Second Edition)-1142	B.K. Wisber	Open	86.00	86.00
86-04-016	Pappy Pawtucket™-1143	B.K. Wisber	Closed	32.00	42.00
86-04-017	Cousin Clara Pawtucket™ (First Edition)-1144	B.K. Wisber	Closed	32.00	42.00
86-04-018	The Little One Bunnies-girl-1145 (First Edition)	B.K. Wisber	Closed	15.00	40.00
94-04-019	The Little One Bunnies-girl-1145 (Second Edition)	B.K. Wisber	Open	33.00	33.00
86-04-020	The Little One Bunnies-boy-1145 (First Edition)	B.K. Wisber	Closed	15.00	20.00
94-04-021	The Little One Bunnies-boy-1145A (Second Edition)	B.K. Wisber	Open	33.00	33.00
87-04-022	Cousin Isabel Pawtucket™-1209	B.K. Wisber	Closed	36.00	43.00
87-04-023	Cousin Alberta Pawtucket™-1210	B.K. Wisber	Closed	36.00	43.00
87-04-024	Sister Clemmie Pawtucket™-1211	B.K. Wisber	Closed	34.00	42.00
87-04-025	Aunt Mabel Pawtucket™-1212	B.K. Wisber	Closed	45.00	54.00
87-04-026	Bunny Bed-1218	B.K. Wisber	Closed	16.00	20.00
88-04-027	Cousin Winnie Pawtucket™-1233	B.K. Wisber	Closed	49.00	59.00
88-04-028	Cousin Jed Pawtucket™-1234	B.K. Wisber	Closed	34.00	42.00
Ladie and Friends™		**The Grummels™ of Log Hollow**			
86-05-001	Cousin Miranda Grummel™-1165	B.K. Wisber	Closed	47.00	60.00
86-05-002	Uncle Hollis Grummel™-1166	B.K. Wisber	Closed	34.00	42.00
86-05-003	Ma Grummel™-1167	B.K. Wisber	Closed	36.00	43.00
86-05-004	Teddy Bear Bed-1168	B.K. Wisber	Closed	15.00	18.00
86-05-005	Aunt Polly Grummel™-1169	B.K. Wisber	Closed	34.00	42.00
86-05-006	Cousin Lottie Grummel™-1170	B.K. Wisber	Closed	36.00	42.00
86-05-007	Aunt Gertie Grummel™-1171	B.K. Wisber	Closed	34.00	42.00
86-05-008	Pa Grummel™-1172	B.K. Wisber	Closed	34.00	42.00
86-05-009	Grandma Grummel™-1173	B.K. Wisber	Closed	45.00	45.00
86-05-010	Aunt Hilda Grummel™-1174	B.K. Wisber	Closed	34.00	42.00
86-05-011	Washline-1175	B.K. Wisber	Closed	15.00	20.00
86-05-012	Grandpa Grummel™-1176	B.K. Wisber	Closed	36.00	42.00
86-05-013	Sister Nora Grummel™-1177	B.K. Wisber	Closed	34.00	42.00
86-05-014	The Little Ones-Grummels™ (boy/girl)-1196	B.K. Wisber	Closed	15.00	20.00
Ladie and Friends™		**The Thanksgiving Play**			
88-06-001	Pilgrim Boy-1242	B.K. Wisber	Open	40.00	42.00
88-06-002	Pilgrim Girl-1243	B.K. Wisber	Open	48.00	50.00
88-06-003	Indian Squaw-1244	B.K. Wisber	Open	36.00	38.00
Ladie and Friends™		**The Christmas Pageant™**			
85-07-001	Mary and Baby Jesus-1118	B.K. Wisber	Open	30.00	37.00
85-07-002	Joseph and Donkey-1119	B.K. Wisber	Open	30.00	37.00
85-07-003	"Peace" Angel-1120	B.K. Wisber	Closed	30.00	42.00
85-07-004	"On" Angel-1121	B.K. Wisber	Closed	30.00	42.00
85-07-005	"Earth" Angel-1122	B.K. Wisber	Closed	30.00	42.00

Company Number	Name	Series Artist	Edition Limit	Issue Price	Quote
89-07-006	"Peace" Angel (Second Edition)-1120	B.K. Wisber	Open	48.00	50.00
85-07-007	"Noel" Angel (First Edition)-1126	B.K. Wisber	Closed	30.00	32.00
89-07-008	"Noel" Angel (Second Edition)-1126	B.K. Wisber	Open	48.00	50.00
85-07-009	Wiseman #1-1123	B.K. Wisber	Open	30.00	37.00
85-07-010	Wiseman #2-1124	B.K. Wisber	Open	30.00	37.00
85-07-011	Wiseman #3-1125	B.K. Wisber	Open	30.00	37.00
85-07-012	Wooden Creche-1132	B.K. Wisber	Open	28.00	31.00
85-07-013	Christmas Wooly Lamb-1133	B.K. Wisber	Closed	11.00	14.00
86-07-014	Shepherd-1193	B.K. Wisber	Open	32.00	37.00
Ladie and Friends™		**The Christmas Concert**			
90-08-001	Claire Valentine-1262	B.K. Wisber	Open	56.00	57.00
92-08-002	Judith High-1292	B.K. Wisber	Open	70.00	71.00
93-08-003	Stephanie Bowman-1309	B.K. Wisber	Open	74.00	74.00
93-08-004	James Valentine-1310	B.K. Wisber	Open	60.00	60.00
Ladie and Friends™		**Lizzie High® Society Members Dolls**			
93-09-001	Audrey High-1301	B.K. Wisber	Closed	59.00	59.00
93-09-002	Becky High-1330	B.K. Wisber	Yr.Iss.	96.00	96.00
Lawtons		**Childhood Classics ®**			
83-01-001	Alice In Wonderland	W. Lawton	Closed	225.00	2000-3000.
84-01-002	Heidi	W. Lawton	Closed	325.00	650-850.00
85-01-003	Hans Brinker	W. Lawton	Closed	325.00	1000-1800.
86-01-004	Anne Of Green Gables	W. Lawton	Closed	325.00	2000-2400.
86-01-005	Pollyanna	W. Lawton	Closed	325.00	1000-1600.
86-01-006	Laura Ingals	W. Lawton	Closed	325.00	500-900.
87-01-007	Mary Lennox	W. Lawton	Closed	325.00	500-950.
87-01-008	Just David	W. Lawton	Closed	325.00	700-1100.
87-01-009	Polly Pepper	W. Lawton	Closed	325.00	450-700.
88-01-010	Rebecca	W. Lawton	Closed	350.00	500-850.
88-01-011	Little Eva	W. Lawton	Closed	350.00	500-1000.
88-01-012	Topsy	W. Lawton	Closed	350.00	750-1200.
89-01-013	Little Princess	W. Lawton	Closed	395.00	650-950.
89-01-014	Honey Bunch	W. Lawton	Closed	350.00	550-800.
90-01-015	Mary Frances	W. Lawton	Closed	350.00	425.00
90-01-016	Poor Little Match Girl	W. Lawton	Closed	350.00	475.00
91-01-017	The Bobbsey Twins: Freddie	W. Lawton	Closed	364.50	364.50
91-01-018	The Bobbsey Twins: Flossie	W. Lawton	Closed	364.50	364.50
91-01-019	Hiawatha	W. Lawton	Closed	395.00	500.00
91-01-020	Little Black Sambo	W. Lawton	Closed	395.00	595.00
Lawtons		**Childhood Classics ® II**			
92-02-001	Peter And The Wolf	W. Lawton	Closed	495.00	495.00
92-02-002	Marigold Garden	W. Lawton	Closed	450.00	450.00
92-02-003	Oliver Twist	W. Lawton	Closed	450.00	450.00
93-02-004	Tom Sawyer	W. Lawton	Closed	395.00	395.00
93-02-005	The Velveteen Rabbit	W. Lawton	Closed	395.00	395.00
94-02-006	Girl of the Limberlost	W. Lawton	500	425.00	425.00
Lawtons		**Sugar 'n' Spice**			
86-03-001	Kimberly	W. Lawton	Closed	250.00	550-800.
86-03-002	Kersten	W. Lawton	Closed	250.00	550-800.
86-03-003	Jason	W. Lawton	Closed	250.00	800-1700.
86-03-004	Jessica	W. Lawton	Closed	250.00	800-1700.
87-03-005	Marie	W. Lawton	Closed	275.00	450.00
87-03-006	Ginger	W. Lawton	Closed	275.00	395-550.
Lawtons		**Newcomer Collection**			
87-04-001	Ellin Elizabeth, Eyes Closed	W. Lawton	Closed	335.00	750-1000.
87-04-002	Ellin Elizabeth, Eyes Open	W. Lawton	Closed	335.00	900-1200.
Lawtons		**Timeless Ballads ®**			
87-05-001	Highland Mary	W. Lawton	Closed	550.00	600-875.
87-05-002	Annabel Lee	W. Lawton	Closed	550.00	600-695.
87-05-003	Young Charlotte	W. Lawton	Closed	550.00	850-900.
88-05-004	She Walks In Beauty	W. Lawton	Closed	550.00	600.00
Lawtons		**One-Of-A Kind Issues**			
89-06-001	Amelia	W. Lawton	1	N/A	N/A
90-06-002	Goldilocks And Baby Bear	W. Lawton	1	N/A	4250.00
91-06-003	Felicity Minds The Quints	W. Lawton	1	N/A	N/A
92-06-004	Little Miss Muffet	W. Lawton	1	3900.00	3900.00
93-06-005	Jack And The Beanstalk	W. Lawton	1	2500.00	2500.00
93-06-006	Curly Locks, Curly Locks	W. Lawton	1	5700.00	5700.00
Lawtons		**Special Edition**			
88-07-001	Marcella And Raggedy Ann	W. Lawton	Closed	395.00	550-595.
93-07-002	Flora McFlimsey	W. Lawton	Closed	895.00	895.00
94-07-003	Mary Chilton	W. Lawton	350	395.00	395.00
Lawtons		**Christmas Dolls**			
88-08-001	Christmas Joy	W. Lawton	Closed	325.00	750-1200.
89-08-002	Noel	W. Lawton	Closed	325.00	325-750.
90-08-003	Christmas Angel	W. Lawton	Closed	325.00	325.00
91-08-004	Yuletide Carole	W. Lawton	Closed	395.00	395.00
Lawtons		**Special Occasion**			
88-09-001	Nanthy	W. Lawton	Closed	325.00	450-525.
89-09-002	First Day Of School	W. Lawton	Closed	325.00	450-550.
90-09-003	First Birthday	W. Lawton	Closed	295.00	350.00
Lawtons		**Seasons**			
88-10-001	Amber Autumn	W. Lawton	Closed	325.00	300.00
89-10-002	Summer Rose	W. Lawton	Closed	325.00	375-475.
90-10-003	Crystal Winter	W. Lawton	Closed	325.00	325.00
91-10-004	Spring Blossom	W. Lawton	Closed	350.00	350.00
Lawtons		**Wee Bits**			
88-11-001	Wee Bit O'Heaven	W. Lawton	Closed	295.00	450-600.
88-11-002	Wee Bit O'Woe	W. Lawton	Closed	295.00	450-700.
88-11-003	Wee Bit O'Sunshine	W. Lawton	Closed	295.00	450-600.
89-11-004	Wee Bit O'Bliss	W. Lawton	Closed	295.00	350.00
89-11-005	Wee Bit O'Wonder	W. Lawton	Closed	295.00	395.00
Lawtons		**Playthings Past**			
89-12-001	Victoria And Teddy	W. Lawton	Closed	395.00	395.00
89-12-002	Edward And Dobbin	W. Lawton	Closed	395.00	495-600.
89-12-003	Elizabeth And Baby	W. Lawton	Closed	395.00	495-650.
Lawtons		**Cherished Customs**			
90-13-001	The Blessing/Mexico	W. Lawton	Closed	395.00	850.00
90-13-002	Midsommar/Sweden	W. Lawton	Closed	395.00	395.00
90-13-003	Girl's Day/Japan	W. Lawton	Closed	395.00	450-600.

Company / Number	Name	Series / Artist	Edition Limit	Issue Price	Quote
90-13-004	High Tea/Great Britain	W. Lawton	Closed	395.00	450-550.
91-13-005	Ndeko/Zaire	W. Lawton	Closed	395.00	550-750.
91-13-006	Frolic/Amish	W. Lawton	Closed	395.00	395.00
92-13-007	Pascha/Ukraine	W. Lawton	Closed	495.00	495.00
92-13-008	Carnival/Brazil	W. Lawton	Closed	425.00	425.00
92-13-009	Cradleboard/Navajo	W. Lawton	Closed	425.00	425.00
93-13-010	Nalauqataq-Eskimo	W. Lawton	Closed	395.00	395.00
93-13-011	Topeng Klana-Java	W. Lawton	Closed	495.00	495.00
94-13-012	Kwanzaa/Africa	W. Lawton	500	425.00	425.00
Lawtons		**Guild Dolls**			
89-14-001	Baa Baa Black Sheep	W. Lawton	Closed	395.00	650.00
90-14-002	Lavender Blue	W. Lawton	Closed	395.00	450-600.
91-14-003	To Market, To Market	W. Lawton	Closed	495.00	495.00
92-14-004	Little Boy Blue	W. Lawton	Closed	395.00	395.00
93-14-005	Lawton Logo Doll	W. Lawton	Closed	350.00	350.00
94-14-006	Wee Handful	W. Lawton	Open	250.00	250.00
Lawtons		**The Children's Hour**			
91-15-001	Grave Alice	W. Lawton	Closed	395.00	475.00
91-15-002	Laughing Allegra	W. Lawton	Closed	395.00	475.00
91-15-003	Edith With Golden Hair	W. Lawton	Closed	395.00	475.00
Lawtons		**Store Exclusives**			
89-16-001	Main Street, USA (Disney World, Lake Buena Vista, FL)	W. Lawton	Closed	350.00	350.00
90-16-002	Liberty Square (Disney World, Lake Buena Vista, FL)	W. Lawton	Closed	350.00	395.00
90-16-003	Little Colonel (Dolly Dears, Birmingham, AL)	W. Lawton	Closed	395.00	395.00
90-16-004	Garden Song Marta (Toy Village, Lansing, MI)	W. Lawton	Closed	335.00	335.00
91-16-005	Tish (Disney World, Lake Buena Vista, FL)	W. Lawton	Closed	395.00	395.00
92-16-006	Karen (Disney World, Lake Buena Vista, FL)	W. Lawton	Closed	395.00	395.00
93-16-007	Brita/Tea Party (Toy Village, Lansing, MI)	W. Lawton	Closed	395.00	395.00
93-16-008	Kellyn (Disneyland, Anaheim, CA)	W. Lawton	Closed	395.00	395.00
93-16-009	A Goofy Little Kid (Disney World, Lake Buena Vista, FL)	W. Lawton	Closed	395.00	395.00
Lawtons		**Christmas Legends™**			
91-17-001	The Legend Of The Poinsettia	W. Lawton	Closed	395.00	395.00
93-17-002	The Little Drummer Boy	W. Lawton	Closed	595.00	595.00
94-17-003	Santa Lucia	W. Lawton	350	425.00	425.00
Lawtons		**Folk Tales And Fairy Stories**			
92-18-001	Little Red Riding Hood	W. Lawton	Closed	450.00	450.00
92-18-002	The Little Emperor's Nightingale	W. Lawton	Closed	425.00	425.00
92-18-003	William Tell, The Younger	W. Lawton	Closed	395.00	395.00
92-18-004	Swan Princess	W. Lawton	Closed	495.00	495.00
93-18-005	Snow White	W. Lawton	Closed	395.00	395.00
93-18-006	Goldilocks And Baby Bear	W. Lawton	Closed	595.00	595.00
94-18-007	Little Gretel	W. Lawton	500	395.00	395.00
Lawtons		**Small Wonders**			
93-19-001	Michael	W. Lawton	Closed	149.95	149.95
93-19-002	Meghan	W. Lawton	Closed	149.95	149.95
93-19-003	Jafry	W. Lawton	Closed	149.95	149.95
93-19-004	Jamilla	W. Lawton	Closed	149.95	149.95
Lawtons		**Memories And Melodies™**			
93-20-001	Lyda Rose	W. Lawton	Closed	295.00	295.00
93-20-002	Apple Blossom Time	W. Lawton	Closed	295.00	295.00
93-20-003	Scarlet Ribbons	W. Lawton	Closed	295.00	295.00
93-20-004	In The Good Ol' Summertime	W. Lawton	Closed	295.00	295.00
94-20-005	Let Me Call You Sweetheart	W. Lawton	250	295.00	295.00
Lawtons		**Classic Playthings™**			
93-21-001	Patricia And Her Patsy ®	W. Lawton	Closed	595.00	595.00
94-21-002	Katie and Her Kewpie	W. Lawton	750	595.00	595.00
Lawtons		**Centerpieces**			
92-22-001	Lotta On Stage (First Lawton Collectors Guild Convention)	W. Lawton	Closed	N/A	N/A
93-22-002	Little Colonel II (Dolly Dears, Birmingham, AL)	W. Lawton	Closed	N/A	N/A
Lawtons		**Early American Portrait**			
94-23-001	Abigail and Jane Augusta	W. Lawton	250	995.00	995.00
Lawtons		**Gentle Pursuits**			
94-24-001	Emily and Her Diary	W. Lawton	350	795.00	795.00
Lawtons		**Once Upon A Rhyme™**			
94-25-001	At Aunty's House	W. Lawton	350	795.00	795.00
Lawtons		**Grand Tour™**			
94-26-001	Springtime in Paris	W. Lawton	250	895.00	895.00
Lawtons		**Treasured Tales**			
94-27-001	The Dreamer	W. Lawton	500	395.00	395.00
Lenox Collections		**Lenox China Dolls**			
84-01-001	Maryanne, 20"	J. Grammer	Closed	425.00	N/A
84-01-002	Abigail, 20"	J. Grammer	Closed	425.00	N/A
84-01-003	Jessica, 20"	J. Grammer	Closed	450.00	N/A
84-01-004	Rebecca, 16"	J. Grammer	Closed	375.00	N/A
84-01-005	Amanda, 16"	J. Grammer	Closed	385.00	N/A
84-01-006	Maggie, 16"	J. Grammer	Closed	375.00	N/A
84-01-007	Melissa, 16"	J. Grammer	Closed	450.00	N/A
84-01-008	Samantha, 16"	J. Grammer	Closed	500.00	N/A
Lenox Collections		**China Dolls - Cloth Bodies**			
85-02-001	Amy, 14"	J. Grammer	Closed	250.00	N/A
85-02-002	Elizabeth, 14"	J. Grammer	Closed	250.00	N/A
85-02-003	Sarah, 14"	J. Grammer	Closed	250.00	N/A
85-02-004	Annabelle, 14"	J. Grammer	Closed	250.00	N/A
85-02-005	Miranda, 14"	J. Grammer	Closed	250.00	N/A
85-02-006	Jennifer, 14"	J. Grammer	Closed	250.00	N/A
Lenox Collections		**Lenox Victorian Dolls**			
89-03-001	The Victorian Bride	Unknown	Open	295.00	295.00
90-03-002	Christmas Doll, Elizabeth	Unknown	Open	195.00	195.00
91-03-003	Victorian Christening Doll	Unknown	Open	295.00	295.00
92-03-004	Lady at Gala	Unknown	Open	295.00	295.00
Lenox Collections		**Children of the World**			
89-04-001	Hannah, The Little Dutch Maiden	Unknown	Open	119.00	119.00
90-04-002	Heather, Little Highlander	Unknown	Open	119.00	119.00
91-04-003	Amma-The African Girl	Unknown	Open	119.00	119.00
91-04-004	Sakura-The Japanese Girl	Unknown	Open	119.00	119.00
92-04-005	Gretchen, German Doll	Unknown	Open	119.00	119.00
Lenox Collections		**Sibling Dolls**			
91-05-001	Skating Lesson	A. Lester	Open	195.00	195.00
Lenox Collections		**Ellis Island Dolls**			
91-06-001	Megan	P. Thompson	Closed	150.00	150.00
91-06-002	Stefan	P. Thompson	Closed	150.00	150.00
92-06-003	Angelina	P. Thompson	Closed	150.00	150.00
92-06-004	Catherine	P. Thompson	Closed	152.00	152.00
92-06-005	Anna	P. Thompson	Closed	152.00	152.00
Lenox Collections		**Musical Baby Dolls**			
91-07-001	Patrick's Lullabye	Unknown	Open	95.00	95.00
Lenox Collections		**Bolshoi Nutcracker Dolls**			
91-08-001	Clara	Unknown	Open	195.00	195.00
Lenox Collections		**Country Decor Dolls**			
91-09-001	Molly	Unknown	Open	150.00	150.00
Lenox Collections		**Children With Toys Dolls**			
91-10-001	Tea For Teddy	Unknown	Open	136.00	136.00
Lenox Collections		**Little Women**			
92-11-001	Amy, The Inspiring Artist	Unknown	Open	152.00	152.00
Lenox Collections		**First Collector Doll**			
92-12-001	Lauren	Unknown	Open	152.00	152.00
Lenox Collections		**Inspirational Doll**			
92-13-001	Blessed Are The Peacemakers	Unknown	Open	119.00	119.00
Lenox Collections		**International Baby Doll**			
92-14-001	Natalia, Russian Baby	Unknown	Open	119.00	119.00
Lenox Collections		**Nutcracker Dolls**			
92-15-001	Sugarplum	Unknown	Open	195.00	195.00
93-15-002	Nutcracker	Unknown	Open	195.00	195.00
Lenox Collections		**Prima Ballerina Collection**			
92-16-001	Odette, Queen of the Swans	Unknown	Closed	195.00	195.00
Seymour Mann Inc.		**Connossieur Doll Collection**			
84-01-001	Miss Debutante Debi	E. Mann	Closed	75.00	180.00
85-01-002	Christmas Cheer-124	E. Mann	Closed	40.00	100.00
85-01-003	Wendy-C120	E. Mann	Closed	45.00	150.00
86-01-004	Camelot Fairy-C-84	E. Mann	Closed	75.00	225.00
87-01-005	Audrina-YK-200	E. Mann	Closed	85.00	140.00
87-01-006	Cynthia-DOM-211	E. Mann	Closed	85.00	85.00
87-01-006	Dawn-C185	E. Mann	Closed	75.00	175.00
87-01-007	Linda-C190	E. Mann	Closed	60.00	120.00
87-01-008	Marcy-YK122	E. Mann	Closed	55.00	100.00
87-01-009	Nirmala-YK-210	E. Mann	Closed	50.00	50.00
87-01-010	Rapunzel-C158	E. Mann	Closed	95.00	165.00
87-01-011	Sabrina-C208	E. Mann	Closed	65.00	95.00
87-01-012	Sailorette-DOM217	E. Mann	Closed	70.00	150.00
87-01-013	Vivian-C-201P	E. Mann	Closed	80.00	80.00
88-01-014	Ashley-C-278	E. Mann	Closed	80.00	80.00
88-01-015	Brittany-TK-5	E. Mann	Closed	120.00	120.00
88-01-016	Cissie-DOM263	E. Mann	Closed	65.00	135.00
88-01-017	Crying Courtney-PS75	E. Mann	Closed	115.00	115.00
88-01-018	Cynthia-DOM-211	E. Mann	3,500	85.00	85.00
88-01-019	Doll Oliver-FH392	E. Mann	Closed	100.00	100.00
88-01-020	Giselle on Goose-FH176	E. Mann	Closed	105.00	225.00
88-01-021	Emily-YK-243V	E. Mann	Closed	70.00	70.00
88-01-022	Frances-C-233	E. Mann	Closed	80.00	125.00
88-01-023	Jessica-DOM-267	E. Mann	Closed	90.00	90.00
88-01-024	Joanne Cry Baby-PS-50	E. Mann	Closed	100.00	100.00
88-01-025	Jolie-C231	E. Mann	Closed	65.00	150.00
88-01-026	Julie-C245A	E. Mann	Closed	65.00	160.00
88-01-027	Juliette Bride Musical-C246LTM	E. Mann	Closed	150.00	150.00
88-01-028	Kirsten-PS-40G	E. Mann	Closed	70.00	70.00
88-01-029	Lionel-FH206B	E. Mann	Closed	50.00	120.00
88-01-030	Lucinda-DOM-293	E. Mann	Closed	90.00	90.00
88-01-031	Michelle & Marcel-YK176	E. Mann	Closed	70.00	150.00
88-01-032	Pauline-YK-230	E. Mann	Closed	90.00	90.00
88-01-033	Sabrina -C-208	E. Mann	Closed	65.00	95.00
88-01-034	Sister Agnes 14"-C250	E. Mann	Closed	75.00	75.00
88-01-035	Sister Ignatius Notre Dame-FH184	E. Mann	Closed	75.00	75.00
88-01-036	Sister Teresa-FH187	E. Mann	Closed	80.00	80.00
88-01-037	Tracy-C-3006	E. Mann	Closed	95.00	150.00
88-01-038	Vivian-C201P	E. Mann	Closed	80.00	80.00
89-01-039	Ashley-C-278	E. Mann	Closed	80.00	80.00
89-01-040	Amber-DOM-281A	E. Mann	Closed	85.00	85.00
89-01-041	Betty-PS27G	E. Mann	Closed	65.00	125.00
89-01-042	Brett-PS27B	E. Mann	Closed	65.00	125.00
89-01-043	Brittany-TK-4	E. Mann	Closed	150.00	150.00
89-01-044	Baby John-PS-49B	E. Mann	Closed	85.00	85.00
89-01-045	Crying Courtney-PS-75	E. Mann	Closed	115.00	115.00
89-01-046	Daphne Ecru/Mint Green-C3025	E. Mann	Closed	85.00	85.00
89-01-047	Elisabeth-OM-32	E. Mann	Closed	120.00	120.00
89-01-048	Elizabeth-C-246P	E. Mann	Closed	150.00	200.00
89-01-049	Emily-PS-48	E. Mann	Closed	110.00	110.00
89-01-050	Frances-C233	E. Mann	Closed	80.00	125.00
89-01-051	Happy Birthday-C3012	E. Mann	Closed	80.00	125.00
89-01-052	Heidi-260	E. Mann	Closed	50.00	95.00
89-01-053	Jaqueline-DOLL-254M	E. Mann	Closed	85.00	85.00
89-01-054	Joanne Cry Baby-PS-50	E. Mann	2,500	100.00	100.00
89-01-055	Kayoko-PS-24	E. Mann	Closed	75.00	175.00
89-01-056	Kirsten-PS-40G	E. Mann	Closed	70.00	70.00
89-01-057	Ling-Ling-PS-87G	E. Mann	Closed	90.00	90.00
89-01-058	Liz -YK-269	E. Mann	Closed	70.00	100.00
89-01-059	Lucinda -DOM-293	E. Mann	Closed	90.00	90.00
89-01-060	Mai-Ling-PS-79	E. Mann	2,500	100.00	100.00
89-01-061	Marcey-YK-4005	E. Mann	3,500	90.00	90.00
89-01-062	Margaret-245	E. Mann	Closed	100.00	150.00
89-01-063	Maureen-PS-84	E. Mann	Closed	90.00	90.00
89-01-064	Meimei-PS22	E. Mann	Closed	75.00	225.00

DOLLS

Company Number	Name	Series Artist	Edition Limit	Issue Price	Quote
89-01-065	Melissa-LL-794	E. Mann	Closed	95.00	95.00
89-01-066	Miss Kim-PS-25	E. Mann	Closed	75.00	175.00
89-01-067	Patricia/Patrick-215GBB	E. Mann	Closed	105.00	135.00
89-01-068	Paula-PS-56	E. Mann	2,500	75.00	75.00
89-01-069	Pauline Bonaparte-OM68	E. Mann	2,500	120.00	120.00
89-01-070	Ramona-PS-31B	E. Mann	2,500	80.00	80.00
89-01-071	Rebecca-PS-34V	E. Mann	2,500	45.00	45.00
89-01-072	Rosie-290M	E. Mann	Closed	55.00	85.00
89-01-073	Sister Mary-C-249	E. Mann	Closed	75.00	125.00
89-01-074	Sunny-PS-59V	E. Mann	Closed	71.00	71.00
89-01-075	Suzie-PS-32	E. Mann	2,500	80.00	80.00
89-01-076	Tatiana Pink Ballerina-OM-60	E. Mann	Closed	120.00	120.00
89-01-077	Terri-PS-104	E. Mann	Closed	85.00	85.00
89-01-078	Wendy-PS-51	E. Mann	2,500	105.00	105.00
90-01-079	Anabelle-C-3080	E. Mann	Closed	85.00	85.00
90-01-080	Angel-DOM-335	E. Mann	2,500	105.00	105.00
90-01-081	Angela-C-3084	E. Mann	2,500	105.00	105.00
90-01-082	Angela-C-3084M	E. Mann	2,500	115.00	115.00
90-01-083	Anita-FH-277G	E. Mann	Closed	65.00	65.00
90-01-084	Ashley-FH-325	E. Mann	Closed	75.00	75.00
90-01-085	Audrey-YK-4089	E. Mann	Closed	125.00	125.00
90-01-086	Baby Betty-YK-4087	E. Mann	3,500	125.00	125.00
90-01-087	Baby Bonnie-SP-341	E. Mann	2,500	55.00	55.00
90-01-088	Baby Brent-EP-15	E. Mann	2,500	85.00	85.00
90-01-089	Baby Ecru-WB-17	E. Mann	2,500	65.00	65.00
90-01-090	Baby Kate-WB-19	E. Mann	2,500	85.00	85.00
90-01-091	Baby Nelly-PS-163	E. Mann	Closed	95.00	95.00
90-01-092	Baby Sue-DOLL-402B	E. Mann	2,500	27.50	27.50
90-01-093	Baby Sunshine-C-3055	E. Mann	Closed	90.00	90.00
90-01-094	Beth-YK-4099A/B	E. Mann	2,500	125.00	125.00
90-01-095	Bettina-TR-4	E. Mann	Closed	125.00	125.00
90-01-096	Beverly-DOLL-335	E. Mann	Closed	110.00	110.00
90-01-097	Billie-YK-4056V	E. Mann	Closed	65.00	65.00
90-01-098	Caillin-DOLL-11PH	E. Mann	Closed	60.00	60.00
90-01-099	Caitlin-YK-4051V	E. Mann	Closed	90.00	90.00
90-01-100	Carole-YK-4085W	E. Mann	Closed	125.00	125.00
90-01-101	Charlene-YK-4112	E. Mann	Closed	90.00	90.00
90-01-102	Chin Fa-C-3061	E. Mann	Closed	95.00	95.00
90-01-103	Chinook-WB-24	E. Mann	Closed	85.00	85.00
90-01-104	Chrissie-WB-2	E. Mann	Closed	75.00	75.00
90-01-105	Daisy-EP-6	E. Mann	Closed	90.00	90.00
90-01-106	Daphne Ecru-C-3025	E. Mann	Closed	85.00	85.00
90-01-107	Dianna-TK-31	E. Mann	Closed	175.00	175.00
90-01-108	Diane-FH-275	E. Mann	Closed	90.00	90.00
90-01-109	Domino-C-3050	E. Mann	Closed	145.00	145.00
90-01-110	Dorri-DOLL-16PH	E. Mann	Closed	85.00	85.00
90-01-111	Dorothy-TR-10	E. Mann	Closed	135.00	135.00
90-01-112	Eileen-FH-367	E. Mann	Closed	100.00	100.00
90-01-113	Felicia-TR-9	E. Mann	Closed	115.00	115.00
90-01-114	Francesca-C-3021	E. Mann	Closed	100.00	175.00
90-01-115	Gerri Beige-YK4094	E. Mann	Closed	95.00	95.00
90-01-116	Ginny-YK-4119	E. Mann	3,500	100.00	100.00
90-01-117	Hope-YK-4118	E. Mann	Closed	90.00	90.00
90-01-118	Hyacinth-DOLL-15PH	E. Mann	Closed	85.00	85.00
90-01-119	Indian Doll-FH-295	E. Mann	Closed	60.00	60.00
90-01-120	Janette-DOLL-385	E. Mann	Closed	85.00	85.00
90-01-121	Jillian-DOLL-41PH	E. Mann	Closed	90.00	90.00
90-01-122	Joanne-TR-12	E. Mann	2,500	175.00	175.00
90-01-123	Julie-WB-35	E. Mann	Closed	70.00	70.00
90-01-124	Karen-PS-198	E. Mann	2,500	150.00	150.00
90-01-125	Kate-C-3060	E. Mann	Closed	95.00	95.00
90-01-126	Kathy w/Bear-TE1	E. Mann	Closed	70.00	70.00
90-01-127	Kiku-EP-4	E. Mann	2,500	100.00	100.00
90-01-128	Laura-DOLL-25PH	E. Mann	Closed	55.00	55.00
90-01-129	Lauren-SP-300	E. Mann	Closed	85.00	85.00
90-01-130	Lavender Blue-YK-4024	E. Mann	Closed	95.00	135.00
90-01-131	Lien Wha-YK-4092	E. Mann	Closed	100.00	100.00
90-01-132	Ling-Ling-DOLL	E. Mann	2,500	50.00	50.00
90-01-133	Lisa-FH-379	E. Mann	Closed	100.00	100.00
90-01-134	Lisa Beige Accordion Pleat-YK4093	E. Mann	Closed	125.00	125.00
90-01-135	Liza-C-3053	E. Mann	Closed	100.00	100.00
90-01-136	Lola-SP-79	E. Mann	2,500	105.00	105.00
90-01-137	Loretta-FH-321	E. Mann	Closed	90.00	90.00
90-01-138	Lori-WB-72BM	E. Mann	2,500	75.00	75.00
90-01-139	Madame De Pompadour-C-3088	E. Mann	2,500	250.00	250.00
90-01-140	Maggie-PS-151P	E. Mann	Closed	90.00	90.00
90-01-141	Maggie-WB-51	E. Mann	2,500	105.00	105.00
90-01-142	Maria-YK-4116	E. Mann	Closed	85.00	85.00
90-01-143	Melanie-YK-4115	E. Mann	Closed	80.00	80.00
90-01-144	Melissa-DOLL-390	E. Mann	Closed	75.00	75.00
90-01-145	Merry Widow-C-3040	E. Mann	3,500	145.00	145.00
90-01-146	Merry Widow 20"-C-3040M	E. Mann	2,500	140.00	140.00
90-01-147	Nanook-WB-23	E. Mann	Closed	75.00	75.00
90-01-148	Natasha-PS-102	E. Mann	Closed	100.00	100.00
90-01-149	Odessa-FH-362	E. Mann	Closed	65.00	65.00
90-01-150	Ping-Ling-DOLL-363RV	E. Mann	Closed	50.00	50.00
90-01-151	Polly-DOLL-22PH	E. Mann	Closed	90.00	90.00
90-01-152	Princess Fair Skies-FH-268B	E. Mann	2,500	75.00	75.00
90-01-153	Princess Red Feather-PS-189	E. Mann	2,500	90.00	90.00
90-01-154	Priscilla-WB-50	E. Mann	2,500	105.00	105.00
90-01-155	Sabrina-C3050	E. Mann	Closed	105.00	105.00
90-01-156	Sally-WB-20	E. Mann	Closed	95.00	95.00
90-01-157	Shirley-WB-37	E. Mann	Closed	65.00	65.00
90-01-158	Sister Mary-WB-15	E. Mann	Closed	70.00	70.00
90-01-159	Sophie-OM-1	E. Mann	Open	65.00	65.00
90-01-160	Stacy-TR-5	E. Mann	2,500	105.00	105.00
90-01-161	Sue Chuen-C-3061G	E. Mann	Closed	95.00	95.00
90-01-162	Sunny-FH-331	E. Mann	Closed	70.00	70.00
90-01-163	Susan-DOLL-364MC	E. Mann	Closed	75.00	75.00
90-01-164	Tania-DOLL-376P	E. Mann	Closed	65.00	65.00
90-01-165	Tina-DOLL-371	E. Mann	Closed	85.00	85.00
90-01-166	Tina-WB-32	E. Mann	Closed	65.00	65.00
90-01-167	Tommy-C-3064	E. Mann	Closed	75.00	75.00
90-01-168	Wendy-TE-3	E. Mann	Closed	75.00	75.00
90-01-169	Wilma-PS-174	E. Mann	Closed	75.00	75.00
90-01-170	Yen Yen-YK-4091	E. Mann	Closed	95.00	95.00
91-01-171	Abigail-EP-3	E. Mann	Closed	100.00	100.00
91-01-172	Abigal-WB-72WM	E. Mann	2,500	75.00	75.00
91-01-173	Abby 16" Pink Dress-C3145	E. Mann	Closed	100.00	100.00
91-01-174	Alexis 24" Beige Lace-EP32	E. Mann	2,500	220.00	220.00
91-01-175	Alicia-YK-4215	E. Mann	3,500	90.00	90.00
91-01-176	Amanda Toast-OM-182	E. Mann	2,500	260.00	260.00
91-01-177	Amelia-TR-47	E. Mann	2,500	105.00	105.00
91-01-178	Amy-C-3147	E. Mann	2,500	135.00	135.00
91-01-179	Ann-TR-52	E. Mann	Closed	135.00	135.00
91-01-180	Annette-TR-59	E. Mann	Closed	130.00	130.00
91-01-181	Annie-YK-4214	E. Mann	3,500	145.00	145.00
91-01-182	Antoinette-FH-452	E. Mann	2,500	100.00	100.00
91-01-183	Arabella-C-3163	E. Mann	2,500	135.00	135.00
91-01-184	Ariel 34" Blue/White-EP-33	E. Mann	Closed	175.00	175.00
91-01-185	Audrey-FH-455	E. Mann	2,500	125.00	125.00
91-01-186	Aurora Gold 22"-OM-181	E. Mann	2,500	260.00	260.00
91-01-187	Azure-AM-15	E. Mann	2,500	175.00	175.00
91-01-188	Baby Beth-DOLL-406P	E. Mann	2,500	27.50	27.50
91-01-189	Baby Bonnie w/Walker Music-DOLL-409	E. Mann	2,500	40.00	40.00
91-01-190	Baby Bonnie-SP-341	E. Mann	Closed	55.00	55.00
91-01-191	Baby Brent-EP-15	E. Mann	Closed	85.00	85.00
91-01-192	Baby Carrie-DOLL-402P	E. Mann	2,500	27.50	27.50
91-01-193	Baby Ecru-WB-17	E. Mann	Closed	65.00	65.00
91-01-194	Baby Ellie Ecru Musical-DOLL-402E	E. Mann	2,500	27.50	27.50
91-01-195	Baby Gloria Black Baby-PS-289	E. Mann	Closed	75.00	75.00
91-01-196	Baby John-PS-498	E. Mann	Closed	85.00	85.00
91-01-197	Baby Linda-DOLL-406E	E. Mann	2,500	27.50	27.50
91-01-198	Baby Sue-DOLL-402B	E. Mann	2,500	27.50	27.50
91-01-199	Belinda-C-3164	E. Mann	2,500	150.00	150.00
91-01-200	Bernetta-EP-40	E. Mann	Closed	115.00	115.00
91-01-201	Betsy-AM-6	E. Mann	Closed	105.00	105.00
91-01-202	Bettina-YK-4144	E. Mann	Closed	105.00	105.00
91-01-203	Blaine-TR-61	E. Mann	Closed	115.00	115.00
91-01-204	Blythe-CH-15V	E. Mann	Closed	135.00	135.00
91-01-205	Bo-Peep w/Lamb-C-3128	E. Mann	Closed	105.00	105.00
91-01-206	Bridget-SP-379	E. Mann	2,500	105.00	105.00
91-01-207	Brooke-FH-461	E. Mann	2,500	115.00	115.00
91-01-208	Bryna-AM-100B	E. Mann	2,500	70.00	70.00
91-01-209	Camellia-FH-457	E. Mann	2,500	100.00	100.00
91-01-210	Caroline-LL-838	E. Mann	2,500	110.00	110.00
91-01-211	Caroline-LL-905	E. Mann	2,500	110.00	110.00
91-01-212	Cheryl-TR-49	E. Mann	2,500	120.00	120.00
91-01-213	Chin Chin-YK-4211	E. Mann	Closed	85.00	85.00
91-01-214	Christina-PS-261	E. Mann	2,500	115.00	115.00
91-01-215	Cindy Lou-FH-464	E. Mann	2,500	85.00	85.00
91-01-216	Cissy-EP-56	E. Mann	2,500	95.00	95.00
91-01-217	Clare-DOLL-465	E. Mann	Open	100.00	100.00
91-01-218	Claudine-C-3146	E. Mann	Closed	95.00	95.00
91-01-219	Colette-WB-7	E. Mann	Closed	65.00	65.00
91-01-220	Colleen-YK-4163	E. Mann	Closed	120.00	120.00
91-01-221	Cookie-GU-6	E. Mann	2,500	110.00	110.00
91-01-222	Courtney-LL-859	E. Mann	2,500	150.00	150.00
91-01-223	Creole-AM-17	E. Mann	2,500	160.00	160.00
91-01-224	Crystal-YK-4237	E. Mann	3,500	125.00	125.00
91-01-225	Danielle-AM-5	E. Mann	Closed	125.00	125.00
91-01-226	Darcy-EP-47	E. Mann	Closed	110.00	110.00
91-01-227	Darcy-FH-451	E. Mann	2,500	105.00	105.00
91-01-228	Daria-C-3122	E. Mann	Closed	110.00	110.00
91-01-229	Darlene-DOLL-444	E. Mann	2,500	75.00	75.00
91-01-230	Dawn-C-3135	E. Mann	Closed	130.00	130.00
91-01-231	Denise-LL-852	E. Mann	2,500	105.00	105.00
91-01-232	Dephine-SP-308	E. Mann	2,500	135.00	135.00
91-01-233	Desiree-LL-898	E. Mann	2,500	120.00	120.00
91-01-234	Duanane-SP-366	E. Mann	Closed	85.00	85.00
91-01-235	Dulcie-YK-4131V	E. Mann	Closed	100.00	100.00
91-01-236	Dwayne-C-3123	E. Mann	2,500	120.00	120.00
91-01-237	Edie -YK-4177	E. Mann	Closed	115.00	115.00
91-01-238	Elisabeth and Lisa-C-3095	E. Mann	2,500	195.00	195.00
91-01-239	Elise -PS-259	E. Mann	Closed	105.00	105.00
91-01-240	Elizabeth-AM-32	E. Mann	2,500	105.00	105.00
91-01-241	Emmaline-OM-191	E. Mann	2,500	300.00	300.00
91-01-242	Emmaline Beige/Lilac-OM-197	E. Mann	Closed	300.00	300.00
91-01-243	Emmy-C-3099	E. Mann	Closed	125.00	125.00
91-01-244	Erin-DOLL-4PH	E. Mann	Closed	60.00	60.00
91-01-245	Evalina-C-3124	E. Mann	Closed	135.00	135.00
91-01-246	Fifi-AM-100F	E. Mann	Closed	70.00	70.00
91-01-247	Fleurette-PS-286	E. Mann	2,500	75.00	75.00
91-01-248	Flora-TR-46	E. Mann	Closed	125.00	125.00
91-01-249	Francesca-AM-14	E. Mann	2,500	175.00	175.00
91-01-250	Georgia-YK-4131	E. Mann	Closed	100.00	100.00
91-01-251	Georgia-YK-4143	E. Mann	Closed	150.00	150.00
91-01-252	Gigi-C-3107	E. Mann	2,500	135.00	135.00
91-01-253	Ginger-LL-907	E. Mann	Closed	115.00	115.00
91-01-254	Gloria-AM-100G	E. Mann	2,500	70.00	70.00
91-01-255	Gloria-YK-4166	E. Mann	Closed	105.00	105.00
91-01-256	Gretchen-DOLL-446	E. Mann	Open	45.00	45.00
91-01-257	Gretel-DOLL-434	E. Mann	Closed	60.00	60.00
91-01-258	Hansel and Gretel-DOLL-448V	E. Mann	Closed	60.00	60.00
91-01-259	Helene-AM-29	E. Mann	2,500	150.00	150.00
91-01-260	Holly-CH-6	E. Mann	Closed	100.00	100.00
91-01-261	Honey-FH-401	E. Mann	Closed	100.00	100.00
91-01-262	Honey Bunny-WB-9	E. Mann	Closed	70.00	70.00
91-01-263	Hope-FH-434	E. Mann	2,500	90.00	90.00
91-01-264	Indira-AM-4	E. Mann	2,500	125.00	125.00
91-01-265	Iris-TR-58	E. Mann	Closed	120.00	120.00
91-01-266	Ivy-PS-307	E. Mann	Closed	75.00	75.00
91-01-267	Jane-PS-243L	E. Mann	Closed	115.00	115.00
91-01-268	Janice-OM-194	E. Mann	2,500	300.00	300.00
91-01-269	Jessica-FH-423	E. Mann	2,500	95.00	95.00
91-01-270	Joy-EP-23V	E. Mann	Closed	130.00	130.00
91-01-271	Joyce-AM-100J	E. Mann	2,500	35.00	35.00
91-01-272	Julia-C-3102	E. Mann	Closed	135.00	135.00
91-01-273	Juliette-OM-192	E. Mann	2,500	300.00	300.00
91-01-274	Karen-EP-24	E. Mann	Closed	115.00	115.00
91-01-275	Karmela-EP-57	E. Mann	2,500	120.00	120.00
91-01-276	Kelly-AM-8	E. Mann	2,500	125.00	125.00
91-01-277	Kerry-FH-396	E. Mann	Closed	100.00	100.00
91-01-278	Kim-AM-100K	E. Mann	2,500	70.00	70.00
91-01-279	Kinesha-SP-402	E. Mann	2,500	110.00	110.00
91-01-280	Kristi-FH-402	E. Mann	Closed	100.00	100.00
91-01-281	Kyla-YK-4137	E. Mann	3,500	95.00	95.00
91-01-282	Laura-WB-110P	E. Mann	Closed	85.00	85.00
91-01-283	Leigh-DOLL-457	E. Mann	2,500	95.00	95.00
91-01-284	Leila-AM-2	E. Mann	Closed	125.00	125.00
91-01-285	Lenore-LL-911	E. Mann	2,500	105.00	105.00
91-01-286	Lenore-YK-4218	E. Mann	3,500	135.00	135.00
91-01-287	Libby-EP-18	E. Mann	Closed	85.00	85.00
91-01-288	Lila-AM-10	E. Mann	2,500	125.00	125.00
91-01-289	Lila-FH-404	E. Mann	2,500	100.00	100.00
91-01-290	Lindsey-C-3127	E. Mann	Closed	135.00	135.00
91-01-291	Linetta-C-3166	E. Mann	Closed	135.00	135.00
91-01-292	Lisa-AM-100L	E. Mann	2,500	70.00	70.00

DOLLS

Company Number	Name	Series Artist	Edition Limit	Issue Price	Quote
91-01-293	Little Boy Blue-C-3159	E. Mann	2,500	100.00	100.00
91-01-294	Liz-C-3150	E. Mann	2,500	100.00	100.00
91-01-295	Liza-YK-4226	E. Mann	3,500	35.00	35.00
91-01-296	Lola-SP-363	E. Mann	2,500	90.00	90.00
91-01-297	Loni-FH-448	E. Mann	2,500	100.00	100.00
91-01-298	Lori-EP-52	E. Mann	2,500	95.00	95.00
91-01-299	Louise-LL-908	E. Mann	2,500	105.00	105.00
91-01-300	Lucy-LL-853	E. Mann	Closed	80.00	80.00
91-01-301	Madeleine-C-3106	E. Mann	Closed	95.00	95.00
91-01-302	Marcy-TR-55	E. Mann	Closed	135.00	135.00
91-01-303	Mariel 18" Ivory-C-3119	E. Mann	Closed	125.00	125.00
91-01-304	Maude-AM-100M	E. Mann	2,500	70.00	70.00
91-01-305	Melissa-AM-9	E. Mann	Closed	120.00	120.00
91-01-306	Melissa-CH-3	E. Mann	Closed	110.00	110.00
91-01-307	Melissa-LL-901	E. Mann	Closed	135.00	135.00
91-01-308	Meredith-FH-391-P	E. Mann	Closed	95.00	95.00
91-01-309	Meryl-FH-463	E. Mann	2,500	95.00	95.00
91-01-310	Michael w/School Books-FH-439B	E. Mann	2,500	95.00	95.00
91-01-311	Michelle Lilac/Green-EP36	E. Mann	Closed	95.00	95.00
91-01-312	Michelle w/School Books-FH-439G	E. Mann	Closed	95.00	95.00
91-01-313	Miranda-DOLL-9PH	E. Mann	Closed	75.00	75.00
91-01-314	Missy-DOLL-464	E. Mann	Closed	70.00	70.00
91-01-315	Missy-PS-258	E. Mann	Closed	90.00	90.00
91-01-316	Mon Yun w/Parasol-TR33	E. Mann	2,500	115.00	115.00
91-01-317	Nancy 21" Pink w/Rabbit-EP-31	E. Mann	Closed	165.00	165.00
91-01-318	Nancy -WB-73	E. Mann	2,500	65.00	65.00
91-01-319	Nellie-EP-1B	E. Mann	Closed	75.00	75.00
91-01-320	Nicole-AM-12	E. Mann	Closed	135.00	135.00
91-01-321	Noelle-PS-239V	E. Mann	Closed	95.00	95.00
91-01-322	Patti-DOLL-440	E. Mann	2,500	65.00	65.00
91-01-323	Patty-YK-4221	E. Mann	3,500	125.00	125.00
91-01-324	Pepper-PS-277	E. Mann	Closed	130.00	130.00
91-01-325	Pia-PS-246L	E. Mann	Closed	115.00	115.00
91-01-326	Princess Summer Winds-FH-427	E. Mann	2,500	120.00	120.00
91-01-327	Prissy White/Blue-C-3140	E. Mann	Closed	100.00	100.00
91-01-328	Rapunzel-C-3157	E. Mann	2,500	150.00	150.00
91-01-329	Red Wing-AM-30	E. Mann	2,500	165.00	165.00
91-01-330	Robin-AM-22	E. Mann	Closed	120.00	120.00
91-01-331	Rosalind-C-3090	E. Mann	Closed	150.00	150.00
91-01-332	Samantha-GU-3	E. Mann	Closed	100.00	100.00
91-01-333	Sandra-DOLL-6-PHE	E. Mann	2,500	65.00	65.00
91-01-334	Scarlett-FH-399	E. Mann	2,500	100.00	100.00
91-01-335	Scarlett-FH-436	E. Mann	2,500	135.00	135.00
91-01-336	Shaka-SP-401	E. Mann	2,500	110.00	110.00
91-01-337	Sharon 21" Blue-EP-34	E. Mann	Closed	120.00	120.00
91-01-338	Shau Chen-GU-2	E. Mann	2,500	85.00	85.00
91-01-339	Shelley-CH-1	E. Mann	2,500	110.00	110.00
91-01-340	Sophie-TR-53	E. Mann	2,500	135.00	135.00
91-01-341	Stacy-DOLL-6PH	E. Mann	Closed	65.00	65.00
91-01-342	Stephanie-AM-11	E. Mann	Closed	105.00	105.00
91-01-343	Stephanie-FH-467	E. Mann	Closed	95.00	95.00
91-01-344	Stephanie Pink & White-OM-196	E. Mann	Closed	300.00	300.00
91-01-345	Summer-AM-33	E. Mann	2,500	200.00	200.00
91-01-346	Sybil 20" Beige-C-3131	E. Mann	Closed	135.00	135.00
91-01-347	Sybil Pink-DOLL-12PHMC	E. Mann	2,500	75.00	75.00
91-01-348	Tamara-OM-187	E. Mann	Closed	135.00	135.00
91-01-349	Terri-TR-62	E. Mann	2,500	75.00	75.00
91-01-350	Tessa-AM-19	E. Mann	2,500	135.00	135.00
91-01-351	Tina-AM-16	E. Mann	Closed	130.00	130.00
91-01-352	Vanessa-AM-34	E. Mann	Closed	90.00	90.00
91-01-353	Vicki-C-3101	E. Mann	Closed	200.00	200.00
91-01-345	Violet-EP-41	E. Mann	Closed	135.00	135.00
91-01-355	Violet-OM-186	E. Mann	2,500	270.00	270.00
91-01-356	Virginia-SP-359	E. Mann	2,500	120.00	120.00
91-01-357	Wah-Ching Watching Oriental Toddler-YK-4175	E. Mann	Closed	110.00	110.00
92-01-358	Alice-JNC-4013	E. Mann	Open	90.00	90.00
92-01-359	Amy-OM-06	E. Mann	2,500	150.00	150.00
92-01-360	Beth-OM-05	E. Mann	Closed	135.00	135.00
92-01-361	Bette-OM-01	E. Mann	2,500	115.00	115.00
92-01-362	Charlotte-FH-484	E. Mann	2,500	115.00	115.00
92-01-363	Chelsea-IND-397	E. Mann	Open	85.00	85.00
92-01-364	Cordelia-OM-009	E. Mann	2,500	250.00	250.00
92-01-365	Cordelia-OM-09	E. Mann	2,500	250.00	250.00
92-01-366	Debbie-JNC-4006	E. Mann	Open	90.00	90.00
92-01-367	Deidre-FH-473	E. Mann	2,500	115.00	115.00
92-01-368	Deidre-YK-4083	E. Mann	Closed	95.00	95.00
92-01-369	Dona-FH-494	E. Mann	2,500	100.00	100.00
92-01-370	Eugenie-OM-225	E. Mann	2,500	300.00	300.00
92-01-371	Giselle-OM-02	E. Mann	Closed	90.00	90.00
92-01-372	Jan-OM-012	E. Mann	9,200	135.00	135.00
92-01-373	Janet-FH-496	E. Mann	2,500	120.00	120.00
92-01-374	Jet-FH-478	E. Mann	2,500	115.00	115.00
92-01-375	Jodie-FH-495	E. Mann	2,500	115.00	115.00
92-01-376	Juliette-OM-08	E. Mann	2,500	175.00	175.00
92-01-377	Laura-OM-010	E. Mann	2,500	250.00	250.00
92-01-378	Laurie-JNC-4004	E. Mann	Open	90.00	90.00
92-01-379	Lydia-OM-226	E. Mann	2,500	250.00	250.00
92-01-380	Maggie-FH-505	E. Mann	Closed	125.00	125.00
92-01-381	Melissa-OM-03	E. Mann	2,500	135.00	135.00
92-01-382	Nancy-JNC-4001	E. Mann	Open	90.00	90.00
92-01-383	Sally-FH-492	E. Mann	2,500	105.00	105.00
92-01-384	Sapphires-OM-223	E. Mann	2,500	250.00	250.00
92-01-385	Sara Ann-FH-474	E. Mann	2,500	115.00	115.00
92-01-386	Scarlett-FH-471	E. Mann	2,500	120.00	120.00
92-01-387	Sonja-FH-486	E. Mann	2,500	125.00	125.00
92-01-388	Sue-JNC-4003	E. Mann	Open	90.00	90.00
92-01-389	Tiffany-OM-014	E. Mann	2,500	150.00	150.00
92-01-390	Trina-OM-011	E. Mann	Closed	165.00	165.00
92-01-391	Violette-FH-503	E. Mann	2,500	120.00	120.00
92-01-392	Yvette-OM-015	E. Mann	2,500	150.00	150.00
93-01-393	Adrienne C-3162	E. Mann	Closed	135.00	135.00
93-01-394	Antonia OM-227	E. Mann	2,500	350.00	350.00
93-01-395	Arlene SP-421	E. Mann	Closed	100.00	100.00
93-01-396	Blaine C-3167	E. Mann	Closed	100.00	100.00
93-01-397	Camille OM-230	E. Mann	2,500	250.00	250.00
93-01-398	Cinnamon JNC-4014	E. Mann	Closed	90.00	90.00
93-01-399	Clare FH-497	E. Mann	2,500	100.00	100.00
93-01-400	Clothilde FH-469	E. Mann	2,500	125.00	125.00
93-01-401	Donna DOLL-447	E. Mann	2,500	85.00	85.00
93-01-402	Ellen YK-4223	E. Mann	3,500	150.00	150.00
93-01-403	Gena OM-229	E. Mann	Closed	250.00	250.00
93-01-404	Happy FH-479	E. Mann	2,500	105.00	105.00
93-01-405	Hedy FH-449	E. Mann	Closed	95.00	95.00
93-01-406	Iris FH-483	E. Mann	2,500	95.00	95.00
93-01-407	Jan Dress-Up OM-12	E. Mann	2,500	135.00	135.00
93-01-408	Jillian SP-428	E. Mann	Closed	165.00	165.00
93-01-409	Juliette OM-8	E. Mann	2,500	175.00	175.00
93-01-410	Kendra FH-481	E. Mann	2,500	115.00	115.00
93-01-411	Kit SP-426	E. Mann	Closed	55.00	55.00
93-01-412	Linda SP-435	E. Mann	Closed	95.00	95.00
93-01-413	Lynn FH-498	E. Mann	2,500	120.00	120.00
93-01-414	Mariah LL-909	E. Mann	Closed	135.00	135.00
93-01-415	Nina YK-4232	E. Mann	3,500	135.00	135.00
93-01-416	Oona TR-57	E. Mann	Closed	135.00	135.00
93-01-417	Rebecca C-3177	E. Mann	2,500	135.00	135.00
93-01-418	Saretta SP-423	E. Mann	2,500	100.00	100.00
93-01-419	Shaka TR-45	E. Mann	2,500	100.00	100.00
93-01-420	Suzie SP-422	E. Mann	2,500	164.00	164.00
94-01-421	Abby YK-4533	E. Mann	3,500	135.00	135.00
94-01-422	Adak PS-412	E. Mann	2,500	150.00	150.00
94-01-423	Alice GU-32	E. Mann	2,500	150.00	150.00
94-01-424	Alice IND-508	E. Mann	2,500	115.00	115.00
94-01-425	Ally FH-556	E. Mann	2,500	115.00	115.00
94-01-426	Alyssa C-3201	E. Mann	2,500	110.00	110.00
94-01-427	Alyssa PP-1	E. Mann	2,500	275.00	275.00
94-01-428	Amy OC-43M	E. Mann	2,500	115.00	115.00
94-01-429	Angel LL-956	E. Mann	2,500	90.00	90.00
94-01-430	Angel SP-460	E. Mann	2,500	140.00	140.00
94-01-431	Angelica FH-291E	E. Mann	2,500	85.00	85.00
94-01-432	Angelina FH-291S	E. Mann	2,500	85.00	85.00
94-01-433	Angeline FH-291WG	E. Mann	2,500	85.00	85.00
94-01-434	Angelita FH-291G	E. Mann	2,500	85.00	85.00
94-01-435	Angelo OC-57	E. Mann	2,500	135.00	135.00
94-01-436	Antonia OM-42	E. Mann	2,500	150.00	150.00
94-01-437	Arilene LL-940	E. Mann	2,500	90.00	90.00
94-01-438	Atanak PS-414	E. Mann	2,500	150.00	150.00
94-01-439	Baby Belle C-3193	E. Mann	2,500	150.00	150.00
94-01-440	Baby Scarlet C-3194	E. Mann	2,500	115.00	115.00
94-01-441	Blair YK-4532	E. Mann	3,500	150.00	150.00
94-01-442	Bobbi NM-30	E. Mann	2,500	135.00	135.00
94-01-443	Brandy YK-4537	E. Mann	3,500	165.00	165.00
94-01-444	Bronwyn IND-517	E. Mann	2,500	140.00	140.00
94-01-445	Cactus Flower Indian LL-944	E. Mann	2,500	105.00	105.00
94-01-446	Callie TR-76	E. Mann	2,500	140.00	140.00
94-01-447	Calypso LL-942	E. Mann	2,500	150.00	150.00
94-01-448	Carmen PS-408	E. Mann	2,500	150.00	150.00
94-01-449	Casey C-3197	E. Mann	2,500	140.00	140.00
94-01-450	Cathy GU-41	E. Mann	2,500	140.00	140.00
94-01-451	Chris FH-561	E. Mann	2,500	85.00	85.00
94-01-452	Chrissie FH-562	E. Mann	2,500	85.00	85.00
94-01-453	Cindy OC-58	E. Mann	2,500	140.00	140.00
94-01-454	Clara IND-518	E. Mann	2,500	140.00	140.00
94-01-455	Clara IND-524	E. Mann	2,500	150.00	150.00
94-01-456	Claudette TR-81	E. Mann	2,500	150.00	150.00
94-01-457	Copper YK-4546C	E. Mann	3,500	150.00	150.00
94-01-458	Cora FH-565	E. Mann	2,500	140.00	140.00
94-01-459	Cory FH-564	E. Mann	2,500	115.00	115.00
94-01-460	Dallas PS-403	E. Mann	2,500	150.00	150.00
94-01-461	Daryl LL-947	E. Mann	2,500	150.00	150.00
94-01-462	Dee LL-948	E. Mann	2,500	110.00	110.00
94-01-463	Delilah C-3195	E. Mann	2,500	150.00	150.00
94-01-464	Faith IND-522	E. Mann	2,500	135.00	135.00
94-01-465	Faith OC-60	E. Mann	2,500	115.00	115.00
94-01-466	Flora FH-583	E. Mann	2,500	115.00	115.00
94-01-467	Florette IND-519	E. Mann	2,500	140.00	140.00
94-01-468	Gardiner PS-405	E. Mann	2,500	150.00	150.00
94-01-469	Georgia IND-510	E. Mann	2,500	220.00	220.00
94-01-470	Georgia SP-456	E. Mann	2,500	115.00	115.00
94-01-471	Hatty/Matty IND-514	E. Mann	2,500	165.00	165.00
94-01-472	Heather YK-4531	E. Mann	3,500	165.00	165.00
94-01-473	Honey LL-945	E. Mann	2,500	150.00	150.00
94-01-474	Hyacinth LL-941	E. Mann	2,500	90.00	90.00
94-01-475	Indian IND-520	E. Mann	2,500	115.00	115.00
94-01-476	Ivy C-3203	E. Mann	2,500	85.00	85.00
94-01-477	Jacqueline C-3202	E. Mann	2,500	150.00	150.00
94-01-478	Jan FH-584R	E. Mann	2,500	115.00	115.00
94-01-479	Janis FH-584B	E. Mann	2,500	115.00	115.00
94-01-480	Jenny OC-36M	E. Mann	2,500	115.00	115.00
94-01-481	Jillian C-3196	E. Mann	2,500	150.00	150.00
94-01-482	Jo YK-4539	E. Mann	3,500	150.00	150.00
94-01-483	Jordan SP-455	E. Mann	2,500	150.00	150.00
94-01-484	Kate OC-55	E. Mann	2,500	150.00	150.00
94-01-485	Katie IND-511	E. Mann	2,500	110.00	110.00
94-01-486	Kelly YK-4536	E. Mann	3,500	150.00	150.00
94-01-487	Kevin MS-25	E. Mann	2,500	150.00	150.00
94-01-488	Kevin YK-4543	E. Mann	3,500	140.00	140.00
94-01-489	Kit YK-4547	E. Mann	3,500	115.00	115.00
94-01-490	Kitten IND-512	E. Mann	2,500	110.00	110.00
94-01-491	Lady Caroline LL-938	E. Mann	2,500	120.00	120.00
94-01-492	Lady Caroline LL-939	E. Mann	2,500	120.00	120.00
94-01-493	Laughing Waters PS-410	E. Mann	2,500	150.00	150.00
94-01-494	Lauren SP-458	E. Mann	2,500	125.00	125.00
94-01-495	Lindsay SP-462	E. Mann	2,500	150.00	150.00
94-01-496	Little Red Riding Hood FH-557	E. Mann	2,500	140.00	140.00
94-01-497	Loretta SP-457	E. Mann	2,500	140.00	140.00
94-01-498	Lucinda PS-406	E. Mann	2,500	150.00	150.00
94-01-499	Magnolia FH-558	E. Mann	2,500	150.00	150.00
94-01-500	Maiden PS-409	E. Mann	2,500	150.00	150.00
94-01-501	Mandy YK-4548	E. Mann	3,500	115.00	115.00
94-01-502	Margaret C-3204	E. Mann	2,500	150.00	150.00
94-01-503	Maria GU-35	E. Mann	2,500	115.00	115.00
94-01-504	Mary OC-56	E. Mann	2,500	135.00	135.00
94-01-505	Mary Ann TR-79	E. Mann	2,500	125.00	125.00
94-01-506	Mary Jo FH-552	E. Mann	2,500	150.00	150.00
94-01-507	Mary Lou FH-565	E. Mann	2,500	135.00	135.00
94-01-508	Megan C-3192	E. Mann	2,500	150.00	150.00
94-01-509	Miss Elizabeth SP-459	E. Mann	2,500	150.00	150.00
94-01-510	Missy FH-567	E. Mann	2,500	140.00	140.00
94-01-511	Morning Dew Indian PS-404	E. Mann	2,500	150.00	150.00
94-01-512	Musical Doll OC-45M	E. Mann	2,500	140.00	140.00
94-01-513	Natalie PP-2	E. Mann	2,500	275.00	275.00
94-01-514	Nikki PS-401	E. Mann	2,500	150.00	150.00
94-01-515	Nikki SP-461	E. Mann	2,500	150.00	150.00
94-01-516	Noel MS-27	E. Mann	2,500	150.00	150.00
94-01-517	Noelle C-3199	E. Mann	2,500	195.00	195.00
94-01-518	Noelle MS-28	E. Mann	2,500	150.00	150.00
94-01-519	Odetta IND-521	E. Mann	2,500	140.00	140.00

Company		Series			
Number	Name	Artist	Edition Limit	Issue Price	Quote
94-01-520	Oriana IND-515	E. Mann	2,500	140.00	140.00
94-01-521	Paige GU-33	E. Mann	2,500	150.00	150.00
94-01-522	Pamela LL-949	E. Mann	2,500	115.00	115.00
94-01-523	Panama OM-43	E. Mann	2,500	195.00	195.00
94-01-524	Patty GU-34	E. Mann	2,500	115.00	115.00
94-01-525	Payson YK-4541	E. Mann	3,500	135.00	135.00
94-01-526	Payton PS-407	E. Mann	2,500	150.00	150.00
94-01-527	Pearl IND-523	E. Mann	2,500	275.00	275.00
94-01-528	Petula C-3191	E. Mann	2,500	140.00	140.00
94-01-529	Pegeen C-3205	E. Mann	2,500	150.00	150.00
94-01-530	Peggy TR-75	E. Mann	2,500	185.00	185.00
94-01-531	Princess Foxfire PS-411	E. Mann	2,500	150.00	150.00
94-01-532	Princess Moonrise YK-4542	E. Mann	3,500	140.00	140.00
94-01-533	Princess Snow Flower PS-402	E. Mann	2,500	150.00	150.00
94-01-534	Priscilla YK-4538	E. Mann	3,500	135.00	135.00
94-01-535	Rebecca C-3177	E. Mann	2,500	135.00	135.00
94-01-536	Regina OM-41	E. Mann	2,500	150.00	150.00
94-01-537	Rita FH-553	E. Mann	2,500	115.00	115.00
94-01-538	Robby NM-29	E. Mann	2,500	135.00	135.00
94-01-539	Saretta SP-423	E. Mann	2,500	100.00	100.00
94-01-540	Shaka TR-45	E. Mann	2,500	100.00	100.00
94-01-541	Sister Suzie IND-509	E. Mann	2,500	95.00	95.00
94-01-542	Southern Belle FH-570	E. Mann	2,500	140.00	140.00
94-01-543	Sparkle OM-40	E. Mann	2,500	150.00	150.00
94-01-544	Stephie OC-41M	E. Mann	2,500	115.00	115.00
94-01-545	Sue Kwei TR-73	E. Mann	2,500	110.00	110.00
94-01-546	Sugar Plum Fairy OM-39	E. Mann	2,500	150.00	150.00
94-01-547	Suzanne LL-943	E. Mann	2,500	105.00	105.00
94-01-548	Suzie GU-38	E. Mann	2,500	135.00	135.00
94-01-549	Suzie SP-422	E. Mann	2,500	164.00	164.00
94-01-550	Taffey TR-80	E. Mann	2,500	150.00	150.00
94-01-551	Tallulah OM-44	E. Mann	2,500	275.00	275.00
94-01-552	Teresa C-3198	E. Mann	2,500	110.00	110.00
94-01-553	Tiffany OC-44M	E. Mann	2,500	140.00	140.00
94-01-554	Tippi LL-946	E. Mann	2,500	110.00	110.00
94-01-555	Todd YK-4540	E. Mann	3,500	45.00	45.00
94-01-556	Topaz TR-74	E. Mann	2,500	195.00	195.00
94-01-557	Trixie TR-77	E. Mann	2,500	110.00	110.00
94-01-558	Virginia TR-78	E. Mann	2,500	195.00	195.00
94-01-559	Wendy MS-26	E. Mann	2,500	150.00	150.00
Seymour Mann Inc.		**Signature Doll Series**			
91-02-001	Amber-MS-1	M. Severino	Closed	95.00	95.00
91-02-002	Becky-MS-2	M. Severino	5,000	95.00	95.00
91-02-003	Bianca-PK-101	P. Kolesar	Closed	120.00	120.00
91-02-004	Bridgette-PK-104	P. Kolesar	Closed	120.00	120.00
91-02-005	Clair-Ann-PK-252	P. Kolesar	5,000	100.00	100.00
91-02-006	Daddy's Little Darling-MS-8	M. Severino	5,000	165.00	165.00
91-02-007	Dozy Elf w/ Featherbed-MAB-100	M.A. Byerly	Closed	110.00	110.00
91-02-008	Duby Elf w/ Featherbed-MAB-103	M.A. Byerly	Closed	110.00	110.00
91-02-009	Dudley Elf w/ Featherbed-MAB-101	M.A. Byerly	Closed	110.00	110.00
91-02-010	Duffy Elf w/ Featherbed-MAB-102	M.A. Byerly	Closed	110.00	110.00
91-02-011	Enoc-PK-100	P. Kolesar	5,000	100.00	100.00
91-02-012	Mikey-MS-3	M. Severino	5,000	95.00	95.00
91-02-013	Mommy's Rays of Sunshine-MS-9	M. Severino	5,000	165.00	165.00
91-02-014	Paulette-PAC-2	P. Aprile	5,000	250.00	250.00
91-02-015	Paulette-PAC-4	P. Aprile	5,000	250.00	250.00
91-02-016	Precious Baby-SB-100	S. Bilotto	5,000	250.00	250.00
91-02-017	Precious Pary Time-SB-102	S. Bilotto	5,000	250.00	250.00
91-02-018	Precious Spring Time-SB-104	S. Bilotto	Closed	250.00	250.00
91-02-019	Shun Lee-PK-102	P. Kolesar	Closed	120.00	120.00
91-02-020	Sparkle-PK-250	P. Kolesar	5,000	100.00	100.00
91-02-021	Stephie-MS-6	M. Severino	Closed	125.00	125.00
91-02-022	Alice-MS-7	M. Severino	5,000	120.00	120.00
91-02-023	Su Lin-MS-5	M. Severino	5,000	105.00	105.00
91-02-024	Susan Marie-PK-103	P. Kolesar	Closed	120.00	120.00
91-02-025	Sweet Pea-PK-251	P. Kolesar	Closed	100.00	100.00
91-02-026	Yawning Kate-MS-4	M. Severino	Closed	105.00	105.00
92-02-027	Abigail-MS-11	M. Severino	5,000	125.00	125.00
92-02-028	Adora-MS-14	M. Severino	5,000	185.00	185.00
92-02-029	Alexandria-PAC-19	P. Aprile	5,000	300.00	300.00
92-02-030	Baby Cakes Crumbs-PK-CRUMBS	P. Kolesar	5,000	17.50	17.50
92-02-031	Baby Cakes Crumbs/Black-PK-CRUMBS/B	P. Kolesar	5,000	17.50	17.50
92-02-032	Bride & Flower Girl-PAC-6	P. Aprile	5,000	600.00	600.00
92-02-033	Cassandra-PAC-8	P. Aprile	Closed	450.00	450.00
92-02-034	Cassie Flower Girl-PAC-9	P. Aprile	Closed	175.00	175.00
92-02-035	Celine-PAC-11	P. Aprile	5,000	165.00	165.00
92-02-036	Clarissa-PAC-3	P. Aprile	5,000	165.00	165.00
92-02-037	Cody-MS-19	M. Severino	Closed	120.00	120.00
92-02-038	Creole Black-HP-202	H. Payne	Closed	250.00	250.00
92-02-039	Cynthia-PAC-10	P. Ap rile	Closed	165.00	165.00
92-02-040	Darla-HP-204	H. Payne	5,000	250.00	250.00
92-02-041	Dulcie-HP-200	H. Payne	Closed	250.00	250.00
92-02-042	Dustin-HP-201	H. Payne	5,000	250.00	250.00
92-02-043	Eugenie Bride-PAC-1	P. Aprile	5,000	165.00	165.00
92-02-044	Evening Star-PAC-5	P. Aprile	Closed	500.00	500.00
92-02-045	Kate-MS-15	M. Severino	Closed	190.00	190.00
92-02-046	Little Match Girl-HP-205	H. Payne	5,000	150.00	150.00
92-02-047	"Little Turtle" Indian-PK-110	P. Kolesar	Closed	150.00	150.00
92-02-048	Megan-MS-12	M. Severino	5,000	125.00	125.00
92-02-049	Melanie-PAC-14	P. Aprile	Closed	300.00	300.00
92-02-050	Nadia-PAC-18	P. Aprile	Closed	175.00	175.00
92-02-051	Olivia-PAC-12	P. Aprile	Closed	300.00	300.00
92-02-052	Pavlova-PAC-17	P. Aprile	5,000	145.00	145.00
92-02-053	Polly-HP-206	H. Payne	5,000	120.00	120.00
92-02-054	Raven Eskimo-PK-106	P. Kolesar	Closed	130.00	130.00
92-02-055	Rebecca Beige Bonnet-MS-17B	M. Severino	5,000	175.00	175.00
92-02-056	Ruby-MS-18	M. Severino	5,000	135.00	135.00
92-02-057	Sally-MS-25	M. Severino	5,000	110.00	110.00
92-02-058	Spanky-HP-25	H. Payne	5,000	250.00	250.00
92-02-059	Stacy-MS-24	M. Severino	Closed	110.00	110.00
92-02-060	Vanessa-PAC-15	P. Aprile	Closed	300.00	300.00
92-02-061	Victoria w/Blanket-MS-10	M. Severino	Closed	110.00	110.00
92-02-062	Violetta-PAC-16	P. Aprile	5,000	165.00	165.00
93-02-063	Bonnett Baby MS-17W	M. Severino	5,000	175.00	175.00
93-02-064	Grace HKH-2	H. Kahl-Hyland	5,000	250.00	250.00
93-02-065	Helene HKH-1	H. Kahl-Hyland	5,000	250.00	250.00
93-02-066	Reilly HKH-3	H. Kahl-Hyland	5,000	260.00	260.00
94-02-067	Sis JAG-110	J. Grammer	5,000	110.00	110.00
94-02-068	Tex JAG-114	J. Grammer	5,000	110.00	110.00
94-02-069	Tracy JAG-111	J. Grammer	5,000	150.00	150.00
94-02-070	Trevor JAG-112	J. Grammer	5,000	115.00	115.00

Company		Series			
Number	Name	Artist	Edition Limit	Issue Price	Quote
Mattel		**Bob Mackie Barbie Dolls**			
90-01-001	Gold Barbie 5405	B. Mackie	Retrd.	144.00	300-600.
91-01-002	Platinum Barbie 2703	B. Mackie	Retrd.	153.00	250-385.
91-01-003	Starlight Splendor Barbie 2704	B. Mackie	Retrd.	135.00	200-400.
92-01-004	Neptune Fantasy Barbie 4248	B. Mackie	Retrd.	160.00	225-300.
92-01-005	Empress Bride Barbie 4247	B. Mackie	Retrd.	232.00	295-350.
Mattel		**Nostalgic Porcelain Barbie Dolls**			
89-02-001	Wedding Day Barbie 2641	Mattel	Retrd.	198.00	450-550.
90-02-002	Sophisticated Lady 5313	Mattel	Retrd.	198.00	200-395.
90-02-003	Solo in the Spotlight 7613	Mattel	Retrd.	198.00	200-295.
Jan McLean Originals		**Flowers of the Heart Collection**			
90-01-001	Pansy	J. McLean	100	2200.00	3000.00
90-01-002	Poppy	J. McLean	100	2200.00	2600.00
91-01-003	Primrose	J. McLean	100	2500.00	2800-3000.
91-01-004	Marigold	J. McLean	100	2400.00	3000.00
Jan McLean Originals		**Jan McLean Originals**			
90-02-001	Phoebe I	J. McLean	25	2700.00	3000.00
91-02-002	Lucrezia	J. McLean	15	6000.00	6000.00
Middleton Doll Company		**Porcelain Limited Edition Series**			
88-01-001	Cherish-1st Edition	L. Middleton	750	350.00	500.00
88-01-002	Sincerity -1st Edition-Nettie/Simplicity	L. Middleton	750	330.00	350-475.
89-01-003	My Lee	L. Middleton	629	500.00	500.00
89-01-004	Devan	L. Middleton	525	500.00	500.00
90-01-005	Baby Grace	L. Middleton	500	500.00	500.00
90-01-006	Johanna	L. Middleton	500	500.00	500.00
91-01-007	Molly Rose	L. Middleton	500	500.00	500.00
94-01-008	Bride	L. Middleton	200	1390.00	1390.00
94-01-009	Tenderness-Petite Pierrot	L. Middleton	250	500.00	500.00
Middleton Doll Company		**Limited Edition Vinyl**			
81-02-001	Little Angel-Kingdom (Hand Painted)	L. Middleton	800	40.00	300.00
85-02-002	Little Angel-King-2 (Hand Painted)	L. Middleton	400	40.00	200.00
89-02-003	Angel Fancy	L. Middleton	10,000	120.00	130.00
90-02-004	Baby Grace	L. Middleton	5,000	190.00	190.00
90-02-005	Sincerity-Apricots n' Cream	L. Middleton	5,000	250.00	250.00
90-02-006	Sincerity-Apples n' Spice	L. Middleton	5,000	250.00	250.00
90-02-007	Forever Cherish	L. Middleton	5,000	170.00	170.00
90-02-008	First Moments-Twin Boy	L. Middleton	5,000	180.00	180.00
90-02-009	First Moments-Twin Girl	L. Middleton	5,000	180.00	180.00
90-02-010	Angel Locks	L. Middleton	10,000	140.00	150.00
90-02-011	Missy- Buttercup	L. Middleton	5,000	160.00	170.00
90-02-012	Dear One-Sunday Best	L. Middleton	5,000	140.00	140.00
91-02-013	Bubba Batboy	L. Middleton	5,000	190.00	190.00
91-02-014	My Lee Candy Cane	L. Middleton	2,500	170.00	170.00
91-02-015	Devan Delightful	L. Middleton	5,000	170.00	170.00
91-02-016	Gracie Mae	L. Middleton	5,000	250.00	250.00
92-02-017	Johanna	L. Middleton	5,000	190.00	190.00
92-02-018	Cottontop Cherish	L. Middleton	5,000	180.00	180.00
92-02-019	Molly Rose	L. Middleton	5,000	196.00	196.00
92-02-020	Gracie Mae (Brown or Blond Hair)	L. Middleton	5,000	250.00	250.00
92-02-021	Serenity Berries & Bows	L. Middleton	1,500	250.00	250.00
92-02-022	Sincerity Petals & Plums	L. Middleton	1,500	250.00	250.00
93-02-023	Amanda Springtime	L. Middleton	2,000	180.00	180.00
94-02-024	Johanna-Newborn	L. Middleton	2,000	180.00	180.00
94-02-025	Joey-Newborn	L. Middleton	1,000	180.00	180.00
Middleton Doll Company		**First Moments Series**			
84-03-001	First Moments (Sleeping)	L. Middleton	41,000	69.00	150.00
86-03-002	First Moments Blue Eyes	L. Middleton	15,000	120.00	150.00
86-03-003	First Moments Brown Eyes	L. Middleton	5,490	120.00	150.00
87-03-004	First Moments Boy	L. Middleton	6,075	130.00	160.00
87-03-005	First Moments Christening (Asleep)	L. Middleton	Open	160.00	180.00
87-03-006	First Moments Christening (Awake)	L. Middleton	Open	160.00	180.00
90-03-007	First Moments Sweetness	L. Middleton	Open	180.00	180.00
92-03-008	First Moments Awake in Pink	L. Middleton	5,000	170.00	170.00
92-03-009	First Moments Awake in Blue	L. Middleton	5,000	170.00	170.00
93-03-010	First Moments Heirloom	L. Middleton	Open	190.00	190.00
94-03-011	Sweetness-Newborn	L. Middleton	Open	190.00	190.00
Middleton Doll Company		**Vinyl Collectors Series**			
86-04-001	Bubba Chubbs	L. Middleton	5,600	100.00	150-200.
88-04-002	Bubba Chubbs Railroader	L. Middleton	Open	140.00	170.00
86-04-003	Little Angel - 3rd Edition	L. Middleton	Open	90.00	110.00
85-04-004	Angel Face	L. Middleton	20,200	90.00	150.00
87-04-005	Missy	L. Middleton	Open	100.00	120.00
87-04-006	Amanda - 1st Edition	L. Middleton	4,200	140.00	160.00
86-04-007	Dear One - 1st Edition	L. Middleton	4,935	90.00	200.00
88-04-008	Cherish	L. Middleton	Open	160.00	160.00
88-04-009	Sincerity - Limited 1st Ed. - Nettie/Simplicity	L. Middleton	4,380	160.00	160.00
89-04-010	My Lee	L. Middleton	Open	170.00	170.00
89-04-011	Devan	L. Middleton	Open	170.00	170.00
89-04-012	Sincerity-Schoolgirl	L. Middleton	Open	180.00	180.00
92-04-013	Little Angel Girl	L. Middleton	Open	130.00	130.00
92-04-014	Little Angel Boy	L. Middleton	Open	130.00	130.00
92-04-015	Beth	L. Middleton	Open	160.00	160.00
92-04-016	Polly Esther	L. Middleton	Open	160.00	160.00
93-04-017	Echo	L. Middleton	Open	180.00	180.00
94-04-018	Angel Kisses Girl	L. Middleton	Open	98.00	98.00
94-04-019	Angel Kisses Boy	L. Middleton	Open	98.00	98.00
94-04-020	Country Girl	L. Middleton	Open	118.00	118.00
94-04-021	Country Boy	L. Middleton	Open	118.00	118.00
94-04-022	Town Girl	L. Middleton	Open	118.00	118.00
94-04-023	Town Boy	L. Middleton	Open	118.00	118.00
94-04-024	Country Girl (Dark Flesh)	L. Middleton	Open	118.00	118.00
94-04-025	Country Boy (Dark Flesh)	L. Middleton	Open	118.00	118.00
94-04-026	Town Girl (Dark Flesh)	L. Middleton	Open	118.00	118.00
94-04-027	Town Boy (Dark Flesh)	L. Middleton	Open	118.00	118.00
Middleton Doll Company		**Littlest Ballet Company**			
88-05-001	April (Dressed in Pink)	S. Wakeen	7,500	100.00	110.00
88-05-002	Melanie (Dressed in Blue)	S. Wakeen	7,500	100.00	110.00
88-05-003	Jeanne (Dressed in White)	S. Wakeen	7,500	100.00	110.00
88-05-004	Lisa (Black Leotards)	S. Wakeen	7,500	100.00	110.00
89-05-005	April (In Leotard)	S. Wakeen	7,500	100.00	110.00
89-05-006	Melanie (In Leotard)	S. Wakeen	7,500	100.00	110.00
89-05-007	Jeannie (In Leotard)	S. Wakeen	7,500	100.00	110.00
Middleton Doll Company		**First Collectibles**			
90-06-001	Sweetest Little Dreamer (Asleep)	L. Middleton	Open	40.00	40.00
90-06-002	Day Dreamer (Awake)	L. Middleton	Open	42.00	42.00

Company / Number	Name	Series / Artist	Edition Limit	Issue Price	Quote
91-06-003	Day Dreamer Sunshine	L. Middleton	Open	49.00	49.00
91-06-004	Teenie	L. Middleton	Open	59.00	59.00
Middleton Doll Company		**Birthday Babies**			
92-07-001	Winter	L. Middleton	3,000	180.00	180.00
92-07-002	Fall	L. Middleton	3,000	170.00	170.00
92-07-003	Summer	L. Middleton	3,000	160.00	160.00
92-07-004	Spring	L. Middleton	3,000	170.00	170.00
Middleton Doll Company		**Wise Penny Collection**			
93-08-001	Jennifer (Peach Dress)	L. Middleton	Open	140.00	140.00
93-08-002	Jennifer (Print Dress)	L. Middleton	Open	140.00	140.00
93-08-003	Molly Jo	L. Middleton	Open	140.00	140.00
93-08-004	Gordon	L. Middleton	Open	140.00	140.00
93-08-005	Ashley (Brown Hair)	L. Middleton	Open	120.00	120.00
93-08-006	Merry	L. Middleton	Open	140.00	140.00
93-08-007	Grace	L. Middleton	Open	140.00	140.00
93-08-008	Ashley (Blond Hair)	L. Middleton	Open	120.00	120.00
93-08-009	Baby Devan	L. Middleton	Open	140.00	140.00
Middleton Doll Company		**Porcelain Collector Series**			
92-09-001	Beloved & Bé Bé	L. Middleton	500	590.00	590.00
92-09-002	Sencerity II - Country Fair	L. Middleton	500	500.00	500.00
93-09-003	Cherish - Lilac & Lace	L. Middleton	500	500.00	500.00
Middleton Doll Company		**Porcelain Bears & Bunny**			
93-10-001	Buster Bear	L. Middleton	Open	250.00	250.00
93-10-002	Baby Buster	L. Middleton	Open	230.00	230.00
93-10-003	Bye Baby Bunting	L. Middleton	Open	270.00	270.00
Middleton Doll Company		**Christmas Angel Collection**			
87-11-001	Christmas Angel 1987	L. Middleton	4,174	130.00	195.00
88-11-002	Christmas Angel 1988	L. Middleton	6,385	130.00	160.00
89-11-003	Christmas Angel 1989	L. Middleton	7,500	150.00	160.00
90-11-004	Christmas Angel 1990	L. Middleton	5,000	150.00	150.00
91-11-005	Christmas Angel 1991	L. Middleton	5,000	180.00	180.00
92-11-006	Christmas Angel 1992	L. Middleton	5,000	190.00	190.00
93-11-007	Christmas Angel 1993-Girl	L. Middleton	4,000	190.00	190.00
93-11-008	Christmas Angel 1993 (set)	L. Middleton	1,000	390.00	390.00
94-11-009	Christmas Angel 1994	L. Middleton	5,000	190.00	190.00
Midwest of Cannon Falls		**Folk Art Gallery Collection**			
94-01-001	Heartfelt Angel 11422-3	S. Hale	Open	37.00	37.00
94-01-002	Heartfelt Angel 11423-0	S. Hale	Open	20.00	20.00
94-01-003	Sitting Santa 11424-7	S. Hale	Open	30.00	30.00
94-01-004	Santa of Christmas Past 12057-6	S. Hale	Open	130.00	130.00
94-01-005	Gardening Girl 11426-1	S. Hale	Open	45.00	45.00
94-01-006	Bewitching Belinda 11425-4	S. Hale	Open	40.00	40.00
94-01-007	Santa Gone Fishing 12029-3	S. Hale	Open	65.00	65.00
Nahrgang Collection		**Porcelain Doll Series**			
89-01-001	Palmer	J. Nahrgang	250	270.00	270.00
90-01-002	Grant (Take Me Out To The Ball Game)	J. Nahrgang	500	390.00	390.00
90-01-003	Maggie	J. Nahrgang	500	295.00	295.00
90-01-004	Kelsey	J. Nahrgang	250	350.00	350.00
90-01-005	Kasey	J. Nahrgang	250	450.00	450.00
90-01-006	Alicia	J. Nahrgang	250	330.00	330.00
90-01-007	Karman (Gypsy)	J. Nahrgang	250	350.00	350.00
90-01-008	Karissa	J. Nahrgang	500	350.00	395.00
91-01-009	McKinsey	J. Nahrgang	250	350.00	350.00
91-01-010	Rae	J. Nahrgang	250	350.00	350.00
91-01-011	Aubry	J. Nahrgang	250	390.00	390.00
91-01-012	Laura	J. Nahrgang	250	450.00	450.00
91-01-013	Sophie	J. Nahrgang	250	450.00	450.00
91-01-014	Carson	J. Nahrgang	250	350.00	350.00
91-01-015	Erin	J. Nahrgang	250	295.00	295.00
91-01-016	Ana Marie	J. Nahrgang	250	390.00	390.00
91-01-017	Holly	J. Nahrgang	175	295.00	295.00
92-01-018	Brooke	J. Nahrgang	250	390.00	390.00
92-01-019	Alexis	J. Nahrgang	250	390.00	390.00
92-01-020	Katie	J. Nahrgang	250	295.00	295.00
92-01-021	Pocahontas	J. Nahrgang	100	395.00	395.00
92-01-022	Molly Pitcher	J. Nahrgang	100	395.00	395.00
92-01-023	Harriet Tubman	J. Nahrgang	100	395.00	395.00
92-01-024	Florence Nightingale	J. Nahrgang	100	395.00	395.00
92-01-025	Dolly Madison	J. Nahrgang	100	395.00	395.00
92-01-026	Annie Sullivan	J. Nahrgang	25	895.00	895.00
92-01-027	Taylor	J. Nahrgang	250	295.00	295.00
93-01-028	Taylor "26	J. Nahrgang	250	395.00	395.00
93-01-029	Taylor "24	J. Nahrgang	500	300.00	300.00
93-01-030	Jordan	J. Nahrgang	250	450.00	450.00
93-01-031	Sean-Patrick	J. Nahrgang	100	495.00	495.00
93-01-032	Cinnamon	J. Nahrgang	50	595.00	595.00
93-01-033	American Beauty	J. Nahrgang	100	295.00	295.00
93-01-034	Tuesday's Child	C. Dutra	500	495.00	495.00
93-01-035	Erin	C. Dutra	500	495.00	495.00
93-01-036	Andi	C. Dutra	500	495.00	495.00
94-01-037	Christmas Taylor	J. Nahrgang	100	299.00	299.00
94-01-038	Taylor 20"	J. Nahrgang	500	299.00	299.00
94-01-039	Angelique	J. Nahrgang	200	380.00	380.00
94-01-040	Natalia	J. Nahrgang	100	380.00	380.00
94-01-041	Mikayla	J. Nahrgang	100	380.00	380.00
94-01-042	Miranda	J. Nahrgang	200	250.00	250.00
94-01-043	Littlest Warrior	J. Nahrgang	200	199.00	199.00
94-01-044	Niki (Eskimo)	J. Nahrgang	200	225.00	225.00
94-01-045	Tori	J. Nahrgang	200	250.00	250.00
94-01-046	Tuesday's Child	C. Dutra	500	495.00	495.00
94-01-047	Giselle	C. Dutra	250	495.00	495.00
94-01-048	Monday's Child	C. Dutra	350	495.00	495.00
94-01-049	Krissy (Baby)	C. Dutra	100	495.00	495.00
94-01-050	Erin	C. Dutra	500	495.00	495.00
94-01-051	He Loves Me Not	H. Payne	200	299.00	299.00
94-01-052	She Loves Me	H. Payne	200	299.00	299.00
94-01-053	Pansy	G. Hoyt	200	390.00	390.00
94-01-054	Atlanta	G. Hoyt	200	390.00	390.00
Nahrgang Collection		**Vinyl Doll Series**			
90-02-001	Karman (Gypsy)	J. Nahrgang	2,000	190.00	190.00
91-02-002	Aubry	J. Nahrgang	1,000	225.00	225.00
91-02-003	Laura	J. Nahrgang	1,000	250.00	250.00
91-02-004	Ann Marie	J. Nahrgang	500	225.00	225.00
91-02-005	Molly	J. Nahrgang	500	190.00	190.00
91-02-006	Alexis	J. Nahrgang	500	250.00	250.00
91-02-007	Brooke	J. Nahrgang	500	250.00	250.00
91-02-008	Beatrix	J. Nahrgang	500	250.00	250.00
91-02-009	Angela	J. Nahrgang	500	190.00	190.00
91-02-010	Vanessa	J. Nahrgang	250	250.00	250.00
91-02-011	Chelsea	J. Nahrgang	250	190.00	190.00
91-02-012	Polly	J. Nahrgang	250	270.00	270.00
92-02-013	Pocahontas	J. Nahrgang	500	199.00	199.00
92-02-014	Molly Pitcher	J. Nahrgang	500	199.00	199.00
92-02-015	Harriet Tubman	J. Nahrgang	500	199.00	199.00
92-02-016	Florence Nightingale	J. Nahrgang	500	199.00	199.00
92-02-017	Dolly Madison	J. Nahrgang	500	199.00	199.00
93-02-018	Tuesday's Child	C. Dutra	1,000	295.00	295.00
94-02-019	Giselle	C. Dutra	500	295.00	295.00
Original Appalachian Artworks		**Little People**			
78-01-001	"Helen" Blue	X. Roberts	Closed	150.00	4500-6000.
78-01-002	"A" Blue	X. Roberts	Closed	125.00	4000.00
78-01-003	"B" Red	X. Roberts	Closed	100.00	2500-3200.
78-01-004	"C" Burgundy	X. Roberts	Closed	100.00	1800.00
79-01-005	"D" Purple	X. Roberts	Closed	100.00	800-1600.
78-01-006	"E" Bronze	X. Roberts	Closed	125.00	750.00
80-01-007	"SP" Preemie	X. Roberts	Closed	100.00	400-700.
80-01-008	Celebrity	X. Roberts	Closed	200.00	400-750.
80-01-009	Grand Edition	X. Roberts	Closed	1000.00	1000.00
80-01-010	"U" Unsigned	X. Roberts	Closed	125.00	450.00
81-01-011	New 'Ears	X. Roberts	Closed	125.00	175.00
81-01-012	"PR II" Preemie	X. Roberts	Closed	130.00	250.00
81-01-013	Standing Edition	X. Roberts	Closed	300.00	375.00
82-01-014	"PE" New 'Ears Preemie	X. Roberts	Closed	140.00	250.00
82-01-015	"U" Unsigned	X. Roberts	Closed	125.00	450.00
Original Appalachian Artworks		**Cabbage Patch Kids International**			
83-02-001	Oriental/Pair	X. Roberts	Closed	300.00	1400.00
83-02-002	American Indian/Pair	X. Roberts	Closed	300.00	1400-1895.
83-02-003	Hispanic/Pair	X. Roberts	Closed	300.00	450-650.
84-02-004	Bavarian/Pair	X. Roberts	Closed	300.00	800-950.
83-02-005	Irish/Pair	X. Roberts	Closed	320.00	320-325.
Original Appalachian Artworks		**Cabbage Patch Kids**			
82-03-001	Amy	X. Roberts	Closed	125.00	700.00
82-03-002	Bobbie	X. Roberts	Closed	125.00	700.00
82-03-003	Billie	X. Roberts	Closed	125.00	700.00
82-03-004	Gilda	X. Roberts	Closed	125.00	700-2500.
82-03-005	Tyler	X. Roberts	Closed	125.00	1500-4000.
82-03-006	Sybil	X. Roberts	Closed	125.00	700.00
82-03-007	Marilyn	X. Roberts	Closed	125.00	700.00
82-03-008	Otis	X. Roberts	Closed	125.00	700.00
82-03-009	Rebecca	X. Roberts	Closed	125.00	700.00
82-03-010	Dorothy	X. Roberts	Closed	125.00	700.00
83-03-011	Andre/Madeira	X. Roberts	Closed	250.00	1500-2000.
84-03-012	Daddy's Darlins' Pun'kin	X. Roberts	Closed	300.00	500-700.
84-03-013	Daddy's Darlins' Tootsie	X. Roberts	Closed	300.00	500-700.
84-03-014	Daddy's Darlins' Princess	X. Roberts	Closed	300.00	500-700.
84-03-015	Daddy's Darlins' Kitten	X. Roberts	Closed	300.00	500-700.
88-03-016	Tiger's Eye-Valentine's Day	X. Roberts	Closed	150.00	200-400.
89-03-017	Tiger's Eye-Mother's Day	X. Roberts	Closed	150.00	150-400.
93-03-018	Unicoi Edition	X. Roberts	1,500	210.00	240.00
93-03-019	Little People Edition 27"	X. Roberts	Closed	300.00	450-650.
Original Appalachian Artworks		**Cabbage Patch Kids Circus Parade**			
87-04-001	Big Top Clown-Baby Cakes	X. Roberts	2,000	180.00	500.00
89-04-002	Happy Hobo-Bashful Billy	X. Roberts	1,000	180.00	450.00
91-04-003	Mitzi	X. Roberts	1,000	220.00	220.00
Original Appalachian Artworks		**Collectors Club Editions**			
87-05-001	Baby Otis	X. Roberts	Closed	250.00	400-550.
89-05-002	Anna Ruby	X. Roberts	Closed	250.00	350-550.
90-05-003	Lee Ann	X. Roberts	Closed	250.00	350-500.
91-05-004	Richard Russell	X. Roberts	Closed	250.00	250-350.
92-05-005	Baby Dodd	X. Roberts	Closed	250.00	250.00
93-05-006	Patti w/ Cabbage Bud Boutonnier	X. Roberts	Closed	280.00	280.00
Original Appalachian Artworks		**Convention Baby**			
89-06-001	Ashley	X. Roberts	Closed	150.00	400-800.
90-06-002	Bradley	X. Roberts	Closed	175.00	600.00
91-06-003	Caroline	X. Roberts	Closed	200.00	500.00
92-06-004	Duke	X. Roberts	Closed	225.00	300-500.
93-06-005	Ellen	X. Roberts	Closed	225.00	250-500.
Original Appalachian Artworks		**Happily Ever After**			
93-07-001	Bride & Groom	X. Roberts	Open	230.00	230-250.
Original Appalachian Artworks		**Christmas Collection**			
79-08-001	X Christmas/Pair	X. Roberts	Closed	300.00	3500-6000.
80-08-002	Christmas-Nicholas/Noel	X. Roberts	Closed	400.00	2500-3500.
82-08-003	Christmas-Baby Rudy/Christy Nicole	X. Roberts	Closed	400.00	1500-2000.
83-08-004	Christmas-Holly/Berry	X. Roberts	Closed	400.00	800-2000.
84-08-005	Christmas-Carole/Chris	X. Roberts	Closed	400.00	1000-1500.
85-08-006	Christmas-Baby Sandy/Claude	X. Roberts	Closed	400.00	400-800.
86-08-007	Christmas-Hilliary/Nigel	X. Roberts	Closed	400.00	500-800.
87-08-008	Christmas-Katrina/Misha	X. Roberts	Closed	500.00	500.00
88-08-009	Christmas-Kelly/Kane	X. Roberts	Closed	500.00	500.00
89-08-010	Christmas-Joy	X. Roberts	Closed	250.00	500-550.
Princeton Gallery		**Little Ladies of Victorian England**			
90-01-001	Victoria Anne	Unknown	Open	59.00	59.00
91-01-002	Abigail	Unknown	Open	59.00	59.00
91-01-003	Valerie	Unknown	Open	58.50	58.50
92-01-004	Caroline	Unknown	Open	58.50	58.50
92-01-005	Heather	Unknown	Open	58.50	58.50
93-01-006	Beverly	Unknown	Open	58.50	58.50
Princeton Gallery		**Best Friend Dolls**			
91-02-001	Sharing Secrets	Unknown	Open	78.00	78.00
Princeton Gallery		**Childhood Songs Dolls**			
91-03-001	It's Raining, It's Pouring	Unknown	Open	78.00	78.00
Princeton Gallery		**Dress Up Dolls**			
91-04-001	Grandma's Attic	Unknown	Open	95.00	95.00
Princeton Gallery		**Fabrique Santa**			
91-05-001	Christmas Dream	Unknown	Open	76.00	76.00

Company Number	Name	Series Artist	Edition Limit	Issue Price	Quote
Princeton Gallery		**Santa Doll**			
91-06-001	Checking His List	Unknown	Open	119.00	119.00
Princeton Gallery		**Rock-N-Roll Dolls**			
91-07-001	Cindy at the Hop	M. Sirko	Open	95.00	95.00
92-07-002	Chantilly Lace	M. Sirko	Open	95.00	95.00
93-07-003	Yellow Dot Bikini	Unknown	Open	95.00	95.00
Princeton Gallery		**Terrible Twos Dolls**			
91-08-001	One Man Band	M. Sirko	Open	95.00	95.00
Princeton Gallery		**Imaginary People**			
92-09-001	Melinda, Tooth Fairy	Unknown	Open	95.00	95.00
Reco International		**Precious Memories of Motherhood**			
90-01-001	Loving Steps	S. Kuck	Yr.Iss.	125.00	150-195.
91-01-002	Lullaby	S. Kuck	Yr.Iss.	125.00	125.00
92-01-003	Expectant Moments	S. Kuck	Yr.Iss.	149.00	149.00
93-01-004	Bedtime	S. Kuck	Yr.Iss.	149.00	149.00
94-01-004	A Kiss Goodnight	S. Kuck	Yr.Iss.	79.00	79.00
Reco International		**Children's Circus Doll Collection**			
91-02-001	Tommy The Clown	J. McClelland	Yr.Iss.	78.00	78.00
91-02-002	Katie The Tightrope Walker	J. McClelland	Yr.Iss.	78.00	78.00
91-02-003	Johnny The Strongman	J. McClelland	Yr.Iss.	83.00	83.00
92-02-004	Maggie The Animal Trainer	J. McClelland	Yr.Iss.	83.00	83.00
Rhodes Studios		**A Norman Rockwell Christmas**			
90-01-001	Scotty Plays Santa	Rockwell-Inspired	Yr.Iss.	48.00	48.00
91-01-002	Scotty Gets His Tree	Rockwell-Inspired	Yr.Iss.	59.00	59.00
Roman, Inc.		**Ellen Williams Doll**			
89-01-001	Noelle	E. Williams	5,000	125.00	125.00
89-01-002	Rebecca 999	E. Williams	7,500	195.00	195.00
Roman, Inc.		**A Christmas Dream**			
90-02-001	Chelsea	E. Williams	5,000	125.00	125.00
90-02-002	Carole	E. Williams	5,000	125.00	125.00
Roman, Inc.		**Tyrolean Treasures: Wood Body, Moveable Joint**			
90-03-001	Nadia	Unkn.	2,000	650.00	650.00
90-03-002	Susie	Unkn.	2,000	650.00	650.00
90-03-003	Verena	Unkn.	2,000	650.00	650.00
90-03-004	Monica	Unkn.	2,000	650.00	650.00
90-03-005	Melissa	Unkn.	2,000	650.00	650.00
90-03-006	Karin	Unkn.	2,000	650.00	650.00
90-03-007	Tina	Unkn.	2,000	650.00	650.00
90-03-008	Ann	Unkn.	2,000	650.00	650.00
90-03-009	Lisa	Unkn.	2,000	650.00	650.00
90-03-010	David	Unkn.	2,000	650.00	650.00
Roman, Inc.		**Tyrolean Treasures: Soft Body, Human Hair**			
90-04-001	Erika	Unkn.	2,000	575.00	575.00
90-04-002	Ellan	Unkn.	2,000	575.00	575.00
90-04-003	Marisa	Unkn.	2,000	575.00	575.00
90-04-004	Sarah	Unkn.	2,000	575.00	575.00
90-04-005	Andrew	Unkn.	2,000	575.00	575.00
90-04-006	Matthew	Unkn.	2,000	575.00	575.00
Roman, Inc.		**Classic Brides of the Century**			
91-05-001	Flora-The 1900's Bride	E. Williams	Yr.Iss.	145.00	145.00
92-05-002	Jennifer-The 1980's Bride	E. Williams	Yr.Iss.	149.00	149.00
93-05-003	Kathleen-The 1930's Bride	E. Williams	Yr.Iss.	149.00	149.00
Roman, Inc.		**Abbie Williams Collection**			
91-06-001	Molly	E. Williams	5,000	155.00	155.00
Sarah's Attic, Inc.		**Angels in The Attic Collection**			
86-01-001	Hope Black Angel 0007	Sarah's Attic	Closed	34.00	34.00
86-01-002	Charity White Angel 0008	Sarah's Attic	Closed	34.00	34.00
86-01-003	Holly Black Angel 0410	Sarah's Attic	Closed	34.00	34.00
89-01-004	Joy Angel 1459	Sarah's Attic	Closed	50.00	55.00
89-01-005	Holly Angel 1460	Sarah's Attic	Closed	50.00	55.00
89-01-006	Peace Angel 1465	Sarah's Attic	Closed	50.00	55.00
89-01-007	Hope Angel 1466	Sarah's Attic	Closed	50.00	55.00
89-01-008	Liberty Angel 1470	Sarah's Attic	Closed	50.00	55.00
89-01-009	Glory Angel 1471	Sarah's Attic	Closed	50.00	55.00
91-01-010	Enos 1822	Sarah's Attic	Closed	90.00	90.00
91-01-011	Adora 1823	Sarah's Attic	Closed	90.00	90.00
92-01-012	Angelle Guardian Angel 3569	Sarah's Attic	Closed	170.00	170.00
92-01-013	Kiah Guardian Angel 3570	Sarah's Attic	Closed	170.00	170.00
94-01-014	Star Black Angel 4107	Sarah's Attic	500	120.00	120.00
94-01-015	Twinkle-White Angel 4108	Sarah's Attic	500	120.00	120.00
Sarah's Attic Inc.		**Beary Adorables Collection**			
86-02-001	Brownie Bear 0001	Sarah's Attic	Closed	36.00	36.00
86-02-002	Buffy Bear 0003	Sarah's Attic	Closed	80.00	80.00
86-02-003	Billy Bear 0004	Sarah's Attic	Closed	80.00	80.00
87-02-004	Benji Bear 0089	Sarah's Attic	Closed	25.00	25.00
90-02-005	Betty Bear-Sunday's Best 1772	Sarah's Attic	Closed	160.00	160.00
90-02-006	Teddy Bear-Sunday's Best 1773	Sarah's Attic	Closed	160.00	160.00
90-02-007	Teddy Bear-School Days 1774	Sarah's Attic	Closed	160.00	160.00
90-02-008	Teddy Bear-Americana 1775	Sarah's Attic	Closed	160.00	160.00
90-02-009	Betty Bear-Christmas 1815	Sarah's Attic	Closed	160.00	160.00
90-02-010	Teddy Bear-Christmas 1816	Sarah's Attic	Closed	160.00	160.00
92-02-011	Betty Bear-Springtime 1826	Sarah's Attic	Closed	160.00	160.00
92-02-012	Teddy Bear-Springtime 1827	Sarah's Attic	Closed	160.00	160.00
Sarah's Attic Inc.		**Black Heritage Collection**			
86-03-001	Judith Ann Black Doll 0010	Sarah's Attic	Closed	34.00	34.00
86-03-002	Sadie Black Doll 0014	Sarah's Attic	Closed	90.00	90.00
86-03-003	Louisa May Black Cloth Doll 0018	Sarah's Attic	Closed	120.00	120.00
87-03-004	Tess Rag Doll 0083	Sarah's Attic	Closed	140.00	140.00
87-03-005	Leroy Black Rag Doll 0105	Sarah's Attic	Closed	54.00	54.00
87-03-006	Lucy Black Rag Doll 0106	Sarah's Attic	Closed	54.00	54.00
88-03-007	Lily-Black Doll 2221	Sarah's Attic	Closed	90.00	90.00
89-03-008	Sassafras-School Days 1680	Sarah's Attic	Closed	140.00	195.00
89-03-009	Sassafras-Sweet Dreams 1681	Sarah's Attic	Closed	140.00	195.00
90-03-010	Sassafras-Playtime 1682	Sarah's Attic	Closed	140.00	150-175.
90-03-011	Sassafras-Beachtime 1683	Sarah's Attic	Closed	140.00	150-175.
90-03-012	Sassafra-Sunday's Best 1684	Sarah's Attic	Closed	150.00	195.00
90-03-013	Sassafra-Americana 1685	Sarah's Attic	Closed	150.00	150-175.
90-03-014	Hickory-School Days 1766	Sarah's Attic	Closed	140.00	195.00
90-03-015	Hickory-Sweet Dreams 1767	Sarah's Attic	Closed	140.00	150-175.

Company Number	Name	Series Artist	Edition Limit	Issue Price	Quote
90-03-016	Hickory-Playtime 1768	Sarah's Attic	Closed	140.00	150-175.
90-03-017	Hickory-Beachtime 1769	Sarah's Attic	Closed	140.00	150-175.
90-03-018	Hickory-Sunday's Best 1770	Sarah's Attic	Closed	150.00	195.00
90-03-019	Hickory-Americana 1771	Sarah's Attic	Closed	150.00	150-175.
91-03-020	Sassafras-Christmas 1809	Sarah's Attic	Closed	150.00	150-175.
91-03-021	Hickory-Christmas 1810	Sarah's Attic	Closed	150.00	150-175.
91-03-022	Sassafras-Springtime 1813	Sarah's Attic	Closed	150.00	195.00
91-03-023	Hickory-Springtime 1814	Sarah's Attic	Closed	150.00	195.00
92-03-024	Edie-Victorian 1833	Sarah's Attic	Closed	170.00	170.00
92-03-025	Edie-Country 1834	Sarah's Attic	Closed	170.00	170.00
92-03-026	Edie-Playtime 1835	Sarah's Attic	Closed	170.00	170.00
92-03-027	Emma-Victorian 1836	Sarah's Attic	Closed	160.00	160.00
92-03-028	Emma-Country 1837	Sarah's Attic	Closed	160.00	160.00
92-03-029	Emma-Playtime 1838	Sarah's Attic	Closed	160.00	160.00
92-03-030	Harpster w/Banjo 3591	Sarah's Attic	Closed	250.00	250.00
92-03-031	Whoopie 3597	Sarah's Attic	Closed	200.00	200.00
92-03-032	Wooster 3602	Sarah's Attic	Closed	160.00	160.00
93-03-033	Granny Quilting Lady Doll 3576	Sarah's Attic	Closed	130.00	130.00
93-03-034	Lilla Quilting Lady Doll 3581	Sarah's Attic	Closed	130.00	130.00
93-03-035	Millie Quilting Lady Doll 3586	Sarah's Attic	Closed	130.00	130.00
Sarah's Attic, Inc.		**Cuddly Critters**			
86-04-001	Trapp the Cat Doll 0740	Sarah's Attic	Closed	36.00	36.00
Sarah's Attic, Inc.		**Cotton Tales**			
87-05-001	Roxie Rabbit Doll 0084	Sarah's Attic	Closed	32.00	32.00
88-05-002	Melville Cloth Bunny 1104	Sarah's Attic	Closed	46.00	46.00
88-05-003	Maybelle Cloth Bunny 1105	Sarah's Attic	Closed	46.00	46.00
Sarah's Attic, Inc.		**Happy Collection**			
88-06-001	Smiley Clown Doll 3050	Sarah's Attic	Closed	126.00	126.00
89-06-002	Harmony-Victorian Clown 1464	Sarah's Attic	Closed	120.00	120.00
89-06-003	Noel-Christmas Clown 1469	Sarah's Attic	Closed	120.00	120.00
89-06-004	Freedom-Americana Clown 1472	Sarah's Attic	Closed	120.00	120.00
Sarah's Attic, Inc.		**Sarah's Neighborhood Friends**			
86-07-001	Amie Amish Doll 0002	Sarah's Attic	Closed	40.00	40.00
86-07-002	Betsy Boo Doll 0005	Sarah's Attic	Closed	40.00	40.00
86-07-003	Jennie White Doll 0006	Sarah's Attic	Closed	44.00	44.00
86-07-004	Priscilla Doll 0030	Sarah's Attic	Closed	140.00	300.00
86-07-005	Peter Doll 0031	Sarah's Attic	Closed	140.00	140.00
86-07-006	Jennie White Angel Doll 0074	Sarah's Attic	Closed	52.00	52.00
86-07-007	Spike Doll 0039G	Sarah's Attic	Closed	32.00	32.00
86-07-008	Nellie Doll 0039H	Sarah's Attic	Closed	32.00	32.00
87-07-009	Patches White Rag Doll 0110	Sarah's Attic	Closed	54.00	54.00
87-07-010	Polly White Rag Doll 0111	Sarah's Attic	Closed	54.00	54.00
87-07-011	Molly Doll 2053	Sarah's Attic	Closed	44.00	44.00
87-07-012	Sunshine Doll 3003	Sarah's Attic	Closed	118.00	118.00
88-07-013	Country Girl Doll 1190	Sarah's Attic	Closed	26.00	26.00
88-07-014	Victorian Girl Doll 1191	Sarah's Attic	Closed	24.00	24.00
88-07-015	Victorian Boy Doll 1192	Sarah's Attic	Closed	24.00	24.00
88-07-016	Ashlee Doll 1193	Sarah's Attic	Closed	20.00	20.00
88-07-017	Albert Doll 1194	Sarah's Attic	Closed	20.00	20.00
88-07-018	Daisy Doll 1195	Sarah's Attic	Closed	20.00	20.00
88-07-019	David Doll 1196	Sarah's Attic	Closed	20.00	20.00
88-07-020	Michael Doll 4015	Sarah's Attic	Closed	44.00	44.00
89-07-021	Becky Doll 1461	Sarah's Attic	Closed	120.00	120.00
89-07-022	Bobby Doll 1462	Sarah's Attic	Closed	120.00	120.00
89-07-023	Victoria Doll 1467	Sarah's Attic	Closed	120.00	120.00
89-07-024	Victor Doll 1468	Sarah's Attic	Closed	120.00	120.00
89-07-025	Beverly Jane-Black Dress 1496	Sarah's Attic	Closed	160.00	160.00
89-07-026	Beverly Jane-Sunday's Best 1666	Sarah's Attic	Closed	160.00	160.00
89-07-027	Beverly Jane-Green Dress 1693	Sarah's Attic	Closed	160.00	160.00
89-07-028	Beverly Jane-Red Dress 1694	Sarah's Attic	Closed	160.00	160.00
89-07-029	Megan Doll 1752	Sarah's Attic	Closed	70.00	70.00
89-07-030	Scott Doll 1753	Sarah's Attic	Closed	70.00	70.00
92-07-031	Emily-Victorian 1829	Sarah's Attic	Closed	250.00	250.00
92-07-032	Emily-Country 1830	Sarah's Attic	Closed	250.00	250.00
92-07-033	Hilary-Victorian 1831	Sarah's Attic	Closed	200.00	200.00
92-07-034	Hilary-Country 1832	Sarah's Attic	Closed	200.00	200.00
Sarah's Attic, Inc.		**Sarah's Gang**			
86-08-001	Twinkie Doll 0039A	Sarah's Attic	Closed	32.00	32.00
86-08-002	Cupcake Doll 0039B	Sarah's Attic	Closed	32.00	32.00
86-08-003	Whimpy Doll 0039E	Sarah's Attic	Closed	32.00	32.00
86-08-004	Katie Doll 0039F	Sarah's Attic	Closed	32.00	32.00
86-08-005	Willie Doll 0039I	Sarah's Attic	Closed	32.00	32.00
86-08-006	Tillie Doll 0039J	Sarah's Attic	Closed	32.00	32.00
87-08-007	Willie Rag Doll 0343	Sarah's Attic	Closed	32.00	32.00
87-08-008	Tillie Rag Doll 0344	Sarah's Attic	Closed	32.00	32.00
94-08-009	Tillie-Clown 4100	Sarah's Attic	1,000	120.00	120.00
94-08-010	Willie-Clown Doll 4105	Sarah's Attic	1,000	120.00	120.00
Sarah's Attic, Inc.		**Matt & Maggie**			
86-09-001	Matt Cloth Doll 0011	Sarah's Attic	Closed	70.00	120.00
86-09-002	Maggie Cloth Doll 0012	Sarah's Attic	Closed	70.00	120.00
86-09-003	Matt Cloth Doll 0039 C	Sarah's Attic	Closed	32.00	32.00
86-09-004	Maggie Cloth Doll 0039 D	Sarah's Attic	Closed	32.00	32.00
Sarah's Attic, Inc.		**Spirit Of Christmas**			
88-10-001	Mrs. Claus Doll 6284	Sarah's Attic	Closed	120.00	120.00
88-10-002	Santa Claus Doll 6337	Sarah's Attic	Closed	120.00	120.00
89-10-003	Spirit of America Santa 1476	Sarah's Attic	Closed	150.00	150.00
92-10-004	Peace on Earth Santa 3564	Sarah's Attic	Closed	175.00	175.00
Sarah's Attic, Inc.		**Tattered 'N Torn**			
91-11-001	All Cloth Opie White Doll 1818	Sarah's Attic	Closed	90.00	90.00
91-11-002	All Cloth Polly White Doll 1819	Sarah's Attic	Closed	90.00	90.00
91-11-003	All Cloth Muffin Black Doll 1820	Sarah's Attic	Closed	90.00	90.00
91-11-004	All Cloth Puffin Black Doll 1821	Sarah's Attic	Closed	90.00	90.00
Sarah's Attic, Inc.		**Daisy Petals**			
93-12-001	Sally Booba Doll 3890	Sarah's Attic	500	130.00	130.00
93-12-002	Jack Boy Doll 3893	Sarah's Attic	500	130.00	130.00
Schmid		**June Amos Grammer**			
88-01-001	Rosamund	J. Amos Grammer	750	225.00	225.00
89-01-002	Katie	J. Amos Grammer	1,000	180.00	180.00
89-01-003	Vanessa	J. Amos Grammer	1,000	180.00	210.00
90-01-004	Lauren	J. Amos Grammer	1,000	279.00	280.00
90-01-005	Jester Love	J. Amos Grammer	1,000	195.00	210.00
90-01-006	Leigh Ann	J. Amos Grammer	1,000	195.00	210.00
90-01-007	Megan	J. Amos Grammer	750	380.00	380.00
91-01-008	Lauren	J. Amos Grammer	1,000	280.00	280.00

Company Number	Name	Series Artist	Edition Limit	Issue Price	Quote
91-01-009	Mitsuko	J. Amos Grammer	1,000	210.00	210.00
91-01-010	Heather	J. Amos Grammer	1,000	210.00	210.00
Timeless Creations		**Barefoot Children**			
87-01-001	Fatou	A. Himstedt	Closed	329.00	925-1800.
87-01-002	Bastian	A. Himstedt	Closed	329.00	700.00
87-01-003	Ellen	A. Himstedt	Closed	329.00	700-1200.
87-01-004	Paula	A. Himstedt	Closed	329.00	700-900.
87-01-005	Lisa	A. Himstedt	Closed	329.00	900-1500.
87-01-006	Kathe	A. Himstedt	Closed	329.00	700-850.
Timeless Creations		**Heartland Series**			
88-02-001	Timi	A. Himstedt	Closed	329.00	500-800.
88-02-002	Toni	A. Himstedt	Closed	329.00	495-800.
Timeless Creations		**Blessed Are The Children**			
88-03-001	Friederike	A. Himstedt	Closed	499.00	1100-1200.
88-03-002	Makimura	A. Himstedt	Closed	499.00	800-2000.
88-03-003	Kasimir	A. Himstedt	Closed	499.00	1500-1900.
88-03-004	Michiko	A. Himstedt	Closed	499.00	1000-2000.
88-03-005	Malin	A. Himstedt	Closed	499.00	1500-2000.
Timeless Creations		**Reflection of Youth**			
89-04-001	Adrienne (France)	A. Himstedt	Closed	558.00	900-1500.
89-04-002	Kai (German)	A. Himstedt	Closed	558.00	800-900.
89-04-003	Janka (Hungry)	A. Himstedt	Closed	558.00	650.00
89-04-004	Ayoka (Africa)	A. Himstedt	Closed	558.00	900-2500.
Timeless Creations		**Fiene And The Barefoot Babies**			
90-05-001	Annchen-German Baby Girl	A. Himstedt	2-Yr.	498.00	500-550.
90-05-002	Taki-Japanese Baby Girl	A. Himstedt	2-Yr.	498.00	600.00
90-05-003	Mo-American Baby Boy	A. Himstedt	2-Yr.	498.00	425-450.
90-05-004	Fiene-Belgian Girl	A. Himstedt	2-Yr.	598.00	695-850.
Timeless Creations		**Faces of Friendship**			
91-06-001	Liliane (Netherlands)	A. Himstedt	2-Yr.	598.00	500-750.
91-06-002	Shireem (Bali)	A. Himstedt	2-Yr.	598.00	450-750.
91-06-003	Neblina (Switzerland)	A. Himstedt	2-Yr.	598.00	500-750.
Timeless Creations		**Summer Dreams**			
92-07-001	Sanga	A. Himstedt	2-Yr.	599.00	599.00
92-07-002	Pemba	A. Himstedt	2-Yr.	599.00	599.00
92-07-003	Jule	A. Himstedt	2-Yr.	599.00	599.00
92-07-004	Enzo	A. Himstedt	2-Yr.	599.00	599.00
Timeless Creations		**Images of Childhood**			
93-08-001	Lona (California)	A. Himstedt	2-Yr.	599.00	599.00
93-08-002	Tara (Germany)	A. Himstedt	2-Yr.	599.00	599.00
93-08-003	Kima (Greenland)	A. Himstedt	2-Yr.	599.00	599.00
Susan Wakeen Doll Co. Inc.		**The Littlest Ballet Company**			
85-01-001	Jeanne	S. Wakeen	375	198.00	800.00
85-01-002	Patty	S. Wakeen	375	198.00	400-500.
85-01-003	Cynthia	S. Wakeen	375	198.00	350.00
85-01-004	Jennifer	S. Wakeen	250	750.00	750.00
87-01-005	Elizabeth	S. Wakeen	250	425.00	1000.00
87-01-006	Marie Ann	S. Wakeen	50	1000.00	1000.00

FIGURINES

Company Number	Name	Series Artist	Edition Limit	Issue Price	Quote
Kurt S. Adler Inc.		**Camelot Steinbach Nutcracker Series**			
91-01-001	Merlin The Magician ES610	KSA/Steinbach	Retrd.	185.00	1070-1500.
92-01-002	King Arthur ES621	KSA/Steinbach	Retrd.	195.00	242-350.
93-01-003	Sir Lancelot ES638	KSA/Steinbach	12,000	225.00	225.00
94-01-004	Sir Galahad ES862	KSA/Steinbach	12,000	225.00	225.00
94-01-005	Sir Lancelot Smoker ES833	KSA/Steinbach	7,500	150.00	150.00
Kurt S. Adler Inc.		**American Presidents Steinbach Nutcracker Series**			
92-02-001	Abraham Lincoln ES622	KSA/Steinbach	12,000	195.00	225.00
92-02-002	George Washington ES623	KSA/Steinbach	12,000	195.00	225.00
93-02-003	Teddy Roosevelt ES644	KSA/Steinbach	10,000	225.00	225.00
Kurt S. Adler Inc.		**American Inventors Steinbach Nutcracker Series**			
93-03-001	Ben Franklin ES622	KSA/Steinbach	12,000	225.00	225.00
Kurt S. Adler Inc.		**Famous Chieftans Steinbach Nutcracker Series**			
93-04-001	Chief Sitting Bull ES637	KSA/Steinbach	8,500	225.00	225.00
94-04-002	Red Cloud ES864	KSA/Steinbach	8,500	225.00	225.00
94-04-003	Chief Sitting Bull Smoker ES834	KSA/Steinbach	7,500	150.00	150.00
Kurt S. Adler Inc.		**Christmas Legends Steinbach Nutcracker Series**			
93-05-001	Father Christmas ES645	KSA/Steinbach	7,500	225.00	225.00
94-05-002	St. Nicholas, The Bishop ES865	KSA/Steinbach	7,500	225.00	225.00
Kurt S. Adler Inc.		**Camelot Steinbach Smoking Figure Series**			
92-06-001	Merlin The Magician ES830	KSA/Steinbach	7,500	150.00	150.00
93-06-002	King Arthur ES832	KSA/Steinbach	7,500	175.00	175.00
Kurt S. Adler Inc.		**Steinbach Nutcracker Collection**			
92-07-001	Happy Santa ES601	KSA/Steinbach	Open	190.00	220.00
Kurt S. Adler Inc.		**Tales of Sherwood Forest**			
92-08-001	Robin Hood ES863	KSA/Steinbach	7,500	225.00	225.00
Kurt S. Adler Inc.		**Zuber Nutcracker Series**			
92-09-001	Bronco Billy The Cowboy EK1	KSA/Zuber	5,000	125.00	125.00
92-09-002	Paul Bunyan The Lumberjack EK2	KSA/Zuber	5,000	125.00	125.00
92-09-003	The Nor' Easter Sea Captain EK3	KSA/Zuber	5,000	125.00	125.00
92-09-004	TheTyrolean EK4	KSA/Zuber	5,000	125.00	125.00
92-09-005	The Golfer EK5	KSA/Zuber	5,000	125.00	125.00
92-09-006	The Chimney Sweep EK6	KSA/Zuber	5,000	125.00	125.00
92-09-007	The Annapolis Midshipman EK7	KSA/Zuber	5,000	125.00	125.00
92-09-008	The West Point Cadet With Canon EK8	KSA/Zuber	5,000	130.00	130.00
92-09-009	Gepetto, The Toymaker EK9	KSA/Zuber	5,000	125.00	125.00
92-09-010	The Pilgrim EK14	KSA/Zuber	5,000	125.00	125.00
92-09-011	The Indian EK15	KSA/Zuber	5,000	135.00	135.00
92-09-012	The Bavarian EK16	KSA/Zuber	5,000	130.00	130.00
92-09-013	The Fisherman EK17	KSA/Zuber	5,000	125.00	125.00
92-09-014	The Gold Prospector EK18	KSA/Zuber	5,000	125.00	125.00
92-09-015	The Country Singer EK19	KSA/Zuber	5,000	125.00	125.00
93-09-016	Herr Drosselmeir Nutcracker EK21	KSA/Zuber	5,000	150.00	150.00
93-09-017	The Pizzamaker EK22	KSA/Zuber	5,000	150.00	150.00
93-09-018	Napoleon Bonaparte EK23	KSA/Zuber	5,000	150.00	150.00
93-09-019	The Ice Cream Vendor EK24	KSA/Zuber	5,000	150.00	150.00

Company Number	Name	Series Artist	Edition Limit	Issue Price	Quote
94-09-020	Jazz Player EK25	KSA/Zuber	2,500	145.00	145.00
94-09-021	The Gardner EK26	KSA/Zuber	2,500	150.00	150.00
94-09-022	Scuba Diver EK27	KSA/Zuber	2,500	150.00	150.00
94-09-023	Kurt the Traveling Salesman EK28	KSA/Zuber	2,500	155.00	155.00
94-09-024	Peter Pan EK28	KSA/Zuber	2,500	145.00	145.00
94-09-025	Soccer Player EK30	KSA/Zuber	2,500	145.00	145.00
94-09-026	Mouse King EK31	KSA/Zuber	2,500	150.00	150.00
Kurt S. Adler Inc.		**Mickey Unlimited**			
92-10-001	Goofy H1216	KSA/Disney	Open	78.00	78.00
92-10-002	Mickey Mouse Sorcerer H1221	KSA/Disney	Open	100.00	100.00
92-10-003	Mickey Mouse Soldier H1194	KSA/Disney	Open	72.00	72.00
93-10-004	Pinnochio H1222	KSA/Disney	Open	110.00	110.00
93-10-005	Donald Duck H1235	KSA/Disney	Open	90.00	90.00
93-10-006	Mickey Mouse With Gift Boxes W1608	KSA/Disney	Open	78.00	78.00
94-10-007	Mickey Santa Nutcracker H1237	KSA/Disney	Open	90.00	90.00
94-10-008	Minnie Mouse Soldier Nutcrackers H1236	KSA/Disney	Open	90.00	90.00
94-10-009	Mickey Bandleader W1669	KSA/Disney	Open	N/A	N/A
94-10-010	Minnie With Cymbals W1670	KSA/Disney	Open	N/A	N/A
94-10-011	Donald Duck Drummer W1671	KSA/Disney	Open	N/A	N/A
Kurt S. Adler Inc.		**Jim Henson's Muppet Nutcrackers**			
93-11-001	Kermit The Frog H1223	KSA/JHP	Open	90.00	90.00
Kurt S. Adler Inc.		**Fabriché™ Holiday Figurines**			
91-12-001	Santa Fiddler W1549	M. Rothenberg	Retrd.	100.00	100.00
92-12-002	Bringin in the Yule Log W1589	M. Rothenberg	5,000	200.00	200.00
92-12-003	Santa's Ice Capades W1588	M. Rothenberg	Open	110.00	110.00
92-12-004	Santa Steals A Kiss & A Cookie W1581	M. Rothenberg	Open	150.00	150.00
92-12-005	An Apron Full of Love W1582	M. Rothenberg	Open	75.00	75.00
92-12-006	Christmas is in the Air W1590	K.S. Adler	Open	110.00	110.00
92-12-007	Bundles of Joy W1578	K.S. Adler	Open	78.00	78.00
92-12-008	Homeward Bound W1568	K.S. Adler	Open	61.00	61.00
92-12-009	Merry Kissmas W1548	M. Rothenberg	Retrd.	140.00	140.00
92-12-010	Santa's Cat Nap W1504	M .Rothenberg	Retrd.	98.00	98.00
92-12-011	St. Nicholas The Bishop W1532	K.S. Adler	Open	78.00	78.00
92-12-012	Hugs and Kisses W1531	K.S. Adler	Open	67.00	67.00
92-12-013	I'm Late, I'm Late J7947	T. Rubel	Open	100.00	100.00
92-12-014	It's Time To Go J7943	T. Rubel	Open	150.00	150.00
92-12-015	He Did It Again J7944	T. Rubel	Open	160.00	160.00
93-12-016	Par For The Claus W1603	K.S. Adler	Open	60.00	60.00
93-12-017	Checking It Twice W1604	K.S. Adler	Open	56.00	56.00
93-12-018	Bringing the Gifts W1605	K.S. Adler	Open	60.00	60.00
93-12-019	Forever Green W1607	K.S. Adler	Open	56.00	56.00
93-12-020	With All The Trimmings W1616	K.S. Adler	Open	76.00	76.00
93-12-021	Playtime For Santa W1619	K.S. Adler	Open	67.00	67.00
93-12-022	All That Jazz W1620	K.S. Adler	Open	67.00	67.00
93-12-023	Here Kitty W1618	M. Rothenberg	Open	90.00	90.00
93-12-024	Stocking Stuffer W1622	K.S. Adler	Open	56.00	56.00
93-12-025	Top Brass W1630	K.S. Adler	Open	67.00	67.00
94-12-026	Schussing Claus W1651	K.S. Adler	Open	78.00	78.00
94-12-027	All Star Santa W1652	K.S. Adler	Open	56.00	56.00
94-12-028	Firefighting Friends W1654	K.S. Adler	Open	72.00	72.00
94-12-029	Star Gazing Santa W1656	M. Rothenberg	Open	120.00	120.00
94-12-030	Checking His List W1643	K.S. Adler	Open	60.00	60.00
94-12-031	Holiday Express W1636	K.S. Adler	Open	100.00	100.00
94-12-032	Santa's Fishtales W1640	K.S. Adler	Open	60.00	60.00
94-12-033	Merry St. Nick W1641	Giordano	Open	100.00	100.00
94-12-034	Mail Must Go Through W1667	KSA/WRG	Open	110.00	110.00
94-12-035	Peace Santa W1631	K.S. Adler	Open	60.00	60.00
94-12-036	Ho, Ho, Ho Santa W1632	K.S. Adler	Open	56.00	56.00
94-12-037	Basket of Goodies W1650	K.S. Adler	Open	60.00	60.00
94-12-038	Friendship W1642	K.S. Adler	Open	65.00	65.00
Kurt S. Adler Inc.		**Fabriché™ Thomas Nast Figurines**			
91-13-001	Hello! Little One W1552	K.S. Adler	12,000	90.00	90.00
92-13-002	Christmas Sing-A-Long W1576	K.S. Adler	12,000	110.00	110.00
92-13-003	Caught in the Act W1577	K.S. Adler	12,000	133.00	133.00
93-13-004	Dear Santa W1602	K.S. Adler	7,500	110.00	110.00
Kurt S. Adler Inc.		**Smithsonian Museum Fabriché™ Series**			
91-14-001	Santa On A Bicycle W1527	KSA/Smithsonian	Open	150.00	150.00
92-14-002	Holiday Drive W1556	KSA/Smithsonian	Open	155.00	155.00
92-14-003	Peace on Earth Angel Treetop W1583	KSA/Smithsonian	Open	52.00	52.00
92-14-004	Peace on Earth Flying Angel W1585	KSA/Smithsonian	Open	49.00	49.00
93-14-005	Holiday Flight W1617	KSA/Smithsonian	Open	144.00	144.00
Kurt S. Adler Inc.		**Fabriché™ Angel Series**			
92-15-001	Heavenly Messenger W1584	K.S. Adler	Open	41.00	41.00
Kurt S. Adler Inc.		**Camelot Fabriché™ Figure Series**			
93-16-001	Merlin the Magician J7966	P. Mauk	7,500	120.00	120.00
93-16-002	Young Arthur J7967	P. Mauk	7,500	120.00	120.00
94-16-003	King Arthur J3372	P. Mauk	7,500	110.00	110.00
Kurt S. Adler Inc.		**Fabriché™ Santa at Home Series**			
93-17-001	Grandpa Santa's Piggyback Ride W1621	M. Rothenberg	7,500	84.00	84.00
94-17-002	The Christmas Waltz 1635	M. Rothenberg	Open	135.00	135.00
94-17-003	Santa's New Friend W1655	M. Rothenberg	Open	110.00	110.00
Kurt S. Adler Inc.		**Fabriché™ Santa's Helpers Series**			
92-18-001	A Stitch in Time W1591	M. Rothenberg	5,000	135.00	135.00
93-18-002	Little Olde Clockmaker W1629	M. Rothenberg	5,000	134.00	134.00
Kurt S. Adler Inc.		**Old World Santa Series**			
92-19-001	Large Black Forest Santa W2717	J. Mostrom	Retrd.	110.00	110.00
92-19-002	Small Grandfather Frost W2718	J. Mostrom	3,000	106.00	106.00
92-19-003	Large Father Christmas W2719	J. Mostrom	Retrd.	106.00	106.00
92-19-004	Patriotic Santa W2720	J. Mostrom	3,000	128.00	128.00
92-19-005	Chelsea Garden Santa W2721	J. Mostrom	5,000	33.50	33.50
92-19-006	Small Father Christmas W2712	J. Mostrom	Retrd.	33.50	33.50
92-19-007	Pere Noel W2723	J. Mostrom	Retrd.	33.50	33.50
92-19-008	Small Black Forest Santa W2712	J. Mostrom	Retrd.	40.00	40.00
92-19-009	St. Nicholas W2713	J. Mostrom	5,000	30.00	30.00
92-19-010	Mrs. Claus W2714	J. Mostrom	5,000	37.00	37.00
92-19-011	Workshop Santa W2715	J. Mostrom	5,000	43.00	43.00
92-19-012	Small Grandfather Frost W2716	J. Mostrom	5,000	43.00	43.00
93-19-013	Medieval King of Christmas W2881	J. Mostrom	3,000	390.00	390.00
93-19-014	Good King Wenceslas W2928	J. Mostrom	3,000	134.00	134.00
Kurt S. Adler Inc.		**Visions Of Santa Series**			
92-20-001	Workshop Santa J825	K.S. Adler	7,500	27.00	27.00
92-20-002	Santa Holding Child J826	K.S. Adler	Retrd.	24.50	24.50
92-20-003	Santa With Sack Holding Toy J827	K.S. Adler	7,500	24.50	24.50

Number	Name	Artist	Edition Limit	Issue Price	Quote
92-20-004	Santa Spilling Bag Of Toys J1022	K.S. Adler	7,500	25.50	25.50
92-20-005	Santa Coming Out Of Fireplace J1023	K.S. Adler	Retrd.	29.00	29.00
92-20-006	Santa With Little Girls On Lap J1024	K.S. Adler	7,500	24.50	24.50
Kurt S. Adler Inc.	**The Fabriché™ Bear & Friends Series**				
92-21-001	Not A Creature Was Stirring W1534	K.S. Adler	Open	67.00	67.00
92-21-002	Laughing All The Way J1567	K.S. Adler	Open	83.00	83.00
93-21-003	Teddy Bear Parade W1601	K.S. Adler	Open	73.00	73.00
Kurt S. Adler Inc.	**Sesame Street Series**				
93-22-001	Big Bird Fabriché Figurine J7928	KSA/JHP	Open	60.00	60.00
93-22-002	Big Bird Nutcracker H1199	KSA/JHP	Open	60.00	60.00
Kurt S. Adler Inc.	**Ho Ho Ho Gang**				
94-23-001	Holy Mackerel J8202	P.F. Bounger	Open	25.00	25.00
94-23-002	Santa Cob J8203	P.F. Bounger	Open	28.00	28.00
94-23-003	Christmas Goose J8201	P.F. Bounger	Open	25.00	25.00
94-23-004	Surprise J8201	P.F. Bounger	Open	25.00	25.00
94-23-005	Will He Make It? J8203	P.F. Bounger	Open	28.00	28.00
Kurt S. Adler Inc.	**Gallery of Angels**				
94-24-001	Guardian Angel M1099	K.S. Adler	2,000	150.00	150.00
94-24-002	Unspoken Word M1100	K.S. Adler	2,000	150.00	150.00
Kurt S. Adler Inc.	**Christmas Legends**				
94-25-001	Aldwyn of the Greenwood J8196	B.F. Bounger	Open	145.00	145.00
94-25-002	Silvanus the Cheerful J8197	B.F. Bounger	Open	165.00	165.00
94-25-003	Berwyn the Grand J8198	B.F. Bounger	Open	175.00	175.00
94-25-004	Caradoc the Kind J8199	B.F. Bounger	Open	70.00	70.00
94-25-005	Florian of the Berry Bush J8199	B.F. Bounger	Open	70.00	70.00
94-25-006	Gustave the Gutsy J8199	B.F. Bounger	Open	70.00	70.00
All God's Children	**All God's Children**				
85-01-001	Abe -1357	M. Holcombe	Retrd.	24.95	950-1000.
89-01-002	Adam - 1526	M. Holcombe	Open	36.00	36.00
87-01-003	Amy - 1405W	M. Holcombe	Open	22.00	26.00
87-01-004	Angel - 1401W	M. Holcombe	Open	19.99	26-36.00
86-01-005	Annie Mae 8 1/2" -1310	M. Holcombe	Retrd.	26.95	78-200.00
86-01-006	Annie Mae 6" -1311	M. Holcombe	Retrd.	18.95	54-125.00
87-01-007	Aunt Sarah - blue -1440	M. Holcombe	Retrd.	45.00	125-200.
87-01-008	Aunt Sarah - red-1440	M. Holcombe	Retrd.	45.00	320-350.
92-01-009	Barney - 1557	M. Holcombe	Open	32.00	32.00
88-01-010	Bean (Clear Water)-1521	M. Holcombe	Retrd.	36.00	117-350.
92-01-011	Bean (Painted Water)-1521	M. Holcombe	Retrd.	36.00	55-100.00
87-01-012	Becky with Patch - 1402W	M. Holcombe	Retrd.	18.95	181-200.
87-01-013	Becky - 1402W	M. Holcombe	Open	22.00	26.00
87-01-014	Ben - 1504	M. Holcombe	Retrd.	21.95	345.00
91-01-015	Bessie & Corkie - 1547	M. Holcombe	Open	70.00	70.00
92-01-016	Beth - 1558	M. Holcombe	Open	32.00	32.00
88-01-017	Betsy (Clear Water)- 1513	M. Holcombe	Retrd.	36.00	120-350.
92-01-018	Betsy (Painted Water)- 1513	M. Holcombe	Retrd.	36.00	55-100.00
89-01-019	Beverly - 1525	M. Holcombe	Retrd.	50.00	220-500.
91-01-020	Billy - 1545	M. Holcombe	Retrd.	36.00	55-100.00
87-01-021	Blossom - blue - 1500	M. Holcombe	Retrd.	59.95	136-253.
87-01-022	Blossom - red- 1500	M. Holcombe	Retrd.	59.95	700.00
89-01-023	Bo - 1530	M. Holcombe	Retrd.	22.00	22.00
85-01-024	Booker T - 1320	M. Holcombe	Retrd.	18.95	850-1250.
88-01-025	Boone - 1510	M. Holcombe	Retrd.	16.00	60-110.00
89-01-026	Bootsie - 1529	M. Holcombe	Retrd.	22.00	22.00
87-01-027	Bonnie & Buttons - 1502	M. Holcombe	Retrd.	24.00	49-100.00
92-01-028	Caitlin - 1554	M. Holcombe	Open	36.00	36.00
85-01-029	Callie 4 1/2" - 1361	M. Holcombe	Retrd.	18.95	375-438.
85-01-030	Callie 2 1/4" - 1362	M. Holcombe	Retrd.	12.00	230.00
88-01-031	Calvin - 777	M. Holcombe	Retrd.	200.00	1625.00
87-01-032	Cassie - 1503	M. Holcombe	Retrd.	21.95	50-125.00
94-01-033	Chantel 1573	M. Holcombe	Open	39.00	39.00
87-01-034	Charity - 1408	M. Holcombe	Open	28.00	28.00
94-01-035	Cheri 1574	M. Holcombe	Open	38.00	38.00
89-01-036	David - 1528	M. Holcombe	Open	28.00	28.00
91-01-037	Dori (green dress) - 1544	M. Holcombe	Retrd.	30.00	335-350.
87-01-038	Eli - 1403W	M. Holcombe	Open	26.00	26.00
85-01-039	Emma - 1322	M. Holcombe	Retrd.	26.95	1775.00
92-01-040	Faith - 1555	M. Holcombe	Retrd.	32.00	42-75.00
87-01-041	Ginnie - 1508	M. Holcombe	Retrd.	22.00	350.00
86-01-042	Grandma - 1323	M. Holcombe	Retrd.	29.95	3525.00
88-01-043	Hannah - 1515	M. Holcombe	Open	36.00	36.00
88-01-044	Hope - 1519	M. Holcombe	Open	36.00	36.00
87-01-045	Jacob - 1407W	M. Holcombe	Open	26.00	26.00
90-01-046	Jerome - 1532	M. Holcombe	Open	30.00	30.00
89-01-047	Jessica and Jeremy -1522-1523	M. Holcombe	Retrd.	195.00	1600-1650.
89-01-048	Jessie - 1501	M. Holcombe	Open	30.00	30.00
87-01-049	Jessie (no base) -1501W	M. Holcombe	Retrd.	18.95	385-400.
88-01-050	John - 1514	M. Holcombe	Retrd.	30.00	74-170.00
90-01-051	Joseph - 1537	M. Holcombe	Open	30.00	30.00
92-01-052	Joy - 1548	M. Holcombe	Open	30.00	30.00
90-01-053	Kacie - 1533	M. Holcombe	Open	38.00	38.00
88-01-054	Kezia - 1518	M. Holcombe	Open	36.00	36.00
86-01-055	Lil' Emmie 4 1/2" -1344	M. Holcombe	Retrd.	17.99	110-125.
86-01-056	Lil' Emmie 3 1/2"-1345	M. Holcombe	Retrd.	13.99	48-100.00
88-01-057	Lisa-1512	M. Holcombe	Retrd.	36.00	100-160.
90-01-058	Mary - 1536	M. Holcombe	Open	30.00	30.00
88-01-059	Maya - 1520	M. Holcombe	Retrd.	36.00	34-85.00
88-01-060	Meg (blue dress, long hair) -1505	M. Holcombe	Retrd.	21.00	350.00
88-01-061	Meg (blue dress, short hair) -1505	M. Holcombe	Retrd.	21.00	325-800.
88-01-062	Meg (beige dress) -1505	M. Holcombe	Retrd.	21.00	1030.00
92-01-063	Melissa - 1556	M. Holcombe	Open	32.00	32.00
92-01-064	Merci - 1559	M. Holcombe	Open	36.00	36.00
88-01-065	Michael & Kim - 1517	M. Holcombe	Open	36.00	36.00
88-01-066	Moe & Pokey - 1552	M. Holcombe	Retrd.	16.00	24.50-35.00
87-01-067	Moses - 1506	M. Holcombe	Retrd.	30.00	79-97.00
93-01-068	Nathaniel-11569	M. Holcombe	Open	36.00	36.00
91-01-069	Nellie - 1546	M. Holcombe	Retrd.	36.00	55-100.00
87-01-070	Paddy Paw & Luke - 1551	M. Holcombe	Open	24.00	24.00
87-01-071	Paddy Paw & Lucy - 1553	M. Holcombe	Open	24.00	24.00
88-01-072	Peanut -1509	M. Holcombe	Retrd.	16.00	52-117.00
90-01-073	Preshus - 1538	M. Holcombe	Open	24.00	24.00
87-01-074	Primas Jones -1377	M. Holcombe	Retrd.	39.95	675-750.
87-01-075	Primas Jones (w/base) -1377	M. Holcombe	Retrd.	39.95	700-730.
87-01-076	Prissy with Yarn Hair (6 strands) -1343	M. Holcombe	Retrd.	18.95	100-200.
87-01-077	Prissy with Yarn Hair (9 strands) -1343	M. Holcombe	Retrd.	18.95	196-400.
87-01-078	Prissy with Basket -1346	M. Holcombe	Retrd.	16.00	78-118.00
86-01-079	Prissy (Moon Pie) - 1557	M. Holcombe	Open	19.99	30.00
86-01-080	Prissy (Bear) - 1558	M. Holcombe	Open	17.99	24.00
87-01-081	Pud- 1550	M. Holcombe	Retrd.	10.99	1200.00

Number	Name	Artist	Edition Limit	Issue Price	Quote
87-01-082	Rachel - 1404W	M. Holcombe	Open	19.99	26.00
92-01-083	Rakiya - 1561	M. Holcombe	Open	36.00	36.00
88-01-084	Sally -1507	M. Holcombe	Retrd.	18.95	59-125.00
91-01-085	Samantha - 1542	M. Holcombe	Open	38.00	38.00
91-01-086	Samuel - 1541	M. Holcombe	Open	32.00	32.00
89-01-087	Sasha - 1531	M. Holcombe	Open	30.00	30.00
86-01-088	Selina Jane (6 strands) -1338	M. Holcombe	Retrd.	21.95	130-185.
86-01-089	Selina Jane (9 strands) -1338	M. Holcombe	Retrd.	21,95	160-450.
93-01-090	Simon & Andrew - 1565	M. Holcombe	Open	45.00	45.00
86-01-091	St. Nicholas-W -1315	M. Holcombe	Retrd.	29.95	54-135.00
86-01-092	St. Nicholas-B -1316	M. Holcombe	Retrd.	29.95	110-135.
92-01-093	Stephen (Nativity Shepherd) - 1563	M. Holcombe	Open	36.00	75-115.00
90-01-094	Sunshine - 1535	M. Holcombe	Open	38.00	38.00
93-01-095	Sylvia - 1564	M. Holcombe	Open	36.00	36.00
88-01-096	Tansi & Tedi (green socks, collar, cuffs)-1516	M. Holcombe	Retrd.	30.00	300.00
88-01-097	Tansy & Tedi - 1516	M. Holcombe	Open	N/A	36.00
89-01-098	Tara - 1527	M. Holcombe	Open	36.00	36.00
90-01-099	Tess - 1534	M. Holcombe	Open	30.00	30.00
90-01-100	Thaliyah- 778	M. Holcombe	Retrd.	150.00	1425.00
92-01-101	Thomas - 1549	M. Holcombe	Open	30.00	300.00
87-01-102	Tiffany - 1511	M. Holcombe	Open	32.00	32.00
94-01-103	Tish 1572	M. Holcombe	Open	38.00	38.00
86-01-104	Toby 4 1/2"- 1331	M. Holcombe	Retrd.	15.99	78-120.00
86-01-105	Toby 3 1/2"- 1332	M. Holcombe	Retrd.	12.99	36-100.00
85-01-106	Tom- 1353	M. Holcombe	Retrd.	15.95	330-350.
86-01-107	Uncle Bud 8 1/2"- 1303	M. Holcombe	Retrd.	26.95	150-260.
86-01-108	Uncle Bud 6"- 1304	M. Holcombe	Retrd.	18.95	110-125.
92-01-109	Valerie - 1560	M. Holcombe	Open	36.00	36.00
87-01-110	Willie - 1406	M. Holcombe	Open	21.95	26.00
87-01-111	Willie (no base)- 1406W	M. Holcombe	Retrd.	19.95	395.00
93-01-112	Zack - 1566	M. Holcombe	Open	34.00	34.00
All God's Children	**Christmas**				
87-02-001	1987 Father Christmas-W -1750	M. Holcombe	Retrd.	145.00	600.00
87-02-002	1987 Father Christmas-B -1751	M. Holcombe	Retrd.	145.00	600.00
88-02-003	1988 Father Christmas-W -1757	M. Holcombe	Retrd.	195.00	475.00
88-02-004	1988 Father Christmas-B -1758	M. Holcombe	Retrd.	195.00	475.00
88-02-005	Santa Claus-W -1767	M. Holcombe	Retrd.	185.00	480.00
88-02-006	Santa Claus-B -1768	M. Holcombe	Retrd.	185.00	480-500.
89-02-007	1989 Father Christmas-W -1769	M. Holcombe	Retrd.	195.00	550.00
89-02-008	1989 Father Christmas-B -1770	M. Holcombe	Retrd.	195.00	550.00
91-02-009	1990-91 Father Christmas-W -1771	M. Holcombe	Retrd.	195.00	525.00
91-02-010	1990-91 Father Christmas-B -1772	M. Holcombe	Retrd.	195.00	225-525.
92-02-011	1991-92 Father Christmas-W -1773	M. Holcombe	Retrd.	195.00	250-360.
92-02-012	1991-92 Father Christmas-B -1774	M. Holcombe	Retrd.	195.00	195-395.
92-02-013	Father Christmas Bust-W -1775	M. Holcombe	Retrd.	145.00	175-200.
92-02-014	Father Christmas Bust-B -1776	M. Holcombe	Retrd.	145.00	200.00.
All God's Children	**Sugar And Spice**				
87-03-001	God is Love (Angel) -1401	M. Holcombe	Retrd.	21.95	500.00
87-03-002	Friend Show Love (Becky) -1402	M. Holcombe	Retrd.	21.95	500.00
87-03-003	Blessed are the Peacemakers (Eli) -1403	M. Holcombe	Retrd.	21.95	500.00
87-03-004	Old Friends are Best (Rachel) -1404	M. Holcombe	Retrd.	21.95	500.00
87-03-005	Jesus Loves Me (Amy) -1405	M. Holcombe	Retrd.	21.95	500.00
87-03-006	Sharing with Friends (Willie) -1406	M. Holcombe	Retrd.	21.95	500.00
87-03-007	Friendship Warms the Heart (Jacob) -1407	M. Holcombe	Retrd.	21.95	500.00
All God's Children	**International Series**				
88-04-001	Juan - 1807	M. Holcombe	Retrd.	26.00	65.00
87-04-002	Kameko - 1802	M. Holcombe	Open.	26.00	26.00
87-04-003	Karl - 1808	M. Holcombe	Open.	26.00	26.00
88-04-004	Katrina - 1803	M. Holcombe	Retrd.	26.00	58-67.00
87-04-005	Kelli - 1805	M. Holcombe	Open	30.00	30.00
87-04-006	Little Chief - 1804	M. Holcombe	Open	32.00	32.00
93-04-007	Minnie - 1568	M. Holcombe	Open	36.00	36.00
87-04-008	Pike - 1806	M. Holcombe	Open	30.00	30.00
87-04-009	Tat - 1801	M. Holcombe	Open	30.00	30.00
All God's Children	**Historical Series**				
89-05-001	Harriet Tubman - 1900	M. Holcombe	Retrd.	65.00	70.00
90-05-002	Sojourner Truth - 1901	M. Holcombe	Open	65.00	65.00
91-05-003	Frederick Douglass - 1902	M. Holcombe	Open	70.00	70.00
92-05-004	Dr. Daniel Williams - 1903	M. Holcombe	Open	70.00	70.00
92-05-005	Mary Bethune - 1904	M. Holcombe	Open	70.00	70.00
92-05-006	Mary Bethune - 1904 (misspelled)	M. Holcombe	Closed	70.00	125-150.
92-05-007	Frances Harper - 1905	M. Holcombe	Open	70.00	70.00
92-05-008	Ida B. Wells - 1906	M. Holcombe	Open	70.00	70.00
92-05-009	George Washington Carver - 1907	M. Holcombe	Open	70.00	70.00
94-05-010	Augustus Walley (Buffalo Soldier) - 1908	M. Holcombe	5/94	95.00	95.00
All God's Children	**Collectors' Club**				
89-06-001	Molly -1524	M. Holcombe	Retrd.	38.00	300-475.
90-06-002	Joey -1539	M. Holcombe	Retrd.	32.00	200-312.
91-06-003	Mandy -1540	M. Holcombe	Retrd.	36.00	72-185.00
92-06-004	Olivia -1562	M. Holcombe	Retrd.	36.00	100.00
93-06-005	Garrett -1567	M. Holcombe	5/94	36.00	36.00
93-06-006	Peek-a-Boo	M. Holcombe	5/94	Gift	N/A
94-06-007	Alexandria -1575	M. Holcombe	5/95	36.00	36.00
94-06-008	Lindy	M. Holcombe	5/95	Gift	N/A
All God's Children	**Angelic Messengers**				
94-07-001	Cieara 2500	M. Holcombe	Open	38.00	38.00
All God's Children	**Event Piece**				
94-08-001	Uriel 2000	M. Holcombe	Yr.Iss.	45.00	45.00
American Artists	**Fred Stone Figurines**				
85-01-001	The Black Stallion, porcelain	F. Stone	2,500	125.00	260.00
85-01-002	The Black Stallion, bronze	F. Stone	1,500	150.00	175.00
86-01-003	Arab Mare & Foal	F. Stone	2,500	150.00	225.00
86-01-004	Tranquility	F. Stone	2,500	175.00	275.00
87-01-005	Rearing Black Stallion (Porcelain)	F. Stone	3,500	150.00	175.00
87-01-006	Rearing Black Stallion (Bronze)	F. Stone	1,250	175.00	195.00
ANRI	**Ferrandiz Shepherds of the Year**				
77-01-001	Friendships, 6"	J. Ferrandiz	Annual	110.00	500-675.
77-01-002	Friendships, 3"	J. Ferrandiz	Annual	53.50	330.00
78-01-003	Spreading the Word, 6"	J. Ferrandiz	Annual	270.50	500.00
78-01-004	Spreading the Word, 3"	J. Ferrandiz	Annual	115.00	250-275.
79-01-005	Drummer Boy, 6"	J. Ferrandiz	Annual	220.00	400-425.
79-01-006	Drummer Boy, 3"	J. Ferrandiz	Annual	80.00	250.00
80-01-007	Freedom Bound, 6"	J. Ferrandiz	Annual	225.00	400.00
80-01-008	Freedom Bound, 3"	J. Ferrandiz	Annual	90.00	225.00
81-01-009	Jolly Piper, 6"	J. Ferrandiz	Closed	225.00	375.00

Company Number	Name	Series Artist	Edition Limit	Issue Price	Quote
82-01-010	Companions, 6"	J. Ferrandiz	Closed	220.00	275-300.
83-01-011	Good Samaritan, 6"	J. Ferrandiz	Closed	220.00	300-320.
84-01-012	Devotion, 6"	J. Ferrandiz	Closed	180.00	200-250.
84-01-013	Devotion, 3"	J. Ferrandiz	Closed	82.50	125.00
ANRI		**Ferrandiz Matching Number Woodcarvings**			
88-02-001	Dear Sweetheart, 6"	J. Ferrandiz	Closed	525.00	900.00
88-02-002	For My Sweetheart, 6"	J. Ferrandiz	Set	Set	Set
88-02-003	Dear Sweetheart, 3"	J. Ferrandiz	Closed	285.00	495.00
88-02-004	For My Sweetheart, 3"	J. Ferrandiz	Set	Set	Set
88-02-005	Extra, Extra!, 6"	J. Ferrandiz	Closed	665.00	665.00
88-02-006	Sunny Skies, 6"	J. Ferrandiz	Set	Set	Set
88-02-007	Extra, Extra!, 3"	J. Ferrandiz	Closed	315.00	315.00
88-02-008	Sunny Skies, 3"	J. Ferrandiz	Set	Set	Set
88-02-009	Picnic for Two, 6"	J. Ferrandiz	Closed	845.00	845.00
88-02-010	Bon Appetit, 6"	J. Ferrandiz	Set	Set	Set
88-02-011	Picnic for Two, 3"	J. Ferrandiz	Closed	390.00	390.00
88-02-012	Bon Appetit, 3"	J. Ferrandiz	Set	Set	Set
89-02-013	Baker / Pastry, 6"	J. Ferrandiz	Closed	680.00	680.00
89-02-014	Baker / Pastry, 3"	J. Ferrandiz	Closed	340.00	340.00
90-02-015	Alpine Music / Friend, 6"	J. Ferrandiz	Closed	900.00	900.00
90-02-016	Alpine Music / Friend, 3"	J. Ferrandiz	Closed	450.00	450.00
91-02-017	Catalonian Boy/Girl, 6"	J. Ferrandiz	Closed	1000.00	1000.00
91-02-018	Catalonian Boy/Girl, 3"	J. Ferrandiz	Closed	455.00	455.00
ANRI		**Ferrandiz Boy and Girl**			
76-03-001	Cowboy, 6"	J. Ferrandiz	Closed	75.00	500-600.
76-03-002	Harvest Girl, 6"	J. Ferrandiz	Closed	75.00	400-800.
77-03-003	Tracker, 6"	J. Ferrandiz	Closed	100.00	400.00
77-03-004	Leading the Way, 6"	J. Ferrandiz	Closed	100.00	300-375
78-03-005	Peace Pipe, 6"	J. Ferrandiz	Closed	140.00	325-450.
78-03-006	Basket of Joy, 6"	J. Ferrandiz	Closed	140.00	350-450.
79-03-007	Happy Strummer, 6"	J. Ferrandiz	Closed	160.00	395.00
79-03-008	First Blossom, 6"	J. Ferrandiz	Closed	135.00	345-375.
80-03-009	Friends, 6"	J. Ferrandiz	Closed	200.00	300-350.
80-03-010	Melody for Two, 6"	J. Ferrandiz	Closed	200.00	350.00
81-03-011	Merry Melody, 6"	J. Ferrandiz	Closed	210.00	300-350.
81-03-012	Tiny Sounds, 6"	J. Ferrandiz	Closed	210.00	300-350.
82-03-013	Guiding Light, 6"	J. Ferrandiz	Closed	225.00	275-350.
82-03-014	To Market, 6"	J. Ferrandiz	Closed	220.00	295.00
83-03-015	Bewildered, 6"	J. Ferrandiz	Closed	196.00	295.00
83-03-016	Admiration, 6"	J. Ferrandiz	Closed	220.00	295.00
84-03-017	Wanderer's Return, 6"	J. Ferrandiz	Closed	196.00	250.00
84-03-018	Wanderer's Return, 3"	J. Ferrandiz	Closed	93.00	135.00
84-03-019	Friendly Faces, 6"	J. Ferrandiz	Closed	210.00	225-295.
84-03-020	Friendly Faces, 3"	J. Ferrandiz	Closed	93.00	110.00
85-03-021	Tender Love, 6"	J. Ferrandiz	Closed	225.00	250.00
85-03-022	Tender Love, 3"	J. Ferrandiz	Closed	100.00	125.00
85-03-023	Peaceful Friends, 6"	J. Ferrandiz	Closed	250.00	295.00
85-03-024	Peaceful Friends, 3"	J. Ferrandiz	Closed	120.00	120.00
86-03-025	Season's Bounty, 6"	J. Ferrandiz	Closed	245.00	245.00
86-03-026	Season's Bounty, 3"	J. Ferrandiz	Closed	125.00	125.00
86-03-027	Golden Sheaves, 6"	J. Ferrandiz	Closed	245.00	245.00
86-03-028	Golden Sheaves, 3"	J. Ferrandiz	Closed	125.00	125.00
87-03-029	Dear Sweetheart, 6"	J. Ferrandiz	Closed	250.00	250.00
87-03-030	Dear Sweetheart, 3"	J. Ferrandiz	Closed	130.00	130.00
87-03-031	For My Sweetheart, 6"	J. Ferrandiz	Closed	250.00	250.00
87-03-032	For My Sweetheart, 3"	J. Ferrandiz	Closed	130.00	130.00
88-03-033	Extra, Extra!, 6"	J. Ferrandiz	Closed	320.00	320.00
88-03-034	Extra, Extra!, 3"	J. Ferrandiz	Closed	145.00	145.00
88-03-035	Sunny Skies, 6"	J. Ferrandiz	Closed	320.00	320.00
88-03-036	Sunny Skies, 3"	J. Ferrandiz	Closed	145.00	145.00
89-03-037	Baker Boy, 6"	J. Ferrandiz	Closed	340.00	340.00
89-03-038	Baker Boy, 3"	J. Ferrandiz	Closed	170.00	170.00
89-03-039	Pastry Girl, 6"	J. Ferrandiz	Closed	340.00	340.00
89-03-040	Pastry Girl, 3"	J. Ferrandiz	Closed	170.00	170.00
89-03-041	Swiss Girl, 6"	J. Ferrandiz	Closed	470.00	470.00
89-03-042	Swiss Girl, 3"	J. Ferrandiz	Closed	200.00	200.00
89-03-043	Swiss Boy, 6"	J. Ferrandiz	Closed	380.00	380.00
89-03-044	Swiss Boy, 3"	J. Ferrandiz	Closed	180.00	180.00
90-03-045	Alpine Music, 6"	J. Ferrandiz	1,500	450.00	580.00
90-03-046	Alpine Music, 3"	J. Ferrandiz	Closed	225.00	225.00
90-03-047	Alpine Friend, 6"	J. Ferrandiz	1,500	450.00	610.00
90-03-048	Alpine Friend, 3"	J. Ferrandiz	1,500	225.00	265.00
91-03-049	Catalonian Boy, 6"	J. Ferrandiz	Closed	500.00	500.00
91-03-050	Catalonian Boy, 3"	J. Ferrandiz	Closed	227.50	227.50
91-03-051	Catalonian Girl, 6"	J. Ferrandiz	Closed	500.00	500.00
91-03-052	Catalonian Girl, 3"	J. Ferrandiz	Closed	227.50	227.50
92-03-053	Waste Not, Want Not, 6"	J. Ferrandiz	1,000	430.00	430.00
92-03-054	Waste Not, Want Not, 3"	J. Ferrandiz	1,000	190.00	200.00
92-03-055	May I, Too?, 6"	J. Ferrandiz	1,000	440.00	440.00
92-03-056	May I, Too?, 3"	J. Ferrandiz	1,000	230.00	230.00
92-03-057	Madonna With Child, 6"	J. Ferrandiz	1,000	370.00	370.00
92-03-058	Madonna With Child, 3"	J. Ferrandiz	1,000	190.00	190.00
92-03-059	Pascal Lamb, 6"	J. Ferrandiz	1,000	460.00	460.00
92-03-060	Pascal Lamb, 3"	J. Ferrandiz	1,000	210.00	210.00
ANRI		**Ferrandiz Woodcarvings**			
69-04-001	Sugar Heart, 6"	J. Ferrandiz	Closed	25.00	525.00
69-04-002	Sugar Heart, 3"	J. Ferrandiz	Closed	12.50	450.00
69-04-003	Angel Sugar Heart, 6"	J. Ferrandiz	Closed	25.00	2500.00
69-04-004	Heavenly Quintet, 6"	J. Ferrandiz	Closed	25.00	2000.00
69-04-005	Heavenly Gardener, 6"	J. Ferrandiz	Closed	25.00	2000.00
69-04-006	Love's Messenger, 6"	J. Ferrandiz	Closed	25.00	2000.00
74-04-007	Greetings, 6"	J. Ferrandiz	Closed	55.00	475.00
74-04-008	Greetings, 3"	J. Ferrandiz	Closed	30.00	300.00
74-04-009	New Friends, 6"	J. Ferrandiz	Closed	55.00	550.00
74-04-010	New Friends, 3"	J. Ferrandiz	Closed	30.00	275.00
74-04-011	Tender Moments, 6"	J. Ferrandiz	Closed	55.00	575.00
74-04-012	Tender Moments, 3"	J. Ferrandiz	Closed	30.00	375.00
74-04-013	Helping Hands, 6"	J. Ferrandiz	Closed	55.00	700.00
74-04-014	Helping Hands, 3"	J. Ferrandiz	Closed	30.00	350.00
74-04-015	Spring Outing, 6"	J. Ferrandiz	Closed	55.00	900.00
74-04-016	Spring Outing, 3"	J. Ferrandiz	Closed	30.00	625.00
73-04-017	Sweeper, 6"	J. Ferrandiz	Closed	75.00	425.00
73-04-018	Sweeper, 3"	J. Ferrandiz	Closed	35.00	130.00
74-04-019	The Bouquet, 6"	J. Ferrandiz	Closed	75.00	325.00
74-04-020	The Bouquet, 3"	J. Ferrandiz	Closed	35.00	175.00
70-04-021	Artist, 6"	J. Ferrandiz	Closed	25.00	350.00
74-04-022	Artist, 3"	J. Ferrandiz	Closed	30.00	195.00
74-04-023	Little Mother, 6"	J. Ferrandiz	Closed	85.00	285.00
74-04-024	Little Mother, 3"	J. Ferrandiz	Closed	136.00	290.00
74-04-025	Romeo, 6"	J. Ferrandiz	Closed	85.00	395.00
74-04-026	Romeo, 3"	J. Ferrandiz	Closed	50.00	250.00
75-04-027	Inspector, 6"	J. Ferrandiz	Closed	80.00	395.00
75-04-028	Inspector, 3"	J. Ferrandiz	Closed	40.00	250.00
76-04-029	Girl with Rooster, 6"	J. Ferrandiz	Closed	60.00	275.00
76-04-030	Girl with Rooster, 3"	J. Ferrandiz	Closed	32.50	175.00
75-04-031	The Gift, 6"	J. Ferrandiz	Closed	70.00	295.00
75-04-032	The Gift, 3"	J. Ferrandiz	Closed	40.00	195.00
75-04-033	Love Gift, 6"	J. Ferrandiz	Closed	70.00	295.00
75-04-034	Love Gift, 3"	J. Ferrandiz	Closed	40.00	175.00
77-04-035	The Blessing, 6"	J. Ferrandiz	Closed	125.00	250.00
77-04-036	The Blessing, 3"	J. Ferrandiz	Closed	45.00	150.00
69-04-037	Love Letter, 6"	J. Ferrandiz	Closed	25.00	250.00
69-04-038	Love Letter, 3"	J. Ferrandiz	Closed	12.50	150.00
75-04-039	Courting, 6"	J. Ferrandiz	Closed	150.00	450.00
75-04-040	Courting, 3"	J. Ferrandiz	Closed	70.00	235.00
75-04-041	Wanderlust, 6"	J. Ferrandiz	Closed	70.00	450.00
76-04-042	Wanderlust, 3"	J. Ferrandiz	Closed	32.50	125.00
76-04-043	Catch a Falling Star, 6"	J. Ferrandiz	Closed	75.00	250.00
76-04-044	Catch a Falling Star, 3"	J. Ferrandiz	Closed	35.00	150.00
75-04-045	Mother and Child, 6"	J. Ferrandiz	Closed	90.00	295.00
75-04-046	Mother and Child, 3"	J. Ferrandiz	Closed	45.00	150.00
77-04-047	Journey, 6"	J. Ferrandiz	Closed	120.00	400.00
77-04-048	Journey, 3"	J. Ferrandiz	Closed	67.50	175.00
77-04-049	Night Night, 6"	J. Ferrandiz	Closed	67.50	250-315.
77-04-050	Night Night, 3"	J. Ferrandiz	Closed	45.00	120.00
76-04-051	Sharing, 6"	J. Ferrandiz	Closed	32.50	225-275.
76-04-052	Sharing, 3"	J. Ferrandiz	Closed	32.50	130.00
82-04-053	Clarinet, 6"	J. Ferrandiz	Closed	175.00	200.00
82-04-054	Clarinet, 3"	J. Ferrandiz	Closed	80.00	100.00
82-04-055	Violin, 6"	J. Ferrandiz	Closed	175.00	195.00
82-04-056	Violin, 3"	J. Ferrandiz	Closed	80.00	95.00
82-04-057	Bagpipe, 6"	J. Ferrandiz	Closed	175.00	190.00
82-04-058	Bagpipe, 3"	J. Ferrandiz	Closed	80.00	95.00
82-04-059	Flute, 6"	J. Ferrandiz	Closed	175.00	190.00
82-04-060	Flute, 3"	J. Ferrandiz	Closed	80.00	95.00
82-04-061	Guitar, 6"	J. Ferrandiz	Closed	175.00	190.00
82-04-062	Guitar, 3"	J. Ferrandiz	Closed	80.00	95.00
82-04-063	Harmonica, 6"	J. Ferrandiz	Closed	175.00	190.00
82-04-064	Harmonica, 3"	J. Ferrandiz	Closed	80.00	95.00
82-04-065	Harmonica, 3"	J. Ferrandiz	Closed	80.00	95.00
82-04-066	Lighting the Way, 6"	J. Ferrandiz	Closed	225.00	295.00
82-04-067	Lighting the Way, 3"	J. Ferrandiz	Closed	105.00	150.00
81-04-068	Musical Basket, 6"	J. Ferrandiz	Closed	200.00	225.00
81-04-069	Musical Basket, 3"	J. Ferrandiz	Closed	90.00	115.00
82-04-070	The Good Life, 6"	J. Ferrandiz	Closed	225.00	295.00
82-04-071	The Good Life, 3"	J. Ferrandiz	Closed	100.00	200.00
82-04-072	Star Bright, 6"	J. Ferrandiz	Closed	250.00	295.00
82-04-073	Star Bright, 3"	J. Ferrandiz	Closed	110.00	125.00
82-04-074	Encore, 6"	J. Ferrandiz	Closed	225.00	235.00
82-04-075	Encore, 3"	J. Ferrandiz	Closed	100.00	115.00
82-04-076	Play It Again, 6"	J. Ferrandiz	Closed	250.00	255.00
82-04-077	Play It Again, 3"	J. Ferrandiz	Closed	100.00	120.00
73-04-078	Girl with Dove, 6"	J. Ferrandiz	Closed	50.00	175-200.
73-04-079	Girl with Dove, 3"	J. Ferrandiz	Closed	30.00	110.00
79-04-080	Stitch in Time, 6"	J. Ferrandiz	Closed	150.00	235.00
79-04-081	Stitch in Time, 3"	J. Ferrandiz	Closed	75.00	125.00
79-04-082	He's My Brother, 6"	J. Ferrandiz	Closed	155.00	240.00
79-04-083	He's My Brother, 3"	J. Ferrandiz	Closed	70.00	130.00
81-04-084	Stepping Out, 6"	J. Ferrandiz	Closed	220.00	275.00
81-04-085	Stepping Out, 3"	J. Ferrandiz	Closed	95.00	110-145.
79-04-086	High Riding, 6"	J. Ferrandiz	Closed	340.00	475.00
79-04-087	High Riding, 3"	J. Ferrandiz	Closed	145.00	200.00
80-04-088	Umpapa, 4"	J. Ferrandiz	Closed	125.00	140.00
81-04-089	Jolly Piper, 3"	J. Ferrandiz	Closed	100.00	120.00
77-04-090	Tracker, 3"	J. Ferrandiz	Closed	70.00	120-200.
81-04-091	Merry Melody, 3"	J. Ferrandiz	Closed	90.00	115.00
82-04-092	Guiding Light, 3"	J. Ferrandiz	Closed	100.00	115-140.
82-04-093	Companions, 3"	J. Ferrandiz	Closed	95.00	115.00
77-04-094	Leading the Way, 3"	J. Ferrandiz	Closed	62.50	120.00
82-04-095	To Market, 3"	J. Ferrandiz	Closed	95.00	115.00
78-04-096	Basket of Joy, 3"	J. Ferrandiz	Closed	65.00	120.00
81-04-097	Tiny Sounds, 3"	J. Ferrandiz	Closed	90.00	105.00
78-04-098	Spring Dance, 12"	J. Ferrandiz	Closed	950.00	1750.00
78-04-099	Spring Dance, 24"	J. Ferrandiz	Closed	4750.00	6200.00
76-04-100	Gardener, 3"	J. Ferrandiz	Closed	32.00	195.00
76-04-101	Gardener, 6"	J. Ferrandiz	Closed	65.00	275-350.
79-04-102	First Blossom, 3"	J. Ferrandiz	Closed	70.00	110.00
81-04-103	Sweet Arrival Pink, 6"	J. Ferrandiz	Closed	225.00	225.00
81-04-104	Sweet Arrival Pink, 3"	J. Ferrandiz	Closed	105.00	110.00
81-04-105	Sweet Arrival Blue, 6"	J. Ferrandiz	Closed	225.00	255.00
81-04-106	Sweet Arrival Blue, 3"	J. Ferrandiz	Closed	105.00	110.00
82-04-107	The Champion, 6"	J. Ferrandiz	Closed	225.00	250.00
82-04-108	The Champion, 3"	J. Ferrandiz	Closed	98.00	110.00
82-04-109	Sweet Melody, 6"	J. Ferrandiz	Closed	198.00	210.00
82-04-110	Sweet Melody, 3"	J. Ferrandiz	Closed	80.00	90.00
73-04-111	Trumpeter, 6"	J. Ferrandiz	Closed	120.00	240.00
73-04-112	Trumpeter, 3"	J. Ferrandiz	Closed	69.00	115.00
80-04-113	Trumpeter, 10"	J. Ferrandiz	Closed	500.00	500.00
84-04-114	Trumpeter, 20"	J. Ferrandiz	Closed	2350.00	3050.00
79-04-115	Peace Pipe, 3"	J. Ferrandiz	Closed	85.00	120.00
83-04-116	Peace Pipe, 10"	J. Ferrandiz	Closed	460.00	495.00
84-04-117	Peace Pipe, 20"	J. Ferrandiz	Closed	2200.00	3500.00
74-04-118	Happy Wanderer, 6"	J. Ferrandiz	Closed	70.00	200.00
74-04-119	Happy Wanderer, 3"	J. Ferrandiz	Closed	40.00	105.00
73-04-120	Happy Wanderer, 10"	J. Ferrandiz	Closed	120.00	500.00
74-04-121	Flight Into Egypt, 6"	J. Ferrandiz	Closed	70.00	500.00
74-04-122	Flight Into Egypt, 3"	J. Ferrandiz	Closed	35.00	125.00
77-04-123	Poor Boy, 6"	J. Ferrandiz	Closed	125.00	215.00
77-04-124	Poor Boy, 3"	J. Ferrandiz	Closed	50.00	110.00
79-04-125	Happy Strummer, 3"	J. Ferrandiz	Closed	75.00	110.00
78-04-126	Harvest Girl, 3"	J. Ferrandiz	Closed	75.00	110-140.
82-04-127	Hitchhiker, 6"	J. Ferrandiz	Closed	125.00	230.00
82-04-128	Hitchhiker, 3"	J. Ferrandiz	Closed	98.00	85-110.00
84-04-129	High Hopes, 6"	J. Ferrandiz	Closed	170.00	255.00
84-04-130	High Hopes, 3"	J. Ferrandiz	Closed	81.00	81-100.00
88-04-131	Abracadabra, 6"	J. Ferrandiz	Closed	315.00	345.00
88-04-132	Abracadabra, 3"	J. Ferrandiz	Closed	145.00	165.00
88-04-133	Peace Maker, 6"	J. Ferrandiz	Closed	360.00	395.00
88-04-134	Peace Maker, 3"	J. Ferrandiz	Closed	180.00	200.00
88-04-135	Picnic for Two, 6"	J. Ferrandiz	Closed	425.00	465.00
88-04-136	Picnic for Two, 3"	J. Ferrandiz	Closed	190.00	210.00
88-04-137	Bon Appetit, 6"	J. Ferrandiz	Closed	395.00	440.00
88-04-138	Bon Appetit, 3"	J. Ferrandiz	Closed	175.00	195.00
69-04-139	The Good Sheperd, 3"	J. Ferrandiz	Closed	12.50	120.50
69-04-140	The Good Shepherd, 6"	J. Ferrandiz	Closed	25.00	236.50

Company Number	Name	Series Artist	Edition Limit	Issue Price	Quote
71-04-141	The Good Shepherd, 10"	J. Ferrandiz	Closed	90.00	90.00
75-04-142	Going Home, 3"	J. Ferrandiz	Closed	40.00	110.00
75-04-143	Going Home, 6"	J. Ferrandiz	Closed	70.00	240.00
75-04-144	Holy Family, 3"	J. Ferrandiz	Closed	75.00	250.00
75-04-145	Holy Family, 6"	J. Ferrandiz	Closed	200.00	670.00
73-04-146	Nature Girl, 3"	J. Ferrandiz	Closed	30.00	30.00
73-04-147	Nature Girl, 6"	J. Ferrandiz	Closed	60.00	272.00
73-04-148	Girl in the Egg, 3"	J. Ferrandiz	Closed	30.00	127.00
73-04-149	Girl in the Egg, 6"	J. Ferrandiz	Closed	60.00	272.00
76-04-150	Flower Girl, 3"	J. Ferrandiz	Closed	40.00	40.00
76-04-151	Flower Girl, 6"	J. Ferrandiz	Closed	90.00	310.00
76-04-152	The Letter, 3"	J. Ferrandiz	Closed	40.00	40.00
76-04-153	The Letter, 6"	J. Ferrandiz	Closed	90.00	600.00
69-04-154	Talking to the Animals, 3"	J. Ferrandiz	Closed	12.50	125.00
69-04-155	Talking to the Animals, 6"	J. Ferrandiz	Closed	45.00	45.00
71-04-156	Talking to the Animals, 10"	J. Ferrandiz	Closed	90.00	90.00
71-04-157	Talking to Animals, 20"	J. Ferrandiz	Closed	Unkn.	3000.00
70-04-158	Duet, 3"	J. Ferrandiz	Closed	36.00	165.00
70-04-159	Duet, 6"	J. Ferrandiz	Closed	Unkn.	355.00
73-04-160	Spring Arrivals, 3"	J. Ferrandiz	Open	30.00	160.00
73-04-161	Spring Arrivals, 6"	J. Ferrandiz	Open	50.00	350.00
80-04-162	Spring Arrivals, 10"	J. Ferrandiz	Open	435.00	770.00
80-04-163	Spring Arrivals, 20"	J. Ferrandiz	250	2,000	3360.00
75-04-164	Summertime, 3"	J. Ferrandiz	Closed	35.00	35.00
75-04-165	Summertime, 6"	J. Ferrandiz	Closed	70.00	258.00
76-04-166	Cowboy, 3"	J. Ferrandiz	Closed	35.00	140-160.
84-04-167	Cowboy, 10"	J. Ferrandiz	Closed	370.00	500.00
83-04-168	Cowboy, 20"	J. Ferrandiz	Closed	2100.00	2100.00
87-04-169	Serenity, 3"	J. Ferrandiz	Closed	125.00	150.50
84-04-170	Bird's Eye View, 3"	J. Ferrandiz	Closed	88.00	129.00
84-04-171	Bird's Eye View, 6"	J. Ferrandiz	Closed	216.00	700.00
86-04-172	God's Little Helper, 2"	J. Ferrandiz	Closed	170.00	255.00
86-04-173	God's Little Helper, 4"	J. Ferrandiz	Closed	425.00	550.00
85-04-174	Butterfly Boy, 3"	J. Ferrandiz	Closed	95.00	140.00
85-04-175	Butterfly Boy, 6"	J. Ferrandiz	Closed	220.00	322.00
84-04-176	Shipmates, 3"	J. Ferrandiz	Closed	81.00	118.50
84-04-177	Shipmates, 6"	J. Ferrandiz	Closed	170.00	247.50
78-04-178	Spreading the Word, 3"	J. Ferrandiz	Closed	115.00	193.50
78-04-179	Spreading the Word, 6"	J. Ferrandiz	Closed	270.00	494.50
82-04-180	Bundle of Joy, 3"	J. Ferrandiz	Closed	100.00	300.00
82-04-181	Bundle of Joy, 6"	J. Ferrandiz	Closed	225.00	322.50
77-04-182	Riding Thru the Rain, 5"	J. Ferrandiz	Open	145.00	450.00
77-04-183	Riding Thru the Rain, 10"	J. Ferrandiz	Open	400.00	1150.00
81-04-184	Sweet Dreams, 3"	J. Ferrandiz	Closed	100.00	140.00
77-04-185	Hurdy Gurdy, 3"	J. Ferrandiz	Closed	53.00	150.00
77-04-186	Hurdy Gurdy, 6"	J. Ferrandiz	Closed	112.00	390.00
77-04-187	Proud Mother, 3"	J. Ferrandiz	Closed	52.50	150.00
77-04-188	Proud Mother, 6"	J. Ferrandiz	Closed	130.00	350.00
80-04-189	Drummer Boy, 3"	J. Ferrandiz	Closed	130.00	200.00
80-04-190	Drummer Boy, 6"	J. Ferrandiz	Closed	300.00	400.00
82-04-191	Circus Serenade, 3"	J. Ferrandiz	Closed	100.00	160.00
82-04-192	Circus Serenade, 6"	J. Ferrandiz	Closed	220.00	220.00
82-04-193	Surprise, 3"	J. Ferrandiz	Closed	100.00	150.00
82-04-194	Surprise, 6"	J. Ferrandiz	Closed	225.00	325.00
75-04-195	Cherub, 2"	J. Ferrandiz	Closed	32.00	90.00
75-04-196	Cherub, 4"	J. Ferrandiz	Closed	32.00	275.00
69-04-197	The Quintet, 3"	J. Ferrandiz	Closed	12.50	140.00
69-04-198	The Quintet, 6"	J. Ferrandiz	Closed	25.00	340.00
71-04-199	The Quintet, 10"	J. Ferrandiz	Closed	100.00	600.00
71-04-200	The Quintet, 20"	J. Ferrandiz	Closed	Unkn.	3000.00
87-04-201	Serenity, 6"	J. Ferrandiz	Closed	245.00	290.50
87-04-202	Nature's Wonder, 3"	J. Ferrandiz	Closed	125.00	150.50
87-04-203	Nature's Wonder, 6"	J. Ferrandiz	Closed	245.00	290.50
87-04-204	Black Forest Boy, 3"	J. Ferrandiz	Closed	125.00	150.50
87-04-205	Black Forest Boy, 6"	J. Ferrandiz	Closed	250.00	301.00
87-04-206	Black Forest Girl, 3"	J. Ferrandiz	Closed	125.00	150.50
87-04-207	Black Forest Girl, 6"	J. Ferrandiz	Closed	250.00	300-350.
87-04-208	Heavenly Concert, 2"	J. Ferrandiz	Closed	200.00	200.00
87-04-209	Heavenly Concert, 4"	J. Ferrandiz	Closed	450.00	550.00
86-04-210	Swiss Girl, 3"	J. Ferrandiz	Closed	122.00	122.00
86-04-211	Swiss Girl, 6"	J. Ferrandiz	Closed	245.00	303.50
86-04-212	Swiss Boy, 3"	J. Ferrandiz	Closed	122.00	161.50
86-04-213	Swiss Boy, 6"	J. Ferrandiz	Closed	245.00	323.50
86-04-214	A Musical Ride, 4"	J. Ferrandiz	Closed	165.00	236.50
86-04-215	A Musical Ride, 8"	J. Ferrandiz	Closed	395.00	559.00
82-04-216	Sweet Dreams, 6"	J. Ferrandiz	Closed	225.00	330.00
83-04-217	Love Message, 3"	J. Ferrandiz	Closed	105.00	150.50
83-04-218	Love Message, 6"	J. Ferrandiz	Closed	240.00	365.50
83-04-219	Edelweiss, 3"	J. Ferrandiz	Open	95.00	190.00
83-04-220	Edelweiss, 6"	J. Ferrandiz	Open	220.00	450.00
86-04-221	Edelweiss, 10"	J. Ferrandiz	Open	500.00	1000.00
86-04-222	Edelweiss, 20"	J. Ferrandiz	250	3300.00	5420.00
83-04-223	Golden Blossom, 3"	J. Ferrandiz	Open	95.00	190.00
83-04-224	Golden Blossom, 6"	J. Ferrandiz	Open	220.00	450.00
86-04-225	Golden Blossom, 10"	J. Ferrandiz	Open	500.00	1000.00
86-04-226	Golden Blossom, 20"	J. Ferrandiz	250	3300.00	5420.00
86-04-227	Golden Blossom, 40"	J. Ferrandiz	Closed	8300.00	12950.00
88-04-228	Winter Memories, 3"	J. Ferrandiz	Closed	180.00	195.00
88-04-229	Winter Memories, 6"	J. Ferrandiz	Closed	398.00	440.00
87-04-230	Among Friends, 3"	J. Ferrandiz	Closed	125.00	150.50
87-04-231	Among Friends, 6"	J. Ferrandiz	Closed	245.00	290.50
89-04-232	Mexican Girl, 3"	J. Ferrandiz	Closed	170.00	175.00
89-04-233	Mexican Girl, 6"	J. Ferrandiz	Closed	340.00	350.00
89-04-234	Mexican Boy, 3"	J. Ferrandiz	Closed	170.00	175.00
89-04-235	Mexican Boy, 6"	J. Ferrandiz	Closed	340.00	350.00
93-04-236	Santa and Teddy, 5"	J. Ferrandiz	750	360.00	380.00
93-04-237	Christmas Time, 5"	J. Ferrandiz	750	360.00	380.00
93-04-238	Holiday Greetings, 3"	J. Ferrandiz	1,000	200.00	200.00
93-04-239	Holiday Greetings, 6"	J. Ferrandiz	1,000	450.00	450.00
93-04-240	Lots of Gifts, 3"	J. Ferrandiz	1,000	200.00	200.00
93-04-241	Lots of Gifts, 6"	J. Ferrandiz	1,000	450.00	450.00
ANRI		**Ferrandiz Message Collection**			
89-05-001	He is the Light, 4 1/2"	J. Ferrandiz	Closed	300.00	300.00
89-05-002	Heaven Sent, 4 1/2"	J. Ferrandiz	Closed	300.00	300.00
89-05-003	God's Precious Gift, 4 1/2"	J. Ferrandiz	Closed	300.00	300.00
89-05-004	Love Knows No Bounds, 4 1/2"	J. Ferrandiz	Closed	300.00	300.00
89-05-005	Love So Powerful, 4 1/2"	J. Ferrandiz	Closed	300.00	300.00
89-05-006	Light From Within, 4 1/2"	J. Ferrandiz	Closed	300.00	300.00
89-05-007	He Guides Us, 4 1/2"	J. Ferrandiz	Closed	300.00	300.00
89-05-008	God's Miracle, 4 1/2"	J. Ferrandiz	Closed	300.00	300.00
89-05-009	He is the Light, 9"	J. Ferrandiz	Closed	600.00	600.00
90-05-010	God's Creation 4 1/2"	J. Ferrandiz	Closed	300.00	300.00
90-05-011	Count Your Blessings, 4 1/2"	J. Ferrandiz	Closed	300.00	300.00

Company Number	Name	Series Artist	Edition Limit	Issue Price	Quote
90-05-012	Christmas Carillon, 4 1/2"	J. Ferrandiz	Closed	299.00	299.00
ANRI		**Ferrandiz Mini Nativity Set**			
84-06-001	Mary, 1 1/2"	J. Ferrandiz	Closed	300.00	540.00
84-06-002	Joseph, 1 1/2"	J. Ferrandiz	Closed	Set	Set
84-06-003	Infant, 1 1/2"	J. Ferrandiz	Closed	Set	Set
84-06-004	Leading the Way, 1 1/2"	J. Ferrandiz	Closed	Set	Set
84-06-005	Ox Donkey, 1 1/2"	J. Ferrandiz	Closed	Set	Set
84-06-006	Sheep Standing, 1 1/2"	J. Ferrandiz	Closed	Set	Set
84-06-007	Sheep Kneeling, 1 1/2"	J. Ferrandiz	Closed	Set	Set
85-06-008	Reverence, 1 1/2"	J. Ferrandiz	Closed	45.00	53.00
85-06-009	Harmony, 1 1/2"	J. Ferrandiz	Closed	45.00	53.00
85-06-010	Rest, 1 1/2"	J. Ferrandiz	Closed	45.00	53.00
85-06-011	Thanksgiving, 1 1/2"	J. Ferrandiz	Closed	45.00	53.00
85-06-012	Small Talk, 1 1/2"	J. Ferrandiz	Closed	45.00	53.00
85-06-013	Camel, 1 1/2"	J. Ferrandiz	Closed	45.00	53.00
85-06-014	Camel Guide, 1 1/2"	J. Ferrandiz	Closed	45.00	53.00
85-06-015	Baby Camel, 1 1/2"	J. Ferrandiz	Closed	45.00	53.00
86-06-016	Mini Melchoir, 1 1/2"	J. Ferrandiz	Closed	45.00	53.00
86-06-017	Mini Caspar, 1 1/2"	J. Ferrandiz	Closed	45.00	53.00
86-06-018	Mini Balthasar, 1 1/2"	J. Ferrandiz	Closed	45.00	53.00
86-06-019	Mini Angel, 1 1/2"	J. Ferrandiz	Closed	45.00	53.00
86-06-020	Mini Free Ride, plus Mini Lamb, 1 1/2"	J. Ferrandiz	Closed	45.00	53.00
86-06-021	Mini Weary Traveller, 1 1/2"	J. Ferrandiz	Closed	45.00	53.00
86-06-022	Mini The Stray, 1 1/2"	J. Ferrandiz	Closed	45.00	53.00
86-06-023	Mini The Hiker, 1 1/2"	J. Ferrandiz	Closed	45.00	53.00
86-06-024	Mini Star Struck, 1 1/2"	J. Ferrandiz	Closed	45.00	53.00
88-06-025	Jolly Gift, 1 1/2"	J. Ferrandiz	Closed	53.00	53.00
88-06-026	Sweet Inspiration, 1 1/2"	J. Ferrandiz	Closed	53.00	53.00
88-06-027	Sweet Dreams, 1 1/2"	J. Ferrandiz	Closed	53.00	53.00
88-06-028	Long Journey, 1 1/2"	J. Ferrandiz	Closed	53.00	53.00
88-06-029	Devotion, 1 1/2"	J. Ferrandiz	Closed	53.00	53.00
ANRI		**Limited Edition Couples**			
85-07-001	Springtime Stroll, 8"	J. Ferrandiz	Closed	590.00	950.00
85-07-002	First Kiss, 8"	J. Ferrandiz	Closed	590.00	950.00
86-07-003	A Tender Touch, 8"	J. Ferrandiz	Closed	590.00	850.00
86-07-004	My Heart Is Yours, 8"	J. Ferrandiz	Closed	590.00	850.00
87-07-005	Heart to Heart, 8"	J. Ferrandiz	Closed	590.00	850.00
88-07-006	A Loving Hand, 8"	J. Ferrandiz	Closed	795.00	850.00
ANRI		**Sarah Kay Figurines**			
83-08-001	Morning Chores,6"	S. Kay	Closed	210.00	550.00
83-08-002	Morning Chores, 4"	S. Kay	Closed	95.00	300.00
83-08-003	Morning Chores, 1 1/2"	S. Kay	Closed	45.00	110.00
83-08-004	Helping Mother, 6"	S. Kay	Closed	210.00	495.00
83-08-005	Helping Mother, 4"	S. Kay	Closed	95.00	300.00
83-08-006	Helping Mother, 1 1/2"	S. Kay	Closed	45.00	110.00
83-08-007	Sweeping, 6"	S. Kay	Closed	195.00	435.00
83-08-008	Sweeping, 4"	S. Kay	Closed	95.00	230.00
83-08-009	Sweeping, 1 1/2"	S. Kay	Closed	45.00	110.00
83-08-010	Playtime, 6"	S. Kay	Closed	195.00	495.00
83-08-011	Playtime, 4"	S. Kay	Closed	95.00	250.00
83-08-012	Playtime, 1 1/2"	S. Kay	Closed	45.00	110.00
83-08-013	Feeding the Chickens, 6"	S. Kay	Closed	195.00	450.00
83-08-014	Feeding the Chickens, 4"	S. Kay	Closed	95.00	250.00
83-08-015	Feeding the Chickens, 1 1/2"	S. Kay	Closed	45.00	110.00
83-08-016	Waiting for Mother, 6"	S. Kay	Closed	195.00	445.00
83-08-017	Waiting for Mother, 4"	S. Kay	Closed	95.00	230.00
83-08-018	Waiting for Mother, 1 1/2"	S. Kay	Closed	45.00	110.00
83-08-019	Waiting for Mother, 11"	S. Kay	Closed	495.00	795.00
83-08-020	Bedtime, 6"	S. Kay	Closed	195.00	435.00
83-08-021	Bedtime, 4"	S. Kay	Closed	95.00	230.00
83-08-022	Bedtime, 1 1/2"	S. Kay	Closed	45.00	110.00
83-08-023	From the Garden, 6"	S. Kay	Closed	195.00	450.00
83-08-024	From the Garden, 4"	S. Kay	Closed	95.00	235.00
83-08-025	From the Garden, 1 1/2"	S. Kay	Closed	45.00	110.00
83-08-026	Wake Up Kiss, 6"	S. Kay	Closed	210.00	550.00
84-08-027	Wake Up Kiss, 4"	S. Kay	Closed	95.00	195.00
84-08-028	Wake Up Kiss, 1 1/2"	S. Kay	Closed	45.00	550.00
84-08-029	Finding R Way, 6"	S. Kay	Closed	210.00	495.00
84-08-030	Finding R Way, 4"	S. Kay	Closed	95.00	245.00
84-08-031	Finding R Way, 1 1/2"	S. Kay	Closed	45.00	135.00
84-08-032	Daydreaming, 6"	S. Kay	Closed	195.00	445.00
84-08-033	Daydreaming, 4"	S. Kay	Closed	95.00	235.00
84-08-034	Daydreaming,1 1/2"	S. Kay	Closed	45.00	125.00
84-08-035	Off to School, 6"	S. Kay	4,000	195.00	450.00
84-08-036	Off to School, 4"	S. Kay	4,000	95.00	240.00
84-08-037	Off to School,1 1/2"	S. Kay	Closed	45.00	125.00
84-08-038	Off to School, 11"	S. Kay	750	Unkn.	880.00
84-08-039	Off to School, 20"	S. Kay	100	Unkn.	4200.00
84-08-040	Flowers for You, 6"	S. Kay	Closed	195.00	450.00
84-08-041	Flowers for You, 4"	S. Kay	Closed	95.00	250.00
84-08-042	Flowers for You, 1 1/2"	S. Kay	Closed	45.00	125.00
84-08-043	Watchful Eye, 6"	S. Kay	Closed	195.00	445.00
84-08-044	Watchful Eye, 4"	S. Kay	Closed	95.00	235.00
84-08-045	Watchful Eye,1 1/2"	S. Kay	Closed	45.00	125.00
84-08-046	Special Delivery, 6"	S. Kay	Closed	195.00	312-350.
84-08-047	Special Delivery, 4"	S. Kay	Closed	95.00	187.00
84-08-048	Special Delivery, 1 1/2"	S. Kay	Closed	45.00	125.00
84-08-049	Tag Along, 6"	S. Kay	Closed	195.00	290.00
84-08-050	Tag Along, 4"	S. Kay	Closed	95.00	225.00
84-08-051	Tag Along,1 1/2"	S. Kay	Closed	45.00	130.00
85-08-052	A Special Day, 6"	S. Kay	Closed	195.00	325.00
85-08-053	A Special Day, 4"	S. Kay	Closed	95.00	195.00
85-08-054	Afternoon Tea, 6"	S. Kay	Closed	195.00	325-365.
85-08-055	Afternoon Tea, 4"	S. Kay	Closed	95.00	185.00
85-08-056	Afternoon Tea, 11"	S. Kay	Closed	Unkn.	770.00
85-08-057	Afternoon Tea, 20"	S. Kay	Closed	Unkn.	3500.00
85-08-058	Nightie Night, 6"	S. Kay	Closed	195.00	325.00
85-08-059	Nightie Night, 4"	S. Kay	Closed	95.00	185.00
85-08-060	Yuletide Cheer, 6"	S. Kay	Closed	210.00	435.00
85-08-061	Yuletide Cheer, 4"	S. Kay	Closed	95.00	250.00
85-08-062	'Tis the Season, 6"	S. Kay	Closed	210.00	425.00
85-08-063	'Tis the Season, 4"	S. Kay	Closed	95.00	250.00
85-08-064	Giddyap!, 6"	S. Kay	Closed	195.00	325.00
85-08-065	Giddyap!, 4"	S. Kay	Closed	95.00	250.00
86-08-066	Our Puppy, 6"	S. Kay	Closed	210.00	355.00
86-08-067	Our Puppy, 4"	S. Kay	Closed	95.00	185.00
86-08-068	Our Puppy, 1 1/2"	S. Kay	Closed	45.00	90.00
86-08-069	Always By My Side, 6"	S. Kay	Closed	195.00	375.00
86-08-070	Always By My Side, 4"	S. Kay	Closed	95.00	195.00
86-08-071	Always By My Side, 1 1/2"	S. Kay	Closed	45.00	95.00
86-08-072	Finishing Touch, 6"	S. Kay	Closed	195.00	312.00

Company Number	Name	Series Artist	Edition Limit	Issue Price	Quote
86-08-073	Finishing Touch, 4"	S. Kay	Closed	95.00	172.00
86-08-074	Finishing Touch, 1 1/2"	S. Kay	Closed	45.00	85.00
86-08-075	Good As New, 6"	S. Kay	4,000	195.00	500.00
86-08-076	Good As New, 4"	S. Kay	4,000	95.00	290.00
86-08-077	Good As New, 1 1/2"	S. Kay	Closed	45.00	90.00
86-08-078	Bunny Hug, 6"	S. Kay	Closed	210.00	395.00
86-08-079	Bunny Hug, 4"	S. Kay	Closed	95.00	172.00
86-08-080	Bunny Hug, 1 1/2"	S. Kay	Closed	45.00	85.00
86-08-081	Sweet Treat, 6"	S. Kay	Closed	195.00	312.00
86-08-082	Sweet Treat, 4"	S. Kay	Closed	95.00	172.00
86-08-083	Sweet Treat, 1 1/2"	S. Kay	Closed	45.00	85.00
86-08-084	To Love And To Cherish, 6"	S. Kay	Closed	195.00	312.00
86-08-085	To Love And To Cherish, 4"	S. Kay	Closed	95.00	172.00
86-08-086	To Love And To Cherish, 1 1/2"	S. Kay	Closed	45.00	85.00
86-08-087	To Love and To Cherish, 11"	S. Kay	Closed	Unkn.	667.00
86-08-088	To Love and To Cherish, 20"	S. Kay	Closed	Unkn.	3600.00
86-08-089	With This Ring, 6"	S. Kay	Closed	195.00	312.00
86-08-090	With This Ring, 4"	S. Kay	Closed	95.00	172.00
86-08-091	With This Ring, 1 1/2"	S. Kay	Closed	45.00	85.00
86-08-092	With This Ring, 11"	S. Kay	Closed	Unkn.	667.50
86-08-093	With This Ring, 20"	S. Kay	Closed	Unkn.	3600.00
87-08-094	All Aboard, 6"	S. Kay	Closed	265.00	355.00
87-08-095	All Aboard, 4"	S. Kay	Closed	130.00	185.00
87-08-096	All Aboard, 1 1/2"	S. Kay	Closed	49.50	90.00
87-08-097	Let's Play, 6"	S. Kay	Closed	265.00	355.00
87-08-098	Let's Play, 4"	S. Kay	Closed	130.00	185.00
87-08-099	Let's Play, 1 1/2"	S. Kay	Closed	49.50	90.00
87-08-100	A Loving Spoonful, 6"	S. Kay	4,000	295.00	550.00
87-08-101	A Loving Spoonful, 4"	S. Kay	4,000	150.00	290.00
87-08-102	A Loving Spoonful, 1 1/2"	S. Kay	Closed	49.50	90.00
87-08-103	Little Nanny, 6"	S. Kay	Closed	295.00	400.00
87-08-104	Little Nanny, 4"	S. Kay	Closed	150.00	200.00
87-08-105	Little Nanny, 1 1/2"	S. Kay	Closed	49.50	90.00
87-08-106	All Mine, 6"	S. Kay	Closed	245.00	465.00
87-08-107	All Mine, 4"	S. Kay	Closed	130.00	225.00
87-08-108	All Mine, 1 1/2"	S. Kay	Closed	49.50	95.00
87-08-109	Cuddles, 6"	S. Kay	Closed	245.00	465.00
87-08-110	Cuddles, 4"	S. Kay	Closed	130.00	225.00
87-08-111	Cuddles, 1 1/2"	S. Kay	Closed	49.50	95.00
88-08-112	My Little Brother, 6"	S. Kay	Closed	375.00	450.00
88-08-113	My Little Brother, 4"	S. Kay	Closed	195.00	225.00
88-08-114	My Little Brother, 1 1/2"	S. Kay	Closed	70.00	90.00
88-08-115	Purrfect Day, 6"	S. Kay	Closed	265.00	455.00
88-08-116	Purrfect Day, 4"	S. Kay	Closed	184.00	215.00
88-08-117	Purrfect Day, 1 1/2"	S. Kay	Closed	70.00	90.00
88-08-118	Penny for Your Thoughts, 6"	S. Kay	Closed	365.00	455.00
88-08-119	Penny for Your Thoughts, 4"	S. Kay	Closed	185.00	215.00
88-08-120	Penny for Your Thoughts, 1 1/2"	S. Kay	Closed	70.00	90.00
88-08-121	New Home, 6"	S. Kay	Closed	365.00	500.00
88-08-122	New Home, 4"	S. Kay	Closed	185.00	240.00
88-08-123	New Home, 1 1/2"	S. Kay	Closed	70.00	90.00
88-08-124	Ginger Snap, 6"	S. Kay	Closed	300.00	355.00
88-08-125	Ginger Snap, 4"	S. Kay	Closed	150.00	185.00
88-08-126	Ginger Snap, 1 1/2"	S. Kay	Closed	70.00	90.00
88-08-127	Hidden Treasures, 6"	S. Kay	Closed	300.00	355.00
88-08-128	Hidden Treasures, 4"	S. Kay	Closed	150.00	185.00
88-08-129	Hidden Treasures, 1 1/2"	S. Kay	Closed	70.00	90.00
89-08-130	First School Day, 6"	S. Kay	2,000	550.00	650.00
89-08-131	First School Day, 4"	S. Kay	2,000	290.00	350.00
89-08-132	First School Day, 1 1/2"	S. Kay	Closed	85.00	95.00
89-08-133	Yearly Check-Up, 6"	S. Kay	Closed	390.00	390.00
89-08-134	Yearly Check-Up, 4"	S. Kay	Closed	190.00	195.00
89-08-135	Yearly Check-Up, 1 1/2"	S. Kay	Closed	85.00	95.00
89-08-136	House Call, 6"	S. Kay	Closed	390.00	390.00
89-08-137	House Call, 4"	S. Kay	Closed	190.00	195.00
89-08-138	House Call, 1 1/2"	S. Kay	Closed	85.00	95.00
89-08-139	Take Me Along, 6"	S. Kay	1,000	440.00	525.00
89-08-140	Take Me Along, 4"	S. Kay	2,000	220.00	285.00
89-08-141	Take Me Along, 1 1/2"	S. Kay	Closed	85.00	95.00
89-08-142	Garden Party, 6"	S. Kay	Closed	440.00	475.00
89-08-143	Garden Party, 4"	S. Kay	2,000	220.00	240.00
89-08-144	Garden Party, 1 1/2"	S. Kay	Closed	85.00	95.00
89-08-145	Fisherboy, 6"	S. Kay	Closed	440.00	475.00
89-08-146	Fisherboy, 4"	S. Kay	2,000	220.00	240.00
89-08-147	Fisherboy, 1 1/2"	S. Kay	Closed	85.00	95.00
89-08-148	Cherish, 6"	S. Kay	2,000	398.00	560.00
89-08-149	Cherish, 4"	S. Kay	2,000	199.00	290.00
89-08-150	Cherish, 1 1/2"	S. Kay	Closed	80.00	95.00
90-08-151	Holiday Cheer, 6"	S. Kay	1,000	450.00	610.00
90-08-152	Holiday Cheer, 4"	S. Kay	2,000	225.00	305.00
90-08-153	Holiday Cheer, 1 1/2"	S. Kay	Closed	90.00	95.00
90-08-154	Tender Loving Care, 6"	S. Kay	Closed	440.00	475.00
90-08-155	Tender Loving Care, 4"	S. Kay	Closed	220.00	240.00
90-08-156	Tender Loving Care, 1 1/2"	S. Kay	Closed	90.00	95.00
90-08-157	Spring Fever, 6"	S. Kay	2,000	450.00	610.00
90-08-158	Spring Fever, 4"	S. Kay	2,000	225.00	305.00
90-08-159	Spring Fever, 1 1/2"	S. Kay	Closed	90.00	95.00
90-08-160	Batter Up, 6"	S. Kay	2,000	440.00	505.00
90-08-161	Batter Up, 4"	S. Kay	2,000	220.00	265.00
90-08-162	Batter Up, 1 1/2"	S. Kay	Closed	90.00	95.00
90-08-163	Seasons Greetings, 6"	S. Kay	1,000	450.00	610.00
90-08-164	Seasons Greetings, 4"	S. Kay	2,000	225.00	305.00
90-08-165	Seasons Greetings, 1 1/2"	S. Kay	Closed	90.00	95.00
90-08-166	Shootin' Hoops, 6"	S. Kay	2,000	440.00	450.00
90-08-167	Shootin' Hoops, 4"	S. Kay	2,000	220.00	225.00
90-08-168	Shootin' Hoops,1 1/2"	S. Kay	Closed	90.00	95.00
91-08-169	Figure Eight, 6"	S. Kay	2,000	550.00	660.00
91-08-170	Figure Eight, 4"	S. Kay	2,000	270.00	365.00
91-08-171	Figure Eight, 1 1/2"	S. Kay	3,750	110.00	110.00
91-08-172	Season's Joy, 6"	S. Kay	1,000	550.00	620.00
91-08-173	Season's Joy, 4"	S. Kay	2,000	270.00	305.00
91-08-174	Season's Joy, 1 1/2"	S. Kay	3,750	110.00	115.00
91-08-175	Winter Surprise, 6"	S. Kay	1,000	550.00	550.00
91-08-176	Winter Surprise, 4"	S. Kay	2,000	270.00	270.00
91-08-177	Winter Surprise, 1 1/2"	S. Kay	3,750	110.00	110.00
91-08-178	Dress Up, 6"	S. Kay	2,000	550.00	550.00
91-08-179	Dress Up, 4"	S. Kay	2,000	270.00	270.00
91-08-180	Dress Up, 1 1/2"	S. Kay	3,750	110.00	110.00
91-08-181	Touch Down, 6"	S. Kay	2,000	550.00	550.00
91-08-182	Touch Down, 4"	S. Kay	2,000	270.00	270.00
91-08-183	Touch Down, 1 1/2"	S. Kay	3,750	110.00	110.00
91-08-184	Fore!!, 6"	S. Kay	2,000	550.00	580.00
91-08-185	Fore!!, 4"	S. Kay	2,000	270.00	325.00
91-08-186	Fore!!, 1 1/2"	S. Kay	3,750	110.00	115.00

Company Number	Name	Series Artist	Edition Limit	Issue Price	Quote
92-08-187	Raindrops, 6"	S. Kay	1,000	640.00	640.00
92-08-188	Raindrops, 4"	S. Kay	1,000	350.00	350.00
92-08-189	Raindrops, 1 1/2"	S. Kay	3,750	110.00	110.00
92-08-190	Free Skating, 6"	S. Kay	1,000	590.00	610.00
92-08-191	Free Skating, 4"	S. Kay	1,000	310.00	325.00
92-08-192	Free Skating, 1 1/2"	S. Kay	3,750	110.00	115.00
92-08-193	Merry Christmas, 6"	S. Kay	1,000	580.00	580.00
92-08-194	Merry Christmas, 4"	S. Kay	1,000	350.00	350.00
92-08-195	Merry Christmas, 1 1/2"	S. Kay	3,750	110.00	115.00
92-08-196	Tulips For Mother, 6"	S. Kay	1,000	590.00	620.00
92-08-197	Tulips For Mother, 4"	S. Kay	1,000	310.00	325.00
92-08-198	Tulips For Mother, 1 1/2"	S. Kay	3,750	110.00	115.00
92-08-199	Winter Cheer, 6"	S. Kay	1,000	580.00	580.00
92-08-200	Winter Cheer, 4"	S. Kay	2,000	300.00	300.00
94-08-201	Christmas Wonder, 6"	S. Kay	1,000	790.00	790.00
94-08-202	Christmas Wonder, 4"	S. Kay	1,000	420.00	420.00
94-08-203	Little Chimney Sweep, 6"	S. Kay	1,000	700.00	700.00
94-08-204	Little Chimney Sweep, 4"	S. Kay	1,000	375.00	375.00
94-08-205	Bubbles & Bows, 6"	S. Kay	1,000	700.00	700.00
94-08-206	Bubbles & Bows, 4"	S. Kay	1,000	360.00	360.00
94-08-203	Clowning Around, 6"	S. Kay	1,000	620.00	620.00
94-08-204	Clowning Around, 4"	S. Kay	1,000	315.00	315.00
94-08-205	Jolly Pair, 6"	S. Kay	1,000	730.00	730.00
94-08-206	Jolly Pair, 4"	S. Kay	1,000	380.00	380.00
ANRI		**Sarah Kay Santas**			
88-09-001	Jolly St. Nick, 6"	S. Kay	Closed	398.00	850.00
88-09-002	Jolly St. Nick, 4"	S. Kay	Closed	199.00	300-550.
88-09-003	Jolly Santa, 6"	S. Kay	Closed	480.00	600.00
88-09-004	Jolly Santa, 4"	S. Kay	Closed	235.00	300-350.
89-09-005	Jolly Santa, 12"	S. Kay	Closed	1300.00	1300.00
89-09-006	Santa, 6"	S. Kay	Closed	480.00	480.00
89-09-007	Santa, 4"	S. Kay	Closed	235.00	350.00
90-09-008	Kris Kringle Santa, 6"	S. Kay	Closed	550.00	550.00
90-09-009	Kris Kringle Santa, 4"	S. Kay	Closed	275.00	350.00
91-09-010	A Friend To All, 6"	S. Kay	750	590.00	590.00
91-09-011	A Friend To All, 4"	S. Kay	750	300.00	300.00
92-09-012	Father Christmas, 6"	S. Kay	750	590.00	590.00
92-09-013	Father Christmas, 4"	S. Kay	750	350.00	350.00
ANRI		**Sarah Kay Mini Santas**			
91-10-001	Jolly St. Nick, 1 1/2"	S. Kay	Closed	110.00	110.00
91-10-002	Jolly Santa, 1 1/2"	S. Kay	Closed	110.00	110.00
91-10-003	Sarah Kay Santa, 1 1/2"	S. Kay	Closed	110.00	110.00
91-10-004	Kris Kringle, 1 1/2"	S. Kay	Closed	110.00	110.00
ANRI		**Sarah Kay 10th Anniversary**			
93-11-001	Mr. Santa, 4"	S. Kay	750	375.00	390.00
93-11-002	Mr. Santa, 6"	S. Kay	750	695.00	730.00
93-11-003	Mrs. Santa, 4"	S. Kay	750	375.00	390.00
93-11-004	Mrs. Santa, 6"	S. Kay	750	695.00	730.00
93-11-005	Joy to the World, 4"	S. Kay	1,000	310.00	290.00
93-11-006	Joy to the World, 6"	S. Kay	1,000	600.00	580.00
93-11-007	Christmas Basket, 4"	S. Kay	1,000	310.00	290.00
93-11-008	Christmas Basket, 6"	S. Kay	1,000	600.00	580.00
93-11-009	Innocence, 4"	S. Kay	1,000	345.00	315.00
93-11-010	Innocence, 6"	S. Kay	1,000	630.00	630.00
93-11-011	My Favorite Doll, 4"	S. Kay	1,000	315.00	315.00
93-11-012	My Favorite Doll, 6"	S. Kay	1,000	630.00	630.00
ANRI		**Club ANRI**			
83-12-001	Welcome 4"	J. Ferrandiz	Closed	110.00	395.00
84-12-002	My Friend 4"	J. Ferrandiz	Closed	110.00	400.00
84-12-003	Apple of My Eye 4 1/2"	S. Kay	Closed	135.00	385.00
85-12-004	Harvest Time 4"	J. Ferrandiz	Closed	125.00	175-385.
85-12-005	Dad's Helper 4 1/2"	S. Kay	Closed	135.00	150-375.
86-12-006	Harvest's Helper 4"	J. Ferrandiz	Closed	135.00	175-335.
86-12-007	Romantic Notions 4"	S. Kay	Closed	135.00	175-310.
86-12-008	Celebration March 5"	J. Ferrandiz	Closed	165.00	225-295.
87-12-009	Will You Be Mine 4"	J. Ferrandiz	Closed	135.00	175-310.
86-12-010	Make A Wish 4"	S. Kay	Closed	165.00	215-325.
87-12-011	A Young Man's Fancy 4"	S. Kay	Closed	135.00	165-265.
88-12-012	Forever Yours 4"	J. Ferrandiz	Closed	170.00	250.00
88-12-013	I've Got a Secret 4"	S. Kay	Closed	170.00	205.00
88-12-014	Maestro Mickey 4 1/2"	Disney Studio	Closed	170.00	200-215.
89-12-015	Diva Minnie 4 1/2"	Disney Studio	Closed	190.00	190.00
89-12-016	I'll Never Tell 4"	S. Kay	Closed	190.00	190.00
89-12-017	Twenty Years of Love 4"	J. Ferrandiz	Closed	190.00	190.00
90-12-018	You Are My Sunshine 4"	J. Ferrandiz	Yr.Iss.	220.00	220.00
90-12-019	A Little Bashful 4"	S. Kay	Yr.Iss.	220.00	220.00
90-12-020	Dapper Donald 4"	Disney Studio	Closed	199.00	199.00
91-12-021	With All My Heart 4"	J. Ferrandiz	N/A	250.00	250.00
91-12-022	Kiss Me 4"	S.Kay	N/A	250.00	250.00
91-12-023	Daisy Duck 4 1/2"	Disney Studio	N/A	250.00	250.00
92-12-024	You Are My All 4"	J. Ferrandiz	N/A	260.00	260.00
92-12-025	My Present For You 4"	S. Kay	N/A	270.00	270.00
ANRI		**Disney Woodcarving**			
87-13-001	Mickey Mouse, 4"	Disney Studio	Closed	150.00	210.00
87-13-002	Minnie Mouse, 4"	Disney Studio	Closed	150.00	210.00
87-13-003	Pinocchio, 4"	Disney Studio	Closed	150.00	195.00
87-13-004	Donald Duck, 4"	Disney Studio	Closed	150.00	195.00
87-13-005	Goofy, 4"	Disney Studio	Closed	150.00	195.00
87-13-006	Mickey & Minnie, 6" (matching numbers)	Disney Studio	Closed	625.00	1650.00
88-13-007	Donald Duck, 6"	Disney Studio	Closed	350.00	700.00
88-13-008	Goofy, 6"	Disney Studio	Closed	380.00	700.00
88-13-009	Mickey Mouse, 4"	Disney Studio	Closed	180.00	199.00
88-13-010	Pluto, 4"	Disney Studio	Closed	180.00	199.00
88-13-011	Pinocchio, 4"	Disney Studio	Closed	180.00	199.00
88-13-012	Donald Duck, 4"	Disney Studio	Closed	180.00	199.00
88-13-013	Goofy, 4"	Disney Studio	Closed	180.00	199.00
88-13-014	Mickey Mouse, 1 3/4"	Disney Studio	Closed	80.00	100.00
88-13-015	Pluto, 1-3/4"	Disney Studio	Closed	80.00	100.00
88-13-016	Pinocchio, 1 3/4"	Disney Studio	Closed	80.00	140.00
88-13-017	Donald Duck, 1 3/4"	Disney Studio	Closed	80.00	100.00
88-13-018	Goofy, 1 3/4"	Disney Studio	Closed	80.00	100.00
89-13-019	Pluto, 4"	Disney Studio	Closed	190.00	205.00
88-13-020	Pluto, 6"	Disney Studio	Closed	350.00	350.00
88-13-021	Goofy, 6"	Disney Studio	Closed	350.00	350.00
89-13-022	Mickey, 4"	Disney Studio	Closed	190.00	205.00
89-13-023	Minnie, 4"	Disney Studio	Closed	190.00	205.00
89-13-024	Donald, 4"	Disney Studio	Closed	190.00	205.00
89-13-025	Daisy, 4"	Disney Studio	Closed	190.00	205.00
89-13-026	Goofy, 4"	Disney Studio	Closed	190.00	205.00

Company / Number	Name	Series / Artist	Edition Limit	Issue Price	Quote
89-13-027	Mini Mickey, 2"	Disney Studio	Closed	85.00	100.00
89-13-028	Mini Minnie, 2"	Disney Studio	Closed	85.00	100.00
89-13-029	Mini Donald, 2"	Disney Studio	Closed	85.00	100.00
89-13-030	Minnie Daisy, 2"	Disney Studio	Closed	85.00	100.00
89-13-031	Mini Goofy, 2"	Disney Studio	Closed	85.00	100.00
89-13-032	Mini Pluto, 2"	Disney Studio	Closed	85.00	100.00
89-13-033	Mickey, 10"	Disney Studio	Closed	700.00	750.00
89-13-034	Minnie, 10"	Disney Studio	Closed	700.00	750.00
89-13-035	Mickey, 20"	Disney Studio	Closed	3500.00	3500.00
89-13-036	Minnie, 20"	Disney Studio	Closed	3500.00	3500.00
89-13-037	Mickey & Minnie, 20" matched set	Disney Studio	Closed	7000.00	7000.00
89-13-038	Mickey & Minnie Set, 6"	Disney Studio	Closed	700.00	700.00
88-13-039	Mickey Sorcerer's Apprentice, 6"	Disney Studio	Closed	350.00	500.00
88-13-040	Mickey Sorcerer's Apprentice, 4"	Disney Studio	Closed	180.00	199.00
88-13-041	Mickey Sorcerer's Apprentice, 2"	Disney Studio	Closed	80.00	100.00
89-13-042	Pinocchio, 6"	Disney Studio	Closed	350.00	350.00
89-13-043	Pinocchio, 4"	Disney Studio	Closed	190.00	199.00
89-13-044	Pinocchio, 2"	Disney Studio	Closed	85.00	100.00
89-13-045	Pinocchio, 10"	Disney Studio	Closed	700.00	700.00
89-13-046	Pinocchio, 20"	Disney Studio	Closed	3500.00	3500.00
90-13-047	Mickey Mouse, 4"	Disney Studio	Closed	199.00	205.00
90-13-045	Mickey Mouse, 2"	Disney Studio	Closed	100.00	100.00
90-13-049	Minnie Mouse, 4"	Disney Studio	Closed	199.00	205.00
90-13-050	Minnie Mouse, 2"	Disney Studio	Closed	100.00	100.00
90-13-051	Chef Goofy, 5"	Disney Studio	Closed	265.00	265.00
90-13-052	Chef Goofy, 2 1/2"	Disney Studio	Closed	125.00	125.00
90-13-053	Donald & Daisy, 6" (Matched Set)	Disney Studio	Closed	700.00	700.00
91-13-054	Mickey Skating, 4"	Disney Studio	Closed	250.00	250.00
91-13-055	Minnie Skating, 4"	Disney Studio	Closed	250.00	250.00
91-13-056	Mickey Skating, 2"	Disney Studio	Closed	120.00	120.00
91-13-057	Minnie Skating, 2"	Disney Studio	Closed	120.00	120.00
91-13-058	Bell Boy Donald, 6"	Disney Studio	Closed	400.00	400.00
91-13-059	Bell Boy Donald, 4"	Disney Studio	Closed	250.00	250.00
ANRI		**Mickey Mouse Thru The Ages**			
90-14-001	Steam Boat Willie, 4"	Disney Studio	Closed	295.00	475-550.
91-14-002	The Mad Dog, 4"	Disney Studio	Closed	500.00	395-500.
Armani		**Wildlife**			
83-01-001	Eagle Bird of Prey 3213	G. Armani	Open	210.00	425.00
83-01-002	Royal Eagle with Babies 3553	G. Armani	Open	215.00	400.00
82-01-003	Snow Bird 5548	G. Armani	Open	100.00	180.00
88-01-004	Peacock 455S	G. Armani	5,000	600.00	675.00
88-01-005	Peacock 458S	G. Armani	5,000	630.00	700.00
88-01-006	Bird Of Paradise 454S	G. Armani	5,000	475.00	500.00
90-01-007	Three Doves 996S	G. Armani	5,000	670.00	750.00
90-01-008	Soaring Eagle 970S	G. Armani	5,000	620.00	700.00
90-01-009	Bird of Paradise 718S	G. Armani	5,000	550.00	575.00
93-01-010	Parrot With Vase 736S	G. Armani	3,000	460.00	460.00
93-01-011	Doves With Vase 204S	G. Armani	3,000	375.00	375.00
93-01-012	Peacock With Vase 735S	G. Armani	3,000	375.00	375.00
93-01-013	Horse Head 205S	G. Armani	Open	140.00	140.00
93-01-014	Galloping Horse 905S	G. Armani	7,500	465.00	465.00
93-01-015	Show Horse 907S	G. Armani	7,500	550.00	550.00
93-01-016	Rearing Horse 909S	G. Armani	7,500	515.00	515.00
Armani		**My Fair Ladies™**			
87-02-001	Lady With Peacock 385C	G. Armani	Retrd.	380.00	1200-1850.
87-02-002	Lady with Compact 386C	G. Armani	Retrd.	300.00	400-800.
87-02-003	Lady with Muff 388C	G. Armani	5,000	250.00	450.00
87-02-004	Lady With Fan 387C	G. Armani	5,000	300.00	400.00
87-02-005	Flamenco Dancer 389C	G. Armani	5,000	400.00	500.00
87-02-006	Lady With Book 384C	G. Armani	5,000	300.00	450.00
87-02-007	Lady With Great Dane 429C	G. Armani	5,000	365.00	475.00
87-02-008	Mother & Child 405C	G. Armani	5,000	410.00	550.00
89-02-009	Lady With Parrot 616C	G. Armani	5,000	400.00	500.00
93-02-010	Fascination 192C	G. Armani	5,000	500.00	500.00
93-02-011	Fascination 192F	G. Armani	Open	250.00	250.00
93-02-012	Morning Rose 193C	G. Armani	5,000	450.00	450.00
93-02-013	Morning Rose 193F	G. Armani	Open	225.00	225.00
93-02-014	Elegance 195C	G. Armani	5,000	525.00	525.00
93-02-015	Elegance 195F	G. Armani	Open	300.00	300.00
93-02-016	Mahogany 194C	G. Armani	5,000	500.00	500.00
93-02-017	Mahogany 194F	G. Armani	Open	360.00	360.00
Armani		**Wedding**			
82-03-001	Wedding Couple 5132	G. Armani	Open	110.00	190.00
87-03-002	Wedding Couple 407C	G. Armani	Open	525.00	550.00
88-03-003	Bride & Groom Wedding 475P	G. Armani	Open	270.00	285.00
89-03-004	Just Married 827C	G. Armani	5,000	950.00	1000.00
91-03-005	Wedding Couple At Threshold 813C	G. Armani	7,500	400.00	400.00
91-03-006	Wedding Couple With Bicycle 814C	G. Armani	7,500	600.00	600.00
91-03-007	Wedding Couple Kissing 815C	G. Armani	7,500	500.00	500.00
92-03-008	Bride With Doves 885C	G. Armani	Open	280.00	280.00
92-03-009	Bride With Doves 885F	G. Armani	Open	220.00	220.00
93-03-010	Carriage Wedding902C	G. Armani	2,500	1000.00	1000.00
93-03-011	Carriage Wedding 902F	G. Armani	Open	500.00	500.00
93-03-012	Garden Wedding 189F	G. Armani	Open	120.00	120.00
93-03-013	Garden Wedding 189C	G. Armani	Open	225.00	225.00
93-03-014	Wedding Flowers To Mary 187C	G. Armani	Open	225.00	225.00
93-03-015	Wedding Flowers To Mary 187F	G. Armani	Open	115.00	115.00
93-03-016	Wedding Couple At Wall 201C	G. Armani	Open	225.00	225.00
93-03-017	Wedding Couple At Wall 201F	G. Armani	Open	115.00	115.00
93-03-018	Wedding Couple Forever 791F	G. Armani	Open	250.00	250.00
94-03-019	Bride With Column & Vase 488C	G. Armani	Open	260.00	260.00
94-03-020	Bride With Column & Vase 488F	G. Armani	Open	200.00	200.00
94-03-021	Bride With Flower Vase 489C	G. Armani	Open	135.00	135.00
94-03-022	Bride With Flower Vase 489F	G. Armani	Open	90.00	90.00
Armani		**Special Times**			
82-04-001	Sledding 5111E	G. Armani	Retrd.	115.00	250.00
82-04-002	Girl with Sheep Dog 5117E	G. Armani	Retrd.	100.00	210.00
82-04-003	Girl with Chicks 5122E	G. Armani	Suspd.	95.00	165.00
82-04-004	Shy Kiss 5138E	G. Armani	Retrd.	125.00	285.00
82-04-005	Soccer Boy 5109	G. Armani	Open	75.00	180.00
82-04-006	Card Players (Cheaters) 3280	G. Armani	Open	400.00	1200.00
91-04-007	Couple in Car 862C	G. Armani	5,000	1000.00	1000.00
91-04-008	Lady with Car 861C	G. Armani	3,000	900.00	900.00
91-04-009	Doctor in Car 848C	G. Armani	2,000	800.00	800.00
94-04-010	The Fairy Tale 219C	G. Armani	Open	335.00	335.00
94-04-011	The Fairy Tale 219F	G. Armani	Open	175.00	175.00
94-04-012	Story Time 250C	G. Armani	Open	275.00	275.00
94-04-013	Grandpa's Nap 251C	G. Armani	Open	225.00	225.00
94-04-014	Old Acquaintance 252C	G. Armani	Open	275.00	275.00

Company / Number	Name	Series / Artist	Edition Limit	Issue Price	Quote
94-04-015	Lady Doctor 249C	G. Armani	Open	200.00	200.00
94-04-016	Lady Doctor 249F	G. Armani	Open	105.00	105.00
94-04-017	Lady Graduate-Lawyer 253C	G. Armani	Open	225.00	225.00
94-04-018	Lady Graduate-Lawyer 253F	G. Armani	Open	120.00	120.00
94-04-019	The Encounter 472F	G. Armani	Open	315.00	315.00
Armani		**Premiere Ballerina**			
88-05-001	Ballerina Group in Flight 518C	G. Armani	Retrd.	810.00	900.00
88-05-002	Ballerina with Drape 504C	G. Armani	Retrd.	450.00	550.00
88-05-003	Ballerina 508C	G. Armani	Retrd.	430.00	530.00
88-05-004	Two Ballerinas 515C	G. Armani	Retrd.	620.00	775.00
88-05-005	Ballerina in Flight 503C	G. Armani	Retrd.	420.00	500.00
88-05-006	Ballerina 517C	G. Armani	Retrd.	325.00	530.00
Armani		**Religious**			
87-06-001	Choir Boys 900	G. Armani	5,000	350.00	620.00
88-06-002	Crucifix 1158C	G. Armani	10,000	155.00	350-375.
90-06-003	Crucifix Plaque 711C	G. Armani	15,000	265.00	265.00
91-06-004	Crucifix 790C	G. Armani	15,000	180.00	180.00
92-06-005	Madonna With Child 787C	G. Armani	Open	425.00	425.00
92-06-006	Madonna With Child 787F	G. Armani	Open	265.00	265.00
92-06-007	Madonna With Child 787B	G. Armani	Open	260.00	260.00
93-06-008	Crucifix 786C	G. Armani	7,500	250.00	250.00
94-06-009	La Pieta 802C	G. Armani	5,000	950.00	950.00
94-06-010	La Pieta 802F	G. Armani	Open	550.00	550.00
94-06-011	Moses 812C	G. Armani	Open	220.00	220.00
94-06-012	Moses 812F	G. Armani	Open	115.00	115.00
Armani		**Pearls Of The Orient**			
89-07-001	Madame Butterfly 610C	G. Armani	10,000	450.00	500.00
89-07-002	Turnadot 611C	G. Armani	10,000	475.00	500.00
89-07-003	Chu Chu San 612C	G. Armani	10,000	500.00	550.00
89-07-004	Lotus Blossom 613C	G. Armani	10,000	450.00	475.00
Armani		**Moonlight Masquerade**			
90-08-001	Harlequin Lady 740C	G. Armani	7,500	450.00	450.00
90-08-002	Lady Pierrot 741C	G. Armani	7,500	390.00	390.00
90-08-003	Lady Clown with Cane 742C	G. Armani	7,500	390.00	390.00
90-08-004	Lady Clown with Doll 743C	G. Armani	7,500	410.00	410.00
90-08-005	Queen of Hearts 744C	G. Armani	7,500	450.00	450.00
Armani		**Renaissance**			
91-09-001	Bust of Eve 590T	G. Armani	Closed	250.00	600-1200.
92-09-002	Abundance 870C	G. Armani	5,000	600.00	600.00
92-09-003	Vanity 871C	G. Armani	5,000	585.00	585.00
92-09-004	Twilight 872C	G. Armani	5,000	560.00	560.00
92-09-005	Dawn 874C	G. Armani	5,000	500.00	500.00
92-09-006	Lilac & Roses-Girl w/Flowers 882C	G. Armani	7,500	410.00	410.00
92-09-007	Lilac & Roses-Girl w/Flowers 882B	G. Armani	Open	220.00	220.00
92-09-008	Aurora-Girl With Doves 884C	G. Armani	7,500	370.00	370.00
92-09-009	Aurora-Girl With Doves 884B	G. Armani	Open	220.00	220.00
92-09-010	Liberty-Girl On Horse 903C	G. Armani	5,000	750.00	750.00
92-09-011	Liberty-Girl On Horse 903B	G. Armani	Open	450.00	450.00
93-09-012	Freedom-Man And Horse 906C	G. Armani	3,000	850.00	850.00
93-09-013	Wind Song-Girl With Sail 904C	G. Armani	5,000	520.00	520.00
94-09-014	Ambrosia 482C	G. Armani	5,000	435.00	435.00
94-09-015	Angelica 484C	G. Armani	5,000	575.00	575.00
Armani		**Special Issues**			
91-10-001	Discovery of America Plaque 867C	G. Armani	2,500	400.00	400.00
93-10-002	Mother's Day Plaque 899C	G. Armani	Closed	100.00	100.00
94-10-003	Mother's Day Plaque-The Swing 254C	G. Armani	Yr. Iss.	120.00	120.00
Armani		**G. Armani Society Members Only Figurine**			
90-11-001	Awakening 591C	G. Armani	Closed	137.50	700-1100.
91-11-002	Ruffles 745E	G. Armani	Closed	139.00	384.00
92-11-003	Ascent 866C	G. Armani	Closed	195.00	293.00
93-11-004	Venus 881C	G. Armani	Closed	225.00	225.00
93-11-005	Lady Rose 197C	G. Armani	Closed	125.00	125.00
93-11-006	Julie (Bonus) 293P	G. Armani	Closed	90.00	225.00
93-11-007	Juliette (Bonus) 294P	G. Armani	Closed	90.00	125.00
Armani		**G. Armani Society Members Only Event**			
90-12-001	My Fine Feathered Friends (Bonus)122S	G. Armani	Closed	175.00	175.00
91-12-002	Peace & Harmony (Bonus) 824C	G. Armani	Closed	300.00	250-400.
92-12-003	Springtime 961C	G. Armani	Closed	250.00	500.00
92-12-004	Boy with Dog 409S	G. Armani	Closed	200.00	200.00
93-12-005	Loving Arms 880E	G. Armani	Closed	250.00	250.00
Armani		**Garden Series**			
91-13-001	Lady with Cornucopie 870C	G. Armani	10,000	600.00	600.00
91-13-002	Lady with Peacock 871C	G. Armani	10,000	585.00	1560.00
91-13-003	Lady with Violin 872C	G. Armani	10,000	560.00	560.00
91-13-004	Lady with Harp 874C	G. Armani	10,000	500.00	500.00
94-13-005	Lady At Well 222C	G. Armani	Open	275.00	275.00
94-13-006	Lady At Well 222F	G. Armani	Open	150.00	150.00
Armani		**Can-Can Dancers**			
89-14-001	Two Can-Can Dancers 516C	G. Armani	Open	820.00	975.00
Armani		**Four Seasons**			
90-15-001	Lady With Bicycle (Spring) 539C	G. Armani	Open	550.00	550.00
90-15-002	Lady With Umbrella (Fall) 541C	G. Armani	Open	475.00	475.00
90-15-003	Lady With Ice Skates (Winter) 542C	G. Armani	Open	400.00	400.00
90-15-004	Lady on Seashore (Summer) 540C	G. Armani	Open	440.00	440.00
92-15-005	Lady With Roses (Spring)181C	G. Armani	Open	275.00	275.00
92-15-006	Lady With Roses (Spring)181B	G. Armani	Open	135.00	135.00
92-15-007	Lady With Fruit (Summer) 182C	G. Armani	Open	275.00	275.00
92-15-008	Lady With Fruit (Summer) 182B	G. Armani	Open	135.00	135.00
92-15-009	Lady With Grapes (Fall) 183C	G. Armani	Open	275.00	275.00
92-15-010	Lady With Grapes (Fall)182B	G. Armani	Open	135.00	135.00
92-15-011	Lady With Vegetables (Winter)183C	G. Armani	Open	275.00	275.00
92-15-012	Lady With Vegetables (Winter)183B	G. Armani	Open	135.00	135.00
Armani		**Special Walt Disney Production**			
92-16-001	Cinderella	G. Armani	Retrd.	500.00	3100-3500.
93-16-002	Snow White 199C	G. Armani	Retrd.	750.00	950-1500.
93-16-003	Dopey	G. Armani	Open	125.00	125.00
Armani		**Motherhood**			
92-17-001	Mother With Child (Mother's Day) 185C	G. Armani	Open	400.00	400.00
92-17-002	Mother With Child (Mother's Day) 185B	G. Armani	Open	235.00	235.00
93-17-003	Garden Maternity 188C	G. Armani	Open	210.00	210.00
93-17-004	Garden Maternity 188F	G. Armani	Open	115.00	115.00

Company / Number	Name	Series / Artist	Edition Limit	Issue Price	Quote
93-17-005	Maternity Embracing 190C	G. Armani	Open	250.00	250.00
93-17-006	Maternity Embracing 190F	G. Armani	Open	160.00	160.00
93-17-007	Mother/Child 792C	G. Armani	Open	385.00	385.00
93-17-008	Mother/Child 792F	G. Armani	Open	250.00	250.00
94-17-009	Kneeling Maternity 216C	G. Armani	Open	275.00	275.00
94-17-010	Kneeling Maternity 216F	G. Armani	Open	135.00	135.00
94-17-011	Mother & Child 470F	G. Armani	Open	150.00	150.00
94-17-012	Mother's Hand 479F	G. Armani	Open	215.00	215.00
Armani		**Sports**			
92-18-001	Lady Equestrian 910C	G. Armani	Open	315.00	315.00
92-18-002	Lady Equestrian 910F	G. Armani	Open	155.00	155.00
92-18-003	Lady Golfer 911C	G. Armani	Open	325.00	325.00
92-18-004	Lady Golfer 911F	G. Armani	Open	170.00	170.00
92-18-005	Lady Tennis 912C	G. Armani	Open	275.00	275.00
92-18-006	Lady Tennis 912F	G. Armani	Open	175.00	175.00
92-18-007	Lady Skater 913C	G. Armani	Open	300.00	300.00
92-18-008	Lady Skater 913F	G. Armani	Open	170.00	170.00
Armani		**Yesteryears**			
93-19-001	Country Doctor In Car 848C	G. Armani	2,000	800.00	800.00
94-19-002	Summertime-Lady on Swing 485C	G. Armani	5,000	650.00	650.00
94-19-003	Summertime-Lady on Swing 485F	G. Armani	Open	450.00	450.00
Armani		**Romantic**			
93-20-001	Lovers 191C	G. Armani	3,000	450.00	450.00
93-20-002	Lovers 879C	G. Armani	3,000	570.00	570.00
93-20-003	Lovers 879F	G. Armani	Open	325.00	325.00
93-20-004	Girl With Ducks 887C	G. Armani	Open	320.00	320.00
93-20-005	Girl With Ducks 887F	G. Armani	Open	160.00	160.00
93-20-006	Lovers With Wheelbarrow 891C	G. Armani	Open	370.00	370.00
93-20-007	Lovers With Wheelbarrow 891F	G. Armani	Open	190.00	370.00
93-20-008	Girl w/Dog At Fence 886C	G. Armani	Open	350.00	350.00
93-20-009	Girl w/Dog At Fence 886F	G. Armani	Open	175.00	175.00
93-20-010	Lovers On A Swing 942C	G. Armani	Open	410.00	410.00
93-20-011	Lovers On A Swing 942F	G. Armani	Open	265.00	265.00
93-20-012	Lovers With Roses 888C	G. Armani	Open	300.00	300.00
93-20-013	Lovers With Roses 888F	G. Armani	Open	155.00	155.00
94-20-014	The Embrace 480C	G. Armani	3,000	1450.00	1450.00
Armani		**Romantic Motherhood**			
93-21-001	Maternity On Swing 941C	G. Armani	Open	360.00	360.00
93-21-002	Maternity On Swing 941F	G. Armani	Open	220.00	220.00
Armani		**Country Series**			
93-22-001	Boy With Flute 890C	G. Armani	Open	175.00	175.00
93-22-002	Boy With Flute 890F	G. Armani	Open	90.00	90.00
93-22-003	Girl With Chicks 889C	G. Armani	Open	155.00	155.00
93-22-004	Girl With Chicks 889F	G. Armani	Open	75.00	75.00
93-22-005	Girl With Wheelbarrow /Flowers 468C	G. Armani	Open	240.00	240.00
93-22-006	Girl Tending Flowers 466C	G. Armani	Open	210.00	210.00
93-22-007	Girl With Sheep 178C	G. Armani	Open	150.00	150.00
93-22-008	Girl With Sheep 178F	G. Armani	Open	65.00	65.00
93-22-009	Boy With Accordion 177C	G. Armani	Open	170.00	170.00
93-22-010	Boy With Accordion 177F	G. Armani	Open	75.00	75.00
94-22-011	Laundry Girl 214C	G. Armani	Open	230.00	230.00
94-22-012	Laundry Girl 214F	G. Armani	Open	120.00	120.00
94-22-013	Country Girl with Grapes 215C	G. Armani	Open	230.00	230.00
94-22-014	Country Girl with Grapes 215F	G. Armani	Open	120.00	120.00
94-22-015	Fresh Fruits 471F	G. Armani	Open	250.00	250.00
94-22-016	Back From the Fields 473F	G. Armani	Open	360.00	360.00
Armani		**Gypsy Series**			
94-23-001	Esmeralda-Gypsy Girl 198C	G. Armani	Open	400.00	400.00
94-23-002	Esmeralda-Gypsy Girl 198F	G. Armani	Open	215.00	215.00
Armani		**Clown Series**			
94-24-001	Sound the Trumpet 476C	G. Armani	Open	300.00	300.00
94-24-002	The Happy Fiddler 478C	G. Armani	Open	360.00	360.00
Armani		**Terra Cotta**			
94-25-001	The Embrace 1011T	G. Armani	Open	930.00	930.00
94-25-002	Ambrosia 1013T	G. Armani	Open	275.00	275.00
94-25-003	Country Boy With Mushrooms 1014T	G. Armani	2,500	135.00	135.00
94-25-004	La Pieta 1015T	G. Armani	Open	550.00	550.00
94-25-005	Angelica 1016T	G. Armani	Open	450.00	450.00
Armani		**The Galleria Collection: Distinguished Dealers**			
93-26-001	The Sea Wave 1006T	G. Armani	1,500	500.00	500.00
93-26-002	Spring Water 1007T	G. Armani	1,500	500.00	500.00
93-26-003	Spring Herald 1009T	G. Armani	1,500	500.00	500.00
93-26-004	Zephyr 1010T	G. Armani	1,500	500.00	500.00
94-26-005	Leda & The Swan 1012T	G. Armani	1,500	500.00	500.00
Armstrong's		**The Red Skelton Collection**			
81-01-001	Freddie in the Bathtub	R. Skelton	7,500	80.00	100.00
81-01-002	Freddie on the Green	R. Skelton	7,500	80.00	100.00
81-01-003	Freddie the Freeloader	R. Skelton	7,500	70.00	150.00
81-01-004	Sheriff Deadeye	R. Skelton	7,500	75.00	150.00
81-01-005	Clem Kadiddlehopper	R. Skelton	7,500	75.00	150.00
81-01-006	Jr., The Mean Widdle Kid	R. Skelton	7,500	75.00	150.00
81-01-007	San Fernando Red	R. Skelton	7,500	75.00	150.00
Armstrong's		**The Red Skelton Porcelain Plaque**			
91-02-001	All American	R. Skelton	1,500	495.00	800-2000.
92-02-002	Independance Day?	R. Skelton	1,500	525.00	525.00
93-02-003	Red & Freddie Both Turned 80	R. Skelton	1,993	595.00	800-900.
Armstrong's		**Armstrong's/Ron Lee**			
84-03-001	Captain Freddie	R. Skelton	7,500	85.00	300.00
84-03-002	Freddie the Torchbearer	R. Skelton	7,500	110.00	350.00
Armstrong's		**Happy Art**			
82-04-001	Woody's Triple Self-Portrait	W. Lantz	5,000	95.00	300.00
Armstrong's		**Ceramic Plaque**			
85-05-001	Flamborough Head	A. D'Estrehan	500	195.00	195.00
85-05-002	Flamborough Head (Artist's Proof)	A. D'Estrehan	50	295.00	295.00
88-05-003	Katrina	L. De Winne	500	195.00	195.00
Armstrong's		**Ceramic Plaque**			
85-06-001	The Stamp Collector	M. Paredes	400	195.00	195.00
85-06-002	The Stamp Collector (Artist's Proof)	M. Paredes	50	295.00	295.00
85-06-003	Mother's Pride	M. Paredes	400	195.00	195.00
85-06-004	Mother's Pride (Artist's Proof)	M. Paredes	50	295.00	295.00
Armstrong's		**Pro Autographed Ceramic Baseball Card Plaque**			
85-07-001	Brett, Garvey, Jackson, Rose, Seaver, auto, 3-1/4X5	Unknown	1,000	149.75	300.00
Armstrong's		**Pro Classic Ceramic Baseball Card Plaques**			
85-08-001	George Brett, 2-1/2" x 3-1/2"	Unknown	Open	9.95	9.95
85-08-002	Steve Garvey, 2-1/2" x 3-1/2"	Unknown	Open	9.95	9.95
85-08-003	Reggie Jackson, 2-1/2" x 3-1/2"	Unknown	Open	9.95	9.95
85-08-004	Pete Rose, 2-1/2" x 3-1/2"	Unknown	Open	9.95	9.95
85-08-005	Tom Seaver, 2-1/2" x 3-1/2"	Unknown	Open	9.95	9.95
Artaffects		**Heavenly Blessings**			
85-01-001	First Step	Unknown	Open	15.00	19.00
85-01-002	Heaven Scent	Unknown	Open	15.00	19.00
85-01-003	Bubbles	Unknown	Open	15.00	19.00
85-01-004	So Soft	Unknown	Open	15.00	19.00
85-01-005	See!	Unknown	Open	15.00	19.00
85-01-006	Listen!	Unknown	Open	15.00	19.00
85-01-007	Happy Birthday	Unknown	Open	15.00	19.00
85-01-008	Day Dreams	Unknown	Open	15.00	19.00
85-01-009	Just Up	Unknown	Open	15.00	19.00
85-01-010	Beddy Bye	Unknown	Open	15.00	19.00
85-01-011	Race You!	Unknown	Open	15.00	19.00
85-01-012	Yum, Yum!	Unknown	Open	15.00	19.00
Artaffects		**Musical Figurines**			
84-02-001	The Wedding	R. Sauber	Open	65.00	70.00
86-02-002	The Anniversary	R. Sauber	Open	65.00	70.00
87-02-003	Home Sweet Home	R. Sauber	Open	65.00	70.00
87-02-004	Newborn	R. Sauber	Open	65.00	70.00
87-02-005	Motherhood	R. Sauber	Open	65.00	70.00
87-02-006	Fatherhood	R. Sauber	Open	65.00	70.00
87-02-007	Sweet Sixteen	R. Sauber	Open	65.00	70.00
Artaffects		**Christian Collection**			
87-03-001	Bring To Me the Children	A. Tobey	Open	65.00	100.00
88-03-002	The Healer	A. Tobey	Open	65.00	65.00
Artaffects		**Reflections of Youth**			
88-04-001	Julia	MaGo	N/A	29.50	70.00
89-04-002	Jessica	MaGo	14-day	29.50	60.00
89-04-003	Sebastian	MaGo	14-day	29.50	40.00
Artaffects		**Single Issue**			
82-05-001	Babysitter Musical Fig.	G. Perillo	2,500	65.00	90.00
Artaffects		**The Professionals**			
80-06-001	The Big Leaguer	G. Perillo	10,000	65.00	150.00
80-06-002	Ballerina's Dilemma	G. Perillo	10,000	65.00	75.00
81-06-003	The Quarterback	G. Perillo	10,000	65.00	75.00
82-06-004	Rodeo Joe	G. Perillo	10,000	80.00	80.00
82-06-005	Major Leaguer	G. Perillo	10,000	65.00	175.00
83-06-006	Hockey Player	G. Perillo	10,000	65.00	125.00
Artaffects		**The Storybook Collection**			
80-07-001	Little Red Ridinghood	G. Perillo	10,000	65.00	95.00
81-07-002	Cinderella	G. Perillo	10,000	65.00	95.00
82-07-003	Hansel and Gretel	G. Perillo	10,000	80.00	110.00
82-07-004	Goldilocks & 3 Bears	G. Perillo	10,000	80.00	110.00
Artaffects		**The Princesses**			
84-08-001	Lily of the Mohawks	G. Perillo	1,500	65.00	155.00
84-08-002	Pocahontas	G. Perillo	1,500	65.00	125.00
84-08-003	Minnehaha	G. Perillo	1,500	65.00	125.00
84-08-004	Sacajawea	G. Perillo	1,500	65.00	125.00
Artaffects		**The Chieftains**			
83-09-001	Sitting Bull	G. Perillo	5,000	65.00	500.00
83-09-002	Joseph	G. Perillo	5,000	65.00	250.00
83-09-003	Red Cloud	G. Perillo	5,000	65.00	275.00
83-09-004	Geronimo	G. Perillo	5,000	65.00	135.00
83-09-005	Crazy Horse	G. Perillo	5,000	65.00	200.00
Artaffects		**Child Life**			
83-10-001	Siesta	G. Perillo	2,500	65.00	75.00
83-10-002	Sweet Dreams	G. Perillo	1,500	65.00	75.00
Artaffects		**Members Only Limited Edition Redemption Offerings**			
83-11-001	Apache Brave (Bust)	G. Perillo	Open	50.00	150.00
86-11-002	Painted Pony	G. Perillo	Open	125.00	125.00
91-11-003	Chief Crazy Horse	G. Perillo	Open	195.00	195.00
Artaffects		**Limited Edition Free Gifts to Members**			
86-12-001	Dolls	G. Perillo	Open	Gift	N/A
91-12-002	Sunbeam	G. Perillo	Open	Gift	N/A
92-12-003	Little Shadow	G. Perillo	Open	Gift	N/A
Artaffects		**The Little Indians**			
82-13-001	Blue Spruce	G. Perillo	10,000	50.00	75.00
82-13-002	White Rabbit	G. Perillo	10,000	50.00	75.00
82-13-003	Tender Love	G. Perillo	10,000	65.00	65.00
90-13-004	Babysitter	G. Perillo	10,000	65.00	65.00
Artaffects		**Special Issue**			
82-14-001	The Peaceable Kingdom	G. Perillo	950	750.00	1500.00
84-14-001	Papoose	G. Perillo	325	500.00	500-975.
84-14-001	Apache Boy Bust	G. Perillo	Open	40.00	75.00
84-14-002	Apache Girl Bust	G. Perillo	Open	40.00	75.00
85-14-001	Lovers	G. Perillo	Open	70.00	125.00
Artaffects		**The War Pony**			
83-15-001	Sioux War Pony	G. Perillo	495	150.00	250.00
83-15-002	Nez Perce War Pony	G. Perillo	495	150.00	250.00
83-15-003	Apache War Pony	G. Perillo	495	150.00	250.00
Artaffects		**The Tribal Ponies**			
84-16-001	Arapaho	G. Perillo	1,500	65.00	200.00
84-16-002	Comanche	G. Perillo	1,500	65.00	200.00
84-16-003	Crow	G. Perillo	1,500	65.00	250.00
Artaffects		**Pride of America's Indians**			
88-17-001	Brave and Free	G. Perillo	10-day	50.00	150.00

Company Number	Name	Series Artist	Edition Limit	Issue Price	Quote
89-17-002	Dark Eyed Friends	G. Perillo	10-day	45.00	75.00
89-17-003	Noble Companions	G. Perillo	10-day	45.00	50.00
89-17-004	Kindred Spirits	G. Perillo	10-day	45.00	50.00
89-17-005	Loyal Alliance	G. Perillo	10-day	45.00	75.00
89-17-006	Small & Wise	G. Perillo	10-day	45.00	50.00
89-17-007	Winter Scouts	G. Perillo	10-day	45.00	50.00
89-17-008	Peaceful Comrades	G. Perillo	10-day	45.00	50.00
Artaffects		**Sagebrush Kids**			
85-18-001	Hail to the Chief	G. Perillo	Closed	19.50	52.00
85-18-002	Dressing Up	G. Perillo	Closed	19.50	52.00
85-18-003	Favorite Kachina	G. Perillo	Closed	19.50	52.00
85-18-004	Message of Joy	G. Perillo	Closed	19.50	52.00
85-18-005	Boots	G. Perillo	Closed	19.50	52.00
85-18-006	Stay Awhile	G. Perillo	Closed	19.50	52.00
85-18-007	Room for Two?	G. Perillo	Closed	19.50	52.00
85-18-008	Blue Bird	G. Perillo	Closed	19.50	52.00
85-18-009	Ouch!	G. Perillo	Closed	19.50	52.00
85-18-010	Take One	G. Perillo	Closed	19.50	52.00
86-18-011	The Long Wait	G. Perillo	Closed	19.50	52.00
86-18-012	Westward Ho!	G. Perillo	Closed	19.50	52.00
86-18-013	Finishing Touches	G. Perillo	Closed	19.50	52.00
86-18-014	Deputies	G. Perillo	Closed	19.50	52.00
86-18-015	Country Music	G. Perillo	Closed	19.50	52.00
86-18-016	Practice Makes Perfect	G. Perillo	Closed	19.50	52.00
86-18-017	The Hiding Place	G. Perillo	Closed	19.50	52.00
86-18-018	Prarie Prayers	G. Perillo	Closed	19.50	52.00
87-18-019	Just Picked	G. Perillo	Closed	19.50	52.00
87-18-020	Row, Row	G. Perillo	Closed	19.50	52.00
87-18-021	My Papoose	G. Perillo	Closed	19.50	52.00
87-18-022	Playing House	G. Perillo	Closed	19.50	52.00
87-18-023	Wagon Train	G. Perillo	Closed	19.50	52.00
87-18-024	Small Talk	G. Perillo	Closed	19.50	52.00
90-18-025	How! Do I Love Thee?	G. Perillo	Closed	39.50	50.00
90-18-026	Easter Offering	G. Perillo	Closed	27.50	50.00
90-18-027	Just Married	G. Perillo	Closed	45.00	45.00
91-18-028	Baby Bronc	G. Perillo	Closed	27.50	80.00
91-18-029	Little Warriors	G. Perillo	Closed	27.50	35.00
91-18-030	Toy Totem	G. Perillo	Closed	27.50	35.00
91-18-031	Just Baked	G. Perillo	Closed	27.50	35.00
91-18-032	Lovin Spoonful	G. Perillo	Closed	27.50	35.00
91-18-033	Teddy Too??	G. Perillo	Closed	27.50	35.00
Artaffects		**Sagebrush Kids-Christmas Caravan**			
87-19-001	Leading the Way	G. Perillo	Open	90.00	120.00
87-19-002	Sleepy Sentinels	G. Perillo	Open	45.00	50.00
87-19-003	Singing Praises	G. Perillo	Open	45.00	50.00
87-19-004	Gold, Frankincense & Gifts	G. Perillo	Open	35.00	35.00
87-19-005	4-Piece Set (Above)	G. Perillo	Open	185.00	255.00
Artaffects		**Sagebrush Kids-Nativity**			
86-20-001	Christ Child	G. Perillo	Open	12.50	13.50
86-20-002	Mary	G. Perillo	Open	17.50	19.50
86-20-003	Joseph	G. Perillo	Open	17.50	19.50
86-20-004	Teepee	G. Perillo	Open	17.50	22.50
86-20-005	4-pc. Set (Above)	G. Perillo	Open	50.00	65.00
86-20-006	King with Corn	G. Perillo	Open	17.50	22.50
86-20-007	King with Pottery	G. Perillo	Open	17.50	22.50
86-20-008	King with Jewelry	G. Perillo	Open	17.50	22.50
86-20-009	Shepherd with Lamb	G. Perillo	Open	17.50	22.50
86-20-010	Shepherd Kneeling	G. Perillo	Open	17.50	22.50
86-20-011	Cow	G. Perillo	Open	12.00	13.50
86-20-012	Donkey	G. Perillo	Open	12.00	13.50
86-20-013	Lamb	G. Perillo	Open	6.00	8.00
86-20-014	Goat	G. Perillo	Open	8.00	9.50
86-20-015	Backdrop Dove	G. Perillo	Open	17.50	21.50
86-20-016	Backdrop Pottery	G. Perillo	Open	17.50	21.50
86-20-017	15 piece Set (Above)	G. Perillo	Open	225.00	245.00
89-20-018	Pig	G. Perillo	Open	15.00	15.00
89-20-019	Racoon	G. Perillo	Open	12.50	12.50
89-20-020	Cactus	G. Perillo	Open	24.50	24.50
89-20-021	Buffalo	G. Perillo	Open	17.50	17.50
90-20-022	Harmony Angel	G. Perillo	Open	37.50	37.50
90-20-023	Melody Angel	G. Perillo	Open	37.50	37.50
91-20-024	Peace Angel	G. Perillo	Open	27.50	27.50
91-20-025	Joy Angel	G. Perillo	Open	27.50	27.50
Artaffects		**Sagebrush Kids-Christmas Treasury**			
90-21-001	Santa's Lullaby	G. Perillo	Open	45.00	45.00
90-21-002	3/Set:Flight Into Egypt (Holy Family /Donkey)	G. Perillo	Open	65.00	65.00
Artaffects		**Sagebrush Kids-Banks**			
90-22-001	Perillo's Piggy Bank	G. Perillo	Open	39.50	39.50
90-22-002	Buckaroo Bank	G. Perillo	Open	39.50	39.50
90-22-003	Wampum Wig-Wam Bank	G. Perillo	Open	39.50	39.50
Artaffects		**Sagebrush Kids-Wedding Party**			
90-23-001	Bride	G. Perillo	Open	24.50	24.50
90-23-002	Groom	G. Perillo	Open	24.50	24.50
90-23-003	Flower Girl	G. Perillo	Open	22.50	22.50
90-23-004	Ring Bearer	G. Perillo	Open	22.50	22.50
90-23-005	Donkey	G. Perillo	Open	22.50	22.50
90-23-006	Chief	G. Perillo	Open	24.50	24.50
90-23-007	Wedding Backdrop	G. Perillo	Open	27.50	27.50
90-23-008	7 Piece Set (Above)	G. Perillo	Open	165.00	165.00
Artaffects		**Perillo Limited Edition Porcelain Figurines**			
91-24-001	One Nation Under God	G. Perillo	5,000	195.00	195.00
91-24-002	Safe And Dry (Umbrella Boy)	G. Perillo	5,000	95.00	95.00
91-24-003	Out Of The Rain (Umbrella Girl)	G. Perillo	5,000	95.00	95.00
91-24-004	Angel of the Plains	G. Perillo	5,000	75.00	75.00
91-24-005	The Sioux Carousel Horse	G. Perillo	5,000	95.00	95.00
91-24-006	The Cheyenne Carousel Horse	G. Perillo	5,000	95.00	95.00
Artaffects		**Musical Figurines**			
89-25-001	A Boy's Prayer	G. Perillo	Open	45.00	65.00
89-25-002	A Girl's Prayer	G. Perillo	Open	45.00	65.00
Artaffects		**Wildlife Figurines**			
90-26-001	Mustang	G. Perillo	Open	85.00	85.00
90-26-002	White-Tailed Deer	G. Perillo	Open	95.00	95.00
90-26-003	Mountain Lion	G. Perillo	Open	75.00	75.00
90-26-004	Bald Eagle	G. Perillo	Open	65.00	65.00
93-26-005	Buffalo	G. Perillo	Open	75.00	75.00
93-26-006	Timber Wolf	G. Perillo	Open	85.00	85.00
93-26-007	Polar Bear	G. Perillo	Open	65.00	65.00
93-26-008	Bighorn Sheep	G. Perillo	Open	75.00	75.00
Artaffects		**The Great Chieftains**			
91-27-001	Crazy Horse (Club Piece)	G. Perillo	Open	195.00	195.00
91-27-002	Sitting Bull	G. Perillo	S/O	195.00	195.00
91-27-003	Red Cloud	G. Perillo	S/O	195.00	195.00
91-27-004	Chief Joseph	G. Perillo	S/O	195.00	195.00
91-27-005	Cochise	G. Perillo	S/O	195.00	195.00
91-27-006	Geronimo	G. Perillo	S/O	195.00	195.00
Artaffects		**The Young Chieftains**			
85-28-001	Young Sitting Bull	G. Perillo	5,000	50.00	50.00
85-28-002	Young Joseph	G. Perillo	5,000	50.00	50.00
85-28-003	Young Red Cloud	G. Perillo	5,000	50.00	50.00
85-28-004	Young Geronimo	G. Perillo	5,000	50.00	50.00
85-28-005	Young Crazy Horse	G. Perillo	5,000	50.00	50.00
Artaffects		**Grand Bronze Collection**			
88-29-001	Free Spirit	G. Perillo	21-day	175.00	175.00
88-29-002	Fresh Waters	G. Perillo	21-day	350.00	350.00
88-29-003	Silhouette	G. Perillo	2,500	300.00	300.00
88-29-004	Partners	G. Perillo	2,500	200.00	200.00
88-29-005	Chief Red Cloud	G. Perillo	2,500	500.00	500.00
88-29-006	Discovery	G. Perillo	2,500	150.00	150.00
88-29-007	Peacemaker	G. Perillo	2,500	300.00	300.00
Artaffects		**American Indian Heritage**			
91-30-001	Cheyenne Nation (bust)	G. Perillo	10-day	55.00	55.00
Artaffects		**Village of the Sun**			
91-31-001	Sunbeam (Club Only)	G. Perillo	Open	Gift	N/A
92-31-002	Little Shadow (Club Renewal Only)	G. Perillo	Open	Gift	N/A
92-31-003	Rolling Thunder (Medicine Man)	G. Perillo	Open	24.00	24.00
92-31-004	Cloud Catcher (Boy with Dog)	G. Perillo	Open	24.00	24.00
92-31-005	Smiling Eyes (Baby with Lamb)	G. Perillo	Open	19.50	19.50
92-31-006	Many Bears (Farmer)	G. Perillo	Open	27.50	27.50
92-31-007	Cactus Flower (Weaver)	G. Perillo	Open	39.50	39.50
92-31-008	Dancing Waters (Tortilla Maker)	G. Perillo	Open	27.50	27.50
92-31-009	Red Bird (Jewelry Maker)	G. Perillo	Open	27.50	27.50
92-31-010	Bright Sky (Cook)	G. Perillo	Open	27.50	27.50
92-31-011	Summer Breeze (Maiden)	G. Perillo	Open	24.00	24.00
92-31-012	Standing Deer (Brave)	G. Perillo	Open	27.50	27.50
92-31-013	Noble Guardian (Horse)	G. Perillo	Open	39.50	39.50
92-31-014	Lambs	G. Perillo	Open	10.00	10.00
92-31-015	Small Cactus (Yellow Flowers)	G. Perillo	Open	7.50	7.50
92-31-016	Small Cactus (Pink Flowers)	G. Perillo	Open	7.50	7.50
92-31-017	Medium Cactus	G. Perillo	Open	10.00	10.00
92-31-018	Large Cactus	G. Perillo	Open	15.00	15.00
92-31-019	Hogan	G. Perillo	Open	59.00	59.00
Artaffects		**The Spirit Dancers**			
94-32-001	Eagle Dancer	G. Perillo	N/A	195.00	195.00
94-32-002	Buffalo Dancer	G. Perillo	N/A	195.00	195.00
Artaffects		**Simple Wonders**			
91-33-001	Joseph	C. Roeda	N/A	45.00	45.00
91-33-002	Joseph (Black)	C. Roeda	N/A	45.00	45.00
91-33-003	Mary	C. Roeda	N/A	40.00	40.00
91-33-004	Mary (Black)	C. Roeda	N/A	40.00	40.00
91-33-005	Baby Jesus	C. Roeda	N/A	35.00	35.00
91-33-006	Baby Jesus (Black)	C. Roeda	N/A	35.00	35.00
91-33-007	Sheep Dog	C. Roeda	N/A	15.00	15.00
91-33-008	Off To School	C. Roeda	N/A	49.50	49.50
91-33-009	Playing Hookey	C. Roeda	N/A	49.50	49.50
91-33-010	Mommy's Best	C. Roeda	N/A	49.50	49.50
91-33-011	Made With Love	C. Roeda	Retrd.	49.50	49.50
91-33-012	Bride	C. Roeda	N/A	55.00	55.00
91-33-013	Groom	C. Roeda	N/A	45.00	45.00
91-33-014	The Littlest Angel	C. Roeda	N/A	29.50	29.50
91-33-015	Star Light, Star Bright	C. Roeda	N/A	35.00	35.00
91-33-016	Lighting the Way	C. Roeda	N/A	39.50	39.50
91-33-017	Forever Friends	C. Roeda	N/A	39.50	39.50
91-33-018	Song of Joy	C. Roeda	N/A	39.50	39.50
91-33-019	I Love Ewe	C. Roeda	Retrd.	37.50	37.50
91-33-020	The Littlest Angel (Black)	C. Roeda	N/A	29.50	29.50
92-33-021	Ten Penny Serenade	C. Roeda	N/A	45.00	45.00
92-33-022	Ten Penny Serenade (Black)	C. Roeda	N/A	45.00	45.00
92-33-023	Rainbow Patrol	C. Roeda	N/A	39.50	39.50
92-33-024	The Three Bears	C. Roeda	N/A	45.00	45.00
92-33-025	Trick or Treat	C. Roeda	N/A	39.50	39.50
92-33-026	A Perfect Fit	C. Roeda	N/A	45.00	45.00
92-33-027	Pocketful of Love	C. Roeda	N/A	35.00	35.00
92-33-028	Pocketful of Love (Black)	C. Roeda	N/A	35.00	35.00
92-33-029	This Too Shall Pass	C. Roeda	N/A	35.00	35.00
92-33-030	Fallen Angel	C. Roeda	N/A	35.00	35.00
92-33-031	Lil' Dumplin	C. Roeda	N/A	25.00	25.00
92-33-032	Lil' Dumplin (Black)	C. Roeda	N/A	25.00	25.00
92-33-033	Little Big Shot	C. Roeda	N/A	35.00	35.00
92-33-034	With Open Arms (Wisechild)	C. Roeda	N/A	39.50	39.50
92-33-035	Following the Star (Wisechild)	C. Roeda	N/A	45.00	45.00
92-33-036	Catch the Spirit (Wisechild)	C. Roeda	N/A	35.00	35.00
93-33-037	Toad Taxi (Black)	C. Roeda	N/A	35.00	35.00
93-33-038	Toad Taxi	C. Roeda	N/A	35.00	35.00
93-33-039	Thumbs Up (Black)	C. Roeda	N/A	29.50	29.50
93-33-040	Thumbs Up	C. Roeda	N/A	29.50	29.50
93-33-041	Catch A Falling Star	C. Roeda	N/A	29.50	29.50
93-33-042	Snuggles (Black)	C. Roeda	N/A	22.50	22.50
93-33-043	Snuggles	C. Roeda	N/A	22.50	22.50
93-33-044	Devine K-9	C. Roeda	N/A	35.00	35.00
93-33-045	Prayer For Peace (Black)	C. Roeda	N/A	35.00	35.00
93-33-046	Prayer For Peace	C. Roeda	N/A	35.00	35.00
93-33-047	Heavenly Lullaby (Black)	C. Roeda	N/A	39.50	39.50
93-33-048	Heavenly Lullaby	C. Roeda	N/A	39.50	39.50
93-33-049	Manna From Heaven (Black)	C. Roeda	N/A	39.50	39.50
93-33-050	Manna From Heaven	C. Roeda	N/A	39.50	39.50
93-33-051	Teamwork	C. Roeda	N/A	29.50	29.50
93-33-052	Lambs Of God	C. Roeda	N/A	29.50	29.50
93-33-053	Francis and Friends	C. Roeda	N/A	37.50	37.50
93-33-054	Multi-Faced Pin	C. Roeda	N/A	12.50	12.50
93-33-055	Asian Angel Pin	C. Roeda	N/A	7.50	7.50
93-33-056	Black Angel Pin	C. Roeda	N/A	7.50	7.50
93-33-057	Angel w/ Blue Ribbon Pin	C. Roeda	N/A	7.50	7.50

Number	Name	Artist	Edition Limit	Issue Price	Quote
Company		**Series**			
93-33-058	Angel w/ Blond Hair Pin	C. Roeda	N/A	7.50	7.50
93-33-059	Angel w/ Brown Hair Pin	C. Roeda	N/A	7.50	7.50
93-33-060	I Love Ewe	C. Roeda	Retrd.	7.50	7.50
93-33-061	Made With Love	C. Roeda	Retrd.	7.50	7.50
93-33-062	Sweet Surprise	C. Roeda	Retrd.	7.50	7.50
94-33-063	Tea For Two (Black)	C. Roeda	N/A	22.50	22.50
94-33-064	Tea For Two	C. Roeda	N/A	22.50	22.50
94-33-065	Pals (Black)	C. Roeda	N/A	20.00	20.00
94-33-066	Pals	C. Roeda	N/A	20.00	20.00
94-33-067	Purrfect Prayer (Black)	C. Roeda	N/A	20.00	20.00
94-33-068	Purrfect Prayer	C. Roeda	N/A	20.00	20.00
94-33-069	What A Catch (Black)	C. Roeda	N/A	20.00	20.00
94-33-070	What A Catch	C. Roeda	N/A	20.00	20.00
94-33-071	Teachers Pet (Black)	C. Roeda	N/A	22.50	22.50
94-33-072	Teachers Pet	C. Roeda	N/A	22.50	22.50
94-33-073	Ewe & Me	C. Roeda	N/A	20.00	20.00
94-33-074	Evergreen Express	C. Roeda	N/A	22.50	22.50
94-33-075	Sunday Best	C. Roeda	N/A	22.50	22.50
Artaffects		**Blue Ribbon Babies**			
92-34-001	Petunia Penguin	Artaffects Studio	Open	19.50	19.50
92-34-002	Penelope Pig	Artaffects Studio	Open	19.50	19.50
92-34-003	Chauncey Camel	Artaffects Studio	Open	19.50	19.50
92-34-004	Siegfried Seal	Artaffects Studio	Open	19.50	19.50
92-34-005	Hortense Hippo	Artaffects Studio	Open	19.50	19.50
92-34-006	Elmont Elephant	Artaffects Studio	Open	19.50	19.50
93-34-007	Mollie Mouse	Artaffects Studio	Open	19.50	19.50
93-34-008	Prescott Panda	Artaffects Studio	Open	19.50	19.50
93-34-009	Oliver Owl	Artaffects Studio	Open	19.50	19.50
93-34-010	Reba Rabbit	Artaffects Studio	Open	19.50	19.50
93-34-011	Clementine Cow	Artaffects Studio	Open	19.50	19.50
93-34-012	Reginald Rhino	Artaffects Studio	Open	19.50	19.50
Artaffects		**Dino Babies**			
94-35-001	Tiny Triceratops	Artaffects Studio	N/A	20.00	20.00
94-35-002	April Apatosaurus	Artaffects Studio	N/A	20.00	20.00
94-35-003	Pickles Pachycephalosaurus	Artaffects Studio	N/A	20.00	20.00
94-35-004	Stanley Stegosaurus	Artaffects Studio	N/A	20.00	20.00
94-35-005	Patti Parasaurolophus	Artaffects Studio	N/A	20.00	20.00
94-35-006	Tyrone Tyrannosaurus	Artaffects Studio	N/A	20.00	20.00
94-35-007	Iggy Iguanadon	Artaffects Studio	N/A	20.00	20.00
94-35-008	Speedy Spinosaurus	Artaffects Studio	N/A	20.00	20.00
94-35-009	Hank Anklysaurus	Artaffects Studio	N/A	20.00	20.00
94-35-010	Alvin Allosaurus	Artaffects Studio	N/A	20.00	20.00
94-35-011	Priscilla Protoceratops	Artaffects Studio	N/A	20.00	20.00
94-35-012	Terri Pterodactyl	Artaffects Studio	N/A	20.00	20.00
Artaffects		**Legacy of the Lands**			
94-36-001	The Tracker (Blackfoot)	Artaffects Studio	N/A	35.00	35.00
94-36-002	Keeping Watch (Pawnee)	Artaffects Studio	N/A	35.00	35.00
94-36-003	The Lookout (Shoshoni)	Artaffects Studio	N/A	35.00	35.00
94-36-004	Thunder in the Ground (Crow)	Artaffects Studio	N/A	35.00	35.00
94-36-005	Hero in the Sun (Comanche)	Artaffects Studio	N/A	35.00	35.00
94-36-006	Moment of Victory (Arapaho)	Artaffects Studio	N/A	35.00	35.00
Artaffects		**Celebrations**			
94-37-001	Russian Celebrations	Artaffects Studio	N/A	35.00	35.00
94-37-002	African American Celebrations	Artaffects Studio	N/A	35.00	35.00
94-37-003	Scandinavian Celebrations	Artaffects Studio	N/A	35.00	35.00
94-37-004	North American Celebrations	Artaffects Studio	N/A	35.00	35.00
94-37-005	Persian Celebrations	Artaffects Studio	N/A	35.00	35.00
Artaffects		**Artaffects Tepee Ornament Collection**			
94-38-001	Buffalo Tepee	Artaffects Studio	N/A	6.00	6.00
94-38-002	Elk Tepee	Artaffects Studio	N/A	6.00	6.00
94-38-003	Eagle Tepee	Artaffects Studio	N/A	6.00	6.00
94-38-004	Dragonfly Tepee	Artaffects Studio	N/A	6.00	6.00
94-38-005	Bear Tepee	Artaffects Studio	N/A	6.00	6.00
94-38-006	Turtle Tepee	Artaffects Studio	N/A	6.00	6.00
94-38-007	Horse Tepee	Artaffects Studio	N/A	6.00	6.00
94-38-008	Wolf Tepee	Artaffects Studio	N/A	6.00	6.00
Artaffects		**Love Bugs**			
94-39-001	Peaches	Artaffects Studio	N/A	30.00	30.00
94-39-002	Blackberry	Artaffects Studio	N/A	30.00	30.00
94-39-003	Blueberry	Artaffects Studio	N/A	30.00	30.00
94-39-004	Raspberry	Artaffects Studio	N/A	30.00	30.00
94-39-005	Cherry	Artaffects Studio	N/A	30.00	30.00
94-39-006	Strawberry	Artaffects Studio	N/A	30.00	30.00
Artists of the World		**DeGrazia Figurine**			
84-01-001	Flower Girl	T. DeGrazia	Susp.	65.00	125-150.
84-01-002	Flower Boy	T. DeGrazia	Closed	65.00	150-250.
84-01-003	Sunflower Boy	T. DeGrazia	Closed	65.00	195-275.
84-01-004	My First Horse	T. DeGrazia	Closed	65.00	195-225.
84-01-005	White Dove	T. DeGrazia	Closed	45.00	110.00
84-01-006	Wondering	T. DeGrazia	Closed	85.00	145-250.
84-01-007	Flower Girl Plaque	T. DeGrazia	Closed	45.00	85-100.00
85-01-008	Little Madonna	T. DeGrazia	Closed	80.00	145.00
86-01-009	The Blue Boy	T. DeGrazia	Open	70.00	110.00
86-01-010	Festival Lights	T. DeGrazia	Open	75.00	110.00
86-01-011	Merry Little Indian	T. DeGrazia	S/O	175.00	185-275.
85-01-012	Pima Drummer Boy	T. DeGrazia	Closed	65.00	125-295.
87-01-013	Love Me	T. DeGrazia	Closed	95.00	145-250.
87-01-014	Wee Three	T. DeGrazia	Closed	180.00	250.00
88-01-015	Christmas Prayer Angel	T. DeGrazia	Closed	70.00	175-295.
88-01-016	Los Niños	T. DeGrazia	S/O	595.00	895-1200.
88-01-017	Beautiful Burden	T. DeGrazia	Closed	175.00	195-250.
88-01-018	Merrily, Merrily, Merrily	T. DeGrazia	Closed	95.00	225-250.
88-01-019	Flower Boy Plaque	T. DeGrazia	Closed	80.00	85-100.00
89-01-020	Two Little Lambs	T. DeGrazia	Closed	70.00	175-195.
89-01-021	My First Arrow	T. DeGrazia	Closed	95.00	135-175.
89-01-022	My Beautiful Rocking Horse	T. DeGrazia	Open	225.00	275.00
89-01-023	Los Ninos (Artist's Edition)	T. DeGrazia	S/O	695.00	1500.00
90-01-024	Alone	T. DeGrazia	Open	395.00	495.00
90-01-025	El Burrito	T. DeGrazia	Open	60.00	90.00
90-01-026	Sunflower Girl	T. DeGrazia	Closed	95.00	125-195.
90-01-027	Crucifixion	T. DeGrazia	Yr.Iss.	295.00	295.00
90-01-028	Navajo Boy	T. DeGrazia	Yr.Iss.	110.00	150.00
90-01-029	Desert Harvest	T. DeGrazia	S/O	135.00	145.00
90-01-030	Biggest Drum	T. DeGrazia	Yr.Iss.	110.00	145-250.
90-01-031	Little Prayer	T. DeGrazia	Yr.Iss.	85.00	125.00
91-01-032	Navajo Mother	T. DeGrazia	3,500	295.00	325.00
91-01-033	Shepherd Boy	T. DeGrazia	Open	95.00	125.00

Number	Name	Artist	Edition Limit	Issue Price	Quote
Company		**Series**			
92-01-034	Sun Showers	T. DeGrazia	5,000	195.00	225.00
92-01-035	Navajo Madonna	T. DeGrazia	Closed	135.00	145.00
92-01-036	Coming Home	T. DeGrazia	3,500	165.00	175.00
92-01-037	Telling Tales	T. DeGrazia	Closed	48.00	48.00
92-01-038	The Listener	T. DeGrazia	Closed	48.00	48.00
93-01-039	Saddle Up	T. DeGrazia	5,000	195.00	215.00
93-01-040	El Toro	T. DeGrazia	Open	95.00	97.50
93-01-041	Little Medicine Man	T. DeGrazia	Open	175.00	185.00
93-01-042	Flowers For Mother	T. DeGrazia	Open	145.00	145.00
93-01-043	Mother Silently Prays	T. DeGrazia	3,500	345.00	345.00
93-01-044	Water Wagon	T. DeGrazia	Open	295.00	295.00
94-01-045	Fresh Flowers	T. DeGrazia	3,500	197.50	197.50
94-01-046	Bearing Gifts	T. DeGrazia	Open	145.00	145.00
94-01-047	Pedro	T. DeGrazia	Open	145.00	145.00
94-01-048	Rio Grande Dance	T. DeGrazia	Open	98.50	98.50
94-01-049	Saguaro Dance	T. DeGrazia	5,000	495.00	495.00
Artists of the World		**DeGrazia Nativity Collection**			
85-02-001	Mary	T. DeGrazia	Open	90.00	100.00
85-02-002	Joseph	T. DeGrazia	Open	100.00	110.00
85-02-003	Jesus	T. DeGrazia	Open	55.00	65.00
85-02-004	Nativity Set-3 pc. (Mary, Joseph, Jesus)	T. DeGrazia	Open	275.00	275.00
93-02-005	Gaspar	T. DeGrazia	Open	135.00	135.00
93-02-006	Balthasar	T. DeGrazia	Open	135.00	135.00
93-02-007	Melchoir	T. DeGrazia	Open	135.00	135.00
Artists of the World		**DeGrazia Annual Christmas Collection**			
92-03-001	Feliz Navidad	T. DeGrazia	1,992	195.00	225.00
93-03-002	Fiesta Angels	T. DeGrazia	1,993	295.00	295.00
94-03-003	Littlest Angel	T. DeGrazia	1,994	150.00	150.00
Artists of the World		**DeGrazia Village Collection**			
93-04-001	Peace Pipe	T. DeGrazia	Open	65.00	65.00
93-04-002	Three Feathers	T. DeGrazia	Open	65.00	65.00
93-04-003	Let's Compromise	T. DeGrazia	Open	65.00	65.00
Artists of the World		**Goebel Miniatures: DeGrazia**			
85-05-001	Flower Girl 501-P	R. Olszewski	Suspd.	85.00	145-200.
85-05-002	Flower Boy 502-P	R. Olszewski	Suspd.	85.00	145-200.
85-05-003	My First Horse 503-P	R. Olszewski	Suspd.	85.00	100-165.
85-05-004	Sunflower Boy 551- P	R. Olszewski	Suspd.	93.00	100-165.
85-05-005	White Dove 504-P	R. Olszewski	Suspd.	80.00	100-125.
85-05-006	Wondering 505-P	R. Olszewski	Suspd.	93.00	100-175.
86-05-007	Little Madonna 552-P	R. Olszewski	Suspd.	93.00	100-225.
86-05-008	Pima Drummer Boy 506-P	R. Olszewski	Suspd.	85.00	155-350.
86-05-009	Festival of Lights 507-P	R. Olszewski	Suspd.	85.00	100-350.
87-05-010	Merry Little Indian 508-P	R. Olszewski	Suspd.	95.00	110-200.
88-05-011	Adobe Display 948D	R. Olszewski	Suspd.	45.00	59.00
89-05-012	Beautiful Burden 554-P	R. Olszewski	Suspd.	110.00	115-200.
90-05-013	Adobe Hacienda (large) Display 958-D	R. Olszewski	Suspd.	85.00	95.00
90-05-014	Chapel Display 971-D	R. Olszewski	Suspd.	95.00	125.00
91-05-015	My Beautiful Rocking Horse 555-P	R. Olszewski	Suspd.	110.00	125-250.
Artists of the World		**DeGrazia Pendants**			
85-06-001	Flower Girl Pendant 561-P	R. Olszewski	Open	125.00	150.00
87-06-002	Festival of Lights 562-P	R. Olszewski	Open	90.00	195.00
Band Creations, Inc.		**Busybodies™**			
93-01-001	Baseball/Homer 80001	T. Madsen	Open	16.00	16.00
93-01-002	Tennis/Ace 80002	T. Madsen	Open	16.00	16.00
93-01-003	Policeperson/Cuffs 80003	T. Madsen	Open	16.00	16.00
93-01-004	Fisherman/Fish Tales 80004	T. Madsen	Open	16.00	16.00
93-01-005	Fireman/Hot Stuff 80005	T. Madsen	Open	16.00	16.00
93-01-006	Chef/Short Order 80006	T. Madsen	Open	16.00	16.00
93-01-007	Football/Spike 80007	T. Madsen	Open	16.00	16.00
93-01-008	Golfer/Slicer 80008	T. Madsen	Open	16.00	16.00
93-01-009	Hunter/Big Shot 80009	T. Madsen	Open	16.00	16.00
93-01-010	Workman/Hard Hat 80010	T. Madsen	Open	16.00	16.00
93-01-011	Nurse/Needles 80011	T. Madsen	Open	16.00	16.00
93-01-012	Doctor/Fixer 80012	T. Madsen	Open	16.00	16.00
Band Creations, Inc.		**Best Friends-Angels Of The Month**			
93-02-001	January UF1	Richards/Penfield	Open	10.00	10.00
93-02-002	February UF2	Richards/Penfield	Open	10.00	10.00
93-02-003	March UF3	Richards/Penfield	Open	10.00	10.00
93-02-004	April UF4	Richards/Penfield	Open	10.00	10.00
93-02-005	May UF5	Richards/Penfield	Open	10.00	10.00
93-02-006	June UF6	Richards/Penfield	Open	10.00	10.00
93-02-007	July UF7	Richards/Penfield	Open	10.00	10.00
93-02-008	August UF8	Richards/Penfield	Open	10.00	10.00
93-02-009	September UF9	Richards/Penfield	Open	10.00	10.00
93-02-010	October UF10	Richards/Penfield	Open	10.00	10.00
93-02-011	November UF11	Richards/Penfield	Open	10.00	10.00
93-02-012	December UF12	Richards/Penfield	Open	10.00	10.00
93-02-013	5pc. Carolers Set UF14 (3 carolers, 1 lamp post, 1 dog)	Richards/Penfield	Open	24.00	24.00
Band Creations, Inc.		**The Nativity**			
93-03-001	Holy Family SC42013	T. Rubel	Open	80.00	80.00
93-03-002	Three Kings SC42014	T. Rubel	Open	136.00	136.00
93-03-003	Gloria SC42015	T. Rubel	Open	45.50	45.50
93-03-004	Angel with Lamb SC42016	T. Rubel	Open	45.50	45.50
93-03-005	Angel with Mandolin SC42017	T. Rubel	Open	45.50	45.50
93-03-006	8 pc. Nativity Scene SC42012	T. Rubel	Open	340.00	340.00
Band Creations, Inc.		**Best Friends**			
93-04-001	Sharing Is Caring 300425	Richards/Penfield	Open	12.00	12.00
93-04-002	Oh So Pretty 300426	Richards/Penfield	Open	14.00	14.00
93-04-003	Grandma's Favorite 300427	Richards/Penfield	Open	15.00	15.00
93-04-004	Quiet Time 300428	Richards/Penfield	Open	15.00	15.00
93-04-005	Purr-Fit Friends 300429	Richards/Penfield	Open	12.00	12.00
93-04-006	Fishing Friends 300430	Richards/Penfield	Open	18.00	18.00
93-04-007	Feathered Friends 300431	Richards/Penfield	Open	13.00	13.00
93-04-008	Dad's Best Pal 300432	Richards/Penfield	Open	15.00	15.00
93-04-009	My Beary Best Friend 300433	Richards/Penfield	Open	12.00	12.00
93-04-010	Castles In The Sand 300434	Richards/Penfield	Open	16.00	16.00
93-04-011	A Wagon Full Of Fun 300435	Richards/Penfield	Open	15.00	15.00
93-04-012	Rainbow Of Friends 300436	Richards/Penfield	Open	24.00	24.00
93-04-013	My Best Friend 300437	Richards/Penfield	Open	24.00	24.00
93-04-014	Santa's First Visit 300438	Richards/Penfield	Open	15.00	15.00
93-04-015	Santa's Surprise 300439	Richards/Penfield	Open	14.00	14.00
93-04-016	Checking It Twice 300440	Richards/Penfield	Open	15.00	15.00

Company Number	Name	Series Artist	Edition Limit	Issue Price	Quote
Band Creations, Inc.		**Li'l Velvets Magical Christmas**			
94-05-001	Tiny Tim SC42044	T. Rubel	Open	21.00	21.00
94-05-002	Spirit of Christmas Future SC42045	T. Rubel	Open	21.00	21.00
94-05-003	Spirit of Christmas Past SC42046	T. Rubel	Open	25.00	25.00
94-05-004	Walking Scrooge SC42047	T. Rubel	Open	25.00	25.00
94-05-005	Scrooge in Robe SC42048	T. Rubel	Open	25.00	25.00
94-05-006	Spirit of Christmas Present SC42049	T. Rubel	Open	25.00	25.00
94-05-007	Scrooge with Carollers SC42051	T. Rubel	Open	75.00	75.00
94-05-008	Cratchit with Tim SC42052	T. Rubel	Open	25.00	25.00
94-05-009	The Cheese is Next SC42041	T. Rubel	Open	25.00	25.00
94-05-010	Velvet with Toys SC42050	T. Rubel	Open	25.00	25.00
94-05-011	Pulling Tree SC42053	T. Rubel	Open	16.00	16.00
94-05-012	Windy Day SC42054	T. Rubel	Open	16.00	16.00
94-05-013	Sleigh Ride SC42065	T. Rubel	Open	25.00	25.00
94-05-014	What a Tree SC42063	T. Rubel	Open	25.00	25.00
94-05-015	Just What I Wanted SC42066	T. Rubel	Open	25.00	25.00
94-05-016	Bucket Full SC42068	T. Rubel	Open	25.00	25.00
94-05-017	Break Time SC42069	T. Rubel	Open	25.00	25.00
94-05-018	Sleepy Time SC42081	T. Rubel	Open	50.00	50.00
94-05-019	Just Right SC42070	T. Rubel	Open	30.00	30.00
Band Creations, Inc.		**Li'l Velvets Magical Christmas Musicals**			
94-06-001	Just Right SC42071	T. Rubel	Open	50.00	50.00
94-06-002	Finishing Touch SC42043	T. Rubel	Open	45.00	45.00
94-06-003	Cheese Block SC42059	T. Rubel	Open	75.00	75.00
94-06-004	Nutcracker (waterglobe) SC42042	T. Rubel	Open	45.00	45.00
94-06-005	Bedtime SC42073	T. Rubel	Open	25.00	25.00
94-06-006	Rocking Horse SC42074	T. Rubel	Open	25.00	25.00
94-06-007	Stocking Stuffer SC42075	T. Rubel	Open	25.00	25.00
Band Creations, Inc.		**Nature's Woods**			
94-07-001	Tower-lighted house SC92001	T. Rubel	Open	30.00	30.00
94-07-002	Workshop-lighted house SC92002	T. Rubel	Open	30.00	30.00
94-07-003	2 Piece-lighted house SC92003	T. Rubel	Open	50.00	50.00
94-07-004	Elf Tying Gift SC92004	T. Rubel	Open	12.00	12.00
94-07-005	Elf with Jack-in-Box SC92005	T. Rubel	Open	10.50	10.50
94-07-006	2 Elves Pulling Sleigh SC92006	T. Rubel	Open	10.50	10.50
94-07-007	Elf Pushing Cart SC92007	T. Rubel	Open	16.00	16.00
94-07-008	Elf Running With Gift SC92008	T. Rubel	Open	10.50	10.50
94-07-009	Elf Walking with Gift SC92009	T. Rubel	Open	10.50	10.50
94-07-010	Train Engine SC92010	T. Rubel	Open	16.00	16.00
94-07-011	Train Car SC92011	T. Rubel	Open	15.00	15.00
94-07-012	Woodswoman Singer SC92012	T. Rubel	Open	5.50	5.50
94-07-013	Woodsman Sax Player SC92013	T. Rubel	Open	5.50	5.50
94-07-014	Woodsman Bandleader SC92014	T. Rubel	Open	5.50	5.50
94-07-015	Woodsman with Trumpet SC92015	T. Rubel	Open	5.50	5.50
94-07-016	Woodsman Singer SC92016	T. Rubel	Open	5.50	5.50
94-07-017	Woodsman with Bell SC92017	T. Rubel	Open	5.50	5.50
94-07-018	Elf Hammering Crate SC92018	T. Rubel	Open	12.000	12.00
94-07-019	Elf with Screwdriver SC92019	T. Rubel	Open	12.00	12.00
94-07-020	2 Elves at Mailbox SC92020	T. Rubel	Open	13.50	13.50
94-07-021	Santa Claus SC92021	T. Rubel	Open	12.00	12.00
94-07-022	Toy Drum, Train, & Books SC92022	T. Rubel	Open	12.00	12.00
94-07-023	Toy Blocks, Soldiers, & Boat SC92025	T. Rubel	Open	12.00	12.00
94-07-024	Toy Clown and Boat SC92028	T. Rubel	Open	5.50	5.50
94-07-025	Toy Rocking Horse SC92029	T. Rubel	Open	7.50	7.50
94-07-026	3 Pine Trees SC92030	T. Rubel	Open	21.00	21.00
94-07-027	3 Oak Trees SC92031	T. Rubel	Open	25.00	25.00
94-07-028	Small Pine Tree SC92032	T. Rubel	Open	6.00	6.00
94-07-029	Small Pine Tree SC92033	T. Rubel	Open	6.00	6.00
Band Creations, Inc.		**Nature's Wood-Musicals**			
94-08-001	4 Woodsmen SC92034	T. Rubel	Open	50.00	50.00
94-08-002	4 Rocking Horses SC92035	T. Rubel	Open	50.00	50.00
94-08-003	4 Elves & Toys SC92036	T. Rubel	Open	50.00	50.00
Band Creations, Inc.		**Celebrations**			
94-09-001	Deck the Halls-Christmas SC62000	T. Rubel	Open	22.00	22.00
94-09-002	L'Amour-Valentine's Day SC62001	T. Rubel	Open	22.00	22.00
94-09-003	Lucky Lady-St. Patrick's Day SC62002	T. Rubel	Open	22.00	22.00
94-09-004	My Someone Special-Mother's Day SC62003	T. Rubel	Open	22.00	22.00
94-09-005	Always on the Ball-Father's Day SC62004	T. Rubel	Open	22.00	22.00
94-09-006	Hop To It-Easter SC62005	T. Rubel	Open	22.00	22.00
94-09-007	It's Only Me-Halloween SC62006	T. Rubel	Open	22.00	22.00
94-09-008	Bountiful Bear-Thanksgiving SC62007	T. Rubel	Open	22.00	22.00
94-09-009	With Honors-Graduation SC62008	T. Rubel	Open	22.00	22.00
94-09-010	Best Friends-First Date SC62009	T. Rubel	Open	22.00	22.00
94-09-011	Happy Days-Anniversary SC62010	T. Rubel	Open	22.00	22.00
94-09-012	Another Year-Birthday SC62011	T. Rubel	Open	22.00	22.00
Band Creations, Inc.		**Celebrations-Musicals**			
94-10-001	Deck the Halls-Christmas SC62050	T. Rubel	Open	42.00	42.00
94-10-002	L'Amour-Valentine's Day SC62051	T. Rubel	Open	42.00	42.00
94-10-003	Lucky Lady-St. Patrick's Day SC62052	T. Rubel	Open	42.00	42.00
94-10-004	My Someone Special-Mother's Day SC62053	T. Rubel	Open	42.00	42.00
94-10-005	Always on the Ball-Father's Day SC62054	T. Rubel	Open	42.00	42.00
94-10-006	Hop To It-Easter SC62055	T. Rubel	Open	42.00	42.00
94-10-007	It's Only Me-Halloween SC62056	T. Rubel	Open	42.00	42.00
94-10-008	Bountiful Bear-Thanksgiving SC62057	T. Rubel	Open	42.00	42.00
94-10-009	With Honors-Graduation SC62058	T. Rubel	Open	42.00	42.00
94-10-010	Best Friends-First Date SC62059	T. Rubel	Open	42.00	42.00
94-10-011	Happy Days-Anniversary SC62060	T. Rubel	Open	42.00	42.00
94-10-012	Another Year-Birthday SC62061	T. Rubel	Open	42.00	42.00
Band Creations, Inc.		**Christmas Animals-Large Musicals**			
94-11-001	Bear SC22011	T. Rubel	Open	32.00	32.00
94-11-002	Horse SC22012	T. Rubel	Open	32.00	32.00
94-11-003	Elephant SC22013	T. Rubel	Open	32.00	32.00
94-11-004	Dalmatian SC22014	T. Rubel	Open	32.00	32.00
94-11-005	Rabbit SC22015	T. Rubel	Open	32.00	32.00
94-11-006	Moose SC22016	T. Rubel	Open	32.00	32.00
Band Creations, Inc.		**Christmas Animals-Small Musicals**			
94-12-001	Fawn SC22017	T. Rubel	Open	25.00	25.00
94-12-002	Camel SC22018	T. Rubel	Open	25.00	25.00
94-12-003	Horse SC22019	T. Rubel	Open	25.00	25.00
94-12-004	Giraffe SC22020	T. Rubel	Open	25.00	25.00
94-12-005	Goose SC22021	T. Rubel	Open	25.00	25.00
94-12-006	Moose SC22022	T. Rubel	Open	25.00	25.00
Band Creations, Inc.		**Wildlife Triples**			
94-13-001	Brown Bears SC32000	T. Rubel	4,500	37.50	37.50
94-13-002	Pandas SC32001	T. Rubel	4,500	37.50	37.50

Company Number	Name	Series Artist	Edition Limit	Issue Price	Quote
Band Creations, Inc.		**Season Animals**			
94-14-001	Fall Elephant SC32051	T. Rubel	Open	18.00	18.00
94-14-002	Summer Elephant SC32052	T. Rubel	Open	18.00	18.00
94-14-003	Spring Elephant SC32053	T. Rubel	Open	18.00	18.00
94-14-004	Fall Dalmatian SC32054	T. Rubel	Open	18.00	18.00
94-14-005	Spring Dalmatian SC32055	T. Rubel	Open	18.00	18.00
Band Creations, Inc.		**Christmas Celebrations-10" Fabrichette**			
94-15-001	Who Turned Out the Lights SC52020	T. Rubel	Open	85.00	85.00
94-15-002	Where to First? SC52021	T. Rubel	Open	85.00	85.00
94-15-003	Work Never Ends SC52022	T. Rubel	Open	85.00	85.00
Band Creations, Inc.		**Christmas Celebrations-6" Cold Cast Figurines**			
94-16-001	Who Turned Out the Lights SC52023	T. Rubel	Open	30.00	30.00
94-16-002	Where to First? SC52024	T. Rubel	Open	30.00	30.00
94-16-003	Work Never Ends SC52025	T. Rubel	Open	30.00	30.00
Band Creations, Inc.		**Christmas Celebrations-Musicals**			
94-17-001	Who Turned Out the Lights SC52026	T. Rubel	Open	50.00	50.00
94-17-002	Where to First? SC52027	T. Rubel	Open	50.00	50.00
94-17-003	Work Never Ends SC52028	T. Rubel	Open	50.00	50.00
Band Creations, Inc.		**Santa Claus-Fabrichette**			
94-18-001	Tannenbaum SC52001	T. Rubel	Open	50.00	50.00
94-18-002	Spirit SC52002	T. Rubel	Open	50.00	50.00
94-18-003	Cornucopia SC52003	T. Rubel	Open	50.00	50.00
Band Creations, Inc.		**Santa Claus-Cold Cast Figurines**			
94-19-001	Tannenbaum SC52004	T. Rubel	Open	45.00	45.00
94-19-002	Spirit SC52005	T. Rubel	Open	45.00	45.00
94-19-003	Cornucopia SC52006	T. Rubel	Open	45.00	45.00
Band Creations, Inc.		**Candyland Mountain**			
94-20-001	Lion SC82008	T. Rubel	Open	18.00	18.00
94-20-002	Bear SC82009	T. Rubel	Open	18.00	18.00
94-20-003	Duck SC82010	T. Rubel	Open	18.00	18.00
94-20-004	Elephant SC82011	T. Rubel	Open	18.00	18.00
94-20-005	Stork SC82012	T. Rubel	Open	18.00	18.00
94-20-006	Cat SC82013	T. Rubel	Open	18.00	18.00
94-20-007	Dog SC82014	T. Rubel	Open	18.00	18.00
94-20-008	Mouse SC82015	T. Rubel	Open	18.00	18.00
Band Creations, Inc.		**Candyland Mountain-Musicals**			
94-21-001	Mouse SC82024	T. Rubel	Open	25.00	25.00
94-21-002	Bear SC82025	T. Rubel	Open	25.00	25.00
94-21-003	Elephant SC82026	T. Rubel	Open	25.00	25.00
94-21-004	Lion, Bear, Duck SC82027	T. Rubel	Open	33.00	33.00
Band Creations, Inc.		**Santa's Animal Kingdom**			
94-22-001	Full Santa SC12001	T. Rubel	2,500	125.00	125.00
94-22-002	Standing Santa SC12002	T. Rubel	Open	50.00	50.00
94-22-003	Poly Santa SC12003	T. Rubel	Open	35.00	35.00
94-22-004	Musical Santa SC12004	T. Rubel	Open	35.00	35.00
94-22-005	Waterglobe SC12005	T. Rubel	Open	75.00	75.00
Boehm Studios		**Bird Sculptures**			
80-01-001	American Avocet 40134	Boehm	300	1400.00	1655.00
81-01-002	American Bald Eagle 40185	Boehm	655	1200.00	1330.00
82-01-003	American Eagle (Commemorative) 40215	Boehm	250	950.00	1150.00
57-01-004	American Eagle, large 428A	Boehm	31	225.00	11200.00
57-01-005	American Eagle, small 428B	Boehm	76	225.00	9200.00
82-01-006	American Eagle (Symbol of Freedom) 40200	Boehm	35	16500.00	18560.00
58-01-007	American Redstarts 447	Boehm	500	350.00	2010.00
80-01-008	American Redstart 40138	Boehm	225	850.00	1090.00
80-01-009	American Wild Turkey 40154	Boehm	75	1800.00	2020.00
80-01-010	American Wild Turkey (life-size) 40115	Boehm	25	15000.00	16940.00
83-01-011	Anna's Hummingbird 10048	Boehm	300	1100.00	1940.00
80-01-012	Arctic Tern 40135	Boehm	350	1400.00	2060.00
79-01-013	Avocet 100-27	Boehm	175	1200.00	1345.00
72-01-014	Barn Owl 1005	Boehm	350	3600.00	5400.00
72-01-015	Black Grouse 1006	Boehm	175	2800.00	3100.00
73-01-016	Blackbirds, pair 100-13	Boehm	75	5400.00	6470.00
84-01-017	Blackburnian Warbler 40253	Boehm	125	925.00	965.00
82-01-018	Black-eared Bushtit (female) 10038	Boehm	100	975.00	1045.00
82-01-019	Black-eared Bushtit (male) 10039	Boehm	100	975.00	1045.00
69-01-020	Black-headed Grosbeak 400-03	Boehm	675	1250.00	1535.00
56-01-021	Black-tailed Bantams, pair 423	Boehm	57	350.00	4800.00
58-01-022	Black-throated Blue Warbler 441	Boehm	500	400.00	1780.00
76-01-023	Black-throated Blue Warbler 400-60	Boehm	200	900.00	1165.00
67-01-024	Blue Grosbeak 489	Boehm	750	1050.00	1530.00
82-01-025	Blue Jay (with Morning Glories) 40218	Boehm	300	975.00	1190.00
81-01-026	Blue Jay (with Wild Raspberries) 40190	Boehm	350	1950.00	2405.00
62-01-027	Blue Jays, pair 466	Boehm	250	2000.00	12300.00
73-01-028	Blue Tits 1008	Boehm	300	3000.00	3250.00
82-01-029	Blue-throated Hummingbird 10040	Boehm	300	1100.00	1440.00
64-01-030	Bobolink 475	Boehm	500	550.00	1520.00
53-01-031	Bob White Quail, pair 407	Boehm	750	400.00	2500.00
81-01-032	Boreal Owl 40172	Boehm	200	1750.00	1875.00
72-01-033	Brown Pelican 400-22	Boehm	100	10500.00	14400.00
80-01-034	Brown Pelican 40161	Boehm	90	2800.00	2860.00
73-01-035	Brown Thrasher 400-26	Boehm	260	1850.00	1930.00
72-01-036	Cactus Wren 400-17	Boehm	225	3000.00	3410.00
57-01-037	California Quail, pair 433	Boehm	500	400.00	2730.00
79-01-038	Calliope Hummingbird 40104	Boehm	200	900.00	1115.00
87-01-039	Calliope Hummingbird 40319	Boehm	500	575.00	595.00
78-01-040	Canada Geese, pair 400-71	Boehm	100	4200.00	4200.00
77-01-041	Cape May Warbler 400-45	Boehm	400	825.00	990.00
55-01-042	Cardinals, pair 415	Boehm	500	550.00	3650.00
77-01-043	Cardinals 400-53	Boehm	200	3500.00	4095.00
57-01-044	Carolina Wrens 422	Boehm	100	750.00	5400.00
65-01-045	Catbird 483	Boehm	500	900.00	2080.00
83-01-046	Catbird 40246	Boehm	111	1250.00	1250.00
80-01-047	Cedar Waxwing 40117	Boehm	325	950.00	1040.00
56-01-048	Cedar Waxwings, pair 418	Boehm	100	600.00	7835.00
57-01-049	Cerulean Warblers 424	Boehm	100	800.00	4935.00
74-01-050	Chaffinch 100-20	Boehm	125	2000.00	2525.00
76-01-051	Chickadees 400-61	Boehm	400	1450.00	1550.00
68-01-052	Common Tern 497	Boehm	500	1400.00	6040.00
85-01-053	Condor 10057	Boehm	2	75000.00	87710.00
79-01-054	Costa's Hummingbird 40103	Boehm	200	1050.00	1200.00
67-01-055	Crested Flycatcher 488	Boehm	500	1650.00	3005.00
74-01-056	Crested Tit 100-18	Boehm	400	1150.00	1310.00
80-01-057	Crimson Topaz Hummingbird 40113	Boehm	310	1400.00	1640.00
83-01-058	Dove of Peace 40236	Boehm	709	750.00	1480.00

Company Number	Name	Series Artist	Edition Limit	Issue Price	Quote
83-01-059	Doves with Cherry Blossoms, pair 10049	Boehm	150	7500.00	10600.00
79-01-060	Downy Woodpecker 40116	Boehm	300	950.00	1000.00
57-01-061	Downy Woodpeckers 427	Boehm	500	450.00	1760.00
76-01-062	Eagle of Freedom I 400-50	Boehm	15	35000.00	51375.00
76-01-063	Eagle of Freedom II 400-70	Boehm	200	7200.00	7370.00
77-01-064	Eastern Bluebird 400-51	Boehm	300	2300.00	2625.00
59-01-065	Eastern Bluebirds, pair 451	Boehm	100	1800.00	12210.00
75-01-066	Eastern Kingbird 400-42	Boehm	100	3500.00	4275.00
83-01-067	Egret (National Audubon Society) 40221	Boehm	1,029	1200.00	1580.00
75-01-068	European Goldfinch 100-22	Boehm	250	1150.00	1400.00
73-01-069	Everglades Kites 400-24	Boehm	50	5800.00	7340.00
87-01-070	Flamingo w/ Young (National Audubon Society) 40316	Boehm	225	1500.00	1525.00
77-01-071	Fledgling Brown Thrashers 400-72A	Boehm	400	500.00	680.00
67-01-072	Fledgling Canada Warbler 491	Boehm	750	550.00	2205.00
65-01-073	Fledgling Great Horned Owl 479	Boehm	750	350.00	1590.00
71-01-074	Flicker 400-16	Boehm	250	2400.00	2770.00
83-01-075	Forster's Tern (Cresting) 40224	Boehm	300	1850.00	2080.00
83-01-076	Forster's Tern (on the Wing) 40223	Boehm	300	1850.00	2080.00
86-01-077	Gannet 40287	Boehm	30	4300.00	4300.00
72-01-078	Goldcrest 1004	Boehm	500	650.00	1210.00
83-01-079	Golden Eagle 10046	Boehm	25	32000.00	36085.00
54-01-080	Golden Pheasant, decorated 414A	Boehm	7	350.00	19235.00
54-01-081	Golden Pheasant, bisque 414B	Boehm	7	200.00	11375.00
56-01-082	Golden-crowned Kinglets 419	Boehm	500	400.00	2320.00
83-01-083	Goldfinch 40245	Boehm	136	1200.00	1200.00
61-01-084	Goldfinches 457	Boehm	500	400.00	1830.00
82-01-085	Great White Egret 40214	Boehm	50	11500.00	15055.00
66-01-086	Green Jays, pair 486	Boehm	400	1850.00	4120.00
82-01-087	Green Jays, pair 40198	Boehm	65	3900.00	3900.00
73-01-088	Green Woodpeckers 100-15	Boehm	50	4200.00	4890.00
79-01-089	Grey Wagtail 100-26	Boehm	150	1050.00	1385.00
74-01-090	Hooded Warbler 400-30	Boehm	100	2400.00	3020.00
73-01-091	Horned Larks 400-25	Boehm	200	3800.00	4435.00
64-01-092	Ivory-billed Woodpeckers 474	Boehm	4	N/A	N/A
68-01-093	Kestrels, pair 492	Boehm	460	2300.00	3160.00
82-01-094	Killdeer 40213	Boehm	125	1075.00	1090.00
64-01-095	Killdeer, pair 473	Boehm	300	1750.00	5160.00
76-01-096	Kingfishers 100-24	Boehm	200	1900.00	2205.00
80-01-097	Kirtland's Warble 40169	Boehm	130	750.00	890.00
73-01-098	Lapwing 100-14	Boehm	100	2600.00	3000.00
74-01-099	Lark Sparrow 400-35	Boehm	150	2100.00	2340.00
73-01-100	Lazuli Buntings 400-23	Boehm	250	1800.00	2455.00
81-01-101	Least Sandpipers 40136	Boehm	350	2100.00	2540.00
79-01-102	Least Tern 40102	Boehm	350	1275.00	3045.00
62-01-103	Lesser Prairie Chickens, pair 464	Boehm	300	1200.00	2390.00
71-01-104	Little Owl 1002	Boehm	350	700.00	1390.00
84-01-105	Long-eared Owl 10052	Boehm	12	6000.00	6260.00
73-01-106	Long Tail Tits 100-11	Boehm	200	2600.00	3000.00
84-01-107	Magnolia Warbler 40258	Boehm	246	1100.00	1100.00
52-01-108	Mallards, pair 406	Boehm	500	650.00	1745.00
57-01-109	Meadowlark 435	Boehm	750	350.00	3180.00
63-01-110	Mearn's Quail, pair 467	Boehm	350	950.00	3635.00
68-01-111	Mergansers, pair 496	Boehm	440	2200.00	2985.00
78-01-112	Mockingbirds 400-52	Boehm	350	2200.00	3045.00
61-01-113	Mockingbirds, pair 459	Boehm	500	650.00	3970.00
81-01-114	Mockingbird's Nest with Bluebonnet 10033	Boehm	55	1300.00	1365.00
63-01-115	Mountain Bluebirds 470	Boehm	300	1900.00	5480.00
81-01-116	Mourning Dove 40189	Boehm	300	2200.00	2325.00
58-01-117	Mourning Doves 443	Boehm	500	550.00	1490.00
82-01-118	Mute Swans, pair 40219	Boehm	115	5800.00	6350.00
71-01-119	Mute Swans, life-size, pair 400-14A	Boehm	3	N/A	N/A
71-01-120	Mute Swans, small size, pair 400-14B	Boehm	400	4000.00	7820.00
74-01-121	Myrtle Warblers 400-28	Boehm	210	1850.00	2105.00
58-01-122	Nonpareil Buntings 446	Boehm	750	250.00	1165.00
81-01-123	Northern Oriole 40194	Boehm	100	1750.00	1900.00
67-01-124	Northern Water Thrush 490	Boehm	500	800.00	1420.00
71-01-125	Nuthatch 1001	Boehm	350	650.00	1130.00
70-01-126	Orchard Orioles 400-11	Boehm	550	1750.00	2305.00
81-01-127	Osprey 10037	Boehm	100	4350.00	4710.00
81-01-128	Osprey 10031	Boehm	25	17000.00	21070.00
70-01-129	Oven-bird 400-04	Boehm	450	1400.00	1790.00
65-01-130	Parula Warblers 484	Boehm	400	1500.00	3370.00
85-01-131	Parula Warblers 40270	Boehm	100	2450.00	2465.00
75-01-132	Pekin Robins 400-37	Boehm	100	7000.00	9680.00
84-01-133	Pelican 40259	Boehm	93	1200.00	1235.00
73-01-134	Peregrine Falcon 100-12	Boehm	350	4400.00	5470.00
81-01-135	Peregrine Falcon with Young 40171	Boehm	105	1850.00	2020.00
80-01-136	Pheasant 40133	Boehm	100	2100.00	2175.00
84-01-137	Pileated Woodpeckers 40250	Boehm	50	2900.00	2925.00
79-01-138	Prince Rudolph's Blue Bird of Paradise 40101	Boehm	10	35000.00	37200.00
62-01-139	Ptarmigans, pair 463	Boehm	350	800.00	3465.00
74-01-140	Purple Martins 400-32	Boehm	50	6700.00	9150.00
79-01-141	Racquet-tail Hummingbird 40105	Boehm	310	1500.00	1965.00
85-01-142	Racquet-tailed Hummingbird 10053	Boehm	350	2100.00	2500.00
75-01-143	Red-billed Blue Magpie 400-44	Boehm	100	4600.00	6230.00
79-01-144	Red-breasted Nuthatch 40118	Boehm	200	800.00	925.00
57-01-145	Red-winged Blackbirds, pair 426	Boehm	100	700.00	5590.00
54-01-146	Ringed-necked Pheasants, pair 409	Boehm	500	650.00	1810.00
76-01-147	Rivoli's Hummingbird 100-23	Boehm	350	950.00	1535.00
68-01-148	Roadrunner 493	Boehm	500	2600.00	3680.00
82-01-149	Roadrunner 40199	Boehm	150	2100.00	2325.00
64-01-150	Robin (Daffodils) 472	Boehm	500	600.00	5650.00
77-01-151	Robin (Nest) 400-65	Boehm	350	1650.00	2080.00
81-01-152	Robin's Nest with Wild Rose 10030	Boehm	90	1300.00	1380.00
81-01-153	Rose-breasted Grosbeak 10032	Boehm	165	1850.00	1880.00
83-01-154	Royal Terns 10047	Boehm	75	4300.00	4845.00
74-01-155	Ruby-throated Hummingbird 100-21	Boehm	200	1900.00	2825.00
60-01-156	Ruffed Grouse, pair 456	Boehm	250	950.00	5080.00
77-01-157	Ruffed Grouse, pair 400-65	Boehm	100	4400.00	4485.00
66-01-158	Rufous Hummingbirds 487	Boehm	500	850.00	2360.00
86-01-159	Sandhill Crane 40286 (National Audubon Society)	Boehm	205	1650.00	1665.00
77-01-160	Scarlet Tanager 400-41	Boehm	4	1800.00	4275.00
85-01-161	Scarlet Tanager 40267	Boehm	125	2100.00	2125.00
77-01-162	Scissor-tailed Flycatcher 400-48	Boehm	100	3200.00	3650.00
79-01-163	Scops Owl 40114	Boehm	300	975.00	1415.00
73-01-164	Screech Owl 100-10	Boehm	500	850.00	1495.00
80-01-165	Screech Owl 40132	Boehm	350	2100.00	3125.00
78-01-166	Siskens 100-25	Boehm	250	2100.00	2405.00
70-01-167	Slate-colored Junco 400-12	Boehm	500	1600.00	2240.00
72-01-168	Snow Buntings 400-21	Boehm	350	2400.00	2700.00
85-01-169	Soaring Eagle (bisque) 40276B	Boehm	304	950.00	960.00
85-01-170	Soaring Eagle (gilded) 40276G	Boehm	35	5000.00	5290.00
56-01-171	Song Sparrows, pair 421	Boehm	50	2000.00	38450.00
74-01-172	Song Thrushes 100-16	Boehm	100	2800.00	3590.00
74-01-173	Stonechats 100-17	Boehm	150	2200.00	2560.00
61-01-174	Sugarbirds 460	Boehm	100	2500.00	14910.00
74-01-175	Swallows 100-19	Boehm	125	3400.00	4320.00
63-01-176	Towhee 471	Boehm	500	350.00	2430.00
83-01-177	Towhee 40244	Boehm	75	975.00	1045.00
72-01-178	Tree Creepers 1007	Boehm	200	3200.00	3200.00
85-01-179	Trumpeter Swan 40266 (National Audubon Society)	Boehm	500	1500.00	1625.00
65-01-180	Tufted Titmice 482	Boehm	500	600.00	2040.00
65-01-181	Varied Buntings 481	Boehm	300	2200.00	4935.00
74-01-182	Varied Thrush 400-29	Boehm	300	2500.00	3115.00
69-01-183	Verdins 400-02	Boehm	575	1150.00	1565.00
69-01-184	Western Bluebirds 400-01	Boehm	300	5500.00	7020.00
71-01-185	Western Meadowlark 400-15	Boehm	350	1425.00	1735.00
84-01-186	Whooping Crane 40254 (National Audubon Society)	Boehm	647	1800.00	2025.00
71-01-187	Winter Robin 1003	Boehm	225	1150.00	1420.00
81-01-188	Wood Ducks 40192	Boehm	90	3400.00	3560.00
51-01-189	Wood Thrush 400	Boehm	2	375.00	N/A
66-01-190	Wood Thrushes, pair 485	Boehm	400	4200.00	8285.00
54-01-191	Woodcock 413	Boehm	500	300.00	2060.00
82-01-192	Wren 10036	Boehm	50	1700.00	1950.00
72-01-193	Yellow-bellied Sapsucker 400-18	Boehm	250	2700.00	3200.00
74-01-194	Yellow-billed Cuckoo 400-31	Boehm	150	2800.00	3055.00
74-01-195	Yellow-headed Blackbird 400-34	Boehm	75	3200.00	3600.00
82-01-196	Yellow-shafted Flicker 40220	Boehm	175	1450.00	1500.00
73-01-197	Yellowhammers 1009	Boehm	350	3300.00	4180.00
80-01-198	Yellow Warbler 40137	Boehm	200	950.00	1070.00
69-01-199	Young American Eagle 498B	Boehm	850	700.00	1520.00
73-01-200	Young American Eagle, Inaugural 498A	Boehm	100	1500.00	2125.00
75-01-201	Young & Spirited 1976 400-49	Boehm	1,121	950.00	1610.00
Boehm Studios		**Animal Sculptures**			
69-02-001	Adios 400-05	Boehm	130	1500.00	1900.00
77-02-002	African Elephant 5006	Boehm	50	9500.00	14630.00
76-02-003	American Mustangs 5005	Boehm	75	3700.00	5665.00
81-02-004	Appaloosa Horse 40193	Boehm	75	975.00	1070.00
80-02-005	Arabian Oryx, pair 50015	Boehm	60	3800.00	4135.00
83-02-006	Arabian Stallion (Prancing) 55007	Boehm	200	1500.00	1565.00
83-02-007	Arabian Stallion (Rearing) 55006	Boehm	200	1500.00	1565.00
80-02-008	Asian Lion 50017	Boehm	100	1500.00	1645.00
79-02-009	Bengel Tiger 500-13	Boehm	12	25000.00	26540.00
78-02-010	Black Rhinoceros 500-11	Boehm	50	9500.00	9920.00
71-02-011	Bobcats 4001	Boehm	200	1600.00	1990.00
82-02-012	Buffalo 50022	Boehm	100	1625.00	1625.00
78-02-013	Camel & Calf 5009	Boehm	50	3500.00	3700.00
80-02-014	Cheetah 50016	Boehm	100	2700.00	3000.00
85-02-015	Elephant (white bisque) 200-44B	Boehm	200	495.00	575.00
79-02-016	Fallow Deer 500-12	Boehm	30	7500.00	7500.00
71-02-017	Foxes 4003	Boehm	200	1800.00	2360.00
75-02-018	Giant Panda 5003	Boehm	100	3800.00	6890.00
78-02-019	Gorilla 5008	Boehm	50	3800.00	4550.00
82-02-020	Greater Kudu 50023	Boehm	75	7500.00	7500.00
79-02-021	Hunter Chase 55001	Boehm	20	4000.00	4085.00
52-02-022	Hunter 203	Boehm	250	600.00	1400.00
81-02-023	Jaguar 50020	Boehm	100	2900.00	3310.00
73-02-024	Nyala Antelope 5001	Boehm	100	4700.00	6560.00
76-02-025	Otter 5004	Boehm	75	1100.00	1505.00
81-02-026	Polar Bear with Cubs 40188	Boehm	65	1800.00	1875.00
57-02-027	Polo Player 206	Boehm	100	850.00	4610.00
82-02-028	Polo Player on Pinto 55005	Boehm	50	3500.00	3500.00
75-02-029	Puma 5002	Boehm	50	5700.00	6560.00
71-02-030	Raccoons 4002	Boehm	200	1600.00	2105.00
72-02-031	Red Squirrels 4004	Boehm	100	2600.00	2770.00
78-02-032	Snow Leopard 5007	Boehm	75	3500.00	4670.00
78-02-033	Thoroughbred with Jockey 400-85	Boehm	25	2600.00	2785.00
84-02-034	White-tailed Buck 50026	Boehm	200	1375.00	1660.00
79-02-035	Young & Free Fawns 50014	Boehm	160	1875.00	2055.00
Boehm Studios		**Floral Sculptures**			
80-03-001	Begonia (pink) 30041	Boehm	500	1250.00	1470.00
80-03-002	Bluebonnets 30050	Boehm	160	650.00	775.00
79-03-003	Cactus Dahlia 300-33	Boehm	300	800.00	970.00
80-03-004	Caprice Iris (pink) 30049	Boehm	235	650.00	725.00
86-03-005	Cherries Jubilee Camellia 10388	Boehm	250	625.00	625.00
83-03-006	Chrysanthemum 30105	Boehm	75	1250.00	1464.00
85-03-007	Chrysanthemum Petal Camellia 30125	Boehm	500	575.00	600.00
72-03-008	Chrysanthemums 3005	Boehm	350	1100.00	2030.00
71-03-009	Daisies 3002	Boehm	350	600.00	1045.00
81-03-010	Daisy (white) 30056	Boehm	75	975.00	995.00
74-03-011	Debutante Camellia 3008	Boehm	500	625.00	865.00
73-03-012	Dogwood 3003	Boehm	250	625.00	1035.00
81-03-013	Dogwood 30045	Boehm	510	875.00	955.00
78-03-014	Double Clematis Centerpiece 300-27	Boehm	150	1500.00	1780.00
74-03-015	Double Peony 3007	Boehm	275	575.00	995.00
82-03-016	Double Peony 30078	Boehm	110	1525.00	1640.00
78-03-017	Edward Boehm Camellia 300-23	Boehm	500	850.00	960.00
75-03-018	Emmett Barnes Camellia 300-11	Boehm	425	550.00	770.00
85-03-019	Emmett Barnes Camellia 30120	Boehm	275	625.00	630.00
83-03-020	Empress Camellia (white) 30109	Boehm	350	1025.00	1050.00
74-03-021	Gentians 3009	Boehm	350	425.00	730.00
86-03-022	Globe of Light Peony 10372	Boehm	125	475.00	505.00
79-03-023	Grand Floral Centerpiece 300-35	Boehm	15	7500.00	8755.00
78-03-024	Helen Boehm Camellia 300-25	Boehm	500	600.00	1110.00
78-03-025	Helen Boehm Daylily 300-20	Boehm	175	975.00	1140.00
78-03-026	Helen Boehm Iris 300-19	Boehm	175	975.00	1190.00
79-03-027	Honeysuckle 300-34	Boehm	200	900.00	1055.00
86-03-028	Icarian Peony Centerpiece 30119	Boehm	33	2800.00	2865.00
81-03-029	Julia Hamiter Camellia 30061	Boehm	300	675.00	745.00
85-03-030	Kama Pua Hibiscus (orange) 30128	Boehm	122	1600.00	1615.00
84-03-031	Lady's Slipper Orchid 30112	Boehm	76	575.00	575.00
82-03-032	Magnolia Centerpiece 30101	Boehm	15	6800.00	6985.00
75-03-033	Magnolia Grandiflora 300-12	Boehm	750	650.00	1525.00
80-03-034	Magnolia Grandiflora 300-47	Boehm	350	1650.00	1935.00
82-03-035	Marigolds 30072	Boehm	150	1275.00	1275.00
84-03-036	Mary Heatley Begonia 30111	Boehm	200	1100.00	1125.00
80-03-037	Miss Indiana Iris (blue) 30049	Boehm	235	650.00	710.00
81-03-038	Nancy Reagan Camellia 30076	Boehm	600	650.00	830.00
80-03-039	Orchid (pink) 30036	Boehm	175	725.00	780.00

Company / Number	Name	Series / Artist	Edition Limit	Issue Price	Quote
80-03-040	Orchid (yellow) 30037	Boehm	130	725.00	780.00
76-03-041	Orchid Cactus 300-15	Boehm	100	650.00	1030.00
84-03-042	Orchid Centerpiece (assorted) 30016	Boehm	150	2600.00	2650.00
84-03-043	Orchid Centerpiece (pink) 30115	Boehm	350	2100.00	2490.00
84-03-044	Orchid, Cymbidium 30114	Boehm	160	575.00	625.00
84-03-045	Orchid, Odontoglossum 30113	Boehm	100	575.00	610.00
80-03-046	Parrot Tulips 30042	Boehm	300	850.00	1000.00
85-03-047	Peonies (white) 30118	Boehm	100	1650.00	1650.00
78-03-048	Pink Lotus 300-21	Boehm	175	975.00	1055.00
81-03-049	Poinsettia 30055	Boehm	200	1100.00	1230.00
82-03-050	Pontiff Iris 30097	Boehm	200	3000.00	3830.00
81-03-051	Poppies 30058	Boehm	325	1150.00	1265.00
76-03-052	Queen of the Night Cactus 300-14	Boehm	125	650.00	895.00
81-03-053	Rhododendron 30064	Boehm	275	825.00	825.00
85-03-054	Rhododendron (pink, yellow) 30122	Boehm	125	1850.00	1895.00
78-03-055	Rhododendron Centerpiece 300-30	Boehm	350	1150.00	1900.00
81-03-056	Rose (yellow in shell) 30059	Boehm	300	1100.00	1160.00
80-03-057	Rose, Alec's Red 30039	Boehm	500	1050.00	1390.00
81-03-058	Rose, Annenberg 30051	Boehm	200	1450.00	1495.00
78-03-059	Rose, Blue Moon 300-28	Boehm	500	650.00	915.00
85-03-060	Rose, Duet 30130	Boehm	200	1525.00	1550.00
80-03-061	Rose, Elizabeth of Glamis 30046	Boehm	500	1650.00	1970.00
81-03-062	Rose Grace de Monaco 30071	Boehm	350	1650.00	1940.00
81-03-063	Rose, Grandpa Dickson 30069	Boehm	225	1200.00	1430.00
85-03-064	Rose, Helen Boehm 30121	Boehm	360	1475.00	1480.00
82-03-065	Rose, Jehan Sadat 30080	Boehm	200	875.00	1030.00
81-03-066	Rose, Just Joey 30052	Boehm	240	1050.00	1050.00
81-03-067	Rose, Lady Helen 30070	Boehm	325	1350.00	1520.00
82-03-068	Rose, Mountbatten 30094	Boehm	50	1525.00	1665.00
81-03-069	Rose, Nancy Reagan 35027	Boehm	1,200	800.00	920.00
78-04-070	Rose, Pascali 300-24	Boehm	500	950.00	1520.00
82-03-071	Rose, Pascali 30093	Boehm	250	1500.00	1710.00
80-03-072	Rose, Peach 30038	Boehm	350	1800.00	2070.00
81-03-073	Rose, Prince Charles & Lady Diana Centerpiece 30065/6	Boehm	100	4800.00	6330.00
81-03-074	Rose, Prince Charles & Lady Diana Floral 30068	Boehm	600	750.00	850.00
82-03-075	Rose, Princess Margaret 30095	Boehm	350	950.00	1170.00
82-03-076	Rose, Queen Elizabeth 30091	Boehm	350	1450.00	1790.00
82-03-077	Rose, Royal Blessing 30099	Boehm	500	1350.00	1715.00
76-03-078	Rose, Supreme Peace 300-16	Boehm	250	850.00	1745.00
76-03-079	Rose, Supreme Yellow 300-17	Boehm	250	850.00	1735.00
78-03-080	Rose, Tropicana 300-22	Boehm	500	475.00	1075.00
81-03-081	Rose, Tropicana in Conch Shell 30060	Boehm	150	1100.00	1100.00
83-03-082	Rose, Yankee Doodle 30108	Boehm	450	650.00	700.00
86-03-083	Rose Centerpiece (yellow) 10370	Boehm	25	5500.00	5625.00
82-03-084	Royal Bouquet 30092	Boehm	125	1500.00	1690.00
82-03-085	Scabious with Japonica 30090	Boehm	50	1550.00	1575.00
85-03-086	Seminole Hibiscus (pink) 30129	Boehm	100	1800.00	1815.00
78-03-087	Spanish Iris 300-29	Boehm	500	600.00	760.00
83-03-088	Spring Centerpiece 30110	Boehm	100	1125.00	1200.00
82-03-089	Stewart's Supreme Camellia 30084	Boehm	350	675.00	710.00
73-03-090	Streptocalyx Poeppigii 3006	Boehm	50	3400.00	4485.00
71-03-091	Swan Centerpiece 3001	Boehm	135	1950.00	2930.00
76-03-092	Swan Lake Camellia 300-13	Boehm	750	825.00	1790.00
71-03-093	Sweet Viburnum 3004	Boehm	35	650.00	1395.00
82-03-094	Tiger Lilies (orange) 30077	Boehm	350	1225.00	1270.00
80-03-095	Tree Peony 30043	Boehm	325	1400.00	1485.00
82-03-096	Tulips 30089	Boehm	180	1050.00	1090.00
74-03-097	Waterlily 300-10	Boehm	350	400.00	725.00
78-03-098	Watsonii Magnolia 300-31	Boehm	250	575.00	680.00
Boehm Studios		**Figurines**			
86-04-001	Amanda with Parasol 10269	Boehm	27	750.00	750.00
86-04-002	Aria 67003	Boehm	100	875.00	875.00
86-04-003	Aurora 67001	Boehm	100	875.00	875.00
77-04-004	Beverly Sills 7006	Boehm	100	950.00	1010.00
86-04-005	Celeste 67002	Boehm	100	875.00	875.00
86-04-006	Devina 67000	Boehm	100	875.00	875.00
77-04-007	Jerome Hines 7007	Boehm	12	825.00	1000.00
86-04-008	Jo, Skating 10267	Boehm	26	750.00	750.00
86-04-009	Mattina 67004	Boehm	100	875.00	875.00
86-04-010	Meg with Basket 10268	Boehm	26	625.00	625.00
Brandywine Collectables		**Hilton Village**			
87-01-001	Georgian House	M. Whiting	Closed	8.50	8.50
87-01-002	Gwen's House	M. Whiting	Closed	8.50	8.50
87-01-003	Dutch House	M. Whiting	Closed	8.50	8.50
87-01-004	English House	M. Whiting	Closed	8.50	8.50
87-01-005	Hilton Firehouse	M. Whiting	Closed	8.50	8.50
Brandywine Collectables		**Yorktown Collection**			
87-02-001	Custom House	M. Whiting	Open	17.50	17.50
87-02-002	Pate House	M. Whiting	Open	19.00	19.00
87-02-003	Moore House	M. Whiting	Open	22.00	22.00
87-02-004	Nelson House	M. Whiting	Open	22.00	22.00
87-02-005	Grace Church	M. Whiting	Open	19.00	19.00
87-02-006	Medical Shop	M. Whiting	Open	13.00	13.00
87-02-007	Swan Tavern	M. Whiting	Open	22.00	22.00
93-02-008	Digges House	M. Whiting	Open	22.00	22.00
Brandywine Collectables		**Old Salem Collection**			
87-03-001	Schultz Shoemaker	M. Whiting	Open	10.50	10.50
87-03-002	Miksch Tobacco Shop	M. Whiting	Open	12.00	12.00
87-03-003	First House	M. Whiting	Open	12.80	12.80
87-03-004	Home Moravian Church	M. Whiting	Open	18.50	18.50
87-03-005	Boys School	M. Whiting	Open	18.50	18.50
87-03-006	Winkler Bakery	M. Whiting	Open	20.50	20.50
87-03-007	Vogler House	M. Whiting	Open	20.50	20.50
87-03-008	Salem Tavern	M. Whiting	Open	20.50	20.50
Brandywine Collectables		**Williamsburg Collection**			
88-04-001	The Magazine	M. Whiting	Open	23.50	23.50
88-04-002	Governor's Palace	M. Whiting	Open	37.50	37.50
88-04-003	Court House of 1770	M. Whiting	Open	26.50	26.50
88-04-004	Wythe House	M. Whiting	Open	25.00	25.00
88-04-005	Colonial Capitol	M. Whiting	Open	43.50	43.50
93-04-006	Kings Arms Tavern	M. Whiting	Open	25.00	25.00
93-04-007	Campbell's Tavern	M. Whiting	Open	28.00	28.00
Brandywine Collectables		**Custom Collection**			
88-05-001	Burgess Museum	M. Whiting	Open	15.50	15.50
88-05-002	Princetown Monument	M. Whiting	Closed	9.70	9.70
89-05-003	Yankee Candle Co.	M. Whiting	Closed	13.50	13.50
89-05-004	Lorain Lighthouse	M. Whiting	Closed	11.00	11.00
90-05-005	Jared Coffin House	M. Whiting	Open	32.00	32.00
90-05-006	Doylestown Public School	M. Whiting	Open	32.00	32.00
91-05-007	Smithfield VA. Courthouse	M. Whiting	Closed	12.00	12.00
91-05-008	Jamestown Tower	M. Whiting	Closed	9.00	9.00
92-05-009	Loudon County Courthouse	M. Whiting	Open	15.00	15.00
92-05-010	Cumberland County Courthouse	M. Whiting	Open	15.00	15.00
Brandywine Collectables		**Victorian Collection**			
89-06-001	Seabreeze Cottage	M. Whiting	Open	15.30	15.30
89-06-002	Serenity Cottage	M. Whiting	Open	15.30	15.30
89-06-003	Hearts Ease Cottage	M. Whiting	Open	15.30	15.30
89-06-004	Broadway House	M. Whiting	Open	22.00	22.00
89-06-005	Peachtree House	M. Whiting	Open	22.50	22.50
89-06-006	Skippack School	M. Whiting	Open	22.50	22.50
89-06-007	Fairplay Church	M. Whiting	Open	19.50	19.50
89-06-008	Elm House	M. Whiting	Open	25.00	25.00
89-06-009	Old Star Hook & Ladder	M. Whiting	Open	23.00	23.00
Brandywine Collectables		**Barnsville Collection**			
90-07-001	Candace Bruce House	M. Whiting	Open	30.00	30.00
90-07-002	Thompson House	M. Whiting	Open	32.00	32.00
90-07-003	Treat-Smith House	M. Whiting	Open	32.00	32.00
90-07-004	Gay 90's Mansion	M. Whiting	Open	32.00	32.00
91-07-005	Bradfield House	M. Whiting	Open	32.00	32.00
91-07-006	B & O Station	M. Whiting	Open	28.00	28.00
91-07-007	Whiteley House	M. Whiting	Open	32.00	32.00
92-07-008	Barnesville Church	M. Whiting	Open	44.00	44.00
92-07-009	Plumtree Bed & Breakfast	M. Whiting	Open	44.00	44.00
Brandywine Collectables		**North Pole Collection**			
91-08-001	Gingerbread House	D. Whiting	Open	24.00	24.00
91-08-002	Claus House	M. Whiting	Open	24.00	24.00
91-08-003	Reindeer Barn	M. Whiting	Open	24.00	24.00
92-08-004	Elves Workshop	M. Whiting	Open	24.00	24.00
92-08-005	Sugarplum Bakery	M. Whiting	Open	24.00	24.00
92-08-006	Snowflake Lodge	M. Whiting	Open	24.00	24.00
92-08-007	3 Winter Trees	D. Whiting	Open	10.50	10.50
92-08-008	Snowman with St. Sign	M. Whiting	Open	11.50	11.50
93-08-009	Teddybear Factory	M. Whiting	Open	24.00	24.00
93-08-010	Elf Club	M. Whiting	Open	24.00	24.00
93-08-011	Candy Cane Factory	M. Whiting	Open	24.00	24.00
93-08-012	Town Christmas Tree	M. Whiting	Open	20.00	20.00
Brandywine Collectables		**Seymour Collection**			
91-09-001	Seymour Church	M. Whiting	Open	19.00	19.00
91-09-002	Seymour Library	M. Whiting	Open	20.00	20.00
91-09-003	Seymour House	M. Whiting	Open	20.00	20.00
91-09-004	Anderson House	M. Whiting	Open	20.00	20.00
92-09-005	Majestic Theater	M. Whiting	Open	22.00	22.00
Brandywine Collectables		**Patriots Collection**			
92-10-001	Washingtons Headquarters	M. Whiting	Open	24.00	24.00
92-10-002	Betsy Ross House	M. Whiting	Open	17.50	17.50
Brandywine Collectables		**Treasured Times**			
94-11-001	Mother's Day House	M. Whiting	750	32.00	32.00
94-11-002	Birthday House	M. Whiting	750	32.00	32.00
94-11-003	New Baby House	M. Whiting	750	32.00	32.00
94-11-004	Anniversary House	M. Whiting	750	32.00	32.00
94-11-005	Halloween House	M. Whiting	750	32.00	32.00
94-11-006	Valentine House	M. Whiting	750	32.00	32.00
Brandywine Collectables		**Hometown I**			
90-12-001	School	M. Whiting	Closed	14.00	14.00
90-12-002	General Store	M. Whiting	Closed	14.00	14.00
90-12-003	Barber Shop	M. Whiting	Closed	14.00	14.00
90-12-004	Toy Store	M. Whiting	Closed	14.00	14.00
Brandywine Collectables		**Hometown II**			
91-13-001	Church	M. Whiting	Closed	14.00	14.00
91-13-002	Dentist	M. Whiting	Closed	14.00	14.00
91-13-003	Ice Cream Shop	M. Whiting	Closed	14.00	14.00
91-13-004	Stitch-N-Sew	M. Whiting	Closed	14.00	14.00
Brandywine Collectables		**Hometown III**			
91-14-001	Dairy	M. Whiting	Closed	15.50	15.50
91-14-002	Library	M. Whiting	Closed	15.50	15.50
91-14-003	Firehouse	M. Whiting	Closed	15.50	15.50
91-14-004	Basket Shop	M. Whiting	Closed	15.50	15.50
Brandywine Collectables		**Hometown IV**			
92-15-001	Country Inn	M. Whiting	Closed	21.50	21.50
92-15-002	Courthouse	M. Whiting	Closed	21.50	21.50
92-15-003	Gas Station	M. Whiting	Closed	21.00	21.00
92-15-004	Bakery	M. Whiting	Closed	21.00	21.00
Brandywine Collectables		**Hometown V**			
92-16-001	Pharmacy	M. Whiting	Open	22.00	22.00
92-16-002	Sporting Goods	M. Whiting	Open	22.00	22.00
92-16-003	Tea Room	M. Whiting	Open	22.00	22.00
92-16-004	Antiques Shop	M. Whiting	Open	22.00	22.00
92-16-005	Gift Shop	M. Whiting	Open	22.00	22.00
Brandywine Collectables		**Hometown VI**			
93-17-001	School	M. Whiting	Open	24.00	24.00
93-17-002	Church	M. Whiting	Open	24.00	24.00
93-17-003	General Store	M. Whiting	Open	24.00	24.00
93-17-004	Train Station	M. Whiting	Open	24.00	24.00
93-17-005	Diner	M. Whiting	Open	24.00	24.00
Brandywine Collectables		**Hometown VII**			
93-18-001	Flower Shop	M. Whiting	Open	24.00	24.00
93-18-002	Dress Shop	M. Whiting	Open	24.00	24.00
93-18-003	Candy Shop	M. Whiting	Open	24.00	24.00
93-18-004	Pet Shop	M. Whiting	Open	24.00	24.00
93-18-005	Post Office	M. Whiting	Open	24.00	24.00
93-18-006	Quilt Shop	M. Whiting	Open	24.00	24.00
Brandywine Collectables		**Hometown VIII**			
94-19-001	Sewing Shop	M. Whiting	Open	26.00	26.00
94-19-002	Country Store	M. Whiting	Open	28.00	28.00
94-19-003	Professional Building	M. Whiting	Open	28.00	28.00
94-19-004	Barber Shop	M. Whiting	Open	28.00	28.00

Company Number	Name	Series Artist	Edition Limit	Issue Price	Quote
94-19-005	Fire Company	M. Whiting	Open	28.00	28.00
Brandywine Collectables		**Accesories**			
87-20-001	Summer Tree with Fence	M. Whiting	Open	7.00	7.00
88-20-002	Flag	M. Whiting	Open	10.00	10.00
88-20-003	Lampost, Wall & Fence	M. Whiting	Open	11.00	11.00
89-20-004	Mailbox, Tree & Fence	M. Whiting	Open	10.00	10.00
89-20-005	Victorian Gas Light	M. Whiting	Open	6.50	6.50
89-20-006	Horse & Carriage	M. Whiting	Open	13.00	13.00
89-20-007	Pumpkin Wagon	M. Whiting	Open	11.50	11.50
90-20-008	Flower Cart	M. Whiting	Open	13.00	13.00
90-20-009	Wishing Well	M. Whiting	Open	10.00	10.00
90-20-010	Bandstand	M. Whiting	Closed	10.50	10.50
90-20-011	Gate & Arbor	M. Whiting	Closed	9.00	9.00
90-20-012	Gooseneck Lamp	M. Whiting	Open	7.50	7.50
91-20-013	Town Clock	M. Whiting	Open	7.50	7.50
91-20-014	Baggage Cart	M. Whiting	Open	10.50	10.50
91-20-015	Street Sign	M. Whiting	Open	8.00	8.00
92-20-016	Apple Tree/Tire Swing	M. Whiting	Open	10.00	10.00
92-20-017	Tree with Birdhouse	M. Whiting	Open	10.00	10.00
94-20-018	Elm Tree with Benches	M. Whiting	Open	16.00	16.00
94-20-019	Lamp with Barber Pole	M. Whiting	Open	10.50	10.50
Byers' Choice Ltd.		**Carolers**			
78-01-001	Traditional Man Caroler	J. Byers	Closed	N/A	300.00
78-01-002	Traditional Lady Caroler (w/ hands)	J. Byers	Closed	N/A	1500.00
82-01-003	Victorian Adult Caroler (1st Version)	J. Byers	Closed	32.00	300.00
82-01-004	Victorian Child Caroler (1st Version)	J. Byers	Closed	32.00	300.00
83-01-005	Victorian Adult Caroler (2nd Version)	J. Byers	Open	35.00	46.00
83-01-006	Victorian Child Caroler (2nd Version)	J. Byers	Open	33.00	46.00
86-01-007	Traditional Grandparents	J. Byers	Open	35.00	42.00
86-01-008	Singing Dogs	J. Byers	Open	13.00	15.00
88-01-009	Victorian Grand Parent Carolers	J. Byers	Open	40.00	45.00
88-01-010	Children with Skates	J. Byers	Open	40.00	47.00
88-01-011	Singing Cats	J. Byers	Open	13.50	15.00
Byers' Choice Ltd.		**Special Characters**			
81-02-001	Thanksgiving Man (Clay Hands)	J. Byers	Closed	Unkn.	2000.00
81-02-002	Thanksgiving Lady (Clay Hands)	J. Byers	Closed	Unkn.	2000.00
82-02-003	Icabod	J. Byers	Closed	32.00	1150.00
82-02-004	Choir Children, boy and girl set	J. Byers	Closed	32.00	500.00
82-02-005	Valentine Boy	J. Byers	Closed	32.00	450.00
82-02-006	Valentine Girl	J. Byers	Closed	32.00	450.00
82-02-007	Easter Boy	J. Byers	Closed	32.00	450.00
82-02-008	Easter Girl	J. Byers	Closed	32.00	450.00
82-02-009	Leprechauns	J. Byers	Closed	34.00	1200.00
82-02-010	Conductor	J. Byers	Closed	32.00	100-110.
82-02-011	Drummer Boy	J. Byers	Closed	34.00	50-120.00
83-02-012	Boy on Rocking Horse	J. Byers	300	85.00	1500.00
84-02-013	Chimney Sweep (Adult)	J. Byers	Closed	36.00	1200.00
85-02-014	Pajama Children	J. Byers	Closed	35.00	120-210.
87-02-015	Boy on Sled	J. Byers	Closed	50.00	175-290.
87-02-016	Caroler with Lamp	J. Byers	Closed	40.00	120-150.
87-02-017	Mother's Day	J. Byers	225	125.00	350.00
88-02-018	Mother's Day (Son)	J. Byers	Closed	125.00	310-330.
88-02-019	Mother's Day (Daughter)	J. Byers	Closed	125.00	330.00
88-02-020	Angel Tree Top	J. Byers	100	Unkn.	160-200.
88-02-021	Mother Holding Baby	J. Byers	Closed	40.00	70.00
89-02-022	Newsboy with Bike	J. Byers	Closed	78.00	100-150.
89-02-023	Girl with Hoop	J. Byers	Closed	44.00	100-115.
89-02-024	Mother's Day (with Carriage)	J. Byers	3,000	75.00	250-325.
90-02-025	Postman	J. Byers	Closed	45.00	50-70.00
90-02-026	Parson	J. Byers	Closed	44.00	46.00
90-02-027	Victorian Girl On Rocking Horse	J. Byers	Closed	70.00	150-210.
91-02-028	Chimney Sweep (Child)	J. Byers	Open	50.00	50.00
91-02-029	Boy W/Tree	J. Byers	Open	49.00	49.00
92-02-030	Schoolteacher	J. Byers	Open	48.00	48.00
92-02-031	Victorian Mother With Toddler (Spr/Sum)	J. Byers	Closed	60.00	125.00
92-02-032	Victorian Mother With Toddler (Fall/Win)	J. Byers	Closed	60.00	125.00
93-02-033	Victorian Mother With Toddler (Spr/Sum)	J. Byers	Closed	61.00	61.00
93-02-034	Victorian Mother With Toddler (Fall/Win)	J. Byers	Closed	61.00	61.00
93-02-035	Choir Director	J. Byers	Open	56.00	56.00
93-02-036	School Kids	J. Byers	Open	48.00	48.00
93-02-037	Lamplighter	J. Byers	Open	48.00	48.00
94-02-038	Constable	J. Byers	Open	53.00	53.00
94-02-039	Sandwich Board Man	J. Byers	Open	52.00	52.00
94-02-040	Nanny	J. Byers	Open	66.00	66.00
94-02-041	Boy With Goose	J. Byers	Open	49.50	49.50
94-02-042	Baby in Basket	J. Byers	Open	7.50	7.50
Byers' Choice Ltd.		**Santas**			
78-03-001	Old World Santa	J. Byers	Closed	33.00	250.00
78-03-002	Velvet Santa	J. Byers	Open	Unkn.	50.00
82-03-003	Santa in a Sleigh (1st Version)	J. Byers	Closed	46.00	800.00
83-03-004	Working Santa	J. Byers	Closed	38.00	100-150.
83-03-005	Velvet Santa w/Tree	J. Byers	Closed	N/A	250.00
84-03-006	Santa in Sleigh (2nd Version)	J. Byers	Closed	70.00	400-675.
84-03-007	Mrs. Claus	J. Byers	Closed	38.00	95-150.00
86-03-008	Mrs. Claus on Rocker	J. Byers	Closed	73.00	400.00
86-03-009	Victorian Santa	J. Byers	Closed	39.00	100-295.
87-03-010	Velvet Mrs. Claus	J. Byers	Open	44.00	44.00
88-03-011	Saint Nicholas	J. Byers	Closed	44.00	60-125.00
88-03-012	Knecht Ruprecht (Black Peter)	J. Byers	Closed	38.00	100-148.
89-03-013	Russian Santa	J. Byers	Closed	85.00	125-350.
90-03-014	Weihnachtsmann (German Santa)	J. Byers	Closed	56.00	115-225.
91-03-015	Father Christmas	J. Byers	Closed	48.00	58-150.00
92-03-016	Mrs. Claus (2nd Version)	J. Byers	Closed	50.00	70.00
92-03-017	Working Santa (2nd Version)	J. Byers	Open	52.00	52.00
93-03-018	Skating Santa	J. Byers	Closed	60.00	90.00
Byers' Choice Ltd.		**Dickens Series**			
83-04-001	Scrooge (1st Edition)	J. Byers	Closed	36.00	1000-2000.
84-04-002	Mrs. Cratchit (1st Edition)	J. Byers	Closed	38.00	1800.00
84-04-003	Scrooge (2nd Edition)	J. Byers	Open	38.00	38.00
85-04-004	Mrs. Fezziwig (1st Edition)	J. Byers	Closed	43.00	385-1100.
85-04-005	Mr. Fezziwig (1st Edition)	J. Byers	Closed	43.00	385-1100.
85-04-006	Mrs. Cratchit (2nd Edition)	J. Byers	Open	39.00	39.00
86-04-007	Marley's Ghost (1st Edition)	J. Byers	Closed	40.00	400-450.
86-04-008	Mrs. Fezziwig (2nd Edition)	J. Byers	Closed	43.00	155-400.
86-04-009	Mr. Fezziwig (2nd Edition)	J. Byers	Closed	43.00	155-400.
87-04-010	Spirit of Christmas Past (1st Edition)	J. Byers	Closed	42.00	125-350.
87-04-011	Marley's Ghost (2nd Edition)	J. Byers	Closed	42.00	96-325.00
88-04-012	Spirit of Christmas Present (1st Edition)	J. Byers	Closed	44.00	125-350.
88-04-013	Spirit of Christmas Past (2nd Edition)	J. Byers	Closed	46.00	140-250.

Company Number	Name	Series Artist	Edition Limit	Issue Price	Quote
89-04-014	Spirit of Christmas Future (1st Edition)	J. Byers	Closed	46.00	156-400.
89-04-015	Spirit of Christmas Present (2nd Edition)	J. Byers	Closed	48.00	140-250.
90-04-016	Bob Cratchit & Tiny Tim (1st Edition)	J. Byers	Closed	84.00	210-225.
90-04-017	Spirit of Christmas Future (2nd Edition)	J. Byers	Closed	48.00	125-210.
91-04-018	Happy Scrooge (1st Edition)	J. Byers	Closed	50.00	60-250.
91-04-019	Bob Cratchit & Tiny Tim (2nd Edition)	J. Byers	Open	86.00	86.00
92-04-020	Happy Scrooge (2nd Edition)	J. Byers	Closed	50.00	85-199.00
Byers' Choice Ltd.		**Musicians**			
83-05-001	Violin Player Man (1st Version)	J. Byers	Closed	38.00	800.00
84-05-002	Violin Player Man (2nd Version)	J. Byers	Closed	38.00	1500.00
85-05-003	Horn Player, chubby face	J. Byers	Closed	37.00	700.00
85-05-004	Horn Player	J. Byers	Closed	38.00	300-400.
86-05-005	Victorian Girl with Violin	J. Byers	Closed	39.00	250.00
89-05-006	Musician with Clarinet	J. Byers	Closed	44.00	300-400.
90-05-007	Musician with Mandolin	J. Byers	Closed	46.00	125-225.
91-05-008	Musician with Accordian	J. Byers	Closed	48.00	125-200.
91-05-009	Boy W/Mandolin	J. Byers	Closed	48.00	180.00
92-05-010	Musician With French Horn	J. Byers	Closed	52.00	70-104.00
Byers' Choice Ltd.		**Nativity**			
87-06-001	Black Angel	J. Byers	Closed	36.00	90.00
87-06-002	Angel-Great Star (Blonde)	J. Byers	Closed	40.00	125.00
87-06-003	Angel-Great Star (Brunette)	J. Byers	Closed	40.00	100.00
87-06-004	Angel-Great Star (Red Head)	J. Byers	Closed	40.00	60-125.00
88-06-005	Shepherds	J. Byers	Closed	37.00	95.00
89-06-006	King Gasper	J. Byers	Closed	40.00	70-100.00
89-06-007	King Melchior	J. Byers	Closed	40.00	60-100.00
89-06-008	King Balthasar	J. Byers	Closed	40.00	95-100.00
90-06-009	Holy Family	J. Byers	Closed	90.00	150-300.
Byers' Choice Ltd.		**Display Figures**			
81-07-001	Display Man	J. Byers	Closed	Unkn.	2000.00
81-07-002	Display Lady	J. Byers	Closed	Unkn.	2000.00
82-07-003	Display Drummer Boy-1st	J. Byers	Closed	96.00	600.00
85-07-004	Display Drummer Boy-2nd	J. Byers	Closed	160.00	300.00
82-07-005	Display Santa	J. Byers	Closed	96.00	600.00
83-07-006	Display Carolers	J. Byers	Closed	200.00	500.00
84-07-007	Display Working Santa	J. Byers	Closed	260.00	500.00
85-07-008	Display Old World Santa	J. Byers	Closed	260.00	500.00
85-07-009	Display Children	J. Byers	Closed	140.00	500.00
86-07-010	Display Adults	J. Byers	Closed	170.00	500.00
87-07-011	Mechanical Boy W/ Drum	J. Byers	Closed	N/A	N/A
90-07-012	Display Santa-red	J. Byers	Closed	250.00	450.00
90-07-013	Display Santa-bayberry	J. Byers	Closed	250.00	450.00
Byers' Choice Ltd.		**Cries Of London**			
91-08-001	Apple Lady	J. Byers	Closed	80.00	420-890.
92-08-002	Baker	J. Byers	Closed	62.00	65-125.00
93-08-003	Chestnut Roaster	J. Byers	Closed	64.00	64-150.00
94-08-004	Flower Vendor	J. Byers	Yr. Iss.	64.00	64.00
Byers' Choice Ltd.		**Skaters**			
91-09-001	Adult Skaters	J. Byers	Open	50.00	50.00
92-09-002	Children Skaters	J. Byers	Open	50.00	50.00
93-09-003	Grandparent Skaters	J. Byers	Open	50.00	50.00
93-09-004	Boy Skater on Log	J. Byers	Closed	55.00	70.00
Byers' Choice Ltd.		**Toddlers**			
91-10-001	Sled with Dog	J. Byers	Closed	30.00	45-60.00
92-10-002	Shovel	J. Byers	Closed	17.00	35.00
92-10-003	Snowball (lg.)	J. Byers	Open	17.00	19.00
92-10-004	Sled	J. Byers	Open	17.00	19.00
93-10-005	Package	J. Byers	Closed	18.50	35.00
93-10-006	Gingerbread Boy	J. Byers	Open	18.50	18.50
93-10-007	Teddy Bear	J. Byers	Closed	18.50	35.00
94-10-008	Skis	J. Byers	Open	19.00	19.00
94-10-009	Tree	J. Byers	Open	18.00	18.00
94-10-010	Snowflake	J. Byers	Open	18.00	18.00
Byers' Choice Ltd.		**Salvation Army Band**			
92-11-001	Woman With Kettle	J. Byers	Open	64.00	64.00
93-11-002	Man With Cornet	J. Byers	Open	54.00	54.00
93-11-003	Woman With Tambourine	J. Byers	Open	58.00	58.00
Byers' Choice Ltd.		**The Nutcracker**			
93-12-001	Marie (1st Edition)	J. Byers	Yr.Iss.	52.00	95.00
94-12-002	Fritz (1st Edition)	J. Byers	Yr.Iss.	56.00	56.00
94-12-003	Marie (2nd Edition)	J. Byers	Yr.Iss.	53.00	53.00
Byers' Choice Ltd.		**Children of The World**			
92-13-001	Dutch Boy	J. Byers	Yr.Iss.	50.00	100-250.
92-13-002	Dutch Girl	J. Byers	Yr.Iss.	50.00	100-250.
93-13-003	Bavarian Boy	J. Byers	Yr.Iss.	50.00	100-290.
Byers' Choice Ltd.		**Wayside Country Store Exclusives**			
86-14-001	Colonial Lamplighter s/n	J. Byers	600	46.00	450.00
87-14-002	Colonial Watchman s/n	J. Byers	600	49.00	400.00
88-14-003	Colonial Lady s/n	J. Byers	600	49.00	350.00
Byers' Choice Ltd.		**Snow Goose Exclusive**			
88-15-001	Man with Goose	J. Byers	600	60.00	300.00
Byers' Choice Ltd.		**Country Christmas Store Exclusive**			
88-16-001	Toymaker	J. Byers	600	59.00	600.00
Byers' Choice Ltd.		**Woodstock Inn Exclusives**			
87-17-001	Skier Boy	J. Byers	200	40.00	250-350.
87-17-002	Skier Girl	J. Byers	200	40.00	250-350.
88-17-003	Woodstock Lady	J. Byers	N/A	41.00	250.00
88-17-004	Woodstock Man	J. Byers	N/A	41.00	250.00
88-17-005	Sugarin Kids (Woodstock)	J. Byers	N/A	41.00	300.00
Byers' Choice Ltd.		**Stacy's Gifts & Collectibles Exclusives**			
87-18-001	Santa in Rocking Chair with Boy	J. Byers	100	130.00	550.00
87-18-002	Santa in Rocking Chair with Girl	J. Byers	100	130.00	450.00
Byers' Choice Ltd.		**Port-O-Call Exclusives**			
87-19-001	Cherub Angel-pink	J. Byers	Closed	N/A	125.00
87-19-002	Cherub Angel-rose	J. Byers	Closed	N/A	125.00
87-19-003	Cherub Angel-blue	J. Byers	Closed	N/A	225.00
87-19-004	Cherub Angel-cream	J. Byers	Closed	N/A	400.00

Company Number	Name	Series Artist	Edition Limit	Issue Price	Quote
Rick Cain Studios		**Master Series**			
85-01-001	Box Turtle	R. Cain	5,000	66.00	66.00
85-01-002	Woodland Spirit	R. Cain	5,000	165.00	165.00
85-01-003	Featherview	R. Cain	Retrd.	151.80	151.80
85-01-004	Catchmaster	R. Cain	Retrd.	184.80	184.80
85-01-005	Nightmaster	R. Cain	Retrd.	184.80	184.80
85-01-006	Tidemaster	R. Cain	5,000	242.00	242.00
85-01-007	Sea View	R. Cain	S/O	70.40	70.40
86-01-008	Wind Horse	R. Cain	S/O	70 .00	70.00
86-01-009	African Youth	R. Cain	5,000	137.00	137.00
86-01-010	Marshkeeper	R. Cain	5,000	231.00	231.00
86-01-011	Tropical Flame	R. Cain	Retrd.	209.00	209.00
86-01-012	Dragon Sprout	R. Cain	S/O	92.50	92.50
86-01-013	Elder	R. Cain	S/O	550.00	550.00
86-01-014	Aerial Hunter	R. Cain	S/O	70.40	70.40
86-01-015	Sandmaster	R. Cain	5,000	93.00	93.00
87-01-016	Habitat	R. Cain	5,000	93.00	93.00
87-01-017	Liquid Universe	R. Cain	5,000	540.00	540.00
87-01-018	Winged Fortress	R. Cain	5,000	363.00	363.00
87-01-019	Sentinel Crest	R. Cain	5,000	121.00	121.00
87-01-020	Teller	R. Cain	Retrd.	308.00	308.00
87-01-021	Yore Castle	R. Cain	Retrd.	165.00	165.00
87-01-022	Dragonflies Dance	R. Cain	Retrd.	55.00	55.00
87-01-023	Dragon Sprout II	R. Cain	5,000	159.00	159.00
88-01-024	Paradise Found	R. Cain	5,000	308.00	308.00
88-01-025	Watercourse Way	R. Cain	5,000	99.00	99.00
88-01-026	Old Man of the Forest	R. Cain	Retrd.	132.00	132.00
88-01-027	Orbist	R. Cain	Retrd.	108.00	108.00
88-01-028	Heron Pass	R. Cain	5,000	231.00	231.00
88-01-029	Lady Reflecting	R. Cain	5,000	93.00	93.00
88-01-030	Fair Atlantis	R. Cain	Retrd.	319.00	319.00
88-01-031	Guardian	R. Cain	Retrd.	325.00	325.00
88-01-032	The Balance	R. Cain	Retrd.	374.00	374.00
88-01-033	Blackberry Summer	R. Cain	5,000	165.00	165.00
89-01-034	Encompass	R. Cain	5,000	104.00	104.00
89-01-035	Innerview	R. Cain	5,000	84.00	84.00
89-01-036	Universes	R. Cain	5,000	115.00	115.00
89-01-037	Domain	R. Cain	Retrd.	187.00	187.00
89-01-038	Hatchling	R. Cain	5,000	85.00	85.00
90-01-039	Wood Flight	R. Cain	S/O	105.50	105.50
90-01-040	Pathfinder	R. Cain	S/O	101.00	101.00
90-01-041	Scarlett Wing	R. Cain	2,000	101.00	101.00
90-01-042	Tropic Array	R. Cain	2,000	100.00	100.00
90-01-043	Falcon Lore	R. Cain	S/O	86.00	86.00
90-01-044	Pondering	R. Cain	2,000	108.00	108.00
90-01-045	Rising Shadow	R. Cain	2,000	187.00	187.00
90-01-046	Dark Feather	R. Cain	2,000	86.00	86.00
90-01-047	Searchers	R. Cain	2,000	174.00	174.00
90-01-048	Dual Motion	R. Cain	2,000	185.00	185.00
90-01-049	Aquarian	R. Cain	2,000	203.00	203.00
90-01-050	Majestic Cradle	R. Cain	900	440.00	440.00
91-01-051	Cain Sign	R. Cain	Open	55.00	55.00
91-01-052	Alpha Sprout	R. Cain	2,000	99.00	99.00
91-01-053	Pride	R. Cain	2,000	105.00	105.00
91-01-054	Cheetah	R. Cain	2,000	105.00	105.00
91-01-055	Soft Wave	R. Cain	2,000	121.00	121.00
91-01-056	Cameo	R. Cain	2,000	154.00	154.00
91-01-057	La Kimono	R. Cain	2,000	176.00	176.00
91-01-058	Spirit Dog	R. Cain	S/O	198.00	198.00
91-01-059	Thunderbowl	R. Cain	2,000	242.00	242.00
91-01-060	Blossom	R. Cain	2,000	99.00	99.00
91-01-061	Jungle Graces	R. Cain	2,000	110.00	110.00
91-01-062	Aerial Victor	R. Cain	2,000	115.00	115.00
92-01-063	Bathing Hole	R. Cain	2,000	102.00	102.00
92-01-064	The Pack	R. Cain	S/O	105.50	105.50
92-01-065	Prairie Thunder	R. Cain	2,000	110.00	110.00
92-01-066	Leading Wolf	R. Cain	S/O	143.00	143.00
92-01-067	Medicine Hawk	R. Cain	2,000	187.00	187.00
92-01-068	Spirit Eagle	R. Cain	S/O	121.00	121.00
92-01-069	Three Bears	R. Cain	2,000	187.00	187.00
92-01-070	Seven Bears	R. Cain	S/O	231.00	231.00
92-01-071	Power of One	R. Cain	2,000	77.00	77.00
92-01-072	Radiance	R. Cain	2,000	132.00	132.00
93-01-073	Wood Song	R. Cain	S/O	143.00	143.00
93-01-074	Wolf Crossing	R. Cain	2,000	715.00	715.00
93-01-075	Fountain of Youth	R. Cain	2,000	132.00	132.00
93-01-076	Rites of Passage	R. Cain	2,000	165.00	165.00
93-01-077	Arctic Moon	R. Cain	S/O	231.00	231.00
93-01-078	Dark Shadow	R. Cain	900	1650.00	1650.00
93-01-079	Wolf Trail	R. Cain	S/O	121.00	121.00
93-01-080	Medicine Bowl	R. Cain	2,000	220.00	220.00
93-01-081	Little Bears	R. Cain	2,000	220.00	220.00
93-01-082	Spirit Totem	R. Cain	S/O	286.00	286.00
93-01-083	Speaks to Strangers	R. Cain	2,000	132.00	132.00
93-01-084	Buffalo's Son	R. Cain	2,000	143.00	143.00
93-01-085	Steppin' Wolf	R. Cain	S/O	210.00	210.00
93-01-086	Where Bear	R. Cain	2,000	253.00	253.00
93-01-087	Arctic Son	R. Cain	S/O	275.00	275.00
94-01-088	Rebirth	R. Cain	2,000	180.00	180.00
94-01-089	Waiting Wolf	R. Cain	S/O	198.00	198.00
94-01-090	Moon Walk	R. Cain	S/O	198.00	198.00
94-01-091	Forest Nimble	R. Cain	2,000	218.00	218.00
94-01-092	Wolf Prince	R. Cain	2,000	325.00	325.00
94-01-093	Four Bears	R. Cain	2,000	1100.00	1100.00
Rick Cain Studios		**Vision Quest**			
91-02-001	Silver Shadow	R. Cain	2,000	176.00	176.00
92-02-002	Alphascape	R. Cain	S/O	210.00	210.00
93-02-003	White Vision	R. Cain	2,000	242.00	242.00
Rick Cain Studios		**Eco-Sculpture**			
91-03-001	Highland Voyager	R. Cain	2,000	132.00	132.00
91-03-002	Orchestration	R. Cain	2,000	132.00	132.00
92-03-003	Polar Eclipse	R. Cain	2,000	110.00	110.00
Rick Cain Studios		**Gallery I**			
92-04-001	Wind Spirit	R. Cain	1,500	1650.00	1650.00
92-04-002	American Dream	R. Cain	500	3300.00	3300.00
93-04-003	Raven Shadow	R. Cain	900	2200.00	2200.00
Rick Cain Studios		**Birds of Prey (Miniatures)**			
92-05-001	Bald Eagle	R. Cain	3,000	49.50	49.50
92-05-002	Golden Eagle	R. Cain	3,000	49.50	49.50
92-05-003	Kestrel Hawk	R. Cain	3,000	49.50	49.50
92-05-004	Night Owl	R. Cain	3,000	49.50	49.50
92-05-005	Peregrine Falcon	R. Cain	3,000	49.50	49.50
92-05-006	Red Tail Hawk	R. Cain	3,000	49.50	49.50
Rick Cain Studios		**Collectors Guild**			
92-06-001	High Point	R. Cain	S/O	82.00	82.00
92-06-002	Visor	R. Cain	Retrd.	Gift	N/A
93-06-003	Strider	R. Cain	S/O	82.00	82.00
93-06-004	Star Shadow	R. Cain	Retrd.	Gift	N/A
94-06-005	Midnight Son	R. Cain	Yr.Iss.	297.00	297.00
94-06-006	Arctic Moon II	R. Cain	Yr.Iss.	Gift	N/A
Calabar Creations		**Little Farmers**			
93-01-001	Playful Kittens LF73016	P. Apsit	5,000	64.00	64.00
93-01-002	Going Home LF73027	P. Apsit	5,000	64.00	64.00
93-01-003	It's Not For You LF73038	P. Apsit	5,000	64.00	64.00
93-01-004	Surprise! LF73046	P. Apsit	5,000	60.00	60.00
93-01-005	Oops! LF73058	P. Apsit	5,000	64.00	64.00
93-01-006	Caring Friend LF73066	P. Apsit	5,000	57.00	57.00
93-01-007	Little Lumber Joe LF73077	P. Apsit	5,000	64.00	64.00
93-01-008	True Love LF73087	P. Apsit	5,000	45.00	45.00
93-01-009	Piggy Ride LF73097	P. Apsit	5,000	45.00	45.00
93-01-010	Between Chores LF73105	P. Apsit	5,000	40.00	40.00
93-01-011	Lunch Express LF73117	P. Apsit	5,000	76.00	76.00
93-01-012	Apple Delivery LF73127	P. Apsit	5,000	54.00	54.00
93-01-013	Vita-Veggie Vendor LF73137	P. Apsit	5,000	62.00	62.00
93-01-014	LF Signature Piece LF73147	P. Apsit	Open	40.00	40.00
Calabar Creations		**Red Moon Children**			
93-02-001	Bashful Brave RM67415	R. Myer	5,000	44.00	44.00
93-02-002	Temptations RM67426	R. Myer	5,000	58.00	58.00
93-02-003	I Said Forward! RM67438	R. Myer	5,000	46.00	46.00
93-02-004	Sunset Duet RM67445	R. Myer	5,000	44.00	44.00
93-02-005	Practice Makes Perfect RM67465	R. Myer	5,000	40.00	40.00
93-02-006	Tickle My Fancy RM67475	R. Myer	5,000	48.00	48.00
93-02-007	Reputable Rainmakers RM67486	R. Myer	5,000	38.00	38.00
93-02-008	I Saw It First RM67496	R. Myer	5,000	44.00	44.00
93-02-009	Tying the Knot RM67506	R. Myer	5,000	44.00	44.00
93-02-010	Deer Talk RM67516	R. Myer	5,000	40.00	40.00
93-02-011	Puzzled RM67525	R. Myer	5,000	44.00	44.00
93-02-012	Big Sister RM67535	R. Myer	5,000	44.00	44.00
Calabar Creations		**Santaventure**			
93-03-001	Cart O' Plenty SV73737	P. Apsit	5,000	66.00	66.00
93-03-002	Pilgrim Santa SV73748	P. Apsit	5,000	59.00	59.00
93-03-003	Hooray For Santa SV73757	P. Apsit	5,000	59.00	59.00
93-03-004	A Pinch of Advice SV73768	P. Apsit	5,000	68.00	68.00
93-03-005	Santa Tested SV73778	P. Apsit	5,000	68.00	68.00
93-03-006	Nuts For You SV73787	P. Apsit	5,000	59.00	59.00
93-03-007	Santa's Sack Attack SV73796	P. Apsit	5,000	60.00	60.00
Calabar Creations		**Tee Club**			
93-04-001	Prac-Tees TC73858	P. Apsit	5,000	66.00	66.00
93-04-002	Putt-Teeing TC73868	P. Apsit	5,000	66.00	66.00
93-04-003	Teed-Off TC73877	P. Apsit	5,000	60.00	60.00
93-04-004	Old Tee-Mer TC73887	P. Apsit	5,000	78.00	78.00
93-04-005	Certain-Tee TC73898	P. Apsit	5,000	100.00	100.00
93-04-006	Naugh-Tee TC73908	P. Apsit	5,000	56.00	56.00
Calabar Creations		**Yesterday's Friends**			
93-05-001	Freewheeling RW74436	P. Apsit	7,500	48.00	48.00
93-05-002	Bluester RW74446	P. Apsit	7,500	44.00	44.00
93-05-003	Bayou Boys RW74456	P. Apsit	3,500	80.00	80.00
93-05-004	Buddies RW74466	P. Apsit	7,500	50.00	50.00
93-05-005	Mike's Magic RW74475	P. Apsit	7,500	37.00	37.00
93-05-006	Jazzy Bubble RW74486	P. Apsit	7,500	37.00	37.00
93-05-007	Dinner For Two RW74496	P. Apsit	7,500	38.00	38.00
93-05-008	Interference RW74506	P. Apsit	7,500	42.00	42.00
93-05-009	Strike So Sweet RW74517	P. Apsit	7,500	42.00	42.00
93-05-010	Hop-a-Long Pete RW74539	P. Apsit	3,500	80.00	80.00
93-05-011	Me Big Chief RW74548	P. Apsit	7,500	56.00	56.00
93-05-012	Tug-a-Leg RW74557	P. Apsit	7,500	56.00	56.00
Cast Art Industries		**Dreamsicles Cherubs**			
92-01-001	Logo Piece-pink-DC001	K. Haynes	Open	33.00	33.00
92-01-002	Logo Piece-blue-DC002	K. Haynes	Open	33.00	33.00
92-01-003	Cherub and Child-DC100	K. Haynes	Open	15.00	15.00
92-01-004	Sitting Pretty-DC101	K. Haynes	Open	10.00	10.00
92-01-005	Forever Friends-DC102	K. Haynes	Open	15.00	15.00
92-01-006	Best Pals-DC103	K. Haynes	Open	15.00	15.00
92-01-007	Mischief Maker-DC105	K. Haynes	Open	10.00	10.00
92-01-008	Heavenly Dreamer-DC106	K. Haynes	Open	11.00	11.00
92-01-009	Wildflower-DC107	K. Haynes	Open	11.00	11.00
92-01-010	Bright Eyes-DC108	K. Haynes	Open	10.00	10.00
92-01-011	Forever Yours-DC110	K. Haynes	Open	50.00	50.00
93-01-012	Limited Edtion Cherub-DC111	K. Haynes	Retrd.	50.00	50.00
92-01-013	Limited Edition Cherub-DC112	K. Haynes	Retrd.	50.00	50.00
92-01-014	Cherub For All Seasons-DC114	K. Haynes	Open	50.00	50.00
92-01-015	Bluebird On My Shoulder-DC115	K. Haynes	Open	20.00	20.00
93-01-016	Me and My Shadow-DC116	K. Haynes	Open	20.00	20.00
92-01-017	Make A Wish-DC118	K. Haynes	Open	15.00	15.00
92-01-018	Life Is Good-DC119	K. Haynes	Open	11.00	11.00
93-01-019	Wishin' On A Star-DC120	K. Haynes	Open	11.00	11.00
92-01-020	My Prayer-DC121	K. Haynes	Open	15.00	15.00
92-01-021	Sleigh Ride-DC122	K. Haynes	Open	16.00	16.00
93-01-022	Teacher's Pet-DC124	K. Haynes	Open	12.00	12.00
93-01-023	Sweet Dreams-DC125	K. Haynes	Open	30.00	30.00
93-01-024	Long Fellow-DC126	K. Haynes	Open	25.00	25.00
93-01-025	Little Dickens-DC127	K. Haynes	Open	25.00	25.00
93-01-026	Bookends-DC128	K. Haynes	Open	48.00	48.00
93-01-027	Thinking Of You-DC129	K. Haynes	Open	45.00	45.00
93-01-028	Love My Kitty-DC130	K. Haynes	Open	15.00	15.00
93-01-029	Love My Puppy-DC 131	K. Haynes	Open	14.00	14.00
93-01-030	Love My Teddy-DC132	K. Haynes	Open	15.00	15.00
93-01-031	Happy Birthday DC133	K. Haynes	Open	15.00	15.00
94-01-032	The Graduate DC135	K. Haynes	Open	17.00	17.00
92-01-033	Dance Ballerina Dance-DC140	K. Haynes	Open	39.00	39.00
93-01-034	Miss Morningstar-DC141	K. Haynes	Open	27.00	27.00
92-01-035	Bundle Of Joy-DC142	K. Haynes	Open	7.50	7.50
92-01-036	Littlest Angel-DC143	K. Haynes	Open	7.50	7.50
92-01-037	Dream A Little Dream-DC144	K. Haynes	Open	7.50	7.50
92-01-038	A Child's Prayer-DC145	K. Haynes	Open	7.50	7.50
92-01-039	Little Darlin'-DC146	K. Haynes	Open	7.50	7.50
92-01-040	Baby Love-DC147	K. Haynes	Open	7.50	7.50

FIGURINES/COTTAGES

Company		Series			
Number	**Name**	**Artist**	**Edition Limit**	**Issue Price**	**Quote**
93-01-041	Tiny Dancer-DC165	K. Haynes	Open	15.00	15.00
93-01-042	Catch A Falling Star-DC166	K. Haynes	Open	13.00	13.00
94-01-043	Sugarfoot DC167	K. Haynes	Open	26.00	26.00
94-01-044	New Born Cherub DC168	K. Haynes	Open	10.00	10.00
94-01-045	Side by Side DC169	K. Haynes	Open	33.00	33.00
94-01-046	You've Got a Friend DC170	K. Haynes	Open	28.00	28.00
94-01-047	Birthday Party DC171	K. Haynes	Open	15.00	15.00
94-01-048	Here's Looking at You DC172	K. Haynes	Open	27.00	27.00
94-01-049	Lullaby DC173	K. Haynes	Open	100.00	100.00
92-01-050	My Funny Valentine-DC201	K. Haynes	Open	17.00	17.00
92-01-051	Cupid's Bow-DC202	K. Haynes	Open	27.00	27.00
93-01-052	P.S. I Love You-DC203	K. Haynes	Open	8.00	8.00
93-01-053	Handful of Hearts-DC204	K. Haynes	Open	8.00	8.00
92-01-054	Caroler-Center Scroll-DC216	K. Haynes	Open	19.00	19.00
92-01-055	Caroler-Right Scroll-DC217	K. Haynes	Open	19.00	19.00
92-01-056	Caroler-Left Scroll-DC218	K. Haynes	Open	19.00	19.00
93-01-057	Flying Lesson Limited Edition-DC251	K. Haynes	Retrd.	80.00	80.00
93-01-058	Teeter Tots Limited Edition-DC252	K. Haynes	Retrd.	100.00	100.00
93-01-059	By the Silvery Moon-Limited Edition DC253	K. Haynes	10,000	100.00	100.00
94-01-060	The Recital-Limited Editon DC254	K. Haynes	10,000	135.00	135.00
Cast Art Industries		**Dreamsicles Christmas**			
92-02-001	Cherub and Child-DX100	K. Haynes	Open	16.00	16.00
92-02-002	Sitting Pretty-DX101	K. Haynes	Open	11.00	11.00
92-02-003	Forever Friends-DX102	K. Haynes	Open	16.00	16.00
92-02-004	Best Pals-DX103	K. Haynes	Open	16.00	16.00
92-02-005	Mischief Maker-DX105	K. Haynes	Open	11.00	11.00
92-02-006	Heavenly Dreamer-DX106	K. Haynes	Open	12.00	12.00
92-02-007	Wildflower-DX107	K. Haynes	Open	12.00	12.00
92-02-008	Bright Eyes-DX108	K. Haynes	Open	11.00	11.00
92-02-009	Forever Yours-DX110	K. Haynes	10,000	50.00	50.00
92-02-010	Bluebird On My Shoulder-DX115	K. Haynes	Open	21.00	21.00
93-02-011	Me and My Shadow-DX116	K. Haynes	Open	21.00	21.00
92-02-012	Make a Wish-DX118	K. Haynes	Open	16.00	16.00
92-02-013	Life is Good-DX119	K. Haynes	Open	12.00	12.00
93-02-014	Wishin' On a Star-DX120	K. Haynes	Open	12.00	12.00
92-02-015	My Prayer-DX121	K. Haynes	Open	16.00	16.00
92-02-016	Sleigh Ride-DX122	K. Haynes	Open	17.00	17.00
93-02-017	Teacher's Pet-DX124	K. Haynes	Open	13.00	13.00
93-02-018	Sweet Dreams-DX125	K. Haynes	Open	31.00	31.00
93-02-019	Long Fellow-DX126	K. Haynes	Open	26.00	26.00
93-02-020	Little Dickens-DX127	K. Haynes	Open	26.00	26.00
93-02-021	Thinking of You-DX129	K. Haynes	Open	46.00	46.00
93-02-022	Love My Kitty-DX130	K. Haynes	Open	16.00	16.00
93-02-023	Love My Puppy-DX131	K. Haynes	Open	15.00	15.00
93-02-024	Love My Teddy-DX132	K. Haynes	Open	16.00	16.00
93-02-025	Miss Morningstar-DX141	K. Haynes	Open	28.00	28.00
92-02-026	Bundle of Joy-DX142	K. Haynes	Open	8.00	8.00
92-02-027	Littlest Angel-DX143	K. Haynes	Open	8.00	8.00
92-02-028	Dream A Little Dream-DX144	K. Haynes	Open	8.00	8.00
92-02-029	A Child's Prayer-DX145	K. Haynes	Open	8.00	8.00
92-02-030	Little Darlin-DX146	K. Haynes	Open	8.00	8.00
92-02-031	Baby Love-DX147	K. Haynes	Open	8.00	8.00
92-02-032	Prancer-DX202	K. Haynes	Open	39.00	39.00
92-02-033	Santa Bunny-DX203	K. Haynes	Open	33.00	33.00
92-02-034	Here Comes Trouble-DX214	K. Haynes	Open	39.00	39.00
92-02-035	Caroler-Center Scroll-DX216	K. Haynes	Open	20.00	20.00
92-02-036	Caroler-Right Scroll-DX217	K. Haynes	Open	20.00	20.00
92-02-037	Caroler-Left Scroll-DX218	K. Haynes	Open	20.00	20.00
92-02-038	Stocking Holder-Snowman-DX219	K. Haynes	Open	26.00	26.00
92-02-039	Stocking Holder-Toboggan-DX220	K. Haynes	Open	22.00	22.00
92-02-040	Stocking Holder-Xmas Tree-DX221	K. Haynes	Open	26.00	26.00
92-02-041	Santa's Elf-DX240	K. Haynes	Open	20.00	20.00
92-02-042	Little Drummer Boy-DX241	K. Haynes	Open	33.00	33.00
92-02-043	Jolly Old Santa-DX244	K. Haynes	Open	28.00	28.00
92-02-044	Here Comes Santa Claus-DX245	K. Haynes	Open	70.00	70.00
93-02-045	Father Christmas-DX246	K. Haynes	Open	45.00	45.00
92-02-046	Santa In Dreamsicle Land-DX247	K. Haynes	Retrd.	85.00	85.00
93-02-047	The Finishing Touches-DX248	K. Haynes	Open	85.00	85.00
92-02-048	Snowman-DX252	K. Haynes	Open	11.00	11.00
92-02-049	Gathering Flowers-DX320	K. Haynes	Open	20.00	20.00
93-02-050	Pierre The Bear-DX453	K. Haynes	Open	15.00	15.00
Cast Art Industries		**Dreamsicles**			
91-03-001	Hanging Cherub on Ribbon-5104	K. Haynes	Retrd.	10.00	10.00
91-03-002	Xmas Cherub on Ribbon-5104C	K. Haynes	Retrd.	10.50	10.50
91-03-003	Cherub Wall Plaque-5130	K. Haynes	Retrd.	15.00	15.00
91-03-004	Cherub Wall Plaque-5131	K. Haynes	Retrd.	15.00	15.00
91-03-005	Musician w/Trumpet-5151	K. Haynes	Retrd.	22.00	22.00
91-03-006	Musician w/Drums-5152	K. Haynes	Retrd.	22.00	22.00
91-03-007	Musician w/Flute-5153	K. Haynes	Retrd.	22.00	22.00
91-03-008	Musician w/Cymbals-5154	K. Haynes	Retrd.	22.00	22.00
91-03-009	Ballerina Box-5700	K. Haynes	Retrd.	9.00	9.00
91-03-010	"I Love You" Box-5701	K. Haynes	Retrd.	9.00	9.00
91-03-011	Bunny Box-5750	K. Haynes	Retrd.	14.00	14.00
91-03-012	Heart Cherub Box-5751	K. Haynes	Retrd.	14.00	14.00
91-03-013	Queen Cherub Box-5804	K. Haynes	Retrd.	26.00	26.00
Cast Art Industries		**Dreamsicles Animals**			
92-04-001	Mr. Bunny-DA107	K. Haynes	Open	27.00	27.00
92-04-002	Mrs. Bunny-DA108	K. Haynes	Open	27.00	27.00
92-04-003	Sir Hareold-DA123	K. Haynes	Open	39.00	39.00
92-04-004	King Rabbit-DA124	K. Haynes	Open	66.00	66.00
92-04-005	Witch-DA660	K. Haynes	Open	17.00	17.00
Cast Art Industries		**Animal Attraction™**			
93-05-001	The Flasher-AA001	S.&G. Hackett	Open	32.00	32.00
93-05-002	Udderly Ridiculous-AA002	S.&G. Hackett	Open	28.00	28.00
93-05-003	Pigs in a Blanket-AA003	S.&G. Hackett	Open	11.00	11.00
93-05-004	Barnyard Shuffle-AA004	S.&G. Hackett	Open	15.00	15.00
93-05-005	Bar-B-Cutie-AA005	S.&G. Hackett	Open	15.00	15.00
93-05-006	Hog Heaven-AA006	S.&G. Hackett	Open	28.00	28.00
93-05-007	Punker Pig-AA007	S.&G. Hackett	Open	11.00	11.00
93-05-008	V. I. Pig-AA008	S.&G. Hackett	Open	11.00	11.00
93-05-009	Bacon in the Sun-AA009	S.&G. Hackett	Open	15.00	15.00
93-05-010	Unexpected Guest-AA010	S.&G. Hackett	Open	17.00	17.00
93-05-011	Honey Bear Blues-AA011	S.&G. Hackett	Open	23.00	23.00
93-05-012	Bear Hug-AA012	S.&G. Hackett	Open	26.00	26.00
93-05-013	Expecting-AA013	S.&G. Hackett	Open	16.50	16.50
93-05-014	Papa's Turn-AA014	S.&G. Hackett	Open	28.00	28.00
93-05-015	Undelivered Mail-AA015	S.&G. Hackett	Open	15.00	15.00
93-05-016	Feeding Time-AA016	S.&G. Hackett	Open	10.00	10.00
93-05-017	Pigrobics-AA017	S.&G. Hackett	Open	15.00	15.00
93-05-018	Animal Attraction Logo-AA018	S.&G. Hackett	Open	32.00	32.00
93-05-019	Great White Hunter-AA019	S.&G. Hackett	Open	32.00	32.00
93-05-020	Bear Back Rider-AA020	S.&G. Hackett	Open	21.00	21.00
93-05-021	Turtle Doves-AA021	S.&G. Hackett	Open	16.00	16.00
93-05-022	This Little Piggie...-AA022	S.&G. Hackett	Open	18.00	18.00
93-05-023	When Pigs Fly-AA023	S.&G. Hackett	Open	15.00	15.00
93-05-024	Bathing Beauty Pig-AA024	S.&G. Hackett	Open	10.00	10.00
93-05-025	Happy As Pigs-AA025	S.&G. Hackett	Open	12.00	12.00
93-05-026	Cat Dancing-AA026	S.&G. Hackett	Open	21.00	21.00
93-05-027	Bear Comes Callin'-AA027	S.&G. Hackett	Open	17.00	17.00
93-05-028	Blind Date Bulldog-AA028	S.&G. Hackett	Open	17.00	17.00
93-05-029	Prom Date Cat-AA029	S.&G. Hackett	Open	16.00	16.00
93-05-030	First Date Mouse-AA030	S.&G. Hackett	Open	12.00	12.00
94-05-031	Grin and Bear It AA031	S.&G. Hackett	Open	18.00	18.00
94-05-032	Olympig AA032	S.&G. Hackett	Open	18.00	18.00
94-05-033	No Pain, No Gain AA033	S.&G. Hackett	Open	15.00	15.00
94-05-034	Over the Threshold AA034	S.&G. Hackett	Open	21.00	21.00
93-05-035	Pig Kahuna AA035	S.&G. Hackett	Open	17.00	17.00
Cast Art Industries		**Story Time Treasures™**			
93-06-001	Three Little Pigs ST001	S.&G. Hackett	Open	28.00	28.00
93-06-002	Goldilocks and the Three Bears ST002	S.&G. Hackett	Open	36.00	36.00
93-06-003	Puff the Magic Dragon ST003	S.&G. Hackett	Open	50.00	50.00
93-06-004	Peter Rabbit ST004	S.&G. Hackett	Open	28.00	28.00
93-06-005	The Frog Prince ST005	S.&G. Hackett	Open	28.00	28.00
93-06-006	Little Red Riding Hood ST006	S.&G. Hackett	Open	28.00	28.00
93-06-007	The Ugly Duckling ST007	S.&G. Hackett	Open	12.00	12.00
93-06-008	Story Time Treasures Logo ST008	S.&G. Hackett	Open	32.00	32.00
94-06-009	Cow Jumped Over the Moon ST009	S.&G. Hackett	Open	28.00	28.00
Cast Art Industries		**Cuckoo Corners™**			
93-07-001	Wolfgang Pluck CC001	K. Haynes	Open	33.00	33.00
93-07-002	Doctor Killbear CC002	K. Haynes	Open	27.00	27.00
93-07-003	Nurse Frazzle CC003	K. Haynes	Open	27.00	27.00
93-07-004	James Vagabond CC004	K. Haynes	Open	33.00	33.00
94-07-005	Slick Hardsell CC005	K. Haynes	Open	27.00	27.00
94-07-006	Sgt. Thursday CC006	K. Haynes	Open	31.00	31.00
94-07-007	Doc Housecall CC007	K. Haynes	Open	31.00	31.00
94-07-008	Shamus O'Shark CC008	K. Haynes	Open	27.00	27.00
94-07-009	Pryce Waterhouse CC009	K. Haynes	Open	27.00	27.00
93-07-010	Davis Kupper CC010	K. Haynes	Open	28.00	28.00
93-07-011	Linda Loveless CC011	K. Haynes	Open	28.00	28.00
94-07-012	Anna Robics CC012	K. Haynes	Open	22.00	22.00
94-07-013	Miles Long CC013	K. Haynes	Open	22.00	22.00
94-07-014	Betty Bunnyhill CC014	K. Haynes	Open	31.00	31.00
94-07-015	Danny Downslope CC015	K. Haynes	Open	31.00	31.00
94-07-016	Stricker Freekick CC016	K. Haynes	Open	22.00	22.00
93-07-017	Rod N. Reel CC021	K. Haynes	Open	33.00	33.00
93-07-018	Yips McDivot CC031	K. Haynes	Open	33.00	33.00
93-07-019	Hy Overpar CC032	K. Haynes	Open	28.00	28.00
93-07-020	Sandy Trapp CC033	K. Haynes	Open	28.00	28.00
93-07-021	Barnum N. Bailey CC041	K. Haynes	Open	40.00	40.00
93-07-022	Sid Sideshow CC042	K. Haynes	Open	40.00	40.00
93-07-023	Sammy Slapstick CC043	K. Haynes	Open	33.00	33.00
93-07-024	Lindy Hopper CC050	K. Haynes	Open	33.00	33.00
93-07-025	Granny Farkle CC051	K. Haynes	Open	35.00	35.00
94-07-026	Priscilla Pirouette CC052	K. Haynes	Open	22.00	22.00
94-07-027	Tex Fritter CC053	K. Haynes	Open	31.00	31.00
93-07-028	Jackie Tar CC060	K. Haynes	Open	22.00	22.00
93-07-029	Dolly House CC061	K. Haynes	Open	22.00	22.00
93-07-030	Faith Flowerpower CC062	K. Haynes	Open	27.00	27.00
93-07-031	Beth Friend CC063	K. Haynes	Open	22.00	22.00
93-07-032	Heidi Hoedown CC064	K. Haynes	Open	27.00	27.00
94-07-033	Dee Tension CC065	K. Haynes	Open	22.00	22.00
93-07-034	Baby Rug Ratz CC070	K. Haynes	Open	16.50	16.50
93-07-035	Baby Pamperdamp CC071	K. Haynes	Open	16.50	16.50
93-07-036	Baby Knickertwist CC072	K. Haynes	Open	16.50	16.50
93-07-037	Baby Fidget CC073	K. Haynes	Open	16.50	16.50
93-07-038	Baby Winsome CC074	K. Haynes	Open	16.50	16.50
93-07-039	Baby Cradlerock CC075	K. Haynes	Open	16.50	16.50
94-07-040	Baby Johnny CC076	K. Haynes	Open	20.00	20.00
94-07-041	Baby Loo CC077	K. Haynes	Open	20.00	20.00
94-07-042	Baby Boomer CC078	K. Haynes	Open	20.00	20.00
The Cat's Meow		**Series I**			
83-01-001	Federal House	F. Jones	Retrd.	8.00	134.00
83-01-002	Inn	F. Jones	Retrd.	8.00	450.00
83-01-003	Garrison House	F. Jones	Retrd.	8.00	100.00
83-01-004	Victorian House	F. Jones	Retrd.	8.00	100.00
83-01-005	School	F. Jones	Retrd.	8.00	100.00
83-01-006	Barbershop	F. Jones	Retrd.	8.00	134.00
83-01-007	Sweetshop	F. Jones	Retrd.	8.00	85-134.00
83-01-008	Book Store	F. Jones	Retrd.	8.00	80-110.00
83-01-009	Antique Shop	F. Jones	Retrd.	8.00	110.00
83-01-010	Florist Shop	F. Jones	Retrd.	8.00	85.00
83-01-011	Toy Shoppe	F. Jones	Retrd.	8.00	85.00
83-01-012	Apothecary	F. Jones	Retrd.	8.00	134.00
83-01-013	Set	F. Jones	Retrd.	96.00	850-3200.
The Cat's Meow		**Series II**			
84-02-001	Grandinere House	F. Jones	Retrd.	8.00	50-80.00
84-02-002	Brocke House	F. Jones	Retrd.	8.00	75.00
84-02-003	Eaton House	F. Jones	Retrd.	8.00	75.00
84-02-004	Church	F. Jones	Retrd.	8.00	50-150.00
84-02-005	Town Hall	F. Jones	Retrd.	8.00	150.00
84-02-006	Music Shop	F. Jones	Retrd.	8.00	50-150.00
84-02-007	Attorney/Bank	F. Jones	Retrd.	8.00	60-100.00
84-02-008	S&T Clothiers	F. Jones	Retrd.	8.00	60.00
84-02-009	Millinery/Quilt	F. Jones	Retrd.	8.00	50-150.00
84-02-010	Tobacconist/Shoemaker	F. Jones	Retrd.	8.00	90-100.00
84-02-011	Set	F. Jones	Retrd.	96.00	750-2500.
The Cat's Meow		**Series III**			
85-03-001	Hobart-Harley House	F. Jones	Retrd.	8.00	28-45.00
85-03-002	Kalorama Guest House	F. Jones	Retrd.	8.00	28-45.00
85-03-003	Allen-Coe House	F. Jones	Retrd.	8.00	28-45.00
85-03-004	Opera House	F. Jones	Retrd.	8.00	28-45.00
85-03-005	Connecticut Ave. FireHouse	F. Jones	Retrd.	8.00	28-45.00
85-03-006	Dry Goods Store	F. Jones	Retrd.	8.00	28-45.00
85-03-007	Fine Jewelers	F. Jones	Retrd.	8.00	28-45.00
85-03-008	Edinburgh Times	F. Jones	Retrd.	8.00	28-45.00
85-03-009	Main St. Carriage Shop	F. Jones	Retrd.	8.00	28-45.00
85-03-010	Ristorante	F. Jones	Retrd.	8.00	28-45.00
85-03-011	Set	F. Jones	Retrd.	80.00	360.00

Company / Number	Name	Series / Artist	Edition Limit	Issue Price	Quote
The Cat's Meow		**Series IV**			
86-04-001	John Belville House	F. Jones	Retrd.	8.00	18-36.00
86-04-002	Westbrook House	F. Jones	Retrd.	8.00	18-36.00
86-04-003	Bennington-Hull House	F. Jones	Retrd.	8.00	18-36.00
86-04-004	Vandenberg House	F. Jones	Retrd.	8.00	18-36.00
86-04-005	Chepachet Union Church	F. Jones	Retrd.	8.00	18-45.00
86-04-006	Chagrin Falls Popcorn Shop	F. Jones	Retrd.	8.00	18-45.00
86-04-007	O'Malley's Livery Stable	F. Jones	Retrd.	8.00	18-45.00
86-04-008	The Little House Giftables	F. Jones	Retrd.	8.00	18-45.00
86-04-009	Jones Bros. Tea Co.	F. Jones	Retrd.	8.00	18-45.00
86-04-010	Village Clock Shop	F. Jones	Retrd.	8.00	18-45.00
86-04-011	Set	F. Jones	Retrd.	80.00	140-220.
The Cat's Meow		**Series V**			
87-05-001	Murray Hotel	F. Jones	Retrd.	8.00	14-27.00
87-05-002	Congruity Tavern	F. Jones	Retrd.	8.00	14-27.00
87-05-003	M. Washington House	F. Jones	Retrd.	8.00	14-27.00
87-05-004	Creole House	F. Jones	Retrd.	8.00	14-27.00
87-05-005	Police Department	F. Jones	Retrd.	8.00	14-27.00
87-05-006	Markethouse	F. Jones	Retrd.	8.00	14-27.00
87-05-007	Southport Bank	F. Jones	Retrd.	8.00	14-27.00
87-05-008	Amish Oak/Dixie Shoe	F. Jones	Retrd.	8.00	14-27.00
87-05-009	Dentist/Physician	F. Jones	Retrd.	8.00	14-27.00
87-05-010	Architect/Tailor	F. Jones	Retrd.	8.00	14-27.00
87-05-011	Set	F. Jones	Retrd.	80.00	180-230.
The Cat's Meow		**Series VI**			
88-06-001	Burton Lancaster House	F. Jones	Retrd.	8.00	12.50-18.00
88-06-002	Ohliger House	F. Jones	Retrd.	8.00	12.50-18.00
88-06-003	Stiffenbody Funeral Home	F. Jones	Retrd.	8.00	12.50-18.00
88-06-004	Pruyn House	F. Jones	Retrd.	8.00	12.50-18.00
88-06-005	First Baptist Church	F. Jones	Retrd.	8.00	12.50-18.00
88-06-006	City Hospital	F. Jones	Retrd.	8.00	12.50-18.00
88-06-007	Lincoln School	F. Jones	Retrd.	8.00	12.50-18.00
88-06-008	Fish/Meat Market	F. Jones	Retrd.	8.00	12.50-18.00
88-06-009	New Masters Gallery	F. Jones	Retrd.	8.00	12.50-18.00
88-06-010	Williams & Sons	F. Jones	Retrd.	8.00	12.50-18.00
The Cat's Meow		**Series VII**			
89-07-001	Thorpe House Bed & Breakfast	F. Jones	5-Yr.	8.00	10.00
89-07-002	Justice of the Peace	F. Jones	5-Yr.	8.00	10.00
89-07-003	Old Franklin Book Shop	F. Jones	5-Yr.	8.00	10.00
89-07-004	Octagonal School	F. Jones	5-Yr.	8.00	10.00
89-07-005	Winkler Bakery	F. Jones	5-Yr.	8.00	10.00
89-07-006	Black Cat Antiques	F. Jones	5-Yr.	8.00	10.00
89-07-007	Village Tinsmith	F. Jones	5-Yr.	8.00	10.00
89-07-008	Williams Apothecary	F. Jones	5-Yr.	8.00	10.00
89-07-009	Handcrafted Toys	F. Jones	5-Yr.	8.00	10.00
89-07-010	Hairdressing Parlor	F. Jones	5-Yr.	8.00	10.00
The Cat's Meow		**Series VIII**			
90-08-001	Puritan House	F. Jones	5-Yr.	8.00	10.00
90-08-002	Haberdashers	F. Jones	5-Yr.	8.00	10.00
90-08-003	Walldorff Furniture	F. Jones	5-Yr.	8.00	10.00
90-08-004	Victoria's Parlour	F. Jones	5-Yr.	8.00	10.00
90-08-005	Globe Corner Bookstore	F. Jones	5-Yr.	8.00	10.00
90-08-006	Medina Fire Department	F. Jones	5-Yr.	8.00	10.00
90-08-007	Piccadilli Pipe & Tobacco	F. Jones	5-Yr.	8.00	10.00
90-08-008	Noah's Ark Veterinary	F. Jones	5-Yr.	8.00	10.00
90-08-009	F.J. Realty Company	F. Jones	5-Yr.	8.00	10.00
90-08-010	Nell's Stems & Stitches	F. Jones	5-Yr.	8.00	10.00
The Cat's Meow		**Series IX**			
91-09-001	Central City Opera House	F. Jones	5-Yr.	8.00	10.00
91-09-002	All Saints Chapel	F. Jones	5-Yr.	8.00	10.00
91-09-003	City Hall	F. Jones	5-Yr.	8.00	10.00
91-09-004	Gov. Snyder Mansion	F. Jones	5-Yr.	8.00	10.00
91-09-005	American Red Cross	F. Jones	5-Yr.	8.00	10.00
91-09-006	The Treble Clef	F. Jones	5-Yr.	8.00	10.00
91-09-007	Osbahr's Upholstery	F. Jones	5-Yr.	8.00	10.00
91-09-008	Spanky's Hardware Co.	F. Jones	5-Yr.	8.00	10.00
91-09-009	CPA/Law Office	F. Jones	5-Yr.	8.00	10.00
91-09-010	Jeweler/Optometrist	F. Jones	5-Yr.	8.00	10.00
The Cat's Meow		**Series X**			
92-10-001	Henyan's Athletic Shop	F. Jones	5-Yr.	8.50	10.00
92-10-002	Grand Haven	F. Jones	5-Yr.	8.50	10.00
92-10-003	Fudge Kitchen	F. Jones	5-Yr.	8.50	10.00
92-10-004	United Church of Acworth	F. Jones	5-Yr.	8.50	10.00
92-10-005	City News	F. Jones	5-Yr.	8.50	10.00
92-10-006	Pure Gas Station	F. Jones	5-Yr.	8.50	10.00
92-10-007	Pickles Pub	F. Jones	5-Yr.	8.50	10.00
92-10-008	Madeline's Dress Shop	F. Jones	5-Yr.	8.50	10.00
92-10-009	Owl And The Pussycat	F. Jones	5-Yr.	8.50	10.00
92-10-010	Leppert's 5 &10¢	F. Jones	5-Yr.	8.50	10.00
The Cat's Meow		**Series XI**			
93-11-001	Shrimplin & Jones Produce	F. Jones	5-Yr.	9.00	10.00
93-11-002	Johann Singer Boots & Shoes	F. Jones	5-Yr.	9.00	10.00
93-11-003	Haddonfield Bank	F. Jones	5-Yr.	9.00	10.00
93-11-004	Stone's Restaurant	F. Jones	5-Yr.	9.00	10.00
93-11-005	U.S. Post Office	F. Jones	5-Yr.	9.00	10.00
93-11-006	Police-Troop C	F. Jones	5-Yr.	9.00	10.00
93-11-007	Immanuel Church	F. Jones	5-Yr.	9.00	10.00
93-11-008	Barbershop/Gallery	F. Jones	5-Yr.	9.00	10.00
93-11-009	U.S. Armed Forces	F. Jones	5-Yr.	9.00	10.00
93-11-010	Pet Shop/Gift Shop	F. Jones	5-Yr.	9.00	10.00
The Cat's Meow		**Series XII**			
94-12-001	Spread Eagle Tavern	F. Jones	5-Yr.	10.00	10.00
94-12-002	Historical Society	F. Jones	5-Yr.	10.00	10.00
94-12-003	Haddon Hts. Train Depot	F. Jones	5-Yr.	10.00	10.00
94-12-004	Arnold-Lynch Funeral Home	F. Jones	5-Yr.	10.00	10.00
94-12-005	Boyd's Drug Strore	F. Jones	5-Yr.	10.00	10.00
94-12-006	Christmas Tree Hill Gifts	F. Jones	5-Yr.	10.00	10.00
94-12-007	Bedford County Courthouse	F. Jones	5-Yr.	10.00	10.00
94-12-008	Foorman-Morrison House	F. Jones	5-Yr.	10.00	10.00
94-12-009	Masonic Temple	F. Jones	5-Yr.	10.00	10.00
94-12-010	Ritz Theater	F. Jones	5-Yr.	10.00	10.00
The Cat's Meow		**Roscoe Village**			
86-13-001	Roscoe General Store	F. Jones	Retrd.	8.00	27-36.00
86-13-002	Jackson Twp. Hall	F. Jones	Retrd.	8.00	27-40.00
86-13-003	Old Warehouse Rest.	F. Jones	Retrd.	8.00	27-36.00
86-13-004	Canal Company	F. Jones	Retrd.	8.00	27-36.00
The Cat's Meow		**Fall**			
86-14-001	Mail Pouch Barn	F. Jones	Retrd.	8.00	27-76.00
86-14-002	Vollant Mills	F. Jones	Retrd.	8.00	27-36.00
86-14-003	Grimm's Farmhouse	F. Jones	Retrd.	8.00	27-45.00
86-14-004	Golden Lamb Buttery	F. Jones	Retrd.	8.00	27-36.00
86-14-005	Set	F. Jones	Retrd.	32.00	125.00
The Cat's Meow		**Nautical**			
87-15-001	Monhegan Boat Landing	F. Jones	Retrd.	8.00	16-27.00
87-15-002	Lorain Lighthouse	F. Jones	Retrd.	8.00	16-27.00
87-15-003	Yacht Club	F. Jones	Retrd.	8.00	16-27.00
87-15-004	H & E Ships Chandlery	F. Jones	Retrd.	8.00	16-27.00
87-15-005	Set	F. Jones	Retrd.	32.00	48.00
The Cat's Meow		**Main St.**			
87-16-001	Historical Museum	F. Jones	Retrd.	8.00	16-33.00
87-16-002	Franklin Library	F. Jones	Retrd.	8.00	16-33.00
87-16-003	Garden Theatre	F. Jones	Retrd.	8.00	16-33.00
87-16-004	Telegraph/Post Office	F. Jones	Retrd.	8.00	16-33.00
87-16-005	Set	F. Jones	Retrd.	32.00	50-90.00
The Cat's Meow		**Nantucket**			
87-17-001	Nantucket Atheneum	F. Jones	Retrd.	8.00	16-40.00
87-17-002	Unitarian Church	F. Jones	Retrd.	8.00	16-27.00
87-17-003	Maria Mitchell House	F. Jones	Retrd.	8.00	16-40.00
87-17-004	Jared Coffin House	F. Jones	Retrd.	8.00	16-27.00
87-17-005	Set	F. Jones	Retrd.	32.00	48.00
The Cat's Meow		**Hagerstown**			
88-18-001	The Yule Cupboard	F. Jones	Retrd.	8.00	18.00
88-18-002	J Hager House	F. Jones	Retrd.	8.00	18.00
88-18-003	Miller House	F. Jones	Retrd.	8.00	18.00
88-18-004	Woman's Club	F. Jones	Retrd.	8.00	18.00
The Cat's Meow		**Tradesman**			
88-19-001	Hermannhof Winery	F. Jones	Retrd.	8.00	18.00
88-19-002	Jenney Grist Mill	F. Jones	Retrd.	8.00	18.00
88-19-003	Buckeye Candy & Tobacco	F. Jones	Retrd.	8.00	18.00
88-19-004	C.O. Wheel Company	F. Jones	Retrd.	8.00	18.00
The Cat's Meow		**Liberty St.**			
88-20-001	County Courthouse	F. Jones	Retrd.	8.00	18.00
88-20-002	Wilton Railway Depot	F. Jones	Retrd.	8.00	18.00
88-20-003	Graf Printing Co.	F. Jones	Retrd.	8.00	18.00
88-20-004	Z. Jones Basketmaker	F. Jones	Retrd.	8.00	18.00
The Cat's Meow		**Painted Ladies**			
88-21-001	Lady Elizabeth	F. Jones	Retrd.	8.00	18.00
88-21-002	Lady Iris	F. Jones	Retrd.	8.00	18.00
88-21-003	Lady Amanda	F. Jones	Retrd.	8.00	18.00
88-21-004	Andrews Hotel	F. Jones	Retrd.	8.00	18.00
The Cat's Meow		**Wild West**			
89-22-001	F.C. Zimmermann's Gun Shop	F. Jones	Retrd.	8.00	18.00
89-22-002	Drink 'em up Saloon	F. Jones	Retrd.	8.00	18.00
89-22-003	Wells, Fargo & Co.	F. Jones	Retrd.	8.00	18.00
89-22-004	Marshal's Office	F. Jones	Retrd.	8.00	18.00
The Cat's Meow		**Market St.**			
89-23-001	Schumacher Mills	F. Jones	Retrd.	8.00	18.00
89-23-002	Seville Hardware Store	F. Jones	Retrd.	8.00	18.00
89-23-003	West India Goods Store	F. Jones	Retrd.	8.00	18.00
89-23-004	Yankee Candle Company	F. Jones	Retrd.	8.00	18.00
The Cat's Meow		**Lighthouse**			
90-24-001	Split Rock Lighthouse	F. Jones	5-Yr.	8.00	10.00
90-24-002	Cape Hatteras Lighthouse	F. Jones	5-Yr.	8.00	10.00
90-24-003	Sandy Hook Lighthouse	F. Jones	5-Yr.	8.00	10.00
90-24-004	Admiralty Head	F. Jones	5-Yr.	8.00	10.00
The Cat's Meow		**Ohio Amish**			
91-25-001	Jonas Troyer Home	F. Jones	5-Yr.	8.00	10.00
91-25-002	Ada Mae's Quilt Barn	F. Jones	5-Yr.	8.00	10.00
91-25-003	Eli's Harness Shop	F. Jones	5-Yr.	8.00	10.00
91-25-004	Brown School	F. Jones	5-Yr.	8.00	10.00
The Cat's Meow		**Washington, D.C.**			
91-26-001	U.S. Capitol	F. Jones	5-Yr.	8.00	10.00
91-26-002	White House	F. Jones	5-Yr.	8.00	10.00
91-26-003	National Archives	F. Jones	5-Yr.	8.00	10.00
91-26-004	U.S. Supreme Court	F. Jones	5-Yr.	8.00	10.00
The Cat's Meow		**American Barns**			
92-27-001	Ohio Barn	F. Jones	5-Yr.	8.50	10.00
92-27-002	Bank Barn	F. Jones	5-Yr.	8.50	10.00
92-27-003	Crib Barn	F. Jones	5-Yr.	8.50	10.00
92-27-004	Vermont Barn	F. Jones	5-Yr.	8.50	10.00
The Cat's Meow		**Chippewa Amusement Park**			
93-28-001	Pavilion	F. Jones	5-Yr.	9.00	10.00
93-28-002	Midway	F. Jones	5-Yr.	9.00	10.00
93-28-003	Bath House	F. Jones	5-Yr.	9.00	10.00
93-28-004	Ballroom	F. Jones	5-Yr.	9.00	10.00
The Cat's Meow		**General Store Series**			
93-29-001	Davoll's General Store	F. Jones	5-Yr.	10.00	10.00
93-29-002	Calef's Country Store	F. Jones	5-Yr.	10.00	10.00
93-29-003	S. Woodstock Country Store	F. Jones	5-Yr.	10.00	10.00
93-29-004	Peltier's Market	F. Jones	5-Yr.	10.00	10.00
The Cat's Meow		**Williamsburg Series**			
93-30-001	Bruton Parish	F. Jones	5-Yr.	10.00	10.00
93-30-002	Raleigh Tavern	F. Jones	5-Yr.	10.00	10.00
93-30-003	Grissell Hay Lodging House	F. Jones	5-Yr.	10.00	10.00
93-30-004	Governor's Palace	F. Jones	5-Yr.	10.00	10.00
The Cat's Meow		**West Coast Lighthouse Series**			
94-31-001	Mukilteo Light	F. Jones	5-Yr.	10.00	10.00
94-31-002	East Brother Lighthouse	F. Jones	5-Yr.	10.00	10.00
94-31-003	Heceta Head Light	F. Jones	5-Yr.	10.00	10.00
94-31-004	Point Pinos Light	F. Jones	5-Yr.	10.00	10.00

Company / Number	Name	Series / Artist	Edition Limit	Issue Price	Quote
The Cat's Meow		**Nursery Rhyme Series**			
94-32-001	Crooked House	F. Jones	5-Yr.	10.00	10.00
94-32-002	Peter, Peter Pumpkin Eater	F. Jones	5-Yr.	10.00	10.00
94-32-003	House That Jack Built	F. Jones	5-Yr.	10.00	10.00
94-32-004	Old Woman in the Shoe	F. Jones	5-Yr.	10.00	10.00
The Cat's Meow		**Firehouse Series**			
94-33-001	Denver No. 1	F. Jones	5-Yr.	10.00	10.00
94-33-002	David Crockett No. 1	F. Jones	5-Yr.	10.00	10.00
94-33-003	Toledo No. 18	F. Jones	5-Yr.	10.00	10.00
94-33-004	Vigilant 1891	F. Jones	5-Yr.	10.00	10.00
The Cat's Meow		**Waterfront Series**			
94-34-001	Seaside Market	F. Jones	5-Yr.	10.00	10.00
94-34-002	Arnold Transit Company	F. Jones	5-Yr.	10.00	10.00
94-34-003	Lowell's Boat Shop	F. Jones	5-Yr.	10.00	10.00
94-34-004	Sand Island Lighthouse	F. Jones	5-Yr.	10.00	10.00
The Cat's Meow		**Elm Street Series**			
94-35-001	Blumenthal's	F. Jones	5-Yr.	10.00	10.00
94-35-002	Jim's Hunting & Fishing	F. Jones	5-Yr.	10.00	10.00
94-35-003	Clyde's Shoe Repair	F. Jones	5-Yr.	10.00	10.00
94-35-004	First Congregational Church	F. Jones	5-Yr.	10.00	10.00
The Cat's Meow		**Duke of Gloucester Series**			
94-36-001	Pasteur & Galt Apothecary	F. Jones	5-Yr.	10.00	10.00
94-36-002	Prentis Shop	F. Jones	5-Yr.	10.00	10.00
94-36-003	Nicolson Store	F. Jones	5-Yr.	10.00	10.00
94-36-004	Cole Shop	F. Jones	5-Yr.	10.00	10.00
The Cat's Meow		**Accessories**			
83-37-001	8" Picket Fence	F. Jones	Retrd.	3.25	12-50.00
83-37-002	5" Hedge	F. Jones	Retrd.	3.00	30-50.00
83-37-003	8" Hedge	F. Jones	Retrd.	3.25	35-60.00
83-37-004	Lilac Bushes	F. Jones	Retrd.	3.00	150.00
83-37-005	5" Iron Fence	F. Jones	Retrd.	3.00	60.00
83-37-006	8" Iron Fence	F. Jones	Retrd.	3.25	60.00
83-37-007	Iron Gate	F. Jones	Retrd.	3.00	65.00
85-37-008	Summer Tree	F. Jones	Retrd.	4.00	40.00
85-37-009	Fall Tree	F. Jones	Retrd.	4.00	26-40.00
85-37-010	Pine Tree	F. Jones	Retrd.	4.00	30.00
85-37-011	Xmas Pine Tree	F. Jones	Retrd.	4.00	30.00
85-37-012	Xmas Pine Tree w/Red Bows	F. Jones	Retrd.	3.00	175-220.
85-37-013	Poplar Tree	F. Jones	Retrd.	4.00	40.00
86-37-014	Dairy Wagon	F. Jones	Retrd.	4.00	10-20.00
86-37-015	Horse & Carriage	F. Jones	Retrd.	4.00	10-20.00
86-37-016	FJ Real Estate Sign	F. Jones	Retrd.	3.00	8-25.00
86-37-017	Chickens	F. Jones	Retrd.	3.25	8-20.00
86-37-018	Ducks	F. Jones	Retrd.	3.25	8-20.00
86-37-019	Cows	F. Jones	Retrd.	4.00	10-20.00
86-37-020	Wells, Fargo Wagon	F. Jones	Retrd.	4.00	10-20.00
86-37-021	Market St. Sign	F. Jones	Retrd.	3.25	8.00
86-37-022	Carolers	F. Jones	Retrd.	4.00	8-20.00
86-37-023	Wishing Well	F. Jones	Retrd.	3.25	10.00
86-37-024	Ice Wagon	F. Jones	Retrd.	4.00	10-20.00
86-37-025	Liberty St. Sign	F. Jones	Retrd.	3.25	8.00
86-37-026	Cable Car	F. Jones	Retrd.	4.00	9.00
87-37-027	Wooden Gate	F. Jones	Retrd.	3.00	50.00
87-37-028	Band Stand	F. Jones	Retrd.	6.50	10-45.00
87-37-029	Horse & Sleigh	F. Jones	Retrd.	4.00	10-12.00
87-37-030	5" Picket Fence	F. Jones	Retrd.	3.00	25.00
87-37-031	FJ Express	F. Jones	Retrd.	4.00	8.00
87-37-032	Railroad Sign	F. Jones	Retrd.	3.00	7.00
87-37-033	Windmill	F. Jones	Retrd.	3.25	8.00-12.50
87-37-034	Butch & T.J.	F. Jones	Retrd.	4.00	7.00-8.50
87-37-035	Charlie & Co.	F. Jones	Retrd.	4.00	8.50
87-37-036	Nanny	F. Jones	Retrd.	4.00	8-15.00
88-37-037	Main St. Sign	F. Jones	Retrd.	3.25	8.00
88-37-038	Colonial Bread Wagon	F. Jones	Retrd.	4.00	7-9.00
88-37-039	Gas Light	F. Jones	Retrd.	4.00	7-9.00
88-37-040	Telephone Booth	F. Jones	Retrd.	4.00	8.00
88-37-041	U.S. Flag	F. Jones	Retrd.	4.00	8.00
88-37-042	Flower Pots	F. Jones	Retrd.	4.00	7.00
88-37-043	Skipjack	F. Jones	Retrd.	6.50	10-13.00
88-37-044	Mail Wagon	F. Jones	Retrd.	4.00	8.00
88-37-045	Street Clock	F. Jones	Retrd.	4.00	8.00
88-37-046	Pony Express Rider	F. Jones	Retrd.	4.00	8.00
89-37-047	Ada Belle	F. Jones	5-Yr.	4.00	4.50
89-37-048	Passenger Train Car	F. Jones	5-Yr.	4.00	4.50
89-37-049	Harry's Hotdogs	F. Jones	5-Yr.	4.00	4.50
89-37-050	Clothesline	F. Jones	5-Yr.	4.00	4.50
89-37-051	Pumpkin Wagon	F. Jones	5-Yr.	3.25	4.50
89-37-052	Rudy & Aldine	F. Jones	5-Yr.	4.00	4.50
89-37-053	Tad & Toni	F. Jones	5-Yr.	4.00	4.50
89-37-054	Snowmen	F. Jones	5-Yr.	4.00	4.50
89-37-055	Rose Trellis	F. Jones	5-Yr.	3.25	4.50
89-37-056	Quaker Oats Train Car	F. Jones	5-Yr.	4.00	4.50
90-37-057	Gerstenslager Buggy	F. Jones	5-Yr.	4.00	4.50
90-37-058	1914 Fire Pumper	F. Jones	5-Yr.	4.00	4.50
90-37-059	1913 Peerless Touring Car	F. Jones	5-Yr.	4.00	4.50
90-37-060	1909 Franklin Limousine	F. Jones	5-Yr.	4.00	4.50
90-37-061	Watkins Wagon	F. Jones	5-Yr.	4.00	4.50
90-37-062	Veterinary Wagon	F. Jones	5-Yr.	4.00	4.50
90-37-063	Amish Buggy	F. Jones	5-Yr.	4.00	4.50
90-37-064	Victorian Outhouse	F. Jones	5-Yr.	4.00	4.50
90-37-065	Bus Stop	F. Jones	5-Yr.	4.00	4.50
90-37-066	Eugene	F. Jones	5-Yr.	4.00	4.50
90-37-067	Christmas Tree Lot	F. Jones	5-Yr.	4.00	4.50
90-37-068	Santa & Reindeer	F. Jones	5-Yr.	4.00	4.50
90-37-069	5" Wrought Iron Fence	F. Jones	5-Yr.	3.00	4.50
90-37-070	Little Red Caboose	F. Jones	5-Yr.	4.00	4.50
90-37-071	Red Maple Tree	F. Jones	5-Yr.	4.00	4.50
90-37-072	Tulip Tree	F. Jones	5-Yr.	4.00	4.50
90-37-073	Blue Spruce	F. Jones	5-Yr.	4.00	4.50
90-37-074	Xmas Spruce	F. Jones	5-Yr.	4.00	4.50
91-37-075	School Bus	F. Jones	5-Yr.	4.00	4.50
91-37-076	Popcorn Wagon	F. Jones	5-Yr.	4.00	4.50
91-37-077	Scarey Harry (Scarecrow)	F. Jones	5-Yr.	4.00	4.50
91-37-078	Amish Garden	F. Jones	5-Yr.	4.00	4.50
91-37-079	Chessie Hopper Car	F. Jones	5-Yr.	4.00	4.50
91-37-080	USMC War Memorial	F. Jones	5-Yr.	6.50	6.50
91-37-081	Village Entrance Sigh	F. Jones	5-Yr.	6.50	6.50
91-37-082	Concert in the Park	F. Jones	5-Yr.	4.00	4.50
91-37-083	Martin House	F. Jones	5-Yr.	3.25	4.50
91-37-084	Marble Game	F. Jones	5-Yr.	4.00	4.50
91-37-085	Barnyard	F. Jones	5-Yr.	4.00	4.50
91-37-086	Ski Party	F. Jones	5-Yr.	4.00	4.50
91-37-087	On Vacation	F. Jones	5-Yr.	4.00	4.50
91-37-088	Jack The Postman	F. Jones	5-Yr.	3.25	4.50
92-37-089	Forsythia Bush	F. Jones	5-Yr.	4.00	4.50
92-37-090	Police Car	F. Jones	5-Yr.	4.00	4.50
92-37-091	Delivery Truck	F. Jones	5-Yr.	4.00	4.50
92-37-092	School Crossing	F. Jones	5-Yr.	4.00	4.50
92-37-093	Mr. Softee Truck	F. Jones	5-Yr.	4.00	4.50
92-37-094	Silo	F. Jones	5-Yr.	4.00	4.50
92-37-095	Springhouse	F. Jones	5-Yr.	3.25	4.50
92-37-096	Nutcracker Billboard	F. Jones	5-Yr.	4.00	4.50
93-37-097	Jennie & George's Wedding	F. Jones	5-Yr.	4.00	4.50
93-37-098	Market Wagon	F. Jones	5-Yr.	4.00	4.50
93-37-099	Chippewa Lake Billboard	F. Jones	5-Yr.	4.00	4.50
93-37-100	Garden House	F. Jones	5-Yr.	3.25	4.50
93-37-101	Johnny Appleseed Statue	F. Jones	5-Yr.	4.00	4.50
93-37-102	Getting Directions	F. Jones	5-Yr.	4.00	4.50
93-37-103	Grape Arbor	F. Jones	5-Yr.	4.00	4.50
93-37-104	Rustic Fence	F. Jones	5-Yr.	4.00	4.50
93-37-105	Cannonball Express	F. Jones	5-Yr.	4.00	4.50
93-37-106	Little Marine	F. Jones	5-Yr.	4.00	4.50
94-37-107	Nativity	F. Jones	5-Yr.	15.00	17.00
94-37-108	Weeping Willow Tree	F. Jones	5-Yr.	4.50	4.50
94-37-109	U.S. Flag	F. Jones	5-Yr.	4.50	4.50
94-37-110	Garden Wall	F. Jones	5-Yr.	4.50	4.50
94-37-111	Lemonade Stand	F. Jones	5-Yr.	4.50	4.50
94-37-112	Street Lamp	F. Jones	5-Yr.	4.50	4.50
94-37-113	Lunch Wagon	F. Jones	5-Yr.	4.50	4.50
94-37-114	Moving Truck	F. Jones	5-Yr.	4.50	4.50
94-37-115	Salvation Army Band	F. Jones	5-Yr.	4.50	4.50
94-37-116	Stock Train Car	F. Jones	5-Yr.	4.50	4.50
94-37-117	Light Ship	F. Jones	5-Yr.	4.50	4.50
94-37-118	Cat & The Fiddle S/2	F. Jones	5-Yr.	4.50	4.50
94-37-119	Apple Tree	F. Jones	5-Yr.	4.50	4.50
94-37-120	Kearsarge Fire Pumper	F. Jones	5-Yr.	4.50	4.50
94-37-121	Wharf	F. Jones	5-Yr.	4.50	4.50
94-37-122	Moving Truck	F. Jones	5-Yr.	4.50	4.50
94-37-123	Yule Tree S/2	F. Jones	5-Yr.	4.50	4.50
94-37-124	Good Humor Man	F. Jones	5-Yr.	4.50	4.50
94-37-125	Gracie (in carriage)	F. Jones	5-Yr.	4.50	4.50
94-37-126	Daily Business (wlbg. people)	F. Jones	5-Yr.	4.50	4.50
The Cat's Meow		**Williamsburg Christmas**			
83-39-001	Christmas Church	F. Jones	Retrd.	6.00	N/A
83-39-002	Garrison House	F. Jones	Retrd.	6.00	N/A
83-39-003	Federal House	F. Jones	Retrd.	6.00	N/A
83-39-004	Georgian House	F. Jones	Retrd.	6.00	450.00
83-39-005	Set	F. Jones	Retrd.	24.00	N/A
The Cat's Meow		**Nantucket Christmas**			
84-40-001	Powell House	F. Jones	Retrd.	6.50	350.00
84-40-002	Shaw House	F. Jones	Retrd.	6.50	350.00
84-40-003	Wintrop House	F. Jones	Retrd.	6.50	N/A
84-40-004	Christmas Shop	F. Jones	Retrd.	6.50	N/A
84-40-005	Set	F. Jones	Retrd.	26.00	400-1350.
The Cat's Meow		**Ohio Western Reserve Christmas**			
85-41-001	Western Reserve Academy	F. Jones	Retrd.	7.00	35-175.00
85-41-002	Olmstead House	F. Jones	Retrd.	7.00	35-175.00
85-41-003	Bellevue House	F. Jones	Retrd.	7.00	35-175.00
85-41-004	Gates Mills Church	F. Jones	Retrd.	7.00	35-175.00
85-41-005	Set	F. Jones	Retrd.	27.00	1250.00
The Cat's Meow		**Savannah Christmas**			
86-42-001	J.J. Dale Row House	F. Jones	Retrd.	7.25	150.00
86-42-002	Liberty Inn	F. Jones	Retrd.	7.25	150.00
86-42-003	Lafayette Square House	F. Jones	Retrd.	7.25	140-150.
86-42-004	Simon Mirault Cottage	F. Jones	Retrd.	7.25	175-300.
86-42-005	Set	F. Jones	Retrd.	29.00	1200.00
The Cat's Meow		**Maine Christmas**			
87-43-001	Damariscotta Church	F. Jones	Retrd.	7.75	300.00
87-43-002	Portland Head Lighthouse	F. Jones	Retrd.	7.75	125-205.
87-43-003	Cappy's Chowder House	F. Jones	Retrd.	7.75	125-200.
87-43-004	Captain's House	F. Jones	Retrd.	7.75	125.00
87-43-005	Set	F. Jones	Retrd.	31.00	750-1350.
The Cat's Meow		**Philadelphia Christmas**			
88-44-001	Graff House	F. Jones	Retrd.	7.75	85.00
88-44-002	Hill-Physick-Keith House	F. Jones	Retrd.	7.75	85.00
88-44-003	Elfreth's Alley	F. Jones	Retrd.	7.75	85.00
88-44-004	The Head House	F. Jones	Retrd.	7.75	85.00
88-44-005	Set	F. Jones	Retrd.	31.00	400-500.
The Cat's Meow		**Christmas In New England**			
89-45-001	The Old South Meeting House	F. Jones	Retrd.	8.00	65.00
89-45-002	Hunter House	F. Jones	Retrd.	8.00	65-85.00
89-45-003	Sheldon's Tavern	F. Jones	Retrd.	8.00	65.00
89-45-004	The Vermont Country Store	F. Jones	Retrd.	8.00	65.00
89-45-005	Set	F. Jones	Retrd.	32.00	300-450.
The Cat's Meow		**Colonial Virginia Christmas**			
90-46-001	Rising Sun Tavern	F. Jones	Retrd.	8.00	55.00
90-46-002	St. John's Church	F. Jones	Retrd.	8.00	55.00
90-46-003	Dulany House	F. Jones	Retrd.	8.00	55.00
90-46-004	Shirley Plantation	F. Jones	Retrd.	8.00	55.00
90-46-005	Set	F. Jones	Retrd.	32.00	350.00
The Cat's Meow		**Rocky Mountain Christmas**			
91-47-001	First Presbyterian Church	F. Jones	Retrd.	8.20	28-40.00
91-47-002	Tabor House	F. Jones	Retrd.	8.20	28-80.00
91-47-003	Western Hotel	F. Jones	Retrd.	8.20	28-60.00
91-47-004	Wheller-Stallard House	F. Jones	Retrd.	8.20	28.00
91-47-005	Set	F. Jones	Retrd.	32.80	100-150.
The Cat's Meow		**Hometown Christmas**			
92-48-001	Wayne Co. Courthouse	F. Jones	Retrd.	8.50	16-20.00
92-48-002	Overholt House	F. Jones	Retrd.	8.50	16-20.00
92-48-003	August Imgard House	F. Jones	Retrd.	8.50	16-20.00
92-48-004	Howey House	F. Jones	Retrd.	8.50	16-20.00
92-48-005	Set	F. Jones	Retrd.	34.00	48-75.00

Company		Series			
Number	**Name**	**Artist**	**Edition Limit**	**Issue Price**	**Quote**
The Cat's Meow		**St. Charles Christmas**			
93-49-001	Newbill-McElhiney House	F. Jones	Retrd.	10.00	10.00
93-49-002	St. Peter's Catholic Church	F. Jones	Retrd.	10.00	10.00
93-49-003	Lewis & Clark Center	F. Jones	Retrd.	10.00	10.00
93-49-004	Stone Row	F. Jones	Retrd.	10.00	10.00
The Cat's Meow		**New Orleans Christmas Series**			
94-50-001	Gallier House	F. Jones	12/94	9.00	9.00
94-50-002	St. Patrick's Church	F. Jones	12/94	9.00	9.00
94-50-003	Beauregard-Keyes House	F. Jones	12/94	9.00	9.00
94-50-004	Hermann-Grima House	F. Jones	12/94	9.00	9.00
The Cat's Meow		**Collector Club Gift - Houses**			
89-51-001	Betsy Ross House	F. Jones	Retrd.	Gift	250.00
90-51-002	Amelia Earhart	F. Jones	Retrd.	Gift	150.00
91-51-003	Limberlost Cabin	F. Jones	Retrd.	Gift	N/A
92-51-004	Abigail Adams Birthplace	F. Jones	Retrd.	Gift	N/A
93-51-005	Pearl S. Buck House	F. Jones	Yr.Iss.	Gift	N/A
93-51-005	Set	F. Jones	Yr.Iss.	Gift	450.00
The Cat's Meow		**Collector Club Pieces - Famous Authors**			
89-52-001	Harriet Beecher Stowe	F. Jones	Retrd.	8.75	85.00
89-52-002	Orchard House	F. Jones	Retrd.	8.75	85.00
89-52-003	Longfellow House	F. Jones	Retrd.	8.75	85.00
89-52-004	Herman Melville's Arrowhead	F. Jones	Retrd.	8.75	85.00
89-52-005	Set	F. Jones	Retrd.	35.00	850.00
The Cat's Meow		**Collector Club Pieces - Great Inventors**			
90-53-001	Thomas Edison	F. Jones	Retrd.	9.25	N/A
90-53-002	Ford Motor Co.	F. Jones	Retrd.	9.25	N/A
90-53-003	Seth Thomas Clock Co.	F. Jones	Retrd.	9.25	N/A
90-53-004	Wright Cycle Co.	F. Jones	Retrd.	9.25	N/A
90-53-005	Set	F. Jones	Retrd.	37.00	500.00
The Cat's Meow		**Collector Club Pieces - American Songwriters**			
91-54-001	Benjamin R. Hanby House	F. Jones	Retrd.	9.25	N/A
91-54-002	Anna Warner House	F. Jones	Retrd.	9.25	N/A
91-54-003	Stephen Foster Home	F. Jones	Retrd.	9.25	N/A
91-54-004	Oscar Hammerstein House	F. Jones	Retrd.	9.25	N/A
91-54-005	Set	F. Jones	Retrd.	37.00	100.00
The Cat's Meow		**Collector Club Pieces - Signers of the Declaration**			
92-55-001	Josiah Bartlett Home	F. Jones	Retrd.	9.75	9.75
92-55-002	George Clymer Home	F. Jones	Retrd.	9.75	9.75
92-55-003	Stephen Hopkins Home	F. Jones	Retrd.	9.75	9.75
92-55-004	John Witherspoon Home	F. Jones	Retrd.	9.75	9.75
The Cat's Meow		**Collector Club Pieces -19th Century Master Builders**			
93-56-001	Henry Hobson Richardson	F. Jones	Yr.Iss.	10.25	10.25
93-56-002	Samuel Sloan	F. Jones	Yr.Iss.	10.25	10.25
93-56-003	Alexander Jackson Davis	F. Jones	Yr.Iss.	10.25	10.25
93-56-004	Andrew Jackson Downing	F. Jones	Yr.Iss.	10.25	10.25
The Cat's Meow		**Collector Club Pieces - Williamsburg Merchants**			
94-57-001	East Carlton Wigmaker	F. Jones	Yr.Iss.	46.50	46.50
94-57-002	J. Geddy Silversmith	F. Jones	Yr.Iss.	set	set
94-57-003	Craig Jeweler	F. Jones	Yr.Iss.	set	set
94-57-004	M. Hunter Millinery	F. Jones	Yr.Iss.	set	set
The Cat's Meow		**Miscellaneous**			
85-58-001	Pencil Holder	F. Jones	Retrd.	3.95	210.00
85-58-002	Recipe Holder	F. Jones	Retrd.	3.95	210.00
The Cat's Meow		**Limited Edition Promotional Items**			
90-59-001	Frycrest Farm Homestead	F. Jones	Retrd.	10.00	10.00
92-59-002	Glen Pine	F. Jones	Retrd.	10.00	10.00
93-59-003	F.J. Factory	F. Jones	Open	12.95	12.95
93-59-004	F.J. Factory/Gold Cat Edition	F. Jones	Retrd.	12.95	12.95
93-59-005	Convention Museum	F. Jones	Retrd.	12.95	12.95
93-59-006	Nativity Cat on the Fence	F. Jones	Retrd.	19.95	19.95
Classic Collectibles by Uniquely Yours		**Limited Edition Santas**			
89-01-001	Kris Kringle	E. Tisa	Closed	178.00	230.00
89-01-002	Father Christmas	E. Tisa	Closed	138.00	190.00
89-01-003	Father Christmas-sm.	E. Tisa	Closed	48.00	56.00
89-01-004	Olde World Santa	E. Tisa	Closed	48.00	56.00
90-01-005	Jolly St. Nick	E. Tisa	250	104.00	130.00
91-01-006	Victorian Santa	E. Tisa	1,500	196.00	230.00
91-01-007	European Santa w/Little Girl	E. Tisa	1,000	118.00	150.00
93-01-008	Olde World Santa	E. Tisa	300	270.00	270.00
93-01-009	Traditional Santa in Sleigh	E. Tisa	400	160.00	170.00
93-01-010	Renaissance Santa	E. Tisa	450	210.00	230.00
93-01-011	Pere Noel	E. Tisa	500	350.00	350.00
94-01-012	Black Santa on Tricycle	E. Tisa	600	160.00	160.00
94-01-013	Santa on Tricycle	E. Tisa	600	160.00	160.00
Classic Collectibles by Uniquely Yours		**Additional Santas**			
89-02-001	Santa at Work	E. Tisa	Open	68.00	98.00
90-02-002	St. Nicholas	E. Tisa	Open	76.00	94.00
91-02-003	Mrs. Claus	E. Tisa	Open	36.00	48.00
93-02-004	Russian Santa	E. Tisa	Open	72.00	72.00
93-02-005	Olde English Santa	E. Tisa	Open	66.00	66.00
Classic Collectibles by Uniquely Yours		**Dicken's-A Christmas Carol**			
86-03-001	Single Woman Caroler	E. Tisa	Closed	N/A	N/A
86-03-002	Single Man Caroler	E. Tisa	Closed	N/A	N/A
86-03-003	Single Girl Caroler	E. Tisa	Closed	N/A	N/A
86-03-004	Single Boy Caroler	E. Tisa	Closed	N/A	N/A
88-03-005	Bob Cratchit and Tiny Tim	E. Tisa	Open	68.00	86.00
88-03-006	Marley's Ghost	E. Tisa	Open	36.00	54.00
88-03-007	Ghost of Christmas Past	E. Tisa	Open	36.00	48.00
88-03-008	Ghost of Christmas Present	E. Tisa	Open	68.00	86.00
88-03-009	Ghost of Christmas Yet To Be	E. Tisa	Open	48.00	72.00
88-03-010	Mr. & Mrs. Fezziwig	E. Tisa	Open	78.00	88.00
88-03-011	Mrs. Crachit	E. Tisa	Open	36.00	48.00
88-03-012	Scrooge	E. Tisa	Open	36.00	48.00
88-03-013	Boy on Sled	E. Tisa	Open	32.00	44.00
88-03-014	Girl in a Sleigh	E. Tisa	Open	36.00	52.00
89-03-015	Adult Carolers	E. Tisa	Open	78.00	88.00
89-03-016	Senior Carolers	E. Tisa	Open	78.00	88.00
89-03-017	Children Carolers	E. Tisa	Open	68.00	84.00
88-03-018	Match Girl	E. Tisa	Closed	68.00	68.00
89-03-019	Victorian Band	E. Tisa	Closed	144.00	144.00
89-03-020	Scrooge & Marley	E. Tisa	Closed	78.00	78.00
89-03-021	Christmas Present (vingette w/feast)	E. Tisa	Closed	90.00	90.00
90-03-022	Lighting the Menorrah	E. Tisa	Closed	96.00	96.00
Classic Collectibles by Uniquely Yours		**Dicken's-A Christmas Carol (Miniatures)**			
87-04-001	Tiny Tim & Bob	E. Tisa	Closed	60.00	60.00
87-04-002	Marley's Ghost	E. Tisa	Closed	40.00	40.00
87-04-003	Christmas Past	E. Tisa	Closed	40.00	40.00
87-04-004	Christmas Present	E. Tisa	Closed	40.00	40.00
87-04-005	Christmas Yet to Be	E. Tisa	Closed	32.00	32.00
87-04-007	Mrs. Fezziwig	E. Tisa	Closed	40.00	40.00
87-04-008	Mr. Fezzziwig	E. Tisa	Closed	40.00	40.00
87-04-009	Scrooge	E. Tisa	Closed	40.00	40.00
87-04-010	Mrs. Cratchit	E. Tisa	Closed	42.00	42.00
87-04-011	Belle	E. Tisa	Closed	40.00	40.00
87-04-012	Father Christmas	E. Tisa	Closed	40.00	40.00
Classic Collectibles by Uniquely Yours		**Victorian**			
89-05-001	Victorian Woman	E. Tisa	Closed	36.00	36.00
89-05-002	Victorian Man	E. Tisa	Closed	40.00	40.00
89-05-003	Victorian Girl	E. Tisa	Closed	36.00	36.00
89-05-004	Victorian Boy w/Hoop	E. Tisa	Closed	36.00	36.00
89-05-005	Victorian Treetop Angel	E. Tisa	Open	80.00	80.00
Classic Collectibles by Uniquely Yours		**Thanksgiving**			
88-06-001	Pilgrim-Woman	E. Tisa	Closed	38.00	38.00
88-06-002	Pilgrim-Man	E. Tisa	Closed	40.00	40.00
Classic Collectibles by Uniquely Yours		**Halloween**			
89-07-001	Trick or Treat-Devil	E. Tisa	Closed	36.00	36.00
89-07-002	Trick or Treat-Witch	E. Tisa	Closed	32.00	32.00
89-07-003	Ghoul	E. Tisa	Closed	38.00	38.00
Classic Collectibles by Uniquely Yours		**Easter**			
89-08-001	Boy w/Easter Basket	E. Tisa	Closed	36.00	36.00
89-08-002	Girl w/Bunnies	E. Tisa	Closed	36.00	36.00
Classic Collectibles by Uniquely Yours		**Valentine's Day**			
90-09-001	Valentine-Girl	E. Tisa	Closed	36.00	36.00
90-09-002	Valentine-Boy	E. Tisa	Closed	36.00	36.00
Classic Collectibles by Uniquely Yours		**Miscellaneous**			
88-10-001	Bride	E. Tisa	Closed	40.00	40.00
88-10-002	Groom	E. Tisa	Closed	40.00	40.00
89-10-003	Mother & Daughter	E. Tisa	Closed	68.00	68.00
89-10-004	African Woman	E. Tisa	Closed	36.00	36.00
89-10-005	African Man	E. Tisa	Closed	40.00	40.00
89-10-006	Christmas Child	E. Tisa	Closed	22.00	22.00
89-10-007	Christmas Shopper	E. Tisa	Closed	26.00	26.00
Creart		**African Wildlife**			
86-01-001	Running Elephant -73	Perez	2,500	260.00	320.00
87-01-002	African Elephant -10	Perez	S/O	410.00	575.00
87-01-003	African Elephant With Leaf -22	Martinez	2,500	230.00	280.00
87-01-004	Giraffe -43	Perez	2,500	250.00	320.00
87-01-005	Cob Antelope -46	Perez	2,500	310.00	370.00
87-01-006	African Lion -61	Martinez	2,500	260.00	320.00
87-01-007	Zebra -67	Perez	2,500	305.00	380.00
87-01-008	White Rhinoceros -136	Perez	2,500	330.00	410.00
90-01-009	Symbol of Power Lion -40	Quezada	2,500	450.00	470.00
90-01-010	Hippopotamus -55	Quezeda	2,500	420.00	420.00
91-01-011	Breaking Away Gazelles -256	Quezeda	1,500	650.00	650.00
91-01-012	Sound of Warning Elephant -268	Perez	2,500	500.00	500.00
92-01-013	Small African Elephant- 271	Perez	2,500	320.00	320.00
93-01-014	Travieso-358	Perez	1,500	198.00	198.00
93-01-015	Cobe Buffalo-412	Contreras	1,500	420.00	420.00
94-01-016	Numa Lion-433	Contreras	2,500	N/A	N/A
94-01-017	Love For Ever Elephant-436	Contreras	2,500	N/A	N/A
94-01-018	Grumbler Cape Buffalo-451	Martinez	1,500	N/A	N/A
Creart		**American Wildlife**			
85-02-001	Pigeons- 64	Perez	Closed	265.00	265.00
86-02-002	Polar Bear- 58	Martinez	2,500	200.00	240.00
86-02-003	Bald Eagle- 70	Martinez	Susp.	730.00	900.00
86-02-004	American Bison- 121	Perez	Susp.	400.00	490.00
87-02-005	Grizzley Bear- 31	Perez	2,500	210.00	270.00
87-02-006	Royal Eagle- 49	Martinez	Closed	545.00	598.00
87-02-007	Puma- 130	Perez	2,500	370.00	470.00
88-02-008	Mammoth-112	Martinez	2,500	450.00	550.00
88-02-009	Flamingo Upright-169	Perez	2,500	230.00	294.00
88-02-010	Flamingo Head Down-172	Perez	2,500	230.00	294.00
88-02-011	Flamingo Flapping-175	Perez	2,500	230.00	298.00
89-02-012	Jaguar- 79	Gonzalez	500	700.00	750.00
89-02-013	Rooster- R40	Martinez	Closed	290.00	290.00
89-02-014	Penguins- R76	Del Valle	Closed	175.00	175.00
90-02-015	The Challenge, Rams- 82	Gonzalez	1,500	698.00	698.00
90-02-016	Over the Clouds Falcon- 85	Martinez	2,500	520.00	520.00
90-02-017	Gray Wolf- 88	Quezada	2,500	365.00	370.00
90-02-018	Dolphin, Front- 142	Perez	2,500	210.00	236.00
90-02-019	Dolphin, Middle- 145	Perez	2,500	210.00	236.00
90-02-020	Dolphin, Back- 148	Perez	2,500	210.00	236.00
90-02-021	White Tail Deer- 151	Martinez	2,500	380.00	460.00
90-02-022	White Tail Doe- 154	Martinez	2,500	330.00	400.00
90-02-023	White Tail Fawn- 157	Martinez	2,500	220.00	280.00
91-02-024	White Hunter Polar Bear- 250	Gonzalez	2,500	380.00	390.00
91-02-025	Royal Eagle With Snake- 259	Martinez	2,500	700.00	700.00
91-02-026	Mischievous Raccoon- 262	Quezada	2,500	370.00	370.00
91-02-027	Playmates Sparrows- 265	Martinez	2,500	500.00	500.00
92-02-028	Soaring Royal Eagle- 52	Martinez	2,500	580.00	580.00
92-02-029	Penguins- 76	Perez	2,500	100.00	100.00
92-02-030	Standing Whitetail Deer- 109	Martinez	2,500	364.00	364.00
92-02-031	California Grizzly- 238	Perez	2,500	270.00	270.00
93-02-032	The Red Fox- 220	Contreras	1,500	199.00	199.00
93-02-033	Howling Coyote- 217	Martinez	1,500	199.00	199.00
93-02-034	Scent of Honey Bear-223	Perez	1,500	398.00	398.00
93-02-035	Buenos Dias Jack Rabbit-229	Martinez	1,500	218.00	218.00
94-02-036	Sky Queen Eagle-436	Martinez	1,500	N/A	N/A
94-02-037	Singing to the Moon I Wolf-439	Perez	1,500	438.00	438.00
94-02-038	Singing to the Moon II Wolf-442	Perez	1,500	N/A	N/A
94-02-039	Waiting in Ambush Puma-445	Perez	1,500	N/A	N/A
94-02-040	Catamountain-603	Estevez	2,500	138.00	138.00
94-02-041	Puffins-606	Estevez	1,500	260.00	260.00
94-02-042	The American Cougar-612	Estevez	1,500	138.00	138.00

Company / Number	Name	Series / Artist	Edition Limit	Issue Price	Quote
Creart		**Wild America Edition**			
92-03-001	Puma Head- 334	Perez	900	320.00	320.00
92-03-002	Twelve Pointer Deer- 337	Perez	900	472.00	472.00
93-03-003	White Blizzard- 331	Perez	1,500	275.00	275.00
93-03-004	American Symbol- 328	Contreras	1,500	246.00	246.00
93-03-005	Wild America Bison-409	Contreras	1,500	338.00	338.00
Creart		**Horses And Cattle**			
85-04-001	Running Horse- 7	Martinez	2,500	360.00	440.00
85-04-002	Arabian Horse- 34	Martinez	2,500	230.00	280.00
85-04-003	Bull- 28	Martinez	Susp.	285.00	285.00
87-04-004	Horse In Passage- 127	Martinez	2,500	500.00	550.00
88-04-005	Horse Head- 139	Martinez	2,500	440.00	448.00
89-04-006	Quarter Horse Recoil- 1	Gonzalez	Closed	310.00	310.00
89-04-007	Brahma Bull- 13	Gonzalez	2,500	420.00	470.00
89-04-008	Arabian Horse- 91	Perez	2,500	260.00	270.00
89-04-009	Lippizzan Horse- 94	Perez	2,500	260.00	270.00
89-04-010	Thoroughbred Horse-97	Perez	2,500	260.00	270.00
89-04-011	Apaloosa Horse- 100	Martinez	2,500	260.00	270.00
89-04-012	Quarter Horse II- 103	Perez	2,500	260.00	270.00
92-04-013	Pegasus- 106	Perez	2,500	420.00	420.00
93-04-014	Rosie Bella-421	Martinez	1,500	758.00	758.00
Creart		**From Asia & Europe**			
85-05-001	Indian Elephant Mother- 25	Perez	Susp.	485.00	490.00
85-05-002	Marco Polo Sheep- 37	Martinez	2,500	270.00	300.00
85-05-003	Tiger- R55	Martinez	Closed	200.00	200.00
86-05-004	Deer- 4	Martinez	Closed	560.00	600.00
86-05-005	Indian Elephant Baby- 16	Perez	Susp.	200.00	200.00
87-05-006	Drover of Camels- 124	Martinez	2,500	650.00	700.00
87-05-007	Royal Owl- 133	Perez	Closed	340.00	370.00
88-05-008	Bengal Tiger- 115	Perez	Closed	440.00	520.00
90-05-009	Giant Panda- 244	Martinez	2,500	280.00	290.00
Creart		**Pets**			
87-06-001	Labrador Retriever- 19	Martinez	2,500	300.00	350.00
89-06-002	Cocker Spaniel American- 184	Martinez	Susp.	100.00	100.00
89-06-003	Boxer- 187	Martinez	Susp.	135.00	135.00
89-06-004	Schnauzer Miniature- 190	Perez	Susp.	110.00	110.00
89-06-005	Great Dane, Brown- 193	Martinez	Susp.	140.00	140.00
89-06-006	Great Dane, Harlequi- 196	Martinez	Susp.	140.00	140.00
89-06-007	Pointer, Brown- 199	Perez	Susp.	132.00	132.00
89-06-008	Pointer, Black- 202	Perez	Susp.	132.00	132.00
89-06-009	Poodle- 205	Perez	Susp.	120.00	120.00
89-06-010	Saint Bernard- 208	Perez	Susp.	130.00	130.00
89-06-011	Labrador, Golden- 211	Martinez	Susp.	130.00	130.00
89-06-012	Labrador, Black- 214	Martinez	Susp.	130.00	130.00
91-06-013	German Shepherd Dog- 253	Martinez	2,500	360.00	370.00
Creart		**Nature's Care Collection**			
93-07-001	Penguin and Chicks- 76	A.Del Valle	2,500	99.00	112.00
93-07-002	Otters- 325	Estevez	2,500	99.00	110.00
93-07-003	Grizzly and Cubs- 340	Contreras	2,500	99.00	110.00
93-07-004	Jack Rabbit and Young- 343	Martinez	2,500	99.00	110.00
93-07-005	Lioness and Cubs- 346	Contreras	2,500	99.00	110.00
93-07-006	Wolf and Pups- 349	Contreras	2,500	99.00	110.00
93-07-007	Doe and Fawns- 355	Contreras	2,500	99.00	134.00
93-07-008	Gorilla and Baby- 394	Contreras	2,500	99.00	100.00
93-07-009	Eagle and Eaglets-352	Contreras	2,500	120.00	120.00
Creart		**Birds of Prey**			
94-08-001	Gyrfalcon-600	Robison	450	1300.00	1300.00
94-08-002	The Vantage Point Eagle-609	Robison	650	780.00	780.00
94-08-003	Urban Release Peregrine Falcon-615	Robison	650	N/A	N/A
Crystal World		**Limited Edition Series**			
85-01-001	Extra Large-Empire State Building	R. Nakai	Closed	1000.00	1300.00
86-01-002	The Eiffel Tower	T. Suzuki	2,000	1000.00	1300.00
86-01-003	Airplane	T. Suzuki	Closed	400.00	500.00
86-01-004	Crucifix	N. Mulargia	Closed	300.00	400.00
87-01-005	Taj Mahal	T. Suzuki	2,000	2000.00	2100.00
87-01-006	Large Empire State	R. Nakai	2,000	650.00	700.00
87-01-007	Large US Capitol Building	T. Suzuki	Closed	1000.00	1100.00
87-01-008	Manhattanscape	G. Veith	Closed	1000.00	1100.00
88-01-009	Small Eiffel Tower	T. Suzuki	2,000	500.00	600.00
89-01-010	Grand Castle	R. Nakai	1,500	2500.00	2500.00
89-01-011	Dream Castle	R. Nakai	500	9000.00	10000.00
89-01-012	Space Shuttle Launch	T. Suzuki	Closed	900.00	1000.00
90-01-013	Tower Bridge	T. Suzuki	Closed	600.00	650.00
91-01-014	Cruise Ship	T. Suzuki	1,000	2000.00	2100.00
91-01-015	Ellis Island	R. Nakai	Closed	450.00	500.00
92-01-016	Santa Maria	N. Mulargia	Closed	1000.00	1050.00
92-01-017	The White House	R. Nakai	Closed	3000.00	3000.00
93-01-018	Country Gristmill	T. Suzuki	1,250	320.00	320.00
93-01-019	Victorian House	N. Mulargia	2,000	190.00	190.00
93-01-020	Enchanted Castle	R. Nakai	750	800.00	800.00
93-01-021	Riverboat	N. Mulargia	350	570.00	570.00
Crystal World		**Bird Collection**			
83-02-001	Large Owl	R. Nakai	Closed	44.00	75.00
83-02-002	Small Owl	R. Nakai	Closed	22.00	36.00
83-02-003	Owl Standing	R. Nakai	Closed	40.00	70.00
84-02-004	Love Bird	R. Nakai	Closed	44.00	65.00
84-02-005	Bird Family	R. Nakai	Closed	22.00	35.00
85-02-006	Extra Large Parrot	R. Nakai	Closed	300.00	450.00
85-02-007	Large Parrot	R. Nakai	Closed	100.00	150.00
85-02-008	Small Parrot	R. Nakai	Closed	30.00	45.00
86-02-009	Love Birds	N. Mulargia	Closed	54.00	75.00
86-02-010	Bird Bath	N. Mulargia	Closed	54.00	75.00
87-02-011	Small Parrot	R. Nakai	Closed	96.00	110.00
87-02-012	Large Parrot	R. Nakai	Closed	130.00	170.00
90-02-013	Tree Top Owls	T. Suzuki	Closed	55.00	75.00
90-02-014	Wise Owl	T. Suzuki	Closed	55.00	65.00
90-02-015	Small Wise Owl	T. Suzuki	Closed	40.00	45.00
90-02-016	Ollie Owl	T. Suzuki	Closed	32.00	40.00
91-02-017	Parrot Couple	R. Nakai	Closed	90.00	100.00
CUI/Carolina Collection/Dram Tree		**Legends of Santa Claus**			
91-01-001	Checkin' it Twice	Christjohn	Retrd.	60.00	60.00
91-01-002	Have You Been a Good Little Boy	Christjohn	Retrd.	60.00	60.00
91-01-003	Have You Been a Good Little Girl	Christjohn	Retrd.	60.00	60.00
91-01-004	Mrs. Claus	Christjohn	Retrd.	60.00	60.00
91-01-005	Won't You Guide My Sleigh Tonight	Christjohn	Retrd.	60.00	60.00
91-01-006	With A Finger Aside His Nose	Christjohn	Retrd.	60.00	60.00

Company / Number	Name	Series / Artist	Edition Limit	Issue Price	Quote
CUI/Carolina Collection/Dram Tree		**Texaco Fire Chief Pups**			
92-02-001	Christmas Dalmations	Unknown	Open	49.50	49.50
93-02-002	Glide Away Starts	Unknown	Open	49.50	49.50
CUI/Carolina Collection/Dram Tree		**First Encounter Series**			
93-03-001	Stand Off	R. Cruwys	Open	49.50	49.50
Cybis		**Animal Kingdom**			
71-01-001	American Bullfrog	Cybis	Closed	250.00	600.00
75-01-002	American White Buffalo	Cybis	250	1250.00	4000.00
71-01-003	Appaloosa Colt	Cybis	Closed	150.00	300.00
80-01-004	Arctic White Fox	Cybis	100	4500.00	4700.00
84-01-005	Australian Greater Sulpher Crested Cockatoo	Cybis	25	9850.00	9850.00
85-01-006	Baxter and Doyle	Cybis	400	450.00	450.00
68-01-007	Bear	Cybis	Closed	85.00	400.00
85-01-008	Beagles, Branigan and Clancy	Cybis	Open	375.00	625.00
81-01-009	Beavers, Egbert and Brewster	Cybis	400	285.00	335.00
68-01-010	Buffalo	Cybis	Closed	115.00	185.00
XX-01-011	Bull	Cybis	100	150.00	4500.00
76-01-012	Bunny, Muffet	Cybis	Closed	85.00	150.00
77-01-013	Bunny Pat-a-Cake	Cybis	Closed	90.00	150.00
85-01-014	Bunny, Snowflake	Cybis	Open	65.00	75.00
84-01-015	Chantilly, Kitten	Cybis	Open	175.00	210.00
76-01-016	Chipmunk w/Bloodroot	Cybis	225	625.00	675.00
69-01-017	Colts, Darby and Joan	Cybis	Closed	295.00	475.00
82-01-018	Dall Sheep	Cybis	50	Unkn.	4250.00
86-01-019	Dapple Grey Foal	Cybis	Open	195.00	250.00
70-01-020	Deer Mouse in Clover	Cybis	Closed	65.00	160.00
78-01-021	Dormouse, Maximillian	Cybis	Closed	250.00	285.00
78-01-022	Dormouse, Maxine	Cybis	Closed	195.00	225.00
68-01-023	Elephant	Cybis	100	600.00	5000.00
85-01-024	Elephant, Willoughby	Cybis	Open	195.00	245.00
61-01-025	Horse	Cybis	100	150.00	2000.00
86-01-026	Huey, the Harmonious Hare	Cybis	Open	175.00	275.00
67-01-027	Kitten, Blue Ribbon	Cybis	Closed	95.00	500.00
75-01-028	Kitten, Tabitha	Cybis	Closed	90.00	150.00
75-01-029	Kitten, Topaz	Cybis	Closed	90.00	150.00
86-01-030	Mick, The Melodious Mutt	Cybis	Open	175.00	275.00
85-01-031	Monday, Rhinoceros	Cybis	Open	85.00	150.00
71-01-032	Nashua	Cybis	100	2000.00	3000.00
78-01-033	Pinky Bunny/Carrot	Cybis	200	200.00	265.00
72-01-034	Pinto Colt	Cybis	Closed	175.00	250.00
76-01-035	Prairie Dog	Cybis	Closed	245.00	345.00
65-01-036	Raccoon, Raffles	Cybis	Closed	110.00	365.00
68-01-038	Snail, Sir Escargot	Cybis	Closed	50.00	300.00
65-01-039	Squirrel, Mr. Fluffy Tail	Cybis	Closed	90.00	350.00
80-01-040	Squirrel, Highrise	Cybis	400	475.00	525.00
68-01-041	Stallion	Cybis	350	475.00	850.00
66-01-042	Thoroughbred	Cybis	350	425.00	1500.00
86-01-043	White Tailed Deer	Cybis	50	9500.00	11500.00
Cybis		**Biblical**			
60-02-001	Exodus	Cybis	50	350.00	2600.00
60-02-002	Flight Into Egypt	Cybis	50	175.00	2500.00
56-02-003	Holy Child of Prague	Cybis	10	1500.00	N/A
XX-02-004	Holywater Font "Holy Ghost"	Cybis	Closed	15.00	145.00
57-02-005	Madonna, House of Gold	Cybis	8	125.00	4000.00
60-02-006	Madonna Lace & Rose	Cybis	Open	15.00	295.00
63-02-007	Moses, The Great Lawgiver	Cybis	750	250.00	5500.00
84-02-008	Nativity, Mary	Cybis	Open	Unkn.	325.00
84-02-009	Nativity, Joseph	Cybis	Open	Unkn.	325.00
84-02-010	Christ Child with Lamb	Cybis	Open	Unkn.	290.00
84-02-011	Nativity, Angel, Color	Cybis	Open	395.00	575.00
84-02-012	Nativity, Camel, Color	Cybis	Open	625.00	825.00
85-02-013	Nativity, Cow, Color	Cybis	Open	175.00	195.00
85-02-014	Nativity, Cow, White	Cybis	Open	125.00	225.00
85-02-015	Nativity, Donkey, Color	Cybis	Open	195.00	225.00
85-02-016	Nativity, Donkey, White	Cybis	Open	130.00	150.00
85-02-017	Nativity, Lamb, Color	Cybis	Open	150.00	195.00
85-02-018	Nativity, Lamb, White	Cybis	Open	115.00	125.00
84-02-019	Nativity, Shepherd, Color	Cybis	Open	395.00	475.00
76-02-020	Noah	Cybis	500	975.00	2800.00
64-02-021	St. Peter	Cybis	500	Unkn.	1250.00
60-02-022	The Prophet	Cybis	50	250.00	3500.00
Cybis		**Birds & Flowers**			
85-03-001	American Bald Eagle	Cybis	300	2900.00	3595.00
72-03-002	American Crested Iris	Cybis	400	975.00	1150.00
76-03-003	American White Turkey	Cybis	75	1450.00	1600.00
76-03-004	American Wild Turkey	Cybis	75	1950.00	2200.00
77-03-005	Apple Blossoms	Cybis	400	350.00	550.00
72-03-006	Autumn Dogwood w/Chickadees	Cybis	350	1100.00	1200.00
XX-03-007	Birds & Flowers	Cybis	250	500.00	4500.00
61-03-008	Blue-Grey Gnatcatchers, pair	Cybis	200	400.00	2500.00
60-03-009	Blue Headed Virio Building Nest	Cybis	Closed	60.00	1100.00
60-03-010	Blue Headed Virio with Lilac	Cybis	275	1200.00	2200.00
XX-03-011	Butterfly w/Dogwood	Cybis	200	Unkn.	350.00
68-03-012	Calla Lily	Cybis	500	750.00	1750.00
65-03-013	Christmas Rose	Cybis	500	250.00	750.00
77-03-014	Clematis	Cybis	Closed	210.00	315.00
69-03-015	Clematis with House Wren	Cybis	350	1300.00	1400.00
76-03-016	Colonial Basket	Cybis	100	2750.00	5500.00
76-03-017	Constancy Flower Basket	Cybis	Closed	345.00	400.00
64-03-018	Dahlia, Yellow	Cybis	350	450.00	1800.00
76-03-019	Devotion Flower Basket	Cybis	Closed	345.00	400.00
62-03-020	Duckling "Baby Brother"	Cybis	Closed	35.00	140.00
77-03-021	Duckling "Buttercup & Daffodil"	Cybis	Closed	165.00	295.00
70-03-022	Dutch Crocus	Cybis	350	550.00	750.00
76-03-023	Felicity Flower Basket	Cybis	Closed	325.00	345.00
61-03-024	Golden Clarion Lily	Cybis	100	250.00	4500.00
74-03-025	Golden Winged Warbler	Cybis	200	1075.00	1150.00
75-03-026	Great Horned Owl, Color	Cybis	50	3250.00	7500.00
75-03-027	Great Horned Owl, White	Cybis	150	1950.00	4500.00
64-03-028	Great White Heron	Cybis	350	850.00	3750.00
77-03-029	Hermit Thrush	Cybis	150	1450.00	1450.00
59-03-030	Hummingbird	Cybis	Closed	95.00	950.00
63-03-031	Iris	Cybis	250	500.00	4500.00
77-03-032	Krestrel	Cybis	175	1875.00	1925.00
78-03-033	Kinglets on Pyracantha	Cybis	175	900.00	1100.00
71-03-034	Little Blue Heron	Cybis	500	425.00	1500.00
63-03-035	Magnolia	Cybis	Closed	350.00	450-1500.
76-03-036	Majesty Flower Basket	Cybis	Closed	345.00	400.00
70-03-037	Mushroom with Butterfly	Cybis	Closed	225.00	450.00

Company Number	Series Name	Artist	Edition Limit	Issue Price	Quote
68-03-038	Narcissus	Cybis	500	350.00	550.00
78-03-039	Nestling Bluebirds	Cybis	Closed	235.00	250.00
72-03-040	Pansies, China Maid	Cybis	1,000	275.00	350.00
75-03-041	Pansies, Chinolina Lady	Cybis	750	295.00	400.00
60-03-042	Pheasant	Cybis	150	750.00	5000.00
XX-03-043	Sandpipers	Cybis	400	700.00	1500.00
85-03-044	Screech Owl & Siblings	Cybis	100	3250.00	3925.00
XX-03-045	Skylarks	Cybis	350	330.00	1800.00
62-03-046	Sparrow on a Log	Cybis	Closed	35.00	450.00
82-03-047	Spring Bouquet	Cybis	200	750.00	750.00
57-03-048	Turtle Doves	Cybis	500	350.00	5000.00
68-03-049	Wood Duck	Cybis	500	325.00	800.00
80-03-050	Yellow Rose	Cybis	Closed	80.00	450.00
80-03-051	Yellow Condesa Rose	Cybis	Closed	Unkn.	255.00
Cybis	**Children to Cherish**				
64-04-001	Alice in Wonderland	Cybis	Closed	50.00	850.00
78-04-002	Alice (Seated)	Cybis	Closed	350.00	550.00
78-04-003	Allegra	Cybis	Closed	310.00	350.00
63-04-004	Ballerina on Cue	Cybis	Closed	150.00	700.00
68-04-005	Ballerina, Little Princess	Cybis	Closed	125.00	750.00
85-04-006	Ballerina, Recital	Cybis	Open	275.00	275.00
60-04-007	Ballerina Red Shoes	Cybis	Closed	75.00	1200.00
85-04-008	Ballerina, Swanilda	Cybis	Open	450.00	725.00
68-04-009	Baby Bust	Cybis	239	375.00	1000.00
85-04-010	Beth	Cybis	Open	235.00	275.00
77-04-011	Boys Playing Marbles	Cybis	Closed	285.00	425.00
84-04-012	The Choirboy	Cybis	Open	325.00	345.00
85-04-013	Clara	Cybis	Open	395.00	395.00
86-04-014	Clarissa	Cybis	Open	165.00	195.00
78-04-015	Edith	Cybis	Closed	310.00	325.00
76-04-016	Elizabeth Ann	Cybis	Closed	195.00	275.00
85-04-017	Felicia	Cybis	Open	425.00	525.00
86-04-018	"Encore" Figure Skater	Cybis	750	625.00	675.00
85-04-019	Figure Eight	Cybis	750	625.00	750.00
XX-04-020	First Bouquet	Cybis	250	150.00	300.00
66-04-021	First Flight	Cybis	Closed	50.00	475.00
81-04-022	Fleurette	Cybis	1,000	725.00	1075.00
73-04-023	Goldilocks	Cybis	Closed	145.00	525.00
74-04-024	Gretel	Cybis	Closed	260.00	425.00
74-04-025	Hansel	Cybis	Closed	270.00	550.00
62-04-026	Heide, White	Cybis	Closed	165.00	550.00
62-04-027	Heide, Color	Cybis	Closed	165.00	550.00
84-04-028	Jack in the Beanstalk	Cybis	750	575.00	575.00
85-04-029	Jody	Cybis	Open	235.00	275.00
86-04-030	Kitri	Cybis	Open	450.00	550.00
78-04-031	Lisa and Lynette	Cybis	Closed	395.00	475.00
78-04-032	Little Boy Blue	Cybis	Closed	425.00	500.00
84-04-033	Little Champ	Cybis	Open	325.00	375.00
80-04-034	Little Miss Muffet	Cybis	Closed	335.00	365.00
73-04-035	Little Red Riding Hood	Cybis	Closed	110.00	475.00
86-04-036	Lullaby, Pink	Cybis	Open	125.00	160.00
86-04-037	Lullaby, Blue	Cybis	Open	125.00	160.00
86-04-038	Lullaby, Ivory	Cybis	Open	125.00	160.00
85-04-039	Marguerite	Cybis	Open	425.00	525.00
74-04-040	Mary, Mary	Cybis	500	475.00	750.00
76-04-041	Melissa	Cybis	Closed	285.00	425.00
84-04-042	Michael	Cybis	Open	235.00	350.00
67-04-043	Pandora Blue	Cybis	Closed	265.00	325.00
58-04-044	Peter Pan	Cybis	Closed	80.00	1000.00
71-04-045	Polyanna	Cybis	Closed	195.00	550.00
75-04-046	Rapunzel, Apricot	Cybis	1,500	475.00	1200.00
78-04-047	Rapunzel, Lilac	Cybis	1,000	675.00	1000.00
72-04-048	Rapunzel, Pink	Cybis	1,000	425.00	1100.00
64-04-049	Rebecca	Cybis	Closed	110.00	360.00
85-04-050	Recital	Cybis	Open	275.00	275.00
82-04-051	Robin	Cybis	1,000	475.00	850.00
82-04-052	Sleeping Beauty	Cybis	750	695.00	1475.00
63-04-053	Springtime	Cybis	Closed	45.00	775.00
57-04-054	Thumbelina	Cybis	Closed	45.00	525.00
59-04-055	Tinkerbell	Cybis	Closed	95.00	1500.00
85-04-056	Vanessa	Cybis	Open	425.00	525.00
75-04-057	Wendy with Flowers	Cybis	Unkn.	250.00	450.00
75-04-058	Yankee Doodle Dandy	Cybis	Closed	275.00	325.00
Cybis	**Commemoratives**				
81-05-001	Arion, Dolphin Rider	Cybis	1,000	575.00	1150.00
69-05-002	Apollo II Moon Mission	Cybis	111	1500.00	2500.00
72-05-003	Chess Set	Cybis	10	30000.00	60000.00
67-05-004	Columbia	Cybis	200	1000.00	2500.00
86-05-005	1986 Commemorative Egg	Cybis	Open	365.00	365.00
67-05-006	Conductor's Hands	Cybis	250	250.00	1500.00
71-05-007	Cree Indian	Cybis	100	2500.00	5500.00
84-05-008	Cree Indian "Magic Boy"	Cybis	200	4250.00	4995.00
75-05-009	George Washington Bust	Cybis	Closed	275.00	350.00
85-05-010	Holiday Ornament	Cybis	Open	75.00	75.00
81-05-011	Kateri Takakwitha	Cybis	100	2875.00	2975.00
86-05-012	Little Miss Liberty	Cybis	Open	295.00	350.00
77-05-013	Oceania	Cybis	200	1250.00	975-1550.
81-05-014	Phoenix	Cybis	100	950.00	950.00
80-05-015	The Bride	Cybis	100	6500.00	10500.00
84-05-016	1984 Cybis Holiday	Cybis	Open	145.00	145.00
85-05-017	Liberty	Cybis	100	1875.00	4000.00
Cybis	**Fantasia**				
74-06-001	Cybele	Cybis	500	675.00	800.00
81-06-002	Desiree, White Deer	Cybis	400	575.00	595.00
84-06-003	Flight and Fancy	Cybis	1,000	975.00	1175.00
80-06-004	Pegasus	Cybis	500	1450.00	3750.00
80-06-005	Pegaus, Free Spirit	Cybis	1,000	675.00	775.00
81-06-006	Prince Brocade Unicorn	Cybis	500	2200.00	2600.00
78-06-007	"Satin" Horse Head	Cybis	500	1100.00	2800.00
77-06-008	Sea King's Steed "Oceania"	Cybis	200	1250.00	1450.00
78-06-009	"Sharmaine" Sea Nymph	Cybis	250	1450.00	1650.00
82-06-010	Theron	Cybis	350	675.00	850.00
69-06-011	Unicorn	Cybis	500	1250.00	3750.00
77-06-012	Unicorns, Gambol and Frolic	Cybis	1,000	425.00	2300.00
85-06-013	Dore'	Cybis	1,000	575.00	1075.00
Cybis	**Land of Chemeric**				
77-07-001	Marigold	Cybis	Closed	185.00	550.00
81-07-002	Melody	Cybis	1,000	725.00	800.00
79-07-003	Pip, Elfin Player	Cybis	1,000	450.00	665.00
77-07-004	Queen Titania	Cybis	750	725.00	2500.00
77-07-005	Tiffin	Cybis	Closed	175.00	550.00
85-07-006	Oberon	Cybis	750	825.00	825.00
Cybis	**North American Indian**				
74-08-001	Apache, "Chato"	Cybis	350	1950.00	3300.00
69-08-002	Blackfeet "Beaverhead Medicine Man"	Cybis	500	2000.00	2775.00
82-08-003	Choctaw "Tasculusa"	Cybis	200	2475.00	4050.00
77-08-004	Crow Dancer	Cybis	200	3875.00	8500.00
69-08-005	Dakota "Minnehaha Laughing Water"	Cybis	500	1500.00	2500.00
73-08-006	Eskimo Mother	Cybis	200	1875.00	2650.00
79-08-007	Great Spirit "Wankan Tanka"	Cybis	200	3500.00	4150.00
73-08-008	Iriquois "At the Council Fire"	Cybis	500	4250.00	4975.00
69-08-009	Onondaga "Haiwatha"	Cybis	500	1500.00	2450.00
71-08-010	Shoshone "Sacajawea"	Cybis	500	2250.00	2775.00
85-08-011	Yaqui "Deer Dancer"	Cybis	200	2095.00	2850.00
Cybis	**Portraits in Porcelain**				
76-09-001	Abigail Adams	Cybis	600	875.00	1300.00
73-09-002	Ballet-Princess Aurora	Cybis	200	1125.00	1500.00
73-09-003	Ballet-Prince Florimond	Cybis	200	975.00	1100.00
84-09-004	Bathsheba	Cybis	500	1975.00	3250.00
65-09-005	Beatrice	Cybis	700	225.00	1800.00
79-09-006	Berengaria	Cybis	500	1450.00	2000-4700.
86-09-007	Carmen	Cybis	500	1675.00	1975.00
82-09-008	Desdemona	Cybis	500	1850.00	4000.00
71-09-009	Eleanor of Aquitaine	Cybis	750	875.00	4250.00
67-09-010	Folk Singer	Cybis	283	300.00	850.00
78-09-011	Good Queen Anne	Cybis	350	975.00	1500.00
67-09-012	Guinevere	Cybis	800	250.00	2400.00
68-09-013	Hamlet	Cybis	500	350.00	2000.00
81-09-014	Jane Eyre	Cybis	500	975.00	1500.00
65-09-015	Juliet	Cybis	800	175.00	4000.00
85-09-016	King Arthur	Cybis	350	2350.00	3450.00
85-09-017	King David	Cybis	350	1475.00	2175.00
72-09-018	Kwan Yin	Cybis	350	1250.00	2000.00
82-09-019	Lady Godiva	Cybis	200	1875.00	3250.00
75-09-020	Lady Macbeth	Cybis	750	850.00	1350.00
79-09-021	Nefertiti	Cybis	500	2100.00	3000.00
69-09-022	Ophelia	Cybis	800	750.00	4500.00
85-09-023	Pagliacci	Cybis	Open	325.00	325.00
82-09-024	Persephone	Cybis	200	3250.00	5250.00
73-09-025	Portia	Cybis	750	825.00	3750.00
76-09-026	Priscilla	Cybis	500	825.00	1500.00
74-09-027	Queen Esther	Cybis	750	925.00	1800.00
85-09-028	Romeo and Juliet	Cybis	500	2200.00	3400.00
68-09-029	Scarlett	Cybis	500	450.00	3250-3500.
85-09-030	Tristan and Isolde	Cybis	200	2200.00	2200.00
Cybis	**Theatre of Porcelain**				
81-10-001	Columbine	Cybis	250	2250.00	2250.00
78-10-002	Court Jester	Cybis	250	1450.00	1750.00
80-10-003	Harlequin	Cybis	250	1575.00	1875.00
81-10-004	Puck	Cybis	250	2300.00	2450.00
Cybis	**Carousel-Circus**				
75-11-001	"Barnaby" Bear	Cybis	Closed	165.00	325.00
81-11-002	Bear, "Bernhard"	Cybis	325	1125.00	1150.00
75-11-003	Bicentennial Horse Ticonderoga	Cybis	350	925.00	4000.00
75-11-004	"Bosun" Monkey	Cybis	Closed	195.00	425.00
81-11-005	Bull, Plutus	Cybis	325	1125.00	2050.00
85-11-006	Carousel Unicorn	Cybis	325	1275.00	2750.00
79-11-007	Circus Rider "Equestrienne Extraordinaire"	Cybis	150	2275.00	3500.00
77-11-008	"Dandy" Dancing Dog	Cybis	Closed	145.00	295.00
81-11-009	Frollo	Cybis	1,000	750.00	825.00
76-11-010	"Funny Face" Child Head/Holly	Cybis	Closed	325.00	750.00
82-11-011	Giraffe	Cybis	750	Unkn.	1750.00
73-11-012	Carousel Goat	Cybis	325	875.00	1750.00
73-11-013	Carousel Horse	Cybis	325	925.00	7500.00
74-11-014	Lion	Cybis	325	1025.00	1350.00
76-11-015	Performing Pony "Poppy"	Cybis	1,000	325.00	1200.00
84-11-016	Phineas, Circus Elephant	Cybis	Open	325.00	425.00
86-11-017	Pierre, the Performing Poodle	Cybis	Open	225.00	275.00
81-11-018	Pony	Cybis	750	975.00	975.00
76-11-019	"Sebastian" Seal	Cybis	Closed	195.00	200.00
74-11-020	Tiger	Cybis	325	925.00	1500.00
85-11-021	Jumbles and Friend	Cybis	750	675.00	725.00
85-11-022	Valentine	Cybis	Open	335.00	375.00
Cybis	**Children of the World**				
72-12-001	Eskimo Child Head	Cybis	Closed	165.00	400.00
75-12-002	Indian Girl Head	Cybis	Closed	325.00	900.00
75-12-003	Indian Boy Head	Cybis	Closed	425.00	900.00
78-12-004	Jason	Cybis	Closed	285.00	375.00
78-12-005	Jennifer	Cybis	Closed	325.00	375.00
77-12-006	Jeremy	Cybis	Closed	315.00	475.00
79-12-007	Jessica	Cybis	Closed	325.00	475.00
Cybis	**Sport Scenes**				
80-13-001	Jogger, Female	Cybis	Closed	345.00	425.00
80-13-002	Jogger, Male	Cybis	Closed	395.00	475.00
Cybis	**Everyone's Fun Time (Limnettes)**				
72-14-001	Country Fair	Cybis	500	125.00	200.00
72-14-002	Windy Day	Cybis	500	125.00	200.00
72-14-003	The Pond	Cybis	500	125.00	200.00
72-14-004	The Seashore	Cybis	500	125.00	200.00
Cybis	**The Wonderful Seasons (Limnettes)**				
72-15-001	Autumn	Cybis	500	125.00	200.00
72-15-002	Spring	Cybis	500	125.00	200.00
72-15-003	Summer	Cybis	500	125.00	200.00
72-15-004	Winter	Cybis	500	125.00	200.00
Cybis	**When Bells are Ringing (Limnettes)**				
72-16-001	Easter Egg Hunt	Cybis	500	125.00	200.00
72-16-002	Independence Celebration	Cybis	500	125.00	200.00
72-16-003	Merry Christmas	Cybis	500	125.00	200.00
72-16-004	Sabbath Morning	Cybis	500	125.00	200.00
Department 56	**Dickens' Village Series**				
84-01-001	The Original Shops of Dickens' Village 6515-3, Set of 7	Department 56	Closed	175.00	1100-1750.
84-01-002	Crowntree Inn 6515-3	Department 56	Closed	25.00	250-450.
84-01-003	Candle Shop 6515-3	Department 56	Closed	25,00	160-300.

Company Number	Name	Series Artist	Edition Limit	Issue Price	Quote
84-01-004	Green Grocer 6515-3	Department 56	Closed	25.00	160-325.
84-01-005	Golden Swan Baker 6515-3	Department 56	Closed	25.00	120-250.
84-01-006	Bean And Son Smithy Shop 6515-3	Department 56	Closed	25.00	160-250.
84-01-007	Abel Beesley Butcher 6515-3	Department 56	Closed	25.00	100-250.
84-01-008	Jones & Co. Brush & Basket Shop 6515-3	Department 56	Closed	25.00	275-335.
84-01-009	Dickens' Village Church (cream) 6516-1	Department 56	Closed	35.00	220-440.
85-01-010	Dickens' Village Church(tan) 6516-1	Department 56	Closed	35.00	145-175.
85-01-011	Dickens' Village Church(green) 6516-1	Department 56	Closed	35.00	209-400.
85-01-012	Dickens' Cottages 6518-8 Set of 3	Department 56	Closed	75.00	865-1500.
85-01-013	Thatched Cottage 6518-8	Department 56	Closed	25.00	155-330.
85-01-014	Stone Cottage 6518-8	Department 56	Closed	25.00	355-488.
85-01-015	Tudor Cottage 6518-8	Department 56	Closed	25.00	330-480.
85-01-016	Dickens' Village Mill 6519-6	Department 56	2,500	35.00	4500-6500.
86-01-017	Christmas Carol Cottages 6500-5, Set of 3 (Fezziwig's Warehouse, Scrooge and Marley Counting House, The Cottage of Bob Cratchit & Tiny Tim)	Department 56	Open	75.00	90.00
86-01-018	Norman Church 6502-1	Department 56	3,500	40.00	2640-3400.
86-01-019	Dickens' Lane Shops 6507-2, Set of 3	Department 56	Closed	80.00	440-725.
86-01-020	Thomas Kersey Coffee House 6507-2	Department 56	Closed	27.00	108-230.
86-01-021	Cottage Toy Shop 6507-2	Department 56	Closed	27.00	180-217.
86-01-022	Tuttle's Pub 6507-2	Department 56	Closed	27.00	190-250.
86-01-023	Blythe Pond Mill House 6508-0	Department 56	Closed	37.00	150-320.
86-01-024	By The Pond Mill House 6508-0	Department 56	Closed	37.00	115-175.
86-01-025	Chadbury Station and Train 6528-5	Department 56	Closed	65.00	300-440.
87-01-026	Barley Bree 5900-5, Set of 2 (Farmhouse, Barn)	Department 56	Closed	60.00	330-500.
87-01-027	The Old Curiosity Shop 5905-6	Department 56	Open	32.00	37.50
87-01-028	Kenilworth Castle 5916-1	Department 56	Closed	70.00	405-500.
87-01-029	Brick Abbey 6549-8	Department 56	Closed	33.00	330-525.
87-01-030	Chesterton Manor House 6568-4	Department 56	7,500	45.00	1400-1800.
88-01-031	Counting House & Silas Thimbleton Barrister 5902-1	Department 56	Closed	32.00	69-135.50
88-01-032	C. Fletcher Public House 5904-8	Department 56	12,500	35.00	525-785.
88-01-033	Cobblestone Shops 5924-2, Set of 3	Department 56	Closed	95.00	275-385.
88-01-034	The Wool Shop 5924-2	Department 56	Closed	32.00	143-230.
88-01-035	Booter and Cobbler 5924-2	Department 56	Closed	32.00	90-165.00
88-01-036	T. Wells Fruit & Spice Shop 5924-2	Department 56	Closed	32.00	70-125.00
88-01-037	Nicholas Nickleby 5925-0, Set of 2	Department 56	Closed	72.00	135-206.
88-01-038	Nicholas Nickleby Cottage 5925-0	Department 56	Closed	36.00	63-115.00
88-01-039	Wackford Squeers Boarding School 5925-0	Department 56	Closed	36.00	65-115.00
88-01-040	Nickolas Nickleby Cottage 5925-0-misspelled	Department 56	Closed	36.00	85-125.00
88-01-041	Nickolas Nickleby set of 2, 5925-0-misspelled	Department 56	Closed	36.00	210-260.
88-01-042	Merchant Shops 5926-9, 5/set,	Department 56	Closed	150.00	216-375.
88-01-043	Poulterer 5926-9	Department 56	Closed	30.00	55-105.00
88-01-044	Geo. Weeton Watchmaker 5926-9	Department 56	Closed	30.00	55-70.00
88-01-045	The Mermaid Fish Shoppe 5926-9	Department 56	Closed	30.00	60-135.00
88-01-046	White Horse Bakery 5926-9	Department 56	Closed	30.00	55-105.00
88-01-047	Walpole Tailors 5926-9	Department 56	Closed	30.00	55-80.50
88-01-048	Ivy Glen Church 5927-7	Department 56	Closed	35.00	65-132.00
89-01-049	David Copperfield 5550-6, Set of 3	Department 56	Closed	125.00	154-287.
89-01-050	Mr. Wickfield Solicitor 5550-6	Department 56	Closed	42.50	72-110.00
89-01-051	Betsy Trotwood's Cottage 5550-6	Department 56	Closed	42.50	41-110.00
89-01-052	Peggotty's Seaside Cottage 5550-6 (green boat)	Department 56	Closed	42.50	47-95.00
89-01-053	David Copperfield 5550-6, Set of 3 with tan boat	Department 56	Closed	125.00	216-373.
89-01-054	Peggotty's Seaside Cottage 5550-6 (tan boat)	Department 56	Closed	42.50	110-195.
89-01-055	Victoria Station 5574-3	Department 56	Open	100.00	100.00
89-01-056	Knottinghill Church 5582-4	Department 56	Open	50.00	50.00
89-01-057	Cobles Police Station 5583-2	Department 56	Closed	37.50	82-145.00
89-01-058	Theatre Royal 5584-0	Department 56	Closed	45.00	56-135.50
89-01-059	Ruth Marion Scotch Woolens 5585-9	Department 56	17,500	65.00	320-475.
89-01-060	Green Gate Cottage 5586-7	Department 56	22,500	65.00	240-400.
89-01-061	The Flat of Ebenezer Scrooge 5587-5	Department 56	Open	37.50	37.50
90-01-062	Bishops Oast House 5567-0	Department 56	Closed	45.00	50-125.00
90-01-063	Kings Road 5568-9, Set of 2 (Tutbury Printer, C.H. Watt Physician)	Department 56	Open	72.00	72.00
91-01-064	Fagin's Hide-A-Way 5552-2	Department 56	Open	68.00	68.00
91-01-065	Oliver Twist 5553-0 Set of 2,	Department 56	Closed	75.00	99-142.00
91-01-066	Brownlow House 5553-0	Department 56	Closed	38.00	66-98.00
91-01-067	Maylie Cottage	Department 56	Closed	38.00	65-92.00
91-01-068	Ashbury Inn 5555-7	Department 56	Open	55.00	55.00
91-01-069	Nephew Fred's Flat 5557-3	Department 56	Open	35.00	35.00
92-01-070	Crown & Cricket Inn (Charles Dickens' Signature Series), 5750-9	Department 56	Closed	100.00	140-267.
92-01-071	Old Michaelchurch, 5562-0	Department 56	Open	42.00	42.00
92-01-072	Hembleton Pewterer, 5800-9	Department 56	Open	72.00	72.00
92-01-073	King's Road Post Office, 5801-7	Department 56	Open	45.00	45.00
93-01-074	The Pied Bull Inn (Charles Dickens' Signature Series), 5751-7	Department 56	Closed	100.00	125-242.
93-01-075	Boarding and Lodging School, 5809-2 (Christmas Carol Commemorative Piece)	Department 56	Closed	48.00	220-365.
93-01-076	Pump Lane Shoppes,5808-4 set of 3 (Bumpstead Nye Cloaks & Canes, Lomas Ltd. Molasses, W.M. Wheat Cakes & Puddings)	Department 56	Open	112.00	112.00
93-01-077	Kingford's Brewhouse, 5811-4	Department 56	Open	45.00	45.00
93-01-078	Great Denton Mill, 5812-2	Department 56	Open	50.00	50.00
94-01-079	Dedlock Arms, 5752-5 (Charles Dickens' Signature Series)	Department 56	Yr.Iss.	100.00	100.00
94-01-080	Boarding & Lodging School 5810-6	Department 56	Open	48.00	48.00
Department 56		**New England Village Series**			
86-02-001	New England Village 6530-7, Set of 7	Department 56	Closed	170.00	900-1320.
86-02-002	Apothecary Shop 6530-7	Department 56	Closed	25.00	75-115.00
86-02-003	General Store 6530-7	Department 56	Closed	25.00	170-375.
86-02-004	Nathaniel Bingham Fabrics 6530-7	Department 56	Closed	25.00	120-160.
86-02-005	Livery Stable & Boot Shop 6530-7	Department 56	Closed	25.00	100-144.
86-02-006	Steeple Church (Original) 6530-7	Department 56	Closed	25.00	175-180.
86-02-007	Brick Town Hall 6530-7	Department 56	Closed	25.00	180-373.
86-02-008	Red Schoolhouse 6530-7	Department 56	Closed	25.00	220-345.
86-02-009	Jacob Adams Farmhouse and Barn 6538-2	Department 56	Closed	65.00	400-632.
86-02-010	Steeple Church (Second Version) 6539-0	Department 56	Closed	30.00	82-135.00
87-02-011	Craggy Cove Lighthouse 5930-7	Department 56	Open	35.00	44.00
87-02-012	Weston Train Station 5931-5	Department 56	Closed	42.00	220-316.
87-02-013	Smythe Woolen Mill 6543-9	Department 56	7,500	42.00	1080-1320.
87-02-014	Timber Knoll Log Cabin 6544-7	Department 56	Closed	28.00	108-155.
88-02-015	Old North Church 5932-3	Department 56	Open	40.00	42.00
88-02-016	Cherry Lane Shops 5939-0, Set of 3	Department 56	Closed	80.00	199-325.
88-02-017	Ben's Barbershop 5939-0	Department 56	Closed	27.00	70-98.00
88-02-018	Otis Hayes Butcher Shop 5939-0	Department 56	Closed	27.00	50-85.00
88-02-019	Anne Shaw Toys 5939-0	Department 56	Closed	27.00	95-150.00

Company Number	Name	Series Artist	Edition Limit	Issue Price	Quote
88-02-020	Ada's Bed and Boarding House (lemon yellow) 5940-4	Department 56	Closed	36.00	132-300.
88-02-021	Ada's Bed and Boarding House (pale yellow) 5940-4	Department 56	Closed	36.00	80-148.00.
89-02-022	Berkshire House (medium blue) 5942-0	Department 56	Closed	40.00	90-165.00
89-02-023	Berkshire House (teal) 5942-0	Department 56	Closed	40.00	75-125.00
89-02-024	Jannes Mullet Amish Farm House 5943-9	Department 56	Closed	32.00	74-135.00
89-02-025	Jannes Mullet Amish Barn 5944-7	Department 56	Closed	48.00	77-135.00
90-02-026	Shingle Creek House 5946-3	Department 56	Open	37.50	37.50
90-02-027	Captain's Cottage 5947-1	Department 56	Open	40.00	40.00
90-02-028	Sleepy Hollow 5954-4, Set of 3	Department 56	Closed	96.00	130-162.
90-02-029	Sleepy Hollow School 5954-4	Department 56	Closed	32.00	60-80.50
90-02-030	Van Tassel Manor 5954-4	Department 56	Closed	32.00	48-80.50
90-02-031	Ichabod Crane's Cottage 5954-4	Department 56	Closed	32.00	48-80.50
90-02-032	Sleepy Hollow Church 5955-2	Department 56	Closed	36.00	50-86.00
91-02-033	McGrebe-Cutters & Sleighs 5640-5	Department 56	Open	45.00	45.00
92-02-034	Bluebird Seed and Bulb, 5642-1	Department 56	Open	48.00	48.00
92-02-035	Yankee Jud Bell Casting 5643-0	Department 56	Open	44.00	44.00
92-02-036	Stoney Brook Town Hall 5644-8	Department 56	Open	42.00	42.00
93-02-037	Blue Star Ice Co., 5647-2	Department 56	Open	45.00	45.00
93-02-038	A. Bieler Farm 5648-0, set of 2 (Pennsylvania Dutch Farmhouse, Pennsylvania Dutch Barn)	Department 56	Open	92.00	92.00
Department 56		**Alpine Village Series**			
86-03-001	Alpine Village 6540-4, 5/set (Bessor Bierkeller, Gasthof Eisl, Apotheke, E. Staubr Backer, Milch-Kase)	Department 56	Open	150.00	185.00
87-03-002	Josef Engel Farmhouse 5952-8	Department 56	Closed	33.00	425-810.
87-03-003	Alpine Church 6541-2	Department 56	Closed	32.00	85-150.00
88-03-004	Grist Mill 5953-6	Department 56	Open	42.00	44.00
90-03-005	Bahnhof 5615-4	Department 56	Closed	42.00	70-135.00
91-03-006	St. Nikolaus Kirche 5617-0	Department 56	Open	37.50	37.50
92-03-007	Alpine Shops 5618-9,2/set (Metterniche Wurst, Kukuck Uhren)	Department 56	Open	75.00	75.00
93-03-008	Sport Laden, 5612-0	Department 56	Open	50.00	50.00
Department 56		**Christmas In the City Series**			
87-04-001	Sutton Place Brownstones 5961-7	Department 56	Closed	80.00	660-1025.
87-04-002	The Cathedral 5962-5	Department 56	Closed	60.00	275-450.
87-04-003	Palace Theatre 5963-3	Department 56	Closed	45.00	825-1112.
87-04-004	Christmas In The City 6512-9, Set of 3	Department 56	Closed	112.00	330-485.
87-04-005	Toy Shop and Pet Store 6512-9	Department 56	Closed	37.50	120-180.
87-04-006	Bakery 6512-9	Department 56	Closed	37.50	72-120.00
87-04-007	Tower Restaurant 6512-9	Department 56	Closed	37.50	121-250.
88-04-008	Chocolate Shoppe 5968-4	Department 56	Closed	40.00	75-135.00
88-04-009	City Hall (standard) 5969-2	Department 56	Closed	65.00	115-300.
88-04-010	City Hall (small) 5969-2	Department 56	Closed	65.00	150-200.
88-04-011	Hank's Market 5970-6	Department 56	Closed	40.00	60-135.00
88-04-012	Variety Store 5972-2	Department 56	Closed	45.00	110-195.
89-04-013	Ritz Hotel 5973-0	Department 56	Open	55.00	55.00
89-04-014	Dorothy's Dress Shop 5974-9	Department 56	12,500	70.00	300-500.
89-04-015	Dorothy's Dress Shop (proof) 5974-9	Department 56	12,500	70.00	325-350.
89-04-016	5607 Park Avenue Townhouse 5977-3	Department 56	Closed	48.00	50-135.00
89-04-017	5609 Park Avenue Townhouse 5978-1	Department 56	Closed	48.00	50-135.00
90-04-018	Red Brick Fire Station 5536-0	Department 56	Open	55.00	55.00
90-04-019	Wong's In Chinatown 5537-9	Department 56	Open	55.00	55.00
91-04-020	Hollydale's Department Store 5534-4	Department 56	Open	75.00	75.00
91-04-021	"Little Italy" Ristorante 5538-7	Department 56	Open	50.00	50.00
91-04-022	All Saints Corner Church 5542-5	Department 56	Open	96.00	96.00
91-04-023	Arts Academy 5543-3	Department 56	Closed	45.00	60-98.00
90-04-024	The Doctor's Office 5544-1	Department 56	Open	60.00	60.00
92-04-025	Cathedral Church of St. Mark 5549-2	Department 56	3,024	120.00	1900-3500.
92-04-026	Uptown Shoppes 5531-0, Set of 3 (Haberdashery, City Clockworks, Music Emporium)	Department 56	Open	150.00	150.00
93-04-027	West Village Shops 5880-7, set of 2 (Potters' Tea Seller, Spring St. Coffee House)	Department 56	Open	90.00	90.00
Department 56		**Little Town of Bethlehem Series**			
87-05-001	Little Town of Bethlehem 5975-7, Set of 12	Department 56	Open	150.00	150.00
Department 56		**The Original Snow Village Collection**			
76-06-001	Mountain Lodge 5001-3	Department 56	Closed	20.00	385-500.
76-06-002	Gabled Cottage 5002-1	Department 56	Closed	20.00	240-400.
76-06-003	The Inn 5003-9	Department 56	Closed	20.00	445-500.
76-06-004	Country Church 5004-7	Department 56	Closed	18.00	220-385.
76-06-005	Steepled Church 5005-4	Department 56	Closed	25.00	480-655.
76-06-006	Small Chalet 5006-2	Department 56	Closed	15.00	300-500.
77-06-007	Victorian House 5007-0	Department 56	Closed	30.00	390-400.
77-06-008	Mansion 5008-8	Department 56	Closed	30.00	600.00
77-06-009	Stone Church (10") 5009-6	Department 56	Closed	35.00	425-660.
78-06-010	Homestead 5011-2	Department 56	Closed	30.00	198-250.
78-06-011	General Store (white) 5012-0	Department 56	Closed	25.00	425-440.
78-06-012	Cape Cod 5013-8	Department 56	Closed	20.00	365-415.
78-06-013	Nantucket 5014-6	Department 56	Closed	25.00	240-310.
78-06-014	Skating Rink, Duck Pond (Set) 5015-3	Department 56	Closed	16.00	1100.00
78-06-015	Small Double Trees w/ red birds 5016-1	Department 56	Closed	13.50	43-69.00
78-06-016	Small Double Trees w/ blue birds 5016-1	Department 56	Closed	13.50	150-165.
79-06-017	Thatched Cottage 5050-0 Meadowland Series	Department 56	Closed	30.00	600.00
79-06-018	Countryside Church 5051-8 Meadowland Series	Department 56	Closed	25.00	700.00
79-06-019	Victorian 5054-2	Department 56	Closed	30.00	358-418.
79-06-020	Knob Hill 5055-9	Department 56	Closed	30.00	300-330.
79-06-021	Knob Hill (gold) 5055-9	Department 56	Closed	30.00	415.00
79-06-022	Brownstone 5056-7	Department 56	Closed	36.00	500-535.
79-06-023	Log Cabin 5057-5	Department 56	Closed	22.00	390-480.
79-06-024	Countryside Church 5058-3	Department 56	Closed	27.50	220-360.
79-06-025	Stone Church (8") 5059-1	Department 56	Closed	32.00	825-908.
79-06-026	School House 5060-9	Department 56	Closed	30.00	341-410.
79-06-027	Tudor House 5061-7	Department 56	Closed	25.00	330-345.
79-06-028	Mission Church 5062-5	Department 56	Closed	30.00	880.00
79-06-029	Mobile Home 5063-3	Department 56	Closed	18.00	1575.00
79-06-030	Giant Trees 5065-8	Department 56	Closed	20.00	290-330.
79-06-031	Adobe House 5066-6	Department 56	Closed	18.00	1990.00
80-06-032	Cathedral Church 5067-4	Department 56	Closed	36.00	1650.00
80-06-033	Stone Mill House 5068-2	Department 56	Closed	30.00	550-661.
80-06-034	Colonial Farm House 5070-9	Department 56	Closed	30.00	286-300.
80-06-035	Town Church 5071-7	Department 56	Closed	33.00	330-358.
80-06-036	Train Station with 3 Train Cars 5085-6	Department 56	Closed	100.00	240-410.
81-06-037	Wooden Clapboard 5072-5	Department 56	Closed	32.00	270-305.
81-06-038	English Cottage 5073-3	Department 56	Closed	25.00	265-305.
81-06-039	Barn 5074-1	Department 56	Closed	32.00	360-488.
81-06-040	Corner Store 5076-8	Department 56	Closed	30.00	150-240.

Company		Series			
Number	**Name**	**Artist**	**Edition Limit**	**Issue Price**	**Quote**
81-06-041	Bakery 5077-6	Department 56	Closed	30.00	150-304.
81-06-042	English Church 5078-4	Department 56	Closed	30.00	335-380.
81-06-043	Large Single Tree 5080-6	Department 56	Closed	17.00	36-55.00
82-06-044	Skating Pond 5017-2	Department 56	Closed	25.00	375-418.
82-06-045	Street Car 5019-9	Department 56	Closed	16.00	320-425.
82-06-046	Centennial House 5020-2	Department 56	Closed	32.00	303-335.
82-06-047	Carriage House 5021-0	Department 56	Closed	28.00	240-362.
82-06-048	Pioneer Church 5022-9	Department 56	Closed	30.00	310-360.
82-06-049	Swiss Chalet 5023-7	Department 56	Closed	28.00	300-375.
82-06-050	Bank 5024-5	Department 56	Closed	32.00	550-575.
82-06-051	Gabled House 5081-4	Department 56	Closed	30.00	303-425.
82-06-052	Flower Shop 5082-2	Department 56	Closed	25.00	360-402.
82-06-053	New Stone Church 5083-0	Department 56	Closed	32.00	300-363.
83-06-054	Town Hall 5000-8	Department 56	Closed	32.00	174-330.
83-06-055	Grocery 5001-6	Department 56	Closed	35.00	275-335.
83-06-056	Victorian Cottage 5002-4	Department 56	Closed	35.00	360.00.
83-06-057	Governor's Mansion 5003-2	Department 56	Closed	32.00	185-220.
83-06-058	Turn of the Century 5004-0	Department 56	Closed	36.00	210-275.
83-06-059	Gingerbread HouseBank (Non-lighted)5025-3	Department 56	Closed	24.00	300-350.
83-06-060	Village Church 5026-1	Department 56	Closed	30.00	385.00
83-06-061	Gothic Church 5028-8	Department 56	Closed	36.00	240-330.
83-06-062	Parsonage 5029-6	Department 56	Closed	35.00	360-460.
83-06-063	Wooden Church 5031-8	Department 56	Closed	30.00	330-425.
83-06-064	Fire Station 5032-6	Department 56	Closed	32.00	600-743.
83-06-065	English Tudor 5033-4	Department 56	Closed	30.00	191-300.
83-06-066	Chateau 5084-9	Department 56	Closed	35.00	324-462.
84-06-067	Main Street House 5005-9	Department 56	Closed	27.00	240-264.
84-06-068	Stratford House 5007-5	Department 56	Closed	28.00	156-220.
84-06-069	Haversham House 5008-3	Department 56	Closed	37.00	240-286.
84-06-070	Galena House 5009-1	Department 56	Closed	32.00	325-360.
84-06-071	River Road House 5010-5	Department 56	Closed	36.00	114-247.
84-06-072	Delta House 5012-1	Department 56	Closed	32.00	300-373.
84-06-073	Bayport 5015-6	Department 56	Closed	30.00	198-232.
84-06-074	Congregational Church 5034-2	Department 45	Closed	28.00	525-550.
84-06-075	Trinity Church 5035-0	Department 56	Closed	32.00	295-307.
84-06-076	Summit House 5036-9	Department 56	Closed	28.00	358-425.
84-06-077	New School House 5037-7	Department 56	Closed	35.00	220-375.
84-06-078	Parish Church 5039-3	Department 56	Closed	32.00	360-431.
85-06-079	Stucco Bungalow 5045-8	Department 56	Closed	30.00	315-374.
85-06-080	Williamsburg House 5046-6	Department 56	Closed	37.00	73-150.
85-06-081	Plantation House 5047-4	Department 56	Closed	37.00	60-172.
85-06-082	Church of the Open Door 5048-2	Department 56	Closed	34.00	85-143.00
85-06-083	Spruce Place 5049-0	Department 56	Closed	33.00	253-345.
85-06-084	Duplex 5050-4	Department 56	Closed	35.00	85-175.00
85-06-085	Depot and Train with 2 Train Cars 5051-2	Department 56	Closed	65.00	110-143.
85-06-086	Ridgewood 5052-0	Department 56	Closed	35.00	110-190.
86-06-087	Waverly Place 5041-5	Department 56	Closed	35.00	286-345.
86-06-088	Twin Peaks 5042-3	Department 56	Closed	32.00	275-501.
86-06-089	2101 Maple 5043-1	Department 56	Closed	32.00	374-400.
86-06-090	Lincoln Park Duplex 5060-1	Department 56	Closed	33.00	87-115.00
86-06-091	Sonoma House 5062-8	Department 56	Closed	33.00	98-115.
86-06-092	Highland Park House 5063-6	Department 56	Closed	35.00	110-125.
86-06-093	Beacon Hill House 5065-2	Department 56	Closed	31.00	90-170.00
86-06-094	Pacific Heights House 5066-0	Department 56	Closed	33.00	90-100.00
86-06-095	Ramsey Hill House 5067-9	Department 56	Closed	36.00	83-138.00
86-06-096	Saint James Church 5068-7	Department 56	Closed	37.00	120-172.
86-06-097	All Saints Church 5070-9	Department 56	Open	38.00	45.00
86-06-098	Carriage House 5071-7	Department 56	Closed	29.00	65-110.00
86-06-099	Toy Shop 5073-3	Department 56	Closed	36.00	60-105.00
86-06-100	Apothecary 5076-8	Department 56	Closed	34.00	77-126.00
86-06-101	Bakery 5077-6	Department 56	Closed	35.00	54-97.00
86-06-102	Mickey's Diner 5078-4	Department 56	Closed	22.00	350-510.
87-06-103	St. Anthony Hotel & Post Office 5006-7	Department 56	Closed	40.00	50-138.00
87-06-104	Snow Village Factory 5013-0	Department 56	Closed	45.00	87-140.00
87-06-105	Cathedral Church 5019-9	Department 56	Closed	50.00	85-125.00
87-06-106	Cumberland House 5024-5	Department 56	Open	42.00	44.00
87-06-107	Springfield House 5027-0	Department 56	Closed	40.00	59-126.00
87-06-108	Lighthouse 5030-0	Department 56	Closed	36.00	275-620.
87-06-109	Red Barn 5081-4	Department 56	Closed	38.00	54-97.00
87-06-110	Jefferson School 5082-2	Department 56	Closed	36.00	90-149.00
87-06-111	Farm House 5089-0	Department 56	Closed	40.00	50-97.00
87-06-112	Fire Station No. 2 5091-1	Department 56	Closed	40.00	138-150.
87-06-113	Snow Village Resort Lodge 5092-0	Department 56	Closed	55.00	95-132.00
88-06-114	Village Market 5044-0	Department 56	Closed	39.00	50-125.00
88-06-115	Kenwood House 5054-7	Department 56	Closed	50.00	70-115.00
88-06-116	Maple Ridge Inn 5121-7	Department 56	Closed	55.00	55-126.00
88-06-117	Village Station and Train 5122-5	Department 56	Closed	65.00	83-96.00
88-06-118	Cobblestone Antique Shop 5123-3	Department 56	Closed	36.00	50-66.00
88-06-119	Corner Cafe 5124-1	Department 56	Closed	37.00	50-99.00
88-06-120	Single Car Garage 5125-0	Department 56	Closed	22.00	33-70.00
88-06-121	Home Sweet Home/House & Windmill5126-8	Department 56	Closed	60.00	88-126.00
88-06-122	Redeemer Church 5127-6	Department 56	Closed	42.00	48-97.00
88-06-123	Service Station 5128-4	Department 56	Closed	37.50	75-130.00
88-06-124	Stonehurst House 5140-3	Department 56	Open	37.50	37.50
88-06-125	Palos Verdes 5141-1	Department 56	Closed	37.50	53-115.00
89-06-126	Jingle Belle Houseboat 5114-4	Department 56	Closed	42.00	66-121.00
89-06-127	Colonial Church 5119-5	Department 56	Closed	60.00	60-103.00
89-06-128	North Creek Cottage 5120-9	Department 56	Closed	45.00	54-90.00
89-06-129	Paramount Theater 5142-0	Department 56	Closed	42.00	43-92.00
89-06-130	Doctor's House 5143-8	Department 56	Closed	56.00	65-85.00
89-06-131	Courthouse 5144-6	Department 56	Closed	65.00	90-144.00
89-06-132	Village Warming House 5145-4	Department 56	Closed	42.00	50-97.00
89-06-133	J. Young's Granary 5149-7	Department 56	Closed	45.00	60-125.00
89-06-134	Pinewood Log Cabin 5150-0	Department 56	Open	37.50	37.50
90-06-135	56 Flavors Ice Cream Parlor 5151-9	Department 56	Closed	42.00	60-110.00
90-06-136	Morningside House 5152-7	Department 56	Closed	45.00	44-97.00
90-06-137	Mainstreet Hardware Store 5153-5	Department 56	Closed	42.00	50-97.00
90-06-138	Village Realty 5154-3	Department 56	Closed	42.00	46-97.00
90-06-139	Spanish Mission Church 5155-1	Department 56	Closed	42.00	51-97.00
90-06-140	Prairie House (American Architecture Series), 5156-0	Department 56	Closed	42.00	44.00
90-06-141	Queen Anne Victorian (American Architecture Series), 5157-8	Department 56	Open	48.00	48.00
91-06-142	Oak Grove Tudor 5400-3	Department 56	Open	42.00	42.00
91-06-143	Honeymooner Motel 5401-1	Department 56	Closed	42.00	66-97.00
91-06-144	The Christmas Shop 5097-0	Department 56	Open	37.50	37.50
91-06-145	Village Greenhouse 5402-0	Department 56	Open	35.00	35.00
91-06-146	Southern Colonial (American Architecture Series), 5403-8	Department 56	Open	48.00	48.00
91-06-147	Gothic Farmhouse (American Architecture Series), 5404-6	Department 56	Open	48.00	48.00
91-06-148	Finklea's Finery: Costume Shop 5405-4	Department 56	Closed	45.00	55-81.00
91-06-149	Jack's Corner Barber Shop 5406-2	Department 56	Open	42.00	42.00
91-06-150	Double Bungalow, 5407-0	Department 56	Open	45.00	45.00
92-06-151	Post Office 5422-4	Department 56	Open	35.00	35.00
92-06-152	Grandma's Cottage 5420-8	Department 56	Open	42.00	42.00
92-06-153	St. Luke's Church 5421-6	Department 56	Open	45.00	45.00
92-06-154	Al's TV Shop 5423-2	Department 56	Open	40.00	40.00
92-06-155	Good Shepherd Chapel & Church School Set of 2 5424-0	Department 56	Open	72.00	72.00
92-06-156	Print Shop & Village News 5425-9	Department 56	Open	37.50	37.50
92-06-157	Hartford House 5426-7	Department 56	Open	55.00	55.00
92-06-158	Village Vet and Pet Shop 5427-5	Department 56	Open	32.00	32.00
92-06-159	Craftsman Cottage (American Architecture Series),5437-2	Department 56	Open	55.00	55.00
92-06-160	Village Station 5438-0	Department 56	Open	65.00	65.00
92-06-161	Airport 5439-9	Department 56	Open	60.00	60.00
93-06-162	Nantucket Renovation 5441-0	Department 56	Closed	55.00	78-125.00
93-06-163	Mount Olivet Church, 5442-9	Department 56	Open	65.00	65.00
93-06-164	Village Public Library, 5443-7	Department 56	Open	55.00	55.00
93-06-165	Woodbury House, 5444-5	Department 56	Open	45.00	45.00
93-06-166	Hunting Lodge, 5445-3	Department 56	Open	50.00	50.00
93-06-169	Dairy Barn, 5446-1	Department 56	Open	55.00	55.00
93-06-170	Dinah's Drive-In, 5447-0	Department 56	Open	45.00	45.00
93-06-171	Snowy Hills Hospital, 5448-8	Department 56	Open	48.00	48.00
Department 56		**North Pole Series**			
90-07-001	Santa's Workshop 5600-6	Department 56	Closed	72.00	100-175.
90-07-002	North Pole 5601-4 Set of 2 (Reindeer Barn, Elf Bunkhouse)	Department 56	Open	70.00	70.00
91-07-003	Neenee's Dolls & Toys 5620-0	Department 56	Open	37.50	36.00
91-07-004	North Pole Shops, Set of 2 5621-9 (Orly's Bell & Harness Supply, Rimpy's Bakery)	Department 56	Open	75.00	75.00
91-07-005	Tassy's Mittens & Hassel's Woolies 5622-7	Department 56	Open	50.00	50.00
92-07-006	North Pole Post Office 5623-5	Department 56	Open	45.00	45.00
92-07-007	Obbie's Books & Letrinka's Candy 5624-3	Department 56	Open	70.00	70.00
92-07-008	Elfie's Sleds & Skates 5625-1	Department 56	Open	48.00	48.00
93-07-009	North Pole Chapel 5626-0	Department 56	Open	45.00	45.00
93-07-010	Express Depot 5627-8	Department 56	Open	48.00	48.00
93-07-011	Santa's Woodworks 5628-6	Department 56	Open	42.00	42.00
93-07-012	Santa's Lookout Tower 5629-4	Department 56	Open	45.00	45.00
Department 56		**Event Piece - Heritage Village Collection Accessory**			
92-08-001	Gate House 5530-1	Department 56	Closed	22.50	55-100.00
Department 56		**Retired Heritage Village Collection Accessories**			
84-09-001	Carolers 6526-9, set of 3 w/ Lamppost(wh)	Department 56	Closed	10.00	65-132.00
84-09-002	Carolers 6526-9, set of 3 w/ Lamppost(bl)	Department 56	Closed	10.00	25-49.00
85-09-003	Village Train Brighton 6527-7, set of 3	Department 56	Closed	12.00	285-395.
86-09-004	Christmas Carol Figures 6501-3, set of 3	Department 56	Closed	12.50	35-60.00
86-09-005	Lighted Tree With Children & Ladder 6510-2	Department 56	Closed	35.00	300-385.
86-09-006	Sleighride 6511-0	Department 56	Closed	19.50	35-69.00
86-09-007	Covered Wooden Bridge 6531-5	Department 56	Closed	10.00	25-46.00
86-09-008	New England Winter Set 6532-3, set of 5	Department 56	Closed	18.00	36-55.00
86-09-009	Porcelain Trees, 6537-4, set of 2	Department 56	Closed	14.00	24-44.00
86-09-010	Alpine Villagers 6542-0, set of 3	Department 56	Closed	13.00	25-38.00
87-09-011	Farm People And Animals 5901-3, set of 5	Department 56	Closed	24.00	50-90.00
87-09-012	Blacksmith 5934-0, set of 3	Department 56	Closed	20.00	32-72.00
87-09-013	City People 5965-0, set of 5	Department 56	Closed	27.50	28-57.00
87-09-014	Silo And Hay Shed 5950-1	Department 56	Closed	18.00	110-150.
87-09-015	Ox Sled (tan pants) 5951-0	Department 56	Closed	20.00	150-220.
87-09-016	Ox Sled (blue pants) 5951-0	Department 56	Closed	20.00	83-140.00
87-09-017	Shopkeepers 5966-8, set of 4	Department 56	Closed	15.00	24-61.00
87-09-018	City Workers 5967-6, set of 4	Department 56	Closed	15.00	28-77.00
87-09-019	Skating Pond 6545-5	Department 56	Closed	24.00	65-85.00
87-09-020	Stone Bridge 6546-3	Department 56	Closed	12.00	64-103.00
87-09-021	Village Well And Holy Cross 6547-1, set /2	Department 56	Closed	13.00	84-160.
87-09-022	Maple Sugaring Shed 6589-7, set of 3	Department 56	Closed	19.00	140-209.
87-09-023	Dover Coach 6590-0	Department 56	Closed	18.00	50-88.00
87-09-024	Dover Coach w/o Mustache 6590-0	Department 56	Closed	18.00	85-150.00
87-09-025	Village Express Train (electric, black),5997-8	Department 56	Closed	89.95	275-350.
87-09-026	Christmas in the City Sign, 5960-9	Department 56	Closed	6.00	8-17.00
87-09-027	Dickens' Village Sign 6569-2	Department 56	Closed	6.00	8-28.00
87-09-028	New England Village Sign 6570-6	Department 56	Closed	6.00	8-18.00
87-09-029	Alpine Village Sign 6571-4	Department 56	Closed	6.00	8-12.00
88-09-030	Fezziwig and Friends 5928-5, set of 3	Department 56	Closed	12.50	38-78.00
88-09-031	Village Train Trestle 5981-1	Department 56	Closed	17.00	30-69.00
88-09-032	Woodcutter And Son 5986-2, set of 2	Department 56	Closed	10.00	22-46.00
88-09-033	Childe Pond and Skaters 5903-0, set of 4	Department 56	Closed	30.00	55-110.00
88-09-034	Nicholas Nickleby Characters 5929-3, set /4	Department 56	Closed	20.00	25-50.00
88-09-035	Village Harvest People 5941-2 set of 4	Department 56	Closed	27.50	32-60.00
88-09-036	City Newsstand 5971-4, set of 4	Department 56	Closed	25.00	25-75.00
88-09-037	City Bus & Milk Truck 5983-8, set of 2	Department 56	Closed	15.00	17-60.00
88-09-038	Salvation Army Band 5985-4, set of 6	Department 56	Closed	24.00	40-66.00
88-09-039	One Horse Open Sleigh 5982-0	Department 56	Closed	20.00	25-57.00
89-09-040	Constables 5579-4, set of 3	Department 56	Closed	17.50	32-75.00
89-09-041	Farm Animals 5945-5, set of 4	Department 56	Closed	15.00	25-51.00
89-09-042	Organ Grinder 5957-9, set of 3	Department 56	Closed	21.00	18-55.00
89-09-043	River Street Ice House Cart 5959-5	Department 56	Closed	20.00	20-50.00
89-09-044	David Copperfield Characters, set of 5 5551-4	Department 56	Closed	32.50	29-50.00
89-09-045	Royal Coach 5578-6	Department 56	Closed	55.00	55-100.00
89-09-046	Violet Vendor/Carolers/Chestnut Vendor set of 3 5580-8	Department 56	Closed	23.00	24-48.00
89-09-047	Popcorn Vendor, set of 3 5958-7	Department 56	Closed	22.00	20-40.00
89-09-048	U.S. Mail Box and Fire Hydrant, 5517-4	Department 56	Closed	5.00	10-45.00
89-09-049	Heritage Village Sign, 9953-8	Department 56	Closed	10.00	10-28.00
90-09-050	Busy Sidewalks, set of 4 5535-2	Department 56	Closed	28.00	27-75.00
90-09-051	Amish Family, set of 3 5948-0	Department 56	Closed	20.00	21-50.00
90-09-052	Amish Family, set of 3 5948-0 w/Moustache	Department 56	Closed	20.00	42-97.00
90-09-053	Amish Buggy 5949-8	Department 56	Closed	22.00	33-57.00
90-09-054	Sleepy Hollow Characters, set of 3 5956-0	Department 56	Closed	27.50	35-73.00
90-09-055	Carolers on the Doorstep, set of 4 5570-0	Department 56	Closed	25.00	33-48.00
90-09-056	Trimming the North Pole 5608-1	Department 56	Closed	10.00	18-28.00
90-09-057	Santa's Little Helpers, set of 3 5610-3	Department 56	Closed	28.00	35-57.00
91-09-058	Market Day, set of 3 5641-3	Department 56	Closed	35.00	37-61.00
91-09-059	All Around the Town, set of 2 5545-0	Department 56	Closed	18.00	29-46.00
91-09-060	Oliver Twist Characters, set of 3, 5554-9	Department 56	Closed	35.00	36-66.00
92-09-061	Churchyard Gate and Fence, 5563-8, set of 3	Department 56	Closed	15.00	40.00
Department 56		**The Original Snow Village Collection Accessories Retired**			
79-10-001	Aspen Trees 5052-6, Meadowland Series	Department 56	Closed	16.00	32.00
79-10-002	Sheep, 9 White, 3 Black 5053-4 Meadowland Series	Department 56	Closed	12.00	24.00
79-10-003	Carolers 5064-1	Department 56	Closed	12.00	105-121.
80-10-004	Ceramic Car 5069-0	Department 56	Closed	5.00	40-55.00
81-10-005	Ceramic Sleigh 5079-2	Department 56	Closed	5.00	48-60.00

Company Number	Name	Series Artist	Edition Limit	Issue Price	Quote
82-10-006	Snowman With Broom 5018-0	Department 56	Closed	3.00	9-15.00
83-10-007	Monks-A-Caroling (butterscotch) 6459-9	Department 56	Closed	6.00	54-86.00
84-10-008	Scottie With Tree 5038-5	Department 56	Closed	3.00	108-133.
84-10-009	Monks-A-Caroling (brown) 5040-7	Department 56	Closed	6.00	22-40.00
85-10-010	Singing Nuns 5053-9	Department 56	Closed	6.00	54-105.00
85-10-011	Snow Kids Sled, Skis 5056-3	Department 56	Closed	11.00	48-50.00
85-10-012	Family Mom/Kids, Goose/Girl 5057-1	Department 56	Closed	11.00	22-42.00
85-10-013	Santa/Mailbox 5059-8	Department 56	Closed	11.00	39-48.00
86-10-014	Girl/Snowman, Boy 5095-4	Department 56	Closed	11.00	36-50.00
86-10-015	Shopping Girls w/Packages (small) 5096-2	Department 56	Closed	11.00	24-57.00
86-10-016	Shopping Girls w/Packages (large) 5096-2	Department 56	Closed	11.00	33-46.00
86-10-017	Kids Around The Tree (small) 5094-6	Department 56	Closed	15.00	24-57.00
86-10-018	Kids Around The Tree (large) 5094-6	Department 56	Closed	15.00	72-95.00
87-10-019	3 Nuns With Songbooks 5102-0	Department 56	Closed	6.00	95-120.00
87-10-020	Praying Monks 5103-9	Department 56	Closed	6.00	30-80.00
87-10-021	Children In Band 5104-7	Department 56	Closed	15.00	17-34.00
87-10-022	Caroling Family 5105-5, set of 3	Department 56	Closed	20.00	22-42.00
87-10-023	Christmas Children 5107-1, set of 4	Department 56	Closed	20.00	22-46.00
87-10-024	Snow Kids 5113-6, set of 4	Department 56	Closed	20.00	42-60.00
88-10-025	Hayride 5117-9	Department 56	Closed	30.00	46-85.00
88-10-026	School Children 5118-7, set of 3	Department 56	Closed	15.00	12-38.00
88-10-027	Apple Girl/Newspaper Boy 5129-2, set of 2	Department 56	Closed	11.00	13-35.00
88-10-028	Woodsman and Boy 5130-6, set of 2	Department 56	Closed	13.00	16-32.00
88-10-029	Woody Station Wagon 5136-5	Department 56	Closed	6.50	18-40.00
88-10-030	Water Tower 5133-0	Department 56	Closed	20.00	40-60.00
88-10-031	School Bus, Snow Plow 5137-3, set of 2	Department 56	Closed	16.00	26-46.00
88-10-032	Sisal Tree Lot 8183-3	Department 56	Closed	45.00	55-97.00
88-10-033	Man On Ladder Hanging Garland 5116-0	Department 56	Closed	7.50	12-20.00
88-10-034	Doghouse/Cat In Garbage Can,set/2 5131-4	Department 56	Closed	15.00	18-31.00
89-10-035	US Special Delivery 5148-9 set of 2	Department 56	Closed	16.00	24-57.00
89-10-036	US Mailbox 5179-9	Department 56	Closed	3.50	10-17.00
89-10-037	Kids Tree House 5168-3	Department 56	Closed	25.00	25-69.00
89-10-038	Skate Faster Mom 5170-5	Department 56	Closed	13.00	17-46.00
89-10-039	Through the Woods 5172-1, set of 2	Department 56	Closed	18.00	20-46.00
89-10-040	Statue of Mark Twain 5173-0	Department 56	Closed	15.00	20-46.00
89-10-041	Calling All Cars 5174-8, set of 2	Department 56	Closed	15.00	22-34.00
89-10-042	Choir Kids 5147-0	Department 56	Closed	15.00	18-28.00
89-10-043	Bringing Home The Tree 5169-1	Department 56	Closed	15.00	18-27.00
90-10-044	Sleighride 5160-8	Department 56	Closed	30.00	37-69.00
90-10-045	Here We Come A Caroling, set/3 5161-6	Department 56	Closed	18.00	17-30.00
90-10-046	Home Delivery, set of 2 5162-4	Department 56	Closed	16.00	24-32.00
90-10-047	SV Special Delivery, set of 2 5197-7	Department 56	Closed	16.00	24-50.00
90-10-048	Kids Decorating the Village Sign, 5134-9	Department 56	Closed	12.50	12-14.00
90-10-049	Down the Chimney He Goes, 5158-6	Department 56	Closed	6.50	14.00
90-10-050	Sno-Jet Snowmobile, 5159-4	Department 56	Closed	15.00	17.00
90-10-051	Fresh Frozen Fish 5163-2, set of 2	Department 56	Closed	20.00	30-46.00
91-10-052	Come Join The Parade 5411-9	Department 56	Closed	12.50	12-46.00
91-10-053	Village Marching Band, set of 3 5412-7	Department 56	Closed	30.00	44-75.00
91-10-054	Winter Fountain, 5409-7	Department 56	Closed	25.00	39-57.00
91-10-055	Snowball Fort 5414-3, set of 3	Department 56	Closed	27.50	27-43.00
91-10-056	Country Harvest, 5415-1	Department 56	Closed	13.00	13.00
Department 56		**Snowbabies**			
86-11-001	Give Me A Push 7955-3	Department 56	Closed	12.00	38-66.00
86-11-002	Hold On Tight 7956-1	Department 56	Open	12.00	12.00
86-11-003	Best Friends 7958-8	Department 56	Closed	12.00	80-132.00
86-11-004	Snowbaby Nite-Lite 7959-6	Department 56	Closed	15.00	220-350.
86-11-005	I'm Making Snowballs 7962-6	Department 56	Closed	12.00	24-50.00
86-11-006	Climbing on Snowball, Bisque Votive w/Candle 7965-0	Department 56	Closed	15.00	53-90.00
86-11-007	Hanging Pair 7966-9	Department 56	Closed	15.00	94-138.00
86-11-008	Snowbaby Holding Picture Frame, set of 2 7970-7	Department 56	Closed	15.00	430-545.
86-11-009	Forest Accessory "Frosty Forest", set of 2 7963-4	Department 56	Open	15.00	15.00
87-11-010	Tumbling In the Snow, set of 5 7957-0	Department 56	Closed	35.00	45-69.00
87-11-011	Down The Hill We Go 7960-0	Department 56	Open	20.00	20.00
87-11-012	Don't Fall Off 7968-5	Department 56	Closed	12.50	35-72.00
87-11-013	Climbing On Tree, set of 2 7971-5	Department 56	Closed	25.00	450-528.
87-11-014	Winter Surprise 7974-0	Department 56	Closed	15.00	27-50.00
88-11-015	Are All These Mine? 7977-4	Department 56	Open	10.00	10.00
88-11-016	Polar Express 7978-2	Department 56	Closed	22.00	41-70.00
88-11-017	Tiny Trio, set of 3 7979-0	Department 56	Closed	20.00	85-120.00
88-11-018	Frosty Frolic 7981-2	Department 56	4,800	35.00	610-770.
89-11-019	Helpful Friends 7982-0	Department 56	Closed	30.00	35-44.00
89-11-020	Frosty Fun 7983-9	Department 56	Closed	27.50	32-75.00
89-11-021	All Fall Down, set of 4 7984-7	Department 56	Closed	36.00	50-80.00
89-11-022	Finding Fallen Stars 7985-5	Department 56	6,000	32.50	140-175.
89-11-023	Penguin Parade 7986-3	Department 56	Closed	25.00	41-69.00
89-11-024	Icy Igloo 7987-1	Department 56	Open	37.50	37.50
90-11-025	Twinkle Little Stars 7942-1, set of 2	Department 56	Closed	37.50	38.50
90-11-026	Wishing on a Star 7943-0	Department 56	Open	20.00	20.00
90-11-027	Read Me a Story 7945-6	Department 56	Open	25.00	25.00
90-11-028	We Will Make it Shine 7946-4	Department 56	Closed	45.00	55-97.00
90-11-029	Playing Games Is Fun 7947-2	Department 56	Closed	30.00	50.00
90-11-030	A Special Delivery 7948-0	Department 56	Open	13.50	13.50
90-11-031	Who Are You? 7949-9	Department 56	12,500	32.50	105-160.
91-11-032	I'll Put Up The Tree 6800-4	Department 56	Open	24.00	24.00
91-11-033	Why Don't You Talk To Me 6801-2	Department 56	Open	24.00	24.00
91-11-034	I Made This Just For You 6802-0	Department 56	Open	15.00	15.00
91-11-035	Is That For Me 6803-9, set of 2	Department 56	Closed	32.50	33-57.00
91-11-036	Snowbaby Polar Sign 6804-7	Department 56	Open	20.00	20.00
91-11-037	This Is Where We Live 6805-5	Department 56	Open	60.00	60.00
91-11-038	Waiting For Christmas 6807-1	Department 56	Closed	27.50	33-46.00
91-11-039	Dancing To a Tune 6808-0, set of 3	Department 56	Open	30.00	30.00
91-11-040	Fishing For Dreams 6809-8	Department 56	Open	28.00	28.00
92-11-041	Can I Help, Too? 6806-3	Department 56	18,500	48.00	70-150.00
92-11-042	I Need A Hug 6813-6	Department 56	Open	20.00	20.00
92-11-043	Let's Go Skiing 6815-2	Department 56	Open	15.00	15.00
92-11-044	Wait For Me 6812-8	Department 56	Open	48.00	48.00
92-11-045	Winken, Blinken, and Nod 6814-4	Department 56	Open	60.00	60.00
92-11-046	This Willl Cheer You Up 6816-0	Department 56	Open	30.00	30.00
92-11-047	Help Me, I'm Stuck 6817-9	Department 56	Open	32.50	32.50
92-11-048	You Can't Find Me! 6818-7	Department 56	Open	45.00	45.00
92-11-049	Look What I Can Do! 6819-5	Department 56	Open	16.50	16.50
92-11-050	Shall I Play For You? 6820-9	Department 56	Open	16.50	16.50
92-11-051	You Didn't Forget Me 6821-7	Department 56	Open	32.50	32.50
92-11-052	Stars-In-A-Row, Tic-Tac-Toe 6822-5	Department 56	Open	32.50	32.50
92-11-053	Just One Little Candle 6823-3	Department 56	Open	15.00	15.00
92-11-054	Join The Parade 6824-1	Department 56	Open	37.50	37.50
92-11-055	Snowbabies Bridge "Over the Milky Way" 6828-4	Department 56	Open	32.00	32.00
92-11-056	Snowbabies Trees "Starry Pines" set of 2, 6829-2	Department 56	Open	17.50	17.50

Company Number	Name	Series Artist	Edition Limit	Issue Price	Quote
93-11-057	Look What I Found 6833-0	Department 56	Open	45.00	45.00
93-11-058	Crossing Starry Skies 6834-9	Department 56	Open	35.00	35.00
93-11-059	I'll Teach You A Trick 6835-7	Department 56	Open	24.00	24.00
93-11-060	I Found Your Mittens, Set of 2, 6836-5	Department 56	Open	30.00	30.00
93-11-061	So Much Work To Do 6837-3	Department 56	Open	18.00	18.00
93-11-062	Can I Open it Now? 6838-1 (Event Piece)	Department 56	Closed	15.00	30-33.00
93-11-063	Now I Lay Me Down to Sleep 6839-0	Department 56	Open	13.50	13.50
93-11-064	Somewhere in Dreamland 6840-3	Department 56	Open	85.00	85.00
93-11-065	Where Did He Go? 6841-1	Department 56	Open	35.00	35.00
93-11-066	I'm Making an Ice Sculpture 6842-0	Department 56	Open	30.00	30.00
93-11-067	We Make a Great Pair 6843-8	Department 56	Open	30.00	30.00
93-11-068	Will it Snow Today? 6844-6	Department 56	Open	45.00	45.00
93-11-069	Let's All Chime In! 6845-4, set of 2	Department 56	Open	37.50	37.50
93-11-070	Snowbabies Picture Frame, Baby's First Smile 6846-2	Department 56	Open	30.00	30.00
Department 56		**Snowbabies Pewter Miniatures**			
89-12-001	Are All These Mine? 7605-8	Department 56	Closed	7.00	10-19.00
89-12-002	Helpful Friends, set of 4 7608-2	Department 56	Closed	13.50	24-34.00
89-12-003	Polar Express, set of 2, 7609-0	Department 56	Closed	13.50	19-34.00
89-12-004	Icy Igloo, w/tree, set of 2 7610-4	Department 56	Closed	7.50	17-22.00
89-12-005	Tumbling in the Snow!, set of 5, 7614-7	Department 56	Closed	30.00	44-77.00
89-12-006	Finding Fallen Stars, set of 2, 7618-0	Department 56	Closed	12.50	18-28.00
89-12-007	Frosty Frolic, set of 4, 7613-9	Department 56	Closed	24.00	24.00
89-12-008	Tiny Trio, set of 3, 7615-5	Department 56	Closed	18.00	18.00
89-12-009	Penguin Parade, set of 4, 7616-3	Department 56	Closed	12.50	12.50
89-12-010	All Fall Down, set of 4, 7617-1	Department 56	Closed	25.00	25.00
90-12-011	Twinkle Little Stars, set of 2, 7621-0	Department 56	Closed	15.00	15.00
90-12-012	Playing Games is Fun!, set of 2, 7623-6	Department 56	Closed	13.50	13.50
90-12-013	A Special Delivery 7624-4	Department 56	Closed	7.00	7.00
91-12-014	Waiting for Christmas, 7629-5	Department 56	Closed	12.50	12.50
91-12-015	Dancing to a Tune, set of 3, 7630-9	Department 56	Closed	18.00	18.00
91-12-016	Is That For Me?, set of 2, 7631-7	Department 56	Closed	12.50	12.50
Department 56		**Village CCP Miniatures**			
87-13-001	Dickens' Village Original, set of 7 6558-7	Department 56	Closed	72.00	200-250.
87-13-002	Crowntree Inn 6558-7	Department 56	Closed	12.00	36.00
87-13-003	Candle Shop 6558-7	Department 56	Closed	12.00	30-40.00
87-13-004	Green Grocer 6558-7	Department 56	Closed	12.00	30-49.00
87-13-005	Golden Swan Baker 6558-7	Department 56	Closed	12.00	30-49.00
87-13-006	Bean and Son Smithy Shop 6558-7	Department 56	Closed	12.00	37.00
87-13-007	Abel Beesley Butcher 6558-7	Department 56	Closed	12.00	22.00
87-13-008	Jones & Co. Brush & Basket Shop 6558-7	Department 56	Closed	12.00	36.00
87-13-009	Dickens' Cottages, set of 3 6559-5	Department 56	Closed	30.00	150-200.
87-13-010	Thatched Cottage 6559-5	Department 56	Closed	10.00	72.00
87-13-011	Stone Cottage 6559-5	Department 56	Closed	10.00	90.00
87-13-012	Tudor Cottage 6559-5	Department 56	Closed	10.00	85-175.00
87-13-013	Dickens' Village Assorted, set of 3 6560-9	Department 56	Closed	48.00	N/A
87-13-014	Dickens Village Church 6560-9	Department 56	Closed	16.00	50.00
87-13-015	Norman Church 6560-9	Department 56	Closed	16.00	55-100.00
87-13-016	Blythe Pond Mill House 6560-9	Department 56	Closed	16.00	36-50.00
87-13-017	Christmas Carol Cottages, set of 3 6561-7	Department 56	Closed	30.00	77-88.00
87-13-018	Fezziwig's Warehouse 6561-7	Department 56	Closed	10.00	25-35.00
87-13-019	Scrooge & Marley Countinghouse 6561-7	Department 56	Closed	10.00	26-33.00
87-13-020	The Cottage of Bob Cratchit & Tiny Tim 6561-7	Department 56	Closed	10.00	36.00
87-13-021	Dickens' Village Assorted, set of 4 6562-5	Department 56	Closed	60.00	N/A
87-13-022	The Old Curiosity Shop 6562-5	Department 56	Closed	15.00	45-58.00
87-13-023	Brick Abbey 6562-5	Department 56	Closed	15.00	23-60.00
87-13-024	Chesterton Manor House 6562-5	Department 56	Closed	15.00	60-75.00
87-13-025	Barley Bree Farmhouse 6562-5	Department 56	Closed	15.00	35.00
88-13-026	Dickens' Kenilworth Castle 6565-0	Department 56	Closed	30.00	89.00
87-13-027	Dickens' Lane Shops, set of 3 6591-9	Department 56	Closed	30.00	100-150.
87-13-028	Thomas Kersey Coffee House 6591-9	Department 56	Closed	10.00	35-65.00
87-13-029	Cottage Toy Shop 6591-9	Department 56	Closed	10.00	37.00
87-13-030	Tuttle's Pub 6591-9	Department 56	Closed	10.00	49.00
87-13-031	Dickens' Chadbury Station & Train 6592-7	Department 56	Closed	27.50	70-75.00
88-13-032	New England Village Original, set of 7 5935-8	Department 56	Closed	72.00	250-425.
88-13-033	Apothecary Shop 5935-8	Department 56	Closed	10.50	30-45.00
88-13-034	General Store 5935-8	Department 56	Closed	10.50	50-60.00
88-13-035	Nathaniel Bingham Fabrics 5935-8	Department 56	Closed	10.50	50.00
88-13-036	Livery Stable & Boot Shop 5935-8	Department 56	Closed	10.50	30-50.00
88-13-037	Steeple Church 5935-8	Department 56	Closed	10.50	40-125.00
88-13-038	Brick Town Hall 5935-8	Department 56	Closed	10.50	40-55.00
88-13-039	Red Schoolhouse 5935-8	Department 56	Closed	10.50	40-65.00
88-13-040	New England Village Assorted, set of 6 5937-4	Department 56	Closed	85.00	225.00
88-13-041	Timber Knoll Log Cabin 5937-4	Department 56	Closed	14.50	30-42.00
88-13-042	Smythe Wollen Mill 5937-4	Department 56	Closed	14.50	65-80.00
88-13-043	Jacob Adams Farmhouse 5937-4	Department 56	Closed	14.50	42-50.00
88-13-044	Jacob Adams Barn 5937-4	Department 56	Closed	14.50	60.00
88-13-045	Craggy Cove Lighthouse 5937-4	Department 56	Closed	14.50	90-150.
88-13-046	Maple Sugaring Shed 5937-4	Department 56	Closed	14.50	32-48.00
87-13-047	Little Town of Bethlehem, set of 12 5976-5	Department 56	Closed	85.00	140-195.
86-13-048	Victorian Miniatures, set of 5 6563-3	Department 56	Closed	65.00	N/A
86-13-049	Victorian Miniatures, set of 2 6564-1	Department 56	Closed	45.00	300.00
86-13-050	Estate 6564-1	Department 56	Closed	22.50	N/A
86-13-051	Church 6564-1	Department 56	Closed	22.50	N/A
86-13-052	Williamsburg Snowhouse Series, set of 6 6566-8	Department 56	Closed	60.00	500-575.
86-13-053	Williamsburg Church, White 6566-8	Department 56	Closed	10.00	40.00
86-13-054	Williamsburg House, Blue 6566-8	Department 56	Closed	10.00	60.00
86-13-055	Williamsburg House, Brown Brick 6566-8	Department 56	Closed	10.00	40.00
86-13-056	Williamsburg House, Brown Clapboard 6566-8	Department 56	Closed	10.00	40.00
86-13-057	Williamsburg House, Red 6566-8	Department 56	Closed	10.00	60.00
86-13-058	Williamsburg House, White 6566-8	Department 56	Closed	10.00	75.00
Department 56		**Easter Collectibles**			
91-14-001	Bisque Lamb, Large 4" 7392-0	Department 56	Closed	7.50	26-46.00
91-14-002	Bisque Lamb, Small 2.5" 7393-8	Department 56	Closed	5.00	20-36.00
91-14-003	Bisque Lamb, set	Department 56	Closed	12.50	31-57.00
92-14-004	Bisque Rabbit, Large 5" 7498-5	Department 56	Closed	8.00	25-28.00
92-14-005	Bisque Rabbit, Small 4" 7499-3	Department 56	Closed	6.00	14-19.00
92-14-006	Bisque Rabbit, set	Department 56	Closed	14.00	34-39.00
93-14-007	Bisque Duckling, Large 3.5" 7282-6	Department 56	Closed	8.50	11-21.00
93-14-008	Bisque Duckling, Small 2.75" 7281-8	Department 56	Closed	6.50	10-18.00
93-14-009	Bisque Duckling, set	Department 56	Closed	15.00	22.00
94-14-010	Bisque Fledgling in Nest, Large 2.75" 2400-7	Department 56	Open	6.00	6.00
94-14-011	Bisque Fledgling in Nest, Small 2.5" 2401-5	Department 56	Open	5.00	5.00
Walt Disney		**Classics Collection-Cinderella**			
92-01-001	Cinderella 6" 41000	Disney Studios	Closed	195.00	282-600.

Company / Number	Name	Series / Artist	Edition Limit	Issue Price	Quote
92-01-002	Lucifer 2 3/5" 41001	Disney Studios	Closed	69.00	100-200.
92-01-003	Bruno 4 2/5" 41002	Disney Studios	Closed	69.00	100-200.
92-01-004	Sewing Book 41003	Disney Studios	Open	69.00	69.00
92-01-005	Needle Mouse 5 4/5" 41004	Disney Studios	Open	69.00	69.00
92-01-006	Birds With Sash 6 2/5" 41005	Disney Studios	Open	149.00	149.00
92-01-007	Chalk Mouse 3 2/5" 41006	Disney Studios	Open	65.00	65.00
92-01-008	Gus 3 2/5" 41007	Disney Studios	Open	65.00	65.00
92-01-009	Jaq 4 1/5" 41008	Disney Studios	Open	65.00	65.00
92-01-010	Cinderella-Opening Title 41009	Disney Studios	Open	29.00	29.00
93-01-011	A Dress For Cinderelly 41030	Disney Studios	Closed	800.00	1600-2500.
Walt Disney		**Classics Collection-Bambi**			
92-02-001	Bambi & Flower 6" 41010	Disney Studios	Closed	298.00	400-700.
92-02-002	Friend Owl 8 3/5" 41011	Disney Studios	Open	195.00	195.00
92-02-003	Field Mouse 5 3/5" 41012	Disney Studios	Closed	195.00	1000-1875.
92-02-004	Thumper 3" 41013	Disney Studios	Open	55.00	55.00
92-02-005	Thumper's Sisters 3 3/5" 41014	Disney Studios	Open	69.00	69.00
92-02-006	Bambi 41033	Disney Studios	Open	195.00	195.00
92-02-007	Flower 41034	Disney Studios	Open	78.00	78.00
92-02-008	Bambi-Opening Title 41015	Disney Studios	Open	29.00	29.00
Walt Disney		**Classics Collection-Fantasia**			
92-03-001	Sorcerer Mickey 5 1/5" 41016	Disney Studios	Open	195.00	195.00
92-03-002	Broom (Two) 5 4/5" 41017	Disney Studios	Open	150.00	150.00
93-03-003	Romantic Reflections-Pink Centaurette 41040	Disney Studios	Open	175.00	175.00
93-03-004	Beauty in Bloom-Blue Centaurette 41041	Disney Studios	Open	195.00	195.00
93-03-005	Love's Little Helpers 41042	Disney Studios	Open	N/A	N/A
92-03-006	Fantasia-Opening Title 41018	Disney Studios	Open	29.00	29.00
Walt Disney		**Classics Collection-The Delivery Boy**			
92-04-001	Mickey 6" 41020	Disney Studios	Open	125.00	125.00
92-04-002	Minnie 6" 41021	Disney Studios	Open	125.00	125.00
92-04-003	Pluto 3 3/5" 41022	Disney Studios	Open	125.00	125.00
92-04-004	Delivery Boy-Opening Title 41019	Disney Studios	Open	29.00	29.00
Walt Disney		**Classics Collection-Mr. Duck**			
93-05-001	Donald & Daisy (cleft) 41024	Disney Studios	5,000	295.00	600-1100.
93-05-002	Donald & Daisy (wheel) 41024	Disney Studios	5,000	295.00	550-1210.
93-05-003	Nephew Duck-Dewey 41025	Disney Studios	Open	65.00	65.00
93-05-004	Nephew Duck-Huey 41049	Disney Studios	Open	65.00	65.00
93-05-005	Nephew Duck-Louie 41050	Disney Studios	Open	65.00	65.00
93-05-006	Mr. Duck Steps Out-Opening Title 41032	Disney Studios	Open	29.00	29.00
Walt Disney		**Classics Collection-Symphony Hour**			
93-06-001	Goofy (wheel) 41026	Disney Studios	Closed	198.00	1210.00
93-06-002	Goofy 41026	Disney Studios	Open	198.00	198.00
93-06-003	Clarabelle 41027	Disney Studios	Open	198.00	198.00
93-06-003	Horace 41028	Disney Studios	Open	198.00	198.00
93-06-004	Mickey Conductor 41029	Disney Studios	Open	185.00	185.00
93-06-005	Symphony Hour-Opening Title 41031	Disney Studios	Open	29.00	29.00
Walt Disney		**Classics Collection-Three Little Pigs**			
93-07-001	Practical Pig 41036	Disney Studios	Open	75.00	75.00
93-07-002	Fifer Pig 41037	Disney Studios	Open	75.00	75.00
93-07-003	Fiddler Pig 41038	Disney Studios	Open	75.00	75.00
93-07-004	Big Bad Wolf 41039	Disney Studios	7,500	295.00	660-1000.
93-07-005	Three Little Pigs-Opening Title 41046	Disney Studios	Open	29.00	29.00
Walt Disney		**Classics Collection-Peter Pan**			
93-08-001	Peter Pan 41043	Disney Studios	Open	165.00	165.00
93-08-002	Captain Hook 41044	Disney Studios	Open	275.00	275.00
93-08-003	The Crocodile 41054	Disney Studios	Open	315.00	315.00
93-08-004	Tinkerbell 41045	Disney Studios	12,500	215.00	215.00
93-08-005	Peter Pan-Opening Title 41047	Disney Studios	Open	29.00	29.00
Walt Disney		**Classics Collection-Special Event**			
93-09-001	Flight of Fancy 41051	Disney Studios	Open	35.00	35.00
Walt Disney		**Classics Collection Collector Club**			
93-10-001	Jiminy Cricket	Disney Studios	Yr.Iss.	Gift	84-140.00
93-10-002	Brave Little Tailor	Disney Studios	Yr.Iss.	160.00	160-293.
94-10-003	Cheshire Cat	Disney Studios	Yr.Iss.	Gift	N/A
Disneyana		**Disneyana Conventions**			
92-01-001	Tinker Bell 022075	Lladro	1,500	350.00	2000-3200.
92-01-002	Two Merry Wanderers 022074	Goebel	1,500	250.00	770-1000.
92-01-003	Big Thunder Mountain A26648	R. Lee	100	1650.00	1650-3000.
92-01-004	Nifty-Nineties Mickey & Minnie 022503	House of Laurenz	250	650.00	1100.00
92-01-005	Carousel Horse 022482	PJ's	250	125.00	330-500.
92-01-006	1947 Mickey Mouse Plush J20967	Gund	1,000	50.00	250.00
92-01-007	Carousel Horse Poster (Lithograph) -A26318	R. Souders	2,000	25.00	N/A
92-01-008	Cinderella 022076	Armani	500	500.00	3100-3500.
92-01-009	Serigraph Diptych Collage (set of 2) -022073	M. Graves	1,000	900.00	N/A
92-01-010	Cruella DeVill Doll-porcelain 22554	J. Wolf	25	3000.00	N/A
92-01-011	Cinderella Castle 022077	John Hine Studio	500	250.00	770-1200.
92-01-012	Pinocchio	R. Wright	250	750.00	N/A
92-01-013	Walt's Convertible (Cel)	Disney Art Ed.	500	950.00	1100.00
93-01-014	Snow White	Armani	2,000	750.00	950-1500.
93-01-015	Dopey	Armani	Open	125.00	125.00
93-01-016	The Band Concert-Bronze	B. Toma	25	650.00	5000-6600.
93-01-017	Alice in Wonderland	Malvern	10	8,000.00	N/A
93-01-018	Barbershop Quartet (Lithograph)	C. Boyer	1,000	350.00	N/A
93-01-019	Family Dinner Figurine	C. Boyer	1,000	600.00	N/A
93-01-020	Two Little Drummers	Goebel	1,500	325.00	495-600.
93-01-021	1947 Minnie Mouse Plush	Gund	1,000	50.00	110-175.
93-01-022	Sleeping Beauty Castle	John Hine Studio	500	250.00	495-700.
93-01-023	Peter Pan	Lladro	2,000	400.00	1050-1650.
93-01-024	Jumper from King Arthur Carousel	PJ's	250	125.00	165-400.
93-01-025	Mickey's Dreams	R. Lee	250	400.00	660-800.
93-01-026	Disneyland Bandstand Poster	R. Souders	2,000	25.00	N/A
93-01-027	Annette Doll	Alexander Doll	1,000	400.00	660.00
93-01-038	Mickey Mouse, the Bandleader	Arribas Brothers	25	700.00	3300-5000.
93-01-029	Walt's Train Celebration	Disney Art Ed.	950	950.00	1650.00
93-01-030	The Band Concert "Maestro Mickey"	Disney Art Ed.	275	2950.00	N/A
Duncan Royale		**History of Santa Claus I**			
83-01-001	St. Nicholas	P. Apsit	Retrd.	175.00	455-1800.
83-01-002	Dedt Moroz	P. Apsit	Retrd.	145.00	285-1000.
83-01-003	Black Peter	P. Apsit	Retrd.	145.00	163-350.
83-01-004	Victorian	P. Apsit	Retrd.	120.00	156-495.
83-01-005	Medieval	P. Apsit	Retrd.	220.00	1500-4500.
83-01-006	Russian	P. Apsit	Retrd.	145.00	450-1000.
83-01-007	Wassail	P. Apsit	Retrd.	90.00	163-500.
83-01-008	Kris Kringle	P. Apsit	Retrd.	165.00	1000-3500.
83-01-009	Soda Pop	P. Apsit	Retrd.	145.00	1500-4500.
83-01-010	Pioneer	P. Apsit	Retrd.	145.00	250-1500.
83-01-011	Civil War	P. Apsit	10,000	145.00	250-495.
83-01-012	Nast	P. Apsit	Retrd.	90.00	2400-6900.
83-01-013	Set/12	P. Apsit	Retrd.	1730.00	7200-15000.
Duncan Royale		**History of Santa Claus II**			
86-02-001	Odin	P. Apsit	10,000	200.00	250.00
86-02-002	Lord of Misrule	P. Apsit	10,000	160.00	200.00
86-02-003	Mongolian/Asian	P. Apsit	10,000	240.00	300.00
86-02-004	The Magi	P. Apsit	10,000	350.00	400.00
86-02-005	St. Lucia	P. Apsit	10,000	180.00	225.00
86-02-006	Befana	P. Apsit	10,000	200.00	250.00
86-02-007	Babouska	P. Apsit	10,000	170.00	200.00
86-02-008	Bavarian	P. Apsit	10,000	250.00	300.00
86-02-009	Alsace Angel	P. Apsit	10,000	250.00	300.00
86-02-010	Frau Holda	P. Apsit	10,000	160.00	180.00
86-02-011	Sir Christmas	P. Apsit	10,000	150.00	175.00
86-02-012	The Pixie	P. Apsit	10,000	140.00	175.00
Duncan Royale		**History of Santa Claus III**			
90-03-001	St. Basil	Duncan Royale	10,000	300.00	300.00
90-03-002	Star Man	Duncan Royale	10,000	300.00	300.00
90-03-003	Julenisse	Duncan Royale	10,000	200.00	200.00
90-03-004	Ukko	Duncan Royale	10,000	250.00	250.00
90-03-005	Druid	Duncan Royale	10,000	250.00	250.00
91-03-006	Saturnalia King	Duncan Royale	10,000	200.00	200.00
91-03-007	Judah Maccabee	Duncan Royale	10,000	300.00	300.00
91-03-008	King Wenceslas	Duncan Royale	10,000	300.00	300.00
91-03-009	Hoteisho	Duncan Royale	10,000	200.00	200.00
91-03-010	Knickerbocker	Duncan Royale	10,000	300.00	300.00
91-03-011	Samichlaus	Duncan Royale	10,000	350.00	350.00
91-03-012	Grandfather Frost & Snow Maiden	Duncan Royale	10,000	400.00	400.00
Duncan Royale		**History Of Santa Claus-Special Releases**			
91-04-001	Signature Piece	Duncan Royale	Open	50.00	50.00
92-04-002	Nast & Sleigh	Duncan Royale	5,000	500.00	500.00
Duncan Royale		**History of Santa Claus I -Wood**			
87-05-001	St. Nicholas-8" wood	P. Apsit	500	450.00	450.00
87-05-002	Dedt Moroz-8" wood	P. Apsit	Retrd.	450.00	450.00
87-05-003	Black Peter-8" wood	P. Apsit	Retrd.	450.00	450.00
87-05-004	Victorian-8" wood	P. Apsit	Retrd.	450.00	450.00
87-05-005	Medieval-8" wood	P. Apsit	500	450.00	450.00
87-05-006	Russian-8" wood	P. Apsit	Retrd.	450.00	450.00
87-05-007	Wassail-8" wood	P. Apsit	Retrd.	450.00	450.00
87-05-008	Kris Kringle-8" wood	P. Apsit	500	450.00	450.00
87-05-009	Soda Pop-8" wood	P. Apsit	Retrd.	450.00	450.00
87-05-010	Pioneer-8" wood	P. Apsit	Retrd.	450.00	450.00
87-05-011	Civil War-8" wood	P. Apsit	500	450.00	450.00
87-05-012	Nast-8" wood	P. Apsit	Retrd.	450.00	450.00
Duncan Royale		**History of Santa Claus (18")**			
89-06-001	St. Nicholas-18"	P. Apsit	1,000	1500.00	1500.00
89-06-002	Medieval-18"	P. Apsit	1,000	1500.00	1500.00
89-06-003	Russian-18"	P. Apsit	1,000	1500.00	1500.00
89-06-004	Kris Kringle-18"	P. Apsit	1,000	1500.00	1500.00
89-06-005	Soda Pop-18"	P. Apsit	1,000	1500.00	1500.00
89-06-006	Nast-18"	P. Apsit	1,000	1500.00	1500.00
Duncan Royale		**History of Santa Claus I (6")**			
88-07-001	St. Nicholas-6" porcelain	P. Apsit	6,000/yr.	70.00	80.00
88-07-002	Dedt Moroz -6" porcelain	P. Apsit	6,000/yr.	70.00	80.00
88-07-003	Black Peter-6" porcelain	P. Apsit	6,000/yr.	70.00	80.00
88-07-004	Victorian-6" porcelain	P. Apsit	6,000/yr.	60.00	80.00
88-07-005	Medieval-6" porcelain	P. Apsit	6,000/yr.	70.00	80.00
88-07-006	Russian-6" porcelain	P. Apsit	6,000/yr.	70.00	80.00
88-07-007	Wassail-6" porcelain	P. Apsit	6,000/yr.	60.00	80.00
88-07-008	Kris Kringle-6" porcelain	P. Apsit	6,000/yr.	60.00	80.00
88-07-009	Soda Pop-6" porcelain	P. Apsit	6,000/yr.	60.00	80.00
88-07-010	Pioneer-6" porcelain	P. Apsit	6,000/yr.	60.00	80.00
88-07-011	Civil War-6" porcelain	P. Apsit	6,000/yr.	60.00	80.00
88-07-012	Nast-6" porcelain	P. Apsit	6,000/yr.	60.00	80.00
Duncan Royale		**History of Santa Claus II (6")**			
88-08-001	Odin-6" porcelain	P. Apsit	6,000/yr.	80.00	90.00
88-08-002	Lord of Misrule-6" porcelain	P. Apsit	6,000/yr.	60.00	80.00
88-08-003	Mongolian/Asian-6" porcelain	P. Apsit	6,000/yr.	80.00	90.00
88-08-004	Magi-6" porcelain	P. Apsit	6,000/yr.	130.00	150.00
88-08-005	St. Lucia-6" porcelain	P. Apsit	6,000/yr.	70.00	80.00
88-08-006	Befana-6" porcelain	P. Apsit	6,000/yr.	70.00	80.00
88-08-007	Babouska-6" porcelain	P. Apsit	6,000/yr.	70.00	80.00
88-08-008	Bavarian-6" porcelain	P. Apsit	6,000/yr.	90.00	100.00
88-08-009	Alsace Angel-6" porcelain	P. Apsit	6,000/yr.	80.00	90.00
88-08-010	Frau Holda-6" porcelain	P. Apsit	6,000/yr.	50.00	80.00
88-08-011	Sir Christmas-6" porcelain	P. Apsit	6,000/yr.	60.00	80.00
88-08-012	Pixie-6" porcelain	P. Apsit	6,000/yr.	50.00	80.00
90-08-013	Bob Hope-6" porcelain	P. Apsit	6,000/yr.	130.00	130.00
Duncan Royale		**History of Classic Entertainers**			
87-09-001	Greco-Roman	P. Apsit	Retrd.	180.00	350.00
87-09-002	Jester	P. Apsit	Retrd.	410.00	600-850.
87-09-003	Pierrot	P. Apsit	Retrd.	180.00	180-350.
87-09-004	Harlequin	P. Apsit	Retrd.	250.00	350.00
87-09-005	Grotesque	P. Apsit	Retrd.	230.00	350.00
87-09-006	Pantalone	P. Apsit	Retrd.	270.00	350.00
87-09-007	Pulcinella	P. Apsit	Retrd.	220.00	350.00
87-09-008	Russian	P. Apsit	Retrd.	190.00	350.00
87-09-009	Auguste	P. Apsit	Retrd.	220.00	350.00
87-09-010	Slapstick	P. Apsit	Retrd.	250.00	350.00
87-09-011	Uncle Sam	P. Apsit	Retrd.	160.00	250-350.
87-09-012	American	P. Apsit	Retrd.	160.00	350.00
Duncan Royale		**History of Classic Entertainers II**			
88-10-001	Goliard	P. Apsit	Retrd.	200.00	200-350.
88-10-002	Touchstone	P. Apsit	Retrd.	200.00	200-350.
88-10-003	Feste	P. Apsit	Retrd.	250.00	200-350.
88-10-004	Tartaglia	P. Apsit	Retrd.	200.00	200-350.
88-10-005	Zanni	P. Apsit	Retrd.	200.00	200-350.
88-10-006	Mountebank	P. Apsit	Retrd.	270.00	200-350.

Company / Number	Series / Name	Artist	Edition Limit	Issue Price	Quote
88-10-007	Pedrolino	P. Apsit	Retrd.	200.00	200-350.
88-10-008	Thomassi	P. Apsit	Retrd.	200.00	200-350.
88-10-009	Tramp	P. Apsit	Retrd.	200.00	200-350.
88-10-010	White Face	P. Apsit	Retrd.	250.00	200-350.
88-10-011	Mime	P. Apsit	Retrd.	200.00	200-350.
88-10-012	Bob Hope	P. Apsit	Retrd.	250.00	250-350.
Duncan Royale	**History of Classic Entertainers-Special Releases**				
88-11-001	Signature Piece	P. Apsit	Retrd.	50.00	50.00
90-11-002	Mime-18"	P. Apsit	Retrd.	1500.00	1500.00
90-11-003	Bob Hope-18"	P. Aspit	Retrd.	1500.00	1500-2200.
Duncan Royale	**Greatest Gift...Love**				
88-12-001	Annunciation, marble	P. Apsit	5,000	270.00	270.00
88-12-002	Annunciation, painted porcelain	P. Apsit	5,000	270.00	270.00
88-12-003	Nativity, marble	P. Apsit	5,000	500.00	500.00
88-12-004	Nativity, painted porcelain	P. Apsit	5,000	500.00	500.00
88-12-005	Crucifixion, marble	P. Apsit	5,000	300.00	300.00
88-12-006	Crucifixion, painted porcelain	P. Apsit	5,000	300.00	300.00
Duncan Royale	**Woodland Fairies**				
88-13-001	Cherry	Duncan Royale	10,000	70.00	70.00
88-13-002	Mulberry	Duncan Royale	10,000	70.00	70.00
88-13-003	Apple	Duncan Royale	10,000	70.00	70.00
88-13-004	Poplar	Duncan Royale	10,000	70.00	70.00
88-13-005	Elm	Duncan Royale	10,000	70.00	70.00
88-13-006	Chestnut	Duncan Royale	10,000	70.00	70.00
88-13-007	Calla Lily	Duncan Royale	10,000	70.00	70.00
88-13-008	Pear Blossom	Duncan Royale	10,000	70.00	70.00
88-13-010	Lime Tree	Duncan Royale	10,000	70.00	70.00
88-13-011	Christmas Tree	Duncan Royale	10,000	70.00	70.00
88-13-012	Sycamore	Duncan Royale	10,000	70.00	70.00
88-13-013	Pine Tree	Duncan Royale	10,000	70.00	70.00
88-13-014	Almond Blossom	Duncan Royale	10,000	70.00	70.00
Duncan Royale	**Calendar Secrets (12")**				
90-14-001	January	D. Aphessetche	5,000	260.00	260.00
90-14-002	February	D. Aphessetche	5,000	370.00	370.00
90-14-003	March	D. Aphessetche	5,000	350.00	350.00
90-14-004	April	D. Aphessetche	5,000	370.00	370.00
90-14-005	May	D. Aphessetche	5,000	390.00	390.00
90-14-006	June	D. Aphessetche	5,000	410.00	410.00
90-14-007	July	D. Aphessetche	5,000	280.00	280.00
90-14-008	August	D. Aphessetche	5,000	300.00	300.00
90-14-009	September	D. Aphessetche	5,000	300.00	300.00
90-14-010	October	D. Aphessetche	5,000	350.00	350.00
90-14-011	November	D. Aphessetche	5,000	410.00	410.00
90-14-012	December	D. Aphessetche	5,000	410.00	410.00
Duncan Royale	**Ebony Collection**				
90-15-001	The Fiddler	Duncan Royale	5,000	90.00	90.00
90-15-002	Harmonica Man	Duncan Royale	5,000	80.00	80.00
90-15-003	Banjo Man	Duncan Royale	5,000	80.00	80.00
91-15-004	Spoons	Duncan Royale	5,000	90.00	90.00
91-15-005	Preacher	Duncan Royale	5,000	90.00	90.00
91-15-006	Female Gospel Singer	Duncan Royale	5,000	90.00	90.00
91-15-007	Male Gospel Singer	Duncan Royale	5,000	90.00	90.00
91-15-008	Jug Man	Duncan Royale	5,000	90.00	90.00
92-15-009	Jug Tooter	Duncan Royale	5,000	90.00	90.00
92-15-010	A Little Magic	Duncan Royale	5,000	80.00	80.00
93-15-011	Ebony Angel	Duncan Royale	5,000	170.00	170.00
Duncan Royale	**Ebony Collection-Jazzman**				
92-16-001	Jazz Man Set	Duncan Royale	5,000	500.00	500.00
92-16-002	Sax	Duncan Royale	5,000	90.00	90.00
92-16-003	Trumpet	Duncan Royale	5,000	90.00	90.00
92-16-004	Bass	Duncan Royale	5,000	90.00	90.00
92-16-005	Piano	Duncan Royale	5,000	130.00	130.00
92-16-006	Bongo	Duncan Royale	5,000	90.00	90.00
Duncan Royale	**Ebony Collection-Jubilee Dancers**				
93-17-001	Fallana	Duncan Royale	5,000	100.00	100.00
93-17-002	Keshia	Duncan Royale	5,000	100.00	100.00
93-17-003	Lottie	Duncan Royale	5,000	100.00	100.00
93-17-004	Wilfred	Duncan Royale	5,000	100.00	100.00
93-17-005	Bliss	Duncan Royale	5,000	100.00	100.00
93-17-006	Lamar	Duncan Royale	5,000	100.00	100.00
Duncan Royale	**Ebony Collection-Special Releases**				
91-18-001	Signature Piece	Duncan Royale	Open	50.00	50.00
Duncan Royale	**Ebony Collection-Buckwheat Collection**				
92-19-001	Petee & Friend	Duncan Royale	5,000	90.00	90.00
92-19-002	Painter	Duncan Royale	5,000	80.00	90.00
92-19-003	O'Tay	Duncan Royale	5,000	70.00	90.00
92-19-004	Smile For The Camera	Duncan Royale	5,000	80.00	90.00
Duncan Royale	**Early American (12")**				
91-20-001	Doctor	Duncan Royale	10,000	150.00	150.00
91-20-002	Accountant	Duncan Royale	10,000	170.00	170.00
91-20-003	Lawyer	Duncan Royale	10,000	170.00	170.00
91-20-004	Nurse	Duncan Royale	10,000	150.00	150.00
91-20-005	Fireman	Duncan Royale	10,000	150.00	150.00
91-20-006	Policeman	Duncan Royale	10,000	150.00	150.00
91-20-007	Dentist	Duncan Royale	10,000	150.00	150.00
91-20-008	Pharmacist	Duncan Royale	10,000	150.00	150.00
91-20-009	Teacher	Duncan Royale	10,000	150.00	150.00
91-20-010	Banker	Duncan Royale	10,000	150.00	150.00
91-20-011	Secretary	Duncan Royale	10,000	150.00	150.00
91-20-012	Chiropractor	Duncan Royale	10,000	150.00	150.00
91-20-013	Set of 12	Duncan Royale	10,000	2290.00	2290.00
Duncan Royale	**Early American (6")**				
93-21-001	6" Set of 12	Duncan Royale	6,000	960.00	960.00
93-21-002	Doctor	Duncan Royale	6,000	80.00	80.00
93-21-003	Accountant	Duncan Royale	6,000	80.00	80.00
93-21-004	Lawyer	Duncan Royale	6,000	80.00	80.00
93-21-005	Nurse	Duncan Royale	6,000	80.00	80.00
93-21-006	Fireman	Duncan Royale	6,000	80.00	80.00
93-21-007	Policeman	Duncan Royale	6,000	80.00	80.00
93-21-008	Dentist	Duncan Royale	6,000	80.00	80.00
93-21-009	Pharmacist	Duncan Royale	6,000	80.00	80.00
93-21-010	Teacher	Duncan Royale	6,000	80.00	80.00
93-21-011	Banker	Duncan Royale	6,000	80.00	80.00
93-21-012	Secretary	Duncan Royale	6,000	80.00	80.00
93-21-013	Chiropractor	Duncan Royale	6,000	80.00	80.00
Duncan Royale	**Christmas Images**				
91-22-001	The Carolers	Duncan Royale	10,000	120.00	120.00
91-22-002	The Christmas Pageant	Duncan Royale	10,000	175.00	175.00
92-22-003	Are You Really Santa?	Duncan Royale	10,000	N/A	N/A
92-22-004	The Midnight Watch	Duncan Royale	10,000	N/A	N/A
92-22-005	The Christmas Angel	Duncan Royale	10,000	110.00	110.00
92-22-006	Sneaking A Peek	Duncan Royale	10,000	N/A	N/A
Duncan Royale	**Painted Pewter Miniatures-Santa 1st Series**				
86-23-001	St. Nicholas	Duncan Royale	500	30.00	30.00
86-23-002	Dedt Moroz	Duncan Royale	500	30.00	30.00
86-23-003	Black Peter	Duncan Royale	500	30.00	30.00
86-23-004	Victorian	Duncan Royale	500	30.00	30.00
86-23-005	Medieval	Duncan Royale	500	30.00	30.00
86-23-006	Russian	Duncan Royale	500	30.00	30.00
86-23-007	Wassail	Duncan Royale	500	30.00	30.00
86-23-008	Kris Kringle	Duncan Royale	500	30.00	30.00
86-23-009	Soda Pop	Duncan Royale	500	30.00	30.00
86-23-010	Pioneer	Duncan Royale	500	30.00	30.00
86-23-011	Civil War	Duncan Royale	500	30.00	30.00
86-23-012	Nast	Duncan Royale	500	30.00	30.00
86-23-013	Set of 12	Duncan Royale	500	360.00	360-495.
Duncan Royale	**Painted Pewter Miniatures-Santa 2nd Series**				
88-24-001	Odin	Duncan Royale	500	30.00	30.00
88-24-002	Lord of Misrule	Duncan Royale	500	30.00	30.00
88-24-003	Mongolian	Duncan Royale	500	30.00	30.00
88-24-004	Magi	Duncan Royale	500	30.00	30.00
88-24-005	St. Lucia	Duncan Royale	500	30.00	30.00
88-24-006	Befana	Duncan Royale	500	30.00	30.00
88-24-007	Babouska	Duncan Royale	500	30.00	30.00
88-24-008	Bavarian	Duncan Royale	500	30.00	30.00
88-24-009	Alsace Angel	Duncan Royale	500	30.00	30.00
88-24-010	Frau Holda	Duncan Royale	500	30.00	30.00
88-24-011	Sir Christmas	Duncan Royale	500	30.00	30.00
88-24-012	Pixie	Duncan Royale	500	30.00	30.00
88-24-013	Set of 12	Duncan Royale	500	360.00	360-495.
Duncan Royale	**Collector Club**				
91-25-001	Today's Nast	Duncan Royale	Retrd.	80.00	100-125.
94-25-002	Winter Santa	Duncan Royale	Yr.Iss.	125.00	125.00
Duncan Royale	**1990 & 1991 Special Event Piece**				
XX-26-001	Nast & Music	Duncan Royale	Retrd.	79.95	79.95
Enchantica	**Retired Enchantica Collection**				
88-01-001	Rattajack - Please-2000	A. Bill	Retrd.	40.00	58-69.00
88-01-002	Rattajack - My Ball-2001	A. Bill	Retrd.	40.00	58-69.00
88-01-003	Rattajack - Terragon Dreams-2002	A. Bill	Retrd.	40.00	58-69.00
88-01-004	Rattajack - Circles-2003	A. Bill	Retrd.	40.00	68-95.00
88-01-005	Jonquil- Dragons Footprint-2004	A. Bill	Retrd.	55.00	115-125.
88-01-006	Snappa Hatches Out-2006	A. Bill	Retrd.	25.00	50-75.00
88-01-007	Snappa's First Feast-2007	A. Bill	Retrd.	25.00	39-50.00
88-01-008	Snappa Climbs High-2008	A. Bill	Retrd.	25.00	39-50.00
88-01-009	Snappa Finds a Collar-2009	A. Bill	Retrd.	25.00	39-70.00
88-01-010	Snappa Plays Ball-2010	A. Bill	Retrd.	25.00	39-50.00
88-01-011	Snappa Dozes Off-2011	A. Bill	Retrd.	25.00	39-50.00
88-01-012	Tarbet with Sack-2012	A. Bill	Retrd.	47.00	N/A
88-01-013	Blick Scoops Crystals-2015	A. Bill	Retrd.	47.00	N/A
88-01-014	Fantazar- Spring Wizard-2016	A. Bill	Retrd.	132.50	275-350.
88-01-015	Gorgoyle - Spring Dragon-2017	A. Bill	Retrd.	132.50	350-370.
89-01-016	Vrorst - The Ice Sorcerer-2018	A. Bill	Retrd.	155.00	400-700.
89-01-017	Grawlfang - Winter Dragon-2019	A. Bill	Retrd.	132.50	450-750.
89-01-018	Hobba, Hellbenders Twin Son-2023	A. Bill	Retrd.	69.00	116.00
90-01-019	Orolan-Summer Wizard-2025	A. Bill	Retrd.	165.00	400.00
90-01-020	Arangast - Summer Dragon-2026	A. Bill	Retrd.	165.00	350-400.
90-01-021	The Swamp Demon-2028	A. Bill	Retrd.	69.00	149.00
90-01-022	Oellandia-Summer Fairy-2029	A. Bill	Retrd.	115.00	150.00
90-01-023	Fossfex - Autumn Fairy-2030	A. Bill	Retrd.	115.00	150.00
91-01-024	Waxifrade - Autumn Wizard-2033	A. Bill	Retrd.	265.00	350.00
91-01-025	Snarlgard - Autumn Dragon-2034	A. Bill	Retrd.	337.00	380-390.
91-01-026	Flight to Danger-2044	A. Bill	Retrd.	3000.00	N/A
91-01-027	Bledderag, Goblin Twin-2048	A. Bill	Retrd.	115.00	N/A
91-01-028	Furza - Carrier Dragon-2050	A. Hull	Retrd.	137.50	N/A
92-01-029	Breen - Carrier Dragon-2053	A. Hull	Retrd.	156.00	N/A
92-01-030	Spring Wizard and Yim-2060	A. Bill	Retrd.	410.00	410.00
92-01-031	Thrace-Gladiator-2061	A. Bill	Retrd.	280.00	280.00
92-01-032	Manu Manu-Peeper-2105	A. Bill	Retrd.	40.00	40.00
94-01-033	Escape (5th Anniversary)-2110	A. Bill	Retrd.	250.00	250.00
Enchantica	**Enchantica Collectors Club**				
91-02-001	Snappa & Mushroom-2101	A. Hull	Retrd.	Gift	65.00
91-02-002	Rattajack with Snail-2102	A. Bill	Retrd.	60.00	N/A
92-02-003	Jonquil-2103	A. Bill	Retrd.	Gift	60.00
92-02-004	Ice Demon-2104	A. Bill	Retrd.	85.00	N/A
92-02-005	Sea Dragon-2106	A. Bill	Retrd.	99.00	200.00
93-02-006	White Dragon-2107	A. Bill	Retrd.	Gift	N/A
93-02-007	Jonquil's Flight-2108	A. Bill	Retrd.	140.00	140.00
94-02-008	Verratus-2111	A. Bill	Yr.Iss.	Gift	N/A
94-02-009	Mimmer-Spring Fairy-2112	A. Bill	Yr.Iss.	100.00	100.00
94-02-010	Gorgoyle Cameo piece	A. Bill	Yr.Iss.	Gift	N/A
Enesco Corporation	**Precious Moments Special Edition**				
81-01-001	Hello, Lord, It's Me Again-PM-811	S. Butcher	Retrd.	25.00	410-495.
82-01-002	Smile, God Loves You-PM-821	S. Butcher	Retrd.	25.00	175-275.
83-01-003	Put on a Happy Face-PM-822	S. Butcher	Retrd.	25.00	120-250.
83-01-004	Dawn's Early Light-PM-831	S. Butcher	Retrd.	27.50	71-95.00
84-01-005	God's Ray of Mercy-PM-841	S. Butcher	Retrd.	25.00	55-85.00
84-01-006	Trust in the Lord to the Finish-PM-842	S. Butcher	Retrd.	25.00	40-75.00
85-01-007	The Lord is My Shepherd-PM-851	S. Butcher	Retrd.	25.00	80-125.00
85-01-008	I Love to Tell the Story-PM-852	S. Butcher	Retrd.	27.50	65-150.00
86-01-009	Grandma's Prayer-PM-861	S. Butcher	Retrd.	25.00	80-100.00
86-01-010	I'm Following Jesus-PM-862	S. Butcher	Retrd.	25.00	85-100.00
87-01-011	Feed My Sheep-PM-871	S. Butcher	Retrd.	25.00	55-95.00
87-01-012	In His Time-PM-872	S. Butcher	Retrd.	25.00	42-95.00
87-01-013	Loving You Dear Valentine-PM-873	S. Butcher	Retrd.	25.00	40-65.00
87-01-014	Loving You Dear Valentine-PM-874	S. Butcher	Retrd.	25.00	45-65.00
88-01-015	God Bless You for Touching My Life-PM-881	S. Butcher	Retrd.	27.50	48-85.00
88-01-016	You Just Can't Chuck A Good Friendship-PM-882	S. Butcher	Retrd.	27.50	50-65.00
89-01-017	You Will Always Be My Choice- PM-891	S. Butcher	Retrd.	27.50	20-55.00

Company Number	Name	Series Artist	Edition Limit	Issue Price	Quote
89-01-018	Mow Power To Ya-PM-892	S. Butcher	Retrd.	27.50	48-80.00
90-01-019	Ten Years And Still Going Strong-PM-901	S. Butcher	Retrd.	30.00	35-60.00
90-01-020	You Are A Blessing To Me-PM-902	S. Butcher	Retrd.	27.50	45-55.00
91-01-021	One Step At A Time-PM-911	S. Butcher	Retrd.	33.00	35-60.00
91-01-022	Lord, Keep Me In TeePee Top Shape-PM-912	S. Butcher	Retrd.	27.50	40-50.00
92-01-023	Only Love Can Make A Home-PM-921	S. Butcher	Retrd.	30.00	45-70.00
92-01-024	Sowing The Seeds of Love-PM-922	S. Butcher	Retrd.	30.00	30-45.00
92-01-025	This Land Is Our Land-527386	S. Butcher	Retrd.	350.00	400-450.
93-01-026	His Little Treasure-PM-931	S. Butcher	Yr.Iss.	30.00	50-60.00
93-01-027	Loving PM-932	S. Butcher	Yr.Iss.	30.00	30.00
Enesco Corporation		**Precious Moments Collectors Club Welcome Gift**			
82-02-001	But Love Goes On Forever-Plaque-E-0202	S. Butcher	Yr.Iss.	Unkn.	65-85.00
83-02-002	Let Us Call the Club to Order-E-0303	S. Butcher	Yr.Iss.	Unkn.	30-60.00
84-02-003	Join in on the Blessings-E-0404	S. Butcher	Yr.Iss.	Unkn.	45-100.00
85-02-004	Seek and Ye Shall Find-E-0005	S. Butcher	Yr.Iss.	Unkn.	20-67.00
86-02-005	Birds of a Feather Collect Together-E-0006	S. Butcher	Yr.Iss.	Unkn.	20-70.00
87-02-006	Sharing Is Universal-E-0007	S. Butcher	Yr.Iss.	Unkn.	20-55.00
88-02-007	A Growing Love-E-0008	S. Butcher	Yr.Iss.	Unkn.	35-49.00
89-02-008	Always Room For One More-C-0009	S. Butcher	Yr.Iss.	Unkn.	25-55.00
90-02-009	My Happiness-C-0010	S. Butcher	Yr.Iss.	Unkn.	35-75.00
91-02-010	Sharing the Good News Together-C-0011	S. Butcher	Yr.Iss.	Unkn.	20-45.00
92-02-011	The Club That's Out Of This World-C-0012	S. Butcher	Yr.Iss.	Unkn.	20-45.00
93-02-012	Loving, Caring, and Sharing Along the Way-C-0013.	S. Butcher	Yr.Iss.	Unkn.	30-45.00
94-02-013	You Are the End of My Rainbow-C-0014	S. Butcher	Yr.Iss.	Unkn.	Unkn.
Enesco Corporation		**Precious Moments Inscribed Charter Member Renewal Gift**			
81-03-001	But Love Goes on Forever-E-0001	S. Butcher	Yr.Iss.	Unkn.	65-199.00
82-03-002	But Love Goes on Forever-Plaque-E-0102	S. Butcher	Yr.Iss.	Unkn.	75-110.00
83-03-003	Let Us Call the Club to Order-E-0103	S. Butcher	Yr.Iss.	25.00	40-90.00
84-03-004	Join in on the Blessings-E-0104	S. Butcher	Yr.Iss.	25.00	50-95.00
85-03-005	Seek and Ye Shall Find-E-0105	S. Butcher	Yr.Iss.	25.00	50-85.00
86-03-006	Birds of a Feather Collect Together-E-0106	S. Butcher	Yr.Iss.	25.00	25-85.00
87-03-007	Sharing Is Universal -E-0107	S. Butcher	Yr.Iss.	25.00	45-50.00
88-03-008	A Growing Love-E-0108	S. Butcher	Yr.Iss.	25.00	20-45.00
89-03-009	Always Room For One More-C-0109	S. Butcher	Yr.Iss.	35.00	40-50.00
90-03-010	My Happiness-C-0110	S. Butcher	Yr.Iss.	Unkn.	38-45.00
91-03-011	Sharing The Good News Together-C-0111	S. Butcher	Yr.Iss.	Unkn.	40-50.00
92-03-012	The Club That's Out Of This World-C-0112	S. Butcher	Yr.Iss.	Unkn.	40-50.00
93-03-013	Loving, Caring, and Sharing Along the Way-C-0113	S. Butcher	Yr.Iss.	Unkn.	40.00
94-03-014	You Are the End of My Rainbow-C-0114	S. Butcher	Yr.Iss.	Unkn.	Unkn.
Enesco Corporation		**Precious Moments Figurines**			
83-04-001	Sharing Our Season Together-E-0501	S. Butcher	Suspd.	50.00	110-145.
83-04-002	Jesus is the Light that Shines-E-0502	S. Butcher	Suspd.	23.00	50-60.00
83-04-003	Blessings from My House to Yours-E-0503	S. Butcher	Suspd.	27.00	60-80.00
83-04-004	Christmastime Is for Sharing-E-0504	S. Butcher	Retrd.	37.00	85.00
83-04-005	Surrounded with Joy-E-0506	S. Butcher	Retrd.	21.00	48-84.00
83-04-006	God Sent His Son-E-0507	S. Butcher	Suspd.	32.50	65-90.00
83-04-007	Prepare Ye the Way of the Lord-E-0508	S. Butcher	Suspd.	75.00	95-125.00
83-04-008	Bringing God's Blessing to You-E-0509	S. Butcher	Suspd.	35.00	70-100.00
83-04-009	Tubby's First Christmas-E-0511	S. Butcher	Suspd.	12.00	16.50-40.00
83-04-010	It's a Perfect Boy-E-0512	S. Butcher	Suspd.	18.50	42-60.00
83-04-011	Onward Christian Soldiers-E-0523	S. Butcher	Open	24.00	35-95.00
83-04-012	You Can't Run Away from God-E-0525	S. Butcher	Retrd.	28.50	75-155.00
83-04-013	He Upholdeth Those Who Fall-E-0526	S. Butcher	Suspd.	35.00	65-120.00
87-04-014	His Eye Is On The Sparrow-E-0530	S. Butcher	Retrd.	28.50	85-125.00
79-04-015	Jesus Loves Me-E-1372B	S. Butcher	Open	7.00	27.50-90.00
79-04-016	Jesus Loves Me-E-1372G	S. Butcher	Open	7.00	25-115.00
79-04-017	Smile, God Loves You-E-1373B	S. Butcher	Retrd.	7.00	50-105.00
79-04-018	Jesus is the Light-E-1373G	S. Butcher	Retrd.	7.00	50-125.00
79-04-019	Praise the Lord Anyhow-E-1374B	S. Butcher	Retrd.	8.00	75-95.00
79-04-020	Make a Joyful Noise-E-1374G	S. Butcher	Open	8.00	28-125.00
79-04-021	Love Lifted Me-E-1375A	S. Butcher	Retrd.	11.00	45-120.00
79-04-022	Prayer Changes Things-E-1375B	S. Butcher	Suspd.	11.00	114-200.
79-04-023	Love One Another-E-1376	S. Butcher	Open	10.00	48-100.00
79-04-024	He Leadeth Me-E-1377A	S. Butcher	Suspd.	9.00	70-144.00
79-04-025	He Careth For You-E-1377B	S. Butcher	Suspd.	9.00	90-102.
79-04-026	God Loveth a Cheerful Giver-E-1378	S. Butcher	Retrd.	11.00	775-1200.
79-04-027	Love is Kind-E-1379A	S. Butcher	Suspd.	8.00	66-130.00
79-04-028	God Understands-E-1379B	S. Butcher	Suspd.	8.00	90-135.00
79-04-029	O, How I Love Jesus-E-1380B	S. Butcher	Retrd.	8.00	80-130.00
79-04-030	His Burden Is Light-E-1380G	S. Butcher	Retrd.	8.00	80-110.00
79-04-031	Jesus is the Answer-E-1381	S. Butcher	Suspd.	11.50	120-150.
79-04-032	We Have Seen His Star-E-2010	S. Butcher	Suspd.	8.00	75-144.00
79-04-033	Come Let Us Adore Him-E-2011	S. Butcher	Retrd.	10.00	250-310.
79-04-034	Jesus is Born-E-2012	S. Butcher	Suspd.	12.00	90-95.00
79-04-035	Unto Us a Child is Born-E-2013	S. Butcher	Suspd.	12.00	85-105.00
82-04-036	May Your Christmas Be Cozy-E-2345	S. Butcher	Suspd.	23.00	60-80.00
82-04-037	May Your Christmas Be Warm-E-2348	S. Butcher	Suspd.	30.00	80-105.00
82-04-038	Tell Me the Story of Jesus-E-2349	S. Butcher	Suspd.	30.00	75-100.00
82-04-039	Dropping in for Christmas-E-2350	S. Butcher	Suspd.	18.00	70-85.00
87-04-040	Holy Smokes-E-2351	S. Butcher	Retrd.	27.00	80-130.00
82-04-041	O Come All Ye Faithful-E-2353	S. Butcher	Retrd.	27.50	65-85.00
82-04-042	I'll Play My Drum for Him-E-2356	S. Butcher	Suspd.	30.00	65-110.00
82-04-043	I'll Play My Drum for Him-E-2360	S. Butcher	Open	16.00	25-95.00
82-04-044	Christmas Joy from Head to Toe-E-2361	S. Butcher	Suspd.	25.00	55-80.00
82-04-045	Camel Figurine-E-2363	S. Butcher	Open	20.00	33-50.00
82-04-046	Goat Figurine-E-2364	S. Butcher	Suspd.	10.00	35-43.00
82-04-047	The First Noel-E-2365	S. Butcher	Suspd.	16.00	35-72.00
82-04-048	The First Noel-E-2366	S. Butcher	Suspd.	16.00	35-69.00
82-04-049	Bundles of Joy-E-2374	S. Butcher	Retrd.	27.50	46-132.00
82-04-050	Dropping Over for Christmas-E-2375	S. Butcher	Retrd.	30.00	75-100.00
82-04-051	Our First Christmas Together-E-2377	S. Butcher	Suspd.	35.00	60-95.00
82-04-052	3 Mini Nativity Houses & Palm Tree-E-2387	S. Butcher	Open	45.00	75-110.00
82-04-053	Come Let Us Adore Him-E-2395(11pc. set)	S. Butcher	Open	80.00	120-175.
80-04-054	Come Let Us Adore Him-E2800(9 pc. set)	S. Butcher	Open	70.00	125-175.
80-04-055	Jesus is Born-E-2801	S. Butcher	Suspd.	37.00	225-350.
80-04-056	Christmas is a Time to Share-E-2802	S. Butcher	Suspd.	20.00	60-100.00
80-04-057	Crown Him Lord of All-E-2803	S. Butcher	Suspd.	20.00	60-95.00
80-04-058	Peace on Earth-E-2804	S. Butcher	Suspd.	20.00	115-140.
80-04-059	Wishing You a Season Filled w/ Joy-E-2805	S. Butcher	Retrd.	20.00	95-125.00
84-04-060	You Have Touched So Many Hearts-E-2821	S. Butcher	Open	25.00	37.50-50.00
84-04-061	This is Your Day to Shine-E-2822	S. Butcher	Retrd.	37.50	50-100.00
84-04-062	To God Be the Glory-E-2823	S. Butcher	Suspd.	40.00	75-85.00
84-04-063	To a Very Special Mom-E-2824	S. Butcher	Open	27.50	37.50-55.00
84-04-064	To a Very Special Sister-E-2825	S. Butcher	Open	37.50	55-65.00
84-04-065	May Your Birthday Be a Blessing-E-2826	S. Butcher	Suspd.	37.50	70-99.00
84-04-066	I Get a Kick Out of You-E-2827	S. Butcher	Suspd.	50.00	85-100.00
84-04-067	Precious Memories-E-2828	S. Butcher	Open	45.00	60-75.00
84-04-068	I'm Sending You a White Christmas-E-2829	S. Butcher	Open	37.50	50-70.00
84-04-069	God Bless the Bride-E-2832	S. Butcher	Open	35.00	50-60.00

Company Number	Name	Series Artist	Edition Limit	Issue Price	Quote
86-04-070	Sharing Our Joy Together-E-2834	S. Butcher	Suspd.	30.00	40-60.00
84-04-071	Baby Figurines (set of 6)-E-2852	S. Butcher	Open	12.00	105-168.00
80-04-072	Blessed Are the Pure in Heart-E-3104	S. Butcher	Suspd.	9.00	25-40.00
80-04-073	He Watches Over Us All-E-3105	S. Butcher	Suspd.	11.00	50-110.00
80-04-074	Mother Sew Dear-E-3106	S. Butcher	Open	13.00	27.50-80.00
80-04-075	Blessed are the Peacemakers-E-3107	S. Butcher	Retrd.	13.00	80-85.00
80-04-076	The Hand that Rocks the Future-E-3108	S. Butcher	Suspd.	13.00	60-95.00
80-04-077	The Purr-fect Grandma-E-3109	S. Butcher	Open	13.00	27.50-75.00
80-04-078	Loving is Sharing-E-3110B	S. Butcher	Retrd.	13.00	45-90.00
80-04-079	Loving is Sharing-E-3110G	S. Butcher	Open	13.00	30-85.00
80-04-080	Be Not Weary In Well Doing-E-3111	S. Butcher	Retrd.	14.00	75-110.00
80-04-081	God's Speed-E-3112	S. Butcher	Retrd.	14.00	60-100.00
80-04-082	Thou Art Mine-E-3113	S. Butcher	Open	16.00	35-65.00
80-04-083	The Lord Bless You and Keep You-E-3114	S. Butcher	Open	16.00	37.50-85.00
80-04-084	But Love Goes on Forever-E-3115	S. Butcher	Open	16.50	35-115.00
80-04-085	Thee I Love-E-3116	S. Butcher	Open	16.50	37.50-100.
80-04-086	Walking By Faith-E-3117	S. Butcher	Open	35.00	70-125.00
80-04-087	Eggs Over Easy-E-3118	S. Butcher	Retrd.	12.00	65-115.00
80-04-088	It's What's Inside that Counts-E-3119	S. Butcher	Suspd.	13.00	70-130.00
80-04-089	To Thee With Love-E-3120	S. Butcher	Suspd.	13.00	57-95.00
81-04-090	The Lord Bless You and Keep You-E-4720	S. Butcher	Suspd.	14.00	32-48.00
81-04-091	The Lord Bless You and Keep You-E-4721	S. Butcher	Open	14.00	30-80.00
81-04-092	Love Cannot Break a True Friendship-E-4722	S. Butcher	Suspd.	22.50	90-130.00
81-04-093	Peace Amid the Storm-E-4723	S. Butcher	Suspd.	22.50	59-105.00
81-04-094	Rejoicing with You-E-4724	S. Butcher	Open	25.00	45-99.00
81-04-095	Peace on Earth-E-4725	S. Butcher	Suspd.	25.00	60-90.00
81-04-096	Bear Ye One Another's Burdens-E-5200	S. Butcher	Suspd.	20.00	80-105.00
81-04-097	Love Lifted Me-E-5201	S. Butcher	Suspd.	25.00	60-97.00
81-04-098	Thank You for Coming to My Ade-E-5202	S. Butcher	Suspd.	22.50	80-130.00
81-04-099	Let Not the Sun Go Down Upon Your Wrath-E-5203	S. Butcher	Suspd.	22.50	100-160.
81-04-100	To A Special Dad-E-5212	S. Butcher	Open	20.00	35-79.00
81-04-101	God is Love-E-5213	S. Butcher	Suspd.	17.00	60-99.00
81-04-102	Prayer Changes Things-E-5214	S. Butcher	Suspd.	35.00	85-150.00
84-04-103	May Your Christmas Be Blessed-E-5376	S. Butcher	Suspd.	37.50	59-75.00
87-04-104	Love is Kind-E-5377	S. Butcher	Retrd.	27.50	78-100.00
84-04-105	Joy to the World-E-5378	S. Butcher	Suspd.	18.00	32-45.00
84-04-106	Isn't He Precious?-E-5379	S. Butcher	Open	20.00	30-45.00
84-04-107	A Monarch is Born-E-5380	S. Butcher	Suspd.	33.00	60-75.00
84-04-108	His Name is Jesus-E-5381	S. Butcher	Suspd.	45.00	70-120.00
84-04-109	For God So Loved the World-E-5382	S. Butcher	Suspd.	70.00	110-135.
84-04-110	Wishing You a Merry Christmas-E-5383	S. Butcher	Yr.Iss.	17.00	40-55.00
84-04-111	I'll Play My Drum for Him-E-5384	S. Butcher	Open	10.00	16-30.00
84-04-112	Oh Worship the Lord-E-5385	S. Butcher	Suspd.	10.00	34-45.00
84-04-113	Oh Worship the Lord-E-5386	S. Butcher	Suspd.	10.00	34-45.00
81-04-114	Come Let Us Adore Him-E-5619	S. Butcher	Suspd.	10.00	30-50.00
81-04-115	Donkey Figurine-E-5621	S. Butcher	Open	6.00	15-35.00
81-04-116	They Followed the Star-E-5624	S. Butcher	Open	130.00	200-270.
81-04-117	Wee Three Kings-E-5635	S. Butcher	Open	40.00	75-125.00
81-04-118	Rejoice O Earth-E-5636	S. Butcher	Open	15.00	30-65.00
81-04-119	The Heavenly Light-E-5637	S. Butcher	Open	15.00	27.50-60.00
81-04-120	Cow with Bell Figurine-E-5638	S. Butcher	Open	16.00	30-50.00
81-04-121	Isn't He Wonderful-E-5639	S. Butcher	Suspd.	12.00	40-72.00
81-04-122	Isn't He Wonderful-E-5640	S. Butcher	Suspd.	12.00	40-72.00
81-04-123	They Followed the Star-E-5641	S. Butcher	Suspd.	75.00	165-185.
81-04-124	Nativity Wall (2 pc. set)-E-5644	S. Butcher	Open	60.00	120-145.
84-04-125	God Sends the Gift of His Love-E-6613	S. Butcher	Suspd.	22.50	60-90.00
82-04-126	God is Love, Dear Valentine-E-7153	S. Butcher	Suspd.	16.00	40-59.00
82-04-127	God is Love, Dear Valentine-E-7154	S. Butcher	Suspd.	16.00	35-65.00
82-04-128	Thanking Him for You-E-7155	S. Butcher	Suspd.	16.00	60-65.00
82-04-129	I Believe in Miracles-E-7156	S. Butcher	Retrd.	17.00	80-140.00
87-04-130	I Believe In Miracles-E-7156R	S. Butcher	Retrd.	22.50	65-90.00
82-04-131	There is Joy in Serving Jesus-E-7157	S. Butcher	Retrd.	17.00	50-90.00
82-04-132	Love Beareth All Things-E-7158	S. Butcher	Open	25.00	40-64.00
82-04-133	Lord Give Me Patience-E-7159	S. Butcher	Suspd.	25.00	45-55.00
82-04-134	The Perfect Grandpa-E-7160	S. Butcher	Suspd.	25.00	45-70.00
82-04-135	His Sheep Am I-E-7161	S. Butcher	Suspd.	25.00	52-55.00
82-04-136	Love is Sharing-E-7162	S. Butcher	Suspd.	25.00	100-162.
82-04-137	God is Watching Over You-E-7163	S. Butcher	Suspd.	27.50	65-85.00
82-04-138	Bless This House-E-7164	S. Butcher	Suspd.	45.00	100-200.
82-04-139	Let the Whole World Know-E-7165	S. Butcher	Suspd.	45.00	80-150.00
83-04-140	If God Be for Us, Who Can Be Against Us-E-9239	S. Butcher	Suspd.	27.50	55-70.00
83-04-141	Love is Patient-E-9251	S. Butcher	Suspd.	35.00	55-85.00
83-04-142	Forgiving is Forgetting-E-9252	S. Butcher	Suspd.	37.50	60-85.00
83-04-143	The End is in Sight-E-9253	S. Butcher	Suspd.	25.00	53-95.00
83-04-144	Praise the Lord Anyhow-E-9254	S. Butcher	Open	35.00	55-75.00
83-04-145	Bless You Two-E-9255	S. Butcher	Open	21.00	37.50-44.00
83-04-146	We are God's Workmanship-E-9258	S. Butcher	Open	19.00	27.50-53.00
83-04-147	We're In It Together-E-9259	S. Butcher	Suspd.	24.00	50-65.00
83-04-148	God's Promises are Sure-E-9260	S. Butcher	Suspd.	30.00	55-75.00
83-04-149	Seek Ye the Lord-E-9261	S. Butcher	Suspd.	21.00	37-54.00
83-04-150	Seek Ye the Lord-E-9262	S. Butcher	Suspd.	21.00	45-55.00
83-04-151	How Can Two Walk Together Except They Agree-E-9263	S. Butcher	Suspd.	35.00	90-139.00
63-04-152	Press On-E-9265	S. Butcher	Open	40.00	55-87.00
73-04-153	Animal Collection, Teddy Bear-E-9267A	S. Butcher	Suspd.	6.50	18-24.30
83-04-154	Animal Collection, Dog W/ Slippers-E-9267B	S. Butcher	Suspd.	6.50	18-24.30
83-04-155	Animal Collection, Bunny W/ Carrot-E-9267C	S. Butcher	Suspd.	6.50	18-24.30
83-04-156	Animal Collection, Kitty With Bow-E-9267D	S. Butcher	Suspd.	6.50	18-24.30
83-04-157	Animal Collection, Lamb With Bird-E-9267E	S. Butcher	Suspd.	6.50	18-24.30
83-04-158	Animal Collection, Pig W/ Patches-E-9267F	S. Butcher	Suspd.	6.50	18-24.30
83-04-159	Nobody's Perfect-E-9268	S. Butcher	Retrd.	21.00	65-85.00
87-04-160	Let Love Reign-E-9273	S. Butcher	Retrd.	27.50	65-90.00
83-04-161	Taste and See that the Lord is Good-E-9274	S. Butcher	Retrd.	22.50	55-95.00
83-04-162	Jesus Loves Me-E-9278	S. Butcher	Open	9.00	16-27.00
83-04-163	Jesus Loves Me-E-9279	S. Butcher	Open	9.00	16-32.00
83-04-164	To Some Bunny Special-E-9282A	S. Butcher	Suspd.	8.00	18-40.00
83-04-165	You're Worth Your Weight In Gold-E-9282B	S. Butcher	Suspd.	8.00	21-40.00
83-04-166	Especially For Ewe-E-9282C	S. Butcher	Suspd.	8.00	20-37.00
83-04-167	Peace on Earth-E-9287	S. Butcher	Suspd.	37.50	60-96.00
83-04-168	Sending You a Rainbow-E-9288	S. Butcher	Suspd.	22.50	55-90.00
83-04-169	Trust in the Lord-E-9289	S. Butcher	Suspd.	21.00	45-65.00
85-04-170	Love Covers All-12009	S. Butcher	Suspd.	27.50	48-65.00
85-04-171	Part of Me Wants to be Good-12149	S. Butcher	Suspd.	19.00	40-65.00
87-04-172	This Is The Day Which The Lord Has Made-12157	S. Butcher	Suspd.	20.00	45-100.00
85-04-173	Get into the Habit of Prayer-12203	S. Butcher	Suspd.	19.00	35-45.00
85-04-174	Miniature Clown-12238A	S. Butcher	Open	13.50	19-29.00
85-04-175	Miniature Clown-12238B	S. Butcher	Open	13.50	19-29.00
85-04-176	Miniature Clown-12238C	S. Butcher	Open	13.50	19-29.00
85-04-177	Miniature Clown-12238D	S. Butcher	Open	13.50	19-29.00
85-04-178	It is Better to Give than to Receive-12297	S. Butcher	Suspd.	19.00	60-110.00
85-04-179	Love Never Fails-12300	S. Butcher	Open	25.00	35-49.00

Company Number	Name	Series Artist	Edition Limit	Issue Price	Quote
85-04-180	God Bless Our Home-12319	S. Butcher	Open	40.00	55-65.00
86-04-181	You Can Fly-12335	S. Butcher	Suspd.	25.00	50-65.00
85-04-182	Jesus is Coming Soon-12343	S. Butcher	Suspd.	22.50	40-70.00
85-04-183	Halo, and Merry Christmas-12351	S. Butcher	Suspd.	40.00	90-135.00
85-04-184	May Your Christmas Be Delightful-15482	S. Butcher	Open	25.00	35-50.00
85-04-185	Honk if You Love Jesus-15490	S. Butcher	Open	13.00	20-35.00
85-04-186	Baby's First Christmas-15539	S. Butcher	Yr.Iss.	13.00	42-45.00
85-04-187	Baby's First Christmas-15547	S. Butcher	Yr.Iss.	13.00	45.00
85-04-188	God Sent His Love-15881	S. Butcher	Yr.Iss.	17.00	30-39.00
86-04-189	To My Favorite Paw-100021	S. Butcher	Suspd.	22.50	50-65.00
87-04-190	To My Deer Friend-100048	S. Butcher	Open	33.00	50-92.00
87-04-191	Sending My Love-100056	S. Butcher	Suspd.	22.50	40-60.00
86-04-192	O Worship the Lord-100064	S. Butcher	Open	24.00	35-49.00
86-04-193	To My Forever Friend-100072	S. Butcher	Open	33.00	50-90.00
87-04-194	He's The Healer Of Broken Hearts-100080	S. Butcher	Open	33.00	50-59.00
87-04-195	Make Me A Blessing-100102	S. Butcher	Retrd.	35.00	70-135.00
86-04-196	Lord I'm Coming Home-100110	S. Butcher	Open	22.50	32.50-72.00
86-04-197	Lord, Keep Me On My Toes-100129	S. Butcher	Retrd.	22.50	85-100.00
86-04-198	The Joy of the Lord is My Strength-100137	S. Butcher	Open	35.00	50-89.00
86-04-199	God Bless the Day We Found You-100145	S. Butcher	Suspd.	37.50	80-110.00
86-04-200	God Bless the Day We Found You-100153	S. Butcher	Suspd.	37.50	62-100.00
86-04-201	Serving the Lord-100161	S. Butcher	Suspd.	19.00	44-65.00
86-04-202	I'm a Possibility-100188	S. Butcher	Retrd.	21.00	35-95.00
87-04-203	The Spirit Is Willing But The Flesh Is Weak-100196	S. Butcher	Retrd.	19.00	60-95.00
87-04-204	The Lord Giveth & the Lord Taketh Away-100226	S. Butcher	Open	33.50	40-49.00
86-04-205	Friends Never Drift Apart-100250	S. Butcher	Open	35.00	55-69.00
86-04-206	Help, Lord, I'm In a Spot-100269	S. Butcher	Retrd.	18.50	55-70.00
86-04-207	He Cleansed My Soul-100277	S. Butcher	Open	24.00	37.50-60.00
86-04-208	Serving the Lord-100293	S. Butcher	Suspd.	19.00	30-47.00
87-04-209	Scent From Above-100528	S. Butcher	Retrd.	19.00	50-80.00
86-04-210	Brotherly Love-100544	S. Butcher	Suspd.	37.00	59-75.00
87-04-211	No Tears Past The Gate-101826	S. Butcher	Open	40.00	60-67.00
87-04-212	Smile Along The Way-101842	S. Butcher	Retrd.	30.00	140-190.
87-04-213	Lord, Help Us Keep Our Act Together-101850	S. Butcher	Retrd.	35.00	115-165.
86-04-214	O Worship the Lord-102229	S. Butcher	Open	24.00	35-42.00
86-04-215	Shepherd of Love-102261	S. Butcher	Open	10.00	16-24.00
86-04-216	Three Mini Animals-102296	S. Butcher	Open	13.50	19-30.00
86-04-217	Wishing You a Cozy Christmas-102342	S. Butcher	Yr.Iss.	17.00	39-45.00
86-04-218	Love Rescued Me-102393	S. Butcher	Open	21.00	32.50-44.00
86-04-219	Angel of Mercy-102482	S. Butcher	Open	19.00	30-39.00
86-04-220	Sharing our Christmas Together-102490	S. Butcher	Suspd.	35.00	65-70.00
87-04-221	We Are All Precious In His Sight-102903	S. Butcher	Yr.Iss.	30.00	75-125.00
86-04-222	God Bless America-102938	S. Butcher	Yr.Iss.	30.00	50-85.00
86-04-223	It's the Birthday of a King-102962	S. Butcher	Suspd.	18.50	35-50.00
87-04-224	I Would Be Sunk Without You-102970	S. Butcher	Open	15.00	19-29.00
87-04-225	My Love Will Never Let You Go-103497	S. Butcher	Open	25.00	35-45.00
86-04-226	I Believe in the Old Rugged Cross-103632	S. Butcher	Open	25.00	35-47.00
86-04-227	Come Let Us Adore Him-104000 (9 pc. set w/cassette)	S. Butcher	Open	95.00	125.00
87-04-228	With this Ring I...-104019	S. Butcher	Open	40.00	55-65.00
87-04-229	Love Is The Glue That Mends-104027	S. Butcher	Suspd.	33.50	50-75.00
87-04-230	Cheers To The Leader-104035	S. Butcher	Open	22.50	30-39.00
87-04-231	Happy Days Are Here Again-104396	S. Butcher	Suspd.	25.00	50-70.00
87-04-232	A Tub Full of Love-104817	S. Butcher	Open	22.50	30-42.00
87-04-233	Sitting Pretty-104825	S. Butcher	Suspd.	22.50	43-60.00
87-04-234	Have I Got News For You-105635	S. Butcher	Suspd.	22.50	30-50.00
88-04-235	Something's Missing When You're Not Around -105643	S. Butcher	Suspd.	32.50	37.50
87-04-236	To Tell The Tooth You're Special-105813	S. Butcher	Suspd.	38.50	65-85.00
88-04-237	Hallelujah Country-105821	S. Butcher	Open	35.00	45-54.00
87-04-238	We're Pulling For You-106151	S. Butcher	Suspd.	40.00	60-75.00
88-04-239	God Bless You Graduate-106194	S. Butcher	Open	20.00	30-35.00
87-04-240	Congratulations Princess-106208	S. Butcher	Open	20.00	30-35.00
87-04-241	Lord Help Me Make the Grade-106216	S. Butcher	Suspd.	25.00	45-70.00
88-04-242	Heaven Bless Your Togetherness-106755	S. Butcher	Open	65.00	80-87.00
88-04-243	Precious Memories-106763	S. Butcher	Open	37.50	50-55.00
88-04-244	Puppy Love Is From Above-106798	S. Butcher	Open	45.00	55-63.00
88-04-245	Happy Birthday Poppy-106836	S. Butcher	Suspd.	27.50	39-49.00
88-04-246	Sew In Love-106844	S. Butcher	Open	45.00	55-60.00
87-04-247	They Followed The Star-108243	S. Butcher	Open	75.00	100-115.00
87-04-248	The Greatest Gift Is A Friend-109231	S. Butcher	Open	30.00	37.50-49.00
88-04-249	Believe the Impossible-109487	S. Butcher	Suspd.	35.00	50-110.00
88-04-250	Happiness Divine-109584	S. Butcher	Retrd.	25.00	50-75.00
87-04-251	Wishing You A Yummy Christmas-109754	S. Butcher	Open	35.00	45-55.00
87-04-252	We Gather Together To Ask The Lord's Blessing-109762	S. Butcher	Open	130.00	150-169.
88-04-253	Meowie Christmas-109800	S. Butcher	Open	30.00	40-65.00
87-04-254	Oh What Fun It Is To Ride-109819	S. Butcher	Open	85.00	110-120.
88-04-255	Wishing You A Happy Easter-109886	S. Butcher	Open	23.00	27.50-34.00
88-04-256	Wishing You A Basket Full Of Blessings-109924	S. Butcher	Open	23.00	27.50-33.00
88-04-257	Sending You My Love-109967	S. Butcher	Open	35.00	45-65.00
88-04-258	Mommy, I Love You-109975	S. Butcher	Open	22.50	27.50-34.00
87-04-259	Love Is The Best Gift of All-110930	S. Butcher	Yr.Iss.	22.50	45-49.00
88-04-260	Faith Takes The Plunge-111155	S. Butcher	Open	27.50	33.50-125.
88-04-261	Tis the Season-111163	S. Butcher	Open	27.50	35-45.00
87-04-262	O Come Let Us Adore Him (4 pc. 9" Nativity)-111333	S. Butcher	Suspd.	200.00	225-275.
88-04-263	Mommy, I Love You-112143	S. Butcher	Open	22.50	27.50-32.00
87-04-264	A Tub Full of Love-112313	S. Butcher	Open	22.50	30-33.00
88-04-265	This Too Shall Pass-114014	S. Butcher	Open	23.00	27.50-37.00
88-04-266	Some Bunny's Sleeping-115274	S. Butcher	Open	15.00	25-40.00
88-04-267	Our First Christmas Together-115290	S. Butcher	Suspd.	50.00	60-80.00
88-04-268	Time to Wish You a Merry Christmas-115339	S. Butcher	Yr.Iss.	24.00	35-48.00
88-04-269	Rejoice O Earth-520268	S. Butcher	Open	13.00	16-22.00
88-04-270	Jesus the Savior Is Born-520357	S. Butcher	Suspd.	25.00	32.50-40.00
92-04-271	The Lord Turned My Life Around-520535	S. Butcher	Open	35.00	35.00
91-04-272	In The Spotlight Of His Grace-520543	S. Butcher	Open	35.00	35.00
90-04-273	Lord, Turn My Life Around-520551	S. Butcher	Open	35.00	35-49.00
92-04-274	You Deserve An Ovation-520578	S. Butcher	Open	35.00	35.00
89-04-275	My Heart Is Exposed With Love-520624	S. Butcher	Open	45.00	50-60.00
89-04-276	A Friend Is Someone Who Cares-520632	S. Butcher	Open	30.00	35-45.00
89-04-277	I'm So Glad You Fluttered Into My Life-520640	S. Butcher	Retrd.	40.00	250-375.
89-04-278	Eggspecially For You-520667	S. Butcher	Open	45.00	50-60.00
89-04-279	Your Love Is So Uplifting-520675	S. Butcher	Open	60.00	65-79.00
89-04-280	Sending You Showers Of Blessings-520683	S. Butcher	Retrd.	32.50	60-110.00
89-04-281	Just A LineTo Wish You A Happy Day-520721	S. Butcher	Open	65.00	70-79.00
89-04-282	Friendship Hits The Spot-520748	S. Butcher	Open	55.00	60-68.00
89-04-283	Jesus Is The Only Way-520756	S. Butcher	Suspd.	40.00	45-50.00
89-04-284	Puppy Love-520764	S. Butcher	Open	12.50	16-22.00
89-04-285	Many Moons In Same Canoe, Blessum You-520772	S. Butcher	Retrd.	50.00	195-234.
89-04-286	Wishing You Roads Of Happiness-520780	S. Butcher	Open	60.00	75.00
89-04-287	Someday My Love-520799	S. Butcher	Retrd.	40.00	48-150.00
89-04-288	My Days Are Blue Without You-520802	S. Butcher	Suspd.	65.00	75-125.00
89-04-289	We Need A Good Friend Through The Ruff Times-520810	S. Butcher	Suspd.	35.00	50-70.00
89-04-290	You Are My Number One-520829	S. Butcher	Open	25.00	27.50-30.00
89-04-291	The Lord Is Your Light To Happiness-520837	S. Bucher	Open	50.00	55-62.00
89-04-292	Wishing You A Perfect Choice-520845	S.Butcher	Open	55.00	60-67.00
89-04-293	I Belong To The Lord-520853	S. Butcher	Suspd.	25.00	35-50.00
90-04-294	Heaven Bless You-520934	S. Butcher	Open	35.00	30-150.00
93-04-295	There Is No Greater Treasure Than To Have A Friend Like You -521000	S. Butcher	Open	30.00	30.00
89-04-296	Hello World-521175	S. Butcher	Open	15.00	16.00
90-04-297	That's What Friends Are For-521183	S. Butcher	Open	45.00	45-49.00
90-04-298	Hope You're Up And OnThe Trail Again-521205	S. Butcher	Suspd.	35.00	35-45.00
93-04-299	The Fruit of the Spirit is Love-521213	S. Butcher	Yr.Iss.	30.00	30.00
91-04-300	Take Heed When You Stand-521272	S. Butcher	Open	55.00	55.00
90-04-301	Happy Trip-521280	S. Butcher	Open	35.00	35-73.00
91-04-302	Hug One Another-521299	S. Butcher	Retrd.	45.00	130-150.
90-04-303	Yield Not To Temptation-521310	S. Butcher	Suspd.	27.50	27.50-40.00
90-04-304	Faith Is A Victory-521396	S. Butcher	Retrd.	25.00	160-190.
90-04-305	I'll Never Stop Loving You-521418	S. Butcher	Open	37.50	37.50-49.00
91-04-306	To A Very Special Mom & Dad-521434	S. Butcher	Suspd.	35.00	35.00
90-04-307	Lord, Help Me Stick To My Job-521450	S. Butcher	Open	30.00	30-40.00
89-04-308	Tell It To Jesus-521477	S. Butcher	Open	35.00	37.50-49.00
91-04-309	There's A Light At The End Of The Tunnel-521485	S. Butcher	Open	55.00	55.00
91-04-310	A Special Delivery-521493	S. Butcher	Open	30.00	30.00
91-04-311	Thumb-body Loves You-521698	S. Butcher	Open	55.00	55-59.00
90-04-312	Sweep All Your Worries Away-521779	S. Butcher	Open	40.00	40-130.00
90-04-313	Good Friends Are Forever-521817	S. Butcher	Open	50.00	50-57.00
90-04-314	Love Is From Above-521841	S. Butcher	Open	45.00	45-59.00
89-04-315	The Greatest of These Is Love-521868	S. Butcher	Suspd.	27.50	40-54.00
90-04-316	Easter's On Its Way-521892	S. Butcher	Open	60.00	65-75.00
91-04-317	Hoppy Easter Friend-521906	S. Butcher	Open	40.00	40-43.00
93-04-318	Safe In The Arms Of Jesus-521922	S. Butcher	Open	30.00	30.00
89-04-319	Wishing You A Cozy Season-521949	S. Butcher	Suspd.	42.50	45-53.00
90-04-320	High Hopes-521957	S. Butcher	Suspd.	30.00	30-40.00
91-04-321	To A Special Mum-521965	S. Butcher	Open	30.00	30-33.00
93-04-322	To The Apple Of God's Eye-522015	S. Butcher	Yr.Iss.	32.50	32.50
79-04-323	May Your Life Be Blessed With Touchdowns-522023	S. Butcher	Open	45.00	50-58.00
89-04-324	Thank You Lord For Everything-522031	S. Butcher	Suspd.	55.00	60-70.00
91-04-325	May Your World Be Trimmed With Joy-522082	S. Butcher	Open	55.00	55.00
90-04-326	There Shall Be Showers Of Blessings-522090	S. Butcher	Open	60.00	70.00
92-04-327	It's No Yolk When I Say I Love You-522104	S. Butcher	Open	60.00	65.00
89-04-328	Don't Let the Holidays Get You Down-522112	S. Butcher	Retrd.	42.50	45-54.00
89-04-329	Wishing You A Very Successful Season-522120	S. Butcher	Open	60.00	65-70.00
89-04-330	Bon Voyage!-522201	S. Butcher	Open	75.00	80-99.00
89-04-331	He Is The Star Of The Morning-522252	S. Butcher	Suspd.	55.00	60-65.00
89-04-332	To Be With You Is Uplifting-522260	S. Butcher	Open	20.00	22.50-30.00
91-04-333	A Reflection Of His Love-522279	S. Butcher	Open	50.00	50.00
90-04-334	Thinking Of You Is What I Really Like To Do-522287	S. Butcher	Open	30.00	30-35.00
89-04-335	Merry Christmas Deer-522317	S. Butcher	Open	50.00	55-65.00
89-04-336	Isn't He Precious-522988	S. Butcher	Suspd.	15.00	16.50-20.00
90-04-337	Some Bunny's Sleeping-522996	S. Butcher	Suspd.	12.00	12-19.00
89-04-338	Jesus Is The Sweetest Name I Know-523097	S. Butcher	Suspd.	22.50	25-29.00
91-04-339	Joy On Arrival-523178	S. Butcher	Open	50.00	50.00
90-04-340	The Good Lord Always Delivers- 523453	S. Butcher	Open	27.50	27.50-35.00
90-04-341	This Day Has Been Made In Heaven-523496	S. Butcher	Open	30.00	30-45.00
90-04-342	God Is Love Dear Valentine-523518	S. Butcher	Open	27.50	27.50-32.00
91-04-343	I Will Cherish The Old Rugged Cross-523534	S. Butcher	Yr.Iss.	27.50	40-45.00
92-04-344	You Are The Type I Love-523542	S. Butcher	Open	40.00	40.00
93-04-345	The Lord Will Provide-523593	S. Butcher	Yr.Iss.	40.00	40.00
91-04-346	Good News Is So Uplifting-523615	S. Butcher	Open	60.00	65.00
94-04-347	I Will Always Be Thinking Of You-523631	S. Butcher	Open	45.00	45.00
90-04-348	Time Heals-523739	S. Butcher	Open	37.50	37.50-40.00
90-04-349	Blessings From Above-523747	S. Butcher	Open	45.00	45-50.00
91-04-350	I Can't Spell Success Without You-523763	S. Butcher	Open	40.00	45-45.00
90-04-351	Once Upon A Holy Night-523836	S. Butcher	Yr.Iss.	25.00	25-29.00
92-04-352	My Warmest Thoughts Are You-524085	S. Butcher	Open	55.00	60.00
91-04-353	Good Friends Are For Always-524123	S. Butcher	Open	27.50	27.50
94-04-354	Lord Teach Us to Pray-524158	S. Butcher	Yr.Iss.	35.00	35.00
91-04-355	May Your Christmas Be Merry-524166	S. Butcher	Yr.Iss.	27.50	30-40.00
91-04-356	He Loves Me -524263	S. Butcher	Yr.Iss.	35.00	35-65.00
92-04-357	Friendship Grows When You Plant A Seed-524271	S. Butcher	Open	40.00	40.00
93-04-358	May Your Every Wish Come True-524298	S. Butcher	Open	50.00	50.00
91-04-359	May Your Birthday Be A Blessing-524301	S. Butcher	Open	30.00	30-35.00
92-04-360	What The World Needs Now-524352	S. Butcher	Open	50.00	50.00
91-04-361	May Only Good Things Come Your Way-524425	S. Butcher	Open	30.00	30-35.00
93-04-362	A Special Chime For Jesus-524468	S. Butcher	Yr.Iss.	32.50	32.50
93-04-363	Sealed With A Kiss-524441	S. Butcher	Open	50.00	50.00
90-04-364	Happy Birthday Dear Jesus-524875	S. Butcher	Suspd.	13.50	13.50-16.00
92-04-365	It's So Uplifting To Have A Friend Like You-524905	S. Butcher	Open	40.00	40.00
90-04-366	We're Going To Miss You-524913	S. Butcher	Open	50.00	50-55.00
91-04-367	Angels We Have Heard On High-524921	S. Butcher	Open	60.00	60.00
92-04-368	Tubby's First Christmas-525278	S. Butcher	Open	10.00	10.00
91-04-369	It's A Perfect Boy-525286	S. Butcher	Open	16.50	17.00
93-04-370	May Your Future Be Blessed-525316	S. Butcher	Open	35.00	35.00
92-04-371	Going Home-525979	S. Butcher	Open	60.00	60.00
92-04-372	I Would Be Lost Without You-526142	S. Butcher	Open	27.50	27.50
94-04-373	Friends 'Til The Very End-526150	S. Butcher	Open	40.00	40.00
92-04-374	You Are My Happiness-526185	S. Butcher	Yr.Iss.	37.50	40-65.00
94-04-395	You Suit Me to a Tee-526193	S. Butcher	Open	35.00	35.00
94-04-376	Sharing Sweet Moments Together-526487	S. Butcher	Open	45.00	45.00
91-04-377	How Could I Ever Forget You-526924	S. Butcher	Open	15.00	16.00
91-04-378	We Have Come From Afar-526959	S. Butcher	Open	17.50	17.50
92-04-379	Let's Be Friends 527270	S. Butcher	Open	15.00	16.00
93-04-379	Bless-Um You-527335	S. Butcher	Open	35.00	35.00
92-04-380	You Are My Favorite Star-527378	S. Butcher	Open	55.00	55.00
92-04-381	Bring The Little Ones To Jesus-527556	S. Butcher	Open	90.00	90.00
92-04-382	God Bless The U.S.A.-527564	S. Butcher	Yr.Iss.	32.50	32.50
93-04-383	Tied Up For The Holidays-527580	S. Butcher	Yr.Iss.	40.00	40.00

Number	Name	Artist	Edition Limit	Issue Price	Quote
93-04-384	Bringing You A Merry Christmas-527599	S. Butcher	Yr.Iss.	45.00	45.00
92-04-385	Wishing You A Ho Ho Ho-527629	S. Butcher	Open	40.00	40.00
92-04-386	But The Greatest of These Is Love-527688	S. Butcher	Yr.Iss.	27.50	27.50
92-04-387	Wishing You A Comfy Christmas-527750	S. Butcher	Open	30.00	30.00
93-04-388	I Only Have Arms For You-527769	S. Butcher	Open	15.00	16.00
92-04-389	This Land Is Our Land-527777	S. Butcher	Yr.Iss.	35.00	40-50.00
94-04-390	To a Very Special Sister-528633	S. Butcher	Open	60.00	60.00
93-04-391	America You're Beautiful-528862	S. Butcher	Yr.Iss.	35.00	35.00
93-04-392	Ring Out The Good News-529966	S. Butcher	Yr.Iss.	27.50	27.50
93-04-393	Wishing You the Sweetest Christmas-530166	S. Butcher	Yr.Iss.	27.50	27.50
94-04-394	Serenity Prayer Girl-530697	S. Butcher	Open	35.00	35.00
94-04-395	Serenity Prayer Boy-530700	S. Butcher	Open	35.00	35.00
94-04-396	The Lord is Counting on You-531707	S. Butcher	Open	32.50	32.50
94-04-397	The Lord Bless You and Keep You-532118	S. Butcher	Open	40.00	40.00
94-04-398	The Lord Bless You and Keep You-532126	S. Butcher	Open	30.00	30.00
94-04-399	The Lord Bless You and Keep You-532134	S. Butcher	Open	30.00	30.00
94-04-400	Nothing Can Dampen The Spirit of Caring -603865	S. Butcher	Open	35.00	35.00
Enesco Corporation	**Precious Moments Bridal Party**				
84-05-001	Bridesmaid-E-2831	S. Butcher	Open	13.50	22.50-30.00
85-05-002	Ringbearer-E-2833	S. Butcher	Open	11.00	17-30.00
85-05-003	Flower Girl-E-2835	S. Butcher	Open	11.00	17-25.00
84-05-004	Groomsman-E-2836	S. Butcher	Open	13.50	22.50-30.00
86-05-005	Groom-E-2837	S. Butcher	Open	13.50	20-40.00
85-05-006	Junior Bridesmaid-E-2845	S. Butcher	Open	12.50	20-30.00
87-05-007	Bride-E-2846	S. Butcher	Open	18.00	25-30.00
87-05-008	God Bless Our Family (Parents of the Groom)-100498	S. Butcher	Open	35.00	50-55.00
87-05-009	God Bless Our Family (Parents of the Bride)-100501	S. Butcher	Open	35.00	50-60.00
87-05-010	Wedding Arch-102369	S. Butcher	Suspd.	22.50	45-65.00
Enesco Corporation	**Precious Moments Baby's First**				
84-06-001	Baby's First Step-E-2840	S. Butcher	Suspd.	35.00	65-90.00
84-06-002	Baby's First Picture-E-2841	S. Butcher	Retrd.	45.00	140-175.
85-06-003	Baby's First Haircut-12211	S. Butcher	Suspd.	32.50	85-115.00
86-06-004	Baby's First Trip-16012	S. Butcher	Suspd.	32.50	75-174.00
89-06-005	Baby's First Pet-520705	S. Butcher	Open	45.00	50-78.00
90-06-006	Baby's First Meal-524077	S. Butcher	Open	35.00	35-45.00
90-06-007	Baby's First Word-527238	S. Butcher	Open	24.00	24-28.00
93-06-008	Baby's First Birthday-524069	S. Butcher	Open	25.00	25.00
Enesco Corporation	**Precious Moments Anniversary Figurines**				
84-07-001	God Blessed Our Years Together With So Much Love And Happiness-E-2853	S. Butcher	Open	35.00	50-60.00
84-07-002	God Blessed Our Year Together With So Much Love And Happiness (1st)-E-2854	S. Butcher	Open	35.00	50-60.00
84-07-003	God Blessed Our Years Together With So Much Love And Happiness (5th)-E-2855	S. Butcher	Open	35.00	50-55.00
84-07-004	God Blessed Our Years Together With So Much Love And Happiness (10th)-E-2856	S. Butcher	Open	35.00	50-55.00
84-07-005	God Blessed Our Years Together With So Much Love And Happiness (25th)-E-2857	S. Butcher	Open	35.00	50-65.00
84-07-006	God Blessed Our Years Together With So Much Love And Happiness (40th)-E-2859	S. Butcher	Open	35.00	50-65.00
84-07-007	God Blessed Our Years Together With So Much Love And Happiness (50th)-E-2860	S. Butcher	Open	35.00	50-65.00
94-07-008	I Still Do-530999	S. Butcher	Open	30.00	30.00
94-07-009	I Still Do-531006	S. Butcher	Open	30.00	30.00
Enesco Corporation	**Precious Moments The Four Seasons**				
85-08-001	The Voice of Spring-12068	S. Butcher	Yr.Iss.	30.00	228-350.
85-08-002	Summer's Joy-12076	S. Butcher	Yr.Iss.	30.00	100-121.
86-08-003	Autumn's Praise-12084	S. Butcher	Yr.Iss.	30.00	60-90.00
86-08-004	Winter's Song-12092	S. Butcher	Yr.Iss.	30.00	100-140.00
86-08-005	Set	S. Butcher	Yr.Iss.	120.00	550.00
Enesco Corporation	**Precious Moments Rejoice in the Lord**				
87-09-001	Lord Keep My Life In Tune - 12165	S. Butcher	Suspd.	37.50	70-100.00
85-09-002	There's a Song in My Heart-12173	S. Butcher	Suspd.	11.00	25-45.00
85-09-003	Happiness is the Lord-12378	S. Butcher	Suspd.	15.00	35-60.00
85-09-004	Lord Give Me a Song-12386	S. Butcher	Suspd.	15.00	30-50.00
85-09-005	He is My Song-12394	S. Butcher	Suspd.	17.50	35-60.00
Enesco Corporation	**Precious Moments Clown**				
XX-10-001	I Get a Bang Out of You-12262	S. Butcher	Open	30.00	45-55.00
86-10-002	Lord Keep Me On the Ball-12270	S. Butcher	Open	30.00	45-55.00
85-10-003	Waddle I Do Without You-12459	S. Butcher	Retrd.	30.00	80-110.00
86-10-004	The Lord Will Carry You Through-12467	S. Butcher	Retrd.	30.00	75-100.00
Enesco Corporation	**Precious Moments Club 5th Anniversary Commemorative Edition**				
85-11-001	God Bless Our Years Together-12440	S. Butcher	Retrd.	175.00	275-350.
Enesco Corporation	**Precious Moments Family Christmas Scene**				
85-12-001	May You Have the Sweetest Christmas-15776	S. Butcher	Suspd.	17.00	37-55.00
85-12-002	The Story of God's Love-15784	S. Butcher	Suspd.	22.50	40-59.00
85-12-003	Tell Me a Story-15792	S. Butcher	Suspd.	10.00	15-49.00
85-12-004	God Gave His Best-15806	S. Butcher	Suspd.	13.00	30-45.00
85-12-005	Silent Night-15814	S. Butcher	Suspd.	37.50	75-120.00
86-12-006	Sharing Our Christmas Together-102490	S. Butcher	Suspd.	40.00	55-80.00
89-12-007	Have A Beary Merry Christmas-522856	S. Butcher	Suspd.	15.00	30-45.00
90-12-008	Christmas Fireplace-524883	S. Butcher	Suspd.	37.50	85-125.00
Enesco Corporation	**Precious Moments Collection 10th Anniv. Commemorative Edition**				
88-13-001	The Good Lord has Blessed Us Tenfold-114022	S. Butcher	Yr.Iss.	90.00	135-250.
Enesco Corporation	**Precious Moments Birthday Train Figurines**				
88-14-001	Isn't Eight Just Great-109460	S. Butcher	Open	18.50	22.50-30.00
88-14-002	Wishing You Grr-eatness-109479	S. Butcher	Open	18.50	22.50-30.00
86-14-003	May Your Birthday Be Warm-15938	S. Butcher	Open	10.00	15-40.00
86-14-004	Happy Birthday Little Lamb-15946	S. Butcher	Open	10.00	15-39.00
86-14-005	Heaven Bless Your Special Day-15954	S. Butcher	Open	11.00	16.50-30.00
86-14-006	God Bless You On Your Birthday-15962	S. Butcher	Open	11.00	16.50-40.00
86-14-007	May Your Birthday Be Gigantic -15970	S. Butcher	Open	12.50	18.50-40.00
86-14-008	This Day Is Something To Roar About-15989	S. Butcher	Open	13.50	20-40.00
86-14-009	Keep Looking Up-15997	S. Butcher	Open	13.50	20-43.00
86-14-010	Bless The Days Of Our Youth-16004	S. Butcher	Open	15.00	22.50-45.00
92-14-011	May Your Birthday Be Mammoth-521825	S. Butcher	Open	25.00	25-40.00
92-14-012	Being Nine Is Just Divine-521833	S. Butcher	Open	25.00	25-40.00
Enesco Corporation	**Precious Moments Birthday Club Figurines**				
86-15-001	Fishing For Friends-BC-861	S. Butcher	Yr.Iss.	10.00	108-195.
87-15-002	Hi Sugar-BC-871	S. Butcher	Yr.Iss.	11.00	80-140.00
88-15-003	Somebunny Cares-BC-881	S. Butcher	Yr.Iss.	13.50	55-100.00
89-15-004	Can't Bee Hive Myself Without You-BC-891	S. Butcher	Yr.Iss.	13.50	35-80.00
90-15-005	Collecting Makes Good Scents-BC-901	S. Butcher	Yr.Iss.	15.00	30-45.00
90-15-006	I'm Nuts Over My Collection-BC-902	S. Butcher	Yr.Iss.	15.00	35-50.00
91-15-007	Love Pacifies-BC-911	S. Butcher	Yr.Iss.	15.00	20-45.00
91-15-008	True Blue Friends-BC-912	S. Butcher	Yr.Iss.	15.00	20-35.00
92-15-009	Every Man's House Is His Castle-BC-921	S. Butcher	Yr.Iss.	16.50	20-25.00
93-15-010	I Got You Under My Skin-BC-922	S. Butcher	Yr.Iss.	16.00	16-35.00
94-15-011	Put a Little Punch In Your Birthday-BC-931	S. Butcher	Yr.Iss.	15.00	30.00
94-15-012	Owl Always Be Your Friend-BC-932	S. Butcher	Yr.Iss.	16.00	16.00
Enesco Corporation	**Precious Moments Birthday Club Welcome Gift**				
86-16-001	Our Club Can't Be Beat-B-0001	S. Butcher	Yr.Iss.	Unkn.	70-100.00
87-16-002	A Smile's The Cymbal of Joy-B-0002	S. Butcher	Yr.Iss.	Unkn.	55-85.00
88-16-003	The Sweetest Club Around-B-0003	S. Butcher	Yr.Iss.	Unkn.	45-70.00
89-16-004	Have A Beary Special Birthday- B-0004	S. Butcher	Yr.Iss.	Unkn.	32-55.00
90-16-005	Our Club Is A Tough Act To Follow-B-0005	S. Butcher	Yr.Iss.	Unkn.	35-75.00
91-16-006	Jest To Let You Know You're Tops-B-0006	S. Butcher	Yr.Iss.	Unkn.	35-40.00
92-16-007	All Aboard For Birthday Club Fun-B-0007	S. Butcher	Yr.Iss.	Unkn.	25-35.00
94-16-008	Happiness Is Belonging-B-0008	S. Butcher	Yr.Iss.	Unkn.	Unkn.
Enesco Corporation	**Birthday Club Inscribed Charter Member Renewal Gift**				
87-17-001	A Smile's the Cymbal of Joy-B-0102	S. Butcher	Yr.Iss.	Unkn.	60-70.00
88-17-002	The Sweetest Club Around-B-0103	S. Butcher	Yr.Iss.	Unkn.	45-55.00
89-17-003	Have A Beary Special Birthday- B-0104	S. Butcher	Yr.Iss.	Unkn.	45-55.00
90-17-004	Our Club Is A Tough Act To Follow-B-0105	S. Butcher	Yr.Iss.	Unkn.	35-40.00
91-17-005	Jest To Let You Know You're Tops-B-0106	S. Butcher	Yr.Iss.	Unkn.	30-40.00
92-17-006	All Aboard For Birthday Club Fun-B-0107	S. Butcher	Yr.Iss.	Unkn.	25.00
94-17-007	Happines is Belonging-B-0108	S. Butcher	Yr.Iss.	Unkn.	Unkn.
Enesco Corporation	**Birthday Series**				
88-18-001	Friends To The End-104418	S. Butcher	Suspd.	15.00	18.50-35.00
87-18-002	Showers Of Blessings-105945	S. Butcher	Retrd.	16.00	40-75.00
88-18-003	Brighten Someone's Day-105953	S. Butcher	Suspd.	12.50	15-30.00
90-18-004	To My Favorite Fan-521043	S. Butcher	Suspd.	16.00	16-50.00
89-18-005	Hello World!-521175	S. Butcher	Open	13.50	15-30.00
93-18-006	Hope You're Over The Hump-521671	S. Butcher	Open	16.00	16.00
90-18-007	Not A Creature Was Stirring-524484	S. Butcher	Open	17.00	17-25.00
91-18-008	Can't Be Without You-524492	S. Butcher	Open	16.00	16-29.00
94-18-009	Oinky Birthday-524506	S. Butcher	Open	13.50	13.50
91-18-010	How Can I Ever Forget You-526924	S. Butcher	Open	15.00	15.00
92-18-011	Let's Be Friends-527270	S. Butcher	Open	15.00	15.00
92-18-012	Happy Birdie-527343	S. Butcher	Open	8.00	8.00
93-18-013	Happy Birthday Jesus-530492	S. Butcher	Open	20.00	20.00
Enesco Corporation	**Precious Moments Events Figurines**				
88-19-001	You Are My Main Event-115231	S. Butcher	Yr.Iss.	30.00	50-110.00
89-19-002	Sharing Begins In The Heart-520861	S. Butcher	Yr.Iss.	25.00	45-80.00
90-19-003	I'm A Precious Moments Fan-523526	S. Butcher	Yr.Iss.	25.00	45-85.00
90-19-004	Good Friends Are Forever-525049	S. Butcher	Yr.Iss.	25.00	25.00
91-19-005	You Can Always Bring A Friend-527122	S. Butcher	Yr.Iss.	27.50	45-65.00
92-19-006	An Event Worth Wading For-527319	S. Butcher	Yr.Iss.	32.50	32.50-55.00
93-19-007	An Event For All Seasons-530158	S. Butcher	Yr.Iss.	30.00	40.00
94-19-008	Memories Are Made of This-529982	S. Butcher	Yr.Iss.	30.00	30.00
Enesco Corporation	**Precious Moments Commemorative Easter Seal Figurines**				
88-20-001	Jesus Loves Me-9" Fig.-104531	S. Butcher	1,000	N/A	1800-2000.
87-20-002	He Walks With Me-107999	S. Butcher	Yr.Iss.	25.00	65-75.00
88-20-003	Blessed Are They That Overcome-115479	S. Butcher	Yr.Iss.	27.50	38-75.00
89-20-004	Make A Joyful Noise-9" Fig.-520322	S. Butcher	1,500	N/A	750-1400.
89-20-005	His Love Will Shine On You-522376	S. Butcher	Yr.Iss.	30.00	50-65.00
90-20-006	You Have Touched So Many Hearts-9" fig.-523283	S. Butcher	2,000	N/A	675-775.
91-20-007	We Are God's Workmanship-9" fig.-523879	S. Butcher	2,000	N/A	725-879.
90-20-008	Always In His Care-524522	S. Butcher	Yr.Iss.	30.00	36-70.00
92-20-009	You Are Such A Purr-fect Friend 9" fig.-526010	S. Butcher	2,000	N/A	600-985.
91-20-010	Sharing A Gift Of Love-527114	S. Butcher	Yr.Iss.	30.00	49-65.00
92-20-011	A Universal Love-527173	S. Butcher	Yr.Iss.	32.50	35-75.00
93-20-012	Gather Your Dreams-9" fig.-529680	S. Butcher	2,000	N/A	N/A
93-20-013	You're My Number One Friend-530026	S. Butcher	Yr.Iss.	30.00	30.00
94-20-014	It's No Secret What God Can Do - 531111	S. Butcher	Yr.Iss.	30.00	30.00
Enesco Corporation	**Precious Moments Musical Figurines**				
83-21-001	Sharing Our Season Together-E-0519	S. Butcher	Retrd.	70.00	100-140.
83-21-002	Wee Three Kings-E-0520	S. Butcher	Suspd.	60.00	90-110.00
83-21-003	Let Heaven And Nature Sing-E-2346	S. Butcher	Suspd.	55.00	115-130.
93-21-004	O Come All Ye Faithful-E-2352	S. Butcher	Open	50.00	50.00
82-21-005	I'll Play My Drum For Him-E-2355	S. Butcher	Suspd.	45.00	110-140.
79-21-006	Christmas Is A Time To Share-E-2806	S. Butcher	Retrd.	35.00	140-170.
79-21-007	Crown Him Lord Of All-E-2807	S. Butcher	Suspd.	35.00	75-110.00
79-21-008	Unto Us A Child Is Born-E-2808	S. Butcher	Suspd.	35.00	65-115.00
80-21-009	Jesus Is Born-E-2809	S. Butcher	Suspd.	35.00	90-120.00
80-21-010	Come Let Us Adore Him-E-2810	S. Butcher	Suspd.	45.00	85-150.00
80-21-011	Peace On Earth-E-4726	S. Butcher	Suspd.	45.00	95-120.00
80-21-012	The Hand That Rocks The Future-E-5204	S. Butcher	Open	30.00	55-85.00
80-21-013	My Guardian Angel-E-5205	S. Butcher	Suspd.	22.50	65-80.00
81-21-014	My Guardian Angel-E-5206	S. Butcher	Suspd.	22.50	55-95.00
84-21-015	Wishing You A Merry Christmas-E-5394	S. Butcher	Suspd.	55.00	80-100.00
80-21-016	Silent Knight-E-5642	S. Butcher	Suspd.	45.00	125-150.
81-21-017	Rejoice O Earth-E-5645	S. Butcher	Retrd.	35.00	80-125.00
81-21-018	The Lord Bless You And Keep You-E-7180	S. Butcher	Open	55.00	80-100.00
81-21-019	Mother Sew Dear-E-7182	S. Butcher	Open	35.00	55-75.00
81-21-020	The Purr-fect Grandma-E-7184	S. Butcher	Suspd.	35.00	55-80.00
81-21-021	Love Is Sharing-E-7185	S. Butcher	Retrd.	40.00	125-165.
81-21-022	Let the Whole World Know-E-7186	S. Butcher	Suspd.	60.00	135.00
93-21-023	Lord Keep My Life In Tune (2/set)-12165	S. Butcher	Open	50.00	50.00
84-21-024	We Saw A Star-12408	S. Butcher	Suspd.	50.00	65-80.00
93-21-025	Lord Keep My Life In Tune (2/set)-12580	S. Butcher	Open	50.00	50.00
93-21-026	God Sent You Just In Time-15504	S. Butcher	Retrd.	60.00	60.00
93-21-027	Silent Night-15814	S. Butcher	Open	55.00	55-75.00
85-21-028	Heaven Bless You-100285	S. Butcher	Suspd.	45.00	69-89.00
86-21-029	Our 1st Christmas Together-101702	S. Butcher	Retrd.	50.00	110-180.00
93-21-030	Let's Keep In Touch-102520	S. Butcher	Open	85.00	85.00
93-21-031	Peace On Earth-109746	S. Butcher	Suspd.	120.00	120.00
87-21-032	I'm Sending You A White Christmas-112402	S. Butcher	Retrd.	55.00	70-75.00
87-21-033	You Have Touched So Many Hearts-112577	S. Butcher	Open	50.00	50-60.00
91-21-034	Lord Keep My Life In Balance-520691	S. Butcher	Suspd.	60.00	68.00
93-21-035	The Light Of The World Is Jesus-521507	S. Butcher	Open	65.00	65.00
92-21-036	Do Not Open Till Christmas-522244	S. Butcher	Open	75.00	75.00
92-21-037	This Day Has Been Made In Heaven-523682	S. Butcher	Open	60.00	60.00

Company / Number	Name	Series / Artist	Edition Limit	Issue Price	Quote
93-21-038	Wishing You Were Here-526916	S. Butcher	Open	100.00	100.00
Enesco Corporation		**Precious Moments Calendar Girl**			
88-22-001	January-109983	S. Butcher	Open	37.50	45-67.00
88-22-002	February-109991	S. Butcher	Open	27.50	33.50-67.00
88-22-003	March-110019	S. Butcher	Open	27.50	33.50-64.00
88-22-004	April-110027	S. Butcher	Open	30.00	35-118.00
88-22-005	May -110035	S. Butcher	Open	25.00	30-150.00
88-22-006	June-110043	S. Butcher	Open	40.00	50-112.00
88-22-007	July-110051	S. Butcher	Open	35.00	45-58.00
88-22-008	August-110078	S. Butcher	Open	40.00	50-57.00
88-22-009	September-110086	S. Butcher	Open	27.50	33.50-49.00
88-22-010	October-110094	S. Butcher	Open	35.00	45-59.00
88-22-011	November-110108	S. Butcher	Open	32.50	37.50-50.00
88-22-012	December-110116	S. Butcher	Open	27.50	35-75.00
Enesco Corporation		**Bless Those Who Serve Their Country**			
91-23-001	Bless Those Who Serve Their Country (Navy) 526568	S. Butcher	Suspd.	32.50	36.00
91-23-002	Bless Those Who Serve Their Country (Army) 526576	S. Butcher	Suspd.	32.50	32.50
91-23-003	Bless Those Who Serve Their Country (Air Force) 526584	S. Butcher	Suspd.	32.50	35.00
91-23-004	Bless Those Who Serve Their Country (Girl Soldier) 527289	S. Butcher	Suspd.	32.50	35.00
91-23-005	Bless Those Who Serve Their Country (Soldier) 527297	S. Butcher	Suspd.	32.50	32.50
91-23-006	Bless Those Who Serve Their Country (Marine) 527521	S. Butcher	Suspd.	32.50	45.00
Enesco Corporation		**Sugartown**			
93-24-001	Sammy-528668	S. Butcher	Open	17.00	17.00
92-24-002	Christmas Tree-528684	S. Butcher	Open	15.00	15.00
93-24-003	Sam Butcher-528842	S. Butcher	Yr.Iss.	22.50	22.50
93-24-004	Dusty-529435	S. Butcher	Open	17.00	17.00
93-24-005	Car-529443	S. Butcher	Open	22.50	22.50
92-24-006	Aunt Ruth & Aunt Dorothy-529486	S. Butcher	Open	20.00	20.00
92-24-007	Philip-529494	S. Butcher	Open	17.00	17.00
92-24-008	Nativity-529508	S. Butcher	Open	20.00	20.00
92-24-009	Grandfather-529516	S. Butcher	Open	15.00	15.00
93-24-010	Katy Lynne-529524	S. Butcher	Open	20.00	20.00
92-24-011	Sam Butcher-529567	S. Butcher	Yr.Iss.	22.50	22.50-50.00
93-24-012	House Night Light 529605	S. Butcher	Open	80.00	80.00
92-24-013	Chapel-529621	S. Butcher	Open	85.00	85.00
93-24-014	Fence-529796	S. Butcher	Open	10.00	10.00
93-24-015	Collector's Set/7-531773	S. Butcher	Open	189.00	189.00
Enesco Corporation		**Spring Catalog Figurine**			
93-25-001	Happiness Is At Our Fingertips-529931	S. Butcher	Retrd.	35.00	140.00
94-25-002	So Glad I Picked You As A Friend-524379	S. Butcher	Yr.Iss.	40.00	40.00
Enesco Corporation		**Two By Two**			
93-26-001	Noah, Noah's Wife, & Noah's Ark (lighted)-530042	S. Butcher	Open	125.00	125.00
93-26-002	Sheep (mini double fig.) -530077	S. Butcher	Open	10.00	10.00
93-26-003	Pigs (mini double fig.) -530085	S. Butcher	Open	12.00	12.00
93-26-004	Giraffes (mini double fig.) -530115	S. Butcher	Open	16.00	16.00
93-26-005	Bunnies (mini double fig.) -530123	S. Butcher	Open	9.00	9.00
93-26-006	Elephants (mini double fig.) -530131	S. Butcher	Open	18.00	18.00
93-26-007	Eight Piece Collector's Set -530948	S. Butcher	Open	190.00	190.00
94-26-008	Llamas-531375	S. Butcher	Open	15.00	15.00
Enesco Corporation		**Precious Moments Collection 15th Anniv. Commemorative Edition**			
93-27-001	15 Happy Years Together: What A Tweet -530786	S. Butcher	Yr.Iss.	100.00	100.00
Enesco Corporation		**Sammy's Circus**			
94-28-001	Markie-528099	S. Butcher	Open	18.50	18.50
94-28-002	Dusty-529176	S. Butcher	Open	22.50	22.50
94-28-003	Katie-529184	S. Butcher	Open	17.00	17.00
94-28-004	Tippy-529192	S. Butcher	Open	12.00	12.00
94-28-005	Collin-529214	S. Butcher	Open	20.00	20.00
94-28-006	Sammy-529222	S. Butcher	Yr.Iss.	20.00	20.00
94-28-007	Circus Ten-528196 (Nite-Lite)	S. Butcher	Open	90.00	90.00
Enesco Corporation		**Memories of Yesterday Special Edition**			
88-28-001	Mommy, I Teared It-523488	M. Attwell	10,000	25.00	175-325.
89-28-002	As Good As His Mother Ever Made-522392	M. Attwell	9,600	32.50	114-150.
90-28-003	A Lapful of Luck -525014	M. Attwell	5,000	30.00	114-180.
90-28-004	Set of Three	M. Attwell	N/A	87.50	735.00
Enesco Corporation		**Memories of Yesterday -Charter 1988**			
88-29-001	Mommy, I Teared It-114480	M. Attwell	Open	25.00	32-143.00
88-29-002	Now I Lay Me Down To Sleep-114499	M. Attwell	Open	20.00	25-65.00
88-29-003	We's Happy! How's Yourself?-114502	M. Attwell	Open	40.00	45-60.00
88-29-004	Hang On To Your Luck!-114510	M. Attwell	Open	25.00	27.50-70.00
88-29-005	How Do You Spell S-O-R-R-Y?-114529	M. Attwell	Retrd.	25.00	50-95.00
88-29-006	What Will I Grow Up To Be?-114537	M. Attwell	Open	40.00	45-72.00
88-29-007	Can I Keep Her Mommy?-114545	M. Attwell	Open	25.00	27.50-70.00
88-29-008	Hush!-114553	M. Attwell	Retrd.	45.00	75-125.00
88-29-009	It Hurts When Fido Hurts-114561	M. Attwell	Retrd.	30.00	32.50-75.00
88-29-010	Anyway, Fido Loves Me-114588	M. Attwell	Open	30.00	32.50-75.00
88-29-011	If You Can't Be Good, Be Careful-114596	M. Attwell	Retrd.	50.00	55-90.00
88-29-012	Mommy, I Teared It, 9"-115924	M. Attwell	Retrd.	85.00	140-195.
88-29-013	Welcome Santa-114960	M. Attwell	Open	45.00	50-100.00
88-29-014	Special Delivery-114979	M. Attwell	Retrd.	30.00	32.50-70.00
88-29-015	How 'bout A Little Kiss?-114987	M. Attwell	Open	25.00	27.50-85.00
88-29-016	Waiting For Santa-114995	M. Attwell	Open	40.00	45-55.00
88-29-017	Dear Santa. . .-115002	M. Attwell	Open	50.00	55-65.00
88-29-018	I Hope Santa Is Home . . .-115010	M. Attwell	Open	30.00	32.50-45.00
88-29-019	It's The Thought That Counts-115029	M. Attwell	Open	25.00	27.50-75.00
88-29-020	Is It Really Santa?-115347	M. Attwell	Open	50.00	55-60.00
88-29-021	He Knows IF You've Been Bad Or Good-115355	M. Attwell	Open	40.00	45-75.00
88-29-022	Now He Can Be Your Friend, Too!-115363	M. Attwell	Open	45.00	50-70.00
88-29-023	We Wish You A Merry Christmas-115371	M. Attwell	Open	70.00	75-125.00
88-29-024	Good Morning Mr. Snowman-115401	M. Attwell	Retrd.	75.00	80-170.00
Enesco Corporation		**Memories of Yesterday Figurines**			
89-30-001	Blow Wind, Blow-520012	M. Attwell	Open	40.00	40.00
89-30-002	Let's Be Nice Like We Was Before-520047	M. Attwell	Open	50.00	50.00
89-30-003	I'se Spoken For-520071	M. Attwell	Retrd.	30.00	50-70.00
89-30-004	Daddy, I Can Never Fill Your Shoes-520187	M. Attwell	Open	30.00	30.00
89-30-005	This One's For You, Dear-520195	M. Attwell	Open	50.00	50.00
89-30-006	Should I . . . ?-520209	M. Attwell	Open	50.00	50.00
89-30-007	Here Comes The Bride-God Bless Her! -9"-5205272	M. Attwell	Retrd.	95.00	95-100.
89-30-008	We's Happy! How's Yourself?-520616	M. Attwell	Retrd.	70.00	85-150.00
89-30-009	Here Comes The Bride & Groom God Bless 'Em-520896	M. Attwell	Open	50.00	50.00
89-30-010	The Long and Short of It-522384	M. Attwell	Open	32.50	32.50
89-30-011	As Good As His Mother Ever Made-522392	M. Attwell	Open	32.50	32.50
89-30-012	Must Feed Them Over Christmas-522406	M. Attwell	Open	38.50	38.50
89-30-013	Knitting You A Warm & Cozy Winter-522414	M. Attwell	Open	37.50	37.50
89-30-014	Joy To You At Christmas-522449	M. Attwell	Open	45.00	45.00
89-30-015	For Fido And Me-522457	M. Attwell	Open	70.00	70.00
90-30-016	Hold It! You're Just Swell-520020	M. Attwell	Open	50.00	50.00
90-30-017	Kiss The Place And Make It Well-520039	M. Attwell	Open	50.00	50.00
90-30-018	Where's Muvver?-520101	M. Attwell	Open	30.00	30.00
90-30-019	Here Comes The Bride And Groom God Bless 'Em!-520136	M. Attwell	Open	80.00	80.00
90-30-020	Luck At Last! He Loves Me-520217	M. Attwell	Retrd.	35.00	36-58.00
90-30-021	I'm Not As Backwards As I Looks-523240	M. Attwell	Open	32.50	32.50
90-30-022	I Pray The Lord My Soul To Keep-523259	M. Attwell	Open	25.00	25.00
90-30-023	He Hasn't Forgotten Me-523267	M. Attwell	Open	30.00	30.00
90-30-024	Time For Bed 9"-523275	M. Attwell	Retrd.	95.00	95-125.00
90-30-025	Got To Get Home For The Holidays-524751	M. Attwell	Open	100.00	100.00
90-30-026	Hush-A-Bye Baby-524778	M. Attwell	Open	80.00	80.00
90-30-027	Let Me Be Your Guardian Angel-524670	M. Attwell	Open	32.50	32.50
90-30-028	I'se Been Painting-524700	M. Attwell	Open	37.50	37.50
90-30-029	A Lapful Of Luck-524689	M. Attwell	Open	15.00	15.00
90-30-030	The Greatest Treasure The World Can Hold-524808	M. Attwell	Open	50.00	50.00
90-30-031	Hoping To See You Soon-524824	M. Attwell	Open	30.00	30.00
90-30-032	A Dash of Something With Something For the Pot-524727	M. Attwell	Open	55.00	55.00
90-30-033	Not A Creature Was Stirrin'-524697	M. Attwell	Open	45.00	45.00
90-30-034	Collection Sign-513156	M. Attwell	Retrd.	7.00	7.00
91-30-035	He Loves Me -9" -525022	M. Attwell	Retrd.	100.00	100.00
91-30-036	Give It Your Best Shot-525561	M. Attwell	Open	35.00	35.00
91-30-037	Wishful Thinking-522597	M. Attwell	Open	45.00	45.00
91-30-038	Them Dishes Nearly Done-524611	M. Attwell	Open	50.00	50.00
91-30-039	Just Thinking 'bout You-523461	M. Attwell	Open	70.00	70.00
91-30-040	Who Ever Told Mother To Order Twins?-520063	M. Attwell	Open	33.50	33.50
91-30-041	Tying The Knot-522678	M. Attwell	Open	60.00	60.00
91-30-042	Pull Yourselves Together Girls, Waists Are In-522783	M. Attwell	Open	30.00	30.00
91-30-043	I Must Be Somebody's Darling-524832	M. Attwell	Retrd.	30.00	30.00
91-30-044	We All Loves A Cuddle-524832	M. Attwell	Retrd.	30.00	35.00
91-30-045	Sitting Pretty-522708	M. Attwell	Retrd.	40.00	40.00
91-30-046	Why Don't You Sing Along?-522600	M. Attwell	Open	55.00	55.00
91-30-047	Wherever I Am, I'm Dreaming of You-522686	M. Attwell	Open	40.00	40.00
91-30-048	Opening Presents Is Much Fun!-524735	M. Attwell	Open	37.50	37.50
91-30-049	I'm As Comfy As Can Be-525480	M. Attwell	Open	50.00	50.00
91-30-050	Friendship Has No Boundaries (Special Understamp)-525545	M. Attwell	Yr.Iss.	30.00	30-55.00
91-30-051	Could You Love Me For Myself Alone?-525618	M. Attwell	Open	30.00	30.00
91-30-052	Good Morning, Little Boo-Boo-525766	M. Attwell	Open	40.00	40.00
91-30-053	S'no Use Lookin' Back Now!-527203	M. Attwell	Open	75.00	75.00
92-30-054	I Pray the Lord My Soul To Keep (Musical)-525596	M. Attwell	Open	65.00	65.00
92-30-055	Time For Bed-527076	M. Attwell	Open	30.00	30.00
92-30-056	Now Be A Good Dog Fido-524581	M. Attwell	Open	45.00	45.00
92-30-057	A Kiss From Fido-523119	M. Attwell	Open	35.00	35.00
92-30-058	I'se Such A Good Little Girl Sometimes-522759	M. Attwell	Open	30.00	30.00
92-30-059	Send All Life's Little Worries Skipping-527505	M. Attwell	Open	30.00	30.00
92-30-060	A Whole Bunch of Love For You-522732	M. Attwell	Open	40.00	40.00
92-30-061	Hurry Up For the Last Train to Fairyland-525863	M. Attwell	Open	40.00	40.00
92-30-062	I'se So Happy You Called-526401	M. Attwell	2-Yr.	100.00	100.00
92-30-063	I'm Hopin' You're Missing Me Too-525499	M. Attwell	Open	55.00	55.00
92-30-064	You'll Always Be My Hero-524743	M. Attwell	Open	50.00	50.00
92-30-065	Things Are Rather Upside Down-522775	M. Attwell	Open	30.00	30.00
92-30-066	The Future-God Bless 'Em!-524719	M. Attwell	Open	37.50	37.50
92-30-067	Making Something Special For You-525472	M. Attwell	Open	45.00	45.00
92-30-068	Home's A Grand Place To Get Back To Musical-525553	M. Attwell	Open	100.00	100.00
92-30-069	Five Years Of Memories-525669 (Five Year Anniversary Figurine)	M. Attwell	Yr.Iss.	50.00	65.00
92-30-070	Good Night and God Bless You In Every Way!-525634	M. Attwell	Open	50.00	50.00
92-30-071	Collection Sign-527300	M. Attwell	Open	30.00	30.00
92-30-072	Merry Christmas, Little Boo-Boo-528803	M. Attwell	Open	37.50	37.50
92-30-073	Five Years Of Memories. Celebrating Our Five Years1992-525669A	M. Attwell	500	N/A	N/A
93-30-074	You Do Make Me Happy-520098	M. Attwell	Open	27.50	27.50
93-30-075	Will You Be Mine?-522694	M. Attwell	Open	30.00	30.00
93-30-076	Here's A Little Song From Me To You Musical-522716	M. Attwell	Open	70.00	70.00
93-30-077	Bringing Good Luck To You-522791	M. Attwell	Open	30.00	30.00
93-30-078	With A Heart That's True, I'll Wait For You-524816	M. Attwell	Open	50.00	50.00
93-30-079	Now I Lay Me Down To Sleep-525413 (musical)	M. Attwell	Open	65.00	65.00
93-30-080	The Jolly Ole Sun Will Shine Again-525502	M. Attwell	Open	55.00	55.00
93-30-081	May Your Flowers Be Even Better Than The Pictures On The Packets-525685	M. Attwell	Open	37.50	37.50
93-30-082	You Won't Catch Me Being A Golf Widow -525715	M. Attwell	Open	30.00	30.00
93-30-083	Having A Wash And Brush Up-527424	M. Attwell	Open	35.00	35.00
93-30-084	A Bit Tied Up Just Now-But Cheerio-527467	M. Attwell	Open	45.00	45.00
93-30-085	Hullo! Did You Come By Underground? -527653	M. Attwell	Yr.Iss.	40.00	40.00
93-30-086	Hullo! Did You Come By Underground? Commemorative Issue: 1913-1993 -527653A	M. Attwell	500	N/A	N/A
93-30-087	Look Out-Something Good Is Coming Your Way!-528781	M. Attwell	Open	37.50	37.50
93-30-088	Strikes Me, I'm Your Match-529656	M. Attwell	Open	27.50	27.50
93-30-089	Wot's All This Talk About Love?-529737	M. Attwell	2-Yr.	100.00	100.00
93-30-090	Do You Know The Way To Fairyland? -530379	M. Attwell	Open	50.00	50.00
94-30-091	Too Shy For Words-525758	M. Attwell	Open	50.00	50.00

Company Number	Name	Series Artist	Edition Limit	Issue Price	Quote
94-30-092	Pleasant Dreams and Sweet Repose-(musical)-526592	M. Attwell	Open	80.00	80.00
94-30-093	Bless 'Em!-523127	M. Attwell	Open	35.00	35.00
94-30-094	Bless 'Em!-523232	M. Attwell	Open	35.00	35.00
94-30-095	Don't Wait For Wishes to Come True-Go Get Them!-527645	M. Attwell	Open	37.50	37.50
94-30-096	There's Nothing in the World I Wouldn't Do For You-529907	M. Attwell	Open	30.00	30.00
94-30-097	The Nativity Pageant-602949	M. Attwell	Open	90.00	90.00
94-30-098	Taking After Mother-525731	M. Attwell	Open	40.00	40.00
94-30-099	Bobbed-526991	M. Attwell	Open	32.50	32.50
94-30-100	Having a Good Ole Laugh-527432	M. Attwell	Open	50.00	50.00
94-30-101	Do Be Friends With Me-529117	M. Attwell	Open	40.00	40.00
94-30-102	Good Morning From One Cheery Soul To Another-529141	M. Attwell	Open	30.00	30.00
94-30-103	May Your Birthday Be Bright And Happy-529575	M. Attwell	Open	35.00	35.00
94-30-104	Thank God For Fido-529753	M. Attwell	2-Yr.	100.00	100.00
94-30-105	Still Going Strong-530344	M. Attwell	Open	27.50	27.50
94-30-106	Comforting Thoughts-531367	M. Attwell	Open	32.50	32.50
Enesco Corporation	**Memories of Yesterday Once Upon A Fairy Tale™...**				
92-31-001	Mother Goose-526428	M. Attwell	18,000	50.00	50.00
92-31-002	Mary Had A Little Lamb-526479	M. Attwell	18,000	45.00	45.00
92-31-003	Simple Simon-526452	M. Attwell	18,000	35.00	35.00
93-31-004	Mary, Mary Quite Contrary-526436	M. Attwell	18,000	45.00	45.00
93-31-005	Little Miss Muffett-526444	M. Attwell	18,000	50.00	50.00
94-31-006	Tweedle Dum & Tweedle Dee-526460	M. Attwell	Yr. Iss.	50.00	50.00
Enesco Corporation	**Memories of Yesterday-Exclusive Membership Figurine**				
91-32-001	We Belong Together-S0001	M. Attwell	Yr.Iss.	Gift	80.00
92-32-002	Waiting For The Sunshine-S0002	M. Attwell	Yr.Iss.	Gift	60.00
93-32-003	I'm The Girl For You-S0003	M. Attwell	Yr.Iss.	Gift	40.00
94-32-004	Blowing a Kiss to a Dear I Miss-S0004	M. Attwell	Yr.Iss.	Gift	N/A
Enesco Corporation	**Memories of Yesterday-Exclusive Charter Membership Figurine**				
92-33-001	Waiting For The Sunshine-S0102	M. Attwell	Yr.Iss.	Gift	N/A
93-33-002	I'm The Girl For You-S0103	M. Attwell	Yr.Iss.	Gift	N/A
94-33-003	Blowing a Kiss to a Dear I Miss-S0104	M. Attwell	Yr.Iss.	Gift	N/A
Enesco Corporation	**Memories of Yesterday-Society Figurines**				
91-34-001	Welcome To Your New Home-M4911	M. Attwell	Yr.Iss.	30.00	85.00
91-34-002	I Love My Friends-MY921	M. Attwell	Yr.Iss.	32.50	60.00
93-34-003	Now I'm The Fairest Of Them All-MY931	M. Attwell	Yr.Iss.	35.00	35.00
93-34-004	A Little Love Song for You-MY941	M. Attwell	Yr.Iss.	35.00	35.00
Enesco Corporation	**Memories of Yesterday-Exclusive Heritage Dealer Figurine**				
91-35-001	A Friendly Chat and a Cup of Tea-525510	M. Attwell	Yr.Iss.	50.00	100.00
93-35-002	I'm Always Looking Out For You-527440	M. Attwell	Yr.Iss.	55.00	55.00
Enesco Corporation	**Memories of Yesterday-Event Item Only**				
94-36-001	I'll Always Be Your Truly Friend-525693	M. Attwell	Yr.Iss.	30.00	30.00
Enesco Corporation	**Memories of Yesterday-Memories Of A Special Day**				
94-37-001	Monday's Child...-531421	M. Attwell	Open	35.00	35.00
94-37-002	Tuesday's Child...-531448	M. Attwell	Open	35.00	35.00
94-37-003	Wednesday's Child...-531405	M. Attwell	Open	35.00	35.00
94-37-004	Thursday's Child...-531413	M. Attwell	Open	35.00	35.00
94-37-005	Friday's Child...-531391	M. Attwell	Open	35.00	35.00
94-37-006	Saturday's Child...-531383	M. Attwell	Open	35.00	35.00
94-37-007	Sunday's Child...-531480	M. Attwell	Open	35.00	35.00
94-37-008	Collector's Commemorative Edition Set of 7, Hand-numbered-528056	M. Attwell	1,994	250.00	250.00
Enesco/Hamilton Gifts Ltd.	**Maud Humphrey Bogart Figurines**				
88-01-001	Tea And Gossip H1301	M. Humphrey	Retrd.	65.00	65-156.00
88-01-002	Cleaning House H1303	M. Humphrey	Retrd.	60.00	65-175.00
88-01-003	Susanna H 1305	M. Humphrey	Retrd.	60.00	161-375.
88-01-004	Little Chickadees H1306	M. Humphrey	Retrd.	65.00	108.00
88-01-005	The Magic Kitten H1308	M. Humphrey	Retrd.	66.00	54-125.00
88-01-006	Seamstress H1309	M. Humphrey	Retrd.	66.00	90-150.00
88-01-007	A Pleasure To Meet You H1310	M. Humphrey	15,000	65.00	178.00
88-01-008	My First Dance H1311	M. Humphrey	Retrd.	60.00	350.00
88-01-009	Sarah H1312	M. Humphrey	Retrd.	60.00	384-440.
89-01-010	The Bride H1313	M. Humphrey	19,500	90.00	65-90.00
89-01-011	Sealed With A Kiss H1316	M. Humphrey	Retrd.	45.00	65-105.00
88-01-012	Special Friends H1317	M. Humphrey	Retrd.	66.00	90-160.00
89-01-013	School Days H1318	M. Humphrey	Retrd.	42.50	59-85.00
89-01-014	Gift Of Love H1319	M. Humphrey	Retrd.	65.00	29-100.00
89-01-015	My 1st Birthday H1320	M. Humphrey	Retrd.	47.00	100.00
90-01-016	A Little Robin H1347	M. Humphrey	19,500	55.00	55.00
90-01-017	Autumn Days H1348	M. Humphrey	24,500	45.00	45.00
90-01-018	Little Playmates H1349	M. Humphrey	19,500	48.00	48.00
89-01-019	No More Tears H1351	M. Humphrey	24,500	44.00	44.00
89-01-020	Winter Fun H1354	M. Humphrey	Retrd.	46.00	72-92.00
89-01-021	Kitty's Lunch H1355	M. Humphrey	19,500	60.00	60.00
90-01-022	School Lesson H1356	M. Humphrey	19,500	77.00	65-77.00
90-01-023	In The Orchard H1373	M. Humphrey	24,500	33.00	33.00
89-01-024	The Little Captive H1374	M. Humphrey	19,500	55.00	55.00
89-01-025	Little Red Riding Hood H1381	M. Humphrey	24,500	42.50	42.50
89-01-026	Little Bo Peep H1382	M. Humphrey	24,500	45.00	45.00
90-01-027	Playtime H1383	M. Humphrey	19,500	60.00	66.00
90-01-028	Kitty's Bath H1384	M. Humphrey	19,500	103.00	103.00
89-01-029	Springtime Gathering H1385	M. Humphrey	7,500	295.00	295.00
89-01-030	A Sunday Outing H1386	M. Humphrey	15,000	135.00	135.00
89-01-031	Spring Beauties H1387	M. Humphrey	15,000	135.00	135.00
89-01-032	The Bride-Porcelain H1388	M. Humphrey	15,000	125.00	128.00
89-01-033	Little Chickadees-Porcelain H1389	M. Humphrey	15,000	125.00	125.00
89-01-034	Special Friends-Porcelain H1390	M. Humphrey	15,000	125.00	128.00
89-01-035	Playing Bridesmaid H5500	M. Humphrey	15,000	125.00	125.00
89-01-036	The Magic Kitten-Porcelain H5543	M. Humphrey	15,000	125.00	125.00
90-01-037	A Special Gift H5550	M. Humphrey	19,500	70.00	90.00
90-01-038	Holiday Surprise H5551	M. Humphrey	24,500	50.00	50.00
90-01-039	Winter Friends H5552	M. Humphrey	19,500	64.00	64.00
90-01-040	Winter Days H5553	M. Humphrey	24,500	50.00	50.00
90-01-041	My Winter Hat H5554	M. Humphrey	24,500	40.00	40.00
91-01-042	The Graduate H5559	M. Humphrey	19,500	75.00	75.00
90-01-043	A Chance Acquaintance H5589	M. Humphrey	19,500	70.00	135.00
91-01-044	Spring Frolic H5590	M. Humphrey	15,000	170.00	170.00
90-01-045	Sarah (Waterball) H5594	M. Humphrey	19,500	75.00	79.00
90-01-046	Susanna (Waterball) H5595	M. Humphrey	19,500	75.00	79.00
91-01-047	Spring Bouquet H5598	M. Humphrey	24,500	44.00	44.00
91-01-048	The Pinwheel H5600	M. Humphrey	24,500	45.00	45.00
91-01-049	Little Boy Blue H5612	M. Humphrey	19,500	55.00	55.00

Company Number	Name	Series Artist	Edition Limit	Issue Price	Quote
91-01-050	Little Miss Muffet H5621	M. Humphrey	24,500	75.00	75.00
91-01-051	My First Dance-Porcelain H5650	M. Humphrey	15,000	110.00	110.00
91-01-052	Sarah-Porcelain H5651	M. Humphrey	15,000	110.00	110.00
91-01-053	Susanna-Porcelain H5652	M. Humphrey	15,000	110.00	110.00
91-01-054	Tea And Gossip-Porcelain H5653	M. Humphrey	15,000	132.00	132.00
91-01-055	Cleaning House (Waterball) H5654	M. Humphrey	19,500	75.00	75.00
91-01-056	My First Dance (Waterball) H5655	M. Humphrey	19,500	75.00	75.00
91-01-057	Hush A Bye Baby H5695	M. Humphrey	19,500	62.00	62.00
91-01-058	All Bundled Up -910015	M. Humphrey	19,500	85.00	85.00
91-01-059	Doubles -910023	M. Humphrey	19,500	70.00	70.00
91-01-060	Melissa -910031	M. Humphrey	24,500	55.00	55.00
91-01-061	My Snow Shovel -910058	M. Humphrey	19,500	7000	70.00
91-01-062	Winter Ride -910066	M. Humphrey	19,500	60.00	60.00
91-01-063	Melissa (Waterball) -910074	M. Humphrey	19,500	40.00	40.00
91-01-064	Winter Days (Waterball) -915130	M. Humphrey	19,500	75.00	75.00
91-01-065	Winter Friends (Waterball) -915149	M. Humphrey	19,500	75.00	75.00
91-01-066	My Winter Hat -921017	M. Humphrey	15,000	80.00	80.00
91-01-067	Winter Fun -921025	M. Humphrey	15,000	90.00	90.00
92-01-068	Spring's Child 910244	M. Humphrey	24,500	50.00	50.00
92-01-069	Summer's Child 910252	M. Humphrey	24,500	50.00	50.00
92-01-070	Autumn's Child 910260	M. Humphrey	24,500	50.00	50.00
92-01-071	Winter's Child 910279	M. Humphrey	24,500	50.00	50.00
92-01-072	Jack and Jill 910155	M. Humphrey	19,500	75.00	75.00
92-01-073	The Young Artist 910228	M. Humphrey	19,500	75.00	75.00
92-01-074	Stars and Stripes Forever 910201	M. Humphrey	Closed	75.00	150.00
92-01-075	New Friends 910171	M. Humphrey	15,000	125.00	125.00
92-01-076	Under The Mistletoe 910309	M. Humphrey	19,500	75.00	75.00
92-01-077	Hollies For You 910317	M. Humphrey	24,500	55.00	55.00
92-01-078	Hush! Santa's Coming 915378	M. Humphrey	19,500	50.00	50.00
92-01-079	A Melody For You 915432	M. Humphrey	Open	60.00	60.00
92-01-080	The Christmas Carol 915823	M. Humphrey	24,500	75.00	50-75.00
92-01-081	Susanna (Musical) 921084	M. Humphrey	7,500	125.00	125.00
92-01-082	Sarah (Musical) 921076	M. Humphrey	7,500	125.00	125.00
92-01-083	Hollies For You (Musical) 921092	M. Humphrey	5,000	125.00	125.00
93-01-084	Tee Time 915386	M. Humphrey	10,000	50.00	50.00
93-01-085	The Entertainer 910562	M. Humphrey	19,500	60.00	60.00
93-01-086	A Basket Full of Blessings 910147	M. Humphrey	15,000	55.00	55.00
93-01-087	Love's First Bloom 910120	M. Humphrey	15,000	50.00	50.00
93-01-088	Bedtime Blessings 910236	M. Humphrey	10,000	60.00	60.00
93-01-089	Flying Lessons 910139	M. Humphrey	15,000	50.00	50.00
93-01-090	Playing Mama 5th Anniv. Figurine 915963	M. Humphrey	Retrd.	80.00	80.00
93-01-091	Playing Mama Event Figurine 915963R	M. Humphrey	Retrd.	80.00	80.00
94-01-092	Marie-Childhood Memories 869619	M. Humphrey	5,000	35.00	35.00
94-01-093	Good As New 914924	M. Humphrey	5,000	100.00	100.00
94-01-094	Poetry Recital 914959	M. Humphrey	5,000	80.00	80.00
94-01-095	Loving Care 914932	M. Humphrey	5,000	60.00	60.00
Enesco/Hamilton Gifts Ltd.	**Maud Humphrey Bogart Gallery Figurines**				
91-02-001	Mother's Treasures H5619	M. Humphrey	15,000	118.00	118.00
91-02-002	Sharing Secrets-910007	M. Humphrey	15,000	120.00	120.00
92-02-003	New Friends-910171	M. Humphrey	15,000	125.00	125.00
92-02-004	A Little Bird Told Me So-910570	M. Humphrey	7,500	120.00	120.00
93-02-005	May I Have This Dance?-915750	M. Humphrey	Yr.Iss.	110.00	110.00
Enesco/Hamilton Gifts Ltd.	**Maud Humphrey Bogart Symbol Of Membership Figurines**				
91-03-001	A Flower For You H5596	M. Humphrey	Closed	Unkn.	26.00
92-03-002	Sunday Best M0002	M. Humphrey	Closed	Unkn.	53.00
93-03-003	Playful Companions M0003	M. Humphrey	Yr.Iss.	Unkn.	Unkn.
Enesco/Hamilton Gifts Ltd.	**Maud Humphrey Bogart Collectors' Club Members Only**				
91-04-001	Friends For Life MH911	M. Humphrey	Closed	60.00	60-200.00
92-04-002	Nature's Little Helper MH921	M. Humphrey	Closed	65.00	65.00
93-04-003	Sitting Pretty	M. Humphrey	Yr.Iss.	60.00	60.00
Enesco/Hamilton Gifts Ltd.	**Maud Humphrey Bogart Victorian Village Mini Figurines**				
93-05-001	No.5 Greenwood-9 11569	M. Humphrey	18,840	50.00	50.00
93-05-002	Village Sign-911542	M. Humphrey	Open	12.00	12.00
93-05-003	No.5 Greenwood Accessories-911534	M. Humphrey	Open	20.00	20.00
93-05-004	A.J. Warner-911518	M. Humphrey	Open	12.00	12.00
93-05-005	Maud Humphrey-911496	M. Humphrey	Open	12.00	12.00
93-05-006	Mabel Humphrey-911933	M. Humphrey	Open	12.00	12.00
93-05-007	No.5 Greenwood Collectors' Proof Set -913804	M. Humphrey	1,868	120.00	120.00
Enesco/Hamilton Gifts Ltd.	**Linen and Lace**				
94-06-001	Capture the Moment 912654	M. Humphrey	2,500	125.00	125.00
94-06-002	A Dream Come True 916048	M. Humphrey	2,500	65.00	65.00
94-06-003	Artist of Her Time 916722	M. Humphrey	2,500	60.00	60.00
Enesco/Hamilton Gifts Ltd.	**Victorian Village**				
94-07-001	Timeless Traditions 655457	M. Humphrey	Yr.Iss.	50.00	50.00
94-07-002	A.J. 654906	M. Humphrey	Yr.Iss.	12.00	12.00
94-07-003	Maud 654892	M. Humphrey	Yr.Iss.	12.00	12.00
94-07-004	Mabel 654884	M. Humphrey	Yr.Iss.	12.00	12.00
94-07-005	Tree, Ottoman, Presents 654914	M. Humphrey	Yr.Iss.	20.00	20.00
94-07-006	Indoor Vignette Set of 7 654876 Collector's Proof Set	M. Humphrey	Yr.Iss.	120.00	120.00
94-07-007	Amazing Grace 911577	M. Humphrey	1,868	55.00	55.00
94-07-008	Elizabeth 911453	M. Humphrey	1,868	12.00	12.00
94-07-009	Sarah 911437	M. Humphrey	1,868	12.00	12.00
94-07-010	James Horvath 911445	M. Humphrey	1,868	12.00	12.00
94-07-011	Clock, Bench, Sign, Lamp 914231	M. Humphrey	1,868	12.00	12.00
94-07-012	Maud Humphrey Village Collector's Proof Set 911577-911445	M. Humphrey	1,868	125.00	125.00
Fenton Art Glass Company	**1983 Connoisseur Collection**				
83-01-001	5 pc. Burmese Epergne Set	Fenton	Closed	200.00	200.00
83-01-002	Vase, 4 1/2" Sculptured Rose Quartz	Fenton	Closed	32.50	32.50
83-01-003	Vase, 7" Sculptured Rose Quartz	Fenton	Closed	50.00	50.00
83-01-004	Basket, 9" Vasa Murrhina	Fenton	Closed	75.00	75.00
83-01-005	Cruet/Stopper Vasa Murrhina	Fenton	Closed	75.00	75.00
83-01-006	Vase, 9" Sculptured Rose Quartz	Fenton	Closed	75.00	75.00
83-01-007	Craftsman Stein, White Satin Carnival	Fenton	Closed	35.00	35.00
Fenton Art Glass Company	**1984 Connoisseur Collection**				
84-02-001	Basket, 10" Plated Amberina Velvet	Fenton	Closed	85.00	85.00
84-02-002	Top Hat, 8" Plated Amberina Velvet	Fenton	Closed	65.00	65.00
84-02-003	Cane, 18" Plated Amberina Velvet	Fenton	Closed	35.00	35.00
84-02-004	Vase, 9" Rose Velvet-Mother/Child	Fenton	Closed	125.00	125.00
84-02-005	3 pc. Covered Candy Box, Blue Burmese	Fenton	Closed	75.00	75.00
84-02-006	Vase, Swan, 8" Gold Azure	Fenton	Closed	65.00	65.00
84-02-007	Vase, 9" Rose Velvet-Floral	Fenton	Closed	75.00	75.00

FIGURINES/COTTAGES

Number	Name	Artist	Edition Limit	Issue Price	Quote
Fenton Art Glass Company		**1985 Connoisseur Collection**			
85-03-001	14 pc. Punch Set Green Opalescent	Fenton	Closed	250.00	250.00
85-03-002	4 pc. Diamond Lace Epergne, Green Opal.	Fenton	Closed	95.00	95.00
85-03-003	Lamp, 22" Burmese-Butterfly/Branch	Fenton	Closed	300.00	300.00
85-03-004	Basket, 8 1/2" Buremese, Handpainted	Fenton	Closed	95.00	95.00
85-03-005	Vase, 12" "Garielle" Scul. French Blue	Fenton	Closed	150.00	150.00
85-03-006	Vase, 7 1/2" Chrysanthemums & Circlet	Fenton	Closed	125.00	125.00
85-03-007	Vase, 7 1/2" Burmese-Shell	Fenton	Closed	135.00	135.00
Fenton Art Glass Company		**1986 Connoisseur Collection**			
86-04-001	4 pc. Vanity Set, Blue Ridge	Fenton	Closed	125.00	125.00
86-04-002	Handled Vase, 7" French Royale	Fenton	Closed	100.00	100.00
86-04-003	Handled Urn, 13" Cranberry Satin	Fenton	Closed	185.00	185.00
86-04-004	Lamp, 20" Burmese-Shells	Fenton	Closed	350.00	350.00
86-04-005	Basket, Top hat Wild Rose/Teal Overlay	Fenton	Closed	49.00	49.00
86-04-006	Boudoir Lamp Cranberry Pearl	Fenton	Closed	145.00	145.00
86-04-007	Cruet/Stopper Cranberry Pearl	Fenton	Closed	75.00	75.00
86-04-008	Vase, 10 1/2" "Misty Morn", Handpainted	Fenton	Closed	95.00	95.00
86-04-009	Vase 7 1/2", "Danielle" Sandcarved	Fenton	Closed	95.00	95.00
Fenton Art Glass Company		**1987 Connoisseur Collection**			
87-05-001	Vase, 7 1/4" Blossom/Bows on Cranberry	Fenton	Closed	95.00	95.00
87-05-002	Pitcher, 8" Enameled Azure	Fenton	Closed	85.00	85.00
Fenton Art Glass Company		**1988 Connoisseur Collection**			
88-06-001	Pitcher, Cased Cranberry/ Opal Teal Ring	Fenton	Closed	60.00	60.00
88-06-002	Vase, 6" Cased Cranberry/Opal Teal/Irid.	Fenton	Closed	50.00	50.00
88-06-003	Basket, Irid. Teal Cased Vasa Murrhina	Fenton	Closed	65.00	65.00
88-06-004	Candy, Wave Crest, Cranberry	Fenton	Closed	95.00	95.00
Fenton Art Glass Company		**1989 Connoisseur Collection**			
89-07-001	Basket, 7" Cranberry w/Crystal Ring	Fenton	Closed	85.00	85.00
89-07-002	Covered candy, Cranberry, Handpainted	Fenton	Closed	85.00	85.00
89-07-003	Vase, Pinch, 8" Vasa Murrhina	Fenton	Closed	65.00	65.00
89-07-004	Pitcher, Diamond Optic, Rosalene	Fenton	Closed	55.00	55.00
89-07-005	5 pc. Epergne, Rosalene	Fenton	Closed	250.00	250.00
89-07-006	Vase, Basketweave, Rosalene	Fenton	Closed	45.00	45.00
89-07-007	Lamp, 21" Handpainted Rosalene Satin	Fenton	Closed	250.00	250.00
Fenton Art Glass Company		**1990-85th Anniversary Collection**			
90-08-001	Basket, 5 1/2" Trees on Burmese	Fenton	Closed	57.50	57.50
90-08-002	Vase, 9" Trees on Burmese	Fenton	Closed	75.00	75.00
90-08-003	Lamp, 21" Raspberry on Burmese	Fenton	Closed	295.00	295.00
90-08-004	7 pc. Water Set Raspberry on Burmese	Fenton	Closed	275.00	275.00
90-08-005	Basket, 7" Raspberry on Burmese	Fenton	Closed	75.00	75.00
90-08-006	2 pc. Epergne Petite Floral on Burmese	Fenton	Closed	125.00	125.00
90-08-007	Cruet/Stopper Petite Floral on Burmese	Fenton	Closed	85.00	85.00
90-08-008	Vase, Fan, 6" Rose Burmese	Fenton	Closed	49.50	49.50
90-08-009	Vase, 6 1/2" Rose Burmese	Fenton	Closed	45.00	45.00
90-08-010	Lamp, 20" Rose Burmese	Fenton	Closed	250.00	250.00
Fenton Art Glass Company		**1991 Connoisseur Collection**			
91-09-001	Vase, Floral on Favrene	Fenton	Closed	125.00	125.00
91-09-002	3 pc. Candy Box, Favrene	Fenton	Closed	90.00	90.00
91-09-003	Vase, Fruit on Favrene	Fenton	Closed	125.00	125.00
91-09-004	Basket, Floral on Rosalene	Fenton	Closed	64.00	64.00
91-09-005	Fish, Paperweight, Rosalene	Fenton	Closed	30.00	30.00
91-09-006	Lamp, 20" Roses on Burmese	Fenton	Closed	275.00	275.00
91-09-007	Vase, 7 1/2" Raspberry Burmese	Fenton	Closed	65.00	65.00
Fenton Art Glass Company		**1992 Connoisseur Collection**			
92-10-001	Vase, 6 1/2" Rasberry Burmese	Fenton	Closed	45.00	45.00
92-10-002	Pitcher, 4 1/2" Berries/Leaves Burmese	Fenton	Closed	65.00	65.00
92-10-003	Vase, 8" "Seascape"	Fenton	Closed	150.00	150.00
92-10-004	Covered Box "Poppy and Daisy"	Fenton	Closed	95.00	95.00
92-10-005	Vase, "Twining Floral" Rosalene Satin	Fenton	Closed	110.00	110.00
92-10-006	Pitcher, 9" Empire on Cranberry	Fenton	Closed	110.00	110.00
Fenton Art Glass Company		**1993 Connoisseur Collection**			
93-11-001	Owl Figurine, 6" Favrene	Fenton	Closed	95.00	95.00
93-11-002	Amphora w/Stand Favrene	Fenton	Closed	285.00	285.00
93-11-003	Perfume/Stopper "Rose Trellis" Rosalene	Fenton	Closed	95.00	95.00
93-11-004	Vase "Victorian Roses" Persian Blue Opal.	Fenton	Closed	125.00	125.00
93-11-005	Bowl, Ruby Stretch w/Gold Scrolls	Fenton	Closed	95.00	95.00
93-11-006	Vase, 9" "Leaves of Gold" Plum Irid.	Fenton	Closed	175.00	175.00
93-11-007	Lamp, "Spring Woods" Reverse Painted	Fenton	Closed	590.00	590.00
Fenton Art Glass Company		**1993 Family Signature Collection**			
93-12-001	Vase, 11" Cranberry Dec.	G. Fenton	Closed	110.00	110.00
93-12-002	Basket, "Lilacs"	B. Fenton	Closed	65.00	65.00
93-12-003	Vase, "Vintage" on Plum	D. Fenton	Closed	80.00	80.00
93-12-004	Vase, Al. Thistle/Ruby Carnival	F. Fenton	Closed	105.00	105.00
93-12-005	Vase, "Cottage Scene"	S. Fenton	Closed	90.00	90.00
Fenton Art Glass Company		**1994 Family Signature Collection**			
94-13-001	Covered Candy "Autumn Leaves"	D. Fenton	Yr.Iss.	60.00	60.00
94-13-002	Vase, Fuschia	G. Fenton	Yr.Iss.	95.00	95.00
94-13-003	Basket "Lilacs"	S. Fenton	Yr.Iss.	65.00	65.00
94-13-004	Vase "Pansies" on Cranberry	B. Fenton	Yr.Iss.	95.00	95.00
94-13-005	Basket, Autumn Gold Opal	F. Fenton	Yr.Iss.	70.00	70.00
94-13-006	Basket, Ruby Carnival	T. Fenton	Yr.Iss.	65.00	65.00
Fenton Art Glass Company		**Collectors Club**			
78-14-001	Cranberry Opalescent Baskets w/variety of spot moulds	Fenton	Closed	20.00	20.00
79-14-002	Vasa Murrhina Vases (Variety of colors)	Fenton	Closed	25.00	25.00
80-14-003	Velva Rose Bubble Optic "Melon" Vases	Fenton	Closed	30.00	30.00
81-14-004	Amethyst w/White Hanging Hearts Vases	Fenton	Closed	37.50	37.50
82-14-005	Overlay Baskets in pastel shades (Swirl Optic)	Fenton	Closed	40.00	40.00
83-14-006	Cranberry Opalescent 1 pc. Fairy Lights	Fenton	Closed	40.00	40.00
84-14-007	Blue Burmese w/peloton Treatment Vases	Fenton	Closed	25.00	25.00
85-14-008	Overlay Vases in Dusty Rose w/Mica Flecks	Fenton	Closed	25.00	25.00
86-14-009	Ruby Iridized Art Glass Vase	Fenton	Closed	30.00	30.00
87-14-010	Dusty Rose Overlay/Peach Blow Interior w/dark blue Crest Vase	Fenton	Closed	38.00	38.00
88-14-011	Teal Green and Milk marble Basket	Fenton	Closed	30.00	30.00
89-14-012	Mulberry Opalescent Basket w/Coin Dot Optic	Fenton	Closed	37.50	37.50
90-14-013	Sea Mist Green Opalescent Fern Optic Basket	Fenton	Closed	40.00	40.00
91-14-014	Rosalene Leaf Basket and Peacock & Dahlia Basket	Fenton	Closed	65.00	65.00
92-14-015	Blue Bubble Optic Vases	Fenton	Closed	35.00	35.00
93-14-016	Cranberry Opalescent "Jonquil" Basket	Fenton	Closed	35.00	35.00

Number	Name	Artist	Edition Limit	Issue Price	Quote
Fitz And Floyd, Inc.		**Wonderland**			
93-01-001	Wonderland Characters, set of 6	R. Havins	3,000	100.00	100.00
Fitz And Floyd, Inc.		**Nutcracker Sweets Collection**			
93-02-001	Nutcracker Figurines, set of 6	R. Havins	2,500	135.00	135.00
Fitz And Floyd, Inc.		**A Christmas Carol Collection**			
93-03-001	Christmas Carol Figurines, set of 11	T. Kerr	2,500	175.00	175.00
Fitz And Floyd, Inc.		**Holiday Hamlet-Lighted Houses**			
93-04-001	Stocking Stuffer's Workshop	V. Balcou	Open	45.00	45.00
93-04-002	Toymaker's Workshop	V. Balcou	Open	45.00	45.00
93-04-003	Doctor's Office	V. Balcou	Open	75.00	75.00
93-04-004	Holiday Manor	V. Balcou	Open	75.00	75.00
93-04-005	Holiday Hamlet Chapel	V. Balcou	Open	75.00	75.00
93-04-006	Dollmaker's Cottage	V. Balcou	Open	125.00	125.00
93-04-007	Tavern in the Woods	V. Balcou	Open	125.00	125.00
93-04-008	Railroad Station	V. Balcou	Closed	125.00	125.00
94-04-009	Christmas Pageant Stage	V. Balcou	Open	75.00	75.00
94-04-010	Snowman Supply Hut	V. Balcou	Open	65.00	65.00
94-04-011	World's Best Snowman	V. Balcou	Open	55.00	55.00
94-04-012	Whistlestop Junction Train Stop	V. Balcou	Open	65.00	65.00
94-04-013	Mr. Winterberry's Pie Shop	V. Balcou	2,500	100.00	100.00
Fitz And Floyd, Inc.		**Holiday Hamlet-Accessories**			
93-05-001	Christmas Tree, small	V. Balcou	Open	30.00	30.00
93-05-002	Christmas Tree, large	V. Balcou	Open	45.00	45.00
93-05-003	Village Sign	V. Balcou	Open	40.00	40.00
93-05-004	Village Square Clock	V. Balcou	Open	50.00	50.00
93-05-005	Silent Night Singers	V. Balcou	Open	30.00	30.00
93-05-006	Carols in the Snow	V. Balcou	Open	30.00	30.00
93-05-007	Blizzard Express Train	V. Balcou	Open	95.00	95.00
94-05-008	Hand Car	V. Balcou	Open	35.00	35.00
Fitz And Floyd, Inc.		**Holiday Hamlet-Figurines**			
93-06-001	Gathering Pine Boughs	V. Balcou	Open	10.00	10.00
93-06-002	Pastry Vendor	V. Balcou	Open	10.00	10.00
93-06-003	Baby Squirrel	V. Balcou	Open	15.00	15.00
93-06-004	Dollmaker's Apprentice	V. Balcou	Open	15.00	15.00
93-06-005	Bell Choir Fox	V. Balcou	Open	10.00	10.00
93-06-006	The Parson	V. Balcou	Open	10.00	10.00
93-06-007	The Conductor	V. Balcou	Open	10.00	10.00
94-06-008	The Porter	V. Balcou	Open	25.00	25.00
93-06-009	Dr. B. Well	V. Balcou	Open	15.00	15.00
93-06-010	Dollmaker	V. Balcou	Open	15.00	15.00
93-06-011	Dr. Quack & Patient	V. Balcou	Open	15.00	15.00
93-06-012	Christmas Treats	V. Balcou	Open	15.00	15.00
93-06-013	Gathering Apples	V. Balcou	Open	15.00	15.00
93-06-014	Bell Choir Bunny	V. Balcou	Open	15.00	15.00
93-06-015	Squirrel Family	V. Balcou	Open	15.00	15.00
93-06-016	Skaters	V. Balcou	Open	20.00	20.00
93-06-017	Welcome Banner	V. Balcou	Open	20.00	20.00
93-06-018	Christmas Carolers	V. Balcou	Open	20.00	20.00
93-06-019	Tying the Christmas Garland	V. Balcou	Open	20.00	20.00
93-06-020	Nanny Rabbit & Bunnies	V. Balcou	Open	20.00	20.00
93-06-021	Delivering Gifts	V. Balcou	Open	20.00	20.00
93-06-022	Old Royal Elf	V. Balcou	Open	20.00	20.00
93-06-023	Santa Claus	V. Balcou	Open	25.00	25.00
93-06-024	Waving Elf	V. Balcou	Open	10.00	10.00
93-06-025	Mrs. Grizzly	V. Balcou	Open	20.00	20.00
93-06-027	Mr. Grizzly	V. Balcou	Open	20.00	20.00
93-06-028	Welcoming Elf	V. Balcou	Open	10.00	10.00
94-06-029	Little Angels	V. Balcou	Open	30.00	30.00
94-06-030	Poor Shepherds	V. Balcou	Open	15.00	15.00
94-06-031	Three Wisemen	V. Balcou	Open	20.00	20.00
94-06-032	Blessed Mother/Joseph Players	V. Balcou	Open	25.00	25.00
94-06-033	Proud Mother/Father	V. Balcou	Open	20.00	20.00
94-06-034	Mr. Winterberry, Pie Vendor	V. Balcou	2,500	25.00	25.00
Fitz And Floyd, Inc.		**Important Women**			
93-07-001	Betsy Ross, teapot	T. Kerr	1,777	75.00	75.00
94-07-002	Queen Victoria, teapot	T. Kerr	1,750	75.00	75.00
Fitz And Floyd, Inc.		**Figures From History**			
92-08-001	Christopher Columbus, teapot	T. Kerr	7,500	60.00	60.00
93-08-002	George Washington, teapot	T. Kerr	5,000	75.00	75.00
94-08-003	Napoleon Boneparte, teapot	T. Kerr	2,250	75.00	75.00
Fitz And Floyd, Inc.		**Famous Landmarks of the World**			
93-09-001	The White House, teapot	T. Kerr	5,000	75.00	75.00
94-09-002	St. Basil's Cathedral, teapot	T. Kerr	5,000	75.00	75.00
Fitz And Floyd, Inc.		**Fables & Fairytales**			
93-10-001	Bremen Town Musicians, teapot	V. Balcou	1,500	75.00	75.00
94-10-002	Three Little Pigs, teapot	T. Kerr	1,500	75.00	75.00
Fitz And Floyd, Inc.		**Musical Maestros**			
93-11-001	Wolfgang Amadeus Mozart, teapot	T. Kerr	5,000	75.00	75.00
94-11-002	Ludwig Van Beethoven, teapot	T. Kerr	2,500	75.00	75.00
Fitz And Floyd, Inc.		**Literary Masters**			
94-12-001	William Shakespeare, teapot	T. Kerr	5,000	75.00	75.00
Fitz And Floyd, Inc.		**Nutcracker Sweets Collection**			
93-13-001	Nutcracker Sweets, waterglobe	R. Havins	Retrd.	45.00	45.00
Fitz And Floyd, Inc.		**Wonderland Collection**			
93-14-001	A Mad Tea Party, waterglobe	R. Havins	Open	75.00	75.00
94-14-002	Queen's Croquet Game, waterglobe	R. Havins	Open	45.00	45.00
Fitz And Floyd, Inc.		**Woodland Santa Collection**			
94-15-001	Woodland Santa, waterglobe	V. Balcou	Open	75.00	75.00
Flambro Imports		**Emmett Kelly, Jr. Figurines**			
81-01-001	Looking Out To See	Undis.	12,000	75.00	960-3200.
81-01-002	Sweeping Up	Undis.	12,000	75.00	1100-1210.
82-01-003	Wet Paint	Undis.	15,000	80.00	600-1000.
82-01-004	The Thinker	Undis.	15,000	60.00	900-1700.
82-01-005	Why Me?	Undis.	15,000	65.00	358-900.
83-01-006	The Balancing Act	Undis.	10,000	75.00	550-950.
83-01-007	Wishful Thinking	Undis.	10,000	65.00	500-700.
83-01-008	Hole In The Sole	Undis.	10,000	75.00	485-600.
83-01-009	Balloons For Sale	Undis.	10,000	75.00	230-700.
83-01-010	Spirit of Christmas I	Undis.	3,500	125.00	1400-3600.

Company Number	Name	Series Artist	Edition Limit	Issue Price	Quote
84-01-011	Eating Cabbage	Undis.	12,000	75.00	174-600.
84-01-012	Big Business	Undis.	9,500	110.00	455-950.
84-01-013	Piano Player	Undis.	9,500	160.00	396-750.
84-01-014	Spirit of Christmas II	Undis.	3,500	270.00	390-685.
85-01-015	Man's Best Friend	Undis.	9,500	98.00	395-600.
85-01-016	No Strings Attached	Undis.	9,500	98.00	220-375.
85-01-017	In The Spotlight	Undis.	12,000	103.00	150-375.
85-01-018	Emmett's Fan	Undis.	12,000	80.00	250-650.
85-01-019	Spirit of Christmas III	Undis.	3,500	220.00	240-700.
86-01-020	The Entertainers	Undis.	12,000	120.00	182-200.
86-01-021	Cotton Candy	Undis.	12,000	98.00	242-275.
86-01-022	Bedtime	Undis.	12,000	98.00	111-225.
86-01-023	Making New Friends	Undis.	9,500	140.00	208-275.
86-01-024	Fair Game	Undis.	2,500	450.00	840-2600
86-01-025	Spirit of Christmas IV	Undis.	3,500	150.00	220-279.
87-01-026	On The Road Again	Undis.	9,500	109.00	163-400.
87-01-027	My Favorite Things	Undis.	9,500	109.00	350-700.
87-01-028	Saturday Night	Undis.	7,500	153.00	455.00
87-01-029	Toothache	Undis.	12,000	98.00	170-199.
87-01-030	Spirit of Christmas V	Undis.	2,400	170.00	500-750.
88-01-031	Over a Barrel	Undis.	9,500	130.00	132-300.
88-01-032	Wheeler Dealer	Undis.	7,500	160.00	239.00
88-01-033	Dining Out	Undis.	12,000	120.00	156-300.
88-01-034	Amen	Undis.	12,000	120.00	175-400.
88-01-035	Spirit of Christmas VI	Undis.	2,400	194.00	200-700.
89-01-036	Making Up	Undis.	7,500	200.00	250.00
89-01-037	No Loitering	Undis	7,500	200.00	264.00
89-01-038	Hurdy-Gurdy Man	Undis.	9,500	150.00	175-250.
89-01-039	65th Birthday Commemorative	Undis.	1,989	275.00	995-2700.
90-01-040	Watch the Birdie	Undis.	9,500	200.00	225.00
90-01-041	Convention-Bound	Undis.	7,500	225.00	242-300.
90-01-042	Balloons for Sale II	Undis.	7,500	250.00	300.00
90-01-043	Misfortune?	Undis.	3,500	400.00	363.00
90-01-044	Spirit Of Christmas VII	Undis.	3,500	275.00	242-350.
91-01-045	Finishing Touch	Undis.	7,500	245.00	245.00
91-01-046	Artist At Work	Undis.	7,500	295.00	295.00
91-01-047	Follow The Leader	Undis.	7,500	200.00	200.00
91-01-048	Spirit Of Christmas VIII	Undis.	3,500	250.00	310.00
92-01-049	No Use Crying	Undis.	7,500	200.00	200.00
92-01-050	Ready-Set-Go	Undis.	7,500	200.00	200.00
92-01-051	Peanut Butter?	Undis.	7,500	200.00	200.00
93-01-052	Kittens For Sale	Undis.	7,500	190.00	190.00
93-01-053	World Traveler	Undis.	7,500	190.00	190.00
93-01-054	After The Parade	Undis.	7,500	190.00	190.00
93-01-055	Spirit of Christmas IX	Undis.	3,500	200.00	200.00
93-01-056	Spirit of Christmas X	Undis.	3,500	200.00	200.00
94-01-057	Spirit of Christmas XI	Undis.	3,500	200.00	200.00
94-01-058	Forest Friends	Undis.	7,500	190.00	190.00
94-01-059	The Lion Tamer	Undis.	7,500	190.00	190.00
94-01-060	Let Him Eat Cake	Undis.	3,500	300.00	300.00
Flambro Imports		**Circus World Museum Clowns**			
85-02-001	Paul Jerome (Hobo)	Undis.	9,500	80.00	80-150.00
85-02-002	Paul Jung (Neat)	Undis.	9,500	80.00	110-120.
85-02-003	Felix Adler (Grotesque)	Undis.	9,500	80.00	80-110.00
87-02-004	Paul Jerome with Dog	Undis.	7,500	90.00	90.00
87-02-005	Paul Jung, Sitting	Undis.	7,500	90.00	90.00
87-02-006	Felix Adler with Balloon	Undis.	7,500	90.00	90.00
87-02-007	Abe Goldstein, Keystone Kop	Undis.	7,500	90.00	90.00
Flambro Imports		**Emmett Kelly, Jr. Miniatures**			
86-03-001	Looking Out To See	Undis.	Retrd.	25.00	98-125.00
86-03-002	Sweeping Up	Undis.	Retrd.	25.00	100.00
86-03-003	Wet Paint	Undis.	Retrd.	25.00	50-75.00
86-03-004	Why Me?	Undis.	Retrd.	25.00	54-65.00
86-03-005	The Thinker	Undis.	Retrd.	25.00	42-65.00
86-03-006	Balancing Act	Undis.	Retrd.	25.00	48-65.00
86-03-007	Hole in the Sole	Undis.	Retrd.	25.00	66.00
86-03-008	Balloons for Sale	Undis.	Retrd.	25.00	50-55.00
86-03-009	Wishful Thinking	Undis.	Retrd.	25.00	55.00
87-03-010	Emmett's Fan	Undis.	Retrd.	30.00	40-50.00
87-03-011	Eating Cabbage	Undis.	Retrd.	30.00	40-65.00
88-03-012	Spirit of Christmas I	Undis.	Retrd.	40.00	84-160.00
88-03-013	Big Business	Undis.	Numbrd.	35.00	38.50
90-03-014	Saturday Night	Undis.	Numbrd.	50.00	50.00
90-03-015	My Favorite Things	Undis.	Numbrd.	45.00	45.00
90-03-016	Spirit Of Christmas III	Undis.	Retrd.	50.00	50.00
89-03-017	Man's Best Friend?	Undis.	Numbrd.	35.00	35.00
89-03-018	Cotton Candy	Undis.	Retrd.	30.00	50.00
91-03-019	In The Spotlight	Undis.	Numbrd.	35.00	35.00
91-03-020	No Strings Attached	Undis.	Numbrd.	35.00	35.00
92-03-021	Spirit of Christmas II	Undis.	Numbrd.	50.00	50.00
92-03-022	Making New Friends	Undis.	Numbrd.	40.00	40.00
92-03-023	Piano Player	Undis.	Numbrd.	50.00	50.00
92-03-024	On the Road Again	Undis.	Numbrd.	35.00	35.00
93-03-025	Spirit of Christmas IV	Undis.	Numbrd.	40.00	40.00
Flambro Imports		**Annual Emmett Kelly Jr. Nutcracker**			
90-04-001	1990 Nutcracker	Undis.	Retrd.	50.00	100.00
Flambro Imports		**Emmett Kelly Jr. Metal Sculptures**			
91-05-001	Carousel Rider	Undis.	5,000	125.00	125.00
91-05-002	The Magician	Undis.	5,000	125.00	125.00
91-05-003	Emmett's Pooches	Undis.	5,000	125.00	125.00
91-05-004	Balancing Act, Too	Undis.	5,000	125.00	125.00
Flambro Imports		**Emmett Kelly Jr. A Day At The Fair**			
90-06-001	Step Right Up	Undis.	Numbrd.	65.00	65.00
90-06-002	Three For A Dime	Undis.	Numbrd.	65.00	65.00
90-06-003	Look At You	Undis.	Retrd.	65.00	65.00
90-06-004	75 Please	Undis.	Numbrd.	65.00	65.00
90-06-005	The Stilt Man	Undis.	Retrd.	65.00	65.00
90-06-006	Ride The Wild Mouse	Undis.	Numbrd.	65.00	65.00
90-06-007	You Can Do It, Emmett	Undis.	Retrd.	65.00	65.00
90-06-008	Thanks Emmett	Undis.	Numbrd.	65.00	65.00
90-06-009	You Go First, Emmett	Undis.	Retrd.	65.00	65.00
91-06-010	The Trouble With Hot Dogs	Undis.	Retrd.	65.00	65.00
91-06-011	Popcorn!	Undis.	Retrd.	65.00	65.00
91-06-012	Coin Toss	Undis.	Retrd.	65.00	65.00
92-06-013	Stilt Man	Undis.	Retrd.	65.00	65.00
Flambro Imports		**Emmett Kelly Jr. Appearance Figurine**			
92-07-001	Now Appearing	Undis.	Open	100.00	100.00
93-07-002	The Vigilante	Undis.	Open	75.00	75.00

Company Number	Name	Series Artist	Edition Limit	Issue Price	Quote
Flambro Imports		**Emmett Kelly Jr. Members Only Figurine**			
90-08-001	Merry-Go-Round	Undis.	Closed	125.00	200-550.
91-08-002	10 Years Of Collecting	Undis.	Closed	100.00	100-180.
92-08-003	All Aboard	Undis.	Closed	75.00	75.00
93-08-004	Ringmaster	Undis.	Closed	125.00	125.00
94-08-005	Birthday Mail	Undis.	Yr.Iss.	100.00	100.00
Flambro Imports		**Emmett Kelly Jr. Real Rags Collection**			
93-09-001	Checking His List	Undis.	Open	100.00	100.00
93-09-002	Thinker II	Undis.	Open	120.00	120.00
93-09-003	Sweeping Up II	Undis.	Open	100.00	100.00
93-09-004	Looking Out To See II	Undis.	Open	100.00	100.00
93-09-005	Big Business II	Undis.	Open	140.00	140.00
Flambro Imports		**Raggedy Ann & Andy**			
88-10-001	70 Years Young	C. Beylon	2,500	95.00	110.00
88-10-002	Giddy Up	C. Beylon	3,500	95.00	110.00
88-10-003	Wet Paint	C. Beylon	3,500	70.00	80.00
88-10-004	Oops!	C. Beylon	3,500	80.00	90.00
Flambro Imports		**Pleasantville 1893**			
90-11-001	Sweet Shoppe & Bakery	J. Berg Victor	Open	40.00	40.00
90-11-002	Toy Store	J. Berg Victor	Open	30.00	30.00
90-11-003	1st Church Of Pleasantville	J. Berg Victor	Open	35.00	35.00
90-11-004	Department Store	J. Berg Victor	Retrd.	25.00	25.00
90-11-005	Pleasantville Library	J. Berg Victor	Open	32.00	32.00
90-11-006	The Band Stand	J. Berg Victor	Retrd.	12.00	12.00
90-11-007	The Gerber House	J. Berg Victor	Retrd.	30.00	30.00
90-11-008	Reverend Littlefield's House	J. Berg Victor	Open	34.00	34.00
90-11-009	Mason's Hotel and Saloon	J. Berg Victor	Open	35.00	35.00
91-11-010	Methodist Church	J. Berg Victor	Open	40.00	40.00
91-11-011	Fire House	J. Berg Victor	Open	40.00	40.00
91-11-012	Court House	J. Berg Victor	Open	36.00	36.00
91-11-013	School Houe	J. Berg Victor	Open	36.00	36.00
92-11-014	Railroad Station	J. Berg Victor	Open	40.00	40.00
92-11-015	Bank/Real Estate Office	J. Berg Victor	Open	36.00	36.00
92-11-016	Apothecary/Ice Cream Shop	J. Berg Victor	Open	36.00	36.00
92-11-017	Tubbs, Jr. House	J. Berg Victor	Open	40.00	40.00
92-11-018	Miss Fountains Boarding House	J. Berg Victor	Open	48.00	48.00
92-11-019	Covered Bridge	J. Berg Victor	Open	36.00	36.00
92-11-020	Library	J. Berg Victor	Open	32.00	32.00
92-11-021	Post Office	J. Berg Victor	Open	40.00	40.00
92-11-022	Ashbey House	J. Berg Victor	Open	40.00	40.00
93-11-023	Balcomb's Farm (out buildings)	J. Berg Victor	Open	40.00	40.00
93-11-024	Balcomb's Barn	J. Berg Victor	Open	40.00	40.00
93-11-025	Balcomb's Farmhouse	J. Berg Victor	Open	40.00	40.00
93-11-026	Blacksmith Shop	J. Berg Victor	Open	40.00	40.00
93-11-027	Livery Stable and Residence	J. Berg Victor	Open	40.00	40.00
93-11-028	Gazebo/Bandstand	J. Berg Victor	Open	25.00	25.00
94-11-029	Sacred Heart Catholic Church	J. Berg Victor	Open	40.00	40.00
94-11-030	Sacred Heart Rectory	J. Berg Victor	Open	40.00	40.00
Flambro Imports		**Daddy Loves You**			
91-12-001	Make You....Giggle!	C. Pracht	2,500	100.00	100.00
91-12-002	You're Sooo....Sweet	C. Pracht	2,500	100.00	100.00
91-12-003	C'mon, Daddy!	C. Pracht	2,500	100.00	100.00
91-12-004	Soo....You Like It?	C. Pracht	2,500	100.00	100.00
Flambro Imports		**Pleasantville 1893 Members Only**			
93-13-001	Pleasantville Gazette Building	Undis.	Open	45.00	45.00
Flambro/Land of Legend		**Pocket Dragons**			
93-01-001	A Big Hug	R. Musgrave	Open	35.00	35.00
94-01-002	A Book My Size	R. Musgrave	Open	30.00	30.00
92-01-003	A Different Drummer	R. Musgrave	Open	32.50	32.50
89-01-004	A Good Egg	R. Musgrave	Retrd.	36.50	101.00
91-01-005	A Joyful Noise	R. Musgrave	Open	16.50	16.50
89-01-006	Attack	R. Musgrave	Retrd.	45.00	42-65.00
89-01-007	Baby Brother	R. Musgrave	Retrd.	19.50	19.50-25.00
93-01-008	Bath Time	R. Musgrave	Open	90.00	90.00
92-01-009	Bubbles	R. Musgrave	Open	55.00	55.00
94-01-010	Candy Cane	R. Musgrave	Open	55.00	55.00
89-01-011	Do I Have To?	R. Musgrave	Open	45.00	45.00
91-01-012	Dragons in the Attic	R. Musgrave	Open	120.00	120.00
89-01-013	Drowsy Dragon	R. Musgrave	Open	27.50	27.50
89-01-014	Flowers For You	R. Musgrave	Retrd.	42.50	60.00
91-01-015	Friends	R. Musgrave	Open	55.00	55.00
93-01-016	Fuzzy Ears	R. Musgrave	Open	16.50	16.50
89-01-017	Gargoyle Hoping For Raspberry Teacakes	R. Musgrave	Retrd.	139.50	385.00
94-01-018	Gargoyles Just Wanna Have Fun	R. Musgrave	Open	30.00	30.00
93-01-019	I Ate the Whole Thing	R. Musgrave	Open	32.50	32.50
91-01-020	I Didn't Mean To	R. Musgrave	Open	32.50	32.50
91-01-021	I'm A Kitty	R. Musgrave	Retrd.	37.50	37.50
94-01-022	In Trouble Again	R. Musgrave	Open	35.00	35.00
94-01-023	It's Dark Out There	R. Musgrave	Open	45.00	45.00
93-01-024	Let's Make Cookies	R. Musgrave	Open	90.00	90.00
93-01-025	Little Bit (lapel pin)	R. Musgrave	Open	16.50	16.50
93-01-026	Little Jewel (brooch)	R. Musgrave	Open	19.50	19.50
89-01-027	Look at Me	R. Musgrave	Retrd.	42.50	115.00
92-01-028	Mitten Toes	R. Musgrave	Open	16.50	16.50
94-01-029	My Big Cookie	R. Musgrave	Open	35.00	35.00
92-01-030	Nap Time	R. Musgrave	Open	15.00	15.00
89-01-031	New Bunny Shoes	R. Musgrave	Retrd.	28.50	28.50-50.00
89-01-032	No Ugly Monsters Allowed	R. Musgrave	Retrd.	47.50	57.50-65.00
93-01-033	Oh Goody!	R. Musgrave	Open	16.50	16.50
90-01-034	One-Size-Fits-All	R. Musgrave	Retrd.	16.50	16.50
92-01-035	Oops!	R. Musgrave	Open	16.50	16.50
89-01-036	Opera Gargoyle	R. Musgrave	Retrd.	85.00	80-195.00
92-01-037	Percy	R. Musgrave	Open	70.00	70.00
91-01-038	Pick Me Up	R. Musgrave	Open	16.50	16.50
89-01-039	Pink 'n' Pretty	R. Musgrave	Retrd.	23.90	35.00
94-01-040	Playing Dress Up	R. Musgrave	Open	30.00	30.00
91-01-041	Playing Footsie	R. Musgrave	Open	16.50	16.50
89-01-042	Pocket Dragon Countersign	R. Musgrave	Retrd.	50.00	100-150.
92-01-043	Pocket Posey	R. Musgrave	Open	16.50	16.50
93-01-044	Pocket Rider (brooch)	R. Musgrave	Open	19.50	19.50
91-01-045	Practice Makes Perfect	R. Musgrave	Retrd.	32.50	32.50
91-01-046	Putt Putt	R. Musgrave	Retrd.	37.50	37.50
94-01-047	Raiding the Cookie Jar	R. Musgrave	Open	200.00	200.00
93-01-048	Reading the Good Parts	R. Musgrave	Open	70.00	70.00
91-01-049	Scales of Injustice	R. Musgrave	Open	45.00	45.00
89-01-050	Scribbles	R. Musgrave	Open	32.50	45.00
89-01-051	Sea Dragon	R. Musgrave	Retrd.	45.00	105.00

FIGURINES/COTTAGES

Company / Number	Name	Series / Artist	Edition Limit	Issue Price	Quote
89-01-052	Sir Nigel Smythebe-Smoke	R. Musgrave	Retrd.	120.00	120.00
91-01-053	Sleepy Head	R. Musgrave	Open	37.50	37.50
89-01-054	Stalking the Cookie Jar	R. Musgrave	Open	27.50	27.50
89-01-055	Storytime at Wizard's House	R. Musgrave	Retrd.	375.00	450.00
90-01-056	Tag-A-Long	R. Musgrave	Retrd.	15.00	50.00
89-01-057	Teddy Magic	R. Musgrave	Retrd.	85.00	81.50-130.
90-01-058	The Apprentice	R. Musgrave	Open	22.50	22.50
93-01-059	The Book End	R. Musgrave	Open	90.00	90.00
89-01-060	The Gallant Defender	R. Musgrave	Retrd.	36.50	42.50-75.00
92-01-061	The Juggler	R. Musgrave	Open	32.50	32.50
92-01-062	The Library Cat	R. Musgrave	Open	38.50	38.50
89-01-063	The Pocket Minstrel	R. Musgrave	Retrd.	36.50	72.00
91-01-064	Thimble Foot	R. Musgrave	Open	38.50	38.50
91-01-065	Tickle	R. Musgrave	Open	27.50	27.50
89-01-066	Toady Goldtrayler	R. Musgrave	Retrd.	55.00	90.00
93-01-067	Treasure	R. Musgrave	Open	90.00	90.00
91-01-068	Twinkle Toes	R. Musgrave	Open	16.50	16.50
92-01-069	Under the Bed	R. Musgrave	2,500	450.00	525-595.
89-01-070	Walkies	R. Musgrave	Retrd.	65.00	50.00
93-01-071	We're Very Brave	R. Musgrave	Open	37.50	37.50
89-01-072	What Cookie?	R. Musgrave	Open	38.50	38.50
89-01-073	Wizardry for Fun and Profit	R. Musgrave	Retrd.	375.00	450.00
93-01-074	You Can't Make Me	R. Musgrave	Open	15.00	15.00
89-01-075	Your Paint is Stirred	R. Musgrave	Retrd.	42.50	55-85.00
92-01-076	Zoom Zoom	R. Musgrave	Open	37.50	37.50
Flambro/Land of Legend		**Christmas Editions**			
92-02-001	A Pocket-Sized Tree	R. Musgrave	Retrd.	18.95	42-65.00
93-02-002	Christmas Angel	R. Musgrave	Retrd.	45.00	45.00
91-02-003	I've Been Very Good	R. Musgrave	Open	37.50	50-65.00
89-02-004	Putting Me on the Tree	R. Musgrave	Retrd.	52.50	65-125.00
94-02-005	Dear Santa	R. Musgrave	Open	50.00	50.00
Flambro/Land of Legend		**Land of Legend Collectors Club Redemption Pieces**			
91-03-001	A Spot of Tea	R. Musgrave	Retrd.	75.00	143-200.
	Won't You Join Us	R. Musgrave	Retrd.	set	set
91-03-002	Wizard's House Print	R. Musgrave	Retrd.	39.95	105.00
92-03-003	Book Nook	R. Musgrave	Retrd.	140.00	165-211.
93-03-004	Pen Pals	R. Musgrave	5/94	90.00	90.00
94-03-005	The Best Seat in the House	R. Musgrave	5/95	N/A	N/A
Flambro/Land of Legend		**Land of Legend Collector Club**			
91-04-001	Collecting Butterflies	R. Musgrave	Retrd.	Gift	59-150.00
92-04-002	The Key to My Heart	R. Musgrave	Retrd.	Gift	40-75.00
93-04-003	Want A Bite?	R. Musgrave	5/94	Gift	N/A
93-04-004	Bitsy	R. Musgrave	5/94	Gift	N/A
94-04-005	Friendship Pin	R. Musgrave	5/95	Gift	N/A
Franklin Mint		**Joys of Childhood**			
76-01-001	Hopscotch	N. Rockwell	3,700	120.00	175.00
76-01-002	The Fishing Hole	N. Rockwell	3,700	120.00	175.00
76-01-003	Dressing Up	N. Rockwell	3,700	120.00	175.00
76-01-004	The Stilt Walker	N. Rockwell	3,700	120.00	175.00
76-01-005	Trick or Treat	N. Rockwell	3,700	120.00	175.00
76-01-006	Time Out	N. Rockwell	3,700	120.00	175.00
76-01-007	The Marble Champ	N. Rockwell	3,700	120.00	175.00
76-01-008	The Nurse	N. Rockwell	3,700	120.00	175.00
76-01-009	Ride 'Em Cowboy	N. Rockwell	3,700	120.00	175.00
76-01-010	Coasting Along	N. Rockwell	3,700	120.00	175.00
Fraser International		**Countryside in Miniature Collection**			
88-01-001	Hawthorn Cottage 01	I. Fraser	Retrd.	21.00	21.00
88-01-002	Irish Cottage 03	I. Fraser	Retrd.	25.00	25.00
88-01-003	Bluebell Cottage 04	I. Fraser	Retrd.	27.00	27.00
88-01-004	Smugglers Cove 05	I. Fraser	Retrd.	25.00	25.00
88-01-005	The Mill 06	I. Fraser	Retrd.	25.00	25.00
88-01-006	Sweet Hope 07	I. Fraser	Retrd.	32.00	32.00
88-01-007	Myrtle Cottage 08	I. Fraser	Retrd.	28.00	28.00
88-01-008	The Blacksmith 09	I. Fraser	Retrd.	28.00	28.00
88-01-009	St. Andrews Church 10 mold #1	I. Fraser	Retrd.	32.00	32.00
90-01-010	St. Andrews Church mold #2	I. Fraser	Retrd.	32.00	32.00
88-01-011	Lake View 11	I. Fraser	Retrd.	28.00	28.00
88-01-012	Highland Croft 12 mold #1	I. Fraser	Retrd.	32.00	32.00
90-01-013	Highland Croft mold #2	I. Fraser	Retrd.	32.00	32.00
88-01-014	Lilac Cottage 13	I. Fraser	Retrd.	34.00	34.00
88-01-015	Rose Cottage 14	I. Fraser	Retrd.	35.75	35.75
88-01-016	Acorn Cottage 15	I. Fraser	Retrd.	34.00	25.00
88-01-017	Sheep Farm 16	I. Fraser	Retrd.	34.00	34.00
88-01-018	Lighthouse 17	I. Fraser	Retrd.	32.00	32.00
88-01-019	Cornish-Tin-Mine 18	I. Fraser	Retrd.	35.75	35.75
88-01-020	Green Gables 19	I. Fraser	Retrd.	39.00	39.00
88-01-021	Cotswold Cottage 20	I. Fraser	Retrd.	39.00	39.00
88-01-022	Old Market 21	I. Fraser	Retrd.	39.00	39.00
88-01-023	Swan Inn 22	I. Fraser	Retrd.	39.00	39.00
88-01-024	Camelot 23 (white)	I. Fraser	Retrd.	44.75	44.75
88-01-025	Camelot 23 (gray)	I. Fraser	Retrd.	44.75	44.75
88-01-026	Camelot 23 (beige)	I. Fraser	Retrd.	44.75	44.75
88-01-027	Lavender Lane 24	I. Fraser	Retrd.	42.00	42.00
88-01-028	Riverside 25	I. Fraser	Retrd.	42.00	42.00
88-01-029	Robert Burns Cottage 26	I. Fraser	Retrd.	45.00	45.00
88-01-030	Preston Mill 27	I. Fraser	Retrd.	45.00	45.00
88-01-031	Sea View 29	I. Fraser	Retrd.	49.50	49.50
89-01-032	Fisherman's Cottage 30	I. Fraser	Retrd.	49.50	49.50
88-01-033	The Chandlery 31 mold #1	I. Fraser	Retrd.	54.00	54.00
89-01-034	The Chandlery 31 mold #2	I. Fraser	Retrd.	54.00	54.00
88-01-035	The Homestead 34	I. Fraser	Retrd.	57.00	57.00
88-01-036	Cornish Cottage 35	I. Fraser	Retrd.	57.00	57.00
88-01-037	Milton Manor 36	I. Fraser	Retrd.	57.00	57.00
88-01-038	Snow Church 37	I. Fraser	Retrd.	59.75	59.75
88-01-039	Oak Tree Inn 39	I. Fraser	Retrd.	69.50	69.50
88-01-040	Kent Oast House 41	I. Fraser	Retrd.	75.00	75.00
88-01-041	The Wedding 45 mold #1	I. Fraser	Retrd.	115.00	115.00
90-01-042	The Wedding 45 mold #2	I. Fraser	Retrd.	115.00	115.00
88-01-043	The Wedding on Plinth 46 mold #1	I. Fraser	Retrd.	135.00	135.00
90-01-044	The Wedding on Plinth 46 mold #2	I. Fraser	Retrd.	135.00	135.00
88-01-045	The Forge 47 mold #1	I. Fraser	Retrd.	115.00	115.00
88-01-046	The Forge 47 mold #2	I. Fraser	Retrd.	115.00	115.00
88-01-047	The Forge on Plinth 48	I. Fraser	Retrd.	135.00	135.00
88-01-048	The Millers 49	I. Fraser	Retrd.	129.00	129.00
88-01-049	The Millers on Plinth 50	I. Fraser	Retrd.	159.00	159.00
88-01-050	The Thatchers 51 mold #1	I. Fraser	Retrd.	124.00	124.00
88-01-051	The Thatchers 51 mold #2	I. Fraser	Retrd.	124.00	124.00
88-01-052	The Thatchers on Plinth 52	I. Fraser	Retrd.	149.50	149.50
88-01-053	Tudor Court 53 mold #1	I. Fraser	Retrd.	129.00	129.00
88-01-054	Tudor Court 53 mold #2	I. Fraser	Retrd.	129.00	129.00
88-01-055	Tudor Court on Plinth 54 mold #1	I. Fraser	Retrd.	149.50	149.50
88-01-056	Tudor Court on Plinth 54 mold #2	I. Fraser	Retrd.	149.50	149.50
88-01-057	Staging Post 55	I. Fraser	Retrd.	389.75	389.75
88-01-058	Hillview Base 56	I. Fraser	Retrd.	137.75	137.75
88-01-059	Harbor Base 57	I. Fraser	Retrd.	140.00	140.00
88-01-060	The Barge's Base 58	I. Fraser	Retrd.	270.00	270.00
88-01-061	Highbury House 59	I. Fraser	Retrd.	101.75	101.75
88-01-062	Ivy Mews 60	I. Fraser	Retrd.	45.00	45.00
88-01-063	Old Antique Shop 61	I. Fraser	Retrd.	42.00	42.00
88-01-064	Summerside 62	I. Fraser	Retrd.	45.00	45.00
88-01-065	Woodcutters Cottage 63	I. Fraser	Retrd.	45.00	45.00
88-01-066	Devon Cottage 64	I. Fraser	Retrd.	34.00	34.00
88-01-067	Springbank 65	I. Fraser	Retrd.	41.75	41.75
88-01-068	Fisherman's Wharf 66	I. Fraser	Retrd.	89.75	25.00
88-01-069	Bridge House 67	I. Fraser	Retrd.	27.00	27.00
88-01-070	Primrose Cottage 68	I. Fraser	Retrd.	33.00	33.00
88-01-071	Rowan Cottage 69	I. Fraser	Retrd.	21.00	21.00
88-01-072	Fern Cottage 70	I. Fraser	Retrd.	21.00	21.00
88-01-073	Shepherd's Cottage 71	I. Fraser	Retrd.	99.50	99.50
88-01-074	Shepherd's Cottage on Plinth 73	I. Fraser	Retrd.	119.50	119.50
88-01-075	Ploughman's Cottage 72	I. Fraser	Retrd.	99.50	99.50
88-01-076	Ploughman's Cottage on Plinth 74	I. Fraser	Retrd.	119.50	119.50
88-01-077	Old Brig Inn 79	I. Fraser	Retrd.	63.50	63.50
88-01-078	Morningside 80	I. Fraser	Retrd.	300.00	300.00
88-01-079	Highland House 81	I. Fraser	Retrd.	63.50	63.50
88-01-080	Cove Cottage 82	I. Fraser	Retrd.	32.00	32.00
88-01-081	Creel Cottage 83	I. Fraser	Retrd.	37.00	37.00
88-01-082	Chester House 84	I. Fraser	Retrd.	75.00	75.00
88-01-083	Drover Cottage 85	I. Fraser	Retrd.	22.50	22.50
88-01-084	Yeoman's Cottage 86	I. Fraser	Retrd.	25.00	25.00
88-01-085	Honeymoon Cottage 87	I. Fraser	Retrd.	25.00	25.00
88-01-086	Somerset Cottage 88	I. Fraser	Retrd.	32.75	32.75
88-01-087	Tweedale Cottage 89	I. Fraser	Retrd.	38.75	38.75
88-01-088	Old Leonach Cottage 90	I. Fraser	Retrd.	41.75	41.75
88-01-089	Boatman's House 91	I. Fraser	Retrd.	39.00	39.00
88-01-090	Greystone Manor 92	I. Fraser	Retrd.	54.00	54.00
88-01-091	Merchant's Court 95	I. Fraser	Retrd.	291.00	291.00
90-01-092	Killarney Cottage 96	I. Fraser	Retrd.	63.50	63.50
90-01-093	Heather Lea 97	I. Fraser	Retrd.	21.00	21.00
90-01-094	Linden Lea 98	I. Fraser	Retrd.	32.00	32.00
90-01-095	Dove Cottage 99	I. Fraser	Retrd.	56.75	56.75
90-01-096	Bull & Bush 100	I. Fraser	Retrd.	54.00	54.00
90-01-097	Castle of Monte Crisco 101	I. Fraser	Retrd.	149.75	149.75
90-01-098	St. Georges Church 102	I. Fraser	Retrd.	32.00	32.00
91-01-099	But 'N' Ben 104	I. Fraser	Retrd.	17.00	17.00
91-01-100	Pebble Cottage 105	I. Fraser	Retrd.	17.00	17.00
91-01-101	Belle Cottage 106	I. Fraser	Retrd.	17.00	17.00
91-01-102	Rock Cliff 107	I. Fraser	Retrd.	17.00	17.00
91-01-103	Grannie's Heiland Home 108	I. Fraser	Retrd.	21.00	21.00
91-01-104	Fishers Wynd 110	I. Fraser	Retrd.	32.00	32.00
91-01-105	Follyfoot 112	I. Fraser	Retrd.	37.00	37.00
91-01-106	Village Post Office 114	I. Fraser	Retrd.	37.00	37.00
91-01-107	Horseshoe Inn 115	I. Fraser	Retrd.	39.00	39.00
91-01-108	Meadowsweet Farm 116	I. Fraser	Retrd.	39.00	39.00
91-01-109	St. David's Church 117	I. Fraser	Retrd.	42.00	42.00
91-01-110	Lifeboat House 118	I. Fraser	Retrd.	54.00	54.00
91-01-111	The Parsonage 119	I. Fraser	Retrd.	63.50	63.50
88-01-112	Black Isle Cottage 121	I. Fraser	Retrd.	32.00	32.00
91-01-113	Tintagel Post Office 122	I. Fraser	Retrd.	42.00	42.00
91-01-114	Kent Oast House 123	I. Fraser	Retrd.	37.00	37.00
88-01-115	Crooked House 171	I. Fraser	Retrd.	37.00	37.00
Fraser International		**The British Heritage Collection**			
87-02-001	Robert Burn's Cottage 02	I. Fraser	Open	23.50	25.00
87-02-002	John Knox House 28	I. Fraser	Open	39.50	47.50
88-02-003	Anne Hathaway's Cottage 32 mold #1	I. Fraser	Retrd.	53.00	53.00
94-02-004	Anne Hathaway's Cottage 32 mold #2	I. Fraser	Open	53.00	59.50
88-02-005	Shakespeare's Birthplace 33 mold #1	I. Fraser	Retrd.	53.00	53.00
94-02-006	Shakespeare's Birthplace 33 mold #2	I. Fraser	Open	53.00	59.50
87-02-007	Holyrood Palace 42	I. Fraser	Open	85.00	95.00
87-02-008	Edinburgh Castle 43	I. Fraser	Open	85.00	95.00
87-02-009	Royal & Ancient Clubhouse 44	I. Fraser	Open	85.00	95.00
87-02-010	The Giant's Causway 75	I. Fraser	Open	19.50	22.50
87-02-010	The Scott Monument 76	I. Fraser	Open	49.50	55.00
88-02-011	The Tower of London 78	I. Fraser	Open	99.50	115.00
87-02-012	Eilean Donan Castle 93	I. Fraser	Open	85.00	95.00
88-02-013	Craigievar Castle 94	I. Fraser	Open	59.50	75.00
88-02-014	Dove Cottage 99	I. Fraser	Open	45.00	49.50
89-02-015	York Minster 103	I. Fraser	Open	99.50	115.00
89-02-016	Cliffords Tower 109	I. Fraser	Open	31.50	35.00
89-02-017	Micklegate Bar 111	I. Fraser	Open	39.50	45.00
89-02-018	Windsor Castle 120	I. Fraser	Open	99.50	115.00
90-02-019	Culzean Castle 124	I. Fraser	Open	115.00	125.00
91-02-020	Caernarfon Castle 125	I. Fraser	Open	85.00	95.00
91-02-021	Leeds Castle 126	I. Fraser	Open	85.00	95.00
90-02-022	Stirling Castle 127	I. Fraser	Open	115.00	125.00
91-02-023	Balmoral Castle 128	I. Fraser	Open	115.00	125.00
91-02-024	Warwick Castle 131	I. Fraser	Open	99.50	115.00
91-02-025	Buckingham Palace 132	I. Fraser	Open	159.50	175.00
91-02-026	Kings College Chapel 133	I. Fraser	Open	115.00	125.00
92-02-027	St. Pauls Cathedral 134	I. Fraser	Open	149.50	165.00
92-02-028	Westminster Abbey 135	I. Fraser	Open	149.50	165.00
92-02-029	The White Tower 151	I. Fraser	Open	59.50	75.00
91-02-030	Cardiff Castle Keep 152	I. Fraser	Open	49.50	55.00
92-02-031	Canterbury Cathedral 153	I. Fraser	Open	149.50	165.00
92-02-032	Big Ben 154	I. Fraser	Open	57.50	65.00
91-02-033	Nelson's Column 156	I. Fraser	Open	39.50	45.00
91-02-034	St. Margaret's Church 157	I. Fraser	Open	39.50	45.00
92-02-035	The Round Tower 158	I. Fraser	Open	59.50	75.00
92-02-036	The Cenotaph 172	I. Fraser	Open	35.00	37.50
92-02-037	The Royal Albert Hall 174	I. Fraser	Open	59.50	75.00
87-02-038	Old Leonach Cottage 178	I. Fraser	Open	35.00	37.50
Fraser International		**German Collection**			
90-03-001	Schless Neuschwanstein 113	I. Fraser	Open	145.00	165.00
91-03-002	Schloss Linderhof 129	I. Fraser	Open	155.00	175.00
92-03-003	Schloss Heidelberg 136	I. Fraser	Open	155.00	175.00
92-03-004	St. Coloman Chapel 138	I. Fraser	Open	39.50	45.00
92-03-005	St. Wilhelm Chapel 139	I. Fraser	Open	39.50	45.00
92-03-006	Altstadter Town Hall 140	I. Fraser	Open	79.50	90.00
92-03-007	Holstein Town Gates 141	I. Fraser	Open	119.50	130.00
92-03-008	Schloss Badinghagen 142	I. Fraser	Open	79.50	90.00
92-03-009	Mayor Toppler's Little House 143	I. Fraser	Open	39.50	45.00

Number	Name	Artist	Edition Limit	Issue Price	Quote
92-03-010	Schloss Heidelburg (with snow) 188	I. Fraser	Open	165.00	185.00

Fraser International — **The British Heritage Miniature Collection**

Number	Name	Artist	Edition Limit	Issue Price	Quote
92-04-001	Edinburgh Castle 159	I. Fraser	Open	39.00	45.00
92-04-002	York Minster 160	I. Fraser	Open	48.00	55.00
92-04-003	Stirling Castle 161	I. Fraser	Open	45.00	49.50
92-04-004	Westminister Abbey 162	I. Fraser	Open	45.00	49.50
92-04-005	St. Pauls Cathedral 163	I. Fraser	Open	45.00	49.50
92-04-006	Windsor Castle 164	I. Fraser	Open	42.00	45.00
92-04-007	Balmoral Castle 165	I. Fraser	Open	42.00	45.00
92-04-008	The Tower of London 166	I. Fraser	Open	42.00	45.00
92-04-009	Warwick Castle 167	I. Fraser	Open	42.00	45.00
92-04-010	Holyrood Palace 168	I. Fraser	Open	42.00	45.00
92-04-011	Buckingham Palace 169	I. Fraser	Open	48.00	55.00
92-04-012	Leeds Castle 170	I. Fraser	Open	42.00	45.00
92-04-013	Ely Cathedral 175	I. Fraser	Open	51.00	55.00
92-04-014	Durham Cathedral 176	I. Fraser	Open	59.50	65.00
92-04-015	Norwich Cathedral 177	I. Fraser	Open	48.00	55.00
92-04-016	Drum Castle 180	I. Fraser	Open	45.00	49.50
92-04-017	Fyvie Castle 182	I. Fraser	Open	48.00	55.00
92-04-018	Castle Fraser 183	I. Fraser	Open	48.00	55.00
92-04-019	Braemar Castle 184	I. Fraser	Open	48.00	55.00
92-04-020	Urquhart Castle 185	I. Fraser	Open	48.00	55.00
92-04-021	Cawdor Castle 186	I. Fraser	Open	54.00	65.00
92-04-022	Crathes Castle 187	I. Fraser	Open	42.00	45.00
93-04-023	Stonehenge 189	I. Fraser	Open	39.50	43.00
93-04-024	Glamis Castle 193	I. Fraser	Open	57.50	65.00
93-04-025	Claypotts 194	I. Fraser	Open	48.00	49.50

Fraser International — **Classic Cottage Collection**

Number	Name	Artist	Edition Limit	Issue Price	Quote
94-05-001	Perriwinkle Cottage C01	I. Fraser	Open	29.50	29.50
94-05-002	Fyne View C02	I. Fraser	Open	35.00	35.00
94-05-003	Clover Cottage C03	I. Fraser	Open	37.50	75.00
94-05-004	Saxmund Smithy C04	I. Fraser	Open	39.50	39.50
94-05-005	Buttermere Tearooms C05	I. Fraser	Open	39.50	39.50
94-05-006	Rock Cliff C06	I. Fraser	Open	39.50	39.50
94-05-007	Ennerdale Farm C07	I. Fraser	Open	47.50	47.50
94-05-008	The Old Curiosity Shop C08	I. Fraser	Open	47.50	47.50
94-05-009	St. Mary's Chapel C09	I. Fraser	Open	47.50	47.50
94-05-010	Ranworth View C10	I. Fraser	Open	47.50	47.50
94-05-011	Rosebank C11	I. Fraser	Open	47.50	47.50
94-05-012	Ivy Cottage C12	I. Fraser	Open	49.50	49.50
94-05-013	Heatherlea Cottage C13	I. Fraser	Open	49.50	49.50
94-05-014	Cheddar View C14	I. Fraser	Open	49.50	49.50
94-05-015	Grannie's Hieland Hame C15	I. Fraser	Open	52.50	52.50
94-05-016	Honeymoon Hideaway C16	I. Fraser	Open	52.50	52.50
94-05-017	The Rose & Crown C17	I. Fraser	Open	52.50	52.50
94-05-018	Birch Cottage C18	I. Fraser	Open	59.50	59.50
94-05-019	Foxglove Cottage C19	I. Fraser	Open	59.50	59.50
94-05-020	Duck Cottage C20	I. Fraser	Open	59.50	59.50
94-05-021	Crail Cottage C21	I. Fraser	Open	62.50	62.50
94-05-022	The Old Anchor Inn C22	I. Fraser	Open	65.00	65.00
94-05-023	Inverbeg Gatehouse C23	I. Fraser	Open	69.50	69.50
94-05-024	Benmore Croft C24	I. Fraser	Open	69.50	69.50
94-05-025	Cullin Croft C25	I. Fraser	Open	69.50	69.50
94-05-026	Langdale Farm C26	I. Fraser	Open	69.50	69.50
94-05-027	The Kings Arms C27	I. Fraser	Open	75.00	75.00
94-05-028	Polperro Cottage C28	I. Fraser	Open	75.00	75.00
94-05-029	Follyfoot Farm C29	I. Fraser	Open	75.00	75.00
94-05-030	Puffin Lighthouse C30	I. Fraser	Open	75.00	75.00
94-05-031	Kilrea Cottage C31	I. Fraser	Open	75.00	75.00
94-05-032	Smugglers Hideaway C32	I. Fraser	Open	75.00	75.00
94-05-033	Whitesand Lighthouse C33	I. Fraser	Open	80.00	80.00
94-05-034	Horseshoe Inn C34	I. Fraser	Open	80.00	80.00
94-05-035	Lomond View C35	I. Fraser	Open	80.00	80.00
94-05-036	Coniston House C36	I. Fraser	Open	87.50	87.50
94-05-037	Gamekeepers Lodge C37	I. Fraser	Open	95.00	95.00
94-05-038	Laurel Bank C38	I. Fraser	Open	95.00	95.00
94-05-039	Crathie Church C39	I. Fraser	Open	95.00	95.00
94-05-040	Lavender Lane C40	I. Fraser	Open	95.00	95.00
94-05-041	Windrush Lane C41	I. Fraser	Open	99.50	99.50
94-05-042	The Wine Merchant C42	I. Fraser	Open	99.50	99.50
94-05-043	Dale Farm C43	I. Fraser	Open	135.00	135.00
94-05-044	Strathmore Loged C44	I. Fraser	Open	135.00	135.00
94-05-045	Glengarry Homestead C45	I. Fraser	Open	175.00	175.00
94-05-046	Northborough Manor C46	I. Fraser	Open	225.00	225.00
94-05-047	St. Andrews Kirk C47	I. Fraser	Open	69.50	69.50
94-05-048	The Red Lion Tavern C48	I. Fraser	Open	495.00	495.00
94-05-049	The Village Post Office C49	I. Fraser	Open	75.00	75.00
94-05-050	Honey Cottage C50	I. Fraser	Open	59.50	59.50
94-05-051	Daisy Cottage C51	I. Fraser	Open	29.50	29.50
94-05-052	Swallow Mill C52	I. Fraser	Open	52.50	52.50
94-05-053	Merchant's Manor C53	I. Fraser	Open	52.50	52.50
94-05-054	Carbis View C54	I. Fraser	Open	29.50	29.50
94-05-055	Coombe Cottage C55	I. Fraser	Open	69.50	69.50

Fraser International — **Collectors' Society**

Number	Name	Artist	Edition Limit	Issue Price	Quote
93-06-001	Granny Smith's Cottage	I. Fraser	Yr.Iss.	25.00	25.00

Ganz/Little Cheesers — **Cheeserville Picnic Collection**

Number	Name	Artist	Edition Limit	Issue Price	Quote
91-01-001	Papa Woodsworth	G.D.A. Group	Open	13.00	13.00
91-01-002	Auntie Marigold Eating Cookie	G.D.A. Group	Open	13.00	13.00
91-01-003	Baby Cicely	G.D.A. Group	Open	8.00	8.00
91-01-004	Medley Meadowmouse With Bouquet	G.D.A. Group	Open	13.00	13.00
91-01-005	Violet With Peaches	G.D.A. Group	Open	13.00	13.00
91-01-006	Baby Truffle	G.D.A. Group	Open	8.00	8.00
91-01-007	Harriet Harvestmouse	G.D.A. Group	Retrd.	13.00	13.00
91-01-008	Grandpapa Thistledown Carrying Basket	G.D.A. Group	Open	13.00	13.00
91-01-009	Jenny Butterfield Kneeling	G.D.A. Group	Open	13.00	13.00
91-01-010	Mama With Rolling Pin	G.D.A. Group	Open	13.00	13.00
91-01-011	Grandmama Thistledown Holding Bread	G.D.A. Group	Open	14.00	14.00
91-01-012	Harley Harvestmouse Waving	G.D.A. Group	Open	13.00	13.00
91-01-013	Cousin Woody With Bread and Fruit	G.D.A. Group	Open	14.00	14.00
91-01-014	Marigold Thistledown Picking Up Jar	G.D.A. Group	Open	14.00	14.00
91-01-015	Little Truffle Eating Grapes	G.D.A. Group	Open	8.00	8.00
91-01-016	Jeremy Butterfield	G.D.A. Group	Open	13.00	13.00
91-01-017	Mama Fixing Sweet Cicely's Hair	G.D.A. Group	Retrd.	16.50	16.50
91-01-018	Picnic Buddies	G.D.A. Group	Open	19.00	19.00
91-01-019	Blossom & Hickory In Love	G.D.A. Group	Open	19.00	19.00
91-01-020	Little Truffle Smelling Flowers	G.D.A. Group	Open	16.50	16.50
91-01-021	Fellow With Picnic Hamper	G.D.A. Group	Retrd.	13.00	13.00
91-01-022	Fellow With Plate Of Cookies	G.D.A. Group	Retrd.	13.00	13.00
91-01-023	Lady With Grapes	G.D.A. Group	Retrd.	14.00	14.00
91-01-024	Mama Woodsworth With Crate	G.D.A. Group	Retrd.	14.00	14.00
93-01-025	Sunday Drive	C.Thammavongsa	Open	40.00	40.00
93-01-026	Sweet Dreams	C.Thammavongsa	Open	27.50	27.50
93-01-027	Willy's Toe-Tappin' Tunes	C.Thammavongsa	Open	15.00	15.00
93-01-028	The Storyteller	C.Thammavongsa	10,000	25.00	25.00
93-01-029	For Someone Special	C.Thammavongsa	Open	13.50	13.50
93-01-030	Words Of Wisdom	C.Thammavongsa	Open	14.00	14.00
93-01-031	Clownin' Around	C.Thammavongsa	Open	10.50	10.50
93-01-032	Chuckles The Clown	C.Thammavongsa	Open	16.00	16.00
93-01-033	Little Cheesers Display Plaque	C.Thammavongsa	Open	25.00	25.00

Ganz/Little Cheesers — **Cheeserville Picnic Collection Mini-Food Accessories**

Number	Name	Artist	Edition Limit	Issue Price	Quote
91-02-001	Food Trolley	G.D.A. Group	Retrd.	12.00	12.00
91-02-002	Set Of Four Bottles	G.D.A. Group	Retrd.	10.00	10.00
91-02-003	Napkin In Can	G.D.A. Group	Retrd.	2.00	2.00
91-02-004	Honey Jar	G.D.A. Group	Retrd.	2.00	2.00
91-02-005	Wine Glass	G.D.A. Group	Open	1.25	1.25
91-02-006	Ice Cream Cup	G.D.A. Group	Open	2.00	2.00
91-02-007	Candy	G.D.A. Group	Open	2.00	2.00
91-02-008	Sundae	G.D.A. Group	Open	2.00	2.00
91-02-009	Egg Tart	G.D.A. Group	Open	1.00	1.00
91-02-010	Hot Dog	G.D.A. Group	Open	2.00	2.25
91-02-011	Basket Of Peaches	G.D.A. Group	Open	2.00	2.00
91-02-012	Cherry Mousse	G.D.A. Group	Open	2.00	2.00
91-02-013	Blueberry Cake	G.D.A. Group	Open	2.50	2.50
91-02-014	Chocolate Cake	G.D.A. Group	Open	2.50	2.50
91-02-015	Chocolate Cheesecake	G.D.A. Group	Open	2.00	2.00
91-02-016	Strawberry Cake	G.D.A. Group	Open	2.00	2.00
91-02-017	Doughnut Basket	G.D.A. Group	Open	2.50	2.50
91-02-018	Bread Basket	G.D.A. Group	Open	2.50	2.50
91-02-019	Basket Of Apples	G.D.A. Group	Open	2.25	2.25
91-02-020	Hazelnut Roll	G.D.A. Group	Retrd.	2.00	2.00
91-02-021	Lemon Cake	G.D.A. Group	Retrd.	2.00	2.00
91-02-022	Cherry Pie	G.D.A. Group	Retrd.	2.00	2.00
91-02-023	Food Basket With Blue Cloth	G.D.A. Group	Open	6.50	6.50
91-02-024	Food Basket With Pink Cloth	G.D.A. Group	Open	6.00	6.00
91-02-025	Food Basket With Green Cloth	G.D.A. Group	Open	7.50	7.50
91-02-026	Food Basket With Purple Cloth	G.D.A. Group	Open	6.00	6.00

Ganz/Little Cheesers — **Cheeserville Picnic Collection Musicals**

Number	Name	Artist	Edition Limit	Issue Price	Quote
91-03-001	Musical Sunflower Base	G.D.A. Group	Retrd.	65.00	65.00
91-03-002	Musical Picnic Base	G.D.A. Group	Open	60.00	60.00
91-03-003	Musical Violet Woodsworth Cookie Jar	G.D.A. Group	Retrd.	75.00	75.00
91-03-004	Musical Medley Meadowmouse Cookie Jar	G.D.A. Group	Retrd.	75.00	75.00
91-03-005	Mama & Sweet Cicely Waterglobe	G.D.A. Group	Retrd.	55.00	55.00
91-03-006	Medley Meadowmouse Waterglobe	G.D.A. Group	Open	47.00	47.00
92-03-007	Sweet Cicely Musical Doll Basket	G.D.A. Group	Open	85.00	85.00
91-03-008	Blossom & HIckory Musical Jewelry Box	G.D.A. Group	Retrd.	65.00	65.00
91-03-009	Musical Basket Trinket Box	G.D.A. Group	Open	30.00	30.00
91-03-010	Musical Floral Trinket Box	G.D.A. Group	Open	32.00	32.00
93-03-011	Musical "Secret Treasures" Trinket Box	C.Thammavongsa	Open	36.00	36.00
93-03-012	Wishing Well Musical	C.Thammavongsa	Open	50.00	50.00

Ganz/Little Cheesers — **The Wedding Collection**

Number	Name	Artist	Edition Limit	Issue Price	Quote
92-04-001	Harley & Harriet Harvestmouse	GDA/Thammavongsa	Open	20.00	20.00
92-04-002	Jenny Butterfield/Sweet Cicely (bridesmaids)	GDA/Thammavongsa	Open	20.00	20.00
92-04-003	Blossom Thistledown (bride)	GDA/Thammavongsa	Open	16.00	16.00
92-04-004	Hickory Harvestmouse (groom)	GDA/Thammavongsa	Open	16.00	16.00
92-04-005	Cousin Woody & Little Truffle	GDA/Thammavongsa	Open	20.00	20.00
92-04-006	Grandmama & Grandpapa Thistledown	GDA/Thammavongsa	Open	20.00	20.00
92-04-007	Pastor Smallwood	GDA/Thammavongsa	Open	16.00	16.00
92-04-008	Little Truffle (ringbearer)	GDA/Thammavongsa	Open	10.00	10.00
92-04-009	Myrtle Meadowmouse With Medley	GDA/Thammavongsa	Retrd.	20.00	20.00
92-04-010	Frowzy Roquefort III With Gramophone	GDA/Thammavongsa	Open	20.00	20.00
92-04-011	Marigold Thistledown & Oscar Bobbins	GDA/Thammavongsa	Open	20.00	20.00
92-04-012	Great Aunt Rose Beside Table	GDA/Thammavongsa	Open	20.00	20.00
92-04-013	Mama & Papa Woodsworth Dancing	GDA/Thammavongsa	Open	20.00	20.00
92-04-014	Wedding Procession	GDA/Thammavongsa	Open	40.00	40.00
93-04-015	The Big Day	C. Thammavongsa	Open	20.00	20.00

Ganz/Little Cheesers — **The Wedding Collection Mini-Food Accessories**

Number	Name	Artist	Edition Limit	Issue Price	Quote
92-05-001	Flour Bag	G.D.A. Group	Retrd.	2.00	2.00
92-05-002	Salt Can	G.D.A. Group	Retrd.	2.00	2.00
92-05-003	Chocolate Pastry	G.D.A. Group	Retrd.	2.00	2.00
92-05-004	Souffle	G.D.A. Group	Retrd.	2.50	2.50
92-05-005	Teddy Mouse	G.D.A. Group	Open	2.00	2.00
92-05-006	Chocolate Pudding	G.D.A. Group	Open	2.50	2.50
92-05-007	Tea Pot Set	G.D.A. Group	Open	3.00	3.00
92-05-008	Honey Pot	G.D.A. Group	Open	2.00	2.00
92-05-009	Candles	G.D.A. Group	Open	3.00	3.00
92-05-010	Big Chocolate Cake	G.D.A. Group	Open	4.50	4.50
92-05-011	Fruit Salad	G.D.A. Group	Open	3.00	3.00
92-05-012	Cherry Jello	G.D.A. Group	Open	3.00	3.00
92-05-013	Ring Cake	G.D.A. Group	Open	3.00	3.00
92-05-014	Soup Pot	G.D.A. Group	Open	3.00	3.00
92-05-015	Flower Vase	G.D.A. Group	Open	3.00	3.00
92-05-016	Groom Candleholder	GDA/Thammavongsa	Open	20.00	20.00
92-05-017	Bride Candleholder	GDA/Thammavongsa	Open	20.00	20.00
92-05-018	Cake Trinket Box	GDA/Thammavongsa	Open	14.00	14.00
92-05-019	Bible Trinket Box	GDA/Thammavongsa	Open	16.50	16.50
92-05-020	Grass Base	GDA/Thammavongsa	Open	3.50	3.50
93-05-021	Wedding Cake	C. Thammavongsa	Open	4.50	4.50
93-05-022	Gooseberry Champagne	C. Thammavongsa	Open	3.00	3.00

Ganz/Little Cheesers — **The Wedding Collection Accesories**

Number	Name	Artist	Edition Limit	Issue Price	Quote
93-06-001	Gazebo Base	C. Thammavongsa	Open	42.00	42.00
93-06-002	Banquet Table	C. Thammavongsa	Open	14.00	14.00

Ganz/Little Cheesers — **The Wedding Collection Musicals**

Number	Name	Artist	Edition Limit	Issue Price	Quote
92-07-001	Musical Wooden Base For Wedding Processional	G.D.A. Group	Open	25.00	25.00
92-07-002	Musical Wedding Base	GDA/Thammavongsa	Open	32.00	32.00
92-07-003	Musical Blossom & Hickory Wedding Weblobe	GDA/Thammavongsa	Open	55.00	55.00
93-07-004	Blossom & Hickory Musical	C. Thammavongsa	Open	50.00	50.00
93-07-005	White Musical Wood Base For Gazebo Base "Evergreen"	C. Thammavongsa	Open	25.00	25.00

Ganz/Little Cheesers — **The Christmas Collection**

Number	Name	Artist	Edition Limit	Issue Price	Quote
91-08-001	Cheeser Snowman	G.D.A. Group	Open	7.50	7.50
91-08-002	Violet With Snowball	G.D.A. Group	Open	8.00	8.00
91-08-003	Medley Playing Drum	G.D.A. Group	Open	8.00	8.00
91-08-004	Little Truffle With Stocking	G.D.A. Group	Open	8.00	8.00
91-08-005	Jeremy With Teddy Bear	G.D.A. Group	Open	12.00	12.00
91-08-006	Santa Cheeser	G.D.A. Group	Open	13.00	13.00

FIGURINES/COTTAGES

Number	Name	Artist	Edition Limit	Issue Price	Quote
Company		**Series**			
91-08-007	Frowzy Roquefort III Skating	G.D.A. Group	Retrd.	14.00	14.00
91-08-008	Jenny On Sleigh	G.D.A. Group	Open	16.00	16.00
91-08-009	Auntie Blossom With Ornaments	G.D.A. Group	Open	14.00	14.00
91-08-010	Mama Pouring Tea	G.D.A. Group	Retrd.	14.00	14.00
91-08-011	Great Aunt Rose With Tray	G.D.A. Group	Open	14.00	14.00
91-08-012	Abner Appleton Ringing Bell	G.D.A. Group	Retrd.	14.00	14.00
91-08-013	Grandpapa Blowing Horn	G.D.A. Group	Open	14.00	14.00
91-08-014	Hickory Playing Cello	G.D.A. Group	Open	14.00	14.00
91-08-015	Myrtle Meadowmouse With Book	G.D.A. Group	Retrd.	14.00	14.00
91-08-016	Cousin Woody Playing Flute	G.D.A. Group	Open	14.00	14.00
91-08-017	Harley & Harriet Dancing	G.D.A. Group	Retrd.	19.00	19.00
91-08-018	Grandpapa & Sweet Cicely	G.D.A. Group	Open	19.00	19.00
91-08-019	Grandmama & Little Truffle	G.D.A..Group	Retrd.	19.00	19.00
91-08-020	Marigold & Oscar Stealing A Christmas Kiss	G.D.A. Group	Open	19.00	19.00
93-08-021	All I Want For Christmas	C.Thammavongsa	Open	18.00	18.00
93-08-022	Christmas Greetings	C.Thammavongsa	Open	16.50	16.50
93-08-023	Sleigh Ride	C.Thammavongsa	Open	11.00	11.00
Ganz/Little Cheesers		**The Christmas Collection Accessories**			
91-09-001	Christmas Tree	G.D.A. Group	Open	9.00	9.00
91-09-002	Lamp Post	G.D.A. Group	Open	8.50	8.50
91-09-003	Parlor Scene Base	G.D.A. Group	Open	37.50	37.50
91-09-004	Outdoor Scene Base	G.D.A. Group	Retrd.	35.00	35.00
93-09-005	Candleholder-Santa Cheeser	C.Thammavongsa	Open	19.00	19.00
93-09-006	Ice Pond Base	C.Thammavongsa	Open	5.50	5.50
93-09-007	Gingerbread House	C.Thammavongsa	Open	3.00	3.00
93-09-008	Toy Train	C.Thammavongsa	Open	3.00	3.00
93-09-009	Christmas Gift	C.Thammavongsa	Open	3.00	3.00
93-09-010	Christmas Stocking	C.Thammavongsa	Open	3.00	3.00
93-09-011	Candy Cane	C.Thammavongsa	Open	2.00	2.00
93-09-012	Toy Soldier	C.Thammavongsa	Open	3.00	3.00
Ganz/Little Cheesers		**The Christmas Collection Musicals**			
92-10-001	Musical Santa Cheeser Roly-Poly	G.D.A. Group	Suspd.	55.00	55.00
92-10-002	Little Truffle Christmas Waterglobe	G.D.A. Group	Open	45.00	45.00
92-10-003	Jenny Butterfield Christmas Waterglobe	GDA/Thammavongsa	Retrd.	55.00	55.00
93-10-004	Round Wood Base "We Wish You a Merry X'mas"	C.Thammavongsa	Open	25.00	25.00
93-10-005	Rotating Round Wood Base "I'll be Home for X'mas"	C.Thammavongsa	Open	30.00	30.00
Ganz/Little Cheesers		**Springtime In Cheeserville Collection**			
92-11-001	Hippity-Hop. It's Eastertime!	C.Thammavongsa	Open	16.00	16.00
92-11-002	A Wheelbarrow Of Sunshine	C.Thammavongsa	Open	17.00	17.00
92-11-003	Springtime Delights	C.Thammavongsa	Open	12.00	12.00
92-11-004	A Basket Full Of Joy	C.Thammavongsa	Open	16.00	16.00
93-11-005	Gift From Heaven	C.Thammavongsa	Open	10.00	10.00
93-11-006	Blossom Has A Little lamb	C.Thammavongsa	Open	16.50	16.50
93-11-007	Ballerina Sweetheart	C.Thammavongsa	Open	10.00	10.00
93-11-008	Playing Cupid	C.Thammavongsa	Open	10.00	10.00
93-11-009	Hugs & Kisses	C.Thammavongsa	Open	11.00	11.00
93-11-010	Gently Down The Stream	C.Thammavongsa	10,000	27.00	27.00
93-11-011	First Kiss	C.Thammavongsa	Open	24.00	24.00
93-11-012	Sunday Stroll	C.Thammavongsa	Open	22.00	22.00
93-11-013	Sugar & Spice	C.Thammavongsa	Open	24.00	24.00
93-11-014	For My Sweatheart	C.Thammavongsa	Open	22.00	22.00
93-11-015	I Love You	C.Thammavongsa	Open	22.00	22.00
93-11-016	Friends Forever	C.Thammavongsa	Open	22.00	22.00
94-11-017	Birthday Party	C.Thammavongsa	Open	22.00	22.00
94-11-018	Hip Hip Hooray	C.Thammavongsa	Open	22.00	22.00
94-11-019	Get Well	C.Thammavongsa	Open	22.00	22.00
Ganz/Little Cheesers		**Springtime In Cheeserville Collection Accessories**			
92-12-001	Decorated With Love	C.Thammavongsa	Open	7.50	7.50
92-12-002	April Showers Bring May Flowers	C.Thammavongsa	Open	7.50	7.50
92-12-003	For Somebunny Special	C.Thammavongsa	Open	7.50	7.50
Ganz/Little Cheesers		**Springtime In Cheeserville Collection Musicals**			
92-13-001	Tulips & Ribbons Musical Trinket Box	GDA/Thammavongsa	Open	28.00	28.00
Ganz/Little Cheesers		**The Cowtown Collection**			
93-14-001	Old MooDonald	C.Thammavongsa	Open	13.50	13.50
93-14-002	Buffalo Bull Cody	C.Thammavongsa	Open	15.00	15.00
93-14-003	Cowlamity Jane	C.Thammavongsa	Open	15.00	15.00
93-14-004	Moo West	C.Thammavongsa	Open	15.00	15.00
93-14-005	Gloria Bovine & Rudolph Bullentino	C.Thammavongsa	Open	20.00	20.00
93-14-006	Daisy Moo	C.Thammavongsa	Open	11.00	11.00
93-14-007	Jethro Bovine	C.Thammavongsa	Open	15.00	15.00
93-14-008	Bull Rogers	C.Thammavongsa	Open	17.00	17.00
93-14-009	Lil' Orphan Angus	C.Thammavongsa	Open	11.00	11.00
93-14-010	Buttermilk & Buttercup	C.Thammavongsa	Open	16.00	16.00
93-14-011	Bull Ruth	C.Thammavongsa	Open	13.00	13.00
93-14-012	Bull Masterson	C.Thammavongsa	Open	15.00	15.00
Ganz/Little Cheesers		**The Pigsville Collection**			
93-15-001	Pig at the Beach	G.D.A. Group	Open	9.00	9.00
93-15-002	Ice Cream Anyone?	G.D.A. Group	Open	9.00	9.00
93-15-003	Tipsy	G.D.A. Group	Open	9.00	9.00
93-15-004	Squeaky Clean	G.D.A. Group	Open	11.00	11.00
93-15-005	Soap Suds	G.D.A. Group	Open	12.00	12.00
93-15-006	Nap Time	G.D.A. Group	Open	11.00	11.00
93-15-007	Mother Love	G.D.A. Group	Open	13.00	13.00
93-15-008	Me & My Ice Cream	G.D.A. Group	Open	17.00	17.00
93-15-009	Prima Ballerina	C.Thammavongsa	Open	11.00	11.00
93-15-010	True Love	C.Thammavongsa	Open	12.00	12.00
93-15-011	Bakin' at the Beach	C.Thammavongsa	Open	11.00	11.00
93-15-012	Wee Little Piggy	C.Thammavongsa	Open	8.00	8.00
93-15-013	P.O.P Display Sign	C.Thammavongsa	Open	8.00	8.00
94-15-014	Pretty Piglet	C.Thammavongsa	Open	8.00	8.00
94-15-015	Bedtime	C.Thammavongsa	Open	9.50	9.50
94-15-016	Birthday Surprise	C.Thammavongsa	Open	9.50	9.50
94-15-017	Sandcastle	C.Thammavongsa	Open	12.00	12.00
94-15-018	Snacktime	C.Thammavongsa	Open	11.50	11.50
94-15-019	Play Ball	C.Thammavongsa	Open	11.50	11.50
94-15-020	Special Treat	C.Thammavongsa	Open	11.50	11.50
94-15-021	Storytime	C.Thammavongsa	Open	13.00	13.00
94-15-022	Wedded Bliss	C.Thammavongsa	Open	16.00	16.00
94-15-023	Ole Fishing Hole	C.Thammavongsa	Open	16.00	16.00
Ganz/Little Cheesers		**The Pigsville Accessories**			
94-16-001	Barn	C.Thammavongsa	Open	35.00	35.00
94-16-002	Silo	C.Thammavongsa	Open	35.00	35.00

Number	Name	Artist	Edition Limit	Issue Price	Quote
Company		**Series**			
Gartlan USA, Inc.		**Plaques**			
85-01-001	Pete Rose-"Desire to Win", signed	T. Sizemore	4,192	75.00	300.00
86-01-002	George Brett-"Royalty in Motion", signed	J. Martin	2,000	85.00	250-275.
86-01-003	Reggie Jackson-"The Roundtripper", signed	J. Martin	500	150.00	325.00
86-01-004	Reggie Jackson Artist Proof- "The Roundtripper", signed	J. Martin	44	175.00	250-475.
87-01-005	Roger Staubach, signed	C. Soileau	1,979	85.00	195.00
Gartlan USA, Inc.		**Baseball/Football/Hockey Card Series**			
85-02-001	Pete Rose Ceramic Baseball Card	T. Sizemore	Open	9.95	18.00
85-02-002	Pete Rose Ceramic Baseball Card, signed	T. Sizemore	4,192	39.00	50.00
86-02-003	George Brett Baseball Rounder	J. Martin	Open	9.95	14.00
86-02-004	George Brett Baseball Rounder, signed	J. Martin	2,000	30.00	50.00
86-02-005	George Brett Ceramic Baseball	J. Martin	Open	20.00	20.00
86-02-006	Geroge Brett Ceramic Baseball, signed	J. Martin	2,000	39.75	95-125.00
87-02-007	Roger Staubach Ceramic Football Card	C. Soileau	Open	9.95	18.00
87-02-008	Roger Staubach Ceramic Football Card, signed	C. Soileau	1,979	39.00	39.00
90-02-009	Wayne Gretzky Ceramic Hockey Card	M. Taylor	Open	16.00	18.00
91-02-010	Joe Montana Ceramic Football Card	M. Taylor	Open	18.00	18.00
92-02-011	Carlton Fisk Ceramic Baseball Card	M. Taylor	Open	18.00	18.00
92-02-012	Tom Seaver	M. Taylor	Open	18.00	18.00
92-02-013	Gordon Howe	M. Taylor	Open	18.00	18.00
92-02-014	Phil Esposito	M. Taylor	Open	18.00	18.00
Gartlan USA, Inc.		**Magic Johnson Gold Rim Collection**			
88-03-001	Magic Johnson Artist Proof-"Magic in Motion", signed	Roger	250	175.00	2500.00
88-03-002	Magic Johnson-"Magic in Motion"	Roger	1,737	125.00	295-500.
88-03-003	Magic Johnson Commemorative	Roger	32	275.00	4500.00
Gartlan USA, Inc.		**Mike Schmidt "500th" Home Run Edition**			
87-04-001	Figurine-signed	Roger	1,987	150.00	750-850.
87-04-002	Figurine-signed, Artist Proof	Roger	20	275.00	1200-1700.
87-04-003	Plaque-"Only Perfect"-signed	Paluso	500	150.00	225.00
87-04-004	Plaque-"Only Perfect", Artist Proof	Paluso	20	200.00	550.00
Gartlan USA, Inc.		**Pete Rose Diamond Collection**			
88-05-001	Farewell Ceramic Baseball Card-signed	Forbes	4,256	39.00	50.00
88-05-002	Farewell Ceramic Baseball Card	Forbes	Open	9.95	18.00
Gartlan USA, Inc.		**Reggie Jackson "500th" Home Run Edition**			
86-06-001	Ceramic Baseball Card, signed	J. Martin	1,986	39.00	50.00
86-06-002	Ceramic Baseball Card	J. Martin	Open	9.95	18.00
Gartlan USA, Inc.		**Kareem Abdul-Jabbar Sky-Hook Collection**			
89-07-001	Kareem Abdul-Jabbar "The Captain"-signed	L. Heyda	1,989	175.00	375-395.
89-07-002	Kareem Abdul-Jabbar, Artist Proof	L. Heyda	100	200.00	575.00
89-07-003	Kareem Abdul-Jabbar, Commemorative	L. Heyda	33	275.00	4000-6000.
Gartlan USA, Inc.		**Signed Figurines**			
85-08-001	Pete Rose-"For the Record", signed	H. Reed	4,192	125.00	1000.00
89-08-002	Carl Yastrzemski-"Yaz"	L. Heyda	1,989	150.00	325.00
89-08-003	Carl Yastrzemski-"Yaz" , Artist Proof	L. Heyda	250	150.00	450-495.
89-08-004	Johnny Bench	L. Heyda	1,989	150.00	325-375.
89-08-005	Johnny Bench, Artist Proof	L. Heyda	250	150.00	425-495.
89-08-006	Joe DiMaggio	L. Heyda	2,214	275.00	895-950.
90-08-007	Joe DiMaggio- Pinstripe Yankee Clipper	L. Heyda	325	695.00	1800-2250.
89-08-008	John Wooden-Coaching Classics	L. Heyda	1,975	175.00	175.00
89-08-009	John Wooden-Coaching Classics, Artist Pr.	L. Heyda	250	350.00	350.00
89-08-010	Ted Williams	L. Heyda	2,654	295.00	395-575.
89-08-011	Ted Williams, Artist Proof	L. Heyda	250	650.00	650.00
89-08-012	Wayne Gretzky	L. Heyda	1,851	225.00	575-795.
89-08-013	Wayne Gretzky, Artist Proof	L. Heyda	300	695.00	1700.00
89-08-014	Yogi Berra	F. Barnum	2,150	225.00	225.00
89-08-015	Yogi Berra, Artist Proof	F. Barnum	250	350.00	350.00
89-08-016	Steve Carlton	L. Heyda	3,290	175.00	175-225.
89-08-017	Steve Carlton, Artist Proof	L. Heyda	300	350.00	350.00
90-08-018	Whitey Ford	S. Barnum	2,360	225.00	225.00
90-08-019	Whitey Ford, Artist Proof	S. Barnum	250	350.00	350.00
90-08-020	Luis Aparicio	J. Slockbower	1,984	225.00	225.00
90-08-021	Darryl Strawberry	L. Heyda	2,500	225.00	225.00
90-08-022	George Brett	F. Barnum	2,250	225.00	225.00
91-08-023	Ken Griffey, Jr	J. Slockbower	1,989	225.00	225.00
91-08-024	Warren Spahn	J. Slockbower	1,973	225.00	225.00
91-08-025	Rod Carew - Hitting Splendor	J. Slockbower	1,991	225.00	225.00
91-08-026	Brett Hull - The Golden Brett	L. Heyda	1,986	250.00	250.00
92-08-027	Brett Hull, Artist Proof	L. Heyda	300	350.00	350.00
91-08-028	Bobby Hull - The Golden Jet	L. Heyda	1,983	250.00	250.00
92-08-029	Bobby Hull, Artist Proof	L. Heyda	300	350.00	350.00
91-08-030	Hull Matched Figurines	L. Heyda	950	500.00	500.00
91-08-031	Al Barlick	V. Bova	1,989	175.00	175.00
91-08-032	Monte Irvin	V. Bova	1,973	225.00	225.00
91-08-033	Joe Montana	F. Barnum	2,250	325.00	325-375.
91-08-034	Joe Montana, Artist Proof	F. Barnum	250	500.00	650.00
92-08-035	Isiah Thomas	J. Slockbower	1,990	225.00	225.00
92-08-036	Hank Aaron	F. Barnum	1,982	225.00	225.00
92-08-037	Carlton Fisk	J. Slockbower	1,972	225.00	225.00
92-08-038	Carlton Fisk, Artist Proof	J. Slockbower	300	350.00	350.00
92-08-039	Gordie Howe	L. Heyda	2,358	225.00	225.00
92-08-040	Gordie Howe, Artist Proof	L. Heyda	250	500.00	500.00
92-08-041	Phil Esposito	L. Heyda	1, 984	225.00	225.00
92-08-042	Phil Esposito, Artist Proof	L. Heyda	250	500.00	500.00
92-08-043	Hank Aaron Commemorative w/display case	F. Barnum	755	275.00	275.00
92-08-044	Hank Aaron, Artist Proof	F. Barnum	300	325.00	325.00
92-08-045	Stan Musial	J. Slockbower	1,969	325.00	325.00
92-08-046	Stan Musial, Artist Proof	J. Slockbower	300	500.00	500.00
92-08-047	Ralph Kiner	J. Slockbower	1,975	225.00	225.00
92-08-048	Tom Seaver	J. Slockbower	1,992	225.00	225.00
93-08-049	Kristi Yamaguchi	K. Ling Sun	950	195.00	195.00
93-08-050	Bob Cousy	L. Heyda	950	225.00	225.00
94-08-051	Sam Snead	L. Cella	950	225.00	225.00
94-08-052	Shaquille O'Neal	R. Sun	1,993	275.00	275.00
94-08-053	Carl Ripken, Jr.	L. Heyda	1,982	225.00	225.00
94-08-054	Troy Aikman	L. Cella	1,993	225.00	225.00
94-08-055	Brian Boitano	R. Sun	950	195.00	195.00
94-08-056	Steve Young	L. Cella	950	225.00	225.00
94-08-057	Eddie Matthews	R. Sun	950	195.00	195.00
Gartlan USA, Inc.		**All-Star Gems Miniature Figurines**			
89-09-001	Carl Yastrzemski	L. Heyda	10,000	75.00	79.00
89-09-002	Johnny Bench	L. Heyda	10,000	75.00	75.00
89-09-003	Ted Williams	L. Heyda	10,000	75.00	79.00
89-09-004	Steve Carlton	L. Heyda	10,000	75.00	79.00

Company Number	 Name	Series Artist	 Edition Limit	 Issue Price	 Quote
90-09-005	John Wooden	L. Heyda	10,000	75.00	79.00
90-09-006	Wayne Gretzky	L. Heyda	10,000	75.00	79.00
90-09-007	Pete Rose	F. Barnum	10,000	75.00	79.00
90-09-008	Mike Schmidt	Roger	10,000	75.00	79.00
90-09-009	Yogi Berra	F. Barnum	10,000	75.00	79.00
90-09-010	George Brett	F. Barnum	10,000	75.00	79.00
90-09-011	Whitey Ford	F. Barnum	10,000	75.00	79.00
90-09-012	Luis Aparicio	J. Slockbower	10,000	75.00	79.00
90-09-013	Darryl Strawberry	L. Heyda	10,000	75.00	79.00
90-09-014	Kareem Abdul-Jabbar	L. Heyda	10,000	75.00	75.00
91-09-015	Ken Griffey, Jr.	J. Slockbower	10,000	75.00	79.00
91-09-016	Warren Spahn	J. Slockbower	10,000	75.00	79.00
91-09-017	Rod Carew	J. Slockbower	10,000	75.00	79.00
91-09-018	Brett Hull	L. Heyda	10,000	75.00	79.00
91-09-019	Bobby Hull	L. Heyda	10,000	75.00	79.00
91-09-020	Monte Irvin	V. Bova	10,000	75.00	79.00
91-09-021	Joe Montana	F. Barnum	10,000	79.00	95.00
92-09-022	Isiah Thomas	J. Slockbower	10,000	79.00	79.00
92-09-023	Hank Aaron	F. Barnum	10,000	79.00	79.00
92-09-024	Carlton Fisk	J. Slockbower	10,000	79.00	79.00
92-09-025	Phil Esposito	L. Heyda	10,000	79.00	79.00
92-09-026	Stan Musial	J. Slockbower	2, 269	99.00	99.00
92-09-027	Tom Seaver	J. Slockbower	10,000	79.00	79.00
92-09-028	Ralph Kiner	J. Slockbower	10,000	79.00	79.00
92-09-029	Gordie Howe	L. Heyda	10,000	79.00	79.00
93-09-030	Kristi Yamaguchi	K. Ling Sun	5,000	79.00	79.00
94-09-031	Bob Cousy	L. Heyda	5,000	79.00	79.00
94-09-032	Sam Snead	L. Cella	5,000	79.00	79.00
94-09-033	Shaquille O'Neal	R. Sun	10,000	79.00	79.00
94-09-034	Carl Ripken, Jr.	L. Heyda	10,000	79.00	79.00
94-09-035	Troy Aikman	L. Cella	10,000	79.00	79.00
94-09-036	Brian Boitano	R. Sun	5,000	79.00	79.00
94-09-037	Steve Young	L. Cella	5,000	79.00	79.00
94-09-038	Eddie Matthews	R. Sun	5,000	79.00	79.00
Gartlan USA, Inc.		**Members Only Figurine**			
90-10-001	Wayne Gretzky-Home Uniform	L. Heyda	N/A	75.00	225-350.
91-10-002	Joe Montana-Road Uniform	F. Barnum	N/A	75.00	175-195.
91-10-003	Kareem Abdul-Jabbar	L. Heyda	N/A	75.00	100-125.
92-10-004	Mike Schmidt	J. Slockbower	N/A	79.00	100.00
93-10-005	Hank Aaron	J. Slockbower	N/A	79.00	79.00
94-10-006	Shaquille O'Neal	L. Cella	N/A	79.00	79.00
Gartlan USA, Inc.		**Club Gift**			
89-11-001	Pete Rose, Plate (8 1/2")	B. Forbes	Closed	Gift	100.00
90-11-002	Al Barlick, Plate (8 1/2")	M. Taylor	Closed	Gift	49.00
91-11-003	Joe Montana (8 1/2")	M. Taylor	Closed	Gift	125.00
92-11-004	Ken Griffey Jr., Plate (8 1/2")	M. Taylor	Closed	30.00	49.00
93-11-005	Gordie Howe, Plate (8 1/2")	M. Taylor	Closed	30.00	30.00
94-11-006	Shaquille O'Neal, Plate (8 1/2")	M. Taylor	Yr.Iss.	30.00	30.00
Gartlan USA, Inc.		**Master's Museum Collection**			
91-12-001	Kareem Abdul-Jabbar	L. Heyda	500	3000.00	3000.00
91-12-002	Wayne Gretzky	L. Heyda	500	set	set
91-12-003	Joe Montana	F. Barnum	500	set	set
91-12-004	Ted Williams	L. Heyda	500	set	set
93-12-005	Stan Musial	J. Slockbower	500	850	850
Gartlan USA, Inc.		**Negro League Series**			
91-13-001	James "Cool Papa" Bell	V. Bova	1,499	195.00	195.00
91-13-002	Ray Dandridge	V. Bova	1,987	195.00	195.00
91-13-003	Buck Leonard	V. Bova	1,972	195.00	195.00
91-13-004	Matched-Number set #1-950	V. Bova	950	500.00	500.00
Goebel		**Goebel Figurines**			
63-01-001	Little Veterinarian (Mysterious Malady)	N. Rockwell	Closed	15.00	400.00
63-01-002	Boyhood Dreams (Adventurers between Adventures)	N. Rockwell	Closed	12.00	400.00
63-01-003	Mother's Helper (Pride of Parenthood)	N. Rockwell	Closed	15.00	400.00
63-01-004	His First Smoke	N. Rockwell	Closed	9.00	400.00
63-01-005	My New Pal (A Boy Meets His Dog)	N. Rockwell	Closed	12.00	400.00
63-01-006	Home Cure	N. Rockwell	Closed	16.00	400.00
63-01-007	Timely Assistance (Love Aid)	N. Rockwell	Closed	16.00	400.00
63-01-008	She Loves Me (Day Dreamer)	N. Rockwell	Closed	8.00	400.00
63-01-009	Buttercup Test (Beguiling Buttercup)	N. Rockwell	Closed	10.00	400.00
63-01-010	First Love (A Scholarly Pace)	N. Rockwell	Closed	30.00	400.00
63-01-011	Patient Anglers (Fisherman's Paradise)	N. Rockwell	Closed	18.00	400.00
63-01-012	Advertising Plaque	N. Rockwell	Closed	Unkn.	600.00
Goebel		**Betsey Clark Figurines**			
72-02-001	Bless You	G. Bochmann	Closed	18.00	275.00
72-02-002	Friends	G. Bochmann	Closed	21.00	400.00
72-02-003	So Much Beauty	G. Bochmann	Closed	24.50	350.00
72-02-004	Little Miracle	G. Bochmann	Closed	24.50	350.00
Goebel		**Co-Boy**			
71-03-001	Robby the Vegetarian	G. Skrobek	Closed	16.00	80.00
71-03-002	Mike the Jam Maker	G. Skrobek	Closed	16.00	72.00
71-03-003	Bit the Bachelor	G. Skrobek	Closed	16.00	28-80.00
71-03-004	Tom the Honey Lover	G. Skrobek	Closed	16.00	28.00
71-03-005	Sam the Gourmet	G. Skrobek	Closed	16.00	28.00
71-03-006	Plum the Pastry Chef	G. Skrobek	Closed	16.00	28-60.00
71-03-007	Wim the Court Supplier	G. Skrobek	Closed	16.00	28.00
71-03-008	Fips the Foxy Fisherman	G. Skrobek	Closed	16.00	80-90.00
72-03-009	Porz the Mushroom Muncher	G. Skrobek	Closed	20.00	28.00
72-03-010	Sepp the Beer Buddy	G. Skrobek	Closed	20.00	72.00
72-03-011	Kuni the Big Dipper	G. Skrobek	Closed	20.00	60-65.00
71-03-012	Fritz the Happy Boozer	G. Skrobek	Closed	16.00	42-50.00
72-03-013	Bob the Bookworm	G. Skrobek	Closed	20.00	42-50.00
72-03-014	Brum the Lawyer	G. Skrobek	Closed	20.00	72.00
72-03-015	Utz the Banker	G. Skrobek	Closed	20.00	80.00
72-03-016	Co-Boy Plaque	G. Skrobek	Closed	20.00	72.00
XX-03-017	Jack the Village Pharmacist	G. Skrobek	Closed	Unkn.	42-50.00
XX-03-018	John the Hawkeye Hunter	G. Skrobek	Closed	Unkn.	72.00
XX-03-019	Petrl the Village Angler	G. Skrobek	Closed	Unkn.	72.00
XX-03-020	Conny the Night Watchman	G. Skrobek	Closed	Unkn.	42-50.00
XX-03-021	Ed the Wine Cellar Steward	G. Skrobek	Closed	Unkn.	42-50.00
XX-03-022	Toni the Skier	G. Skrobek	Closed	Unkn.	72.00
XX-03-023	Candy the Baker's Delight	G. Skrobek	Closed	Unkn.	78.00
XX-03-024	Mark-Safety First	G. Skrobek	Closed	Unkn.	78.00
XX-03-025	Bert the Soccer Star	G. Skrobek	Closed	Unkn.	50.00
XX-03-026	Jim the Bowler	G. Skrobek	Closed	Unkn.	50.00
XX-03-027	Max the Boxing Champ	G. Skrobek	Closed	Unkn.	50.00
78-03-028	Gil the Goalie	G. Skrobek	Closed	34.00	50.00
78-03-029	Pat the Pitcher	G. Skrobek	Closed	34.00	50.00
78-03-030	Tommy Touchdown	G. Skrobek	Closed	34.00	50.00
80-03-031	Ted the Tennis Player	G. Skrobek	Closed	49.00	50.00
80-03-032	Herb the Horseman	G. Skrobek	Closed	49.00	90.00
80-03-033	Monty the Mountain Climber	G. Skrobek	Closed	49.00	72.00
80-03-034	Carl the Chef	G. Skrobek	Closed	49.00	72-80.00
80-03-035	Doc the Doctor	G. Skrobek	Closed	49.00	72.00
80-03-036	Gerd the Diver	G. Skrobek	Closed	49.00	125-175.
81-03-037	George the Gourmand	G. Skrobek	Closed	45.00	72.00
81-03-038	Greg the Gourmet	G. Skrobek	Closed	45.00	50.00
81-03-039	Ben the Blacksmith	G. Skrobek	Closed	45.00	50.00
81-03-040	Al the Trumpet Player	G. Skrobek	Closed	45.00	50.00
81-03-041	Peter the Accordionist	G. Skrobek	Closed	45.00	50.00
81-03-042	Niels the Strummer	G. Skrobek	Closed	45.00	50.00
81-03-043	Greta the Happy Housewife	G. Skrobek	Closed	45.00	50.00
81-03-044	Nick the Nightclub Singer	G. Skrobek	Closed	45.00	50.00
81-08-045	Walter the Jogger	G. Skrobek	Closed	45.00	50.00
84-03-046	Rudy the World Traveler	G. Skrobek	Closed	45.00	100.00
84-03-047	Sid the Vintner	G. Skrobek	Closed	45.00	50.00
84-03-048	Herman the Butcher	G. Skrobek	Closed	45.00	50.00
84-03-049	Rick the Fireman	G. Skrobek	Closed	45.00	50-80.00
84-03-050	Chuck the Chimney Sweep	G. Skrobek	Closed	45.00	50.00
84-03-051	Chris the Shoemaker	G. Skrobek	Closed	45.00	50.00
84-03-052	Felix the Baker	G. Skrobek	Closed	45.00	85.00
84-03-053	Marthe the Nurse	G. Skrobek	Closed	45.00	50.00
84-03-054	Paul the Dentist	G. Skrobek	Closed	45.00	80.00
84-03-055	Homer the Driver	G. Skrobek	Closed	45.00	50-80.00
84-03-056	Brad the Clockmaker	G. Skrobek	Closed	75.00	125.00
87-03-057	Clock-Cony the Watchman	G. Skrobek	Closed	125.00	125.00
87-03-058	Clock-Sepp and the Beer Keg	G. Skrobek	Closed	125.00	125.00
87-03-059	Bank-Pete the Pirate	G. Skrobek	Closed	80.00	80.00
87-03-060	Bank-Utz the Money Bags	G. Skrobek	Closed	80.00	80.00
87-03-061	Chuck on His Pig	G. Skrobek	Closed	75.00	75.00
Goebel		**Co-Boys-Culinary**			
94-04-001	Mike the Jam Maker 301050	Welling/Skrobek	Open	30.00	30.00
94-04-002	Sepp the Drunkard 301051	Welling/Skrobek	Open	30.00	30.00
94-04-003	Plum the Sweets Maker 301052	Welling/Skrobek	Open	30.00	30.00
94-04-004	Tom the Sweet Tooth 301053	Welling/Skrobek	Open	30.00	30.00
94-04-005	Robby the Vegetarian 301054	Welling/Skrobek	Open	30.00	30.00
Goebel		**Co-Boys-Sports**			
94-05-001	Petri the Fisherman 301055	Welling/Skrobek	Open	30.00	30.00
94-05-002	Toni the Skier 301056	Welling/Skrobek	Open	30.00	30.00
94-05-003	Jim the Bowler 301057	Welling/Skrobek	Open	30.00	30.00
94-05-004	Ted the Tennis Player 301058	Welling/Skrobek	Open	30.00	30.00
94-05-005	Bert the Soccer Player 301059	Welling/Skrobek	Open	30.00	30.00
Goebel		**Co-Boys-Professionals**			
94-06-001	Brum the Lawyer 301060	Welling/Skrobek	Open	30.00	30.00
94-06-002	Utz the Banker 301061	Welling/Skrobek	Open	30.00	30.00
94-06-003	Conny the Nightwatchman 301062	Welling/Skrobek	Open	30.00	30.00
94-06-004	John the Hunter 301063	Welling/Skrobek	Open	30.00	30.00
94-06-005	Doc the Doctor 301064	Welling/Skrobek	Open	30.00	30.00

Goebel/DeGrazia: See Artists of the World

Number	Name	Artist	Edition Limit	Issue Price	Quote
Goebel/M.I. Hummel		**M.I. Hummel Collectibles Figurines**			
88-01-001	A Budding Maestro 477	M.I. Hummel	Open	Unkn.	95.00
XX-01-002	A Fair Measure 345	M.I. Hummel	Open	Unkn.	165-260.
93-01-003	A Free Flight 569	M.I. Hummel	Open	Unkn.	185.00
XX-01-004	A Gentle Glow 439	M.I. Hummel	Open	Unkn.	190.00
91-01-005	A Nap 534	M.I. Hummel	Open	Unkn.	70-110.00
XX-01-006	Accordion Boy 185	M.I. Hummel	12/94	Unkn.	180.00
XX-01-007	Adoration 23/I	M.I. Hummel	Open	Unkn.	215-325.
XX-01-008	Adoration 23/III	M.I. Hummel	Open	Unkn.	510.00
XX-01-009	Adventure Bound 347	M.I. Hummel	Open	Unkn.	3500.00
89-01-010	An Apple A Day 403	M.I. Hummel	Open	Unkn.	260.00
XX-01-011	Angel Duet 261	M.I. Hummel	Open	Unkn.	195.00
XX-01-012	Angel Serenade 214/0	M.I. Hummel	Open	Unkn.	80.00
XX-01-013	Angel Serenade with Lamb 83	M.I. Hummel	Open	Unkn.	170-175.
XX-01-014	Angel with Accordion 238/B	M.I. Hummel	Open	Unkn.	50.00
XX-01-015	Angel with Lute 238/A	M.I. Hummel	Open	Unkn.	50.00
XX-01-016	Angel With Trumpet 238/C	M.I. Hummel	Open	Unkn.	50.00
XX-01-017	Angelic Song 144	M.I. Hummel	Open	Unkn.	135.00
XX-01-018	Apple Tree Boy 142/3/0	M.I. Hummel	Open	Unkn.	90-130.00
XX-01-019	Apple Tree Boy 142/I	M.I. Hummel	Open	Unkn.	250.00
XX-01-020	Apple Tree Boy 142/V	M.I. Hummel	Open	Unkn.	1080.00
XX-01-021	Apple Tree Girl 141/3/0	M.I. Hummel	Open	Unkn.	174.00
XX-01-022	Apple Tree Girl 141/I	M.I. Hummel	Open	Unkn.	245.00
XX-01-023	Apple Tree Girl 141/V	M.I. Hummel	Open	Unkn.	1080.00
91-01-024	Art Critic 318	M.I. Hummel	Open	Unkn.	260.00
XX-01-025	Artist, The 304	M.I. Hummel	Open	Unkn.	220.00
XX-01-026	Auf Wiedersehen 153/0	M.I. Hummel	Open	Unkn.	220.00
XX-01-027	Auf Wiedersehen 153/I	M.I. Hummel	Open	Unkn.	270.00
XX-01-028	Autumn Harvest 355	M.I. Hummel	Open	Unkn.	195.00
XX-01-029	Baker 128	M.I. Hummel	Open	Unkn.	175.00
XX-01-030	Baking Day 330	M.I. Hummel	Open	Unkn.	240.00
XX-01-031	Band Leader 129	M.I. Hummel	Open	Unkn.	180.00
XX-01-032	Band Leader 129/4/0	M.I. Hummel	Open	Unkn.	90.00
XX-01-033	Barnyard Hero 195/2/0	M.I. Hummel	Open	Unkn.	150.00
XX-01-034	Barnyard Hero 195/I	M.I. Hummel	Open	Unkn.	290.00
XX-01-035	Bashful 377	M.I. Hummel	Open	Unkn.	180.00
90-01-036	Bath Time 412	M.I. Hummel	Open	Unkn.	350.00
XX-01-037	Begging His Share 9	M.I. Hummel	Open	Unkn.	220.00
XX-01-038	Be Patient 197/2/0	M.I. Hummel	Open	Unkn.	175-182.
XX-01-039	Be Patient 197/I	M.I. Hummel	Open	Unkn.	260.00
XX-01-040	Big Housecleaning 363	M.I. Hummel	Open	Unkn.	260.00
XX-01-041	Bird Duet 169	M.I. Hummel	Open	Unkn.	90-130.00
XX-01-042	Bird Watcher 300	M.I. Hummel	Open	Unkn.	205.00
89-01-043	Birthday Cake 338	M.I. Hummel	Open	Unkn.	130.00
94-01-044	Birthday Present (Special Event)	M.I. Hummel	Open	140.00	140.00
XX-01-045	Birthday Serenade 218/2/0	M.I. Hummel	Open	Unkn.	160.00
XX-01-046	Birthday Serenade 218/0	M.I. Hummel	Open	Unkn.	270.00
XX-01-047	Blessed Event 333	M.I. Hummel	Open	Unkn.	300.00
XX-01-048	Bookworm 8	M.I. Hummel	Open	Unkn.	195.00
XK-01-049	Bookworm 3/I	M.I. Hummel	Open	Unkn.	270.00
XX-01-050	Boots 143/0	M.I. Hummel	Open	Unkn.	180.00
XX-01-051	Boots 143/I	M.I. Hummel	Open	Unkn.	300.00
XX-01-052	Botanist, The 351	M.I. Hummel	Open	Unkn.	195.00
XX-01-053	Boy with Accordion 390	M.I. Hummel	Open	Unkn.	75.00
XX-01-054	Boy with Horse 239C	M.I. Hummel	Open	Unkn.	50.00
XX-01-055	Boy with Toothache 217	M.I. Hummel	Open	Unkn.	200.00
XX-01-056	Brother 95	M.I. Hummel	Open	Unkn.	180.00

Company Number	Series Name	Artist	Edition Limit	Issue Price	Quote
XX-01-057	Builder, The 305	M.I. Hummel	Open	Unkn.	220.00
XX-01-058	Busy Student 367	M.I. Hummel	Open	Unkn.	150.00
XX-01-059	Call to Glory 739	M.I. Hummel	Open	250.00	250.00
XX-01-060	Carnival 328	M.I. Hummel	Open	Unkn.	205.00
XX-01-061	Celestial Musician 188/0	M.I. Hummel	Open	Unkn.	195.00
XX-01-062	Celestial Musician 188/I	M.I. Hummel	Open	Unkn.	230.00
93-01-063	Celestial Musician (mini) 188/4/0	M.I. Hummel	Open	Unkn.	90.00
XX-01-064	Chick Girl 57/2/0	M.I. Hummel	Open	Unkn.	135.00
XX-01-065	Chick Girl 57/0	M.I. Hummel	Open	Unkn.	155-164.
XX-01-066	Chick Girl 57/I	M.I. Hummel	Open	Unkn.	250.00
XX-01-067	Chicken-Licken 385	M.I. Hummel	Open	Unkn.	260.00
XX-01-068	Chicken-Licken 385/4	M.I. Hummel	Open	Unkn.	90.00
XX-01-069	Chimney Sweep 12/2/0	M.I. Hummel	Open	Unkn.	110.00
XX-01-070	Chimney Sweep 12/I	M.I. Hummel	Open	Unkn.	195-218.
89-01-071	Christmas Angel 301	M.I. Hummel	Open	Unkn.	230.00
XX-01-072	Christmas Song 343	M.I. Hummel	Open	Unkn.	195.00
XX-01-073	Cinderella 337	M.I. Hummel	Open	Unkn.	260.00
XX-01-074	Close Harmony 336	M.I. Hummel	Open	Unkn.	260.00
XX-01-075	Confidentially 314	M.I. Hummel	Open	Unkn.	260.00
XX-01-076	Congratulations 17/0	M.I. Hummel	Open	Unkn.	180.00
XX-01-077	Coquettes 179	M.I. Hummel	Open	Unkn.	260.00
XX-01-078	Crossroads (Original) 331	M.I. Hummel	Open	Unkn.	255-380.
XX-01-079	Crossroads (Commemorative) 331	M.I. Hummel	10,000	Unkn.	500-1200.
XX-01-080	Culprits 56/A	M.I. Hummel	Open	Unkn.	265.00
89-01-081	Daddy's Girls 371	M.I. Hummel	Open	Unkn.	150-220.
XX-01-082	Doctor 127	M.I. Hummel	Open	Unkn.	101-145.
XX-01-083	Doll Bath 319	M.I. Hummel	Open	Unkn.	260.00
XX-01-084	Doll Mother 67	M.I. Hummel	Open	Unkn.	190.00
XX-01-085	Duet 130	M.I. Hummel	Open	Unkn.	250.00
XX-01-086	Easter Greetings 378	M.I. Hummel	Open	Unkn.	195.00
XX-01-087	Easter Time 384	M.I. Hummel	Open	Unkn.	240.00
92-01-088	Evening Prayer 495	M.I. Hummel	Open	Unkn.	67-105.00
XX-01-089	Eventide 99	M.I. Hummel	Open	Unkn.	315.00
XX-01-090	Farm Boy 66	M.I. Hummel	Open	Unkn.	205.00
XX-01-091	Favorite Pet 361	M.I. Hummel	Open	Unkn.	260.00
XX-01-092	Feathered Friends 344	M.I. Hummel	Open	Unkn.	240.00
XX-01-093	Feeding Time 199/0	M.I. Hummel	Open	Unkn.	175.00
XX-01-094	Feeding Time 199/I	M.I. Hummel	Open	Unkn.	240.00
XX-01-095	Festival Harmony, with Mandolin 172/0	M.I. Hummel	Open	Unkn.	280.00
94-01-096	Festival Harmony w/Mandolin 172	M.I. Hummel	Open	95.00	95.00
XX-01-097	Festival Harmony, with Flute 173/0	M.I. Hummel	Open	Unkn.	245-280.
XX-01-098	Flower Vendor 381	M.I. Hummel	Open	Unkn.	220.00
XX-01-099	Follow the Leader 369	M.I. Hummel	Open	Unkn.	1100.00
XX-01-100	For Father 87	M.I. Hummel	Open	Unkn.	195.00
XX-01-101	For Mother 257/2/0	M.I. Hummel	Open	Unkn.	110.00
XX-01-102	For Mother 257	M.I. Hummel	Open	Unkn.	130-185.
XX-01-103	Forest Shrine 183	M.I. Hummel	Open	Unkn.	495.00
91-01-104	Friend Or Foe 434	M.I. Hummel	Open	Unkn.	195.00
XX-01-105	Friends 136/I	M.I. Hummel	Open	Unkn.	195.00
XX-01-106	Friends 136/V	M.I. Hummel	Open	Unkn.	1080.00
93-01-107	Friends Together 662/I	M.I. Hummel	25,000	475.00	475.00
93-01-108	Friends Together 662/0	M.I. Hummel	Open	260.00	260.00
XX-01-109	Gay Adventure 356	M.I. Hummel	Open	Unkn.	175.00
XX-01-110	Girl with Doll 239/B	M.I. Hummel	Open	Unkn.	50.00
XX-01-111	Girl with Nosegay 239/A	M.I. Hummel	Open	Unkn.	50.00
XX-01-112	Girl with Sheet Music 389	M.I. Hummel	Open	Unkn.	75.00
XX-01-113	Girl with Trumpet 391	M.I. Hummel	Open	Unkn.	75.00
XX-01-114	Going Home 383	M.I. Hummel	Open	Unkn.	280.00
XX-01-115	Going to Grandma's 52/0	M.I. Hummel	Open	Unkn.	250.00
XX-01-116	Good Friends 182	M.I. Hummel	Open	Unkn.	175.00
XX-01-117	Good Hunting 307	M.I. Hummel	Open	Unkn.	220.00
XX-01-118	Good Night 214/C	M.I. Hummel	Open	Unkn.	80.00
XX-01-119	Good Shepherd 42/0	M.I. Hummel	Open	Unkn.	220.00
XX-01-120	Goose Girl 47/3/0	M.I. Hummel	Open	Unkn.	155-161.
XX-01-121	Goose Girl 47/0	M.I. Hummel	Open	Unkn.	205.00
XX-01-122	Goose Girl 47/II	M.I. Hummel	Open	Unkn.	380.00
XX-01-123	Grandma's Girl 561	M.I. Hummel	Open	Unkn.	135.00
XX-01-124	Grandpa's Boy 562	M.I. Hummel	Open	Unkn.	135.00
XX-01-125	Guiding Angel 357	M.I. Hummel	Open	Unkn.	80.00
XX-01-126	Happiness 86	M.I. Hummel	Open	Unkn.	120.00
XX-01-127	Happy Birthday 176/0	M.I. Hummel	Open	Unkn.	195.00
XX-01-128	Happy Birthday 176/I	M.I. Hummel	Open	Unkn.	270.00
XX-01-129	Happy Days 150/2/0	M.I. Hummel	Open	Unkn.	160.00
XX-01-130	Happy Days 150/0	M.I. Hummel	Open	Unkn.	270.00
XX-01-131	Happy Days 150/I	M.I. Hummel	Open	Unkn.	430.00
XX-01-132	Happy Pastime 69	M.I. Hummel	Open	Unkn.	145.00
XX-01-133	Happy Traveller 109/0	M.I. Hummel	Open	Unkn.	130.00
XX-01-134	Hear Ye! Hear Ye! 15/0	M.I. Hummel	Open	Unkn.	180-280.
XX-01-135	Hear Ye! Hear Ye! 15/I	M.I. Hummel	Open	Unkn.	225.00
XX-01-136	Hear Ye! Hear Ye! 15/II	M.I. Hummel	Open	Unkn.	400.00
XX-01-137	Hear Ye! Hear Ye! 15/2/0	M.I. Hummel	Open	Unkn.	135.00
XX-01-138	Heavenly Angel 21/0	M.I. Hummel	Open	Unkn.	110.00
XX-01-139	Heavenly Angel 21/0/1/2	M.I. Hummel	Open	Unkn.	190-263.
XX-01-140	Heavenly Angel 21/I	M.I. Hummel	Open	Unkn.	230.00
XX-01-141	Heavenly Angel 21/II	M.I. Hummel	Open	Unkn.	390.00
XX-01-142	Heavenly Lullaby 262	M.I. Hummel	Open	Unkn.	170.00
XX-01-143	Heavenly Protection 88/I	M.I. Hummel	Open	Unkn.	350-395.
XX-01-144	Heavenly Protection 88/II	M.I. Hummel	Open	Unkn.	590.00
XX-01-145	Hello 124/0	M.I. Hummel	Open	Unkn.	195-210.
XX-01-146	Home from Market 198/2/0	M.I. Hummel	Open	Unkn.	130.00
XX-01-147	Home from Market 198/I	M.I. Hummel	Open	Unkn.	195.00
XX-01-148	Homeward Bound 334	M.I. Hummel	Open	Unkn.	320.00
90-01-149	Horse Trainer 423	M.I. Hummel	Open	Unkn.	200.00
89-01-150	Hosanna 480	M.I. Hummel	Open	Unkn.	90.00
89-01-151	I'll Protect Him 483	M.I. Hummel	Open	Unkn.	75.00
94-01-152	I'm Care Free 633	M.I. Hummel	Open	365.00	365.00
89-01-153	I'm Here 478	M.I. Hummel	Open	Unkn.	95.00
89-01-154	In D Major 430	M.I. Hummel	Open	Unkn.	180.00
XX-01-155	In The Meadow 459	M.I. Hummel	Open	Unkn.	180.00
XX-01-156	In Tune 414	M.I. Hummel	Open	Unkn.	250.00
XX-01-157	Is It Raining? 420	M.I. Hummel	Open	Unkn.	240.00
XX-01-158	Joyful 53	M.I. Hummel	Open	Unkn.	110.00
XX-01-159	Joyous News 27/III	M.I. Hummel	Open	Unkn.	158-195.
XX-01-160	Just Fishing 373	M.I. Hummel	Open	Unkn.	140-205.
XX-01-161	Just Resting 112/3/0	M.I. Hummel	Open	Unkn.	135.00
XX-01-162	Just Resting 112/I	M.I. Hummel	Open	Unkn.	250.00
XX-01-163	Kindergartner 467	M.I. Hummel	Open	Unkn.	180.00
XX-01-164	Kiss Me 311	M.I. Hummel	Open	Unkn.	168-260.
XX-01-165	Knitting Lesson 256	M.I. Hummel	Open	Unkn.	475.00
XX-01-166	Knit One, Purl One 432	M.I. Hummel	Open	Unkn.	105.00
92-01-167	Land in Sight 530	M.I. Hummel	30,000	Unkn.	780-1600.
XX-01-168	Latest News 184/0	M.I. Hummel	Open	Unkn.	260.00
XX-01-169	Let's Sing 110/0	M.I. Hummel	Open	Unkn.	115.00
XX-01-170	Let's Sing 110/I	M.I. Hummel	Open	Unkn.	155.00
XX-01-171	Letter to Santa Claus 340	M.I. Hummel	Open	Unkn.	225-305.
93-01-172	Little Architect 410/I	M.I. Hummel	Open	Unkn.	290.00
XX-01-173	Little Bookkeeper 306	M.I. Hummel	Open	Unkn.	260.00
XX-01-174	Little Cellist 89/I	M.I. Hummel	Open	Unkn.	195.00
XX-01-175	Little Cellist 89/II	M.I. Hummel	Open	Unkn.	380.00
XX-01-176	Little Drummer 240	M.I. Hummel	Open	Unkn.	135.00
XX-01-177	Little Fiddler 2/4/0	M.I. Hummel	Open	Unkn.	90.00
XX-01-178	Little Fiddler 4	M.I. Hummel	Open	Unkn.	185.00
XX-01-179	Little Fiddler 2/0	M.I. Hummel	Open	Unkn.	205.00
XX-01-180	Little Fiddler 2/I	M.I. Hummel	Open	Unkn.	370.00
XX-01-181	Little Gabriel 32	M.I. Hummel	Open	Unkn.	125.00
XX-01-182	Little Gardener 74	M.I. Hummel	Open	Unkn.	110.00
XX-01-183	Little Goat Herder 200/0	M.I. Hummel	Open	Unkn.	175.00
XX-01-184	Little Goat Herder 200/I	M.I. Hummel	Open	Unkn.	220.00
XX-01-185	Little Guardian 145	M.I. Hummel	Open	Unkn.	135.00
XX-01-186	Little Helper 73	M.I. Hummel	Open	Unkn.	110.00
XX-01-187	Little Hiker 16/2/0	M.I. Hummel	Open	Unkn.	110.00
XX-01-188	Little Hiker 16/I	M.I. Hummel	Open	Unkn.	200.00
XX-01-189	Little Nurse 376	M.I. Hummel	Open	Unkn.	108-225.
XX-01-190	Little Pharmacist 322	M.I. Hummel	Open	Unkn.	220.00
XX-01-191	Little Scholar 80	M.I. Hummel	Open	Unkn.	195.00
XX-01-192	Little Shopper 96	M.I. Hummel	Open	Unkn.	130.00
XX-01-193	Little Sweeper 171/4/0	M.I. Hummel	Open	Unkn.	90.00
88-01-194	Little Sweeper 171	M.I. Hummel	Open	Unkn.	126.00
XX-01-195	Little Tailor 308	M.I. Hummel	Open	Unkn.	220.00
XX-01-196	Little Thrifty 118	M.I. Hummel	Open	Unkn.	130.00
XX-01-197	Little Tooter 214/H	M.I. Hummel	Open	Unkn.	95.00
XX-01-198	Little Tooter 214/H	M.I. Hummel	Open	Unkn.	110.00
XX-01-199	Lost Sheep 68/2/0	M.I. Hummel	Open	Unkn.	125.00
XX-01-200	Lost Sheep 68/0	M.I. Hummel	Open	Unkn.	180.00
XX-01-201	Lost Stocking 374	M.I. Hummel	Open	Unkn.	130.00
XX-01-202	Mail is Here 226	M.I. Hummel	Open	Unkn.	505.00
89-01-203	Make A Wish 475	M.I. Hummel	Open	Unkn.	175.00
XX-01-204	March Winds 43	M.I. Hummel	Open	Unkn.	145.00
XX-01-205	Max and Moritz 123	M.I. Hummel	Open	Unkn.	205.00
XX-01-206	Meditation 13/2/0	M.I. Hummel	Open	Unkn.	130.00
XX-01-207	Meditation 13/0	M.I. Hummel	Open	Unkn.	205.00
XX-01-208	Merry Wanderer 11/2/0	M.I. Hummel	Open	Unkn.	125.00
XX-01-209	Merry Wanderer 11/0	M.I. Hummel	Open	Unkn.	175.00
XX-01-210	Merry Wanderer 7/0	M.I. Hummel	Open	Unkn.	245.00
XX-01-211	Merry Wanderer 7/I	M.I. Hummel	Open	Unkn.	360.00
XX-01-212	Merry Wanderer 7/II	M.I. Hummel	Open	Unkn.	1100.00
XX-01-213	Mischief Maker 342	M.I. Hummel	Open	Unkn.	240.00
94-01-214	Morning Stroll 375	M.I. Hummel	Open	170.00	170.00
XX-01-215	Mother's Darling 175	M.I. Hummel	Open	Unkn.	195.00
XX-01-216	Mother's Helper 133	M.I. Hummel	Open	Unkn.	175.00
XX-01-217	Mountaineer 315	M.I. Hummel	Open	Unkn.	145-195.
XX-01-218	Not For You 317	M.I. Hummel	Open	Unkn.	220.00
89-01-219	One For You, One For Me 482	M.I. Hummel	Open	Unkn.	95.00
93-01-220	One Plus One 556	M.I. Hummel	Open	Unkn.	115.00
XX-01-221	On Holiday 350	M.I. Hummel	Open	Unkn.	160.00
XX-01-222	On Secret Path 386	M.I. Hummel	Open	Unkn.	225.00
XX-01-223	Out of Danger 56/B	M.I. Hummel	Open	Unkn.	265.00
93-01-224	Parade Of Lights 616	M.I. Hummel	Open	Unkn.	235.00
XX-01-225	Photographer 178	M.I. Hummel	Open	Unkn.	260.00
XX-01-226	Playmates 58/2/0	M.I. Hummel	Open	Unkn.	135.00
XX-01-227	Playmates 58/0	M.I. Hummel	Open	Unkn.	155.00
XX-01-228	Playmates 58/I	M.I. Hummel	Open	Unkn.	250.00
XX-01-229	Postman 119	M.I. Hummel	Open	Unkn.	180.00
89-01-230	Postman 119/2/0	M.I. Hummel	Open	Unkn.	90-125.00
XX-01-231	Prayer Before Battle 20	M.I. Hummel	Open	Unkn.	155.00
XX-01-232	Retreat to Safety 201/2/0	M.I. Hummel	Open	Unkn.	150.00
XX-01-233	Retreat to Safety 201/I	M.I. Hummel	Open	Unkn.	275.00
XX-01-234	Ride into Christmas 396/2/0	M.I. Hummel	Open	Unkn.	220.00
XX-01-235	Ride into Christmas 396/I	M.I. Hummel	Open	Unkn.	280-390.
XX-01-236	Ring Around the Rosie 348	M.I. Hummel	Open	Unkn.	2500.00
XX-01-237	Run-A-Way 327	M.I. Hummel	Open	Unkn.	225.00
XX-01-238	St. George 55	M.I. Hummel	Open	Unkn.	300.00
92-01-239	Scamp 553	M.I. Hummel	Open	Unkn.	105.00
XX-01-240	School Boy 82/2/0	M.I. Hummel	Open	Unkn.	130.00
XX-01-241	School Boy 82/0	M.I. Hummel	Open	Unkn.	175.00
XX-01-242	School Boy 82/II	M.I. Hummel	Open	Unkn.	415.00
XX-01-243	School Boys 170/I	M.I. Hummel	Open	Unkn.	1100.00
XX-01-244	School Girl 81/2/0	M.I. Hummel	Open	Unkn.	130.00
XX-01-245	School Girl 81/0	M.I. Hummel	Open	Unkn.	175.00
XX-01-246	School Girls 177/I	M.I. Hummel	Open	Unkn.	1100.00
XX-01-247	Sensitive Hunter 6/0	M.I. Hummel	Open	Unkn.	175.00
XX-01-248	Sensitive Hunter 6/I	M.I. Hummel	Open	Unkn.	230.00
XX-01-249	Sensitive Hunter 6/2/0	M.I. Hummel	Open	Unkn.	135.00
XX-01-250	Serenade 85/0	M.I. Hummel	Open	Unkn.	120.00
XX-01-251	Serenade 85/4/0	M.I. Hummel	Open	Unkn.	90.00
XX-01-252	Serenade 85/II	M.I. Hummel	Open	Unkn.	410.00
XX-01-253	She Loves Me, She Loves Me Not 174	M.I. Hummel	Open	Unkn.	170.00
XX-01-254	Shepherd's Boy 214/G/II	M.I. Hummel	Open	Unkn.	120.00
XX-01-255	Shepherd's Boy 64	M.I. Hummel	Open	Unkn.	200.00
XX-01-256	Shining Light 358	M.I. Hummel	Open	Unkn.	80.00
XX-01-257	Sing Along 433	M.I. Hummel	Open	Unkn.	260.00
XX-01-258	Singing Lesson 63	M.I. Hummel	Open	Unkn.	110.00
XX-01-259	Sing With Me 405	M.I. Hummel	Open	Unkn.	280.00
XX-01-260	Sister 98/2/0	M.I. Hummel	Open	Unkn.	130.00
XX-01-261	Sister 98/0	M.I. Hummel	Open	Unkn.	180.00
XX-01-262	Skier 59	M.I. Hummel	Open	Unkn.	195.00
90-01-263	Sleep Tight 424	M.I. Hummel	Open	Unkn.	200.00
XX-01-264	Smart Little Sister 346	M.I. Hummel	Open	Unkn.	225.00
XX-01-265	Soldier Boy 332	M.I. Hummel	Open	Unkn.	195.00
XX-01-266	Soloist 135/4/0	M.I. Hummel	Open	Unkn.	90.00
XX-01-267	Soloist 135	M.I. Hummel	Open	Unkn.	120.00
88-01-268	Song of Praise 454	M.I. Hummel	Open	Unkn.	90.00
88-01-269	Sound the Trumpet 457	M.I. Hummel	Open	Unkn.	90.00
88-01-270	Sounds of the Mandolin 438	M.I. Hummel	Open	Unkn.	110.00
XX-01-271	Spring Dance 353/0	M.I. Hummel	Open	Unkn.	280.00
XX-01-272	Star Gazer 132	M.I. Hummel	Open	Unkn.	195.00
XX-01-273	Stitch in Time 255	M.I. Hummel	Open	Unkn.	260.00
XX-01-274	Stitch in Time 255	M.I. Hummel	Open	Unkn.	85.00
XX-01-275	Stormy Weather 71/I	M.I. Hummel	Open	Unkn.	415.00
XX-01-276	Stormy Weather 71/2/0	M.I. Hummel	Open	Unkn.	187-270.
92-01-277	Storybook Time 458	M.I. Hummel	Open	Unkn.	231-360.
XX-01-278	Street Singer 131	M.I. Hummel	Open	Unkn.	170.00
XX-01-279	Surprise 94/3/0	M.I. Hummel	Open	Unkn.	140.00
XX-01-280	Surprise 94/I	M.I. Hummel	Open	Unkn.	260.00
XX-01-281	Sweet Greetings 352	M.I. Hummel	Open	Unkn.	195.00
XX-01-282	Sweet Music 186	M.I. Hummel	Open	Unkn.	180.00
XX-01-283	Telling Her Secret 196/0	M.I. Hummel	Open	Unkn.	270.00
88-01-284	The Accompanist 453	M.I. Hummel	Open	Unkn.	90.00

Number	Name	Artist	Edition Limit	Issue Price	Quote
91-01-285	The Guardian 455	M.I. Hummel	Open	Unkn.	155.00
94-01-286	The Poet 397	M.I. Hummel	Open	220.00	220.00
92-01-287	The Professor 320/0	M.I. Hummel	Open	Unkn.	195.00
XX-01-288	Thoughtful 415	M.I. Hummel	Open	Unkn.	205.00
XX-01-289	Timid Little Sister 394	M.I. Hummel	Open	Unkn.	390.00
XX-01-290	To Market 49/3/0	M.I. Hummel	Open	Unkn.	150.00
XX-01-291	To Market 49/0	M.I. Hummel	Open	Unkn.	250.00
XX-01-292	Trumpet Boy 97	M.I. Hummel	Open	Unkn.	120.00
89-01-293	Tuba Player 437	M.I. Hummel	Open	Unkn.	240.00
XX-01-294	Tuneful Angel 359	M.I. Hummel	Open	Unkn.	80.00
XX-01-295	Umbrella Boy 152/0/A	M.I. Hummel	Open	Unkn.	333-530.
XX-01-296	Umbrella Boy 152/II/A	M.I. Hummel	Open	Unkn.	1300.00
XX-01-297	Umbrella Girl 152/0/B	M.I. Hummel	Open	Unkn.	530.00
XX-01-298	Umbrella Girl 152/II/B	M.I. Hummel	Open	Unkn.	1300.00
XX-01-299	Village Boy 51/3/0	M.I. Hummel	Open	Unkn.	110.00
XX-01-300	Village Boy 51/2/0	M.I. Hummel	Open	Unkn.	125.00
XX-01-301	Village Boy 51/0	M.I. Hummel	Open	Unkn.	220.00
XX-01-302	Visiting an Invalid 382	M.I. Hummel	Open	Unkn.	195.00
XX-01-303	Volunteers 50/2/0	M.I. Hummel	Open	Unkn.	205.00
XX-01-304	Volunteers 50/0	M.I. Hummel	Open	Unkn.	270.00
XX-01-305	Waiter 154/0	M.I. Hummel	Open	Unkn.	195.00
XX-01-306	Waiter 154/I	M.I. Hummel	Open	Unkn.	260.00
XX-01-307	Wash Day 321	M.I. Hummel	Open	Unkn.	260.00
89-01-308	Wash Day 321/4/0	M.I. Hummel	Open	Unkn.	90.00
XX-01-309	Watchful Angel 194	M.I. Hummel	Open	Unkn.	290.00
XX-01-310	Wayside Devotion 28/II	M.I. Hummel	Open	Unkn.	395.00
XX-01-311	Wayside Devotion 28/III	M.I. Hummel	Open	Unkn.	520.00
XX-01-312	Wayside Harmony 111/3/0	M.I. Hummel	Open	Unkn.	135.00
XX-01-313	Wayside Harmony 111/I	M.I. Hummel	Open	Unkn.	245.00
XX-01-314	Weary Wanderer 204	M.I. Hummel	Open	Unkn.	225.00
XX-01-315	We Congratulate 214/E/II	M.I. Hummel	Open	Unkn.	150.00
XX-01-316	We Congratulate 220	M.I. Hummel	Open	Unkn.	145.00
90-01-317	What's New? 418	M.I. Hummel	Open	Unkn.	260.00
XX-01-318	Which Hand? 258	M.I. Hummel	Open	Unkn.	180.00
92-01-319	Whistler's Duet 413	M.I. Hummel	Open	Unkn.	250.00
XX-01-320	Whitsuntide 163	M.I. Hummel	Open	Unkn.	290.00
88-01-321	Winter Song 476	M.I. Hummel	Open	Unkn.	100.00
XX-01-322	With Loving Greetings 309	M.I. Hummel	Open	Unkn.	175.00
XX-01-323	Worship 84/0	M.I. Hummel	Open	Unkn.	145.00

Goebel/M.I. Hummel — **M.I. Hummel's Temp. Out of Production**

Number	Name	Artist	Edition Limit	Issue Price	Quote
XX-02-001	Angel Serenade 260/E	M.I. Hummel	Suspd.	Unkn.	N/A
XX-02-002	Apple Tree Boy 142/X	M.I. Hummel	Suspd.	Unkn.	17000.00
XX-02-003	Apple Tree Girl 141/X	M.I. Hummel	Suspd.	Unkn.	17000.00
XX-02-004	Blessed Child 78/I/83	M.I. Hummel	Suspd.	Unkn.	35.00
XX-02-005	Blessed Child 78/II/83	M.I. Hummel	Suspd.	Unkn.	40.00
XX-02-006	Blessed Child 78/III/83	M.I. Hummel	Suspd.	Unkn.	50.00
XX-02-007	Bookworm 3/II	M.I. Hummel	Suspd.	Unkn.	900-1200.
XX-02-008	Bookworm 3/III	M.I. Hummel	Suspd.	Unkn.	975-1300.
XX-02-009	Christ Child 18	M.I. Hummel	Suspd.	Unkn.	120-300.
XX-02-010	Donkey 260/L	M.I. Hummel	Suspd.	Unkn.	115.00
XX-02-011	Festival Harmony, with Mandolin 172/II	M.I. Hummel	Suspd.	Unkn.	325-400.
XX-02-012	Festival Harmony ,with Flute 173/II	M.I. Hummel	Suspd.	Unkn.	325-400.
XX-02-013	Flower Madonna, color 10/III/II	M.I. Hummel	Suspd.	Unkn.	375-475.
XX-02-014	Flower Madonna, white 10/III/W	M.I. Hummel	Suspd.	Unkn.	250-310.
XX-02-015	Going to Grandma's 52/I	M.I. Hummel	Suspd.	Unkn.	325-390.
XX-02-016	Good Night 260/D	M.I. Hummel	Suspd.	Unkn.	120.00
XX-02-017	Happy Traveler 109/II	M.I. Hummel	Suspd.	Unkn.	350-750.
XX-02-018	Hello 124/I	M.I. Hummel	Suspd.	Unkn.	160-230.
XX-02-019	Holy Child 70	M.I. Hummel	Suspd.	Unkn.	135-160.
XX-02-020	"Hummel" Display Plaque 187	M.I. Hummel	Suspd.	Unkn.	150-200.
XX-02-021	King, Kneeling 260/P	M.I. Hummel	Suspd.	Unkn.	430.00
XX-02-022	King, Moorish 260/N	M.I. Hummel	Suspd.	Unkn.	450.00
XX-02-023	King, Standing 260/O	M.I. Hummel	Suspd.	Unkn.	450.00
XX-02-024	Little Band 392	M.I. Hummel	Suspd.	Unkn.	132-225.
XX-02-025	Little Fiddler 2/II	M.I. Hummel	Suspd.	Unkn.	900-1200.
XX-02-026	Little Fiddler 2/III	M.I. Hummel	Suspd.	Unkn.	975-1300.
XX-02-027	Little Tooter 260/K	M.I. Hummel	Suspd.	Unkn.	140.00
XX-02-028	Lullaby 24/III	M.I. Hummel	Suspd.	Unkn.	285-450.
XX-02-029	Madonna w/o Halo, color 46/I/6	M.I. Hummel	Suspd.	Unkn.	N/A
XX-02-030	Madonna w/o Halo,white 46/I/W	M.I. Hummel	Suspd.	Unkn.	N/A
XX-02-031	Madonna Praying, color 46/III/6	M.I. Hummel	Suspd.	Unkn.	155.00
XX-02-032	Madonna Praying, white 46/0/W	M.I. Hummel	Suspd.	Unkn.	45.00
XX-02-033	Madonna Praying, white 46/I/W	M.I. Hummel	Suspd.	Unkn.	75-95.00
XX-02-034	Meditation 13/II	M.I. Hummel	Suspd.	Unkn.	275-360.
XX-02-035	Meditation 13/V	M.I. Hummel	Suspd.	Unkn.	975-1250.
XX-02-036	Merry Wanderer 7/III	M.I. Hummel	Suspd.	Unkn.	875-1200.
XX-02-037	Merry Wanderer 7/X	M.I. Hummel	Suspd.	Unkn.	17000.00
XX-02-038	Ox 260/M	M.I. Hummel	Suspd.	Unkn.	130.00
XX-02-039	School Boys 170/III	M.I. Hummel	Suspd.	Unkn.	1850-5000.
XX-02-040	School Girls 177/III	M.I. Hummel	Suspd.	Unkn.	1850-5000.
XX-02-041	Sensitive Hunter 6/II	M.I. Hummel	Suspd.	Unkn.	300-400.
XX-02-042	Sheep (Lying) 260/R	M.I. Hummel	Suspd.	Unkn.	40.00
XX-02-043	Sheep (Standing) w/ Lamb 260/H	M.I. Hummel	Suspd.	Unkn.	80.00
XX-02-044	Shepherd, Standing 260/G	M.I. Hummel	Suspd.	Unkn.	475.00
XX-02-045	Shepherd Boy, Kneeling 260/J	M.I. Hummel	Suspd.	Unkn.	270.00
XX-02-046	Spring Cheer 72	M.I. Hummel	Suspd.	Unkn.	150-200.
XX-02-047	Spring Dance 353/I	M.I. Hummel	Suspd.	Unkn.	265-500.
XX-02-048	Telling Her Secret 196/I	M.I. Hummel	Suspd.	Unkn.	240-375.
XX-02-049	To Market 49/I	M.I. Hummel	Suspd.	Unkn.	240-420.
XX-02-050	Volunteers 50/I	M.I. Hummel	Suspd.	Unkn.	240-425.
XX-02-051	Village Boy 51/I	M.I. Hummel	Suspd.	Unkn.	110-250.
XX-02-052	We Congratulate 260/F	M.I. Hummel	Suspd.	Unkn.	330.00
XX-02-053	Worship 84/V	M.I. Hummel	Suspd.	Unkn.	925-1050.
XX-02-054	16-Pc. Set Figs. only, Color, 214/A/M/I, B/I, A/K/I, C/I, D/I, E/I, F/I, G/I, H/I, J/I, K/I, L/I, M/I, N/I, O/I, 366/I	M.I. Hummel	Suspd.	Unkn.	1820.00
XX-02-055	17-Pc. Set large color 16 Figs.& Wooden Stable 260 A-R	M.I. Hummel	Suspd.	Unkn.	4540.00

Goebel/M.I. Hummel — **M.I. Hummel Collectibles Figurines Retired**

Number	Name	Artist	Edition Limit	Issue Price	Quote
XX-03-001	Jubilee 416	M.I. Hummel	Closed	200.00	204-400.
XX-03-002	Supreme Protection 364	M.I. Hummel	Closed	150.00	250.00
XX-03-003	Puppy Love I	M.I. Hummel	Closed	125.00	200-400.
XX-03-004	Strolling Along 5	M.I. Hummel	Closed	115.00	225-400.
XX-03-005	Signs Of Spring 203/2/0	M.I. Hummel	Closed	120.00	190.00
XX-03-006	Signs Of Spring 203/I	M.I. Hummel	Closed	155.00	200-900.
XX-03-007	Globe Trotter 79	M.I. Hummel	Closed	Unkn.	200-400.
XX-03-008	Farewell 65	M.I. Hummel	Closed	Unkn.	240.00

Goebel/M.I. Hummel — **M.I. Hummel Collectibles-Century Collection**

Number	Name	Artist	Edition Limit	Issue Price	Quote
86-04-001	Chapel Time 442	M.I. Hummel	Closed	500.00	850-1900.
87-04-002	Pleasant Journey 406	M.I. Hummel	Closed	500.00	1200-1895.
88-04-003	Call to Worship 441	M.I. Hummel	Closed	600.00	660-950.
89-04-004	Harmony in Four Parts 471	M.I. Hummel	Closed	850.00	1080-2000.
90-04-005	Let's Tell the World 487	M.I. Hummel	Closed	875.00	900.00
91-04-006	We Wish You The Best 600	M.I. Hummel	Closed	1300.00	1300-1500.
92-04-007	On Our Way 472	M.I. Hummel	Closed	950.00	950.00
93-04-008	Welcome Spring 635	M.I. Hummel	Closed	1085.00	1085.00
94-04-009	Rock-A-Bye 111	M.I. Hummel	Yr.Iss.	1150.00	1150.00

Goebel/M.I. Hummel — **M.I. Hummel Collectibles Nativity Components**

Number	Name	Artist	Edition Limit	Issue Price	Quote
XX-05-001	Madonna 214/A/M/0	M.I. Hummel	Open	Unkn.	120.00
XX-05-002	Infant Jesus 214/A/K/0	M.I. Hummel	Open	Unkn.	40.00
XX-05-003	St. Joseph 214/B/0	M.I. Hummel	Open	Unkn.	120.00
XX-05-004	Shepherd Standing 214/F/0	M.I. Hummel	Open	Unkn.	145.00
XX-05-005	Shepherd Kneeling 214/G/0	M.I. Hummel	Open	Unkn.	110.00
XX-05-006	Donkey 214/J/0	M.I. Hummel	Open	Unkn.	50.00
XX-05-007	Ox,214/K/0	M.I. Hummel	Open	Unkn.	50.00
XX-05-008	King, Moorish 214/L/0	M.I. Hummel	Open	Unkn.	140.00
XX-05-009	King, Kneeling 214M/0	M.I. Hummel	Open	Unkn.	130.00
XX-05-010	King, Kneeling w/ Box 214/N/0	M.I. Hummel	Open	Unkn.	131.00
XX-05-011	Lamb 214/0/0	M.I. Hummel	Open	Unkn.	17.00
XX-05-012	Flying Angel 366/0	M.I. Hummel	Open	Unkn.	85.00
XX-05-013	Little Tooter 214/14/0	M.I. Hummel	Open	Unkn.	95.00
XX-05-014	Small Camel Standing	Goebel	Open	Unkn.	160.00
XX-05-015	Small Camel Lying	Goebel	Open	Unkn.	160.00
XX-05-016	Small Camel Kneeling	Goebel	Open	Unkn.	160.00
XX-05-017	Madonna 214/A/M/I	M.I. Hummel	Open	Unkn.	160.00
XX-05-018	Infant Jesus 214/A/K/I	M.I. Hummel	Open	Unkn.	60.00
XX-05-019	St. Joseph color 214/B/I	M.I. Hummel	Open	Unkn.	160.00
XX-05-020	Good Night 214/C/I	M.I. Hummel	Open	Unkn.	80.00
XX-05-021	Angel Serenade 214/D/I	M.I. Hummel	Open	Unkn.	80.00
XX-05-022	We Congratulate 214/E/I	M.I. Hummel	Open	Unkn.	150.00
XX-05-023	Shepherd with Sheep-1 piece 214/F/I	M.I. Hummel	Open	Unkn.	165.00
XX-05-024	Shepherd Boy 214/G/I	M.I. Hummel	Open	Unkn.	120.00
XX-05-025	Little Tooter 214/H/I	M.I. Hummel	Open	Unkn.	110.00
XX-05-026	Donkey 214/J/I	M.I. Hummel	Open	Unkn.	65.00
XX-05-027	Ox 214/K/I	M.I. Hummel	Open	Unkn.	65.00
XX-05-028	King, Moorish 214/L/I	M.I. Hummel	Open	Unkn.	170.00
XX-05-029	King, Kneeling 214/M/I	M.I. Hummel	Open	Unkn.	160.00
XX-05-030	King, Kneeling w/Box 214/N/I	M.I. Hummel	Open	Unkn.	150.00
XX-05-031	Lamb 214/0/I	M.I. Hummel	Open	Unkn.	20.00
XX-05-032	Flying Angel/color 366/I	M.I. Hummel	Open	Unkn.	115.00
XX-05-033	Camel Standing	Goebel	Open	Unkn.	205.00
XX-05-034	Camel Lying	Goebel	Open	Unkn.	205.00
XX-05-035	Camel Kneeling	Goebel	Open	Unkn.	205.00
XX-05-036	Madonna-260/A	M.I. Hummel	Open	Unkn.	590.00
XX-05-037	St. Joseph 260/B	M.I. Hummel	Open	Unkn.	590.00
XX-05-038	Infant Jesus 260/C	M.I. Hummel	Open	Unkn.	120.00
XX-05-039	Good Night 260/D	M.I. Hummel	Suspd.	Unkn.	120.00
XX-05-040	Angel Serenade 260/E	M.I. Hummel	Suspd.	Unkn.	115.00
XX-05-041	We Congratulate 260/F	M.I. Hummel	Suspd.	Unkn.	330.00
XX-05-042	Shepherd, Standing 260/G	M.I. Hummel	Suspd.	Unkn.	475.00
XX-05-043	Sheep (Standing) w/ Lamb 260/H	M.I. Hummel	Suspd.	Unkn.	80.00
XX-05-044	Shepherd Boy, Kneeling 260/J	M.I. Hummel	Suspd.	Unkn.	270.00
XX-05-045	Little Tooter 260/K	M.I. Hummel	Suspd.	Unkn.	140.00
XX-05-046	Donkey 260/L	M.I. Hummel	Suspd.	Unkn.	115.00
XX-05-047	Ox 260/M	M.I. Hummel	Suspd.	Unkn.	130.00
XX-05-048	King, Moorish 260/N	M.I. Hummel	Suspd.	Unkn.	450.00
XX-05-049	King, Standing 260/O	M.I. Hummel	Suspd.	Unkn.	450.00
XX-05-050	King, Kneeling 260/P	M.I. Hummel	Suspd.	Unkn.	430.00
XX-05-051	Sheep (Lying) 260/R	M.I. Hummel	Suspd.	Unkn.	40.00
XX-05-052	Holy Family,3 Pcs., Color 214/A/M/0, B/0, A/K/0	M.I. Hummel	Open	Unkn.	270.00
XX-05-053	Holy Family 3 Pcs.,Color 214/A/M/I, B/I, A/K/I	M.I. Hummel	Open	Unkn.	380.00
XX-05-054	12-Pc. Set Figs. only, Color, 214/A/M/I, B/I, A/K/I, F/I,G/I,J/I K/I, L/I, M/I, N/I, O/I, 366/I	M.I. Hummel	Open	Unkn.	1350.00
XX-05-055	16-Pc. Set Figs. only, Color, 214/A/M/I, B/I, A/K/I, C/I, D/I, E/I, F/I, G/I, H/I, J/I, K/I, L/I, M/I, N/I, O/I, 366/I	M.I. Hummel	Suspd.	Unkn.	1820.00
XX-05-056	17-Pc. Set Large Color 16 Figs.& Wooden Stable 260 A-R	M.I. Hummel	Suspd.	Unkn.	4540.00
XX-05-057	Stable only, fits 3-pc. HUM214 Set	M.I. Hummel	Open	Unkn.	45.00
XX-05-058	Stable only, fits12 or16-pc. HUM 214/II Set	M.I. Hummel	Open	Unkn.	100.00
XX-05-059	Stable only, fits 16-piece HUM260 Set	M.I. Hummel	Open	Unkn.	400.00

Goebel/M.I. Hummel — **M.I. Hummel Collectibles-Madonna Figurines**

Number	Name	Artist	Edition Limit	Issue Price	Quote
XX-06-001	Flower Madonna, color 10/I/II	M.I. Hummel	Open	Unkn.	390.00
XX-06-002	Flower Madonna, white 10/I/W	M.I. Hummel	Open	Unkn.	165.00
XX-06-003	Madonna Holding Child, color 151/II	M.I. Hummel	Open	Unkn.	115.00
XX-06-004	Madonna Holding Child, white 151/W	M.I. Hummel	Open	Unkn.	320.00
XX-06-005	Madonna with Halo, color 45/I/6	M.I. Hummel	Open	Unkn.	115.00
XX-06-006	Madonna with Halo, white 45/I/W	M.I. Hummel	Open	Unkn.	70.00
XX-06-007	Madonna without Halo, color 46/I/6	M.I. Hummel	Suspd.	Unkn.	75.00
XX-06-008	Madonna without Halo, white 46/I/W	M.I. Hummel	Suspd.	Unkn.	50.00

Goebel/M.I. Hummel — **M.I. Hummel Collectibles-Christmas Angels**

Number	Name	Artist	Edition Limit	Issue Price	Quote
93-07-001	Angel in Cloud 585	M.I. Hummel	Open	25.00	25.00
93-07-002	Angel with Lute 580	M.I. Hummel	Open	25.00	25.00
93-07-003	Angel with Trumpet 586	M.I. Hummel	Open	25.00	25.00
93-07-004	Celestial Musician 578	M.I. Hummel	Open	25.00	25.00
93-07-005	Festival Harmony with Flute 577	M.I. Hummel	Open	25.00	25.00
93-07-006	Festival Harmony with Mandolin 576	M.I. Hummel	Open	25.00	25.00
93-07-007	Gentle Song 582	M.I. Hummel	Open	25.00	25.00
93-07-008	Heavenly Angel 575	M.I. Hummel	Open	25.00	25.00
93-07-009	Prayer of Thanks 581	M.I. Hummel	Open	25.00	25.00
93-07-010	Song of Praise 579	M.I. Hummel	Open	25.00	25.00

Goebel/M.I. Hummel — **First Edition M.I. Hummel Miniatures**

Number	Name	Artist	Edition Limit	Issue Price	Quote
91-08-001	Accordion Boy -37225	M.I. Hummel	Suspd.	105.00	105.00
89-08-002	Apple Tree Boy -37219	M.I. Hummel	Suspd.	115.00	125-250.
90-08-003	Baker -37222	M.I. Hummel	Suspd.	100.00	105-125.
92-08-004	Bavarian Church (Display) -37370	M.I. Hummel	Retrd.	60.00	60.00
88-08-005	Bavarian Cottage (Display) -37355	M.I. Hummel	Retrd.	60.00	64.00
90-08-006	Bavarian Marketsquare Bridge(Dsply) -37358	M.I. Hummel	Retrd.	110.00	110.00
88-08-007	Bavarian Village (Display) -37356	M.I. Hummel	Retrd.	100.00	100.00
91-08-008	Busy Student -37226	M.I. Hummel	Suspd.	105.00	105.00
91-08-009	Countryside School (Display) -37365	M.I. Hummel	Retrd.	100.00	100.00
90-08-010	Cinderella -37223	M.I. Hummel	Suspd.	115.00	115-175.
89-08-011	Doll Bath -37214	M.I. Hummel	Suspd.	95.00	115-175.
92-08-012	Goose Girl -37238	M.I. Hummel	Suspd.	130.00	150-168.
89-08-013	Little Fiddler -37211	M.I. Hummel	Suspd.	90.00	120-200.
89-08-014	Little Sweeper -37212	M.I. Hummel	Suspd.	90.00	125-200.
90-08-015	Marketsquare Hotel (Display)-37359	M.I. Hummel	Retrd.	70.00	100.00
90-08-016	Marketsquare Flower Stand (Display) -37360	M.I. Hummel	Retrd.	35.00	45.00

Company Number	Name	Series Artist	Edition Limit	Issue Price	Quote
89-08-017	Merry Wanderer -37213	M.I. Hummel	Suspd.	95.00	120-200.
91-08-018	Merry Wanderer Dealer Plaque -37229	M.I. Hummel	Retrd.	130.00	130.00
89-08-019	Postman -37217	M.I. Hummel	Suspd.	95.00	100-200.
91-08-020	Roadside Shrine (Display)-37366	M.I. Hummel	Retrd.	60.00	60.00
92-08-021	School Boy -37236	M.I. Hummel	Suspd.	120.00	150-170.
91-08-022	Serenade -37228	M.I. Hummel	Suspd.	105.00	105.00
92-08-023	Snow-Covered Mountain (Display)-37371	M.I. Hummel	Retrd.	100.00	100.00
89-08-024	Stormy Weather -37215	M.I. Hummel	Suspd.	115.00	175-250.
92-08-025	Trees (Display)-37369	M.I. Hummel	Retrd.	40.00	40.00
89-08-026	Visiting an Invalid -37218	M.I. Hummel	Suspd.	105.00	115-140.
90-08-027	Waiter -37221	M.I. Hummel	Suspd.	100.00	125-250.
92-08-028	Wayside Harmony -37237	M.I. Hummel	Suspd.	140.00	140.00
91-08-029	We Congratulate -37227	M.I. Hummel	Suspd.	130.00	130.00
Goebel/M.I. Hummel		**M.I. Hummel Collectors Club Exclusives**			
77-09-001	Valentine Gift 387	M.I. Hummel	Closed	45.00	340-400.
78-09-002	Smiling Through Plaque 690	M.I. Hummel	Closed	50.00	80-275.
79-09-003	Bust of Sister-M.I.Hummel HU-3	G. Skrobek	Closed	75.00	210.00
80-09-004	Valentine Joy 399	M.I. Hummel	Closed	95.00	166-275.
81-09-005	Daisies Don't Tell 380	M.I. Hummel	Closed	80.00	150-200.
82-09-005	It's Cold 421	M.I. Hummel	Closed	80.00	150-193.
83-09-007	What Now? 422	M.I. Hummel	Closed	90.00	150.00
83-09-008	Valentine Gift Mini Pendant	R. Olszewski	Closed	85.00	180-250.
84-09-009	Coffee Break 409	M.I. Hummel	Closed	90.00	150.00
85-09-010	Smiling Through 408/0	M.I. Hummel	Closed	125.00	200.00
86-09-011	Birthday Candle 440	M.I. Hummel	Closed	95.00	133.00
86-09-012	What Now? Mini Pendant	R. Olszewski	Closed	125.00	275.00
87-09-013	Morning Concert 447	M.I. Hummel	Closed	98.00	155.00
87-09-014	Little Cocopah Indian Girl	T. DeGrazia	Closed	140.00	175-300.
88-09-015	The Surprise 431	M.I. Hummel	Closed	125.00	295.00
89-09-016	Mickey and Minnie	H. Fischer	Closed	275.00	350-500.
89-09-017	Hello World 429	M.I. Hummel	Closed	130.00	200-250.
90-09-018	I Wonder 486	M.I. Hummel	Closed	140.00	175-250.
91-09-019	Gift From A Friend 485	M.I. Hummel	Closed	160.00	160.00
91-09-020	Miniature Morning Concert w/ Display	R. Olszewski	Closed	175.00	190.00
92-09-021	My Wish Is Small 463/0	M.I. Hummel	5/94	170.00	170.00
92-09-022	Cheeky Fellow 554	M.I. Hummel	5/94	120.00	120.00
93-09-023	I Didn't Do It 623	M.I. Hummel	5/95	175.00	175.00
93-09-024	Sweet As Can Be 541	M.I. Hummel	5/95	127.00	127.00
94-09-025	Little Visitor 563	M.I. Hummel	5/96	210.00	210.00
94-09-026	Little Troubadour 558	M.I. Hummel	5/96	145.00	145.00
94-09-027	Miniature Honey Lover Pendant	M.I. Hummel	5/96	N/A	N/A
Goebel/M.I. Hummel		**Special Edition M.I. Hummel Anniversary Figurine For 5 & 10 & 15 Year Club Members**			
90-10-001	Flower Girl 548 (5 year)	M.I. Hummel	Open	105.00	120.00
90-10-002	The Little Pair 449 (10 year)	M.I. Hummel	Open	170.00	190.00
91-10-003	Honey Lover 312 (15 year)	M.I. Hummel	Open	190.00	196.00
Goebel/M.I. Hummel		**M.I. Hummel Tree Toppers**			
94-11-001	Heavenly Angel 755	M.I. Hummel	Open	450.00	450.00
Goebel Miniatures		**Children's Series**			
80-01-001	Blumenkinder-Courting 630-P	R. Olszewski	Closed	55.00	480.00
81-01-002	Summer Days 631-P	R. Olszewski	Closed	65.00	290.00
82-01-003	Out and About 632-P	R. Olszewski	Closed	85.00	300.00
83-01-004	Backyard Frolic 633-P	R. Olszewski	Closed	65.00	100-250.
85-01-005	Snow Holiday 635-P	R. Olszewski	Closed	75.00	100-125.
86-01-006	Clowning Around 636-P	R. Olszewski	Closed	85.00	195.00
87-01-007	Carrousel Days 637-P	R. Olszewski	Closed	85.00	165-245.
88-01-008	Little Ballerina 638-P	R. Olszewski	Closed	85.00	100-150.
88-01-009	Children's Display (small)	R. Olszewski	Closed	45.00	60.00
84-01-010	Grandpa 634-P	R. Olszewski	Closed	75.00	125-165.
90-01-011	Building Blocks Castle (large) 968-D	R. Olszewski	Closed	75.00	100.00
Goebel Miniatures		**Wildlife Series**			
80-02-001	Chipping Sparrow 620-P	R. Olszewski	Open	55.00	85.00
81-02-002	Owl-Daylight Encounter 621-P	R. Olszewski	Closed	65.00	320-340.
82-02-003	Western Bluebird 622-P	R. Olszewski	Closed	65.00	195.00
83-02-004	Red-Winged Blackbird 623-P	R. Olszewski	Closed	65.00	150-245.
84-02-005	Winter Cardinal 624-P	R. Olszewski	Closed	65.00	200.00
85-02-006	American Goldfinch 625-P	R. Olszewski	Open	65.00	90-120.00
86-02-007	Autumn Blue Jay 626-P	R. Olszewski	Open	65.00	135-205.
87-02-008	Mallard Duck 627-P	R. Olszewski	Open	75.00	185.00
88-02-009	Spring Robin 628-P	R. Olszewski	Closed	75.00	165-195.
87-02-010	Country Display (small) 940-D	R. Olszewski	Open	45.00	65.00
90-02-011	Wildlife Display (large) 957-D	R. Olszewski	Open	85.00	110.00
89-02-012	Hooded Oriole 629-P	R. Olszewski	Open	80.00	115-175.
90-02-013	Hummingbird 696-P	R. Olszewski	Closed	85.00	125.00
Goebel Miniatures		**Women's Series**			
80-03-001	Dresden Dancer 610-P	R. Olszewski	Closed	55.00	520.00
81-03-002	The Hunt With Hounds 611-P	R. Olszewski	Closed	75.00	385.00
82-03-003	Precious Years 612-P	R. Olszewski	Closed	65.00	250.00
83-03-004	On The Avenue 613-P	R. Olszewski	Closed	65.00	95-150.00
84-03-005	Roses 614-P	R. Olszewski	Closed	65.00	95-150.00
86-03-006	I Do 615-P	R. Olszewski	Closed	85.00	100-235.
89-03-007	Women's Display (small) 950-D	R. Olszewski	Closed	40.00	65.00
Goebel Miniatures		**Historical Series**			
80-04-001	Capodimonte 600-P	R. Olszewski	Closed	90.00	535.00
81-04-002	Masquerade-St. Petersburg 601-P	R. Olszewski	Closed	65.00	260.00
83-04-003	The Cherry Pickers 602-P	R. Olszewski	Closed	85.00	290.00
84-04-004	Moor With Spanish Horse 603-P	R. Olszewski	Open	85.00	110-200.
85-04-005	Floral Bouquet Pompadour 604-P	R. Olszewski	Open	85.00	115-130.
87-04-006	Meissen Parrot 605-P	R. Olszewski	Open	85.00	110-150.
88-04-007	Minton Rooster 606-P	R. Olszewski	7,500	85.00	110-195.
89-04-008	Farmer w/Doves 607-P	R. Olszewski	Open	85.00	110-150.
90-04-009	Gentleman Fox Hunt 616-P	R. Olszewski	Open	145.00	180.00
88-04-010	Historical Display 943-D	R. Olszewski	Suspd.	45.00	60.00
90-04-011	English Country Garden 970-D	R. Olszewski	Open	85.00	105.00
92-04-012	Poultry Seller 608-G	R. Olszewski	Open	200.00	230.00
Goebel Miniatures		**Oriental Series**			
80-05-001	Kuan Yin 640-W	R. Olszewski	Closed	40.00	245.00
82-05-002	The Geisha 641-P	R. Olszewski	Closed	65.00	150-250.
85-05-003	Tang Horse 642-P	R. Olszewski	Open	65.00	95-175.00
86-05-004	The Blind Men and the Elephant 643-P	R. Olszewski	Open	70.00	100-175.
87-05-005	Chinese Water Dragon 644-P	R. Olszewski	Closed	70.00	165-175.
87-05-006	Oriental Display (small) 945-D	R. Olszewski	Suspd.	45.00	65.00
89-05-007	Tiger Hunt 645-P	R. Olszewski	Open	85.00	100-105.
90-05-008	Chinese Temple Lion 646-P	R. Olszewski	Open	90.00	110-125.
90-05-009	Empress' Garden Display 967-D	R. Olszewski	Open	95.00	130.00

Company Number	Name	Series Artist	Edition Limit	Issue Price	Quote
Goebel Miniatures		**Americana Series**			
81-06-001	The Plainsman 660-B	R. Olszewski	Closed	45.00	240.00
82-06-002	American Bald Eagle 661-B	R. Olszewski	Closed	45.00	285.00
83-06-003	She Sounds the Deep 662-B	R. Olszewski	Closed	45.00	70-145.00
84-06-004	Eyes on the Horizon 663-B	R. Olszewski	Closed	45.00	70-125.00
85-06-005	Central Park Sunday 664-B	R. Olszewski	Closed	45.00	70-115.00
86-06-006	Carrousel Ride 665-B	R. Olszewski	Closed	45.00	70-115.00
87-06-007	To The Bandstand 666-B	R. Olszewski	Closed	45.00	70-110.00
89-06-008	Blacksmith 676-B	R. Olszewski	Closed	55.00	145-165.
86-06-009	Americana Display 951-D	R. Olszewski	Suspd.	80.00	105.00
Goebel Miniatures		**The American Frontier Collection**			
87-07-001	The End of the Trail 340-B	Frazier	Closed	80.00	80-125.00
87-07-002	The First Ride 330-B	Rogers	Open	85.00	100.00
87-07-003	Eight Count 310-B	Pounder	Open	75.00	90.00
87-07-004	Grizzly's Last Stand 320-B	Jonas	Open	65.00	65-85.00
87-07-005	Indian Scout and Buffalo 300-B	Bonheur	Closed	95.00	95-135.00
87-07-006	The Bronco Buster 350-B	Remington	Closed	80.00	80.00
87-07-007	American Frontier Museum Display 947-D	R. Olszewski	Open	80.00	110.00
Goebel Miniatures		**Portrait of America/Saturday Evening Post (Pewter)**			
88-08-001	The Doctor and the Doll 361-P	N. Rockwell	Suspd.	85.00	100.00
88-08-002	No Swimming 360-P	N. Rockwell	Open	85.00	85.00
88-08-003	Marbles Champion 362-P	N. Rockwell	Open	85.00	85.00
88-08-004	Check-Up 363-P	N. Rockwell	Open	85.00	85.00
88-08-005	Triple Self-Portrait 364-P	N. Rockwell	Suspd.	85.00	100.00
88-08-006	Bottom of the Sixth 365-P	N. Rockwell	Suspd.	85.00	100.00
89-08-007	Bottom Drawer 366-P	N. Rockwell	7,500	85.00	85.00
88-08-008	Rockwell Display-952-D	N. Rockwell	Open	80.00	100.00
91-08-009	Soldier 368-P	N. Rockwell	Open	85.00	100.00
91-08-010	Mother 369-P	N. Rockwell	Open	85.00	100.00
91-08-011	Home Coming Vignette-Soldier/Mother 990-D	N. Rockwell	Closed	200.00	300.00
Goebel Miniatures		**Disney-Snow White**			
87-09-001	Sneezy 161-P	R. Olszewski	Closed	60.00	85.00
87-09-002	Doc 162-P	R. Olszewski	Closed	60.00	85-200.00
87-09-003	Sleepy 163-P	R. Olszewski	Closed	60.00	85.00
87-09-004	Happy 164-P	R. Olszewski	Closed	60.00	85.00
87-09-005	Bashful 165-P	R. Olszewski	Closed	60.00	85.00
87-09-006	Grumpy 166-P	R. Olszewski	Closed	60.00	85.00
87-09-007	Dopey 167-P	R. Olszewski	Closed	60.00	250-300.
87-09-008	Snow White 168-P	R. Olszewski	Closed	60.00	95-120.00
90-09-009	Snow White's Prince 170-P	R. Olszewski	19,500	80.00	115.00
87-09-010	Cozy Cottage Display 941-D	R. Olszewski	Closed	35.00	320.00
88-09-011	House In The Woods Display 944-D	R. Olszewski	Open	60.00	110.00
90-09-012	The Wishing Well Display 969-D	R. Olszewski	Open	65.00	85.00
91-09-013	Castle Courtyard Display 981-D	R. Olszewski	Open	105.00	125.00
92-09-014	Snow White's Witch 183-P	R. Olszewski	Open	100.00	115.00
92-09-015	Snow White's Queen 182-P	R. Olszewski	Open	100.00	115.00
92-09-016	Path In The Woods 996-D	R. Olszewski	Open	140.00	150.00
Goebel Miniatures		**Disney-Pinocchio**			
90-10-001	Geppetto/Figaro 682-P	R. Olszewski	Open	90.00	110.00
90-10-002	Gideon 683-P	R. Olszewski	Open	75.00	100.00
90-10-003	J. Worthington Foulfellow 684-P	R. Olszewski	Open	95.00	115.00
90-10-004	Jiminy Cricket 685-P	R. Olszewski	Open	75.00	100.00
90-10-005	Pinocchio 686-P	R. Olszewski	Open	75.00	110.00
91-10-006	Little Street Lamp Display 964-D	R. Olszewski	Open	65.00	80.00
90-10-007	Geppetto's Toy Shop Display 965-D	R. Olszewski	Open	95.00	120.00
91-10-008	Stromboli 694-P	R. Olszewski	Open	95.00	120.00
91-10-009	Blue Fairy 693-P	R. Olszewski	Open	95.00	120.00
91-10-010	Stromboli's Street Wagon 979-D	R. Olszewski	Open	105.00	125.00
92-10-011	Monstro The Whale 985-D	R. Olszewski	Open	120.00	130.00
Goebel Miniatures		**Disney-Cinderella**			
91-11-001	Anastasia 172-P	R.Olszewski	Open	85.00	100.00
91-11-002	Jaq 173-P	R.Olszewski	Open	80.00	90.00
91-11-003	Drizella 174-P	R.Olszewski	Open	85.00	100.00
91-11-004	Lucifer 175-P	R.Olszewski	Open	80.00	90.00
91-11-005	Cinderella 176-P	R.Olszewski	Open	85.00	105.00
91-11-006	Gus 177-P	R.Olszewski	Open	80.00	90.00
91-11-007	Stepmother 178-P	R.Olszewski	Open	85.00	100.00
91-11-008	Prince Charming 179-P	R.Olszewski	Open	85.00	100.00
91-11-009	Fairy Godmother 180-P	R.Olszewski	Open	85.00	100.00
91-11-010	Footman 181-P	R.Olszewski	Open	85.00	100.00
91-11-011	Cinderella's Dream Castle 976-D	R.Olszewski	Open	95.00	115.00
91-11-012	Cinderella's Coach Display 978-D	R.Olszewski	Open	95.00	120.00
Goebel Miniatures		**Mickey Mouse**			
90-12-001	The Sorcerer's Apprentice 171-P	R. Olszewski	Suspd.	80.00	165-200.00
90-12-002	Fantasia Living Brooms 972-D	R. Olszewski	Suspd.	85.00	165.00
Goebel Miniatures		**Night Before Christmas (1st Edition)**			
90-13-001	Sugar Plum Boy 687-P	R. Olszewski	5,000	70.00	95.00
90-13-002	Yule Tree 688-P	R. Olszewski	5,000	90.00	105.00
90-13-003	Sugar Plum Girl 689-P	R. Olszewski	5,000	70.00	95.00
90-13-004	St. Nicholas 690-P	R. Olszewski	5,000	95.00	120.00
90-13-005	Eight Tiny Reindeer 691-P	R. Olszewski	5,000	110.00	130.00
90-13-006	Mama & Papa 692-P	R. Olszewski	5,000	110.00	125.00
91-13-007	Up To The Housetop 966-D	R. Olszewski	5,000	95.00	105.00
Goebel Miniatures		**Special Release-Alice in Wonderland**			
82-14-001	Alice In the Garden 670-P	R. Olszewski	Closed	60.00	835.00
83-14-002	Down the Rabbit Hole 671-P	R. Olszewski	Closed	75.00	540.00
84-14-003	The Cheshire Cat 672-P	R. Olszewski	Closed	75.00	520.00
Goebel Miniatures		**Special Release-Wizard of Oz**			
84-15-001	Scarecrow 673-P	R. Olszewski	Closed	75.00	455.00
85-15-002	Tinman 674-P	R. Olszewski	Closed	80.00	355.00
86-15-003	The Cowardly Lion 675-P	R. Olszewski	Closed	85.00	160-325.
87-15-004	The Wicked Witch 676-P	R. Olszewski	Closed	85.00	105.00
88-15-005	The Munchkins 677-P	R. Olszewski	Closed	85.00	100.00
87-15-006	Oz Display 942-D	R. Olszewski	Closed	45.00	45.00
XX-15-007	Oz Display Set	R. Olszewski	Closed	410.00	1900-2000.
92-15-008	Dorothy/Glinda 695-P	R. Olszewski	Closed	135.00	155.00
92-15-009	Good-Bye to Oz Display 980-D	R. Olszewski	Closed	110.00	160.00
Goebel Miniatures		**Three Little Pigs**			
89-16-001	Little Sticks Pig 678-P	R. Olszewski	7,500	75.00	105.00
90-16-002	Little Straw Pig 679-P	R. Olszewski	7,500	75.00	105.00
91-16-003	Little Bricks Pig 680-P	R. Olszewski	Closed	75.00	105.00
91-16-004	The Hungry Wolf 681-P	R. Olszewski	Closed	80.00	105.00
89-16-005	Three Little Pigs House 956-D	R. Olszewski	7,500	50.00	125.00

Company Number	Name	Series Artist	Edition Limit	Issue Price	Quote
Goebel Miniatures		**Pendants**			
90-17-001	Hummingbird 697-P	R. Olszewski	Open	125.00	150.00
91-17-002	Rose Pendant 220-P	R. Olszewski	Open	135.00	150.00
91-17-003	Daffodil Pendant 221-P	R. Olszewski	Open	135.00	150.00
91-17-004	Chrysanthemum Pendant 222-P	R. Olszewski	Open	135.00	150.00
91-17-005	Poinsettia Pendant 223-P	R. Olszewski	Open	135.00	150.00
Goebel Miniatures		**Nativity Collection**			
91-18-001	Mother/Child 440-P	R. Olszewski	10,000	120.00	150.00
91-18-002	Joseph 401-P	R. Olszewski	10,000	95.00	125.00
91-18-003	Joyful Cherubs 403-P	R. Olszewski	10,000	130.00	175.00
91-18-004	The Stable Donkey 402-P	R. Olszewski	10,000	95.00	125.00
91-18-005	Holy Family Display 982-D	R. Olszewski	10,000	85.00	90.00
92-18-006	Balthazar 405-P	R. Olszewski	10,000	135.00	195.00
92-18-007	Melchoir 404-P	R. Olszewski	10,000	135.00	195.00
92-18-008	Gaspar 406-P	R. Olszewski	10,000	135.00	195.00
92-18-009	3 Kings Display 987-D	R. Olszewski	10,000	85.00	100.00
94-18-010	Guardian Angel 407-P	R. Olszewski	10,000	200.00	200.00
94-18-011	Final Nativity Display 991-D	R. Olszewski	10,000	260.00	260.00
Goebel Miniatures		**Special Releases**			
91-19-001	Portrait Of The Artist 658-P	R. Olszewski	Open	195.00	210.00
92-19-002	Summer Days Collector Plaque 659-P	R. Olszewski	Open	130.00	155.00
94-19-003	Dresden Timepiece 450-P	R. Olszewski	750	1250.00	1250.00
Goebel Miniatures		**Disney-Peter Pan**			
92-20-001	Peter Pan 184-P	R. Olszewski	Open	90.00	125.00
92-20-002	Wendy 185-P	R. Olszewski	Open	90.00	110.00
92-20-003	John 186-P	R. Olszewski	Open	90.00	110.00
92-20-004	Michael 187-P	R. Olszewski	Open	90.00	110.00
92-20-005	Nana 189-P	R. Olszewski	Open	95.00	110.00
92-20-006	Peter Pan's London 986-D	R. Olszewski	Open	125.00	135.00
94-20-007	Neverland Display 997-D	R. Olszewski	Open	150.00	150.00
94-20-008	Captain Hook 188-P	R. Olszewski	Open	160.00	160.00
94-20-009	Smee 190-P	R. Olszewski	Open	140.00	140.00
94-20-010	Lost Boy-Fox 191-P	R. Olszewski	Open	130.00	130.00
94-20-011	Lost Boy-Rabbit 192-P	R. Olszewski	Open	130.00	130.00
Goebel Miniatures		**Archive Releases**			
92-21-001	Autumn Blue Jay 626-P	R. Olszewski	Open	125.00	125.00
93-21-002	Cherry Pickers 602-P	R. Olszewski	Open	175.00	175.00
93-21-003	Kuan Yin 640-W	R. Olszewski	Open	100.00	100.00
Goebel Miniatures		**Jack & The Beanstalk**			
94-22-001	Jack & The Beanstalk Display 999-D	R. Olszewski	Open	225.00	250.00
94-22-002	Jack's Mom 741-P	R. Olszewski	Open	145.00	175.00
Gorham		**A Boy And His Dog (Four Seasons)**			
72-01-001	A Boy Meets His Dog	N. Rockwell	2,500	200.00	1575.00
72-01-002	Adventurers Between Adventures	N. Rockwell	2,500	Set	Set
72-01-003	The Mysterious Malady	N. Rockwell	2,500	Set	Set
72-01-004	Pride of Parenthood	N. Rockwell	2,500	Set	Set
Gorham		**Young Love (Four Seasons)**			
73-02-001	Downhill Daring	N. Rockwell	2,500	250.00	1100.00
73-02-002	Beguiling Buttercup	N. Rockwell	2,500	Set	Set
73-02-003	Flying High	N. Rockwell	2,500	Set	Set
73-02-004	A Scholarly Pace	N. Rockwell	2,500	Set	Set
Gorham		**Four Ages of Love (Four Seasons)**			
74-03-001	Gaily Sharing Vintage Times	N. Rockwell	2,500	300.00	1600.00
74-03-002	Sweet Song So Young	N. Rockwell	2,500	Set	Set
74-03-003	Flowers In Tender Bloom	N. Rockwell	2,500	Set	Set
74-03-004	Fondly Do We Remember	N. Rockwell	2,500	Set	Set
Gorham		**Grandpa and Me (Four Seasons)**			
75-04-001	Gay Blades	N. Rockwell	2,500	300.00	1000.00
75-04-002	Day Dreamers	N. Rockwell	2,500	Set	Set
75-04-003	Goin' Fishing	N. Rockwell	2,500	Set	Set
75-04-004	Pensive Pals	N. Rockwell	2,500	Set	Set
Gorham		**Me and My Pal (Four Seasons)**			
76-05-001	A Licking Good Bath	N. Rockwell	2,500	300.00	1250.00
76-05-002	Young Man's Fancy	N. Rockwell	2,500	Set	Set
76-05-003	Fisherman's Paradise	N. Rockwell	2,500	Set	Set
76-05-004	Disastrous Daring	N. Rockwell	2,500	Set	Set
Gorham		**Grand Pals (Four Seasons)**			
77-06-001	Snow Sculpturing	N. Rockwell	2,500	350.00	675.00
77-06-002	Soaring Spirits	N. Rockwell	2,500	Set	Set
77-06-003	Fish Finders	N. Rockwell	2,500	Set	Set
77-06-004	Ghostly Gourds	N. Rockwell	2,500	Set	Set
Gorham		**Going On Sixteen (Four Seasons)**			
78-07-001	Chilling Chore	N. Rockwell	2,500	400.00	675.00
78-07-002	Sweet Serenade	N. Rockwell	2,500	Set	Set
78-07-003	Shear Agony	N. Rockwell	2,500	Set	Set
78-07-004	Pilgrimage	N. Rockwell	2,500	Set	Set
Gorham		**Tender Years (Four Seasons)**			
79-08-001	New Year Look	N. Rockwell	2,500	500.00	550.00
79-08-002	Spring Tonic	N. Rockwell	2,500	Set	Set
79-08-003	Cool Aid	N. Rockwell	2,500	Set	Set
79-08-004	Chilly Reception	N. Rockwell	2,500	Set	Set
Gorham		**A Helping Hand (Four Seasons)**			
80-09-001	Year End Court	N. Rockwell	2,500	650.00	700.00
80-09-002	Closed For Business	N. Rockwell	2,500	Set	Set
80-09-003	Swatter's Right	N. Rockwell	2,500	Set	Set
80-09-004	Coal Seasons Coming	N. Rockwell	2,500	Set	Set
Gorham		**Dad's Boy (Four Seasons)**			
81-10-001	Ski Skills	N. Rockwell	2,500	750.00	800.00
81-10-002	In His Spirit	N. Rockwell	2,500	Set	Set
81-10-003	Trout Dinner	N. Rockwell	2,500	Set	Set
81-10-004	Careful Aim	N. Rockwell	2,500	Set	Set
Gorham		**Rockwell**			
74-11-001	Weighing In	N. Rockwell	Closed	40.00	125.00
74-11-002	Missing Tooth	N. Rockwell	Closed	30.00	75.00
74-11-003	Tiny Tim	N. Rockwell	Closed	30.00	75.00
74-11-004	At The Vets	N. Rockwell	Closed	25.00	65.00
74-11-005	Fishing	N. Rockwell	Closed	50.00	100.00
74-11-006	Batter Up	N. Rockwell	Closed	40.00	90.00

Company Number	Name	Series Artist	Edition Limit	Issue Price	Quote
74-11-007	Skating	N. Rockwell	Closed	37.50	85.00
74-11-008	Captain	N. Rockwell	Closed	45.00	95.00
75-11-009	Boy And His Dog	N. Rockwell	Closed	37.50	85.00
75-11-010	No Swimming	N. Rockwell	Closed	35.00	80.00
75-11-011	Old Mill Pond	N. Rockwell	Closed	45.00	95.00
76-11-012	Saying Grace	N. Rockwell	Closed	75.00	120.00
76-11-013	God Rest Ye Merry Gentlemen	N. Rockwell	Closed	50.00	800.00
76-11-014	Tackled (Ad Stand)	N. Rockwell	Closed	35.00	85.00
76-11-015	Independence	N. Rockwell	Closed	40.00	150.00
76-11-016	Marriage License	N. Rockwell	Closed	50.00	175.00
76-11-017	The Occultist	N. Rockwell	Closed	50.00	145-175.
81-11-018	Day in the Life Boy II	N. Rockwell	Closed	75.00	85.00
81-11-019	Wet Sport	N. Rockwell	Closed	85.00	85.00
82-11-020	April Fool's (At The Curiosity Shop)	N. Rockwell	Closed	55.00	110.00
82-11-021	Tackled (Rockwell Name Signed)	N. Rockwell	Closed	45.00	70.00
82-11-022	A Day in the Life Boy III	N. Rockwell	Closed	85.00	85.00
82-11-023	A Day in the Life Girl III	N. Rockwell	Closed	85.00	85.00
81-11-024	Christmas Dancers	N. Rockwell	7,500	130.00	130.00
82-11-025	Marriage License	N. Rockwell	5,000	110.00	400.00
82-11-026	Saying Grace	N. Rockwell	5,000	110.00	450.00
82-11-027	Triple Self Portrait	N. Rockwell	5,000	300.00	500.00
80-11-028	Jolly Coachman	N. Rockwell	7,500	75.00	125.00
82-11-029	Merrie Christmas	N. Rockwell	7,500	75.00	75.00
83-11-030	Facts of Life	N. Rockwell	7,500	110.00	120.00
83-11-031	Antique Dealer	N. Rockwell	7,500	130.00	130.00
83-11-032	Christmas Goose	N. Rockwell	7,500	75.00	75.00
84-11-033	Serenade	N. Rockwell	7,500	95.00	95.00
84-11-034	Card Tricks	N. Rockwell	7,500	110.00	110.00
84-11-035	Santa's Friend	N. Rockwell	7,500	75.00	75.00
85-11-036	Puppet Maker	N. Rockwell	7,500	130.00	130.00
85-11-037	The Old Sign Painter	N. Rockwell	7,500	130.00	130.00
86-11-038	Drum For Tommy	N. Rockwell	Annual	90.00	90.00
87-11-039	Santa Planning His Annual Visit	N. Rockwell	7,500	95.00	95.00
88-11-040	Home for the Holidays	N. Rockwell	7,500	100.00	100.00
88-11-041	Gary Cooper in Hollywood	N. Rockwell	15,000	90.00	90.00
88-11-042	Cramming	N. Rockwell	15,000	80.00	80.00
88-11-043	Dolores & Eddie	N. Rockwell	15,000	75.00	75.00
88-11-044	Confrontation	N. Rockwell	15,000	75.00	75.00
88-11-045	The Diary	N. Rockwell	15,000	80.00	80.00
Gorham		**Miniature Christmas Figurines**			
79-12-001	Tiny Tim	N. Rockwell	Yr.Iss.	15.00	20.00
80-12-002	Santa Plans His Trip	N. Rockwell	Yr.Iss.	15.00	15.00
81-12-003	Yuletide Reckoning	N. Rockwell	Yr.Iss.	20.00	20.00
82-12-004	Checking Good Deeds	N. Rockwell	Yr.Iss.	20.00	20.00
83-12-005	Santa's Friend	N. Rockwell	Yr.Iss.	20.00	20.00
84-12-006	Downhill Daring	N. Rockwell	Yr.Iss.	20.00	20.00
85-12-007	Christmas Santa	T. Nast	Yr.Iss.	20.00	20.00
86-12-008	Christmas Santa	T. Nast	Yr.Iss.	25.00	25.00
87-12-009	Annual Thomas Nast Santa	T. Nast	Yr.Iss.	25.00	25.00
Gorham		**Miniatures**			
81-13-001	Young Man's Fancy	N. Rockwell	Closed	55.00	55.00
81-13-002	Beguiling Buttercup	N. Rockwell	Closed	45.00	45.00
81-13-003	Gay Blades	N. Rockwell	Closed	45.00	70.00
81-13-004	Sweet Song So Young	N. Rockwell	Closed	55.00	55.00
81-13-005	Snow Sculpture	N. Rockwell	Closed	45.00	70.00
81-13-006	Sweet Serenade	N. Rockwell	Closed	45.00	45.00
81-13-007	At the Vets	N. Rockwell	Closed	27.50	39.50
81-13-008	Boy Meets His Dog	N. Rockwell	Closed	37.50	37.50
81-13-009	Downhill Daring	N. Rockwell	Closed	45.00	70.00
81-13-010	Flowers in Tender Bloom	N. Rockwell	Closed	60.00	60.00
82-13-011	Triple Self Portrait	N. Rockwell	Closed	60.00	175.00
82-13-012	Marriage License	N. Rockwell	Closed	60.00	75.00
82-13-013	The Runaway	N. Rockwell	Closed	50.00	50.00
82-13-014	Vintage Times	N. Rockwell	Closed	50.00	50.00
82-13-015	The Annual Visit	N. Rockwell	Closed	50.00	75.00
83-13-016	Trout Dinner	N. Rockwell	15,000	60.00	60.00
84-13-017	Ghostly Gourds	N. Rockwell	Closed	60.00	60.00
84-13-018	Years End Court	N. Rockwell	Closed	60.00	60.00
84-13-019	Shear Agony	N. Rockwell	Closed	60.00	60.00
84-13-020	Pride of Parenthood	N. Rockwell	Closed	50.00	50.00
84-13-021	Goin Fishing	N. Rockwell	Closed	60.00	60.00
84-13-022	Careful Aims	N. Rockwell	Closed	55.00	55.00
84-13-023	In His Spirit	N. Rockwell	Closed	60.00	60.00
85-13-024	To Love & Cherish	N. Rockwell	Closed	32.50	32.50
85-13-025	Spring Checkup	N. Rockwell	Closed	60.00	60.00
85-13-026	Engineer	N. Rockwell	Closed	55.00	55.00
85-13-027	Best Friends	N. Rockwell	Closed	27.50	27.50
85-13-028	Muscle Bound	N. Rockwell	Closed	30.00	30.00
85-13-029	New Arrival	N. Rockwell	Closed	32.50	32.50
85-13-030	Little Red Truck	N. Rockwell	Closed	25.00	25.00
86-13-031	The Old Sign Painter	N. Rockwell	Closed	70.00	75.00
86-13-032	The Graduate	N. Rockwell	Closed	30.00	30.00
86-13-033	Football Season	N. Rockwell	Closed	60.00	60.00
86-13-034	Lemonade Stand	N. Rockwell	Closed	60.00	60.00
86-13-035	Welcome Mat	N. Rockwell	Closed	70.00	70.00
86-13-036	Shoulder Ride	N. Rockwell	Closed	50.00	60.00
86-13-037	Morning Walk	N. Rockwell	Closed	60.00	60.00
86-13-038	Little Angel	N. Rockwell	Closed	50.00	60.00
87-13-039	Starstruck	N. Rockwell	15,000	75.00	75.00
87-13-040	The Prom Dress	N. Rockwell	15,000	75.00	75.00
87-13-041	The Milkmaid	N. Rockwell	15,000	80.00	85.00
87-13-042	Cinderella	N. Rockwell	15,000	70.00	75.00
87-13-043	Springtime	N. Rockwell	15,000	65.00	65.00
87-13-044	Babysitter	N. Rockwell	15,000	75.00	75.00
87-13-045	Between The Acts	N. Rockwell	15,000	60.00	60.00
Gorham		**Old Timers (Four Seasons Miniatures)**			
82-14-001	Canine Solo	N. Rockwell	2,500	250.00	250.00
82-14-002	Sweet Surprise	N. Rockwell	2,500	Set	Set
82-14-003	Lazy Days	N. Rockwell	2,500	Set	Set
82-14-004	Fancy Footwork	N. Rockwell	2,500	Set	Set
Gorham		**Life With Father (Four Seasons Miniatures)**			
83-15-001	Big Decision	N. Rockwell	2,500	250.00	250.00
83-15-002	Blasting Out	N. Rockwell	2,500	Set	Set
83-15-003	Cheering The Champs	N. Rockwell	2,500	Set	Set
83-15-004	A Tough One	N. Rockwell	2,500	Set	Set
Gorham		**Old Buddies (Four Seasons)**			
84-16-001	Shared Success	N. Rockwell	2,500	250.00	250.00
84-16-002	Hasty Retreat	N. Rockwell	2,500	Set	Set
84-16-003	Final Speech	N. Rockwell	2,500	Set	Set

Company Number	Name	Series Artist	Edition Limit	Issue Price	Quote
84-16-004	Endless Debate	N. Rockwell	2,500	Set	Set
Gorham		**Traveling Salesman (Four Seasons)**			
85-17-001	Horse Trader	N. Rockwell	2,500	275.00	275.00
85-17-002	Expert Salesman	N. Rockwell	2,500	Set	Set
85-17-003	Traveling Salesman	N. Rockwell	2,500	Set	Set
85-17-004	Country Pedlar	N. Rockwell	2,500	Set	Set
Granget		**Granget Wood Carvings**			
XX-01-001	Barn Owl, 20 inches	G. Granget	250	2000.00	N/A
73-01-002	Black Grouse, large	G. Granget	250	2800.00	N/A
73-01-003	Golden Eagle, large	G. Granget	250	2000.00	N/A
73-01-004	Lynx, large	G. Granget	250	1600.00	N/A
73-01-005	Mallard, large	G. Granget	250	2000.00	N/A
XX-01-006	Peregrine Falcon, large	G. Granget	250	2250.00	N/A
73-01-007	Rooster, large	G. Granget	250	2400.00	N/A
73-01-008	Black Grouse, small	G. Granget	1,000	700.00	N/A
73-01-009	Fox, small	G. Granget	1,000	650.00	N/A
73-01-010	Golden Eagle, small	G. Granget	1,000	550.00	N/A
73-01-011	Lynx, small	G. Granget	1,000	400.00	N/A
73-01-012	Mallard, small	G. Granget	1,000	500.00	N/A
73-01-013	Partridge, small	G. Granget	1,000	550.00	N/A
XX-01-014	Peregrine Falcon, small	G. Granget	1,000	500.00	N/A
73-01-015	Rooster, small	G. Granget	1,000	600.00	N/A
73-01-016	Wild Boar, small	G. Granget	1,000	275.00	N/A
XX-01-017	Wild Sow with Young, large	G. Granget	1,000	2800.00	N/A
73-01-018	Fox, large	G. Granget	200	2800.00	N/A
73-01-019	Partridge. large	G. Granget	200	2400.00	N/A
73-01-020	Wild Boar, large	G. Granget	200	2400.00	N/A
XX-01-021	Wild Sow with Young, small	G. Granget	200	600.00	N/A
XX-01-022	Barn Owl, 10 inches	G. Granget	2,500	600.00	N/A
XX-01-023	Barn Owl, 12.5 inches	G. Granget	1,500	700.00	N/A
XX-01-024	Peregrine Falcon, medium	G. Granget	1,500	700.00	N/A
XX-01-025	Ring-necked Pheasant, large	G. Granget	Unkn.	2250.00	N/A
XX-01-026	Ring-necked Pheasant, small	G. Granget	Unkn.	500.00	N/A
Great American Taylor Collectibles		**Old World Santas**			
88-01-001	Jangle Claus-Ireland 335s	L. Smith	Retrd.	20.00	N/A
88-01-002	Hans Von Claus-Germany 337s	L. Smith	Retrd.	20.00	N/A
88-01-003	Ching Chang Claus-China 338s	L. Smith	Retrd.	20.00	N/A
88-01-004	Kris Kringle Claus-Switzerland 339s	L. Smith	Retrd.	20.00	N/A
88-01-005	Jingle Claus-England 336s	L. Smith	Retrd.	20.00	N/A
89-01-006	Rudy Claus-Austria 410s	L. Smith	Retrd.	20.00	30-45.00
89-01-007	Noel Claus-Belguim 412s	L. Smith	Retrd.	20.00	30-45.00
89-01-008	Pierre Claus-France 414s	L. Smith	Retrd.	20.00	30-45.00
89-01-009	Nicholai Claus-Russia 413s	L. Smith	Retrd.	20.00	30-45.00
89-01-010	Yule Claus-Germany 411s	L. Smith	Retrd.	20.00	30-45.00
90-01-011	Matts Claus-Sweden 430s	L. Smith	Retrd.	20.00	30-65.00
90-01-012	Vander Claus-Holland 433s	L. Smith	Retrd.	20.00	30-65.00
90-01-013	Sven Claus-Norway 432s	L. Smith	Retrd.	20.00	30-65.00
90-01-014	Cedric Claus-England 434s	L. Smith	Retrd.	20.00	30-65.00
90-01-015	Mario Claus-Italy 431s	L. Smith	Retrd.	20.00	30-65.00
91-01-016	Mitch Claus-England 437s	L. Smith	Retrd.	25.00	31-49.00
91-01-017	Samuel Claus-USA 436s	L. Smith	Retrd.	25.00	31-49.00
91-01-018	Duncan Claus-Scotland 439s	L. Smith	Retrd.	25.00	31-49.00
91-01-019	Benjamin Claus-Israel 438s	L. Smith	Retrd.	25.00	31-49.00
91-01-020	Boris Claus-Russia 435s	L. Smith	Retrd.	25.00	31-49.00
92-01-021	Mickey Claus-Ireland 701s	L. Smith	12/94	25.00	25.00
92-01-022	Jacques Claus-France 702s	L. Smith	12/94	25.00	25.00
92-01-023	Terry Claus-Denmark 703s	L. Smith	12/94	25.00	25.00
92-01-024	José Claus-Spain 704s	L. Smith	12/94	25.00	25.00
92-01-025	Stu Claus-Poland 705s	L. Smith	12/94	25.00	25.00
93-01-026	Otto Claus-Germany 707s	L. Smith	12/95	27.50	27.50
93-01-027	Franz Claus-Switzerland 706s	L. Smith	12/95	27.50	27.50
93-01-028	Bjorn Claus-Sweden 709s	L. Smith	12/95	27.50	27.50
93-01-029	Ryan Claus-Canada 710s	L. Smith	12/95	27.50	27.50
93-01-030	Vito Claus-Italy 708s	L. Smith	12/95	27.50	27.50
94-01-031	Angus Claus-Scotland 713s	L. Smith	12/96	29.00	29.00
94-01-032	Ivan Claus-Russia 712s	L. Smith	12/96	29.00	29.00
94-01-033	Desmond Claus-England 715s	L. Smith	12/96	29.00	29.00
94-01-034	Gord Claus-Canada 714s	L. Smith	12/96	29.00	29.00
94-01-035	Wilhelm Claus-Holland 711s	L. Smith	12/96	29.00	29.00
Great American Taylor Collectibles		**Collectors' Guild**			
93-02-001	William Claus-USA 700s	L. Smith	12/94	35.00	35.00
Dave Grossman Creations		**Saturday Evening Post**			
90-01-001	No Swimming NRP-901	Rockwell-Inspired	Open	50.00	50.00
90-01-002	Daydreamer NRP-902	Rockwell-Inspired	Open	55.00	55.00
90-01-003	Prom Dress NRP-903	Rockwell-Inspired	Open	60.00	60.00
90-01-004	Bedside Manner NRP-904	Rockwell-Inspired	Open	65.00	65.00
90-01-005	Runaway NRP-905	Rockwell-Inspired	Open	130.00	130.00
90-01-006	Big Moment NRP-906	Rockwell-Inspired	Retrd.	100.00	100.00
90-01-007	Doctor and Doll NRP-907	Rockwell-Inspired	Retrd.	110.00	150.00
90-01-008	Bottom of the Sixth NRP-908	Rockwell-Inspired	Open	165.00	165.00
91-01-009	Catching The Big One NRP-909	Rockwell-Inspired	Open	75.00	75.00
91-01-010	Gramps NRP-910	Rockwell-Inspired	Open	85.00	85.00
91-01-011	The Pharmacist NRP-911	Rockwell-Inspired	Open	70.00	70.00
92-01-012	Choosin Up NRP-912	Rockwell-Inspired	7,500	110.00	110.00
92-01-013	Missed NRP-914	Rockwell-Inspired	Open	110.00	110.00
92-01-014	Gone Fishing NRP-915	Rockwell-Inspired	Open	65.00	65.00
92-01-015	After the Prom NRP-916	Rockwell-Inspired	Open	75.00	75.00
92-01-016	Locomotive NRC-603	Rockwell-Inspired	Open	110.00	110.00
93-01-017	Baby's First Step NRC-604	Rockwell-Inspired	Open	100.00	100.00
93-01-018	Bride & Groom NRC-605	Rockwell-Inspired	Open	100.00	100.00
93-01-019	Bed Time NRC-606	Rockwell-Inspired	Open	100.00	100.00
94-01-020	Little Mother NRC-607	Rockwell-Inspired	Open	75.00	75.00
94-01-021	For A Good Boy NRC-608	Rockwell-Inspired	Open	100.00	100.00
94-01-022	Almost Grown Up NRC-609	Rockwell-Inspired	Open	75.00	75.00
94-01-023	A Visit with Rockwell (100th Aniversary) -NRP-100	Rockwell-Inspired	1,994	100.00	100.00
Dave Grossman Creations		**Saturday Evening Post-Miniatures**			
91-02-001	A Boy Meets His Dog BMR-01	Rockwell-Inspired	Retrd.	35.00	35.00
91-02-002	Downhill Daring BMR-02	Rockwell-Inspired	Retrd.	40.00	40.00
91-02-003	Flowers in Tender Bloom BMR-03	Rockwell-Inspired	Retrd.	32.00	32.00
91-02-004	Fondly Do We Remember BMR-04	Rockwell-Inspired	Retrd.	30.00	30.00
91-02-005	In His Spirit BMR-05	Rockwell-Inspired	Retrd.	30.00	30.00
91-02-006	Pride of Parenthood BMR-06	Rockwell-Inspired	Retrd.	35.00	35.00
91-02-007	Sweet Serenade BMR-07	Rockwell-Inspired	Retrd.	32.00	32.00
91-02-008	Sweet Song So Young BMR-08	Rockwell-Inspired	Retrd.	30.00	30.00
Dave Grossman Creations		**Norman Rockwell America Collection-Large Limited Edition**			
89-03-001	Doctor and Doll NRP-300	Rockwell-Inspired	Retrd.	150.00	150.00
89-03-002	Bottom of the Sixth NRP-307	Rockwell-Inspired	Retrd.	190.00	190.00
89-03-003	Runaway NRP-310	Rockwell-Inspired	Retrd.	190.00	190.00
89-03-004	Weigh-In NRP-311	Rockwell-Inspired	Retrd.	160.00	175.00
Dave Grossman Creations		**Norman Rockwell America Collection**			
89-04-001	Doctor and Doll NRP-600	Rockwell-Inspired	Retrd.	90.00	90.00
89-04-002	Locomotive NRC-603	Rockwell-Inspired	Retrd.	110.00	110.00
89-04-003	First Haircut NRC-604	Rockwell-Inspired	Retrd.	75.00	75.00
89-04-004	First Visit NRC-605	Rockwell-Inspired	Retrd.	110.00	110.00
89-04-005	First Day Home NRC-606	Rockwell-Inspired	Retrd.	80.00	80.00
89-04-006	Bottom of the Sixth NRC-607	Rockwell-Inspired	Retrd.	140.00	140.00
89-04-007	Runaway NRC-610	Rockwell-Inspired	Retrd.	140.00	140.00
89-04-008	Weigh-In NRC-611	Rockwell-Inspired	Retrd.	120.00	120.00
93-04-009	Missed NRP-914	Rockwell-Inspired	7,500	110.00	110.00
93-04-010	Gone Fishing NRP-915	Rockwell-Inspired	7,500	65.00	65.00
93-04-011	After The Prom NRP-916	Rockwell-Inspired	7,500	75.00	75.00
Dave Grossman Creations		**Norman Rockwell America Collection-Miniatures**			
89-05-001	First Haircut MRC-904	Rockwell-Inspired	Retrd.	45.00	45.00
89-05-002	First Day Home MRC-906	Rockwell-Inspired	Retrd.	45.00	45.00
Dave Grossman Creations		**Emmett Kelly-Circus Collection**			
86-06-001	I Love You EK-601	B. Leighton-Jones	15,000	30.00	30.00
86-06-002	Wallstreet EK-602	B. Leighton-Jones	15,000	35.00	35.00
86-06-003	Spotlight EK-603	B. Leighton-Jones	15,000	34.00	34.00
86-06-004	Thinker EK-604	B. Leighton-Jones	15,000	34.00	34.00
86-06-005	Feels Like Rain EK-605	B. Leighton-Jones	Retrd.	34.00	34.00
86-06-006	The Titanic EK-606	B. Leighton-Jones	Retrd.	50.00	50.00
86-06-007	All Washed Up EK-607	B. Leighton-Jones	Retrd.	48.00	48.00
86-06-008	The Cheaters EK-608	B. Leighton-Jones	Retrd.	70.00	70.00
86-06-009	Till Death Do Us Part EK-609	B. Leighton-Jones	Retrd.	48.00	48.00
86-06-010	Where Did I Go Wrong EK-610	B. Leighton-Jones	Retrd.	80.00	80.00
86-06-011	Fore EK-611	B. Leighton-Jones	15,000	30.00	30.00
86-06-012	Christmas Carol EK-612	B. Leighton-Jones	Retrd.	35.00	35.00
87-06-013	Cabbage Routine EK-613	B. Leighton-Jones	Retrd.	30.00	30.00
87-06-014	Fisherman EK-614	B. Leighton-Jones	15,000	40.00	40.00
87-06-015	Big Game Hunter EK-615	B. Leighton-Jones	15,000	35.00	35.00
87-06-016	Wagon Wheel EK-616	B. Leighton-Jones	Retrd.	40.00	40.00
87-06-017	Self-Portrait EK-617	B. Leighton-Jones	15,000	50.00	50.00
88-06-018	Dressing Room EK-618	B. Leighton-Jones	15,000	55.00	55.00
88-06-019	Feather Act EK-619	B. Leighton-Jones	15,000	35.00	35.00
89-06-020	Missing Parents EK-620	B. Leighton-Jones	15,000	35.00	35.00
89-06-021	Cotton Candy EK-621	B. Leighton-Jones	15,000	55.00	55.00
89-06-022	Choosing Sides EK-622	B. Leighton-Jones	15,000	50.00	50.00
90-06-023	A Dog's Life EK-623	B. Leighton-Jones	15,000	52.00	52.00
90-06-024	The Proposal EK-624	B. Leighton-Jones	Retrd.	65.00	65.00
90-06-025	With This Ring EK-625	B. Leighton-Jones	Retrd.	65.00	65.00
91-06-026	Emmett The Snowman-EK626	B. Leighton-Jones	15,000	45.00	45.00
91-06-027	Artful Dodger EK-627	B. Leighton-Jones	15,000	35.00	35.00
91-06-028	Emmett At Bat EK-628	B. Leighton-Jones	15,000	35.00	35.00
92-06-029	Christmas Tunes EK-629	B. Leighton-Jones	15,000	40.00	40.00
92-06-030	Emmett The Caddy EK-630	B. Leighton-Jones	15,000	45.00	45.00
92-06-031	Emmett At the Organ EK-631	B. Leighton-Jones	15,000	50.00	50.00
92-06-032	Emmett At Work EK-632	B. Leighton-Jones	15,000	45.00	45.00
92-06-033	Look At The Birdie EK-633	B. Leighton-Jones	15,000	40.00	40.00
92-06-034	Hard Time EK-634	B. Leighton-Jones	15,000	45.00	45.00
92-06-035	Lion Tamer EK-635	B. Leighton-Jones	15,000	55.00	55.00
92-06-036	Sunday Driver EK-636	B. Leighton-Jones	15,000	55.00	55.00
92-06-037	Dear Emmett Ek-637	B. Leighton-Jones	15,000	45.00	45.00
94-06-038	Stuck on Bowling Ek-638	B. Leighton-Jones	15,000	45.00	45.00
94-06-039	Parenthood Ek-639	B. Leighton-Jones	15,000	55.00	55.00
94-06-040	I've Got It Ek-640	B. Leighton-Jones	15,000	45.00	45.00
Dave Grossman Creations		**Native American Series**			
91-07-001	Lone Wolf	E. Roberts	7,500	55.00	55.00
92-07-002	Tortoise Lady	E. Roberts	7,500	60.00	60.00
Dave Grossman Creations		**Gone With The Wind Series**			
87-08-001	Tara GWW-5	Unknown	Retrd.	70.00	70.00
88-08-002	Mammy GWW-6	Unknown	Retrd.	70.00	70.00
91-08-003	Prissy GWW-8	Unknown	Open	50.00	50.00
92-08-004	Scarlett in Green Dress GWW-9	Unknown	Open	70.00	70.00
93-08-005	Belle Waiting GWW-10	Unknown	Open	70.00	70.00
93-08-006	Rhett & Bonnie GWW-11	Unknown	Open	80.00	80.00
93-08-007	Rhett in White Suit GWW-12	Unknown	Open	70.00	70.00
94-08-008	Scarlett in Bar B Que Dress GWW-14	Unknown	Open	70.00	70.00
94-08-009	Gerald O'Hara GWW-15	Unknown	Open	70.00	70.00
Dave Grossman Creations		**6" Gone With The Wind Series**			
94-09-001	Scarlett GWW-101	Unknown	Open	40.00	40.00
94-09-002	Ashley GWW-102	Unknown	Open	40.00	40.00
94-09-003	Rhett GW-104	Unknown	Open	40.00	40.00
Dave Grossman Designs		**Norman Rockwell Collection**			
73-01-001	Redhead NR-01	Rockwell-Inspired	Retrd.	20.00	150.00
73-01-002	Back To School NR-02	Rockwell-Inspired	Retrd.	20.00	35.00
73-01-003	Caroller NR-03	Rockwell-Inspired	Retrd.	22.50	35.00
73-01-004	Daydreamer NR-04	Rockwell-Inspired	Retrd.	22.50	50.00
73-01-005	No Swimming NR-05	Rockwell-Inspired	Retrd.	25.00	50.00
73-01-006	Love Letter NR-06	Rockwell-Inspired	Retrd.	25.00	60.00
73-01-007	Lovers NR-07	Rockwell-Inspired	Retrd.	45.00	66.00
73-01-008	Lazybones NR-08	Rockwell-Inspired	Retrd.	30.00	450.00
73-01-009	Leapfrog NR-09	Rockwell-Inspired	Retrd.	50.00	550-750.
73-01-010	Schoolmaster NR-10	Rockwell-Inspired	Retrd.	55.00	300.00
73-01-011	Marble Players NR-11	Rockwell-Inspired	Retrd.	60.00	450-1100.
73-01-012	Doctor & Doll NR-12	Rockwell-Inspired	Retrd.	65.00	150.00
74-01-013	Friends In Need NR-13	Rockwell-Inspired	Retrd.	45.00	100.00
74-01-014	Springtime '33 NR-14	Rockwell-Inspired	Retrd.	30.00	45.00
74-01-015	Summertime '33 NR-15	Rockwell-Inspired	Retrd.	45.00	45.00
74-01-016	Baseball NR-16	Rockwell-Inspired	Retrd.	45.00	125-150.
74-01-017	See America First NR-17	Rockwell-Inspired	Retrd.	50.00	85.00
74-01-018	Take Your Medicine NR-18	Rockwell-Inspired	Retrd.	50.00	95.00
75-01-019	Discovery NR-20	Rockwell-Inspired	Retrd.	55.00	160.00
75-01-020	Big Moment NR-21	Rockwell-Inspired	Retrd.	60.00	120.00
75-01-021	Circus NR-22	Rockwell-Inspired	Retrd.	55.00	100.00
75-01-022	Barbershop Quartet NR-23	Rockwell-Inspired	Retrd.	100.00	950.00
76-01-023	Drum For Tommy NRC-24	Rockwell-Inspired	Retrd.	40.00	80.00
77-01-024	Springtime '35 NR-19	Rockwell-Inspired	Retrd.	50.00	55.00
77-01-025	Pals NR-25	Rockwell-Inspired	Retrd.	60.00	75.00
78-01-026	Young Doctor NRD-26	Rockwell-Inspired	Retrd.	100.00	175.00
78-01-027	First Day of School NR-27	Rockwell-Inspired	Retrd.	100.00	135.00
78-01-028	Magic Potion NR-28	Rockwell-Inspired	Retrd.	84.00	100.00
78-01-029	At the Doctor NR-29	Rockwell-Inspired	Retrd.	108.00	160.00
79-01-030	Teacher's Pet NRA-30	Rockwell-Inspired	Retrd.	35.00	80.00

Number	Name	Artist	Edition Limit	Issue Price	Quote
79-01-031	Dreams of Long Ago NR-31	Rockwell-Inspired	Retrd.	100.00	160.00
79-01-032	Grandpa's Ballerina NR-32	Rockwell-Inspired	Retrd.	100.00	110.00
79-01-033	Back From Camp NR-33	Rockwell-Inspired	Retrd.	96.00	110.00
80-01-034	The Toss NR-34	Rockwell-Inspired	Retrd.	110.00	110.00
80-01-035	Exasperated Nanny NR-35	Rockwell-Inspired	Retrd.	96.00	96.00
80-01-036	Hankerchief NR-36	Rockwell-Inspired	Retrd.	110.00	110.00
80-01-037	Santa's Good Boys NR-37	Rockwell-Inspired	Retrd.	90.00	90.00
81-01-038	Spirit of Education NR-38	Rockwell-Inspired	Retrd.	96.00	110.00
82-01-039	A Visit With Rockwell NR-40	Rockwell-Inspired	Retrd.	120.00	120.00
82-01-040	Croquet NR-41	Rockwell-Inspired	Retrd.	100.00	110.00
82-01-041	American Mother NRG-42	Rockwell-Inspired	Retrd.	100.00	110.00
83-01-042	Country Critic NR-43	Rockwell-Inspired	Retrd.	75.00	75.00
83-01-043	Graduate NR-44	Rockwell-Inspired	Retrd.	30.00	35.00
83-01-044	Scotty's Surprise NRS-20	Rockwell-Inspired	Retrd.	25.00	25.00
84-01-045	Scotty's Home Plate NR-46	Rockwell-Inspired	Retrd.	30.00	40.00
86-01-046	Red Cross NR-47	Rockwell-Inspired	Retrd.	67.00	75.00
87-01-047	Young Love NR-48	Rockwell-Inspired	Retrd.	70.00	70.00
88-01-048	Wedding March NR-49	Rockwell-Inspired	Retrd.	110.00	110.00

Dave Grossman Designs — **Norman Rockwell Collection Miniatures**

Number	Name	Artist	Edition Limit	Issue Price	Quote
79-02-001	Redhead NR-201	Rockwell-Inspired	Retrd.	18.00	50.00
79-02-002	Back To School NR-202	Rockwell-Inspired	Retrd.	18.00	25.00
79-02-003	Caroller NR-203	Rockwell-Inspired	Retrd.	20.00	25.00
79-02-004	Daydreamer NR-204	Rockwell-Inspired	Retrd.	20.00	30.00
79-02-005	No Swimming NR-205	Rockwell-Inspired	Retrd.	22.00	30.00
79-02-006	Love Letter NR-206	Rockwell-Inspired	Retrd.	26.00	30.00
79-02-007	Lovers NR-207	Rockwell-Inspired	Retrd.	28.00	30.00
79-02-008	Lazybones NR-208	Rockwell-Inspired	Retrd.	22.00	30.00
79-02-009	Leapfrog NR-209	Rockwell-Inspired	Retrd.	32.00	32.00
79-02-010	Schoolmaster NR-210	Rockwell-Inspired	Retrd.	34.00	40.00
79-02-011	Marble Players NR-211	Rockwell-Inspired	Retrd.	36.00	38.00
79-02-012	Doctor and Doll NR-212	Rockwell-Inspired	Retrd.	40.00	40.00
80-02-013	Friends In Need NR-213	Rockwell-Inspired	Retrd.	30.00	40.00
80-02-014	Springtime '33 NR-214	Rockwell-Inspired	Retrd.	24.00	80.00
80-02-015	Summertime '33 NR-215	Rockwell-Inspired	Retrd.	22.00	25.00
80-02-016	Baseball NR-216	Rockwell-Inspired	Retrd.	40.00	50.00
80-02-017	See America First NR-217	Rockwell-Inspired	Retrd.	28.00	40.00
80-02-018	Take Your Medicine NR-218	Rockwell-Inspired	Retrd.	36.00	40.00
82-02-019	Springtime '35 NR-219	Rockwell-Inspired	Retrd.	24.00	30.00
82-02-020	Discovery NR-220	Rockwell-Inspired	Retrd.	35.00	45.00
82-02-021	Big Moment NR-221	Rockwell-Inspired	Retrd.	36.00	40.00
82-02-022	Circus NR-222	Rockwell-Inspired	Retrd.	35.00	40.00
82-02-023	Barbershop Quartet NR-223	Rockwell-Inspired	Retrd.	40.00	50.00
82-02-024	Drum For Tommy NRC-224	Rockwell-Inspired	Retrd.	25.00	30.00
83-02-025	Santa On the Train NR-245	Rockwell-Inspired	Retrd.	35.00	55.00
84-02-026	Pals NR-225	Rockwell-Inspired	Retrd.	25.00	25.00
84-02-027	Young Doctor NRD-226	Rockwell-Inspired	Retrd.	30.00	50.00
84-02-028	First Day of School NR-227	Rockwell-Inspired	Retrd.	35.00	35.00
84-02-029	Magic Potion NR-228	Rockwell-Inspired	Retrd.	30.00	40.00
84-02-030	At the Doctor's NR-229	Rockwell-Inspired	Retrd.	35.00	35.00
84-02-031	Dreams of Long Ago NR-231	Rockwell-Inspired	Retrd.	30.00	30.00

Dave Grossman Designs — **Norman Rockwell Collection-Large Limited Editions**

Number	Name	Artist	Edition Limit	Issue Price	Quote
74-03-001	Doctor and Doll NR-100	Rockwell-Inspired	Retrd.	300.00	1600.00
74-03-002	See America First NR-103	Rockwell-Inspired	Retrd.	100.00	395.00
75-03-003	No Swimming NR-101	Rockwell-Inspired	Retrd.	150.00	450.00
75-03-004	Baseball NR-102	Rockwell-Inspired	Retrd.	125.00	450.00
79-03-005	Leapfrog NR-104	Rockwell-Inspired	Retrd.	440.00	750.00
81-03-006	Dreams of Long Ago NR-105	Rockwell-Inspired	Retrd.	500.00	750.00
82-03-007	Circus NR-106	Rockwell-Inspired	Retrd.	500.00	550.00
84-03-008	Marble Players NR-107	Rockwell-Inspired	Retrd.	500.00	750.00

Dave Grossman Designs — **Norman Rockwell Collection-American Rockwell Series**

Number	Name	Artist	Edition Limit	Issue Price	Quote
81-04-001	Breaking Home Ties NRV-300	Rockwell-Inspired	Retrd.	2000.00	2300.00
82-04-002	Lincoln NRV-301	Rockwell-Inspired	Retrd.	300.00	375.00
82-04-003	Thanksgiving NRV-302	Rockwell-Inspired	Retrd.	2500.00	2650.00

Dave Grossman Designs — **Norman Rockwell Collection-Lladro Series**

Number	Name	Artist	Edition Limit	Issue Price	Quote
82-05-001	Lladro Love Letter RL-400	Rockwell-Inspired	Retrd.	650.00	925-1200.
82-05-002	Summer Stock RL-401	Rockwell-Inspired	Retrd.	750.00	775-950.
82-05-003	Practice Makes Perfect RL-402	Rockwell-Inspired	Retrd.	725.00	795.00
82-05-004	Young Love RL-403	Rockwell-Inspired	Retrd.	450.00	975.00
82-05-005	Daydreamer RL-404	Rockwell-Inspired	Retrd.	450.00	1500.00
82-05-006	Court Jester RL-405	Rockwell-Inspired	Retrd.	600.00	900.00
82-05-007	Springtime RL-406	Rockwell-Inspired	Retrd.	450.00	1050-1800.

Dave Grossman Designs — **Norman Rockwell Collection-Rockwell Club Series**

Number	Name	Artist	Edition Limit	Issue Price	Quote
81-06-001	Young Artist RCC-01	Rockwell-Inspired	Retrd.	96.00	105.00
82-06-002	Diary RCC-02	Rockwell-Inspired	Retrd.	35.00	50.00
83-06-003	Runaway Pants RCC-03	Rockwell-Inspired	Retrd.	65.00	75.00
84-06-004	Gone Fishing RCC-04	Rockwell-Inspired	Retrd.	30.00	55.00

Dave Grossman Designs — **Norman Rockwell Collection-Tom Sawyer Series**

Number	Name	Artist	Edition Limit	Issue Price	Quote
75-07-001	Whitewashing the Fence TS-01	Rockwell-Inspired	Retrd.	60.00	200.00
76-07-002	First Smoke TS-02	Rockwell-Inspired	Retrd.	60.00	200.00
77-07-003	Take Your Medicine TS-03	Rockwell-Inspired	Retrd.	63.00	170.00
78-07-004	Lost In Cave TS-04	Rockwell-Inspired	Retrd.	70.00	145.00

Dave Grossman Designs — **Norman Rockwell Collection-Tom Sawyer Miniatures**

Number	Name	Artist	Edition Limit	Issue Price	Quote
83-08-001	Whitewashing the Fence TSM-01	Rockwell-Inspired	Retrd.	40.00	50.00
83-08-002	First Smoke TSM-02	Rockwell-Inspired	Retrd.	40.00	45.00
83-08-003	Take Your Medicine TSM-04	Rockwell-Inspired	Retrd.	40.00	45.00
83-08-004	Lost In Cave TSM-05	Rockwell-Inspired	Retrd.	40.00	45.00

Dave Grossman Designs — **Norman Rockwell Collection-Huck Finn Series**

Number	Name	Artist	Edition Limit	Issue Price	Quote
79-09-001	The Secret HF-01	Rockwell-Inspired	Retrd.	110.00	130.00
80-09-002	Listening HF-02	Rockwell-Inspired	Retrd.	110.00	120.00
80-09-003	No Kings HF-03	Rockwell-Inspired	Retrd.	110.00	110.00
80-09-004	Snake Escapes HF-04	Rockwell-Inspired	Retrd.	110.00	120.00

Dave Grossman Designs — **Norman Rockwell Collection-Boy Scout Series**

Number	Name	Artist	Edition Limit	Issue Price	Quote
81-10-001	Can't Wait BSA-01	Rockwell-Inspired	Retrd.	30.00	50.00
81-10-002	Scout Is Helpful BSA-02	Rockwell-Inspired	Retrd.	38.00	45.00
81-10-003	Physically Strong BSA-03	Rockwell-Inspired	Retrd.	56.00	60.00
81-10-004	Good Friends BSA-04	Rockwell-Inspired	Retrd.	58.00	65.00
81-10-005	Good Turn BSA-05	Rockwell-Inspired	Retrd.	65.00	100.00
81-10-006	Scout Memories BSA-06	Rockwell-Inspired	Retrd.	65.00	70.00
82-10-007	Guiding Hand BSA-07	Rockwell-Inspired	Retrd.	58.00	60.00
83-10-008	Tomorrow's Leader BSA-08	Rockwell-Inspired	Retrd.	45.00	55.00

Dave Grossman Designs — **Norman Rockwell Collection-Country Gentlemen Series**

Number	Name	Artist	Edition Limit	Issue Price	Quote
82-11-001	Turkey Dinner CG-01	Rockwell-Inspired	Retrd.	85.00	90.00
82-11-002	Bringing Home the Tree CG-02	Rockwell-Inspired	Retrd.	60.00	75.00
82-11-003	Pals CG-03	Rockwell-Inspired	Retrd.	36.00	45.00
82-11-004	The Catch CG-04	Rockwell-Inspired	Retrd.	50.00	60.00
82-11-005	On the Ice CG-05	Rockwell-Inspired	Retrd.	50.00	60.00
82-11-006	Thin Ice CG-06	Rockwell-Inspired	Retrd.	50.00	60.00

Dave Grossman Designs — **Norman Rockwell Collection-Select Collection, Ltd.**

Number	Name	Artist	Edition Limit	Issue Price	Quote
82-12-001	Boy & Mother With Puppies SC-1001	Rockwell-Inspired	Retrd.	27.50	N/A
82-12-002	Girl With Dolls In Crib SC-1002	Rockwell-Inspired	Retrd.	26.50	N/A
82-12-003	Young Couple SC-1003	Rockwell-Inspired	Retrd.	27.50	N/A
82-12-004	Football Player SC-1004	Rockwell-Inspired	Retrd.	22.00	N/A
82-12-005	Father With Child SC-1005	Rockwell-Inspired	Retrd.	22.00	N/A
82-12-006	Girl Bathing Dog SC-1006	Rockwell-Inspired	Retrd.	26.50	N/A
82-12-007	Helping Hand SC-1007	Rockwell-Inspired	Retrd.	32.00	N/A
82-12-008	Lemonade Stand SC-1008	Rockwell-Inspired	Retrd.	32.00	N/A
82-12-009	Shaving Lesson SC-1009	Rockwell-Inspired	Retrd.	30.00	N/A
82-12-010	Save Me SC-1010	Rockwell-Inspired	Retrd.	35.00	N/A

Dave Grossman Designs — **Norman Rockwell Collection-Pewter Figurines**

Number	Name	Artist	Edition Limit	Issue Price	Quote
80-13-001	Back to School FP-02	Rockwell-Inspired	Retrd.	25.00	N/A
80-13-002	Caroller FP-03	Rockwell-Inspired	Retrd.	25.00	N/A
80-13-003	No Swimming FP-05	Rockwell-Inspired	Retrd.	25.00	N/A
80-13-004	Lovers FP-07	Rockwell-Inspired	Retrd.	25.00	N/A
80-13-005	Doctor and Doll FP-12	Rockwell-Inspired	Retrd.	25.00	N/A
80-13-006	See America First FP-17	Rockwell-Inspired	Retrd.	25.00	N/A
80-13-007	Take Your Medicine FP-18	Rockwell-Inspired	Retrd.	25.00	N/A
80-13-008	Big Moment FP-21	Rockwell-Inspired	Retrd.	25.00	N/A
80-13-009	Circus FP-22	Rockwell-Inspired	Retrd.	25.00	N/A
80-13-010	Barbershop Quartet FP-23	Rockwell-Inspired	Retrd.	25.00	N/A
80-13-011	Magic Potion FP-28	Rockwell-Inspired	Retrd.	25.00	N/A
80-13-012	Grandpa's Ballerina FP-32	Rockwell-Inspired	Retrd.	25.00	N/A
80-13-013	Figurine Display Rack FDR-01	Rockwell-Inspired	Retrd.	60.00	N/A

Hallmark Galleries — **Moustershire**

Number	Name	Artist	Edition Limit	Issue Price	Quote
92-01-001	Andrew Allsgood- Honorable Citizen	D. Rhodus	Open	10.00	10.00
92-01-002	Chelsea Goforth- Ingenue	D. Rhodus	Open	10.00	10.00
92-01-003	Miles Fielding- Farmer	D. Rhodus	Open	10.00	10.00
92-01-004	Colin Tuneman- Musician of Note	D. Rhodus	Open	10.00	10.00
92-01-005	Olivia Puddingsby- Baker	D. Rhodus	Open	10.00	10.00
92-01-006	Hillary Hemstitch- Seamstress	D. Rhodus	Open	10.00	10.00
92-01-007	L.E. Hosten- Innkeeper	D. Rhodus	Open	10.00	10.00
92-01-008	Malcolm Cramwell- Mouserly Scholar	D. Rhodus	Open	10.00	10.00
92-01-009	Acorn Inn/Timothy Duzmuch	D. Rhodus	9,500	65.00	65.00
92-01-010	Bakery/Dunne Eaton	D. Rhodus	9,500	55.00	55.00
92-01-011	Bandstand/Cyrus & Cecilia Sunnyside	D. Rhodus	9,500	50.00	50.00
92-01-012	Nigel Puffmore- Talented Tubist	D. Rhodus	19,500	10.00	10.00
92-01-013	Robin Ripengood- Grocer	D. Rhodus	19,500	28.00	28.00
92-01-014	Claire Lovencare- Nanny	D. Rhodus	19,500	18.00	18.00
92-01-015	Hattie Chapeau- Milliner	D. Rhodus	19,500	15.00	15.00
92-01-016	Trio	D. Rhodus	19,500	23.00	23.00
92-01-017	The Picnic/Tree	D. Rhodus	9,500	50.00	50.00
92-01-018	The Park Gate	D. Rhodus	9,500	60.00	60.00
92-01-019	Acorn Inn Customers	D. Rhodus	9,500	28.00	28.00
92-01-020	Hyacinth House	D. Rhodus	9,500	65.00	65.00
92-01-021	Peter Philpott- Gardener	D. Rhodus	19,500	12.00	12.00
92-01-022	Village/Bay Crossroads Sign	D. Rhodus	19,500	10.00	10.00
92-01-023	Tess Tellingtale/Well	D. Rhodus	19,500	28.00	28.00
92-01-024	Michael McFogg/Lighthouse	D. Rhodus	9,500	55.00	55.00
92-01-025	Henrietta Seaworthy	D. Rhodus	19,500	15.00	15.00
93-01-026	Henrietta Seaworthy-Junior Sailorette	D. Rhodus	19,500	15.00	15.00
93-01-027	Michael McFogg At Lighthouse	D. Rhodus	9,500	55.00	55.00

Hallmark Galleries — **Times to Cherish**

Number	Name	Artist	Edition Limit	Issue Price	Quote
92-02-001	The Joys of Fatherhood	T. Andrews	4,500	60.00	60.00
92-02-002	Dancer's Dream	T. Andrews	4,500	50.00	50.00
92-02-003	Daily Devotion	T. Andrews	4,500	40.00	40.00
92-02-004	Beautiful Dreamer	T. Andrews	4,500	65.00	65.00
92-02-005	Sister Time	T. Andrews	4,500	55.00	55.00
92-02-006	Mother's Blessing	T. Andrews	4,500	65.00	65.00
92-02-007	The Embrace	T. Andrews	4,500	60.00	60.00
92-02-008	A Child's Prayer	T. Andrews	4,500	35.00	35.00
92-02-009	A Mother's Touch	T. Andrews	4,500	60.00	60.00
93-02-010	Spring Tulip Lidded Box	P. Andrews	4,500	25.00	25.00
93-02-011	Showing The Way	P. Andrews	4,500	45.00	45.00

Hallmark Galleries — **Birds of North America**

Number	Name	Artist	Edition Limit	Issue Price	Quote
92-03-001	House Wren	G.&G. Dooly	2,500	85.00	85.00
92-03-002	Ovenbird	G.&G. Dooly	2,500	95.00	95.00
92-03-003	American Goldfinch	G.&G. Dooly	2,500	85.00	85.00
92-03-004	American Robins	G.&G. Dooly	2,500	175.00	175.00
92-03-005	Dark-eyed Junco	G.&G. Dooly	2,500	85.00	85.00
92-03-006	Cedar Waxwing	G.&G. Dooly	2,500	120.00	120.00
92-03-007	Cardinal	G.&G. Dooly	2,500	110.00	110.00
92-03-008	Red-breasted Nuthatch	G.&G. Dooly	2,500	95.00	95.00

Hallmark Galleries — **Lou Rankin's Creations**

Number	Name	Artist	Edition Limit	Issue Price	Quote
92-04-001	Orangutan -The Thinker	L. Rankin	19,500	38.00	38.00
92-04-002	Seated Rabbit	L. Rankin	19,500	30.00	30.00
92-04-003	Squirrel I -Satisfied	L. Rankin	19,500	25.00	25.00
92-04-004	Squirrel II -Sassy	L. Rankin	19,500	20.00	20.00
92-04-005	Happy Frog -Feelin' Fine	L. Rankin	19,500	35.00	35.00
92-04-006	Two Otters -Two's Company	L. Rankin	9,500	45.00	45.00
92-04-007	Seated Bear	L. Rankin	19,500	30.00	30.00
92-04-008	Reclining Bear	L. Rankin	19,500	35.00	35.00
92-04-009	Basset Hound -Faithful Friend	L. Rankin	19,500	38.00	38.00
92-04-010	Shih Tzu -The Sophisticate	L. Rankin	19,500	30.00	30.00
92-04-011	Bulldog and Beagle -Best Buddies	L. Rankin	9,500	48.00	48.00
92-04-012	Reclining Cat -Feline Fatale	L. Rankin	19,500	30.00	30.00
92-04-013	Pair of Pigs -Happy Hogs	L. Rankin	19,500	38.00	38.00
92-04-014	Pig with Head Raised - Little Porker	L. Rankin	19,500	35.00	35.00
93-04-015	Fairbanks Polar Bear	L. Rankins	12,500	70.00	70.00
93-04-016	Slowpoke Turtle	L. Rankins	19,500	30.00	30.00
93-04-017	Lucille Seal	L. Rankins	19,500	32.00	32.00
93-04-018	Backyard Bandit Raccoon	L. Rankins	19,500	30.00	30.00
93-04-019	Mini Paws Happy-Looking Cat	L. Rankins	19,500	25.00	25.00
94-04-020	Frog Pucker Up Baby 3500QHG9923	L. Rankins	19,500	35.00	35.00
94-04-021	Cocker Spaniel Pal 3500QHG9924	L. Rankins	19,500	35.00	35.00
94-04-022	Two Pigs 3000QHG9925	L. Rankins	19,500	30.00	30.00
94-04-023	Bulldog 3500QHG9926	L. Rankins	19,500	35.00	35.00
94-04-024	Otter 4500QHG9927	L. Rankins	19,500	45.00	45.00

Hallmark Galleries — **Eileen's Richardson's Enchanted Garden**

Number	Name	Artist	Edition Limit	Issue Price	Quote
92-05-001	Enchanted Garden (vase)	E. Richardson	1,200	115.00	115.00
92-05-002	Bunny Abundance (vase)	E. Richardson	9,500	75.00	75.00
92-05-003	Milk Bath (vase)	E. Richardson	9,500	80.00	80.00
92-05-004	Everybunny Can Fly (vase)	E. Richardson	9,500	70.00	70.00

Company Number	 Name	Series Artist	 Edition Limit	 Issue Price	 Quote
92-05-005	Baby Bunny Hop (bowl)	E. Richardson	9,500	85.00	85.00
92-05-006	Promenade (bowl)	E. Richardson	9,500	65.00	65.00
92-05-007	Let Them Eat Carrots (pitcher)	E. Richardson	9,500	70.00	70.00
93-05-008	Peaceable Kingdom Lidded Box	E. Richardson	9,500	38.00	38.00
Hallmark Galleries		**Days to Remember-The Art of Norman Rockwell**			
92-06-001	Saying Grace	D. Unruh	1,500	375.00	375.00
92-06-002	Sleeping Children	D. Unruh	7,500	105.00	105.00
92-06-003	The Truth About Santa	D. Unruh	7,500	85.00	85.00
92-06-004	Santa and His Helpers	D. Unruh	7,500	95.00	95.00
92-06-005	The Fiddler	D. Unruh	4,500	95.00	95.00
92-06-006	Marbles Champion	D. Unruh	4,500	75.00	75.00
92-06-007	Low and Outside	D. Unruh	4,500	95.00	95.00
92-06-008	Springtime 1927	D. Unruh	4,500	95.00	95.00
92-06-009	Little Spooners	D. Unruh	4,500	70.00	70.00
93-06-010	Secrets	D. Unruh	7,500	70.00	70.00
93-06-011	A Child's Prayer	D. Unruh	7,500	75.00	75.00
94-06-012	No Swimming 6500QHG9725	D. Unruh	4,500	65.00	65.00
Hallmark Galleries		**Innocent Wonders**			
92-07-001	Pockets	T. Blackshear	4,500	125.00	125.00
92-07-002	Dinky Toot	T. Blackshear	4,500	125.00	125.00
92-07-003	Bobo Bipps	T. Blackshear	2,500	150.00	150.00
92-07-004	Pippy Lou	T. Blackshear	4,500	150.00	150.00
92-07-005	Pinkie Poo	T. Blackshear	2,500	135.00	135.00
92-07-006	Zip Doodle	T. Blackshear	4,500	125.00	125.00
92-07-007	Waggletag	T. Blackshear	7,500	125.00	125.00
93-07-008	Twinky Wink	T. Blackshear	4,500	115.00	115.00
Hallmark Galleries		**Tobin Fraley Carousels**			
92-08-001	Musical Premier Horse	T. Fraley	1,200	275.00	275.00
92-08-002	Charles Carmel, circa 1914/musical	T. Fraley	4,500	40.00	40.00
92-08-003	Philadelphia Toboggan Co/1910/musical	T. Fraley	4,500	40.00	40.00
92-08-004	Stein & Goldstein/1914/musical	T. Fraley	2,500	60.00	60.00
92-08-005	Philadelphia Toboggan Co/1928/musical	T. Fraley	2,500	60.00	60.00
92-08-006	Playland Carousel/musical	T. Fraley	Retrd.	195.00	195.00
92-08-007	Revolving Brass/Wood Display	T. Fraley	4,500	40.00	40.00
92-08-008	M.C. Illions & Sons/1910/musical	T. Fraley	2,500	60.00	60.00
92-08-009	Charles Looff/1915/musical	T. Fraley	2,500	60.00	60.00
92-08-010	M.C. Illions & Sons/1910/musical	T. Fraley	4,500	40.00	40.00
92-08-011	C.W. Parker/1922/musical	T. Fraley	4,500	40.00	40.00
92-08-012	C.W. Parker/1922	T. Fraley	4,500	30.00	30.00
92-08-013	Charles Looff/1915	T. Fraley	4,500	50.00	50.00
92-08-014	M.C. Illions & Sons/1910	T. Fraley	4,500	50.00	50.00
92-08-015	Charles Carmel/1914	T. Fraley	4,500	30.00	30.00
92-08-016	Philadelphia Toboggan Co/1928	T. Fraley	4,500	50.00	50.00
92-08-017	Philadelphia Toboggan Co/1910	T. Fraley	4,500	30.00	30.00
92-08-018	Stein & Goldstein/1914	T. Fraley	4,500	50.00	50.00
92-08-019	M.C. Illions & Sons/1910	T. Fraley	4,500	30.00	30.00
93-08-020	Magical Ride	Unkn.	9,500	35.00	35.00
94-08-021	Armour 6000QHG25	T. Fraley	4,500	60.00	60.00
94-08-022	Patriot 6000QHG26	T. Fraley	4,500	60.00	60.00
94-08-023	Floral 6000QHG27	T. Fraley	4,500	60.00	60.00
94-08-024	Indian 6000QHG28	T. Fraley	4,500	60.00	60.00
94-08-025	M-G-R Phil Toboggan Co. 19500QHG29	T. Fraley	2,500	195.00	195.00
Hallmark Galleries		**Majestic Wilderness**			
92-09-001	Bison	M. Newman	4,500	120.00	120.00
92-09-002	Red Fox	M. Newman	4,500	75.00	75.00
92-09-003	American Bald Eagle	M. Newman	Retrd.	195.00	195.00
92-09-004	Mountain Lion	M. Newman	4,500	75.00	75.00
92-09-005	Grizzly Mother with Cub	M. Newman	2,500	135.00	135.00
92-09-006	White-tailed Doe with Fawn	M. Newman	2,500	135.00	135.00
92-09-007	White-tailed Buck	M. Newman	2,500	135.00	135.00
92-09-008	Male Grizzly	M. Newman	2,500	145.00	145.00
92-09-009	Bighorn Sheep	M. Newman	4,500	125.00	125.00
92-09-010	Timber Wolves	M. Newman	2,500	135.00	135.00
93-09-011	American Wilderness Environment Set	M. Newman	2,500	225.00	225.00
93-09-012	Mini Black Bear	M. Newman	14,500	28.00	28.00
93-09-013	Mini Mule Deer	M. Newman	14,500	28.00	28.00
93-09-014	Mini Eagle	M. Newman	14,500	28.00	28.00
93-09-015	Mini Cottontail Rabbits	M. Newman	14,500	20.00	20.00
93-09-016	Mini Raccoons	M. Newman	14,500	20.00	20.00
93-09-017	Mini Red Fox	M. Newman	14,500	20.00	20.00
93-09-018	American Wilderness Mini Environment With Dome	M. Newman	Open	80.00	80.00
93-09-019	Large Base	M. Newman	Open	3.50	3.50
93-09-020	Small Base	M. Newman	Open	2.50	2.50
93-09-021	The Launch	M. Newman	2,500	165.00	165.00
94-09-022	Arctic Wolves 13000QHG2031	M. Newman	4,500	130.00	130.00
94-09-023	Elk in Water 12000QHG2032	M. Newman	4,500	120.00	120.00
94-09-024	Winter Environment 6000QHG2033	M. Newman	Open	60.00	60.00
94-09-025	Mini Snow Owl 2500QHG2034	M. Newman	14,500	25.00	25.00
94-09-026	Mini Lynx 2500QHG2035	M. Newman	14,500	25.00	25.00
94-09-027	Mini Deer 2500QHG2036	M. Newman	14,500	25.00	25.00
94-09-028	Mini Snowshoe Rabbits 2500QHG2037	M. Newman	14,500	25.00	25.00
94-09-029	Winter Environment Set 16000QHG2038	M. Newman	2,500	160.00	160.00
Hallmark Galleries		**Tender Touches**			
88-10-001	Rabbits with Cake	E. Seale	Retrd.	20.00	40.00
88-10-002	Baby Raccoon	E. Seale	Retrd.	20.00	40.00
88-10-003	Raccoon with Cake	E. Seale	Retrd.	18.00	36.00
88-10-004	Raccoons Playing Ball	E. Seale	Retrd.	18.00	36.00
88-10-005	Squirrels with Bandage	E. Seale	Retrd.	18.00	18.00
88-10-006	Mouse with Heart	E. Seale	Retrd.	18.00	18.00
88-10-007	Mice at Tea Party	E. Seale	Retrd.	23.00	23.00
88-10-008	Rabbits at Juice Stand	E. Seale	Open	23.00	23.00
88-10-009	Teacher with Student	E. Seale	Open	18.00	18.00
88-10-010	Mice in Rocking Chair	E. Seale	Open	18.00	18.00
88-10-011	Raccoons Fishing	E. Seale	Open	18.00	18.00
88-10-012	Bear with Umbrella	E. Seale	Open	16.00	16.00
88-10-013	Rabbit with Ribbon	E. Seale	Open	15.00	15.00
89-10-014	Bunny in Flowers	E. Seale	Retrd.	16.00	26.00
89-10-015	Chipmunk With Roses	E. Seale	Retrd.	16.00	26.00
89-10-016	Mouse with Violin	E. Seale	Retrd.	16.00	28.00
89-10-017	Halloween Trio	E. Seale	Retrd.	18.00	26.00
89-10-018	Pilgrim Mouse	E. Seale	Retrd.	16.00	30.00
89-10-019	Santa Mouse in Chair	E. Seale	Retrd.	20.00	28.00
89-10-020	Mouse at Desk	E. Seale	Retrd.	18.00	28.00
89-10-021	Rabbits Ice Skating	E. Seale	Retrd.	18.00	28.00
89-10-022	Chipmunk Praying	E. Seale	Retrd.	18.00	28.00
89-10-023	Bride & Groom	E. Seale	Open	20.00	20.00
89-10-024	Birthday Mouse	E. Seale	Retrd.	16.00	16.00
89-10-025	Bear Decorating Tree	E. Seale	Retrd.	18.00	18.00
89-10-026	Rabbit Painting Egg	E. Seale	Open	18.00	18.00
90-10-027	Dad and Son Bears	E. Seale	Retrd.	23.00	33.00
90-10-028	Teacher and Student Chipmunks	E. Seale	Retrd.	20.00	30.00
90-10-029	Bunny With Stocking	E. Seale	Retrd.	15.00	25.00
90-10-030	Mice With Mistletoe	E. Seale	Retrd.	20.00	30.00
90-10-031	Mouse in Pumpkin	E. Seale	Retrd.	18.00	28.00
90-10-032	Bears WIth Gift	E. Seale	Retrd.	18.00	28.00
90-10-033	Bear Praying	E. Seale	Retrd.	18.00	28.00
90-10-034	Baby Bear in Backpack	E. Seale	Retrd.	16.00	26.00
90-10-035	Mice in Red Car	E. Seale	Retrd.	20.00	30.00
90-10-036	Easter Egg Hunt	E. Seale	Retrd.	18.00	28.00
90-10-037	Romeo and Julie Mice	E. Seale	Retrd.	25.00	35.00
90-10-038	Tucking Baby in Bed	E. Seale	Retrd.	18.00	18.00
90-10-039	Bunnies with Slide	E. Seale	Open	20.00	20.00
90-10-040	Mice with Quilt	E. Seale	Open	20.00	20.00
90-10-041	Raccoon Watering Roses	E. Seale	Open	20.00	20.00
90-10-042	Bears Playing Baseball	E. Seale	Open	20.00	20.00
90-10-043	Bunnies Eating Ice Cream	E. Seale	Retrd.	20.00	20.00
90-10-044	Bunny Pulling Wagon	E. Seale	Open	23.00	23.00
90-10-045	Raccoons with Wagon	E. Seale	Retrd.	23.00	23.00
90-10-046	Raccoons with Flag	E. Seale	Open	23.00	23.00
90-10-047	Bunny in Boat	E. Seale	Open	18.00	18.00
90-10-048	Raccoon Mail Carrier	E. Seale	Open	16.00	16.00
90-10-049	Mouse Nurse	E. Seale	Open	15.00	15.00
90-10-050	Bear Graduate	E. Seale	Open	15.00	15.00
90-10-051	Bunny Hiding Valentine	E. Seale	Open	16.00	16.00
90-10-052	Beavers with Tree	E. Seale	Open	23.00	23.00
90-10-053	Santa in Chimney	E. Seale	Open	18.00	18.00
90-10-054	Bunny Cheerleader	E. Seale	Open	16.00	16.00
90-10-055	Bunny with Ice Cream	E. Seale	Open	15.00	15.00
90-10-056	Bear's Easter Parade	E. Seale	Open	23.00	23.00
91-10-057	Mouse Couple Sharing Soda	E. Seale	Retrd.	23.00	23.00
91-10-058	Bunny in High Chair	E. Seale	Retrd.	16.00	16.00
91-10-059	Bunny with Large Eggs	E. Seale	Retrd.	16.00	16.00
91-10-060	Mice Couple Slow Waltzing	E. Seale	Retrd.	20.00	20.00
91-10-061	First Christmas Mice @ Piano	E. Seale	Retrd.	23.00	23.00
91-10-062	Baby's 1st Bear Riding Rocking Bear	E. Seale	Retrd.	16.00	16.00
91-10-063	Father Bear Barbequing	E. Seale	Open	23.00	23.00
91-10-064	Foxes in Rowboat	E. Seale	Open	23.00	23.00
91-10-065	Mother Raccoon Reading Bible Stories	E. Seale	Open	20.00	20.00
91-10-066	Love-American Gothic-Farmer Raccoons	E. Seale	Open	20.00	20.00
91-10-067	Christmas Bunny Skiing	E. Seale	Open	18.00	18.00
91-10-068	Raccoon Witch	E. Seale	Open	16.00	16.00
92-10-069	Racoon in Bath	E. Seale	Retrd.	18.00	18.00
92-10-070	Swingtime Love	E. Seale	Retrd.	21.00	21.00
92-10-071	Building a Pumpkin Man	E. Seale	Open	18.00	18.00
92-10-072	Sweet Sharing	E. Seale	Open	20.00	20.00
92-10-073	Waiting for Santa	E. Seale	Open	20.00	20.00
92-10-074	Stealing a Kiss	E. Seale	19,500	23.00	23.00
92-10-075	Fitting Gift	E. Seale	Open	23.00	23.00
92-10-076	Delightful Fright	E. Seale	19,500	23.00	23.00
92-10-077	New World, Ahoy!	E. Seale	Open	55.00	55.00
92-10-078	Tender Touches Tree House	E. Seale	9,500	55.00	55.00
92-10-079	Raccoons on Bridge	E. Seale	19,500	25.00	25.00
92-10-080	Thanksgiving Family Around Table	E. Seale	Open	25.00	25.00
92-10-081	Chatting Mice	E. Seale	19,500	23.00	23.00
92-10-082	Soapbox Racer	E. Seale	19,500	23.00	23.00
92-10-083	Beaver Growth Chart	E. Seale	19,500	20.00	20.00
92-10-084	Bunny with Kite	E. Seale	19,500	19.00	19.00
92-10-085	Newsboy Bear	E. Seale	Open	16.00	16.00
92-10-086	Chipmunks with Album	E. Seale	Open	23.00	23.00
92-10-087	Beaver with Double Bass	E. Seale	Open	18.00	18.00
92-10-088	Breakfast in Bed	E. Seale	Open	18.00	18.00
92-10-089	Bear Family Christmas	E. Seale	9,500	45.00	45.00
92-10-090	Younger Than Springtime	E. Seale	19,500	35.00	35.00
93-10-091	The Old Swimming Hole 6000QHG7086	E. Seale	9,500	45.00	60.00
93-10-092	Woodland Americana-Patriot George	E. Seale	Open	25.00	25.00
93-10-093	Woodland Americana-Stitching the Stars and Stripes	E. Seale	Open	21.00	21.00
93-10-094	Woodland Americana-Liberty Mouse	E. Seale	Open	21.00	21.00
93-10-095	Ensemble Chipmunk Kettledrum 1800QHG7087	E. Seale	Open	18.00	18.00
93-10-096	Teeter For Two	E. Seale	Open	23.00	23.00
93-10-097	Handling a Big Thirst	E. Seale	Open	21.00	21.00
93-10-098	Garden Capers	E. Seale	Open	20.00	20.00
93-10-099	Mr. Repair Bear	E. Seale	Open	18.00	18.00
93-10-100	Playground Go-Round 2300QHG7089	E. Seale	Open	23.00	23.00
93-10-101	Making A Splash 2000QHG7088	E. Seale	Open	20.00	20.00
93-10-102	Downhill Dash	E. Seale	Open	23.00	23.00
93-10-103	Sculpting Santa	E. Seale	Open	20.00	20.00
93-10-104	Love at First Sight 2300QHG7085	E. Seale	Open	23.00	23.00
93-10-105	Easter Stroll 2100QHG7084	E. Seale	Open	21.00	21.00
94-10-106	Fireman 2300QHG7090	E. Seale	Open	23.00	23.00
94-10-107	Golfing 2100QHG7091	E. Seale	Open	21.00	21.00
94-10-108	"Happy Campers" 2500QHG7092	E. Seale	Open	25.00	25.00
94-10-109	Halloween 2300QHG7093	E. Seale	Open	23.00	23.00
94-10-110	Jesus, Mary, Joseph 2300QHG7094	E. Seale	Open	23.00	23.00
94-10-111	Daniel Boone Raccoon 2300QHG7097	E. Seale	Open	23.00	23.00
Hallmark Galleries		**Kiddie Car Classics**			
92-11-001	1941 Spitfire Airplane 5000QHG9009	E. Weirick	Retrd.	50.00	50-100.00
92-11-002	1955 Red Champion 4500QHG9002	E. Weirick	Retrd.	45.00	45-100.00
92-11-003	1955 Murray Fire Truck 5000QHG9010	E. Weirick	Retrd.	50.00	50-100.00
92-11-004	1955 Murray Dump Truck 4800QHG9011	E. Weirick	Retrd.	48.00	48-100.00
92-11-005	Murray Tractor and Trailer	E. Weirick	14,500	55.00	55.00
93-11-006	Murray Boat Jolly Roger	E. Weirick	19,500	50.00	50.00
93-11-007	Murray Fire Chief	E. Weirick	19,500	45.00	45.00
93-11-008	Murray Ranch Wagon 4800QHG9007	E. Weirick	19,500	48.00	48.00
94-11-009	1961 Speedway Pace Car 4500QHG9013	E. Weirick	19,500	45.00	45.00
94-11-010	1961 Circus Car 4800QHG9014	E. Weirick	19,500	48.00	48.00
94-11-011	1936 Lincoln Zephyr 5000QHG9015	E. Weirick	19,500	50.00	50.00
94-11-012	1956 Dragnet Police Car 5000QHG9016	E. Weirick	19,500	50.00	50.00
94-11-013	1956 Murray Garton Kiddilac (Special Edition) 5000QHG9017	E. Weirick	Yr.Iss.	50.00	50.00
94-11-014	1958 Murray Atomic Missile 5000QHG9018	E. Weirick	19,500	50.00	50.00
94-11-015	1961 Garton Casey Jones 5500QHG9019	E. Weirick	19,500	55.00	55.00
94-11-016	1950 Murray Torpedo 4500QHG9020	E. Weirick	19,500	45.00	45.00
94-11-017	1935 Auburn 4500QHG9021	E. Weirick	19,500	45.00	45.00
94-11-018	1956 Garton Ranch Wagon 4800QHG9022	E. Weirick	19,500	48.00	48.00
Hallmark Galleries		**Victorian Memories**			
92-12-001	Tea Set	J. Greene	9,500	35.00	35.00
92-12-002	Rebecca-cold cast	J. Lyle	9,500	60.00	60.00
92-12-003	Rabbit (on wheels)	J. Greene	4,500	65.00	65.00

Company		Series			
Number	**Name**	**Artist**	**Edition Limit**	**Issue Price**	**Quote**
92-12-004	Wooden Rocking Horse	J. Greene	4,500	75.00	75.00
92-12-005	Wicker Rocker	J. Greene	4,500	45.00	45.00
92-12-006	Sarah-cold cast	J. Lyle	9,500	60.00	60.00
92-12-007	Lillian-cold cast	J. Lyle	9,500	55.00	55.00
92-12-008	Wooden Horse Pull Toy-miniature	J. Greene	9,500	18.00	18.00
92-12-009	Wooden Train-miniature	J. Greene	9,500	15.00	15.00
92-12-010	Wooden Noah's Ark-miniature	J. Greene	9,500	15.00	15.00
92-12-011	Wooden Doll Carriage-miniature	J. Greene	9,500	20.00	20.00
93-12-012	Gloria Summer Figurine	Greene/Lyle	9,500	60.00	60.00
93-12-013	Mini Snow Globe	J. Greene	9,500	18.00	18.00
93-12-014	Toy Cradle	J. Greene	9,500	20.00	20.00
93-12-015	Hobby Horse	J. Greene	9,500	18.00	18.00
94-12-016	Mini Sailboat 1200QHG1034	J. Greene	9,500	12.00	12.00
94-12-017	Shoo-Fly Rocking Horse 1800QHG1036	J. Greene	9,500	18.00	18.00
94-12-018	Victorian Toy Cupboard 7500QHG1038	J. Greene	7,500	75.00	75.00
94-12-019	Bunny in Rompers 6000QHG1040	J. Greene	4,500	60.00	60.00
94-12-020	Skittle 2500QHG1043	J. Greene	9,500	25.00	25.00
Hallmark Galleries		**Little Creations**			
94-13-001	Shih Tzu-Daddy's Girl 750QEC1293	L. Rankin	Open	7.50	7.50
94-13-002	Sitting Pig 1200QEC1224	L. Rankin	Open	12.00	12.00
94-13-003	Polar Bear 1000QEC1226	L. Rankin	Open	10.00	10.00
94-13-004	Cat 750QEC1227	L. Rankin	Open	7.50	7.50
94-13-005	Orangutan 850QEC1228	L. Rankin	Open	8.50	8.50
Hallmark Galleries		**1994 Heartland Merry Miniatures**			
94-14-001	Mailbox 675QSM8023	Hallmark	Open	6.75	6.75
94-14-002	Chipmunk With Kite 375QSM8003	Hallmark	Open	3.75	3.75
94-14-003	Bear Mail Man 375QSM8006	Hallmark	Open	3.75	3.75
94-14-004	Beaver With Card 375QSM8013	Hallmark	Open	3.75	3.75
94-14-005	Raccoon With Cutout Heart 350QSM8062	Hallmark	Open	3.50	3.50
94-14-006	Rabbit With Heart Cutouts 325QSM8016	Hallmark	Open	3.25	3.25
94-14-007	Tree Stump and Paint Can 300QSM8075	Hallmark	Open	3.00	3.00
94-14-008	Owl in Stump 275QSM8085	Hallmark	Open	2.75	2.75
94-14-009	Dog With Balloon Heart 250QSM8092	Hallmark	Open	2.50	2.50
Hallmark Galleries		**1994 Easter Egg Hunt Merry Miniatures**			
94-15-001	Egg Wishing Well 675QSM8033	Hallmark	Open	6.75	6.75
94-15-002	Chick in Wagon 375QSM8123	Hallmark	Open	3.75	3.75
94-15-003	Birds in Nest 375QSM8116	Hallmark	Open	3.75	3.75
94-15-004	Rabbit with Croquet 375QSM8113	Hallmark	Open	3.75	3.75
94-15-005	Lamb in Flower Patch 325QSM8132	Hallmark	Open	3.25	3.25
94-15-006	Rabbit with Egg-Shaped Watering Can 325QSM8083	Hallmark	Open	3.25	3.25
94-15-007	Duck with Egg on Spoon 300QSM8135	Hallmark	Open	3.00	3.00
94-15-008	Bunny with Cracked Egg 300QSM8125	Hallmark	Open	3.00	3.00
94-15-009	Mouse with Flower 275QSM8243	Hallmark	Open	2.75	2.75
94-15-010	Easter Basket 250QSM8145	Hallmark	Open	2.50	2.50
Hallmark Galleries		**1994 Patriotic Merry Miniatures**			
94-16-001	Flag 675QSM8056	Hallmark	Open	6.75	6.75
94-16-002	Bear with Flag 375QSM8043	Hallmark	Open	3.75	3.75
94-16-003	Eagle with Hat 375QSM8036	Hallmark	Open	3.75	3.75
94-16-004	Hedgehog with Fife 350QSM8492	Hallmark	Open	3.50	3.50
94-16-005	Lamb Betsy Ross with Flag 350QSM8482	Hallmark	Open	3.50	3.50
94-16-006	Mouse Statue of Liberty 300QSM8475	Hallmark	Open	3.00	3.00
94-16-007	Goat Uncle Sam 300QSM8472	Hallmark	Open	3.00	3.00
94-16-008	Document 275QSM8053	Hallmark	Open	2.75	2.75
Hallmark Galleries		**1994 At The Beach Merry Miniatures**			
94-17-001	Dock 675QSM8076	Hallmark	Open	6.75	6.75
94-17-002	Raccoon with Scuba Gear 375QSM8063	Hallmark	Open	3.75	3.75
94-17-003	Bear with Surfboard 350QSM8015	Hallmark	Open	3.50	3.50
94-17-004	Chipmunk on Inflated Horse 350QSM8002	Hallmark	Open	3.50	3.50
94-17-005	Hippo in Inner Tube 300QSM8032	Hallmark	Open	3.00	3.00
94-17-006	Hedgehog Eating Hot Dog 300QSM8026	Hallmark	Open	3.00	3.00
94-17-007	Rabbit with Ice Cream Cone 275QSM8066	Hallmark	Open	2.75	2.75
94-17-008	Pail of Seashells 275QSM8052	Hallmark	Open	2.75	2.75
94-17-009	Mouse with Sunglasses 250QSM8035	Hallmark	Open	2.50	2.50
Hallmark Galleries		**1994 Thanksgiving Feast Merry Miniatures**			
94-18-001	Corn Stalk 675QFM8363	Hallmark	Open	6.75	6.75
94-18-002	Beaver with Apple 375QFM8336	Hallmark	Open	3.75	3.75
94-18-003	Pilgrim Girl Bunny 375QFM8343	Hallmark	Open	3.75	3.75
94-18-004	Indian Bear with Honey 350QFM8162	Hallmark	Open	3.50	3.50
94-18-005	Indian Chickadee with Corn 325QFM8346	Hallmark	Open	3.25	3.25
94-18-006	Pilgrim Mouse Praying 300QFM8175	Hallmark	Open	3.00	3.00
94-18-007	Indian Squirrel with Pie 300QFM8182	Hallmark	Open	3.00	3.00
94-18-008	Cute Indian Bunny 275QFM8353	Hallmark	Open	2.75	2.75
94-18-009	Basket of Apples 275QFM8356	Hallmark	Open	2.75	2.75
Hallmark Galleries		**1994 Haunted House Party Merry Miniatures**			
94-19-001	Fence with Lantern 675QFM8283	Hallmark	Open	6.75	6.75
94-19-002	Squirrel Dressed as Clown 375QFM8263	Hallmark	Open	3.75	3.75
94-19-003	Bunny Alien 375QFM8266	Hallmark	Open	3.75	3.75
94-19-004	Cute Black Kitten 325QFM8273	Hallmark	Open	3.25	3.25
94-19-005	Bear Dressed as Bat 300QFM8285	Hallmark	Open	3.00	3.00
94-19-006	Mouse Dressed as Witch 300QFM8292	Hallmark	Open	3.00	3.00
94-19-007	Bunny Super Hero 300QFM8422	Hallmark	Open	3.00	3.00
94-19-008	Pumpkin with Hat 275QFM8276	Hallmark	Open	2.75	2.75
94-19-009	Ghost on Tombstone 250QFM8282	Hallmark	Open	2.50	2.50
Hallmark Galleries		**1994 A North Pole Christmas Merry Miniatures**			
94-20-001	North Pole Sign 675QFM8333	Hallmark	Open	6.75	6.75
94-20-002	Mrs. Claus 375QFM8286	Hallmark	Open	3.75	3.75
94-20-003	Polar Bear on Skates 375QFM8293	Hallmark	Open	3.75	3.75
94-20-004	White Arctic Fox on Skates 375QFM8303	Hallmark	Open	3.75	3.75
94-20-005	Baby Whale with Hat 350QFM8222	Hallmark	Open	3.50	3.50
94-20-006	Sled Dog with Candy Cane 325QFM8306	Hallmark	Open	3.25	3.25
94-20-007	Polar Snuggle Bears 325QFM8323	Hallmark	Open	3.25	3.25
94-20-008	Walrus in Hat with Gifts 300QFM8232	Hallmark	Open	3.00	3.00
94-20-009	Penguin Throwing Snowball 275QFM8313	Hallmark	Open	2.75	2.75
94-20-010	Snowman 275QFM8316	Hallmark	Open	2.75	2.75
94-20-011	Tree 275QFM8326	Hallmark	Open	2.75	2.75
94-20-012	Seal with Earmuffs 250QFM8272	Hallmark	Open	2.50	2.50
Hamilton/Boehm		**Roses of Distinction**			
83-01-001	Peace Rose	Boehm	9,800	135.00	195.00
83-01-002	White Masterpiece Rose	Boehm	9,800	135.00	180.00
83-01-003	Angel Face Rose	Boehm	9,800	135.00	175.00
83-01-004	Queen Elizabeth Rose	Boehm	9,800	135.00	175.00
83-01-005	Elegance Rose	Boehm	9,800	135.00	175.00
83-01-006	Royal Highness Rose	Boehm	9,800	135.00	175.00
83-01-007	Tropicana Rose	Boehm	9,800	135.00	175.00
83-01-008	Mr. Lincoln Rose	Boehm	9,800	135.00	175.00
Hamilton/Boehm		**Favorite Garden Flowers**			
85-02-001	Morning Glory	Boehm	9,800	195.00	225.00
85-02-002	Hibiscus	Boehm	9,800	195.00	225.00
85-02-003	Tulip	Boehm	9,800	195.00	225.00
85-02-004	Sweet Pea	Boehm	9,800	195.00	225.00
85-02-005	Rose	Boehm	9,800	195.00	225.00
85-02-006	Carnation	Boehm	9,800	195.00	225.00
85-02-007	California Poppy	Boehm	9,800	195.00	225.00
85-02-008	Daffodil	Boehm	9,800	195.00	225.00
Hamilton Collection		**American Wildlife Bronze Collection**			
79-01-001	Cougar	H./N. Deaton	7,500	60.00	125.00
79-01-002	White-Tailed Deer	H./N. Deaton	7,500	60.00	105.00
79-01-003	Bobcat	H./N. Deaton	7,500	60.00	75.00
80-01-004	Beaver	H./N. Deaton	7,500	60.00	65.00
80-01-005	Polar Bear	H./N. Deaton	7,500	60.00	65.00
80-01-006	Sea Otter	H./N. Deaton	7,500	60.00	65.00
Hamilton Collection		**Rockwell Home of The Brave**			
82-02-001	Reminiscing	N. Rockwell	7,500	75.00	52.50-75.00
82-02-002	Hero's Welcome	N. Rockwell	7,500	75.00	52.50-75.00
82-02-003	Uncle Sam Takes Wings	N. Rockwell	7,500	75.00	52.50-75.00
82-02-004	Back to His Old Job	N. Rockwell	7,500	75.00	52.50-75.00
82-02-005	Willie Gillis in Church	N. Rockwell	7,500	75.00	52.50-75.00
82-02-006	Taking Mother over the Top	N. Rockwell	7,500	75.00	52.50-75.00
Hamilton Collection		**Ringling Bros. Circus Animals**			
83-03-001	Miniature Show Horse	P. Cozzolino	9,800	49.50	68.00
83-03-002	Baby Elephant	P. Cozzolino	9,800	49.50	55.00
83-03-003	Acrobatic Seal	P. Cozzolino	9,800	49.50	49.50
83-03-004	Skating Bear	P. Cozzolino	9,800	49.50	49.50
83-03-005	Mr. Chimpanzee	P. Cozzolino	9,800	49.50	49.50
83-03-006	Performing Poodles	P. Cozzolino	9,800	49.50	49.50
84-03-007	Roaring Lion	P. Cozzolino	9,800	49.50	49.60
84-03-008	Parade Camel	P. Cozzolino	9,800	49.50	49.50
Hamilton Collection		**Great Animals of the American Wilderness**			
83-04-001	Mountain Lion	H. Deaton	7,500	75.00	75.00
83-04-002	Grizzly Bear	H. Deaton	7,500	75.00	75.00
83-04-003	Timber Wolf	H. Deaton	7,500	75.00	75.00
83-04-004	Pronghorn Antelope	H. Deaton	7,500	75.00	75.00
83-04-005	Plains Bison	H. Deaton	7,500	75.00	75.00
83-04-006	Elk	H. Deaton	7,500	75.00	75.00
83-04-007	Mustang	H. Deaton	7,500	75.00	75.00
83-04-008	Bighorn Sheep	H. Deaton	7,500	75.00	75.00
Hamilton Collection		**American Garden Flowers**			
87-05-001	Camelia	D. Fryer	9,800	55.00	75.00
87-05-002	Gardenia	D. Fryer	15,000	75.00	75.00
87-05-003	Azalea	D. Fryer	15,000	75.00	75.00
87-05-004	Rose	D. Fryer	15,000	75.00	75.00
88-05-005	Day Lily	D. Fryer	15,000	75.00	75.00
88-05-006	Petunia	D. Fryer	15,000	75.00	75.00
88-05-007	Calla Lilly	D. Fryer	15,000	75.00	75.00
89-05-008	Pansy	D. Fryer	15,000	75.00	75.00
Hamilton Collection		**Celebration of Opera**			
86-06-001	Cio-Cio-San	J. Villena	7,500	95.00	95.00
86-06-002	Carmen	J. Villena	7,500	95.00	95.00
87-06-003	Figaro	J. Villena	7,500	95.00	95.00
88-06-004	Mimi	J. Villena	7,500	95.00	95.00
88-06-005	Aida	J. Villena	7,500	95.00	95.00
88-06-006	Canio	J. Villena	7,500	95.00	95.00
Hamilton Collection		**Exotic Birds of the World**			
84-07-001	The Cockatoo	Francesco	7,500	75.00	115.00
84-07-002	The Budgerigar	Francesco	7,500	75.00	105.00
84-07-003	The Rubenio Parakeet	Francesco	7,500	75.00	95.00
84-07-004	The Quetzal	Francesco	7,500	75.00	95.00
84-07-005	The Red Lorg	Francesco	7,500	75.00	95.00
84-07-006	The Fisher's Whydah	Francesco	7,500	75.00	95.00
84-07-007	The Diamond Dove	Francesco	7,500	75.00	95.00
84-07-008	The Peach-faced Lovebird	Francesco	7,500	75.00	95.00
Hamilton Collection		**Majestic Wildlife of North America**			
85-08-001	White-tailed Deer	H. Deaton	7,500	75.00	75.00
85-08-002	Ocelot	H. Deaton	7,500	75.00	75.00
85-08-003	Alaskan Moose	H. Deaton	7,500	75.00	75.00
85-08-004	Black Bear	H. Deaton	7,500	75.00	75.00
85-08-005	Mountain Goat	H. Deaton	7,500	75.00	75.00
85-08-006	Coyote	H. Deaton	7,500	75.00	75.00
85-08-007	Barren Ground Caribou	H. Deaton	7,500	75.00	75.00
85-08-008	Harbour Seal	H. Deaton	7,500	75.00	75.00
Hamilton Collection		**Magnificent Birds of Paradise**			
85-09-001	Emperor of Germany	Francesco	12,500	75.00	95.00
85-09-002	Greater Bird of Paradise	Francesco	12,500	75.00	95.00
85-09-003	Magnificent Bird of Paradise	Francesco	12,500	75.00	95.00
85-09-004	Raggiana Bird of Paradise	Francesco	12,500	75.00	95.00
85-09-005	Princess Stephanie Bird of Paradise	Francesco	12,500	75.00	95.00
85-09-006	Goldie's Bird of Paradise	Francesco	12,500	75.00	95.00
85-09-007	Blue Bird of Paradise	Francesco	12,500	75.00	95.00
85-09-008	Black Sickle-Billed Bird of Paradise	Francesco	12,500	75.00	95.00
Hamilton Collection		**Legendary Flowers of the Orient**			
85-10-001	Iris	Ito	15,000	55.00	55.00
85-10-002	Lotus	Ito	15,000	55.00	55.00
85-10-003	Chinese Peony	Ito	15,000	55.00	55.00
85-10-004	Gold Band Lily	Ito	15,000	55.00	55.00
85-10-005	Chrysanthemum	Ito	15,000	55.00	55.00
85-10-006	Cherry Blossom	Ito	15,000	55.00	55.00
85-10-007	Japanese Orchid	Ito	15,000	55.00	55.00
85-10-008	Wisteria	Ito	15,000	55.00	55.00
Hamilton Collection		**The Splendor of Ballet**			
87-11-001	Juliet	E. Daub	15,000	95.00	95.00
87-11-002	Odette	E. Daub	15,000	95.00	95.00
87-11-003	Giselle	E. Daub	15,000	95.00	95.00
87-11-004	Kitri	E. Daub	15,000	95.00	95.00
88-11-005	Aurora	E. Daub	15,000	95.00	95.00
89-11-006	Swanilda	E. Daub	15,000	95.00	95.00
89-11-007	Firebird	E. Daub	15,000	95.00	95.00

Company Number	Name	Series Artist	Edition Limit	Issue Price	Quote
89-11-008	Clara	E. Daub	15,000	95.00	95.00
Hamilton Collection		**The Noble Swan**			
85-12-001	The Noble Swan	G. Granget	5,000	295.00	295.00
Hamilton Collection		**The Gibson Girls**			
86-13-001	The Actress	Unknown	Open	75.00	75.00
87-13-002	The Career Girl	Unknown	Open	75.00	75.00
87-13-003	The College Girl	Unknown	Open	75.00	75.00
87-13-004	The Bride	Unknown	Open	75.00	75.00
87-13-005	The Sportswoman	Unknown	Open	75.00	75.00
88-13-006	The Debutante	Unknown	Open	75.00	75.00
88-13-007	The Artist	Unknown	Open	75.00	75.00
88-13-008	The Society Girl	Unknown	Open	75.00	75.00
Hamilton Collection		**The Romance of Flowers**			
87-14-001	Springtime Bouquet	Maruri	15,000	95.00	95.00
87-14-002	Summer Bouquet	Maruri	15,000	95.00	95.00
88-14-003	Autumn Bouquet	Maruri	15,000	95.00	95.00
88-14-004	Winter Bouquet	Maruri	15,000	95.00	95.00
Hamilton Collection		**Wild Ducks of North America**			
87-15-001	Common Mallard	C. Burgess	15,000	95.00	95.00
87-15-002	Wood Duck	C. Burgess	15,000	95.00	95.00
87-15-003	Green Winged Teal	C. Burgess	15,000	95.00	95.00
87-15-004	Hooded Merganser	C. Burgess	15,000	95.00	95.00
88-15-005	Northern Pintail	C. Burgess	15,000	95.00	95.00
88-15-006	Ruddy Duck Drake	C. Burgess	15,000	95.00	95.00
88-15-007	Bufflehead	C. Burgess	15,000	95.00	95.00
88-15-008	American Widgeon	C. Burgess	15,000	95.00	95.00
Hamilton Collection		**Snuggle Babies**			
88-16-001	Baby Bunnies	Jacqueline B.	Open	35.00	35.00
88-16-002	Baby Bears	Jacqueline B.	Open	35.00	35.00
88-16-003	Baby Skunks	Jacqueline B.	Open	35.00	35.00
88-16-004	Baby Foxes	Jacqueline B.	Open	35.00	35.00
89-16-005	Baby Chipmunks	Jacqueline B.	Open	35.00	35.00
89-16-006	Baby Raccoons	Jacqueline B.	Open	35.00	35.00
89-16-007	Baby Squirrels	Jacqueline B.	Open	35.00	35.00
89-16-008	Baby Fawns	Jacqueline B.	Open	35.00	35.00
Hamilton Collection		**Tropical Treasures**			
89-17-001	Sail-finned Surgeonfish	M. Wald	Open	37.50	37.50
89-17-002	Flag-tail Surgeonfish	M. Wald	Open	37.50	37.50
89-17-003	Pennant Butterfly Fish	M. Wald	Open	37.50	37.50
89-17-004	Sea Horse	M. Wald	Open	37.50	37.50
90-17-005	Zebra Turkey Fish	M. Wald	Open	37.50	37.50
90-17-006	Spotted Angel Fish	M. Wald	Open	37.50	37.50
90-17-007	Blue Girdled Angel Fish	M. Wald	Open	37.50	37.50
90-17-008	Beaked Coral Butterfly Fish	M. Wald	Open	37.50	37.50
Hamilton Collection		**A Celebration of Roses**			
89-18-001	Tiffany	N/A	Open	55.00	55.00
89-18-002	Color Magic	N/A	Open	55.00	55.00
89-18-003	Honor	N/A	Open	55.00	55.00
89-18-004	Brandy	N/A	Open	55.00	55.00
89-18-005	Miss All-American Beauty	N/A	Open	55.00	55.00
90-18-006	Oregold	N/A	Open	55.00	55.00
91-18-007	Paradise	N/A	Open	55.00	55.00
91-18-008	Ole'	N/A	Open	55.00	55.00
Hamilton Collection		**Heroes of Baseball-Porcelain Baseball Cards**			
90-19-001	Brooks Robinson	N/A	Open	19.50	19.50
90-19-002	Roberto Clemente	N/A	Open	19.50	19.50
90-19-003	Willie Mays	N/A	Open	19.50	19.50
90-19-004	Duke Snider	N/A	Open	19.50	19.50
91-19-005	Whitey Ford	N/A	Open	19.50	19.50
91-19-006	Gil Hodges	N/A	Open	19.50	19.50
91-19-007	Mickey Mantle	N/A	Open	19.50	19.50
91-19-008	Casey Stengel	N/A	Open	19.50	19.50
91-19-009	Jackie Robinson	N/A	Open	19.50	19.50
91-19-010	Ernie Banks	N/A	Open	19.50	19.50
91-19-011	Yogi Berra	N/A	Open	19.50	19.50
91-19-012	Satchel Page	N/A	Open	19.50	19.50
Hamilton Collection		**Little Night Owls**			
90-20-001	Tawny Owl	D.T. Lyttleton	Open	45.00	45.00
90-20-002	Barn Owl	D.T. Lyttleton	Open	45.00	45.00
90-20-003	Snowy Owl	D.T. Lyttleton	Open	45.00	45.00
91-20-004	Barred Owl	D.T. Lyttleton	Open	45.00	45.00
91-20-005	Great Horned Owl	D.T. Lyttleton	Open	45.00	45.00
91-20-006	White-Faced Owl	D.T. Lyttleton	Open	45.00	45.00
91-20-007	Great Grey Owl	D.T. Lyttleton	Open	45.00	45.00
91-20-008	Short-Eared Owl	D.T. Lyttleton	Open	45.00	45.00
Hamilton Collection		**Puppy Playtime Sculpture Collection**			
90-21-001	Double Take	J. Lamb	Open	29.50	29.50
91-21-002	Catch of the Day	J. Lamb	Open	29.50	29.50
91-21-003	Cabin Fever	J. Lamb	Open	29.50	29.50
91-21-004	Weekend Gardner	J. Lamb	Open	29.50	29.50
91-21-005	Hanging Out	J. Lamb	Open	29.50	29.50
91-21-006	Getting Acquainted	J. Lamb	Open	29.50	29.50
91-21-007	A New Leash on Life	J. Lamb	Open	29.50	29.50
91-21-008	Fun and Games	J. Lamb	Open	29.50	29.50
Hamilton Collection		**Freshwater Challenge**			
91-22-001	The Strike	M. Wald	Open	75.00	75.00
91-22-002	Rainbow Lure	M. Wald	Open	75.00	75.00
91-22-003	Sun Catcher	M. Wald	Open	75.00	75.00
92-22-004	Prized Catch	M. Wald	Open	75.00	75.00
Hamilton Collection		**Puss in Boots**			
92-23-001	Caught Napping	P. Cooper	Open	35.00	35.00
92-23-002	Sweet Dreams	P. Cooper	Open	35.00	35.00
93-23-003	Hide'n Go Seek	P. Cooper	Open	35.00	35.00
93-23-004	All Dressed Up	P. Cooper	Open	35.00	35.00
Hamilton Collection		**International Santa**			
92-24-001	Father Christmas	N/A	Open	55.00	55.00
92-24-002	Santa Claus	N/A	Open	55.00	55.00
92-24-003	Grandfather Frost	N/A	Open	55.00	55.00
93-24-004	Belsnickel	N/A	Open	55.00	55.00
93-24-005	Kris Kringle	N/A	Open	55.00	55.00
93-24-006	Jolly Old St. Nick	N/A	Open	55.00	55.00
93-24-007	Pére Santa	N/A	Open	55.00	55.00
93-24-008	Yuletide Santa	N/A	Open	55.00	55.00
Hamilton Collection		**Noble American Indian Women**			
93-25-001	Sacajawea	N/A	Open	55.00	55.00
93-25-002	White Rose	N/A	Open	55.00	55.00
94-25-003	Falling Star	N/A	Open	55.00	55.00
94-25-004	Minnehaha	N/A	Open	55.00	55.00
Hamilton Collection		**Noble Warriors**			
93-26-001	Deliverance	N/A	Open	135.00	135.00
94-26-002	Spirit of the Plains	N/A	Open	135.00	135.00
Hamilton Collection		**Visions of Christmas**			
93-27-001	Santa's Delivery	M. Griffin	Open	135.00	135.00
93-27-002	Toys in Progress	M. Griffin	Open	135.00	135.00
Hamilton Collection		**Santa Clothtique**			
92-28-001	Checking His List	Possible Dreams	Open	95.00	95.00
93-28-002	'Twas the Nap Before Christmas	Possible Dreams	Open	95.00	95.00
93-28-003	Last Minute Details	Possible Dreams	Open	95.00	95.00
Hamilton Collection		**The Nolan Ryan Collectors Edition-Porcelain Baseball Cards**			
93-29-001	Mets 1968-C #177	N/A	Open	19.50	19.50
93-29-002	Rangers 1990-C #1	N/A	Open	19.50	19.50
93-29-003	Mets 1969-C #533	N/A	Open	19.50	19.50
93-29-004	Angels 1972-C #595	N/A	Open	19.50	19.50
93-29-005	Rangers 1992-C #1	N/A	Open	19.50	19.50
93-29-006	Astros 1985-C #7	N/A	Open	19.50	19.50
Hamilton Gifts/Maud Humphrey Bogart: See Enesco/Hamilton Gifts Ltd.					
Harbour Lights		**Original Collection**			
91-01-001	Admiralty Head 101	Harbour Lights	5,500	60.00	60.00
91-01-002	Cape Hatteras 102	Harbour Lights	Retrd.	60.00	60.00
92-01-003	Cape Hatteras 102R	Harbour Lights	Retrd.	60.00	60.00
91-01-004	West Quoddy Head 103	Harbour Lights	5,500	60.00	60.00
91-01-005	Sandy Hook 104	Harbour Lights	5,500	60.00	60.00
91-01-006	Point Loma 105	Harbour Lights	5,500	60.00	60.00
91-01-007	North Head 106	Harbour Lights	5,500	60.00	60.00
91-01-008	Umpqua River 107	Harbour Lights	5,500	60.00	60.00
91-01-009	Burrows Island 108	Harbour Lights	5,500	60.00	60.00
91-01-010	Cape Blanco 109	Harbour Lights	5,500	60.00	60.00
91-01-011	Yaquina Head 110	Harbour Lights	5,500	60.00	60.00
91-01-012	Coquille River 111	Harbour Lights	Retrd.	60.00	60.00
91-01-013	Sand Island 112	Harbour Lights	5,500	60.00	60.00
91-01-014	Port Niagara 113	Harbour Lights	5,500	60.00	60.00
91-01-015	Gt. Captain's Island 114	Harbour Lights	5,500	60.00	60.00
91-01-016	St. George's Reef 115	Harbour Lights	5,500	60.00	60.00
91-01-017	Castle Hill 116	Harbour Lights	5,500	60.00	60.00
91-01-018	Boston Harbor 117	Harbour Lights	5,500	60.00	60.00
Harbour Lights		**Great Lakes Series**			
92-02-001	Old Mackinac Point 118	Harbour Lights	5,500	65.00	65.00
92-02-002	Cana Island 119	Harbour Lights	5,500	60.00	60.00
92-02-003	Grosse Point 120	Harbour Lights	5,500	60.00	60.00
92-02-004	Marblehead 121	Harbour Lights	5,500	50.00	50.00
92-02-005	Buffalo 122	Harbour Lights	5,500	60.00	60.00
92-02-006	Michigan City123	Harbour Lights	5,500	60.00	60.00
92-02-007	Split Rock 124	Harbour Lights	5,500	60.00	60.00
Harbour Lights		**New England Series**			
92-03-001	Portland Head 125	Harbour Lights	5,500	65.00	65.00
92-03-002	Nauset 126	Harbour Lights	5,500	65.00	65.00
92-03-003	Whaleback127	Harbour Lights	5,500	60.00	60.00
92-03-004	Southeast Block Island128	Harbour Lights	5,500	70.00	70.00
92-03-005	New London Ledge 129	Harbour Lights	5,500	65.00	65.00
92-03-006	Portland Breakwater 130	Harbour Lights	5,500	60.00	60.00
92-03-007	Minot's Ledge131	Harbour Lights	5,500	60.00	60.00
Harbour Lights		**Southern Belles**			
93-04-001	Ponce de Leon, FL 132	Harbour Lights	5,500	60.00	60.00
93-04-002	Tybee, GA 133	Harbour Lights	5,500	60.00	60.00
93-04-003	Key West, FL 134	Harbour Lights	5,500	60.00	60.00
93-04-004	Ocracoke, NC 135	Harbour Lights	5,500	60.00	60.00
93-04-005	Hilton Head, SC 136	Harbour Lights	5,500	60.00	60.00
93-04-006	St. Simons, GA 137	Harbour Lights	5,500	65.00	65.00
93-04-007	St. Augustine, FL 138	Harbour Lights	5,500	70.00	70.00
Harbour Lights		**New Releases**			
93-05-001	Barnegat, NJ 139	Harbour Lights	5,500	60.00	60.00
93-05-002	Diamond Head, HI 140	Harbour Lights	5,500	60.00	60.00
93-05-003	Cape Neddick (Nubble), ME 141	Harbour Lights	5,500	65.00	65.00
93-05-004	Holland (Big Red), MI 142	Harbour Lights	5,500	60.00	60.00
Hawthorne		**Concord: The Hometown of American Literature**			
92-01-001	Hawthorne's Wayside Retreat	K.&H. LeVan	Closed	39.90	39.90
92-01-002	Emerson's Old Manse	K.&H. LeVan	7/94	39.90	39.90
93-01-003	Alcott's Orchard House	K.&H. LeVan	10/94	39.90	39.90
Hawthorne		**Victorian Grove Collection**			
92-02-001	Lilac Cottage	K.&H. LeVan	Closed	34.90	34.90
92-02-002	Rose Haven	K.&H. LeVan	9/94	34.90	34.90
93-02-003	Cherry Blossom	K.&H. LeVan	11/94	34.90	34.90
Hawthorne		**Stonefield Valley**			
92-03-001	Springbridge Cottage	K.&H. LeVan	Closed	34.90	34.90
92-03-002	Meadowbrook School	K.&H. LeVan	5/94	34.90	34.90
92-03-003	Weaver's Cottage	K.&H. LeVan	9/94	37.90	37.90
92-03-004	Church in the Glen	K.&H. LeVan	11/94	37.90	37.90
93-03-005	Parson's Cottage	K.&H. LeVan	1/95	37.90	37.90
93-03-006	Hillside Country Store	K.&H. LeVan	Open	37.90	37.90
93-03-007	Ferryman's Cottage	K.&H. LeVan	Open	39.90	39.90
Hawthorne		**Strolling Through Colonial America**			
91-04-001	Jefferson's Ordinance	K.&H. LeVan	Closed	34.90	34.90
92-04-002	Millrace Store	K.&H. LeVan	Closed	34.90	34.90
92-04-003	Higgins' Grist Mill	K.&H. LeVan	Closed	37.90	37.90
92-04-004	Eastbrook Church	K.&H. LeVan	Closed	37.90	37.90
92-04-005	Court House on the Green	K.&H. LeVan	Closed	37.90	37.90
92-04-006	Captain Lee's Grammar School	K.&H. LeVan	Closed	37.90	37.90
92-04-007	The Village Smithy	K.&H. LeVan	Closed	39.90	39.90
93-04-008	Everette's Joiner Shop	K.&H. LeVan	5/94	39.90	39.90

Company		Series			
Number	Name	Artist	Edition Limit	Issue Price	Quote
Hawthorne		**Lost Victorians of Old San Francisco**			
92-05-001	The Grande Dame of Nob Hill	R. Brouillette	Closed	34.90	34.90
92-05-002	The Empress of Russian Hill	R. Brouillette	9/94	34.90	34.90
93-05-003	The Princess of Pacific Heights	R. Brouillette	11/94	34.90	34.90
Hawthorne		**Rockwell's Home for the Holidays**			
92-06-001	Christmas Eve at the Studio	Unkn.	Closed	34.90	34.90
92-06-002	Bringing Home the Tree	Unkn.	8/94	34.90	34.90
92-06-003	Carolers In The Church Yard	Unkn.	12/94	37.90	37.90
93-06-004	Three-Day Pass	Unkn.	6/94	37.90	37.90
Hawthorne		**Gone With theWInd Collection**			
92-07-001	Tara . . .Scarlett's Pride	K.&H. LeVan	12/94	39.90	39.90
92-07-002	Twelve Oaks: The Romance Begins	K.&H. LeVan	3/95	39.90	39.90
93-07-003	Rhett Returns	K.&H. LeVan	6/95	39.90	39.90
93-07-004	Against Her Will	K.&H. LeVan	3/95	42.90	42.90
Hawthorne		**Chestnut Hill Station**			
93-08-001	Wishing Well Cottage	K.&H. LeVan	Open	29.90	29.90
93-08-002	Parkside Cafe	K.&H. LeVan	Open	29.90	29.90
Hawthorne		**Thatcher's Crossing**			
93-09-001	Rose Arbour Cottage	Unknown	Open	29.90	29.90
93-09-002	Midsummer's Cottage	Unknown	Open	29.90	29.90
Hawthorne		**Kinkade's Candlelight Cottages**			
93-10-001	Olde Porterfield Tea Room	Kinkade-Inspired	Open	24.90	24.90
93-10-002	Swanbrooke Cottage	Kinkade-Inspired	Open	24.90	24.90
93-10-003	Chandler's Cottage	Kinkade-Inspired	Open	24.90	24.90
Hawthorne		**Rockwell's Home for the Holidays**			
93-11-001	Over the River	Unknown	9/95	37.90	37.90
93-11-002	School's Out	Unknown	11/95	39.90	39.90
93-11-003	A Room at the Inn	Unknown	12/95	39.90	39.90
Hawthorne		**Kinkade's Candlelight Cottages (Illuminated)**			
93-12-001	Olde Porterfield Tea Room	Kinkade-Inspired	Open	29.90	29.90
93-12-002	Chandler's Cottage	Kinkade-Inspired	Open	29.90	29.90
Hawthorne		**Rockwell's Christmas in Stockbridge (Illuminated)**			
93-13-001	Rockwell's Studio	Rockwell-Inspired	Open	29.90	29.90
93-13-002	Country Store	Rockwell-Inspired	Open	29.90	29.90
93-13-003	Antique Shop	Rockwell-Inspired	Open	29.90	29.90
93-13-004	Town Offices	Rockwell-Inspired	Open	29.90	29.90
93-13-005	Bank	Rockwell-Inspired	Open	29.90	29.90
93-13-006	Library	Rockwell-Inspired	Open	29.90	29.90
93-13-007	Red Lion Inn	Rockwell-Inspired	Open	29.90	29.90
Hawthorne		**Gone With the Wind (Illuminated)**			
93-14-001	Tara	Rockwell-Inspired	Open	39.90	39.90
John Hine N.A. Ltd.		**David Winter Cottages**			
80-01-001	Rose Cottage	D. Winter	Open	28.90	52.00
80-01-002	Market Street	D. Winter	Open	48.80	84.00
81-01-003	Triple Oast	D. Winter	Open	59.90	112.00
81-01-004	Stratford House	D. Winter	Open	74.80	124.00
81-01-005	The Village	D. Winter	Open	362.00	575.00
82-01-006	Drover's Cottage	D. Winter	Open	22.00	32.00
82-01-007	Sussex Cottage	D. Winter	Open	22.00	40.00
82-01-008	The Village Shop	D. Winter	Open	22.00	32.00
82-01-009	Cotswold Cottage	D. Winter	Open	22.00	32.00
83-01-010	The Bakehouse	D. Winter	Open	31.40	56.00
83-01-011	The Bothy	D. Winter	Open	31.40	56.00
83-01-012	Fisherman's Wharf	D. Winter	Open	31.40	56.00
83-01-013	The Green Dragon Inn	D. Winter	Open	31.40	56.00
84-01-014	The Parsonage	D. Winter	Open	390.00	556.00
85-01-015	Kent Cottage	D. Winter	Open	48.80	98.00
85-01-016	The Schoolhouse	D. Winter	Open	24.10	44.00
85-01-017	Craftsmen's Cottages	D. Winter	Open	24.10	40.00
85-01-018	The Vicarage	D. Winter	Open	24.10	40.00
85-01-019	The Hogs Head Tavern	D. Winter	Open	24.10	44.00
85-01-020	Blackfriars Grange	D. Winter	Open	24.10	40.00
85-01-021	Shirehall	D. Winter	Open	24.10	44.00
85-01-022	The Apothecary Shop	D. Winter	Open	24.10	44.00
85-01-023	Yeoman's Farmhouse	D. Winter	Open	24.10	40.00
85-01-024	Meadowbank Cottages	D. Winter	Open	24.10	40.00
85-01-025	St. George's Church	D. Winter	Open	24.10	44.00
87-01-026	Smuggler's Creek	D. Winter	Open	390.00	514.00
87-01-027	Devoncombe	D. Winter	Open	73.00	112.00
87-01-028	Tamar Cottage	D. Winter	Open	45.30	74.00
87-01-029	There was a Crooked House	D. Winter	Open	96.90	152.00
87-01-030	Devon Creamery	D. Winter	Open	62.90	98.00
88-01-031	Windmill	D. Winter	Open	37.50	52.00
88-01-032	Lock-keepers Cottage	D. Winter	Open	65.00	84.00
88-01-033	Derbyshire Cotton Mill	D. Winter	Open	65.00	84.00
88-01-034	Gunsmiths	D. Winter	Open	78.00	98.00
88-01-035	Coal Miner's Row	D. Winter	Open	90.00	112.00
88-01-036	Lacemaker's Cottage	D. Winter	Open	120.00	152.00
88-01-037	Cornish Harbour	D. Winter	Open	120.00	152.00
88-01-038	Cornish Engine House	D. Winter	Open	120.00	152.00
91-01-039	Inglenook Cottage	D. Winter	Open	60.00	70.00
91-01-040	The Weaver's Lodgings	D. Winter	Open	65.00	76.00
91-01-041	The Printers and The Bookbinders	D. Winter	Open	120.00	138.00
91-01-042	Moonlight Haven	D. Winter	Open	120.00	138.00
91-01-043	Castle in the Air	D. Winter	Open	675.00	708.00
93-01-044	Horatio Pernickety's Amorous Intent	D. Winter	9,999	375.00	375.00
John Hine N.A. Ltd.		**David Winter Retired Cottages**			
89-02-001	A Christmas Carol (Xmas '89)	D. Winter	Closed	135.00	81-375.00
83-02-002	The Alms Houses	D. Winter	Closed	59.90	465-550.
92-02-003	Audrey's Tea Room	D. Winter	Closed	90.00	120-400.
92-02-004	Audrey's Tea Shop	D. Winter	Closed	90.00	150-370.
82-02-005	Blacksmith's Cottage	D. Winter	Closed	22.00	550.00
88-02-006	Bottle Kilns	D. Winter	Closed	78.00	47-105.00
82-02-007	Brookside Hamlet	D. Winter	Closed	74.80	100-195.
84-02-008	Castle Gate	D. Winter	Closed	154.90	120-500.
81-02-009	Castle Keep	D. Winter	Closed	30.00	1200-2000.
84-02-010	The Chapel	D. Winter	Closed	48.80	95-125.00
81-02-011	Chichester Cross	D. Winter	Closed	50.00	3400-3600.
80-02-012	The Coaching Inn	D. Winter	Closed	165.00	3900.00
85-02-013	The Cooper's Cottage	D. Winter	Closed	57.90	78-125.00
82-02-014	Cornish Cottage	D. Winter	Closed	30.00	900.00
83-02-015	Cornish Tin Mine	D. Winter	Closed	22.00	48-125.00
82-02-016	Cotswold Village	D. Winter	Closed	59.90	85-125.00
83-02-017	The Cotton Mill	D. Winter	Closed	41.30	408-625.
86-02-018	Crofter's Cottage	D. Winter	Closed	51.00	59-125.00
81-02-019	Double Oast	D. Winter	Closed	60.00	3300.00
80-02-020	Dove Cottage	D. Winter	Closed	60.00	1200-2000.
82-02-021	The Dower House	D. Winter	Closed	22.00	60-200.00
87-02-022	Ebenezer Scrooge's Counting House (Xmas '87)	D. Winter	Closed	96.90	100-550.
82-02-023	Fairytale Castle	D. Winter	Closed	115.40	180-695.
86-02-024	Falstaff's Manor	D. Winter	Closed	242.00	350-700.
80-02-025	The Forge	D. Winter	Closed	60.00	1600.00
91-02-026	Fred's Home: "A Merry Christmas, Uncle Ebenezer," said Scrooge's Nephew Fred, "and a Happy New Year." (Xmas '91)	D. Winter	Closed	145.00	160-250.
88-02-027	The Grange	D. Winter	Closed	120.00	900-1800.
82-02-028	The Haybarn	D. Winter	Closed	22.00	250-450.
85-02-029	Hermit's Humble Home	D. Winter	Closed	87.00	250-375.
83-02-030	Hertford Court	D. Winter	Closed	87.00	150-175.
88-02-031	Hogmanay (Xmas '88)	D. Winter	Closed	100.00	150-200.
84-02-032	House of the Master Mason	D. Winter	Closed	74.80	250-350.
82-02-033	The House on Top	D. Winter	Closed	92.30	250-375.
82-02-034	Ivy Cottage	D. Winter	Closed	22.00	50-100.00
88-02-035	Jim'll Fixit	D. Winter	Closed	350.00	2100-3500.
88-01-036	John Benbow's Farmhouse	D. Winter	Closed	78.00	92-150.00
80-02-037	Little Forge	D. Winter	Closed	40.00	2500-5000.
80-01-038	Little Market	D. Winter	Closed	28.90	28-75.00
80-02-039	Little Mill	D. Winter	Closed	40.00	1700-2300.
80-02-040	Little Mill-remodeled	D. Winter	Closed	Unkn.	Unkn.
92-02-041	Mad Baron Fourthrite's Folly	D. Winter	Closed	275.00	220-495.
80-02-042	Mill House	D. Winter	Closed	50.00	2000-2800.
80-02-043	Mill House-remodeled	D. Winter	Closed	Unkn.	Unkn.
82-02-044	Miner's Cottage	D. Winter	Closed	22.00	182-365.
82-02-045	Moorland Cottage	D. Winter	Closed	22.00	235.00
90-02-046	Mr. Fezziwig's Emporium (Xmas '90)	D. Winter	Closed	135.00	90-300.00
81-02-047	The Old Curiosity Shop	D. Winter	Closed	40.00	1200-4000.
82-02-048	The Old Distillery	D. Winter	Closed	312.20	400-650.
91-01-049	Old Joe's Beetling Shop A Veritable Den of Iniquity! (Xmas '93)	D. Winter	Closed	175.00	175.00
92-06-050	Only A Span Apart	D. Winter	Closed	80.00	85.00
87-02-050	Orchard Cottage	D. Winter	Closed	91.30	128-300.
83-02-051	Pilgrim's Rest	D. Winter	Closed	48.80	80-115.00
80-02-052	Quayside	D. Winter	Closed	60.00	1400.00
82-02-053	Sabrina's Cottage	D. Winter	Closed	30.00	1995.00
92-02-054	Scrooge's School (Xmas '92)	D. Winter	Closed	160.00	160-260.
92-06-055	Secret Shebeen	D. Winter	Closed	70.00	75-140.00
81-01-056	Single Oast	D. Winter	Closed	22.00	75.00
84-02-057	Snow Cottage	D. Winter	Closed	74.80	105-175.
84-02-058	Spinner's Cottage	D. Winter	Closed	28.90	60-105.00
85-02-059	Squires Hall	D. Winter	Closed	92.30	105-250.
81-02-060	St. Paul's Cathedral	D. Winter	Closed	40.00	2000-2800.
85-02-061	Suffolk House	D. Winter	Closed	48.80	60-175.00
80-02-062	Three Ducks Inn	D. Winter	Closed	60.00	2000-3000.
84-02-063	Tollkeeper's Cottage	D. Winter	Closed	87.00	125-190.
81-02-064	Tudor Manor House	D. Winter	Closed	48.80	95-275.00
81-02-065	Tythe Barn	D. Winter	Closed	39.30	1500.00
82-02-066	William Shakespeare's Birthplace(large)	D. Winter	Closed	60.00	1080-1400.
80-02-067	The Wine Merchant	D. Winter	Closed	28.90	50-100.00
83-02-068	Woodcutter's Cottage	D. Winter	Closed	87.00	240-495.
John Hine N.A. Ltd.		**David Winter Retired Cottages-Tiny Series**			
80-03-001	William Shakespeare's Birthplace	D. Winter	Closed	Unkn.	750-1000.
80-03-002	Ann Hathaway's Cottage	D. Winter	Closed	Unkn.	750.00
80-03-003	Sulgrave Manor	D. Winter	Closed	Unkn.	1000.00
80-03-004	Cotswold Farmhouse	D. Winter	Closed	Unkn.	550-875.
80-03-005	Crown Inn	D. Winter	Closed	Unkn.	940.00
80-03-006	St. Nicholas' Church	D. Winter	Closed	Unkn.	1000-1500.
John Hine N.A. Ltd.		**Collectors Guild Exclusives**			
87-04-001	The Village Scene	D. Winter	Closed	Gift	180-350.
87-04-002	Robin Hood's Hideaway	D. Winter	Closed	54.00	330-700.
88-04-003	Queen Elizabeth Slept Here	D. Winter	Closed	183.00	240-500.
88-04-004	Black Bess Inn	D. Winter	Closed	60.00	108-200.
88-04-005	The Pavillion	D. Winter	Closed	52.00	110-215.
89-04-006	Street Scene	D. Winter	Closed	Gift	120-185.
89-04-007	Homeguard	D. Winter	Closed	105.00	118-350.
89-04-008	Coal Shed	D. Winter	Closed	112.00	155-450.
90-04-009	Plucked Duck	D. Winter	Closed	Gift	75-145.00
90-04-010	The Cobblers	D. Winter	Closed	40.00	65-200.00
90-04-011	The Pottery	D. Winter	Closed	40.00	65-250.00
90-04-012	Cartwrights Cottage	D. Winter	Closed	45.00	80-125.
91-04-013	Pershore Mill	D. Winter	Closed	Gift	85-200.00
91-04-014	Tomfool's Cottage	D. Winter	Closed	100.00	125-228
91-04-015	Will O' The Wisp	D. Winter	Closed	120.00	114-190.
92-04-016	Irish Water Mill	D. Winter	Closed	Gift	75-125.00
92-04-017	Patrick's Water Mill	D. Winter	Closed	Gift	225-315.
92-04-018	Candle Maker's	D. Winter	Closed	65.00	125.00
92-04-019	Bee Keeper's	D. Winter	Closed	65.00	125.00
93-04-020	On The River Bank	D. Winter	Yr.Iss.	Gift	80.00
93-04-021	Thameside	D. Winter	Yr.Iss.	79.00	79.00
93-04-022	Swan Upping Cottage	D. Winter	Yr.Iss.	69.00	69.00
94-04-023	15 Lawnside Road	D. Winter	Yr.Iss.	Gift	Gift
94-04-024	While Away Cottage?	D. Winter	Yr.Iss.	70.00	70.00
94-04-025	Ashe Cottage	D. Winter	Yr.Iss.	67.00	67.00
John Hine N.A. Ltd.		**Scottish Collection**			
89-05-001	Scottish Crofter	D. Winter	Open	42.00	56.00
89-05-002	House on the Loch	D. Winter	Open	65.00	84.00
89-05-003	Gillie's Cottage	D. Winter	Open	65.00	84.00
89-05-004	Gatekeeper's	D. Winter	Open	65.00	84.00
89-05-005	MacBeth's Castle	D. Winter	Open	200.00	256.00
John Hine N.A. Ltd.		**Irish Collection**			
92-06-001	Irish Round Tower	D. Winter	Open	65.00	68.00
92-06-002	Fogartys	D. Winter	Open	75.00	78.00
92-06-003	Murphys	D. Winter	Open	100.00	106.00
92-06-004	O'Donovan's Castle	D. Winter	Open	145.00	152.00
John Hine N.A. Ltd.		**British Traditions**			
90-07-001	Burns' Reading Room	D. Winter	Open	31.00	36.00
90-07-002	Stonecutters Cottage	D. Winter	Open	48.00	54.00
90-07-003	The Boat House	D. Winter	Open	37.50	44.00
90-07-004	Pudding Cottage	D. Winter	Open	78.00	90.00
90-07-005	Blossom Cottage	D. Winter	Open	59.00	64.00
90-07-006	Knight's Castle	D. Winter	Open	59.00	68.00
90-07-007	St. Anne's Well	D. Winter	Open	48.00	54.00

FIGURINES/COTTAGES

Company		Series			
Number	Name	Artist	Edition Limit	Issue Price	Quote
90-07-008	Grouse Moor Lodge	D. Winter	Open	48.00	54.00
90-07-009	Staffordshire Vicarage	D. Winter	Open	48.00	54.00
90-07-010	Harvest Barn	D. Winter	Open	31.00	36.00
90-07-011	Guy Fawkes	D. Winter	Open	31.00	36.00
90-07-012	Bull & Bush	D. Winter	Open	37.50	44.00
John Hine N.A. Ltd.		**David Winter Cameos**			
92-08-001	Brooklet Bridge	D. Winter	Open	12.50	14.00
92-08-002	Poultry Ark	D. Winter	Open	12.50	14.00
92-08-003	The Potting Shed	D. Winter	Open	12.50	14.00
92-08-004	Lych Gate	D. Winter	Open	12.50	14.00
92-08-005	One Man Jail	D. Winter	Open	12.50	14.00
92-08-006	Market Day	D. Winter	Open	12.50	14.00
92-08-007	Welsh Pig Pen	D. Winter	Open	12.50	14.00
92-08-008	The Privy	D. Winter	Open	12.50	14.00
92-08-009	Greenwood Wagon	D. Winter	Open	12.50	14.00
92-08-010	Saddle Steps	D. Winter	Open	12.50	14.00
92-08-011	Barley Malt Kilns	D. Winter	Open	12.50	14.00
92-08-012	Penny Wishing Well	D. Winter	Open	12.50	14.00
92-08-013	Diorama-Light	D. Winter	Closed	30.00	30.00
92-08-014	Diorama-Bright	D. Winter	Open	52.00	52.00
John Hine N.A. Ltd.		**David Winter Scenes**			
92-09-001	At The Bothy Vignette Base	D. Winter	5,000	39.00	39.00
92-09-002	Farmer And Plough	Cameo Guild	5,000	60.00	60.00
92-09-003	Farm Hand And Spade	Cameo Guild	5,000	40.00	40.00
92-09-004	Farmer's Wife	Cameo Guild	5,000	45.00	45.00
92-09-005	Goose Girl	Cameo Guild	5,000	45.00	45.00
92-09-006	At The Bake House Vignette	D. Winter	5,000	35.00	35.00
92-09-007	Hot Cross Bun Seller	Cameo Guild	5,000	60.00	60.00
92-09-008	Woman At Pump	Cameo Guild	5,000	45.00	45.00
92-09-009	Lady Customer	Cameo Guild	5,000	45.00	45.00
92-09-010	Small Boy And Dog	Cameo Guild	5,000	45.00	45.00
92-09-011	Girl Selling Eggs	Cameo Guild	5,000	30.00	30.00
92-09-012	At Rose cottage Vignette	D. Winter	5,000	39.00	39.00
92-09-013	Mother	Cameo Guild	5,000	50.00	50.00
92-09-014	Father	Cameo Guild	5,000	45.00	45.00
92-09-015	Son	Cameo Guild	5,000	30.00	30.00
92-09-016	Daughter	D. Winter	5,000	30.00	30.00
93-09-017	Miss Belle	Cameo Guild	5,000	35.00	35.00
93-09-018	Bob Cratchit And Tiny Tim	Cameo Guild	5,000	50.00	50.00
93-09-019	Fred	Cameo Guild	5,000	35.00	35.00
93-09-020	Mrs. Fezziwig	Cameo Guild	5,000	35.00	35.00
93-09-021	Tom The Street Shoveler	Cameo Guild	5,000	60.00	60.00
93-09-022	Ebenezer Scrooge	Cameo Guild	5,000	45.00	45.00
93-09-023	Snow Vignette base	D. Winter	5,000	50.00	50.00
John Hine N.A. Ltd.		**Shires Collection**			
93-10-001	Oxfordshire Goat Yard	D. Winter	Open	32.00	32.00
93-10-002	Shropshire Pig Shelter	D. Winter	Open	32.00	32.00
93-10-003	Hampshire Hutches	D. Winter	Open	34.00	34.00
93-10-004	Wiltshire Waterwheel	D. Winter	Open	34.00	34.00
93-10-005	Cheshire Kennels	D. Winter	Open	36.00	36.00
93-10-006	Derbyshire Dovecote	D. Winter	Open	36.00	36.00
93-10-007	Staffordshire Stable	D. Winter	Open	36.00	36.00
93-10-008	Berkshire Milking Byre	D. Winter	Open	38.00	38.00
93-10-009	Buckinghamshire Bull Pen	D. Winter	Open	38.00	38.00
93-10-010	Lancashire Donkey Shed	D. Winter	Open	38.00	38.00
93-10-011	Yorkshire Sheep Fold	D. Winter	Open	38.00	38.00
93-10-012	Gloucestershire Greenhouse	D. Winter	Open	40.00	40.00
John Hine N.A. Ltd.		**Welsh Collection**			
93-11-001	Pen Y Graig	D. Winter	Open	88.00	88.00
93-11-002	Tyddyn Siriol	D. Winter	Open	88.00	88.00
93-11-003	Y Ddraig Goch	D. Winter	Open	88.00	88.00
93-11-004	A Bit of Nonsense	D. Winter	Open	52.00	52.00
John Hine N.A. Ltd.		**The English Village**			
94-12-001	Post Office	D. Winter	Open	53.00	53.00
94-12-002	Rectory	D. Winter	Open	55.00	55.00
94-12-003	Smithy	D. Winter	Open	50.00	50.00
94-12-004	Tannery	D. Winter	Open	50.00	50.00
94-12-005	Hall	D. Winter	Open	55.00	55.00
94-12-006	One Acre Cottage	D. Winter	Open	55.00	55.00
94-12-007	Cat & Pipe	D. Winter	Open	53.00	53.00
94-12-008	Quack's Cottage	D. Winter	Open	57.00	57.00
94-12-009	Constabulatory	D. Winter	Open	60.00	60.00
94-12-010	Crystal Cottage	D. Winter	Open	53.00	53.00
94-12-011	Chandlery	D. Winter	Open	53.00	53.00
94-12-012	Seminary	D. Winter	Open	57.00	57.00
94-12-013	Church & Vestry	D. Winter	Open	57.00	57.00
94-12-014	Glebe Cottage	D. Winter	Open	53.00	53.00
94-12-015	The Engine House	D. Winter	Open	55.00	55.00
John Hine N.A. Ltd.		**David Winter Special Event Pieces**			
93-13-001	Birthstone Wishing Well	D. Winter	Closed	40.00	40.00
93-13-002	Birthday Cottage	D. Winter	6/94	55.00	55.00
John Hine N.A. Ltd.		**David Winter Tour Special Event Piece**			
93-14-001	Arches Thrice	D. Winter	Closed	150.00	120-250.
John Hine N.A. Ltd.		**American Collection**			
89-15-001	The Out House	M. Wideman	Closed	15.00	12-16.00
89-15-002	Colonial Wellhouse	M. Wideman	Closed	15.00	16.00
89-15-003	Wisteria	M. Wideman	Closed	15.00	12-45.00
89-15-004	The Blockhouse	M. Wideman	Closed	25.00	25.00
89-15-005	Garconniere	M. Wideman	Closed	25.00	70.00
89-15-006	The Log Cabin	M. Wideman	Closed	45.00	40-56.00
89-15-007	Cherry Hill School	M. Wideman	Closed	45.00	56.00
89-15-008	The Maple Sugar Shack	M. Wideman	Closed	50.00	56.00
89-15-009	The Kissing Bridge	M. Wideman	Closed	50.00	56.00
89-15-010	The Gingerbread House	M. Wideman	Closed	60.00	72.00
89-15-011	The New England Church	M. Wideman	Closed	79.00	115.00
89-15-012	The Opera House	M. Wideman	Closed	89.00	100.00
89-15-013	The Pacific Lighthouse	M. Wideman	Closed	89.00	80-155.00
89-15-014	King William Tavern	M. Wideman	Closed	99.00	100-200.
89-15-015	The Mission	M. Wideman	Closed	99.00	110.00
89-15-016	New England Lighthouse	M. Wideman	Closed	99.00	115.00
89-15-017	The River Bell	M. Wideman	Closed	99.00	120.00
89-15-018	Plantation House	M. Wideman	Closed	119.00	185.00
89-15-019	Town Hall	M. Wideman	Closed	129.00	95-144.00
89-15-020	Dog House	M. Wideman	Closed	10.00	8-12.00
89-15-021	Star Cottage	M. Wideman	Closed	30.00	34.00
89-15-022	Sod House	M. Wideman	Closed	40.00	62.00
89-15-023	Barber Shop	M. Wideman	Closed	40.00	44.00
89-15-024	Octagonal House	M. Wideman	Closed	40.00	44.00
89-15-025	Cajun Cottage	M. Wideman	Closed	50.00	56.00
89-15-026	Prairie Forge	M. Wideman	Closed	65.00	72.00
89-15-027	Oxbow Saloon	M. Wideman	Closed	90.00	100.00
89-15-028	Sierra Mine	M. Wideman	Closed	120.00	149.00
89-15-029	California Winery	M. Wideman	Closed	180.00	198.00
89-15-030	Railhead Inn	M. Wideman	Closed	250.00	165-276.00
89-15-031	Haunted House	M. Wideman	Closed	100.00	80-110.00
89-15-032	Tobacconist	M. Wideman	Closed	45.00	50.00
89-15-033	Hawaiian Grass Hut	M. Wideman	Closed	45.00	50.00
89-15-034	The Old Mill	M. Wideman	Closed	100.00	110.00
89-15-035	Band Stand	M. Wideman	Closed	90.00	100.00
89-15-036	Seaside Cottage	M. Wideman	Closed	225.00	248.00
89-15-037	Tree House	M. Wideman	Closed	45.00	36-50.00
89-15-038	Hacienda	M. Wideman	Closed	51.00	52-56.00
89-15-039	Sweetheart Cottage	M. Wideman	Closed	45.00	50.00
89-15-040	Forty-Niner Cabin	M. Wideman	Closed	50.00	40-56.00
91-15-041	Desert Storm Tent	M. Wideman	Closed	75.00	125-150.
91-15-042	Paul Revere's House	M. Wideman	Closed	90.00	100.00
91-15-043	Mo At Work	M. Wideman	Closed	35.00	35-70.00
91-15-044	Church in the Dale	M. Wideman	Closed	130.00	144.00
91-15-045	Milk House	M. Wideman	Closed	20.00	22.00
91-15-046	Moe's Diner	M. Wideman	Closed	100.00	400.00
91-15-047	Fire Station	M. Wideman	Closed	160.00	176.00
91-15-048	Joe's Service Station	M. Wideman	Closed	90.00	72-100.00
92-15-049	News Stand	M. Wideman	Closed	30.00	24-30.00
92-15-050	Village Mercantile	M. Wideman	Closed	60.00	60.00
92-15-051	Grain Elevator	M. Wideman	Closed	110.00	110.00
92-15-052	Telephone Booth	M. Wideman	Closed	15.00	12-32.00
92-15-053	Topper's Drive-In	M. Wideman	Closed	120.00	110-200.
John Hine N.A. Ltd.		**First Nation Collection**			
93-16-001	The First Nation Collection, set of 8	M. Wideman	Closed	500.00	1200-1500.
93-16-002	Elm Bark Longhouse	M. Wideman	Closed	56.00	56.00
93-16-003	Igloo	M. Wideman	Closed	60.00	120-175.
93-16-004	Mandan Earth Lodge	M. Wideman	Closed	56.00	300.00
93-16-005	Plains Teepee	M. Wideman	Closed	68.00	300.00
93-16-006	Stilt House	M. Wideman	Closed	60.00	60-90.00
93-16-007	Sweat Lodge	M. Wideman	Closed	34.00	100.00
93-16-008	West Coast Longhouse	M. Wideman	Closed	100.00	100.00
93-16-009	Wigwam	M. Wideman	Closed	65.00	300.00
John Hine N.A. Ltd.		**Wideman**			
92-17-001	Moe's Clubhouse	M. Wideman	Closed	40.00	250-300.
John Hine N.A. Ltd.		**Mushrooms**			
89-18-001	Royal Bank of Mushland	C. Lawrence	2,500	235.00	235.00
89-18-002	The Elders Mushroom	C. Lawrence	2,500	175.00	175.00.
89-18-003	The Cobblers	C. Lawrence	2,500	265.00	265.00
89-18-004	The Mush Hospital for Malingerers	C. Lawrence	2,500	250.00	250.00
89-18-005	The Ministry	C. Lawrence	2,500	185.00	185.00
89-18-006	The Gift Shop	C. Lawrence	1,200	350.00	420.00
89-18-007	The Constables	C. Lawrence	2,500	200.00	200.00
89-18-008	The Princess Palace	C. Lawrence	750	600.00	730.00
John Hine N.A. Ltd.		**Bugaboos**			
89-19-001	Arnold	John Hine Studio	Closed	45.00	45.00
89-19-002	Edna	John Hine Studio	Closed	45.00	45.00
89-19-003	Wilbur	John Hine Studio	Closed	45.00	45.00
89-19-004	Beryl	John Hine Studio	Closed	45.00	45.00
89-19-005	Gerald	John Hine Studio	Closed	45.00	45.00
89-19-006	Wesley	John Hine Studio	Closed	45.00	45.00
89-19-007	Oscar	John Hine Studio	Closed	45.00	45.00
89-19-008	Lizzie	John Hine Studio	Closed	45.00	45.00
89-19-009	Enid	John Hine Studio	Closed	45.00	45.00
John Hine N.A. Ltd.		**Great British Pubs**			
89-20-001	Smith's Arms	M. Cooper	Open	28.00	28.00
89-20-002	The Plough	M. Cooper	Open	28.00	28.00
89-20-003	King's Arms	M. Cooper	Closed	28.00	28.00
89-20-004	White Tower	M. Cooper	Open	35.00	35.00
89-20-005	Old Bridge House	M. Cooper	Open	37.50	37.50
89-20-006	White Horse	M. Cooper	Open	39.50	39.50
89-20-007	Jamaica Inn	M. Cooper	Open	39.50	39.50
89-20-008	The George	M. Cooper	Open	57.50	57.50
89-20-009	Montague Arms	M. Cooper	Open	57.50	57.50
89-20-010	Blue Bell	M. Cooper	Open	57.50	57.50
89-20-011	The Lion	M. Cooper	Open	57.50	57.50
89-20-012	Coach & Horses	M. Cooper	Open	79.50	79.50
89-20-013	Ye Olde Spotted Horse	M. Cooper	Open	79.50	79.50
89-20-014	The Crown Inn	M. Cooper	Open	79.50	79.50
89-20-015	The Bell	M. Cooper	Closed	79.50	100-350.
89-20-016	Black Swan	M. Cooper	Closed	79.50	100-350.
89-20-017	Ye Grapes	M. Cooper	Open	87.50	87.50
89-20-018	Old Bull Inn	M. Cooper	Open	87.50	87.50
89-20-019	Dickens Inn	M. Cooper	Open	100.00	100.00
89-20-020	Sherlock Holmes	M. Cooper	Closed	100.00	200.00
89-20-021	George Somerset	M. Cooper	Open	100.00	100.00
89-20-022	The Feathers	M. Cooper	Open	200.00	200.00
89-20-023	Hawkeshead	M. Cooper	Open	Unkn.	900.00
John Hine N.A. Ltd.		**Great British Pubs-Yard of Pubs**			
89-21-001	Grenadier	M. Cooper	Closed	25.00	25.00
89-21-002	Black Friars	M. Cooper	Closed	25.00	25.00
89-21-003	Falkland Arms	M. Cooper	Closed	25.00	25.00
89-21-004	George & Pilgrims	M. Cooper	Closed	25.00	25.00
89-21-005	Dirty Duck	M. Cooper	Closed	25.00	25.00
89-21-006	Wheatsheaf	M. Cooper	Closed	35.00	35.00
89-21-007	Lygon Arms	M. Cooper	Closed	35.00	35.00
89-21-008	Suffolk Bull	M. Cooper	Closed	35.00	35.00
89-21-009	The Swan	M. Cooper	Closed	35.00	35.00
89-21-010	The Falstaff	M. Cooper	Closed	35.00	35.00
89-21-011	The Eagle	M. Cooper	Closed	35.00	35.00
89-21-012	The Green Man	M. Cooper	Closed	Unkn.	75.00
John Hine N.A. Ltd.		**The Shoemaker's Dream**			
91-22-001	The Jester Boot	J. Herbert	Open	29.00	29.00
91-22-002	The Crooked Boot	J. Herbert	Open	35.00	35.00
91-22-003	Rosie's Cottage	J. Herbert	Open	40.00	40.00
91-22-004	Baby Booty (pink)	J. Herbert	Open	45.00	45.00
91-22-005	Baby Booty (blue)	J. Herbert	Open	45.00	45.00
91-22-006	Shoemaker's Palace	J. Herbert	Open	50.00	50.00
91-22-007	Tavern Boot	J. Herbert	Open	55.00	55.00

Number	Name	Artist	Edition Limit	Issue Price	Quote
91-22-008	River Shoe Cottage	J. Herbert	Open	55.00	55.00
91-22-009	The Chapel	J. Herbert	Open	55.00	55.00
91-22-010	Castle Boot	J. Herbert	Open	55.00	55.00
91-22-011	The Clocktower Boot	J. Herbert	Open	60.00	60.00
91-22-012	Watermill Boot	J. Herbert	Open	60.00	60.00
91-22-013	Windmill Boot	J. Herbert	Open	65.00	65.00
91-22-014	The Gate Lodge	J. Herbert	Open	65.00	65.00
92-22-015	Wishing Well Shoe	J. Herbert	Open	32.00	32.00
92-22-016	The Golf Shoe	J. Herbert	Open	35.00	35.00
92-22-017	The Sports Shoe	J. Herbert	Open	35.00	35.00
92-22-018	Clown Boot	J. Herbert	Open	45.00	45.00
92-22-019	Upside Down Boot	J. Herbert	Open	45.00	45.00
92-22-020	Christmas Boot	J. Herbert	Open	55.00	55.00
93-22-021	Wedding Bells	J. Herbert	Open	45.00	50.00
93-22-022	Shiver me Timbers	J. Herbert	Open	45.00	55.00
93-22-023	The Woodcutter's Shoe	J. Herbert	Open	40.00	40.00
John Hine N.A. Ltd.		**Animal Antics**			
93-23-001	Sir Mouse	J. Herbert	Open	20.00	20.00
93-23-002	Lady Mouse	J. Herbert	Open	20.00	20.00
93-23-003	You're Bone Idle	J. Herbert	Open	30.00	30.00
93-23-004	Real Cool Carrot	J. Herbert	Open	30.00	30.00
93-23-005	Tabby Tabitha	J. Herbert	Open	37.00	37.00
93-23-006	Lucky Dragon	J. Herbert	Open	40.00	40.00
93-23-007	Slow Progress	J. Herbert	Open	40.00	40.00
93-23-008	Bird Brain	J. Herbert	Open	32.00	32.00
93-23-009	Snail Place	J. Herbert	Open	37.00	37.00
John Hine N.A. Ltd.		**Heartstrings**			
92-24-001	Hush, It's Sleepytime	S. Kuck	15,000	97.50	97.50
92-24-002	Taking Tea	S. Kuck	15,000	92.50	92.50
92-24-003	Day Dreaming	S. Kuck	15,000	92.50	92.50
92-24-004	Watch Me Waltz	S. Kuck	15,000	97.50	97.50
John Hine N.A. Ltd.		**Santa's Big Day**			
92-25-001	Booting Up	J. King	Closed	40.00	40.00
92-25-002	Home Rudolph	J. King	Closed	50.00	50.00
92-25-003	Reindeer Breakfast	J. King	Closed	50.00	50.00
92-25-004	Feet First	J. King	Closed	55.00	55.00
92-25-005	Santa's Night Ride	J. King	Closed	55.00	55.00
92-25-006	Tight Fit!	J. King	Closed	55.00	55.00
92-25-007	Wakey, Wakey!	J. King	Closed	55.00	55.00
92-25-008	Rest-a-while	J. King	Closed	60.00	60.00
92-25-009	Whoops!	J. King	Closed	60.00	60.00
92-25-010	Heave Ho!	J. King	Closed	70.00	70.00
92-25-011	Ready Boys?	J. King	Closed	80.00	80.00
92-25-012	Zzzzz...	J. King	Closed	85.00	85.00
John Hine N.A. Ltd.		**Father Christmas**			
88-26-001	Standing	J. King	Closed	70.00	70.00
88-26-002	Feet	J. King	Closed	70.00	70.00
88-26-003	Falling	J. King	Closed	70.00	70.00
John Hine N.A. Ltd.		**London By Gaslight**			
92-27-001	Starter Packet (Knightsbridge Mansion, Banker's House in the City, end pieces, and transformer)	B. Russell	Open	150.00	155.00
92-27-002	Piccadilly Chambers	B. Russell	Open	65.00	80.00
92-27-003	St. Bartholomew's Church Gate	B. Russell	Open	75.00	75.00
92-27-004	Chelsea Townhouse	B. Russell	Open	60.00	80.00
92-27-005	Streatham South of Thames	B. Russell	Open	55.00	70.00
92-27-006	Belgravia Mews Cottage	B. Russell	Open	50.00	55.00
92-27-007	Cockney's Corner Shop and The Iron Duke, Blackfriars	B. Russell	Open	100.00	135.00
92-27-008	Weaver's Warehouse, Holborn	B. Russell	Open	50.00	60.00
92-27-009	Clothfriar Road, Smithfield	B. Russell	Open	55.00	70.00
92-27-010	Thameside Walk	B. Russell	Open	60.00	75.00
92-27-011	Regency House in St. James	B. Russell	Open	70.00	85.00
92-27-012	Birdcage Walk, Westminster	B. Russell	Open	70.00	85.00
John Hine N.A. Ltd.		**London By Gaslight- Accessories**			
92-28-001	Fire Engine	A. Stadden	Open	15.00	15.00
92-28-002	Hanson Cab (empty)	A. Stadden	Open	12.00	13.00
92-28-003	Hanson Cab	A. Stadden	Open	12.00	13.00
92-28-004	Organ Grinder	A. Stadden	Open	9.00	9.00
92-28-005	Goods Wagon	A. Stadden	Open	12.00	12.00
92-28-006	Five Men; Four Men	A. Stadden	Open	13.50	16.40
92-28-007	Police w/Two Children/Children Playing	A. Stadden	Open	9.00	14.50
92-28-008	Woman w/Baby/Three Drunks	A. Stadden	Open	9.00	14.00
92-28-009	Couple Walking/Two Couples Walking	A. Stadden	Open	11.00	15.00
92-28-010	Jack the Ripper/Victim/Holmes/Watson	A. Stadden	Open	15.00	15.40
92-28-011	Borrowman/Woman/Milk Float/Man/Trolley	A. Stadden	Open	15.00	22.00
92-28-012	Flower Seller/Gas Lamp Lighter/Post Box	A. Stadden	Open	9.00	16.20
92-28-013	Dog Cart/Stick Up Man/Wheelbarrow	A. Stadden	Open	11.00	16.00
92-28-014	Tree	A. Stadden	Open	16.20	16.20
Historical Miniatures		**American Heritage:Charleston**			
94-01-001	Rutledge House	M. Weisser	Open	50.00	50.00
94-01-002	The Pink House	M. Weisser	Open	36.00	36.00
94-01-003	Rainbow Row:Blue #1	M. Weisser	Open	36.00	36.00
94-01-004	Rainbow Row:Green #1	M. Weisser	Open	36.00	36.00
Historical Miniatures		**American Heritage: New Orleans**			
94-02-001	Royal Cafe	M. Weisser	Open	39.00	39.00
94-02-002	Chart House	M. Weisser	Open	34.00	34.00
Historical Miniatures		**American Heritage:Miami Beach: Deco District**			
94-03-001	Hotel Taft	M. Weisser	Open	29.90	29.90
94-03-002	Hotel Carlyle	M. Weisser	Open	36.00	36.00
94-03-003	Hotel Century	M. Weisser	Open	31.00	31.00
Hutschenreuther		**American Limited Edition Collection**			
XX-01-001	A Family Affair	Granget	200	Unkn.	3700.00
XX-01-002	Take Cover	Granget	125	Unkn.	14000.00
XX-01-003	The Challenge	Granget	150	Unkn.	14000.00
XX-01-004	Heading South	Granget	150	Unkn.	14000.00
XX-01-005	First Lesson	Granget	175	Unkn.	3550.00
XX-01-006	Safe at Home	Granget	350	Unkn.	9000.00
XX-01-007	Off Season	Granget	125	Unkn.	4125.00
XX-01-008	Disdain-Owl	Granget	175	Unkn.	5200.00
XX-01-009	Friendly Enemies-Woodpecker	Granget	175	Unkn.	5200.00
XX-01-010	Engaged	Granget	250	Unkn.	1750.00
XX-01-011	Spring is Here	Granget	175	Unkn.	4500.00
XX-01-012	Anxious Moment	Granget	175	Unkn.	5225.00
XX-01-013	It's Spring Again	Granget	250	Unkn.	3475.00
XX-01-014	Freedom in Flight	Granget	200	Unkn.	9000.00
XX-01-015	Reluctant Fledgling	Granget	350	Unkn.	3475.00
XX-01-016	Proud Parent	Granget	250	Unkn.	13750.00
XX-01-017	Joe-Stag	Granget	150	Unkn.	12000.00
XX-01-018	Olympic Champion	Granget	500	Unkn.	3650.00
XX-01-019	The Sentinel-Springbok	Granget	150	Unkn.	5200.00
XX-01-020	Sea Frolic-Sea Lion	Granget	500	Unkn.	3500.00
XX-01-021	The Dance-Crowncrested Crane	Granget	25	Unkn.	30000.00
XX-01-022	The Contest	Granget	100	Unkn.	14000.00
XX-01-023	The Fish Hawk	Granget	500	Unkn.	12000.00
XX-01-024	To Ride the Wind	Granget	500	Unkn.	8650.00
XX-01-025	Decorated Sea Lions	Granget	100	Unkn.	6000.00
XX-01-026	Dolphin Group	Granget	500	Unkn.	4000.00
XX-01-027	Silver Heron	Netzsch	500	Unkn.	5000.00
XX-01-028	Sparrowhawk w/Kingbird	Granget	500	Unkn.	8250.00
XX-01-029	Saw Whet Owl	Granget	750	Unkn.	3575.00
XX-01-030	Pygmy Owls	Granget	650	Unkn.	6225.00
XX-01-031	Arabian Stallion	Achtziger	300	Unkn.	8525.00
XX-01-032	Whooping Cranes	Netzsch	300	Unkn.	8000.00
XX-01-033	Wren on Wild Rose	Netzsch	250	Unkn.	1675.00
XX-01-034	Redstart on Quince Branch	Netzsch	250	Unkn.	1300.00
XX-01-035	Linnet on Ear of Rye	Netzsch	250	Unkn.	1175.00
XX-01-036	Quince	Netzsch	375	Unkn.	2850.00
XX-01-037	Water Lily	O'Hara	375	Unkn.	4150.00
XX-01-038	Christmas Rose	O'Hara	375	Unkn.	3050.00
XX-01-039	Blue Dolphins	Granget	100	Unkn.	10000.00
Iris Arc Crystal		**1981 Introductions**			
81-01-001	Octopus	P. Hale	Open	32.00	50.00
81-01-002	Kitten	T. Holliman	Retrd.	40.00	48.00
81-01-003	Dachshund	P. Hale	Retrd.	48.00	58.00
81-01-004	Mushrooms	T. Holliman	Retrd.	50.00	60.00
81-01-005	Miniature Snail (Silver)	P. Hale	Retrd.	20.00	24.00
81-01-006	Miniature Snail (Rainbow)	P. Hale	Open	20.00	27.00
81-01-007	Miniature Koala	T. Holliman	Retrd.	24.00	29.00
81-01-008	Miniature Dragonfly	T. Holliman	Retrd.	20.00	24.00
81-01-009	Miniature Bunny	T. Holliman	Retrd.	28.00	33 .75
81-01-010	Miniature Frog	P. Hale	Retrd.	20.00	24.00
81-01-011	Miniature Firefly (Silver)	T. Holliman	Retrd.	20.00	24.00
81-01-012	Miniature Firefly (Rainbow)	T. Holliman	Retrd.	20.00	24.00
81-01-013	Miniature Angel	T. Holliman	Retrd.	24.00	29.00
Iris Arc Crystal		**1982 Introductions**			
82-02-001	Seal (Silver)	P. Hale	Retrd.	32.00	38.00
82-02-002	Seal (Rainbow)	P. Hale	Open	32.00	35.00
82-02-003	Hippo	P. Hale	Retrd.	64.00	77.00
82-02-004	Small Teddy Bear w/Heart (Silver)	P. Hale	Retrd.	36.00	43.00
82-02-005	Small Teddy Bear w/Heart (Rose)	P. Hale	Open	36.00	45.00
82-02-006	Polar Bear	P. Hale	Retrd.	32.00	39.00
82-02-007	Koala	T. Holliman	Retrd.	44.00	53.00
82-02-008	Squirrel	P. Hale	Retrd.	36.00	43.00
82-02-009	Small Mouse	Iris Arc	Retrd.	38.00	46.00
82-02-010	Large Mouse	Iris Arc	Retrd.	48.00	58.00
82-02-011	Swan Lake	P. Hale	Retrd.	40.00	48.00
82-02-012	Small Elephant	P. Hale	Retrd.	70.00	84.00
82-02-013	Arc Angel	Iris Arc	Retrd.	40.00	48.00
82-02-014	Birdbath	T. Holliman	Retrd.	60.00	90.00
82-02-015	Snowman	P. Hale	Retrd.	42.00	51.00
82-02-016	Siamese Cat	T. Holliman	Retrd.	48.00	58.00
82-02-017	Unicorn	P. Hale	Retrd.	76.00	91.00
82-02-018	Small Butterfly	T. Holliman	Retrd.	44.00	53.00
82-02-019	Large Butterfly	T. Holliman	Retrd.	56.00	67.00
82-02-020	Miniature Swan	T. Holliman	Retrd.	20.00	27.00
Iris Arc Crystal		**1983 Introductions**			
83-03-001	Panda	P. Hale	Retrd.	56.00	67.00
83-03-002	Kangaroo	P. Hale	Retrd.	36.00	43.00
83-03-003	Otter (Silver)	P. Hale	Retrd.	36.00	43.00
83-03-004	Otter (Rainbow)	P. Hale	Retrd.	36.00	43.00
83-03-005	Turtle	Iris Arc	Retrd.	48.00	58.00
83-03-006	Crab	P. Hale	Retrd.	32.00	38.00
83-03-007	Camel	T. Holliman	Retrd.	136.00	163.00
83-03-008	Miniature Turtle	P. Hale	Open	20.00	27.00
83-03-009	Miniature Dove	P. Hale	Retrd.	20.00	24.00
83-03-010	Miniature Owl	P. Patruno	Retrd.	24.00	29.00
83-03-011	Miniature Frog	P. Hale	Retrd.	20.00	24.00
Iris Arc Crystal		**1984 Introductions**			
84-04-001	Enchanted Castle	T. Holliman	Retrd.	1200.00	1440.00
84-04-002	Dragon Slayer	P. Hale	Retrd.	120.00	144.00
84-04-003	Dragon	P. Hale	Retrd.	190.00	228.00
84-04-004	Pegasus	P. Hale	Retrd.	100.00	120.00
84-04-005	Knight	P. Hale	Retrd.	56.00	67.00
84-04-006	Jester	P. Hale	Retrd.	50.00	60.00
84-04-007	Fairy	P. Hale	Retrd.	32.00	39.00
84-04-008	Maiden	P. Hale	Retrd.	56.00	67.00
84-04-009	Wizard	P. Hale	Retrd.	64.00	77.00
84-04-010	Med. Teddy Bear w/Heart (Silver)	P. Hale	Retrd.	56.00	67.00
84-04-011	Med. Teddy Bear w/Heart (Rose)	P. Hale	Retrd.	56.00	70.00
84-04-012	Mini Teddy Bear w/Heart (Silver)	P. Hale	Retrd.	18.00	22.00
84-04-013	Mini Teddy Bear w/Heart (Rose)	P. Hale	Open	18.00	25.00
84-04-014	Panda w/Heart	P. Hale	Retrd.	58.00	70.00
84-04-015	Miniature Panda	P. Hale	Retrd.	18.00	22.00
84-04-016	Mini Panda w/Heart	P. Hale	Open	20.00	27.00
84-04-017	Koala w/Heart	P. Hale	Retrd.	46.00	55.00
84-04-018	Mini Koala w/Heart	P. Hale	Retrd.	13.00	16.00
84-04-019	Large Giraffe	P. Hale	Retrd.	240.00	288.00
84-04-020	Small Giraffe	P. Hale	Retrd.	100.00	120.00
84-04-021	Medium Elephant	P. Hale	Retrd.	150.00	180.00
84-04-022	Kangaroo	P. Hale	Retrd.	48.00	58.00
84-04-023	Rhino	P. Hale	Retrd.	56.00	67.00
84-04-024	Lion w/Heart	P. Hale	Retrd.	70.00	84.00
84-04-025	Peacock	P. Hale	Retrd.	140.00	168.00
84-04-026	Dog w/Bone	P. Hale	Retrd.	50.00	60.00
84-04-027	Kitten w/Ball	P. Hale	Retrd.	50.00	60.00
84-04-028	Dolphin	P. Hale	Retrd.	48.00	58.00
84-04-029	Whale	P. Hale	Retrd.	44.00	53.00
84-04-030	Penguin	P. Hale	Retrd.	32.00	39.00
84-04-031	Miniature Rabbit	P. Hale	Retrd.	18.00	22.00
84-04-032	Miniature Kitten	P. Hale	Open	18.00	27.00
84-04-033	Miniature Puppy	P. Hale	Retrd.	18.00	22.00
84-04-034	Miniature Robin	P. Hale	Retrd.	18.00	21.00

Company Number	Name	Series Artist	Edition Limit	Issue Price	Quote
Iris Arc Crystal		**1985 Introductions**			
85-05-001	Rainbow Juggler	P. Hale	Retrd.	100.00	120.00
85-05-002	Small Rainbow Juggler	P. Hale	Retrd.	50.00	60.00
85-05-003	Nativity Scene	P. Hale	Retrd.	130.00	156.00
85-05-004	Baby Bunny with Carrot	P. Hale	Open	45.00	60.00
85-05-005	Small Unicorn	P. Hale	Retrd.	45.00	54.00
85-05-006	Ballerina	P. Hale	Retrd.	70.00	84.00
85-05-007	Rudolph the Rednose Reindeer®	P. Hale	Retrd.	100.00	120.00
85-05-008	Christmas Tree	P. Hale	Retrd.	150.00	180.00
85-05-009	Small Camel	P. Hale	Retrd.	88.00	106.00
85-05-010	Small Lion with Heart	P. Hale	Retrd.	45.00	54.00
85-05-011	Small Peacock	P. Hale	Retrd.	50.00	60.00
85-05-012	Small AB Peacock	P. Hale	Open	60.00	120.00
85-05-013	Medium AB Peacock	P. Hale	Retrd.	160.00	200.00
85-05-014	Large Peacock	P. Hale	Retrd.	700.00	840.00
85-05-015	Large Swan Lake	P. Hale	Retrd.	170.00	204.00
85-05-016	Poodle	P. Hale	Retrd.	150.00	180.00
85-05-017	Bunny with Carrot	P. Hale	Retrd.	65.00	78.00
85-05-018	Medium Turtle	P. Hale	Retrd.	55.00	66.00
85-05-019	Medium Swan	P. Hale	Retrd.	60.00	72.00
85-05-020	Large Swan	P. Hale	Retrd.	350.00	420.00
85-05-021	Feeding Time	P. Hale	Retrd.	120.00	144.00
85-05-022	Wildflower with Hummingbird	P. Hale	Open	240.00	390.00
85-05-023	Wildflower	P. Hale	Retrd.	190.00	228.00
85-05-024	Large Owl	P. Hale	Retrd.	140.00	168.00
85-05-025	Small Owl	P. Hale	Retrd.	55.00	66.00
Iris Arc Crystal		**1986 Introductions**			
86-06-001	Rainbow Cloud Castle	P. Hale	Open	350.00	400.00
86-06-002	Lovebirds	P. Hale	Retrd.	150.00	180.00
86-06-003	Caprice Carousel Horse	P. Hale	Retrd.	100.00	130.00
86-06-004	Angel with Cymbals	P. Hale	Open	30.00	35.00
86-06-005	Angel with Flute	P. Hale	Open	30.00	35.00
86-06-006	Angel with Guitar	P. Hale	Open	30.00	35.00
86-06-007	Angel with Harp	P. Hale	Open	30.00	35.00
86-06-008	Angel Singing	P. Hale	Open	30.00	35.00
86-06-009	Angel Gabriel	P. Hale	Open	30.00	35.00
86-06-010	Santa	P. Hale	Retrd.	90.00	108.00
86-06-011	Small Snowman	P. Hale	Open	36.00	45.00
86-06-012	Large Snowman	J. Mulroy	Retrd.	56.00	67.25
86-06-013	Guardian Angel	P. Hale	Retrd.	50.00	65.00
86-06-014	Moose	P. Hale	Open	60.00	90.00
86-06-015	Large Parrot	P. Hale	Retrd.	350.00	420.00
86-06-016	Parrot	P. Hale	Retrd.	120.00	144.00
86-06-017	Baby Elephant	P. Hale	Open	52.00	65.00
86-06-018	Beaver	P. Hale	Retrd.	48.00	58.00
86-06-019	Small Swan	P. Hale	Open	30.00	40.00
86-06-020	U.S. Space Shuttle	P. Hale	Retrd.	250.00	300.00
86-06-021	Pig	P. Hale	Retrd.	65.00	78.00
86-06-022	Baby Butterfly	P. Hale	Retrd.	40.00	48.00
86-06-023	Small Butterfly	P. Hale	Retrd.	90.00	108.00
86-06-024	Medium Butterfly	P. Hale	Retrd.	130.00	156.00
86-06-025	Large Butterfly	P. Hale	Retrd.	170.00	204.00
86-06-026	Small Sailboat	P. Hale	Open	65.00	85.00
86-06-027	Medium Sailboat	P. Hale	Retrd.	170.00	204.00
86-06-028	Large Sailboat	P. Hale	Retrd.	230.00	276.00
Iris Arc Crystal		**1987 Introductions**			
87-07-001	Calliope Carousel Horse	P. Hale	Retrd.	110.00	132.00
87-07-002	Cleanup Clown	P. Hale	Retrd.	72.00	87.00
87-07-003	"Happy Birthday" Clown	P. Hale	Retrd.	50.00	60.00
87-07-004	"Have a Happy Day" Clown	P. Hale	Retrd.	50.00	60.00
87-07-005	"Congratulations" Clown	P. Hale	Retrd.	50.00	60.00
87-07-006	"I Love You" Clown	P. Hale	Retrd.	50.00	60.00
87-07-007	"Merry Christmas" Clown	P. Hale	Retrd.	50.00	60.00
87-07-008	Flower Clown	M. Goena	Retrd.	80.00	96.00
87-07-009	Airplane	P. Hale	Open	48.00	55.00
87-07-010	Horse and Rider	P. Hale	Retrd.	130.00	156.00
87-07-011	Bison/Buffalo	M. Goena	Retrd.	50.00	60.00
87-07-012	Mother and Baby Bear	P. Hale	Retrd.	60.00	72.00
87-07-013	Small Santa	P. Hale	Retrd.	30.00	36.00
87-07-014	Sweetie Bear Couple	T. Holliman	Retrd.	140.00	168.00
87-07-015	Sweetie Bear Dancer	T. Holliman	Retrd.	72.00	87.00
87-07-016	Medium AB Swan	P. Hale	Open	100.00	100.00
87-07-017	Carousel Reindeer	P. Hale	Retrd.	120.00	144.00
87-07-018	Grand Duckling	P. Hale	Retrd.	300.00	360.00
87-07-019	Ram	M. Goena	Retrd.	60.00	72.00
87-07-020	Gazelle	M. Goena	Retrd.	130.00	156.00
87-07-021	Allegro Caousel Horse	P. Hale	Retrd.	170.00	204.00
87-07-022	Golf Cart	P. Hale	Retrd.	75.00	90.00
87-07-023	Roadster	P. Hale	Retrd.	60.00	72.00
87-07-024	Pickup Truck	P. Hale	Retrd.	60.00	72.00
87-07-025	Locomotive	P. Hale	Retrd.	90.00	108.00
87-07-026	Passenger Car	P. Hale	Retrd.	80.00	96.00
87-07-027	Coal Car	P. Hale	Retrd.	80.00	96.00
87-07-028	Semi Truck	P. Hale	Retrd.	100.00	120.00
87-07-029	Miniature Duckling	P. Hale	Retrd.	20.00	24.00
Iris Arc Crystal		**1988 Introductions**			
88-08-001	Bullfrog	M. Goena	Retrd.	30.00	36.00
88-08-002	Tambourine Gator	M. Goena	Retrd.	120.00	144.00
88-08-003	Drummer Gator	M. Goena	Retrd.	140.00	168.00
88-08-004	Banjo Gator	M. Goena	Retrd.	120.00	144.00
88-08-005	Lighthouse	P. Hale	Retrd.	150.00	150.00
88-08-006	Rocking Horse	P. Hale	Retrd.	120.00	135.00
88-08-007	Bunny with Flowers	P. Hale	Open	55.00	60.00
88-08-008	Basket of Violets	M. Goena	Open	50.00	60.00
88-08-009	Bear with Honey	M. Goena	Retrd.	80.00	96.00
88-08-010	Bear with Milk and Cookies	M. Goena	Retrd.	80.00	96.00
88-08-011	Bear with Candle	M. Goena	Retrd.	80.00	96.00
88-08-012	Miniature Frog	M. Goena	Open	23.00	27.00
88-08-013	Small Enchanted Castle®	P. Hale	Open	50.00	75.00
88-08-014	Medium Enchanted Castle®	P. Hale	Open	100.00	150.00
88-08-015	Large Enchanted Castle®	P. Hale	Open	180.00	250.00
88-08-016	Clown with Dog	M. Goena	Retrd.	90.00	108.00
88-08-017	Computer Bear	M. Goena	Retrd.	80.00	95.00
88-08-018	Angel Bear	M. Goena	Retrd.	60.00	72.00
88-08-019	Golf Bag	M. Goena/P. Hale	Open	100.00	130.00
88-08-020	Cable Car	M. Goena/P. Hale	Retrd.	70.00	84.00
Iris Arc Crystal		**1989 Introductions**			
89-09-001	Small Mouse	P. Hale	Retrd.	45.00	50.00
89-09-002	Blue Whale	M. Goena	Retrd.	32.00	39.00
89-09-003	Magic Bunny	P. Hale	Retrd.	48.00	58.00
89-09-004	Flower Cart	P. Hale	Open	90.00	95.00
89-09-005	Big Hearted Bunny	M. Goena	Open	55.00	60.00
89-09-006	Golfing Bear	P. Hale	Open	70.00	75.00
89-09-007	Basket of Bunnies	P. Hale	Retrd.	100.00	120.00
89-09-008	Gingerbread Cottage	M. Goena	Open	130.00	170.00
89-09-009	Miniature Clown	M. Goena	Retrd.	23.00	27.00
89-09-010	Miniature Lion	M. Goena	Retrd.	23.00	27.00
89-09-011	Miniature Mouse	M. Goena	Open	23.00	27.00
89-09-012	Miniature Angel	M. Goena	Open	23.00	27.00
89-09-013	Miniature Sailboat	M. Goena	Retrd.	23.00	27.00
89-09-014	Miniature Bunny with Carrot	P. Hale	Open	23.00	27.00
89-09-015	Rudolph the Red Nosed Reindeer®	M. Goena	Retrd.	80.00	96.00
89-09-016	Santa Claus	M. Goena	Open	55.00	60.00
89-09-017	Ski Bunny	M. Goena	Open	55.00	70.00
89-09-018	Train Set	M. Goena	Open	100.00	120.00
89-09-019	Dragon	M. Goena	Open	70.00	95.00
89-09-020	Wizard	M. Goena	Retrd.	80.00	96.00
89-09-021	Miniature Dog	M. Goena	Open	23.00	27.00
89-09-022	Miniature Pig	M. Goena	Open	23.00	27.00
89-09-023	Miniature Moose	M. Goena	Open	23.00	27.00
89-09-024	Miniature Butterfly AB	M. Goena	Open	23.00	27.00
89-09-025	Miniature Butterfly MV	M. Goena	Open	23.00	27.00
89-09-026	Miniature Oyster with Pearl	M. Goena	Open	23.00	27.00
Iris Arc Crystal		**1990 Introductions**			
90-10-001	Snuggle Bunnies	M. Goena	Open	40.00	45.00
90-10-002	Lovebirds	M. Goena	Open	90.00	100.00
90-10-003	Wishing Well	M. Goena	Open	130.00	150.00
90-10-004	Toy Chest	P. Hale	Open	60.00	60.00
90-10-005	Tennis Bear	P. Hale	Open	70.00	75.00
90-10-006	Large Rainbow Butterfly	M. Goena	Retrd.	80.00	96.00
90-10-007	Legendary Castle	P. Hale	Open	200.00	220.00
90-10-008	American Beauty Rose	P. Hale	Retrd.	90.00	95.00
90-10-009	Baby Carriage	M. Goena	Open	50.00	50.00
90-10-010	Miniature Koala with Heart	M. Goena	Open	23.00	27.00
90-10-011	Miniature Castle	M. Goena	Open	23.00	27.00
90-10-012	Vase of Red Roses	M. Goena	Open	20.00	25.00
90-10-013	Small Flower Cart	P. Hale	Open	40.00	45.00
90-10-014	Lotus	P. Hale	Open	60.00	60.00
90-10-015	Crab	P. Hale	Open	40.00	45.00
90-10-016	Dog	M. Goena	Open	70.00	75.00
90-10-017	Cat	M. Goena	Open	70.00	75.00
90-10-018	Hummingbird	M. Goena	Open	85.00	90.00
90-10-019	Loveboat	P. Hale	Open	55.00	60.00
90-10-020	Carousel	C. Hughes	Retrd.	100.00	120.00
90-10-021	Medium Legendary Castle	P. Hale	Open	140.00	150.00
90-10-022	Mushroom Cottage	C. Hughes	Retrd.	130.00	156.00
90-10-023	Space Shuttle	M. Goena	Retrd.	140.00	168.00
90-10-024	Jazz Piano	C. Hughes	Retrd.	150.00	160.00
90-10-025	Miniature Vase of Flowers	P. Hale	Retrd.	25.00	27.00
Iris Arc Crystal		**1991 Introductions**			
91-11-001	Snuggle Bears	M. Goena	Open	40.00	45.00
91-11-002	Bride and Groom	P. Hale	Retrd.	130.00	150.00
91-11-003	Honeymoon Cottage	P. Hale	Open	120.00	130.00
91-11-004	Courting Bears	M. Goena	Open	90.00	90.00
91-11-005	Mouse Mobile	M. Goena	Retrd.	120.00	144.00
91-11-006	Beach Bunnies	M. Goena	Open	120.00	125.00
91-11-007	Red Wagon	P. Hale	Open	70.00	75.00
91-11-008	Jack in the Box	C. Hughes	Open	40.00	40.00
91-11-009	Mother and Baby Bunny	C. Hughes	Retrd.	65.00	78.00
91-11-010	Oyster with Pearl RB	M. Goena	Open	40.00	40.00
91-11-011	Pelican	P. Hale	Retrd.	75.00	90.00
91-11-012	Otter	P. Hale	Open	35.00	40.00
91-11-013	Small Legendary Castle	P. Hale	Open	90.00	95.00
91-11-014	Baseball Bear	M. Goena	Open	75.00	75.00
91-11-015	Speedboat Bunnies	P. Hale	Open	90.00	100.00
91-11-016	Miniature Whale	M. Goena	Open	25.00	27.00
91-11-017	Miniature Mushrooms	C. Hughes	Retrd.	25.00	27.00
91-11-018	Miniature Bunny with Heart	M. Goena	Open	25.00	27.00
91-11-019	Miniature Elephant	M. Goena	Open	25.00	27.00
91-11-020	Miniature Bud Vase	M. Goena	Retrd.	25.00	27.00
91-11-021	Miniature Penguin	M. Goena	Open	25.00	27.00
91-11-022	Miniature Bluebird	M. Goena	Open	25.00	27.00
91-11-023	Miniature Chistmas Tree	C. Hughes	Open	25.00	27.00
91-11-024	Miniature School of Fish	M. Goena	Open	125.00	135.00
91-11-025	Storybook Cottage	P. Hale	Retrd.	80.00	80.00
91-11-026	Teeter Totter	C. Hughes	Retrd.	80.00	96.00
91-11-027	Cat and Fishbowl	P. Hale	Open	70.00	70.00
91-11-028	Mice and Cheese	P. Hale	Open	70.00	75.00
91-11-029	Turtle Grotto	C. Hughes	Open	130.00	135.00
91-11-030	Happy Campers	C. Hughes	Retrd.	110.00	120.00
91-11-031	Country Church	M. Goena	Open	150.00	170.00
91-11-032	Small Mushroom Cottage	C. Hughes	Retrd.	80.00	85.00
91-11-033	Tea for Two	C. Hughes	Retrd.	85.00	90.00
91-11-034	Christmas Morning	C. Hughes	Retrd.	80.00	90.00
91-11-035	Small Gingerbread Cottage	M. Goena	Open	55.00	55.00
91-11-036	Basket of Roses	P. Hale	Open	60.00	60.00
91-11-037	Bouquet Basket	P. Hale	Retrd.	80.00	85.00
91-11-038	Fishing Bear	C. Hughes	Retrd.	50.00	50.00
Iris Arc Crystal		**1992 Introductions**			
92-12-001	Tunnel of Love	C. Hughes	Open	150.00	150.00
92-12-002	Love Doves	M. Goena	Open	40.00	45.00
92-12-003	Video Bear	C. Hughes	Open	75.00	80.00
92-12-004	Bible Bear	C. Hughes	Retrd.	100.00	100.00
92-12-005	Rainbow Apple	M. Goena	Open	45.00	50.00
92-12-006	School House	M. Goena	Open	180.00	180.00
92-12-007	Windmill	C. Hughes	Open	100.00	100.00
92-12-008	Guitar with Stand	C. Hughes	Open	100.00	100.00
92-12-009	Grand Piano	C. Hughes	Open	150.00	150.00
92-12-010	Baby Grand Piano	C. Hughes	Open	50.00	50.00
92-12-011	Small Bouquet Basket	M. Goena	Open	50.00	50.00
92-12-012	Kitty in a Basket	M. Goena	Open	60.00	60.00
92-12-013	Birdhouse	M. Goena	Open	180.00	180.00
92-12-014	Kitten with Ball	M. Goena	Open	55.00	55.00
92-12-015	Treasure Chest	C. Hughes	Open	55.00	55.00
92-12-016	Golf Cart	M. Goena	Open	80.00	85.00
92-12-017	Basketball Bears	C. Hughes	Open	100.00	100.00
92-12-018	Teddy Bear with Blocks	C. Hughes	Open	55.00	60.00
92-12-019	Miniature Baby Carriage	M. Goena	Open	25.00	27.00
92-12-020	Miniature Vase of Pink Flowers	M. Goena	Open	25.00	27.00
92-12-021	Miniature Vase of Violets	M. Goena	Open	25.00	27.00
92-12-022	Miniature Oyster with Pearl AB	M. Goena	Open	25.00	27.00

Number	Name	Artist	Edition Limit	Issue Price	Quote
92-12-023	Snuggle Kittens	M. Goena	Open	40.00	45.00
92-12-024	Romeo and Juliet	C. Hughes	Open	130.00	130.00
92-12-025	Home Sweet Home	C. Hughes	Retrd.	150.00	150.00
92-12-026	Mouse House	C. Hughes	Retrd.	170.00	170.00
92-12-027	Billiards Bunny	C. Hughes	Open	75.00	75.00
92-12-028	Surfin' USA	M. Goena	Open	100.00	100.00
92-12-029	Cruise Ship	M. Goena	Open	100.00	100.00
92-12-030	Cluster of Butterflies	M. Goena	Open	125.00	135.00
92-12-031	Miniature Owl	M. Goena	Open	25.00	27.00
92-12-032	Miniature Bumblebee	M. Goena	Open	25.00	27.00
92-12-033	Nativity Scene	C. Hughes	Open	130.00	130.00

Iris Arc Crystal — **1993 Introductions**

Number	Name	Artist	Edition Limit	Issue Price	Quote
93-13-001	Balloon Bears	M. Goena	Open	130.00	130.00
93-13-002	Mountain Chapel	C. Hughes	Open	135.00	135.00
93-13-003	Business Bear	C. Hughes	Open	75.00	75.00
93-13-004	Antique Telephone	C. Hughes	Open	40.00	40.00
93-13-005	Dice	M. Goena	Open	45.00	45.00
93-13-006	Slot Machine	M. Goena	Open	100.00	100.00
93-13-007	Basket of Mice	C. Hughes	Open	55.00	55.00
93-13-008	Hide-N-Seek	C. Hughes	Open	70.00	70.00
93-13-009	Hockey Bear	C. Hughes	Open	90.00	90.00
93-13-010	Pacifier	M. Goena	Open	45.00	45.00
93-13-011	Kitty Cariage	C. Hughes	Open	70.00	70.00
93-13-012	Baby Seal	C. Hughes	Open	35.00	35.00
93-13-013	Miniature Rainbow Apple	M. Goena	Open	27.00	27.00
93-13-014	Table for Two	M. Goena	Open	75.00	75.00
93-13-015	Sunday Drive	M. Goena	Open	65.00	65.00
93-13-016	Small Lovebirds	R. Barrera	Open	65.00	65.00
93-13-017	"I Love You" Hearts	M. Goena	Open	75.00	75.00
93-13-018	Empire State Building	M. Goena	Retrd.	90.00	90.00
93-13-019	Cactus	C. Hughes	Open	55.00	55.00
93-13-020	Pineapple	M. Goena	Open	30.00	30.00
93-13-021	Blue Bird Nest	C. Hughes	Open	50.00	50.00
93-13-022	Cat and Bird	C. Hughes	Open	55.00	55.00
93-13-023	Small Cloud Castle	M. Goena	Open	150.00	150.00
93-13-024	Ping Pong Bears	C. Hughes	Open	75.00	75.00
93-13-025	Birthday Cake	M. Goena	Open	75.00	75.00
93-13-026	Dolphin	C. Hughes	Open	90.00	90.00
93-13-027	Kissing Fish	M. Goena	Open	55.00	55.00
93-13-028	T-Rex	C. Hughes	Open	130.00	130.00
93-13-029	Miniature Rainbow Apple	M. Goena	Open	25.00	25.00
93-13-030	Rainbow Church	M. Goena	Open	50.00	50.00
93-13-031	Small Red Dice	M. Goena	Open	40.00	40.00
93-13-032	Black Dice	M. Goena	Open	45.00	45.00
93-13-033	Small Slot Machine	M. Goena	Open	55.00	55.00
93-13-034	Choir Bears	C. Hughes	Open	90.00	90.00
93-13-035	Charmer Jack in the Box	C. Hughes	Open	14.00	14.00
93-13-036	Charmer Basket of Flowers	C. Hughes	Open	14.00	14.00
93-13-037	Charmer AB Hearts	C. Hughes	Open	14.00	14.00
93-13-038	Charmer Turtle	C. Hughes	Open	14.00	14.00
93-13-039	Charmer Cactus	C. Hughes	Open	14.00	14.00
93-13-040	Charmer Angel	C. Hughes	Open	14.00	14.00
93-13-041	Charmer Flower Vase	M. Goena	Open	14.00	14.00
93-13-042	Charmer Aladdin's Lamp	M. Goena	Open	14.00	14.00
93-13-043	Charmer Oyster w/ Pearl AB	M. Goena	Open	14.00	14.00
93-13-044	Charmer Oyster w/ Pearl Pink Ice	M. Goena	Open	14.00	14.00
93-13-045	Charmer Pacifer	C. Hughes	Open	14.00	14.00
93-13-046	Charmer Kitten	C. Hughes	Open	19.00	19.00
93-13-047	Charmer Telephone	M. Goena	Open	19.00	19.00
93-13-048	Charmer Teddy Bear with Heart	M. Goena	Open	19.00	19.00
93-13-049	Charmer Bunny with Heart	M. Goena	Open	19.00	19.00
93-13-050	Charmer Seal with Ball	M. Goena	Open	19.00	19.00
93-13-051	Charmer Snail RB	M. Goena	Open	19.00	19.00
93-13-052	Charmer Sailboat	C. Hughes	Open	19.00	19.00
93-13-053	Charmer Bluebird	M. Goena	Open	19.00	19.00
93-13-054	Charmer Butterfly	M. Goena	Open	19.00	19.00

Iris Arc Crystal — **1994 Introductions**

Number	Name	Artist	Edition Limit	Issue Price	Quote
94-14-001	Blue Dolphin	C. Hughes	Open	40.00	40.00
94-14-002	Kitty Jack in the Box	C. Hughes	Open	45.00	45.00
94-14-003	Baby Cradle	C. Hughes	Open	90.00	90.00
94-14-004	Catamaran	C. Hughes	Open	70.00	70.00
94-14-005	Wedding Bears	C. Hughes	Open	80.00	80.00
94-14-006	Skyscraper	M. Goena	Open	90.00	90.00
94-14-007	Charmer Oyster w/ Pearl RB	M. Goena	Open	14.95	14.95
94-14-008	Charmer Mushrooms	M. Goena	Open	19.95	19.95
94-14-009	Charmer Candle	M. Goena	Open	19.95	19.95
94-14-010	Charmer Rainbow Apple	M. Goena	Open	19.95	19.95

Iris Arc Crystal — **Limited Editions**

Number	Name	Artist	Edition Limit	Issue Price	Quote
83-15-001	Teddy Bear with Heart (Silver)	P. Hale	Retrd.	170.00	204.00
83-15-002	Teddy Bear with Heart (Rose)	P. Hale	Retrd.	170.00	204.00
83-15-003	Elephant	P. Hale	Retrd.	190.00	228.00
83-15-004	Peacock	P. Hale	Retrd.	140.00	168.00
86-15-005	Classic Car	T. Holliman	Retrd.	500.00	600.00
87-15-006	Carousel	T. Holliman	Retrd.	600.00	720.00
87-15-007	Eagle	P. Hale	Retrd.	700.00	840.00
88-15-008	Horse and Foal	M. Goena	Retrd.	1000.00	1200.00
89-15-009	Angel	M. Goena	Retrd.	180.00	240.00
90-15-010	Rainbow Enchanted Castle®	C. Hughes	500	1500.00	1500.00
91-15-011	Vase of Flowers	P. Hale	750	250.00	250.00
91-15-012	Country Cottage	M. Goena	300	1500.00	1500.00
91-15-013	Basket of Flowers	M. Goena	Retrd.	250.00	300.00
92-15-014	Victorian House	C. Hughes	750	270.00	290.00
92-15-015	Water Mill	M. Goena	350	900.00	950.00
92-15-016	Rainbow Cathedral	M. Goena	150	2500.00	2500.00
93-15-017	Country Church	M. Goena	350	590.00	590.00
93-15-018	Basket of Violets	M. Goena	750	190.00	190.00
93-15-019	Birdbath	M. Goena	750	190.00	190.00
93-15-020	Nob Hill Victorian	C. Hughes	250	1000.00	1000.00
94-15-021	Bluebird Basket	M. Goena	1,000	190.00	190.00
94-15-022	Mystic Star Castle	M. Goena	500	390.00	390.00

Iris Arc Crystal — **Collector's Society Edition**

Number	Name	Artist	Edition Limit	Issue Price	Quote
92-16-001	Gramophone	C. Hughes	Retrd.	100.00	180.00
93-16-002	Classic Telephone	C. Hughes	Open	150.00	150.00

Kaiser — **Birds of America Collection**

Number	Name	Artist	Edition Limit	Issue Price	Quote
72-01-001	Blue Bird-496, color/base	W. Gawantka	2,500	120.00	480.00
73-01-002	Blue Jay-503, color/base	W. Gawantka	1,500	475.00	1198.00
76-01-003	Baltimore Oriole-536, color/base	G. Tagliariol	1,000	280.00	746.00
73-01-004	Cardinal-504, color/base	W. Gawantka	1,500	60.00	600.00
75-01-005	Sparrow-516, color/base	G. Tagliariol	1,500	300.00	596.00
70-01-006	Scarlet Tanager, color/base	Kaiser	Closed	60.00	90.00
XX-01-007	Sparrow Hawk-749, color/base	Kaiser	3,000	575.00	906.00
82-01-008	Hummingbird Group-660, color/base	G. Tagliariol	3,000	650.00	1232.00
81-01-009	Kingfisher-639, color/base	G. Tagliariol	Closed	45.00	60.00
73-01-010	Robin-502, color/base	W. Gawantka	1,500	340.00	718.00
XX-01-011	Robin II-537, color/base	Kaiser	1,000	260.00	888.00
XX-01-012	Robin & Worm, color/base	Kaiser	Closed	60.00	90.00
XX-01-013	Baby Titmice-501, white/base	W. Gawantka	1,200	200.00	754.00
XX-01-014	Baby Titmice-501, color/base	W. Gawantka	Closed	400.00	500.00
78-01-015	Baby Titmice-601, color/base	G. Tagliariol	2,000	Unkn.	956.00
78-01-016	Baby Titmice-601, white/base	G. Tagliariol	2,000	Unkn.	562.00
68-01-017	Pidgeon Group-475, white/base	U. Netzsch	2,000	60.00	412.00
68-01-018	Pidgeon Group-475, color/base	U. Netzsch	1,500	150.00	812.00
76-01-019	Pheasant-556, color/base	G. Tagliariol	1,500	3200.00	6020.00
84-01-020	Pheasant-715, color/base	G. Tagliariol	1,500	1000.00	1962.00
76-01-021	Pelican-534, color/base	G. Tagliariol	1,200	925.00	1768.00
XX-01-022	Pelican-534, white/base	G. Tagliariol	Closed	Unkn.	625.00
84-01-023	Peregrine Falcon-723, color/base	M. Tandy	1,500	850.00	4946.00
72-01-024	Goshawk-491, white/base	W. Gawantka	1,500	850.00	1992.00
72-01-025	Goshawk-491, color/base	W. Gawantka	1,500	2400.00	4326.00
XX-01-026	Roadrunner-492, color/base	Kaiser	Closed	350.00	900.00
72-01-027	Seagull-498, white/base	W. Gawantka	700	550.00	1586.00
72-01-028	Seagull-498, color/base	W. Gawantka	Closed	850.00	1150.00
73-01-028	Seagull-498, color bisque	W. Gawantka	Closed	Unkn.	1150.00
75-01-029	Woodpeckers-515, color/base	G. Tagliariol	800	900.00	1762.00
76-01-030	Screech Owl-532, white/base	W. Gawantka	Closed	175.00	199.00
76-01-031	Screech Owl-532, color bisque	W. Gawantka	Closed	Unkn.	175.00
XX-01-032	Horned Owl II-524, white/base	G. Tagliariol	1,000	Unkn.	918.00
XX-01-033	Horned Owl II- 524, color/base	G. Tagliariol	1,000	650.00	2170.00
69-01-034	Owl-476, color bisque	W. Gawantka	Closed	Unkn.	550.00
69-01-035	Owl -476, white bisque	W. Gawantka	Closed	Unkn.	180.00
77-01-036	Owl IV-559, color/base	G. Tagliariol	1,000	Unkn.	1270.00
XX-01-037	Snowy Owl -776, white/base	Kaiser	1,500	Unkn.	668.00
XX-01-038	Snowy Owl -776, color/base	Kaiser	1,500	Unkn.	1146.00
68-01-039	Pair of Mallards-456, white/base	U. Netzsch	2,000	75.00	518.00
68-01-040	Pair of Mallards-456, color/base	U. Netzsch	Closed	150.00	500.00
78-01-041	Pair of Mallards II-572, color/base	G. Tagliariol	1,500	Unkn.	1156.00
78-01-042	Pair of Mallards II-572, white/base	G. Tagliariol	1,500	Unkn.	2366.00
75-01-043	Wood Ducks-514, color/base	G. Tagliariol	800	Unkn.	2804.00
85-01-044	Pintails-747, white/base	Kaiser	1,500	Unkn.	364.00
85-01-045	Pintails-747, color/base	Kaiser	1,500	Unkn.	838.00
76-01-046	Canadian Geese-550, white/base	G. Tagliariol	1,500	1500.00	3490.00
81-01-047	Quails-640, color/base	G. Tagliariol	1,500	Unkn.	2366.00
79-01-048	Swan-602, color/base	G. Tagliariol	2,000	Unkn.	1370.00
69-01-049	Bald Eagle I -464, color	U. Netzsch	Closed	Unkn.	650.00
69-01-050	Bald Eagle I -464, white	U. Netzsch	Closed	Unkn.	250.00
73-01-051	Bald Eagle II -497, color bisque	G. Tagliariol	Closed	Unkn.	1300.00
74-01-052	Bald Eagle III -513, color bisque	W. Gawantka	Closed	Unkn.	850.00
74-01-053	Bald Eagle III -513,white bisque	W. Gawantka	Closed	Unkn.	378.00
76-01-054	Bald Eagle IV-552, white/base	W. Gawantka	1,500	210.00	572.00
76-01-055	Bald Eagle IV-552, color/base	W. Gawantka	1,500	450.00	998.00
78-01-056	Bald Eagle V-600, color/base	G. Tagliariol	1,500	Unkn.	3848.00
80-01-057	Bald Eagle VI-634, white/base	W. Gawantka	3,000	Unkn.	672.00
XX-01-058	Bald Eagle VII-637, color/base	G. Tagliariol	200	Unkn.	20694.00
82-01-059	Bald Eagle VIII-656, color/base	G. Tagliariol	Closed	800.00	880.00
82-01-060	Bald Eagle VIII-656, white/base	G. Tagliariol	1,000	400.00	904.00
84-01-061	Bald Eagle IX-714, white/base	W. Gawantka	4,000	190.00	374.00
84-01-062	Bald Eagle IX-714, color/base	W. Gawantka	3,500	500.00	850.00
85-01-063	Bald Eagle X-746, white/base	W. Gawantka	1,500	375.00	672.00
85-01-064	Bald Eagle X-746, color/base	W. Gawantka	1,500	Unkn.	1198.00
85-01-065	Bald Eagle XI-751, white/base	W. Gawantka	1,000	Unkn.	902.00
85-01-066	Bald Eagle XI-751, color/base	W. Gawantka	1,000	880.00	1422.00
81-01-067	Rooster-642, white/base	G. Tagliariol	1,500	380.00	688.00
81-01-068	Rooster-642, color/base	G. Tagliariol	1,500	860.00	1304.00
74-01-069	Falcon-507, color/base	W. Gawantka	1,500	820.00	1928.00
86-01-070	Sparrow Hawk-777, white bisque	M. Tandy	1,000	440.00	716.00
86-01-071	Sparrow Hawk-777, colored bisque	M. Tandy	10,000	950.00	1336.00
XX-01-072	Bald Eagle II-497, Colored	Kaiser	Closed	Unkn.	1300.00
XX-01-073	Paradise Bird-318, white bisque	Kaiser	Closed	Unkn.	135.00
XX-01-074	Fighting Peacocks -337, color glaze	G. Bochman	Closed	Unkn.	340.00
XX-01-075	Wild Ducks-456, color bisque	Kaiser	Closed	Unkn.	500.00
68-01-076	Wild Ducks-456, white bisque	Kaiser	2,000	Unkn.	175.00
72-01-077	Roadrunner-492, color bisque	W. Gawantka	1,000	175.00	199.00

Kaiser — **Horse Sculpture**

Number	Name	Artist	Edition Limit	Issue Price	Quote
69-02-001	Arabian Stallion-Comet, color/bisque	W. Gawantka	Closed	Unkn.	850.00
76-02-002	Hassan/Arabian-553, white/base	W. Gawantka	Closed	250.00	600.00
76-02-003	Hassan/Arabian-553, color/base	W. Gawantka	1,500	600.00	1100-1200.
80-02-004	Orion/Arabian-629, color/base	W. Gawantka	2,000	600.00	1038.00
80-02-005	Orion/Arabian-629, white/base	W. Gawantka	2,000	250.00	442.00
78-02-006	Capitano/Lipizzaner- 597, white	W. Gawantka	Closed	275.00	574.00
78-02-007	Capitano/Lipizzaner- 597, color	W. Gawantka	1,500	625.00	1496.00
75-02-008	Mare & Foal II-510, color/base	W. Gawantka	Closed	650.00	775.00
75-02-009	Mare & Foal II-510, white/bisque	W. Gawantka	Closed	Unkn.	775.00
80-02-010	Mare & Foal III-636, white/base	W. Gawantka	1,500	300.00	646.00
80-02-011	Mare & Foal III-636, color/base	W. Gawantka	1,500	950.00	1632.00
71-02-012	Pony Group-488, white/base	W. Gawantka	2,500	50.00	418.00
71-02-013	Pony Group-488, color/base	W. Gawantka	Closed	Unkn.	350.00
71-02-014	Pony Group-488, color bisque	W. Gawantka	Closed	Unkn.	350.00
87-02-015	Trotter-780, white/base	W. Gawantka	1,500	574.00	652.00
87-02-016	Trotter-780, color/base	W. Gawantka	1,500	1217.00	1350.00
87-02-017	Pacer-792, white/base	W. Gawantka	1,500	574.00	652.00
87-02-018	Pacer-792, color/base	W. Gawantka	1,500	1217.00	1350.00
90-02-019	Argos-633101/wht. bisq./base	W. Gawantka	1,000	578.00	672.00
90-02-020	Argos-633103/lt. color/base	W. Gawantka	1,000	1194.00	1388.00
90-02-021	Argos-633143/color/base	W. Gawantka	1,000	1194.00	1388.00
75-02-022	Lipizzaner/Maestoso-517/color bisque	W. Gawantka	Closed	Unkn.	1150.00
75-02-023	Lipizzaner/Maestoso-517white bisque	W. Gawantka	Closed	Unkn.	750.00

Kaiser — **Animals**

Number	Name	Artist	Edition Limit	Issue Price	Quote
75-03-001	German Shepherd-528, white bisque	W. Gawantka	Closed	185.00	420.00
75-03-002	German Shepherd-528, color bisque	W. Gawantka	Closed	250.00	652.00
76-03-003	Irish Setter-535, color bisque	W. Gawantka	1,000	290.00	652.00
76-03-004	Irish Setter-535, white/base	W. Gawantka	1,500	Unkn.	424.00
79-03-005	Bear & Cub-521, white bisque	W. Gawantka	Closed	125.00	378.00
79-03-006	Bear & Cub-521, color bisque	W. Gawantka	900	400.00	1072.00
85-03-007	Trout-739, color bisque	W. Gawantka	Open	95.00	488.00
85-03-008	Rainbow Trout-739, color bisque	W. Gawantka	Open	250.00	488.00
85-03-009	Brook Trout-739, color bisque	W. Gawantka	Open	250.00	488.00
85-03-010	Pike-737, color bisque	W. Gawantka	Open	350.00	682.00
69-03-011	Porpoise Group (3)-478, white bisque	W. Gawantka	Closed	85.00	375.00
78-03-012	Dolphin Group (4)-596/4, white bisque	W. Gawantka	4,500	75.00	956.00
75-03-013	Dolphin Group (4)-508, white bisque	W. Gawantka	Closed	Unkn.	575.00
75-03-014	Dolphin Group (5)-520/5, white bisque	W. Gawantka	800	850.00	3002.00

Company / Number	Name	Series / Artist	Edition Limit	Issue Price	Quote
78-03-015	Killer Whale-579, color/bisque	W. Gawantka	2,000	420.00	798.00
78-03-016	Killer Whale-579, white/bisque	W. Gawantka	2,000	85.00	404.00
78-03-017	Killer Whales (2)-594, color	W. Gawantka	2,000	925.00	2008.00
78-03-018	Killer Whales (2)-594, white	W. Gawantka	2,000	425.00	1024.00
82-03-019	Two wild Boars-664, color bisque	H. Liederly	1,000	650.00	890.00
80-03-020	Bison-630, color bisque	G. Tagliariol	2,000	620.00	1044.00
80-03-021	Bison-690, white bisque	G. Tagliariol	2,000	350.00	488.00
91-03-022	Lion-701203, color bisque	W. Gawantka	1,500	1300.00	1300.00
91-03-023	Lion-701201, white bisque	W. Gawantka	1,500	650.00	650.00
Kaiser		**Human Figures**			
82-04-001	Father & Son-659, white/base	W. Gawantka	2,500	100.00	384.00
82-04-002	Father & Son-659, color/base	W. Gawantka	2,500	400.00	712.00
83-04-003	Mother & Child/bust-696, white	W. Gawantka	4,000	225.00	428.00
83-04-004	Mother & Child/bust-696, color	W. Gawantka	3,500	500.00	1066.00
XX-04-005	Father & Daughter-752, white	Kaiser	2,500	175.00	362.00
XX-04-006	Father & Daughter-752, color	Kaiser	2,500	390.00	710.00
82-04-007	Swan Lake Ballet-641, white	W. Gawantka	2,500	200.00	974.00
82-04-008	Swan Lake Ballet-641, color	W. Gawantka	2,500	650.00	1276.00
82-04-009	Ice Princess-667, white	W. Gawantka	5,000	200.00	416.00
82-04-010	Ice Princess-667, color	W. Gawantka	5,000	375.00	732.00
XX-04-011	Mother & Child-757, white	Kaiser	4,000	300.00	430.00
XX-04-012	Mother & Child-757, color	Kaiser	3,500	600.00	864.00
XX-04-013	Mother & Child-775, white	Kaiser	4,000	300.00	430.00
XX-04-014	Mother & Child-775, color	Kaiser	3,500	600.00	864.00
60-04-015	Mother & Child-398, white bisque	G. Bochmann	Open	Unkn.	312.00
Lalique Society of America		**Lalique Society Annual Series**			
89-01-001	Degas Box 10585	R. Lalique	Yr.Iss.	295.00	500-725.
90-01-002	Hestia Medallion 61051	M.C. Lalique	Yr.Iss.	295.00	450.00
91-01-003	Lily of Valley 61053	R. Lalique	Yr.Iss.	275.00	400.00
92-01-004	La Patineuse 61054	M.C. Lalique	Yr.Iss.	325.00	325.00
93-01-005	Enchantment 61055	M.C. Lalique	Yr.Iss.	395.00	395.00
Lance Corporation		**Chilmark Pewter American West**			
74-01-001	Cheyenne	D. Polland	S/O	200.00	2700-3000.
74-01-002	Counting Coup	D. Polland	S/O	225.00	1600-2000.
74-01-003	Crow Scout	D. Polland	S/O	250.00	1000-1700.
75-01-004	Maverick Calf	D. Polland	S/O	250.00	1300-1700.
76-01-005	Cold Saddles, Mean Horses	D. Polland	S/O	200.00	1100-1600.
75-01-006	The Outlaws	D. Polland	S/O	450.00	900-1180.
76-01-007	Buffalo Hunt	D. Polland	S/O	300.00	1625.00
76-01-008	Rescue	D. Polland	S/O	275.00	1150.00
76-01-009	Painting the Town	D. Polland	S/O	300.00	1550-1700.
76-01-010	Monday Morning Wash	D. Polland	S/O	200.00	1300-1800.
78-01-011	Dangerous Encounter	B. Rodden	Retrd.	475.00	600-950.
79-01-012	Border Rustlers	D. Polland	S/O	1295.00	1500.00
79-01-013	Mandan Hunter	D. Polland	S/O	65.00	780-900.
79-01-014	Getting Acquainted	D. Polland	S/O	215.00	500-1100.
79-01-015	Cavalry Officer	D. LaRocca	S/O	125.00	400-650.
79-01-016	Cowboy	D. LaRocca	S/O	125.00	500-750.
79-01-017	Mountain Man	D. LaRocca	Retrd.	95.00	500-650.
79-01-018	Indian Warrior	D. LaRocca	Retrd.	95.00	400.00
79-01-019	Running Battle	B. Rodden	Retrd.	400.00	750-900.
81-01-020	Buffalo Robe	D. Polland	2,500	235.00	335.00
81-01-021	When War Chiefs Meet	D. Polland	S/O	300.00	800.00
81-01-022	War Party	D. Polland	Retrd.	550.00	975-1150.
81-01-023	Dog Soldier	D. Polland	2,500	235.00	315.00
81-01-024	Enemy Tracks	D. Polland	S/O	225.00	700-725.
81-01-025	Ambushed	D. Polland	Retrd.	2370.00	2700.00
81-01-026	U.S. Marshal	D. Polland	S/O	95.00	450-600.
81-01-027	Plight of the Huntsman	M. Boyette	S/O	495.00	850.00
82-01-028	Last Arrow	D. Polland	S/O	95.00	370-400.
82-01-029	Sioux War Chief	D. Polland	S/O	95.00	375-480.
82-01-030	Navajo Kachina Dancer	D. Polland	2,500	95.00	115.00
82-01-031	Arapaho Drummer	D. Polland	2,500	95.00	115.00
82-01-032	Apache Hostile	D. Polland	2,500	95.00	115.00
82-01-033	Buffalo Prayer	D. Polland	S/O	95.00	225-400.
82-01-034	Jemez Eagle Dancer	D. Polland	S/O	95.00	250-450.
82-01-035	Flathead War Dancer	D. Polland	2,500	95.00	115.00
82-01-036	Hopi Kachina Dancer	D. Polland	2,500	95.00	115.00
82-01-037	Apache Gan Dancer	D. Polland	2,500	95.00	115.00
82-01-038	Crow Medicine Dancer	D. Polland	2,500	95.00	115.00
82-01-039	Comanche Plaines Drummer	D. Polland	2,500	95.00	115.00
82-01-040	Yakima Salmon Fisherman	D. Polland	S/O	200.00	900.00
82-01-041	Mustanger	D. Polland	2,500	425.00	580.00
82-01-042	Blood Brothers	M. Boyett	Retrd.	250.00	610-995.
83-01-043	Line Rider	D. Polland	S/O	195.00	975.00
83-01-044	Bounty Hunter	D. Polland	S/O	250.00	300-600.
83-01-045	The Wild Bunch	D. Polland	S/O	200.00	225-400.
83-01-046	Too Many Aces	D. Polland	Retrd.	400.00	495.00
83-01-047	Eye to Eye	D. Polland	2,500	350.00	500.00
83-01-048	Now or Never	D. Polland	Retrd.	265.00	800.00
84-01-049	Flat Out for Red River Station	M. Boyett	S/O	3000.00	4500-7200.
85-01-050	Postal Exchange	S. York	Retrd.	300.00	400-600.
85-01-051	Bear Meet	S. York	Retrd.	500.00	600-800.
85-01-052	Horse of A Different Color	S. York	Retrd.	500.00	600-800.
87-01-053	Cool Waters	F. Barnum	Suspd.	350.00	395.00
87-01-054	Treed	F. Barnum	Suspd.	300.00	345.00
88-01-055	Custer's Last Stand	F. Barnum	Suspd.	350.00	395.00
88-01-056	Father Farewell	F. Barnum	S/O	150.00	225.00
90-01-057	Pequot Wars	D. Polland	S/O	395.00	450-800.
90-01-058	Tecumseh's Rebellion	D. Polland	S/O	350.00	700.00
90-01-059	Red River Wars	D. Polland	S/O	425.00	700-850.
90-01-060	Buffalo Spirit	D. Polland	S/O	110.00	110.00
90-01-061	Eagle Dancer (deNatura)	D. Polland	Retrd.	300.00	300.00
90-01-062	Running Wolf (deNatura)	D. Polland	Retrd.	350.00	350.00
91-01-063	Kiowa Princess (deNatura)	D. Polland	Retrd.	300.00	300.00
91-01-064	Yellow Boy (deNatura)	D. Polland	Retrd.	350.00	350.00
Lance Corporation		**Chilmark Pewter American West Annual Specials**			
83-02-001	The Chief	D. Polland	Yr.Iss.	275.00	1650-2700.
84-02-002	Unit Colors	D. Polland	Yr.Iss.	250.00	1250-1700.
85-02-003	Oh Great Spirit	D. Polland	Yr.Iss.	300.00	1000-1300.
86-02-004	Eagle Catcher	M. Boyett	Yr.Iss.	300.00	850-1200.
87-02-005	Surprise Encounter	F. Barnum	Yr.Iss.	250.00	600-800.
88-02-006	I Will Fight No More Forever (Chief Joseph)	D. Polland	Yr.Iss.	350.00	700-750.
89-02-007	Geronimo	D. Polland	Yr.Iss.	375.00	700-875.
90-02-008	Cochise	D. Polland	Yr.Iss.	400.00	600.00
91-02-009	Crazy Horse	D. Polland	Yr.Iss.	295.00	600-750.
92-02-010	Strong Hearts to the Front	D. Polland	Yr.Iss.	425.00	600.00
Lance Corporation		**Chilmark Pewter American West Christmas Special**			
91-03-001	Merry Christmas Neighbor	D. Polland	Annual	395.00	625.00
92-03-002	Merry Christmas My Love	D. Polland	Annual	350.00	350-450.
93-03-003	Almost Home	D. Polland	Annual	375.00	375.00
Lance Corporation		**Chilmark Pewter American West Event Specials**			
91-04-001	Uneasy Truce	D. Polland	Annual	125.00	175-195.
92-04-002	Irons In The Fire	D. Polland	Annual	125.00	125.00
Lance Corporation		**Chilmark Pewter Civil War Annual Specials**			
89-05-001	Lee To The Rear	F. Barnum	Yr.Iss.	300.00	600-900.
90-05-002	Lee And Jackson	F. Barnum	Yr.Iss.	375.00	500-800.
91-05-003	Stonewall Jackson	F. Barnum	Yr.Iss.	295.00	500.00
92-05-004	Zouaves 1st Manassas	F. Barnum	Yr.Iss.	375.00	375.00
93-05-005	Letter to Sarah	F. Barnum	Yr.Iss.	395.00	395.00
Lance Corporation		**Chilmark Pewter Civil War Event Specials**			
91-06-001	Boots and Saddles	F. Barnum	Annual	95.00	200.00
92-06-002	140th NY Zouave	F. Barnum	Annual	95.00	150.00
93-06-003	Johnny Reb	F. Barnum	Annual	95.00	95.00
Lance Corporation		**Chilmark Pewter Civil War Christmas Specials**			
92-07-001	Merry Christmas Yank	F. Barnum	Annual	350.00	435.00
93-07-002	Silent Night	F. Barnum	Annual	350.00	350.00
Lance Corporation		**Chilmark Pewter Wildlife**			
78-08-001	Buffalo	B. Rodden	S/O	170.00	375-400.
79-08-002	Elephant	D. Polland	S/O	315.00	450-550.
79-08-003	Giraffe	D. Polland	S/O	145.00	145.00
79-08-004	Kudu	D. Polland	S/O	160.00	160.00
79-08-005	Rhino	D. Polland	S/O	135.00	135-550.
80-08-006	Ruby-Throated Hummingbird	V. Hayton	S/O	275.00	350.00
80-08-007	Prairie Sovereign	M. Boyett	Retrd.	550.00	800.00
80-08-008	Duel of the Bighorns	M. Boyett	Retrd.	650.00	1200.00
80-08-009	Lead Can't Catch Him	M. Boyett	Retrd.	645.00	845.00
80-08-010	Voice of Experience	M. Boyett	Retrd.	645.00	850.00
88-08-011	The Patriarch	F. Barnum	Suspd.	350.00	395.00
88-08-012	Fishing Lesson	F. Barnum	Suspd.	325.00	365.00
89-08-013	Summit	F. Barnum	Suspd.	250.00	265.00
Lance Corporation		**Chilmark Pewter Horses**			
76-09-001	Stallion	B. Rodden	S/O	75.00	260.00
76-09-002	Running Free	B. Rodden	S/O	75.00	300.00
77-09-003	Rise and Shine	B. Rodden	S/O	135.00	200.00
77-09-004	The Challenge	B. Rodden	S/O	175.00	250-300.
78-09-005	Paddock Walk	A. Petito	Retrd.	85.00	215.00
80-09-006	Born Free	B. Rodden	S/O	250.00	500-680.
80-09-007	Affirmed	M. Jovine	Retrd.	850.00	1275.00
81-09-008	Clydesdale Wheel Horse	C. Keim	Retrd.	120.00	430.00
82-09-009	Tender Persuasion	J. Mootry	Retrd.	950.00	1250.00
85-09-010	Fighting Stallions	D. Polland	2,500	225.00	300.00
85-09-011	Wild Stallion	D. Polland	Retrd.	145.00	350.00
Lance Corporation		**Chilmark Pewter Rodeo**			
85-10-001	Saddle Bronc Rider	D. Polland	2,500	250.00	315.00
85-10-002	Bareback Rider	D. Polland	2,500	225.00	315.00
85-10-003	Bull Rider	D. Polland	2,500	265.00	350.00
85-10-004	Steer Wrestling	D. Polland	2,500	500.00	635.00
85-10-005	Team Roping	D. Polland	2,500	500.00	660.00
85-10-006	Calf Roper	D. Polland	2,500	300.00	395.00
85-10-007	Barrel Racer	D. Polland	2,500	275.00	345.00
Lance Corporation		**Chilmark Pewter Legacy of Courage**			
81-11-001	Apache Signals	M. Boyett	Retrd.	175.00	550-575.
81-11-002	Iroquois Warfare	M. Boyett	Retrd.	125.00	600.00
81-11-003	Victor Cheyenne	M. Boyett	Retrd.	175.00	500.00
81-11-004	Buffalo Stalker	M. Boyett	Retrd.	175.00	560.00
81-11-005	Comanche	M. Boyett	Retrd.	175.00	530-670.
81-11-006	Unconquered Seminole	M. Boyett	Retrd.	175.00	540.00
81-11-007	Blackfoot Snow Hunter	M. Boyett	Retrd.	175.00	650.00
82-11-008	Shoshone Eagle Catcher	M. Boyett	S/O	225.00	1650-2040.
82-11-009	Plains Talk-Pawnee	M. Boyett	Retrd.	195.00	625.00
82-11-010	Kiowa Scout	M. Boyett	Retrd.	195.00	525.00
82-11-011	Mandan Buffalo Dancer	M. Boyett	Retrd.	195.00	450-600.
82-11-012	Listening For Hooves	M. Boyett	Retrd.	150.00	400.00
82-11-013	Arapaho Sentinel	M. Boyett	Retrd.	195.00	500.00
82-11-014	Dance of the Eagles	M. Boyett	Retrd.	150.00	215.00
82-11-015	The Tracker Nez Perce	M. Boyett	Retrd.	150.00	575.00
83-11-016	Moment of Truth	M. Boyett	Retrd.	295.00	550-620.
83-11-017	Winter Hunt	M. Boyett	Retrd.	295.00	400.00
83-11-018	Along the Cherokee Trace	M. Boyett	Retrd.	295.00	720.00
83-11-019	Forest Watcher	M. Boyett	Retrd.	215.00	540.00
83-11-020	Rite of the Whitetail	M. Boyett	Retrd.	295.00	400.00
83-11-021	Circling the Enemy	M. Boyett	Retrd.	295.00	395.00
83-11-022	A Warrior's Tribute	M. Boyett	Retrd.	335.00	635.00
Lance Corporation		**Chilmark Pewter OffCanvas™**			
90-12-001	Smoke Signal	A. T. McGrory	S/O	345.00	550-700.
90-12-002	Vigil	A. T. McGrory	S/O	345.00	500-700.
90-12-003	Warrior	A. T. McGrory	S/O	300.00	350-600.
91-12-004	Blanket Signel	A. T. McGrory	S/O	750.00	850.00
Lance Corporation		**Chilmark Pewter Sculptures**			
79-13-001	Unicorn	R. Sylvan	S/O	115.00	550.00
79-13-002	Carousel	R. Sylvan	S/O	115.00	115.00
79-13-003	Moses	B. Rodden	S/O	140.00	235.00
79-13-004	Pegasus	R. Sylvan	Retrd.	95.00	175.00
80-13-005	Charge of the 7th Cavalry	B. Rodden	Retrd.	600.00	950.00
81-13-006	Budweiser Wagon	C. Keim	Retrd.	2000.00	3000.00
83-13-007	Dragon Slayer	D. LaRocca	Retrd.	385.00	500.00
84-13-008	Garden Unicorn	J. Royce	Retrd.	160.00	200.00
86-13-009	Camelot Chess Set	P. Jackson	Retrd.	2250.00	2250.00
92-13-010	Christopher Columbus	D. LaRocca	Retrd.	295.00	295.00
Lance Corporation		**Chilmark Pewter The Sorcerer's Apprentice Collectors Series**			
90-14-001	The Sorcerer's Apprentice	Disney Studios	2,500	225.00	240.00
90-14-002	The Incantation	Disney Studios	2,500	150.00	160.00
90-14-003	The Dream	Disney Studios	2,500	225.00	240.00
90-14-004	The Whirlpool	Disney Studios	2,500	225.00	250.00
90-14-005	The Repentant Apprentice	Disney Studios	2,500	195.00	205.00
Lance Corporation		**Chilmark Pewter Disney Figurines**			
89-15-001	Hollywood Mickey	Disney Studios	Suspd.	165.00	250-350.
89-15-002	"Gold Edition" Hollywood Mickey	Disney Studios	Retrd.	200.00	200.00
91-15-003	Mickey's Carousel Ride	Disney Studios	2,500	150.00	160.00
92-15-004	Minnie's Carousel Ride	Disney Studios	2,500	150.00	160.00

Number	Name	Artist	Edition Limit	Issue Price	Quote
Company		**Series**			
94-15-005	Mouse in a Million (Bronze)	Disney Studios	S/O	1250.00	1250.00
94-15-006	Mouse in a Million (MetalART))	Disney Studios	S/O	650.00	650.00
94-15-007	Mouse in a Million (Pewter)	Disney Studios	S/O	500.00	500.00
94-15-008	Jitterbugging	Disney Studios	S/O	450.00	450.00
Lance Corporation		**Chilmark Pewter Generations of Mickey**			
87-16-001	Antique Mickey	Disney Studios	S/O	95.00	550-650.
89-16-002	Steamboat Willie	Disney Studios	S/O	165.00	200-350.
89-16-003	Sorcerer's Apprentice	Disney Studios	S/O	150.00	225.00
89-16-004	Mickey's Gala Premiere	Disney Studios	2,500	150.00	160.00
90-16-005	Disneyland Mickey	Disney Studios	2,500	150.00	160.00
90-16-006	The Band Concert	Disney Studios	2,500	185.00	195.00
90-16-007	The Band Concert (Painted)	Disney Studios	S/O	215.00	250-400.
91-16-008	Plane Crazy-1928	Disney Studios	2,500	175.00	185.00
91-16-009	The Mouse-1935	Disney Studios	1,200	185.00	195.00
Lance Corporation		**Chilmark Pewter The Adversaries**			
91-17-001	Robert E. Lee	F. Barnum	S/O	350.00	750-1300.
92-17-002	Ulysses S. Grant	F. Barnum	S/O	350.00	435-750.
92-17-003	Stonewall Jackson	F. Barnum	S/O	375.00	375-850.
93-17-004	Wm. Tecumseh Sherman	F. Barnum	S/O	375.00	375-750.
Lance Corporation		**Chilmark Pewter Civil War**			
87-18-001	Saving The Colors	F. Barnum	Retrd.	350.00	700.00
88-18-002	Johnny Shiloh	F. Barnum	S/O	100.00	220.00
92-18-003	Kennesaw Mountain	F. Barnum	S/O	650.00	765-1300.
92-18-004	Parson's Battery	F. Barnum	S/O	495.00	500-575.
93-18-005	Abraham Lincoln Bust (Bronze)	F. Barnum	S/O	2000.00	2250.00
94-18-006	Gentleman Soldier (Bronze)	F. Barnum	S/O	1500.00	1500.00
Lance Corporation		**Chilmark Pewter Eagles**			
81-19-001	Freedom Eagle	G. deLodzia	S/O	195.00	750-900.
82-19-002	Wings of Liberty	M. Boyett	S/O	625.00	1565.00
87-19-003	Winged Victory	J. Mullican	Suspd.	275.00	315.00
89-19-004	High and Mighty	A. McGrory	Suspd.	185.00	200.00
91-19-005	Cry of Freedom	S. Knight	Suspd.	395.00	395.00
Lance Corporation		**Chilmark Pewter Masters of the American West**			
84-20-001	Cheyenne (Remington)	C. Rousell	Retrd.	400.00	600.00
85-20-002	Bronco Buster (Large)	C. Rousell	Retrd.	400.00	400.00
86-20-003	Buffalo Hunt	A. McGrory	Retrd.	550.00	800.00
88-20-004	End of the Trail (Mini)	A. McGrory	S/O	225.00	250.00
89-20-005	Trooper of the Plains	A. McGrory	Suspd.	250.00	265.00
89-20-006	The Triumph	A. McGrory	Suspd.	275.00	290.00
90-20-007	Remington Self Portrait	A. McGrory	Suspd.	275.00	275.00
Lance Corporation		**Chilmark Pewter The Cavalry Generals**			
92-21-001	J.E.B. Stuart	F. Barnum	S/O	375.00	375.00
Lance Corporation		**Chilmark Pewter World War II**			
90-22-001	Navy Pearl Harbor	D. LaRocca	Suspd.	425.00	450.00
90-22-002	Army Corregidor	D. LaRocca	Suspd.	315.00	325.00
90-22-003	Air Corps Hickam Field	D. LaRocca	Suspd.	200.00	210.00
90-22-004	Marines Wake Island	D. LaRocca	Suspd.	200.00	210.00
91-22-005	Marines In Solomons	D. LaRocca	Suspd.	275.00	275.00
91-22-006	Army North Africa	D. LaRocca	Suspd.	375.00	375.00
91-22-007	Navy North Atlantic	D. LaRocca	Suspd.	375.00	375.00
91-22-008	Air Corps Tokyo Raid	D. LaRocca	Suspd.	350.00	350.00
Lance Corporation		**Chilmark Pewter Beautiful Women**			
84-23-001	Sibyl	A. Kann	Suspd.	150.00	165-375.
84-23-002	Adrienne	A. Kann	Suspd.	175.00	195.00
84-23-003	Clarisse	A. Kann	Suspd.	195.00	200.00
84-23-004	Desiree	A. Kann	Suspd.	195.00	200.00
85-23-005	Giselle	A. Kann	Suspd.	225.00	225.00
89-23-006	Michelle	A. Kann	Suspd.	350.00	365.00
Lance Corporation		**Chilmark Pewter The Ballet**			
89-24-001	Nadia	S. Feldman	Suspd.	250.00	275.00
89-24-002	The Pair	S. Feldman	Suspd.	300.00	315.00
89-24-003	Anna	S. Feldman	Suspd.	350.00	375.00
Lance Corporation		**Chilmark MetalART™ The Great Chiefs**			
92-25-001	Chief Joseph	J. Slockbower	S/O	975.00	1900-1500.
92-25-002	Geronimo	J. Slockbower	S/O	975.00	975.00
Lance Corporation		**Chilmark Pewter/MetalART™ The Warriors**			
92-26-001	Spirit of the Wolf (pewter)	D. Polland	S/O	350.00	850.00
93-26-002	Son of the Morning Star (pewter)	D. Polland	S/O	375.00	460.00
Lance Corporation		**Chilmark Pewter/MetalART™ The Medicine Men**			
92-27-001	False Face (pewter)	D. Polland	S/O	375.00	375.00
Lance Corporation		**Chilmark Pewter/MetalART™ To The Great Spirit**			
92-27-001	Shooting Star	Sullivan	S/O	750.00	750.00
Lance Corporation		**Chilmark MetalART™ On the Road**			
92-28-001	Cruising	Disney Studios	S/O	275.00	990-1100.
93-28-002	Sunday Drive	Disney Studios	S/O	325.00	880.00
94-28-003	Beach Bound	Disney Studios	S/O	350.00	350.00
Lance Corporation		**Chilmark MetalART™ The Seekers**			
92-29-001	Buffalo Vision	A. McGrory	S/O	1075.00	1075.00
Lance Corporation		**Chilmark Pewter Turning Points**			
93-30-001	The High Tide	F. Barnum	S/O	600.00	900.00
Lance Corporation		**Chilmark Pewter Mickey & Co. Christmas**			
93-31-001	Checking it Twice	Disney Studios	Yr.Iss.	195.00	195.00
93-31-002	Hanging the Stockings	Disney Studios	Yr.Iss.	295.00	295.00
Lance Corporation		**Cp smithshire™**			
93-32-001	St. Nicholai	C. Smith	Yr.Iss.	75.00	75.00
94-32-002	Santa and Nicky	C. Smith	Yr.Iss.	90.00	90.00
Lance Corporation		**Cp smithshire Event Figurine**			
93-33-001	Sap	C. Smith	Yr.Iss.	60.00	60.00
Lance Corporation		**Pangaean Society Member Only Redemption Specials**			
93-34-001	Dentzel	C. Smith	Yr.Iss.	90.00	90.00
Lance Corporation		**Pangaean Society Membership Figurines**			
93-35-001	Fellowship Inn	C. Smith	Yr.Iss.	Gift	N/A

Number	Name	Artist	Edition Limit	Issue Price	Quote
Company		**Series**			
Lance Corporation		**Summer Villagers**			
94-36-001	Ring Around the Rosie	Hudson Studios	1,500	110.00	110.00
Lance Corporation		**Sebastian Miniature Figurines**			
83-37-001	Harry Hood	P.W. Baston, Jr.	S/O	Unkn.	200-250.
85-37-002	It's Hoods (Wagon)	P.W. Baston, Jr.	S/O	Unkn.	150-175.
86-37-003	Statue of Liberty (AT & T)	P.W. Baston, Jr.	S/O	Unkn.	175-200.
87-37-004	White House (Gold, Oval Base)	P.W. Baston, Jr.	S/O	17.00	75-100.00
91-37-005	America Salutes Desert Storm-painted	P.W. Baston, Jr.	S/O	49.50	200-325.
91-37-006	America Salutes Desert Storm-bronze	P.W. Baston, Jr.	1,641	26.50	100.00
91-37-007	Happy Hood Holidays	P.W. Baston, Jr.	2,000	32.50	85.00
92-37-008	Firefighter	P.W. Baston, Jr.	S/O	28.00	50.00
92-37-009	I Know I Left It Here Somewhere	P.W. Baston, Jr.	1,000	28.50	28.50
Lance Corporation		**Sebastian Miniatures Children At Play**			
78-38-001	Sidewalk Days Boy	P.W. Baston	S/O	19.50	35-50.00
78-38-002	Sidewalk Days Girl	P.W. Baston	S/O	19.50	30-50.00
79-38-003	Building Days Boy	P.W. Baston	S/O	19.50	20-40.00
79-38-004	Building Days Girl	P.W. Baston	S/O	19.50	20-40.00
80-38-005	Snow Days Boy	P.W. Baston	S/O	19.50	20-40.00
80-38-006	Snow Days Girl	P.W. Baston	S/O	19.50	20-40.00
81-38-007	Sailing Days Boy	P.W. Baston	S/O	19.50	20-30.00
81-38-008	Sailing Days Girl	P.W. Baston	S/O	19.50	20-30.00
82-38-009	School Days Boy	P.W. Baston	S/O	19.50	20-30.00
82-38-010	School Days Girl	P.W. Baston	S/O	19.50	20-30.00
Lance Corporation		**Sebastian Miniatures America Remembers**			
79-39-001	Family Sing	P.W. Baston	Yr.Iss.	29.50	75-125.00
80-39-002	Family Picnic	P.W. Baston	Yr.Iss.	29.50	30-60.00
81-39-003	Family Reads Aloud	P.W. Baston	Yr.Iss.	34.50	34.50
82-39-004	Family Fishing	P.W. Baston	Yr.Iss.	34.50	34.50
83-39-005	Family Feast	P.W. Baston	Yr.Iss.	37.50	100-150.
Lance Corporation		**Sebastian Miniatures Jimmy Fund**			
83-40-001	Schoolboy	P.W. Baston	Yr.Iss.	24.50	35-75.00
84-40-002	Catcher	P.W. Baston	Yr.Iss.	24.50	35-75.00
85-40-003	Hockey Player	P.W. Baston,Jr.	Yr.Iss.	24.50	35-50.00
86-40-004	Soccer Player	P.W. Baston,Jr.	Yr.Iss.	25.00	25.00
87-40-005	Football Player	P.W. Baston,Jr.	Yr.Iss.	26.50	26.50
88-40-006	Santa	P.W. Baston,Jr.	Closed	32.50	32.50
Lance Corporation		**Sebastian Miniatures Exchange Figurines**			
83-41-001	Newspaper Boy	P.W. Baston	Yr.Iss.	28.50	45-60.00
84-41-002	First Things First	P.W. Baston,Jr.	Yr.Iss.	30.00	45.00
85-41-003	Newstand	P.W. Baston,Jr.	Yr.Iss.	30.00	40.00
86-41-004	News Wagon	P.W. Baston,Jr.	Yr.Iss.	35.00	40.00
87-41-005	It's About Time	P.W. Baston,Jr.	Yr.Iss.	25.00	35.00
Lance Corporation		**Sebastian Miniatures Washington Irving-Member Only**			
80-42-001	Rip Van Winkle	P.W. Baston	Closed	19.50	19.50
81-42-002	Dame Van Winkle	P.W. Baston	Closed	19.50	19.50
81-42-003	Ichabod Crane	P.W. Baston	Closed	19.50	19.50
82-42-004	Katrina Van Tassel	P.W. Baston	Closed	19.50	19.50
82-42-005	Brom Bones(Headless Horseman)	P.W. Baston	Closed	22.50	22.50
83-42-006	Diedrich Knickerbocker	P.W. Baston	Closed	22.50	22.50
Lance Corporation		**Sebastian Miniatures Shakespearean-Member Only**			
84-43-001	Henry VIII	P.W. Baston	Yr.Iss.	19.50	19.50
84-43-002	Anne Boyeln	P.W. Baston	6 month	17.50	17.50
85-43-003	Falstaff	P.W. Baston	Yr.Iss.	19.50	19.50
85-43-004	Mistress Ford	P.W. Baston	6 month	17.50	17.50
86-43-005	Romeo	P.W. Baston	Yr.Iss.	19.50	19.50
86-43-006	Juliet	P.W. Baston	6 month	17.50	17.50
87-43-007	Malvolio	P.W. Baston	Yr.Iss.	21.50	21.50
87-43-008	Countess Olivia	P.W. Baston	6 month	19.50	19.50
88-43-009	Touchstone	P.W. Baston	Yr.Iss.	22.50	22.50
88-43-010	Audrey	P.W. Baston	6 month	22.50	22.50
89-43-011	Mark Anthony	P.W. Baston	Yr.Iss.	27.00	27.00
89-43-012	Cleopatra	P.W. Baston	6 month	27.00	27.00
88-43-013	Shakespeare	P.W. Baston,Jr.	Yr.Iss.	23.50	23.50
Lance Corporation		**Sebastian Miniatures Member Only**			
89-44-001	The Collectors	P.W. Baston,Jr.	Yr.Iss.	39.50	39.50
92-44-002	Christopher Columbus	P.W. Baston,Jr.	Yr.Iss.	28.50	28.50
Lance Corporation		**Sebastian Miniatures Holiday Memories-Member Only**			
90-45-001	Thanksgiving Helper	P.W. Baston,Jr.	Yr.Iss.	39.50	39.50
90-45-002	Leprechaun	P.W. Baston,Jr.	Yr.Iss.	27.50	27.50
91-45-003	Trick or Treat	P.W. Baston,Jr.	Yr.Iss.	25.50	25.50
93-45-004	Father Time	P.W. Baston,Jr.	Yr.Iss.	27.50	27.50
Lance Corporation		**Sebastian Miniatures Collectors Society**			
80-46-001	S.M.C. Society Plaque ('80 Charter)	P.W. Baston	Yr.Iss.	Unkn.	50-75.00
81-46-002	S.M.C. Society Plaque	P.W. Baston	Yr.Iss.	Unkn.	20-30.00
82-46-003	S.M.C. Society Plaque	P.W. Baston	Yr.Iss.	Unkn.	20-30.00
83-46-004	S.M.C. Society Plaque	P.W. Baston	Yr.Iss.	Unkn.	20-30.00
84-46-005	S.M.C. Society Plaque	P.W. Baston	Yr.Iss.	Unkn.	20-30.00
84-46-006	Self Portrait	P.W. Baston	Open	34.50	45.00
Lance Corporation		**Sebastian Miniatures Christmas**			
93-47-001	Caroling With Santa	P.W. Baston,Jr.	1,000	29.00	29.00
93-47-002	Harmonizing With Santa	P.W. Baston,Jr.	1,000	27.00	27.00

Also see Sebastian Studios

Number	Name	Artist	Edition Limit	Issue Price	Quote
Lance Corporation		**Hudson Pewter Figures**			
69-48-001	George Washington (Cannon)	P.W. Baston	Closed	35.00	75-100.00
69-48-002	John Hancock	P.W. Baston	Closed	15.00	100-125.
69-48-003	Colonial Blacksmith	P.W. Baston	Closed	30.00	100-125.
69-48-004	Betsy Ross	P.W. Baston	Closed	30.00	100-125.
72-48-005	Benjamin Franklin	P.W. Baston	Closed	15.00	75-100.00
72-48-006	Thomas Jefferson	P.W. Baston	Closed	15.00	75-100.00
72-48-007	George Washington	P.W. Baston	Closed	15.00	75-100.00
72-48-008	John Adams	P.W. Baston	Closed	15.00	75-100.00
72-48-009	James Madison	P.W. Baston	Closed	15.00	50-75.00
75-48-010	Declaration Wall Plaque	P.W. Baston	Closed	Unkn.	300-500.
75-48-011	Washington's Letter of Acceptance	P.W. Baston	Closed	Unkn.	300-400.
75-48-012	Lincoln's Gettysburg Address	P.W. Baston	Closed	Unkn.	300-400.
75-48-013	Lee's Ninth General Order	P.W. Baston	Closed	Unkn.	300-400.
75-48-014	The Favored Scholar	P.W. Baston	Closed	Unkn.	600-1000.
75-48-015	Neighboring Pews	P.W. Baston	Closed	Unkn.	600-1000.
75-48-016	Weighing the Baby	P.W. Baston	Closed	Unkn.	600-1000.
75-48-017	Spirit of '76	P.W. Baston	Closed	Unkn.	750-1500.
76-48-018	Great Horned Owl	H. Wilson	Closed	Unkn.	41.50

Number	Name	Artist	Edition Limit	Issue Price	Quote
76-48-019	Bald Eagle	H. Wilson	Closed	100.00	112.50
Lance Corporation		**Hudson Pewter Crystals of Zorn**			
88-49-001	Guarding the Crystal	D. Liberty	950	450.00	460.00
88-49-002	Charging the Stone	D. Liberty	950	375.00	395.00
88-49-003	USS Strikes Back	D. Liberty	500	650.00	675.00
88-49-004	Response of Ornic Force	D. Liberty	950	275.00	285.00
88-49-005	Battle on the Plains of Xenon	D. Liberty	950	250.00	265.00
88-49-006	Restoration	D. Liberty	950	425.00	435.00
90-49-007	Struggle For Supremacy	D. Liberty	950	395.00	400.00
90-49-008	Asmund's Workshop	D. Liberty	950	275.00	275.00
90-49-009	Vesting The Grail	D. Liberty	950	200.00	200.00
Lance Corporation		**Military Commemoratives**			
91-50-001	Desert Liberator (Pewter)	D. LaRocca	Retrd.	295.00	295.00
91-50-002	Desert Liberator (Painted Porcelain)	D. LaRocca	Retrd.	125.00	125.00
Lance Corporation		**Hudson Pewter The Villagers**			
87-51-001	Mr. Bosworth	Hudson Studios	Retrd.	35.00	35.00
87-51-002	Emily	Hudson Studios	Retrd.	23.00	23.00
87-51-003	Reginald	Hudson Studios	Retrd.	23.00	23.00
87-51-004	Oliver	Hudson Studios	Retrd.	20.00	20.00
87-51-005	Jenny	Hudson Studios	Retrd.	20.00	20.00
87-51-006	Thomas	Hudson Studios	Retrd.	20.00	20.00
88-51-007	Melissa	Hudson Studios	Retrd.	18.00	18.00
88-51-008	Tully's Pond	Hudson Studios	Retrd.	49.00	49.00
88-51-009	Main Street	Hudson Studios	Retrd.	47.00	47.00
88-51-010	Bosworth Manor	Hudson Studios	Retrd.	57.00	57.00
88-51-011	Santa	Hudson Studios	Retrd.	28.00	28.00
89-51-012	Grandpa Todd	Hudson Studios	Retrd.	23.00	23.00
89-51-013	Grandma Todd & Sarah	Hudson Studios	Retrd.	29.00	29.00
89-51-014	Rascal	Hudson Studios	Retrd.	25.00	25.00
89-51-015	Seated Santa	Hudson Studios	Yr.Iss.	25.00	25.00
89-51-016	Creche	Hudson Studios	Retrd.	15.00	15.00
89-51-017	Ben Torpey	Hudson Studios	Retrd.	28.00	28.00
89-51-018	Villagers Plaque	Hudson Studios	Retrd.	27.00	27.00
89-51-019	Danny	Hudson Studios	Retrd.	19.00	19.00
90-51-020	Santa & Holly	Hudson Studios	Yr.Iss.	32.00	32.00
90-51-021	Toy Shop	Hudson Studios	Retrd.	60.00	60.00
90-51-022	Sweet Shop	Hudson Studios	Retrd.	50.00	50.00
90-51-023	Cliff	Hudson Studios	Retrd.	37.00	37.00
90-51-024	Johnny Hart	Hudson Studios	Retrd.	24.00	24.00
90-51-025	Mrs. Bosworth	Hudson Studios	Retrd.	29.00	29.00
90-51-026	Mrs. Fearnley	Hudson Studios	Retrd.	24.00	24.00
90-51-027	Mr. Whiteaker	Hudson Studios	Retrd.	24.00	24.00
90-51-028	Jay & Jodi	Hudson Studios	Retrd.	24.00	24.00
87-51-029	Mr. Hazen	Hudson Studios	Retrd.	24.00	24.00
91-51-030	Santa and Matthew	Hudson Studios	Yr.Iss.	35.00	35.00
92-51-031	Crack the Whip	Hudson Studios	S/O	95.00	95.00
92-51-032	1992 Annual Santa	Hudson Studios	Yr.Iss.	32.00	32.00
93-51-033	1993 Santa	Hudson Studios	Yr.Iss.	32.00	32.00
93-51-034	Toboggan Ride	Hudson Studios	1,500	110.00	110.00
93-51-035	Family Caroling	Hudson Studios	1,500	95.00	95.00
Lance Corporation		**Hudson Pewter Noah's Ark**			
81-52-001	Monkey Pair	Hudson Studios	Retrd.	16.50	16.50
81-52-002	Pelican Pair	Hudson Studios	Retrd.	16.50	16.50
81-52-003	Female Hippo	Hudson Studios	Retrd.	12.00	12.00
81-52-004	Male Hippo	Hudson Studios	Retrd.	12.00	12.00
82-52-005	Toucan Pair	Hudson Studios	Retrd.	18.00	18.00
82-52-006	Male Horse	Hudson Studios	Retrd.	12.00	12.00
82-52-007	Female Horse	Hudson Studios	Retrd.	12.00	12.00
81-52-008	Male Turtle	Hudson Studios	Retrd.	12.00	12.00
81-52-009	Female Turtle	Hudson Studios	Retrd.	12.00	12.00
83-52-010	Male Rhino	Hudson Studios	Retrd.	13.00	13.00
83-52-011	Female Rhino	Hudson Studios	Retrd.	13.00	13.00
83-52-012	Panda Pair	Hudson Studios	Retrd.	18.00	18.00
84-52-013	Male Tiger	Hudson Studios	Retrd.	13.00	13.00
84-52-014	Female Tiger	Hudson Studios	Retrd.	13.00	13.00
84-52-015	Male Deer	Hudson Studios	Retrd.	13.00	13.00
84-52-016	Female Deer	Hudson Studios	Retrd.	13.00	13.00
84-52-017	Mice Pair	Hudson Studios	Retrd.	14.00	14.00
84-52-018	Raccoon Pair	Hudson Studios	Retrd.	14.00	14.00
87-52-019	Cat Pair	Hudson Studios	Retrd.	18.00	18.00
87-52-020	Female Dog	Hudson Studios	Retrd.	13.00	13.00
87-52-021	Male Dog	Hudson Studios	Retrd.	16.00	16.00
87-52-022	Ram	Hudson Studios	Retrd.	16.00	16.00
87-52-023	Ewe	Hudson Studios	Retrd.	16.00	16.00
88-52-024	Geese Pair	Hudson Studios	Retrd.	18.00	18.00
89-52-025	Male Bear	Hudson Studios	Retrd.	16.00	16.00
89-52-026	Female Bear	Hudson Studios	Retrd.	16.00	16.00
Land of Legends: See Flambro/Land of Legends					
Ron Lee's World of Clowns		**The Original Ron Lee Collection-1976**			
76-01-001	Pinky Upside Down 111	R. Lee	Closed	25.00	150.00
76-01-002	Pinky Lying Down 112	R. Lee	Closed	25.00	150.00
76-01-003	Hobo Joe Hitchiking 116	R. Lee	Closed	55.00	65.00
76-01-004	Hobo Joe with Umbrella 117	R. Lee	Closed	58.00	65-160.00
76-01-005	Pinky Sitting 119	R. Lee	Closed	25.00	150.00
76-01-006	Hobo Joe with Balloons 120	R. Lee	Closed	63.00	90.00
76-01-007	Hobo Joe with Pal 115	R. Lee	Closed	63.00	85-170.00
76-01-008	Clown and Dog Act 101	R. Lee	Closed	48.00	78-140.00
76-01-009	Clown Tightrope Walker 104	R. Lee	Closed	50.00	82-155.00
76-01-010	Clown and Elephant Act 107	R. Lee	Closed	56.00	85-140.00
76-01-011	Pinky Standing 118	R. Lee	Closed	25.00	45-100.00
76-01-012	Owl With Guitar 500	R. Lee	Closed	15.00	35-78.00
76-01-013	Turtle On Skateboard 501	R. Lee	Closed	15.00	35-78.00
76-01-014	Frog Surfing 502	R. Lee	Closed	15.00	35-78.00
76-01-015	Penguin on Snowskis 503	R. Lee	Closed	15.00	35-78.00
76-01-016	Alligator Bowling 504	R. Lee	Closed	15.00	35-78.00
76-01-017	Hippo on Scooter 505	R. Lee	Closed	15.00	35-78.00
76-01-018	Rabbit Playing Tennis 507	R. Lee	Closed	15.00	35-78.00
76-01-019	Kangaroos Boxing 508	R. Lee	Closed	15.00	35-78.00
76-01-020	Pig Playing Violin 510	R. Lee	Closed	15.00	35-78.00
76-01-021	Bear Fishing 511	R. Lee	Closed	15.00	35-78.00
76-01-022	Dog Fishing 512	R. Lee	Closed	15.00	35-78.00
Ron Lee's World of Clowns		**The Original Ron Lee Collection-1977**			
77-02-001	Koala Bear In Tree 514	R. Lee	Closed	15.00	35-78.00
77-02-002	Koala Bear With Baby 515	R. Lee	Closed	15.00	35-78.00
77-02-003	Koala Bear On Log 516	R. Lee	Closed	15.00	35-78.00
77-02-004	Mr. Penguin 518	R. Lee	Closed	18.00	39-85.00
77-02-005	Owl Graduate 519	R. Lee	Closed	22.00	44-90.00

Number	Name	Artist	Edition Limit	Issue Price	Quote
77-02-006	Mouse and Cheese 520	R. Lee	Closed	18.00	30-80.00
77-02-007	Monkey With Banana 521	R. Lee	Closed	18.00	30-80.00
77-02-008	Pelican and Python 522	R. Lee	Closed	18.00	30-80.00
77-02-009	Bear On Rock 523	R. Lee	Closed	18.00	30-80.00
Ron Lee's World of Clowns		**The Original Ron Lee Collection-1978**			
78-03-001	Polly, the Parrot & Crackers 201	R. Lee	Closed	63.00	100-170.
78-03-002	Corky, the Drummer Boy 202	R. Lee	Closed	53.00	85-130.00
78-03-003	Tinker Bowing 203	R. Lee	Closed	37.00	55-110.00
78-03-004	Bobbi on Unicyle 204	R. Lee	Closed	45.00	65-98.00
78-03-005	Clara-Bow 205	R. Lee	Closed	52.00	70-120.00
78-03-006	Sparky Skating 206	R. Lee	Closed	55.00	72-260.00
78-03-007	Pierrot Painting 207	R. Lee	Closed	50.00	80-170.00
78-03-008	Cuddles 208	R. Lee	Closed	37.00	55-110.00
78-03-009	Poppy with Puppet 209	R. Lee	Closed	60.00	75-140.00
78-03-010	Clancy, the Cop 210	R. Lee	Closed	55.00	72-130.00
78-03-011	Driver the Golfer 211	R. Lee	Closed	55.00	200-275.
78-03-012	Sad Sack 212	R. Lee	Closed	48.00	62-210.00
78-03-013	Elephant on Stand 213	R. Lee	Closed	26.00	42-80.00
78-03-014	Elephant on Ball 214	R. Lee	Closed	26.00	42-80.00
78-03-015	Elephant Sitting 215	R. Lee	Closed	26.00	42-80.00
78-03-016	Fireman with Hose 216	R. Lee	Closed	62.00	85-140.00
78-03-017	Tobi-Hands Outstretched 217	R. Lee	Closed	70.00	98-260.00
78-03-018	Coco-Hands on Hips 218	R. Lee	Closed	70.00	95-150.00
78-03-019	Jeri In a Barrel 219	R. Lee	Closed	75.00	110-180.
78-03-020	Hey Rube 220	R. Lee	Closed	35.00	53-92.00
78-03-021	Jocko with Lollipop 221	R. Lee	Closed	67.50	93-215.00
78-03-022	Bow Tie 222	R. Lee	Closed	67.50	93-215.00
78-03-023	Oscar On Stilts 223	R. Lee	Closed	55.00	90-120.00
78-03-024	Fancy Pants 224	R. Lee	Closed	55.00	90-120.00
78-03-025	Skippy Swinging 239	R. Lee	Closed	52.00	65-85.00
78-03-026	Sailfish 524	R. Lee	Closed	18.00	40-95.00
78-03-027	Dolphins 525	R. Lee	Closed	22.00	40-85.00
78-03-028	Prince Frog 526	R. Lee	Closed	22.00	40-85.00
78-03-029	Seagull 527	R. Lee	Closed	22.00	40-85.00
78-03-030	Hummingbird 528	R. Lee	Closed	22.00	40-85.00
78-03-031	Butterfly and Flower 529	R. Lee	Closed	22.00	40-85.00
78-03-032	Turtle on Rock 530	R. Lee	Closed	22.00	40-85.00
78-03-033	Sea Otter on Back 531	R. Lee	Closed	22.00	40-85.00
78-03-034	Sea Otter on Rock 532	R. Lee	Closed	22.00	40-85.00
Ron Lee's World of Clowns		**The Original Ron Lee Collection-1979**			
79-04-001	Timmy Tooting 225	R. Lee	Closed	35.00	52-85.00
79-04-002	Tubby Tuba 226	R. Lee	Closed	35.00	55-90.00
79-04-003	Lilli 227	R. Lee	Closed	75.00	105-145.
79-04-004	Doctor Sawbones 228	R. Lee	Closed	75.00	110-150.
79-04-005	Buttons Bicycling 229	R. Lee	Closed	75.00	110-150.
79-04-006	Kelly in Kar 230	R. Lee	Closed	164.00	210-380.
79-04-007	Kelly's Kar 231	R. Lee	Closed	75.00	90-230.00
79-04-008	Carousel Horse 232	R. Lee	Closed	119.00	130-195.
79-04-009	Harry and the Hare 233	R. Lee	Closed	69.00	102-180.
79-04-010	Fearless Fred in Cannon 234	R. Lee	Closed	80.00	105-300.
79-04-011	Darby with Flower 235	R. Lee	Closed	35.00	60-140.00
79-04-012	Darby with Umbrella 236	R. Lee	Closed	35.00	60-140.00
79-04-013	Darby With Violin 237	R. Lee	Closed	35.00	60-140.00
79-04-014	Darby Tipping Hat 238	R. Lee	Closed	35.00	60-140.00
79-04-015	Kelly at the Piano 241	R. Lee	Closed	185.00	280-510.
Ron Lee's World of Clowns		**The Original Ron Lee Collection-1980**			
80-05-001	Cubby Holding Balloon 240	R. Lee	Closed	50.00	65-70.00
80-05-002	Jingles Telling Time 242	R. Lee	Closed	75.00	90-190.00
80-05-003	Donkey What 243	R. Lee	Closed	60.00	92-250.00
80-05-004	Chuckles Juggling 244	R. Lee	Closed	98.00	105-150
80-05-005	P. T. Dinghy 245	R. Lee	Closed	65.00	80-190.00
80-05-006	Roni Riding Horse 246	R. Lee	Closed	115.00	180-290.
80-05-007	Peanuts Playing Concertina 247	R. Lee	Closed	65.00	150-285.
80-05-008	Carousel Horse 248	R. Lee	Closed	88.00	115-285.
80-05-009	Carousel Horse 249	R. Lee	Closed	88.00	115-285.
80-05-010	Jo-Jo at Make-up Mirror 250	R. Lee	Closed	86.00	125-185
80-05-011	Monkey 251	R. Lee	Closed	60.00	85-210.00
80-05-012	Dennis Playing Tennis 252	R. Lee	Closed	74.00	95-185.00
80-05-013	Jaque Downhill Racer 253	R. Lee	Closed	74.00	90-210.00
80-05-014	Ruford 254	R. Lee	Closed	43.00	82-190.00
80-05-015	Happy Waving 255	R. Lee	Closed	43.00	82-190.00
80-05-016	Zach 256	R. Lee	Closed	43.00	82-190.00
80-05-017	Emile 257	R. Lee	Closed	43.00	82-190.00
80-05-018	Banjo Willie 258	R. Lee	Closed	68.00	85-195.00
80-05-019	Hobo Joe in Tub 259	R. Lee	Closed	96.00	105-125
80-05-020	Doctor Jawbones 260	R. Lee	Closed	85.00	110-305.
80-05-021	Alexander's One Man Band 261	R. Lee	Closed	N/A	N/A
80-05-022	The Menagerie 262	R. Lee	Closed	N/A	N/A
80-05-023	Horse Drawn Chariot 263	R. Lee	Closed	N/A	N/A
Ron Lee's World of Clowns		**The Original Ron Lee Collection-1981**			
81-06-001	Executive Reading 264	R. Lee	Closed	23.00	45-110.00
81-06-002	Executive with Umbrella 265	R. Lee	Closed	23.00	45-110.00
81-06-003	Executive Resting 266	R. Lee	Closed	23.00	45-110.00
81-06-004	Executive Hitchiking 267	R. Lee	Closed	23.00	45-110.00
81-06-005	Louie on Park Bench 268	R. Lee	Closed	56.00	85-160.00
81-06-006	Louie Hitching A Ride 269	R. Lee	Closed	47.00	58-135.00
81-06-007	Louie On Railroad Car 270	R. Lee	Closed	77.00	95-180.00
81-06-008	Elephant Reading 271	R. Lee	Closed	N/A	N/A
81-06-009	Pistol Pete 272	R. Lee	Closed	76.00	85-180.00
81-06-010	Barbella 273	R. Lee	Closed	N/A	N/A
81-06-011	Larry and His Hotdogs 274	R. Lee	Closed	76.00	90-200.00
81-06-012	Cashew On One Knee 275	R. Lee	Closed	N/A	N/A
81-06-013	Bojangles 276	R. Lee	Closed	N/A	N/A
81-06-014	Bozo Playing Cymbols 277	R. Lee	Closed	28.00	49-185.00
81-06-015	Bozo Riding Car 278	R. Lee	Closed	28.00	49-185.00
81-06-016	Bozo On Unicycle 279	R. Lee	Closed	28.00	49-185.00
81-06-017	Carousel Horse 280	R. Lee	Closed	88.00	125-240.
81-06-018	Carousel Horse 281	R. Lee	Closed	88.00	125-240.
81-06-019	Ron Lee Trio 282	R. Lee	Closed	144.00	280-435.
81-06-020	Kevin at the Drums 283	R. Lee	Closed	50.00	92-150.00
81-06-021	Al at the Bass 284	R. Lee	Closed	48.00	52-112.00
81-06-022	Ron at the Piano 285	R. Lee	Closed	46.00	55-110.00
81-06-023	Timothy In Big Shoes 286	R. Lee	Closed	37.00	50-95.00
81-06-024	Perry Sitting With Balloon 287	R. Lee	Closed	37.00	50-95.00
81-06-025	Perry Standing With Balloon 288	R. Lee	Closed	37.00	50-95.00
81-06-026	Nicky Sitting on Ball 289	R. Lee	Closed	39.00	48-92.00
81-06-027	Nicky Standing on Ball 290	R. Lee	Closed	39.00	48-92.00
81-06-028	Mickey With Umbrella 291	R. Lee	Closed	50.00	75-140.00
81-06-029	Mickey Tightrope Walker 292	R. Lee	Closed	50.00	75-140.00
81-06-030	Mickey Upside Down 293	R. Lee	Closed	50.00	75-140.00

Company Number	Name	Series Artist	Edition Limit	Issue Price	Quote
81-06-031	Rocketman 294	R. Lee	Closed	77.00	92-180.00
81-06-032	My Son Darren 295	R. Lee	Closed	57.00	72-140.00
81-06-033	Harpo 296	R. Lee	Closed	120.00	190-350.
81-06-034	Pickles and Pooch 297	R. Lee	Closed	90.00	140-240.
81-06-035	Hobo Joe Praying 298	R. Lee	Closed	57.00	65-85.00
81-06-036	Bosom Buddies 299	R. Lee	Closed	135.00	90-280.00
81-06-037	Carney and Seal Act 300	R. Lee	Closed	63.00	75-140.00
Ron Lee's World of Clowns		**The Original Ron Lee Collection-1982**			
82-07-001	Ron Lee Carousel	R. Lee	Closed	10000.00	12500.00
82-07-002	Carney and Dog Act 301	R. Lee	Closed	63.00	75-149.00
82-07-003	Georgie Going Anywhere 302	R. Lee	Closed	95.00	125-256.
82-07-004	Fireman Watering House 303	R. Lee	Closed	99.00	99-180.00
82-07-005	Quincy Lying Down 304	R. Lee	Closed	80.00	92-210.00
82-07-006	Denny Eating Ice Cream 305	R. Lee	Closed	39.00	50-170.00
82-07-007	Denny Holding Gift Box 306	R. Lee	Closed	39.00	50-170.00
82-07-008	Denny Juggling Ball 307	R. Lee	Closed	39.00	50-170.00
82-07-009	Buster in Barrel 308	R. Lee	Closed	85.00	90-120.00
82-07-010	Sammy Riding Elephant 309	R. Lee	Closed	90.00	102-250.
82-07-011	Benny Pulling Car 310	R. Lee	Closed	190.00	235-360.
82-07-012	Dr. Painless and Patient 311	R. Lee	Closed	195.00	240-385.
82-07-013	Too Loose-L'Artiste 312	R. Lee	Closed	150.00	180-290.
82-07-014	Slim Charging Bull 313	R. Lee	Closed	195.00	265-410.
82-07-015	Norman Painting Dumbo 314	R. Lee	Closed	126.00	150-210.
82-07-016	Barnum Feeding Bacon 315	R. Lee	Closed	120.00	160-270.
82-07-017	Kukla and Friend 316	R. Lee	Closed	100.00	140-210.
82-07-018	Marion With Marrionette 317	R. Lee	Closed	105.00	135-225.
82-07-019	Two Man Valentinos 318	R. Lee	Closed	45.00	60-130.00
82-07-020	Three Man Valentinos 319	R. Lee	Closed	55.00	70-120.00
82-07-021	Captain Cranberry 320	R. Lee	Closed	115.00	145-180.
82-07-022	Charlie in the Rain 321	R. Lee	Closed	80.00	90-160.00
82-07-023	Hobo Joe on Cycle 322	R. Lee	Closed	125.00	170-280.
82-07-024	Tou Tou 323	R. Lee	Closed	70.00	90-190.00
82-07-025	Toy Soldier 324	R. Lee	Closed	95.00	140-270.
82-07-026	Herbie Dancing 325	R. Lee	Closed	26.00	40-110.00
82-07-027	Herbie Hands Outstretched 326	R. Lee	Closed	26.00	40-110.00
82-07-028	Herbie Balancing Hat 327	R. Lee	Closed	26.00	40-110.00
82-07-029	Herbie Lying Down 328	R. Lee	Closed	26.00	40-110.00
82-07-030	Herbie Legs in Air 329	R. Lee	Closed	26.00	40-110.00
82-07-031	Herbie Touching Ground 330	R. Lee	Closed	26.00	40-110.00
82-07-032	Clarence - The Lawyer 331	R. Lee	Closed	100.00	140-230.
82-07-033	Pinball Pal 332	R. Lee	Closed	150.00	195-287.
82-07-034	Clancy, the Cop and Dog 333	R. Lee	Closed	115.00	140-250.
82-07-035	Burrito Bandito 334	R. Lee	Closed	150.00	190-260.
82-07-036	Ali on His Magic Carpet 335	R. Lee	Closed	105.00	150-210.
82-07-037	Chico Playing Guitar 336	R. Lee	Closed	70.00	95-180.00
82-07-038	Murphy On Unicycle 337	R. Lee	Closed	115.00	160-288.
82-07-039	Robin Resting 338	R. Lee	Closed	110.00	125-210.
82-07-040	Nappy Snoozing 346	R. Lee	Closed	110.00	125-210.
82-07-041	Laurel & Hardy 700	R. Lee	Closed	225.00	290-500.
82-07-042	Charlie Chaplain 701	R. Lee	Closed	230.00	285-650.
82-07-044	Self Portrait 702	R. Lee	Closed	355.00	550-816.
82-07-045	Captain Mis-Adventure 703	R. Lee	Closed	250.00	300-550.
82-07-046	Steppin' Out 704	R. Lee	Closed	325.00	390-700.
82-07-047	Limousine Service 705	R. Lee	Closed	330.00	375-750.
82-07-048	Pig Brick Layer 800	R. Lee	Closed	23.00	35-92.00
82-07-049	Rabbit With Egg 801	R. Lee	Closed	23.00	35-92.00
82-07-050	Smokey, the Bear 802	R. Lee	Closed	23.00	35-92.00
82-07-051	Fish With Shoe 803	R. Lee	Closed	23.00	35-92.00
82-07-052	Seal Blowing His Horns 804	R. Lee	Closed	23.00	35-92.00
82-07-053	Dog Playing Guitar 805	R. Lee	Closed	23.00	35-92.00
82-07-054	Fox In An Airplane 806	R. Lee	Closed	23.00	35-92.00
82-07-055	Beaver Playing Accordian 807	R. Lee	Closed	23.00	35-92.00
82-07-056	Rooster With Barbell 808	R. Lee	Closed	23.00	35-92.00
82-07-057	Parrot Rollerskating 809	R. Lee	Closed	23.00	35-92.00
82-07-058	Walrus With Umbrella 810	R. Lee	Closed	23.00	35-92.00
82-07-059	Turtle With Gun 811	R. Lee	Closed	57.00	75-150.00
82-07-060	Reindeer 812	R. Lee	Closed	57.00	75-150.00
82-07-061	Ostrich 813	R. Lee	Closed	57.00	75-150.00
82-07-062	Tiger 814	R. Lee	Closed	57.00	75-150.00
82-07-063	Rooster 815	R. Lee	Closed	57.00	75-150.00
82-07-064	Giraffe 816	R. Lee	Closed	57.00	75-150.00
82-07-065	Lion 817	R. Lee	Closed	57.00	75-150.00
82-07-066	Camel 818	R. Lee	Closed	57.00	75-150.00
82-07-067	Horse 819	R. Lee	Closed	57.00	75-150.00
Ron Lee's World of Clowns		**The Original Ron Lee Collection-1983**			
83-08-001	Clyde Juggling 339	R. Lee	Closed	39.00	100-115.
83-08-002	Clyde Upside Down 340	R. Lee	Closed	39.00	105-115.
83-08-003	Little Horse - Head Up 341	R. Lee	Closed	29.00	72.00
83-08-004	Little Horse - Head Down 342	R. Lee	Closed	29.00	72.00
83-08-005	Rufus and His Refuse 343	R. Lee	Closed	65.00	160.00
83-08-006	Hobi in His Hammock 344	R. Lee	Closed	85.00	175-250.
83-08-007	Flipper Diving 345	R. Lee	Closed	115.00	200-350.
83-08-008	Ride 'em Roni 347	R. Lee	Closed	125.00	200-375.
83-08-009	Little Saturday Night 348	R. Lee	Closed	53.00	140-160.
83-08-010	Tottie Scottie 349	R. Lee	Closed	39.00	75-115.00
83-08-011	Teeter Tottie Scottie 350	R. Lee	Closed	55.00	105-165.
83-08-012	Casey Cruising 351	R. Lee	Closed	57.00	95-170.00
83-08-013	Tatters and Balloons 352	R. Lee	Closed	65.00	125-200.
83-08-014	Bumbles Selling Balloons 353	R. Lee	Closed	80.00	170-240.
83-08-015	Cecil and Sausage 354	R. Lee	Closed	90.00	200-270.
83-08-016	On The Road Again 355	R. Lee	Closed	220.00	300-650.
83-08-017	Engineer Billie 356	R. Lee	Closed	190.00	275-550.
83-08-018	My Daughter Deborah 357	R. Lee	Closed	63.00	125-185.
83-08-019	Beethoven's Fourth Paws 358	R. Lee	Closed	59.00	110-165.
83-08-020	Say It With Flowers 359	R. Lee	Closed	35.00	95-110.00
83-08-021	I Love You From My Heart 360	R. Lee	Closed	35.00	95-105.00
83-08-022	Chef's Cuisine 361	R. Lee	Closed	57.00	100-170.
83-08-023	Singin' In The Rain 362	R. Lee	Closed	105.00	225-300.
83-08-024	Buster and His Balloons 363	R. Lee	Closed	47.00	90-125.00
83-08-025	Up, Up and Away 364	R. Lee	Closed	50.00	100-150.
83-08-026	Lou Proposing 365	R. Lee	Closed	57.00	120-170.
83-08-027	Knickers Balancing Feather 366	R. Lee	Closed	47.00	120-135.
83-08-028	Daring Dudley 367	R. Lee	Closed	65.00	100-200.
83-08-029	Wilt the Stilt 368	R. Lee	Closed	49.00	100-155.
83-08-030	Coco and His Compact 369	R. Lee	Closed	55.00	145-175.
83-08-031	Josephine 370	R. Lee	Closed	55.00	145-175.
83-08-032	The Jogger 372	R. Lee	Closed	75.00	120-220.
83-08-033	Door to Door Dabney 373	R. Lee	Closed	100.00	200-285.
83-08-034	Riches to Rags 374	R. Lee	Closed	55.00	200-265.
83-08-035	Captain Freddy 375	R. Lee	Closed	85.00	200-425.
83-08-036	Gilbert Tee'd Off 376	R. Lee	Closed	60.00	100-200.
83-08-037	Cotton Candy 377	R. Lee	Closed	150.00	200-400.

Company Number	Name	Series Artist	Edition Limit	Issue Price	Quote
83-08-038	Matinee Jitters 378	R. Lee	Closed	175.00	200-450.
83-08-039	The Last Scoop 379	R. Lee	Closed	175.00	300-475.
83-08-040	Cimba the Elephant 706	R. Lee	Closed	225.00	300-550.
83-08-041	The Bandwagon 707	R. Lee	Closed	900.00	1500-2700.
83-08-042	Catch the Brass Ring 708	R. Lee	Closed	510.00	900-1350.
83-08-043	The Last Scoop 900	R. Lee	Closed	325.00	300-725.
83-08-044	Matinee Jitters 901	R. Lee	Closed	325.00	350-500.
83-08-045	No Camping or Fishing 902	R. Lee	Closed	325.00	350-600.
83-08-046	Black Carousel Horse 1001	R. Lee	Closed	450.00	450-600.
83-08-047	Chestnut Carousel Horse 1002	R. Lee	Closed	450.00	700-1100.
83-08-048	White Carousel Horse 1003	R. Lee	Closed	450.00	700-1100.
83-08-049	Gazebo 1004	R. Lee	Closed	750.00	1300-1750.
Ron Lee's World of Clowns		**The Original Ron Lee Collection-1984**			
84-09-001	No Camping or Fishing 380	R. Lee	Closed	175.00	275-450.
84-09-002	Wheeler Sheila 381	R. Lee	Closed	75.00	175-225.
84-09-003	Mortimer Fishing 382	R. Lee	Closed	N/A	N/A
84-09-004	Give a Dog a Bone 383	R. Lee	Closed	95.00	95-182.00
84-09-005	The Peppermints 384	R. Lee	Closed	150.00	180-250.
84-09-006	T.K. and OH!! 385	R. Lee	Closed	85.00	200-325.
84-09-007	Just For You 386	R. Lee	Closed	110.00	150-250.
84-09-008	Baggy Pants 387	R. Lee	Closed	98.00	250-300.
84-09-009	Look at the Birdy 388	R. Lee	Closed	138.00	200-300.
84-09-010	Bozo's Seal of Approval 389	R. Lee	Closed	138.00	200-350.
84-09-011	A Bozo Lunch 390	R. Lee	Closed	148.00	250-400.
84-09-012	My Fellow Americans 391	R. Lee	Closed	138.00	250-425.
84-09-013	No Loitering 392	R. Lee	Closed	113.00	150-250.
84-09-014	Tisket and Tasket 393	R. Lee	Closed	93.00	150-250.
84-09-015	White Circus Horse 709	R. Lee	Closed	305.00	350-520.
84-09-016	Chestnut Circus Horse 710A	R. Lee	Closed	305.00	350-520.
84-09-017	Black Circus Horse 711A	R. Lee	Closed	305.00	350-520.
84-09-018	Rudy Holding Balloons 713	R. Lee	Closed	230.00	300-550.
84-09-019	Saturday Night 714	R. Lee	Closed	250.00	600-825.
Ron Lee's World of Clowns		**The Original Ron Lee Collection-1985**			
85-10-001	From Riches to Rags 374	R. Lee	Closed	108.00	250.00
85-10-002	Gilbert Tee'd OFF 376	R. Lee	Closed	63.00	55-63.00
85-10-003	'Twas the Night Before 408	R. Lee	Closed	235.00	405.00
85-10-004	The Finishing Touch 409	R. Lee	Closed	178.00	305.00
85-10-005	Bull-Can-Rear-You 422	R. Lee	Closed	120.00	206.00
85-10-006	Giraffe Getting a Bath 428	R. Lee	Closed	160.00	235-450.
85-10-007	Rosebuds 433	R. Lee	Closed	155.00	315.00
85-10-008	Pee Wee With Umbrella 434	R. Lee	Closed	50.00	100.00
85-10-009	Pee Wee With Balloons 435	R. Lee	Closed	50.00	100.00
85-10-010	Catch of the Day 441	R. Lee	Closed	170.00	305.00
85-10-011	Ham Track 451	R. Lee	Closed	240.00	430.00
85-10-012	Get the Picture 456	R. Lee	Closed	70.00	140.00
85-10-013	Dr. Sigmund Fraud 457	R. Lee	Closed	98.00	190.00
85-10-014	Yo Yo Stravinsky-Attoney at Law 458	R. Lee	Closed	98.00	185.00
85-10-015	Dr. Timothy DeCay 459	R. Lee	Closed	98.00	185.00
85-10-016	Duster Buster 461	R. Lee	Closed	43.00	90.00
85-10-017	Hi Ho Blinky 462	R. Lee	Closed	53.00	105.00
85-10-018	One Wheel Winky 464	R. Lee	Closed	43.00	83.00
85-10-019	Cannonball 466	R. Lee	Closed	43.00	83.00
85-10-020	Whiskers Sweeping 744	R. Lee	Closed	240.00	500-800.
85-10-021	Whiskers Hitchhiking 745	R. Lee	Closed	240.00	500-800.
85-10-022	Whiskers Holding Balloons 746	R. Lee	Closed	265.00	500-800.
85-10-023	Whiskers Holding Umbrella 747	R. Lee	Closed	265.00	500-800.
85-10-024	Whiskers Bathing 749	R. Lee	Closed	305.00	500-800.
85-10-025	Whiskers On The Beach 750	R. Lee	Closed	230.00	500-800.
85-10-026	Clowns of the Caribbean PS101	R. Lee	Closed	1250.00	2000-2800.
85-10-027	Fred Figures 903	R. Lee	Closed	175.00	340.00
85-10-028	Policy Paul 904	R. Lee	Closed	175.00	310.00
Ron Lee's World of Clowns		**The Original Ron Lee Collection-1986**			
86-11-001	Wet Paint 436	R. Lee	Closed	80.00	100-200.
86-11-002	Bathing Buddies 450	R. Lee	Closed	145.00	250-375.
86-11-003	Hari and Hare 454	R. Lee	Closed	57.00	85-135.00
86-11-004	Ride 'Em Peanuts 463	R. Lee	Closed	55.00	70-135.00
86-11-005	Captain Cranberry 469	R. Lee	Closed	140.00	175-335.
86-11-006	Getting Even 485	R. Lee	Closed	85.00	125-225.00
86-11-007	Bums Day at the Beach L105	R. Lee	Closed	97.00	N/A
86-11-008	The Last Stop L106	R. Lee	Closed	99.00	N/A
86-11-009	Christmas Morning Magic L107	R. Lee	Closed	99.00	N/A
86-11-010	Most Requested Toy L108	R. Lee	Closed	264.00	N/A
86-11-011	High Above the Big Top L112	R. Lee	Closed	162.00	N/A
86-11-012	Puppy Love's Portrait L113	R. Lee	Closed	168.00	N/A
Ron Lee's World of Clowns		**The Original Ron Lee Collection-1987**			
87-12-001	Heartbroken Harry L101	R. Lee	Closed	63.00	125-225.
87-12-002	Lovable Luke L102	R. Lee	Closed	70.00	70.00
87-12-003	Puppy Love L103	R. Lee	Closed	71.00	71.00
87-12-004	Would You Like To Ride? L104	R. Lee	Closed	246.00	300-475.
87-12-005	Sugarland Express L109	R. Lee	Closed	342.00	400-600.
87-12-006	First & Main L110	R. Lee	Closed	368.00	500-725.
87-12-007	Show of Shows L115	R. Lee	Closed	175.00	N/A
87-12-008	Happines Is L116	R. Lee	Closed	155.00	N/A
Ron Lee's World of Clowns		**The Original Ron Lee Collection-1988**			
88-13-001	New Ron Lee Carousel	R. Lee	Closed	7000.00	9500.00
88-13-002	The Fifth Wheel L117	R. Lee	Closed	250.00	375.00
88-13-003	Bozorina L118	R. Lee	Closed	95.00	N/A
88-13-004	Dinner for Two L119	R. Lee	Closed	140.00	N/A
88-13-005	Anchors-A-Way L120	R. Lee	Closed	195.00	N/A
88-13-006	Pumpkuns Galore L121	R. Lee	Closed	135.00	N/A
88-13-007	Fore! L122	R. Lee	Closed	135.00	N/A
88-13-008	Tunnel of Love L123	R. Lee	Closed	490.00	600-800.
88-13-009	Boulder Bay L124	R. Lee	Closed	700.00	N/A
88-13-010	Cactus Pete L125	R. Lee	Closed	495.00	N/A
88-13-011	Together Again L126	R. Lee	Closed	130.00	N/A
88-13-012	To The Rescue L127	R. Lee	Closed	130.00	160-550.
88-13-013	When You're Hot, You're Hot! L128	R. Lee	Closed	221.00	250-800.
Ron Lee's World of Clowns		**The Original Ron Lee Collection-1989**			
89-14-001	Be It Ever So Humble L111	R. Lee	Closed	900.00	950-1250.
89-14-002	Wishful Thinking L114	R. Lee	Closed	230.00	250-500.
89-14-003	No Fishing L130	R. Lee	Closed	247.00	N/A
89-14-004	Get Well L131	R. Lee	Closed	79.00	N/A
89-14-005	Maestro L132	R. Lee	Closed	173.00	N/A
89-14-006	If I Were A Rich Man L133	R. Lee	Closed	315.00	400-600.
89-14-007	I Pledge Allegiance L134	R. Lee	Closed	131.00	150-250.
89-14-008	In Over My Head L135	R. Lee	Closed	95.00	125-190.
89-14-009	Eye Love You L136	R. Lee	Closed	68.00	N/A
89-14-010	My Heart Beats For You L137	R. Lee	Closed	74.00	N/A

Company Number	Name	Series Artist	Edition Limit	Issue Price	Quote
89-14-011	Just Carried Away L138	R. Lee	Closed	135.00	N/A
89-14-012	O' Solo Mia L139	R. Lee	Closed	85.00	90-150.00
89-14-013	Beauty Is In The Eye Of L140	R. Lee	Closed	190.00	N/A
89-14-014	Tee for Two L141	R. Lee	Closed	125.00	150.00
89-14-015	My Money's OnThe Bull L142	R. Lee	Closed	187.00	N/A
89-14-016	Circus Little L143	R. Lee	Closed	990.00	1250.00
89-14-017	Hughie Mungus L144	R. Lee	Closed	250.00	300-825.
89-14-018	Not A Ghost Of A Chance L145	R. Lee	Closed	195.00	N/A
89-14-019	Sh-h-h-h! L146	R. Lee	Closed	210.00	400-1000.
89-14-020	Today's Catch L147	R. Lee	Closed	230.00	245-325.
89-14-021	Catch A Falling Star L148	R. Lee	Closed	57.00	N/A
89-14-022	Rest Stop L149	R. Lee	Closed	47.00	N/A
89-14-023	Marcelle L150	R. Lee	Closed	47.00	N/A
89-14-024	Butt-R-Fly L151	R. Lee	Closed	47.00	N/A
89-14-025	Stormy Weathers L152	R. Lee	Closed	47.00	N/A
89-14-026	I Just Called! L153	R. Lee	Closed	47.00	N/A
89-14-027	Sunflower L154	R. Lee	Closed	47.00	N/A
89-14-028	Candy Apple L155	R. Lee	Closed	47.00	N/A
89-14-029	Just Go! L156	R. Lee	Closed	47.00	N/A
89-14-030	My Affections L157	R. Lee	Closed	47.00	N/A
89-14-031	Wintertime Pals L158	R. Lee	Closed	90.00	N/A
89-14-032	Merry Xmas L159	R. Lee	Closed	94.00	N/A
89-14-033	Santa's Dilemma L160	R. Lee	Closed	97.00	N/A
89-14-034	My First Tree L161	R. Lee	Closed	92.00	N/A
89-14-035	Happy Chanakah L162	R. Lee	Closed	106.00	N/A
89-14-036	Snowdrifter L163	R. Lee	Closed	230.00	275-450.
89-14-037	If That's Your Drive How's Your Putts L164	R. Lee	Closed	260.00	N/A
89-14-038	The Policeman L165	R. Lee	Closed	68.00	100-200.
89-14-039	The Pharmacist L166	R. Lee	Closed	65.00	N/A
89-14-040	The Salesman L167	R. Lee	Closed	68.00	N/A
89-14-041	The Nurse L168	R. Lee	Closed	65.00	N/A
89-14-042	The Fireman L169	R. Lee	Closed	68.00	150-200.
89-14-043	The Doctor L170	R. Lee	Closed	65.00	150-200.
89-14-044	The Lawyer 171	R. Lee	Closed	68.00	150-200.
89-14-045	The Photographer L172	R. Lee	Closed	68.00	150-200.
89-14-046	The Accountant L173	R. Lee	Closed	68.00	150-200.
89-14-047	The Optometrist L174	R. Lee	Closed	65.00	150-200.
89-14-048	The Dentist L175	R. Lee	Closed	65.00	150-200.
89-14-049	The Plumber L176	R. Lee	Closed	65.00	150-200.
89-14-050	The Real Estate Man L177	R. Lee	Closed	65.00	150-200.
89-14-051	The Chef L178	R. Lee	Closed	65.00	150-200.
89-14-052	The Secretary L179	R. Lee	Closed	65.00	150-200.
89-14-053	The Chiropractor L180	R. Lee	Closed	68.00	150-200.
89-14-054	The Housewife L181	R. Lee	Closed	75.00	150-200.
89-14-055	The Veterinarian L182	R. Lee	Closed	72.00	150-200.
89-14-056	The Beautician L183	R. Lee	Closed	68.00	150-200.
89-14-057	The Mechanic L184	R. Lee	Closed	68.00	150-200.
89-14-058	The Real Estate Lady L185	R. Lee	Closed	70.00	150-200.
89-14-059	The Football Player L186	R. Lee	Closed	65.00	150-200.
89-14-060	The Basketball Player L187	R. Lee	Closed	68.00	150-200.
89-14-061	The Golfer L188	R. Lee	Closed	72.00	150-200.
89-14-062	The Baseball Player L189	R. Lee	Closed	72.00	150-200.
89-14-063	The Tennis Player L190	R. Lee	Closed	72.00	150-200.
89-14-064	The Bowler L191	R. Lee	Closed	68.00	150-200.
89-14-065	The Surfer L192	R. Lee	Closed	72.00	150-200.
89-14-066	The Skier L193	R. Lee	Closed	75.00	150-200.
89-14-067	The Fisherman L194	R. Lee	Closed	72.00	150-200.
89-14-068	I Ain't Got No Money L195	R. Lee	Closed	325.00	N/A
89-14-069	I Should've When I Could've L196	R. Lee	Closed	325.00	N/A
89-14-070	Memories L197	R. Lee	Closed	325.00	N/A
89-14-071	Be Happy L198	R. Lee	Closed	160.00	N/A
89-14-072	Two a.m. Blues L199	R. Lee	Closed	125.00	N/A
89-14-073	Dang It L200	R. Lee	Closed	47.00	N/A
89-14-074	Hot Diggity Dog L201	R. Lee	Closed	47.00	N/A
89-14-075	The Serenade L202	R. Lee	Closed	47.00	N/A
89-14-076	Rain Bugs Me L203	R. Lee	Closed	225.00	N/A
89-14-077	Butterflies Are Free L204	R. Lee	Closed	225.00	N/A
89-14-078	She Loves Me Not L205	R. Lee	Closed	225.00	N/A
89-14-079	Birdbrain L206	R. Lee	Closed	110.00	N/A
89-14-080	Jingles With Umbrella L207	R. Lee	Closed	90.00	N/A
89-14-081	Jingles Holding Balloon L208	R. Lee	Closed	90.00	N/A
89-14-082	Jingles Hitchhiking L209	R. Lee	Closed	90.00	N/A
89-14-083	The Greatest Little Shoe On Earth L210	R. Lee	Closed	165.00	200-300.
89-14-084	Slots Of Luck L211	R. Lee	Closed	90.00	N/A
89-14-085	Craps L212	R. Lee	Closed	530.00	N/A
89-14-086	My Last Chip L213	R. Lee	Closed	550.00	N/A
89-14-087	Over 21 L214	R. Lee	Closed	550.00	N/A
89-14-088	I-D-D-D-Do! L215	R. Lee	Closed	180.00	N/A
89-14-089	You Must Be Kidding L216	R. Lee	Closed	N/A	850.00
89-14-090	Candy Man L217	R. Lee	Closed	350.00	360.00
89-14-091	The New Self Portrait L218	R. Lee	Closed	800.00	950.00
Ron Lee's World of Clowns		**The Original Ron Lee Collection-1990**			
90-15-001	Carousel Horse L219	R. Lee	Closed	150.00	N/A
90-15-002	Carousel Horse L220	R. Lee	Closed	150.00	N/A
90-15-003	Carousel Horse L221	R. Lee	Closed	150.00	N/A
90-15-004	Carousel Horse L222	R. Lee	Closed	150.00	N/A
90-15-005	Flapper Riding Carousel L223	R. Lee	Closed	190.00	N/A
90-15-006	Peaches Riding Carousel L224	R. Lee	Closed	190.00	N/A
90-15-007	Rascal Riding Carousel L225	R. Lee	Closed	190.00	N/A
90-15-008	Jo-Jo Riding Carousel L226	R. Lee	Closed	190.00	N/A
90-15-009	New Pinky Upside Down L227	R. Lee	8,500	42.00	42.00
90-15-010	New Pinky Lying Down L228	R. Lee	8,500	42.00	42.00
90-15-011	New Pinky Standing L229	R. Lee	8,500	42.00	42.00
90-15-012	New Pinky Sitting L230	R. Lee	8,500	42.00	42.00
90-15-013	Me Too!! L231	R. Lee	Closed	70.00	70-80.00
90-15-014	Par Three L232	R. Lee	2,750	144.00	144.00
90-15-015	Heartbroken Hobo L233	R. Lee	Closed	116.00	160.00
90-15-016	Scooter L234	R. Lee	Closed	240.00	275.00
90-15-017	Tandem Mania L235	R. Lee	Closed	360.00	360.00
90-15-018	The Big Wheel L236	R. Lee	Closed	240.00	240.00
90-15-019	Uni-Cycle L237	R. Lee	Closed	240.00	240.00
90-15-020	All Show No Go L238	R. Lee	1,500	285.00	285.00
90-15-021	Skiing My Way L239	R. Lee	2,500	400.00	400.00
90-15-022	My Heart's on for You L240	R. Lee	5,500	55.00	55.00
90-15-023	Swinging on a Star L241	R. Lee	5,500	55.00	55.00
90-15-024	I Love You L242	R. Lee	5,500	55.00	55.00
90-15-025	Stuck on Me L243	R. Lee	5,500	55.00	55.00
90-15-026	Loving You L244	R. Lee	5,500	55.00	55.00
90-15-027	L-O-V-E L245	R. Lee	5,500	55.00	55.00
90-15-028	Heart of My Heart L246	R. Lee	5,500	55.00	55.00
90-15-029	Watch Your Step L247	R. Lee	2,500	78.00	78.00
90-15-030	Fill'er Up L248	R. Lee	Closed	280.00	300.00
90-15-031	Push and Pull L249	R. Lee	Closed	260.00	375.00
90-15-032	Snowdrifter II L250	R. Lee	Closed	340.00	340-350.
90-15-033	Kiss! Kiss! L251	R. Lee	Closed	37.00	37.00
90-15-034	Na! Na! L252	R. Lee	Closed	33.00	33.00
90-15-035	I.Q. Two L253	R. Lee	2,750	33.00	33.00
90-15-036	Your Heaviness L254	R. Lee	2,750	37.00	37.00
90-15-037	Same To "U" L255	R. Lee	2,750	37.00	37.00
90-15-038	Yo Mama L256	R. Lee	2,750	35.00	35.00
90-15-039	Q.T. Pie L257	R. Lee	2,750	37.00	37.00
90-15-040	Squirt L258	R. Lee	2,750	37.00	37.00
90-15-041	Paddle L259	R. Lee	2,750	33.00	33.00
90-15-042	Henry 8-3/4 L260	R. Lee	Closed	37.00	50.00
90-15-043	Pitch L261	R. Lee	2,750	35.00	35.00
90-15-044	Horsin' Around L262	R. Lee	Closed	37.00	37-50.00
Ron Lee's World of Clowns		**The Original Ron Lee Collection-1991**			
91-16-001	The Visit L263	R. Lee	1,750	100.00	100.00
91-16-002	Tender-Lee L264	R. Lee	1,750	96.00	96.00.
91-16-003	Cruising L265	R. Lee	Closed	170.00	170-175.
91-16-004	Business is Business L266	R. Lee	Closed	110.00	110.00
91-16-005	Refugee L267	R. Lee	1,750	88.00	88.00
91-16-006	I'm Singin' In The Rain L268	R. Lee	Closed	135.00	150.00
91-16-007	Anywhere? L269	R. Lee	Closed	125.00	125-145.
91-16-008	Gilbert's Dilemma L270	R. Lee	Closed	90.00	125.00
91-16-009	Marcelle I L271	R. Lee	2,250	50.00	50.00
91-16-010	Marcelle II L272	R. Lee	2,250	50.00	50.00
91-16-011	Marcelle III L273	R. Lee	2,250	50.00	50.00
91-16-012	Marcelle IV L274	R. Lee	2,250	50.00	50.00
91-16-013	Puppy Love Scootin' L275	R. Lee	Closed	73.00	73-80.00
91-16-014	Puppy Love's Free Ride L276	R. Lee	Closed	73.00	73-80.00
91-16-015	Puppy Love's Treat L277	R. Lee	Closed	73.00	73-80.00
91-16-016	Happy Birthday Puppy Love L278	R. Lee	Closed	73.00	73-80.00
91-16-017	Winter L279	R. Lee	1,500	115.00	115-125.
91-16-018	Spring L280	R. Lee	1,500	95.00	95-100.00
91-16-019	Summer L281	R. Lee	1,500	95.00	95-110.00
91-16-020	Fall L282	R. Lee	1,500	120.00	120-125.
91-16-021	Makin Tracks L283	R. Lee	1,500	142.00	142.00
91-16-022	Soap Suds Serenade L284	R. Lee	1,750	85.00	85.00
91-16-023	IRS or Bust L285	R. Lee	1,500	122.00	122.00
91-16-024	Tootie Tuba L286	R. Lee	1,750	42.00	42.00
91-16-025	Truly Trumpet L287	R. Lee	1,750	42.00	42.00
91-16-026	Trusty Trombone L288	R. Lee	1,750	42.00	42.00
91-16-027	Clarence Clarinet L289	R. Lee	1,750	42.00	42.00
91-16-028	Droopy Drummer L290	R. Lee	1,750	42.00	42.00
91-16-029	Harley Horn L291	R. Lee	1,750	42.00	42.00
91-16-030	Banjo Willie L293	R. Lee	1,750	90.00	90.00
91-16-031	TA DA L294	R. Lee	Closed	220.00	220-225.
91-16-032	Trash Can Sam L295	R. Lee	1,750	118.00	118.00
91-16-033	This Won't Hurt L296	R. Lee	1,750	110.00	110.00
91-16-034	Two For Fore L297	R. Lee	1,750	120.00	120.00
91-16-035	Lit'l Snowdrifter L298	R. Lee	1,750	70.00	85-115.00
91-16-036	Hobi Daydreaming L299	R. Lee	1,750	112.00	112.00
91-16-037	Surf's Up L300	R. Lee	1,750	80.00	80.00
91-16-038	Sand Trap L301	R. Lee	1,750	100.00	100.00
91-16-039	Strike!!! L302	R. Lee	1,750	76.00	76.00
91-16-040	Hook, Line and Sinker L303	R. Lee	1,750	100.00	100.00
91-16-041	Geronimo L304	R. Lee	1,750	127.00	127.00
91-16-042	New Harpo L305	R. Lee	1,250	130.00	130.00
91-16-043	New Toy Soldier L306	R. Lee	1,250	115.00	115.00
91-16-044	New Darby with Flower L307	R. Lee	1,250	57.00	57.00
91-16-045	New Darby with Umbrella L308	R. Lee	1,250	57.00	57.00
91-16-046	New Darby with Violin L309	R. Lee	1,250	57.00	57.00
91-16-047	New Darby Tipping Hat L310	R. Lee	1,250	57.00	57.00
91-16-048	Eight Ball-Corner Pocket L311	R. Lee	1,750	224.00	224.00
91-16-049	Our Nation's Pride L312	R. Lee	Closed	150.00	150.00
91-16-050	Give Me Liberty L313	R. Lee	Closed	155.00	155-165.
91-16-051	United We Stand L314	R. Lee	Closed	150.00	150.00
91-16-052	Ain't No Havana L315	R. Lee	500	230.00	230.00
91-16-053	Hot Dawg! L316	R. Lee	500	255.00	255.00
Ron Lee's World of Clowns		**The Original Ron Lee Collection-1992**			
92-17-001	Snowdrifter Blowin' In Wind L317	R. Lee	1,750	77.50	77.50
92-17-002	Snowdrifter's Special Delivery L318	R. Lee	1,750	136.00	136.00
92-17-003	Scrub-A- Dub-Dub L319	R. Lee	Closed	185.00	185.00
92-17-004	Hippolong Cassidy L320	R. Lee	Closed	166.00	166.00
92-17-005	Handy Standy L321	R. Lee	2,500	26.00	27.00
92-17-006	Cyclin' Around L322	R. Lee	2,500	26.00	27.00
92-17-007	Strike Out L323	R. Lee	2,500	26.00	27.00
92-17-008	Shake Jake L324	R. Lee	2,500	26.00	27.00
92-17-009	Howdy L325	R. Lee	2,500	26.00	27.00
92-17-010	Lolly L326	R. Lee	2,500	26.00	27.00
92-17-011	To-Tee L327	R. Lee	2,500	26.00	27.00
92-17-012	Dunkin' L328	R. Lee	2,500	26.00	27.00
92-17-013	Heel's Up L329	R. Lee	2,500	26.00	27.00
92-17-014	Twirp Chirp L330	R. Lee	2,500	26.00	27.00
92-17-015	Stop Cop L331	R. Lee	2,500	26.00	27.00
92-17-016	Dreams L332	R. Lee	2,500	26.00	27.00
92-17-017	Penny Saver L333	R. Lee	2,500	26.00	27.00
92-17-018	My Pal L334	R. Lee	2,500	26.00	27.00
92-17-019	Break Point L335	R. Lee	2,500	26.00	27.00
92-17-020	Clar-A-Bow L336	R. Lee	2,500	26.00	27.00
92-17-021	Myak Kyak L337	R. Lee	2,500	26.00	27.00
92-17-022	Steamer L338	R. Lee	2,500	26.00	27.00
92-17-023	Hi-Five L339	R. Lee	2,500	26.00	27.00
92-17-024	Flyin' High L340	R. Lee	2,500	26.00	27.00
92-17-025	Forget Me Not L341	R. Lee	2,500	26.00	27.00
92-17-026	Beau Regards L342	R. Lee	2,500	26.00	27.00
92-17-027	Shufflin' L343	R. Lee	2,500	26.00	27.00
92-17-028	Go Man Go L344	R. Lee	2,500	26.00	27.00
92-17-029	Ship Ahoy L345	R. Lee	2,500	26.00	27.00
92-17-030	Struttin' L346	R. Lee	2,500	26.00	27.00
92-17-031	Juggles L347	R. Lee	2,500	26.00	27.00
92-17-032	On My Way L348	R. Lee	2,500	26.00	27.00
92-17-033	Little Pard L349	R. Lee	2,500	26.00	27.00
92-17-034	Baloony L350	R. Lee	2,500	26.00	27.00
92-17-035	Wrong Hole Clown L351	R. Lee	1,750	125.00	125.00
92-17-036	Birdy The Hard Way L352	R. Lee	1,750	85.00	85.00
92-17-037	Vincent Van Clown L353	R. Lee	Closed	160.00	160.00
92-17-038	My Portrait L354	R. Lee	Closed	315.00	315.00
92-17-039	Love Ya' Baby L355	R. Lee	1,250	190.00	190.00
92-17-040	Seven's Up L356	R. Lee	1,250	165.00	165.00
92-17-041	Beats Nothin' L357	R. Lee	1,500	145.00	145.00
92-17-042	Fish in Pail L358	R. Lee	1,500	130.00	130.00
92-17-043	Buster Too PC100	R. Lee	1,500	65.00	65.00
92-17-044	Miles PC105	R. Lee	1,500	65.00	65.00

Company / Number	Name	Series / Artist	Edition Limit	Issue Price	Quote
92-17-045	Topper PC110	R. Lee	1,500	65.00	65.00
92-17-046	Webb-ster PC115	R. Lee	1,500	65.00	65.00
92-17-047	Popcorn & Cotton Candy RLC1001	R. Lee	1,750	70.00	70.00
92-17-048	Jo-Jo Juggling RLC1002	R. Lee	1,750	70.00	70.00
92-17-049	Bo-Bo Balancing RLC1003	R. Lee	1,750	75.00	75.00
92-17-050	Gassing Up RLC1004	R. Lee	1,750	70.00	70.00
92-17-051	Big Wheel Kop RLC1005	R. Lee	1,750	65.00	65.00
92-17-052	Brokenhearted Huey RLC1006	R. Lee	1,750	65.00	65.00
92-17-053	Sure-Footed Freddie RLC1007	R. Lee	1,750	80.00	80.00
92-17-054	Cannonball RLC1009	R. Lee	1,750	95.00	95.00
92-17-055	Dudley's Dog Act RLC1010	R. Lee	1,750	75.00	75.00
92-17-056	Walking A Fine Line RMB7000	R. Lee	1,750	65.00	65.00
Ron Lee's World of Clowns		**The Original Ron Lee Collection-1993**			
93-18-001	Tinker And Toy L359	R. Lee	950	95.00	95.00
93-18-002	Dave Bomber L360	R. Lee	950	90.00	90.00
93-18-003	Scrubs L361	R. Lee	950	87.00	87.00
93-18-004	Yo-Yo L362	R. Lee	950	87.00	87.00
93-18-005	Lollipop L363	R. Lee	950	87.00	87.00
93-18-006	Andy Jackson L364	R. Lee	950	87.00	87.00
93-18-007	Bo-Bo L365	R. Lee	950	95.00	95.00
93-18-008	Sailin' L366	R. Lee	950	95.00	95.00
93-18-009	Skittles L367	R. Lee	950	95.00	95.00
93-18-010	Buster L368	R. Lee	950	87.00	87.00
93-18-011	Happy Trails L369	R. Lee	950	90.00	90.00
93-18-012	Honk Honk L370	R. Lee	950	90.00	90.00
93-18-013	Wagone Hes L371	R. Lee	750	210.00	210.00
93-18-014	Pretzels L372	R. Lee	750	195.00	195.00
93-18-015	Sho-Sho L373	R. Lee	750	115.00	115.00
93-18-016	Chattanooga Choo-Choo L374	R. Lee	750	420.00	420.00
93-18-017	Sole-Full L375	R. Lee	750	250.00	250.00
93-18-018	Hot Buns L376	R. Lee	750	175.00	175.00
93-18-019	Britches L377	R. Lee	750	205.00	205.00
93-18-020	Taxi L378	R. Lee	750	470.00	470.00
93-18-021	Piggy Backin' L379	R. Lee	750	205.00	205.00
93-18-022	Moto Kris L380	R. Lee	750	255.00	255.00
93-18-023	Charkles L381	R. Lee	750	220.00	220.00
93-18-024	Blinky Standing L382	R. Lee	1,200	45.00	45.00
93-18-025	Blinky Sitting L383	R. Lee	1,200	45.00	45.00
93-18-026	Blinky Lying Down L384	R. Lee	1,200	45.00	45.00
93-18-027	Blinky Upside Down L385	R. Lee	1,200	45.00	45.00
93-18-028	Bellboy L390	R. Lee	950	80.00	80.00
93-18-029	North Pole L396	R. Lee	950	75.00	75.00
93-18-030	Anywhere Warm L398	R. Lee	950	90.00	90.00
93-18-031	Snoozin' L399	R. Lee	950	90.00	90.00
93-18-032	Soft Shoe L400	R. Lee	750	275.00	275.00
93-18-033	Wanderer L401	R. Lee	750	255.00	255.00
93-18-034	Special Occasion L402	R. Lee	750	280.00	280.00
93-18-035	Bumper Fun L403	R. Lee	750	330.00	330.00
93-18-036	Shriner Cop L404	R. Lee	750	175.00	175.00
93-18-037	Merry Go Clown L405	R. Lee	750	375.00	375.00
Ron Lee's World of Clowns		**The Ron Lee Disney Collection Exclusives**			
90-19-001	The Bandleader MM100	R. Lee	Closed	75.00	75.00
90-19-002	The Sorcerer MM200	R. Lee	Closed	85.00	120.00
90-19-003	Steamboat Willie MM300	R. Lee	2,750	95.00	95.00
90-19-004	Mickey's Christmas MM400	R. Lee	2,750	95.00	95.00
90-19-005	Pinocchio MM500	R. Lee	2,750	85.00	85.00
90-19-006	Dumbo MM600	R. Lee	2,750	110.00	110.00
90-19-007	Uncle Scrooge MM700	R. Lee	2,750	110.00	110.00
90-19-008	Snow White & Grumpy MM800	R. Lee	2,750	140.00	140.00
91-19-009	Goofy MM110	R. Lee	2,750	115.00	115.00
91-19-010	Dopey MM120	R. Lee	2,750	80.00	80.00
91-19-011	The Witch MM130	R. Lee	2,750	115.00	115.00
91-19-012	Two Gun Mickey MM140	R. Lee	2,750	115.00	115.00
91-19-013	Mickey's Adventure MM150	R. Lee	2,750	195.00	195.00
91-19-014	Mt. Mickey MM900	R. Lee	2,750	175.00	175.00
91-19-015	Tugboat Mickey MM160	R. Lee	2,750	180.00	180.00
91-19-016	Minnie Mouse MM170	R. Lee	2,750	80.00	80.00
91-19-017	Mickey & Minnie at the Piano MM180	R. Lee	2,750	195.00	195.00
91-19-018	Decorating Donald MM210	R. Lee	2,750	60.00	60.00
91-19-019	Mickey's Delivery MM220	R. Lee	2,750	70.00	70.00
91-19-020	Goofy's Gift MM230	R. Lee	2,750	70.00	70.00
91-19-021	Pluto's Treat MM240	R. Lee	2,750	60.00	60.00
91-19-022	Jiminy's List MM250	R. Lee	2,750	60.00	60.00
91-19-023	Lady and the Tramp MM280	R. Lee	1,500	295.00	295.00
91-19-024	Lion Around MM270	R. Lee	2,750	140.00	140.00
91-19-025	The Tea Cup Ride (Disneyland Exclusive) MM260	R. Lee	1,250	225.00	225.00
92-19-026	Sorcerer's Apprentice MM290	R. Lee	2,750	125.00	125.00
92-19-027	Little Mermaid MM310	R. Lee	2,750	230.00	230.00
92-19-028	Captain Hook MM320	R. Lee	2,750	175.00	175.00
92-19-029	Bambi MM330	R. Lee	2,750	195.00	195.00
92-19-030	Litt'l Sorcerer MM340	R. Lee	2,750	57.00	57.00
92-19-031	Lumiere & Cogsworth MM350	R. Lee	2,750	145.00	145.00
92-19-032	Mrs. Potts & Chip MM360	R. Lee	2,750	125.00	125.00
92-19-033	The Dinosaurs MM370	R. Lee	2,750	195.00	195.00
92-19-034	Workin' Out MM380	R. Lee	2,750	95.00	95.00
92-19-035	Winnie The Pooh & Tigger MM390	R. Lee	2,750	105.00	105.00
92-19-036	Stocking Stuffer MM410	R. Lee	1,500	63.00	63.00
92-19-037	Christmas '92 MM420	R. Lee	1,500	145.00	145.00
92-19-038	Wish Upon A Star MM430	R. Lee	1,500	80.00	80.00
92-19-039	Finishing Touch MM440	R. Lee	1,500	85.00	85.00
92-19-040	Genie MM450	R. Lee	2,750	110.00	110.00
92-19-041	Big Thunder Mountain MM460	R. Lee	250	1650.00	1650-3000.
93-19-042	Darkwing Duck MM470	R. Lee	1,750	105.00	105.00
93-19-043	Winnie The Pooh MM480	R. Lee	1,750	125.00	125.00
93-19-044	Tinker Bell MM490	R. Lee	1,750	85.00	85.00
93-19-045	Cinderella's Slipper MM510	R. Lee	1,750	115.00	115.00
93-19-046	Mickey's Dream MM520	R. Lee	250	400.00	400.00
93-19-047	Flying With Dumbo MM530	R. Lee	1,000	330.00	330.00
93-19-048	Santa's Workshop MM540	R. Lee	1,500	170.00	170.00
93-19-049	Letters to Santa MM550	R. Lee	1,500	170.00	170.00
93-19-050	Aladdin MM560	R. Lee	500	550.00	550.00
92-19-051	Beauty & The Beast (shadow box) DIS100	R. Lee	500	1650.00	1650.00
93-19-052	Snow White & The Seven Dwarfs (shadow box) DIS200	R. Lee	250	1800.00	1800.00
Ron Lee's World of Clowns		**The Ron Lee Emmett Kelly, Sr. Collection**			
91-20-001	That-A-Way EK201	R. Lee	Closed	125.00	125.00
91-20-002	Help Yourself EK202	R. Lee	Closed	145.00	145.00
91-20-003	Spike's Uninvited Guest EK203	R. Lee	Closed	165.00	165.00
91-20-004	Love at First Sight EK204	R. Lee	Closed	197.00	197.00
91-20-005	Time for a Change EK205	R. Lee	Closed	190.00	400.00

Company / Number	Name	Series / Artist	Edition Limit	Issue Price	Quote
91-20-006	God Bless America EK206	R. Lee	Closed	130.00	130.00
91-20-007	My Protege EK207	R. Lee	Closed	160.00	160.00
91-20-008	Emmett Kelly, Sr. Sign E208	R. Lee	Closed	110.00	110.00
Ron Lee's World of Clowns		**The Ron Lee Warner Bros. Collection**			
91-21-001	The Maltese Falcon WB100	R. Lee	Closed	175.00	175.00
91-21-002	Robin Hood Bugs WB200	R. Lee	1,000	190.00	190.00
92-21-003	Yankee Doodle Bugs WB300	R. Lee	850	195.00	195.00
92-21-004	Dickens' Christmas WB400	R. Lee	850	198.00	198.00
93-21-005	Hare Under Par WB001	R. Lee	1,000	102.00	102.00
93-21-006	Gridiron Glory WB002	R. Lee	1,000	102.00	102.00
93-21-007	Courtly Gent WB003	R. Lee	1,000	102.00	102.00
93-21-008	Home Plate Heroes WB004	R. Lee	1,000	102.00	102.00
93-21-009	Duck Dodgers WB005	R. Lee	1,000	300.00	300.00
93-21-010	Hair-Raising Hare WB006	R. Lee	1,000	300.00	300.00
Ron Lee's World of Clowns		**The Flintstones**			
91-22-001	The Flinstones HB100	R. Lee	2,750	410.00	410.00
91-22-002	Yabba-Dabba-Doo HB110	R. Lee	2,750	230.00	230.00
91-22-003	Saturday Blues HB120	R. Lee	2,750	105.00	105.00
91-22-004	Bedrock Serenade HB130	R. Lee	2,750	250.00	250.00
91-22-005	Joyride-A-Saurus HB140	R. Lee	2,750	107.00	107.00
91-22-006	Bogey Buddies HB150	R. Lee	2,750	143.00	143.00
91-22-007	Vac-A-Saurus HB160	R. Lee	2,750	105.00	110.00
91-22-008	Buffalo Brothers HB170	R. Lee	2,750	134.00	134.00
Ron Lee's World of Clowns		**The Jetsons**			
91-23-001	The Jetsons HB500	R. Lee	2,750	500.00	500.00
91-23-002	The Cosmic Couple HB510	R. Lee	2,750	105.00	105.00
91-23-003	Astro: Cosmic Canine HB520	R. Lee	2,750	275.00	275.00
91-23-004	I Rove Roo HB530	R. Lee	2,750	105.00	105.00
91-23-005	Scare-D-Dog HB540	R. Lee	2,750	160.00	160.00
91-23-006	4 O'Clock Tea HB550	R. Lee	2,750	203.00	203.00
Ron Lee's World of Clowns		**The Classics**			
91-24-001	Yogi Bear & Boo Boo HB800	R. Lee	2,750	95.00	95.00
91-24-002	Quick Draw McGraw HB805	R. Lee	2,750	90.00	90.00
91-24-003	Scooby Doo & Shaggy HB810	R. Lee	2,750	114.00	114.00
91-24-004	Huckleberry Hound HB815	R. Lee	2,750	90.00	90.00
Ron Lee's World of Clowns		**The Ron Lee Collector's Club Gifts**			
87-25-001	Hooping It Up CCG1	R. Lee	Closed	Gift	N/A
88-25-002	Pudge CCG2	R. Lee	Closed	Gift	N/A
89-25-003	Pals CCG3	R. Lee	Closed	Gift	N/A
90-25-004	Potsie CCG4	R. Lee	Closed	Gift	N/A
91-25-005	Hi! Ya! CCG5	R. Lee	Closed	Gift	N/A
92-25-006	Bashful Beau CCG6	R. Lee	Closed	Gift	N/A
93-25-007	Lit'l Mate CCG7	R. Lee	Yr.Iss.	Gift	N/A
Ron Lee's World of Clowns		**The Ron Lee Collector's Club Renewal Sculptures**			
87-26-001	Doggin' Along CC1	R. Lee	Yr.Iss.	75.00	115.00
88-26-002	Midsummer's Dream CC2	R. Lee	Yr.Iss.	97.00	140.00
89-26-003	Peek-A-Boo Charlie CC3	R. Lee	Yr.Iss.	65.00	100.00
90-26-004	Get The Message CC4	R. Lee	Yr.Iss.	65.00	65.00
91-26-005	I'm So Pretty CC5	R. Lee	Yr.Iss.	65.00	65.00
92-26-006	It's For You CC6	R. Lee	Yr.Iss.	65.00	65.00
93-26-007	My Son Keven CC7	R. Lee	Yr.Iss.	70.00	70.00
Ron Lee's World of Clowns		**Rocky & Bullwinkle And Friends Collection**			
92-27-001	Rocky & Bullwinkle RB600	R. Lee	1,750	120.00	120.00
92-27-002	The Swami RB605	R. Lee	1,750	175.00	175.00
92-27-003	Dudley Do-Right RB610	R. Lee	1,750	175.00	175.00
92-27-004	My Hero RB615	R. Lee	1,750	275.00	275.00
92-27-005	KA-BOOM! RB620	R. Lee	1,750	175.00	175.00
Ron Lee's World of Clowns		**The Wizard of Oz Collection**			
92-28-001	Kansas WZ400	R. Lee	750	550.00	550.00
92-28-002	The Munchkins WZ405	R. Lee	750	620.00	620.00
92-28-003	The Ruby Slippers WZ410	R. Lee	750	620.00	620.00
92-28-004	The Scarecrow WZ415	R. Lee	750	510.00	510.00
92-28-005	The Tin Man WZ420	R. Lee	750	530.00	530.00
92-28-006	The Cowardly Lion WZ425	R. Lee	750	620.00	620.00
Ron Lee's World of Clowns		**The Woody Woodpecker And Friends Collection**			
92-29-001	Birdy for Woody WL005	R. Lee	1,750	117.00	117.00
92-29-002	Peck of My Heart WL010	R. Lee	1,750	370.00	370.00
92-29-003	Woody Woodpecker WL015	R. Lee	1,750	73.00	73.00
92-29-004	1940 Woody Woodpecker WL020	R. Lee	1,750	73.00	73.00
92-29-005	Andy and Miranda Panda WL025	R. Lee	1,750	140.00	140.00
92-29-006	Pals WL030	R. Lee	1,750	179.00	179.00
Ron Lee's World of Clowns		**The Popeye Collection**			
92-30-001	Liberty P001	R. Lee	1,750	184.00	184.00
92-30-002	Men!!! P002	R. Lee	1,750	230.00	230.00
92-30-003	Strong to The Finish P003	R. Lee	1,750	95.00	95.00
92-30-004	That's My Boy P004	R. Lee	1,750	145.00	145.00
92-30-005	Oh Popeye P005	R. Lee	1,750	230.00	230.00
92-30-006	Par Excellence P006	R. Lee	1,750	220.00	220.00
Ron Lee's World of Clowns		**The Ron Lee Looney Tunes Collection**			
91-31-001	Western Daffy Duck LT105	R. Lee	Closed	87.00	87-90.00
91-31-002	Michigan J. Frog LT110	R. Lee	Closed	115.00	115.00
91-31-003	Porky Pig LT115	R. Lee	Closed	97.00	97-100.00
91-31-004	Tasmanian Devil LT120	R. Lee	Closed	105.00	105.00
91-31-005	Elmer Fudd LT125	R. Lee	Closed	87.00	87-90.00
91-31-006	Yosemite Sam LT130	R. Lee	Closed	110.00	110.00
91-31-007	Sylvester & Tweety LT135	R. Lee	Closed	110.00	110-115.
91-31-008	Daffy Duck LT140	R. Lee	Closed	80.00	80-85.00
91-31-009	Pepe LePew & Penelope LT145	R. Lee	Closed	115.00	115.00
91-31-010	Bugs Bunny LT150	R. Lee	Closed	123.00	125.00
91-31-011	Tweety LT155	R. Lee	Closed	110.00	110-115.
91-31-012	Foghorn Leghorn & Henry Hawk LT160	R. Lee	Closed	115.00	115.00
91-31-013	1940 Bugs Bunny LT165	R. Lee	Closed	85.00	85.00
91-31-014	Marvin the Martian LT170	R. Lee	Closed	75.00	75.00
91-31-015	Wile E. Coyote & Roadrunner LT175	R. Lee	Closed	165.00	165-175.
91-31-016	Mt. Yosemite LT180	R. Lee	850	160.00	160-300.
Ron Lee's World of Clowns		**The Ron Lee Looney Tunes II Collection**			
92-32-001	Speedy Gonzales LT185	R. Lee	2,750	73.00	73.00
92-32-002	For Better or Worse LT190	R. Lee	1,500	285.00	285.00
92-32-003	What The ...? LT195	R. Lee	1,500	240.00	240.00
92-32-004	Ditty Up LT200	R. Lee	2,750	110.00	110.00
92-32-005	Leopold & Giovanni LT205	R. Lee	1,500	225.00	225.00
92-32-006	No Pain No Gain LT210	R. Lee	950	270.00	270.00

Company Number	Name	Series Artist	Edition Limit	Issue Price	Quote
92-32-007	What's up Doc? LT215	R. Lee	950	950.00	950.00
92-32-008	Beep Beep LT220	R. Lee	1,500	115.00	115.00
92-32-009	Rackin' Frackin' Varmint LT225	R. Lee	950	260.00	260.00
92-32-010	Van Duck LT230	R. Lee	950	335.00	335.00
92-32-011	The Virtuosos LT235	R. Lee	950	350.00	350.00
Ron Lee's World of Clowns		**The Ron Lee Looney Tunes III Collection**			
92-33-001	Bugs Bunny w/ Horse LT245	R. Lee	1,500	105.00	105.00
92-33-002	Sylvester w/ Horse LT250	R. Lee	1,500	105.00	105.00
92-33-003	Tasmanian Devil w/ Horse LT255	R. Lee	1,500	105.00	105.00
92-33-004	Porky Pig w/ Horse LT260	R. Lee	1,500	105.00	105.00
92-33-005	Yosemite Sam w/ Horse LT265	R. Lee	1,500	105.00	105.00
92-33-006	Elmer Fudd w/ Horse LT270	R. Lee	1,500	105.00	105.00
92-33-007	Daffy Duck w/ Horse LT275	R. Lee	1,500	105.00	105.00
92-33-008	Wile E. Coyote w/ Horse LT280	R. Lee	1,500	105.00	105.00
92-33-009	Pepe Le Pew w/ Horse LT285	R. Lee	1,500	105.00	105.00
92-33-010	Cowboy Bugs LT290	R. Lee	1,500	70.00	70.00
Ron Lee's World of Clowns		**The Ron Lee Looney Tunes IV Collection**			
93-34-001	Me Deliver LT295	R. Lee	1,200	110.00	110.00
93-34-002	Yo-Ho-Ho- LT300	R. Lee	1,200	105.00	105.00
93-34-003	Martian's Best Friend LT305	R. Lee	1,200	140.00	140.00
93-34-004	The Essence of Love LT310	R. Lee	1,200	145.00	145.00
93-34-005	The Rookie LT315	R. Lee	1,200	75.00	75.00
93-34-006	A Christmas Carrot LT320	R. Lee	1,200	175.00	175.00
93-34-007	Puttin' on the Glitz LT325	R. Lee	1,200	79.00	79.00
93-34-008	Bugs LT330	R. Lee	1,200	79.00	79.00
Ron Lee's World of Clowns		**The Ron Lee Looney Tunes V Collection**			
94-35-001	Smashing LT335	R. Lee	1,200	80.00	80.00.
94-35-002	Ma Cherie LT340	R. Lee	1,200	185.00	185.00
94-35-003	Guilty LT345	R. Lee	1,200	80.00	80.00
94-35-004	A Carrot a Day LT350	R. Lee	1,200	85.00	85.00
94-35-005	No H20 LT355	R. Lee	1,200	160.00	160.00
94-35-006	Taz On Ice	R. Lee	1,200	115.00	115.00
94-35-007	Puttin' on the Glitz LT325	R. Lee	1,200	79.00	79.00
94-35-008	Bugs LT330	R. Lee	1,200	79.00	79.00
Ron Lee's World of Clowns		**The Betty Boop Collection**			
92-36-001	Harvest Moon BB700	R. Lee	1,500	93.00	93.00
92-36-002	Boop Oop A Doop BB705	R. Lee	1,500	97.00	97.00
92-36-003	Spicy Dish BB710	R. Lee	1,500	215.00	215.00
92-36-004	Bamboo Isle BB715	R. Lee	1,500	240.00	240.00
92-36-005	Max's Cafe BB720	R. Lee	1,500	99.00	99.00
Ron Lee's World of Clowns		**The E.T. Collection**			
92-37-001	E.T. ET100	R. Lee	1,500	94.00	94.00
92-37-002	It's Mee...E.T. ET105	R. Lee	1,500	94.00	94.00
93-37-003	Friends ET110	R. Lee	1,500	125.00	125.00
93-37-004	Flight ET115	R. Lee	1,500	325.00	325.00
Ron Lee's World of Clowns		**Around the World With Hobo Joe**			
94-38-001	Hobo Joe in Italy L406	R. Lee	750	110.00	110.00
94-38-002	Hobo Joe in France L407	R. Lee	750	110.00	110.00
94-38-003	Hobo Joe in Japan L408	R. Lee	750	110.00	110.00
94-38-004	Hobo Joe in the U.S.A L409	R. Lee	750	110.00	110.00
94-38-005	Hobo Joe in Tahiti L410	R. Lee	750	110.00	110.00
94-38-006	Hobo Joe in England L411	R. Lee	750	110.00	110.00
94-38-007	Hobo Joe in Caribbean L412	R. Lee	750	110.00	110.00
94-38-008	Hobo Joe in Norway L413	R. Lee	750	110.00	110.00
94-38-009	Hobo Joe in Spain L414	R. Lee	750	110.00	110.00
94-38-010	Hobo Joe in Egypt L415	R. Lee	750	110.00	110.00
Ron Lee's World of Clowns		**Musical Clowns in Harmony**			
94-39-001	Puddles L-416	R. Lee	750	175.00	175.00
94-39-002	Daisy L-417	R. Lee	750	175.00	175.00
94-39-003	Hot Dog L-418	R. Lee	750	175.00	175.00
94-39-004	Kandy L-419	R. Lee	750	175.00	175.00
94-39-005	Poodles L-420	R. Lee	750	175.00	175.00
94-39-006	Carpet Bagger L-421	R. Lee	750	175.00	175.00
94-39-007	Bubbles L-422	R. Lee	750	175.00	175.00
94-39-008	Barella L-423	R. Lee	750	175.00	175.00
94-39-009	Aristocrat L-424	R. Lee	750	175.00	175.00
94-39-010	Snacks L-425	R. Lee	750	175.00	175.00
Ron Lee's World of Clowns		**Premier Dealer Collection**			
92-40-001	Framed Again PD001	R. Lee	Closed	110.00	110.00
92-40-002	Dream On PD002	R. Lee	Closed	125.00	125.00
92-40-003	Nest to Nothing PD003	R. Lee	Closed	110.00	115.00
92-40-004	Moonlighting PD004	R. Lee	Closed	125.00	125.00
93-40-005	Pockets PD005	R. Lee	500	175.00	175.00
93-40-006	Jake-A-Juggling Cylinder PD006	R. Lee	500	85.00	85.00
93-40-007	Jake-A-Juggling Clubs PD007	R. Lee	500	85.00	85.00
93-35-008	Jake-A-Juggling Balls PD008	R. Lee	500	85.00	85.00
Geo. Zoltan Lefton Company		**Colonial Village**			
86-01-001	Original Set of 6	Lefton	Unkn.	210.00	N/A
86-01-002	Nelson House 05891	Lefton	Closed	35.00	110-130.
86-01-003	McCauley House 05892	Lefton	Closed	35.00	110-130.
86-01-004	Old Stone Church 05825	Lefton	Open	35.00	47.00
86-01-015	Charity Chapel 05895	Lefton	Closed	35.00	85-112.00
86-01-006	King's Cottage 05890	Lefton	Open	35.00	50.00
86-01-007	The Welcome Home 05824	Lefton	Open	35.00	47.00
86-01-008	Original Set of 6	Lefton	Unkn.	210.00	N/A
86-01-009	General Store 05823	Lefton	Closed	35.00	110-130.
86-01-010	Lil Red School House 05821	Lefton	Closed	35.00	110-130.
86-01-011	Penny House 05893	Lefton	Open	35.00	50.00
86-01-012	Church of the Golden Rule 05820	Lefton	Open	35.00	50.00
86-01-013	General Store 05823	Lefton	Closed	35.00	110-130.
86-01-014	Ritter House 05894	Lefton	Closed	35.00	110-130.
88-01-015	Faith Church 06333	Lefton	Closed	40.00	85-120.00
88-01-016	Friendship Chapel 06334	Lefton	Closed	40.00	47.00
88-01-017	Old Time Station 06335	Lefton	Open	40.00	50.00
88-01-018	Trader Tom's Gen'l Store 06336	Lefton	Open	40.00	47.00
88-01-019	House of Blue Gables 06337	Lefton	Open	40.00	47.00
88-01-020	The Stone House 06338	Lefton	Open	40.00	47.00
88-01-021	Greystone House 06339	Lefton	Open	40.00	47.00
88-01-022	City Hall 06340	Lefton	Suspd.	40.00	45.00
88-01-023	The Ritz Hotel 06341	Lefton	Suspd.	40.00	45.00
88-01-024	Engine Co. No. 5 Firehouse 06342	Lefton	Open	40.00	50.00
88-01-025	First Post Office 06343	Lefton	Open	40.00	50.00
88-01-026	Village Police Station 06344	Lefton	Open	40.00	50.00
88-01-027	The State Bank 06345	Lefton	Open	40.00	50.00
88-01-028	Johnson's Antiques 06346	Lefton	Closed	40.00	200.00

Company Number	Name	Series Artist	Edition Limit	Issue Price	Quote
88-01-029	New Hope Church (Musical) 06470	Lefton	Closed	40.00	75-88.00
89-01-030	Gull's Nest Lighthouse 06747	Lefton	Open	40.00	47.00
89-01-031	Maple St. Church 06748	Lefton	Closed	40.00	250.00
89-01-032	Village School 06749	Lefton	Closed	40.00	100.00
89-01-033	Cole's Barn 06750	Lefton	Closed	40.00	47.00
89-01-034	Sweetheart's Bridge 06751	Lefton	Open	40.00	47.00
89-01-035	Village Library 06752	Lefton	Open	40.00	47.00
89-01-036	Bijou Theatre 06897	Lefton	Closed	40.00	125.00
89-01-037	The Village Bakery 06898	Lefton	Open	40.00	47.00
89-01-038	Quincy's Clock Shop 06899	Lefton	Open	40.00	47.00
89-01-039	Victorian Apothecary 06900	Lefton	Closed	40.00	105-130.
89-01-040	Village Barber Shop 06901	Lefton	Open	40.00	47.00
89-01-041	The Major's Manor 06902	Lefton	Open	40.00	47.00
89-01-042	Cobb's Bootery 06903	Lefton	Suspd.	40.00	45.00
89-01-043	Capper's Millinery 06904	Lefton	Suspd.	40.00	45.00
89-01-044	Miller Bros. Silversmiths 06905	Lefton	Suspd.	40.00	45.00
90-01-045	The First Church 07333	Lefton	Open	45.00	47.00
90-01-046	Fellowship Church 07334	Lefton	Open	45.00	47.00
90-01-047	The Victorian House 07335	Lefton	Closed	45.00	250.00
90-01-048	Hampshire House 07336	Lefton	Open	45.00	50.00
90-01-049	The Nob Hill 07337	Lefton	Open	45.00	47.00
90-01-050	The Ardmore House 07338	Lefton	Open	45.00	47.00
90-01-051	Ship's Chandler's Shop 07339	Lefton	Open	45.00	47.00
90-01-052	Village Hardware 07340	Lefton	Open	45.00	50.00
90-01-053	Country Post Office 07341	Lefton	Closed	45.00	47.00
90-01-054	Coffee & Tea Shoppe 07342	Lefton	Open	45.00	47.00
90-01-055	Pierpont-Smithe's Curios 07343	Lefton	Closed	45.00	200.00
90-01-056	Mulberry Station 07344	Lefton	Open	50.00	65.00
90-01-057	Ryman Auditorium-Special Edition 08010	Lefton	Open	50.00	55.00
90-01-058	Hillside Church 11991	Lefton	Closed	60.00	180-230.
91-01-059	Smith's Smithy 07476	Lefton	Closed	45.00	100.00
91-01-060	The Toy Maker's Shop 07477	Lefton	Open	45.00	47.00
91-01-061	Daisy's Flower Shop 07478	Lefton	Open	45.00	47.00
91-01-062	Watt's Candle Shop 07479	Lefton	Closed	45.00	47.00
91-01-063	Wig Shop 07480	Lefton	Suspd.	45.00	45.00
91-01-064	Sweet Shop 07481	Lefton	Open	45.00	47.00
91-01-065	Belle-Union Saloon 07482	Lefton	Closed	45.00	47.00
91-01-066	Victorian Gazebo 07925	Lefton	Open	45.00	45.00
91-01-067	Sanderson's Mill 07927	Lefton	Open	45.00	47.00
92-01-068	Northpoint School 07960	Lefton	Open	45.00	50.00
92-01-069	Brenner's Apothecary 07961	Lefton	Open	45.00	50.00
92-01-070	The Village Inn 07962	Lefton	Open	45.00	50.00
92-01-071	Village Green Gazebo 00227	Lefton	Open	22.00	22.00
92-01-072	Stearn's Stable 00228	Lefton	Open	45.00	50.00
92-01-073	Windmilll 00229	Lefton	Open	45.00	47.00
92-01-074	Main St. Church 00230	Lefton	Open	45.00	50.00
92-01-075	San Sebastian Mission 00231	Lefton	Open	45.00	50.00
92-01-076	Elegant Lady Dress Shop 00232	Lefton	Open	45.00	50.00
92-01-077	County Courthouse 00233	Lefton	Open	45.00	50.00
92-01-078	Lakehurst House 11992	Lefton	Closed	55.00	145-300.
93-01-079	St. Peter's Church w/Speaker 00715	Lefton	Open	60.00	60.00
93-01-080	Kirby House-CVRA Exclusive 00716	Lefton	Open	50.00	50.00
93-01-081	Burnside 00717	Lefton	Open	50.00	50.00
93-01-082	Joseph House 00718	Lefton	Open	50.00	50.00
93-01-083	Mark Hall 00719	Lefton	Open	50.00	50.00
93-01-084	Blacksmith 00720	Lefton	Open	47.00	47.00
93-01-085	Doctor's Office 00721	Lefton	Open	50.00	50.00
93-01-086	Baldwin's Fine Jewelry 00722	Lefton	Open	50.00	50.00
93-01-087	Antiques & Curiosities 00723	Lefton	Open	50.00	50.00
93-01-088	Dentist's Office 00724	Lefton	Open	50.00	50.00
93-01-089	Green's Grocery 00725	Lefton	Open	50.00	50.00
93-01-090	St. James Cathedral 11993	Lefton	Closed	75.00	162-230.
94-01-091	Rosamond 00988	Lefton	Open	50.00	50.00
94-01-092	Springfield 00989	Lefton	Open	50.00	50.00
94-01-093	Brown's Book Shop 01001	Lefton	Open	50.00	50.00
94-01-094	Black Sheep Tavern 01003	Lefton	Open	50.00	50.00
94-01-095	Village Hospital 01004	Lefton	Open	50.00	50.00
94-01-096	White's Butcher Shop 01005	Lefton	Open	50.00	50.00
94-01-097	Drug Store 01007	Lefton	Open	50.00	50.00
94-01-098	Real Estate Office -CVRA Exclusive 01006	Lefton	Open	50.00	50.00
Legends		**The Legendary West Premier Edition**			
88-01-001	Red Cloud's Coup	C. Pardell	S/O	480.00	2700-4500.
89-01-002	Pursued	C. Pardell	S/O	750.00	1995-3300.
89-01-003	Songs of Glory	C. Pardell	S/O	850.00	2600-3895.
90-01-004	Crow Warrior	C. Pardell	S/O	1225.00	1995-3600.
91-01-005	Triumphant	C. Pardell	S/O	1150.00	1395-2000.
92-01-006	The Final Charge	C. Pardell	S/O	1250.00	1250-1500.
Legends		**The Legacies Of The West Premier Edition**			
90-02-001	Mystic Vision	C. Pardell	S/O	990.00	2000-4000.
90-02-002	Victorious	C. Pardell	S/O	1275.00	2195-4000.
91-02-003	Defiant Comanche	C. Pardell	S/O	1300.00	1595-2800.
91-02-004	No More, Forever	C. Pardell	S/O	1500.00	1700-2850.
92-02-005	Esteemed Warrior	C. Pardell	S/O	1750.00	1750-2900.
92-02-006	Rebellious	C. Pardell	950	1500.00	1500-1700.
93-02-007	Eminent Crow	C. Pardell	950	1500.00	1500.00
94-02-008	Enduring	C. Pardell	950	1250.00	1250.00
Legends		**The Legendary West Collection**			
87-03-001	Pony Express (Bronze)	C. Pardell	S/O	320.00	450.00
87-03-002	Pony Express (Pewter)	C. Pardell	S/O	320.00	450.00
89-03-003	White Feather's Vision	C. Pardell	S/O	390.00	550-900.
89-03-004	Johnson's Last Fight	C. Pardell	S/O	590.00	725-1000.
89-03-005	Tables Turned	C. Pardell	2,500	680.00	680.00
89-03-006	Bustin' A Herd Quitter	C. Pardell	2,500	590.00	590.00
89-03-007	Eagle Dancer	C. Pardell	2,500	370.00	370.00
89-03-008	Pony Express (Mixed Media)	C. Pardell	2,500	390.00	390.00
89-03-009	Sacajawea	C. Pardell	2,500	380.00	380.00
90-03-010	Unbridled	C. Pardell	2,500	290.00	290.00
90-03-011	Shhh	C. Pardell	2,500	390.00	390.00
90-03-012	Stand of the Sash Wearer	C. Pardell	2,500	390.00	390.00
90-03-013	Keeper of Eagles	C. Pardell	2,500	370.00	370.00
91-03-014	Warning	C. Pardell	2,500	390.00	390.00
92-03-015	Crazy Horse	C. Pardell	S/O	390.00	495-875.
92-03-016	Beating Bad Odds	C. Pardell	2,500	390.00	390.00
93-03-017	Cliff Hanger	C. Pardell	2,500	990.00	990.00
93-03-018	Hunter's Brothers	C. Pardell	2,500	590.00	590.00
Legends		**American West Premier Edition**			
91-04-001	Unexpected Rescuer	C. Pardell	S/O	990.00	1300-2795.
91-04-002	First Coup	C. Pardell	S/O	1150.00	1150.00
92-04-003	American Horse	C. Pardell	950	1300.00	1300.00
92-04-004	Defending the People	C. Pardell	950	1350.00	1350.00

Company / Number	Name	Series / Artist	Edition Limit	Issue Price	Quote
93-04-005	Four Bears' Challenge	C. Pardell	950	990.00	990.00
Legends		**The Endangered Wildlife Collection**			
90-05-001	Forest Spirit	K. Cantrell	S/O	290.00	600-950.
90-05-002	Savannah Prince	K. Cantrell	950	290.00	290.00
91-05-003	Mountain Majesty	K. Cantrell	950	350.00	350.00
91-05-004	Old Tusker	K. Cantrell	950	390.00	390.00
92-05-005	Plains Monarch	K. Cantrell	950	350.00	350.00
92-05-006	Spirit Song	K. Cantrell	S/O	350.00	400-700.
92-05-007	Unchallenged	K. Cantrell	950	350.00	350.00
92-05-008	Songs of Autumn	K. Cantrell	950	390.00	390.00
93-05-009	Big Pine Survivor	K. Cantrell	950	390.00	390.00
93-05-010	Silvertip	K. Cantrell	950	370.00	370.00
XX-05-011	Prairie Phantom	K. Cantrell	950	N/A	N/A
XX-05-012	Twilight	K. Cantrell	950	N/A	N/A
Legends		**Endangered Wildlife Eagle Series**			
89-06-001	Sentinel	K. Cantrell	S/O	280.00	350-595.
89-06-002	Unbounded	K. Cantrell	2,500	280.00	280.00
89-06-003	Outpost	K. Cantrell	2,500	280.00	280.00
89-06-004	Aquila Libre	K. Cantrell	2,500	280.00	280.00
92-06-005	Food Fight	K. Cantrell	2,500	650.00	650.00
92-06-006	Sunday Brunch	K. Cantrell	2,500	550.00	550.00
93-06-007	Defiance	K. Cantrell	2,500	350.00	350.00
93-06-008	Spiral Flight	K. Cantrell	2,500	290.00	290.00
Legends		**Annual Collectors Edition**			
90-07-001	The Night Before	C. Pardell	S/O	990.00	1200-1500.
91-07-002	Medicine Gift of Manhood	C. Pardell	S/O	990.00	1400-2300.
92-07-003	Spirit of the Wolf	C. Pardell	S/O	950.00	1100-2100.
93-07-004	Tomorrow's Warrior	C. Pardell	S/O	590.00	690-1500.
Legends		**The Great Outdoorsman**			
88-08-001	Both Are Hooked (Bronze)	C. Pardell	Retrd.	320.00	320.00
88-08-002	Both Are Hooked (Pewter)	C. Pardell	Retrd.	320.00	320.00
Legends		**Classic Equestrian Collection**			
88-09-001	Lippizzaner (Bronze)	C. Pardell	Retrd.	200.00	200.00
Legends		**Wild Realm Collection**			
88-10-001	Fly Fisher (Bronze)	C. Pardell	Retrd.	330.00	330.00
88-10-002	Fly Fisher (Pewter)	C. Pardell	Retrd.	330.00	330.00
Legends		**Wild Realm Premier Edition**			
89-11-001	High Spirit	C. Pardell	1,600	870.00	870.00
91-11-002	Speed Incarnate	C. Pardell	Retrd.	790.00	790.00
Legends		**Indian Arts Collection**			
90-12-001	Chief's Blanket	C. Pardell	S/O	350.00	450-690.
90-12-002	Kachina Carver	C. Pardell	S/O	270.00	370-500.
90-12-003	Story Teller	C. Pardell	S/O	290.00	500-795.
90-12-004	Indian Maiden	C. Pardell	1,500	240.00	240.00
90-12-005	Indian Potter	C. Pardell	1,500	260.00	260.00
Legends		**Gallery Editions**			
92-13-001	Resolute	C. Pardell	S/O	7950.00	7950-14500.
93-13-002	Visionary	C. Pardell	350	7500.00	7500.00
93-13-003	Over the Rainbow	K. Cantrell	600	2900.00	1900.00
93-13-004	The Wanderer	K. Cantrell	350	3500.00	3500.00
94-13-005	Center Fire	W. Whitten	350	2500.00	2500.00
Legends		**Oceanic World**			
89-14-001	Freedom's Beauty (Bronze)	D. Medina	Retrd.	330.00	330.00
89-14-002	Freedom's Beauty (Pewter)	D. Medina	Retrd.	130.00	130.00
89-14-003	Together (Bronze)	D. Medina	Retrd.	140.00	140.00
89-14-004	Together (Pewter)	D. Medina	Retrd.	130.00	130.00
Legends		**North American Wildlife**			
88-15-001	Double Trouble (Bronze)	D. Edwards	Retrd.	300.00	300.00
88-15-002	Double Trouble (Pewter)	D. Edwards	Retrd.	320.00	320.00
88-15-003	Grizzly Solitude (Bronze)	D. Edwards	Retrd.	310.00	310.00
88-15-004	Grizzly Solitude (Pewter)	D. Edwards	Retrd.	330.00	330.00
88-15-005	Defenders of Freedom (Bronze)	D. Edwards	Retrd.	340.00	340.00
88-15-006	Defenders of Freedom (Pewter)	D. Edwards	Retrd.	370.00	370.00
88-15-007	The Proud American (Bronze)	D. Edwards	Retrd.	330.00	330.00
88-15-008	The Proud American (Pewter)	D. Edwards	Retrd.	340.00	340.00
88-15-009	Downhill Run (Bronze)	D. Edwards	Retrd.	330.00	330.00
88-15-010	Downhill Run (Pewter)	D. Edwards	Retrd.	340.00	340.00
88-15-011	Sudden Alert (Bronze)	D. Edwards	Retrd.	300.00	300.00
88-15-012	Sudden Alert (Pewter)	D. Edwards	Retrd.	320.00	320.00
88-15-013	Ridge Runners (Bronze)	D. Edwards	Retrd.	300.00	300.00
88-15-014	Ridge Runners (Pewter)	D. Edwards	Retrd.	310.00	310.00
88-15-015	Last Glance (Bronze)	D. Edwards	Retrd.	300.00	300.00
88-15-016	Last Glance (Pewter)	D. Edwards	Retrd.	320.00	320.00
Legends		**American Heritage**			
87-16-001	Grizz Country (Bronze)	D. Edwards	Retrd.	350.00	350.00
87-16-002	Grizz Country (Pewter)	D. Edwards	Retrd.	370.00	370.00
87-16-003	Winter Provisions (Bronze)	D. Edwards	Retrd.	340.00	340.00
87-16-004	Winter Provisions (Pewter)	D. Edwards	Retrd.	370.00	370.00
87-16-005	Wrangler's Dare (Bronze)	D. Edwards	Retrd.	630.00	630.00
87-16-006	Wrangler's Dare (Pewter)	D. Edwards	Retrd.	660.00	660.00
Legends		**Special Commissions**			
87-17-001	Mama's Joy (Bronze)	D. Edwards	Retrd.	200.00	200.00
87-17-002	Mama's Joy (Pewter)	D. Edwards	Retrd.	250.00	250.00
87-17-003	Wild Freedom (Bronze)	D. Edwards	Retrd.	320.00	320.00
87-17-004	Wild Freedom (Pewter)	D. Edwards	Retrd.	330.00	330.00
88-17-005	Alpha Pair (Bronze)	C. Pardell	Retrd.	330.00	330.00
88-17-006	Alpha Pair (Pewter)	C. Pardell	Retrd.	330.00	330.00
88-17-007	Alpha Pair (Mixed Media)	C. Pardell	S/O	390.00	600.00
91-17-008	Symbols of Freedom	K. Cantrell	2,500	490.00	490.00
92-17-009	Yellowstone Bound	K. Cantrell	600	2500.00	2500.00
Legends		**American Indian Dance Premier Edition**			
93-18-001	Drum Song	C. Pardell	750	2800.00	2800.00
94-18-002	Image of the Eagle	C. Pardell	750	1900.00	1900.00
Legends		**Kachina Dancers Collection**			
91-19-001	Angakchina	C. Pardell	2,500	370.00	370.00
91-19-002	Ahote	C. Pardell	2,500	370.00	370.00
91-19-003	Koyemsi	C. Pardell	2,500	370.00	370.00
91-19-004	Hilili	C. Pardell	2,500	390.00	390.00
92-19-005	Tawa	C. Pardell	2,500	390.00	390.00
92-19-006	Kwahu	C. Pardell	2,500	390.00	390.00
93-19-007	Koshari	C. Pardell	2,500	370.00	370.00
93-19-008	Mongwa	C. Pardell	2,500	390.00	390.00
94-19-009	Palhik Mana	C. Pardell	2,500	390.00	390.00
94-19-010	Eototo	C. Pardell	2,500	390.00	390.00
Legends		**Way of the Warrior Collection**			
91-20-001	Rite of Manhood	C. Pardell	1,600	170.00	170.00
91-20-002	Seeker of Visions	C. Pardell	1,600	170.00	170.00
91-20-003	Tribal Defender	C. Pardell	1,600	170.00	170.00
91-20-004	Medicine Dancer	C. Pardell	1,600	170.00	170.00
91-20-005	Clan Leader	C. Pardell	1,600	170.00	170.00
91-20-006	Elder Chief	C. Pardell	1,600	170.00	170.00
Legends		**Way of the Wolf Collection**			
93-21-001	Courtship	K. Cantrell	S/O	590.00	590.00
94-21-002	Renewal	K. Cantrell	500	700.00	700.00
Legends		**Warriors of the Sacred Circle**			
92-22-001	Dog Soldier	K. Cantrell	950	450.00	450.00
92-22-002	Peace Offering	K. Cantrell	950	550.00	550.00
93-22-003	Coup Feather	K. Cantrell	950	450.00	450.00
93-22-004	Yellow Boy	K. Cantrell	950	450.00	450.00
Legends		**Relics of the Americas**			
93-23-001	Dream Medicine	W. Whitten	950	1150.00	1150.00
94-23-002	Flared Glory	W. Whitten	950	N/A	N/A
Legends		**The North & South Collection**			
92-24-001	Victory at Hand	W. Whitten	950	390.00	390.00
93-24-002	The Noble Heart	W. Whitten	950	450.00	450.00
93-24-003	Brother Against Brother	W. Whitten	950	550.00	550.00
94-24-004	Stonewall	W. Whitten	950	450.00	450.00
Legends		**Mystical Quest Collection**			
92-25-001	Vision Quest	D. Medina	950	990.00	990.00
93-25-002	Hunter's Quest	D. Medina	950	990.00	990.00
Legends		**Clear Visions**			
93-26-001	Salmon Falls	W. Whitten	950	950.00	950.00
94-26-002	Saving Their Skins	C. Pardell	950	1590.00	1590.00
Legends		**Collectors Only**			
93-27-001	Give Us Peace	C. Pardell	Retrd.	270.00	270.00
Legends		**Happy Trails Collection**			
94-28-001	Cowboy Soul	W. Whitten	750	450.00	450.00
Legends		**The North American Collection**			
94-29-001	Spirit of the Wolf	K. Cantrell	2,500	150.00	150.00
94-29-002	Eagles Realm	K. Cantrell	2,500	150.00	150.00
94-29-003	Buffalo Spirit	K. Cantrell	2,500	150.00	150.00
94-29-004	Elusive	K. Cantrell	2,500	150.00	150.00
Legends		**Genesis Aquatics**			
94-30-001	Sea Wolves (Killer Whales)	K. Cantrell	950	950.00	950.00
94-30-002	Old Men of the Sea (Sea Otters)	K. Cantrell	950	990.00	990.00
94-30-003	Ancient Mariner (Sea Turtles)	K. Cantrell	950	950.00	950.00
94-30-004	Bringing Up Baby (Humpback Whales)	K. Cantrell	950	950.00	950.00
94-30-005	Splish Splash (Dolphins)	K. Cantrell	950	950.00	950.00
Legends		**Genesis River Dwellers**			
94-31-001	Construction Crew (Beavers)	K. Cantrell	950	990.00	990.00
Legends		**Genesis Ocean Realm**			
94-32-001	Dophins (Dolphins in Lucite)	K. Cantrell	1,250	240.00	240.00
Lenox Collections		**American Fashion**			
83-01-001	Springtime Promenade	Unknown	Open	95.00	95.00
84-01-002	Tea at the Ritz	Unknown	Open	95.00	95.00
84-01-003	First Waltz	Unknown	Open	95.00	95.00
85-01-004	Governor's Garden Party	Unknown	Open	95.00	95.00
86-01-005	Grand Tour	Unknown	Open	95.00	95.00
86-01-006	Belle of the Ball	Unknown	Open	95.00	95.00
87-01-007	Centennial Bride	Unknown	Open	95.00	95.00
87-01-008	Gala at the Whitehouse	Unknown	Open	95.00	95.00
92-01-009	Royal Reception	Unknown	Open	95.00	95.00
Lenox Collections		**Wildlife of the Seven Continents**			
84-02-001	North American Bighorn Sheep	Unknown	Open	120.00	120.00
85-02-002	Australian Koala	Unknown	Open	120.00	120.00
85-02-003	Asian Elephant	Unknown	Open	120.00	120.00
86-02-004	South American Puma	Unknown	Open	120.00	120.00
87-02-005	European Red Deer	Unknown	Open	136.00	136.00
87-02-006	Antarctic Seals	Unknown	Open	136.00	136.00
88-02-007	African Lion	Unknown	Open	136.00	136.00
Lenox Collections		**Legendary Princesses**			
85-03-001	Rapunzel	Unknown	Open	119.00	136.00
86-03-002	Sleeping Beauty	Unknown	Open	119.00	136.00
87-03-003	Snow Queen	Unknown	Open	119.00	136.00
88-03-004	Cinderella	Unknown	Open	136.00	136.00
89-03-005	Swan Princess	Unknown	Open	136.00	136.00
89-03-006	Snow White	Unknown	Open	136.00	136.00
90-03-007	Juliet	Unknown	Open	136.00	136.00
90-03-008	Guinevere	Unknown	Open	136.00	136.00
90-03-009	Cleopatra	Unknown	Open	136.00	136.00
91-03-010	Peacock Maiden	Unknown	Open	136.00	136.00
91-03-011	Pocohontas	Unknown	9,500	136.00	136.00
92-03-012	Firebird	Unknown	Open	156.00	156.00
92-03-013	Sheherezade	Unknown	Open	156.00	156.00
93-03-014	Little Mermaid	Unknown	Open	156.00	156.00
93-03-015	Princess and the Pea	Unknown	Open	156.00	156.00
93-03-016	Princes Beauty	Unknown	Open	156.00	156.00
94-03-017	Maid Marion	Unknown	Open	156.00	156.00
94-03-018	Frog Princess	Unknown	Open	156.00	156.00
Lenox Collections		**Carousel Animals**			
87-04-001	Carousel Horse	Unknown	Open	136.00	152.00
88-04-002	Carousel Unicorn	Unknown	Open	136.00	152.00
89-04-003	Carousel Circus Horse	Unknown	Open	136.00	152.00
89-04-004	Carousel Reindeer	Unknown	Open	136.00	152.00

Company Number	 Name	Series Artist	 Edition Limit	 Issue Price	 Quote
90-04-005	Carousel Elephant	Unknown	Open	136.00	152.00
90-04-006	Carousel Lion	Unknown	Open	136.00	152.00
90-04-007	Carousel Charger	Unknown	Open	136.00	152.00
91-04-008	Carousel Polar Bear	Unknown	Open	152.00	152.00
91-04-009	Pride of America	Unknown	Closed	152.00	152.00
91-04-010	Western Horse	Unknown	Open	152.00	152.00
92-04-011	Camelot Horse	Unknown	Open	152.00	152.00
92-04-012	Statement Piece	Unknown	Open	395.00	395.00
92-04-013	Victorian Romance Horse	Unknown	Open	156.00	156.00
92-04-014	Tropical Horse	Unknown	Open	156.00	156.00
92-04-015	Christmas Horse	Unknown	Open	156.00	156.00
93-04-016	Nautical Horse	Unknown	Open	156.00	156.00
Lenox Collections		**Nativity**			
86-05-001	Holy Family	Unknown	Open	119.00	136.00
87-05-002	Three Kings	Unknown	Open	119.00	152.00
88-05-003	Shepherds	Unknown	Open	119.00	152.00
88-05-004	Animals of the Nativity	Unknown	Open	119.00	152.00
89-05-005	Angels of Adoration	Unknown	Open	136.00	152.00
90-05-006	Children of Bethlehem	Unknown	Open	136.00	152.00
91-05-007	Townspeople of Bethlehem	Unknown	Open	136.00	152.00
91-05-008	Standing Camel & Driver	Unknown	9,500	152.00	152.00
Lenox Collections		**Garden Birds**			
85-06-001	Chickadee	Unknown	Open	39.00	45.00
86-06-002	Blue Jay	Unknown	Open	39.00	45.00
86-06-003	Eastern Bluebird	Unknown	Open	39.00	45.00
86-06-004	Tufted Titmouse	Unknown	Open	39.00	45.00
87-06-005	Red-Breasted Nuthatch	Unknown	Open	39.00	45.00
87-06-006	Cardinal	Unknown	Open	39.00	45.00
87-06-007	Turtle Dove	Unknown	Open	39.00	45.00
87-06-008	American Goldfinch	Unknown	Open	39.00	45.00
88-06-009	Hummingbird	Unknown	Open	39.00	45.00
88-06-010	Cedar Waxwing	Unknown	Open	39.00	45.00
89-06-011	Robin	Unknown	Open	39.00	45.00
89-06-012	Downy Woodpecker	Unknown	Open	39.00	45.00
89-06-013	Saw Whet Owl	Unknown	Open	45.00	45.00
90-06-014	Baltimore Oriole	Unknown	Open	45.00	45.00
90-06-015	Marsh Wren	Unknown	Open	45.00	45.00
90-06-016	Chipping Sparrow	Unknown	Open	45.00	45.00
90-06-017	Wood Duck	Unknown	Open	45.00	45.00
91-06-018	Purple Finch	Unknown	Open	45.00	45.00
91-06-019	Golden Crowned Kinglet	Unknown	Open	45.00	45.00
91-06-020	Dark Eyed Junco	Unknown	Open	45.00	45.00
91-06-021	Broadbilled Hummingbird	Unknown	Open	45.00	45.00
91-06-022	Rose Grosbeak	Unknown	Open	45.00	45.00
92-06-023	Scarlet Tanger	Unknown	Open	45.00	45.00
92-06-024	Magnificent Hummingbird	Unknown	Open	45.00	45.00
92-06-025	Western Meadowlark	Unknown	Open	45.00	45.00
93-06-026	Statement Piece	Unknown	Open	345.00	345.00
93-06-027	Mockingbird	Unknown	Open	45.00	45.00
93-06-028	Barn Swallow	Unknown	Open	45.00	45.00
93-06-029	Indigo Bunting	Unknown	Open	45.00	45.00
93-06-030	Chipping Sparrow	Unknown	Open	45.00	45.00
93-06-031	Red Winged Blackbird	Unknown	Open	45.00	45.00
93-06-032	Female Cardinal	Unknown	Open	45.00	45.00
94-06-033	Christmas Dove	Unknown	Yr.Iss.	45.00	45.00
94-06-034	Vermillion Flycatcher	Unknown	Open	45.00	45.00
Lenox Collections		**Floral Sculptures**			
86-07-001	Rubrum Lily	Unknown	Open	119.00	136.00
87-07-002	Iris	Unknown	Open	119.00	136.00
88-07-003	Magnolia	Unknown	Open	119.00	136.00
88-07-004	Peace Rose	Unknown	Open	119.00	136.00
Lenox Collections		**Garden Flowers**			
88-08-001	Tea Rose	Unknown	Open	39.00	45.00
88-08-002	Cattleya Orchid	Unknown	Open	39.00	45.00
88-08-003	Parrot Tulip	Unknown	Open	39.00	39.00
89-08-004	Iris	Unknown	Open	45.00	45.00
90-08-005	Day Lily	Unknown	Open	45.00	45.00
90-08-006	Carnation	Unknown	Open	45.00	45.00
90-08-007	Daffodil	Unknown	Open	45.00	45.00
91-08-008	Morning Glory	Unknown	Open	45.00	45.00
91-08-009	Magnolia	Unknown	Open	45.00	45.00
91-08-010	Calla Lily	Unknown	Open	45.00	45.00
91-08-011	Camelia	Unknown	Open	45.00	45.00
91-08-012	Poinsettia	Unknown	Open	39.00	39.00
Lenox Collections		**Mother & Child**			
86-09-001	Cherished Moment	Unknown	Open	119.00	119.00
86-09-002	Sunday in the Park	Unknown	Open	119.00	119.00
87-09-003	Storytime	Unknown	Open	119.00	119.00
88-09-004	The Present	Unknown	Open	119.00	119.00
89-09-005	Christening	Unknown	Open	119.00	119.00
90-09-006	Bedtime Prayers	Unknown	Open	119.00	119.00
91-09-007	Afternoon Stroll	Unknown	7,500	136.00	136.00
91-09-008	Evening Lullaby	Unknown	7,500	136.00	136.00
92-09-009	Morning Playtime	Unknown	Open	136.00	136.00
Lenox Collections		**Owls of America**			
88-10-001	Snowy Owl	Unknown	Open	136.00	136.00
89-10-002	Barn Owl	Unknown	Open	136.00	136.00
90-10-003	Screech Owl	Unknown	Open	136.00	136.00
91-10-004	Great Horned Owl	Unknown	9,500	136.00	136.00
Lenox Collections		**International Horse Sculptures**			
88-11-001	Arabian Knight	Unknown	Open	136.00	136.00
89-11-002	Thoroughbred	Unknown	Open	136.00	136.00
90-11-003	Lippizan	Unknown	Open	136.00	136.00
90-11-004	Appaloosa	Unknown	Open	136.00	136.00
Lenox Collections		**Nature's Beautiful Butterflies**			
89-12-001	Blue Temora	Unknown	Open	39.00	45.00
90-12-002	Yellow Swallowtail	Unknown	Open	39.00	45.00
90-12-003	Monarch	Unknown	Open	39.00	45.00
90-12-004	Purple Emperor	Unknown	Open	45.00	45.00
91-12-005	Malachite	Unknown	Open	45.00	45.00
91-12-006	Adonis	Unknown	Open	45.00	45.00
93-12-007	Black Swallowtail	Unknown	Open	45.00	45.00
93-12-008	Great Orange Wingtip	Unknown	Open	45.00	45.00
Lenox Collections		**Kings of the Sky**			
89-13-001	American Bald Eagle	Unknown	Open	195.00	195.00
91-13-002	Golden Eagle	Unknown	Open	234.00	234.00
91-13-003	Defender of Freedom	Unknown	Closed	234.00	234.00
92-13-004	Take Off	Unknown	Open	234.00	234.00
94-13-005	Golden Conquerors	Unknown	Open	295.00	295.00
Lenox Collections		**Endangered Baby Animals**			
90-14-001	Panda	Unknown	Open	39.00	39.00
91-14-002	Elephant	Unknown	Open	57.00	57.00
91-14-003	Baby Florida Panther	Unknown	Open	57.00	57.00
91-14-004	Baby Grey Wolf	Unknown	Open	57.00	57.00
92-14-005	Baby Rhinocerous	Unknown	Open	57.00	57.00
93-14-006	Indian Elephant Calf	Unknown	Open	57.00	57.00
Lenox Collections		**Lenox Baby Book**			
90-15-001	Baby's First Shoes	Unknown	Open	57.00	57.00
91-15-002	Baby's First Steps	Unknown	Open	57.00	57.00
91-15-003	Baby's First Christmas	Unknown	Open	57.00	57.00
92-15-004	Baby's First Portrait	Unknown	Open	57.00	57.00
Lenox Collections		**Lenox Puppy Collection**			
90-16-001	Beagle	Unknown	Open	76.00	76.00
91-16-002	Cocker Spaniel	Unknown	Open	76.00	76.00
92-16-003	Poodle	Unknown	Open	76.00	76.00
94-16-004	German Shepherd	Unknown	Open	75.00	75.00
Lenox Collections		**International Brides**			
90-17-001	Russian Bride	Unknown	Open	136.00	136.00
92-17-002	Japanese Bride, Kiyoshi	Unknown	Open	136.00	136.00
Lenox Collections		**Life of Christ**			
90-18-001	The Children's Blessing	Unknown	Open	95.00	95.00
90-18-002	Madonna And Child	Unknown	Open	95.00	95.00
90-18-003	The Good Shepherd	Unknown	Open	95.00	95.00
91-18-004	The Savior	Unknown	Open	95.00	95.00
91-18-005	Jesus, The Teacher	Unknown	9,500	95.00	95.00
92-18-006	A Child's Prayer	Unknown	Open	95.00	95.00
92-18-007	Childrens's Devotion (Painted)	Unknown	Open	195.00	195.00
92-18-008	Mary & Christ Child (Painted)	Unknown	Open	195.00	195.00
92-18-009	A Child's Comfort	Unknown	Open	95.00	95.00
93-18-010	Jesus, The Carpenter	Unknown	Open	95.00	95.00
Lenox Collections		**North American Bird Pairs**			
90-19-001	Hummingbirds	Unknown	Open	119.00	119.00
91-19-002	Chickadees	Unknown	Open	119.00	119.00
91-19-003	Blue Jay Pairs	Unknown	Open	119.00	119.00
92-19-004	Cardinal	Unknown	Open	119.00	119.00
Lenox Collections		**Santa Claus Collections**			
90-20-001	Father Christmas	Unknown	Open	136.00	136.00
91-20-002	Americana Santa	Unknown	Open	136.00	136.00
91-20-003	Kris Kringle	Unknown	Open	136.00	136.00
92-20-004	Grandfather Frost	Unknown	Open	136.00	136.00
92-20-005	Pere Noel	Unknown	Open	136.00	136.00
93-20-006	St. Nick	Unknown	Open	136.00	136.00
Lenox Collections		**Woodland Animals**			
90-21-001	Red Squirrel	Unknown	Open	39.00	39.00
90-21-002	Raccoon	Unknown	Open	39.00	39.00
91-21-003	Chipmunk	Unknown	Open	39.00	39.00
92-21-004	Rabbit	Unknown	Open	39.00	39.00
93-21-005	Fawn	Unknown	Open	39.00	39.00
93-21-006	Deer	Unknown	Open	45.00	45.00
94-21-007	Mouse	Unknown	Open	45.00	45.00
Lenox Collections		**Gentle Majesty**			
90-22-001	Bear Hug Polar Bear	Unknown	Open	76.00	76.00
90-22-002	Penguins	Unknown	Open	76.00	76.00
91-22-003	Keeping Warm (Foxes)	Unknown	Open	76.00	76.00
Lenox Collections		**Street Crier Collection**			
90-23-001	French Flower Maiden	Unknown	Open	136.00	136.00
91-23-002	Belgian Lace Maker	Unknown	Open	136.00	136.00
Lenox Collections		**Country Kids**			
91-24-001	Goose Girl	Unknown	Open	75.00	75.00
Lenox Collections		**Doves & Roses**			
91-25-001	Love's Promise	Unknown	Open	95.00	95.00
91-25-002	Dove's of Peace	Unknown	Open	95.00	95.00
92-25-003	Dove's of Honor	Unknown	Open	119.00	119.00
Lenox Collections		**Exotic Birds**			
91-26-001	Cockatoo	Unknown	Open	45.00	45.00
93-26-002	Parakeet	Unknown	Open	49.50	49.50
Lenox Collections		**Jessie Willcox Smith**			
91-27-001	Rosebuds	J.W.Smith	Open	60.00	60.00
91-27-002	Feeding Kitty	J.W.Smith	Open	60.00	60.00
Lenox Collections		**Baby Bears**			
91-28-001	Polar Bear	Unknown	Open	45.00	45.00
Lenox Collections		**Baby Bird Pairs**			
91-29-001	Robins	Unknown	Open	64.00	64.00
92-29-002	Orioles	Unknown	Open	64.00	64.00
92-29-003	Chickadee	Unknown	Open	64.00	64.00
Lenox Collections		**Lenox Sea Animals**			
91-30-001	Dance of the Dolphins	Unknown	Open	119.00	119.00
93-30-002	Flight of the Dolphins	Unknown	Open	119.00	119.00
Lenox Collections		**North American Wildlife**			
91-31-001	White Tailed Deer	Unknown	Open	195.00	195.00
Lenox Collections		**Porcelain Duck Collection**			
91-32-001	Wood Duck	Unknown	Open	45.00	45.00
91-32-002	Mallard Duck	Unknown	Open	45.00	45.00
92-32-003	Blue Winged Teal Duck	Unknown	Open	45.00	45.00
93-32-004	Pintail Duck	Unknown	Open	45.00	45.00
Lenox Collections		**Biblical Characters**			
92-33-001	Moses, The Lawgiver	Unknown	Open	95.00	95.00

Company / Number	Name	Series / Artist	Edition Limit	Issue Price	Quote
Lenox Collections		**Parent & Child Bird Pairs**			
92-34-001	Blue Jay Pairs	Unknown	Open	119.00	119.00
Lenox Collections		**Renaissance Nativity**			
91-35-001	Holy Family	Unknown	Open	195.00	195.00
91-35-002	Shepherds of Bethlehem	Unknown	Open	195.00	195.00
91-35-003	Three Kings	Unknown	Open	195.00	195.00
91-35-004	Animals of the Nativity	Unknown	Open	195.00	195.00
91-35-005	Angels	Unknown	Open	195.00	195.00
Lenox Collections		**International Songbirds**			
92-36-001	European Goldfinch	Unknown	Open	152.00	152.00
92-36-002	American Goldfinch	Unknown	Open	152.00	152.00
Lenox Collections		**Challenge of the Eagles**			
93-37-001	Double Eagle	Unknown	Open	275.00	275.00
Lenox Collections		**Classical Goddesses**			
92-38-001	Aphrodite, Painted	Unknown	Open	136.00	136.00
92-38-002	Aphrodite	Unknown	Open	95.00	95.00
Lilliput Lane Ltd.		**Lilliput Lane Cottage Collection-English Cottages**			
82-01-001	Old Mine	D. Tate	Retrd.	15.95	6500.00
82-01-002	Drapers	D. Tate	Retrd.	15.95	3400-4000.
82-01-003	Dale House	D. Tate	Retrd.	25.00	840.00
82-01-004	Sussex Mill	D. Tate	Retrd.	25.00	325-500.
82-01-005	Lakeside House-Mold 1	D. Tate	Retrd.	40.00	1500.00
82-01-006	Lakeside House-Mold 2	D. Tate	Retrd.	40.00	770-940.
82-01-007	Stone Cottage-Mold 1	D. Tate	Retrd.	40.00	1500.00
82-01-008	Stone Cottage-Mold 2	D. Tate	Retrd.	40.00	275.00
82-01-009	Acorn Cottage-Mold 1	D. Tate	Retrd.	30.00	125-400.
83-01-010	Acorn Cottage-Mold 2	D. Tate	Retrd.	30.00	80-125.00
82-01-011	Bridge House	D. Tate	Retrd.	15.95	50-200.00
82-01-012	April Cottage	D. Tate	Retrd.	Unkn.	80-125.00
82-01-013	Honeysuckle	D. Tate	Retrd.	45.00	85-350.00
82-01-014	Oak Lodge	D. Tate	Retrd.	40.00	72-170.00
82-01-015	Dale Farm	D. Tate	Retrd.	30.00	875.00
82-01-016	The Old Post Office	D. Tate	Retrd.	35.00	475-670.
82-01-017	Coach House	D. Tate	Retrd.	100.00	1000-1875.
82-01-018	Castle Street	D. Tate	Retrd.	130.00	245-525.
82-01-019	Holly Cottage	D. Tate	Retrd.	42.50	95-110.00
82-01-020	Burnside	D. Tate	Retrd.	30.00	550.00
83-01-021	Coopers	D. Tate	Retrd.	15.00	440-825.
83-01-022	Millers	D. Tate	Retrd.	15.00	150-275.
83-01-023	Miners	D. Tate	Retrd.	15.00	375-455.
83-01-024	Toll House	D. Tate	Retrd.	15.00	125-200.
83-01-025	Woodcutters	D. Tate	Retrd.	15.00	125.00
83-01-026	Tuck Shop	D. Tate	Retrd.	35.00	550-875.
83-01-027	Warwick Hall-Mold 1	D. Tate	Retrd.	185.00	3000-4000.
83-01-028	Warwick Hall-Mold 2	D. Tate	Retrd.	185.00	1200-1800.
82-01-029	Anne Hathaway's-Mold 1	D. Tate	Retrd.	40.00	1400-2650.
83-01-030	Anne Hathaway's-Mold 2	D. Tate	Retrd.	40.00	400-600.
84-01-031	Anne Hathaway's-Mold 3	D. Tate	Retrd.	40.00	375.00
89-01-032	Anne Hathaway's-Mold 4	D. Tate	Open	130.00	150.00
82-01-033	William Shakespeare-Mold 1	D. Tate	Retrd.	55.00	3000.00
83-01-034	William Shakespeare-Mold 2	D. Tate	Retrd.	55.00	200.00
86-01-035	William Shakespeare-Mold 3	D. Tate	Retrd.	55.00	215.00
89-01-036	William Shakespeare-Mold 4	D. Tate	Retrd.	130.00	150.00
83-01-037	Red Lion	D. Tate	Retrd.	125.00	264-400.
83-01-038	Thatcher's Rest	D. Tate	Retrd.	185.00	225.00
83-01-039	Troutbeck Farm	D. Tate	Retrd.	125.00	210-300.
83-01-040	Dove Cottage-Mold 1	D. Tate	Retrd.	35.00	1800.00
84-01-041	Dove Cottage-Mold 2	D. Tate	Retrd.	35.00	85-200.00
84-01-042	Old School House	D. Tate	Retrd.	Unkn.	1000-1440.
84-01-043	Tintagel	D. Tate	Retrd.	39.50	175-250.
85-01-044	Old Curiosity Shop	D. Tate	Retrd.	62.50	59-125.00
85-01-045	St. Mary's Church	D. Tate	Retrd.	40.00	85-160.00
85-01-046	Clare Cottage	D. Tate	Retrd.	30.00	63.00
85-01-047	Fisherman's Cottage	D. Tate	Retrd.	30.00	70-95.00
85-01-048	Sawrey Gill	D. Tate	Retrd.	30.00	175-200.
85-01-049	Ostlers Keep	D. Tate	Retrd.	55.00	66-100.00
85-01-050	Moreton Manor	D. Tate	Retrd.	55.00	75-150.00
85-01-051	Kentish Oast	D. Tate	Retrd.	55.00	60-125.00
85-01-052	Watermill	D. Tate	Retrd.	40.00	85.00
85-01-053	Bronte Parsonage	D. Tate	Retrd.	72.00	105-190.
85-01-054	Farriers	D. Tate	Retrd.	40.00	75-110.00
86-01-055	Dale Head	D. Tate	Retrd.	75.00	72-150.00
86-01-056	Bay View	D. Tate	Retrd.	39.50	125.00
86-01-057	Cobblers Cottage	D. Hall	Open	42.00	65.00
86-01-058	Three Feathers	D. Tate	Retrd.	115.00	220-250.
86-01-059	Spring Bank	D. Tate	Retrd.	42.00	70.00
86-01-060	Scroll on the Wall	D. Tate	Retrd.	55.00	115-175.
86-01-061	Tudor Court	Lilliput Lane	Retrd.	260.00	345.00
87-01-062	Beacon Heights	Lilliput Lane	Retrd.	125.00	175-235.
87-01-063	Wealden House	D. Tate	Retrd.	125.00	165-600.
87-01-064	The Gables	Lilliput Lane	Retrd.	145.00	175-260.
87-01-065	Secret Garden	M. Adkinson	Open	145.00	220.00
87-01-066	Rydal View	D. Tate	Retrd.	220.00	240-325.
87-01-067	Stoneybeck	D. Tate	Retrd.	45.00	75.00
87-01-068	Riverview	D. Tate	Open	27.50	40.00
87-01-069	Clover Cottage	D. Tate	Open	27.50	40.00
87-01-070	Inglewood	D. Tate	Open	27.50	40.00
87-01-071	Tanners Cottage	D. Tate	Retrd.	27.50	65.00
87-01-072	Holme Dyke	D. Tate	Retrd.	50.00	90-250.
87-01-073	Saddlers Inn	M. Adkinson	Retrd.	50.00	70-165.00
87-01-074	Four Seasons	M. Adkinson	Retrd.	70.00	100-140.
87-01-075	Magpie Cottage	D. Tate	Retrd.	70.00	85-300.
87-01-076	Izaak Waltons Cottage	D. Tate	Retrd.	75.00	80-200.
87-01-077	Keepers Lodge	D. Tate	Retrd.	75.00	105-130.
87-01-078	Summer Haze	D. Tate	Retrd.	90.00	105-130.
87-01-079	Street Scene No. 1	Unknown	Retrd.	40.00	120-240.
87-01-080	Street Scene No. 2	Unknown	Retrd.	45.00	120-240.
87-01-081	Street Scene No. 3	Unknown	Retrd.	45.00	120-240.
87-01-082	Street Scene No. 4	Unknown	Retrd.	45.00	120-240.
87-01-083	Street Scene No. 5	Unknown	Retrd.	40.00	120-240.
87-01-084	Street Scene No. 6	Unknown	Retrd.	40.00	120-240.
87-01-085	Street Scene No. 7	Unknown	Retrd.	40.00	120-240.
87-01-086	Street Scene No. 8	Unknown	Retrd.	40.00	120-240.
87-01-087	Street Scene No. 9	Unknown	Retrd.	45.00	120-240.
87-01-088	Street Scene No. 10	Unknown	Retrd.	45.00	120-240.
88-01-089	Brockbank	D. Tate	Open	58.00	80.00
88-01-090	St. Marks	D. Tate	Retrd.	75.00	125.00
88-01-091	Swift Hollow	D. Tate	Retrd.	75.00	100-300.
88-01-092	Pargetters Retreat	D. Tate	Retrd.	75.00	70-300.
88-01-093	Swan Inn	D. Tate	Retrd.	120.00	170-225.
88-01-094	Ship Inn	Lilliput Lane	Retrd.	210.00	228-325.
88-01-095	Saxon Cottage	D. Tate	Retrd.	245.00	175-400.
88-01-096	Smallest Inn	D. Tate	Retrd.	42.50	65-150.00
88-01-097	Rising Sun	D. Tate	Retrd.	58.00	84-105.00
88-01-098	Crown Inn	D. Tate	Retrd.	120.00	120-215.
88-01-099	Royal Oak	D. Tate	Retrd.	145.00	114-325.
88-01-100	Bredon House	D. Tate	Retrd.	145.00	150-315.
89-01-101	Chine Cot	D. Tate	Open	36.00	50.00
89-01-102	Fiveways	D. Tate	Open	42.50	55.00
89-01-103	Ash Nook	D. Tate	Open	47.50	60.00
89-01-104	The Briary	D. Tate	Open	47.50	60.00
89-01-105	Victoria Cottage	D. Tate	Open	52.50	65.00
89-01-106	Butterwick	D. Tate	Open	52.50	70.00
89-01-107	Greensted Church	D. Tate	Open	72.50	95.00
89-01-108	Beehive Cottage	D. Tate	Open	72.50	95.00
89-01-109	Tanglewood Lodge	D. Tate	Retrd.	97.00	145-185.
89-01-110	St. Peter's Cove	D. Tate	Retrd.	1375.00	1400-3375.
89-01-111	Wight Cottage	D. Tate	Open	52.50	65.00
89-01-112	Helmere	D. Tate	Open	65.00	80.00
89-01-113	Titmouse Cottage	D. Tate	Open	92.50	120.00
89-01-114	St. Lawrence Church	D. Tate	Open	110.00	140.00
89-01-115	Olde York Toll	D. Tate	Retrd.	95.00	95.00
90-01-116	Strawberry Cottage	D. Tate	Open	36.00	45.00
90-01-117	Buttercup Cottage	D. Tate	Retrd.	40.00	46.50
90-01-118	Bramble Cottage	D. Tate	Open	55.00	70.00
90-01-119	Mrs. Pinkerton's Post Office	D. Tate	Open	72.50	85.00
90-01-120	Sulgrave Manor	D. Tate	Retrd.	120.00	140-200.
90-01-121	Periwinkle Cottage	D. Tate	Open	165.00	220.00
90-01-122	Robin's Gate	D. Tate	Open	33.50	45.00
90-01-123	Cherry Cottage	D. Tate	Open	33.50	45.00
90-01-124	Otter Reach	D. Tate	Open	33.50	45.00
90-01-125	Runswick House	D. Tate	Open	62.50	80.00
90-01-126	The King's Arms	D. Tate	Open	450.00	550.00
90-01-127	Convent in The Woods	D. Tate	Open	175.00	220.00
91-01-128	Armada House	D. Tate	Open	175.00	185.00
91-01-129	Moonlight Cove	D. Tate	Open	82.50	85.00
91-01-130	Pear Tree House	D. Tate	Open	82.50	85.00
91-01-131	Lapworth Lock	D. Tate	Open	82.50	85.00
91-01-132	Micklegate Antiques	D. Tate	Open	90.00	95.00
91-01-133	Bridge House 1991	D. Tate	Open	25.00	30.00
91-01-134	Tillers Green	D. Tate	Open	60.00	65.00
91-01-135	Wellington Lodge	D. Tate	Open	55.00	60.00
91-01-136	Primrose Hill	D. Tate	Open	46.50	50.00
91-01-137	Daisy Cottage	D. Tate	Open	37.50	40.00
91-01-138	Farthing Lodge	D. Tate	Open	37.50	40.00
91-01-139	Dovetails	D. Tate	Open	90.00	95.00
91-01-140	Lace Lane	D. Tate	Open	90.00	95.00
91-01-141	The Flower Sellers	D. Tate	Open	110.00	120.00
91-01-142	Witham Delph	D. Tate	Open	110.00	120.00
91-01-143	Village School	D. Tate	Open	120.00	130.00
91-01-144	Hopcroft Cottage	D. Tate	Open	120.00	130.00
91-01-145	John Barleycorn Cottage	D. Tate	Open	130.00	140.00
91-01-146	Paradise Lodge	D. Tate	Open	130.00	140.00
91-01-147	The Priest's House	D. Tate	Open	180.00	195.00
91-01-148	Old Shop at Bignor	D. Tate	Open	215.00	220.00
91-01-149	Chatsworth View	D. Tate	Open	250.00	275.00
91-01-150	Anne of Cleves	D. Tate	Open	360.00	395.00
91-01-151	Saxham St. Edmunds	D. Tate	4,500	1550.00	1650.00
92-01-152	Bow Cottage	D. Tate	Open	127.50	135.00
92-01-153	Granny Smiths	D. Tate	Open	60.00	65.00
92-01-154	Oakwood Smithy	D. Tate	Open	450.00	475.00
92-01-155	Pixie House	D. Tate	Open	55.00	60.00
92-01-156	Puffin Row	D. Tate	Open	127.50	135.00
92-01-157	Rustic Root House	D. Tate	Open	110.00	120.00
92-01-158	Wheyside Cottage	Lilliput Lane	Open	46.50	50.00
92-01-159	Wedding Bells	Lilliput Lane	Open	75.00	80.00
92-01-160	Derwent-le-Dale	Lilliput Lane	Open	75.00	80.00
92-01-161	The Nutshell	Lilliput Lane	Open	75.00	80.00
92-01-162	Finchingfields	Lilliput Lane	Open	82.50	95.00
92-01-163	The Chocolate House	Lilliput Lane	Open	130.00	140.00
92-01-164	Grantchester Meadows	Lilliput Lane	Open	275.00	275.00
92-01-165	High Ghyll Farm	Lilliput Lane	Open	360.00	395.00
93-01-166	Cat's Coombe Cottage	Lilliput Lane	Open	95.00	95.00
93-01-167	Cley-next-the-sea	Lilliput Lane	2,500	725.00	725.00
93-01-168	Foxglove Fields	Lilliput Lane	Open	130.00	130.00
93-01-169	Junk and Disorderly	Lilliput Lane	Open	150.00	150.00
93-01-170	Purbeck Stores	Lilliput Lane	Open	55.00	55.00
93-01-171	Stocklebeck Mill	Lilliput Lane	Open	325.00	325.00
93-01-172	Stradling Priory	Lilliput Lane	Open	130.00	130.00
93-01-173	Birdlip Bottom	Lilliput Lane	Open	80.00	80.00
93-01-174	Marigold Meadow	Lilliput Lane	Open	120.00	120.00
93-01-175	Old Mother Hubbard's	Lilliput Lane	Open	185.00	185.00
93-01-176	Titwillow Cottage	Lilliput Lane	Open	70.00	70.00
94-01-177	Applejack Cottage	Lilliput Lane	Open	45.00	45.00
94-01-178	Camomile Lawn	Lilliput Lane	Open	125.00	125.00
94-01-179	Gulliver's Gate	Lilliput Lane	Open	45.00	45.00
94-01-180	Orchard Farm Cottage	Lilliput Lane	Open	145.00	145.00
94-01-181	Saffron House	Lilliput Lane	Open	220.00	220.00
94-01-182	Teacaddy Cottage	Lilliput Lane	Open	79.00	79.00
94-01-183	Waterside Mill	Lilliput Lane	Open	65.00	65.00
Lilliput Lane Ltd.		**Collectors Club Specials**			
86-02-001	Packhorse Bridge	D. Tate	Retrd.	Gift	600-950.
86-02-002	Crendon Manor	D. Tate	Retrd.	285.00	800-1000.
86-02-003	Gulliver	Unknown	Retrd.	65.00	95-228.00
87-02-004	Little Lost Dog	D. Tate	Retrd.	Gift	220-290.
87-02-005	Yew Tree Farm	D. Tate	Retrd.	160.00	225.00
88-02-006	Wishing Well	D. Tate	Retrd.	Gift	100.00
89-02-007	Dovecot	D. Tate	Retrd.	Gift	100-160.
89-02-008	Wenlock Rise	D. Tate	Retrd.	175.00	190-400.
90-02-009	Cosy Corner	D. Tate	Retrd.	Gift	75-125.00
90-02-010	Lavender Cottage	D. Tate	Retrd.	50.00	95-190.00
90-02-011	Bridle Way	D. Tate	Retrd.	100.00	195-250.
91-02-012	Puddlebrook	D. Tate	Retrd.	Gift	59-100.00
91-02-013	Gardeners Cottage	D. Tate	Retrd.	120.00	118-250.
91-02-014	Wren Cottage	D. Tate	Retrd.	13.95	125-200.
92-02-015	Pussy Willow	D. Tate	Retrd.	Gift	60-200.00
92-02-016	Forget-Me-Not	D. Tate	Retrd.	130.00	83-225.00
93-02-017	The Spinney	Lilliput Lane	Retrd.	Gift	N/A
93-02-018	Heaven Lea Cottage	Lilliput Lane	Retrd.	150.00	150.00
93-02-019	Curlew Cottage	Lilliput Lane	Retrd.	18.95	18.95
94-02-020	Petticoat Cottage	Lilliput Lane	4/95	Gift	N/A
94-02-021	Woodman's Retreat	Lilliput Lane	4/95	135.00	135.00

Company / Number	Name	Series / Artist	Edition Limit	Issue Price	Quote
Lilliput Lane Ltd.		**German Collection**			
87-03-001	Meersburger Weinstube	D. Tate	Open	82.50	95.00
87-03-002	Jaghutte	D. Tate	Open	82.50	95.00
87-03-003	Das Gebirgskirchlein	D. Tate	Open	120.00	140.00
87-03-004	Nurnberger Burgerhaus	D. Tate	Open	140.00	160.00
87-03-005	Schwarzwaldhaus	D. Tate	Open	140.00	160.00
87-03-006	Moselhaus	D. Tate	Open	140.00	160.00
87-03-007	Haus Im Rheinland	D. Tate	Open	220.00	250.00
88-03-008	Der Familienschrein	D. Tate	Retrd.	52.50	100.00
88-03-009	Das Rathaus	D. Tate	Open	140.00	160.00
88-03-010	Die Kleine Backerei	D. Tate	Open	68.00	80.00
92-03-011	Alte Schmiede	D. Tate	Open	175.00	185.00
92-03-012	Der Bücherwurm	D. Tate	Open	140.00	160.00
92-03-013	Rosengartenhaus	D. Tate	Open	120.00	130.00
92-03-014	Strandvogthaus	D. Tate	Open	120.00	130.00
Lilliput Lane Ltd.		**Christmas Collection**			
88-04-001	Deer Park Hall	D. Tate	Retrd.	120.00	176-500.
89-04-002	St. Nicholas Church	D. Tate	Retrd.	130.00	165-225.
90-04-003	Yuletide Inn	D. Tate	Retrd.	145.00	175-285.
91-04-004	The Old Vicarage at Christmas	D. Tate	Retrd.	180.00	170-400.
92-04-005	Chestnut Cottage	Lilliput Lane	Open	46.50	50.00
92-04-006	Cranberry Cottage	Lilliput Lane	Open	46.50	50.00
92-04-007	Hollytree House	Lilliput Lane	Open	46.50	50.00
93-04-008	The Gingerbread Shop	Lilliput Lane	Open	50.00	50.00
93-04-009	Partridge Cottage	Lilliput Lane	Open	50.00	50.00
93-04-010	St. Joseph's Church	Lilliput Lane	Open	70.00	70.00
94-04-011	Ring O' Bells	Lilliput Lane	Open	50.00	50.00
94-04-012	St. Joseph's School	Lilliput Lane	Open	50.00	50.00
94-04-013	The Vicarage	Lilliput Lane	Open	50.00	50.00
Lilliput Lane Ltd.		**Christmas Lodge Collection**			
92-05-001	Highland Lodge	Lilliput Lane	Retrd.	180.00	119-500.
93-05-002	Eamont Lodge	Lilliput Lane	Retrd.	185.00	250.00
94-05-003	Snowdon Lodge	Lilliput Lane	Yr.Iss.	175.00	175.00
Lilliput Lane Ltd.		**Blaise Hamlet Collection**			
89-06-001	Diamond Cottage	D. Tate	Open	110.00	135.00
89-06-002	Oak Cottage	D. Tate	Open	110.00	135.00
89-06-003	Circular Cottage	D. Tate	Open	110.00	135.00
90-06-004	Dial Cottage	D. Tate	Open	110.00	135.00
90-06-005	Vine Cottage	D. Tate	Open	110.00	135.00
90-06-006	Sweetbriar Cottage	D. Tate	Open	110.00	135.00
91-06-007	Double Cottage	D. Tate	Open	200.00	220.00
91-06-008	Jasmine Cottage	D. Tate	Open	140.00	150.00
91-06-009	Rose Cottage	D. Tate	Open	140.00	150.00
Lilliput Lane Ltd.		**Irish Cottages**			
87-07-001	Donegal Cottage	D. Tate	Retrd.	29.00	80.00
89-07-002	Kennedy Homestead	D. Tate	Open	33.50	45.00
89-07-003	Magilligans	D. Tate	Open	33.50	45.00
89-07-004	St. Columba's School	D. Tate	Open	47.50	60.00
89-07-005	St. Kevin's Church	D. Tate	Open	55.00	70.00
89-07-006	O'Lacey's Store	D. Tate	Open	68.00	85.00
89-07-007	Hegarty's Home	D. Tate	Retrd.	68.00	110.00
89-07-008	Kilmore Quay	D. Tate	Retrd.	68.00	200.00
89-07-009	Quiet Cottage	D. Tate	Retrd.	72.50	220.00
89-07-010	Thoor Ballylee	D. Tate	Retrd.	105.00	170.00
89-07-011	Pat Cohan's Bar	D. Tate	Open	110.00	140.00
89-07-012	Limerick House	D. Tate	Retrd.	110.00	160-170.
89-07-013	St. Patrick's Church	D. Tate	Open	185.00	220.00
89-07-014	Ballykerne Croft	D. Tate	Open	75.00	95.00
Lilliput Lane Ltd.		**Scottish Collection**			
82-08-001	The Croft (without sheep)	D. Tate	Retrd.	29.00	800-1250.
84-08-002	The Croft (renovated)	D. Tate	Retrd.	36.00	75-200.00
85-08-003	Preston Mill	D. Tate	Retrd.	45.00	175-200.
85-08-004	Burns Cottage	D. Tate	Retrd.	35.00	98-125.00
85-08-005	7 St. Andrews Square	A. Yarrington	Retrd.	15.95	125.00
87-08-006	East Neuk	D. Tate	Retrd.	29.00	60-75.00
87-08-007	Preston Mill (renovated)	D. Tate	Retrd.	62.50	78.00
89-08-008	Culloden Cottage	D. Tate	Open	36.00	45.00
89-08-009	Inverlochie Hame	D. Tate	Open	47.50	60.00
89-08-010	Carrick House	D. Tate	Open	47.50	60.00
89-08-011	Stockwell Tenement	D. Tate	Open	62.50	80.00
89-08-012	John Knox House	D. Tate	Retrd.	68.00	79-250.00
89-08-013	Claypotts Castle	D. Tate	Open	72.50	95.00
89-08-014	Kenmore Cottage	D. Tate	Retrd.	87.00	110.00
89-08-015	Craigievar Castle	D. Tate	Retrd.	185.00	265-300.
89-08-016	Blair Atholl	D. Tate	Retrd.	275.00	400-700.
90-08-017	Fishermans Bothy	D. Tate	Open	36.00	45.00
90-08-018	Hebridean Hame	D. Tate	Retrd.	55.00	65-120.00
90-08-019	Kirkbrae Cottage	D. Tate	Retrd.	55.00	70-95.00
90-08-020	Kinlochness	D. Tate	Retrd.	79.00	85-125.00
90-08-021	Glenlochie Lodge	D. Tate	Open	110.00	120.00
90-08-022	Eilean Donan	D. Tate	Open	145.00	185.00
90-08-023	Cawdor Castle	D. Tate	Retrd.	295.00	560-690.
92-08-024	Culross House	D. Tate	Open	90.00	95.00
92-08-025	Duart Castle	D. Tate	3,000	450.00	475.00
92-08-026	Eriskay Croft	D. Tate	Open	50.00	55.00
92-08-027	Mair Haven	D. Tate	Open	46.50	50.00
93-08-028	Edzell Summer House	Lilliput Lane	N/A	110.00	110.00
Lilliput Lane Ltd.		**Lakeland Bridge Plaques**			
89-09-001	Aira Force	D. Simpson	Retrd.	35.00	35.00
89-09-002	Birks Bridge	D. Simpson	Retrd.	35.00	35.00
89-09-003	Stockley Bridge	D. Simpson	Retrd.	35.00	35.00
89-09-004	Hartsop Packhorse	D. Simpson	Retrd.	35.00	35.00
89-09-005	Bridge House	D. Simpson	Retrd.	35.00	105-120.
89-09-006	Ashness Bridge	D. Simpson	Retrd.	35.00	35.00
Lilliput Lane Ltd.		**Countryside Scene Plaques**			
89-10-001	Country Inn	D. Simpson	Retrd.	49.50	49.50
89-10-002	Norfolk Windmill	D. Simpson	Retrd.	49.50	49.50
89-10-003	Watermill	D. Simpson	Retrd.	49.50	49.50
89-10-004	Parish Church	D. Simpson	Retrd.	49.50	49.50
89-10-005	Bottle Kiln	D. Simpson	Retrd.	49.50	49.50
89-10-006	Cornish Tin Mine	D. Simpson	Retrd.	49.50	49.50
89-10-007	Lighthouse	D. Simpson	Retrd.	49.50	49.50
89-10-008	Cumbrian Farmhouse	D. Simpson	Retrd.	49.50	49.50
89-10-009	Post Office	D. Simpson	Retrd.	49.50	49.50
89-10-010	Village School	D. Simpson	Retrd.	49.50	49.50
89-10-011	Old Smithy	D. Simpson	Retrd.	49.50	49.50
89-10-012	Oasthouse	D. Simpson	Retrd.	49.50	49.50

Company / Number	Name	Series / Artist	Edition Limit	Issue Price	Quote
Lilliput Lane Ltd.		**Framed Scottish Plaques**			
90-11-001	Preston Oat Mill	D. Tate	Retrd.	59.50	59.50
90-11-002	Barra Black House	D. Tate	Retrd.	59.50	59.50
90-11-003	Kyle Point	D. Tate	Retrd.	59.50	59.50
90-11-004	Fife Ness	D. Tate	Retrd.	59.50	59.50
Lilliput Lane Ltd.		**Unframed Plaques**			
89-12-001	Small Stoney Wall Lea	D. Tate	Retrd.	47.50	47.50
89-12-002	Small Woodside Farm	D. Tate	Retrd.	47.50	47.50
89-12-003	Medium Cobble Combe Cottage	D. Tate	Retrd.	68.00	68.00
89-12-004	Medium Wishing Well	D. Tate	Retrd.	75.00	75.00
89-12-005	Large Lower Brockhampton	D. Tate	Retrd.	120.00	120.00
89-12-006	Large Somerset Springtime	D. Tate	Retrd.	130.00	130.00
Lilliput Lane Ltd.		**London Plaques**			
89-13-001	Buckingham Palace	D. Simpson	Retrd.	39.50	39.50
89-13-002	Trafalgar Square	D. Simpson	Retrd.	39.50	39.50
89-13-003	Tower Bridge	D. Simpson	Retrd.	39.50	39.50
89-13-004	Tower of London	D. Simpson	Retrd.	39.50	39.50
89-13-005	Big Ben	D. Simpson	Retrd.	39.50	39.50
89-13-006	Piccadilly Circus	D. Simpson	Retrd.	39.50	39.50
Lilliput Lane Ltd.		**Framed Irish Plaques**			
90-14-001	Ballyteag House	D. Tate	Retrd.	59.50	59.50
90-14-002	Shannons Bank	D. Tate	Retrd.	59.50	59.50
90-14-003	Pearses Cottages	D. Tate	Retrd.	59.50	59.50
90-14-004	Crockuna Croft	D. Tate	Retrd.	59.50	59.50
Lilliput Lane Ltd.		**Framed English Plaques**			
90-15-001	Huntingdon House	D. Tate	Retrd.	59.50	59.50
90-15-002	Coombe Cot	D. Tate	Retrd.	59.50	59.50
90-15-003	Ashdown Hall	D. Tate	Retrd.	59.50	59.50
90-15-004	Flint Fields	D. Tate	Retrd.	59.50	59.50
90-15-005	Fell View	D. Tate	Retrd.	59.50	59.50
90-15-006	Cat Slide Cottage	D. Tate	Retrd.	59.50	59.50
90-15-007	Battleview	D. Tate	Retrd.	59.50	59.50
90-15-008	Stowside	D. Tate	Retrd.	59.50	59.50
90-15-009	Jubilee Lodge	D. Tate	Retrd.	59.50	59.50
90-15-010	Trevan Cove	D. Tate	Retrd.	59.50	59.50
Lilliput Lane Ltd.		**Special Event Collection**			
89-16-001	Commemorative Medallion-1989 South Bend	D. Tate	Retrd.	N/A	130-220.
90-16-002	Rowan Lodge-1990 South Bend	D. Tate	Retrd.	N/A	370.00
91-16-003	Gamekeepers Cottage-1991 South Bend	D. Tate	Retrd.	N/A	150-200.
92-16-004	Ashberry Cottage-1992 South Bend	D. Tate	Retrd.	N/A	150-275.
93-16-005	Magnifying Glass-1993 South Bend	Lilliput Lane	Retrd.	N/A	N/A
Lilliput Lane Ltd.		**Specials**			
83-17-001	Cliburn School	D. Tate	Retrd.	22.50	6000-7200.
83-17-002	Bridge House Dealer Sign	D. Tate	Retrd.	N/A	345.00
85-17-003	Bermuda Cottage (3 Colors)	D. Tate	Retrd.	29.00	30.00
86-17-004	Seven Dwarf's Cottage	D. Tate	Retrd.	N/A	275-475.
87-17-005	Clockmaker's Cottage	D. Tate	Retrd.	40.00	200-275.
87-17-006	Guildhall	D. Tate	Retrd.	N/A	175-275.
88-17-007	Chantry Chapel	D. Tate	Retrd.	N/A	200-325.
89-17-008	Chiltern Mill	D. Tate	Open	87.50	110.00
89-17-009	Mayflower House	D. Tate	Retdr.	79.50	150-240.
89-17-010	Olde York Toll	D. Tate	Retrd.	82.50	110.00
90-17-011	Rowan Lodge	D. Tate	Retrd.	50.00	120-200.
91-17-012	Gamekeeper's Cottage	Lilliput Lane	Retrd.	75.00	100-140.
92-17-013	Ploughman's Cottage	Lilliput Lane	Retrd.	75.00	75.00
93-17-014	Aberford Gate	Lilliput Lane	Retrd.	95.00	95.00
Lilliput Lane Ltd.		**American Landmark Series**			
89-18-001	Countryside Barn	R. Day	Retrd.	75.00	120-150.
89-18-002	Mail Pouch Barn	R. Day	Open	75.00	110.00
89-18-003	Falls Mill	R. Day	Retrd.	130.00	98-225.
90-18-004	Sign Of The Times	R. Day	Open	27.50	35.00
90-18-005	Pioneer Barn	R. Day	Retrd.	30.00	65-150.
90-18-006	Great Point Light	R. Day	Open	39.50	55.00
90-18-007	Hometown Depot	R. Day	Open	68.00	95.00
90-18-008	Country Church	R. Day	Retrd.	82.50	140.00
90-18-009	Riverside Chapel	R. Day	Open	82.50	130.00
90-18-010	Pepsi Cola Barn	R. Day	Retrd.	87.00	190-250.
90-18-011	Roadside Coolers	R. Day	Open	75.00	110.00
90-18-012	Covered Memories	R. Day	Open	110.00	160.00
91-18-013	Rambling Rose	R. Day	Open	60.00	65.00
91-18-014	School Days	R. Day	Open	60.00	80.00
91-18-015	Fire House 1	R. Day	Open	87.50	110.00
91-18-016	Victoriana	R. Day	Retrd.	295.00	350-1000.
92-18-017	Home Sweet Home	R. Day	Open	120.00	130.00
92-18-018	Small Town Library	R. Day	Open	130.00	140.00
92-18-019	16.9 Cents Per Gallon	R. Day	Open	150.00	160.00
92-18-020	Gold Miners' Claim	R. Day	Open	110.00	120.00
92-18-021	Winnie's Place	R. Day	Closed	395.00	420-1000.
93-18-022	Simply Amish	R. Day	Open	160.00	160.00
93-18-023	See Rock City	R. Day	N/A	60.00	60.00
93-18-024	Shave and A Haircut	R. Day	N/A	160.00	160.00
94-18-025	Birdsong	R. Day	Open	120.00	120.00
94-18-026	Harvest Mill	R. Day	3,500	395.00	395.00
Lilliput Lane Ltd.		**American Collection**			
84-19-001	Adobe Church	D. Tate	Retrd.	22.50	450-650.
84-19-002	Adobe Village	D. Tate	Retrd.	60.00	1045-1500.
84-19-003	Cape Cod	D. Tate	Retrd.	22.50	570.00
84-19-004	Covered Bridge	D. Tate	Retrd.	22.50	3200.00
84-19-005	Country Church	D. Tate	Retrd.	22.50	500-800.
84-19-006	Forge Barn	D. Tate	Retrd.	22.50	550-660.
84-19-007	Grist Mill	D. Tate	Retrd.	22.50	500-785.
84-19-008	Log Cabin	D. Tate	Retrd.	22.50	500-1000.
84-19-009	General Store	D. Tate	Retrd.	22.50	840-2800.
84-19-010	Light House	D. Tate	Retrd.	22.50	700-1000.
84-19-011	Midwest Barn	D. Tate	Retrd.	22.50	250-450.
84-19-012	Wallace Station	D. Tate	Retrd.	22.50	350-1000.
84-19-013	San Francisco House	D. Tate	Retrd.	22.50	400-1000.
Lilliput Lane Ltd.		**Welsh Collection**			
85-20-001	Hermitage	D. Tate	Retrd.	30.00	250.00
87-20-002	Hermitage Renovated	D. Tate	Retrd.	42.50	85.00
86-20-003	Brecon Bach	D. Tate	Retrd.	42.00	65.00
91-20-004	Tudor Merchant	D. Tate	Open	90.00	95.00
91-20-005	Ugly House	D. Tate	Open	55.00	60.00
91-20-006	Bro Dawel	D. Tate	Open	37.50	40.00
92-20-007	St. Govan's Chapel	Lilliput Lane	Open	75.00	80.00

Company Number	Name	Series Artist	Edition Limit	Issue Price	Quote
Lilliput Lane Ltd.		**Dutch Collection**			
91-21-001	Aan de Amstel	D. Tate	Open	79.00	85.00
91-21-002	Begijnhof	D. Tate	Open	55.00	60.00
91-21-003	Bloemenmarkt	D. Tate	Open	79.00	85.00
91-21-004	De Branderij	D. Tate	Open	72.50	80.00
91-21-005	De Diamantair	D. Tate	Open	79.00	85.00
91-21-006	De Pepermolen	D. Tate	Open	55.00	60.00
91-21-007	De Wolhandelaar	D. Tate	Open	72.50	80.00
91-21-008	De Zijdewever	D. Tate	Open	79.00	85.00
91-21-009	Rembrant van Rijn	D. Tate	Open	120.00	130.00
91-21-010	Rozengracht	D. Tate	Open	72.50	80.00
Lilliput Lane Ltd.		**French Collection**			
91-22-001	L' Auberge d'Armorique	D. Tate	Open	220.00	250.00
91-22-002	La Bergerie du Perigord	D. Tate	Open	230.00	250.00
91-22-003	La Cabane du Gardian	D. Tate	Open	55.00	60.00
91-22-004	La Chaumiere du Verger	D. Tate	Open	120.00	130.00
91-22-005	La Maselle de Nadaillac	D. Tate	Open	130.00	140.00
91-22-006	La Porte Schoenenberg	D. Tate	Open	75.00	85.00
91-22-007	Le Manoir de Champfleuri	D. Tate	Open	265.00	295.00
91-22-008	Le Mas du Vigneron	D. Tate	Open	120.00	130.00
91-22-009	Le Petite Montmartre	D. Tate	Open	130.00	140.00
91-22-010	Locmaria	D. Tate	Open	65.00	80.00
Lilliput Lane Ltd.		**Village Shop Collection**			
92-23-001	The Greengrocers	D. Tate	Open	120.00	130.00
92-23-002	Penny Sweets	Lilliput Lane	Open	130.00	130.00
93-23-003	Jones The Butcher	Lilliput Lane	Open	120.00	120.00
Lilliput Lane Ltd.		**Blaise Hamlet Classics**			
93-24-001	Jasmine Cottage	Lilliput Lane	Open	95.00	95.00
93-24-002	Double Cottage	Lilliput Lane	Open	95.00	95.00
93-24-003	Vine Cottage	Lilliput Lane	Open	95.00	95.00
93-24-004	Circular Cottage	Lilliput Lane	Open	95.00	95.00
93-24-005	Diamond Cottage	Lilliput Lane	Open	95.00	95.00
93-24-006	Dial Cottage	Lilliput Lane	Open	95.00	95.00
93-24-007	Rose Cottage	Lilliput Lane	Open	95.00	95.00
93-24-008	Sweet Briar Cottage	Lilliput Lane	Open	95.00	95.00
93-24-009	Oak Cottage	Lilliput Lane	Open	95.00	95.00
Lilliput Lane Ltd.		**Anniversary Special**			
92-25-001	Honeysuckle Cottage	Lilliput Lane	Yr.Iss.	195.00	220-350.
93-25-002	Cotman Cottage	Lilliput Lane	Yr.Iss.	220.00	265.00
94-25-003	Watermeadows	Lilliput Lane	Yr.Iss.	189.00	189.00
Lladro		**Capricho**			
87-01-001	Orchid Arrangement C1541	Lladro	Closed	500.00	1700-2100.
87-01-002	Iris Arrangement C1542	Lladro	Closed	800.00	1000-1250.
87-01-003	Fan C1546	Lladro	Closed	650.00	900-1600.
87-01-004	Fan C1546.3	Lladro	Closed	650.00	900-1600.
87-01-005	Iris with Vase C1551	Lladro	Closed	110.00	375.00
88-01-006	Bust w/ Black Veil & base C1538	Lladro	Open	650.00	835.00
88-01-007	Small Bust w/ Veil & base C1539	Lladro	Open	225.00	357.00
87-01-008	Flowers Chest C1572	Lladro	Open	550.00	693.00
87-01-009	Flat Basket with Flowers C1575	Lladro	Closed	450.00	750.00
89-01-010	Romantic Lady / Black Veil w/base C1666	Lladro	Closed	420.00	520.00
XX-01-011	White Bust w/ Veil & base C5927	Lladro	Open	550.00	730.00
Lladro		**Lladro**			
69-02-001	Shepherdess with Goats L1001M	Lladro	Closed	80.00	460.00
69-02-002	Girl's Head L1003M	Lladro	Closed	150.00	700-900.
69-02-003	Girl With Lamb L1010G	Lladro	Closed	26.00	180.00
69-02-004	Girl With Pig L1011G	Lladro	Open	13.00	85.00
69-02-005	Centaur Girl L1012M	Lladro	Closed	45.00	350.00
69-02-006	Centaur Boy L1013M	Lladro	Closed	425.00	425-450.
69-02-007	Dove L1015 G	Lladro	Open	21.00	105.00
69-02-008	Dove L1016 G	Lladro	Open	36.00	180.00
69-02-009	Idyl L1017G	Lladro	Closed	115.00	615.00
69-02-010	Idyl L1017M	Lladro	Closed	115.00	550-615.
69-02-011	King Gaspar L1018M	Lladro	Open	345.00	1895.00
69-02-012	King Melchior L1019M	Lladro	Open	345.00	1850.00
69-02-013	King Baltasar L1020M	Lladro	Open	345.00	1850.00
69-02-014	Horse Group L1021G	Lladro	Closed	950.00	1950.00
69-02-015	Horse Group/All White L1022M	Lladro	Open	465.00	2100.00
69-02-016	Flute Player L1025G	Lladro	Closed	73.00	700.00
69-02-017	Clown with Concertina L1027G	Lladro	Open	95.00	735.00
69-02-018	Don Quixote w/Stand L1030G	Lladro	Open	225.00	1450.00
69-02-019	Sancho Panza L1031G	Lladro	Closed	65.00	475-525.
69-02-020	Old Folks L1033G	Lladro	Closed	140.00	1600.00
69-02-021	Girl with Basket L1034	Lladro	Closed	30.00	275.00
69-02-022	Girl with Geese L1035G	Lladro	Open	37.50	180.00
69-02-023	Girl With Geese L1035M	Lladro	Closed	37.50	165.00
69-02-024	Violinist and Girl L1039G	Lladro	Closed	120.00	1000-1200.
69-02-025	Violinist and Girl L1039M	Lladro	Closed	120.00	825.00
69-02-026	Hunters L1048	Lladro	Closed	115.00	1100-2000.
69-02-027	Del Monte (Boy) L1050	Lladro	Closed	65.00	N/A
69-02-028	Girl with Duck L1052G	Lladro	Open	30.00	205.00
69-02-029	Girl with Duck L1052M	Lladro	Closed	30.00	190.00
69-02-030	Girl with Pheasant L1055G	Lladro	Closed	105.0 0	N/A
69-02-031	Panchito L1059	Lladro	Closed	28.00	N/A
69-02-032	Deer L1064	Lladro	Closed	27.50	N/A
69-02-033	Fox and Cub L1065	Lladro	Closed	17.50	350-500.
69-02-034	Afghan (sitting) L1069G	Lladro	Closed	36.00	492-550.
70-02-035	Beagle Puppy L1070	Lladro	Closed	16.50	200.00
69-02-036	Beagle Puppy L1071G	Lladro	Closed	16.50	200.00
69-02-037	Beagle Puppy L1071M	Lladro	Closed	16.50	200.00
69-02-038	Beagle Puppy L1072G	Lladro	Closed	16.50	250.00
69-02-039	Dutch Girl L1077	Lladro	Closed	57.50	135.00
69-02-040	Girl With Brush L1081	Lladro	Closed	14.50	300.00
69-02-041	Girl Manicuring L1082	Lladro	Closed	14.50	300.00
69-02-042	Girl With Doll L1083	Lladro	Closed	14.50	300.00
69-02-043	Girl with Mother's Shoe L1084	Lladro	Closed	14.50	300.00
69-02-044	Girl Seated with Flowers L1088G	Lladro	Closed	45.00	650.00
71-02-045	Lawyer (Face) L1089G	Lladro	Closed	35.00	N/A
69-02-046	Beggar L1094	Lladro	Closed	65.00	N/A
71-02-047	Pelusa Clown L1125	Lladro	Closed	70.00	875-1150.
71-02-048	Clown with Violin L1126	Lladro	Closed	71.00	1200.00
71-02-049	Puppy Love L1127G	Lladro	Open	50.00	285.00
71-02-050	Dog in the Basket L1128G	Lladro	Closed	17.50	450.00
71-02-051	Dog and Snail L1139G	Lladro	Closed	40.00	270.00
71-02-052	Dog's Head L1149G	Lladro	Closed	27.50	N/A
71-02-053	Elephants (3) L1150G	Lladro	Open	100.00	795.00
71-02-054	Elephants (2) L1151G	Lladro	Open	45.00	390.00
71-02-055	Dog Playing Bass Fiddle L1154G	Lladro	Closed	36.50	400.00
71-02-056	Dog w/Microphone L1155G	Lladro	Closed	35.00	325-475.
71-02-057	Kissing Doves L1169 G	Lladro	Open	32.00	140.00
71-02-058	Kissing Doves L1170 G	Lladro	Closed	25.00	250.00
71-02-059	Girl With Flowers L1172 G	Lladro	Open	27.00	295.00
71-02-060	Girl With Domino L1175G	Lladro	Closed	34.00	350.00
71-02-061	Clown on Domino L1179G	Lladro	Closed	34.00	350.00
71-02-062	Platero and Marcelino L1181G	Lladro	Closed	50.00	400.00
72-02-063	Little Girl with Cat L1187G	Lladro	Closed	37.00	350-450.
72-02-064	Boy Meets Girl L1188	Lladro	Closed	310.00	400.00
72-02-065	Eskimo L1195G	Lladro	Open	30.00	135.00
72-02-066	Bear, White L1207G	Lladro	Open	16.00	75.00
72-02-067	Bear, White L1208G	Lladro	Open	16.00	75.00
72-02-068	Bear, White L1209G	Lladro	Open	16.00	75.00
72-02-069	Round Fish L1210G	Lladro	Closed	35.00	N/A
72-02-070	Girl With Doll L1211G	Lladro	Open	72.00	440.00
72-02-071	Woman Carrying Water L1212	Lladro	Closed	100.00	400.00
72-02-072	Young Harlequin L1229G	Lladro	Open	70.00	520.00
72-02-073	Friendship L1230G	Lladro	Closed	68.00	325.00
72-02-074	Friendship L1230M	Lladro	Closed	68.00	325.00
72-02-075	Angel with Lute L1231	Lladro	Closed	60.00	400.00
72-02-076	Angel with Clarinet L1232	Lladro	Closed	60.00	400.00
72-02-077	Angel with Flute L1233	Lladro	Closed	60.00	400.00
73-02-078	Christmas Carols L1239G	Lladro	Closed	125.00	800-900.
73-02-079	Girl with Wheelbarrow L1245	Lladro	Closed	75.00	500-600.
72-02-080	Caress and Rest L1246	Lladro	Closed	50.00	300.00
74-02-081	Honey Lickers L1248G	Lladro	Closed	100.00	575.00
74-02-082	The Race L1249G	Lladro	Closed	450.00	1800-2250.
74-02-083	Lovers from Verona L 1250G	Lladro	Closed	330.00	900-1050.
74-02-084	Shepherd L1252	Lladro	Closed	100.00	N/A
74-02-085	Sad Chimney Sweep L1253G	Lladro	Closed	180.00	1200.00
74-02-086	Hamlet and Yorick L1254G	Lladro	Closed	325.00	1100-1175.
74-02-087	Seesaw L1255G	Lladro	Open	110.00	550.00
74-02-088	Mother with Pups L1257	Lladro	Closed	50.00	700.00
74-02-089	Playing Poodles L1258	Lladro	Closed	47.50	700.00
74-02-090	Poodle L1259G	Lladro	Closed	27.50	375-500.
74-02-091	Flying Duck L1263G	Lladro	Open	20.00	90.00
74-02-092	Flying Duck L1264G	Lladro	Open	20.00	90.00
74-02-093	Flying Duck L1265G	Lladro	Open	20.00	90.00
74-02-094	Girl with Ducks L1267G	Lladro	Open	55.00	260.00
74-02-095	Reminiscing L1270G	Lladro	Closed	975.00	1375.00
74-02-096	Thoughts L1272G	Lladro	Open	87.50	3200.00
74-02-097	Lovers in the Park L1274G	Lladro	Open	450.00	1365.00
74-02-098	Feeding Time L1277G	Lladro	Closed	120.00	380.00
74-02-099	Devotion L1278G	Lladro	Closed	140.00	475.00
74-02-100	The Wind L1279M	Lladro	Open	250.00	795.00
74-02-101	Playtime L1280G	Lladro	Closed	160.00	475-725.
74-02-102	Afghan Standing L1282G	Lladro	Closed	45.00	350-475.
74-02-103	Little Gardener L1283G	Lladro	Open	250.00	785.00
74-02-104	"My Flowers" L1284G	Lladro	Open	200.00	550.00
74-02-105	"My Goodness" L1285G	Lladro	Open	190.00	415.00
74-02-106	Flower Harvest L1286G	Lladro	Open	200.00	495.00
74-02-107	Picking Flowers L1287G	Lladro	Open	170.00	440.00
74-02-108	Aggressive Duck L1288G	Lladro	Open	170.00	475.00
74-02-109	Victorian Girl on Swing L1297G	Lladro	Closed	520.00	2100.00
74-02-110	Valencian Lady with Flowers L1304G	Lladro	Open	200.00	625.00
74-02-111	"On the Farm" L1306	Lladro	Closed	130.00	240.00
74-02-112	Ducklings L1307G	Lladro	Open	47.50	150.00
74-02-113	Girl with Cats L1309G	Lladro	Open	120.00	310.00
74-02-114	Girl with Puppies in Basket L1311G	Lladro	Open	120.00	345.00
74-02-115	Schoolgirl L1313G	Lladro	Closed	200.50	575-650.
76-02-116	Collie L1316G	Lladro	Closed	45.00	400.00
76-02-117	IBIS L1319G	Lladro	Open	1550.00	2625.00
77-02-118	Angel with Tamborine L1320G	Lladro	Closed	125.00	375-500.
77-02-119	Angel with Lyre L1321G	Lladro	Closed	125.00	375-500.
77-02-120	Angel with Song L1322G	Lladro	Closed	125.00	375-500.
77-02-121	Angel with Accordian L1323	Lladro	Closed	125.00	370-450.
77-02-122	Angel with Mandolin L1324G	Lladro	Closed	125.00	375-500.
76-02-123	The Helmsman L1325M	Lladro	Closed	600.00	6400.00
76-02-124	Playing Cards L1327 M, numbered series	Lladro	Open	3800.00	6600.00
77-02-125	Dove Group L1335G	Lladro	Closed	950.00	1100.00
77-02-126	Blooming Roses L1339G	Lladro	Closed	325.00	425.00
77-02-127	Male Jockey L1341G	Lladro	Closed	120.00	450.00
77-02-128	Wrath of Don Quixote L1343G	Lladro	Closed	250.00	850.00
77-02-129	Derby L1344G	Lladro	Closed	1125.00	2500.00
78-02-130	Under the Willow L1346G	Lladro	Closed	1600.00	2000.00
78-02-131	Mermaid on Wave L1347G	Lladro	Closed	425.00	425.00
78-02-132	Nautical Vision L1349G	Lladro	Closed	Unkn.	3000.00
78-02-133	In the Gondola L1350G, numbered series	Lladro	Open	1850.00	3250.00
78-02-134	Growing Roses L1354G	Lladro	Closed	485.00	635.00
78-02-135	Phyllis L1356G	Lladro	Open	75.00	170.00
78-02-136	Shelley L1357G	Lladro	Open	75.00	170.00
78-02-137	Beth L1358G	Lladro	Open	75.00	170.00
78-02-138	Heather L1359G	Lladro	Open	75.00	170.00
78-02-139	Laura L1360G	Lladro	Open	75.00	170.00
78-02-140	Julia L1361G	Lladro	Open	75.00	170.00
78-02-141	Swinging L1366G	Lladro	Closed	825.00	1375.00
78-02-142	Spring Birds L1368G	Lladro	Closed	1600.00	2500.00
78-02-143	Anniversary Waltz L1372G	Lladro	Open	260.00	545.00
78-02-144	Chestnut Seller L1373G	Lladro	Closed	800.00	N/A
78-02-145	Waiting in the Park L1374G	Lladro	Open	235.00	450.00
78-02-146	Watering Flowers L1376G	Lladro	Closed	400.00	700-1000.
78-02-147	Suzy and Her Doll L1378G	Lladro	Closed	215.00	600-800.
78-02-148	Debbie and Her Doll L1379G	Lladro	Closed	215.00	600-825.
78-02-149	Cathy and Her Doll L1380G	Lladro	Closed	215.00	570-950.
78-02-150	Princess Sitting L1381G	Lladro	Closed	11.75	400-600.
78-02-151	Medieval Girl L1381G	Lladro	Closed	11.75	600.00
78-02-152	Medieval Boy L1382G	Lladro	Closed	235.00	600-700.
78-02-153	A Rickshaw Ride L1383G	Lladro	Open	1500.00	2150.00
78-02-154	The Brave Knight L1385G	Lladro	Closed	350.00	750.00
81-02-155	St. Joseph L1386G	Lladro	Open	250.00	385.00
81-02-156	Mary L1387G	Lladro	Open	240.00	385.00
81-02-157	Baby Jesus L1388G	Lladro	Open	85.00	140.00
81-02-158	Donkey L1389G	Lladro	Open	95.00	200.00
81-02-159	Cow L1390G	Lladro	Open	95.00	180.00
82-02-160	Holy Mary, L1394G, numbered series	Lladro	Open	1000.00	1450.00
82-02-161	Full of Mischief L1395G	Lladro	Open	420.00	765.00
82-02-162	Appreciation L1396G	Lladro	Open	420.00	765.00
82-02-163	Second Thoughts L1397G	Lladro	Open	420.00	750.00
82-02-164	Reverie L1398G	Lladro	Open	490.00	895.00
82-02-165	Dutch Woman with Tulips L1399G	Lladro	Closed	750.00	750.00
82-02-166	Valencian Boy L1400G	Lladro	Closed	297.50	400.00
82-02-167	Sleeping Nymph L1401G	Lladro	Closed	210.00	600-875.
82-02-168	Daydreaming Nymph L1402G	Lladro	Closed	210.00	525-625.
82-02-169	Butterfly Girl L1403G	Lladro	Closed	210.00	550.00

Company Number	Name	Series Artist	Edition Limit	Issue Price	Quote
82-02-170	Matrimony L1404G	Lladro	Open	320.00	585.00
82-02-171	Illusion L1413G	Lladro	Open	115.00	245.00
82-02-172	Fantasy L1414G	Lladro	Open	115.00	240.00
82-02-173	Mirage L1415G	Lladro	Open	115.00	240.00
82-02-174	From My Garden L1416G	Lladro	Open	140.00	275.00
82-02-175	Nature's Bounty L1417G	Lladro	Open	160.00	310.00
82-02-176	Flower Harmony L1418G	Lladro	Open	130.00	245.00
82-02-177	A Barrow of Blossoms L1419G	Lladro	Open	390.00	675.00
82-02-178	Born Free w/base L1420G	Lladro	Open	1520.00	2850.00
82-02-179	Mariko w/base L1421G	Lladro	Open	860.00	1575.00
82-02-180	Miss Valencia L1422G	Lladro	Open	175.00	350.00
82-02-181	King Melchor L1423G	Lladro	Open	225.00	440.00
82-02-182	King Gaspar L1424G	Lladro	Open	265.00	475.00
82-02-183	King Baltasar L1425G	Lladro	Open	315.00	585.00
82-02-184	Male Tennis Player L1426M	Lladro	Closed	200.00	300-400.
82-02-185	Female Tennis Player L1427M	Lladro	Closed	200.00	375-425.
82-02-186	Afternoon Tea L1428G	Lladro	Open	115.00	250.00
82-02-187	Afternoon Tea L1428M	Lladro	Open	115.00	250.00
82-02-188	Winter Wonderland w/base L1429G	Lladro	Open	1025.00	1925.00
82-02-189	High Society L1430G	Lladro	Open	305.00	595.00
82-02-190	The Debutante L1431G	Lladro	Open	115.00	245.00
82-02-191	The Debutante L1431M	Lladro	Open	115.00	245.00
83-02-192	Vows L1434G	Lladro	Closed	600.00	950.00
83-02-193	Blue Moon L1435G	Lladro	Closed	98.00	450.00
83-02-194	Moon Glow L1436	Lladro	Closed	98.00	375.00
83-02-195	Moon Light L1437	Lladro	Closed	98.00	375.00
83-02-196	Full Moon L1438	Lladro	Closed	115.00	500.00
83-02-197	"How Do You Do!" L1439G	Lladro	Open	185.00	295.00
83-02-198	Pleasantries L1440G	Lladro	Closed	960.00	1900.00
83-02-199	A Litter of Love L1441G	Lladro	Open	385.00	645.00
83-02-200	Kitty Confrontation L1442G	Lladro	Open	155.00	285.00
83-02-201	Bearly Love L1443G	Lladro	Open	55.00	98.00
83-02-202	Purr-Fect L1444G	Lladro	Open	350.00	615.00
83-02-203	Springtime in Japan L1445G	Lladro	Open	965.00	1800.00
83-02-204	"Here Comes the Bride" L1446G	Lladro	Open	517.50	965.00
83-02-205	Michiko L1447G	Lladro	Open	235.00	460.00
83-02-206	Yuki L1448G	Lladro	Open	285.00	550.00
83-02-207	Mayumi L1449G	Lladro	Open	235.00	460.00
83-02-208	Kiyoko L1450G	Lladro	Open	235.00	460.00
83-02-209	Teruko L1451G	Lladro	Open	235.00	460.00
83-02-210	On the Town L1452G	Lladro	Open	220.00	440.00
83-02-211	Golfing Couple L1453G	Lladro	Open	248.00	485.00
83-02-212	Flowers of the Season L1454G	Lladro	Open	1460.00	2550.00
83-02-213	Reflections of Hamlet L1455G	Lladro	Closed	1000.00	1260.00
83-02-214	Cranes w/base L1456G	Lladro	Open	1000.00	1950.00
85-02-215	A Boy and His Pony L1460G	Lladro	Closed	285.00	800.00
85-02-216	Carefree Angel with Flute L1463G	Lladro	Closed	220.00	575-650.
85-02-217	Carefree Angel with Lyre L1464G	Lladro	Closed	220.00	575.00
85-02-218	Girl on Carousel Horse L1469G	Lladro	Open	470.00	835.00
85-02-219	Boy on Carousel Horse L1470G	Lladro	Open	470.00	850.00
85-02-220	Wishing On A Star L1475G	Lladro	Closed	130.00	600.00
85-02-221	Star Light Star Bright L1476G	Lladro	Closed	130.00	350.00
85-02-222	Star Gazing L1477G	Lladro	Closed	130.00	375.00
85-02-223	Hawaiian Dancer/Aloha! L1478G	Lladro	Open	230.00	440.00
85-02-224	In a Tropical Garden L1479G	Lladro	Open	230.00	440.00
85-02-225	Aroma of the Islands L1480G	Lladro	Open	260.00	480.00
85-02-226	Sunning L1481G	Lladro	Closed	145.00	525.00
85-02-227	Eve L1482	Lladro	Closed	145.00	650.00
85-02-228	Free As a Butterfly L1483G	Lladro	Closed	145.00	450.00
86-02-229	Lady of the East L1488G	Lladro	Open	625.00	1100.00
86-02-230	Valencian Children L1489G	Lladro	Open	700.00	1225.00
86-02-231	My Wedding Day L1494G	Lladro	Open	800.00	1450.00
86-02-232	A Lady of Taste L1495G	Lladro	Open	575.00	1025.00
86-02-233	Don Quixote & The Windmill L1497G	Lladro	Open	1100.00	2050.00
86-02-234	Tahitian Dancing Girls L1498G	Lladro	Open	750.00	1325.00
86-02-235	Blessed Family L1499G	Lladro	Open	200.00	360.00
86-02-236	Ragamuffin L1500G	Lladro	Closed	125.00	200.00
86-02-237	Ragamuffin L1500M	Lladro	Closed	125.00	300.00
86-02-238	Rag Doll L1501G	Lladro	Closed	125.00	200.00
86-02-239	Rag Doll L1501M	Lladro	Closed	125.00	300.00
86-02-240	Forgotten L1502G	Lladro	Closed	125.00	200.00
86-02-241	Forgotten L1502M	Lladro	Closed	125.00	300.00
86-02-242	Neglected L1503G	Lladro	Closed	125.00	200.00
86-02-243	Neglected L1503M	Lladro	Closed	125.00	300.00
86-02-243	The Reception L1504G	Lladro	Closed	625.00	1050.00
86-02-244	Nature Boy L1505G	Lladro	Closed	100.00	250.00
86-02-245	Nature Boy L1505M	Lladro	Closed	100.00	N/A
86-02-246	A New Friend L1506G	Lladro	Closed	110.00	180.00
86-02-247	A New Friend L1506M	Lladro	Closed	110.00	N/A
86-02-248	Boy & His Bunny L1507G	Lladro	Closed	90.00	120-160.
86-02-249	Boy & His Bunny L1507M	Lladro	Closed	90.00	N/A
86-02-250	In the Meadow L1508G	Lladro	Closed	100.00	180.00
86-02-251	In the Meadow L1508M	Lladro	Closed	100.00	N/A
86-02-253	Spring Flowers L1509G	Lladro	Closed	100.00	246.00
86-02-254	Spring Flowers L1509M	Lladro	Closed	100.00	N/A
87-02-255	Cafe De Paris L1511G	Lladro	Open	1900.00	2950.00
87-02-256	Hawaiian Beauty L1512G	Lladro	Closed	575.00	950-1100.
87-02-257	A Flower for My Lady L1513G	Lladro	Closed	1150.00	1375.00
87-02-258	Gaspar 's Page L1514G	Lladro	Closed	275.00	450.00
87-02-259	Melchior's Page L1515G	Lladro	Closed	290.00	400-500.
87-02-260	Balthasar's Page L1516G	Lladro	Closed	275.00	700.00
87-02-261	Circus Train L1517G	Lladro	Open	2900.00	4350.00
87-02-262	Valencian Garden L1518G	Lladro	Closed	1100.00	1650.00
87-02-263	Stroll in the Park L1519G	Lladro	Open	1600.00	2600.00
87-02-264	The Landau Carriage L1521G	Lladro	Open	2500.00	3850.00
87-02-265	I am Don Quixote! L1522G	Lladro	Open	2600.00	3950.00
87-02-266	Valencian Bouquet L1524G	Lladro	Closed	250.00	400.00
87-02-267	Valencian Dreams L1525G	Lladro	Closed	240.00	450.00
87-02-268	Valencian Flowers L1526G	Lladro	Closed	375.00	550.00
87-02-270	Tenderness L1527G	Lladro	Open	260.00	415.00
87-02-271	I Love You Truly L1528G	Lladro	Open	375.00	575.00
87-02-272	Momi L1529G	Lladro	Closed	275.00	340.00
87-02-273	Leilani L1530G	Lladro	Closed	275.00	500.00
87-02-274	Malia L1531G	Lladro	Closed	275.00	340.00
87-02-275	Lehua L1532G	Lladro	Closed	275.00	575.00
87-02-276	Not So Fast! L1533G	Lladro	Open	175.00	245.00
88-02-277	Little Sister L1534G	Lladro	Open	180.00	240.00
88-02-278	Sweet Dreams L1535G	Lladro	Open	150.00	195.00
88-02-279	Stepping Out L1537G	Lladro	Open	230.00	310.00
87-02-280	Wild Stallions w/base L1566G	Lladro	Open	1100.00	1465.00
87-02-281	Running Free w/base L1567G	Lladro	Open	1500.00	1525.00
87-02-282	Grand Dame L1568G	Lladro	Open	290.00	395.00
89-02-283	Fluttering Crane L1598G	Lladro	Open	115.00	145.00
89-02-284	Nesting Crane L1599G	Lladro	Open	95.00	115.00
89-02-285	Landing Crane L1600G	Lladro	Open	115.00	145.00
89-02-286	Rock Nymph L1601G	Lladro	Open	665.00	795.00
89-02-287	Spring Nymph L1602G	Lladro	Open	665.00	825.00
89-02-288	Latest Addition L1606G	Lladro	Open	385.00	480.00
89-02-289	Flight Into Egypt w/base L1610G	Lladro	Open	885.00	1150.00
89-02-290	Courting Cranes L1611G	Lladro	Open	565.00	695.00
89-02-291	Preening Crane L1612G	Lladro	Open	385.00	485.00
89-02-292	Bowing Crane L1613G	Lladro	Open	385.00	485.00
89-02-293	Dancing Crane L1614G	Lladro	Open	385.00	485.00
88-02-294	Cellist L1700M	Lladro	Closed	1200.00	1200.00
88-02-295	Saxophone Player L1701M	Lladro	Closed	835.00	835.00
88-02-296	Boy at the Fair (Decorated) L1708M	Lladro	Closed	650.00	650.00
88-02-297	Exodus L1709M	Lladro	Closed	875.00	875.00
88-02-298	School Boy L1710M	Lladro	Closed	750.00	750.00
88-02-299	School Girl L1711M	Lladro	Closed	950.00	950.00
88-02-300	Nanny L1714M	Lladro	Closed	700.00	700.00
88-02-301	Harlequin with Puppy L1716M	Lladro	Closed	825.00	825.00
88-02-302	Harlequin with Dove L1717M	Lladro	Closed	900.00	900.00
88-02-303	Dress Rehearsal L1718M	Lladro	Closed	1150.00	1150.00
89-02-304	Back From the Fair L1719M	Lladro	Closed	1825.00	1825.00
90-02-305	Sprite w/base L1720G	Lladro	Open	1200.00	1400.00
90-02-306	Leprechaun w/base L1721G	Lladro	Open	1200.00	1395.00
89-02-307	Group Discussion L1722M	Lladro	Closed	1500.00	1500.00
89-02-308	Belle Epoque L1724M	Lladro	Closed	700.00	700.00
89-02-309	Young Lady with Parasol L1725M	Lladro	Closed	950.00	950.00
89-02-310	Young Lady with Fan L1726M	Lladro	Closed	750.00	750.00
89-02-311	Pose L1727M	Lladro	Closed	725.00	725.00
91-02-312	Nativity L1730M	Lladro	Open	725.00	725.00
70-02-314	Shepherdess with Lamb L2005M	Lladro	Closed	100.00	710.00
70-02-315	Water Carrier Girl Lamp L2006	Lladro	Closed	30.00	600.00
71-02-316	Girl with Dog L2013M	Lladro	Closed	300.00	N/A
71-02-317	Little Eagle Owl L2020	Lladro	Closed	15.00	425.00
71-02-318	Boy/Girl Eskimo L2038.3M	Lladro	Closed	100.00	275-455.
74-02-319	Setter's Head L2045M	Lladro	Closed	42.50	550.00
74-02-320	Magistrates L2052M	Lladro	Closed	135.00	1200.00
74-02-321	Oriental L2056M	Lladro	Open	35.00	100.00
74-02-322	Oriental L2057M	Lladro	Open	30.00	100.00
74-02-323	Thailandia L2058M	Lladro	Open	650.00	1725.00
74-02-324	Muskateer L2059M	Lladro	Closed	900.00	750.00
77-02-325	Monk L2060M	Lladro	Open	60.00	130.00
71-02-326	Dogs-Bust L2067M	Lladro	Closed	280.00	800.00
77-02-327	Thai Dancers L2069M	Lladro	Open	300.00	725.00
77-02-328	A New Hairdo L2070M	Lladro	Closed	1060.00	1430.00
77-02-329	Graceful Duo L2073M	Lladro	Open	775.00	1650.00
77-02-330	Nuns L2075M	Lladro	Open	90.00	230.00
78-02-331	Lonely L2076M	Lladro	Open	72.50	185.00
78-02-332	Rain in Spain L2077M	Lladro	Closed	190.00	550.00
78-02-333	Don Quixote Dreaming L2084M	Lladro	Closed	550.00	1800.00
78-02-334	The Little Kiss L2086M	Lladro	Closed	180.00	475.00
78-02-335	Saint Francis L2090	Lladro	Closed	565.00	N/A
78-02-336	Holy Virgin L2092M	Lladro	Closed	200.00	N/A
78-02-337	Girl Waiting L2093M	Lladro	Open	90.00	185.00
78-02-338	Tenderness L2094M	Lladro	Open	100.00	205.00
78-02-339	Duck Pulling Pigtail L2095M	Lladro	Open	110.00	275.00
78-02-340	Nosy Puppy L2096M	Lladro	Open	190.00	410.00
78-02-341	Laundress L2109M	Lladro	Closed	325.00	325-650.
80-02-342	Marujita with Two Ducks L2113M	Lladro	Open	240.00	295.00
80-02-343	Kissing Father L2114M	Lladro	Closed	575.00	450.00
80-02-344	Mother's Kiss L2115M	Lladro	Closed	575.00	450.00
80-02-345	The Whaler L2121M	Lladro	Closed	820.00	1050.00
81-02-346	Lost in Thought L2125M	Lladro	Closed	210.00	250.00
83-02-347	American Heritage L2127M	Lladro	Closed	525.00	650-950.
83-02-348	Venus L2128M	Lladro	Closed	650.00	1150.00
83-02-349	Egyptian Cat L2130M	Lladro	Closed	75.00	500.00
83-02-350	Mother & Son L2131M, numbered series	Lladro	Open	850.00	1425.00
83-02-349	Spring Sheperdess L2132M	Lladro	Closed	450.00	N/A
83-02-350	Autumn Sheperdess L2133M	Lladro	Closed	285.00	N/A
84-02-351	Nautical Watch L2134M	Lladro	Closed	450.00	750.00
84-02-352	Mystical Joseph L2135M	Lladro	Closed	427.50	700.00
84-02-353	The King L2136M	Lladro	Closed	510.00	710.00
84-02-354	Fairy Ballerina L2137M	Lladro	Closed	500.00	625.00
84-02-355	Friar Juniper L2138M	Lladro	Open	160.00	275.00
84-02-356	Aztec Indian L2139M	Lladro	Closed	552.50	600.00
84-02-357	Pepita wth Sombrero L2140M	Lladro	Open	97.50	185.00
84-02-358	Pedro with Jug L2141M	Lladro	Open	100.00	185.00
84-02-359	Sea Harvest L2142M	Lladro	Closed	535.00	700.00
84-02-360	Aztec Dancer L2143M	Lladro	Closed	462.50	650.00
84-02-361	Leticia L2144M	Lladro	Open	100.00	170.00
84-02-362	Gabriela L2145M	Lladro	Open	100.00	170.00
84-02-363	Desiree L2146M	Lladro	Open	100.00	170.00
84-02-364	Alida L2147M	Lladro	Open	100.00	170.00
84-02-365	Head of Congolese Woman L2148M	Lladro	Closed	55.00	300-500.
85-02-366	Young Madonna L2149M	Lladro	Closed	400.00	675.00
85-02-367	A Tribute to Peace w/base L2150M	Lladro	Open	470.00	850.00
85-02-368	A Bird on Hand L2151M	Lladro	Open	117.50	230.00
85-02-369	Chinese Girl L2152M	Lladro	Closed	90.00	200-250.
85-02-370	Chinese Boy L2153	Lladro	Closed	90.00	200-250.
85-02-371	Hawaiian Flower Vendor L2154M	Lladro	Open	245.00	420.00
85-02-372	Arctic inter L2156M	Lladro	Open	75.00	140.00
85-02-373	Eskimo Girl with Cold Feet L2157M	Lladro	Open	140.00	260.00
85-02-374	Pensive Eskimo Girl L2158M	Lladro	Open	100.00	190.00
85-02-375	Pensive Eskimo Boy L2159M	Lladro	Open	100.00	190.00
85-02-376	Flower Vendor L2160M	Lladro	Open	110.00	200.00
85-02-377	Fruit Vendor L2161M	Lladro	Open	120.00	230.00
85-02-378	Fish Vendor L2162M	Lladro	Open	110.00	205.00
87-02-379	Mountain Shepherd L2163M	Lladro	Open	120.00	190.00
87-02-380	My Lost Lamb L2164M	Lladro	Open	100.00	165.00
87-02-381	Chiquita L2165M	Lladro	Open	100.00	170.00
87-02-382	Paco L2166M	Lladro	Open	100.00	170.00
87-02-383	Fernando L2167M	Lladro	Open	100.00	170.00
87-02-384	Julio L2168M	Lladro	Open	100.00	170.00
87-02-385	Repose L2169M	Lladro	Open	120.00	175.00
87-02-386	Spanish Dancer L2170M	Lladro	Open	190.00	315.00
87-02-387	Ahoy Tere L2173M	Lladro	Open	190.00	295.00
88-02-388	Harvest Helpers L2178M	Lladro	Open	190.00	250.00
88-02-389	Sharing the Harvest L2179M	Lladro	Open	190.00	250.00
88-02-390	Dreams of Peace w/base L2180M	Lladro	Open	880.00	1025.00
88-02-391	Bathing Nymph w/base L2181M	Lladro	Open	560.00	760.00
88-02-392	Daydreamer w/base L2182M	Lladro	Open	560.00	760.00
89-02-393	Wakeup Kitty L2183M	Lladro	Open	225.00	270.00
89-02-394	Angel and Friend L2184M	Lladro	Open	150.00	185.00
89-02-395	Devoted Reader L2185M	Lladro	Open	125.00	160.00
89-02-396	The Greatest Love L2186M	Lladro	Open	235.00	290.00
89-02-397	Jealous Friend L2187M	Lladro	Open	275.00	340.00

Company Number	Series Name	Artist	Edition Limit	Issue Price	Quote
90-02-398	Mother's Pride L2189M	Lladro	Open	300.00	350.00
80-02-399	To The Well L2190M	Lladro	Open	250.00	295.00
90-02-400	Forest Born L2191M	Lladro	Closed	230.00	400.00
80-02-401	King Of The Forest L2192M	Lladro	Closed	290.00	310.00
80-02-402	Heavenl Strings L2194M	Lladro	Open	170.00	195.00
90-02-403	Heavenly Sounds L2195M	Lladro	Open	170.00	195.00
90-02-404	Heavenly Solo L2196M	Lladro	Open	170.00	195.00
90-02-405	Heavenly Song L2197M	Lladro	Open	175.00	185.00
90-02-406	A King is Born w/base L2198M	Lladro	Open	750.00	880.00
90-02-407	Devoted Friends w/base L2199M	Lladro	Open	700.00	825.00
90-02-408	A Big Hug! L2200M	Lladro	Open	250.00	295.00
90-02-409	Our Daily Bread L2201M	Lladro	Open	150.00	185.00
90-02-410	A Helping Hand L2202M	Lladro	Open	150.00	185.00
90-02-411	Afternoon Chores L2203M	Lladro	Open	150.00	185.00
90-02-412	Farmyard Grace L2204M	Lladro	Open	180.00	210.00
90-02-413	Prayerful Stitch L2200M	Lladro	Open	160.00	190.00
90-02-414	Sisterly Love L2206M	Lladro	Open	300.00	350.00
90-02-415	What A Day! L2207M	Lladro	Open	550.00	630.00
90-02-416	Let's Rest L2208M	Lladro	Open	550.00	630.00
91-02-417	Long Dy L2209M	Lladro	Open	295.00	315.00
91-02-418	Lazy Day L2210M	Lladro	Open	240.00	260.00
91-02-419	Patrol Leader L2212M	Lladro	Open	390.00	420.00
91-02-420	Nature's Friend L2213M	Lladro	Open	390.00	420.00
91-02-421	Seaside Angel L2214M	Lladro	Open	150.00	165.00
91-02-422	Friends in Flight L2215M	Lladro	Open	165.00	180.00
91-02-423	Laundry Day L2216M	Lladro	Open	350.00	385.00
91-02-424	Gentle Play L2217M	Lladro	Open	380.00	415.00
91-02-425	Costumed Couple L2218M	Lladro	Open	680.00	750.00
92-02-426	Underfoot L2219M	Lladro	Open	360.00	375.00
92-02-427	Free Spirit L2220M	Lladro	Open	235.00	245.00
92-02-428	Spring Beauty L2221M	Lladro	Open	285.00	295.00
92-02-429	Tender Moment L2222M	Lladro	Open	400.00	420.00
92-02-430	New Lamb L2223M	Lladro	Open	365.00	385.00
92-02-431	Cherish L2224M	Lladro	Open	1750.00	1850.00
92-02-432	FriendlySparrow L2225M	Lladro	Open	295.00	310.00
92-02-433	Boy's Best Friend L2226M	Lladro	Open	390.00	410.00
92-02-434	Artic Allies L2227M	Lladro	Open	585.00	615.00
92-02-435	Snowy Sunday L2228M	Lladro	Open	550.00	575.00
92-02-436	Seasonal Gifts L2229M	Lladro	Open	450.00	475.00
92-02-437	Mary's Child L2230M	Lladro	Open	525.00	550.00
92-02-438	Afternoon Verse L2231M	Lladro	Open	580.00	595.00
92-02-439	Poor Little Bear L2232M	Lladro	Open	250.00	265.00
92-02-450	Guess What I Have L2233M	Lladro	Open	340.00	360.00
92-02-451	Playful Push L2234M	Lladro	Open	850.00	875.00
93-02-452	Adoring Mother L2235M	Lladro	Open	405.00	405.00
93-02-453	Frosty Outing L2236M	Lladro	Open	375.00	375.00
93-02-454	The Old Fishing Hole L2237M	Lladro	Open	625.00	625.00
93-02-455	Learning Together L2238M	Lladro	Open	500.00	500.00
93-02-456	Valencian Courtship L2239M	Lladro	Open	880.00	880.00
93-02-457	WingedLove L2240M	Lladro	Open	285.00	285.00
93-02-458	Winged Harmony L2241M	Lladro	Open	285.00	285.00
93-02-459	Away to School L2242M	Lladro	Open	465.00	465.00
93-02-460	Lion Tamer L2246M	Lladro	Open	375.00	375.00
93-02-461	Just Us L2247M	Lladro	Open	650.00	650.00
93-02-462	Noella L2251M	Lladro	Open	405.00	405.00
93-02-463	Waiting For Father L2252M	Lladro	Open	660.00	660.00
93-02-464	Noisy Friend L2253M	Lladro	Open	280.00	280.00
93-02-465	Step Aside L2254M	Lladro	Open	280.00	280.00
78-02-466	Native L3502M	Lladro	Open	700.00	2450.00
78-02-467	Letters to Dulcinea L3509M, numbered series	Lladro	Open	875.00	2050.00
78-02-468	Horse Heads L3511M	Lladro	Closed	260.00	700.00
78-02-469	Girl With Pails L3512M	Lladro	Open	140.00	285.00
78-02-470	A Wintry Day L3513M	Lladro	Closed	525.00	750.00
78-02-471	Pensive w/ base L3514M	Lladro	Open	500.00	1050.00
78-02-472	Jesus Christ L3516M	Lladro	Closed	1050.00	1450.00
78-02-473	Nude with Rose w/ base L3517M	Lladro	Open	225.00	760.00
80-02-474	Lady Macbeth L3518M	Lladro	Closed	385.00	425-1000.
80-02-475	Mother's Love L3521M	Lladro	Closed	1000.00	1100.00
81-02-476	Weary w/ base L3525M	Lladro	Open	360.00	625.00
82-02-477	Contemplation w/ base L3526M	Lladro	Open	265.00	540.00
82-02-478	Stormy Sea w/base L3554M	Lladro	Open	675.00	1325.00
84-02-479	Innocence w/base/green L3558M	Lladro	Closed	960.00	1650.00
84-02-480	Innocence w/base/red L3558.3M	Lladro	Closed	960.00	1200.00
85-02-481	Peace Offering w/base L3559M	Lladro	Open	397.00	665.00
69-02-482	Marketing Day L4502G	Lladro	Closed	40.00	300.00
69-02-483	Girl with Lamb L4505G	Lladro	Open	20.00	110.00
69-02-484	Boy with Kid L4506M	Lladro	Closed	22.50	400.00
69-02-485	Girl with Parasol and Geese L4510G	Lladro	Open	40.00	245.00
69-02-486	Nude L4511M	Lladro	Closed	45.00	900.00
69-02-487	Man on Horse L4515G	Lladro	Closed	180.00	N/A
69-02-488	Female Equestrian L4516G	Lladro	Open	170.00	695.00
69-02-489	Flamenco Dancers L4519G	Lladro	Open	150.00	1100.00
70-02-490	Boy With Dog L4522M	Lladro	Closed	25.00	155.00
69-02-491	Girl With Slippers L4523G	Lladro	Open	17.00	100.00
69-02-492	Girl With Slippers L4523M	Lladro	Open	17.00	100.00
69-02-493	Donkey in Love L4524G	Lladro	Closed	15.00	450.00
69-02-494	Donkey in Love L4524M	Lladro	Closed	15.00	350.00
69-02-495	Joseph L4533G	Lladro	Open	60.00	100.00
69-02-496	Joseph L4533M	Lladro	Open	60.00	100.00
69-02-497	Mary L4534G	Lladro	Open	60.00	85.00
69-02-498	Mary L4534M	Lladro	Open	60.00	85.00
71-02-499	Baby Jesus L4535.3G	Lladro	Open	60.00	70.00
69-02-500	Baby Jesus L4535.3M	Lladro	Open	60.00	70.00
69-02-501	Angel, Chinese L4536G	Lladro	Open	45.00	90.00
69-02-502	Angel, Chinese L4536M	Lladro	Open	45.00	90.00
69-02-503	Angel, Black L4537G	Lladro	Open	13.00	90.00
69-02-504	Angel, Black L4537M	Lladro	Open	13.00	90.00
69-02-505	Angel, Praying L4538G	Lladro	Open	13.00	90.00
69-02-506	Angel, Praying L4538M	Lladro	Open	13.00	90.00
69-02-507	Angel, Thinking L4539G	Lladro	Open	13.00	90.00
69-02-508	Angel, Thinking L4539M	Lladro	Open	13.00	90.00
69-02-509	Angel with Horn L4540G	Lladro	Open	13.00	90.00
69-02-510	Angel with Horn L4540M	Lladro	Open	13.00	90.00
69-02-511	Angel Reclining L4541G	Lladro	Open	13.00	90.00
69-02-512	Angel Reclining L4541M	Lladro	Open	13.00	90.00
69-02-513	Group of Angels L4542G	Lladro	Open	31.00	185.00
69-02-514	Group of Angels L4542M	Lladro	Open	31.00	185.00
69-02-515	Geese Group L4549G	Lladro	Open	28.50	210.00
69-02-516	Geese Group L4549M	Lladro	Closed	28.50	200.00
69-02-517	Flying Dove L4550G	Lladro	Open	47.50	245.00
69-02-518	Flying Dove L4550M	Lladro	Closed	47.50	225.00
69-02-519	Ducks,set of 3 asst. L4551-3G	Lladro	Open	18.00	140.00
69-02-520	Shepherd L4554	Lladro	Closed	69.00	N/A
69-02-521	Sad Harlequin L4558G	Lladro	Open	110.00	550.00
69-02-522	Waiting Backstage L4559G	Lladro	Open	110.00	440.00
69-02-523	Couple with Parasol L4563G	Lladro	Closed	180.00	625.00
69-02-524	Girl with Geese L4568G	Lladro	Open	45.00	220.00
69-02-525	Girl With Turkey L4569G	Lladro	Closed	28.50	375.00
69-02-526	Girl with Piglets L4572G	Lladro	Closed	70.00	400.00
69-02-527	Girl with Piglets L4572M	Lladro	Closed	70.00	400.00
69-02-528	Mother & Child L4575G	Lladro	Open	50.00	265.00
69-02-529	New Shepherdess L4576G	Lladro	Closed	37.50	300.00
69-02-530	Girl with Sheep L4584G	Lladro	Open	27.00	170.00
69-02-531	Holy Family L4585G	Lladro	Open	18.00	135.00
69-02-532	Holy Family L4585M	Lladro	Closed	18.00	125.00
69-02-533	Madonna L4586G	Lladro	Closed	32.50	350.00
69-02-534	White Cockeral L4588G	Lladro	Closed	17.50	200.00
69-02-535	Shepherdess with Basket L4591G	Lladro	Open	20.00	140.00
69-02-536	Fairy L4595G	Lladro	Open	27.50	140.00
69-02-537	Playfull Horses L4597	Lladro	Closed	240.00	925-1000.
69-02-538	Doctor L4602.3G	Lladro	Open	33.00	185.00
69-02-539	Nurse-L4603.3G	Lladro	Open	35.00	190.00
69-02-549	Clown with Girl L4605	Lladro	Closed	160.00	1050-1200.
69-02-541	Accordian Player L4606	Lladro	Closed	60.00	550-775.
69-02-542	Cupid L4607	Lladro	Closed	15.00	N/A
69-02-543	Cook in Trouble L4608	Lladro	Closed	27.50	500-650.
69-02-544	Nuns L4611G	Lladro	Open	37.50	155.00
69-02-545	Nuns L4611M	Lladro	Open	37.50	155.00
69-02-546	Girl Singer L4612G	Lladro	Closed	14.00	450.00
69-02-547	Boy With Cymbals L4613G	Lladro	Closed	14.00	400.00
69-02-548	Boy With Drum L4616G	Lladro	Closed	16.50	400.00
69-02-549	Clown L4618G	Lladro	Open	70.00	415.00
69-02-550	Sea Captain L4621G	Lladro	Open	45.00	265.00
69-02-551	Angel with Child L4635G	Lladro	Open	15.00	95.00
69-02-552	Honey Peddler L4638G	Lladro	Closed	60.00	575.00
69-02-553	Cow With Pig L4640	Lladro	Closed	42.50	540.00
69-02-554	Pekinese L4641G	Lladro	Closed	20.00	575.00
69-02-555	Skye Terrier L4643	Lladro	Closed	15.00	375-650.
69-02-556	Andalucians Group L4647G	Lladro	Closed	412.00	1400.00
69-02-557	Valencian Couple on Horseback L4648	Lladro	Closed	900.00	1200.00
69-02-558	Madonna Head L4649G	Lladro	Open	25.00	145.00
69-02-559	Madonna Head L4649M	Lladro	Open	25.00	145.00
69-02-560	Girl with Calla Lillies L4650G	Lladro	Open	18.00	135.00
69-02-561	Cellist L4651G	Lladro	Closed	70.00	800.00
69-02-562	Happy Travelers L4652	Lladro	Closed	115.00	650.00
69-02-563	Orchestra Conductor L4653G	Lladro	Closed	95.00	850.00
69-02-564	Horses L4655G	Lladro	Open	110.00	760.00
69-02-565	Shepherdess L4660G	Lladro	Open	21.00	175.00
69-02-566	Maja Head L4668G	Lladro	Closed	50.00	550.00
69-02-567	Baby Jesus L4670BG	Lladro	Open	18.00	50.00
69-02-568	Mary L4671G	Lladro	Open	33.00	75.00
69-02-569	St. Joseph L4672G	Lladro	Open	33.00	90.00
69-02-570	King Melchior L4673G	Lladro	Open	35.00	95.00
69-02-571	King Gaspar L4674G	Lladro	Open	35.00	95.00
69-02-572	King Balthasar L4675G	Lladro	Open	35.00	95.00
69-02-573	Shepherd with Lamb L4676G	Lladro	Open	14.00	95.00
69-02-574	Girl with Rooster L4677G	Lladro	Open	14.00	90.00
69-02-575	Girl with Basket L4678G	Lladro	Open	13.00	90.00
69-02-576	Donkey L4679G	Lladro	Open	36.50	100.00
69-02-577	Cow L4680G	Lladro	Open	36.50	90.00
70-02-578	Girl with Milkpail L4682	Lladro	Closed	28.00	350.00
70-02-579	Hebrew Student L4684G	Lladro	Closed	33.00	575-700.
70-02-580	Dressmaker L4700G	Lladro	Open	45.00	360.00
70-02-581	Mother & Child L4701G	Lladro	Open	45.00	295.00
70-02-582	Bird Watcher L4730	Lladro	Closed	35.00	375.00
71-02-583	Romeo and Juliet L4750G	Lladro	Open	150.00	1250.00
71-02-584	Doncel With Roses L4757G	Lladro	Closed	35.00	500.00
74-02-585	Lady with Dog L4761G	Lladro	Open	60.00	260.00
71-02-586	Dentist L4762	Lladro	Closed	36.00	500.00
71-02-587	Dentist (Reduced) L4762. 3G	Lladro	Closed	30.00	500-600.
71-02-588	Obstetrician L4763.3G	Lladro	Open	40.00	235.00
71-02-589	Rabbit L4772G	Lladro	Open	17.50	135.00
71-02-590	Rabbit L4773G	Lladro	Open	17.50	130.00
71-02-591	Children, Praying L4779G	Lladro	Open	36.00	180.00
71-02-592	Children, Praying L4779M	Lladro	Closed	36.00	N/A
71-02-593	Boy with Goat L4780	Lladro	Closed	80.00	475.00
72-02-594	Gypsy with Brother L4800G	Lladro	Closed	36.00	350-400.
72-02-595	Girl with Dog L4806G	Lladro	Closed	80.00	N/A
72-02-596	Geisha L4807G	Lladro	Open	190.00	440.00
72-02-597	Wedding L4808G	Lladro	Open	50.00	175.00
72-02-598	Wedding L4808M	Lladro	Open	50.00	175.00
72-02-599	Going Fishing L4809G	Lladro	Open	33.00	160.00
72-02-600	Young Sailor L4810G	Lladro	Open	33.00	165.00
72-02-601	Boy with Pails L4811	Lladro	Closed	30.00	350-425.
72-02-602	Getting Her Goat L4812G	Lladro	Closed	55.00	450.00
72-02-603	Girl with Geese L4815G	Lladro	Closed	72.00	275-295.
72-02-604	Girl with Geese L4815M	Lladro	Closed	72.00	295.00
74-02-605	Pery Girl with Baby L4822	Lladro	Closed	65.00	775.00
74-02-606	Legionary L4823	Lladro	Closed	55.00	N/A
72-02-607	Male Golfer L4824G	Lladro	Open	66.00	285.00
72-02-608	Veterinarian L4825	Lladro	Closed	48.00	400-500.
72-02-609	Girl Feeding Rabbit L4826G	Lladro	Open	40.00	185.00
72-02-610	Caressing Calf L4827G	Lladro	Closed	55.00	475.00
72-02-611	Cinderella L4828G	Lladro	Open	47.00	225.00
75-02-612	Swan L4829G	Lladro	Closed	16.00	275-500.
73-02-613	Clean Up Time L4838G	Lladro	Open	36.00	170.00
73-02-614	Clean Up Time L4838M	Lladro	Closed	36.00	155.00
72-02-615	Shepherdess L4835G	Lladro	Closed	42.00	225.00
73-02-616	Oriental Flower Arranger/Girl L4840G	Lladro	Open	90.00	490.00
73-02-617	Oriental Flower Arranger/Girl L4840M	Lladro	Open	90.00	490.00
74-02-618	Girl from Valencia L4841G	Lladro	Open	35.00	205.00
73-02-619	Pharmacist L4844	Lladro	Closed	70.00	1500.00
73-02-620	Classic Dance L4847G	Lladro	Closed	80.00	600.00
73-02-621	Feeding The Ducks L4849G	Lladro	Open	60.00	250.00
73-02-622	Feeding The Ducks L4849M	Lladro	Closed	60.00	230.00
73-02-623	Aesthetic Pose L4850G	Lladro	Closed	110.00	650.00
73-02-624	Lady Golfer L4851M	Lladro	Closed	70.00	235.00
73-02-625	Gardner in Trouble L4852	Lladro	Closed	65.00	500.00
74-02-626	Cobbler L4853G	Lladro	Closed	100.00	500-650.
73-02-627	Don Quixote L4854G	Lladro	Open	40.00	205.00
73-02-628	Ballerina L4855G	Lladro	Open	45.00	330.00
83-02-629	Ballerina, white L4855.3	Lladro	Closed	110.00	250.00
74-02-630	Dog L4857G	Lladro	Closed	40.00	N/A
74-02-631	Peddler L4859G	Lladro	Closed	180.00	750-1000.
74-02-632	Embroiderer L4865G	Lladro	Open	115.00	645.00
74-02-633	Girl with Swan and Dog L4866G	Lladro	Open	26.00	205.00
74-02-634	Seesaw L4867G	Lladro	Open	55.00	350.00
74-02-635	Girl with Candle L4868G	Lladro	Open	13.00	90.00

Company Number	Name	Series Artist	Edition Limit	Issue Price	Quote
74-02-636	Girl with Candle L4868M	Lladro	Closed	13.00	80.00
74-02-637	Boy Kissing L4869G	Lladro	Open	13.00	90.00
74-02-638	Boy Kissing L4869M	Lladro	Closed	13.00	175.00
74-02-639	Boy Yawning L4870G	Lladro	Open	13.00	90.00
74-02-640	Boy Yawning L4870M	Lladro	Closed	13.00	175.00
74-02-641	Girl with Guitar L4871G	Lladro	Open	13.00	90.00
74-02-642	Girl with Guitar L4871M	Lladro	Closed	13.00	80.00
74-02-643	Girl Stretching L4872G	Lladro	Open	13.00	90.00
74-02-644	Girl Stretching L4872M	Lladro	Closed	13.00	80.00
74-02-645	Girl Kissing L4873G	Lladro	Open	13.00	90.00
74-02-646	Girl Kissing L4873M	Lladro	Closed	13.00	80.00
74-02-647	Boy & Girl L4874G	Lladro	Open	25.00	150.00
74-02-648	Boy & Girl L4874M	Lladro	Closed	25.00	135.00
74-02-649	Girl with Jugs L4875	Lladro	Closed	40.00	N/A
74-02-650	Boy Thinking L4876G	Lladro	Open	20.00	135.00
74-02-651	Boy Thinking L4876M	Lladro	Closed	20.00	120.00
74-02-652	Lady with Parasol L4879G	Lladro	Open	48.00	300.00
74-02-653	Carnival Couple L4882G	Lladro	Open	60.00	300.00
74-02-654	The Kiss L4888G	Lladro	Closed	150.00	700.00
79-02-655	Spanish Policeman L4889	Lladro	Closed	55.00	360.00
76-02-656	"My Dog" L4893G	Lladro	Open	85.00	210.00
74-02-657	Ducks L4895G	Lladro	Open	45.00	90.00
74-02-658	Ducks L4895M	Lladro	Closed	45.00	85.00
74-02-659	Boy with Snails L4896G	Lladro	Closed	50.00	400.00
74-02-660	Boy From Madrid L4898G	Lladro	Open	55.00	145.00
74-02-661	Boy From Madrid L4898M	Lladro	Closed	55.00	130.00
75-02-662	Boy with Smoking Jacket L4900	Lladro	Closed	45.00	N/A
74-02-663	Barrister L4908G	Lladro	Closed	100.00	425.00
74-02-664	Girl With Dove L4909G	Lladro	Closed	70.00	450.00
74-02-665	Young Lady in Trouble L4912G	Lladro	Closed	110.00	450.00
75-02-666	Lady with Shawl L4914G	Lladro	Open	220.00	685.00
75-02-667	Girl with Pigeons L4915	Lladro	Closed	110.00	215.00
76-02-668	Chinese Noblewoman L4916G	Lladro	Closed	300.00	2000.00
76-02-669	Gypsy Woman L4919G	Lladro	Closed	165.00	975-1200.
74-02-670	Country Lass with Dog L4920G	Lladro	Open	185.00	495.00
74-02-671	Country Lass with Dog L4920M	Lladro	Closed	185.00	450.00
74-02-672	Windblown Girl L4922G	Lladro	Open	150.00	375.00
74-02-673	Lanquid Clown L4924G	Lladro	Closed	200.00	675.00
74-02-674	Sisters L4930	Lladro	Closed	250.00	625.00
74-02-675	Children with Fruits L4931G	Lladro	Closed	210.00	400.00
74-02-676	Dainty Lady L4934G	Lladro	Closed	60.00	350.00
74-02-677	"Closing Scene" L4935G	Lladro	Open	180.00	520.00
83-02-678	"Closing Scene"/white L4935.3M	Lladro	Closed	212.50	265.00
74-02-679	Spring Breeze L4936G	Lladro	Open	145.00	410.00
76-02-680	Baby's Outing L4938G	Lladro	Open	250.00	725.00
77-02-681	Missy L4951M	Lladro	Closed	300.00	600-850.
77-02-682	Meditation L4952M	Lladro	Closed	200.00	N/A
77-02-683	Tavern Drinkers L4956G	Lladro	Closed	1125.00	2800-3500.
77-02-684	Attentive Dogs L4957G	Lladro	Closed	350.00	N/A
77-02-685	Cherub, Puzzled L4959G	Lladro	Open	40.00	98.00
77-02-686	Cherub, Smiling L4960G	Lladro	Open	40.00	98.00
77-02-687	Cherub, Dreaming L4961G	Lladro	Open	40.00	98.00
77-02-688	Cherub, Wondering L4962G	Lladro	Open	40.00	98.00
77-02-689	Cherub, Wondering L4962M	Lladro	Closed	40.00	98.00
77-02-690	Infantile Candour L4963G	Lladro	Closed	285.00	675.00
77-02-691	Little Red Riding Hood L4965G	Lladro	Closed	210.00	600-825.
77-02-692	Tennis Player Puppet L4966G	Lladro	Closed	60.00	500-900.
77-02-693	Soccer Puppet L4967G	Lladro	Closed	65.00	500.00
77-02-694	Cowboy & Sherriff Puppet L4969G	Lladro	Closed	85.00	800.00
77-02-695	Skier Puppet L4970G	Lladro	Closed	85.00	500-900.
77-02-696	Hunter Puppet L4971G	Lladro	Closed	95.00	550-900.
77-02-697	Girl with Calla Lillies sitting L4972G	Lladro	Open	65.00	170.00
77-02-698	Choir Lesson L4973G	Lladro	Closed	350.00	1175.00.
77-02-699	Augustina of Aragon L4976G	Lladro	Closed	475.00	1500-1800.
77-02-700	Harlequin Serenade L4977	Lladro	Closed	185.00	675.00
78-02-701	Naughty Dog L4982G	Lladro	Open	130.00	250.00
78-02-702	Gossip L4984G	Lladro	Closed	260.00	750-900.
78-02-703	Oriental Spring L4988G	Lladro	Open	125.00	325.00
78-02-704	Sayonara L4989G	Lladro	Open	125.00	300.00
78-02-705	Chrysanthemum L4990G	Lladro	Open	125.00	310.00
78-02-706	Butterfly L4991G	Lladro	Open	125.00	295.00
78-02-707	Gypsy Venders L4993G	Lladro	Closed	165.00	475.00
78-02-708	Don Quixote & Sancho L4998G	Lladro	Closed	875.00	3300.00
78-02-709	Reading L5000G	Lladro	Open	150.00	255.00
78-02-710	Elk Family L5001G	Lladro	Closed	550.00	700-1500.
78-02-711	Sunny Day L5003	Lladro	Open	192.50	360.00
78-02-712	Naughty L5006G	Lladro	Open	55.00	140.00
78-02-713	Bashful L5007G	Lladro	Open	55.00	140.00
78-02-714	Static-Girl w/Straw Hat L5008G	Lladro	Open	55.00	140.00
78-02-715	Curious-Girl w/Straw Hat L5009G	Lladro	Open	55.00	140.00
78-02-716	Coiffure-Girl w/Straw Hat L5010G	Lladro	Open	55.00	140.00
78-02-717	Trying on a Straw Hat L5011G	Lladro	Open	55.00	140.00
78-02-718	Daughters L5013G	Lladro	Closed	425.00	900.00
78-02-719	Woman With Scarf L5024G	Lladro	Closed	140.90	450.00
79-02-720	Flower Curtsy L5027G	Lladro	Open	230.00	470.00
80-02-721	Boy with Tricycle & Flowers L5029G	Lladro	Closed	675.00	1250-1350.
80-02-722	Wildflower L5030G	Lladro	Open	360.00	695.00
79-02-723	Little Friskies L5032G	Lladro	Open	107.50	220.00
79-02-724	Avoiding the Goose L5033G	Lladro	Open	160.00	350.00
79-02-725	Goose Trying To Eat L5034G	Lladro	Open	135.00	290.00
80-02-726	Act II w/base L5035G	Lladro	Open	700.00	1425.00
79-02-727	Jockey with Lass L5036G	Lladro	Open	950.00	2050.00
80-02-728	Sleighride w/base L5037G	Lladro	Open	585.00	1045.00
80-02-729	Candid L5039G	Lladro	Closed	145.00	425-500.
79-02-730	Girl Walking L5040G	Lladro	Closed	150.00	425.00
80-02-731	Ladies Talking L5042G	Lladro	Closed	385.00	575-1000.
80-02-732	Hind and Baby Deer L5043G	Lladro	Closed	650.00	3600.00
80-02-733	Girl with Toy Wagon L5044G	Lladro	Open	115.00	220.00
80-02-734	Belinda with Doll L5045G	Lladro	Open	115.00	205.00
80-02-735	Organ Grinder L5046G	Lladro	Closed	327.50	1200.00
79-02-736	Dancer L5050G	Lladro	Open	85.00	190.00
80-02-737	Samson and Delilah L5051G	Lladro	Closed	350.00	1600.00
80-02-738	Clown and Girl/ At the Circus L5052G	Lladro	Closed	525.00	1200-1500.
80-02-739	Festival Time L5053G	Lladro	Closed	250.00	400.00
80-02-740	Little Senorita L5054G	Lladro	Closed	235.00	600.00
80-02-741	Ship-Boy with Baskets L5055G	Lladro	Closed	140.00	400.00
80-02-742	Clown with Clock L5056G	Lladro	Closed	290.00	750-950.
80-02-743	Clown with Violin and Top Hat L5057G	Lladro	Closed	270.00	690.00
80-02-744	Clown with Concertina L5058G	Lladro	Closed	290.00	690.00
80-02-745	Clown with Saxaphone L5059G	Lladro	Closed	320.00	690.00
80-02-746	Girl Clown with Trumpet L5060G	Lladro	Closed	290.00	800.00
80-02-747	Girl Bending/March Wind L5061G	Lladro	Closed	370.00	325-400.
80-02-748	Dutch Girl with Hands in Back L5062G	Lladro	Closed	225.00	400.00
80-02-749	Dutch Girl With Braids L5063G	Lladro	Closed	265.00	425-450.
80-02-750	Gretel L5064G	Lladro	Closed	255.00	650.00
80-02-751	Ingrid L5065G	Lladro	Closed	370.00	400.00
80-02-752	Ilsa L5066G	Lladro	Closed	275.00	300.00
81-02-753	Halloween L5067G	Lladro	Closed	450.00	1300.00
80-02-754	Fairy Queen L5068G	Lladro	Closed	625.00	1200.00
80-02-755	Choir Boy L5070G	Lladro	Closed	240.00	400-600.
80-02-756	Nostalgia L5071G	Lladro	Open	185.00	310.00
80-02-757	Courtship L5072	Lladro	Closed	327.00	525.00
80-02-758	My Hungry Brood L5074G	Lladro	Open	295.00	415.00
80-02-759	Harlequin L5076G	Lladro	Closed	185.00	400.00
80-02-760	Teasing the Dog L5078G	Lladro	Closed	300.00	750.00
80-02-761	Woman Painting Vase L5079G	Lladro	Closed	300.00	600-750.
80-02-762	Boy Pottery Seller L5080G	Lladro	Closed	320.00	650-700.
80-02-763	Girl Pottery Seller L5081G	Lladro	Closed	300.00	550-600.
80-02-764	Flower Vendor L5082G	Lladro	Closed	750.00	1700-2500.
80-02-765	A Good Book L5084G	Lladro	Closed	175.00	350-525.
80-02-766	Mother Amabilis L5086G	Lladro	Closed	275.00	425.00
80-02-767	Roses for My Mom L5088G	Lladro	Closed	645.00	1150.00
80-02-768	Scare-Dy Cat/Playful Cat L5091G	Lladro	Open	65.00	95.00
80-02-769	Ballet Bowing L5095G	Lladro	Closed	165.00	375.00
89-02-770	Her Ladyship, L5097G, numbered series	Lladro	Closed	5900.00	6700.00
82-02-771	Playful Tot L5099G	Lladro	Closed	58.00	N/A
82-02-772	Cry Baby L5100G	Lladro	Closed	58.00	N/A
82-02-773	Learning to Crawl L5101G	Lladro	Closed	58.00	275.00
82-02-774	Teething L5102G	Lladro	Closed	58.00	275.00
82-02-775	Time for a Nap L5103G	Lladro	Closed	58.00	275.00
82-02-776	Natalia L5106G	Lladro	Closed	85.00	350.00
82-02-777	Little Ballet Girl L5108G	Lladro	Closed	85.00	400.00
82-02-778	Little Ballet Girl L5109G	Lladro	Closed	85.00	400.00
82-02-779	Dog Sniffing L5110G	Lladro	Closed	50.00	500.00
82-02-780	Play with Me L5112G	Lladro	Open	40.00	80.00
82-02-781	Feed Me L5113G	Lladro	Open	40.00	80.00
82-02-782	Pet Me L5114G	Lladro	Open	40.00	80.00
82-02-783	Little Boy Bullfighter L5115G	Lladro	Closed	122.50	400.00
82-02-784	A Victory L5116G	Lladro	Closed	123.00	400-500.
82-02-785	Proud Matador L5117G	Lladro	Closed	123.00	425-500.
82-02-786	Girl in Green Dress L5118G	Lladro	Closed	170.00	475.00
82-02-787	Lilly (Bluish Dress w/ Flowers) L5119G	Lladro	Closed	170.00	540.00
82-02-788	August Moon L5122G	Lladro	Open	185.00	310.00
82-02-789	My Precious Bundle L5123G	Lladro	Open	150.00	230.00
82-02-790	Dutch Couple with Tulips L5124G	Lladro	Closed	310.00	900.00
82-02-791	Amparo L5125G	Lladro	Closed	130.00	330-350.
82-02-792	Sewing A Trousseau L5126G	Lladro	Closed	185.00	300.00
82-02-793	Marcelina L5127G	Lladro	Closed	255.00	N/A
82-02-794	Lost Love L5128G	Lladro	Closed	400.00	650-750.
82-02-795	Jester w/base L5129G	Lladro	Open	220.00	405.00
82-02-796	Pensive Clown w/base L5130G	Lladro	Open	250.00	415.00
82-02-797	Cervantes L5132G	Lladro	Closed	925.00	1175.00
82-02-798	Trophy with Base L5133G	Lladro	Closed	250.00	425-600.
82-02-799	Girl Soccer Player L5134G	Lladro	Closed	140.00	575-900.
82-02-800	Billy Football Player L5135G	Lladro	Closed	140.00	525-900.
82-02-801	Billy Skier L5136G	Lladro	Closed	140.00	750-900.
82-02-802	Billy Baseball Player L5137G	Lladro	Closed	140.00	800-900.
82-02-803	A New Doll House L5139G	Lladro	Closed	185.00	525.00
82-02-804	Feed Her Son L5140G	Lladro	Closed	170.00	280.00
82-02-805	Balloons for Sale L5141G	Lladro	Open	145.00	250.00
82-02-806	Comforting Daughter L5142G	Lladro	Closed	195.00	475.00
82-02-807	Scooting L5143G	Lladro	Closed	575.00	850-1000.
82-02-808	Amy L5145G	Lladro	Closed	110.00	1060-1500.
82-02-809	Ellen L5146G	Lladro	Closed	110.00	1200.00
82-02-810	Ivy L5147G	Lladro	Closed	100.00	600.00
82-02-811	Olivia L5148G	Lladro	Closed	100.00	450-500
82-02-812	Ursula L5149G	Lladro	Closed	100.00	400-500
82-02-813	Girl's Head L5151G	Lladro	Closed	380.00	575.00
82-02-814	Girl's Head L5153G	Lladro	Closed	475.00	575.00
82-02-815	First Prize L5154G	Lladro	Closed	90.00	N/A
82-02-816	Monks at Prayer L5155M	Lladro	Open	130.00	250.00
82-02-817	Susan and the Doves L5156G	Lladro	Closed	202.50	325-360.
82-02-818	Bongo Beat L5157G	Lladro	Open	135.00	230.00
82-02-819	A Step In Time L5158G	Lladro	Open	90.00	180.00
82-02-820	Harmony L5159G	Lladro	Open	270.00	495.00
82-02-821	Rhumba L5160G	Lladro	Open	112.50	185.00
82-02-822	Cycling To A Picnic L5161G	Lladro	Closed	2000.00	2800.00
82-02-823	Mouse Girl/Mindy L5162G	Lladro	Closed	125.00	400-450.
82-02-824	Bunny Girl/Bunny L5163G	Lladro	Closed	125.00	400-450.
82-02-825	Cat Girl/Kitty L5164G	Lladro	Closed	125.00	400-450.
82-02-826	A Toast by Sancho L5165	Lladro	Closed	100.00	300-475.
82-02-827	Sea Fever L5166M	Lladro	Closed	130.00	235.00
82-02-828	Jesus L5167G	Lladro	Open	130.00	265.00
82-02-829	King Solomon L5168G	Lladro	Closed	205.00	750-850.
82-02-830	Abraham L5169G	Lladro	Closed	155.00	600-900.
82-02-831	Moses L5170G	Lladro	Open	175.00	360.00
82-02-832	Madonna with Flowers L5171G	Lladro	Open	172.50	310.00
82-02-833	Fish A'Plenty L5172G	Lladro	Open	190.00	385.00
82-02-834	Pondering L5173G	Lladro	Closed	300.00	495.00
82-02-835	Roaring 20's L5174G	Lladro	Closed	172.50	295.00
82-02-836	Flapper L5175G	Lladro	Open	185.00	365.00
82-02-837	Rhapsody in Blue L5176G	Lladro	Closed	325.00	1250.00
82-02-838	Dante L5177G	Lladro	Closed	263.00	550-600.
82-02-840	Stubborn Mule L5178G	Lladro	Closed	250.00	420.00
83-02-841	Three Pink Roses w/base L5179M	Lladro	Closed	70.00	110.00
83-02-842	Dahlia L5180M	Lladro	Closed	65.00	140.00
83-02-843	Japanese Camelia w/base L5181M	Lladro	Closed	60.00	90.00
83-02-844	White Peony L5182M	Lladro	Closed	85.00	125.00
83-02-845	Two Yellow Roses L5183M	Lladro	Closed	57.50	85.00
83-02-846	White Carnation L5184M	Lladro	Closed	65.00	100.00
83-02-847	Lactiflora Peony L5185M	Lladro	Closed	65.00	100.00
83-02-848	Begonia L5186M	Lladro	Closed	67.50	100.00
83-02-849	Rhododendrom L5187M	Lladro	Closed	67.50	100.00
83-02-850	Miniature Begonia L5188M	Lladro	Closed	80.00	120.00
83-02-851	Chrysanthemum L5189M	Lladro	Closed	100.00	150.00
83-02-852	California Poppy L5190M	Lladro	Closed	97.50	180.00
85-02-853	Predicting the Future L5191G	Lladro	Closed	135.00	400.00
84-02-854	Lolita L5192G	Lladro	Open	80.00	155.00
84-02-855	Juanita L5193G	Lladro	Open	80.00	155.00
84-02-856	Roving Photographer L5194G	Lladro	Closed	145.00	750.00
83-02-857	Say "Cheese!" L5195G	Lladro	Closed	170.00	550.00
83-02-858	"Maestro, Music Please!" L5196G	Lladro	Closed	135.00	675.00
83-02-859	Female Physician L5197	Lladro	Open	120.00	240.00
84-02-860	Boy Graduate L5198G	Lladro	Open	160.00	275.00
84-02-861	Girl Graduate L5199G	Lladro	Open	160.00	260.00
83-02-862	Male Soccer Player L5200G	Lladro	Closed	155.00	475.00
84-02-863	Special Male Soccer Player L5200.3G	Lladro	Closed	150.00	450.00
83-02-864	Josefa Feeding Duck L5201G	Lladro	Closed	125.00	250.00

Company Number	Name	Series Artist	Edition Limit	Issue Price	Quote
83-02-865	Aracely with Ducks L5202G	Lladro	Closed	125.00	250-300.
84-02-866	Little Jester L5203G	Lladro	Closed	75.00	140.00
84-02-867	Little Jester L5203M	Lladro	Closed	75.00	125.00
83-02-868	Sharpening the Cutlery L5204	Lladro	Closed	210.00	700.00
83-02-869	Lamplighter L5205G	Lladro	Open	170.00	360.00
83-02-870	Yachtsman L5206G	Lladro	Open	110.00	210.00
83-02-871	A Tall Yarn L5207G	Lladro	Open	260.00	515.00
83-02-872	Professor L5208G	Lladro	Closed	205.00	450-750.
83-02-873	School Marm L5209G	Lladro	Closed	205.00	834.00
84-02-874	Jolie L5210G	Lladro	Open	105.00	195.00
84-02-875	Angela L5211G	Lladro	Open	105.00	195.00
84-02-876	Evita L5212G	Lladro	Open	105.00	195.00
83-02-877	Lawyer L5213G	Lladro	Open	250.00	520.00
83-02-878	Architect L5214G	Lladro	Closed	140.00	625.00
83-02-879	Fishing with Gramps w/base L5215G	Lladro	Open	410.00	775.00
83-02-880	On the Lake L5216G	Lladro	Closed	660.00	825.00
83-02-881	Spring L5217G	Lladro	Open	90.00	170.00
83-02-882	Spring L5217M	Lladro	Open	90.00	170.00
83-02-883	Autumn L5218G	Lladro	Open	90.00	170.00
83-02-884	Autumn L5218M	Lladro	Open	90.00	170.00
83-02-885	Summer L5219G	Lladro	Open	90.00	170.00
83-02-886	Summer L5219M	Lladro	Open	90.00	170.00
83-02-887	Winter L5220G	Lladro	Open	90.00	170.00
83-02-888	Winter L5220M	Lladro	Open	90.00	170.00
83-02-889	Sweet Scent L5221G	Lladro	Open	80.00	130.00
83-02-890	Sweet Scent L5221M	Lladro	Open	80.00	130.00
83-02-891	Pretty Pickings L5222G	Lladro	Open	80.00	130.00
83-02-892	Pretty Pickings L5222M	Lladro	Open	80.00	130.00
83-02-893	Spring is Here L5223G	Lladro	Open	80.00	130.00
83-02-894	Spring is Here L5223M	Lladro	Open	80.00	130.00
84-02-895	The Quest L5224G	Lladro	Open	125.00	275.00
84-02-896	Male Candleholder L5226	Lladro	Closed	660.00	660-1000.
84-02-897	Playful Piglets L5228G	Lladro	Open	80.00	135.00
83-02-898	Storytime L5229G	Lladro	Closed	245.00	850.00
84-02-899	Graceful Swan L5230G	Lladro	Open	35.00	80.00
84-02-900	Swan with Wings Spread L5231G	Lladro	Open	50.00	115.00
83-02-901	Playful Kittens L5232G	Lladro	Open	130.00	255.00
84-02-902	Charlie the Tramp L5233G	Lladro	Closed	150.00	850.00
84-02-903	Artistic Endeavor L5234G	Lladro	Closed	225.00	750.00
84-02-904	Ballet Trio L5235G	Lladro	Open	785.00	1525.00
84-02-905	Cat and Mouse L5236G	Lladro	Open	55.00	98.00
84-02-906	Cat and Mouse L5236M	Lladro	Closed	55.00	95.00
84-02-907	School Chums L5237G	Lladro	Open	225.00	440.00
84-02-908	Eskimo Boy with Pet L5238G	Lladro	Open	55.00	105.00
84-02-909	Eskimo Boy with Pet L5238M	Lladro	Closed	55.00	95.00
84-02-910	Wine Taster L5239G	Lladro	Open	190.00	360.00
84-02-911	Lady from Majorca L5240G	Lladro	Closed	120.00	400.00
84-02-912	Best Wishes L5244G	Lladro	Closed	185.00	275.00
84-02-913	St. Christopher L5246	Lladro	Closed	265.00	600.00
84-02-914	Penguin L5247G	Lladro	Closed	70.00	325.00
84-02-915	Exam Day L5250G	Lladro	Open	115.00	210.00
84-02-916	Torch Bearer L5251G	Lladro	Closed	100.00	550.00
84-02-917	Dancing the Polka L5252G	Lladro	Closed	205.00	385.00
84-02-918	Cadet L5253G	Lladro	Closed	150.00	350-400.
84-02-919	Making Paella L5254G	Lladro	Closed	215.00	400.00
84-02-920	Spanish Soldier L5255G	Lladro	Closed	185.00	400-650.
84-02-921	Folk Dancing L5256	Lladro	Closed	205.00	300.00
85-02-922	Bust of Lady from Elche L5269M	Lladro	Closed	432.00	750.00
85-02-923	Racing Motor Cyclist L5270G	Lladro	Closed	360.00	550-750.
85-02-924	Gazelle L5271G	Lladro	Closed	205.00	400.00
85-02-925	Biking in the Country L5272G	Lladro	Closed	295.00	775.00
85-02-926	Wedding Day L5274G	Lladro	Open	240.00	415.00
85-02-927	Weary Ballerina L5275G	Lladro	Open	175.00	295.00
85-02-928	Weary Ballerina L5275M	Lladro	Closed	175.00	275.00
85-02-929	Sailor Serenades His Girl L5276G	Lladro	Closed	315.00	475.00
85-02-930	Pierrot with Puppy L5277G	Lladro	Open	95.00	160.00
85-02-931	Pierrot with Puppy and Ball L5278G	Lladro	Open	95.00	160.00
85-02-932	Pierrot with Concertina L5279G	Lladro	Open	95.00	160.00
85-02-933	Hiker L5280G	Lladro	Closed	195.00	425.00
85-02-934	Nativity Scene "Haute Relief" L5281M	Lladro	Closed	210.00	450.00
85-02-935	Over the Threshold L5282G	Lladro	Open	150.00	270.00
85-02-936	Socialite of the Twenties L5283G	Lladro	Open	175.00	340.00
85-02-937	Glorious Spring L5284G	Lladro	Open	355.00	650.00
85-02-938	Summer on the Farm L5285G	Lladro	Open	235.00	440.00
85-02-939	Fall Clean-up L5286G	Lladro	Open	295.00	550.00
85-02-940	Winter Frost L5287G	Lladro	Open	270.00	520.00
85-02-941	Mallard Duck L5288G	Lladro	Open	310.00	520.00
85-02-942	Love in Bloom L5292G	Lladro	Open	225.00	425.00
85-02-943	Mother and Child and Lamb L5299G	Lladro	Closed	180.00	450.00
85-02-944	Medieval Courtship L5300G	Lladro	Closed	735.00	850.00
85-02-945	Waiting to Tee Off L5301G	Lladro	Open	145.00	285.00
85-02-946	Playing with Ducks at the Pond L5303	Lladro	Closed	425.00	700.00
85-02-947	Children at Play L5304	Lladro	Closed	220.00	450-550.
85-02-948	A Visit with Granny L5305G	Lladro	Closed	275.00	515.00
85-02-949	Young Street Musicians L5306	Lladro	Closed	300.00	950.00
85-02-950	Mini Kitten L5307G	Lladro	Closed	35.00	70.00
85-02-951	Mini Cat L5308G	Lladro	Closed	35.00	70.00
85-02-952	Mini Cocker Spaniel Pup L5309G	Lladro	Closed	35.00	70.00
85-02-953	Mini Cocker Spaniel L5310G	Lladro	Closed	35.00	70.00
85-02-954	Mini Puppies L5311G	Lladro	Closed	65.00	200.00
85-02-955	Mini Bison Resting L5312G	Lladro	Closed	50.00	162.50
85-02-956	Mini Bison Attacking L5313G	Lladro	Closed	57.50	162.50
85-02-957	Mini Seal Family L5318G	Lladro	Closed	77.50	275.00
85-02-958	Wistful Centaur Girl L5319	Lladro	Closed	157.00	340.00
85-02-959	Demure Centaur Girl L5320	Lladro	Closed	157.00	300.00
85-02-960	Parisian Lady L5321G	Lladro	Open	192.50	325.00
85-02-961	Viennese Lady L5322G	Lladro	Open	160.00	295.00
85-02-962	Milanese Lady L5323G	Lladro	Open	180.00	340.00
85-02-963	English Lady L5324G	Lladro	Open	225.00	410.00
85-02-964	Ice Cream Vendor L5325G	Lladro	Open	380.00	650.00
85-02-965	The Tailor L5326G	Lladro	Closed	335.00	850.00
85-02-966	Nippon Lady L5327G	Lladro	Open	325.00	545.00
85-02-967	Lady Equestrian L5328G	Lladro	Closed	160.00	550.00
85-02-968	Gentleman Equestrian L5329G	Lladro	Closed	160.00	525.00
85-02-969	Concert Violinist L5330G	Lladro	Closed	220.00	500.00
85-02-970	Aerobics Push-Up L5334G	Lladro	Closed	110.00	N/A
85-02-971	"La Giaconda" L5337G	Lladro	Closed	350.00	400.00
86-02-972	A Stitch in Time L5344G	Lladro	Open	425.00	745.00
86-02-973	A New Hat L5345G	Lladro	Closed	200.00	375.00
86-02-974	Nature Girl L5346G	Lladro	Closed	450.00	950-1350.
86-02-975	Bedtime L5347G	Lladro	Open	300.00	545.00
86-02-976	On Guard L5350G	Lladro	Closed	50.00	450.00
86-02-977	Woe is Me L5351G	Lladro	Closed	45.00	70.00
86-02-978	Hindu Children L5352G	Lladro	Open	250.00	410.00
86-02-979	Eskimo Riders L5353G	Lladro	Open	150.00	250.00
86-02-980	Eskimo Riders L5353M	Lladro	Open	150.00	250.00
86-02-981	A Ride in the Country L5354G	Lladro	Closed	225.00	415.00
86-02-982	Consideration L5355M	Lladro	Closed	100.00	225.00
86-02-983	Wolf Hound L5356G	Lladro	Closed	45.00	55.00
86-02-984	Oration L5357G	Lladro	Open	170.00	275.00
86-02-985	Little Sculptor L5358	Lladro	Closed	160.00	300.00
86-02-986	El Greco L5359G	Lladro	Closed	300.00	675.00
86-02-987	Sewing Circle L5360G	Lladro	Closed	600.00	1000.00
86-02-988	Try This One L5361G	Lladro	Open	225.00	385.00
86-02-989	Still Life L5363G	Lladro	Open	180.00	365.00
86-02-990	Litter of Fun L5364G	Lladro	Open	275.00	465.00
86-02-991	Sunday in the Park L5365G	Lladro	Open	375.00	625.00
86-02-992	Can Can L5370G	Lladro	Closed	700.00	1100-1400.
86-02-993	Family Roots L5371G	Lladro	Open	575.00	895.00
86-02-994	Lolita L5372G	Lladro	Closed	120.00	200.00
86-02-995	Carmencita L5373G	Lladro	Closed	120.00	200.00
86-02-996	Pepita L5374G	Lladro	Closed	120.00	200.00
86-02-997	Teresita L5375G	Lladro	Closed	120.00	200.00
86-02-998	This One's Mine L5376G	Lladro	Open	300.00	520.00
86-02-999	A Touch of Class L5377G	Lladro	Open	475.00	795.00
86-02-1000	Time for Reflection L5378G	Lladro	Open	425.00	745.00
86-02-1001	Children's Games L5379G	Lladro	Closed	325.00	475.00
86-02-1002	Sweet Harvest L5380G	Lladro	Closed	450.00	900.00
86-02-1003	Serenade L5381	Lladro	Closed	450.00	625.00
86-02-1004	Lovers Serenade L5382G	Lladro	Closed	350.00	850.00
86-02-1005	Petite Maiden L5383	Lladro	Closed	110.00	350.00
86-02-1006	Petite Pair L5384	Lladro	Closed	225.00	400.00
86-02-1007	Scarecrow & the Lady L5385G	Lladro	Open	350.00	625.00
86-02-1008	St. Vincent L5387	Lladro	Closed	190.00	350.00
86-02-1009	Sidewalk Serenade L5388G	Lladro	Closed	750.00	1100-1300.
86-02-1010	Deep in Thought L5389G	Lladro	Closed	170.00	300-350.
86-02-1011	Spanish Dancer L5390	Lladro	Closed	170.00	340.00
86-02-1012	A Time to Rest L5391G	Lladro	Closed	170.00	300-350.
86-02-1013	Balancing Act L5392G	Lladro	Closed	35.00	150.00
86-02-1014	Curiosity L5393G	Lladro	Closed	25.00	40.00
86-02-1015	Poor Puppy L5394G	Lladro	Closed	25.00	40.00
86-02-1016	Valencian Boy L5395G	Lladro	Closed	200.00	325.00
86-02-1017	The Puppet Painter L5396G	Lladro	Open	500.00	850.00
86-02-1020	The Poet L5397G	Lladro	Closed	425.00	550.00
86-02-1021	At the Ball L5398G	Lladro	Closed	375.00	700.00
87-02-1022	Time To Rest L5399G	Lladro	Closed	175.00	295.00
87-02-1023	The Wanderer L5400G	Lladro	Open	150.00	245.00
87-02-1024	My Best Friend L5401G	Lladro	Open	150.00	240.00
87-02-1025	Desert Tour L5402G	Lladro	Closed	950.00	1050.00
87-02-1026	The Drummer Boy L5403G	Lladro	Closed	225.00	320-550.
87-02-1027	Cadet Captain L5404G	Lladro	Closed	175.00	325-360.
87-02-1028	The Flag Bearer L5405G	Lladro	Closed	200.00	450.00
87-02-1029	The Bugler L5406G	Lladro	Closed	175.00	300-400.
87-02-1030	At Attention L5407G	Lladro	Closed	175.00	325.00
87-02-1031	Sunday Stroll L5408G	Lladro	Closed	250.00	600.00
87-02-1032	Courting Time L5409	Lladro	Closed	425.00	550.00
87-02-1033	Pilar L5410G	Lladro	Closed	200.00	375.00
87-02-1034	Teresa L5411G	Lladro	Closed	225.00	430.00
87-02-1035	Isabel L5412G	Lladro	Closed	225.00	350-500.
87-02-1036	Mexican Dancers L5415G	Lladro	Open	800.00	1150.00
87-02-1037	In the Garden L5416G	Lladro	Open	200.00	325.00
87-02-1038	Artist's Model L5417	Lladro	Closed	425.00	475.00
87-02-1039	Short Eared Owl L5418G	Lladro	Closed	200.00	360.00
87-02-1040	Great Gray Owl L5419G	Lladro	Closed	190.00	195-225.
87-02-1041	Horned Owl L5420G	Lladro	Closed	150.00	300.00
87-02-1042	Barn Owl L5421G	Lladro	Closed	120.00	275.00
87-02-1043	Hawk Owl L5422G	Lladro	Closed	120.00	145.00
87-02-1044	Intermezzo L5424	Lladro	Closed	325.00	500.00
87-02-1045	Studying in the Park L5425G	Lladro	Closed	675.00	950.00
87-02-1046	Studying in the Park L5425M	Lladro	Closed	675.00	950.00
87-02-1047	One, Two, Three L5426G	Lladro	Open	240.00	365.00
87-02-1048	Saint Nicholas L5427G	Lladro	Closed	425.00	600.00
87-02-1049	Feeding the Pigeons L5428	Lladro	Closed	490.00	700.00
87-02-1050	Happy Birthday L5429G	Lladro	Open	100.00	155.00
87-02-1051	Music Time L5430G	Lladro	Closed	500.00	610.00
87-02-1052	Midwife L5431	Lladro	Closed	175.00	380.00
87-02-1053	Monkey L5432G	Lladro	Closed	60.00	100-150.
87-02-1054	Kangaroo L5433G	Lladro	Closed	65.00	150.00
87-02-1055	Miniature Polar Bear L5434G	Lladro	Open	65.00	100.00
87-02-1056	Cougar L5435G	Lladro	Closed	65.00	450.00
87-02-1057	Lion L5436G	Lladro	Closed	50.00	150.00
87-02-1058	Rhino L5437G	Lladro	Closed	50.00	150.00
87-02-1059	Elephant L5438G	Lladro	Closed	50.00	100-150.
87-02-1060	The Bride L5439G	Lladro	Open	250.00	385.00
87-02-1061	Poetry of Love L5442G	Lladro	Open	500.00	825.00
87-02-1062	Sleepy Trio L5443G	Lladro	Open	190.00	305.00
87-02-1063	Will You Marry Me? L5447G	Lladro	Open	750.00	1250.00
87-02-1064	Naptime L5448G	Lladro	Open	135.00	225.00
87-02-1065	Naptime L5448M	Lladro	Open	135.00	225.00
87-02-1066	Goodnight L5449	Lladro	Open	225.00	350.00
87-02-1067	I Hope She Does L5450G	Lladro	Open	190.00	315.00
88-02-1068	Study Buddies L5451G	Lladro	Open	225.00	295.00
88-02-1069	Masquerade Ball L5452G	Lladro	Closed	220.00	290.00
88-02-1070	Masquerade Ball L5452M	Lladro	Closed	220.00	265.00
88-02-1071	For You L5453G	Lladro	Open	450.00	595.00
88-02-1072	For Me? L5454G	Lladro	Open	290.00	380.00
88-02-1073	Bashful Bather L5455G	Lladro	Open	150.00	190.00
88-02-1074	Bashful Bather L5455M	Lladro	Closed	150.00	180.00
88-02-1075	New Playmates L5456G	Lladro	Open	160.00	210.00
88-02-1076	New Playmates L5456M	Lladro	Closed	160.00	190.00
88-02-1077	Bedtime Story L5457G	Lladro	Open	275.00	355.00
88-02-1078	Bedtime Story L5457M	Lladro	Closed	275.00	330.00
88-02-1079	A Barrow of Fun L5460G	Lladro	Open	370.00	485.00
88-02-1080	A Barrow of Fun L5460M	Lladro	Closed	370.00	450.00
88-02-1081	Koala Love L5461G	Lladro	Closed	115.00	150.00
88-02-1082	Practice Makes Perfect L5462G	Lladro	Open	375.00	495.00
88-02-1083	Look At Me! L5465G	Lladro	Open	375.00	475.00
88-02-1084	Look At Me! L5465M	Lladro	Closed	375.00	435.00
88-02-1085	Chit-Chat L5466G	Lladro	Open	150.00	190.00
88-02-1086	Chit-Chat L5466M	Lladro	Closed	150.00	180.00
88-02-1087	May Flowers L5467G	Lladro	Open	160.00	195.00
88-02-1088	May Flowers L5467M	Lladro	Closed	160.00	190.00
88-02-1089	Who's The Fairest? L5468G	Lladro	Open	150.00	195.00
88-02-1090	Who's The Fairest? L5468M	Lladro	Closed	150.00	180.00
88-02-1091	Lambkins L5469G	Lladro	Closed	150.00	210.00
88-02-1092	Lambkins L5469M	Lladro	Closed	150.00	195.00
88-02-1093	Tea Time L5470G	Lladro	Open	280.00	360.00
88-02-1094	Sad Sax L5471G	Lladro	Open	175.00	205.00

Company		Series			
Number	Name	Artist	Edition Limit	Issue Price	Quote
88-02-1095	Circus Sam L5472G	Lladro	Open	175.00	205.00
88-02-1096	How You've Grown! L5474G	Lladro	Open	180.00	235.00
88-02-1097	How You've Grown! L5474M	Lladro	Closed	180.00	215.00
88-02-1098	A Lesson Shared L5475G	Lladro	Open	150.00	180.00
88-02-1099	A Lesson Shared L5475M	Lladro	Closed	150.00	170.00
88-02-1100	St. Joseph L5476G	Lladro	Open	210.00	270.00
88-02-1101	Mary L5477G	Lladro	Open	130.00	165.00
88-02-1102	Baby Jesus L5478G	Lladro	Open	55.00	75.00
88-02-1103	King Melchior L5479G	Lladro	Open	210.00	265.00
88-02-1104	King Gaspar L5480G	Lladro	Open	210.00	265.00
88-02-1105	King Balthasar L5481G	Lladro	Open	210.00	265.00
88-02-1106	Ox L5482G	Lladro	Open	125.00	165.00
88-02-1107	Donkey L5483G	Lladro	Open	125.00	165.00
88-02-1108	Lost Lamb L5484G	Lladro	Open	100.00	140.00
88-02-1109	Shepherd Boy L5485G	Lladro	Open	140.00	180.00
88-02-1110	Debutantes L5486G	Lladro	Open	490.00	695.00
88-02-1111	Debutantes L5486M	Lladro	Closed	490.00	635.00
88-02-1112	Ingenue L5487G	Lladro	Open	110.00	140.00
88-02-1113	Ingenue L5487M	Lladro	Closed	110.00	130.00
88-02-1114	Sandcastles L5488G	Lladro	Closed	160.00	220.00
88-02-1115	Sandcastles L5488M	Lladro	Closed	160.00	200.00
88-02-1116	Justice L5489G	Lladro	Closed	675.00	825.00
88-02-1117	Flor Maria L5490G	Lladro	Open	500.00	635.00
88-02-1118	Heavenly Strings L5491G	Lladro	Open	140.00	185.00
88-02-1119	Heavenly Cellist L5492G	Lladro	Open	240.00	315.00
88-02-1120	Angel with Lute L5493G	Lladro	Open	140.00	185.00
88-02-1121	Angel with Clarinet L5494G	Lladro	Open	140.00	185.00
88-02-1122	Angelic Choir L5495G	Lladro	Open	300.00	395.00
88-02-1123	Recital L5496G	Lladro	Open	190.00	265.00
88-02-1124	Dress Rehearsal L5497G	Lladro	Open	290.00	385.00
88-02-1125	Opening Night L5498G	Lladro	Open	190.00	260.00
88-02-1126	Pretty Ballerina L5499G	Lladro	Open	190.00	260.00
88-02-1127	Prayerful Moment (blue) L5500G	Lladro	Open	90.00	110.00
88-02-1128	Time to Sew (blue) L5501G	Lladro	Open	90.00	110.00
88-02-1129	Meditation (blue) L5502G	Lladro	Open	90.00	110.00
88-02-1130	Hurry Now L5503G	Lladro	Open	180.00	240.00
88-02-1131	Hurry Now L5503M	Lladro	Closed	180.00	240.00
89-02-1132	Flowers for Sale L5537G	Lladro	Open	1200.00	1550.00
89-02-1133	Puppy Dog Tails L5539G	Lladro	Open	1200.00	1550.00
89-02-1134	An Evening Out L5540G	Lladro	Closed	350.00	400.00
89-02-1135	Melancholy w/base L5542G	Lladro	Open	375.00	440.00
89-02-1136	"Hello Flowers" L5543G	Lladro	Closed	385.00	485.00
89-02-1137	Reaching the Goal L5546G	Lladro	Open	215.00	275.00
89-02-1138	Only the Beginning L5547G	Lladro	Open	215.00	275.00
89-02-1139	Pretty Posies L5548G	Lladro	Open	425.00	530.00
89-02-1140	My New Pet L5549G	Lladro	Open	150.00	185.00
89-02-1141	Serene Moment (blue) L5550G	Lladro	Closed	115.00	150.00
89-02-1142	Serene Moment (white) L5550.3G	Lladro	Closed	115.00	135.00
89-02-1143	Serene Moment (white) L5550.3M	Lladro	Closed	115.00	135.00
89-02-1144	Call to Prayer (blue) L5551G	Lladro	Closed	100.00	135.00
89-02-1145	Call to Prayer (white) L5551.3G	Lladro	Closed	100.00	120.00
89-02-1146	Call to Prayer (white) L5551.3M	Lladro	Closed	100.00	120.00
89-02-1147	Morning Chores (blue) L5552G	Lladro	Open	115.00	140.00
89-02-1148	Wild Goose Chase L5553G	Lladro	Open	175.00	230.00
89-02-1149	Pretty and Prim L5554G	Lladro	Open	215.00	270.00
89-02-1150	"Let's Make Up" L5555G	Lladro	Open	215.00	265.00
89-02-1151	Sad Parting L5583G	Lladro	Closed	375.00	525.00
89-02-1152	Daddy's Girl/Father's Day L5584G	Lladro	Open	315.00	395.00
89-02-1153	Fine Melody w/base L5585G	Lladro	Closed	225.00	295.00
89-02-1154	Sad Note w/base L5586G	Lladro	Closed	185.00	275.00
89-02-1155	Wedding Cake L5587G	Lladro	Open	595.00	750.00
89-02-1156	Blustery Day L5588G	Lladro	Closed	185.00	230.00
89-02-1157	Pretty Pose L5589G	Lladro	Closed	185.00	230.00
89-02-1158	Spring Breeze L5590G	Lladro	Closed	185.00	230.00
89-02-1159	Garden Treasures L5591G	Lladro	Closed	185.00	230.00
89-02-1160	Male Siamese Dancer L5592G	Lladro	Closed	345.00	420.00
89-02-1161	Siamese Dancer L5593G	Lladro	Closed	345.00	420.00
89-02-1162	Playful Romp L5594G	Lladro	Open	215.00	270.00
89-02-1163	Joy in a Basket L5595G	Lladro	Open	215.00	270.00
89-02-1164	A Gift of Love L5596G	Lladro	Open	400.00	495.00
89-02-1165	Summer Soiree L5597G	Lladro	Open	150.00	180.00
89-02-1166	Bridesmaid L5598G	Lladro	Open	150.00	180.00
89-02-1167	Coquette L5599G	Lladro	Open	150.00	180.00
89-02-1168	The Blues w/base L5600G	Lladro	Closed	265.00	340.00
89-02-1169	Ole L5601G	Lladro	Open	365.00	450.00
89-02-1170	Close To My Heart L5603G	Lladro	Open	125.00	165.00
89-02-1171	Spring Token L5604G	Lladro	Open	175.00	230.00
89-02-1172	Floral Treasures L5605G	Lladro	Open	195.00	250.00
89-02-1173	Quiet Evening L5606G	Lladro	Closed	125.00	165.00
89-02-1174	Calling A Friend L5607G	Lladro	Open	125.00	165.00
89-02-1175	Baby Doll L5608G	Lladro	Open	150.00	180.00
89-02-1176	Playful Friends L5609G	Lladro	Open	135.00	170.00
89-02-1177	Star Struck w/base L5610G	Lladro	Open	335.00	420.00
89-02-1178	Sad Clown w/base L5611G	Lladro	Open	335.00	420.00
89-02-1179	Reflecting w/base L5612G	Lladro	Open	335.00	420.00
90-02-1180	Cat Nap L5640G	Lladro	Open	125.00	145.00
90-02-1181	The King's Guard w/base L5642G	Lladro	Closed	950.00	1100.00
90-02-1182	Cathy L5643G	Lladro	Open	200.00	335.00
90-02-1183	Susan L5644G	Lladro	Open	190.00	215.00
90-02-1184	Elizabeth L5645G	Lladro	Open	190.00	215.00
90-02-1185	Cindy L5646G	Lladro	Open	190.00	215.00
90-02-1186	Sara L5647G	Lladro	Open	200.00	230.00
90-02-1187	Courtney L5648G	Lladro	Open	200.00	230.00
90-02-1188	Nothing To Do L5649G	Lladro	Open	190.00	220.00
90-02-1189	Anticipation L5650G	Lladro	Closed	300.00	340.00
90-02-1190	Musical Muse L5651G	Lladro	Open	375.00	440.00
90-02-1191	Venetian Carnival L5658G	Lladro	Closed	500.00	575.00
90-02-1192	Barnyard Scene L5659G	Lladro	Open	200.00	235.00
90-02-1193	Sunning In Ipanema L5660G	Lladro	Closed	370.00	420.00
90-02-1194	Traveling Artist L5661G	Lladro	Open	250.00	290.00
90-02-1195	May Dance L5662G	Lladro	Open	170.00	190.00
90-02-1196	Spring Dance L5663G	Lladro	Open	170.00	195.00
90-02-1197	Giddy Up L5664G	Lladro	Open	190.00	230.00
90-02-1198	Hang On! L5665G	Lladro	Open	225.00	260.00
90-02-1199	Trino At The Beach L5666G	Lladro	Open	390.00	460.00
90-02-1200	Valencian Harvest L5668G	Lladro	Closed	175.00	205.00
90-02-1201	Valencian FLowers L5669G	Lladro	Closed	370.00	420.00
90-02-1202	Valencian Beauty L5670G	Lladro	Closed	175.00	205.00
90-02-1203	Little Dutch Gardener L5671G	Lladro	Closed	400.00	475.00
90-02-1204	Hi There! L5672G	Lladro	Open	450.00	520.00
90-02-1205	A Quiet Moment L5673G	Lladro	Open	450.00	520.00
90-02-1206	A Faun And A Friend L5674G	Lladro	Open	450.00	520.00
90-02-1207	Tee Time L5675G	Lladro	Closed	280.00	315.00
90-02-1208	Wandering Minstrel L5676G	Lladro	Closed	270.00	310.00
90-02-1209	Twilight Years L5677G	Lladro	Open	370.00	420.00
90-02-1210	I Feel Pretty L5678G	Lladro	Open	190.00	230.00
90-02-1211	In No Hurry L5679G	Lladro	Open	550.00	640.00
90-02-1212	Traveling In Style L5680G	Lladro	Open	425.00	495.00
90-02-1213	On The Road L5681G	Lladro	Closed	320.00	500.00
90-02-1214	Breezy Afternoon L5682G	Lladro	Open	180.00	195.00
90-02-1215	Breezy Afternoon L5682M	Lladro	Open	180.00	195.00
90-02-1216	Beautiful Burro L5683G	Lladro	Closed	280.00	396.00
90-02-1217	Barnyard Reflections L5684G	Lladro	Closed	460.00	525.00
90-02-1218	Promenade L5685G	Lladro	Open	275.00	325.00
90-02-1219	On The Avenue L5686G	Lladro	Open	275.00	325.00
90-02-1220	Afternoon Stroll L5687G	Lladro	Open	275.00	325.00
90-02-1221	Dog's Best Friend L5688G	Lladro	Open	250.00	295.00
90-02-1222	Can I Help? L5689G	Lladro	Open	250.00	295.00
90-02-1223	Marshland Mates w/base L5691G	Lladro	Open	950.00	1200.00
90-02-1224	Street Harmonies w/base L5692G	Lladro	Closed	3200.00	3750.00
90-02-1225	Circus Serenade L5694G	Lladro	Open	300.00	360.00
90-02-1226	Concertina L5695G	Lladro	Open	300.00	360.00
90-02-1227	Mandolin Serenade L5696G	Lladro	Open	300.00	360.00
90-02-1228	Over The Clouds L5697G	Lladro	Open	275.00	310.00
90-02-1229	Don't Look Down L5698G	Lladro	Open	330.00	375.00
90-02-1230	Sitting Pretty L5699G	Lladro	Open	300.00	340.00
90-02-1231	Southern Charm L5700G	Lladro	Open	675.00	1025.00
90-02-1232	Just A Little Kiss L5701G	Lladro	Open	320.00	375.00
90-02-1233	Back To School L5702G	Lladro	Closed	350.00	405.00
90-02-1234	Behave! L5703G	Lladro	Open	230.00	265.00
90-02-1235	Swan Song L5704G	Lladro	Open	350.00	410.00
90-02-1236	The Swan And The Princess L5705G	Lladro	Open	350.00	410.00
90-02-1237	We Can't Play L5706G	Lladro	Open	200.00	235.00
90-02-1238	After School L5707G	Lladro	Closed	280.00	315.00
90-02-1239	My First Class L5708G	Lladro	Closed	280.00	315.00
90-02-1240	Between Classes L5709G	Lladro	Closed	280.00	315.00
90-02-1241	Fantasy Friend L5710G	Lladro	Closed	420.00	495.00
90-02-1242	A Christmas Wish L5711G	Lladro	Open	350.00	410.00
90-02-1243	Sleepy Kitten L5712G	Lladro	Open	110.00	130.00
90-02-1244	The Snow Man L5713G	Lladro	Open	300.00	350.00
90-02-1245	First Ballet L5714G	Lladro	Open	370.00	420.00
90-02-1246	Mommy, it's Cold!L5715G	Lladro	Open	360.00	415.00
90-02-1247	Land of The Giants L5716G	Lladro	Open	275.00	315.00
90-02-1248	Rock A Bye Baby L5717G	Lladro	Open	300.00	350.00
90-02-1249	Sharing Secrets L5720G	Lladro	Open	290.00	335.00
90-02-1250	Once Upon A Time L5721G	Lladro	Open	550.00	615.00
90-02-1251	Follow Me L5722G	Lladro	Open	140.00	160.00
90-02-1252	Heavenly Chimes L5723G	Lladro	Open	100.00	120.00
90-02-1253	Angelic Voice L5724G	Lladro	Open	125.00	145.00
90-02-1254	Making A Wish L5725G	Lladro	Open	125.00	145.00
90-02-1255	Sweep Away The Clouds L5726G	Lladro	Open	125.00	145.00
90-02-1256	Angel Care L5727G	Lladro	Open	190.00	210.00
90-02-1257	Heavenly Dreamer L5728G	Lladro	Open	100.00	120.00
91-02-1258	Carousel Charm L5731G	Lladro	Open	1700.00	1850.00
91-02-1259	Carousel Canter L5732G	Lladro	Open	1700.00	1850.00
91-02-1260	Horticulturist L5733G	Lladro	Closed	450.00	495.00
91-02-1261	Pilgrim Couple L5734G	Lladro	Closed	490.00	525.00
91-02-1262	Big Sister L5735G	Lladro	Open	650.00	685.00
91-02-1263	Puppet Show L5736G	Lladro	Open	280.00	295.00
91-02-1264	Little Prince L5737G	Lladro	Closed	295.00	315.00
91-02-1265	Best Foot Forward L5738G	Lladro	Open	280.00	305.00
91-02-1266	Lap Full Of Love L5739G	Lladro	Open	275.00	295.00
91-02-1267	Alice In Wonderland L5740G	Lladro	Open	440.00	485.00
91-02-1268	Dancing Class L5741G	Lladro	Open	340.00	365.00
91-02-1269	Bridal Portrait L5742G	Lladro	Open	480.00	525.00
91-02-1270	Don't Forget Me L5743G	Lladro	Open	150.00	160.00
91-02-1271	Bull & Donkey L5744G	Lladro	Open	250.00	275.00
91-02-1272	Baby Jesus L5745G	Lladro	Open	170.00	185.00
91-02-1273	St. Joseph L5746G	Lladro	Open	350.00	375.00
91-02-1274	Mary L5747G	Lladro	Open	275.00	295.00
91-02-1275	Shepherd Girl L5748G	Lladro	Open	150.00	165.00
91-02-1276	Shepherd Boy L5749G	Lladro	Open	225.00	245.00
91-02-1277	Little Lamb L5750G	Lladro	Open	40.00	42.00
91-02-1278	Walk With Father L5751G	Lladro	Open	375.00	410.00
91-02-1279	Little Virgin L5752G	Lladro	Open	295.00	325.00
91-02-1280	Hold Her Still L5753G	Lladro	Closed	650.00	695.00
91-02-1281	Singapore Dancers L5754G	Lladro	Closed	950.00	1025.00
91-02-1282	Claudette L5755G	Lladro	Closed	265.00	285.00
91-02-1283	Ashley L5756G	Lladro	Closed	265.00	290.00
91-02-1284	Beautiful Tresses L5757G	Lladro	Closed	725.00	785.00
91-02-1285	Sunday Best L5758G	Lladro	Open	725.00	785.00
91-02-1286	Presto! L5759G	Lladro	Closed	275.00	295.00
91-02-1287	Interrupted Nap L5760G	Lladro	Open	325.00	350.00
91-02-1288	Out For A Romp L5761G	Lladro	Open	375.00	410.00
91-02-1289	Checking The Time L5762G	Lladro	Open	560.00	595.00
91-02-1290	Musical Partners L5763G	Lladro	Open	625.00	675.00
91-02-1291	Seeds Of Laughter L5764G	Lladro	Open	525.00	575.00
91-02-1292	Hats Off To Fun L5765G	Lladro	Open	475.00	510.00
91-02-1293	Charming Duet L5766G	Lladro	Open	575.00	625.00
91-02-1294	First Sampler L5767G	Lladro	Open	625.00	680.00
91-02-1295	Academy Days L5768G	Lladro	Closed	280.00	310.00
91-02-1296	Faithful Steed L5769G	Lladro	Open	370.00	395.00
91-02-1297	Out For A Spin L5770G	Lladro	Open	390.00	420.00
91-02-1298	The Magic Of Laughter L5771G	Lladro	Open	950.00	995.00
91-02-1299	Little Dreamers L5772G	Lladro	Open	230.00	240.00
91-02-1300	Little Dreamers L5772M	Lladro	Open	230.00	240.00
91-02-1301	Graceful Offering L5773G	Lladro	Open	850.00	895.00
91-02-1302	Nature's Gifts L5774G	Lladro	Open	900.00	975.00
91-02-1303	Gift Of Beauty L5775G	Lladro	Open	850.00	895.00
91-02-1304	Lover's Paradise L5779G	Lladro	Open	2250.00	2450.00
91-02-1305	Walking The Fields L5780G	Lladro	Closed	725.00	795.00
91-02-1306	Not Too Close L5781G	Lladro	Open	365.00	395.00
91-02-1307	My Chores L5782G	Lladro	Open	325.00	355.00
91-02-1308	Special Delivery L5783G	Lladro	Open	525.00	550.00
91-02-1309	A Cradle Of Kittens L5784G	Lladro	Open	360.00	385.00
91-02-1310	Ocean Beauty L5785G	Lladro	Open	625.00	665.00
91-02-1311	Story Hour L5786G	Lladro	Open	550.00	585.00
91-02-1312	Sophisticate L5787G	Lladro	Open	185.00	195.00
91-02-1313	Talk Of The Town L5788G	Lladro	Open	185.00	195.00
91-02-1314	The Flirt L5789G	Lladro	Open	185.00	195.00
91-02-1315	Carefree L5790G	Lladro	Open	300.00	325.00
91-02-1316	Fairy Godmother L5791G	Lladro	Open	375.00	410.00
91-02-1317	Reverent Moment L5792G	Lladro	Open	295.00	320.00
91-02-1318	Precocious Ballerina L5793G	Lladro	Open	575.00	625.00
91-02-1319	Precious Cargo L5794G	Lladro	Open	460.00	495.00
91-02-1320	Floral Getaway L5795G	Lladro	Closed	625.00	685.00
91-02-1321	Holy Night L5796G	Lladro	Open	330.00	360.00
91-02-1322	Come Out And Play L5797G	Lladro	Open	275.00	295.00

Company Number	Name	Series Artist	Edition Limit	Issue Price	Quote
91-02-1323	Milkmaid L5798G	Lladro	Closed	450.00	495.00
91-02-1324	Shall We Dance? L5799G	Lladro	Closed	600.00	650.00
91-02-1325	Elegant Promenade L5802G	Lladro	Open	775.00	825.00
91-02-1326	Playing Tag L5804G	Lladro	Closed	170.00	190.00
91-02-1327	Tumbling L5805G	Lladro	Closed	130.00	140.00
91-02-1328	Tumbling L5805M	Lladro	Open	130.00	130.00
91-02-1329	Tickling L5806G	Lladro	Open	130.00	145.00
91-02-1330	Tickling L5806M	Lladro	Open	130.00	130.00
91-02-1331	My Puppies L5807G	Lladro	Closed	325.00	360.00
91-02-1332	Musically Inclined L5810G	Lladro	Closed	235.00	250.00
91-02-1333	Littlest Clown L5811G	Lladro	Open	225.00	240.00
91-02-1334	Tired Friend L5812G	Lladro	Open	225.00	245.00
91-02-1335	Having A Ball L5813G	Lladro	Open	225.00	240.00
91-02-1336	Curtain Call L5814G	Lladro	Open	490.00	520.00
91-02-1337	Curtain Call L5814M	Lladro	Open	490.00	520.00
91-02-1338	In Full Relave L5815G	Lladro	Open	490.00	520.00
91-02-1339	In Full Relave L5815M	Lladro	Open	490.00	520.00
91-02-1340	Prima Ballerina L5816G	Lladro	Open	490.00	520.00
91-02-1341	Prima Ballerina L5816M	Lladro	Open	490.00	520.00
91-02-1342	Backstage Preparation L5817G	Lladro	Open	490.00	520.00
91-02-1343	Backstage Preparation L5817M	Lladro	Open	490.00	520.00
91-02-1344	On Her Toes L5818G	Lladro	Open	490.00	520.00
91-02-1345	On Her Toes L5818M	Lladro	Open	490.00	520.00
91-02-1346	Allegory Of Liberty L5819G	Lladro	Open	1950.00	2100.00
91-02-1347	Dance Of Love L5820G	Lladro	Closed	575.00	625.00
91-02-1348	Minstrel's Love L5821G	Lladro	Closed	525.00	575.00
91-02-1349	Little Unicorn L5826G	Lladro	Open	275.00	295.00
91-02-1350	Little Unicorn L5826M	Lladro	Open	275.00	295.00
91-02-1351	I've Got It L5827G	Lladro	Open	170.00	180.00
91-02-1352	Next At Bat L5828G	Lladro	Open	170.00	180.00
91-02-1353	Jazz Horn L5832G	Lladro	Open	295.00	295.00
91-02-1354	Jazz Sax L5833G	Lladro	Open	295.00	295.00
91-02-1355	Jazz Bass L5834G	Lladro	Open	395.00	405.00
91-02-1356	I Do L5835G	Lladro	Open	165.00	175.00
91-02-1357	Sharing Sweets L5836G	Lladro	Open	220.00	245.00
91-02-1358	Sing With Me L5837G	Lladro	Open	240.00	250.00
91-02-1359	On The Move L5838G	Lladro	Open	340.00	365.00
92-02-1360	A Quiet Afternoon L5843G	Lladro	Open	1050.00	1100.00
92-02-1361	Flirtatious Jester L5844G	Lladro	Open	890.00	925.00
92-02-1362	Dressing The Baby L5845G	Lladro	Open	295.00	295.00
92-02-1363	All Tuckered Out L5846G	Lladro	Open	220.00	225.00
92-02-1364	All Tuckered Out L5846M	Lladro	Open	220.00	225.00
92-02-1365	The Loving Family L5848G	Lladro	Open	950.00	985.00
92-02-1366	Inspiring Muse L5850G	Lladro	Open	1200.00	1250.00
92-02-1367	Feathered Fantasy L5851G	Lladro	Open	1200.00	1250.00
92-02-1368	Easter Bonnets L5852G	Lladro	Closed	265.00	275.00
92-02-1369	Floral Admiration L5853G	Lladro	Open	690.00	725.00
92-02-1370	Floral Fantasy L5854G	Lladro	Open	690.00	710.00
92-02-1371	Afternoon Jaunt L5855G	Lladro	Closed	420.00	440.00
92-02-1372	Circus Concert L5856G	Lladro	Open	570.00	585.00
92-02-1373	Grand Entrance L5857G	Lladro	Open	265.00	275.00
92-02-1374	Waiting to Dance L5858G	Lladro	Open	295.00	310.00
92-02-1375	At The Ball L5859G	Lladro	Open	295.00	295.00
92-02-1376	Fairy Garland L5860G	Lladro	Open	630.00	650.00
92-02-1377	Fairy Flowers L5861G	Lladro	Open	630.00	655.00
92-02-1378	Fragrant Bouquet L5862G	Lladro	Open	350.00	360.00
92-02-1379	Dressing For The Ballet L5865G	Lladro	Open	395.00	415.00
92-02-1380	Final Touches L5866G	Lladro	Open	395.00	415.00
92-02-1381	Serene Valenciana L5867G	Lladro	Open	365.00	385.00
92-02-1382	Loving Valenciana L5868G	Lladro	Open	365.00	385.00
92-02-1383	Fallas Queen L5869G	Lladro	Open	420.00	440.00
92-02-1384	Olympic Torch w/Fantasy Logo L5870G	Lladro	Open	165.00	145.00
92-02-1385	Olympic Champion w/Fantasy Logo L5871G	Lladro	Open	165.00	145.00
92-02-1386	Olympic Pride w/Fantasy Logo L5872G	Lladro	Open	165.00	495.00
92-02-1387	Modern Mother L5873G	Lladro	Open	325.00	335.00
92-02-1388	Off We Go L5874G	Lladro	Open	365.00	385.00
92-02-1389	Guest Of Honor L5877G	Lladro	Open	195.00	195.00
92-02-1390	Sister's Pride L5878G	Lladro	Open	595.00	615.00
92-02-1391	Shot On Goal L5879G	Lladro	Open	1100.00	1150.00
92-02-1392	Playful Unicorn L5880G	Lladro	Open	295.00	295.00
92-02-1393	Playful Unicorn L5880M	Lladro	Open	295.00	310.00
92-02-1394	Mischievous Mouse L5881G	Lladro	Open	285.00	295.00
92-02-1395	Restful Mouse L5882G	Lladro	Open	285.00	295.00
92-02-1396	Loving Mouse L5883G	Lladro	Open	285.00	295.00
92-02-1397	From This Day Forward L5885G	Lladro	Open	265.00	265.00
92-02-1398	Hippity Hop L5886G	Lladro	Open	95.00	95.00
92-02-1399	Washing Up L5887G	Lladro	Open	95.00	95.00
92-02-1400	That Tickles! L5888G	Lladro	Open	95.00	95.00
92-02-1401	Snack Time L5889G	Lladro	Open	95.00	95.00
92-02-1402	The Aviator L5891G	Lladro	Open	375.00	380.00
92-02-1403	Circus Magic L5892G	Lladro	Open	470.00	495.00
92-02-1404	Friendship In Bloom L5893G	Lladro	Open	650.00	685.00
92-02-1405	Precious Petals L5894G	Lladro	Open	395.00	415.00
92-02-1406	Bouquet of Blossoms L5895G	Lladro	Open	295.00	295.00
92-02-1407	The Loaves & Fishes L5896G	Lladro	Open	695.00	710.00
92-02-1408	Trimming The Tree L5897G	Lladro	Open	900.00	925.00
92-02-1409	Spring Splendor L5898G	Lladro	Open	440.00	450.00
92-02-1410	Just One More L5899G	Lladro	Open	450.00	460.00
92-02-1411	Sleep Tight L5900G	Lladro	Open	450.00	465.00
92-02-1412	Surprise L5901G	Lladro	Open	325.00	335.00
92-02-1413	Easter Bunnies L5902G	Lladro	Open	240.00	250.00
92-02-1415	Down The Aisle L5903G	Lladro	Open	295.00	295.00
92-02-1416	Sleeping Bunny L5904G	Lladro	Open	75.00	75.00
92-02-1417	Attentive Bunny L5905G	Lladro	Open	75.00	75.00
92-02-1418	Preening Bunny L5906G	Lladro	Open	75.00	75.00
92-02-1419	Sitting Bunny L5907G	Lladro	Open	75.00	75.00
92-02-1420	Just A Little More L5908G	Lladro	Open	370.00	380.00
92-02-1421	All Dressed Up L5909G	Lladro	Open	440.00	450.00
92-02-1422	Making A Wish L5910G	Lladro	Open	790.00	825.00
92-02-1423	Swans Take Flight L5912G	Lladro	Open	2850.00	2950.00
92-02-1424	Rose Ballet L5919G	Lladro	Open	210.00	215.00
92-02-1425	Swan Ballet L5920G	Lladro	Open	210.00	215.00
92-02-1426	Take Your Medicine L5921G	Lladro	Open	360.00	370.00
92-02-1427	Jazz Clarinet L5928G	Lladro	Open	295.00	295.00
92-02-1428	Jazz Drums L5929G	Lladro	Open	595.00	610.00
92-02-1429	Jazz Duo L5930G	Lladro	Open	795.00	810.00
93-02-1430	The Ten Commandments w/Base L5933G	Lladro	Open	930.00	930.00
93-02-1431	The Holy Teacher L5934G	Lladro	Open	375.00	375.00
93-02-1432	Nutcracker Suite L5935G	Lladro	Open	620.00	620.00
93-02-1433	Little Skipper L5936G	Lladro	Open	320.00	320.00
93-02-1434	Riding The Waves L5941G	Lladro	Open	405.00	405.00
93-02-1435	World of Fantasy L5943G	Lladro	Open	295.00	295.00
93-02-1436	The Great Adventure L5944G	Lladro	Open	325.00	325.00
93-02-1437	A Mother's Way L5946G	Lladro	Open	1350.00	1350.00

Company Number	Name	Series Artist	Edition Limit	Issue Price	Quote
93-02-1438	General Practitioner L5947G	Lladro	Open	360.00	360.00
93-02-1439	Physician L5948G	Lladro	Open	360.00	360.00
93-02-1440	Angel Candleholder w/Lyre L5949G	Lladro	Open	295.00	295.00
93-02-1441	Angel Candleholder w/Tambourine L5950G	Lladro	Open	295.00	295.00
93-02-1442	Sounds of Summer L5953G	Lladro	Open	125.00	125.00
93-02-1443	Sounds of Winter L5954G	Lladro	Open	125.00	125.00
93-02-1444	Sounds of Fall L5955G	Lladro	Open	125.00	125.00
93-02-1445	Sounds of Spring L5956G	Lladro	Open	125.00	125.00
93-02-1446	The Glass Slipper L5957G	Lladro	Open	475.00	475.00
93-02-1447	Country Ride w/base L5958G	Lladro	Open	2850.00	2850.00
93-02-1448	It's Your Turn L5959G	Lladro	Open	365.00	365.00
93-02-1449	On Patrol L5960G	Lladro	Open	395.00	395.00
93-02-1450	The Great Teacher w/base L5961G	Lladro	Open	850.00	850.00
93-02-1451	The Clipper Ship w/base L5965M	Lladro	Open	240.00	240.00
93-02-1452	Flowers Forever w/base L5966G	Lladro	Open	4150.00	4150.00
93-02-1453	Honeymoon Ride w/base L5968G	Lladro	Open	2750.00	2750.00
93-02-1454	A Special Toy L5971G	Lladro	Open	815.00	815.00
93-02-1455	Before the Dance w/base L5972G	Lladro	Open	3550.00	3550.00
93-02-1456	Before the Dance w/base L5972M	Lladro	Open	3550.00	3550.00
93-02-1457	Family Outing w/base L5974G	Lladro	Open	4275.00	4275.00
93-02-1458	Up and Away w/base L5975G	Lladro	Open	2850.00	2850.00
93-02-1459	The Fireman L5976G	Lladro	Open	395.00	395.00
93-02-1460	Revelation w/base (white) L5977G	Lladro	Open	310.00	310.00
93-02-1461	Revelation w/base (black) L5978M	Lladro	Open	310.00	310.00
93-02-1462	Revelation w/base (sand) L5979M	Lladro	Open	310.00	310.00
93-02-1463	The Past w/base (white) L5980G	Lladro	Open	310.00	310.00
93-02-1464	The Past w/base (black) L5981M	Lladro	Open	310.00	310.00
93-02-1465	The Past w/base (sand) L5982M	Lladro	Open	310.00	310.00
93-02-1466	Beauty w/base (white) L5983G	Lladro	Open	310.00	310.00
93-02-1467	Beauty w/base (black) L5984M	Lladro	Open	310.00	310.00
93-02-1468	Beauty w/base (sand) L5985M	Lladro	Open	310.00	310.00
93-02-1469	Sunday Sermon L5986G	Lladro	Open	425.00	425.00
93-02-1470	Talk to Me L5987G	Lladro	Open	145.00	145.00
93-02-1471	Taking Time L5988G	Lladro	Open	145.00	145.00
93-02-1472	A Mother's Touch L5989G	Lladro	Open	470.00	470.00
93-02-1473	Thoughtful Caress L5990G	Lladro	Open	225.00	225.00
93-02-1474	Love Story L5991G	Lladro	Open	2800.00	2800.00
93-02-1475	Unicorn and Friend L5993G	Lladro	Open	355.00	355.00
93-02-1476	Unicorn and Friend L5993M	Lladro	Open	355.00	355.00
93-02-1477	Meet My Friend L5994G	Lladro	Open	695.00	695.00
93-02-1478	Soft Meow L5995G	Lladro	Open	480.00	480.00
93-02-1479	Bless the Child L5996G	Lladro	Open	465.00	465.00
93-02-1480	One More Try L5997G	Lladro	Open	715.00	715.00
93-02-1481	My Dad L6001G	Lladro	Open	550.00	550.00
93-02-1482	Down You Go L6002G	Lladro	Open	815.00	815.00
93-02-1483	Ready To Learn L6003G	Lladro	Open	650.00	650.00
93-02-1484	Bar Mitzvah Day L6004G	Lladro	Open	395.00	395.00
93-02-1485	Christening Day w/base L6005G	Lladro	Open	1425.00	1425.00
93-02-1486	Oriental Colonade w/base L6006G	Lladro	Open	1875.00	1875.00
93-02-1487	The Goddess & the Unicorn w/base L6007G	Lladro	Open	1675.00	1675.00
93-02-1488	Joyful Event L6008G	Lladro	Open	825.00	825.00
93-02-1489	Monday's Child (Boy) L6011G	Lladro	Open	245.00	245.00
93-02-1490	Monday's Child (Girl) L6012G	Lladro	Open	260.00	260.00
93-02-1491	Tuesday's Child (Boy) L6013G	Lladro	Open	225.00	225.00
93-02-1492	Tuesday's Child (Girl) L6014G	Lladro	Open	245.00	245.00
93-02-1493	Wednesday's Child (Boy) L6015G	Lladro	Open	245.00	245.00
93-02-1494	Wednesday's Child (Girl) L6016G	Lladro	Open	245.00	245.00
93-02-1495	Thursday's Child (Boy) L6017G	Lladro	Open	225.00	225.00
93-02-1496	Thursday's Child (Girl) L6018G	Lladro	Open	245.00	245.00
93-02-1497	Friday's Child (Boy) L6019G	Lladro	Open	225.00	225.00
93-02-1498	Friday's Child (Girl) L6020G	Lladro	Open	225.00	225.00
93-02-1499	Saturday's Child (Boy) L6021G	Lladro	Open	245.00	245.00
93-02-1500	Saturday's Child (Girl) L6022G	Lladro	Open	245.00	245.00
93-02-1501	Sunday's Child (Boy) L6023G	Lladro	Open	225.00	225.00
93-02-1502	Sunday's Child (Girl) L6024G	Lladro	Open	225.00	225.00
93-02-1503	Barnyard See Saw L6025G	Lladro	Open	500.00	500.00
93-02-1504	My Turn L6026G	Lladro	Open	515.00	515.00
93-02-1505	Hanukah Lights L6027G	Lladro	Open	345.00	345.00
93-02-1506	Mazel Tov! L6028G	Lladro	Open	380.00	380.00
93-02-1507	Hebrew Scholar L6029G	Lladro	Open	225.00	225.00
93-02-1508	On The Go L6031G	Lladro	Open	475.00	475.00
93-02-1509	On The Green L6032G	Lladro	Open	645.00	645.00
93-02-1510	Monkey Business L6034G	Lladro	Open	745.00	745.00
93-02-1511	Young Princess L6036G	Lladro	Open	240.00	240.00
85-02-1512	Lladro Plaque L7116	Lladro	Open	17.50	18.00
85-02-1513	Lladro Plaque L7118	Lladro	Closed	*17.00	*18.00
92-02-1514	Special Torch L7513G	Lladro	Open	165.00	165.00
92-02-1515	Special Champion L7514G	Lladro	Open	165.00	165.00
92-02-1516	Special Pride L7515G	Lladro	Open	165.00	165.00
93-02-1517	Courage L7522G	Lladro	Open	195.00	195.00
85-02-1518	Lladro Plaque w/ Blue Writing L7601G	Lladro	Closed	35.00	150.00
89-02-1519	Starting Forward/Lolo L7605G	Lladro	Closed	125.00	350.00
Lladro		**Limited Edition**			
71-03-001	Hamlet LL1144	Lladro	Closed	250.00	2500.00
71-03-002	Othello and Desdemona LL1145	Lladro	Closed	275.00	2500-3300.
71-03-003	Antique Auto LL1146	Lladro	Closed	1000.00	16000.00
71-03-004	Floral LL1184	Lladro	Closed	400.00	2200.00
71-03-005	Floral LL1185	Lladro	Closed	475.00	1800.00
71-03-006	Floral LL1186	Lladro	Closed	575.00	2200.00
72-03-007	Eagles LL1189	Lladro	Closed	900.00	3200.00
72-03-008	Sea Birds with Nest LL1194	Lladro	Closed	600.00	2750.00
72-03-009	Turkey Group LL1196	Lladro	Closed	650.00	1800.00
72-03-010	Peace LL1202	Lladro	Closed	550.00	7500.00
72-03-011	Eagle Owl LL1223	Lladro	Closed	450.00	1050.00
72-03-012	Hansom Carriage LL1225	Lladro	Closed	1250.00	10-12000
73-03-013	Hunting Scene LL1238	Lladro	Closed	800.00	3000.00
73-03-014	Turtle Doves LL1240	Lladro	Closed	500.00	2300-2500.
73-03-015	The Forest LL1243	Lladro	Closed	1250.00	3300.00
74-03-016	Soccer Players LL1266	Lladro	Closed	2000.00	7500.00
74-03-017	Man From LaMancha LL1269	Lladro	Closed	700.00	4000-5000.
74-03-018	Queen Elizabeth II LL1275	Lladro	Closed	3650.00	5000.00
74-03-019	Judge LL1281	Lladro	Closed	325.00	1200-1400.
74-03-020	The Hunt LL1308	Lladro	Closed	4750.00	6900.00
74-03-021	Ducks at Pond LL1317	Lladro	Closed	4250.00	6900.00
76-03-022	Impossible Dream LL1318	Lladro	Closed	2400.00	5000.00
76-03-023	Comforting Baby LL1329	Lladro	Closed	700.00	1050.00
76-03-024	Mountain Country Lady LL1330	Lladro	Closed	900.00	1850.00
76-03-025	My Baby LL1331	Lladro	Closed	550.00	2000.00
78-03-026	Flight of Gazelles LL1352	Lladro	Closed	2450.00	3100.00
78-03-027	Car in Trouble LL1375	Lladro	Closed	3000.00	7600.00
78-03-028	Fearful Flight LL1377	Lladro	750	7000.00	14200.00
78-03-029	Henry VIII LL1384	Lladro	Closed	650.00	940.00
81-03-030	Venus and Cupid LL1392	Lladro	Closed	1100.00	200-2800.

Company		Series			
Number	**Name**	**Artist**	**Edition Limit**	**Issue Price**	**Quote**
82-03-031	First Date w/base LL1393	Lladro	1,500	3800.00	5900.00
82-03-032	Columbus LL1432	Lladro	Closed	535.00	1200-1500.
83-03-033	Venetian Serenade LL1433	Lladro	Closed	2600.00	3750.00
85-03-034	Festival in Valencia w/base LL1457	Lladro	3,000	1475.00	2350.00
85-03-035	Camelot LL1458	Lladro	3,000	1000.00	1650.00
85-03-036	Napoleon Planning Battle w/base LL1459	Lladro	1,500	875.00	1450.00
85-03-037	Youthful Beauty w/base LL1461	Lladro	5,000	800.00	1200.00
85-03-038	Flock of Birds w/base LL1462	Lladro	1,500	1125.00	1750.00
85-03-039	Classic Spring LL1465	Lladro	Closed	650.00	1100-1400.
85-03-040	Classic Fall LL1466	Lladro	Closed	650.00	1000.00
85-03-041	Valencian Couple on Horse LL1472	Lladro	3,000	1175.00	1550.00
85-03-042	Coach XVIII Century w/base LL1485	Lladro	500	14000.00	25500.00
86-03-043	The New World w/base LL1486	Lladro	4,000	700.00	1350.00
86-03-044	Fantasia w/base LL1487	Lladro	5,000	1500.00	2700.00
86-03-045	Floral Offering w/base LL1490	Lladro	3,000	2500.00	4450.00
86-03-046	Oriental Music w/base LL1491	Lladro	5,000	1350.00	2400.00
86-03-047	Three Sisters w/base LL1492	Lladro	3,000	1850.00	3250.00
86-03-048	At the Stroke of Twelve w/base LL1493	Lladro	1,500	4250.00	7500.00
86-03-049	Hawaiian Festival w/base LL1496	Lladro	4,000	1850.00	3150.00
87-03-050	A Sunday Drive w/base LL1510	Lladro	1,000	2600.00	5250.00
87-03-051	Listen to Don Quixote w/base LL1520	Lladro	750	1800.00	2900.00
87-03-052	A Happy Encounter LL1523	Lladro	1,500	2900.00	4900.00
88-03-053	Garden Party w/base LL1578	Lladro	500	5500.00	7250.00
88-03-054	Blessed Lady w/base LL1579	Lladro	Closed	1150.00	1500.00
88-03-055	Return to La Mancha w/base LL1580	Lladro	500	6400.00	8350.00
89-03-056	Southern Tea LL1597	Lladro	1,000	1775.00	2300.00
89-03-057	Kitakami Cruise w/base LL1605	Lladro	500	5800.00	7350.00
89-03-058	Mounted Warriors w/base LL1608	Lladro	500	2850.00	3450.00
89-03-059	Circus Parade w/base LL1609	Lladro	1,000	5200.00	6550.00
89-03-060	"Jesus the Rock" w/baseLL1615	Lladro	1,000	1175.00	1550.00
88-02-061	On Our Way Home (Decorated) LL1715	Lladro	Closed	2000.00	2000.00
89-02-062	Hopeful Group LL1723	Lladro	Closed	1825.00	1825.00
91-03-063	Valencian Cruise LL1731	Lladro	1,000	2700.00	2950.00
91-03-064	Venice Vows LL1732	Lladro	1,500	3750.00	4100.00
91-03-065	Liberty Eagle LL1738	Lladro	1,500	1000.00	1100.00
91-03-066	Heavenly Swing LL1739	Lladro	1,000	1900.00	2050.00
91-03-067	Columbus, Two Routes LL1740	Lladro	1,000	1500.00	1650.00
91-03-068	Columbus Reflecting LL1741	Lladro	1,000	1850.00	1995.00
91-03-069	Onward! LL1742	Lladro	1,000	2500.00	2700.00
91-03-070	The Prophet LL1743	Lladro	300	800.00	875.00
90-03-071	My Only Friend LL1744	Lladro	Closed	2950.00	2400.00
91-03-072	Dawn LL1745	Lladro	Closed	1200.00	1260.00
91-03-073	Champion LL1746	Lladro	300	1800.00	1950.00
91-03-074	Nesting Doves LL1747	Lladro	300	800.00	875.00
91-03-075	Comforting News LL1748	Lladro	300	1200.00	1325.00
91-03-076	Baggy Pants LL1749	Lladro	300	1500.00	1650.00
91-03-077	Circus Show LL1750	Lladro	300	1400.00	1525.00
91-03-078	Maggie LL1751	Lladro	300	900.00	990.00
91-03-079	Apple Seller LL1752	Lladro	300	900.00	990.00
91-03-080	The Student LL1753	Lladro	300	1300.00	1425.00
91-03-081	Tree Climbers LL1754	Lladro	300	1500.00	1650.00
91-03-082	The Princess And The Unicorn LL1755	Lladro	Closed	1750.00	1860.00
91-03-083	Outing In Seville LL1756	Lladro	500	23000.00	24500.00
92-03-084	Hawaiian Ceremony LL1757	Lladro	1,000	9800.00	10250.00
92-03-085	Circus Time LL1758	Lladro	2,500	9200.00	9650.00
92-03-086	Tea In The Garden LL1759	Lladro	2,000	9500.00	9750.00
93-03-087	Paella Valenciano w/base LL1762	Lladro	500	10000.00	10000.00
93-03-088	Trusting Friends w/base LL1763	Lladro	350	1200.00	1200.00
93-03-089	He's My Brother w/base LL1764	Lladro	350	1500.00	1500.00
93-03-090	The Course of Adventure LL1765	Lladro	250	1625.00	1625.00
93-03-091	Ties That Bind LL1766	Lladro	250	1700.00	1700.00
93-03-092	Motherly Love LL1767	Lladro	250	1330.00	1330.00
93-03-093	Travellers' Respite w/base LL1768	Lladro	250	1825.00	1825.00
93-03-094	Fruitful Harvest LL1769	Lladro	350	1300.00	1300.00
93-03-095	Gypsy Dancers LL1770	Lladro	250	2250.00	2250.00
93-03-096	Country Doctor w/base LL1771	Lladro	250	1475.00	1475.00
93-03-097	Back To Back LL1772	Lladro	350	1450.00	1450.00
93-03-098	Mischevous Musician LL1773	Lladro	350	975.00	975.00
93-03-099	A Treasured Moment w/base LL1774	Lladro	350	950.00	950.00
93-03-100	Oriental Garden w/base LL1775	Lladro	750	22500.00	22500.00
70-03-101	Girl with Guitar LL2016	Lladro	Closed	650.00	1800.00
70-03-102	Madonna with Child LL2018	Lladro	Closed	450.00	1750.00
71-03-103	Oriental Man LL2021	Lladro	Closed	500.00	1850.00
71-03-104	Three Girls LL2028	Lladro	Closed	950.00	3500.00
71-03-105	Eve at Tree LL2029	Lladro	Closed	450.00	3000.00
71-03-106	Oriental Horse LL2030	Lladro	Closed	1100.00	3500-5000.
71-03-107	Lyric Muse LL2031	Lladro	Closed	750.00	2100.00
71-03-108	Madonna and Child LL2043	Lladro	Closed	400.00	1500.00
73-03-109	Peasant Woman LL2049	Lladro	Closed	400.00	1300.00
73-03-110	Passionate Dance LL2051	Lladro	Closed	450.00	2750.00
77-03-111	St. Theresa LL2061	Lladro	Closed	775.00	1600.00
77-03-112	Concerto LL2063	Lladro	Closed	1000.00	1235.00
77-03-113	Flying Partridges LL2064	Lladro	Closed	3500.00	4300.00
87-03-114	Christopher Columbus w/base LL2176	Lladro	1,000	1000.00	1350.00
90-03-115	Invincible w/base LL2188	Lladro	300	1100.00	1250.00
93-03-116	Flight of Fancy w/base LL2243	Lladro	300	1400.00	1400.00
93-03-117	The Awakening w/base LL2244	Lladro	300	1200.00	1200.00
93-03-118	Inspired Voyage w/base LL2245	Lladro	1,000	4800.00	4800.00
93-03-119	Days of Yore w/base LL2248	Lladro	1,000	2050.00	2050.00
93-03-120	Holiday Glow w/base LL2249	Lladro	1,500	750.00	750.00
93-03-121	Autumn Glow w/base LL2250	Lladro	1,500	750.00	750.00
93-03-122	Humble Grace w/base LL2255	Lladro	2,000	2150.00	2150.00
83-03-123	Dawn w/base LL3000	Lladro	300	325.00	550.00
83-03-124	Monks w/base LL3001	Lladro	Closed	1675.00	2550.00
83-03-125	Waiting w/base LL3002	Lladro	Closed	1550.00	1900.00
83-03-126	Indolence LL3003	Lladro	Closed	1465.00	2100.00
83-03-127	Venus in the Bath LL3005	Lladro	Closed	1175.00	1450.00
87-03-128	Classic Beauty w/base LL3012	Lladro	500	1300.00	1750.00
87-03-129	Youthful Innocence w/base LL3013	Lladro	500	1300.00	1750.00
87-03-130	The Nymph w/base LL3014	Lladro	250	1000.00	1450.00
87-03-131	Dignity w/base LL3015	Lladro	150	1400.00	1900.00
88-03-132	Passion w/base LL3016	Lladro	750	865.00	1100.00
88-03-133	Muse w/base LL3017	Lladro	Closed	650.00	875.00
88-03-134	Cellist w/base LL3018	Lladro	Closed	650.00	875.00
88-03-135	True Affection w/base LL3019	Lladro	300	750.00	975.00
89-03-136	Demureness w/base LL3020	Lladro	Closed	400.00	650.00
90-03-137	Daydreaming w/base LL3022	Lladro	500	550.00	775.00
90-03-138	After The Bath w/base LL3023	Lladro	Closed	350.00	750-1000.
90-03-139	Discoveries w/Base LL3024	Lladro	Closed	1500.00	1750.00
91-03-140	Resting Nude LL3025	Lladro	Closed	650.00	725.00
91-03-141	Unadorned Beauty LL3026	Lladro	200	1700.00	1850.00
82-03-142	Elk LL3501	Lladro	Closed	950.00	1200.00
78-03-143	Nude with Dove LL3503	Lladro	Closed	500.00	1400.00
81-03-144	The Rescue LL3504	Lladro	Closed	3500.00	4450.00
78-03-145	St. Michael w/base LL3515	Lladro	1,500	2200.00	4300.00
80-03-146	Turtle Dove Nest w/base LL3519	Lladro	1,200	3600.00	6050.00
80-03-147	Turtle Dove Group w/base LL3520	Lladro	750	6800.00	11500.00
81-03-148	Philippine Folklore LL3522	Lladro	1,500	1450.00	2400.00
81-03-149	Nest of Eagles w/base LL3523	Lladro	300	6900.00	11500.00
81-03-150	Drum Beats/Watusi Queen w/base LL3524	Lladro	1,500	1875.00	3050.00
82-03-151	Togetherness LL3527	Lladro	Closed	750.00	975.00
82-03-152	Wrestling LL3528	Lladro	Closed	950.00	1125.00
83-03-153	Companionship w/base LL3529	Lladro	Closed	1000.00	1700.00
83-03-154	Anxiety w/base LL3530	Lladro	Closed	1075.00	1875.00
83-03-155	Victory LL3531	Lladro	Closed	1500.00	1800.00
83-03-156	Plentitude LL3532	Lladro	Closed	1000.00	1375.00
83-03-157	The Observe w/baser LL3533	Lladro	Closed	900.00	1650.00
83-03-158	In the Distance LL3534	Lladro	Closed	525.00	1275.00
83-03-159	Slave LL3535	Lladro	Closed	950.00	1150.00
83-03-160	Relaxation LL3536	Lladro	Closed	525.00	1000.00
83-03-161	Dreaming w/base LL3537	Lladro	Closed	950.00	1475.00
83-03-162	Youth LL3538	Lladro	Closed	525.00	1120.00
83-03-163	Dantiness LL3539	Lladro	Closed	1000.00	1400.00
83-03-164	Pose LL3540	Lladro	Closed	1250.00	1450.00
83-03-165	Tranquility LL3541	Lladro	Closed	1000.00	1400.00
83-03-166	Yoga LL3542	Lladro	Closed	650.00	900.00
83-03-167	Demure LL3543	Lladro	Closed	1250.00	1700.00
83-03-168	Reflections w/base LL3544	Lladro	Closed	650.00	1050.00
83-03-169	Adoration LL3545	Lladro	Closed	1050.00	1600.00
83-03-170	African Woman LL3546	Lladro	Closed	1300.00	2000.00
83-03-171	Reclining Nude LL3547	Lladro	Closed	650.00	875.00
83-03-172	Serenity w/base LL3548	Lladro	Closed	925.00	1550.00
83-03-173	Reposing LL3549	Lladro	Closed	425.00	575.00
83-03-174	Boxer w/base LL3550	Lladro	Closed	850.00	1450.00
83-03-175	Bather LL3551	Lladro	Closed	975.00	1300.00
82-03-176	Blue God LL3552	Lladro	1,500	900.00	1575.00
82-03-177	Fire Bird LL3553	Lladro	1,500	800.00	1350.00
82-03-178	Desert People w/base LL3555	Lladro	Closed	1680.00	3000.00
82-03-179	Road to Mandalay LL3556	Lladro	Closed	1390.00	2500.00
82-03-180	Jesus in Tiberias w/base LL3557	Lladro	1,200	2600.00	4500.00
92-03-181	The Reader LL3560	Lladro	200	2650.00	2750.00
93-02-182	Trail Boss LL3561M	Lladro	1,500	2450.00	2450.00
93-02-183	Indian Brave LL3562M	Lladro	1,500	2250.00	2250.00
80-03-184	Successful Hunt LL5098	Lladro	Closed	5200.00	5200.00
85-03-185	Napoleon Bonaparte LL 5338	Lladro	5,000	275.00	495.00
85-03-186	Beethoven w/base LL 5339	Lladro	Closed	800.00	1300.00
85-03-187	Thoroughbred Horse w/base LL5340	Lladro	1,000	625.00	1050.00
85-03-188	I Have Found Thee, Dulcinea LL5341	Lladro	Closed	1850.00	2000-3000.
85-03-189	Pack of Hunting Dogs w/base LL5342	Lladro	3,000	925.00	1650.00
85-03-190	Love Boat w/base LL5343	Lladro	3,000	825.00	1350.00
86-03-191	Fox Hunt w/base LL5362	Lladro	1,000	5200.00	8750.00
86-03-192	Rey De Copas w/base LL5366	Lladro	Closed	325.00	600.00
86-03-193	Rey De Oros w/base LL5367	Lladro	Closed	325.00	600.00
86-03-194	Rey De Espadas w/base LL5368	Lladro	Closed	325.00	600.00
86-03-195	Rey De Bastos w/base LL5369	Lladro	Closed	325.00	600.00
86-03-196	Pastoral Scene w/base LL5386	Lladro	750	1100.00	2100.00
87-03-197	Inspiration LL5413	Lladro	Closed	1200.00	2100.00
87-03-198	Carnival Time w/base LL5423	Lladro	Closed	2400.00	3900.00
89-03-199	"Pious" LL5541	Lladro	Closed	1075.00	2000-2200.
89-03-200	Freedom LL5602	Lladro	Closed	875.00	950.00
90-03-201	A Ride In The Park LL5718	Lladro	Closed	3200.00	3895.00
91-03-202	Youth LL5800	Lladro	Closed	650.00	725.00
91-03-203	Charm LL5801	Lladro	Closed	650.00	725.00
91-03-204	New World Medallion LL5808	Lladro	5,000	200.00	215.00
92-03-205	The Voyage of Columbus LL5847	Lladro	Closed	1450.00	1325-2200.
92-03-206	Sorrowful Mother LL5849	Lladro	1,500	1750.00	1850.00
92-03-207	Justice Eagle LL5863	Lladro	1,500	1700.00	1800.00
92-03-208	Maternal Joy LL5864	Lladro	1,500	1600.00	1700.00
92-03-209	Motoring In Style LL5884	Lladro	1,500	3700.00	3850.00
92-03-210	The Way Of The Cross LL5890	Lladro	2,000	975.00	1050.00
92-03-211	Presenting Credentials LL5911	Lladro	1,500	19500.00	20500.00
92-03-212	Young Mozart LL5915	Lladro	Closed	500.00	1800-2000.
93-03-213	Jester's Serenade w/base LL5932	Lladro	3,000	1995.00	1995.00
93-03-214	The Blessing w/base LL5942	Lladro	2,000	1345.00	1345.00
93-03-215	Our Lady of Rocio w/base LL5951	Lladro	2,000	3500.00	3500.00
93-03-216	Where to Sir w/base LL5952	Lladro	1,500	5250.00	5250.00
93-03-217	Discovery Mug LL5967	Lladro	1,992	90.00	90.00
93-03-218	Graceful Moment w/base LL6033	Lladro	3,000	1475.00	1475.00
93-03-219	The Hand of Justice w/base LL6033	Lladro	1,000	1250.00	1250.00
92-03-220	Tinkerbell LL7518	Lladro	1,000	350.00	2000-3200.
93-03-221	Peter Pan LL7529	Lladro	3,000	400.00	1050-1650.
Lladro		**Lladro Collectors Society**			
85-04-001	Little Pals S7600G	Lladro	Closed	95.00	2150-4000.
86-04-002	Little Traveler S7602G	Lladro	Closed	95.00	950-2400.
87-04-003	Spring Bouquets S7603G	Lladro	Closed	125.00	690-1150.
88-04-004	School Days S7604G	Lladro	Closed	125.00	360-700.
88-04-005	Flower Song S7607G	Lladro	Closed	175.00	460-850.
89-04-006	My Buddy S7609G	Lladro	Closed	145.00	210-750.
90-04-007	Can I Play? S7610G	Lladro	Closed	150.00	295-700.
91-04-008	Summer Stroll S7611G	Lladro	Closed	195.00	275-600.
91-04-009	Picture Perfect S7612G	Lladro	Closed	350.00	360-750.
92-04-010	All Aboard S7619G	Lladro	Closed	165.00	200-700.
93-04-011	Best Friend S7620G	Lladro	Closed	195.00	195.00
94-04-012	Basket of Love S7622G	Lladro	Yr.Iss.	225.00	225.00
Lladro		**Lladro Event Figurines**			
91-05-001	Garden Classic L7617G	Lladro	Closed	295.00	325-550.
92-05-002	Garden Song L7618G	Lladro	Closed	295.00	375-675.
93-05-003	Pick of the Litter L7621G	Lladro	Closed	350.00	425.00
94-05-004	Little Riders L7623P	Lladro	Closed	250.00	250.00
Lladro		**Lladro Limited Edition Egg Series**			
93-06-001	1993 Limited Edition Egg L6083M	Lladro	Yr.Iss.	145.00	170-375.
94-06-002	1994 Limited Edition Egg L7532M	Lladro	Yr.Iss.	150.00	150.00

Also see Dave Grossman: Series 05 for Lladro Norman Rockwell

Company		Series			
Seymour Mann, Inc.		**Wizard Of Oz - 40th Anniversary**			
79-01-001	Dorothy, Scarecrow, Lion, Tinman	E. Mann	Closed	7.50	45.00
79-01-002	Dorothy, Scarecrow, Lion, Tinman, Musical	E. Mann	Closed	12.50	75.00
Seymour Mann, Inc.		**Christmas In America**			
88-02-001	Doctor's Office Lite Up	E. Mann	Open	27.50	27.50
88-02-002	Set Of 3, Capitol, White House, Mt. Vernon	E. Mann	Closed	75.00	150.00
89-02-003	Santa in Sleigh	E. Mann	Open	25.00	45.00
90-02-004	Cart With People	E. Mann	Open	25.00	35.00
91-02-005	New England Church Lite Up House MER-375	J. White	Open	27.50	27.50

Company Number	Name	Series Artist	Edition Limit	Issue Price	Quote
91-02-006	New England General Store Lite Up House MER-377	J. White	Open	27.50	27.50
Seymour Mann, Inc.		**Christmas Village**			
91-03-001	Away, Away	L. Sciola	Open	30.00	30.00
91-03-002	The Fire Station	L. Sciola	Open	60.00	60.00
91-03-003	Curiosity Shop	L. Sciola	Open	45.00	45.00
91-03-004	Scrooge/Marley's Counting House	L. Sciola	Open	45.00	45.00
91-03-005	The Playhouse	L. Sciola	Open	60.00	60.00
91-03-006	Ye Old Gift Shoppe	L. Sciola	Open	50.00	50.00
91-03-007	Emily's Toys	L. Sciola	Open	45.00	45.00
91-03-008	Counsil House	L. Sciola	Open	60.00	60.00
91-03-009	Public Library	L. Sciola	Open	50.00	50.00
91-03-010	On Thin Ice	L. Sciola	Open	30.00	30.00
91-03-011	Story Teller	L. Sciola	Open	20.00	20.00
Seymour Mann, Inc.		**Christmas Collection**			
85-04-001	Trumpeting Angel w/Jesus XMAS-527	J. White	Open	40.00	40.00
85-04-002	Virgin w/Christ Musical XMAS-528	J. White	Open	33.50	33.50
86-04-003	Antique Santa Musical XMAS-364	J. White	Closed	20.00	20.00
86-04-004	Jumbo Santa/Toys XMAS-38	J. White	Closed	45.00	45.00
89-04-005	Cat in Teacup Musical XMAS-600	J. White	Open	30.00	30.00
89-04-006	Santa in Sled w/Reindeer CJ-3	Jaimy	Open	25.00	25.00
89-04-007	Santa Musicals CJ-1/4	Jaimy	Open	27.50	27.50
89-04-008	Santa on Horse CJ-33A	Jaimy	Open	33.50	33.50
89-04-009	Santa w/List CJ-23	Jaimy	Open	27.50	27.50
90-04-010	Antique Shope Lite Up House MER-376	J. White	Open	27.50	27.50
90-04-011	Bakery Lite Up House MER-373	J. White	Open	27.50	27.50
90-04-012	Bethlehem Lite Up Set 3 CP-59893	J. White	Open	120.00	120.00
90-04-013	Brick Church Lite Up House MER-360C	J. White	Closed	35.00	35.00
90-04-014	Cathedral Lite Up House MER-362	J. White	Closed	37.50	37.50
90-04-015	Church Lite Up House MER-310	J. White	Closed	27.50	27.50
90-04-016	Deep Gold Church Lite Up House MER-360D	J. White	Closed	35.00	35.00
90-04-017	Double Store Lite Up House MER-311	J. White	Closed	27.50	27.50
90-04-018	Fire Station Lite Up House XMS-1550C	E.Mann	Closed	25.00	25.00
90-04-019	Grist Mill Lite Up House MER-372	J. White	Open	27.50	27.50
90-04-020	Inn Lite Up House MER-316	J. White	Closed	27.50	27.50
90-04-021	Leatherworks Lite Up House MER-371	J. White	Open	27.50	27.50
90-04-022	Library Lite Up House MER-317	J. White	Closed	27.50	27.50
90-04-023	Light House Lite Up House MER-370	J. White	Closed	27.50	27.50
90-04-024	Mansion Lite Up House MER-319	J. White	Closed	27.50	27.50
90-04-025	Mr/Mrs Santa Musical CJ-281	Jaimy	Open	37.50	37.50
90-04-026	New England Church Lite Up House MER-375	J. White	Open	27.50	27.50
90-04-027	New England General Store Lite Up House MER-377	J. White	Open	27.50	27.50
90-04-028	Railroad Station Lite Up House MER-374	J. White	Open	27.50	27.50
90-04-029	Roly Poly Santa 3 Asst. CJ-253/4/7	Jaimy	Open	17.50	17.50
90-04-030	Santa on Chimney Musical CJ-212	Jaimy	Open	33.50	33.50
90-04-031	Santa on See Saw TR-14	E. Mann	Closed	30.00	30.00
90-04-032	Santa Packing Bag CJ-210	Jaimy	Open	33.50	33.50
90-04-033	Santa w/List CJ-23	Jaimy	Closed	27.50	27.50
90-04-034	School Lite Up House MER-320	J. White	Closed	27.50	27.50
90-04-035	Town Hall Lite Up House MER-315	J. White	Closed	27.50	27.50
91-04-036	Apothecary Lite Up CJ-128	Jaimy	Open	33.50	33.50
91-04-037	Beige Church Lite Up House MER-360A	Jaimy	Closed	35.00	35.00
91-04-038	Boy and Girl on Bell CJ-132	Jaimy	Open	13.50	13.50
91-04-039	Boy on Horse CJ-457	Jaimy	Open	6.00	6.00
91-04-040	Carolers Under Lamppost CJ-114A	Jaimy	Open	7.50	7.50
91-04-041	Church Lite Up MER-410	J. White	Open	17.50	17.50
91-04-042	Church w/Blue Roof Lite Up House MER-360E	J. White	Closed	35.00	35.00
91-04-043	Covered Bridge CJ-101	Jaimy	Open	27.50	27.50
91-04-044	Elf w/Doll House CB-14	E. Mann	Open	30.00	30.00
91-04-045	Elf w/Hammer CB-11	E. Mann	Open	30.00	30.00
91-04-046	Elf w/Reindeer CJ-422	Jaimy	Open	9.00	9.00
91-04-047	Elf w/Rocking Horse CB-10	E. Mann	Open	30.00	30.00
91-04-048	Elf w/Teddy Bear CB-12	E. Mann	Open	30.00	30.00
91-04-049	Emily's Toys CJ-127	Jaimy	Open	35.00	35.00
91-04-050	Father and Mother w/Daughter CJ-133	Jaimy	Open	13.50	13.50
91-04-051	Father Christmas CJ-233	Jaimy	Open	33.50	33.50
91-04-052	Father Christmas w/Holly CJ-239	Jaimy	Open	35.00	35.00
91-04-053	Fire Station CJ-129	Jaimy	Open	50.00	50.00
91-04-054	Four Men Talking CJ-138	Jaimy	Closed	27.50	27.50
91-04-055	Gift Shop Lite Up CJ-125	Jaimy	Open	33.50	33.50
91-04-056	Girls w/Instruments CJ-131	Jaimy	Open	13.50	13.50
91-04-057	Horse and Coach CJ-207	Jaimy	Open	25.00	25.00
91-04-058	Kids Building Igloo CJ-137	Jaimy	Open	13.50	13.50
91-04-059	Lady w/Dogs CJ-208	Jaimy	Open	13.50	13.50
91-04-060	Man w/Wheelbarrow CJ-134	Jaimy	Open	13.50	13.50
91-04-061	Newsboy Under Lamppost CJ-144B	Jaimy	Closed	15.00	15.00
91-04-062	Old Curiosity Lite Up CJ-201	Jaimy	Open	37.50	37.50
91-04-063	Playhouse Lite Up CJ-122	Jaimy	Open	50.00	50.00
91-04-064	Public Library Lite Up CJ-121	Jaimy	Open	45.00	45.00
91-04-065	Reindeer Barn Lite Up House CJ-421	Jaimy	Open	55.00	55.00
91-04-066	Restaurant Lite Up House MER-354	J. White	Open	27.50	27.50
91-04-067	Santa Cat Roly Poly CJ-252	Jaimy	Open	17.50	17.50
91-04-068	Santa Fixing Sled CJ-237	Jaimy	Open	35.00	35.00
91-04-069	Santa In Barrel Waterball CJ-243	Jaimy	Open	33.50	33.50
91-04-070	Santa In Toy Shop CJ-441	Jaimy	Open	33.50	33.50
91-04-071	Santa On Train CJ-458	Jaimy	Open	6.00	6.00
91-04-072	Santa On White Horse CJ-338	E. Mann	Open	33.50	33.50
91-04-073	Santa Packing Bag CJ-210	Jaimy	Open	33.50	33.50
91-04-074	Santa Packing Bag CJ-236	Jaimy	Open	35.00	35.00
91-04-075	Santa Sleeping Musical CJ-214	Jaimy	Open	30.00	30.00
91-04-076	Santa w/Bag and List CJ-431	Jaimy	Open	33.50	33.50
91-04-077	Santa w/Deer Musical CJ-21R	Jaimy	Open	33.50	33.50
91-04-078	Santa w/Girl Waterball CJ-241	Jaimy	Open	33.50	33.50
91-04-079	Santa w/Lantern Musical CJ-211	Jaimy	Open	33.50	33.50
91-04-080	Santa w/List CJ-23R	Jaimy	Open	27.50	27.50
91-04-081	Snowball Fight CJ-124B	Jaimy	Open	25.00	25.00
91-04-082	Soup Seller Waterball CJ-209	Jaimy	Open	25.00	25.00
91-04-083	Stone Cottage Lite Up CJ-100	Jaimy	Open	37.50	37.50
91-04-084	Stone House Lite Up CJ-102	Jaimy	Open	45.00	45.00
91-04-085	Teddy Bear On Wheels CB-42	E. Mann	Open	25.00	25.00
91-04-086	The Skaters CJ-205	Jaimy	Open	25.00	25.00
91-04-087	The Story Teller CJ-204	Jaimy	Open	20.00	20.00
91-04-088	The Toy Seller CJ-206	Jaimy	Closed	13.50	13.50
91-04-089	Three Ladies w/Food CJ-136	Jaimy	Open	13.50	13.50
91-04-090	Trader Santa Musical CJ-442	Jaimy	Open	30.00	30.00
91-04-091	Train Set MER-378	J. White	Open	25.00	25.00
91-04-092	2 Tone Stone Church MER-360B	J. White	Closed	35.00	35.00
91-04-093	Toy Store Lite Up House MER-355	J. White	Open	27.50	27.50
91-04-094	Two Old Men Talking CJ-107	Jaimy	Open	13.50	13.50

Company Number	Name	Series Artist	Edition Limit	Issue Price	Quote
91-04-095	Village Mill Lite Up CJ-104	Jaimy	Open	30.00	30.00
91-04-096	Village People CJ-116A	Jaimy	Open	60.00	60.00
91-04-097	Woman w/Cow CJ-135	Jaimy	Open	15.00	15.00
91-04-098	Ye Olde Town Tavern CJ-130	Jaimy	Open	45.00	45.00
Seymour Mann, Inc.		**Dickens Collection**			
89-05-001	Cratchits Lite Up XMS-7000A	J. White	Open	30.00	30.00
89-05-002	Fezziwigs Lite Up XMS-7000C	J. White	Open	30.00	30.00
89-05-003	Gift Shoppe Lite Up XMS-7000D	J. White	Open	30.00	30.00
89-05-004	Scrooge/Marley Lite Up XMS-7000B	J. White	Open	30.00	30.00
90-05-005	Black Swan Inn Lite Up XMS-7000E	J. White	Open	30.00	30.00
90-05-006	Cratchit Family MER-121	J. White	Closed	37.50	37.50
90-05-007	Hen Poultry Lite Up XMS-7000H	J. White	Open	30.00	30.00
90-05-008	Tea and Spice Lite Up XMS-7000F	J. White	Open	30.00	30.00
90-05-009	Waite Fish Store Lite Up XMS-7000G	J. White	Open	30.00	30.00
90-05-010	Cratchit/Tiny Tim Musical MER-105	J. White	Closed	33.50	33.50
91-05-011	Cratchit/Tiny Tim Musical CJ-117	Jaimy	Open	33.50	33.50
91-05-012	Cratchit's Lite Up House CJ-200	Jaimy	Open	37.50	37.50
91-05-013	Scrooge/Marley Counting House CJ-202	Jaimy	Open	37.50	37.50
91-05-014	Scrooge Musical CJ-118	Jaimy	Open	30.00	30.00
Seymour Mann, Inc.		**Gingerbread Christmas Collection**			
91-06-001	Gingerbread Angel CJ-411	J. Sauerbrey	Open	7.50	7.50
91-06-002	Gingerbread Church Lite Up House CJ-403	J. Sauerbrey	Open	65.00	65.00
91-06-003	Gingerbread House CJ-416	J. Sauerbrey	Open	7.50	7.50
91-06-004	Gingerbread House Lite Up CJ-404	J. Sauerbrey	Open	65.00	65.00
91-06-005	Gingerbread Man CJ-415	J. Sauerbrey	Open	7.50	7.50
91-06-006	Gingerbread Mansion Lite Up CJ-405	J. Sauerbrey	Open	70.00	70.00
91-06-007	Gingerbread Mouse/Boot CJ-409	J. Sauerbrey	Open	7.50	7.50
91-06-008	Gingerbread Mrs. Claus CJ-414	J. Sauerbrey	Open	7.50	7.50
91-06-009	Gingerbread Reindeer CJ-410	J. Sauerbrey	Open	7.50	7.50
91-06-010	Gingerbread Rocking Horse Music CJ-460	J. Sauerbrey	Open	33.50	33.50
91-06-011	Gingerbread Santa CJ-408	J. Sauerbrey	Open	7.50	7.50
91-06-012	Gingerbread Sleigh CJ-406	J. Sauerbrey	Open	7.50	7.50
91-06-013	Gingerbread Snowman CJ-412	J. Sauerbrey	Open	7.50	7.50
91-06-014	Gingerbread Swan Musical CJ-462	J. Sauerbrey	Closed	33.50	33.50
91-06-015	Gingerbread Sweet Shop Lite Up House CJ-417	J. Sauerbrey	Open	60.00	60.00
91-06-016	Gingerbread Teddy Bear Music CJ-461	J. Sauerbrey	Closed	33.50	33.50
91-06-017	Gingerbread Toy Shop Lite Up House CJ-402	J. Sauerbrey	Open	60.00	60.00
91-06-018	Gingerbread Tree CJ-407	J. Sauerbrey	Open	7.50	7.50
91-06-019	Gingerbread Village Lite Up House CJ-400	J. Sauerbrey	Open	60.00	60.00
Seymour Mann, Inc.		**Victorian Christmas Collection**			
90-07-001	Toy/Doll House Lite Up MER-314	J. White	Closed	27.50	27.50
90-07-002	Victorian House Lite Up House MER-312	J. White	Closed	27.50	27.50
90-07-003	Yarn Shop Lite Up House MER-313	J. White	Closed	27.50	27.50
91-07-004	Antique Shop Lite Up House MER-353	J. White	Closed	27.50	27.50
91-07-005	Beige Church Lite Up House MER-351	J. White	Closed	35.00	35.00
91-07-006	Book Store Lite Up House MER-351	J. White	Closed	27.50	27.50
91-07-007	Church Lite Up House MER-350	J. White	Closed	37.50	37.50
91-07-008	Country Store Lite Up House MER-356	J. White	Closed	27.50	27.50
91-07-009	Inn Lite Up House MER-352	J. White	Closed	27.50	27.50
91-07-010	Little Match Girl CJ-419	Jaimy	Closed	9.00	9.00
90-07-011	Two Boys w/Snowman CJ-106	Jaimy	Closed	12.00	12.00
93-07-012	Couple Against Wind CJ-420	Jaimy	Closed	15.00	15.00
Seymour Mann, Inc.		**Cat Musical Figurines**			
85-08-001	Cats Ball Shape MH-303A/G	Kenji	Closed	25.00	25.00
86-08-002	Cats w/Ribbon MH-481A/C	Kenji	Open	30.00	30.00
87-08-003	Brown Cat in Teacup MH-600VGB16	Kenji	Open	30.00	30.00
87-08-004	Cat in Garbage Can MH-490	Kenji	Open	35.00	35.00
87-08-005	Cat on Tipped Garbage Can MH-498	Kenji	Open	35.00	35.00
87-08-006	Cat in Rose Teacup MH-600VG	Kenji	Open	30.00	30.00
87-08-007	Cat in Teapot Brown MH-600VGB	Kenji	Open	30.00	30.00
87-08-008	Cat in Teacup MH-600VGG	Kenji	Open	30.00	30.00
87-08-009	Valentine Cat in Teacup MH-600VLT	Kenji	Open	33.50	33.50
87-08-010	Musical Bear MH-602	Kenji	Closed	27.50	27.50
87-08-011	Kittens w/Balls of Yarn MH-612	Kenji	Open	30.00	30.00
87-08-012	Cat in Bag MH-614	Kenji	Open	30.00	30.00
87-08-013	Cat in Bag MH-617	Kenji	Open	30.00	30.00
87-08-014	Brown Cat in Bag MH-617B/6	Kenji	Open	30.00	30.00
87-08-015	Valentine Cat in Bag Musical MH-600	Kenji	Open	33.50	33.50
87-08-016	Teapot Cat MH-631	Kenji	Open	30.00	30.00
88-08-017	Cat in Hat Box MH-634	Kenji	Open	35.00	35.00
88-08-018	Cat in Hat MH-634B	Kenji	Open	35.00	35.00
88-08-019	Brown Cat in Hat MH-634B/6	Kenji	Open	35.00	35.00
89-08-020	Cat w/Coffee Cup Musical MH-706	Kenji	Open	35.00	35.00
89-08-021	Cat in Flower MH-709	Kenji	Open	35.00	35.00
89-08-022	Cat w/Swing Musical MH-710	Kenji	Open	35.00	35.00
89-08-023	Cat in Water Can Musical MH-712	Kenji	Closed	35.00	35.00
89-08-024	Cat on Basket MH-713	Kenji	Closed	35.00	35.00
89-08-025	Cat in Basinet MH-714	Kenji	Closed	35.00	35.00
89-08-026	Cat in Basket MH-713B	Kenji	Open	35.00	35.00
89-08-027	Cat in Gift Box Musical MH-732	Kenji	Open	40.00	40.00
89-08-028	Cat in Shoe MH-718	Kenji	Open	30.00	30.00
89-08-029	Cats in Basket XMAS-664	E. Mann	Closed	7.50	7.50
90-08-030	Bride/Groom Cat MH-738	Kenji	Open	37.50	37.50
90-08-031	Cat in Bootie MH-728	Kenji	Open	35.00	35.00
90-08-032	Grey Cat in Bootie MH-728G/6	Kenji	Open	35.00	35.00
90-08-033	Cat Sailor in Rocking Boat MH-734	Kenji	Open	45.00	45.00
90-08-034	Cat Asleep MH-735	Kenji	Open	17.50	17.50
90-08-035	Cat on Gift Box Music MH-740	Kenji	Open	40.00	40.00
90-08-036	Cat on Pillow MH-731	Kenji	Open	17.50	17.50
90-08-037	Cat w/Bow on Pink Pillow MH-741P	Kenji	Open	33.50	33.50
90-08-038	Cat w/Parrot MH-730	Kenji	Open	37.50	37.50
90-08-039	Kitten Trio in Carriage MH-742	Kenji	Open	37.50	37.50
90-08-040	Cat Calico in Easy Chair MH-743VG	Kenji	Open	27.50	27.50
90-08-041	Cats Graduation MH-745	Kenji	Open	27.50	27.50
90-08-042	Cat in Dress MH-751VG	Kenji	Open	37.50	37.50
91-08-043	Brown Cat in Bag	Kenji	Open	30.00	30.00
91-08-044	Brown Cat in Hat	Kenji	Open	35.00	35.00
91-08-045	Brown Cat in Teacup	Kenji	Open	30.00	30.00
91-08-046	Cat in Bag	Kenji	Open	30.00	30.00
91-08-047	Cat in Bag	Kenji	Open	30.00	30.00
91-08-048	Cat in Bootie	Kenji	Open	35.00	35.00
91-08-049	Cat in Garbage Can	Kenji	Open	35.00	35.00
91-08-050	Cat in Hat	Kenji	Open	35.00	35.00
91-08-051	Cat in Hat Box	Kenji	Open	35.00	35.00
91-08-052	Cat in Rose Teacup	Kenji	Open	30.00	30.00
91-08-053	Cat in Teacup	Kenji	Open	30.00	30.00
91-08-054	Cat in Teapot Brown	Kenji	Open	30.00	30.00
91-08-055	Cat Momma MH-758	Kenji	Open	35.00	35.00
91-08-056	Cat on Tipped Garbage Can	Kenji	Open	35.00	35.00

Company / Number	Name	Series / Artist	Edition Limit	Issue Price	Quote
91-08-057	Cats Ball Shape	Kenji	Open	25.00	25.00
91-08-058	Cats w/Ribbon	Kenji	Open	30.00	30.00
91-08-059	Grey Cat in Bootie	Kenji	Open	35.00	35.00
91-08-060	Kittens w/Balls of Yarn	Kenji	Open	30.00	30.00
91-08-061	Musical Bear	Kenji	Open	27.50	27.50
91-08-062	Teapot Cat	Kenji	Open	30.00	30.00
91-08-063	Cat in Basket MH-768	Kenji	Open	35.00	35.00
91-08-064	Cat Watching Butterfly MH-784	Kenji	Open	17.50	17.50
91-08-065	Cat Watching Canary MH-783	Kenji	Open	25.00	25.00
91-08-066	Cat With Bow on Pink Pillow MH-741P	Kenji	Open	33.50	33.50
91-08-067	Family Cat MH-770	Kenji	Open	35.00	35.00
91-08-068	Kitten Picking Tulips MH-756	Kenji	Open	40.00	40.00
91-08-069	Revolving Cat with Butterfly MH-759	Kenji	Open	40.00	40.00
Seymour Mann, Inc.		**Bunny Musical Figurines**			
91-09-001	Bunny In Teacup MH-781	Kenji	Open	25.00	25.00
91-09-002	Bunny In Teapot MH-780	Kenji	Open	25.00	25.00
Maruri USA		**Birds of Prey**			
81-01-001	Screech Owl	W. Gaither	300	960.00	960.00
81-01-002	American Bald Eagle I	W. Gaither	Closed	165.00	1750.00
82-01-003	American Bald Eagle II	W. Gaither	Closed	245.00	2750.00
83-01-004	American Bald Eagle III	W. Gaither	Closed	445.00	1750.00
84-01-005	American Bald Eagle IV	W. Gaither	Closed	360.00	1750.00
86-01-006	American Bald Eagle V	W. Gaither	Closed	325.00	1250.00
Maruri USA		**North American Waterfowl I**			
81-02-001	Blue Winged Teal	W. Gaither	200	980.00	980.00
81-02-002	Wood Duck, decoy	W. Gaither	950	480.00	480.00
81-02-003	Flying Wood Ducks	W. Gaither	Closed	880.00	880.00
81-02-004	Canvasback Ducks	W. Gaither	300	780.00	780.00
81-02-005	Mallard Drake	W. Gaither	Closed	2380.00	2380.00
Maruri USA		**North American Waterfowl II**			
81-03-001	Mallard Ducks Pair	W. Gaither	1,500	225.00	225.00
82-03-002	Goldeneye Ducks Pair	W. Gaither	Closed	225.00	225.00
82-03-003	Bufflehead Ducks Pair	W. Gaither	1,500	225.00	225.00
82-03-004	Widgeon, male	W. Gaither	Closed	225.00	225.00
82-03-005	Widgeon, female	W. Gaither	Closed	225.00	225.00
82-03-006	Pintail Ducks Pair	W. Gaither	1,500	225.00	225.00
83-03-007	Loon	W. Gaither	Closed	245.00	245.00
Maruri USA		**North American Songbirds**			
82-04-001	Cardinal, male	W. Gaither	Closed	95.00	95.00
82-04-002	Chickadee	W. Gaither	Closed	95.00	95.00
82-04-003	Bluebird	W. Gaither	Closed	95.00	95.00
82-04-004	Mockingbird	W. Gaither	Closed	95.00	95.00
82-04-005	Carolina Wren	W. Gaither	Closed	95.00	95.00
83-04-006	Cardinal, female	W. Gaither	Closed	95.00	95.00
83-04-007	Robin	W. Gaither	Closed	95.00	95.00
Maruri USA		**North American Game Birds**			
81-05-001	Canadian Geese, pair	W. Gaither	Closed	2000.00	2000.00
81-05-002	Eastern Wild Turkey	W. Gaither	Closed	300.00	300.00
82-05-003	Ruffed Grouse	W. Gaither	Closed	1745.00	1745.00
83-05-004	Bobtail Quail, male	W. Gaither	Closed	375.00	375.00
83-05-005	Bobtail Quail, female	W. Gaither	Closed	375.00	375.00
83-05-006	Wild Turkey Hen with Chicks	W. Gaither	Closed	300.00	300.00
Maruri USA		**Baby Animals**			
81-06-001	African Lion Cubs	W. Gaither	1,500	195.00	195.00
81-06-002	Wolf Cubs	W. Gaither	Closed	195.00	195.00
81-06-003	Black Bear Cubs	W. Gaither	Closed	195.00	195.00
Maruri USA		**Upland Birds**			
81-07-001	Mourning Doves	W. Gaither	Closed	780.00	780.00
Maruri USA		**Americana**			
81-08-001	Grizzley Bear and Indian	W. Gaither	Closed	650.00	650.00
82-08-002	Sioux Brave and Bison	W. Gaither	Closed	985.00	985.00
Maruri USA		**Stump Animals**			
82-09-001	Red Fox	W. Gaither	Closed	175.00	175.00
83-09-002	Raccoon	W. Gaither	Closed	175.00	175.00
83-09-003	Owl	W. Gaither	Closed	175.00	175.00
84-09-004	Gray Squirrel	W. Gaither	1,200	175.00	175.00
84-09-005	Chipmunk	W. Gaither	Closed	175.00	175.00
84-09-006	Bobcat	W. Gaither	Closed	175.00	175.00
Maruri USA		**Shore Birds**			
84-10-001	Pelican	W. Gaither	Closed	260.00	260.00
84-10-002	Sand Piper	W. Gaither	Closed	285.00	285.00
Maruri USA		**North American Game Animals**			
84-11-001	White Tail Deer	W. Gaither	950	285.00	285.00
Maruri USA		**African Safari Animals**			
83-12-001	African Elephant	W. Gaither	Closed	3500.00	3500.00
83-12-002	Southern White Rhino	W. Gaither	150	3200.00	3200.00
83-12-003	Cape Buffalo	W. Gaither	Closed	2200.00	2200.00
83-12-004	Black Maned Lion	W. Gaither	Closed	1450.00	1450.00
83-12-005	Southern Leopard	W. Gaither	300	1450.00	1450.00
83-12-006	Southern Greater Kudu	W. Gaither	Closed	1800.00	1800.00
83-12-007	Southern Impala	W. Gaither	Closed	1200.00	1200.00
81-12-008	Nyala	W. Gaither	300	1450.00	1450.00
83-12-009	Sable	W. Gaither	Closed	1200.00	1200.00
83-12-010	Grant's Zebras, pair	W. Gaither	500	1200.00	1200.00
Maruri USA		**Special Commissions**			
81-13-001	White Bengal Tiger	W. Gaither	240	340.00	340.00
82-13-002	Cheetah	W. Gaither	Closed	995.00	995.00
83-13-003	Orange Bengal Tiger	W. Gaither	240	340.00	340.00
Maruri USA		**Signature Collection**			
85-14-001	American Bald Eagle	W. Gaither	Closed	60.00	60.00
85-14-002	Canada Goose	W. Gaither	Closed	60.00	60.00
85-14-003	Hawk	W. Gaither	Closed	60.00	60.00
85-14-004	Snow Goose	W. Gaither	Closed	60.00	60.00
85-14-005	Pintail Duck	W. Gaither	Closed	60.00	60.00
85-14-006	Swallow	W. Gaither	Closed	60.00	60.00
Maruri USA		**Legendary Flowers of the Orient**			
85-15-001	Iris	Ito	15,000	45.00	55.00
85-15-002	Lotus	Ito	15,000	45.00	45.00
85-15-003	Chinese Peony	Ito	15,000	45.00	55.00
85-15-004	Lily	Ito	15,000	45.00	55.00
85-15-005	Chrysanthemum	Ito	15,000	45.00	55.00
85-15-006	Cherry Blossom	Ito	15,000	45.00	55.00
85-15-007	Orchid	Ito	15,000	45.00	55.00
85-15-008	Wisteria	Ito	15,000	45.00	55.00
Maruri USA		**American Eagle Gallery**			
85-16-001	E-8501	Maruri Studios	Closed	45.00	75.00
85-16-002	E-8502	Maruri Studios	Open	55.00	65.00
85-16-003	E-8503	Maruri Studios	Open	60.00	65.00
85-16-004	E-8504	Maruri Studios	Open	65.00	75.00
85-16-005	E-8505	Maruri Studios	Closed	65.00	150.00
85-16-006	E-8506	Maruri Studios	Open	75.00	90.00
85-16-007	E-8507	Maruri Studios	Open	75.00	90.00
85-16-008	E-8508	Maruri Studios	Closed	75.00	85.00
85-16-009	E-8509	Maruri Studios	Closed	85.00	125.00
85-16-010	E-8510	Maruri Studios	Open	85.00	95.00
85-16-011	E-8511	Maruri Studios	Closed	85.00	125.00
85-16-012	E-8512	Maruri Studios	Open	295.00	325.00
87-16-013	E-8721	Maruri Studios	Open	40.00	50.00
87-16-014	E-8722	Maruri Studios	Open	45.00	55.00
87-16-015	E-8723	Maruri Studios	Closed	55.00	60.00
87-16-016	E-8724	Maruri Studios	Open	175.00	195.00
89-16-017	E-8931	Maruri Studios	Open	55.00	60.00
89-16-018	E-8932	Maruri Studios	Open	75.00	80.00
89-16-019	E-8933	Maruri Studios	Open	95.00	95.00
89-16-020	E-8934	Maruri Studios	Open	135.00	140.00
89-16-021	E-8935	Maruri Studios	Open	175.00	185.00
89-16-022	E-8936	Maruri Studios	Open	185.00	195.00
91-16-023	E-9141 Eagle Landing	Maruri Studios	Open	60.00	60.00
91-16-024	E-9142 Eagle w/ Totem Pole	Maruri Studios	Open	75.00	75.00
91-16-025	E-9143 Pair in Flight	Maruri Studios	Open	95.00	95.00
91-16-026	E-9144 Eagle w/Salmon	Maruri Studios	Open	110.00	110.00
91-16-027	E-9145 Eagle w/Snow	Maruri Studios	Open	135.00	135.00
91-16-028	E-9146 Eagle w/Babies	Maruri Studios	Open	145.00	145.00
Maruri USA		**Wings of Love Doves**			
87-17-001	D-8701 Single Dove	Maruri Studios	Open	45.00	55.00
87-17-002	D-8702 Double Dove	Maruri Studios	Open	55.00	65.00
87-17-003	D-8703 Single Dove	Maruri Studios	Open	65.00	70.00
87-17-004	D-8704 Double Dove	Maruri Studios	Open	75.00	85.00
87-17-005	D-8705 Single Dove	Maruri Studios	Open	95.00	95.00
87-17-006	D-8706 Double Dove	Maruri Studios	Open	175.00	195.00
90-17-007	D-9021 Double Dove	Maruri Studios	Open	50.00	55.00
90-17-008	D-9022 Double Dove	Maruri Studios	Open	75.00	75.00
90-17-009	D-9023 Double Dove	Maruri Studios	Open	115.00	120.00
90-17-010	D-9024 Double Dove	Maruri Studios	Open	150.00	160.00
Maruri USA		**Majestic Owls of the Night**			
87-18-001	Burrowing Owl	D. Littleton	15,000	55.00	55.00
88-18-002	Barred Owl	D. Littleton	15,000	55.00	55.00
88-18-003	Elf Owl	D. Littleton	15,000	55.00	55.00
Maruri USA		**Studio Collection**			
90-19-001	Majestic Eagles-MS100	Maruri Studios	Closed	350.00	800.00
91-19-002	Delicate Motion-MS200	Maruri Studios	3,500	325.00	325.00
92-19-003	Imperial Panda-MS300	Maruri Studios	3,500	350.00	350.00
93-19-004	Wild Wings-MS400	Maruri Studios	Closed	395.00	450.00
Maruri USA		**Polar Expedition**			
90-20-001	Baby Emperor Penguin-P-9001	Maruri Studios	Open	45.00	50.00
90-20-002	Baby Arctic Fox-P-9002	Maruri Studios	Open	50.00	55.00
90-20-003	Polar Bear Cub Sliding-P-9003	Maruri Studios	Open	50.00	55.00
90-20-004	Polar Bear Cubs Playing-P-9004	Maruri Studios	Open	60.00	65.00
90-20-005	Baby Harp Seals-P-9005	Maruri Studios	Open	65.00	70.00
90-20-006	Mother & Baby Emperor Penguins -P-9006	Maruri Studios	Open	80.00	85.00
90-20-007	Mother & Baby Harp Seals-P-9007	Maruri Studios	Open	90.00	95.00
90-20-008	Mother & Baby Polar Bears-P-9008	Maruri Studios	Open	125.00	130.00
90-20-009	Polar Expedition Sign-PES-001	Maruri Studios	Open	18.00	18.00
92-20-010	Baby Harp Seal-P-9221	Maruri Studios	Open	55.00	55.00
92-20-011	Emperor Penguins-P-9222	Maruri Studios	Open	60.00	60.00
92-20-012	Arctic Fox Cubs Playing-P-9223	Maruri Studios	Open	65.00	65.00
92-20-013	Polar Bear Family-P-9224	Maruri Studios	Open	90.00	90.00
Maruri USA		**Eyes Of The Night**			
90-21-001	Single Screech Owl-O-8801	Maruri Studios	Closed	50.00	55.00
90-21-002	Single Snowy Owl-O-8802	Maruri Studios	Closed	50.00	55.00
90-21-003	Single Great Horned Owl-O-8803	Maruri Studios	Closed	60.00	65.00
90-21-004	Single Tawny Owl-O-8804	Maruri Studios	Closed	60.00	65.00
90-21-005	Single Snowy Owl-O-8805	Maruri Studios	Closed	80.00	85.00
90-21-006	Single Screech Owl-O-8806	Maruri Studios	Closed	90.00	95.00
90-21-007	Double Barn Owl 0-8807	Maruri Studios	Closed	125.00	130.00
90-21-008	Single Great Horned Owl-O-8808	Mauurl Studios	Closed	145.00	150.00
90-21-009	Double Snowy Owl-O-8809	Maruri Studios	Closed	245.00	250.00
Maruri USA		**Songbirds Of Beauty**			
91-22-001	Chickadee With Roses SB-9101	Maruri Studios	Open	85.00	85.00
91-22-002	Goldfinch With Hawthorne SB-9102	Maruri Studios	Open	85.00	85.00
91-22-003	Cardinal With Cherry Blossom SB-9103	Maruri Studios	Open	85.00	85.00
91-22-004	Robin With Lilies SB-9104	Maruri Studios	Open	85.00	85.00
91-22-005	Bluebird With Apple Blossom SB-9105	Maruri Studios	Open	85.00	85.00
91-22-006	Robin & Baby With Azalea SB-9106	Maruri Studios	Open	115.00	115.00
91-22-007	Dbl. Bluebird With Peach Blossom SB-9107	Maruri Studios	Open	145.00	145.00
91-22-008	Dbl. Cardinal With Dogwood SB-9108	Maruri Studios	Open	145.00	145.00
Maruri USA		**Hummingbirds**			
91-23-001	Rufous w/Trumpet Creeper H-8901	Maruri Studios	Open	70.00	75.00
89-23-002	White-eared w/Morning Glory H-8902	Maruri Studios	Open	85.00	85.00
89-23-003	Violet-crowned w/Gentian H-8903	Maruri Studios	Open	90.00	90.00
89-23-004	Calliope w/Azalea H-8904	Maruri Studios	Open	120.00	120.00
91-23-005	Anna's w/Lily H-8905	Maruri Studios	Open	160.00	160.00
91-23-006	Allew's w/Hibiscus H-8906	Maruri Studios	Open	195.00	195.00
91-23-007	Ruby-Throated w/Azalea H-8911	Maruri Studios	Open	75.00	75.00
91-23-008	White-Eared w/Morning Glory H-8912	Maruri Studios	Open	75.00	75.00
91-23-009	Violet-Crowned w/Gentian H-8913	Maruri Studios	Open	75.00	75.00
91-23-010	Ruby-Throated w/Orchid H-8914	Maruri Studios	Open	150.00	150.00
Maruri USA		**Graceful Reflections**			
91-24-001	Single Mute Swan SW-9151	Maruri Studios	Closed	85.00	85.00
91-24-002	Mute Swan w/Baby SW-9152	Maruri Studios	Closed	95.00	95.00
91-24-003	Pair-Mute Swan SW-9153	Maruri Studios	Closed	145.00	145.00
91-24-004	Pair-Mute Swan SW-9154	Maruri Studios	Closed	195.00	195.00

Number	Name	Artist	Edition Limit	Issue Price	Quote
Maruri USA		**Precious Panda**			
92-25-001	Snack Time PP-9201	Maruri Studios	Open	60.00	60.00
92-25-002	Lazy Lunch PP-9202	Maruri Studios	Open	60.00	60.00
92-25-003	Tug Of War PP-9203	Maruri Studios	Open	70.00	70.00
92-25-004	Mother's Cuddle-PP-9204	Maruri Studios	Open	120.00	120.00
Maruri USA		**Gentle Giants**			
92-26-001	Baby Elephant Standing GG-9251	Maruri Studios	Open	50.00	50.00
92-26-002	Baby Elephant Sitting GG-9252	Maruri Studios	Open	65.00	65.00
92-26-003	Elephant Pair Playing GG-9253	Maruri Studios	Open	80.00	80.00
92-26-004	Mother & Baby Elephant GG-9254	Maruri Studios	Open	160.00	160.00
92-26-005	Elephant Pair GG-9255	Maruri Studios	Open	220.00	220.00
Maruri USA		**Horses Of The World**			
93-27-001	Clydesdale HW-9351	Maruri Studios	Open	145.00	145.00
93-27-002	Thoroughbred HW-9352	Maruri Studios	Open	145.00	145.00
93-27-003	Quarter Horse HW-9353	Maruri Studios	Open	145.00	145.00
93-27-004	Camargue HW-9354	Maruri Studios	Open	150.00	150.00
93-27-005	Paint Horse HW-9355	Maruri Studios	Open	160.00	160.00
93-27-006	Arabian HW-9356	Maruri Studios	Open	175.00	175.00
Maruri USA		**National Parks**			
93-28-001	Baby Bear NP-9301	Maruri Studios	Open	60.00	60.00
93-28-002	Cougar Cubs NP-9302	Maruri Studios	Open	70.00	70.00
93-28-003	Deer Family NP-9303	Maruri Studios	Open	120.00	120.00
93-28-004	Bear Family NP-9304	Maruri Studios	Open	160.00	160.00
93-28-005	Howling Wolves NP-9305	Maruri Studios	Open	165.00	165.00
93-28-006	Buffalo NP-9306	Maruri Studios	Open	170.00	170.00
93-28-007	Eagle NP-9307	Maruri Studios	Open	180.00	180.00
93-28-008	Falcon NP-9308	Maruri Studios	Open	195.00	195.00
June McKenna Collectibles, Inc.		**Limited Edition**			
83-01-001	Father Christmas	J. McKenna	Closed	90.00	2800-6000.
84-01-002	Old Saint Nick	J. McKenna	Closed	100.00	1500-3000.
85-01-003	Woodland	J. McKenna	Closed	140.00	1500-3000.
86-01-004	Victorian	J. McKenna	Closed	150.00	1000-1500.
87-01-005	Christmas Eve	J. McKenna	Closed	170.00	1200-1600.
87-01-006	Kris Kringle	J. McKenna	Closed	350.00	900.00
88-01-007	Bringing Home Christmas	J. McKenna	Closed	170.00	500-1300.
88-01-008	Remembrance of Christmas Past	J. McKenna	4,000	400.00	450.00
89-01-009	Seasons Greetings	J. McKenna	Closed	200.00	225-350.
89-01-010	Santa's Wardrobe	J. McKenna	Closed	750.00	750-1200.
90-01-011	Wilderness	J. McKenna	Closed	200.00	270.00
90-01-012	Night Before Christmas	J. McKenna	Closed	750.00	750.00
91-01-013	Coming to Town	J. McKenna	4,000	220.00	220.00
91-01-014	Santa's Hot Air Balloon	J. McKenna	Closed	800.00	800.00
92-01-015	Christmas Gathering	J. McKenna	4,000	220.00	220.00
93-01-016	The Patriot	J. McKenna	4,000	250.00	250.00
94-01-017	St. Nicholas	J. McKenna	4,000	240.00	240.00
June McKenna Collectibles, Inc.		**Registered Edition**			
86-02-001	Colonial	J. McKenna	Closed	150.00	300-350.
87-02-002	White Christmas	J. McKenna	Closed	170.00	1500.00
88-02-003	Jolly Ole St. Nick	J. McKenna	Closed	170.00	250-350.
89-02-004	Traditional	J. McKenna	Closed	180.00	300.00
90-02-005	Toy Maker	J. McKenna	Closed	200.00	250.00
91-02-006	Checking His List	J. McKenna	Open	230.00	240.00
92-02-007	Forty Winks	J. McKenna	Open	250.00	250.00
93-02-008	Tomorrow's Christmas	J. McKenna	Open	250.00	250.00
94-02-009	Say Cheese, Please	J. McKenna	Open	N/A	N/A
June McKenna Collectibles, Inc.		**Special Limited Edition**			
89-03-001	Santa & His Magic Sleigh	J. McKenna	Closed	280.00	280-450.
89-03-002	Last Gentle Nudge	J. McKenna	Closed	280.00	280-400.
90-03-003	Up On The Rooftop	J. McKenna	Closed	280.00	280-425.
90-03-004	Santa's Reindeer	J. McKenna	Closed	400.00	400-600.
90-03-005	Christmas Dreams	J. McKenna	Closed	280.00	280.00
91-03-006	Bedtime Stories	J. McKenna	2,000	500.00	500.00
92-03-007	Santa's Arrival	J. McKenna	2,000	300.00	300.00
93-03-008	Baking Cookies	J. McKenna	2,000	450.00	450.00
94-03-009	Welcome to the World	J. McKenna	2,000	400.00	400.00
94-03-010	All Aboard-North Pole Express	J. McKenna	Open	500.00	500.00
June McKenna Collectibles, Inc.		**June McKenna Figurines**			
84-04-001	Tree Topper	J. McKenna	Closed	70.00	195.00
85-04-002	Soldier	J. McKenna	Closed	40.00	150-200.
85-04-003	Father Times - 3D	J. McKenna	Closed	40.00	N/A
86-04-004	Male Angel	J. McKenna	Closed	44.00	1000-2000.
86-04-005	Little St. Nick	J. McKenna	Closed	50.00	75-150.00
87-04-006	Patriotic Santa	J. McKenna	Closed	50.00	195.00
87-04-007	Name Plaque	J. McKenna	Closed	50.00	50.00
87-04-008	Country Rag Boy	J. McKenna	Closed	40.00	40.00
87-04-009	Country Rag Girl	J. McKenna	Closed	40.00	40.00
88-04-010	Mrs. Santa	J. McKenna	Closed	50.00	125-300.
88-04-011	Mr. Santa - 3D	J. McKenna	Closed	44.00	80-150.00
89-04-012	16th Century Santa - 3D	J. McKenna	Closed	60.00	60-130.00
89-04-013	17th Century Santa - 3D	J. McKenna	Closed	70.00	70-95.00
89-04-014	Jolly Ole Santa - 3D	J. McKenna	Closed	44.00	44-90.00
90-04-015	Noel - 3D	J. McKenna	Closed	50.00	70.00
92-04-016	Taking A Break	J. McKenna	Open	60.00	70.00
92-04-017	Christmas Santa	J. McKenna	Closed	60.00	70.00
92-04-018	Choir of Angels	J. McKenna	Closed	60.00	60.00
92-04-019	Let It Snow	J. McKenna	Open	60.00	60.00
93-04-020	A Good Night's Sleep	J. McKenna	Open	70.00	70.00
93-04-021	Santa and Friends	J. McKenna	Open	70.00	70.00
93-04-022	Mr. Snowman	J. McKenna	Open	40.00	40.00
93-04-023	The Snow Family	J. McKenna	Open	40.00	40.00
93-04-024	Santa Name Plaque	J. McKenna	Open	70.00	70.00
93-04-025	Angel Name Plaque	J. McKenna	Open	70.00	70.00
93-04-026	Children Ice Skaters	J. McKenna	Open	60.00	60.00
94-04-027	Snowman and Child	J. McKenna	Open	60.00	60.00
94-04-028	Star of Bethlehem-Angel	J. McKenna	Open	40.00	40.00
June McKenna Collectibles, Inc.		**Carolers**			
85-05-001	Man Caroler	J. McKenna	Closed	36.00	65.00
85-05-002	Woman Caroler	J. McKenna	Closed	36.00	65.00
85-05-003	Girl Caroler	J. McKenna	Closed	36.00	65.00
85-05-004	Boy Caroler	J. McKenna	Closed	36.00	65.00
91-05-005	Carolers, Man With Girl	J. McKenna	Open	50.00	50.00
91-05-006	Carolers, Woman With Boy	J. McKenna	Open	50.00	50.00
92-05-007	Carolers, Grandparents	J. McKenna	Open	70.00	70.00
94-05-008	Children Carolers	J. McKenna	Open	N/A	N/A
June McKenna Collectibles, Inc.		**Limited Edition Flatback**			
88-06-001	Toys of Joy	J. McKenna	Closed	30.00	30-75.00
88-06-002	Mystical Santa	J. McKenna	Closed	30.00	30-75.00
89-06-003	Blue Christmas	J. McKenna	Closed	32.00	50-100.00
89-06-004	Victorian	J. McKenna	Closed	32.00	50-75.00
90-06-006	Old Time Santa	J. McKenna	Closed	34.00	45-60.00
90-06-007	Medieval Santa	J. McKenna	Closed	34.00	60.00
91-06-008	Farewell Santa	J. McKenna	Closed	34.00	40.00
91-06-009	Bag of Stars	J. McKenna	Closed	34.00	40.00
92-06-010	Good Tidings	J. McKenna	10,000	34.00	40.00
92-06-011	Deck The Halls	J. McKenna	10,000	34.00	40.00
93-06-012	Bells of Christmas	J. McKenna	10,000	40.00	40.00
93-06-013	Santa's Love	J. McKenna	10,000	40.00	40.00
94-06-014	Not Once But Twice	J. McKenna	10,000	40.00	40.00
June McKenna Collectibles, Inc.		**7" Limited Edition**			
88-07-001	Joyful Christmas	J. McKenna	Closed	90.00	150.00
88-07-002	Christmas Memories	J. McKenna	Closed	90.00	150.00
89-07-003	Old Fashioned Santa	J. McKenna	Closed	100.00	130-150.
89-07-004	Santa's Bag of Surprises	J. McKenna	Closed	100.00	175.00
90-07-005	Christmas Delight	J. McKenna	Closed	100.00	100.00
90-07-006	Ethnic Santa	J. McKenna	Closed	100.00	130.00
91-07-007	Christmas Bishop	J. McKenna	Closed	110.00	120.00
92-07-008	Christmas Wizard	J. McKenna	7,500	110.00	120.00
93-07-009	Christmas Cheer 1st ed.	J. McKenna	Closed	120.00	450.00
93-07-010	Christmas Cheer 2nd. ed.	J. McKenna	7,500	120.00	120.00
94-07-011	Santa's One Man Band	J. McKenna	7,500	120.00	120.00
94-07-012	Mrs. Claus, Dancing to the Tune	J. McKenna	7,500	120.00	120.00
June McKenna Collectibles, Inc.		**Nativity Set**			
88-08-001	Nativity - 6 Pieces	J. McKenna	Open	130.00	150.00
89-08-002	Three Wise Men	J. McKenna	Open	60.00	90.00
91-08-003	Sheep With Shepherds - 2 Pieces	J. McKenna	Open	60.00	60.00
June McKenna Collectibles, Inc.		**Black Folk Art**			
85-09-001	Mammie With Kids - 3D	J. McKenna	Closed	90.00	N/A
85-09-002	Kids in a Tub - 3D	J. McKenna	Closed	30.00	90.00
85-09-003	Toaster Cover	J. McKenna	Closed	50.00	N/A
85-09-004	Kissing Cousins - sill sitter	J. McKenna	Closed	36.00	65-85.00
83-09-005	Black Boy With Watermelon	J. McKenna	Closed	12.00	100.00
83-09-006	Black Girl With Watermelon	J. McKenna	Closed	12.00	100.00
84-09-007	Black Man With Pig	J. McKenna	Closed	13.00	40.00
84-09-008	Black Woman With Broom	J. McKenna	Closed	13.00	110.00
84-09-009	Mammie Cloth Doll	J. McKenna	Closed	90.00	N/A
84-09-010	Remus Cloth Doll	J. McKenna	Closed	90.00	N/A
85-09-011	Watermelon Patch Kids	J. McKenna	Closed	24.00	63.00
85-09-012	Mammie With Spoon	J. McKenna	Closed	13.00	N/A
86-09-013	Black Butler	J. McKenna	Closed	13.00	40.00
87-09-014	Aunt Bertha - 3D	J. McKenna	Closed	36.00	72.00
87-09-015	Uncle Jacob- 3D	J. McKenna	Closed	36.00	50-72.00
87-09-016	Lil' Willie -3D	J. McKenna	Closed	36.00	50-72.00
87-09-017	Sweet Prissy -3D	J. McKenna	Closed	36.00	72.00
88-09-018	Renty	J. McKenna	Closed	16.00	40.00
88-09-019	Netty	J. McKenna	Closed	16.00	40.00
89-09-020	Jake	J. McKenna	Closed	16.00	40.00
89-09-021	Delia	J. McKenna	Closed	16.00	30-40.00
90-09-022	Tasha	J. McKenna	Closed	17.00	40.00
90-09-023	Tyree	J. McKenna	Closed	17.00	40.00
90-09-024	Let's Play Ball -3D	J. McKenna	Closed	45.00	N/A
90-09-025	Sunday's Best -3D	J. McKenna	Closed	45.00	N/A
92-09-026	Fishing John -3D	J. McKenna	1,000	160.00	160.00
92-09-027	Sweet Sister Sue -3D	J. McKenna	1,000	160.00	160.00
June McKenna Collectibles, Inc.		**Victorian Limited Edition**			
90-10-001	Edward - 3D	J. McKenna	Closed	180.00	300-750.
90-10-002	Elizabeth - 3D	J. McKenna	Closed	180.00	300-750.
90-10-003	Joseph - 3D	J. McKenna	Closed	50.00	50-250.00
90-10-004	Victoria - 3D	J. McKenna	Closed	50.00	50-250.00
Michael's Limited		**Brian Baker's Deja Vu Collection**			
87-01-001	Hotel Couronne (original)white/brown 1000	B. Baker	Retrd.	49.00	49.00
87-01-002	Parisian Apartment-golden brown 1001	B. Baker	Retrd.	53.00	53.00
87-01-003	The Bernese Guesthouse-golden brown 1010	B. Baker	Retrd.	49.00	49.00
87-01-004	Bavarian Church-yellow 1020	B. Baker	Retrd.	38.00	38.00
87-01-005	Bavarian Church-white 1021	B. Baker	Retrd.	38.00	38.00
87-01-006	Japanese House-white/brown 1100	B. Baker	Retrd.	47.00	47.00
87-01-007	Snow Cabin-brown/white 1500	B. Baker	Open	51.00	51.00
87-01-008	Colonial House-blue 1510	B. Baker	Retrd.	49.00	49.00
87-01-009	Colonial House-wine 1511	B. Baker	Retrd.	40.00	40.00
87-01-010	Colonial Store-brick 1512	B. Baker	Retrd.	53.00	53.00
87-01-011	Old West General Store-white/grey 1520	B. Baker	Retrd.	50.00	68.00
87-01-012	Old West General Store-yellow 1521	B. Baker	Retrd.	50.00	50.00
87-01-013	The Farm House-beige/blue 1525	B. Baker	Retrd.	49.00	49.00
87-01-014	The Farm House-spiced tan 1526	B. Baker	Retrd.	49.00	49.00
87-01-015	The Cottage House-white 1530	B. Baker	Retrd.	47.00	47.00
87-01-016	The Cottage House-blue 1531	B. Baker	Retrd.	42.00	42.00
87-01-017	The Lighthouse-white 1535	B. Baker	Retrd.	53.00	60.00
87-01-018	Queen Ann Victorian-peach/green 1540	B. Baker	Retrd.	53.00	53.00
87-01-019	Queen Ann Victorian-rose 1541	B. Baker	Retrd.	53.00	53.00
87-01-020	Queen Ann Victorian-rust/green 1542	B. Baker	Retrd.	49.00	49.00
87-01-021	Italianate Victorian-brown 1543	B. Baker	Retrd.	51.00	51.00
87-01-022	Italianate Victorian-rust/blue 1544	B. Baker	Retrd.	49.00	49.00
87-01-023	Italianate Victorian-mauve/blue 1545	B. Baker	Retrd.	49.00	49.00
87-01-024	Turreted Victorian-beige/blue 1546	B. Baker	Retrd.	55.00	55.00
87-01-025	Turreted Victorian-peach 1547	B. Baker	Retrd.	55.00	55.00
87-01-026	Ultimate Victorian-maroon/slate 1548	B. Baker	Retrd.	60.00	60.00
87-01-027	Ultimate Victorian-lt. blue/rose 1549	B. Baker	Retrd.	60.00	60.00
87-01-028	Italianate Victorian-lavendar 1550	B. Baker	Retrd.	45.00	45.00
88-01-029	Roeder Gate, Rothenburg-brown 1022	B. Baker	Retrd.	49.00	49.00
88-01-030	Hampshire House-brick 1040	B. Baker	Retrd.	49.00	49.00
88-01-031	Andulusian Village-white 1060	B. Baker	Retrd.	53.00	63.00
88-01-032	Fairy Tale Cottage-white/brown 1200	B. Baker	Retrd.	46.00	46.00
88-01-033	Christmas House-blue 1225	B. Baker	Retrd.	51.00	51.00
88-01-034	Casa Chiquita-natural 1400	B. Baker	Retrd.	53.00	60.00
88-01-035	Georgian Colonial House-white/blue 1514	B. Baker	Retrd.	53.00	53.00
88-01-036	Adam Colonial Cottage-blue/white 1515	B. Baker	Retrd.	53.00	53.00
88-01-037	French Colonial Cottage-beige 1516	B. Baker	Retrd.	42.00	42.00
88-01-038	Antebellum Mansion-peach 1517	B. Baker	Retrd.	49.00	49.00
88-01-039	Antebellum Mansion-white/green 1518	B. Baker	Retrd.	49.00	49.00
88-01-040	Antebellum Mansion-blue/white 1519	B. Baker	Retrd.	49.00	49.00
88-01-041	Country Church-white/blue 1522	B. Baker	Open	49.00	49.00
88-01-042	One Room School House-red 1524	B. Baker	Retrd.	53.00	53.00
88-01-043	Gothic Victorian-peach 1536	B. Baker	Retrd.	51.00	51.00
88-01-044	Gothic Victorian-sea green 1537	B. Baker	Retrd.	47.00	47.00

Company / Number	Name	Series / Artist	Edition Limit	Issue Price	Quote
88-01-045	Second Empire House-white/blue 1538	B. Baker	Retrd.	54.00	54.00
88-01-046	Second Empire House-sea grn./desert 1539	B. Baker	Retrd.	50.00	50.00
88-01-047	Stone Victorians-browns 1554	B. Baker	Open	56.00	56.00
89-01-048	Parisian Apartment-beige/blue 1002	B. Baker	Retrd.	53.00	53.00
89-01-049	Hotel Couronne-white/brown 1003	B. Baker	Retrd.	55.00	55.00
89-01-050	Blumen Shop-white/brown 1023	B. Baker	Retrd.	53.00	53.00
89-01-051	Windmill on the Dike-beige/green 1034	B. Baker	Open	60.00	60.00
89-01-052	Hampshire House-brick 1041	B. Baker	Retrd.	49.00	49.00
89-01-053	Henry VIII Pub-white/brown 1043	B. Baker	Retrd.	56.00	56.00
89-01-054	Swedish House-Swed.red 1050	B. Baker	Retrd.	51.00	51.00
89-01-055	Norwegian House-brown 1051	B. Baker	Retrd.	51.00	51.00
89-01-056	Antebellum Mansion-blue/rose 1505	B. Baker	Retrd.	53.00	53.00
89-01-057	Antebellum Mansion-peach 1506	B. Baker	Retrd.	49.00	49.00
89-01-058	Country Barn-red 1527	B. Baker	Retrd.	53.00	53.00
89-01-059	Country Barn-blue 1528	B. Baker	Retrd.	49.00	49.00
89-01-060	Italianate Victorian-rose/blue 1551	B. Baker	Retrd.	51.00	51.00
89-01-061	Italianate Victorian-peach/teal 1552	B. Baker	Retrd.	51.00	55.00
89-01-062	Ultimate Victorian-peach/green 1553	B. Baker	Retrd.	60.00	60.00
89-01-063	Deja Vu Sign-ivory/brown 1600	B. Baker	Retrd.	21.00	21.00
90-01-064	Palm Villa-white/blue 1420	B. Baker	Open	54.00	54.00
90-01-065	Palm Villa-desert/green 1421	B. Baker	Open	54.00	54.00
90-01-066	Old Country Cottage-blue 1502	B. Baker	Retrd.	51.00	51.00
90-01-067	Old Country Cottage-red 1503	B. Baker	Retrd.	51.00	51.00
90-01-068	Old Country Cottage-peach 1504	B. Baker	Retrd.	47.00	47.00
90-01-069	Gothic Victorian-blue/mauve 1534	B. Baker	Retrd.	47.00	47.00
90-01-070	Classic Victorian-blue/white 1555	B. Baker	Open	60.00	60.00
90-01-071	Classic Victorian-rose/blue 1556	B. Baker	Open	60.00	60.00
90-01-072	Classic Victorian-peach 1557	B. Baker	Open	60.00	60.00
90-01-073	Victorian Country Estate-desert/brown 1560	B. Baker	Open	62.00	62.00
90-01-074	Victorian Country Estate-rose/blue 1561	B. Baker	Open	62.00	62.00
90-01-075	Victorian Country Estate-peach/blue 1562	B. Baker	Open	62.00	62.00
91-01-076	Wind and Roses-brick 1470	B. Baker	Open	63.00	63.00
91-01-077	Log Cabin-brown 1501	B. Baker	Open	55.00	55.00
91-01-078	Colonial Color-brown 1508	B. Baker	Retrd.	62.00	62.00
91-01-079	Colonial Cottage-white/bue 1509	B. Baker	Open	59.00	59.00
91-01-080	Victorian Farmhouse-goldenbrown 1565	B. Baker	Open	59.00	59.00
91-01-081	Teddy's Place-teal/rose 1570	B. Baker	Open	61.00	61.00
91-01-082	Mayor's Mansion-blue/peach 1585	B. Baker	Open	57.00	57.00
92-01-083	Alpine Ski Lodge-brown/white 1012	B. Baker	Retrd.	62.00	62.00
92-01-084	Firehouse-brick 1140	B. Baker	Open	60.00	60.00
92-01-085	Flower Store-tan/green 1145	B. Baker	Open	67.00	67.00
92-01-086	Country Station-blue/rust 1156	B. Baker	Open	64.00	64.00
92-01-087	Tropical Fantasy-blue/coral 1410	B. Baker	Open	67.00	67.00
92-01-088	Tropical Fantasy-rose/blue 1411	B. Baker	Open	67.00	67.00
92-01-089	Tropical Fantasy-yellow/teal 1412	B. Baker	Open	67.00	67.00
92-01-090	Rose Cottage-grey 1443	B. Baker	Open	59.00	59.00
92-01-091	Looks Like Nantucket-grey 1451	B. Baker	Open	62.00	62.00
92-01-092	Victorian Tower House-blue/maroon 1558	B. Baker	Open	63.00	63.00
92-01-093	Victorian Tower House-peach/blue 1559	B. Baker	Open	63.00	63.00
92-01-094	Victorian Bay View-rose/blue 1563	B. Baker	Open	63.00	63.00
92-01-095	Victorian Bay View-cream/teal 1564	B. Baker	Open	63.00	63.00
92-01-096	Angel of the Sea-mauve/white 1586	B. Baker	Open	67.00	67.00
92-01-097	Angel of the Sea-blue/white 1587	B. Baker	Open	67.00	67.00
92-01-098	Victorian Charm-cream 1588	B. Baker	Open	61.00	61.00
92-01-099	Victorian Charm-mauve 1589	B. Baker	Open	61.00	61.00
92-01-100	Deja Vu Sign-ivory/brown 1999	B. Baker	Open	21.00	21.00
93-01-101	Dinard Mansion-beige/brick 1005	B. Baker	Open	67.00	67.00
93-01-102	Old West Hotel-cream 1120	B. Baker	Open	62.00	62.00
93-01-103	Corner Grocery-brick 1141	B. Baker	Open	67.00	67.00
93-01-104	Post Office-light green 1146	B. Baker	Open	60.00	60.00
93-01-105	Enchanted Cottage-natural 1205	B. Baker	Open	63.00	63.00
93-01-106	Homestead Christmas-red 1224	B. Baker	Open	57.00	57.00
93-01-107	Monday's Wash-white/blue 1449	B. Baker	Open	62.00	62.00
93-01-108	Monday's Wash-cream/blue 1450	B. Baker	Open	62.00	62.00
93-01-109	The Stone House-stone/blue 1453	B. Baker	Open	63.00	63.00
93-01-110	Grandpa's Barn-brown 1498	B. Baker	Open	63.00	63.00
93-01-111	Sunday Afternoon-brick 1523	B. Baker	Open	62.00	62.00
93-01-112	Smuggler's Cove-grey/brown 1529	B. Baker	Open	72.00	72.00
93-01-113	Admiralty Head Lighthouse-white 1532	B. Baker	Open	62.00	62.00
93-01-114	Charlestone Single House-blue/white 1583	B. Baker	Open	60.00	60.00
93-01-115	Charlestone Single House-peach/white 1584	B. Baker	Open	60.00	60.00
93-01-116	Mansard Lady-blue/rose 1606	B. Baker	Open	64.00	64.00
93-01-117	Mansard Lady-tan/green 1607	B. Baker	Open	64.00	64.00
93-01-118	Steiner Street-peach/green 1674	B. Baker	Open	63.00	63.00
93-01-119	Steiner Street-rose/blue 1675	B. Baker	Open	63.00	63.00
94-01-120	Craftsman Cottage-grey 1477	B. Baker	Open	56.00	56.00
94-01-121	Craftsman Cottage-cream 1478	B. Baker	Open	56.00	56.00
94-01-122	Riverside Mill 1507	B. Baker	Open	65.00	65.00
94-01-123	Mukilteo Lighthouse 1569	B. Baker	Open	55.00	55.00
94-01-124	Paris by the Bay 1004	B. Baker	Open	55.00	55.00
94-01-125	Police Station 1147	B. Baker	Open	55.00	55.00
94-01-126	Towered Lady-blue/rose 1688	B. Baker	Open	65.00	65.00
94-01-127	Towered Lady-rose 1689	B. Baker	Open	65.00	65.00
94-01-128	Barber Shop 1164	B. Baker	Open	53.00	53.00
94-01-129	Ellis Island 1250	B. Baker	Open	62.00	62.00
94-01-130	Covered Bridge 1513	B. Baker	Open	69.00	69.00
94-01-131	Cabbagetown 1704	B. Baker	Open	65.00	65.00
94-01-132	Christmas at Church 1223	B. Baker	Open	63.00	63.00
94-01-133	Orleans Cottage-white/blue 1447	B. Baker	Open	63.00	63.00
94-01-134	Orleans Cottage-white/red 1448	B. Baker	Open	63.00	63.00
94-01-135	San Francisco Stick-cream/blue 1624	B. Baker	Open	61.00	61.00
94-01-136	San Francisco Stick-brick/teal 1625	B. Baker	Open	61.00	61.00
94-01-137	Castle in the Clouds 1090	B. Baker	Open	75.00	75.00
94-01-138	Country Store 1435	B. Baker	Open	61.00	61.00
94-01-139	Mission Dolores 1435	B. Baker	Open	47.00	47.00
94-01-140	The Old School House 1439	B. Baker	Open	61.00	61.00
Michael's Limited		**Limited Editions From Brian Baker**			
87-02-001	Amsterdam Canal-brown, S/N 1030	B. Baker	Retrd.	79.00	83-100.00
93-02-002	James River Plantation-brick, Numbrd.1454	B. Baker	Retrd.	108.00	200.00
93-02-003	American Classic-rose, Numbrd.1566	B. Baker	Retrd.	99.00	250-260.
94-02-004	Painted Ladies 1190	B. Baker	1,200	125.00	125.00
94-02-005	White Point 1596	B. Baker	700	100.00	100.00
94-02-006	Hill Top Mansion 1598	B. Baker	1,200	97.00	97.00
Michael's Limited		**Collectors' Corner**			
93-03-001	City Cottage (Membership House)-rose/grn. 1682	B. Baker	Retrd.	35.00	35.00
93-03-002	Brian's House (Redemption House)-red1496	B. Baker	Retrd.	71.00	71.00
94-03-003	Gothic Cottage (Membership Sculpture) 1571	B. Baker	Yr.Iss.	35.00	35.00
94-03-004	Duke of Gloucester Street 1459 (Redemption House)	B. Baker	Yr.Iss.	35.00	35.00
Midwest of Cannon Falls		**Christian Ulbricht Nutcracker Collection**			
86-01-001	Pilgrim Nutcracker, 16 1/2" 00393-0	C. Ulbricht	Open	145.00	155.00
93-01-002	Mrs. Claus Nutcracker 09587-4	C. Ulbricht	5,000	180.00	185.00
93-01-003	Mr. Claus Nutcracker 09588-1	C. Ulbricht	5,000	180.00	185.00
93-01-004	Leprechaun Nutcracker 09110-4	C. Ulbricht	Open	170.00	170.00
94-01-005	Prince on Rocking Horse Nutcracker 12964-7	C. Ulbricht	Open	160.00	160.00
Midwest of Cannon Falls		**Christian Ulbricht "Traditional Santa Series" Nutcracker Collection**			
92-02-001	Father Christmas Nutcracker 07094-9	C. Ulbricht	Retrd.	190.00	190.00
93-02-002	Toymaker Nutcracker 09531-7	C. Ulbricht	2,500	220.00	250.00
94-02-003	Victorian Santa Nutcracker 12961-1	C. Ulbricht	2,500	220.00	220.00
Midwest of Cannon Falls		**Christian Ulbricht "A Christmas Carol" Nutcrackers**			
93-03-001	Bob Cratchit and Tiny Tim Nutcracker 09577-5	C. Ulbricht	6,000	240.00	240.00
93-03-002	Scrooge Nutcracker 09584-3	C. Ulbricht	6,000	210.00	220.00
94-03-003	Ghost of Christmas Present Nutcracker 12041-5	C. Ulbricht	5,000	190.00	190.00
Midwest of Cannon Falls		**Christian Ulbricht "Nutcracker Fantasy" Nutcrackers**			
91-04-001	Herr Drosselmeyer Nutcracker, 16 1/4" 03656-3	C. Ulbricht	Open	170.00	187.00
91-04-002	Clara Nutcracker, 11 1/2" 03657-0	C. Ulbricht	Open	125.00	145.00
91-04-003	Prince Nutcracker, 17" 03665-5	C. Ulbricht	Open	160.00	177.00
91-04-004	Toy Soldier, 14" 03666-2	C. Ulbricht	Open	160.00	177.00
91-04-005	Mouse King Nutcracker, 13 1/2" 04510-7	C. Ulbricht	Open	170.00	184.00
Midwest of Cannon Falls		**Christian Ulbricht "American Folk Hero" Nutcracker Collection**			
94-05-001	Johnny Appleseed Nutcracker 12959-3	C. Ulbricht	2,500	196.00	196.00
94-05-002	Davy Crockett Nutcracker 12960-9	C. Ulbricht	2,500	185.00	185.00
Midwest of Cannon Falls		**Ore Mountain Nutcracker Collection**			
92-06-001	Christopher Columbus Nutcracker 00152-3	Midwest	Closed	80.00	80.00
84-06-002	Pinocchio Nutcracker 00160-8	Midwest	Open	60.00	65.00
92-06-003	Victorian Santa Nutcracker 00187-5	Midwest	Open	130.00	140.00
92-06-004	Pilgrim Nutcracker 00188-2	Midwest	Open	96.00	100.00
92-06-005	Indian Nutcracker 00195-0	Midwest	Open	96.00	100.00
92-06-006	Ringmaster Nutcracker 00196-7	Midwest	Closed	135.00	137.00
92-06-007	Cowboy Nutcracker 00298-8	Midwest	Open	97.00	133.00
92-06-008	Farmer Nutcracker 01109-6	Midwest	Open	65.00	77.00
92-06-009	Santa with Skis Nutcracker 01305-2	Midwest	Open	100.00	110.00
91-06-010	Clown Nutcracker 03561-0	Midwest	Open	115.00	118.00
91-06-011	Nutcracker-Maker Nutcracker 03601-3	Midwest	Closed	62.00	65.00
90-06-012	Elf Nutcracker 04154-3	Midwest	Closed	70.00	73.00
90-06-013	Sea Captain Nutcracker 04157-4	Midwest	Open	86.00	95.00
90-06-014	Witch Nutcracker 04159-8	Midwest	Open	75.00	76.00
90-06-015	Windsor Club Nutcracker 04160-4	Midwest	Open	85.00	86.50
90-06-016	Woodland Santa Nutcracker 04191-8	Midwest	Open	105.00	132.00
90-06-017	Uncle Sam Nutcracker 04206-9	Midwest	Closed	50.00	61.50
90-06-018	Merlin the Magician Nutcracker 04207-6	Midwest	Open	67.00	70.00
88-06-019	Santa with Tree & Toys Nutcracker 07666-8	Midwest	Closed	76.00	87.00
88-06-020	Nordic Santa Nutcracker 08872-2	Midwest	Open	84.00	110.00
89-06-021	Golfer Nutcracker 09325-2	Midwest	Open	85.00	90.00
89-06-022	Country Santa Nutcracker 09326-9	Midwest	Open	95.00	132.00
89-06-023	Fisherman Nutcracker 09327-6	Midwest	Open	90.00	100.00
93-06-024	Fireman with Dog Nutcracker 06592-1	Midwest	Open	134.00	134.00
93-06-025	Gepetto Santa Nutcracker 09417-4	Midwest	Open	115.00	115.00
93-06-026	Santa with Animals Nutcracker 09424-2	Midwest	Open	117.00	117.00
93-06-027	Cat Witch Nutcracker 09426-6	Midwest	Open	93.00	93.00
93-06-028	White Santa Nutcracker 09533-1	Midwest	Open	100.00	100.00
94-06-029	Miner Nutcracker 10493-4	Midwest	Open	110.00	110.00
94-06-030	Cavalier Nutcracker 12953-1	Midwest	Open	65.00	65.00
94-06-031	Cavalier Nutcracker 12952-4	Midwest	Open	80.00	80.00
94-06-032	Cavalier Nutcracker 12958-6	Midwest	Open	57.00	57.00
94-06-033	Regal Prince Nutcracker 10452-1	Midwest	Open	140.00	140.00
94-06-034	Prince Charming Nutcracker 10457-6	Midwest	Open	125.00	125.00
94-06-035	Santa with Basket Nutcracker 10472-9	Midwest	Open	80.00	80.00
94-06-036	Pinecone Santa Nutcracker 10461-3	Midwest	Open	92.00	92.00
94-06-037	Black Santa Nutcracker 10460-6	Midwest	Open	74.00	74.00
94-06-038	Santa in Nightshirt Nutcracker 10462-0	Midwest	Open	108.00	108.00
94-06-039	Sorcerer Nutcracker 10471-2	Midwest	Open	100.00	100.00
94-06-040	Snow King Nutcracker 10470-5	Midwest	Open	108.00	108.00
94-06-041	Sultan King Nutcracker 10455-2	Midwest	Open	130.00	130.00
94-06-042	Toy Vendor Nutcracker 11987-7	Midwest	Open	124.00	124.00
94-06-043	Engineer Nutcracker 10454-5	Midwest	Open	108.00	108.00
94-06-044	Gardening Lady Nutcracker 10450-7	Midwest	Open	104.00	104.00
94-06-045	Nature Lover Nutcracker 10446-0	Midwest	Open	112.00	112.00
94-06-046	Baseball Player Nutcracker 10459-0	Midwest	Open	111.00	111.00
94-06-047	Soccer Player Nutcracker 10494-1	Midwest	Open	97.00	97.00
94-06-048	Union Soldier Nutcracker 12836-7	Midwest	Open	93.00	93.00
94-06-049	Confederate Soldier Nutcracker 12837-4	Midwest	Open	93.00	93.00
94-06-050	Pumpkin Head Scarecrow Nutcracker 10451-1	Midwest	Open	127.00	127.00
94-06-051	Annie Oakley Nutcracker 10464-4	Midwest	Open	128.00	128.00
Midwest of Cannon Falls		**Ore Mountain Easter Nutcrackers**			
91-07-001	Bunny with Egg Nutcracker 00145-5	Midwest	Open	77.00	80.00
84-07-002	March Hare Nutcracker 00312-1	Midwest	Closed	77.00	80.00
92-07-003	Bunny Painter Nutcracker 06480-1	Midwest	Closed	77.00	80.00
Midwest of Cannon Falls		**Ore Mountain "Nutcracker Fantasy" Nutcrackers**			
91-08-001	Clara Nutcracker, 8" 01254-3	Midwest	Open	77.00	85.00
88-08-002	Herr Drosselmeyer Nutcracker, 14 1/2" 07506-7	Midwest	Open	75.00	100.00
88-08-003	The Prince Nutcracker, 12 3/4" 07507-4	Midwest	Open	75.00	90.00
88-08-004	The Toy Soldier Nutcracker, 11" 07508-1	Midwest	Open	70.00	80.00
88-08-005	The Mouse King Nutcracker, 10" 07509-8	Midwest	Open	60.00	70.00
93-08-006	The Mouse King Nutcracker 05350-8	Midwest	5,000	100.00	110.00
94-08-007	Herr Drosselmeyer Nutcracker 10456-9	Midwest	5,000	110.00	110.00
94-08-008	Nutcracker Prince Nutcracker 11001-0	Midwest	5,000	104.00	104.00
Midwest of Cannon Falls		**Ore Mountain "A Christmas Carol" Nutcrackers**			
93-09-001	Ghost of Christmas Present Nutcracker 05520-5	Midwest Importers	5,000	116.00	120.00
93-09-002	Scrooge Nutcracker 05522-9	Midwest Importers	5,000	104.00	110.00
93-09-003	Bob Cratchit Nutcracker 09421-1	Midwest Importers	5,000	120.00	130.00
94-09-004	Ghost of Christmas Past Nutcracker 10447-7	Midwest Importers	4,000	116.00	116.00
94-09-005	Marley's Ghost Nutcracker 10448-4	Midwest Importers	4,000	116.00	116.00
94-09-006	Ghost of Christmas Future Nutcracker 10449-1	Midwest Importers	4,000	116.00	116.00
Midwest of Cannon Falls		**Wendt and Kuhn Collection**			
79-10-001	Angel Playing Violin 00403-6	Wendt/Kuhn	Open	34.00	35.00
83-10-002	Angel Percussion Musicians, set/6 00443-2	Wendt/Kuhn	Open	110.00	120.00

Number	Name	Artist	Edition Limit	Issue Price	Quote
84-10-003	Angels Bearing Toys, set/6 00451-7	Wendt/Kuhn	Open	97.00	100.00
83-10-004	Angel String Musicians, set/6 00455-5	Wendt/Kuhn	Open	105.00	112.00
83-10-005	Angel String & Woodwind Musicians, set/6 00465-4	Wendt/Kuhn	Open	108.00	115.00
83-10-006	Angel Conductor on Stand 00469-2	Wendt/Kuhn	Open	21.00	23.00
83-10-007	Angel Brass Musicians, set/6 00470-8	Wendt/Kuhn	Open	92.00	100.00
79-10-008	Angel Trio, set/3 00471-5	Wendt/Kuhn	Open	140.00	150.00
76-10-009	Santa with Angel 00473-9	Wendt/Kuhn	Open	50.00	52.00
83-10-010	Margarita Birthday Angels, set/3 00480-7	Wendt/Kuhn	Open	44.00	50.00
80-10-011	Angel Pulling Wagon 00553-8	Wendt/Kuhn	Open	43.00	46.00
81-10-012	Angel w/Tree & Basket 11908	Wendt/Kuhn	Closed	24.00	25.00
81-10-013	Santa w/Angel in Sleigh 01192-8	Wendt/Kuhn	Open	52.00	55.00
81-10-014	Angels at Cradle, set/4 01193-5	Wendt/Kuhn	Open	73.00	76.00
83-10-015	Girl w/Wagon 01196-6	Wendt/Kuhn	Open	27.00	29.00
79-10-016	Girl w/Scissors 01197-3	Wendt/Kuhn	Open	25.00	32.00
79-10-017	Girl w/Porridge Bowl 01198-0	Wendt/Kuhn	Open	29.00	32.00
91-10-018	Girl with Doll 01200-0	Wendt/Kuhn	Open	31.50	32.00
91-10-019	Boy on Rocking Horse, 2 asst. 01202-4	Wendt/Kuhn	Open	35.00	36.00
79-10-020	Girl w/Cradle, set/2 01203-1	Wendt/Kuhn	Open	37.50	40.00
91-10-021	White Angel with Violin 01205-5	Wendt/Kuhn	Closed	25.50	26.50
78-10-022	Madonna w/Child 01207-9	Wendt/Kuhn	Open	120.00	125.00
91-10-023	Birdhouse 01209-3	Wendt/Kuhn	Open	22.50	23.00
91-10-024	Flower Children, set/6 01213-0	Wendt/Kuhn	Open	130.00	137.00
91-10-025	Display Base for Wendt und Kuhn Figures, 12 1/2 x2" 01214-7	Wendt/Kuhn	Open	32.00	35.00
79-10-026	Pied Piper and Children, set/7 02843-8	Wendt/Kuhn	Open	120.00	130.00
79-10-027	Bavarian Moving Van 02854-4	Wendt/Kuhn	Open	133.50	140.00
79-10-028	Magarita Angels, set/6 02938-1	Wendt/Kuhn	Open	94.00	100.00
76-10-029	Angel with Sled 02940-4	Wendt/Kuhn	Open	36.50	38.00
80-10-030	Little People Napkin Rings, 6 asst. 03504-7	Wendt/Kuhn	Open	21.00	23.00
90-10-031	Angel Duet in Celestial Stars 04158-1	Wendt/Kuhn	Open	60.00	63.00
87-10-032	Child on Skis, 2 asst. 06083-4	Wendt/Kuhn	Open	28.00	29.00
87-10-033	Child on Sled 06085-8	Wendt/Kuhn	Open	25.50	26.50
92-10-034	Wendt und Kuhn Display Sign w/ Sitting Angel 07535-7	Wendt/Kuhn	Open	20.00	23.00
88-10-035	Lucia Parade Figures, set/3 07667-5	Wendt/Kuhn	Open	75.00	80.00
88-10-036	Children Carrying Lanterns Procession, set/6 07669-9	Wendt/Kuhn	Open	117.00	127.00
89-10-037	Angel at Piano 09403-7	Wendt/Kuhn	Open	31.00	35.00
94-10-038	Busy Elf, 3 asst. 12856-5	Wendt/Kuhn	Open	22.00	22.00
94-10-039	Santa with Tree 12942-5	Wendt/Kuhn	Open	29.00	29.00
94-10-040	Sun, Moon, Star Set 12943-2	Wendt/Kuhn	Open	69.00	69.00
94-10-041	Child with Flowers Set 12947-0	Wendt/Kuhn	Open	45.00	45.00

Midwest of Cannon Falls — **Wendt and Kuhn Figurines Candleholders**

Number	Name	Artist	Edition Limit	Issue Price	Quote
76-11-001	Angel Candleholder Pair 00472-2	Wendt/Kuhn	Open	70.00	75.00
91-11-002	Angel with Friend Candleholder 01191-1	Wendt/Kuhn	Open	33.30	34.00
91-11-003	Small Angel Candleholder Pair 01195-9	Wendt/Kuhn	Open	60.00	63.00
80-11-004	Large Angel Candleholder Pair 01201-7	Wendt/Kuhn	Open	270.00	277.00
86-11-005	Pair of Angels Candleholder 01204-8	Wendt/Kuhn	Open	30.00	32.00
91-11-006	White Angel Candleholder 01206-2	Wendt/Kuhn	Open	28.00	29.00
87-11-007	Santa Candleholder 06082-7	Wendt/Kuhn	Open	53.00	54.00
94-11-008	Angei with Wagon Candleholder 12860-2	Wendt/Kuhn	Open	35.00	35.00

Midwest of Cannon Falls — **Wendt and Kuhn Collection Music Boxes**

Number	Name	Artist	Edition Limit	Issue Price	Quote
91-12-001	Angels & Santa Around Tree 01211-6	Wendt/Kuhn	Open	300.00	300.00
78-12-002	Rotating Angels 'Round Cradle 01911-5	Wendt/Kuhn	Open	270.00	270.00
78-12-003	Angel at Pipe Organ 01929-0	Wendt/Kuhn	Open	176.00	190.00
76-12-004	Girl Rocking Cradle 09215-6	Wendt/Kuhn	Open	180.00	190.00
94-12-005	Angel Under Stars Crank Music Box 12974-6	Wendt/Kuhn	Closed	150.00	150.00

Midwest of Cannon Falls — **Belenes Puig Nativity Collection**

Number	Name	Artist	Edition Limit	Issue Price	Quote
85-13-001	Nativity, set/6: Holy Family, Angel, Animals 6 3/4" 00205-6	J.P. Llobera	Open	250.00	250.00
85-13-002	Shepherd, set/2 00458-6	J.P. Llobera	Open	110.00	110.00
85-13-003	Wise Men, set/3 00459-3	J.P. Llobera	Open	185.00	185.00
86-13-004	Sheep, set/3 00475-3	J.P. Llobera	Open	28.00	28.00
89-13-005	Wise Man with Gold on Camel 02075-3	J.P. Llobera	Open	155.00	155.00
89-13-006	Wise Man with Myrrh on Camel 02076-0	J.P. Llobera	Open	155.00	155.00
89-13-007	Wise Man with Frankincense on Camel 02077-7	J.P. Llobera	Open	155.00	155.00
89-13-008	Donkey 02082-1	J.P. Llobera	Open	26.00	26.00
89-13-009	Ox 02083-8	J.P. Llobera	Open	26.00	26.00
89-13-010	Mother Mary 02084-5	J.P. Llobera	Open	62.00	62.00
89-13-011	Baby Jesus 02085-2	J.P. Llobera	Open	62.00	62.00
89-13-012	Joseph 02086-9	J.P. Llobera	Open	62.00	62.00
89-13-013	Angel 02087-6	J.P. Llobera	Open	50.00	50.00
89-13-014	Wise Man with Frankincense 02088-3	J.P. Llobera	Open	66.00	66.00
89-13-015	Wise Man with Gold 02089-0	J.P. Llobera	Open	66.00	66.00
89-13-016	Wise Man with Myrrh 02090-6	J.P. Llobera	Open	66.00	66.00
89-13-017	Shepherd with Staff 02091-3	J.P. Llobera	Open	56.00	56.00
89-13-018	Shepherd Carrying Lamb 02092-0	J.P. Llobera	Open	56.00	56.00
90-13-019	Resting Camel 04025-6	J.P. Llobera	Open	115.00	115.00
87-13-020	Shepherd & Angel Scene, set/7 06084-1	J.P. Llobera	Open	305.00	305.00
88-13-021	Standing Camel 08792-3	J.P. Llobera	Open	115.00	115.00

Midwest of Cannon Falls — **Leo R. Smith III Collection**

Number	Name	Artist	Edition Limit	Issue Price	Quote
91-14-001	Stars and Stripes Santa 01743-2	L.R. Smith	5,000	190.00	200.00
91-14-002	Woodsman Santa 03310-4	L.R. Smith	5,000	230.00	250.00
91-14-003	Pilgrim Riding Turkey 03312-8	L.R. Smith	5,000	230.00	250.00
91-14-004	Milkmaker 03541-2	L.R. Smith	5,000	170.00	184.00
91-14-005	'Tis a Witching Time 03544-3	L.R. Smith	Retrd.	140.00	600.00
91-14-006	Toymaker 03540-5	L.R. Smith	5,000	120.00	130.00
91-14-007	Cossack Santa 01092-1	L.R. Smith	Retrd.	95.00	103.00
91-14-008	Pilgrim Man 03313-5	L.R. Smith	5,000	78.00	84.00
91-14-009	Pilgrim Woman 03315-9	L.R. Smith	5,000	78.00	84.00
91-14-010	Fisherman Santa 03311-1	L.R. Smith	5,000	270.00	290.00
92-14-011	Dreams of Night Buffalo 07999-7	L.R. Smith	5,000	250.00	270.00
92-14-012	Santa of Peace 07328-5	L.R. Smith	5,000	250.00	270.00
92-14-013	Great Plains Santa 08049-8	L.R. Smith	5,000	270.00	293.00
92-14-014	Ms. Liberty 07866-2	L.R. Smith	5,000	190.00	210.00
92-14-015	Woodland Brave 07867-9	L.R. Smith	Retrd.	87.00	94.00
92-14-016	Leo Smith Name Plaque 07881-5	Midwest	Open	12.00	12.00
93-14-017	Gnome Santa on Deer 05206-8	L.R. Smith	5,000	270.00	270.00
93-14-018	Folk Angel 05444-4	L.R. Smith	5,000	145.00	145.00
93-14-019	Santa Fisherman 08979-8	L.R. Smith	5,000	250.00	250.00
93-14-020	Dancing Santa 09042-8	L.R. Smith	5,000	170.00	170.00
93-14-021	Voyageur 09043-5	L.R. Smith	5,000	170.00	170.00
94-14-022	Santa Skier 12054-5	L.R. Smith	1,500	190.00	190.00
94-14-023	Gift Giver Santa 12056-9	L.R. Smith	1,500	180.00	180.00
94-14-024	Old-World Santa 12053-8	L.R. Smith	1,500	75.00	75.00
94-14-025	Star of the Roundup Cowboy 11966-1	L.R. Smith	1,500	100.00	100.00
94-14-026	Weatherwise Angel 12055-2	L.R. Smith	1,500	150.00	150.00

Midwest of Cannon Falls — **Heritage Santa Collection**

Number	Name	Artist	Edition Limit	Issue Price	Quote
90-15-001	Scanda Klaus 00536-1	Midwest	Open	26.50	27.50
90-15-002	Herr Kristmas 00537-8	Midwest	Retrd.	26.50	27.50
90-15-003	MacNicholas 00538-5	Midwest	Open	26.50	27.50
90-15-004	Papa Frost 00539-2	Midwest	Open	26.50	27.50
91-15-005	Father Christmas 01798-2	Midwest	Open	26.50	27.50
91-15-006	Santa Niccolo 01792-5	Midwest	Retrd.	26.50	27.50
92-15-007	Santa Nykolai 06772-7	Midwest	Retrd.	26.50	26.50
92-15-008	Pere Noel 06771-0	Midwest	Retrd.	26.50	26.50
93-15-009	Santa España 07368-1	Midwest	Open	25.00	26.50
93-15-010	Santa O'Nicholas 07370-4	Midwest	Open	25.00	26.50
94-15-011	American Santa 11622-7	Midwest	Yr. Iss.	20.00	20.00

Midwest of Cannon Falls — **Heritage Santa Roly-Polys**

Number	Name	Artist	Edition Limit	Issue Price	Quote
90-16-001	Scanda Klaus Roly-Poly 00528-6	Midwest	Retrd.	24.00	25.00
90-16-002	Herr Kristmas Roly-Poly 00529-3	Midwest	Retrd.	24.00	25.00
90-16-003	MacNicholas Roly-Poly 00530-9	Midwest	Open	24.00	25.00
90-16-004	Papa Frost Roly-Poly 00531-6	Midwest	Open	24.00	25.00
91-16-005	Father Christmas Roly-Poly 01796-8	Midwest	Open	24.00	25.00
91-16-006	Santa Niccolo Roly-Poly 01795-1	Midwest	Retrd.	24.00	25.00
92-16-007	Santa Nykolai Roly-Poly 06769-7	Midwest	Open	24.00	24.00
92-16-008	Pere Noel Roly-Poly 06768-0	Midwest	Retrd.	24.00	24.00
93-16-009	Santa España Roly-Poly 07373-5	Midwest	Open	20.00	24.00
93-16-010	Santa O'Nicholas Roly-Poly 07375-9	Midwest	Open	20.00	24.00
94-16-011	American Santa Roly-Poly 11620-3	Midwest	Yr. Iss.	17.00	17.00

Midwest of Cannon Falls — **Heritage Santa Collection Fabric Mache**

Number	Name	Artist	Edition Limit	Issue Price	Quote
90-17-001	Scanda Klaus Fabric Mache set 00514-9	Midwest	Retrd.	160.00	170.00
90-17-002	Herr Kristmas Fabric Mache set 00515-6	Midwest	Retrd.	160.00	170.00
90-17-003	MacNicholas Fabric Mache set 00516-3	Midwest	Open	160.00	180.00
90-17-004	Papa Frost Fabric Mache set 00517-0	Midwest	Retrd.	160.00	170.00
91-17-005	Father Christmas Fabric Mache set 01800-2	Midwest	Open	160.00	180.00
91-17-006	Santa Niccolo Fabric Mache set 01799-9	Midwest	Open	160.00	180.00
92-17-007	Santa Nykolai Fabric Mache set 06767-3	Midwest	Open	160.00	180.00
92-17-008	Pere Noel Fabric Mache set 06766-6	Midwest	Open	160.00	180.00
93-17-009	Santa España Fabric Mache set 07357-5	Midwest	Open	170.00	180.00
93-17-010	Santa O'Nicholas Fabric Mache set 07365-0	Midwest	Open	170.00	180.00
94-17-011	Fabric Mache Santa Claus Set 11944-0	Midwest	Yr. Iss.	180.00	180.00

Midwest of Cannon Falls — **Heritage Santa Collection Music Boxes**

Number	Name	Artist	Edition Limit	Issue Price	Quote
90-18-001	Scanda Klaus Music Box 00532-3	Midwest	Open	53.00	59.00
90-18-002	Herr Kristmas Music Box 00533-1	Midwest	Retrd.	53.00	56.00
90-18-003	MacNicholas Music Box 00534-7	Midwest	Retrd.	53.00	59.00
90-18-004	Papa Frost Music Box 00535-4	Midwest	Open	53.00	59.00
91-18-005	Father Christmas Music Box 01802-6	Midwest	Retrd.	53.00	59.00
91-18-006	Santa Niccolo Music Box 01801-9	Midwest	Retrd.	53.00	56.00
92-18-007	Santa Nykolai Music Box 06790-1	Midwest	Retrd.	53.00	59.00
92-18-008	Pere Noel Music Box 06789-5	Midwest	Retrd.	53.00	59.00
93-18-009	Santa España Music Box 07366-7	Midwest	Open	56.00	59.00
93-18-010	Santa O'Nicholas Music Box 07367-4	Midwest	Open	56.00	59.00
94-18-011	American Santa Music Box 11618-0	Midwest	Yr. Iss.	59.00	59.00

Midwest of Cannon Falls — **Heritage Santa Collection Snowglobes**

Number	Name	Artist	Edition Limit	Issue Price	Quote
90-19-001	Scanda Klaus Snowglobe 00524-8	Midwest	Retrd.	40.00	45.00
90-19-002	Herr Kristmas Snowglobe 00525-5	Midwest	Retrd.	40.00	43.00
90-19-003	MacNicholas Snowglobe 00526-2	Midwest	Open	40.00	45.00
90-19-004	Papa Frost Snowglobe 00527-9	Midwest	Retrd.	40.00	43.00
91-19-005	Father Christmas Snowglobe 01794-4	Midwest	Open	40.00	45.00
91-19-006	Santa Niccolo Snowglobe 01793-7	Midwest	Retrd.	40.00	43.00
92-19-007	Santa Nykolai Snowglobe 06783-3	Midwest	Retrd.	40.00	43.00
92-19-008	Pere Noel Snowglobe 06778-9	Midwest	Open	40.00	45.00
93-19-009	Santa España Snowglobe 07371-1	Midwest	Open	43.00	45.00
93-19-010	Santa O'Nicholas Snowglobe 07372-8	Midwest	Open	43.00	45.00
94-19-011	American Santa Waterglobe 11623-4	Midwest	Yr. Iss.	45.00	45.00

Midwest of Cannon Falls — **Creepy Hollow Houses**

Number	Name	Artist	Edition Limit	Issue Price	Quote
93-20-001	Witches Cove (lighted) 01665-7	Midwest	Open	40.00	40.00
93-20-002	Mummy's Mortuary (lighted) 01641-1	Midwest	Open	40.00	40.00
93-20-003	Dracula's Castle (lighted) 01627-5	Midwest	Open	40.00	40.00
93-20-004	Dr. Frankenstein's House (lighted) 01621-3	Midwest	Open	40.00	40.00
93-20-005	Haunted Hotel (lighted) 08549-3	Midwest	Open	40.00	40.00
93-20-006	Blood Bank (lighted) 08548-6	Midwest	Open	40.00	40.00
93-20-007	Shoppe of Horrors (lighted) 08850-9	Midwest	Open	40.00	40.00
94-20-008	Phantom's Opera (lighted) 10650-1	Midwest	Open	40.00	40.00
94-20-009	Cauldron Cafe (lighted) 10649-5	Midwest	Open	40.00	40.00
94-20-010	Medical Ghoul School (lighted) 10651-8	Midwest	Open	40.00	40.00

Midwest of Cannon Falls — **Creepy Hollow Figurines and Accessories**

Number	Name	Artist	Edition Limit	Issue Price	Quote
93-21-001	Witch 06706-2	Midwest	Open	6.00	6.00
93-21-002	Pumpkin Patch Sign, 2 asst. 05898-5	Midwest	Open	6.50	6.50
93-21-003	Hinged Dracula's Coffin 08545-5	Midwest	Open	11.00	11.00
93-21-004	Trick or Treater, 3 asst. 08591-2	Midwest	Open	5.50	5.50
93-21-005	Halloween Sign, 2 asst. 06709-3	Midwest	Open	6.00	6.00
93-21-006	Resin Skeleton 06651-5	Midwest	Open	5.50	5.50
93-21-007	Pumpkin Head Ghost 06661-4	Midwest	Open	5.50	5.50
93-21-008	Haunted Tree, 2 asst. 05892-3	Midwest	Open	7.00	7.00
94-21-009	Mad Scientist 10646-4	Midwest	Open	6.00	6.00
94-21-010	Phantom of the Opera 10645-7	Midwest	Open	6.00	6.00
94-21-011	Werewolf 10643-4	Midwest	Open	6.00	6.00
94-21-012	Street Sign, 2 asst. 10644-0	Midwest	Open	5.70	5.70
94-21-013	Outhouse 10648-8	Midwest	Open	7.00	7.00
94-21-014	Creepy Hollow Sign 10647-1	Midwest	Open	5.50	5.50
94-21-015	Tombstone Sign, 3 asst. 10642-6	Midwest	Open	3.50	3.50
94-21-016	Black Picket Fence 10685-3	Midwest	Open	13.50	13.50
94-21-017	Ghost, 3 asst. 10652-5	Midwest	Open	6.00	6.00

Midwest of Cannon Falls — **Cottontail Lane Houses**

Number	Name	Artist	Edition Limit	Issue Price	Quote
93-22-001	Church (lighted) 01385-4	Midwest	Rtrd.	42.00	42.00
93-22-002	Cottontail Inn (lighted) 01394-6	Midwest	Open	43.00	43.00
93-22-003	Schoolhouse (lighted) 01378-6	Midwest	Open	43.00	43.00
93-22-004	Painting Studio (lighted) 01395-5	Midwest	Open	43.00	43.00
93-22-005	Rose Cottage (lighted) 01386-1	Midwest	Open	43.00	43.00
93-22-006	Bakery (lighted) 01396-0	Midwest	Open	43.00	43.00
93-22-007	Confectionary Shop (lighted) 06335-5	Midwest	Open	43.00	43.00
93-22-008	Springtime Cottage (lighted) 06329-8	Midwest	Open	43.00	43.00
93-22-009	Flower Shop (lighted) 06333-9	Midwest	Open	43.00	43.00
93-22-010	Victorian House (lighted) 06332-1	Midwest	Open	43.00	43.00
93-22-011	Chapel (lighted) 00331-2	Midwest	Open	43.00	43.00
93-22-012	Bed & Breakfast House (lighted) 00337-4	Midwest	Open	43.00	43.00
93-22-013	General Store (lighted) 00340-4	Midwest	Open	43.00	43.00
93-22-014	Train Station (lighted) 00330-5	Midwest	Open	43.00	43.00

Company Number	Series Name	Artist	Edition Limit	Issue Price	Quote

Midwest of Cannon Falls — **Cottontail Lane Figurines and Accessories**

Number	Name	Artist	Edition Limit	Issue Price	Quote
94-23-001	Wedding Bunny Couple, 2 asst. 00347-3	Midwest	Open	4.20	4.20
94-23-002	Cobblestone Road 10072-1	Midwest	Open	9.00	9.00
94-23-003	Bunny Shopping Couple, 2 asst. 10362-3	Midwest	Open	4.20	4.20
94-23-004	Easter Bunny Figure, 2 asst. 00356-5	Midwest	Open	4.20	4.20
94-23-005	Tree & Shrub, 2 asst. 00382-4	Midwest	Open	5.00	5.00
94-23-006	Bunny Couple on Bicycle 02978-7	Midwest	Open	5.30	5.30
94-23-007	Train Station Couple, 2 asst. 00357-2	Midwest	Open	4.20	4.20
94-23-008	Policeman, Conductor Bunny, 2 asst. 00367-1	Midwest	Open	4.20	4.20
94-23-009	Trees, 3 asst. 02194-1	Midwest	Open	6.20	6.20
94-23-010	Strolling Bunny, 2 asst. 02976-3	Midwest	Open	4.20	4.20
94-23-011	Bunny Child Collecting Eggs, 2 asst. 02880-3	Midwest	Open	4.20	4.20
94-23-012	Bunny Marching Band, 6 asst. 00355-8	Midwest	Open	4.20	4.20
94-23-013	Cone-Shaped Tree Set 10369-2	Midwest	Open	7.50	7.50
94-23-014	Topiary Trees, 3 asst. 00346-6	Midwest	Open	2.50	2.50
94-23-015	Bunny Preparing for Easter, 3 asst. 02971-8	Midwest	Open	4.20	4.20
94-23-016	Egg Stand & Flower Cart, 2 asst. 10354-8	Midwest	Open	6.00	6.00
94-23-017	Birdhouse, Sundial & Fountain, 3 asst. 00371-8	Midwest	Open	4.50	4.50
94-23-018	Birdbath, Bench & Mailbox, 02184-2	Midwest	Open	4.00	4.00
94-23-019	Bridge & Gazebo, 2 asst. 02182-9	Midwest	Open	11.50	11.50
94-23-020	Cottontail Lane Sign 10063-9	Midwest	Open	5.00	5.00
94-23-021	Arbor w/ Fence Set 02188-0	Midwest	Open	14.00	14.00
94-23-022	Lamppost, Birdhouse & Mailbox, 3 asst. 02187-3	Midwest	Open	4.50	4.50
94-23-023	Sweeper & Flower Peddler Bunny Couple, 2 asst. 00359-6	Midwest	Open	4.20	4.20

Midwest of Cannon Falls — **Cannon Valley Houses**

Number	Name	Artist	Edition Limit	Issue Price	Quote
94-24-001	Family Farmhouse (lighted) 11292-2	Midwest	Open	43.00	43.00
94-24-002	Red Barn (lighted) 11296-0	Midwest	Open	43.00	43.00
94-24-003	Hen House (lighted) 11294-6	Midwest	Open	33.00	33.00
94-24-004	General Store (lighted) 11295-3	Midwest	Open	43.00	43.00
94-24-005	Little Red Schoolhouse (lighted) 11293-9	Midwest	Yr. Iss.	43.00	43.00

Midwest of Cannon Falls — **Cannon Valley Figurines and Accessories**

Number	Name	Artist	Edition Limit	Issue Price	Quote
94-25-001	Cannon Valley Sign 11297-7	Midwest	Open	5.50	5.50
94-25-002	Hay Wagon and Horse Set 11303-5	Midwest	Open	19.00	19.00
94-25-003	Farm Tractor 11305-9	Midwest	Open	9.50	9.50
94-25-004	Farm Couple, 2 asst. 11458-2	Midwest	Open	5.50	5.50
94-25-005	Children, 2 asst. 11461-2	Midwest	Open	5.50	5.50
94-25-006	Pig and Piglets 11302-8	Midwest	Open	5.30	5.30
94-25-007	Cow, 3 asst. 11309-7	Midwest	Open	5.50	5.50
94-25-008	Horse, 2 asst. 11485-8	Midwest	Open	10.00	10.00
94-25-009	Chicken, 3 asst. 11299-1	Midwest	Open	2.00	2.00
94-25-010	Mailbox and Water Pump, 2 asst. 11301-1	Midwest	Open	4.00	4.00
94-25-011	Farm Town Windmill 11306-6	Midwest	Open	9.50	9.50
94-25-012	Apple Tree 2 asst. 11484-1	Midwest	Open	10.00	10.00
94-25-013	Pickup Truck 11304-2	Midwest	Open	12.00	12.00
94-25-014	Teacher and Children, 3 asst. 11460-5	Midwest	Open	5.50	5.50
94-25-015	Storekeeper 11459-9	Midwest	Open	5.50	5.50
94-25-016	Flagpole 11300-4	Midwest	Open	5.30	5.30

Midwest of Cannon Falls — **MouseKins Figurines**

Number	Name	Artist	Edition Limit	Issue Price	Quote
94-26-001	Florence Burroughs in Rocker Knitting 12128-3	Midwest	Open	11.00	11.00
94-26-002	Nicholas and Florence Preparing Gifts for Christmas, 2 asst. 12129-0	Midwest	Open	10.00	10.00
94-26-003	Burroughs Children in Bed 12130-6	Midwest	Open	11.50	11.50
94-26-004	Heather and Heathcliff Grey Playing, 2 asst. 12133-7	Midwest	Open	9.00	9.00
94-26-005	Prudence Grey Serving Food 12134-4	Midwest	Open	9.50	9.50
94-26-006	Sterling Grey Toasting Good Holiday Cheer 12135-1	Midwest	Open	9.50	9.50
94-26-007	Holly and J.D. Burroughs Playing with Sewing Needle and Thread, 2 asst. 12141-2	Midwest	Open	9.50	9.50
94-26-008	Burroughs Children Nativity Pageant Set 12142-9	Midwest	Open	30.00	30.00
94-26-009	Nicholas Burroughs Telling Story to Children on Bench 12144-3	Midwest	Open	12.00	12.00
94-26-010	Santa Mouse Gift Giver 12148-1	Midwest	Open	10.00	10.00
94-26-011	Sterling and Prudence Grey with Mistletoe Set 12149-8	Midwest	Open	19.00	19.00
94-26-012	Fireplace 12153-5	Midwest	Open	10.00	10.00
94-26-013	Table with Food 12154-2	Midwest	Open	9.50	9.50
94-26-014	Decorated Christmas Tree 12155-9	Midwest	Open	9.50	9.50

Midwest of Cannon Falls — **Farmyard Buddies**

Number	Name	Artist	Edition Limit	Issue Price	Quote
94-27-001	Barn 11799-6	Midwest	Open	21.00	21.00
94-27-002	Chicken Coop 11797-2	Midwest	Open	18.00	18.00
94-27-003	Farmhouse 11798-9	Midwest	Open	24.00	24.00
94-27-004	Corky and Clover Easy Rider, 2 asst. 11795-8	Midwest	Open	10.00	10.00
94-27-005	Farmyard Buddies Sign 12035-4	Midwest	Open	12.00	12.00
94-27-006	Curly, Corky and Clover Hangin' Out, 3 asst. 11787-3	Midwest	Open	7.00	7.00
94-27-007	Curly, Corky and Clover Playin' Hooky, 3 asst. 11794-1	Midwest	Open	9.00	9.00
94-27-008	Corky and Clover Hittin' the Hay, 2 asst. 11788-0	Midwest	Open	7.50	7.50
94-27-009	Corky and Clover Cheerful Chores, 2 asst. 11789-7	Midwest	Open	7.50	7.50
94-27-010	Earl and Pearl Square Dancin' Sitabouts, 2 asst. 11785-2	Midwest	Open	6.00	6.00
94-27-011	Corky, Clover and Curly Perfect Harmony Band, 3 asst. 11785-9	Midwest	Open	7.00	7.00

Midwest of Cannon Falls — **The Littlest Angel Collection**

Number	Name	Artist	Edition Limit	Issue Price	Quote
94-28-001	Angel Chime Candleholder 11626-5	Midwest	Open	11.50	11.50
94-28-002	Angel Chorus, 3 asst. 11627-2	Midwest	Open	11.50	11.50
94-28-003	Kneeling Angel, 2 asst. 11628-9	Midwest	Open	11.50	11.50
94-28-004	Angel Shelf-sitter 11630-2	Midwest	Open	10.50	10.50
94-28-005	Nativity Set 11633-3	Midwest	Open	31.00	31.00
94-28-006	Angel Music Box 11634-0	Midwest	Open	29.00	29.00
94-28-007	Angel Night Light 11635-7	Midwest	Open	33.00	33.00

Midwest of Cannon Falls — **Folk Art Gallery Collection**

Number	Name	Artist	Edition Limit	Issue Price	Quote
94-29-001	Just in Time for Christmas 11418-6	P. Schifferl	Open	110.00	110.00
94-29-002	Snowball Santa 11482-7	P. Schifferl	Open	30.00	30.00
94-29-003	Merry Christmas to All 11417-9	L. Schifferl	Open	115.00	115.00
94-29-004	Mother Goose on the Loose 11938-9	L. Schifferl	Open	95.00	95.00
94-29-005	Santa's Greeting Box 11480-3	L. Schifferl	Open	37.00	37.00
94-29-006	Dancing for Joy 11479-7	L. Schifferl	Open	70.00	70.00
94-29-007	Santa's Joy Ride 11468-1	R. Tate	Open	50.00	50.00
94-29-008	Holiday Fun Gameboard 11470-4	R. Tate	Open	65.00	65.00
94-29-009	Santa Hits the Trail 11466-7	R. Tate	Open	20.00	20.00
94-29-010	Birds at Home 11471-1	R. Tate	Open	57.00	57.00
94-29-011	Jack-O-Lantern Scarecrow Whirligig 11467-4	R. Tate	Open	47.00	47.00
94-29-012	All Aboard Santa's Ark Set 11472-8	R. Tate	Open	77.00	77.00
94-29-013	Santa's Magic Nutcracker 11469-8	R. Tate	Open	48.00	48.00
94-29-014	Wiggling Witch 11465-0	R. Tate	Open	19.00	19.00
94-29-015	Old Father Christmas 12981-4	R. Jones	Open	60.00	60.00
94-29-016	Woodland Roly-Poly Santa 12978-4	R. Jones	Open	30.00	30.00
94-29-017	Milkin' the Cow 11955-6	R. Jones	Open	19.00	19.00
94-29-018	Santa the Birdwatcher 12979-1	R. Jones	Open	37.00	37.00
94-29-019	The Night Before Christmas 12980-7	R. Jones	Open	60.00	60.00
94-29-020	Halloween Folk Witch 11821-4	R. Jones	Open	55.00	55.00
94-29-021	Brightest Star Mirror 12060-6	Origin by Sticks	Open	64.00	64.00
94-29-022	Birds of a Feather Photo Frame 12062-0	Origin by Sticks	Open	50.00	50.00
94-29-023	Sailing Through 12079-8	Origin by Sticks	Open	110.00	110.00
94-29-024	"For the Birds" Box 12070-5	Origin by Sticks	Open	70.00	70.00
94-29-025	Santa's Hours of Hard Work 12058-3	Origin by Sticks	Open	130.00	130.00
94-29-026	Santa's Magic Walking Stick 12066-8	Origin by Sticks	Open	59.00	59.00
94-29-027	Fish and Fowl Tic-Tac-Toe 12059-0	Origin by Sticks	Open	56.00	56.00
94-29-028	Thinking of Christmas 12067-5	Origin by Sticks	Open	144.00	144.00

Museum Collections, Inc. — **American Family I**

Number	Name	Artist	Edition Limit	Issue Price	Quote
79-01-001	Baby's First Step	N. Rockwell	22,500	90.00	220.00
80-01-002	Happy Birthday, Dear Mother	N. Rockwell	22,500	90.00	150.00
80-01-003	Sweet Sixteen	N. Rockwell	22,500	90.00	90.00
80-01-004	First Haircut	N. Rockwell	22,500	90.00	195.00
80-01-005	First Prom	N. Rockwell	22,500	90.00	90.00
80-01-006	Wrapping Christmas Presents	N. Rockwell	22,500	90.00	110.00
80-01-007	The Student	N. Rockwell	22,500	110.00	140.00
80-01-008	Birthday Party	N. Rockwell	22,500	110.00	150.00
80-01-009	Little Mother	N. Rockwell	22,500	110.00	110.00
80-01-010	Washing Our Dog	N. Rockwell	22,500	110.00	110.00
81-01-011	Mother's Little Helpers	N. Rockwell	22,500	110.00	110.00
81-01-012	Bride and Groom	N. Rockwell	22,500	110.00	180.00

Museum Collections, Inc. — **Christmas**

Number	Name	Artist	Edition Limit	Issue Price	Quote
80-02-001	Checking His List	N. Rockwell	Yr.Iss.	65.00	85.00
81-02-002	Ringing in Good Cheer	N. Rockwell	Yr.Iss.	95.00	95.00
82-02-003	Waiting for Santa	N. Rockwell	Yr.Iss.	95.00	95.00
83-02-004	High Hopes	N. Rockwell	Yr.Iss.	95	95.00
84-02-005	Space Age Santa	N. Rockwell	Yr.Iss.	65.00	65.00

Museum Collections, Inc. — **Classic**

Number	Name	Artist	Edition Limit	Issue Price	Quote
80-03-001	Lighthouse Keeper's Daughter	N. Rockwell	Closed	65.00	100.00
80-03-002	The Cobbler	N. Rockwell	Closed	65.00	85.00
80-03-003	The Toymaker	N. Rockwell	Closed	65.00	85.00
80-03-004	Bedtime	N. Rockwell	Closed	65.00	95.00
80-03-005	Memories	N. Rockwell	Closed	65.00	65.00
80-03-006	For A Good Boy	N. Rockwell	Closed	65.00	75.00
81-03-007	A Dollhouse for Sis	N. Rockwell	Closed	65.00	65.00
81-03-008	Music Master	N. Rockwell	Closed	65.00	65.00
81-03-009	The Music Lesson	N. Rockwell	Closed	65.00	65.00
81-03-010	Puppy Love	N. Rockwell	Closed	65.00	65.00
81-03-011	While The Audience Waits	N. Rockwell	Closed	65.00	65.00
81-03-012	Off to School	N. Rockwell	Closed	65.00	65.00
82-03-013	The Country Doctor	N. Rockwell	Closed	65.00	65.00
82-03-014	Spring Fever	N. Rockwell	Closed	65.00	65.00
82-03-015	Words of Wisdom	N. Rockwell	Closed	65.00	65.00
82-03-016	The Kite Maker	N. Rockwell	Closed	65.00	65.00
82-03-017	Dreams in the Antique Shop	N. Rockwell	Closed	65.00	65.00
83-03-018	Winter Fun	N. Rockwell	Closed	65.00	65.00
83-03-019	A Special Treat	N. Rockwell	Closed	65.00	65.00
83-03-020	High Stepping	N. Rockwell	Closed	65.00	65.00
83-03-021	Bored of Education	N. Rockwell	Closed	65.00	65.00
83-03-022	A Final Touch	N. Rockwell	Closed	65.00	65.00
83-03-023	Braving the Storm	N. Rockwell	Closed	65.00	65.00
84-03-024	Goin' Fishin'	N. Rockwell	Closed	65.00	65.00
84-03-025	The Big Race	N. Rockwell	Closed	65.00	65.00
84-03-026	Saturday's Hero	N. Rockwell	Closed	65.00	65.00
84-03-027	All Wrapped Up	N. Rockwell	Closed	65.00	65.00

Museum Collections, Inc. — **Commemorative**

Number	Name	Artist	Edition Limit	Issue Price	Quote
81-04-001	Norman Rockwell Display	N. Rockwell	5,000	125.00	150.00
82-04-002	Spirit of America	N. Rockwell	5,000	125.00	125.00
83-04-003	Norman Rockwell, America's Artist	N. Rockwell	5,000	125.00	125.00
84-04-004	Outward Bound	N. Rockwell	5,000	125.00	125.00
85-04-005	Another Masterpiece by Norman Rockwell	N. Rockwell	5,000	125.00	150.00
86-04-006	The Painter and the Pups	N. Rockwell	5,000	125.00	150.00

Napoleon U.S.A. — **Capodimonte Porcelain Flowers**

Number	Name	Artist	Edition Limit	Issue Price	Quote
89-01-001	Double Mistere Rose, pink-100350	E. Guerra	Open	32.50	32.50
89-01-002	Double Mistere Rose, yellow-100302	E. Guerra	Open	32.50	32.50
89-01-003	Double Mistere Rose, tea-100303	E. Guerra	Open	32.50	32.50
89-01-004	Double Mistere Rose, red-100305	E. Guerra	Open	32.50	32.50
89-01-005	Double Mistere Rose, aurora-100331	E. Guerra	Open	32.50	32.50
89-01-006	Double Mistere Rose, bicolor-100335	E. Guerra	Open	32.50	32.50
89-01-007	Double Mistere Rose, raspberry-100347	E. Guerra	Open	32.50	32.50
89-01-008	Rose & Bud, pink-100450	E. Guerra	Open	29.00	29.00
89-01-009	Rose & Bud, yellow-100402	E. Guerra	Open	29.00	29.00
89-01-010	Rose & Bud, tea-100403	E. Guerra	Open	29.00	29.00
89-01-012	Rose & Bud, red-100405	E. Guerra	Open	30.00	30.00
89-01-013	Rose & Bud, aurora-100431	E. Guerra	Open	29.00	29.00
89-01-014	Rose & Bud, raspberry-100447	E. Guerra	Open	30.00	30.00
89-01-015	Dogwood Single, pink-100901	E. Guerra	Open	15.00	15.00
89-01-016	Dogwood Single, white-100910	E. Guerra	Open	15.00	15.00
89-01-017	Dogwood Single, pink-100911	E. Guerra	Open	15.00	15.00
89-01-018	My Love Single, red-101105	E. Guerra	Open	72.00	72.00
89-01-019	Wild Rose Single, aurora-101331	E. Guerra	Open	75.00	75.00
89-01-020	Dogwood Double, pink-101401	E. Guerra	Open	22.00	22.00
89-01-021	Dogwood Double, white-101410	E. Guerra	Open	22.00	22.00
89-01-022	Dogwood Double, pink-101411	E. Guerra	Open	22.00	22.00
89-01-023	Clarissa Rose, pink-101550	E. Guerra	Open	185.00	185.00
89-01-024	Clarissa Rose, red-101505	E. Guerra	Open	190.00	190.00
89-01-025	Clarissa Rose, aurora-101531	E. Guerra	Open	185.00	185.00
89-01-026	Single Poppy, orange-102007	E. Guerra	Open	22.50	22.50
89-01-027	Single Rose Med., pink-103050	E. Guerra	Open	25.00	25.00
89-01-028	Single Rose Med., tea-103003	E. Guerra	Open	25.00	25.00
89-01-029	Single Rose Med., red-103005	E. Guerra	Open	25.00	25.00

Company Number	Name	Series Artist	Edition Limit	Issue Price	Quote
89-01-030	Single Rose Med., aurora-103031	E. Guerra	Open	25.00	25.00
89-01-031	Single Rose Med., bicolor-103035	E. Guerra	Open	25.00	25.00
89-01-032	Single Rose Med., raspberry-103047	E. Guerra	Open	25.00	25.00
89-01-033	Tulip, pink-103101	E. Guerra	Open	65.00	65.00
89-01-034	Queen Rose 2/bud, pink-110150	E. Guerra	Open	47.00	47.00
89-01-035	Queen Rose 2/bud, red-110105	E. Guerra	Open	48.00	48.00
89-01-036	Queen Rose 2/bud, aurora-110131	E. Guerra	Open	47.00	47.00
89-01-037	Queen Rose 2/bud, raspberry-110147	E. Guerra	Open	47.00	47.00
89-01-038	Poinsettia Sm., red-112806	E. Guerra	Open	30.00	30.00
89-01-039	Poinsettia Med., red-113106	E. Guerra	Open	44.00	44.00
89-01-040	Single Daffodil, yellow-113202	E. Guerra	Open	29.00	29.00
89-01-041	Single Daffodil, yel./wht.-113220	E. Guerra	Open	29.00	29.00
89-01-042	Daffodil Stem, yellow-113502	E. Guerra	Open	62.00	62.00
89-01-043	Triple Daffodil, yellow-113602	E. Guerra	Open	115.00	115.00
89-01-044	Triple Daffodil, yel.wht.-113620	E. Guerra	Open	115.00	115.00
89-01-045	Camellia, pale pink-113911	E. Guerra	Open	75.00	75.00
89-01-046	Magnolia, white-114910	E. Guerra	Open	36.00	36.00
89-01-047	Poinsettia Plant, red-115406	E. Guerra	500	525.00	525.00
89-01-048	Hibiscus Group, purple-121232	E. Guerra	Open	210.00	210.00
89-01-049	Magnolia Large, white-122510	E. Guerra	Open	80.00	80.00
89-01-050	Queen Rose w/2 buds, red-122805	E. Guerra	Open	90.00	90.00
89-01-051	Queen Rose w/2 buds, aurora-122831	E. Guerra	Open	90.00	90.00
89-01-052	Queen Rose w/2 buds, bicolor-122835	E. Guerra	Open	90.00	90.00
89-01-053	Queen Rose w/2 buds, raspberry-122847	E. Guerra	Open	90.00	90.00
89-01-054	Large Rose 2/buds, red-126805	E. Guerra	Open	80.00	80.00
89-01-055	Large Rose 2/buds, aurora-126831	E. Guerra	Open	80.00	80.00
89-01-056	Large Rose 2/buds, bicolor-126835	E. Guerra	Open	80.00	80.00
89-01-057	High Rose Composition, red-126905	E. Guerra	Open	285.00	285.00
89-01-058	High Rose Composition, aurora-126931	E. Guerra	Open	285.00	285.00
89-01-059	High Rose Composition, bicolor-126935	E. Guerra	Open	285.00	285.00
89-01-060	Lying Rose Composition, red-127005	E. Guerra	Open	275.00	275.00
89-01-061	Lying Rose Composition, aurora-127031	E. Guerra	Open	275.00	275.00
89-01-062	Lying Rose Composition, bicolor-127035	E. Guerra	Open	275.00	275.00
89-01-063	Double Crocus, violet-128608	E. Guerra	Open	47.00	47.00
89-01-064	Holly Poinsettia, red-129906	E. Guerra	Open	90.00	90.00
89-01-065	Rose Long Stem, pink-133901	E. Guerra	Open	45.00	45.00
89-01-066	Rose Long Stem, yellow-133902	E. Guerra	Open	45.00	45.00
89-01-067	Rose Long Stem, red-133905	E. Guerra	Open	45.00	45.00
89-01-068	Rose Long Stem, aurora-133931	E. Guerra	Open	45.00	45.00
89-01-069	Rose Long Stem, bicolor-133935	E. Guerra	Open	45.00	45.00
89-01-070	Rose Long Stem, raspberry-133947	E. Guerra	Open	45.00	45.00
89-01-071	Single Iris, violet-134618	E. Guerra	Open	80.00	80.00
89-01-072	Single Iris, white-134620	E. Guerra	Open	80.00	80.00
89-01-073	Iris Stem, violet-134818	E. Guerra	Open	55.00	55.00
89-01-074	Single Hibiscus Large, red-137006	E. Guerra	Open	50.00	50.00
89-01-075	Single Hibiscus, red-137606	E. Guerra	Open	32.00	32.00
89-01-076	Single Hibiscus, purple-137632	E. Guerra	Open	30.00	30.00
89-01-077	Single Hibiscus, white-137611	E. Guerra	Open	30.00	30.00
89-01-078	Double Hibiscus, red-137706	E. Guerra	Open	75.00	75.00
89-01-079	Double Hibiscus, purple-137732	E. Guerra	Open	75.00	75.00
89-01-080	Double Hibiscus, white-137711	E. Guerra	Open	75.00	75.00
89-01-081	Mascotte Rose Branch, red-138205	E. Guerra	Open	75.00	75.00
89-01-082	Azalea, pink-141033	E. Guerra	Open	185.00	185.00
89-01-083	Azalea, yellow-141020	E. Guerra	Open	185.00	185.00
89-01-084	Single Rose Large, pink-141450	E. Guerra	Open	35.00	35.00
89-01-085	Single Rose Large, yellow-141402	E. Guerra	Open	35.00	35.00
89-01-086	Single Rose Large, tea-141403	E. Guerra	Open	35.00	35.00
89-01-087	Single Rose Large, red-141405	E. Guerra	Open	35.00	35.00
89-01-088	Single Rose Large, aurora-141431	E. Guerra	Open	35.00	35.00
89-01-089	Single Rose Large, bicolor-141435	E. Guerra	Open	35.00	35.00
89-01-090	Single Rose Large, raspberry-141447	E. Guerra	Open	35.00	35.00
89-01-091	Small Rose Stem, red-142705	E. Guerra	Open	27.50	27.50
89-01-092	Small Rose Stem, aurora-142731	E. Guerra	Open	27.50	27.50
89-01-093	Trunk Rose, pink-143101	E. Guerra	Open	60.00	60.00
89-01-094	Princess Orchid Group, pink-143511	E. Guerra	Open	200.00	200.00
89-01-095	Double Iris, white-143720	E. Guerra	Open	175.00	175.00
89-01-096	Double Iris, violet--143718	E. Guerra	Open	175.00	175.00
89-01-097	Rose & Bud Candle Holder, pink-150950	E. Guerra	Open	28.00	28.00
89-01-098	Rose & Bud Candle Holder, red-150905	E. Guerra	Open	28.00	28.00
89-01-099	Rose & Bud Candle Holder, aurora-150931	E. Guerra	Open	28.00	28.00
89-01-100	Double Rose Candle Holder, pink-151401	E. Guerra	Open	45.00	45.00
89-01-101	Double Rose Candle Holder, red-151405	E. Guerra	Open	45.00	45.00
89-01-102	Double Rose Candle Holder, aurora-151431	E. Guerra	Open	45.00	45.00
89-01-103	Jenny Rose w/ buds, red-151505	E. Guerra	Open	65.00	65.00
89-01-104	Jenny Rose w/ buds, bicolor-151535	E. Guerra	Open	65.00	65.00
89-01-105	Double Rose Trunk, aurora-151631	E. Guerra	Open	75.00	75.00
89-01-106	Mistere Rose Plant, red-151905	E. Guerra	Open	185.00	185.00
89-01-107	Garden Rose Composition, bicolor-152035	E. Guerra	Open	200.00	200.00
89-01-108	Large Camellia, pink-152811	E. Guerra	Open	55.00	55.00
89-01-109	Three Princess Orchids, yellow-153112	E. Guerra	Open	250.00	250.00
89-01-110	Small Double Azalea, white/yel.-154120	E. Guerra	Open	42.00	42.00
89-01-111	Small Double Azalea, pink-154133	E. Guerra	Open	42.00	42.00
89-01-112	Single Pansy, yellow-157002	E. Guerra	Open	38.00	38.00
89-01-113	Single Pansy, purple-157008	E. Guerra	Open	38.00	38.00
89-01-114	Pansy w/ Cherry Blossom , purple-157108	E. Guerra	Open	60.00	60.00
89-01-115	Double Pansy, purple-157208	E. Guerra	Open	75.00	75.00
89-01-116	Triple Pansy, purple-157308	E. Guerra	Open	95.00	95.00
89-01-117	Rose Plant, spec.pink-158935	E. Guerra	300	1300.00	1300.00
89-01-118	Lily High Branch, pink-159401	E. Guerra	300	1600.00	1600.00
89-01-119	Hibiscus Plant, red-160009	E. Guerra	300	1500.00	1500.00
89-01-120	Double Large Rose, pink-160250	E. Guerra	Open	50.00	50.00
89-01-121	Double Large Rose, yellow-160202	E. Guerra	Open	50.00	50.00
89-01-122	Double Large Rose, tea-160203	E. Guerra	Open	50.00	50.00
89-01-123	Double Large Rose, red-160205	E. Guerra	Open	50.00	50.00
89-01-124	Double Large Rose, aurora-160231	E. Guerra	Open	50.00	50.00
89-01-125	Double Large Rose, bicolor-160235	E. Guerra	Open	50.00	50.00
89-01-126	Double Large Rose, raspberry-160247	E. Guerra	Open	50.00	50.00
89-01-127	Iris Group, violet-160618	E. Guerra	Open	300.00	300.00
89-01-128	Baroness Rose Group, pink-160750	E. Guerra	Open	310.00	310.00
89-01-129	Baroness Rose Group, aurora-160731	E. Guerra	Open	310.00	310.00
89-01-130	Fragrant Rose Composition, red/wht-161205	E. Guerra	Open	350.00	350.00
89-01-131	Queen Rose on Fence, aurora-161431	E. Guerra	Open	260.00	260.00
89-01-132	May Rose, special pink-161535	E. Guerra	500	400.00	400.00
89-01-133	Poinsettia on Branch, red-162106	E. Guerra	Open	68.00	68.00
89-01-134	Trunk Rose & Bud, red-168705	E. Guerra	Open	110.00	110.00
89-01-135	Trunk Rose & Bud, aurora-168731	E. Guerra	Open	110.00	110.00
89-01-136	Small Branch Rose, red-175205	E. Guerra	Open	40.00	40.00
89-01-137	Small Branch Rose, aurora-175231	E. Guerra	Open	40.00	40.00
89-01-138	Small Branch Rose, bicolor-175235	E. Guerra	Open	40.00	40.00
89-01-139	Small Branch Rose, raspberry-175247	E. Guerra	Open	40.00	40.00
89-01-140	Fragrant Rose w/ bud, red-175405	E. Guerra	Open	37.50	37.50
89-01-141	Silver Jubilee Rose, aurora-175731	E. Guerra	Open	35.00	35.00
89-01-142	Rose & bud w/stem, pink-180250	E. Guerra	Open	32.00	32.00
89-01-143	Rose & bud w/stem, tea-180203	E. Guerra	Open	32.00	32.00

Company Number	Name	Series Artist	Edition Limit	Issue Price	Quote
89-01-144	Rose & bud w/stem, red-180205	E. Guerra	Open	35.00	35.00
89-01-145	Rose & bud w/stem, aurora-180231	E. Guerra	Open	32.00	32.00
89-01-146	Rose & bud w/stem, bicolor-180235	E. Guerra	Open	32.00	32.00
89-01-147	Rose & bud w/stem, raspberry-180247	E. Guerra	Open	35.00	35.00
89-01-148	Small Branch Orchid, pink-180811	E. Guerra	Open	50.00	50.00
89-01-149	Two Princess Orchid, yellow-181012	E. Guerra	Open	110.00	110.00
89-01-150	Double Orchid, violet-181118	E. Guerra	Open	115.00	115.00
89-01-151	Daffodil Group, yellow-181902	E. Guerra	Open	200.00	200.00
89-01-152	Daffodil Group, yel./wht.-181920	E. Guerra	Open	200.00	200.00
89-01-153	Single Princess Orchid, white-183010	E. Guerra	Open	45.00	45.00
89-01-154	Typhoon Rose Plant, aurora-183131	E. Guerra	Open	190.00	190.00
89-01-155	Cattleya Orchid, violet-183318	E. Guerra	Open	95.00	95.00
89-01-156	Single Cattleya, violet-183518	E. Guerra	Open	55.00	55.00
89-01-157	May Rose Basket, special pink-190135	E. Guerra	500	650.00	650.00
Old World Christmas		**Night Lights**			
85-01-001	Santa 529701	E.M. Merck	Retrd.	37.00	135.00
86-01-002	Angel 529703	E.M. Merck	Retrd.	18.00	65.00
86-01-003	Santa in Chimney 529707	E.M. Merck	Retrd.	37.00	115.00
86-01-004	Snowman 529709	E.M. Merck	Retrd.	37.00	55.00
86-01-005	Teddy Bear 529711	E.M. Merck	Retrd.	37.00	65.00
86-01-006	ABC Block 529713	E.M. Merck	Open	37.00	37.00
87-01-007	Santa with Tree 529715	E.M. Merck	Retrd.	39.50	110.00
88-01-008	Santa Hugging Tree 529717	E.M. Merck	Retrd.	42.00	110.00
89-01-009	Santa on Locomotive 529719	E.M. Merck	Retrd.	42.00	85.00
90-01-010	Father Christmas 529721	E.M. Merck	Retrd.	45.00	65.00
91-01-011	Santa with Stocking 529723	E.M. Merck	Retrd.	45.00	65.00
92-01-012	Santa with Nutcracker 529725	E.M. Merck	Retrd.	45.00	75.00
93-01-013	Father Christmas with Toys 529727	E.M. Merck	Open	48.50	48.50
Old World Christmas		**Smoking Men**			
85-02-001	Toy Peddler Smoker 70020	K.W.O.	Open	55.00	55.00
85-02-002	Large Toy Peddler Smoker 70020-9	K.W.O.	Open	280.00	280.00
85-02-003	Woodsman Smoker 70021	K.W.O.	Open	50.00	50.00
85-02-004	Large Hunter 70021-9	K.W.O.	Open	250.00	250.00
85-02-005	Nightwatchman Smoker 70022	K.W.O.	Open	48.50	48.50
85-02-006	Hunter 70023	K.W.O.	Open	49.50	49.50
85-02-007	Chimney Sweep 70024	K.W.O.	Open	47.50	47.50
85-02-008	Gardener 70040	K.W.O.	Open	57.00	57.00
87-02-009	Blacksmith 70041	K.W.O.	Open	50.00	50.00
87-02-010	Fisherman 70042	K.W.O.	Open	49.50	49.50
87-02-011	Woodcarver 70043	K.W.O.	Retrd.	40.00	40.00
87-02-012	Tailor 70044	K.W.O.	Open	50.00	50.00
87-02-013	Shepherd 70045	K.W.O.	Open	49.00	49.00
88-02-014	Bird Seller 70046	K.W.O.	Open	56.00	56.00
88-02-015	Artist 70047	K.W.O.	Open	50.00	50.00
88-02-016	Postman 70048	K.W.O.	Open	48.50	48.50
88-02-017	Antique Style Cook 70052	K.W.O.	Retrd.	27.50	27.50
88-02-018	Antique Style Coachman 70053	K.W.O.	Retrd.	28.00	28.00
91-02-019	Santa with Toys 70060	K.W.O.	Open	57.00	57.00
91-02-020	Cook 70061	K.W.O.	Open	49.00	49.00
92-02-021	Coachman 70062	K.W.O.	Open	50.00	50.00
92-02-022	White Santa 70063	K.W.O.	Open	60.00	60.00
92-02-023	Red Santa 70064	K.W.O.	Open	60.00	60.00
94-02-024	Large Red Santa 70064-9	K.W.O.	Open	270.00	270.00
92-02-025	Teal Santa 70065	K.W.O.	Open	60.00	60.00
92-02-026	Peddler 70066	K.W.O.	Open	59.50	59.50
93-02-027	Large Peddler 70066-9	K.W.O.	Open	295.00	295.00
93-02-028	Poacher 70068	K.W.O.	Open	47.50	47.50
93-02-029	Basket Peddler 70069	K.W.O.	Open	58.50	58.50
93-02-030	Highwayman 70070	K.W.O.	Open	50.00	50.00
94-02-031	Mushroom Collector 70071	K.W.O.	Open	50.00	50.00
94-02-032	Grandpa at Oven 70073	K.W.O.	Open	72.00	72.00
94-02-033	Grandpa with Accordion 70076	K.W.O.	Open	59.50	59.50
94-02-034	Grandma 70077	K.W.O.	Open	59.50	59.50
94-02-035	Sitting Hunter 70082	K.W.O.	Open	60.00	60.00
94-02-036	Zither Player 70083	K.W.O.	Open	63.00	63.00
86-02-037	Hunter 701	O.W.C.	Retrd.	30.00	30.00
86-02-038	Father Christmas with Toys 7010	O.W.C.	Retrd.	60.00	60.00
86-02-039	Carved Hunter 70100	O.W.C.	Retrd.	90.00	90.00
93-02-040	Large Clock Peddler 70101	K.W.O.	Open	120.00	120.00
93-02-041	Large Flower Peddler 70103	K.W.O.	Open	120.00	120.00
93-02-042	Large Pottery Peddler 70104	K.W.O.	Open	120.00	120.00
92-02-043	Small Santa 7011	O.W.C.	Open	37.50	37.50
92-02-044	Father Christmas 70113-1	O.W.C.	Retrd.	45.00	45.00
91-02-045	Natural Father Christmas 7012	O.W.C.	Retrd.	60.00	60.00
91-02-046	Woodsman 7013	O.W.C..	Retrd.	60.00	60.00
91-02-047	Bird Seller 7014	O.W.C..	Retrd.	50.00	50.00
92-02-048	Carved Woodsman 7015	O.W.C.	Open	67.50	67.50
94-02-049	Father Christmas 70150	K.W.O.	Open	110.00	110.00
91-02-050	Gardner 7016	E.M. Merck	Retrd.	55.00	55.00
89-02-051	Chimney Sweep 7017	E.M. Merck	Retrd.	55.00	55.00
91-02-052	Hunter 7018	E.M. Merck	Retrd.	55.00	55.00
91-02-053	Woodsman 7019	E.M. Merck	Retrd.	55.00	55.00
86-02-054	Father Christmas 702	O.W.C.	Open	60.00	60.00
86-02-055	Artist 7020	E.M. Merck	Retrd.	55.00	55.00
86-02-056	Small Old World Santa 70202	O.W.C.	Retrd.	37.50	37.50
86-02-057	Large Old World Santa 70203	O.W.C.	Retrd.	77.50	77.50
86-02-058	Old World Santa 70204	O.W.C.	Retrd.	42.50	42.50
92-02-059	Hunter with Crate 7021	O.W.C.	Open	150.00	150.00
92-02-060	Robber with Crate 7022	O.W.C.	Open	150.00	150.00
92-02-061	St. Peter 70228	O.W.C.	Retrd.	95.00	95.00
92-02-062	King 70229	E.M. Merck	Retrd.	95.00	95.00
92-02-063	Farmer with Crate 7023	O.W.C.	Open	150.00	150.00
91-02-064	Cook 7025	O.W.C.	Retrd.	55.00	55.00
92-02-065	Farmer 7026	O.W.C.	Retrd.	55.00	55.00
92-02-066	Tyrolian 702613	O.W.C.	Retrd.	45.00	45.00
85-02-067	Grandpa 702615	O.W.C.	Open	42.50	42.50
86-02-068	Skier 702616	O.W.C.	Retrd.	54.00	54.00
85-02-069	Snowman 702621	O.W.C.	Retrd.	30.00	30.00
92-02-070	Grandma 702622	O.W.C.	Retrd.	42.50	42.50
92-02-071	Innkeeper 70268	O.W.C.	Retrd.	54.00	54.00
91-02-072	Nightwatchman 7027	O.W.C.	Retrd.	55.00	55.00
91-02-073	Postman 7028	O.W.C.	Retrd.	55.00	55.00
91-02-074	Fisherman 7029	O.W.C.	Retrd.	55.00	55.00
91-02-075	Frosty Snowman 703	O.W.C.	Retrd.	22.50	22.50
91-02-076	Toy Peddler 7030	O.W.C.	Retrd.	60.00	60.00
91-02-077	Wood Worker 7031	O.W.C.	Open	79.50	79.50
91-02-078	Bavarian Hunter 7032	O.W.C.	Open	79.50	79.50
91-02-079	Beer Drinker 7033	O.W.C.	Open	67.50	67.50
85-02-080	Nightwatchman 7034	O.W.C.	Retrd.	32.50	32.50
92-02-081	Carved Santa 7035	O.W.C.	Open	67.50	67.50
91-02-082	Mountain Climber 7036	O.W.C.	Open	67.50	67.50
91-02-083	Innkeeper 7037	O.W.C.	Open	60.00	60.00

Company Number	Name	Series Artist	Edition Limit	Issue Price	Quote
91-02-084	Ice Skater 7038	E.M. Merck.	Retrd.	60.00	60.00
92-02-085	Clock Salesman 7039	O.W.C.	Retrd.	275.00	275.00
86-02-086	Santa Smoker/Candleholder 704	O.W.C.	Open	55.00	55.00
92-02-087	Basket Peddler 7040	O.W.C.	Retrd.	130.00	130.00
91-02-088	Champion Archer 7041	O.W.C.	Open	67.50	67.50
91-02-089	Butcher 7043	O.W.C.	Retrd.	49.50	49.50
91-02-090	Baker 7044	O.W.C.	Retrd.	49.50	49.50
91-02-091	Gardener 7045	O.W.C.	Retrd.	49.50	49.50
91-02-092	Santa Claus 705	O.W.C.	Retrd.	45.00	45.00
91-02-093	Father Christmas 7051	O.W.C.	Open	79.95	79.95
92-02-094	Captain 7052	O.W.C.	Open	79.95	79.95
92-02-095	Carved Shepherd 7053	O.W.C.	Retrd.	150.00	150.00
92-02-096	Carved Hunter 7054	O.W.C.	Retrd.	200.00	200.00
92-02-097	Witch 70543	E.M. Merck	Retrd.	49.50	49.50
91-02-098	Toy Peddler 7055	O.W.C.	Retrd.	60.00	60.00
91-02-099	Prussian Soldier 7056	O.W.C.	Retrd.	60.00	60.00
91-02-100	Coachman 7057	O.W.C.	Retrd.	60.00	60.00
92-02-101	Alpenhorn Player 7058	O.W.C.	Open	70.00	70.00
92-02-102	Skier 7059	O.W.C.	Open	59.50	59.50
91-02-103	Natural Santa 706	O.W.C.	Retrd.	40.00	40.00
92-02-104	Toy Peddler 7060	O.W.C.	Open	110.00	110.00
92-02-105	Minstrel 7061	O.W.C.	Open	85.00	85.00
92-02-106	Angler with Crate 7062	O.W.C.	Open	150.00	150.00
93-02-107	Father Christmas 7063	O.W.C.	Retrd.	45.00	45.00
92-02-108	Santa in Crate 707	O.W.C.	Open	165.00	165.00
92-02-109	Carved King 7072	O.W.C.	Open	68.50	68.50
88-02-110	Snowman with Bird 708	O.W.C.	Open	26.00	26.00
89-02-111	Santa 7086	O.W.C.	Retrd.	55.00	55.00
92-02-112	Christmas Tree Vendor 709	O.W.C.	Open	150.00	150.00
91-02-113	Snowman on Skis 7092	O.W.C.	Retrd.	30.00	30.00
87-02-114	Chimney Sweep 72014	K.W.O.	Open	48.50	48.50
87-02-115	Guard Nutcracker 72015	K.W.O.	Open	52.50	52.50
94-02-116	Small Cook Nutcracker 72020	E.M. Merck	Open	42.00	42.00
94-02-117	Small Skier Nutcracker 72021	E.M. Merck	Open	44.00	44.00
94-02-118	Small Toy Peddler Nutcracker 72022	E.M. Merck	Open	44.00	44.00
94-02-119	Small Gardener Nutcracker 72023	E.M. Merck	Open	44.00	44.00
94-02-120	Small Santa Nutcracker 72024	E.M. Merck	Open	42.00	42.00
94-02-121	Small Chimney Sweep Nutcracker 72025	E.M. Merck	Open	42.00	42.00
87-02-122	Small King Nutcracker 72030	K.W.O.	Open	39.95	39.95
87-02-123	King Nutcracker 72031	K.W.O.	Open	50.00	50.00
93-02-124	Large King Nutcracker 72033	K.W.O.	Open	79.95	79.95
93-02-125	Stained King with Crown Nutcracker 72034	K.W.O.	Open	65.00	65.00
87-02-126	Dutch Guard Nutcracker 72040	K.W.O.	Open	55.00	55.00
87-02-127	British Guard Nutcracker 72041	K.W.O.	Open	60.00	60.00
87-02-128	British General Nutcracker 72042	K.W.O.	Open	55.00	55.00
87-02-129	Austrian General Nutcracker 72043	K.W.O.	Open	57.50	57.50
87-02-130	Prussian Hussar Nutcracker 72044	K.W.O.	Open	60.00	60.00
87-02-131	Prussian Sergeant Nutcracker 72045	K.W.O.	Open	60.00	60.00
87-02-132	Spanish Guard Nutcracker 72046	K.W.O.	Open	65.00	65.00
87-02-133	Austrian Musketeer Nutcracker 72048	K.W.O.	Open	57.50	57.50
87-02-134	Saxon Guard Nutcracker 72049	K.W.O.	Open	65.00	65.00
89-02-135	British Major Nutcracker 72050	K.W.O.	Open	65.00	65.00
92-02-136	Saxonian Officer Nutcracker 72051	K.W.O.	Open	65.00	65.00
92-02-137	Prussian Officer Nutcracker 72052	K.W.O.	Open	65.00	65.00
92-02-138	French Officer Nutcracker 72053	K.W.O.	Open	67.50	67.50
92-02-139	Portuguese Guard Nutcracker 72055	K.W.O.	Open	65.00	65.00
92-02-140	Swedish Officer Nutcracker 72056	K.W.O.	Open	67.50	67.50
92-02-141	Austrian Hussar Nutcracker 72058	K.W.O.	Open	62.50	62.50
92-02-142	Hungarian Hussar Nutcracker 72059	K.W.O.	Open	62.50	62.50
92-02-143	Farmer Nutcracker 72064	K.W.O.	Open	62.50	62.50
93-02-144	Traditional Erzgebirge Nutcracker 72067	K.W.O.	Open	62.50	62.50
93-02-145	Hunter Nutcracker 72070	K.W.O.	Open	59.50	59.50
91-02-146	Large Carved Hunter Nutcracker 721	K.W.O.	Open	175.00	175.00
91-02-147	Inlaid Natural King Nutcracker 7214	O.W.C.	Retrd.	150.00	150.00
92-02-148	Large Dutch Guard Nutcracker 72140	K.W.O.	Open	90.00	90.00
92-02-149	Large British Guard 72141	K.W.O.	Open	90.00	90.00
92-02-150	Large Prussian Hussar Nutcracker 72144	K.W.O.	Open	90.00	90.00
92-02-151	Large Prussian Sargeant 72145	K.W.O.	Open	90.00	90.00
92-02-152	Large Austrian Musketeer Nutcracker 72148	K.W.O.	Open	87.50	87.50
92-02-153	Carved Hunter Nutcracker 72213	O.W.C.	Retrd.	150.00	150.00
92-02-154	Large Carved Santa Nutcracker 7223	K.W.O.	Open	175.00	175.00
92-02-155	Large Fireman Nutcracker 72240	K.W.O.	Open	99.50	99.50
92-02-156	Large Saxon Duke Nutcracker 72241	K.W.O.	Open	129.50	129.50
92-02-157	Large Bavarian Duke Nutcracker 72242	K.W.O.	Open	129.50	129.50
92-02-158	Large Austrian King Nutcracker 72243	K.W.O..	Open	129.50	129.50
92-02-159	Large Prussian King Nutcracker 72244	K.W.O.	Open	129.50	129.50
91-02-160	Inlaid Natural Muskateer 7225	O.W.C.	Retrd.	150.00	150.00
91-02-161	Large Hunter Nutcracker 7228	K.W.O.	Open	97.50	97.50
92-02-162	Exceptional King Nutcracker 7230	E.M. Merck	50	950.00	950.00
93-02-163	Exceptional Guard Nutcracker 7231	K.W.O.	50	995.00	995.00
92-02-164	Large Traditional Red King Nutcracker 7237	K.W.O.	Open	115.00	115.00
93-02-165	Brandenburger Guard Nutcracker 7250	E.M. Merck	Retrd.	110.00	110.00
93-02-166	Prussian King Nutcracker 7251	E.M. Merck	Open	110.00	110.00
93-02-167	Rostocker Pirate Nutcracker 7252	E.M. Merck	Open	110.00	110.00
93-02-168	Berliner Baker Nutcracker 7253	E.M. Merck	Open	110.00	110.00
93-02-169	Waldheimer Hunter Nutcracker 7254	E.M. Merck	Open	110.00	110.00
93-02-170	Chemnitzer Clown 7255	E.M. Merck	Open	110.00	110.00
93-02-171	Sonnenberger Toy Peddler Nutcracker 7256	E.M. Merck	Open	110.00	110.00
93-02-172	Seiffener Santa Nutcracker 7257	E.M. Merck	Retrd.	110.00	110.00
93-02-173	Tegernsee Golfer Nutcracker 7259	E.M. Merck	Open	135.00	135.00
93-02-174	Freitaler Fisherman Nutcracker 7260	E.M. Merck	Open	110.00	110.00
93-02-175	Falkensteiner Wizard 7261	E.M. Merck	Open	110.00	110.00
93-02-176	Saalfelder Shepherd Nutcracker 7263	E.M. Merck	Open	110.00	110.00
93-02-177	Bohemian Beekeeper Nutcracker 7264	E.M. Merck	Open	110.00	110.00
93-02-178	Coburger Chimney Sweep Nutcracker 7265	E.M. Merck	Open	110.00	110.00
93-02-179	Altenburger Grandma Nutcracker 7266	E.M. Merck	Open	135.00	135.00
93-02-180	Altenburger Grandpa Nutcracker 7267	E.M. Merck	Open	135.00	135.00
93-02-181	Wittlicher Witch Nutcracker 7268	E.M. Merck	Open	135.00	135.00
93-02-182	Bremer Sea Captain Nutcracker 7269	E.M. Merck	Open	110.00	110.00
93-02-183	Kulmbacher Beer Drinker Nutcracker 7270	E.M. Merck	Open	110.00	110.00
93-02-184	Schneeberger Skier Nutcracker 7271	E.M. Merck	Open	135.00	135.00
93-02-185	Neustadter Nurse Nutcracker 7272	E.M. Merck	Open	135.00	135.00
93-02-186	Berchtesgaden Doctor Nutcracker 7273	E.M. Merck	Open	110.00	110.00
93-02-187	Fuessen Father Christmas Nutcracker 7274	E.M. Merck	Open	135.00	135.00
94-02-188	Salzburger St. Nicholas Nutcracker 7275	E.M. Merck	Open	140.00	140.00
94-02-189	Waldkirchen Father Christmas 7276	E.M. Merck	Open	140.00	140.00
92-02-190	Large Snow Prince Nutcracker 7277	E.M. Merck	Retrd.	100.00	100.00
94-02-184	Giessener Gardener Nutcracker 7278	E.M. Merck	Open	110.00	110.00
94-02-191	Partinkirchen Bride 7279	E.M. Merck	Open	140.00	140.00
94-02-192	Garmish Groom Nutcracker 7280	E.M. Merck	Open	110.00	110.00
94-02-193	Neuschwanstein Knight 7281	E.M. Merck	Open	110.00	110.00
94-02-194	Nuremberger Nightwatchman 7282	E.M. Merck	Open	110.00	110.00
94-02-195	Wyker Viking Nutcracker 7283	E.M. Merck	Open	110.00	110.00
92-02-196	Natural Guard Nutcracker 72915	K.W.O.	Open	52.50	52.50

Company Number	Name	Series Artist	Edition Limit	Issue Price	Quote
92-02-197	Skier Nutcracker 7294	E.M. Merck	Retrd.	82.50	82.50
93-02-198	Snowman Nutcracker 7295	E.M. Merck	Open	110.00	110.00
93-02-199	Teddy Bear Nutcracker 7296	E.M. Merck	Open	135.00	135.00
94-02-200	Easter Bunny Nutcracker 7297	E.M. Merck	Open	140.00	140.00
94-02-201	Black Cat Nutcracker 7298	E.M. Merck	Open	140.00	140.00
Old World Christmas		**Collectibles**			
91-03-001	Noah's Ark 861	O.W.C.	Open	250.00	250.00
92-03-002	Weather House 86109	O.W.C.	Open	31.50	31.50
92-03-003	Large Seiffener Candle Arch 8616	O.W.C.	Open	450.00	450.00
92-03-004	Candle Arch with Church 862	O.W.C.	Retrd.	28.50	28.50
Old World Christmas		**Pyramids**			
86-04-001	Angel Musicians Pyramid 88001	K.W.O.	Open	58.50	58.50
91-04-002	Deer in Forest Pyramid 8810	O.W.C.	Open	97.50	97.50
91-04-003	Camel Caravan Pyramid 8812	O.W.C.	Open	92.50	92.50
91-04-004	Musical 4-Tier Pyramid 8815	O.W.C.	Retrd.	775.00	775.00
91-04-005	White 3-Tier Pyramid 8816	O.W.C.	Retrd.	225.00	225.00
91-04-006	Santa with Train 8817	O.W.C.	Retrd.	62.50	62.50
91-04-007	3-Tier Painted Nativity Pyramid 8818	O.W.C.	Retrd.	225.00	225.00
92-04-008	Mini Natural Angel 8819	O.W.C.	Open	42.50	42.50
92-04-009	3-Tier Forest Pyramid 882	O.W.C.	Open	225.00	225.00
92-04-010	Mini-Pyramid, Santa 8820	O.W.C.	Open	32.50	32.50
92-04-011	Natural Pyramid with Deer 8821	O.W.C.	Open	65.00	65.00
92-04-012	Small Nativity 8822	O.W.C.	Open	110.00	110.00
92-04-013	Mini Painted Angel 8823	O.W.C.	Open	47.50	47.50
92-04-014	White Pyramid with Angels 8824	O.W.C.	Retrd.	55.00	55.00
92-04-015	Traditional 3-Tier Pyramid 8826	K.W.O.	Open	175.00	175.00
92-04-016	3 Tier Nativity Pyramid 883	O.W.C.	Open	250.00	250.00
92-04-017	Traditional 4-Tier Pyramid 8836	K.W.O.	Open	225.00	225.00
92-04-018	4-Tier White Pyramid with Music 8837	K.W.O.	Open	550.00	550.00
92-04-019	Miniature Forest Pyramid 884	O.W.C.	Open	35.00	35.00
92-04-020	6ft Hand-Carved Pyramid 884006	O.W.C.	Retrd.	4000.00	4000.00
92-04-021	5ft Hand-Carved Pyramid 884007	O.W.C.	Retrd.	1295.00	1295.00
92-04-022	Miniature Choir Pyramid 885	O.W.C.	Open	35.00	35.00
92-04-023	Detailed Nativity Pyramid 8851	O.W.C.	Retrd.	175.00	175.00
92-04-024	Miniature Music Band Pyramid 886	O.W.C.	Retrd.	30.00	30.00
92-04-025	Santa with Angels Pyramid 887	O.W.C.	Retrd.	175.00	175.00
92-04-026	Small Choir Pyramid 8879	O.W.C.	Retrd.	68.50	68.50
92-04-027	Fairytale Pyramid 888	O.W.C.	Open	175.00	175.00
92-04-028	Small Nativity Pyramid 889	O.W.C.	Retrd.	82.00	82.00
Old World Christmas		**Candleholders**			
89-05-001	Rocking Horse 9011	E.M. Merck	Open	7.50	7.50
89-05-002	Santa 9012	E.M. Merck	Retrd.	7.55	7.55
89-05-003	Hummingbird 9013	E.M. Merck	Open	7.50	7.50
89-05-004	Teddy Bear 9014	E.M. Merck	Open	7.50	7.50
89-05-005	Angel 9015	E.M. Merck	Open	7.50	7.50
89-05-006	Nutcracker 9016	E.M. Merck	Open	7.50	7.50
Old World Christmas		**Halloween**			
87-06-001	Pumpkin Light with Ghosts 9201	E.M. Merck	Open	39.50	39.50
87-06-002	Pumpkin Light with Scarecrow 9202	E.M. Merck	Retrd.	37.00	37.00
87-06-003	Haunted House with Lights 9203	E.M. Merck.	Open	99.50	99.50
87-06-004	Lighted Ghost Dish 9204	E.M. Merck	Open	45.00	45.00
87-06-005	Ghost Light 9205	E.M. Merck	Retrd.	37.00	37.00
88-06-006	Haunted House Waterglobe 9206	E.M. Merck	Retrd.	22.50	22.50
88-06-007	Pumpkin Head on Wire 9207	E.M. Merck	Retrd.	7.35	7.35
88-06-008	Black Cat on Wire 9208	E.M. Merck	Retrd.	8.35	8.35
89-06-009	Ghost Votive 9211	E.M. Merck	Open	8.50	8.50
89-06-010	Witch on Moon Night Light 9212	E.M. Merck	Open	37.50	37.50
89-06-011	Cast Iron Scarecrow 9218	E.M. Merck	Open	32.50	32.50
89-06-012	Black Cat/Witch with Cart (A) 9251	E.M. Merck	Open	10.00	10.00
88-06-013	Pumpkin Votive 9271	E.M. Merck	Retrd.	8.90	8.90
88-06-014	Pumpkin Taper Holder 9272	E.M. Merck	Retrd.	5.65	5.65
88-06-015	Large Pumpkin Bowl 9273	E.M. Merck	Open	18.50	18.50
88-06-016	Witch Votive Holder 9281	E.M. Merck	Open	29.50	29.50
88-06-017	Witch Taper Holder 9282	E.M. Merck	Retrd.	11.00	11.00
Old World Christmas		**Porcelain Christmas**			
87-07-001	Santa Head Votive 9411	E.M. Merck	Retrd.	10.00	10.00
87-07-002	Santa Head Night Light 9412	E.M. Merck	Retrd.	19.00	19.00
87-07-003	Santa in Chimney Music Box 9413	E.M. Merck.	Retrd.	44.00	44.00
87-07-004	Santa Head Stocking Holder 9414	E.M. Merck	Retrd.	18.00	18.00
87-07-005	Cast Iron Santa on Horse 9418	E.M. Merck	Retrd.	37.50	37.50
87-07-006	Cast Iron Santa 9419	E.M. Merck	Retrd.	35.00	35.00
87-07-007	Angels, set of 3 9421	E.M. Merck	Retrd.	15.45	15.45
87-07-008	Roly-Poly Santa 9440	E.M. Merck	Retrd.	27.00	27.00
87-07-009	Four Castles of Germany 9450	E.M. Merck	Retrd.	31.00	31.00
88-07-010	Santa on Polar Bear 9471	E.M. Merck	Retrd.	6.25	6.25
88-07-011	Santa Visiting Lighthouse 9472	E.M. Merck	Retrd.	6.25	6.25
88-07-012	Santa in Swing 9473	E.M. Merck	Retrd.	6.25	6.25
88-07-013	Santa with Angel 9474	E.M. Merck	Retrd.	6.25	6.25
88-07-014	Santa on Teeter-Totter 9475	E.M. Merck	Retrd.	6.25	6.25
88-07-015	Santa Visiting Igloo 9476	E.M. Merck	Retrd.	6.25	6.25
88-07-016	Bunny on Skies Music Box 9491	E.M. Merck	Retrd.	44.00	44.00
88-07-017	Bear on Skates Music Box 9492	E.M. Merck	Retrd.	44.00	44.00
88-07-018	Penguin with Gifts Music Box 9493	E.M. Merck	Retrd.	44.00	44.00
Old World Christmas		**Paper Mache**			
88-08-001	Father Christmas (A) 9600	E.M. Merck	Retrd.	19.50	19.50
88-08-002	Red Father Christmas 9601	E.M. Merck	Retrd.	19.50	19.50
88-08-003	Blue Father Christmas 9602	E.M. Merck	Retrd.	19.50	19.50
88-08-004	White Father Christmas 9603	E.M. Merck	Retrd.	19.50	19.50
88-08-005	Father Christmas with Gifts 9610	E.M. Merck	Retrd.	32.50	32.50
89-08-006	Father Christmas 9612	E.M. Merck	Retrd.	38.50	38.50
88-08-007	Assorted Father Christmas 9615	E.M. Merck	Retrd.	44.00	44.00
88-08-008	White Father Christmas 9616	E.M. Merck	Retrd.	50.00	50.00
89-08-009	Father Christmas with Pack 9638	E.M. Merck	Retrd.	40.00	40.00
88-08-010	52 cm. Father Christmas 9652	E.M. Merck	Retrd.	175.00	175.00
88-08-011	Traditional Belznickel 9661	E.M. Merck	Open	40.00	40.00
88-08-012	Small Traditional Belznickel 9662	E.M. Merck	Open	35.00	35.00
89-08-013	Santa in Sleigh 9672	E.M. Merck	Retrd.	39.50	39.50
89-08-014	Assorted Santas 9691	E.M. Merck	Retrd.	35.00	35.00
Pemberton & Oakes		**Zolan's Children**			
82-01-001	Erik and the Dandelion	D. Zolan	17,000	48.00	90.00
83-01-002	Sabina in the Grass	D. Zolan	6,800	48.00	130.00
84-01-003	Winter Angel	D. Zolan	8,000	28.00	150.00
85-01-004	Tender Moment	D. Zolan	10,000	29.00	75.00
PenDelfin		**Nursery Rhymes**			
85-01-001	Apple Barrel	J. Heap	Retrd.	N/A	N/A
63-01-002	Aunt Agatha	J. Heap	Retrd.	N/A	N/A

Number	Name	Artist	Edition Limit	Issue Price	Quote
55-01-003	Balloon Woman	J. Heap	Retrd.	1.00	N/A
55-01-004	Bell Man	J. Heap	Retrd.	1.00	N/A
84-01-005	Blossom	D. Roberts	Retrd.	16.50	35.00
56-01-006	Bobbin Woman	J. Heap	Retrd.	N/A	N/A
64-01-007	Bongo	D. Roberts	Retrd.	31.00	N/A
66-01-008	Cakestand	J. Heap	Retrd.	2.00	200.00
53-01-009	Cauldron Witch	J. Heap	Retrd.	3.50	N/A
59-01-010	Cha Cha	J. Heap	Retrd.	N/A	N/A
62-01-011	Cornish Prayer (Corny)	J. Heap	Retrd.	N/A	N/A
80-01-012	Crocker	D. Roberts	Retrd.	20.00	42.00
63-01-013	Cyril Squirrel	J. Heap	Retrd.	N/A	N/A
56-01-014	Desmond Duck	J. Heap	Retrd.	2.50	N/A
55-01-015	Elf	J. Heap	Retrd.	1.00	N/A
61-01-016	Father Mouse	J. Heap	Retrd.	N/A	N/A
55-01-017	Flying Witch	J. Heap	Retrd.	1.00	N/A
60-01-018	Gussie	J. Heap	Retrd.	N/A	N/A
56-01-019	Little Bo Peep	J. Heap	Retrd.	2.00	N/A
56-01-020	Little Jack Horner	J. Heap	Retrd.	2.00	N/A
61-01-021	Lollipop (Mouse)	J. Heap	Retrd.	N/A	N/A
60-01-022	Lucy Pocket	J. Heap	Retrd.	4.20	350.00
56-01-023	Manx Kitten	J. Heap	Retrd.	2.00	N/A
55-01-024	Margot	J. Heap	Retrd.	2.00	N/A
56-01-025	Mary Mary Quite Contrary	J. Heap	Retrd.	2.00	N/A
67-01-026	Maud	J. Heap	Retrd.	N/A	300.00
61-01-027	Megan	J. Heap	Retrd.	3.00	N/A
56-01-028	Midge (Replaced by Picnic Midge)	J. Heap	Retrd.	2.00	N/A
66-01-029	Milk Jug Stand	J. Heap	Retrd.	2.00	N/A
56-01-030	Miss Muffet	J. Heap	Retrd.	2.00	N/A
60-01-031	Model Stand	J. Heap	Retrd.	4.00	N/A
61-01-032	Mother Mouse	J. Heap	Retrd.	N/A	N/A
65-01-033	Mouse House	J. Heap	Retrd.	N/A	N/A
65-01-034	Muncher	D. Roberts	Retrd.	26.00	N/A
81-01-035	Nipper	D. Roberts	Retrd.	20.50	35.00
55-01-036	Old Adam	J. Heap	Retrd.	4.00	N/A
55-01-037	Old Father	J. Heap	Retrd.	6.25	900.00
57-01-038	Old Mother	J. Heap	Retrd.	6.25	N/A
56-01-039	Original Robert	J. Heap	Retrd.	2.50	N/A
53-01-040	Pendle Witch	J. Heap	Retrd.	4.00	N/A
67-01-041	Phumf	J. Heap	Retrd.	24.00	N/A
55-01-042	Phynnodderee (Commissioned-Exclusive)	J. Heap	Retrd.	1.00	N/A
66-01-043	Picnic Basket	J. Heap	Retrd.	2.00	N/A
65-01-044	Picnic Stand	J. Heap	Retrd.	62.50	N/A
67-01-045	Picnic Table	J. Heap	Retrd.	N/A	N/A
66-01-046	Pieface	D. Roberts	Retrd.	31.00	95.00
65-01-047	Pixie Bods	J. Heap	Retrd.	N/A	N/A
53-01-048	Pixie House	J. Heap	Retrd.	N/A	N/A
62-01-049	Pooch	D. Roberts	Retrd.	24.50	N/A
58-01-050	Rabbit Book Ends	J. Heap	Retrd.	10.00	N/A
54-01-051	Rhinegold Lamp	J. Heap	Retrd.	21.00	N/A
67-01-052	Robert	D. Roberts	Retrd.	12.00	100.00
57-01-053	Romeo & Juliet	J. Heap	Retrd.	11.00	N/A
60-01-054	Shiner	J. Heap	Retrd.	2.50	N/A
60-01-055	Squeezy	J. Heap	Retrd.	2.50	N/A
57-01-056	Tammy	D. Roberts	Retrd.	24.50	N/A
67-01-057	The Bath Tub	J. Heap	Retrd.	4.50	N/A
69-01-058	The Gallery Series: Wakey, Pieface, Poppet, Robert, Dodger	J. Heap	Retrd.	N/A	N/A
56-01-059	Timber Stand	J. Heap	Retrd.	35.00	N/A
53-01-060	Tipsy Witch	J. Heap	Retrd.	3.50	N/A
56-01-061	Tom Tom the Piper's Son	J. Heap	Retrd.	2.00	N/A
55-01-062	Toper	J. Heap	Retrd.	1.00	N/A
71-01-063	Totty	J. Heap	Retrd.	21.00	N/A
59-01-064	Uncle Soames	J. Heap	Retrd.	105.00	300.00
56-01-065	Wee Willie Winkie	J. Heap	Retrd.	2.00	N/A
PenDelfin		**Bed Series**			
XX-02-001	Dodger	J. Heap	Open	24.00	24.00
XX-02-002	Peeps	J. Heap	Open	21.00	21.00
XX-02-003	Poppet	D. Roberts	Open	23.00	23.00
XX-02-004	Snuggles	J. Heap	Open	20.00	20.00
XX-02-005	Twins	J. Heap	Open	25.00	25.00
XX-02-006	Wakey	J. Heap	Open	24.00	24.00
XX-02-007	Victoria	J. Heap	Open	47.50	47.50
XX-02-008	Parsley	D. Roberts	Open	25.00	25.00
XX-02-009	Chirpy	D. Roberts	Retrd.	31.50	60.00
XX-02-010	Snuggles Awake	J. Heap	Open	60.00	60.00
92-02-011	Sunny	D. Roberts	Open	40.00	40.00
93-02-012	Forty Winks	D. Roberts	Open	57.00	57.00
PenDelfin		**Band Series**			
XX-03-001	Rocky	J. Heap	Open	32.00	32.00
XX-03-002	Rolly	J. Heap	Open	17.50	17.50
XX-03-003	Thumper	J. Heap	Open	25.00	25.00
XX-03-004	Piano	D. Roberts	Open	25.00	25.00
XX-03-005	Casanova	J. Heap	Open	35.00	35.00
XX-03-006	Clanger	J. Heap	Open	35.00	35.00
XX-03-007	Rosa	J. Heap	Open	40.00	40.00
XX-03-008	Solo	D. Roberts	Retrd.	40.00	40.00
XX-03-009	Jingles	D. Roberts	Retrd.	11.25	22.50
XX-03-010	Bandstand	J. Heap	Open	70.00	70.00
94-03-011	Mike	D. Roberts	Open	55.00	55.00
PenDelfin		**Picnic Series**			
XX-04-001	Picnic Midge	J. Heap	Open	25.00	25.00
XX-04-002	Barrow Boy	J. Heap	Open	35.00	35.00
XX-04-003	Oliver	D. Roberts	Open	25.00	25.00
XX-04-004	Apple Barrel	D. Roberts	Retrd.	7.50	15.00
XX-04-005	Scrumpy	J. Heap	Open	35.00	35.00
XX-04-006	Picnic Island	J. Heap	Open	85.00	85.00
93-04-007	Vanilla	D. Roberts	Open	41.00	41.00
94-04-008	Pipkin	J. Heap	Open	50.00	50.00
PenDelfin		**Toy Shop Series**			
XX-05-001	Jacky	D. Roberts	Open	45.00	45.00
XX-05-002	The Toy Shop	D. Roberts	Open	325.00	325.00
PenDelfin		**Fisherman Series**			
XX-06-001	Whopper	D. Roberts	Open	35.00	35.00
XX-06-002	Jim-Lad	D. Roberts	Retrd.	22.50	45.00
XX-06-003	Little Mo	D. Roberts	Open	35.00	35.00
XX-06-004	The Raft	J. Heap	Open	70.00	70.00
XX-06-005	Shrimp Stand	D. Roberts	Open	70.00	70.00
XX-06-006	The Jetty	J. Heap	Open	180.00	180.00

Number	Name	Artist	Edition Limit	Issue Price	Quote
PenDelfin		**Sport Series**			
XX-07-001	Birdie	J. Heap	Open	47.50	47.50
XX-07-002	Tennyson	D. Roberts	Open	35.00	35.00
XX-07-003	Humphrey Go-Kart	J. Heap	Open	70.00	70.00
XX-07-004	Rambler	D. Roberts	Open	65.00	65.00
XX-07-005	Scout	D. Roberts	Open	N/A	N/A
93-07-006	Campfire	D. Roberts	Open	30.00	30.00
PenDelfin		**School Series**			
XX-08-001	Boswell	J. Heap	Open	37.50	37.50
XX-08-002	Euclid	J. Heap	Open	35.00	35.00
XX-08-003	Digit	D. Roberts	Open	35.00	35.00
XX-08-004	Duffy	J. Heap	Open	50.00	50.00
XX-08-005	Old School House	J. Heap	Open	250.00	250.00
XX-08-006	Angelo	J. Heap	Open	90.00	90.00
XX-08-007	New Boy	D. Roberts	Open	50.00	50.00
XX-08-008	Wordsworth	D. Roberts	Retrd.	60.00	60.00
PenDelfin		**Various**			
XX-09-001	Dandy	D. Roberts	Open	50.00	50.00
XX-09-002	Barney	J. Heap	Open	18.00	18.00
XX-09-003	Honey	D. Roberts	Retrd.	40.00	40.00
XX-09-004	Charlotte	D. Roberts	Retrd.	25.00	50.00
XX-09-005	Butterfingers	D. Roberts	Open	55.00	55.00
XX-09-006	Scoffer	D. Roberts	Open	55.00	55.00
XX-09-007	Mother with baby	J. Heap	Open	150.00	150.00
55-09-008	Original Father	J. Heap	Retrd.	150.00	150.00
93-09-009	Cousin Beau	D. Roberts	Open	55.00	55.00
85-09-010	Christmas Set	D. Roberts	Retrd.	N/A	N/A
55-09-011	Daisy Duck	J. Leap	Retrd.	N/A	N/A
54-09-012	Fairy Jardiniere	N/A	Retrd.	N/A	N/A
PenDelfin		**Village Series**			
XX-10-001	Fruit Shop	J. Heap	Open	125.00	125.00
XX-10-002	Castle Tavern	D. Roberts	Open	120.00	120.00
XX-10-003	Caravan	D. Roberts	Open	350.00	350.00
XX-10-004	Large House	J. Heap	Open	275.00	275.00
XX-10-005	Cobble Cottage	D. Roberts	Open	80.00	80.00
XX-10-006	Curiosity Shop	J. Heap	Open	350.00	350.00
XX-10-007	Balcony Scene	D. Roberts	Open	175.00	175.00
XX-10-008	Grand Stand	J. Heap	Retrd.	150.00	150.00
53-10-009	The Fairy Shop	J. Heap	Retrd.	N/A	N/A
PenDelfin		**PenDelfin Family Circle Collectors' Club**			
93-11-001	Herald	J. Heap	Closed	30.00	30.00
94-11-002	Buttons	J. Heap	Yr. Iss.	Gift	N/A
94-11-003	Puffer	J. Heap	Yr. Iss.	85.00	85.00
Polland Studios		**Collectible Bronzes**			
67-01-001	Bull Session	D. Polland	11	200.00	1200.00
69-01-002	Blowin' Cold	D. Polland	30	375.00	1250.00
69-01-003	The Breed	D. Polland	30	350.00	975.00
68-01-004	Buffalo Hunt	D. Polland	30	450.00	1250.00
69-01-005	Comanchero	D. Polland	30	350.00	750.00
69-01-006	Dancing Indian with Lance	D. Polland	50	250.00	775.00
69-01-007	Dancing Indian with Tomahawk	D. Polland	50	250.00	775.00
69-01-008	Dancing Medicine Man	D. Polland	50	250.00	775.00
69-01-009	Drawn Sabers	D. Polland	50	2000.00	5650.00
69-01-010	Lookouts	D. Polland	30	375.00	1300.00
69-01-011	Top Money	D. Polland	30	275.00	800.00
69-01-012	Trail Hazzard	D. Polland	30	700.00	1750.00
69-01-013	War Cry	D. Polland	30	350.00	975.00
69-01-014	When Enemies Meet	D. Polland	30	700.00	2350.00
70-01-015	Coffee Time	D. Polland	50	1200.00	2900.00
70-01-016	The Lost Dispatch	D. Polland	50	1200.00	2950.00
70-01-017	Wanted	D. Polland	50	400.00	1150.00
70-01-018	Dusted	D. Polland	50	400.00	1175.00
71-01-019	Ambush at Rock Canyon	D. Polland	5	20000.00	45000.00
71-01-020	Oh Sugar!	D. Polland	40	700.00	1525.00
71-01-021	Shakin' Out a Loop	D. Polland	40	500.00	1075.00
72-01-022	Buffalo Robe	D. Polland	50	1000.00	2350.00
73-01-023	Bunch Quitter	D. Polland	60	750.00	1975.00
73-01-024	Challenge	D. Polland	60	750.00	1800.00
73-01-025	War Party	D. Polland	60	1500.00	5500.00
73-01-026	Tracking	D. Polland	60	500.00	1150.00
75-01-027	Cheyenne	D. Polland	6	1300.00	1800.00
75-01-028	Counting Coup	D. Polland	6	1450.00	1950.00
75-01-029	Crow Scout	D. Polland	6	1300.00	1800.00
75-01-030	Buffalo Hunt	D. Polland	6	2200.00	3500.00
76-01-031	Rescue	D. Polland	6	2400.00	3000.00
76-01-032	Painting the Town	D. Polland	6	3000.00	4200.00
76-01-033	Monday Morning Wash	D. Polland	6	2800.00	2800.00
76-01-034	Mandan Hunter	D. Polland	12	775.00	775.00
80-01-035	Buffalo Prayer	D. Polland	25	375.00	675.00
Polland Studios		**Collector Society**			
87-02-001	I Come In Peace	D. Polland	Closed	35.00	400-600.
87-02-002	Silent Trail	D. Polland	Closed	300.00	1300.00
87-02-003	I Come In Peace, Silent Trail-Matched Numbered Set	D. Polland	Closed	335.00	1500-1895.
88-02-004	The Hunter	D. Polland	Closed	35.00	545.00
88-02-005	Disputed Trail	D. Polland	Closed	300.00	700-1045.
88-02-006	The Hunter, Disputed Trail-Matched Numbered Set	D. Polland	Closed	335.00	1100-1450.
89-02-007	Crazy Horse	D. Polland	Closed	35.00	300-470.
89-02-008	Apache Birdman	D. Polland	Closed	300.00	700-970.
89-02-009	Crazy Horse, Apache Birdman-Matched Numbered Set	D. Polland	Closed	335.00	1300-1700.
90-02-010	Chief Pontiac	D. Polland	Closed	35.00	420.00
90-02-011	Buffalo Pony	D. Polland	Closed	300.00	600-800.
90-02-012	Chief Pontiac, Buffalo Pony-Matched Numbered Set	D. Polland	Closed	335.00	900-1350.
91-02-013	War Drummer	D. Polland	Closed	35.00	330.00
91-02-014	The Signal	D. Polland	Closed	350.00	730.00
91-02-015	War Drummer, The Signal-Matched Numbered Set	D. Polland	Closed	385.00	900-1150.
92-02-016	Cabinet Sign	D. Polland	Closed	35.00	125.00
92-02-017	Warrior's Farewell	D. Polland	Closed	350.00	400.00
92-02-018	Cabinet Sign, Warrior's Farewell-Matched Numbered Set	D. Polland	Closed	385.00	465.00
93-02-019	Mountain Man	D. Polland	Closed	35.00	125.00
93-02-020	Blue Bonnets & Yellow Ribbon	D. Polland	Closed	350.00	350-400.
93-02-021	Mountain Man, Blue Bonnets & Yellow Ribbon-Matched Numbered Set	D. Polland	Closed	385.00	385.00

Company		Series			
Number	**Name**	**Artist**	**Edition Limit**	**Issue Price**	**Quote**
94-02-022	The Wedding Robe	D. Polland	Yr.Iss.	45.00	45.00
94-02-023	The Courtship Race	D. Polland	Yr.Iss.	375.00	375.00
94-02-024	The Wedding Robe, The Courtside Race-Matched Numbered Set	D. Polland	Yr.Iss.	385.00	420.00
Possible Dreams®	**Clothtique® The Saturday Evening Post Norman Rockwell Collection**				
89-01-001	Dear Santa-3050	N. Rockwell	Closed	160.00	180.00
89-01-002	Santa with Globe-3051	N. Rockwell	Closed	154.00	175.00
90-01-003	Hobo-3052	N. Rockwell	Open	159.00	167.00
90-01-004	Love Letters-3053	N. Rockwell	Open	172.00	180.00
91-01-005	Gone Fishing-3054	N. Rockwell	Open	250.00	263.00
91-01-006	Doctor and Doll-3055	N. Rockwell	Open	196.00	206.00
91-01-007	Springtime-3056	N. Rockwell	Open	130.00	137.00
91-01-008	The Gift-3057	N. Rockwell	Open	160.00	168.00
91-01-009	Gramps at the Reins-3058	N. Rockwell	Open	290.00	305.00
91-01-010	Man with Geese-3059	N. Rockwell	Open	120.00	126.00
91-01-011	Plotting His Course-3060	N. Rockwell	Open	160.00	168.00
92-01-012	Triple Self Portrait-3061	N. Rockwell	Open	230.00	242.00
92-01-013	Marriage License-3062	N. Rockwell	Open	195.00	205.00
92-01-014	Santa's Helpers-3063	N. Rockwell	Open	170.00	179.00
92-01-015	Balancing the Budget-3064	N. Rockwell	Open	120.00	126.00
Possible Dreams®	**Clothtique® The Saturday Evening Post J.C. Leyendecker Collection**				
90-02-001	Traditional Santa-3600	J. Leyendecker	Closed	100.00	175.00
91-02-002	Hugging Santa-3599	J. Leyendecker	Closed	129.00	150.00
92-02-003	Santa on Ladder-3598	J. Leyendecker	Open	135.00	142.00
Possible Dreams®	**Clothtique® The American Artist Collection**				
91-03-001	Magic of Christmas-15001	L. Bywaters	Closed	132.00	139.00
91-03-002	A Peaceful Eve-15002	L. Bywaters	Closed	99.50	105.00
91-03-003	Alpine Christmas-15003	J. Brett	Closed	129.00	135.00
91-03-004	Traditions-15004	T. Blackshear	Closed	50.00	53.00
91-03-005	A Friendly Visit-15005	T. Browning	Closed	99.50	105.00
91-03-006	Santa's Cuisine-15006	T. Browning	Closed	137.50	145.50
91-03-007	Father Christmas-15007	J. Vaillancourt	Closed	59.50	63.00
92-03-008	An Angel's Kiss-15008	J. Griffith	Open	85.00	89.00
92-03-009	Peace on Earth-15009	M. Alvin	Open	87.50	92.00
92-03-010	Lighting the Way-15012	L. Bywaters	Open	85.00	89.00
92-03-011	Out of the Forrest-15013	J. Vaillancourt	Open	60.00	63.00
92-03-012	Heralding the Way-15014	J. Griffith	Open	72.00	75.00
92-03-013	Music Makers-15010	T. Browning	Open	135.00	142.00
92-03-014	Santa in Rocking Chair-713090	M. Monteiro	Open	85.00	89.00
92-03-015	Christmas Company-15011	T. Browning	Open	77.00	77.00
93-03-016	Strumming the Lute-15015	M. Alvin	Open	79.00	83.00
93-03-017	Nature's Love-15016	M. Alvin	Open	75.00	79.00
93-03-018	Father Earth-15017	M. Monteiro	Open	77.00	80.00
93-03-019	Easy Putt-15018	T. Browning	Open	110.00	115.00
93-03-020	The Workshop-15019	T. Browning	Open	140.00	147.00
93-03-021	The Tree Planter-15020	J. Griffith	Open	79.50	84.00
93-03-022	A Beacon of Light-15022	J. Vaillancourt	Open	60.00	63.00
93-03-023	Just Scooting Along-15023	J. Vaillancourt	Open	79.50	83.00
93-03-024	A Brighter Day-15024	J. St. Denis	Open	67.50	70.00
93-03-025	Ice Capers-15025	T. Browning	Open	99.50	105.00
94-03-026	And Feathered Friend-15026	D. Wenzel	Open	84.00	84.00
94-03-027	A Touch of Magic-15027	T. Browning	Open	95.00	95.00
94-03-028	Spirit of Santa-15028	T. Browning	Open	68.00	68.00
94-03-029	Captain Claus-15030	M. Monteiro	Open	77.00	77.00
94-03-030	The Gentle Craftsman-15031	J. Griffith	Open	81.00	81.00
94-03-031	Gifts from the Garden-15032	J. Griffith	Open	77.00	77.00
94-03-032	Chrstmas Surprise-15033	M. Alvin	Open	88.00	88.00
94-03-033	Tea Time-15034	M. Alvin	Open	90.00	90.00
94-03-034	Spirit of Christmas Past-15036	J. Vaillancourt	Open	79.00	79.00
94-03-035	Teddy Love-15037	J. Griffith	Open	89.00	89.00
Possible Dreams®	**Clothtique® Limited Edition Santas**				
88-04-001	Patriotic Santa-3000	Unknown	Closed	240.00	240.00
88-04-002	Father Christmas-3001	Unknown	Closed	240.00	240.00
88-04-003	Kris Kringle-3002	Unknown	Closed	240.00	240.00
89-04-004	Traditional Santa 40's-3003	Unknown	Closed	240.00	252.00
Possible Dreams®	**Clothtique® Pepsi® Santa Collection**				
90-05-001	Pepsi Cola Santa 1940's-3601	Unknown	Open	68.00	74.00
91-05-002	Rockwell Pepsi Santa 1952-3602	N. Rockwell	Closed	75.00	82.00
92-05-003	Pepsi Santa Sitting-3603	Unknown	Closed	84.00	88.00
94-05-004	Pepsi Holiday Host-3605	Unknown	Open	62.00	62.00
Possible Dreams®	**Clothtique® Santas Collection**				
87-06-001	Traditional Santa-713028	Unknown	Closed	34.50	34.50
87-06-002	Ukko-713031	Unknown	Closed	38.00	38.00
87-06-003	Colonial Santa-713032	Unknown	Closed	38.00	39.50
87-06-004	Christmas Man-713027	Unknown	Closed	34.50	34.50
87-06-005	Santa with Pack-713026	Unknown	Closed	34.50	34.50
87-06-006	Traditional Deluxe Santa-713030	Unknown	Closed	38.00	38.00
88-06-007	Frontier Santa-713034	Unknown	Closed	40.00	42.00
88-06-008	St. Nicholas-713035	Unknown	Closed	40.00	42.00
88-06-009	Weihnachtsman-713037	Unknown	Closed	40.00	43.00
88-06-010	Carpenter Santa-713033	Unknown	Closed	38.00	44.00
88-06-011	Russian St. Nicholas-713036	Unknown	Closed	40.00	43.00
89-06-012	Traditional Santa-713038	Unknown	Closed	42.00	43.00
89-06-013	Pelze Nichol-713039	Unknown	Closed	40.00	47.00
89-06-014	Mrs. Claus w/doll-713041	Unknown	Closed	42.00	43.00
89-06-015	Baby's First Christmas-713042	Unknown	Closed	42.00	46.00
89-06-016	Exhausted Santa-713043	Unknown	Closed	60.00	65.00
89-06-017	Santa with Embroidered Coat-713040	Unknown	Closed	43.00	43.00
90-06-018	Workbench Santa-713044	Unknown	Closed	72.00	75.50
90-06-019	Santa "Please Stop Here"-713045	Unknown	Closed	63.00	66.00
90-06-020	Harlem Santa-713046	Unknown	Closed	46.00	55.00
90-06-021	Santa Skiing-713047	Unknown	Closed	62.00	65.00
90-06-022	Santa With Blue Robe-713048	Unknown	Closed	46.00	50.00
91-06-023	The True Spirit of Christmas-713075	Unknown	Closed	97.00	97.00
91-06-024	Santa in Bed-713076	Unknown	Closed	76.00	83.00
91-06-025	Siberian Santa-713077	Unknown	Closed	49.00	51.50
91-06-026	Mrs. Claus in Coat -713078	Unknown	Open	47.00	52.00
91-06-027	Decorating the Tree-713079	Unknown	Closed	60.00	60.00
91-06-028	Father Christmas-713087	Unknown	Open	43.00	47.00
91-06-029	Kris Kringle-713088	Unknown	Closed	43.00	45.20
91-06-030	Santa Shelf Sitter-713089	Unknown	Open	55.50	60.00
92-06-031	1940's Traditional Santa-713049	Unknown	Closed	44.00	46.00
92-06-032	Santa on Sled-713050	Unknown	Closed	75.00	79.00
92-06-033	Nicholas-713052	Unknown	Open	57.50	60.00
92-06-034	Fireman Santa-713053	Unknown	Open	60.00	63.00
92-06-035	African American Santa-713056	Unknown	Open	65.00	68.00
92-06-036	Engineer Santa-713057	Unknown	Open	130.00	137.00
92-06-037	Santa on Reindeer-713058	Unknown	Open	75.00	83.00

Company		Series			
Number	**Name**	**Artist**	**Edition Limit**	**Issue Price**	**Quote**
92-06-038	Santa on Sleigh-713091	Unknown	Open	79.00	83.00
92-06-039	Santa on Motorbike-713054	Unknown	Closed	115.00	120.00
93-06-040	European Santa-713095	Unknown	Open	53.00	55.00
93-06-041	May Your Wishes Come True-713096	Unknown	Open	59.00	62.00
93-06-042	Victorian Santa-713097	Unknown	Open	55.50	58.00
93-06-043	His Favorite Color-713098	Unknown	Open	48.00	50.00
93-06-044	Santa w/Groceries-713099	Unknown	Open	47.50	50.00
93-06-045	Afro Santa & Doll-713102	Unknown	Open	40.00	42.00
93-06-046	The Modern Shopper-713103	Unknown	Open	40.00	42.00
93-06-047	Nigel as Santa-713427	Unknown	Open	53.50	56.00
93-06-048	A Long Trip-713105	A. Gilberts	Open	95.00	100.00
93-06-049	Fireman & Child-713106	Unknown	Open	55.00	58.00
94-06-050	Good Tidings-713107	Unknown	Open	51.00	51.00
94-06-051	Yuletide Journey-713108	Unknown	Open	58.00	58.00
94-06-052	Christmas Cheer-713109	Unknown	Open	58.00	58.00
94-06-053	Holiday Friend-713110	Unknown	Open	104.00	104.00
94-06-054	Playmates-713111	Unknown	Open	104.00	104.00
94-06-055	A Christmas Guest-713112	Unknown	Open	79.00	79.00
94-06-056	Welcome Visitor-713113	Unknown	Open	63.00	63.00
94-06-057	A Welcome Visit-713114	Unknown	Open	62.00	62.00
94-06-058	Christmas is for Children-713115	Unknown	Open	62.00	62.00
94-06-059	Our Hero-713116	Unknown	Open	62.00	62.00
94-06-060	Puppy Love-713117	Unknown	Open	62.00	62.00
94-06-061	Mrs. Claus-713118	Unknown	Open	58.00	58.00
Possible Dreams®	**The Citizens of Londonshire®**				
92-07-001	Beth-713417	Unknown	Open	35.00	37.00
92-07-002	Albert-713426	Unknown	Open	65.00	68.00
89-07-003	Lady Ashley-713405	Unknown	Open	65.00	68.00
89-07-004	Lord Winston of Riverside-713403	Unknown	Open	65.00	68.00
89-07-005	Sir Robert-713401	Unknown	Open	65.00	68.00
89-07-006	Rodney-713404	Unknown	Open	65.00	68.00
90-07-007	Dr. Isaac-713409	Unknown	Closed	65.00	68.00
90-07-008	Admiral Waldo-713407	Unknown	Open	65.00	68.00
91-07-009	Sir Red-713415	Unknown	Open	72.00	76.00
91-07-010	Bernie-713414	Unknown	Open	68.00	71.00
92-07-011	Tiffany Sorbet-713416	Unknown	Open	65.00	68.00
90-07-012	Margaret of Foxcroft-713408	Unknown	Open	65.00	68.00
90-07-013	Officer Kevin-713406	Unknown	Open	65.00	68.00
89-07-014	Lord Nicholas-713402	Unknown	Open	72.00	76.00
92-07-015	Countess of Hamlett-713419	Unknown	Open	65.00	68.00
89-07-016	Earl of Hamlett-713400	Unknown	Closed	65.00	68.00
92-07-017	Rebecca-713424	Unknown	Open	35.00	37.00
90-07-018	Dianne-713413	Unknown	Open	33.00	35.00
90-07-019	Phillip-713412	Unknown	Open	33.00	35.00
90-07-020	Walter-713410	Unknown	Open	33.00	35.00
90-07-021	Wendy-713411	Unknown	Open	33.00	35.00
92-07-022	Jean Claude-713421	Unknown	Open	35.00	37.00
92-07-023	Nicole-713420	Unknown	Open	35.00	37.00
92-07-024	David-713423	Unknown	Open	37.50	39.00
92-07-025	Debbie-713422	Unknown	Open	37.50	39.00
92-07-026	Christopher-713418	Unknown	Open	35.00	37.00
92-07-027	Richard-713425	Unknown	Open	35.00	37.00
93-07-028	Nigel As Santa-713427	Unknown	Open	53.50	56.00
94-07-029	Maggie-713428	Unknown	Open	60.00	60.00
Possible Dreams®	**Santa Claus Network Collectors Club**				
92-08-001	The Gift Giver	Unknown	Closed	Gift	40.00
93-08-002	Santa's Special Friend	Unknown	Closed	59.00	59.00
93-08-003	Special Delivery	Unknown	7/94	Gift	N/A
94-08-004	On a Winter's Eve	Unknown	Yr. Iss.	65.00	65.00
Possible Dreams®	**The Thickets at Sweetbriar**				
93-09-001	Maude Tweedy-350100	B. Ross	Open	26.25	26.25
93-09-002	Clovis Buttons-350101	B. Ross	Open	24.15	24.15
93-09-003	Peablossom Thorndike-350102	B. Ross	Open	26.25	26.25
93-09-004	Orchid Beasley-350103	B. Ross	Open	26.25	26.25
93-09-005	Morning Glory-350104	B. Ross	Open	30.45	30.45
93-09-006	Lily Blossom-350105	B. Ross	Open	36.75	36.75
93-09-007	Jewel Blossom-350106	B. Ross	Open	36.75	36.75
93-09-008	Rose Blossom-350107	B. Ross	Open	36.75	36.75
93-09-009	Raindrop-350108	B. Ross	Open	47.25	47.25
93-09-010	Mr. Claws-350109	B. Ross	Open	34.00	34.00
93-09-011	Mrs. Claws-350110	B. Ross	Open	34.00	34.00
93-09-012	The Groom-Oliver Doone-350111	B. Ross	Open	30.00	30.00
93-09-013	The Bride-Emily Feathers-350112	B. Ross	Open	30.00	30.00
94-09-014	Morning Dew-350113	B. Ross	Open	30.00	30.00
94-09-015	Sweetie Flowers-350114	B. Ross	Open	33.00	33.00
94-09-016	Precious Petals-350115	B. Ross	Open	34.00	34.00
94-09-017	Lady Slipper-350116	B. Ross	Open	20.00	20.00
94-09-018	Sunshine-350118	B. Ross	Open	33.00	33.00
Precious Art/Panton	**World of Krystonia**				
87-01-001	Small Graffyn/Grunch -1012	Panton	Retrd.	45.00	240-350.
87-01-002	Owhey -1071	Panton	Retrd.	32.00	85-175.
87-01-003	Small N'Borg -1091	Panton	Retrd.	50.00	375.00
87-01-004	Large Rueggan -1701	Panton	Retrd.	55.00	400.00
87-01-005	Medium Stoope -1101	Panton	Retrd.	52.00	250.00
87-01-006	Small Shepf -1152	Panton	Retrd.	40.00	200.00
87-01-007	Large Wodema -1301	Panton	Retrd.	50.00	350.00
87-01-008	Large Krak N'Borg -3001	Panton	Retrd.	240.00	735.00
87-01-009	Large Moplos -1021	Panton	Retrd.	90.00	204-400.
87-01-010	Large Myzer -1201	Panton	Retrd.	50.00	66-250.00
87-01-011	Large Turfen -1601	Panton	Retrd.	50.00	96-250.00
87-01-012	Large Haapf -1901	Panton	Retrd.	38.00	200.00
87-01-013	Small Groc -1042B	Panton	Retrd.	24.00	4600.00
87-01-014	Large Graffyn on Grumblypeg Grunch -1011	Panton	Retrd.	52.00	165.00
87-01-015	Grumblypeg Grunch -1081	Panton	Retrd.	52.00	200.00
87-01-016	Spyke -1061	Panton	Retrd.	50.00	72.00
87-01-017	Medium Wodema -1302	Panton	Retrd.	44.00	66.00
87-01-018	Small N' Tormett -2602	Panton	Retrd.	44.00	50.00
87-01-019	Small Krak N' Borg -3003	Panton	Retrd.	60.00	140.00
88-01-020	Medium Rueggan -1702	Panton	Retrd.	48.00	66.00
88-01-021	Large N'Grall -2201	Panton	Retrd.	108.00	400.00
88-01-022	Small Tulan Captain -2502	Panton	Retrd.	44.00	100-175.
88-01-023	Tarnhold-Med. -3202	Panton	Retrd.	120.00	280.00
89-01-024	Caught At Last! -1107	Panton	Retrd.	150.00	350.00
89-01-025	Stoope (waterglobe) -9003	Panton	Retrd.	40.00	156.00
89-01-026	Graffyn on Grunch (waterglobe) -9006	Panton	Retrd.	42.00	78.00
89-01-027	Krystonia Sign -701	Panton	Retrd.	N/A	N/A
Precious Art/Panton	**Krystonia Collector's Club**				
89-02-001	Pultzr	Panton	Retrd.	55.00	225.00
89-02-002	Key	Panton	Retrd.	Gift	55-150.00

Number	Name	Artist	Edition Limit	Issue Price	Quote
91-02-003	Dragons Play	Panton	Retrd.	65.00	200-350.
91-02-004	Kephrens Chest	Panton	Retrd.	Gift	65-100.00
92-02-005	Vaaston	Panton	Retrd.	65.00	95-125.00
92-02-006	Lantern	Panton	Retrd.	Gift	30-40.00
93-02-007	Sneaking A Peek	Panton	Retrd.	Gift	N/A
93-02-008	Spreading His Wings	Panton	Retrd.	60.00	60.00
94-02-009	All Tuckered Out	Panton	Yr.Iss.	65.00	65.00
94-02-010	Fill-Er-Up	Panton	Yr.Iss.	Gift	N/A
Princeton Gallery		**Unicorn Collection**			
90-01-001	Love's Delight	Unknown	Open	75.00	75.00
90-01-002	Love's Sweetness	Unknown	Open	75.00	75.00
91-01-003	Love's Devotion	Unknown	Open	119.00	119.00
91-01-004	Love's Purity	Unknown	Open	95.00	95.00
91-01-005	Love's Majesty	Unknown	Open	95.00	95.00
91-01-006	Christmas Unicorn	Unknown	Yr.Iss.	85.00	85.00
92-01-007	Love's Fancy	Unknown	Open	95.00	95.00
93-01-008	Love's Courtship	Unknown	Open	95.00	95.00
Princeton Gallery		**Playful Pups**			
90-02-001	Dalmation-Where's The Fire	Unknown	Open	19.50	19.50
90-02-002	Beagle	Unknown	Open	19.50	19.50
91-02-003	St. Bernard	Unknown	Open	19.50	19.50
91-02-004	Labrador Retriever	Unknown	Open	19.50	19.50
91-02-005	Wrinkles (Shar Pei)	Unknown	Open	19.50	19.50
Princeton Gallery		**Garden Capers**			
90-03-001	Any Mail?	Unknown	Open	29.50	29.50
91-03-002	Blue Jays	Unknown	Open	29.50	29.50
91-03-003	Robin	Unknown	Open	29.50	29.50
92-03-004	Goldfinch, Home Sweet Home	Unknown	Open	29.50	29.50
92-03-005	Bluebird, Spring Planting	Unknown	Open	29.50	29.50
Princeton Gallery		**Baby bird Trios**			
91-04-001	Woodland Symphony (Bluebirds)	Unknown	Open	45.00	45.00
91-04-002	Cardinals	Unknown	Open	45.00	45.00
Princeton Gallery		**Pegasus**			
92-05-001	Wings of Magic	Unknown	Open	95.00	95.00
Princeton Gallery		**Enchanted Nursery**			
92-06-001	Caprice	Unknown	Open	57.00	57.00
93-06-002	Pegasus	Unknown	Open	57.00	57.00
Princeton Gallery		**Lady And The Unicorn**			
92-07-001	Love's Innocence	Unknown	Open	119.00	119.00
Rawcliffe Corporation		**Garden Fairies™**			
93-01-001	The Fairy Slipper RF145	J. deStefano	4,500	115.00	115.00
93-01-002	The Dream Fairy RF146	J. deStefano	4,500	115.00	115.00
93-01-003	The Dew Fairy RF147	J. deStefano	4,500	115.00	115.00
93-01-004	The Illusive Fairy RF148	J. deStefano	4,500	115.00	115.00
Rawcliffe Corporation		**Baby Bubble Fairies™**			
92-02-001	Turquoise-January RF161	J. deStefano	6,700	70.00	70.00
92-02-002	Magenta-February RF162	J. deStefano	6,700	70.00	70.00
92-02-003	Blush-March RF163	J. deStefano	6,700	70.00	70.00
92-02-004	Chartreuse-April RF164	J. deStefano	6,700	70.00	70.00
92-02-005	Violet-May RF165	J. deStefano	6,700	70.00	70.00
92-02-006	Coral-June RF167	J. deStefano	6,700	70.00	70.00
92-02-007	Saffron-July RF166	J. deStefano	6,700	70.00	70.00
92-02-008	Azure-August RF168	J. deStefano	6,700	70.00	70.00
92-02-009	Lavender-September RF169	J. deStefano	6,700	70.00	70.00
92-02-010	Amber-October RF170	J. deStefano	6,700	70.00	70.00
92-02-011	Vermilion-November RF171	J. deStefano	6,700	70.00	70.00
92-02-012	Emerald-December RF172	J. deStefano	6,700	70.00	70.00
Rawcliffe Corporation		**Four Seasons Fairies™**			
91-03-001	Snow-Winter RF173	J. deStefano	9,500	95.00	95.00
91-03-002	Petal-Spring RF174	J. deStefano	9,500	95.00	95.00
91-03-003	Aria-Summer RF175	J. deStefano	9,500	95.00	95.00
91-03-004	Harvest-Fall RF176	J. deStefano	9,500	95.00	95.00
Rawcliffe Corporation		**Original Bubble Fairy™ Collection**			
88-04-001	Luna-Large Bubble Fairy RF177	J. deStefano	Open	145.00	145.00
88-04-002	Meadow-Large Bubble Fairy RF178	J. deStefano	Retrd.	145.00	145.00
88-04-003	Mist-Large Bubble Fairy RF179	J. deStefano	Retrd.	145.00	145.00
88-04-004	Sky-Large Bubble Fairy RF180	J. deStefano	Open	145.00	145.00
88-04-005	Bliss-Small Bubble Fairy RF181	J. deStefano	Open	85.00	85.00
88-04-006	Breeze-Small Bubble Fairy RF182	J. deStefano	Retrd.	85.00	85.00
88-04-007	Echo-Small Bubble Fairy RF183	J. deStefano	Open	85.00	85.00
88-04-008	Twilight-Small Bubble Fairy RF186	J. deStefano	Open	85.00	85.00
88-04-009	Whisper-Small Bubble Fairy RF187	J. deStefano	Open	85.00	85.00
88-04-010	Wishes-Small Bubble Fairy RF188	J. deStefano	Retrd.	85.00	85.00
88-04-011	Nimbus-Small Bubble Fairy RF197	J. deStefano	Retrd.	85.00	85.00
88-04-012	Sunbeam-Small Bubble Fairy RF198	J. deStefano	Retrd.	85.00	85.00
Rawcliffe Corporation		**Wish Fairy™ Collection**			
94-05-001	Fun RF1310	J. deStefano	Open	30.00	30.00
94-05-002	Dreams RF1311	J. deStefano	Open	30.00	30.00
94-05-003	Happiness RF1312	J. deStefano	Open	30.00	30.00
94-05-004	Rainbows RF1313	J. deStefano	Open	30.00	30.00
94-05-005	Love RF1314	J. deStefano	Open	30.00	30.00
94-05-006	Good Fortune RF1315	J. deStefano	Open	30.00	30.00
94-05-007	Health RF1316	J. deStefano	Open	30.00	30.00
94-05-008	Good Luck RF1317	J. deStefano	Open	30.00	30.00
94-05-009	Friendship RF1318	J. deStefano	Open	30.00	30.00
94-05-010	Success RF1319	J. deStefano	Open	30.00	30.00
94-05-011	Sunshine RF1320	J. deStefano	Open	30.00	30.00
94-05-012	Laughter RF1321	J. deStefano	Open	30.00	30.00
Rawcliffe Corporation		**Star Trek™ Starships**			
93-06-001	USS Enterprise RF797 (The Next Generation)	M. Schwabe	15,000	100.00	100.00
Rawcliffe Corporation		**Star Wars™ Starships**			
93-07-001	Darth Vader Tie Fighter Ship RF950	M. Schwabe	15,000	135.00	135.00
93-07-002	Millenium Falcon RF951	M. Schwabe	15,000	115.00	115.00
93-07-003	X-Wing Fighter RF952	M. Schwabe	15,000	95.00	95.00
Reco International		**Granget Crystal Sculpture**			
73-01-001	Long Earred Owl, Asio Otus	G. Granget	350	2250.00	2250.00
XX-01-002	Ruffed Grouse	G. Granget	350	1000.00	1000.00

Number	Name	Artist	Edition Limit	Issue Price	Quote
Reco International		**Porcelains in Miniature by John McClelland**			
XX-02-001	John	J. McClelland	10,000	34.50	34.50
XX-02-002	Alice	J. McClelland	10,000	34.50	34.50
XX-02-003	Chimney Sweep	J. McClelland	10,000	34.50	34.50
XX-02-004	Dressing Up	J. McClelland	10,000	34.50	34.50
XX-02-005	Autumn Dreams	J. McClelland	Open	29.50	29.50
XX-02-006	Tuck-Me-In	J. McClelland	Open	29.50	29.50
XX-02-007	Country Lass	J. McClelland	Open	29.50	29.50
XX-02-008	Sudsie Suzie	J. McClelland	Open	29.50	29.50
XX-02-009	Smooth Smailing	J. McClelland	Open	29.50	29.50
XX-02-010	The Clown	J. McClelland	Open	29.50	29.50
XX-02-011	The Baker	J. McClelland	Open	29.50	29.50
XX-02-012	Quiet Moments	J. McClelland	Open	29.50	29.50
XX-02-013	The Farmer	J. McClelland	Open	29.50	29.50
XX-02-014	The Nurse	J. McClelland	Open	29.50	29.50
XX-02-015	The Policeman	J. McClelland	Open	29.50	29.50
XX-02-016	The Fireman	J. McClelland	Open	29.50	29.50
XX-02-017	Winter Fun	J. McClelland	Open	29.50	29.50
XX-02-018	Cowgirl	J. McClelland	Open	29.50	29.50
XX-02-019	Cowboy	J. McClelland	Open	29.50	29.50
XX-02-020	Doc	J. McClelland	Open	29.50	29.50
XX-02-021	Lawyer	J. McClelland	Open	29.50	29.50
XX-02-022	Farmer's Wife	J. McClelland	Open	29.50	29.50
XX-02-023	First Outing	J. McClelland	Open	29.50	29.50
XX-02-024	Club Pro	J. McClelland	Open	29.50	29.50
XX-02-025	Batter Up	J. McClelland	Open	29.50	29.50
XX-02-026	Love 40	J. McClelland	Open	29.50	29.50
XX-02-027	The Painter	J. McClelland	Open	29.50	29.50
XX-02-028	Special Delivery	J. McClelland	Open	29.50	29.50
XX-02-029	Center Ice	J. McClelland	Open	29.50	29.50
XX-02-030	First Solo	J. McClelland	Open	29.50	29.50
XX-02-031	Highland Fling	J. McClelland	7,500	34.50	34.50
XX-02-032	Cheerleader	J. McClelland	Open	29.50	29.50
Reco International		**The Reco Clown Collection**			
85-03-001	Whoopie	J. McClelland	Open	12.00	13.00
85-03-002	The Professor	J. McClelland	Open	12.00	13.00
85-03-003	Top Hat	J. McClelland	Open	12.00	13.00
85-03-004	Winkie	J. McClelland	Open	12.00	13.00
85-03-005	Scamp	J. McClelland	Open	12.00	13.00
85-03-006	Curly	J. McClelland	Open	12.00	13.00
85-03-007	Bow Jangles	J. McClelland	Open	12.00	13.00
85-03-008	Sparkles	J. McClelland	Open	12.00	13.00
85-03-009	Ruffles	J. McClelland	Open	12.00	13.00
85-03-010	Arabesque	J. McClelland	Open	12.00	13.00
85-03-011	Hobo	J. McClelland	Open	12.00	13.00
85-03-012	Sad Eyes	J. McClelland	Open	12.00	13.00
87-03-013	Love	J. McClelland	Open	12.00	13.00
87-03-014	Mr. Big	J. McClelland	Open	12.00	13.00
87-03-015	Twinkle	J. McClelland	Open	12.00	13.00
87-03-016	Disco Dan	J. McClelland	Open	12.00	13.00
87-03-017	Smiley	J. McClelland	Open	12.00	13.00
87-03-018	The Joker	J. McClelland	Open	12.00	13.00
87-03-019	Jolly Joe	J. McClelland	Open	12.00	13.00
87-03-020	Zany Jack	J. McClelland	Open	12.00	13.00
87-03-021	Domino	J. McClelland	Open	12.00	13.00
87-03-022	Happy George	J. McClelland	Open	12.00	13.00
87-03-023	Tramp	J. McClelland	Open	12.00	13.00
87-03-024	Wistful	J. McClelland	Open	12.00	13.00
Reco International		**The Reco Angel Collection**			
86-04-001	Innocence	J. McClelland	Open	12.00	12.00
86-04-002	Harmony	J. McClelland	Open	12.00	12.00
86-04-003	Love	J. McClelland	Open	12.00	12.00
86-04-004	Gloria	J. McClelland	Open	12.00	12.00
86-04-005	Praise	J. McClelland	Open	20.00	20.00
86-04-006	Devotion	J. McClelland	Open	15.00	15.00
86-04-007	Faith	J. McClelland	Open	24.00	24.00
86-04-008	Joy	J. McClelland	Open	15.00	15.00
86-04-009	Adoration	J. McClelland	Open	24.00	24.00
86-04-010	Peace	J. McClelland	Open	24.00	24.00
86-04-011	Serenity	J. McClelland	Open	24.00	24.00
86-04-012	Hope	J. McClelland	Open	24.00	24.00
88-04-013	Reverence	J. McClelland	Open	12.00	12.00
88-04-014	Minstral	J. McClelland	Open	12.00	12.00
Reco International		**Sophisticated Ladies Figurines**			
87-05-001	Felicia	A. Fazio	9,500	29.50	32.50
87-05-002	Samantha	A. Fazio	9,500	29.50	32.50
87-05-003	Phoebe	A. Fazio	9,500	29.50	32.50
87-05-004	Cleo	A. Fazio	9,500	29.50	32.50
87-05-005	Cerissa	A. Fazio	9,500	29.50	32.50
87-05-006	Natasha	A. Fazio	9,500	29.50	32.50
87-05-007	Bianka	A. Fazio	9,500	29.50	32.50
87-05-008	Chelsea	A. Fazio	9,500	29.50	32.50
Reco International		**Clown Figurines by John McClelland**			
87-06-001	Mr. Tip	J. McClelland	9,500	35.00	35.00
87-06-002	Mr. Cure-All	J. McClelland	9,500	35.00	35.00
87-06-003	Mr. One-Note	J. McClelland	9,500	35.00	35.00
87-06-004	Mr. Lovable	J. McClelland	9,500	35.00	35.00
88-06-005	Mr. Magic	J. McClelland	9,500	35.00	35.00
88-06-006	Mr. Cool	J. McClelland	9,500	35.00	35.00
88-06-007	Mr. Heart-Throb	J. McClelland	9,500	35.00	35.00
Reco International		**The Reco Angel Collection Miniatures**			
87-07-001	Innocence	J. McClelland	Open	7.50	7.50
87-07-002	Harmony	J. McClelland	Open	7.50	7.50
87-07-003	Love	J. McClelland	Open	7.50	7.50
87-07-004	Gloria	J. McClelland	Open	7.50	7.50
87-07-005	Devotion	J. McClelland	Open	7.50	7.50
87-07-006	Joy	J. McClelland	Open	7.50	7.50
87-07-007	Adoration	J. McClelland	Open	10.00	10.00
87-07-008	Peace	J. McClelland	Open	10.00	10.00
87-07-009	Serenity	J. McClelland	Open	10.00	10.00
87-07-010	Hope	J. McClelland	Open	10.00	10.00
87-07-011	Praise	J. McClelland	Open	10.00	10.00
87-07-012	Faith	J. McClelland	Open	10.00	10.00
Reco International		**Faces of Love**			
88-08-001	Cuddles	J. McClelland	Open	29.50	32.50
88-08-002	Sunshine	J. McClelland	Open	29.50	32.50

Company / Number	Name	Series / Artist	Edition Limit	Issue Price	Quote
Reco International		**Reco Creche Collection**			
87-09-001	Holy Family (3 Pieces)	J. McClelland	Open	49.00	49.00
87-09-002	Lamb	J. McClelland	Open	9.50	9.50
87-09-003	Shepherd-Kneeling	J. McClelland	Open	22.50	22.50
87-09-004	Shepherd-Standing	J. McClelland	Open	22.50	22.50
88-09-005	King/Frankincense	J. McClelland	Open	22.50	22.50
88-09-006	King/Myrrh	J. McClelland	Open	22.50	22.50
88-09-007	King/Gold	J. McClelland	Open	22.50	22.50
88-09-008	Donkey	J. McClelland	Open	16.50	16.50
88-09-009	Cow	J. McClelland	Open	15.00	15.00
Reco International		**The Reco Collection Clown Busts**			
88-10-001	Hobo	J. McClelland	5,000	40.00	40.00
88-10-002	Love	J. McClelland	5,000	40.00	40.00
88-10-003	Sparkles	J. McClelland	5,000	40.00	40.00
88-10-004	Bow Jangles	J. McClelland	5,000	40.00	40.00
88-10-005	Domino	J. McClelland	5,000	40.00	40.00
Reco International		**Wedding Gifts**			
91-11-001	Cake Topper Bride & Groom	J. McClelland	Open	35.00	35.00
91-11-002	Bride & Groom- Musical	J. McClelland	Open	90.00	90.00
91-11-003	Bride-Blond-Musical	J. McClelland	Open	80.00	80.00
91-11-004	Bride-Brunette-Musical	J. McClelland	Open	80.00	80.00
91-11-005	Bride & Groom	J. McClelland	Open	85.00	85.00
91-11-006	Bride-Blond	J. McClelland	Open	60.00	60.00
91-11-007	Bride-Brunette	J. McClelland	Open	60.00	60.00
Rhodes Studio		**Rockwell's Main Street**			
90-01-001	Rockwell's Studio	Rockwell-Inspired	150-day	28.00	85.00
90-01-002	The Antique Shop	Rockwell-Inspired	150-day	28.00	36.00
90-01-003	The Town Offices	Rockwell-Inspired	150-day	32.00	36.00
90-01-004	The Country Store	Rockwell-Inspired	150-day	32.00	36.00
91-01-005	The Library	Rockwell-Inspired	150-day	36.00	36.00
91-01-006	The Bank	Rockwell-Inspired	150-day	36.00	36.00
91-01-007	Red Lion Inn	Rockwell-Inspired	150-day	39.00	39.00
Rhodes Studio		**Rockwell's Hometown**			
91-02-001	Rockwell's Residence	Rhodes	Closed	34.95	34.95
91-02-002	Greystone Church	Rhodes	Closed	34.95	34.95
91-02-003	Bell Tower	Rockwell-Inspired	Closed	36.95	36.95
91-02-004	Firehouse	Rockwell-Inspired	Closed	36.95	36.95
91-02-005	Church On The Green	Rockwell-Inspired	Closed	39.95	39.95
92-02-006	Town Hall	Rockwell-Inspired	Closed	39.95	39.95
92-02-007	Citizen's Hall	Rockwell-Inspired	Closed	42.95	42.95
92-02-008	The Berkshire Playhouse	Rockwell-Inspired	6/94	42.95	42.95
92-02-009	Mission House	Rockwell-Inspired	9/94	42.95	42.95
92-02-010	Old Corner House	Rockwell-Inspired	12/94	42.95	42.95
Rhodes Studio		**Rockwell's Heirloom Santa Collection**			
90-03-001	Santa's Workshop	Rockwell-Inspired	150-day	49.95	49.95
91-03-002	Christmas Dream	Rockwell-Inspired	150-day	49.95	49.95
92-03-003	Making His List	Rockwell-Inspired	Closed	49.95	49.95
Rhodes Studio		**Rockwell's Age of Wonder**			
91-04-001	Splish Splash	Rockwell-Inspired	Closed	34.95	34.95
91-04-002	Hush-A-Bye	Rockwell-Inspired	Closed	34.95	34.95
91-04-003	Stand by Me	Rockwell-Inspired	Closed	36.95	36.95
91-04-004	School Days	Rockwell-Inspired	Closed	36.95	36.95
91-04-005	Summertime	Rockwell-Inspired	Closed	39.95	39.95
92-04-006	The Birthday Party	Rockwell-Inspired	Closed	39.95	39.95
Rhodes Studios		**Rockwell's Beautiful Dreamers**			
91-05-001	Sitting Pretty	Rockwell-Inspired	Closed	37.95	37.95
91-05-002	Dear Diary	Rockwell-Inspired	Closed	37.95	37.95
91-05-003	Secret Sonnets	Rockwell-Inspired	Closed	39.95	39.95
91-05-004	Springtime Serenade	Rockwell-Inspired	Closed	39.95	39.95
92-05-005	Debutante's Dance	Rockwell-Inspired	Closed	42.95	42.95
92-05-006	Walk in the Park	Rockwell-Inspired	6/94	42.95	42.95
Rhodes Studio		**Rockwell's Gems of Wisdom**			
91-06-001	Love Cures All	Rockwell-Inspired	Closed	39.95	39.95
91-06-002	Practice Makes Perfect	Rockwell-Inspired	Closed	39.95	39.95
91-06-003	A Stitch In Time	Rockwell-Inspired	Closed	42.95	42.95
Also see Norman Rockwell Gallery					
River Shore		**Loveable-Baby Animals**			
78-01-001	Akiku-Seal	R. Brown	15,000	37.50	150.00
78-01-002	Alfred-Raccoon	R. Brown	15,000	42.50	45.00
79-01-003	Scooter-Chipmunk	R. Brown	15,000	45.00	55.00
79-01-004	Matilda-Koala	R. Brown	15,000	45.00	45.00
River Shore		**Wildlife Baby Animals**			
78-02-001	Fanny-Fawn	R. Brown	15,000	45.00	90.00
79-02-002	Roosevelt-Bear	R. Brown	15,000	50.00	65.00
79-02-003	Roscoe-Red Fox	R. Brown	15,000	50.00	50.00
80-02-004	Priscilla-Skunk	R. Brown	15,000	50.00	50.00
River Shore		**Rockwell Single Issues**			
81-03-001	Looking Out To Sea	N. Rockwell	9,500	85.00	225.00
82-03-002	Grandpa's Guardian	N. Rockwell	9,500	125.00	125.00
River Shore		**Babies of Endangered Species**			
84-04-001	Sidney (Cougar)	R. Brown	15,000	45.00	45.00
84-04-002	Baxter (Bear)	R. Brown	15,000	45.00	45.00
84-04-003	Caroline (Antelope)	R. Brown	15,000	45.00	45.00
84-04-004	Webster (Timberwolf)	R. Brown	15,000	45.00	45.00
84-04-005	Violet (Otter)	R. Brown	15,000	45.00	45.00
84-04-006	Chester (Prairie Dog)	R. Brown	15,000	45.00	45.00
84-04-007	Trevor (Fox)	R. Brown	15,000	45.00	45.00
84-04-008	Daisy (Wood Bison)	R. Brown	15,000	45.00	45.00
River Shore		**Wilderness Babies**			
85-05-001	Penelope (Deer)	R. Brown	15,000	45.00	45.00
85-05-002	Carmen (Burro)	R. Brown	15,000	45.00	45.00
85-05-003	Rocky (Bobcat)	R. Brown	15,000	45.00	45.00
85-05-004	Abercrombie (Polar Bear)	R. Brown	15,000	45.00	45.00
85-05-005	Elrod (Fox)	R. Brown	15,000	45.00	45.00
85-05-006	Reggie (Raccoon)	R. Brown	15,000	45.00	45.00
85-05-007	Arianne (Rabbit)	R. Brown	15,000	45.00	45.00
85-05-008	Annabel (Mountain Goat)	R. Brown	15,000	45.00	45.00
River Shore		**Lovable Teddies Musical Figurine Collection**			
87-06-001	Gilbert	M. Hague	Open	29.50	29.50
87-06-002	William	M. Hague	Open	29.50	29.50
87-06-003	Austin	M. Hague	Open	29.50	29.50
87-06-004	April	M. Hague	Open	29.50	29.50
88-06-005	Henry	M. Hague	Open	29.50	29.50
88-06-006	Harvey	M. Hague	Open	29.50	29.50
88-06-007	Adam	M. Hague	Open	29.50	29.50
88-06-008	Katie	M. Hague	Open	29.50	29.50
Also See Rhodes Studio					
Rohn		**Around the World**			
71-01-001	Coolie	E. Rohn	100	700.00	1200.00
72-01-002	Gypsy	E. Rohn	125	1450.00	1850.00
73-01-003	Matador	E. Rohn	90	2400.00	3100.00
73-01-004	Sherif	E. Rohn	100	1500.00	2250.00
74-01-005	Aussie-Hunter	E. Rohn	90	1000.00	1300.00
Rohn		**Clowns-Big Top Series**			
79-02-001	White Face	E. Rohn	100	1000.00	3500.00
80-02-002	Tramp	E. Rohn	100	1200.00	2500.00
81-02-003	Auguste	E. Rohn	100	1400.00	1700.00
83-02-004	Sweetheart	E. Rohn	200	925.00	1500.00
Rohn		**Famous People**			
75-03-001	Harry S. Truman	E. Rohn	75	2400.00	4000.00
79-03-002	Norman Rockwell	E. Rohn	200	1950.00	2300.00
81-03-003	Ronald Reagan	E. Rohn	200	3000.00	3000.00
85-03-004	Sherlock Holmes	E. Rohn	2,210	155.00	190.00
86-03-005	Dr. John Watson	E. Rohn	2,210	155.00	155.00
Rohn		**Remember When**			
71-04-001	Riverboat Captain	E. Rohn	100	1000.00	2400.00
71-04-002	American GI	E. Rohn	100	600.00	1750.00
73-04-003	Apprentice	E. Rohn	175	500.00	850.00
74-04-004	Recruit (set w/FN-5)	E. Rohn	250	250.00	500.00
74-04-005	Missy	E. Rohn	250	250.00	500.00
77-04-006	Flapper	E. Rohn	500	325.00	500.00
77-04-007	Sou' Wester	E. Rohn	450	300.00	500.00
77-04-008	Casey	E. Rohn	300	275.00	500.00
77-04-009	Wally	E. Rohn	250	250.00	500.00
73-04-010	Jazz Man	E. Rohn	150	750.00	3500.00
80-04-011	Showman (W.C. Fields)	E. Rohn	300	220.00	500.00
81-04-012	Clown Prince	E. Rohn	25	2000.00	2400.00
Rohn		**Religious & Biblical**			
77-05-001	Zaide	E. Rohn	70	1950.00	5000.00
78-05-002	Sabbath	E. Rohn	70	1825.00	5000.00
85-05-003	The Mentor	E. Rohn	15	9500.00	9500.00
Rohn		**Small World Series**			
74-06-001	Big Brother	E. Rohn	250	90.00	90.00
74-06-002	Burglers	E. Rohn	250	120.00	120.00
74-06-003	Quackers	E. Rohn	250	75.00	75.00
74-06-004	Knee Deep	E. Rohn	500	60.00	60.00
75-06-005	Field Mushrooms	E. Rohn	250	90.00	90.00
75-06-006	Oyster Mushroom	E. Rohn	250	140.00	140.00
XX-06-007	Johnnie's	E. Rohn	1,500	90.00	90.00
Rohn		**Western**			
71-07-001	Trail-Hand	E. Rohn	100	1200.00	1600.00
71-07-002	Crow Indian	E. Rohn	100	800.00	1500.00
71-07-003	Apache Indian	E. Rohn	125	800.00	2000.00
71-07-004	Chosen One (Indian Maid)	E. Rohn	125	850.00	2000.00
Rohn		**Clowns-Hey Rube**			
79-08-001	Whiteface	E. Rohn	300	190.00	350.00
79-08-002	Tramp	E. Rohn	300	190.00	350.00
79-08-003	Auguste	E. Rohn	300	190.00	350.00
Rohn		**Famous People-Bisque**			
79-09-001	Norman Rockwell	E. Rohn	Yr.Iss.	100.00	200.00
79-09-002	Lincoln	E. Rohn	500	100.00	500.00
81-09-003	Reagan	E. Rohn	2,500	140.00	200.00
83-09-004	J. F. Kennedy	E. Rohn	500	140.00	400.00
Rohn		**Wild West**			
82-10-001	Rodeo Clown	E. Rohn	100	2600.00	3500.00
Roman, Inc.		**Fontanini, The Collectible Creche**			
73-01-001	10cm., (15 piece Set)	E. Simonetti	Closed	63.60	88.50
73-01-002	12cm., (15 piece Set)	E. Simonetti	Closed	76.50	102.00
79-01-003	16cm., (15 piece Set)	E. Simonetti	Closed	178.50	285.00
82-01-004	17cm., (15 piece Set)	E. Simonetti	Closed	189.00	305.00
73-01-005	19cm., (15 piece Set)	E. Simonetti	Closed	175.50	280.00
80-01-006	30cm., (15 piece Set)	E. Simonetti	Closed	670.00	758.50
Roman, Inc.		**A Child's World 1st Edition**			
80-02-001	Nighttime Thoughts	F. Hook	Closed	25.00	65.00
80-02-002	Kiss Me Good Night	F. Hook	15,000	29.00	40.00
80-02-003	Sounds of the Sea	F. Hook	15,000	45.00	140.00
80-02-004	Beach Buddies, signed	F. Hook	15,000	29.00	600.00
80-02-005	My Big Brother	F. Hook	Closed	39.00	200.00
80-02-006	Helping Hands	F. Hook	Closed	45.00	75.00
80-02-007	Beach Buddies, unsigned	F. Hook	15,000	29.00	450.00
Roman, Inc.		**A Child's World 2nd Edition**			
81-03-001	Making Friends	F. Hook	15,000	42.00	46.00
81-03-002	Cat Nap	F. Hook	15,000	42.00	100.00
81-03-003	The Sea and Me	F. Hook	15,000	39.00	43.00
81-03-004	Sunday School	F. Hook	15,000	39.00	70.00
81-03-005	I'll Be Good	F. Hook	15,000	36.00	70.00
81-03-006	All Dressed Up	F. Hook	15,000	36.00	70.00
Roman, Inc.		**A Child's World 3rd Edition**			
81-04-001	Pathway to Dreams	F. Hook	15,000	47.00	50.00
81-04-002	Road to Adventure	F. Hook	15,000	47.00	50.00
81-04-003	Sisters	F. Hook	15,000	64.00	69.00
81-04-004	Bear Hug	F. Hook	15,000	42.00	45.00
81-04-005	Spring Breeze	F. Hook	15,000	37.50	40.00
81-04-006	Youth	F. Hook	15,000	37.50	40.00
Roman, Inc.		**A Child's World 4th Edition**			
82-05-001	All Bundled Up	F. Hook	15,000	37.50	40.00
82-05-002	Bedtime	F. Hook	15,000	35.00	38.00

Company / Number	Name	Series / Artist	Edition Limit	Issue Price	Quote
82-05-003	Birdie	F. Hook	15,000	37.50	40.00
82-05-004	My Dolly!	F. Hook	15,000	39.00	40.00
82-05-005	Ring Bearer	F. Hook	15,000	39.00	40.00
82-05-006	Flower Girl	F. Hook	15,000	42.00	45.00
Roman, Inc.		**A Child's World 5th Edition**			
83-06-001	Ring Around the Rosie	F. Hook	15,000	99.00	105.00
83-06-002	Handful of Happiness	F. Hook	15,000	36.00	40.00
83-06-003	He Loves Me...	F. Hook	15,000	49.00	55.00
83-06-004	Finish Line	F. Hook	15,000	39.00	42.00
83-06-005	Brothers	F. Hook	15,000	64.00	70.00
83-06-006	Puppy's Pal	F. Hook	15,000	39.00	42.00
Roman, Inc.		**A Child's World 6th Edition**			
84-07-001	Good Doggie	F. Hook	15,000	47.00	50.00
84-07-002	Sand Castles	F. Hook	15,000	37.50	40.00
84-07-003	Nature's Wonders	F. Hook	15,000	29.00	31.00
84-07-004	Let's Play Catch	F. Hook	15,000	33.00	35.00
84-07-005	Can I Help?	F. Hook	15,000	37.50	40.00
84-07-006	Future Artist	F. Hook	15,000	42.00	45.00
Roman, Inc.		**A Child's World 7th Edition**			
85-08-001	Art Class	F. Hook	15,000	99.00	105.00
85-08-002	Please Hear Me	F. Hook	15,000	29.00	30.00
85-08-003	Don't Tell Anyone	F. Hook	15,000	49.00	50.00
85-08-004	Mother's Helper	F. Hook	15,000	45.00	50.00
85-08-005	Yummm!	F. Hook	15,000	36.00	39.00
85-08-006	Look at Me!	F. Hook	15,000	42.00	45.00
Roman, Inc.		**A Child's World 8th Edition**			
85-09-001	Private Ocean	F. Hook	15,000	29.00	31.00
85-09-002	Just Stopped By	F. Hook	15,000	36.00	40.00
85-09-003	Dress Rehearsal	F. Hook	15,000	33.00	35.00
85-09-004	Chance of Showers	F. Hook	15,000	33.00	35.00
85-09-005	Engine	F. Hook	15,000	36.00	40.00
85-09-006	Puzzling	F. Hook	15,000	36.00	40.00
Roman, Inc.		**A Child's World 9th Edition**			
87-10-001	Li'l Brother	F. Hook	15,000	60.00	65.00
87-10-002	Hopscotch	F. Hook	15,000	67.50	70.00
Roman, Inc.		**Rohn's Clowns**			
84-11-001	White Face	E. Rohn	7,500	95.00	95.00
84-11-002	Auguste	E. Rohn	7,500	95.00	95.00
84-11-003	Hobo	E. Rohn	7,500	95.00	95.00
Roman, Inc.		**The Masterpiece Collection**			
79-12-001	Adoration	F. Lippe	5,000	73.00	73.00
80-12-002	Madonna with Grapes	P. Mignard	5,000	85.00	85.00
81-12-003	The Holy Family	G. delle Notti	5,000	98.00	98.00
82-12-004	Madonna of the Streets	R. Ferruzzi	5,000	65.00	65.00
Roman, Inc.		**Ceramica Excelsis**			
77-13-001	Madonna and Child with Angels	Unknown	5,000	60.00	60.00
77-13-002	What Happened to Your Hand?	Unknown	5,000	60.00	60.00
77-13-003	Madonna with Child	Unknown	5,000	65.00	65.00
77-13-004	St. Francis	Unknown	5,000	60.00	60.00
77-13-005	Christ Knocking at the Door	Unknown	5,000	60.00	60.00
78-13-006	Infant of Prague	Unknown	5,000	37.50	60.00
78-13-007	Christ in the Garden of Gethsemane	Unknown	5,000	40.00	60.00
78-13-008	Flight into Egypt	Unknown	5,000	59.00	90.00
78-13-009	Christ Entering Jerusalem	Unknown	5,000	96.00	96.00
78-13-010	Holy Family at Work	Unknown	5,000	96.00	96.00
78-13-011	Assumption Madonna	Unknown	5,000	56.00	56.00
78-13-012	Guardian Angel with Girl	Unknown	5,000	69.00	69.00
78-13-013	Guardian Angel with Boy	Unknown	5,000	69.00	69.00
79-13-014	Moses	Unknown	5,000	77.00	77.00
79-13-015	Noah	Unknown	5,000	77.00	77.00
79-13-016	Jesus Speaks in Parables	Unknown	5,000	90.00	90.00
80-13-017	Way to Emmaus	Unknown	5,000	155.00	155.00
80-13-018	Daniel in the Lion's Den	Unknown	5,000	80.00	80.00
80-13-019	David	Unknown	5,000	77.00	77.00
81-13-020	Innocence	Unknown	5,000	95.00	95.00
81-13-021	Journey to Bethlehem	Unknown	5,000	89.00	89.00
81-13-022	Way of the Cross	Unknown	5,000	59.00	59.00
81-13-023	Sermon on the Mount	Unknown	5,000	56.00	56.00
83-13-024	Good Shepherd	Unknown	5,000	49.00	49.00
83-13-025	Holy Family	Unknown	5,000	72.00	72.00
83-13-026	St. Francis	Unknown	5,000	59.50	59.50
83-13-027	St. Anne	Unknown	5,000	49.00	49.00
83-13-028	Jesus with Children	Unknown	5,000	74.00	74.00
83-13-029	Kneeling Santa	Unknown	5,000	95.00	95.00
Roman, Inc.		**Hook**			
82-14-001	Sailor Mates	F. Hook	2,000	290.00	315.00
82-14-002	Sun Shy	F. Hook	2,000	290.00	315.00
Roman, Inc.		**Frances Hook's Four Seasons**			
84-15-001	Winter	F. Hook	12,500	95.00	100.00
85-15-002	Spring	F. Hook	12,500	95.00	100.00
85-15-003	Summer	F. Hook	12,500	95.00	100.00
85-15-004	Fall	F. Hook	12,500	95.00	100.00
Roman, Inc.		**Jam Session**			
85-16-001	Trombone Player	E. Rohn	7,500	145.00	145.00
85-16-002.	Bass Player	E. Rohn	7,500	145.00	145.00
85-16-003	Banjo Player	E. Rohn	7,500	145.00	145.00
85-16-004	Coronet Player	E. Rohn	7,500	145.00	145.00
85-16-005	Clarinet Player	E. Rohn	7,500	145.00	145.00
85-16-006	Drummer	E. Rohn	7,500	145.00	145.00
Roman, Inc.		**Spencer**			
85-17-001	Moon Goddess	I. Spencer	5,000	195.00	195.00
85-17-002	Flower Princess	I. Spencer	5,000	195.00	195.00
Roman, Inc.		**Hook**			
86-18-001	Carpenter Bust	F. Hook	Yr.Iss.	95.00	95.00
86-18-002	Carpenter Bust-Heirloom Edition	F. Hook	Yr.Iss.	95.00	95.00
87-18-003	Madonna and Child	F. Hook	15,000	39.50	39.50
87-18-004	Little Children, Come to Me	F. Hook	15,000	45.00	45.00
Roman, Inc.		**Catnippers**			
85-19-001	The Paw that Refreshes	I. Spencer	15,000	45.00	45.00

Company / Number	Name	Series / Artist	Edition Limit	Issue Price	Quote
85-19-002	A Christmas Mourning	I. Spencer	15,000	45.00	49.50
85-19-003	A Tail of Two Kitties	I. Spencer	15,000	45.00	45.00
85-19-004	Sandy Claws	I. Spencer	15,000	45.00	45.00
85-19-005	Can't We Be Friends	I. Spencer	15,000	45.00	45.00
85-19-006	A Baffling Yarn	I. Spencer	15,000	45.00	45.00
85-19-007	Flying Tiger-Retired	I. Spencer	15,000	45.00	45.00
85-19-008	Flora and Felina	I. Spencer	15,000	45.00	49.50
Roman, Inc.		**Heartbeats**			
86-20-001	Miracle	I. Spencer	5,000	145.00	145.00
87-20-002	Storytime	I. Spencer	5,000	145.00	145.00
Roman, Inc.		**Classic Brides of the Century**			
89-21-001	1900-Flora	E. Williams	5,000	175.00	175.00
89-21-002	1910-Elizabeth Grace	E. Williams	5,000	175.00	175.00
89-21-003	1920-Mary Claire	E. Williams	5,000	175.00	175.00
89-21-004	1930-Kathleen	E. Williams	5,000	175.00	175.00
89-21-005	1940-Margaret	E. Williams	5,000	175.00	175.00
89-21-006	1950-Barbara Ann	E. Williams	5,000	175.00	175.00
89-21-007	1960-Dianne	E. Williams	5,000	175.00	175.00
89-21-008	1970-Heather	E. Williams	5,000	175.00	175.00
89-21-009	1980-Jennifer	E. Williams	5,000	175.00	175.00
92-21-010	1990-Stephanie Helen	E. Williams	5,000	175.00	175.00
Roman Inc.		**Dolfi Original-5" Wood**			
89-22-001	My First Kitten	L. Martin	5,000	230.00	230.00
89-22-002	Flower Child	L. Martin	5,000	230.00	230.00
89-22-003	Pampered Puppies	L. Martin	5,000	230.00	230.00
89-22-004	Wrapped In Love	L. Martin	5,000	230.00	230.00
89-22-005	Garden Secrets	L. Martin	5,000	230.00	230.00
89-22-006	Puppy Express	L. Martin	5,000	230.00	230.00
89-22-007	Sleepyhead	L. Martin	5,000	230.00	230.00
89-22-008	Mother Hen	L. Martin	5,000	230.00	230.00
89-22-009	Holiday Herald	L. Martin	5,000	230.00	230.00
89-22-010	Birdland Cafe	L. Martin	5,000	230.00	230.00
89-22-011	My First Cake	L. Martin	5,000	230.00	230.00
89-22-012	Mud Puddles	L. Martin	5,000	230.00	230.00
89-22-013	Study Break	L. Martin	5,000	250.00	250.00
89-22-014	Dress Rehearsal	L. Martin	5,000	375.00	375.00
89-22-015	Friends & Flowers	L. Martin	5,000	300.00	300.00
89-22-016	Merry Little Light	L. Martin	5,000	250.00	250.00
89-22-017	Mary & Joey	L. Martin	5,000	375.00	375.00
89-22-018	Little Santa	L. Martin	5,000	250.00	250.00
89-22-019	Sing a Song of Joy	L. Martin	5,000	300.00	300.00
89-22-020	Barefoot In Spring	L. Martin	5,000	300.00	300.00
89-22-021	My Favorite Things	L. Martin	5,000	300.00	300.00
89-22-022	Have I Been That Good	L. Martin	5,000	375.00	375.00
89-22-023	A Shoulder to Lean On	L. Martin	5,000	300.00	300.00
89-22-024	Big Chief Sitting Dog	L. Martin	5,000	250.00	250.00
Roman, Inc.		**Dolfi Original-7" Stoneart**			
89-23-001	My First Kitten	L. Martin	Open	110.00	110.00
89-23-002	Flower Child	L. Martin	Open	110.00	110.00
89-23-003	Pampered Puppies	L. Martin	Open	110.00	110.00
89-23-004	Wrapped in Love	L. Martin	Open	110.00	110.00
89-23-005	Garden Secrets	L. Martin	Open	110.00	110.00
89-23-006	Puppy Express	L. Martin	Open	110.00	110.00
89-23-007	Sleepyhead	L. Martin	Open	110.00	110.00
89-23-008	Mother Hen	L. Martin	Open	110.00	110.00
89-23-009	Holiday Herald	L. Martin	Open	110.00	110.00
89-23-010	Birdland Cafe	L. Martin	Open	110.00	110.00
89-23-011	My First Cake	L. Martin	Open	110.00	110.00
89-23-012	Mud Puddles	L. Martin	Open	110.00	110.00
89-23-013	Study Break	L. Martin	Open	120.00	120.00
89-23-014	Dress Rehearsal	L. Martin	Open	185.00	185.00
89-23-015	Friends & Flowers	L. Martin	Open	150.00	150.00
89-23-016	Merry Little Light	L. Martin	Open	120.00	120.00
89-23-017	Mary & Joey	L. Martin	Open	185.00	185.00
89-23-018	Little Santa	L. Martin	Open	120.00	120.00
89-23-019	Sing a Song of Joy	L. Martin	Open	150.00	150.00
89-23-020	Barefoot In Spring	L. Martin	Open	150.00	150.00
89-23-021	My Favorite Things	L. Martin	Open	150.00	150.00
89-23-022	Have I Been That Good	L. Martin	Open	185.00	185.00
89-23-023	A Shoulder to Lean On	L. Martin	Open	150.00	150.00
89-23-024	Big Chief Sitting Dog	L. Martin	Open	120.00	120.00
Roman, Inc.		**Dolfi Original-10" Stoneart**			
89-24-001	My First Kitten	L. Martin	Open	300.00	300.00
89-24-002	Flower Child	L. Martin	Open	300.00	300.00
89-24-003	Pampered Puppies	L. Martin	Open	300.00	300.00
89-24-004	Wrapped in Love	L. Martin	Open	300.00	300.00
89-24-005	Garden Secrets	L. Martin	Open	300.00	300.00
89-24-006	Puppy Express	L. Martin	Open	300.00	300.00
89-24-007	Sleepyhead	L. Martin	Open	300.00	300.00
89-24-008	Mother Hen	L. Martin	Open	300.00	300.00
89-24-009	Holiday Herald	L. Martin	Open	300.00	300.00
89-24-010	Birdland Cafe	L. Martin	Open	300.00	300.00
89-24-011	My First Cake	L. Martin	Open	300.00	300.00
89-24-012	Mud Puddles	L. Martin	Open	300.00	300.00
89-24-013	Study Break	L. Martin	Open	325.00	325.00
89-24-014	Dress Rehearsal	L. Martin	Open	495.00	495.00
89-24-015	Friends & Flowers	L. Martin	Open	400.00	400.00
89-24-016	Merry Little Light	L. Martin	Open	325.00	325.00
89-24-017	Mary & Joey	L. Martin	Open	495.00	495.00
89-24-018	Little Santa	L. Martin	Open	325.00	325.00
89-24-019	Sing a Song of Joy	L. Martin	Open	400.00	400.00
89-24-020	Barefoot In Spring	L. Martin	Open	400.00	400.00
89-24-021	My Favorite Things	L. Martin	Open	400.00	400.00
89-24-022	Have I Been That Good	L. Martin	Open	495.00	495.00
89-24-023	A Shoulder to Lean On	L. Martin	Open	400.00	400.00
89-24-024	Big Chief Sitting Dog	L. Martin	Open	325.00	325.00
Roman, Inc.		**Dolfi Original-10" Wood**			
89-25-001	My First Kitten	L. Martin	2,000	750.00	750.00
89-25-002	Flower Child	L. Martin	2,000	750.00	750.00
89-25-003	Pampered Puppies	L. Martin	2,000	750.00	750.00
89-25-004	Wrapped in Love	L. Martin	2,000	750.00	750.00
89-25-005	Garden Secrets	L. Martin	2,000	750.00	750.00
89-25-006	Puppy Express	L. Martin	2,000	750.00	750.00
89-25-007	Sleepyhead	L. Martin	2,000	750.00	750.00
89-25-008	Mother Hen	L. Martin	2,000	750.00	750.00
89-25-009	Holiday Herald	L. Martin	2,000	750.00	750.00
89-25-010	Birdland Cafe	L. Martin	2,000	750.00	750.00

Company Number	Name	Series Artist	Edition Limit	Issue Price	Quote
89-25-011	My First Cake	L. Martin	2,000	750.00	750.00
89-25-012	Mud Puddles	L. Martin	2,000	750.00	750.00
89-25-013	Study Break	L. Martin	2,000	825.00	825.00
89-25-014	Dress Rehearsal	L. Martin	2,000	1250.00	1250.00
89-25-015	Friends & Flowers	L. Martin	2,000	1000.00	1000.00
89-25-016	Merry Little Light	L. Martin	2,000	825.00	825.00
89-25-017	Mary & Joey	L. Martin	2,000	1250.00	1250.00
89-26-018	Little Santa	L. Martin	2,000	825.00	825.00
89-25-019	Sing a Song of Joy	L. Martin	2,000	1000.00	1000.00
89-25-020	Barefoot In Spring	L. Mariin	2,000	1000.00	1000.00
89-25-021	My Favorite Things	L. Martin	2,000	1000.00	1000.00
89-25-022	Have I Been That Good	L. Martin	2,000	1250.00	1250.00
89-25-023	A Shoulder to Lean On	L. Martin	2,000	1000.00	1000.00
89-25-024	Big Chief Sitting Dog	L. Martin	2,000	825.00	825.00
Roman, Inc.	**The Museum Collection by Angela Tripi**				
90-26-001	The Mentor	A. Tripi	1,000	290.00	290.27
91-26-002	The Fiddler	A. Tripi	1,000	175.00	175.27
91-26-003	Christopher Columbus	A. Tripi	1,000	250.00	250.00
91-26-004	St. Francis of Assisi	A. Tripi	1,000	175.00	175.00
91-26-005	The Caddie	A. Tripi	1,000	135.00	135.00
91-26-006	A Gentleman's Game	A. Tripi	1,000	175.00	175.00
91-26-007	Tee Time at St. Andrew's	A. Tripi	1,000	175.00	175.00
92-26-008	Prince of the Plains	A. Tripi	1,000	175.00	175.00
92-26-009	The Fur Trapper	A. Tripi	1,000	175.00	175.00
92-26-010	Justice for All	A. Tripi	1,000	95.00	95.00
92-26-011	Flying Ace	A. Tripi	1,000	95.00	95.00
92-26-012	Our Family Doctor	A. Tripi	1,000	95.00	95.00
92-26-013	To Serve and Protect	A. Tripi	1,000	95.00	95.00
92-26-014	Ladies' Day	A. Tripi	1,000	175.00	175.00
92-26-015	Ladies' Tee	A. Tripi	1,000	250.00	250.00
92-26-016	The Tap In	A. Tripi	1,000	175.00	175.00
92-26-017	Fore!	A. Tripi	1,000	175.00	175.00
92-26-018	Checking It Twice	A. Tripi	2,500	95.00	95.00
92-26-019	The Tannenbaum Santa	A. Tripi	2,500	95.00	95.00
92-26-020	This Way, Santa	A. Tripi	2,500	95.00	95.00
92-26-021	The Gift Giver	A. Tripi	2,500	95.00	95.00
92-26-022	8-pc. Nativity Set	A. Tripi	2,500	425.00	425.00
93-26-023	Small Tripi Crucifix	A. Tripi	Open	27.50	27.50
93-26-024	Medium Tripi Crucifix	A. Tripi	Open	35.00	35.00
93-26-025	Large Tripi Crucifix	A. Tripi	Open	59.00	59.00
93-26-026	Jesus, The Good Shepherd	A. Tripi	1,000	95.00	95.00
93-26-027	Preacher of Peace	A. Tripi	1,000	175.00	175.00
93-26-028	Public Protector	A. Tripi	1,000	95.00	95.00
93-26-029	Right on Schedule	A. Tripi	1,000	95.00	95.00
93-26-030	Be a Clown	A. Tripi	1,000	95.00	95.00
93-26-031	Road Show	A. Tripi	1,000	95.00	95.00
93-26-032	One Man Band Clown	A. Tripi	1,000	95.00	95.00
93-26-033	For My Next Trick	A. Tripi	1,000	95.00	95.00
94-26-034	Rhapsody	A. Tripi	1,000	95.00	95.00
94-26-035	Serenade	A. Tripi	1,000	95.00	95.00
94-26-036	Sonata	A. Tripi	1,000	95.00	95.00
94-26-037	Native American Woman	A. Tripi	1,000	95.00	95.00
94-26-038	Native American Chief	A. Tripi	1,000	95.00	95.00
94-26-039	Native American Warrior	A. Tripi	1,000	95.00	95.00
Roman, Inc.	**Bristol Falls Carolers Society**				
93-27-001	Catherine Lucy Lancaster	E. Simonetti	Open	23.50	24.50
93-27-002	Timothy Palmer	E. Simonetti	Open	27.50	29.50
93-27-003	Elizabeth Anne Abbot & Stephen	E. Simonetti	Open	23.50	24.50
93-27-004	James Fisk Cushing	E. Simonetti	Open	27.50	29.50
93-27-005	Chester Adams	E. Simonetti	Open	23.50	24.50
93-27-006	Amos Eleazor Whipple	E. Simonetti	Open	23.50	24.50
94-27-007	Mayor Jeremiah Bradshaw Smith	E. Simonetti	Open	23.50	24.50
94-27-008	Margaret Louise Winslow Smith	E. Simonetti	Open	23.50	24.50
94-27-009	Mary Beth Lancaster	E. Simonetti	Open	23.50	24.50
94-27-010	Albert Sinclair	E. Simonetti	Open	23.50	24.50
94-27-011	Jack O'Halloran	E. Simonetti	Open	23.50	24.50
94-27-012	Caroline Williams	E. Simonetti	Open	23.50	29.50
Roman, Inc.	**Fontanini Heirloom Nativity**				
74-28-001	5" Mary (5")	E. Simonetti	Closed	2.50	9.50
74-28-002	Jesus (5")	E. Simonetti	Closed	2.50	9.50
74-28-003	Joseph (5")	E. Simonetti	Closed	2.50	9.50
79-28-004	Gabriel (5")	E. Simonetti	Retrd.	11.50	11.50
79-28-005	Melchior (5")	E. Simonetti	Retrd.	11.50	11.50
79-28-006	Gaspar (5")	E. Simonetti	Retrd.	11.50	11.50
79-28-007	Balthazar (5")	E. Simonetti	Retrd.	11.50	11.50
91-28-008	New (5") Joseph	E. Simonetti	Open	11.50	11.50
91-28-009	New (5") Mary	E. Simonetti	Open	11.50	11.50
91-28-010	New (5") Jesus	E. Simonetti	Open	11.50	11.50
93-28-011	New Gabriel (5")	E. Simonetti	Open	11.50	11.50
93-28-012	New Melchior (5")	E. Simonetti	Open	11.50	11.50
93-28-013	New Gaspar (5")	E. Simonetti	Open	11.50	11.50
93-28-014	New Balthazar (5")	E. Simonetti	Open	11.50	11.50
Roman, Inc.	**Fontanini Heirloom Nativity Limited Edition Figurines**				
92-29-001	Ariel	E. Simonetti	Yr.Iss.	29.50	29.50
93-29-002	Jeshua & Adin	E. Simonetti	Yr.Iss.	29.50	29.50
93-29-003	Abigail & Peter	E. Simonetti	25,000	29.50	29.50
Roman, Inc.	**Fontanini Collectors' Club Member's Only**				
91-30-001	The Pilgrimage	E. Simonetti	Yr.Iss.	24.95	24.95
92-30-002	She Rescued Me	E. Simonetti	Yr.Iss.	23.50	23.50
93-30-003	Christmas Symphony	E. Simonetti	Yr.Iss.	13.50	13.50
94-30-004	Sweet Harmony	E. Simonetti	Yr.Iss.	13.50	13.50
Roman, Inc.	**First Year Fontanini Collectors' Club Welcome Gift**				
90-31-001	I Found Him	E. Simonetti	Open	Gift	N/A
Roman, Inc.	**Fontanini Collectors' Club Special Event Piece**				
90-32-001	Gideon	E. Simonetti	Open	15.00	15.00
Roman, Inc.	**Fontanini Collector Club Renewal Gift**				
93-33-001	He Comforts Me	E. Simonetti	Yr.Iss.	12.50	12.50
94-33-002	I'm Heaven Bound	E. Simonetti	Yr.Iss.	12.50	12.50
Roman, Inc.	**Fontanini 5" Collection**				
94-34-001	Aaron (Resculptured)	E. Simonetti	Open	11.50	11.50
94-34-002	Len (Resculptured)	E. Simonetti	Open	11.50	11.50
94-34-003	Miriam (Resculptured)	E. Simonetti	Open	11.50	11.50
94-34-004	Josiah (Resculptured)	E. Simonetti	Open	11.50	11.50
94-34-005	Jeremiah	E. Simonetti	Open	11.50	11.50
94-34-006	Rachel (Resculptured)	E. Simonetti	Open	11.50	11.50

Company Number	Name	Series Artist	Edition Limit	Issue Price	Quote
Roman, Inc.	**Fontanini 7.5" Collection**				
94-35-001	Gariel (Resculptured)	E. Simonetti	Open	24.50	24.50
94-35-002	Mary (Resculptured)	E. Simonetti	Open	24.50	24.50
94-35-003	Joseph (Resculptured)	E. Simonetti	Open	24.50	24.50
94-35-004	Jesus (Resculptured)	E. Simonetti	Open	24.50	24.50
94-35-005	Miriam	E. Simonetti	Open	24.50	24.50
94-35-006	Deborah	E. Simonetti	Open	24.50	24.50
94-35-007	Michael	E. Simonetti	Open	24.50	24.50
94-35-008	Eli	E. Simonetti	Open	24.50	24.50
94-35-009	Rachel	E. Simonetti	Open	24.50	24.50
Roman, Inc.	**The Richard Judson Zolan Collection**				
92-36-001	Summer at the Seashore	R.J. Zolan	1,200	125.00	125.00
94-36-002	Terrace Dancing	R.J. Zolan	1,200	175.00	175.00
Roman, Inc.	**Tender Expressions**				
92-37-001	You Are Always in the Thoughts That Fill My Day	B. Sargent	Open	27.50	27.50
92-37-002	I Even Love the Rain When You Share My Umbrella	B. Sargent	Open	27.50	27.50
92-37-003	I Tell Everyone How Special You Are	B. Sargent	Open	27.50	27.50
92-37-004	The Greatest Love Shines From A Mother's Face	B. Sargent	Open	27.50	27.50
92-37-005	I Count My Blessings...And There You Are!	B. Sargent	Open	27.50	27.50
92-37-006	Thoughts Of You Are In My Heart	B. Sargent	Open	27.50	27.50
94-37-007	Life Gives Us Precious Moments To Fill Our Hearts With Joy	B. Sargent	Open	39.50	39.50
94-37-008	Each Day is Special...And So Are You	B. Sargent	Open	29.50	29.50
94-37-009	Tender Moments Last Forever	B. Sargent	Open	29.50	29.50
94-37-010	The Tiniest Flower Blossoms With Love	B. Sargent	Open	29.50	29.50
94-37-011	Know What's Special About You?... Everything	B. Sargent	Open	29.50	29.50
94-37-012	I'm On Top of the World When I'm With You	B. Sargent	Open	29.50	29.50
94-37-013	Magic Happens When You Smile	B. Sargent	Open	29.50	29.50
94-37-014	I Saved A Place For You In My Heart	B. Sargent	Open	29.50	29.50
94-37-015	You're In Every Little Prayer (Boy)	B. Sargent	Open	29.50	29.50
94-37-016	You're In Every Little Prayer (Girl)	B. Sargent	Open	29.50	29.50
94-37-017	You Fill My Days With Tiny Blessings	B. Sargent	Open	39.50	39.50
94-37-018	Safely Rest, By Angels Blessed	B. Sargent	Open	32.50	32.50
94-37-019	Home Is In Mother's Heart	B. Sargent	Open	32.50	32.50
Roman, Inc.	**Bill Jauquet Americana Collection**				
93-38-001	Sunday Driver	B. Jauquet	Open	395.00	395.00
93-38-002	Sunrise Ride	B. Jauquet	Open	175.00	175.00
93-38-003	Last Train Out	B. Jauquet	Open	125.00	125.00
Roman, Inc.	**Divine Servant**				
93-39-001	Divine Servant, porcelain sculpture	M. Greiner Jr.	Open	59.50	59.50
93-39-002	Divine Servant, resin sculpture	M. Greiner Jr.	Open	250.00	250.00
93-39-003	Divine Servant, pewter sculpture	M. Greiner Jr.	Open	200.00	200.00
Royal Doulton	**Royal Doulton Figurines**				
24-01-001	Tony Weller HN684	C. Noke	Closed	N/A	1800.00
33-01-002	Beethoven	R. Garbe	25	N/A	6500.00
75-01-003	The Milkmaid HN2057A	L. Harradine	Closed	N/A	225.00
87-01-004	Life Boatman HN2764	W. Harper	Closed	N/A	300.00
Royal Doulton	**Royalty**				
73-02-001	Queen Elizabeth II HN2502	P. Davis	750	N/A	1800.00
80-02-002	Queen Mother HN2882	P. Davies	1,500	650.00	1250.00
81-02-003	Duke Of Edinburgh HN2386	P. Davies	750	395.00	700.00
81-02-004	Prince Of Wales HN2883	E. Griffiths	1,500	395.00	750.00
81-02-005	Prince Of Wales HN2884	E. Griffiths	1,500	750.00	1000.00
82-02-006	Queen Elizabeth II HN2878	E. Griffiths	2,500	N/A	N/A
82-02-007	Lady Diana Spencer HN2885	E. Griffiths	1,500	395.00	600.00
82-02-008	Princess Of Wales HN2887	E. Griffiths	1,500	750.00	1200.00
86-02-009	Duchess Of York HN3086	E. Griffiths	1,500	495.00	750.00
89-02-010	Queen Elizabeth, the Queen Mother as the Duchess of York HN3230	P. Parsons	9,500	N/A	N/A
90-02-011	Queen Elizabeth, the Queen Mother HN3189	E. Griffiths	2,500	N/A	N/A
92-02-012	Queen Elizabeth II, 2nd. Version HN3440	P. Gee	3,500	460.00	460.00
Royal Doulton	**Lady Musicians**				
70-03-001	Cello HN2331	P. Davies	750	250.00	1000.00
71-03-002	Virginals HN2427	P. Davies	750	250.00	1200-1500.
72-03-003	Lute HN2431	P. Davies	750	250.00	950.00
72-03-004	Violin HN2432	P. Davies	750	250.00	900-950.
73-03-005	Harp HN2482	P. Davies	750	250.00	1500-1800.
73-03-006	Flute HN2483	P. Davies	750	250.00	950-1100.
74-03-007	Chitarrone HN2700	P. Davies	750	250.00	700.00
74-03-008	Cymbals HN2699	P. Davies	750	325.00	700.00
75-03-009	Dulcimer HN2798	P. Davies	750	375.00	700.00
75-03-010	Hurdy Gurdy HN2796	P. Davies	750	375.00	700.00
76-03-011	French Horn HN2795	P. Davies	750	400.00	650.00
76-03-012	Viola d'Amore HN2797	P. Davies	750	400.00	650.00
Royal Doulton	**Dancers Of The World**				
77-04-001	Dancers, Indian Temple HN2830	M. Davies	750	400.00	1000-1200.
77-04-002	Dancers, Flamenco HN2831	M. Davies	750	400.00	1200-1500.
78-04-003	Dancers, Philippine HN2439	M. Davies	750	450.00	750-900.
78-04-004	Dancers, Scottish HN2436	M. Davies	750	450.00	850-1200.
79-04-005	Dancers, Kurdish HN2867	M. Davies	750	550.00	550-650.
79-04-006	Dancers, Mexican HN2866	M. Davies	750	550.00	550-650.
80-04-007	Dancers, Polish HN2836	M. Davies	750	750.00	850-950.
80-04-008	Dancers, Chinese HN2840	M. Davies	750	750.00	750-800.
81-04-009	Dancers, Breton HN2383	M. Davies	750	850.00	650-750.
81-04-010	Dancers, West Indian HN2384	M. Davies	750	850.00	600.00
82-04-011	Dancers, Balinese HN2808	M. Davies	750	950.00	600.00
82-04-012	Dancers, No. American Indian HN2809	M. Davies	750	950.00	600.00
Royal Doulton	**Soldiers of The Revolution**				
75-05-001	Soldiers, Georgia HN2779	E. Griffiths	350	750.00	850.00
75-05-002	Soldiers, New Hampshire HN2780	E. Griffiths	350	750.00	750.00
75-05-003	Soldiers, New Jersey HN2752	E. Griffiths	350	750.00	2000.00
75-05-004	Soldiers, South Carolina HN2717	E. Griffiths	350	750.00	850.00
76-05-005	Soldiers, New York HN2260	E. Griffiths	350	750.00	750.00
76-05-006	Soldiers, North Carolina HN2754	E. Griffiths	350	750.00	750.00
76-05-007	Soldiers, Maryland HN2815	E. Griffiths	350	750.00	750.00
77-05-008	Soldiers, Delaware HN2761	E. Griffiths	350	750.00	750.00
77-05-009	Soldiers, Massachusetts HN2760	E. Griffiths	350	750.00	750.00
77-05-010	Soldiers, Rhode Island HN2759	E. Griffiths	350	750.00	750.00
78-05-011	Soldiers, Connecticut HN2845	E. Griffiths	350	750.00	750.00
78-05-012	Soldiers, Pennsylvania HN2846	E. Griffiths	350	750.00	750.00
78-05-013	Soldiers, Virginia HN2844	E. Griffiths	350	1500.00	2700.00

Number	Name	Artist	Edition Limit	Issue Price	Quote
Royal Doulton		**Femmes Fatales**			
79-06-001	Cleopatra HN2868	P. Davies	750	750.00	1350.00
81-06-002	Helen of Troy HN2387	P. Davies	750	1250.00	1250-1400.
82-06-003	Queen of Sheba HN2328	P. Davies	750	1250.00	1250-1400.
83-06-004	Tz'u-Hsi HN2391	P. Davies	750	1250.00	1250.00
84-06-005	Eve HN2466	P. Davies	750	1250.00	1250.00
85-06-006	Lucrezia Borgia HN2342	P. Davies	750	1250.00	1250.00
Royal Doulton		**Myths & Maidens**			
82-07-001	Lady & Unicorn HN2825	R. Jefferson	S/O	2500.00	2500-3500.
83-07-002	Leda & Swan HN2826	R. Jefferson	300	2950.00	2950-3200.
84-07-003	Juno & Peacock HN2827	R. Jefferson	300	2950.00	2950-3200.
85-07-004	Europa & Bull HN2828	R. Jefferson	300	2950.00	2950-3200.
86-07-005	Diana The Huntress HN2829	R. Jefferson	300	2950.00	2950-3200.
Royal Doulton		**Gentle Arts**			
84-08-001	Spinning HN2390	P. Davies	750	1250.00	1250-1400.
85-08-002	Tapestry Weaving HN3048	P. Parsons	750	1250.00	1250.00
86-08-003	Writing HN3049	P. Parsons	750	1350.00	1350.00
87-08-004	Painting HN3012	P. Parsons	750	1350.00	1350.00
88-08-006	Flower Arranging HN3040	P. Parsons	750	1350.00	1350.00
89-08-005	Adornment HN3015	P. Parsons	750	1350.00	1350.00
Royal Doulton		**Ships Figureheads**			
80-09-001	Ajax HN2908	S. Keenan	950	N/A	550-700.
80-09-002	Benmore HN2909	S. Keenan	950	N/A	550-700.
81-09-003	Lalla Rookh HN2910	S. Keenan	950	N/A	750.00
81-09-004	Lord Nelson HN2928	S. Keenan	950	N/A	850.00
82-09-005	Pocahontas HN2930	S. Keenan	950	N/A	950.00
82-09-006	Chieftain HN2929	S. Keenan	950	N/A	850.00
83-09-007	Hibernia HN2932	S. Keenan	950	N/A	950.00
83-09-008	Mary, Queen of Scots HN2931	S. Keenan	950	N/A	1200.00
Royal Doulton		**Les Saisons**			
86-10-001	Automne HN3068	R. Jefferson	300	850.00	950.00
87-10-002	Printemps HN3061	R. Jefferson	300	850.00	850.00
88-10-003	L'Hiver HN3069	R. Jefferson	300	850.00	850.00
89-10-004	L'Ete HN3067	R. Jefferson	300	850.00	895.00
Royal Doulton		**Queens of Realm**			
86-11-001	Queen Elizabeth I HN3099	P. Parsons	S/O	495.00	495-650.
87-11-002	Queen Victoria HN3125	P Parsons	S/O	495.00	850-1000.
88-11-003	Queen Anne HN3141	P. Parsons	Retrd.	525.00	550.00
89-11-004	Mary, Queen of Scots HN3142	P. Parsons	S/O	550.00	850-950.
Royal Doulton		**Gainsborough Ladies**			
90-12-001	Mary, Countess Howe HN3007	P. Gee	5,000	650.00	650-700.
91-12-002	Lady Sheffield HN3008	P. Gee	5,000	650.00	650-700.
91-12-003	Hon Frances Duncombe HN3009	P. Gee	5,000	650.00	650-700.
91-12-004	Countess of Sefton HN3010	P. Gee	5,000	650.00	650-700.
Royal Doulton		**Reynolds Collection**			
91-13-001	Lady Worsley HN3318	P. Gee	5,000	550.00	600.00
92-13-002	Countess Harrington HN3317	P. Gee	5,000	550.00	595-700.
92-13-003	Mrs. Hugh Bonfoy HN3319	P. Gee	5,000	550.00	595-700.
93-13-004	Countess Spencer HN3320	P. Gee	5,000	595.00	600.00
Royal Doulton		**Age of Innocence**			
91-14-001	Feeding Time HN3373	N. Pedley	9,500	245.00	290.00
91-14-002	Making Friends HN3372	N. Pedley	9,500	270.00	310.00
91-14-003	Puppy Love HN3371	N. Pedley	9,500	270.00	310.00
92-14-004	First Outing HN3377	N. Pedley	9,500	275.00	310.00
Royal Doulton		**Prestige Figures**			
50-15-001	King Charles HN2084	C.J. Noke	N/A	2500.00	2500.00
52-15-002	Jack Point HN2080	C.J. Noke	N/A	2900.00	3100.00
52-15-003	Princess Badoura HN2081	N/A	N/A	28000.00	30000.00
52-15-004	The Moor HN2082	C.J. Noke	N/A	2500.00	2700.00
64-15-005	Matador and Bull HN2324	M. Davis	N/A	21500.00	23000.00
64-15-006	Indian Brave HN2376	M. Davis	500	2500.00	5700.00
64-15-007	The Palio HN2428	M. Davis	500	2500.00	6500.00
78-15-008	St George and Dragon HN2856	W.K. Harper	N/A	13600.00	14500.00
82-15-009	Columbine HN2738	D. Tootle	N/A	1250.00	1350.00
82-15-010	Harlequin HN2737	D. Tootle	N/A	1250.00	1350.00
Royal Doulton		**Figure of the Year**			
91-16-001	Amy HN3316	P. Gee	Closed	195.00	300-550.
92-16-002	Mary HN3375	P. Gee	Closed	225.00	300.00
93-16-003	Patricia HN3365	V. Annand	Closed	250.00	250.00
94-16-004	Jennifer HN3447	P. Gee	Yr.Iss.	250.00	250.00
Royal Doulton		**British Sporting Heritage**			
93-17-001	Henley HN3367	V. Annand	5,000	475.00	475.00
94-17-002	Ascot HN3471	V. Annand	5,000	475.00	475.00
Royal Doulton		**Williamsburg**			
60-18-001	Blacksmith HN2240	M. Davies	Closed	N/A	175-320.
60-18-002	Hostess HN2209	M. Davies	Closed	N/A	175-320.
60-18-003	Silversmith HN2208	M. Davies	Closed	N/A	200-320.
60-18-004	Boy HN2183	M. Davies	Closed	N/A	125.00
60-18-005	Gentleman From Williamsburg HN2227	M. Davies	Closed	N/A	N/A
60-18-006	Lady From Williamsburg HN2228	M. Davies	Closed	N/A	N/A
60-18-007	Royal Govenor's Cook HN2233	M. Davies	Closed	N/A	N/A
60-18-008	Wigmaker of Williamsburg HN2239	M. Davies	Closed	N/A	N/A
64-18-009	Child of Williamsburg HN2154	M. Davies	Closed	N/A	N/A
Royal Doulton		**Limited Editions**			
92-19-001	Christopher Columbus HN3392	A. Maslankowski	1,492	1950.00	1950.00
92-19-002	Napoleon at Waterloo HN3429	A. Maslankowski	1,500	1900.00	1900.00
93-19-003	Lt. General Ulysses S. Grant HN3403	R. Tabbenor	5,000	1175.00	1175.00
93-19-004	General Robert E. Lee HN3404	R. Tabbenor	5,000	1175.00	1175.00
93-19-005	Duke of Wellington HN3432	A. Maslankowski	1,500	1750.00	1750.00
93-19-006	Winston S. Churchill HN3433	A. Maslankowski	5,000	595.00	595.00
93-19-007	Vice Admiral Lord Nelson HN3489	A. Maslankowski	950	1750.00	1750.00
94-19-008	Field Marshal Montgomery HN3405	N/A	1,944	1100.00	1100.00
Royal Doulton		**Great Lovers**			
93-20-001	Romeo and Juliet HN3113	R. Jefferson	150	5250.00	5250.00
Royal Doulton		**Classic Heroes**			
93-21-001	Long John Silver	A. Maslankowski	N/A	250.00	250.00
93-21-002	Captain Hook	R. Tabbenor	N/A	250.00	250.00
93-21-003	Robin Hood	A. Maslankowski	N/A	250.00	250.00
93-21-004	Dick Turpin	R. Tabbenor	N/A	250.00	250.00
94-21-005	D' Artagnan	R. Tabbenor	N/A	260.00	260.00
94-21-006	Pied Piper	A. Maslankowski	N/A	260.00	260.00
Royal Doulton		**Images**			
91-22-001	Bride & Groom HN3281	R. Tabbenor	Open	85.00	85.00
91-22-002	Bridesmaid HN3280	R. Tabbenor	Open	90.00	90.00
91-22-003	Brothers HN3191	E. Griffiths	Open	90.00	90.00
93-22-004	Brother & Sister HN3460	A. Hughes	Retrd.	52.50	52.50
81-22-005	Family HN2720	E. Griffiths	Open	210.00	210.00
88-22-006	First Love HN2747	D. Tootle	Open	170.00	170.00
91-22-007	First Steps HN3282	R. Tabbenor	Open	142.00	142.00
XX-22-008	Gift of Freedom HN3443	N/A	Retrd.	90.00	90.00
89-22-009	Happy Anniversary HN3254	D. Tootle	Open	315.00	315.00
81-22-010	Lovers HN2762	D. Tootle	Retrd.	205.00	205.00
80-22-011	Mothers & Daughters HN2841	E. Griffiths	Open	210.00	210.00
XX-22-012	Our First Christmas HN3452	N/A	Open	185.00	185.00
89-22-013	Over the Threshold HN3274	R. Tabbenor	Open	310.00	310.00
83-22-014	Sisters HN3018	P. Parson	Open	90.00	90.00
87-22-015	Wedding Day HN2748	D. Tootle	Open	205.00	205.00
Royal Doulton		**Limited Edition Character Jugs**			
88-23-001	Sir Francis Drake D6805	P .Gee	Closed	N/A	100.00
90-23-002	Henry VIII	N/A	Closed	450.00	175-450.
91-23-003	Henry VIII	W. Harper	1,991	395.00	950.00
91-23-004	Santa Claus Miniature D6900	N/A	5,000	50.00	55.00
91-23-005	Jester	S. Taylor	2,500	125.00	150.00
92-23-006	Mrs. Claus Miniature D6922	N/A	2,500	50.00	55.00
92-23-007	King Charles I D6917	W. Harper	2,500	450.00	450.00
92-23-008	Town Crier D6895	S. Taylor	2,500	175.00	175.00
92-23-009	William Shakespeare D6933	W. Harper	2,500	625.00	625.00
92-23-010	Abraham Lincoln D6936	S. Taylor	2,500	190.00	190.00
93-23-011	Napoleon (Large size) D6941	S. Taylor	2,000	225.00	225.00
94-23-012	Thomas Jefferson	N/A	2,500	200.00	200.00
93-23-013	Clown Toby	N/A	3,000	175.00	175.00
XX-23-014	Father Christmas Toby	N/A	3,500	125.00	125.00
94-23-015	Leprechaun Toby	N/A	2,500	150.00	150.00
XX-23-016	Snake Charmer	N/A	2,500	210.00	210.00
93-23-017	Elf Miniature D6942	N/A	2,500	55.00	55.00
Royal Doulton		**Character Jug of the Year**			
91-24-001	Fortune Teller D6824	S. Taylor	Closed	130.00	225.00
92-24-002	Winston Churchill D6907	S. Taylor	Closed	195.00	195.00
93-24-003	Vice-Admiral Lord Nelson D6932	S. Taylor	Closed	225.00	225.00
94-24-004	Captain Hook	N/A	Yr.Iss.	235.00	235.00
Royal Doulton		**Star Crossed Lovers Character Jugs**			
85-25-001	Anthony & Cleopatra D6728	M. Abberley	S/O	195.00	195.00
86-25-002	Napoleon & Josephine D6750	M. Abberley	S/O	195.00	195.00
88-25-003	Samson & Delilah D6787	S. Taylor	9,500	195.00	195.00
89-25-004	King Arthur & Guinevere D6836	S. Taylor	9,500	195.00	195.00
Royal Doulton		**Antagonists Character Jugs**			
83-26-001	Ulysses S. Grant & Robert E. Lee D6698	M. Abberley	9,500	N/A	100-295.
84-26-002	Chief Sitting Bull & George Armstrong Custer -D6712	M. Abberley	9,500	N/A	100-150.
85-26-003	Davey Crockett & Santa Anna D6729	M. Abberley	9,500	N/A	100-125.
86-26-004	George Washington & George III D6749	M. Abberley	9,500	195.00	150-195.
Royal Doulton		**Character Jugs**			
XX-27-001	Airman, sm.	N/A	Open	82.50	82.50
XX-27-002	Angler, sm.	N/A	Open	82.50	82.50
XX-27-003	Beefeater, lg.	N/A	Open	150.00	150.00
XX-27-004	Beefeater, sm.	N/A	Open	82.50	82.50
XX-27-005	Columbus, lg.	N/A	Open	160.00	160.00
XX-27-006	Clown, lg.	N/A	Open	205.00	205.00
XX-27-007	D'Artagnan, lg.	N/A	Open	150.00	150.00
XX-27-008	D'Artagnan, sm.	N/A	Open	82.50	82.50
XX-27-009	Equestrian, sm.	N/A	Open	82.50	82.50
XX-27-010	George Washington, lg.	N/A	Open	150.00	150.00
XX-27-011	Golfer, lg.	N/A	Open	150.00	150.00
XX-27-012	Graduate-Male, sm.	N/A	Open	85.00	85.00
XX-27-013	Guardsman, lg.	N/A	Open	150.00	150.00
XX-27-014	Gurardsman, sm.	N/A	Open	82.50	82.50
XX-27-015	Guy Fawkes, lg.	N/A	Open	150.00	150.00
XX-27-016	Henry VIII, lg.	N/A	Open	150.00	150.00
XX-27-017	Henry VIII, sm.	N/A	Open	82.50	82.50
XX-27-018	Jockey, sm.	N/A	Open	82.50	82.50
XX-27-019	Lawyer, lg.	N/A	Open	150.00	150.00
XX-27-020	Lawyer, sm.	N/A	Open	82.50	82.50
XX-27-021	Leprechaun, lg	N/A	Open	205.00	205.00
XX-27-022	Leprechaun, sm.	N/A	Open	85.00	85.00
XX-27-023	London Bobby, lg.	N/A	Open	150.00	150.00
XX-27-024	London Bobby, sm.	N/A	Open	82.50	82.50
XX-27-025	Long John Silver, lg.	N/A	Open	150.00	150.00
XX-27-026	Long John Silver, sm.	N/A	Open	82.50	82.50
XX-27-027	Merlin, lg.	N/A	Open	150.00	150.00
XX-27-028	Merlin, sm.	N/A	Open	82.50	82.50
XX-27-029	Modern Golfer, sm.	N/A	Open	82.50	82.50
XX-27-030	Rip Van Winkle, lg.	N/A	Open	150.00	150.00
XX-27-031	Rip Van Winkle, sm.	N/A	Open	82.50	82.50
XX-27-032	Sailor, sm.	N/A	Open	82.50	82.50
XX-27-033	Santa Claus, lg.	N/A	Open	150.00	150.00
XX-27-034	Santa Claus, sm.	N/A	Open	82.50	82.50
XX-27-034	Shakespeare, sm.	N/A	Open	99.00	99.00
XX-27-035	The Sleuth, lg.	N/A	Open	150.00	150.00
XX-27-036	The Sleuth, sm.	N/A	Open	82.50	82.50
XX-27-037	Snooker Player, sm.	N/A	Open	82.50	82.50
XX-27-038	Soldier, sm.	N/A	Open	82.50	82.50
XX-27-039	Town Crier, lg.	N/A	Open	170.00	170.00
XX-27-040	Winston Churchill, sm.	N/A	Open	99.00	99.00
XX-27-041	Wizard, lg.	N/A	Open	175.00	175.00
XX-27-042	Wizard, sm.	N/A	Open	85.00	85.00
XX-27-043	Yeoman of the Guard, lg.	N/A	Open	150.00	150.00
Royal Doulton		**Diamond Anniversary Tinies**			
XX-28-001	John Barleycorn	N/A	2,500	350.00	350.00
XX-28-002	Dick Turpin	N/A	2,500	Set	Set
XX-28-003	Jester	N/A	2,500	Set	Set
XX-28-004	Granny	N/A	2,500	Set	Set
XX-28-005	Parson Brown	N/A	2,500	Set	Set
XX-28-006	The Cellarer	N/A	2,500	Set	Set
Royal Doulton		**Bunnykins**			
XX-29-001	Be Prepared	N/A	Open	40.00	40.00

Company	Series				
Number	**Name**	**Artist**	**Edition Limit**	**Issue Price**	**Quote**
XX-29-002	Bed Time	N/A	Open	40.00	40.00
XX-29-003	Bride	N/A	Open	40.00	40.00
XX-29-004	Brownie	N/A	Retrd.	39.00	39.00
XX-29-005	Cook	N/A	Open	35.00	35.00
XX-29-006	Father, Mother, Victoria	N/A	Open	40.00	40.00
XX-29-007	Fireman	N/A	Open	40.00	40.00
XX-29-008	Fisherman	N/A	Retrd.	39.00	39.00
XX-29-009	Groom	N/A	Open	40.00	40.00
XX-29-010	Halloween Bunnykin	N/A	Retrd.	50.00	50.00
XX-29-011	Happy Birthday	N/A	Open	40.00	40.00
XX-29-012	Harry	N/A	Retrd.	34.00	34.00
XX-29-013	Helping Mother	N/A	Retrd.	34.00	34.00
XX-29-014	Home Run	N/A	Retrd.	39.00	39.00
XX-29-015	Ice Cream	N/A	Retrd.	39.00	39.00
XX-29-016	Mr. Bunnykin Easter Parade	N/A	Retrd.	39.00	39.00
XX-29-017	Mrs. Bunnykin Easter Parade	N/A	Open	40.00	40.00
XX-29-018	Nurse	N/A	Open	35.00	35.00
XX-29-019	Paper Boy	N/A	Retrd.	39.00	39.00
XX-29-020	Playtime	N/A	Retrd.	34.00	34.00
XX-29-021	Policeman	N/A	Open	40.00	40.00
XX-29-022	Polly	N/A	Retrd.	34.00	34.00
XX-29-023	Santa Bunnykins	N/A	Open	40.00	40.00
XX-29-024	School Days	N/A	Open	40.00	40.00
XX-29-025	School Master	N/A	Open	40.00	40.00
XX-29-026	Sleigh Ride	N/A	Open	40.00	40.00
XX-29-027	Sleepytime	N/A	Retrd.	39.00	39.00
XX-29-028	Story Time	N/A	Open	35.00	35.00
XX-29-029	Susan	N/A	Retrd.	34.00	34.00
XX-29-030	Sweetheart Bunnykin	N/A	Open	40.00	40.00
XX-29-031	Tom	N/A	Retrd.	34.00	34.00
XX-29-032	Uncle Sam	N/A	Open	40.00	40.00
XX-29-033	William	N/A	Retrd.	3400	34.00
Royal Doulton	**Beatrix Potter Figures**				
XX-30-001	And This Pig Had None P3319	N/A	Open	29.95	29.95
XX-30-002	Appley Dapply P2333	N/A	Open	29.95	29.95
XX-30-003	Aunt Pettitoes P2276	N/A	Retrd.	29.95	29.95
XX-30-004	Babbity Bumble P2971	N/A	Retrd.	29.95	29.95
XX-30-005	Benjamin Bunny P1105	N/A	Open	29.95	29.95
XX-30-006	Benjamin Ate a Lettuce Leaf P3317	N/A	Open	29.95	29.95
XX-30-007	Benjamin Bunny Sat on a Bank P2803	N/A	Open	29.95	29.95
XX-30-008	Benjamin Wakes Up P3234	N/A	Open	29.95	29.95
XX-30-009	Cecily Parsley P1941	N/A	Retrd.	29.95	29.95
XX-30-010	Chippy Hackee P2627	N/A	Retrd.	29.95	29.95
XX-30-011	Cottontail at Lunchtime P2878	N/A	Open	29.95	29.95
XX-30-012	Cousin Ribby P2284	N/A	Retrd.	29.95	29.95
XX-30-013	Diggory Diggory Delvet P2713	N/A	Open	29.95	29.95
XX-30-014	Fierce Bad Rabbit P2586	N/A	Open	29.95	29.95
XX-30-015	Flopsy Mopsy and Cottontail P1274	N/A	Open	29.95	29.95
XX-30-016	Foxy Whiskered Gentleman P1277	N/A	Open	29.95	29.95
XX-30-017	Gentleman Mouse Made a Bow P3200	N/A	Open	29.95	29.95
XX-30-018	Goody Tiptoes P1675	N/A	Open	29.95	29.95
XX-30-019	Hunca Munca P1198	N/A	Open	29.95	29.95
XX-30-020	Hunca Munca Spills the Beas P3288	N/A	Open	29.95	29.95
XX-30-021	Hunca Munca Sweeping P2584	N/A	Open	29.95	29.95
XX-30-022	Jemima Puddleduck P1092	N/A	Open	29.95	29.95
XX-30-023	Jemima Puddleduck Made a Feather Nest -P2823	N/A	Open	29.95	29.95
XX-30-024	Jeremy Fisher P1157	N/A	Open	29.95	29.95
XX-30-025	John Joiner P2965	N/A	Open	29.95	29.95
XX-30-026	Johnny Townmouse P1276	N/A	Retrd.	29.95	29.95
XX-30-027	Lady Mouse P1183	N/A	Open	29.95	29.95
XX-30-028	Lady Mouse Made a Curtsy P3220	N/A	Open	29.95	29.95
XX-30-029	Little Black Rabbit P2585	N/A	Open	29.95	29.95
XX-30-030	Little Pig Robinson Spying P3031	N/A	Retrd.	29.95	29.95
XX-30-031	Mother Ladybird P2966	N/A	Open	29.95	29.95
XX-30-032	Mr. Alderman Ptolemy P2424	N/A	Open	29.95	29.95
XX-30-033	Mr. Benjamin Bunny P1940	N/A	Open	29.95	29.95
XX-30-034	Mr. Drake Puddleduck P2628	N/A	Open	29.95	29.95
XX-30-035	Mr. Jackson P2453	N/A	Open	29.95	29.95
XX-30-036	Mr. Tod P3091	N/A	Retrd.	29.95	29.95
XX-30-037	Mrs. Flopsy Bunny P1942	N/A	Open	29.95	29.95
XX-30-038	Mrs. Rabbit P1200	N/A	Open	29.95	29.95
XX-30-039	Mrs. Rabbit Cooking P3278	N/A	Open	29.95	29.95
XX-30-040	Mrs. Rabbit with Bunnies P2543	N/A	Open	29.95	29.95
XX-30-041	Mrs. Ribby P1199	N/A	Open	29.95	29.95
XX-30-042	Mrs. Tittlemouse P1103	N/A	Retrd.	29.95	29.95
XX-30-043	No More Twist P3325	N/A	Open	29.95	29.95
XX-30-044	Old Mr. Bouncer P2956	N/A	Open	29.95	29.95
XX-30-045	Old Mr. Brown P1796	N/A	Open	29.95	29.95
XX-30-046	Old Woman Who Lived in a Shoe P1545	N/A	Open	29.95	29.95
XX-30-047	Old Woman Who Lived in a Shoe, Knitting P2804	N/A	Open	29.95	29.95
XX-30-048	Peter Rabbit P1098	N/A	Open	29.95	29.95
XX-30-049	Pig Robinson P1104	N/A	Open	29.95	29.95
XX-30-050	Pigling Bland P1365	N/A	Open	29.95	29.95
XX-30-051	Poorly Peter Rabbit P2560	N/A	Open	29.95	29.95
XX-30-052	Rebeccah Puddleduck P2647	N/A	Open	29.95	29.95
XX-30-053	Ribby and the Patty Pan P3280	N/A	Open	29.95	29.95
XX-30-054	Sally Henry Penney P2452	N/A	Retrd.	29.95	29.95
XX-30-055	Samuel Whiskers P1106	N/A	Open	29.95	29.95
XX-30-056	Squirrel Nutkin P1102	N/A	Open	29.95	29.95
XX-30-057	Tabitha Twitchitt P1678	N/A	Open	29.95	29.95
XX-30-058	Tabitha Twitchitt with Miss Moppett P2544	N/A	Retrd.	29.95	29.95
XX-30-059	Tailor Gloucester P1108	N/A	Open	29.95	29.95
XX-30-060	Tiggy Windle P1107	N/A	Open	29.95	29.95
XX-30-061	Tiggy Winkle Takes Tea P2877	N/A	Open	29.95	29.95
XX-30-062	Timmy Tiptoes P1101	N/A	Open	29.95	29.95
XX-30-063	Timmie Willie P1109	N/A	Retrd.	29.95	29.95
XX-30-064	Timmie Willie Sleeping P2996	N/A	Open	29.95	29.95
XX-30-065	Tom Kitten P1100	N/A	Open	29.95	29.95
XX-30-066	Tom Thumb P2989	N/A	Open	29.95	29.95
XX-30-067	Tommy Brock P1348	N/A	Open	29.95	29.95
Royal Doulton	**Beatrix Potter Figures**				
XX-31-001	Benjamin Bunny with Peter Rabbit P2509	N/A	Open	50.00	50.00
XX-31-002	Christmas Stocking P3257	N/A	Open	65.00	65.00
XX-31-003	Cottontail at Lunchtime P2878	N/A	Open	34.00	34.00
XX-31-004	Foxy Reading Country News P3219	N/A	Open	55.00	55.00
XX-31-005	Goody and Timmy Tiptoes P2957	N/A	Open	55.00	55.00
XX-31-006	Hunca Munca Spills the Beads P3288	N/A	Open	34.00	34.00
XX-31-007	Jemema Puddleduck -Foxy Whiskered Gentleman P3193	N/A	Open	80.00	80.00
XX-31-008	Jemima Puddleduck-Large size P3373	N/A	Open	65.00	65.00

Company	Series				
Number	**Name**	**Artist**	**Edition Limit**	**Issue Price**	**Quote**
XX-31-009	Jeremy Fisher Digging P3090	N/A	Open	80.00	80.00
XX-31-010	Johnny Townmouse with Bag P3094	N/A	Open	50.00	50.00
XX-31-011	Miss Dormouse P3251	N/A	Open	65.00	65.00
XX-31-012	Mittens & Moppet P3197	N/A	Open	50.00	50.00
XX-31-013	Mother Ladybird P2966	N/A	Open	34.00	34.00
XX-31-014	Old Mr. Bouncer P2956	N/A	Open	34.00	34.00
XX-31-015	Peter Rabbit-Large size P3356	N/A	Open	65.00	65.00
XX-31-016	Peter & The Red Handkerchief P3242	N/A	Open	45.00	45.00
XX-31-017	Peter Rabbit in the Gooseberry Net P3157	N/A	Open	50.00	50.00
XX-31-018	Pigling Eats Porridge P3252	N/A	Open	50.00	50.00
XX-31-019	Tom Kittten and Butterfly P3030	N/A	Open	50.00	50.00
Royal Doulton	**Royal Doulton Collectors' Club**				
80-32-001	John Doulton Jug (8 O'Clock) D6656	N/A	Yr.Iss.	70.00	125-150.
81-32-002	Sleepy Darling Figure HN2953	N/A	Yr.Iss.	100.00	250.00
82-32-003	Dog of Fo-Flambe	N/A	Yr.Iss.	50.00	150.00
82-32-004	Prized Possessions Figure HN2942	N/A	Yr.Iss.	125.00	600.00
83-32-005	Loving Cup	N/A	Yr.Iss.	75.00	225.00
83-32-006	Springtime HN3033	N/A	Yr.Iss.	125.00	300.00
84-32-007	Sir Henry Doulton Jug D6703	N/A	Yr.Iss.	50.00	150.00
84-32-008	Pride & Joy Figure HN2945	N/A	Yr.Iss.	125.00	275.00
85-32-009	Top of the Hill Plate HN2126	N/A	Yr.Iss.	34.95	100.00
85-32-010	Wintertime Figure HN3060	N/A	Yr.Iss.	125.00	225.00
86-32-011	Albert Sagger Toby Jug	N/A	Yr.Iss.	34.95	85.00
86-32-012	Auctioneer Figure HN2988	N/A	Yr.Iss.	150.00	250.00
87-32-013	Collector Bunnykins	N/A	Yr.Iss.	40.00	350.00
87-32-014	Summertime Figurine HN3137	N/A	Yr.Iss.	140.00	225.00
88-32-015	Top of the Hill Miniature Figurine HN2126	N/A	Yr.Iss.	95.00	125.00
88-32-016	Beefeater Tiny Jug	N/A	Yr.Iss.	25.00	125.00
88-32-017	Old Salt Tea Pot	N/A	Yr.Iss.	135.00	250.00
89-32-018	Geisha Flambe Figure HN3229	N/A	Yr.Iss.	195.00	200-250.
89-32-019	Flower Sellers Children Plate	N/A	Yr.Iss.	65.00	125.00
90-32-020	Autumntime Figure HN3231	N/A	Yr.Iss.	190.00	225.00
90-32-021	Jester Mini Figure HN3196	N/A	Yr.Iss.	115.00	125-150.
90-32-022	Old King Cole Tiny Jug	N/A	Yr.Iss.	35.00	140.00
91-32-023	Bunny's Bedtime Figure HN3370	N/A	Yr.Iss.	195.00	195.00
91-32-024	Charles Dickens Jug D6901	N/A	Yr.Iss.	100.00	100.00
91-32-025	L'Ambiteuse Figure (Tissot Lady)	N/A	Yr.Iss.	295.00	300.00
91-32-026	Christopher Columbus Jug D6911	N/A	Yr.Iss.	95.00	200.00
92-32-027	Discovery Figure HN3428	N/A	Yr.Iss.	160.00	160.00
92-32-028	King Edward Jug D6923	N/A	Yr.Iss.	250.00	95-250.00
92-32-029	Master Potter Bunnykins DB131	N/A	Yr.Iss.	50.00	95.00
92-32-030	Eliza Farren Prestige Figure HN3442	N/A	Yr.Iss.	335.00	335.00
93-32-031	Barbara Figure	N/A	Yr.Iss.	285.00	285.00
93-32-032	Lord Mountbatten L/S Jug	N/A	N/A	225.00	225.00
93-32-033	Punch & Judy Double Sided Jug	N/A	2,500	400.00	400.00
93-32-034	Flambe Dragon HN3552	R. Tabbenor	N/A	260.00	260.00
94-32-035	Diane HN3604	N/A	N/A	250.00	250.00
Royal Worcester	**Dorothy Doughty Porcelains**				
35-01-001	American Redstarts and Hemlock	D. Doughty	66	Unkn.	5500.00
41-01-002	Apple Blossoms	D. Doughty	250	400.00	1400-3750.
63-01-003	Audubon Warblers	D. Doughty	500	1350.00	2100-4200.
38-01-004	Baltimore Orioles	D. Doughty	250	350.00	Unkn.
56-01-005	Bewick's Wrens & Yellow Jasmine	D. Doughty	500	600.00	2100-3800.
36-01-006	Bluebirds	D. Doughty	350	500.00	8500-9000.
64-01-007	Blue Tits & Pussy Willow	D. Doughty	500	250.00	3000.00
40-01-008	Bobwhite Quail	D. Doughty	22	275.00	11000.
59-01-009	Cactus Wrens	D. Doughty	500	1250.00	1700-4500.
60-01-010	Canyon Wrens	D. Doughty	500	750.00	2000-4000.
37-01-011	Cardinals	D. Doughty	500	500.00	20000-9250.
68-01-012	Carolina Paroquet, Color	D. Doughty	350	1200.00	1900-2200.
68-01-013	Carolina Paroquet, White	D. Doughty	75	600.00	Unkn.
65-01-014	Cerulean Warblers & Red Maple	D. Doughty	500	1350.00	1400-3000.
38-01-015	Chickadees & Larch	D. Doughty	300	350.00	8500-8900.
65-01-016	Chuffchaff	D. Doughty	500	1500.00	1300-2900.
42-01-017	Crabapple Blossom Sprays And A Butterfly	D. Doughty	250	Unkn.	800.00
40-01-018	Crabapples	D. Doughty	250	400.00	3700-4250.
67-01-019	Downy Woodpecker & Pecan, Color	D. Doughty	400	1500.00	1000-2400.
67-01-020	Downy Woodpecker & Pecan, White	D. Doughty	75	1000.00	1900.00
59-01-021	Elf Owl	D. Doughty	500	875.00	Unkn.
55-01-022	Gnatcatchers	D. Doughty	500	600.00	2700-4900.
72-01-023	Goldcrests, Pair	D. Doughty	500	4200.00	Unkn.
36-01-024	Goldfinches & Thistle	D. Doughty	250	350.00	2000-7000.
68-01-025	Gray Wagtail	D. Doughty	500	600.00	Unkn.
61-01-026	Hooded Warblers	D. Doughty	500	950.00	4300.00
50-01-027	Hummingbirds And Fuchsia	D. Doughty	500	Unkn.	2800.00
42-01-028	Indigo Bunting And Plum Twig	D. Doughty	5,000	Unkn.	Unkn.
42-01-029	Indigo Buntings, Blackberry Sprays	D. Doughty	500	375.00	1700-3500.
65-01-030	Kingfisher Cock & Autumn Beech	D. Doughty	500	1250.00	1900-2300.
52-01-031	Kinglets & Noble Pine	D. Doughty	500	450.00	1300-4800.
66-01-032	Lark Sparrow	D. Doughty	500	750.00	Unkn.
62-01-033	Lazuli Bunting & Chokecherries, Color	D. Doughty	500	1350.00	3000-4500.
62-01-034	Lazuli Bunting & Chokecherries, White	D. Doughty	100	1350.00	2600-3000.
64-01-035	Lesser Whitethroats	D. Doughty	500	350.00	1200-4000.
50-01-036	Magnolia Warbler	D. Doughty	150	1100.00	1900-3600.
77-01-037	Meadow Pipit	D. Doughty	500	1800.00	1800.00
50-01-038	Mexican Feijoa	D. Doughty	250	600.00	2600-4900.
40-01-039	Mockingbirds	D. Doughty	500	450.00	7200-7750.
42-01-040	Mockingbirds and Peach Blossom	D. Doughty	500	Unkn.	Unkn.
64-01-041	Moorhen Chick	D. Doughty	500	1000.00	Unkn.
64-01-042	Mountain Bluebirds	D. Doughty	500	950.00	1700-2300.
55-01-043	Myrtle Warblers	D. Doughty	500	550.00	1300-4000.
71-01-044	Nightingale & Honeysuckle	D. Doughty	500	2500.00	2500-2750.
47-01-045	Orange Blossoms & Butterfly	D. Doughty	250	500.00	4200-4500.
57-01-046	Ovenbirds	D. Doughty	250	650.00	4500.00
57-01-047	Parula Warblers	D. Doughty	500	600.00	1700-3600.
58-01-048	Phoebes On Flame Vine	D. Doughty	500	750.00	2200-5500.
52-01-049	Red-Eyed Vireos	D. Doughty	500	450.00	2000.00
68-01-050	Redstarts & Gorse	D. Doughty	500	1900.00	2300.00
64-01-051	Robin	D. Doughty	500	750.00	Unkn.
56-01-052	Scarlet Tanagers	D. Doughty	500	675.00	3000-4200.
62-01-053	Scissor-Tailed Flycatcher, Color	D. Doughty	250	950.00	Unkn.
62-01-054	Scissor-Tailed Flycatcher, White	D. Doughty	75	950.00	1300-1600.
63-01-055	Vermillion Flycatchers	D. Doughty	500	250.00	1100-3400.
64-01-056	Wrens & Burnet Rose	D. Doughty	500	650.00	1000.00
52-01-057	Yellow-Headed Blackbirds	D. Doughty	350	650.00	2000-2400.
58-01-058	Yellowthroats on Water Hyacinth	D. Doughty	350	750.00	1700-4000.
Royal Worcester	**Ronald Van Ruyckevelt Porcelains**				
XX-02-001	Alice	R. Van Ruyckevelt	500	1875.00	1875.00
70-02-002	American Pintail, Pair	R. Van Ruyckevelt	500	Unkn.	3000.00
69-02-003	Argenteuil A-108	R. Van Ruyckevelt	338	Unkn.	Unkn.
68-02-004	Blue Angel Fish	R. Van Ruyckevelt	500	375.00	900.00

Number	Name	Artist	Edition Limit	Issue Price	Quote
67-02-005	Bluefin Tuna	R. Van Ruyckevelt	500	500.00	Unkn.
65-02-006	Blue Marlin	R. Van Ruyckevelt	500	500.00	1000.00
69-02-007	Bobwhite Quail, Pair	R. Van Ruyckevelt	500	Unkn.	2000.00
67-02-008	Butterfly Fish	R. Van Ruyckevelt	500	375.00	1600.00
69-02-009	Castelneau Pink	R. Van Ruyckevelt	429	Unkn.	825-875.
69-02-010	Castelneau Yellow	R. Van Ruyckevelt	163	Unkn.	825-875.
XX-02-011	Cecilia	R. Van Ruyckevelt	500	1875.00	1875.00
68-02-012	Dolphin	R. Van Ruyckevelt	500	500.00	900.00
71-02-013	Elaine	R. Van Ruyckevelt	750	600.00	600-650.
62-02-014	Flying Fish	R. Van Ruyckevelt	300	400.00	450.00
71-02-015	Green-Winged Teal	R. Van Ruyckevelt	500	1450.00	1450.00
62-02-016	Hibiscus	R. Van Ruyckevelt	500	300.00	350.00
56-02-017	Hogfish & Sergeant Major	R. Van Ruyckevelt	500	375.00	650.00
68-02-018	Honfleur A-105	R. Van Ruyckevelt	290	Unkn.	600.00
68-02-019	Honfleur A-106	R. Van Ruyckevelt	290	Unkn.	600.00
71-02-020	Languedoc	R. Van Ruyckevelt	216	Unkn.	1150.00
68-02-021	Mallards	R. Van Ruyckevelt	500	Unkn.	2000.00
68-02-022	Mennecy A-101	R. Van Ruyckevelt	338	Unkn.	675-725.
68-02-023	Mennecy A-102	R. Van Ruyckevelt	334	Unkn.	675-725.
61-02-024	Passionflower	R. Van Ruyckevelt	500	300.00	400.00
76-02-025	Picnic	R. Van Ruyckevelt	250	2850.00	2850.00
76-02-026	Queen Elizabeth I	R. Van Ruyckevelt	250	3850.00	3850.00
77-02-027	Queen Elizabeth II	R. Van Ruyckevelt	250	Unkn.	Unkn.
76-02-028	Queen Mary I	R. Van Ruyckevelt	250	4850.00	4850.00
68-02-029	Rainbow Parrot Fish	R. Van Ruyckevelt	500	1500.00	1500.00
58-02-030	Red Hind	R. Van Ruyckevelt	500	375.00	900.00
68-02-031	Ring-Necked Pheasants	R. Van Ruyckevelt	500	Unkn.	3200-3400.
64-02-032	Rock Beauty	R. Van Ruyckevelt	500	425.00	850.00
62-02-033	Sailfish	R. Van Ruyckevelt	500	400.00	550.00
69-02-034	Saint Denis A-109	R. Van Ruyckevelt	500	Unkn.	925-950.
61-02-035	Squirrelfish	R. Van Ruyckevelt	500	400.00	9000.00
66-02-036	Swordfish	R. Van Ruyckevelt	500	575.00	650.00
64-02-037	Tarpon	R. Van Ruyckevelt	500	500.00	975.00
72-02-038	White Doves	R. Van Ruyckevelt	25	3600.00	27850.00
Royal Worcester		**Ruth Van Ruyckevelt Porcelains**			
60-03-001	Beatrice	R. Van Ruyckevelt	500	125.00	Unkn.
69-03-002	Bridget	R. Van Ruyckevelt	500	300.00	600-700.
60-03-003	Caroline	R. Van Ruyckevelt	500	125.00	Unkn.
68-03-004	Charlotte and Jane	R. Van Ruyckevelt	500	1000.00	1500-1650.
67-03-005	Elizabeth	R. Van Ruyckevelt	750	300.00	750-800.
69-03-006	Emily	R. Van Ruyckevelt	500	300.00	600.00
78-03-007	Esther	R. Van Ruyckevelt	500	Unkn.	Unkn.
71-03-008	Felicity	R. Van Ruyckevelt	750	600.00	600.00
59-03-009	Lisette	R. Van Ruyckevelt	500	100.00	Unkn.
62-03-010	Louisa	R. Van Ruyckevelt	500	400.00	975.00
68-03-011	Madeline	R. Van Ruyckevelt	500	300.00	750-800.
68-03-012	Marion	R. Van Ruyckevelt	500	275.00	575-625.
64-03-013	Melanie	R. Van Ruyckevelt	500	150.00	Unkn.
59-03-014	Penelope	R. Van Ruyckevelt	500	100.00	Unkn.
64-03-015	Rosalind	R. Van Ruyckevelt	500	150.00	Unkn.
63-03-016	Sister of London Hospital	R. Van Ruyckevelt	500	Unkn.	475-500.
63-03-017	Sister of St. Thomas Hospital	R. Van Ruyckevelt	500	Unkn.	475-500.
70-03-018	Sister of the Red Cross	R. Van Ruyckevelt	750	Unkn.	525-500.
66-03-019	Sister of University College Hospital	R. Van Ruyckevelt	500	Unkn.	475-500.
64-03-020	Tea Party	R. Van Ruyckevelt	250	400.00	7000.00
Royal Worcester		**Equestrians**			
XX-04-001	Winner Brown/Bay	D. Linder	Closed	1721.00	1721.00
XX-04-002	Winner Grey/Bay	D. Linder	Closed	1721.00	1721.00
36-04-003	At The Meet	D. Linder	Closed	944.00	944.00
36-04-004	Cantering to the Post	D. Linder	Closed	944.00	944.00
36-04-005	Hog Hunting	D. Linder	Closed	1277.00	1277.00
36-04-006	Huntsman and Hounds	D. Linder	Closed	1110.00	1110.00
36-04-007	Over the Sticks	D. Linder	Closed	944.00	944.00
36-04-008	Polo Player	D. Linder	Closed	1055.00	1055.00
36-04-009	Three Circus Horses Rearing	D. Linder	Closed	4440.00	4440.00
50-04-010	Two Galloping Horses	D. Linder	Closed	2553.00	2553.00
60-04-011	Foxhunter	D. Linder	Closed	1200.00	1200.00
61-04-012	Officer Royal Horse Guards	D. Linder	Closed	1400.00	1400.00
62-04-013	Quarter Horse	D. Linder	Closed	900.00	900.00
63-04-014	Merand	D. Linder	Closed	1550.00	1550.00
64-04-015	Shire Stallion	D. Linder	Closed	1500.00	1500.00
65-04-016	Hyperion	D. Linder	Closed	1000.00	1000.00
66-04-017	Percheron	D. Linder	Closed	1450.00	1450.00
66-04-018	Royal Canadian Policeman	D. Linder	Closed	1700.00	1700.00
68-04-019	Duke of Edinburgh	D. Linder	Closed	2400.00	2400.00
69-04-020	Appaloosa	D. Linder	Closed	1350.00	1350.00
69-04-021	Suffolk Punch	D. Linder	Closed	1350.00	1350.00
71-04-022	Palomino	D. Linder	Closed	1350.00	1350.00
71-04-023	Prince's Grace & Foal (colored)	D. Linder	Closed	2700.00	2700.00
71-04-024	Prince's Grace & Foal (white)	D. Linder	Closed	2600.00	2600.00
72-04-025	Nijinsky	D. Linder	Closed	2300.00	2300.00
72-04-026	M Coakes Mould on Stroller	D. Linder	Closed	1600.00	1600.00
73-04-027	American Saddle Horse	D. Linder	Closed	1525.00	1525.00
73-04-028	Princess Anne on Doublet	D. Linder	Closed	8000.00	8000.00
74-04-029	Galloping in Winter	D. Linder	Closed	8500.00	8500.00
74-04-030	Galloping Ponies (colored)	D. Linder	Closed	4600.00	4600.00
74-04-031	Galloping Ponies (white)	D. Linder	Closed	2900.00	2900.00
75-04-032	Meade on Laurieston	D. Linder	Closed	3600.00	3600.00
75-04-033	Mill Reef	D. Linder	Closed	2300.00	2300.00
76-04-034	Hackney Pony	D. Linder	Closed	2000.00	2000.00
76-04-035	New Born (colored)	D. Linder	Closed	2700.00	2700.00
76-04-036	New Born (white)	D. Linder	Closed	1600.00	1600.00
76-04-037	Red Rum	D. Linder	Closed	2000.00	2000.00
77-04-038	Clydesdale	D. Linder	Closed	2300.00	2300.00
77-04-039	Grundy	D. Linder	Closed	3400.00	3400.00
Royal Worcester		**Bicentennial L.E. Commemoratives**			
73-05-001	Potter	P.W. Baston	500	Unkn.	300-400.
73-05-002	Cabinetmaker	P.W. Baston	500	Unkn.	300-400.
73-05-003	Blacksmith	P.W. Baston	500	Unkn.	500.00
75-05-004	Clockmaker	P.W. Baston	Unkn.	Unkn.	500.00
R.R. Creations		**Colonial Collection Series I**			
89-01-001	Colonial Inn 8903	D. Ross	Retrd.	8.95	8.95
89-01-002	Tavern 8908	D. Ross	Retrd.	8.95	8.95
89-01-003	Silversmith 8909	D. Ross	Retrd.	8.95	8.95
89-01-004	Boot & Shoemaker 8910	D. Ross	Retrd.	8.95	8.95
89-01-005	Large Lampost 8911	D. Ross	Open	2.75	2.75
89-01-006	Easton House 8918	D. Ross	Retrd.	8.95	8.95
92-01-007	Pine Tree 9250	D. Ross	Open	3.50	3.50

Number	Name	Artist	Edition Limit	Issue Price	Quote
R.R. Creations		**Colonial Collection Series II**			
89-02-001	C.L. Edwards 8901	D. Ross	12/94	8.95	8.95
89-02-002	Kiistner 8902	D. Ross	12/94	8.95	8.95
89-02-003	Dry Good 8904	D. Ross	12/94	8.95	8.95
89-02-004	Town Hall 8906	D. Ross	12/94	8.95	8.95
89-02-005	G. Dressmaker 8920	D. Ross	12/94	8.95	8.95
91-02-006	4" Fence w/Tree 9124	D. Ross	Open	7.25	7.25
92-02-007	Pine Tree 9250	D. Ross	Open	3.50	3.50
92-02-008	Small Lamp Post 9254	D. Ross	Open	2.95	2.95
R.R. Creations		**Court House Collection**			
89-03-001	Chase Country 8924	D. Ross	Retrd.	8.95	8.95
90-03-002	Mount Holly 9010	D. Ross	Retrd.	8.95	8.95
90-03-003	Franklin County 9011	D. Ross	Retrd.	8.95	8.95
90-03-004	Large Flag Pole 9017	D. Ross	Open	2.95	2.95
92-03-005	Pine Tree 9250	D. Ross	Open	3.50	3.50
R.R. Creations		**In The Country Series I**			
89-04-001	Church 8905	D. Ross	Retrd.	8.95	8.95
89-04-002	School 8907	D. Ross	Retrd.	8.95	8.95
90-04-003	Grist Mill 9001	D. Ross	Retrd.	8.95	8.95
90-04-004	Large Flag Pole 9017	D. Ross	Open	2.95	2.95
91-04-005	Oak Tree 9123	D. Ross	Open	3.50	3.50
91-04-006	4" Fence w/ Tree 9124	D. Ross	Open	3.65	3.65
92-04-007	Pine Tree 9250	D. Ross	Open	3.50	3.50
R.R. Creations		**In The Country Series II**			
93-05-001	Toll House 9301	D. Ross	12/95	8.95	8.95
93-05-002	Country Livin Shop 9307	D. Ross	12/95	8.95	8.95
93-05-003	Country Church 9322	D. Ross	12/95	8.95	8.95
90-05-004	Sunflower 9016	D. Ross	Open	2.80	2.80
91-05-005	4" Fence w/ Tree 9124	D. Ross	Open	7.25	7.25
92-05-006	Pine Tree 9250	D. Ross	Open	3.50	3.50
R.R. Creations		**Main Street Collection Series I**			
89-06-001	Kingman Firehouse 8919	D. Ross	Retrd.	8.95	8.95
89-06-002	Myerstown Depot 8921	D. Ross	Retrd.	8.95	8.95
89-06-003	Barron Theatre 8922	D. Ross	Retrd.	8.95	8.95
89-06-004	Gas Station 8923	D. Ross	Retrd.	8.95	8.95
90-06-005	Santa Fe Depot 9006	D. Ross	Retrd.	8.95	8.95
90-06-006	Library 9007	D. Ross	Retrd.	8.95	8.95
90-06-007	Main Street Sign 9018	D. Ross	Open	2.75	2.75
90-06-008	Large Flag Pole 9017	D. Ross	Open	2.95	2.95
91-06-009	Telephone Company 9107	D. Ross	Retrd.	8.95	8.95
91-06-010	Oak Tree 9123	D. Ross	Open	3.50	3.50
91-06-011	4" Fence w/ Tree 9124	D. Ross	Open	3.65	3.65
92-06-012	Pine Tree 9250	D. Ross	Open	3.50	3.50
R.R. Creations		**Main Street Collection Series II**			
89-07-001	Harold's Hardware 8925	D. Ross	12/94	8.95	8.95
91-07-002	Chautaqua Hills Jelly 9105	D. Ross	12/94	8.95	8.95
92-07-003	Beauty Shop 9209	D. Ross	12/94	8.95	8.95
92-07-004	Bank 9211	D. Ross	12/94	8.95	8.95
92-07-005	Bakery 9212	D. Ross	12/94	8.95	8.95
92-07-006	Oak Brook Fire Co. 9207	D. Ross	12/94	8.95	8.95
R.R. Creations		**Historical Collection Series I**			
92-08-001	Smith-Bly 9201	D. Ross	12/94	8.95	8.95
92-08-002	Canfield 9205	D. Ross	12/94	8.95	8.95
92-08-003	Hexagon 9208	D. Ross	12/94	8.95	8.95
92-08-004	Lincoln 9217	D. Ross	12/94	8.95	8.95
92-08-005	Susan B. Anthony 9222	D. Ross	12/94	8.95	8.95
90-08-006	Main Street Sign 9018	D. Ross	Open	2.75	2.75
91-08-007	4" Fence w/ Tree 9124	D. Ross	Open	7.25	7.25
R.R. Creations		**Historical Collection Series II**			
93-09-001	Betsy Ross 9305	D. Ross	12/95	8.95	8.95
93-09-002	Kennedy Home 9308	D. Ross	12/95	8.95	8.95
93-09-003	Stone House 9319	D. Ross	12/95	8.95	8.95
89-09-004	Lamp Post 8911	D. Ross	Open	2.75	2.75
91-09-005	Oak Tree 9123	D. Ross	Open	3.50	3.50
92-09-006	Pine Tree 9250	D. Ross	Open	3.50	3.50
R.R. Creations		**Williamsburg Collection Series I**			
92-10-001	Davidson Shop 9213	D. Ross	12/94	8.95	8.95
92-10-002	Orrell House 9214	D. Ross	12/94	8.95	8.95
92-10-003	Tarpley's Shop 9215	D. Ross	12/94	8.95	8.95
92-10-004	Small Lamp Post 9254	D. Ross	Open	2.95	2.95
91-10-005	Oak Tree 9123	D. Ross	Open	3.50	3.50
92-10-006	Pine Tree 9250	D. Ross	Open	3.50	3.50
R.R. Creations		**Williamsburg Collection Series II**			
93-11-001	Court House 9302	D. Ross	12/95	8.95	8.95
93-11-002	Capitol 9303	D. Ross	12/95	8.95	8.95
93-11-003	Governors Palace 9304	D. Ross	12/95	8.95	8.95
91-11-004	4" Fence w/ Tree 9124	D. Ross	Open	7.25	7.25
92-11-005	Pine Tree 9250	D. Ross	Open	3.50	3.50
R.R. Creations		**Victorian Collection**			
91-12-001	Victorian Michigan 9106	D. Ross	12/94	8.95	8.95
92-12-002	Queen Anne 9203	D. Ross	12/94	8.95	8.95
92-12-003	Chapline 9206	D. Ross	12/94	8.95	8.95
92-12-004	Trolley 9255	D. Ross	Open	5.95	5.95
90-12-005	Main Street Sign 9018	D. Ross	Open	2.75	2.75
91-12-006	4" Fence w/ Tree 9124	D. Ross	Open	7.25	7.25
91-12-007	Oak Tree 9123	D. Ross	Open	3.50	3.50
R.R. Creations		**Christmas Memories Series I**			
92-13-001	Christmas Chapel 9216	D. Ross	12/94	8.95	8.95
92-13-002	Christmas F Douglass 9218	D. Ross	12/94	8.95	8.95
92-13-003	Daniel Boone 9219	D. Ross	12/94	8.95	8.95
89-13-004	Lamp Post 8911	D. Ross	Open	2.75	2.75
92-13-005	Pine Tree 9250	D. Ross	Open	3.50	3.50
92-13-006	Sister Sled 9252	D. Ross	Open	5.95	5.95
R.R. Creations		**Christmas Memories Series II**			
93-14-001	Christmas Church 9318	D. Ross	12/95	8.95	8.95
93-14-002	Boscobel 9320	D. Ross	12/95	8.95	8.95
93-14-003	Dell House 9321	D. Ross	12/95	8.95	8.95
89-14-004	4" Picket Fence 8917	D. Ross	Open	3.65	3.65
92-14-005	Sister Sled 9252	D. Ross	Open	5.95	5.95
89-14-006	Lamp Post 8911	D. Ross	Open	2.75	2.75
92-14-007	Pine Tree 9250	D. Ross	Open	3.50	3.50

Number	Name	Artist	Edition Limit	Issue Price	Quote
R.R. Creations		**Amish Collection Series I**			
87-15-001	Windmill 8725	D. Ross	Open	3.60	3.60
90-15-002	Amish Buggy 9013	D. Ross	Open	4.40	4.40
90-15-003	Wheat 9015	D. Ross	Open	2.80	2.80
90-15-004	Sunflower 9016	D. Ross	Open	2.80	2.80
91-15-005	Amish House 9101	D. Ross	12/94	8.95	8.95
91-15-006	Amish Barn 9102	D. Ross	12/94	8.95	8.95
91-15-007	Amish School 9103	D. Ross	12/94	8.95	8.95
91-15-008	Amish Outhouse 9104	D. Ross	Open	4.25	4.25
91-15-009	Amish Family 9120	D. Ross	Open	4.40	4.40
91-15-010	Slow Vehicle 9121	D. Ross	Open	2.95	2.95
92-15-011	Quilt Shop 9204	D. Ross	12/94	8.95	8.95
92-15-012	Barn Raising 9220	D. Ross	12/94	8.95	8.95
92-15-013	Clothesline 9253	D. Ross	Open	2.95	2.95
R.R. Creations		**Amish Collection Series II**			
93-16-001	Troyer Bakery 9328	D. Ross	12/95	8.95	8.95
93-16-002	Blacksmith 9329	D. Ross	12/95	8.95	8.95
93-16-003	Amish Garden 9330	D. Ross	Open	5.95	5.95
93-16-004	Harness & Buggy 9331	D. Ross	12/95	8.95	8.95
91-16-005	Amish Family 9120	D. Ross	Open	4.40	4.40
91-16-006	4" Fence w/ Tree 9124	D. Ross	Open	7.25	7.25
92-16-007	Pine Tree 9250	D. Ross	Open	3.50	3.50
R.R. Creations		**Grandpa's Farm Collection Series I**			
87-17-001	Farm House 8720	D. Ross	Retrd.	8.95	8.95
87-17-002	Barn 8721	D. Ross	Retrd.	8.95	8.95
87-17-003	Chicken Coop 8722	D. Ross	Retrd.	6.50	6.50
87-17-004	Wash House 8723	D. Ross	Retrd.	6.00	6.00
87-17-005	Outhouse 8724	D. Ross	Retrd.	4.25	4.25
R.R. Creations		**Grandpa's Farm Collection Series II**			
93-18-001	Hofacre House 9323	D. Ross	12/95	8.95	8.95
93-18-002	New Barn 9324	D. Ross	12/95	8.95	8.95
93-18-003	Wash House 9325	D. Ross	12/95	6.50	6.50
93-18-004	Chicken Coop 9326	D. Ross	12/95	6.50	6.50
87-18-005	Windmill 8725	D. Ross	Open	3.60	3.60
90-18-006	Wheat 9015	D. Ross	Open	2.80	2.80
92-18-007	Pine Tree 9250	D. Ross	Open	3.50	3.50
92-18-008	Outhouse 9327	D. Ross	Open	4.25	4.25
R.R. Creations		**On the Square I**			
87-19-001	Antique Shop 8708	D. Ross	Retrd.	8.95	8.95
87-19-002	Book Store 8709	D. Ross	Retrd.	8.95	8.95
87-19-003	Bakery 8710	D. Ross	Retrd.	8.95	8.95
87-19-004	Craft Shop 8711	D. Ross	Retrd.	8.95	8.95
87-19-005	Candle Shop 8712	D. Ross	Retrd.	8.95	8.95
88-19-006	Ice Cream Parlor 8806	D. Ross	Retrd.	8.95	8.95
88-19-007	Flower Shop 8807	D. Ross	Retrd.	8.95	8.95
88-19-008	Hardesty House 8808	D. Ross	Retrd.	8.95	8.95
R.R. Creations		**On the Square II**			
93-20-001	Book Store 9309	D. Ross	12/95	8.95	8.95
93-20-002	Ice Cream Shop 9310	D. Ross	12/95	9.95	9.95
93-20-003	Flower Shop 9311	D. Ross	12/95	9.95	9.95
93-20-004	Candle Shop 9312	D. Ross	12/95	8.95	8.95
93-20-005	Craft Shop 9313	D. Ross	12/95	8.95	8.95
93-20-006	Antique Shop 9314	D. Ross	12/95	8.95	8.95
90-20-007	Flag Pole 9017	D. Ross	Open	2.95	2.95
91-20-008	Oak Tree 9123	D. Ross	Open	3.50	3.50
92-20-009	Small Lamp Pole 9254	D. Ross	Open	2.95	2.95
R.R. Creations		**Accessories**			
87-21-001	Welcome Mat 8717	D. Ross	Open	1.80	1.80
87-21-002	Windmill 8725	D. Ross	Open	3.60	3.60
89-21-003	Large Lamp Post 8911	D. Ross	Open	2.75	2.75
90-21-004	Sunflower 9016	D. Ross	Open	2.80	2.80
90-21-005	Mainstreet Sign 9018	D. Ross	Open	2.75	2.75
91-21-006	Oak Tree 9123	D. Ross	Open	3.50	3.50
91-21-007	4" Fence w/ Tree 9124	D. Ross	Open	7.25	7.25
89-21-008	4" Fence 8917	D. Ross	Open	3.65	3.65
90-21-009	Large Flag Pole 9017	D. Ross	Open	2.95	2.95
92-21-010	Pine Tree 9250	D. Ross	Open	3.50	3.50
92-21-011	Sisters Sled 9252	D. Ross	Open	5.95	5.95
92-21-012	Small Lamp Post 9254	D. Ross	Open	2.95	2.95
92-21-013	Small Flag 9251	D. Ross	Open	2.95	2.95
92-21-014	Trolley 9255	D. Ross	Open	5.95	5.95
93-21-015	Welcome R.R. Sign 9332	D. Ross	Open	4.50	4.50
93-21-016	Honey Pine Shelf 9333	D. Ross	Open	9.95	9.95
Salvino Inc.		**Brooklyn Dodger**			
89-01-001	Sandy Koufax	Salvino	S/O	195.00	225.00
89-01-002	Sandy Koufax AP	Salvino	500	250.00	250-325.
89-01-003	Don Drysdale	Salvino	S/O	185.00	250-275.
89-01-004	Don Drysdale AP	Salvino	300	200.00	350.00
90-01-005	Roy Campanella	Salvino	2,000	395.00	395.00
90-01-006	Roy Campanella (Special Edition)	Salvino	S/O	550.00	650.00
93-01-007	Duke Snider	Salvino	1,000	275.00	275.00
Salvino Inc.		**Heroes of the Diamond**			
91-02-001	Rickey Henderson (Home)	Salvino	S/O	275.00	275.00
91-02-002	Rickey Henderson (Away)	Salvino	600	275.00	275.00
91-02-003	Rickey Henderson (Special Edition)	Salvino	550	375.00	375.00
92-02-004	Mickey Mantle Fielding	Salvino	S/O	395.00	495-600.
92-02-005	Mickey Mantle Batting	Salvino	S/O	395.00	495-600.
92-02-006	Willie Mays New York	Salvino	750	395.00	395.00
92-02-007	Willie Mays San Francisco	Salvino	750	395.00	395.00
93-02-008	Brooks Robinson	Salvino	1,000	275.00	275.00
Salvino Inc.		**Boxing Greats**			
90-03-001	Muhammed Ali	Salvino	S/O	250.00	350.00
90-03-002	Muhammed Ali (Special Edition)	Salvino	S/O	375.00	375-575.
Salvino Inc.		**NFL Superstar**			
90-04-001	Jim Brown	Salvino	S/O	275.00	275-550.
90-04-002	Jim Brown (Special Edition)	Salvino	S/O	525.00	525-750.
90-04-003	Joe Montana	Salvino	S/O	275.00	275-325.
90-04-004	Joe Montana (Special Edition)	Salvino	S/O	395.00	375-475.
90-04-005	Joe Namath	Salvino	2,500	275.00	275.00
90-04-006	Joe Namath (Special Edition)	Salvino	500	375.00	375-475.
90-04-007	OJ Simpson	Salvino	1,000	250.00	250-275.
93-04-008	Joe Montana 49'er	Salvino	1,000	275.00	275.00
93-04-009	Joe Montana Chiefs	Salvino	450	275.00	275.00
Salvino Inc.		**Pittsburgh Steeler Greats**			
92-05-001	Terry Bradshaw	Salvino	S/O	275.00	275.00
Salvino Inc.		**Chicago Bears Great**			
92-06-001	Gale Sayers	Salvino	1,000	275.00	275.00
Salvino Inc.		**Green Bay Packer Legends**			
92-07-001	Bart Starr	Salvino	500	250.00	250.00
92-07-002	Paul Hornung	Salvino	500	250.00	250.00
92-07-003	Jim Taylor	Salvino	500	250.00	250.00
Salvino Inc.		**NBA Laker Legends**			
91-08-001	Elgin Baylor	Salvino	700	250.00	250.00
91-08-002	Elgin Baylor (Special Edition)	Salvino	300	350.00	350.00
91-08-003	Jerry West	Salvino	700	250.00	250.00
91-08-004	Jerry West (Special Edition)	Salvino	300	350.00	350.00
Salvino Inc.		**Boston Celtic Greats**			
91-09-001	Larry Bird	Salvino	S/O	285.00	425.00
93-09-001	Larry Bird (Special Edition)	Salvino	S/O	375.00	450.00
Salvino Inc.		**Hockey Greats**			
91-10-001	Mario Lemieux	Salvino	S/O	275.00	375-600.
92-10-002	Mario Lemieux (Special Editon)	Salvino	S/O	285.00	385-600.
94-10-003	Wayne Gretzky	Salvino	S/O	395.00	525-550.
Salvino Inc.		**Racing Legends**			
91-11-001	Richard Petty	Salvino	S/O	250.00	250.00
91-11-002	Richard Petty (Special Edition)	Salvino	S/O	279.00	350-400.
91-11-003	AJ Foyt	Salvino	S/O	250.00	250.00
91-11-004	Darrell Waltrip	Salvino	S/O	250.00	250.00
93-11-005	Richard Petty Farewell Tour	Salvino	2,500	275.00	275.00
Salvino Inc.		**Dealer Special Series**			
92-12-001	Joe Namath	Salvino	S/O	700.00	700.00
92-12-002	Mickey Mantle #6	Salvino	S/O	700.00	700.00
92-12-003	Mickey Mantle #7	Salvino	S/O	700.00	700.00
93-12-004	Willie Mays	Salvino	S/O	700.00	700.00
Salvino Inc.		**Collegiate Series**			
92-13-001	OJ Simpson	Salvino	1,000	275.00	275.00
92-13-002	Joe Montana	Salvino	S/O	275.00	275.00
Salvino Inc.		**Tennis Greats**			
93-14-001	Bjorn Borg	Salvino	500	275.00	275.00
Salvino Inc.		**Unsigned Collection**			
93-15-001	Richard Petty 6" hand-painted	Salvino	2,500	69.95	69.95
93-15-002	Mario Lemieux 6" hand-painted	Salvino	S/O	69.95	69.95
93-15-003	Richard Petty 8" cold-cast pewter	Salvino	2,500	99.95	99.95
93-15-004	Mario Lemieux 8" cold-cast pewter	Salvino	S/O	99.95	99.95
93-15-005	Richard Petty 6" cold-cast pewter	Salvino	5,000	43.95	43.95
93-15-006	Mario Lemieux 6" cold-cast pewter	Salvino	S/O	43.95	43.95
93-15-007	Richard Petty cold-cast pewter plaque	Salvino	5,000	24.95	24.95
93-15-008	Mario Lemieux cold-cast pewter plaque	Salvino	S/O	24.95	24.95
94-15-009	Roberto Clemente	Salvino	1,750	125.00	125.00
Salvino Inc.		**Collector Club Figurines**			
93-16-001	6" Mario Lemieux-Painted Away Uniform (Unsigned)	Salvino	Closed	69.95	90.00
93-16-002	Joe Montana-"KC" Away Uniform (Hand Signed)	Salvino	Closed	275.00	275.00
Sarah's Attic, Inc.		**Angels In The Attic**			
88-01-001	Small Angel Resin Candle 3071	Sarah's Attic	Closed	9.00	9.00
89-01-002	St. Gabbe 2322	Sarah's Attic	Closed	30.00	33.00
89-01-003	St. Anne 2323	Sarah's Attic	Closed	29.00	32.00
89-01-004	Wendall-Angel 2324	Sarah's Attic	Closed	10.00	14.00
89-01-005	Winnie-Angel 2325	Sarah's Attic	Closed	10.00	14.00
89-01-006	Wendy-Angel 2326	Sarah's Attic	Closed	10.00	14.00
89-01-007	Wilbur-Angel 2327	Sarah's Attic	Closed	10.00	21.50
89-01-008	Bonnie-Angel 2328	Sarah's Attic	Closed	17.00	20.00
89-01-009	Clyde-Angel 2329	Sarah's Attic	Closed	17.00	20.00
89-01-010	Floppy-Angel 2330	Sarah's Attic	Closed	10.00	20.00
89-01-011	Edie-Angel 2331	Sarah's Attic	Closed	10.00	10.00
89-01-012	Jessica-Angel 2332	Sarah's Attic	Closed	14.00	14.00
89-01-013	Jeffrey-Angel 2333	Sarah's Attic	Closed	14.00	14.00
89-01-014	Amelia-Angel 2334	Sarah's Attic	Closed	10.00	14.00
89-01-015	Alex-Angel 2335	Sarah's Attic	Closed	10.00	14.00
89-01-016	Abbee-Angel-2336	Sarah's Attic	Closed	10.00	13.00
89-01-017	Ashbee-Angel 2337	Sarah's Attic	Closed	10.00	13.00
89-01-018	Rayburn-Angel 2338	Sarah's Attic	Closed	12.00	19.00
89-01-019	Reggie-Angel 2339	Sarah's Attic	Closed	12.00	15.00
89-01-020	Reba-Angel 2340	Sarah's Attic	Closed	12.00	12.00
89-01-021	Ruthie-Angel 2341	Sarah's Attic	Closed	12.00	12.00
89-01-022	Daisy Angel 2352	Sarah's Attic	Closed	14.00	14.00
89-01-023	Patsy Angel 2353	Sarah's Attic	Closed	13.00	13.00
89-01-024	Ashlee Angel 2354	Sarah's Attic	Closed	14.00	14.00
89-01-025	Shooter Angel 2355	Sarah's Attic	Closed	12.00	18.00
89-01-026	Grams Angel 2356	Sarah's Attic	Closed	17.00	35.00
89-01-027	Gramps Angel 2357	Sarah's Attic	Closed	17.00	95.00
89-01-028	Dusty Angel 2358	Sarah's Attic	Closed	12.00	95.00
89-01-029	Emmy Lou Angel 2359	Sarah's Attic	Closed	12.00	12.00
89-01-030	Saint Willie Bill 2360	Sarah's Attic	Closed	30.00	40.00
89-01-031	Bevie Angel 2361	Sarah's Attic	Closed	10.00	10.00
89-01-032	Angelica Angel 3201	Sarah's Attic	Closed	25.00	25.00
89-01-033	Regina 3208	Sarah's Attic	Closed	24.00	24.00
89-01-034	St. George 3211	Sarah's Attic	Closed	60.00	65.00
89-01-035	Heavenly Guardian 3213	Sarah's Attic	Closed	40.00	40.00
90-01-036	Enos Boy Angel Sitting 3275	Sarah's Attic	Closed	33.00	33.00
90-01-037	Adora Girl Angel Standing 3276	Sarah's Attic	Closed	35.00	35.00
90-01-038	Angel Rabbit in Basket 3293	Sarah's Attic	Closed	25.00	25.00
90-01-039	Angel Bear in Basket 3294	Sarah's Attic	Closed	23.00	23.00
90-01-040	Billie Angel 3295	Sarah's Attic	Closed	18.00	22.00
90-01-041	Cindi Angel 3296	Sarah's Attic	Closed	18.00	22.00
90-01-042	Lena Angel 3297	Sarah's Attic	Closed	36.00	40.00
90-01-043	Trudy Angel 3298	Sarah's Attic	Closed	36.00	36.00
90-01-044	Trapper Angel 3299	Sarah's Attic	Closed	17.00	20.00
90-01-045	Louise Angel 3300	Sarah's Attic	Closed	17.00	20.00
90-01-046	Flossy Angel 3301	Sarah's Attic	Closed	15.00	15.00
90-01-047	Buster Angel 3302	Sarah's Attic	Closed	15.00	15.00
91-01-031	Crate of Love-White 2403	Sarah's Attic	Closed	40.00	40.00
91-01-048	Angel Adora With Bunny 3390	Sarah's Attic	Closed	50.00	50.00
91-01-049	Angel Enos With Frog 3391	Sarah's Attic	Closed	50.00	50.00

Company		Series			
Number	**Name**	**Artist**	**Edition Limit**	**Issue Price**	**Quote**
91-01-050	Donald Angel 3415	Sarah's Attic	Closed	50.00	50.00
91-01-051	Bert Angel 3416	Sarah's Attic	Closed	60.00	60.00
91-01-052	Crate of Love-Black 3496	Sarah's Attic	Closed	40.00	40.00
92-01-053	Love-Grandpa Harold 3501	Sarah's Attic	Closed	80.00	80.00
92-01-054	Contentment-Grandma Bill 3500	Sarah's Attic	Closed	100.00	100.00
92-01-055	Priscilla Angel 3511	Sarah's Attic	Closed	46.00	46.00
92-01-056	Angel Pup 3519	Sarah's Attic	Closed	14.00	14.00
92-01-057	Hope Angel 3659	Sarah's Attic	12/94	40.00	40.00
92-01-058	Heavenly Caring 3661	Sarah's Attic	Closed	70.00	70.00
92-01-059	Heavenly Sharing 3662	Sarah's Attic	Closed	70.00	70.00
92-01-060	Heavenly Giving 3663	Sarah's Attic	Closed	70.00	70.00
92-01-061	Heavenly Loving 3664	Sarah's Attic	Closed	70.00	70.00
92-01-062	Enos & Adora-Small 3671	Sarah's Attic	Closed	35.00	35.00
92-01-063	Harmony Angel 3710	Sarah's Attic	3,500	26.00	26.00
92-01-064	Joy Angel 3711	Sarah's Attic	3,500	26.00	26.00
92-01-065	Noble Angel 3712	Sarah's Attic	3,500	24.00	24.00
92-01-066	Sincerity Angel 3713	Sarah's Attic	3,500	24.00	24.00
93-01-067	Heavenly Uniting 3794	Sarah's Attic	2,500	45.00	45.00
93-01-068	Heavenly Protecting 3795	Sarah's Attic	2,500	40.00	40.00
93-01-069	Heavenly Peace 3833	Sarah's Attic	2,500	47.00	47.00
93-01-070	Faith-Black Angel 3953	Sarah's Attic	1,994	40.00	40.00
93-01-071	Grace-White Angel 3954	Sarah's Attic	1,994	40.00	40.00
93-01-072	Mr. Ward-Happy Me 3971	Sarah's Attic	500	40.00	40.00
94-01-073	Adora w/Harp 4137	Sarah's Attic	4,000	26.00	26.00
94-01-074	Enos w/Horn 4138	Sarah's Attic	4,000	26.00	26.00
Sarah's Attic, Inc.		**Spirit of America**			
88-02-001	Betsy Ross 3024	Sarah's Attic	Closed	40.00	40.00
88-02-002	Indian Brave 4007	Sarah's Attic	Closed	10.00	10.00
88-02-003	Indian Girl 4008	Sarah's Attic	Closed	10.00	10.00
88-02-004	Pilgrim Boy 4009	Sarah's Attic	Closed	12.00	12.00
88-02-005	Pilgrim Girl 4010	Sarah's Attic	Closed	12.00	12.00
91-02-006	Iron Hawk Father Indian 3344	Sarah's Attic	Closed	70.00	140.00
91-02-007	Bright Sky Mother Indian 3345	Sarah's Attic	Closed	70.00	140.00
91-02-008	Little Dove Girl Indian 3346	Sarah's Attic	Closed	40.00	80.00
91-02-009	Spotted Eagle Boy Indian 3347	Sarah's Attic	Closed	30.00	60.00
91-02-010	Forever in Our Hearts 3413	Sarah's Attic	10,000	90.00	90.00
92-02-011	Gray Wolf Father Indian 3692	Sarah's Attic	2,000	46.00	46.00
92-02-012	Morning Flower Indian 3693	Sarah's Attic	2,000	46.00	46.00
92-02-013	Red Feather Boy Indian 3694	Sarah's Attic	2,000	30.00	30.00
92-02-014	Moon Dance Girl Indian 3695	Sarah's Attic	2,000	30.00	30.00
93-02-015	Abraham Lincoln 3876	Sarah's Attic	1,863	60.00	60.00
93-02-016	Lincoln's Birth House 3877	Sarah's Attic	1,863	34.00	34.00
93-02-017	George Washington 3878	Sarah's Attic	1,789	60.00	60.00
93-02-018	George Washington's Birth House 3879	Sarah's Attic	1,789	45.00	45.00
93-02-019	Tallman House 3900	Sarah's Attic	1,856	50.00	50.00
93-02-020	Democrat Donkey 3955	Sarah's Attic	1,840	40.00	40.00
93-02-021	Republican Elephant 3956	Sarah's Attic	1,854	40.00	40.00
94-02-022	Asthon-Mother Indian 3977	Sarah's Attic	1,000	40.00	40.00
94-02-023	Hosteen-Father Indian 3978	Sarah's Attic	1,000	40.00	40.00
94-02-024	Siyah-Girl Indian 3979	Sarah's Attic	1,000	25.00	25.00
94-02-025	Shine-Boy Indian 3980	Sarah's Attic	1,000	25.00	50.00
94-02-026	Hogan-Indian House 3981	Sarah's Attic	1,000	40.00	40.00
94-02-027	Daniel Boone 4109	Sarah's Attic	1,769	60.00	60.00
94-02-028	Benjamin Franklin 4124	Sarah's Attic	1,776	70.00	70.00
Sarah's Attic, Inc.		**Beary Adorables Collection**			
86-03-001	Bear Resin Candle 2022	Sarah's Attic	Closed	12.00	12.00
86-03-002	Collectible Bear 2035	Sarah's Attic	Closed	14.00	14.00
87-03-003	Alex Bear 2003	Sarah's Attic	Closed	10.00	11.50
87-03-004	Amelia Bear 2004	Sarah's Attic	Closed	8.00	11.50
87-03-005	Abbee Bear 2005	Sarah's Attic	Closed	6.00	10.00
87-03-006	Ashbee Bear 2006	Sarah's Attic	Closed	6.00	10.00
87-03-007	Double Bear on Swing 5114	Sarah's Attic	Closed	20.00	20.00
87-03-008	Bear on Trunk 5126	Sarah's Attic	Closed	16.00	20.00
87-03-009	Bear with Bow 5130	Sarah's Attic	Closed	8.00	8.00
87-03-010	Double Bears w/Wood Heart 5400	Sarah's Attic	Closed	10.00	10.00
88-03-011	Americana Bear w/Bow 2072	Sarah's Attic	Closed	10.00	10.00
88-03-012	Americana Bear w/Jacket 2073	Sarah's Attic	Closed	10.00	10.00
88-03-013	Americana Collectible Bear 2074	Sarah's Attic	Closed	18.00	18.00
88-03-014	Girl Bear Resin Candle 3027	Sarah's Attic	Closed	11.00	11.00
88-03-015	Ghost Bear 3028	Sarah's Attic	Closed	9.00	12.00
88-03-016	Americana Bear 3047	Sarah's Attic	Closed	50.00	50.00
88-03-017	Lefty Bear in Stocking 3049	Sarah's Attic	Closed	70.00	70.00
88-03-018	Bear in Basket 4022	Sarah's Attic	Closed	48.00	48.00
88-03-019	Einstein Bear 6266	Sarah's Attic	Closed	8.00	8.50
88-03-020	Benni Bear 6267	Sarah's Attic	Closed	7.00	7.00
88-03-021	Bear Clown 6276	Sarah's Attic	Closed	12.00	12.50
88-03-022	Honey Ma Bear 6316	Sarah's Attic	Closed	16.00	20.00
88-03-023	Rufus Pa Bear 6317	Sarah's Attic	Closed	15.00	20.00
88-03-024	Marti Girl Bear 6318	Sarah's Attic	Closed	12.00	20.00
88-03-025	Arti Boy Bear 6319	Sarah's Attic	Closed	7.00	15.00
88-03-026	Boy Bear Resin Candle 3070	Sarah's Attic	Closed	12.00	12.00
89-03-027	Mini Girl Bear 2315	Sarah's Attic	Closed	5.00	5.00
89-03-028	Mini Boy Bear 2316	Sarah's Attic	Closed	5.00	5.00
89-03-029	Mini Sleeping Bear 2317	Sarah's Attic	Closed	5.00	5.00
89-03-030	Sid Papa Bear 3092	Sarah's Attic	Closed	18.00	25.00
89-03-031	Sophie Mama Bear 3093	Sarah's Attic	Closed	18.00	25.00
89-03-032	Sarah's Bear 3096	Sarah's Attic	Closed	14.50	14.50
89-03-033	Betsy Bear w/Flag 3097	Sarah's Attic	Closed	22.00	22.00
89-03-034	Colonial Bear w/Hat 3098	Sarah's Attic	Closed	22.00	22.00
89-03-035	Daisey Bear 3101	Sarah's Attic	Closed	48.00	55.00
89-03-036	Griswald Bear 3102	Sarah's Attic	Closed	48.00	55.00
89-03-037	Missy Bear 3103	Sarah's Attic	Closed	26.00	30.00
89-03-038	Mikey Bear 3104	Sarah's Attic	Closed	26.00	30.00
89-03-039	Angel Bear 3105	Sarah's Attic	Closed	24.00	24.50
89-03-040	Spice Bear Crawling 3109	Sarah's Attic	Closed	12.00	15.00
89-03-041	Mini Teddy Bear 3110	Sarah's Attic	Closed	5.00	5.00
89-03-042	Sammy Boy Bear 3111	Sarah's Attic	Closed	12.00	15.00
89-03-043	Sugar Bear Sitting 3112	Sarah's Attic	Closed	12.00	12.00
90-03-044	Bailey 50's Papa Bear 3250	Sarah's Attic	Closed	30.00	30.00
90-03-045	Beulah 50's Mama Bear 3251	Sarah's Attic	Closed	30.00	30.00
90-03-046	Birkey 50's Boy Bear Teddy 3252	Sarah's Attic	Closed	25.00	25.00
90-03-047	Belinda 50's Girl Bear 3253	Sarah's Attic	Closed	25.00	25.00
91-03-048	Miss Love Bear 3354	Sarah's Attic	Closed	42.00	42.00
91-03-049	Dudley Bear 3355	Sarah's Attic	Closed	32.00	32.00
91-03-050	Margie Bear 3356	Sarah's Attic	Closed	32.00	32.00
91-03-051	Joey Bear 3357	Sarah's Attic	Closed	32.00	32.00
91-03-052	Franny Bear 3358	Sarah's Attic	Closed	32.00	32.00
91-03-053	Oliver Bear 3359	Sarah's Attic	Closed	32.00	32.00
93-03-054	Beary Huggable Bear 3760	Sarah's Attic	Open	18.00	18.00
93-03-055	Miss You Beary Much Bear 3761	Sarah's Attic	Open	18.00	18.00
93-03-056	You're Beary Special Bear 3762	Sarah's Attic	Open	18.00	18.00
93-03-057	I'm Beary Sorry Bear 3763	Sarah's Attic	Open	18.00	18.00
93-03-058	I Love You Bears 3812	Sarah's Attic	Open	22.00	22.00
93-03-059	Beary Happy Halloween 3830	Sarah's Attic	Open	18.00	18.00
93-03-060	Beary Merry Christmas 3831	Sarah's Attic	Open	20.00	20.00
93-03-061	Beary Special Sister Bear 3872	Sarah's Attic	Open	18.00	18.00
93-03-062	Beary Special Brother Bear 3873	Sarah's Attic	Open	18.00	18.00
93-03-063	Beary Special Mother Bear 3874	Sarah's Attic	Open	18.00	18.00
93-03-064	Beary Special Father Bear 3875	Sarah's Attic	Open	22.00	22.00
93-03-065	Professor Bear 3906	Sarah's Attic	Open	24.00	24.00
93-03-066	Tommy's Bear 3907	Sarah's Attic	Open	24.00	24.00
93-03-067	Irish Bear 3908	Sarah's Attic	Open	24.00	24.00
93-03-068	Just Ted Bear 3909	Sarah's Attic	Open	24.00	24.00
93-03-069	Dowager Twins Bear 3910	Sarah's Attic	Open	24.00	24.00
93-03-070	Me and My Shadow Bear 3911	Sarah's Attic	Open	26.00	26.00
93-03-071	Second Hand-Rose Bear 3912	Sarah's Attic	Open	24.00	24.00
93-03-072	Witchie Bear 3913	Sarah's Attic	Open	24.00	24.00
93-03-073	Bellhop Bear 3914	Sarah's Attic	Open	24.00	24.00
93-03-074	Eddie Bear 3915	Sarah's Attic	Open	24.00	24.00
93-03-075	Librarian Bear 3916	Sarah's Attic	Open	24.00	24.00
93-03-076	Aunt Eunice Bear 3917	Sarah's Attic	Open	24.00	24.00
93-03-077	Eddie w/Trunk 3918	Sarah's Attic	Open	40.00	40.00
93-03-078	Librarian w/Desk 3919	Sarah's Attic	Open	40.00	40.00
93-03-079	Bellhop & Second-Hand Rose 3920	Sarah's Attic	Open	40.00	40.00
93-03-080	Witchie w/Pot 3921	Sarah's Attic	Open	40.00	40.00
93-03-081	Tommy w/Dog 3922	Sarah's Attic	Open	40.00	40.00
93-03-082	Just Ted w/Mirror 3923	Sarah's Attic	Open	40.00	40.00
93-03-083	Aunt Eunice Bathtime 3924	Sarah's Attic	Open	40.00	40.00
93-03-084	Professor w/Board 3925	Sarah's Attic	Open	40.00	40.00
93-03-085	Me and My Shadow w/Chair 3926	Sarah's Attic	Open	45.00	45.00
93-03-086	Dowager Twins on Couch 3927	Sarah's Attic	Open	60.00	60.00
93-03-087	Irish Bear at Pub 3928	Sarah's Attic	Open	40.00	40.00
93-03-088	Michaud Bear Sign 3929	Sarah's Attic	Open	35.00	35.00
94-03-089	Beary Special Friend Bear 3961	Sarah's Attic	Open	20.00	20.00
94-03-090	Beary Special Birthday Bear 3962	Sarah's Attic	Open	20.00	20.00
94-03-091	Get Well Soon Bear 3992	Sarah's Attic	Open	20.00	20.00
Sarah's Attic, Inc.		**Black Heritage Collection**			
89-04-001	Quilting Ladies 3099	Sarah's Attic	Closed	90.00	275.00
89-04-002	Pappy Jake 3100	Sarah's Attic	Closed	40.00	100-150.
90-04-003	Susie Mae 3231	Sarah's Attic	Open	22.00	22.00
90-04-004	Caleb-Lying Down 3232	Sarah's Attic	Open	23.00	23.00
90-04-005	Hattie-Knitting 3233	Sarah's Attic	Closed	40.00	100-135.
90-04-006	Whoopie & Wooster 3255	Sarah's Attic	Closed	50.00	275-310.
90-04-007	Portia Reading Book 3256	Sarah's Attic	Closed	30.00	65-85.00
90-04-008	Harpster W/Banjo 3257	Sarah's Attic	Closed	60.00	275-310.
90-04-009	Libby w/Overalls 3259	Sarah's Attic	Closed	36.00	150.00
90-04-010	Lucas w/Overalls 3260	Sarah's Attic	Closed	36.00	150.00
90-04-011	Praise the Lord I (Preacher I) 3277	Sarah's Attic	Closed	55.00	100.00
90-04-012	Pearl-Black Girl Dancing 3291	Sarah's Attic	Closed	45.00	75.00
90-04-013	Percy-Black Boy Dancing 3292	Sarah's Attic	Closed	45.00	75.00
90-04-014	Brotherly Love 3336	Sarah's Attic	Closed	80.00	80-120.00
91-04-015	Nighttime Pearl 3362	Sarah's Attic	Closed	50.00	55.00
91-04-016	Nighttime Percy 3363	Sarah's Attic	Closed	50.00	50.00
91-04-017	Sadie & Osie Mae 3365	Sarah's Attic	Closed	70.00	70.00
91-04-018	Corporal Pervis 3366	Sarah's Attic	Closed	60.00	60.00
91-04-019	Portia-Victorian Dress 3373	Sarah's Attic	Closed	35.00	35.00
91-04-020	Wester-Victorian Suit 3374	Sarah's Attic	Closed	35.00	35.00
91-04-021	Caleb W/Vegetables 3375	Sarah's Attic	Closed	50.00	50.00
91-04-022	Praise the Lord II w/Kids 3376	Sarah's Attic	5,000	100.00	100.00
91-04-023	Harpster W/Harmonica II 3384	Sarah's Attic	Closed	60.00	60.00
91-04-024	Whoopie & Wooster II 3385	Sarah's Attic	Closed	70.00	70.00
91-04-025	Libby W/Puppy 3386	Sarah's Attic	Closed	50.00	65.00
91-04-026	Lucas W/Dog 3387	Sarah's Attic	Closed	50.00	65.00
91-04-027	Black Baby Tansy 3388	Sarah's Attic	Closed	40.00	50.00
91-04-028	Uncle Reuben 3389	Sarah's Attic	Closed	70.00	110.00
91-04-029	Pappy Jake & Susie Mae 3482	Sarah's Attic	Closed	60.00	60.00
91-04-030	Hattie Quilting 3483	Sarah's Attic	Closed	60.00	60.00
91-04-031	Portia Quilting 3484	Sarah's Attic	Closed	40.00	40.00
91-04-032	Caleb With Football 3485	Sarah's Attic	Closed	40.00	40.00
92-04-033	Muffy-Prayer Time 3509	Sarah's Attic	Closed	46.00	46.00
92-04-034	Calvin Prayer Time 3510	Sarah's Attic	Closed	46.00	46.00
92-04-035	Buffalo Soldier 3524	Sarah's Attic	Closed	80.00	80.00
92-04-036	Porter 3525	Sarah's Attic	Closed	80.00	80.00
92-04-037	Music Masters 3533	Sarah's Attic	Closed	300.00	300.00
92-04-038	Granny Wynne & Olivia 3535	Sarah's Attic	5,000	85.00	85.00
92-04-039	Esther w/Butter Churn 3536	Sarah's Attic	5,000	70.00	70.00
92-04-040	Rhythm & Blues 3620	Sarah's Attic	5,000	80.00	80.00
92-04-041	Music Masters II 3621	Sarah's Attic	1,000	250.00	250.00
92-04-042	Sojourner Truth 3629	Sarah's Attic	Closed	80.00	80.00
92-04-043	Ida B. Wells & Frederick Douglass 3642	Sarah's Attic	Closed	160.00	160.00
92-04-044	Booker T. Washington 3648	Sarah's Attic	Closed	80.00	80.00
92-04-045	Jomo-African Boy 3652	Sarah's Attic	4,000	27.00	27.00
92-04-046	Boys Night Out 3660	Sarah's Attic	2,000	350.00	350.00
92-04-047	Kaminda-African Woman 3679	Sarah's Attic	4,000	50.00	50.00
92-04-048	Shamba-African Man 3680	Sarah's Attic	4,000	50.00	50.00
92-04-049	Nurturing with Love-3686	Sarah's Attic	Closed	60.00	60.00
92-04-050	Harriet Tubman 3687	Sarah's Attic	Closed	60.00	60.00
93-04-051	Waldo Dog Gospel Singer 3751	Sarah's Attic	2,500	10.00	10.00
93-04-052	Miles Boy Angel 3752	Sarah's Attic	2,500	27.00	27.00
93-04-053	Praise the Lord III 3753	Sarah's Attic	2,500	44.00	44.00
93-04-054	Bessie Gospel Singer 3754	Sarah's Attic	2,500	40.00	40.00
93-04-055	Jesse Gospel Singer 3755	Sarah's Attic	2,500	40.00	40.00
93-04-056	Vanessa Gospel Singer 3756	Sarah's Attic	2,500	40.00	40.00
93-04-057	Claudia w/Tamborine Singer 3757	Sarah's Attic	2,500	27.00	27.00
93-04-058	Brewster Clapping Singer 3758	Sarah's Attic	2,500	27.00	27.00
93-04-059	Moriah Girl Angel 3759	Sarah's Attic	2,500	27.00	27.00
93-04-060	Nat Love Cowboy (Isom Dart) 3792	Sarah's Attic	2,500	45.00	45.00
93-04-061	Otis Redding 3793	Sarah's Attic	Closed	70.00	70.00
93-04-062	Carter Woodson 3845	Sarah's Attic	3,000	45.00	45.00
93-04-063	Phillis Wheatley 3846	Sarah's Attic	3,000	45.00	45.00
93-04-064	Mary McLeod Bethune 3847	Sarah's Attic	3,000	45.00	45.00
93-04-065	George Washington Carver 3848	Sarah's Attic	3,000	45.00	45.00
93-04-066	Madame CJ Walker 3849	Sarah's Attic	3,000	45.00	45.00
94-04-067	Harriet Tubman 4110	Sarah's Attic	2,500	50.00	50.00
94-04-068	Nat Love w/Saddle 4121	Sarah's Attic	2,500	60.00	60.00
94-04-069	Mary Church Terrell 4122	Sarah's Attic	2,500	50.00	50.00
94-04-070	W.E.B. DuBois 4123	Sarah's Attic	2,500	60.00	60.00
94-04-071	Libby w/Jacks 4139	Sarah's Attic	4,000	26.00	26.00
94-04-072	Lucas w/Papers 4140	Sarah's Attic	4,000	26.00	26.00
94-04-073	Kitty w/Microphone 4141	Sarah's Attic	2,000	50.00	50.00
94-04-074	Music Master III 4142	Sarah's Attic	2,000	80.00	80.00
94-04-075	Coretta Scott King 4178	Sarah's Attic	12/96	60.00	60.00
94-04-076	Martin Luther King, Jr. 4179	Sarah's Attic	12/96	65.00	65.00

Number	Name	Artist	Edition Limit	Issue Price	Quote
Sarah's Attic, Inc.		**Cuddly Critters Collection**			
86-05-001	Goose Resin Candle 2021	Sarah's Attic	Closed	12.00	12.00
87-05-002	Small Duck 0062	Sarah's Attic	Closed	2.00	2.00
87-05-003	Small Long Neck Goose 2007	Sarah's Attic	Closed	5.00	5.00
87-05-004	Large Long Neck Goose 2008	Sarah's Attic	Closed	8.00	8.00
87-05-005	Small Sitting Goose 2009	Sarah's Attic	Closed	3.00	3.00
87-05-006	Medium Sitting Goose 2010	Sarah's Attic	Closed	4.00	4.00
87-05-007	Large Sitting Goose 2011	Sarah's Attic	Closed	7.00	7.00
87-05-008	Goose 2037	Sarah's Attic	Closed	14.00	14.00
87-05-009	Snapper-Turtle 5109	Sarah's Attic	Closed	8.00	8.00
87-05-010	Sheep Sitting 5132	Sarah's Attic	Closed	6.00	6.00
87-05-011	Sheep Standing 5133	Sarah's Attic	Closed	6.00	6.00
87-05-012	Cat on Heart 5138	Sarah's Attic	Closed	6.00	6.00
87-05-013	Goose on Heart 5147	Sarah's Attic	Closed	6.00	6.00
87-05-014	Pig on Heart 5161	Sarah's Attic	Closed	6.00	6.00
88-05-015	Americana Sparky 2075	Sarah's Attic	Closed	12.00	12.00
88-05-016	Cow w/Bell 3023	Sarah's Attic	Closed	28.00	28.00
88-05-017	Rocking Horse 6150	Sarah's Attic	Closed	44.00	44.00
88-05-018	Mini Duck 6218	Sarah's Attic	Closed	5.00	5.00
88-05-019	Mini Pig 6219	Sarah's Attic	Closed	5.00	5.00
88-05-020	Mini Sheep 6220	Sarah's Attic	Closed	6.00	6.00
88-05-021	Mini Chicken 6221	Sarah's Attic	Closed	5.00	5.00
88-05-022	Mini Rabbit 6222	Sarah's Attic	Closed	5.00	5.00
88-05-023	Mini Cow 6223	Sarah's Attic	Closed	8.00	8.00
88-05-024	Lazy-cat On Back 6265	Sarah's Attic	Closed	13.00	13.00
88-05-025	Clown Puppy 6273	Sarah's Attic	Closed	8.00	8.00
88-05-026	Buster Boy Cat 6275	Sarah's Attic	Closed	14.00	14.00
88-05-027	Flossy Girl Cat 6277	Sarah's Attic	Closed	10.00	10.00
88-05-028	Trapper Papa Cat 6278	Sarah's Attic	Closed	20.00	25.00
88-05-029	Louise Mama Cat 6279	Sarah's Attic	Closed	20.00	25.00
88-05-030	Sheep on Wheels 6280	Sarah's Attic	Closed	16.00	16.00
88-05-031	Pig on Wheels 6281	Sarah's Attic	Closed	16.00	16.00
88-05-032	Sleeping Cat 6315	Sarah's Attic	Closed	6.00	6.00
88-05-033	Carousel Horse 6332	Sarah's Attic	Closed	31.00	31.00
88-05-034	Kitty Cat w/Bonnet 2283	Sarah's Attic	Closed	10.00	10.00
88-05-035	Grady Pa Mouse 3075	Sarah's Attic	Closed	13.00	13.00
88-05-036	Lila Mom Mouse 4000	Sarah's Attic	Closed	18.00	27.00
88-05-037	Lucky Boy Mouse 4001	Sarah's Attic	Closed	13.00	20.00
88-05-038	Lucy Girl Mouse 4002	Sarah's Attic	Closed	12.00	20.00
88-05-039	Myrtle The Pig 6504	Sarah's Attic	Closed	38.00	45.00
89-05-040	Brown Cow 2113	Sarah's Attic	Closed	18.00	18.00
89-05-041	Madam Donna 2321	Sarah's Attic	Closed	36.00	45.00
89-05-042	Maggie's Puppy 3091	Sarah's Attic	Closed	8.00	8.00
89-05-043	Whiskers Boy Cat 3106	Sarah's Attic	Closed	10.00	10.00
89-05-044	Puddin Girl Cat 3107	Sarah's Attic	Closed	10.00	10.00
89-05-045	Otis Pa Cat 3108	Sarah's Attic	Closed	13.00	13.00
89-05-046	Messieur Pierre 2346	Sarah's Attic	Closed	36.00	45.00
89-05-047	Wiggley Pig 3205	Sarah's Attic	Closed	17.00	17.00
90-05-048	Sherman Pa Squirrel 3221	Sarah's Attic	Closed	19.00	29.00
90-05-049	Sasha Ma Squirrel 3222	Sarah's Attic	Closed	19.00	29.00
90-05-050	Sonny Boy Squirrel 3223	Sarah's Attic	Closed	18.00	28.00
90-05-051	Sis Girl Squirrel 3224	Sarah's Attic	Closed	18.00	18.00
90-05-052	Horace & Sissy Dogs 3330	Sarah's Attic	Closed	50.00	50.00
90-05-053	Rebecca Mom Dog 3331	Sarah's Attic	Closed	40.00	40.00
90-05-054	Penny Girl Dog 3332	Sarah's Attic	Closed	35.00	35.00
90-05-055	Scooter Boy Dog 3333	Sarah's Attic	Closed	30.00	30.00
90-05-056	Jasper Dad Cat 3337	Sarah's Attic	Closed	36.00	36.00
90-05-057	Winnie Mom Cat 3338	Sarah's Attic	Closed	36.00	36.00
90-05-058	Scuffy Boy Cat 3339	Sarah's Attic	Closed	26.00	26.00
90-05-059	Lulu Girl Cat 3340	Sarah's Attic	Closed	26.00	26.00
92-05-060	Jiggs Sleeping Cat 3537	Sarah's Attic	Open	10.00	10.00
92-05-061	Banjo Dog 3622	Sarah's Attic	Closed	100.00	100.00
92-05-062	Banjo's Dog Bowl 3732	Sarah's Attic	Closed	10.00	10.00
93-05-063	Ducks on Base 3944	Sarah's Attic	1,994	12.00	12.00
93-05-064	Chicks in Crate 3945	Sarah's Attic	1,994	10.00	10.00
93-05-065	Bunnies w/Eggs 3946	Sarah's Attic	1,994	15.00	15.00
93-05-066	Lambs on Base 3947	Sarah's Attic	1,994	16.00	16.00
93-05-067	Thelma-Easter 3948	Sarah's Attic	1,994	26.00	26.00
93-05-068	Thomas-Easter 3949	Sarah's Attic	1,994	26.00	26.00
93-05-069	Tessy-Easter 3950	Sarah's Attic	1,994	24.00	24.00
93-05-070	Toby-Easter 3951	Sarah's Attic	1,994	24.00	24.00
94-05-071	Cheri-Mom Cat 3964	Sarah's Attic	12/94	30.00	30.00
94-05-072	Chester-Dad Cat 3965	Sarah's Attic	12/94	30.00	30.00
94-05-073	Stinky-Boy Cat 3966	Sarah's Attic	12/94	22.00	22.00
94-05-074	Sweetie-Girl Cat 3967	Sarah's Attic	12/94	16.00	16.00
94-05-075	Dottie-Mom Dog 3973	Sarah's Attic	12/94	30.00	30.00
94-05-076	Duke-Dad Dog 3974	Sarah's Attic	12/94	30.00	30.00
94-05-077	Dixie-Girl Dog 3975	Sarah's Attic	12/94	20.00	20.00
94-05-078	Dusty-Boy Dog 3976	Sarah's Attic	12/94	18.00	18.00
94-05-079	Lamb-lying down 3982	Sarah's Attic	Open	4.00	4.00
94-05-080	Meadow-Horses 3991	Sarah's Attic	500	40.00	40.00
94-05-081	Blaze-Fire Dog 3993	Sarah's Attic	Open	24.00	24.00
94-05-082	Bumbers-Cat Sleeping 3994	Sarah's Attic	Open	18.00	18.00
94-05-083	Gizmo-Cat w/Bow 3995	Sarah's Attic	Open	22.00	22.00
94-05-084	Popper-Dog 3996	Sarah's Attic	Open	14.00	14.00
94-05-085	Winkie-Cat 3997	Sarah's Attic	Open	14.00	14.00
94-05-086	Look at Me Cat 4134	Sarah's Attic	Open	25.00	25.00
Sarah's Attic, Inc.		**Classroom Memories**			
88-06-001	Miss Pritchett	Sarah's Attic	Open	28.00	35.00
91-06-002	Achieving Our Goals	Sarah's Attic	10,000	80.00	80.00
Sarah's Attic, Inc.		**Cotton Tale Collection**			
86-07-001	Winnie Rabbit 2036	Sarah's Attic	Closed	14.00	14.00
87-07-002	Wendall Rabbit 5285	Sarah's Attic	Closed	14.00	25.00
87-07-003	Wendy Rabbit 5286	Sarah's Attic	Closed	15.00	25.00
87-07-004	Wilbur Rabbit 5287	Sarah's Attic	Closed	13.00	25.00
87-07-005	Bonnie 5727	Sarah's Attic	Closed	30.00	30.00
87-07-006	Clyde 5728	Sarah's Attic	Closed	30.00	30.00
87-07-007	Floppy 5729	Sarah's Attic	Closed	19.00	19.00
88-07-008	Girl Rabbit Resin candle 3025	Sarah's Attic	Closed	9.00	9.00
88-07-009	Boy Rabbit Resin Candle 3026	Sarah's Attic	Closed	9.00	9.00
88-07-010	Lizzy Hare 3037	Sarah's Attic	Closed	8.00	8.00
88-07-011	Izzy Hare 3038	Sarah's Attic	Closed	8.00	8.00
88-07-012	Maddy Hare 3039	Sarah's Attic	Closed	11.00	11.00
88-07-013	Amos Hare 3040	Sarah's Attic	Closed	11.00	11.00
88-07-014	Americana Bunny 3048	Sarah's Attic	Closed	58.00	58.00
88-07-015	Bunny in Basket 4021	Sarah's Attic	Closed	48.00	55.00
88-07-016	Bunny w/Wreath 6262	Sarah's Attic	Closed	8.00	8.00
88-07-017	Wendall Mini Rabbit 6268	Sarah's Attic	Closed	8.00	8.00
88-07-018	Wilbur Mini Rabbit 6269	Sarah's Attic	Closed	8.00	8.00
88-07-019	Wendy Mini Rabbit 6270	Sarah's Attic	Closed	8.00	8.00
88-07-020	Winnie Mini Rabbit 6271	Sarah's Attic	Closed	8.00	8.00
88-07-021	Cindi Rabbit 6282	Sarah's Attic	Closed	27.00	35.00
88-07-022	Billi Rabbit 6283	Sarah's Attic	Closed	27.00	35.00
89-07-023	Crumb Rabbit 3077	Sarah's Attic	Closed	29.00	35-43.00
89-07-024	Cookie Rabbit 3078	Sarah's Attic	Closed	29.00	35-43.00
89-07-025	Papa Rabbit 3079	Sarah's Attic	Closed	50.00	60-75.00
89-07-026	Nana Rabbit 3080	Sarah's Attic	Closed	50.00	60-75.00
89-07-027	Thelma Rabbit 3084	Sarah's Attic	Closed	33.00	40.00
89-07-028	Thomas Rabbit 3085	Sarah's Attic	Closed	33.00	40.00
89-07-029	Tessy Rabbit 3086	Sarah's Attic	Closed	15.00	20.00
89-07-030	Toby Rabbit 3087	Sarah's Attic	Closed	17.00	20.00
89-07-031	Sleepy Rabbit 3088	Sarah's Attic	Closed	16.00	16.00
90-07-032	Zeb Pa Rabbit w/Carrots 3217	Sarah's Attic	Closed	18.00	32.00
90-07-033	Zelda Ma Rabbit w/Carrots 3218	Sarah's Attic	Closed	18.00	32.00
90-07-034	Zeke Boy Rabbit w/Carrots 3219	Sarah's Attic	Closed	17.00	32.00
87-07-035	Zoe Girl Rabbit w/Carrots 3220	Sarah's Attic	Closed	17.00	32.00
90-07-036	Ollie Rabbit w/Vest 3239	Sarah's Attic	Closed	75.00	75.00
90-07-037	Molly Rabbit w/Vest 3240	Sarah's Attic	Closed	75.00	75.00
90-07-038	Henry Dad Rabbit w/Pipe 3263	Sarah's Attic	Closed	32.00	32.00
90-07-039	Zeb Sailor Dad 3319	Sarah's Attic	Closed	28.00	28.00
90-07-040	Zelda Sailor Mom 3320	Sarah's Attic	Closed	28.00	28.00
90-07-041	Zeke Sailor Boy 3321	Sarah's Attic	Closed	26.00	26.00
90-07-042	Zoe Sailor Girl 3322	Sarah's Attic	Closed	26.00	26.00
90-07-043	Snowball Rabbit 3329	Sarah's Attic	Closed	8.00	8.00
91-07-044	Papa Rabbit w/Hat 3348	Sarah's Attic	Closed	80.00	80.00
91-07-045	Nana Rabbit w/Washboard 3349	Sarah's Attic	Closed	100.00	100.00
91-07-046	Chuckles Rabbit 3350	Sarah's Attic	Closed	53.00	53.00
91-07-047	Cookie Rabbit 3351	Sarah's Attic	Closed	47.00	47.00
91-07-048	Crumb Rabbit 3352	Sarah's Attic	Closed	53.00	53.00
91-07-049	Sleepy Rabbit 3353	Sarah's Attic	Closed	35.00	35.00
91-07-050	Thomas Victorian Rabbit 3367	Sarah's Attic	Closed	60.00	60.00
91-07-051	Thelma Victorian Rabbit 3368	Sarah's Attic	Closed	60.00	60.00
91-07-052	Toby Victorian Rabbit 3369	Sarah's Attic	Closed	40.00	40.00
91-07-053	Tessy Victorian Rabbit 3370	Sarah's Attic	Closed	20.00	20.00
91-07-054	Tabitha Victorian Rabbit 3371	Sarah's Attic	Closed	30.00	30.00
91-07-055	Tucker Victorian Rabbit 3372	Sarah's Attic	Closed	37.00	37.00
92-07-056	Toby w/Train-Small 3673	Sarah's Attic	Closed	35.00	35.00
92-07-057	Tabitha Christmas 3688	Sarah's Attic	2,500	24.00	24.00
92-07-058	Toby w/Hobby Horse 3689	Sarah's Attic	2,500	32.00	32.00
92-07-059	Flower Girl Rabbit 3699	Sarah's Attic	Closed	32.00	32.00
92-07-060	Dustin Boy Rabbit 3700	Sarah's Attic	Closed	32.00	32.00
92-07-061	Petals Girl Rabbit 3701	Sarah's Attic	2,500	30.00	30.00
92-07-062	Pockets Boy Rabbit 3702	Sarah's Attic	2,500	30.00	30.00
92-07-063	Higgins Dad Rabbit 3703	Sarah's Attic	2,500	40.00	40.00
92-07-064	Annabelle Mom Rabbit 3704	Sarah's Attic	2,500	40.00	40.00
93-07-065	Hannah w/Muff 3733	Sarah's Attic	Closed	30.00	30.00
93-07-066	Henry w/Wreath 3734	Sarah's Attic	Closed	30.00	30.00
93-07-067	Hether in Sled 3735	Sarah's Attic	Closed	30.00	30.00
93-07-068	Herbie Sitting 3736	Sarah's Attic	Closed	25.00	25.00
93-07-069	Toby with Book/Christmas 3737	Sarah's Attic	2,500	20.00	20.00
93-07-070	Tabitha Cowgirl 3738	Sarah's Attic	2,500	30.00	30.00
94-07-071	Tabitha-Valentine 4117	Sarah's Attic	12/94	24.00	24.00
94-07-072	Toby-Valentine 4118	Sarah's Attic	12/94	24.00	24.00
Sarah's Attic, Inc.		**Daisy Collection**			
89-08-001	Sally Booba 2344	Sarah's Attic	Closed	40.00	40.00
90-08-002	Jack Boy Ball & Glove 3249	Sarah's Attic	Closed	40.00	40.00
90-08-003	Sparky-Mark 3307	Sarah's Attic	Closed	55.00	55.00
90-08-004	Spike-Tim 3308	Sarah's Attic	Closed	46.00	46.00
90-08-005	Bomber-Tom 3309	Sarah's Attic	Closed	52.00	52.00
90-08-006	Jewel-Julie 3310	Sarah's Attic	Closed	62.00	62.00
90-08-007	Stretch-Mike 3311	Sarah's Attic	Closed	52.00	52.00
93-08-008	Jack Boy w/Broken Arm 3970	Sarah's Attic	2,000	30.00	30.00
Sarah's Atttic, Inc.		**Ginger Babies Collection**			
89-09-001	Ginger 3202	Sarah's Attic	Closed	17.00	17.00
89-09-002	Molasses 3203	Sarah's Attic	Closed	17.00	17.00
89-09-003	Ginger Basket 3204	Sarah's Attic	Closed	6.00	6.00
90-09-004	Cinnamon 3226	Sarah's Attic	Closed	16.00	16.00
90-09-005	Nutmeg 3227	Sarah's Attic	Closed	16.00	16.00
92-09-006	Home Sweet Home 3608	Sarah's Attic	Closed	100.00	100.00
92-09-007	Ginger Cookie 3909	Sarah's Attic	Closed	50.00	50.00
92-09-008	Ginger Bench 3910	Sarah's Attic	Closed	10.00	10.00
92-09-009	Ginger Fence 3611	Sarah's Attic	Closed	13.00	13.00
92-09-010	Vanilla 3612	Sarah's Attic	Closed	18.00	18.00
92-09-011	Almond 3613	Sarah's Attic	Closed	18.00	18.00
92-09-012	Cinnamon & Nutmeg 3614	Sarah's Attic	Closed	36.00	36.00
92-09-013	Ginger Tree 3615	Sarah's Attic	Closed	20.00	20.00
Sarah's Attic, Inc.		**Happy Collection**			
87-10-001	Large Happy Clown 5113	Sarah's Attic	Closed	20.00	20.00
87-10-002	Mini. Happy Clown 5139	Sarah's Attic	Closed	8.00	8.00
87-10-003	Sitting Happy 3008	Sarah's Attic	Closed	19.00	19.00
87-10-004	Happy w/Balloons 3009	Sarah's Attic	Closed	14.00	14.00
87-10-005	Clown w/Twine 5404	Sarah's Attic	Closed	10.00	10.00
87-10-006	Clown Necklace 5407	Sarah's Attic	Closed	10.00	10.00
88-10-007	Americana Clown 4025	Sarah's Attic	Closed	80.00	80.00
88-10-007	Christmas Clown 4026	Sarah's Attic	Closed	88.00	88.00
88-10-008	Clown Handstand X 6243	Sarah's Attic	Closed	10.00	10.00
88-10-009	Clown Sitting Y 6244	Sarah's Attic	Closed	10.00	10.00
88-10-010	Sitting Clown Z 6259	Sarah's Attic	Closed	10.00	10.00
88-10-011	Lady Clown 6313	Sarah's Attic	Closed	20.00	20.00
89-10-012	Curly Circus Clown 3148	Sarah's Attic	Closed	23.00	23.00
90-10-013	Encore Clown w/Dog 3306	Sarah's Attic	Closed	100.00	100.00
Sarah's Attic, Inc.		**Matt & Maggie**			
86-11-001	Matt Candle Holder	Sarah's Attic	Closed	12.00	12.00
86-11-002	Maggie Candle Holder	Sarah's Attic	Closed	12.00	12.00
86-11-003	Maggie	Sarah's Attic	Closed	14.00	14.00
86-11-004	Matt	Sarah's Attic	Closed	14.00	14.00
87-11-005	Standing Matt	Sarah's Attic	Closed	11.00	11.00
87-11-006	Standing Maggie	Sarah's Attic	Closed	11.00	11.00
87-11-007	Matt on Heart	Sarah's Attic	Closed	9.00	9.00
87-11-008	Maggie on Heart	Sarah's Attic	Closed	9.00	9.00
87-11-009	Matt & Maggie w/ Bear	Sarah's Attic	Closed	100.00	100.00
88-11-010	Large Matt	Sarah's Attic	Closed	48.00	48.00
88-11-012	Small Sitting Matt	Sarah's Attic	Closed	11.50	11.50
88-11-013	Small Sitting Maggie	Sarah's Attic	Closed	11.50	11.50
89-11-014	Mini Matt	Sarah's Attic	Closed	6.00	6.00
89-11-015	Mini Maggie	Sarah's Attic	Closed	6.00	6.00
89-11-016	Matt Bench Sitter	Sarah's Attic	Closed	32.00	32.00
89-11-017	Maggie Bench Sitter	Sarah's Attic	Closed	32.00	32.00
Sarah's Attic, Inc.		**Sarah's Neighborhood Friends**			
87-12-001	Bevie 5103	Sarah's Attic	Closed	14.00	14.00
87-12-002	Gramps 5104	Sarah's Attic	Closed	16.00	16.00

Company Number	Name	Series Artist	Edition Limit	Issue Price	Quote
87-12-003	Grams 5105	Sarah's Attic	Closed	16.00	16.00
87-12-004	Dusty 5106	Sarah's Attic	Closed	19.00	19.00
87-12-005	Willie Bill 5108	Sarah's Attic	Closed	20.00	20.00
87-12-006	Shooter 5110	Sarah's Attic	Closed	20.00	20.00
87-12-007	Emmy Lou 5112	Sarah's Attic	Closed	14.00	14.00
87-12-008	Cheerleader 5120	Sarah's Attic	Closed	19.00	19.00
87-12-009	Eddie 5337	Sarah's Attic	Closed	14.00	14.00
87-12-010	Ashlee 5726	Sarah's Attic	Closed	44.00	44.00
87-12-011	Corky-Boy Sailor Suit 5793	Sarah's Attic	Closed	12.00	12.00
87-12-012	Clementine-Girl Sailor Suit 5794	Sarah's Attic	Closed	12.00	12.00
87-12-013	Butch-Boy Book sitting 5795	Sarah's Attic	Closed	14.00	14.00
87-12-014	Blondie-Girl doll sitting 5796	Sarah's Attic	Closed	14.00	14.00
87-12-015	Amber-Small Girl standing 5797	Sarah's Attic	Closed	14.00	14.00
87-12-016	Archie-Small Boy standing 5798	Sarah's Attic	Closed	14.00	14.00
87-12-017	Bare Bottom Baby 5799	Sarah's Attic	Closed	8.00	8.00
87-12-018	Beau-Cupie Boy 5861	Sarah's Attic	Closed	20.00	20.00
87-12-019	Buttons-Cupie Girl 5862	Sarah's Attic	Closed	20.00	20.00
88-12-020	Americana Beau 2076	Sarah's Attic	Closed	25.00	25.00
88-12-021	Americana Buttons 2077	Sarah's Attic	Closed	25.00	25.00
88-12-022	Jeffrey Boy w/Clown 6151	Sarah's Attic	Closed	26.00	26.00
89-12-023	Lamp Post 3212	Sarah's Attic	Closed	14.00	14.00
89-12-024	Moose Boy sitting 3215	Sarah's Attic	Closed	20.00	20.00
90-12-025	Bubba w/Lantern 3268	Sarah's Attic	Closed	40.00	40.00
90-12-026	Pansy w/Sled 3269	Sarah's Attic	Closed	35.00	35.00
90-12-027	Bud w/Book 3270	Sarah's Attic	Closed	40.00	40.00
90-12-028	Weasel w/Cap 3271	Sarah's Attic	Closed	40.00	40.00
90-12-029	Annie w/Violin 3272	Sarah's Attic	Closed	40.00	40.00
90-12-030	Hewett w/Drum 3273	Sarah's Attic	Closed	40.00	40.00
90-12-031	Waldo Dog 3274	Sarah's Attic	Closed	11.00	11.00
90-12-032	Tyler Victorian Boy 3327	Sarah's Attic	Closed	40.00	40.00
90-12-033	Tiffany Victorian Girl 3328	Sarah's Attic	Closed	40.00	40.00
91-12-034	Hewett w/Apples 3377	Sarah's Attic	Closed	40.00	40.00
91-12-035	Bud w/Newspaper 3378	Sarah's Attic	Closed	40.00	40.00
91-12-036	Waldo w/Flowers 3379	Sarah's Attic	Closed	14.00	14.00
91-12-037	Annie w/Flower Basket 3380	Sarah's Attic	Closed	56.00	56.00
91-12-038	Pansy Pushing Carriage 3381	Sarah's Attic	Closed	50.00	50.00
91-12-039	Bubba w/Lemonade Stand 3382	Sarah's Attic	Closed	54.00	54.00
91-12-040	Weasel w/Newspaper 3383	Sarah's Attic	Closed	40.00	40.00
91-12-041	Dolly Nativity (Jesus) 3418	Sarah's Attic	12/94	20.00	20.00
91-12-042	Annie Nativity (Mary) 3419	Sarah's Attic	12/94	30.00	30.00
91-12-043	Bud Nativity (Joseph) 3420	Sarah's Attic	12/94	34.00	34.00
91-12-044	Kit Nativity 3421	Sarah's Attic	12/94	15.00	15.00
91-12-045	Bubba-Nativity King 3422	Sarah's Attic	12/94	40.00	40.00
91-12-046	Weasel-Nativity King 3423	Sarah's Attic	12/94	40.00	40.00
91-12-047	Hewitt-Nativity King 3424	Sarah's Attic	12/94	40.00	40.00
91-12-048	Pansy-Nativity Angel 3425	Sarah's Attic	12/94	30.00	30.00
91-12-049	Waldo-Nativity 3426	Sarah's Attic	12/94	15.00	15.00
91-12-050	Babes-Nativity Jesus 3427	Sarah's Attic	12/94	20.00	20.00
91-12-051	Noah-Nativity Jesus 3428	Sarah's Attic	12/94	36.00	36.00
91-12-052	Shelby-Nativity Mary 3429	Sarah's Attic	12/94	30.00	30.00
92-12-053	Emily & Gideon-Small 3670	Sarah's Attic	Closed	40.00	40.00
94-12-054	Peaches-Clown 4135	Sarah's Attic	4,000	29.00	29.00
94-12-055	Pug-Clown 4136	Sarah's Attic	4,000	29.00	29.00
Sarah's Attic, Inc.		**Memory Lane Collection**			
89-13-001	Fire Station	Sarah's Attic	Closed	20.00	20.00
89-13-002	Post Office	Sarah's Attic	Closed	25.00	25.00
89-13-003	Mini Depot	Sarah's Attic	Closed	7.00	7.00
89-13-004	Mini Bank	Sarah's Att!c	Closed	6.00	6.00
89-13-005	Briton Church	Sarah's Attic	Closed	25.00	25.00
87-13-006	House W/Dormers	Sarah's Attic	Closed	15.00	15.00
87-13-007	Barn	Sarah's Attic	Closed	16.50	16.50
87-13-008	Mill	Sarah's Attic	Closed	16.50	16.50
87-13-009	Cottage	Sarah's Attic	Closed	13.00	13.00
87-13-010	Barber Shop	Sarah's Attic	Closed	13.00	13.00
87-13-011	Grandma's House	Sarah's Attic	Closed	13.00	13.00
87-13-012	Church	Sarah's Attic	Closed	19.00	19.00
87-13-013	School	Sarah's Attic	Closed	14.00	14.00
87-13-014	General Store	Sarah's Attic	Closed	13.00	13.00
87-13-015	Drug Store	Sarah's Attic	Closed	13.00	13.00
88-13-016	Mini Barber Shop	Sarah's Attic	Closed	6.50	6.50
88-13-017	Mini Drug Store	Sarah's Attic	Closed	6.00	6.00
88-13-018	Mini General Store	Sarah's Attic	Closed	6.00	6.00
88-13-019	Mini Salt Box	Sarah's Attic	Closed	6.00	6.00
88-13-020	Mini Church	Sarah's Attic	Closed	6.50	6.50
88-13-021	Mini School	Sarah's Attic	Closed	6.50	6.50
88-13-022	Mini Barn	Sarah's Attic	Closed	6.00	6.00
88-13-023	Mini Grandma's House	Sarah's Attic	Closed	7.00	7.00
88-13-024	Mini Mill	Sarah's Attic	Closed	6.50	6.50
88-13-025	Bank	Sarah's Attic	Closed	13.00	13.00
88-13-026	Train Depot	Sarah's Attic	Closed	13.50	13.50
Sarah's Attic		**Dreams of Tomorrow**			
87-14-001	Baseball Player 5802	Sarah's Attic	Closed	24.00	24.00
87-14-002	Football Player 5803	Sarah's Attic	Closed	24.00	24.00
87-14-003	Woman Golfer 5804	Sarah's Attic	Closed	24.00	24.00
87-14-004	Man Golfer 5805	Sarah's Attic	Closed	24.00	24.00
88-14-005	Bowler 6152	Sarah's Attic	Closed	24.00	24.00
88-14-006	Basketball Player 6314	Sarah's Attic	Closed	24.00	24.00
91-14-007	Charity Sewing Flags 3486	Sarah's Attic	Closed	46.00	46.00
91-14-008	Benjamin w/Drums 3487	Sarah's Attic	Closed	46.00	46.00
91-14-009	Susie Painting Train 3488	Sarah's Attic	Closed	46.00	46.00
91-14-010	Skip Building Houses 3489	Sarah's Attic	Closed	50.00	50.00
92-14-011	Blossom 3502	Sarah's Attic	Closed	50.00	50.00
92-14-012	Madge-Farmer 3503	Sarah's Attic	Closed	50.00	50.00
92-14-013	Marty-Farmer 3504	Sarah's Attic	Closed	50.00	50.00
92-14-014	Pansy-Nurse 3505	Sarah's Attic	Closed	46.00	46.00
92-14-015	Bubba-Doctor 3506	Sarah's Attic	Closed	60.00	60.00
92-14-016	Annie-Teacher 3507	Sarah's Attic	Closed	55.00	55.00
92-14-017	Noah-Executive 3508	Sarah's Attic	Closed	46.00	46.00
92-14-018	Cupcake-Nurse 3514	Sarah's Attic	Closed	46.00	46.00
92-14-019	Twinkie-Doctor 3515	Sarah's Attic	Closed	50.00	50.00
92-14-020	Tillie-Teacher 3520	Sarah's Attic	Closed	50.00	50.00
92-14-021	Whimpy-Executive 3521	Sarah's Attic	Closed	46.00	46.00
92-14-022	Cricket-Graduate 3531	Sarah's Attic	Closed	46.00	46.00
92-14-023	Chips-Graduate 3532	Sarah's Attic	Closed	46.00	46.00
92-14-024	Katie-Executive 3665	Sarah's Attic	Closed	46.00	46.00
92-14-025	Shelby-Executive 3666	Sarah's Attic	Closed	46.00	46.00
92-14-026	Willie-Fireman 3667	Sarah's Attic	Closed	46.00	46.00
92-14-027	Bud-Fireman 3668	Sarah's Attic	Closed	50.00	50.00
92-14-028	Pansy-Ballerina 3682	Sarah's Attic	Closed	46.00	46.00
92-14-029	Cupcake-Ballerina 3683	Sarah's Attic	Closed	46.00	46.00
92-14-030	Twinkie-Policeman 3684	Sarah's Attic	Closed	46.00	46.00
92-14-031	Bubba-Policeman 3685	Sarah's Attic	Closed	46.00	46.00

Company Number	Name	Series Artist	Edition Limit	Issue Price	Quote
93-14-032	Lottie-White Girl Graduate 3739	Sarah's Attic	Closed	35.00	35.00
93-14-033	Logan-White Boy Graduate 3740	Sarah's Attic	Closed	35.00	35.00
93-14-034	Tillie-Girl Basketball 3774	Sarah's Attic	Open	32.00	32.00
93-14-035	Willie-Boy Baseball 3775	Sarah's Attic	Open	32.00	32.00
93-14-036	Champ-White Boy Baseball 3776	Sarah's Attic	Open	32.00	32.00
93-14-037	Jojo-White Girl Basketball 3777	Sarah's Attic	Open	32.00	32.00
93-14-038	Pansy-Black Waitress 3778	Sarah's Attic	2,000	40.00	40.00
93-14-039	Dana-White Waitress 3779	Sarah's Attic	2,000	34.00	34.00
93-14-040	Noah-Black Pharmacist 3780	Sarah's Attic	2,000	34.00	34.00
93-14-041	Jack-Boy White Pharmacist 3781	Sarah's Attic	2,000	34.00	34.00
93-14-042	Willie-Pilot 3868	Sarah's Attic	2,000	27.00	27.00
93-14-043	Twinkie-Pilot 3869	Sarah's Attic	2,000	27.00	35.00
93-14-044	Tillie-Photographer 3870	Sarah's Attic	2,000	27.00	32.00
93-14-045	Rachel-Photographer 3871	Sarah's Attic	2,000	27.00	32.00
93-14-046	Cody-Cowboy 3886	Sarah's Attic	2,000	30.00	30.00
93-14-047	Josh-Jogger 3887	Sarah's Attic	2,000	25.00	25.00
93-14-048	Katie-Pharmacist 3898	Sarah's Attic	2,000	32.00	32.00
93-14-049	Pansy-Pharmacist 3899	Sarah's Attic	2,000	32.00	32.00
94-14-050	Sally Booba-Graduate 3983	Sarah's Attic	3,000	30.00	30.00
94-14-051	Jack Boy-Graduate 3984	Sarah's Attic	3,000	30.00	30.00
94-14-052	Tillie-Graduate 3985	Sarah's Attic	3,000	30.00	30.00
94-14-053	Willie-Graduate 3986	Sarah's Attic	3,000	30.00	30.00
94-14-054	Katie-Nurse 3987	Sarah's Attic	3,000	33.00	33.00
94-14-055	Whimpy-Doctor 3988	Sarah's Attic	3,000	33.00	33.00
94-14-056	Tillie-Nurse 3989	Sarah's Attic	3,000	33.00	33.00
94-14-057	Willie-Doctor 3990	Sarah's Attic	3,000	33.00	33.00
94-14-058	Dedication-White Doctor 4111	Sarah's Attic	3,000	38.00	38.00
94-14-059	Devotion-Black Doctor 4112	Sarah's Attic	3,000	33.00	33.00
94-14-060	Peaches-Dentist 4113	Sarah's Attic	3,000	33.00	33.00
94-14-061	Pug-Dentist 4114	Sarah's Attic	3,000	33.00	33.00
94-14-062	Twinkie-White Dentist 4115	Sarah's Attic	3,000	33.00	33.00
94-14-063	Cupcake-Dentist 4116	Sarah's Attic	12/94	33.00	33.00
94-14-064	John-Farmer w/Tractor 4119	Sarah's Attic	3,000	36.00	36.00
94-14-065	Joe-Farmer w/Basket 4120	Sarah's Attic	3,000	33.00	33.00
94-14-066	Shelby-Nurse 4127	Sarah's Attic	3,000	33.00	33.00
94-14-067	Annie-Nurse 4128	Sarah's Attic	3,000	33.00	33.00
94-14-068	Juliana-Teacher 4129	Sarah's Attic	3,000	34.00	34.00
94-14-069	Boyd-Teacher 4130	Sarah's Attic	3,000	34.00	34.00
94-14-066	Judy-Teacher 4131	Sarah's Attic	3,000	38.00	38.00
94-14-067	Bernie-Teacher 4132	Sarah's Attic	3,000	38.00	38.00
94-14-068	Calvin-Black Golfer 4161	Sarah's Attic	3,000	35.00	35.00
94-14-069	Spike-White Golfer 4162	Sarah's Attic	3,000	35.00	35.00
Sarah's Attic, Inc.		**Snowflake Collection**			
89-15-001	Flurry 2342	Sarah's Attic	Closed	12.00	12.00
89-15-002	Boo Mini Snowman 3200	Sarah's Attic	Closed	6.00	6.00
89-15-003	Winter Frolic 3209	Sarah's Attic	Closed	70.00	70.00
90-15-004	Old Glory Snowman 3225	Sarah's Attic	Closed	26.00	26.00
92-15-005	Crystal Mother Snowman 3721	Sarah's Attic	3,500	20.00	20.00
92-15-006	Topper Father Snowman 3722	Sarah's Attic	3,500	20.00	20.00
92-15-007	Sparkles Baby Snowman 3723	Sarah's Attic	3,500	14.00	14.00
93-15-008	Sparkles & Topper on Log 3840	Sarah's Attic	4,000	28.00	28.00
93-15-009	Cruiser Snowwman on Bike 3865	Sarah's Attic	4,000	23.00	23.00
93-15-010	Blizzard Snowman News 3866	Sarah's Attic	4,000	20.00	20.00
93-15-011	Bottles Snowman Milkman 3867	Sarah's Attic	4,000	20.00	20.00
Sarah's Attic, Inc.		**Sarah's Gang Collection**			
86-16-001	Willie Resin Candle 2023	Sarah's Attic	Closed	12.00	12.00
86-16-002	Tillie Resin Candle 2024	Sarah's Attic	Closed	12.00	12.00
86-16-003	Tillie-Original 2027	Sarah's Attic	Closed	14.00	20.00
86-16-004	Willie-Original 2028	Sarah's Attic	Closed	14.00	20-75.00
86-16-005	Whimpy-Original 2031	Sarah's Attic	Closed	14.00	20.00
86-16-006	Katie-Original 2032	Sarah's Attic	Closed	14.00	20.00
86-16-007	Twinkie-Original 2033	Sarah's Attic	Closed	14.00	20.00
86-16-008	Cupcake-Original 2034	Sarah's Attic	Closed	14.00	20-75.00
87-16-009	Whimpy Sitting 2001	Sarah's Attic	Closed	14.00	20.00
87-16-010	Katie Sitting 2002	Sarah's Attic	Closed	14.00	20.00
87-16-011	Sparky 2012	Sarah's Attic	Closed	10.00	10.00
87-16-012	Twinkie w/Pole 5107	Sarah's Attic	Closed	20.00	20.00
87-16-013	Cupcake w/Rope 5119	Sarah's Attic	Closed	16.00	16.00
87-16-014	Cupcake On Heart 5140	Sarah's Attic	Closed	9.00	20.00
87-16-015	Katie On Heart 5141	Sarah's Attic	Closed	9.00	20.00
87-16-016	Whimpy on Heart 5142	Sarah's Attic	Closed	9.00	20.00
87-16-017	Twinkie On Heart 5143	Sarah's Attic	Closed	9.00	20.00
87-16-018	Tillie On Heart 5150	Sarah's Attic	Closed	9.00	20.00
87-16-019	Willie On Heart 5151	Sarah's Attic	Closed	9.00	20.00
88-16-020	Cupcake 4027	Sarah's Attic	Open	20.00	20.00
88-16-021	Twinkie 4028	Sarah's Attic	Open	20.00	20.00
88-16-022	Katie 4029	Sarah's Attic	Open	20.00	20.00
88-16-023	Whimpy 4030	Sarah's Attic	Open	20.00	20.00
88-16-024	Willie 4031	Sarah's Attic	Open	20.00	20.00
88-16-025	Tillie 4032	Sarah's Attic	Open	20.00	20.00
89-16-026	Willie-Americana 2300	Sarah's Attic	Closed	21.00	21.00
89-16-027	Tillie-Americana 2301	Sarah's Attic	Closed	21.00	21.00
89-16-028	Katie-Americana 2302	Sarah's Attic	Closed	21.00	21.00
89-16-029	Whimpy-Americana 2303	Sarah's Attic	Closed	21.00	21.00
89-16-030	Cupcake-Americana 2304	Sarah's Attic	Closed	21.00	21.00
89-16-031	Twinkie-Americana 2305	Sarah's Attic	Closed	21.00	21.00
89-16-032	Baby Rachel 2306	Sarah's Attic	Open	20.00	20.00
89-16-033	Katie-Small Sailor 2307	Sarah's Attic	Closed	14.00	20.00
89-16-034	Whimpy-Small Sailor 2308	Sarah's Attic	Closed	14.00	20.00
89-16-035	Cupcake-Small School 2309	Sarah's Attic	Closed	11.00	20.00
89-16-036	Twinkie-Small School 2310	Sarah's Attic	Closed	11.00	20.00
89-16-037	Willie-Small Country 2311	Sarah's Attic	Closed	18.00	18.00
89-16-038	Tillie-Small Country 2312	Sarah's Attic	Closed	18.00	18.00
89-16-039	Cupcake Clown 3144	Sarah's Attic	Closed	21.00	21.00
89-16-040	Twinkie Clown 3145	Sarah's Attic	Closed	19.00	19.00
90-16-041	Katie & Whimpy-Beachtime 3243	Sarah's Attic	Closed	60.00	60-75.00
90-16-042	Cupcake-Beachtime 3244	Sarah's Attic	Closed	35.00	35.00
90-16-043	Twinkie-Beachtime 3245	Sarah's Attic	Closed	35.00	35.00
90-16-044	Willie-Beachtime 3246	Sarah's Attic	Closed	35.00	35.00
90-16-045	Tillie-Beachtime 3247	Sarah's Attic	Closed	35.00	35.00
90-16-046	Baby Rachel-Beachtime 3248	Sarah's Attic	Closed	35.00	35.00
90-16-047	Katie-Witch 3312	Sarah's Attic	Closed	40.00	40.00
90-16-048	Whimpy-Scarecrow 3313	Sarah's Attic	Closed	40.00	40.00
90-16-049	Cupcake-Devil 3314	Sarah's Attic	Closed	40.00	40.00
90-16-050	Twinkie-Devil 3315	Sarah's Attic	Closed	40.00	40.00
90-16-051	Tillie-Clown 3316	Sarah's Attic	Closed	40.00	40.00
90-16-052	Willie-Clown 3317	Sarah's Attic	Closed	40.00	40.00
90-16-053	Rachel-Pumpkin 3318	Sarah's Attic	Closed	40.00	40.00
91-16-054	Rachel-Americana 3364	Sarah's Attic	Closed	30.00	30.00
91-16-055	Tillie Masquerade 3412	Sarah's Attic	Closed	45.00	45.00
91-16-056	Whimpy-Groom 3430	Sarah's Attic	12/94	47.00	47.00
91-16-057	Katie-Bride 3431	Sarah's Attic	12/94	47.00	47.00

Company Number	Name	Series Artist	Edition Limit	Issue Price	Quote
91-16-058	Rachel-Flower Girl 3432	Sarah's Attic	12/94	40.00	40.00
91-16-059	Tyler-Ring Bearer 3433	Sarah's Attic	12/94	40.00	40.00
91-16-060	Cracker Cocker Dog 3434	Sarah's Attic	12/94	9.00	9.00
91-16-061	Twinkie-Minister 3435	Sarah's Attic	12/94	50.00	50.00
91-16-062	Tillie-Bride 3436	Sarah's Attic	12/94	47.00	47.00
91-16-063	Willie-Groom 3437	Sarah's Attic	12/94	47.00	47.00
91-16-064	Peaches-Flower Girl 3438	Sarah's Attic	12/94	40.00	40.00
91-16-065	Pug-Ringbearer 3439	Sarah's Attic	12/94	40.00	40.00
91-16-066	Percy-Minister 3440	Sarah's Attic	12/94	50.00	50.00
91-16-067	Katie-Thanksgiving 3468	Sarah's Attic	Closed	32.00	32.00
91-16-068	Whimpy-Thanksgiving 3469	Sarah's Attic	Closed	32.00	32.00
91-16-069	Tillie-Thanksgiving 3472	Sarah's Attic	Closed	32.00	32.00
91-16-070	Willie-Thanksgiving 3473	Sarah's Attic	Closed	32.00	32.00
91-16-071	Rachel-Thanksgiving 3474	Sarah's Attic	Closed	32.00	32.00
92-16-072	Tillie On Log 3705	Sarah's Attic	2,500	35.00	35.00
92-16-073	Willie w/Skates 3706	Sarah's Attic	2,500	35.00	35.00
92-16-074	Katie On Sled 3707	Sarah's Attic	2,500	35.00	35.00
92-16-075	Whimpy w/Book 3708	Sarah's Attic	2,500	35.00	35.00
93-16-076	Katie & Rachel in Chair 3764	Sarah's Attic	12/94	60.00	60.00
93-16-077	Twinkie w/Football 3765	Sarah's Attic	12/94	28.00	28.00
93-16-078	Cupcake on Bench 3766	Sarah's Attic	12/94	28.00	28.00
93-16-079	Whimpy w/Train 3767	Sarah's Attic	12/94	28.00	28.00
93-16-080	Willie Lying w/Pillow 3768	Sarah's Attic	12/94	28.00	28.00
93-16-081	Tillie w/Bear 3769	Sarah's Attic	12/94	28.00	28.00
93-16-082	Twinkie w/Snowballs 3821	Sarah's Attic	2,500	35.00	35.00
93-16-083	Cupcake w/Snowman 3822	Sarah's Attic	2,500	35.00	35.00
93-16-084	Rachel in Snowsuit 3823	Sarah's Attic	2,500	25.00	25.00
93-16-085	Sparky Dog in Sweater 3824	Sarah's Attic	2,500	8.00	8.00
93-16-086	Whimpy-Spring 3934	Sarah's Attic	1,994	28.00	28.00
93-16-087	Katie-Spring 3935	Sarah's Attic	1,994	28.00	28.00
93-16-088	Twinkie-Spring 3936	Sarah's Attic	1,994	28.00	28.00
93-16-089	Cupcake-Spring 3937	Sarah's Attic	1,994	30.00	30.00
93-16-086	Tillie-Spring 3938	Sarah's Attic	1,994	30.00	30.00
93-16-087	Willie-Spring 3939	Sarah's Attic	1,994	28.00	28.00
93-16-088	Rachel-Spring 3940	Sarah's Attic	1,994	30.00	30.00
Sarah's Attic, Inc.		**Santas Of The Month-Series A**			
88-17-001	January White Santa	Sarah's Attic	Closed	50.00	135-150.
88-17-002	January Black Santa	Sarah's Attic	Closed	50.00	200-300.
88-17-003	February White Santa	Sarah's Attic	Closed	50.00	135-150.
88-17-004	February Black Santa	Sarah's Attic	Closed	50.00	200-300.
88-17-005	March White Santa	Sarah's Attic	Closed	50.00	135-150.
88-17-006	March Black Santa	Sarah's Attic	Closed	50.00	200-300.
88-17-007	April White Santa	Sarah's Attic	Closed	50.00	135-150.
88-17-008	April Black Santa	Sarah's Attic	Closed	50.00	200-300.
88-17-009	May White Santa	Sarah's Attic	Closed	50.00	135-150.
88-17-010	May Black Santa	Sarah's Attic	Closed	50.00	200-300.
88-17-011	June White Santa	Sarah's Attic	Closed	50.00	135-150.
88-17-012	June Black Santa	Sarah's Attic	Closed	50.00	200-300.
88-17-013	July White Santa	Sarah's Attic	Closed	50.00	175.00
88-17-014	July Black Santa	Sarah's Attic	Closed	50.00	200-300.
88-17-015	August White Santa	Sarah's Attic	Closed	50.00	135-150.
88-17-016	August Black Santa	Sarah's Attic	Closed	50.00	200-300.
88-17-017	September White Santa	Sarah's Attic	Closed	50.00	135-150.
88-17-018	September Black Santa	Sarah's Attic	Closed	50.00	200-300.
88-17-019	October White Santa	Sarah's Attic	Closed	50.00	135-150.
88-17-020	October Black Santa	Sarah's Attic	Closed	50.00	200-300.
88-17-021	November White Santa	Sarah's Attic	Closed	50.00	135-150.
88-17-022	November Black Santa	Sarah's Attic	Closed	50.00	200-300.
88-17-023	December White Santa	Sarah's Attic	Closed	50.00	135-150.
88-17-024	December Black Santa	Sarah's Attic	Closed	50.00	225-375.
88-17-025	Mini January White Santa	Sarah's Attic	Closed	14.00	33-35.00
88-17-026	Mini January Black Santa	Sarah's Attic	Closed	14.00	35.00
88-17-027	Mini February White Santa	Sarah's Attic	Closed	14.00	33-35.00
88-17-028	Mini February Black Santa	Sarah's Attic	Closed	14.00	35.00
88-17-029	Mini March White Santa	Sarah's Attic	Closed	14.00	33-35.00
88-17-030	Mini March Black Santa	Sarah's Attic	Closed	14.00	35.00
88-17-031	Mini April White Santa	Sarah's Attic	Closed	14.00	33-35.00
88-17-032	Mini April Black Santa	Sarah's Attic	Closed	14.00	35.00
88-17-033	Mini May White Santa	Sarah's Attic	Closed	14.00	33-35.00
88-17-034	Mini May Black Santa	Sarah's Attic	Closed	14.00	35.00
88-17-035	Mini June White Santa	Sarah's Attic	Closed	14.00	33-35.00
88-17-036	Mini June Black Santa	Sarah's Attic	Closed	14.00	35.00
88-17-037	Mini July White Santa	Sarah's Attic	Closed	14.00	33-35.00
88-17-038	Mini July Black Santa	Sarah's Attic	Closed	14.00	35.00
88-17-039	Mini August White Santa	Sarah's Attic	Closed	14.00	33-35.00
88-17-040	Mini August Black Santa	Sarah's Attic	Closed	14.00	35.00
88-17-041	Mini September White Santa	Sarah's Attic	Closed	14.00	33-35.00
88-17-042	Mini September Black Santa	Sarah's Attic	Closed	14.00	35.00
88-17-043	Mini October White Santa	Sarah's Attic	Closed	14.00	33-35.00
88-17-044	Mini October Black Santa	Sarah's Attic	Closed	14.00	35.00
88-17-045	Mini November White Santa	Sarah's Attic	Closed	14.00	33-35.00
88-17-046	Mini November Black Santa	Sarah's Attic	Closed	14.00	35.00
88-17-047	Mini December White Santa	Sarah's Attic	Closed	14.00	33-35.00
88-17-048	Mini December Black Santa	Sarah's Attic	Closed	14.00	35.00
Sarah's Attic, Inc.		**Santas Of The Month-Series B**			
90-18-001	Jan. Santa Winter Fun	Sarah's Attic	Closed	80.00	80.00
90-18-002	Feb. Santa Cupids Help	Sarah's Attic	Closed	120.00	120.00
90-18-003	Mar. Santa Irish Delight	Sarah's Attic	Closed	120.00	120.00
90-18-004	Apr. Santa Spring/Joy	Sarah's Attic	Closed	150.00	150.00
90-18-005	May Santa Par For Course	Sarah's Attic	Closed	100.00	100.00
90-18-006	June Santa Graduation	Sarah's Attic	Closed	70.00	70.00
90-18-007	July Santa God Bless	Sarah's Attic	Closed	100.00	100.00
90-18-008	Aug. Santa Summers Trn.	Sarah's Attic	Closed	110.00	110.00
90-18-009	Sep. Santa Touchdown	Sarah's Attic	Closed	90.00	90.00
90-18-010	Oct. Santa Seasons Plenty	Sarah's Attic	Closed	120.00	120.00
90-18-011	Nov. Santa Give Thanks	Sarah's Attic	Closed	100.00	100.00
90-18-012	Dec. Santa Peace	Sarah's Attic	Closed	120.00	120.00
90-18-013	Mrs. January	Sarah's Attic	Closed	80.00	80.00
90-18-014	Mrs. February	Sarah's Attic	Closed	110.00	110.00
90-18-015	Mrs. March	Sarah's Attic	Closed	80.00	80.00
90-18-016	Mrs. April	Sarah's Attic	Closed	110.00	110.00
90-18-017	Mrs. May	Sarah's Attic	Closed	80.00	80.00
90-18-018	Mrs. June	Sarah's Attic	Closed	70.00	70.00
90-18-019	Mrs. July	Sarah's Attic	Closed	100.00	100.00
90-18-020	Mrs. August	Sarah's Attic	Closed	90.00	90.00
90-18-021	Mrs. September	Sarah's Attic	Closed	90.00	90.00
90-18-022	Mrs. October	Sarah's Attic	Closed	90.00	90.00
90-18-023	Mrs. November	Sarah's Attic	Closed	90.00	90.00
90-18-024	Mrs. December	Sarah's Attic	Closed	110.00	110.00
Sarah's Attic, Inc.		**Santas Of The Month-Series C**			
90-19-001	Jan. Fruits of Love	Sarah's Attic	12/94	90.00	90.00
90-19-002	Feb. From The Heart	Sarah's Attic	12/94	90.00	90.00
90-19-003	Mar. Irish Love	Sarah's Attic	12/94	100.00	100.00
90-19-004	Apr. Spring Time	Sarah's Attic	12/94	90.00	90.00
90-19-005	May Caddy Chatter	Sarah's Attic	12/94	100.00	100.00
90-19-006	June Homerun	Sarah's Attic	12/94	90.00	90.00
90-19-007	July Celebrate Amer.	Sarah's Attic	12/94	90.00	90.00
90-19-008	Aug. Fun In The Sun	Sarah's Attic	12/94	90.00	90.00
90-19-009	Sept. Lessons In Love	Sarah's Attic	12/94	90.00	90.00
90-19-010	Oct. Masquerade	Sarah's Attic	12/94	120.00	120.00
90-19-011	Nov. Harvest Of Love	Sarah's Attic	12/94	120.00	120.00
90-19-012	Dec. A Gift Of Peace	Sarah's Attic	12/94	90.00	90.00
Sarah's Attic, Inc.		**Santas Of The Month-Series D**			
93-20-001	January White Wintertime Santa	Sarah's Attic	12/94	35.00	35.00
93-20-002	February White Valentine Santa	Sarah's Attic	12/94	35.00	35.00
93-20-003	March White St. Patrick's Santa	Sarah's Attic	12/94	35.00	35.00
93-20-004	April White Easter Santa	Sarah's Attic	12/94	35.00	35.00
93-20-005	May White Springtime Santa	Sarah's Attic	12/94	35.00	35.00
93-20-006	June White Summertime Santa	Sarah's Attic	12/94	35.00	35.00
93-20-007	July White Americana Santa	Sarah's Attic	12/94	35.00	35.00
93-20-008	August White Beachtime Santa	Sarah's Attic	12/94	35.00	35.00
93-20-009	September White Classroom Santa	Sarah's Attic	12/94	35.00	35.00
92-20-010	Oct. White Halloween Santa	Sarah's Attic	12/94	35.00	35.00
92-20-011	Nov. White Harvest Santa	Sarah's Attic	12/94	35.00	35.00
92-20-012	Dec. White Father X-Mas Santa	Sarah's Attic	12/94	35.00	35.00
Sarah's Attic, Inc.		**Santas Of The Month-Series E**			
93-21-001	January Black Wintertime Santa	Sarah's Attic	12/94	35.00	35.00
93-21-002	February Black Valentine Santa	Sarah's Attic	12/94	35.00	35.00
93-21-003	March Black St. Patrick's Santa	Sarah's Attic	12/94	35.00	35.00
93-21-004	April Black Easter Santa	Sarah's Attic	12/94	35.00	35.00
93-21-005	May Black Springtime Santa	Sarah's Attic	12/94	35.00	35.00
93-21-006	June Black Summertime Santa	Sarah's Attic	12/94	35.00	35.00
93-21-007	July Black Americana Santa	Sarah's Attic	12/94	35.00	35.00
93-21-008	August Black Beachtime Santa	Sarah's Attic	12/94	35.00	35.00
93-21-009	September Black Classroom Santa	Sarah's Attic	12/94	35.00	35.00
92-21-010	Oct. Black Halloween Santa	Sarah's Attic	12/94	35.00	35.00
92-21-011	Nov. Black Harvest Santa	Sarah's Attic	12/94	35.00	35.00
92-21-012	Dec. Black Father X-Mas Santa	Sarah's Attic	12/94	35.00	35.00
Sarah's Attic, Inc.		**Tender Moments**			
87-22-001	Daisy 3002	Sarah's Attic	Closed	24.00	24.00
88-22-002	Trudy with Teacup 3042	Sarah's Attic	Closed	34.00	34.00
88-22-003	Lena with Doll 3043	Sarah's Attic	Closed	40.00	40.00
88-22-004	Jessica 4033	Sarah's Attic	Closed	30.00	30.00
89-22-005	Mini Baby Doll 2318	Sarah's Attic	Closed	5.00	5.00
89-22-006	Jennifer & Max 2319	Sarah's Attic	Closed	57.00	57.00
89-22-007	Sweet Rose 3214	Sarah's Attic	Closed	50.00	50.00
90-22-008	Cody Victorian Boy 3229	Sarah's Attic	Closed	46.00	46.00
90-22-009	Adair Victorian Boy w/Instrument 3230	Sarah's Attic	Closed	29.00	29.00
91-22-010	Baby Tansy-White 2402	Sarah's Attic	Closed	40.00	40.00
92-22-011	Black Baby Boy Birth 3516	Sarah's Attic	Closed	50.00	50.00
92-22-012	Black Baby Girl 1-2 3517	Sarah's Attic	Closed	50.00	50.00
92-22-013	Black Baby Boy 1-2 3518	Sarah's Attic	Closed	50.00	50.00
92-22-014	Black Baby Girl Birth 3526	Sarah's Attic	Closed	50.00	50.00
92-22-015	Whte Baby Boy 1 3527	Sarah's Attic	Closed	60.00	60.00
92-22-016	White Baby Girl 1 3528	Sarah's Attic	Closed	60.00	60.00
92-22-017	White Girl 1-2 3529	Sarah's Attic	Closed	60.00	60.00
92-22-018	White Boy 1-2 3530	Sarah's Attic	Closed	60.00	60.00
92-22-019	Misty 3616	Sarah's Attic	Closed	60.00	60.00
92-22-020	White Girl 2-3 3623	Sarah's Attic	Closed	60.00	60.00
92-22-021	White Boy 2-3 3624	Sarah's Attic	Closed	60.00	60.00
92-22-022	Small Black Girl 2-3 3675	Sarah's Attic	Closed	50.00	50.00
92-22-023	Small Black Boy 2-3 3676	Sarah's Attic	Closed	50.00	50.00
92-22-024	White Girl 3-4 3690	Sarah's Attic	Closed	50.00	50.00
92-22-025	White Boy 3-4 3691	Sarah's Attic	Closed	50.00	50.00
93-22-026	Black Girl 3-4/Tricycle 3744	Sarah's Attic	Open	40.00	60.00
93-22-027	Black Boy 3-4/In Wagon 3745	Sarah's Attic	Open	40.00	40.00
93-22-028	Grams With Rolling Pin 3782	Sarah's Attic	Closed	50.00	50.00
93-22-029	Rosie on Crate 3783	Sarah's Attic	Closed	50.00	50.00
93-22-030	Ellie Girl w/Cookbook 3784	Sarah's Attic	Closed	28.00	28.00
93-22-031	Evan Boy w/Bowl 3785	Sarah's Attic	Closed	28.00	28.00
93-22-032	Cookie Jar w/Pan 3786	Sarah's Attic	Closed	6.00	6.00
93-22-033	Squeaks Dog 3787	Sarah's Attic	Closed	7.00	7.00
93-22-034	Love of Life-Black Couple 3788	Sarah's Attic	Closed	70.00	70.00
93-22-035	True Love-White Couple 3789	Sarah's Attic	1,000	70.00	70.00
93-22-036	New Beginning White Pregnant Woman 3790	Sarah's Attic	1,000	55.00	55.00
93-22-037	Joy of Motherhood Black Pregnant Woman -3791	Sarah's Attic	1,000	55.00	55.00
93-22-038	Gentle Touch Black Girls 3825	Sarah's Attic	2,500	40.00	40.00
93-22-039	Special Times White Girls 3826	Sarah's Attic	2,500	40.00	40.00
93-22-040	Catch of Love White Men Fishing 3827	Sarah's Attic	4,000	50.00	50.00
93-22-041	Days to Remember Black Men Fishing 3828	Sarah's Attic	4,000	50.00	50.00
93-22-042	Always & Forever White Wedding 3834	Sarah's Attic	4,000	60.00	60.00
93-22-043	Promise of Love Black Wedding 3835	Sarah's Attic	4,000	60.00	60.00
93-22-044	Bless This Child White Couple 3838	Sarah's Attic	2,500	60.00	60.00
93-22-045	Little Blessing Black Couple 3839	Sarah's Attic	2,500	75.00	75.00
93-22-046	Special White Girl in Wheelchair 3968	Sarah's Attic	Open	38.00	38.00
93-22-047	Special Black Boy in Wheelchair 3969	Sarah's Attic	Open	38.00	38.00
94-22-048	Black Girl on Horse 4-5 3957	Sarah's Attic	Open	37.00	37.00
94-22-049	Black Boy w/Hobby Horse 4-5 3958	Sarah's Attic	Open	33.00	33.00
94-22-050	White Girl w/Trunk 4-5 3959	Sarah's Attic	Open	40.00	40.00
94-22-051	White Boy w/Fire Truck 4-5 3960	Sarah's Attic	Open	40.00	40.00
94-22-052	Special White Boy 4125	Sarah's Attic	Open	38.00	38.00
94-22-053	Special Black Girl 4126	Sarah's Attic	Open	38.00	38.00
Sarah's Attic, Inc.		**Tattered n' Torn Collection**			
90-23-001	Opie Boy Rag Doll 3241	Sarah's Attic	Closed	50.00	50.00
90-23-002	Polly Girl Rag Daoll 3242	Sarah's Attic	Closed	50.00	50.00
90-23-003	Muffin Rag Doll 3335	Sarah's Attic	Closed	30.00	30.00
90-23-004	Puffin Rag Doll 3343	Sarah's Attic	Closed	30.00	30.00
91-23-005	Prissy & Peanut-White 2400	Sarah's Attic	Closed	120.00	120.00
91-23-006	Muffin & Puffin-White 2401	Sarah's Attic	Closed	55.00	55.00
91-23-007	Prissy & Peanut 3360	Sarah's Attic	Closed	120.00	120.00
91-23-008	Muffin & Puffin w/Trunk 3361	Sarah's Attic	Closed	55.00	55.00
94-23-009	Jellie-Girl Rag Doll 4163	Sarah's Attic	2,500	30.00	30.00
94-23-010	Beanie-Boy Rag Doll 4164	Sarah's Attic	2,500	30.00	30.00
94-23-011	Belle-Girl Rag Doll 4180	Sarah's Attic	2,500	30.00	30.00
94-23-012	Britches-Boy Rag Doll 4181	Sarah's Attic	2,500	30.00	30.00
Sarah's Attic, Inc.		**Spirit of Christmas Collection**			
87-24-001	Santa Sitting 5122	Sarah's Attic	Closed	18.00	18.00
87-24-002	Mini Santa w/Cane 5123	Sarah's Attic	Closed	8.00	8.00
87-24-003	Large Santa w/Cane 5124	Sarah's Attic	Closed	27.00	27.00

Company / Number	Name	Series / Artist	Edition Limit	Issue Price	Quote
87-24-004	Small Santa w/Tree 5125	Sarah's Attic	Closed	14.00	14.00
87-24-005	Mary 5134	Sarah's Attic	Closed	12.00	12.00
87-24-006	Joseph 5135	Sarah's Attic	Closed	12.00	12.00
87-24-007	Jesus 5136	Sarah's Attic	Closed	11.00	11.00
87-24-008	Mini Angel 5274	Sarah's Attic	Closed	6.00	6.00
87-24-009	Mrs. Claus 5289	Sarah's Attic	Closed	26.00	26.00
87-24-010	Naughty or Nice 2048	Sarah's Attic	Closed	100.00	100.00
87-24-011	Father Snow 2049	Sarah's Attic	Closed	42.00	42.00
87-24-012	Jingle Bells 2050	Sarah's Attic	Closed	20.00	20.00
87-24-013	Long Journey 2051	Sarah's Attic	Closed	19.00	19.00
87-24-014	St. Nick 3005	Sarah's Attic	Closed	28.00	28.00
87-24-015	Santa's Workshop 3006	Sarah's Attic	Closed	50.00	50.00
87-24-016	Colonel Santa 3007	Sarah's Attic	Closed	30.00	30.00
87-24-017	Kris Kringle 5860	Sarah's Attic	Closed	100.00	100.00
88-24-018	Mary-Natural 2080	Sarah's Attic	Closed	11.00	11.00
88-24-019	Joseph-Natural 2081	Sarah's Attic	Closed	11.00	11.00
88-24-020	Baby Jesus-Natural 2082	Sarah's Attic	Closed	7.00	7.00
88-24-021	Mini Mary-Natural 2087	Sarah's Attic	Closed	5.00	5.00
88-24-022	Mini Joseph-Natural 2088	Sarah's Attic	Closed	5.00	5.00
88-24-023	Mini-Jesus 2089	Sarah's Attic	Closed	4.00	4.00
88-24-024	Cow/Ox-Natural 2105	Sarah's Attic	Closed	16.00	16.00
88-24-025	Sheep-Natural 2106	Sarah's Attic	Closed	8.00	8.00
88-24-026	Mary-Mini 3034	Sarah's Attic	Closed	6.00	6.00
88-24-027	Mini Joseph-Natural 3035	Sarah's Attic	Closed	6.00	6.00
88-24-028	Mini Jesus 3036	Sarah's Attic	Closed	4.00	4.00
88-24-029	Elf Grabbing Hat 3041	Sarah's Attic	Closed	8.00	8.00
88-24-030	Ho Ho Santa w/Elf 3053	Sarah's Attic	Closed	84.00	84.00
88-24-031	Santa in Chimney 4020	Sarah's Attic	Closed	110.00	110.00
88-24-032	Sitting Elf 6238	Sarah's Attic	Closed	7.00	7.00
88-24-033	Elf w/Gift 6239	Sarah's Attic	Closed	8.00	8.00
88-24-034	Small sitting Santa 6258	Sarah's Attic	Closed	11.00	11.00
88-24-035	Mrs. Claus Small 6272	Sarah's Attic	Closed	11.00	11.00
88-24-036	Mary 6307	Sarah's Attic	Closed	19.00	19.00
88-24-037	Joseph 6308	Sarah's Attic	Closed	19.00	19.00
88-24-038	Jesus 6309	Sarah's Attic	Closed	11.00	11.00
88-24-039	Cow/Ox 6310	Sarah's Attic	Closed	13.00	13.00
88-24-040	Sheep 6311	Sarah's Attic	Closed	10.00	10.00
88-24-041	Large Santa Resin Candle 3068	Sarah's Attic	Closed	11.00	11.00
88-24-042	Large Mrs. Claus Resin Candle 3069	Sarah's Attic	Closed	11.00	11.00
88-24-043	Small Santa Resin Candle 3072	Sarah's Attic	Closed	10.00	10.00
88-24-044	Small Mrs. Claus Resin Candle 3073	Sarah's Attic	Closed	10.00	10.00
88-24-045	Mini Santa Resin Candle 3074	Sarah's Attic	Closed	7.00	7.00
88-24-046	Santa Kneeling 4011	Sarah's Attic	Closed	22.00	22.00
88-24-047	Old Reindeer 4012	Sarah's Attic	Closed	6.00	6.00
88-24-048	Young Reindeer 4013	Sarah's Attic	Closed	6.00	6.00
88-24-049	Red Reindeer 4014	Sarah's Attic	Closed	6.00	6.00
89-24-050	Spirit of Christmas Santa 2320	Sarah's Attic	Closed	80.00	80.00
89-24-051	Silent Night 2343	Sarah's Attic	Closed	33.00	33.00
89-24-052	Woodland Santa 2345	Sarah's Attic	Closed	100.00	100.00
89-24-053	Jolly II 2347	Sarah's Attic	Closed	17.00	17.00
89-24-054	Yule Tiding II 2348	Sarah's Attic	Closed	23.00	23.00
89-24-055	St. Nick II 2349	Sarah's Attic	Closed	43.00	43.00
89-24-056	Blessed Christmas 2350	Sarah's Attic	Closed	100.00	100.00
89-24-057	Father Snow II 2351	Sarah's Attic	Closed	36.00	36.00
89-24-058	Christmas Joy 3177	Sarah's Attic	Closed	32.00	32.00
89-24-059	Jingle Bells II 3178	Sarah's Attic	Closed	26.00	26.00
89-24-060	Colonel Santa II 3179	Sarah's Attic	Closed	35.00	35.00
89-24-061	Papa Santa Sitting 3180	Sarah's Attic	Closed	30.00	30.00
89-24-062	Mama Santa sitting 3181	Sarah's Attic	Closed	30.00	30.00
89-24-063	Papa Santa Stocking 3182	Sarah's Attic	Closed	50.00	50.00
89-24-064	Mama Santa Stocking 3183	Sarah's Attic	Closed	50.00	50.00
89-24-065	Long Journey II 3184	Sarah's Attic	Closed	35.00	35.00
89-24-066	Stinky Elf sitting 3185	Sarah's Attic	Closed	16.00	16.00
89-24-067	Winky Elf Letter 3186	Sarah's Attic	Closed	16.00	16.00
89-24-068	Blinkey Elf Ball 3187	Sarah's Attic	Closed	16.00	16.00
89-24-069	Colonel Santa-Mini 3188	Sarah's Attic	Closed	14.00	14.00
89-24-070	St. Nick-Mini 3189	Sarah's Attic	Closed	14.00	14.00
89-24-071	Jingle Bells-Mini 3190	Sarah's Attic	Closed	16.00	16.00
89-24-072	Father Snow-Mini 3191	Sarah's Attic	Closed	16.00	16.00
89-24-073	Long Journey-Mini 3192	Sarah's Attic	Closed	11.00	11.00
89-24-074	Jolly-Mini 3193	Sarah's Attic	Closed	10.00	10.00
89-24-075	Naughty or Nice-Mini 3210	Sarah's Attic	Closed	20.00	20.00
90-24-076	Christmas Wonder Santa 3278	Sarah's Attic	Closed	50.00	50.00
90-24-077	Santa Claus Express 3304	Sarah's Attic	Closed	150.00	150.00
90-24-078	Christmas Music 3305	Sarah's Attic	Closed	60.00	60.00
90-24-079	Love the Children 3324	Sarah's Attic	5,000	75.00	75.00
90-24-080	Christmas Wishes 3325	Sarah's Attic	5,000	50.00	50.00
90-24-081	Bells of Christmas 3326	Sarah's Attic	Closed	35.00	35.00
91-24-082	Santa Tex 3392	Sarah's Attic	Closed	30.00	30.00
91-24-083	Treasures of Love Santa 3490	Sarah's Attic	Closed	140.00	140.00
91-24-084	Sharing Love Santa 3491	Sarah's Attic	Closed	120.00	120.00
92-24-085	Donkey 3656	Sarah's Attic	Closed	26.00	26.00
92-24-086	Cow 3657	Sarah's Attic	Closed	30.00	30.00
92-24-087	Sheep 3658	Sarah's Attic	Closed	20.00	20.00
92-24-088	Blessed Christmas-Small 3669	Sarah's Attic	Closed	40.00	40.00
92-24-089	Love the Children-Small 3672	Sarah's Attic	Closed	35.00	35.00
92-24-090	Christmas Love-Small 3674	Sarah's Attic	Closed	30.00	30.00
92-24-091	Gifts of Christmas Santa 3677	Sarah's Attic	Closed	90.00	90.00
92-24-092	Gifts of Love Santa 3678	Sarah's Attic	Closed	90.00	90.00
92-24-093	Snow Base 3718	Sarah's Attic	Open	40.00	40.00
92-24-094	Evergreen Tree 3719	Sarah's Attic	Open	10.00	10.00
92-24-095	Lamp Post w/Sign 3720	Sarah's Attic	Open	10.00	10.00
92-24-096	Barrel of Love 3724	Sarah's Attic	Open	10.00	10.00
92-24-097	Cart of Love 3725	Sarah's Attic	Open	13.00	13.00
92-24-098	Mandy Mother Bear 3726	Sarah's Attic	3,500	20.00	20.00
92-24-099	Andy Father Bear 3727	Sarah's Attic	3,500	20.00	20.00
92-24-100	Brandy Baby Bear 3728	Sarah's Attic	3,500	14.00	14.00
93-24-101	Let There Be Love Santa 3796	Sarah's Attic	2,000	70.00	70.00
93-24-102	Let The Be Peace Santa 3797	Sarah's Attic	2,000	70.00	70.00
93-24-103	Been Good Santa/Boy 3813	Sarah's Attic	2,500	60.00	60.00
93-24-104	Oh My! Santa/Girl 3814	Sarah's Attic	2,500	55.00	55.00
93-24-105	Christmas Rabbit 3852	Sarah's Attic	Closed	23.00	23.00
93-24-106	Christmas Bear 3853	Sarah's Attic	Closed	23.00	23.00
93-24-107	Christmas Jeb 3854	Sarah's Attic	Closed	25.00	25.00
93-24-108	Christmas Christine 3855	Sarah's Attic	Closed	30.00	30.00
93-24-109	Christmas Jaleesa 3856	Sarah's Attic	Closed	25.00	25.00
93-24-110	Christmas Justin 3857	Sarah's Attic	Closed	25.00	25.00
93-24-111	Christmas Jessica 3858	Sarah's Attic	Closed	25.00	25.00
93-24-112	Christmas Holly Santa 3859	Sarah's Attic	Closed	50.00	50.00
93-24-113	Christmas Proclaim. Love Santa 3860	Sarah's Attic	Closed	50.00	50.00
93-24-114	Christmas Basket 3862	Sarah's Attic	Closed	4.00	4.00
93-24-115	Christmas Tree 3863	Sarah's Attic	Closed	30.00	30.00
93-24-116	Christmas Fireplace 3864	Sarah's Attic	Closed	40.00	40.00
94-24-117	Gift of Love-Black Santa 4145	Sarah's Attic	2,000	60.00	60.00
94-24-118	Gift of Christmas-White Santa 4146	Sarah's Attic	2,000	60.00	60.00
94-24-119	Jessica-Christmas 4147	Sarah's Attic	12/94	28.00	28.00
94-24-120	Justin-Christmas 4148	Sarah's Attic	12/94	30.00	30.00
94-24-121	Christine-Christmas 4149	Sarah's Attic	12/94	24.00	24.00
94-24-122	Sarah Elizabeth Christmas 4150	Sarah's Attic	12/94	27.00	27.00
94-24-123	Labor of Love-Christmas 4151	Sarah's Attic	12/94	30.00	30.00
94-24-124	Tree of Love-Christmas 4152	Sarah's Attic	12/94	30.00	30.00
94-24-125	Potbelly Stove-Christmas 4153	Sarah's Attic	12/94	22.00	22.00
94-24-126	Jalessa-Christmas 4154	Sarah's Attic	12/94	28.00	28.00
94-24-127	Jeb-Christmas 4155	Sarah's Attic	12/94	28.00	28.00
94-24-128	Teapot-Christmas 4156	Sarah's Attic	12/94	4.00	4.00
94-24-129	Christmas Bear 4157	Sarah's Attic	12/94	23.00	23.00
94-24-130	Christmas Rabbit 4158	Sarah's Attic	12/94	23.00	23.00
94-24-131	Deck the Halls-Black Santa 4159	Sarah's Attic	3,000	30.00	30.00
94-24-132	Rejoice-White Santa 4160	Sarah's Attic	3,000	34.00	34.00
Sarah's Attic Inc.		**United Hearts Collection**			
91-25-001	Tillie-January 3441	Sarah's Attic	Closed	32.00	32.00
91-25-002	Willie-January 3442	Sarah's Attic	Closed	32.00	32.00
91-25-003	Chilly Snowman-January 3443	Sarah's Attic	Closed	33.00	33.00
91-25-004	Prissy w/Shaggy-February 3444	Sarah's Attic	Closed	36.00	36.00
91-25-005	Peanut-February 3445	Sarah's Attic	Closed	32.00	32.00
91-25-006	Shelby w/Shamrock-March 3446	Sarah's Attic	Closed	36.00	36.00
91-25-007	Noah w/Pot of Gold-March 3447	Sarah's Attic	Closed	36.00	36.00
91-25-008	Hewett w/Leprechaun-March 3448	Sarah's Attic	Closed	56.00	56.00
91-25-009	Tabitha March 3449	Sarah's Attic	Closed	32.00	32.00
91-25-010	Toby & Tessie-March 3450	Sarah's Attic	Closed	44.00	44.00
91-25-011	Wooly Lamb-March 3451	Sarah's Attic	Closed	16.00	16.00
91-25-012	Emily-Springtime April 3452	Sarah's Attic	Closed	53.00	53.00
91-25-013	Gideon-Springtime April 3453	Sarah's Attic	Closed	40.00	40.00
91-25-014	Sally Booba Graduation-June 3454	Sarah's Attic	Closed	45.00	45.00
91-25-015	Jack Boy Graduation-June 3455	Sarah's Attic	Closed	40.00	40.00
91-25-016	Sparky Dog Graduation-June 3456	Sarah's Attic	Closed	16.00	16.00
91-25-017	Bibi-Miss Liberty Bear-July 3457	Sarah's Attic	Closed	30.00	30.00
91-25-018	Papa Barney & Biff-July 3458	Sarah's Attic	Closed	64.00	64.00
91-25-019	Pansy Beach-August 3459	Sarah's Attic	Closed	34.00	34.00
91-25-020	Annie & Waldo Beach-August 3460	Sarah's Attic	Closed	40.00	40.00
91-25-021	Bubba Beach-August 3461	Sarah's Attic	Closed	34.00	34.00
91-25-022	Cookie w/Kitten-September 3462	Sarah's Attic	Closed	28.00	28.00
91-25-023	Crumb on Stool-September 3463	Sarah's Attic	Closed	32.00	32.00
91-25-024	Chuckles-September 3464	Sarah's Attic	Closed	26.00	26.00
91-25-025	School Desk w/Book 3465	Sarah's Attic	Closed	15.00	15.00
91-25-026	Barney the Great-October 3466	Sarah's Attic	Closed	40.00	40.00
91-25-027	Bibi & Biff Clowns-October 3467	Sarah's Attic	Closed	35.00	35.00
91-25-028	Cupcake-Thanksgiving 3470	Sarah's Attic	Closed	36.00	36.00
91-25-029	Twinkie-Thanksgiving 3471	Sarah's Attic	Closed	32.00	32.00
91-25-030	Adora Christmas-December 3479	Sarah's Attic	Closed	36.00	36.00
91-25-031	Enos Christmas-December 3480	Sarah's Attic	Closed	36.00	36.00
91-25-032	Christmas Tree-December 3481	Sarah's Attic	Closed	40.00	40.00
92-25-034	Heather-January 3617	Sarah's Attic	Closed	26.00	26.00
92-25-035	Herbie-January 3618	Sarah's Attic	Closed	26.00	26.00
92-25-036	Carrotman-January 3619	Sarah's Attic	Closed	30.00	30.00
92-25-037	Fluffy Bear-February 3625	Sarah's Attic	Closed	35.00	35.00
92-25-038	Puffy Bear-Febuary 3626	Sarah's Attic	Closed	35.00	35.00
92-25-039	Young Kim-March 3627	Sarah's Attic	Closed	40.00	40.00
92-25-040	Kyu Lee-March 3628	Sarah's Attic	Closed	40.00	40.00
92-25-041	Jewels-April 3630	Sarah's Attic	Closed	60.00	60.00
92-25-042	Stretch-April 3631	Sarah's Attic	Closed	50.00	50.00
92-25-043	Adora Angel-May 3632	Sarah's Attic	Closed	50.00	50.00
92-25-044	Enos Angel-May 3633	Sarah's Attic	Closed	50.00	50.00
92-25-045	May Pole 3634	Sarah's Attic	Closed	35.00	35.00
92-25-046	Toby w/Bat-June 3635	Sarah's Attic	Closed	34.00	34.00
92-25-047	Tabitha w/Glove-June 3636	Sarah's Attic	Closed	34.00	34.00
92-25-048	Tessie w/Ball-June 3637	Sarah's Attic	Closed	34.00	34.00
92-25-049	Cookie-July 3638	Sarah's Attic	Closed	34.00	34.00
92-25-050	Crumb-July 3639	Sarah's Attic	Closed	34.00	34.00
92-25-051	Zena Angel-August 3640	Sarah's Attic	Closed	46.00	46.00
92-25-052	Ethan Angel-August 3641	Sarah's Attic	Closed	46.00	46.00
92-25-053	Katie-September 3643	Sarah's Attic	Closed	35.00	35.00
92-25-054	Willie-September 3644	Sarah's Attic	Closed	35.00	35.00
92-25-055	September Desk 3645	Sarah's Attic	Closed	36.00	36.00
92-25-056	Pug-October 3646	Sarah's Attic	Closed	47.00	47.00
92-25-057	Peaches-October 3647	Sarah's Attic	Closed	30.00	30.00
92-25-058	Cupcake-November 3649	Sarah's Attic	Closed	35.00	35.00
92-25-059	Twinkie-November 3650	Sarah's Attic	Closed	35.00	35.00
92-25-060	Haystack-November 3651	Sarah's Attic	Closed	23.00	23.00
92-25-061	Mrs. Claus December 3653	Sarah's Attic	Closed	45.00	45.00
92-25-062	Santa-December 3654	Sarah's Attic	Closed	45.00	45.00
92-25-063	December Tree 3655	Sarah's Attic	Closed	40.00	40.00
Sarah's Attic Inc.		**Collector's Club Promotion**			
91-26-001	Diamond 3497	Sarah's Attic	Closed	36.00	100.00
91-26-002	Ruby 3498	Sarah's Attic	Closed	42.00	100.00
92-26-003	Christmas Love Santa 3522	Sarah's Attic	Closed	45.00	45.00
92-26-004	Forever Frolicking Friends 3523	Sarah's Attic	Closed	Gift	50-80.00
92-26-005	Love One Another 3561	Sarah's Attic	Closed	60.00	60.00
92-26-006	Sharing Dreams 3562	Sarah's Attic	Closed	75.00	150.00
92-26-007	Life Time Friends 3563	Sarah's Attic	Closed	75.00	75.00
92-26-008	Love Starts With Children 3607	Sarah's Attic	Closed	Gift	70.00
93-26-009	First Forever Friend Celebration 3903	Sarah's Attic	Closed	50.00	50.00
93-26-010	Pledge of Allegiance 3749	Sarah's Attic	Closed	45.00	45.00
93-26-011	I Love America Heart 3832	Sarah's Attic	Closed	Gift	N/A
93-26-012	Love Starts With Children II 3837	Sarah's Attic	5/94	Gift	60.00
93-26-013	Gem White Girl w/Basket 3842	Sarah's Attic	7/94	33.00	33.00
93-26-014	Rocky Black Boy w/Marbles 3843	Sarah's Attic	7/94	25.00	25.00
Schmid/B.F.A.		**Don Polland Figurines I**			
83-01-001	Young Bull	D. Polland	2,750	125.00	250.00
83-01-002	Escape	D. Polland	2,500	175.00	650.00
83-01-003	Fighting Bulls	D. Polland	2,500	200.00	600.00
83-01-004	Hot Pursuit	D. Polland	2,500	225.00	550.00
83-01-005	The Hunter	D. Polland	2,500	225.00	500.00
83-01-006	Downed	D. Polland	2,500	250.00	600.00
83-01-007	Challenge	D. Polland	2,000	275.00	600.00
83-01-008	A Second Chance	D. Polland	2,000	350.00	650.00
83-01-009	Dangerous Moment	D. Polland	2,000	250.00	350.00
83-01-010	The Great Hunt	D. Polland	350	3750.00	3750.00
86-01-011	Running Wolf-War Chief	D. Polland	2,500	170.00	295.00
86-01-012	Eagle Dancer	D. Polland	2,500	170.00	295.00
86-01-013	Plains Warrior	D. Polland	1,250	350.00	550.00
86-01-014	Second Chance	D. Polland	2,000	125.00	650.00
86-01-015	Shooting the Rapids	D. Polland	2,500	195.00	495.00
86-01-016	Down From The High Country	D. Polland	2,250	225.00	295.00
86-01-017	War Trophy	D. Polland	2,250	225.00	500.00

Company Number	Name	Series Artist	Edition Limit	Issue Price	Quote
Schmid/B.F.A.		**RFD America**			
79-02-001	Country Road 25030	L. Davis	Closed	100.00	700-750.
79-02-002	Ignorance is Bliss 25031	L. Davis	Closed	165.00	1250-1300.
79-02-003	Blossom 25032	L. Davis	Closed	180.00	1800.00
79-02-004	Fowl Play 25033	L. Davis	Closed	100.00	275-325.
79-02-005	Slim Pickins 25034	L. Davis	Closed	165.00	825-850.
79-02-006	Broken Dreams 25035	L. Davis	Closed	165.00	1000-1300.
80-02-007	Good, Clean Fun 25020	L. Davis	Closed	40.00	125-160.
80-02-008	Strawberry Patch 25021	L. Davis	Closed	25.00	59-95.00
80-02-009	Forbidden Fruit 25022	L. Davis	Closed	25.00	120-175.
80-02-010	Milking Time 25023	L. Davis	Closed	20.00	200-240.
80-02-011	Sunday Afternoon 25024	L. Davis	Closed	22.50	225-250.
80-02-012	New Day 25025	L. Davis	Closed	20.00	165.00
80-02-013	Wilbur 25029	L. Davis	Closed	100.00	600-750.
80-02-014	Itching Post 25037	L. Davis	Closed	30.00	50-115.00
80-02-015	Creek Bank Bandit 25038	L. Davis	Closed	37.50	400.00
81-02-016	Split Decision 25210	L. Davis	Closed	45.00	175-325.
81-02-017	Double Trouble 25211	L. Davis	Closed	35.00	475.00
81-02-018	Under the Weather 25212	L. Davis	Closed	25.00	85.00
81-02-019	Country Boy 25213	L. Davis	Closed	37.50	250-375.
81-02-020	Hightailing It 25214	L. Davis	Closed	50.00	375-500.
81-02-021	Studio Mouse 25215	L. Davis	Closed	60.00	275-325.
81-02-022	Dry as a Bone 25216	L. Davis	Closed	45.00	275-325.
81-02-023	Rooted Out 25217	L. Davis	Closed	45.00	85-115.00
81-02-024	Up To No Good 25218	L. Davis	Closed	200.00	850-950.
81-02-025	Punkin' Seeds 25219	L. Davis	Closed	225.00	1200-1750.
81-02-026	Scallawags 25221	L. Davis	Closed	65.00	125-200.
82-02-027	Baby Bobs 25222	L. Davis	Closed	47.50	200-250.
82-02-028	Stray Dog 25223	L. Davis	Closed	35.00	75.00
82-02-029	Two's Company 25224	L. Davis	Closed	43.50	200-250.
82-02-030	Moving Day 25225	L. Davis	Closed	43.50	225-300.
82-02-031	Brand New Day 25226	L. Davis	Closed	23.50	150-175.
82-02-032	Baby Blossom 25227	L. Davis	Closed	40.00	175-300.
82-02-033	When Mama Gets Mad 25228	L. Davis	Closed	37.50	300-375.
82-02-034	A Shoe to Fill 25229	L. Davis	Closed	37.50	150-175.
82-02-035	Idle Hours 25230	L. Davis	Closed	37.50	225-300.
82-02-036	Thinking Big 25231	L. Davis	Closed	35.00	68.00
82-02-037	Country Crook 25280	L. Davis	Closed	37.50	300-400.
82-02-038	Waiting for His Master 25281	L. Davis	Closed	50.00	225-300.
82-02-039	Moon Raider 25325	L. Davis	Closed	190.00	325-400.
82-02-040	Blossom and Calf 25326	L. Davis	Closed	250.00	700-1000.
82-02-041	Treed 25327	L. Davis	Closed	155.00	250-300.
83-02-042	Woman's Work 25232	L. Davis	Closed	35.00	90-95.00
83-02-043	Counting the Days 25233	L. Davis	Closed	40.00	60.00
83-02-044	Licking Good 25234	L. Davis	Closed	35.00	200-250.
83-02-045	Mama's Prize Leghorn 25235	L. Davis	Closed	55.00	100-135.
83-02-046	Fair Weather Friend 25236	L. Davis	Closed	25.00	75.00
83-02-047	False Alarm 25237	L. Davis	Closed	65.00	150-185.
83-02-048	Makin' Tracks 25238	L. Davis	Closed	70.00	125-185.
83-02-049	Hi Girls, The Name's Big Jack 25328	L. Davis	Closed	200.00	354.00
83-02-050	City Slicker 25329	L. Davis	Closed	150.00	300-375.
83-02-051	Happy Hunting Ground 25330	L. Davis	Closed	160.00	240.00
83-02-052	Stirring Up Trouble 25331	L. Davis	Closed	160.00	250.00
83-02-053	His Eyes Are Bigger Than His Stomach 25332	L. Davis	Closed	235.00	325-350.
84-02-054	Courtin' 25220	L. Davis	Closed	45.00	120-135.
84-02-055	Anybody Home 25239	L. Davis	Closed	35.00	90-130.00
84-02-056	Headed Home 25240	L. Davis	Closed	25.00	50.00
84-02-057	One for the Road 25241	L. Davis	Open	37.50	60-70.00
84-02-058	Huh? 25242	L. Davis	Closed	40.00	60-95.00
84-02-059	Gonna Pay for His Sins 25243	L. Davis	Open	27.50	90.00
84-02-060	His Master's Dog 25244	L. Davis	Closed	45.00	120-175.
84-02-061	Pasture Pals 25245	L. Davis	Closed	52.00	75.00
84-02-062	Country Kitty 25246	L. Davis	Closed	52.00	115-125.
84-02-063	Catnapping Too? 25247	L. Davis	Closed	70.00	100-125.
84-02-064	Gossips 25248	L. Davis	Closed	110.00	250.00
84-02-066	Prairie Chorus 25333	L. Davis	Closed	135.00	1000-1500.
84-02-067	Mad As A Wet Hen 25334	L. Davis	Closed	185.00	700-800.
85-02-068	Country Crooner 25256	L. Davis	Open	25.00	65.00
85-02-069	Barn Cats 25257	L. Davis	Open	39.50	80.00
85-02-070	Don't Play with Your Food 25258	L. Davis	Open	28.50	80.00
85-02-071	Out-of-Step 25259	L. Davis	Open	45.00	90.00
85-02-072	Renoir 25261	L. Davis	Closed	45.00	80.00
85-02-073	Too Good to Waste on Kids 25262	L. Davis	Open	70.00	130.00
85-02-074	Ozark Belle 25264	L. Davis	Closed	35.00	80.00
85-02-075	Will You Still Respect Me in the Morning 25265	L. Davis	Open	35.00	70.00
85-02-076	Country Cousins 25266	L. Davis	Open	42.50	80.00
85-02-077	Love at First Sight 25267	L. Davis	Open	70.00	105.00
85-02-078	Feelin' His Oats 25275	L. Davis	1,500	150.00	275-300.
85-02-079	Furs Gonna Fly 25335	L. Davis	1,500	145.00	175-225.
85-02-080	Hog Heaven 25336	L. Davis	1,500	165.00	260-450.
86-02-081	Comfy? 25273	L. Davis	Open	40.00	80.00
86-02-082	Mama? 25277	L. Davis	Closed	15.00	40.00
86-02-083	Bit Off More Than He Could Chew 25279	L. Davis	Open	15.00	60.00
87-02-084	Mail Order Bride 25263	L. Davis	Closed	150.00	150.00
87-02-085	Glutton for Punishment 25268	L. Davis	Closed	95.00	150.00
87-02-086	Easy Pickins 25269	L. Davis	Closed	45.00	85.00
87-02-087	Bottoms Up 25270	L. Davis	Open	80.00	90-105.00
87-02-088	The Orphans 25271	L. Davis	Open	50.00	85.00
87-02-089	When the Cat's Away 25276	L. Davis	Open	40.00	60.00
87-02-090	Two in the Bush 25337	L. Davis	Closed	150.00	245-350.
87-02-091	Chicken Thief 25338	L. Davis	Closed	200.00	300.00
88-02-092	Sawin' Logs 25260	L. Davis	Open	85.00	105.00
88-02-093	Fleas 25272	L. Davis	Open	20.00	24.00
88-02-094	Making a Bee Line 25274	L. Davis	Closed	75.00	125.00
88-02-095	Missouri Spring 25278	L. Davis	Open	115.00	130.00
88-02-096	Perfect Ten 25282	L. Davis	Closed	95.00	105-177.
88-02-097	Goldie and Her Peeps 25283	L. Davis	Open	25.00	36.50
88-02-098	In a Pickle 25284	L. Davis	Open	40.00	50.00
88-02-099	Wishful Thinking 25285	L. Davis	Open	55.00	70.00
88-02-100	Brothers 25286	L. Davis	Closed	55.00	85.00
88-02-101	Happy Hour 25287	L. Davis	Open	57.50	65-80.00
88-02-102	When Three Foot's a Mile 25315	L. Davis	Closed	230.00	286.00
88-02-103	No Private Time 25316	L. Davis	Closed	200.00	250-325.
88-02-104	Wintering Lamb 25317	L. Davis	Closed	200.00	225.00
89-02-105	New Friend 25288	L. Davis	Open	45.00	60.00
89-02-106	Family Outing 25289	L. Davis	Open	45.00	60.00
89-02-107	Left Overs 25290	L. Davis	Open	90.00	100.00
89-02-108	Coon Capers 25291	L. Davis	Open	67.50	90.00
89-02-109	Mother Hen 25292	L. Davis	Open	37.50	50.00
89-02-110	Meeting of Sheldon 25293	L. Davis	Open	120.00	150.00
89-02-111	Boy's Night Out 25339	L. Davis	1,500	190.00	225.00
89-02-112	A Tribute to Hooker 25340	L. Davis	Closed	180.00	200-300.
89-02-113	Woodscolt 25342	L. Davis	Closed	300.00	350-500.
90-02-114	Corn Crib Mouse 25295	L. Davis	Closed	35.00	45.00
90-02-115	Seein' Red (Gus w/shoes) 25296	L. Davis	Open	35.00	47.00
90-02-116	Little Black Lamb (Baba) 25297	L. Davis	Closed	30.00	37.50
90-02-117	Hanky Panky 25298	L. Davis	Closed	65.00	100.00
90-02-118	Finder's Keepers 25299	L. Davis	Open	39.50	45.00
90-02-119	Foreplay 25300	L. Davis	Closed	59.50	80.00
90-02-120	The Last Straw 25301	L. Davis	Open	125.00	147-162.50
90-02-121	Long Days, Cold Nights 25344	L. Davis	Closed	175.00	190.00
90-02-122	Piggin' Out 25345	L. Davis	Closed	190.00	250.00
90-02-123	Tricks Of The Trade 25346	L. Davis	Closed	300.00	300-375.
91-02-124	First Offense 25304	L. Davis	Closed	70.00	70.00
91-02-125	Gun Shy 25305	L. Davis	Closed	70.00	70.00
91-02-126	Heading For The Persimmon Grove 25306	L. Davis	Closed	80.00	80.00
91-02-127	Kissin' Cousins 25307	L. Davis	Closed	80.00	80.00
91-02-128	Washed Ashore 25308	L. Davis	Closed	70.00	70.00
91-02-129	Long, Hot Summer 25343	L. Davis	1,950	250.00	250.00
91-02-130	Cock Of The Walk 25347	L. Davis	2,500	300.00	300.00
91-02-131	Sooieee 25360	L. Davis	1,500	350.00	350.00
92-02-132	Ozark's Vittles 25318	L. Davis	Open	60.00	60.00
92-02-133	Don't Play With Fire 25319	L. Davis	Open	120.00	120.00
92-02-134	Safe Haven 25320	L. Davis	Open	95.00	95.00
92-02-135	Free Lunch 25321	L. Davis	Open	85.00	85.00
92-02-136	Headed South 25327	L. Davis	Open	45.00	45.00
92-02-137	My Favorite Chores 25362	L. Davis	1,500	750.00	750.00
92-02-138	OH Sheeeit . . . 25363	L. Davis	Open	120.00	120.00
92-02-139	She Lay Low 25364	L. Davis	Open	120.00	120.00
92-02-140	Snake Doctor 25365	L. Davis	Open	70.00	70.00
92-02-141	The Grass is Always Greener 25367	L. Davis	Open	195.00	195.00
92-02-142	School Yard Dogs 25369	L. Davis	Open	100.00	100.00
92-02-143	The Honeymoon's Over 25370	L. Davis	1,950	300.00	300.00
93-02-144	Sweet Tooth 25373	L. Davis	Open	60.00	60.00
93-02-145	Dry Hole 25374	L. Davis	Open	30.00	30.00
93-02-146	No Hunting 25375	L. Davis	1,000	95.00	95.00
93-02-147	Peep Show 25376	L. Davis	Open	35.00	35.00
93-02-148	If You Can't Beat Em Join Em 25379	L. Davis	1,750	250.00	250.00
93-02-149	King of The Mountain 25380	L. Davis	750	500.00	500.00
93-02-150	Sheep Sheerin Time 25388	L. Davis	1,200	500.00	500.00
93-02-151	Happy Birthday My Sweet 27560	L. Davis	Open	35.00	35.00
93-02-152	Be My Valentine 27561	L. Davis	Open	35.00	35.00
93-02-153	Don't Open Till Christmas 27562	L. Davis	Open	35.00	35.00
93-02-154	I'm Thankful For You 27563	L. Davis	Open	35.00	35.00
93-02-155	You're a Basket Full of Fun 27564	L. Davis	Open	35.00	35.00
93-02-156	Trick or Treat 27565	L. Davis	Open	35.00	35.00
93-02-157	Oh Where is He Now 95041	L. Davis	1,250	250.00	250.00
93-02-158	The Freeloaders 95042	L. Davis	1,250	230.00	230.00
Schmid/B.F.A.		**Farm Set**			
85-03-001	Privy 25348	L. Davis	Closed	12.50	40.00
85-03-002	Windmill 25349	L. Davs	Closed	25.00	50.00
85-03-003	Remus' Cabin 25350	L. Davis	Closed	42.50	45-65.00
85-03-004	Main House 25351	L. Davis	Closed	42.50	125-150.
85-03-005	Barn 25352	L. Davis	Closed	47.50	350-400.
85-03-006	Goat Yard and Studio 25353	L. Davis	Closed	32.50	45-75.00
85-03-007	Corn Crib and Sheep Pen 25354	L. Davis	Closed	25.00	50-85.00
85-03-008	Hog House 25355	L. Davis	Closed	27.50	60-85.00
85-03-009	Hen House 25356	L. Davis	Closed	32.50	50-85.00
85-03-010	Smoke House 25357	L. Davis	Closed	12.50	30-65.00
85-03-011	Chicken House 25358	L. Davis	Closed	19.00	65.00
85-03-012	Garden and Wood Shed 25359	L. Davis	Closed	25.00	65.00
Schmid/B.F.A.		**Davis Cat Tales Figurines**			
82-04-001	Right Church, Wrong Pew 25204	L. Davis	Closed	70.00	350-400.
82-04-002	Company's Coming 25205	L. Davis	Closed	60.00	225-275.
82-04-003	On the Move 25206	L. Davis	Closed	70.00	650-675.
82-04-004	Flew the Coop 25207	L. Davis	Closed	60.00	275-325.
Schmid/B.F.A.		**Davis Special Edition Figurines**			
83-05-001	The Critics 23600	L. Davis	Closed	400.00	1350-1650.
85-05-002	Home from Market 23601	L. Davis	Closed	400.00	1500.00
89-05-003	From A Friend To A Friend 23602	L. Davis	1,200	750.00	1500-1600.
90-05-004	What Rat Race? 23603	L. Davis	1,200	800.00	950.00
92-05-005	Last Laff 23604	L. Davis	1,200	900.00	900.00
Schmid/B.F.A.		**Davis Country Christmas Figurines**			
83-06-001	Hooker at Mailbox with Presents 23550	L. Davis	Closed	80.00	750.00
84-06-002	Country Christmas 23551	L. Davis	Closed	80.00	450.00
85-06-003	Christmas at Fox Fire Farm 23552	L. Davis	Closed	80.00	200-350.
86-06-004	Christmas at Red Oak 23553	L. Davis	Closed	80.00	150-225.
87-06-005	Blossom's Gift 23554	L. Davis	Closed	150.00	350-500.
88-06-006	Cutting the Family Christmas Tree 23555	L. Davis	Closed	80.00	300-350.
89-06-007	Peter and the Wren 23556	L. Davis	Closed	165.00	300-450.
90-06-008	Wintering Deer 23557	L. Davis	Closed	165.00	250.00
91-06-009	Christmas At Red Oak II 23558	L. Davis	Closed	250.00	250.00
92-06-010	Born on a Starry Night 23559	L. Davis	2,500	225.00	225.00
93-06-011	Waiting For Mr. Lowell 23606	L. Davis	2,500	250.00	250.00
Schmid/B.F.A.		**Little Critters**			
89-07-001	Gittin' a Nibble 25294	L. Davis	Open	50.00	57.00
90-07-002	Outing With Grandpa 25502	L. Davis	Closed	200.00	250.00
90-07-003	Home Squeezins 25504	L. Davis	Closed	90.00	90.00
90-07-004	Punkin' Pig 25505	L. Davis	2,500	250.00	350.00
90-07-005	Private Time 25506	L. Davis	Closed	18.00	40.00
91-07-006	Great American Chicken Race 25500	L. Davis	2,500	225.00	275.00
91-07-007	Punkin' Wine 25501	L. Davis	Closed	100.00	150.00
91-07-008	Milk Mouse 25503	L. Davis	2,500	175.00	228.00
91-07-009	When Coffee Never Tasted So Good 25507	L. Davis	1,250	800.00	800.00
91-07-010	Toad Strangler 25509	L. Davis	Open	57.00	57.00
91-07-011	Hittin' The Sack 25510	L. Davis	Open	70.00	70.00
91-07-012	Itiskit, Itasket 25511	L. Davis	Open	45.00	45.00
91-07-013	Christopher Critter 25514	L. Davis	Closed	150.00	150.00
92-07-014	Double Yolker 25516	L. Davis	Yr.Iss.	70.00	70.00
92-07-015	Miss Private Time 25517	L. Davis	Yr.Iss.	35.00	35.00
92-07-016	A Wolf in Sheep's Clothing 25518	L. Davis	Yr.Iss.	110.00	110.00
92-07-017	Charivari 25707	L. Davis	950	250.00	250.00
Schmid/B.F.A.		**Lowell Davis Farm Club**			
85-08-001	The Bride 221001 / 20993	L. Davis	Closed	45.00	375-475.
87-08-002	The Party's Over 221002 / 20994	L. Davis	Closed	50.00	100-190.
88-08-003	Chow Time 221003 / 20995	L. Davis	Closed	55.00	125-150.
89-08-004	Can't Wait 221004 / 20996	L. Davis	Closed	75.00	125.00
90-08-005	Pit Stop 221005 / 20997	L. Davis	Closed	75.00	125-150.
91-08-006	Arrival Of Stanley 221006 / 20998	L. Davis	Yr.Iss.	100.00	100.00
91-08-007	Don't Pick The Flowers 221007 / 21007	L. Davis	Yr.Iss.	100.00	143.00

Company Number	Name	Series Artist	Edition Limit	Issue Price	Quote
92-08-008	Hog Wild	L. Davis	Yr.Iss.	100.00	100.00
92-08-009	Check's in the Mail	L. Davis	Yr.Iss.	100.00	100.00
93-08-010	The Survivor 25371	L. Davis	Yr.Iss.	70.00	70.00
Schmid/B.F.A.		**Lowell Davis Farm Club Renewal Figurine**			
85-09-001	Thirsty? 892050 / 92050	L. Davis	Yr.Iss.	Gift	N/A
87-09-002	Cackle Berries 892051 / 92051	L. Davis	Yr.Iss.	Gift	N/A
88-09-003	Ice Cream Churn 892052 / 92052	L. Davis	Yr.Iss.	Gift	50.00
90-09-004	Not A Sharing Soul 892053 / 92053	L. Davis	Yr.Iss.	Gift	40.00
91-09-005	New Arrival 892054 / 92054	L. Davis	Yr.Iss.	Gift	40.00
92-09-006	Garden Toad 92055	L. Davis	Yr.Iss.	Gift	N/A
93-09-007	Luke 12:6 25372	L. Davis	Yr.Iss.	Gift	N/A
Schmid/B.F.A.		**Country Pride**			
81-10-001	Surprise in the Cellar 25200	L. Davis	Closed	100.00	900-1200.
81-10-002	Plum Tuckered Out 25201	L. Davis	Closed	100.00	600-950.
81-10-003	Bustin' with Pride 25202	L. Davis	Closed	100.00	225-250.
81-10-004	Duke's Mixture 25203	L. Davis	Closed	100.00	375-450.
Schmid/B.F.A.		**Uncle Remus**			
81-11-001	Brer Fox 25250	L. Davis	Closed	70.00	900-950.
81-11-002	Brer Bear 25251	L. Davis	Closed	80.00	900-1200.
81-11-003	Brer Rabbit 25252	L. Davis	Closed	85.00	1500-2000.
81-11-004	Brer Wolf 25253	L. Davis	Closed	85.00	425-475.
81-11-005	Brer Weasel 25254	L. Davis	Closed	80.00	475-700.
81-11-006	Brer Coyote 25255	L. Davis	Closed	80.00	425-475.
Schmid/B.F.A.		**Promotional Figurine**			
91-12-001	Leavin' The Rat Race 225512	L. Davis	N/A	125.00	120-125.
92-12-002	Hen Scratch Prom 225968	L. Davis	N/A	95.00	95.00
Schmid/B.F.A.		**Route 66**			
91-13-001	Just Check The Air 25600	L. Davis	350	700.00	900-1400.
91-13-002	Nel's Diner 25601	L. Davis	350	700.00	1600.00
91-13-003	Little Bit Of Shade 25602	L. Davis	Open	100.00	100.00
91-13-004	Just Check The Air 25603	L. Davis	2,500	550.00	550.00
91-13-005	Nel's Diner 25604	L. Davis	2,500	550.00	550.00
92-13-006	Relief 25605	L. Davis	Open	80.00	80.00
92-13-007	Welcome Mat (w/ wooden base)25606	L. Davis	1,500	400.00	400-500.
92-13-008	Fresh Squeezed? 25608	L. Davis	2,500	450.00	450.00
92-13-009	Fresh Squeezed? (w/ wooden base) 25609	L. Davis	350	600.00	600.00
92-13-010	Quiet Day at Maple Grove 25618	L. Davis	Open	130.00	130.00
92-13-011	Going To Grandma's 25619	L. Davis	Open	80.00	80.00
92-13-012	What Are Pals For? 25620	L. Davis	Open	100.00	100.00
93-13-013	Home For Christmas 25621	L. Davis	Open	80.00	80.00
93-13-014	Kickin' Himself 25622	L. Davis	Open	80.00	80.00
93-13-015	Summer Days 25607	L. Davis	Yr.Iss.	100.00	100.00
Schmid/B.F.A.		**Friends of Mine**			
89-14-001	Sun Worshippers 23620	L. Davis	Closed	120.00	134.00
89-14-002	Sun Worshippers Mini Figurine 23621	L. Davis	Closed	32.50	32.50
90-14-003	Sunday Afternoon Treat 23625	L. Davis	Closed	120.00	130-170.
90-14-004	Sunday Afternoon Treat Mini Figurine 23626	L. Davis	Closed	32.50	37.50
91-14-005	Warm Milk 23629	L. Davis	Closed	120.00	200.00
91-14-006	Warm Milk Mini Figurine 23630	L. Davis	Closed	32.50	37.50
92-14-007	Cat and Jenny Wren 23633	L. Davis	5,000	170.00	175.00
92-14-008	Cat and Jenny Wren Mini Figurine 23634	L. Davis	Open	35.00	35.00
Schmid/B.F.A.		**Pen Pals**			
93-15-001	The Old Home Place Mini Figurine 25801	L. Davis	Open	30.00	30.00
93-15-002	The Old Home Place 25802	L. Davis	1,200	200.00	200.00
Schmid/B.F.A.		**Dealer Counter Signs**			
80-16-001	RFD America 888902	L. Davis	Closed	40.00	175-275.
81-16-002	Uncle Remus 888904	L. Davis	Closed	30.00	300.00
85-16-003	Fox Fire Farm 888907	L. Davis	Closed	30.00	150-275.
90-16-004	Mr. Lowell's Farm 25302	L. Davis	Open	50.00	55-70.00
92-16-005	Little Critters 25515	L. Davis	Open	50.00	50.00
Schmid/B.F.A.		**Tour Figurines**			
92-17-001	Leapin Lizard 25969	L. Davis	Open	80.00	90-100.00
Schmid/B.F.A.		**Kitty Cucumber Musical Figurine**			
92-18-001	Dance 'Round the Maypole 30215	M. Lillemoe	5,000	55.00	55.00
92-18-002	Butterfly 30221	M. Lillemoe	5,000	50.00	50.00
Sebastian Studios: See also Lance Corporation					
Sebastian Studios		**Large Ceramastone Figures**			
39-01-001	Paul Revere Plaque	P.W. Baston	Closed	Unkn.	400-500.
40-01-002	Jesus	P.W. Baston	Closed	Unkn.	300-400.
40-01-003	Mary	P.W. Baston	Closed	Unkn.	600-1000.
40-01-004	Caroler	P.W. Baston	Closed	Unkn.	300-400.
40-01-005	Candle Holder	P.W. Baston	Closed	Unkn.	300-400.
40-01-006	Lamb	P.W. Baston	Closed	Unkn.	300-400.
40-01-007	Basket	P.W. Baston	Closed	Unkn.	300-400.
40-01-008	Horn of Plenty	P.W. Baston	Closed	Unkn.	300-400.
40-01-009	Breton Man	P.W. Baston	Closed	Unkn.	1000-1500.
40-01-010	Breton Woman	P.W. Baston	Closed	Unkn.	1000-1500.
47-01-011	Large Victorian Couple	P.W. Baston	Closed	Unkn.	600-1000.
48-01-012	Woody at Three	P.W. Baston	Closed	Unkn.	600-1000.
56-01-013	Jell-O Cow Milk Pitcher	P.W. Baston	Closed	Unkn.	175-225.
58-01-014	Swift Instrument Girl	P.W. Baston	Closed	Unkn.	500-750.
59-01-015	Wasp Plaque	P.W. Baston	Closed	Unkn.	500-750.
63-01-016	Henry VIII	P.W. Baston	Closed	Unkn.	600-1000.
63-01-017	Anne Boleyn	P.W. Baston	Closed	Unkn.	600-1000.
63-01-018	Tom Sawyer	P.W. Baston	Closed	Unkn.	600-1000.
63-01-019	Mending Time	P.W. Baston	Closed	Unkn.	600-1000.
63-01-020	David Copperfield	P.W. Baston	Closed	Unkn.	600-1000.
63-01-021	Dora	P.W. Baston	Closed	Unkn.	600-1000.
63-01-022	George Washington Toby Jug	P.W. Baston	Closed	Unkn.	600-1000.
63-01-023	Abraham Lincoln Toby Jug	P.W. Baston	Closed	Unkn.	600-1000.
63-01-024	John F. Kennedy Toby Jug	P.W. Baston	Closed	Unkn.	600-1000.
64-01-025	Colonial Boy	P.W. Baston	Closed	Unkn.	600-1000.
64-01-026	Colonial Man	P.W. Baston	Closed	Unkn.	600-1000.
64-01-027	Colonial Woman	P.W. Baston	Closed	Unkn.	600-1000.
64-01-028	Colonial Girl	P.W. Baston	Closed	Unkn.	600-1000.
64-01-029	IBM Mother	P.W. Baston	Closed	Unkn.	600-1000.
64-01-030	IBM Father	P.W. Baston	Closed	Unkn.	600-1000.
64-01-031	IBM Son	P.W. Baston	Closed	Unkn.	600-1000.
64-01-032	IBM Woman	P.W. Baston	Closed	Unkn.	600-1000.
64-01-033	IBM Photographer	P.W. Baston	Closed	Unkn.	600-1000.
65-01-034	N.E. Home For Little Wanderers	P.W. Baston	Closed	Unkn.	600-1000.
65-01-035	Stanley Music Box	P.W. Baston	Closed	Unkn.	300-500.

Company Number	Name	Series Artist	Edition Limit	Issue Price	Quote
65-01-036	The Dentist	P.W. Baston	Closed	Unkn.	600-1000.
66-01-037	Guitarist	P.W. Baston	Closed	Unkn.	600-1000.
67-01-038	Infant of Prague	P.W. Baston	Closed	Unkn.	600-1000.
73-01-039	Potter	P.W. Baston	Closed	Unkn.	300-400.
73-01-040	Cabinetmaker	P.W. Baston	Closed	Unkn.	300-400.
73-01-041	Blacksmith	P.W. Baston	Closed	Unkn.	300-400.
73-01-042	Clockmaker	P.W. Baston	Closed	Unkn.	600-1000.
75-01-043	Minuteman	P.W. Baston	Closed	Unkn.	600-1000.
78-01-044	Mt. Rushmore	P.W. Baston	Closed	Unkn.	400-500.
XX-01-045	Santa Fe...All The Way	P.W. Baston	Closed	Unkn.	600-1000.
XX-01-046	St. Francis (Plaque)	P.W. Baston	Closed	Unkn.	600-1000.
Sebastian Studios		**Sebastian Miniatures**			
38-02-001	Shaker Man	P.W. Baston	Closed	Unkn.	50-100.00
38-02-002	Shaker Lady	P.W. Baston	Closed	Unkn.	50-100.00
39-02-003	George Washington	P.W. Baston	Closed	Unkn.	35-75.00
39-02-004	Martha Washington	P.W. Baston	Closed	Unkn.	35-75.00
39-02-005	John Alden	P.W. Baston	Closed	Unkn.	35-50.00
39-02-006	Priscilla	P.W. Baston	Closed	Unkn.	35-50.00
39-02-007	Williamsburg Governor	P.W. Baston	Closed	Unkn.	75-100.00
39-02-008	Williamsburg Lady	P.W. Baston	Closed	Unkn.	75-100.00
39-02-009	Benjamin Franklin	P.W. Baston	Closed	Unkn.	75-100.00
39-02-010	Deborah Franklin	P.W. Baston	Closed	Unkn.	75-100.00
39-02-011	Gabriel	P.W. Baston	Closed	Unkn.	100-125.
39-02-012	Evangeline	P.W. Baston	Closed	Unkn.	100-125.
39-02-013	Coronado	P.W. Baston	Closed	Unkn.	75-100.00
39-02-014	Coronado's Senora	P.W. Baston	Closed	Unkn.	75-100.00
39-02-015	Sam Houston	P.W. Baston	Closed	Unkn.	75-100.00
39-02-016	Margaret Houston	P.W. Baston	Closed	Unkn.	75-100.00
39-02-017	Indian Warrior	P.W. Baston	Closed	Unkn.	100-125.
39-02-018	Indian Maiden	P.W. Baston	Closed	Unkn.	100-125.
40-02-019	Jean LaFitte	P.W. Baston	Closed	Unkn.	75-100.00
40-02-020	Catherine LaFitte	P.W. Baston	Closed	Unkn.	75-100.00
40-02-021	Dan'l Boone	P.W. Baston	Closed	Unkn.	75-100.00
40-02-022	Mrs. Dan'l Boone	P.W. Baston	Closed	Unkn.	75-100.00
40-02-023	Peter Stvyvesant	P.W. Baston	Closed	Unkn.	75-100.00
40-02-024	Ann Stvyvesant	P.W. Baston	Closed	Unkn.	75-100.00
40-02-025	John Harvard	P.W. Baston	Closed	Unkn.	125-150.
40-02-026	Mrs. Harvard	P.W. Baston	Closed	Unkn.	125-150.
40-02-027	John Smith	P.W. Baston	Closed	Unkn.	75-150.00
40-02-028	Pocohontas	P.W. Baston	Closed	Unkn.	75-150.00
40-02-029	William Penn	P.W. Baston	Closed	Unkn.	100-150.
40-02-030	Hannah Penn	P.W. Baston	Closed	Unkn.	100-150.
40-02-031	Buffalo Bill	P.W. Baston	Closed	Unkn.	75-100.00
40-02-032	Annie Oakley	P.W. Baston	Closed	Unkn.	75-100.00
40-02-033	James Monroe	P.W. Baston	Closed	Unkn.	150-175.
40-02-034	Elizabeth Monroe	P.W. Baston	Closed	Unkn.	150-175.
41-02-035	Rooster	P.W. Baston	Closed	Unkn.	600-1000.
41-02-036	Ducklings	P.W. Baston	Closed	Unkn.	600-1000.
41-02-037	Peacock	P.W Baston	Closed	Unkn.	600-1000.
41-02-038	Doves	P.W. Baston	Closed	Unkn.	600-1000.
41-02-039	Pheasant	P.W. Baston	Closed	Unkn.	600-1000.
41-02-040	Swan	P.W. Baston	Closed	Unkn.	600-1000.
41-02-041	Secrets	P.W. Baston	Closed	Unkn.	600-1000.
41-02-042	Kitten (Sleeping)	P.W. Baston	Closed	Unkn.	600-1000.
41-02-043	Kitten (Sitting)	P.W. Baston	Closed	Unkn.	600-1000.
42-02-044	Majorette	P.W. Baston	Closed	Unkn.	325.-375.
42-02-045	Cymbals	P.W. Baston	Closed	Unkn.	325-375.
42-02-046	Horn	P.W. Baston	Closed	Unkn.	325-375.
42-02-047	Tuba	P.W. Baston	Closed	Unkn.	325-375.
42-02-048	Drum	P.W. Baston	Closed	Unkn.	325-375.
42-02-049	Accordion	P.W. Baston	Closed	Unkn.	325-375.
46-02-050	Puritan Spinner	P.W. Baston	Closed	Unkn.	500-1000.
46-02-051	Satchel-Eye Dyer	P.W. Baston	Closed	Unkn.	125-150.
47-02-052	Down East	P.W. Baston	Closed	Unkn.	125-150.
47-02-053	First Cookbook Author	P.W. Baston	Closed	Unkn.	125-150.
47-02-054	Fisher Pair PS	P.W. Baston	Closed	Unkn.	400-1000.
47-02-055	Mr. Beacon Hill	P.W. Baston	Closed	Unkn.	50-75.00
47-02-056	Mrs. Beacon Hill	P.W. Baston	Closed	Unkn.	50-75.00
47-02-057	Dahl's Fisherman	P.W. Baston	Closed	Unkn.	150-175.
47-02-058	Dilemma	P.W. Baston	Closed	Unkn.	275-300.
47-02-059	Princess Elizabeth	P.W. Baston	Closed	Unkn.	200-300.
47-02-060	Prince Philip	P.W. Baston	Closed	Unkn.	200-300.
47-02-061	Howard Johnson Pieman	P.W. Baston	Closed	Unkn.	300-450.
47-02-062	Tollhouse Town Crier	P.W. Baston	Closed	Unkn.	125-175.
48-02-063	Slalom	P.W. Baston	Closed	Unkn.	175-200.
48-02-064	Sitzmark	P.W. Baston	Closed	Unkn.	175-200.
48-02-065	Mr. Rittenhouse Square	P.W. Baston	Closed	Unkn.	150-175.
48-02-066	Mrs. Rittenhouse Square	P.W. Baston	Closed	Unkn.	150-175.
48-02-067	Swedish Boy	P.W. Baston	Closed	Unkn.	250-500.
48-02-068	Swedish Girl	P.W. Baston	Closed	Unkn.	250-500.
48-02-069	Democratic Victory	P.W. Baston	Closed	Unkn.	350-500.
48-02-070	Republican Victory	P.W. Baston	Closed	Unkn.	600-1000.
48-02-071	Nathaniel Hawthorne	P.W. Baston	Closed	Unkn.	175-200.
48-02-072	Jordan Marsh Observer	P.W. Baston	Closed	Unkn.	150-175.
48-02-073	Mr. Sheraton	P.W. Baston	Closed	Unkn.	400-500.
48-02-074	A Harvey Girl	P.W. Baston	Closed	Unkn.	250-300.
48-02-075	Mary Lyon	P.W. Baston	Closed	Unkn.	250-300.
49-02-076	Uncle Mistletoe	P.W. Baston	Closed	Unkn.	250-300.
49-02-077	Eustace Tilly	P.W. Baston	Closed	Unkn.	750-1500.
49-02-078	Menotomy Indian	P.W. Baston	Closed	Unkn.	175-250.
49-02-079	Boy Scout Plaque	P.W. Baston	Closed	Unkn.	300-350.
49-02-080	Patrick Henry	P.W. Baston	Closed	Unkn.	100-125.
49-02-081	Sarah Henry	P.W. Baston	Closed	Unkn.	100-125.
49-02-082	Paul Bunyan	P.W. Baston	Closed	Unkn.	150-250.
49-02-083	Emmett Kelly	P.W. Baston	Closed	Unkn.	200-300.
49-02-084	Giant Royal Bengal Tiger	P.W. Baston	Closed	Unkn.	1000-1500.
49-02-085	The Thinker	P.W. Baston	Closed	Unkn.	175-250.
49-02-086	The Mark Twain Home in Hannibal, MO	P.W. Baston	Closed	Unkn.	600-1000.
49-02-087	Dutchman's Pipe	P.W. Baston	Closed	Unkn.	175-225.
49-02-088	Gathering Tulips	P.W. Baston	Closed	Unkn.	225-250.
50-02-089	Phoebe, House of 7 Gables	P.W. Baston	Closed	Unkn.	150-175.
50-02-090	Mr. Obocell	P.W. Baston	Closed	Unkn.	75-125.00
50-02-091	National Diaper Service	P.W. Baston	Closed	Unkn.	250-300.
51-02-092	Judge Pyncheon	P.W. Baston	Closed	Unkn.	175-225.
51-02-093	Seb. Dealer Plaque (Marblehead)	P.W. Baston	Closed	Unkn.	300-350.
51-02-094	Great Stone Face	P.W. Baston	Closed	Unkn.	600-1000.
51-02-095	Christopher Columbus	P.W. Baston	Closed	Unkn.	250-300.
51-02-096	Sir Frances Drake	P.W. Baston	Closed	Unkn.	250-300.
51-02-097	Jesse Buffman (WEEI)	P.W. Baston	Closed	Unkn.	200-350.
51-02-098	Carl Moore (WEEI)	P.W. Baston	Closed	Unkn.	200-300.
51-02-099	Caroline Cabot (WEEI)	P.W. Baston	Closed	Unkn.	200-350.
51-02-100	Mother Parker (WEEI)	P.W. Baston	Closed	Unkn.	200-350.
51-02-101	Charles Ashley (WEEI)	P.W. Baston	Closed	Unkn.	200-350.

Company Number	Name	Series Artist	Edition Limit	Issue Price	Quote
51-02-102	E. B. Rideout (WEEI)	P.W. Baston	Closed	Unkn.	200-350.
51-02-103	Priscilla Fortesue (WEEI)	P.W. Baston	Closed	Unkn.	200-350.
51-02-104	Chiquita Banana	P.W. Baston	Closed	Unkn.	350-400.
51-02-105	Mit Seal	P.W. Baston	Closed	Unkn.	350-425.
51-02-106	The Observer & Dame New England.	P.W. Baston	Closed	Unkn.	325-375.
51-02-107	Jordon Marsh Observer Rides the A.W. Horse	P.W. Baston	Closed	Unkn.	300-325.
51-02-108	The Iron Master's House	P.W. Baston	Closed	Unkn.	350-500.
51-02-109	Chief Pontiac	P.W. Baston	Closed	Unkn.	400-700.
52-02-110	The Favored Scholar	P.W. Baston	Closed	Unkn.	200-300.
52-02-111	Neighboring Pews	P.W. Baston	Closed	Unkn.	200-300.
52-02-112	Weighing the Baby	P.W. Baston	Closed	Unkn.	200-300.
52-02-113	The First House, Plimoth Plantation	P.W. Baston	Closed	Unkn.	150-195.
52-02-114	Scottish Girl (Jell-O)	P.W. Baston	Closed	Unkn.	350-375.
52-02-115	Lost in the Kitchen (Jell-O)	P.W. Baston	Closed	Unkn.	350-375.
52-02-116	The Fat Man (Jell-O)	P.W. Baston	Closed	Unkn.	525-600.
52-02-117	Baby (Jell-O)	P.W. Baston	Closed	Unkn.	525-600.
52-02-118	Stork (Jell-O)	P.W. Baston	Closed	Unkn.	425-525.
52-02-119	Tabasco Sauce	P.W. Baston	Closed	Unkn.	400-500.
52-02-120	Aerial Tramway	P.W. Baston	Closed	Unkn.	300-600.
52-02-121	Marblehead High School Plaque	P.W. Baston	Closed	Unkn.	200-300.
52-02-122	St. Joan d'Arc	P.W. Baston	Closed	Unkn.	300-350.
52-02-123	St. Sebastian	P.W. Baston	Closed	Unkn.	300-350.
52-02-124	Our Lady of Good Voyage	P.W. Baston	Closed	Unkn.	200-250.
52-02-125	Old Powder House	P.W. Baston	Closed	Unkn.	250-300.
53-02-126	Holgrave the Daguerrotypist	P.W. Baston	Closed	Unkn.	200-250.
53-02-127	St. Teresa of Lisieux	P.W. Baston	Closed	Unkn.	225-275.
53-02-128	Darned Well He Can	P.W. Baston	Closed	Unkn.	300-350.
53-02-129	R.H. Stearns Chestnut Hill Mall	P.W. Baston	Closed	Unkn.	225-275.
53-02-130	Boy Jesus in the Temple	P.W. Baston	Closed	Unkn.	350-400.
53-02-131	Blessed Julie Billart	P.W. Baston	Closed	Unkn.	400-500.
53-02-132	"Old Put" Enjoys a Licking	P.W. Baston	Closed	Unkn.	300-350.
53-02-133	Lion (Jell-O)	P.W. Baston	Closed	Unkn.	350-375.
53-02-134	The Schoolboy of 1850	P.W. Baston	Closed	Unkn.	350-400.
54-02-135	Whale (Jell-O)	P.W. Baston	Closed	Unkn.	350-375.
54-02-136	Rabbit (Jell-O)	P.W. Baston	Closed	Unkn.	350-375.
54-02-137	Moose (Jell-O)	P.W. Baston	Closed	Unkn.	350-375.
54-02-138	Scuba Diver	P.W. Baston	Closed	Unkn.	400-450.
54-02-139	Stimalose (Woman)	P.W. Baston	Closed	Unkn.	175-200.
54-02-140	Stimalose (Men)	P.W. Baston	Closed	Unkn.	600-1000.
54-02-141	Bluebird Girl	P.W. Baston	Closed	Unkn.	400-450.
54-02-142	Campfire Girl	P.W. Baston	Closed	Unkn.	400-450.
54-02-143	Horizon Girl	P.W. Baston	Closed	Unkn.	400-450.
54-02-144	Kernel-Fresh Ashtray	P.W. Baston	Closed	Unkn.	400-450.
54-02-145	William Penn	P.W. Baston	Closed	Unkn.	175-225.
54-02-146	St. Pius X	P.W. Baston	Closed	Unkn.	400-475.
54-02-147	Resolute Ins. Co. Clipper PS	P.W. Baston	Closed	Unkn.	300-325.
54-02-148	Dachshund (Audiovox)	P.W. Baston	Closed	Unkn.	300-350.
54-02-149	Our Lady of Laleche	P.W. Baston	Closed	Unkn.	300-350.
54-02-150	Swan Boat Brooch-Empty Seats	P.W. Baston	Closed	Unkn.	600-1000.
54-02-151	Swan Boat Brooch-Full Seats	P.W. Baston	Closed	Unkn.	600-1000.
55-02-152	Davy Crockett	P.W. Baston	Closed	Unkn.	225-275.
55-02-153	Giraffe (Jell-O)	P.W. Baston	Closed	Unkn.	350-375.
55-02-154	Old Woman in the Shoe (Jell-O)	P.W. Baston	Closed	Unkn.	500-600.
55-02-155	Santa (Jell-O)	P.W. Baston	Closed	Unkn.	500-600.
55-02-156	Captain Doliber	P.W. Baston	Closed	Unkn.	300-350.
55-02-157	Second Bank-State St. Trust PS	P.W. Baston	Closed	Unkn.	300-325.
55-02-158	Horse Head PS	P.W. Baston	Closed	Unkn.	350-375.
56-02-159	Robin Hood & Little John	P.W. Baston	Closed	Unkn.	400-500.
56-02-160	Robin Hood & Friar Tuck	P.W. Baston	Closed	Unkn.	400-500.
56-02-161	77th Bengal Lancer (Jell-O)	P.W. Baston	Closed	Unkn.	600-1000.
56-02-162	Three Little Kittens (Jell-O)	P.W. Baston	Closed	Unkn.	375-400.
56-02-163	Texcel Tape Boy	P.W. Baston	Closed	Unkn.	350-425.
56-02-164	Permacel Tower of Tape Ashtray	P.W. Baston	Closed	Unkn.	600-1000.
56-02-165	Arthritic Hands (J & J)	P.W. Baston	Closed	Unkn.	600-1000.
56-02-166	Rarical Blacksmith	P.W. Baston	Closed	Unkn.	300-500.
56-02-167	Praying Hands	P.W. Baston	Closed	Unkn.	250-300.
56-02-168	Eastern Paper Plaque	P.W. Baston	Closed	Unkn.	350-400.
56-02-169	Girl on Diving Board	P.W. Baston	Closed	Unkn.	400-450.
56-02-170	Elsie the Cow Billboard	P.W. Baston	Closed	Unkn.	600-1000.
56-02-171	Mrs. Obocell	P.W. Baston	Closed	Unkn.	400-450.
56-02-172	Alike, But Oh So Different	P.W. Baston	Closed	Unkn.	300-350.
56-02-173	NYU Grad School of Bus. Admin. Bldg.	P.W. Baston	Closed	Unkn.	300-350.
56-02-174	The Green Giant	P.W. Baston	Closed	Unkn.	400-500.
56-02-175	Michigan Millers PS	P.W. Baston	Closed	Unkn.	200-275.
57-02-176	Mayflower PS	P.W. Baston	Closed	Unkn.	300-325.
57-02-177	Jamestown Church	P.W. Baston	Closed	Unkn.	400-450.
57-02-178	Olde James Fort	P.W. Baston	Closed	Unkn.	250-300.
57-02-179	Jamestown Ships	P.W. Baston	Closed	Unkn.	350-475.
57-02-180	IBM 305 Ramac	P.W. Baston	Closed	Unkn.	400-450.
57-02-181	Colonial Fund Doorway PS	P.W. Baston	Closed	Unkn.	600-1000.
57-02-182	Speedy Alka Seltzer	P.W. Baston	Closed	Unkn.	600-1000.
57-02-183	Nabisco Spoonmen	P.W. Baston	Closed	Unkn.	600-1000.
57-02-184	Nabisco Buffalo Bee	P.W. Baston	Closed	Unkn.	600-1000.
57-02-185	Borden's Centennial (Elsie the Cow)	P.W. Baston	Closed	Unkn.	600-1000.
57-02-186	Along the Albany Road PS	P.W. Baston	Closed	Unkn.	600-1000.
58-02-187	Romeo & Juliet	P.W. Baston	Closed	Unkn.	400-500.
58-02-188	Mt. Vernon	P.W. Baston	Closed	Unkn.	400-500.
58-02-189	Hannah Duston PS	P.W. Baston	Closed	Unkn.	250-325.
58-02-190	Salem Savings Bank	P.W. Baston	Closed	Unkn.	250-300.
58-02-191	CBS Miss Columbia PS	P.W. Baston	Closed	Unkn.	600-1000.
58-02-192	Connecticut Bank & Trust	P.W. Baston	Closed	Unkn.	225-275.
58-02-193	Jackie Gleason	P.W. Baston	Closed	Unkn.	600-1000.
58-02-194	Harvard Trust Colonial Man	P.W. Baston	Closed	Unkn.	275-325.
58-02-195	Jordan Marsh Observer	P.W. Baston	Closed	Unkn.	175-275.
58-02-196	Cliquot Club Eskimo PS	P.W. Baston	Closed	Unkn.	1000-2300.
58-02-197	Commodore Stephen Decatur	P.W. Baston	Closed	Unkn.	125-175.
59-02-198	Siesta Coffee PS	P.W. Baston	Closed	Unkn.	600-1000.
59-02-199	Harvard Trust Co. Town Crier	P.W. Baston	Closed	Unkn.	350-400.
59-02-200	Mrs. S.O.S.	P.W. Baston	Closed	Unkn.	300-350.
59-02-201	H.P. Hood Co. Cigar Store Indian	P.W. Baston	Closed	Unkn.	600-1000.
59-02-202	Alexander Smith Weaver	P.W. Baston	Closed	Unkn.	350-425.
59-02-203	Fleischman's Margarine PS	P.W. Baston	Closed	Unkn.	225-325.
59-02-204	Alcoa Wrap PS	P.W. Baston	Closed	Unkn.	350-400.
59-02-205	Fiorello LaGuardia	P.W. Baston	Closed	Unkn.	125-175.
59-02-206	Henry Hudson	P.W. Baston	Closed	Unkn.	125-175.
59-02-207	Giovanni Verrazzano	P.W. Baston	Closed	Unkn.	125-175.
60-02-208	Peter Stvyvesant	P.W. Baston	Closed	Unkn.	125-175.
60-02-209	Masonic Bible	P.W. Baston	Closed	Unkn.	300-400.
60-02-210	Son of the Desert	P.W. Baston	Closed	Unkn.	200-275.
60-02-211	Metropolitan Life Tower PS	P.W. Baston	Closed	Unkn.	350-400.
60-02-212	Supp-Hose Lady	P.W. Baston	Closed	Unkn.	300-350.
60-02-213	Marine Memorial	P.W. Baston	Closed	Unkn.	300-400.
60-02-214	The Infantryman	P.W. Baston	Closed	Unkn.	600-1000.
61-02-215	Tony Piet	P.W. Baston	Closed	Unkn.	600-1000.
61-02-216	Bunky Knudsen	P.W. Baston	Closed	Unkn.	600-1000.
61-02-217	Merchant's Warren Sea Capt.	P.W. Baston	Closed	Unkn.	200-250.
61-02-218	Pope John 23rd	P.W. Baston	Closed	Unkn.	400-450.
61-02-219	St. Jude Thaddeus	P.W. Baston	Closed	Unkn.	400-500.
62-02-220	Seaman's Bank for Savings	P.W. Baston	Closed	Unkn.	300-350.
62-02-221	Yankee Clipper Sulfide	P.W. Baston	Closed	Unkn.	600-1000.
62-02-222	Big Brother Bob Emery	P.W. Baston	Closed	Unkn.	600-1000.
62-02-223	Blue Belle Highlander	P.W. Baston	Closed	Unkn.	200-250.
63-02-224	John F. Kennedy Toby Jug	P.W. Baston	Closed	Unkn.	600-1000.
63-02-225	Jackie Kennedy Toby Jug	P.W. Baston	Closed	Unkn.	600-1000.
63-02-226	Naumkeag Indian	P.W. Baston	Closed	Unkn.	225-275.
63-02-227	Dia-Mel Fat Man	P.W. Baston	Closed	Unkn.	375-400.
65-02-228	Pope Paul VI	P.W. Baston	Closed	Unkn.	400-500.
65-02-229	Henry Wadsworth Longfellow	P.W. Baston	Closed	Unkn.	275-325.
65-02-230	State Street Bank Globe	P.W. Baston	Closed	Unkn.	250-300.
65-02-231	Panti-Legs Girl PS	P.W. Baston	Closed	Unkn.	250-300.
66-02-232	Paul Revere Plaque (W.T. Grant)	P.W. Baston	Closed	Unkn.	300-350.
66-02-233	Massachusetts SPCA	P.W. Baston	Closed	Unkn.	250-350.
66-02-234	Little George	P.W. Baston	Closed	Unkn.	350-450.
66-02-235	Gardeners (Thermometer)	P.W. Baston	Closed	Unkn.	300-400.
66-02-236	Gardener Man	P.W. Baston	Closed	Unkn.	250-300.
66-02-237	Gardener Women	P.W. Baston	Closed	Unkn.	250-300.
66-02-238	Town Lyne Indian	P.W. Baston	Closed	Unkn.	600-1000.
67-02-239	Doc Berry of Berwick (yellow shirt)	P.W. Baston	Closed	Unkn.	300-350.
67-02-240	Ortho-Novum	P.W. Baston	Closed	Unkn.	600-1000.
68-02-241	Captain John Parker	P.W. Baston	Closed	Unkn.	300-350.
68-02-242	Watermill Candy Plaque	P.W. Baston	Closed	Unkn.	600-1000.
70-02-243	Uncle Sam in Orbit	P.W. Baston	Closed	Unkn.	350-400.
71-02-244	Town Meeting Plaque	P.W. Baston	Closed	Unkn.	350-400.
71-02-245	Boston Gas Tank	P.W. Baston	Closed	Unkn.	300-500.
72-02-246	George & Hatchet	P.W. Baston	Closed	Unkn.	400-450.
72-02-247	Martha & the Cherry Pie	P.W. Baston	Closed	Unkn.	350-400.
XX-02-248	The King	P.W. Baston	Closed	Unkn.	600-1000.
XX-02-249	Bob Hope	P.W. Baston	Closed	Unkn.	600-1000.
XX-02-250	Coronation Crown	P.W. Baston	Closed	Unkn.	600-1000.
XX-02-251	Babe Ruth	P.W. Baston	Closed	Unkn.	600-1000.
XX-02-252	Sylvania Electric-Bulb Display	P.W. Baston	Closed	Unkn.	600-1000.
XX-02-252	Ortho Gynecic	P.W. Baston	Closed	Unkn.	600-1000.
XX-02-254	Eagle Plaque	P.W. Baston	Closed	Unkn.	1000-1500.
Shelia's Collectibles		**Painted Ladies I**			
90-01-001	San Francisco Stick House-yellow LAD01	S.Thompson	Retrd.	10.00	40-100.00
90-01-002	San Francisco Stick House-blue LAD02	S.Thompson	Retrd.	10.00	40-100.00
90-01-003	San Francisco Italianate-yellow LAD03	S.Thompson	Retrd.	10.00	100.00
90-01-004	Colorado Queen Anne LAD04	S.Thompson	Retrd.	10.00	50-100.00
90-01-005	Cincinnati Gothic LAD05	S.Thompson	Retrd.	10.00	30-100.00
90-01-006	Illinois Queen Anne LAD06	S.Thompson	Retrd.	10.00	50-125.00
90-01-007	Atlanta Queen Anne LAD07	S.Thompson	Retrd.	10.00	100.00
90-01-008	Cape May Gothic Revival LAD08	S.Thompson	Retrd.	10.00	26-100.00
Shelia's Collectibles		**Painted Ladies II**			
92-02-001	The Gingerbread Mansion LAD09	S.Thompson	Retrd.	15.00	15.00
92-02-002	The Gingerbread Mansion II LAD09	S.Thompson	Open	15.00	15.00
92-02-003	Pitkin House LAD10	S.Thompson	Open	15.00	15.00
92-02-004	The Young-Larson House LAD11	S.Thompson	Open	15.00	15.00
92-02-005	Queen Anne Townhouse LAD12	S.Thompson	Open	15.00	15.00
92-02-006	Pink Gothic LAD13	S.Thompson	Open	15.00	15.00
92-02-007	The Victorian Blue Rose LAD14	S.Thompson	Open	15.00	15.00
92-02-008	Morningstar Inn LAD15	S.Thompson	Open	15.00	15.00
92-02-009	Cape May Victorian Pink House LAD16	S.Thompson	Open	15.00	15.00
Shelia's Collectibles		**Painted Ladies III**			
93-03-001	Cape May Linda Lee LAD17	S.Thompson	Open	16.00	16.00
93-03-002	Cape May Tan Stockton Row LAD18	S.Thompson	Open	16.00	16.00
93-03-003	Cape May Pink Stockton Row LAD19	S.Thompson	Open	16.00	16.00
93-03-004	Cape May Green Stockton Row LAD20	S.Thompson	Open	16.00	16.00
Shelia's Collectibles		**Dicken's Village**			
91-04-001	Scrooge & Marley's Shop XMS01	S.Thompson	Retrd.	15.00	20-25.00
91-04-002	Victorian Apartment Building XMS02	S.Thompson	Retrd.	15.00	20-25.00
91-04-003	Butcher Shop XMS03	S.Thompson	Retrd.	15.00	20-25.00
91-04-004	Toy Shoppe XMS04	S.Thompson	Retrd.	15.00	20-25.00
91-04-005	Scrooge's Home XMS05	S.Thompson	Retrd.	15.00	20-25.00
91-04-006	Gazebo & Carolers XMS06	S.Thompson	Retrd.	12.00	20-25.00
91-04-007	Victorian Skaters XMS07	S.Thompson	Retrd.	12.00	20.00
91-04-008	Evergreen Tree XMS08	S.Thompson	Retrd.	11.00	20.00
92-04-009	Victorian Church XMS09	S.Thompson	Retrd.	15.00	20.00
92-04-010	Set	S.Thompson	Retrd.	125.00	160-185.
Shelia's Collectibles		**Charleston**			
88-06-001	Rainbow Row-rust CHS31	S.Thompson	Retrd.	9.00	16-20.00
88-06-002	Rainbow Row-cream CHS32	S.Thompson	Retrd.	9.00	16-20.00
88-06-003	Rainbow Row-tan CHS33	S.Thompson	Retrd.	9.00	16-20.00
88-06-004	Rainbow Row-green CHS34	S.Thompson	Retrd.	9.00	16-20.00
88-06-005	Rainbow Row-lavender CHS35	S.Thompson	Retrd.	9.00	16-20.00
88-06-006	Rainbow Row-pink CHS36	S.Thompson	Retrd.	9.00	16-20.00
88-06-007	Rainbow Row-blue CHS37	S.Thompson	Retrd.	9.00	16-20.00
88-06-008	Rainbow Row-lt. yellow CHS38	S.Thompson	Retrd.	9.00	16-20.00
88-06-009	Rainbow Row-lt. pink CHS39	S.Thompson	Retrd.	9.00	16-20.00
89-06-010	Powder Magazine CHS16	S.Thompson	Retrd.	9.00	75-100.00
89-06-011	Middleton Plantation CHS19	S.Thompson	Retrd.	9.00	125-130.
90-06-012	Manigault House CHS01	S.Thompson	Retrd.	15.00	17-23.00
90-06-013	Heyward-Washington House CHS02	S.Thompson	Retrd.	15.00	23.00
90-06-014	Magnolia Plantation House CHS03	S.Thompson	Open	16.00	16.00
90-06-015	Edmonston-Alston CHS04	S.Thompson	Open	15.00	15.00
90-06-016	St. Philip's Church CHS05	S.Thompson	Open	15.00	15.00
90-06-017	#2 Meeting Street CHS06	S.Thompson	Open	15.00	15.00
90-06-018	City Market I CHS07	S.Thompson	Retrd.	15.00	20.00
90-06-019	Dock Street Theater I CHS08	S.Thompson	Retrd.	15.00	17-22.00
90-06-020	St. Michael's Church CHS14	S.Thompson	Open	15.00	15.00
90-06-021	Exchange Building CHS15	S.Thompson	Open	15.00	15.00
90-06-022	90 Church St. CHS17	S.Thompson	Retrd.	12.00	15-22.00
90-06-023	Pink House CHS18	S.Thompson	Retrd.	12.00	15-22.00
90-06-024	Beth Elohim Temple CHS20	S.Thompson	Retrd.	15.00	17-23.00
92-06-025	City Market II CHS07	S.Thompson	Open	15.00	15.00
92-06-026	Dock Street Theater II CHS08	S.Thompson	Retrd.	15.00	15.00
93-06-027	City Hall CHS21	S.Thompson	Retrd.	15.00	16-30.00
93-06-028	The Citadel CHS22	S.Thompson	Open	16.00	16.00
93-06-029	Single Side Porch CHS30	S.Thompson	Open	16.00	16.00
93-06-030	Single Side Porch, AP CHS30	S.Thompson	102	20.00	20.00
93-06-031	College of Charleston CHS40	S.Thompson	Open	16.00	16.00
93-06-032	College of Charleston, AP CHS40	S.Thompson	54	20.00	20.00
93-06-033	Rainbow Row-aurora CHS41	S.Thompson	Open	13.00	13.00
93-06-034	Rainbow Row-off-white CHS42	S.Thompson	Open	13.00	13.00

Number	Name	Artist	Edition Limit	Issue Price	Quote
Company		**Series**			
93-06-035	Rainbow Row-cream CHS43	S.Thompson	Open	13.00	13.00
93-06-036	Rainbow Row-green CHS44	S.Thompson	Open	13.00	13.00
93-06-037	Rainbow Row-lavender CHS45	S.Thompson	Open	13.00	13.00
93-06-038	Rainbow Row-pink CHS46	S.Thompson	Open	13.00	13.00
93-06-039	Rainbow Row-blue CHS47	S.Thompson	Open	13.00	13.00
93-06-040	Rainbow Row-yellow CHS48	S.Thompson	Open	13.00	13.00
93-06-041	Rainbow Row-gray CHS49	S.Thompson	Open	13.00	13.00
93-06-042	John Rutledge CHS50	S.Thompson	Open	16.00	16.00
93-06-043	Ashe House CHS51	S.Thompson	Open	16.00	16.00
Shelia's Collectibles		**Charleston Gold Seal**			
88-07-001	Rainbow Row-rust (gold seal) CHS31	S.Thompson	Retrd.	9.00	N/A
88-07-002	Rainbow Row-tan (gold seal) CHS32	S.Thompson	Retrd.	9.00	N/A
88-07-003	Rainbow Row-cream (gold seal) CHS33	S.Thompson	Retrd.	9.00	N/A
88-07-004	Rainbow Row-green (gold seal) CHS34	S.Thompson	Retrd.	9.00	N/A
88-07-005	Rainbow Row-lavender (gold seal) CHS35	S.Thompson	Retrd.	9.00	N/A
88-07-006	Rainbow Row-pink (gold seal) CHS36	S.Thompson	Retrd.	9.00	N/A
88-07-007	Rainbow Row-blue (gold seal) CHS37	S.Thompson	Retrd.	9.00	N/A
88-07-008	Rainbow Row-lt. yellow (gold seal) CHS38	S.Thompson	Retrd.	9.00	N/A
88-07-009	Rainbow Row-lt. pink (gold seal) CHS39	S.Thompson	Retrd.	9.00	N/A
88-07-010	90 Church St. (gold seal) CHS17	S.Thompson	Retrd.	9.00	N/A
88-07-011	Pink House (gold seal) CHS18	S.Thompson	Retrd.	9.00	N/A
89-07-012	St. Michael's Church (gold seal) CHS14	S.Thompson	Retrd.	9.00	N/A
89-07-013	Exchange Building (gold seal) CHS15	S.Thompson	Retrd.	9.00	N/A
89-07-014	Powder Magazine (gold seal) CHS16	S.Thompson	Retrd.	9.00	65-85.00
89-07-015	Middleton Plantation (gold seal) CHS19	S.Thompson	Retrd.	9.00	100.00
Shelia's Collectibles		**Texas**			
90-08-001	The Alamo TEX01	S.Thompson	Retrd.	15.00	22-25.00
90-08-002	Mission San Jose' TEX02	S.Thompson	Retrd.	15.00	25.00
90-08-003	Mission San Francisco TEX03	S.Thompson	Retrd.	15.00	25.00
90-08-004	Mission Concepcion TEX04	S.Thompson	Retrd.	15.00	25.00
Shelia's Collectibles		**New England**			
90-09-001	Longfellow's House NEW01	S.Thompson	Retrd.	15.00	23-25.00
90-09-002	Motif #1 Boathouse NEW02	S.Thompson	Retrd.	15.00	54.00
90-09-003	Paul Revere's Home MEW03	S.Thompson	Retrd.	15.00	23-25.00
90-09-004	Old North Church NEW04	S.Thompson	Retrd.	15.00	23-25.00
90-09-005	Malden Mass. Victorian Inn NEW05	S.Thompson	Retrd.	10.00	50-100.00
90-09-006	President Bush's Home NEW07	S.Thompson	Retrd.	15.00	23-50.00
90-09-007	Wedding Cake House NEW08	S.Thompson	Retrd.	15.00	23-30.00
90-09-008	Faneuil Hall NEW09	S.Thompson	Retrd.	15.00	65.00
90-09-009	Martha's Vineyard Cottage-blue/mauve -MAR06	S.Thompson	Retrd.	15.00	25-65.00
90-09-010	Martha's Vineyard Cottage-blue/orange MAR05	S.Thompson	Retrd.	15.00	25-65.00
Shelia's Collectibles		**Williamsburg**			
90-10-001	Governor's Palace WIL04	S.Thompson	Open	15.00	15.00
90-10-002	Printer-Bookbinder WIL05	S.Thompson	Retrd.	12.00	22.00
90-10-003	Milliner WIL06	S.Thompson	Retrd.	12.00	14.00
90-10-004	Silversmith WIL07	S.Thompson	Retrd.	12.00	14.00
90-10-005	Nicolson Store WIL08	S.Thompson	Retrd.	12.00	14.00
90-10-006	Apothecary WIL09	S.Thompson	Retrd.	12.00	14.00
90-10-007	King's Arm Tavern WIL10	S.Thompson	Open	15.00	15.00
90-10-008	Courthouse WIL11	S.Thompson	Open	15.00	15.00
90-10-009	Homesite WIL12	S.Thompson	Open	15.00	15.00
93-10-010	Bruton Parish Church WIL13	S.Thompson	Open	15.00	15.00
Shelia's Collectibles		**Philadelphia**			
90-11-001	Carpenter's Hall PHI01	S.Thompson	Retrd.	15.00	20.00
90-11-002	Market St. Post Office PHI02	S.Thompson	Retrd.	15.00	20.00
90-11-003	Betsy Ross House PHI03	S.Thompson	Retrd.	15.00	20-25.00
90-11-004	Independence Hall PHI04	S.Thompson	Retrd.	15.00	20.00
90-11-005	Elphreth's Alley PHI05	S.Thompson	Retrd.	15.00	20.00
90-11-006	Old Tavern PHI06	S.Thompson	Retrd.	15.00	20-25.00
90-11-007	Graff House PHI07	S.Thompson	Retrd.	15.00	25.00
90-11-008	Old City Hall PHI08	S.Thompson	Retrd.	15.00	20.00
Shelia's Collectibles		**Washington D.C.**			
92-12-001	National Archives DC001	S.Thompson	Retrd.	16.00	20-22.00
92-12-002	Library of Congress DC002	S.Thompson	Retrd.	16.00	20-22.00
92-12-003	White House DC003	S.Thompson	Retrd.	16.00	20-22.00
92-12-004	Washington Monument DC004	S.Thompson	Retrd.	16.00	20-46.00
92-12-005	Cherry Trees DC005	S.Thompson	Retrd.	12.00	20-46.00
Shelia's Collectibles		**North Carolina**			
91-13-001	Josephus Hall House NC101	S.Thompson	Retrd.	15.00	20-25.00
91-13-002	Presbyterian Bell Tower NC102	S.Thompson	Retrd.	15.00	20-22.00
91-13-003	The Tryon Palace NC104	S.Thompson	Retrd.	15.00	20-22.00
Shelia's Collectibles		**South Carolina**			
90-14-001	The Hermitage SC101	S.Thompson	Open	15.00	15.00
90-14-002	The Governor's Mansion SC102	S.Thompson	Open	15.00	15.00
90-14-003	The Lace House SC103	S.Thompson	Open	15.00	15.00
90-14-004	The State House SC104	S.Thompson	Open	15.00	15.00
90-14-005	All Saints' Church SC105	S.Thompson	Retrd.	15.00	20-25.00
Shelia's Collectibles		**St. Augustine**			
90-15-001	The "Oldest House" FL101	S.Thompson	Retrd.	15.00	20-23.00
90-15-002	Old City Gates FL102	S.Thompson	Retrd.	15.00	20-23.00
90-15-003	Anastasia Lighthousekeeper's House FL104	S.Thompson	Retrd.	15.00	20-23.00
90-15-004	Mission Nombre deDios FL105	S.Thompson	Retrd.	15.00	20-23.00
Shelia's Collectibles		**Savannah**			
90-16-001	Olde Pink House SAV01	S.Thompson	Open	15.00	15.00
90-16-002	Andrew Low Mansion SAV02	S.Thompson	Retrd.	15.00	16-20.00
90-16-003	Davenport House SAV03	S.Thompson	Retrd.	15.00	16-20.00
90-16-004	Juliette Low House SAV04	S.Thompson	Open	15.00	15.00
90-16-005	Herb House SAV05	S.Thompson	Retrd.	15.00	17-28.00
90-16-006	Mikve Israel Temple SAV06	S.Thompson	Retrd.	15.00	16-20.00
90-16-007	Savannah Gingerbread House I SAV08	S.Thompson	Retrd.	15.00	100-150.
90-16-008	Savannah Gingerbread House II SAV08	S.Thompson	Retrd.	15.00	N/A
92-16-009	Catherdral of St. John SAV09	S.Thompson	Open	16.00	16.00
93-16-010	Owens Thomas House SAV10	S.Thompson	Open	16.00	16.00
93-16-011	Owens Thomas House AP SAV10	S.Thompson	60	20.00	20.00
Shelia's Collectibles		**Lighthouse Series**			
90-17-001	Tybee Lighthouse SAV07	S.Thompson	Retrd.	15.00	16-20.00
90-17-002	Stage Harbor Lighthouse NEW06	S.Thompson	Retrd.	15.00	19.00
91-17-003	Cape Hatteras Lighthouse NC103	S.Thompson	Open	15.00	15.00
91-17-004	Anastasia Lighthouse FL103	S.Thompson	Open	15.00	15.00
93-17-005	Morris Island Lighthouse LTS01	S.Thompson	Open	15.00	15.00

Number	Name	Artist	Edition Limit	Issue Price	Quote
Company		**Series**			
94-17-006	Thomas Point Light LTS05	S.Thompson	Open	17.00	17.00
94-17-007	Thomas Point Light, AP LTS05	S.Thompson	95	20.00	20.00
94-17-008	Round Island Light LTS06	S.Thompson	Open	17.00	17.00
94-17-009	Round Island Light, AP LTS06	S.Thompson	49	20.00	20.00
94-17-010	Assateague Island Light LTS07	S.Thompson	Open	17.00	17.00
94-17-011	Assateague Island Light, AP LTS07	S.Thompson	88	20.00	20.00
94-17-012	New London Ledge Light LTS08	S.Thompson	Open	17.00	17.00
94-17-013	New London Ledge Light, AP LTS08	S.Thompson	92	20.00	20.00
Shelia's, Inc.		**Martha's Vineyard**			
93-18-001	Golden Campground Cottage MAR07	S.Thompson	Open	16.00	16.00
93-18-002	Golden Campground Cottage, AP MAR07	S.Thompson	102	20.00	20.00
93-18-003	Alice's Wonderland MAR08	S.Thompson	Open	16.00	16.00
93-18-004	Alice's Wonderland, AP MAR08	S.Thompson	111	20.00	20.00
93-18-005	Gingerbread Cottage-grey MAR09	S.Thompson	Open	16.00	16.00
93-18-006	Gingerbread Cottage-grey AP MAR09	S.Thompson	116	20.00	20.00
93-18-007	Wood Valentine MAR10	S.Thompson	Open	16.00	16.00
93-18-008	Wood Valentine, AP MAR10	S.Thompson	108	20.00	20.00
Shelia's, Inc.		**Amish Village**			
93-19-001	Amish Home AMS01	S.Thompson	Open	17.00	17.00
93-19-002	Amish Home, AP AMS101	S.Thompson	77	20.00	20.00
93-19-003	Amish School AMS102	S.Thompson	Open	15.00	15.00
93-19-004	Amish School, AP AMS02	S.Thompson	81	20.00	20.00
93-19-005	Covered Bridge AMS03	S.Thompson	Open	16.00	16.00
93-19-006	Covered Bridge, AP AMS03	S.Thompson	66	20.00	20.00
93-19-007	Amish Barn AMS04	S.Thompson	Open	17.00	17.00
93-19-008	Amish Barn, AP AMS04	S.Thompson	54	20.00	20.00
93-19-009	Amish Buggy AMS05	S.Thompson	Open	12.00	12.00
93-19-010	Amish Buggy, AP AMS05	S.Thompson	79	16.00	16.00
Shelia's, Inc.		**Collectible Accessories**			
91-20-001	Wrought Iron Gate With Magnolias COL01	S.Thompson	Retrd.	11.00	22.00
91-20-002	Gazebo With Victorian Lady COL02	S.Thompson	Open	11.00	11.00
91-20-003	Oak Bower COL03	S.Thompson	Retrd.	11.00	15.00
92-20-004	Fence 5" COL04	S.Thompson	Retrd.	9.00	9.00
92-20-005	Fence 8" COL05	S.Thompson	Open	10.00	10.00
92-20-006	Lake With Swan COL06	S.Thompson	Retrd.	11.00	11.00
92-20-007	Tree With Bush COL07	S.Thompson	Open	10.00	10.00
93-20-008	Dogwood COL08	S.Thompson	Open	12.00	12.00
93-20-009	Apple Tree COL09	S.Thompson	Open	12.00	12.00
94-20-010	Sunrise At 80 Meeting COL10	S.Thompson	1,500	18.00	18.00
94-20-011	Victorian Arbor COL11	S.Thompson	1,500	18.00	18.00
94-20-012	Amish Quilt Line COL12	S.Thompson	1,500	18.00	18.00
94-20-013	Formal Garden COL13	S.Thompson	1,500	18.00	18.00
Shelia's, Inc.		**Victorian Springtime**			
94-21-001	Ralston House VST01	S.Thompson	Open	17.00	17.00
94-21-002	Ralston House, AP VST01	S.Thompson	85	20.00	20.00
94-21-003	Sessions House VST02	S.Thompson	Open	17.00	17.00
94-21-004	Sessions House ,AP VST02	S.Thompson	88	20.00	20.00
94-21-005	Heffron House VST03	S.Thompson	Open	17.00	17.00
94-21-006	Heffron House, AP VST03	S.Thompson	92	20.00	20.00
94-21-007	Jacobsen House VST04	S.Thompson	Open	17.00	17.00
94-21-008	Jacobsen House, AP VST04	S.Thompson	99	20.00	20.00
94-21-009	Set of 4, AP	S.Thompson	Retrd.	100.00	100-140.
Shelia's, Inc.		**Inventor Series**			
93-22-001	Ford Motor Company INV01	S.Thompson	Open	17.00	17.00
93-22-002	Ford Motor Company, AP INV01	S.Thompson	83	20.00	20.00
93-22-003	Menlo Park Laboratory INV02	S.Thompson	Open	16.00	16.00
93-22-004	Menlo Park Laboratory, AP INV02	S.Thompson	77	20.00	20.00
93-22-005	Noah Webster House INV03	S.Thompson	Open	15.00	15.00
93-22-006	Noah Webster House, AP INV03	S.Thompson	79	20.00	20.00
93-22-007	Wright Cycle Shop INV04	S.Thompson	Open	17.00	17.00
93-22-008	Wright Cycle Shop, AP INV04	S.Thompson	83	20.00	20.00
Shelia's, Inc.		**American Gothic**			
93-23-001	Gothic Revival Cottage ACL01	S.Thompson	Retrd.	20.00	20.00
93-23-002	Perkins House ACL02	S.Thompson	Retrd.	20.00	20.00
93-23-003	Roseland Cottage ACL03	S.Thompson	Retrd.	20.00	20.00
93-23-004	Mele House ACL04	S.Thompson	Retrd.	20.00	20.00
93-23-005	Rose Arbor ACL05	S.Thompson	Retrd.	14.00	14.00
93-23-006	Set of 5	S.Thompson	Retrd.	94.00	125.00
Shelia's, Inc.		**Shelia's Collectors' Society**			
93-24-001	Susan B. Anthony CGA93	S.Thompson	5/94	Gift	N/A
93-24-002	Anne Peacock House SOC01	S.Thompson	5/94	16.00	16.00
94-24-003	Helen Keller's Birthplace-Ivy Green CGA94	S.Thompson	5/95	Gift	N/A
94-24-004	Seaview Cottage SOC02	S.Thompson	5/95	17.00	17.00
Silver Deer, Ltd.		**Crystal Collectibles**			
84-01-001	Pinocchio, 120mm -02059	G. Truex	Closed	195.00	195-320.00
90-01-002	Joe Cool Cruisin'- 02018	G. Truex	Closed	165.00	165.00
90-01-003	Snoopy's Suppertime- 01973	G. Truex	Closed	160.00	160.00
90-01-004	Romance- 02002	S. Dailey	Closed	250.00	290.00
92-01-005	Proud Spirit- 02823	S. Dailey	Closed	550.00	580.00
92-01-006	Joe Cool 'Vette- 02807	S. Dailey	Closed	165.00	175.00
92-01-007	Checkmate- 02812	S. Dailey	Closed	130.00	137.50
93-01-008	Morning Star Muse- 03558	G. Truex	Closed	3,000.00	3,000.00
93-01-009	Lady of the Fountains- 03559	G. Truex	Closed	420.00	420.00
93-01-010	Pool of Flowers- 03560	G. Truex	Closed	230.00	230.00
93-01-011	Literary Ace Comic- 03800	G. Truex	Closed	40.00	40.00
93-01-012	Literary Ace Comic w/Snoopy- 03801	G. Truex	Closed	130.00	130.00
93-01-013	Card Game- 03805	G. Truex	Closed	300.00	300.00
93-01-014	U.S.S. Enterprise- 03812	G. Truex	Closed	375.00	375.00
Silver Deer, Ltd.		**Crystal Zoo Collectors' Club**			
91-02-001	Le Printemps	S. Dailey	Closed	Gift	N/A
91-02-002	Victoriana (Redemption)	S. Dailey	Closed	195.00	195.00
92-02-003	Garden Party	S. Dailey	Closed	Gift	N/A
92-02-004	Garden Guest (Redemption)	S. Dailey	Closed	175.00	175.00
93-02-005	Busy Bee	G. Truex	Closed	Gift	N/A
93-02-006	Debonair Bear (Redemption)	G. Truex	Closed	125.00	125.00
94-02-007	Springtime Teddy	G. Truex	12/94	Gift	Gift
94-02-008	Provocative Polly (Redemption)	G Truex	12/94	125.00	125.00
Silver Deer, Ltd.		**Ark Collectors' Club**			
91-03-001	Christmas Puppy	T. Rubel	Closed	Gift	N/A
91-03-002	Snowy Egret (Redemption)	T. Rubel	Closed	75.00	75.00
92-03-003	Snowball	T. Rubel	Closed	Gift	N/A

Company Number	Name	Series Artist	Edition Limit	Issue Price	Quote
Sports Impressions/Enesco		**Baseball Superstar Figurines**			
87-01-001	Wade Boggs	S. Impressions	Closed	90-125.	150-225.
88-01-002	Jose Canseco	S. Impressions	Closed	90-125.	125-200.
89-01-003	Will Clark	S. Impressions	Closed	90-125.	125-250.
88-01-004	Andre Dawson	S. Impressions	2,500	90-125.	125-200.
88-01-005	Bob Feller	S. Impressions	2,500	90-125.	125-200.
89-01-006	Kirk Gibson	S. Impressions	Closed	90-125.	125-200.
87-01-007	Keith Hernandez	S. Impressions	2,500	90-125.	125-200.
88-01-008	Reg Jackson (Yankees)	S. Impressions	Closed	90-125.	125-200.
89-01-009	Reg Jackson (Angels)	S. Impressions	Closed	90-125.	125-250.
88-01-010	Al Kaline	S. Impressions	2,500	90-125.	125-250.
87-01-011	Mickey Mantle	S. Impressions	Closed	90-125.	175-295.
87-01-012	Don Mattingly	S. Impressions	Closed	90-125.	250.00
87-01-013	Don Mattingly (Flanklin glove variation)	S. Impressions	Closed	90-125.	750.00
88-01-014	Paul Molitor	S. Impressions	2,500	90-125.	125.00
89-01-015	Duke Snider	S. Impressions	2,500	90-125.	125.00
89-01-016	Alan Trammell	S. Impressions	2,500	90-125.	125.00
89-01-017	Frank Viola	S. Impressions	2,500	90-125.	125.00
87-01-018	Ted Williams	S. Impressions	Closed	90-125.	200-375.
Sports Impressions/Enesco		**Collectors' Club Members Only**			
90-02-001	The Mick-Mickey Mantle 5000-1	S. Impressions	Yr.Iss.	75.00	95.00
91-02-002	Rickey Henderson-Born to Run 5001-11	S. Impressions	Yr.Iss.	49.95	49.95
91-02-003	Nolan Ryan-300 Wins 5002-01	S. Impressions	Yr.Iss.	195.00	195.00
91-02-004	Willie, Mickey & Duke plate 5003-04	S. Impressions	Yr.Iss.	39.95	39.95
92-02-005	Babe Ruth 5006-11	S. Impressions	Yr.Iss.	40.00	40.00
92-02-006	Walter Payton 5015-01	S. Impressions	Yr.Iss.	50.00	50.00
93-02-007	The 1927 Yankees plate	R.Tanenbaum	Yr.Iss.	60.00	60.00
Sports Impressions/Enesco		**Collectors' Club Symbol of Membership**			
91-03-001	Mick/7 plate 5001-02	S. Impressions	Yr.Iss.	Gift	N/A
92-03-002	USA Basketball team plate 5008-30	S. Impressions	Yr.Iss.	Gift	N/A
93-03-003	Nolan Ryan porcelain card	S. Impressions	Yr.Iss.	Gift	N/A
Summerhill Crystal		**Summerhill Crystal**			
92-01-001	Venus A261S	Summerhill	Retrd.	96.00	96.00
92-01-002	Sacre Coeur A266S	Summerhill	5,000	190.00	190.00
92-01-003	L'arc du Triomphe A267S	Summerhill	5,000	220.00	220.00
92-01-004	Bicycle A270S	Summerhill	Retrd.	64.00	64.00
92-01-005	Princess Coach A758S	Summerhill	1,500	700.00	700.00
92-01-006	Large Dragon A875S	Summerhill	1,500	320.00	320.00
93-01-007	Fairy Blue Coach Jr. A372S	Summerhill	Open	65.00	65.00
93-01-008	Fairy Blue Coach A374S	Summerhill	Open	125.00	125.00
93-01-009	Royal Blue Coach A0099S	Summerhill	Retrd.	N/A	2800.00
92-01-010	Princess Coach - pink center A758S	Summerhill	1,500	750.00	800.00
92-01-011	Princess Coach - pink center SE	Summerhill	Retrd.	800.00	800.00
93-01-012	Cherub Heart A506S	Summerhill	Open	120.00	120.00
93-01-013	Cherub Wish A501S	Summerhill	Open	120.00	120.00
93-01-014	Cherub Star-light A507S	Summerhill	Open	120.00	120.00
93-01-015	Cherub Dream A498S	Summerhill	Open	120.00	120.00
93-01-016	Mini Crystal Coach A741S	Summerhill	Open	90.00	90.00
93-01-017	Coach Jr. A752S	Summerhill	Open	60.00	60.00
Summerhill Crystal		**Disney Collection**			
92-02-001	Mickey Mouse, Lg. A671S	Summerhill	Retrd.	295.00	425.00
92-02-002	Mickey Mouse, Med. A672S	Summerhill	Retrd.	165.00	165.00
92-02-003	Minnie Mouse, Lg. A673S	Summerhill	Retrd.	295.00	425.00
92-02-004	Minnie Mouse, Med. A674S	Summerhill	Retrd.	165.00	165.00
92-02-005	Epcot Center, Lg. A687S	Summerhill	Open	245.00	245.00
92-02-006	Epcot Center, Med. A686S	Summerhill	Open	110.00	110.00
92-02-007	Epcot Center, Sm. A685S	Summerhill	Open	75.00	75.00
93-02-008	Aladdin's Lamp A684S	Summerhill	2,500	70.00	75.00
93-02-009	Classic Mickey A676S	Summerhill	Open	325.00	325.00
93-02-010	Medium Classic Mickey A677S	Summerhill	Open	185.00	185.00
93-02-011	Classic Minnie A678S	Summerhill	Open	325.00	325.00
93-02-012	Medium Classic Minnie A679S	Summerhill	Open	185.00	185.00
93-02-013	Pinocchio A675S	Summerhill	Open	180.00	180.00
94-02-014	The Sorcerer A668S	Summerhill	N/A	N/A	N/A
93-02-015	Winnie the Pooh A682S	Summerhill	2,500	145.00	145.00
93-02-016	Small Cinderella Coach A759S	Summerhill	Open	65.00	65.00
93-02-017	Cinderella Coach A764S	Summerhill	Open	125.00	125.00
Summerhill Crystal		**Warner Brothers Collection**			
92-03-001	Tasmanian Devil A634S	Summerhill	2,750	220.00	220.00
92-03-002	Speedy Gonzales A633S	Summerhill	2,750	164.00	164.00
92-03-003	Tweety Bird A631S	Summerhill	Retrd.	120.00	120.00
92-03-004	Bugs Bunny A652S	Summerhill	Retrd.	203.00	203.00
92-03-005	Large Porky Pig A635S	Summerhill	Open	273.00	273.00
92-03-006	Small Yosemite Sam A641S	Summerhill	Open	123.00	123.00
92-03-007	Small Tasmanian Devil A639S	Summerhill	Open	125.00	125.00
92-03-008	Small Porky Pig A649S	Summerhill	Open	165.00	165.00
92-03-009	Small Speedy Gonzales A638S	Summerhill	Open	813.00	81.00
92-03-010	Bugs Bunny "What's Up Doc?" A654S	Summerhill	Open	150.00	150.00
92-03-011	Tweety on a Perch A653S	Summerhill	Open	90.00	90.00
Summerhill Crystal		**United Media Collection**			
93-04-001	Garfield© 3" A690S	Summerhill	Open	300.00	300.00
93-04-002	Odie© A691S	Summerhill	Open	224.00	224.00
93-04-003	Pookie© 1 1/4" A692S	Summerhill	Open	80.00	80.00
93-04-004	Pookie© 1 5/8" A694S	Summerhill	Open	115.00	115.00
93-04-005	Pookie© 2 1/2" A693S	Summerhill	Open	190.00	190.00
93-04-006	Garfield© 2 1/4" A689S	Summerhill	Open	120.00	120.00
93-04-007	Pookie© Standing 1 1/2" A695S	Summerhill	Open	90.00	90.00
93-04-008	Pookie© Standing Med.2 1/4" A696S	Summerhill	Open	120.00	120.00
93-04-009	Odie© Med. 2 3/4" A703S	Summerhill	Open	160.00	160.00
Summerhill Crystal		**Turner Inc.**			
93-05-001	Tom© 4 1/4" A272S	Summerhill	Open	308.00	308.00
93-05-002	Jerry© 2 3/4" A272S	Summerhill	Open	154.00	154.00
93-05-003	Tom med.© 2 3/4" A273S	Summerhill	Open	140.00	140.00
Summerhill Crystal		**Collector Society**			
92-06-001	Robbie Rabbit A183S	Summerhill	Retrd.	125.00	125.00
Summerhill Crystal		**American Birds Collection**			
93-07-001	Quail A515S	Summerhill	Open	65.00	65.00
93-07-002	Quail Jr. A518S	Summerhill	Open	36.00	36.00
93-07-003	Night Owl on Branch A381S	Summerhill	Open	60.00	60.00
93-07-004	Baby Bird A396S	Summerhill	Open	38.00	38.00
93-07-005	Cardinal A514S	Summerhill	Open	60.00	60.00
Summerhill Crystal		**Tropical Bird Collection**			
93-08-001	Toucan 2 A519S	Summerhill	Open	112.00	112.00

Company Number	Name	Series Artist	Edition Limit	Issue Price	Quote
Swarovski America		**Our Woodland Friends**			
79-01-001	Mini Owl	M. Schreck	Open	16.00	29.50
79-01-002	Small Owl	M. Schreck	Open	59.00	85.00
79-01-003	Large Owl	M. Schreck	Open	90.00	120.00
83-01-004	Giant Owl	M. Schreck	Open	1200.00	2000.00
85-01-005	Mini Bear	M. Schreck	Open	16.00	55.00
82-01-006	Small Bear	M. Schreck	Open	44.00	75.00
81-01-007	Large Bear	M. Schreck	Open	75.00	95.00
87-01-008	Fox	A. Stocker	Open	50.00	75.00
88-01-009	Mini Sitting Fox	A. Stocker	Open	35.00	42.50
88-01-010	Mini Running Fox	A. Stocker	Open	35.00	42.50
85-01-011	Squirrel	M. Schreck	Open	35.00	55.00
89-01-012	Mushrooms	A. Stocker	Open	35.00	42.50
Swarovski America		**African Wildlife**			
89-02-001	Small Elephant	A. Stocker	Open	50.00	65.00
88-02-002	Large Elephant	A. Stocker	Open	70.00	95.00
89-02-003	Small Hippopotamus	A. Stocker	Open	70.00	75.00
90-02-004	Small Rhinoceros	A. Stocker	Open	70.00	75.00
Swarovski America		**Kingdom Of Ice And Snow**			
86-03-001	Mini Baby Seal	A. Stocker	Open	30.00	42.50
85-03-002	Large Seal	M. Schreck	Open	44.00	85.00
84-03-003	Mini Penguin	M. Schreck	Open	16.00	37.50
84-03-004	Large Penguin	M. Schreck	Open	44.00	95.00
86-03-005	Large Polar Bear	A. Stocker	Open	140.00	195.00
Swarovski America		**In A Summer Meadow**			
87-04-001	Small Hedgehog	M. Schreck	Open	50.00	55.00
85-04-002	Medium Hedgehog	M. Schreck	Open	70.00	85.00
85-04-003	Large Hedgehog	M. Schreck	Open	120.00	135.00
88-04-004	Mini Lying Rabbit	A. Stocker	Open	35.00.	42.50
88-04-005	Mini Sitting Rabbit	A. Stocker	Open	35.00	42.50
88-04-006	Mother Rabbit	A. Stocker	Open	60.00	75.00
76-04-007	Medium Mouse	M. Schreck	Open	48.00	85.00
86-04-008	Mini Butterfly	Team	Open	16.00	42.50
82-04-009	Butterfly	Team	Open	44.00	85.00
86-04-010	Snail	M. Stamey	Open	35.00	55.00
91-04-011	Field Mouse	A. Stocker	Open	47.50	49.50
92-04-012	Sparrow	Schneiderbauer	Open	29.50	29.50
Swarovski America		**Beauties of the Lake**			
89-05-001	Small Swan	M. Schreck	Open	35.00	49.50
77-05-002	Medium Swan	M. Schreck	Open	44.00	75.00
77-05-003	Large Swan	M. Schreck	Open	55.00	95.00
86-05-004	Mini Standing Duck	A. Stocker	Open	22.00	37.50
86-05-005	Mini Swimming Duck	M. Schreck	Open	16.00	37.50
83-05-006	Mini Drake	M. Schreck	Open	20.00	42.50
86-05-007	Mallard	M. Schreck	Open	80.00	135.00
89-05-008	Giant Mallard	M. Stamey	Open	2000.00	4500.00
Swarovski America		**Silver Crystal City**			
90-06-001	Silver Crystal City-Cathedral	G. Stamey	Open	95.00	120.00
90-06-002	Silver Crystal City-Houses I& II(Set of 2)	G. Stamey	Open	75.00	75.00
90-06-003	Silver Crystal City-Houses III & IV(Set of 2)	G. Stamey	Open	75.00	75.00
90-06-004	Silver Crystal City-Poplars (Set of 3)	G. Stamey	Open	40.00	49.50
91-06-005	City Tower	G. Stamey	Open	37.50	42.50
91-06-006	City Gates	G. Stamey	Open	95.00	95.00
Swarovski America		**When We Were Young**			
88-07-001	Locomotive	G. Stamey	Open	150.00	150.00
88-07-002	Tender	G. Stamey	Open	55.00	55.00
88-07-003	Wagon	G. Stamey	Open	85.00	85.00
90-07-004	Petrol Wagon	G. Stamey	Open	75.00	85.00
89-07-005	Old Timer Automobile	G. Stamey	Open	130.00	150.00
90-07-006	Airplane	A. Stocker	Open	135.00	150.00
91-07-007	Santa Maria	G. Stamey	Open	375.00	375.00
93-07-008	Tipping Wagon	G. Stamey	Open	95.00	95.00
Swarovski America		**Exquisite Accents**			
80-08-001	Birdbath	M. Schreck	Open	150.00	195.00
87-08-002	Birds' Nest	Team	Open	90.00	120.00
87-08-003	Small Dinner Bell	M. Schreck	Open	60.00	65.00
87-08-004	Medium Dinner Bell	M. Schreck	Open	80.00	95.00
Swarovski America		**Sparkling Fruit**			
86-09-001	Small Pineapple/Gold	M. Schreck	Open	55.00	85.00
81-09-002	Large Pineapple/Gold	M. Schreck	Open	150.00	250.00
81-09-003	Giant Pineapple/Gold	M. Schreck	Open	1750.00	3250.00
85-09-004	Small Grapes	Team	Open	200.00	250.00
85-09-005	Medium Grapes	Team	Open	300.00	375.00
91-09-006	Apple	M. Stamey	Open	175.00	175.00
91-09-007	Pear	M. Stamey	Open	175.00	175.00
Swarovski America		**Pet's Corner**			
90-10-001	Beagle Puppy	A. Stocker	Open	40.00	49.50
90-10-002	Scotch Terrier	A. Stocker	Open	60.00	75.00
87-10-003	Mini Dachshund	A. Stocker	Open	20.00	49.50
91-10-004	Sitting Cat	M. Stamey	Open	75.00	75.00
91-10-005	Kitten	M. Stamey	Open	47.50	49.50
92-10-006	Poodle	A. Stocker	Open	125.00	135.00
93-10-007	Beagle Playing	A. Stocker	Open	49.50	49.50
93-10-008	Sitting Poodle	A. Stocker	Open	85.00	85.00
Swarovski America		**South Sea**			
91-11-001	South Sea Shell	M. Stamey	Open	110.00	120.00
88-11-002	Open Shell With Pearl	M. Stamey	Open	120.00	165.00
87-11-003	Mini Blowfish	Team	Open	22.00	29.50
86-11-004	Small Blowfish	Team	Open	35.00	55.00
91-11-005	Butterfly Fish	M. Stamey	Open	150.00	165.00
93-11-006	Three South Sea Fish	M. Stamey	Open	135.00	135.00
93-11-007	Sea Horse	M. Stamey	Open	85.00	85.00
Swarovski America		**Endangered Species**			
91-12-001	Kiwi	M. Stamey	Open	37.50	37.50
89-12-002	Mini Koala	A. Stocker	Open	35.00	42.50
87-12-003	Koala	A. Stocker	Open	50.00	65.00
77-12-004	Small Turtle	M. Schreck	Open	35.00	49.50
77-12-005	Large Turtle	M. Schreck	Open	48.00	75.00
81-12-006	Giant Turtle	M. Schreck	Open	2500.00	4500.00
92-12-007	Mother Beaver	A. Stocker	Open	110.00	120.00
92-12-008	Sitting Baby Beaver	A. Stocker	Open	47.50	49.50
92-12-009	Lying Baby Beaver	A. Stocker	Open	47.50	49.50
93-12-010	Baby Panda	A. Stocker	Open	24.50	24.50

Company / Number	Name	Series / Artist	Edition Limit	Issue Price	Quote
93-12-011	Mother Panda	A. Stocker	Open	120.00	120.00
93-12-012	Mother Kangaroo with Baby	G. Stamey	Open	95.00	95.00
Swarovski America		**Barnyard Friends**			
82-13-001	Mini Pig	M. Schreck	Open	16.00	29.50
84-13-002	Medium Pig	M. Schreck	Open	35.00	55.00
88-13-003	Mini Chicks (Set of 3)	G. Stamey	Open	35.00	37.50
87-13-004	Mini Rooster	G. Stamey	Open	35.00	55.00
87-13-005	Mini Hen	G. Stamey	Open	35.00	42.50
Swarovski America		**Game of Kings**			
84-14-001	Chess Set	M. Schreck	Open	950.00	1375.00
Swarovski America		**Among Flowers And Foliage**			
92-15-001	Hummingbird	Schneiderbauer	Open	195.00	195.00
92-15-002	Bumblebee	Schneiderbauer	Open	85.00	85.00
Swarovski America		**Our Candleholders**			
85-16-001	Small Water Lily 7600NR124	M. Schreck	Open	100.00	165.00
83-16-002	Medium Water Lily 7600NR123	M. Schreck	Open	150.00	250.00
85-16-003	Large Water Lily 7600NR125	M. Schreck	Open	200.00	375.00
89-16-004	Medium Star 7600NR143001	Team	Open	200.00	250.00
87-16-005	Large Star 7600NR143	Team	Open	250.00	375.00
Swarovski America		**Decorative Items For The Desk (Paperweights)**			
87-17-001	Small Chaton 7433NR50	M. Schreck	Open	50.00	65.00
87-17-002	Large Chaton 7433NR80	M. Schreck	Open	190.00	250.00
90-17-003	Giant Chaton 7433NR180000	M. Schreck	Open	3900.00	4500.00
87-17-004	Small Pyramid Crystal Cal.7450NR40	M. Schreck	Open	100.00	120.00
87-17-005	Small Pyramid Vitrail Med.7450NR40	M. Schreck	Open	100.00	120.00
Swarovski America		**Crystal Melodies**			
92-18-001	Lute	M. Zendron	Open	125.00	135.00
92-18-002	Harp	M. Zendron	Open	175.00	195.00
93-18-003	Grand Piano w/ Stool	M. Zendron	Open	250.00	250.00
Swarovski America		**Feathered Friends**			
93-19-001	Pelican	A. Hirzinger	Open	37.50	37.50
Swarovski America		**Collectors Society Editions**			
87-20-001	Togetherness-The Lovebirds	Schreck/Stocker	Retrd.	150.00	2400-3750.
88-20-002	Sharing-The Woodpeckers	A. Stocker	Retrd.	165.00	1000-1900.
89-20-003	Amour-The Turtledoves	A. Stocker	Retrd.	195.00	600-1400.
90-20-004	Lead Me-The Dolphins	M. Stamey	Retrd.	225.00	800-1800.
91-20-005	Save Me-The Seals	M. Stamey	Retrd.	225.00	400-925.
92-20-006	Care For Me - The Whales	M. Stamey	Retrd.	265.00	375-800.
91-20-008	Dolphin Brooch	Team	Retrd.	75.00	100-300.
92-20-007	5th Anniversary Edition-The Birthday Cake	G. Stamey	Retrd.	85.00	125-300.
93-20-009	Inspiration Africa-The Elephant	M. Zendron	Retrd.	325.00	375-600.
93-20-010	Elephant Brooch	Team	12/94	85.00	85.00
94-20-011	Inspiration Africa-The Kudu	M. Stamey	12/94	295.00	295.00
Swarovski America		**Retired**			
XX-21-001	Giant Size Bear 7637NR112	M. Schreck	Retrd.	125.00	1080-1200.
XX-21-002	King Size Bear7637NR92	M. Schreck	Retrd.	95.00	900-935.
84-21-003	Mini Bear 7670NR32	M. Schreck	Retrd.	16.00	60-125.00
84-21-004	Large Blowfish 7644NR41	Team	Retrd.	40.00	90-156.00
XX-21-005	Mini Butterfly 7671NR30	Team	Retrd.	16.00	48-130.00
77-21-006	Large Cat 7634NR70	M. Schreck	Retrd.	44.00	90.00
XX-21-007	Medium Cat 7634NR52	Team	Retrd.	38.00	130-357.
82-21-008	Mini Cat 7659NR31	M. Schreck	Retrd.	16.00	30-85.00
XX-21-009	Mini Chicken 7651NR20	Team	Retrd.	16.00	30-100.00
84-21-010	Dachshund 7641NR75	M. Schreck	Retrd.	48.00	54-95.00
XX-21-011	Mini Dachshund 7672NR42	A. Stocker	Retrd.	20.00	53-125.00
XX-21-012	Dog 7635NR70	Team	Retrd.	44.00	48-85.00
XX-21-013	Large Duck 7653NR75	Team	Retrd.	44.00	150-250.
XX-21-014	Medium Duck 7653NR55	Team	Retrd.	38.00	78-120.00
XX-21-015	Mini Duck 7653NR45	Team	Retrd.	16.00	54-100.00
XX-21-016	Elephant 7640NR55	Team	Retrd.	90.00	150-250.
84-21-017	Large Falcon Head 7645NR100	M. Schreck	Retrd.	600.00	795-1200.
86-21-018	Small Falcon Head 7645NR45	M. Schreck	Retrd.	60.00	125.00
84-21-019	Frog 7642NR48	M. Schreck	Retrd.	30.00	65-105.00
XX-21-020	King Size Hedgehog 7630NR60	M. Schreck	Retrd.	98.00	242-330.
XX-21-021	Large Hedgehog 7630NR50	M. Schreck	Retrd.	65.00	160-300.
XX-21-022	Medium Hedgehog 7630NR40	M. Schreck	Retrd.	44.00	108-250.
XX-21-023	Small Hedgehog 7630NR30	M. Schreck	Retrd.	38.00	275-450.
88-21-024	Hippopotamus 7626NR65	A. Stocker	Retrd.	70.00	125.00
90-21-025	Kingfisher 7621NR000001	M. Stamey	Retrd.	75.00	78-120.00
XX-21-026	King Size Mouse 7631NR60	M. Schreck	Retrd.	95.00	414-650.
XX-21-027	Large Mouse 7631NR50	M. Schreck	Retrd.	69.00	144-250.
XX-21-028	Small Mouse 7631NR30	M. Schreck	Retrd.	35.00	48-60.00
XX-21-029	Mini Mouse 7655NR23	Team	Retrd.	16.00	48-125.00
89-21-030	Parrot 7621NR000004	M. Stamey	Retrd.	70.00	88-125.00
87-21-031	Partridge 7625NR50	A. Stocker	Retrd.	85.00	200.00
XX-21-032	Large Pig 7638NR65	M. Schreck	Retrd.	50.00	180-200.
89-21-033	Owl 7621NR000003	M. Stamey	Retrd.	70.00	84-125.00
XX-21-034	Large Rabbit 7652NR45	Team	Retrd.	38.00	144-192.
XX-21-035	Mini Rabbit 7652NR20	Team	Retrd.	16.00	54-100.00
88-21-036	Rhinoceros 7622NR70	A. Stocker	Retrd.	70.00	66-125.00
XX-21-037	Large Sparrow 7650NR32	Team	Retrd.	38.00	95-125.00
79-21-038	Mini Sparrow7650NR20	M. Schreck	Retrd.	16.00	30-60.00
XX-21-039	Mini Swan 7658NR27	M. Schreck	Retrd.	16.00	75-125.00
89-21-040	Toucan 7621NR000002	M. Stamey	Retrd.	70.00	80-125.00
XX-21-041	King Size Turtle 7632NR75	M. Schreck	Retrd.	58.00	165-200.
89-21-042	Walrus 7620NR100000	M. Stamey	Retrd.	120.00	135.00
88-21-043	Whale 7628NR80	M. Stamey	Retrd.	70.00	85-140.00
XX-21-044	Sm. Apple Photo Stand(Gold) 7504NR030G	Team	Retrd.	40.00	250.00
XX-21-045	Sm. Apple Photo Stand 7504NR030R	Team	Retrd.	40.00	250.00
XX-21-046	Lg. Apple Photo Stand(Gold) 7504NR050G	Team	Retrd.	80.00	450.00
XX-21-047	Lg. Apple Photo Stand 7504NR050R	Team	Retrd.	80.00	150-375.
XX-21-048	Kg Sz Apple Photo Stand(Gold) 7504NR060G	Team	Retrd.	120.00	475.00
XX-21-049	Large Grapes 7550NR30015	Team	Retrd.	250.00	600-995.
85-21-050	Butterfly (Gold) 7551NR100	Team	Retrd.	200.00	525-1100.
85-21-051	Butterfly (Rhodium) 7551NR200	Team	Retrd.	200.00	1500.00
85-21-052	Hummingbird (Gold) 7552NR100	Team	Retrd.	200.00	700-1200.
85-21-053	Hummingbird (Rhodium) 7552NR200	Team	Retrd.	200.00	1800-2000.
85-21-054	Bee (Gold) 7553NR100	Team	Retrd.	200.00	680-1100.
85-21-055	Bee (Rhodium) 7553NR200	Team	Retrd.	200.00	960-1500.
87-21-056	Sm. Pineapple/Rhodium 7507NR060002	M. Schreck	Retrd.	55.00	200.00
82-21-057	Lg. Pineapple/Rhodium 7507NR105002	M. Schreck	Retrd.	150.00	450.00
85-21-058	Giant Pineapple/Rhodium 7507NR26002	M. Schreck	Retrd.	1750.00	3500.00
81-21-059	Large Dinner Bell 7467NR071000	M. Schreck	Retrd.	80.00	125-130.
XX-21-060	Rd. Pprwgt-Green 7404NR40	Team	Retrd.	20.00	150-500.
XX-21-061	Rd. Pprwgt-Sahara 7404NR40	Team	Retrd.	20.00	150-500.
XX-21-062	Rd. Pprwgt-Berm Blue 7404NR40	Team	Retrd.	20.00	150-500.
XX-21-063	Rd. Pprwgt-Green 7404NR30	Team	Retrd.	15.00	150-500.
XX-21-064	Rd. Pprwgt-Sahara 7404NR30	Team	Retrd.	15.00	150-500.
XX-21-065	Rd. Pprwgt-Berm. Blue 7404NR30	Team	Retrd.	15.00	150-500.
XX-21-066	Rd. Pprwgt-Green 7404NR50	Team	Retrd.	40.00	150-500.
XX-21-067	Rd. Pprwgt-Sahara 7404NR50	Team	Retrd.	40.00	150-500.
XX-21-068	Rd. Pprwgt-Berm. Blue 7404NR50	Team	Retrd.	40.00	150-500.
XX-21-069	Carousel Pprwgt-Vitrl Med 7451NR60087	Team	Retrd.	80.00	1195-1600.
XX-21-070	Carousel Pprwgt-Crystal Cal 7451NR60095	Team	Retrd.	80.00	1195-1600.
XX-21-071	Atomic Pprwgt-Vitrl Med 7454NR60087	Team	Retrd.	80.00	1150-1650.
XX-21-072	Atomic Pprwgt-Crystal Cal 7454NR60095	Team	Retrd.	80.00	1195-1650.
XX-21-073	Barrel Pprwgt 7453NR60087 Vitrl Med	Team	Retrd.	80.00	360-400.
XX-21-074	Barrel Pprwgt 7453NR60095 Crystal Cal	Team	Retrd.	80.00	400.00
XX-21-075	Rd. Pprwgt-Crystal Cal 7404NR30095	Team	Retrd.	15.00	75.00
XX-21-076	Rd. Pprwgt-Vitrl Med 7404NR30087	Team	Retrd.	15.00	75.00
XX-21-077	Rd. Pprwgt-Crystal Cal 7404NR40095	Team	Retrd.	20.00	95.00
XX-21-078	Rd. Pprwgt-Vitrl Med 7404NR40087	Team	Retrd.	20.00	95.00
XX-21-079	Rd. Pprwgt-Crystal Cal 7404NR50095	Team	Retrd.	40.00	200.00
XX-21-080	Rd. Pprwgt-Vitrl Med 7404NR50087	Team	Retrd.	40.00	200.00
XX-21-081	Rd. Pprwgt-Crystal Cal 7404NR60095	Team	Retrd.	50.00	250.00
XX-21-082	Rd. Pprwgt-Vitrl Med 7404NR60087	Team	Retrd.	50.00	250.00
XX-21-083	Geometric Pprwgt 7432NR57002n	Team	Retrd.	75.00	300.00
XX-21-084	One Ton Pprwgt 7495NR65	Team	Retrd.	75.00	125-175.
XX-21-085	Octron Pprwgt 7456NR41	Team	Retrd.	75.00	150.00
XX-21-086	Octron Pprwgt 7456NR1087	Team	Retrd.	90.00	150.00
XX-21-087	Candleholder 7600NR101	Team	Retrd.	23.00	350.00
XX-21-088	Candleholder 7600NR102	Team	Retrd.	35.00	125.00
XX-21-089	Candleholder 7600NR103	Team	Retrd.	40.00	175.00
XX-21-090	Candleholder European Style 7600NR103	Team	Retrd.	N/A	750.00
XX-21-091	Candleholder 7600NR104	Team	Retrd.	95.00	300.00
XX-21-092	Candleholder 7600NR106	Team	Retrd.	85.00	400.00
XX-21-093	Candleholder 7600NR107	Team	Retrd.	100.00	360-400.
XX-21-094	Candleholder European Style 7600NR108	Team	Retrd.	N/A	850.00
XX-21-095	Candleholder 7600NR109	Team	Retrd.	37.00	115-125.
XX-21-096	Candleholder 7600NR110	Team	Retrd.	40.00	150-160.
XX-21-097	Candleholder 7600NR111	Team	Retrd.	100.00	400.00
XX-21-098	Candleholder 7600NR112	Team	Retrd.	75.00	300.00
XX-21-099	Candleholder 7600NR114	Team	Retrd.	37.00	200.00
XX-21-100	Candleholder 7600NR115	Team	Retrd.	185.00	400.00
XX-21-101	Candleholder 7600NR116	Team	Retrd.	350.00	1500.00
XX-21-102	Candleholder 7600NR119	Team	Retrd.	N/A	500.00
XX-21-103	Sm.Candleholder w/ Flowers 7600NR120	Team	Retrd.	60.00	215-250.
XX-21-104	Baroque Candleholder 7600NR121	Team	Retrd.	150.00	240-450.
XX-21-105	Candleholder 7600NR122	Team	Retrd.	85.00	155-200.
XX-21-106	Sm.Candleholder w/ Leaves 7600NR126	Team	Retrd.	100.00	190-300.
XX-21-107	Candleholder 7600NR127	Team	Retrd.	65.00	160-200.
XX-21-108	Candleholder 7600NR128	Team	Retrd.	100.00	180-250.
XX-21-109	Candleholder 7600NR129	Team	Retrd.	120.00	205-300.
XX-21-110	Candleholder 7600NR130	Team	Retrd.	275.00	1500.00
XX-21-111	Candleholder 7600NR131(Set of 6)	Team	Retrd.	43.00	900.00
XX-21-112	Small Global Candleholder (4) 7600NR132	Team	Retrd.	60.00	115-250.
XX-21-113	Med. Global Candleholder (2) 7600NR133	Team	Retrd.	40.00	75-100.00
XX-21-114	Large Global Candleholder 7600NR134	Team	Retrd.	40.00	80.00
XX-21-115	Kingsize Global Candleholder 7600NR135	Team	Retrd.	50.00	200.00
XX-21-116	Pineapple Candleholder 7600NR136	Team	Retrd.	150.00	450.00
XX-21-117	Large Candleholderw/Flowers 7600NR137	Team	Retrd.	150.00	300.00
XX-21-118	Candleholder 7600NR138	Team	Retrd.	160.00	360-500.
XX-21-119	Candleholder 7600NR139	Team	Retrd.	140.00	245-400.
XX-21-120	Candleholder 7600NR140	Team	Retrd.	120.00	355-400.
XX-21-121	Candleholder European Style 7600NR141	Team	Retrd.	N/A	750.00
XX-21-122	Candleholder European Style 7600NR142	Team	Retrd.	N/A	500.00
90-21-123	Sm. Neo-Classic Candlehldr7600NR144070	A. Stocker	Retrd.	170.00	200.00
90-21-124	Med. Neo-ClassicCandlehldr7600NR144080	A. Stocker	Retrd.	190.00	225.00
90-21-125	Large Neo-Classic Candlehldr7600NR144090	A. Stocker	Retrd.	220.00	250.00
XX-21-126	Beetle Bottle Opener (Rodium) 7505NR76	Team	Retrd.	80.00	1650.00
XX-21-127	Beetle Bottle Opener (Gold) 7505NR76	Team	Retrd.	80.00	1320-2000.
XX-21-128	Table Magnifyer 7510NR01	Team	Retrd.	80.00	1210-1650.
XX-21-129	Treasure Box (Round/Butterfly) 7464NR50/10	Team	Retrd.	80.00	210-250.
XX-21-130	Treasure Box (Heart/Flower)7465NR52	Team	Retrd.	80.00	250.00
XX-21-131	Treasure Box (Oval/Butterfly)7466NR063100	Team	Retrd.	80.00	250-300.
XX-21-132	Salt and Pepper Shakers 7508NR068034	Team	Retrd.	80.00	240-350.
XX-21-133	Picture Frame/Oval 7505NR75G	Team	Retrd.	90.00	200-210.
XX-21-134	Picture Frame/Square 7506NR60G	Team	Retrd.	100.00	215-250.
XX-21-135	Treasure Box (Round/Flower) 7464NR50	Team	Retrd.	80.00	250.00
XX-21-136	Treasure Box (Heart/Butterfly)7465NR52/100	Team	Retrd.	80.00	165-250.
XX-21-137	Treasure Box (Oval/Flower) 7466NR063000	Team	Retrd.	80.00	250.00
XX-21-138	Vase 7511NR70	Team	Retrd.	50.00	125.00
XX-21-139	Schnapps Glasses, Set of 6-7468NR039000	Team	Retrd.	150.00	235-350.
XX-21-140	Ashtray 7461NR100	Team	Retrd.	45.00	225-330.
XX-21-141	Lighter 7462NR062	Team	Retrd.	160.00	225-360.
XX-21-142	Cigarette Holder 7463NR062	Team	Retrd.	85.00	150-175.
XX-21-143	Small Cardholders, Set of 4 -7403NR20095	Team	Retrd.	25.00	80-150.00
XX-21-144	Large Cardholders, Set of 4 -7403NR30095	Team	Retrd.	45.00	180-400.
82-21-145	Cone Vitrail Medium 7452NR60087	M. Schreck	Retrd.	80.00	225.00
82-21-146	Cone Crystal Cal 7452NR60095	M. Schreck	Retrd.	80.00	225.00
81-21-147	Egg 7458NR63069	M. Schreck	Retrd.	60.00	125-150.
81-21-148	Chess Set/Wooden Board	Team	Retrd.	950.00	3000.00
87-21-149	Large Pyramid Crystal Cal 7450NR50095	M. Schreck	Retrd.	90.00	195.00
87-21-150	Large Pyramid Vitrail Medium 7450NR50087	M. Schreck	Retrd.	90.00	195.00
91-21-151	Holy Family With Arch 7475NR001	Team	Retrd.	250.00	250.00
92-21-152	Wise Men (Set of 3) 7475NR200000	Team	Retrd.	175.00	175.00
92-21-153	Shepherd 7475NR000007	Team	Retrd.	65.00	65.00
92-21-154	Angel 6475NR000009	Team	Retrd.	65.00	65.00
Swarovski America		**Commemorative Single Issues**			
90-22-001	Elephant*(Introduced by Swarovski America as a commemorative item test during Design Celebration/January '90 in Walt Disney World)	Team	Closed	125.00	1210-1815.
93-22-002	Elephant*(Introduced by Swarovski America as a commemorative item during Design Celebration/January '93 in Walt Disney World)	Team	Open	150.00	150.00
United Design Corp.		**Legend of Santa Claus**			
86-01-001	Santa At Rest CF-001	L. Miller	Retrd.	70.00	500-1000.
86-01-002	Kris Kringle CF-002	L. Miller	Retrd.	60.00	175.00
86-01-003	Santa With Pups CF-003	S. Bradford	Retrd.	65.00	570.00
86-01-004	Rooftop Santa CF-004	S. Bradford	Retrd.	65.00	170.00
86-01-005	Elf Pair CF-005	L. Miller	Retrd.	60.00	125.00
87-01-006	Mrs. Santa CF-006	S. Bradford	Retrd.	60.00	195.00
87-01-007	On Santa's Knee-CF007	S. Bradford	15,000	65.00	90.00
87-01-008	Dreaming Of Santa CF-008	S. Bradford	Retrd.	65.00	325.00

Company		Series			
Number	**Name**	**Artist**	**Edition Limit**	**Issue Price**	**Quote**
87-01-009	Checking His List CF-009	L. Miller	15,000	75.00	100.00
87-01-010	Loading Santa's Sleigh CF-010	L. Miller	Retrd.	100.00	110.00
87-01-011	Santa On Horseback CF-011	S. Bradford	Retrd.	75.00	270.00
88-01-012	St. Nicholas CF-015	L. Miller	Retrd.	75.00	135.00
88-01-013	Load 'Em Up CF-016	S. Bradford	Retrd.	79.00	350.00
88-01-014	Assembly Required CF-017	L. Miller	7,500	79.00	110.00
88-01-015	Father Christmas CF-018	S. Bradford	Retrd.	75.00	100.00
89-01-016	A Purrr-Fect Christmas CF-019	S. Bradford	7,500	95.00	110.00
89-01-017	Christmas Harmony CF-020	S. Bradford	Retrd.	85.00	140.00
89-01-018	Hitching Up CF-021	L. Miller	Retrd.	90.00	100.00
90-01-019	Puppy Love CF-024	L. Miller	7,500	100.00	130.00
90-01-020	Forest Friends CF-025	L. Miller	Retrd.	90.00	110.00
90-01-021	Waiting For Santa CF-026	S. Bradford	7,500	100.00	130.00
90-01-022	Safe Arrival CF-027	Memoli/Jonas	7,500	150.00	175.00
90-01-023	Victorian Santa CF-028	S. Bradford	Retrd.	125.00	350.00
91-01-024	For Santa CF-029	L. Miller	7,500	99.00	135.00
91-01-025	Santa At Work CF-030	L. Miller	7,500	99.00	110.00
91-01-026	Reindeer Walk CF-031	K. Memoli	7,500	150.00	165.00
91-01-027	Blessed Flight CF-032	K. Memoli	7,500	159.00	185.00
91-01-028	Victorian Santa w/ Teddy CF-033	S. Bradford	7,500	150.00	160.00
92-01-029	Arctic Santa CF-035	S. Bradford	7,500	90.00	100.00
92-01-030	Letters to Santa CF-036	L. Miller	7,500	125.00	130.00
92-01-031	Santa and Comet CF-037	L. Miller	7,500	110.00	110.00
92-01-032	The Christmas Tree CF-038	L. Miller	7,500	90.00	90.00
92-01-031	Santa and Mrs. Claus CF-039	K. Memoli	7,500	150.00	150.00
92-01-032	Earth Home Santa CF-040	S. Bradford	7,500	135.00	140.00
92-01-033	Loads of Happiness CF-041	K. Memoli	7,500	100.00	110.00
92-01-034	Santa and Mrs. Claus, Victorian CF-042	K. Memoli	7,500	135.00	140.00
93-01-035	The Night Before Christmas CF-043	L. Miller	7,500	75.00	100.00
93-01-036	Santa's Friends CF-044	L. Miller	7,500	85.00	100.00
93-01-037	Jolly St. Nick CF-045	K. Memoli	7,500	100.00	130.00
93-01-038	Dear Santa CF-046	K. Memoli	7,500	159.00	170.00
93-01-039	Northwoods Santa CF-047	S. Bradford	7,500	85.00	100.00
93-01-040	Victorian Lion & Lamb Santa CF-048	S. Bradford	7,500	64.00	100.00
93-01-041	Jolly St. Nick, Victorian CF-050	K. Memoli	7,500	100.00	120.00
94-01-042	The Story of Christmas CF-051	K. Memoli	7,500	90.00	90.00
94-01-043	Longstocking Dilemma CF-052	K. Memoli	7,500	85.00	85.00
94-01-044	Santa Riding Dove CF-053	L. Miller	7,500	60.00	60.00
94-01-045	Star Santa w/ Polar Bear CF-054	S. Bradford	7,500	65.00	65.00
94-01-046	Long Stocking Dilemma, Victorian CF-055	K. Memoli	7,500	85.00	85.00

United Design Corp.		**Legend Of The Little People**			
89-02-001	Woodland Cache LL-001	L. Miller	Retrd.	35.00	50.00
89-02-002	Adventure Bound LL-002	L. Miller	Retrd.	35.00	50.00
89-02-003	A Friendly Toast LL-003	L. Miller	Retrd.	35.00	50.00
89-02-004	Treasure Hunt LL-004	L. Miller	Retrd.	45.00	50.00
89-02-005	Magical Discovery LL-005	L. Miller	Retrd.	45.00	50.00
89-02-006	Spring Water Scrub LL-006	L. Miller	Retrd.	35.00	50.00
89-02-007	Caddy's Helper LL-007	L. Miller	Retrd.	35.00	50.00
90-02-008	Husking Acorns LL-008	L. Miller	Retrd.	60.00	65.00
90-02-009	Traveling Fast LL-009	L. Miller	Retrd.	45.00	50.00
90-02-010	Hedgehog In Harness LL-010	L. Miller	Retrd.	45.00	50.00
90-02-011	Woodland Scout LL-011	L. Miller	Retrd.	40.00	50.00
90-02-012	Fishin' Hole LL-012	L. Miller	Retrd.	35.00	50.00
90-02-013	A Proclamation LL-013	L. Miller	Retrd.	45.00	55.00
90-02-014	Gathering Acorns LL-014	L. Miller	Retrd.	100.00	100.00
90-02-015	A Look Through The Spyglass LL-015	L. Miller	Retrd.	40.00	50.00
90-02-016	Writing The Legend LL-016	L. Miller	Retrd.	35.00	65.00
90-02-017	Ministral Magic LL-017	L. Miller	Retrd.	45.00	50.00
90-02-018	A Little Jig LL-018	L. Miller	Retrd.	45.00	50.00
91-02-019	Viking LL-019	L. Miller	Retrd.	45.00	50.00
91-02-020	The Easter Bunny's Cart LL-020	L. Miller	Retrd.	45.00	50.00
91-02-021	Got It LL-021	L. Miller	Retrd.	45.00	50.00
91-02-022	It's About Time LL-022	L. Miller	Retrd.	55.00	60.00
91-02-023	Fire it Up LL-023	L. Miller	Retrd.	50.00	55.00

United Design Corp.		**Music Makers**			
89-03-001	Santa's Sleigh MM-004	L. Miller	Retrd.	69.00	69.00
89-03-002	Evening Carolers MM-005	D. Kennicutt	Retrd.	69.00	69.00
89-03-003	Teddy Drummers MM-009	D. Kennicutt	Retrd.	69.00	69.00
89-03-004	Herald Angel MM-011	S. Bradford	Retrd.	79.00	79.00
89-03-005	Teddy Bear Band MM-012	S. Bradford	Retrd.	99.00	100.00
91-03-006	Dashing Through The Snow MM-013	D. Kennicutt	Retrd.	59.00	59.00
91-03-007	A Christmas Gift MM-015	D. Kennicutt	Retrd.	59.00	59.00
91-03-008	Crystal Angel MM-017	D. Kennicutt	Retrd.	59.00	59.00
91-03-009	Teddy Soldiers MM-018	D. Kennicutt	Open	69.00	84.00
91-03-010	Teddy Bear Band #2 MM-023	D. Kennicutt	Open	90.00	90.00
91-03-011	Nutcracker MM-024	P.J. Jonas	Retrd.	69.00	69.00
91-03-012	Peace Descending MM-025	P.J. Jonas	Retrd.	69.00	69.00
91-03-013	Victorian Santa MM-026	L. Miller	Retrd.	69.00	69.00
91-03-014	Renaissance Angel MM-028	P.J. Jonas	Retrd.	69.00	69.00

United Design Corp.		**Easter Bunny Family**			
88-04-001	Bunnies, Basket Of SEC-001	D. Kennicutt	Retrd.	13.00	17.50
88-04-002	Bunny Boy W/Duck SEC-002	D. Kennicutt	Retrd.	13.00	17.50
88-04-003	Bunny, Easter SEC-003	D. Kennicutt	Retrd.	15.00	17.50
88-04-004	Bunny Girl W/Hen SEC-004	D. Kennicutt	Retrd.	13.00	17.50
88-04-005	Rabbit, Grandma SEC-005	D. Kennicutt	Retrd.	15.00	20.00
88-04-006	Rabbit, Grandpa SEC-006	D. Kennicutt	Retrd.	15.00	20.00
88-04-007	Rabbit, Momma w/Bonnet SEC-007	D. Kennicutt	Retrd.	15.00	20.00
89-04-008	Auntie Bunny SEC-008	D. Kennicutt	Retrd.	20.00	23.00
89-04-009	Little Sis W/Lolly SEC-009	D. Kennicutt	Retrd.	14.50	17.50
89-04-010	Bunny W/Prize Egg SEC-010	D. Kennicutt	Retrd.	19.50	20.00
89-04-011	Sis & Bubba Sharing SEC-011	D. Kennicutt	Open	22.50	24.50
89-04-012	Easter Egg Hunt SEC-012	D. Kennicutt	Open	16.50	22.00
89-04-013	Rock-A-Bye Bunny SEC-013	D. Kennicutt	Open	20.00	24.50
89-04-014	Ducky W/Bonnet, Pink SEC-014	D. Kennicutt	Retrd.	10.00	12.00
89-04-015	Ducky W/Bonnet,Blue SEC-015	D. Kennicutt	Retrd.	10.00	12.00
90-04-016	Bubba w/Wagon SEC-016	D. Kennicutt	Retrd.	16.50	17.50
90-04-017	Easter Bunny w/Crystal SEC-017	D. Kennicutt	Open	23.00	24.50
90-04-018	Hen w/Chick SEC-018	D. Kennicutt	Retrd.	23.00	23.00
90-04-019	Momma Making Basket SEC-019	D. Kennicutt	Retrd.	23.00	23.00
90-04-020	Mother Goose SEC-020	D. Kennicutt	Retrd.	16.50	20.00
91-04-021	Bubba In Wheelbarrow SEC-021	D. Kennicutt	Retrd.	20.00	20.00
91-04-022	Lop-Ear W/Crystal SEC-022	D. Kennicutt	Open	23.00	24.50
91-04-023	Nest of Bunny Eggs SEC-023	D. Kennicutt	Open	17.50	22.00
91-04-024	Victorian Momma SEC-024	D. Kennicutt	Retrd.	20.00	20.00
91-04-025	Bunny Boy W/Basket SEC-025	D. Kennicutt	Retrd.	20.00	20.00
91-04-026	Victorian Auntie Bunny SEC-026	D. Kennicutt	Retrd.	20.00	20.00
91-04-027	Baby in Buggy, Boy SEC-027R	D. Kennicutt	Retrd.	20.00	22.00
91-04-028	Fancy Find SEC-028	D. Kennicutt	Open	20.00	22.00
91-04-029	Baby in Buggy, Girl SEC-029R	D. Kennicutt	Retrd.	20.00	22.00
92-04-030	Easter Bunny w/Back Pack SEC-030	D. Kennicutt	Open	20.00	22.00
92-04-031	Grandma w/ Bible SEC-031	D. Kennicutt	Open	20.00	22.00
92-04-032	Grandpa w/Carrots SEC-032R	D. Kennicutt	Retrd.	20.00	22.00
92-04-033	Auntie Bunny w/Cake SEC-033R	D. Kennicutt	Retrd.	20.00	22.00
92-04-034	Boy Bunny w/Large Egg SEC-034R	D. Kennicutt	Retrd.	20.00	22.00
92-04-035	Girl Bunny w/Large Egg SEC-035R	D. Kennicutt	Retrd.	20.00	22.00
93-04-036	Egg Roll SEC-036	D. Kennicutt	Open	23.00	24.50
93-04-037	Grandma & Quilt SEC-037	D. Kennicutt	Open	23.00	24.50
93-04-038	Rocking Horse SEC-038	D. Kennicutt	Open	20.00	22.00
93-04-039	Girl Bunny w/Basket SEC-039	D. Kennicutt	Open	20.00	22.00
93-04-040	Christening Day SEC-040	D. Kennicutt	Open	20.00	22.00
93-04-041	Easter Bunny, Chocolate Egg SEC-041	D. Kennicutt	Open	23.00	24.50
93-04-042	Lop Ear Dying Eggs SEC-042	D. Kennicutt	Open	23.00	24.50
93-04-043	Mom Storytime SEC-043	D. Kennicutt	Open	20.00	22.00
94-04-044	Bath Time SEC-044	D. Kennicutt	Open	24.50	24.50
94-04-045	All Hidden SEC-045	D. Kennicutt	Open	24.50	24.50
94-04-046	Gift Carrot SEC-046	D. Kennicutt	Open	22.00	22.00
94-04-047	Large Prize Egg SEC-047	D. Kennicutt	Open	22.00	22.00
94-04-048	First Steps SEC-048	D. Kennicutt	Open	24.50	24.50
94-04-049	Babysitter SEC-049	D. Kennicutt	Open	24.50	24.50
94-04-050	Wheelbarrow SEC-050	D. Kennicutt	Open	24.50	24.50

United Design Corp.		**Easter Bunny Family Miniatures**			
93-05-001	Bunny under Bonnet SEC-500	P.J. Jonas	Open	7.50	7.50
93-05-002	Girl Bunny with Carrots SEC-501	P.J. Jonas	Open	8.50	8.50
93-05-003	Girl Bunny with Hen mini SEC-502	P.J. Jonas	Open	7.50	7.50
93-05-004	Lop Ear and Paint Bucket SEC-503	D. Newburn	Open	8.50	8.50
93-05-005	Basket of Bunnies mini SEC-504	P.J. Jonas	Open	7.50	7.50
93-05-006	Bubba with Goose mini SEC-505	D. Newburn	Open	7.50	7.50
93-05-007	Boy Bunny with Blocks SEC-506	P.J. Jonas	Open	8.50	8.50
93-05-008	Grandma Rabbit mini SEC-507	P.J. Jonas	Open	8.50	8.50
93-05-009	Grandpa Rabbit mini SEC-508	P.J. Jonas	Open	8.50	8.50
93-05-010	Lop Ear Girl with Egg SEC-509	D. Newburn	Open	7.50	7.50
93-05-011	Easter Bunny mini SEC-510	D. Newburn	Open	8.50	8.50
93-05-012	Momma Rabbit mini SEC-511	D. Newburn	Open	8.50	8.50
93-05-013	Baby Boy with Pail SEC-512	D. Newburn	Open	8.50	8.50
93-05-014	Baby Girl with Bunny SEC-513	D. Newburn	Open	7.50	7.50
93-05-015	Lilly mini SEC-514	D. Newburn	Open	7.50	7.50
93-05-016	Baby in Cradle SEC-515	P.J. Jonas	Open	7.50	7.50
94-05-017	Bunny and Goose Reading SEC-516	P.J. Jonas	Open	8.50	8.50
94-05-018	Mini Momma with Basket SEC-517	P.J. Jonas	Open	8.50	8.50
94-05-019	Victorian Momma Bunny mini SEC-518	D. Newburn	Open	8.50	8.50
94-05-020	Little Sis with Lolly mini SEC-519	D. Newburn	Open	8.50	8.50
94-05-021	Little Lop Artist SEC-520	D. Newburn	Open	8.50	8.50
94-05-022	Victorian Auntie Bunny mini SEC-521	P.J. Jonas	Open	7.50	7.50
94-05-023	Spring Showers SEC-522	P.J. Jonas	Open	8.50	8.50
94-05-024	Easter Bonnet (Lop Ear) SEC-523	D. Newburn	Open	7.50	7.50
94-05-025	Mini Prize Egg SEC-524	P.J. Jonas	Open	7.50	7.50
94-05-026	Auntie Bunny mini SEC-525	D. Newburn	Open	8.50	8.50
94-05-027	Lop Ear Boy with Wagon SEC-526	D. Newburn	Open	7.50	7.50
94-05-028	Bunny with Toy Cow SEC-527	P.J. Jonas	Open	7.50	7.50

United Design Corp.		**Easter Bunny Family Babies**			
94-06-001	Girl with Blanket SEC-800	D. Kennicutt	Open	6.50	6.50
94-06-002	Boy with Baseball Bat SEC-801	D. Kennicutt	Open	6.50	6.50
94-06-003	Boy with Basket and Egg SEC-802	D. Kennicutt	Open	6.50	6.50
94-06-004	Boy with Stick Horse SEC-803	D. Kennicutt	Open	6.50	6.50
94-06-005	Girl with Toy Rabbit SEC-804	D. Kennicutt	Open	6.50	6.50
94-06-006	Boy Baby with Blocks SEC-805	D. Kennicutt	Open	6.50	6.50
94-06-007	Girl with Big Egg SEC-806	D. Kennicutt	Open	6.50	6.50
94-06-008	Baby on Blanket, Naptime SEC-807	D. Kennicutt	Open	6.50	6.50

United Design Corp.		**Backyard Birds**			
88-07-001	Bluebird, Small BB-001	S. Bradford	Open	10.00	10.50
88-07-002	Cardinal, Small BB-002	S. Bradford	Open	10.00	10.50
88-07-003	Chickadee, Small BB-003	S. Bradford	Open	10.00	10.50
88-07-004	Hummingbird Flying, Small BB-004	S. Bradford	Open	10,00	10.50
88-07-005	Hummingbird Female, Small BB-005	S. Bradford	Retrd.	10.00	10.00
88-07-006	Robin Baby, Small BB-006	S. Bradford	Open	10.00	10.50
88-07-007	Sparrow, Small BB-007	S. Bradford	Open	10.00	10.50
88-07-008	Robin Babies BB-008	S. Bradford	Open	15.00	19.00
88-07-009	Bluebird BB-009	S. Bradford	Open	15.00	21.00
88-07-010	Chickadee BB-010	S. Bradford	Open	15.00	18.00
88-07-011	Cardinal, Female BB-011	S. Bradford	Open	15.00	17.00
88-07-012	Humingbird BB-012	S. Bradford	Open	15.00	18.00
88-07-013	Cardinal, Male BB-013	S. Bradford	Open	15.00	18.00
88-07-014	Red-winged Blackbird BB-014	S. Bradford	Retrd.	15.00	16.50
88-07-015	Robin BB-015	S. Bradford	Open	15.00	21.00
88-07-016	Sparrow BB-016	S. Bradford	Open	15.00	17.00
88-07-017	Bluebird Hanging BB-017	S. Bradford	Retrd.	11.00	16.50
88-07-018	Cardinal Hanging BB-018	S. Bradford	Retrd.	11.00	11.00
88-07-019	Chickadee Hanging BB-019	S. Bradford	Retrd.	11.00	11.00
88-07-020	Robin Hanging BB-020	S. Bradford	Retrd.	11.00	11.00
88-07-021	Sparrow Hanging BB-021	S. Bradford	Retrd.	11.00	11.00
88-07-022	Hummingbird Sm., Hanging BB-022	S. Bradford	Retrd.	11.00	11.00
88-07-023	Humingbird, Lg., Hanging BB-023	S. Bradford	Retrd.	15.00	15.00
89-07-024	Baltimore Oriole BB-024	S. Bradford	Open	19.50	22.00
89-07-025	Hoot Owl BB-025	S. Bradford	Open	15.00	20.00
89-07-026	Blue Jay BB-026	S. Bradford	Open	19.50	22.00
89-07-027	Blue Jay, Baby BB-027	S. Bradford	Open	15.00	15.00
89-07-028	Goldfinch BB-028	S. Bradford	Open	16.50	20.00
89-07-029	Saw-Whet Owl BB-029	S. Bradford	Open	15.00	18.00
89-07-030	Woodpecker BB-030	S. Bradford	Open	16.50	20.00
90-07-031	Bluebird (Upright) BB-031	S. Bradford	Open	20.00	20.00
90-07-032	Cedar Waxwing BB-032	S. Bradford	Open	20.00	20.00
90-07-033	Cedar Waxwing Babies BB-033	S. Bradford	Open	22.00	22.00
90-07-034	Indigo Bunting BB-036	S. Bradford	Open	20.00	20.00
90-07-035	Indigo Bunting, Female BB-039	S. Bradford	Open	20.00	20.00
90-07-036	Nuthatch, White-throated BB-037	S. Bradford	Open	20.00	20.00
90-07-037	Painted Bunting BB-040	S. Bradford	Open	20.00	20.00
90-07-038	Painted Bunting, Female BB-041	S. Bradford	Open	20.00	20.00
90-07-039	Purple Finch BB-038	S. Bradford	Open	20.00	20.00
90-07-040	Rose Breasted Grosbeak BB-042	S. Bradford	Open	20.00	20.00
90-07-041	Evening Grosbeak BB-034	S. Bradford	Open	22.00	22.00
94-07-042	Broadbill on Trumpet Vine BB-043	P.J. Jonas	Open	22.00	22.00
94-07-043	Allen's on Pink Flowers BB-044	P.J. Jonas	Open	22.00	22.00
94-07-044	Rubythroat on Yellow Flowers BB-045	P.J. Jonas	Open	22.00	22.00
94-07-045	Magnificent Pair on Trumpet Vine BB-046	P.J. Jonas	Open	30.00	30.00
94-07-046	Rubythroat Pair on Pink Flowers BB-047	P.J. Jonas	Open	30.00	30.00
94-07-047	Broadbill Pair on Yellow FlowersBB-048	P.J. Jonas	Open	30.00	30.00
94-07-048	Rubythroat on Thistle BB-049	P.J. Jonas	Open	16.50	16.50
94-07-049	Allen's on Purple Morning Glory BB-051	P.J. Jonas	Open	22.00	22.00
94-07-050	Rubythroat on Red Morning Glory BB-052	P.J. Jonas	Open	22.00	22.00
94-07-051	Broadbill on Blue Morning Gloryk BB-053	P.J. Jonas	Open	22.00	22.00
94-07-052	Rubythroat on Pink Fuscia BB-054	P.J. Jonas	Open	22.00	22.00
94-07-053	Broadbill on Yellow Fuscia BB-055	P.J. Jonas	Open	22.00	22.00

Company Number	Name	Series Artist	Edition Limit	Issue Price	Quote
United Design Corp.		**PenniBears™**			
89-08-001	Bouquet Girl PB-001	P.J. Jonas	Retrd.	20.00	45-50.00
89-08-002	Honey Bear PB-002	P.J. Jonas	Retrd.	20.00	45-50.00
89-08-003	Bouquet Boy PB-003	P.J. Jonas	Retrd.	20.00	45-50.00
89-08-004	Beautiful Bride PB-004	P.J. Jonas	Retrd.	20.00	45-50.00
89-08-005	Butterfly Bear PB-005	P.J. Jonas	Retrd.	20.00	45-50.00
89-08-006	Cookie Bandit PB-006	P.J. Jonas	Retrd.	20.00	22.00
89-08-007	Baby Hugs PB-007	P.J. Jonas	Retrd.	20.00	35.00
89-08-008	Doctor Bear PB-008	P.J. Jonas	Retrd.	20.00	22.00
89-08-009	Lazy Days PB-009	P.J. Jonas	Retrd.	20.00	22.00
89-08-010	Petite Mademoiselle PB-010	P.J. Jonas	Retrd.	20.00	45.00
90-08-011	Giddiap Teddy PB-011	P.J. Jonas	Retrd.	20.00	45-50.00
90-08-012	Buttons & Bows PB-012	P.J. Jonas	Retrd.	20.00	45-50.00
90-08-013	Country Spring PB-013	P.J. Jonas	Retrd.	20.00	45-50.00
90-08-014	Garden Path PB-014	P.J. Jonas	Retrd.	20.00	45-50.00
89-08-015	Handsome Groom PB-015	P.J. Jonas	Retrd.	20.00	45.00
89-08-016	Nap Time PB-016	P.J. Jonas	Retrd.	20.00	22.00
89-08-017	Nurse Bear PB-017	P.J. Jonas	Retrd.	20.00	22.00
89-08-018	Birthday Bear PB-018	P.J. Jonas	Retrd.	20.00	40.00
89-08-019	Attic Fun PB-019	P.J. Jonas	Retrd.	20.00	22.00
89-08-020	Puppy Bath PB-020	P.J. Jonas	Retrd.	20.00	22.00
89-08-021	Puppy Love PB-021	P.J. Jonas	Retrd.	20.00	22.00
89-08-022	Tubby Teddy PB-022	P.J. Jonas	Retrd.	20.00	22.00
89-08-023	Bathtime Buddies PB-023	P.J. Jonas	Retrd.	20.00	22.00
89-08-024	Southern Belle PB-024	P.J. Jonas	Retrd.	20.00	45-50.00
90-08-025	Boooo Bear PB-025	P.J. Jonas	Retrd.	20.00	22.00
90-08-026	Sneaky Snowball PB-026	P.J. Jonas	Retrd.	20.00	22.00
90-08-027	Count Bearacula PB-027	P.J. Jonas	Retrd.	22.00	24.00
90-08-028	Dress Up Fun PB-028	P.J. Jonas	Retrd.	22.00	24.00
90-08-029	Scarecrow Teddy PB-029	P.J. Jonas	Retrd.	24.00	24.00
90-08-030	Country Quilter PB-030	P.J. Jonas	Retrd.	22.00	26.00
90-08-031	Santa Bear-ing Gifts PB-031	P.J. Jonas	Retrd.	24.00	26.00
90-08-032	Stocking Surprise PB-032	P.J. Jonas	Retrd.	22.00	26.00
91-08-033	Bearly Awake PB-033	P.J. Jonas	Retrd.	22.00	22.00
91-08-034	Lil' Mer-teddy PB-034	P.J. Jonas	Retrd.	24.00	24.00
91-08-035	Bump-bear-Crop PB-035	P.J. Jonas	Retrd.	26.00	26.00
91-08-036	Country Lullabye PB-036	P.J. Jonas	Retrd.	24.00	24.00
91-08-037	Bear Footin' it PB-037	P.J. Jonas	Retrd.	24.00	24.00
91-08-038	Windy Day PB-038	P.J. Jonas	Retrd.	24.00	24.00
91-08-039	Summer Sailing PB-039	P.J. Jonas	Retrd.	26.00	26.00
91-08-040	Goodnight Sweet Princess PB-040	P.J. Jonas	Retrd.	26.00	26.00
91-08-041	Goodnight Little Prince PB-041	P.J. Jonas	Retrd.	26.00	26.00
91-08-042	Bunny Buddies PB-042	P.J. Jonas	Retrd.	22.00	22.00
91-08-043	Baking Goodies PB-043	P.J. Jonas	Retrd.	26.00	26.00
91-08-044	Sweetheart Bears PB-044	P.J. Jonas	Retrd.	28.00	28.00
91-08-045	Bountiful Harvest PB-045	P.J. Jonas	Retrd.	24.00	24.00
91-08-046	Christmas Reinbear PB-046	P.J. Jonas	Retrd.	28.00	28.00
91-08-047	Pilgrim Provider PB-047	P.J. Jonas	Retrd.	32.00	32.00
91-08-048	Sweet Lil 'Sis PB-048	P.J. Jonas	Retrd.	22.00	22.00
91-08-049	Curtain Call PB-049	P.J. Jonas	Retrd.	24.00	24.00
91-08-050	Boo Hoo Bear PB-050	P.J. Jonas	Retrd.	22.00	22.00
91-08-051	Happy Hobo PB-051	P.J. Jonas	Retrd.	26.00	26.00
91-08-052	A Wild Ride PB-052	P.J. Jonas	Retrd.	26.00	26.00
92-08-053	Spanish Rose PB-053	P.J. Jonas	12/94	24.00	24.00
92-08-054	Tally Ho! PB-054	P.J. Jonas	12/94	22.00	22.00
92-08-055	Smokey's Nephew PB-055	P.J. Jonas	12/94	22.00	22.00
92-08-056	Cinderella PB-056	P.J. Jonas	12/94	22.00	22.00
92-08-057	Puddle Jumper PB-057	P.J. Jonas	12/94	24.00	24.00
92-08-058	After Every Meal PB-058	P.J. Jonas	12/94	22.00	22.00
92-08-059	Pot O' Gold PB-059	P.J. Jonas	12/94	22.00	22.00
92-08-050	"I Made It" Girl PB-060	P.J. Jonas	12/94	22.00	22.00
92-08-061	"I Made It" Boy PB-061	P.J. Jonas	12/94	22.00	22.00
92-08-062	Dust Bunny Roundup PB-062	P.J. Jonas	12/94	22.00	22.00
92-08-063	Sandbox Fun PB-063	P.J. Jonas	12/94	22.00	22.00
92-08-064	First Prom PB-064	P.J. Jonas	12/94	22.00	22.00
92-08-065	Clowning Around PB-065	P.J. Jonas	12/94	22.00	22.00
92-08-066	Batter Up PB-066	P.J. Jonas	12/94	22.00	22.00
92-08-067	Will You Be Mine? PB-067	P.J. Jonas	12/94	22.00	22.00
92-08-068	On Your Toes PB-068	P.J. Jonas	12/94	24.00	24.00
92-08-069	Apple For Teacher PB-069	P.J. Jonas	12/94	24.00	24.00
92-08-070	Downhill Thrills PB-070	P.J. Jonas	12/94	24.00	24.00
92-08-071	Lil' Devil PB-071	P.J. Jonas	12/94	24.00	24.00
92-08-072	Touchdown PB-072	P.J. Jonas	12/94	22.00	22.00
92-08-073	Bear-Capade PB-073	P.J. Jonas	12/94	22.00	22.00
92-08-074	Lil' Sis Makes Up PB-074	P.J. Jonas	12/94	22.00	22.00
92-08-075	Christmas Cookies PB-075	P.J. Jonas	12/94	22.00	22.00
92-08-076	Decorating The Wreath PB-076	P.J. Jonas	12/94	22.00	22.00
93-08-077	A Happy Camper PB-077	P.J. Jonas	12/95	28.00	28.00
93-08-078	My Forever Love PB-078	P.J. Jonas	12/95	28.00	28.00
93-08-079	Rest Stop PB-079	P.J. Jonas	12/95	24.00	24.00
93-08-080	May Joy Be Yours PB-080	P.J. Jonas	12/95	24.00	24.00
93-08-081	Santa's Helper PB-081	P.J. Jonas	12/95	28.00	28.00
93-08-082	Gotta Try Again PB-082	P.J. Jonas	12/95	24.00	24.00
93-08-083	Little Bear Peep PB-083	P.J. Jonas	12/95	24.00	24.00
93-08-084	Happy Birthday PB-084	P.J. Jonas	12/95	26.00	26.00
93-08-085	Getting 'Round On My Own PB-085	P.J. Jonas	12/95	26.00	26.00
93-08-086	Summer Belle PB-086	P.J. Jonas	12/95	24.00	24.00
93-08-087	Making It Better PB-087	P.J. Jonas	12/95	24.00	24.00
93-08-088	Big Chief Little Bear PB-088	P.J. Jonas	12/95	28.00	28.00
United Design Corp.		**PenniBears™ Collector's Club Members Only Editions**			
91-09-001	First Collection PB-C90	P.J. Jonas	Retrd.	26.00	100-125.
92-09-002	Collecting Makes Cents PB-C91	P.J. Jonas	Retrd.	26.00	75-150.00
92-09-003	Today's Pleasures, Tomorrow's Treasures	P.J. Jonas	Retrd.	26.00	100.00
93-09-004	Chalkin Up Another Year PBC-93	P.J. Jones	Retrd.	26.00	26.00
94-09-005	Artist's Touch-Collector's Treasure PBC-94	P.J. Jones	Yr.Iss.	26.00	26.00
United Design Corp.		**Party Animals™**			
84-10-001	Democratic Donkey ('84)	D. Kennicutt	Retrd.	14.50	16.00
84-10-002	GOP Elephant ('84)	L. Miller	Retrd.	14.50	16.00
86-10-003	Democratic Donkey ('86)	L. Miller	Retrd.	14.50	14.50
86-10-004	GOP Elephant ('86)	L. Miller	Retrd.	14.50	14.50
88-10-005	Democratic Donkey ('88)	L. Miller	Retrd.	14.50	16.00
88-10-006	GOP Elephant ('88)	L. Miller	Retrd.	14.50	16.00
90-10-007	Democratic Donkey ('90)	D. Kennicutt	Open	16.00	16.00
90-10-008	GOP Elephant ('90)	D. Kennicutt	Retrd.	16.00	16.00
92-10-009	Democratic Donkey ('92)	K. Memoli	Open	20.00	20.00
92-10-010	GOP Elephant ('92)	K. Memol	Open	20.00	20.00
United Design Corp.		**Angels Collection**			
91-11-001	Christmas Angel AA-003	S. Bradford	10,000	125.00	125.00
91-11-002	Trumpeter Angel AA-004	S. Bradford	10,000	99.00	99.00
91-11-003	Classical Angel AA-005	S. Bradford	10,000	79.00	79.00
91-11-004	Messenger of Peace AA-006	S. Bradford	10,000	75.00	79.00
91-11-005	Winter Rose Angel AA-007	S. Bradford	10,000	65.00	65.00
91-11-006	Heavenly Shepherdess AA-008	S. Bradford	10,000	99.00	99.00
91-11-007	The Gift AA-009	S. Bradford	Retrd.	135.00	350-475.
91-11-008	Peace Descending Angel AA-013	P.J. Jonas	Open	20.00	20.00
92-11-009	Joy To The World AA-016	D. Newburn	10,000	90.00	95.00
92-11-010	Peaceful Encounter AA-017	D. Newburn	10,000	100.00	100.00
92-11-011	The Gift '92 AA-018	S. Bradford	Retrd.	140.00	180-200.
92-11-012	Winter Angel AA-019	D. Newburn	10,000	75.00	75.00
92-11-013	Angel, Lion & Lamb AA-020	K. Memoli	10,000	135.00	135.00
92-11-014	Angel, Lamb & Critters AA-021	S. Bradford	10,000	90.00	95.00
92-11-015	Crystal Angel AA-022	P.J. Jonas	Open	20.00	20.00
92-11-016	Rose Of Sharon AA-023	P.J. Jonas	Open	20.00	20.00
92-11-017	Victorian Angel AA-024	P.J. Jonas	Open	20.00	20.00
92-11-018	Star Glory AA-025	P.J. Jonas	Open	20.00	20.00
93-11-019	Madonna AA-031	K. Memoli	10,000	65.00	100.00
93-11-020	Angel of Flight AA-032	K. Memoli	10,000	79.00	100.00
93-11-021	Angel w/ Lillies-033	D. Newburn	10,000	55.00	80.00
93-11-022	Angel w/ Birds AA-034	D. Newburn	10,000	55.00	75.00
93-11-023	Angel w/ Leaves AA-035	D. Newburn	10,000	55.00	70.00
93-11-024	The Gift '93 AA-037	S. Bradford	3,500	100.00	120.00
93-11-025	Angel w/ Leaves, Emerald AA-041	D. Newburn	10,000	55.00	70.00
93-11-026	Angel w/Lillies, Crimson AA-040	D. Newburn	10,000	80.00	80.00
94-11-027	Angel, Roses and Bluebirds AA-054	D. Newburn	10,000	32.50	32.50
94-11-028	The Gift AA-057	D. Newburn	3,500	70.00	70.00
94-11-029	Angel w/Book AA-058	D. Newburn	10,000	42.00	42.00
94-11-030	Earth Angel AA-059	S. Bradford	10,000	42.00	42.00
94-11-031	Dreaming of Angels AA-060	K. Memoli	10,000	60.00	60.00
94-11-032	Angel w/Christ Child AA-061	K. Memoli	10,000	42.00	42.00
94-11-033	Harvest Angel AA-063	S. Bradford	10,000	42.00	42.00
United Design Corp.		**Lil' Dolls**			
91-12-001	The Nutcracker LD-006	P.J. Jonas	Retrd.	35.00	35.00
92-12-002	Clara & The Nutcracker LD-017	D. Newburn	Retrd.	35.00	35.00
United Design Corp.		**Storytime Rhymes & Tales**			
91-13-001	Mother Goose SL-001	H. Henriksen	Retrd.	64.00	64.00
91-13-002	Mistress Mary SL-002	H. Henriksen	Retrd.	64.00	64.00
91-13-003	Simple Simon SL-003	H. Henriksen	Retrd.	90.00	90.00
91-13-004	Owl & Pussy Cat SL-004	H. Henriksen	Retrd.	100.00	100.00
91-13-005	Three Little Pigs SL-005	H. Henriksen	Retrd.	100.00	100.00
91-13-006	Little Miss Muffet SL-006	H. Henriksen	Retrd.	64.00	64.00
91-13-007	Little Jack Horner SL-007	H. Henriksen	Retrd.	50.00	50.00
91-13-008	Humpty Dumpty SL-008	H. Henriksen	Retrd.	64.00	64.00
VickiLane		**Sweet Thumpins**			
87-01-001	Bunny Sleeping in a Basket	V. Anderson	Retrd.	18.00	18.00
88-01-002	Girl Bunny with a Hat and Doll	V. Anderson	Retrd.	18.00	18.00
88-01-003	Farmer Bunny with Carrots	V. Anderson	Retrd.	18.00	18.00
90-01-004	Venture into Sweet Thumpins	V. Anderson	Retrd.	60.00	73.00
91-01-005	Tea Time	V. Anderson	1,000	79.00	82.00
91-01-006	Making Memories	V. Anderson	1,000	70.00	73.00
92-01-007	Cookie Peddler	V. Anderson	750	90.00	90.00
VickiLane		**Mice Memories**			
90-02-001	Happiness Together	V. Anderson	1,000	65.00	73.00
90-02-002	Mouse on the Beach	V. Anderson	Retrd.	28.00	28.00
VickiLane		**Time For Teddy**			
89-03-001	Boy Teddy Building Sandcastles	V. Anderson	Retrd.	17.00	17.00
89-03-002	Girl Teddy Sunbathing	V. Anderson	Retrd.	18.00	18.00
93-03-003	Bear Holding His Foot	V. Anderson	Retrd.	14.00	14.00
93-03-004	Teddy Bear with a Bow	V. Anderson	Retrd.	14.00	14.00
VickiLane		**Collector Club Series**			
93-04-001	Sweet Secrets	V. Anderson	Retrd.	30.00	30.00
94-04-002	Take Me Home	V. Anderson	Yr.Iss.	28.00	28.00
WACO Products Corp.		**Melody In Motion/Willie**			
85-01-001	Willie The Trumpeter	S. Nakane	Open	130.00	148.00
85-01-002	Willie The Hobo	S. Nakane	Open	130.00	148.00
85-01-003	Willie The Whistler	S. Nakane	Open	130.00	148.00
87-01-004	Lamppost Willie	S. Nakane	Open	110.00	135.00
91-01-005	Willie The Fisherman	S. Nakane	Open	150.00	170.00
92-01-006	Dockside Willie	S. Nakane	Open	160.00	170.00
92-01-007	Wild West Willie	S. Nakane	Open	175.00	190.00
93-01-008	Lamp Light Willie	S. Nakane	Open	240.00	240.00
93-01-009	Willie The Golfer	S. Nakane	Open	240.00	240.00
93-01-010	The Artist	S. Nakane	Open	240.00	240.00
93-01-011	Heartbreak Willie	S. Nakane	Open	180.00	180.00
WACO Products Corp.		**Melody In Motion/Vendor**			
87-02-001	Organ Grinder	S. Nakane	Open	130.00	160.00
89-02-002	Peanut Vendor	S. Nakane	Open	140.00	170.00
89-02-003	Ice Cream Vendor	S. Nakane	Open	140.00	170.00
WACO Products Corp.		**Melody In Motion/Santa**			
86-03-001	Santa Claus-1986	S. Nakane	Retrd.	100.00	N/A
87-03-002	Santa Claus-1987	S. Nakane	Retrd.	130.00	N/A
88-03-003	Santa Claus-1988	S. Nakane	Retrd.	130.00	N/A
89-03-004	Willie The Santa-1989	S. Nakane	Retrd.	130.00	N/A
90-03-005	Santa Claus-1990	S. Nakane	Retrd.	150.00	225.00
91-03-006	Santa Claus-1991	S. Nakane	Retrd.	150.00	N/A
92-03-007	Santa Claus -1992	S. Nakane	11,000	160.00	160.00
93-03-008	Coca-Cola Santa Claus-1993	S. Nakane	6,000	180.00	180.00
WACO Products Corp.		**Melody In Motion/Madame**			
88-04-001	Madame Violin Player	S. Nakane	Retrd.	130.00	130.00
88-04-002	Madame Mandolin Player	S. Nakane	Retrd.	130.00	130.00
88-04-003	Madame Cello Player	S. Nakane	Retrd.	130.00	130.00
88-04-004	Madame Flute Player	S. Nakane	Retrd.	130.00	130.00
88-04-005	Madame Harp Player	S. Nakane	Open	130.00	170.00
88-04-006	Madame Harpsichord Player	S. Nakane	Retrd.	130.00	130.00
88-04-007	Madame Lyre Player	S. Nakane	Retrd.	130.00	130.00
88-04-008	Madame Cello Player (glazed)	S. Nakane	Open	170.00	170.00
88-04-009	Madame Flute Player (glazed)	S. Nakane	Open	170.00	170.00
88-04-010	Madame Harp Player (glazed)	S. Nakane	Open	190.00	190.00
88-04-011	Madame Harpsichord Player (glazed)	S. Nakane	Open	170.00	170.00
WACO Products Corp.		**Melody In Motion/Spotlight Clown**			
89-05-001	Spotlight Clown Cornet	S. Nakane	Retrd.	85.00	85.00
89-05-002	Spotlight Clown Banjo	S. Nakane	Retrd.	85.00	85.00
89-05-003	Spotlight Clown Trombone	S. Nakane	Retrd.	85.00	100.00
89-05-004	Spotlight Clown With Bingo The Dog	S. Nakane	Retrd.	85.00	85.00
89-05-005	Spotlight Clown Tuba	S. Nakane	Retrd.	85.00	85.00

Company Number	Name	Series Artist	Edition Limit	Issue Price	Quote
89-05-006	Spotlight Clown With Upright Bass	S. Nakane	Retrd.	85.00	90.00
WACO Products Corp.		**Melody In Motion/Various**			
85-06-001	Salty 'N' Pepper	S. Nakane	Retrd.	88.00	275.00
86-06-002	The Cellist	S. Nakane	Open	130.00	152.00
86-06-003	The Guitarist	S. Nakane	Open	130.00	152.00
86-06-004	The Fiddler	S. Nakane	Open	130.00	152.00
87-06-005	Violin Clown	S. Nakane	Retrd.	84.00	84.00
87-06-006	Clarinet Clown	S. Nakane	Retrd.	110.00	110.00
87-06-007	Saxophone Clown	S. Nakane	Retrd.	110.00	110.00
87-06-008	Accordion Clown	S. Nakane	Retrd.	110.00	110.00
87-06-009	Balloon Clown	S. Nakane	Open	110.00	135.00
87-06-010	The Carousel	S. Nakane	Open	240.00	260.00
89-06-011	The Grand Carousel	S. Nakane	Open	3000.00	3000.00
90-06-012	Shoemaker	S. Nakane	Retrd.	110.00	120.00
90-06-013	Blacksmith	S. Nakane	Retrd.	110.00	120.00
90-06-014	Woodchopper	S. Nakane	Retrd.	110.00	120.00
90-06-015	Accordion Boy	S. Nakane	Retrd.	120.00	125.00
90-06-016	Hunter	S. Nakane	Open	110.00	150.00
91-06-017	Robin Hood	C. Johnson	Retrd.	180.00	180.00
91-06-018	Little John	C. Johnson	Retrd.	180.00	180.00
91-06-019	Victoria Park Carousel	S. Nakane	Open	300.00	330.00
92-06-020	King of Clown Carousel	S. Nakane	Open	740.00	800.00
91-06-021	The Carousel (2nd Edition)	S. Nakane	Open	240.00	260.00
92-06-022	King of Clowns	S. Nakane	Open	700.00	800.00
93-06-023	South of the Border	S. Nakane	Open	180.00	180.00
94-06-024	Low Pressure Job	S. Nakane	Open	240.00	240.00
94-06-025	Day's End	S. Nakane	Open	240.00	240.00
94-06-026	When I Grow Up	S. Nakane	Open	200.00	200.00
94-06-027	Campfire Cowboy	S. Nakane	Open	180.00	180.00
94-06-028	Blue Danube Carousel	S. Nakane	Open	280.00	280.00
94-06-029	Coca-Cola Santa 1994	S. Nakane	N/A	N/A	N/A
WACO Products Corp.		**Melody In Motion/Timepiece**			
89-07-001	Clockpost Willie	S. Nakane	Open	150.00	190.00
89-07-002	Lull'aby Willie	S. Nakane	Retrd.	170.00	170.00
90-07-003	Grandfather's Clock	S. Nakane	Open	200.00	250.00
91-07-004	Hunter Timepiece	S. Nakane	Open	250.00	320.00
92-07-005	Wall Street Willie	S. Nakane	Open	180.00	185-210.
92-07-006	Golden Mountain Clock	S. Nakane	Open	250.00	300.00
WACO Products Corp.		**The Herman Collection**			
90-08-001	Tennis/Wife	J. Unger	Open	20.00	20.00
90-08-002	Doctor/High Cost	J. Unger	Retrd.	20.00	20.00
90-08-003	Bowling/Wife	J. Unger	Open	20.00	20.00
90-08-004	Husband/Check	J. Unger	Open	20.00	20.00
90-08-005	Birthday Cake	J. Unger	Open	20.00	20.00
90-08-006	Doctor/Fat Man	J. Unger	Open	20.00	20.00
90-08-007	Fry Pan/Fisherman	J. Unger	Retrd.	20.00	20.00
90-08-008	Stop Smoking	J. Unger	Open	20.00	20.00
90-08-009	Husband/Newspaper	J. Unger	Open	20.00	20.00
90-08-010	Wedding Ring	J. Unger	Retrd.	20.00	20.00
90-08-011	Golf/Camel	J. Unger	Retrd.	20.00	20.00
90-08-012	Lawyer/Cabinet	J. Unger	Retrd.	20.00	20.00
WACO Products Corp.		**Whimsicals**			
92-09-001	Just For You	S. Nakane	Open	60.00	60.00
92-09-002	The Entertainer	S. Nakane	Open	60.00	60.00
92-09-003	Cheers	S. Nakane	Open	60.00	60.00
92-09-004	Happy Endings	S. Nakane	Open	60.00	60.00
92-09-005	Pals	S. Nakane	Open	60.00	60.00
92-09-006	The Merrymakers	S. Nakane	Open	60.00	60.00
92-09-007	Showtime	S. Nakane	Open	60.00	60.00
92-09-008	Pampered Pets	S. Nakane	Open	60.00	60.00
92-09-009	Apple Pickin' Time	S. Nakane	Open	60.00	60.00
92-09-010	Special Delivery	S. Nakane	Open	60.00	60.00
92-09-011	Tea Time	S. Nakane	Open	60.00	60.00
92-09-012	Bon Voyage	S. Nakane	Open	60.00	60.00
92-09-013	Storytime	S. Nakane	Open	60.00	60.00
Walt Disney: See Disney					
Wee Forest Folk		**Animals**			
73-01-001	Miss Ducky D-1	A. Petersen	Closed	8.00	N/A
74-01-002	Miss Hippo H-1	A. Petersen	Closed	8.00	N/A
74-01-003	Baby Hippo H-2	A. Petersen	Closed	7.00	N/A
74-01-004	Miss and Baby Hippo H-3	A. Petersen	Closed	15.00	800-1000.
75-01-005	Seedy Rat R-1	A. Petersen	Closed	11.50	200-400.
75-01-006	"Doc" Rat R-2	W. Petersen	Closed	5.25	200-400.
77-01-007	Nutsy Squirrel SQ-1	W. Petersen	Closed	6.00	400-500.
78-01-008	Beaver Wood Cutter BV-1	W. Petersen	Closed	8.00	250-475.
78-01-009	Mole Scout MO-1	A. Petersen	Closed	4.25	225-400.
79-01-010	Turtle Jogger TS-1	A. Petersen	Closed	4.00	300-400.
92-01-011	Mr. Mole M1	A. Petersen	Open	65.00	65.00
Wee Forest Folk		**Bears**			
77-02-001	Blueberry Bears BR-1	A. Petersen	Closed	8.75	500-700.
77-02-002	Girl Blueberry Bear BR-2	A. Petersen	Closed	4.25	250-400.
77-02-003	Boy Blueberry Bear BR-3	A. Petersen	Closed	4.50	250-400.
78-02-004	Big Lady Bear BR-4	A. Petersen	Closed	7.50	N/A
78-02-005	Traveling Bear BR-5	A. Petersen	Closed	8.00	250-375.
Wee Forest Folk		**Book / Figurine**			
88-03-001	Tom & Eon BK-1	W. Petersen	Suspd.	45.00	185-250.
Wee Forest Folk		**Bunnies**			
72-04-001	Double Bunnies B-1	A. Petersen	Closed	4.25	400.00
72-04-002	Housekeeping Bunny B-2	A. Petersen	Closed	4.50	400.00
73-04-003	Sir Rabbit B-3	W. Petersen	Closed	4.50	300-400.
73-04-004	The Professor B-4	A. Petersen	Closed	4.75	350-400.
73-04-005	Sunday Bunny B-5	A. Petersen	Closed	4.75	N/A
73-04-006	Broom Bunny B-6	A. Petersen	Closed	9.50	N/A
73-04-007	Muff Bunny B-7	A. Petersen	Closed	9.00	N/A
73-04-008	Market Bunny B-8	A. Petersen	Closed	9.00	N/A
77-04-009	Batter Bunny B-9	A. Petersen	Closed	4.50	275.00
78-04-010	Wedding Bunnies B-10	W. Petersen	Closed	12.50	450-600.
80-04-011	Professor Rabbit B-11	W. Petersen	Closed	14.00	400-500.
85-04-012	Tiny Easter Bunny B-12	D. Petersen	Closed	25.00	80.00
92-04-013	Windy Day! B-13	D. Petersen	Open	37.00	38.00
77-04-014	Tennis Bunny BS-1	A. Petersen	Closed	3.75	250-350.
Wee Forest Folk		**Christmas Carol Series**			
87-05-001	Scrooge CC-1	A. Petersen	Open	23.00	30.00
87-05-002	Bob Cratchit and Tiny Tim CC-2	A. Petersen	Open	36.00	45.00
87-05-003	Marley's Ghost CC-3	A. Petersen	Open	24.00	31.00
87-05-004	Ghost of Christmas Past CC-4	A. Petersen	Open	24.00	31.00
87-05-005	Ghost of Christmas Present CC-5	A. Petersen	Open	54.00	61.00
87-05-006	Ghost of Christmas Yet to Come CC-6	A. Petersen	Open	24.00	30.00
88-05-007	The Fezziwigs CC-7	A. Petersen	Open	65.00	82.00
Wee Forest Folk		**Cinderella Series**			
88-06-001	Cinderella's Slipper (with Prince) C-1	A. Petersen	Suspd.	62.00	150-235.
89-06-002	Cinderella's Slipper C-1a	A. Petersen	Open	32.00	38.00
88-06-003	The Ugly Stepsisters C-2	A. Petersen	Open	62.00	70.00
88-06-004	The Mean Stepmother C-3	A. Petersen	Open	32.00	39.00
88-06-005	The Flower Girls C-4	A. Petersen	Open	42.00	52.00
88-06-006	Cinderella's Wedding C-5	A. Petersen	Open	62.00	73.00
88-06-007	Flower Girl C-6	A. Petersen	Open	22.00	28.00
89-06-008	The Fairy Godmother C-7	A. Petersen	Open	69.00	83.00
Wee Forest Folk		**Fairy Tale Series**			
80-07-001	Red Riding Hood & Wolf FT-1	A. Petersen	Closed	29.00	1200.00
80-07-002	Red Riding Hood FT-2	A. Petersen	Closed	13.00	500-750.
Wee Forest Folk		**Forest Scene**			
88-08-001	Woodland Serenade FS-1	W. Petersen	Open	125.00	132.00
89-08-002	Hearts and Flowers FS-2	W. Petersen	Open	110.00	112.00
90-08-003	Mousie Comes A-Calling FS-3	W. Petersen	Open	128.00	132.00
91-08-004	Mountain Stream FS-4	W. Petersen	Open	128.00	130.00
92-08-005	Love Letter FS-5	W. Petersen	Open	98.00	98.00
93-08-006	Picnic on the Riverbank FS-6	A. Petersen	Open	150.00	150.00
Wee Forest Folk		**Foxes**			
77-09-001	Fancy Fox FX-1	A. Petersen	Closed	4.75	350-475.
77-09-002	Dandy Fox FX-2	A. Petersen	Closed	6.00	450-500.
78-09-003	Barrister Fox FX-3	A. Petersen	Closed	7.50	450-500.
Wee Forest Folk		**Frogs**			
74-10-001	Prince Charming F-1	W. Petersen	Closed	7.50	400-500.
74-10-002	Frog on Rock F-2	A. Petersen	Closed	6.00	N/A
77-10-003	Frog Friends F-3	W. Petersen	Closed	5.75	350-450.
77-10-004	Spring Peepers F-4	A. Petersen	Closed	3.50	N/A
77-10-005	Grampa Frog F-5	W. Petersen	Closed	6.00	350-450.
78-10-006	Singing Frog F-6	A. Petersen	Closed	5.50	250-300.
Wee Forest Folk		**Limited Edition**			
81-11-001	Beauty and the Beast BB-1	W. Petersen	Closed	89.00	1500-2000.
84-11-002	Postmouster LTD-1	W. Petersen	Closed	46.00	700-755..
85-11-002	Helping Hand LTD-2	A. Petersen	Closed	62.00	650.00
87-11-003	Statue in the Park LTD-3	W. Petersen	Closed	93.00	655-750.
88-11-004	Uncle Sammy LTD-4	A. Petersen	Closed	85.00	240-275.
Wee Forest Folk		**Mice**			
77-12-001	King "Tut" Mouse TM-1	A. Petersen	Closed	4.50	450-600.
77-12-002	Queen "Tut" Mouse TM-2	A. Petersen	Closed	4.50	450-600.
72-12-003	Miss Mouse M-1	A. Petersen	Closed	4.25	300-350.
72-12-004	Market Mouse M-1a	A. Petersen	Closed	4.25	175-350.
72-12-005	Miss Mousey M-2	A. Petersen	Closed	4.00	250-350.
72-12-006	Miss Mousey w/ Straw Hat M-2a	A. Petersen	Closed	4.25	250-350.
72-12-007	Miss Mousey w/ Bow Hat M-2b	A. Petersen	Closed	4.25	250-350.
73-12-008	Miss Nursey Mouse M-3	A. Petersen	Closed	4.00	275-400.
74-12-009	Good Knight Mouse M-4	W. Petersen	Closed	7.50	350-500.
74-12-010	Farmer Mouse M-5	A. Petersen	Closed	3.75	350-450.
74-12-011	Wood Sprite M-6a	A. Petersen	Closed	4.00	350-500.
74-12-012	Wood Sprite M-6b	A. Petersen	Closed	4.00	350-500.
74-12-013	Wood Sprite M-6c	A. Petersen	Closed	4.00	350-500.
75-12-014	Two Mice with Candle M-7	A. Petersen	Closed	4.50	350-450.
75-12-015	Two Tiny Mice M-8	A. Petersen	Closed	4.50	350-500.
75-12-016	Bride Mouse M-9	A. Petersen	Closed	4.00	400-500.
76-12-017	Fan Mouse M-10	A. Petersen	Closed	5.75	450-500.
76-12-018	Tea Mouse M-11	A. Petersen	Closed	5.75	450-500.
76-12-019	May Belle M-12	A. Petersen	Closed	4.25	225-375.
76-12-020	June Belle M-13	A. Petersen	Closed	4.25	350-400.
76-12-021	Nightie Mouse M-14	A. Petersen	Closed	4.75	350-500.
76-12-022	Mrs. Mousey M-15	A. Petersen	Closed	4.00	N/A
76-12-023	Mrs. Mousey w/ Hat M-15a	A. Petersen	Closed	4.25	N/A
76-12-024	Mouse with Muff M-16	A. Petersen	Closed	9.00	N/A
76-12-025	Shawl Mouse M-17	A. Petersen	Closed	9.00	N/A
76-12-026	Mama Mouse with Baby M-18	A. Petersen	Closed	6.00	350-450.
77-12-027	Baby Sitter M-19	A. Petersen	Closed	5.75	275.00
78-12-028	Bridge Club Mouse M-20	A. Petersen	Closed	6.00	300-700.
78-12-029	Bridge Club Mouse Partner M-21	A. Petersen	Closed	6.00	300-700.
78-12-030	Secretary, Miss Spell/Miss Pell M-22	A. Petersen	Closed	4.50	375-500.
78-12-031	Picnic Mice M-23	W. Petersen	Closed	7.25	375-600.
78-12-032	Wedding Mice M-24	W. Petersen	Closed	7.50	375-750.
78-12-033	Cowboy Mouse M-25	A. Petersen	Closed	6.00	300-600.
78-12-034	Chief Nip-a-Way Mouse M-26	A. Petersen	Closed	7.00	300-600.
78-12-035	Pirate Mouse M-27	A. Petersen	Closed	6.50	400-1000.
78-12-036	Town Crier Mouse M-28	A. Petersen	Closed	10.50	500-1000.
79-12-037	Mouse Duet M-29	A. Petersen	Closed	25.00	550-700.
79-12-038	Mouse Pianist M-30	A. Petersen	Closed	17.00	300-550.
79-12-039	Mouse Violinist M-31	A. Petersen	Closed	9.00	300.00
79-12-040	Chris-Miss M-32	A. Petersen	Closed	9.00	175-225.
79-12-041	Chris-Mouse M-33	A. Petersen	Closed	9.00	230.00
79-12-042	Mousey Baby, heart book M-34	A. Petersen	Closed	9.50	250-450.
79-12-043	Rock-a-bye Baby Mouse M-35	A. Petersen	Closed	17.00	350-450.
79-12-044	Raggedy and Mouse M-36	A. Petersen	Closed	12.00	250-350.
79-12-045	Gardener Mouse M-37	A. Petersen	Closed	12.00	400-800.
79-12-046	Mouse Ballerina M-38	A. Petersen	Closed	12.50	400-450.
79-12-047	Mouse Artiste M-39	A. Petersen	Closed	12.50	300-450.
80-12-048	Miss Bobbin M-40	A. Petersen	Open	22.00	56.00
80-12-049	Fishermouse M-41	A. Petersen	Closed	16.00	500-700.
80-12-050	Commo-Dormouse M-42	W. Petersen	Closed	14.00	500-900.
80-12-051	Santa Mouse M-43	A. Petersen	Closed	12.00	200-250.
80-12-052	Witch Mouse M-44	A. Petersen	Closed	12.00	150-200.
80-12-053	Miss Teach M-45	A. Petersen	Closed	18.00	400-500.
80-12-054	Miss Polly Mouse M-46	A. Petersen	Closed	23.00	300-475.
80-12-055	Pirate Mouse M-47	W. Petersen	Closed	16.00	1225.00
80-12-056	Photographer Mouse M-48	W. Petersen	Closed	23.00	400-700.
80-12-057	Carpenter Mouse M-49	A. Petersen	Closed	15.00	400-700.
80-12-058	Mrs. Tidy and Helper M-50	A. Petersen	Closed	24.00	500-700.
80-12-059	Mrs. Tidy M-51	A. Petersen	Closed	19.50	350-500.
81-12-060	Mother's Helper M-52	A. Petersen	Closed	11.00	200-300.
81-12-061	Flower Girl M-53	A. Petersen	Closed	15.00	275-375.
81-12-062	Nurse Mousey M-54	A. Petersen	Closed	14.00	300.00
81-12-063	Doc Mouse & Patient M-55	W. Petersen	Closed	14.00	1200.00
81-12-064	School Marm Mouse M-56	A. Petersen	Closed	19.50	500-700.
81-12-065	Barrister Mouse M-57	A. Petersen	Closed	16.00	400-600.

Company Number	Name	Series Artist	Edition Limit	Issue Price	Quote
81-12-066	Graduate Mouse M-58	A. Petersen	Closed	15.00	85-130.00
81-12-067	Pearl Knit Mouse M-59	A. Petersen	Closed	20.00	200-250.
81-12-068	Mom and Squeaky Clean M-60	A. Petersen	Open	27.00	52.00
81-12-069	Little Devil M-61	A. Petersen	Open	12.50	28.00
81-12-070	Blue Devil M-61	A. Petersen	Closed	12.50	125.00
81-12-071	Little Ghost M-62	A. Petersen	Open	8.50	19.00
81-12-072	The Carolers M-63	A. Petersen	Closed	29.00	400-600.
81-12-073	Lone Caroler M-64	A. Petersen	Closed	15.50	375-575.
81-12-074	Mousey Express M-65	A. Petersen	Suspd.	22.00	105.00.
82-12-075	Baby Sitter M-66	A. Petersen	Suspd.	23.50	130.00
82-12-076	Wedding Mice M-67	W. Petersen	Suspd.	29.50	110-170.
82-12-077	Office Mousey M-68	A. Petersen	Closed	23.00	300-575.
82-12-078	Beddy-bye Mousey M-69	A. Petersen	Open	29.00	49.00
82-12-079	Me and Raggedy Ann M-70	A. Petersen	Open	18.50	33.00
82-12-080	Arty Mouse M-71	A. Petersen	Closed	19.00	95.00
82-12-081	Say "Cheese" M-72	W. Petersen	Closed	15.50	605.00
82-12-082	Miss Teach & Pupil M-73	A. Petersen	Closed	29.50	110-300.
82-12-083	Tea for Two M-74	A. Petersen	Closed	26.00	300-450.
82-12-084	Mousey's Teddy M-75	A. Petersen	Closed	29.00	300-350.
82-12-085	Beach Mousey M-76	A. Petersen	Suspd.	19.00	95-140.00
82-12-086	Little Fire Chief M-77	W. Petersen	Closed	29.00	350-500.
82-12-087	Moon Mouse M-78	A. Petersen	Closed	15.50	405.00
82-12-088	Sweethearts M-79	A. Petersen	Closed	26.00	375-500.
82-12-089	Girl Sweetheart M-80	A. Petersen	Open	13.50	22.00
82-12-090	Boy Sweetheart M-81	A. Petersen	Closed	13.50	350-500.
82-12-091	Easter Bunny Mouse M-82	A. Petersen	Open	18.00	33.00
82-12-092	Happy Birthday! M-83	A. Petersen	Open	17.50	31.00
82-12-093	Snowmouse & Friend M-84	A. Petersen	Closed	23.50	300-475.
82-12-094	Little Sledders M-85	A. Petersen	Closed	24.00	150-250.
82-12-095	Lamplight Carolers M-86	A. Petersen	Closed	35.00	250-350.
82-12-096	Holly Mouse M-87	A. Petersen	Open	13.50	28.00
82-12-097	Littlest Angel M-88	A. Petersen	Closed	15.00	100-125.
82-12-098	Poorest Angel M-89	A. Petersen	Closed	15.00	100-125.
83-12-099	Merry Chris-Miss M-90	A. Petersen	Closed	17.00	175-250.
83-12-100	Merry Chris-Mouse M-91	A. Petersen	Closed	16.00	175-250.
83-12-101	Christmas Morning M-92	A. Petersen	Closed	35.00	175-225.
83-12-102	First Christmas M-93	A. Petersen	Closed	16.00	200-250.
83-12-103	Cupid Mouse M-94	W. Petersen	Open	22.00	38.00
83-12-104	Mousey Nurse M-95	A. Petersen	Open	15.00	27.00
83-12-105	Get Well Soon! M-96	A. Petersen	Closed	15.00	225-350.
83-12-106	Mouse Call M-97	W. Petersen	Closed	24.00	250-400.
83-12-107	Clown Mouse M-98	A. Petersen	Closed	22.00	250-350.
83-12-108	Birthday Girl M-99	A. Petersen	Open	18.50	30.00
83-12-109	Mousey's Cone M-100	A. Petersen	Open	22.00	34.00
83-12-110	Mousey's Tricycle M-101	A. Petersen	Open	24.00	44.00
83-12-111	Mousey's Dollhouse M-102	A. Petersen	Closed	30.00	275-400.
83-12-112	Rocking Tot M-103	A. Petersen	Closed	19.00	50-80.00
83-12-113	Harvest Mouse M-104	W. Petersen	Closed	23.00	250-375.
83-12-114	Wash Day M-105	A. Petersen	Closed	23.00	300-350.
83-12-115	Pack Mouse M-106	W. Petersen	Closed	19.00	300-375.
83-12-116	Chief Geronimouse M-107a	A. Petersen	Open	21.00	38.00
83-12-117	Running Doe/Little Deer M-107b	A. Petersen	Open	35.00	40.00
83-12-118	Rope 'em Mousey M-108	A. Petersen	Closed	19.00	200-350.
84-12-119	Campfire Mouse M-109	W. Petersen	Closed	26.00	300-350.
84-12-120	Traveling Mouse M-110	A. Petersen	Closed	28.00	250-300.
84-12-121	Spring Gardener M-111	A. Petersen	Open	26.00	39.00
84-12-122	First Day of School M-112	A. Petersen	Closed	27.00	300-450.
84-12-123	Tidy Mouse M-113	A. Petersen	Closed	38.00	300-400.
84-12-124	Pen Pal Mousey M-114	A. Petersen	Closed	26.00	300-425.
84-12-125	Mom & Ginger Baker M-115	W. Petersen	Open	38.00	59.00
84-12-126	Santa's Trainee M-116	W. Petersen	Closed	36.50	400-600.
84-12-127	Chris-Mouse Pageant M-117	A. Petersen	Open	38.00	54.00
84-12-128	Peter's Pumpkin M-118	A. Petersen	Closed	19.00	65.00
84-12-129	Prudence Pie Maker M-119	A. Petersen	Closed	18.50	65.00
84-12-130	Witchy Boo! M-120	A. Petersen	Open	21.00	34.00
85-12-131	Pageant Wiseman M-121	A. Petersen	Closed	58.00	125-200.
85-12-132	Wise Man with Turban M-121a	A. Petersen	Open	28.00	34.00
85-12-133	Wise Man in Robe M-121b	A. Petersen	Open	26.00	32.00
85-12-134	Wise Man Kneeling M-121c	A. Petersen	Open	29.00	35.00
85-12-135	Pageant Shepherds M-122	A. Petersen	Closed	35.00	100-200.
85-12-136	Shepherd Kneeling M-122a	A. Petersen	Open	20.00	27.00
85-12-137	Shepherd Standing M-122b	A. Petersen	Open	20.00	27.00
85-12-138	Under the Chris-Mouse Tree M-123	A. Petersen	Open	48.00	74.00
85-12-139	Chris-Mouse Tree M-124	A. Petersen	Open	28.00	43.00
85-12-140	Quilting Bee M-125	W. Petersen	Open	30.00	40.00
85-12-141	Attic Treasure M-126	A. Petersen	Open	42.00	55.00
85-12-142	Family Portrait M-127	A. Petersen	Closed	54.00	225-300.
85-12-143	Strolling with Baby M-128	A. Petersen	Open	42.00	55.00
85-12-144	Piggy-Back Mousey M-129	W. Petersen	Closed	28.00	250-300.
85-12-145	Mouse Talk M-130	A. Petersen	Suspd.	44.00	75-125.00
85-12-146	Come Play! M-131	A. Petersen	Closed	18.00	50-100.00
85-12-147	Sunday Drivers M-132	W. Petersen	Open	58.00	110.00
85-12-148	Field Mouse M-133	W. Petersen	Open	46.00	82.00
86-12-149	First Date M-134	W. Petersen	Open	60.00	65.00
86-12-150	Waltzing Matilda M-135	W. Petersen	Suspd.	48.00	120-250.
86-12-151	Sweet Dreams M-136	A. Petersen	Closed	58.00	125-225.
92-12-152	Tuckered Out! M-136a	A. Petersen	Suspd.	46.00	46.00
86-12-153	First Haircut M-137	W. Petersen	Closed	58.00	125-200.
86-12-154	Fun Float M-138	W. Petersen	Open	34.00	36.00
86-12-155	Mouse on Campus M-139	W. Petersen	Closed	25.00	85-125.00
86-12-156	Just Checking M-140	A. Petersen	Open	34.00	39.00
86-12-157	Come & Get It! M-141	A. Petersen	Closed	34.00	100-165.
86-12-158	Christ-Mouse Stocking M-142	A. Petersen	Open	34.00	39.00
86-12-159	Down the Chimney M-143	A. Petersen	Closed	48.00	175-250.
87-12-160	Pageant Stable M-144	A. Petersen	Open	56.00	66.00
87-12-161	Pageant Angel M-145	A. Petersen	Open	19.00	23.00
87-12-162	Miss Noel M-146	A. Petersen	Open	32.00	38.00
87-12-163	Choir Mouse M-147	W. Petersen	Closed	23.00	50-75.00
87-12-164	Tooth Fairy M-148	A. Petersen	Open	32.00	37.00
87-12-165	Don't Cry! M-149	A. Petersen	Closed	33.00	75-100.00
87-12-166	Market Mouse M-150	W. Petersen	Suspd.	49.00	120.00
87-12-167	The Red Wagon M-151	W. Petersen	Closed	54.00	150-175.
87-12-168	Scooter Mouse M-152	W. Petersen	Open	34.00	39.00
87-12-169	Trumpeter M-153a	W. Petersen	Closed	29.00	50-90.00
87-12-170	Drummer M-153b	W. Petersen	Closed	29.00	50-90.00
87-12-171	Tuba Player M-153c	W. Petersen	Closed	29.00	50-90.00
87-12-172	Bat Mouse M-154	A. Petersen	Open	25.00	30.00
87-12-173	Littlest Witch and Skeleton M-155	A. Petersen	Open	49.00	57.00
87-12-174	Littlest Witch M-156	A. Petersen	Suspd.	24.00	28.00
87-12-175	Skeleton Mousey M-157	A. Petersen	Suspd.	27.00	72.00
88-12-176	Aloha! M-158	A. Petersen	Open	32.00	36.00
88-12-177	Forty Winks M-159	W. Petersen	Open	36.00	42.00
88-12-178	Mousey's Easter Basket M-160	A. Petersen	Suspd.	32.00	36.00
89-12-179	Commencement Day M-161	W. Petersen	Open	28.00	32.00
89-12-180	Prima Ballerina M-162	A. Petersen	Open	35.00	39.00
89-12-181	Elf Tales M-163	A. Petersen	Open	48.00	49.00
89-12-182	Father Chris-Mouse M-164	A. Petersen	Open	34.00	37.00
89-12-183	Haunted Mouse House M-165	D. Petersen	Open	125.00	168.00
90-12-184	Chris-Mouse Slipper M-166	A. Petersen	Open	35.00	38.00
90-12-185	Colleen O'Green M-167	A. Petersen	Open	40.00	44.00
90-12-186	Stars & Stripes M-168	A. Petersen	Open	34.00	37.00
90-12-187	Hans & Greta M-169	A. Petersen	Closed	64.00	100-160.
92-12-188	Hans M-169a	A. Petersen	Suspd.	35.00	75.00
92-12-189	Greta M-169b	A. Petersen	Suspd.	35.00	35.00
90-12-190	Polly's Parasol M-170	A. Petersen	Suspd.	39.00	42.00
90-12-191	Zelda M-171	A. Petersen	Open	37.00	42.00
91-12-192	Red Riding Hood at Grandmother's House M-172	D. Petersen	Open	295.00	295.00
91-12-193	Silent Night M-173	A. Petersen	Open	64.00	69.00
91-12-194	The Nutcracker M-174	D. Petersen	Open	49.00	53.00
91-12-195	Mousie's Egg Factory M-175	A. Petersen	Open	73.00	82.00
91-12-196	Grammy-Phone M-176	A. Petersen	Open	75.00	80.00
91-12-197	Tea For Three M-177	D. Petersen	Open	135.00	148.00
91-12-198	Night Prayer M-178	A. Petersen	Open	52.00	57.00
91-12-199	Sea Sounds M-179	A. Petersen	Open	34.00	37.00
91-12-200	April Showers M-180	A. Petersen	Open	27.00	31.00
91-12-201	Little Squirt M-181	W. Petersen	Open	49.00	52.00
92-12-202	Miss Daisy M-182	A. Petersen	Open	42.00	43.00
92-12-203	Peekaboo! M-183	D. Petersen	Open	52.00	52.00
92-12-204	Mrs. Mousey's Studio M-184	W. Petersen	Open	150.00	150.00
92-12-205	The Old Black Stove M-185	D. Petersen	Open	130.00	132.00
92-12-206	High on the Hog M-186	A. Petersen	Open	52.00	53.00
92-12-207	Adam's Apples M-187	A. Petersen	Open	148.00	148.00
92-12-208	Snow Buddies M-188	D. Petersen	Open	58.00	59.00
93-12-209	Little Mice Who Lived in a Shoe M-189	D. Petersen	Open	395.00	395.00
93-12-210	Peter Pumpkin Eater M-190	A. Petersen	Open	98.00	98.00
93-12-211	Christmas Eve M-191	A. Petersen	Open	145.00	145.00
93-12-212	First Kiss! M-192	A. Petersen	Open	65.00	65.00
93-12-213	Welcome Chick! M-193	A. Petersen	Open	64.00	64.00
93-12-214	The Mummy M-194	A. Petersen	Open	34.00	34.00
93-12-215	Lord & Lady Mousebatten M-195	A. Petersen	Open	85.00	85.00
93-12-216	One-Mouse Band M-196	A. Petersen	Open	95.00	95.00
Wee Forest Folk		**Minutemice**			
74-13-001	Mouse on Drum with Fife MM-1	A. Petersen	Closed	9.00	N/A
74-13-002	Mouse on Drum with Fife Wood Base MM-1a	A. Petersen	Closed	9.00	N/A
74-13-003	Mouse on Drum with Black Hat MM-2	A. Petersen	Closed	9.00	N/A
74-13-004	Mouse Carrying Large Drum MM-3	A. Petersen	Closed	8.00	N/A
74-13-005	Concordian On Drum with Glasses MM-4	A. Petersen	Closed	9.00	N/A
74-13-006	Concordian Wood Base w/Tan Coat MM-4a	A. Petersen	Closed	7.50	N/A
74-13-007	Concordian Wood Base w/Hat MM-4b	A. Petersen	Closed	8.00	N/A
74-13-008	Little Fifer on Drum with Fife MM-5	A. Petersen	Closed	8.00	N/A
74-13-009	Little Fifer on Wood Base MM-5a	A. Petersen	Closed	8.00	N/A
74-13-010	Little Fifer on Drum MM-5b	A. Petersen	Closed	8.00	N/A
79-13-011	Minute Mouse and Red Coat MM-9	W. Petersen	Open	28.00	28.00
79-13-012	Concord Minute Mouse MM-10	W. Petersen	Open	14.00	14-95.00
79-13-013	Red Coat Mouse MM-11	W. Petersen	Open	14.00	14-95.00
Wee Forest Folk		**Mouse Sports**			
75-14-001	Bobsled Three MS-1	A. Petersen	Closed	12.00	400-500.
75-14-002	Skater Mouse MS-2	A. Petersen	Closed	4.50	650.00
76-14-003	Mouse Skier MS-3	A. Petersen	Closed	4.25	300-400.
76-14-004	Tennis Star MS-4	A. Petersen	Closed	3.75	150-300.
76-14-005	Tennis Star MS-5	A. Petersen	Closed	3.75	150-300.
77-14-006	Skating Star Mouse MS-6	A. Petersen	Closed	3.75	250-400.
77-14-007	Golfer Mouse MS-7	A. Petersen	Closed	5.25	356.00
80-14-008	Skater Mouse MS-8	A. Petersen	Closed	16.50	250-450.
80-14-009	Skier Mouse MS-9	A. Petersen	Open	13.00	37.00
80-14-010	Skier Mouse (Red/Yellow, Red/Green) MS-9	A. Petersen	N/A	13.00	225-400.
81-14-011	Golfer Mouse MS-10	A. Petersen	Closed	15.50	250-350.
82-14-012	Two in a Canoe MS-11	W. Petersen	Open	29.00	57.00
84-14-013	Land Ho! MS-12	A. Petersen	Closed	36.50	182.00
84-14-014	Tennis Anyone? MS-13	A. Petersen	Closed	18.00	92-195.00
85-14-015	Fishin' Chip MS-14	W. Petersen	Closed	46.00	150-266.
89-14-016	Joe Di'Mousio MS-15	A. Petersen	Open	39.00	44.00
Wee Forest Folk		**Owls**			
74-15-001	Mr. and Mrs. Owl O-1	A. Petersen	Closed	6.00	300-400.
74-15-002	Mrs. Owl O-2	A. Petersen	Closed	3.00	150-300.
74-15-003	Mr. Owl O-3	A. Petersen	Closed	3.25	150-300.
75-15-004	Colonial Owls O-4	A. Petersen	Closed	11.50	350-500.
79-15-005	"Grad" Owl O-5	W. Petersen	Closed	4.25	350-550.
80-15-006	Graduate Owl (On Books) O-6	W. Petersen	Closed	12.00	330-500.
Wee Forest Folk		**Piggies**			
78-16-001	Miss Piggy School Marm P-1	A. Petersen	Closed	4.50	225-325.
78-16-002	Piggy Baker P-2	A. Petersen	Closed	4.50	225-425.
78-16-003	Jolly Tar Piggy P-3	A. Petersen	Closed	4.50	200-250.
78-16-004	Picnic Piggies P-4	A. Petersen	Closed	7.75	200-300.
78-16-005	Girl Piglet/Picnic Piggy P-5	A. Petersen	Closed	4.00	100-150.
78-16-006	Boy Piglet/ Picnic Piggy P-6	A. Petersen	Closed	4.00	100-150.
80-16-007	Piggy Ballerina P-7	A. Petersen	Closed	15.50	200-275.
80-16-008	Piggy Policeman P-8	A. Petersen	Closed	17.50	200-350.
80-16-009	Pig O' My Heart P-9	A. Petersen	Closed	12.00	200-275.
80-16-010	Nurse Piggy P-10	A. Petersen	Closed	15.50	200-225.
81-16-011	Holly Hog P-11	A. Petersen	Closed	25.00	350-425.
78-16-012	Piggy Jogger PS-1	A. Petersen	Closed	4.50	125-200.
Wee Forest Folk		**Raccoons**			
77-17-001	Mother Raccoon RC-1	A. Petersen	Closed	4.50	300-475.
77-17-002	Hiker Raccoon RC-2	A. Petersen	Closed	4.50	606.00
78-17-003	Bird Watcher Raccoon RC-3	A. Petersen	Closed	6.50	411.00
78-17-004	Raccoon Skater RCS-1	A. Petersen	Closed	4.75	250-400.
78-17-005	Raccoon Skier RCS-2	A. Petersen	Closed	6.00	350-450.
Wee Forest Folk		**Robin Hood Series**			
90-18-001	Robin Hood RH-1	A. Petersen	Open	37.00	40.00
90-18-002	Maid Marion RH-2	A. Petersen	Open	32.00	35.00
90-18-003	Friar Tuck RH-3	A. Petersen	Open	32.00	35.00
Wee Forest Folk		**Single Issues**			
72-19-001	Party Mouse in Sailor Suit	A. Petersen	Closed	N/A	N/A
72-19-002	Party Mouse with Bow Tie	A. Petersen	Closed	N/A	N/A
72-19-003	Party Mouse in Plain Dress	A. Petersen	Closed	N/A	N/A
72-19-004	Party Mouse in Polka-Dot Dress	A. Petersen	Closed	N/A	N/A
79-19-005	Ezra Ripley	A. Petersen	Open	40.00	40-95.00
79-19-006	Sarah Ripley	A. Petersen	Open	48.00	48-110.00
80-19-007	Cave Mouse	W. Petersen	Closed	N/A	500-600.

Company / Number	Name	Series / Artist	Edition Limit	Issue Price	Quote
80-19-008	Cave Mouse with Baby	W. Petersen	Closed	26.00	N/A
83-19-009	Wee Forest Folk Display Piece	A. Petersen	Open	70.00	70.00
Wee Forest Folk		**Tiny Teddies**			
83-20-001	Tiny Teddy TT-1	D. Petersen	Closed	16.00	100-200.
84-20-002	Little Teddy T-1	D. Petersen	Suspd.	20.00	186.00
84-20-003	Sailor Teddy T-2	D. Petersen	Suspd.	20.00	95-150.00
84-20-004	Boo Bear T-3	D. Petersen	Suspd.	20.00	100-155.
84-20-005	Drummer Bear T-4	D. Petersen	Suspd.	22.00	78-100.00
84-20-006	Santa Bear T-5	D. Petersen	Suspd.	27.00	100-150.
85-20-007	Ride 'em Teddy! T-6	D. Petersen	Suspd.	32.00	78-120.00
85-20-008	Seaside Teddy T-7	D. Petersen	Suspd.	28.00	78-100.00
86-20-009	Huggy Bear T-8	D. Petersen	Suspd.	26.00	78-100.00
87-20-010	Wedding Bears T-9	D. Petersen	Suspd.	54.00	104-150.
87-20-011	Christmas Teddy T-10	D. Petersen	Suspd.	26.00	78-90.00
88-20-012	Hansel & Gretel Bears@Witch's House T-11	D. Petersen	Suspd.	175.00	245.00
89-20-013	Momma Bear T-12	D. Petersen	Suspd.	27.00	36.00
Wee Forest Folk		**Wind in the Willows**			
82-21-001	Mole WW-1	A. Petersen	Closed	18.00	200-400.
82-21-002	Badger WW-2	A. Petersen	Closed	18.00	200-400.
82-21-003	Toad WW-3	W. Petersen	Closed	18.00	200-400.
82-21-004	Ratty WW-4	A. Petersen	Closed	18.00	200-400.

GRAPHICS

Company / Number	Name	Series / Artist	Edition Limit	Issue Price	Quote
American Artist		**Fred Stone**			
79-01-001	Affirmed, Steve Cauthen Up	F. Stone	750	100.00	600.00
88-01-002	Alysheba	F. Stone	950	195.00	650.00
92-01-003	The American Triple Crown I, 1948-1978	F. Stone	1,500	325.00	325.00
93-01-004	The American Triple Crown II, 1937-1946	F. Stone	1,500	325.00	325.00
93-01-005	The American Triple Crown III, 1919-1935	F. Stone	1,500	225.00	225.00
83-01-006	Andalusian, The	F. Stone	750	150.00	350.00
81-01-007	Arabians, The	F. Stone	750	115.00	525.00
89-01-008	Battle For The Triple Crown	F. Stone	950	225.00	650.00
80-01-009	Belmont-Bold Forbes, The	F. Stone	500	100.00	375.00
91-01-010	Black Stallion	F. Stone	1,500	225.00	250.00
88-01-011	Cam-Fella	F. Stone	950	175.00	350.00
81-01-012	Contentment	F. Stone	750	115.00	525.00
92-01-013	Dance Smartly-Pat Day Up	F. Stone	950	225.00	325.00
83-01-014	Duel, The	F. Stone	750	150.00	400.00
85-01-015	Eternal Legacy	F. Stone	950	175.00	950.00
80-01-016	Exceller-Bill Shoemaker	F. Stone	500	90.00	800.00
90-01-017	Final Tribute- Secretariat	F. Stone	1,150	265.00	1300.00
87-01-018	First Day, The	F. Stone	950	175.00	225.00
91-01-019	Forego	F. Stone	1,150	225.00	250.00
86-01-020	Forever Friends	F. Stone	950	175.00	725.00
85-01-021	Fred Stone Paints the Sport of Kings (Book)	F. Stone	750	265.00	750.00
80-01-022	Genuine Risk	F. Stone	500	100.00	700.00
91-01-023	Go For Wand-A Candle in the Wind	F. Stone	1,150	225.00	225.00
86-01-024	Great Match Race-Ruffian & Foolish Pleasure	F. Stone	950	175.00	375.00
81-01-025	John Henry-Bill Shoemaker Up	F. Stone	595	160.00	1500.00
85-01-026	John Henry-McCarron Up	F. Stone	750	175.00	500-750.
85-01-027	Kelso	F. Stone	950	175.00	750.00
80-01-028	Kentucky Derby, The	F. Stone	750	100.00	650.00
80-01-029	Kidnapped Mare-Franfreluche	F. Stone	750	115.00	575.00
87-01-030	Lady's Secret	F. Stone	950	175.00	425.00
82-01-031	Man O'War "Final Thunder"	F. Stone	750	175.00	2500-3100.
79-01-032	Mare and Foal	F. Stone	500	90.00	500.00
79-01-033	Moment After, The	F. Stone	500	90.00	350.00
86-01-034	Nijinski II	F. Stone	950	175.00	275.00
84-01-035	Northern Dancer	F. Stone	950	175.00	625.00
82-01-036	Off and Running	F. Stone	750	125.00	250-350.
90-01-037	Old Warriors Shoemaker-John Henry	F. Stone	1,950	265.00	595.00
79-01-038	One, Two, Three	F. Stone	500	100.00	1000.00
80-01-039	Pasture Pest, The	F. Stone	500	100.00	875.00
79-01-040	Patience	F. Stone	1,000	90.00	1200.00
89-01-041	Phar Lap	F. Stone	950	195.00	275.00
82-01-042	Power Horses, The	F. Stone	750	125.00	250.00
87-01-043	Rivalry-Alysheba and Bet Twice, The	F. Stone	950	195.00	550.00
79-01-044	Rivals-Affirmed & Alydar, The	F. Stone	500	90.00	500.00
83-01-045	Ruffian-For Only a Moment	F. Stone	750	175.00	1100.00
83-01-046	Secretariat	F. Stone	950	175.00	995-1200.
89-01-047	Shoe Bald Eagle	F. Stone	950	195.00	675.00
81-01-048	Shoe-8,000 Wins, The	F. Stone	395	200.00	7000.00
80-01-049	Spectacular Bid	F. Stone	500	65.00	350-400.
XX-01-050	Sunday Silence	F. Stone	950	195.00	425.00
81-01-051	Thoroughbreds, The	F. Stone	750	115.00	425.00
83-01-052	Tranquility	F. Stone	750	150.00	525.00
84-01-053	Turning For Home	F. Stone	750	150.00	425.00
82-01-054	Water Trough, The	F. Stone	750	125.00	575.00
Artaffects		**Perillo**			
77-01-001	Madre, S/N	G. Perillo	500	125.00	250-950.
78-01-002	Madonna of the Plains, S/N	G. Perillo	500	125.00	200-600.
78-01-003	Snow Pals, S/N	G. Perillo	500	125.00	150-550.
79-01-004	Sioux Scout and Buffalo Hunt, matched set	G. Perillo	500	150.00	250-850.
80-01-005	Babysitter, S/N	G. Perillo	3,000	45.00	125-350.
80-01-006	Puppies, S/N	G. Perillo	3,000	45.00	200-450.
81-01-007	Peaceable Kingdom, S/N	G. Perillo	950	100.00	375-800.
82-01-008	Tinker, S/N	G. Perillo	3,000	45.00	100-350.
82-01-009	Tender Love, S/N	G. Perillo	950	75.00	125-450.
82-01-010	Lonesome Cowboy, S/N	G. Perillo	950	75.00	100-450.
82-01-011	Chief Pontiac, S/N	G. Perillo	950	75.00	100.00
82-01-012	Hoofbeats, S/N	G. Perillo	950	100.00	150.00
82-01-013	Indian Style, S/N	G. Perillo	950	75.00	100.00
82-01-014	Maria, S/N	G. Perillo	550	150.00	350.00
82-01-015	Papoose, S/N	G. Perillo	950	125.00	125.00
83-01-016	The Moment Poster, S/N	G. Perillo	495	20.00	60.00
84-01-017	Out of the Forest, S/N	G. Perillo	Unkn.	Unkn.	450.00
84-01-018	Navajo Love, S/N	G. Perillo	300	125.00	700.00
85-01-019	Chief Crazy Horse, S/N	G. Perillo	950	125.00	450.00
85-01-020	Chief Sitting Bull, S/N	G. Perillo	500	125.00	350.00
85-01-021	Marigold, S/N	G. Perillo	500	125.00	150-450.
85-01-022	Whirlaway, S/N	G. Perillo	950	125.00	150.00
85-01-023	Secretariat, S/N	G. Perillo	950	125.00	150.00
86-01-024	The Rescue, S/N	G. Perillo	325	150.00	200-550.
86-01-025	War Pony, S/N	G. Perillo	325	150.00	250.00
86-01-026	Learning His Ways, S/N	G. Perillo	325	150.00	250.00
86-01-027	The Pout, S/N	G. Perillo	325	150.00	200-450.
88-01-028	Magnificent Seven, S/N	G. Perillo	950	125.00	125.00
88-01-029	By the Stream, S/N	G. Perillo	950	100.00	150.00
90-01-030	The Pack, S/N	G. Perillo	950	150.00	250.00

Company / Number	Name	Series / Artist	Edition Limit	Issue Price	Quote
Artaffects		**Grand Gallery Collection (Framed)**			
88-02-001	Tender Love	G. Perillo	2,500	75.00	90.00
88-02-002	Brave & Free	G. Perillo	2,500	75.00	175.00
88-02-003	Noble Heritage	G. Perillo	2,500	75.00	90.00
88-02-004	Chief Crazy Horse	G. Perillo	2,500	75.00	90.00
88-02-005	The Cheyenne Nation	G. Perillo	2,500	75.00	90.00
88-02-006	Late Mail	G. Perillo	2,500	75.00	90.00
88-02-007	The Peaceable Kingdom	G. Perillo	2,500	75.00	100.00
88-02-008	Chief Red Cloud	G. Perillo	2,500	75.00	90.00
88-02-009	The Last Frontier	G. Perillo	2,500	75.00	95.00
88-02-010	Native American	G. Perillo	2,500	75.00	90.00
88-02-011	Blackfoot Hunter	G. Perillo	2,500	75.00	90.00
88-02-012	Lily of the Mohawks	G. Perillo	2,500	75.00	90.00
88-02-013	Amy	MaGo	2,500	75.00	90.00
88-02-014	Mischief	MaGo	2,500	75.00	90.00
88-02-015	Tomorrows	MaGo	2,500	75.00	90.00
88-02-016	Lauren	MaGo	2,500	75.00	90.00
88-02-017	Visiting the Doctor	R. Sauber	2,500	75.00	90.00
88-02-018	Home Sweet Home	R. Sauber	2,500	75.00	90.00
88-02-019	God Bless America	R. Sauber	2,500	75.00	90.00
88-02-020	The Wedding	R. Sauber	2,500	75.00	90.00
88-02-021	Motherhood	R. Sauber	2,500	75.00	90.00
88-02-022	Venice	L. Marchetti	2,500	75.00	90.00
88-02-023	Paris	L. Marchetti	2,500	75.00	90.00
Artaffects		**Captured On Canvas**			
91-03-001	Brave and Free	G. Perillo	Open	195.00	195.00
Artaffects		**Members Only Limited Edition Redemption Offerings**			
84-04-001	Out of the Forest (Litho)	G. Perillo	Yr.Iss.	50.00	50.00
Artaffects		**Limited Edition Free Gifts to Members**			
83-05-001	Perillo/Cougar (Poster)	G. Perillo	Yr.Iss.	Gift	N/A
85-05-002	Litte Plum Blossom (Poster)	G. Perillo	Yr.Iss.	Gift	N/A
Artaffects		**Sauber**			
82-06-001	Butterfly	R. Sauber	3,000	45.00	100.00
Artaffects		**Mago**			
88-07-001	Serenity	Mago	950	95.00	200.00
88-07-002	Beth	Mago	950	95.00	200.00
88-07-003	Jessica	Mago	550	225.00	325.00
88-07-004	Sebastian	Mago	Pair	Pair	Pair
Artaffects		**Deneen**			
88-08-001	Twentieth Century Limited	J. Deneen	950	75.00	75.00
88-08-002	Santa Fe	J. Deneen	950	75.00	75.00
88-08-003	Empire Builder	J. Deneen	950	75.00	75.00
Marty Bell		**Limited Edition Lithographs**			
87-01-001	Alderton Village	M. Bell	S/O	235.00	750-899.
88-01-002	Allington Castle, Kent	M. Bell	S/O	540.00	540.00
92-01-003	Antiques of Rye	M. Bell	1,100	220.00	220.00
90-01-004	Arbor Cottage	M. Bell	S/O	130.00	150-250.
93-01-005	Arundel Row	M. Bell	750	130.00	130.00
91-01-006	Bay Tree Cottage, Rye	M. Bell	S/O	230.00	230-520.
81-01-007	Bibury Cottage	M. Bell	S/O	280.00	800-1000.
81-01-008	Big Daddy's Shoe	M. Bell	S/O	64.00	150-300.
88-01-009	Bishop's Roses, The	M. Bell	S/O	220.00	300-500.
89-01-010	Blush of Spring	M. Bell	S/O	96.00	120-160.
88-01-011	Bodiam Twilight	M. Bell	S/O	520.00	900-1100.
92-01-012	Briarwood	M. Bell	S/O	220.00	220.00
93-01-013	Broadway Cottage	M. Bell	750	330.00	330.00
87-01-014	Broughton Village	M. Bell	S/O	128.00	400-500.
84-01-015	Brown Eyes	M. Bell	S/O	296.00	296.00
90-01-016	Bryants Puddle Thatch	M. Bell	S/O	130.00	150-295.
86-01-017	Burford Village Store	M. Bell	S/O	106.00	500-1500.
93-01-018	Byfleet	M. Bell	900	180.00	180.00
94-01-019	Canterbury Roses	M. Bell	750	180.00	180.00
81-01-020	Castle Combe Cottage	M. Bell	S/O	230.00	795.00
93-01-021	Castle Tearoom, The	M. Bell	S/O	88.00	88.00
87-01-022	Chaplains Garden, The	M. Bell	S/O	235.00	1000-2000.
92-01-023	Chelsea Roses	M. Bell	750	298.00	298.00
89-01-024	Cherry Tree Thatch	M. Bell	2,400	88.00	88.00
91-01-025	Childswickham Morning	M. Bell	S/O	396.00	396.00
87-01-026	Chippenham Farm	M. Bell	S/O	120.00	300-900.
88-01-027	Clove Cottage	M. Bell	S/O	128.00	225-600.
88-01-028	Clover Lane Cottage	M. Bell	S/O	272.00	750-1400.
91-01-029	Cobblestone	M. Bell	1,200	374.00	374.00
93-01-030	Coln St. Aldwyn's	M. Bell	1,000	730.00	730.00
86-01-031	Cotswold Parish Church	M. Bell	S/O	98.00	500-1500.
88-01-032	Cotswold Twilight	M. Bell	S/O	128.00	200-495.
93-01-033	Cottontail Lodge	M. Bell	700	375.00	375.00
93-01-034	Craigton Cottage	M. Bell	500	130.00	130.00
82-01-035	Crossroads Cottage	M. Bell	S/O	38.00	200.00
92-01-036	Devon Cottage	M. Bell	900	374.00	374.00
91-01-037	Devon Roses	M. Bell	S/O	78.00	195-500.
91-01-038	Dorset Roses	M. Bell	S/O	96.00	195.00
87-01-039	Dove Cottage Garden	M. Bell	S/O	260.00	304-495.
87-01-040	Driftstone Manor	M. Bell	S/O	440.00	2500.00
87-01-041	Ducksbridge Cottage	M. Bell	S/O	400.00	2000-2400.
87-01-042	Eashing Cottage	M. Bell	S/O	120.00	200-400.
92-01-043	East Sussex Roses (Archival)	M. Bell	S/O	184.00	184.00
89-01-044	Elegance of Spring	M. Bell	1,800	396.00	396.00
89-01-045	Fernbank Cottage	M. Bell	2,400	96.00	88.00
85-01-046	Fiddleford Cottage	M. Bell	S/O	78.00	1950.00
89-01-047	Fireside Christmas	M. Bell	S/O	136.00	750.00
93-01-048	Flower Box, The	M. Bell	900	300.00	300.00
88-01-049	Friday Street Lane	M. Bell	S/O	280.00	450.00
89-01-050	The Game Keeper's Cottage	M. Bell	S/O	560.00	1800-2000.
92-01-051	Garlands Flower Shop	M. Bell	S/O	220.00	220.00
88-01-052	Ginger Cottage	M. Bell	S/O	320.00	550-800.
89-01-053	Glory Cottage	M. Bell	S/O	96.00	96.00
89-01-054	Goater's Cottage	M. Bell	S/O	368.00	400-560.
90-01-055	Gomshall Flower Shop	M. Bell	S/O	396.00	1200-2000
93-01-056	Graffam House	M. Bell	900	180.00	180.00
87-01-057	Halfway Cottage	M. Bell	S/O	260.00	300-550.
92-01-058	Happy Heart Cottage	M. Bell	1,200	368.00	368.00
89-01-059	Hideaway Cottage	M. Bell	2,400	88.00	88.00
92-01-060	Hollybush	M. Bell	1,200	560.00	560.00
91-01-061	Horsham Farmhouse	M. Bell	1,200	180.00	180.00
86-01-062	Housewives Choice	M. Bell	S/O	98.00	750-1000.
88-01-063	Icomb Village Garden	M. Bell	S/O	620.00	1350-1500.
88-01-064	Jasmine Thatch	M. Bell	S/O	272.00	495.00

Company Number	Name	Series Artist	Edition Limit	Issue Price	Quote
89-01-065	Larkspur Cottage	M. Bell	S/O	220.00	495.00
85-01-066	Little Boxford	M. Bell	S/O	156.00	300-900.
91-01-067	Little Bromley Lodge	M. Bell	1,200	456.00	456.00
91-01-068	Little Timbers	M. Bell	S/O	130.00	130.00
87-01-069	Little Tulip Thatch	M. Bell	S/O	120.00	400-700.
90-01-070	Little Well Thatch	M. Bell	S/O	130.00	150-250.
90-01-071	Longparish Cottage	M. Bell	S/O	368.00	300-550.
90-01-072	Longstock Lane	M. Bell	S/O	130.00	150-250.
86-01-073	Lorna Doone Cottage	M. Bell	S/O	380.00	8000-9000.
90-01-074	Lower Brockhampton Manor	M. Bell	S/O	640.00	1750-1800.
88-01-075	Lullabye Cottage	M. Bell	S/O	220.00	300-400.
90-01-076	Martin's Market, Rye	M. Bell	1,100	304.00	304.00
87-01-077	May Cottage	M. Bell	S/O	120.00	200-699.
88-01-078	Meadow School	M. Bell	S/O	220.00	350.00
85-01-079	Meadowlark Cottage	M. Bell	S/O	156.00	450-699.
90-01-080	Mermaid Inn, Rye, The	M. Bell	1,100	560.00	560.00
87-01-081	Millpond, Stockbridge, The	M. Bell	S/O	120.00	1000-1699.
92-01-082	Miss Hathaway's Garden	M. Bell	1,800	694.00	694.00
87-01-083	Morning Glory Cottage	M. Bell	S/O	120.00	450-599.
88-01-084	Morning's Glow	M. Bell	S/O	280.00	320-650.
88-01-085	Murrle Cottage	M. Bell	S/O	320.00	450-650.
83-01-086	Nestlewood	M. Bell	S/O	300.00	2500.00.
89-01-087	Northcote Lane	M. Bell	S/O	88.00	88.00
89-01-088	Old Beams Cottage	M. Bell	S/O	368.00	650.00
88-01-089	Old Bridge, Grasmere	M. Bell	S/O	640.00	640.00
90-01-090	Old Hertfordshire Thatch	M. Bell	S/O	396.00	700-1500.
93-01-091	Old Mother Hubbard's Cottage	M. Bell	2-Yr.	230.00	230.00
89-01-092	Overbrook	M. Bell	S/O	220.00	220.00
92-01-093	Pangbourne on Thames	M. Bell	900	304.00	304.00
84-01-094	Penshurst Tea Rooms (Archival)	M. Bell	S/O	335.00	950.00
84-01-095	Penshurst Tea Rooms (Canvas)	M. Bell	S/O	335.00	1500-3600.
89-01-096	Periwinkle Tea Rooms, The	M. Bell	S/O	694.00	694.00
89-01-097	Pride of Spring	M. Bell	S/O	96.00	200-400.
89-01-098	Primrose Cottage	M. Bell	2,400	88.00	88.00
88-01-099	Rodway Cottage	M. Bell	S/O	694.00	700-1500.
89-01-100	Rose Bedroom, The	M. Bell	S/O	388.00	388.00
90-01-101	Sanctuary	M. Bell	S/O	220.00	350.00
82-01-102	Sandhills Cottage	M. Bell	S/O	38.00	38.00
88-01-103	Sandy Lane Thatch	M. Bell	S/O	380.00	500.00
82-01-104	School Lane Cottage	M. Bell	S/O	38.00	38.00
93-01-105	Selborne Cottage	M. Bell	750	300.00	300.00
92-01-106	Sheffield Roses	M. Bell	750	298.00	298.00
88-01-107	Shere Village Antiques	M. Bell	S/O	272.00	304-699.
93-01-108	Simon the Pieman, Rye	M. Bell	1,100	240.00	240.00
91-01-109	Somerset Inn	M. Bell	1,200	180.00	180.00
93-01-110	Speldhurst Farm	M. Bell	900	248.00	248.00
81-01-111	Spring in the Santa Ynez	M. Bell	S/O	400.00	950.00
91-01-112	Springtime at Scotney	M. Bell	S/O	730.00	950-1200.
89-01-113	St. Martin's Ashurst	M. Bell	S/O	344.00	344.00
92-01-114	Strand Quay, Rye, The	M. Bell	1,100	248.00	248.00
90-01-115	Summer's Garden	M. Bell	S/O	78.00	400-800.
85-01-116	Summers Glow	M. Bell	S/O	98.00	600-1000.
87-01-117	Sunrise Thatch	M. Bell	S/O	120.00	200-300.
85-01-118	Surrey Garden House	M. Bell	S/O	98.00	850-1499.
91-01-119	Swan Cottage Tea Room, Rye	M. Bell	1,100	176.00	176.00
89-01-120	Sweet Blue	M. Bell	1,800	396.00	396.00
90-01-121	Sweetheart Thatch	M. Bell	S/O	220.00	220.00
85-01-122	Sweet Pine Cottage	M. Bell	S/O	78.00	350-1499.
88-01-123	Sweet Twilight	M. Bell	S/O	220.00	350-600.
91-01-124	Tea Time	M. Bell	S/O	130.00	130-350.
82-01-125	Thatchcolm Cottage	M. Bell	S/O	38.00	38.00
89-01-126	Thimble Pub, The	M. Bell	S/O	344.00	344.00
93-01-127	Tithe Barn Cottage	M. Bell	900	368.00	368.00
93-01-128	Umbrella Cottage	M. Bell	900	176.00	176.00
91-01-129	Upper Chute	M. Bell	S/O	496.00	850-1500.
92-01-130	Valentine Cottage	M. Bell	900	304.00	304.00
87-01-131	The Vicar's Gate	M. Bell	S/O	110.00	600-1500.
87-01-132	Wakehurst Place	M. Bell	S/O	480.00	2000-2500.
87-01-133	Well Cottage, Sandy Lane	M. Bell	S/O	440.00	650-1500.
91-01-134	Wepham Cottage	M. Bell	S/O	396.00	1200.00
84-01-135	West Kington Dell	M. Bell	S/O	215.00	480-999.
94-01-136	Westminster Roses	M. Bell	750	180.00	180.00
90-01-137	Weston Manor	M. Bell	900	694.00	694.00
92-01-138	West Sussex Roses (Archival)	M. Bell	S/O	184.00	184.00
87-01-139	White Lilac Thatch	M. Bell	S/O	260.00	400-700.
92-01-140	Wild Rose Cottage	M. Bell	S/O	248.00	248.00
85-01-141	Windsong Cottage	M. Bell	S/O	156.00	350-799.
91-01-142	Windward Cottage, Rye	M. Bell	S/O	228.00	550-635.
91-01-143	Ye Olde Bell, Rye	M. Bell	1,100	196.00	196.00
86-01-144	York Garden Shop	M. Bell	S/O	98.00	250-999.
Marty Bell		**Members Only Collectors Club**			
91-02-001	Little Thatch Twilight	M. Bell	Closed	288.00	320-380.
91-02-002	Charter Rose, The	M. Bell	Closed	Gift	N/A
92-02-003	Candle At Eventide	M. Bell	Closed	Gift	N/A
92-02-004	Blossom Lane	M. Bell	Closed	288.00	288.00
93-02-005	Laverstoke Lodge	M. Bell	Closed	328.00	328.00
93-02-006	Chideock Gate	M. Bell	Closed	Gift	N/A
94-02-007	Hummingbird Hill	M. Bell	Yr.Iss.	320.00	320.00
94-02-008	The Hummingbird	M. Bell	Yr.Iss.	Gift	N/A
Marty Bell		**America the Beautiful**			
93-03-001	Abbey, The	M. Bell	750	400.00	400.00
94-03-002	Bayside Morning	M. Bell	750	400.00	400.00
93-03-003	Idaho Hideaway	M. Bell	750	400.00	400.00
94-03-004	Jones Victorian	M. Bell	750	400.00	400.00
94-03-005	Love Tide	M. Bell	750	400.00	400.00
94-03-006	My Garden	M. Bell	750	430.00	430.00
93-03-007	Turlock Spring	M. Bell	500	700.00	700.00
Marty Bell		**Christmas**			
90-04-001	Ready For Christmas	M. Bell	S/O	148.00	495.00
91-04-002	Christmas in Rochester	M. Bell	S/O	148.00	275-350.
92-04-003	McCoy's Toy Shoppe	M. Bell	S/O	148.00	350.00
93-04-004	Christmas Treasures	M. Bell	900	200.00	200.00
Circle Fine Art		**Rockwell**			
XX-01-001	American Family Folio	N. Rockwell	200	Unkn.	17500.00
XX-01-002	The Artist at Work	N. Rockwell	130	Unkn.	3500.00
XX-01-003	At the Barber	N. Rockwell	200	Unkn.	4900.00
XX-01-004	Autumn	N. Rockwell	200	Unkn.	3500.00
XX-01-005	Autumn/Japon	N. Rockwell	25	Unkn.	3600.00
XX-01-006	Aviary	N. Rockwell	200	Unkn.	4200.00
XX-01-007	Barbershop Quartet	N. Rockwell	200	Unkn.	4200.00

Company Number	Name	Series Artist	Edition Limit	Issue Price	Quote
XX-01-008	Baseball	N. Rockwell	200	Unkn.	3600.00
XX-01-009	Ben Franklin's Philadelphia	N. Rockwell	200	Unkn.	3600.00
XX-01-010	Ben's Belles	N. Rockwell	200	Unkn.	3500.00
XX-01-011	The Big Day	N. Rockwell	200	Unkn.	3400.00
XX-01-012	The Big Top	N. Rockwell	148	Unkn.	2800.00
XX-01-013	Blacksmith Shop	N. Rockwell	200	Unkn.	6300.00
XX-01-014	Bookseller	N. Rockwell	200	Unkn.	2700.00
XX-01-015	Bookseller/Japon	N. Rockwell	25	Unkn.	2750.00
XX-01-016	The Bridge	N. Rockwell	200	Unkn.	3100.00
XX-01-017	Cat	N. Rockwell	200	Unkn.	3400.00
XX-01-018	Cat/Collotype	N. Rockwell	200	Unkn.	4000.00
XX-01-019	Cheering	N. Rockwell	200	Unkn.	3600.00
XX-01-020	Children at Window	N. Rockwell	200	Unkn.	3600.00
XX-01-021	Church	N. Rockwell	200	Unkn.	3400.00
XX-01-022	Church/Collotype	N. Rockwell	200	Unkn.	4000.00
XX-01-023	Circus	N. Rockwell	200	Unkn.	2650.00
XX-01-024	County Agricultural Agent	N. Rockwell	200	Unkn.	3900.00
XX-01-025	The Critic	N. Rockwell	200	Unkn.	4650.00
XX-01-026	Day in the Life of a Boy	N. Rockwell	200	Unkn.	6200.00
XX-01-027	Day in the Life of a Boy/Japon	N. Rockwell	25	Unkn.	6500.00
XX-01-028	Debut	N. Rockwell	200	Unkn.	3600.00
XX-01-029	Discovery	N. Rockwell	200	Unkn.	5900.00
XX-01-030	Doctor and Boy	N. Rockwell	200	Unkn.	9400.00
XX-01-031	Doctor and Doll-Signed	N. Rockwell	200	Unkn.	11900.00
XX-01-032	Dressing Up/Pencil	N. Rockwell	200	Unkn.	3700.00
XX-01-033	Dressing Up/Ink	N. Rockwell	60	Unkn.	4400.00
XX-01-034	The Drunkard	N. Rockwell	200	Unkn.	3600.00
XX-01-035	The Expected and Unexpected	N. Rockwell	200	Unkn.	3700.00
XX-01-036	Family Tree	N. Rockwell	200	Unkn.	5900.00
XX-01-037	Fido's House	N. Rockwell	200	Unkn.	3600.00
XX-01-038	Football Mascot	N. Rockwell	200	Unkn.	3700.00
XX-01-039	Four Seasons Folio	N. Rockwell	200	Unkn.	13500.00
XX-01-040	Four Seasons Folio/Japon	N. Rockwell	25	Unkn.	14000.00
XX-01-041	Freedom from Fear-Signed	N. Rockwell	200	Unkn.	6400.00
XX-01-042	Freedom from Want-Signed	N. Rockwell	200	Unkn.	6400.00
XX-01-043	Freedom of Speech-Signed	N. Rockwell	200	Unkn.	6400.00
XX-01-044	Freedom of Religion-Signed	N. Rockwell	200	Unkn.	6400.00
XX-01-045	Gaiety Dance Team	N. Rockwell	200	Unkn.	4300.00
XX-01-046	Girl at Mirror-Signed	N. Rockwell	200	Unkn.	8400.00
XX-01-047	The Golden Age	N. Rockwell	200	Unkn.	3500.00
XX-01-048	Golden Rule-Signed	N. Rockwell	200	Unkn.	4400.00
XX-01-049	Golf	N. Rockwell	200	Unkn.	3600.00
XX-01-050	Gossips	N. Rockwell	200	Unkn.	5000.00
XX-01-051	Gossips/Japon	N. Rockwell	25	Unkn.	5100.00
XX-01-052	Grotto	N. Rockwell	200	Unkn.	3400.00
XX-01-053	Grotto/Collotype	N. Rockwell	200	Unkn.	4000.00
XX-01-054	High Dive	N. Rockwell	200	Unkn.	3400.00
XX-01-055	The Homecoming	N. Rockwell	200	Unkn.	3700.00
XX-01-056	The House	N. Rockwell	200	Unkn.	3700.00
XX-01-057	Huck Finn Folio	N. Rockwell	200	Unkn.	35000.00
XX-01-058	Ichabod Crane	N. Rockwell	200	Unkn.	6700.00
XX-01-059	The Inventor	N. Rockwell	200	Unkn.	4100.00
XX-01-060	Jerry	N. Rockwell	200	Unkn.	4700.00
XX-01-061	Jim Got Down on His Knees	N. Rockwell	200	Unkn.	4500.00
XX-01-062	Lincoln	N. Rockwell	200	Unkn.	11400.00
XX-01-063	Lobsterman	N. Rockwell	200	Unkn.	5500.00
XX-01-064	Lobsterman/Japon	N. Rockwell	25	Unkn.	5750.00
XX-01-065	Marriage License	N. Rockwell	200	Unkn.	6900.00
XX-01-066	Medicine	N. Rockwell	200	Unkn.	3400.00
XX-01-067	Medicine/Color Litho	N. Rockwell	200	Unkn.	4000.00
XX-01-068	Miss Mary Jane	N. Rockwell	200	Unkn.	4500.00
XX-01-069	Moving Day	N. Rockwell	200	Unkn.	3900.00
XX-01-070	My Hand Shook	N. Rockwell	200	Unkn.	4500.00
XX-01-071	Music Hath Charms	N. Rockwell	200	Unkn.	4200.00
XX-01-072	Out the Window	N. Rockwell	200	Unkn.	3400.00
XX-01-073	Out the Window/ Collotype	N. Rockwell	200	Unkn.	4000.00
XX-01-074	Outward Bound-Signed	N. Rockwell	200	Unkn.	7900.00
XX-01-075	Poor Richard's Almanac	N. Rockwell	200	Unkn.	24000.00
XX-01-076	Prescription	N. Rockwell	200	Unkn.	4900.00
XX-01-077	Prescription/Japon	N. Rockwell	25	Unkn.	5000.00
XX-01-078	The Problem We All Live With	N. Rockwell	200	Unkn.	4500.00
XX-01-079	Puppies	N. Rockwell	200	Unkn.	3700.00
XX-01-080	Raliegh the Dog	N. Rockwell	200	Unkn.	3900.00
XX-01-081	Rocket Ship	N. Rockwell	200	Unkn.	3650.00
XX-01-082	The Royal Crown	N. Rockwell	200	Unkn.	3500.00
XX-01-083	Runaway	N. Rockwell	200	Unkn.	3800.00
XX-01-084	Runaway/Japon	N. Rockwell	200	Unkn.	5700.00
XX-01-085	Safe and Sound	N. Rockwell	200	Unkn.	3800.00
XX-01-086	Saturday People	N. Rockwell	200	Unkn.	3300.00
XX-01-087	Save Me	N. Rockwell	200	Unkn.	3600.00
XX-01-088	Saying Grace-Signed	N. Rockwell	200	Unkn.	7400.00
XX-01-089	School Days Folio	N. Rockwell	200	Unkn.	14000.00
XX-01-090	Schoolhouse	N. Rockwell	200	Unkn.	4500.00
XX-01-091	Schoolhouse/Japon	N. Rockwell	25	Unkn.	4650.00
XX-01-092	See America First	N. Rockwell	200	Unkn.	5650.00
XX-01-093	See America First/Japon	N. Rockwell	25	Unkn.	6100.00
XX-01-094	Settling In	N. Rockwell	200	Unkn.	3600.00
XX-01-095	Shuffelton's Barbershop	N. Rockwell	200	Unkn.	7400.00
XX-01-096	Smoking	N. Rockwell	200	Unkn.	3400.00
XX-01-097	Smoking/Collotype	N. Rockwell	200	Unkn.	4000.00
XX-01-098	Spanking	N. Rockwell	200	Unkn.	3400.00
XX-01-099	Spanking/ Collotype	N. Rockwell	200	Unkn.	4000.00
XX-01-100	Spelling Bee	N. Rockwell	200	Unkn.	6500.00
XX-01-101	Spring	N. Rockwell	200	Unkn.	3500.00
XX-01-102	Spring/Japon	N. Rockwell	25	Unkn.	3600.00
XX-01-103	Spring Flowers	N. Rockwell	200	Unkn.	5200.00
XX-01-104	Study for the Doctor's Office	N. Rockwell	200	Unkn.	6000.00
XX-01-105	Studying	N. Rockwell	200	Unkn.	3600.00
XX-01-106	Summer	N. Rockwell	200	Unkn.	3500.00
XX-01-107	Summer/Japon	N. Rockwell	25	Unkn.	3600.00
XX-01-108	Summer Stock	N. Rockwell	200	Unkn.	4900.00
XX-01-109	Summer Stock/Japon	N. Rockwell	25	Unkn.	5000.00
XX-01-110	The Teacher	N. Rockwell	200	Unkn.	3400.00
XX-01-111	The Teacher/Japon	N. Rockwell	25	Unkn.	3500.00
XX-01-112	Teacher's Pet	N. Rockwell	200	Unkn.	3600.00
XX-01-113	The Texan	N. Rockwell	200	Unkn.	3700.00
XX-01-114	Then For Three Minutes	N. Rockwell	200	Unkn.	4500.00
XX-01-115	Then Miss Watson	N. Rockwell	200	Unkn.	4500.00
XX-01-116	There Warn't No Harm	N. Rockwell	200	Unkn.	4500.00
XX-01-117	Three Farmers	N. Rockwell	200	Unkn.	3600.00
XX-01-118	Ticketseller	N. Rockwell	200	Unkn.	4200.00
XX-01-119	Ticketseller/Japon	N. Rockwell	25	Unkn.	4400.00
XX-01-120	Tom Sawyer Color Suite	N. Rockwell	200	Unkn.	30000.00
XX-01-121	Tom Sawyer Folio	N. Rockwell	200	Unkn.	26500.00

Number	Name	Artist	Edition Limit	Issue Price	Quote
XX-01-122	Top of the World	N. Rockwell	200	Unkn.	4200.00
XX-01-123	Trumpeter	N. Rockwell	200	Unkn.	3900.00
XX-01-124	Trumpeter/Japon	N. Rockwell	25	Unkn.	4100.00
XX-01-125	Two O'Clock Feeding	N. Rockwell	200	Unkn.	3600.00
XX-01-126	The Village Smithy	N. Rockwell	200	Unkn.	3500.00
XX-01-127	Welcome	N. Rockwell	200	Unkn.	3500.00
XX-01-128	Wet Paint	N. Rockwell	200	Unkn.	3800.00
XX-01-129	When I Lit My Candle	N. Rockwell	200	Unkn.	4500.00
XX-01-130	White Washing	N. Rockwell	200	Unkn.	3400.00
XX-01-131	Whitewashing the Fence/Collotype	N. Rockwell	200	Unkn.	4000.00
XX-01-132	Window Washer	N. Rockwell	200	Unkn.	4800.00
XX-01-133	Winter	N. Rockwell	200	Unkn.	3500.00
XX-01-134	Winter/Japon	N. Rockwell	25	Unkn.	3600.00
XX-01-135	Ye Old Print Shoppe	N. Rockwell	200	Unkn.	3500.00
XX-01-136	Your Eyes is Lookin'	N. Rockwell	200	Unkn.	4500.00
Cross Gallery, Inc.		**Limited Edition Prints**			
83-01-001	Isbaaloo Eetshiileehcheek(Sorting Her Beads)	P.A. Cross	S/O	150.00	1750.00
83-01-002	Ayla-Sah-Xuh-Xah (Pretty Colours, Many Designs)	P.A. Cross	S/O	150.00	450.00
84-01-003	Blue Beaded Hair Ties	P.A. Cross	S/O	85.00	330.00
84-01-004	Profile of Caroline	P.A. Cross	S/O	85.00	185.00
84-01-005	Whistling Water Clan Girl: Crow Indian	P.A. Cross	S/O	85.00	85.00
84-01-006	Thick Lodge Clan Boy: Crow Indian	P.A. Cross	475	85.00	85.00
85-01-007	The Water Vision	P.A. Cross	S/O	150.00	325.00
86-01-008	The Winter Shawl	P.A. Cross	S/O	150.00	1600.00
86-01-009	The Red Capote	P.A. Cross	S/O	150.00	850.00
86-01-010	Grand Entry	P.A. Cross	S/O	85.00	85.00
84-01-011	Winter Morning	P.A. Cross	S/O	185.00	1450.00
84-01-012	Dii-tah-shteh Ee-wihza-ahook (A Coat of much Value)	P.A. Cross	S/O	90.00	740.00
87-01-013	Caroline	P.A. Cross	S/O	45.00	145.00
87-01-014	Tina	P.A. Cross	S/O	45.00	110.00
87-01-015	The Red Necklace	P.A. Cross	S/O	90.00	210.00
87-01-016	The Elkskin Robe	P.A. Cross	S/O	190.00	640.00
88-01-017	Ma-a-luppis-she-La-dus (She is above everything, nothing can touch her)	P.A. Cross	S/O	190.00	525.00
88-01-018	Dance Apache	P.A. Cross	S/O	190.00	360.00
89-01-019	The Dreamer	P.A. Cross	S/O	190.00	600.00
89-01-020	Chey-ayjeh: Prey	P.A. Cross	S/O	190.00	325-600.
89-01-021	Teesa Waits To Dance	P.A. Cross	S/O	135.00	180.00
89-01-022	Biaachee-itah Bah-achbeh	P.A. Cross	S/O	225.00	525.00
90-01-023	Baape Ochia (Night Wind, Turquoise)	P.A. Cross	S/O	185.00	370.00
90-01-024	Ishia-Kahda #1 (Quiet One)	P.A. Cross	S/O	185.00	400.00
90-01-025	Eshte	P.A. Cross	S/O	185.00	200.00
91-01-026	The Blue Shawl	P.A. Cross	S/O	185.00	275.00
91-01-027	Ashpahdua Hagay Ashae-Gyoke (My Home & Heart Is Crow)	P.A. Cross	S/O	225.00	225-350.
94-01-028	Winter Girl Bride	P.A. Cross	1,730	225.00	225.00
Cross Gallery, Inc		**Star Quilt Series**			
85-02-001	Winter Warmth	P.A. Cross	S/O	150.00	900-1215.
86-02-002	Reflections	P.A. Cross	S/O	185.00	865.00
88-02-003	The Quilt Makers	P.A. Cross	S/O	190.00	1200.00
Cross Gallery, Inc.		**Wolf Series**			
85-03-001	Dii-tah-shteh Bii-wik; Chedah-bah liidah	P.A. Cross	S/O	185.00	3275.00
87-03-002	The Morning Star Gives Long Otter His Hoop Medicine Power	P.A. Cross	S/O	190.00	1800-2500.
89-03-003	Biagoht Eecuebeh Hehsheesh-Checah: (Red Ridinghood and Her Wolves), Gift I	P.A. Cross	S/O	225.00	1500-2500.
90-03-004	Agninaug Amaguut;Inupiag (Women With Her Wolves)	P.A. Cross	S/O	325.00	350-750.
93-03-005	Ahmah-ghut, Tuhtu-loo; Eelahn-nuht Kah-auhk (Wolves and Caribou; My Furs and My Friends)	P.A. Cross	1,050	255.00	255.00.
Cross Gallery, Inc.		**Half Breed Series**			
89-04-001	Ach-hua Dlubh: (Body Two), Half Breed	P.A. Cross	S/O	190.00	1450.00
89-04-002	Ach-hua Dlubh: (Body Two), Half Breed II	P.A. Cross	S/O	225.00	800-1100.
90-04-003	Ach-hua Dlubh: (Body Two), Half Breed III	P.A. Cross	S/O	225.00	850.00
Cross Gallery, Inc.		**Limited Edition Original Graphics**			
87-05-001	Caroline, Stone Lithograph	P.A. Cross	S/O	300.00	600.00
88-05-002	Maidenhood Hopi, Stone Lithograph	P.A. Cross	S/O	950.00	1150.00
89-05-003	The Red Capote, Serigraph	P.A. Cross	S/O	750.00	1150.00
89-05-004	Rosapina, Etching	P.A. Cross	74	1200.00	1200.00
90-05-005	Nighteyes, I, Serigraph	P.A. Cross	S/O	225.00	425.00
Cross Gallery, Inc.		**Miniature Line**			
91-06-001	BJ	P.A. Cross	447	80.00	80.00
91-06-002	Watercolour Study #2 For Half Breed	P.A. Cross	447	80.00	80.00
91-06-003	The Floral Shawl	P.A. Cross	447	80.00	80.00
91-06-004	Kendra	P.A. Cross	447	80.00	80.00
93-06-005	Sundown	P.A. Cross	447	80.00	80.00
93-06-006	Daybreak	P.A. Cross	447	80.00	80.00
93-06-007	Ponytails	P.A. Cross	447	80.00	80.00
93-06-008	Braids	P.A. Cross	447	80.00	80.00
Cross Gallery, Inc.		**The Painted Ladies' Suite**			
92-07-001	The Painted Ladies	P.A. Cross	S/O	225.00	1200.00
92-07-002	Avisola	P.A. Cross	475	185.00	185.00
92-07-003	Itza-chu (Apache; The Eagle)	P.A. Cross	475	185.00	185.00
92-07-004	Kel'hoya (Hopi; Little Sparrow Hawk)	P.A. Cross	475	185.00	185.00
92-07-005	Dah-say (Crow; Heart)	P.A. Cross	475	185.00	185.00
92-07-006	Tze-go-juni (Chiricahua Apache)	P.A. Cross	447	80.00	80.00
92-07-007	Sus(h)gah-daydus(h) (Crow; Quick)	P.A. Cross	447	80.00	80.00
92-07-008	Acoria (Crow; Seat of Honor)	P.A. Cross	475	185.00	185.00
Cross Gallery, Inc.		**The Gift**			
89-08-001	B' Achua Dlubh-bia Bii Noskiiyahi The Gift, Part II	P.A. Cross	S/O	225.00	650.00
93-08-002	The Gift, Part III	P.A. Cross	S/O	225.00	350-1000.
Gartlan USA		**Lithograph**			
86-01-001	George Brett-"The Swing"	J. Martin	2,000	85.00	150.00
87-01-002	Roger Staubach	C. Soileau	1,979	85.00	125.00
89-01-003	Kareem Abdul Jabbar-The Record Setter	M. Taylor	1,989	85.00	175-225.
90-01-004	Darryl Strawberry	M. Taylor	500	295.00	295.00
91-01-005	Darryl Strawberry, signed Artist Proof	M. Taylor	50	395.00	395.00
91-01-006	Joe Montana	M. Taylor	500	495.00	495.00
91-01-007	Negro League 1st World Series (print)	Unknown	1,924	109.00	109.00

Number	Name	Artist	Edition Limit	Issue Price	Quote
Gartlan USA		**Gallery Series I**			
92-02-001	Wayne Gretzky (16x20) Tri-Cut	M. Taylor	500	195.00	195.00
92-02-002	Ken Griffey Jr. (16x20) Tri-Cut	M. Taylor	500	195.00	195.00
92-02-003	Joe Montana (16x20) Tri-Cut	M. Taylor	500	195.00	195.00
92-02-004	Brett Hull (16x20) Tri-Cut	M. Taylor	500	195.00	195.00
Gartlan USA		**Gallery Series 2**			
92-03-001	Yogi Berra (12x20 w/8 1/2" plate)	M. Taylor	950	89.00	89.00
92-03-002	Rod Carew (12x20 w/8 1/2" plate)	M. Taylor	950	89.00	89.00
92-03-003	Carlton Fisk (12x20 w/8 1/2" plate)	M. Taylor	950	89.00	89.00
92-03-004	Whitey Ford (12x20 w/8 1/2" plate)	M. Taylor	950	89.00	89.00
92-03-005	Wayne Gretzky (12x20 w/8 1/2" plate)	M. Taylor	950	89.00	89.00
92-03-006	Ken Griffey Jr. (12x20 w/8 1/2" plate)	M. Taylor	950	89.00	89.00
92-03-007	Gordy Howe (12x20 w/8 1/2" plate)	M. Taylor	950	89.00	89.00
92-03-008	Joe Montana (12x20 w/8 1/2" plate)	M. Taylor	950	89.00	89.00
92-03-009	Tom Seaver (12x20 w/8 1/2" plate)	M. Taylor	950	89.00	89.00
92-03-010	John Wooden (12x20 w/8 1/2" plate)	M. Taylor	950	89.00	89.00
92-03-011	Carl Yastrzemski (12x20 w/8 1/2" plate)	M. Taylor	950	89.00	89.00
92-03-012	Brett & Bobby Hull (12x20 w/8 1/2" plate)	M. Taylor	950	89.00	89.00
Gartlan USA		**Gallery Series 3**			
92-04-001	Wayne Gretzky (12x16 w/photo)	M. Taylor	Open	79.00	79.00
92-04-002	Ken Griffey, Jr. (12x16 w/photo)	M. Taylor	Open	79.00	79.00
92-04-003	Joe Montana (12x16 w/photo)	M. Taylor	Open	79.00	79.00
92-04-004	Brett Hull (12x16 w/photo)	M. Taylor	Open	79.00	79.00
Gartlan USA		**Gallery Series 4**			
92-05-001	Wayne Gretzky (8x10 w/mini fig.)	M. Taylor	950	89.00	89.00
92-05-002	Carlton Fisk (8x10 w/mini fig.)	M. Taylor	950	89.00	89.00
92-05-003	Ken Griffey, Jr. (8x10 w/mini fig.)	M. Taylor	950	89.00	89.00
92-05-004	Brett Hull (8x10 w/mini fig.)	M. Taylor	950	89.00	89.00
92-05-005	Gordie Howe (8x10 w/mini fig.)	M. Taylor	950	89.00	89.00
92-05-006	Joe Montana (8x10 w/mini fig.)	M. Taylor	950	89.00	89.00
92-05-007	Tom Seaver (8x10 w/mini fig.)	M. Taylor	950	89.00	89.00
92-05-008	Carl Yastrzemski (8x10 w/mini fig.)	M. Taylor	950	89.00	89.00
92-05-009	George Brett (8x10 w/mini fig. & signed rounder)	J. Martin	300	125.00	125.00
Gartlan USA		**Gallery Series 5**			
92-06-001	Carlton Fisk (8x10)	M. Taylor	950	69.00	69.00
92-06-002	Wayne Gretzky (8x10)	M. Taylor	950	69.00	69.00
92-06-003	Ken Griffey, Jr. (8x10)	M. Taylor	950	69.00	69.00
92-06-004	Brett Hull (8x10)	M. Taylor	950	69.00	69.00
92-06-005	Gordie Howe (8x10)	M. Taylor	950	69.00	69.00
92-06-006	Joe Montana (8x10)	M. Taylor	950	69.00	69.00
92-06-007	Tom Seaver (8x10)	M. Taylor	950	69.00	69.00
92-06-008	Carl Yastrzemski (8x10)	M. Taylor	950	69.00	69.00
92-06-009	George Brett (8x10)	J. Martin	3,000	59.00	59.00
94-06-010	Wayne Gretzky & Gordie Howe (8x10)	M. Taylor	999	69.00	69.00
Greenwich Workshop		**Doolittle**			
79-01-001	Pintos	B. Doolittle	1,000	65.00	8000.00
80-01-002	Good Omen, The	B. Doolittle	1,000	85.00	5000.00
80-01-003	Bugged Bear	B. Doolittle	1,000	85.00	2000.00
80-01-004	Whoo !?	B. Doolittle	1,000	75.00	1500.00
81-01-005	Woodland Encounter	B. Doolittle	1,500	145.00	8000.00
81-01-006	Unknown Presence	B. Doolittle	1,500	150.00	2200.00
81-01-007	Spirit of the Grizzly	B. Doolittle	1,500	150.00	3000.00
82-01-008	Eagle's Flight	B. Doolittle	1,500	185.00	3000.00
83-01-009	Escape by a Hare	B. Doolittle	1,500	80.00	600.00
83-01-010	Rushing War Eagle	B. Doolittle	1,500	150.00	1000.00
83-01-011	Art of Camouflage, signed	B. Doolittle	2,000	55.00	450.00
83-01-012	Runs With Thunder	B. Doolittle	1,500	150.00	1500.00
83-01-013	Christmas Day, Give or Take a Week	B. Doolittle	4,581	80.00	1700.00
84-01-014	Let My Spirit Soar	B. Doolittle	1,500	195.00	3500.00
84-01-015	Forest Has Eyes, The	B. Doolittle	8,544	175.00	4000.00
85-01-016	Wolves of the Crow	B. Doolittle	2,650	225.00	1650.00
85-01-017	Two Indian Horses	B. Doolittle	12,253	225.00	3000.00
86-01-018	Where Silence Speaks, Doolittle The Art of Bev Doolittle	B. Doolittle	3,500	650.00	3300.00
86-01-019	Two Bears of the Blackfeet	B. Doolittle	2,650	225.00	1000.00
87-01-020	Guardian Spirits	B. Doolittle	13,238	295.00	1000.00
87-01-021	Calling the Buffalo	B. Doolittle	8,500	245.00	1200.00
87-01-022	Season of the Eagle	B. Doolittle	36,548	245.00	650.00
88-01-023	Doubled Back	B. Doolittle	15,000	245.00	1200.00
89-01-024	Sacred Ground	B. Doolittle	69,996	265.00	600.00
90-01-025	Hide and Seek Suite	B. Doolittle	25,000	1200.00	1200.00
90-01-025	Hide and Seek (Composite & Video)	B. Doolittle	25,000	300.00	300.00
91-01-026	The Sentinel	B. Doolittle	35,000	275.00	650.00
91-01-027	Sacred Circle (Print & Video)	B. Doolittle	40,192	325.00	325.00
92-01-028	Walk Softly (Chapbook)	B. Doolittle	40,192	225.00	225.00
92-01-029	Eagle Heart	B. Doolittle	48,000	285.00	285.00
93-01-030	Wilderness? Wilderness!	B. Doolittle	50,000	65.00	65.00
93-01-031	Prayer for the Wild Things	B. Doolittle	65,000	325.00	350.00
Greenwich Workshop		**McCarthy**			
74-02-001	Lone Sentinel	F. McCarthy	1,000	55.00	1465-1800.
74-02-002	Long Column	F. McCarthy	1,000	75.00	450.00
74-02-003	The Hunt	F. McCarthy	1,000	75.00	620-930.
74-02-004	The Night They Needed a Good Ribbon Man	F. McCarthy	1,000	65.00	350-475.
75-02-005	The Survivor	F. McCarthy	1,000	65.00	350.00
75-02-006	Waiting for the Escort	F. McCarthy	1,000	75.00	225-250.
75-02-007	Smoke Was Their Ally	F. McCarthy	1,000	75.00	425-550.
75-02-008	Returning Raiders	F. McCarthy	1,000	75.00	450.00
76-02-009	Packing In	F. McCarthy	1,000	65.00	500.00
76-02-010	Sioux Warriors	F. McCarthy	650	55.00	375-450..
76-02-011	The Warrior	F. McCarthy	650	50.00	450-600.
76-02-012	The Hostiles	F. McCarthy	1,000	75.00	600.00
77-02-013	The Beaver Men	F. McCarthy	1,000	75.00	500-710.
77-02-014	Distant Thunder	F. McCarthy	1,500	75.00	650-900.
77-02-015	Comanche Moon	F. McCarthy	1,000	75.00	300.00
77-02-016	Robe Signal	F. McCarthy	850	60.00	420-500.
77-02-017	Dust Stained Posse	F. McCarthy	1,000	75.00	600.00
77-02-018	An Old Time Mountain Man	F. McCarthy	1,000	65.00	275.00
78-02-019	The Fording	F. McCarthy	1,000	75.00	300-360.
78-02-020	To Battle	F. McCarthy	1,000	75.00	370.00
78-02-021	Single File	F. McCarthy	1,000	75.00	300-490.
78-02-022	Before the Norther	F. McCarthy	1,000	90.00	400-525.
78-02-023	Night Crossing	F. McCarthy	1,000	75.00	200-250.
78-02-024	In The Pass	F. McCarthy	1,500	90.00	200.00
78-02-025	Ambush, The	F. McCarthy	1,000	125.00	300-345.
79-02-026	The Loner	F. McCarthy	1,000	75.00	350.00
79-02-027	The Prayer	F. McCarthy	1,500	90.00	550-600.
79-02-028	Retreat to Higher Ground	F. McCarthy	2,000	90.00	350-500.

Company		Series			
Number	**Name**	**Artist**	**Edition Limit**	**Issue Price**	**Quote**
79-02-029	On the Warpath	F. McCarthy	1,000	75.00	195-250.
80-02-030	Snow Moon	F. McCarthy	1,000	115.00	250-300.
80-02-031	Before the Charge	F. McCarthy	1,000	115.00	200-400.
80-02-032	Burning the Way Station	F. McCarthy	1,000	175.00	375-500.
80-02-033	The Trooper	F. McCarthy	1,000	90.00	295.00
80-02-034	Forbidden Land	F. McCarthy	1,000	125.00	225.00
80-02-035	Roar of the Norther	F. McCarthy	1,000	90.00	250-450.
80-02-036	A Time Of Decision	F. McCarthy	1,150	125.00	250.00
81-02-037	Under Hostile Fire	F. McCarthy	1,000	150.00	210-250.
81-02-038	The Coup	F. McCarthy	1,000	125.00	375-450.
81-02-039	Headed North	F. McCarthy	1,000	150.00	225-275.
81-02-040	Surrounded	F. McCarthy	1,000	150.00	195-275.
81-02-041	Race with the Hostiles	F. McCarthy	1,000	135.00	170-225.
81-02-042	Crossing the Divide (The Old West)	F. McCarthy	1,500	850.00	1100.00
82-02-043	Alert	F. McCarthy	1,000	135.00	160.00
82-02-044	The Warriors	F. McCarthy	1,000	150.00	200.00
82-02-045	Attack on the Wagon Train	F. McCarthy	1,400	150.00	220-395.
82-02-046	Apache Scout	F. McCarthy	1,000	165.00	175-190.
82-02-047	The Challenge	F. McCarthy	1,000	175.00	425.00
82-02-048	Whirling He Raced to Meet the Challenge	F. McCarthy	1,000	175.00	275-340.
83-02-049	Out Of The Mist They Came	F. McCarthy	1,000	165.00	225-325.
83-02-050	Moonlit Trail	F. McCarthy	1,000	90.00	210.00
83-02-051	Blackfeet Raiders	F. McCarthy	1,000	90.00	250.00
83-02-052	Under Attack	F. McCarthy	5,676	125.00	295-350.
83-02-053	In The Land Of The Sparrow Hawk People	F. McCarthy	1,000	165.00	180.00
84-02-054	Along the West Fork	F. McCarthy	1,000	175.00	225-285.
84-02-055	Hostiles, signed	F. McCarthy	1,000	55.00	55.00
84-02-056	Leading the Charge, signed	F. McCarthy	1,000	55.00	55.00
84-02-057	Watching the Wagons	F. McCarthy	1,400	175.00	440.00
84-02-058	The Decoys	F. McCarthy	450	325.00	500.00
84-02-059	The Savage Taunt	F. McCarthy	1,000	225.00	250-375.
84-02-060	After the Dust Storm	F. McCarthy	1,000	145.00	165.00
85-02-061	The Long Knives	F. McCarthy	1,000	175.00	300.00
85-02-062	The Fireboat	F. McCarthy	1,000	175.00	200.00
85-02-063	Charging the Challenger	F. McCarthy	1,000	150.00	200-300.
85-02-064	Scouting The Long Knives	F. McCarthy	1,400	195.00	250-300.
85-02-065	The Last Crossing	F. McCarthy	550	350.00	450-500.
85-02-066	The Traders	F. McCarthy	1,000	195.00	195-275.
86-02-067	Comanche War Trail	F. McCarthy	1,000	165.00	165-225.
86-02-068	The Buffalo Runners	F. McCarthy	1,000	195.00	195-250.
86-02-069	The Drive (C)	F. McCarthy	1,000	95.00	95-175.
86-02-070	Children of the Raven	F. McCarthy	1,000	185.00	550.00
86-02-071	Where Tracks Will Be Lost	F. McCarthy	550	350.00	350-375.
86-02-072	Spooked	F. McCarthy	1,400	195.00	200.00
86-02-073	Red Bull's War Party	F. McCarthy	1,000	165.00	225-275.
87-02-074	Following the Herds	F. McCarthy	1,000	195.00	250-300.
87-02-075	When Omens Turn Bad	F. McCarthy	1,000	165.00	400.00
87-02-076	Chiricahua Raiders	F. McCarthy	1,000	165.00	165-275.
87-02-077	In The Land Of The Winter Hawk	F. McCarthy	1,000	225.00	350-525.
87-02-078	From the Rim	F. McCarthy	1,000	225.00	225-310.
88-02-079	The Hostile Land	F. McCarthy	1,000	225.00	235.00
88-02-080	Saber Charge	F. McCarthy	2,250	225.00	225-250.
88-02-081	In Pursuit of the White Buffalo	F. McCarthy	1,500	225.00	900.00
88-02-082	Turning The Leaders	F. McCarthy	1,500	225.00	240.00
88-02-083	Apache Trackers (C)	F. McCarthy	1,000	95.00	135-150.
89-02-084	The Coming Of The Iron Horse	F. McCarthy	1,500	225.00	225-375.
89-02-085	The Coming Of The Iron Horse (Print/Pewter Train Special Publ. Ed.)	F. McCarthy	100	1500.00	1650-2150.
89-02-086	The Last Stand: Little Big Horn	F. McCarthy	2,250	225.00	225-250.
89-02-087	Big Medicine	F. McCarthy	1,000	225.00	500.00
89-02-088	Los Diablos	F. McCarthy	1,250	225.00	225-275.
89-02-089	Down From The Mountains	F. McCarthy	1,500	245.00	245-290.
89-02-090	Canyon Lands	F. McCarthy	1,250	225.00	235.00
90-02-091	Winter Trail	F. McCarthy	1,500	235.00	235-300.
90-02-092	On The Old North Trail (Triptych)	F. McCarthy	650	550.00	550.00.
90-02-093	Below The Breaking Dawn	F. McCarthy	1,250	225.00	185-225.
90-02-094	Hoka Hey: Sioux War Cry	F. McCarthy	1,250	225.00	225.00
90-02-095	Out Of The Windswept Ramparts	F. McCarthy	1,250	225.00	225.00
91-02-096	Pony Express	F. McCarthy	1,000	225.00	225.00
91-02-097	The Pursuit	F. McCarthy	650	550.00	550.00
91-02-098	The Wild Ones	F. McCarthy	1,000	225.00	225.00
91-02-099	The Chase	F. McCarthy	1,000	225.00	225.00
92-02-100	Where Others Has Passed	F. McCarthy	1,000	245.00	300.00
92-02-101	Where Ancient Ones Had Hunted	F. McCarthy	1,000	245.00	300.00
92-02-102	When the Land Was Theirs	F. McCarthy	1,000	225.00	225.00
92-02-103	Navajo Ponies Comanchie Warriors	F. McCarthy	1,000	225.00	225.00
92-02-104	The Art of Frank McCarthy	F. McCarthy	10,418	60.00	60.00
92-02-105	Breaking the Moonlit Silence	F. McCarthy	650	375.00	300-375.
92-02-106	Heading Back	F. McCarthy	1,000	225.00	200-225.
92-02-107	In the Land of the Ancient Ones	F. McCarthy	1,250	245.00	300.00
93-02-108	Sighting the Intruders	F. McCarthy	1,000	225.00	225.00
93-02-109	By the Ancient Trails They Passed	F. McCarthy	1,000	245.00	245.00
93-02-110	With Pistols Drawn	F. McCarthy	1,000	195.00	195.00
93-02-111	Shadows of Warriors (3 Print Suite)	F. McCarthy	1,000	225.00	225.00
94-02-112	Show of Defiance	F. McCarthy	1,000	195.00	195.00
Greenwich Workshop		**Wysocki**			
79-03-001	Fox Run	C. Wysocki	1,000	75.00	1700.00
79-03-002	Butternut Farms	C. Wysocki	1,000	75.00	975-1300.
79-03-003	Shall We?	C. Wysocki	1,000	75.00	500.00
79-03-004	Fairhaven by the Sea	C. Wysocki	1,000	75.00	700.00
80-03-005	Derby Square	C. Wysocki	1,000	90.00	1100.00
80-03-006	Jolly Hill Farms	C. Wysocki	1,000	75.00	850.00
80-03-007	Caleb's Buggy Barn	C. Wysocki	1,000	80.00	300.00
84-03-008	Yankee Wink Hollow	C. Wysocki	1,000	95.00	1300.00
81-03-009	Page's Bake Shoppe	C. Wysocki	1,000	115.00	500.00
81-03-010	Prairie Wind Flowers	C. Wysocki	1,000	125.00	1800.00
81-03-011	Olde America	C. Wysocki	1,500	125.00	700.00
81-03-012	Carver Coggins	C. Wysocki	1,000	145.00	900.00
82-03-013	Sunset Hills, Texas Wildcatters	C. Wysocki	1,000	125.00	150.00
82-03-014	Sleepy Town West	C. Wysocki	1,500	150.00	500.00
82-03-015	The Nantucket	C. Wysocki	1,000	145.00	400.00
82-03-016	Christmas Print, 1982	C. Wysocki	2,000	80.00	700.00
83-03-017	Amish Neighbors	C. Wysocki	1,000	150.00	500.00
83-03-018	Commemorative Print, 1983	C. Wysocki	2,000	55.00	55.00
83-03-019	Tea by the Sea	C. Wysocki	1,000	145.00	1500.00
83-03-020	Plum Island Sound, signed	C. Wysocki	1,000	55.00	55.00
83-03-021	Plum Island Sound, unsigned	C. Wysocki	Open	40.00	40.00
83-03-022	Applebutter Makers	C. Wysocki	1,000	135.00	500.00
83-03-023	Country Race	C. Wysocki	1,000	150.00	400.00
83-03-024	Commemorative Print, 1984	C. Wysocki	2,000	55.00	55.00
84-03-025	Sweetheart Chessmate	C. Wysocki	1,000	95.00	350.00
84-03-026	Cape Cod Cold Fish Party	C. Wysocki	1,000	150.00	150.00
84-03-027	Cotton Country	C. Wysocki	1,000	150.00	200.00
84-03-028	Chumbuddies, signed	C. Wysocki	1,000	55.00	55.00
84-03-029	The Gang's All Here	C. Wysocki	Open	65.00	65.00
84-03-030	The Gang's All Here, remarque	C. Wysocki	250	90.00	90.00
84-03-031	Storin' Up	C. Wysocki	450	325.00	1000.00
84-03-032	Bird House (C)	C. Wysocki	1,000	85.00	450.00
84-03-033	The Foxy Fox Outfoxes the Fox Hunters	C. Wysocki	1,500	150.00	600.00
84-03-034	Commemorative Print, 1985	C. Wysocki	2,000	55.00	55.00
84-03-035	A Warm Christmas Love	C. Wysocki	3,951	80.00	350.00
85-03-036	Salty Witch Bay	C. Wysocki	475	350.00	2400.00
85-03-037	Clammers at Hodge's Horn	C. Wysocki	1,000	150.00	1500.00
85-03-038	I Love America	C. Wysocki	2,000	20.00	20.00
85-03-039	Birds of a Feather	C. Wysocki	1,250	145.00	400.00
85-03-040	Merrymakers Serenade	C. Wysocki	1,250	135.00	135.00
85-03-041	Commemorative Print, 1986	C. Wysocki	2,000	55.00	55.00
86-03-042	Carnival Capers	C. Wysocki	620	200.00	200.00
86-03-043	Devilstone Harbor/An American Celebration (Print & Book))	C. Wysocki	3,500	195.00	400.00
86-03-044	Hickory Haven Canal	C. Wysocki	1,500	165.00	800.00
86-03-045	Devilbelly Bay	C. Wysocki	1,000	145.00	300.00
86-03-046	Daddy's Coming Home	C. Wysocki	1,250	150.00	1100.00
86-03-047	Lady Liberty's Independence Day Enterprising Immigrants	C. Wysocki	1,500	140.00	200-300.
86-03-048	Mr. Swallobark	C. Wysocki	2,000	145.00	1500.00
86-03-049	Dancing Pheasant Farms	C. Wysocki	1,750	165.00	350.00
87-03-050	Yearning For My Captain	C. Wysocki	2,000	150.00	285-300.
87-03-051	Dahalia Dinalhaven Makes a Dory Deal	C. Wysocki	2,250	150.00	250.00
87-03-052	Bach's Magnificat in D Minor	C. Wysocki	2,250	150.00	500.00
87-03-053	You've Been So Long at Sea, Horatio	C. Wysocki	2,500	150.00	200.00
87-03-054	'Twas the Twilight Before Christmas	C. Wysocki	7,500	95.00	150.00
88-03-055	Home Is My Sailor	C. Wysocki	2,500	150.00	150.00
88-03-056	Feathered Critics	C. Wysocki	2,500	150.00	150-195.
88-03-057	The Americana Bowl	C. Wysocki	3,500	295.00	295.00
89-03-058	Bostonians And Beans (PC)	C. Wysocki	6,711	225.00	565-600.
89-03-059	The Memory Maker	C. Wysocki	2,500	165.00	165.00
89-03-060	Dreamers	C. Wysocki	3,000	175.00	350.00
89-03-061	Another Year At Sea	C. Wysocki	2,500	175.00	250-410.
89-03-062	Christmas Greeting	C. Wysocki	11,000	125.00	100.00
89-03-063	Fun Lovin' Silly Folks	C. Wysocki	3,000	185.00	300-400.
90-03-064	Belly Warmers	C. Wysocki	2,500	150.00	195-200.
90-03-065	Wednesday Night Checkers	C. Wysocki	2,500	175.00	175.00
90-03-066	Robin Hood	C. Wysocki	2,000	165.00	165.00
90-03-067	Where The Bouys Are	C. Wysocki	2,750	175.00	200.00
90-03-068	Jingle Bell Teddy and Friends	C. Wysocki	5,000	125.00	125.00
91-03-069	Rockland Breakwater Light	C. Wysocki	2,500	165.00	275-280.
91-03-070	Beauty And The Beast	C. Wysocki	2,000	125.00	125.00
91-03-071	Sea Captain's Wife Abiding	C. Wysocki	1,500	150.00	150.00
91-03-072	West Quoddy Head Light, Maine	C. Wysocki	2,500	165.00	165.00.
91-03-073	Whistle Stop Christmas	C. Wysocki	5,000	125.00	100.00
92-03-074	Frederick the Literate	C. Wysocki	6,500	150.00	1600.00
92-03-075	Gay Head Light	C. Wysocki	2,500	165.00	165.00
92-03-076	Proud Little Angler	C. Wysocki	2,750	150.00	150.00
92-03-077	Ethel the Gourmet	C. Wysocki	10,179	150.00	400.00
92-03-078	Love Letter From Laramie	C. Wysocki	1,500	150.00	150.00
93-03-079	The Three Sisters of Nauset, 1880	C. Wysocki	2,500	165.00	200.00
94-03-080	Remington w/Book-Heartland	C. Wysocki	15,000	195.00	195.00
Greenwich Workshop		**Lyman**			
83-04-001	End Of The Ridge	S. Lyman	850	95.00	900.00
83-04-002	The Pass	S. Lyman	850	95.00	400-575.
83-04-003	Early Winter In The Mountains	S. Lyman	850	95.00	400.00
84-04-004	Free Flight	S. Lyman	850	70.00	70-120.00
84-04-005	Noisy Neighbors	S. Lyman	650	95.00	1000.00
84-04-006	Noisy Neighbors, remarque	S.Lyman	25	215.00	520-1800.
85-04-007	Autumn Gathering	S. Lyman	850	115.00	250.00
85-04-008	Bear & Blossoms (C)	S. Lyman	850	75.00	75-220.00
86-04-009	Colors of Twilight	S. Lyman	850	N/A	N/A
86-04-010	Morning Solitude	S. Lyman	850	115.00	150-250.
86-04-011	Snowy Throne (C)	S. Lyman	850	85.00	85-295.
86-04-012	High Trail At Sunset	S Lyman	1,000	125.00	700.00
87-04-013	Twilight Snow (C)	S. Lyman	950	85.00	85-225.
87-04-014	High Creek Crossing	S. Lyman	1,000	165.00	800.00
87-04-015	New Territory (Grizzly & Cubs)	S.Lyman	1,000	135.00	210-235.
87-04-016	An Elegant Couple (Wood Ducks)	S. Lyman	1,000	125.00	150-235.
87-04-017	Canadian Autumn	S.Lyman	1,500	165.00	175.00
87-04-018	Moon Shadows	S. Lyman	1,500	135.00	135-185.
88-04-019	Snow Hunter	S.Lyman	1,500	135.00	135.00
88-04-020	Return Of The Falcon	S. Lyman	1,500	150.00	500.00
88-04-021	Uzumati: Great Bear of Yosemite	S. Lyman	1,750	150.00	500.00
88-04-022	The Intruder	S. Lyman	1,500	150.00	150.00
88-04-023	The Raptor's Watch	S. Lyman	1,500	150.00	600.00
89-04-024	Quiet Rain	S. Lyman	1,500	165.00	475-600.
89-04-025	High Light	S. Lyman	1,250	165.00	200-350.
89-04-026	Last Light of Winter	S. Lyman	1,500	175.00	1400.00
89-04-027	Color In The Snow (Pheasant)	S. Lyman	1,500	165.00	1700.00
90-04-028	A Mountain Campfire	S. Lyman	1,500	195.00	2400.00
90-04-029	Among The Wild Brambles	S. Lyman	1,750	185.00	180-275.
90-04-030	Silent Snows	S.Lyman	1,750	210.00	400.00
90-04-031	Evening Light	S. Lyman	2,500	225.00	1700.00
91-04-032	Dance of Cloud and Cliff	S. Lyman	1,500	225.00	500.00
91-04-033	Embers at Dawn	S. Lyman	3,500	225.00	1100.00
91-04-034	Secret Watch (Lynx)	S. Lyman	2,250	150.00	150.00
91-04-035	Dance of Water and Light	S. Lyman	3,000	225.00	225.00
92-04-036	River of Light (Geese)	S. Lyman	2,950	225.00	225.00
92-04-037	Warmed by the View	S. Lyman	8,500	235.00	345-400.
92-04-038	Wildflower Suite (Hummingbird)	S. Lyman	2,250	175.00	175.00
92-04-039	Wilderness Welcome	S. Lyman	8,500	235.00	400-550.
92-04-040	Lantern Light Print w Firelight Chapbook	S. Lyman	10,000	195.00	195.00
92-04-041	Woodland Haven	S. Lyman	2,500	195.00	195.00
93-04-042	Lake of the Shining Rocks	S. Lyman	2,250	235.00	325.00
93-04-043	Riparian Riches	S. Lyman	2,500	235.00	235.00
93-04-044	Fire Dance	S. Lyman	8,500	235.00	235.00
93-04-045	The Spirit of Christmas	S. Lyman	2,750	165.00	165.00
94-04-046	New Kid on the Rock	S. Lyman	2,250	185.00	185.00
Greenwich Workshop		**Bama**			
74-05-001	Ken Hunder, Working Cowboy	J. Bama	1,000	55.00	55.00
74-05-002	Shoshone Chief	J. Bama	1,000	65.00	65.00
75-05-003	Chuck Wagon in the Snow	J. Bama	1,000	50.00	50.00
76-05-004	Sage Grinder	J. Bama	1,000	65.00	65.00
77-05-005	Timber Jack Joe	J. Bama	1,000	65.00	65.00
77-05-006	A Crow Indian	J. Bama	1,000	65.00	65.00
78-05-007	A Mountain Ute	J. Bama	1,000	75.00	75.00
78-05-008	Contemporary Sioux Indian	J. Bama	1,000	75.00	75.00
78-05-009	Rookie Bronc Rider	J. Bama	1,000	75.00	75.00

GRAPHICS

Company		Series			
Number	**Name**	**Artist**	**Edition Limit**	**Issue Price**	**Quote**
78-05-010	Mountain Man	J. Bama	1,000	75.00	75.00
78-05-011	Indian at Crow Fair	J. Bama	1,500	75.00	75.00
79-05-012	Pre-Columbian Indian with Atlatl	J. Bama	1,500	75.00	75.00
79-05-013	Heritage	J. Bama	1,500	75.00	75.00
79-05-014	Little Star	J. Bama	1,500	80.00	80.00
79-05-015	Mountain Man and His Fox	J. Bama	1,500	90.00	90.00
80-05-016	Ken Blackbird	J. Bama	1,500	95.00	95.00
80-05-017	Old Sod House	J. Bama	1,500	80.00	80.00
80-05-018	Mountain Man 1820-1840 Period	J. Bama	1,500	115.00	115.00
80-05-019	Old Saddle in the Snow	J. Bama	1,500	75.00	75.00
80-05-020	Young Plains Indian	J. Bama	1,500	125.00	125.00
80-05-021	Sheep Skull in Drift	J. Bama	1,500	75.00	75.00
81-05-022	Portrait of a Sioux	J. Bama	1,500	135.00	135.00
81-05-023	At a Mountain Man Wedding	J. Bama	1,500	145.00	145.00
81-05-024	At Burial Gallager and Blind Bill	J. Bama	1,500	135.00	135.00
81-05-025	Old Arapaho Story-Teller	J. Bama	1,500	135.00	135.00
81-05-026	Winter Trapping	J. Bama	1,500	150.00	150.00
81-05-027	Oldest Living Crow Indian	J. Bama	1,500	135.00	135.00
82-05-028	Sioux Indian with Eagle Feather	J. Bama	1,250	150.00	150.00
82-05-029	Crow Indian Dancer	J. Bama	1,250	150.00	150.00
82-05-030	Mountain Man with Rifle	J. Bama	1,250	135.00	135.00
83-05-031	Don Walker-Bareback Rider	J. Bama	1,250	85.00	85.00
83-05-032	The Davilla Brothers-Bronc Riders	J. Bama	1,250	145.00	145.00
83-05-033	Southwest Indian Father and Son	J. Bama	1,250	145.00	145.00
87-05-034	Winter on Trout Creek	J. Bama	1,000	150.00	150.00
87-05-035	Buck Norris-Crossed Sabres Ranch	J. Bama	1,000	195.00	195.00
88-05-036	Indian Wearing War Medicine Bonnet	J. Bama	1,000	225.00	225.00
88-05-037	Dan-Mountain Man	J. Bama	1,250	195.00	195.00
88-05-038	Crow Indian From Lodge Grass	J. Bama	1,250	225.00	225.00
88-05-039	The Volunteer	J. Bama	1,500	225.00	225.00
88-05-040	Bittin' Up-Rimrock Ranch	J. Bama	1,250	195.00	195.00
89-05-041	Little Fawn-Cree Indian Girl	J. Bama	1,250	195.00	195.00
90-05-042	Ridin' the Rims	J. Bama	1,250	210.00	210.00
90-05-043	Buffalo Bill	J. Bama	1,250	210.00	210.00
90-05-044	Newman/Butch Cassidy & Video	J. Bama	1,000	375.00	375.00
90-05-045	Young Sheepherder	J. Bama	1,500	225.00	225.00
90-05-046	Paul Newman as Butch Cassidy & Video	J. Bama	2,000	250.00	250.00
91-05-047	The Drift on Skull Creek Pass	J. Bama	1,500	225.00	225.00
91-05-048	Ceremonial Lance	J. Bama	1,250	225.00	225.00
91-05-049	Chuck Wagon	J. Bama	1,000	225.00	225.00
91-05-050	Ready to Rendezvous	J. Bama	1,000	225.00	225.00
91-05-051	Riding the High Country	J. Bama	1,250	225.00	225.00
92-05-052	Coming' Round the Bend	J. Bama	1,000	195.00	195.00
92-05-053	Northern Cheyene Wolf Scout	J. Bama	1,000	195.00	195.00
92-05-054	Crow Cavalry Scout	J. Bama	1,000	195.00	195.00
92-05-055	Blackfeet War Robe	J. Bama	1,000	195.00	195.00
92-05-056	Sioux Subchief	J. Bama	1,000	195.00	195.00
93-05-057	Making Horse Medicine	J. Bama	1,000	225.00	225.00
93-05-058	Magua-"The Last of the Mohicans"	J. Bama	1,000	225.00	225.00
93-05-059	Art of James Bama Book with Chester Medicine Crow Fathers Flag Print	J. Bama	2,500	345.00	345.00
93-05-060	The Buffalo Dance	J. Bama	1,000	195.00	195.00
93-05-061	On the North Fork of the Shoshoni	J. Bama	1,000	195.00	195.00
Greenwich Workshop		**Christensen**			
85-06-001	The Gift For Mrs. Claus	J. Christensen	3,500	80.00	425-600.
86-06-002	Olde World Santa	J. Christensen	3,500	80.00	500.00
86-06-003	Your Plaice, or Mine?	J. Christensen	850	125.00	125.00
86-06-004	Jonah	J. Christensen	850	95.00	400.00
87-06-005	Old Man with a Lot on His Mind	J. Christensen	850	85.00	600.00
87-06-006	Voyage of the Basset w/Journal	J. Christensen	850	225.00	1800.00
87-06-007	Low Tech	J. Christensen	2,000	35.00	35.00
88-06-008	The Widows Mite	J. Christensen	850	145.00	1500.00
88-06-009	The Man Who Minds the Moon	J. Christensen	850	145.00	950.00
89-06-010	The Fish Walker (Bronze)	J. Christensen	100	711.00	711.00
89-06-011	The Annunciation	J. Christensen	850	175.00	175.00
90-06-012	The Burden of the Responsible Man	J. Christensen	850	145.00	1500.00
90-06-013	Two Sisters	J. Christensen	650	325.00	325.00
90-06-014	Rhymes & Reasons w/Booklet, remarque	J. Christensen	500	208.00	600.00
90-06-015	Rhymes & Reasons w/Booklet	J. Christensen	3,000	150.00	150.00
90-06-016	The Candleman, AP (Bronze)	J. Christensen	100	737.00	737.00
91-06-017	The Candleman	J. Christensen	850	160.00	250.00
91-06-018	Pelican King	J. Christensen	850	115.00	350-435.
91-06-019	Once Upon a Time	J. Christensen	1,500	175.00	1600.00
91-06-020	Once Upon a Time, remarque	J. Christensen	500	220.00	2000.00
91-06-021	Lawrence and a Bear	J. Christensen	850	145.00	310-400.
91-06-022	Three Blind Mice-Etching	J. Christensen	75	210.00	210.00
91-06-023	Three Wise Men of Gotham-Etching	J. Christensen	75	210.00	210.00
91-06-024	Man in the Moon-Etching	J. Christensen	75	210.00	210.00
91-06-025	Diggery Diggery Dar- Etching	J. Christensen	75	210.00	210.00
91-06-026	Jack Be Nimble-Etching	J. Christensen	75	210.00	210.00
91-06-027	Peter Peter Pumpkin Eater-Etching	J. Christensen	75	210.00	210.00
91-06-028	Tweedle Dee & Tweedle Dum-Etching	J. Christensen	75	210.00	210.00
91-06-029	Mother Goose-Etching	J. Christensen	75	210.00	210.00
92-06-030	The Reponsible Woman	J. Christensen	2,500	175.00	190.00
92-06-031	The Royal Processional	J. Christensen	1,500	185.00	500-550.
92-06-032	The Royal Processional, remarque	J. Christensen	500	252.50	800.00
92-06-033	The Oldest Angel	J. Christensen	850	125.00	650.00
93-06-034	Waiting for the Tide	J. Christensen	2,250	150.00	150.00
93-06-035	College of Magical Knowledge	J. Christensen	4,500	185.00	300-325.
93-06-036	College of Magical Knowledge, remarque	J. Christensen	500	252.50	600.00
93-06-037	The Scholar	J. Christensen	3,250	125.00	125.00
93-06-038	Getting it Right	J. Christensen	4,000	185.00	185.00
93-06-039	The Royal Music Barque	J. Christensen	2,750	375.00	375.00
94-06-040	Six Bird Hunters-Full Camouflage	J. Christensen	Open	165.00	165.00
94-06-041	Bird Hunters (Bronze) 1 of 4	J. Christensen	50	750.00	750.00
94-06-042	Bird Hunters (Bronze) 2 or 4	J. Christensen	50	750.00	750.00
94-06-043	Bird Hunters (Bronze) 3 of 4	J. Christensen	50	750.00	750.00
94-06-044	Bird Hunters (Bronze) 4 of 4	J. Christensen	50	750.00	750.00
Greenwich Workshop		**Combes**			
80-07-001	Facing the Wind	S. Combes	1,500	75.00	75.00
80-07-002	Solitary Hunter	S. Combes	1,500	75.00	75.00
80-07-003	Interlude	S. Combes	1,500	85.00	85.00
80-07-004	Manyara Afternoon	S. Combes	1,500	75.00	75.00
80-07-005	Serengeti Monarch	S. Combes	1,500	85.00	85.00
81-07-006	Leopard Cubs	S. Combes	1,000	95.00	95.00
81-07-007	Alert	S. Combes	1,000	95.00	95.00
83-07-008	Chui	S. Combes	275	250.00	250.00
85-07-009	Tension at Dawn	S. Combes	825	145.00	145.00
85-07-010	Tension at Dawn, remarque	S. Combes	25	275.00	275.00
86-07-011	The Wildebeest Migration	S. Combes	450	350.00	350.00
87-07-012	The Angry One	S. Combes	850	95.00	95.00
87-07-013	Tall Shadows	S. Combes	850	150.00	150.00
88-07-014	Confrontation	S. Combes	850	145.00	145.00
88-07-015	Bushwhacker	S. Combes	850	145.00	145.00
88-07-016	Simba	S. Combes	850	125.00	125.00
88-07-017	The Crossing	S. Combes	1,250	245.00	245.00
89-07-018	Masai-Longonot, Kenya	S. Combes	850	145.00	145.00
89-07-019	Mountain Gorillas	S. Combes	550	135.00	135.00
89-07-020	The Watering Hole	S. Combes	850	225.00	225.00
90-07-021	The Guardian (Silverback)	S. Combes	1,000	185.00	185.00
90-07-022	Standoff	S. Combes	850	375.00	375.00
91-07-023	Kilimanjaro Morning	S. Combes	850	185.00	185.00
91-07-024	Study in Concentration	S. Combes	850	185.00	185.00
92-07-025	Midday Sun (Lioness & Cubs)	S. Combes	850	125.00	125.00
92-07-026	African Oasis	S. Combes	650	375.00	375.00
92-07-027	The Hypnotist	S. Combes	1,250	145.00	145.00
92-07-028	Lookout	S. Combes	1,250	95.00	95.00
93-07-029	Fearful Symmetry	S. Combes	850	110.00	110.00
Greenwich Workshop		**Ferris**			
82-08-001	Sunrise Encounter	K. Ferris	1,000	145.00	145.00
83-08-002	Little Willie Coming Home	K. Ferris	1,000	145.00	145.00
90-08-003	The Circus Outbound	K. Ferris	1,000	225.00	225.00
91-08-004	Linebacker in the Buff	K. Ferris	1,000	225.00	225.00
91-08-005	Farmer's Nightmare	K. Ferris	850	185.00	185.00
91-08-006	Too Little, Too Late w/Video	K. Ferris	1,000	245.00	245.00
93-08-007	A Test of Courage	K. Ferris	850	185.00	185.00
Greenwich Workshop		**Frederick**			
84-09-001	From Timber's Edge	R. Frederick	850	125.00	125.00
84-09-002	Misty Morning Sentinel	R. Frederick	850	125.00	125.00
84-09-003	First Moments of Gold	R. Frederick	825	145.00	145.00
84-09-004	First Moments of Gold, remarque	R. Frederick	25	172.50	172.50
85-09-005	High Society	R. Frederick	950	115.00	115.00
85-09-006	Early Evening Gathering	R. Frederick	475	325.00	325.00
85-09-007	Los Colores De Chiapas	R. Frederick	950	85.00	85.00
85-09-008	Misty Morning Lookout	R. Frederick	950	145.00	145.00
86-09-009	Winter's Call	R. Frederick	1,250	165.00	165.00
86-09-010	Winter's Call Raptor, AP	R. Frederick	100	165.00	165.00
86-09-011	Out on a Limb	R. Frederick	1,250	145.00	145.00
86-09-012	Great Horned Owl	R. Frederick	1,250	115.00	115.00
86-09-013	Sounds of Twilight	R. Frederick	1,500	135.00	135.00
87-09-014	Northern Light	R. Frederick	1,500	165.00	165.00
87-09-015	Evening Shadows (White-Tail Deer)	R. Frederick	1,500	125.00	125.00
87-09-016	Tundra Watch (Snowy Owl)	R. Frederick	1,500	145.00	145.00
87-09-017	Woodland Crossing (Caribou)	R. Frederick	1,500	145.00	145.00
87-09-018	Before the Storm (Diptych)	R. Frederick	550	350.00	350.00
87-09-019	Winter's Brilliance (Cardinal)	R. Frederick	1,500	135.00	135.00
88-09-020	The Nesting Call	R. Frederick	2,500	150.00	150.00
88-09-021	The Nesting Call, remarque	R. Frederick	1,000	165.00	165.00
88-09-022	World of White	R. Frederick	2,500	150.00	150.00
88-09-023	Rim Walk	R. Frederick	1,500	90.00	90.00
88-09-024	Shadows of Dusk	R. Frederick	1,500	165.00	165.00
88-09-025	Glimmer of Solitude	R. Frederick	1,500	145.00	145.00
88-09-026	Timber Ghost w/Mini Wine Label	R. Frederick	3,000	150.00	150.00
88-09-027	Gifts of the Land w/Wine & Wine Label	R. Frederick	500	150.00	150.00
89-09-028	Colors of Home	R. Frederick	1,500	165.00	165.00
89-09-029	Monarch of the North	R. Frederick	2,000	150.00	150.00
89-09-030	Gifts of the Land #2	R. Frederick	500	150.00	150.00
89-09-031	Barely Spring	R. Frederick	1,500	165.00	165.00
90-09-032	Autumn Leaves	R. Frederick	1,250	175.00	175.00
90-09-033	Echoes of Sunset	R. Frederick	1,750	235.00	235.00
90-09-034	Silent Watch (High Desert Museum)	R. Frederick	2,000	35.00	35.00
90-09-035	Morning Surprise	R. Frederick	1,750	165.00	165.00
90-09-036	Snowy Reflections (Snowy Egret)	R. Frederick	1,500	150.00	150.00
91-09-037	Morning Thunder	R. Frederick	1,750	185.00	185.00
91-09-038	The Long Run	R. Frederick	1,750	235.00	235.00
91-09-039	The Long Run, AP	R. Frederick	200	167.50	167.50
91-09-040	Summer's Song (Triptych)	R. Frederick	2,500	225.00	225.00
91-09-041	Breaking the Ice	R. Frederick	2,750	235.00	235.00
92-09-042	Fire and Ice (Suite of 2)	R. Frederick	1,750	175.00	175.00
92-09-043	Fast Break	R. Frederick	2,250	235.00	235.00
92-09-044	Rain Forest Rendezvous	R. Frederick	1,500	225.00	225.00
92-09-045	Snowstorm	R. Frederick	1,750	195.00	195.00
92-09-046	An Early Light Breakfast	R. Frederick	1,750	235.00	235.00
93-09-047	Glory Days	R. Frederick	1,750	115.00	115.00
93-09-048	New Heights	R. Frederick	1,950	195.00	195.00
93-09-049	Temple of the Jaguar	R. Frederick	1,500	225.00	225.00
93-09-050	Point of View	R. Frederick	1,000	235.00	235.00
94-09-051	Tropic Moon	R. Frederick	850	165.00	165.00
Greenwich Workshop		**Gurney**			
90-10-001	Dinosaur Parade, remarque	J. Gurney	150	130.00	3000.00
90-10-002	Morning in Treetown	J. Gurney	1,500	175.00	600.00
90-10-003	Seaside Romp	J. Gurney	1,000	175.00	600.00
91-10-004	Waterfall City	J. Gurney	3,000	125.00	125.00
91-10-005	Waterfall City, remarque	J. Gurney	250	186.00	900.00
91-10-006	Dinosaur Boulevard	J. Gurney	2,000	125.00	125.00
91-10-007	Dinosaur Boulevard, remarque	J. Gurney	250	196.00	900.00
92-10-008	Dream Canyon	J. Gurney	N/A	125.00	125.00
92-10-009	Dream Canyon, remarque	J. Gurney	150	196.00	100.00
92-10-010	Skyback Print w/Dinotopia Book	J. Gurney	3,500	295.00	295.00
92-10-011	Birthday Pageant	J. Gurney	2,500	60.00	60.00
92-10-012	Birthday Pageant, remarque	J. Gurney	300	275.00	600.00
93-10-013	Ring Riders	J. Gurney	2,500	175.00	175.00
93-10-014	Palace in the Clouds	J. Gurney	3,500	175.00	175.00
93-10-015	The Excursion	J. Gurney	3,500	175.00	175.00
93-10-016	Garden of Hope	J. Gurney	3,500	175.00	175.00
Greenwich Workshop		**Gustafson**			
93-11-001	Humpty Dumpty	S. Gustafson	3,500	125.00	125.00
93-11-002	Goldilocks and the Three Bears	S. Gustafson	3,500	125.00	125.00
93-11-003	Little Red Riding Hood	S. Gustafson	3,500	125.00	300.00
93-11-004	Snow White and the Seven Dwarfs	S. Gustafson	3,500	165.00	500.00
Greenwich Workshop		**Kennedy**			
88-12-001	Distant Relations	S. Kennedy	950	200.00	600.00
88-12-002	Eager to Run	S. Kennedy	950	200.00	1500.00
88-12-003	After Dinner Music	S. Kennedy	2,500	175.00	400.00
89-12-004	Up a Creek	S. Kennedy	2,500	185.00	185.00
89-12-005	Snowshoes	S. Kennedy	4,000	185.00	185.00
90-12-006	Fish Tales	S. Kennedy	5,500	225.00	225.00
90-12-007	On the Edge	S. Kennedy	4,000	225.00	225.00
91-12-008	In Training	S. Kennedy	3,350	165.00	165.00
91-12-009	In Training, remarque	S. Kennedy	150	215.50	215.50
91-12-010	A Breed Apart	S. Kennedy	2,750	225.00	225.00

Number	Name	Artist	Edition Limit	Issue Price	Quote
Company		**Series**			
92-12-011	Cabin Fever	S. Kennedy	2,250	175.00	175.00
92-12-012	Aurora	S. Kennedy	2,250	195.00	195.00
93-12-013	Never Alone	S. Kennedy	2,250	225.00	225.00
93-12-014	Never Alone, remarque	S. Kennedy	250	272.50	600.00
93-12-015	Midnight Eyes	S. Kennedy	1,750	125.00	125.00
93-12-016	The Touch	S. Kennedy	1,500	115.00	115.00
94-12-017	Spruce and Fur	S. Kennedy	1,500	165.00	165.00
Greenwich Workshop		**Kodera**			
86-13-001	The A Team (K10)	C. Kodera	850	145.00	145.00
87-13-002	Fifty Years a Lady	C. Kodera	550	150.00	150.00
87-13-003	Voyager: The Skies Yield	C. Kodera	1,500	225.00	225.00
88-13-004	Moonlight Intruders	C. Kodera	1,000	125.00	125.00
88-13-005	The Great Greenwich Balloon Race	C. Kodera	1,000	145.00	145.00
89-13-006	Springtime Flying in the Rockies	C. Kodera	550	95.00	95.00
90-13-007	Green Light-Jump!	C. Kodera	650	145.00	145.00
90-13-008	A Moment's Peace	C. Kodera	1,250	150.00	150.00
91-13-009	Darkness Visible (Stealth)	C. Kodera	2,671	40.00	40.00
91-13-010	This is No Drill w/Video	C. Kodera	1,000	225.00	225.00
92-13-011	Thirty Seconds Over Tokyo	C. Kodera	1,000	275.00	275.00
92-13-012	Looking For Nagumo	C. Kodera	1,000	225.00	225.00
92-13-013	Memphis Belle/Dauntless Dotty	C. Kodera	1,250	245.00	245.00
92-13-014	Halsey's Surprise	C. Kodera	850	95.00	95.00
93-13-015	Tiger's Bite	C. Kodera	850	150.00	150.00
94-13-016	This is No Time to Lose an Engine	C. Kodera	850	150.00	150.00
Greenwich Workshop		**Landry**			
84-14-001	Regatta	P. Landry	500	75.00	75.00
84-14-002	Regatta, remarque	P. Landry	50	97.50	97.50
85-14-003	The Skaters	P. Landry	500	75.00	75.00
85-14-004	The Skaters, remarque	P. Landry	50	97.50	97.50
86-14-005	Seaside Mist	P. Landry	450	85.00	400.00
87-14-006	Bluenose Country	P. Landry	550	115.00	115.00
88-14-007	Flower Boxes	P. Landry	550	75.00	75.00
88-14-008	Seaside Cottage	P. Landry	550	125.00	125.00
89-14-009	Summer Garden	P. Landry	850	125.00	700.00
89-14-010	Cape Cod Welcome	P. Landry	850	75.00	700.00
89-14-011	A Canadian Christmas	P. Landry	1,250	125.00	125.00
90-14-012	The Captain's Garden	P. Landry	1,000	165.00	500.00
90-14-013	Morning Papers	P. Landry	1,250	135.00	135.00
90-14-014	Seaside Carousel	P. Landry	1,500	165.00	165.00
90-14-015	Christmas Treasures	P. Landry	2,500	165.00	165.00
90-14-016	Flower Wagon	P. Landry	1,500	165.00	165.00
91-14-017	Flower Market	P. Landry	1,500	185.00	735-1100.
91-14-018	Victorian Memories	P. Landry	1,500	150.00	150.00
91-14-019	Summer Concert	P. Landry	1,500	195.00	195.00
91-14-020	Nantucket Colors	P. Landry	1,500	150.00	150.00
91-14-021	The Toymaker	P. Landry	1,500	165.00	165.00
92-14-022	Apple Orchard	P. Landry	1,250	150.00	150.00
92-14-023	Boardwalk Promenade	P. Landry	1,250	175.00	175.00
92-14-024	Cottage Garden	P. Landry	1,250	160.00	160.00
92-14-025	Sunflowers	P. Landry	1,250	125.00	125.00
92-14-026	Christmas at the Flower Market	P. Landry	2,500	125.00	125.00
92-14-027	Aunt Martha's Country Farm	P. Landry	1,500	185.00	185.00
93-14-028	The Antique Shop	P. Landry	1,250	125.00	125.00
93-14-029	Hometown Parade	P. Landry	1,250	165.00	165.00
93-14-030	A Place in the Park	P. Landry	1,500	185.00	185.00
93-14-031	Christmas at Mystic Seaport	P. Landry	2,000	125.00	125.00
93-14-032	Paper Boy	P. Landry	1,500	150.00	150.00
Greenwich Workshop		**Marris**			
85-15-001	The Fishing Lesson	B. Marris	1,000	145.00	145.00
85-15-002	Kenai Dusk	B. Marris	1,000	145.00	145.00
86-15-003	Best Friends	B. Marris	850	85.00	85.00
86-15-004	Other Footsteps	B. Marris	950	75.00	75.00
87-15-005	Desperados	B. Marris	850	135.00	135.00
87-15-006	Honey Creek Whitetales	B. Marris	850	145.00	145.00
87-15-007	Above the Glacier	B. Marris	850	145.00	145.00
88-15-008	Courtship	B. Marris	850	145.00	145.00
88-15-009	Waiting For the Freeze	B. Marris	1,000	125.00	125.00
89-15-010	Bittersweet	B. Marris	1,000	135.00	135.00
89-15-011	The Playgroud Showoff	B. Marris	850	165.00	165.00
89-15-012	New Beginnings	B. Marris	1,000	175.00	175.00
90-15-013	Bugles and Trumpets!	B. Marris	1,000	175.00	175.00
90-15-014	Mom's Shadow	B. Marris	1,000	165.00	165.00
90-15-015	Of Myth and Magic	B. Marris	1,500	175.00	175.00
91-15-016	Cops & Robbers	B. Marris	1,000	165.00	165.00
91-15-017	The Stillness (Grizzly & Cubs)	B. Marris	1,000	165.00	165.00
91-15-018	Under the Morning Star	B. Marris	1,500	175.00	175.00
91-15-019	End of the Season	B. Marris	1,000	165.00	165.00
92-15-020	The Comeback	B. Marris	1,250	175.00	175.00
92-15-021	Security Blanket	B. Marris	1,250	175.00	175.00
92-15-022	To Stand and Endure	B. Marris	1,000	195.00	195.00
92-15-023	Sun Bath	B. Marris	1,000	95.00	95.00
93-15-024	Spring Fever	B. Marris	1,000	165.00	165.00
94-15-025	Lady Marmalade's Bed & Breakfast	B. Marris	1,000	125.00	125.00
Greenwich Workshop		**Mitchell**			
92-16-001	Rowena	D. Mitchell	550	195.00	195.00
93-16-002	Psalms 4:1	D. Mitchell	550	195.00	195.00
93-16-003	Country Church	D. Mitchell	550	175.00	175.00
94-16-004	Bonding Years	D. Mitchell	550	175.00	175.00
Greenwich Workshop		**Phillips**			
82-17-001	Advantage Eagle	W. Phillips	1,000	135.00	400.00
82-17-002	Welcome Home Yank	W. Phillips	1,000	135.00	1100.00
83-17-003	Two Down, One to Go	W. Phillips	3,000	15.00	15.00
83-17-004	Those Clouds Won't Help You Now	W. Phillips	625	135.00	135.00
83-17-005	Those Clouds Won't Help You Now, remarque	W. Phillips	25	275.00	275.00
83-17-006	The Giant Begins to Stir	W. Phillips	1,250	185.00	2500.00
84-17-007	Into the Teeth of the Tiger	W. Phillips	975	135.00	1200.00
84-17-008	Into the Teeth of the Tiger, remarque	W. Phillips	25	167.50	2000.00
84-17-009	Hellfire Corner	W. Phillips	1,225	185.00	1000.00
84-17-010	Hellfire Corner, remarque	W. Phillips	25	225.82	225.82
85-17-011	The Phantoms and the Wizard	W. Phillips	850	145.00	850.00
85-17-012	Lest We Forget	W. Phillips	1,250	195.00	195.00
85-17-013	Heading For Trouble	W. Phillips	1,000	125.00	500.00
86-17-014	Thunder in the Canyon	W. Phillips	1,000	165.00	1000.00
86-17-015	Changing of the Guard	W. Phillips	500	100.00	100.00
86-17-016	Top Cover for the Straggler	W. Phillips	1,000	145.00	145.00
86-17-017	Confrontation at Beachy Head	W. Phillips	1,000	150.00	150.00
86-17-018	Next Time Get 'Em All	W. Phillips	1,500	225.00	550.00
87-17-019	Range Wars	W. Phillips	1,000	160.00	160.00
87-17-020	Sunward We Climb	W. Phillips	1,000	175.00	175.00

Number	Name	Artist	Edition Limit	Issue Price	Quote
Company		**Series**			
87-17-021	Shore Birds at Point Lobos	W. Phillips	1,250	175.00	175.00
87-17-022	Those Last Critical Moments	W. Phillips	1,250	185.00	550.00
88-17-023	America on the Move	W. Phillips	1,500	185.00	210.00
88-17-024	The Long Green Line	W. Phillips	3,500	185.00	185.00
89-17-025	Sierra Hotel	W. Phillips	1,250	175.00	175.00
89-17-026	Over the Top	W. Phillips	1,000	165.00	165.00
89-17-027	No Flying Today	W. Phillips	1,500	185.00	185.00
89-17-028	Time to Head Home	W. Phillips	1,500	165.00	165.00
89-17-029	No Empty Bunks Tonight	W. Phillips	1,500	165.00	165.00
90-17-030	Going in Hot w/Book	W. Phillips	1,500	250.00	250.00
90-17-031	Hunter Becomes the Hunted	W. Phillips	1,500	265.00	265.00
90-17-032	A Time of Eagles	W. Phillips	1,250	245.00	245.00
91-17-033	Fifty Miles Out	W. Phillips	1,000	175.00	175.00
91-17-034	When You See Zeros, Fight Em'	W. Phillips	1,000	245.00	245.00
91-17-035	Low Pass For the Home Folks, BP	W. Phillips	1,000	175.00	175.00
91-17-036	Last Chance	W. Phillips	1,000	165.00	165.00
91-17-037	Dauntless Against a Rising Sun	W. Phillips	850	195.00	195.00
91-17-038	Intruder Outbound	W. Phillips	1,000	225.00	225.00
92-17-039	I Could Never Be So Lucky Again	W. Phillips	850	295.00	800.00
92-17-040	The Long Ride Home (P-51D)	W. Phillips	850	195.00	195.00
92-17-041	Ploesti: Into the Fire and Fury	W. Phillips	850	195.00	195.00
92-17-042	Alone No More	W. Phillips	850	195.00	195.00
93-17-043	And Now the Trap	W. Phillips	850	175.00	175.00
93-17-044	Chasing the Daylight	W. Phillips	850	185.00	185.00
93-17-045	When Prayers are Answered	W. Phillips	850	245.00	400.00
93-17-046	If Only in My Dreams	W. Phillips	1,000	175.00	260.00
93-17-047	Threading the Eye of the Needle	W. Phillips	1,000	195.00	195.00
94-17-048	Lethal Encounter	W. Phillips	1,000	225.00	225.00
Greenwich Workshop		**Terpning**			
81-18-001	Stones that Speak	H. Terpning	1,000	150.00	1400.00
81-18-002	Small Comfort	H. Terpning	1,000	135.00	135.00
81-18-003	The Spectators	H. Terpning	1,000	135.00	1400.00
81-18-004	The Victors	H. Terpning	1,000	150.00	700.00
81-18-005	Sioux Flag Carrier	H. Terpning	1,000	125.00	125.00
82-18-006	Search For the Renegades	H. Terpning	1,000	150.00	150.00
82-18-007	Chief Joseph Rides to Surrender	H. Terpning	1,000	150.00	3500.00
82-18-008	CA Set Pony Soldiers/Warriors	H. Terpning	1,000	200.00	200.00
82-18-009	Shield of Her Husband	H. Terpning	1,000	150.00	1400.00
83-18-010	Shoshonis	H. Terpning	1,250	85.00	85.00
83-18-011	Crossing Medicine Lodge Creek	H. Terpning	1,000	150.00	1000.00
83-18-012	Staff Carrier	H. Terpning	1,250	90.00	90.00
83-18-013	Paints	H. Terpning	1,000	140.00	140.00
84-18-014	The Long Shot, signed	H. Terpning	1,000	55.00	55.00
84-18-015	Woman of the Sioux	H. Terpning	1,000	165.00	165.00
84-18-016	Crow Pipe Holder	H. Terpning	1,000	150.00	150.00
84-18-017	Medicine Man of the Cheyene	H. Terpning	450	350.00	4000.00
85-18-018	One Man's Castle	H. Terpning	1,000	150.00	150.00
85-18-019	The Scouts of General Crook	H. Terpning	1,000	175.00	175.00
85-18-020	The Warning	H. Terpning	1,650	175.00	175.00
85-18-021	The Signal	H. Terpning	1,250	90.00	625-800.
85-18-022	The Cache	H. Terpning	1,000	175.00	175.00
85-18-023	Blackfeet Spectators	H. Terpning	475	350.00	350.00
86-18-024	Status Symbols	H. Terpning	1,000	185.00	1200-1450.
86-18-025	Thunderpipe and the Holy Man	H. Terpning	550	350.00	350.00
86-18-026	Watching the Column	H. Terpning	1,250	90.00	90.00
86-18-027	Comanche Spoilers	H. Terpning	1,000	195.00	195.00
87-18-028	The Ploy	H. Terpning	1,000	195.00	1100.00
87-18-029	Preparing for the Sun Dance	H. Terpning	1,000	175.00	175.00
87-18-030	Winter Coat	H. Terpning	1,250	95.00	95.00
87-18-031	Blackfeet Among the Aspen	H. Terpning	1,000	225.00	225.00
88-18-032	Search For the Pass	H. Terpning	1,000	225.00	225.00
88-18-033	Hope Springs Eternal-Ghost Dance	H. Terpning	2,250	225.00	225.00
88-18-034	Blood Man	H. Terpning	1,250	95.00	95.00
88-18-035	Sunday Best	H. Terpning	1,250	195.00	195.00
88-18-036	Pride of the Cheyene	H. Terpning	1,250	195.00	195.00
89-18-037	Scout's Report	H. Terpning	1,250	225.00	225.00
89-18-038	Shepherd of the Plains	H. Terpning	1,250	125.00	125.00
89-18-039	The Storyteller w/Video & Book	H. Terpning	1,500	950.00	950.00
90-18-040	When Careless Spelled Disaster	H. Terpning	1,000	225.00	225.00
90-18-041	Cree Finery	H. Terpning	1,000	225.00	225.00
90-18-042	Telling of the Legends	H. Terpning	1,250	225.00	1200.00
91-18-043	The Last Buffalo	H. Terpning	1,000	225.00	225.00
91-18-044	Transferring the Medicine Shield	H. Terpning	850	375.00	1800.00
91-18-045	Leader of Men	H. Terpning	1,250	235.00	235.00
91-18-046	Digging in at Sappa Creek MW	H. Terpning	650	375.00	375.00
92-18-047	Prairie Knights	H. Terpning	1,000	225.00	225.00
92-18-048	Four Sacred Drummers	H. Terpning	1,000	225.00	225.00
92-18-049	The Strength of Eagles	H. Terpning	1,250	235.00	235.00
92-18-050	Passing Into Womanhood	H. Terpning	650	375.00	400.00
92-18-051	Against the Coldmaker	H. Terpning	1,000	195.00	195.00
92-18-052	Capture of the Horse Bundle	H. Terpning	1,250	235.00	235.00
92-18-053	Crow Camp, 1864	H. Terpning	1,000	235.00	400.00
93-18-054	Army Regulations	H. Terpning	1,000	235.00	235.00
93-18-055	Medicine Pipe	H. Terpning	1,000	150.00	150.00
93-18-056	Profile of Wisdom	H. Terpning	1,000	175.00	175.00
93-18-057	The Apache Fire Makers	H. Terpning	1,000	235.00	235.00
93-18-058	Soldier Hat	H. Terpning	1,000	235.00	235.00
Greenwich Workshop		**Townsend**			
92-19-001	Riverbend	B. Townsend	1,000	185.00	185.00
92-19-002	Open Ridge	B. Townsend	1,500	225.00	225.00
93-19-003	Out of the Shadows	B. Townsend	1,500	195.00	195.00
93-19-004	Hailstorm Creek	B. Townsend	1,250	195.00	195.00
93-19-005	Dusk	B. Townsend	1,250	195.00	195.00
94-19-006	Autumn Hillside	B. Townsend	1,000	175.00	175.00
Greenwich Workshop		**Weiss**			
82-20-001	Lab Puppies	J. Weiss	1,000	65.00	65.00
82-20-002	Rebel & Soda	J. Weiss	1,000	45.00	45.00
83-20-003	Golden Retriever Puppies	J. Weiss	1,000	65.00	65.00
84-20-004	Basset Hound Puppies	J. Weiss	1,000	65.00	65.00
84-20-005	Cocker Spaniel Puppies	J. Weiss	1,000	75.00	75.00
84-20-006	Old English Sheepdog Puppies	J. Weiss	1,000	65.00	65.00
85-20-007	Persian Kitten	J. Weiss	1,000	65.00	65.00
86-20-008	One Morning in October	J. Weiss	850	125.00	125.00
88-20-009	Goldens at the Shore	J. Weiss	850	145.00	145.00
88-20-010	Yellow Labrador Head Study	J. Weiss	1,000	90.00	90.00
88-20-011	Black Labrador Head Study	J. Weiss	1,000	90.00	90.00
91-20-012	Wake Up Call	J. Weiss	850	165.00	165.00
92-20-013	No Swimming Lessons Today	J. Weiss	1,000	140.00	140.00
92-20-014	Cuddle Time	J. Weiss	850	95.00	95.00
93-20-015	A Feeling of Warmth	J. Weiss	1,000	165.00	165.00
93-20-016	Old Friends	J. Weiss	1,000	95.00	95.00

Company Number	Name	Series Artist	Edition Limit	Issue Price	Quote
Guildhall, Inc.		**De Haan**			
79-01-001	Foggy Mornin' Wait	C. De Haan	650	75.00	2525.00
80-01-002	Texas Panhandle	C. De Haan	650	75.00	1525.00
81-01-003	MacTavish	C. De Haan	650	75.00	1000.00
81-01-004	Forgin' The Keechi	C. De Haan	650	85.00	725.00
81-01-005	Surprise Encounter	C. De Haan	750	85.00	475.00
82-01-006	O' That Strawberry Roan	C. De Haan	750	85.00	125.00
83-01-007	Ridin' Ol' Paint	C. De Haan	750	85.00	625.00
83-01-008	Crossin' Horse Creek	C. De Haan	650	100.00	625.00
83-01-009	Keep A Movin' Dan	C. De Haan	750	85.00	125.00
84-01-010	Jake	C. De Haan	650	100.00	600.00
84-01-011	Spooked	C. De Haan	650	95.00	1825.00
85-01-012	Up the Chisholm	C. De Haan	750	85.00	125.00
85-01-013	Keechi Country	C. De Haan	750	100.00	375.00
85-01-014	Oklahoma Paints	C. De Haan	750	100.00	425.00
85-01-015	Horsemen of the West (Suite of 3)	C. De Haan	650	145.00	975.00
86-01-016	The Mustangers	C. De Haan	750	100.00	400.00
86-01-017	The Searchers	C. De Haan	650	100.00	375.00
86-01-018	Moon Dancers	C. De Haan	750	100.00	165.00
86-01-019	The Loner (with matching buckle)	C. De Haan	750	145.00	425.00
87-01-020	Snow Birds	C. De Haan	750	100.00	350.00
87-01-021	Murphy's Law	C. De Haan	750	100.00	225.00
87-01-022	Crow Ceremonial Dress	C. De Haan	750	100.00	175.00
87-01-023	Supremacy	C. De Haan	750	100.00	175.00
88-01-024	Mornin' Gather	C. DeHaan	750	100.00	350.00
88-01-025	Stage To Deadwood	C. DeHaan	750	100.00	275.00
88-01-026	Water Breakin'	C. DeHaan	750	125.00	600.00
89-01-027	Kentucky Blue	C. DeHaan	750	125.00	575.00
89-01-028	Village Markers	C. DeHaan	750	125.00	525.00
89-01-029	The Quarter Horse	C. DeHaan	800	125.00	325.00
89-01-030	Crows	C. DeHaan	800	135.00	525.00
90-01-031	War Cry	C. DeHaan	925	135.00	275.00
90-01-032	Crow Autumn	C. DeHaan	925	135.00	250.00
90-01-033	Escape	C. DeHaan	925	135.00	200.00
90-01-034	High Plains Drifters	C. DeHaan	925	140.00	200.00
90-01-035	The Pipe Carrier	C. DeHaan	925	140.00	175.00
91-01-036	The Encounter	C. DeHaan	925	140.00	300.00
91-01-037	Sundance	C. DeHaan	925	140.00	175.00
91-01-038	The Prideful Ones (Set of 2)	C. DeHaan	925	150.00	200.00
92-01-039	Crossing At The Big Trees	C. DeHaan	925	140.00	200.00
92-01-040	Silent Trail Talk	C. DeHaan	925	140.00	175.00
92-01-041	73° In Amarillo...Yesterday	C. DeHaan	925	140.00	140.00
93-01-042	The Return	C. DeHaan	925	150.00	150.00
93-01-043	Appeasing The Water People	C. DeHaan	925	150.00	150.00
93-01-044	As The Buffalo Leave	C. DeHaan	925	150.00	150.00
93-01-045	Goosed	C. DeHaan	925	150.00	150.00
Hadley House		**Franca**			
88-01-001	Sitting Bull	O. Franca	950	70.00	250.00
88-01-002	The Apache	O. Franca	950	70.00	175.00
88-01-003	Slow Bull	O. Franca	950	70.00	250.00
88-01-004	Cacique	O. Franca	950	70.00	175.00
88-01-005	The Red Shawl	O. Franca	600	80.00	300.00
88-01-006	Feathered Hair Ties	O. Franca	600	80.00	300.00
89-01-007	Young Warrior	O. Franca	999	80.00	425.00
89-01-008	Navajo Fantasy	O. Franca	999	80.00	150.00
89-01-009	Winter	O. Franca	999	80.00	220.00
89-01-010	Pink Navajo	O. Franca	999	80.00	250.00
90-01-011	Cecy	O. Franca	1,500	125.00	225.00
90-01-012	Santa Fe	O. Franca	1,500	125.00	300.00
90-01-013	Blue Navajo	O. Franca	1,500	125.00	125.00
90-01-014	Destiny	O. Franca	999	100.00	100.00
90-01-015	Blue Tranquility	O. Franca	999	100.00	100.00
90-01-016	Wind Song	O. Franca	999	100.00	425.00
90-01-017	Navajo Summer	O. Franca	999	100.00	240.00
90-01-018	Feathered Hair Ties II	O. Franca	999	100.00	300.00
90-01-019	Turqoise Necklace	O. Franca	999	100.00	450.00
91-01-020	Early Morning	O. Franca	3,600	125.00	225.00
91-01-021	Red Wolf	O. Franca	1,500	125.00	225.00
91-01-022	Olympia	O. Franca	1,500	125.00	250.00
91-01-023	The Lovers	O. Franca	2,400	125.00	500-650.
91-01-024	The Model	O. Franca	1,500	125.00	400.00
92-01-025	Navajo Reflection	O. Franca	4,000	80.00	225.00
92-01-026	Wind Song II	O. Franca	4,000	80.00	150.00
92-01-027	Navajo Daydream	O. Franca	3,600	175.00	300.00
92-01-028	Navajo Meditating	O. Franca	4,000	80.00	125.00
93-01-029	Evening In Taos	O. Franca	4,000	80.00	80.00
Hadley House		**Hanks**			
90-02-001	Contemplation	S. Hanks	999	100.00	150.00
90-02-002	Quiet Rapport	S. Hanks	999	150.00	300.00
90-02-003	Emotional Appeal	S. Hanks	999	150.00	200.00
91-02-004	Duet	S. Hanks	999	150.00	250.00
91-02-005	A World For Our Children	S. Hanks	999	125.00	475.00
91-02-006	Sunday Afternoon	S. Hanks	Open	40.00	40.00
92-02-007	Stepping Stones	S. Hanks	999	150.00	250.00
92-02-008	An Innocent View	S. Hanks	999	150.00	350.00
92-02-009	Sometimes It's the Little Things	S. Hanks	999	125.00	225.00
92-02-010	Things Worth Keeping	S. Hanks	999	125.00	1500.00
92-02-011	Conferring With the Sea	S. Hanks	999	125.00	250.00
93-02-012	Gathering Thoughts	S. Hanks	1,500	150.00	150.00
93-02-013	The Thinkers	S. Hanks	1,500	150.00	150.00
93-02-014	The New Arrival	S. Hanks	1,500	150.00	300.00
93-02-015	Places I Remember	S. Hanks	1,500	150.00	150.00
93-02-016	Catching The Sun	S. Hanks	999	150.00	250.00
Hadley House		**Redlin**			
77-03-001	Apple River Mallards	T. Redlin	Open	10.00	150.00
77-03-002	Over the Blowdown	T. Redlin	Open	20.00	70.00
77-03-003	Winter Snows	T. Redlin	Open	20.00	100.00
78-03-004	Back from the Fields	T. Redlin	720	40.00	325.00
78-03-005	Backwater Mallards	T. Redlin	720	40.00	900.00
78-03-006	Old Loggers Trail	T. Redlin	720	40.00	550.00
78-03-007	Over the Rushes	T. Redlin	720	40.00	400.00
78-03-008	Quiet Afternoon	T. Redlin	720	40.00	400.00
78-03-009	Startled	T. Redlin	720	30.00	400.00
79-03-010	Ageing Shoreline	T. Redlin	960	40.00	250.00
79-03-011	Colorful Trio	T. Redlin	960	40.00	400.00
79-03-012	Fighting a Headwind	T. Redlin	960	30.00	250.00
79-03-013	Morning Chores	T. Redlin	960	40.00	1100.00
79-03-014	The Loner	T. Redlin	960	40.00	200.00
79-03-015	Whitecaps	T. Redlin	960	40.00	375.00
80-03-016	Autumn Run	T. Redlin	960	60.00	450.00
80-03-017	Breaking Away	T. Redlin	960	60.00	300.00
80-03-018	Clearing the Rail	T. Redlin	960	60.00	350.00
80-03-019	Country Road	T. Redlin	960	60.00	375.00
80-03-020	Drifting	T. Redlin	960	60.00	300.00
80-03-021	The Homestead	T. Redlin	960	60.00	375.00
80-03-022	Intruders	T. Redlin	960	60.00	200.00
80-03-023	Night Watch	T. Redlin	2,400	60.00	700.00
80-03-024	Rusty Refuge	T. Redlin	960	60.00	475.00
80-03-025	Secluded Pond	T. Redlin	960	60.00	250.00
80-03-026	Silent Sunset	T. Redlin	960	60.00	850.00
80-03-027	Spring Thaw	T. Redlin	960	60.00	350.00
80-03-028	Squall Line	T. Redlin	960	60.00	300.00
81-03-029	1981 Mn Duck Stamp Print	T. Redlin	7,800	125.00	200.00
81-03-030	All Clear	T. Redlin	960	150.00	350.00
81-03-031	April Snow	T. Redlin	960	100.00	450.00
81-03-032	Broken Covey	T. Redlin	960	100.00	325.00
81-03-033	High Country	T. Redlin	960	100.00	450.00
81-03-034	Hightailing	T. Redlin	960	75.00	200.00
81-03-035	The Landmark	T. Redlin	960	100.00	400.00
81-03-036	Morning Retreat (AP)	T. Redlin	240	400.00	2700.00
81-03-037	Passing Through	T. Redlin	960	100.00	225.00
81-03-038	Rusty Refuge II	T. Redlin	960	100.00	375.00
81-03-039	Sharing the Bounty	T. Redlin	960	100.00	550.00
81-03-040	Soft Shadows	T. Redlin	960	100.00	225.00
81-03-041	Spring Run-Off	T. Redlin	1,700	125.00	350.00
82-03-042	1982 Mn Trout Stamp Print	T. Redlin	960	125.00	600.00
82-03-043	Evening Retreat (AP)	T. Redlin	300	400.00	2500.00
82-03-044	October Evening	T. Redlin	960	100.00	450.00
82-03-045	Reflections	T. Redlin	960	100.00	400.00
82-03-046	Seed Hunters	T. Redlin	960	100.00	450.00
82-03-047	Spring Mapling	T. Redlin	960	100.00	450.00
82-03-048	The Birch Line	T. Redlin	960	100.00	500.00
82-03-049	The Landing	T. Redlin	Open	30.00	80.00
82-03-050	Whitewater	T. Redlin	960	100.00	400.00
82-03-051	Winter Haven	T. Redlin	500	85.00	800.00
83-03-052	1983 ND Duck Stamp Print	T. Redlin	3,438	135.00	135.00
83-03-053	Autumn Shoreline	T. Redlin	Open	50.00	200.00
83-03-054	Backwoods Cabin	T. Redlin	960	150.00	675.00
83-03-055	Evening Glow	T. Redlin	960	150.00	1400.00
83-03-056	Evening Surprise	T. Redlin	960	150.00	900.00
83-03-057	Hidden Point	T. Redlin	960	150.00	350.00
83-03-058	On the Alert	T. Redlin	960	125.00	400.00
83-03-059	Peaceful Evening	T. Redlin	960	100.00	350.00
83-03-060	Prairie Springs	T. Redlin	960	150.00	325.00
83-03-061	Rushing Rapids	T. Redlin	960	125.00	400.00
84-03-062	1984 Quail Conservation	T. Redlin	1,500	135.00	135.00
84-03-063	Bluebill Point (AP)	T. Redlin	240	300.00	400.00
84-03-064	Changing Seasons-Summer	T. Redlin	960	150.00	800.00
84-03-065	Closed for the Season	T. Redlin	960	150.00	300.00
84-03-066	Leaving the Sanctuary	T. Redlin	960	150.00	475.00
84-03-067	Morning Glow	T. Redlin	960	150.00	1200.00
84-03-068	Night Harvest	T. Redlin	960	150.00	575.00
84-03-069	Nightflight (AP)	T. Redlin	360	600.00	2200-2800.
84-03-070	Prairie Skyline	T. Redlin	960	150.00	550.00
84-03-071	Rural Route	T. Redlin	960	150.00	350.00
84-03-072	Rusty Refuge III	T. Redlin	960	150.00	400.00
84-03-073	Silent Wings Suite (set of 4)	T. Redlin	960	200.00	450.00
84-03-074	Sundown	T. Redlin	960	300.00	575.00
84-03-075	Sunny Afternoon	T. Redlin	960	150.00	375.00
84-03-076	Winter Windbreak	T. Redlin	960	150.00	450.00
85-03-077	1985 MN Duck Stamp	T. Redlin	4,385	135.00	135.00
85-03-078	Afternoon Glow	T. Redlin	960	150.00	1000.00
85-03-079	Breaking Cover	T. Redlin	960	150.00	325.00
85-03-080	Brousing	T. Redlin	960	150.00	350.00
85-03-081	Clear View	T. Redlin	1,500	300.00	450.00
85-03-082	Delayed Departure	T. Redlin	1,500	150.00	450.00
85-03-083	Evening Company	T. Redlin	960	150.00	450.00
85-03-084	Night Light	T. Redlin	1,500	300.00	600.00
85-03-085	Riverside Pond	T. Redlin	960	150.00	525.00
85-03-086	Rusty Refuge IV	T. Redlin	960	150.00	500.00
85-03-087	The Sharing Season	T. Redlin	Open	60.00	150.00
85-03-088	Whistle Stop	T. Redlin	960	150.00	550.00
85-03-089	Back to the Sanctuary	T. Redlin	960	150.00	450.00
86-03-090	Changing Seasons-Autumn	T. Redlin	960	150.00	400.00
86-03-091	Changing Seasons-Winter	T. Redlin	960	200.00	400.00
86-03-092	Coming Home	T. Redlin	2,400	100.00	1200.00
86-03-093	Hazy Afternoon	T. Redlin	2,560	200.00	650.00
86-03-094	Night Mapling	T. Redlin	960	200.00	550.00
86-03-095	Prairie Monuments	T. Redlin	960	200.00	400.00
86-03-096	Sharing Season II	T. Redlin	Open	60.00	150.00
86-03-097	Silent Flight	T. Redlin	960	150.00	250.00
86-03-098	Stormy Weather	T. Redlin	1,500	200.00	550.00
86-03-099	Sunlit Trail	T. Redlin	960	150.00	325.00
86-03-100	Twilight Glow	T. Redlin	960	200.00	700.00
87-03-101	Autumn Afternoon	T. Redlin	4,800	100.00	750.00
87-03-102	Changing Seasons-Spring	T. Redlin	960	200.00	450.00
87-03-103	Deer Crossing	T. Redlin	2,400	200.00	450.00
87-03-104	Evening Chores (print & book)	T. Redlin	2,400	400.00	500.00
87-03-105	Evening Harvest	T. Redlin	960	200.00	475.00
87-03-106	Golden Retreat (AP)	T. Redlin	500	800.00	1600.00
87-03-107	Prepared for the Season	T. Redlin	Open	70.00	100.00
87-03-108	Sharing the Solitude	T. Redlin	2,400	125.00	700.00
87-03-109	That Special Time	T. Redlin	2,400	125.00	650.00
87-03-110	Together for the Season	T. Redlin	Open	70.00	150.00
88-03-111	Boulder Ridge	T. Redlin	4,800	150.00	150-200.
88-03-112	Catching the Scent	T. Redlin	2,400	200.00	150-250.
88-03-113	Country Neighbors	T. Redlin	4,800	150.00	350.00
88-03-114	Homeward Bound	T. Redlin	Open	70.00	125.00
88-03-115	Lights of Home	T. Redlin	9,500	125.00	275-750.
88-03-116	Moonlight Retreat (A/P)	T. Redlin	530	1000.00	1000.00
88-03-117	Prairie Morning	T. Redlin	4,800	150.00	250.00
88-03-118	Quiet of the Evening	T. Redlin	4,800	150.00	850.00
88-03-119	The Master's Domain	T. Redlin	2,400	225.00	700.00
88-03-120	Wednesday Afternoon	T. Redlin	6,800	175.00	400.00
88-03-121	House Call	T. Redlin	6,800	175.00	450.00
89-03-122	Office Hours	T. Redlin	6,800	175.00	450.00
89-03-123	Morning Rounds	T. Redlin	6,800	175.00	175-350.
89-03-124	Indian Summer	T. Redlin	4,800	200.00	300.00
89-03-125	Aroma of Fall	T. Redlin	6,800	200.00	1300.00
89-03-126	Homeward Bound	T. Redlin	Open	80.00	100.00
89-03-127	Special Memories (AP Only)	T. Redlin	570	1000.00	1000.00
90-03-128	Family Traditions	T. Redlin	Open	80.00	100.00
90-03-129	Pure Contentment	T. Redlin	9,500	150.00	475.00
90-03-130	Master of the Valley	T. Redlin	6,800	200.00	200.00
90-03-131	Evening Solitude	T. Redlin	9,500	200.00	500-650.

Company / Number	Name	Series / Artist	Edition Limit	Issue Price	Quote
90-03-132	Best Friends (AP Only)	T. Redlin	570	1000.00	1000.00
90-03-133	Heading Home	T. Redlin	Open	80.00	100.00
90-03-134	Welcome to Paradise	T. Redlin	14,500	150.00	400.00
90-03-135	Evening With Friends	T. Redlin	19,500	225.00	475-975.
91-03-136	Morning Solitude	T. Redlin	12,107	250.00	400-475.
91-03-137	Flying Free	T. Redlin	14,500	200.00	200.00
91-03-138	Hunter's Haven (A/P Only)	T. Redlin	N/A	175.00	175.00
91-03-140	Pleasures of Winter	T. Redlin	24,500	150.00	200-275.
91-03-141	Comforts of Home	T. Redlin	22,900	175.00	350.00
92-03-142	Summertime	T. Redlin	24,900	225.00	225.00
92-03-143	Oh Beautiful for Spacious Skies	T. Redlin	29,500	250.00	250.00
92-03-144	Winter Wonderland	T. Redlin	29,500	150.00	150-200.
93-03-145	The Conservationists	T. Redlin	29,500	175.00	175.00
93-03-146	For Amber Waves of Grain	T. Redlin	29,500	250.00	250.00
93-03-147	For Purple Mountains Majesty	T. Redlin	29,500	250.00	250.00
93-03-148	Autumn Evening	T. Redlin	29,500	250.00	250.00
Hadley House		**Casper**			
92-04-001	Comes the Dawn	M. Casper	600	100.00	100.00
92-04-002	Silence Unbroken	M. Casper	600	100.00	100.00
92-04-003	The Watch	M. Casper	600	100.00	350.00
92-04-004	Reflections	M. Casper	600	100.00	100.00
93-04-005	Skyline Serenade	M. Casper	600	100.00	100.00
93-04-006	Pickets & Vines	M. Casper	999	100.00	100.00
93-04-007	Whispering Wings	M. Casper	1,500	100.00	100.00
Hadley House		**Daniel**			
92-05-001	Puppy Love	K. Daniel	850	75.00	75.00
92-05-002	Nightwatch	K. Daniel	999	150.00	225.00
92-05-003	Forever Friends	K. Daniel	850	185.00	185.00
92-05-004	Lone Drifter	K. Daniel	999	150.00	200.00
93-05-005	Mystic Point	K. Daniel	999	150.00	150.00
Hadley House		**Hulings**			
88-06-001	Ile de la Cite-Paris	C. Hulings	580	150.00	300.00
88-06-002	Onteniente	C. Hulings	580	150.00	425.00
88-06-003	Three Cats on a Grapevine	C. Hulings	580	65.00	225.00
89-06-004	Chechaquene-Morocco Market Square	C. Hulings	999	150.00	150.00
89-06-005	Portuguese Vegetable Woman	C. Hulings	999	85.00	85.00
90-06-006	The Lonely Man	C. Hulings	999	150.00	150.00
90-06-007	Spanish Shawl	C. Hulings	999	125.00	175.00
90-06-008	Ancient French Farmhouse	C. Hulings	999	150.00	240.00
91-06-009	Place des Ternes	C. Hulings	580	195.00	700.00
92-06-010	Cuernavaca Flower Market	C. Hulings	580	225.00	325.00
92-06-011	Sunday Afternoon	C. Hulings	580	195.00	300.00
93-06-012	Spring Flowers	C. Hulings	580	225.00	300.00
93-06-013	Washday In Provence	C. Hulings	580	225.00	225.00
Hallmark Galleries		**Innocent Wonders**			
92-01-001	Pinkie Poo	T. Blackshear	9,500	75.00	75.00
Hallmark Galleries		**Majestic Wilderness**			
92-02-001	White-tailed Deer	M. Newman	9,500	75.00	75.00
92-02-002	Timber Wolves	M. Newman	9,500	75.00	75.00
Hallmark Galleries		**Tobin Fraley Carousel Collection**			
93-03-001	Magical Ride	Fraley/ Taylor Bruce	9,500	75.00	75.00
John Hine		**Rambles**			
89-01-001	Two for Joy	A. Wyatt	Closed	59.90	59.90
89-01-002	Riverbank	A. Wyatt	Closed	59.90	59.90
89-01-003	Waters Edge	A. Wyatt	Closed	59.90	59.90
89-01-004	Summer Harvest	A. Wyatt	Closed	59.90	59.90
89-01-005	Garden Gate	A. Wyatt	Closed	59.90	59.90
89-01-006	Hedgerow	A. Wyatt	Closed	59.90	59.90
89-01-007	Frog	A. Wyatt	Closed	33.00	33.00
89-01-008	Wren	A. Wyatt	Closed	33.00	33.00
89-01-009	Kingfisher	A. Wyatt	Closed	33.00	33.00
89-01-010	Blue Tit	A. Wyatt	Closed	33.00	33.00
89-01-011	Lobster Pot	A. Wyatt	Closed	50.00	50.00
89-01-012	Puffin Rock	A. Wyatt	Closed	50.00	50.00
89-01-013	Otter's Holt	A. Wyatt	Closed	50.00	50.00
89-01-014	Bluebell Cottage	A. Wyatt	Closed	50.00	50.00
89-01-015	Shirelarm	A. Wyatt	Closed	42.00	42.00
89-01-016	St. Mary's Church	A. Wyatt	Closed	42.00	42.00
89-01-017	The Swan	A. Wyatt	Closed	42.00	42.00
89-01-018	Castle Street	A. Wyatt	Closed	42.00	42.00
Lightpost Group Inc./ Lightpost Publishing		**Canvas Editions-Framed**			
91-01-001	Afternoon Light, Dogwood S/N	T. Kinkade	Closed	495.00	695-850.
91-01-002	Afternoon Light, Dogwood A/P	T. Kinkade	Closed	595.00	1050.00
92-01-003	Amber Afternoon S/N	T. Kinkade	Closed	595.00	950-1500.
92-01-004	Amber Afternoon A/P	T. Kinkade	200	695.00	1700.00
91-01-005	The Autumn Gate S/N	T. Kinkade	Closed	595.00	995.00
91-01-006	The Autumn Gate A/P	T. Kinkade	Closed	695.00	1700.00
93-01-007	Beside Still Waters S/N	T. Kinkade	Closed	495.00	695-950.
93-01-008	Beside Still Waters A/P	T. Kinkade	Closed	695.00	1150.00
93-01-009	Beyond Autumn Gate S/N	T. Kinkade	Closed	815.00	925-1350.
93-01-010	Beyond Autumn Gate A/P	T. Kinkade	Closed	915.00	1400.00
93-01-011	The Blessings of Autumn S/N	T. Kinkade	1,250	615.00	615.00
93-01-012	The Blessings of Autumn A/P	T. Kinkade	300	715.00	715.00
92-01-013	Blossom Hill Church S/N	T. Kinkade	980	595.00	615.00
92-01-014	Blossom Hill Church A/P	T. Kinkade	200	695.00	715.00
91-01-015	Boston S/N	T. Kinkade	Closed	495.00	815-850.
91-01-016	Boston A/P	T. Kinkade	Closed	595.00	1050.00
92-01-017	Broadwater Bridge S/N	T. Kinkade	Closed	495.00	695-2000.
92-01-018	Broadwater BridgeA/P	T. Kinkade	Closed	595.00	1450.00
89-01-019	Carmel, Ocean Avenue S/N	T. Kinkade	Closed	645.00	3800-5000.
89-01-020	Carmel, Ocean Avenue A/P	T. Kinkade	Closed	745.00	5200.00
91-01-021	Carmel, Delores Street and the Tuck Box Tea Room S/N	T. Kinkade	Closed	645.00	995-1500.
91-01-022	Carmel, Delores Street and the Tuck Box Tea Room A/P	T. Kinkade	Closed	745.00	1400.00
91-01-023	Cedar Nook Cottage S/N	T. Kinkade	Closed	195.00	295-750.
90-01-024	Chandler's Cottage S/N	T. Kinkade	Closed	495.00	1800.00
92-01-025	Christmas At the Ahwahnee S/N	T. Kinkade	980	495.00	515.00
92-01-026	Christmas At the Ahwahnee A/P	T. Kinkade	200	595.00	615.00
90-01-027	Christmas Cottage 1990 S/N	T. Kinkade	Closed	295.00	995-1600.
90-01-028	Christmas Cottage 1990 A/P	T. Kinkade	Closed	295.00	1600.00
90-01-029	Christmas Eve S/N	T. Kinkade	Closed	395.00	595-1700.
90-01-030	Christmas Eve A/P	T. Kinkade	Closed	495.00	1900.00
92-01-031	Cottage-By-The-Sea S/N	T. Kinkade	Closed	595.00	895-2000.
92-01-032	Cottage-By-The-Sea A/P	T. Kinkade	Closed	695.00	1150.00
92-01-033	Country Memories S/N	T. Kinkade	Closed	395.00	495-1350.
92-01-034	Country Memories A/P	T. Kinkade	Closed	495.00	1550.00
93-01-035	The End of a Perfect Day S/N	T. Kinkade	Closed	515.00	700-1000.
93-01-036	The End of a Perfect Day A/P	T. Kinkade	Closed	615.00	1150.00
93-01-037	The End of a Perfect Day G/P	T. Kinkade	Closed	665.00	895-1250.
94-01-038	The End of a Perfect Day II S/N	T. Kinkade	Closed	815.00	815.00
94-01-039	The End of a Perfect Day II A/P	T. Kinkade	Closed	965.00	965.00
89-01-040	Entrance to the Manor House S/N	T. Kinkade	Closed	495.00	850-2200.
89-01-041	Entrance to the Manor House A/P	T. Kinkade	Closed	595.00	1200.00
89-01-042	Evening at Merritt's Cottage S/N	T. Kinkade	Closed	495.00	2000-2200.
89-01-043	Evening at Merritt's Cottage A/P	T. Kinkade	Closed	595.00	2200.00
92-01-044	Evening at Swanbrooke Cottage Thomashire S/N	T. Kinkade	Closed	495.00	615-1700.
92-01-045	Evening at Swanbrooke Cottage Thomashire A/P	T. Kinkade	Closed	595.00	1900.00
92-01-046	Evening Carolers S/N	T. Kinkade	1960	295.00	315.00
92-01-047	Evening Carolers A/P	T. Kinkade	200	395.00	415.00
93-01-048	Fisherman's Wharf; San Francisco S/N	T. Kinkade	Closed	965.00	965-1750.
93-01-049	Fisherman's Wharf; San Francisco A/P	T. Kinkade	Closed	1065.00	1950.
91-01-050	Flags Over The Capitol S/N	T. Kinkade	980	595.00	615.00
91-01-051	Flags Over The Capitol A/P	T. Kinkade	200	695.00	715.00
93-01-052	The Garden of Promise S/N	T. Kinkade	1,250	615.00	615.00
93-01-053	The Garden of Promise A/P	T. Kinkade	400	715.00	715.00
92-01-054	The Garden Party S/N	T. Kinkade	980	495.00	515.00
92-01-055	The Garden Party A/P	T. Kinkade	200	595.00	615.00
93-01-056	Glory of Morning S/N	T. Kinkade	1,960	315.00	315.00
93-01-057	Glory of Morning A/P	T. Kinkade	400	415.00	415.00
93-01-058	Glory of Evening S/N	T. Kinkade	1,960	315.00	315.00
93-01-059	Glory of Evening A/P	T. Kinkade	400	415.00	415.00
93-01-060	Glory of Winter S/N	T. Kinkade	1,250	615.00	615.00
93-01-061	Glory of Winter A/P	T. Kinkade	300	715.00	715.00
93-01-062	Heather's Hutch A/P	T. Kinkade	1,250	415.00	415.00
93-01-063	Heather's Hutch S/N	T. Kinkade	400	515.00	515.00
90-01-064	Hidden Cottage S/N	T. Kinkade	Closed	495.00	1250-4500.
90-01-065	Hidden Cottage A/P	T. Kinkade	Closed	595.00	4700.00
93-01-066	Hidden Cottage II S/N	T. Kinkade	1,480	515.00	515.00
93-01-067	Hidden Cottage II A/P	T. Kinkade	400	615.00	615.00
94-01-068	Hidden Gazebo S/N	T. Kinkade	Closed	515.00	515.00
94-01-069	Hidden Gazebo A/P	T. Kinkade	Closed	665.00	665.00
92-01-070	Home is Where the Heart Is S/N	T. Kinkade	Closed	595.00	995-2500.
92-01-071	Home is Where the Heart Is A/P	T. Kinkade	Closed	695.00	2700.00
91-01-072	Home For The Evening S/N	T. Kinkade	Closed	195.00	295-1300.
91-01-073	Home For The Evening A/P	T. Kinkade	200	295.00	1500.00
91-01-074	Home For The Holidays S/N	T. Kinkade	Closed	595.00	1000-2000.
91-01-075	Home For The Holidays A/P	T. Kinkade	Closed	695.00	2200.00
93-01-076	Homestead House S/N	T. Kinkade	1,250	615.00	615.00
93-01-077	Homestead House A/P	T. Kinkade	300	715.00	715.00
92-01-078	Julianne's Cottage S/N	T. Kinkade	Closed	395.00	595-2250.
92-01-079	Julianne's Cottage A/P	T. Kinkade	Closed	495.00	2450.00
92-01-080	Julianne's Cottage G/P	T. Kinkade	Closed	565.00	895-2350.
93-01-081	Lamplight Brooke S/N	T. Kinkade	Closed	615.00	858-1350.
93-01-082	Lamplight Brooke A/P	T. Kinkade	Closed	715.00	1550.00
93-01-083	Lamplight Brooke G/P	T. Kinkade	Closed	765.00	895-1450.
93-01-084	Lamplight Lane S/N	T. Kinkade	Closed	595.00	1495-3500.
93-01-085	Lamplight Lane A/P	T. Kinkade	Closed	695.00	3700.00
91-01-086	The Lit Path S/N	T. Kinkade	1,960	195.00	215.00
91-01-087	The Lit Path A/P	T. Kinkade	200	295.00	315.00
91-01-088	McKenna's Cottage S/N	T. Kinkade	980	495.00	515.00
91-01-089	McKenna's Cottage A/P	T. Kinkade	100	595.00	615.00
92-01-090	Miller's Cottage,Thomashire S/N	T. Kinkade	980	495.00	695-2200.
92-01-091	Miller's Cottage, Thomashire A/P	T. Kinkade	200	595.00	2400.00
94-01-092	Moonlight Lane I S/N	T. Kinkade	2,400	515.00	515.00
94-01-093	Moonlight Lane I A/P	T. Kinkade	240	665.00	665.00
92-01-094	Moonlit Sleigh Ride S/N	T. Kinkade	1960	295.00	315.00
92-01-095	Moonlit Sleigh Ride A/P	T. Kinkade	200	395.00	415.00
90-01-096	Morning Light A/P	T. Kinkade	Closed	695.00	1150-1600.
92-01-097	Olde Porterfield Gift Shoppe S/N	T. Kinkade	980	495.00	515.00
92-01-098	Olde Porterfield Gift Shoppe A/P	T. Kinkade	200	595.00	615.00
91-01-099	Olde Porterfield Tea Room S/N	T. Kinkade	Closed	495.00	695-2500.
91-01-100	Olde Porterfield Tea Room A/P	T. Kinkade	Closed	595.00	2700.00
91-01-101	Open Gate, Sussex S/N	T. Kinkade	980	195.00	215.00
91-01-102	Open Gate, Sussex A/P	T. Kinkade	100	295.00	315.00
93-01-103	Paris, City of Lights S/N	T. Kinkade	Closed	715.00	795-2700.
93-01-104	Paris, City of Lights A/P	T. Kinkade	600	815.00	2900.00
91-01-105	Pye Corner Cottage S/N	T. Kinkade	1,960	195.00	215.00
91-01-106	Pye Corner Cottage A/P	T. Kinkade	200	295.00	315.00
90-01-107	Rose Arbor S/N	T. Kinkade	Closed	495.00	495-900.
90-01-108	Rose Arbor A/P	T. Kinkade	Closed	595.00	1100.00
92-01-109	San Francisco, Nob Hill (California St.) S/N	T. Kinkade	Closed	645.00	2200-3500.
92-01-110	San Francisco, Nob Hill (California St.) A/P	T. Kinkade	Closed	715.00	3700.00
92-01-111	San Francisco, Nob Hill (California St.) P/P	T. Kinkade	Closed	815.00	2900.00
89-01-112	San Francisco, Union Square S/N	T. Kinkade	Closed	595.00	3000-5000.
89-01-113	San Francisco, Union Square A/P	T. Kinkade	Closed	595.00	5200.00
92-01-114	Silent Night S/N	T. Kinkade	Closed	395.00	495-1200.
92-01-115	Silent Night A/P	T. Kinkade	Closed	495.00	1400.00
90-01-116	Spring At Stonegate S/N	T. Kinkade	550	295.00	415.00
90-01-117	Spring At Stonegate A/P	T. Kinkade	50	395.00	515.00
93-01-118	Stonehearth Hutch S/N	T. Kinkade	Closed	415.00	415-750.
93-01-119	Stonehearth Hutch A/P	T. Kinkade	Closed	515.00	515-950.
93-01-120	St. Nicholas Circle S/N	T. Kinkade	1,750	615.00	615.00
93-01-121	St. Nicholas Circle A/P	T. Kinkade	420	715.00	715.00
93-01-122	Studio in the Garden S/N	T. Kinkade	1,480	415.00	415.00
93-01-123	Studio in the GardenA/P	T. Kinkade	400	515.00	515.00
92-01-124	Sunday at Apple Hill S/N	T. Kinkade	Closed	495.00	695-1250.
92-01-125	Sunday at Apple Hill A/P	T. Kinkade	Closed	595.00	1450.00
93-01-126	Sunday Outing S/N	T. Kinkade	Closed	495.00	695-800.
93-01-127	Sunday Outing A/P	T. Kinkade	Closed	595.00	1000.00
92-01-128	Sweetheart Cottage S/N	T. Kinkade	Closed	495.00	695-1600.
92-01-129	Sweetheart Cottage A/P	T. Kinkade	Closed	595.00	1800.00
93-01-130	Sweetheart Cottage II S/N	T. Kinkade	Closed	595.00	650-1200.
93-01-131	Sweetheart Cottage II A/P	T. Kinkade	Closed	695.00	1400.00
94-01-132	Sweetheart Cottage III S/N	T. Kinkade	Closed	515.00	515.00
94-01-133	Sweetheart Cottage III A/P	T. Kinkade	Closed	615.00	615.00
92-01-134	Victorian Christmas S/N	T. Kinkade	Closed	595.00	995-1500.
92-01-135	Victorian Christmas A/P	T. Kinkade	Closed	695.00	1700.00
92-01-136	Victorian Christmas II S/N	T. Kinkade	Closed	615.00	795-1200.
92-01-137	Victorian Christmas II A/P	T. Kinkade	Closed	715.00	1400.00
91-01-138	Victorian Evening	T. Kinkade	Closed	495.00	495-1200.
92-01-139	Victorian Garden S/N	T. Kinkade	Closed	795.00	995-2000.
92-01-140	Victorian Garden A/P	T. Kinkade	Closed	895.00	2200.00
93-01-141	Village Inn S/N	T. Kinkade	1,200	515.00	515.00
93-01-142	Village Inn A/P	T. Kinkade	400	615.00	615.00
92-01-143	Weathervane Hutch S/N	T. Kinkade	1,960	295.00	315.00
92-01-144	Weathervane Hutch A/P	T. Kinkade	200	395.00	415.00
93-01-145	Winter's End S/N	T. Kinkade	1,450	615.00	615.00

Company Number	Name	Series Artist	Edition Limit	Issue Price	Quote
93-01-146	Winter's End A/P	T. Kinkade	400	715.00	715.00
91-01-147	Woodman's Thatch S/N	T. Kinkade	1,960	195.00	215.00
91-01-148	Woodman's Thatch A/P	T. Kinkade	200	295.00	315.00
92-01-149	Yosemite S/N	T. Kinkade	980	595.00	615.00
92-01-150	Yosemite A/P	T. Kinkade	200	695.00	715.00
Lightpost Group Inc./ Lightpost Publishing		**Archival Paper-UnFramed**			
91-02-001	Afternoon Light, Dogwood	T. Kinkade	980	185.00	195.00
92-02-002	Amber Afternoon	T. Kinkade	980	225.00	235.00
91-02-003	The Autumn Gate	T. Kinkade	980	225.00	235-500.
93-02-004	Beside Still Waters	T. Kinkade	1,280	185.00	185.00
93-02-005	Beyond Autumn Gate	T. Kinkade	1,750	285.00	285.00
85-02-006	Birth of a City	T. Kinkade	Closed	150.00	595.00
93-02-007	The Blessings of Autumn	T. Kinkade	1,250	235.00	235.00
92-02-008	Blossom Hill Church	T. Kinkade	980	225.00	235.00
91-02-009	Boston	T. Kinkade	550	175.00	195.00
92-02-010	Broadwater Bridge	T. Kinkade	980	225.00	235.00
89-02-011	Carmel, Ocean Avenue	T. Kinkade	Closed	225.00	1200-1350.
91-02-012	Carmel, Delores Street and the Tuck Box Tea Room	T. Kinkade	980	275.00	285.00
90-02-013	Chandler's Cottage	T. Kinkade	Closed	125.00	595.00
92-02-014	Christmas At the Ahwahnee	T. Kinkade	980	175.00	175.00
90-02-015	Christmas Cottage 1990	T. Kinkade	Closed	95.00	595.00
91-02-016	Christmas Eve	T. Kinkade	980	125.00	175.00
92-02-017	Cottage-By-The-Sea	T. Kinkade	980	250.00	250.00
92-02-018	Country Memories	T. Kinkade	980	185.00	185.00
84-02-019	Dawson	T. Kinkade	Closed	150.00	300-595.
93-02-020	The End of a Perfect Day	T. Kinkade	1,250	195.00	195.00
94-02-021	The End of a Perfect Day II, S/N	T. Kinkade	2,750	285.00	285.00
89-02-022	Entrance to the Manor House	T. Kinkade	Closed	125.00	600-800.
89-02-023	Evening at Merritt's Cottage	T. Kinkade	Closed	125.00	675.00
92-02-024	Evening at Swanbrooke Cottage	T. Kinkade	980	250.00	250.00
85-02-025	Evening Service	T. Kinkade	Closed	90.00	495.00
91-02-026	Flags Over The Capitol	T. Kinkade	1,991	195.00	235.00
93-02-027	The Garden of Promise	T. Kinkade	1,250	235.00	235.00
92-02-028	The Garden Party	T. Kinkade	980	175.00	195.00
93-02-029	Glory of Winter	T. Kinkade	1,250	235.00	235.00
93-02-030	Heather's Hutch	T. Kinkade	1,250	175.00	195.00
90-02-031	Hidden Cottage	T. Kinkade	Closed	125.00	650.00
94-02-032	Hidden Gazebo, S/N	T. Kinkade	2,400	195.00	195.00
93-02-033	Sweetheart Cottage II	T. Kinkade	980	150.00	150.00
91-02-034	Home For The Evening	T. Kinkade	Closed	100.00	110.00
91-02-035	Home For The Holidays	T. Kinkade	980	225.00	235.00
92-02-036	Home is Where the Heart Is	T. Kinkade	980	225.00	235.00
93-02-037	Homestead House	T. Kinkade	1,250	235.00	235.00
92-02-038	Julianne's Cottage	T. Kinkade	Closed	185.00	395.00
93-02-039	Lamplight Brook	T. Kinkade	1,650	235.00	235.00
93-02-040	Lamplight Lane	T. Kinkade	Closed	225.00	235.00
91-02-041	McKenna's Cottage	T. Kinkade	Closed	150.00	195.00
92-02-042	Miller's Cottage	T. Kinkade	980	175.00	195.00
94-02-043	Moonlight Lane I S/N	T. Kinkade	2,400	195.00	195.00
85-02-044	Moonlight on the Waterfront	T. Kinkade	Closed	150.00	495.00
86-02-045	New York, 6th Avenue	T. Kinkade	Closed	150.00	995.00
92-02-046	Olde Porterfield Gift Shoppe	T. Kinkade	980	175.00	195.00
91-02-047	Olde Porterfield Tea Room	T. Kinkade	980	150.00	195.00
91-02-048	Open Gate, Sussex	T. Kinkade	980	100.00	110.00
93-02-049	Paris, City of Lights	T. Kinkade	1,980	285.00	285.00
84-02-050	Placerville, 1916	T. Kinkade	Closed	90.00	1200.00
88-02-051	Room with a View	T. Kinkade	Closed	150.00	650-950.
90-02-052	Rose Arbor	T. Kinkade	Closed	125.00	300.00
86-02-053	San Francisco, 1909	T. Kinkade	Closed	150.00	1800-1900.
93-02-054	San Francisco, Fisherman's Wharf	T. Kinkade	2,750	305.00	305.00
92-02-055	San Francisco, Nob Hill (California St.)	T. Kinkade	Closed	285.00	400-995.
89-02-056	San Francisco, Union Square	T. Kinkade	Closed	225.00	1200-1350.
92-02-057	Silent Night	T. Kinkade	980	185.00	185.00
90-02-058	Spring At Stonegate	T. Kinkade	550	95.00	95.00
93-02-059	St. Nicholas Circle	T. Kinkade	1,750	235.00	235.00
93-02-060	Stonehearth Hutch	T. Kinkade	1,650	175.00	175.00
93-02-061	Studio in the Garden	T. Kinkade	980	175.00	175.00
92-02-062	Sunday At Apple Hill	T. Kinkade	980	175.00	195.00
93-02-063	Sunday Outing	T. Kinkade	980	175.00	195.00
92-02-064	Sweetheart Cottage	T. Kinkade	980	150.00	150.00
93-02-065	Sweetheart Cottage II	T. Kinkade	980	150.00	150.00
93-02-066	Sweetheart Cottage III S/N	T. Kinkade	1,650	235.00	235.00
92-02-067	Victorian Christmas	T. Kinkade	980	250.00	250.00
93-02-068	Victorian Christmas II	T. Kinkade	1,650	235.00	235.00
91-02-069	Victorian Evening	T. Kinkade	980	150.00	150.00
92-02-070	Victorian Garden	T. Kinkade	980	275.00	285.00
93-02-071	Village Inn	T. Kinkade	1,200	195.00	195.00
93-02-072	Winter's End	T. Kinkade	875	235.00	235.00
92-02-073	Yosemite	T. Kinkade	980	225.00	235.00
Lightpost Group Inc./ Lightpost Publishing		**Archival Paper/Canvas-Combined Edition-Framed**			
90-03-001	Blue Cottage(Paper)	T. Kinkade	Closed	125.00	125.00
90-03-002	Blue Cottage(Canvas)	T. Kinkade	Closed	495.00	495.00
90-03-003	Moonlit Village(Paper)	T. Kinkade	Closed	225.00	1500.00
90-03-004	Moonlit Village(Canvas)	T. Kinkade	Closed	595.00	2000-3000.
90-03-005	New York, 1932(Paper)	T. Kinkade	Closed	225.00	1200.00
90-03-006	New York, 1932(Canvas)	T. Kinkade	Closed	595.00	2900.00
90-03-007	Skating in the Park(Paper)	T. Kinkade	750	275.00	275.00
90-03-008	Skating in the Park(Canvas)	T. Kinkade	Combined	645.00	645.00
Lightpost Group Inc./ Lightpost Publishing		**Member's Only Collectors' Society**			
92-04-001	Skater's Pond	T. Kinkade	Closed	295.00	295.00
92-04-002	Morning Lane	T. Kinkade	Closed	Gift	N/A
94-04-003	Collector's Cottage I	T. Kinkade	Yr.Iss.	315.00	315.00
94-04-004	Painter of Light Book	T. Kinkade	Yr.Iss.	Gift	N/A
Lightpost Group Inc./ Recollections by Lightpost		**Cinema Classics Collection-Framed**			
93-05-001	Over The Rainbow	Recollections	7,500	240.00	240.00
93-05-002	Not A Marrying Man	Recollections	12,500	240.00	240.00
93-05-003	You Do Waltz Divinely	Recollections	12,500	299.00	299.00
93-05-004	Scarlett & Her Beaux	Recollections	12,500	240.00	240.00
93-05-005	You Need Kissing	Recollections	12,500	299.00	299.00
94-05-006	Frankly My Dear	Recollections	Open	39.95	39.95
94-05-007	As God As My Witness	Recollections	Open	39.95	39.95
94-05-008	The Kiss	Recollections	Open	39.95	39.95
94-05-009	A Dream Remembered	Recollections	Open	44.95	44.95
94-05-010	Gone With the Wind-Movie Ticket	Recollections	Open	39.95	39.95
94-05-011	We're Off to See the Wizard	Recollections	Open	39.95	39.95
94-05-012	Follow the Yellow Brick Road	Recollections	Open	39.95	39.95
94-05-013	The Ruby Slippers	Recollections	Open	39.95	39.95
94-05-014	The Emerald City	Recollections	Open	39.95	39.95

Company Number	Name	Series Artist	Edition Limit	Issue Price	Quote
Lightpost Group Inc./ Recollections by Lightpost		**American Heroes Collection-Framed**			
93-06-001	Babe Ruth	Recollections	2,250	136.00	136.00
93-06-002	A Nation United	Recollections	1,000	154.00	154.00
93-06-003	Ben Franklin	Recollections	1,000	136.00	136.00
93-06-004	Mark Twain	Recollections	7,500	190.00	190.00
93-06-005	Abraham Lincoln	Recollections	7,500	190.00	190.00
93-06-006	George Washington	Recollections	7,500	190.00	190.00
93-06-007	John F. Kennedy	Recollections	7,500	190.00	190.00
94-06-008	Eternal Love (Civil War)	Recollections	1,861	195.00	195.00
94-06-009	A Nation Divided	Recollections	1,000	154.00	154.00
Lightpost Group Inc./ Recollections by Lightpost		**The Elvis Collection**			
94-07-001	Public Image/Private Man	Recollections	Open	39.95	39.95
94-07-002	Vulgar Shoman/Serious Musician	Recollections	Open	39.95	39.95
94-07-003	Dreams Remembered/Dreams Realized	Recollections	Open	39.95	39.95
94-07-004	Celebrity Soldier/Regular G.I.	Recollections	Open	39.95	39.95
94-07-005	Elvis the Pelvis	Recollections	2,750	295.00	295.00
94-07-006	Elvis the Pelvis, PP	Recollections	250	495.00	495.00
94-07-007	Elvis the King	Recollections	2,750	295.00	295.00
94-07-008	Elvis the King, PP	Recollections	250	495.00	495.00
Mill Pond Press		**Bateman**			
86-01-001	A Resting Place-Cape Buffalo	R. Bateman	950	265.00	265.00
82-01-002	Above the River-Trumpeter Swans	R. Bateman	950	200.00	850-925.
84-01-003	Across the Sky-Snow Geese	R. Bateman	950	220.00	650-750.
80-01-004	African Amber-Lioness Pair	R. Bateman	950	175.00	525-900.
79-01-005	Afternoon Glow-Snowy Owl	R. Bateman	950	125.00	550-625.
90-01-006	Air, The Forest and The Watch	R. Bateman	42,558	325.00	325-400.
84-01-007	Along the Ridge-Grizzly Bears	R. Bateman	950	200.00	700-950.
84-01-008	American Goldfinch-Winter Dress	R. Bateman	950	75.00	200-300.
79-01-009	Among the Leaves-Cottontail Rabbit	R. Bateman	950	75.00	1200.00
80-01-010	Antarctic Elements	R. Bateman	950	125.00	150.00
91-01-011	Arctic Cliff-White Wolves	R. Bateman	13,000	325.00	600-800.
82-01-012	Arctic Evening-White Wolf	R. Bateman	950	185.00	950-1200.
80-01-013	Arctic Family-Polar Bears	R. Bateman	950	150.00	1400.00
82-01-014	Arctic Portrait-White Gyrfalcon	R. Bateman	950	175.00	250.00
85-01-015	Arctic Tern Pair	R. Bateman	950	175.00	200.00
81-01-016	Artist and His Dog	R. Bateman	950	150.00	550.00
80-01-017	Asleep on the Hemlock-Screech Owl	R. Bateman	950	125.00	600.00
91-01-018	At the Cliff-Bobcat	R. Bateman	12,500	325.00	325.00
87-01-019	At the Nest-Secretary Birds	R. Bateman	950	290.00	290.00
82-01-020	At the Roadside-Red-Tailed Hawk	R. Bateman	950	185.00	550.00
80-01-021	Autumn Overture-Moose	R. Bateman	950	245.00	1450.00
80-01-022	Awesome Land-American Elk	R. Bateman	950	245.00	1450.00
89-01-023	Backlight-Mute Swan	R. Bateman	950	275.00	600.00
83-01-024	Bald Eagle Portrait	R. Bateman	950	185.00	350.00
82-01-025	Baobab Tree and Impala	R. Bateman	950	245.00	350.00
80-01-026	Barn Owl in the Churchyard	R. Bateman	950	125.00	950.00
89-01-027	Barn Swallow and Horse Collar	R. Bateman	950	225.00	225.00
82-01-028	Barn Swallows in August	R. Bateman	950	245.00	425.00
92-01-029	Beach Grass and Tree Frog	R. Bateman	1,250	345.00	350.00
85-01-030	Beaver Pond Reflections	R. Bateman	950	185.00	225.00
84-01-031	Big Country, Pronghorn Antelope	R. Bateman	950	185.00	200.00
86-01-032	Black Eagle	R. Bateman	950	200.00	200.00
86-01-033	Black-Tailed Deer in the Olympics	R. Bateman	950	245.00	300.00
86-01-034	Blacksmith Plover	R. Bateman	950	185.00	185.00
91-01-035	Bluebird and Blossoms	R. Bateman	4,500	235.00	235.00
91-01-036	Bluebird and Blossoms-Prestige Ed.	R. Bateman	450	625.00	625.00
80-01-037	Bluffing Bull-African Elephant	R. Bateman	950	135.00	1125.00
81-01-038	Bright Day-Atlantic Puffins	R. Bateman	950	175.00	875.00
89-01-039	Broad-Tailed Hummingbird Pair	R. Bateman	950	225.00	225.00
80-01-040	Brown Pelican and Pilings	R. Bateman	950	165.00	950.00
79-01-041	Bull Moose	R. Bateman	950	125.00	1275.00
78-01-042	By the Tracks-Killdeer	R. Bateman	950	75.00	1200.00
83-01-043	Call of the Wild-Bald Eagle	R. Bateman	950	200.00	250.00
81-01-044	Canada Geese-Nesting	R. Bateman	950	295.00	2950.00
85-01-045	Canada Geese Family(stone lithograph)	R. Bateman	260	350.00	1000.00
85-01-046	Canada Geese Over the Escarpment	R. Bateman	950	135.00	175.00
86-01-047	Canada Geese With Young	R. Bateman	950	195.00	325.00
93-01-048	Cardinal and Sumac	R. Bateman	2,510	235.00	235.00
88-01-049	Cardinal and Wild Apples	R. Bateman	950	235.00	225.00
89-01-050	Catching The Light-Barn Owl	R. Bateman	2,000	295.00	295.00
88-01-051	Cattails, Fireweed and Yellowthroat	R. Bateman	950	235.00	275.00
89-01-052	Centennial Farm	R. Bateman	950	295.00	450.00
80-01-053	Chapel Doors	R. Bateman	950	135.00	375.00
86-01-054	Charging Rhino	R. Bateman	950	325.00	500.00
88-01-055	Cherrywood with Juncos	R. Bateman	950	245.00	245-345.
82-01-056	Cheetah Profile	R. Bateman	950	245.00	500.00
78-01-057	Cheetah With Cubs	R. Bateman	950	95.00	450.00
90-01-058	Chinstrap Penguin	R. Bateman	810	150.00	150.00
92-01-059	Clan of the Raven	R. Bateman	950	235.00	600.00
81-01-060	Clear Night-Wolves	R. Bateman	950	245.00	6500-8100.
88-01-061	Colonial Garden	R. Bateman	950	245.00	245.00
87-01-062	Continuing Generations-Spotted Owls	R. Bateman	950	525.00	1150.00
91-01-063	Cottage Lane-Red Fox	R. Bateman	950	285.00	285.00
84-01-064	Cougar Portrait	R. Bateman	950	95.00	200.00
79-01-065	Country Lane-Pheasants	R. Bateman	950	85.00	300.00
81-01-066	Courting Pair-Whistling Swans	R. Bateman	950	245.00	550.00
81-01-067	Courtship Display-Wild Turkey	R. Bateman	950	175.00	175.00
80-01-068	Coyote in Winter Sage	R. Bateman	950	245.00	3600.00
92-01-069	Cries of Courtship-Red Crowned Cranes	R. Bateman	950	350.00	350.00
80-01-070	Curious Glance-Red Fox	R. Bateman	950	135.00	1200.00
86-01-071	Dark Gyrfalcon	R. Bateman	950	225.00	325.00
93-01-072	Day Lilies and Dragonflies	R. Bateman	1,250	345.00	345.00
82-01-073	Dipper By the Waterfall	R. Bateman	950	165.00	225.00
89-01-074	Dispute Over Prey	R. Bateman	950	325.00	325.00
89-01-075	Distant Danger-Raccoon	R. Bateman	1,600	225.00	225.00
84-01-076	Down for a Drink-Morning Dove	R. Bateman	950	135.00	200.00
78-01-077	Downy Woodpecker on Goldenrod Gall	R. Bateman	950	50.00	1425.00
88-01-078	Dozing Lynx	R. Bateman	950	335.00	1900.00
86-01-079	Driftwood Perch-Striped Swallows	R. Bateman	950	195.00	250.00
83-01-080	Early Snowfall-Ruffed Grouse	R. Bateman	950	195.00	225.00
83-01-081	Early Spring-Bluebird	R. Bateman	950	185.00	450.00
81-01-082	Edge of the Ice-Ermine	R. Bateman	950	175.00	475.00
82-01-083	Edge of the Woods-Whitetail Deer, w/Book	R. Bateman	950	745.00	1400.00
91-01-084	Elephant Cow and Calf	R. Bateman	950	300.00	300.00
86-01-085	Elephant Herd and Sandgrouse	R. Bateman	950	235.00	235.00
91-01-086	Encounter in the Bush-African Lions	R. Bateman	950	295.00	325.00
87-01-087	End of Season-Grizzly	R. Bateman	950	325.00	500.00
91-01-088	Endangered Spaces-Grizzly	R. Bateman	4,008	325.00	350.00
85-01-089	Entering the Water-Common Gulls	R. Bateman	950	195.00	200.00
86-01-090	European Robin and Hydrangeas	R. Bateman	950	130.00	225.00
89-01-091	Evening Call-Common Loon	R. Bateman	950	235.00	525.00
80-01-092	Evening Grosbeak	R. Bateman	950	125.00	1175.00

GRAPHICS

Company		Series			
Number	Name	Artist	Edition Limit	Issue Price	Quote
83-01-093	Evening Idyll-Mute Swans	R. Bateman	950	245.00	525.00
81-01-094	Evening Light-White Gyrfalcon	R. Bateman	950	245.00	1100.00
79-01-095	Evening Snowfall-American Elk	R. Bateman	950	150.00	1900.00
87-01-096	Everglades	R. Bateman	950	360.00	360.00
80-01-097	Fallen Willow-Snowy Owl	R. Bateman	950	200.00	950.00
87-01-098	Farm Lane and Blue Jays	R. Bateman	950	225.00	450.00
86-01-099	Fence Post and Burdock	R. Bateman	950	130.00	130.00
91-01-100	Fluid Power-Orca	R. Bateman	290	2500.00	2500.00
80-01-101	Flying High-Golden Eagle	R. Bateman	950	150.00	975.00
82-01-102	Fox at the Granary	R. Bateman	950	165.00	225.00
82-01-103	Frosty Morning-Blue Jay	R. Bateman	950	185.00	1000.00
82-01-104	Gallinule Family	R. Bateman	950	135.00	135.00
81-01-105	Galloping Herd-Giraffes	R. Bateman	950	175.00	1200.00
85-01-106	Gambel's Quail Pair	R. Bateman	950	95.00	350.00
82-01-107	Gentoo Penguins and Whale Bones	R. Bateman	950	205.00	300.00
83-01-108	Ghost of the North-Great Gray Owl	R. Bateman	950	200.00	2675.00
82-01-109	Golden Crowned Kinglet and Rhododendron	R. Bateman	950	150.00	2575.00
79-01-110	Golden Eagle	R. Bateman	950	150.00	250.00
85-01-111	Golden Eagle Portrait	R. Bateman	950	115.00	175.00
89-01-112	Goldfinch In the Meadow	R. Bateman	1,600	150.00	200.00
83-01-113	Goshawk and Ruffed Grouse	R. Bateman	950	185.00	400-700.
88-01-114	Grassy Bank-Great Blue Heron	R. Bateman	950	285.00	285.00
81-01-115	Gray Squirrel	R. Bateman	950	180.00	1250.00
79-01-116	Great Blue Heron	R. Bateman	950	125.00	1300.00
87-01-117	Great Blue Heron in Flight	R. Bateman	950	295.00	550.00
88-01-118	Great Crested Grebe	R. Bateman	950	135.00	135.00
87-01-119	Great Egret Preening	R. Bateman	950	315.00	500.00
83-01-120	Great Horned Owl in the White Pine	R. Bateman	950	225.00	575.00
87-01-121	Greater Kudu Bull	R. Bateman	950	145.00	145.00
93-01-122	Grizzly and Cubs	R. Bateman	2,250	335.00	335.00
91-01-123	Gulls on Pilings	R. Bateman	1,950	265.00	265.00
88-01-124	Hardwood Forest-White-Tailed Buck	R. Bateman	950	345.00	2100.00
88-01-125	Harlequin Duck-Bull Kelp-Executive Ed.	R. Bateman	950	550.00	550.00
88-01-126	Harlequin Duck-Bull Kelp-Gold Plated	R. Bateman	950	300.00	300.00
80-01-127	Heron on the Rocks	R. Bateman	950	75.00	300.00
81-01-128	High Camp at Dusk	R. Bateman	950	245.00	300.00
79-01-129	High Country-Stone Sheep	R. Bateman	950	125.00	325.00
87-01-130	High Kingdom-Snow Leopard	R. Bateman	950	325.00	675-850.
90-01-131	Homage to Ahmed	R. Bateman	290	3300.00	3300.00
84-01-132	Hooded Mergansers in Winter	R. Bateman	950	210.00	650-700.
84-01-133	House Finch and Yucca	R. Bateman	950	95.00	175.00
86-01-134	House Sparrow	R. Bateman	950	125.00	150.00
87-01-135	House Sparrows and Bittersweet	R. Bateman	950	220.00	400.00
86-01-136	Hummingbird Pair Diptych	R. Bateman	950	330.00	475.00
87-01-137	Hurricane Lake-Wood Ducks	R. Bateman	950	135.00	200.00
81-01-138	In for the Evening	R. Bateman	950	150.00	1500.00
84-01-139	In the Brier Patch-Cottontail	R. Bateman	950	165.00	350.00
86-01-140	In the Grass-Lioness	R. Bateman	950	245.00	245.00
85-01-141	In the Highlands-Golden Eagle	R. Bateman	950	235.00	425.00
85-01-142	In the Mountains-Osprey	R. Bateman	950	95.00	125.00
92-01-143	Intrusion-Mountain Gorilla	R. Bateman	2,250	325.00	325.00
90-01-144	Ireland House	R. Bateman	950	265.00	318.00
85-01-145	Irish Cottage and Wagtail	R. Bateman	950	175.00	175.00
90-01-146	Keeper of the Land	R. Bateman	290	3300.00	3300.00
93-01-147	Kestrel and Grasshopper	R. Bateman	1,250	335.00	335.00
79-01-148	King of the Realm	R. Bateman	950	125.00	675.00
87-01-149	King Penguins	R. Bateman	950	130.00	135.00
81-01-150	Kingfisher and Aspen	R. Bateman	950	225.00	600.00
80-01-151	Kingfisher in Winter	R. Bateman	950	175.00	825.00
80-01-152	Kittiwake Greeting	R. Bateman	950	75.00	550.00
81-01-153	Last Look-Bighorn Sheep	R. Bateman	950	195.00	225.00
87-01-154	Late Winter-Black Squirrel	R. Bateman	950	165.00	165.00
81-01-155	Laughing Gull and Horseshoe Crab	R. Bateman	950	125.00	125.00
82-01-156	Leopard Ambush	R. Bateman	950	245.00	600.00
88-01-157	Leopard and Thomson Gazelle Kill	R. Bateman	950	275.00	275.00
85-01-158	Leopard at Seronera	R. Bateman	950	175.00	280.00
80-01-159	Leopard in a Sausage Tree	R. Bateman	950	150.00	1250.00
84-01-160	Lily Pads and Loon	R. Bateman	950	200.00	1875.00
87-01-161	Lion and Wildebeest	R. Bateman	950	265.00	265.00
80-01-162	Lion at Tsavo	R. Bateman	950	150.00	275.00
78-01-163	Lion Cubs	R. Bateman	950	125.00	800.00
87-01-164	Lioness at Serengeti	R. Bateman	950	325.00	325.00
85-01-165	Lions in the Grass	R. Bateman	950	265.00	1250.00
81-01-166	Little Blue Heron	R. Bateman	950	95.00	275.00
82-01-167	Lively Pair-Chickadees	R. Bateman	950	160.00	450.00
83-01-168	Loon Family	R. Bateman	950	200.00	750.00
90-01-169	Lunging Heron	R. Bateman	1,250	225.00	225.00
78-01-170	Majesty on the Wing-Bald Eagle	R. Bateman	950	150.00	2650.00
88-01-171	Mallard Family at Sunset	R. Bateman	950	235.00	235.00
86-01-172	Mallard Family-Misty Marsh	R. Bateman	950	130.00	175.00
86-01-173	Mallard Pair-Early Winter	R. Bateman	41,740	135.00	200.00
86-01-174	Mallard Pair-Early Winter Gold Plated	R. Bateman	7,691	250.00	375.00
85-01-175	Mallard Pair-Early Winter 24K Gold	R. Bateman	950	1650.00	2000.00
89-01-176	Mangrove Morning-Roseate Spoonbills	R. Bateman	2,000	325.00	325.00
91-01-177	Mangrove Shadow-Common Egret	R. Bateman	1,250	285.00	285.00
93-01-178	Marbled Murrelet	R. Bateman	55	1200.00	1200.00
86-01-179	Marginal Meadow	R. Bateman	950	220.00	350.00
79-01-180	Master of the Herd-African Buffalo	R. Bateman	950	150.00	2250.00
84-01-181	May Maple-Scarlet Tanager	R. Bateman	950	175.00	825.00
82-01-182	Meadow's Edge-Mallard	R. Bateman	950	175.00	900.00
82-01-183	Merganser Family in Hiding	R. Bateman	950	200.00	525.00
89-01-184	Midnight-Black Wolf	R. Bateman	25,352	325.00	1500-2200.
80-01-185	Mischief on the Prowl-Raccoon	R. Bateman	950	85.00	350.00
80-01-186	Misty Coast-Gulls	R. Bateman	950	135.00	600.00
84-01-187	Misty Lake-Osprey	R. Bateman	950	95.00	300.00
81-01-188	Misty Morning-Loons	R. Bateman	950	150.00	3000.00
86-01-189	Moose at Water's Edge	R. Bateman	950	130.00	225.00
90-01-190	Morning Cove-Common Loon	R. Bateman	950	165.00	165.00
85-01-191	Morning Dew-Roe Deer	R. Bateman	950	175.00	175.00
83-01-192	Morning on the Flats-Bison	R. Bateman	950	200.00	300.00
84-01-193	Morning on the River-Trumpeter Swans	R. Bateman	950	185.00	300.00
90-01-194	Mossy Branches-Spotted Owl	R. Bateman	4,500	300.00	525.00
90-01-195	Mowed Meadow	R. Bateman	950	190.00	190.00
86-01-196	Mule Deer in Aspen	R. Bateman	950	175.00	175.00
83-01-197	Mule Deer in Winter	R. Bateman	950	200.00	275-350.
88-01-198	Muskoka Lake-Common Loons	R. Bateman	950	265.00	450.00
89-01-199	Near Glenburnie	R. Bateman	950	265.00	265.00
83-01-200	New Season-American Robin	R. Bateman	950	200.00	450.00
86-01-201	Northern Reflections-Loon Family	R. Bateman	8,631	255.00	2100.00
85-01-202	Old Whaling Base and Fur Seals	R. Bateman	950	195.00	550.00
87-01-203	Old Willow and Mallards	R. Bateman	950	325.00	390.00
80-01-204	On the Alert-Chipmunk	R. Bateman	950	60.00	500.00
93-01-205	On the Brink-River Otters	R. Bateman	1,250	345.00	345.00
85-01-206	On the Garden Wall	R. Bateman	950	115.00	300.00
85-01-207	Orca Procession	R. Bateman	950	245.00	2525.00
81-01-208	Osprey Family	R. Bateman	950	245.00	325.00
83-01-209	Osprey in the Rain	R. Bateman	950	110.00	650.00
87-01-210	Otter Study	R. Bateman	950	235.00	375.00
81-01-211	Pair of Skimmers	R. Bateman	950	150.00	150.00
88-01-212	Panda's At Play (stone lithograph)	R. Bateman	160	400.00	2500.00
84-01-213	Peregrine and Ruddy Turnstones	R. Bateman	950	200.00	350.00
85-01-214	Peregrine Falcon and White-Throated Swifts	R. Bateman	950	245.00	550.00
87-01-215	Peregrine Falcon on the Cliff-Stone Litho	R. Bateman	525	350.00	625.00
83-01-216	Pheasant in Cornfield	R. Bateman	950	200.00	375.00
88-01-217	Pheasants at Dusk	R. Bateman	950	325.00	525.00
82-01-218	Pileated Woodpecker on Beech Tree	R. Bateman	950	175.00	525.00
90-01-219	Pintails in Spring	R. Bateman	9,651	135.00	135.00
82-01-220	Pioneer Memories-Magpie Pair	R. Bateman	950	175.00	250.00
87-01-221	Plowed Field-Snowy Owl	R. Bateman	950	145.00	400.00
90-01-222	Polar Bear	R. Bateman	290	3300.00	3300.00
82-01-223	Polar Bear Profile	R. Bateman	950	210.00	2350.00
82-01-224	Polar Bears at Bafin Island	R. Bateman	950	245.00	875.00
90-01-225	Power Play-Rhinoceros	R. Bateman	950	320.00	320.00
80-01-226	Prairie Evening-Short-Eared Owl	R. Bateman	950	150.00	200.00
94-01-227	Predator Portfolio/Black Bear	R. Bateman	950	475.00	475.00
92-01-228	Predator Portfolio/Cougar	R. Bateman	950	465.00	465.00
93-01-229	Predator Portfolio/Grizzly	R. Bateman	950	475.00	475.00
93-01-230	Predator Portfolio/Polar Bear	R. Bateman	950	485.00	485.00
93-01-231	Predator Portfolio/Wolf	R. Bateman	950	475.00	475.00
88-01-232	Preening Pair-Canada Geese	R. Bateman	950	235.00	300.00
87-01-233	Pride of Autumn-Canada Goose	R. Bateman	950	135.00	245.00
86-01-234	Proud Swimmer-Snow Goose	R. Bateman	950	185.00	185.00
89-01-235	Pumpkin Time	R. Bateman	950	195.00	195.00
82-01-236	Queen Anne's Lace and AmericanGoldfinch	R. Bateman	950	150.00	1000.00
84-01-237	Ready for Flight-Peregrine Falcon	R. Bateman	950	185.00	500.00
82-01-238	Ready for the Hunt-Snowy Owl	R. Bateman	950	245.00	550.00
93-01-239	Reclining Snow Leopard	R. Bateman	1,250	335.00	335.00
88-01-240	Red Crossbills	R. Bateman	950	125.00	125.00
84-01-241	Red Fox on the Prowl	R. Bateman	950	245.00	1500.00
82-01-242	Red Squirrel	R. Bateman	950	175.00	700.00
86-01-243	Red Wolf	R. Bateman	950	250.00	525.00
81-01-244	Red-Tailed Hawk by the Cliff	R. Bateman	950	245.00	550.00
81-01-245	Red-Winged Blackbird and Rail Fence	R. Bateman	950	195.00	225.00
84-01-246	Reeds	R. Bateman	950	185.00	575.00
86-01-247	Resting Place-Cape Buffalo	R. Bateman	950	265.00	265.00
87-01-248	Rhino at Ngoro Ngoro	R. Bateman	950	325.00	325.00
93-01-049	River Otter	R. Bateman	290	1500.00	1500.00
86-01-250	Robins at the Nest	R. Bateman	950	185.00	225.00
87-01-251	Rocky Point-October	R. Bateman	950	195.00	275.00
80-01-252	Rocky Wilderness-Cougar	R. Bateman	950	175.00	1425.00
90-01-253	Rolling Waves-Lesser Scaup	R. Bateman	3,330	125.00	125.00
93-01-254	Rose-breasted Grosbeak	R. Bateman	290	450.00	450.00
81-01-255	Rough-Legged Hawk in the Elm	R. Bateman	950	175.00	250.00
81-01-256	Royal Family-Mute Swans	R. Bateman	950	245.00	1100.00
83-01-257	Ruby Throat and Columbine	R. Bateman	950	150.00	2200.00
87-01-258	Ruddy Turnstones	R. Bateman	950	175.00	175.00
94-01-259	Salt Spring Sheep	R. Bateman	1,250	235.00	235.00
81-01-260	Sarah E. with Gulls	R. Bateman	950	245.00	2625.00
93-01-261	Saw Whet Owl and Wild Grapes	R. Bateman	950	185.00	185.00
91-01-262	Sea Otter Study	R. Bateman	950	150.00	150.00
81-01-263	Sheer Drop-Mountain Goats	R. Bateman	950	245.00	2800.00
93-01-264	Shadow of the Rain Forest	R. Bateman	9,000	345.00	345.00
88-01-265	Shelter	R. Bateman	950	325.00	1000.00
92-01-266	Siberian Tiger	R. Bateman	4,500	325.00	325.00
84-01-267	Smallwood	R. Bateman	950	200.00	500.00
90-01-268	Snow Leopard	R. Bateman	290	2500.00	3500.00
85-01-269	Snowy Hemlock-Barred Owl	R. Bateman	950	245.00	400.00
94-01-270	Snowy Nap-Tiger	R. Bateman	950	185.00	185.00
87-01-271	Snowy Owl and Milkweed	R. Bateman	950	235.00	950.00
83-01-272	Snowy Owl on Driftwood	R. Bateman	950	245.00	1450.00
83-01-273	Spirits of the Forest	R. Bateman	950	170.00	1750.00
86-01-274	Split Rails-Snow Buntings	R. Bateman	950	220.00	220.00
80-01-275	Spring Cardinal	R. Bateman	950	125.00	600.00
82-01-276	Spring Marsh-Pintail Pair	R. Bateman	950	200.00	275.00
80-01-277	Spring Thaw-Killdeer	R. Bateman	950	85.00	150.00
82-01-278	Still Morning-Herring Gulls	R. Bateman	950	200.00	250.00
87-01-279	Stone Sheep Ram	R. Bateman	950	175.00	175.00
85-01-280	Stream Bank June	R. Bateman	950	160.00	175.00
84-01-281	Stretching-Canada Goose	R. Bateman	950	225.00	3600-3900.
85-01-282	Strutting-Ring-Necked Pheasant	R. Bateman	950	225.00	325.00
85-01-283	Sudden Blizzard-Red-Tailed Hawk	R. Bateman	950	245.00	600.00
84-01-284	Summer Morning-Loon	R. Bateman	950	185.00	1250.00
90-01-285	Summer Morning Pasture	R. Bateman	950	175.00	175.00
86-01-286	Summertime-Polar Bears	R. Bateman	950	225.00	475.00
79-01-287	Surf and Sanderlings	R. Bateman	950	65.00	450.00
81-01-288	Swift Fox	R. Bateman	950	175.00	350.00
86-01-289	Swift Fox Study	R. Bateman	950	115.00	150.00
87-01-290	Sylvan Stream-Mute Swans	R. Bateman	950	125.00	125.00
84-01-291	Tadpole Time	R. Bateman	950	135.00	475.00
88-01-292	Tawny Owl In Beech	R. Bateman	950	325.00	600.00
92-01-293	Tembo (African Elephant)	R. Bateman	1,550	350.00	350.00
88-01-294	The Challenge-Bull Moose	R. Bateman	10,671	325.00	325.00
91-01-295	The Scolding-Chickadees & Screech Owl	R. Bateman	12,500	235.00	235.00
84-01-296	Tiger at Dawn	R. Bateman	950	225.00	2500.00
83-01-297	Tiger Portrait	R. Bateman	950	130.00	400.00
88-01-298	Tree Swallow over Pond	R. Bateman	950	290.00	290.00
91-01-299	Trumpeter Swan Family	R. Bateman	290	2500.00	2500.00
85-01-300	Trumpeter Swans and Aspen	R. Bateman	950	245.00	550.00
79-01-301	Up in the Pine-Great Horned Owl	R. Bateman	950	150.00	550.00
80-01-302	Vantage Point	R. Bateman	950	245.00	1300.00
93-01-303	Vigilance	R. Bateman	9,500	330.00	330.00
89-01-304	Vulture And Wildebeest	R. Bateman	550	295.00	295.00
81-01-305	Watchful Repose-Black Bear	R. Bateman	950	245.00	700.00
85-01-306	Weathered Branch-Bald Eagle	R. Bateman	950	115.00	300.00
91-01-307	Whistling Swan-Lake Erie	R. Bateman	1,950	325.00	325.00
85-01-308	White-Breasted Nuthatch on a Beech Tree	R. Bateman	950	175.00	300.00
80-01-309	White Encounter-Polar Bear	R. Bateman	950	245.00	4200-4800.
80-01-310	White-Footed Mouse in Wintergreen	R. Bateman	950	60.00	650.00
82-01-311	White-Footed Mouse on Aspen	R. Bateman	950	90.00	180.00
92-01-312	White-Tailed Deer Through the Birches	R. Bateman	10,000	335.00	335.00
84-01-313	White-Throated Sparrow and Pussy Willow	R. Bateman	950	150.00	580.00
90-01-314	White on White-Snowshoe Hare	R. Bateman	950	195.00	590.00
82-01-315	White World-Dall Sheep	R. Bateman	950	200.00	450.00
91-01-316	Wide Horizon-Tundra Swans	R. Bateman	2,862	325.00	350-450.
91-01-317	Wide Horizon-Tundra Swans Companion	R. Bateman	2,862	325.00	325.00
86-01-318	Wildbeest	R. Bateman	950	185.00	185.00
82-01-319	Willet on the Shore	R. Bateman	950	125.00	225.00
79-01-320	Wily and Wary-Red Fox	R. Bateman	950	125.00	1500.00

Company / Number	Name	Series / Artist	Edition Limit	Issue Price	Quote
84-01-321	Window into Ontario	R. Bateman	950	265.00	1500.00
83-01-322	Winter Barn	R. Bateman	950	170.00	400.00
79-01-323	Winter Cardinal	R. Bateman	950	75.00	3550.00
85-01-324	Winter Companion	R. Bateman	950	175.00	500.00
80-01-325	Winter Elm-American Kestrel	R. Bateman	950	135.00	600.00
86-01-326	Winter in the Mountains-Raven	R. Bateman	950	200.00	200.00
83-01-327	Winter-Lady Cardinal	R. Bateman	950	200.00	1500.00
81-01-328	Winter Mist-Great Horned Owl	R. Bateman	950	245.00	900.00
79-01-329	Winter-Snowshoe Hare	R. Bateman	950	95.00	1200.00
80-01-330	Winter Song-Chickadees	R. Bateman	950	95.00	900.00
84-01-331	Winter Sunset-Moose	R. Bateman	950	245.00	2700.00
81-01-332	Winter Wren	R. Bateman	950	135.00	250.00
87-01-333	Wise One, The	R. Bateman	950	325.00	800.00
79-01-334	Wolf Pack in Moonlight	R. Bateman	950	95.00	3000.00
83-01-335	Wolves on the Trail	R. Bateman	950	225.00	700.00
85-01-336	Wood Bison Portrait	R. Bateman	950	165.00	200.00
83-01-337	Woodland Drummer-Ruffed Grouse	R. Bateman	950	185.00	250.00
81-01-338	Wrangler's Campsite-Gray Jay	R. Bateman	950	195.00	550.00
79-01-339	Yellow-Rumped Warbler	R. Bateman	950	50.00	575.00
78-01-340	Young Barn Swallow	R. Bateman	950	75.00	700.00
83-01-341	Young Elf Owl-Old Saguaro	R. Bateman	950	95.00	250.00
91-01-342	Young Giraffe	R. Bateman	290	850.00	850.00
89-01-343	Young Kittiwake	R. Bateman	950	195.00	195.00
88-01-344	Young Sandhill-Cranes	R. Bateman	950	325.00	325.00
89-01-345	Young Snowy Owl	R. Bateman	950	195.00	195.00
Mill Pond Press		**Brenders**			
88-02-001	A Hunter's Dream	C. Brenders	950	165.00	750-875.
90-02-002	A Threatened Symbol	C. Brenders	1,950	145.00	300.00
88-02-003	Apple Harvest	C. Brenders	950	115.00	295.00
87-02-004	Autumn Lady	C. Brenders	950	150.00	375.00
89-02-005	A Young Generation	C. Brenders	1,250	165.00	375-425.
86-02-006	Black-Capped Chickadees	C. Brenders	950	40.00	450.00
93-02-007	Black Sphinx	C. Brenders	950	235.00	235.00
90-02-008	Blond Beauty	C. Brenders	1,950	185.00	185.00
86-02-009	Bluebirds	C. Brenders	950	40.00	200-350.
91-02-010	Calm Before the Challenge-Moose	C. Brenders	1,950	225.00	225.00
87-02-011	Close to Mom	C. Brenders	950	150.00	900-1450.
93-02-012	Collectors Group (Butterfly Collections)	C. Brenders	290	375.00	375.00
86-02-013	Colorful Playground-Cottontails	C. Brenders	950	75.00	475.00
92-02-014	Den Mother-Pencil Sketch	C. Brenders	2,500	135.00	135.00
92-02-015	Den Mother-Wolf Family	C. Brenders	25,000	250.00	400.00
86-02-016	Disturbed Daydreams	C. Brenders	950	95.00	425.00
87-02-017	Double Trouble-Raccoons	C. Brenders	950	120.00	500-750.
93-02-018	Exotic Group (Butterfly Collections)	C. Brenders	290	375.00	375.00
93-02-019	European Group (Butterfly Collections)	C. Brenders	290	375.00	375.00
88-02-020	Forest Sentinel-Bobcat	C. Brenders	950	135.00	500.00
90-02-021	Full House-Fox Family	C. Brenders	20,106	235.00	400.00
90-02-022	Ghostly Quiet-Spanish Lynx	C. Brenders	1,950	200.00	200.00
86-02-023	Golden Season-Gray Squirrel	C. Brenders	950	85.00	450-525.
86-02-024	Harvest Time-Chipmunk	C. Brenders	950	65.00	150-250.
88-02-025	Hidden In the Pines-Immature Great Hor	C. Brenders	950	175.00	1500.00
88-02-026	High Adventure-Black Bear Cubs	C. Brenders	950	105.00	375.00
93-02-027	In Northern Hunting Grounds	C. Brenders	1,750	375.00	375.00
87-02-028	Ivory-Billed Woodpecker	C. Brenders	950	95.00	500.00
88-02-029	Long Distance Hunters	C. Brenders	950	175.00	2250.00
89-02-030	Lord of the Marshes	C. Brenders	1,250	135.00	175.00
86-02-031	Meadowlark	C. Brenders	950	40.00	150.00
89-02-032	Merlins at the Nest	C. Brenders	1,250	165.00	300-375.
85-02-033	Mighty Intruder	C. Brenders	950	95.00	275.00
87-02-034	Migration Fever-Barn Swallows	C. Brenders	950	150.00	295-350.
93-02-035	Mother of Pearls	C. Brenders	5,000	275.00	275.00
90-02-036	Mountain Baby-Bighorn Sheep	C. Brenders	1,950	165.00	165.00
87-02-037	Mysterious Visitor-Barn Owl	C. Brenders	950	150.00	295-375.
93-02-038	Narrow Escape-Chipmunk	C. Brenders	1,750	150.00	150.00
91-02-039	The Nesting Season-House Sparrow	C. Brenders	1,950	195.00	200-250.
89-02-040	Northern Cousins-Black Squirrels	C. Brenders	950	150.00	250.00
84-02-041	On the Alert-Red Fox	C. Brenders	950	95.00	475.00
90-02-042	On the Old Farm Door	C. Brenders	1,500	225.00	450.00
91-02-043	One to One-Gray Wolf	C. Brenders	10,000	245.00	450-550.
92-02-044	Pathfinder-Red Fox	C. Brenders	5,000	245.00	300.00
84-02-045	Playful Pair-Chipmunks	C. Brenders	950	60.00	400.00
94-02-046	Power and Grace	C. Brenders	2,500	265.00	265.00
92-02-047	Red Fox Study	C. Brenders	1,250	125.00	125.00
86-02-048	Robins	C. Brenders	950	40.00	125.00
93-02-049	Rocky Camp-Cougar Family	C. Brenders	5,000	275.00	275.00
93-02-050	Rocky Camp-Cubs	C. Brenders	950	225.00	225.00
92-02-051	Rocky Kingdom-Bighorn Sheep	C. Brenders	1,750	255.00	255.00
91-02-052	Shadows in the Grass-Young Cougars	C. Brenders	1,950	235.00	235.00
90-02-053	Shoreline Quartet-White Ibis	C. Brenders	1,950	265.00	265.00
84-02-054	Silent Hunter-Great Horned Owl	C. Brenders	950	95.00	450.00
84-02-055	Silent Passage	C. Brenders	950	150.00	495.00
90-02-056	Small Talk	C. Brenders	1,500	125.00	150-250.
90-02-057	Spring Fawn	C. Brenders	1,500	125.00	300.00
90-02-058	Squirrel's Dish	C. Brenders	1,950	110.00	110.00
89-02-059	Steller's Jay	C. Brenders	1,250	135.00	175.00
91-02-060	Study for One to One	C. Brenders	1,950	120.00	200.00
93-02-061	Summer Roses-Winter Wren	C. Brenders	1,500	250.00	250.00
88-02-062	Talk on the Old Fence	C. Brenders	950	165.00	525-725.
86-02-063	The Acrobat's Meal-Red Squirrel	C. Brenders	950	65.00	275.00
89-02-064	The Apple Lover	C. Brenders	1,500	125.00	275.00
91-02-065	The Balance of Nature	C. Brenders	1,950	225.00	225.00
89-02-066	The Companions	C. Brenders	18,036	200.00	900-1250.
89-02-067	The Predator's Walk	C. Brenders	1,250	150.00	375.00
89-02-068	The Survivors-Canada Geese	C. Brenders	1,500	225.00	850-950.
84-02-069	Waterside Encounter	C. Brenders	950	95.00	1000.00
87-02-070	White Elegance-Trumpeter Swans	C. Brenders	950	115.00	390.00
92-02-071	Wolf Scout #1	C. Brenders	2,500	105.00	105.00
92-02-072	Wolf Scout #2	C. Brenders	2,500	105.00	105.00
91-02-073	Wolf Study	C. Brenders	950	125.00	125.00
87-02-074	Yellow-Bellied Marmot	C. Brenders	950	95.00	425.00
Mill Pond Press		**Calle**			
84-03-001	A Brace for the Spit	P. Calle	950	110.00	275.00
83-03-002	A Winter Surprise	P. Calle	950	195.00	800.00
81-03-003	Almost Home	P. Calle	950	150.00	150.00
91-03-004	Almost There	P. Calle	950	165.00	165.00
89-03-005	And A Good Book For Company	P. Calle	950	135.00	190.00
93-03-006	And A Gizzly Claw Necklace	P. Calle	750	150.00	150.00
81-03-007	And Still Miles to Go	P. Calle	950	245.00	300.00
81-03-008	Andrew At The Falls	P. Calle	950	150.00	175.00
89-03-009	The Beaver Men	P. Calle	950	125.00	125.00
80-03-010	Caring for the Herd	P. Calle	950	110.00	110.00
84-03-011	Chance Encounter	P. Calle	950	225.00	300.00
81-03-012	Chief High Pipe (Color)	P. Calle	950	265.00	275.00
80-03-013	Chief High Pipe (Pencil)	P. Calle	950	75.00	165.00
80-03-014	Chief Joseph-Man of Peace	P. Calle	950	135.00	150.00
90-03-015	Children of Walpi	P. Calle	350	160.00	160.00
90-03-016	The Doll Maker	P. Calle	950	95.00	95.00
82-03-017	Emerging from the Woods	P. Calle	950	110.00	110-160.
81-03-018	End of a Long Day	P. Calle	950	150.00	150-190.
84-03-019	Fate of the Late Migrant	P. Calle	950	110.00	300.00
83-03-020	Free Spirits	P. Calle	950	195.00	325.00
83-03-021	Free Trapper Study	P. Calle	550	75.00	125-300.
81-03-022	Fresh Tracks	P. Calle	950	150.00	165.00
81-03-023	Friend of Foe	P. Calle	950	125.00	125.00
81-03-024	Friends	P. Calle	950	150.00	150.00
89-03-025	The Fur Trapper	P. Calle	550	75.00	175.00
82-03-026	Generations in the Valley	P. Calle	950	245.00	245.00
85-03-027	Grandmother, The	P. Calle	950	150.00	150.00
92-03-028	Hunter of Geese	P. Calle	950	125.00	125.00
93-03-029	I Call Him Friend	P. Calle	950	235.00	235.00
83-03-030	In Search of Beaver	P. Calle	950	225.00	600.00
91-03-031	In the Beginning . . . Friends	P. Calle	1,250	250.00	250.00
87-03-032	In the Land of the Giants	P. Calle	950	245.00	780.00
90-03-033	Interrupted Journey	P. Calle	1,750	265.00	265.00
90-03-034	Interrupted Journey-Prestige Ed.	P. Calle	290	465.00	465.00
87-03-035	Into the Great Alone	P. Calle	950	245.00	600.00
81-03-036	Just Over the Ridge	P. Calle	950	245.00	325.00
80-03-037	Landmark Tree	P. Calle	950	125.00	225.00
91-03-038	Man of the Fur Trade	P. Calle	550	110.00	110.00
84-03-039	Mountain Man	P. Calle	950	95.00	250-550.
89-03-040	Navajo Madonna	P. Calle	650	95.00	95.00
81-03-041	One With The Land	P. Calle	950	245.00	325.00
81-03-042	Pause at the Lower Falls	P. Calle	950	110.00	125.00
80-03-043	Prayer to the Great Mystery	P. Calle	950	245.00	400.00
82-03-044	Return to Camp	P. Calle	950	245.00	400.00
80-03-045	Sioux Chief	P. Calle	950	85.00	85-140.00
90-03-046	Son of Sitting Bull	P. Calle	950	95.00	95.00
86-03-047	Snow Hunter	P. Calle	950	150.00	250-410.
80-03-048	Something for the Pot	P. Calle	950	175.00	1000.00
85-03-049	Storyteller of the Mountains	P. Calle	950	225.00	575.00
83-03-050	Strays From the Flyway	P. Calle	950	195.00	250-340.
81-03-051	Teton Friends	P. Calle	950	150.00	200.00
91-03-052	The Silenced Honkers	P. Calle	1,250	250.00	250.00
91-03-053	They Call Me Matthew	P. Calle	950	125.00	125.00
92-03-054	Through the Tall Grass	P. Calle	950	175.00	175.00
82-03-055	Two from the Flock	P. Calle	950	245.00	400.00
80-03-056	View from the Heights	P. Calle	950	245.00	350.00
80-03-057	When Snow Came Early	P. Calle	950	85.00	250-340.
84-03-058	When Trails Cross	P. Calle	950	245.00	750.00
91-03-059	When Trails Grow Cold	P. Calle	2,500	265.00	265.00
91-03-060	When Trails Grow Cold-Prestige Ed.	P. Calle	290	465.00	465-600.
94-03-061	When Trappers Meet	P. Calle	750	165.00	165.00
81-03-062	Winter Hunter (Color)	P. Calle	950	245.00	725.00
80-03-063	Winter Hunter (Pencil)	P. Calle	950	65.00	450.00
Mill Pond Press		**Cross**			
93-04-001	Ever Green	T. Cross	750	135.00	135.00
93-04-002	Flame Catcher	T. Cross	750	185.00	185.00
93-04-003	Flicker, Flash and Twirl	T. Cross	525	165.00	165.00
92-04-004	Shell Caster	T. Cross	750	150.00	150.00
93-04-005	Shepards of Magic	T. Cross	750	135.00	135.00
93-04-006	Spellbound	T. Cross	750	85.00	85.00
92-04-007	Star Weaver	T. Cross	750	150.00	150.00
93-04-008	The Summons...And Then They Are One	T. Cross	750	195.00	195.00
94-04-009	When Water Takes to Air	T. Cross	750	135.00	135.00
93-04-010	Wind Sifter	T. Cross	750	150.00	150.00
Mill Pond Press		**Daly**			
91-05-001	A New Beginning	J. Daly	5,000	125.00	125.00
90-05-002	The Big Moment	J. Daly	1,500	125.00	125.00
91-05-003	Cat's Cradle Prestige Edition	J. Daly	950	450.00	450.00
90-05-004	Confrontation	J. Daly	1,500	85.00	85.00
90-05-005	Contentment	J. Daly	1,500	95.00	275.00
92-05-006	Dominoes	J. Daly	1,500	155.00	155.00
86-05-007	Flying High	J. Daly	950	50.00	350.00
93-05-008	Good Company	J. Daly	1,500	155.00	155.00
92-05-009	Her Secret Place	J. Daly	1,500	135.00	250.00
91-05-010	Home Team: Zero	J. Daly	1,500	150.00	150.00
91-05-011	Homemade	J. Daly	1,500	125.00	125.00
90-05-012	Honor and Allegiance	J. Daly	1,500	110.00	110.00
90-05-013	The Ice Man	J. Daly	1,500	125.00	125.00
89-05-014	In the Doghouse	J. Daly	1,500	75.00	250.00
90-05-015	It's That Time Again	J. Daly	1,500	120.00	120.00
92-05-016	Left Out	J. Daly	1,500	110.00	110.00
89-05-017	Let's Play Ball	J. Daly	1,500	75.00	150.00
90-05-018	Make Believe	J. Daly	1,500	75.00	125.00
93-05-019	New Citizen, The	J. Daly	5,000	125.00	125.00
91-05-020	Pillars of a Nation-Charter Edition	J. Daly	20,000	175.00	175.00
92-05-021	Playmates	J. Daly	1,500	155.00	350.00
90-05-022	Radio Daze	J. Daly	1,500	150.00	150.00
83-05-022	Saturday Night	J. Daly	950	85.00	1125.00
90-05-023	The Scholar	J. Daly	1,500	110.00	110.00
93-05-024	Secret Admirer	J. Daly	1,500	150.00	150.00
94-05-025	Slugger	J. Daly	950	75.00	75.00
82-05-026	Spring Fever	J. Daly	950	85.00	750.00
93-05-027	Sunday Afternoon	J. Daly	1,500	150.00	150.00
89-05-028	The Thief	J. Daly	1,500	95.00	175.00
92-05-029	The Flying Horse	J. Daly	950	325.00	325.00
91-05-030	Time-Out	J. Daly	1,500	125.00	125.00
93-05-031	To All a Good Night	J. Daly	1,500	160.00	160.00
93-05-032	When I Grow Up	J. Daly	1,500	175.00	175.00
94-05-033	Wind-Up, The	J. Daly	950	75.00	75.00
Mill Pond Press		**Morrissey**			
93-06-001	Charting the Skies	D. Morrissey	1,250	195.00	195.00
93-06-002	Charting the Skies-Caprice Edition	D. Morrissey	550	375.00	375.00
93-06-003	Draft of Drem	D. Morrissey	175	250.00	250.00
94-06-004	The Dreamer's Trunk	D. Morrissey	1,500	195.00	195.00
93-06-005	Drifting Closer	D. Morrissey	1,250	175.00	175.00
93-06-006	The Mystic Mariner	D. Morrissey	750	150.00	250.00
93-06-007	The Redd Rocket	D. Morrissey	1,250	175.00	375.00
92-06-008	The Sandman's Ship of Dreams	D. Morrissey	750	150.00	150.00
93-06-009	Sleeper Flight	D. Morrissey	1,250	195.00	195.00
93-06-010	The Telescope of Time	D. Morrissey	5,000	195.00	195.00

Company		Series			
Number	**Name**	**Artist**	**Edition Limit**	**Issue Price**	**Quote**
Mill Pond Press		**Olsen**			
93-07-001	Angels of Christmas	G. Olsen	750	135.00	135.00
93-07-002	Dress Rehearseal	G. Olsen	750	165.00	825.00
93-07-003	The Fraternity Tree	G. Olsen	750	195.00	195.00
94-07-004	Little Girls Will Mothers Be	G. Olsen	750	135.00	135.00
94-07-005	Mother's Love	G. Olsen	750	165.00	165.00
Mill Pond Press		**Seerey-Lester**			
94-08-001	Abandoned	J. Seerey-Lester	950	175.00	175.00
86-08-002	Above the Treeline-Cougar	J. Seerey-Lester	950	130.00	175.00
87-08-003	Alpenglow-Artic Wolf	J. Seerey-Lester	950	200.00	275.00
84-08-004	Among the Cattails-Canada Geese	J. Seerey-Lester	950	130.00	425.00
84-08-005	Artic Procession-Willow Ptarmigan	J. Seerey-Lester	950	220.00	600.00
90-08-006	Artic Wolf Pups	J. Seerey-Lester	290	500.00	500.00
87-08-007	Autumn Mist-Barred Owl	J. Seerey-Lester	950	160.00	225.00
92-08-008	Banyan Ambush- Black Panther	J. Seerey-Lester	950	235.00	400.00
84-08-009	Basking-Brown Pelicans	J. Seerey-Lester	950	115.00	125.00
90-08-010	Bittersweet Winter-Cardinal	J. Seerey-Lester	1,250	150.00	275.00
92-08-011	Black Jade	J. Seerey-Lester	1,950	275.00	275.00
92-08-012	Black Magic-Panther	J. Seerey-Lester	750	195.00	195.00
87-08-013	Canyon Creek-Cougar	J. Seerey-Lester	950	195.00	450.00
94-08-014	Child of the Outback	J. Seerey-Lester	950	175.00	175.00
85-08-015	Children of the Forest-Red Fox Kits	J. Seerey-Lester	950	110.00	150.00
85-08-016	Children of the Tundra-Artic Wolf Pup	J. Seerey-Lester	950	110.00	225.00
84-08-017	Close Encounter-Bobcat	J. Seerey-Lester	950	130.00	190.00
83-08-018	Cool Retreat-Lynx	J. Seerey-Lester	950	85.00	100.00
89-08-019	Cougar Run	J. Seerey-Lester	950	185.00	350-450.
90-08-020	Dawn Majesty	J. Seerey-Lester	1,250	185.00	185.00
93-08-021	Dark Encounter	J. Seerey-Lester	3,500	200.00	200.00
91-08-022	Denali Family-Grizzly Bear	J. Seerey-Lester	950	195.00	195.00
88-08-023	Edge of the Forest-Timber Wolves	J. Seerey-Lester	950	500.00	700.00
89-08-024	Evening Duet-Snowy Egrets	J. Seerey-Lester	1,250	185.00	185.00
91-08-025	Evening Encounter-Grizzly & Wolf	J. Seerey-Lester	1,250	185.00	185.00
91-08-026	Face to Face	J. Seerey-Lester	1,250	200.00	200.00
85-08-027	Fallen Birch-Chipmunk	J. Seerey-Lester	950	60.00	250.00
85-08-028	First Light-Gray Jays	J. Seerey-Lester	950	130.00	200.00
83-08-029	First Snow-Grizzly Bears	J. Seerey-Lester	950	95.00	250.00
93-08-030	Freedom I	J. Seerey-Lester	350	500.00	500.00
93-08-031	Frozen Moonlight	J. Seerey-Lester	2,500	225.00	225.00
85-08-032	Gathering-Gray Wolves, The	J. Seerey-Lester	950	165.00	350.00
89-08-033	Gorilla	J. Seerey-Lester	290	400.00	600.00
93-08-034	Grizzly Impact	J. Seerey-Lester	950	225.00	225.00
90-08-035	Grizzly Litho	J. Seerey-Lester	290	400.00	600.00
89-08-036	Heavy Going-Grizzly	J. Seerey-Lester	950	175.00	300.00
86-08-037	Hidden Admirer-Moose	J. Seerey-Lester	950	165.00	275.00
89-08-038	High and Mighty-Gorilla	J. Seerey-Lester	950	185.00	225.00
86-08-039	High Country Champion-Grizzly	J. Seerey-Lester	950	175.00	275.00
84-08-040	High Ground-Wolves	J. Seerey-Lester	950	130.00	325.00
84-08-041	Icy Outcrop-White Gyrfalcon	J. Seerey-Lester	950	115.00	200.00
90-08-042	In Their Presence	J. Seerey-Lester	1,250	200.00	200.00
85-08-043	Island Sanctuary-Mallards	J. Seerey-Lester	950	95.00	175.00
83-08-044	Lone Fisherman-Great Blue Heron	J. Seerey-Lester	950	85.00	300.00
93-08-045	Loonlight	J. Seerey-Lester	1,500	225.00	225.00
84-08-046	Lying Low-Cougar	J. Seerey-Lester	950	85.00	450.00
91-08-047	Monsoon-White Tiger	J. Seerey-Lester	950	195.00	195.00
91-08-048	Moonlight Chase-Cougar	J. Seerey-Lester	1,250	195.00	195-220.
88-08-049	Morning Display-Common Loons	J. Seerey-Lester	950	135.00	300.00
93-08-050	Morning Glory	J. Seerey-Lester	1,250	225.00	225.00
84-08-051	Morning Mist-Snowy Owl	J. Seerey-Lester	950	95.00	95-180.00
90-08-052	Mountain Cradle	J. Seerey-Lester	1,250	200.00	300.00
90-08-053	Night Run-Artic Wolves	J. Seerey-Lester	1,250	200.00	250.00
93-08-054	Night Specter	J. Seerey-Lester	1,250	195.00	195.00
87-08-055	Out of the Blizzard-Timber Wolves	J. Seerey-Lester	950	215.00	350.00
92-08-056	Out of the Darkness	J. Seerey-Lester	290	200.00	200.00
91-08-057	Out on a Limb-Young Barred Owl	J. Seerey-Lester	950	185.00	185.00
91-08-058	Panda Trilogy	J. Seerey-Lester	950	375.00	375.00
93-08-059	Phantoms of the Tundra	J. Seerey-Lester	950	235.00	235.00
90-08-060	The Plunge-Northern Sea Lions	J. Seerey-Lester	1,250	200.00	200.00
86-08-061	Racing the Storm-Artic Wolves	J. Seerey-Lester	950	200.00	350.00
93-08-062	The Rains-Tiger	J. Seerey-Lester	950	225.00	225.00
92-08-063	Ranthambhore Rush	J. Seerey-Lester	950	225.00	225.00
92-08-064	Regal Majesty	J. Seerey-Lester	290	200.00	200.00
90-08-065	Seasonal Greeting-Cardinal	J. Seerey-Lester	1,250	150.00	150.00
93-08-066	Seeking Attention	J. Seerey-Lester	950	200.00	200.00
91-08-067	Sisters-Artic Wolves	J. Seerey-Lester	1,250	185.00	185.00
89-08-068	Sneak Peak	J. Seerey-Lester	950	185.00	185.00
89-08-069	Softly, Softly-White Tiger	J. Seerey-Lester	950	220.00	490.00
91-08-070	Something Stirred (Bengal Tiger)	J. Seerey-Lester	950	195.00	195.00
84-08-071	Spirit of the North-White Wolf	J. Seerey-Lester	950	130.00	185.00
90-08-072	Spout	J. Seerey-Lester	290	500.00	500.00
86-08-073	Spring Mist Chickadees	J. Seerey-Lester	950	105.00	150.00
89-08-074	Spring Flurry-Adelie Penguins	J. Seerey-Lester	950	185.00	185.00
90-08-075	Suitors-Wood Ducks	J. Seerey-Lester	3,313	135.00	135.00
90-08-076	Summer Rain-Common Loons	J. Seerey-Lester	4,500	200.00	200.00
90-08-077	Summer Rain-Common Loons (Prestige)	J. Seerey-Lester	450	425.00	425.00
92-08-078	The Chase-Snow Leopard	J. Seerey-Lester	950	200.00	200.00
83-08-079	The Refuge-Raccoon	J. Seerey-Lester	950	85.00	300.00
90-08-080	Their First Season	J. Seerey-Lester	1,250	200.00	200.00
90-08-081	Togetherness	J. Seerey-Lester	1,250	125.00	185.00
85-08-082	Under the Pines-Bobcat	J. Seerey-Lester	950	95.00	275.00
89-08-083	Water Sport-Bobcat	J. Seerey-Lester	950	185.00	185.00
90-08-084	Whitetail Spring	J. Seerey-Lester	1,250	185.00	185.00
83-08-084	Winter Lookout-Cougar	J. Seerey-Lester	950	85.00	500.00
86-08-086	Winter Perch-Cardinal	J. Seerey-Lester	950	85.00	175.00
85-08-087	Winter Rendezvous-Coyotes	J. Seerey-Lester	950	140.00	225.00
93-08-088	Wolong Whiteout	J. Seerey-Lester	950	225.00	225.00
Mill Pond Press		**Smith**			
93-09-001	African Ebony-Black Leopard	D. Smith	1,250	195.00	195.00
92-09-002	Armada	D. Smith	950	195.00	195.00
93-09-003	Catching the Scent-Polar Bear	D. Smith	950	175.00	175.00
91-09-004	Dawn's Early Light-Bald Eagles	D. Smith	950	185.00	185.00
93-09-005	Echo Bay-Loon Family	D. Smith	1,150	185.00	185.00
92-09-006	Eyes of the North	D. Smith	2,500	225.00	225.00
93-09-007	Guardians of the Den	D. Smith	1,500	195.00	325.00
92-09-008	Night Moves-Cougar	D. Smith	950	185.00	185.00
93-09-009	Shrouded Forest-Bald Eagle	D. Smith	950	150.00	750.00
91-09-010	Twilight's Calling-Common Loons	D. Smith	950	175.00	375.00
93-09-011	What's Bruin	D. Smith	1,750	185.00	325.00
New Masters Publishing		**Bannister**			
78-01-001	Bandstand	P. Bannister	S/O	75.00	450.00
80-01-002	Dust of Autumn	P. Bannister	S/O	200.00	1225.00
80-01-003	Faded Glory	P. Bannister	S/O	200.00	1225.00
80-01-004	Gift of Happiness	P. Bannister	S/O	200.00	2000.00
80-01-005	Girl on the Beach	P. Bannister	S/O	200.00	1200.00
80-01-006	The Silver Bell	P. Bannister	S/O	200.00	2000.00
81-01-007	April	P. Bannister	S/O	200.00	1100.00
81-01-008	Easter	P. Bannister	S/O	260.00	950.00
81-01-009	Juliet	P. Bannister	S/O	260.00	5000.00
81-01-010	My Special Place	P. Bannister	S/O	260.00	1850.00
81-01-011	Porcelain Rose	P. Bannister	S/O	260.00	2000.00
81-01-012	Rehearsal	P. Bannister	S/O	260.00	1850.00
81-01-013	Sea Haven	P. Bannister	S/O	260.00	1100.00
81-01-014	Titania	P. Bannister	S/O	260.00	900.00
82-01-015	Amaryllis	P. Bannister	S/O	285.00	1900.00
82-01-016	Emily	P. Bannister	S/O	285.00	800.00
82-01-017	Ivy	P. Bannister	S/O	285.00	700.00
82-01-018	Jasmine	P. Bannister	S/O	285.00	650.00
82-01-019	Mail Order Brides	P. Bannister	S/O	325.00	2300.00
82-01-020	Memories	P. Bannister	S/O	235.00	500.00
82-01-021	Nuance	P. Bannister	S/O	235.00	470.00
82-01-022	The Present	P. Bannister	S/O	260.00	800.00
83-01-023	The Duchess	P. Bannister	S/O	250.00	1800.00
84-01-024	The Fan Window	P. Bannister	S/O	195.00	450.00
84-01-025	Window Seat	P. Bannister	S/O	150.00	600.00
83-01-026	Ophelia	P. Bannister	S/O	150.00	675.00
84-01-027	Scarlet Ribbons	P. Bannister	S/O	150.00	325.00
83-01-028	Mementos	P. Bannister	S/O	150.00	1400.00
84-01-029	April Light	P. Bannister	S/O	150.00	600.00
84-01-030	Make Believe	P. Bannister	S/O	150.00	600.00
88-01-031	Summer Choices	P. Bannister	S/O	250.00	800.00
88-01-032	Guinevere	P. Bannister	S/O	265.00	1000.00
88-01-033	Love Seat	P. Bannister	S/O	230.00	500.00
88-01-034	Apples and Oranges	P. Bannister	S/O	265.00	600.00
89-01-035	Daydreams	P. Bannister	S/O	265.00	530.00
86-01-036	Pride & Joy	P. Bannister	S/O	150.00	300.00
87-01-037	September Harvest	P. Bannister	S/O	150.00	300.00
87-01-038	Quiet Corner	P. Bannister	S/O	115.00	300.00
87-01-039	First Prize	P. Bannister	S/O	115.00	175.00
88-01-040	Floribunda	P. Bannister	S/O	265.00	550.00
89-01-041	March Winds	P. Bannister	S/O	265.00	530.00
89-01-042	Peace	P. Bannister	S/O	265.00	1100.00
89-01-043	The Quilt	P. Bannister	S/O	265.00	900.00
89-01-044	Low Tide	P. Bannister	S/O	265.00	550.00
89-01-045	Chapter One	P. Bannister	S/O	265.00	1300.00
90-01-046	Lavender Hill	P. Bannister	S/O	265.00	625.00
90-01-047	Rendezvous	P. Bannister	S/O	265.00	650.00
90-01-048	Sisters	P. Bannister	S/O	265.00	950.00
90-01-049	Seascapes	P. Bannister	S/O	265.00	550.00
90-01-050	Songbird	P. Bannister	S/O	265.00	550.00
90-01-051	Good Friends	P. Bannister	S/O	265.00	750.00
91-01-052	String of Pearls	P. Bannister	S/O	265.00	850.00
91-01-053	Wildflowers	P. Bannister	S/O	295.00	590.00
91-01-054	Crossroads	P. Bannister	S/O	295.00	590.00
91-01-055	Teatime	P. Bannister	S/O	295.00	600.00
91-01-056	Celebration	P. Bannister	S/O	350.00	700.00
91-01-057	Pudding & Pies	P. Bannister	S/O	265.00	265.00
92-01-058	Morning Mist	P. Bannister	S/O	265.00	265.00
92-01-059	Love Letters	P. Bannister	S/O	265.00	265.00
92-01-060	Crystal Bowl	P. Bannister	S/O	265.00	265.00
93-01-061	Deja Vu	P. Bannister	S/O	265.00	265.00
93-01-062	Crowning Glory	P. Bannister	S/O	265.00	265.00
Past Impressions		**Maley**			
84-01-001	Secluded Garden	A. Maley	Closed	150.00	970.00
84-01-002	Glorious Summer	A. Maley	Closed	150.00	725.00
85-01-003	Secret Thoughts	A. Maley	Closed	150.00	,850.00
85-01-004	Passing Elegance	A. Maley	Closed	150.00	750.00
86-01-005	Winter Romance	A. Maley	Closed	150.00	600.00
86-01-006	Tell Me	A. Maley	Closed	150.00	850.00
88-01-007	Opening Night	A. Maley	Closed	250.00	2000.00
67-01-008	Love Letter	A. Maley	Closed	200.00	300-550.
87-01-009	The Promise	A. Maley	450	200.00	315.00
88-01-010	Day Dreams	A. Maley	500	200.00	350-450.
88-01-011	The Boardwalk	A. Maley	500	250.00	340.00
88-01-012	Tranquil Moment	A. Maley	Closed	250.00	315.00
88-01-013	Joys of Childhood	A. Maley	500	250.00	250.00
88-01-014	Victorian Trio	A. Maley	500	250.00	340.00
89-01-015	English Rose	A. Maley	750	250.00	285.00
89-01-016	Winter Impressions	A. Maley	750	250.00	315.00
89-01-017	In Harmony	A. Maley	750	250.00	250.00
90-01-018	Festive Occasion	A. Maley	750	250.00	250.00
90-01-019	Summer Pastime	A. Maley	750	250.00	250.00
90-01-020	Cafe Royale	A. Maley	750	275.00	275.00
90-01-021	Romantic Engagement	A. Maley	750	275.00	275.00
90-01-022	Gracious Era	A. Maley	750	275.00	275.00
90-01-023	Evening Performance	A. Maley	750	150.00	150.00
91-01-024	Between Friends	A. Maley	750	275.00	275.00
91-01-025	Summer Carousel	A. Maley	750	200.00	200.00
91-01-026	Sunday Afternoon	A. Maley	750	275.00	275.00
91-01-027	Winter Carousel	A. Maley	750	200.00	200.00
92-01-028	Evening Performance	A. Maley	750	150.00	150.00
92-01-029	Intimate Moment	A. Maley	750	250.00	250.00
92-01-030	A Walk in the Park	A. Maley	500	260.00	260.00
92-01-031	An Elegant Affair	A. Maley	500	260.00	260.00
92-01-032	Circle of Love	A. Maley	500	250.00	250.00
94-01-033	The Recital	A. Maley	500	275.00	275.00
94-01-034	Visiting The Nursery	A. Maley	500	250.00	250.00
Pemberton & Oakes		**Zolan's Children-Lithographs**			
82-01-001	By Myself	D. Zolan	880	98.00	250-289.
82-01-002	Erik and the Dandelion	D. Zolan	880	98.00	400-460.
84-01-003	Sabina in the Grass	D. Zolan	880	98.00	640-710.
86-01-004	Tender Moment	D. Zolan	880	98.00	375-450.
87-01-005	Touching the Sky	D. Zolan	880	98.00	290-350.
88-01-006	Tiny Treasures	D. Zolan	450	150.00	175-275.
88-01-007	Winter Angel	D. Zolan	980	98.00	325-400.
88-01-009	Small Wonder	D. Zolan	880	98.00	312.00
88-01-010	Day Dreamer	D. Zolan	1,000	35.00	150.00
88-01-011	Waiting to Play	D. Zolan	1,000	35.00	130-195.
89-01-012	Christmas Prayer	D. Zolan	880	98.00	175-245.
89-01-013	Almost Home	D. Zolan	880	98.00	275-309.
89-01-014	Brotherly Love	D. Zolan	880	98.00	360.00
89-01-015	Daddy's Home	D. Zolan	880	98.00	305.00
89-01-016	Grandma's Mirror	D. Zolan	880	98.00	170.00
89-01-017	Mother's Angels	D. Zolan	880	98.00	310.00
89-01-018	Rodeo Girl	D. Zolan	880	98,00	170.00

Company Number	Name	Series Artist	Edition Limit	Issue Price	Quote
89-01-019	Snowy Adventure	D. Zolan	880	98.00	295.00
89-01-020	Summer's Child	D. Zolan	880	98.00	98.00
90-01-021	Colors of Spring	D. Zolan	880	98.00	185-325.
90-01-022	Crystal's Creek	D. Zolan	880	98.00	195-325.
90-01-023	First Kiss	D. Zolan	880	98.00	260.00
90-01-024	Laurie and the Creche	D. Zolan	880	98.00	98.00
91-01-025	Autumn Leaves	D. Zolan	880	98.00	175.00
91-01-026	Flowers for Mother	D. Zolan	880	98.00	98.00
91-01-027	Summer Suds	D. Zolan	880	98.00	98.00
92-01-028	Enchanted Forest	D. Zolan	880	98.00	98.00
92-01-029	New Shoes	D. Zolan	880	98.00	98.00
93-01-030	The Big Catch	D. Zolan	880	98.00	98.00
93-01-031	Grandma's Garden	D. Zolan	880	98.00	98.00
Pemberton & Oakes		**Zolan's Children-Miniature Lithographs**			
91-02-001	Morning Discovery	D. Zolan	Yr.Iss.	35.00	35.00
92-02-002	The Little Fisherman	D. Zolan	Yr.Iss.	35.00	35.00
92-02-003	Colors of Spring	D. Zolan	Yr.Iss.	35.00	35.00
92-02-004	Forest & Fairytales	D. Zolan	Yr.Iss.	22.00	22.00
Pemberton & Oakes		**Grandparents Day-Miniature Lithographs**			
92-03-001	Letter to Grandma	D. Zolan	Yr.Iss.	35.00	35.00
Pemberton & Oakes		**Single Issues-Miniature Lithographs**			
91-04-001	Tender Moment	D. Zolan	Yr.Iss.	35.00	35.00
93-04-002	1993 A Christmas Prayer	D. Zolan	Yr.Iss.	35.00	27-35.00
93-04-003	Daddy's Home	D. Zolan	Yr.Iss.	22.00	22.00
93-04-004	Letter To Grandma	D. Zolan	Yr.Iss.	22.00	27.00
93-04-005	First Kiss	D. Zolan	Yr.Iss.	22.00	22.00
Pemberton & Oakes		**Miniature Replicas of Oils**			
90-05-001	Brotherly Love	D. Zolan	Yr.Iss.	24.40	24.40
90-05-002	Daddy's Home	D. Zolan	Yr.Iss.	24.40	24.40
91-05-003	Crystal's Creek	D. Zolan	Yr.Iss.	24.40	24.40
92-05-004	It's Grandma & Grandpa	D. Zolan	Yr.Iss.	24.40	24.40
92-05-005	Mother's Angels	D. Zolan	Yr.Iss.	24.40	24.40
92-05-006	Touching the Sky	D. Zolan	Yr.Iss.	24.40	30.00
Pemberton & Oakes		**Canvas Replicas**			
92-06-001	Quiet Time	D. Zolan	Yr.Iss.	18.80	24.00
92-06-002	September Girl	D. Zolan	Yr.Iss.	18.80	18.80
92-06-003	Summer Garden	D. Zolan	Yr.Iss.	18.80	30.00
Pemberton & Oakes		**Quiet Moments -Miniature Lithographs**			
92-07-001	92 One Summer Day	D. Zolan	Yr.Iss.	22.00	27.00
93-07-002	Crystal's Creek	D. Zolan	Yr.Iss.	22.00	22.00
93-07-003	Birthday Greetings	D. Zolan	Yr.Iss.	22.00	22.00
93-07-004	Country Kitten	D. Zolan	Yr.Iss.	22.00	22.00
Pemberton & Oakes		**Membership-Miniature Lithographs**			
92-08-001	Brotherly Love	D. Zolan	Yr.Iss.	18.00	18.00
93-08-002	New Shoes	D. Zolan	Yr.Iss.	18.00	18.00
93-08-003	Country Walk	D. Zolan	Yr.Iss.	22.00	22.00
Pemberton & Oakes		**Canvas Transfer**			
92-09-001	Daisy Days	D. Zolan	Yr.Iss.	24.20	24.20
93-09-002	It's Grandma & Grandpa	D. Zolan	Yr.Iss.	24.20	24.20
93-09-003	Spring Duet	D. Zolan	Yr.Iss.	24.40	24.40
Reco International		**Limited Edition Print**			
84-01-001	Jessica	S. Kuck	500	60.00	400.00
85-01-002	Heather	S. Kuck	500	75.00	150.00
86-01-003	Ashley	S. Kuck	500	85.00	150.00
Reco International		**McClelland**			
XX-02-001	Olivia	J. McClelland	300	175.00	175.00
XX-02-002	Sweet Dreams	J. McClelland	300	145.00	145.00
XX-02-003	Just for You	J. McClelland	300	155.00	155.00
XX-02-004	Reverie	J. McClelland	300	110.00	110.00
XX-02-005	I Love Tammy	J. McClelland	500	75.00	100.00
Reco International		**Fine Art Canvas Reproduction**			
90-03-001	Beach Play	J. McClelland	350	80.00	80.00
91-03-002	Flower Swing	J. McClelland	350	100.00	100.00
91-03-003	Summer Conversation	J. McClelland	350	80.00	80.00
Roman, Inc.		**Hook**			
81-01-001	The Carpenter	F. Hook	Yr.Iss	100.00	1000.00
81-01-002	The Carpenter (remarque)	F. Hook	Yr.Iss	100.00	3000.00
82-01-003	Frolicking	F. Hook	1,200	60.00	350.00
82-01-004	Gathering	F. Hook	1,200	60.00	350-450.
82-01-005	Poulets	F. Hook	1,200	60.00	350.00
82-01-006	Bouquet	F. Hook	1,200	70.00	350.00
82-01-007	Surprise	F. Hook	1,200	50.00	350.00
82-01-008	Posing	F. Hook	1,200	70.00	350.00
82-01-009	Little Children, Come to Me	F. Hook	1,950	50.00	500.00
82-01-010	Little Children, Come to Me, remarque	F. Hook	50	100.00	500.00
Roman, Inc.		**Portraits of Love**			
88-02-001	Sharing	F. Hook	2,500	25.00	25.00
88-02-002	Expectation	F. Hook	2,500	25.00	25.00
88-02-003	Remember When...	F. Hook	2,500	25.00	25.00
88-02-004	My Kitty	F. Hook	2,500	25.00	25.00
88-02-005	In Mother's Arms	F. Hook	2,500	25.00	25.00
88-02-006	Sunkissed Afternoon	F. Hook	2,500	25.00	25.00
Roman, Inc.		**Abbie Williams**			
88-03-001	Mary, Mother of the Carpenter	A. Williams	Closed	100.00	100.00
Roman, Inc.		**The Discovery of America Miniature Art Print**			
91-04-001	The Discovery of America	I. Spencer	Open	2.00	2.00
Roman, Inc.		**Divine Servant**			
93-05-001	Divine Servant, print of drawing	M. Greiner Jr.	Open	35.00	35.00
94-05-002	Divine Servant, print of painting	M. Greiner Jr.	Yr.Iss.	75.00	75.00
94-05-003	Divine Servant, print of painting w/remarque	M. Greiner Jr.	Yr.Iss.	75.00	75.00
94-05-004	Divine Servant, print of painting	M. Greiner Jr.	Yr.Iss.	150.00	150.00
94-05-005	Divine Servant, print of painting w/remarque	M. Greiner Jr.	Yr.Iss.	150.00	150.00
Schmid		**Lowell Davis Lithographs**			
81-01-001	Surprise in the Cellar, remarque	L. Davis	101	100.00	400.00
81-01-002	Surprise in the Cellar, regular edition	L. Davis	899	75.00	375.00
81-01-003	Plum Tuckered Out, remarque	L. Davis	101	100.00	350.00
81-01-004	Plum Tuckered Out, regular edition	L. Davis	899	75.00	400.00

Company Number	Name	Series Artist	Edition Limit	Issue Price	Quote
81-01-005	Duke's Mixture, remarque	L. Davis	101	150.00	350.00
81-01-006	Duke's Mixture, regular edition	L. Davis	899	75.00	125.00
82-01-007	Bustin' with Pride, remarque	L. Davis	101	150.00	250.00
82-01-008	Bustin' with Pride, regular edition	L. Davis	899	75.00	125.00
82-01-009	Birth of a Blossom, remarque	L. Davis	50	200.00	450.00
82-01-010	Birth of a Blossom, regular edition	L. Davis	400	125.00	300.00
82-01-011	Suppertime, remarque	L. Davis	50	200.00	450.00
82-01-012	Suppertime, regular edition	L. Davis	400	125.00	300.00
82-01-013	Foxfire Farm, remarque	L. Davis	100	200.00	250.00
82-01-014	Foxfire Farm, regular edition	L. Davis	800	125.00	125.00
85-01-015	Self Portrait	L. Davis	450	75.00	192.00
87-01-016	Blossom's Gift	L. Davis	450	75.00	300.00
89-01-017	Sun Worshippers	L. Davis	750	100.00	100.00
90-01-018	Sunday Afternoon Treat	L. Davis	750	100.00	100.00
91-01-019	Warm Milk	L. Davis	750	100.00	179.00
92-01-020	Cat and Jenny Wren	L. Davis	750	100.00	100.00
93-01-021	The Old Home Place	L. Davis	750	130.00	130.00
Schmid		**Berta Hummel Lithographs**			
80-02-001	Moonlight Return	B. Hummel	900	150.00	850.00
80-02-002	1984 American Visit	B. Hummel	5	550.00	1000.00
81-02-003	A Time to Remember	B. Hummel	720	150.00	300.00
81-02-004	1984 American Visit	B. Hummel	5	550.00	1100.00
81-02-005	Remarqued	B. Hummel	180	250.00	1250.00
81-02-006	1984 American Visit	B. Hummel	2	1100.00	1700.00
82-02-007	Poppies	B. Hummel	450	150.00	650.00
82-02-008	1984 American Visit	B. Hummel	3	250.00	850.00
83-02-009	Angelic Messenger, 75th Anniversary	B. Hummel	195	375.00	700.00
83-02-010	Angelic Messenger, Christmas Message	B. Hummel	400	275.00	450.00
83-02-011	1984 American Visit	B. Hummel	10	275.00	600.00
83-02-012	Regular	B. Hummel	100	175.00	350.00
83-02-013	1984 American Visit	B. Hummel	10	175.00	400.00
85-02-014	Birthday Bouquet, Edition 1	B. Hummel	195	450.00	550.00
85-02-015	Birthday Bouquet, Edition 2	B. Hummel	225	375.00	375.00
85-02-016	Birthday Bouquet, Edition 3	B. Hummel	100	195.00	395.00
Schmid		**Ferrandiz Lithographs**			
80-03-001	Most Precious Gift, remarque	J. Ferrandiz	50	225.00	2800.00
80-03-002	Most Precious Gift, regular edition	J. Ferrandiz	425	125.00	1200.00
80-03-003	My Star, remarque	J. Ferrandiz	75	175.00	1800.00
80-03-004	My Star, regular edition	J. Ferrandiz	675	100.00	650.00
81-03-005	Heart of Seven Colors, remarque	J. Ferrandiz	75	175.00	1300.00
81-03-006	Heart of Seven Colors, regular edition	J. Ferrandiz	600	100.00	395.00
82-03-007	Oh Small Child, remarque	J. Ferrandiz	50	225.00	1450.00
82-03-008	Oh Small Child, regular edition	J. Ferrandiz	450	125.00	495.00
82-03-009	Spreading the Word, remarque	J. Ferrandiz	75	225.00	1075.00
82-03-010	Spreading the Word, regular edition	J. Ferrandiz	675	125.00	190-250.
82-03-011	On the Threshold of Life, remarque	J. Ferrandiz	50	275.00	1350.00
82-03-012	On the Threshold of Life, regular edition	J. Ferrandiz	425	150.00	450.00
82-03-013	Riding Through the Rain, remarque	J. Ferrandiz	100	300.00	950.00
82-03-014	Riding Through the Rain, regular edition	J. Ferrandiz	900	165.00	350.00
82-03-015	Mirror of the Soul, regular edition	J. Ferrandiz	225	150.00	425.00
82-03-016	Mirror of the Soul, remarque	J. Ferrandiz	35	250.00	2400.00
82-03-017	He Seems to Sleep, regular edition	J. Ferrandiz	450	150.00	700.00
82-03-018	He Seems to Sleep, remarque	J. Ferrandiz	25	300.00	3200.00
83-03-019	Friendship, remarque	J. Ferrandiz	15	1200.00	2300.00
83-03-020	Friendship, regular edition	J. Ferrandiz	460	165.00	450.00
84-03-021	Star in the Teapot; regular edition	J. Ferrandiz	410	165.00	165.00
84-03-022	Star in the Teapot; remarque	J. Ferrandiz	15	1200.00	2100.00
V.F. Fine Arts		**Kuck**			
86-01-001	Tender Moments, proof	S. Kuck	50	80.00	295.00
86-01-002	Tender Moments, S/N	S. Kuck	500	70.00	250.00
86-01-003	Summer Reflections, proof	S. Kuck	90	70.00	300.00
86-01-004	Summer Reflections, S/N	S. Kuck	900	60.00	250.00
86-01-005	Silhouette, proof	S. Kuck	25	90.00	250.00
86-01-006	Silhouette, S/N	S. Kuck	250	80.00	220.00
87-01-007	Le Papillion, remarque	S. Kuck	7	150.00	250.00
87-01-008	Le Papillion, proof	S. Kuck	35	110.00	175.00
87-01-009	Le Papillion, S/N	S. Kuck	350	90.00	150.00
87-01-010	The Reading Lesson, proof	S. Kuck	90	70.00	190-250.
87-01-011	The Reading Lesson, S/N	S. Kuck	900	60.00	200.00
87-01-012	The Daisy, proof	S. Kuck	90	40.00	100.00
87-01-013	The Daisy, S/N	S. Kuck	900	30.00	75.00
87-01-014	The Loveseat, proof	S. Kuck	90	40.00	50-75.00
87-01-015	The Loveseat, S/N	S. Kuck	900	30.00	50.00
87-01-016	A Quiet Time, proof	S. Kuck	90	50.00	75.00
87-01-017	A Quiet Time, S/N	S. Kuck	900	40.00	50.00
87-01-018	The Flower Girl, proof	S. Kuck	90	50.00	75.00
87-01-019	The Flower Girl, S/N	S. Kuck	900	40.00	50-60.00
87-01-020	Mother's Love, proof	S. Kuck	12	225.00	1800.00
87-01-021	Mother's Love, S/N	S. Kuck	150	195.00	1200.00
88-01-022	My Dearest, S/N	S. Kuck	350	160.00	775.00
88-01-023	My Dearest, proof	S. Kuck	50	200.00	900.00
88-01-024	My Dearest, remarque	S. Kuck	25	325.00	1100.00
88-01-025	The Kitten, S/N	S. Kuck	350	120.00	1200.00
88-01-026	The Kitten, proof	S. Kuck	50	150.00	1300.00
88-01-027	The Kitten, remarque	S. Kuck	25	250.00	950-1450.
88-01-028	Wild Flowers, S/N	S. Kuck	350	160.00	250.00
88-01-029	Wild Flowers, proof	S. Kuck	50	175.00	300.00
88-01-030	Wild Flowers, remarque	S. Kuck	25	250.00	350.00
88-01-031	Little Ballerina, S/N	S. Kuck	150	110.00	300.00
88-01-032	Little Ballerina, proof	S. Kuck	25	150.00	350.00
88-01-033	Little Ballerina, remarque	S. Kuck	25	225.00	450.00
88-01-034	First Recital, S/N	S. Kuck	150	200.00	900.00
88-01-035	First Recital, proof	S. Kuck	25	250.00	1000.00
88-01-036	First Recital, remarque	S. Kuck	25	400.00	1200.00
89-01-037	Sisters, S/N	S. Kuck	900	95.00	190.00
89-01-038	Sisters, proof	S. Kuck	90	150.00	395.00
89-01-039	Sisters, remarque	S. Kuck	50	200.00	375.00
89-01-040	Rose Garden, S/N	S. Kuck	500	95.00	400.00
89-01-041	Rose Garden, proof	S. Kuck	50	150.00	450.00
89-01-042	Rose Garden, remarque	S. Kuck	50	200.00	600.00
89-01-043	Sonatina, S/N	S. Kuck	900	150.00	350.00
89-01-044	Sonatina, proof	S. Kuck	90	225.00	450.00
89-01-045	Sonatina, remarque	S. Kuck	50	300.00	600.00
89-01-046	Puppy, S/N	S. Kuck	500	120.00	600.00
89-01-047	Puppy, proof	S. Kuck	50	180.00	650.00
89-01-048	Puppy, remarque	S. Kuck	50	240.00	750-950.
89-01-049	Innocence, S/N	S. Kuck	900	150.00	200.00
89-01-050	Innocence, proof	S. Kuck	90	225.00	250.00
89-01-051	Innocence, remarque	S. Kuck	50	300.00	350.00
89-01-052	Bundle of Joy, S/N	S. Kuck	1,000	125.00	250.00
89-01-053	Day Dreaming, S/N	S. Kuck	900	150.00	200.00

Number	Name	Artist	Edition Limit	Issue Price	Quote
89-01-054	Day Dreaming, proof	S. Kuck	90	225.00	225.00
89-01-055	Day Dreaming, remarque	S. Kuck	50	300.00	300.00
90-01-056	Lilly Pond, S/N	S. Kuck	750	150.00	150.00
90-01-057	Lilly Pond, proof	S. Kuck	75	200.00	200.00
90-01-058	Lilly Pond, color remarque	S. Kuck	125	500.00	500.00
90-01-059	First Snow, S/N	S. Kuck	500	95.00	225.00
90-01-060	First Snow, proof	S. Kuck	50	150.00	275.00
90-01-061	First Snow, remarque	S. Kuck	25	200.00	325.00
90-01-062	Le Beau, S/N	S. Kuck	1,500	80.00	160.00
90-01-063	Le Beau, proof	S. Kuck	150	120.00	200.00
90-01-064	Le Beau, remarque	S. Kuck	25	160.00	250.00
90-01-065	Chopsticks, S/N	S. Kuck	1,500	80.00	80.00
90-01-066	Chopsticks, proof	S. Kuck	150	120.00	120.00
90-01-067	Chopsticks, remarque	S. Kuck	25	160.00	160.00
91-01-068	Memories, S/N	S. Kuck	5,000	195.00	195.00
91-01-069	God's Gift, proof	S. Kuck	150	150.00	150.00
91-01-070	God's Gift, S/N	S. Kuck	1,500	95.00	95.00
92-01-071	Joyous Day, S/N	S. Kuck	1,200	125.00	125.00
92-01-072	Joyous Day, proof	S. Kuck	120	175.00	175.00
92-01-073	Joyous Day, Canvas Transfer	S. Kuck	250	250.00	250.00
92-01-074	Yesterday, S/N	S. Kuck	950	95.00	95.00
92-01-075	Yesterday, proof	S. Kuck	95	150.00	150.00
92-01-076	Yesterday, Canvas Framed	S. Kuck	550	195.00	195.00
92-01-077	Duet, S/N	S. Kuck	950	125.00	125.00
92-01-078	Duet, proof	S. Kuck	95	175.00	175.00
92-01-079	Duet, Canvas Framed	S. Kuck	500	255.00	255.00
93-01-080	Good Morning, S/N	S. Kuck	2,500	145.00	145.00
93-01-081	Good Morning, proof	S. Kuck	50	175.00	175.00
93-01-082	Good Morning, Canvas	S. Kuck	250	500.00	500.00
93-01-083	Best Friends, S/N	S. Kuck	2,500	145.00	145.00
93-01-084	Best Friend, proof	S. Kuck	250	175.00	175.00
93-01-085	Best Friends, Cansvas Transfer	S. Kuck	250	500.00	500.00
93-01-086	Thinking of You, S/N	S. Kuck	2,500	145.00	145.00
93-01-087	Thinking of You, Canvas Transfer	S. Kuck	250	500.00	500.00
93-01-088	Buttons & Bows, S/N	S. Kuck	950	95.00	95.00
93-01-089	Buttons & Bows, proof	S. Kuck	95	125.00	125.00
93-01-090	Good Morning, S/N	S. Kuck	2,500	145.00	145.00
93-01-091	Good Morning, proof	S. Kuck	250	175.00	175.00
93-01-092	Good Morning, Canvas Transfer	S. Kuck	250	500.00	500.00
94-01-093	Garden Memories, S/N	S. Kuck	2,500	145.00	145.00
94-01-094	Garden Memories, Canvas Transfer	S. Kuck	250	500.00	500.00
World Art Editions		**Masseria**			
80-01-001	Eduardo	F. Masseria	300	275.00	2700.00
80-01-002	Rosanna	F. Masseria	300	275.00	3200.00
80-01-003	Nina	F. Masseria	300	325.00	1950.00
80-01-004	First Kiss	F. Masseria	300	375.00	2200.00
81-01-005	Selene	F. Masseria	300	325.00	2200.00
81-01-006	First Flower	F. Masseria	300	325.00	2200.00
81-01-007	Elisa with Flower	F. Masseria	300	325.00	2200.00
81-01-008	Solange	F. Masseria	300	325.00	2200.00
81-01-009	Susan Sewing	F. Masseria	300	375.00	2500.00
81-01-010	Jessica	F. Masseria	300	375.00	2300.00
81-01-011	Eleanor	F. Masseria	300	375.00	1900.00
81-01-012	Julie	F. Masseria	300	375.00	950.00
82-01-013	Robin	F. Masseria	300	425.00	975.00
82-01-014	Jodie	F. Masseria	300	425.00	950.00
82-01-015	Jill	F. Masseria	300	425.00	750.00
82-01-016	Jamie	F. Masseria	300	425.00	750.00
82-01-017	Yasmin	F. Masseria	300	425.00	720.00
82-01-018	Yvette	F. Masseria	300	425.00	620.00
82-01-019	Judith	F. Masseria	300	425.00	750.00
82-01-020	Amy	F. Masseria	300	425.00	720.00
83-01-021	Tara	F. Masseria	300	450.00	1100.00
83-01-022	Antonio	F. Masseria	300	450.00	1100.00
84-01-023	Memoirs	F. Masseria	300	450.00	700.00
84-01-024	Christopher	F. Masseria	300	450.00	700.00
84-01-025	Bettina	F. Masseria	250	550.00	700.00
84-01-026	Vincente	F. Masseria	360	550.00	1000.00
85-01-027	Christina	F. Masseria	300	500.00	700.00
85-01-028	Jorgito	F. Masseria	300	500.00	700.00
84-01-029	Regina	F. Masseria	950	395.00	495.00
84-01-030	Peter	F. Masseria	950	395.00	495.00
85-01-031	Marquerita	F. Masseria	950	495.00	495.00
85-01-032	To Catch a Butterfly	F. Masseria	950	495.00	495.00

PLATES

Number	Name	Artist	Edition Limit	Issue Price	Quote
American Artists		**The Horses of Fred Stone**			
82-01-001	Patience	F. Stone	9,500	55.00	145.00
82-01-002	Arabian Mare and Foal	F. Stone	9,500	55.00	125.00
82-01-003	Safe and Sound	F. Stone	9,500	55.00	80-120.00
83-01-004	Contentment	F. Stone	9,500	55.00	70-120.00
American Artists		**The Stallion Series**			
83-02-001	Black Stallion	F. Stone	19,500	49.50	100.00
83-02-002	Andalusian	F. Stone	19,500	49.50	80.00
American Artists		**Sport of Kings Series**			
84-03-001	Man O'War	F. Stone	9,500	65.00	200-275.
84-03-002	Secretariat	F. Stone	9,500	65.00	295.00
85-03-003	John Henry	F. Stone	9,500	65.00	100.00
86-03-004	Seattle Slew	F. Stone	9,500	65.00	65.00
American Artists		**Mare and Foal Series**			
86-04-001	Water Trough	F. Stone	12,500	49.50	125.00
86-04-002	Tranquility	F. Stone	12,500	49.50	65.00
86-04-003	Pasture Pest	F. Stone	12,500	49.50	100.00
87-04-004	The Arabians	F. Stone	12,500	49.50	49.50
American Artists		**Mare and Foal Series II**			
89-05-001	The First Day	F. Stone	Open	35.00	35.00
89-05-002	Diamond in the Rough	F. Stone	Retrd.	35.00	35.00
American Artists		**Fred Stone Classic Series**			
86-06-001	The Shoe-8,000 Wins	F. Stone	9,500	75.00	95.00
86-06-002	The Eternal Legacy	F. Stone	9,500	75.00	95.00
88-06-003	Forever Friends	F. Stone	9,500	75.00	85.00
89-06-004	Alysheba	F. Stone	9,500	75.00	85.00
American Artists		**Famous Fillies Series**			
87-07-001	Lady's Secret	F. Stone	9,500	65.00	85.00
88-07-002	Ruffian	F. Stone	9,500	65.00	85.00
88-07-003	Genuine Risk	F. Stone	9,500	65.00	85.00

Number	Name	Artist	Edition Limit	Issue Price	Quote
92-07-004	Go For The Wand	F. Stone	9,500	65.00	85.00
American Artists		**Racing Legends**			
89-08-001	Phar Lap	F. Stone	9,500	75.00	75.00
89-08-002	Sunday Silence	F. Stone	9,500	75.00	75.00
90-08-003	John Henry-Shoemaker	F. Stone	9,500	75.00	75.00
American Artists		**Gold Signature Series**			
90-09-001	Secretariat Final Tribute, signed	F. Stone	4,500	150.00	150.00
90-09-002	Secretariat Final Tribute, unsigned	F. Stone	7,500	75.00	75.00
91-09-003	Old Warriors, signed	F. Stone	4,500	150.00	150.00
91-09-004	Old Warriors, unsigned	F. Stone	7,500	75.00	75.00
American Artists		**Gold Signature Series II**			
91-10-001	Northern Dancer, double signature	F. Stone	1,500	175.00	175.00
91-10-002	Northern Dancer, single signature	F. Stone	3,000	150.00	150.00
91-10-003	Northern Dancer, unsigned	F. Stone	7,500	75.00	75.00
91-10-004	Kelso, double signature	F. Stone	1,500	175.00	175.00
91-10-005	Kelso, single signature	F. Stone	3,000	150.00	150.00
91-10-006	Kelso, unsigned	F. Stone	7,500	75.00	75.00
American Artists		**Gold Signature Series III**			
92-11-001	Dance Smartly-Pat Day, Up, double signature	F. Stone	1,500	175.00	175.00
92-11-002	Dance Smartly-Pat Day, Up, single signature	F. Stone	3,000	150.00	150.00
92-11-003	Dance Smartly-Pat Day, Up, unsigned	F. Stone	7,500	75.00	75.00
93-11-004	American Triple Crown-1937-1946, signed	F. Stone	2,500	195.00	195.00
93-11-005	American Triple Crown-1937-1946, unsigned	F. Stone	7,500	75.00	75.00
93-11-006	American Triple Crown-1948-1978, signed	F. Stone	2,500	195.00	195.00
93-11-007	American Triple Crown-1948-1978, unsigned	F. Stone	7,500	75.00	75.00
94-11-008	American Triple Crown-1919-1935, signed	F. Stone	2,500	95.00	95.00
94-11-009	American Triple Crown-1919-1935, unsigned	F. Stone	7,500	75.00	75.00
American Artists		**The Best of Fred Stone-Mares & Foals Series (6 1/2 ")**			
91-12-001	Patience	F. Stone	19,500	25.00	25.00
92-12-002	Water Trough	F. Stone	19,500	25.00	25.00
92-12-003	Pasture Pest	F. Stone	19,500	25.00	25.00
92-12-004	Kidnapped Mare	F. Stone	19,500	25.00	25.00
93-12-005	Contentment	F. Stone	19,500	25.00	25.00
93-12-006	Arabian Mare & Foal	F. Stone	19,500	25.00	25.00
American Rose Society		**All-American Rose**			
75-01-001	Oregold	Unknown	9,800	39.00	142.00
75-01-002	Arizona	Unknown	9,800	39.00	142.00
75-01-003	Rose Parade	Unknown	9,800	39.00	137.00
76-01-004	Yankee Doodle	Unknown	9,800	39.00	135.50
76-01-005	America	Unknown	9,800	39.00	135.50
76-01-006	Cathedral	Unknown	9,800	39.00	135.50
76-01-007	Seashell	Unknown	9,800	39.00	135.50
77-01-008	Double Delight	Unknown	9,800	39.00	115.00
77-01-009	Prominent	Unknown	9,800	39.00	115.00
77-01-010	First Edition	Unknown	9,800	39.00	115.00
78-01-011	Color Magic	Unknown	9,800	39.00	107.00
78-01-012	Charisma	Unknown	9,800	39.00	58-89.00
79-01-013	Paradise	Unknown	9,800	39.00	39-58.00
79-01-014	Sundowner	Unknown	9,800	39.00	67-75.00
79-01-015	Friendship	Unknown	9,800	39.00	74-79.00
80-01-016	Love	Unknown	9,800	49.00	80.00
80-01-017	Honor	Unknown	9,800	49.00	55-77.00
80-01-018	Cherish	Unknown	9,800	49.00	80.00
81-01-019	Bing Crosby	Unknown	9,800	49.00	49.00
81-01-020	White Lightnin'	Unknown	9,800	49.00	69.00
81-01-021	Marina	Unknown	9,800	49.00	61-69.00
82-01-022	Shreveport	Unknown	9,800	49.00	50-54.00
82-01-023	French Lace	Unknown	9,800	49.00	54.00
82-01-024	Brandy	Unknown	9,800	49.00	69.00
82-01-025	Mon Cheri	Unknown	9,800	49.00	49.00
83-01-026	Sun Flare	Unknown	9,800	49.00	69.00
83-01-027	Sweet Surrender	Unknown	9,800	49.00	55.00
84-01-028	Impatient	Unknown	9,800	49.00	55.00
84-01-029	Olympiad	Unknown	9,800	49.00	55.00
84-01-030	Intrigue	Unknown	9,800	49.00	58.00
85-01-031	Showbiz	Unknown	9,800	49.50	49.50
85-01-032	Peace	Unknown	9,800	49.50	49.50
85-01-033	Queen Elizabeth	Unknown	9,800	49.50	49.50
Anheuser-Busch, Inc.		**Holiday Plate Series**			
89-01-001	Winters Day N2295	B. Kemper	Retrd.	30.00	75.00
90-01-002	An American Tradition N2767	S. Sampson	Retrd.	30.00	40.00
91-01-003	The Season's Best N3034	S. Sampson	25-day	30.00	30.00
92-01-004	A Perfect Christmas N3440	S. Sampson	25-day	27.50	27.50
93-01-005	Special Delivery N4002	N. Koerber	25-day	27.50	27.50
Anheuser-Busch, Inc.		**Man's Best Friend Series**			
90-02-001	Buddies N2615	M. Urdahl	Retrd.	30.00	60-75.00
90-02-002	Six Pack N3005	M. Urdahl	Retrd.	30.00	40.00
92-02-003	Something's Brewing N3147	M. Urdahl	25-day	30.00	30.00
93-02-004	Outstanding in Their Field N4003	M. Urdahl	25-day	27.50	27.50
Anheuser-Busch, Inc.		**1992 Olympic Team Series**			
91-03-001	1992 Olympic Team Winter Plate N3180	A-Busch, Inc.	25-day	35.00	30-35.00
92-03-002	1992 Olympic Team Summer Plate N3122	A-Busch, Inc.	25-day	35.00	30-35.00
Anheuser-Busch, Inc.		**Civil War Series**			
92-04-001	General Grant N3478	D. Langeneckert	25-day	45.00	45.00
93-04-002	General Robert E. Lee N3590	D. Langeneckert	25-day	45.00	45.00
93-04-003	President Abraham Lincoln N3591	D. Langeneckert	25-day	45.00	45.00
Anheuser-Busch, Inc.		**Archives Plate Series**			
92-05-001	1893 Columbian Exposition N3477	D. Langeneckert	25-day	27.50	27.50
92-05-002	Ganymede	D. Langeneckert	25-day	27.50	27.50
Anna-Perenna Porcelain		**Uncle Tad's Cats**			
79-01-001	Oliver's Birthday	T. Krumeich	5,000	75.00	220.00
80-01-002	Peaches & Cream	T. Krumeich	5,000	75.00	80.00
81-01-003	Princess Aurora	T. Krumeich	5,000	80.00	85.00
81-01-004	Walter's Window	T. Krumeich	5,000	80.00	95.00
Anna-Perenna Porcelain		**Annual Christmas Plate**			
84-02-001	Noel, Noel	P. Buckley Moss	5,000	67.50	325.00
85-02-002	Helping Hands	P. Buckley Moss	5,000	67.50	225.00
86-02-003	Night Before Christmas	P. Buckley Moss	5,000	67.50	150.00
87-02-004	Christmas Sleigh	P. Buckley Moss	5,000	75.00	95.00
88-02-005	Christmas Joy	P. Buckley Moss	7,500	75.00	75.00
89-02-006	Christmas Carol	P. Buckley Moss	7,500	80.00	95.00

PLATES

Company / Number	Name / Series	Artist	Edition Limit	Issue Price	Quote
90-02-007	Christmas Eve	P. Buckley Moss	7,500	80.00	80.00
91-02-008	The Snowman	P. Buckley Moss	7,500	80.00	80.00
92-02-009	Christmas Warmth	P. Buckley Moss	7,500	85.00	85.00
Anna-Perenna Porcelain	**American Silhouettes-Childrens Series**				
81-03-001	Fiddlers Two	P. Buckley Moss	5,000	75.00	95.00
83-03-002	Mary With The Lambs	P. Buckley Moss	5,000	75.00	85.00
84-03-003	Ring-Around-the-Rosie	P. Buckley Moss	5,000	75.00	200.00
84-03-004	Waiting For Tom	P. Buckley Moss	5,000	75.00	175.00
Anna-Perenna Porcelain	**The Celebration Series**				
86-04-001	Wedding Joy	P. Buckley Moss	5,000	100.00	200-350.
87-04-002	The Christening	P. Buckley Moss	5,000	100.00	175.00
88-04-003	The Anniversary	P. Buckley Moss	5,000	100.00	120-190.
89-04-004	Family Reunion	P. Buckley Moss	5,000	100.00	150.00
Anna-Perenna Porcelain	**American Silhouettes Family Series**				
81-05-001	Family Outing	P. Buckley Moss	5,000	75.00	95.00
82-05-002	John and Mary	P. Buckley Moss	5,000	75.00	95.00
82-05-003	Homemakers Quilting	P. Buckley Moss	5,000	75.00	85-195.00
84-05-004	Leisure Time	P. Buckley Moss	5,000	75.00	85.00
Anna-Perenna Porcelain	**American Silhouettes Valley Series**				
81-06-001	Frosty Frolic	P. Buckley Moss	5,000	75.00	85-95.00
82-06-002	Hay Ride	P. Buckley Moss	5,000	75.00	85.00
83-06-003	Sunday Ride	P. Buckley Moss	5,000	75.00	85-100.00
84-06-004	Market Day	P. Buckley Moss	5,000	75.00	120.00
ANRI	**Ferrandiz Christmas**				
72-01-001	Christ In The Manger	J. Ferrandiz	Closed	35.00	230.00
73-01-002	Christmas	J. Ferrandiz	Unkn.	40.00	225.00
74-01-003	Holy Night	J. Ferrandiz	Unkn.	50.00	100.00
75-01-004	Flight into Egypt	J. Ferrandiz	Unkn.	60.00	95.00
76-01-005	Tree of Life	J. Ferrandiz	Unkn.	60.00	85.00
76-01-006	Girl with Flowers	J. Ferrandiz	Closed	65.00	185.00
78-01-007	Leading the Way	J. Ferrandiz	Closed	77.50	180.00
79-01-008	The Drummer	J. Ferrandiz	Closed	120.00	175.00
80-01-009	Rejoice	J. Ferrandiz	Closed	150.00	160.00
81-01-010	Spreading the Word	J. Ferrandiz	Closed	150.00	150.00
82-01-011	The Shepherd Family	J. Ferrandiz	Closed	150.00	150.00
83-01-012	Peace Attend Thee	J. Ferrandiz	Closed	150.00	150.00
ANRI	**Ferrandiz Mother's Day Series**				
72-02-001	Mother Sewing	J. Ferrandiz	Closed	35.00	200.00
73-02-002	Alpine Mother & Child	J. Ferrandiz	Closed	40.00	150.00
74-02-003	Mother Holding Child	J. Ferrandiz	Closed	50.00	150.00
75-02-004	Dove Girl	J. Ferrandiz	Closed	60.00	150.00
76-02-005	Mother Knitting	J. Ferrandiz	Closed	60.00	200.00
77-02-006	Alpine Stroll	J. Ferrandiz	Closed	65.00	125.00
78-02-007	The Beginning	J. Ferrandiz	Closed	75.00	150.00
79-02-008	All Hearts	J. Ferrandiz	Closed	120.00	170.00
80-02-009	Spring Arrivals	J. Ferrandiz	Closed	150.00	165.00
81-02-010	Harmony	J. Ferrandiz	Closed	150.00	150.00
82-02-011	With Love	J. Ferrandiz	Closed	150.00	150.00
ANRI	**Ferrandiz Wooden Wedding Plates**				
72-03-001	Boy and Girl Embracing	J. Ferrandiz	Unkn.	40.00	150.00
73-03-002	Wedding Scene	J. Ferrandiz	Unkn.	40.00	150.00
74-03-003	Wedding	J. Ferrandiz	Unkn.	48.00	150.00
75-03-004	Wedding	J. Ferrandiz	Unkn.	60.00	150.00
76-03-005	Wedding	J. Ferrandiz	Unkn.	60.00	90-150.00
ANRI	**Christmas**				
71-04-001	St. Jakob in Groden	J. Malfertheiner	Closed	37.50	65.00
72-04-002	Pipers at Alberobello	J. Malfertheiner	Closed	45.00	75.00
73-04-003	Alpine Horn	J. Malfertheiner	Closed	45.00	390.00
74-04-004	Young Man and Girl	J. Malfertheiner	Closed	50.00	95.00
75-04-005	Christmas in Ireland	J. Malfertheiner	Closed	60.00	60.00
76-04-006	Alpine Christmas	J. Malfertheiner	Closed	65.00	190.00
77-04-007	Legend of Heligenblut	J. Malfertheiner	Closed	65.00	91.00
78-04-008	Klockler Singers	J. Malfertheiner	Closed	80.00	80.00
79-04-009	Moss Gatherers	Unknown	Closed	135.00	177.00
80-04-010	Wintry Churchgoing	Unknown	Closed	165.00	165.00
81-04-011	Santa Claus in Tyrol	Unknown	Closed	165.00	200.00
82-04-012	The Star Singers	Unknown	Closed	165.00	165.00
83-04-013	Unto Us a Child is Born	Unknown	Closed	165.00	310.00
84-04-014	Yuletide in the Valley	Unknown	Closed	165.00	170.00
85-04-015	Good Morning, Good Cheer	J. Malfertheiner	Closed	165.00	165.00
86-04-016	A Groden Christmas	J. Malfertheiner	Closed	165.00	200.00
87-04-017	Down From the Alps	J. Malfertheiner	Closed	195.00	250.00
88-04-018	Christkindl Markt	J. Malfertheiner	Closed	220.00	230.00
88-04-019	Flight Into Egypt	J. Malfertheiner	Closed	275.00	275.00
90-04-020	Holy Night	J. Malfertheiner	Closed	300.00	300.00
ANRI	**ANRI Mother's Day**				
72-05-001	Alpine Mother & Children	Unknown.	Closed	35.00	50.00
73-05-002	Alpine Mother & Children	Unknown	Closed	40.00	50.00
74-05-003	Alpine Mother & Children	Unknown	Closed	50.00	55.00
75-05-004	Alpine Stroll	Unknown	Closed	60.00	65.00
76-05-005	Knitting	Unknown	Closed	60.00	65.00
ANRI	**ANRI Father's Day**				
72-06-001	Alpine Father & Children	Unknown	Closed	35.00	100.00
73-06-002	Alpine Father & Children	Unknown	Closed	40.00	95.00
74-06-003	Cliff Gazing	Unknown	Closed	50.00	100.00
76-06-004	Sailing	Unknown	Closed	60.00	90.00
ANRI	**Disney Four Star Collection**				
89-07-001	Mickey Mini Plate	Disney Studios	Closed	40.00	45.00
90-07-002	Minnie Mini Plate	Disney Studios	Closed	40.00	45.00
91-07-003	Donald Mini Plate	Disney Studios	Closed	50.00	50.00
Armstrong's	**Infinite Love**				
87-01-001	A Pair of Dreams	S. Etem	14-day	24.50	24.50
87-01-002	The Eyes Say "I Love You"	S. Etem	14-day	24.50	24.50
87-01-003	Once Upon a Smile	S. Etem	14-day	24.50	24.50
87-01-004	Kiss a Little Giggle	S. Etem	14-day	24.50	24.50
88-01-005	Love Goes Forth in Little Feet	S. Etem	14-day	24.50	24.50
88-01-006	Bundle of Joy	S. Etem	14-day	24.50	24.50
88-01-007	Grins For Grandma	S. Etem	14-day	24.50	24.50
89-01-008	A Moment to Cherish	S. Etem	14-day	24.50	24.50
Armstrong's	**Statue of Liberty**				
86-02-001	Dedication	A. D'Estrehan	10,000	39.50	49.50
86-02-002	The Immigrants	A. D'Estrehan	10,000	39.50	49.50
86-02-003	Independence	A. D'Estrehan	10,000	39.50	49.50
86-02-004	Re-Dedication	A. D'Estrehan	10,000	39.50	49.50
Armstrong's	**Commemorative Issues**				
83-03-001	70 Years Young (10 1/2")	R. Skelton	15,000	85.00	125.00
84-03-002	Freddie the Torchbearer (8 1/2")	R. Skelton	15,000	62.50	85.00
Armstrong's	**The Signature Collection**				
86-04-001	Anyone for Tennis?	R. Skelton	9,000	62.50	62.50
86-04-002	Anyone for Tennis? (signed)	R. Skelton	1,000	125.00	650.00
87-04-003	Ironing the Waves	R. Skelton	9,000	62.50	75.00
87-04-004	Ironing the Waves (signed)	R. Skelton	1,000	125.00	175.00
88-04-005	The Cliffhanger	R. Skelton	9,000	62.50	65.00
88-04-006	The Cliffhanger (signed)	R. Skelton	1,000	150.00	150.00
88-04-007	Hooked on Freddie	R. Skelton	9,000	62.50	62.50
88-04-008	Hooked on Freddie (signed)	R. Skelton	1,000	175.00	175.00
Armstrong's	**Happy Art Series**				
81-05-001	Woody's Triple Self-Portrait, Signed	W. Lantz	1,000	100.00	100.00
81-05-002	Woody's Triple Self-Portrait	W. Lantz	9,000	39.50	39.50
83-05-003	Gothic Woody, Signed	W. Lantz	1,000	100.00	100.00
83-05-004	Gothic Woody	W. Lantz	9,000	39.50	39.50
84-05-005	Blue Boy Woody, Signed	W. Lantz	1,000	100.00	100.00
84-05-006	Blue Boy Woody	W. Lantz	9,000	39.50	39.50
Armstrong's	**The Constitution Series**				
87-06-001	U.S. Constitution vs. Guerriere	A. D'Estrehan	10,000	39.50	45.00
87-06-002	U.S. Constitution vs. Tripoli	A. D'Estrehan	10,000	39.50	45.00
87-06-003	U.S. Constitution vs. Java	A. D'Estrehan	10,000	39.50	45.00
87-06-004	The Great Chase	A. D'Estrehan	10,000	39.50	45.00
Armstrong's	**The Mischief Makers**				
86-07-001	Puddles	S. Etem	10,000	39.95	39.95
86-07-002	Buckles	S. Etem	10,000	39.95	39.95
87-07-003	Trix	S. Etem	10,000	39.95	39.95
88-07-004	Naps	S. Etem	10,000	39.95	45.00
Armstrong's	**Faces of the World**				
88-08-001	Erin (Ireland)	L. De Winne	14-day	24.50	24.50
88-08-002	Clara (Belgium)	L. De Winne	14-day	24.50	24.50
88-08-003	Luisa (Spain)	L. De Winne	14-day	24.50	24.50
88-08-004	Tamiko (Japan)	L. De Winne	14-day	24.50	24.50
88-08-005	Colette (France)	L. De Winne	14-day	24.50	24.50
88-08-006	Heather (England)	L. De Winne	14-day	24.50	24.50
88-08-007	Greta (Austria)	L. De Winne	14-day	24.50	24.50
88-08-008	Maria (Italy)	L. De Winne	14-day	24.50	24.50
Armstrong's	**Freedom Collection of Red Skelton**				
90-09-001	The All American, (signed)	R. Skelton	1,000	195.00	195.00
90-09-002	The All American	R. Skelton	9,000	62.50	62.50
91-09-003	Independence Day? (signed)	R. Skelton	1,000	195.00	350.00
91-09-004	Independence Day?	R. Skelton	9,000	62.50	65.00
92-09-005	Let Freedom Ring, (signed)	R. Skelton	1,000	195.00	200.00
92-09-006	Let Freedom Ring	R. Skelton	9,000	62.50	65.00
93-09-007	Freddie's Gift of Life, (signed)	R. Skelton	1,000	195.00	195.00
93-09-008	Freddie's Gift of Life	R. Skelton	9,000	62.50	62.50
Armstrong's/Crown Parlan	**Freddie The Freeloader**				
78-01-001	Freddie the Freeloader	R. Skelton	10,000	60.00	400.00
79-01-002	Freddie in the Bathtub	R. Skelton	10,000	60.00	215-300.
80-01-003	Freddie's Shack	R. Skelton	10,000	60.00	95.00
81-01-004	Freddie on the Green	R. Skelton	10,000	60.00	80.00
82-01-005	Love that Freddie	R. Skelton	10,000	60.00	70.00
Armstrong's/Crown Parlan	**Freddie's Adventures**				
82-02-001	Captain Freddie	R. Skelton	15,000	60.00	225.00
82-02-002	Bronco Freddie	R. Skelton	15,000	60.00	65-75.00
83-02-003	Sir Freddie	R. Skelton	15,000	62.50	65-79.00
84-02-004	Gertrude and Heathcliffe	R. Skelton	15,000	62.50	70.00
Artaffects	**Portraits of American Brides**				
86-01-001	Caroline	R. Sauber	10-day	29.50	75-85.00
86-01-002	Jacqueline	R. Sauber	10-day	29.50	30-45.00
87-01-003	Elizabeth	R. Sauber	10-day	29.50	37-45.00
87-01-004	Emily	R. Sauber	10-day	29.50	45.00
87-01-005	Meredith	R. Sauber	10-day	29.50	45-55.00
87-01-006	Laura	R. Sauber	10-day	29.50	45.00
87-01-007	Sarah	R. Sauber	10-day	29.50	46.00
87-01-008	Rebecca	R. Sauber	10-day	29.50	64.00
Artaffects	**How Do I Love Thee?**				
82-02-001	Alaina	R. Sauber	19,500	39.95	60.00
82-02-002	Taylor	R. Sauber	19,500	39.95	60.00
83-02-003	Rendezvouse	R. Sauber	19,500	39.95	60.00
83-02-004	Embrace	R. Sauber	19,500	39.95	60.00
Artaffects	**Childhood Delights**				
83-03-001	Amanda	R. Sauber	7,500	45.00	75.00
Artaffects	**Songs of Stephen Foster**				
84-04-001	Oh! Susannah	R. Sauber	3,500	60.00	80.00
84-04-002	Jeanie with the Light Brown Hair	R. Sauber	3,500	60.00	80.00
84-04-003	Beautiful Dreamer	R. Sauber	3,500	60.00	80.00
Artaffects	**Times of Our Lives Collection**				
84-05-001	Happy Birthday-(10 1/4")	R. Sauber	Open	37.50	39.50
88-05-002	Happy Birthday-(6 1/2")	R. Sauber	Open	19.50	22.50
85-05-003	Home Sweet Home-(10 1/4")	R. Sauber	Open	37.50	39.50
88-05-004	Home Sweet Home-(6 1/2")	R. Sauber	Open	19.50	22.50
82-05-005	The Wedding-(10 1/4")	R. Sauber	Open	37.50	39.50
88-05-006	The Wedding-(6 1/2")	R. Sauber	Open	19.50	22.50
86-05-007	The Anniversary-(10 1/4")	R. Sauber	Open	37.50	39.50
88-05-008	The Anniversary-(6 1/2")	R. Sauber	Open	19.50	22.50
86-05-009	Sweethearts-(10 1/4")	R. Sauber	Open	37.50	49.00
88-05-010	Sweethearts-(6 1/2")	R. Sauber	Open	19.50	22.50
86-05-011	The Christening-(10 1/4")	R. Sauber	Open	37.50	39.50
88-05-012	The Christening-(6 1/2")	R. Sauber	Open	19.50	22.50
85-05-013	All Adore Him-(10 1/4")	R. Sauber	Open	37.50	39.50
88-05-014	All Adore Him-(6 1/2")	R. Sauber	Open	19.50	22.50
87-05-015	Motherhood-(10 1/4")	R. Sauber	Open	37.50	39.50
88-05-016	Motherhood-(6 1/2")	R. Sauber	Open	19.50	22.50
87-05-017	Fatherhood-(10 1/4")	R. Sauber	Open	37.50	39.50
88-05-018	Fatherhood-(6 1/2")	R. Sauber	Open	19.50	22.50

Company Number	Name	Series Artist	Edition Limit	Issue Price	Quote
87-05-019	Sweet Sixteen-(10 1/4")	R. Sauber	Open	37.50	39.50
89-05-020	God Bless America-(10 1/4")	R. Sauber	14-day	39.50	39.50
89-05-021	God Bless America-(6 1/4")	R. Sauber	14-day	21.50	22.50
89-05-022	Visiting the Doctor-(10 1/4")	R. Sauber	14-day	39.50	39.50
90-05-023	Mother's Joy-(6 1/2")	R. Sauber	Open	22.50	22.50
90-05-024	Mother's Joy-(10 1/4")	R. Sauber	Open	39.50	39.50
Artaffects		**Timeless Love**			
89-06-001	The Proposal	R. Sauber	14-day	35.00	38.00
89-06-002	Sweet Embrace	R. Sauber	14-day	35.00	35.00
90-06-003	Afternoon Light	R. Sauber	14-day	35.00	35.00
90-06-004	Quiet Moments	R. Sauber	14-day	35.00	35.00
Artaffects		**Winter Mindscape**			
89-07-001	Peaceful Village	R. Sauber	14-day	29.50	65.00
89-07-002	Snowbound	R. Sauber	14-day	29.50	40.00
90-07-003	Papa's Surprise	R. Sauber	14-day	29.50	40.00
90-07-004	Well Traveled Road	R. Sauber	14-day	29.50	40.00
90-07-005	First Freeze	R. Sauber	14-day	29.50	40.00
90-07-006	Country Morning	R. Sauber	14-day	29.50	40.00
90-07-007	Sleigh Ride	R. Sauber	14-day	29.50	40.00
90-07-008	January Thaw	R. Sauber	14-day	29.50	40.00
Artaffects		**Baby's Firsts**			
89-08-001	Visiting the Doctor (6 1/2")	R. Sauber	14-day	21.50	22.50
89-08-002	Baby's First Step (6 1/2")	R. Sauber	14-day	21.50	22.50
89-08-003	First Birthday (6 1/2")	R. Sauber	14-day	21.50	22.50
89-08-004	Christmas Morn (6 1/2")	R. Sauber	14-day	21.50	22.50
89-08-005	Picture Perfect (6 1/2")	R. Sauber	14-day	21.50	22.50
Artaffects		**American Blues Special Occasions**			
92-09-001	Happily Ever After (Wedding)	R. Sauber	N/A	35.00	35.00
92-09-002	The Perfect Tree (Christmas)	R. Sauber	N/A	35.00	35.00
92-09-003	My Sunshine (Motherhood)	R. Sauber	N/A	35.00	35.00
Artaffects		**An Old Fashioned Christmas**			
93-10-001	Up On The Roof Top	R. Sauber	N/A	29.50	29.50
94-10-002	The Toy Shoppe	R. Sauber	N/A	29.50	29.50
94-10-003	Christmas Delight	R. Sauber	N/A	29.50	29.50
94-10-004	Christmas Eve	R. Sauber	N/A	29.50	29.50
Artaffects		**Masterpieces of Rockwell**			
80-11-001	After the Prom	N. Rockwell	17,500	42.50	150.00
80-11-002	The Challenger	N. Rockwell	17,500	50.00	75.00
82-11-003	Girl at the Mirror	N. Rockwell	17,500	50.00	100.00
82-11-004	Missing Tooth	N. Rockwell	17,500	50.00	75.00
Artaffects		**Rockwell Americana**			
81-12-001	Shuffleton's Barbershop	N. Rockwell	17,500	75.00	150.00
82-12-002	Breaking Home Ties	N. Rockwell	17,500	75.00	125.00
83-12-003	Walking to Church	N. Rockwell	17,500	75.00	125.00
Artaffects		**Rockwell Trilogy**			
81-13-001	Stockbridge in Winter 1	N. Rockwell	Open	35.00	50-65.00
82-13-002	Stockbridge in Winter 2	N. Rockwell	Open	35.00	50-65.00
82-13-003	Stockbridge in Winter 3	N. Rockwell	Open	35.00	50-75.00
Artaffects		**Simpler Times Series**			
84-14-001	Lazy Daze	N. Rockwell	7,500	35.00	75.00
84-14-002	One for the Road	N. Rockwell	7,500	35.00	75.00
Artaffects		**On the Road Series**			
84-15-001	Pride of Stockbridge	N. Rockwell	Open	35.00	75.00
84-15-002	City Pride	N. Rockwell	Open	35.00	75.00
84-15-003	Country Pride	N. Rockwell	Open	35.00	75.00
Artaffects		**Special Occasions**			
82-16-001	Bubbles	F. Tipton Hunter	Open	29.95	50.00
82-16-002	Butterflies	F. Tipton Hunter	Open	29.95	50.00
Artaffects		**Masterpieces of Impressionism**			
80-17-001	Woman with Parasol	Monet/Cassat	17,500	35.00	75.00
81-17-002	Young Mother Sewing	Monet/Cassat	17,500	35.00	60.00
82-17-003	Sara in Green Bonnet	Monet/Cassat	17,500	35.00	60.00
83-17-004	Margot in Blue	Monet/Cassat	17,500	35.00	50.00
Artaffects		**Magical Moment**			
81-18-001	Happy Dreams	B. P. Gutmann	Open	29.95	100.00
81-18-002	Harmony	B. P. Gutmann	Open	29.95	90.00
82-18-003	His Majesty	B. P. Gutmann	Open	29.95	60.00
83-18-003	The Lullaby	B. P. Gutmann	Open	29.95	50.00
82-18-004	Waiting for Daddy	B. P Gutmann	Open	29.95	50.00
82-18-005	Thank You God	B. P .Gutmann	Open	29.95	50.00
Artaffects		**Mother's Love**			
84-19-001	Daddy's Here	B. P. Gutmann	Open	29.95	60.00
Artaffects		**Bessie's Best**			
84-20-001	Oh! Oh! A Bunny	B. P. Gutmann	Open	29.95	65.00
84-20-002	The New Love	B. P. Gutmann	Open	29.95	65.00
84-20-003	My Baby	B. P. Gutmann	Open	29.95	65.00
84-20-004	Looking for Trouble	B. P. Gutmann	Open	29.95	65.00
84-20-005	Taps	B. P. Gutmann	Open	29.95	65.00
Artaffects		**Masterpieces of the West**			
80-21-001	Texas Night Herder	Johnson	17,500	35.00	75.00
80-21-002	Indian Trapper	Remington	17,500	35.00	100.00
82-21-003	Cowboy Style	Leigh	17,500	35.00	75.00
82-21-004	Indian Style	Perillo	17,500	35.00	150.00
Artaffects		**Playful Pets**			
82-22-001	Curiosity	J. H. Dolph	7,500	45.00	75.00
82-22-002	Master's Hat	J. H. Dolph	7,500	45.00	75.00
Artaffects		**The Tribute Series**			
82-23-001	I Want You	J. M. Flagg	Open	29.95	50.00
82-23-002	Gee, I Wish	H. C. Christy	Open	29.95	50.00
83-23-003	Soldier's Farewell	N. Rockwell	Open	29.95	50.00
Artaffects		**The Carnival Series**			
82-24-001	Knock em' Down	T. Newsom	19,500	35.00	50.00
82-24-002	Carousel	T. Newsom	19,500	35.00	50.00

Company Number	Name	Series Artist	Edition Limit	Issue Price	Quote
Artaffects		**The Adventures of Peter Pan**			
90-25-001	Flying Over London	T. Newsom	14-day	29.50	40.00
90-25-002	Look At Me	T. Newsom	14-day	29.50	40.00
90-25-003	The Encounter	T. Newsom	14-day	29.50	40.00
90-25-004	Never land	T. Newsom	14-day	29.50	40.00
Artaffects		**Nursery Pair**			
83-26-001	In Slumberland	C. Becker	Open	25.00	60.00
83-26-002	The Awakening	C. Becker	Open	25.00	60.00
Artaffects		**Becker Babies**			
83-27-001	Snow Puff	C. Becker	Open	29.95	60.00
84-27-002	Smiling Through	C. Becker	Open	29.95	60.00
84-27-003	Pals	C. Becker	Open	29.95	60.00
Artaffects		**Melodies of Childhood**			
83-28-001	Twinkle, Twinkle Little Star	H. Garrido	19,500	35.00	50.00
83-28-002	Row, Row, Row Your Boat	H. Garrido	19,500	35.00	50.00
83-28-003	Mary had a Little Lamb	H. Garrido	19,500	35.00	50.00
Artaffects		**Unicorn Magic**			
83-29-001	Morning Encounter	J. Terreson	7,500	50.00	60.00
83-29-002	Afternoon Offering	J. Terreson	7,500	50.00	60.00
Artaffects		**Baker Street**			
83-30-001	Sherlock Holmes	M. Hooks	9,800	55.00	55-95.00
83-30-002	Watson	M. Hooks	9,800	55.00	55-75.00
Artaffects		**Angler's Dream**			
83-31-001	Brook Trout	J. Eggert	9,800	55.00	75.00
83-31-002	Striped Bass	J. Eggert	9,800	55.00	75.00
83-31-003	Largemouth Bass	J. Eggert	9,800	55.00	75.00
83-31-004	Chinook Salmon	J. Eggert	9,800	55.00	75.00
Artaffects		**Portrait Series**			
86-32-001	Chantilly	J. Eggert	14-day	24.50	40.00
86-32-002	Dynasty	J. Eggert	14-day	24.50	40.00
86-32-003	Velvet	J. Eggert	14-day	24.50	40.00
86-32-004	Jambalaya	J. Eggert	14-day	24.50	40.00
Artaffects		**The Great Trains**			
85-33-001	Santa Fe	J. Deneen	7,500	35.00	100.00
85-33-002	Twentieth Century Ltd.	J. Deneen	7,500	35.00	100.00
86-33-003	Empire Builder	J. Deneen	7,500	35.00	100.00
Artaffects		**Classic American Trains**			
88-34-001	Homeward Bound	J. Deneen	14-day	35.00	53.00
88-34-002	A Race Against Time	J. Deneen	14-day	35.00	63.00
88-34-003	Midday Stop	J. Deneen	14-day	35.00	55.00
88-34-004	The Silver Bullet	J. Deneen	14-day	35.00	65.00
88-34-005	Traveling in Style	J. Deneen	14-day	35.00	50-66.00
88-34-006	Round the Bend	J. Deneen	14-day	35.00	56.00
88-34-007	Taking the High Road	J. Deneen	14-day	35.00	45-56.00
88-34-008	Competition	J. Deneen	14-day	35.00	40-55.00
Aftaffects		**Classic American Cars**			
89-35-001	Duesenberg	J. Deneen	14-day	35.00	40.00
89-35-002	Cadillac	J. Deneen	14-day	35.00	35.00
89-35-003	Cord	J. Deneen	14-day	35.00	35.00
89-35-004	Ruxton	J. Deneen	14-day	35.00	35.00
90-35-005	Lincoln	J. Deneen	14-day	35.00	35.00
90-35-006	Packard	J. Deneen	14-day	35.00	35.00
90-35-007	Hudson	J. Deneen	14-day	35.00	35.00
90-35-008	Pierce-Arrow	J. Deneen	14-day	35.00	35.00
Artaffects		**Great American Trains**			
92-36-001	The Alton Limited	J. Deneen	75-day	27.00	27.00
92-36-002	The Capitol Limited	J. Deneen	75-day	27.00	27.00
92-36-003	The Merchants Limited	J. Deneen	75-day	27.00	27.00
92-36-004	The Broadway Limited	J. Deneen	75-day	27.00	27.00
92-36-005	The Southwestern Limited	J. Deneen	75-day	27.00	27.00
92-36-006	The Blackhawk Limited	J. Deneen	75-day	27.00	27.00
92-36-007	The Sunshine Special Limited	J. Deneen	75-day	27.00	27.00
92-36-008	The Panama Special Limited	J. Deneen	75-day	27.00	27.00
Artaffects		**Sailing Through History**			
86-37-001	Flying Cloud	K. Soldwedel	14-day	29.50	60.00
86-37-002	Santa Maria	K. Soldwedel	14-day	29.50	60.00
86-37-003	Mayflower	K. Soldwedel	14-day	29.50	60.00
Artaffects		**American Maritime Heritage**			
87-38-001	U.S.S. Constitution	K. Soldwedel	14 Day	35.00	35.00
Artaffects		**Christian Collection**			
87-39-001	Bring to Me the Children	A. Tobey	Unkn.	35.00	35.00
87-39-002	Wedding Feast at Cana	A. Tobey	Unkn.	35.00	35.00
87-39-003	The Healer	A. Tobey	Unkn.	35.00	35.00
Artaffects		**Reflections of Youth**			
88-40-001	Julia	Mago	14-day	29.50	45-55.00
88-40-002	Jessica	Mago	14-day	29.50	35.00
88-40-003	Sebastian	Mago	14-day	29.50	35.00
88-40-004	Michelle	Mago	14-day	29.50	55.00
88-40-005	Andrew	Mago	14-day	29.50	35.00
88-40-006	Beth	Mago	14-day	29.50	39.00
88-40-007	Amy	Mago	14-day	29.50	39.00
88-40-008	Lauren	Mago	14-day	29.50	39.00
Artaffects		**MaGo's Motherhood**			
90-41-001	Serenity	MaGo	14-day	50.00	50.00
Artaffects		**Studies of Early Childhood**			
90-42-001	Christopher & Kate	MaGo	150-day	34.90	35.00
90-42-002	Peek-A-Boo	MaGo	150-day	34.90	35.00
90-42-003	Anybody Home?	MaGo	150-day	34.90	32.00
90-42-004	Three-Part Harmony	MaGo	150-day	34.90	53.00
Artaffects		**Heavenly Angels**			
92-43-001	Hush-A-Bye	MaGo	75-day	27.00	27.00
92-43-002	Heavenly Helper	MaGo	75-day	27.00	27.00
92-43-003	Heavenly Light	MaGo	75-day	27.00	27.00
92-43-004	The Angel's Kiss	MaGo	75-day	27.00	27.00
92-43-005	Caught In The Act	MaGo	75-day	27.00	27.00
92-43-006	My Angel	MaGo	75-day	27.00	27.00

PLATES

Company Number	Name	Series Artist	Edition Limit	Issue Price	Quote
92-43-007	Angel Cake	MaGo	75-day	27.00	27.00
92-43-008	Sleepy Sentinel	MaGo	75-day	27.00	27.00
Artaffects		**Bring Unto Me the Children**			
94-44-001	Love's Blessing	MaGo	75-day	29.50	29.50
94-44-002	Heavenly Embrace	MaGo	75-day	29.50	29.50
94-44-003	Sweet Serenity	MaGo	75-day	29.50	29.50
94-44-004	The Lord's Prayer	MaGo	75-day	29.50	29.50
94-44-005	Communion	MaGo	75-day	29.50	29.50
94-44-006	The Baptism	MaGo	75-day	29.50	29.50
94-44-007	A Little Love Song	MaGo	75-day	29.50	29.50
94-44-008	Sweet Dreams	MaGo	75-day	29.50	29.50
Artaffects		**Special Issue**			
94-45-001	Divine Intervention	MaGo	75-day	35.00	35.00
Artaffects		**Good Sports**			
89-46-001	Purrfect Game (6 1/2")	S. Miller-Maxwell	14-day	22.50	25.00
89-46-002	Alley Cats (6 1/2")	S. Miller-Maxwell	14-day	22.50	25.00
89-46-003	Tee Time (6 1/2")	S. Miller-Maxwell	14-day	22.50	25.00
89-46-004	Two/Love (6 1/2")	S. Miller-Maxwell	14-day	22.50	25.00
89-46-005	What's the Catch (6 1/2")	S. Miller-Maxwell	14-day	22.50	25.00
89-46-006	Quaterback Sneak (6 1/2")	S. Miller-Maxwell	14-day	22.50	25.00
Artaffects		**Romantic Cities of Europe**			
89-47-001	Venice	L. Marchetti	14-day	35.00	65.00
89-47-002	Paris	L. Marchetti	14-day	35.00	50.00
90-47-003	London	L. Marchetti	14-day	35.00	50.00
90-47-004	Moscow	L. Marchetti	14-day	35.00	35.00
Artaffects		**The Life of Jesus**			
92-48-001	The Last Supper	L. Marchetti	25-day	27.00	27.00
92-48-002	The Sermon on the Mount	L. Marchetti	25-day	27.00	27.00
92-48-003	The Agony in the Garden	L. Marchetti	25-day	27.00	27.00
92-48-004	The Entry Into Jerusalem	L. Marchetti	25-day	27.00	27.00
92-48-005	The Blessing of the Children	L. Marchetti	25-day	27.00	27.00
92-48-006	The Resurrection	L. Marchetti	25-day	27.00	27.00
92-48-007	The Healing of the Sick	L. Marchetti	25-day	27.00	27.00
92-48-008	The Descent from the Cross	L. Marchetti	25-day	27.00	27.00
Artaffects		**Backstage**			
90-49-001	The Runaway	B. Leighton-Jones	14-day	29.50	29.50
90-49-002	The Letter	B. Leighton-Jones	14-day	29.50	29.50
90-49-003	Bubbling Over	B. Leighton-Jones	14-day	29.50	29.50
Artaffects		**Rose Wreaths**			
93-50-001	Summer's Bounty	Knox/Robertson	N/A	27.00	27.00
93-50-002	Victorian Fantasy	Knox/Robertson	N/A	27.00	27.00
93-50-003	Gentle Persuasion	Knox/Robertson	N/A	27.00	27.00
93-50-004	Sunset Splendor	Knox/Robertson	N/A	27.00	27.00
94-50-005	Sweethearts Delight	Knox/Robertson	N/A	27.00	27.00
94-50-006	Sweet Sunshine	Knox/Robertson	N/A	27.00	27.00
94-50-007	Floral Fascination	Knox/Robertson	N/A	27.00	27.00
94-50-008	Love's Embrace	Knox/Robertson	N/A	27.00	27.00
Artaffects		**Christmas Celebrations Of Yesterday**			
93-51-001	Christmas On Main Street	M. Leone	N/A	27.00	27.00
93-51-002	Christmas On The Farm	M. Leone	N/A	27.00	27.00
93-51-003	Christmas Eve	M. Leone	N/A	27.00	27.00
93-51-004	Wreath Maker	M. Leone	N/A	27.00	27.00
93-51-005	Christmas Party	M. Leone	N/A	27.00	27.00
93-51-006	Trimming The Tree	M. Leone	N/A	27.00	27.00
93-51-007	Christmas Blessings	M. Leone	N/A	27.00	27.00
93-51-008	Home For Christmas	M. Leone	N/A	27.00	27.00
Artaffects		**Lands Before Time**			
94-52-001	Pharoah's Return	A. Chesterman	75-day	29.50	29.50
94-52-002	Roman Holiday	A. Chesterman	75-day	29.50	29.50
94-52-003	Imperial Dynasty	A. Chesterman	75-day	29.50	29.50
94-52-004	Knights in Shining Armour	A. Chesterman	75-day	29.50	29.50
Artaffects		**Chieftains I**			
79-53-001	Chief Sitting Bull	G. Perillo	7,500	65.00	400.00
79-53-002	Chief Joseph	G. Perillo	7,500	65.00	175.00
80-53-003	Chief Red Cloud	G. Perillo	7,500	65.00	135-175.
80-53-004	Chief Geronimo	G. Perillo	7,500	65.00	175.00
81-53-005	Chief Crazy Horse	G. Perillo	7,500	65.00	150-250.
Artaffects		**The Plainsmen**			
78-54-001	Buffalo Hunt (Bronze)	G. Perillo	2,500	350.00	500.00
79-54-002	The Proud One (Bronze)	G. Perillo	2,500	350.00	800.00
Artaffects		**The Professionals**			
79-55-001	The Big Leaguer	G. Perillo	15,000	29.95	33-55.00
80-55-002	Ballerina's Dilemma	G. Perillo	15,000	32.50	33-55.00
81-55-003	Quarterback	G. Perillo	15,000	32.50	40-55.00
81-55-004	Rodeo Joe	G. Perillo	15,000	35.00	40.00
82-55-005	Major Leaguer	G. Perillo	15,000	35.00	40-55.00
83-55-006	The Hockey Player	G. Perillo	15,000	35.00	40-55.00
Artaffects		**Pride of America's Indians**			
86-56-001	Brave and Free	G. Perillo	10-day	24.50	65.00
86-56-002	Dark-Eyed Friends	G. Perillo	10-day	24.50	50-85.00
86-56-003	Noble Companions	G. Perillo	10-day	24.50	50-65.00
87-56-004	Kindred Spirits	G. Perillo	10-day	24.50	50-75.00
87-56-005	Loyal Alliance	G. Perillo	10-day	24.50	85-100.00
87-56-006	Small and Wise	G. Perillo	10-day	24.50	35-50.00
87-56-007	Winter Scouts	G. Perillo	10-day	24.50	40.00
87-56-008	Peaceful Comrades	G. Perillo	10-day	24.50	50-75.00
Artaffects		**Legends of the West**			
82-57-001	Daniel Boone	G. Perillo	10,000	65.00	80.00
83-57-002	Davy Crockett	G. Perillo	10,000	65.00	80.00
83-57-003	Kit Carson	G. Perillo	10,000	65.00	80.00
83-57-004	Buffalo Bill	G. Perillo	10,000	65.00	80.00
Artaffects		**Chieftains II**			
83-58-001	Chief Pontiac	G. Perillo	7,500	70.00	85.00
83-58-002	Chief Victorio	G. Perillo	7,500	70.00	85.00
84-58-003	Chief Tecumseh	G. Perillo	7,500	70.00	85.00
84-58-004	Chief Cochise	G. Perillo	7,500	70.00	85.00
84-58-005	Chief Black Kettle	G. Perillo	7,500	70.00	110.00
Artaffects		**Child's Life**			
83-59-001	Siesta	G. Perillo	10,000	45.00	50.00
84-59-002	Sweet Dreams	G. Perillo	10,000	45.00	50.00
Artaffects		**Indian Nations**			
83-60-001	Blackfoot	G. Perillo	7,500	140.00	350-500.
83-60-002	Cheyenne	G. Perillo	7,500	Set	Set
83-60-003	Apache	G. Perillo	7,500	Set	Set
83-60-004	Sioux	G. Perillo	7,500	Set	Set
Artaffects		**Storybook Collection**			
80-61-001	Little Red Riding Hood	G. Perillo	18-day	29.95	30-52.00
81-61-002	Cinderella	G. Perillo	18-day	29.95	30-60.00
81-61-003	Hansel & Gretel	G. Perillo	18-day	29.95	30-52.00
82-61-004	Goldilocks & 3 Bears	G. Perillo	18-day	29.95	30-60.00
Artaffects		**Perillo Santas**			
80-62-001	Santa's Joy	G. Perillo	Open	29.95	50.00
81-62-002	Santa's Bundle	G. Perillo	Open	29.95	48.00
Artaffects		**The Princesses**			
82-63-001	Lily of the Mohawks	G. Perillo	7,500	50.00	85.00
82-63-002	Pocahontas	G. Perillo	7,500	50.00	50-65.00
82-63-003	Minnehaha	G. Perillo	7,500	50.00	65.00
82-63-004	Sacajawea	G. Perillo	7,500	50.00	85.00
Artaffects		**Nature's Harmony**			
82-64-001	The Peaceable Kingdom	G. Perillo	12,500	100.00	200-250.
82-64-002	Zebra	G. Perillo	12,500	50.00	60.00
82-64-003	Bengal Tiger	G. Perillo	12,500	50.00	60.00
83-64-004	Black Panther	G. Perillo	12,500	50.00	70.00
83-64-005	Elephant	G. Perillo	12,500	50.00	80.00
Artaffects		**Arctic Friends**			
82-65-001	Siberian Love	G. Perillo	7,500	100.00	175.00
82-65-002	Snow Pals	G. Perillo	7,500	Set	Set
Artaffects		**Motherhood Series**			
83-66-001	Madre	G. Perillo	10,000	50.00	75.00
84-66-002	Madonna of the Plains	G. Perillo	3,500	50.00	75-100.00
85-66-003	Abuela	G. Perillo	3,500	50.00	75.00
86-66-004	Nap Time	G. Perillo	3,500	50.00	75.00
Artaffects		**The War Ponies**			
83-67-001	Sioux War Pony	G. Perillo	7,500	60.00	95-125.00
83-67-002	Nez Perce War Pony	G. Perillo	7,500	60.00	149-195.
83-67-003	Apache War Pony	G. Perillo	7,500	60.00	95-125.00
Artaffects		**The Tribal Ponies**			
84-68-001	Arapaho Tribal Pony	G. Perillo	3,500	65.00	150.00
84-68-002	Comanche Tribal Pony	G. Perillo	3,500	65.00	150.00
84-68-003	Crow Tribal Pony	G. Perillo	3,500	65.00	200.00
Artaffects		**The Thoroughbreds**			
84-69-001	Whirlaway	G. Perillo	9,500	50.00	250.00
84-69-002	Secretariat	G. Perillo	9,500	50.00	350.00
84-69-003	Man o' War	G. Perillo	9,500	50.00	150.00
84-69-004	Seabiscuit	G. Perillo	9,500	50.00	150.00
Artaffects		**Special Issue**			
81-70-001	Apache Boy	G. Perillo	5,000	95.00	175.00
83-70-002	Papoose	G. Perillo	3,000	100.00	125.00
83-70-003	Indian Style	G. Perillo	17,500	50.00	50.00
84-69-004	The Lovers	G. Perillo	Open	50.00	100.00
84-70-005	Navajo Girl	G. Perillo	3,500	95.00	350.00
86-70-006	Navajo Boy	G. Perillo	3,500	95.00	150-250.
87-70-007	We The People	H.C. Christy	Open	35.00	35.00
Artaffects		**The Arabians**			
86-71-001	Silver Streak	G. Perillo	3,500	95.00	150.00
Artaffects		**The Colts**			
85-72-001	Appaloosa	G. Perillo	5,000	40.00	100.00
85-72-002	Pinto	G. Perillo	5,000	40.00	110.00
85-72-003	Arabian	G. Perillo	5,000	40.00	100.00
85-72-004	Thoroughbred	G. Perillo	5,000	40.00	100.00
Artaffects		**Tender Moments**			
85-73-001	Sunset	G. Perillo	2,000	150.00	250.00
85-73-002	Winter Romance	G. Perillo	2,000	Set	Set
Artaffects		**Young Emotions**			
86-74-001	Tears	G. Perillo	5,000	75.00	250.00
86-74-002	Smiles	G. Perillo	5,000	Set	Set
Artaffects		**The Maidens**			
85-75-001	Shimmering Waters	G. Perillo	5,000	60.00	150.00
85-75-002	Snow Blanket	G. Perillo	5,000	60.00	150.00
85-75-003	Song Bird	G. Perillo	5,000	60.00	150.00
Artaffects		**The Young Chieftains**			
85-76-001	Young Sitting Bull	G. Perillo	5,000	50.00	75-150.00
85-76-002	Young Joseph	G. Perillo	5,000	50.00	100.00
86-76-003	Young Red Cloud	G. Perillo	5,000	50.00	100.00
86-76-004	Young Geronimo	G. Perillo	5,000	50.00	100.00
86-76-005	Young Crazy Horse	G. Perillo	5,000	50.00	100.00
Artaffects		**Perillo Christmas**			
87-77-001	Shining Star	G. Perillo	Yr.Iss.	29.50	125-300.
88-77-002	Silent Light	G. Perillo	Yr.Iss.	35.00	50-200.00
89-77-003	Snow Flake	G. Perillo	Yr.Iss.	35.00	50.00
90-77-004	Bundle Up	G. Perillo	Yr.Iss.	39.50	75.00
91-77-005	Christmas Journey	G. Perillo	Yr.Iss.	39.50	50.00
Artaffects		**America's Indian Heritage**			
87-78-001	Cheyenne Nation	G. Perillo	10-day	24.50	45-85.00
88-78-002	Arapaho Nation	G. Perillo	10-day	24.50	45.00
88-78-003	Kiowa Nation	G. Perillo	10-day	24.50	45.00
88-78-004	Sioux Nation	G. Perillo	10-day	24.50	55-80.00
88-78-005	Chippewa Nation	G. Perillo	10-day	24.50	50.00
88-78-006	Crow Nation	G. Perillo	10-day	24.50	60.00
88-78-007	Nez Perce Nation	G. Perillo	10-day	24.50	55.00
88-78-008	Blackfoot Nation	G. Perillo	10-day	24.50	95.00

Number	Name	Artist	Edition Limit	Issue Price	Quote
Artaffects		**Mother's Love**			
88-79-001	Feelings	G. Perillo	Yr.Iss.	35.00	90.00
89-79-002	Moonlight	G. Perillo	Yr.Iss.	35.00	65.00
90-79-003	Pride & Joy	G. Perillo	Yr.Iss.	39.50	50.00
91-79-004	Little Shadow	G. Perillo	Yr.Iss.	39.50	45.00
Artaffects		**North American Wildlife**			
89-80-001	Mustang	G. Perillo	14-day	29.50	45.00
89-80-002	White-Tailed Deer	G. Perillo	14-day	29.50	35.00
89-80-003	Mountain Lion	G. Perillo	14-day	29.50	45.00
90-80-004	American Bald Eagle	G. Perillo	14-day	29.50	29.50
90-80-005	Timber Wolf	G. Perillo	14-day	29.50	35.00
90-80-006	Polar Bear	G. Perillo	14-day	29.50	39.00
90-80-007	Buffalo	G. Perillo	14-day	29.50	39.00
90-80-008	Bighorn Sheep	G. Perillo	14-day	29.50	39.00
Artaffects		**Portraits By Perillo-Mini Plates**			
89-81-001	Smiling Eyes-(4 1/4")	G. Perillo	9,500	19.50	19.50
89-81-002	Bright Sky-(4 1/4")	G. Perillo	9,500	19.50	19.50
89-81-003	Running Bear-(4 1/4")	G. Perillo	9,500	19.50	19.50
89-81-004	Little Feather-(4 1/4")	G. Perillo	9,500	19.50	19.50
90-81-005	Proud Eagle-(4 1/4")	G. Perillo	9,500	19.50	19.50
90-81-006	Blue Bird-(4 1/4")	G. Perillo	9,500	19.50	19.50
90-81-007	Wildflower-(4 1/4")	G. Perillo	9,500	19.50	19.50
90-81-008	Spring Breeze-(4 1/4")	G. Perillo	9,500	19.50	19.50
Artaffects		**March of Dimes: Our Children, Our Future**			
89-82-001	A Time to Be Born	G. Perillo	150-day	29.00	30.00
Artaffects		**Indian Bridal**			
90-83-001	Yellow Bird (6 1/2")	G. Perillo	14-day	25.00	25.00
90-83-002	Autumn Blossom (6 1/2")	G. Perillo	14-day	25.00	25.00
90-83-003	Misty Waters (6 1/2")	G. Perillo	14-day	25.00	25.00
90-83-004	Sunny Skies (6 1/2")	G. Perillo	14-day	25.00	25.00
Artaffects		**Proud Young Spirits**			
90-84-001	Protector of the Plains	G. Perillo	14-day	29.50	45-65.00
90-84-002	Watchful Eyes	G. Perillo	14-day	29.50	55.00
90-84-003	Freedom's Watch	G. Perillo	14-day	29.50	35-45.00
90-84-004	Woodland Scouts	G. Perillo	14-day	29.50	35-45.00
90-84-005	Fast Friends	G. Perillo	14-day	29.50	35-45.00
90-84-006	Birds of a Feather	G. Perillo	14-day	29.50	35-45.00
90-84-007	Prairie Pals	G. Perillo	14-day	29.50	35-45.00
90-84-008	Loyal Guardian	G. Perillo	14-day	29.50	35-45.00
Artaffects		**Perillo's Four Seasons**			
91-85-001	Summer (6 1/2")	G. Perillo	14-day	25.00	25.00
91-85-002	Autumn (6 1/2")	G. Perillo	14-day	25.00	25.00
91-85-003	Winter (6 1/2")	G. Perillo	14-day	25.00	25.00
91-85-004	Spring (6 1/2")	G. Perillo	14-day	25.00	25.00
Artaffects		**Council of Nations**			
92-86-001	Strength of the Sioux	G. Perillo	14-day	29.50	45.00
92-86-002	Pride of the Cheyenne	G. Perillo	14-day	29.50	29.50
92-86-003	Dignity of the Nez Perce	G. Perillo	14-day	29.50	29.50
92-86-004	Courage of the Arapaho	G. Perillo	14-day	29.50	29.50
92-86-005	Power of the Blackfoot	G. Perillo	14-day	29.50	29.50
92-86-006	Nobility of the Algonquin	G. Perillo	14-day	29.50	29.50
92-86-007	Wisdom of the Cherokee	G. Perillo	14-day	29.50	29.50
92-86-008	Boldness of the Seneca	G. Perillo	14-day	29.50	29.50
Artaffects		**War Ponies of the Plains**			
92-87-001	Nightshadow	G. Perillo	75-day	27.00	27.00
92-87-002	Windcatcher	G. Perillo	75-day	27.00	27.00
92-87-003	Prairie Prancer	G. Perillo	75-day	27.00	27.00
92-87-004	Thunderfoot	G. Perillo	75-day	27.00	27.00
92-87-005	Proud Companion	G. Perillo	75-day	27.00	27.00
92-87-006	Sun Dancer	G. Perillo	75-day	27.00	27.00
92-87-007	Free Spirit	G. Perillo	75-day	27.00	27.00
92-87-008	Gentle Warrior	G. Perillo	75-day	27.00	27.00
Artaffects		**Living In Harmony**			
91-88-001	Peaceable Kingdom	G. Perillo	75-day	29.50	29.50
Artaffects		**Studies in Black and White-Collector's Club Only (Miniatures)**			
92-89-001	Dignity	G. Perillo	Yr. Iss.	75/Set	75/Set
92-89-002	Determination	G. Perillo	Yr. Iss.	Set	Set
92-89-003	Diligence	G. Perillo	Yr. Iss.	Set	Set
92-89-004	Devotion	G. Perillo	Yr. Iss.	Set	Set
Artaffects		**Club Member Limited Edition Redemption Offerings**			
92-90-001	The Pencil	G. Perillo	Yr. Iss.	35.00	75.00
92-90-002	Studies in Black and White (Set of 4)	G. Perillo	Yr. Iss.	75/Set	75/Set
93-90-003	Watcher of the Wilderness	G. Perillo	Yr. Iss.	60.00	60.00
Artaffects		**Spirits of Nature**			
93-91-001	Protector of the Nations	G. Perillo	3,500	60.00	60.00
93-91-002	Defender of the Mountain	G. Perillo	3,500	60.00	60.00
93-91-003	Spirit of the Plains	G. Perillo	3,500	60.00	60.00
93-91-004	Guardian of Safe Passage	G. Perillo	3,500	60.00	60.00
93-91-005	Keeper of the Forest	G. Perillo	3,500	60.00	60.00
Artaffects		**Children Of The Prairie**			
93-92-001	Tender Loving Care	G. Perillo	N/A	29.50	29.50
93-92-002	Daydreamers	G. Perillo	N/A	29.50	29.50
93-92-003	Play Time	G. Perillo	N/A	29.50	29.50
93-92-004	The Sentinal	G. Perillo	N/A	29.50	29.50
93-92-005	Beach Comber	G. Perillo	N/A	29.50	29.50
93-92-006	Watchful Waiting	G. Perillo	N/A	29.50	29.50
93-92-007	Patience	G. Perillo	N/A	29.50	29.50
93-92-008	Sisters	G. Perillo	N/A	29.50	29.50
Artaffects		**Native American Christmas**			
93-93-001	The Little Shepherd (Single Issue '93)	G. Perillo	Annual	35.00	35.00
94-93-002	Joy to the World (Single Issue '94)	G. Perillo	Annual	45.00	45.00
Artaffects		**Tribal Images**			
94-94-001	Sioux Cheiftans	G. Perillo	75-day	35.00	35.00
94-94-002	Crow Cheiftans	G. Perillo	75-day	35.00	35.00
94-94-003	Cheyenne Cheiftans	G. Perillo	75-day	35.00	35.00
94-94-004	Blackfoot Cheiftans	G. Perillo	75-day	35.00	35.00
Artaffects		**Perillo's Favorites**			
94-95-001	Buffalo and the Brave	G. Perillo	75-day	45.00	45.00

Number	Name	Artist	Edition Limit	Issue Price	Quote
Artaffects		**Special Edition**			
94-96-001	Home of the Brave and Free	G. Perillo	75-day	35.00	35.00
Artists of the World		**Holiday**			
76-01-001	Festival of Lights	T. DeGrazia	9,500	45.00	108.00
77-01-002	Bell of Hope	T. DeGrazia	9,500	45.00	48-75.00
78-01-003	Little Madonna	T. DeGrazia	9,500	45.00	50-59.00
79-01-004	The Nativity	T. DeGrazia	9,500	50.00	78-90.00
80-01-005	Little Pima Drummer	T. DeGrazia	9,500	50.00	50-60.00
81-01-006	A Little Prayer	T. DeGrazia	9,500	55.00	35-65.00
82-01-007	Blue Boy	T. DeGrazia	10,000	60.00	36-65.00
83-01-008	Heavenly Blessings	T. DeGrazia	10,000	65.00	30-65.00
84-01-009	Navajo Madonna	T. DeGrazia	10,000	65.00	28-65.00
85-01-010	Saguaro Dance	T. DeGrazia	10,000	65.00	40-65.00
Artists of the World		**Holiday (Signed)**			
76-02-001	Festival of Lights, signed	T. DeGrazia	500	100.00	350.00
77-02-002	Bell of Hope, signed	T. DeGrazia	500	100.00	200.00
78-02-003	Little Madonna, signed	T. DeGrazia	500	100.00	350.00
79-02-004	The Nativity, signed	T. DeGrazia	500	100.00	200.00
80-02-005	Little Pima Drummer, signed	T. DeGrazia	500	100.00	200.00
81-02-006	A Little Prayer, signed	T. DeGrazia	500	100.00	200.00
82-02-007	Blue Boy, signed	T. DeGrazia	96	100.00	200.00
Artists of the World		**Holiday Mini-Plates**			
80-03-001	Festival of Lights	T. DeGrazia	5,000	15.00	250.00
81-03-002	Bell of Hope	T. DeGrazia	5,000	15.00	95.00
82-03-003	Little Madonna	T. DeGrazia	5,000	15.00	95.00
82-03-004	The Nativity	T. DeGrazia	5,000	15.00	95.00
83-03-005	Little Pima Drummer	T. DeGrazia	5,000	15.00	25.00
83-03-006	Little Prayer	T. DeGrazia	5,000	20.00	25.00
84-03-007	Blue Boy	T. DeGrazia	5,000	20.00	25.00
84-03-008	Heavenly Blessings	T. DeGrazia	5,000	20.00	25.00
85-03-009	Navajo Madonna	T. DeGrazia	5,000	20.00	25.00
85-03-010	Saguaro Dance	T. DeGrazia	5,000	20.00	25.00
Artists of the World		**Children**			
76-04-001	Los Ninos	T. DeGrazia	5,000	35.00	900-1000.
77-04-002	White Dove	T. DeGrazia	5,000	40.00	60-100.00
78-04-003	Flower Girl	T. DeGrazia	9,500	45.00	85.00
79-04-004	Flower Boy	T. DeGrazia	9,500	45.00	62.00
80-04-005	Little Cocopah	T. DeGrazia	9,500	50.00	65.00
81-04-006	Beautiful Burden	T. DeGrazia	9,500	50.00	48.00
82-04-007	Merry Little Indian	T. DeGrazia	9,500	55.00	50.00
83-04-008	Wondering	T. DeGrazia	10,000	60.00	33-60.00
84-04-009	Pink Papoose	T. DeGrazia	10,000	65.00	26-65.00
85-04-010	Sunflower Boy	T. DeGrazia	10,000	65.00	25-65.00
Artists of the World		**Children (Signed)**			
78-05-001	Los Ninos, signed	T. DeGrazia	500	100.00	900.00
78-05-002	White Dove, signed	T. DeGrazia	500	100.00	450.00
78-05-003	Flower Girl, signed	T. DeGrazia	500	100.00	450.00
79-05-004	Flower Boy, signed	T. DeGrazia	500	100.00	450.00
80-05-005	Little Cocopah Girl, signed	T. DeGrazia	500	100.00	320.00
81-05-006	Beautiful Burden, signed	T. DeGrazia	500	100.00	320.00
81-05-007	Merry Little Indian, signed	T. DeGrazia	500	100.00	450.00
Artists of the World		**Children Mini-Plates**			
80-06-001	Los Ninos	T. DeGrazia	5,000	15.00	300.00
81-06-002	White Dove	T. DeGrazia	5,000	15.00	35.00
82-06-003	Flower Girl	T. DeGrazia	5,000	15.00	35.00
82-06-004	Flower Boy	T. DeGrazia	5,000	15.00	35.00
83-06-005	Little Cocopah Indian Girl	T. DeGrazia	5,000	15.00	25.00
83-06-006	Beautiful Burden	T. DeGrazia	5,000	20.00	53.00
84-06-007	Merry Little Indian	T. DeGrazia	5,000	20.00	25.00
84-06-008	Wondering	T. DeGrazia	5,000	20.00	25.00
85-06-009	Pink Papoose	T. DeGrazia	5,000	20.00	25.00
85-06-010	Sunflower Boy	T. DeGrazia	5,000	20.00	25.00
Artists of the World		**Children at Play**			
85-07-001	My First Horse	T. DeGrazia	15,000	65.00	65.00
86-07-002	Girl With Sewing Machine	T. DeGrazia	15,000	65.00	65.00
87-07-003	Love Me	T. DeGrazia	15,000	65.00	65.00
88-07-004	Merrily, Merrily, Merrily	T. DeGrazia	15,000	65.00	65.00
89-07-005	My First Arrow	T. DeGrazia	15,000	65.00	85.00
90-07-006	Away With My Kite	T. DeGrazia	15,000	65.00	75.00
Artists of the World		**Western**			
86-08-001	Morning Ride	T. DeGrazia	5,000	65.00	85.00
87-08-002	Bronco	T. DeGrazia	5,000	65.00	85.00
88-08-003	Apache Scout	T. DeGrazia	5,000	65.00	85.00
89-08-004	Alone	T. DeGrazia	5,000	65.00	85.00
Artists of the World		**Children of the Sun**			
87-09-001	Spring Blossoms	T. DeGrazia	150-day	34.50	45.00
87-09-002	My Little Pink Bird	T. DeGrazia	150-day	34.50	45.00
87-09-003	Bright Flowers of the Desert	T. DeGrazia	150-day	37.90	45.00
88-09-004	Gifts from the Sun	T. DeGrazia	150-day	37.90	45.00
88-09-005	Growing Glory	T. DeGrazia	150-day	37.90	45.00
88-09-006	The Gentle White Dove	T. DeGrazia	150-day	37.90	45.00
88-09-007	Sunflower Maiden	T. DeGrazia	150-day	39.90	45.00
89-09-008	Sun Showers	T. DeGrazia	150-day	39.90	45.00
Artists of the World		**Fiesta of the Children**			
90-10-001	Welcome to the Fiesta	T. DeGrazia	150-day	34.50	38.00
90-10-002	Castanets in Bloom	T. DeGrazia	150-day	34.50	45.00
91-10-003	Fiesta Flowers	T. DeGrazia	150-day	34.50	45.00
91-10-004	Fiesta Angels	T. DeGrazia	150-day	34.50	38.00
Artists of the World		**Celebration Series**			
93-11-001	The Lord's Candle	T. DeGrazia	5,000	39.50	39.50
93-11-002	Pinata Party	T. DeGrazia	5,000	39.50	39.50
93-11-003	Holiday lullaby	T. DeGrazia	5,000	39.50	39.50
93-11-004	Caroling	T. DeGrazia	5,000	39.50	39.50
Artists of the World		**Children of Aberdeen**			
79-12-001	Girl with Little Brother	K. Fung Ng	Undis.	50.00	50.00
80-12-002	Sampan Girl	K. Fung Ng	Undis.	50.00	50.00
81-12-003	Girl with Little Sister	K. Fung Ng	Undis.	55.00	58.00
82-12-004	Girl with Seashells	K. Fung Ng	Undis.	60.00	60.00
83-12-005	Girl with Seabirds	K. Fung Ng	Undis.	60.00	60.00
84-12-006	Brother and Sister	K. Fung Ng	Undis.	60.00	60.00

PLATES

Number	Name	Artist	Edition Limit	Issue Price	Quote
Band Creations		**Santa's Animal Kingdom**			
94-01-001	Santa with Animals	T. Rubel	5,000	30.00	30.00
Bareuther		**Christmas**			
67-01-001	Stiftskirche	H. Mueller	10,000	12.00	85.00
68-01-002	Kapplkirche	H. Mueller	10,000	12.00	25.00
69-01-003	Christkindlesmarkt	H. Mueller	10,000	12.00	18.00
70-01-004	Chapel in Oberndorf	H. Mueller	10,000	12.50	22.00
71-01-005	Toys for Sale From Drawing By	L. Richter	10,000	12.75	27.00
72-01-006	Christmas in Munich	H. Mueller	10,000	14.50	25.00
73-01-007	Sleigh Ride	H. Mueller	10,000	15.00	35.00
74-01-008	Black Forest Church	H. Mueller	10,000	19.00	19.00
75-01-009	Snowman	H. Mueller	10,000	21.50	30.00
76-01-010	Chapel in the Hills	H. Mueller	10,000	23.50	26.00
77-01-011	Story Time	H. Mueller	10,000	24.50	40.00
78-01-012	Mittenwald	H. Mueller	10,000	27.50	31.00
79-01-013	Winter Day	H. Mueller	10,000	35.00	35.00
80-01-014	Mittenberg	H. Mueller	10,000	37.50	39.00
81-01-015	Walk in the Forest	H. Mueller	10,000	39.50	39.50
82-01-016	Bad Wimpfen	H. Mueller	10,000	39.50	43.00
83-01-017	The Night before Christmas	H. Mueller	10,000	39.50	39.50
84-01-018	Zeil on the River Main	H. Mueller	10,000	42.50	45.00
85-01-019	Winter Wonderland	H. Mueller	10,000	42.50	57.00
86-01-020	Christmas in Forchheim	H. Mueller	10,000	42.50	70.00
87-01-021	Decorating the Tree	H. Mueller	10,000	42.50	85.00
88-01-022	St. Coloman Church	H. Mueller	10,000	52.50	65.00
89-01-023	Sleigh Ride	H. Mueller	10,000	52.50	80-90.00
90-01-024	The Old Forge in Rothenburg	H. Mueller	10,000	52.50	52.50
91-01-025	Christmas Joy	H. Mueller	10,000	56.50	56.50
92-01-026	Market Place in Heppenheim	H. Mueller	10,000	59.50	59.50
93-01-027	Winter Fun	H. Mueller	10,000	59.50	59.50
94-01-028	Coming Home For Christmas	H. Mueller	10,000	59.50	59.50
Belleek		**Christmas**			
70-01-001	Castle Caldwell	Unknown	7,500	25.00	70-85.00
71-01-002	Celtic Cross	Unknown	7,500	25.00	60.00
72-01-003	Flight of the Earls	Unknown	7,500	30.00	35.00
73-01-004	Tribute To Yeats	Unknown	7,500	38.50	40.00
74-01-005	Devenish Island	Unknown	7,500	45.00	190.00
75-01-006	The Celtic Cross	Unknown	7,500	48.00	80.00
76-01-007	Dove of Peace	Unknown	7,500	55.00	55.00
77-01-008	Wren	Unknown	7,500	55.00	55.00
Belleek		**Holiday Scenes in Ireland**			
91-02-001	Traveling Home	Unknown	7,500	75.00	75.00
92-02-002	Bearing Gifts	Unknown	7,500	75.00	75.00
Berlin Design		**Christmas**			
70-01-001	Christmas in Bernkastel	Unknown	4,000	14.50	125.00
71-01-002	Christmas in Rothenburg	Unknown	20,000	14.50	45.00
72-01-003	Christmas in Michelstadt	Unknown	20,000	15.00	55.00
73-01-004	Christmas in Wendlestein	Unknown	20,000	20.00	55.00
74-01-005	Christmas in Bremen	Unknown	20,000	25.00	53.00
75-01-006	Christmas in Dortland	Unknown	20,000	30.00	35.00
76-01-007	Christmas in Augsburg	Unknown	20,000	32.00	75.00
77-01-008	Christmas in Hamburg	Unknown	20,000	32.00	32.00
78-01-009	Christmas in Berlin	Unknown	20,000	36.00	85.00
79-01-010	Christmas in Greetsiel	Unknown	20,000	47.50	60.00
80-01-011	Christmas in Mittenberg	Unknown	20,000	50.00	55.00
81-01-012	Christmas Eve In Hahnenklee	Unknown	20,000	55.00	55.00
82-01-013	Christmas Eve In Wasserberg	Unknown	20,000	55.00	50.00
83-01-014	Christmas in Oberndorf	Unknown	20,000	55.00	65.00
84-01-015	Christmas in Ramsau	Unknown	20,000	55.00	55.00
85-01-016	Christmas in Bad Wimpfen	Unknown	20,000	55.00	59.00
86-01-017	Christmas Eve in Gelnhaus	Unknown	20,000	65.00	65.00
87-01-018	Christmas Eve in Goslar	Unknown	20,000	65.00	65.00
88-01-019	Christmas Eve in Ruhpolding	Unknown	20,000	65.00	90.00
89-01-020	Christmas Eve in Friedechsdadt	Unknown	20,000	80.00	80.00
90-01-021	Christmas Eve in Partenkirchen	Unknown	20,000	80.00	80.00
91-01-022	Christmas Eve in Allendorf	Unknown	20,000	80.00	80.00
Bing & Grondahl		**Christmas**			
95-01-001	Behind The Frozen Window	F.A. Hallin	Annual	.50	5000-7500.
96-01-002	New Moon	F.A. Hallin	Annual	.50	1200-1700.
97-01-003	Sparrows	F.A. Hallin	Annual	.75	1090-1900.
98-01-004	Roses and Star	F. Garde	Annual	.75	675-900.
99-01-005	Crows	F. Garde	Annual	.75	800-1325.
00-01-006	Church Bells	F. Garde	Annual	.75	800-1090.
01-01-007	Three Wise Men	S. Sabra	Annual	1.00	450-495.
02-01-008	Gothic Church Interior	D. Jensen	Annual	1.00	300-400.
03-01-009	Expectant Children	M. Hyldahl	Annual	1.00	370-400.
04-01-010	Fredericksberg Hill	C. Olsen	Annual	1.00	150-225.
05-01-011	Christmas Night	D. Jensen	Annual	1.00	170-210.
06-01-012	Sleighing to Church	D. Jensen	Annual	1.00	98-105.00
07-01-013	Little Match Girl	E. Plockross	Annual	1.00	150.00
08-01-014	St. Petri Church	P. Jorgensen	Annual	1.00	80-87.00
09-01-015	Yule Tree	Aarestrup	Annual	1.50	100-104.00
10-01-016	The Old Organist	C. Ersgaard	Annual	1.50	76-95.00
11-01-017	Angels and Shepherds	H. Moltke	Annual	1.50	95.00
12-01-018	Going to Church	E. Hansen	Annual	1.50	88-95.00
13-01-019	Bringing Home the Tree	T. Larsen	Annual	1.50	88-95.00
14-01-020	Amalienborg Castle	T. Larsen	Annual	1.50	77-80.00
15-01-021	Dog Outside Window	D. Jensen	Annual	1.50	120-156.
16-01-022	Sparrows at Christmas	P. Jorgensen	Annual	1.50	80.00
17-01-023	Christmas Boat	A. Friis	Annual	1.50	80.00
18-01-024	Fishing Boat	A. Friis	Annual	1.50	80-82.00
19-01-025	Outside Lighted Window	A. Friis	Annual	2.00	75-80.00
20-01-026	Hare in the Snow	A. Friis	Annual	2.00	60-118.00
21-01-027	Pigeons	A. Friis	Annual	2.00	60-93.00
22-01-028	Star of Bethlehem	A. Friis	Annual	2.00	60-64.00
23-01-029	The Ermitage	A. Friis	Annual	2.00	60-66.00
24-01-030	Lighthouse	A. Friis	Annual	2.50	60-80.00
25-01-031	Child's Christmas	A. Friis	Annual	2.50	60-90.00
26-01-032	Churchgoers	A. Friis	Annual	2.50	60-89.00
27-01-033	Skating Couple	A. Friis	Annual	2.50	90-100.00
28-01-034	Eskimos	A. Friis	Annual	2.50	61-65.00
29-01-035	Fox Outside Farm	A. Friis	Annual	2.50	75-84.00
30-01-036	Town Hall Square	H. Flugenring	Annual	2.50	87-95.00
31-01-037	Christmas Train	A. Friis	Annual	2.50	80-105.00
32-01-038	Life Boat	H. Flugenring	Annual	2.50	78-85.00
33-01-039	Korsor-Nyborg Ferry	H. Flugenring	Annual	3.00	70-81.00
34-01-040	Church Bell in Tower	H. Flugenring	Annual	3.00	70-87.00
35-01-041	Lillebelt Bridge	O. Larson	Annual	3.00	65-76.00
36-01-042	Royal Guard	O. Larson	Annual	3.00	65-84.00
37-01-043	Arrival of Christmas Guests	O. Larson	Annual	3.00	80-96.00
38-01-044	Lighting the Candles	I. Tjerne	Annual	3.00	125-143.
39-01-045	Old Lock-Eye, The Sandman	I. Tjerne	Annual	3.00	150-238.
40-01-046	Christmas Letters	O. Larson	Annual	4.00	130-366.
41-01-047	Horses Enjoying Meal	O. Larson	Annual	4.00	150-200.
42-01-048	Danish Farm	O. Larson	Annual	4.00	140-228.
43-01-049	Ribe Cathedral	O. Larson	Annual	5.00	140-200.
44-01-050	Sorgenfri Castle	O. Larson	Annual	5.00	85-142.00
45-01-051	The Old Water Mill	O. Larson	Annual	5.00	95-145.00
46-01-052	Commemoration Cross	M. Hyldahl	Annual	5.00	75.00
47-01-053	Dybbol Mill	M. Hyldahl	Annual	5.00	75-122.00
48-01-054	Watchman	M. Hyldahl	Annual	5.50	65-82.00
49-01-055	Landsoldaten	M. Hyldahl	Annual	5.50	60-90.00
50-01-056	Kronborg Castle	M. Hyldahl	Annual	5.50	95-126.00
51-01-057	Jens Bang	M. Hyldahl	Annual	6.00	74-94.00
52-01-058	Thorsvaldsen Museum	B. Pramvig	Annual	6.00	65-107.00
53-01-059	Snowman	B. Pramvig	Annual	7.50	65-90.00
54-01-060	Royal Boat	K. Bonfils	Annual	7.00	83-90.00
55-01-061	Kaulundorg Church	K. Bonfils	Annual	8.00	70-113.00
56-01-062	Christmas in Copenhagen	K. Bonfils	Annual	8.50	90-148.00
57-01-063	Christmas Candles	K. Bonfils	Annual	9.00	110-140.
58-01-064	Santa Claus	K. Bonfils	Annual	9.50	95-114.00
59-01-065	Christmas Eve	K. Bonfils	Annual	10.00	128-142.
60-01-066	Village Church	K. Bonfils	Annual	10.00	130-160.
61-01-067	Winter Harmony	K. Bonfils	Annual	10.50	75-95.00
62-01-068	Winter Night	K. Bonfils	Annual	11.00	53-65.00
63-01-069	The Christmas Elf	H. Thelander	Annual	11.00	80-105.00
64-01-070	The Fir Tree and Hare	H. Thelander	Annual	11.50	34-60.00
65-01-071	Bringing Home the Tree	H. Thelander	Annual	12.00	34-65.00
66-01-072	Home for Christmas	H. Thelander	Annual	12.00	25-50.00
67-01-073	Sharing the Joy	H. Thelander	Annual	13.00	23-50.00
68-01-074	Christmas in Church	H. Thelander	Annual	14.00	18-45.00
69-01-075	Arrival of Guests	H. Thelander	Annual	14.00	12-35.00
70-01-076	Pheasants in Snow	H. Thelander	Annual	14.50	9-25.00
71-01-077	Christmas at Home	H. Thelander	Annual	15.00	9-20.00
72-01-078	Christmas in Greenland	H. Thelander	Annual	16.50	8-20.00
73-01-079	Country Christmas	H. Thelander	Annual	19.50	16-30.00
74-01-080	Christmas in the Village	H. Thelander	Annual	22.00	12-30.00
75-01-081	Old Water Mill	H. Thelander	Annual	27.50	14-28.00
76-01-082	Christmas Welcome	H. Thelander	Annual	27.50	19-28.00
77-01-083	Copenhagen Christmas	H. Thelander	Annual	29.50	16-28.00
78-01-084	Christmas Tale	H. Thelander	Annual	32.00	24-28.00
79-01-085	White Christmas	H. Thelander	Annual	36.50	22-35.00
80-01-086	Christmas in Woods	H. Thelander	Annual	42.50	19-45.00
81-01-087	Christmas Peace	H. Thelander	Annual	49.50	34-39.00
82-01-088	Christmas Tree	H. Thelander	Annual	54.50	30-35.00
83-01-089	Christmas in Old Town	H. Thelander	Annual	54.50	39.00
84-01-090	The Christmas Letter	E. Jensen	Annual	54.50	24-39.00
85-01-091	Christmas Eve at the Farmhouse	E. Jensen	Annual	54.50	30-39.00
86-01-092	Silent Night, Holy Night	E. Jensen	Annual	54.50	40-48.00
87-01-093	The Snowman's Christmas Eve	E. Jensen	Annual	59.50	45-48.00
88-01-094	In the Kings Garden	E. Jensen	Annual	64.50	34-45.00
89-01-095	Christmas Anchorage	E. Jensen	Annual	59.50	35-59.00
90-01-096	Changing of the Guards	E. Jensen	Annual	64.50	48-65.00
91-01-097	Copenhagen Stock Exchange	E. Jensen	Annual	69.50	45-60.00
92-01-098	Christmas At the Rectory	J. Steensen	Annual	69.50	55-95.00
93-01-099	Father Christmas in Copenhagen	J. Nielson	Annual	69.50	69.50-75.00
94-01-100	A Day At The Deer Park	J. Nielson	Annual	72.50	72.50
Bing & Grondahl		**Jubilee-5 Year Cycle**			
15-02-001	Frozen Window	F.A. Hallin	Annual	Unkn.	155.00
20-02-002	Church Bells	F. Garde	Annual	Unkn.	65.00
25-02-003	Dog Outside Window	D. Jensen	Annual	Unkn.	130.00
30-02-004	The Old Organist	C. Ersgaard	Annual	Unkn.	169.00
35-02-005	Little Match Girl	E. Plockross	Annual	Unkn.	720.00
40-02-006	Three Wise Men	S. Sabra	Annual	Unkn.	1839.00
45-02-007	Amalienborg Castle	T. Larsen	Annual	Unkn.	199.00
50-02-008	Eskimos	A. Friis	Annual	Unkn.	199.00
55-02-009	Dybbol Mill	M. Hyldahl	Annual	Unkn.	210.00
60-02-010	Kronborg Castle	M. Hyldahl	Annual	25.00	129.00
65-02-011	Chruchgoers	A. Friis	Annual	25.00	69.00
70-02-012	Amalienborg Castle	T. Larsen	Annual	30.00	30.00
75-02-013	Horses Enjoying Meal	O. Larson	Annual	40.00	50.00
80-02-014	Yule Tree	Aarestrup	Annual	60.00	60.00
85-02-015	Lifeboat at Work	H. Flugenring	Annual	65.00	93.00
90-02-016	The Royal Yacht Dannebrog	J. Bonfils	Annual	95.00	95.00
Bing & Grondahl		**Mother's Day**			
69-03-001	Dogs and Puppies	H. Thelander	Annual	9.75	350-450.
70-03-002	Bird and Chicks	H. Thelander	Annual	10.00	11-35.00
71-03-003	Cat and Kitten	H. Thelander	Annual	11.00	9-25.00
72-03-004	Mare and Foal	H. Thelander	Annual	12.00	12-20.00
73-03-005	Duck and Ducklings	H. Thelander	Annual	13.00	9-20.00
74-03-006	Bear and Cubs	H. Thelander	Annual	16.50	10-20.00
75-03-007	Doe and Fawns	H. Thelander	Annual	19.50	9-20.00
76-03-008	Swan Family	H. Thelander	Annual	22.50	18-25.00
77-03-009	Squirrel and Young	H. Thelander	Annual	23.50	15-25.00
78-03-010	Heron	H. Thelander	Annual	24.50	12-25.00
79-03-011	Fox and Cubs	H. Thelander	Annual	27.50	30-45.00
80-03-012	Woodpecker and Young	H. Thelander	Annual	29.50	28-30.00
81-03-013	Hare and Young	H. Thelander	Annual	36.50	20-30.00
82-03-014	Lioness and Cubs	H. Thelander	Annual	39.50	30-42.00
83-03-015	Raccoon and Young	H. Thelander	Annual	39.50	30-35.00
84-03-016	Stork and Nestlings	H. Thelander	Annual	39.50	35-40.00
85-03-017	Bear and Cubs	H. Thelander	Annual	39.50	34-40.00
86-03-018	Elephant with Calf	H. Thelander	Annual	39.50	35-40.00
87-03-019	Sheep with Lambs	H. Thelander	Annual	42.50	88-90.00
88-03-020	Crested Ployer & Young	H. Thelander	Annual	47.50	40-80.00
88-03-021	Lapwing Mother with Chicks	H. Thelander	Annual	49.50	40-60.00
89-03-022	Cow With Calf	H. Thelander	Annual	49.50	56-65.00
90-03-023	Hen with Chicks	L. Jensen	Annual	52.50	45-50.00
91-03-024	The Nanny Goat and her Two Frisky Kids	L. Jensen	Annual	54.50	50-95.00
92-03-025	Panda With Cubs	L. Jensen	Annual	59.50	45-69.00
93-03-026	St. Bernard Dog and Puppies	A. Therkelsen	Annual	59.50	59.50-83.00
94-03-027	Cat with Kittens	A. Therkelsen	Annual	59.50	59.50
Bing & Grondahl		**Children's Day Plate Series**			
85-04-001	The Magical Tea Party	C. Roller	Annual	24.50	35.00
86-04-002	A Joyful Flight	C. Roller	Annual	26.50	35.00
86-04-003	The Little Gardeners	C. Roller	Annual	29.50	85.00
88-04-004	Wash Day	C. Roller	Annual	34.50	50.00
89-04-005	Bedtime	C. Roller	Annual	37.00	55.00
90-04-006	My Favorite Dress	S. Vestergaard	Annual	37.00	45.00
91-04-007	Fun on the Beach	S. Vestergaard	Annual	45.00	35-45.00

Company Number	Name	Series Artist	Edition Limit	Issue Price	Quote
92-04-008	A Summer Day in the Meadow	S. Vestergaard	Annual	45.00	39.50-45.00
93-04-009	The Carousel	S. Vestergaard	Annual	45.00	45.00
94-04-010	The Little Fisherman	S. Vestergaard	Annual	45.00	45.00
Bing & Grondahl		**Statue of Liberty**			
85-05-001	Statue of Liberty	Unknown	10,000	60.00	100.00
Bing & Grondahl		**Christmas In America**			
86-06-001	Christmas Eve in Williamsburg	J. Woodson	Annual	29.50	95-150.00
87-06-002	Christmas Eve at the White House	J. Woodson	Annual	34.50	35.00
88-06-003	Christmas Eve at Rockefeller Center	J. Woodson	Annual	34.50	49.00
89-06-004	Christmas In New England	J. Woodson	Annual	37.00	49.00
90-06-005	Christmas Eve at the Capitol	J. Woodson	Annual	39.50	40-55.00
91-06-006	Christmas Eve at Independence Hall	J. Woodson	Annual	45.00	45.00
92-06-007	Christmas in San Francisco	J. Woodson	Annual	47.50	40-47.50
93-06-008	Coming Home For Christmas	J. Woodson	Annual	47.50	47.50
94-06-009	Christmas Eve In Alaska	J. Woodson	Annual	47.50	47.50
Bing & Grondahl		**Santa Claus Collection**			
89-07-001	Santa's Workshop	H. Hansen	Annual	59.50	60-90.00
90-07-002	Santa's Sleigh	H. Hansen	Annual	59.50	59.50
91-07-003	Santa's Journey	H. Hansen	Annual	69.50	60-69.50
92-07-004	Santa's Arrival	H. Hansen	Annual	74.50	74.50
93-07-005	Santa's Gifts	H. Hansen	Annual	74.50	74.50
94-07-006	Christmas Stories	H. Hansen	Annual	74.50	74.50
Bing & Grondahl		**Young Adventurer Plate**			
90-08-001	The Little Viking	S. Vestergaard	Annual	52.50	65.00
Bing & Grondahl		**Christmas in America Anniversary Plate**			
91-09-001	Christmas Eve in Williamsburg	J. Woodson	Annual	69.50	69.50
Bing & Grondahl		**Centennial Collection**			
91-10-001	Crows Enjoying Christmas	D. Jensen	Annual	59.50	47.50
92-10-002	Copenhagen Christmas	H. Vlugenring	Annual	59.50	47.50
93-10-003	Christmas Elf	H. Thelander	Annual	59.50	59.50
94-10-004	Christmas in Church	H. Thelander	Annual	59.50	59.50
95-10-005	Behind The Frozen Window	A. Hallin	Annual	59.50	59.50
Boehm Studios		**Panda**			
82-01-001	Panda, Harmony	Boehm	5,000	65.00	65.00
82-01-002	Panda, Peace	Boehm	5,000	65.00	65.00
The Bradford Exchange/China		**Echoes of Tranquility**			
93-01-001	Red Paradise	J. Lung	95-day	29.90	29.90
The Bradford Exchange/Russia		**The Nutcracker**			
93-02-001	Marie's Magical Gift	N. Zaitseva	95-day	39.87	39.87
The Bradford Exchange/United States		**Lincoln's Portraits of Valor**			
93-03-001	The Gettysburg Address	B. Maguire	95-day	29.90	29.90
The Bradford Exchange/United States		**Superstars of Country Music**			
93-04-001	Dolly Parton: I Will Always Love You	N. Giorgro	95-day	29.90	29.90
The Bradford Exchange/United States		**Elvis: Young & Wild**			
93-05-001	The King of Creole	B. Emmett	95-day	29.90	29.90
The Bradford Exchange/United States		**Great Moments in Baseball**			
93-06-001	Joe DiMaggio: The Streak	S. Gardner	95-day	29.90	29.90
The Bradford Exchange/United States		**America's Triumph in Space**			
93-07-001	The Eagle Has Landed	R. Schaar	95-day	29.90	29.90
The Bradford Exchange/United States		**New Horizons**			
93-08-001	Building For a New Generation	R. Copple	95-day	29.90	29.90
The Bradford Exchange/United States		**Mystic Guardians**			
93-09-001	Soul Mates	S. Hill	95-day	29.90	29.90
The Bradford Exchange/United States		**When All Hearts Come Home**			
93-10-01	Oh Christmas Tree	J. Barnes	95-day	29.90	29.90
The Bradford Exchange/United States		**Promise of a Savior**			
93-11-001	An Angel's Message	Various	95-day	29.90	29.90
The Bradford Exchange/United States		**Footsteps of the Brave**			
93-12-001	Noble Quest	H. Schaare	95-day	24.90	24.90
93-12-001	At Storm's Passage	H. Schaare	95-day	24.90	24.90
The Bradford Exchange/United States		**The Eyes Have It**			
93-13-001	Little Blue Eyes	T. Humphrey	95-day	29.90	29.90
The Bradford Exchange/United States		**Old Fashioned Christmas with Thomas Kinkade**			
93-14-001	All Friends Are Welcome	T. Kinkade	95-day	29.90	29.90
The Bradford Exchange/United States		**Alice in Wonderland**			
93-15-001	The Mad Tea Party	S. Gustafson	95-day	29.90	29.90
The Bradford Exchange/United States		**Notorious Disney Villains**			
93-16-001	The Wicked Queen	Disney-Studios	95-day	29.90	29.90
The Bradford Exchange/United States		**Hideaway Lake**			
93-17-001	Rusty's Retreat	R. Rust	95-day	34.90	34.90
The Bradford Exchange/United States		**Vanishing Paradises**			
93-18-001	The Rainforest	G. Dieckhoner	95-day	29.90	29.90
The Bradford Exchange/United States		**A Hidden World**			
93-19-001	Two by Night, Two by Light	R. Rust	95-day	29.90	29.90
93-19-002	Two by Steam, Two in Dream	R. Rust	95-day	29.90	29.90
The Bradford Exchange/United States		**Dog Days**			
93-20-001	Sweet Dreams	J. Gadmus	95-day	29.90	29.90
The Bradford Exchange/United States		**Baskets of Love**			
93-21-001	Andrew and Abbey	A. Isakov	95-day	29.90	29.90
93-21-002	Cody and Courtney	A. Isakov	95-day	29.90	29.90
The Bradford Exchange/United States		**Keepsakes of the Heart**			
93-22-001	Forever Friends	C. Layton	95-day	29.90	29.90
93-22-002	Afternoon Tea	C. Layton	95-day	29.90	29.90
The Bradford Exchange/United States		**Charles Wysocki's Peppercricket Grove**			
93-23-001	Peppercricket Farms	C. Wysocki	95-day	24.90	24.90
The Bradford Exchange/United States		**Trains of the Great West**			
93-24-001	Moonlit Journey	K. Randle	95-day	29.90	29.90
93-24-002	Mountain Hideaway	K. Randle	95-day	29.90	29.90
The Bradford Exchange/United States		**Kingdom of the Unicorn**			
93-25-001	The Magic Begins	M. Ferraro	95-day	29.90	29.90
93-25-002	In Crystal Waters	M. Ferraro	95-day	29.90	29.90
The Bradford Exchange/United States		**Christmas Memories**			
93-26-001	A Winter's Tale	J. Tanton	95-day	29.90	29.90
The Bradford Exchange/United States		**Little Bandits**			
93-27-001	Handle With Care	C. Jagodits	95-day	29.90	29.90
93-27-002	All Tied Up	C. Jagodits	95-day	29.90	29.90
93-27-003	Everything's Coming Up Daisies	C. Jagodits	95-day	32.90	32.90
The Bradford Exchange/United States		**Pathways of the Heart**			
93-28-001	October Radiance	J. Barnes	95-day	29.90	29.90
The Bradford Exchange/United States		**Panda Bear Hugs**			
93-29-001	Rock-a-Bye	W. Nelson	3/95	39.00	39.00
The Bradford Exchange/United States		**Aladdin**			
93-30-001	Magic Carpet Ride	Disney-Studios	95-day	29.90	29.90
The Bradford Exchange/United States		**Family Circles**			
93-31-001	Great Gray Owl Family	R. Rust	95-day	29.90	29.90
The Bradford Exchange/United States		**Peace on Earth**			
93-32-001	Winter Lullaby	D. Geisness	95-day	29.90	29.90
The Bradford Exchange/United States		**A Christmas Carol**			
93-33-001	God Bless Us Everyone	L. Garrison	95-day	29.90	29.90
The Bradford Exchange/United States		**Windows on a World of Suns**			
93-34-001	The Library: Cardinals	K. Daniel	95-day	34.90	34.90
The Bradford Exchange/United States		**America's Favorite Classic Cars**			
93-35-001	1957 Corvette	D. Everhart	3/95	54.00	54.00
93-35-002	1956 Thunderbird	D. Everhart	5/95	54.00	54.00
The Bradford Exchange/United States		**Untamed Spirits**			
93-36-001	Wild Hearts	P. Weirs	95-day	29.90	29.90
The Bradford Exchange/United States		**Sacred Circle**			
93-37-001	Before the Hunt	K. Randle	95-day	29.90	29.90
The Bradford Exchange/United States		**American Frontier**			
93-38-001	Timberline Jack's Trading Post	C. Wysocki	95-day	29.90	29.90
The Bradford Exchange/United States		**Sovreigns of the Wild**			
93-39-001	The Snow Queen	D. Grant	95-day	29.90	29.90
The Bradford Exchange/United States		**101 Dalmations**			
93-40-001	Watch Dogs	Disney-Studios	95-day	29.90	29.90
The Bradford Exchange/United States		**A Hidden Garden**			
93-41-001	Curious Kittens	T. Clausnitzer	95-day	29.90	29.90
Curator Collection: See Artaffects					
CUI/Carolina Collection/Dram Tree		**Native American Series**			
91-01-001	Hunt for the Buffalo Edition I	P. Kethley	Retrd.	39.50	39.50
CUI/Carolina Collection/Dram Tree		**Christmas Series**			
91-02-001	Checkin' it Twice Edition I	CUI	Retrd.	39.50	39.50
CUI/Carolina Collection/Dram Tree		**Environmental Series**			
91-03-001	Rainforest Magic Edition I	C. L. Bragg	Retrd.	39.50	39.50
92-03-002	First Breath	M. Hoffman	Retrd.	40.00	40.00
CUI/Carolina Collection/Dram Tree		**Girl In The Moon**			
91-04-001	Miller Girl in the Moon Edition I	CUI	9,950	39.50	39.50
CUI/Carolina Collection/Dram Tree		**DU Great American Sporting Dogs**			
92-05-001	Black Lab Edition I	J. Killen	20,000	40.00	40.00
93-05-002	Golden Retriever Edition II	J. Killen	28-day	40.00	40.00
93-05-003	Springer Spaniel Edition III	J. Killen	28-day	40.00	40.00
93-05-004	Yellow Labrador Edition IV	J. Killen	28-day	40.00	40.00
93-05-005	English Setter Edition V	J. Killen	28-day	40.00	40.00
93-05-006	Brittany Spaniel Edition VI	J. Killen	28-day	40.00	40.00
CUI/Carolina Collection/Dram Tree		**Classic Car Series**			
92-06-001	1957 Chevy	G. Geivette	Retrd.	40.00	40.00
CUI/Carolina Collection/Dram Tree		**Corvette Series**			
92-07-001	1953 Corvette	G. Geivette	28-day	40.00	40.00
CUI/Carolina Collection/Dram Tree		**Coors Winterfest**			
92-08-001	Skating Party	T. Stortz	Retrd.	29.50	29.50
CUI/Carolina Collection/Dram Tree		**Coors Factory Plate**			
92-09-001	First Edition	Unknown	45-day	29.50	29.50
93-09-002	Second Edition	Unknown	45-day	29.50	29.50
CUI/Carolina Collection/Dram Tree		**First Encounter**			
93-10-001	Stand Off	R. Cruwys	45-day	29.50	29.50
94-10-002	Class Clown	R. Cruwys	45-day	29.50	29.50
D'Arceau Limoges		**Lafayette**			
73-01-001	The Secret Contract	A. Restieau	Unkn.	14.82	20.00
73-01-002	North Island Landing	A. Restieau	Unkn.	19.82	22.00
74-01-003	City Tavern Meeting	A. Restieau	Unkn.	19.82	22.00
74-01-004	Battle of Brandywine	A. Restieau	Unkn.	19.82	22.00
75-01-005	Messages to Franklin	A. Restieau	Unkn.	19.82	23.00
75-01-006	Siege at Yorktown	A. Restieau	Unkn.	19.82	20.00
Delphi		**Elvis Presley: Looking At A Legend**			
88-01-001	Elvis at/Gates of Graceland	B. Emmett	150-day	24.75	124-129.
89-01-002	Jailhouse Rock	B. Emmett	150-day	24.75	130-149.
89-01-003	The Memphis Flash	B. Emmett	150-day	27.75	59-69.00

PLATES

Company Number	Series Name	Artist	Edition Limit	Issue Price	Quote
89-01-004	Homecoming	B. Emmett	150-day	27.75	60-69.00
90-01-005	Elvis and Gladys	B. Emmett	150-day	27.75	50-59.00
90-01-006	A Studio Session	B. Emmett	150-day	27.75	34-39.00
90-01-007	Elvis in Hollywood	B. Emmett	150-day	29.75	41-49.00
90-01-008	Elvis on His Harley	B. Emmett	150-day	29.75	60-69.00
90-01-009	Stage Door Autographs	B. Emmett	150-day	29.75	49-59.00
91-01-010	Christmas at Graceland	B. Emmett	150-day	32.75	59-69.00
91-01-011	Entering Sun Studio	B. Emmett	150-day	32.75	49-59.00
91-01-012	Going for the Black Belt	B. Emmett	150-day	32.75	55-59.00
91-01-013	His Hand in Mine	B. Emmett	150-day	32.75	52-59.00
91-01-014	Letters From Fans	B. Emmett	150-day	32.75	32.75-59.00
91-01-015	Closing the Deal	B. Emmett	150-day	34.75	34.75
92-01-016	Elvis Returns to the Stage	B. Emmett	150-day	34.75	34.75
Delphi	**Elvis Presley: In Performance**				
90-02-001	'68 Comeback Special	B. Emmett	150-day	24.75	55-84.00
91-02-002	King of Las Vegas	B. Emmett	150-day	24.75	50-82.00
91-02-003	Aloha From Hawaii	B. Emmett	150-day	27.75	69-79.00
91-02-004	Back in Tupelo, 1956	B. Emmett	150-day	27.75	46-55.00
91-02-005	If I Can Dream	B. Emmett	150-day	27.75	28-69.00
91-02-006	Benefit for the USS Arizona	B. Emmett	150-day	29.75	30-42.00
91-02-007	Madison Square Garden, 1972	B. Emmett	150-day	29.75	29.75
91-02-008	Tampa, 1955	B. Emmett	150-day	29.75	29.75
91-02-009	Concert in Baton Rouge, 1974	B. Emmett	150-day	29.75	29.75
92-02-010	On Stage in Wichita, 1974	B. Emmett	150-day	31.75	31.75
92-02-011	In the Spotlight: Hawaii, '72	B. Emmett	150-day	31.75	31.75
92-02-012	Tour Finale: Indianapolis 1977	B. Emmett	150-day	31.75	31.75
Delphi	**Portraits of the King**				
91-03-001	Love Me Tender	D. Zwierz	150-day	27.75	27.75
91-03-002	Are You Lonesome Tonight?	D. Zwierz	150-day	27.75	27.75
91-03-003	I'm Yours	D. Zwierz	150-day	30.75	30.75
91-03-004	Treat Me Nice	D. Zwierz	150-day	30.75	30.75
92-03-005	The Wonder of You	D. Zwierz	150-day	30.75	30.75
92-03-006	You're a Heartbreaker	D. Zwierz	150-day	32.75	32.75
92-03-007	Just Because	D. Zwierz	150-day	32.75	32.75
92-03-008	Follow That Dream	D. Zwierz	150-day	32.75	32.75
Delphi	**The Elvis Presley Hit Parade**				
92-04-001	Heartbreak Hotel	N. Giorgio	150-day	29.75	29.75
92-04-002	Blue Suede Shoes	N. Giorgio	150-day	29.75	29.75
92-04-003	Hound Dog	N. Giorgio	150-day	32.75	32.75
92-04-004	Blue Christmas	N. Giorgio	150-day	32.75	32.75
92-04-005	Return to Sender	N. Giorgio	150-day	32.75	32.75
93-04-006	Teddy Bear	N. Giorgio	150-day	34.75	34.75
93-04-007	Always on My Mind	N. Giorgio	150-day	34.75	34.75
93-04-008	Mystery Train	N. Giorgio	150-day	34.75	34.75
93-04-009	Blue Moon of Kentucky	N. Giorgio	150-day	34.75	34.75
Delphi	**Elvis on the Big Screen**				
92-05-001	Elvis in Loving You	B. Emmett	150-day	29.75	29.75
92-05-002	Elvis in G.I. Blues	B. Emmett	150-day	29.75	29.75
92-05-003	Viva Las Vegas	B. Emmett	150-day	32.75	32.75
93-05-004	Elvis in Blue Hawaii	B. Emmett	150-day	32.75	32.75
93-05-005	Elvis in Jailhouse Rock	B. Emmett	150-day	32.75	32.75
93-05-006	Elvis in Spinout	B. Emmett	150-day	34.75	34.75
93-05-007	Elvis in Speedway	B. Emmett	150-day	34.75	34.75
Delphi	**Dream Machines**				
88-06-001	'56 T-Bird	P. Palma	150-day	24.75	42-49.00
88-06-002	'57 'Vette	P. Palma	150-day	24.75	30.00
89-06-003	'58 Biarritz	P. Palma	150-day	27.75	28.00
89-06-004	'56 Continental	P. Palma	150-day	27.75	28.00
89-06-005	'57 Bel Air	P. Palma	150-day	27.75	49.00
89-06-006	'57 Chrysler 300C	P. Palma	150-day	27.75	35.00
Delphi	**Indiana Jones**				
89-07-001	Indiana Jones	V. Gadino	150-day	24.75	25.00
89-07-002	Indiana Jones and His Dad	V. Gadino	150-day	24.75	35.00
90-07-003	Indiana Jones/Dr. Schneider	V. Gadino	150-day	27.75	28.00
90-07-004	A Family Discussion	V. Gadino	150-day	27.75	32.00
90-07-005	Young Indiana Jones	V. Gadino	150-day	27.75	35.00
91-07-006	Indiana Jones/The Holy Grail	V. Gadino	150-day	27.75	45.00
Delphi	**The Marilyn Monroe Collection**				
89-08-001	Marilyn Monroe/7 Year Itch	C. Notarile	150-day	24.75	80-89.00
90-08-002	Diamonds/Girls Best Friend	C. Notarile	150-day	24.75	65-79.00
91-08-003	Marilyn Monroe/River of No Return	C. Notarile	150-day	27.75	58-72.00
92-08-004	How to Marry a Millionaire	C. Notarile	150-day	27.75	52-69.00
92-08-005	There's No Business/Show Business	C. Notarile	150-day	27.75	45-75.00
92-08-006	Marilyn Monroe in Niagra	C. Notarile	150-day	29.75	48-66.00
92-08-007	My Heart Belongs to Daddy	C. Notarile	150-day	29.75	42-49.00
92-08-008	Marilyn Monroe as Cherie in Bus Stop	C. Notarile	150-day	29.75	30-60.00
92-08-009	Marilyn Monroe in All About Eve	C. Notarile	150-day	29.75	30-39.00
92-08-010	Marilyn Monroe in Monkey Business	C. Notarile	150-day	31.75	31.75
92-08-011	Marilyn Monroe in Don't Bother to Knock	C. Notarile	150-day	31.75	31.75
92-08-012	Marilyn Monroe in We're Not Married	C. Notarile	150-day	31.75	31.75
Delphi	**The Magic of Marilyn**				
92-09-001	For Our Boys in Korea, 1954	C. Notarile	150-day	24.75	24.75
92-09-002	Opening Night	C. Notarile	150-day	24.75	24.75
93-09-003	Rising Star	C. Notarile	150-day	27.75	27.75
93-09-004	Stopping Traffic	C. Notarile	150-day	27.75	27.75
93-09-005	Strasberg's Class	C. Notarile	150-day	27.75	27.75
93-09-006	Photo Opportunity	C. Notarile	150-day	29.75	29.75
Delphi	**The Beatles Collection**				
91-10-001	The Beatles, Live In Concert	N. Giorgio	150-day	24.75	24.75
91-10-002	Hello America	N. Giorgio	150-day	24.75	24.75
91-10-003	A Hard Day's Night	N. Giorgio	150-day	27.75	27.75
92-10-004	Beatles '65	N. Giorgio	150-day	27.75	27.75
92-10-005	Help	N. Giorgio	150-day	27.75	27.75
92-10-006	The Beatles at Shea Stadium	N. Giorgio	150-day	29.75	29.75
92-10-007	Rubber Soul	N. Giorgio	150-day	29.75	29.75
92-10-008	Yesterday and Today	N. Giorgio	150-day	29.75	29.75
Delphi	**The Beatles '67-'70**				
92-11-001	Sgt. Pepper the 25th Anniversary	D. Sivavec	150-day	27.75	27.75
92-11-002	All You Need is Love	D. Sivavec	150-day	27.75	27.75
93-11-003	Magical Mystery Tour	D. Sivavec	150-day	30.75	30.75
93-11-004	Hey Jude	D. Sivavec	150-day	30.75	30.75
Delphi	**Legends of Baseball**				
92-12-001	Babe Ruth: The Called Shot	B. Benger	150-day	24.95	24.95

Company Number	Series Name	Artist	Edition Limit	Issue Price	Quote
92-12-002	Lou Gehrig: The Luckiest Man	J. Barson	150-day	24.75	24.75
93-12-003	Ty Cobb: The Georgia Peach	J. Barson	150-day	27.95	27.95
93-12-004	Cy Young: The Perfect Game	J. Barson	150-day	27.75	27.75
Delphi	**Commemorating The King**				
93-13-001	The Rock and Roll Legend	M. Stutzman	95-day	29.75	29.75
93-13-002	Las Vegas, Live	M. Stutzman	95-day	29.75	29.75
93-13-003	Blues and Black Leather	M. Stutzman	95-day	32.75	32.75
Delphi	**Take Me Out To The Ballgame**				
93-14-001	Wrigley Field: The Friendly Confines	D. Henderson	95-day	29.75	29.75
93-14-002	Yankee Stadium: House that Ruth Built	D. Henderson	95-day	29.75	29.75
93-14-003	Fenway Park: Home of the Green Monster	D. Henderson	95-day	32.75	32.75
Delphi	**Fabulous Cars of the '50's**				
93-15-001	'57 Red Corvette	G. Angelini	95-day	24.75	24.75
93-15-002	'57 White T-Bird	G. Angelini	95-day	24.75	24.75
Delphi	**In theFootsteps of the King**				
93-16-001	Graceland: Memphis, Tenn.	D. Sivavec	95-day	27.75	27.75
Department 56	**Dickens' Village**				
87-01-001	Dickens' Village Porcelain Plates, 5917-0 Set of 4	Department 56	Closed	140.00	220.00
Department 56	**A Christmas Carol**				
91-02-001	The Cratchit's Christmas Pudding, 5706-1	R. Innocenti	18,000	60.00	60-85.00
92-02-002	Marley's Ghost Appears To Scrooge, 5721-5	R. Innocenti	18,000	60.00	48-60.00
93-02-003	The Spirit of Christmas Present, 5722-3	R. Innocenti	18,000	60.00	60.00
94-02-004	Visions of Christmas Past 5723-1	R. Innocenti	18,000	60.00	60.00
Duncan Royale	**History of Santa Claus I**				
85-01-001	Medieval	S. Morton	Retrd.	40.00	50.00
85-01-002	Kris Kringle	S. Morton	Retrd.	40.00	65.00
85-01-003	Pioneer	S. Morton	10,000	40.00	40.00
86-01-004	Russian	S. Morton	Retrd.	40.00	40.00
86-01-005	Soda Pop	S. Morton	Retrd.	40.00	65.00
86-01-006	Civil War	S. Morton	10,000	40.00	40.00
86-01-007	Nast	S. Morton	Retrd.	40.00	75.00
87-01-008	St. Nicholas	S. Morton	Retrd.	40.00	75.00
87-01-009	Dedt Moroz	S. Morton	10,000	40.00	40.00
87-01-010	Black Peter	S. Morton	10,000	40.00	40.00
87-01-011	Victorian	S. Morton	Retrd.	40.00	40.00
87-01-012	Wassail	S. Morton	Retrd.	40.00	40.00
XX-01-013	Collection of 12 Plates	S. Morton	Retrd.	480.00	480.00
Enesco Corporation	**Precious Moments Inspired Thoughts**				
85-01-001	Love One Another-E-5215	S. Butcher	15,000	40.00	66.00
82-01-002	Make a Joyful Noise-E-7174	S. Butcher	15,000	40.00	40-55.00
83-01-003	I Believe In Miracles-E-9257	S. Butcher	15,000	40.00	45.00
84-01-004	Love is Kind-E-2847	S. Butcher	15,000	40.00	48.00
Enesco Corporation	**Precious Moments Mother's Love**				
81-02-001	Mother Sew Dear-E-5217	S. Butcher	15,000	40.00	72.00
82-02-002	The Purr-fect Grandma-E-7173	S. Butcher	15,000	40.00	48.00
83-02-003	The Hand that Rocks the Future-E-9256	S. Butcher	15,000	40.00	48.00
84-02-004	Loving Thy Neighbor-E-2848	S. Butcher	15,000	40.00	40-45.00
Enesco Corporation	**Precious Moments Christmas Collection**				
81-03-001	Come Let Us Adore Him-E-5646	S. Butcher	15,000	40.00	48-65.00
82-03-002	Let Heaven and Nature Sing-E-2347	S. Butcher	15,000	40.00	45-49.00
83-03-003	Wee Three Kings-E-0538	S. Butcher	15,000	40.00	50.00
84-03-004	Unto Us a Child Is Born-E-5395	S. Butcher	15,000	40.00	40-45.00
Enesco Corporation	**Precious Moments Joy of Christmas**				
82-04-001	I'll Play My Drum For Him-E-2357	S. Butcher	Yr.Iss.	40.00	90-93.00
83-04-002	Christmastime is for Sharing-E-0505	S. Butcher	Yr.Iss.	40.00	95-110.00
84-04-003	The Wonder of Christmas-E-5396	S. Butcher	Yr.Iss.	40.00	70-75.00
85-04-004	Tell Me the Story of Jesus-15237	S. Butcher	Yr.Iss.	40.00	90-105.00
Enesco Corporation	**Precious Moments The Four Seasons**				
85-05-001	The Voice of Spring-12106	S. Butcher	Yr.Iss.	40.00	87.00
85-05-002	Summer's Joy-12114	S. Butcher	Yr.Iss.	40.00	80.00
86-05-003	Autumn's Praise-12122	S. Butcher	Yr.Iss.	40.00	53.00
86-05-004	Winter's Song-12130	S. Butcher	Yr.Iss.	40.00	58.00
Enesco Corporation	**Precious Moments Open Editions**				
82-06-001	Our First Christmas Together-E-2378	S. Butcher	Suspd.	30.00	45-55.00
81-06-002	The Lord Bless You and Keep You-E-5216	S. Butcher	Suspd.	30.00	40-45.00
82-06-003	Rejoicing with You-E-7172	S. Butcher	Suspd.	30.00	40.00
83-06-004	Jesus Loves Me-E-9275	S. Butcher	Suspd.	30.00	45-48.00
83-06-005	Jesus Loves Me-E-9276	S. Butcher	Suspd.	30.00	45-48.00
94-06-006	Bring The Little Ones To Jesus-531359	S. Butcher	Yr.Iss.	50.00	50.00
Enesco Corporation	**Precious Moments Christmas Love**				
86-07-001	I'm Sending You a White Christmas-101834	S. Butcher	Yr.Iss.	45.00	48-76.50
87-07-002	My Peace I Give Unto Thee-102954	S. Butcher	Yr.Iss.	45.00	90.00
88-07-003	Merry Christmas Deer-520284	S. Butcher	Yr.Iss.	50.00	80.00
89-07-004	May Your Christmas Be A Happy Home-523003	S. Butcher	Yr.Iss.	50.00	50-75.00
Enesco Corporation	**Precious Moments Christmas Blessings**				
90-08-001	Wishing You A Yummy Christmas-523801	S. Butcher	Yr.Iss.	50.00	70.00
91-08-002	Blessings From Me To Thee-523860	S. Butcher	Yr.Iss.	50.00	60.00
92-08-003	But The Greatest of These Is Love-527742	S. Butcher	Yr.Iss.	50.00	50.00
93-08-004	Wishing You the Sweetest Christmas-530204	S. Butcher	Yr.Iss.	50.00	50.00
Enesco Corporation	**Precious Moments Mother's Day**				
93-09-001	Thinking of You is What I Really Like to Do 531766	S. Butcher	Yr.Iss.	50.00	50.00
Enesco Corporation	**Memories of Yesterday Dated Plate Series**				
93-10-001	Look Out-Something Good Is Coming Your Way!-530298	S. Butcher	Yr.Iss.	50.00	50.00
94-10-002	Pleasant Dreams and Sweet Repose-528102	M. Atwell	Yr.Iss.	50.00	50.00
Ernst Enterprises	**Women of the West**				
79-01-001	Expectations	D. Putnam	10,000	39.50	39.50
81-01-002	Silver Dollar Sal	D. Putnam	10,000	39.50	45.00
82-01-003	School Marm	D. Putnam	10,000	39.50	39.50
83-01-004	Dolly	D. Putnam	10,000	39.50	39.50
Ernst Enterprises	**A Beautiful World**				
81-02-001	Tahitian Dreamer	S. Morton	27,500	27.50	30.00

Number	Name	Artist	Edition Limit	Issue Price	Quote
Company		**Series**			
82-02-002	Flirtation	S. Morton	27,500	27.50	27.50
84-02-003	Elke of Oslo	S. Morton	27,500	27.50	27.50
Ernst Enterprises		**Seems Like Yesterday**			
81-03-001	Stop & Smell the Roses	R. Money	10-day	24.50	24.50
82-03-002	Home by Lunch	R. Money	10-day	24.50	24.50
82-03-003	Lisa's Creek	R. Money	10-day	24.50	24.50
83-03-004	It's Got My Name on It	R. Money	10-day	24.50	24.50
83-03-005	My Magic Hat	R. Money	10-day	24.50	24.50
84-03-006	Little Prince	R. Money	10-day	24.50	24.50
Ernst Enterprises		**Turn of The Century**			
81-04-001	Riverboat Honeymoon	R. Money	10-day	35.00	35.00
82-04-002	Children's Carousel	R. Money	10-day	35.00	37.50
84-04-003	Flower Market	R. Money	10-day	35.00	35.00
85-04-004	Balloon Race	R. Money	10-day	35.00	35.00
Ernst Enterprises		**Hollywood Greats**			
81-05-001	John Wayne	S. Morton	27,500	29.95	50-165.00
81-05-002	Gary Cooper	S. Morton	27,500	29.95	32.50
82-05-003	Clark Gable	S. Morton	27,500	29.95	65-85.00
84-05-004	Alan Ladd	S. Morton	27,500	29.95	95.00
Ernst Enterprises		**Commemoratives**			
81-06-001	John Lennon	S. Morton	30-day	39.50	155.00
82-06-002	Elvis Presley	S. Morton	30-day	39.50	148-150.
82-06-003	Marilyn Monroe	S. Morton	30-day	39.50	75.00
83-06-004	Judy Garland	S. Morton	30-day	39.50	75.00
84-06-005	John Wayne	S. Morton	2,500	39.50	75.00
Ernst Enterprises		**Classy Cars**			
82-07-001	The 26T	S. Kuhnly	20-day	24.50	32.00
82-07-002	The 31A	S. Kuhnly	20-day	24.50	30.00
83-07-003	The Pickup	S. Kuhnly	20-day	24.50	27.50
84-07-004	Panel Van	S. Kuhnly	20-day	24.50	35.00
Ernst Enterprises		**Star Trek**			
84-08-001	Mr. Spock	S. Morton	Retrd.	29.50	150-199.
85-08-002	Dr. McCoy	S. Morton	Retrd.	29.50	50-99.00
85-08-003	Sulu	S. Morton	Retrd.	29.50	50-80.00
85-08-004	Scotty	S. Morton	Retrd.	29.50	50-80.00
85-08-005	Uhura	S. Morton	Retrd.	29.50	50.00
85-08-006	Chekov	S. Morton	Retrd.	29.50	50.00
85-08-007	Captain Kirk	S. Morton	Retrd.	29.50	50-150.00
85-08-008	Beam Us Down Scotty	S. Morton	Retrd.	29.50	100.00
85-08-009	The Enterprise	S. Morton	Retrd.	39.50	50-150.00
Ernst Enterprises		**Star Trek: Commemorative Collection**			
87-09-001	The Trouble With Tribbles	S. Morton	Retrd.	29.50	150.00
87-09-002	Mirror, Mirror	S. Morton	Retrd.	29.50	169-175.
87-09-003	A Piece of the Action	S. Morton	Retrd.	29.50	75-149.00
87-09-004	The Devil in the Dark	S. Morton	Retrd.	29.50	75-135.00
87-09-005	Amok Time	S. Morton	Retrd.	29.50	75-135.00
87-09-006	The City on the Edge of Forever	S. Morton	Retrd.	29.50	165-250.
87-09-007	Journey to Babel	S. Morton	Retrd.	29.50	75-175.00
87-09-008	The Menagerie	S. Morton	Retrd.	29.50	75-179.00
Ernst Enterprises		**Elvira**			
86-09-001	Night Rose	S. Morton	90-day	29.50	29.50
Fairmont		**Spencer Special**			
78-01-001	Hug Me	I. Spencer	10,000	55.00	150.00
78-01-002	Sleep Little Baby	I. Spencer	10,000	65.00	125.00
Fairmont		**Famous Clowns**			
76-02-001	Freddie the Freeloader	R. Skelton	10,000	55.00	450.00
77-02-002	W. C. Fields	R. Skelton	10,000	55.00	45.00
78-02-003	Happy	R. Skelton	10,000	55.00	75.00
79-02-004	The Pledge	R. Skelton	10,000	55.00	70.00
Fenton Art Glass		**American Craftsman Carnival**			
70-01-001	Glassmaker	Unknown	600	10.00	140.00
70-01-002	Glassmaker	Unknown	200	10.00	220.00
70-01-003	Glassmaker	Unknown	Annual	10.00	68.00
71-01-004	Printer	Unknown	Annual	10.00	80.00
72-01-005	Blacksmith	Unknown	Annual	10.00	150.00
73-01-006	Shoemaker	Unknown	Annual	12.50	70.00
74-01-007	Cooper	Unknown	Annual	12.50	55.00
75-01-008	Silversmith Revere	Unknown	Annual	12.50	60.00
76-01-009	Gunsmith	Unknown	Annual	15.00	45.00
77-01-010	Potter	Unknown	Annual	15.00	35.00
78-01-011	Wheelwright	Unknown	Annual	15.00	25.00
79-01-012	Cabinetmaker	Unknown	Annual	15.00	23.00
80-01-013	Tanner	Unknown	Annual	16.50	20.00
81-01-014	Housewright	Unknown	Annual	17.50	18.00
Fitz and Floyd, Inc.		**Annual Christmas Plate**			
92-01-001	Nutcracker Sweets "The Magic of the Nutcracker"	R. Havins	Closed	65.00	65.00
93-01-002	A Dickens Christmas	T. Kerr	5,000	75.00	75.00
94-01-003	Night Before Christmas	T. Kerr	7,500	75.00	75.00
Fitz and Floyd, Inc.		**Wonderland**			
93-02-001	A Mad Tea Party	R. Havins	5,000	70.00	70.00
Fitz and Floyd, Inc.		**The Twelve Days of Christmas**			
93-03-001	Twelve Days of Christmas	R. Havins	5,000	75.00	75.00
Fitz and Floyd, Inc.		**The Myth of Santa Claus**			
93-04-001	Father Frost	R. Havins	5,000	70.00	70.00
Flambro Imports		**Emmett Kelly, Jr. Plates**			
83-01-001	Why Me? Plate I	C. Kelly	10,000	40.00	450.00
84-01-002	Balloons For Sale Plate II	C. Kelly	10,000	40.00	350.00
85-01-003	Big Business Plate III	C. Kelly	10,000	40.00	350.00
86-01-004	And God Bless America IV	C. Kelly	10,000	40.00	325.00
88-01-005	Tis the Season	D. Rust	10,000	40.00	40-75.00
89-01-006	Looking Back- 65th Birthday	D. Rust	6,500	50.00	250.00
91-01-007	Winter	D. Rust	10,000	60.00	60.00
92-01-008	Spring	D. Rust	10,000	60.00	60.00
92-01-009	Summer	D. Rust	10,000	60.00	60.00
92-01-010	Autumn	D. Rust	10,000	60.00	60.00
93-01-011	Santa's Stowaway	D. Rust	10,000	30.00	30.00
94-01-010	70th Birthday Commemorative	D. Rust	10,000	30.00	30.00
Flambro Imports		**Raggedy Ann & Andy**			
88-02-001	70 Years Young	C. Beylon	10,000	35.00	55-59.00
Fountainhead		**The Wings of Freedom**			
85-01-001	Courtship Flight	M. Fernandez	2,500	250.00	2400.00
86-01-002	Wings of Freedom	M. Fernandez	2,500	250.00	1100.00
Fountainhead		**As Free As The Wind**			
89-02-001	As Free As The Wind	M. Fernandez	Unkn.	295.00	300-600.
Gartlan USA, Inc.		**Pete Rose Platinum Edition**			
85-01-001	Pete Rose "The Best of Baseball"(3 1/4")	T. Sizemore	Open	12.95	20.00
85-01-002	Pete Rose "The Best of Baseball"(10 1/4")	T. Sizemore	4,192	100.00	325-450.
85-01-003	Pete Rose "The Best of Baseball"(10 1/4") (signed & dated)	T. Sizemore	50	100.00	675.00
Gartlan USA, Inc.		**The Round Tripper**			
86-02-001	Reggie Jackson (3 1/4" diameter)	J. Martin	Open	12.95	20.00
Gartlan USA, Inc.		**George Brett Gold Crown Collection**			
86-03-001	George Brett "Baseball's All Star" (3 1/4")	J. Martin	Open	12.95	20.00
86-03-002	George Brett "Baseball's All Star" (10 1/4") signed	J. Martin	2,000	100.00	200.00
Gartlan USA, Inc.		**Roger Staubach Sterling Collection**			
87-04-001	Roger Staubach (3 1/4" diameter)	C. Soileau	Open	12.95	20.00
87-04-002	Roger Staubach (10 1/4" diameter) signed	C. Soileau	1,979	100.00	125-195.
Gartlan USA, Inc.		**Magic Johnson Gold Rim Collection**			
87-05-001	Magic Johnson "The Magic Show" (10 1/4") signed	R. Winslow	1,987	100.00	400-500.
87-05-002	Magic Johnson "The Magic Show" (3 1/4")	R. Winslow	Closed	14.50	25-35.00
Gartlan USA, Inc.		**Mike Schmidt "500th" Home Run Edition**			
87-06-001	Mike Schmidt "Power at the Plate" (10 1/4") signed	C. Paluso	1,987	100.00	395.00
87-06-002	Mike Schmidt "Power at the Plate" (3 1/4")	C. Paluso	Open	14.50	19.00
87-06-003	Mike Schmidt Artist Proof	C. Paluso	56	150.00	150.00
87-06-004	Mike Schmidt (signed & dated)	C. Paluso	50	100.00	595.00
Gartlan USA, Inc.		**Pete Rose Diamond Collection**			
88-07-001	Pete Rose "The Reigning Legend" (10 1/4") signed	Forbes	950	195.00	275-295.
88-07-002	Pete Rose "The Reigning Legend" (10 1/4") signed Artist Proof	Forbes	50	300.00	395.00
88-07-003	Pete Rose "The Reigning Legend"(3 1/4")	Forbes	Open	14.50	19.00
Gartlan USA, Inc		**Kareem Abdul-Jabbar Sky-Hook Collection**			
89-08-001	Kareem Abdul-Jabbar "Path of Glory" (10 1/4"), signed	M. Taylor	1,989	100.00	195-225.
89-08-002	Collector plate (3 1/4")	M. Taylor	Closed	16.00	30.00
Gartlan USA, Inc.		**Johnny Bench**			
89-09-001	Collector Plate (10 1/4") signed	M. Taylor	1,989	100.00	200.00
89-09-002	Collector Plate (3 1/4")	M. Taylor	Open	16.00	19.00
Gartlan USA, Inc.		**Coaching Classics-John Wooden**			
89-10-001	Collector Plate (10 1/4") signed	M. Taylor	1,975	100.00	100.00
89-10-002	Collector Plate (8 1/2")	M. Taylor	10,000	45.00	45.00
89-10-003	Collector Plate (3 1/4")	M. Taylor	Open	16.00	19.00
Gartlan USA, Inc.		**Wayne Gretzky**			
89-11-001	Collector Plate (10 1/4") signed by Gretzky and Howe	M. Taylor	1,851	225.00	275-300.
89-11-002	Collector Plate (10 1/4") Artist Proof signed by Gretzky and Howe	M. Taylor	300	300.00	425.00
89-11-003	Collector Plate (8 1/2")	M. Taylor	10,000	45.00	45-50.00
89-11-004	Collector Plate (3 1/4")	M. Taylor	Open	16.00	20.00
Gartlan USA, Inc.		**Yogi Berra**			
89-12-001	Collector Plate (10 1/4") signed	M. Taylor	2,150	125.00	125-150.
89-12-002	Collector Plate (10 1/4") signed Artist Proof	M. Taylor	250	175.00	175.00
89-12-003	Collector Plate (3 1/4")	M. Taylor	Open	16.00	20.00
89-12-004	Collector Plate (8 1/2")	M. Taylor	10,000	45.00	45.00
Gartlan USA, Inc.		**Whitey Ford**			
90-13-001	Signed Plate (10 1/4")	M. Taylor	2,360	125.00	125-150.
90-13-002	Signed Plate (10 1/4") Artist Proof	M. Taylor	250	175.00	175.00
90-13-003	Plate (8 1/2")	M. Taylor	10,000	45.00	45.00
90-13-004	Plate (3 1/4")	M. Taylor	Open	16.00	20.00
Gartlan USA, Inc.		**Darryl Strawberry**			
90-14-001	Signed Plate (10 1/4")	M. Taylor	2,500	125.00	125.00
90-14-002	Plate (8 1/2")	M. Taylor	10,000	45.00	45.00
90-14-003	Plate (3 1/4")	M. Taylor	Open	16.00	20.00
Gartlan USA, Inc.		**Luis Aparicio**			
90-15-001	Signed Plate (10 1/4")	M. Taylor	1,984	125.00	125.00
90-15-002	Signed Plate (10 1/4") Artist Proof	M. Taylor	250	150.00	150.00
90-15-003	Plate (8 1/2")	M. Taylor	10,000	45.00	45.00
90-15-004	Plate (3 1/4")	M. Taylor	Open	16.00	20.00
Gartlan USA, Inc.		**Rod Carew**			
91-16-001	Hitting For The Hall(10 1/4") signed	M. Taylor	950	150.00	150.00
91-16-002	Hitting For The Hall(8 1/2")	M. Taylor	10,000	45.00	45.00
91-16-003	Hitting For The Hall(3 1/4")	M. Taylor	Open	16.00	20.00
Gartlan USA, Inc.		**Brett & Bobby Hull**			
91-17-001	Hockey's Golden Boys (10 1/4") signed	M. Taylor	950	250.00	250.00
92-17-002	Plate Artist Proof	M. Taylor	300	350.00	350.00
91-17-003	Hockey's Golden Boys (8 1/2")	M. Taylor	10,000	45.00	45.00
91-17-004	Hockey's Golden Boys (3 1/4")	M. Taylor	Open	16.00	20.00
Gartlan USA, Inc.		**Joe Montana**			
91-18-001	Signed Plate (10 1/4")	M. Taylor	2,250	125.00	125.00
91-18-002	Signed Plate (10 1/4") Artist Proof	M. Taylor	250	195.00	195.00
91-18-003	Plate (8 1/2")	M. Taylor	10,000	45.00	45.00
91-18-004	Plate (3 1/4")	M. Taylor	Open	16.00	20.00
Gartlan USA, Inc.		**Al Barlick**			
91-19-001	Plate (3 1/4")	M. Taylor	Open	16.00	19.00
Gartlan USA, Inc.		**Carlton Fisk**			
92-20-001	Signed Plate (10 1/4")	M. Taylor	950	150.00	150.00

Company		Series			
Number	**Name**	**Artist**	**Edition Limit**	**Issue Price**	**Quote**
92-20-002	Signed Plate (10 1/4") Artist Proof	M. Taylor	300	175.00	225.00
92-20-003	Plate (8 1/2")	M. Taylor	10,000	45.00	45.00
92-20-004	Plate (3 1/4")	M. Taylor	Open	19.00	19.00
Gartlan USA, Inc.		**Ken Griffey Jr.**			
92-21-001	Signed Plate (10 1/4")	M. Taylor	1,989	125.00	125.00
92-21-002	Signed Plate (10 1/2") Artist Proof	M. Taylor	300	195.00	195.00
92-21-003	Plate (8 1/2")	M. Taylor	10,000	45.00	45.00
92-21-004	Plate (3 1/4")	M. Taylor	Open	19.00	19.00
Gartlan USA, Inc.		**Phil Esposito**			
92-22-001	Signed Plate (10 1/4")	M. Taylor	1,984	150.00	150.00
92-22-002	Signed Plate (10 1/2") Artist Proof	M. Taylor	300	195.00	195.00
92-22-003	Plate (8 1/2")	M. Taylor	10,000	49.00	49.00
92-22-004	Plate (3 1/4")	M. Taylor	Open	19.00	19.00
Gartlan USA, Inc.		**Tom Seaver**			
92-23-001	Signed Plate (10 1/4")	M. Taylor	1,992	150.00	150.00
92-23-002	Signed Plate (10 1/4") Artist Proof	M. Taylor	250	195.00	195.00
92-23-003	Signed Plate (8 1/2")	M. Taylor	10,000	45.00	45.00
92-23-004	Signed Plate (3 1/4")	M. Taylor	Open	19.00	19.00
Gartlan USA, Inc.		**Gordie Howe**			
92-24-001	Signed Plate (10 1/4")	M. Taylor	2,358	150.00	150.00
92-24-002	Signed Plate (10 1/4") Artist Proof	M. Taylor	250	195.00	195.00
92-24-003	Signed Plate (8 1/2")	M. Taylor	10,000	45.00	45.00
92-24-004	Signed Plate (3 1/4")	M. Taylor	Open	19.00	19.00
Gartlan USA, Inc.		**Carl Yastrzemski-The Impossible Dream**			
93-25-001	Signed Plate (10 1/4")	M. Taylor	950	175.00	150.00
93-25-002	Plate (8 1/2")	M. Taylor	10,000	49.00	49.00
93-25-003	Plate (3 1/4")	M. Taylor	Open	19.00	19.00
Gartlan USA, Inc.		**Bob Cousy**			
93-26-001	Signed Plate (10 1/4")	M. Taylor	950	150.00	150.00
93-26-002	Plate (8 1/2")	M. Taylor	5,000	49.00	49.00
93-26-003	Plate (3 1/4")	M. Taylor	Open	19.00	19.00
Gartlan USA, Inc.		**Sam Sneed**			
93-27-001	Signed Plate (10 1/4")	M. Taylor	950	175.00	175.00
93-27-002	Plate (8 1/2")	M. Taylor	5,000	49.00	49.00
93-27-003	Plate (3 1/4")	M. Taylor	Open	19.00	19.00
Gartlan USA, Inc.		**Kristi Yamaguchi**			
93-28-001	Signed Plate (10 1/4")	M. Taylor	950	150.00	150.00
93-28-002	Plate (8 1/2")	M. Taylor	5,000	49.00	49.00
93-28-003	Plate (3 1/4")	M. Taylor	Open	19.00	19.00
Gartlan USA, Inc.		**Shaquille O'Neal**			
94-29-001	Signed Plate (10 1/4")	M. Taylor	1,993	195.00	195.00
94-29-002	Plate (8 1/2")	M. Taylor	10,000	49.00	49.00
Gartlan USA, Inc.		**Carl Ripken Jr.**			
94-30-001	Signed Plate (10 1/4")	M. Taylor	1,982	150.00	150.00
94-30-002	Plate (8 1/2")	M. Taylor	10,000	49.00	49.00
Gartlan USA, Inc.		**Troy Aikman**			
94-31-001	Signed Plate (10 1/4")	M. Taylor	1,993	150.00	150.00
94-31-002	Plate (8 1/2")	M. Taylor	10,000	49.00	49.00
Gartlan USA, Inc.		**Brian Boitano**			
94-32-001	Signed Plate (10 1/4")	M. Taylor	950	150.00	150.00
94-32-002	Plate (8 1/2")	M. Taylor	5,000	49.00	49.00
Gartlan USA, Inc.		**Steve Young**			
94-33-001	Signed Plate (10 1/4")	M. Taylor	950	150.00	150.00
94-33-002	Plate (8 1/2")	M. Taylor	5,000	49.00	49.00
Gartlan USA, Inc.		**Hank Aaron**			
94-34-002	Plate (8 1/2")	M. Taylor	715	69.00	69.00
W. S. George		**Gone With the Wind: Golden Anniversary**			
88-01-001	Scarlett and Her Suitors	H. Rogers	150-day	24.50	65-80.00
88-01-002	The Burning of Atlanta	H. Rogers	150-day	24.50	64-73.00
88-01-003	Scarlett and Ashley After the War	H. Rogers	150-day	27.50	70-95.00
88-01-004	The Proposal	H. Rogers	150-day	27.50	79-105.00
89-01-005	Home to Tara	H. Rogers	150-day	27.50	48.00
89-01-006	Strolling in Atlanta	H. Rogers	150-day	27.50	55-62.00
89-01-007	A Question of Honor	H. Rogers	150-day	29.50	40-53.00
89-01-008	Scarlett's Resolve	H. Rogers	150-day	29.50	56.00
89-01-009	Frankly My Dear	H. Rogers	150-day	29.50	35-45.00
89-01-010	Melane and Ashley	H. Rogers	150-day	32.50	50.00
90-01-011	A Toast to Bonnie Blue	H. Rogers	150-day	32.50	50.00
90-01-012	Scarlett and Rhett's Honeymoon	H. Rogers	150-day	32.50	50.00
W. S. George		**Scenes of Christmas Past**			
87-02-001	Holiday Skaters	L. Garrison	150-day	27.50	50.00
88-02-002	Christmas Eve	L. Garrison	150-day	27.50	35-50.00
89-02-003	The Homecoming	L. Garrison	150-day	30.50	31.00
90-02-004	The Toy Store	L. Garrison	150-day	30.50	31.00
91-02-005	The Carollers	L. Garrison	150-day	30.50	30.00
92-02-006	Family Traditions	L. Garrison	150-day	32.50	55.00
93-02-007	Holiday Past	L. Garrison	150-day	32.50	32.50
W. S. George		**On Gossamer Wings**			
88-03-001	Monarch Butterflies	L. Liu	150-day	24.50	25-50.00
88-03-002	Western Tiger Swallowtails	L. Liu	150-day	24.50	28-47.00
88-03-003	Red-Spotted Purple	L. Liu	150-day	27.50	30-49.00
88-03-004	Malachites	L. Liu	150-day	27.50	29-40.00
88-03-005	White Peacocks	L. Liu	150-day	27.50	40-45.00
89-03-006	Eastern Tailed Blues	L. Liu	150-day	27.50	28-49.00
89-03-007	Zebra Swallowtails	L. Liu	150-day	29.50	30-37.50
89-03-008	Red Admirals	L. Liu	150-day	29.50	30-35.00
W. S. George		**Flowers of Your Garden**			
88-04-001	Roses	V. Morley	150-day	24.50	75.00
88-04-002	Lilacs	V. Morley	150-day	24.50	48.00
88-04-003	Daisies	V. Morley	150-day	27.50	40.00
88-04-004	Peonies	V. Morley	150-day	27.50	28.00
88-04-005	Chrysanthemums	V. Morley	150-day	27.50	28.00
89-04-006	Daffodils	V. Morley	150-day	27.50	28.00
89-04-007	Tulips	V. Morley	150-day	29.50	30.00
89-04-008	Irises	V. Morley	150-day	29.50	34.00

Company		Series			
Number	**Name**	**Artist**	**Edition Limit**	**Issue Price**	**Quote**
W. S. George		**Beloved Hymns of Childhood**			
88-05-001	The Lord's My Shepherd	C. Barker	150-day	29.50	47.00
88-05-002	Away In a Manger	C. Barker	150-day	29.50	30.00
89-05-003	Now Thank We All Our God	C. Barker	150-day	32.50	33.00
89-05-004	Love Divine	C. Barker	150-day	32.50	33.00
89-05-005	I Love to Hear the Story	C. Barker	150-day	32.50	33.00
89-05-006	All Glory, Laud and Honour	C. Barker	150-day	32.50	33.00
90-05-007	All People on Earth Do Dwell	C. Barker	150-day	34.50	35.00
90-05-008	Loving Shepherd of Thy Sheep	C. Barker	150-day	34.50	35.00
W. S. George		**Classic Waterfowl: The Ducks Unlimited**			
88-06-001	Mallards at Sunrise	L. Kaatz	150-day	36.50	40.00
88-06-002	Geese in the Autumn Fields	L. Kaatz	150-day	36.50	37.00
89-06-003	Green Wings/Morning Marsh	L. Kaatz	150-day	39.50	40.00
89-06-004	Canvasbacks, Breaking Away	L. Kaatz	150-day	39.50	40.00
89-06-005	Pintails in Indian Summer	L. Kaatz	150-day	39.50	40.00
90-06-006	Wood Ducks Taking Flight	L. Kaatz	150-day	39.50	40.00
90-06-007	Snow Geese Against November Skies	L. Kaatz	150-day	41.50	42.00
90-06-008	Bluebills Coming In	L. Kaatz	150-day	41.50	42.00
W. S. George		**The Elegant Birds**			
88-07-001	The Swan	J. Faulkner	150-day	32.50	33.00
88-07-002	Great Blue Heron	J. Faulkner	150-day	32.50	33.00
89-07-003	Snowy Egret	J. Faulkner	150-day	32.50	36.00
89-07-004	The Anhinga	J. Faulkner	150-day	35.50	36.00
89-07-005	The Flamingo	J. Faulkner	150-day	35.50	38.00
90-07-006	Sandhill and Whooping Crane	J. Faulkner	150-day	35.50	36.00
W. S. George		**Last of Their Kind: The Endangered Species**			
88-08-001	The Panda	W. Nelson	150-day	27.50	45.00
89-08-002	The Snow Leopard	W. Nelson	150-day	27.50	45-50.00
89-08-003	The Red Wolf	W. Nelson	150-day	30.50	31.00
89-08-004	The Asian Elephant	W. Nelson	150-day	30.50	31.00
90-08-005	The Slender-Horned Gazelle	W. Nelson	150-day	30.50	31.00
90-08-006	The Bridled Wallaby	W. Nelson	150-day	30.50	25-30.50
90-08-007	The Black-Footed Ferret	W. Nelson	150-day	33.50	34.00
90-08-008	The Siberian Tiger	W. Nelson	150-day	33.50	35.00
91-08-009	The Vicuna	W. Nelson	150-day	33.50	34.00
91-08-010	Przewalski's Horse	W. Nelson	150-day	33.50	34.00
W. S. George		**America the Beautiful**			
88-09-001	Yosemite Falls	H. Johnson	150-day	34.50	35.00
89-09-002	The Grand Canyon	H. Johnson	150-day	34.50	35.00
89-09-003	Yellowstone River	H. Johnson	150-day	37.50	38.00
89-09-004	The Great Smokey Mountains	H. Johnson	150-day	37.50	38.00
90-09-005	The Everglades	H. Johnson	150-day	37.50	38.00
90-09-006	Acadia	H. Johnson	150-day	37.50	40.00
90-09-007	The Grand Tetons	H. Johnson	150-day	39.50	54.00
90-09-008	Crater Lake	H. Johnson	150-day	39.50	40.00
W. S. George		**Bonds of Love**			
89-10-001	Precious Embrace	B. Burke	150-day	29.50	35.00
90-10-002	Cherished Moment	B. Burke	150-day	29.50	30.00
91-10-003	Tender Caress	B. Burke	150-day	32.50	50.00
92-10-004	Loving Touch	B. Burke	150-day	32.50	40.00
92-10-005	Treasured Kisses	B. Burke	150-day	32.50	44.00
W. S. George		**The Golden Age of the Clipper Ships**			
89-11-001	The Twilight Under Full Sail	C. Vickery	150-day	29.50	30.00
89-11-002	The Blue Jacket at Sunset	C. Vickery	150-day	29.50	30.00
89-11-003	Young America, Homeward	C. Vickery	150-day	32.50	33.00
90-11-004	Flying Cloud	C. Vickery	150-day	32.50	32.00
90-11-005	Davy Crocket at Daybreak	C. Vickery	150-day	32.50	35-48.00
90-11-006	Golden Eagle Conquers Wind	C. Vickery	150-day	32.50	35.00
90-11-007	The Lightning in Lifting Fog	C. Vickery	150-day	34.50	35.00
90-11-008	Sea Witch, Mistress/Oceans	C. Vickery	150-day	34.50	45.00
W. S. George		**Romantic Gardens**			
89-12-001	The Woodland Garden	C. Smith	150-day	29.50	30.00
89-12-002	The Plantation Garden	C. Smith	150-day	29.50	30.00
90-12-003	The Cottage Garden	C. Smith	150-day	32.50	25-32.50
90-12-004	The Colonial Garden	C. Smith	150-day	32.50	29-32.50
W. S. George		**Country Nostalgia**			
89-13-001	The Spring Buggy	M. Harvey	150-day	29.50	30.00
89-13-002	The Apple Cider Press	M. Harvey	150-day	29.50	40.00
89-13-003	The Vintage Seed Planter	M. Harvey	150-day	29.50	40.00
89-13-004	The Old Hand Pump	M. Harvey	150-day	32.50	55.00
90-13-005	The Wooden Butter Churn	M. Harvey	150-day	32.50	47.00
90-13-006	The Dairy Cans	M. Harvey	150-day	32.50	35.00
90-13-007	The Forgotten Plow	M. Harvey	150-day	34.50	37.00
90-13-008	The Antique Spinning Wheel	M. Harvey	150-day	34.50	35.00
W. S. George		**Hollywood's Glamour Girls**			
89-14-001	Jean Harlow-Dinner at Eight	E. Dzenis	150-day	24.50	43.00
90-14-002	Lana Turner-Postman Ring Twice	E. Dzenis	150-day	29.50	30-49.00
90-14-003	Carol Lombard-The Gay Bride	E. Dzenis	150-day	29.50	30-40.00
90-14-004	Greta Garbo-In Grand Hotel	E. Dzenis	150-day	29.50	30-60.00
W. S. George		**Purebred Horses of the Americas**			
89-15-001	The Appalosa	D. Schwartz	150-day	34.50	35.00
89-15-002	The Tenessee Walker	D. Schwartz	150-day	34.50	35.00
90-15-003	The Quarterhorse	D. Schwartz	150-day	37.50	38.00
90-15-004	The Saddlebred	D. Schwartz	150-day	37.50	50.00
90-15-005	The Mustang	D. Schwartz	150-day	37.50	39.00
90-15-006	The Morgan	D. Schwartz	150-day	37.50	70.00
W. S. George		**Nature's Poetry**			
89-16-001	Morning Serenade	L. Liu	150-day	24.50	45.00
89-16-002	Song of Promise	L. Liu	150-day	24.50	48.00
90-16-003	Tender Lullaby	L. Liu	150-day	27.50	28.00
90-16-004	Nature's Harmony	L. Liu	150-day	27.50	55.00
90-16-005	Gentle Refrain	L. Liu	150-day	27.50	35.00
90-16-006	Morning Chorus	L. Liu	150-day	27.50	35.00
90-16-007	Melody at Daybreak	L. Liu	150-day	29.50	30.00
91-16-008	Delicate Accord	L. Liu	150-day	29.50	35.00
91-16-009	Lyrical Beginnings	L. Liu	150-day	29.50	35.00
91-16-010	Song of Spring	L. Liu	150-day	32.50	40.00
91-16-011	Mother's Melody	L. Liu	150-day	32.50	50.00
91-16-012	Cherub Chorale	L. Liu	150-day	32.50	78.00
W. S. George		**Art Deco**			
89-17-001	A Flapper With Greyhounds	M. McDonald	150-day	39.50	50.00
90-17-002	Tango Dancers	M. McDonald	150-day	39.50	80.00

Number	Name	Artist	Edition Limit	Issue Price	Quote
Company	**Series**				
90-17-003	Arriving in Style	M. McDonald	150-day	39.50	90.00
90-17-004	On the Town	M. McDonald	150-day	39.50	79.00
W. S. George	**Our Woodland Friends**				
89-18-001	Fascination	C. Brenders	150-day	29.50	35.00
90-18-002	Beneath the Pines	C. Brenders	150-day	29.50	32.00
90-18-003	High Adventure	C. Brenders	150-day	32.50	33.00
90-18-004	Shy Explorers	C. Brenders	150-day	32.50	44.00
91-18-005	Golden Season:Gray Squirrel	C. Brenders	150-day	32.50	35.00
91-18-006	Full House Fox Family	C. Brenders	150-day	32.50	60.00
91-18-007	A Jump Into Life: Spring Fawn	C. Brenders	150-day	34.50	50.00
91-18-008	Forest Sentinel:Bobcat	C. Brenders	150-day	34.50	55.00
W. S. George	**The Federal Duck Stamp Plate Collection**				
90-19-001	The Lesser Scaup	N. Anderson	150-day	27.50	40.00
90-19-002	Mallard	N. Anderson	150-day	27.50	55.00
90-19-003	The Ruddy Ducks	N. Anderson	150-day	30.50	31.00
90-19-004	Canvasbacks	N. Anderson	150-day	30.50	42.00
91-19-005	Pintails	N. Anderson	150-day	30.50	31.00
91-19-006	Wigeons	N. Anderson	150-day	30.50	35.00
91-19-007	Cinnamon Teal	N. Anderson	150-day	32.50	34.00
91-19-008	Fulvous Wistling Duck	N. Anderson	150-day	32.50	45.00
91-19-009	The Redheads	N. Anderson	150-day	32.50	55.00
91-19-010	Snow Goose	N. Anderson	150-day	32.50	32.50
W. S. George	**Dr. Zhivago**				
90-20-001	Zhivago and Lara	G. Bush	150-day	39.50	40.00
91-20-002	Love Poems For Lara	G. Bush	150-day	39.50	40.00
91-20-003	Zhivago Says Farewell	G. Bush	150-day	39.50	40.00
91-20-004	Lara's Love	G. Bush	150-day	39.50	65.00
W. S. George	**Blessed Are The Children**				
90-21-001	Let the/Children Come To Me	W. Rane	150-day	29.50	52.00
90-21-002	I Am the Good Shepherd	W. Rane	150-day	29.50	40.00
91-21-003	Whoever Welcomes/Child	W. Rane	150-day	32.50	50.00
91-21-004	Hosanna in the Highest	W. Rane	150-day	32.50	40.00
91-21-005	Jesus Had Compassion on Them	W. Rane	150-day	32.50	35.00
91-21-006	Blessed are the Peacemakers	W. Rane	150-day	34.50	57.00
91-21-007	I am the Vine, You are the Branches	W. Rane	150-day	34.50	60.00
91-21-008	Seek and You Will Find	W. Rane	150-day	34.50	34.50
W. S. George	**The Vanishing Gentle Giants**				
91-22-001	Jumping For Joy	A. Casay	150-day	32.50	44.00
91-22-002	Song of the Humpback	A. Casay	150-day	32.50	45.00
91-22-003	Monarch of the Deep	A. Casay	150-day	35.50	45.00
91-22-004	Travelers of the Sea	A. Casay	150-day	35.50	60.00
91-22-005	White Whale of the North	A. Casay	150-day	35.50	58.00
91-22-006	Unicorn of the Sea	A. Casay	150-day	35.50	55.00
W. S. George	**Spirit of Christmas**				
90-23-001	Silent Night	J. Sias	150-day	29.50	34.00
91-23-002	Jingle Bells	J. Sias	150-day	29.50	30.00
91-23-003	Deck The Halls	J. Sias	150-day	32.50	45.00
91-23-004	I'll Be Home For Christmas	J. Sias	150-day	32.50	47.00
91-23-005	Winter Wonderland	J. Sias	150-day	32.50	40.00
91-23-006	O Christmas Tree	J. Sias	150-day	32.50	33.00
W. S. George	**Flowers From Grandma's Garden**				
90-24-001	Country Cuttings	G. Kurz	150-day	24.50	58.00
90-24-002	The Morning Bouquet	G. Kurz	150-day	24.50	49.00
91-24-003	Homespun Beauty	G. Kurz	150-day	27.50	34.00
91-24-004	Harvest in the Meadow	G. Kurz	150-day	27.50	30.00
91-24-005	Gardener's Delight	G. Kurz	150-day	27.50	65.00
91-24-006	Nature's Bounty	G. Kurz	150-day	27.50	49.00
91-24-007	A Country Welcome	G. Kurz	150-day	29.50	50.00
91-24-008	The Springtime Arrangement	G. Kurz	150-day	29.50	48.00
W. S. George	**The Secret World Of The Panda**				
90-25-001	A Mother's Care	J. Bridgett	150-day	27.50	32.00
91-25-002	A Frolic in the Snow	J. Bridgett	150-day	27.50	28.00
91-25-003	Lazy Afternoon	J. Bridgett	150-day	30.50	31.00
91-25-004	A Day of Exploring	J. Bridgett	150-day	30.50	37.00
91-25-005	A Gentle Hug	J. Bridgett	150-day	32.50	38.00
91-25-006	A Bamboo Feast	J. Bridgett	150-day	32.50	75.00
W. S. George	**Wonders Of The Sea**				
91-26-001	Stand By Me	R.Harm	150-day	34.50	35.00
91-26-002	Heart to Heart	R.Harm	150-day	34.50	35.00
91-26-003	Warm Embrace	R.Harm	150-day	34.50	44.00
91-26-004	A Family Affair	R.Harm	150-day	34.50	34.50
W. S. George	**Critic's Choice: Gone With The Wind**				
91-27-001	Marry Me, Scarlett	P. Jennis	150-day	27.50	45-49.00
91-27-002	Waiting for Rhett	P. Jennis	150-day	27.50	57.00
91-27-003	A Declaration of Love	P. Jennis	150-day	30.50	31-75.00
91-27-004	The Paris Hat	P. Jennis	150-day	30.50	80.00
91-27-005	Scarlett Asks a Favor	P. Jennis	150-day	30.50	30.50
92-27-006	Scarlett Gets Her Way	P. Jennis	150-day	32.50	32.50
92-27-007	The Smitten Suitor	P. Jennis	150-day	32.50	32.50
92-27-008	Scarlett's Shopping Spree	P. Jennis	150-day	32.50	32.50
92-27-009	The Buggy Ride	P. Jennis	150-day	32.50	32.50
92-27-010	Scarlett Gets Down to Business	P. Jennis	150-day	34.50	34.50
W. S. George	**Gone With The Wind: The Passions of Scarlett O'Hara**				
92-28-001	Fiery Embrace	P. Jennis	150-day	29.50	29.50-69.00
92-28-002	Pride and Passion	P. Jennis	150-day	29.50	29.50-80.00
92-28-003	Dreams of Ashley	P. Jennis	150-day	32.50	32.50
92-28-004	The Fond Farewell	P. Jennis	150-day	32.50	32.50
W. S. George	**Victorian Cat**				
90-29-001	Mischief With The Hatbox	H. Bonner	150-day	24.50	54.00
91-29-002	String Quartet	H. Bonner	150-day	24.50	35.00
91-29-003	Daydreams	H. Bonner	150-day	27.50	30.00
91-29-004	Frisky Felines	H. Bonner	150-day	27.50	53.00
91-29-005	Kittens at Play	H. Bonner	150-day	27.50	54.00
91-29-006	Playing in the Parlor	H. Bonner	150-day	29.50	68.00
91-29-007	Perfectly Poised	H. Bonner	150-day	29.50	75.00
92-29-008	Midday Repose	H. Bonner	150-day	29.50	30.00
W. S. George	**Victorian Cat Capers**				
92-30-001	Who's the Fairest of Them All?	F. Paton	150-day	24.50	24.50
92-30-002	Puss in Boots	Unknown	150-day	24.50	24.50
92-30-003	My Bowl is Empty	W. Hepple	150-day	27.50	27.50
92-30-004	A Curious Kitty	W. Hepple	150-day	27.50	27.50
92-30-005	Vanity Fair	W. Hepple	150-day	27.50	27.50
92-30-006	Forbidden Fruit	W. Hepple	150-day	29.50	29.50
93-30-007	The Purr-fect Pen Pal	W. Hepple	150-day	29.50	29.50
93-30-008	The Kitten Express	W. Hepple	150-day	29.50	29.50
W. S. George	**Glorious Songbirds**				
91-31-001	Cardinals on a Snowy Branch	R. Cobane	150-day	29.50	35.00
91-31-002	Indigo Buntings and/Blossoms	R. Cobane	150-day	29.50	32.00
91-31-003	Chickadees Among The Lilacs	R. Cobane	150-day	32.50	32.00
91-31-004	Goldfinches in/Thistle	R. Cobane	150-day	32.50	33.00
91-31-005	Cedar Waxwing/Winter Berries	R. Cobane	150-day	32.50	34.00
91-31-006	Bluebirds in a Blueberry Bush	R. Cobane	150-day	34.50	35.00
91-31-007	Baltimore Orioles/Autumn Leaves	R. Cobane	150-day	34.50	35.00
91-31-008	Robins with Dogwood in Bloom	R. Cobane	150-day	34.50	35.00
W. S. George	**Nature's Lovables**				
90-32-001	The Koala	C. Frace	150-day	27.50	50.00
91-32-002	New Arrival	C. Frace	150-day	27.50	40.00
91-32-003	Chinese Treasure	C. Frace	150-day	27.50	28.00
91-32-004	Baby Harp Seal	C. Frace	150-day	30.50	70.00
91-32-005	Bobcat: Nature's Dawn	C. Frace	150-day	30.50	31.00
91-32-006	Clouded Leopard	C. Frace	150-day	32.50	35.00
91-32-007	Zebra Foal	C. Frace	150-day	32.50	60.00
91-32-008	Bandit	C. Frace	150-day	32.50	41.00
W. S. George	**Soaring Majesty**				
91-33-001	Freedom	C. Frace	150-day	29.50	54.00
91-33-002	The Northern Goshhawk	C. Frace	150-day	29.50	45.00
91-33-003	Peregrine Falcon	C. Frace	150-day	32.50	33.00
91-33-004	Red-Tailed Hawk	C. Frace	150-day	32.50	33.00
91-33-005	The Ospray	C. Frace	150-day	32.50	33.00
91-33-006	The Gyrfalcon	C. Frace	150-day	34.50	48.00
91-33-007	The Golden Eagle	C. Frace	150-day	34.50	34.50
92-33-008	Red-Shouldered Hawk	C. Frace	150-day	34.50	34.50
W. S. George	**The World's Most Magnificent Cats**				
91-34-001	Fleeting Encounter	C. Frace	150-day	24.50	85.00
91-34-002	Cougar	C. Frace	150-day	24.50	90.00
91-34-003	Royal Bengal	C. Frace	150-day	27.50	53.00
91-34-004	Powerful Presence	C. Frace	150-day	27.50	60.00
91-34-005	Jaguar	C. Frace	150-day	27.50	75.00
91-34-006	The Clouded Leopard	C. Frace	150-day	29.50	139.00
91-34-007	The African Leopard	C. Frace	150-day	29.50	75.00
91-34-008	Mighty Warrior	C. Frace	150-day	29.50	95.00
92-34-009	The Cheetah	C. Frace	150-day	31.50	32.00
92-34-010	Siberian Tiger	C. Frace	150-day	31.50	31.50
W. S. George	**A Loving Look: Duck Families**				
90-35-001	Family Outing	B. Langton	150-day	34.50	34.50
91-35-002	Sleepy Start	B. Langton	150-day	34.50	34.50
91-35-003	Quiet Moment	B. Langton	150-day	37.50	37.50
91-35-004	Safe and Sound	B. Langton	150-day	37.50	37.50
91-35-005	Spring Arrivals	B. Langton	150-day	37.50	73.00
91-35-006	The Family Tree	B. Langton	150-day	37.50	50-60.00
W. S. George	**Nature's Legacy**				
90-36-001	Blue Snow at Half Dome	J. Sias	150-day	24.50	30.00
91-36-002	Misty Morning/Mt. McKinley	J. Sias	150-day	24.50	25-53.00
91-36-003	Mount Ranier	J. Sias	150-day	27.50	28-55.00
91-36-004	Havasu Canyon	J. Sias	150-day	27.50	27.50
91-36-005	Autumn Splendor in the Smoky Mts.	J. Sias	150-day	27.50	27.50
91-36-006	Winter Peace in Yellowstone Park	J. Sias	150-day	29.50	29.50
91-36-007	Golden Majesty/Rocky Mountains	J. Sias	150-day	29.50	29.50
91-36-008	Radiant Sunset Over the Everglades	J. Sias	150-day	29.50	29.50
W. S. George	**Symphony of Shimmering Beauties**				
91-37-001	Iris Quartet	L. Liu	150-day	29.50	49.00
91-37-002	Tulip Ensemble	L. Liu	150-day	29.50	29.50
91-37-003	Poppy Pastorale	L. Liu	150-day	32.50	32.50
91-37-004	Lily Concerto	L. Liu	150-day	32.50	32.50
91-37-005	Peony Prelude	L. Liu	150-day	32.50	32.50
91-37-006	Rose Fantasy	L. Liu	150-day	34.50	34.50
91-37-007	Hibiscus Medley	L. Liu	150-day	34.50	34.50
92-37-008	Dahlia Melody	L. Liu	150-day	34.50	34.50
92-37-009	Hollyhock March	L. Liu	150-day	34.50	34.50
92-37-010	Carnation Serenade	L. Liu	150-day	36.50	36.50
92-37-011	Gladiolus Romance	L. Liu	150-day	36.50	36.50
92-37-012	Zinnia Finale	L. Liu	150-day	36.50	36.50
W. S. George	**Portraits of Christ**				
91-38-001	Father, Forgive Them	J. Salamanca	150-day	29.50	90.00
91-38-002	Thy Will Be Done	J. Salamanca	150-day	29.50	98.00
91-38-003	This is My Beloved Son	J. Salamanca	150-day	32.50	75.00
91-38-004	Lo, I Am With You	J. Salamanca	150-day	32.50	32.50
91-38-005	Become as Little Children	J. Salamanca	150-day	32.50	75.00
91-38-006	Peace I Leave With You	J. Salamanca	150-day	34.50	65.00
92-38-007	For God So Loved the World	J. Salamanca	150-day	34.50	34.50
92-38-008	I Am the Way, the Truth and the Life	J. Salamanca	150-day	34.50	34.50
92-38-009	Weep Not For Me	J. Salamanca	150-day	34.50	34.50
92-38-010	Follow Me	J. Salamanca	150-day	34.50	34.50
W. S. George	**Portraits of Exquisite Birds**				
90-39-001	Backyard Treasure/Chickadee	C. Brenders	150-day	29.50	29.50-50.00
90-39-002	The Beautiful Bluebird	C. Brenders	150-day	29.50	35-61.00
91-39-003	Summer Gold: The Robin	C. Brenders	150-day	32.50	35.00
91-39-004	The Meadowlark's Song	C. Brenders	150-day	32.50	32.50
91-39-005	Ivory-Billed Woodpecker	C. Brenders	150-day	32.50	32.50
91-39-006	Red-Winged Blackbird	C. Brenders	150-day	32.50	32.50
W. S. George	**Alaska: The Last Frontier**				
91-40-001	Icy Majesty	H. Lambson	150-day	34.50	34.50
91-40-002	Autumn Grandeur	H. Lambson	150-day	34.50	34.50
92-40-003	Mountain Monarch	H. Lambson	150-day	37.50	37.50
92-40-004	Down the Trail	H. Lambson	150-day	37.50	37.50
92-40-005	Moonlight Lookout	H. Lambson	150-day	37.50	37.50
92-40-006	Graceful Passage	H. Lambson	150-day	39.50	39.50
92-40-007	Arctic Journey	H. Lambson	150-day	39.50	39.50
92-40-008	Summit Domain	H. Lambson	150-day	39.50	39.50
W. S. George	**On Wings of Snow**				
91-41-001	The Swans	L. Liu	150-day	34.50	34.50
91-41-002	The Doves	L. Liu	150-day	34.50	34.50
91-41-003	The Peacocks	L. Liu	150-day	37.50	37.50
91-41-004	The Egrets	L. Liu	150-day	37.50	37.50

Company / Number	Name	Series / Artist	Edition Limit	Issue Price	Quote
91-41-005	The Cockatoos	L. Liu	150-day	37.50	37.50
92-41-006	The Herons	L. Liu	150-day	37.50	37.50
W. S. George		**Nature's Playmates**			
91-42-001	Partners	C. Frace	150-day	29.50	45.00
91-42-002	Secret Heights	C. Frace	150-day	29.50	57.00
91-42-003	Recess	C. Frace	150-day	32.50	32.50
91-42-004	Double Trouble	C. Frace	150-day	32.50	32.50
91-42-005	Pals	C. Frace	150-day	32.50	32.50
92-42-006	Curious Trio	C. Frace	150-day	34.50	34.50
92-42-007	Playmates	C. Frace	150-day	34.50	34.50
92-42-008	Surprise	C. Frace	150-day	34.50	34.50
92-42-009	Peace On Ice	C. Frace	150-day	36.50	36.50
92-42-010	Ambassadors	C. Frace	150-day	36.50	36.50
W. S. George		**Field Birds of North America**			
91-43-001	Winter Colors: Ring-Necked Pheasant	D. Bush	150-day	39.50	45.00
91-43-002	In Display: Ruffed Goose	D. Bush	150-day	39.50	60.00
91-43-003	Morning Light: Bobwhite Quail	D. Bush	150-day	42.50	62.00
91-43-004	Misty Clearing: Wild Turkey	D. Bush	150-day	42.50	42.50
92-43-005	Autumn Moment: American Woodcock	D. Bush	150-day	42.50	42.50
92-43-006	Season's End: Willow Ptarmigan	D. Bush	150-day	42.50	42.50
W. S. George		**Country Bouquets**			
91-44-001	Morning Sunshine	G. Kurz	150-day	29.50	50.00
91-44-002	Summer Perfume	G. Kurz	150-day	29.50	40.00
91-44-003	Warm Welcome	G. Kurz	150-day	32.50	35.00
91-44-004	Garden's Bounty	G. Kurz	150-day	32.50	35.00
W. S. George		**Gentle Beginnings**			
91-45-001	Tender Loving Care	W. Nelson	150-day	34.50	34.50
91-45-002	A Touch of Love	W. Nelson	150-day	34.50	34.50
91-45-003	Under Watchful Eyes	W. Nelson	150-day	37.50	37.50
91-45-004	Lap of Love	W. Nelson	150-day	37.50	37.50
92-45-005	Happy Together	W. Nelson	150-day	37.50	37.50
92-45-006	First Steps	W. Nelson	150-day	37.50	37.50
W. S. George		**Garden of the Lord**			
92-46-001	Love One Another	C. Gillies	150-day	29.50	29.50
92-46-002	Perfect Peace	C. Gillies	150-day	29.50	29.50
92-46-003	Trust In the Lord	C. Gillies	150-day	32.50	32.50
92-46-004	The Lord's Love	C. Gillies	150-day	32.50	32.50
92-46-005	The Lord Bless You	C. Gillies	150-day	32.50	32.50
92-46-006	Ask In Prayer	C. Gillies	150-day	34.50	34.50
93-46-007	Peace Be With You	C. Gillies	150-day	34.50	34.50
93-46-008	Give Thanks To The Lord	C. Gillies	150-day	34.50	34.50
W. S. George		**The Majestic Horse**			
92-47-001	Classic Beauty: Thoroughbred	P. Wildermuth	150-day	34.50	50.00
92-47-002	American Gold: The Quarterhorse	P. Wildermuth	150-day	34.50	35.00
92-47-003	Regal Spirit: The Arabian	P. Wildermuth	150-day	34.50	50.00
92-47-004	Western Favorite: American Paint Horse	P. Wildermuth	150-day	34.50	45.00
W. S. George		**Columbus Discovers America: The 500th Anniversary**			
92-48-001	Under Full Sail	J. Penalva	150-day	29.50	30.00
92-48-002	Ashore at Dawn	J. Penalva	150-day	29.50	47.00
92-48-003	Columbus Raises the Flag	J. Penalva	150-day	32.50	54.00
92-48-004	Bringing Together Two Cultures	J. Penalva	150-day	32.50	55.00
92-48-005	The Queen's Approval	J. Penalva	150-day	32.50	33.00
92-48-006	Treasures From The New World	J. Penalva	150-day	32.50	33.00
W. S. George		**Lena Liu's Basket Bouquets**			
92-49-001	Roses	L. Liu	150-day	29.50	29.50
92-49-002	Pansies	L. Liu	150-day	29.50	29.50
92-49-003	Tulips and Lilacs	L. Liu	150-day	32.50	32.50
92-49-004	Irises	L. Liu	150-day	32.50	32.50
92-49-005	Lilies	L. Liu	150-day	32.50	32.50
92-49-006	Parrot Tulips	L. Liu	150-day	32.50	32.50
92-49-007	Peonies	L. Liu	150-day	32.50	32.50
93-49-008	Begonias	L. Liu	150-day	32.50	32.50
93-49-009	Magnolias	L. Liu	150-day	32.50	32.50
93-49-010	Calla Lilies	L. Liu	150-day	32.50	32.50
W. S. George		**Tomorrow's Promise**			
92-50-001	Curiosity: Asian Elephants	W. Nelson	150-day	29.50	40.00
92-50-002	Playtime Pandas	W. Nelson	150-day	29.50	29.50
92-50-003	Innocence: Rhinos	W. Nelson	150-day	32.50	55.00
92-50-004	Friskiness: Kit Foxes	W. Nelson	150-day	32.50	32.50
W. S. George		**Sonnets in Flowers**			
92-51-001	Sonnet of Beauty	G. Kurz	150-day	29.50	40.00
92-51-002	Sonnet of Happiness	G. Kurz	150-day	34.50	34.50
92-51-003	Sonnet of Love	G. Kurz	150-day	34.50	34.50
92-51-004	Sonnet of Peace	G. Kurz	150-day	34.50	34.50
W. S. George		**The Sound of Music: Silver Anniversary**			
91-52-001	The Hills are Alive	V. Gadino	150-day	29.50	29.50
92-52-002	Let's Start at the Very Beginning	V. Gadino	150-day	29.50	29.50
92-52-003	Something Good	V. Gadino	150-day	32.50	32.50
92-52-004	Maria's Wedding Day	V. Gadino	150-day	32.50	32.50
W. S. George		**On the Wing**			
92-53-001	Winged Splendor	T. Humphrey	150-day	29.50	29.50
92-53-002	Rising Mallard	T. Humphrey	150-day	29.50	29.50
92-53-003	Glorious Ascent	T. Humphrey	150-day	32.50	32.50
92-53-004	Taking Wing	T. Humphrey	150-day	32.50	32.50
92-53-005	Upward Bound	T. Humphrey	150-day	32.50	32.50
93-53-006	Wondrous Motion	T. Humphrey	150-day	34.50	34.50
93-53-007	Springing Forth	T. Humphrey	150-day	34.50	34.50
W. S. George		**Grand Safari: Images of Africa**			
92-54-001	A Moment's Rest	C. Frace	150-day	34.50	34.50
92-54-002	Elephant's of Kilimanjaro	C. Frace	150-day	34.50	34.50
92-54-003	Undivided Attention	C. Frace	150-day	37.50	37.50
93-54-004	Quiet Time in Samburu	C. Frace	150-day	37.50	37.50
93-54-005	Lone Hunter	C. Frace	150-day	37.50	37.50
93-54-006	The Greater Kudo	C. Frace	150-day	37.50	37.50
W. S. George		**A Treasury of Songbirds**			
92-55-001	Springtime Splendor	R. Stine	150-day	29.50	29.50
92-55-002	Morning's Glory	R. Stine	150-day	29.50	29.50
92-55-003	Golden Daybreak	R. Stine	150-day	32.50	32.50
92-55-004	Afternoon Calm	R. Stine	150-day	32.50	32.50
92-55-005	Dawn's Radiance	R. Stine	150-day	32.50	32.50
93-55-006	Scarlet Sunrise	R. Stine	150-day	34.50	34.50
93-55-007	Sapphire Dawn	R. Stine	150-day	34.50	34.50
93-55-008	Alluring Daylight	R. Stine	150-day	34.50	34.50
W. S. George		**Heart of the Wild**			
91-56-001	A Gentle Touch	G. Beecham	150-day	29.50	29.50
92-56-002	Mother's Pride	G. Beecham	150-day	29.50	29.50
92-56-003	An Afternoon Together	G. Beecham	150-day	32.50	32.50
92-56-004	Quiet Time?	G. Beecham	150-day	32.50	32.50
W. S. George		**Spirits of the Sky**			
92-57-001	Twilight Glow	C. Fisher	150-day	29.50	29.50
92-57-002	First Light	C. Fisher	150-day	29.50	29.50
92-57-003	Evening Glimmer	C. Fisher	150-day	32.50	32.50
92-57-004	Golden Dusk	C. Fisher	150-day	32.50	32.50
93-57-005	Sunset Splendor	C. Fisher	150-day	32.50	32.50
93-57-006	Amber Flight	C. Fisher	150-day	34.50	34.50
93-57-007	Winged Radiance	C. Fisher	150-day	34.50	34.50
W. S. George		**Poetic Cottages**			
92-58-001	Garden Paths of Oxfordshire	C. Valente	150-day	29.50	29.50
92-58-002	Twilight at Woodgreen Pond	C. Valente	150-day	29.50	29.50
92-58-003	Stonewall Brook Blossoms	C. Valente	150-day	32.50	32.50
92-58-004	Bedfordshire Evening Sky	C. Valente	150-day	32.50	32.50
93-58-005	Wisteria Summer	C. Valente	150-day	32.50	32.50
93-58-006	Wiltshire Rose Arbor	C. Valente	150-day	32.50	32.50
93-58-007	Alderbury Gardens	C. Valente	150-day	32.50	32.50
93-58-008	Hampshire Spring Splendor	C. Valente	150-day	32.50	32.50
W. S. George		**Memories of a Victorian Childhood**			
92-59-001	You'd Better Not Pout	Unknown	150-day	29.50	29.50
92-59-002	Sweet Slumber	Unknown	150-day	29.50	29.50
92-59-003	Through Thick and Thin	Unknown	150-day	32.50	32.50
92-59-004	An Armful of Treasures	Unknown	150-day	32.50	32.50
93-59-005	A Trio of Bookworms	Unknown	150-day	32.50	32.50
93-59-006	Pugnacious Playmate	Unknown	150-day	32.50	32.50
W. S. George		**Petal Pals**			
92-60-001	Garden Discovery	L. Chang	150-day	24.50	24.50
92-60-002	Flowering Fascination	L. Chang	150-day	24.50	24.50
93-60-003	Alluring Lilies	L. Chang	150-day	24.50	24.50
93-60-004	Springtime Oasis	L. Chang	150-day	24.50	24.50
93-60-005	Blossoming Adventure	L. Chang	150-day	24.50	24.50
93-60-006	Dancing Daffodils	L. Chang	150-day	24.50	24.50
93-60-007	Summer Surprise	L. Chang	150-day	24.50	24.50
W. S. George		**Lena Liu's Hummingbird Treasury**			
92-61-001	The Ruby-Throated Hummingbird	L. Liu	150-day	29.50	29.50
92-61-002	Anna's Hummingbird	L. Liu	150-day	29.50	29.50
92-61-003	Violet-Crowned Hummingbird	L. Liu	150-day	32.50	32.50
92-61-004	The Rufous Hummingbird	L. Liu	150-day	32.50	32.50
93-61-005	White-Eared Hummingbird	L. Liu	150-day	32.50	32.50
93-61-006	Broad-Billed Hummingbird	L. Liu	150-day	34.50	34.50
93-61-007	Calliope Hummingbird	L. Liu	150-day	34.50	34.50
W. S. George		**The Christmas Story**			
92-62-001	Gifts of the Magi	H. Garrido	150-day	29.50	29.50
93-62-002	Rest on the Flight into Egypt	H. Garrido	150-day	29.50	29.50
93-62-003	Journey of the Magi	H. Garrido	150-day	29.50	29.50
93-62-004	The Nativity	H. Garrido	150-day	29.50	29.50
93-62-005	The Annunciation	H. Garrido	150-day	29.50	29.50
93-62-006	Adoration of the Shepherds	H. Garrido	150-day	29.50	29.50
W. S. George		**Winter's Majesty**			
92-63-001	The Quest	C. Frace	150-day	34.50	34.50
92-63-002	The Chase	C. Frace	150-day	34.50	34.50
93-63-003	Alaskan Friend	C. Frace	150-day	34.50	34.50
93-63-004	American Cougar	C. Frace	150-day	34.50	34.50
93-63-005	On Watch	C. Frace	150-day	34.50	34.50
93-63-006	Solitude	C. Frace	150-day	34.50	34.50
W. S. George		**America's Pride**			
92-64-001	Misty Fjords	R. Richert	150-day	29.50	42.00
92-64-002	Rugged Shores	R. Richert	150-day	29.50	29.50
93-64-003	Mighty Summit	R. Richert	150-day	32.50	32.50
93-64-004	Lofty Reflections	R. Richert	150-day	32.50	32.50
93-64-005	Tranquil Waters	R. Richert	150-day	32.50	32.50
93-64-006	Mountain Majesty	R. Richert	150-day	34.50	34.50
93-64-007	Canyon Climb	R. Richert	150-day	34.50	34.50
W. S. George		**A Black Tie Affair: The Penguin**			
92-65-001	Little Explorer	C. Jagodits	150-day	29.50	29.50
92-65-002	Penguin Parade	C. Jagodits	150-day	29.50	29.50
93-65-003	Baby-Sitters	C. Jagodits	150-day	29.50	29.50
93-65-004	Belly Flopping	C. Jagodits	150-day	29.50	29.50
W. S. George		**The Faces of Nature**			
92-66-001	Canyon of the Cat	J. Kramer Cole	150-day	29.50	29.50
92-66-002	Wolf Ridge	J. Kramer Cole	150-day	29.50	29.50
93-66-003	Trail of the Talisman	J. Kramer Cole	150-day	29.50	29.50
93-66-004	Wolfpack of the Ancients	J. Kramer Cole	150-day	29.50	29.50
93-66-005	Two Bears Camp	J. Kramer Cole	150-day	29.50	29.50
93-66-006	Wintering With the Wapiti	J. Kramer Cole	150-day	29.50	29.50
93-66-007	Within Sunrise	J. Kramer Cole	150-day	29.50	29.50
93-66-008	Wambli Okiye	J. Kramer Cole	150-day	29.50	29.50
W. S. George		**Wings of Winter**			
92-67-001	Moonlight Retreat	D. Rust	150-day	29.50	29.50
93-67-002	Twilight Serenade	D. Rust	150-day	29.50	29.50
93-67-003	Silent Sunset	D. Rust	150-day	29.50	29.50
93-67-004	Night Lights	D. Rust	150-day	29.50	29.50
93-67-005	Winter Haven	D. Rust	150-day	29.50	29.50
93-67-006	Full Moon Companions	D. Rust	150-day	29.50	29.50
93-67-007	White Night	D. Rust	150-day	29.50	29.50
93-67-008	Winter Reflections	D. Rust	150-day	29.50	29.50
W. S. George		**Gardens of Paradise**			
92-68-001	Tranquility	L. Chang	150-day	29.50	29.50
92-68-002	Serenity	L. Chang	150-day	29.50	29.50
93-68-003	Splendor	L. Chang	150-day	32.50	32.50
93-68-004	Harmony	L. Chang	150-day	32.50	32.50
93-68-005	Beauty	L. Chang	150-day	32.50	32.50
93-68-006	Elegance	L. Chang	150-day	32.50	32.50

Company		Series			
Number	**Name**	**Artist**	**Edition Limit**	**Issue Price**	**Quote**
W. S. George		**The Passions of Scarlett O'Hara**			
92-69-001	Fiery Embrace	P. Jennis	150-day	29.50	68.00
92-69-002	Pride and Passion	P. Jennis	150-day	29.50	29.50
92-69-003	Dreams of Ashley	P. Jennis	150-day	32.50	32.50
92-69-004	The Fond Farewell	P. Jennis	150-day	32.50	32.50
92-69-005	The Waltz	P. Jennis	150-day	32.50	32.50
92-69-006	As God Is My Witness	P. Jennis	150-day	34.50	34.50
93-69-007	Brave Scarlett	P. Jennis	150-day	34.50	34.50
93-69-008	Nightmare	P. Jennis	150-day	34.50	34.50
W. S. George		**Little Angels**			
92-70-001	Angels We Have Heard on High	B. Burke	150-day	29.50	29.50
92-70-002	O Tannenbaum	B. Burke	150-day	29.50	29.50
93-70-003	Joy to the World	B. Burke	150-day	32.50	32.50
93-70-004	Hark the Herald Angels Sing	B. Burke	150-day	32.50	32.50
93-70-005	It Came Upon a Midnight Clear	B. Burke	150-day	32.50	32.50
W. S. George		**Wild Spirits**			
92-71-001	Solitary Watch	T. Hirata	150-day	29.50	29.50
92-71-002	Timber Ghost	T. Hirata	150-day	29.50	29.50
92-71-003	Mountain Magic	T. Hirata	150-day	32.50	32.50
93-71-004	Silent Guard	T. Hirata	150-day	32.50	32.50
93-71-005	Sly Eyes	T. Hirata	150-day	32.50	32.50
93-71-006	Mighty Presence	T. Hirata	150-day	34.50	34.50
93-71-007	Quiet Vigil	T. Hirata	150-day	34.50	34.50
W. S. George		**Paw Prints: Baby Cats of the Wild**			
92-72-001	Morning Mischief	C. Frace	95-day	29.50	29.50
93-72-002	Togetherness	C. Frace	95-day	29.50	29.50
93-72-003	The Buddy System	C. Frace	95-day	32.50	32.50
93-72-004	Nap Time	C. Frace	95-day	32.50	32.50
W. S. George		**A Delicate Balance: Vanishing Wildlife**			
92-73-001	Tomorrow's Hope	G. Beecham	95-day	29.50	29.50
93-73-002	Today's Future	G. Beecham	95-day	29.50	29.50
93-73-003	Present Dreams	G. Beecham	95-day	32.50	32.50
93-73-004	Eyes on the New Day	G. Beecham	95-day	32.50	32.50
W. S. George		**Bear Tracks**			
92-74-001	Denali Family	J. Seerey-Lester	150-day	29.50	29.50
93-74-002	Their First Season	J. Seerey-Lester	150-day	29.50	29.50
93-74-003	High Country Champion	J. Seerey-Lester	150-day	29.50	29.50
93-74-004	Heavy Going	J. Seerey-Lester	150-day	29.50	29.50
93-74-005	Breaking Cover	J. Seerey-Lester	150-day	29.50	29.50
93-74-006	Along the Ice Flow	J. Seerey-Lester	150-day	29.50	29.50
W. S. George		**Hometown Memories**			
93-75-001	Moonlight Skaters	H.T. Becker	150-day	29.50	29.50
93-75-002	Mountain Sleigh Ride	H.T. Becker	150-day	29.50	29.50
93-75-003	Heading Home	H.T. Becker	150-day	29.50	29.50
93-75-004	A Winter Ride	H.T. Becker	150-day	29.50	29.50
W. S. George		**Wild Innocents**			
93-76-001	Reflections	C. Frace	95-day	29.50	29.50
93-76-002	Spiritual Heir	C. Frace	95-day	29.50	29.50
W. S. George		**A Flash of Cats**			
93-77-001	Moonlight Chase: Cougar	J. Seerey-Lester	150-day	29.50	29.50
W. S. George		**Rare Encounters**			
93-78-001	Softly, Softly	J. Seerey-Lester	95-day	29.50	29.50
93-78-002	Black Magic	J. Seerey-Lester	95-day	29.50	29.50
93-78-003	Future Song	J. Seerey-Lester	95-day	32.50	32.50
93-78-004	High and Mighty	J. Seerey-Lester	95-day	32.50	32.50
W. S. George		**Along an English Lane**			
93-79-001	Summer's Bright Welcome	M. Harvey	95-day	29.50	29.50
93-79-002	Greeting the Day	M. Harvey	95-day	29.50	29.50
93-79-003	Friends and Flowers	M. Harvey	95-day	29.50	29.50
93-79-004	Cottage Around the Bend	M. Harvey	95-day	29.50	29.50
W. S. George		**Romantic Harbors**			
93-80-001	Advent of the Golden Bough	C. Vickery	95-day	34.50	34.50
93-80-002	Christmas Tree Schooner	C. Vickery	95-day	34.50	34.50
93-80-003	Prelude to the Journey	C. Vickery	95-day	37.50	37.50
W. S. George		**Lena Liu's Flower Fairies**			
93-81-001	Magic Makers	L. Liu	95-day	29.50	29.50
93-81-002	Petal Playmates	L. Liu	95-day	29.50	29.50
W. S. George		**Touching the Spirit**			
93-82-001	Running With the Wind	J. Kramer Cole	95-day	29.50	29.50
93-82-002	Kindred Spirits	J. Kramer Cole	95-day	29.50	29.50
93-82-003	The Marking Tree	J. Kramer Cole	95-day	29.50	29.50
93-82-004	Wakan Tanka	J. Kramer Cole	95-day	29.50	29.50
W. S. George		**Eyes of the Wild**			
93-83-001	Eyes in the Mist	D. Pierce	95-day	29.50	29.50
93-83-002	Eyes in the Pines	D. Pierce	95-day	29.50	29.50
93-83-003	Eyes on the Sly	D. Pierce	95-day	29.50	29.50
93-83-004	Eyes of Gold	D. Pierce	95-day	29.50	29.50
W. S. George		**Enchanted Garden**			
93-84-001	A Peaceful Retreat	E. Antonaccio	95-day	24.50	24.50
93-84-002	Pleasant Pathways	E. Antonaccio	95-day	24.50	24.50
93-84-003	A Place to Dream	E. Antonaccio	95-day	24.50	24.50
93-84-004	Tranquil Hideaway	E. Antonaccio	95-day	24.50	24.50
W. S. George		**Feline Fancy**			
93-85-001	Globetrotters	H. Ronner	95-day	34.50	34.50
93-85-002	Little Athletes	H. Ronner	95-day	34.50	34.50
93-85-003	Young Adventurers	H. Ronner	95-day	34.50	34.50
93-85-004	The Geographers	H. Ronner	95-day	34.50	34.50
W. S. George		**'Tis the Season**			
93-86-001	A World Dressed in Snow	J. Sias	95-day	29.50	29.50
93-86-002	A Time for Tradition	J. Sias	95-day	29.50	29.50
93-86-003	We Shall Come Rejoining	J. Sias	95-day	29.50	29.50
93-86-004	Our Family Tree	J. Sias	95-day	29.50	29.50
W.S. George		**Floral Fancies**			
93-87-001	Sitting Softly	C. Callos	95-day	34.50	34.50
93-87-002	Sitting Pretty	C. Callos	95-day	34.50	34.50
W.S. George		**Melodies in the Mist**			
93-88-001	Early Morning Rain	A. Sakhavarz	95-day	34.50	34.50
93-88-002	Among the Dewdrops	A. Sakhavarz	95-day	34.50	34.50
W.S. George		**On Golden Wings**			
93-89-001	Morning Light	W. Goebel	95-day	29.50	29.50
93-89-002	Early Risers	W. Goebel	95-day	29.50	29.50
W. S. George		**Romantic Roses**			
93-90-001	Victorian Beauty	V. Morley	95-day	29.50	29.50
93-90-002	Old-Fashioned Grace	V. Morley	95-day	29.50	29.50
93-90-003	Country Charm	V. Morley	95-day	32.50	32.50
93-90-004	Summer Romance	V. Morley	95-day	32.50	32.50
Georgetown		**Hearts in Song**			
93-01-001	Buffalo Child	C. Theroux	35-day	29.95	29.95
Goebel/M.I. Hummel		**M.I. Hummel Collectibles-Annual Plates**			
71-01-001	Heavenly Angel 264	M.I. Hummel	Closed	25.00	486-765.
72-01-002	Hear Ye, Hear Ye 265	M.I. Hummel	Closed	30.00	36-53.00
73-01-003	Glober Trotter 266	M.I. Hummel	Closed	32.50	74-120.00
74-01-004	Goose Girl 267	M.I. Hummel	Closed	40.00	44-74.00
75-01-005	Ride into Christmas 268	M.I. Hummel	Closed	50.00	39-75.00
76-01-006	Apple Tree Girl 269	M.I. Hummel	Closed	50.00	39-65.00
77-01-007	Apple Tree Boy 270	M.I. Hummel	Closed	52.50	59-64.00
78-01-008	Happy Pastime 271	M.I. Hummel	Closed	65.00	36.00
79-01-009	Singing Lesson 272	M.I. Hummel	Closed	90.00	24-90.00
80-01-010	School Girl 273	M.I. Hummel	Closed	100.00	49-59.00
81-01-011	Umbrella Boy 274	M.I. Hummel	Closed	100.00	60.00
82-01-012	Umbrella Girl 275	M.I. Hummel	Closed	100.00	98-118.00
83-01-013	The Postman 276	M.I. Hummel	Closed	108.00	156-190.
84-01-014	Little Helper 277	M.I. Hummel	Closed	108.00	58.00
85-01-015	Chick Girl 278	M.I. Hummel	Closed	110.00	78-93.00
86-01-016	Playmates 279	M.I. Hummel	Closed	125.00	140-185.
87-01-017	Feeding Time 283	M.I. Hummel	Closed	135.00	270-375.
88-01-018	Little Goat Herder 284	M.I. Hummel	Closed	145.00	65-120.
89-01-019	Farm Boy 285	M.I. Hummel	Closed	160.00	120.00
90-01-020	Shepherd's Boy 286	M.I. Hummel	Closed	170.00	166-200.
91-01-021	Just Resting 287	M.I. Hummel	Closed	196.00	130-150.
92-01-022	Wayside Harmony 288	M.I. Hummel	Closed	210.00	210-250.
93-01-023	Doll Bath 289	M.I. Hummel	Yr.Iss.	210.00	250-310.
94-01-024	Doctor 290	M.I. Hummel	Yr.Iss.	225.00	225.00
Goebel/M.I. Hummel		**M.I. Hummel Collectibles Anniversary Plates**			
75-02-001	Stormy Weather 280	M.I. Hummel	Closed	100.00	62.00
80-02-002	Spring Dance 281	M.I. Hummel	Closed	225.00	54.00
85-02-003	Auf Wiedersehen 282	M.I. Hummel	Closed	225.00	220.00
Goebel/M.I. Hummel		**M.I. Hummel-Little Music Makers**			
84-03-001	Little Fiddler 744	M.I. Hummel	Closed	30.00	70-125.00
85-03-002	Serenade 741	M.I. Hummel	Closed	30.00	70-125.00
86-03-003	Soloist 743	M.I. Hummel	Closed	35.00	70-125.00
87-03-004	Band Leader 742	M.I. Hummel	Closed	40.00	70-125.00
Goebel/M.I. Hummel		**M.I. Hummel Club Exclusive-Celebration**			
86-04-001	Valentine Gift (Hum 738)	M.I. Hummel	Closed	90.00	100-150.
87-04-002	Valentine Joy (Hum 737)	M.I. Hummel	Closed	98.00	130-150.
88-04-003	Daisies Don't Tell (Hum 736)	M.I. Hummel	Closed	115.00	130-150.
89-04-004	It's Cold (Hum 735)	M.I. Hummel	Closed	120.00	130-150.
Goebel/M.I. Hummel		**M.I. Hummel-The Little Homemakers**			
88-05-001	Little Sweeper (Hum 745)	M.I. Hummel	Closed	45.00	28-45.00
89-05-002	Wash Day (Hum 746)	M.I. Hummel	Closed	50.00	24-50.00
90-05-003	A Stitch in Time (Hum 747)	M.I. Hummel	Closed	50.00	70-90.00
91-05-004	Chicken Licken (Hum 748)	M.I. Hummel	Closed	70.00	70-99.00
Goebel/M.I. Hummel		**M.I. Hummel-Friends Forever**			
92-06-001	Meditation 292	M.I. Hummel	Open	180.00	180.00
93-06-002	For Father 293	M.I. Hummel	Open	195.00	195.00
94-06-003	Sweet Greetings 294	M.I. Hummel	Open	205.00	205.00
Gorham		**Christmas**			
74-01-001	Tiny Tim	N. Rockwell	Annual	12.50	35.00
75-01-002	Good Deeds	N. Rockwell	Annual	17.50	35.00
76-01-003	Christmas Trio	N. Rockwell	Annual	19.50	20.00
77-01-004	Yuletide Reckoning	N. Rockwell	Annual	19.50	30.00
78-01-005	Planning Christmas Visit	N. Rockwell	Annual	24.50	24.50
79-01-006	Santa's Helpers	N. Rockwell	Annual	24.50	24.50
80-01-007	Letter to Santa	N. Rockwell	Annual	27.50	32.00
81-01-008	Santa Plans His Visit	N. Rockwell	Annual	29.50	50.00
82-01-009	Jolly Coachman	N. Rockwell	Annual	29.50	30.00
83-01-010	Christmas Dancers	N. Rockwell	Annual	29.50	35.00
84-01-011	Christmas Medley	N. Rockwell	17,500	29.95	29.95
85-01-012	Home For The Holidays	N. Rockwell	17,500	29.95	30.00
86-01-013	Merry Christmas Grandma	N. Rockwell	17,500	29.95	65.00
87-01-014	The Homecoming	N. Rockwell	17,500	35.00	52.00
88-01-015	Discovery	N. Rockwell	17,500	37.50	37.50
Gorham		**A Boy and His Dog Four Seasons Plates**			
71-02-001	Boy Meets His Dog	N. Rockwell	Annual	50.00	180.00
71-02-002	Adventures Between Adventures	N. Rockwell	Annual	Set	Set
71-02-003	The Mysterious Malady	N. Rockwell	Annual	Set	Set
71-02-004	Pride of Parenthood	N. Rockwell	Annual	Set	Set
Gorham		**Young Love Four Seasons Plates**			
72-03-001	Downhill Daring	N. Rockwell	Annual	60.00	125.00
72-03-002	Beguiling Buttercup	N. Rockwell	Annual	Set	Set
72-03-003	Flying High	N. Rockwell	Annual	Set	Set
72-03-004	A Scholarly Pace	N. Rockwell	Annual	Set	Set
Gorham		**Four Ages of Love**			
73-04-001	Gaily Sharing Vintage Time	N. Rockwell	Annual	60.00	130.00
73-04-002	Flowers in Tender Bloom	N. Rockwell	Annual	Set	Set
73-04-003	Sweet Song So Young	N. Rockwell	Annual	Set	Set
73-04-004	Fondly We Do Remember	N. Rockwell	Annual	Set	Set
Gorham		**Grandpa and Me Four Seasons Plates**			
74-05-001	Gay Blades	N. Rockwell	Annual	60.00	85.00
74-05-002	Day Dreamers	N. Rockwell	Annual	Set	Set
74-05-003	Goin' Fishing	N. Rockwell	Annual	Set	Set
74-05-004	Pensive Pals	N. Rockwell	Annual	Set	Set
Gorham		**Me and My Pals Four Seasons Plates**			
75-06-001	A Lickin' Good Bath	N. Rockwell	Annual	70.00	115.00

Company Number	Name	Series Artist	Edition Limit	Issue Price	Quote
75-06-002	Young Man's Fancy	N. Rockwell	Annual	Set	Set
75-06-003	Fisherman's Paradise	N. Rockwell	Annual	Set	Set
75-06-004	Disastrous Daring	N. Rockwell	Annual	Set	Set
Gorham		**Grand Pals Four Seasons Plates**			
76-07-001	Snow Sculpturing	N. Rockwell	Annual	70.00	118.00
76-07-002	Soaring Spirits	N. Rockwell	Annual	Set	Set
76-07-003	Fish Finders	N. Rockwell	Annual	Set	Set
76-07-004	Ghostly Gourds	N. Rockwell	Annual	Set	Set
Gorham		**Going on Sixteen Four Seasons Plates**			
77-08-001	Chilling Chore	N. Rockwell	Annual	75.00	95.00
77-08-002	Sweet Serenade	N. Rockwell	Annual	Set	Set
77-08-003	Shear Agony	N. Rockwell	Annual	Set	Set
77-08-004	Pilgrimage	N. Rockwell	Annual	Set	Set
Gorham		**Tender Years Four Seasons Plates**			
78-09-001	New Year Look	N. Rockwell	Annual	100.00	60.00
78-09-002	Spring Tonic	N. Rockwell	Annual	Set	Set
78-09-003	Cool Aid	N. Rockwell	Annual	Set	Set
78-09-004	Chilly Reception	N. Rockwell	Annual	Set	Set
Gorham		**A Helping Hand Four Seasons Plates**			
79-10-001	Year End Court	N. Rockwell	Annual	100.00	44.00
79-10-002	Closed for Business	N. Rockwell	Annual	Set	Set
79-10-003	Swatter's Rights	N. Rockwell	Annual	Set	Set
79-10-004	Coal Season's Coming	N. Rockwell	Annual	Set	Set
Gorham		**Dad's Boys Four Seasons Plates**			
80-11-001	Ski Skills	N. Rockwell	Annual	135.00	98.00
80-11-002	In His Spirits	N. Rockwell	Annual	Set	Set
80-11-003	Trout Dinner	N. Rockwell	Annual	Set	Set
80-11-004	Careful Aim	N. Rockwell	Annual	Set	Set
Gorham		**Old Timers Four Seasons Plates**			
81-12-001	Canine Solo	N. Rockwell	Annual	100.00	100.00
81-12-002	Sweet Surprise	N. Rockwell	Annual	Set	Set
81-12-003	Lazy Days	N. Rockwell	Annual	Set	Set
81-12-004	Fancy Footwork	N. Rockwell	Annual	Set	Set
Gorham		**Life with Father Four Seasons Plates**			
82-13-001	Big Decision	N. Rockwell	Annual	100.00	200-300.
82-13-002	Blasting Out	N. Rockwell	Annual	Set	Set
82-13-003	Cheering the Champs	N. Rockwell	Annual	Set	Set
82-13-004	A Tough One	N. Rockwell	Annual	Set	Set
Gorham		**Old Buddies Four Seasons Plates**			
83-14-001	Shared Success	N. Rockwell	Annual	115.00	115.00
83-14-002	Endless Debate	N. Rockwell	Annual	Set	Set
83-14-003	Hasty Retreat	N. Rockwell	Annual	Set	Set
83-14-004	Final Speech	N. Rockwell	Annual	Set	Set
Gorham		**Bas Relief**			
81-15-001	Sweet Song So Young	N. Rockwell	Undis.	100.00	100.00
81-15-002	Beguiling Buttercup	N. Rockwell	Undis.	62.50	70.00
82-15-003	Flowers in Tender Bloom	N. Rockwell	Undis.	100.00	100.00
82-15-004	Flying High	N. Rockwell	Undis.	62.50	65.00
Gorham		**Single Release**			
74-16-001	Weighing In	N. Rockwell	Annual	12.50	80-99.00
Gorham		**Single Release**			
74-17-001	The Golden Rule	N. Rockwell	Annual	12.50	30.00
Gorham		**Single Release**			
75-18-001	Ben Franklin	N. Rockwell	Annual	19.50	35.00
Gorham		**Boy Scout Plates**			
75-19-001	Our Heritage	N. Rockwell	18,500	19.50	40.00
76-19-002	A Scout is Loyal	N. Rockwell	18,500	19.50	55.00
77-19-003	The Scoutmaster	N. Rockwell	18,500	19.50	60.00
77-19-004	A Good Sign	N. Rockwell	18,500	19.50	50.00
78-19-005	Pointing the Way	N. Rockwell	18,500	19.50	50.00
78-19-006	Campfire Story	N. Rockwell	18,500	19.50	25.00
80-19-007	Beyond the Easel	N. Rockwell	18,500	45.00	45.00
Gorham		**Single Release**			
76-20-001	The Marriage License	N. Rockwell	Numbrd	37.50	52-75.00
Gorham		**Presidential**			
76-21-001	John F. Kennedy	N. Rockwell	9,800	30.00	65.00
76-21-002	Dwight D. Eisenhower	N. Rockwell	9,800	30.00	35.00
Gorham		**Single Release**			
78-22-001	Triple Self Portrait Memorial Plate	N. Rockwell	Annual	37.50	60.00
Gorham		**Four Seasons Landscapes**			
80-23-001	Summer Respite	N. Rockwell	Annual	45.00	80.00
81-23-002	Autumn Reflection	N. Rockwell	Annual	45.00	65.00
82-23-003	Winter Delight	N. Rockwell	Annual	50.00	62.50
83-23-004	Spring Recess	N. Rockwell	Annual	60.00	60.00
Gorham		**Single Release**			
80-24-001	The Annual Visit	N. Rockwell	Annual	32.50	70.00
Gorham		**Single Release**			
81-25-001	Day in Life of Boy	N. Rockwell	Annual	50.00	80.00
81-25-002	Day in Life of Girl	N. Rockwell	Annual	50.00	80-108.00
Gorham		**Gallery of Masters**			
71-26-001	Man with a Gilt Helmet	Rembrandt	10,000	50.00	50.00
72-26-002	Self Portrait with Saskia	Rembrandt	10,000	50.00	50.00
73-26-003	The Honorable Mrs. Graham	Gainsborough	7,500	50.00	50.00
Gorham		**Barrymore**			
71-27-001	Quiet Waters	Barrymore	15,000	25.00	25.00
72-27-002	San Pedro Harbor	Barrymore	15,000	25.00	25.00
Gorham		**Barrymore**			
72-28-001	Nantucket, Sterling	Barrymore	1,000	100.00	100.00
72-28-002	Little Boatyard, Sterling	Barrymore	1,000	100.00	145.00
Gorham		**Pewter Bicentennial**			
71-29-001	Burning of the Gaspee	R. Pailthorpe	5,000	35.00	35.00

Company Number	Name	Series Artist	Edition Limit	Issue Price	Quote
72-29-002	Boston Tea Party	R. Pailthorpe	5,000	35.00	35.00
Gorham		**Vermeil Bicentennial**			
72-30-001	1776 Plate	Gorham	250	750.00	800.00
Gorham		**Silver Bicentennial**			
72-31-001	1776 Plate	Gorham	500	500.00	500.00
72-31-002	Burning of the Gaspee	R. Pailthorpe	750	500.00	500.00
73-31-003	Boston Tea Party	R. Pailthorpe	750	550.00	575.00
Gorham		**China Bicentennial**			
72-32-001	1776 Plate	Gorham	18,500	17.50	35.00
76-32-002	1776 Bicentennial	Gorham	8,000	17.50	35.00
Gorham		**Remington Western**			
73-33-001	A New Year on the Cimarron	F. Remington	Annual	25.00	35-50.00
73-33-002	Aiding a Comrade	F. Remington	Annual	25.00	30-125.00
73-33-003	The Flight	F. Remington	Annual	25.00	30-95.00
73-33-004	The Fight for the Water Hole	F. Remington	Annual	25.00	30-125.00
75-33-005	Old Ramond	F. Remington	Annual	20.00	35-60.00
75-33-006	A Breed	F. Remington	Annual	20.00	35-65.00
76-33-007	Cavalry Officer	F. Remington	5,000	37.50	60-75.00
76-33-008	A Trapper	F. Remington	5,000	37.50	60-75.00
Gorham		**Moppet Plates-Christmas**			
73-34-001	M. Plate Christmas	Unknown	Annual	10.00	35.00
74-34-002	M. Plate Christmas	Unknown	Annual	12.00	12.00
75-34-003	M. Plate Christmas	Unknown	Annual	13.00	13.00
76-34-004	M. Plate Christmas	Unknown	Annual	13.00	15.00
77-34-005	M. Plate Christmas	Unknown	Annual	13.00	14.00
78-34-006	M. Plate Christmas	Unknown	Annual	10.00	10.00
79-34-007	M. Plate Christmas	Unknown	Annual	12.00	12.00
80-34-008	M. Plate Christmas	Unknown	Annual	12.00	12.00
81-34-009	M. Plate Christmas	Unknown	Annual	12.00	12.00
82-34-010	M. Plate Christmas	Unknown	Annual	12.00	12.00
83-34-011	M. Plate Christmas	Unknown	Annual	12.00	12.00
Gorham		**Moppet Plates-Mother's Day**			
73-35-001	M. Plate Mother's Day	Unknown	Annual	10.00	30.00
74-35-002	M. Plate Mother's Day	Unknown	Annual	12.00	20.00
75-35-003	M. Plate Mother's Day	Unknown	Annual	13.00	15.00
76-35-004	M. Plate Mother's Day	Unknown	Annual	13.00	15.00
77-35-005	M. Plate Mother's Day	Unknown	Annual	13.00	15.00
78-35-006	M. Plate Mother's Day	Unknown	Annual	10.00	10.00
Gorham		**Moppet Plates-Anniversary**			
76-36-001	M. Plate Anniversary	Unknown	20,000	13.00	13.00
Gorham		**Julian Ritter, Fall In Love**			
77-37-001	Enchantment	J. Ritter	5,000	100.00	100.00
77-37-002	Frolic	J. Ritter	5,000	Set	Set
77-37-003	Gutsy Gal	J. Ritter	5,000	Set	Set
77-37-004	Lonely Chill	J. Ritter	5,000	Set	Set
Gorham		**Julian Ritter**			
77-38-001	Christmas Visit	J. Ritter	9,800	24.50	29.00
Gorham		**Julian Ritter, To Love a Clown**			
78-39-001	Awaited Reunion	J. Ritter	5,000	120.00	120.00
78-39-002	Twosome Time	J. Ritter	5,000	120.00	120.00
78-39-003	Showtime Beckons	J. Ritter	5,000	120.00	120.00
78-39-004	Together in Memories	J. Ritter	5,000	120.00	120.00
Gorham		**Julian Ritter**			
78-40-001	Valentine, Fluttering Heart	J. Ritter	7,500	45.00	45.00
Gorham		**Christmas/Children's Television Workshop**			
81-41-001	Sesame Street Christmas	Unknown	Annual	17.50	17.50
82-41-002	Sesame Street Christmas	Unknown	Annual	17.50	17.50
83-41-003	Sesame Street Christmas	Unknown	Annual	19.50	19.50
Gorham		**Pastoral Symphony**			
82-42-001	When I Was a Child	B. Felder	7,500	42.50	50.00
82-42-002	Gather the Children	B. Felder	7,500	42.50	50.00
84-42-003	Sugar and Spice	B. Felder	7,500	42.50	50.00
XX-42-004	He Loves Me	B. Felder	7,500	42.50	50.00
Gorham		**Encounters, Survival and Celebrations**			
82-43-001	A Fine Welcome	J. Clymer	7,500	50.00	75.00
83-43-002	Winter Trail	J. Clymer	7,500	50.00	125.00
83-43-003	Alouette	J. Clymer	7,500	62.50	62.50
83-43-004	The Trader	J. Clymer	7,500	62.50	62.50
83-43-005	Winter Camp	J. Clymer	7,500	62.50	75.00
83-43-006	The Trapper Takes a Wife	J. Clymer	7,500	62.50	62.50
Gorham		**Charles Russell**			
80-44-001	In Without Knocking	C. Russell	9,800	38.00	75.00
81-44-002	Bronc to Breakfast	C. Russell	9,800	38.00	75-115.00
82-44-003	When Ignorance is Bliss	C. Russell	9,800	45.00	75-115.00
83-44-004	Cowboy Life	C. Russell	9,800	45.00	100.00
Gorham		**Gorham Museum Doll Plates**			
84-45-001	Lydia	Gorham	5,000	29.00	125.00
84-45-002	Belton Bebe	Gorham	5,000	29.00	55.00
84-45-003	Christmas Lady	Gorham	7,500	32.50	32.50
85-45-004	Lucille	Gorham	5,000	29.00	35.00
85-45-005	Jumeau	Gorham	5,000	29.00	29.00
Gorham		**Time Machine Teddies Plates**			
86-46-001	Miss Emily, Bearing Up	B. Port	5,000	32.50	32.50
87-46-002	Big Bear, The Toy Collector	B. Port	5,000	32.50	32.50
88-46-003	Hunny Munny	B. Port	5,000	37.50	37.50
Gorham		**Leyendecker Annual Christmas Plates**			
88-47-001	Christmas Hug	J. C. Leyendecker	10,000	37.50	50.00
Gorham		**Single Release**			
76-48-001	The Black Regiment 1778	F. Quagon	7,500	25.00	58.00
Gorham		**American Artist**			
76-49-001	Apache Mother & Child	R. Donnelly	9,800	25.00	56.00
Dave Grossman Creations		**Emmett Kelly Plates**			
86-01-001	Christmas Carol	B. Leighton-Jones	Yr.Iss.	20.00	20.00

PLATES

Company Number	Name	Series Artist	Edition Limit	Issue Price	Quote
87-01-002	Christmas Wreath	B. Leighton-Jones	Yr.Iss.	20.00	20.00
88-01-003	Christmas Dinner	B. Leighton-Jones	Yr.Iss.	20.00	49.00
89-01-004	Christmas Feast	B. Leighton-Jones	Yr.Iss.	20.00	39.00
90-01-005	Just What I Needed	B. Leighton-Jones	Yr.Iss.	24.00	39.00
91-01-006	Emmett The Snowman	B. Leighton-Jones	Yr.Iss.	25.00	45.00
92-01-007	Christmas Tunes	B. Leighton-Jones	Yr.Iss.	25.00	25.00
93-01-008	Downhill-Christmas Plate	B. Leighton-Jones	Yr.Iss.	30.00	30.00
Dave Grossman Creations		**Saturday Evening Post Collection**			
91-02-001	Downhill Daring BRP-91	Rockwell-Inspired	Yr.Iss.	25.00	25.00
91-02-002	Missed BRP-101	Rockwell-Inspired	Yr.Iss.	25.00	25.00
92-02-003	Choosin Up BRP-102	Rockwell-Inspired	Yr.Iss.	25.00	25.00
Dave Grossman Creations		**Native American Series**			
91-03-001	Lone Wolf	E. Roberts	10,000	45.00	50.00
92-03-002	Tortoise Lady	E. Roberts	10,000	45.00	50.00
Dave Grossman Designs		**Norman Rockwell Collection**			
79-01-001	Leapfrog NRP-79	Rockwell-Inspired	Retrd.	50.00	50.00
80-01-002	Lovers NRP-80	Rockwell-Inspired	Retrd.	60.00	60.00
81-01-003	Dreams of Long Ago NRP-81	Rockwell-Inspired	Retrd.	60.00	60.00
82-01-004	Doctor and Doll NRP-82	Rockwell-Inspired	Retrd.	65.00	95.00
83-01-005	Circus NRP-83	Rockwell-Inspired	Retrd.	65.00	65.00
84-01-006	Visit With Rockwell NRP-84	Rockwell-Inspired	Retrd.	65.00	65.00
80-01-007	Christmas Trio RXP-80	Rockwell-Inspired	Retrd.	75.00	75.00
81-01-008	Santa's Good Boys RXP-81	Rockwell-Inspired	Retrd.	75.00	75.00
82-01-009	Faces of Christmas RXP-82	Rockwell-Inspired	Retrd.	75.00	75.00
83-01-010	Christmas Chores RXP-83	Rockwell-Inspired	Retrd.	75.00	75.00
84-01-011	Tiny Tim RXP-84	Rockwell-Inspired	Retrd.	75.00	75.00
80-01-012	Back To School RMP-80	Rockwell-Inspired	Retrd.	24.00	24.00
81-01-013	No Swimming RMP-81	Rockwell-Inspired	Retrd.	25.00	25.00
82-01-014	Love Letter RMP-82	Rockwell-Inspired	Retrd.	27.00	30.00
83-01-015	Doctor and Doll RMP-83	Rockwell-Inspired	Retrd.	27.00	27.00
84-01-016	Big Moment RMP-84	Rockwell-Inspired	Retrd.	27.00	27.00
79-01-017	Butterboy RP-01	Rockwell-Inspired	Retrd.	40.00	40.00
82-01-018	American Mother RGP-42	Rockwell-Inspired	Retrd.	45.00	45.00
83-01-019	Dreamboat RGP-83	Rockwell-Inspired	Retrd.	24.00	30.00
78-01-020	Young Doctor RDP-26	Rockwell-Inspired	Retrd.	50.00	65.00
Dave Grossman Designs		**Norman Rockwell Collection-Tom Sawyer Plates**			
75-02-001	Whitewashing the Fence TSP-01	Rockwell-Inspired	Retrd.	26.00	35.00
76-02-002	First Smoke TSP-02	Rockwell-Inspired	Retrd.	26.00	35.00
77-02-003	Take Your Medicine TSP-03	Rockwell-Inspired	Retrd.	26.00	40.00
78-02-004	Lost in Cave TSP-04	Rockwell-Inspired	Retrd.	26.00	40.00
Dave Grossman Designs		**Norman Rockwell Collection-Huck Finn Plates**			
79-03-001	Secret HFP-01	Rockwell-Inspired	Retrd.	40.00	40.00
80-03-002	ListeningHFP-02	Rockwell-Inspired	Retrd.	40.00	40.00
80-03-003	No Kings HFP-03	Rockwell-Inspired	Retrd.	40.00	40.00
81-03-004	Snake Escapes HFP-04	Rockwell-Inspired	Retrd.	40.00	40.00
Dave Grossman Designs		**Norman Rockwell Collection-Boy Scout Plates**			
81-04-001	Can't Wait BSP-01	Rockwell-Inspired	Retrd.	30.00	45.00
82-04-002	Guiding Hand BSP-02	Rockwell-Inspired	Retrd.	30.00	35.00
83-04-003	Tomorrow's Leader BSP-03	Rockwell-Inspired	Retrd.	30.00	45.00
Grande Copenhagen		**Christmas**			
75-01-001	Alone Together	Unknown	Undis.	24.50	24.50
76-01-002	Christmas Wreath	Unknown	Undis.	24.50	24.50
77-01-003	Fishwives at Gammelstrand	Unknown	Undis.	26.50	26.50
78-01-004	Hans Christian Anderson	Unknown	Undis.	32.50	32.50
79-01-005	Pheasants	Unknown	Undis.	34.50	56.00
80-01-006	Snow Queen in the Tivoli	Unknown	Undis.	39.50	39.50
81-01-007	Little Match Girl in Nyhavn	Unknown	Undis.	42.50	43.00
82-01-008	Shepherdess/Chimney Sweep	Unknown	Undis.	45.00	49.00
83-01-009	Little Mermaid Near Kronborg	Unknown	Undis.	45.00	104.00
84-01-010	Sandman at Amalienborg	Unknown	Undis.	45.00	50.00
Hadley House		**Glow Series**			
85-01-001	Evening Glow	T. Redlin	5,000	55.00	450-500.
85-01-002	Morning Glow	T. Redlin	5,000	55.00	200-250.
85-01-003	Twilight Glow	T. Redlin	5,000	55.00	90-125.00
88-01-004	Afternoon Glow	T. Redlin	5,000	55.00	55.00
Hadley House		**Retreat Series**			
87-02-001	Morning Retreat	T. Redlin	9,500	65.00	90-125.00
87-02-002	Evening Retreat	T. Redlin	9,500	65.00	65-75.00
88-02-003	Golden Retreat	T. Redlin	9,500	65.00	95.00
89-02-004	Moonlight Retreat	T. Redlin	9,500	65.00	65.00
Hadley House		**American Memories Series**			
87-03-001	Coming Home	T. Redlin	9,500	85.00	85.00
88-03-002	Lights of Home	T. Redlin	9,500	85.00	85.00
89-03-003	Homeward Bound	T. Redlin	9,500	85.00	85.00
91-03-004	Family Traditions	T. Redlin	9,500	85.00	85.00
Hadley House		**Annual Christmas Series**			
91-04-001	Heading Home	T. Redlin	9,500	65.00	65.00
92-04-002	Pleasures Of Winter	T. Redlin	19,500	65.00	65.00
93-04-003	Winter Wonderland	T. Redlin	19,500	65.00	65.00
Hadley House		**Windows To The Wild**			
90-05-001	Master's Domain	T. Redlin	9,500	65.00	65.00
91-05-002	Winter Windbreak	T. Redlin	9,500	65.00	65.00
92-05-003	Evening Company	T. Redlin	9,500	65.00	65.00
94-05-004	Night Mapling	T. Redlin	9,500	65.00	65.00
Hadley House		**That Special Time**			
91-06-001	Evening Solitude	T. Redlin	9,500	65.00	65.00
92-06-002	Aroma of Fall	T. Redlin	9,500	65.00	65.00
93-06-003	Welcome To Paradise	T. Redlin	9,500	65.00	65.00
Hadley House		**Lovers Collection**			
92-07-001	Lovers	O. Franca	9,500	50.00	50.00
Hadley House		**Navajo Woman Series**			
90-08-001	Feathered Hair Ties	O. Franca	5,000	50.00	50.00
91-08-002	Navajo Summer	O. Franca	5,000	50.00	50.00
92-08-003	Turquoise Necklace	O. Franca	5,000	50.00	50.00
93-08-004	Pink Navajo	O. Franca	5,000	50.00	50.00
Hadley House		**Navajo Visions Suite**			
93-09-001	Navajo Fantasy	O. Franca	5,000	50.00	50.00
93-09-002	Young Warrior	O. Franca	5,000	50.00	50.00

Company Number	Name	Series Artist	Edition Limit	Issue Price	Quote
Hallmark Galleries		**Enchanted Garden**			
92-01-001	Swan Lake (tile)	E. Richardson	9,500	35.00	35.00
92-01-002	Fairy Bunny Tale: The Beginning (tile)	E. Richardson	14,500	25.00	25.00
92-01-003	Fairy Bunny Tale: Beginning II (tile)	E. Richardson	14,500	35.00	35.00
92-01-004	Neighborhood Dreamer	E. Richardson	9,500	45.00	45.00
Hallmark Galleries		**Days to Remember-The Art of Norman Rockwell**			
92-02-001	Sweet Song So Young (pewter medallion)	Rockwell-Inspired	9,500	45.00	45.00
92-02-002	Sleeping Children (pewter medallion)	Rockwell-Inspired	9,500	45.00	45.00
92-02-003	A Boy Meets His Dog (pewter medallion)	Rockwell-Inspired	9,500	45.00	45.00
92-02-004	Fisherman's Paradise (pewter medallion)	Rockwell-Inspired	9,500	45.00	45.00
93-02-005	Breaking Home Ties	Rockwell-Inspired	9,500	35.00	35.00
94-02-006	After the Prom	Rockwell-Inspired	9,500	35.00	35.00
94-02-007	"No Swimming" 6500QHG9725	Rockwell-Inspired	4,500	65.00	65.00
94-02-008	Growing Years 3500QHG9724	Rockwell-Inspired	9,500	35.00	35.00
Hallmark Galleries		**Innocent Wonders**			
92-03-001	Dinky Toot	T. Blackshear	9,500	35.00	35.00
92-03-002	Pinky Poo	T. Blackshear	9,500	35.00	35.00
93-03-003	Pockets	T. Blackshear	9,500	35.00	35.00
94-03-004	Twinky Wink	T. Blackshear	9,500	35.00	35.00
Hallmark Galleries		**Tobin Fraley Carousels**			
92-04-001	Philadelphia Toboggan Co/1920 (pewter medallion)	T. Fraley	9,500	45.00	45.00
93-04-002	Magical Ride 3500QHG30	T. Fraley	9,500	35.00	35.00
94-04-003	Riding to Adventure	T. Fraley	9,500	35.00	35.00
Hallmark Galleries		**Majestic Wilderness**			
92-05-001	Vixen & Kits	M. Newman	9,500	35.00	35.00
92-05-002	Timber Wolves (porcelain)	M. Newman	9,500	35.00	35.00
94-05-003	Fawn 3500QHG2030	M. Newman	9,500	35.00	35.00
Hallmark Galleries		**Easter Plate**			
94-06-001	Collector's Plate-First Ed. 775QEO8233	L. Votruba	Yr.Iss.	7.75	7.75
Hamilton/Boehm		**Award Winning Roses**			
79-01-001	Peace Rose	Boehm	15,000	45.00	62.50
79-01-002	White Masterpiece Rose	Boehm	15,000	45.00	62.50
79-01-003	Tropicana Rose	Boehm	15,000	45.00	62.50
79-01-004	Elegance Rose	Boehm	15,000	45.00	62.50
79-01-005	Queen Elizabeth Rose	Boehm	15,000	45.00	62.50
79-01-006	Royal Highness Rose	Boehm	15,000	45.00	62.50
79-01-007	Angel Face Rose	Boehm	15,000	45.00	62.50
79-01-008	Mr. Lincoln Rose	Boehm	15,000	45.00	62.50
Hamilton/Boehm		**Owl Collection**			
80-02-001	Boreal Owl	Boehm	15,000	45.00	75.00
80-02-002	Snowy Owl	Boehm	15,000	45.00	62.50
80-02-003	Barn Owl	Boehm	15,000	45.00	62.50
80-02-004	Saw Whet Owl	Boehm	15,000	45.00	62.50
80-02-005	Great Horned Owl	Boehm	15,000	45.00	62.50
80-02-006	Screech Owl	Boehm	15,000	45.00	62.50
80-02-007	Short Eared Owl	Boehm	15,000	45.00	62.50
80-02-008	Barred Owl	Boehm	15,000	45.00	62.50
Hamilton/Boehm		**Hummingbird Collection**			
80-03-001	Calliope	Boehm	15,000	62.50	80.00
80-03-002	Broadbilled	Boehm	15,000	62.50	62.50
80-03-003	Rufous Flame Bearer	Boehm	15,000	62.50	80.00
80-03-004	Broadtail	Boehm	15,000	62.50	62.50
80-03-005	Streamertail	Boehm	15,000	62.50	80.00
80-03-006	Blue Throated	Boehm	15,000	62.50	80.00
80-03-007	Crimson Topaz	Boehm	15,000	62.50	62.50
80-03-008	Brazilian Ruby	Boehm	15,000	62.50	80.00
Hamilton/Boehm		**Water Birds**			
81-04-001	Canada Geese	Boehm	15,000	62.50	75.00
81-04-002	Wood Ducks	Boehm	15,000	62.50	62.50
81-04-003	Hooded Merganser	Boehm	15,000	62.50	87.00
81-04-004	Ross's Geese	Boehm	15,000	62.50	62.50
81-04-005	Common Mallard	Boehm	15,000	62.50	62.50
81-04-006	Canvas Back	Boehm	15,000	62.50	62.50
81-04-007	Green Winged Teal	Boehm	15,000	62.50	62.50
81-04-008	American Pintail	Boehm	15,000	62.50	62.50
Hamilton/Boehm		**Gamebirds of North America**			
84-05-001	Ring-Necked Pheasant	Boehm	15,000	62.50	62.50
84-05-002	Bob White Quail	Boehm	15,000	62.50	62.50
84-05-003	American Woodcock	Boehm	15,000	62.50	62.50
84-05-004	California Quail	Boehm	15,000	62.50	62.50
84-05-005	Ruffed Grouse	Boehm	15,000	62.50	62.50
84-05-006	Wild Turkey	Boehm	15,000	62.50	62.50
84-05-007	Willow Partridge	Boehm	15,000	62.50	62.50
84-05-008	Prairie Grouse	Boehm	15,000	62.50	62.50
Hamilton Collection		**Precious Portraits**			
87-01-001	Sunbeam	B. P. Gutmann	14-day	24.50	36.00
87-01-002	Mischief	B. P. Gutmann	14-day	24.50	30.00
87-01-003	Peach Blossom	B. P. Gutmann	14-day	24.50	36.00
87-01-004	Goldilocks	B. P. Gutmann	14-day	24.50	30.00
87-01-005	Fairy Gold	B. P. Gutmann	14-day	24.50	36.00
87-01-006	Bunny	B. P. Gutmann	14-day	24.50	30.00
Hamilton Collection		**Bundles of Joy**			
88-02-001	Awakening	B. P. Gutmann	14-day	24.50	75.00
88-02-002	Happy Dreams	B. P. Gutmann	14-day	24.50	60-99.00
88-02-003	Tasting	B. P. Gutmann	14-day	24.50	36-59.00
88-02-004	Sweet Innocence	B. P. Gutmann	14-day	24.50	30.00
88-02-005	Tommy	B. P. Gutmann	14-day	24.50	30.00
88-02-006	A Little Bit of Heaven	B. P. Gutmann	14-day	24.50	75.00
88-02-007	Billy	B. P. Gutmann	14-day	24.50	30-59.00
88-02-008	Sun Kissed	B. P. Gutmann	14-day	24.50	30-35.00
Hamilton Collection		**The Nutcracker Ballet**			
78-03-001	Clara	S. Fisher	28-day	19.50	36.00
79-03-002	Godfather	S. Fisher	28-day	19.50	15-19.50
79-03-003	Sugar Plum Fairy	S. Fisher	28-day	19.50	45.00
79-03-004	Snow Queen and King	S. Fisher	28-day	19.50	40.00
80-03-005	Waltz of the Flowers	S. Fisher	28-day	19.50	19.50
80-03-006	Clara and the Prince	S. Fisher	28-day	19.50	45.00
Hamilton Collection		**Precious Moments Plates**			
79-04-001	Friend in the Sky	T. Utz	28-day	21.50	50.00

Company		Series			
Number	Name	Artist	Edition Limit	Issue Price	Quote
80-04-002	Sand in her Shoe	T. Utz	28-day	21.50	27.00
80-04-003	Snow Bunny	T. Utz	28-day	21.50	18.00
80-04-004	Seashells	T. Utz	28-day	21.50	37.50
81-04-005	Dawn	T. Utz	28-day	21.50	27.00
82-04-006	My Kitty	T. Utz	28-day	21.50	36.00
Hamilton Collection		**The Greatest Show on Earth**			
81-05-001	Clowns	F. Moody	10-day	30.00	45.00
81-05-002	Elephants	F. Moody	10-day	30.00	30.00
81-05-003	Aerialists	F. Moody	10-day	30.00	30.00
81-05-004	Great Parade	F. Moody	10-day	30.00	30.00
81-05-005	Midway	F. Moody	10-day	30.00	30.00
81-05-006	Equestrians	F. Moody	10-day	30.00	30.00
82-05-007	Lion Tamer	F. Moody	10-day	30.00	30.00
82-05-008	Grande Finale	F. Moody	10-day	30.00	30.00
Hamilton Collection		**Rockwell Home of the Brave**			
81-06-001	Reminiscing	N. Rockwell	18,000	35.00	52.50
81-06-002	Hero's Welcome	N. Rockwell	18,000	35.00	52.50
81-06-003	Back to his Old Job	N. Rockwell	18,000	35.00	52.50
81-06-004	War Hero	N. Rockwell	18,000	35.00	35.00
82-06-005	Willie Gillis in Church	N. Rockwell	18,000	35.00	52.50
82-06-006	War Bond	N. Rockwell	18,000	35.00	35.00
82-06-007	Uncle Sam Takes Wings	N. Rockwell	18,000	35.00	75.00
82-06-008	Taking Mother over the Top	N. Rockwell	18,000	35.00	35.00
Hamilton Collection		**Japanese Floral Calendar**			
81-07-001	New Year's Day	Shuho/Kage	10-day	32.50	32.50
82-07-002	Early Spring	Shuho/Kage	10-day	32.50	32.50
82-07-003	Spring	Shuho/Kage	10-day	32.50	32.50
82-07-004	Girl's Doll Day Festival	Shuho/Kage	10-day	32.50	32.50
82-07-005	Buddha's Birthday	Shuho/Kage	10-day	32.50	32.50
82-07-006	Early Summer	Shuho/Kage	10-day	32.50	32.50
82-07-007	Boy's Doll Day Festival	Shuho/Kage	10-day	32.50	32.50
82-07-008	Summer	Shuho/Kage	10-day	32.50	32.50
82-07-009	Autumn	Shuho/Kage	10-day	32.50	32.50
83-07-010	Festival of the Full Moon	Shuho/Kage	10-day	32.50	32.50
83-07-011	Late Autumn	Shuho/Kage	10-day	32.50	32.50
83-07-012	Winter	Shuho/Kage	10-day	32.50	32.50
Hamilton Collection		**Portraits of Childhood**			
81-08-001	Butterfly Magic	T. Utz	28-day	24.95	13.50-24.95
82-08-002	Sweet Dreams	T. Utz	28-day	24.95	24.95
83-08-003	Turtle Talk	T. Utz	28-day	24.95	36.00
84-08-004	Friends Forever	T. Utz	28-day	24.95	24.95
Hamilton Collection		**Carefree Days**			
82-09-001	Autumn Wanderer	T. Utz	10-day	24.50	18.00-24.50
82-09-002	Best Friends	T. Utz	10-day	24.50	30.00
82-09-003	Feeding Time	T. Utz	10-day	24.50	24.50
82-09-004	Bathtime Visitor	T. Utz	10-day	24.50	30.00
82-09-005	First Catch	T. Utz	10-day	24.50	30.00
82-09-006	Monkey Business	T. Utz	10-day	24.50	30.00
82-09-007	Touchdown	T. Utz	10-day	24.50	24.50
82-09-008	Nature Hunt	T. Utz	10-day	24.50	24.50
Hamilton Colletion		**Utz Mother's Day**			
83-10-001	A Gift of Love	T. Utz	N/A	27.50	37.50
83-10-002	Mother's Helping Hand	T. Utz	N/A	27.50	27.50
83-10-003	Mother's Angel	T. Utz	N/A	27.50	27.50
Hamilton Collection		**Single Issues**			
83-11-001	Princess Grace	T. Utz	21-day	39.50	60.00
93-11-002	The Official Honeymooner's Commemorative Plate	D. Bobnick	28-day	37.50	37.50
Hamilton Collection		**Summer Days of Childhood**			
83-12-001	Mountain Friends	T. Utz	10-day	29.50	29.50
83-12-002	Garden Magic	T. Utz	10-day	29.50	29.50
83-12-003	Little Beachcomber	T. Utz	10-day	29.50	29.50
83-12-004	Blowing Bubbles	T. Utz	10-day	29.50	29.50
83-12-005	The Birthday Party	T. Utz	10-day	29.50	29.50
83-12-006	Playing Doctor	T. Utz	10-day	29.50	29.50
83-12-007	A Stolen Kiss	T. Utz	10-day	29.50	29.50
83-12-008	Kitty's Bathtime	T. Utz	10-day	29.50	29.50
83-12-009	Cooling Off	T. Utz	10-day	29.50	29.50
83-12-010	First Customer	T. Utz	10-day	29.50	29.50
83-12-011	A Jumping Contest	T. Utz	10-day	29.50	29.50
83-12-012	Balloon Carnival	T. Utz	10-day	29.50	29.50
Hamilton Collection		**Passage to China**			
83-13-001	Empress of China	R. Massey	15,000	55.00	55.00
83-13-002	Alliance	R. Massey	15,000	55.00	55.00
83-13-003	Grand Turk	R. Massey	15,000	55.00	55.00
85-13-004	Sea Witch	R. Massey	15,000	55.00	55.00
85-13-005	Flying Cloud	R. Massey	15,000	55.00	55.00
85-13-006	Romance of the Seas	R. Massey	15,000	55.00	55.00
85-13-007	Sea Serpent	R. Massey	15,000	55.00	55.00
85-13-008	Challenge	R. Massey	15,000	55.00	55.00
Hamilton Collection		**Springtime of Life**			
85-14-001	Teddy's Bathtime	T. Utz	14-day	29.50	29.50
85-14-002	Just Like Mommy	T. Utz	14-day	29.50	29.50
85-14-003	Among the Daffodils	T. Utz	14-day	29.50	29.50
85-14-004	My Favorite Dolls	T. Utz	14-day	29.50	29.50
85-14-005	Aunt Tillie's Hats	T. Utz	14-day	29.50	29.50
85-14-006	Little Emily	T. Utz	14-day	29.50	29.50
85-14-007	Granny's Boots	T. Utz	14-day	29.50	29.50
85-14-008	My Masterpiece	T. Utz	14-day	29.50	29.50
Hamilton Collection		**A Child's Best Friend**			
85-15-001	In Disgrace	B. P. Gutmann	14-day	24.50	90-199.00
85-15-002	The Reward	B. P. Gutmann	14-day	24.50	60-149.00
85-15-003	Who's Sleepy	B. P. Gutmann	14-day	24.50	90-99.00
85-15-004	Good Morning	B. P. Gutmann	14-day	24.50	75.00
85-15-005	Sympathy	B. P. Gutmann	14-day	24.50	54.00
85-15-006	On the Up and Up	B. P. Gutmann	14-day	24.50	75-99.00
85-15-007	Mine	B. P. Gutmann	14-day	24.50	90.00
85-15-008	Going to Town	B. P. Gutmann	14-day	24.50	60-95.00
Hamilton Collection		**A Country Summer**			
85-16-001	Butterfly Beauty	N. Noel	10-day	29.50	36.00
85-16-002	The Golden Puppy	N. Noel	10-day	29.50	29.50

Company		Series			
Number	Name	Artist	Edition Limit	Issue Price	Quote
86-16-003	The Rocking Chair	N. Noel	10-day	29.50	36.00
86-16-004	My Bunny	N. Noel	10-day	29.50	33.00
88-16-005	The Piglet	N. Noel	10-day	29.50	29.50
88-16-006	Teammates	N. Noel	10-day	29.50	29.50
Hamilton Collection		**The Little Rascals**			
85-17-001	Three for the Show	Unknown	10-day	24.50	30-50.00
85-17-002	My Gal	Unknown	10-day	24.50	24.50
85-17-003	Skeleton Crew	Unknown	10-day	24.50	24.50
85-17-004	Roughin' It	Unknown	10-day	24.50	24.50
85-17-005	Spanky's Pranks	Unknown	10-day	24.50	24.50
85-17-006	Butch's Challenge	Unknown	10-day	24.50	24.50
85-17-007	Darla's Debut	Unknown	10-day	24.50	24.50
85-17-008	Pete's Pal	Unknown	10-day	24.50	24.50
Hamilton Collection		**The Japanese Blossoms of Autumn**			
85-18-001	Bellflower	Koseki/Ebihara	10-day	45.00	45.00
85-18-002	Arrowroot	Koseki/Ebihara	10-day	45.00	45.00
85-18-003	Wild Carnation	Koseki/Ebihara	10-day	45.00	45.00
85-18-004	Maiden Flower	Koseki/Ebihara	10-day	45.00	45.00
85-18-005	Pampas Grass	Koseki/Ebihara	10-day	45.00	45.00
85-18-006	Bush Clover	Koseki/Ebihara	10-day	45.00	45.00
85-18-007	Purple Trousers	Koseki/Ebihara	10-day	45.00	45.00
Hamilton Collection		**Kitten Classics**			
85-18-001	Cat Nap	P. Cooper	14-day	29.50	36.00
85-18-002	Purrfect Treasure	P. Cooper	14-day	29.50	29.50
85-18-003	Wild Flower	P. Cooper	14-day	29.50	29.50
85-18-004	Birdwatcher	P. Cooper	14-day	29.50	29.50
85-18-005	Tiger's Fancy	P. Cooper	14-day	29.50	33.00
85-18-006	Country Kitty	P. Cooper	14-day	29.50	33.00
85-18-007	Little Rascal	P. Cooper	14-day	29.50	29.50
85-18-008	First Prize	P. Cooper	14-day	29.50	29.50
Hamilton Collection		**The Star Wars Plate Collection**			
87-19-001	Hans Solo	T. Blackshear	14-day	29.50	45-79.00
87-19-002	R2-D2 and Wicket	T. Blackshear	14-day	29.50	45-79.00
87-19-003	Luke Skywalker and Darth Vader	T. Blackshear	14-day	29.50	60-79.00
87-19-004	Princess Leia	T. Blackshear	14-day	29.50	60-150.00
87-19-005	The Imperial Walkers	T. Blackshear	14-day	29.50	60-150.00
87-19-006	Luke and Yoda	T. Blackshear	14-day	29.50	60-75.00
88-19-007	Space Battle	T. Blackshear	14-day	29.50	275.00
88-19-008	Crew in Cockpit	T. Blackshear	14-day	29.50	60-150.00
Hamilton Collection		**America's Greatest Sailing Ships**			
88-20-001	USS Constitution	T. Freeman	14-day	29.50	36.00
88-20-002	Great Republic	T. Freeman	14-day	29.50	36.00
88-20-003	America	T. Freeman	14-day	29.50	45.00
88-20-004	Charles W. Morgan	T. Freeman	14-day	29.50	36.00
88-20-005	Eagle	T. Freeman	14-day	29.50	48.00
88-20-006	Bonhomme Richard	T. Freeman	14-day	29.50	36.00
88-20-007	Gertrude L. Thebaud	T. Freeman	14-day	29.50	45.00
88-20-008	Enterprise	T. Freeman	14-day	29.50	36.00
Hamilton Collection		**Noble Owls of America**			
86-21-001	Morning Mist	J. Seerey-Lester	15,000	55.00	55.00
87-21-002	Prairie Sundown	J. Seerey-Lester	15,000	55.00	55.00
87-21-003	Winter Vigil	J. Seerey-Lester	15,000	55.00	55.00
87-21-004	Autumn Mist	J. Seerey-Lester	15,000	55.00	75.00
87-21-005	Dawn in the Willows	J. Seerey-Lester	15,000	55.00	55.00
87-21-006	Snowy Watch	J. Seerey-Lester	15,000	55.00	60.00
88-21-007	Hiding Place	J. Seerey-Lester	15,000	55.00	55.00
88-21-008	Waiting for Dusk	J. Seerey-Lester	15,000	55.00	55.00
Hamilton Collection		**Treasured Days**			
87-22-001	Ashley	H. Bond	14-day	29.50	60.00
87-22-002	Christopher	H. Bond	14-day	24.50	45.00
87-22-003	Sara	H. Bond	14-day	24.50	30.00
87-22-004	Jeremy	H. Bond	14-day	24.50	45.00
87-22-005	Amanda	H. Bond	14-day	24.50	45.00
88-22-006	Nicholas	H. Bond	14-day	24.50	45.00
88-22-007	Lindsay	H. Bond	14-day	24.50	45.00
88-22-008	Justin	H. Bond	14-day	24.50	45.00
Hamilton Collection		**Butterfly Garden**			
87-23-001	Spicebush Swallowtail	P. Sweany	14-day	29.50	45.00
87-23-002	Common Blue	P. Sweany	14-day	29.50	37.50
87-23-003	Orange Sulphur	P. Sweany	14-day	29.50	30.00
87-23-004	Monarch	P. Sweany	14-day	29.50	37.50
87-23-005	Tiger Swallowtail	P. Sweany	14-day	29.50	30.00
87-23-006	Crimson Patched Longwing	P. Sweany	14-day	29.50	37.50
88-23-007	Morning Cloak	P. Sweany	14-day	29.50	29.50
88-23-008	Red Admiral	P. Sweany	14-day	29.50	37.50
Hamilton Collection		**The Golden Classics**			
87-24-001	Sleeping Beauty	C. Lawson	10-day	37.50	37.50
87-24-002	Rumpelstiltskin	C. Lawson	10-day	37.50	37.50
87-24-003	Jack and the Beanstalk	C. Lawson	10-day	37.50	37.50
87-24-004	Snow White and Rose Red	C. Lawson	10-day	37.50	37.50
87-24-005	Hansel and Gretel	C. Lawson	10-day	37.50	37.50
88-24-006	Cinderella	C. Lawson	10-day	37.50	37.50
88-24-007	The Golden Goose	C. Lawson	10-day	37.50	37.50
88-24-008	The Snow Queen	C. Lawson	10-day	37.50	37.50
Hamilton Collection		**Children of the American Frontier**			
86-25-001	In Trouble Again	D. Crook	10-day	24.50	35.00
86-25-002	Tubs and Suds	D. Crook	10-day	24.50	27.00
86-25-003	A Lady Needs a Little Privacy	D. Crook	10-day	24.50	24.50
86-25-004	The Desperadoes	D. Crook	10-day	24.50	27.00
86-25-005	Riders Wanted	D. Crook	10-day	24.50	30.00
87-25-006	A Cowboy's Downfall	D. Crook	10-day	24.50	24.50
87-25-007	Runaway Blues	D. Crook	10-day	24.50	24.50
87-25-008	A Special Patient	D. Crook	10-day	24.50	24.50
Hamilton Collection		**Puppy Playtime**			
87-25-001	Double Take-Cocker Spaniels	J. Lamb	14-day	24.50	75.00
87-25-002	Catch of the Day-Golden Retrievers	J. Lamb	14-day	24.50	45.00
87-25-003	Cabin Fever-Black Labradors	J. Lamb	14-day	24.50	45.00
87-25-004	Weekend Gardener-Lhasa Apsos	J. Lamb	14-day	24.50	36.00
87-25-005	Getting Acquainted-Beagles	J. Lamb	14-day	24.50	36.00
87-25-006	Hanging Out-German Shepherd	J. Lamb	14-day	24.50	45.00
87-25-007	New Leash on Life-Mini Schnauzer	J. Lamb	14-day	24.50	45.00
87-25-008	Fun and Games-Poodle	J. Lamb	14-day	24.50	36.00

Number	Name	Artist	Edition Limit	Issue Price	Quote
Company		**Series**			
Hamilton Collection		**The Official Honeymooners Plate Collection**			
87-26-001	The Honeymooners	D. Kilmer	14-day	24.50	60-129.00
87-26-002	The Hucklebuck	D. Kilmer	14-day	24.50	90-150.00
87-26-003	Baby, You're the Greatest	D. Kilmer	14-day	24.50	60-175.00
88-26-004	The Golfer	D. Kilmer	14-day	24.50	99-149.00
88-26-005	The TV Chefs	D. Kilmer	14-day	24.50	120-129.
88-26-006	Bang! Zoom!	D. Kilmer	14-day	24.50	60-129.00
88-26-007	The Only Way to Travel	D. Kilmer	14-day	24.50	120.00
88-26-008	The Honeymoon Express	D. Kilmer	14-day	24.50	150-299.
Hamilton Collection		**North American Waterbirds**			
88-27-001	Wood Ducks	R. Lawrence	14-day	37.50	54.00
88-27-002	Hooded Mergansers	R. Lawrence	14-day	37.50	54.00
88-27-003	Pintails	R. Lawrence	14-day	37.50	45.00
88-27-004	Canada Geese	R. Lawrence	14-day	37.50	45.00
89-27-005	American Widgeons	R. Lawrence	14-day	37.50	54.00
89-27-006	Canvasbacks	R. Lawrence	14-day	37.50	55.00
89-27-007	Mallard Pair	R. Lawrence	14-day	37.50	60.00
89-27-008	Snow Geese	R. Lawrence	14-day	37.50	45.00
Hamilton Collection		**Nature's Quiet Moments**			
88-28-001	A Curious Pair	R. Parker	14-day	37.50	37.50
88-28-002	Northern Morning	R. Parker	14-day	37.50	37.50
88-28-003	Just Resting	R. Parker	14-day	37.50	37.50
89-28-004	Waiting Out the Storm	R. Parker	14-day	37.50	37.50
89-28-005	Creekside	R. Parker	14-day	37.50	37.50
89-28-006	Autumn Foraging	R. Parker	14-day	37.50	37.50
89-28-007	Old Man of the Mountain	R. Parker	14-day	37.50	37.50
89-28-008	Mountain Blooms	R. Parker	14-day	37.50	37.50
Hamilton Collection		**Wizard of Oz Commemorative**			
88-29-001	We're Off to See the Wizard	T. Blackshear	14-day	24.50	156-250.
88-29-002	Dorothy Meets the Scarecrow	T. Blackshear	14-day	24.50	90-135.00
89-29-003	The Tin Man Speaks	T. Blackshear	14-day	24.50	105-150.
89-29-004	A Glimpse of the Munchkins	T. Blackshear	14-day	24.50	90-135.00
89-29-005	The Witch Casts A Spell	T. Blackshear	14-day	24.50	100-175.
89-29-006	If I Were King Of The Forest	T. Blackshear	14-day	24.50	120-175.
89-29-007	The Great and Powerful Oz	T. Blackshear	14-day	24.50	120-165.
89-29-008	There's No Place Like Home	T. Blackshear	14-day	24.50	120-189.
Hamilton Collection		**Petals and Purrs**			
88-30-001	Blushing Beauties	B. Harrison	14-day	24.50	45.00
88-30-002	Spring Fever	B. Harrison	14-day	24.50	37.50
88-30-003	Morning Glories	B. Harrison	14-day	24.50	36.00
88-30-004	Forget-Me-Not	B. Harrison	14-day	24.50	36.00
89-30-005	Golden Fancy	B. Harrison	14-day	24.50	30.00
89-30-006	Pink Lillies	B. Harrison	14-day	24.50	30.00
89-30-007	Summer Sunshine	B. Harrison	14-day	24.50	30.00
89-30-008	Siamese Summer	B. Harrison	14-day	24.50	30.00
Hamilton Collection		**The Jeweled Hummingbirds Plate Collection**			
89-31-001	Ruby-throated Hummingbirds	J. Landenberger	14-day	37.50	37.50
89-31-002	Great Sapphire Wing Hummingbirds	J. Landenberger	14-day	37.50	37.50
89-31-003	Ruby-Topaz Hummingbirds	J. Landenberger	14-day	37.50	37.50
89-31-004	Andean Emerald Hummingbirds	J. Landenberger	14-day	37.50	37.50
89-31-005	Garnet-throated Hummingbirds	J. Landenberger	14-day	37.50	37.50
89-31-006	Blue-Headed Sapphire Hummingbirds	J. Landenberger	14-day	37.50	37.50
89-31-007	Pearl Coronet Hummingbirds	J. Landenberger	14-day	37.50	37.50
89-31-008	Amethyst-throated Sunangels	J. Landenberger	14-day	37.50	37.50
Hamilton Collection		**Stained Glass Gardens**			
89-32-001	Peacock and Wisteria	Unknown	15,000	55.00	55.00
89-32-002	Garden Sunset	Unknown	15,000	55.00	55.00
89-32-003	The Cockatoo's Garden	Unknown	15,000	55.00	55.00
89-32-004	Waterfall and Iris	Unknown	15,000	55.00	55.00
90-32-005	Roses and Magnolias	Unknown	15,000	55.00	55.00
90-32-006	A Hollyhock Sunrise	Unknown	15,000	55.00	55.00
90-32-007	Peaceful Waters	Unknown	15,000	55.00	55.00
90-32-008	Springtime in the Valley	Unknown	15,000	55.00	55.00
Hamilton Collection		**The I Love Lucy Plate Collection**			
89-33-001	California, Here We Come	J. Kritz	14-day	29.50	54-120.00
89-33-002	It's Just Like Candy	J. Kritz	14-day	29.50	60-110.00
90-33-003	The Big Squeeze	J. Kritz	14-day	29.50	59-95.00
90-33-004	Eating the Evidence	J. Kritz	14-day	29.50	83-135.00
90-33-005	Two of a Kind	J. Kritz	14-day	29.50	45-85.00
91-33-006	Queen of the Gypsies	J. Kritz	14-day	29.50	54-90.00
92-33-007	Night at the Copa	J. Kritz	14-day	29.50	39-105.00
92-33-008	A Rising Problem	J. Kritz	14-day	29.50	48-100.00
Hamilton Collection		**Great Fighter Planes Of World War II**			
92-34-001	Old Crow	R. Waddey	14-day	29.50	29.50
92-34-002	Big Hog	R. Waddey	14-day	29.50	29.50
92-34-003	P-47 Thunderbolt	R. Waddey	14-day	29.50	29.50
92-34-004	P-40 Flying Tiger	R. Waddey	14-day	29.50	29.50
92-34-005	F4F Wildcat	R. Waddey	14-day	29.50	29.50
92-34-006	P-38F Lightning	R. Waddey	14-day	29.50	29.50
93-34-007	F6F Hellcat	R. Waddey	14-day	29.50	29.50
93-34-008	P-39M Airacobra	R. Waddey	14-day	29.50	29.50
Hamilton Collection		**Birds of the Temple Gardens**			
89-35-001	Doves of Fidelity	J. Cheng	14-day	29.50	29.50
89-35-002	Cranes of Eternal Life	J. Cheng	14-day	29.50	29.50
89-35-003	Honorable Swallows	J. Cheng	14-day	29.50	29.50
89-35-004	Oriental White Eyes of Beauty	J. Cheng	14-day	29.50	29.50
89-35-005	Pheasants of Good Fortune	J. Cheng	14-day	29.50	29.50
89-35-006	Imperial Goldcrest	J. Cheng	14-day	29.50	29.50
89-35-007	Goldfinches of Virtue	J. Cheng	14-day	29.50	29.50
89-35-008	Magpies: Birds of Good Omen	J. Cheng	14-day	29.50	29.50
Hamilton Collection		**Winter Wildlife**			
89-36-001	Close Encounters	J. Seerey-Lester	15,000	55.00	55.00
89-36-002	Among the Cattails	J. Seerey-Lester	15,000	55.00	55.00
89-36-003	The Refuge	J. Seerey-Lester	15,000	55.00	55.00
89-36-004	Out of the Blizzard	J. Seerey-Lester	15,000	55.00	55.00
89-36-005	First Snow	J. Seerey-Lester	15,000	55.00	55.00
89-36-006	Lying In Wait	J. Seerey-Lester	15,000	55.00	55.00
89-36-007	Winter Hiding	J. Seerey-Lester	15,000	55.00	55.00
89-36-008	Early Snow	J. Seerey-Lester	15,000	55.00	55.00
Hamilton Collection		**Big Cats of the World**			
89-37-001	African Shade	D. Manning	14-day	29.50	29.50
89-37-002	View from Above	D. Manning	14-day	29.50	29.50

Number	Name	Artist	Edition Limit	Issue Price	Quote
Company		**Series**			
90-37-003	On The Prowl	D. Manning	14-day	29.50	29.50
90-37-004	Deep In The Jungle	D. Manning	14-day	29.50	29.50
90-37-005	Spirit Of The Mountain	D. Manning	14-day	29.50	29.50
90-37-006	Spotted Sentinel	D. Manning	14-day	29.50	29.50
90-37-007	Above the Treetops	D. Manning	14-day	29.50	29.50
90-37-008	Mountain Dweller	D. Manning	14-day	29.50	29.50
92-37-009	Jungle Habitat	D. Manning	14-day	29.50	29.50
92-37-010	Solitary Sentry	D. Manning	14-day	29.50	29.50
Hamilton Collection		**Mixed Company**			
90-38-001	Two Against One	P. Cooper	14-day	29.50	36.00
90-38-002	A Sticky Situation	P. Cooper	14-day	29.50	36.00
90-38-003	What's Up	P. Cooper	14-day	29.50	29.50
90-38-004	All Wrapped Up	P. Cooper	14-day	29.50	36.00
90-38-005	Picture Perfect	P. Cooper	14-day	29.50	29.50
91-38-006	A Moment to Unwind	P. Cooper	14-day	29.50	33.00
91-38-007	Ole	P. Cooper	14-day	29.50	33.00
91-38-008	Picnic Prowlers	P. Cooper	14-day	29.50	29.50
Hamilton Collection		**Portraits From Oz**			
89-39-001	Dorothy	T. Blackshear	14-day	29.50	75-139.00
89-39-002	Scarecrow	T. Blackshear	14-day	29.50	75-99.00
89-39-003	Tin Man	T. Blackshear	14-day	29.50	75-125.00
90-39-004	Cowardly Lion	T. Blackshear	14-day	29.50	75-120.00
90-39-005	Glinda	T. Blackshear	14-day	29.50	75-115.00
90-39-006	Wizard	T. Blackshear	14-day	29.50	75-115.00
90-39-007	Wicked Witch	T. Blackshear	14-day	29.50	90-250.00
90-39-008	Toto	T. Blackshear	14-day	29.50	150-250.
Hamilton Collection		**Delights of Childhood**			
89-40-001	Crayon Creations	J. Lamb	14-day	29.50	29.50
89-40-002	Little Mother	J. Lamb	14-day	29.50	29.50
90-40-003	Bathing Beauty	J. Lamb	14-day	29.50	29.50
90-40-004	Is That You, Granny?	J. Lamb	14-day	29.50	36.00
90-40-005	Nature's Little Helper	J. Lamb	14-day	29.50	29.50
90-40-006	So Sorry	J. Lamb	14-day	29.50	33.00
90-40-007	Shower Time	J. Lamb	14-day	29.50	33.00
90-40-008	Storytime Friends	J. Lamb	14-day	29.50	29.50
Hamilton Collection		**Classic Sporting Dogs**			
89-41-001	Golden Retrievers	B. Christie	14-day	24.50	54.00
89-41-002	Labrador Retrievers	B. Christie	14-day	24.50	60.00
89-41-003	Beagles	B. Christie	14-day	24.50	36.00
89-41-004	Pointers	B. Christie	14-day	24.50	30.00
89-41-005	Springer Spaniels	B. Christie	14-day	24.50	39.00
90-41-006	German Short-Haired Pointers	B. Christie	14-day	24.50	54.00
90-41-007	Irish Setters	B. Christie	14-day	24.50	36.00
90-41-008	Brittany Spaniels	B. Christie	14-day	24.50	48.00
Hamilton Collection		**Majesty of Flight**			
89-42-001	The Eagle Soars	T. Hirata	14-day	37.50	48.00
89-42-002	Realm of the Red-Tail	T. Hirata	14-day	37.50	39.00
89-42-003	Coastal Journey	T. Hirata	14-day	37.50	45.00
89-42-004	Sentry of the North	T. Hirata	14-day	37.50	48.00
89-42-005	Commanding the Marsh	T. Hirata	14-day	37.50	37.50-45.00
90-42-006	The Vantage Point	T. Hirata	14-day	29.50	45.00
90-42-007	Silent Watch	T. Hirata	14-day	29.50	48.00
90-42-008	Fierce and Free	T. Hirata	14-day	29.50	45.00
Hamilton Collection		**The Proud Nation**			
89-43-001	Navajo Little One	R. Swanson	14-day	24.50	45.00
89-43-002	In a Big Land	R. Swanson	14-day	24.50	24.50
89-43-003	Out with Mama's Flock	R. Swanson	14-day	24.50	24.50
89-43-004	Newest Little Sheepherder	R. Swanson	14-day	24.50	30.00
89-43-005	Dressed Up for the Powwow	R. Swanson	14-day	24.50	30.00
89-43-006	Just a Few Days Old	R. Swanson	14-day	24.50	30.00
89-43-007	Autumn Treat	R. Swanson	14-day	24.50	30.00
89-43-008	Up in the Red Rocks	R. Swanson	14-day	24.50	24.50
Hamilton Collection		**Thornton Utz 10th Anniversary Commemorative Plate Collection**			
89-44-001	Dawn	T. Utz	14-day	29.50	29.50
89-44-002	Just Like Mommy	T. Utz	14-day	29.50	29.50
89-44-003	Playing Doctor	T. Utz	14-day	29.50	29.50
89-44-004	My Kitty	T. Utz	14-day	29.50	29.50
89-44-005	Turtle Talk	T. Utz	14-day	29.50	29.50
89-44-006	Best Friends	T. Utz	14-day	29.50	29.50
89-44-007	Among the Daffodils	T. Utz	14-day	29.50	39.00
89-44-008	Friends in the Sky	T. Utz	14-day	29.50	29.50
89-44-009	Teddy's Bathtime	T. Utz	14-day	29.50	29.50
89-44-010	Little Emily	T. Utz	14-day	29.50	29.50
Hamilton Collection		**Country Kitties**			
89-45-001	Mischief Makers	G. Gerardi	14-day	24.50	45.00
89-45-002	Table Manners	G. Gerardi	14-day	24.50	36.00
89-45-003	Attic Attack	G. Gerardi	14-day	24.50	45.00
89-45-004	Rock and Rollers	G. Gerardi	14-day	24.50	40.00
89-45-005	Just For the Fern of It	G. Gerardi	14-day	24.50	40.00
89-45-006	All Washed Up	G. Gerardi	14-day	24.50	39.00
89-45-007	Stroller Derby	G. Gerardi	14-day	24.50	39.00
89-45-008	Captive Audience	G. Gerardi	14-day	24.50	39.00
Hamilton Collection		**Winged Reflections**			
89-46-001	Following Mama	R. Parker	14-day	37.50	37.50
89-46-002	Above the Breakers	R. Parker	14-day	37.50	37.50
89-46-003	Among the Reeds	R. Parker	14-day	37.50	37.50
89-46-004	Freeze Up	R. Parker	14-day	37.50	37.50
89-46-005	Wings Above the Water	R. Parker	14-day	37.50	37.50
90-46-006	Summer Loon	R. Parker	14-day	29.50	29.50
90-46-007	Early Spring	R. Parker	14-day	29.50	29.50
90-46-008	At The Water's Edge	R. Parker	14-day	29.50	29.50
Hamilton Collection		**Elvis Remembered**			
89-47-001	Loving You	S. Morton	90-day	37.50	75-99.00
89-47-002	Early Years	S. Morton	90-day	37.50	75-99.00
89-47-003	Tenderly	S. Morton	90-day	37.50	75-99.00
89-47-004	The King	S. Morton	90-day	37.50	75-129.00
89-47-005	Forever Yours	S. Morton	90-day	37.50	75-99.00
89-47-006	Rockin in the Moonlight	S. Morton	90-day	37.50	75-99.00
89-47-007	Moody Blues	S. Morton	90-day	37.50	75-99.00
89-47-008	Elvis Presley	S. Morton	90-day	37.50	125-129.
Hamilton Collection		**Fifty Years of Oz**			
89-48-001	Fifty Years of Oz	T. Blackshear	14-day	37.50	120-175.

Company / Number	Name	Series / Artist	Edition Limit	Issue Price	Quote
Hamilton Collection		**Small Wonders of the Wild**			
89-49-001	Hideaway	C. Frace	14-day	29.50	45.00
90-49-002	Young Explorers	C. Frace	14-day	29.50	36.00
90-49-003	Three of a Kind	C. Frace	14-day	29.50	75.00
90-49-004	Quiet Morning	C. Frace	14-day	29.50	29.50
90-49-005	Eyes of Wonder	C. Frace	14-day	29.50	29.50
90-49-006	Ready for Adventure	C. Frace	14-day	29.50	29.50
90-49-007	Uno	C. Frace	14-day	29.50	29.50
90-49-008	Exploring a New World	C. Frace	14-day	29.50	29.50
Hamilton Collection		**Dear to My Heart**			
90-50-001	Cathy	J. Hagara	14-day	29.50	29.50
90-50-002	Addie	J. Hagara	14-day	29.50	29.50
90-50-003	Jimmy	J. Hagara	14-day	29.50	29.50
90-50-004	Dacy	J. Hagara	14-day	29.50	29.50
90-50-005	Paul	J. Hagara	14-day	29.50	29.50
91-50-006	Shelly	J. Hagara	14-day	29.50	29.50
91-50-007	Jenny	J. Hagara	14-day	29.50	29.50
91-50-008	Joy	J. Hagara	14-day	29.50	29.50
Hamilton Collection		**North American Gamebirds**			
90-51-001	Ring-necked Pheasant	J. Killen	14-day	37.50	37.50
90-51-002	Bobwhite Quail	J. Killen	14-day	37.50	45.00
90-51-003	Ruffed Grouse	J. Killen	14-day	37.50	37.50
90-51-004	Gambel Quail	J. Killen	14-day	37.50	42.00
90-51-005	Mourning Dove	J. Killen	14-day	37.50	45.00
90-51-006	Woodcock	J. Killen	14-day	37.50	45.00
91-51-007	Chukar Partridge	J. Killen	14-day	37.50	45.00
91-51-008	Wild Turkey	J. Killen	14-day	37.50	45.00
Hamilton Collection		**The Saturday Evening Post Plate Collection**			
89-52-001	The Wonders of Radio	N. Rockwell	14-day	35.00	35.00
89-52-002	Easter Morning	N. Rockwell	14-day	35.00	60.00
89-52-003	The Facts of Life	N. Rockwell	14-day	35.00	35.00
90-52-004	The Window Washer	N. Rockwell	14-day	35.00	45.00
90-52-005	First Flight	N. Rockwell	14-day	35.00	54.00
90-52-006	Traveling Companion	N. Rockwell	14-day	35.00	35.00
90-52-007	Jury Room	N. Rockwell	14-day	35.00	35.00
90-52-008	Furlough	N. Rockwell	14-day	35.00	35.00
Hamilton Collection		**Favorite American Songbirds**			
89-53-001	Blue Jays of Spring	D. O'Driscoll	14-day	29.50	36.00
89-53-002	Red Cardinals of Winter	D. O'Driscoll	14-day	29.50	36.00
89-53-003	Robins & Apple Blossoms	D. O'Driscoll	14-day	29.50	36.00
89-53-004	Goldfinches of Summer	D. O'Driscoll	14-day	29.50	36.00
90-53-005	Autumn Chickadees	D. O'Driscoll	14-day	29.50	36.00
90-53-006	Bluebirds and Morning Glories	D. O'Driscoll	14-day	29.50	36.00
90-53-007	Tufted Titmouse and Holly	D. O'Driscoll	14-day	29.50	29.50
91-53-008	Carolina Wrens of Spring	D. O'Driscoll	14-day	29.50	29.50
Hamilton Collection		**Coral Paradise**			
89-54-001	The Living Oasis	H. Bond	14-day	29.50	29.50
90-54-002	Riches of the Coral Sea	H. Bond	14-day	29.50	29.50
90-54-003	Tropical Pageantry	H. Bond	14-day	29.50	36.00
90-54-004	Caribbean Spectacle	H. Bond	14-day	29.50	33.00
90-54-005	Undersea Village	H. Bond	14-day	29.50	36.00
90-54-006	Shimmering Reef Dwellers	H. Bond	14-day	29.50	36.00
90-54-007	Mysteries of the Galapagos	H. Bond	14-day	29.50	33.00
90-54-008	Forest Beneath the Sea	H. Bond	14-day	29.50	29.50
Hamilton Collection		**Noble American Indian Women**			
89-55-001	Sacajawea	D. Wright	14-day	29.50	45.00
90-55-002	Pocahontas	D. Wright	14-day	29.50	45.00
90-55-003	Minnehaha	D. Wright	14-day	29.50	36.00
90-55-004	Pine Leaf	D. Wright	14-day	29.50	45.00
90-55-005	Lily of the Mohawk	D. Wright	14-day	29.50	36.00
90-55-006	White Rose	D. Wright	14-day	29.50	45.00
91-55-007	Lozen	D. Wright	14-day	29.50	33.00
91-55-008	Falling Star	D. Wright	14-day	29.50	45.00
Hamilton Collection		**Little Ladies**			
89-56-001	Playing Bridesmaid	M.H. Bogart	14-day	29.50	60-100.00
90-56-002	The Seamstress	M.H. Bogart	14-day	29.50	45-60.00
90-56-003	Little Captive	M.H. Bogart	14-day	29.50	45.00
90-56-004	Playing Mama	M.H. Bogart	14-day	29.50	54.00
90-56-005	Susanna	M.H. Bogart	14-day	29.50	45-60.00
90-56-006	Kitty's Bath	M.H. Bogart	14-day	29.50	54-65.00
90-56-007	A Day in the Country	M.H. Bogart	14-day	29.50	45-60.00
91-56-008	Sarah	M.H. Bogart	14-day	29.50	45.00
91-56-009	First Party	M.H. Bogart	14-day	29.50	29.50
91-56-010	The Magic Kitten	M.H. Bogart	14-day	29.50	29.50
Hamilton Collection		**A Country Season of Horses**			
90-57-001	First Day of Spring	J.M. Vass	14-day	29.50	36.00
90-57-002	Summer Splendor	J.M. Vass	14-day	29.50	33.00
90-57-003	A Winter's Walk	J.M. Vass	14-day	29.50	33.00
90-57-004	Autumn Grandeur	J.M. Vass	14-day	29.50	29.50
90-57-005	Cliffside Beauty	J.M. Vass	14-day	29.50	29.50
90-57-006	Frosty Morning	J.M. Vass	14-day	29.50	29.50
90-57-007	Crisp Country Morning	J.M. Vass	14-day	29.50	29.50
90-57-008	River Retreat	J.M. Vass	14-day	29.50	29.50
Hamilton Collection		**Good Sports**			
90-58-001	Wide Retriever	J. Lamb	14-day	29.50	45.00
90-58-002	Double Play	J. Lamb	14-day	29.50	36.00
90-58-003	Hole in One	J. Lamb	14-day	29.50	60.00
90-58-004	The Bass Masters	J. Lamb	14-day	29.50	36.00
90-58-005	Spotted on the Sideline	J. Lamb	14-day	29.50	36.00
90-58-006	Slap Shot	J. Lamb	14-day	29.50	36.00
91-58-007	Net Play	J. Lamb	14-day	29.50	45.00
91-58-008	Bassetball	J. Lamb	14-day	29.50	36.00
92-58-009	Boxer Rebellion	J. Lamb	14-day	29.50	33.00
92-58-010	Great Try	J. Lamb	14-day	29.50	39.00
Hamilton Collection		**Curious Kittens**			
90-59-001	Rainy Day Friends	B. Harrison	14-day	29.50	36.00
90-59-002	Keeping in Step	B. Harrison	14-day	29.50	36.00
91-59-003	Delightful Discovery	B. Harrison	14-day	29.50	36.00
91-59-004	Chance Meeting	B. Harrison	14-day	29.50	36.00
91-59-005	All Wound Up	B. Harrison	14-day	29.50	36.00
91-59-006	Making Tracks	B. Harrison	14-day	29.50	36.00
91-59-007	Playing Cat and Mouse	B. Harrison	14-day	29.50	36.00
91-59-008	A Paw's in the Action	B. Harrison	14-day	29.50	36.00
92-59-009	Little Scholar	B. Harrison	14-day	29.50	36.00
92-59-010	Cat Burglar	B. Harrison	14-day	29.50	36.00
Hamilton Collection		**The American Civil War**			
90-60-001	General Robert E. Lee	D. Prechtel	14-day	37.50	48.00
90-60-002	Generals Grant and Lee At Appomattox	D. Prechtel	14-day	37.50	48.00
90-60-003	General Thomas "Stonewall" Jackson	D. Prechtel	14-day	37.50	54.00
90-60-004	Abraham Lincoln	D. Prechtel	14-day	37.50	60.00
91-60-005	General J.E.B. Stuart	D. Prechtel	14-day	37.50	45.00
91-60-006	General Philip Sheridan	D. Prechtel	14-day	37.50	45.00
91-60-007	A Letter from Home	D. Prechtel	14-day	37.50	60.00
91-60-008	Going Home	D. Prechtel	14-day	37.50	45.00
92-60-009	Assembling The Troop	D. Prechtel	14-day	37.50	45.00
92-60-010	Standing Watch	D. Prechtel	14-day	37.50	45.00
Hamilton Collection		**Growing Up Together**			
90-61-001	My Very Best Friends	P. Brooks	14-day	29.50	36.00
90-61-002	Tea for Two	P. Brooks	14-day	29.50	29.50
90-61-003	Tender Loving Care	P. Brooks	14-day	29.50	29.50
90-61-004	Picnic Pals	P. Brooks	14-day	29.50	29.50
91-61-005	Newfound Friends	P. Brooks	14-day	29.50	29.50
91-61-006	Kitten Caboodle	P. Brooks	14-day	29.50	29.50
91-61-007	Fishing Buddies	P. Brooks	14-day	29.50	29.50
91-61-008	Bedtime Blessings	P. Brooks	14-day	29.50	29.50
Hamilton Collection		**Classic TV Westerns**			
90-62-001	The Lone Ranger and Tonto	K. Milnazik	14-day	29.50	69.00
90-62-002	Bonanza ™	K. Milnazik	14-day	29.50	60-65.00
90-62-003	Roy Rogers and Dale Evans	K. Milnazik	14-day	29.50	60-69.00
91-62-004	Rawhide	K. Milnazik	14-day	29.50	36-69.00
91-62-005	Wild Wild West	K. Milnazik	14-day	29.50	60-69.00
91-62-006	Have Gun, Will Travel	K. Milnazik	14-day	29.50	36-69.00
91-62-007	The Virginian	K. Milnazik	14-day	29.50	29.50-69.00
91-62-008	Hopalong Cassidy	K. Milnazik	14-day	29.50	60-79.00
Hamilton Collection		**Timeless Expressions of the Orient**			
90-63-001	Fidelity	M. Tsang	15,000	75.00	95.00
91-63-002	Femininity	M. Tsang	15,000	75.00	75.00
91-63-003	Longevity	M. Tsang	15,000	75.00	75.00
91-63-004	Beauty	M. Tsang	15,000	55.00	55.00
92-63-005	Courage	M. Tsang	15,000	55.00	55.00
Hamilton Collection		**Star Wars 10th Anniversary Commemorative**			
90-64-001	Star Wars 10th Anniversary Commemorative Plates	T. Blackshear	14-day	39.50	89-95.00
Hamilton Collection		**Romantic Castles of Europe**			
90-65-001	Ludwig's Castle	D. Sweet	19,500	55.00	55.00
91-65-002	Palace of the Moors	D. Sweet	19,500	55.00	55.00
91-65-003	Swiss Isle Fortress	D. Sweet	19,500	55.00	55.00
91-65-004	The Legendary Castle of Leeds	D. Sweet	19,500	55.00	55.00
91-65-005	Davinci's Chambord	D. Sweet	19,500	55.00	55.00
91-65-006	Eilean Donan	D. Sweet	19,500	55.00	55.00
92-65-007	Eltz Castle	D. Sweet	19,500	55.00	55.00
92-65-008	Kylemore Abbey	D. Sweet	19,500	55.00	55.00
Hamilton Collection		**The American Rose Garden**			
88-66-001	American Spirit	P.J. Sweany	14-day	29.50	29.50
88-66-002	Peace Rose	P.J. Sweany	14-day	29.50	29.50
89-66-003	White Knight	P.J. Sweany	14-day	29.50	36.00
89-66-004	American Heritage	P.J. Sweany	14-day	29.50	36.00
89-66-005	Eclipse	P.J. Sweany	14-day	29.50	33.00
89-66-006	Blue Moon	P.J. Sweany	14-day	29.50	36.00
89-66-007	Coral Cluster	P.J. Sweany	14-day	29.50	33.00
89-66-008	President Herbert Hoover	P.J. Sweany	14-day	29.50	29.50
Hamilton Collection		**English Country Cottages**			
90-67-001	Periwinkle Tea Room	M. Bell	14-day	29.50	45.00
91-67-002	Gamekeeper's Cottage	M. Bell	14-day	29.50	75.00
91-67-003	Ginger Cottage	M. Bell	14-day	29.50	60.00
91-67-004	Larkspur Cottage	M. Bell	14-day	29.50	36.00
91-67-005	The Chaplain's Garden	M. Bell	14-day	29.50	33.00
91-67-006	Lorna Doone Cottage	M. Bell	14-day	29.50	29.50
91-67-007	Murrle Cottage	M. Bell	14-day	29.50	29.50
91-67-008	Lullabye Cottage	M. Bell	14-day	29.50	29.50
Hamilton Collection		**The Angler's Prize**			
91-68-001	Trophy Bass	M. Susinno	14-day	29.50	36.00
91-68-002	Blue Ribbon Trout	M. Susinno	14-day	29.50	33.00
91-68-003	Sun Dancers	M. Susinno	14-day	29.50	36.00
91-68-004	Freshwater Barracuda	M. Susinno	14-day	29.50	36.00
91-68-005	Bronzeback Fighter	M. Susinno	14-day	29.50	36.00
91-68-006	Autumn Beauty	M. Susinno	14-day	29.50	36.00
92-68-007	Old Mooneyes	M. Susinno	14-day	29.50	36.00
92-68-008	Silver King	M. Susinno	14-day	29.50	33.00
Hamilton Collection		**Woodland Encounters**			
91-69-001	Want to Play?	G. Giordano	14-day	29.50	29.50
91-69-002	Peek-a-boo!	G. Giordano	14-day	29.50	29.50
91-69-003	Lunchtime Visitor	G. Giordano	14-day	29.50	33.00
91-69-004	Anyone for a Swim?	G. Giordano	14-day	29.50	36.00
91-69-005	Nature Scouts	G. Giordano	14-day	29.50	33.00
91-69-006	Meadow Meeting	G. Giordano	14-day	29.50	33.00
91-69-007	Hi Neighbor	G. Giordano	14-day	29.50	29.50
92-69-008	Field Day	G. Giordano	14-day	29.50	36.00
Hamilton Collection		**Childhood Reflections**			
91-70-001	Harmony	B.P. Gutmann	14-day	29.50	45-100.00
91-70-002	Kitty's Breakfast	B.P. Gutmann	14-day	29.50	29.50
91-70-003	Friendly Enemies	B.P. Gutmann	14-day	29.50	36.00
91-70-004	Smile, Smile, Smile	B.P. Gutmann	14-day	29.50	29.50
91-70-005	Lullaby	B.P. Gutmann	14-day	29.50	29.50
91-70-006	Oh! Oh! A Bunny	B.P. Gutmann	14-day	29.50	29.50
91-70-007	Little Mother	B.P. Gutmann	14-day	29.50	29.50
91-70-008	Thank You, God	B.P. Gutmann	14-day	29.50	36.00
Hamilton Collection		**Great Mammals of the Sea**			
91-71-001	Orca Trio	Wyland	14-day	35.00	45.00
91-71-002	Hawaii Dolphins	Wyland	14-day	35.00	37.50
91-71-003	Orca Journey	Wyland	14-day	35.00	43.00
91-71-004	Dolphin Paradise	Wyland	14-day	35.00	45.00
91-71-005	Children of the Sea	Wyland	14-day	35.00	60.00
91-71-006	Kissing Dolphins	Wyland	14-day	35.00	39.00
91-71-007	Islands	Wyland	14-day	35.00	45.00
91-71-008	Orcas	Wyland	14-day	35.00	45.00

Company / Number	Name	Series / Artist	Edition Limit	Issue Price	Quote
Hamilton Collection		**The West of Frank McCarthy**			
91-72-001	Attacking the Iron Horse	F. McCarthy	14-day	37.50	60.00
91-72-002	Attempt on the Stage	F. McCarthy	14-day	37.50	45.00
91-72-003	The Prayer	F. McCarthy	14-day	37.50	54.00
91-72-004	On the Old North Trail	F. McCarthy	14-day	37.50	48.00
91-72-005	The Hostile Threat	F. McCarthy	14-day	37.50	45.00
91-72-006	Bringing Out the Furs	F. McCarthy	14-day	37.50	45.00
91-72-007	Kiowa Raider	F. McCarthy	14-day	37.50	45.00
91-72-008	Headed North	F. McCarthy	14-day	37.50	37.50
Hamilton Collection		**The Quilted Countryside: A Signature Collection by Mel Steele**			
91-73-001	The Old Country Store	M. Steele	14-day	29.50	36.00
91-73-002	Winter's End	M. Steele	14-day	29.50	29.50
91-73-003	The Quilter's Cabin	M. Steele	14-day	29.50	33.00
91-73-004	Spring Cleaning	M. Steele	14-day	29.50	29.50
91-73-005	Summer Harvest	M. Steele	14-day	29.50	29.50
91-73-006	The Country Merchant	M. Steele	14-day	29.50	29.50
92-73-007	Wash Day	M. Steele	14-day	29.50	29.50
92-73-008	The Antiques Store	M. Steele	14-day	29.50	29.50
Hamilton Collection		**Sporting Generation**			
91-74-001	Like Father, Like Son	J. Lamb	14-day	29.50	29.50
91-74-002	Golden Moments	J. Lamb	14-day	29.50	29.50
91-74-003	The Lookout	J. Lamb	14-day	29.50	29.50
92-74-004	Picking Up The Scent	J. Lamb	14-day	29.50	29.50
92-74-005	First Time Out	J. Lamb	14-day	29.50	29.50
92-74-006	Who's Tracking Who	J. Lamb	14-day	29.50	29.50
92-74-007	Springing Into Action	J. Lamb	14-day	29.50	29.50
92-74-008	Point of Interest	J. Lamb	14-day	29.50	29.50
Hamilton Collection		**Seasons of the Bald Eagle**			
91-75-001	Autumn in the Mountains	J. Pitcher	14-day	37.50	37.50
91-75-002	Winter in the Valley	J. Pitcher	14-day	37.50	37.50
91-75-003	Spring on the River	J. Pitcher	14-day	37.50	37.50
91-75-004	Summer on the Seacoast	J. Pitcher	14-day	37.50	37.50
Hamilton Collection		**The STAR TREK 25th Anniversary Commemorative Collection**			
91-76-001	SPOCK	T. Blackshear	14-day	35.00	35-99.00
91-76-002	Kirk	T. Blackshear	14-day	35.00	35-75.00
92-76-003	McCoy	T. Blackshear	14-day	35.00	35.00
92-76-004	Uhura	T. Blackshear	14-day	35.00	35.00
92-76-005	Scotty	T. Blackshear	14-day	35.00	35.00
93-76-006	Sulu	T. Blackshear	14-day	35.00	35.00
93-76-007	Chekov	T. Blackshear	14-day	35.00	35.00
Hamilton Collection		**The Spock® Commemorative Wall Plaque**			
93-77-001	Spock® Commemorative Wall Plaque	N/A	2,500	195.00	195.00
Hamilton Collection		**STAR TREK 25th Anniversary Commemorative Plate**			
91-78-001	STAR TREK 25th Anniversary Commemorative Plate	T. Blackshear	14-day	37.50	60-99.00
Hamilton Collection		**Vanishing Rural America**			
91-79-001	Quiet Reflections	J. Harrison	14-day	29.50	45.00
91-79-002	Autumn's Passage	J. Harrison	14-day	29.50	45.00
91-79-003	Storefront Memories	J. Harrison	14-day	29.50	45.00
91-79-004	Country Path	J. Harrison	14-day	29.50	36.00
91-79-005	When the Circus Came To Town	J. Harrison	14-day	29.50	36.00
91-79-006	Covered in Fall	J. Harrison	14-day	29.50	45.00
91-79-007	America's Heartland	J. Harrison	14-day	29.50	33.00
91-79-008	Rural Delivery	J. Harrison	14-day	29.50	33.00
Hamilton Collection		**North American Ducks**			
91-80-001	Autumn Flight	R. Lawrence	14-day	29.50	36.00
91-80-002	The Resting Place	R. Lawrence	14-day	29.50	29.50
91-80-003	Twin Flight	R. Lawrence	14-day	29.50	29.50
92-80-004	Misty Morning	R. Lawrence	14-day	29.50	29.50
92-80-005	Springtime Thaw	R. Lawrence	14-day	29.50	29.50
92-80-006	Summer Retreat	R. Lawrence	14-day	29.50	29.50
92-80-007	Overcast	R. Lawrence	14-day	29.50	29.50
92-80-008	Perfect Pintails	R. Lawrence	14-day	29.50	29.50
Hamilton Collection		**Proud Indian Families**			
91-81-001	The Storyteller	K. Freeman	14-day	29.50	29.50
91-81-002	The Power of the Basket	K. Freeman	14-day	29.50	29.50
91-81-003	The Naming Ceremony	K. Freeman	14-day	29.50	29.50
92-81-004	Playing With Tradition	K. Freeman	14-day	29.50	29.50
92-81-005	Preparing the Berry Harvest	K. Freeman	14-day	29.50	29.50
92-81-006	Ceremonial Dress	K. Freeman	14-day	29.50	29.50
92-81-007	Sounds of the Forest	K. Freeman	14-day	29.50	29.50
92-81-008	The Marriage Ceremony	K. Freeman	14-day	29.50	29.50
93-81-009	The Jewelry Maker	K. Freeman	14-day	29.50	29.50
93-81-010	Beautiful Creations	K. Freeman	14-day	29.50	29.50
Hamilton Collection		**Little Shopkeepers**			
90-82-001	Sew Tired	G. Gerardi	14-day	29.50	29.50
91-82-002	Break Time	G. Gerardi	14-day	29.50	29.50
91-82-003	Purrfect Fit	G. Gerardi	14-day	29.50	29.50
91-82-004	Toying Around	G. Gerardi	14-day	29.50	36.00
91-82-005	Chain Reaction	G. Gerardi	14-day	29.50	45.00
91-82-006	Inferior Decorators	G. Gerardi	14-day	29.50	36.00
91-82-007	Tulip Tag	G. Gerardi	14-day	29.50	36.00
91-82-008	Candy Capers	G. Gerardi	14-day	29.50	36.00
Hamilton Collection		**Our Cherished Seas**			
92-83-001	Whale Song	S. Barlowe	48-day	37.50	37.50
92-83-002	Lions of the Sea	S. Barlowe	48-day	37.50	37.50
92-83-003	Flight of the Dolphins	S. Barlowe	48-day	37.50	37.50
92-83-004	Palace of the Seals	S. Barlowe	48-day	37.50	37.50
93-83-005	Orca Ballet	S. Barlowe	48-day	37.50	37.50
93-83-006	Emperors of the Ice	S. Barlowe	48-day	37.50	37.50
93-83-007	Sea Turtles	S. Barlowe	48-day	37.50	37.50
93-83-008	Splendor of the Sea	S. Barlowe	48-day	37.50	37.50
Hamilton Collection		**Republic Pictures Film Library Collection**			
92-84-001	Show With Laredo	S. Morton	28-day	37.50	37.50
92-84-002	The Ride Home	S. Morton	28-day	37.50	37.50
92-84-003	Attack at Tarawa	S. Morton	28-day	37.50	37.50
92-84-004	Thoughts of Angelique	S. Morton	28-day	37.50	37.50
92-84-005	War of the Wildcats	S. Morton	28-day	37.50	37.50
92-84-006	The Fighting Seabees	S. Morton	28-day	37.50	37.50
92-84-007	The Quiet Man	S. Morton	28-day	37.50	37.50
93-84-008	Angel & The Badman	S. Morton	28-day	37.50	37.50
93-84-009	Sands of Iwo Jima	S. Morton	28-day	37.50	37.50
93-84-010	Flying Tigers	S. Morton	28-day	39.50	39.50
Hamilton Collection		**Unbridled Spirit**			
92-85-001	Surf Dancer	C. DeHaan	28-day	29.50	29.50
92-85-002	Winter Renegade	C. DeHaan	28-day	29.50	29.50
92-85-003	Desert Shadows	C. DeHaan	28-day	29.50	29.50
93-85-004	Painted Sunrise	C. DeHaan	28-day	29.50	29.50
93-85-005	Desert Duel	C. DeHaan	28-day	29.50	29.50
93-85-006	Midnight Run	C. DeHaan	28-day	29.50	29.50
93-85-007	Moonlight Majesty	C. DeHaan	28-day	29.50	29.50
93-85-008	Autumn Reverie	C. DeHaan	28-day	29.50	29.50
93-85-009	Blizzard's Peril	C. DeHaan	28-day	29.50	29.50
93-85-010	Sunrise Surprise	C. DeHaan	28-day	29.50	29.50
Hamilton Collection		**Victorian Playtime**			
91-86-001	A Busy Day	M. H. Bogart	14-day	29.50	29.50
92-86-002	Little Masterpiece	M. H. Bogart	14-day	29.50	29.50
92-86-003	Playing Bride	M. H. Bogart	14-day	29.50	29.50
92-86-004	Waiting for a Nibble	M. H. Bogart	14-day	29.50	29.50
92-86-005	Tea and Gossip	M. H. Bogart	14-day	29.50	29.50
92-86-006	Cleaning House	M. H. Bogart	14-day	29.50	29.50
92-86-007	A Little Persuasion	M. H. Bogart	14-day	29.50	29.50
92-86-008	Peek-a-Boo	M. H. Bogart	14-day	29.50	29.50
Hamilton Collection		**Winter Rails**			
92-87-001	Winter Crossing	T. Xaras	28-day	29.50	29.50
93-87-002	Coal Country	T. Xaras	28-day	29.50	29.50
93-87-003	Daylight Run	T. Xaras	28-day	29.50	29.50
93-87-004	By Sea or Rail	T. Xaras	28-day	29.50	29.50
93-87-005	Country Crossroads	T. Xaras	28-day	29.50	29.50
93-87-006	Timber Line	T. Xaras	28-day	29.50	29.50
93-87-007	The Long Haul	T. Xaras	28-day	29.50	29.50
93-87-008	Darby Crossing	T. Xaras	28-day	29.50	29.50
Hamilton Collection		**Farmyard Friends**			
92-88-001	Mistaken Identity	J. Lamb	28-day	29.50	29.50
92-88-002	Little Cowhands	J. Lamb	28-day	29.50	29.50
93-88-003	Shreading the Evidence	J. Lamb	28-day	29.50	29.50
93-88-004	Partners in Crime	J. Lamb	28-day	29.50	29.50
93-88-005	Fowl Play	J. Lamb	28-day	29.50	29.50
93-88-006	Follow The Leader	J. Lamb	28-day	29.50	29.50
93-88-007	Pony Tales	J. Lamb	28-day	29.50	29.50
93-88-008	An Apple A Day	J. Lamb	28-day	29.50	29.50
Hamilton Collection		**Man's Best Friend**			
92-89-001	Special Delivery	L. Picken	28-day	29.50	29.50
92-89-002	Making Waves	L. Picken	28-day	29.50	29.50
92-89-003	Good Catch	L. Picken	28-day	29.50	29.50
93-89-004	Time For a Walk	L. Picken	28-day	29.50	29.50
93-89-005	Faithful Friend	L. Picken	28-day	29.50	29.50
93-89-006	Let's Play Ball	L. Picken	28-day	29.50	29.50
93-89-007	Sitting Pretty	L. Picken	28-day	29.50	29.50
93-89-008	Bedtime Story	L. Picken	28-day	29.50	29.50
93-89-009	Trusted Companion	L. Picken	28-day	29.50	29.50
Hamilton Collection		**Nature's Nightime Realm**			
92-90-001	Bobcat	G. Murray	28-day	29.50	29.50
92-90-002	Cougar	G. Murray	28-day	29.50	29.50
93-90-003	Jaguar	G. Murray	28-day	29.50	29.50
93-90-004	White Tiger	G. Murray	28-day	29.50	29.50
93-90-005	Lynx	G. Murray	28-day	29.50	29.50
93-90-006	Lion	G. Murray	28-day	29.50	29.50
93-90-007	Snow Leopard	G. Murray	28-day	29.50	29.50
93-90-008	Cheetah	G. Murray	28-day	29.50	29.50
Hamilton Collection		**Precious Moments Bible Story**			
91-91-001	Come Let Us Adore Him	S. Butcher	28-day	29.50	29.50
92-91-002	They Followed The Star	S. Butcher	28-day	29.50	29.50
92-91-003	The Flight Into Egypt	S. Butcher	28-day	29.50	29.50
92-91-004	The Carpenter Shop	S. Butcher	28-day	29.50	29.50
92-91-005	Jesus In The Temple	S. Butcher	28-day	29.50	29.50
92-91-006	The Crucifixion	S. Butcher	28-day	29.50	29.50
93-91-007	He Is Not Here	S. Butcher	28-day	29.50	29.50
Hamilton Collection		**The Wonder Of Christmas**			
91-92-001	Santa's Secret	J. McClelland	28-day	29.50	29.50
92-92-002	My Favorite Ornament	J. McClelland	28-day	29.50	29.50
92-92-003	Waiting For Santa	J. McClelland	28-day	29.50	29.50
93-92-004	The Caroler	J. McClelland	28-day	29.50	29.50
Hamilton Collection		**Romantic Victorian Keepsake**			
92-93-001	Dearest Kiss	J. Grossman	28-day	35.00	35.00
93-93-002	First Love	J. Grossman	28-day	35.00	35.00
93-93-003	As Fair as a Rose	J. Grossman	28-day	35.00	35.00
93-93-004	Springtime Beauty	J. Grossman	28-day	35.00	35.00
93-93-005	Summertime Fancy	J. Grossman	28-day	35.00	35.00
93-93-006	Bonnie Blue Eyes	J. Grossman	28-day	35.00	35.00
93-93-007	Precious Friends	J. Grossman	28-day	35.00	35.00
94-93-008	Bonnets and Bouquets	J. Grossman	28-day	35.00	35.00
Hamilton Collection		**The World Of Zolan**			
92-94-001	First Kiss	D. Zolan	28-day	29.50	29.50
92-94-002	Morning Discovery	D. Zolan	28-day	29.50	29.50
93-94-003	Little Fisherman	D. Zolan	28-day	29.50	29.50
93-94-004	Letter to Grandma	D. Zolan	28-day	29.50	29.50
93-94-005	Twilight Prayer	D. Zolan	28-day	29.50	29.50
93-94-006	Flowers for Mother	D. Zolan	28-day	29.50	29.50
Hamilton Collection		**Mystic Warriors**			
92-95-001	Deliverance	C. Ren	28-day	29.50	29.50
92-95-002	Mystic Warrior	C. Ren	28-day	29.50	29.50
92-95-003	Sun Seeker	C. Ren	28-day	29.50	29.50
92-95-004	Top Gun	C. Ren	28-day	29.50	29.50
92-95-005	Man Who Walks Alone	C. Ren	28-day	29.50	29.50
92-95-006	Windrider	C. Ren	28-day	29.50	29.50
92-95-007	Spirit of the Plains	C. Ren	28-day	29.50	29.50
93-95-008	Blue Thunder	C. Ren	28-day	29.50	29.50
93-95-009	Sun Glow	C. Ren	28-day	29.50	29.50
93-95-010	Peace Maker	C. Ren	28-day	29.50	29.50
Hamilton Collection		**Andy Griffith**			
92-96-001	Sheriff Andy Taylor	R. Tanenbaum	28-day	29.50	29.50
92-96-002	A Startling Conclusion	R. Tanenbaum	28-day	29.50	29.50
93-96-003	Mayberry Sing-a-long	R. Tanenbaum	28-day	29.50	29.50

PLATES

Company / Number	Name	Series / Artist	Edition Limit	Issue Price	Quote
93-96-004	Aunt Bee's Kitchen	R. Tanenbaum	28-day	29.50	29.50
93-96-005	Surprise! Surprise!	R. Tanenbaum	28-day	29.50	29.50
93-96-006	An Explosive Situation	R. Tanenbaum	28-day	29.50	29.50
93-96-007	Meeting Aunt Bee	R. Tanenbaum	28-day	29.50	29.50
93-96-008	Opie's Big Catch	R. Tanenbaum	28-day	29.50	29.50
Hamilton Collection		**Madonna And Child**			
92-97-001	Madonna Della Seida	R. Sanzio	28-day	37.50	37.50
92-97-002	Virgin of the Rocks	L. DaVinci	28-day	37.50	37.50
93-97-003	Madonna of Rosary	B. E. Murillo	28-day	37.50	37.50
93-97-004	Sistine Madonna	R. Sanzio	28-day	37.50	37.50
93-97-005	Virgin Adoring Christ Child	A. Correggio	28-day	37.50	37.50
93-97-006	Virgin of the Grape	P. Mignard	28-day	37.50	37.50
93-97-007	Madonna del Magnificat	S. Botticelli	28-day	37.50	37.50
93-97-008	Madonna col Bambino	S. Botticelli	28-day	37.50	37.50
Hamilton Collection		**Council Of Nations**			
91-98-001	Strength of the Sioux	G. Perillo	28-day	29.50	29.50
92-98-002	Pride of the Cheyenne	G. Perillo	28-day	29.50	29.50
92-98-003	Dignity of the Nez Parce	G. Perillo	28-day	29.50	29.50
92-98-004	Courage of the Arapaho	G. Perillo	28-day	29.50	29.50
92-98-005	Power of the Blackfoot	G. Perillo	28-day	29.50	29.50
92-98-006	Nobility of the Algonqui	G. Perillo	28-day	29.50	29.50
92-98-007	Wisdom of the Cherokee	G. Perillo	28-day	29.50	29.50
92-98-008	Boldness of the Seneca	G. Perillo	28-day	29.50	29.50
Hamilton Collection		**Beauty Of Winter**			
92-99-001	Silent Night	N/A	28-day	19.50	19.50
93-99-002	Moonlight Sleighride	N/A	28-day	19.50	19.50
Hamilton Collection		**Bialosky®& Friends**			
92-100-001	Family Addition	P./A.Bialosky	28-day	29.50	29.50
93-100-002	Sweetheart	P./A.Bialosky	28-day	29.50	29.50
93-100-003	Let's Go Fishing	P./A.Bialosky	28-day	29.50	29.50
93-100-004	U.S. Mail	P./A.Bialosky	28-day	29.50	29.50
93-100-005	Sleigh Ride	P./A.Bialosky	28-day	29.50	29.50
93-100-006	Honey For Sale	P./A.Bialosky	28-day	29.50	29.50
93-100-007	Breakfast In Bed	P./A.Bialosky	28-day	29.50	29.50
93-100-008	My First Two-Wheeler	P./A.Bialosky	28-day	29.50	29.50
Hamilton Collection		**Country Garden Cottages**			
92-101-001	Riverbank Cottage	E. Dertner	28-day	29.50	29.50
92-101-002	Sunday Outing	E. Dertner	28-day	29.50	29.50
92-101-003	Shepherd's Cottage	E. Dertner	28-day	19.50	19.50
93-101-004	Daydream Cottage	E. Dertner	28-day	19.50	19.50
93-101-005	Garden Glorious	E. Dertner	28-day	29.50	29.50
93-101-006	This Side of Heaven	E. Dertner	28-day	29.50	29.50
93-101-007	Summer Symphony	E. Dertner	28-day	29.50	29.50
93-101-008	April Cottage	E. Dertner	28-day	29.50	29.50
Hamilton Collection		**Quiet Moments Of Childhood**			
91-102-001	Elizabeth's Afternoon Tea	D. Green	14-day	29.50	33.00
91-102-002	Christina's Secret Garden	D. Green	14-day	29.50	29.50
91-102-003	Eric & Erin's Storytime	D. Green	14-day	29.50	29.50
92-102-004	Jessica's Tea Party	D. Green	14-day	29.50	33.00
92-102-005	Megan & Monique's Bakery	D. Green	14-day	29.50	36.00
92-102-006	Children's Day By The Sea	D. Green	14-day	29.50	29.50
92-102-007	Jordan's Playful Pups	D. Green	14-day	29.50	29.50
92-102-008	Daniel's Morning Playtime	D. Green	14-day	29.50	29.50
Hamilton Collection		**Star Trek: The Next Generation**			
93-103-001	Captain Jean-Luc Picard	T. Blackshear	28-day	35.00	35.00
93-103-002	Commander William Riker	T. Blackshear	28-day	35.00	35.00
94-103-003	Lieutenant Commander Data	T. Blackshear	28-day	35.00	35.00
94-103-004	Lieutenant Warf	T. Blackshear	28-day	35.00	35.00
Hamilton Collection		**Portraits of the Bald Eagle**			
93-104-001	Ruler of the Sky	J. Pitcher	28-day	37.50	37.50
93-104-002	In Bold Defiance	J. Pitcher	28-day	37.50	37.50
93-104-003	Master Of The Summer Skies	J. Pitcher	28-day	37.50	37.50
93-104-004	Spring's Sentinel	J. Pitcher	28-day	37.50	37.50
Hamilton Collection		**A Lisi Martin Christmas**			
92-105-001	Santa's Littlest Reindeer	L. Martin	28-day	29.50	29.50
93-105-002	Not A Creature Was Stirring	L. Martin	28-day	29.50	29.50
93-105-003	Christmas Dreams	L. Martin	28-day	29.50	29.50
93-105-004	The Christmas Story	L. Martin	28-day	29.50	29.50
93-105-005	Trimming The Tree	L. Martin	28-day	29.50	29.50
93-105-006	A Taste Of The Holidays	L. Martin	28-day	29.50	29.50
93-105-007	The Night Before Christmas	L. Martin	28-day	29.50	29.50
93-105-008	Christmas Watch	L. Martin	28-day	29.50	29.50
Hamilton Collection		**Glory of Christ**			
92-106-001	The Ascension	C. Micarelli	48-day	29.50	29.50
93-106-002	Jesus Teaching	C. Micarelli	48-day	29.50	29.50
93-106-003	Lost Supper	C. Micarelli	48-day	29.50	29.50
93-106-004	The Nativity	C. Micarelli	48-day	29.50	29.50
93-106-005	The Baptism of Christ	C. Micarelli	48-day	29.50	29.50
93-106-006	Jesus Heals the Sick	C. Micarelli	48-day	29.50	29.50
Hamilton Collection		**Star Wars Trilogy**			
93-107-001	Star Wars	M. Weistling	28-day	37.50	37.50
93-107-002	The Empire Strikes Back	M. Weistling	28-day	37.50	37.50
93-107-003	Return Of The Jedi	M. Weistling	28-day	37.50	37.50
Hamilton Collection		**Norman Rockwell's Saturday Evening Post Baseball Plate Collection**			
92-108-001	100th Year of Baseball	N. Rockwell	Open	19.50	19.50
93-108-002	The Rookie	N. Rockwell	Open	19.50	19.50
93-108-003	The Dugout	N. Rockwell	Open	19.50	19.50
93-108-004	Bottom of the Sixth	N. Rockwell	Open	19.50	19.50
Hamilton Collection		**Cameo Kittens**			
93-109-001	Ginger Snap	Q. Lemonds	28-day	29.50	29.50
93-109-002	Cat Tails	Q. Lemonds	28-day	29.50	29.50
93-109-003	Lady Blue	Q. Lemonds	28-day	29.50	29.50
93-109-004	Tiny Heart Stealer	Q. Lemonds	28-day	29.50	29.50
93-109-005	Blossom	Q. Lemonds	28-day	29.50	29.50
94-109-006	Whisker Antics	Q. Lemonds	28-day	29.50	29.50
94-109-007	Tiger's Temptation	Q. Lemonds	28-day	29.50	29.50
Hamilton Collection		**Princesses of the Plains**			
93-110-001	Prairie Flower	D. Wright	28-day	29.50	29.50
93-110-002	Snow Princess	D. Wright	28-day	29.50	29.50
93-110-003	Wild Flower	D. Wright	28-day	29.50	29.50
93-110-004	Noble Beauty	D. Wright	28-day	29.50	29.50
93-110-005	Winter's Rose	D. Wright	28-day	29.50	29.50
93-110-006	Gentle Beauty	D. Wright	28-day	29.50	29.50
94-110-007	Nature's Guardian	D. Wright	28-day	29.50	29.50
94-110-008	Mountain Princess	D. Wright	28-day	29.50	29.50
Hamilton Collection		**Victorian Christmas Memories**			
92-111-001	A Visit from St. Nicholas	J. Grossman	28-day	29.50	29.50
93-111-002	Christmas Delivery	J. Grossman	28-day	29.50	29.50
93-111-003	Christmas Angels	J. Grossman	28-day	29.50	29.50
92-111-004	With Visions of Sugar Plums	J. Grossman	28-day	29.50	29.50
93-111-005	Merry Olde Kris Kringle	J. Grossman	28-day	29.50	29.50
93-111-006	Grandfather Frost	J. Grossman	28-day	29.50	29.50
Hamilton Collection		**Daughters Of The Sun**			
93-112-001	Sun Dancer	K. Thayer	28-day	29.50	29.50
93-112-002	Shining Feather	K. Thayer	28-day	29.50	29.50
93-112-003	Delighted Dancer	K. Thayer	28-day	29.50	29.50
93-112-004	Evening Dancer	K. Thayer	28-day	29.50	29.50
93-112-005	A Secret Glance	K. Thayer	28-day	29.50	29.50
93-112-006	Chippewa Charmer	K. Thayer	28-day	29.50	29.50
94-112-007	Pride of the Yakima	K. Thayer	28-day	29.50	29.50
94-112-008	Radiant Beauty	K. Thayer	28-day	29.50	29.50
Hamilton Collection		**The Best Of Baseball**			
93-113-001	The Legendary Mickey Mantle	R. Tanenbaum	28-day	29.50	29.50
93-113-002	The Immortal Babe Ruth	R. Tanenbaum	28-day	29.50	29.50
93-113-003	The Great Willie Mays	R. Tanenbaum	28-day	29.50	29.50
93-113-004	The Unbeatable Duke Snider	R. Tanenbaum	28-day	29.50	29.50
93-113-005	The Extraordinary Lou Gehrig	R. Tanenbaum	28-day	29.50	29.50
93-113-006	The Phenomenal Roberto Clemente	R. Tanenbaum	28-day	29.50	29.50
93-113-007	The Remarkable Johnny Bench	R. Tanenbaum	28-day	29.50	29.50
93-113-008	The Incredible Nolan Ryan	R. Tanenbaum	28-day	29.50	29.50
Hamilton Collection		**Lore Of The West**			
93-114-001	A Mile In His Mocassins	L. Danielle	28-day	29.50	29.50
93-114-002	Path of Honor	L. Danielle	28-day	29.50	29.50
93-114-003	A Chief's Pride	L. Danielle	28-day	29.50	29.50
94-114-004	Pathways of the Pueblo	L. Danielle	28-day	29.50	29.50
94-114-005	In Her Seps	L. Danielle	28-day	29.50	29.50
94-114-006	Growing Up Brave	L. Danielle	28-day	29.50	29.50
Hamilton Collection		**The Fierce And The Free**			
92-115-001	Big Medicine	F. McCarthy	28-day	29.50	29.50
93-115-002	Land of the Winter Hawk	F. McCarthy	28-day	29.50	29.50
93-115-003	Warrior of Savage Splendor	F. McCarthy	28-day	29.50	29.50
94-115-004	War Party	F. McCarthy	28-day	29.50	29.50
94-115-005	The Challenge	F. McCarthy	28-day	29.50	29.50
Hamilton Collection		**Year Of The Wolf**			
93-116-001	Broken Silence	A. Agnew	28-day	29.50	29.50
93-116-002	Leader of the Pack	A. Agnew	28-day	29.50	29.50
93-116-003	Solitude	A. Agnew	28-day	29.50	29.50
94-116-004	Tundra Light	A. Agnew	28-day	29.50	29.50
Hamilton Collection		**Precious Moments Classics**			
93-117-001	God Loveth A Cheerful Giver	S. Butcher	28-day	35.00	35.00
93-117-002	Make A Joyful Noise	S. Butcher	28-day	35.00	35.00
Hamilton Collection		**The Golden Age of American Railroads**			
91-118-001	The Blue Comet	T. Xaras	14-day	29.50	45.00
91-118-002	The Morning Local	T. Xaras	14-day	29.50	60.00
91-118-003	The Pennsylvania K-4	T. Xaras	14-day	29.50	70.00
91-118-004	Above the Canyon	T. Xaras	14-day	29.50	90.00
91-118-005	Portrait in Steam	T. Xaras	14-day	29.50	75.00
91-118-006	The Santa Fe Super Chief	T. Xaras	14-day	29.50	105.00
91-118-007	Big Boy	T. Xaras	14-day	29.50	60.00
91-118-008	The Empire Builder	T. Xaras	14-day	29.50	60.00
92-118-009	An American Classic	T. Xaras	14-day	29.50	33.00
92-118-010	Final Destination	T. Xaras	14-day	29.50	36.00
Hamilton Collection		**Lucy Collage**			
93-119-001	Lucy	M. Weistling	28-day	37.50	37.50
Hamilton Collection		**The Last Warriors**			
93-120-001	Winter of '41	C. Ren	28-day	29.50	29.50
93-120-002	Morning of Reckoning	C. Ren	28-day	29.50	29.50
93-120-003	Twilights Last Gleaming	C. Ren	28-day	29.50	29.50
93-120-004	Lone Winter Journey	C. Ren	28-day	29.50	29.50
Hamilton Collection		**Classic American Santas**			
93-121-001	A Christmas Eve Visitor	G. Hinke	28-day	29.50	29.50
Hamilton Collection		**Nature's Majestic Cats**			
93-122-001	Siberian Tiger	M. Richter	28-day	29.50	29.50
93-122-002	Himalayan Snow Leopard	M. Richter	28-day	29.50	29.50
93-122-003	African Lion	M. Richter	28-day	29.50	29.50
Hamilton Collection		**Enchanted Seascapes**			
93-123-001	Sanctuary of the Dolphin	J. Enright	28-day	29.50	29.50
94-123-002	Rhapsody of Hope	J. Enright	28-day	29.50	29.50
Hamilton Collection		**Call to Adventure**			
93-124-001	USS Constitution	R. Cross	28-day	29.50	29.50
93-124-002	The Bounty	R. Cross	28-day	29.50	29.50
94-124-003	Bonhomme Richard	R. Cross	28-day	29.50	29.50
94-124-004	Old Nantucket	R. Cross	28-day	29.50	29.50
Hamilton Collection		**All in a Day's Work**			
94-125-001	Where's the Fire?	J. Lamb	28-day	29.50	29.50
Hamilton Collection		**Forging New Frontiers**			
94-126-001	The Race is On	J. Deneen	28-day	29.50	29.50
Hamilton Collection		**Romance of the Rails**			
94-127-001	Starlight Limited	D. Tutwiler	28-day	29.50	29.50
94-127-002	Portland Rose	D. Tutwiler	28-day	29.50	29.50
Haviland		**Twelve Days of Christmas**			
70-01-001	Partridge	R. Hetreau	30,000	25.00	54.00
71-01-002	Two Turtle Doves	R. Hetreau	30,000	25.00	25.00
72-01-003	Three French Hens	R. Hetreau	30,000	27.50	27.50
73-01-004	Four Calling Birds	R. Hetreau	30,000	28.50	30.00
74-01-005	Five Golden Rings	R. Hetreau	30,000	30.00	30.00

PLATES

Company / Number	Name	Series / Artist	Edition Limit	Issue Price	Quote
75-01-006	Six Geese a'laying	R. Hetreau	30,000	32.50	32.50
76-01-007	Seven Swans	R. Hetreau	30,000	38.00	38.00
77-01-008	Eight Maids	R. Hetreau	30,000	40.00	40.00
78-01-009	Nine Ladies Dancing	R. Hetreau	30,000	45.00	67.00
79-01-010	Ten Lord's a'leaping	R. Hetreau	30,000	50.00	50.00
80-01-011	Eleven Pipers Piping	R. Hetreau	30,000	55.00	65.00
81-01-012	Twelve Drummers	R. Hetreau	30,000	60.00	60.00
Haviland & Parlon		**Christmas Madonnas**			
72-01-001	By Raphael	Raphael	5,000	35.00	42.00
73-01-002	By Feruzzi	Feruzzi	5,000	40.00	78.00
74-01-003	By Raphael	Raphael	5,000	42.50	42.50
75-01-004	By Murillo	Murillo	7,500	42.50	42.50
76-01-005	By Botticelli	Botticelli	7,500	45.00	45.00
77-01-006	By Bellini	Bellini	7,500	48.00	48.00
78-01-007	By Lippi	Lippi	7,500	48.00	53.00
79-01-008	Madonna of The Eucharist	Botticelli	7,500	49.50	112.00
Edna Hibel Studios		**Mother and Child**			
73-01-001	Colette & Child	E. Hibel	15,000	40.00	725.00
74-01-002	Sayuri & Child	E. Hibel	15,000	40.00	425.00
75-01-003	Kristina & Child	E. Hibel	15,000	50.00	400.00
76-01-004	Marilyn & Child	E. Hibel	15,000	55.00	400.00
77-01-005	Lucia & Child	E. Hibel	15,000	60.00	350.00
81-01-006	Kathleen & Child	E. Hibel	15,000	85.00	275.00
Edna Hibel Studios		**Oriental Gold**			
75-02-001	Yasuko	E. Hibel	2,000	275.00	3000.00
76-02-002	Mr. Obata	E. Hibel	2,000	275.00	2100.00
78-02-003	Sakura	E. Hibel	2,000	295.00	1800.00
79-02-004	Michio	E. Hibel	2,000	325.00	1500.00
Edna Hibel Studios		**Nobility Of Children**			
76-03-001	La Contessa Isabella	E. Hibel	12,750	120.00	425.00
77-03-002	Le Marquis Maurice Pierre	E. Hibel	12,750	120.00	225.00
78-03-003	Baronesse Johanna-Maryke Van Vollendam Tot Marken	E. Hibel	12,750	130.00	225.00
79-03-004	Chief Red Feather	E. Hibel	12,750	140.00	200.00
Edna Hibel Studios		**Museum Commemorative**			
77-04-001	Flower Girl of Provence	E. Hibel	12,750	175.00	425.00
80-04-002	Diana	E. Hibel	3,000	350.00	395.00
Edna Hibel Studios		**David Series**			
79-05-001	Wedding of David & Bathsheba	E. Hibel	5,000	250.00	650.00
80-05-002	David, Bathsheba & Solomon	E. Hibel	5,000	275.00	425.00
82-05-003	David the King	E. Hibel	5,000	275.00	295.00
82-05-004	David the King, cobalt A/P	E. Hibel	25	275.00	1200.00
84-05-005	Bathsheba	E. Hibel	5,000	275.00	295.00
84-05-006	Bathsheba, cobalt A/P	E. Hibel	100	275.00	1200.00
Edna Hibel Studios		**Allegro**			
78-06-001	Plate & Book	E. Hibel	7,500	120.00	135.00
Edna Hibel Studios		**Arte Ovale**			
80-07-001	Takara, gold	E. Hibel	300	1000.00	4200.00
80-07-002	Takara, blanco	E. Hibel	700	450.00	1200.00
80-07-003	Takara, cobalt blue	E. Hibel	1,000	595.00	2350.00
84-07-004	Taro-kun, gold	E. Hibel	300	1000.00	2700.00
84-07-005	Taro-kun, blanco	E. Hibel	700	450.00	825.00
84-07-006	Taro-kun, cobalt blue	E. Hibel	1,000	995.00	1050.00
Edna Hibel Studios		**The World I Love**			
81-08-001	Leah's Family	E. Hibel	17,500	85.00	225.00
82-08-002	Kaylin	E. Hibel	17,500	85.00	375.00
83-08-003	Edna's Music	E. Hibel	17,500	85.00	195.00
83-08-004	O' Hana	E. Hibel	17,500	85.00	195.00
Edna Hibel Studios		**Famous Women & Children**			
80-09-001	Pharaoh's Daughter & Moses, gold	E. Hibel	2,500	350.00	625.00
80-09-002	Pharaoh's Daughter & Moses, cobalt blue	E. Hibel	500	350.00	1350.00
82-09-003	Cornelia & Her Jewels, gold	E. Hibel	2,500	350.00	495.00
82-09-004	Cornelia & Her Jewels, cobalt blue	E. Hibel	500	350.00	1350.00
82-09-005	Anna & The Children of the King of Siam, gold	E. Hibel	2,500	350.00	495.00
82-09-006	Anna & The Children of the King of Siam, cobalt blue	E. Hibel	500	350.00	1350.00
84-09-007	Mozart & The Empress Marie Theresa, gold	E. Hibel	2,500	350.00	395.00
84-09-008	Mozart & The Empress Marie Theresa, cobalt blue	E. Hibel	500	350.00	975.00
Edna Hibel Studios		**Tribute To All Children**			
84-10-001	Giselle	E. Hibel	19,500	55.00	95.00
84-10-002	Gerard	E. Hibel	19,500	55.00	95.00
85-10-003	Wendy	E. Hibel	19,500	55.00	125.00
86-10-004	Todd	E. Hibel	19,500	55.00	125.00
Edna Hibel Studios		**International Mother Love German**			
82-11-001	Gesa Und Kinder	E. Hibel	5,000	195.00	195.00
83-11-002	Alexandra Und Kinder	E. Hibel	5,000	195.00	195.00
Edna Hibel Studios		**International Mother Love French**			
85-12-001	Yvette Avec Ses Enfants	E. Hibel	5,000	125.00	225.00
91-12-002	Liberte, Egalite, Fraternite	E. Hibel	5,000	95.00	95.00
Edna Hibel Studios		**Mother's Day Annual**			
84-13-001	Abby & Lisa	E. Hibel	Yr.Iss.	29.50	400.00
85-13-002	Erica & Jamie	E. Hibel	Yr.Iss.	29.50	250.00
86-13-003	Emily & Jennifer	E. Hibel	Yr.Iss.	29.50	325.00
87-13-004	Catherine & Heather	E. Hibel	Yr.Iss.	34.50	275.00
88-13-005	Sarah & Tess	E. Hibel	Yr.Iss.	34.90	175-225
89-13-006	Jessica & Kate	E. Hibel	Yr.Iss.	34.90	125.00
90-13-007	Elizabeth, Jorday & Janie	E. Hibel	Yr.Iss.	36.90	95.00
91-13-008	Michele & Anna	E. Hibel	Yr.Iss.	36.90	55.00
Edna Hibel Studios		**Flower Girl Annual**			
85-14-001	Lily	E. Hibel	15,000	79.00	300.00
86-14-002	Iris	E. Hibel	15,000	79.00	225.00
87-14-003	Rose	E. Hibel	15,000	79.00	175.00
88-14-004	Camellia	E. Hibel	15,000	79.00	165.00
89-14-005	Peony	E. Hibel	15,000	79.00	95.00
92-14-006	Wisteria	E. Hibel	15,000	79.00	79.00

Company / Number	Name	Series / Artist	Edition Limit	Issue Price	Quote
Edna Hibel Studios		**Christmas Annual**			
85-15-001	The Angels' Message	E. Hibel	Yr.Iss.	45.00	225.00
86-15-002	Gift of the Magi	E. Hibel	Yr.Iss.	45.00	275.00
87-15-003	Flight Into Egypt	E. Hibel	Yr.Iss.	49.00	250.00
88-15-004	Adoration of the Shepherds	E. Hibel	Yr.Iss.	49.00	175.00
89-15-005	Peaceful Kingdom	E. Hibel	Yr.Iss.	49.00	165.00
90-15-006	The Nativity	E. Hibel	Yr.Iss.	49.00	150.00
Edna Hibel Studios		**To Life Annual**			
86-16-001	Golden's Child	E. Hibel	5,000	99.00	275.00
87-16-002	Triumph! Everyone A Winner	E. Hibel	19,500	55.00	55-75.00
88-16-003	The Whole Earth Bloomed as a Sacred Place	E. Hibel	15,000	85.00	90.00
89-16-004	Lovers of the Summer Palace	E. Hibel	5,000	65.00	75.00
92-16-005	People of the Fields	E. Hibel	5,000	49.00	49.00
Edna Hibel Studios		**Scandinavian Mother & Child**			
87-17-001	Pearl & Flowers	E. Hibel	7,500	55.00	225.00
89-17-002	Anemone & Violet	E. Hibel	7,500	75.00	90.00
90-17-003	Holly & Talia	E. Hibel	7,500	75.00	85.00
Edna Hibel Studios		**Nordic Families**			
87-18-001	A Tender Moment	E. Hibel	7,500	79.00	95.00
Edna Hibel Studios		**March of Dimes: Our Children, Our Future**			
90-19-001	A Time To Embrace	E. Hibel	150-day	29.00	29.00
Edna Hibel Studios		**Eroica**			
90-20-001	Compassion	E. Hibel	10,000	49.50	65.00
92-20-002	Darya	E. Hibel	10,000	49.50	49.50
Edna Hibel Studios		**Edna Hibel Holiday**			
91-21-001	The First Holiday	E. Hibel	Yr.Iss.	49.00	90.00
91-21-002	The First Holiday, gold	E. Hibel	1,000	99.00	150.00
92-21-003	The Christmas Rose	E. Hibel	Yr.Iss.	49.00	49.00
92-21-004	The Christmas Rose, gold	E. Hibel	1,000	99.00	99.00
Edna Hibel Studios		**Mother's Day**			
92-22-001	Molly & Annie	E. Hibel	Yr.Iss.	39.00	39.00
92-22-002	Molly & Annie, gold	E. Hibel	2,500	95.00	150.00
92-22-003	Molly & Annie, platinum	E. Hibel	500	275.00	275.00
John Hine N.A. Ltd.		**David Winter Plate Collection**			
91-01-001	A Christmas Carol	M. Fisher	10,000	30.00	30.00
91-01-002	Cotswold Village Plate	M. Fisher	10,000	30.00	30.00
92-01-003	Chichester Cross Plate	M. Fisher	10,000	30.00	30.00
92-01-004	Little Mill Plate	M. Fisher	10,000	30.00	30.00
92-01-005	Old Curiosity Shop	M. Fisher	10,000	30.00	30.00
92-01-006	Scrooge's Counting House	M. Fisher	10,000	30.00	30.00
93-01-007	Dove Cottage	M. Fisher	10,000	30.00	30.00
93-01-008	Little Forge	M. Fisher	10,000	30.00	30.00
94-01-009	House on Top	M. Fisher	10,000	30.00	30.00
94-01-010	Tytne Barn	M. Fisher	10,000	30.00	30.00
Hutschenreuther		**Gunther Granget**			
72-01-001	American Sparrows	G. Granget	5,000	50.00	150.00
72-01-002	European Sparrows	G. Granget	5,000	30.00	65.00
73-01-003	American Kildeer	G. Granget	2,250	75.00	90.00
73-01-004	American Squirrel	G. Granget	2,500	75.00	75.00
73-01-005	European Squirrel	G. Granget	2,500	35.00	50.00
74-01-006	American Partridge	G. Granget	2,500	75.00	90.00
75-01-007	American Rabbits	G. Granget	2,500	90.00	90.00
76-01-008	Freedom in Flight	G. Granget	5,000	100.00	100.00
76-01-009	Wrens	G. Granget	2,500	100.00	110.00
76-01-010	Freedom in Flight, Gold	G. Granget	200	200.00	200.00
77-01-011	Bears	G. Granget	2,500	100.00	100.00
78-01-012	Foxes' Spring Journey	G. Granget	1,000	125.00	200.00
Hutschenreuther		**The Glory of Christmas**			
82-02-001	The Nativity	W./C. Hallett	25,000	80.00	125.00
83-02-002	The Annunciation	W./C. Hallett	25,000	80.00	115.00
84-02-003	The Shepherds	W./C. Hallett	25,000	80.00	100.00
85-02-004	The Wiseman	W./C. Hallett	25,000	80.00	100.00
Imperial Ching-te Chen		**Beauties of the Red Mansion**			
86-01-001	Pao-chai	Z. HuiMin	115-day	27.92	30.00
86-01-002	Yuan-chun	Z. HuiMin	115-day	27.92	25.00
87-01-003	Hsi-feng	Z. HuiMin	115-day	30.92	30.00
87-01-004	Hsi-chun	Z. HuiMin	115-day	30.92	31-35.00
88-01-005	Miao-yu	Z. HuiMin	115-day	30.92	20.00
88-01-006	Ying-chun	Z. HuiMin	115-day	30.92	35.00
88-01-007	Tai-yu	Z. HuiMin	115-day	32.92	33.00
88-01-008	Li-wan	Z. HuiMin	115-day	32.92	33-35.00
88-01-009	Ko-Ching	Z. HuiMin	115-day	32.92	34.00
88-01-010	Hsiang-yun	Z. HuiMin	115-day	34.92	35.00
89-01-011	Tan-Chun	Z. HuiMin	115-day	34.92	35-55.00
89-01-012	Chiao-chieh	Z. HuiMin	115-day	34.92	35.00
Imperial Ching-te Chen		**Scenes from the Summer Palace**			
88-02-001	The Marble Boat	Z. Song Mao	175-day	29.92	30.00
88-02-002	Jade Belt Bridge	Z. Song Mao	175-day	29.92	30.00
89-02-003	Hall that Dispels the Clouds	Z. Song Mao	175-day	32.92	33.00
89-02-004	The Long Promenade	Z. Song Mao	175-day	32.92	33.00
89-02-005	Garden/Harmonious Pleasure	Z. Song Mao	175-day	32.92	33.00
89-02-006	The Great Stage	Z. Song Mao	175-day	32.92	33.00
89-02-007	Seventeen Arch Bridge	Z. Song Mao	175-day	34.92	35.00
89-02-008	Boaters on Kumming Lake	Z. Song Mao	175-day	34.92	35.00
Imperial Ching-te Chen		**Blessings From a Chinese Garden**			
88-03-001	The Gift of Purity	Z. Song Mao	175-day	39.92	40.00
89-03-002	The Gift of Grace	Z. Song Mao	175-day	39.92	40.00
89-03-003	The Gift of Beauty	Z. Song Mao	175-day	42.92	43.00
89-03-004	The Gift of Happiness	Z. Song Mao	175-day	42.92	43.00
90-03-005	The Gift of Truth	Z. Song Mao	175-day	42.92	43.00
90-03-006	The Gift of Joy	Z. Song Mao	175-day	42.92	43.00
Imperial Ching-te Chen		**Legends of West Lake**			
89-04-001	Lady White	J. Xue-Bing	175-day	29.92	30.00
90-04-002	Lady Silkworm	J. Xue-Bing	175-day	29.92	30.00
90-04-003	Laurel Peak	J. Xue-Bing	175-day	29.92	33.00
90-04-004	Rising Sun Terrace	J. Xue-Bing	175-day	32.92	33.00
90-04-005	The Apricot Fairy	J. Xue-Bing	175-day	32.92	33.00
90-04-006	Bright Pearl	J. Xue-Bing	175-day	32.92	33.00
90-04-007	Thread of Sky	J. Xue-Bing	175-day	34.92	35.00

Number	Name	Artist	Edition Limit	Issue Price	Quote
91-04-008	Phoenix Mountain	J. Xue-Bing	175-day	34.92	40.00
91-04-009	Ancestors of Tea	J. Xue-Bing	175-day	34.92	62.00
91-04-010	Three Pools Mirroring/Moon	J. Xue-Bing	175-day	36.92	75.00
91-04-011	Fly-In Peak	J. Xue-Bing	175-day	36.92	50.00
91-04-012	The Case of the Folding Fans	J. Xue-Bing	175-day	36.92	50.00
Imperial Ching-te Chen		**Flower Goddesses of China**			
91-05-001	The Lotus Goddess	Z. HuiMin	175-day	34.92	40.00
91-05-002	The Chrysanthemum Goddess	Z. HuiMin	175-day	34.92	35.00
91-05-003	The Plum Blossom Goddess	Z. HuiMin	175-day	37.92	38.00
91-05-004	The Peony Goddess	Z. HuiMin	175-day	37.92	52.00
91-05-005	The Narcissus Goddess	Z. HuiMin	175-day	37.92	50.00
91-05-006	The Camellia Goddess	Z. HuiMin	175-day	37.92	45.00
Imperial Ching-te Chen		**The Forbidden City**			
90-06-001	Pavilion of 10,000 Springs	S. Fu	150-day	39.92	40.00
90-06-002	Flying Kites/Spring Day	S. Fu	150-day	39.92	40.00
90-06-003	Pavilion/Floating Jade Green	S. Fu	150-day	42.92	44.00
91-06-004	The Lantern Festival	S. Fu	150-day	42.92	43.00
91-06-005	Nine Dragon Screen	S. Fu	150-day	42.92	60.00
91-06-006	The Hall of the Cultivating Mind	S. Fu	150-day	42.92	45.00
91-06-007	Dressing the Empress	S. Fu	150-day	45.92	50.00
91-06-008	Pavilion of Floating Cups	S. Fu	150-day	45.92	50.00
Imperial Ching-te Chen		**Maidens of the Folding Sky**			
92-07-001	Lady Lu	J. Xue-Bing	175-day	29.92	30.00
92-07-002	Mistress Yang	J. Xue-Bing	175-day	29.92	30.00
92-07-003	Bride Yen Chun	J. Xue-Bing	175-day	32.92	32.92
93-07-004	Parrot Maiden	J. Xue-Bing	175-day	32.92	32.92
Imperial Ching-te Chen		**Garden of Satin Wings**			
92-08-001	A Morning Dream	J. Xue-Bing	115-day	29.92	29.92
93-08-002	An Evening Mist	J. Xue-Bing	115-day	29.92	29.92
93-08-003	A Garden Whisper	J. Xue-Bing	115-day	29.92	29.92
International Silver		**Bicentennial**			
72-01-001	Signing Declaration	M. Deoliveira	7,500	40.00	310.00
73-01-002	Paul Revere	M. Deoliveira	7,500	40.00	160.00
74-01-003	Concord Bridge	M. Deoliveira	7,500	40.00	115.00
75-01-004	Crossing Delaware	M. Deoliveira	7,500	50.00	80.00
76-01-005	Valley Forge	M. Deoliveira	7,500	50.00	65.00
77-01-006	Surrender at Yorktown	M. Deoliveira	7,500	50.00	60.00
Kaiser		**Christmas Plates**			
70-01-001	Waiting for Santa Claus	T. Schoener	Closed	12.50	25.00
71-01-002	Silent Night	K. Bauer	Closed	13.50	23.00
72-01-003	Welcome Home	K. Bauer	Closed	16.50	43.00
73-01-004	Holy Night	T. Schoener	Closed	18.00	44.00
74-01-005	Christmas Carolers	K. Bauer	Closed	25.00	30.00
75-01-006	Bringing Home the Tree	J. Northcott	Closed	25.00	30.00
76-01-007	Christ/Saviour Born	C. Maratti	Closed	25.00	35.00
77-01-008	The Three Kings	T. Schoener	Closed	25.00	25.00
78-01-009	Shepherds in The Field	T. Schoener	Closed	30.00	30.00
79-01-010	Christmas Eve	H. Blum	Closed	32.00	45.00
80-01-011	Joys of Winter	H. Blum	Closed	40.00	43.00
81-01-012	Adoration by Three Kings	K. Bauer	Closed	40.00	41.00
82-01-013	Bringing Home the Tree	K. Bauer	Closed	40.00	45.00
Kaiser		**Mother's Day**			
71-02-001	Mare and Foal	T. Schoener	Closed	13.00	25.00
72-02-002	Flowers for Mother	T. Schoener	Closed	16.50	20.00
73-02-003	Cats	T. Schoener	Closed	17.00	40.00
74-02-004	Fox	T. Schoener	Closed	20.00	40.00
75-02-005	German Shepherd	T. Schoener	Closed	25.00	100.00
76-02-006	Swan and Cygnets	T. Schoener	Closed	25.00	27.50
77-02-007	Mother Rabbit and Young	T. Schoener	Closed	25.00	30.00
78-02-008	Hen and Chicks	T. Schoener	Closed	30.00	50.00
79-02-009	A Mother's Devotion	N. Peterner	Closed	32.00	40.00
80-02-010	Raccoon Family	J. Northcott	Closed	40.00	45.00
81-02-011	Safe Near Mother	H. Blum	Closed	40.00	40.00
82-02-012	Pheasant Family	K. Bauer	Closed	40.00	44.00
83-02-013	Tender Care	K. Bauer	Closed	40.00	65.00
Kaiser		**King Tut**			
78-03-001	King Tut	Unknown	Closed	65.00	100.00
Kaiser		**Egyptian**			
80-04-001	Nefertiti	Unknown	10,000	275.00	458.00
80-04-002	Tutankhamen	Unknown	10,000	275.00	458.00
Kaiser		**Bicentennial Plate**			
76-05-001	Signing Declaration	J. Trumball	Closed	75.00	150.00
Edwin M. Knowles		**Wizard of Oz**			
77-01-001	Over the Rainbow	J. Auckland	100-day	19.00	45.00
78-01-002	If I Only Had a Brain	J. Auckland	100-day	19.00	35.00
78-01-003	If I Only Had a Heart	J. Auckland	100-day	19.00	38.00
78-01-004	If I Were King of the Forest	J. Auckland	100-day	19.00	40.00
79-01-005	Wicked Witch of the West	J. Auckland	100-day	19.00	50.00
79-01-006	Follow the Yellow Brick Road	J. Auckland	100-day	19.00	40.00
79-01-007	Wonderful Wizard of Oz	J. Auckland	100-day	19.00	44.00
80-01-008	The Grand Finale	J. Auckland	100-day	24.00	45.00
Edwin M. Knowles		**Gone with the Wind**			
78-02-001	Scarlett	R. Kursar	100-day	21.50	220-250.
79-02-002	Ashley	R. Kursar	100-day	21.50	120.00.
80-02-003	Melanie	R. Kursar	100-day	21.50	55-59.00
81-02-004	Rhett	R. Kursar	100-day	23.50	38-45.00
82-02-005	Mammy Lacing Scarlett	R. Kursar	100-day	23.50	68-75.00
83-02-006	Melanie Gives Birth	R. Kursar	100-day	23.50	85-94.00
84-02-007	Scarlet's Green Dress	R. Kursar	100-day	25.50	75.00
85-02-008	Rhett and Bonnie	R. Kursar	100-day	25.50	75-94.00
85-02-009	Scarlett and Rhett: The Finale	R. Kursar	100-day	29.50	75-81.00
Edwin M. Knowles		**Csatari Grandparent**			
80-03-001	Bedtime Story	J. Csatari	100-day	18.00	18.00
81-03-002	The Skating Lesson	J. Csatari	100-day	20.00	20.00
82-03-003	The Cookie Tasting	J. Csatari	100-day	20.00	20.00
83-03-004	The Swinger	J. Csatari	100-day	20.00	20.00
84-03-005	The Skating Queen	J. Csatari	100-day	22.00	22-25.00
85-03-006	The Patriot's Parade	J. Csatari	100-day	22.00	22.00
86-03-007	The Home Run	J. Csatari	100-day	22.00	22.00
87-03-008	The Sneak Preview	J. Csatari	100-day	22.00	22.00

Number	Name	Artist	Edition Limit	Issue Price	Quote
Edwin M. Knowles		**Americana Holidays**			
78-04-001	Fourth of July	D. Spaulding	Yr.Iss.	26.00	26.00
79-04-002	Thanksgiving	D. Spaulding	Yr.Iss.	26.00	26.00
80-04-003	Easter	D. Spaulding	Yr.Iss.	26.00	26.00
81-04-004	Valentine's Day	D. Spaulding	Yr.Iss.	26.00	26.00
82-04-005	Father's Day	D. Spaulding	Yr.Iss.	26.00	26.00
83-04-006	Christmas	D. Spaulding	Yr.Iss.	26.00	26.00
84-04-007	Mother's Day	D. Spaulding	Yr.Iss.	26.00	27.00
Edwin M. Knowles		**Annie**			
83-05-001	Annie and Sandy	W. Chambers	100-day	19.00	19.00
83-05-002	Daddy Warbucks	W. Chambers	100-day	19.00	19.00
83-05-003	Annie and Grace	W. Chambers	100-day	19.00	19.00
84-05-004	Annie and the Orphans	W. Chambers	100-day	21.00	21.00
85-05-005	Tomorrow	W. Chambers	100-day	21.00	21.00
86-05-006	Annie and Miss Hannigan	W. Chambers	100-day	21.00	21.00
86-05-007	Annie, Lily and Rooster	W. Chambers	100-day	24.00	24.00
86-05-008	Grand Finale	W. Chambers	100-day	24.00	24.00
Edwin M. Knowles		**The Four Ancient Elements**			
84-06-001	Earth	G. Lambert	75-day	27.50	28.00
84-06-002	Water	G. Lambert	75-day	27.50	28.00
85-06-003	Air	G. Lambert	75-day	29.50	30.00
85-06-004	Fire	G. Lambert	75-day	29.50	45.00
Edwin M. Knowles		**Biblical Mothers**			
83-07-001	Bathsheba and Solomon	E. Licea	Yr.Iss.	39.50	40.00
84-07-002	Judgment of Solomon	E. Licea	Yr.Iss.	39.50	40.00
84-07-003	Pharaoh's Daughter and Moses	E. Licea	Yr.Iss.	39.50	40.00
85-07-004	Mary and Jesus	E. Licea	Yr.Iss.	39.50	40.00
85-07-005	Sarah and Isaac	E. Licea	Yr.Iss.	44.50	44.00
86-07-006	Rebekah, Jacob and Esau	E. Licea	Yr.Iss.	44.50	45.00
Edwin M. Knowles		**Hibel Mother's Day**			
84-08-001	Abby and Lisa	E. Hibel	Yr.Iss.	29.50	32.00
85-08-002	Erica and Jamie	E. Hibel	Yr.Iss.	29.50	30.00
86-08-003	Emily and Jennifer	E. Hibel	Yr.Iss.	29.50	50.00
87-08-004	Catherine and Heather	E. Hibel	Yr.Iss.	34.50	54-59.00
88-08-005	Sarah and Tess	E. Hibel	Yr.Iss.	34.90	35.00
89-08-006	Jessica and Kate	E. Hibel	Yr.Iss.	34.90	35.00
90-08-007	Elizabeth, Jordan & Janie	E. Hibel	Yr.Iss.	36.90	37.00
91-08-008	Michele and Anna	E. Hibel	Yr.Iss.	36.90	37.00
Edwin M. Knowles		**Friends I Remember**			
83-09-001	Fish Story	J. Down	97-day	17.50	17.50
84-09-002	Office Hours	J. Down	97-day	17.50	17.50
85-09-003	A Coat of Paint	J. Down	97-day	17.50	17.50
85-09-004	Here Comes the Bride	J. Down	97-day	19.50	19.50
85-09-005	Fringe Benefits	J. Down	97-day	19.50	19.50
86-09-006	High Society	J. Down	97-day	19.50	19.50
86-09-007	Flower Arrangement	J. Down	97-day	21.50	22-29.00
86-09-008	Taste Test	J. Down	97-day	21.50	21.50
Edwin M. Knowles		**Father's Love**			
84-10-001	Open Wide	B. Bradley	100-day	19.50	20.00
84-10-002	Batter Up	B. Bradley	100-day	19.50	20.00
85-10-003	Little Shaver	B. Bradley	100-day	19.50	20.00
85-10-004	Swing Time	B. Bradley	100-day	22.50	23.00
Edwin M. Knowles		**The King and I**			
84-11-001	A Puzzlement	W. Chambers	150-day	19.50	20.00
85-11-002	Shall We Dance?	W. Chambers	150-day	19.50	30.00
85-11-003	Getting to Know You	W. Chambers	150-day	19.50	20.00
85-11-004	We Kiss in a Shadow	W. Chambers	150-day	19.50	20-25.00
Edwin M. Knowles		**Ency. Brit. Birds of Your Garden**			
85-12-001	Cardinal	K. Daniel	100-day	19.50	35.00
85-12-002	Blue Jay	K. Daniel	100-day	19.50	27.00
85-12-003	Oriole	K. Daniel	100-day	22.50	28.00
86-12-004	Chickadees	K. Daniel	100-day	22.50	37.00
86-12-005	Bluebird	K. Daniel	100-day	22.50	30.00
86-12-006	Robin	K. Daniel	100-day	22.50	20.00
86-12-007	Hummingbird	K. Daniel	100-day	24.50	25.00
87-12-008	Goldfinch	K. Daniel	100-day	24.50	30.00
87-12-009	Downy Woodpecker	K. Daniel	100-day	24.50	25.00
87-12-010	Cedar Waxwing	K. Daniel	100-day	24.90	25.00
Edwin M. Knowles		**Frances Hook Legacy**			
85-13-001	Fascination	F. Hook	100-day	19.50	19.50
85-13-002	Daydreaming	F. Hook	100-day	19.50	19.50
86-13-003	Discovery	F. Hook	100-day	22.50	22.50
86-13-004	Disappointment	F. Hook	100-day	22.50	22.50
86-13-005	Wonderment	F. Hook	100-day	22.50	22.50
87-13-006	Expectation	F. Hook	100-day	22.50	22.50
Edwin M. Knowles		**Hibel Christmas**			
85-14-001	The Angel's Message	E. Hibel	Yr.Iss.	45.00	45.00
86-14-002	The Gifts of the Magi	E. Hibel	Yr.Iss.	45.00	45.00
87-14-003	The Flight Into Egypt	E. Hibel	Yr.Iss.	49.00	49.00
88-14-004	Adoration of the Shepherd	E. Hibel	Yr.Iss.	49.00	49.00
89-14-005	Peaceful Kingdom	E. Hibel	Yr.Iss.	49.00	49.00
90-14-006	Nativity	E. Hibel	Yr.Iss.	49.00	59.00
Edwin M. Knowles		**Upland Birds of North America**			
86-15-001	The Pheasant	W. Anderson	150-day	24.50	25.00
86-15-002	The Grouse	W. Anderson	150-day	24.50	25.00
87-15-003	The Quail	W. Anderson	150-day	27.50	28.00
87-15-004	The Wild Turkey	W. Anderson	150-day	27.50	28.00
87-15-005	The Gray Partridge	W. Anderson	150-day	27.50	28.00
87-15-006	The Woodcock	W. Anderson	150-day	27.90	28.00
Edwin M. Knowles		**Oklahoma!**			
85-16-001	Oh, What a Beautiful Mornin'	M. Kunstler	150-day	19.50	19.50
86-16-002	Surrey with the Fringe on Top'	M. Kunstler	150-day	19.50	19.50
86-16-003	I Cain't Say No	M. Kunstler	150-day	19.50	19.50
86-16-004	Oklahoma	M. Kunstler	150-day	19.50	19.50
Edwin M. Knowles		**Sound of Music**			
86-17-001	Sound of Music	T. Crnkovich	150-day	19.50	20.00
86-17-002	Do-Re-Mi	T. Crnkovich	150-day	19.50	20.00
86-17-003	My Favorite Things	T. Crnkovich	150-day	22.50	23.00
86-17-004	Laendler Waltz	T. Crnkovich	150-day	22.50	26-36.00
87-17-005	Edelweiss	T. Crnkovich	150-day	22.50	30-48.00
87-17-006	I Have Confidence	T. Crnkovich	150-day	22.50	23-25.00

PLATES

Company Number	Name	Series Artist	Edition Limit	Issue Price	Quote
87-17-007	Maria	T. Crnkovich	150-day	24.90	30-33.00
87-17-008	Climb Ev'ry Mountain	T. Crnkovich	150-day	24.90	42.00
Edwin M. Knowles		**American Innocents**			
86-18-001	Abigail in the Rose Garden	Marsten/Mandrajji	100-day	19.50	19.50
86-18-002	Ann by the Terrace	Marsten/Mandrajji	100-day	19.50	19.50
86-18-003	Ellen and John in the Parlor	Marsten/Mandrajji	100-day	19.50	19.50
86-18-004	William on the Rocking Horse	Marsten/Mandrajji	100-day	19.50	48.00
Edwin M. Knowles		**J. W. Smith Childhood Holidays**			
86-19-001	Easter	J. W. Smith	97-day	19.50	21.00
86-19-002	Thanksgiving	J. W. Smith	97-day	19.50	21.00
86-19-003	Christmas	J. W. Smith	97-day	19.50	24.00
86-19-004	Valentine's Day	J. W. Smith	97-day	22.50	25.00
87-19-005	Mother's Day	J. W. Smith	97-day	22.50	25.00
87-19-006	Fourth of July	J. W. Smith	97-day	22.50	25-30.00
Edwin M. Knowles		**Living with Nature-Jerner's Ducks**			
86-20-001	The Pintail	B. Jerner	150-day	19.50	34.00
86-20-002	The Mallard	B. Jerner	150-day	19.50	35.00
87-20-003	The Wood Duck	B. Jerner	150-day	22.50	36.00
87-20-004	The Green-Winged Teal	B. Jerner	150-day	22.50	30.00
87-20-005	The Northern Shoveler	B. Jerner	150-day	22.90	35.00
87-20-006	The American Widgeon	B. Jerner	150-day	22.90	25.00
87-20-007	The Gadwall	B. Jerner	150-day	24.90	30.00
88-20-008	The Blue-Winged Teal	B. Jerner	150-day	24.90	25.00
Edwin M. Knowles		**Lincoln Man of America**			
86-21-001	The Gettysburg Address	M. Kunstler	150-day	24.50	24.50
87-21-002	The Inauguration	M. Kunstler	150-day	24.50	24.50
87-21-003	The Lincoln-Douglas Debates	M. Kunstler	150-day	27.50	27.50
87-21-004	Beginnings in New Salem	M. Kunstler	150-day	27.90	27.90
88-21-005	The Family Man	M. Kunstler	150-day	27.90	27.90
88-21-006	Emancipation Proclamation	M. Kunstler	150-day	27.90	27.90
Edwin M. Knowles		**Portraits of Motherhood**			
87-22-001	Mother's Here	W. Chambers	150-day	29.50	35.00
88-22-002	First Touch	W. Chambers	150-day	29.50	32.00
Edwin M. Knowles		**A Swan is Born**			
87-23-001	Hopes and Dreams	L. Roberts	150-day	24.50	24.50
87-23-002	At the Barre	L. Roberts	150-day	24.50	17.00
87-23-003	In Position	L. Roberts	150-day	24.50	27.00
88-23-004	Just For Size	L. Roberts	150-day	24.50	45.00
Edwin M. Knowles		**South Pacific**			
87-24-001	Some Enchanted Evening	E. Gignilliat	150-day	24.50	24.50
87-24-002	Happy Talk	E. Gignilliat	150-day	24.50	24.50
87-24-003	Dites Moi	E. Gignilliat	150-day	24.90	24.50
88-24-004	Honey Bun	E. Gignilliat	150-day	24.90	24.90
Edwin M. Knowles		**Tom Sawyer**			
87-25-001	Whitewashing the Fence	W. Chambers	150-day	27.50	27.50
87-25-002	Tom and Becky	W. Chambers	150-day	27.90	27.90
87-25-003	Tom Sawyer the Pirate	W. Chambers	150-day	27.90	27.90
88-25-004	First Pipes	W. Chambers	150-day	27.90	27.90
Edwin M. Knowles		**Friends of the Forest**			
87-26-001	The Rabbit	K. Daniel	150-day	24.50	26.00
87-26-002	The Raccoon	K. Daniel	150-day	24.50	35.00
87-26-003	The Squirrel	K. Daniel	150-day	27.90	28.00
88-26-004	The Chipmunk	K. Daniel	150-day	27.90	28.00
88-26-005	The Fox	K. Daniel	150-day	27.90	28.00
88-26-006	The Otter	K. Daniel	150-day	27.90	28.00
Edwin M. Knowles		**Amy Brackenbury's Cat Tales**			
87-27-001	A Chance Meeting: White American Shorthairs	A. Brackenbury	150-day	21.50	31.00
87-27-002	Gone Fishing: Maine Coons	A. Brackenbury	150-day	21.50	75.00
88-27-003	Strawberries and Cream: Cream Persians	A. Brackenbury	150-day	24.90	70.00
88-27-004	Flower Bed: British Shorthairs	A. Brackenbury	150-day	24.90	25.00
88-27-005	Kittens and Mittens: Silver Tabbies	A. Brackenbury	150-day	24.90	29.00
88-27-006	All Wrapped Up: Himalayans	A. Brackenbury	150-day	24.90	48.00
Edwin M. Knowles		**The Story of Christmas by Eve Licea**			
87-28-001	The Annunciation	E. Licea	Yr.Iss.	44.90	45.00
88-28-002	The Nativity	E. Licea	Yr.Iss.	44.90	45.00
89-28-003	Adoration Of The Shepherds	E. Licea	Yr.Iss.	49.90	50.00
90-28-004	Journey Of The Magi	E. Licea	Yr.Iss.	49.90	48.00
91-28-005	Gifts Of The Magi	E. Licea	Yr.Iss.	49.90	50.00
92-28-006	Rest on the Flight into Egypt	E. Licea	Yr.Iss.	49.90	50.00
Edwin M. Knowles		**Carousel**			
87-29-001	If I Loved You	D. Brown	150-day	24.90	25.00
88-29-002	Mr. Snow	D. Brown	150-day	24.90	25.00
88-29-003	The Carousel Waltz	D. Brown	150-day	24.90	45.00
88-29-004	You'll Never Walk Alone	D. Brown	150-day	24.90	35.00
Edwin M. Knowles		**Field Puppies**			
87-30-001	Dog Tired-The Springer Spaniel	L. Kaatz	150-day	24.90	55-58.00
87-30-002	Caught in the Act-The Golden Retriever	L. Kaatz	150-day	24.90	60.00
88-30-003	Missing/Point/Irish Setter	L. Kaatz	150-day	27.90	28.00
88-30-004	A Perfect Set-Labrador	L. Kaatz	150-day	27.90	48.00
88-30-005	Fritz's Folly-German Shorthaired Pointer	L. Kaatz	150-day	27.90	42.00
88-30-006	Shirt Tales: Cocker Spaniel	L. Kaatz	150-day	27.90	51-53.00
89-30-007	Fine Feathered Friends-English Setter	L. Kaatz	150-day	29.90	30-32.00
89-30-008	Command Performance/ Wiemaraner	L. Kaatz	150-day	29.90	35.00
Edwin M. Knowles		**The American Journey**			
87-31-001	Westward Ho	M. Kunstler	150-day	29.90	29.90
88-31-002	Kitchen With a View	M. Kunstler	150-day	29.90	32.00
88-31-003	Crossing the River	M. Kunstler	150-day	29.90	29.90
88-31-004	Christmas at the New Cabin	M. Kunstler	150-day	29.90	29.90
Edwin M. Knowles		**Precious Little Ones**			
88-32-001	Little Red Robins	M. T. Fangel	150-day	29.90	29.90
88-32-002	Little Fledglings	M. T. Fangel	150-day	29.90	29.90
88-32-003	Saturday Night Bath	M. T. Fangel	150-day	29.90	33.00
88-32-004	Peek-A-Boo	M. T. Fangel	150-day	29.90	38.00
Edwin M. Knowles		**Aesop's Fables**			
88-33-001	The Goose That Laid the Golden Egg	M. Hampshire	150-day	27.90	28.00
88-33-002	The Hare and the Tortoise	M. Hampshire	150-day	27.90	28.00
88-33-003	The Fox and the Grapes	M. Hampshire	150-day	30.90	31.00

Company Number	Name	Series Artist	Edition Limit	Issue Price	Quote
89-33-004	The Lion And The Mouse	M. Hampshire	150-day	30.90	40.00
89-33-005	The Milk Maid And Her Pail	M. Hampshire	150-day	30.90	32.00
89-33-006	The Jay And The Peacock	M. Hampshire	150-day	30.90	33.00
Edwin M. Knowles		**Not So Long Ago**			
88-34-001	Story Time	J. W. Smith	150-day	24.90	24.90
88-34-002	Wash Day for Dolly	J. W. Smith	150-day	24.90	24.90
88-34-003	Suppertime for Kitty	J. W. Smith	150-day	24.90	35.00
88-34-004	Mother's Little Helper	J. W. Smith	150-day	24.90	30.00
Edwin M. Knowles		**Jerner's Less Travelled Road**			
88-35-001	The Weathered Barn	B. Jerner	150-day	29.90	29.90
88-35-002	The Murmuring Stream	B. Jerner	150-day	29.90	29.90
88-35-003	The Covered Bridge	B. Jerner	150-day	32.90	36.00
89-35-004	Winter's Peace	B. Jerner	150-day	32.90	40.00
89-35-005	The Flowering Meadow	B. Jerner	150-day	32.90	33.00
89-35-006	The Hidden Waterfall	B. Jerner	150-day	32.90	33.00
Edwin M. Knowles		**Once Upon a Time**			
88-36-001	Little Red Riding Hood	K. Pritchett	150-day	24.90	24.90
88-36-002	Rapunzel	K. Pritchett	150-day	24.90	24.90
88-36-003	Three Little Pigs	K. Pritchett	150-day	27.90	28.00
89-36-004	The Princess and the Pea	K. Pritchett	150-day	27.90	28.00
89-36-005	Goldilocks and the Three Bears	K. Pritchett	150-day	27.90	29.00
89-36-006	Beauty and the Beast	K. Pritchett	150-day	27.90	45.00
Edwin M. Knowles		**Majestic Birds of North America**			
88-37-001	The Bald Eagle	D. Smith	150-day	29.90	30.00
88-37-002	Peregrine Falcon	D. Smith	150-day	29.90	37.00
88-37-003	The Great Horned Owl	D. Smith	150-day	32.90	33.00
89-37-004	The Red-Tailed Hawk	D. Smith	150-day	32.90	33.00
89-37-005	The White Gyrfalcon	D. Smith	150-day	32.90	33.00
89-37-006	The American Kestral	D. Smith	150-day	32.90	33.00
90-37-007	The Osprey	D. Smith	150-day	34.90	35.00
90-37-008	The Golden Eagle	D. Smith	150-day	34.90	35.00
Edwin M. Knowles		**Cinderella**			
88-38-001	Bibbidi, Bobbidi, Boo	Disney Studios	150-day	29.90	74.00
88-38-002	A Dream Is A Wish Your Heart Makes	Disney Studios	150-day	29.90	80.00
89-38-003	Oh Sing Sweet Nightingale	Disney Studios	150-day	32.90	45.00
89-38-004	A Dress For Cinderelly	Disney Studios	150-day	32.90	71-89.00
89-38-005	So This Is Love	Disney Studios	150-day	32.90	50-52.00
90-38-006	At The Stroke Of Midnight	Disney Studios	150-day	32.90	51-54.00
90-38-007	If The Shoe Fits	Disney Studios	150-day	34.90	45.00
90-38-008	Happily Ever After	Disney Studios	150-day	34.90	35.00
Edwin M. Knowles		**Mary Poppins**			
89-40-001	Mary Poppins	M. Hampshire	150-day	29.90	30.00
89-40-002	A Spoonful of Sugar	M. Hampshire	150-day	29.90	30.00
90-40-003	A Jolly Holiday With Mary	M. Hampshire	150-day	32.90	41.00
90-40-004	We Love To Laugh	M. Hampshire	150-day	32.90	50.00
91-40-005	Chim Chim Cher-ee	M. Hampshire	150-day	32.90	39.00
91-40-006	Tuppence a Bag	M. Hampshire	150-day	32.90	55.00
Edwin M. Knowles		**Home Sweet Home**			
89-41-001	The Victorian	R. McGinnis	150-day	39.90	39.90
89-41-002	The Greek Revival	R. McGinnis	150-day	39.90	30-39.90
89-41-003	The Georgian	R. McGinnis	150-day	39.90	39.90
90-41-004	The Mission	R. McGinnis	150-day	39.90	39.90
Edwin M. Knowles		**My Fair Lady**			
89-42-001	Opening Day at Ascot	W. Chambers	150-day	24.90	25.00
89-42-002	I Could Have Danced All Night	W. Chambers	150-day	24.90	25.00
89-42-003	The Rain in Spain	W. Chambers	150-day	27.90	28.00
89-42-004	Show Me	W. Chambers	150-day	27.90	27.00
90-42-005	Get Me To/Church On Time	W. Chambers	150-day	27.90	28.00
90-42-006	I've Grown Accustomed/Face	W. Chambers	150-day	27.90	41.00
Edwin M. Knowles		**Sundblom Santas**			
89-43-001	Santa By The Fire	H. Sundblom	Closed	27.90	45.00
90-43-002	Christmas Vigil	H. Sundblom	Closed	27.90	47.00
91-43-003	To All A Good Night	H. Sundblom	Closed	32.90	45.00
92-43-004	Santa's on His Way	H. Sundblom	Closed	32.90	63.00
Edwin M. Knowles		**Great Cats Of The Americas**			
89-44-001	The Jaguar	L. Cable	150-day	29.90	70.00
89-44-002	The Cougar	L. Cable	150-day	29.90	50.00
89-44-003	The Lynx	L. Cable	150-day	32.90	33.00
90-44-004	The Ocelot	L. Cable	150-day	32.90	33.00
90-44-005	The Bobcat	L. Cable	150-day	32.90	33.00
90-44-006	The Jaguarundi	L. Cable	150-day	32.90	35.00
90-44-007	The Margay	L. Cable	150-day	34.90	35.00
91-44-008	The Pampas Cat	L. Cable	150-day	34.90	35.00
Edwin M. Knowles		**Heirlooms And Lace**			
89-45-001	Anna	C. Layton	150-day	34.90	55.00
89-45-002	Victoria	C. Layton	150-day	34.90	54.00
90-45-003	Tess	C. Layton	150-day	37.90	84.00
90-45-004	Olivia	C. Layton	150-day	37.90	125.00
91-45-005	Bridget	C. Layton	150-day	37.90	120.00
91-45-006	Rebecca	C. Layton	150-day	37.90	100.00
Edwin M. Knowles		**Stately Owls**			
89-46-001	The Snowy Owl	J. Beaudoin	150-day	29.90	47.00
89-46-002	The Great Horned Owl	J. Beaudoin	150-day	29.90	35.00
90-46-003	The Barn Owl	J. Beaudoin	150-day	32.90	31.00
90-46-004	The Screech Owl	J. Beaudoin	150-day	32.90	34.00
90-46-005	The Short-Eared Owl	J. Beaudoin	150-day	32.90	33.00
90-46-006	The Barred Owl	J. Beaudoin	150-day	32.90	50.00
90-46-007	The Great Grey Owl	J. Beaudoin	150-day	34.90	34.90
91-46-008	The Saw-Whet Owl	J. Beaudoin	150-day	34.90	35.00
Edwin M. Knowles		**Singin' In The Rain**			
90-47-001	Singin' In The Rain	M. Skolsky	150-day	32.90	33.00
90-47-002	Good Morning	M. Skolsky	150-day	32.90	33.00
91-47-003	Broadway Melody	M. Skolsky	150-day	32.90	40.00
91-47-004	We're Happy Again	M. Skolsky	150-day	32.90	32.00
Edwin M. Knowles		**Pinocchio**			
89-48-001	Gepetto Creates Pinocchio	Disney Studios	150-day	29.90	60-80.00
90-48-002	Pinocchio And The Blue Fairy	Disney Studios	150-day	29.90	75.00
90-48-003	It's an Actor's Life For Me	Disney Studios	150-day	32.90	40.00
90-48-004	I've Got No Strings On Me	Disney Studios	150-day	32.90	48.00
91-48-005	Pleasure Island	Disney Studios	150-day	32.90	45.00

Number	Name	Artist	Edition Limit	Issue Price	Quote
91-48-006	A Real Boy	Disney Studios	150-day	32.90	57.00
Edwin M. Knowles		**Nature's Child**			
90-49-001	Sharing	M. Jobe	150-day	29.90	31.00
90-49-002	The Lost Lamb	M. Jobe	150-day	29.90	29.00
90-49-003	Seems Like Yesterday.	M. Jobe	150-day	32.90	35.00
90-49-004	Faithful Friends	M. Jobe	150-day	32.90	33.00
90-49-005	Trusted Companion	M. Jobe	150-day	32.90	55.00
91-49-006	Hand in Hand	M. Jobe	150-day	32.90	45.00
Edwin M. Knowles		**Fantasia: (The Sorcerer's Apprentice) Golden Anniversary**			
90-50-001	The Apprentice's Dream	Disney Studios	150-day	29.90	50.00
90-50-002	Mischievous Apprentice	Disney Studios	150-day	29.90	50.00
91-50-003	Dreams of Power	Disney Studios	150-day	32.90	68.00
91-50-004	Mickey's Magical Whirlpool	Disney Studios	150-day	32.90	48.00
91-50-005	Wizardry Gone Wild	Disney Studios	150-day	32.90	32.90
91-50-006	Mickey Makes Magic	Disney Studios	150-day	34.90	34.90
91-50-007	The Penitent Apprentice	Disney Studios	150-day	34.90	34.90
92-50-008	An Apprentice Again	Disney Studios	150-day	34.90	34.90
Edwin M. Knowles		**Casablanca**			
90-51-001	Here's Looking At You, Kid	J. Griffin	150-day	34.90	47.00
90-51-002	We'll Always Have Paris	J. Griffin	150-day	34.90	42.00
91-51-003	We Loved Each Other Once	J. Griffin	150-day	37.90	39.00
91-51-004	Rick's Cafe Americain	J. Griffin	150-day	37.90	42.00
91-51-005	A Franc For Your Thoughts	J. Griffin	150-day	37.90	58.00
91-51-006	Play it Sam	J. Griffin	150-day	37.90	50-58.00
Edwin M. Knowles		**Field Trips**			
90-52-001	Gone Fishing	L. Kaatz	150-day	24.90	24.90
91-52-002	Ducking Duty	L. Kaatz	150-day	24.90	24.90
91-52-003	Boxed In	L. Kaatz	150-day	27.90	32.00
91-52-004	Pups 'N Boots	L. Kaatz	150-day	27.90	35.00
91-52-005	Puppy Tales	L. Kaatz	150-day	27.90	27.90
91-52-006	Pail Pals	L. Kaatz	150-day	29.90	29.90
91-52-007	Chesapeake Bay Retrievers	L. Kaatz	150-day	29.90	29.90
91-52-008	Hat Trick	L. Kaatz	150-day	29.90	29.90
Edwin M. Knowles		**The Old Mill Stream**			
90-53-001	New London Grist Mill	C. Tennant	150-day	39.90	39.90
91-53-002	Wayside Inn Grist Mill	C. Tennant	150-day	39.90	49.00
91-53-003	Old Red Mill	C. Tennant	150-day	39.90	54.00
91-53-004	Glade Creek Grist Mill	C. Tennant	150-day	39.90	58.00
Edwin M. Knowles		**Birds of the Seasons**			
90-54-001	Cardinals In Winter	S. Timm	150-day	24.90	50.00
90-54-002	Bluebirds In Spring	S. Timm	150-day	24.90	40.00
91-54-003	Nuthatches In Fall	S. Timm	150-day	27.90	27.00
91-54-004	Baltimore Orioles In Summer	S. Timm	150-day	27.90	32.00
91-54-005	Blue Jays In Early Fall	S. Timm	150-day	27.90	35.00
91-54-006	Robins In Early Spring	S. Timm	150-day	27.90	30.00
91-54-007	Cedar Waxwings in Fall	S. Timm	150-day	29.90	40.00
91-54-008	Chickadees in Winter	S. Timm	150-day	29.90	40.00
Edwin M. Knowles		**Cozy Country Corners**			
90-55-001	Lazy Morning	H. H. Ingmire	150-day	24.90	58.00
90-55-002	Warm Retreat	H. H. Ingmire	150-day	24.90	47.00
91-55-003	A Sunny Spot	H. H. Ingmire	150-day	27.90	44.00
91-55-004	Attic Afternoon	H. H. Ingmire	150-day	27.90	50.00
91-55-005	Mirror Mischief	H. H. Ingmire	150-day	27.90	60.00
91-55-006	Hide and Seek	H. H. Ingmire	150-day	29.90	60.00
91-55-007	Apple Antics	H. H. Ingmire	150-day	29.90	50.00
91-55-008	Table Trouble	H. H. Ingmire	150-day	29.90	50.00
Edwin M. Knowles		**Jewels of the Flowers**			
91-56-001	Sapphire Wings	T.C. Chiu	150-day	29.90	37.00
91-56-002	Topaz Beauties	T.C. Chiu	150-day	29.90	44.00
91-56-003	Amethyst Flight	T.C. Chiu	150-day	32.90	44.00
91-56-004	Ruby Elegance	T.C. Chiu	150-day	32.90	32.90
91-56-005	Emerald Pair	T.C. Chiu	150-day	32.90	32.90
91-56-006	Opal Splendor	T.C. Chiu	150-day	34.90	34.90
92-56-007	Pearl Luster	T.C. Chiu	150-day	34.90	34.90
92-56-008	Aquamarine Glimmer	T.C. Chiu	150-day	34.90	34.90
Edwin M. Knowles		**Pussyfooting Around**			
91-57-001	Fish Tales	C. Wilson	150-day	24.90	25.00
91-57-002	Teatime Tabbies	C. Wilson	150-day	24.90	25.00
91-57-003	Yarn Spinners	C. Wilson	150-day	24.90	24.90
91-57-004	Two Maestros	C. Wilson	150-day	24.90	24.90
Edwin M. Knowles		**Baby Owls of North America**			
91-58-001	Peek-A-Whoo:Screech Owls	J. Thornbrugh	150-day	27.90	45.00
91-58-002	Forty Winks: Saw-Whet Owls	J. Thornbrugh	150-day	29.90	44.00
91-58-003	The Tree House: Northern Pygmy Owls	J. Thornbrugh	150-day	30.90	31.00
91-58-004	Three of a Kind: Great Horned Owls	J. Thornbrugh	150-day	30.90	30.90
91-58-005	Out on a Limb: Great Gray Owls	J. Thornbrugh	150-day	30.90	30.90
91-58-006	Beginning to Explore: Boreal Owls	J. Thornbrugh	150-day	32.90	32.90
92-58-007	Three's Company: Long Eared Owls	J. Thornbrugh	150-day	32.90	32.90
92-58-008	Whoo's There: Barred Owl	J. Thornbrugh	150-day	32.90	32.90
Edwin M. Knowles		**Season For Song**			
91-59-001	Winter Concert	M. Jobe	150-day	34.90	58.00
91-59-002	Snowy Symphony	M. Jobe	150-day	34.90	58.00
91-59-003	Frosty Chorus	M. Jobe	150-day	34.90	38.00
91-59-004	Silver Serenade	M. Jobe	150-day	34.90	35.00
Edwin M. Knowles		**Garden Cottages of England**			
91-60-001	Chandler's Cottage	T. Kinkade	150-day	27.90	45.00
91-60-002	Cedar Nook Cottage	T. Kinkade	150-day	27.90	28.00
91-60-003	Candlelit Cottage	T. Kinkade	150-day	30.90	30.90
91-60-004	Open Gate Cottage	T. Kinkade	150-day	30.90	30.90
91-60-005	McKenna's Cottage	T. Kinkade	150-day	30.90	30.90
91-60-006	Woodsman's Thatch Cottage	T. Kinkade	150-day	32.90	32.90
92-60-007	Merritt's Cottage	T. Kinkade	150-day	32.90	32.90
92-60-008	Stonegate Cottage	T. Kinkade	150-day	32.90	32.90
Edwin M. Knowles		**Sleeping Beauty**			
91-61-001	Once Upon A Dream	Disney Studios	150-day	39.90	39.90
91-61-002	Awakened by a Kiss	Disney Studios	150-day	39.90	39.90
91-61-003	Happy Birthday Briar Rose	Disney Studios	150-day	42.90	42.90
92-61-004	Together At Last	Disney Studios	150-day	42.90	42.90
Edwin M. Knowles		**Snow White and the Seven Dwarfs**			
91-62-001	The Dance of Snow White/Seven Dwarfs	Disney Studios	150-day	29.90	29.90

Number	Name	Artist	Edition Limit	Issue Price	Quote
91-62-002	With a Smile and a Song	Disney Studios	150-day	29.90	29.90
91-62-003	A Special Treat	Disney Studios	150-day	32.90	32.90
92-62-004	A Kiss for Dopey	Disney Studios	150-day	32.90	32.90
92-62-005	The Poison Apple	Disney Studios	150-day	32.90	32.90
92-62-006	Fireside Love Story	Disney Studios	150-day	34.90	34.90
92-62-007	Stubborn Grumpy	Disney Studios	150-day	34.90	34.90
92-62-008	A Wish Come True	Disney Studios	150-day	34.90	34.90
92-62-009	Time To Tidy Up	Disney Studios	150-day	34.50	34.50
93-62-010	May I Have This Dance?	Disney Studios	150-day	36.90	36.90
93-62-011	A Surprise in the Clearing	Disney Studios	150-day	36.50	36.50
93-62-012	Happy Ending	Disney Studios	150-day	36.90	36.90
Edwin M. Knowles		**Classic Fairy Tales**			
91-63-001	Goldilocks and the Three Bears	S. Gustafson	150-day	29.90	60.00
91-63-002	Little Red Riding Hood	S. Gustafson	150-day	29.90	50.00
91-63-003	The Three Little Pigs	S. Gustafson	150-day	32.90	33.00
91-63-004	The Frog Prince	S. Gustafson	150-day	32.90	32.90
92-63-005	Jack and the Beanstalk	S. Gustafson	150-day	32.90	32.90
92-63-006	Hansel and Gretel	S. Gustafson	150-day	34.90	34.90
92-63-007	Puss in Boots	S. Gustafson	150-day	34.90	34.90
92-63-008	Tom Thumb	S. Gustafson	150-day	34.90	34.90
Edwin M. Knowles		**Wizard of Oz: A National Treasure**			
91-64-001	Yellow Brick Road	R. Laslo	150-day	29.90	29.90
92-64-002	I Haven't Got a Brain	R. Laslo	150-day	29.90	29.90
92-64-003	I'm a Little Rusty Yet	R. Laslo	150-day	32.90	32.90
92-64-004	I Even Scare Myself	R. Laslo	150-day	32.90	32.90
92-64-005	We're Off To See the Wizard	R. Laslo	150-day	32.90	32.90
92-64-006	I'll Never Get Home	R. Laslo	150-day	34.90	34.90
92-64-007	I'm Melting	R. Laslo	150-day	34.90	34.90
92-64-008	There's No Place Like Home	R. Laslo	150-day	34.90	34.90
Edwin M. Knowles		**First Impressions**			
91-65-001	Taking a Gander	J. Giordano	150-day	29.90	30.00
91-65-002	Two's Company	J. Giordano	150-day	29.90	25.00
91-65-003	Fine Feathered Friends	J. Giordano	150-day	32.90	35.00
91-65-004	What's Up?	J. Giordano	150-day	32.90	35.00
91-65-005	All Ears	J. Giordano	150-day	32.90	35.00
92-65-006	Between Friends	J. Giordano	150-day	32.90	40.00
Edwin M. Knowles		**Santa's Christmas**			
91-66-001	Santa's Love	T. Browning	150-day	29.90	30.00
91-66-002	Santa's Cheer	T. Browning	150-day	29.90	45-50.00
91-66-003	Santa's Promise	T. Browning	150-day	32.90	59-65.00
91-66-004	Santa's Gift	T. Browning	150-day	32.90	35-63.00
92-66-005	Santa's Surprise	T. Browning	150-day	32.90	50.00
92-66-006	Santa's Magic	T. Browning	150-day	32.90	95.00
Edwin M. Knowles		**Home for the Holidays**			
91-67-001	Sleigh Ride Home	T. Kinkade	150-day	29.90	59-63.00
91-67-002	Home to Grandma's	T. Kinkade	150-day	29.90	50-55.00
91-67-003	Home Before Christmas	T. Kinkade	150-day	32.90	60-65.00
91-67-004	The Warmth of Home	T. Kinkade	150-day	32.90	40.00
92-67-005	Homespun Holiday	T. Kinkade	150-day	32.90	33.00
92-67-006	Hometime Yuletide	T. Kinkade	150-day	34.90	34.90
92-67-007	Home Away From Home	T. Kinkade	150-day	34.90	34.90
92-67-008	The Journey Home	T. Kinkade	150-day	34.90	34.90
Edwin M. Knowles		**Call of the Wilderness**			
91-68-001	First Outing	K. Daniel	150-day	29.90	29.90
91-68-002	Howling Lesson	K. Daniel	150-day	29.90	29.90
91-68-003	Silent Watch	K. Daniel	150-day	32.90	32.90
91-68-004	Winter Travelers	K. Daniel	150-day	32.90	32.90
92-68-005	Ahead of the Pack	K. Daniel	150-day	32.90	32.90
92-68-006	Northern Spirits	K. Daniel	150-day	34.90	34.90
92-68-007	Twilight Friends	K. Daniel	150-day	34.90	34.90
92-68-008	A New Future	K. Daniel	150-day	34.90	34.90
92-68-009	Morning Mist	K. Daniel	150-day	36.90	36.90
92-68-010	The Silent One	K. Daniel	150-day	36.90	36.90
Edwin M. Knowles		**Old-Fashioned Favorites**			
91-69-001	Apple Crisp	M. Weber	150-day	29.90	60.00
91-69-002	Blueberry Muffins	M. Weber	150-day	29.90	55.00
91-69-003	Peach Cobbler	M. Weber	150-day	29.90	60.00
91-69-004	Chocolate Chip Oatmeal Cookies	M. Weber	150-day	29.90	78.00
Edwin M. Knowles		**Songs of the American Spirit**			
91-70-001	The Star Spangled Banner	H. Bond	150-day	29.90	30.00
91-70-002	Battle Hymn of the Republic	H. Bond	150-day	29.90	30.00
91-70-003	America the Beautiful	H. Bond	150-day	29.90	35.00
91-70-004	My Country 'Tis of Thee	H. Bond	150-day	29.90	40.00
Edwin M. Knowles		**Backyard Harmony**			
91-71-001	The Singing Lesson	J. Thornbrugh	150-day	27.90	28.00
91-71-002	Welcoming a New Day	J. Thornbrugh	150-day	27.90	27.90
91-71-003	Announcing Spring	J. Thornbrugh	150-day	30.90	30.90
92-71-004	The Morning Harvest	J. Thornbrugh	150-day	30.90	30.90
92-71-005	Spring Time Pride	J. Thornbrugh	150-day	30.90	30.90
92-71-006	Treetop Serenade	J. Thornbrugh	150-day	32.90	32.90
92-71-007	At The Peep Of Day	J. Thornbrugh	150-day	32.90	32.90
92-71-008	Today's Discoveries	J. Thornbrugh	150-day	32.90	32.90
Edwin M. Knowles		**Bambi**			
92-72-001	Bashful Bambi	Disney Studios	150-day	34.90	34.90
92-72-002	Bambi's New Friends	Disney Studios	150-day	34.90	34.90
92-72-003	Hello Little Prince	Disney Studios	150-day	37.90	37.90
92-72-004	Bambi's Morning Greetings	Disney Studios	150-day	37.90	37.90
92-72-005	Bambi's Skating Lesson	Disney Studios	150-day	37.90	37.90
93-72-006	What's Up Possums?	Disney Studios	150-day	37.90	37.90
Edwin M. Knowles		**Purrfect Point of View**			
92-73-001	Unexpected Visitors	J. Giordano	150-day	29.90	30.00
92-73-002	Wistful Morning	J. Giordano	150-day	29.90	30.00
92-73-003	Afternoon Catnap	J. Giordano	150-day	29.90	29.90
92-73-004	Cozy Company	J. Giordano	150-day	29.90	29.90
Edwin M. Knowles		**China's Natural Treasures**			
92-74-001	The Siberian Tiger	T.C. Chiu	150-day	29.90	45.00
92-74-002	The Snow Leopard	T.C. Chiu	150-day	29.90	30.00
92-74-003	The Giant Panda	T.C. Chiu	150-day	32.90	32.90
92-74-004	The Tibetan Brown Bear	T.C. Chiu	150-day	32.90	32.90
92-74-005	The Asian Elephant	T.C. Chiu	150-day	32.90	32.90
92-74-006	The Golden Monkey	T.C. Chiu	150-day	34.90	34.90

Company Number	Name	Series Artist	Edition Limit	Issue Price	Quote
Edwin M. Knowles		**Under Mother's Wing**			
92-75-001	Arctic Spring: Snowy Owls	J. Beaudoin	150-day	29.90	39.00
92-75-002	Forest's Edge: Great Gray Owls	J. Beaudoin	150-day	29.90	47.00
92-75-003	Treetop Trio: Long-Eared Owls	J. Beaudoin	150-day	32.90	45.00
92-75-004	Woodland Watch: Spotted Owls	J. Beaudoin	150-day	32.90	35.00
92-75-005	Vast View: Saw Whet Owls	J. Beaudoin	150-day	32.90	32.90
92-75-006	Lofty-Limb: Great Horned Owl	J. Beaudoin	150-day	34.90	34.90
93-75-007	Perfect Perch: Barred Owls	J. Beaudoin	150-day	34.90	34.90
93-75-008	Happy Home: Short-Eared Owl	J. Beaudoin	150-day	34.90	34.90
Edwin M. Knowles		**Classic Mother Goose**			
92-76-001	Little Miss Muffet	S. Gustafson	150-day	29.90	30.00
92-76-002	Mary had a Little Lamb	S. Gustafson	150-day	29.90	29.90
92-76-003	Mary, Mary, Quite Contrary	S. Gustafson	150-day	29.90	29.90
92-76-004	Little Bo Peep	S. Gustafson	150-day	29.90	29.90
Edwin M. Knowles		**Keepsake Rhymes**			
92-77-001	Humpty Dumpty	S. Gustafson	150-day	29.90	29.90
93-77-002	Peter Pumpkin Eater	S. Gustafson	150-day	29.90	29.90
93-77-003	Pat-a-Cake	S. Gustafson	150-day	29.90	29.90
93-77-004	Old King Cole	S. Gustafson	150-day	29.90	29.90
Edwin M. Knowles		**Thomas Kinkade's Thomashire**			
92-78-001	Olde Porterfield Tea Room	T. Kinkade	150-day	29.90	29.90
92-78-002	Olde Thomashire Mill	T. Kinkade	150-day	29.90	29.90
92-78-003	Swanbrook Cottage	T. Kinkade	150-day	32.90	32.90
92-78-004	Pye Corner Cottage	T. Kinkade	150-day	32.90	32.90
93-78-005	Blossom Hill Church	T. Kinkade	150-day	32.90	32.90
93-78-006	Olde Garden Cottage	T. Kinkade	150-day	32.90	32.90
Edwin M. Knowles		**Small Blessings**			
92-79-001	Now I Lay Me Down to Sleep	C. Layton	150-day	29.90	29.90
92-79-002	Bless Us O Lord For These, Thy Gifts	C. Layton	150-day	29.90	29.90
92-79-003	Jesus Loves Me, This I Know	C. Layton	150-day	32.90	32.90
92-79-004	This Little Light of Mine	C. Layton	150-day	32.90	32.90
92-79-005	Blessed Are The Pure In Heart	C. Layton	150-day	32.90	32.90
93-79-006	Bless Our Home	C. Layton	150-day	32.90	32.90
Edwin M. Knowles		**Seasons of Splendor**			
92-80-001	Autumn's Grandeur	K. Randle	150-day	29.90	49.00
92-80-002	School Days	K. Randle	150-day	29.90	50.00
92-80-003	Woodland Mill Stream	K. Randle	150-day	32.90	35.00
92-80-004	Harvest Memories	K. Randle	150-day	32.90	35.00
92-80-005	A Country Weekend	K. Randle	150-day	32.90	33.00
93-80-006	Indian Summer	K. Randle	150-day	32.90	33.00
Edwin M. Knowles		**Lady and the Tramp**			
92-81-001	First Date	Disney Studios	150-day	34.90	34.90
92-81-002	Puppy Love	Disney Studios	150-day	34.90	34.90
92-81-003	Dog Pound Blues	Disney Studios	150-day	37.90	37.90
92-81-004	Merry Christmas To All	Disney Studios	150-day	37.90	37.90
93-81-005	Double Siamese Trouble	Disney Studios	150-day	37.90	37.90
Edwin M. Knowles		**Sweetness and Grace**			
92-82-001	God Bless Teddy	J. Welty	150-day	34.90	38.00
92-82-002	Sunshine and Smiles	J. Welty	150-day	34.90	34.90
92-82-003	Favorite Buddy	J. Welty	150-day	34.90	34.90
92-82-004	Sweet Dreams	J. Welty	150-day	34.90	34.90
Edwin M. Knowles		**Thomas Kinkade's Yuletide Memories**			
92-83-001	The Magic of Christmas	T. Kinkade	150-day	29.90	29.90
92-83-002	A Beacon of Faith	T. Kinkade	150-day	29.90	29.90
93-83-003	Moonlit Sleighride	T. Kinkade	150-day	29.90	29.90
93-83-004	Silent Night	T. Kinkade	150-day	29.90	29.90
93-83-005	Olde Porterfield Gift Shoppe	T. Kinkade	150-day	29.90	29.90
93-83-006	The Wonder of the Season	T. Kinkade	150-day	29.90	29.90
93-83-007	A Winter's Walk	T. Kinkade	150-day	29.90	29.90
93-83-008	Skater's Delight	T. Kinkade	150-day	32.90	32.90
Edwin M. Knowles		**It's a Dog's Life**			
92-84-001	We've Been Spotted	L. Kaatz	150-day	29.90	29.90
92-84-002	Literary Labs	L. Kaatz	150-day	29.90	29.90
93-84-003	Retrieving Our Dignity	L. Kaatz	150-day	32.90	32.90
93-84-004	Lodging a Complaint	L. Kaatz	150-day	32.90	32.90
93-84-005	Barreling Along	L. Kaatz	150-day	32.90	32.90
93-84-006	Play Ball	L. Kaatz	150-day	34.90	34.90
93-84-007	Dogs and Suds	L. Kaatz	150-day	34.90	34.90
Edwin M. Knowles		**Mickey's Christmas Carol**			
92-85-001	Bah Humbug	Disney Studios	150-day	29.90	29.90
92-85-002	What's So Merry About Christmas?	Disney Studios	150-day	29.90	29.90
93-85-003	God Bless Us Every One	Disney Studios	150-day	32.90	32.90
93-85-004	A Christmas Surprise	Disney Studios	150-day	32.90	32.90
93-85-005	Yuletide Greetings	Disney Studios	150-day	32.90	32.90
93-85-006	Marley's Warning	Disney Studios	150-day	34.90	34.90
Edwin M. Knowles		**The Disney Treasured Moments Collection**			
92-86-001	Cinderella	Disney Studios	150-day	29.90	29.90
92-86-002	Snow White and the Seven Dwarves	Disney Studios	150-day	29.90	29.90
93-86-003	Alice in Wonderland	Disney Studios	150-day	32.90	32.90
93-86-004	Sleeping Beauty	Disney Studios	150-day	32.90	32.90
93-86-005	Peter Pan	Disney Studios	150-day	32.90	32.90
Edwin M. Knowles		**Christmas in the City**			
92-87-001	A Christmas Snowfall	A. Leimanis	150-day	34.90	35.00
92-87-002	Yuletide Celebration	A. Leimanis	150-day	34.90	35.00
93-87-003	Holiday Cheer	A. Leimanis	150-day	34.90	34.90
93-87-004	The Magic of Christmas	A. Leimanis	150-day	34.90	35.00
Edwin M. Knowles		**Romantic Age of Steam**			
92-88-001	The Empire Builder	R.B. Pierce	150-day	29.90	29.90
92-88-002	The Broadway Limited	R.B. Pierce	150-day	29.90	29.90
92-88-003	Twentieth Century Limited	R.B. Pierce	150-day	32.90	32.90
92-88-004	The Chief	R.B. Pierce	150-day	32.90	32.90
92-88-005	The Crescent Limited	R.B. Pierce	150-day	32.90	32.90
93-88-006	The Overland Limited	R.B. Pierce	150-day	34.90	34.90
93-88-007	The Jupiter	R.B. Pierce	150-day	34.90	34.90
Edwin M. Knowles		**The Comforts of Home**			
92-89-001	Sleepyheads	H. Hollister Ingmire	150-day	24.90	24.90
92-89-002	Curious Pair	H. Hollister Ingmire	150-day	24.90	24.90
93-89-003	Mother's Retreat	H. Hollister Ingmire	150-day	27.90	27.90
93-89-004	Welcome Friends	H. Hollister Ingmire	150-day	27.90	27.90
93-89-005	Playtime	H. Hollister Ingmire	150-day	27.90	27.90
93-89-006	Feline Frolic	H. Hollister Ingmire	150-day	29.90	29.90
Edwin M. Knowles		**Free as the Wind**			
92-90-001	Skyward	M. Budden	150-day	29.90	29.90
92-90-002	Aloft	M. Budden	150-day	29.90	29.90
92-90-003	Airborne	M. Budden	150-day	32.90	32.90
93-90-004	Flight	M. Budden	150-day	32.90	32.90
93-90-005	Ascent	M. Budden	150-day	32.90	32.90
93-90-006	Heavenward	M. Budden	150-day	32.90	32.90
Edwin M. Knowles		**Yesterday's Innocents**			
92-91-001	My First Book	J. Wilcox Smith	150-day	29.90	30.00
92-91-002	Time to Smell the Roses	J. Wilcox Smith	150-day	29.90	30.00
93-91-003	Hush, Baby's Sleeping	J. Wilcox Smith	150-day	32.90	32.90
93-91-004	Ready and Waiting	J. Wilcox Smith	150-day	32.90	32.90
Edwin M. Knowles		**Home is Where the Heart Is**			
92-92-001	Home Sweet Home	T. Kinkade	150-day	29.90	29.90
92-92-002	A Warm Welcome Home	T. Kinkade	150-day	29.90	29.90
92-92-003	A Carriage Ride Home	T. Kinkade	150-day	32.90	32.90
93-92-004	Amber Afternoon	T. Kinkade	150-day	32.90	32.90
93-92-005	Country Memories	T. Kinkade	150-day	32.90	32.90
93-92-006	The Twilight Cafe	T. Kinkade	150-day	34.90	34.90
93-92-007	Our Summer Home	T. Kinkade	150-day	34.90	34.90
Edwin M. Knowles		**Shadows and Light: Winter's Wildlife**			
93-93-001	Winter's Children	N. Glazier	150-day	29.90	50.00
93-93-002	Cub Scouts	N. Glazier	150-day	29.90	55.00
93-93-003	Little Snowman	N. Glazier	150-day	29.90	40.00
93-93-004	The Snow Cave	N. Glazier	150-day	29.90	29.90
Edwin M. Knowles		**Beauty and the Beast**			
93-94-001	Love's First Dance	Disney Studios	150-day	29.90	29.90
93-94-002	A Blossoming Romance	Disney Studios	150-day	29.90	29.90
93-94-003	Warming Up	Disney Studios	150-day	32.90	32.90
93-94-004	Learning to Love	Disney Studios	150-day	32.90	32.90
Edwin M. Knowles		**Nature's Nursery**			
92-95-001	Testing the Waters	J. Thornbrugh	150-day	29.90	29.90
93-95-002	Taking the Plunge	J. Thornbrugh	150-day	29.90	29.90
93-95-003	Race Ya Mom	J. Thornbrugh	150-day	29.90	29.90
93-95-004	Time to Wake Up	J. Thornbrugh	150-day	29.90	29.90
93-95-005	Hide and Seek	J. Thornbrugh	150-day	29.90	29.90
93-95-006	Piggyback Ride	J. Thornbrugh	150-day	29.90	29.90
Edwin M. Knowles		**Proud Sentinels of the American West**			
93-96-001	Youngblood	N. Glazier	150-day	29.90	29.90
93-96-002	Cat Nap	N. Glazier	150-day	29.90	29.90
93-96-003	Desert Bighorn-Mormon Ridge	N. Glazier	150-day	32.90	32.90
93-96-004	Crown Prince	N. Glazier	150-day	32.90	32.90
Edwin M. Knowles		**Garden Secrets**			
93-97-001	Nine Lives	B. Higgins Bond	150-day	24.90	24.90
93-97-002	Floral Purr-fume	B. Higgins Bond	150-day	24.90	24.90
93-97-003	Bloomin' Kitties	B. Higgins Bond	150-day	24.90	24.90
93-97-004	Kitty Corner	B. Higgins Bond	150-day	24.90	24.90
93-97-005	Flower Fanciers	B. Higgins Bond	150-day	24.90	24.90
93-97-006	Meadow Mischief	B. Higgins Bond	150-day	24.90	24.90
93-97-007	Pussycat Potpourri	B. Higgins Bond	150-day	24.90	24.90
Edwin M. Knowles		**Windows of Glory**			
93-98-001	King of Kings	J. Welty	95-day	29.90	29.90
93-98-002	Prince of Peace	J. Welty	95-day	29.90	29.90
93-98-003	The Messiah	J. Welty	95-day	32.90	32.90
Edwin M. Knowles		**Nature's Garden**			
93-99-001	Springtime Friends	C. Decker	95-day	29.90	29.90
93-99-002	A Morning Splash	C. Decker	95-day	29.90	29.90
Edwin M. Knowles		**The Little Mermaid**			
93-100-001	A Song From the Sea	Disney Studios	95-day	29.90	29.90
93-100-002	A Visit to the Surface	Disney Studios	95-day	29.90	29.90
Edwin M. Knowles		**Enchanted Cottages**			
93-101-001	Fallbrooke Cottage	T. Kinkade	95-day	29.90	29.90
93-101-002	Julianne's Cottage	T. Kinkade	95-day	29.90	29.90
93-101-003	Seaside Cottage	T. Kinkade	95-day	29.90	29.90
93-101-004	Sweetheart Cottage	T. Kinkade	95-day	29.90	29.90
Edwin M. Knowles		**Musical Moments From the Wizard of Oz**			
93-102-001	Over the Rainbow	K. Milnazik	95-day	29.90	29.90
93-102-002	We're Off to See the Wizard	K. Milnazik	95-day	29.90	29.90
KPM-Royal Berlin		**Christmas**			
69-01-001	Christmas Star	Unknown	5,000	28.00	380.00
70-01-002	Three Kings	Unknown	5,000	28.00	300.00
71-01-003	Christmas Tree	Unknown	5,000	28.00	290.00
72-01-004	Christmas Angel	Unknown	5,000	31.00	300.00
73-01-005	Christ Child on Sled	Unknown	5,000	33.00	280.00
74-01-006	Angel and Horn	Unknown	5,000	35.00	180.00
75-01-007	Shepherds	Unknown	5,000	40.00	165.00
76-01-008	Star of Bethlehem	Unknown	5,000	43.00	140.00
77-01-009	Mary at Crib	Unknown	5,000	46.00	100.00
78-01-010	Three Wise Men	Unknown	5,000	49.00	54.00
79-01-011	The Manger	Unknown	5,000	55.00	55.00
80-01-012	Shepherds in Fields	Unknown	5,000	55.00	55.00
Lalique		**Annual**			
65-01-001	Deux Oiseaux (Two Birds)	M. Lalique	2,000	25.00	1400.00
66-01-002	Rose de Songerie (Dream Rose)	M. Lalique	5,000	25.00	120.00
67-01-003	Ballet de Poisson (Fish Ballet)	M. Lalique	5,000	25.00	104.00
68-01-004	Gazelle Fantaisie (Gazelle Fantasy)	M. Lalique	5,000	25.00	75.00
69-01-005	Papillon (Butterfly)	M. Lalique	5,000	30.00	48.00
70-01-006	Paon (Peacock)	M. Lalique	5,000	30.00	59.00
71-01-007	Hibou (Owl)	M. Lalique	5,000	35.00	69.00
72-01-008	Coquillage (Shell)	M. Lalique	5,000	40.00	74.00
73-01-009	Petit Geai (Jayling)	M. Lalique	5,000	42.50	104.00
74-01-010	Sous d'Argent (Silver Pennies)	M. Lalique	5,000	47.50	99.00
75-01-011	Duo de Poisson (Fish Duet)	M. Lalique	5,000	50.00	145.00
76-01-012	Aigle (Eagle)	M. Lalique	5,000	60.00	90.00
Lance Corporation		**Sebastian Plates**			
78-01-001	Motif No. 1	P.W. Baston	Closed	75.00	50-75.00
79-01-002	Grand Canyon	P.W. Baston	Closed	75.00	50-75.00

Number	Name	Artist	Edition Limit	Issue Price	Quote
80-01-003	Lone Cypress	P.W. Baston	Closed	75.00	150-175.
80-01-004	In The Candy Store	P.W. Baston	Closed	39.50	39.50
81-01-005	The Doctor	P.W. Baston	Closed	39.50	39.50
83-01-006	Little Mother	P.W. Baston	Closed	39.50	39.50
84-01-007	Switching The Freight	P.W. Baston	Closed	42.50	80-100.00
Lance Corporaton	**Miscellaneous (Hudson Pewter)**				
74-02-001	Spirit of '76 9"	P.W. Baston	Retrd.	27.50	75.00
76-02-002	Declaration of Independence 8 1/2"	Unknown	Retrd.	25.00	50.00
78-02-003	Zodiac 8"	Unknown	Retrd.	60.00	75.00
Lance Corporation	**The American Expansion (Hudson Pewter)**				
75-03-001	Spirit of '76 (6" Plate)	P.W. Baston	Closed	Unkn.	100-120.
75-03-002	American Independence	P.W. Baston	Closed	Unkn.	100-125.
75-03-003	American Expansion	P.W. Baston	Closed	Unkn.	50-75.00
75-03-004	The American War Between the States	P.W. Baston	Closed	Unkn.	150-200.
Lance Corporaton	**American Commemoratives (Hudson Pewter)**				
75-04-001	Mt. Vernon 6"	R. Lamb	Retrd.	N/A	55.00
75-04-002	Monticello 6"	R. Lamb	Retrd.	N/A	55.00
75-04-003	Log Cabin 6"	R. Lamb	Retrd.	N/A	55.00
75-04-004	Hyde Park 6"	R. Lamb	Retrd.	N/A	55.00
75-04-005	Spirit of '76 6"	R. Lamb	Retrd.	N/A	55.00
Lance Corporaton	**Sailing Ships (Hudson Pewter)**				
78-05-001	Flying Cloud 6"	A. Petito	Retrd.	35.00	55.00
78-05-002	America 6"	A. Petito	Retrd.	35.00	55.00
78-05-003	Morgan 6"	A. Petito	Retrd.	35.00	55.00
78-05-004	Constitution 6"	A. Petito	Retrd.	35.00	55.00
Lance Corporaton	**Songbirds of the Four Seasons (Hudson Pewter)**				
78-06-001	Cardinal (Winter) 6"	Hollis/Yourdon	Retrd.	35.00	55.00
78-06-002	Hummingbird (Summer) 6"	Hollis/Yourdon	Retrd.	35.00	55.00
78-06-003	Sparrow (Autumn) 6"	Hollis/Yourdon	Retrd.	35.00	55.00
78-06-004	Wood Thrush (Spring) 6"	Hollis/Yourdon	Retrd.	35.00	55.00
Lance Corporaton	**America's Favorite Birds (Hudson Pewter/Crystal)**				
78-07-001	Crystal Wren 8"	C. Terris	Retrd.	79.50	79.50
Lance Corporation	**A Child's Christmas (Hudson Pewter)**				
78-08-001	Bedtime Story	A. Petitto	Suspd.	35.00	60.00
79-08-002	Littlest Angels	A. Petitto	Suspd.	35.00	60.00
80-08-003	Heaven's Christmas Tree	A. Petitto	Suspd.	42.50	60.00
81-08-004	Filling The Sky	A. Petitto	Suspd.	47.50	60.00
Lance Corporaton	**Mother's Day (Hudson Pewter)**				
79-09-001	Cherished 6"	A. Petito	Retrd.	42.50	55.00
80-09-002	1980 Mother's Day 6"	A. Petito	Retrd.	42.50	55.00
Lance Corporaton	**Twas The Night Before Christmas (Hudson Pewter)**				
82-10-001	Not A Creature Was Stirring	A. Hollis	Suspd.	47.50	60.00
83-10-002	Visions Of Sugar Plums	A. Hollis	Suspd.	47.50	60.00
84-10-003	His Eyes How They Twinkled	A. Hollis	Suspd.	47.50	60.00
85-10-004	Happy Christmas To All	A. Hollis	Suspd.	47.50	60.00
Lance Corporation	**Walt Disney (Hudson Pewter)**				
86-11-001	God Bless Us, Every One	D. Everhart	Suspd.	47.50	60.00
87-11-002	Jolly Old Saint Nick	D. Everhart	Suspd.	55.00	60.00
88-11-003	He's Checking It Twice	D. Everhart	Suspd.	50.00	60.00
Lance Corporaton	**The Songs of Christmas (Hudson Pewter)**				
88-12-001	Silent Night	A. McGrory	Suspd.	55.00	60.00
89-12-002	Hark! The Herald Angels Sing	A. McGrory	Suspd.	60.00	60.00
90-12-003	The First Noel	A. McGrory	Suspd.	60.00	60.00
91-12-004	We Three Kings	A. McGrory	Suspd.	60.00	60.00
Lance Corporaton	**Christmas (Hudson Pewter)**				
86-13-001	Bringing Home The Tree	J. Wanat	Suspd.	47.50	60.00
87-13-002	The Caroling Angels	A. Petitto	Suspd.	47.50	60.00
93-13-003	Crack the Whip	A. McGrory	950	55.00	55.00
Lance Corporaton	**Mother's Day (Chilmark Pewter)**				
74-14-001	Flowers of the Field 8"	Unknown	Retrd.	65.00	75.00
80-14-002	1980 Mother's Day	Unknown	Retrd.	90.00	90.00
Lance Corporaton	**Christmas (Chilmark Pewter)**				
77-15-001	Currier & Ives Christmas 8"	Unknown	Retrd.	60.00	75.00
78-15-002	Trimming the Tree 8"	Unknown	Retrd.	65.00	75.00
79-15-003	Three Wisemen 8"	Unknown	Retrd.	65.00	75.00
Lance Corporaton	**Twelve Days of Christmas (Chilmark Pewter/Stained Glass)**				
79-16-001	Partridge in a Pear Tree 8"	Unknown	Retrd.	99.50	99.50
80-16-002	Two Turtle Doves 8"	Unknown	Retrd.	99.50	99.50
LCS Products	**Early Innings**				
93-01-001	Ebbets Field	LCS	25-day	29.95	29.95
Lenox China	**Boehm Birds**				
70-01-001	Wood Thrush	E. Boehm	Yr.Iss.	35.00	100.00
71-01-002	Goldfinch	E. Boehm	Yr.Iss.	35.00	53.00
72-01-003	Mountain Bluebird	E. Boehm	Yr.Iss.	37.50	50.00
73-01-004	Meadowlark	E. Boehm	Yr.Iss.	50.00	30.00
74-01-005	Rufous Hummingbird	E. Boehm	Yr.Iss.	45.00	49.00
75-01-006	American Redstart	E. Boehm	Yr.Iss.	50.00	25.00
76-01-007	Cardinals	E. Boehm	Yr.Iss.	53.00	80.00
77-01-008	Robins	E. Boehm	Yr.Iss.	55.00	45.00
78-01-009	Mockingbirds	E. Boehm	Yr.Iss.	58.00	59.00
79-01-010	Golden-Crowned Kinglets	E. Boehm	Yr.Iss.	65.00	95.00
80-01-011	Black-Throated Blue Warblers	E. Boehm	Yr.Iss.	80.00	109.00
81-01-012	Eastern Phoebes	E. Boehm	Yr.Iss.	92.50	100.00
Lenox China	**Boehm Woodland Wildlife**				
73-02-001	Racoons	E. Boehm	Yr.Iss.	50.00	50.00
74-02-002	Red Foxes	E. Boehm	Yr.Iss.	52.50	52.50
75-02-003	Cottontail Rabbits	E. Boehm	Yr.Iss.	58.50	58.50
76-02-004	Eastern Chipmunks	E. Boehm	Yr.Iss.	62.50	62.50
77-02-005	Beaver	E. Boehm	Yr.Iss.	67.50	67.50
78-02-006	Whitetail Deer	E. Boehm	Yr.Iss.	70.00	70.00
79-02-007	Squirrels	E. Boehm	Yr.Iss.	76.00	76.00
80-02-008	Bobcats	E. Boehm	Yr.Iss.	82.50	82.50
81-02-009	Martens	E. Boehm	Yr.Iss.	100.00	150.00
82-02-010	River Otters	E. Boehm	Yr.Iss.	100.00	180.00

Number	Name	Artist	Edition Limit	Issue Price	Quote
Lenox China	**Colonial Christmas Wreath**				
81-03-001	Colonial Virginia	Unknown	Yr.Iss.	65.00	76.00
82-03-002	Massachusetts	Unknown	Yr.Iss.	70.00	93.00
83-03-003	Maryland	Unknown	Yr.Iss.	70.00	79.00
84-03-004	Rhode Island	Unknown	Yr.Iss.	70.00	82.00
85-03-005	Connecticut	Unknown	Yr.Iss.	70.00	75.00
86-03-006	New Hampshire	Unknown	Yr.Iss.	70.00	75.00
87-03-007	Pennsylvania	Unknown	Yr.Iss.	70.00	75.00
88-03-008	Delaware	Unknown	Yr.Iss.	70.00	70.00
89-03-009	New York	Unknown	Yr.Iss.	75.00	82.00
90-03-010	New Jersey	Unknown	Yr.Iss.	75.00	78.00
91-03-011	South Carolina	Unknown	Yr.Iss.	75.00	75.00
92-03-012	North Carolina	Unknown	Yr.Iss.	75.00	75.00
Lenox Collections	**American Wildlife**				
82-01-001	Red Foxes	N. Adams	9,500	65.00	65.00
82-01-002	Ocelots	N. Adams	9,500	65.00	65.00
82-01-003	Sea Lions	N. Adams	9,500	65.00	65.00
82-01-004	Raccoons	N. Adams	9,500	65.00	65.00
82-01-005	Dall Sheep	N. Adams	9,500	65.00	65.00
82-01-006	Black Bears	N. Adams	9,500	65.00	65.00
82-01-007	Mountain Lions	N. Adams	9,500	65.00	65.00
82-01-008	Polar Bears	N. Adams	9,500	65.00	65.00
82-01-009	Otters	N. Adams	9,500	65.00	65.00
82-01-010	White Tailed Deer	N. Adams	9,500	65.00	65.00
82-01-011	Buffalo	N. Adams	9,500	65.00	65.00
82-01-012	Jack Rabbits	N. Adams	9,500	65.00	65.00
Lenox Collections	**Garden Bird Plate Collection**				
88-02-001	Chickadee	Unknown	Open	48.00	48.00
88-02-002	Bluejay	Unknown	Open	48.00	48.00
89-02-003	Hummingbird	Unknown	Open	48.00	48.00
91-02-004	Dove	Unknown	Open	48.00	48.00
91-02-005	Cardinal	Unknown	Open	48.00	48.00
92-02-006	Goldfinch	Unknown	Open	48.00	48.00
Lenox Collections	**Christmas Trees Around the World**				
91-03-001	Germany	Unknown	Yr.Iss.	75.00	75.00
92-03-002	France	Unknown	Yr.Iss.	75.00	75.00
Lenox Collections	**Annual Christmas Plates**				
92-04-001	Sleigh	Unknown	Yr.Iss.	75.00	75.00
93-04-002	Midnight Sleighride	L. Bywater	90-day	119.00	119.00
Lenox Collections	**Nature's Collage**				
92-05-001	Cedar Waxwing, Among The Berries	C. McClung	Open	34.50	34.50
92-05-002	Gold Finches, Golden Splendor	C. McClung	Open	34.50	34.50
93-05-003	Bluebirds, Summer Interlude	C. McClung	90-day	39.50	39.50
93-05-004	Chickadees, Rose Morning	C. McClung	90-day	39.50	39.50
93-05-005	Bluejays, Winter Song	C. McClung	90-day	39.50	39.50
93-05-006	Cardinals, Spring Courtship	C. McClung	90-day	39.50	39.50
93-05-007	Hummingbirds, Jeweled Glory	C. McClung	90-day	39.50	39.50
93-05-008	Indigo Buntings, Indigo Evening	C. McClung	90-day	39.50	39.50
Lenox Collections	**Children of the Sun & Moon**				
93-06-001	Desert Blossom	D. Crowley	Open	39.50	39.50
93-06-002	Shy One	D. Crowley	Open	39.50	39.50
93-06-003	Feathers & Furs	D. Crowley	Open	39.50	39.50
Lenox Collections	**Dolphins of the Seven Seas**				
93-07-001	Bottlenose Dolphins	J. Holderby	Open	39.50	39.50
Lenox Collections	**Whale Conservation**				
93-08-001	Orca	J. Holderby	Open	39.50	39.50
Lenox Collections	**Pierced Nativity**				
93-09-001	Holy Family	Unknown	Open	45.00	45.00
Lenox Collections	**International Victorian Santas**				
92-10-001	Kris Kringle	R. Hoover	90-day	39.50	39.50
93-10-002	Father Christmas	R. Hoover	90-day	39.50	39.50
94-10-003	Grandfather Frost	R. Hoover	90-day	39.50	39.50
95-10-004	American Santa Claus	R. Hoover	90-day	39.50	39.50
Lenox Collections	**Hopes & Dreams**				
93-11-001	Daddy's Dream	D. McCammon	90-day	39.50	39.50
Lenox Collections	**Owls of North America**				
93-12-001	Spirit of the Arctic, Snowy Owl	L. Laffin	Open	39.50	39.50
Lenox Collections	**Magic of Christmas**				
93-13-001	Santa of the Northen Forest	L. Bywaters	Open	39.50	39.50
93-13-002	Santa's Gift of Peace	L. Bywaters	Open	39.50	39.50
93-13-003	Gifts For All	L. Bywaters	Open	39.50	39.50
94-13-004	Coming Home	L. Bywaters	Open	39.50	39.50
94-13-005	Santa's Sentinels	L. Bywaters	Open	39.50	39.50
94-13-006	Wonder of Wonders	L. Bywaters	Open	39.50	39.50
94-13-007	A Berry Merry Christmas	L. Bywaters	Open	39.50	39.50
Lenox Collections	**Big Cats of the World**				
93-14-001	Black Panther	Q. Lemonds	Open	39.50	39.50
93-14-002	Chinese Leopard	Q. Lemonds	Open	39.50	39.50
93-14-003	Cougar	Q. Lemonds	Open	39.50	39.50
93-14-004	Bobcat	Q. Lemonds	Open	39.50	39.50
93-14-005	White Tiger	Q. Lemonds	Open	39.50	39.50
93-14-006	Tiger	Q. Lemonds	Open	39.50	39.50
93-14-007	Lion	Q. Lemonds	Open	39.50	39.50
93-14-008	Snow Leopard	Q. Lemonds	Open	39.50	39.50
Lenox Collections	**Eagle Conservation**				
93-15-001	Soaring the Peaks	R. Kelley	Open	39.50	39.50
93-15-002	Solo Flight	R. Kelley	Open	39.50	39.50
93-15-003	Northern Heritage	R. Kelley	Open	39.50	39.50
93-15-004	Lone Sentinel	R. Kelley	Open	39.50	39.50
93-15-005	River Scout	R. Kelley	Open	39.50	39.50
93-15-006	Eagles on Mt. McKinley	R. Kelley	Open	39.50	39.50
93-15-007	Daybreak on River's Edge	R. Kelley	Open	39.50	39.50
93-15-008	Northwood's Legend	R. Kelley	Open	39.50	39.50
Lenox Collections	**Great Cats of the World**				
93-16-001	Siberian Tiger	G. Coleach	Open	39.50	39.50
93-16-002	Lion	G. Coleach	Open	39.50	39.50
93-16-003	Lioness	G. Coleach	Open	39.50	39.50
93-16-004	Snow Leopard	G. Coleach	Open	39.50	39.50

Company Number	Name	Series Artist	Edition Limit	Issue Price	Quote
93-16-005	White Tiger	G. Coleach	Open	39.50	39.50
93-16-006	Jaquar	G. Coleach	Open	39.50	39.50
93-16-007	Cougar	G. Coleach	Open	39.50	39.50
93-16-008	Chinese Leopard	G. Coleach	Open	39.50	39.50
Lenox Collections		**Cubs of the Big Cats**			
93-17-001	Jaquar Cub	Q. Lemonds	90-day	29.50	29.50
Lenox Collections		**Darling Dalmations**			
93-18-001	Three Alarm Fire	L. Picken	90-day	29.50	29.50
93-18-002	All Fired Up	L. Picken	90-day	29.50	29.50
93-18-003	Fire Brigade	L. Picken	90-day	29.50	29.50
93-18-004	Pup in Boots	L. Picken	90-day	29.50	29.50
93-18-005	Caught in the Act	L. Picken	90-day	29.50	29.50
93-18-006	Please Don't Pick the Flowers	L. Picken	90-day	29.50	29.50
Lenox Collections		**Actic Wolves**			
93-19-001	Far Country Crossing	J. VanZyle	90-day	29.50	29.50
93-19-002	Cry of the Wild	J. VanZyle	90-day	29.50	29.50
93-19-003	Nightwatch	J. VanZyle	90-day	29.50	29.50
93-19-004	Midnight Renegade	J. VanZyle	90-day	29.50	29.50
93-19-005	On the Edge	J. VanZyle	90-day	29.50	29.50
93-19-006	Picking Up the Trail	J. VanZyle	90-day	29.50	29.50
Lenox Collections		**Rainbow Valley of the Unicorn**			
92-20-001	Hidden Glade of Unicorn	R. Sanderson	90-day	29.50	29.50
92-20-002	Secret Garden of Unicorn	R. Sanderson	90-day	29.50	29.50
93-20-003	Joyful Meadow of Unicorn	R. Sanderson	90-day	29.50	29.50
93-20-004	Misty Hills of Unicorn	R. Sanderson	90-day	29.50	29.50
93-20-005	Tropical Paradise of Unicorn	R. Sanderson	90-day	29.50	29.50
93-20-006	Springtime Pasture of Unicorn	R. Sanderson	90-day	29.50	29.50
Lenox Collections		**Birds of the Garden**			
92-21-001	Spring Glory, Cardinals	W. Mumm	Open	39.50	39.50
93-21-002	Sunbright Songbirds, Goldfinch	W. Mumm	Open	39.50	39.50
93-21-003	Bluebirds Haven, Bluebirds	W. Mumm	Open	39.50	39.50
93-21-004	Blossoming Bough, Chickadees	W. Mumm	Open	39.50	39.50
93-21-005	Jewels of the Garden, Hummingbirds	W. Mumm	Open	39.50	39.50
93-21-006	Indigo Meadow, Indigo Buntings	W. Mumm	Open	39.50	39.50
93-21-007	Scarlet Tanagers	W. Mumm	Open	39.50	39.50
Lihs Linder		**Christmas**			
72-01-001	Little Drummer Boy	J. Neubauer	6,000	25.00	35.00
73-01-002	Carolers	J. Neubauer	6,000	25.00	25.00
74-01-003	Peace	J. Neubauer	6,000	25.00	25.00
75-01-004	Christmas Cheer	J. Neubauer	6,000	30.00	34.00
76-01-005	Joy of Christmas	J. Neubauer	6,000	30.00	30.00
77-01-006	Holly Jolly Christmas	J. Neubauer	6,000	30.00	30.00
78-01-007	Holy Night	J. Neubauer	6,000	40.00	40.00
Lightpost Publishing		**Thomas Kinkade Signature Collection**			
91-01-001	Chandler's Cottage	T. Kinkade	2,500	49.95	49.95
91-01-002	Cedar Nook	T. Kinkade	2,500	49.95	49.95
91-01-003	Sleigh Ride Home	T. Kinkade	2,500	49.95	49.95
91-01-004	Home To Grandma's	T. Kinkade	2,500	49.95	49.95
Lilliput Lane, Ltd.		**American Landmarks Collection**			
90-01-001	Country Church	R. Day	5,000	35.00	35.00
90-01-002	Riverside Chapel	R. Day	5,000	35.00	35.00
Lladro		**Lladro Plate Collection**			
93-01-001	The Great Voyage L5964G	Lladro	Open	50.00	50.00
93-01-002	Looking Out L5998G	Lladro	Open	38.00	38.00
93-01-003	Swinging L5999G	Lladro	Open	38.00	38.00
93-01-004	Duck Plate L6000G	Lladro	Open	38.00	38.00
March of Dimes		**Our Children, Our Future**			
89-01-001	A Time for Peace	D. Zolan	150-day	29.00	29.00
89-01-002	A Time To Love	S. Kuck	150-day	29.00	43.00
89-01-003	A Time To Plant	J. McClelland	150-day	29.00	30.00
89-01-004	A Time To Be Born	G. Perillo	150-day	29.00	30.00
90-01-005	A Time To Embrace	E. Hibel	150-day	29.00	30.00
90-01-006	A Time To Laugh	A. Williams	150-day	29.00	30.00
Maruri USA		**Eagle Plate Series**			
84-01-001	Free Flight	W. Gaither	Closed	150.00	150-198.
Museum Collections, Inc.		**American Family I**			
79-01-001	Baby's First Step	N. Rockwell	9,900	28.50	48.00
79-01-002	Happy Birthday Dear Mother	N. Rockwell	9,900	28.50	45.00
79-01-003	Sweet Sixteen	N. Rockwell	9,900	28.50	35.00
79-01-004	First Haircut	N. Rockwell	9,900	28.50	60.00
79-01-005	First Prom	N. Rockwell	9,900	28.50	35.00
79-01-006	Wrapping Christmas Presents	N. Rockwell	9,900	28.50	35.00
79-01-007	The Student	N. Rockwell	9,900	28.50	35.00
79-01-008	Birthday Party	N. Rockwell	9,900	28.50	35.00
79-01-009	Little Mother	N. Rockwell	9,900	28.50	35.00
79-01-010	Washing Our Dog	N. Rockwell	9,900	28.50	35.00
79-01-011	Mother's Little Helpers	N. Rockwell	9,900	28.50	35.00
79-01-012	Bride and Groom	N. Rockwell	9,900	28.50	35.00
Museum Collections, Inc.		**American Family II**			
80-02-001	New Arrival	N. Rockwell	22,500	35.00	55.00
80-02-002	Sweet Dreams	N. Rockwell	22,500	35.00	37.50
80-02-003	Little Shaver	N. Rockwell	22,500	35.00	40.00
80-02-004	We Missed You Daddy	N. Rockwell	22,500	35.00	37.50
80-02-005	Home Run Slugger	N. Rockwell	22,500	35.00	37.50
80-02-006	Giving Thanks	N. Rockwell	22,500	35.00	37.50
80-02-007	Space Pioneers	N. Rockwell	22,500	35.00	37.50
80-02-008	Little Salesman	N. Rockwell	22,500	35.00	37.50
80-02-009	Almost Grown up	N. Rockwell	22,500	35.00	37.50
80-02-010	Courageous Hero	N. Rockwell	22,500	35.00	37.50
81-02-011	At the Circus	N. Rockwell	22,500	35.00	37.50
81-02-012	Good Food, Good Friends	N. Rockwell	22,500	35.00	37.50
Museum Collections, Inc.		**Christmas**			
79-03-001	Day After Christmas	N. Rockwell	Yr.Iss	75.00	75.00
80-03-002	Checking His List	N. Rockwell	Yr.Iss	75.00	75.00
81-03-003	Ringing in Good Cheer	N. Rockwell	Yr.Iss	75.00	75.00
82-03-004	Waiting for Santa	N. Rockwell	Yr.Iss	75.00	75.00
83-03-005	High Hopes	N. Rockwell	Yr.Iss	75.00	75.00
84-03-006	Space Age Santa	N. Rockwell	Yr.Iss	55.00	55.00

Company Number	Name	Series Artist	Edition Limit	Issue Price	Quote
Pemberton & Oakes		**Zolan's Children**			
78-01-001	Erik and Dandelion	D. Zolan	22-day	19.00	240.00
79-01-002	Sabina in the Grass	D. Zolan	22-day	22.00	250.00
80-01-003	By Myself	D. Zolan	22-day	24.00	54.00
81-01-004	For You	D. Zolan	22-day	24.00	36.00
Pemberton & Oakes		**Wonder of Childhood**			
82-02-001	Touching the Sky	D. Zolan	22-day	19.00	25-39.00
83-02-002	Spring Innocence	D. Zolan	22-day	19.00	30-45.00
84-02-003	Winter Angel	D. Zolan	22-day	22.00	43-60.00
85-02-004	Small Wonder	D. Zolan	22-day	22.00	34-45.00
86-02-005	Grandma's Garden	D. Zolan	22-day	22.00	39-48.00
87-02-006	Day Dreamer	D. Zolan	22-day	22.00	30-36.00
Pemberton & Oakes		**Children and Pets**			
84-03-001	Tender Moment	D. Zolan	28-day	19.00	50-85.00
84-03-002	Golden Moment	D. Zolan	28-day	19.00	29-45.00
85-03-003	Making Friends	D. Zolan	28-day	19.00	29-45.00
85-03-004	Tender Beginning	D. Zolan	28-day	19.00	35-45.00
86-03-005	Backyard Discovery	D. Zolan	28-day	19.00	32-39.00
86-03-006	Waiting to Play	D. Zolan	28-day	19.00	36-45.00
Pemberton & Oakes		**Children at Christmas**			
81-04-001	A Gift for Laurie	D. Zolan	15,000	48.00	70-75.00
82-04-002	Christmas Prayer	D. Zolan	15,000	48.00	80-90.00
83-04-003	Erik's Delight	D. Zolan	15,000	48.00	66-95.00
84-04-004	Christmas Secret	D. Zolan	15,000	48.00	50-66.00
85-04-005	Christmas Kitten	D. Zolan	15,000	48.00	50-75.00
86-04-006	Laurie and the Creche	D. Zolan	15,000	48.00	75-78.00
Pemberton & Oakes		**Special Moments of Childhood Collection**			
88-05-001	Brotherly Love	D. Zolan	19-day	19.00	60-75.00
88-05-002	Sunny Surprise	D. Zolan	19-day	19.00	28-51.00
89-05-003	Summer's Child	D. Zolan	19-day	22.00	38-45.00
90-05-004	Meadow Magic	D. Zolan	19-day	22.00	29-36.00
90-05-005	Cone For Two	D. Zolan	19-day	24.60	25-30.00
90-05-006	Rodeo Girl	D. Zolan	19-day	24.60	24.60
Pemberton & Oakes		**Childhood Friendship Collection**			
86-06-001	Beach Break	D. Zolan	17-day	19.00	55.00
87-06-002	Little Engineers	D. Zolan	17-day	19.00	66.00
88-06-003	Tiny Treasures	D. Zolan	17-day	19.00	48.00
88-06-004	Sharing Secrets	D. Zolan	17-day	19.00	60.00
88-06-005	Dozens of Daisies	D. Zolan	17-day	19.00	40.00
90-06-006	Country Walk	D. Zolan	17-day	19.00	36.00
Pemberton & Oakes		**Tenth Anniversary**			
88-07-001	Ribbons and Roses	D. Zolan	19-day	24.40	54.00
Pemberton & Oakes		**Father's Day**			
86-08-001	Daddy's Home	D. Zolan	19-day	19.00	120.00
Pemberton & Oakes		**Mother's Day**			
88-09-001	Mother's Angels	D. Zolan	19-day	19.00	75.00
Pemberton & Oakes		**Grandparent's Day**			
90-10-001	It's Grandma & Grandpa	D. Zolan	19-day	24.40	36.00
93-10-002	Grandpa's Fence	D. Zolan	13-day	24.40	24.40
Pemberton & Oakes		**Adventures of Childhood Collection**			
89-11-001	Almost Home	D. Zolan	44-day	19.60	60.00
89-11-002	Crystal's Creek	D. Zolan	44-day	19.60	45.00
89-11-003	Summer Suds	D. Zolan	44-day	22.00	27.00
90-11-004	Snowy Adventure	D. Zolan	44-day	22.00	24.00
91-11-005	Forests & Fairy Tales	D. Zolan	44-day	24.40	24.40
Pemberton & Oakes		**Thanksgiving**			
81-12-001	I'm Thankful Too	D. Zolan	19-day	19.00	70.00
Pemberton & Oakes		**Nutcracker II**			
81-13-001	Grand Finale	S. Fisher	Undis.	24.40	36.00
82-13-002	Arabian Dancers	S. Fisher	Undis.	24.40	67.50
83-13-003	Dew Drop Fairy	S. Fisher	Undis.	24.40	40-70.00
84-13-004	Clara's Delight	S. Fisher	Undis.	24.40	45.00
85-13-005	Bedtime for Nutcracker	S. Fisher	Undis.	24.40	45.00
86-13-006	The Crowning of Clara	S. Fisher	Undis.	24.40	36.00
87-13-007	Dance of the Snowflakes	D. Zolan	Undis.	24.40	50.00
88-13-008	The Royal Welcome	R. Anderson	Undis.	24.40	24.40
89-13-009	The Spanish Dancer	M. Vickers	Undis.	24.40	24.40
Pemberton & Oakes		**March of Dimes: Our Children, Our Future**			
89-14-001	A Time for Peace	D. Zolan	150-day	29.00	45-50.00
Pemberton & Oakes		**Christmas**			
91-15-001	Candlelight Magic	D. Zolan	Open	24.80	24.80
Pemberton & Oakes		**Companion to Brotherly Love**			
89-16-001	Sisterly Love	D. Zolan	19-day	22.00	42.00
Pemberton & Oakes		**Single Issue Day to Day Spode**			
91-17-001	Daisy Days	D. Zolan	15,000	48.00	48.00
Pemberton & Oakes		**Plaques-Single Issues**			
91-18-001	Flowers for Mother	D. Zolan	Yr.Iss.	16.80	45.00
Pemberton & Oakes		**Heirloom Ovals**			
92-19-001	My Kitty	D. Zolan	Yr.Iss.	18.80	40.00
Pemberton & Oakes		**Single Issue**			
93-20-001	Winter Friends	D. Zolan	19-day	18.80	18.80
Pemberton & Oakes		**The Best of Zolan in Miniature**			
85-21-001	Sabina	D. Zolan	22-day	12.50	112-145.
86-21-002	Erik and Dandelion	D. Zolan	22-day	12.50	96-102.00
86-21-003	Tender Moment	D. Zolan	22-day	12.50	65-84.00
86-21-004	Touching the Sky	D. Zolan	22-day	12.50	65-79.00
87-21-005	A Gift for Laurie	D. Zolan	22-day	12.50	78.00
87-21-006	Small Wonder	D. Zolan	22-day	12.50	76.00
Pemberton & Oakes		**Childhood Discoveries (Miniature)**			
90-22-001	Colors of Spring	D. Zolan	19-day	14.40	49.00
90-22-002	Autumn Leaves	D. Zolan	19-day	14.40	35-45.00
91-22-003	Enchanted Forest	D. Zolan	19-day	16.60	30-45.00
91-22-004	Just Ducky	D. Zolan	19-day	16.60	35.00

PLATES

Company / Number	Name	Series / Artist	Edition Limit	Issue Price	Quote
91-22-005	Rainy Day Pals	D. Zolan	19-day	16.60	35.00
92-22-006	Double Trouble	D. Zolan	19-day	16.60	35.00
Pemberton & Oakes		**Valentine's Day (Miniature)**			
90-23-001	First Kiss	D. Zolan	19-day	14.40	49-59.00
93-23-002	Peppermint Kiss	D. Zolan	19-day	16.60	24-36.00
Pemberton & Oakes		**Easter (Miniature)**			
91-24-001	Easter Morning	D. Zolan	19-day	16.60	30-35.00
Pemberton & Oakes		**Mother's Day (Miniature)**			
90-25-001	Flowers for Mother	D. Zolan	19-day	14.40	45-50.00
92-25-002	Twilight Prayer	D. Zolan	19-day	16.60	30-35.00
93-25-003	Jessica's Field	D. Zolan	11-day	16.60	24-35.00
94-25-004	One Summer Day	D. Zolan	11-day	16.60	16.60
Pemberton & Oakes		**Moments To Remember (Miniature)**			
92-26-001	Just We Two	D. Zolan	19-day	16.60	27-30.00
92-26-002	Almost Home	D. Zolan	19-day	16.60	21.00
93-26-003	Tiny Treasures	D. Zolan	19-day	16.60	19.00
93-26-004	Forest Friends	D. Zolan	19-day	16.60	19.00
Pemberton & Oakes		**Single Issues (Miniature)**			
86-27-001	Backyard Discovery	D. Zolan	22-day	12.50	55-85.00
86-27-002	Daddy's Home	D. Zolan	19-day	12.50	810.00
89-27-003	Sunny Surprise	D. Zolan	19-day	12.50	62.00
89-27-004	My Pumpkin	D. Zolan	19-day	14.40	54.00
91-27-005	Backyard Buddies	D. Zolan	19-day	16.60	35-40.00
91-27-006	The Thinker	D. Zolan	19-day	16.60	30-37.00
93-27-007	Quiet Time	D. Zolan	19-day	16.60	16.60
Pemberton & Oakes		**Plaques**			
91-28-001	New Shoes	D. Zolan	Yr.Iss.	18.80	69.00
92-28-002	Grandma's Garden	D. Zolan	Yr.Iss.	18.80	35.00
92-28-003	Small Wonder	D. Zolan	Yr.Iss.	18.80	42.00
92-28-004	Easter Morning	D. Zolan	Yr.Iss.	18.80	35.00
Pemberton & Oakes		**Membership (Miniature)**			
87-29-001	For You	D. Zolan	19-day	12.50	46-100.00
88-29-002	Making Friends	D. Zolan	19-day	12.50	75.00
89-29-003	Grandma's Garden	D. Zolan	19-day	12.50	65-71.00
90-29-004	A Christmas Prayer	D. Zolan	19-day	14.40	50-95.00
91-29-005	Golden Moment	D. Zolan	19-day	15.00	35-44.00
92-29-006	Brotherly Love	D. Zolan	19-day	15.00	65.00
93-29-007	New Shoes	D. Zolan	19-day	17.00	17.00
94-29-008	My Kitty	D. Zolan	19-day	Gift	N/A
Pemberton & Oakes		**Single Issue Bone China (Miniature)**			
92-30-001	Window of Dreams	D. Zolan	19-day	18.80	30-39.00
Pemberton & Oakes		**Times To Treasure Bone China (Miniature)**			
93-31-001	Little Traveler	D. Zolan	19-day	16.60	16.60-37.00
93-31-002	Garden Swing	D. Zolan	19-day	16.60	16.60
94-31-003	Summer Garden	D. Zolan	19-day	16.60	16.60
Pemberton & Oakes		**Members Only Single Issue (Miniature)**			
90-32-001	By Myself	D. Zolan	19-day	14.40	61.00
93-32-002	Summer's Child	D. Zolan	10-day	16.60	16.60
94-32-003	Little Slugger	D. Zolan	10-day	16.60	16.60
Pemberton & Oakes		**Christmas (Miniature)**			
93-33-001	Snowy Adventure	D. Zolan	19-day	16.60	16.60
Pemberton & Oakes		**Thanksgiving (Miniature)**			
93-34-001	I'm Thankful Too	D. Zolan	19-day	16.60	21.00
Pemberton & Oakes		**Father's Day (Miniature)**			
94-35-001	Two of a Kind	D. Zolan	19-day	16.60	16.60
Pemberton & Oakes		**Yesterday's Children (Miniature)**			
94-36-001	Little Friends	D. Zolan	19-day	16.60	16.60
PenDelfin		**Plate Series**			
XX-01-001	Mother With Baby	J. Heap	Retrd.	40.00	200.00
XX-01-002	Father	J. Heap	7,500	40.00	40.00
XX-01-003	Whopper	D. Roberts	7,500	50.00	50.00
XX-01-004	Gingerbread Day	J. Heap	7,500	55.00	55.00
XX-01-005	Caravan	D. Roberts	7,500	60.00	60.00
XX-01-006	Old Schoolhouse	J. Heap	7,500	60.00	60.00
Pickard		**Mother's Love**			
80-01-001	Miracle	I. Spencer	7,500	95.00	95.00
81-01-002	Story Time	I. Spencer	7,500	110.00	110.00
82-01-003	First Edition	I. Spencer	7,500	115.00	115.00
83-01-004	Precious Moment	I. Spencer	7,500	120.00	145.00
Pickard		**Symphony of Roses**			
82-02-001	Wild Irish Rose	I. Spencer	10,000	85.00	95.00
83-02-002	Yellow Rose of Texas	I. Spencer	10,000	90.00	100-110.
84-02-003	Honeysuckle Rose	I. Spencer	10,000	95.00	135.00
85-02-004	Rose of Washington Square	I. Spencer	10,000	100.00	175.00
Princeton Gallery		**Circus Friends Collection**			
89-01-001	Don't Be Shy	R. Sanderson	Unkn.	29.50	29.50
90-01-002	Make Me A Clown	R. Sanderson	Unkn.	29.50	29.50
90-01-003	Looks Like Rain	R. Sanderson	Unkn.	29.50	29.50
90-01-004	Cheer Up Mr. Clown	R. Sanderson	Unkn.	29.50	29.50
Princeton Gallery		**Cubs Of The Big Cats**			
90-02-001	Cougar Cub	Q. Lemond	Unkn.	29.50	29.50
91-02-002	Lion Cub	Q. Lemond	90-day	29.50	29.50
91-02-003	Snow Leopard	Q. Lemond	90-day	29.50	29.50
91-02-004	Cheetah	Q. Lemond	90-day	29.50	29.50
91-02-005	Tiger	Q. Lemond	90-day	29.50	29.50
92-02-006	Lynx Cub	Q. Lemond	90-day	29.50	29.50
92-02-007	White Tiger Cub	Q. Lemond	90-day	29.50	29.50
Princeton Gallery		**Arctic Wolves**			
91-03-001	Song of the Wilderness	J. Van Zyle	90-day	29.50	29.50
92-03-002	In The Eye of the Moon	J. Van Zyle	90-day	29.50	29.50
Princeton Gallery		**Enchanted World of the Unicorn**			
91-04-001	Rainbow Valley	R. Sanderson	90-day	29.50	29.50
92-04-002	Golden Shore	R. Sanderson	90-day	29.50	29.50

Company / Number	Name	Series / Artist	Edition Limit	Issue Price	Quote
Princeton Gallery		**Darling Dalmatians**			
91-05-001	Dalmatian	L. Picken	90-day	29.50	29.50
92-05-002	Firehouse Frolic	L. Picken	90-day	29.50	29.50
Reco International		**Bohemian Annuals**			
74-01-001	1974	Unknown	500	130.00	155.00
75-01-002	1975	Unknown	500	140.00	160.00
76-01-003	1976	Unknown	500	150.00	160.00
Reco International		**Americanna**			
72-02-001	Gaspee Incident	S. Devlin	1,500	200.00	325.00
Reco International		**Dresden Christmas**			
71-03-001	Shepherd Scene	Unknown	3,500	15.00	50.00
72-03-002	Niklas Church	Unknown	6,000	15.00	25.00
73-03-003	Schwanstein Church	Unknown	6,000	18.00	35.00
74-03-004	Village Scene	Unknown	5,000	20.00	30.00
75-03-005	Rothenburg Scene	Unknown	5,000	24.00	30.00
76-03-006	Village Church	Unknown	5,000	26.00	35.00
77-03-007	Old Mill (Issue Closed)	Unknown	5,000	28.00	30.00
Reco International		**Dresden Mother's Day**			
72-04-001	Doe and Fawn	Unknown	8,000	15.00	20.00
73-04-002	Mare and Colt	Unknown	6,000	16.00	25.00
74-04-003	Tiger and Cub	Unknown	5,000	20.00	23.00
75-04-004	Dachshunds	Unknown	5,000	24.00	28.00
76-04-005	Owl and Offspring	Unknown	5,000	26.00	30.00
77-04-006	Chamois (Issue Closed)	Unknown	5,000	28.00	30.00
Reco International		**Furstenberg Christmas**			
71-05-001	Rabbits	Unknown	7,500	15.00	30.00
72-05-002	Snowy Village	Unknown	6,000	15.00	20.00
73-05-003	Christmas Eve	Unknown	4,000	18.00	35.00
74-05-004	Sparrows	Unknown	4,000	20.00	30.00
75-05-005	Deer Family	Unknown	4,000	22.00	30.00
76-05-006	Winter Birds	Unknown	4,000	25.00	25.00
Reco International		**Furstenberg Deluxe Christmas**			
71-06-001	Wise Men	E. Grossberg	1,500	45.00	45.00
72-06-002	Holy Family	E. Grossberg	2,000	45.00	45.00
73-06-003	Christmas Eve	E. Grossberg	2,000	60.00	65.00
Reco International		**Furstenberg Easter**			
71-07-001	Sheep	Unknown	3,500	15.00	150.00
72-07-002	Chicks	Unknown	6,500	15.00	60.00
73-07-003	Bunnies	Unknown	4,000	16.00	80.00
74-07-004	Pussywillow	Unknown	4,000	20.00	32.50
75-07-005	Easter Window	Unknown	4,000	22.00	30.00
76-07-006	Flower Collecting	Unknown	4,000	25.00	25.00
Reco International		**Furstenberg Mother's Day**			
72-08-001	Hummingbirds, Fe	Unknown	6,000	15.00	45.00
73-08-002	Hedgehogs	Unknown	5,000	16.00	40.00
74-08-003	Doe and Fawn	Unknown	4,000	20.00	30.00
75-08-004	Swans	Unknown	4,000	22.00	23.00
76-08-005	Koala Bears	Unknown	4,000	25.00	30.00
Reco International		**Furstenberg Olympic**			
72-09-001	Munich	J. Poluszynski	5,000	20.00	75.00
76-09-002	Montreal	J. Poluszynski	5,000	37.50	37.50
Reco International		**Grafburg Christmas**			
75-10-001	Black-Capped Chickadee	Unknown	5,000	20.00	60.00
76-10-002	Squirrels	Unknown	5,000	22.00	22.00
Reco International		**King's Christmas**			
73-11-001	Adoration	Merli	1,500	100.00	265.00
74-11-002	Madonna	Merli	1,500	150.00	250.00
75-11-003	Heavenly Choir	Merli	1,500	160.00	235.00
76-11-004	Siblings	Merli	1,500	200.00	225.00
Reco International		**King's Flowers**			
73-12-001	Carnation	A. Falchi	1,000	85.00	130.00
74-12-002	Red Rose	A. Falchi	1,000	100.00	145.00
75-12-003	Yellow Dahlia	A. Falchi	1,000	110.00	162.00
76-12-004	Bluebells	A. Falchi	1,000	130.00	165.00
77-12-005	Anemones	A. Falchi	1,000	130.00	175.00
Reco International		**King's Mother's Day**			
73-13-001	Dancing Girl	Merli	1,500	100.00	225.00
74-13-002	Dancing Boy	Merli	1,500	115.00	250.00
75-13-003	Motherly Love	Merli	1,500	140.00	225.00
76-13-004	Maiden	Merli	1,500	180.00	200.00
Reco International		**Four Seasons**			
73-14-001	Spring	J. Poluszynski	2,500	50.00	75.00
73-14-002	Summer	J. Poluszynski	2,500	50.00	75.00
73-14-003	Fall	J. Poluszynski	2,500	50.00	75.00
73-14-004	Winter	J. Poluszynski	2,500	50.00	75.00
Reco International		**Marmot Father's Day**			
70-15-001	Stag	Unknown	3,500	12.00	100.00
71-15-002	Horse	Unknown	3,500	12.50	40.00
Reco International		**Marmot Christmas**			
70-16-001	Polar Bear, Fe	Unknown	5,000	13.00	60.00
71-16-002	Buffalo Bill	Unknown	6,000	16.00	55.00
72-16-003	Boy and Grandfather	Unknown	5,000	20.00	50.00
71-16-004	American Buffalo	Unknown	6,000	14.50	35.00
73-16-005	Snowman	Unknown	3,000	22.00	45.00
74-16-006	Dancing	Unknown	2,000	24.00	30.00
75-16-007	Quail	Unknown	2,000	30.00	40.00
76-16-008	Windmill	Unknown	2,000	40.00	40.00
Reco International		**Marmot Mother's Day**			
72-17-001	Seal	Unknown	6,000	16.00	60.00
73-17-002	Bear with Cub	Unknown	3,000	20.00	140.00
74-17-003	Penguins	Unknown	2,000	24.00	50.00
75-17-004	Raccoons	Unknown	2,000	30.00	45.00
76-17-005	Ducks	Unknown	2,000	40.00	40.00
Reco International		**Moser Christmas**			
70-18-001	Hradcany Castle	Unknown	400	75.00	170.00
71-18-002	Karlstein Castle	Unknown	1,365	75.00	80.00

Number	Name	Artist	Edition Limit	Issue Price	Quote
72-18-003	Old Town Hall	Unknown	1,000	85.00	85.00
73-18-004	Karlovy Vary Castle	Unknown	500	90.00	100.00
Reco International		**Moser Mother's Day**			
71-19-001	Peacocks	Unknown	350	75.00	100.00
72-19-002	Butterflies	Unknown	750	85.00	90.00
73-19-003	Squirrels	Unknown	500	90.00	95.00
Reco International		**Royale**			
69-20-001	Apollo Moon Landing	Unknown	2,000	30.00	80.00
Reco International		**Royale Christmas**			
69-21-001	Christmas Fair	Unknown	6,000	12.00	125.00
70-21-002	Vigil Mass	Unknown	10,000	13.00	110.00
71-21-003	Christmas Night	Unknown	8,000	16.00	50.00
72-21-004	Elks	Unknown	8,000	16.00	45.00
73-21-005	Christmas Down	Unknown	6,000	20.00	37.50
74-21-006	Village Christmas	Unknown	5,000	22.00	60.00
75-21-007	Feeding Time	Unknown	5,000	26.00	35.00
76-21-008	Seaport Christmas	Unknown	5,000	27.50	30.00
77-21-009	Sledding	Unknown	5,000	30.00	30.00
Reco International		**Royal Mother's Day**			
70-22-001	Swan and Young	Unknown	6,000	12.00	80.00
71-22-002	Doe and Fawn	Unknown	9,000	13.00	55.00
72-22-003	Rabbits	Unknown	9,000	16.00	40.00
73-22-004	Owl Family	Unknown	6,000	18.00	40.00
74-22-005	Duck and Young	Unknown	5,000	22.00	40.00
75-22-006	Lynx and Cubs	Unknown	5,000	26.00	40.00
76-22-007	Woodcock and Young	Unknown	5,000	27.50	32.50
77-22-008	Koala Bear	Unknown	5,000	30.00	30.00
Reco International		**Royale Father's Day**			
70-23-001	Frigate Constitution	Unknown	5,000	13.00	80.00
71-23-002	Man Fishing	Unknown	5,000	13.00	35.00
72-23-003	Mountaineer	Unknown	5,000	16.00	55.00
73-23-004	Camping	Unknown	4,000	18.00	45.00
74-23-005	Eagle	Unknown	2,500	22.00	35.00
75-23-006	Regatta	Unknown	2,500	26.00	35.00
76-23-007	Hunting	Unknown	2,500	27.50	32.50
77-23-008	Fishing	Unknown	2,500	30.00	30.00
Reco International		**Royale Game Plates**			
72-24-001	Setters	J. Poluszynski	500	180.00	200.00
73-24-002	Fox	J. Poluszynski	500	200.00	250.00
74-24-003	Osprey	W. Schiener	250	250.00	250.00
75-24-004	California Quail	W. Schiener	250	265.00	265.00
Reco International		**Royale Germania Christmas Annual**			
70-25-001	Orchid	Unknown	600	200.00	650.00
71-25-002	Cyclamen	Unknown	1,000	200.00	325.000
72-25-003	Silver Thistle	Unknown	1,000	250.00	290.00
73-25-004	Tulips	Unknown	600	275.00	310.00
74-25-005	Sunflowers	Unknown	500	300.00	320.00
75-25-006	Snowdrops	Unknown	350	450.00	500.00
Reco Inernational		**Royale Germania Crystal Mother's Day**			
71-26-001	Roses	Unknown	250	135.00	650.00
72-26-002	Elephant and Youngster	Unknown	750	180.00	250.00
73-26-003	Koala Bear and Cub	Unknown	600	200.00	225.00
74-26-004	Squirrels	Unknown	500	240.00	250.00
75-26-005	Swan and Young	Unknown	350	350.00	360.00
Reco International		**Western**			
74-27-001	Mountain Man	E. Berke	1,000	165.00	165.00
Reco International		**The World of Children**			
77-28-001	Rainy Day Fun	J. McClelland	10,000	50.00	32.00
78-28-002	When I Grow Up	J. McClelland	15,000	50.00	29.00
79-28-003	You're Invited	J. McClelland	15,000	50.00	30.00
80-28-004	Kittens for Sale	J. McClelland	15,000	50.00	17.00
Reco International		**Mother Goose**			
79-29-001	Mary, Mary	J. McClelland	Yr.Iss.	22.50	99.00
80-29-002	Little Boy Blue	J. McClelland	Yr.Iss.	22.50	30.00
81-29-003	Little Miss Muffet	J. McClelland	Yr.Iss.	24.50	25.00
82-29-004	Little Jack Horner	J. McClelland	Yr.Iss.	24.50	25.00
83-29-005	Little Bo Peep	J. McClelland	Yr.Iss.	24.50	24.50
84-29-006	Diddle, Diddle Dumpling	J. McClelland	Yr.Iss.	24.50	24.50
85-29-007	Mary Had a Little Lamb	J. McClelland	Yr.Iss.	27.50	28.00
86-29-008	Jack and Jill	J. McClelland	Yr.Iss.	27.50	30.00
Reco International		**The McClelland Children's Circus Collection**			
82-30-001	Tommy the Clown	J. McClelland	100-day	29.50	49.00
82-30-002	Katie, the Tightrope Walker	J. McClelland	100-day	29.50	49.00
83-30-003	Johnny the Strongman	J. McClelland	100-day	29.50	39.00
84-30-004	Maggie the Animal Trainer	J. McClelland	100-day	29.50	30.00
Reco International		**Becky's Day**			
85-31-001	Awakening	J. McClelland	90-day	24.50	29.00
85-31-002	Getting Dressed	J. McClelland	90-day	24.50	29.00
86-31-003	Breakfast	J. McClelland	90-day	27.50	35.00
86-31-004	Learning is Fun	J. McClelland	90-day	27.50	27.50
86-31-005	Muffin Making	J. McClelland	90-day	27.50	27.50
86-31-006	Tub Time	J. McClelland	90-day	27.50	35.00
86-31-007	Evening Prayer	J. McClelland	90-day	27.50	27.50
Reco International		**Treasured Songs of Childhood**			
87-32-001	Twinkle, Twinkle, Little Star	J. McClelland	150-day	29.50	30.00
88-32-002	A Tisket, A Tasket	J. McClelland	150-day	29.50	30.00
88-32-003	Baa, Baa, Black Sheep	J. McClelland	150-day	32.90	33.00
89-32-004	Round The Mulberry Bush	J. McClelland	150-day	32.90	33.00
89-32-005	Rain, Rain Go Away	J. McClelland	150-day	32.90	33.00
89-32-006	I'm A Little Teapot	J. McClelland	150-day	32.90	33.00
89-32-007	Pat-A-Cake	J. McClelland	150-day	34.90	35.00
90-32-008	Hush Little Baby	J. McClelland	150-day	34.90	35.00
Reco International		**The Wonder of Christmas**			
91-33-001	Santa's Secret	J. McClelland	48-day	29.50	29.50
92-33-002	My Favorite Ornament	J. McClelland	48-day	29.50	29.50
92-33-003	Waiting For Santa	J. McClelland	48-day	29.50	29.50
93-33-004	Candlelight Christmas	J. McClelland	48-day	29.50	29.50

Number	Name	Artist	Edition Limit	Issue Price	Quote
Reco International		**The Premier Collection**			
91-34-001	Love	J. McClelland	7,500	75.00	75.00
Reco International		**Golf Collection**			
92-35-001	Par Excellence	J. McClelland	180-day	35.00	35.00
Reco International		**The Children's Garden**			
93-36-001	Garden Friends	J. McClelland	120-day	29.50	29.50
93-36-002	Tea for Three	J. McClelland	120-day	29.50	29.50
93-36-003	Puppy Love	J. McClelland	120-day	29.50	29.50
Reco International		**March of Dimes: Our Children, Our Future**			
89-37-001	A Time to Love (2nd in Series)	S. Kuck	150-day	29.00	45.00
89-37-002	A Time to Plant (3rd in Series)	J. McClelland	150-day	29.00	50.00
Reco International		**Games Children Play**			
79-38-001	Me First	S. Kuck	10,000	45.00	50.00
80-38-002	Forever Bubbles	S. Kuck	10,000	45.00	48.00
81-38-003	Skating Pals	S. Kuck	10,000	45.00	47.50
82-38-004	Join Me	S. Kuck	10,000	45.00	45.00
Reco International		**The Grandparent Collector's Plates**			
81-39-001	Grandma's Cookie Jar	S. Kuck	Yr.Iss.	37.50	37.50
81-39-002	Grandpa and the Dollhouse	S. Kuck	Yr.Iss.	37.50	37.50
Reco International		**Little Professionals**			
82-40-001	All is Well	S. Kuck	10,000	39.50	43-65.00
83-40-002	Tender Loving Care	S. Kuck	10,000	39.50	50-75.00
84-40-003	Lost and Found	S. Kuck	10,000	39.50	45.00
85-40-004	Reading, Writing and...	S. Kuck	10,000	39.50	45.00
Reco International		**Days Gone By**			
83-41-001	Sunday Best	S. Kuck	14-day	29.50	39.00
83-41-002	Amy's Magic Horse	S. Kuck	14-day	29.50	36.00
84-41-003	Little Anglers	S. Kuck	14-day	29.50	30.00
84-41-004	Afternoon Recital	S. Kuck	14-day	29.50	74-85.00
84-41-005	Little Tutor	S. Kuck	14-day	29.50	24.00
85-41-006	Easter at Grandma's	S. Kuck	14-day	29.50	24.00
85-41-007	Morning Song	S. Kuck	14-day	29.50	14.00
85-41-008	The Surrey Ride	S. Kuck	14-day	29.50	40.00
Reco International		**A Childhood Almanac**			
85-42-001	Fireside Dreams-January	S. Kuck	14-day	29.50	45-49.00
85-42-002	Be Mine-February	S. Kuck	14-day	29.50	45.00
86-42-003	Winds of March-March	S. Kuck	14-day	29.50	45-49.00
85-42-004	Easter Morning-April	S. Kuck	14-day	29.50	55.00
85-42-005	For Mom-May	S. Kuck	14-day	29.50	45.00
85-42-006	Just Dreaming-June	S. Kuck	14-day	29.50	55.00
85-42-007	Star Spangled Sky-July	S. Kuck	14-day	29.50	45.00
85-42-008	Summer Secrets-August	S. Kuck	14-day	29.50	49-55.00
85-42-009	School Days-September	S. Kuck	14-day	29.50	55-60.00
86-42-010	Indian Summer-October	S. Kuck	14-day	29.50	45.00
86-42-011	Giving Thanks-November	S. Kuck	14-day	29.50	45-49.00
85-42-012	Christmas Magic-December	S. Kuck	14-day	35.00	45-55.00
Reco International		**Mother's Day Collection**			
85-43-001	Once Upon a Time	S. Kuck	Yr.Iss.	29.50	55-75.00
86-43-002	Times Remembered	S. Kuck	Yr.Iss.	29.50	50-75.00
87-43-003	A Cherished Time	S. Kuck	Yr.Iss.	29.50	55.00
88-43-004	A Time Together	S. Kuck	Yr.Iss.	29.50	59.00
Reco International		**A Children's Christmas Pageant**			
86-44-001	Silent Night	S. Kuck	Yr.Iss.	32.50	35-55.00
87-44-002	Hark the Herald Angels Sing	S. Kuck	Yr.Iss.	32.50	35.00
88-44-003	While Shepherds Watched...	S. Kuck	Yr.Iss.	32.50	32.50
89-44-004	We Three Kings	S. Kuck	Yr.Iss.	32.50	32.50
Reco International		**Barefoot Children**			
87-45-001	Night-Time Story	S. Kuck	14-day	29.50	40.00
87-45-002	Golden Afternoon	S. Kuck	14-day	29.50	40.00
88-45-003	Little Sweethearts	S. Kuck	14-day	29.50	40.00
88-45-004	Carousel Magic	S. Kuck	14-day	29.50	49.00
88-45-005	Under the Apple Tree	S. Kuck	14-day	29.50	40.00
88-45-006	The Rehearsal	S. Kuck	14-day	29.50	45-55.00
88-45-007	Pretty as a Picture	S. Kuck	14-day	29.50	45.00
88-45-008	Grandma's Trunk	S. Kuck	14-day	29.50	45.00
Reco International		**Special Occasions by Reco**			
88-46-001	The Wedding	S. Kuck	Open	35.00	35.00
89-46-002	Wedding Day (6 1/2")	S. Kuck	Open	25.00	25.00
90-46-003	The Special Day	S. Kuck	Open	25.00	25.00
Reco International		**Victorian Mother's Day**			
89-47-001	Mother's Sunshine	S. Kuck	Yr.Iss.	35.00	45-85.00
90-47-002	Reflection Of Love	S. Kuck	Yr.Iss.	35.00	50-80.00
91-47-003	A Precious Time	S. Kuck	Yr.Iss.	35.00	45-75.00
92-47-004	Loving Touch	S. Kuck	Yr.Iss.	35.00	45-49.00
Reco International Corp.		**Plate Of The Month Collection**			
90-48-001	January	S. Kuck	28-day	25.00	25.00
90-48-002	February	S. Kuck	28-day	25.00	25.00
90-48-003	March	S. Kuck	28-day	25.00	25.00
90-48-004	April	S. Kuck	28-day	25.00	25.00
90-48-005	May	S. Kuck	28-day	25.00	25.00
90-48-006	June	S. Kuck	28-day	25.00	25.00
90-48-007	July	S. Kuck	28-day	25.00	25.00
90-48-008	August	S. Kuck	28-day	25.00	25.00
90-48-009	September	S. Kuck	28-day	25.00	25.00
90-48-010	October	S. Kuck	28-day	25.00	25.00
90-48-011	November	S. Kuck	28-day	25.00	25.00
90-48-012	December	S. Kuck	28-day	25.00	25.00
Reco International Corp.		**Premier Collection**			
91-49-001	Puppy	S. Kuck	7,500	95.00	125-150.
91-49-002	Kitten	S. Kuck	7,500	95.00	150-200.
92-49-003	La Belle	S. Kuck	7,500	95.00	95.00
92-49-004	Le Beau	S. Kuck	7,500	95.00	95.00
Reco International Corp.		**Hearts And Flowers**			
91-50-001	Patience	S. Kuck	120-day	29.50	29.50
91-50-002	Tea Party	S. Kuck	120-day	29.50	29.50
92-50-003	Cat's In The Cradle	S. Kuck	120-day	32.50	32.50
92-50-004	Carousel of Dreams	S. Kuck	120-day	32.50	32.50
92-50-005	Storybook Memories	S. Kuck	120-day	32.50	32.50

Number	Name	Artist	Edition Limit	Issue Price	Quote
93-50-006	Delightful Bundle	S. Kuck	120-day	34.50	34.50
93-50-007	Easter Morning Visitor	S. Kuck	120-day	34.50	34.50
93-50-008	Me and My Pony	S. Kuck	120-day	34.50	34.50
Reco International Corp.		**Gift of Love Mother's Day Collection**			
93-51-001	Morning Glory	S. Kuck	10,000	65.00	65.00
94-51-002	Memories From The Heart	S. Kuck	10,000	65.00	65.00
Reco International Corp.		**Tidings Of Joy**			
92-52-001	Peace on Earth	S. Kuck	N/A	35.00	35.00
93-52-002	Rejoice	S. Kuck	N/A	35.00	35.00
Reco International		**Little Angel Plate Collection**			
94-53-001	Angel of Charity	S. Kuck	95-day	29.50	29.50
94-53-002	Angel of Joy	S. Kuck	95-day	29.50	29.50
94-53-003	Angel of Grace	S. Kuck	95-day	29.50	29.50
94-53-004	Angel of Hope	S. Kuck	95-day	29.50	29.50
Reco International		**The Sophisticated Ladies Collection**			
85-54-001	Felicia	A. Fazio	21-day	29.50	32.50
85-54-002	Samantha	A. Fazio	21-day	29.50	32.50
85-54-003	Phoebe	A. Fazio	21-day	29.50	32.50
85-54-004	Cleo	A. Fazio	21-day	29.50	32.50
86-54-005	Cerissa	A. Fazio	21-day	29.50	32.50
86-54-006	Natasha	A. Fazio	21-day	29.50	32.50
86-54-007	Bianka	A. Fazio	21-day	29.50	32.50
86-54-008	Chelsea	A. Fazio	21-day	29.50	32.50
Reco International		**Gardens of Beauty**			
88-55-001	English Country Garden	D. Barlowe	14-day	29.50	29.50
88-55-002	Dutch Country Garden	D. Barlowe	14-day	29.50	29.50
88-55-003	New England Garden	D. Barlowe	14-day	29.50	29.50
88-55-004	Japanese Garden	D. Barlowe	14-day	29.50	29.50
89-55-005	Italian Garden	D. Barlowe	14-day	29.50	29.50
89-55-006	Hawaiian Garden	D. Barlowe	14-day	29.50	29.50
89-55-007	German Country Garden	D. Barlowe	14-day	29.50	29.50
89-55-008	Mexican Garden	D. Barlowe	14-day	29.50	29.50
Reco International		**Gardens of America**			
92-56-001	Colonial Splendor	D. Barlowe	48-day	29.50	29.50
Reco International		**Vanishing Animal Kingdoms**			
86-57-001	Rama the Tiger	S. Barlowe	21,500	35.00	35.00
86-57-002	Olepi the Buffalo	S. Barlowe	21,500	35.00	35.00
87-57-003	Coolibah the Koala	S. Barlowe	21,500	35.00	42.00
87-57-004	Ortwin the Deer	S. Barlowe	21,500	35.00	39.00
87-57-005	Yen-Poh the Panda	S. Barlowe	21,500	35.00	40.00
88-57-006	Mamakuu the Elephant	S. Barlowe	21,500	35.00	59.00
Reco International Corp.		**Town And Country Dogs**			
90-58-001	Fox Hunt	S. Barlowe	36-day	35.00	35.00
91-58-002	The Retrieval	S. Barlowe	36-day	35.00	35.00
91-58-003	Golden Fields (Golden Retriever)	S. Barlowe	36-day	35.00	35.00
93-58-004	Faithful Companions (Cocker Spaniel)	S. Barlowe	36-day	35.00	35.00
Reco International		**Our Cherished Seas**			
91-59-001	Whale Song	S. Barlowe	48-day	37.50	37.50
91-59-002	Lions of the Sea	S. Barlowe	48-day	37.50	37.50
91-59-003	Flight of the Dolphins	S. Barlowe	48-day	37.50	37.50
92-59-004	Palace of the Seals	S. Barlowe	48-day	37.50	37.50
92-59-005	Orca Ballet	S. Barlowe	48-day	37.50	37.50
93-59-006	Emperors of the Ice	S. Barlowe	48-day	37.50	37.50
93-59-007	Turtle Treasure	S. Barlowe	48-day	37.50	37.50
93-59-008	Splendor of the Sea	S. Barlowe	48-day	37.50	37.50
Reco International		**Great Stories from the Bible**			
87-60-001	Moses in the Bulrushes	G. Katz	14-day	29.50	35.00
87-60-002	King Saul & David	G. Katz	14-day	29.50	35.00
87-60-003	Moses and the Ten Commandments	G. Katz	14-day	29.50	38.00
87-60-004	Joseph's Coat of Many Colors	G. Katz	14-day	29.50	35.00
88-60-005	Rebekah at the Well	G. Katz	14-day	29.50	35.00
88-60-006	Daniel Reads the Writing on the Wall	G. Katz	14-day	29.50	35.00
88-60-007	The Story of Ruth	G. Katz	14-day	29.50	35.00
88-60-008	King Solomon	G. Katz	14-day	29.50	35.00
Reco International		**The Nutcracker Ballet**			
89-61-001	Christmas Eve Party	C. Micarelli	14-day	35.00	35.00
90-61-002	Clara And Her Prince	C. Micarelli	14-day	35.00	37.00
90-61-003	The Dream Begins	C. Micarelli	14-day	35.00	35.00
91-61-004	Dance of the Snow Fairies	C. Micarelli	14-day	35.00	35.00
92-61-005	The Land of Sweets	C. Micarelli	14-day	35.00	35.00
92-61-006	The Sugar Plum Fairy	C. Micarelli	14-day	35.00	35.00
Reco International		**Special Occasions-Wedding**			
91-62-001	From This Day Forward (9 1/2")	C. Micarelli	Open	35.00	35.00
91-62-002	From This Day Forward (6 1/2")	C. Micarelli	Open	25.00	25.00
91-62-003	To Have And To Hold (9 1/2")	C. Micarelli	Open	35.00	35.00
91-62-004	To Have And To Hold (6 1/2")	C. Micarelli	Open	25.00	25.00
Reco International		**The Glory Of Christ**			
92-63-001	The Ascension	C. Micarelli	48-day	29.50	29.50
93-63-002	Jesus Teaching	C. Micarelli	48-day	29.50	29.50
93-63-003	The Last Supper	C. Micarelli	48-day	29.50	29.50
93-63-004	The Nativity	C. Micarelli	48-day	29.50	29.50
93-63-005	The Baptism Of Christ	C. Micarelli	48-day	29.50	29.50
93-63-006	Jesus Heals The Sick	C. Micarelli	48-day	29.50	29.50
94-63-007	Jesus Walks On Water	C. Micarelli	48-day	29.50	29.50
94-63-008	Descent From The Cross	C. Micarelli	48-day	29.50	29.50
Reco International		**J. Bergsma Mother's Day Series**			
90-64-001	The Beauty Of Life	J. Bergsma	14-day	35.00	35.00
92-64-002	Life's Blessing	J. Bergsma	14-day	35.00	35.00
93-64-003	My Greatest Treasures	J. Bergsma	14-day	35.00	35.00
94-64-004	Forever In My Heart	J. Bergsma	14-day	35.00	35.00
Reco International		**Guardians Of The Kingdom**			
90-65-001	Rainbow To Ride On	J. Bergsma	17,500	35.00	37.00
90-65-002	Special Friends Are Few	J. Bergsma	17,500	35.00	35.00
90-65-003	Guardians Of The Innocent Children	J. Bergsma	17,500	35.00	38.00
90-65-004	The Miracle Of Love	J. Bergsma	17,500	35.00	37.00
91-65-005	The Magic Of Love	J. Bergsma	17,500	35.00	35.00
91-65-006	Only With The Heart	J. Bergsma	17,500	35.00	35.00
91-65-007	To Fly Without Wings	J. Bergsma	17,500	35.00	35.00
91-65-008	In Faith I Am Free	J. Bergsma	17,500	35.00	35.00

Number	Name	Artist	Edition Limit	Issue Price	Quote
Reco International		**Castles & Dreams**			
92-66-001	The Birth of a Dream	J. Bergsma	48-day	29.50	29.50
92-66-002	Dreams Come True	J. Bergsma	48-day	29.50	29.50
93-66-003	Believe In Your Dreams	J. Bergsma	48-day	29.50	29.50
94-66-004	Follow Your Dreams	J. Bergsma	48-day	29.50	29.50
Reco International		**The Christmas Series**			
90-67-001	Down The Glistening Lane	J. Bergsma	14-day	35.00	39.00
91-67-002	A Child Is Born	J. Bergsma	14-day	35.00	35.00
92-67-003	Christmas Day	J. Bergsma	14-day	35.00	35.00
93-67-004	I Wish You An Angel	J. Bergsma	14-day	35.00	35.00
Reco International		**God's Own Country**			
90-68-001	Daybreak	I. Drechsler	14-day	30.00	30.00
90-68-002	Coming Home	I. Drechsler	14-day	30.00	30.00
90-68-003	Peaceful Gathering	I. Drechsler	14-day	30.00	30.00
90-68-004	Quiet Waters	I. Drechsler	14-day	30.00	30.00
Reco International		**The Flower Fairies Year Collection**			
90-69-001	The Red Clover Fairy	C.M. Barker	14-day	29.50	29.50
90-69-002	The Wild Cherry Blossom Fairy	C.M. Barker	14-day	29.50	29.50
90-69-003	The Pine Tree Fairy	C.M. Barker	14-day	29.50	29.50
90-69-004	The Rose Hip Fairy	C.M. Barker	14-day	29.50	29.50
Reco International		**Oscar & Bertie's Edwardian Holiday**			
91-70-001	Snapshot	P.D. Jackson	48-day	29.50	29.50
92-70-002	Early Rise	P.D. Jackson	48-day	29.50	29.50
92-70-003	All Aboard	P.D. Jackson	48-day	29.50	29.50
92-70-004	Learning To Swim	P.D. Jackson	48-day	29.50	29.50
Reco International		**In The Eye of The Storm**			
91-71-001	First Strike	W. Lowe	120-day	29.50	29.50
92-71-002	Night Force	W. Lowe	120-day	29.50	29.50
92-71-003	Tracks Across The Sand	W. Lowe	120-day	29.50	29.50
92-71-004	The Storm Has Landed	W. Lowe	120-day	29.50	29.50
Reco International		**Celebration of Love**			
92-72-001	Happy Anniversary (9 1/4")	J. Hall	Open	35.00	35.00
92-72-002	10th (9 1/4")	J. Hall	Open	35.00	35.00
92-72-003	25th (9 1/4")	J. Hall	Open	35.00	35.00
92-72-004	50th (9 1/4")	J. Hall	Open	35.00	35.00
92-72-005	Happy Anniversary (6 1/2")	J. Hall	Open	25.00	35.00
92-72-006	10th (6 1/2")	J. Hall	Open	25.00	35.00
92-72-007	25th (6 1/2")	J. Hall	Open	25.00	35.00
92-72-008	50th (6 1/2")	J. Hall	Open	25.00	35.00
Reco International		**The Heart of the Family**			
92-73-001	Sharing Secrets	J. York	48-day	29.50	29.50
93-73-002	Spinning Dreams	J. York	48-day	29.50	29.50
Reco International		**The Enchanted Norfin Trolls**			
93-74-001	Troll Maiden	C. Hopkins	75-day	19.50	19.50
93-74-002	The Wizard Troll	C. Hopkins	75-day	19.50	19.50
93-74-003	The Troll and His Dragon	C. Hopkins	75-day	19.50	19.50
94-74-004	Troll in Shinning Armor	C. Hopkins	75-day	19.50	19.50
94-74-005	Minstrel Troll	C. Hopkins	75-day	19.50	19.50
Reco International		**Sugar and Spice**			
93-75-001	Best Friends	S. Kuck	95-day	29.90	29.90
93-75-002	Sisters	S. Kuck	95-day	29.90	29.90
94-75-003	Little One	S. Kuck	95-day	32.90	32.90
Reco International		**Noble and Free**			
94-76-001	Gathering Storm	Kelly	95-day	29.50	29.50
Reco International		**Memories Of Yesterday**			
93-77-001	Hush	M. Attwell	Open	29.50	29.50
93-77-002	Time For Bed	M. Attwell	Open	29.50	29.50
93-77-003	I'se Been Painting	M. Attwell	Open	29.50	29.50
93-77-004	Just Looking Pretty	M. Attwell	Open	29.50	29.50
94-77-005	Give it Your Best Shot	M. Attwell	Open	29.50	29.50
94-77-006	I Pray The Lord My Soul to Keep	M. Attwell	Open	29.50	29.50
94-77-007	Just Thinking About You	M. Attwell	Open	29.50	29.50
94-77-008	What Will I Grow Up To Be	M. Attwell	Open	29.50	29.50
Reco International		**Trains of the Orient**			
93-78-001	The Golden Arrow-England	R. Johnson	N/A	29.50	29.50
94-78-002	Austria	R. Johnson	N/A	29.50	29.50
94-78-003	Bavaria	R. Johnson	N/A	29.50	29.50
94-78-004	Rumania	R. Johnson	N/A	29.50	29.50
94-78-005	Greece	R. Johnson	N/A	29.50	29.50
94-78-006	Frankonia	R. Johnson	N/A	29.50	29.50
94-78-007	Turkey	R. Johnson	N/A	29.50	29.50
94-78-008	France	R. Johnson	N/A	29.50	29.50
River Shore		**Famous Americans**			
76-01-001	Brown's Lincoln	Rockwell-Brown	9,500	40.00	40.00
77-01-002	Rockwell's Triple Self-Portrait	Rockwell-Brown	9,500	45.00	45.00
78-01-003	Peace Corps	Rockwell-Brown	9,500	45.00	45.00
79-01-004	Spirit of Lindbergh	Rockwell-Brown	9,500	50.00	50.00
River Shore		**Norman Rockwell Single Issue**			
79-02-001	Spring Flowers	N. Rockwell	17,000	75.00	145.00
80-02-002	Looking Out to Sea	N. Rockwell	17,000	75.00	195.00
82-02-003	Grandpa's Guardian	N. Rockwell	17,000	80.00	80.00
82-02-004	Grandpa's Treasures	N. Rockwell	17,000	80.00	80.00
River Shore		**Baby Animals**			
79-03-001	Akiku	R. Brown	20,000	50.00	80.00
80-03-002	Roosevelt	R. Brown	20,000	50.00	90.00
81-03-003	Clover	R. Brown	20,000	50.00	65.00
82-03-004	Zuela	R. Brown	20,000	50.00	65.00
River Shore		**Rockwell Four Freedoms**			
81-04-001	Freedom of Speech	N. Rockwell	17,000	65.00	80-99.00
82-04-002	Freedom of Worship	N. Rockwell	17,000	65.00	80.00
82-04-003	Freedom from Fear	N. Rockwell	17,000	65.00	65-200.00
82-04-004	Freedom from Want	N. Rockwell	17,000	65.00	65-425.00
River Shore		**Puppy Playtime**			
87-05-001	Double Take	J. Lamb	14-day	24.50	32-35.00
88-05-002	Catch of the Day	J. Lamb	14-day	24.50	24.50
88-05-003	Cabin Fever	J. Lamb	14-day	24.50	24.50
88-05-004	Weekend Gardener	J. Lamb	14-day	24.50	24.50

Company / Number	Name	Series / Artist	Edition Limit	Issue Price	Quote
88-05-005	Getting Acquainted	J. Lamb	14-day	24.50	24.50
88-05-006	Hanging Out	J. Lamb	14-day	24.50	24.50
88-05-007	A New Leash On Life	J. Lamb	14-day	24.50	29.50
87-05-008	Fun and Games	J. Lamb	14-day	24.50	29.50
River Shore		**Lovable Teddies**			
85-06-001	Bedtime Blues	M. Hague	10-day	21.50	21.50
85-06-002	Bearly Frightful	M. Hague	10-day	21.50	21.50
85-06-003	Caught in the Act	M. Hague	10-day	21.50	21.50
85-06-004	Fireside Friends	M. Hague	10-day	21.50	21.50
85-06-005	Harvest Time	M. Hague	10-day	21.50	21.50
85-06-006	Missed a Button	M. Hague	10-day	21.50	21.50
85-06-007	Tender Loving Bear	M. Hague	10-day	21.50	21.50
85-06-008	Sunday Stroll	M. Hague	10-day	21.50	21.50
River Shore		**Little House on the Prairie**			
85-07-001	Founder's Day Picnic	E. Christopherson	10-day	29.50	50.00
85-07-002	Women's Harvest	E. Christopherson	10-day	29.50	45.00
85-07-003	Medicine Show	E. Christopherson	10-day	29.50	45.00
85-07-004	Caroline's Eggs	E. Christopherson	10-day	29.50	45.00
85-07-005	Mary's Gift	E. Christopherson	10-day	29.50	45.00
85-07-006	A Bell for Walnut Grove	E. Christopherson	10-day	29.50	45.00
85-07-007	Ingall's Family	E. Christopherson	10-day	29.50	45.00
85-07-008	The Sweetheart Tree	E. Christopherson	10-day	29.50	45.00
River Shore		**We the Children**			
87-08-001	The Freedom of Speech	D. Crook	14-day	24.50	24.50
88-08-002	Right to Vote	D. Crook	14-day	24.50	24.50
88-08-003	Unreasonable Search and Seizure	D. Crook	14-day	24.50	24.50
88-08-004	Right to Bear Arms	D. Crook	14-day	24.50	24.50
88-08-005	Trial by Jury	D. Crook	14-day	24.50	24.50
88-08-006	Self Incrimination	D. Crook	14-day	24.50	24.50
88-08-007	Cruel and Unusual Punishment	D. Crook	14-day	24.50	24.50
88-08-008	Quartering of Soldiers	D. Crook	14-day	24.50	24.50
Norman Rockwell Gallery		**Rockwell's Christmas Legacy**			
92-01-001	Santa's Workshop	Rockwell Inspired	Closed	49.90	49.90
93-01-002	Making a List	Rockwell Inspired	6/94	49.90	49.90
93-01-003	While Santa Slumbers	Rockwell Inspired	8/94	54.90	54.90
93-01-004	Visions of Santa	Rockwell Inspired	10/94	54.90	54.90
Norman Rockwell Gallery		**Norman Rockwell Centennial**			
93-02-001	The Toymaker	Rockwell Inspired	3/95	39.90	39.90
93-02-002	The Cobbler	Rockwell Inspired	3/95	39.90	39.90
Rockwell Society		**Christmas**			
74-01-001	Scotty Gets His Tree	N. Rockwell	Yr.Iss.	24.50	100.00
75-01-002	Angel with Black Eye	N. Rockwell	Yr.Iss.	24.50	35-75.00
76-01-003	Golden Christmas	N. Rockwell	Yr.Iss.	24.50	35-49.00
77-01-004	Toy Shop Window	N. Rockwell	Yr.Iss.	24.50	25.00
78-01-005	Christmas Dream	N. Rockwell	Yr.Iss.	24.50	25.00
79-01-006	Somebody's Up There	N. Rockwell	Yr.Iss.	24.50	25.00
80-01-007	Scotty Plays Santa	N. Rockwell	Yr.Iss.	24.50	24.50
81-01-008	Wrapped Up in Christmas	N. Rockwell	Yr.Iss.	25.50	26.50
82-01-009	Christmas Courtship	N. Rockwell	Yr.Iss.	25.50	25.50
83-01-010	Santa in the Subway	N. Rockwell	Yr.Iss.	25.50	25.50-32.50
84-01-011	Santa in the Workshop	N. Rockwell	Yr.Iss.	27.50	27.50
85-01-012	Grandpa Plays Santa	N. Rockwell	Yr.Iss.	27.90	35.00
86-01-013	Dear Santy Claus	N. Rockwell	Yr.Iss.	27.90	27.90
87-01-014	Santa's Golden Gift	N. Rockwell	Yr.Iss.	27.90	27.90
88-01-015	Santa Claus	N. Rockwell	Yr.Iss.	29.90	29.90
89-01-016	Jolly Old St. Nick	N. Rockwell	Yr.Iss.	29.90	29.90
90-01-017	A Christmas Prayer	N. Rockwell	Yr.Iss.	29.90	29.90
91-01-018	Santa's Helpers	N. Rockwell	Yr.Iss.	32.90	32.90
92-01-019	The Christmas Surprise	N. Rockwell	Yr.Iss.	32.90	40.00
93-01-020	The Tree Brigade	N. Rockwell	Yr.Iss.	32.90	32.90
Rockwell Society		**Mother's Day**			
76-02-001	A Mother's Love	N. Rockwell	Yr.Iss.	24.50	75.00
77-02-002	Faith	N. Rockwell	Yr.Iss.	24.50	50.00
78-02-003	Bedtime	N. Rockwell	Yr.Iss.	24.50	34.00
79-02-004	Reflections	N. Rockwell	Yr.Iss.	24.50	24.50
80-02-005	A Mother's Pride	N. Rockwell	Yr.Iss.	24.50	24.50
81-02-006	After the Party	N. Rockwell	Yr.Iss.	24.50	24.50
82-02-007	The Cooking Lesson	N. Rockwell	Yr.Iss.	24.50	26.00
83-02-008	Add Two Cups and Love	N. Rockwell	Yr.Iss.	25.50	26.00
84-02-009	Grandma's Courting Dress	N. Rockwell	Yr.Iss.	25.50	26.00
85-02-010	Mending Time	N. Rockwell	Yr.Iss.	27.50	28.00
86-02-011	Pantry Raid	N. Rockwell	Yr.Iss.	27.90	28.00
87-02-012	Grandma's Surprise	N. Rockwell	Yr.Iss.	29.90	30.00
88-02-013	My Mother	N. Rockwell	Yr.Iss.	29.90	29.90
89-02-014	Sunday Dinner	N. Rockwell	Yr.Iss.	29.90	30.00
90-02-015	Evening Prayers	N. Rockwell	Yr.Iss.	29.90	30.00
91-02-016	Building Our Future	N. Rockwell	Yr.Iss.	32.90	33.00
91-02-017	Gentle Reassurance	N. Rockwell	Yr.Iss.	32.90	34.00
92-02-018	A Special Delivery	N. Rockwell	Yr.Iss.	32.90	48.00
Rockwell Society		**Heritage**			
77-03-001	Toy Maker	N. Rockwell	Yr.Iss.	14.50	97.00
78-03-002	Cobbler	N. Rockwell	Yr.Iss.	19.50	54.00
79-03-003	Lighthouse Keeper's Daughter	N. Rockwell	Yr.Iss.	19.50	21-30.00
80-03-004	Ship Builder	N. Rockwell	Yr.Iss.	19.50	20.00
81-03-005	Music maker	N. Rockwell	Yr.Iss.	19.50	19.50
82-03-006	Tycoon	N. Rockwell	Yr.Iss.	19.50	19.50
83-03-007	Painter	N. Rockwell	Yr.Iss.	19.50	19.50
84-03-008	Storyteller	N. Rockwell	Yr.Iss.	19.50	19.50
85-03-009	Gourmet	N. Rockwell	Yr.Iss.	19.50	19.50
86-03-010	Professor	N. Rockwell	Yr.Iss.	22.90	22.90
87-03-011	Shadow Artist	N. Rockwell	Yr.Iss.	22.90	30.00
88-03-012	The Veteran	N. Rockwell	Yr.Iss.	22.90	23.00
88-03-013	The Banjo Player	N. Rockwell	Yr.Iss.	22.90	25-31.00
90-03-014	The Old Scout	N. Rockwell	Yr.Iss.	24.90	27.00
91-03-015	The Young Scholar	N. Rockwell	Yr.Iss.	24.90	30.00
91-03-016	The Family Doctor	N. Rockwell	Yr.Iss.	27.90	40.00
92-03-017	The Jeweler	N. Rockwell	Yr.Iss.	27.90	27.90
93-03-018	Halloween Frolic	N. Rockwell	Yr.Iss.	27.90	27.90
Rockwell Society		**Rockwell's Rediscovered Women**			
84-04-001	Dreaming in the Attic	N. Rockwell	100-day	19.50	20.00
84-04-002	Waiting on the Shore	N. Rockwell	100-day	22.50	23.00
84-04-003	Pondering on the Porch	N. Rockwell	100-day	22.50	23.00
84-04-004	Making Believe at the Mirror	N. Rockwell	100-day	22.50	23-30.00
84-04-005	Waiting at the Dance	N. Rockwell	100-day	22.50	23.00
84-04-006	Gossiping in the Alcove	N. Rockwell	100-day	22.50	23.00
84-04-007	Standing in the Doorway	N. Rockwell	100-day	22.50	20-35.00
84-04-008	Flirting in the Parlor	N. Rockwell	100-day	22.50	23-35.00
84-04-009	Working in the Kitchen	N. Rockwell	100-day	22.50	23.00
84-04-010	Meeting on the Path	N. Rockwell	100-day	22.50	23.00
84-04-011	Confiding in the Den	N. Rockwell	100-day	22.50	23.00
84-04-012	Reminiscing in the Quiet	N. Rockwell	100-day	22.50	22.50
XX-04-013	Complete Collection	N. Rockwell	100-day	267.00	267.00
Rockwell Society		**Rockwell on Tour**			
83-05-001	Walking Through Merrie Englande	N. Rockwell	150-day	16.00	16.00
83-05-002	Promenade a Paris	N. Rockwell	150-day	16.00	16.00
83-05-003	When in Rome	N. Rockwell	150-day	16.00	16.00
84-05-004	Die Walk am Rhein	N. Rockwell	150-day	16.00	16.00
Rockwell Society		**Rockwell's Light Compaign**			
83-06-001	This is the Room that Light Made	N. Rockwell	150-day	19.50	20.00
84-06-002	Grandpa's Treasure Chest	N. Rockwell	150-day	19.50	20.00
84-06-003	Father's Help	N. Rockwell	150-day	19.50	19.50
84-06-004	Evening's Ease	N. Rockwell	150-day	19.50	19.50
84-06-005	Close Harmony	N. Rockwell	150-day	21.50	21.50
84-06-006	The Birthday Wish	N. Rockwell	150-day	21.50	21.50
Rockwell Society		**Rockwell's American Dream**			
85-07-001	A Young Girl's Dream	N. Rockwell	150-day	19.90	20.00
85-07-002	A Couple's Commitment	N. Rockwell	150-day	19.90	20.00
85-07-003	A Family's Full Measure	N. Rockwell	150-day	22.90	22.90
86-07-004	A Mother's Welcome	N. Rockwell	150-day	22.90	28.00
86-07-005	A Young Man's Dream	N. Rockwell	150-day	22.90	28.00
86-07-006	The Musician's Magic	N. Rockwell	150-day	22.90	24.00
87-07-007	An Orphan's Hope	N. Rockwell	150-day	24.90	25.00
87-07-008	Love's Reward	N. Rockwell	150-day	24.90	41.00
Rockwell Society		**Colonials-The Rarest Rockwells**			
85-08-001	Unexpected Proposal	N. Rockwell	150-day	27.90	27.90
86-08-002	Words of Comfort	N. Rockwell	150-day	27.90	27.90
86-08-003	Light for the Winter	N. Rockwell	150-day	30.90	30.90
87-08-004	Portrait for a Bridegroom	N. Rockwell	150-day	30.90	30.90
87-08-005	The Journey Home	N. Rockwell	150-day	30.90	30.90
87-08-006	Clinching the Deal	N. Rockwell	150-day	30.90	30.90
88-08-007	Sign of the Times	N. Rockwell	150-day	32.90	32.90
88-08-008	Ye Glutton	N. Rockwell	150-day	32.90	32.90
Rockwell Society		**A Mind of Her Own**			
86-09-001	Sitting Pretty	N. Rockwell	150-day	24.90	25.00
87-09-002	Serious Business	N. Rockwell	150-day	24.90	25.00
87-09-003	Breaking the Rules	N. Rockwell	150-day	24.90	32.00
87-09-004	Good Intentions	N. Rockwell	150-day	27.90	28.00
88-09-005	Second Thoughts	N. Rockwell	150-day	27.90	27.90
88-09-006	World's Away	N. Rockwell	150-day	27.90	28.00
88-09-007	Kiss and Tell	N. Rockwell	150-day	29.90	29.90
88-09-008	On My Honor	N. Rockwell	150-day	29.90	30.00
Rockwell Society		**Rockwell's Golden Moments**			
87-10-001	Grandpa's Gift	N. Rockwell	150-day	19.90	10.00
87-10-002	Grandma's Love	N. Rockwell	150-day	19.90	25.00
88-10-003	End of day	N. Rockwell	150-day	22.90	23.00
88-10-004	Best Friends	N. Rockwell	150-day	22.90	23.00
89-10-005	Love Letters	N. Rockwell	150-day	22.90	23.00
89-10-006	Newfound Worlds	N. Rockwell	150-day	22.90	23.00
89-10-007	Keeping Company	N. Rockwell	150-day	24.90	24.90
89-10-008	Evening's Repose	N. Rockwell	150-day	24.90	24.90
Rockwell Society		**Rockwell's The Ones We Love**			
88-11-001	Tender Loving Care	N. Rockwell	150-day	19.90	38.00
89-11-002	A Time to Keep	N. Rockwell	150-day	19.90	19.90
89-11-003	The Inventor And The Judge	N. Rockwell	150-day	22.90	22.90
89-11-004	Ready For The World	N. Rockwell	150-day	22.90	22.90
89-11-005	Growing Strong	N. Rockwell	150-day	22.90	22.90
90-11-006	The Story Hour	N. Rockwell	150-day	22.90	22.90
90-11-007	The Country Doctor	N. Rockwell	150-day	24.90	24.90
90-11-008	Our Love of Country	N. Rockwell	150-day	24.90	24.90
90-11-009	The Homecoming	N. Rockwell	150-day	24.90	24.90
91-11-010	A Helping Hand	N. Rockwell	150-day	24.90	24.90
Rockwell Society		**Coming Of Age**			
90-12-001	Back To School	N. Rockwell	150-day	29.90	29.90
90-12-002	Home From Camp	N. Rockwell	150-day	29.90	29.90
90-12-003	Her First Formal	N. Rockwell	150-day	32.90	44.00
90-12-004	The Muscleman	N. Rockwell	150-day	32.90	44.00
90-12-005	A New Look	N. Rockwell	150-day	32.90	36.00
91-12-006	A Balcony Seat	N. Rockwell	150-day	32.90	32.90
91-12-007	Men About Town	N. Rockwell	150-day	34.90	35.00
91-12-008	Paths of Glory	N. Rockwell	150-day	34.90	35.00
91-12-009	Doorway to the Past	N. Rockwell	150-day	34.90	55.00
91-12-010	School's Out!	N. Rockwell	150-day	34.90	90.00
Rockwell Society		**Innocence and Experience**			
91-13-001	The Sea Captain	N. Rockwell	150-day	29.90	29.90
91-13-002	The Radio Operator	N. Rockwell	150-day	29.90	32.00
91-13-003	The Magician	N. Rockwell	150-day	32.90	38.00
92-13-004	The American Heroes	N. Rockwell	150-day	32.90	39.00
Rockwell Society		**Rockwell's Treasured Memories**			
91-14-001	Quiet Reflections	N. Rockwell	150-day	29.90	29.90
91-14-002	Romantic Reverie	N. Rockwell	150-day	29.90	29.90
91-14-003	Tender Romance	N. Rockwell	150-day	32.90	32.90
91-14-004	Evening Passage	N. Rockwell	150-day	32.90	32.90
91-14-005	Heavenly Dreams	N. Rockwell	150-day	32.90	32.90
91-14-006	Sentimental Shores	N. Rockwell	150-day	32.90	32.90
Roman, Inc.		**The Masterpiece Collection**			
79-01-001	Adoration	F. Lippe	5,000	65.00	65.00
80-01-002	Madonna with Grapes	P. Mignard	5,000	87.50	87.50
81-01-003	The Holy Family	G. Delle Notti	5,000	95.00	95.00
82-01-004	Madonna of the Streets	R. Ferruzzi	5,000	85.00	85.00
Roman, Inc.		**A Child's World**			
80-02-001	Little Children, Come to Me	F. Hook	15,000	45.00	49.00
Roman, Inc.		**A Child's Play**			
82-03-001	Breezy Day	F. Hook	30-day	29.95	39.00
82-03-002	Kite Flying	F. Hook	30-day	29.95	39.00
84-03-003	Bathtub Sailor	F. Hook	30-day	29.95	35.00
84-03-004	The First Snow	F. Hook	30-day	29.95	35.00

PLATES

Company / Number	Name	Series / Artist	Edition Limit	Issue Price	Quote
Roman, Inc.		**Frances Hook Collection-Set I**			
82-04-001	I Wish, I Wish	F. Hook	15,000	24.95	35-39.00
82-04-002	Baby Blossoms	F. Hook	15,000	24.95	35-39.00
82-04-003	Daisy Dreamer	F. Hook	15,000	24.95	35-39.00
82-04-004	Trees So Tall	F. Hook	15,000	24.95	35-39.00
Roman, Inc.		**Frances Hook Collection-Set II**			
83-05-001	Caught It Myself	F. Hook	15,000	24.95	25.00
83-05-002	Winter Wrappings	F. Hook	15,000	24.95	25.00
83-05-003	So Cuddly	F. Hook	15,000	24.95	25.00
83-05-004	Can I Keep Him?	F. Hook	15,000	24.95	25.00
Roman, Inc.		**Pretty Girls of the Ice Capades**			
83-06-001	Ice Princess	G. Petty	30-day	24.50	24.50
Roman, Inc.		**The Ice Capades Clown**			
83-07-001	Presenting Freddie Trenkler	G. Petty	30-day	24.50	24.50
Roman, Inc.		**Roman Memorial**			
84-08-001	The Carpenter	F. Hook	Yr.Iss.	100.00	135.00
Roman, Inc.		**Roman Cats**			
84-09-001	Grizabella	Unknown	30-day	29.50	29.50
84-09-002	Mr. Mistoffelees	Unknown	30-day	29.50	29.50
84-09-003	Rum Rum Tugger	Unknown	30-day	29.50	29.50
Roman, Inc.		**The Magic of Childhood**			
85-10-001	Special Friends	A. Williams	10-day	24.50	35.00
85-10-002	Feeding Time	A. Williams	10-day	24.50	35.00
85-10-003	Best Buddies	A. Williams	10-day	24.50	35.00
85-10-004	Getting Acquainted	A. Williams	10-day	24.50	35.00
86-10-005	Last One In	A. Williams	10-day	24.50	35.00
86-10-006	A Handful Of Love	A. Williams	10-day	24.50	35.00
86-10-007	Look Alikes	A. Williams	10-day	24.50	35.00
86-10-008	No Fair Peeking	A. Williams	10-day	24.50	35.00
Roman, Inc.		**Frances Hook Legacy**			
85-11-001	Fascination	F. Hook	100-day	19.50	35-39.00
85-11-002	Daydreaming	F. Hook	100-day	19.50	35-39.00
85-11-003	Discovery	F. Hook	100-day	22.50	35-39.00
85-11-004	Disappointment	F. Hook	100-day	22.50	35-39.00
85-11-005	Wonderment	F. Hook	100-day	22.50	35-39.00
85-11-006	Expectation	F. Hook	100-day	22.50	35-39.00
Roman, Inc.		**The Lord's Prayer**			
86-12-001	Our Father	A. Williams	10-day	24.50	24.50
86-12-002	Thy Kingdom Come	A. Williams	10-day	24.50	24.50
86-12-003	Give Us This Day	A. Williams	10-day	24.50	24.50
86-12-004	Forgive Our Trespasses	A. Williams	10-day	24.50	34.00
86-12-005	As We Forgive	A. Williams	10-day	24.50	24.50
86-12-006	Lead Us Not	A. Williams	10-day	24.50	24.50
86-12-007	Deliver Us From Evil	A. Williams	10-day	24.50	24.50
86-12-008	Thine Is The Kingdom	A. Williams	10-day	24.50	24.50
Roman, Inc.		**The Sweetest Songs**			
86-13-001	A Baby's Prayer	I. Spencer	30-day	39.50	45.00
86-13-002	This Little Piggie	I. Spencer	30-day	39.50	39.50
88-13-003	Long, Long Ago	I. Spencer	30-day	39.50	39.50
89-13-004	Rockabye	I. Spencer	30-day	39.50	39.50
Roman, Inc.		**Fontanini Annual Christmas Plate**			
86-14-001	A King Is Born	E. Simonetti	Yr.Iss.	60.00	60.00
87-14-002	O Come, Let Us Adore Him	E. Simonetti	Yr.Iss.	60.00	65.00
88-14-003	Adoration of the Magi	E. Simonetti	Yr.Iss.	70.00	75.00
89-14-004	Flight Into Egypt	E. Simonetti	Yr.Iss.	75.00	85.00
Roman, Inc.		**The Love's Prayer**			
88-15-001	Love Is Patient and Kind	A. Williams	14-day	29.50	29.50
88-15-002	Love Is Never Jealous or Boastful	A. Williams	14-day	29.50	29.50
88-15-003	Love Is Never Arrogant or Rude	A. Williams	14-day	29.50	29.50
88-15-004	Love Does Not Insist on Its Own Way	A. Williams	14-day	29.50	29.50
88-15-005	Love Is Never Irritable or Resentful	A. Williams	14-day	29.50	29.50
88-15-006	Love Rejoices In the Right	A. Williams	14-day	29.50	29.50
88-15-007	Love Believes All Things	A. Williams	14-day	29.50	29.50
88-15-008	Love Never Ends	A. Williams	14-day	29.50	29.50
Roman, Inc.		**March of Dimes: Our Children, Our Future**			
90-16-001	A Time To Laugh	A. Williams	150-day	29.00	39-49.00
Roman, Inc.		**Abbie Williams Collection**			
91-17-001	Legacy of Love	A. Williams	Open	29.50	29.50
91-17-002	Bless This Child	A. Williams	Open	29.50	29.50
Roman, Inc.		**Catnippers**			
86-18-001	Christmas Mourning	I. Spencer	9,500	34.50	34.50
92-18-002	Happy Holidaze	I. Spencer	9,500	34.50	34.50
Roman, Inc.		**God Bless You, Little One**			
91-19-001	Baby's First Birthday (Girl)	A. Williams	Open	29.50	29.50
91-19-002	Baby's First Birthday (Boy)	A. Williams	Open	29.50	29.50
91-19-003	Baby's First Smile	A. Williams	Open	19.50	19.50
91-19-004	Baby's First Word	A. Williams	Open	19.50	19.50
91-19-005	Baby's First Step	A. Williams	Open	19.50	19.50
91-19-006	Baby's First Tooth	A. Williams	Open	19.50	19.50
Roman, Inc.		**Millenium Series**			
92-20-001	Silent Night	Morcaldo/Lucchesi	Closed	49.50	49.50
93-20-002	The Annunciation	Morcaldo/Lucchesi	5,000	49.50	49.50
94-20-003	Peace On Earth	Morcaldo/Lucchesi	5,000	49.50	49.50
Roman, Inc.		**Tender Expressions**			
92-21-001	Thoughts of You Are In My Heart	B. Sargent	100-day	29.50	29.50
Roman, Inc.		**The Richard Judson Zolan Collection**			
92-22-001	The Butterfly Net	R.J. Zolan	100-day	29.50	29.50
94-22-002	The Ring	R.J. Zolan	100-day	29.50	29.50
94-22-003	Terrace Dancing	R.J. Zolan	100-day	29.50	29.50
Roman, Inc.		**Precious Children**			
93-23-001	Bless Baby Brother	A. Williams	N/A	29.50	29.50
93-23-002	Blowing Bubbles	A. Williams	N/A	29.50	29.50
93-23-003	Don't Worry, Mother Duck	A. Williams	N/A	29.50	29.50
93-23-004	Treetop Discovery	A. Williams	N/A	29.50	29.50
93-23-005	The Tea Party	A. Williams	N/A	29.50	29.50
93-23-006	Mother's Little Angel	A. Williams	N/A	29.50	29.50
93-23-007	Picking Daisies	A. Williams	N/A	29.50	29.50
93-23-008	Let's Say Grace	A. Williams	N/A	29.50	29.50
Roman, Inc.		**Promise of a Savior**			
93-24-001	An Angel's Message	Unknown	95-day	29.90	29.90
93-24-002	Gifts to Jesus	Unknown	95-day	29.90	29.90
93-24-003	The Heavenly King	Unknown	95-day	29.90	29.90
93-24-004	Angels Were Watching	Unknown	95-day	29.90	29.90
93-24-005	Holy Mother & Child	Unknown	95-day	29.90	29.90
93-24-006	A Child is Born	Unknown	95-day	29.90	29.90
Roman, Inc.		**Single Releases**			
87-25-001	The Christening	A. Williams	Open	29.50	29.50
90-25-002	The Dedication	A. Williams	Open	29.50	29.50
90-25-003	The Baptism	A. Williams	Open	29.50	29.50
Rorstrand		**Christmas**			
68-01-001	Bringing Home the Tree	G. Nylund	Annual	12.00	500.00
69-01-002	Fisherman Sailing Home	G. Nylund	Annual	13.50	18-30.00
70-01-003	Nils with His Geese	G. Nylund	Annual	13.50	13.50-15.00
71-01-004	Nils in Lapland	G. Nylund	Annual	15.00	15.00
72-01-005	Dalecarlian Fiddler	G. Nylund	Annual	15.00	20-22.00
73-01-006	Farm in Smaland	G. Nylund	Annual	16.00	60.00
74-01-007	Vadslena	G. Nylund	Annual	19.00	43.00
75-01-008	Nils in Vastmanland	G. Nylund	Annual	20.00	35.00
76-01-009	Nils in Uppland	G. Nylund	Annual	20.00	43-49.00
77-01-010	Nils in Varmland	G. Nylund	Annual	29.50	29.50
78-01-011	Nils in Fjallbacka	G. Nylund	Annual	32.50	49.00
79-01-012	Nils in Vaestergoetland	G. Nylund	Annual	38.50	38.50
80-01-013	Nils in Halland	G. Nylund	Annual	55.00	60.00
81-01-014	Nils in Gotland	G. Nylund	Annual	55.00	45.00
82-01-015	Nils at Skansen	G. Nylund	Annual	47.50	40.00
83-01-016	Nils in Oland	G. Nylund	Annual	42.50	55.00
84-01-017	Angerman land	G. Nylund	Annual	42.50	35.00
85-01-018	Nils in Jamtland	G. Nylund	Annual	42.50	70.00
86-01-019	Nils in Karlskr	G. Nylund	Annual	42.50	50.00
87-01-020	Dalsland, Forget-Me-Not	G. Nylund	Annual	47.50	150.00
88-01-021	Nils in Halsingland	G. Nylund	Annual	55.00	60.00
89-01-022	Nils Visits Gothenborg	G. Nylund	Annual	60.00	61.00
90-01-023	Nils in Kvikkjokk	G. Nylund	Annual	75.00	75.00
91-01-024	Nils in Medelpad	G. Nylund	Annual	85.00	85.00
92-01-025	Gastrikland, Lily of the Valley	G. Nylund	Annual	92.50	92.50
93-01-026	Narke's Castle	G. Nylund	Annual	92.50	92.50
Rosenthal		**Christmas**			
10-01-001	Winter Peace	Unknown	Annual	Unkn.	550.00
11-01-002	Three Wise Men	Unknown	Annual	Unkn.	325.00
12-01-003	Stardust	Unknown	Annual	Unkn.	255.00
13-01-004	Christmas Lights	Unknown	Annual	Unkn.	235.00
14-01-005	Christmas Song	Unknown	Annual	Unkn.	350.00
15-01-006	Walking to Church	Unknown	Annual	Unkn.	180.00
16-01-007	Christmas During War	Unknown	Annual	Unkn.	240.00
17-01-008	Angel of Peace	Unknown	Annual	Unkn.	200.00
18-01-009	Peace on Earth	Unknown	Annual	Unkn.	200.00
19-01-010	St. Christopher with Christ Child	Unknown	Annual	Unkn.	225.00
20-01-011	Manger in Bethlehem	Unknown	Annual	Unkn.	325.00
21-01-012	Christmas in Mountains	Unknown	Annual	Unkn.	200.00
22-01-013	Advent Branch	Unknown	Annual	Unkn.	200.00
23-01-014	Children in Winter Woods	Unknown	Annual	Unkn.	200.00
24-01-015	Deer in the Woods	Unknown	Annual	Unkn.	200.00
25-01-016	Three Wise Men	Unknown	Annual	Unkn.	200.00
26-01-017	Christmas in Mountains	Unknown	Annual	Unkn.	195.00
27-01-018	Station on the Way	Unknown	Annual	Unkn.	200.00
28-01-019	Chalet Christmas	Unknown	Annual	Unkn.	185.00
29-01-020	Christmas in Alps	Unknown	Annual	Unkn.	225.00
30-01-021	Group of Deer Under Pines	Unknown	Annual	Unkn.	225.00
31-01-022	Path of the Magi	Unknown	Annual	Unkn.	225.00
32-01-023	Christ Child	Unknown	Annual	Unkn.	185.00
33-01-024	Thru the Night to Light	Unknown	Annual	Unkn.	190.00
34-01-025	Christmas Peace	Unknown	Annual	Unkn.	190.00
35-01-026	Christmas by the Sea	Unknown	Annual	Unkn.	190.00
36-01-027	Nurnberg Angel	Unknown	Annual	Unkn.	195.00
37-01-028	Berchtesgaden	Unknown	Annual	Unkn.	195.00
38-01-029	Christmas in the Alps	Unknown	Annual	Unkn.	195.00
39-01-030	Schneekoppe Mountain	Unknown	Annual	Unkn.	195.00
40-01-031	Marien Chruch in Danzig	Unknown	Annual	Unkn.	250.00
41-01-032	Strassburg Cathedral	Unknown	Annual	Unkn.	250.00
42-01-033	Marianburg Castle	Unknown	Annual	Unkn.	300.00
43-01-034	Winter Idyll	Unknown	Annual	Unkn.	300.00
44-01-035	Wood Scape	Unknown	Annual	Unkn.	300.00
45-01-036	Christmas Peace	Unknown	Annual	Unkn.	400.00
46-01-037	Christmas in an Alpine Valley	Unknown	Annual	Unkn.	240.00
47-01-038	Dillingen Madonna	Unknown	Annual	Unkn.	985.00
48-01-039	Message to the Shepherds	Unknown	Annual	Unkn.	875.00
49-01-040	The Holy Family	Unknown	Annual	Unkn.	185.00
50-01-041	Christmas in the Forest	Unknown	Annual	Unkn.	185.00
51-01-042	Star of Bethlehem	Unknown	Annual	Unkn.	450.00
52-01-043	Christmas in the Alps	Unknown	Annual	Unkn.	195.00
53-01-044	The Holy Light	Unknown	Annual	Unkn.	195.00
54-01-045	Christmas Eve	Unknown	Annual	Unkn.	195.00
55-01-046	Christmas in a Village	Unknown	Annual	Unkn.	195.00
56-01-047	Christmas in the Alps	Unknown	Annual	Unkn.	195.00
57-01-048	Christmas by the Sea	Unknown	Annual	Unkn.	195.00
58-01-049	Christmas Eve	Unknown	Annual	Unkn.	195.00
59-01-050	Midnight Mass	Unknown	Annual	Unkn.	195.00
60-01-051	Christmas in a Small Village	Unknown	Annual	Unkn.	195.00
61-01-052	Solitary Christmas	Unknown	Annual	Unkn.	225.00
62-01-053	Christmas Eve	Unknown	Annual	Unkn.	195.00
63-01-054	Silent Night	Unknown	Annual	Unkn.	195.00
64-01-055	Christmas Market in Nurnberg	Unknown	Annual	Unkn.	225.00
65-01-056	Christmas Munich	Unknown	Annual	Unkn.	185.00
66-01-057	Christmas in Ulm	Unknown	Annual	Unkn.	275.00
67-01-058	Christmas in Reginburg	Unknown	Annual	Unkn.	185.00
68-01-059	Christmas in Bremen	Unknown	Annual	Unkn.	195.00
69-01-060	Christmas in Rothenburg	Unknown	Annual	Unkn.	220.00
70-01-061	Christmas in Cologne	Unknown	Annual	Unkn.	175.00
71-01-062	Christmas in Garmisch	Unknown	Annual	42.00	100.00
72-01-063	Christmas in Franconia	Unknown	Annual	50.00	95.00
73-01-064	Lubeck-Holstein	Unknown	Annual	77.00	105.00
74-01-065	Christmas in Wurzburg	Unknown	Annual	85.00	100.00
Rosenthal		**Wiinblad Christmas**			
71-02-001	Maria & Child	B. Wiinblad	Undis.	100.00	700.00

Company / Number	Name	Series / Artist	Edition Limit	Issue Price	Quote
72-02-002	Caspar	B. Wiinblad	Undis.	100.00	290.00
73-02-003	Melchior	B. Wiinblad	Undis.	125.00	335.00
74-02-004	Balthazar	B. Wiinblad	Undis.	125.00	300.00
75-02-005	The Annunciation	B. Wiinblad	Undis.	195.00	195.00
76-02-006	Angel with Trumpet	B. Wiinblad	Undis.	195.00	195.00
77-02-007	Adoration of Shepherds	B. Wiinblad	Undis.	225.00	225.00
78-02-008	Angel with Harp	B. Wiinblad	Undis.	275.00	295.00
79-02-009	Exodus from Egypt	B. Wiinblad	Undis.	310.00	310.00
80-02-010	Angel with Glockenspiel	B. Wiinblad	Undis.	360.00	360.00
81-02-011	Christ Child Visits Temple	B. Wiinblad	Undis.	375.00	375.00
82-02-012	Christening of Christ	B. Wiinblad	Undis.	375.00	375.00
Rosenthal		**Nobility of Children**			
76-03-001	La Contessa Isabella	E. Hibel	12,750	120.00	120.00
77-03-002	La Marquis Maurice-Pierre	E. Hibel	12,750	120.00	120.00
78-03-003	Baronesse Johanna	E. Hibel	12,750	130.00	140.00
79-03-004	Chief Red Feather	E. Hibel	12,750	140.00	180.00
Rosenthal		**Oriental Gold**			
76-04-001	Yasuko	E. Hibel	2,000	275.00	650.00
77-04-002	Mr. Obata	E. Hibel	2,000	275.00	500.00
78-04-003	Sakura	E. Hibel	2,000	295.00	400.00
79-04-004	Michio	E. Hibel	2,000	325.00	375.00
Royal Copenhagen		**Christmas**			
08-01-001	Madonna and Child	C. Thomsen	Annual	1.00	3200.00
09-01-002	Danish Landscape	S. Ussing	Annual	1.00	170.00
10-01-003	The Magi	C. Thomsen	Annual	1.00	135.00
11-01-004	Danish Landscape	O. Jensen	Annual	1.00	148.00
12-01-005	Christmas Tree	C. Thomsen	Annual	1.00	148.00
13-01-006	Frederik Church Spire	A. Boesen	Annual	1.50	126.00
14-01-007	Holy Spirit Church	A. Boesen	Annual	1.50	126.00
15-01-008	Danish Landscape	A. Krog	Annual	1.50	126.00
16-01-009	Shepherd at Christmas	R. Bocher	Annual	1.50	96.00
17-01-010	Our Savior Church	O. Jensen	Annual	2.00	96.00
18-01-011	Sheep and Shepherds	O. Jensen	Annual	2.00	96.00
19-01-012	In the Park	O. Jensen	Annual	2.00	96.00
20-01-013	Mary and Child Jesus	G. Rode	Annual	2.00	96.00
21-01-014	Aabenraa Marketplace	O. Jensen	Annual	2.00	81.00
22-01-015	Three Singing Angels	E. Selschau	Annual	2.00	74.00
23-01-016	Danish Landscape	O. Jensen	Annual	2.00	74.00
24-01-017	Sailing Ship	B. Olsen	Annual	2.00	110.00
25-01-018	Christianshavn	O. Jensen	Annual	2.00	88.00
26-01-019	Christianshavn Canal	R. Bocher	Annual	2.00	88.00
27-01-020	Ship's Boy at Tiller	B. Olsen	Annual	2.00	126.00
28-01-021	Vicar's Family	G. Rode	Annual	2.00	90.00
29-01-022	Grundtvig Church	O. Jensen	Annual	2.00	90.00
30-01-023	Fishing Boats	B. Olsen	Annual	2.50	100.00
31-01-024	Mother and Child	G. Rode	Annual	2.50	100.00
32-01-025	Frederiksberg Gardens	O. Jensen	Annual	2.50	100.00
33-01-026	Ferry and the Great Belt	B. Olsen	Annual	2.50	145.00
34-01-027	The Hermitage Castle	O. Jensen	Annual	2.50	118.00
35-01-028	Kronborg Castle	B. Olsen	Annual	2.50	175.00
36-01-029	Roskilde Cathedral	R. Bocher	Annual	2.50	145.00
37-01-030	Main Street Copenhagen	N. Thorsson	Annual	2.50	160.00
38-01-031	Round Church in Osterlars	H. Nielsen	Annual	3.00	255.00
39-01-032	Greenland Pack-Ice	S. Nielsen	Annual	3.00	285.00
40-01-033	The Good Shepherd	K. Lange	Annual	3.00	390.00
41-01-034	Danish Village Church	T. Kjolner	Annual	3.00	350.00
42-01-035	Bell Tower	N. Thorsson	Annual	4.00	350.00
43-01-036	Flight into Egypt	N. Thorsson	Annual	4.00	450.00
44-01-037	Danish Village Scene	V. Olson	Annual	4.00	250.00
45-01-038	A Peaceful Motif	R. Bocher	Annual	4.00	395.00
46-01-039	Zealand Village Church	N. Thorsson	Annual	4.00	150.00
47-01-040	The Good Shepherd	K. Lange	Annual	4.50	200.00
48-01-041	Nodebo Church	T. Kjolner	Annual	4.50	175.00
49-01-042	Our Lady's Cathedral	H. Hansen	Annual	5.00	190.00
50-01-043	Boeslunde Church	V. Olson	Annual	5.00	198.00
51-01-044	Christmas Angel	R. Bocher	Annual	5.00	328.00
52-01-045	Christmas in the Forest	K. Lange	Annual	5.00	125.00
53-01-046	Frederiksberg Castle	T. Kjolner	Annual	6.00	125.00
54-01-047	Amalienborg Palace	K. Lange	Annual	6.00	125.00
55-01-048	Fano Girl	K. Lange	Annual	7.00	190.00
56-01-049	Rosenborg Castle	K. Lange	Annual	7.00	167.00
57-01-050	The Good Shepherd	H. Hansen	Annual	8.00	115-129.
58-01-051	Sunshine over Greenland	H. Hansen	Annual	9.00	80-135.00
59-01-052	Christmas Night	H. Hansen	Annual	9.00	120-130.
60-01-053	The Stag	H. Hansen	Annual	10.00	109-160.
61-01-054	Training Ship	K. Lange	Annual	10.00	99-152.00
62-01-055	The Little Mermaid	Unknown	Annual	11.00	140-250.
63-01-056	Hojsager Mill	K. Lange	Annual	11.00	49-52.00
64-01-057	Fetching the Tree	K. Lange	Annual	11.00	42-81.00
65-01-058	Little Skaters	K. Lange	Annual	12.00	44-81.00
66-01-059	Blackbird	K. Lange	Annual	12.00	27-81.00
67-01-060	The Royal Oak	K. Lange	Annual	13.00	23-55.00
68-01-061	The Last Umiak	K. Lange	Annual	13.00	19-35.00
69-01-062	The Old Farmyard	K. Lange	Annual	14.00	19-48.00
70-01-063	Christmas Rose and Cat	K. Lange	Annual	14.00	19-45.00
71-01-064	Hare In Winter	K. Lange	Annual	15.00	10-30.00
72-01-065	In the Desert	K. Lange	Annual	16.00	13-30.00
73-01-066	Train Homeward Bound	K. Lange	Annual	22.00	20-40.00
74-01-067	Winter Twilight	K. Lange	Annual	22.00	14-35.00
75-01-068	Queen's Palace	K. Lange	Annual	27.50	15-35.00
76-01-069	Danish Watermill	S. Vestergaard	Annual	27.50	30-45.00
77-01-070	Immervad Bridge	K. Lange	Annual	32.00	16-45.00
78-01-071	Greenland Scenery	K. Lange	Annual	35.00	18-45.00
79-01-072	Choosing Christmas Tree	K. Lange	Annual	42.50	45-90.00
80-01-073	Bringing Home the Tree	K. Lange	Annual	49.50	21-45.00
81-01-074	Admiring Christmas Tree	K. Lange	Annual	52.50	19-55.00
82-01-075	Waiting for Christmas	K. Lange	Annual	54.50	40-60.00
83-01-076	Merry Christmas	K. Lange	Annual	54.50	45-58.00
84-01-077	Jingle Bells	K. Lange	Annual	54.50	45-54.00
85-01-078	Snowman	K. Lange	Annual	54.50	50-85.00
86-01-079	Christmas Vacation	K. Lange	Annual	54.50	48-58.00
87-01-080	Winter Birds	S. Vestergaard	Annual	59.50	49-75.00
88-01-081	Christmas Eve in Copenhagen	S. Vestergaard	Annual	59.50	45-55.00
89-01-082	The Old Skating Pond	S. Vestergaard	Annual	59.50	30-89.00
90-01-083	Christmas at Tivoli	S. Vestergaard	Annual	64.50	100-125.
91-01-084	The Festival of Santa Lucia	S. Vestergaard	Annual	69.50	45-69.00
92-01-085	The Queen's Carriage	S. Vestergaard	Annual	69.50	55-60.00
93-01-086	Christmas Guests	S. Vestergaard	Annual	69.50	55-73.00
94-01-087	Christmas Shopping	S. Vestergaard	Annual	72.50	72.50

Company / Number	Name	Series / Artist	Edition Limit	Issue Price	Quote
Royal Copenhagen		**Nature's Children**			
93-02-001	The Robins	J. Nielsen	Annual	39.50	39.50
94-02-002	The Fawn	J. Nielsen	Annual	39.50	39.50
Royal Copenhagen		**Christmas in Denmark**			
91-03-001	Bringing Home the Tree	H. Hansen	Annual	72.50	72.50
92-03-002	Christmas Shopping	H. Hansen	Annual	72.50	72.50
93-03-003	The Skating Party	H. Hansen	Annual	74.50	74.50
94-03-004	The Sleigh Ride	H. Hansen	Annual	74.50	74.50
Royal Copenhagen		**American Mother's Day**			
88-04-001	Western Trail	S. Vestergaard	Annual	34.50	34.50
89-04-002	Indian Love Call	S. Vestergaard	Annual	37.00	37.00
90-04-003	Southern Belle	S. Vestergaard	Annual	39.50	39.50
91-04-004	Mother's Day at the Mission	S. Vestergaard	Annual	42.50	42.50
92-04-005	Turn of the Century Boston	S. Vestergaard	Annual	45.00	45.00
94-04-006	Tropical Paradise	S. Vestergaard	Annual	47.50	47.50
Royal Devon		**Rockwell Christmas**			
75-01-001	Downhill Daring	N. Rockwell	Yr.Iss.	24.50	30.00
76-01-002	The Christmas Gift	N. Rockwell	Yr.Iss.	24.50	35.00
77-01-003	The Big Moment	N. Rockwell	Yr.Iss.	27.50	50.00
78-01-004	Puppets for Christmas	N. Rockwell	Yr.Iss.	27.50	27.50
79-01-005	One Present Too Many	N. Rockwell	Yr.Iss.	31.50	31.50
80-01-006	Gramps Meets Gramps	N. Rockwell	Yr.Iss.	33.00	33.00
Royal Devon		**Rockwell Mother's Day**			
75-02-001	Doctor and Doll	N. Rockwell	Yr.Iss.	23.50	50.00
76-02-002	Puppy Love	N. Rockwell	Yr.Iss.	24.50	104.00
77-02-003	The Family	N. Rockwell	Yr.Iss.	24.50	85.00
78-02-004	Mother's Day Off	N. Rockwell	Yr.Iss.	27.00	35.00
79-02-005	Mother's Evening Out	N. Rockwell	Yr.Iss.	30.00	32.00
80-02-006	Mother's Treat	N. Rockwell	Yr.Iss.	32.50	35.00
Royal Doulton		**Family Christmas Plates**			
91-01-001	Dad Plays Santa	N/A	Yr.Iss.	60.00	60.00
Royal Doulton		**Christmas Plates**			
93-02-001	Royal Doulton-Together For Christmas	N/A	N/A	45.00	45.00
93-02-002	Royal Albert-Sleighride	N/A	N/A	45.00	45.00
Royal Worcester		**Birth Of A Nation**			
72-01-001	Boston Tea Party	P.W. Baston	10,000	45.00	140-275.
73-01-002	Paul Revere	P.W. Baston	10,000	45.00	140-250.
74-01-003	Concord Bridge	P.W. Baston	10,000	50.00	140.00
75-01-004	Signing Declaration	P.W. Baston	10,000	65.00	140.00
76-01-005	Crossing Delaware	P.W. Baston	10,000	65.00	140.00
77-01-006	Washington's Inauguration	P.W. Baston	1,250	65.00	140.00
Royal Worcester		**Currier and Ives Plates**			
74-02-001	Road in Winter	P.W. Baston	5,570	59.50	55-100.00
75-02-002	Old Grist Mill	P.W. Baston	3,200	59.50	55-100.00
76-02-003	Winter Pastime	P.W. Baston	1,500	59.50	55-125.00
77-02-004	Home to Thanksgiving	P.W. Baston	546	59.50	200-250.
Royal Worcester		**Water Birds of North America**			
85-03-001	Mallards	J. Cooke	15,000	55.00	55.00
85-03-002	Canvas Backs	J. Cooke	15,000	55.00	55.00
85-03-003	Wood Ducks	J. Cooke	15,000	55.00	55.00
85-03-004	Snow Geese	J. Cooke	15,000	55.00	55.00
85-03-005	American Pintails	J. Cooke	15,000	55.00	55.00
85-03-006	Green Winged Teals	J. Cooke	15,000	55.00	55.00
85-03-007	Hooded Mergansers	J. Cooke	15,000	55.00	55.00
85-03-008	Canada Geese	J. Cooke	15,000	55.00	55.00
Royal Worcester		**Kitten Encounters**			
87-04-001	Fishful Thinking	P. Cooper	14-day	29.50	30-54.00
87-04-002	Puppy Pal	P. Cooper	14-day	29.50	36.00
87-04-003	Just Ducky	P. Cooper	14-day	29.50	36.00
87-04-004	Bunny Chase	P. Cooper	14-day	29.50	30.00
87-04-005	Flutter By	P. Cooper	14-day	29.50	30.00
87-04-006	Bedtime Buddies	P. Cooper	14-day	29.50	30.00
88-04-007	Cat and Mouse	P. Cooper	14-day	29.50	33.00
88-04-008	Stablemates	P. Cooper	14-day	29.50	48.00
Royal Worcester		**Kitten Classics**			
85-05-001	Cat Nap	P. Cooper	14-day	29.50	36.00
85-05-002	Purrfect Treasure	P. Cooper	14-day	29.50	29.50
85-05-003	Wild Flower	P. Cooper	14-day	29.50	29.50
85-05-004	Birdwatcher	P. Cooper	14-day	29.50	29.50
85-05-005	Tiger's Fancy	P. Cooper	14-day	29.50	33.00
85-05-006	Country Kitty	P. Cooper	14-day	29.50	33.00
85-05-007	Little Rascal	P. Cooper	14-day	29.50	29.50
86-05-008	First Prize	P. Cooper	14-day	29.50	29.50
Sarah's Attic		**Classroom Memories**			
91-01-001	Classroom Memories	Sarah's Attic	Closed	80.00	80.00
Schmid		**Davis Red Oak Sampler**			
86-01-001	General Store	L. Davis	5,000	45.00	150.00
87-01-002	Country Wedding	L. Davis	5,000	45.00	110.00
89-01-003	Country School	L. Davis	5,000	45.00	75.00
90-01-004	Blacksmith Shop	L. Davis	5,000	52.50	60.00
Schmid		**Davis Country Pride Plates**			
81-02-001	Surprise in the Cellar	L. Davis	7,500	35.00	230.00
81-02-002	Plum Tuckered Out	L. Davis	7,500	35.00	200.00
81-02-003	Duke's Mixture	L. Davis	7,500	35.00	190.00
82-02-004	Bustin' with Pride	L. Davis	7,500	35.00	100-125.
Schmid		**Davis Cat Tales Plates.**			
82-03-001	Right Church, Wrong Pew	L. Davis	12,500	37.50	190.00
82-03-002	Company's Coming	L. Davis	12,500	37.50	180.00
82-03-003	On the Move	L. Davis	12,500	37.50	145.00
82-03-004	Flew the Coop	L. Davis	12,500	37.50	145.00
Schmid		**Davis Special Edition Plates**			
83-04-001	The Critics	L. Davis	12,500	45.00	145.00
84-04-002	Good Ole Days Privy Set 2	L. Davis	5,000	60.00	185.00
86-04-003	Home From Market	L. Davis	7,500	55.00	145.00
Schmid		**Davis Christmas Plates**			
83-05-001	Hooker at Mailbox With Present	L. Davis	7,500	45.00	125.00
84-05-002	Country Christmas	L. Davis	7,500	45.00	125.00

Number	Name	Artist	Edition Limit	Issue Price	Quote
85-05-003	Christmas at Foxfire Farm	L. Davis	7,500	45.00	135.00
86-05-004	Christmas at Red Oak	L. Davis	7,500	45.00	125.00
87-05-005	Blossom's Gift	L. Davis	7,500	47.50	100.00
88-05-006	Cutting the Family Christmas Tree	L. Davis	7,500	47.50	100.00
89-05-007	Peter and the Wren	L. Davis	7,500	47.50	75.00
90-05-008	Wintering Deer	L. Davis	7,500	47.50	47.50
91-05-009	Christmas at Red Oak II	L. Davis	7,500	55.00	75.00
92-05-010	Born On A Starry Night	L. Davis	7,500	55.00	55.00
93-05-011	Waiting For Mr. Lowell	L. Davis	5,000	55.00	55.00
Schmid		**Friends of Mine**			
89-06-001	Sun Worshippers	L. Davis	7,500	53.00	53.00
90-06-002	Sunday Afternoon Treat	L. Davis	7,500	53.00	53.00
91-06-003	Warm Milk	L. Davis	7,500	55.00	55.00
92-06-004	Cat and Jenny Wren	L. Davis	7,500	55.00	55.00
Schmid		**Pen Pals**			
93-07-001	The Old Home Place	L. Davis	5,000	50.00	50.00
Schmid		**Disney Annual**			
83-08-001	Sneak Preview	Disney Studios	20,000	22.50	22.50
84-08-002	Command Performance	Disney Studios	20,000	22.50	22.50
85-08-003	Snow Biz	Disney Studios	20,000	22.50	22.50
86-08-004	Tree For Two	Disney Studios	20,000	22.50	22.50
87-08-005	Merry Mouse Medley	Disney Studios	20,000	25.00	25.00
88-08-006	Warm Winter Ride	Disney Studios	20,000	25.00	25.00
89-08-007	Merry Mickey Claus	Disney Studios	20,000	32.50	60.00
90-08-008	Holly Jolly Christmas	Disney Studios	20,000	32.50	32.50
91-08-009	Mickey and Minnie's Rockin' Christmas	Disney Studios	20,000	37.00	37.00
Schmid		**Disney Christmas**			
73-09-001	Sleigh Ride	Disney Studio	Annual	10.00	325.00
74-09-002	Decorating The Tree	Disney Studio	Annual	10.00	84.00
75-09-003	Caroling	Disney Studio	Annual	12.50	14.00
76-09-004	Building A Snowman	Disney Studio	Annual	13.00	15.00
77-09-005	Down The Chimney	Disney Studio	Annual	13.00	14.00
78-09-006	Night Before Christmas	Disney Studio	Annual	15.00	31.00
79-09-007	Santa's Suprise	Disney Studio	15,000	17.50	27.00
80-09-008	Sleigh Ride	Disney Studio	15,000	17.50	33.00
81-09-009	Happy Holidays	Disney Studio	15,000	17.50	20.00
82-09-010	Winter Games	Disney Studio	15,000	18.50	25.00
Schmid		**Disney Mother's Day**			
74-10-001	Flowers For Mother	Disney Studio	Annual	10.00	45.00
75-10-002	Snow White & Dwarfs	Disney Studio	Annual	12.50	50.00
76-10-003	Minnie Mouse	Disney Studio	Annual	13.00	25.00
77-10-004	Pluto's Pals	Disney Studio	Annual	13.00	18.00
78-10-005	Flowers For Bambi	Disney Studio	Annual	15.00	40.00
79-10-006	Happy Feet	Disney Studio	10,000	17.50	20.00
80-10-007	Minnie's Surprise	Disney Studio	10,000	17.50	30.00
81-10-008	Playmates	Disney Studio	10,000	17.50	35.00
82-10-009	A Dream Come True	Disney Studio	10,000	18.50	40.00
Schmid		**Disney Special Edition Plates**			
78-11-001	Mickey Mouse At Fifty	Disney Studios	15,000	25.00	65-100.00
80-11-002	Happy Birthday Pinocchio	Disney Studios	7,500	17.50	25-60.00
81-11-003	Alice in Wonderland	Disney Studios	7,500	17.50	17.50
82-11-004	Happy Birthday Pluto	Disney Studios	7,500	17.50	39.00
82-11-005	Goofy's Golden Jubilee	Disney Studios	7,500	18.50	29.00
87-11-006	Snow White Golden Anniversary	Disney Studios	5,000	47.50	47.50
88-11-007	Mickey Mouse & Minnie Mouse 60th	Disney Studios	10,000	50.00	95-125.00
89-11-008	Sleeping Beauty 30th Anniversary	Disney Studios	5,000	80.00	95.00
90-11-009	Fantasia-Sorcerer's Apprentice	Disney Studios	5,000	59.00	59-99.00
90-11-010	Pinocchio's Friend	Disney Studios	Annual	25.00	25.00
90-11-011	Fantasia Relief Plate	Disney Studios	20,000	25.00	39.00
Schmid		**Ferrandiz Music Makers Porcelain Plates**			
81-12-001	The Flutist	J. Ferrandiz	10,000	25.00	29.00
81-12-002	The Entertainer	J. Ferrandiz	10,000	25.00	29.00
82-12-003	Magical Medley	J. Ferrandiz	10,000	25.00	29.00
82-12-004	Sweet Serenade	J. Ferrandiz	10,000	25.00	32.00
Schmid		**Ferrandiz Beautiful Bounty Porcelain Plates**			
82-13-001	Summer's Golden Harvest	J. Ferrandiz	10,000	40.00	40.00
82-13-002	Autumn's Blessing	J. Ferrandiz	10,000	40.00	40.00
82-13-003	A Mid-Winter's Dream	J. Ferrandiz	10,000	40.00	42.50
82-13-004	Spring Blossoms	J. Ferrandiz	10,000	40.00	40.00
Schmid		**Ferrandiz Wooden Birthday Plates**			
72-14-001	Boy	J. Ferrandiz	Unkn.	15.00	150.00
72-14-002	Girl	J. Ferrandiz	Unkn.	15.00	160.00
73-14-003	Boy	J. Ferrandiz	Unkn.	20.00	200.00
73-14-004	Girl	J. Ferrandiz	Unkn.	20.00	150.00
74-14-005	Boy	J. Ferrandiz	Unkn.	22.00	160.00
74-14-006	Girl	J. Ferrandiz	Unkn.	22.00	160.00
Schmid		**Juan Ferrandiz Porcelain Christmas Plates**			
72-15-001	Christ in the Manger	J. Ferrandiz	Unkn.	30.00	179.00
73-15-002	Christmas	J. Ferrandiz	Unkn.	30.00	229.00
Schmid		**Christmas**			
71-16-001	Angel	B. Hummel	Annual	15.00	19-39.00
72-16-002	Angel With Flute	B. Hummel	Annual	15.00	15.00
73-16-003	The Nativity	B. Hummel	Annual	15.00	73.00
74-16-004	The Guardian Angel	B. Hummel	Annual	18.50	18.50
75-16-005	Christmas Child	B. Hummel	Annual	25.00	25.00
76-16-006	Sacred Journey	B. Hummel	Annual	27.50	32.00
77-16-007	Herald Angel	B. Hummel	Annual	27.50	32.00
78-16-008	Heavenly Trio	B. Hummel	Annual	32.50	32.50
79-16-009	Starlight Angel	B. Hummel	Annual	38.00	38.00
80-16-010	Parade Into Toyland	B. Hummel	Annual	45.00	45.00
81-16-011	A Time To Remember	B. Hummel	Annual	45.00	45.00
82-16-012	Angelic Procession	B. Hummel	Annual	45.00	49.00
83-16-013	Angelic Messenger	B. Hummel	Annual	45.00	45.00
84-16-014	A Gift from Heaven	B. Hummel	Annual	45.00	48.00
85-16-015	Heavenly Light	B. Hummel	Annual	45.00	46.50
86-16-016	Tell The Heavens	B. Hummel	Annual	45.00	56.00
87-16-017	Angelic Gifts	B. Hummel	Annual	47.50	47.50
88-16-018	Cheerful Cherubs	B. Hummel	Annual	53.00	66.00
89-16-019	Angelic Musician	B. Hummel	Annual	53.00	53.00
90-16-020	Angel's Light	B. Hummel	Annual	53.00	57.00
91-16-021	Message From Above	B. Hummel	Annual	60.00	60.00
92-16-022	Sweet Blessings	B. Hummel	Annual	65.00	65.00

Number	Name	Artist	Edition Limit	Issue Price	Quote
Schmid		**Mother's Day**			
72-17-001	Playing Hooky	B. Hummel	Annual	15.00	15.00
73-17-002	Little Fisherman	B. Hummel	Annual	15.00	33.00
74-17-003	Bumblebee	B. Hummel	Annual	18.50	20.00
75-17-004	Message of Love	B. Hummel	Annual	25.00	29.00
76-17-005	Devotion For Mother	B. Hummel	Annual	27.50	30.00
77-17-006	Moonlight Return	B. Hummel	Annual	27.50	29.00
78-17-007	Afternoon Stroll	B. Hummel	Annual	32.50	32.50
79-17-008	Cherub's Gift	B. Hummel	Annual	38.00	38.00
80-17-009	Mother's Little Helpers	B. Hummel	Annual	45.00	52.00
81-17-010	Playtime	B. Hummel	Annual	45.00	52.00
82-17-011	The Flower Basket	B. Hummel	Annual	45.00	47.50
83-17-012	Spring Bouquet	B. Hummel	Annual	45.00	54.00
84-17-013	A Joy to Share	B. Hummel	Annual	45.00	45.00
85-17-014	A Mother's Journey	B. Hummel	Annual	45.00	45.00
86-17-015	Home From School	B. Hummel	Annual	45.00	55.00
88-17-016	Young Reader	B. Hummel	Annual	52.50	81.00
89-17-017	Pretty as a Picture	B. Hummel	Annual	53.00	75.00
90-17-018	Mother's Little Athlete	B. Hummel	Annual	53.00	53.00
91-17-019	Soft & Gentle	B. Hummel	Annual	55.00	55.00
Schmid		**The Littlest Night**			
93-18-001	The Littlest Night	B. Hummel	Annual	25.00	25.00
Schmid		**Paddington Bear/Musician's Dream Plates**			
83-19-001	The Beat Goes On	Unknown	10,000	17.50	22.50
83-19-002	Knowing the Score	Unknown	10,000	17.50	20.00
83-19-003	Perfect Harmony	Unknown	10,000	17.50	17.50
83-19-004	Tickling The Ivory	Unknown	10,000	17.50	17.50
Schmid		**A Year With Paddington Bear Plates**			
79-20-001	Pyramid of Presents	Unknown	25,000	12.50	27.50
80-20-002	Springtime	Unknown	25,000	12.50	25.00
81-20-003	Sandcastles	Unknown	25,000	12.50	22.50
82-20-004	School Days	Unknown	25,000	12.50	12.50
Schmid		**Peanuts Mother's Day Plates**			
72-21-001	Linus	C. Schulz	Unkn.	10.00	10.00
73-21-002	Mom?	C. Schulz	Unkn.	10.00	10.00
74-21-003	Snoopy/Woodstock/Parade	C. Schulz	Unkn.	10.00	10.00
75-21-004	A Kiss for Lucy	C. Schulz	Unkn.	12.50	10.00
76-21-005	Linus and Snoopy	C. Schulz	Unkn.	13.00	35.00
77-21-006	Dear Mom	C. Schulz	Unkn.	13.00	30.00
78-21-007	Thoughts That Count	C. Schulz	Unkn.	15.00	25.00
79-21-008	A Special Letter	C. Schulz	Unkn.	17.50	22.50
80-21-009	A Tribute to Mom	C. Schulz	Unkn.	17.50	22.50
81-21-010	Mission for Mom	C. Schulz	Unkn.	17.50	20.00
82-21-011	Which Way to Mother	C. Schulz	Unkn.	18.50	18.50
Schmid		**Peanuts Valentine's Day Plates**			
77-22-001	Home Is Where the Heart is	C. Schulz	Unkn.	13.00	32.50
78-22-002	Heavenly Bliss	C. Schulz	Unkn.	13.00	30.00
79-22-003	Love Match	C. Schulz	Unkn.	17.50	27.50
80-22-004	From Snoopy, With Love	C. Schulz	Unkn.	17.50	25.00
81-22-005	Hearts-A-Flutter	C. Schulz	Unkn.	17.50	20.00
82-22-006	Love Patch	C. Schulz	Unkn.	17.50	17.50
Schmid		**Peanuts World's Greatest Athlete**			
82-23-001	Go Deep	C. Schulz	10,000	17.50	25.00
82-23-002	The Puck Stops Here	C. Schulz	10,000	17.50	22.50
82-23-003	The Way You Play The Game	C. Schulz	10,000	17.50	20.00
82-23-004	The Crowd Went Wild	C. Schulz	10,000	17.50	17.50
Schmid		**Peanuts Special Edition Plate**			
76-24-001	Bi-Centennial	C. Schulz	Unkn.	13.00	30.00
Schmid		**Peanuts Christmas**			
72-25-001	Snoopy Guides the Sleigh	C. Schulz	Annual	10.00	40.00
73-25-002	Christmas Eve at Doghouse	C. Schulz	Annual	10.00	88.00
74-25-003	Christmas At Fireplace	C. Schulz	Annual	10.00	30.00
75-25-004	Woodstock and Santa Claus	C. Schulz	Annual	12.50	10.00
76-25-005	Woodstock's Christmas	C. Schulz	Annual	13.00	20.00
77-25-006	Deck The Doghouse	C. Schulz	Annual	13.00	19.00
78-25-007	Filling the Stocking	C. Schulz	Annual	15.00	15.00
79-25-008	Christmas at Hand	C. Schulz	15,000	17.50	24.00
80-25-009	Waiting for Santa	C. Schulz	15,000	17.50	30.00
81-25-010	A Christmas Wish	C. Schulz	15,000	17.50	28.00
82-25-011	Perfect Performance	C. Schulz	15,000	18.50	50.00
Schmid		**Raggedy Ann Annual Plates**			
80-26-001	The Sunshine Wagon	Unknown	10,000	17.50	80-100.00
81-26-002	The Raggedy Shuffle	Unknown	10,000	17.50	27.50-75.00
82-26-003	Flying High	Unknown	10,000	18.50	18.50
83-26-004	Winning Streak	Unknown	10,000	22.50	22.50
84-26-005	Rocking Rodeo	Unknown	10,000	22.50	22.50
Schmid		**Raggedy Ann Bicentennial Plate**			
76-27-001	Bicentennial Plate	Unknown	Unkn.	13.00	30-60.00
Schmid		**Raggedy Ann Christmas Plates**			
75-28-001	Gifts of Love	Unknown	Unkn.	12.50	45.00
76-28-002	Merry Blades	Unknown	Unkn.	13.00	37.50
77-28-003	Christmas Morning	Unknown	Unkn.	13.00	22.50
78-28-004	Checking the List	Unknown	Unkn.	15.00	20.00
79-28-005	Little Helper	Unknown	Unkn.	17.50	19.50
Schmid		**Raggedy Ann Valentine's Day Plates**			
78-29-001	As Time Goes By	Unknown	Unkn.	13.00	25.00
79-29-002	Daisies Do Tell	Unknown	Unkn.	17.50	20.00
Schmid		**Kitty Cucumber Annual**			
89-30-001	Ring Around the Rosie	M. Lillemoe	20,000	25.00	45.00
90-30-002	Swan Lake	M. Lillemoe	20,000	25.00	45.00
91-30-003	Tea Party	M. Lillemoe	2,500	25.00	45.00
92-30-004	Dance 'Round the Maypole	M. Lillemoe	2,500	25.00	45.00
Sports Impressions/Enesco		**Gold Edition Plates**			
86-01-001	Larry Bird	R. Simon	Closed	125.00	150.00
86-01-002	Wade Boggs	B. Johnson	Closed	125.00	150.00
86-01-003	Mickey Mantle At Night	R. Simon	Closed	125.00	250.00
86-01-004	Keith Hernandez	R. Simon	Closed	125.00	175.00
86-01-005	Don Mattingly	B. Johnson	Closed	125.00	175.00
87-01-006	Darryl Strawberry #1	R. Simon	Closed	125.00	125.00
87-01-007	Ted Williams	R. Simon	Closed	125.00	495.00

Number	Name	Artist	Edition Limit	Issue Price	Quote
87-01-008	Carl Yastrzemski	R. Simon	Closed	125.00	175.00
87-01-009	Mickey, Willie, & Duke	R. Simon	Closed	150.00	225.00
88-01-010	Brooks Robinson	R. Simon	Closed	125.00	225.00
88-01-011	Larry Bird	R. Simon	Closed	125.00	275.00
88-01-012	Magic Johnson	R. Simon	Closed	125.00	350.00
88-01-013	Yankee Tradition	J. Catalano	Closed	150.00	150.00
89-01-014	Mantle Switch Hitter	J. Catalano	Closed	150.00	150.00
89-01-015	Will Clark	J. Catalano	Closed	125.00	150.00
89-01-016	Darryl Strawberry #2	T. Fogerty	Closed	125.00	125.00
91-01-017	Larry Bird	J. Catalano	Closed	150.00	195.00
91-01-018	Magic Johnson	W.C. Mundy	Closed	150.00	225.00
91-01-019	Michael Jordan	J. Catalano	Closed	150.00	275.00
91-01-020	Dream Team (1st Ten Chosen)	L. Salk	Closed	150.00	275.00
92-01-021	Dream Team	R.Tanenbaum	Closed	150.00	150-175.
92-01-022	Michael Jordan	R.Tanenbaum	Closed	150.00	200.00
93-01-023	Magic Johnson	T. Fogerty	Closed	150.00	175.00
93-01-024	Magic Johnson (4042-04)	R.Tanenbaum	Closed	150.00	200.00

Vague Shadows: See Artaffects

V-Palekh Art Studios — **Russian Legends**

Number	Name	Artist	Edition Limit	Issue Price	Quote
88-01-001	Ruslan and Ludmilla	G. Lubimov	195-day	29.87	33-40.00
88-01-002	The Princess/Seven Bogatyrs	A. Kovalev	195-day	29.87	35-38.00
88-01-003	The Golden Cockerel	V. Vleshko	195-day	32.87	32.87
88-01-004	Lukomorya	R. Belousov	195-day	32.87	32.87
89-01-005	Fisherman and the Magic Fish	N. Lopatin	195-day	32.87	38.00
89-01-006	Tsar Saltan	G. Zhiryakova	195-day	32.87	47.00
89-01-007	The Priest and His Servant	O. An	195-day	34.87	42.00
90-01-008	Stone Flower	V. Bolshakova	195-day	34.87	40.00
90-01-009	Sadko	E. Populor	195-day	34.87	34.87
90-01-010	The Twelve Months	N. Lopatin	195-day	36.87	36.87
90-01-011	Silver Hoof	S. Adeyanor	195-day	36.87	36.87
90-01-012	Morozko	N. Lopatin	195-day	36.87	36.87

Villeroy & Boch — **Russian Fairytales Snow Maiden**

Number	Name	Artist	Edition Limit	Issue Price	Quote
80-01-001	The Snow Maiden	B. Zvorykin	27,500	70.00	130.00
81-01-002	Snegurochka at the Court of Tsar Berendei	B. Zvorykin	27,500	70.00	70.00
81-01-003	Snegurochka and Lei, the Shepherd Boy	B. Zvorykin	27,500	70.00	73.00

Villeroy & Boch — **Russian Fairytales The Red Knight**

Number	Name	Artist	Edition Limit	Issue Price	Quote
81-02-001	The Red Knight	B. Zvorykin	27,500	70.00	70-135.00
81-02-002	Vassilissa and Her Stepsisters	B. Zvorykin	27,500	70.00	77.00
81-02-003	Vassilissa is Presented to the Tsar	B. Zvorykin	27,500	70.00	75.00

Villeroy & Boch — **Russian Fairytales The Firebird**

Number	Name	Artist	Edition Limit	Issue Price	Quote
81-03-001	In Search of the Firebird	B. Zvorykin	27,500	70.00	120.00
81-03-002	Ivan and Tsarevna on the Grey Wolf	B. Zvorykin	27,500	70.00	78.00
81-03-003	The Wedding of Tsarevna Elena the Fair	B. Zvorykin	27,500	70.00	100-118.

Villeroy & Boch — **Russian Fairytales Maria Morevna**

Number	Name	Artist	Edition Limit	Issue Price	Quote
82-04-001	Maria Morevna and Tsarevich Ivan	B. Zvorykin	27,500	70.00	70.00
82-04-002	Koshchey Carries Off Maria Morevna	B. Zvorykin	27,500	70.00	81.00
82-04-003	Tsarevich Ivan and the Beautiful Castle	B. Zvorykin	27,500	70.00	95-115.00

Villeroy & Boch — **Flower Fairy**

Number	Name	Artist	Edition Limit	Issue Price	Quote
79-05-001	Lavender	C. Barker	21-day	35.00	125.00
80-05-002	Sweet Pea	C. Barker	21-day	35.00	125.00
80-05-003	Candytuft	C. Barker	21-day	35.00	89.00
81-05-004	Heliotrope	C. Barker	21-day	35.00	75.00
81-05-005	Blackthorn	C. Barker	21-day	35.00	75.00
81-05-006	Appleblossom	C. Barker	21-day	35.00	95.00

Waterford Wedgwood USA — **Wedgwood Christmas**

Number	Name	Artist	Edition Limit	Issue Price	Quote
69-01-001	Windsor Castle	T. Harper	Annual	25.00	200.00
70-01-002	Trafalgar Square	T. Harper	Annual	30.00	60.00
71-01-003	Picadilly Circus	T. Harper	Annual	30.00	50.00
72-01-004	St. Paul's Cathedral	T. Harper	Annual	35.00	50.00
73-01-005	Tower of London	T. Harper	Annual	40.00	90.00
74-01-006	Houses of Parliament	T. Harper	Annual	40.00	40.00
75-01-007	Tower Bridge	T. Harper	Annual	45.00	45.00
76-01-008	Hampton Court	T. Harper	Annual	50.00	50.00
77-01-009	Westminister Abbey	T. Harper	Annual	55.00	60.00
78-01-010	Horse Guards	T. Harper	Annual	60.00	60.00
79-01-011	Buckingham Palace	Unknown	Annual	65.00	65.00
80-01-012	St. James Palace	Unknown	Annual	70.00	70.00
81-01-013	Marble Arch	Unknown	Annual	75.00	75.00
82-01-014	Lambeth Palace	Unknown	Annual	80.00	90.00
83-01-015	All Souls, Langham Palace	Unknown	Annual	80.00	80.00
84-01-016	Constitution Hill	Unknown	Annual	80.00	80.00
85-01-017	The Tate Gallery	Unknown	Annual	80.00	80.00
86-01-018	The Albert Memorial	Unknown	Annual	80.00	150.00
87-01-019	Guildhall	Unknown	Annual	80.00	85.00
88-01-020	The Observatory/Greenwich	Unknown	Annual	80.00	90.00
89-01-021	Winchester Cathedral	Unknown	Annual	88.00	88.00

Waterford Wedgwood USA — **Bicentennial**

Number	Name	Artist	Edition Limit	Issue Price	Quote
72-03-001	Boston Tea Party	Unknown	Annual	40.00	40.00
73-03-002	Paul Revere's Ride	Unknown	Annual	40.00	115.00
74-03-003	Battle of Concord	Unknown	Annual	40.00	55.00
75-03-004	Across the Delaware	Unknown	Annual	40.00	105.00
75-03-005	Victory at Yorktown	Unknown	Annual	45.00	53.00
76-03-006	Declaration Signed	Unknown	Annual	45.00	45.00

STEINS

Anheuser-Busch, Inc. — **Specialty Steins**

Number	Name	Artist	Edition Limit	Issue Price	Quote
75-01-001	Bud Man CS1	A-Busch,Inc.	Retrd.	N/A	350-550.
75-01-002	A&Eagle CS2	A-Busch,Inc.	Retrd.	N/A	225-275.
75-01-003	A&Eagle Lidded CSL2 (Reference CS28)	A-Busch,Inc.	Retrd.	N/A	275-375.
75-01-004	Katakombe CS3	A-Busch,Inc.	Retrd.	N/A	200-275.
75-01-005	Katakombe Lidded CSL3	A-Busch,Inc.	Retrd.	N/A	350.00
75-01-006	German Olympia CS4	A-Busch,Inc.	Retrd.	N/A	75-150.00
75-01-007	Senior Grande Lidded CSL4	A-Busch,Inc.	Retrd.	N/A	650.00
75-01-008	German Pilique CS5	A-Busch,Inc.	Retrd.	N/A	350-375.
75-01-009	German Pilique Lidded CSL5	A-Busch,Inc.	Retrd.	N/A	450-550.
75-01-010	Senior Grande CS6	A-Busch,Inc.	Retrd.	N/A	550-700.
75-01-011	German Olympia Lidded CSL6	A-Busch,Inc.	Retrd.	N/A	250-300.
75-01-012	Miniature Bavarian CS7	A-Busch,Inc.	Retrd.	N/A	225-300.
76-01-013	Budweiser Centennial Lidded CSL7	A-Busch,Inc.	Retrd.	N/A	475-500.
76-01-014	U.S. Bicentennial Lidded CSL8	A-Busch,Inc.	Retrd.	N/A	475-500.
76-01-015	Natural Light CS9	A-Busch,Inc.	Retrd.	N/A	225-250.
76-01-016	Clydesdales Hofbrau Lidded CSL9	A-Busch,Inc.	Retrd.	N/A	250-350.
76-01-017	Blue Delft CS11	A-Busch,Inc.	Retrd.	N/A	2400.00
76-01-018	Clydesdales CS12	A-Busch,Inc.	Retrd.	N/A	450.00
76-01-019	Budweiser Centennial CS13	A-Busch,Inc.	Retrd.	N/A	350-475.
76-01-020	U.S. Bicentennial CS14	A-Busch,Inc.	Retrd.	N/A	350-475.
76-01-021	Clydesdales Grants Farm CS15	A-Busch,Inc.	Retrd.	N/A	200-300.
76-01-022	German Cities (6 assorted) CS16	A-Busch,Inc.	Retrd.	N/A	1500-1800.
76-01-023	Americana CS17	A-Busch,Inc.	Retrd.	N/A	350-550.
76-01-024	Budweiser Label CS18	A-Busch,Inc.	Retrd.	N/A	450-625.
80-01-025	Budweiser Ladies (4 assorted) CS20	A-Busch,Inc.	Retrd.	N/A	2000-2500.
77-01-026	Budweiser Girl CS21	A-Busch,Inc.	Retrd.	N/A	500.00
76-01-027	Budweiser Centennial CS22	A-Busch,Inc.	Retrd.	N/A	400-475.
77-01-028	A&Eagle CS24	A-Busch,Inc.	Retrd.	N/A	450.00
76-01-029	A&Eagle Barrel CS26	A-Busch,Inc.	Retrd.	N/A	125-175.
76-01-030	Michelob CS27	A-Busch,Inc.	Retrd.	N/A	150-250.
76-01-031	A&Eagle Lidded CS28 (Reference CSL2)	A-Busch,Inc.	Retrd.	N/A	375.00
76-01-032	Clydesdales Lidded CS29	A-Busch,Inc.	Retrd.	N/A	350.00
76-01-033	Coracao Decanter Set (7 piece) CS31	A-Busch,Inc.	Retrd.	N/A	560-750.
76-01-034	Geraman Wine Set (7 piece) CS32	A-Busch,Inc.	Retrd.	N/A	400-500.
76-01-035	Clydesdales Decanter CS33	A-Busch,Inc.	Retrd.	N/A	1000-1200.
76-01-036	Holanda Brown Decanter Set (7 piece) CS34	A-Busch,Inc.	Retrd.	N/A	275.00
76-01-037	Holanda Blue Decanter Set (7 piece) CS35	A-Busch,Inc.	Retrd.	N/A	750.00
76-01-038	Canteen Decanter Set (7 piece) CS36	A-Busch,Inc.	Retrd.	N/A	N/A
76-01-039	St. Louis Decanter CS37	A-Busch,Inc.	Retrd.	N/A	400.00
76-01-040	St. Louis Decanter Set (7 piece) CS38	A-Busch,Inc.	Retrd.	N/A	1000-1200.
80-01-041	Wurzburger Hofbrau CS39	A-Busch,Inc.	Retrd.	N/A	350-450.
80-01-042	Budweiser Chicago Skyline CS40	A-Busch,Inc.	Retrd.	N/A	135-225.
78-01-043	Busch Gardens CS41	A-Busch,Inc.	Retrd.	N/A	250-350.
80-01-044	Oktoberfest-- "The Old Country" CS42	A-Busch,Inc.	Retrd.	N/A	350.00
80-01-045	Natural Light Label CS43	A-Busch,Inc.	Retrd.	N/A	125-175.
80-01-046	Busch Label CS44	A-Busch,Inc.	Retrd.	N/A	150-200.
80-01-047	Michelob Label CS45	A-Busch,Inc.	Retrd.	N/A	100-125.
80-01-048	Budweiser Label CS46	A-Busch,Inc.	Retrd.	N/A	125-150.
81-01-049	Budweiser Chicagoland CS51	A-Busch,Inc.	Retrd.	N/A	50.00
81-01-050	Budweiser Texas CS52	A-Busch,Inc.	Retrd.	N/A	40-60.00
81-01-051	Budweiser California CS56	A-Busch,Inc.	Retrd.	N/A	45-55.00
83-01-052	Budweiser San Francisco CS59	A-Busch,Inc.	Retrd.	N/A	170-200.
84-01-053	Budweiser Olympic Games CS60	A-Busch,Inc.	Retrd.	N/A	15-50.00
83-01-054	Bud Light Baron CS61	A-Busch,Inc.	Retrd.	N/A	30-50.00
87-01-055	Santa Claus CS79	A-Busch,Inc.	Retrd.	N/A	57-75.00
87-01-056	King Cobra CS80	A-Busch,Inc.	Retrd.	N/A	225.00
87-01-057	Winter Olympic Games, Lidded CS81	A-Busch,Inc.	Retrd.	49.95	75-85.00
88-01-058	Budweiser Winter Olympic Games CS85	A-Busch,Inc.	Retrd.	24.95	20-27.00
88-01-059	Summer Olympic Games, Lidded CS91	A-Busch,Inc.	Retrd.	54.95	50-65.00
88-01-060	Budweiser Summer Olympic Games CS92	A-Busch,Inc.	Retrd.	54.95	20-54.95
88-01-061	Budweiser/ Field&Stream Set (4 piece) CS95	A-Busch,Inc.	Retrd.	69.95	225-275.
89-01-062	Bud Man CS100	A-Busch,Inc.	Retrd.	29.95	25-45.00
90-01-063	Baseball Cardinal Stein CS125	A-Busch,Inc.	Retrd.	30.00	25-30.00
91-01-064	Bevo Fox Stein CS160	A-Busch,Inc.	Retrd.	250.00	195-250.

Anheuser-Busch, Inc. — **Clydesdales Holiday Series**

Number	Name	Artist	Edition Limit	Issue Price	Quote
80-02-001	1st Holiday CS19	A-Busch,Inc.	Retrd.	9.95	95-125.
76-02-002	Budweiser Champion Clydesdales CS19A	A-Busch,Inc.	Retrd.	N/A	N/A
81-02-003	2nd Holiday CS50	A-Busch,Inc.	Retrd.	9.95	215-275.
82-02-004	3rd Holiday CS57 50th Anniversary	A-Busch,Inc.	Retrd.	9.95	75-95.00
83-02-005	4th Holiday CS58	A-Busch,Inc.	Retrd.	9.95	25-35.00
84-02-006	5th Holiday CS62	A-Busch,Inc.	Retrd.	9.95	10-20.00
85-02-007	6th Holiday CS63	A-Busch,Inc.	Retrd.	9.95	12-20.00
86-02-008	7th Holiday CS66	A-Busch,Inc.	Retrd.	9.95	20-25.00
87-02-009	8th Holiday CS70	A-Busch,Inc.	Retrd.	9.95	10-25.00
88-02-010	9th Holiday CS88	A-Busch,Inc.	Retrd.	9.95	10-15.00
89-02-011	10th Holiday CS89	A-Busch,Inc.	Retrd.	12.95	10-15.00

Anheuser-Busch, Inc. — **Horseshoe Series**

Number	Name	Artist	Edition Limit	Issue Price	Quote
86-03-001	Horseshoe CS68	A-Busch,Inc.	Retrd.	14.95	30-50.00
87-03-002	Horsehead CS76	A-Busch,Inc.	Retrd.	16.00	20-40.00
86-03-003	Horseshoe CS77	A-Busch,Inc.	Retrd.	16.00	40-75.00
87-03-004	Horsehead CS78	A-Busch,Inc.	Retrd.	14.95	40-75.00
88-03-005	Harness CS94	A-Busch,Inc.	Retrd.	16.00	75-80.00

Anheuser-Busch, Inc. — **Limited Edition Series**

Number	Name	Artist	Edition Limit	Issue Price	Quote
85-04-001	Ltd. Ed. I Brewing & Fermenting CS64	A-Busch,Inc.	Retrd.	29.95	175-200.
86-04-002	Ltd. Ed. II Aging & Cooperage CS65	A-Busch,Inc.	Retrd.	29.95	50-75.00
87-04-003	Ltd. Ed. III Transportation CS71	A-Busch,Inc.	Retrd.	29.95	35-50.00
88-04-004	Ltd. Ed. IV Taverns & Public Houses CS75	A-Busch,Inc.	Retrd.	29.95	28-35.00
89-04-005	Ltd. Ed.V Festival Scene CS98	A-Busch,Inc.	Retrd.	34.95	28-35.00

Anheuser-Busch, Inc. — **Historical Landmark Series**

Number	Name	Artist	Edition Limit	Issue Price	Quote
86-05-001	Brew House CS67 (First)	A-Busch,Inc.	Retrd.	19.95	30-40.00
87-05-002	Stables CS73 (Second)	A-Busch,Inc.	Retrd.	19.95	20-25.00
88-05-003	Grant Cabin CS83 (Third)	A-Busch,Inc.	Retrd.	19.95	30-40.00
88-05-004	Old School House CS84 (Fourth)	A-Busch,Inc.	Retrd.	19.95	20-25.00

Anheuser-Busch, Inc. — **Classic Series**

Number	Name	Artist	Edition Limit	Issue Price	Quote
88-06-001	1st Edition CS93	A-Busch,Inc.	Retrd.	34.95	135-160.
89-06-002	2nd Edition CS104	A-Busch,Inc.	Retrd.	54.95	95-110.00
90-06-003	3rd Edition CS113	A-Busch,Inc.	Retrd.	75.00	75-100.00
91-06-004	4th Edition CS130	A-Busch,Inc.	Retrd.	75.00	54-75.00

Anheuser-Busch, Inc. — **Wholesaler Holiday Series**

Number	Name	Artist	Edition Limit	Issue Price	Quote
90-07-001	An American Tradition, CS112, 1990	S. Sampson	Retrd.	13.50	13-15.00
90-07-002	An American Tradition, CS112-SE Signature Edition, 1990	S. Sampson	Retrd.	24.00	65-80.00
91-07-003	The Season's Best, CS133, 1991	S. Sampson	Retrd.	14.50	13-15.00
91-07-004	The Season's Best, CS133-SE Signature Edition, 1991	S. Sampson	Retrd.	25.00	45.00
92-07-005	The Perfect Christmas, CS167, 1992	S. Sampson	Open	14.50	14.50
92-07-006	The Perfect Christmas, CS167-SE Signature Edition, 1992	S. Sampson	Open	25.00	25.00
93-07-007	Special Delivery, CS192, 1993	N. Koerber	Open	15.00	15.00
93-07-008	Special Delivery, CS192-SE Signature Edition, 1993	N. Koerber	Retrd.	30.00	85-125.00

Anheuser-Busch, Inc. — **Giftware Edition**

Number	Name	Artist	Edition Limit	Issue Price	Quote
92-08-001	U.S. Olympic Team CS168	A-Busch,Inc.	Open	16.00	19.00
92-08-002	1992 Rodeo CS184	A-Busch,Inc.	Open	18.00	25.00
93-08-003	Bud Man Character Stein CS213	A-Busch,Inc.	Open	45.00	45.00
94-08-004	Budweiser Golf Bag Stein CS225	A-Busch,Inc.	Open	16.00	16.00

Anheuser-Busch, Inc. — **Clydesdales Series-Giftware Edition**

Number	Name	Artist	Edition Limit	Issue Price	Quote
87-09-001	Eight Horse Hitch CS74	A-Busch,Inc.	Retrd.	9.95	20-25.00
88-09-002	Mare & Foal CS90	A-Busch,Inc.	Retrd.	11.50	20-25.00
89-09-003	Parade Dress CS99	A-Busch,Inc.	Retrd.	11.50	35-40.00
91-09-004	Training Hitch CS131	A-Busch,Inc.	Retrd.	13.00	11-25.00
92-09-005	Clydesdales on Parade CS161	A-Busch,Inc.	Open	16.00	16.00
94-09-006	Proud and Free CS223	A-Busch,Inc.	Open	17.00	17.00

STEINS

Number	Name	Artist	Edition Limit	Issue Price	Quote
Anheuser-Busch, Inc.	**Sports History Series-Giftware Edition**				
90-10-001	Baseball, America's Favorite Pastime CS124	A-Busch,Inc.	Retrd.	20.00	25-30.00
90-10-002	Football, Gridiron Legacy CS128	A-Busch,Inc.	Retrd.	20.00	17-22.00
91-10-003	Auto Racing, Chasing The Checkered Flag CS132	A-Busch,Inc.	100,000	22.00	22.00
91-10-004	Basketball, Heroes of the Hardwood CS134	A-Busch,Inc.	100,000	22.00	22.00
92-10-005	Golf, Par For The Course CS165	A-Busch,Inc.	100,000	22.00	22.00
93-10-006	Hockey, Center Ice CS209	A-Busch,Inc.	100,000	22.00	22.00
Anheuser-Busch, Inc.	**Bud Label Series-Giftware Edition**				
89-11-001	Budweiser Label CS101	A-Busch,Inc.	Open	N/A	13-16.00
90-11-002	Antique Label II CS127	A-Busch,Inc.	Retrd.	14.00	14-16.00
90-11-003	Bottled Beer III CS136	A-Busch,Inc.	Open	15.00	15.00
Anheuser-Busch, Inc.	**St. Patrick's Day Series-Giftware Edition**				
91-12-001	1991 St. Patrick's Day CS109	A-Busch,Inc.	Retrd.	15.00	37-45.00
92-12-002	1992 St. Patrick's Day CS166	A-Busch,Inc.	100,000	15.00	15.00
93-12-003	1993 St. Patrick's Day CS193	A-Busch,Inc.	Retrd.	15.30	25.00
94-12-004	Luck O' The Irish CS210	A-Busch,Inc.	Open	18.00	18.00
Anheuser-Busch, Inc.	**Logo Series Steins-Giftware Edition**				
91-13-001	Budweiser CS143	A-Busch,Inc.	Open	16.00	16.00
91-13-002	Bud Light CS144	A-Busch,Inc.	Open	16.00	16.00
91-13-003	Michelob CS145	A-Busch,Inc.	Retrd.	16.00	16.00
91-13-004	Michelob Dry CS146	A-Busch,Inc.	Open	16.00	16.00
91-13-005	Busch CS147	A-Busch,Inc.	Open	16.00	16.00
91-13-006	A&Eagle CS148	A-Busch,Inc.	Open	16.00	16.00
91-13-007	Bud Dry Draft CS156	A-Busch,Inc.	Open	16.00	16.00
Anheuser-Busch, Inc.	**A & Eagle Historical Trademark Series-Giftware Edition**				
93-14-001	The 1872 Edition CS191, boxed	D. Langeneckert	Retrd.	22.00	22-35.00
93-14-002	The 1872 Edition CS201, tin	D. Langeneckert	Retrd.	31.00	30-40.00
93-14-003	The 1890 Edition CS218, tin	A-Busch,Inc.	30,000	24.00	24.00
94-14-004	The 1890 Edition CS219, boxed	A-Busch,Inc.	20,000	24.00	24.00
Anheuser-Busch, Inc.	**Octoberfest Series-Giftware Edition**				
92-15-001	1992 Octoberfest CS185	A-Busch,Inc.	35,000	16.00	16.00
93-15-002	1993 Octoberfest CS202	A-Busch,Inc.	35,000	18.00	18.00
Anheuser-Busch, Inc.	**Budweiser Racing Series-Giftware Edition**				
92-16-001	Budweiser Racing-Elliot/Johnson N3553	T. Watts	Retrd.	18.00	30-45.00
93-16-002	Budweiser RacingTeam CS194	H. Droog	Open	19.00	19.00
Anheuser-Busch, Inc.	**Budweiser Military Series-Giftware Edition**				
94-17-001	Army CS224	H. Droog	Open	19.00	19.00
Anheuser-Busch, Inc.	**Marine Conservation Series-Collector Edition**				
94-18-001	Manatee Stein CS203	B. Kemper	25,000	33.50	33.50
Anheuser-Busch, Inc.	**Endangered Species Series-Collector Edition**				
89-19-001	Bald Eagle CS106(First)	A-Busch,Inc.	Retrd.	24.95	175-275.
90-19-002	Asian Tiger CS126 (Second)	A-Busch,Inc.	Retrd.	27.50	30-50.00
91-19-003	African Elephant CS135 (Third)	A-Busch,Inc.	100,000	29.00	29.00
92-19-004	Giant Panda CS173(Fourth)	B. Kemper	100,000	29.00	29.00
92-19-005	Grizzly CS199(Fifth)	B. Kemper	100,000	29.50	29.50
Anheuser-Busch, Inc.	**Discover America Series-Collector Edition**				
90-20-001	Nina CS107	A-Busch,Inc.	100,000	40.00	40.00
91-20-002	Pinta CS129	A-Busch,Inc.	100,000	40.00	40.00
92-20-003	Santa Maria CS138	A-Busch,Inc.	100,000	40.00	40.00
Anheuser-Busch, Inc.	**Sports Legend Series-Collector Edition**				
91-21-001	Babe Ruth CS142	A-Busch,Inc.	50,000	85.00	85.00
92-21-002	Jim Thorpe CS171	M. Caito	50,000	85.00	85.00
93-21-003	Joe Louis CS206	M. Caito	50,000	85.00	85.00
Anheuser-Busch, Inc.	**1992 Olympic Team Series-Collector Edition**				
91-22-001	1992 Winter Olympic Stein CS162	A-Busch,Inc.	25,000	85.00	85.00
92-22-002	1992 Summer Olympic Stein CS163	A-Busch,Inc.	25,000	85.00	85.00
Anheuser-Busch, Inc.	**Archives Series-Collector Edition**				
92-23-001	1893 Columbian Exposition CS169	A-Busch,Inc.	75,000	35.00	35.00
92-23-002	Ganymede CS190	D. Langeneckert	75,000	35.00	35.00
Anheuser-Busch, Inc.	**Sea World Series-Collector Edition**				
92-24-001	Killer Whale CS186	A-Busch, Inc.	25,000	100.00	100.00
92-24-002	Dolphin CS187	A-Busch, Inc.	22,500	90.00	90.00
Anheuser-Busch, Inc.	**Hunter's Companion Series-Collector Edition**				
93-25-001	Labrador Retriever CS195	L. Freeman	50,000	32.50	32.50
94-25-002	The Setter Stein CS205	S. Ryan	50,000	32.50	32.50
94-25-003	Budweiser World Cup Stein CS230	J. Tull.	25,000	40.00	40.00
Anheuser-Busch, Inc.	**Porcelain Heritage Series-Premier Edition**				
90-26-001	Berninghaus CS105	Berninghaus	Retrd.	75.00	54-75.00
91-26-002	After The Hunt CS155	A-Busch,Inc.	25,000	100.00	100.00
92-26-003	Cherub CS182	D. Langeneckert	25,000	100.00	100.00
Anheuser-Busch, Inc.	**Birds of Prey Series-Premier Edition**				
91-27-001	American Bald Eagle CS164	P. Ford	25,000	125.00	125.00
92-27-002	Peregrine Falcon CS183	P. Ford	25,000	125.00	125.00
94-27-003	Osprey CS212	P. Ford	25,000	135.00	135.00
Anheuser-Busch, Inc.	**Civil War Series-Premier Edition**				
92-28-001	General Grant CS181	D. Langeneckert	25,000	150.00	150.00
93-28-002	General Robert E. Lee CS188	D. Langeneckert	25,000	150.00	150.00
93-28-003	President Abraham Lincoln CS189	D. Langeneckert	25,000	150.00	150.00
Anheuser-Busch, Inc.	**Anheuser-Busch Founder Series-Premier Collection**				
93-29-001	Adophus Busch CS216	A-Busch,Inc.	10,000	180.00	180.00
93-29-002	Bill Elliott CS196	H. Droog	25,000	150.00	150.00
93-29-003	Bill Elliott CS196SE	H. Droog	1,500	295.00	295.00
Anheuser-Busch, Inc./Gerz Meisterwerke Collection	**First Hunt Series**				
92-30-001	Golden Retriever GM-2	P. Ford	10,000	150.00	150.00
94-30-002	Springer Spaniel GM-5	P. Ford	10,000	170.00	170.00
Anheuser-Busch, Inc./Gerz Meisterwerke Collection	**Saturday Evening Post Collection**				
93-31-001	Santa's Mailbag GM-1	Gerz	Retrd.	195.00	225-300.
93-31-002	Santa's Helper GM-3	Gerz	7,500	200.00	200.00
Anheuser-Busch, Inc./Gerz Meisterwerke Collection	**American Heritage Collection**				
93-32-001	John F. Kennedy Stein-GM-4	Gerz	10,000	200.00	200.00
Anheuser Busch, Inc./Gerz Meisterwerke Collection	**Gerz Meisterwerke Collection**				
94-33-001	Norman Rockwell-Triple Self Portrait GM6	A-Busch,Inc.	5,000	250.00	250.00
Anheuser Busch, Inc./Gerz Collectowerke	**Favorite Past Times Collection**				
93-34-001	The Dugout-GL1	Gerz	10,000	110.00	110.00
94-34-002	Winchester Stein-GL2	A-Busch,Inc.	10,000	120.00	120.00
Artaffects	**Perillo Steins**				
89-01-001	Buffalo Hunt	G. Perillo	5,000	125.00	125.00
91-01-002	Hoofbeats	G. Perillo	5,000	125.00	125.00
CUI/Carolina Collection/Dram Tree	**Ducks Unlimited**				
87-01-001	Wood Duck Edition I	K. Bloom	Retrd.	80.00	175.00
88-01-002	Mallard Edition II	M. Bradford	Retrd.	80.00	100.00
89-01-003	Canvasbacks Edition III	L. Barnicle	Retrd.	80.00	89.00
90-01-004	Pintails Edition IV	R. Plasschaert	20,000	80.00	80.00
91-01-005	Canada Geese Edition V	J. Meger	20,000	80.00	80.00
CUI/Carolina Collection/Dram Tree	**Federal Duck Stamp**				
90-02-001	Lesser Scaup Edition I	N. Anderson	6,950	80.00	80.00
91-02-002	Black Bellied Whistling Duck Edition II	J. Hautman	6,950	80.00	80.00
92-02-003	King Eiders Edition III	N. Howe	Retrd.	80.00	80.00
93-02-004	Spectacled Eiders	J. Hautman	6,950	80.00	80.00
93-02-005	50th Anniversary Commemorative	W.C. Morris	6,950	85.00	85.00
94-02-006	Canvasbacks	B. Miller	6,950	80.00	80.00
CUI/Carolina Collection/Dram Tree	**National Wild Turkey Federation**				
90-03-001	The Apprentice Edition I	M.T. Noe	9,950	125.00	125.00
91-03-002	Sultan's Sunrise Edition II	A. Agnew	6,950	100.00	100.00
92-03-003	Double Gobble Edition III	J.S. Eberhardt	6,950	100.00	100.00
93-02-004	Tempting Trio	J. Kasper	6,950	100.00	105.50
CUI/Carolina Collection/Dram Tree	**North American Hunting Club**				
90-04-001	Deer Crossing Edition I	R. McGovern	6,950	85.00	85.00
92-04-002	Yukon Grizzly Edition II	L. Anderson	6,950	74.00	74.00
93-04-003	Interrupted Crossing	J. Kasper	6,950	74.00	74.00
94-04-004	Untouchables	H. Lambson	2,950	74.00	74.00
CUI/Carolina Collection/Dram Tree	**Nat'l. Foundation to Protect America's Eagles**				
91-05-001	Great American Patriots Edition I	R.J. McDonald	6,950	80.00	80.00
CUI/Carolina Collection/Dram Tree	**American Angler Series Limited Edition**				
90-06-001	Large Mouth Bass	J.R. Hook	Retrd.	25.00	25.00
CUI/Carolina Collection/Dram Tree	**Pheasants Forever**				
91-07-001	Jumping Ringnecks Edition I	J. Killen	Retrd.	100.00	100.00
92-07-002	Foggy Morning Magic Edition II	P. Crowe	Retrd.	100.00	100.00
CUI/Carolina Collection/Dram Tree	**Trout Unlimited**				
91-08-001	Rainbow Edition I	M. Stidham	6,950	90.00	90.00
92-08-002	Downstream & Across Edition II	E. Hardle	6,950	90.00	90.00
94-08-003	Williams Fork River	CUI	6,950	85.00	85.00
CUI/Carolina Collection/Dram Tree	**Quail Unlimited**				
91-09-001	Hedgerow Bobs Edition I	D. Chapple	Retrd.	90.00	90.00
92-09-002	California Trio Edition II	J. Garcia	Retrd.	90.00	90.00
CUI/Carolina Collection/Dram Tree	**Whitetails Unlimited**				
91-10-001	Last Glance at Trails End	J. Paluh	Retrd.	90.00	90.00
92-10-002	Indian Summer Flight Edition II	B. Miller	6,950	90.00	90.00
CUI/Carolina Collection/Dram Tree	**Jack Russell Terrier**				
91-11-001	Jack Russell Terrier Edition I	B.B. Atwater	6,950	90.00	90.00
CUI/Carolina Collection/Dram Tree	**Statue of Liberty**				
91-12-001	Lady Liberty	CUI	Open	50.00	50.00
86-12-002	Statue of Liberty	CUI	Retrd.	42.50	42.50
93-12-003	Ellis Island	CUI	Open	25.00	25.00
CUI/Carolina Collection/Dram Tree	**Civil War**				
91-13-001	Firing on Fort Sumter Edition I	CUI	4,950	125.00	125.00
92-13-002	Stonewall Jackson Edition II	CUI	4,950	125.00	125.00
92-13-003	J.E.B. Stuart Edition III	CUI	4,950	128.00	128.00
93-13-004	Robert E. Lee Edition IV	CUI	4,950	128.00	128.00
CUI/Carolina Collection/Dram Tree	**Native American Series**				
91-14-001	Hunt for the Buffalo Edition I	P. Kethley	Retrd.	100.00	100.00
92-14-002	Story Teller	P. Kethley	Retrd.	50.00	50.00
CUI/Carolina Collection/Dram Tree	**Christmas Series**				
91-15-001	Checkin' It Twice Edition I	CUI	Retrd.	125.00	125.00
92-15-002	With A Finger Aside His Nose	CUI	Retrd.	125.00	128.00
93-15-003	Mrs. Claus	CUI	Retrd.	128.00	128.00
CUI/Carolina Collection/Dram Tree	**Environmental Series**				
91-16-001	Rain Forest Magic Edition I	C.L. Bragg	4,950	90.00	90.00
92-16-002	First Breath Edition II	M. Hoffman	4,950	90.00	90.00
93-16-003	Humpback Whale	CUI	4,950	95.00	95.00
CUI/Carolina Collection/Dram Tree	**Miller Girl in the Moon**				
90-17-001	Miller Girl in the Moon	CUI	Open	50.00	50.00
CUI/Carolina Collection/Dram Tree	**Miller Girl in the Moon Miniatures**				
94-18-001	The Original Toast	CUI	Open	25.00	25.00
94-18-002	Twilight Gazebo	CUI	Open	25.00	25.00
94-18-003	Moonbeam Girl Over the Water	CUI	Open	25.00	25.00
94-18-004	Celestial Beer Garden Escape	CUI	Open	25.00	25.00
CUI/Carolina Collection/Dram Tree	**Wild Life Series**				
94-19-001	Timber Wolf	A. Agnew	Open	30.00	30.00
94-19-002	Eagle	R. McGovern	Open	30.00	30.00
94-19-003	Mallards	R. Cruwys	Open	30.00	30.00
94-19-004	Whitetail Deer	R. Cruwys	Open	30.00	30.00
CUI/Carolina Collection/Dram Tree	**Great American Achievements**				
86-20-001	First Successful Flight Edition I	CUI	Retrd.	10.95	75-95.00
87-20-002	The Model T Edition II	CUI	Retrd.	12.95	30-55.00
88-20-003	First Transcontinental Railway Edition III	CUI	Retrd.	15.95	28-55.00
89-20-004	The First River Steamer Edition IV	CUI	Retrd.	25.00	25.00
90-20-005	Man's First Walk on the Moon Edition V	CUI	Retrd.	25.00	25.00
CUI/Carolina Collection/Dram Tree	**Birth of a Nation**				
91-21-001	Paul Revere's Ride Edition I	CUI	Retrd.	25.00	25.00
91-21-002	Paul Revere's Ride Lidded Edition I	CUI	Retrd.	70.00	70.00

Number	Name	Artist	Edition Limit	Issue Price	Quote
92-21-003	Signing Of The Declaration Of Independence-Edition II	CUI	Retrd.	25.00	25.00
92-21-004	Signing Of The Declaration Of Independence-Special Pewter Lidden Edition II	CUI	Retrd.	70.00	70.00
93-21-005	George Washington Crossing the Delaware Edition III	CUI	Open	25.00	25.00
93-21-006	George Washington Crossing the Delaware-Special Lidded Edition III	CUI	10,000	70.00	70.00
CUI/Carolina Collection/Dram Tree		**Miller Plank Road**			
91-22-001	Miller Plank Road Edition I	CUI	Retrd.	90.00	90.00
CUI/Carolina Collection/Dram Tree		**Miller Historical Collection**			
90-23-001	Frederic Miller Edition I	CUI	Retrd.	136.00	136.00
91-23-002	Miller's Delivery Wagon Edition II	CUI	Retrd.	130.00	130.00
92-23-003	Coopersmith Edition III	CUI	9,950	130.00	130.00
CUI/Carolina Collection/Dram Tree		**Miller Holiday Series**			
91-24-001	Milwaukee Waterfront Edition I	CUI	9,950	50.00	50.00
92-24-002	Christmas on Old World Third St. Edition II	CUI	9,950	50.00	50.00
92-24-003	Miller Inn Edition III	CUI	9,950	50.00	50.00
93-24-004	Plank Road Christmas	CUI	9,950	50.00	50.00
CUI/Carolina Collection/Dram Tree		**Coors Historical Collection**			
88-25-001	Rocky Mountain Brewry Edition I	CUI	Retrd.	15.95	15.95
89-25-002	Old Time Delivery Wagon Edition II	CUI	Retrd.	16.95	16.95
90-25-003	Waterfall Edition III	CUI	Retrd.	25.00	25.00
CUI/Carolina Collection/Dram Tree		**Rocky Mountain Legends**			
91-26-001	Skier Edition I	CUI	Open	25.00	25.00
91-26-002	Skier Lidded Edition I	CUI	10,000	70.00	70.00
92-26-003	White Water Rafting Edition II	CUI	Retrd.	25.00	25.00
92-26-004	White Water Rafting Special Lidded Edition II	CUI	Retrd.	70.00	70.00
93-26-005	Fly Fishing Edition III	CUI	Open	25.00	25.00
93-26-006	Fly Fishing Special Lidded Edition III	CUI	10,000	70.00	70.00
CUI/Carolina Collection/Dram Tree		**Coors Rodeo Collection**			
91-27-001	Jack Hammer Edition I	M.H. Scott	20,000	90.00	90.00
92-27-002	Born To Buck Edition II	M.H. Scott	20,000	90.00	90.00
93-27-003	Bulldogger Edition III	M.H. Scott	20,000	90.00	90.00
93-27-004	Ride on the Wild Side Edition IV	M.H. Scott	20,000	90.00	90.00
93-27-005	Teamwork Edition V	M.H. Scott	20,000	90.00	90.00
93-27-006	Turning Tight Edition VI	M.H. Scott	20,000	90.00	90.00
CUI/Carolina Collection/Dram Tree		**Winterfest**			
89-28-001	Outdoor Skating Edition I	T. Stortz	9,950	50.00	50.00
90-28-002	Christmas Square Edition II	T. Stortz	9,950	50.00	50.00
91-28-003	Horsedrawn Sleighs Edition III	T. Stortz	9,950	50.00	50.00
92-28-004	Skating Party Edition IV	T. Stortz	9,950	50.00	50.00
93-28-005	Awaiting the Train Edition V	T. Stortz	9,950	50.00	50.00
CUI/Carolina Collection/Dram Tree		**Coors Legacy Series**			
91-29-001	Coors Rams Head Edition I	CUI	Retrd.	130.00	130.00
92-29-002	Bock Beer Edition II	CUI	6,950	120.00	120.00
93-29-003	Bock Beer Edition III	CUI	6,950	120.00	120.00
CUI/Carolina Collection/Dram Tree		**Miller Racing Team**			
91-30-001	Penske/Wallace	CUI	6,950	50.00	50.00
92-30-002	Bobby Rahal	CUI	6,950	53.00	53.00
CUI/Carolina Collection/Dram Tree		**Ruffed Grouse Society**			
90-31-001	Northwoods Grouse Edition I	G. Moss	Retrd.	50.00	50.00
91-31-002	Edition II	Z. Jones	Retrd.	50.00	50.00
CUI/Carolina Collection/Dram Tree		**Phillip Morris**			
91-32-001	London's Bond St. Edition I	D. Hilburn	9,950	50.00	50.00
CUI/Carolina Collection/Dram Tree		**The Fleet Reserve**			
91-33-001	The Arizona Edition I	T. Freeman	6,950	60.00	60.00
92-33-002	Old Salts Edition II	F. Collinyswood	6,950	63.50	63.50
CUI/Carolina Collection/Dram Tree		**Experimental Aircraft Association**			
91-34-001	Into the Teeth of a Tiger Edition I	W.S. Phillips	4,950	80.00	80.00
92-34-002	Tokyo Raiders Ready For Launch Edition II	J. Dietz	4,950	80.00	80.00
93-34-003	305th Schweinfurt Bound	J. Dietz	4,950	80.00	80.00
CUI/Carolina Collection/Dram Tree		**National Football League**			
91-35-001	First NFL Championship Game Edition I -Pewter Edition	CUI	4,950	80.00	80.00
CUI/Carolina Collection/Dram Tree		**N.F.L. National Football League**			
91-36-001	Historically Speaking Pewter Edition I	CUI	Retrd.	80.00	80.00
CUI/Carolina Collection/Dram Tree		**N.B.A. National Basketball Association**			
91-37-001	100 Years of Basketball-Pewter Edition I	CUI	Retrd.	80.00	80.00
CUI/Carolina Collection/Dram Tree		**Stroh Heritage Collection**			
84-38-001	Horsedrawn Wagon - Heritage I	CUI	Retrd.	11.95	15-25.00
85-38-002	Kirn Inn Germany - Heritage II	CUI	Retrd.	12.95	15-22.00
86-38-003	Lion Brewing Company - Heritage III	CUI	Retrd.	13.95	25-35.00
87-38-004	Bohemian Beer - Heritage IV	CUI	Retrd.	14.95	19-22.00
88-38-005	Delivery Vehicles - Heritage V	CUI	Retrd.	25.00	25.00
89-38-006	Fire Brewed - Heritage V I	CUI	Retrd.	16.95	19.00
CUI/Carolina Collection/Dram Tree		**Stroh Bavaria Collection**			
90-39-001	Dancers Edition I - Bavaria I	CUI	Retrd.	45.00	45.00
90-39-002	Dancers Pewter Figure Edition I - Bavaria I	CUI	Retrd.	70.00	70.00
91-39-003	Barrel Pusher Edition II - Bavaria II	CUI	Retrd.	45.00	45.00
91-39-004	Barrel Pusher Pewter Edition II - Bavaria II	CUI	Retrd.	70.00	70.00
92-39-005	The Aging Cellar-Edition III	CUI	Retrd.	45.00	45.00
92-39-006	The Aging Cellar-Pewter Edition III	CUI	Retrd.	70.00	70.00
93-39-007	Bandwagon Street Party-Pewter Edition II	CUI	Retrd.	70.00	70.00
93-39-008	Bandwagon Street Party-Edition IV	CUI	Retrd.	45.00	45.00
CUI/Carolina Collection/Dram Tree		**Beck's**			
90-40-001	Beck's Purity Law Edition I	CUI	Retrd.	115.00	115.00
CUI/Carolina Collection/Dra Tree		**Northern Solitude**			
90-41-001	Moosehead Northern Solitude	N. Anderson	Retrd.	72.00	72.00
CUI/Carolina Collection/Dram Tree		**Big Game Series**			
90-42-001	Wind Blown-Big Horn Sheep	J. Antolik	3,950	70.00	70.00
92-42-002	Heat of the Kalahari-Lions	J. Antolik	3,950	70.00	70.00
93-42-003	Spring Back-Polar Bears	J. Morgan	3,950	70.00	70.00
CUI/Carolina Collection/Dram Tree		**Team of the Decade - NFL**			
90-43-001	NFL 49ers	CUI	Retrd.	60.00	60.00
CUI/Carolina Collection/Dram Tree		**SuperBowl XXV - NFL**			
91-44-001	NFL	CUI	Retrd.	60.00	60.00
CUI/Carolina Collection/Dram Tree		**SuperBowl Champions - NFL**			
91-45-001	NY Giants - NFL	CUI	Retrd.	60.00	60.00
92-45-002	Washington Redskins - NFL	CUI	Retrd.	60.00	60.00
CUI/Carolina Collection/Dram Tree		**World Series Champions - MLB**			
90-46-001	Cincinnati Reds - MLB	CUI	Retrd.	60.00	60.00
91-46-002	Minnesota Twins - MLB	CUI	Retrd.	60.00	60.00
92-46-003	Toronto Blue Jays-MLB	CUI	Retrd.	60.00	60.00
CUI/Carolina Collection/Dram Tree		**Stanley Cup Champions - NHL**			
91-47-001	Pittsburgh Penguins - NHL	CUI	Retrd.	60.00	60.00
92-47-002	Pittsburgh Penguins - NHL	CUI	Retrd.	60.00	60.00
93-47-003	Montreal Canadians-NHL	CUI	4,950	60.00	60.00
CUI/Carolina Collection/Dram Tree		**World Champions - NBA**			
91-48-001	Chicago Bulls - NBA	CUI	Retrd.	60.00	60.00
92-48-002	Chicago Bulls - NBA	CUI	Retrd.	60.00	60.00
93-48-003	Chicago Bulls - NBA	CUI	Retrd.	60.00	60.00
CUI/Carolina Collection/Dram Tree		**Anniversary Series**			
91-49-001	Chicago Bulls 25th Anniversary	CUI	Retrd.	60.00	60.00
92-49-002	Philadelphia Eagles 60th Anniversary	CUI	Retrd.	60.00	60.00
92-49-003	Cincinnati Bengals 25th Anniversary	CUI	Retrd.	60.00	60.00
92-49-004	Pittsburgh Steelers 60th Anniversary	CUI	Open	60.00	60.00
93-49-005	Greenbay Packers-75th Anniversary	CUI	4,950	60.00	60.00
CUI/Carolina Collection/Dram Tree		**Ducks Unlimited Classic Decoy Series**			
92-50-001	1930's Bert Graves Mallard Decoys Edition I	D. Boncela	Retrd.	100.00	100.00
CUI/Carolina Collection/Dram Tree		**North American Fishing Club**			
92-51-001	Jumpin' Hog	V. Beck	6,950	90.00	90.00
93-51-002	Rainbow Trout	R. Cruwys	6,950	90.00	90.00
93-51-003	On the Take	R. Cruwys	6,950	91.00	91.00
CUI/Carolina Collection/Dram Tree		**Lighthouse Collectors Series**			
92-52-001	Boston Light Edition I	CUI	4,950	100.00	100.00
92-52-002	Cape Hatteras Lighthouse Edition II	CUI	4,950	100.00	100.00
93-52-003	Split Rock Edition III	CUI	4,950	100.00	100.00
94-52-004	Old Point Loma Lighthouse IV	CUI	4,950	100.00	100.00
CUI/Carolina Collection/Dram Tree		**American Conference Champion - NFL**			
92-53-001	Buffalo Bills-91 ACC	CUI	Retrd.	60.00	60.00
CUI/Carolina Collection/Dram Tree		**National League Champion - MLB**			
92-54-001	Atlanta Braves-91 NLC	CUI	Retrd.	60.00	60.00
CUI/Carolina Collection/Dram Tree		**Ducks Unlimited Waterfowl of North America**			
93-55-001	Into the Wind	T. Burleson	45-day	60.00	60.00
CUI/Carolina Collection/Dram Tree		**Classic Car Series**			
92-56-001	1957 Chevy	G. Geivette	6,950	100.00	100.00
93-56-002	Classic T-Birds	K. Eberts	6,950	100.00	100.00
CUI/Carolina Collection/Dram Tree		**The Corvette Series**			
92-57-001	1953 Corvette	G. Geivette	6,950	100.00	100.00
93-57-002	1963 Corvette	K. Eberts	6,950	100.00	100.00
CUI/Carolina Collection/Dram Tree		**Moosehead**			
92-58-001	Moosehead 125th Anniversary	CUI	Retrd.	100.00	100.00
CUI/Carolina Collection/Dram Tree		**Quarterback Legends**			
92-59-001	Hall of Fame - John Unitas Edition I	CUI	4,950	175.00	175.00
92-59-002	Hall of Fame - Y.A. Tittle Edition II	CUI	4,950	175.00	175.00
92-59-003	Hall of Fame - Bart Starr	CUI	4,950	175.00	175.00
CUI/Carolina Collection/Dram Tree		**Cooperstown Collection**			
92-60-001	St. Louis Cardinals 100th Anniversary	CUI	Retrd.	70.00	70.00
93-60-002	Ebbets Field	CUI	Open	75.00	75.00
94-60-003	Polo Grounds	CUI	Open	75.00	75.00
CUI/Carolina Collection/Dram Tree		**Cooperstown Team Collection**			
92-61-001	Brooklyn Dodgers	CUI	Retrd.	60.00	60.00
92-61-002	Boston Braves	CUI	Retrd.	60.00	60.00
92-61-003	Washington Senators	CUI	Retrd.	60.00	60.00
CUI/Carolina Collection/Dram Tree		**The History of Billiards**			
93-62-001	Brooklyn Dodgers	Trouvian	2,450	39.50	39.50
93-62-002	Boston Braves	Unknown	2,450	39.50	39.50
93-62-003	Indifference -1823	D. Egerton	2,450	39.50	39.50
93-62-004	First Major Stake Match -1859	Unknown	2,450	39.50	39.50
93-62-005	Grand Union Hotel, Saratoga NY -1875	Unknown	2,450	39.50	39.50
93-62-006	Untitled Print-1905	M. Neuman	2,450	39.50	39.50
CUI/Carolina Collection/Dram Tree		**Coors Racing**			
92-63-001	Keystone/Wally Dallenbach, Jr.	CUI	Retrd.	53.00	53.00
CUI/Carolina Collection/Dram Tree		**Still the King**			
92-64-001	Elvis Presley Postage Stamp	Unknown	45-day	60.00	60.00
93-64-002	'68 Comeback Special	CUI	45-day	60.00	60.00
94-64-003	Gates of Graceland	Unknown	45-day	60.00	60.00
CUI/Carolina Collection/Dram Tree		**Texaco Heritage Collection**			
92-65-001	Return From a Holiday	Unknown	9,950	90.00	90.00
93-65-002	Companions on a Winter Journey Edition II	Unknown	9,950	100.00	100.00
CUI/Carolina Collection/Dram Tree		**West End Brewing**			
92-66-001	Baseball	Unknown	2,450	95.00	95.00
93-66-002	Picnic	Unknown	2,450	95.00	95.00
CUI/Carolina Collection/Dram Tree		**David Mann Easy Riders**			
93-67-001	Limited Edition Holiday	D. Mann	4,950	70.00	70.00
CUI/Carolina Collection/Dram Tree		**Sheffield Pewter**			
93-68-001	Robin Hood	Unknown	Open	95.00	95.00

Company Number	Name	Series Artist	Edition Limit	Issue Price	Quote
CUI/Carolina Collection/Dram Tree		**Special Edition Series**			
93-69-001	Killer Whale	CUI	Open	70.00	70.00
93-69-002	Pintails in the Shallows	CUI	499	58.50	58.50
94-69-003	Great Locomotive Chase: The General	CUI	Open	70.00	70.00
94-69-004	Mallard Decoy	R. Cruwys	Open	50.00	50.00
94-69-005	First Man on the Moon Anniversary	CUI	1,969	70.00	70.00
CUI/Carolina Collection/Dram Tree		**DU Waterfowl of North America**			
93-70-001	Early Flight Canvasbacks	R. Plasschaert	45-day	73.00	73.00
94-70-002	Pintail Trio	R. Leslie	45-day	73.00	73.00
CUI/Carolina Collection/Dram Tree		**Life of Elvis Hoffbrau**			
93-71-001	Elvis Presley-Postage Stamp	Unknown	45-day	39.50	39.50
93-71-002	Elvis Presley '68 Comeback Special	Unknown	45-day	39.50	39.50
94-71-003	Elvis Presley-Army Days	Unknown	45-day	39.50	39.50
94-71-004	Elvis Presley-Gates of Graceland	Unknown	45-day	39.50	39.50
94-71-005	Elvis Presley -Young Elvis	Unknown	45-day	39.50	39.50
94-71-006	Elvis Presley-Las Vegas	Unknown	45-day	39.50	39.50
CUI/Carolina Collection/Dram Tree		**Elvis Presley Deluxe Series**			
93-72-001	Comeback Special-25th Anniversary	Unknown	1,968	130.00	130.00
94-72-002	Life of Elvis Deluxe	Unknown	1,977	130.00	130.00
CUI/Carolina Collection/Dram Tree		**Oktoberfest**			
93-73-001	Dancing Pair	CUI	Open	39.95	39.95
CUI/Carolina Collection/Dram Tree		**Nostalgic Golf Series**			
93-74-001	Down the Middle	CUI	6,950	65.00	65.00
CUI/Carolina Collection/Dram Tree		**Sailing Series**			
93-75-001	Blythe Spirit	CUI	Open	25.00	25.00
CUI/Carolina Collection/Dram Tree		**First Encounter**			
94-76-001	Stand Off	R. Cruwys	Open	50.00	50.00
CUI/Carolina Collection/Dram Tree		**NASCAR Relief Hoffbrau**			
94-77-001	Rusty Wallace/Miller Genuine Draft	Unknown	Open	25.00	25.00
Hamilton Collection		**Warriors of the Plains Tankerds**			
92-01-001	Thundering Hooves	G. Stewart	Open	125.00	125.00
LCS Products		**Early Innings**			
93-01-001	Ebbets Field	LCS	25,000	59.95	59.95

NOTES

❖ NOTES ❖